World Map:

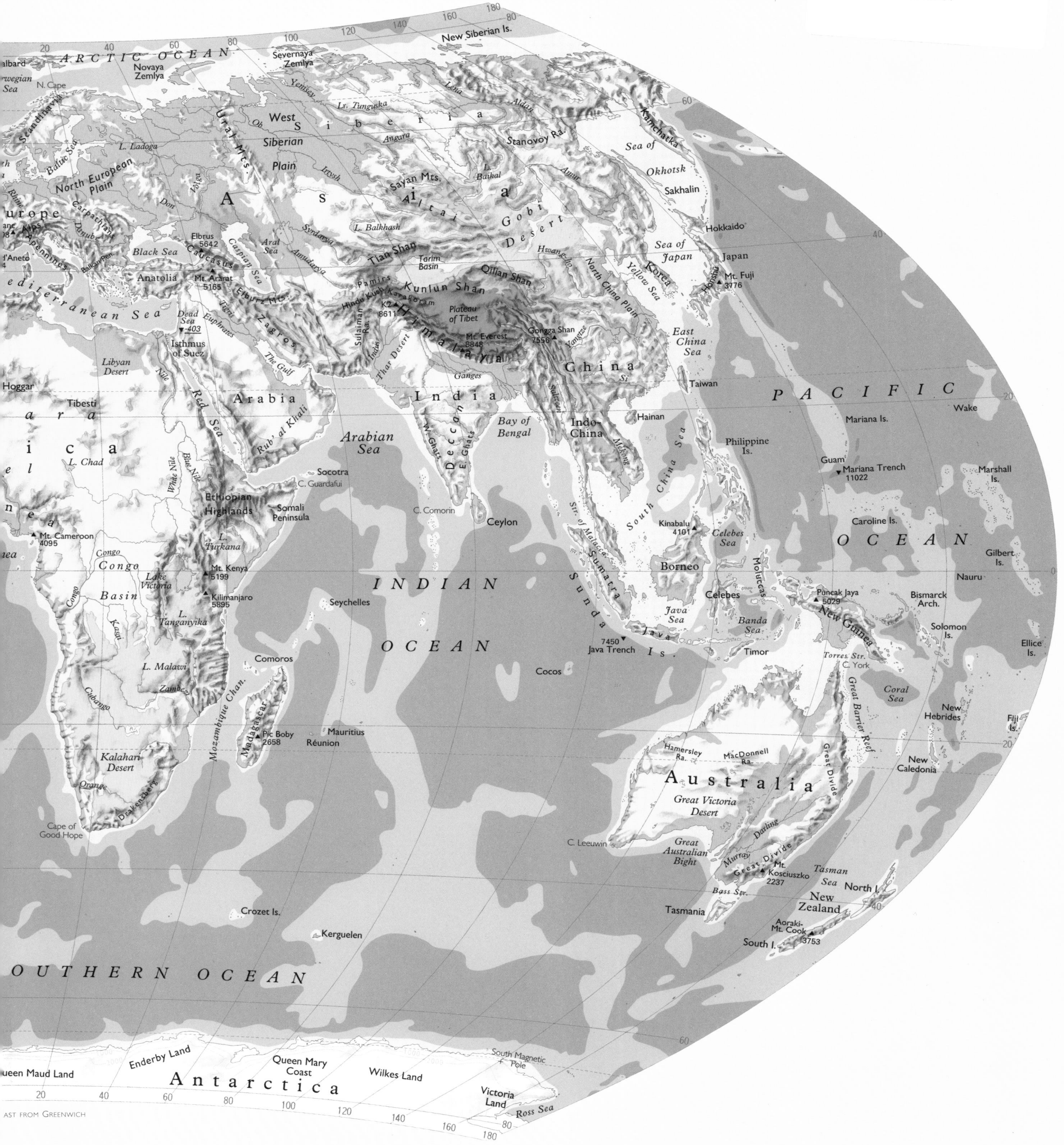

ARCTIC OCEAN
New Siberian Is.
Severnaya Zemlya
Novaya Zemlya
N. Cape
Scandinavia
Baltic Sea
L. Ladoga
North European Plain
Europe
Alps
Carpathians
Danube
Apennines
Balkan Pen.
Black Sea
Mediterranean Sea
Anatolia
Caucasus
Elbrus 5642
Mt. Ararat 5165
Caspian Sea
Aral Sea
Elburz Mts.
Zagros
Dead Sea -403
Isthmus of Suez
Libyan Desert
Hoggar
Tibesti
Africa
L. Chad
Nile
White Nile
Blue Nile
Red Sea
Arabia
Rub' al Khali
The Gulf
Ural Mts.
Volga
Don
Ob
Yenisey
Lr. Tunguska
Angara
Irtysh
West Siberian Plain
Siberia
Asia
Sayan Mts.
Altai
L. Baikal
Lena
Aldan
Stanovoy Ra.
Amur
Sea of Okhotsk
Kamchatka
Sakhalin
Hokkaido
Sea of Japan
Japan
Honshu
Mt. Fuji 3776
Korea
Yellow Sea
North China Plain
Hwang Ho
Gobi Desert
L. Balkhash
Syrdarya
Amudarya
Tian Shan
Tarim Basin
Pamirs
Hindu Kush
Karakoram
K2 8611
Kunlun Shan
Qilian Shan
Plateau of Tibet
Himalaya
Mt. Everest 8848
Gongga Shan 7556
Yangtze
Sulaiman Ra.
Indus
Thar Desert
Ganges
India
Deccan
W. Ghats
E. Ghats
Bay of Bengal
Arabian Sea
Socotra
C. Guardafui
C. Comorin
Ceylon
China
East China Sea
Taiwan
Hainan
Indo-China
Mekong
Salween
South China Sea
Philippine Is.
PACIFIC OCEAN
Mariana Is.
Guam
Mariana Trench 11022
Wake
Marshall Is.
Caroline Is.
Gilbert Is.
Nauru
Kinabalu 4101
Celebes Sea
Borneo
Celebes
Moluccas
Str. of Malacca
Sumatra
Sunda Is.
Java Sea
Java
Banda Sea
Timor
Java Trench 7450
Cocos
Puncak Jaya 5029
New Guinea
Bismarck Arch.
Solomon Is.
Ellice Is.
Torres Str.
C. York
Coral Sea
Great Barrier Reef
New Hebrides
Fiji Is.
New Caledonia
Hamersley Ra.
MacDonnell Ra.
Australia
Great Victoria Desert
Great Dividing Range
Darling
Murray
C. Leeuwin
Great Australian Bight
Mt. Kosciuszko 2237
Bass Str.
Tasmania
Tasman Sea
New Zealand
North I.
South I.
Aoraki-Mt. Cook 3753
Ethiopian Highlands
Somali Peninsula
Mt. Cameroon 4095
Congo
Congo Basin
L. Turkana
Lake Victoria
Mt. Kenya 5199
Kilimanjaro 5895
L. Tanganyika
Kasai
L. Malawi
Zambezi
Cubango
Mozambique Chan.
Madagascar
Pic Boby 2658
Comoros
Seychelles
INDIAN OCEAN
Mauritius
Réunion
Kalahari Desert
Orange
Drakensberg
Cape of Good Hope
Crozet Is.
Kerguelen
SOUTHERN OCEAN
Queen Maud Land
Enderby Land
Queen Mary Coast
Wilkes Land
South Magnetic Pole
Antarctica
Victoria Land
Ross Sea

EAST FROM GREENWICH

PROJECTION: HAMMER EQUAL AREA

PHILIP'S

GREAT WORLD ATLAS

SEVENTH EDITION

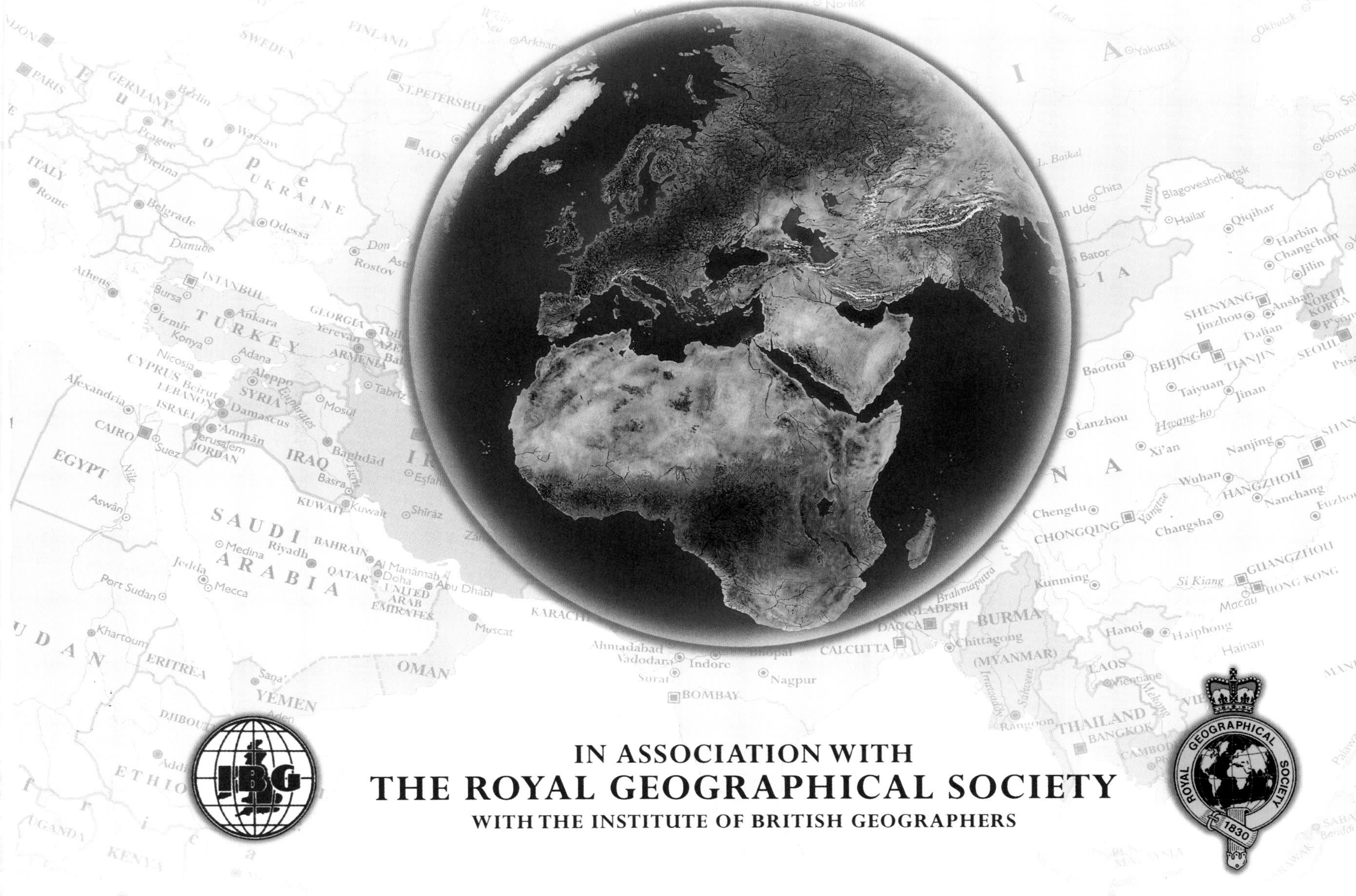

IN ASSOCIATION WITH

THE ROYAL GEOGRAPHICAL SOCIETY

WITH THE INSTITUTE OF BRITISH GEOGRAPHERS

Specialist Geography Consultants

Philip's is grateful to the following people for acting as specialist geography consultants on the '*Introduction to World Geography*' front section:

Professor D. Brunsden, Kings College, University of London, UK
Dr C. Clarke, Oxford University, UK
Professor P. Haggett, University of Bristol, UK
Professor M-L. Hsu, University of Minnesota, Minnesota, USA
Professor K. McLachlan, Geopolitical and International Boundaries Research Centre, School of Oriental and African Studies, University of London, UK
Professor M. Monmonier, Syracuse University, New York, USA
Professor M. J. Tooley, University of St Andrews, UK
Dr T. Unwin, Royal Holloway, University of London, UK

Philip's would also like to thank:

Keith Lye
Robin Scagell
Dr I. S. Evans, Durham University, UK
Dr Andrew Tatham, The Royal Geographical Society

Images of Earth (pages ix–xvi)
All satellite images in this section courtesy of NPA Group Limited, Edenbridge, Kent (www.satmaps.com)

Introduction to World Geography
Picture Acknowledgements
Courtesy of NPA Group, Edenbridge, UK 9, 48
Science Photo Library /Earth Satellite Corporation 20, /NOAA 22 bottom left and bottom right

Illustrations
Stefan Chabluk
William Donohoe
Bernard Thornton Artists /Steve Seymour

Star charts
John Cox and Richard Monkhouse

Cartography by Philip's

Published in Great Britain in 2000
by George Philip Limited,
a division of Octopus Publishing Group Ltd,
2–4 Heron Quays, London E14 4JP

ISBN 0-540-07921-9

A CIP catalogue record for this book is available from the British Library.

Printed in Spain

Details of other Philip's titles and services can be found on our website at: www.philips-maps.co.uk

Philip's is proud to announce that its World Atlases are now published in association with The Royal Geographical Society (with The Institute of British Geographers).

The Society was founded in 1830 and given a Royal Charter in 1859 for 'the advancement of geographical science'. It holds historical collections of national and international importance, many of which relate to the Society's association with and support for scientific exploration and research from the 19th century onwards. It was pivotal in establishing geography as a teaching and research discipline in British universities close to the turn of the century, and has played a key role in geographical and environmental education ever since.

Today the Society is a leading world centre for geographical learning – supporting education, teaching, research and expeditions, and promoting public understanding of the subject.

The Society welcomes those interested in geography as members. For further information, please visit the website at: www.rgs.org

Philip's World Maps

The reference maps which form the main body of this atlas have been prepared in accordance with the highest standards of international cartography to provide an accurate and detailed representation of the Earth. The scales and projections used have been carefully chosen to give balanced coverage of the world, while emphasizing the most densely populated and economically significant regions. A hallmark of Philip's mapping is the use of hill shading and relief colouring to create a graphic impression of landforms: this makes the maps exceptionally easy to read. However, knowledge of the key features employed in the construction and presentation of the maps will enable the reader to derive the fullest benefit from the atlas.

Map Sequence

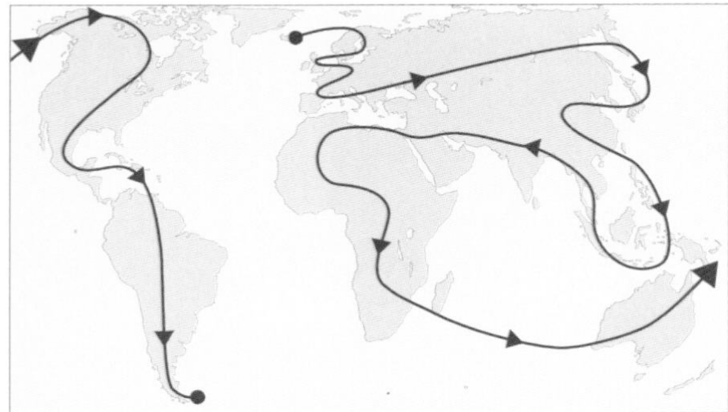

The atlas covers the Earth continent by continent: first Europe; then its land neighbour Asia (mapped north before south, in a clockwise sequence), then Africa, Australia and Oceania, North America and South America. This is the classic arrangement adopted by most cartographers since the 16th century. For each continent, there are maps at a variety of scales. First, physical relief and political maps of the whole continent; then a series of larger-scale maps of the regions within the continent, each followed, where required, by still larger-scale maps of the most important or densely populated areas. The governing principle is that by turning the pages of the atlas, the reader moves steadily from north to south through each continent, with each map overlapping its neighbours. A key map showing this sequence, and the area covered by each map, can be found on the endpapers of the atlas.

Map Presentation

With very few exceptions (e.g. for the Arctic and Antarctic), the maps are drawn with north at the top, regardless of whether they are presented upright or sideways on the page. In the borders will be found the map title; a locator diagram showing the area covered and the page numbers for maps of adjacent areas; the scale; the projection used; the degrees of latitude and longitude; and the letters and figures used in the index for locating place names and geographical features. Physical relief maps also have a height reference panel identifying the colours used for each layer of contouring.

Map Symbols

Each map contains a vast amount of detail which can only be conveyed clearly and accurately by the use of symbols. Points and circles of varying sizes locate and identify the relative importance of towns and cities; different styles of type are employed for administrative, geographical and regional place names to aid identification. A variety of pictorial symbols denote landforms such as glaciers, marshes and coral reefs, and man-made structures including roads, railways, airports and canals. International borders are shown by red lines. Where neighbouring countries are in dispute, for example in parts of the Middle East, the maps show the *de facto* boundary between nations, regardless of the legal or historical situation. The symbols are explained on the first page of the World Maps section of the atlas.

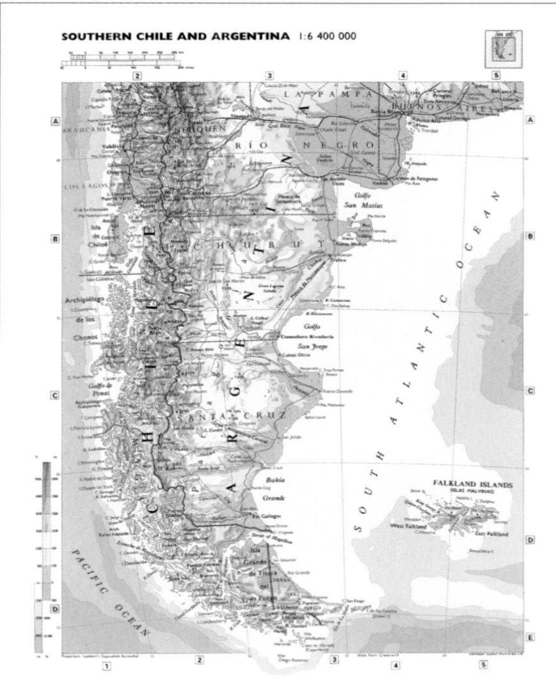

Map Scales

1:16 000 000 1 inch = 252 statute miles

The scale of each map is given in the numerical form known as the 'representative fraction'. The first figure is always one, signifying one unit of distance on the map; the second figure, usually in millions, is the number by which the map unit must be multiplied to give the equivalent distance on the Earth's surface. Calculations can easily be made in centimetres and kilometres, by dividing the Earth units figure by 100 000 (i.e. deleting the last five 0s). Thus 1:1 000 000 means 1 cm = 10 km. The calculation for inches and miles is more laborious, but 1 000 000 divided by 63 360 (the number of inches in a mile) shows that 1:1 000 000 means approximately 1 inch = 16 miles. The table below provides distance equivalents for scales down to 1:50 000 000.

LARGE SCALE		
1:1 000 000	1 cm = 10 km	1 inch = 16 miles
1:2 500 000	1 cm = 25 km	1 inch = 39.5 miles
1:5 000 000	1 cm = 50 km	1 inch = 79 miles
1:6 000 000	1 cm = 60 km	1 inch = 95 miles
1:8 000 000	1 cm = 80 km	1 inch = 126 miles
1:10 000 000	1 cm = 100 km	1 inch = 158 miles
1:15 000 000	1 cm = 150 km	1 inch = 237 miles
1:20 000 000	1 cm = 200 km	1 inch = 316 miles
1:50 000 000	1 cm = 500 km	1 inch = 790 miles
SMALL SCALE		

Measuring Distances

Although each map is accompanied by a scale bar, distances cannot always be measured with confidence because of the distortions involved in portraying the curved surface of the Earth on a flat page. As a general rule, the larger the map scale, the more accurate and reliable will be the distance measured. On small-scale maps such as those of the world and of entire continents, measurement may only be accurate along the 'standard parallels', or central axes, and should not be attempted without considering the map projection.

Map Projections

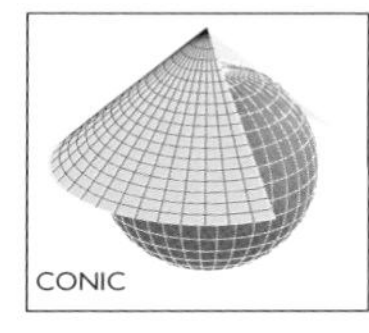

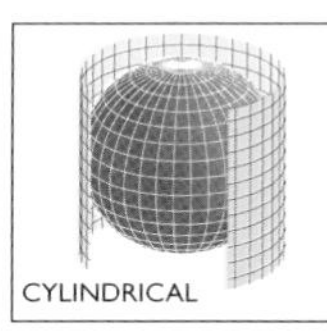

Unlike a globe, no flat map can give a true scale representation of the world in terms of area, shape and position of every region. Each of the numerous systems that have been devised for projecting the curved surface of the Earth on to a flat page involves the sacrifice of accuracy in one or more of these elements. The variations in shape and position of landmasses such as Alaska, Greenland and Australia, for example, can be quite dramatic when different projections are compared.

For this atlas, the guiding principle has been to select projections that involve the least distortion of size and distance. The projection used for each map is noted in the border. Most fall into one of three categories – conic, cylindrical or azimuthal – whose basic concepts are shown above. Each involves plotting the forms of the Earth's surface on a grid of latitude and longitude lines, which may be shown as parallels, curves or radiating spokes.

Latitude and Longitude

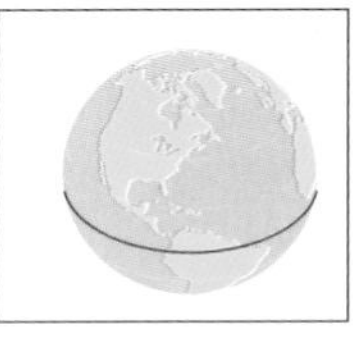

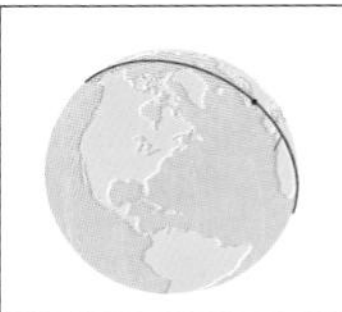

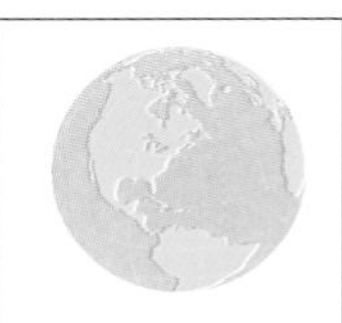

Accurate positioning of individual points on the Earth's surface is made possible by reference to the geometrical system of latitude and longitude. Latitude parallels are drawn west–east around the Earth and numbered by degrees north and south of the Equator, which is designated 0° of latitude. Longitude meridians are drawn north–south and numbered by degrees east and west of the prime meridian, 0° of longitude, which passes through Greenwich in England. By referring to these co-ordinates and their subdivisions of minutes (1/60th of a degree) and seconds (1/60th of a minute), any place on Earth can be located to within a few hundred metres. Latitude and longitude are indicated by blue lines on the maps; they are straight or curved according to the projection employed. Reference to these lines is the easiest way of determining the relative positions of places on different maps, and for plotting compass directions.

Name Forms

For ease of reference, both English and local name forms appear in the atlas. Oceans, seas and countries are shown in English throughout the atlas; country names may be abbreviated to their commonly accepted form (e.g. Germany, not The Federal Republic of Germany). Conventional English forms are also used for place names on the smaller-scale maps of the continents. However, local name forms are used on all large-scale and regional maps, with the English form given in brackets only for important cities – the large-scale map of Russia and Central Asia thus shows Moskva (Moscow). For countries which do not use a Roman script, place names have been transcribed according to the systems adopted by the British and US Geographic Names Authorities. For China, the Pin Yin system has been used, with some more widely known forms appearing in brackets, as with Beijing (Peking). Both the English and local names appear in the index, the English form being cross-referenced to the local form.

Contents

World Statistics

Countries VI

Physical Dimensions VII

Regions in the News VIII

Images of Earth

Crete IX

Rhône Valley X

Abu Dhabi XI

Singapore XII

Sydney XIII

San Francisco XIV

Chicago XV

New York XVI

Introduction to World Geography

The Universe 2–3

The Solar System 4–5

Time and Motion 6–7

Oceans 8–9

Geology 10–11

Landforms 12–13

Atmosphere and Weather 14–15

Climate 16–17

Water and Vegetation 18–19

The Natural Environment 20–21

People and the Environment 22–23

Population 24–25

Cities 26–27

The Human Family 28–29

Conflict and Co-operation 30–31

Agriculture 32–33

Energy 34–35

Minerals 36–37

Manufacturing 38–39

Trade 40–41

Health 42–43

Wealth 44–45

Standards of Living 46–47

World Maps

Map Symbols 1

The World: Political 2–3
1:80 000 000

Arctic Ocean 4
1:29 400 000

Antarctica 5
1:29 400 000

Europe

Europe: Physical 6
1:16 800 000

Europe: Political 7
1:16 800 000

Scandinavia 8–9
1:4 200 000

Denmark and Southern Sweden 10–11
1:2 100 000

England and Wales 12–13
1:1 700 000

Scotland 14
1:1 700 000

Ireland 15
1:1 700 000

British Isles 16
1:4 200 000

Netherlands, Belgium and Luxembourg 17
1:2 100 000

Northern France 18–19
1:2 100 000

Southern France 20–21
1:2 100 000

Middle Europe 22–23
1:4 200 000

Germany and Swizerland 24–25
1:2 100 000

Austria, Czech Republic and Slovak Republic 26–27
1:2 100 000

Northern Italy, Slovenia and Croatia 28–29
1:2 100 000

Southern Italy 30–31
1:2 100 000

Eastern Spain 32–33
1:2 100 000

Western Spain and Portugal 34–35
1:2 100 000

Malta, Crete, Corfu, Rhodes and Cyprus 36
1:1 100 000

The Balearics, the Canaries and Madeira 37
1:1 100 000

Southern Greece and Western Turkey 38–39
1:2 100 000

Northern Greece, Bulgaria and Yugoslavia 40–41
1:2 100 000

Hungary, Romania and the Lower Danube 42–43
1:2 100 000

Poland and the Southern Baltic 44–45
1:2 100 000

Baltic States, Belarus and Ukraine 46–47
1:4 200 000

The Volga Basin and the Caucasus 48–49
1:4 200 000

Asia

Russia and Central Asia 50–51
1:16 800 000

Asia: Physical 52
1:42 000 000

Asia: Political 53
1:42 000 000

Japan 54–55
1:4 200 000

Northern China and Korea 56–57
1:5 000 000

Southern China 58–59
1:5 000 000

China 60
1:16 800 000

The Philippines 61
1:6 300 000

Indonesia and the Philippines 62–63
1:10 500 000

Mainland South-east Asia 64–65
1:5 000 000

South Asia 66–67
1:8 400 000

The Indo-Gangetic Plain 68–69
1:5 000 000

The Middle East 70–71
1:5 900 000

Turkey and Transcaucasia 72–73
1:4 200 000

Arabia and the Horn of Africa 74
1:12 600 000

The Near East 75
1:2 100 000

Africa

Africa: Physical 76
1:33 600 000

Africa: Political 77
1:33 600 000

Northern Africa 78–79
1:12 600 000

The Nile Valley and the Nile Delta 80–81
1:6 700 000 / 1:3 400 000

West Africa 82–83
1:6 700 000

Central and Southern Africa 84–85
1:12 600 000

East Africa 86–87
1:6 700 000

Southern Africa 88–89
1:6 700 000

Australia and Oceania

Australia and Oceania: Physical and Political 90
1:33 600 000

New Zealand and Samoa, Fiji and Tonga 91
1:5 000 000 / 1:10 100 000

Western Australia 92–93
1:6 700 000

Eastern Australia 94–95
1:6 700 000

Pacific Ocean 96–97
1:45 100 000

North America

North America: Physical 98
1:29 400 000

North America: Political 99
1:29 400 000

Canada and Alaska 100–101
1:12 600 000 / 1:25 200 000

Eastern Canada 102–103
1:5 900 000

Western Canada 104–105
1:5 900 000

United States and Hawaii 106–107
1:10 100 000 / 1:8 400 000

Eastern United States 108–109
1:5 000 000

North-eastern United States 110–111
1:2 100 000

Middle United States 112–113
1:5 000 000

Western United States 114–115
1:5 000 000

Central and Southern California and Western Washington 116–117
1:2 100 000

Mexico 118–119
1:6 700 000

Central America and the West Indies 120–121
1:6 700 000

South America

South America: Physical 122
1:25 200 000

South America: Political 123
1:25 200 000

South America – North 124–125
1:13 400 000

Central South America 126–127
1:6 700 000

South America – South 128
1:13 400 000

Index to World Maps 129–224

World Statistics: Countries

This alphabetical list includes all the countries and territories of the world. If a territory is not completely independent, then the country it is associated with is named. The area figures give the total area of land, inland water and ice. Units for areas and populations are thousands. The population figures are 2000 estimates. The annual income is the Gross National Product per capita in US dollars. The figures are the latest available, usually 1998.

Country/Territory	Area km² Thousands	Area miles² Thousands	Population Thousands	Capital	Annual Income US $
Afghanistan	652	252	26,511	Kabul	800
Albania	28.8	11.1	3,795	Tirana	810
Algeria	2,382	920	32,904	Algiers	1,550
American Samoa (US)	0.20	0.08	39	Pago Pago	2,600
Andorra	0.45	0.17	49	Andorra La Vella	18,000
Angola	1,247	481	13,295	Luanda	340
Anguilla (UK)	0.1	0.04	8	The Valley	6,800
Antigua & Barbuda	0.44	0.17	79	St John's	8,300
Argentina	2,767	1,068	36,238	Buenos Aires	8,970
Armenia	29.8	11.5	3,968	Yerevan	480
Aruba (Netherlands)	0.19	0.07	58	Oranjestad	22,000
Australia	7,687	2,968	18,855	Canberra	20,300
Austria	83.9	32.4	7,613	Vienna	26,850
Azerbaijan	86.6	33.4	8,324	Baku	490
Azores (Portugal)	2.2	0.87	238	Ponta Delgada	–
Bahamas	13.9	5.4	295	Nassau	20,100
Bahrain	0.68	0.26	683	Manama	7,660
Bangladesh	144	56	150,589	Dhaka	350
Barbados	0.43	0.17	265	Bridgetown	7,890
Belarus	207.6	80.1	10,697	Minsk	2,200
Belgium	30.5	11.8	9,832	Brussels	25,380
Belize	23	8.9	230	Belmopan	2,610
Benin	113	43	6,369	Porto-Novo	380
Bermuda (UK)	0.05	0.02	62	Hamilton	34,000
Bhutan	47	18.1	1,906	Thimphu	1,000
Bolivia	1,099	424	9,724	La Paz/Sucre	1,000
Bosnia-Herzegovina	51	20	4,601	Sarajevo	1,720
Botswana	582	225	1,822	Gaborone	3,600
Brazil	8,512	3,286	179,487	Brasília	4,570
Brunei	5.8	2.2	333	Bandar Seri Begawan	24,000
Bulgaria	111	43	9,071	Sofia	1,230
Burkina Faso	274	106	12,092	Ouagadougou	240
Burma (= Myanmar)	677	261	51,129	Rangoon	1,200
Burundi	27.8	10.7	7,358	Bujumbura	140
Cambodia	181	70	10,046	Phnom Penh	280
Cameroon	475	184	16,701	Yaoundé	610
Canada	9,976	3,852	28,488	Ottawa	20,020
Canary Is. (Spain)	7.3	2.8	1,494	Las Palmas/Santa Cruz	–
Cape Verde Is.	4	1.6	515	Praia	1,060
Cayman Is. (UK)	0.26	0.10	35	George Town	20,000
Central African Republic	623	241	4,074	Bangui	300
Chad	1,284	496	7,337	Ndjaména	230
Chile	757	292	15,272	Santiago	4,810
China	9,597	3,705	1,299,180	Beijing	750
Colombia	1,139	440	39,397	Bogotá	2,600
Comoros	2.2	0.86	670	Moroni	370
Congo	342	132	3,167	Brazzaville	690
Congo (Dem. Rep. of the)	2,345	905	49,190	Kinshasa	110
Cook Is. (NZ)	0.24	0.09	17	Avarua	900
Costa Rica	51.1	19.7	3,711	San José	2,780
Croatia	56.5	21.8	4,960	Zagreb	4,520
Cuba	111	43	11,504	Havana	1,560
Cyprus	9.3	3.6	762	Nicosia	13,000
Czech Republic	78.9	30.4	10,500	Prague	5,040
Denmark	43.1	16.6	5,153	Copenhagen	33,260
Djibouti	23.2	9	552	Djibouti	1,200
Dominica	0.75	0.29	87	Roseau	3,010
Dominican Republic	48.7	18.8	8,621	Santo Domingo	1,770
Ecuador	284	109	13,319	Quito	1,530
Egypt	1,001	387	64,210	Cairo	1,290
El Salvador	21	8.1	6,739	San Salvador	1,850
Equatorial Guinea	28.1	10.8	455	Malabo	1,500
Eritrea	94	36	4,523	Asmara	200
Estonia	44.7	17.3	1,647	Tallinn	3,390
Ethiopia	1,128	436	61,841	Addis Ababa	100
Faroe Is. (Denmark)	1.4	0.54	49	Tórshavn	16,000
Fiji	18.3	7.1	883	Suva	2,110
Finland	338	131	5,077	Helsinki	24,110
France	552	213	58,145	Paris	24,940
French Guiana (France)	90	34.7	130	Cayenne	6,000
French Polynesia (France)	4	1.5	268	Papeete	10,800
Gabon	268	103	1,612	Libreville	3,950
Gambia, The	11.3	4.4	1,119	Banjul	340
Georgia	69.7	26.9	5,777	Tbilisi	930
Germany	357	138	76,962	Berlin	25,850
Ghana	239	92	20,564	Accra	390
Gibraltar (UK)	0.007	0.003	32	Gibraltar Town	5,000
Greece	132	51	10,193	Athens	11,650
Greenland (Denmark)	2,176	840	60	Nuuk (Godthåb)	16,100
Grenada	0.34	0.13	83	St George's	3,170
Guadeloupe (France)	1.7	0.66	365	Basse-Terre	9,200
Guam (US)	0.55	0.21	128	Agana	19,000
Guatemala	109	42	12,222	Guatemala City	1,640
Guinea	246	95	7,830	Conakry	540
Guinea-Bissau	36.1	13.9	1,197	Bissau	160
Guyana	215	83	891	Georgetown	770
Haiti	27.8	10.7	8,003	Port-au-Prince	410
Honduras	112	43	6,846	Tegucigalpa	730
Hong Kong (China)	1.1	0.40	6,336	–	23,670
Hungary	93	35.9	10,531	Budapest	4,510
Iceland	103	40	274	Reykjavik	28,010
India	3,288	1,269	1,041,543	New Delhi	430
Indonesia	1,905	735	218,661	Jakarta	680
Iran	1,648	636	68,759	Tehran	1,770
Iraq	438	169	26,339	Baghdad	2,400
Ireland	70.3	27.1	4,086	Dublin	18,340
Israel	27	10.3	5,321	Jerusalem	15,940
Italy	301	116	57,195	Rome	20,250
Ivory Coast (Côte d'Ivoire)	322	125	17,600	Yamoussoukro	700
Jamaica	11	4.2	2,735	Kingston	1,680
Japan	378	146	128,470	Tokyo	32,380
Jordan	89.2	34.4	5,558	Amman	1,520
Kazakstan	2,717	1,049	19,006	Astana	1,310
Kenya	580	224	35,060	Nairobi	330
Kiribati	0.72	0.28	72	Tarawa	1,180
Korea, North	121	47	26,117	Pyŏngyang	1,000
Korea, South	99	38.2	46,403	Seoul	7,970
Kuwait	17.8	6.9	2,639	Kuwait City	22,700
Kyrgyzstan	198.5	76.6	5,403	Bishkek	350
Laos	237	91	5,463	Vientiane	330
Latvia	65	25	2,768	Riga	2,430
Lebanon	10.4	4	3,327	Beirut	3,360
Lesotho	30.4	11.7	2,370	Maseru	570
Liberia	111	43	3,575	Monrovia	1,000
Libya	1,760	679	6,500	Tripoli	6,700
Liechtenstein	0.16	0.06	28	Vaduz	50,000
Lithuania	65.2	25.2	3,935	Vilnius	2,440
Luxembourg	2.6	1	377	Luxembourg	43,570
Macau (China)	0.02	0.006	656	Macau	16,000
Macedonia (F.Y.R.O.M.)	25.7	9.9	2,157	Skopje	1,290
Madagascar	587	227	16,627	Antananarivo	260
Madeira (Portugal)	0.81	0.31	253	Funchal	–
Malawi	118	46	12,458	Lilongwe	200
Malaysia	330	127	21,983	Kuala Lumpur	3,600
Maldives	0.30	0.12	283	Malé	1,230
Mali	1,240	479	12,685	Bamako	250
Malta	0.32	0.12	366	Valletta	9,440
Marshall Is.	0.18	0.07	70	Dalap-Uliga-Darrit	1,540
Martinique (France)	1.1	0.42	362	Fort-de-France	10,700
Mauritania	1,030	412	2,702	Nouakchott	410
Mauritius	2.0	0.72	1,201	Port Louis	3,700
Mayotte (France)	0.37	0.14	141	Mamoundzou	1,430
Mexico	1,958	756	107,233	Mexico City	3,970
Micronesia, Fed. States of	0.70	0.27	110	Palikir	1,800
Moldova	33.7	13	4,707	Chişinău	410
Monaco	0.002	0.0001	30	Monaco	25,000
Mongolia	1,567	605	2,847	Ulan Bator	400
Montserrat (UK)	0.10	0.04	13	Plymouth	4,500
Morocco	447	172	31,559	Rabat	1,250
Mozambique	802	309	20,493	Maputo	210
Namibia	825	318	2,437	Windhoek	1,940
Nauru	0.02	0.008	10	Yaren District	10,000
Nepal	141	54	24,084	Katmandu	210
Netherlands	41.5	16	15,829	Amsterdam/The Hague	24,760
Netherlands Antilles (Neths)	0.99	0.38	203	Willemstad	11,500
New Caledonia (France)	18.6	7.2	195	Nouméa	11,400
New Zealand	269	104	3,662	Wellington	14,700
Nicaragua	130	50	5,261	Managua	390
Niger	1,267	489	10,752	Niamey	190
Nigeria	924	357	105,000	Abuja	300
Northern Mariana Is. (US)	0.48	0.18	50	Saipan	11,500
Norway	324	125	4,331	Oslo	34,330
Oman	212	82	2,176	Muscat	7,900
Pakistan	796	307	162,409	Islamabad	480
Palau	0.46	0.18	18	Koror	5,000
Panama	77.1	29.8	2,893	Panama City	3,080
Papua New Guinea	463	179	4,845	Port Moresby	890
Paraguay	407	157	5,538	Asunción	1,760
Peru	1,285	496	26,276	Lima	2,460
Philippines	300	116	77,473	Manila	1,050
Poland	313	121	40,366	Warsaw	3,900
Portugal	92.4	35.7	10,587	Lisbon	10,690
Puerto Rico (US)	9	3.5	3,836	San Juan	9,000
Qatar	11	4.2	499	Doha	17,100
Réunion (France)	2.5	0.97	692	Saint-Denis	4,800
Romania	238	92	24,000	Bucharest	1,390
Russia	17,075	6,592	155,096	Moscow	2,300
Rwanda	26.3	10.2	10,200	Kigali	230
St Kitts & Nevis	0.36	0.14	44	Basseterre	6,130
St Lucia	0.62	0.24	177	Castries	3,410
St Vincent & Grenadines	0.39	0.15	128	Kingstown	2,420
Samoa	2.8	1.1	171	Apia	1,020
San Marino	0.06	0.02	25	San Marino	20,000
São Tomé & Príncipe	0.96	0.37	151	São Tomé	280
Saudi Arabia	2,150	830	20,697	Riyadh	9,000
Senegal	197	76	8,716	Dakar	530
Seychelles	0.46	0.18	75	Victoria	6,450
Sierra Leone	71.7	27.7	5,437	Freetown	140
Singapore	0.62	0.24	3,000	Singapore	30,060
Slovak Republic	49	18.9	5,500	Bratislava	3,700
Slovenia	20.3	7.8	2,055	Ljubljana	9,760
Solomon Is.	28.9	11.2	429	Honiara	750
Somalia	638	246	9,736	Mogadishu	600
South Africa	1,220	471	43,666	C. Town/Pretoria/Bloem.	2,880
Spain	505	195	40,667	Madrid	14,080
Sri Lanka	65.6	25.3	19,416	Colombo	810
Sudan	2,506	967	33,625	Khartoum	290
Surinam	163	63	497	Paramaribo	1,660
Swaziland	17.4	6.7	1,121	Mbabane	1,400
Sweden	450	174	8,560	Stockholm	25,620
Switzerland	41.3	15.9	6,762	Bern	40,080
Syria	185	71	17,826	Damascus	1,020
Taiwan	36	13.9	22,000	Taipei	12,400
Tajikistan	143.1	55.2	7,041	Dushanbe	350
Tanzania	945	365	39,639	Dodoma	210
Thailand	513	198	63,670	Bangkok	2,200
Togo	56.8	21.9	4,861	Lomé	330
Tonga	0.75	0.29	92	Nuku'alofa	1,690
Trinidad & Tobago	5.1	2	1,484	Port of Spain	4,430
Tunisia	164	63	9,924	Tunis	2,050
Turkey	779	301	66,789	Ankara	3,160
Turkmenistan	488.1	188.5	4,585	Ashkhabad	1,630
Turks & Caicos Is. (UK)	0.43	0.17	12	Cockburn Town	5,000
Tuvalu	0.03	0.01	11	Fongafale	600
Uganda	236	91	26,958	Kampala	320
Ukraine	603.7	233.1	52,558	Kiev	850
United Arab Emirates	83.6	32.3	1,951	Abu Dhabi	18,220
United Kingdom	243.3	94	58,393	London	21,400
United States of America	9,373	3,619	266,096	Washington, DC	29,340
Uruguay	177	68	3,274	Montevideo	6,180
Uzbekistan	447.4	172.7	26,044	Tashkent	870
Vanuatu	12.2	4.7	206	Port-Vila	1,270
Venezuela	912	352	24,715	Caracas	350
Vietnam	332	127	82,427	Hanoi	330
Virgin Is. (UK)	0.15	0.06	15	Road Town	–
Virgin Is. (US)	0.34	0.13	135	Charlotte Amalie	12,500
Wallis & Futuna Is. (France)	0.20	0.08	26	Mata-Utu	–
Western Sahara	266	103	228	El Aaiún	300
Yemen	528	204	13,219	Sana	300
Yugoslavia	102.3	39.5	10,761	Belgrade	2,300
Zambia	753	291	12,267	Lusaka	330
Zimbabwe	391	151	13,123	Harare	610

World Statistics: Physical Dimensions

Each topic list is divided into continents and within a continent the items are listed in order of size. The bottom part of many of the lists is selective in order to give examples from as many different countries as possible. The order of the continents is the same as in the atlas, beginning with Europe and ending with South America. The figures are rounded as appropriate.

World, Continents, Oceans

	km²	miles²	%
The World	509,450,000	196,672,000	–
Land	149,450,000	57,688,000	29.3
Water	360,000,000	138,984,000	70.7
Asia	44,500,000	17,177,000	29.8
Africa	30,302,000	11,697,000	20.3
North America	24,241,000	9,357,000	16.2
South America	17,793,000	6,868,000	11.9
Antarctica	14,100,000	5,443,000	9.4
Europe	9,957,000	3,843,000	6.7
Australia & Oceania	8,557,000	3,303,000	5.7
Pacific Ocean	179,679,000	69,356,000	49.9
Atlantic Ocean	92,373,000	35,657,000	25.7
Indian Ocean	73,917,000	28,532,000	20.5
Arctic Ocean	14,090,000	5,439,000	3.9

Ocean Depths

Atlantic Ocean	m	ft
Puerto Rico (Milwaukee) Deep	9,220	30,249
Cayman Trench	7,680	25,197
Gulf of Mexico	5,203	17,070
Mediterranean Sea	5,121	16,801
Black Sea	2,211	7,254
North Sea	660	2,165
Indian Ocean	m	ft
Java Trench	7,450	24,442
Red Sea	2,635	8,454
Pacific Ocean	m	ft
Mariana Trench	11,022	36,161
Tonga Trench	10,882	35,702
Japan Trench	10,554	34,626
Kuril Trench	10,542	34,587
Arctic Ocean	m	ft
Molloy Deep	5,608	18,399

Mountains

Europe		m	ft
Elbrus	*Russia*	5,642	18,510
Mont Blanc	*France/Italy*	4,807	15,771
Monte Rosa	*Italy/Switzerland*	4,634	15,203
Dom	*Switzerland*	4,545	14,911
Liskamm	*Switzerland*	4,527	14,852
Weisshorn	*Switzerland*	4,505	14,780
Taschorn	*Switzerland*	4,490	14,730
Matterhorn/Cervino	*Italy/Switzerland*	4,478	14,691
Mont Maudit	*France/Italy*	4,465	14,649
Dent Blanche	*Switzerland*	4,356	14,291
Nadelhorn	*Switzerland*	4,327	14,196
Grandes Jorasses	*France/Italy*	4,208	13,806
Jungfrau	*Switzerland*	4,158	13,642
Grossglockner	*Austria*	3,797	12,457
Mulhacén	*Spain*	3,478	11,411
Zugspitze	*Germany*	2,962	9,718
Olympus	*Greece*	2,917	9,570
Triglav	*Slovenia*	2,863	9,393
Gerlachovka	*Slovak Republic*	2,655	8,711
Galdhöpiggen	*Norway*	2,468	8,100
Kebnekaise	*Sweden*	2,117	6,946
Ben Nevis	*UK*	1,343	4,406
Asia		m	ft
Everest	*China/Nepal*	8,850	29,035
K2 (Godwin Austen)	*China/Kashmir*	8,611	28,251
Kanchenjunga	*India/Nepal*	8,598	28,208
Lhotse	*China/Nepal*	8,516	27,939
Makalu	*China/Nepal*	8,481	27,824
Cho Oyu	*China/Nepal*	8,201	26,906
Dhaulagiri	*Nepal*	8,172	26,811
Manaslu	*Nepal*	8,156	26,758
Nanga Parbat	*Kashmir*	8,126	26,660
Annapurna	*Nepal*	8,078	26,502
Gasherbrum	*China/Kashmir*	8,068	26,469
Broad Peak	*China/Kashmir*	8,051	26,414
Xixabangma	*China*	8,012	26,286
Kangbachen	*India/Nepal*	7,902	25,925
Trivor	*Pakistan*	7,720	25,328
Pik Kommunizma	*Tajikistan*	7,495	24,590
Demavend	*Iran*	5,604	18,386
Ararat	*Turkey*	5,165	16,945
Gunong Kinabalu	*Malaysia (Borneo)*	4,101	13,455
Fuji-San	*Japan*	3,776	12,388
Africa		m	ft
Kilimanjaro	*Tanzania*	5,895	19,340
Mt Kenya	*Kenya*	5,199	17,057
Ruwenzori (Margherita)	*Ug./Congo (D.R.)*	5,109	16,762
Ras Dashan	*Ethiopia*	4,620	15,157
Meru	*Tanzania*	4,565	14,977
Karisimbi	*Rwanda/Congo (D.R.)*	4,507	14,787
Mt Elgon	*Kenya/Uganda*	4,321	14,176
Batu	*Ethiopia*	4,307	14,130
Toubkal	*Morocco*	4,165	13,665
Mt Cameroon	*Cameroon*	4,070	13,353
Oceania		m	ft
Puncak Jaya	*Indonesia*	5,029	16,499
Puncak Trikora	*Indonesia*	4,750	15,584
Puncak Mandala	*Indonesia*	4,702	15,427
Mt Wilhelm	*Papua New Guinea*	4,508	14,790
Mauna Kea	*USA (Hawaii)*	4,205	13,796
Mauna Loa	*USA (Hawaii)*	4,169	13,681
Mt Cook (Aoraki)	*New Zealand*	3,753	12,313
Mt Kosciuszko	*Australia*	2,237	7,339
North America		m	ft
Mt McKinley (Denali)	*USA (Alaska)*	6,194	20,321
Mt Logan	*Canada*	5,959	19,551
Citlaltepetl	*Mexico*	5,700	18,701
Mt St Elias	*USA/Canada*	5,489	18,008
Popocatepetl	*Mexico*	5,452	17,887
Mt Foraker	*USA (Alaska)*	5,304	17,401
Ixtaccihuatl	*Mexico*	5,286	17,342
Lucania	*Canada*	5,227	17,149
Mt Steele	*Canada*	5,073	16,644
Mt Bona	*USA (Alaska)*	5,005	16,420
Mt Whitney	*USA*	4,418	14,495
Tajumulco	*Guatemala*	4,220	13,845
Chirripó Grande	*Costa Rica*	3,837	12,589
Pico Duarte	*Dominican Rep.*	3,175	10,417
South America		m	ft
Aconcagua	*Argentina*	6,960	22,834
Bonete	*Argentina*	6,872	22,546
Ojos del Salado	*Argentina/Chile*	6,863	22,516
Pissis	*Argentina*	6,779	22,241
Mercedario	*Argentina/Chile*	6,770	22,211
Huascaran	*Peru*	6,768	22,204
Llullaillaco	*Argentina/Chile*	6,723	22,057
Nudo de Cachi	*Argentina*	6,720	22,047
Yerupaja	*Peru*	6,632	21,758
Sajama	*Bolivia*	6,542	21,463
Chimborazo	*Ecuador*	6,267	20,561
Pico Colon	*Colombia*	5,800	19,029
Pico Bolivar	*Venezuela*	5,007	16,427
Antarctica		m	ft
Vinson Massif		4,897	16,066
Mt Kirkpatrick		4,528	14,855

Rivers

Europe		km	miles
Volga	*Caspian Sea*	3,700	2,300
Danube	*Black Sea*	2,850	1,770
Ural	*Caspian Sea*	2,535	1,575
Dnepr (Dnipro)	*Black Sea*	2,285	1,420
Kama	*Volga*	2,030	1,260
Don	*Black Sea*	1,990	1,240
Petchora	*Arctic Ocean*	1,790	1,110
Oka	*Volga*	1,480	920
Dnister (Dniester)	*Black Sea*	1,400	870
Vyatka	*Kama*	1,370	850
Rhine	*North Sea*	1,320	820
N. Dvina	*Arctic Ocean*	1,290	800
Elbe	*North Sea*	1,145	710
Asia		km	miles
Yangtze	*Pacific Ocean*	6,380	3,960
Yenisey–Angara	*Arctic Ocean*	5,550	3,445
Huang He	*Pacific Ocean*	5,464	3,395
Ob–Irtysh	*Arctic Ocean*	5,410	3,360
Mekong	*Pacific Ocean*	4,500	2,795
Amur	*Pacific Ocean*	4,400	2,730
Lena	*Arctic Ocean*	4,400	2,730
Irtysh	*Ob*	4,250	2,640
Yenisey	*Arctic Ocean*	4,090	2,540
Ob	*Arctic Ocean*	3,680	2,285
Indus	*Indian Ocean*	3,100	1,925
Brahmaputra	*Indian Ocean*	2,900	1,800
Syrdarya	*Aral Sea*	2,860	1,775
Salween	*Indian Ocean*	2,800	1,740
Euphrates	*Indian Ocean*	2,700	1,675
Amudarya	*Aral Sea*	2,540	1,575
Africa		km	miles
Nile	*Mediterranean*	6,670	4,140
Congo	*Atlantic Ocean*	4,670	2,900
Niger	*Atlantic Ocean*	4,180	2,595
Zambezi	*Indian Ocean*	3,540	2,200
Oubangi/Uele	*Congo (D.R.)*	2,250	1,400
Kasai	*Congo (D.R.)*	1,950	1,210
Shaballe	*Indian Ocean*	1,930	1,200
Orange	*Atlantic Ocean*	1,860	1,155
Cubango	*Okavango Swamps*	1,800	1,120
Limpopo	*Indian Ocean*	1,600	995
Senegal	*Atlantic Ocean*	1,600	995
Australia		km	miles
Murray–Darling	*Indian Ocean*	3,750	2,330
Darling	*Murray*	3,070	1,905
Murray	*Indian Ocean*	2,575	1,600
Murrumbidgee	*Murray*	1,690	1,050
North America		km	miles
Mississippi–Missouri	*Gulf of Mexico*	6,020	3,740
Mackenzie	*Arctic Ocean*	4,240	2,630
Mississippi	*Gulf of Mexico*	3,780	2,350
Missouri	*Mississippi*	3,780	2,350
Yukon	*Pacific Ocean*	3,185	1,980
Rio Grande	*Gulf of Mexico*	3,030	1,880
Arkansas	*Mississippi*	2,340	1,450
Colorado	*Pacific Ocean*	2,330	1,445
Red	*Mississippi*	2,040	1,270
Columbia	*Pacific Ocean*	1,950	1,210
Saskatchewan	*Lake Winnipeg*	1,940	1,205
South America		km	miles
Amazon	*Atlantic Ocean*	6,450	4,010
Paraná–Plate	*Atlantic Ocean*	4,500	2,800
Purus	*Amazon*	3,350	2,080
Madeira	*Amazon*	3,200	1,990
São Francisco	*Atlantic Ocean*	2,900	1,800
Paraná	*Plate*	2,800	1,740
Tocantins	*Atlantic Ocean*	2,750	1,710
Paraguay	*Paraná*	2,550	1,580
Orinoco	*Atlantic Ocean*	2,500	1,550
Pilcomayo	*Paraná*	2,500	1,550
Araguaia	*Tocantins*	2,250	1,400

Lakes

Europe		km²	miles²
Lake Ladoga	*Russia*	17,700	6,800
Lake Onega	*Russia*	9,700	3,700
Saimaa system	*Finland*	8,000	3,100
Vänern	*Sweden*	5,500	2,100
Asia		km²	miles²
Caspian Sea	*Asia*	371,800	143,550
Lake Baykal	*Russia*	30,500	11,780
Aral Sea	*Kazakstan/Uzbekistan*	28,687	11,086
Tonlé Sap	*Cambodia*	20,000	7,700
Lake Balqash	*Kazakstan*	18,500	7,100
Africa		km²	miles²
Lake Victoria	*East Africa*	68,000	26,000
Lake Tanganyika	*Central Africa*	33,000	13,000
Lake Malawi/Nyasa	*East Africa*	29,600	11,430
Lake Chad	*Central Africa*	25,000	9,700
Lake Turkana	*Ethiopia/Kenya*	8,500	3,300
Lake Volta	*Ghana*	8,500	3,300
Australia		km²	miles²
Lake Eyre	*Australia*	8,900	3,400
Lake Torrens	*Australia*	5,800	2,200
Lake Gairdner	*Australia*	4,800	1,900
North America		km²	miles²
Lake Superior	*Canada/USA*	82,350	31,800
Lake Huron	*Canada/USA*	59,600	23,010
Lake Michigan	*USA*	58,000	22,400
Great Bear Lake	*Canada*	31,800	12,280
Great Slave Lake	*Canada*	28,500	11,000
Lake Erie	*Canada/USA*	25,700	9,900
Lake Winnipeg	*Canada*	24,400	9,400
Lake Ontario	*Canada/USA*	19,500	7,500
Lake Nicaragua	*Nicaragua*	8,200	3,200
South America		km²	miles²
Lake Titicaca	*Bolivia/Peru*	8,300	3,200
Lake Poopo	*Peru*	2,800	1,100

Islands

Europe		km²	miles²
Great Britain	*UK*	229,880	88,700
Iceland	*Atlantic Ocean*	103,000	39,800
Ireland	*Ireland/UK*	84,400	32,600
Novaya Zemlya (N.)	*Russia*	48,200	18,600
Sicily	*Italy*	25,500	9,800
Corsica	*France*	8,700	3,400
Asia		km²	miles²
Borneo	*Southeast Asia*	744,360	287,400
Sumatra	*Indonesia*	473,600	182,860
Honshu	*Japan*	230,500	88,980
Sulawesi (Celebes)	*Indonesia*	189,000	73,000
Java	*Indonesia*	126,700	48,900
Luzon	*Philippines*	104,700	40,400
Hokkaido	*Japan*	78,400	30,300
Africa		km²	miles²
Madagascar	*Indian Ocean*	587,040	226,660
Socotra	*Indian Ocean*	3,600	1,400
Réunion	*Indian Ocean*	2,500	965
Oceania		km²	miles²
New Guinea	*Indonesia/Papua NG*	821,030	317,000
New Zealand (S.)	*Pacific Ocean*	150,500	58,100
New Zealand (N.)	*Pacific Ocean*	114,700	44,300
Tasmania	*Australia*	67,800	26,200
Hawaii	*Pacific Ocean*	10,450	4,000
North America		km²	miles²
Greenland	*Atlantic Ocean*	2,175,600	839,800
Baffin Is.	*Canada*	508,000	196,100
Victoria Is.	*Canada*	212,200	81,900
Ellesmere Is.	*Canada*	212,000	81,800
Cuba	*Caribbean Sea*	110,860	42,800
Hispaniola	*Dominican Rep./Haiti*	76,200	29,400
Jamaica	*Caribbean Sea*	11,400	4,400
Puerto Rico	*Atlantic Ocean*	8,900	3,400
South America		km²	miles²
Tierra del Fuego	*Argentina/Chile*	47,000	18,100
Falkland Is. (E.)	*Atlantic Ocean*	6,800	2,600

World: Regions in the News

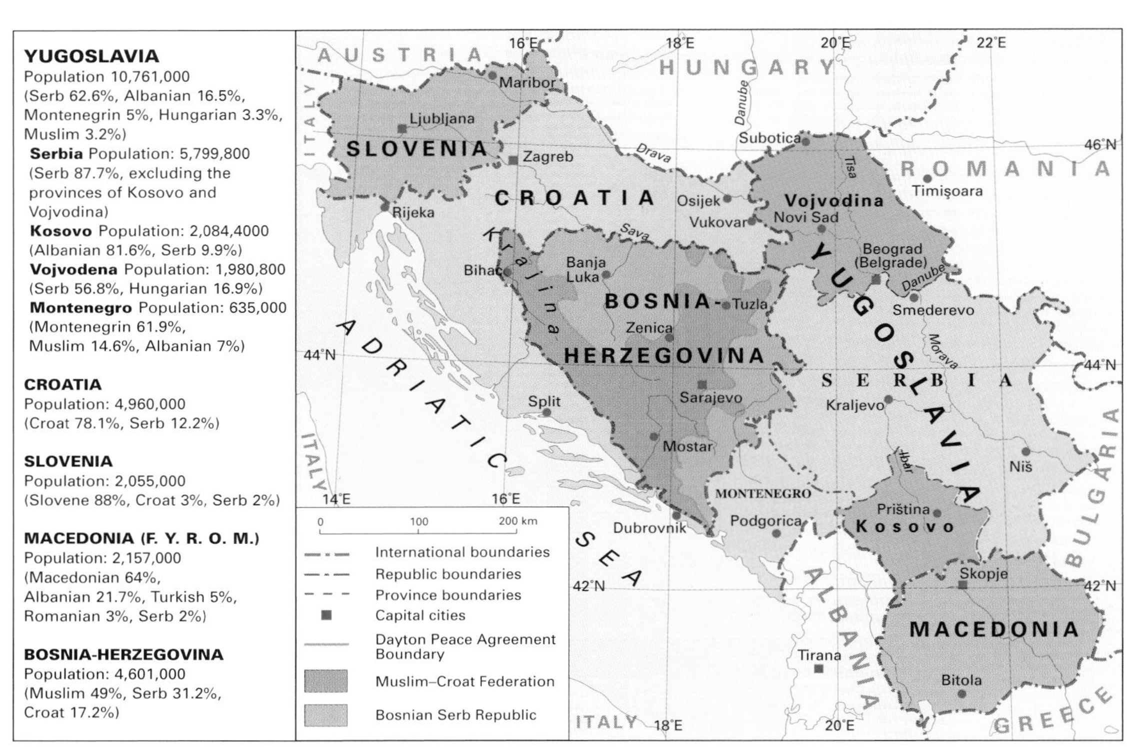

FORMER YUGOSLAVIA AND KOSOVO

The former Yugoslavia, a federation of six republics, split apart in 1991–92. Fearing Serb domination, Croatia, Slovenia, Macedonia and Bosnia-Herzegovina declared themselves independent. This left two states, Serbia and Montenegro, to continue as Yugoslavia. The presence in Croatia and Bosnia-Herzegovina of Orthodox Christian Serbs, Roman Catholic Croats, and Muslims led to civil war and 'ethnic cleansing'. In 1995, the war ended when the Dayton Peace Accord affirmed Bosnia-Herzegovina as a single state partitioned into a Muslim–Croat Federation and a Serbian Republic.

But the status of Kosovo, a former autonomous Yugoslav region, remained unresolved. Kosovo's autonomy had been abolished in 1989 and the Albanian-speaking, Muslim Kosovars were forced to accept direct Serbian rule. After 1995, support grew for the rebel Kosovo Liberation Army. The Serbs hit back and thousands of Kosovars were forced to flee their homes. In March 1999, NATO launched an aerial offensive in an attempt to halt the 'ethnic cleansing'. A Serb military withdrawal from Kosovo was finally agreed in June 1999.

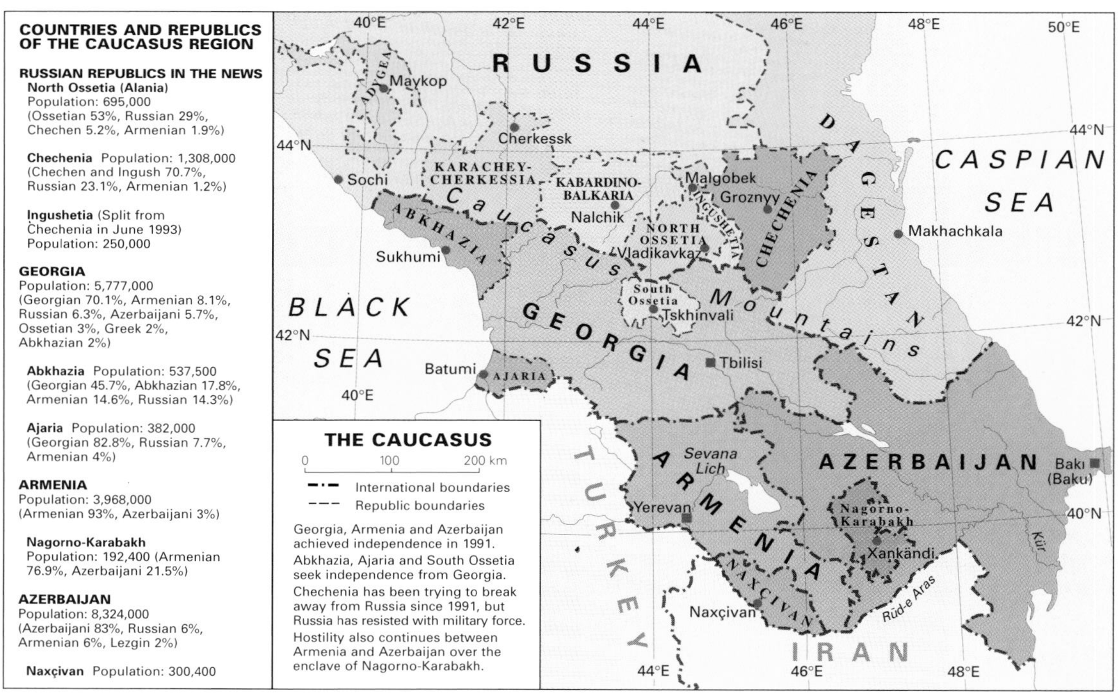

COUNTRIES AND REPUBLICS OF THE CAUCASUS REGION
RUSSIAN REPUBLICS IN THE NEWS
North Ossetia (Alania)
Population: 695,000
(Ossetian 53%, Russian 29%, Chechen 5.2%, Armenian 1.9%)
Chechenia Population: 1,308,000
(Chechen and Ingush 70.7%, Russian 23.1%, Armenian 1.2%)
Ingushetia (Split from Chechenia in June 1993)
Population: 250,000
GEORGIA
Population: 5,777,000
(Georgian 70.1%, Armenian 8.1%, Russian 6.3%, Azerbaijani 5.7%, Ossetian 3%, Greek 2%, Abkhazian 2%)
Abkhazia Population: 537,500
(Georgian 45.7%, Abkhazian 17.8%, Armenian 14.6%, Russian 14.3%)
Ajaria Population: 382,000
(Georgian 82.8%, Russian 7.7%, Armenian 4%)
ARMENIA
Population: 3,968,000
(Armenian 93%, Azerbaijani 3%)
Nagorno-Karabakh
Population: 192,400 (Armenian 76.9%, Azerbaijani 21.5%)
AZERBAIJAN
Population: 8,324,000
(Azerbaijani 83%, Russian 6%, Armenian 6%, Lezgin 2%)
Naxçivan Population: 300,400
RUSSIA
CASPIAN SEA
BLACK SEA
GEORGIA
ARMENIA
AZERBAIJAN
TURKEY
IRAN
THE CAUCASUS
0 100 200 km
International boundaries
Republic boundaries
Georgia, Armenia and Azerbaijan achieved independence in 1991. Abkhazia, Ajaria and South Ossetia seek independence from Georgia. Chechenia has been trying to break away from Russia since 1991, but Russia has resisted with military force. Hostility also continues between Armenia and Azerbaijan over the enclave of Nagorno-Karabakh.

ISRAEL
Population: 5,321,000 (inc. East Jerusalem and Jewish settlers in the areas under Israeli administration. Jewish 82%, Arab Muslim 13.8%, Arab Christian 2.5%, Druze 1.7%)

West Bank
Population: 1,122,900 (Palestinian Arabs 97% [of whom Arab Muslim 85%, Jewish 7%, Christian 8%])

Gaza Strip
Population: 748,400 (Arab 98%)

JORDAN
Population: 5,558,000 (Arab 99% [of whom about 50% are Palestinian Arab])

LEBANON
Population: 3,327,000 (Arab 93% [of whom 83% are Lebanese Arab and 10% Palestinian Arab])

IMAGES OF EARTH

Crete, Mediterranean Sea IX
Rhône Valley, France X
Abu Dhabi, UAE XI
Singapore, Malay Peninsula XII
Sydney, NSW, Australia XIII
San Francisco, California, USA XIV
Chicago, Illinois, USA XV
New York, NY, USA XVI

Rhône Valley, France

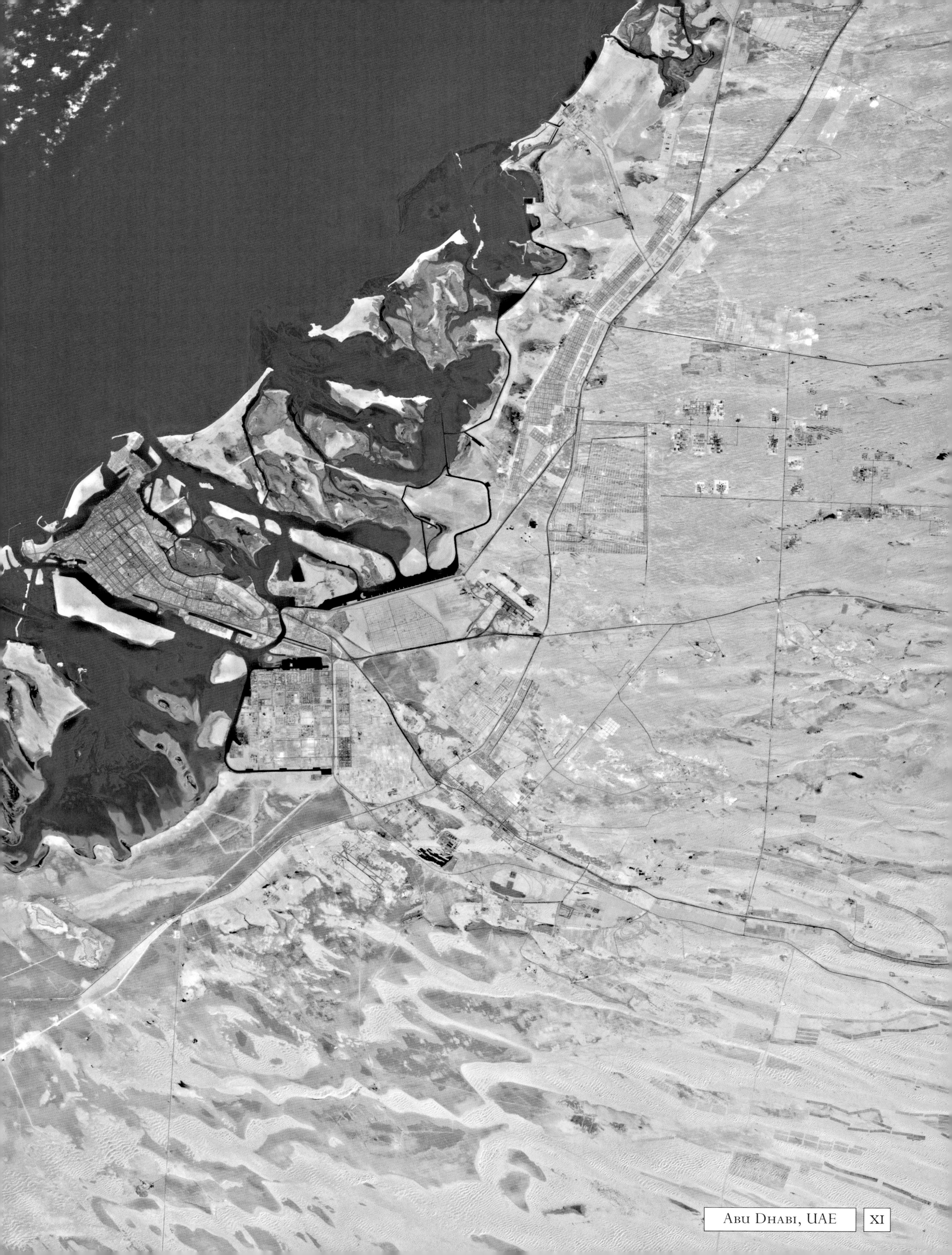
Abu Dhabi, UAE

XII | Singapore, Malay Peninsula

Sydney, NSW, Australia XIII

XIV San Francisco, California, USA

Chicago, Illinois, USA

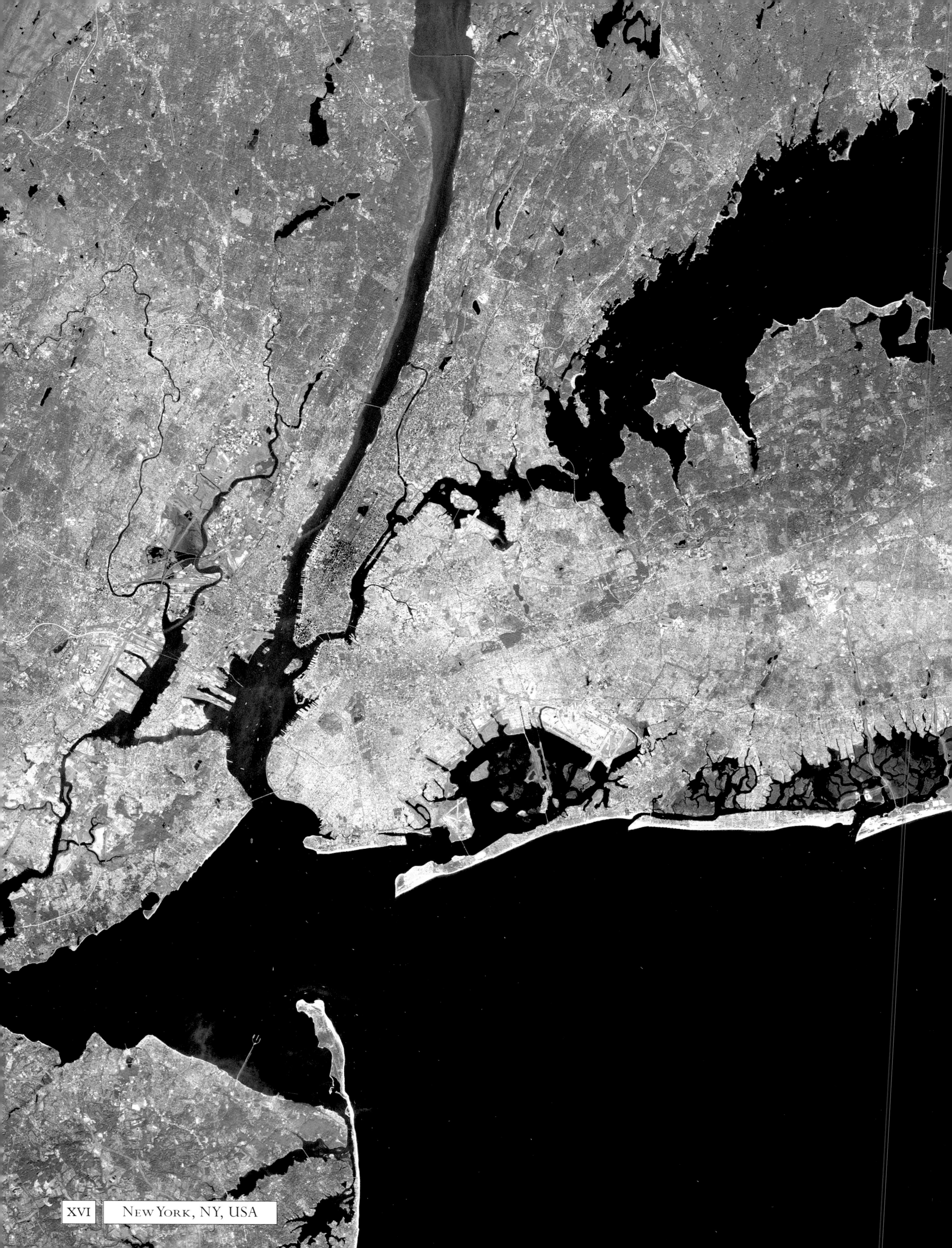
XVI
New York, NY, USA

INTRODUCTION TO WORLD GEOGRAPHY

The Universe 2
The Solar System 4
Time and Motion 6
Oceans 8
Geology 10
Landforms 12
Atmosphere and Weather 14
Climate 16
Water and Vegetation 18
The Natural Environment 20
People and the Environment 22
Population 24
Cities 26
The Human Family 28
Conflict and Co-operation 30
Agriculture 32
Energy 34
Minerals 36
Manufacturing 38
Trade 40
Health 42
Wealth 44
Standards of Living 46

The Universe

For more information:
4 Orbits of the planets
Planetary data

About 15 billion years ago, time and space began with the most colossal explosion in cosmic history: the so-called 'Big Bang' that is believed to have initiated the universe. According to current theory, in the first millionth of a second of its existence it expanded from a dimensionless point of infinite mass and density into a fireball about 30 billion kilometres across; and it has been expanding ever since.

It took almost a million years for the primal fireball to cool enough for atoms to form. They were mostly hydrogen, still the most abundant material in the universe. But the new matter was not evenly distributed around the young universe, and a few billion years later atoms in relatively dense regions began to cling together under the influence of gravity, forming distinct masses of gas separated by vast expanses of empty space. To begin with, these first proto-galaxies were dark places: the universe had cooled. But gravitational attraction continued, condensing matter into coherent lumps inside the galactic gas clouds. About three billion years later, some of these masses had contracted so much that internal pressure produced the high temperatures necessary to bring about nuclear fusion: the first stars were born.

There were several generations of stars, each feeding on the wreckage of its extinct predecessors as well as the original galactic gas swirls. With each new generation, progressively larger atoms were forged in stellar furnaces and the galaxy's range of elements, once restricted to hydrogen, grew larger. About 10 billion years after the Big Bang, a star formed on the outskirts of our galaxy with enough matter left over to create a retinue of planets. Nearly five billion years after that human beings evolved.

The Sun is one of more than 100 billion stars in the home galaxy alone. Our galaxy, in turn, forms part of a local group of approximately 30 similar structures, some much larger than our own; there are at least 100 billion other galaxies in the universe as a whole. The most distant ever observed, a highly energetic galactic core known only as quasar PC 1247 +3406, lies about 12 billion light-years away.

Life of a Star

For most of its existence, a star produces energy by the nuclear fusion of hydrogen into helium at its core. The duration of this hydrogen-burning period – known as the main sequence – depends on the star's mass; the greater the mass, the higher the core temperatures and the sooner the star's supply of hydrogen is exhausted. Dim, dwarf stars consume their hydrogen slowly, eking it out over 1,000 billion years or more. The Sun, like other stars of its mass, should spend about 10 billion years on the main sequence; since it was formed less than five billion years ago, it still has half its life left.

Once all a star's core hydrogen has been fused into helium, nuclear activity moves outwards into layers of unconsumed hydrogen. For a time, energy production sharply increases: the star grows hotter and expands enormously, turning into a so-called red giant. Its energy output will increase a thousandfold, and it will swell to a hundred times its present diameter.

After a few hundred million years, helium in the core will become sufficiently compressed to initiate a new cycle of nuclear fusion: from helium to carbon. The star will contract somewhat, before beginning its last expansion, in the Sun's case engulfing the Earth and perhaps Mars. In this bloated condition, the Sun's outer layers will break off into space, leaving a tiny inner core, mainly of carbon, that shrinks progressively under the force of its own gravity: dwarf stars can attain a density more than 10,000 times that of normal matter, with crushing surface gravities to match. Gradually, the nuclear fires will die down, and the Sun will reach its terminal stage: a black dwarf, emitting insignificant amounts of energy.

However, stars more massive than the Sun may undergo another transformation. The additional mass allows gravitational collapse to continue indefinitely: eventually, all the star's remaining matter shrinks to a point, and its density approaches infinity – a state that will not permit even subatomic structures to survive.

The star has become a black hole: an anomalous 'singularity' in the fabric of space and time. Although vast coruscations of radiation will be emitted by any matter falling into its grasp, the singularity itself has an escape velocity that exceeds the speed of light, and nothing can ever be released from it. Within the boundaries of the black hole, the laws of physics are suspended, but no physicist can ever observe the extraordinary events that may occur.

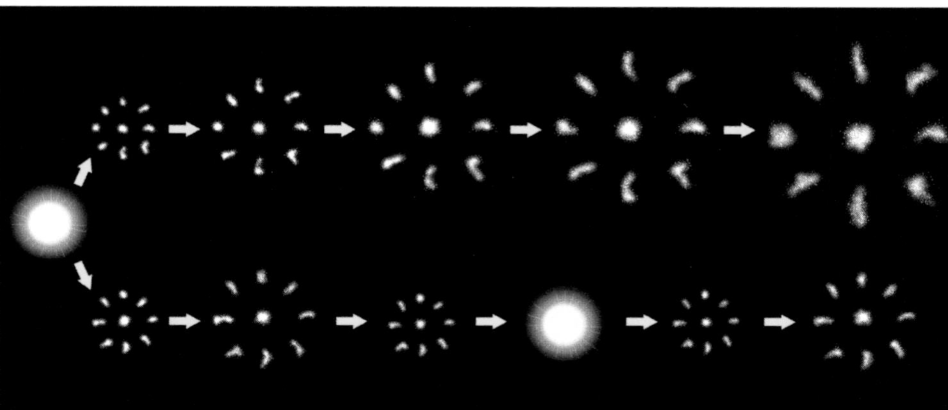

The End of the Universe

The likely fate of the universe is disputed. One theory (shown top left) dictates that the expansion begun at the time of the Big Bang will continue 'indefinitely', with ageing galaxies moving further and further apart in an immense, dark graveyard.

Alternatively, gravity may overcome the expansion (bottom left). Galaxies will fall back together until everything is again concentrated at a single point, followed by a new Big Bang and a new expansion, in an endlessly repeated cycle.

The first of these theories is supported by the amount of visible matter in the universe; the second theory assumes that there is enough dark material to bring about the gravitational collapse.

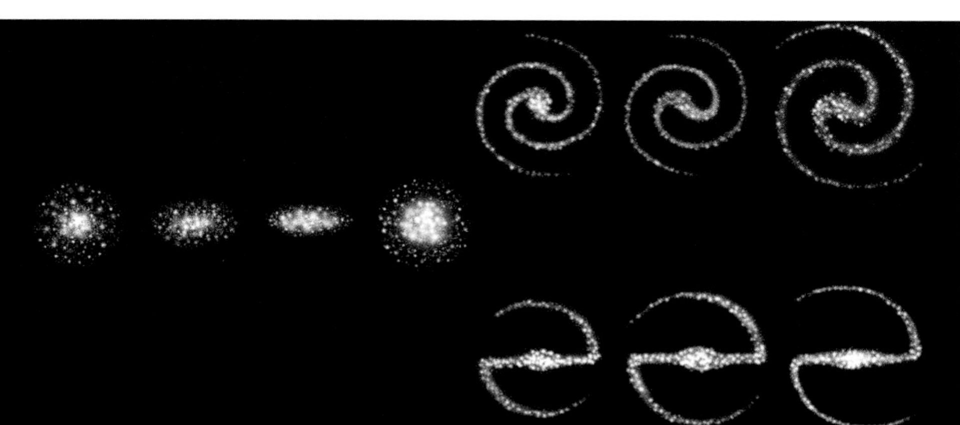

Galactic Structures

Many of the universe's 100 billion galaxies show clear structural patterns, originally classified by the American astronomer Edwin Hubble in 1925. Spiral galaxies like our own (top row) have a central, almost spherical bulge and a surrounding disk composed of spiral arms. Barred spirals (bottom row) have a central bar of stars across the nucleus, with spiral arms trailing from the ends of the bar. Elliptical galaxies (far left) have a uniform appearance, ranging from a flattened disk to a near sphere. So-called SO galaxies (left row, right) have a central bulge, but no spiral arms. Most galaxies, however, have no obvious structure at all.

Galaxies also vary enormously in size, from dwarfs only 2,000 light-years across to great assemblies of stars 80 or more times larger.

The Home Galaxy

The Sun and its planets are located in one of the spiral arms, a little less than 28,000 light-years from the galactic centre and orbiting around it in a period of 200 million years. The centre is invisible from the Earth, masked by vast, light-absorbing clouds of interstellar dust. The galaxy is probably around 12 billion years old and, like other spiral galaxies, has three distinct regions. The central bulge is about 30,000 light-years in diameter. The disk in which the Sun is located is not much more than 1,000 light-years thick but 100,000 light-years from end to end. Around the galaxy is the halo, a spherical zone 300,000 light-years across, studded with globular star-clusters and sprinkled with individual suns.

Star Charts

Star charts are drawn as projections of a vast, hollow sphere with the observer in the middle. Each circle below represents slightly more than one hemisphere, centred on the north and south celestial poles respectively – projections of the Earth's poles in the heavens. At the present era, the north pole is marked by the star Polaris; the south pole has no such convenient reference point.

Astronomical co-ordinates are normally given in terms of 'Right Ascension' for longitude and 'Declination' for latitude or altitude. Since the stars appear to rotate around the Earth once every 24 hours, Right Ascension is measured eastwards – anticlockwise – in hours and minutes and is marked around the edge of the map. One hour is equivalent to 15 angular degrees; zero on the scale is the point at which the Sun crosses the celestial equator at the spring equinox, known to astronomers as the First Point in Aries. Unlike the Sun, stars always rise and set at the same point on the horizon. Declination measures (in degrees) a star's angular distance above or below the celestial equator and is marked on the vertical line.

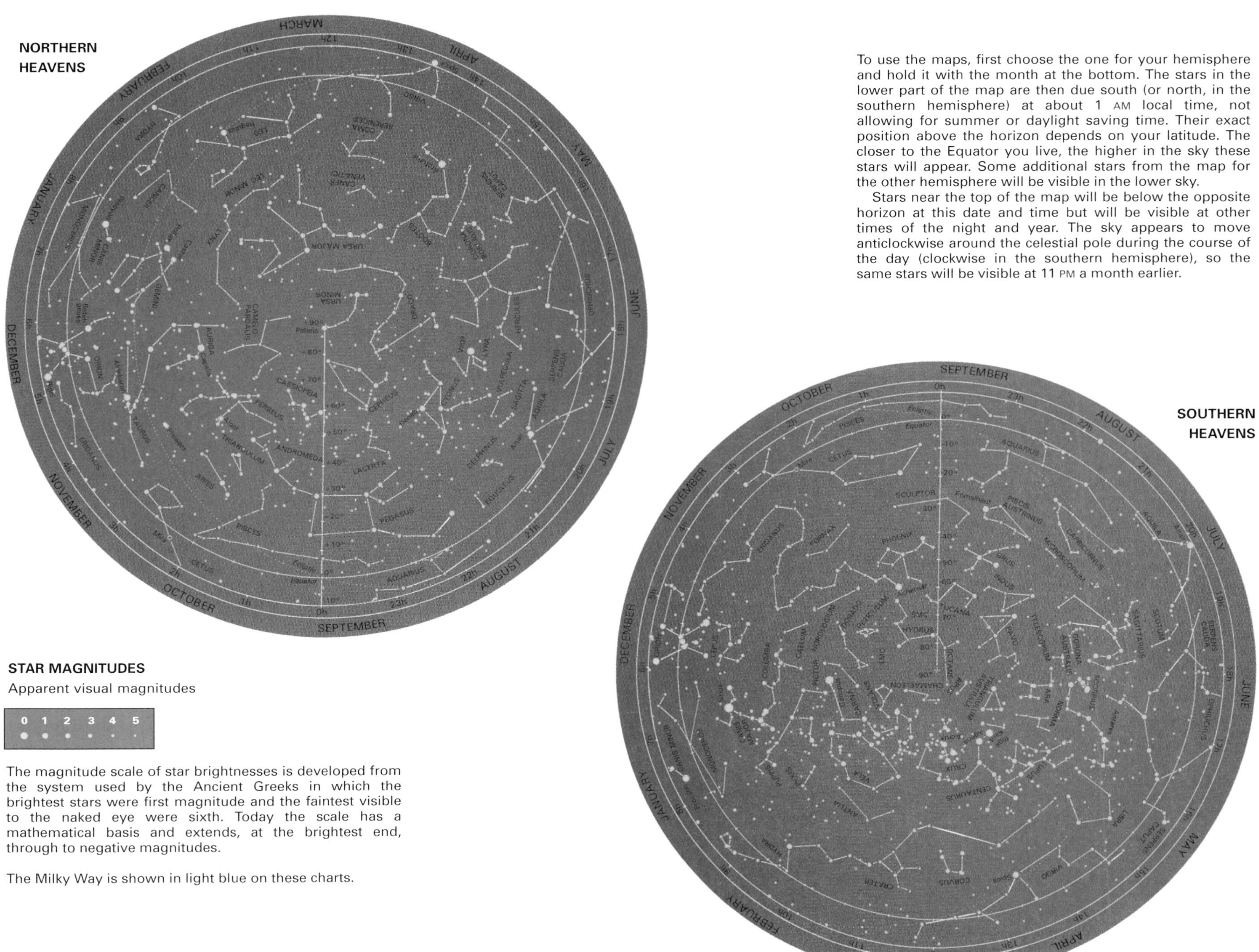

To use the maps, first choose the one for your hemisphere and hold it with the month at the bottom. The stars in the lower part of the map are then due south (or north, in the southern hemisphere) at about 1 AM local time, not allowing for summer or daylight saving time. Their exact position above the horizon depends on your latitude. The closer to the Equator you live, the higher in the sky these stars will appear. Some additional stars from the map for the other hemisphere will be visible in the lower sky.

Stars near the top of the map will be below the opposite horizon at this date and time but will be visible at other times of the night and year. The sky appears to move anticlockwise around the celestial pole during the course of the day (clockwise in the southern hemisphere), so the same stars will be visible at 11 PM a month earlier.

STAR MAGNITUDES

Apparent visual magnitudes

0 1 2 3 4 5

The magnitude scale of star brightnesses is developed from the system used by the Ancient Greeks in which the brightest stars were first magnitude and the faintest visible to the naked eye were sixth. Today the scale has a mathematical basis and extends, at the brightest end, through to negative magnitudes.

The Milky Way is shown in light blue on these charts.

THE NEAREST STARS

The 20 nearest stars, excluding the Sun, with their distance from Earth in light-years*

Proxima Centauri	4.25
Alpha Centauri A	4.3
Alpha Centauri B	4.3
Barnard's Star	6.0
Wolf 359	7.8
Lalande 21185	8.3
Sirius A	8.7
Sirius B	8.7
UV Ceti A	8.7
UV Ceti B	8.7
Ross 154	9.4
Ross 248	10.3
Epsilon Eridani	10.7
Ross 128	10.9
61 Cygni A	11.1
61 Cygni B	11.1
Epsilon Indi	11.2
Groombridge 34A	11.2
Groombridge 34B	11.2
L789-6	11.2
Procyon A	11.4
Procyon B	11.4

Many of the nearest stars, like Alpha Centauri A and B, are doubles, orbiting about the common centre of gravity and to all intents and purposes equidistant from Earth. Many of them are dim objects, with no name other than the designation given by the astronomers who investigated them. However, they include Sirius, the brightest star in the sky, and Procyon, the seventh brightest. Both are far larger than the Sun; of the nearest stars, only Epsilon Eridani is similar in size and luminosity.

* A light-year equals approx. 9,500,000,000,000 kilometres

THE CONSTELLATIONS

The constellations and their English names

Andromeda	Andromeda	Circinus	Compasses	Lacerta	Lizard	Piscis Austrinus	Southern Fish
Antlia	Air Pump	Columba	Dove	Leo	Lion	Puppis	Ship's Stern
Apus	Bird of Paradise	Coma Berenices	Berenice's Hair	Leo Minor	Little Lion	Pyxis	Mariner's Compass
Aquarius	Water Carrier	Corona Australis	Southern Crown	Lepus	Hare	Reticulum	Net
Aquila	Eagle	Corona Borealis	Northern Crown	Libra	Scales	Sagitta	Arrow
Ara	Altar	Corvus	Crow	Lupus	Wolf	Sagittarius	Archer
Aries	Ram	Crater	Cup	Lynx	Lynx	Scorpius	Scorpion
Auriga	Charioteer	Crux	Southern Cross	Lyra	Lyre	Sculptor	Sculptor
Boötes	Herdsman	Cygnus	Swan	Mensa	Table	Scutum	Shield
Caelum	Chisel	Delphinus	Dolphin	Microscopium	Microscope	Serpens	Serpent
Camelopardalis	Giraffe	Dorado	Swordfish	Monoceros	Unicorn	Sextans	Sextant
Cancer	Crab	Draco	Dragon	Musca	Fly	Taurus	Bull
Canes Venatici	Hunting Dogs	Equuleus	Little Horse	Norma	Level	Telescopium	Telescope
Canis Major	Great Dog	Eridanus	Eridanus	Octans	Octant	Triangulum	Triangle
Canis Minor	Little Dog	Fornax	Furnace	Ophiuchus	Serpent Bearer	Triangulum Australe	Southern Triangle
Capricornus	Goat	Gemini	Twins	Orion	Orion	Tucana	Toucan
Carina	Keel	Grus	Crane	Pavo	Peacock	Ursa Major	Great Bear
Cassiopeia	Cassiopeia	Hercules	Hercules	Pegasus	Winged Horse	Ursa Minor	Little Bear
Centaurus	Centaur	Horologium	Clock	Perseus	Perseus	Vela	Sails
Cepheus	Cepheus	Hydra	Water Snake	Phoenix	Phoenix	Virgo	Virgin
Cetus	Whale	Hydrus	Sea Serpent	Pictor	Easel	Volans	Flying Fish
Chamaeleon	Chameleon	Indus	Indian	Pisces	Fishes	Vulpecula	Fox

The Solar System

For more information:
2 The home galaxy
6 The seasons
Day and night
7 The Moon

Lying 28,000 light-years from the centre of one of billions of galaxies that comprise the observable universe, our Solar System contains nine planets and their moons, innumerable asteroids and comets, and a miscellany of dust and gas, all tethered by the immense gravitational field of the Sun, the middling-sized star whose thermonuclear furnaces provide them all with heat and light. The Solar System was formed about 4,600 million years ago, when a spinning cloud of gas, mostly hydrogen but seeded with other, heavier elements, condensed enough to ignite a nuclear reaction and create a star. The Sun still accounts for almost 99.9% of the system's total mass; one planet, Jupiter, contains most of the remainder.

By composition as well as distance, the planetary array divides neatly in two: an inner system of four small, solid planets, including the Earth, and an outer system, from Jupiter to Neptune, of four much larger planets composed of lighter materials, such as gas, liquid and ice. Between the two groups lies a scattering of rocky asteroids, perhaps as many as 400,000. They may be debris left over from the inner solar system's formation. The outermost planet, Pluto, may simply be the largest of a number of bodies composed of rock and ice orbiting beyond Neptune, similarly left over from the formation of the outer solar system.

By the 1990s, however, the Solar System also included some newer anomalies: several thousand spacecraft. Most were in orbit around the Earth, but some had probed far and wide around the system. The valuable information beamed back by these robotic investigators has transformed our knowledge of our celestial environment.

Much of the early history of science is the story of people trying to make sense of the errant points of light that were all they knew of the planets. Now, men have stood on the Earth's Moon; probes have landed on Mars and Venus, and orbiting radars have mapped far distant landscapes with astonishing accuracy. In the 1980s, the US *Voyagers* skimmed all four major planets of the outer system, bringing new revelations with each close approach. Only Pluto, inscrutably distant in an orbit that takes it 50 times the Earth's distance from the Sun, remains unvisited by our messengers.

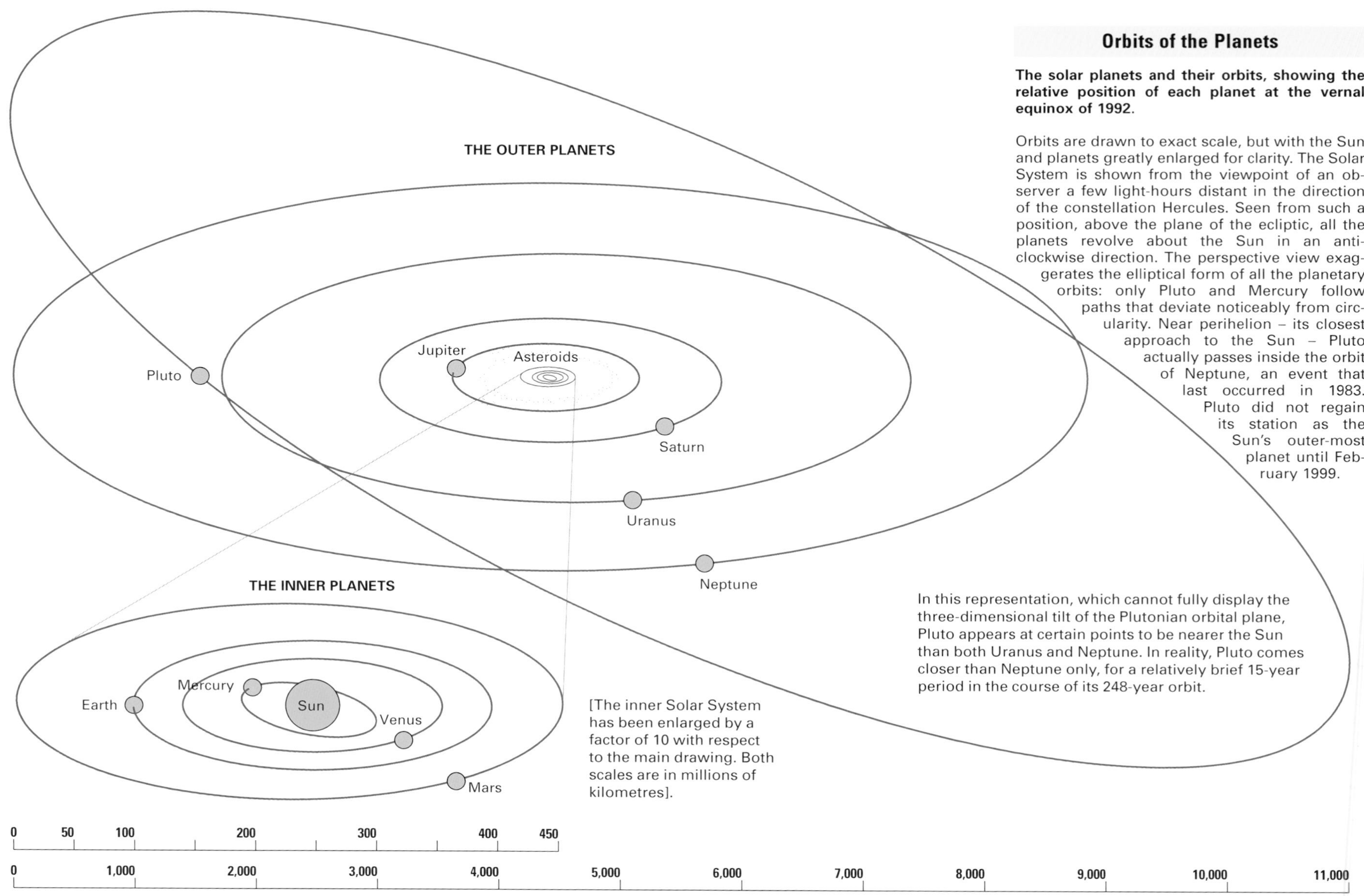

Orbits of the Planets

The solar planets and their orbits, showing the relative position of each planet at the vernal equinox of 1992.

Orbits are drawn to exact scale, but with the Sun and planets greatly enlarged for clarity. The Solar System is shown from the viewpoint of an observer a few light-hours distant in the direction of the constellation Hercules. Seen from such a position, above the plane of the ecliptic, all the planets revolve about the Sun in an anticlockwise direction. The perspective view exaggerates the elliptical form of all the planetary orbits: only Pluto and Mercury follow paths that deviate noticeably from circularity. Near perihelion – its closest approach to the Sun – Pluto actually passes inside the orbit of Neptune, an event that last occurred in 1983. Pluto did not regain its station as the Sun's outer-most planet until February 1999.

In this representation, which cannot fully display the three-dimensional tilt of the Plutonian orbital plane, Pluto appears at certain points to be nearer the Sun than both Uranus and Neptune. In reality, Pluto comes closer than Neptune only, for a relatively brief 15-year period in the course of its 248-year orbit.

[The inner Solar System has been enlarged by a factor of 10 with respect to the main drawing. Both scales are in millions of kilometres].

Planetary Data

	Mean distance from Sun (million km)	Mass (Earth = 1)	Period of orbit (Earth years)	Period of rotation (Earth days)	Equatorial diameter (km)	Average density (water = 1)	Surface gravity (Earth = 1)	Escape velocity (km/sec)	Number of known satellites
Sun	–	*332,946*	–	*25.38*	*1,392,000*	*1.41*	*27.9*	*617.5*	–
Mercury	57.9	0.06	0.241	58.67	4,878	5.43	0.38	4.25	0
Venus	108.2	0.8	0.615	243.00	12,100	5.24	0.90	10.36	0
Earth	149.6	1.0	1.00	1.00	12,756	5.52	1.00	11.18	1
Mars	227.9	0.1	1.88	1.02	6,794	3.93	0.38	5.03	2
Jupiter	778.3	317.8	11.86	0.41	142,800	1.33	2.69	59.60	16
Saturn	1,426.8	95.2	29.46	0.42	120,000	0.706	1.16	35.60	18
Uranus	2,869.4	14.5	84.01	0.45	52,400	1.25	0.93	21.10	15
Neptune	4,496.3	17.1	164.79	0.71	48,400	1.77	1.21	24.60	8
Pluto	5,900.1	0.002	247.7	6.39	2,445	1.40	0.05	1.20	1

Planetary days are given in sidereal time – that is, with respect to the stars rather than the Sun. Most of the information in the table was confirmed by spacecraft and often obtained from photographs and other data transmitted back to the Earth. In the case of Pluto, however, only earthbound observations have been made, and no spacecraft will encounter it until well into the 21st century. Given the planet's small size and great distance, figures for its diameter and rotation period have only recently been confirmed.

Pluto is not massive enough to account for the perturbations in the orbits of Uranus and Neptune that led to its 1930 discovery, but it is now widely believed that these perturbations can be explained away as observational errors made by the earlier observers.

The Planets

Mercury is the closest planet to the Sun and hence the fastest-moving. It is very hot with a cratered, wrinkled surface very similar to that of Earth's Moon. It is small and has no gravity, hence there is no significant atmosphere.

Venus has much the same physical dimensions as Earth. Its dense atmosphere is composed of 97% CO_2 resulting in a runaway greenhouse effect that makes the Venusian surface, at 475°C, the hottest of all the planets in the Solar System. Radar mapping shows relatively level land with volcanic regions whose sulphurous discharges explain the sulphuric acid rains reported by soft-landing space probes before they succumbed to Venus' fierce climate.

Earth seen from space is easily the most beautiful of the inner planets; it is also, and more objectively, the largest, as well as the only home of known life. Living things are the main reason why the Earth is able to retain a substantial proportion of corrosive and highly reactive oxygen in its atmosphere, a state of affairs that contradicts the laws of chemical equilibrium; the oxygen in turn supports the life that constantly regenerates it.

Mars, smaller and cooler than the Earth, is nevertheless the most likely planet other than Earth where life may have formed. Vast water channels show that it was once warmer and wetter; there may still be traces of former simple life forms, though whether life could thrive in its current cold, dry and thin atmosphere is doubtful. The ice caps are mainly frozen carbon dioxide, and whatever oxygen the planet once possessed is now locked up in the iron-bearing rock that covers its cratered surface and gives it its characteristic red hue. Mars is a dustbowl with occasional storms whirling the dust high into the air.

Jupiter masses almost three times as much as all the other planets combined; had it scooped up rather more matter during its formation, it might have evolved into a small companion star for the Sun. The planet is mostly gas, under intense pressure in the lower atmosphere above a core of fiercely compressed hydrogen and helium. The upper layers form strikingly-coloured rotating belts, the outward sign of the intense storms created by Jupiter's rapid diurnal rotation. Close approaches by spacecraft have shown an orbiting ring system and discovered several previously unknown moons: Jupiter has at least 16 moons.

Saturn is structurally similar to Jupiter, rotating fast enough to produce an obvious bulge at its equator. It is composed of 89% hydrogen and 11% helium, and has wind velocities in the outer atmosphere of 500 metres per second. Ever since the invention of the telescope, however, Saturn's rings have been the feature that has attracted most observers. *Voyager* probes in 1980 and 1981 sent back detailed pictures that showed them to be composed of thousands of separate ringlets, each in turn made up of tiny icy particles.

Uranus was unknown to the ancients. Although it is faintly visible to the naked eye, it was not discovered until 1781. Its interior is largely water, with an atmosphere of hydrogen, helium and some methane, which gives the planet its blue-green colour. Observations in 1977 suggested the presence of a faint ring system, amply confirmed when *Voyager 2* swung past the planet in 1986.

Neptune is always more than 4,000 million km from Earth, and despite its diameter of almost 50,000 km, it can only be seen by telescope. Its 1846 discovery was the result of mathematical predictions by astronomers seeking to explain irregularities in the orbit of Uranus, but until *Voyager 2* closed with the planet in 1989, little was known of it. Like Uranus, it has a ring system; *Voyager*'s photographs revealed a total of eight moons.

Pluto is the most mysterious of the solar planets, if only because even the most powerful telescopes can scarcely resolve it from a point of light to a disk. It was discovered as recently as 1930, like Neptune as the result of perturbations in the orbits of the two then outermost planets. Its small size, as well as its eccentric and highly tilted orbit, has led to suggestions that it is a former satellite of Neptune, somehow liberated from its primary. In 1978 Pluto was found to have a moon of its own, Charon, apparently half the size of Pluto itself.

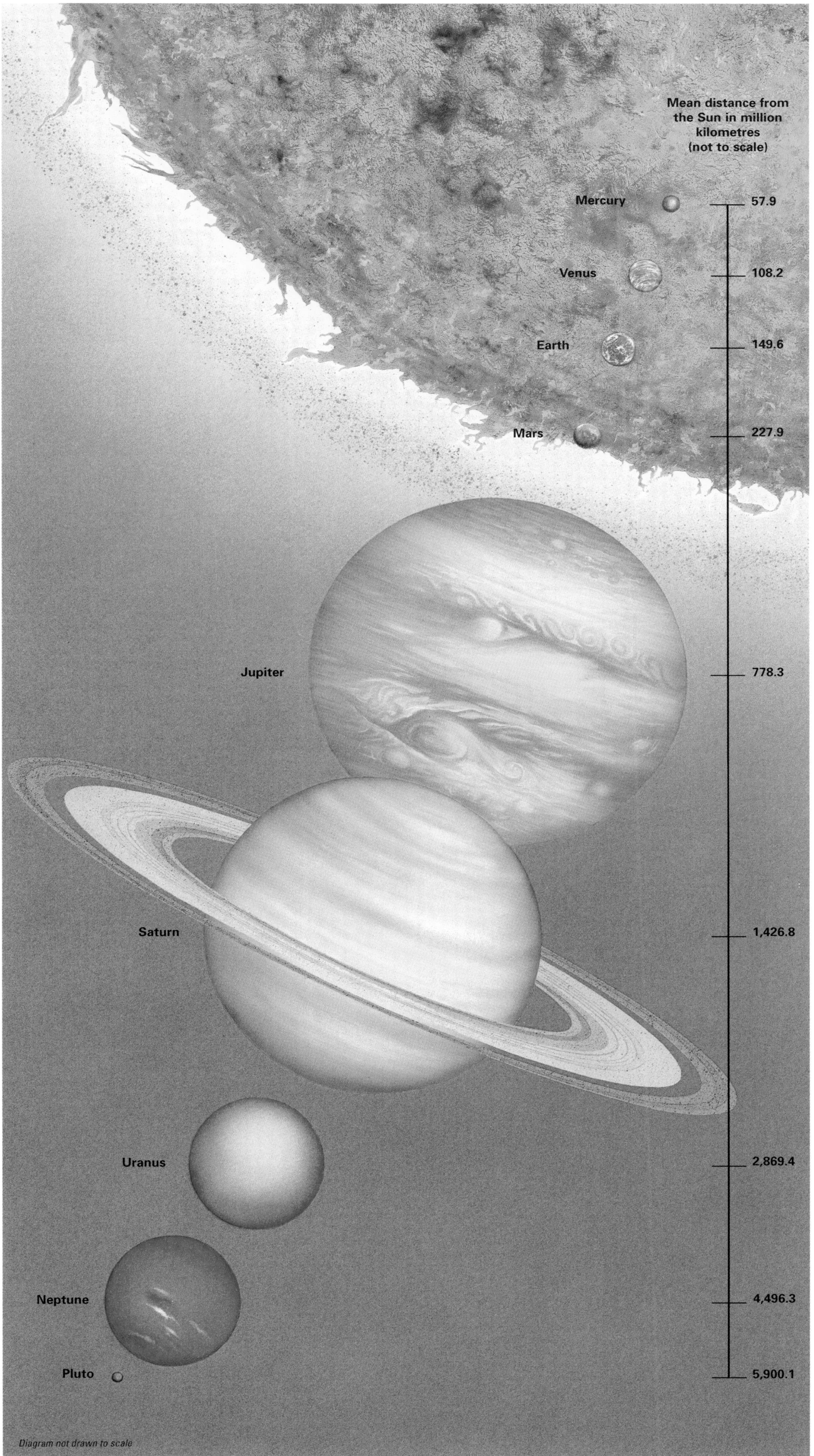

Time and Motion

For more information:

4 Orbits of the planets
9 Ocean currents
14 Circulation of the air
16 Climate

The basic unit of time measurement is the day, that is, one rotation of the Earth on its axis. Our present calendar is based on the solar year of 365.24 days, the time taken by the Earth to orbit the Sun.

Calendars based on the movements of the Sun and Moon have been used since ancient times. The average length of the year, according to the Julian Calendar introduced by Julius Caesar, was about 11 minutes too long. The cumulative error was rectified in 1582 by the Gregorian Calendar, when Pope Gregory XIII decreed that the day following 4 October was 15 October, and in that century years did not count as leap years unless they were divisible by 400. England finally adopted the reformed calendar in 1752, when it was 11 days behind the European mainland.

The rotation of the Earth on its axis causes day and night. Because the Earth rotates through 360° every 24 hours, the world is divided into 24 time zones centred on lines of longitude at 15° longitude.

The tilt of the Earth's axis, also called the obliquity of the ecliptic, accounts for the seasons which are so familiar in the middle latitudes. But geological evidence shows that, over long periods of time, climates change and the advances and retreats of the ice during the Pleistocene Ice Age may have been caused by regular variations in the Earth's tilt, its orbit around the Sun, and changes in the season when it is closest to the Sun (perihelion).

Earth Data

Aphelion (maximum distance from Sun): 152,007,016 km

Perihelion (minimum distance from Sun): 147,000,830 km

Angle of tilt (obliquity of the ecliptic): 23° 27′ 08″

Length of year – solar tropical (equinox to equinox): 365.24 days

Length of year: 365 days, 5 hours, 48 minutes, 46 seconds of mean solar time

Superficial area: 510,000,000 sq km

Land surface: 149,000,000 sq km (29.2%)

Water surface: 361,000,000 sq km (70.8%)

Equatorial circumference: 40,077 km

Polar circumference: 40,009 km

Equatorial diameter: 12,756.8 km

Polar diameter: 12,713.8 km

Equatorial radius: 6,378.4 km

Polar radius: 6,356.9 km

Volume of the Earth: 1,083,230 x 10^6 cu km

Mass of the Earth: 5.9 x 10^{21} tonnes

Spring/Vernal Equinox
Northern spring, southern autumn
Equinox is one of the two times in the year when day and night are of equal length due to the Sun being overhead at the Equator
Summer Solstice
Winter Solstice
21 March
21 June
SUN
22 December
23 September
Northern summer, southern winter
Northern winter, southern summer
Autumnal Equinox
Northern autumn, southern spring
Solstice is one of the two times in the year when the Sun is overhead at one of the Tropics, 23½° north or south of the Equator

The Seasons

Seasons occur because the Earth's axis is tilted at a constant angle of 23½°. When the northern hemisphere is tilted to a maximum extent towards the Sun, on 21 June, the Sun is overhead at the Tropic of Cancer (latitude 23½° North). This is midsummer, or the summer solstice, in the northern hemisphere.

On 22 or 23 September, the Sun is overhead at the Equator, and day and night are of equal length throughout the world. This is the autumn equinox in the northern hemisphere. On 21 or 22 December, the Sun is overhead at the Tropic of Capricorn (23½° South), the winter solstice in the northern hemisphere. The overhead Sun then tracks north until, on 21 March, it is overhead at the Equator. This is the spring (vernal) equinox in the northern hemisphere.

In the southern hemisphere, the seasons are the reverse of those in the north.

Day and Night

The Sun appears to rise in the east, reach its highest point at noon, and then set in the west, to be followed by night. In reality, it is not the Sun that is moving but the Earth rotating from west to east. The moment when the Sun's upper limb first appears above the horizon is termed sunrise; the moment when the Sun's upper limb disappears below the horizon is sunset.

At the summer solstice in the northern hemisphere (21 June), the Arctic has total daylight and the Antarctic total darkness. The opposite occurs at the winter solstice (21 or 22 December). At the Equator, the length of day and night are almost equal all year.

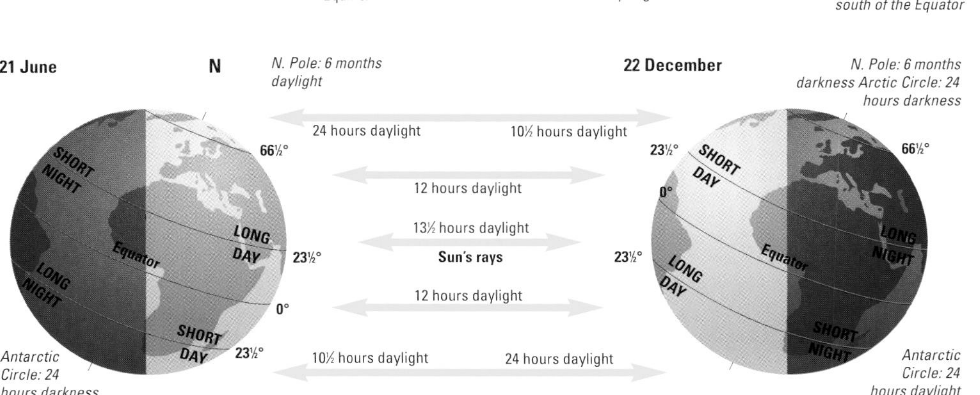

The Sun's Path

The diagrams on the right illustrate the apparent path of the Sun at (A) the Equator, (B) in mid-latitude (45°), (C) at the Arctic Circle (66½°), and (D) at the North Pole, where there are six months of continuous daylight and six months of continuous night.

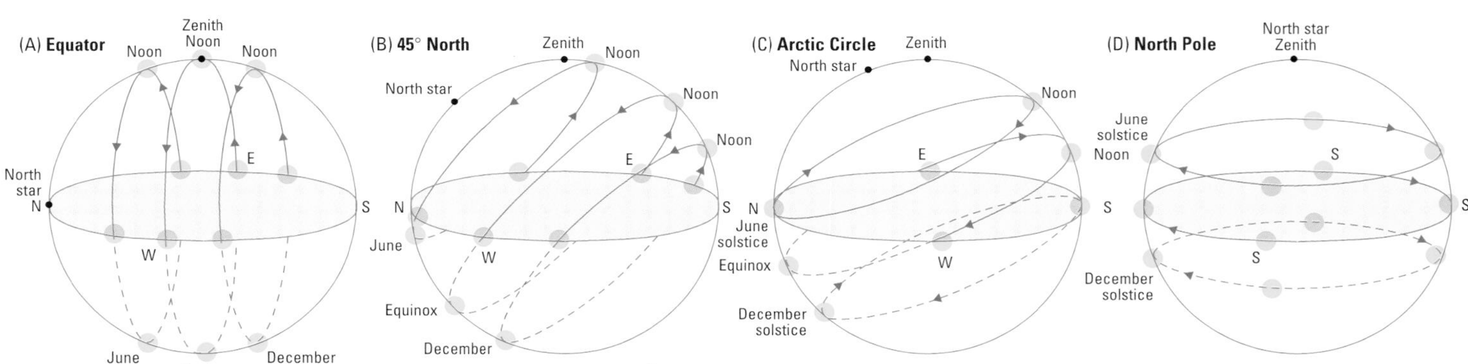

Sunrise and Sunset

The term equinox comes from two Latin words meaning 'equal night'. At the spring and autumn equinoxes, the Sun is vertically overhead at the Equator and all places on Earth have 12 hours of darkness and 12 of daylight. The graphs showing sunrise and sunset show that these occasions occur on 21 March and on 22 or 23 September. The graphs also show that, because the Sun remains high in the sky throughout the year, the length of the day and night at the Equator remain roughly the same throughout the year, with sunrise occurring around 6 AM and sunset at around 6 PM. The further north or south one travels, the greater the difference between the number of hours of daylight and darkness. For example, the graph, right, shows that at latitude 60°N, sunrise varies from just after 9 AM in midwinter (on 22 or 23 December) to about 2.30 AM in midsummer (around the summer solstice on 21 June). By contrast, the second graph, far right, shows that sunset at latitude 60°N occurs at about 2.45 PM in midwinter and 9.20 PM in midsummer.

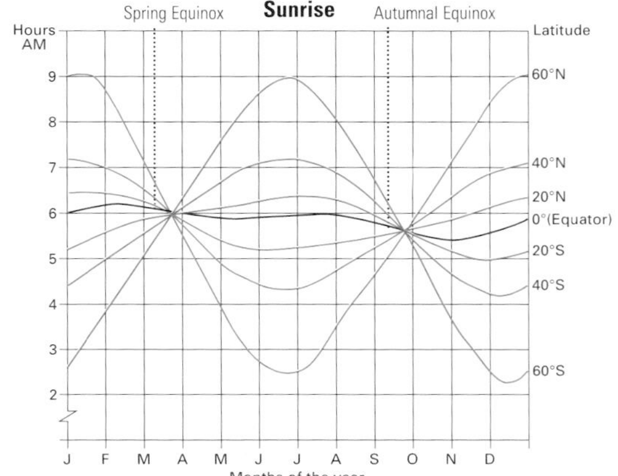

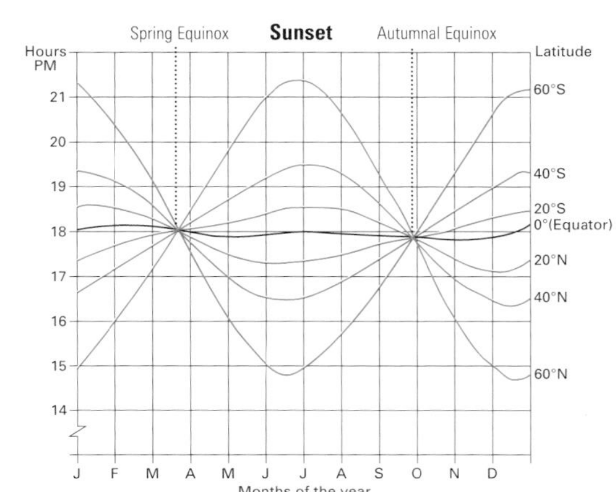

The Moon

The Moon rotates more slowly than the Earth, making one complete turn on its axis in just over 27 days. Since this corresponds to its period of revolution around the Earth, the Moon always presents the same hemisphere or face to us, and we never see 'the dark side'. The interval between one full Moon and the next (and between new Moons) is about 29½ days – a lunar month. The apparent changes in the shape of the Moon are caused by its changing position in relation to the Earth; like the planets, it produces no light of its own and shines by reflecting the rays of the Sun.

Phases of the Moon

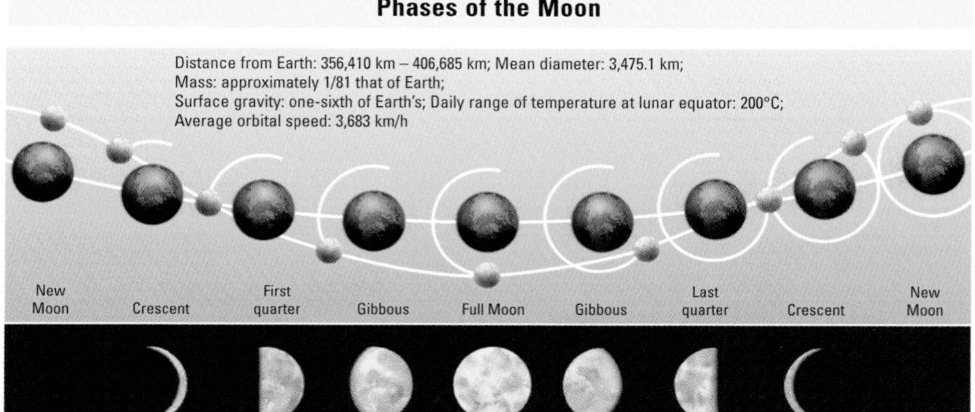

Moon Data

Distance from Earth

The Moon orbits at a mean distance of 384,199.1 km, at an average speed of 3,683 km/h in relation to the Earth.

Size and mass

The average diameter of the Moon is 3,475.1 km. It is 400 times smaller than the Sun but is about 400 times closer to the Earth, so we see them as the same size. The Moon has a mass of 7,348 x 10^{19} tonnes, with a density 3.344 times that of water.

Visibility

Only 59% of the Moon's surface is directly visible from Earth. Reflected light takes 1.25 seconds to reach Earth – compared to 8 minutes 27.3 seconds for light to reach us from the Sun.

Temperature

With the Sun overhead, the temperature on the lunar equator can reach 117.2°C [243°F]. At night it can sink to –162.7°C [–261°F].

Eclipses

When the Moon passes between the Sun and the Earth it causes a partial eclipse of the Sun (1) if the Earth passes through the Moon's outer shadow (P), or a total eclipse (2) if the inner cone shadow crosses the Earth's surface. In a lunar eclipse, the Earth's shadow crosses the Moon and, again, provides either a partial or total eclipse.

Eclipses of the Sun and the Moon do not occur every month because of the 5° difference between the plane of the Moon's orbit and the plane in which the Earth moves. In the 1990s only 14 lunar eclipses were possible, for example, seven partial and seven total; each was visible only from certain, and variable, parts of the world. The same period witnessed 13 solar eclipses – six partial (or annular) and seven total.

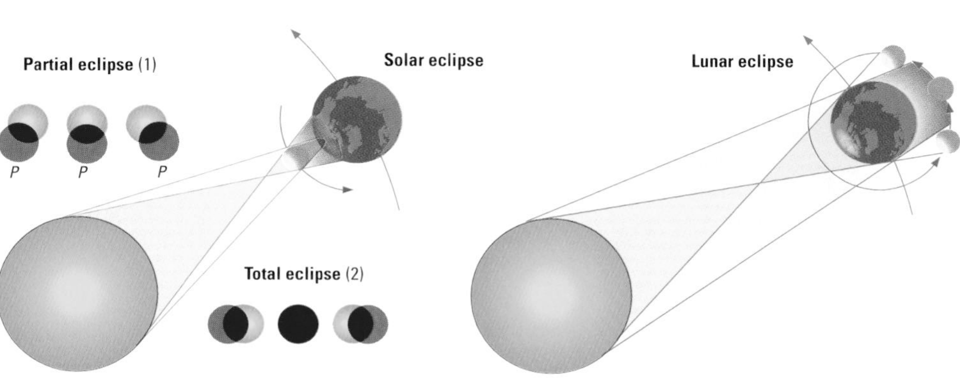

Tides

The daily rise and fall of the ocean's tides are the result of the gravitational pull of the Moon and that of the Sun, though the effect of the latter is only 46.6% as strong as that of the Moon. This effect is greatest on the hemisphere facing the Moon and causes a tidal 'bulge'. When the Sun, Earth and Moon are in line, tide-raising forces are at a maximum and Spring tides occur: high tide reaches the highest values, and low tide falls to low levels. When lunar and solar forces are least coincidental with the Sun and Moon at an angle (near the Moon's first and third quarters), Neap tides occur, which have a small tidal range.

Spring tide
Neap tide
Spring tide
Last quarter
New Moon
Full Moon
Neap tide
Gravitational pull by the Sun
First quarter

Time Zones

The Earth rotates through 360° in 24 hours, and so moves 15° every hour. The world is divided into 24 standard time zones, each centred on lines of longitude at 15° intervals. At the centre of the first zone is the Prime meridian or Greenwich meridian. All places to the west of Greenwich are one hour behind for every 15° of longitude; places to the east are ahead by one hour for every 15°. When it is 12 noon at the Greenwich meridian, 180° east it is midnight of the same day – while 180° west the day is just beginning. To overcome this, the International Date Line was established, approximately following the 180° meridian. Thus, if you travelled eastwards from Japan (140° East) to Samoa (170° West), you would pass from Sunday night into Sunday morning.

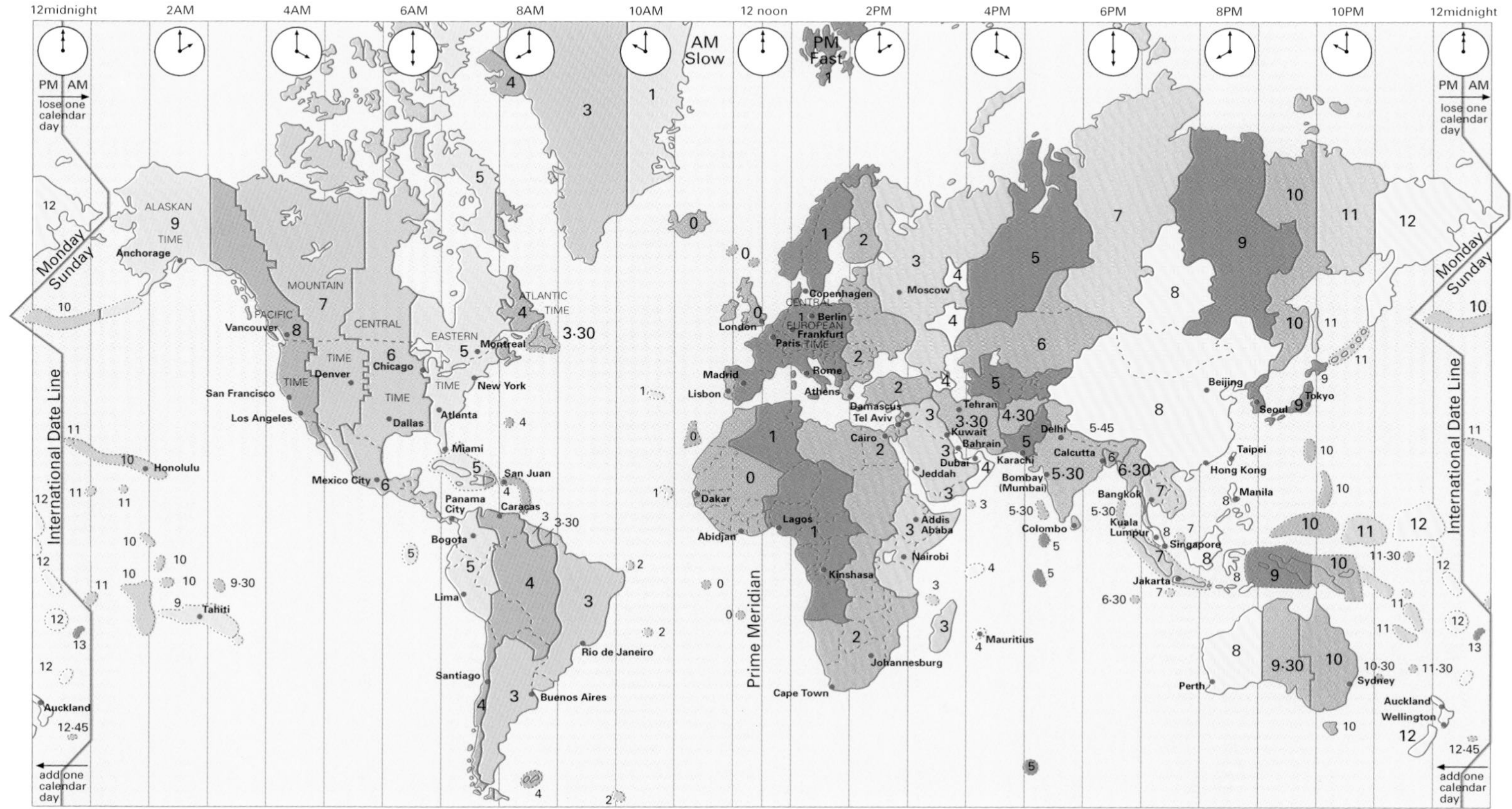

Projection: Mercator

Oceans

For more information:
- 7 Tides
- 10 The spreading Earth
- 14 Atmosphere
- 18 Hydrological cycle
  Water distribution
- 19 Watersheds
- 23 Water pollution
- 41 Shipping

The last 40 years have been described as the 'Space Age', but another exciting and perhaps even more important area of discovery, proceeding at the same time, has been the exploration of 'inner space', namely the oceans which cover more than 70% of our planet. The study of the ocean floor and oceanic islands has revealed features that help to explain how continents move, and how the movements are related to earthquakes and volcanic activity.

Manned submersibles have established that life exists even in the deepest trenches, where the pressure reaches 1,000 atmospheres, the equivalent of the force of one tonne bearing down on every square centimetre. Further exploration in the pitch-black environment of the ocean ridges has revealed strange forms of marine life around scalding hot vents. The creatures include giant tubeworms, blind shrimps, and bacteria, some of which are genetically very different from any other known life forms. In 1996, an analysis of one micro-organism revealed that at least half of its 1,700 or so genes were hitherto unknown. This environment, which is based on chemicals, not sunlight, may resemble the places where life on Earth first began.

Another vital area of contemporary research concerns the interactions between the oceans and the atmosphere, as exemplified in the El Niño–Southern Oscillation (ENSO), and the bearing that these have on climatic change.

Most geographers divide the world's ocean waters into four areas: the Pacific, Atlantic, Indian and Arctic oceans. The most active zone in the oceans is the sunlit upper layer, where the water is moved around by wind-blown currents. It is the home of most sea life and acts as a membrane through which the ocean breathes, absorbing great quantities of carbon dioxide and partly exchanging it for oxygen.

As the depth increases, so light fades and temperatures fall until just before 1,000 metres where there is a marked temperature change at the thermocline, the boundary between the warm surface zone and the cold deep zone. Below the thermocline, slow currents are caused by density differences between bodies of water with varying temperatures and salinity.

Seawater

The chemical composition of the sea, by percentage, excluding the elements of water itself

Chloride (Cl)	55.04%
Sodium (Na)	30.61%
Sulphate (SO_4)	7.69%
Magnesium (Mg)	3.69%
Calcium (Ca)	1.16%
Potassium (K)	1.10%
Bicarbonate (HCO_3)	0.41%
Bromide (Br)	0.19%
Boric Acid (H_3BO_3)	0.07%
Strontium (Sr)	0.04%
Fluoride (Fl)	0.003%
Lithium (Li)	trace
Rubidium (Rb)	trace
Phosphorus (P)	trace
Iodine (I)	trace
Barium (Ba)	trace
Arsenic (As)	trace
Cesium (Cs)	trace

Eleven constituents account for over 99% of the salt content of seawater, but seawater also contains virtually every other element. In natural conditions, its composition is broadly consistent across the world's seas and oceans; but in coastal areas especially, variations are sometimes substantial. The oceans are about 35 parts water to one part salt.

Life in the Oceans

An imaginary profile of the typical coastal and oceanic zones is shown, with a selection of the life forms that might occur in the water off the Pacific Coast of Central America. The animals illustrated are not drawn to scale as the range of sizes is too great. Most marine life is confined to the first 200 metres, the upper sunlit (photic) zone, where sunlight can still penetrate. Plant and animal plankton, the basis of life in the ocean, occur in great quantities in all zones.

In the pelagic environment (open sea), vertical gradients, including those of light, temperature and salinity, determine the distribution of organisms. From the tidal zone at the coastline, the continental shelf, geologically still part of the continental landmass, drops gently to about 200 metres – the sunlit zone. At the end of the shelf, the seabed falls away in the steeper angle of the continental slope. The subsequent descent to the deep ocean floor, known as the continental rise, is more gentle, with gradients between 1 in 100 and 1 in 700 until the abyssal plains and hills between 2,500 and 6,000 metres below the surface.

The deep sea floor contains seamounts, some of which are capped by coral reefs, ocean ridges, the longest mountain chains on Earth, and deep ocean trenches, especially in the Pacific Ocean where six trenches reach depths of more than 10,000 metres, including the 11,022-metre deep Mariana Trench.

Each of these zones contains a distinctive community of species adapted to the different conditions of salinity, temperature and light intensity. Indeed, a few organisms have been found even in the abyssal darkness of the great ocean trenches.

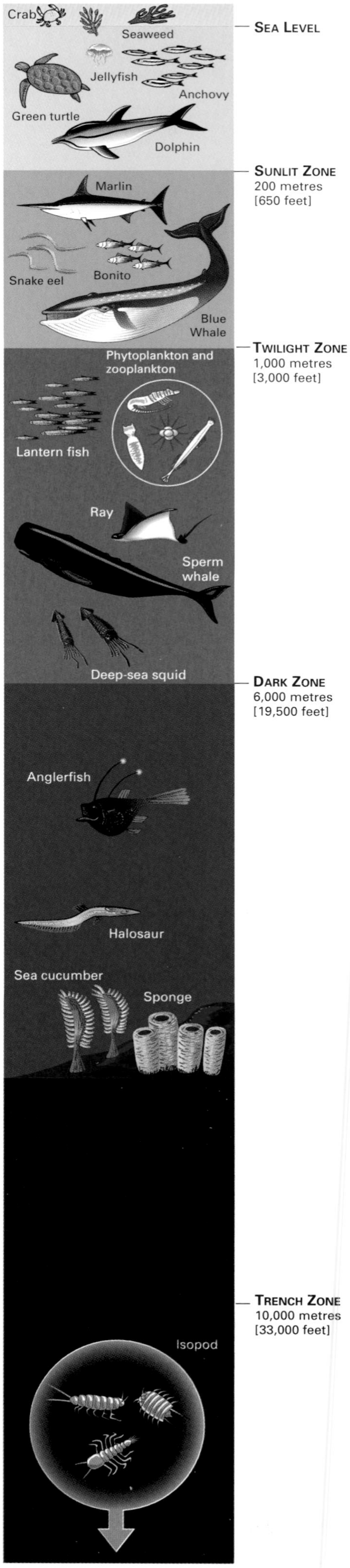

Crab
Seaweed
Jellyfish
Anchovy
Green turtle
Dolphin
SEA LEVEL
Marlin
Snake eel
Bonito
Blue Whale
SUNLIT ZONE 200 metres [650 feet]
Phytoplankton and zooplankton
Lantern fish
Ray
Sperm whale
Deep-sea squid
TWILIGHT ZONE 1,000 metres [3,000 feet]
Anglerfish
Halosaur
Sea cucumber
Sponge
DARK ZONE 6,000 metres [19,500 feet]
Isopod
TRENCH ZONE 10,000 metres [33,000 feet]

Atoll Building

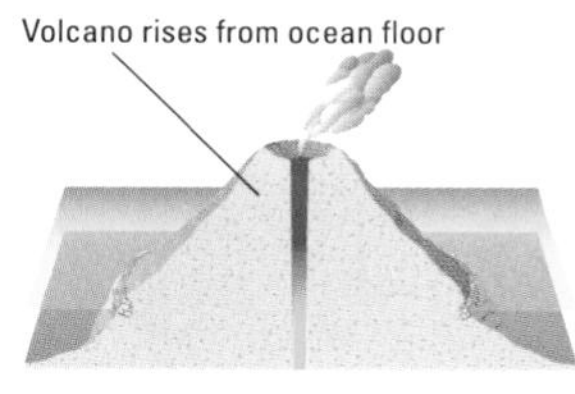

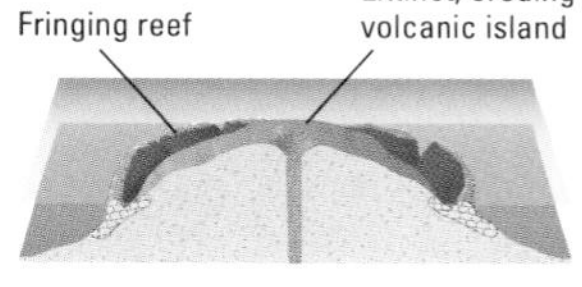

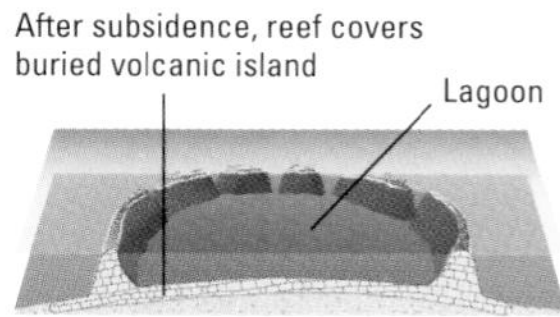

A coral atoll usually begins existence as a bare volcanic peak, thrusting above the surface of the ocean. A colony of coral – organisms with calcium carbonate skeletons – forms itself in the shallow water around the peak. The volcano is eroded and slowly sinks, leaving the coral forming a ring of hard limestone around its remnant. In time, the barrier reef of an atoll is all that remains.

The El Niño Phenomenon

The importance of the ocean–atmosphere interaction is nowhere more dramatically demonstrated than the El Niño phenomenon in the southern Pacific Ocean.

Under normal conditions, shown in the diagram, top right, surface water flows eastwards from South America under the influence of trade winds while, near the coast, cold, nutrient-rich water (dark blue) rises to the surface and spreads westwards. In the western Pacific, sea surface temperatures reach 28°C or more and warm air rises, creating a low pressure air system and causing heavy rains. The rising warm air spreads out and some of it descends over South America and the eastern Pacific creating a high pressure air system from which winds blow westwards. This rotating system is called a Walker Circulation Cell.

An El Niño event, also called an El Niño–Southern Oscillation cycle, or ENSO cycle, is characterized by a reversal of currents whereby the eastward-moving South Equatorial Current extends much further eastwards and the trade winds weaken. The upwelling of cold water off South America is greatly reduced and surface water temperatures rise, causing a drastic reduction in fish life. The heaviest rainfall is over the eastern Pacific, while South-east Asia is much drier than usual. Warm air rises in the east and spreads out, descending in the western Pacific, which then becomes a high pressure area, as shown on the second diagram, below right.

During an intense El Niño, such as in 1982–83 when sea temperatures in the eastern Pacific rose by 6°C, the effects of the current and wind reversals affect the weather around the world. In Australia and South-east Asia, the monsoon rainfall is reduced, while, in 1983–84, a severe drought occurred in the Sahel, south of the Sahara, and also in southern Africa. The south-east coast of the United States also suffered storms and heavy rainfall, and even Europe experienced changes in weather patterns, possibly as a result of consequent changes in the course of the jet stream.

Scientists have found evidence that the frequency of the El Niño event, which normally occurs every two to seven years, may have increased in recent years with warm conditions persisting in the eastern Pacific from 1990 until mid-1995, an unprecedented length of time during the 114 years for which data exist. Another intense El Niño occurred in 1997–98, with resultant freak weather conditions across the entire Pacific region. Scientists do not know the causes of the El Niño event, though some researchers are investigating possible connections between major volcanic eruptions in the tropical Pacific region, the ENSO cycle and atmospheric circulation.

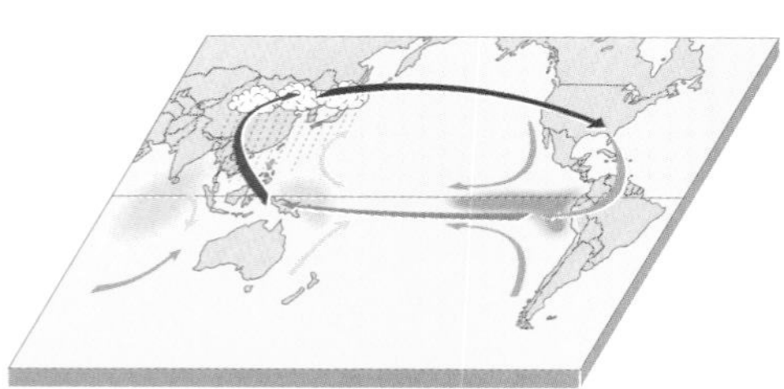

Normal year – Walker Circulation Cell

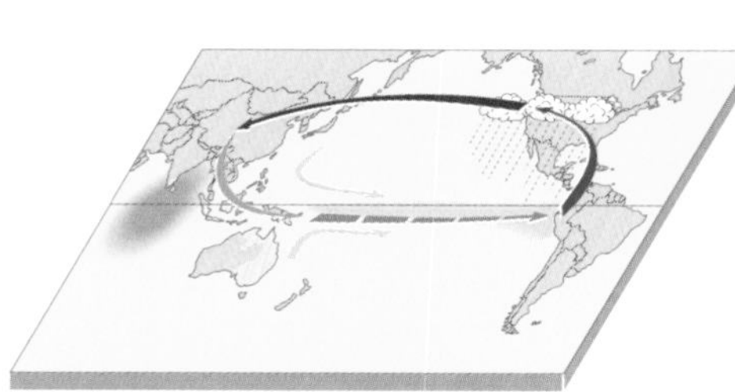
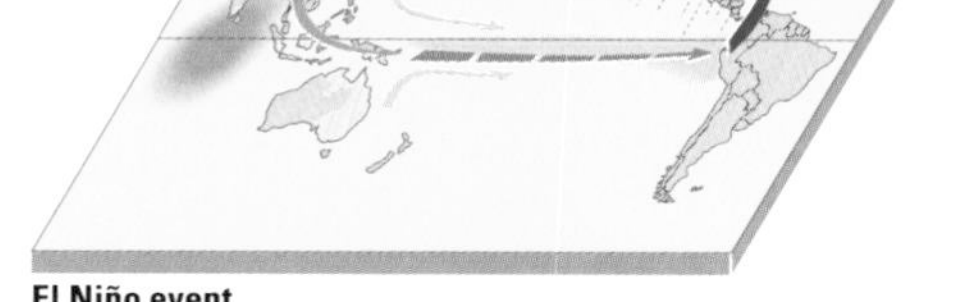

El Niño event

Ocean Currents

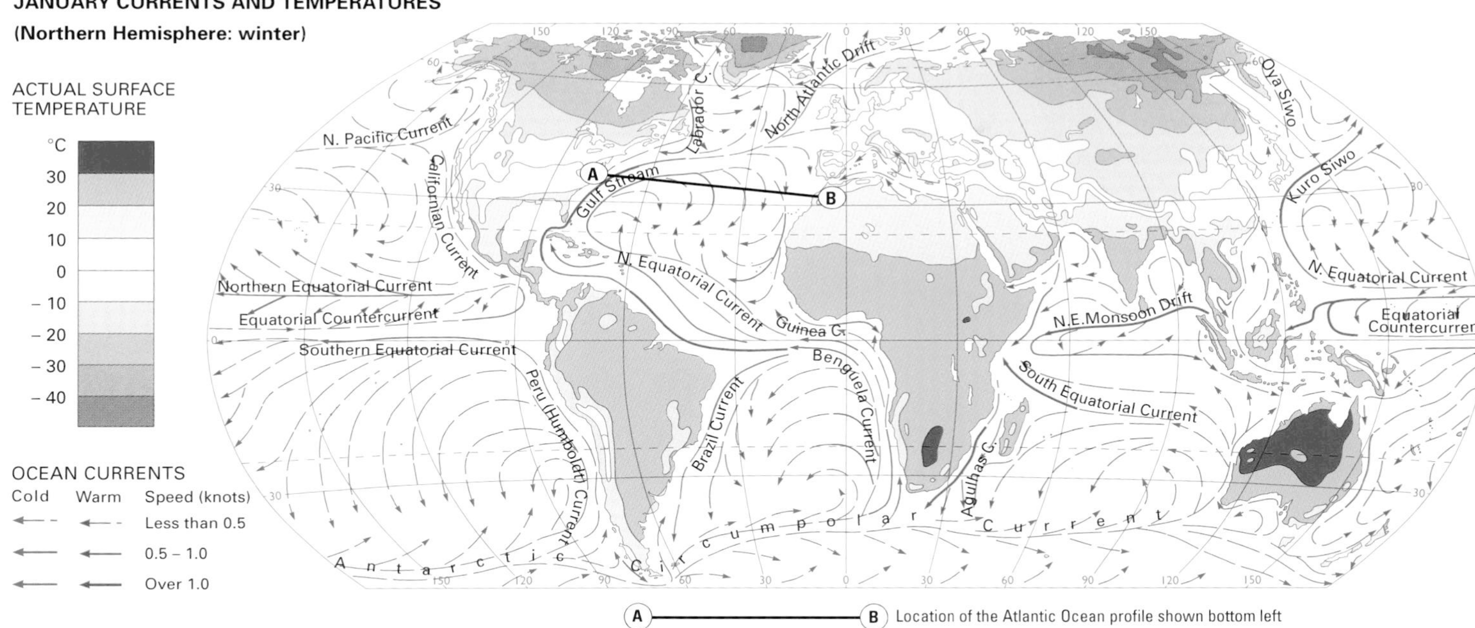

A — B Location of the Atlantic Ocean profile shown bottom left

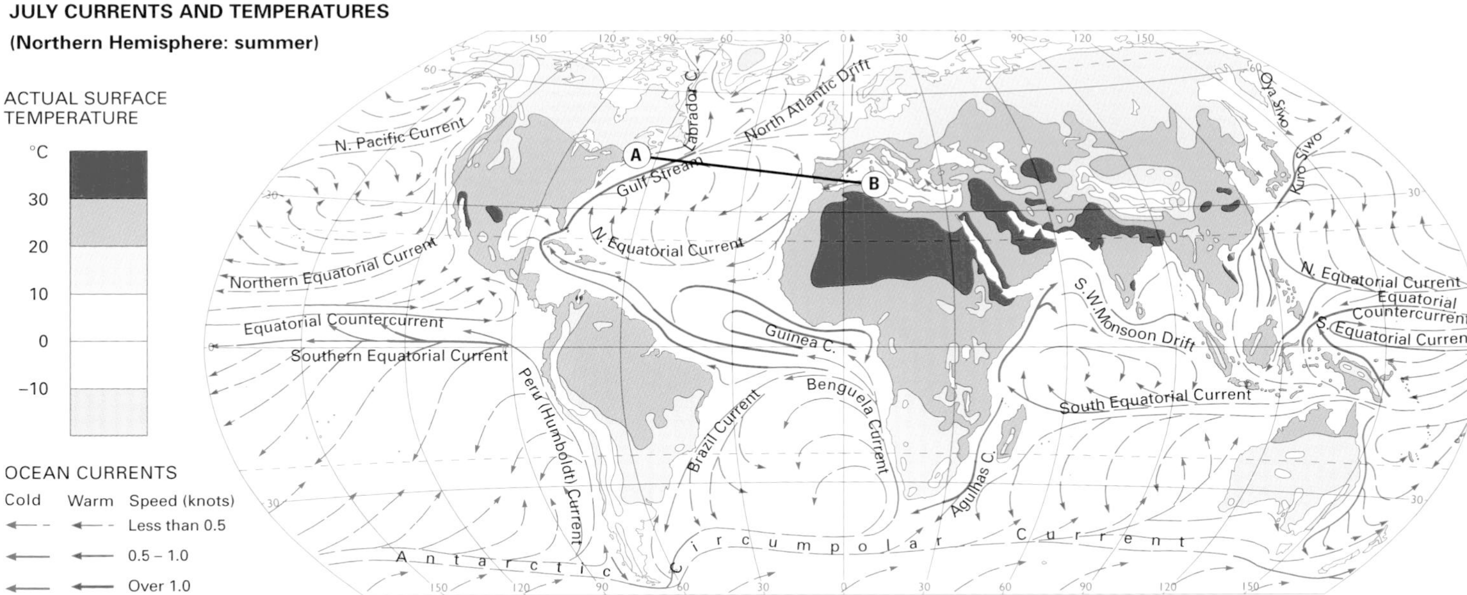

Moving immense quantities of energy as well as billions of tonnes of water every hour, the ocean currents are a vital part of the great heat engine that drives the Earth's climate. They themselves are produced by a twofold mechanism. At the surface, winds push huge masses of water before them; in the deep ocean, below an abrupt temperature gradient that separates the churning surface waters from the still depths, density variations cause slow vertical movements.

The pattern of circulation of the great surface currents is determined by the displacement known as the Coriolis effect. As the Earth turns beneath a moving object – whether it is a tennis ball or a vast mass of water – it appears to be deflected to one side. The deflection is most obvious near the Equator, where the Earth's surface is spinning eastwards at 1,700 km/h; currents moving polewards are curved clockwise in the northern hemisphere and anti-clockwise in the southern.

The result is a system of spinning circles known as gyres. Warm currents move constantly from the Equator towards the poles, while cold water moves in the reverse direction. In this way, ocean currents act like a thermostat, helping to regulate temperatures around the world.

Depending on the annual movements of the prevailing wind belts, some currents on or near the Equator may reverse their direction in the course of the year, a variation on which Asia's monsoon rains depend and whose occasional failure has brought disaster to millions of people.

Topography of the Ocean Floor

Profile of the Atlantic Ocean

The deep ocean floor was once believed to be flat, but maps compiled from readings made by sonar equipment show that it is no more uniform than the surface of the continents. The profile, below, shows some of the features on the Atlantic Ocean floor between Massachusetts in North America and Gibraltar (for location of profile, see maps above). Around the continents are shallow continental shelves composed of rocks which are less dense than the underlying oceanic crust. The continents end at the top of the steep continental slope, which descends to the abyss via the continental rise, made up of sediments washed down from the continental shelves. The abyss contains large plains overlain by oozes but the plains are broken by volcanic seamounts and guyots (flat-topped seamounts), a few of which reach the surface as islands. The other main feature is the Mid-Atlantic Ridge, through which runs a rift valley where new crustal rock is being formed as the plates on either side move apart.

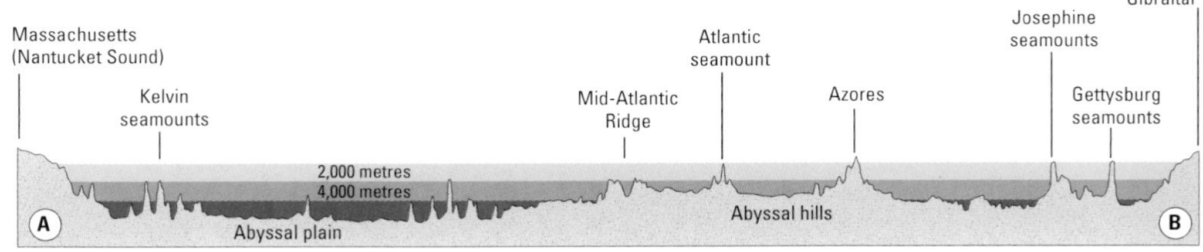

Topography of the ocean floor around Australia

In the image on the right, land areas are shown in grey, with shaded relief. The colours represent sea depth, with red representing the shallowest areas, through yellow and green to dark blue (the deepest). The data for the sea topography are from the Seasat radar satellite. The deep blue area in the upper left is the Java Trench which forms the boundary between the Indo-Australian plate and the Eurasian plate. In the top right, the New Guinea trench, which has a maximum depth of 9,103 metres, forms the border of the Indo-Australian and Pacific plates. Alongside the trenches are volcanic islands formed from magma, created as the edge of the Indo-Australian plate is subducted and melted.

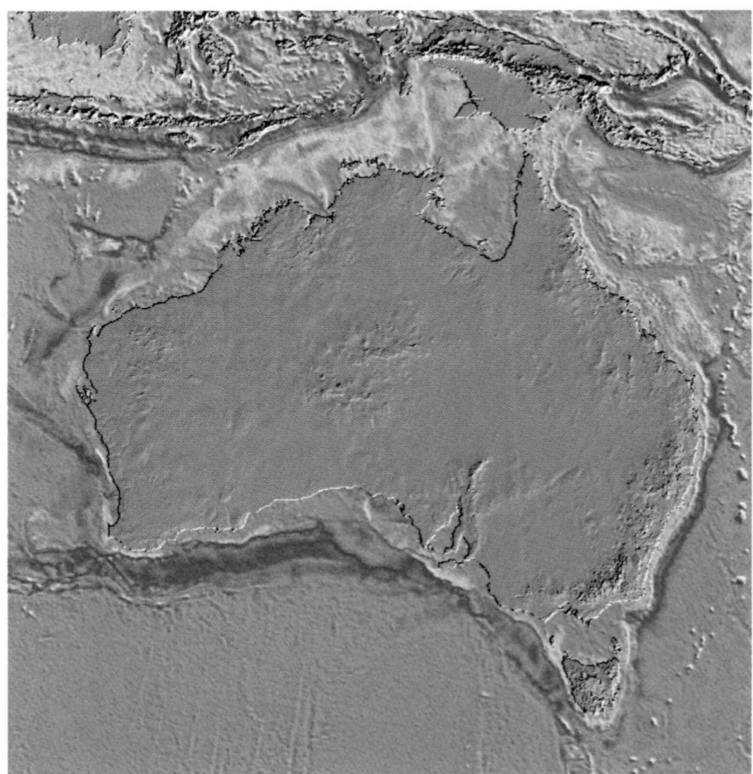

Geology of the Earth

For more information:
12 Types of rock
Mountain building
13 Surface processes
21 The carbon cycle
36 Minerals

Every year, earthquakes and volcanic eruptions cause much destruction throughout the world. Such phenomena were once thought to be unconnected but since the late 1960s, scientists have understood that these events are surface manifestations of the tremendous forces operating in the Earth's interior that are slowly but constantly changing the face of our planet.

The Earth is divided into three zones. The crust, a brittle, low-density zone, overlies the dense mantle. Separating the crust from the mantle is a distinct boundary called the Mohorovičić (or Moho) discontinuity. Enclosed by the mantle is the Earth's core, which consists mainly of iron and nickel.

Temperatures inside the Earth range from about 870°C in the upper mantle to perhaps 5,000°C in the core. Heat creates convection currents in a semi-molten part of the mantle called the asthenosphere. Above the asthenosphere is the lithosphere, a solid layer about 70 km thick, consisting of the crust and part of the mantle. The lithosphere is divided into rigid plates, moved around by the currents in the asthenosphere, a process named plate tectonics.

The Earth was formed around 4.6 billion years ago. Lighter elements floated towards the surface, where they formed crustal rocks. The oldest rocks so far discovered are nearly 4 billion years old, while the oldest fossils occur in rocks formed around 3.5 billion years ago. An explosion of life occurred at the start of the Cambrian period, 570 million years ago. The fossil record since the start of the Cambrian has enabled scientists to piece together the story of life on Earth.

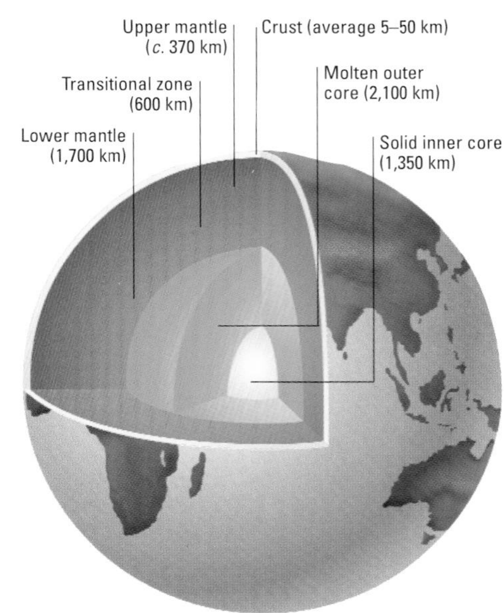

Plate Tectonics

In the early 20th century, the German scientist Alfred Wegener and others noticed similarities between the shapes of the continents. From a study of rocks and fossils in widely separated continents, they suggested that the continents had once been joined together and that somehow they had drifted apart. But no one knew of a mechanism that might cause continents to drift. However, in the 1950s and 1960s, evidence from studies of the ocean floor suggested that the low-density continents rest on huge slow-moving plates.

Sea-floor spreading in the Indian Ocean and continental plate collision

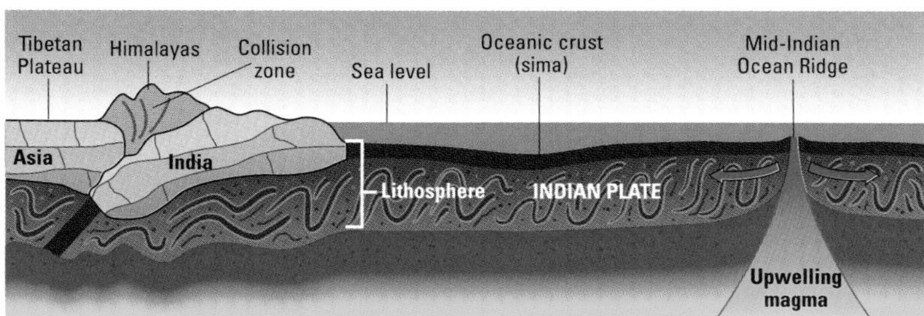

Sea-floor spreading in the Atlantic Ocean and plate collision

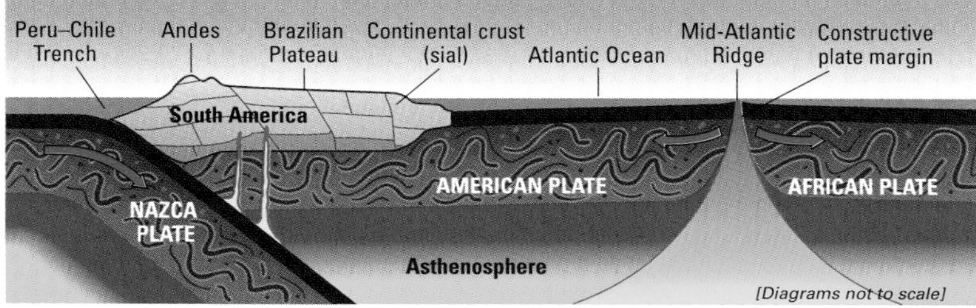

The huge ridges that run through the oceans represent boundaries between plates. Here plates are diverging at rates of 20–41 mm a year. Molten magma from the mantle rises along a central rift valley to form new crustal rock. These ocean ridges, which are active zones where earthquakes and volcanic eruptions are common, are called constructive plate margins. Destructive plate margins, which occur when two plates converge, are marked by deep ocean trenches as one plate is forced under the other. The descending plate is melted to produce the magma that fuels volcanoes alongside the trenches. Movements of descending plates are often sudden and violent, triggering earthquakes in overlying continental areas. Where two continents collide, their margins are buckled up to form fold mountain ranges. A third type of plate margin, the transform fault, is not illustrated above. Along these plate margins, such as California's San Andreas fault, plates are moving parallel to each other.

The debate about plate tectonics is not over. Questions still arise as to why some active volcanoes lie far from plate margins, and why major earthquakes occur in mid-plate areas.

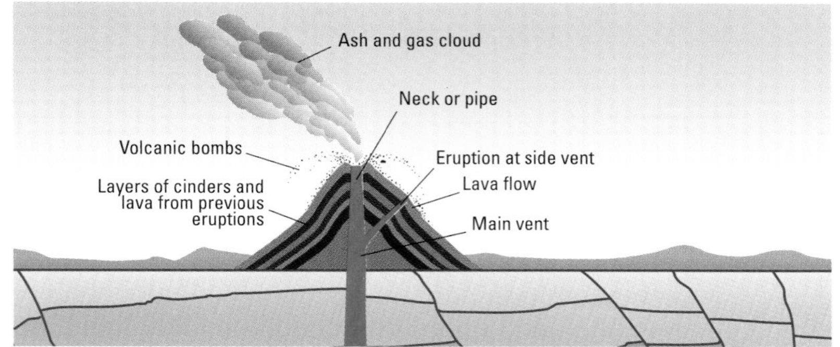

Continental Drift

In 1915, Alfred Wegener produced a series of world maps proposing that, around 200 million years ago, the continents had been joined together in a supercontinent which he called Pangaea. This landmass started to break up about 180 million years ago and the parts drifted to their present positions. The arrows on the present day world map shows that the continents are still on the move.

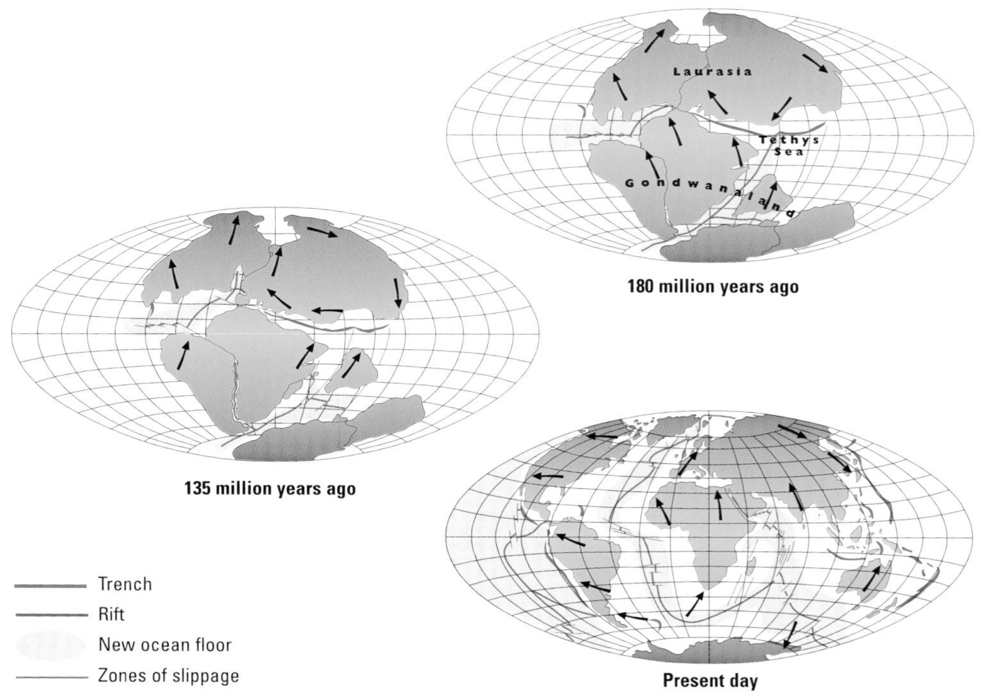

180 million years ago

135 million years ago

Present day

Distribution of Volcanoes

Volcanoes occur when hot liquefied rock beneath the Earth's crust is pushed up by pressure to the surface as molten lava. There are some 550 known active volcanoes, around 20 of which are erupting at any one time.

▲ Land volcanoes active since 1700
• Submarine volcanoes
◆ Geysers
Direction of movement (cm/year)
Boundaries of tectonic plates

AMERICAN PLATE
PACIFIC PLATE
NAZCA PLATE
AMERICAN PLATE
EURASIAN PLATE
AFRICAN PLATE
PACIFIC PLATE
INDIAN PLATE
ANTARCTIC PLATE

Geological Time

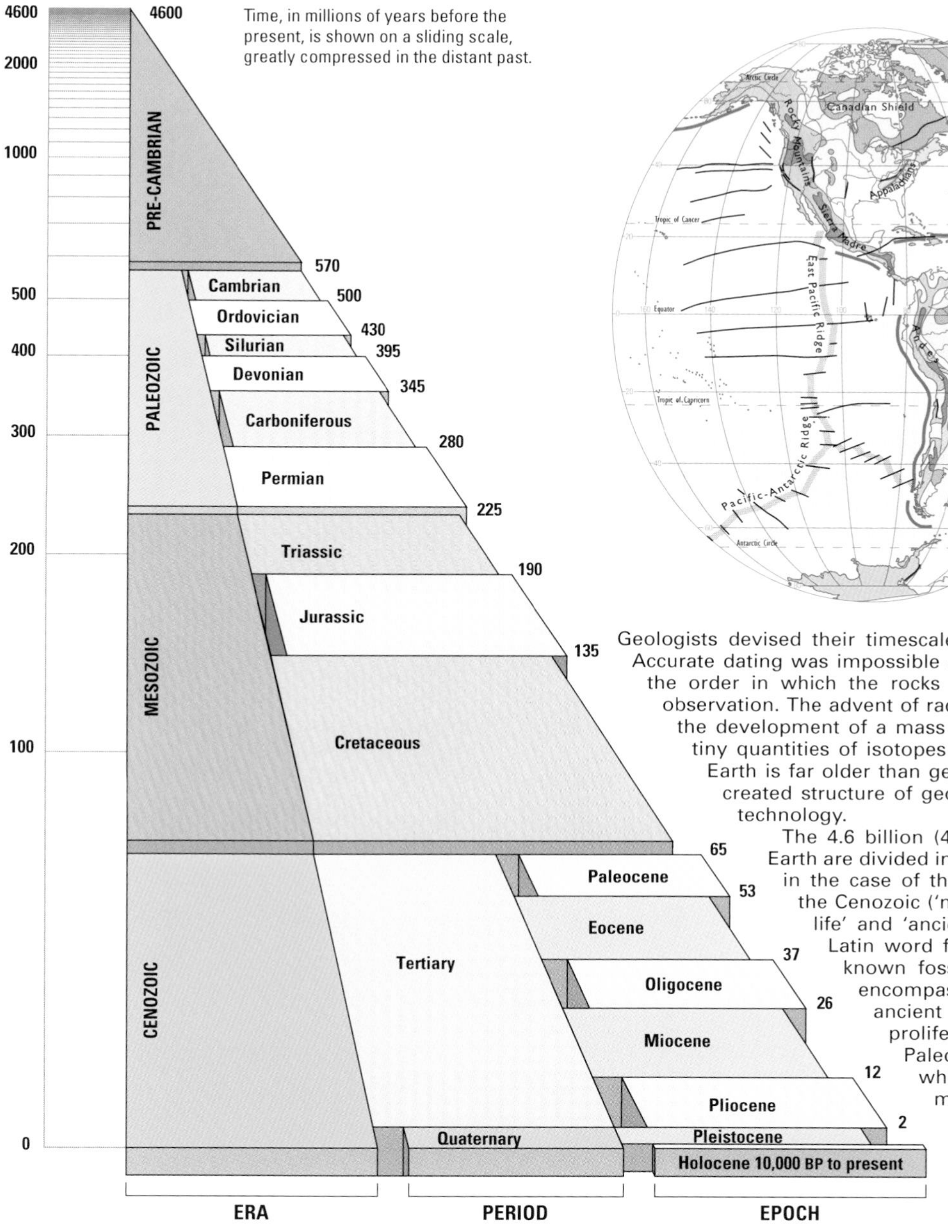

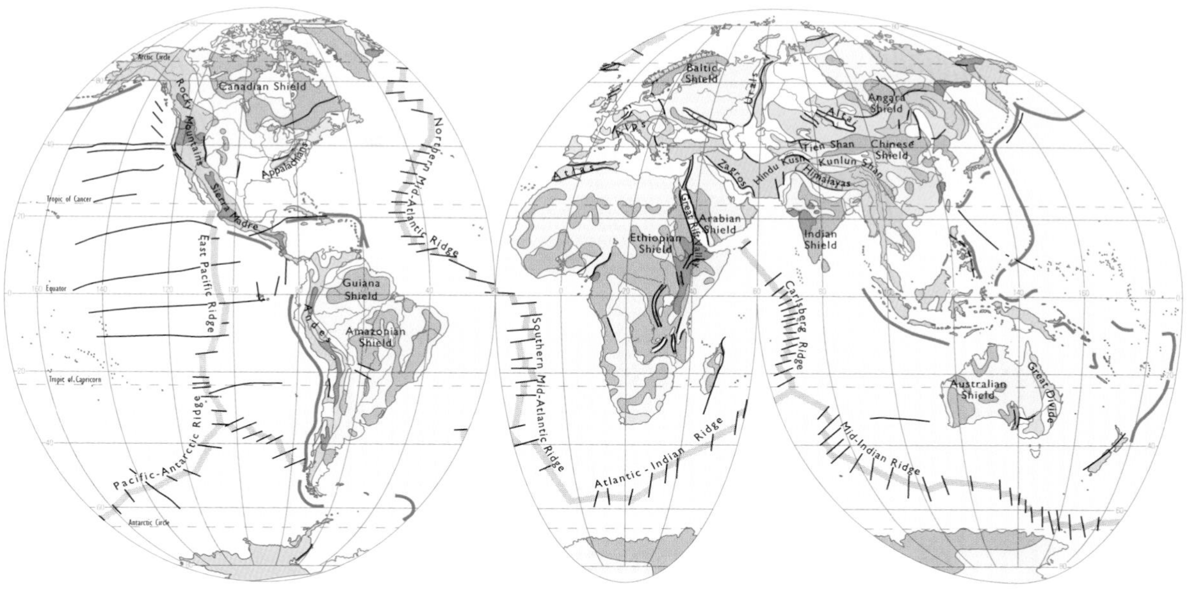

Time, in millions of years before the present, is shown on a sliding scale, greatly compressed in the distant past.

4600
2000
1000
500
400
300
200
100
0

PRE-CAMBRIAN 4600
570
PALEOZOIC
Cambrian
500
Ordovician
430
Silurian
395
Devonian
345
Carboniferous
280
Permian
225
MESOZOIC
Triassic
190
Jurassic
135
Cretaceous
65
CENOZOIC
Tertiary
Paleocene
53
Eocene
37
Oligocene
26
Miocene
12
Pliocene
2
Quaternary
Pleistocene
Holocene 10,000 BP to present

ERA
PERIOD
EPOCH

Canadian Shield
Rocky Mountains
Appalachians
Sierra Madre
Norse Mid-Atlantic Ridge
East Pacific Ridge
Guiana Shield
Amazonian Shield
Andes
Southern Mid-Atlantic Ridge
Pacific-Antarctic Ridge
Tropic of Cancer
Equator
Tropic of Capricorn
Antarctic Circle
Baltic Shield
Alps
Urals
Atlas
Angara Shield
Tien Shan
Chinese Shield
Kunlun Shan
Hindu Kush
Zagros
Himalayas
Arabian Shield
Ethiopian Shield
Indian Shield
Carlsberg Ridge
Atlantic-Indian Ridge
Mid-Indian Ridge
Australian Shield
Great Divide

Geologists devised their timescale on the basis of relative, not calendar, ages. Accurate dating was impossible and estimates were often bitterly disputed, but the order in which the rocks were formed could be deduced from careful observation. The advent of radioactive dating – culminating in the 1950s with the development of a mass spectrometer capable of accurately measuring tiny quantities of isotopes – appears to have settled the arguments. The Earth is far older than geologists first imagined, but their painstakingly-created structure of geological time has withstood the advent of high technology.

The 4.6 billion (4,600 million) years since the formation of the Earth are divided into four great eras, further split into periods and, in the case of the most recent era, epochs. The present era is the Cenozoic ('new life'), extending backwards through 'middle life' and 'ancient life' to the Pre-Cambrian, named after the Latin word for Wales, the location of some of the earliest known fossils. Most of the Earth's geological history is encompassed by the Pre-Cambrian: though traces of ancient life have since been found, it was largely the proliferation of fossils from the beginning of the Paleozoic era onwards, some 570 million years ago, which first allowed precise subdivisions to be made.

Like the Cambrian, most are named after regions exemplifying a period's geology. Others – such as the Carboniferous ('coal-bearing') or the Cretaceous ('chalk-bearing') – are more directly descriptive.

Pre-Cambrian shields
Sedimentary cover on Pre-Cambrian shields
Paleozoic (Caledonian and Hercynian) folding
Sedimentary cover on Paleozoic folding
Mesozoic folding
Sedimentary cover on Mesozoic folding
Cenozoic (Alpine) folding
Sedimentary cover on Cenozoic folding
Intensive Mesozoic and Cenozoic vulcanism
Principal faults
Oceanic marginal troughs
Mid-oceanic ridges
Overthrust faults

Earthquakes

Earthquake magnitude is usually rated according to either the Richter or the Modified Mercalli scale, both devised by seismologists in the 1930s. The Richter scale measures absolute earthquake power with mathematical precision: each step upwards represents a ten-fold increase in the amplitude of the shockwave. Theoretically, there is no upper limit, but the largest earthquakes measured have been rated at between 8.8 and 8.9. The 12-point Mercalli scale, based on observed effects, is often more meaningful, ranging from I (earthquakes noticed only by seismographs) to XII (total destruction); intermediate points include V (people awakened at night; unstable objects overturned), VII (collapse of ordinary buildings; chimneys and monuments fall) and IX (conspicuous cracks in ground; serious damage to reservoirs).

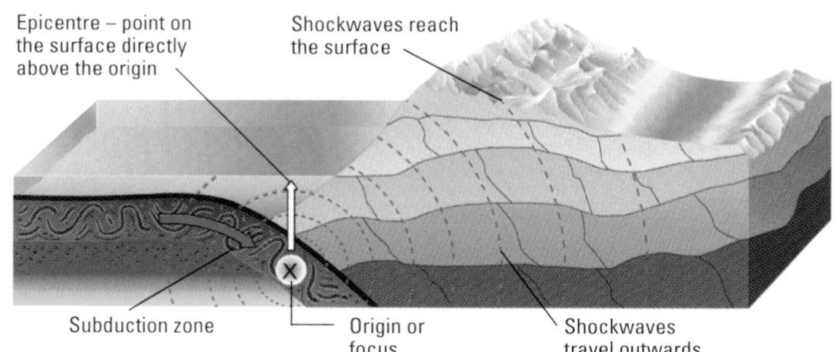

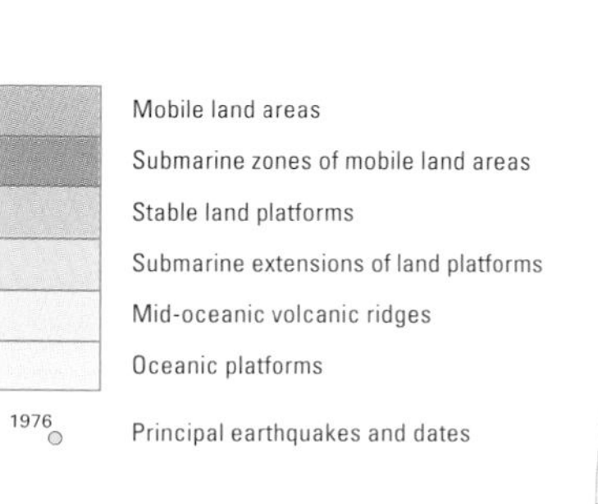

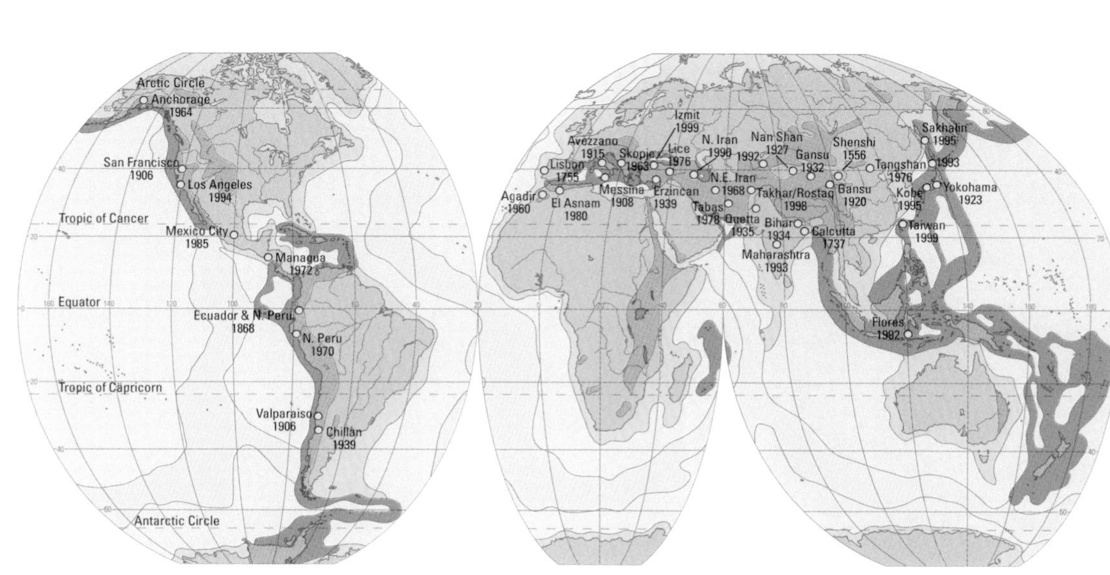

Earthquakes are a series of rapid vibrations originating from the slipping or faulting of parts of the Earth's crust when stresses within build up to breaking point. They usually happen at depths varying from 8 km to 30 km. Severe earthquakes cause extensive damage when they take place in populated areas, destroying structures and severing communications. Most initial loss of life occurs due to secondary causes such as falling masonry, fires and flooding.

Notable Earthquakes Since 1900

Year	Location	Mag.	Deaths
1906	San Francisco, USA	8.3	503
1906	Valparaiso, Chile	8.6	22,000
1908	Messina, Italy	7.5	83,000
1915	Avezzano, Italy	7.5	30,000
1920	Gansu (Kansu), China	8.6	180,000
1923	Yokohama, Japan	8.3	143,000
1927	Nan Shan, China	8.3	200,000
1932	Gansu (Kansu), China	7.6	70,000
1933	Sanriku, Japan	8.9	2,990
1934	Bihar, India/Nepal	8.4	10,700
1935	Quetta, India*	7.5	60,000
1939	Chillan, Chile	8.3	28,000
1939	Erzincan, Turkey	7.9	30,000
1960	Agadir, Morocco	5.8	12,000
1962	Khorasan, Iran	7.1	12,230
1968	N.E. Iran	7.4	12,000
1970	N. Peru	7.7	66,794
1972	Managua, Nicaragua	6.2	5,000
1974	N. Pakistan	6.3	5,200
1976	Guatemala	7.5	22,778
1976	Tangshan, China	8.2	255,000
1978	Tabas, Iran	7.7	25,000
1980	El Asnam, Algeria	7.3	20,000
1980	S. Italy	7.2	4,800
1985	Mexico City, Mexico	8.1	4,200
1988	N.W. Armenia	6.8	55,000
1990	N. Iran	7.7	36,000
1992	Flores, Indonesia	6.8	1,895
1993	Maharashtra, India	6.4	30,000
1994	Los Angeles, USA	6.6	51
1995	Kobe, Japan	7.2	5,000
1995	Sakhalin Is., Russia	7.5	2,000
1996	Yunnan, China	7.0	240
1997	N.E. Iran	7.1	2,400
1998	Takhar, Afghanistan	6.1	4,200
1998	Rostaq, Afghanistan	7.0	5,000
1999	Izmit, Turkey	7.4	15,000
1999	Tapei, Taiwan	7.6	1,700

The most devastating quake ever was at Shaanxi (Shenshi) province, central China, on 3 January 1556, when an estimated 830,000 people were killed.

* now Pakistan

Landforms

For more information:
8 Oceans
10 The Earth's structure
Plate tectonics
Volcanoes
11 Geological time
18 Hydrological cycle
37 Structural regions

The theory of plate tectonics has offered new insights as to how the Earth works, elucidating mysteries concerning continental drift, volcanic eruptions and earthquakes. It has also contributed to our understanding of how plate collisions can squeeze up layers of sediments on seabeds into fold mountain ranges, such as the Himalayas.

Yet even as mountains rise, natural forces are wearing them away. In hot, dry climates, mechanical weathering, a result of rapid temperature changes, causes the outer layers of rocks to peel away, while, in cold mountain regions, boulders are prised apart when water freezes in cracks in rocks. Chemical weathering is responsible for hollowing out limestone caves and decomposing granites.

Climatic conditions have a great bearing on the principle agent of erosion in any area. Running water is most important in moist temperate regions. In cold regions, ice is the major agent of erosion, and in many mountain ranges, U-shaped valleys are evidence of the erosive power of valley glaciers. Ice sheets moulded much of the Earth's surface during the Ice Ages, the most recent of which, in the northern hemisphere, ended 10,000 years ago. Polar climates also shape the scenery of periglacial areas that border bodies of ice. Such areas are subject to constant freeze-thaw action, which creates such features as pingos (domed mounds).

Climatic change has also affected many of the landforms in hot deserts, which were shaped by running water at a time when the deserts enjoyed much wetter climates. However, the major agent of erosion in deserts today is wind-blown sand which erodes rock strata to form mushroom-shaped rocks and caves.

The surface of the Earth is under constant assault from tectonic processes and the agents of erosion. The products of erosion, fragments of rock such as sand, are deposited to form sedimentary rocks. Metamorphic rocks are created when igneous or sedimentary rocks are buried and metamorphosed by heat and pressure. Eventually the rocks are recycled to form magma, which rises upwards to start the rock cycle all over again.

The Rock Cycle

James Hutton first proposed the rock cycle in the late 1700s after he observed the slow but steady effects of erosion.

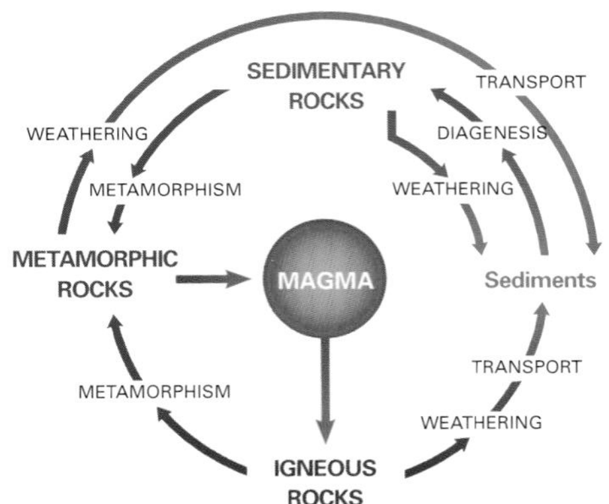

Rocks are divided into three types, according to the way in which they are formed:

Igneous rocks, including granite and basalt, are formed by the cooling of magma from within the Earth's crust.

Metamorphic rocks, such as slate, marble and quartzite, are formed below the Earth's surface by the compression or baking of existing rocks.

Sedimentary rocks, like sandstone and limestone, are formed on the surface of the Earth from the remains of living organisms and eroded fragments of older rocks.

Mountain Building

Mountains are formed when pressures on the Earth's crust caused by continental drift become so intense that the surface buckles or cracks. This happens where oceanic crust is subducted by continental crust or, more dramatically, where two tectonic plates collide: the Rockies, Andes, Alps, Urals and Himalayas resulted from such impacts. These are all known as fold mountains because they were formed by the compression of the rocks, forcing the surface to bend and fold like a crumpled rug. The Himalayas are formed from the folded former sediments of the Tethys Sea which was trapped in the collision zone between the Indian and Eurasian plates.

The other main mountain-building process occurs when the crust fractures to create faults, allowing rock to be forced upwards in large blocks; or when the pressure of magma within the crust forces the surface to bulge into a dome, or erupts to form a volcano. Large mountain ranges may reveal a combination of those features; the Alps, for example, have been compressed so violently that the folds are fragmented by numerous faults and intrusions of molten igneous rock.

Over millions of years, even the greatest mountain ranges can be reduced by the agents of erosion (especially rivers) to a low rugged landscape known as a peneplain.

Types of faults: Faults occur where the crust is being stretched or compressed so violently that the rock strata break in a horizontal or vertical movement. They are classified by the direction in which the blocks of rock have moved. A normal fault results when a vertical movement causes the surface to break apart; compression causes a reverse fault. Horizontal movement causes shearing, known as a strike-slip fault. When the rock breaks in two places, the central block may be pushed up in a horst fault, or sink (creating a rift valley) in a graben fault.

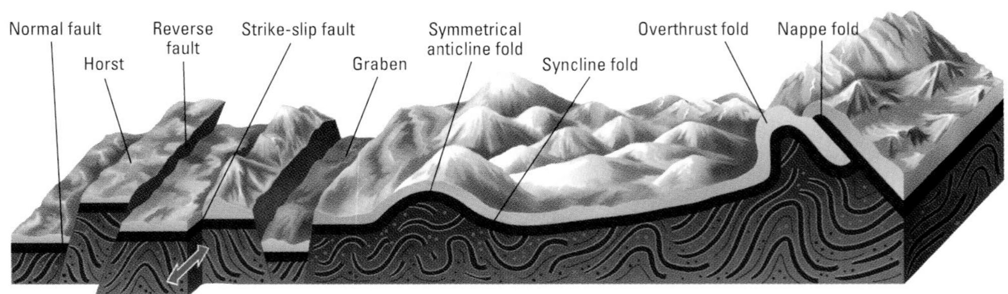

Types of fold: Folds occur when rock strata are squeezed and compressed. They are common, therefore, at destructive plate margins and where plates have collided, forcing the rocks to buckle into mountain ranges. Geographers give different names to the degrees of fold that result from continuing pressure on the rock. A simple fold may be symmetric, with even slopes on either side, but as the pressure builds up, one slope becomes steeper and the fold becomes asymmetric. Later, the ridge or 'anticline' at the top of the fold may slide over the lower ground or 'syncline' to form a recumbent fold. Eventually, the rock strata may break under the pressure to form an overthrust and finally a nappe fold.

Annual Fluctuations for Selected Glaciers

Glacier name and location	Change in mass balance 1970–90
Wolverine, USA	+2,320
Storglaciaren, Sweden	–120
Djankuat, Russia	–1,890
Grasubreen, Norway	–2,530
Ürümqi, China	–3,828
Golubin, Kyrgyzstan	–7,105
Gries, Switzerland	–10,600
Careser, Italy	–11,610
Abramov, Tajikistan	–13,700
Sarennes, France	–15,020
Place, Canada	–15,175

The mass balance is defined as the difference between glacier accumulation and ablation (melting), and is expressed as water equivalent in millimetres. A minus indicates a reduction in the depth or length of a glacier. As can be seen from this geographically diverse selection, glaciers are retreating in many areas worldwide. The most dramatic and serious example of this phenomenon is the continuing distintegration of several large Antarctic ice-shelves.

The extent to which glacial retreat is due to global warming, or to longer term climatic fluctuations, remains a matter for debate.

Continental Glaciation

Many landforms in the northern hemisphere were shaped by ice sheets and meltwater during the Pleistocene Ice Age, which began about two million years ago. During the Ice Age, the ice sheets periodically advanced and retreated. The first map shows the ice cover at its greatest extent about 200,000 years BP (before the present), when it covered about 30% of the land surface, as compared with 10% today. About 18,000 years BP, the ice covered most of Canada and as far south as the Bristol Channel in England. Around the ice sheets, land areas experienced periglacial conditions.

200,000 years BP

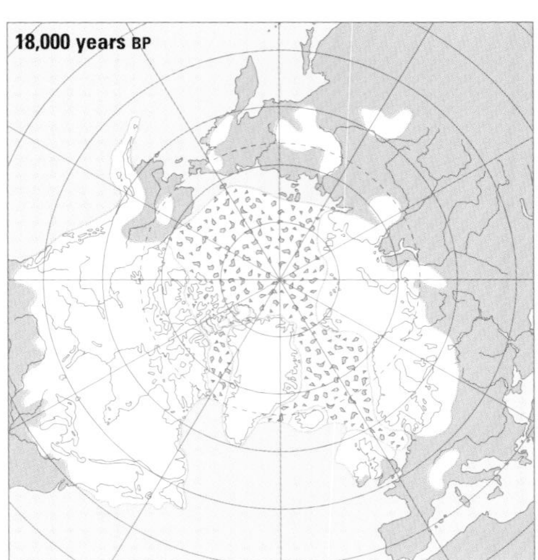

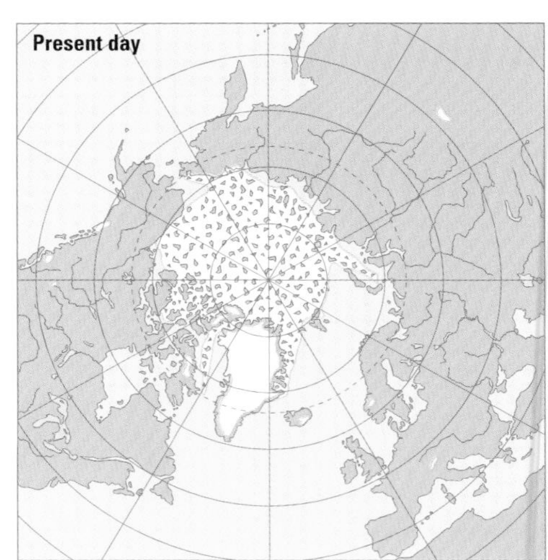

Natural Landforms

Natural landforms reflect the influence of plate tectonics through mountain-building and the generation of new rocks from the interior, together with the agents of erosion: running water, ice, winds and coastal waves. Over millions of years, mountains are gradually eroded, producing landforms that reflect the major forces that have been at work, as well as the underlying geology, the climatic conditions, which often vary over time, and the vegetation cover. The stylized diagram, below, shows some major natural landforms found in the mid-latitudes.

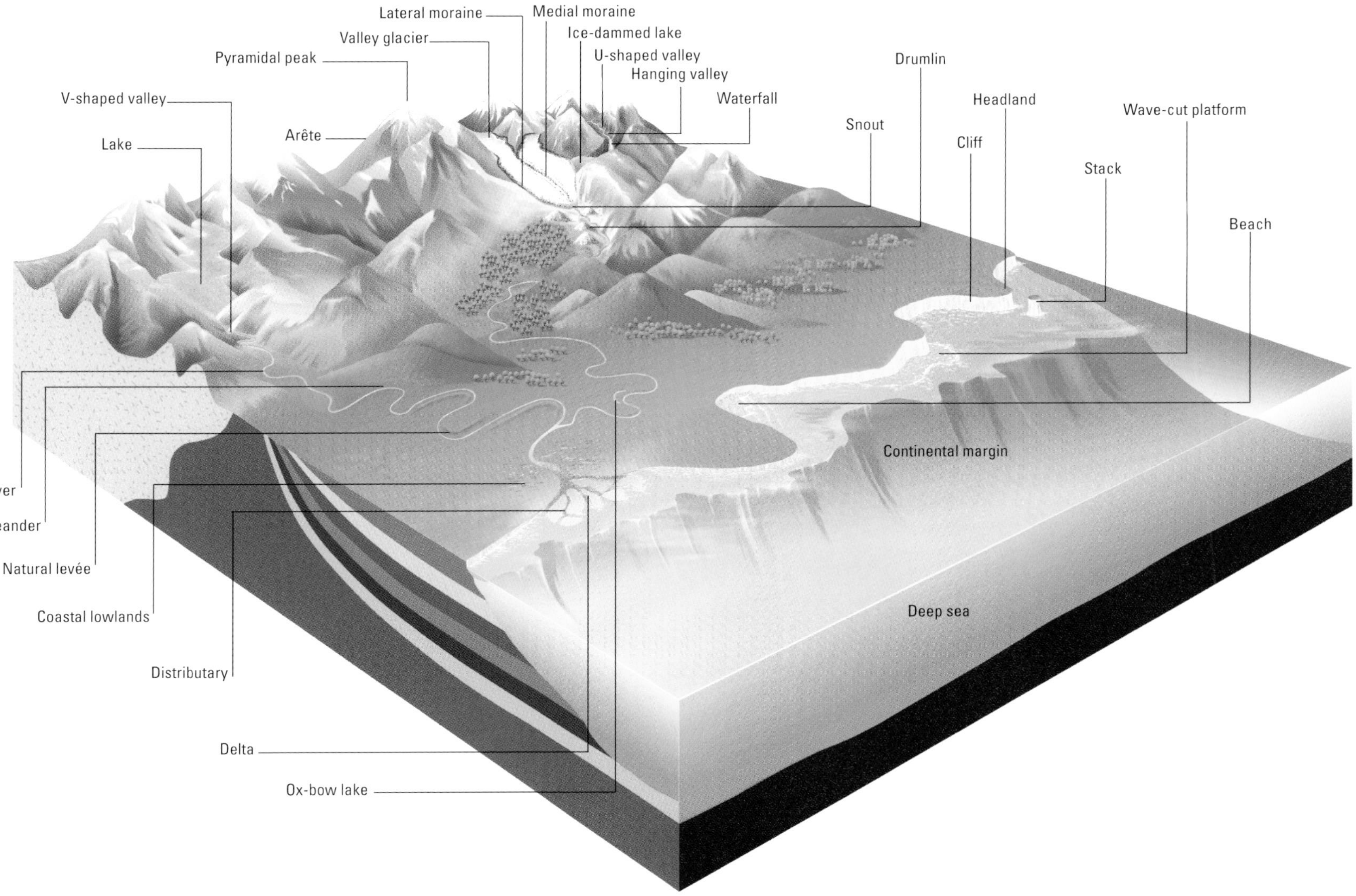

Lateral moraine
Medial moraine
Ice-dammed lake
Valley glacier
U-shaped valley
Hanging valley
Pyramidal peak
Drumlin
V-shaped valley
Waterfall
Headland
Wave-cut platform
Snout
Arête
Lake
Cliff
Stack
Beach
Continental margin
River
Meander
Natural levée
Coastal lowlands
Deep sea
Distributary
Delta
Ox-bow lake

Desert Landforms

Deserts are defined as places with an average annual precipitation of 250 mm per year, though places with a higher rainfall and a high evaporation rate may also qualify as deserts. The three types of desert landforms are known by their Arabic names, a reflection of the fact that the Sahara in North Africa is the world's largest desert. Sand desert, called erg, covers about one-fifth of the world's deserts. The rest is divided between hammada (areas of bare rock) and reg (broad plains covered by loose gravel or pebbles).

The shapes of dunes in sand deserts reflect the character of local winds. Where winds are constant in direction, the sand often piles up in crescent-shaped dunes, called barchans. Barchans are constantly on the move and their forward march, unless halted by vegetation, may overwhelm settlements at oases. Seif dunes, named after the Arabic word for sword, are long ridges of sand which lie parallel to the direction of the wind, but where winds are variable, the sand sheets are often featureless.

Wind-blown sand is an effective agent of erosion but because of the weight of sand grains, this type of erosion is confined to within two metres of the land surface, creating caves and mushroom-shaped rocks.

In assessing desert landforms, it is important to remember that other processes were at work in the past when the climate was very different from today. For example, cave paintings suggest that the Sahara had a much wetter climate after the end of the Ice Age and only began to dry up after about 5000 BC. However, human action, including overgrazing and the cutting down of trees for firewood, can turn a grassland region into desert – a process known as desertification.

Erg

Hammada

Reg

Surface Processes

Catastrophic changes to landforms are periodically caused by such phenomena as avalanches, landslides and volcanic eruptions, but most of the processes that shape the Earth's surface operate extremely slowly in human terms. One estimate, based on a study of landforms in the United States, suggests that, on average, one metre of land is removed from the entire surface of the country every 29,500 years. However, the terrain and the climate have a great effect on the erosion rate. For example, on cold plains, such as the Hudson Bay lowlands, the rate drops to around one metre for every 154,200 years, while in wet, tropical mountain areas, the rate may reach one metre for every 1,300 years.

Chemical weathering is at its greatest in warm, humid regions, while mechanical weathering, or the physical break-up of rocks, predominates in cold mountain or hot desert regions. The most familiar type of chemical weathering is caused by the reaction of rainwater containing dissolved carbon dioxide on limestone. This leads to the creation of labyrinthine cave networks dissolved by groundwater. Mechanical weathering includes frost action, while in hot deserts, rapid temperature changes cause the outer layers of rocks to expand and contract until they crack and peel away, a process called exfoliation.

The most important product of weathering is soil, which consists of rock fragments and humus, the decayed remains of plants and animals, together with living organisms, including vast numbers of micro-organisms. Soils vary in character according to the climate, ranging from the heavily leached, red laterite soils of wet tropical areas to the fertile, brown soils of dry grasslands. Soils are important because they support plants, which in turn anchor the soil and act as a protection against erosion. Soil erosion is greatest on sloping land because the steeper the slope, the greater the tendency for the soil to creep or flow downhill. The degree of movement of soil and rock downhill under the influence of gravity, called mass wasting, depends on a slope's stability. The stability may be disturbed by earthquakes or by heavy rain (water acts as a lubricant and increases the weight of the overlying material) which may trigger flows, slides or large falls of rock.

Running water is probably the world's leading agent of erosion and transportation. The energy of a river depends on several factors, including its velocity and volume, and its erosive power is at its peak when it is in full flood, sweeping soil, pebbles and even boulders along its course, cutting downwards into the bedrock or widening its valley. Sea waves also exert tremendous erosive power during storms when they hurl pebbles and large rocks against the shore, undercutting cliffs and hollowing out caves. Headlands are often attacked on both sides, forming caves, then a natural arch and eventually an isolated stack.

Glacier ice forms in mountain hollows, called cirques, and spills out to form valley glaciers, which transport rocks shattered by frost action. As a glacier moves, rocks embedded in the base and sides scrape away bedrock, eroding steep-sided, flat-bottomed, U-shaped valleys. Evidence of past glaciation in mountain regions includes cirques, knife-edged ridges, or arêtes, and pyramidal peaks, or horns.

Geologists once considered that landforms evolved from 'young', newly uplifted mountainous areas, through a 'mature' hilly stage, to an 'old age' stage when the land was reduced to an almost flat plain, or peneplain. This theory, called the 'cycle of erosion', fell into disuse when it became evident that so many factors, including the effects of plate tectonics and climatic change, constantly interrupt the cycle, which takes no account of the highly complex interactions that shape the surface of our planet.

The Atmosphere

For more information:

9 Ocean currents
17 Beaufort wind scale
Climate change
Monsoon
21 Solar energy
Greenhouse effect
22 Greenhouse power
23 Acid rain

The atmosphere is a meteor shield, a radiation deflector, a thermal blanket and a source of chemical energy for the Earth's diverse life forms. Five-sixths of its mass is in the lowest layer, the troposphere which ranges in thickness from 18 to 10 km between the Equator and the poles. Powered by the Sun, the air is always on the move, flowing generally from high- to low-pressure areas. The troposphere is the layer where nearly all weather phenomena, including clouds, precipitation and winds, occur. Above the troposphere is the stratosphere, which contains the ozone layer and extends to 50 km above the Earth's surface. Beyond 100 km, the density is lower than most laboratory vacuums.

Structure of the Atmosphere

Hubble Space Telescope 600 km [370 miles] — 600 km

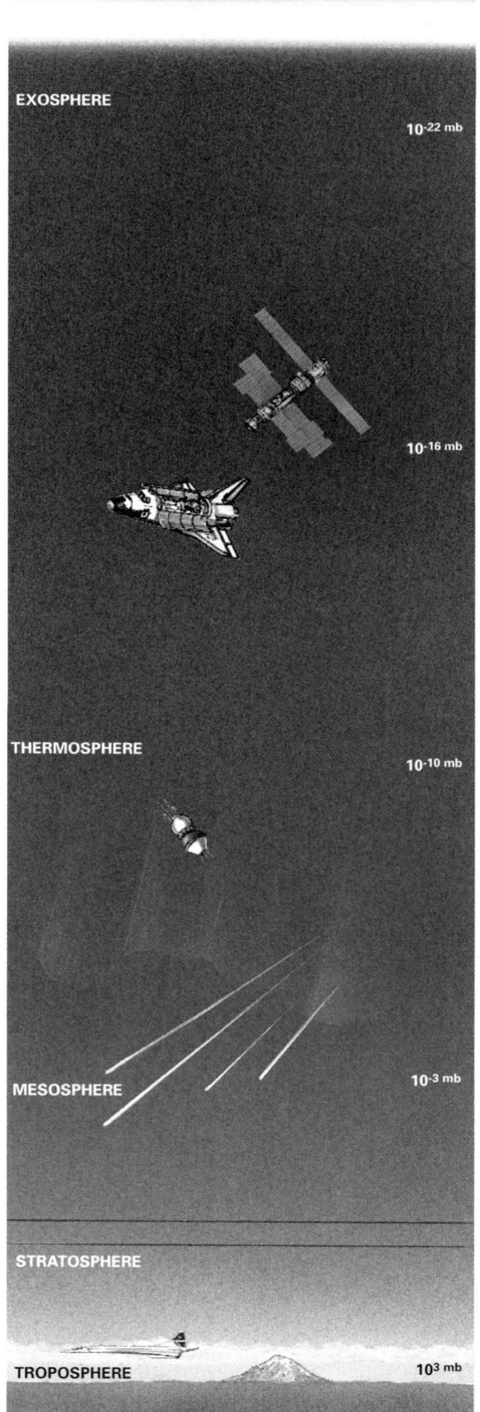

350 km

Mir Space Station 325 km [200 miles]

300 km

Space Shuttle 275 km [170 miles]

250 km

200 km

Vostock Manned Capsule (first manned space flight, 1961) 175 km [110 miles]

150 km

Aurorae

100 km

Meteor trails

50 km

Ozone layer

10 km

Concorde

Mount Everest 8,848 m [29,029 ft]

Circulation of the Air

N

S

EASTERLY WINDS

SOUTH-WESTERLY WINDS

NORTH-EASTERLY TRADES

DOLDRUMS

SOUTH-EASTERLY TRADES

NORTH-WESTERLY WINDS

EASTERLY WINDS

60°

30°

0°

30°

60°

FRONTAL RAIN

ITCZ

CONVECTIONAL THUNDERSTORM

FRONTAL RAIN

1, 2, 3

- High pressure
- Low pressure
- Warm air
- Cold air
- Surface winds
- Clouds

1 Hadley Cell
2 Ferrel Cell
3 Polar Cell

ITCZ Intertropical convergence zone

Chemical Composition

Gaseous composition of the principal atmospheric layers

Exosphere: 50–100% hydrogen; 25–50% helium

Helium vanishes with increasing altitude. Above 2,400 km the exosphere is almost entirely composed of hydrogen.

Mesosphere: 70% nitrogen; 15% oxygen; 15% helium

The high energy of mesospheric gas gives it a notional temperature of more than 2,000°C, although its density is negligible.

Stratosphere: 80% nitrogen; 18% oxygen; 1% argon; 1% ozone

Stratospheric air contains enough ozone to make it poisonous, although it is in any case too rarified to breathe.

Troposphere: 78% nitrogen; 21% oxygen; 1% argon

The narrowest of all the layers, this thin region contains about 85% of the atmosphere's total mass and almost all of its water vapour. It is also the realm of the Earth's weather.

Frontal Systems

Depressions, or cyclones, form along the polar front where dense polar easterlies meet warm subtropical westerlies. Depressions occur when warm air flows into waves in the polar front, while cold air flows in behind it, creating rotating air systems that bring changeable weather. Along the warm front (the boundary on the ground between the warm and cold air), the warm air flows upwards over the cold air, producing a sequence of clouds which help forecasters to predict a depression's advance. Along the cold front, the advancing cold air forces warm air to rise steeply. Towering cumulonimbus clouds form in the rising air. When the cold front overtakes the warm front, the warm air is pushed above ground level to form an occluded front. Cloud and rain persist along occlusions until temperatures equalize, the air mixes, and the depression dies out.

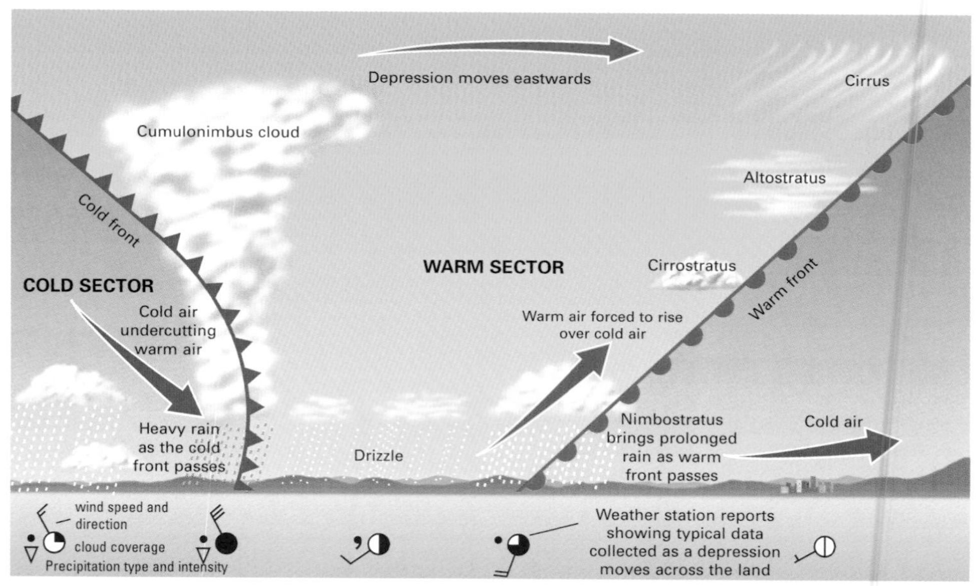

Air Masses

Air masses are bodies of air whose characteristics are broadly the same over a large area. Around the Equator, where the Sun's heat creates relatively high surface temperatures, warm air rises to create a zone of low pressure called the doldrums. The air cools and finally spreads out towards the poles. Around latitudes 30° north and south, the air sinks back to the surface, becoming warmer as it descends and creating zones of high pressure called the horse latitudes.

The high- and low-pressure zones are both areas of comparative calm, but between them lie the prevailing trade wind belts. Air also flows north and south from the high-pressure horse latitudes and these air flows meet up with cold, dense air flowing from the poles along the polar front. This basic circulatory system is complicated by the Coriolis effect, brought about by the spinning Earth. Because of the Coriolis effect, the prevailing winds do not flow directly north–south but are deflected to the right in the northern hemisphere and to the left in the southern. Along the polar front, depressions form where the polar easterlies meet the westerlies.

The first classification of clouds was developed by a London chemist, Luke Howard, in 1803, and it was later modified by the World Meteorological Organization. The main types are divided into three groups according to their altitude, and into subgroups according to their shape, which vary from hairlike filaments (cirrus), heaps or piles (cumulus), and layers (stratus). Each cloud carries some kind of message, though not always a clear one, to weather forecasters.

Classification of Clouds

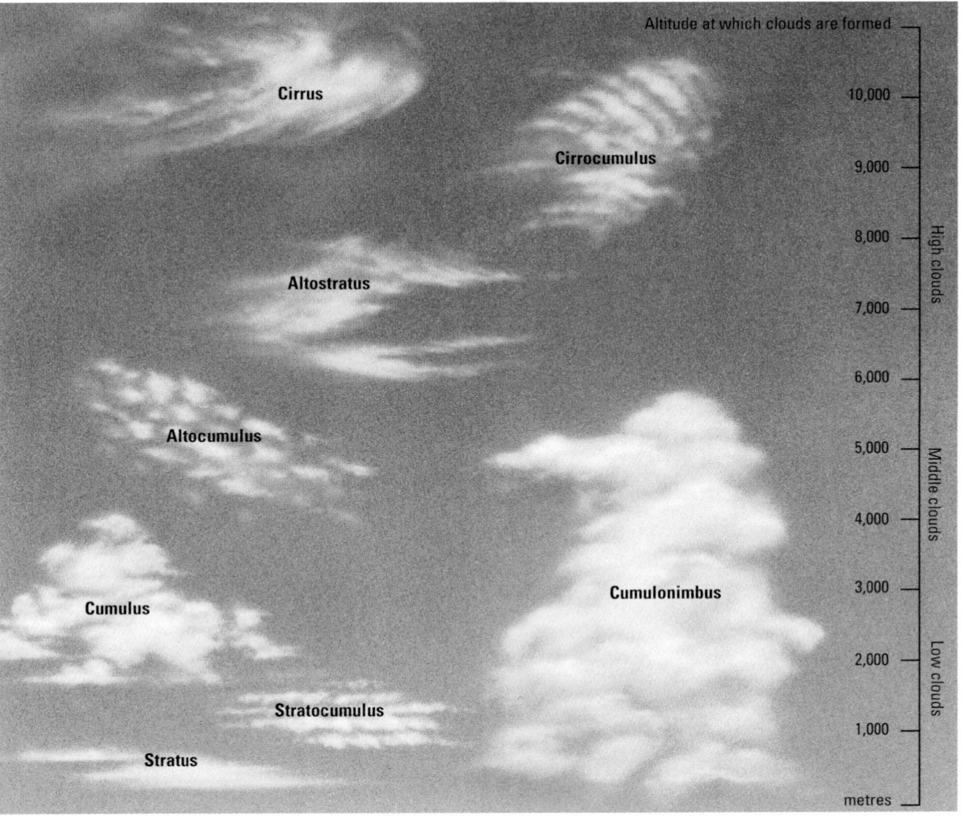

Clouds form when damp, usually rising, air is cooled. Thus they form when a wind rises to cross hills or mountains; when a mass of air rises over, or is pushed up by, another mass of denser air; or when local heating of the ground causes convection currents.

The types of clouds are classified according to altitude as high, middle or low. The high ones, composed of ice crystals, are cirrus, cirrostratus and cirrocumulus. The middle clouds are altostratus, a grey or bluish striated, fibrous or uniform sheet producing light drizzle, and altocumulus, a thicker and fluffier version of cirrocumulus.

Low clouds include nimbostratus, a dark grey layer that brings rain or snow; cumulus, a detached heap, dark at the base; stratus, which forms dull, overcast skies at low levels; and stratocumulus, which consists of fluffy greyish-white layers.

Cumulonimbus, associated with storms and rains, heavy and dense with a flat base and a high, fluffy outline, can be tall enough to occupy middle as well as low altitudes.

Pressure and Surface Winds

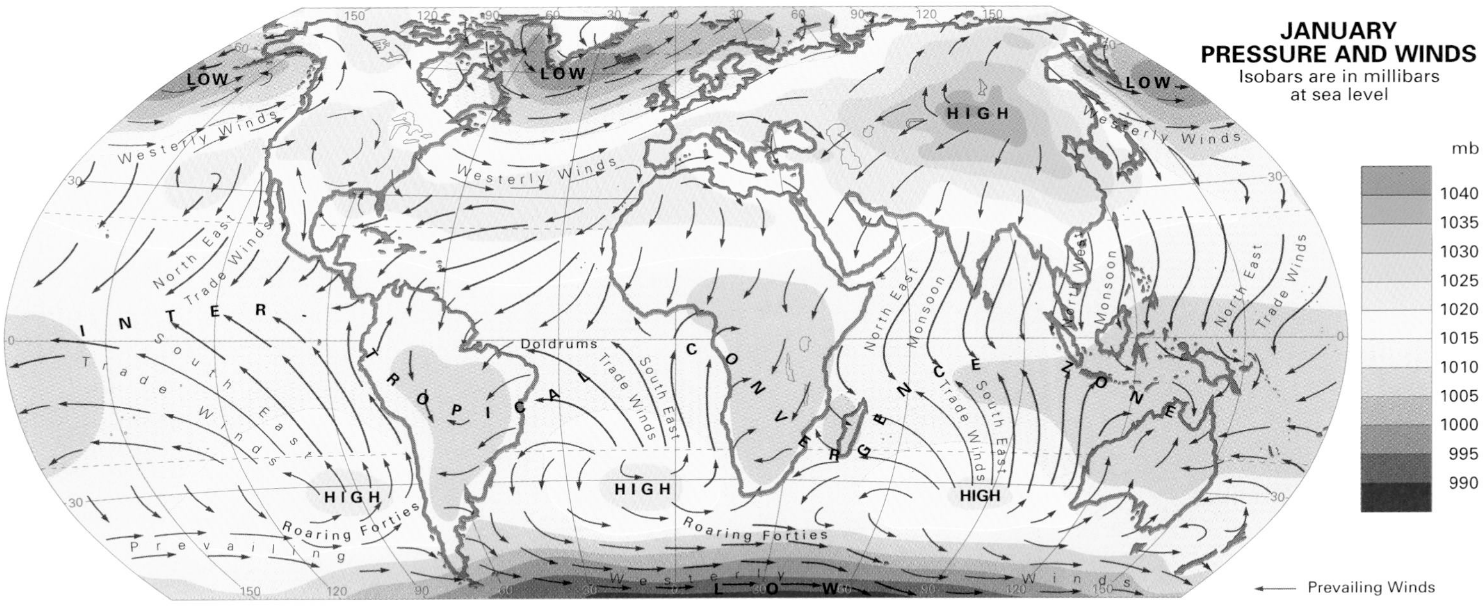

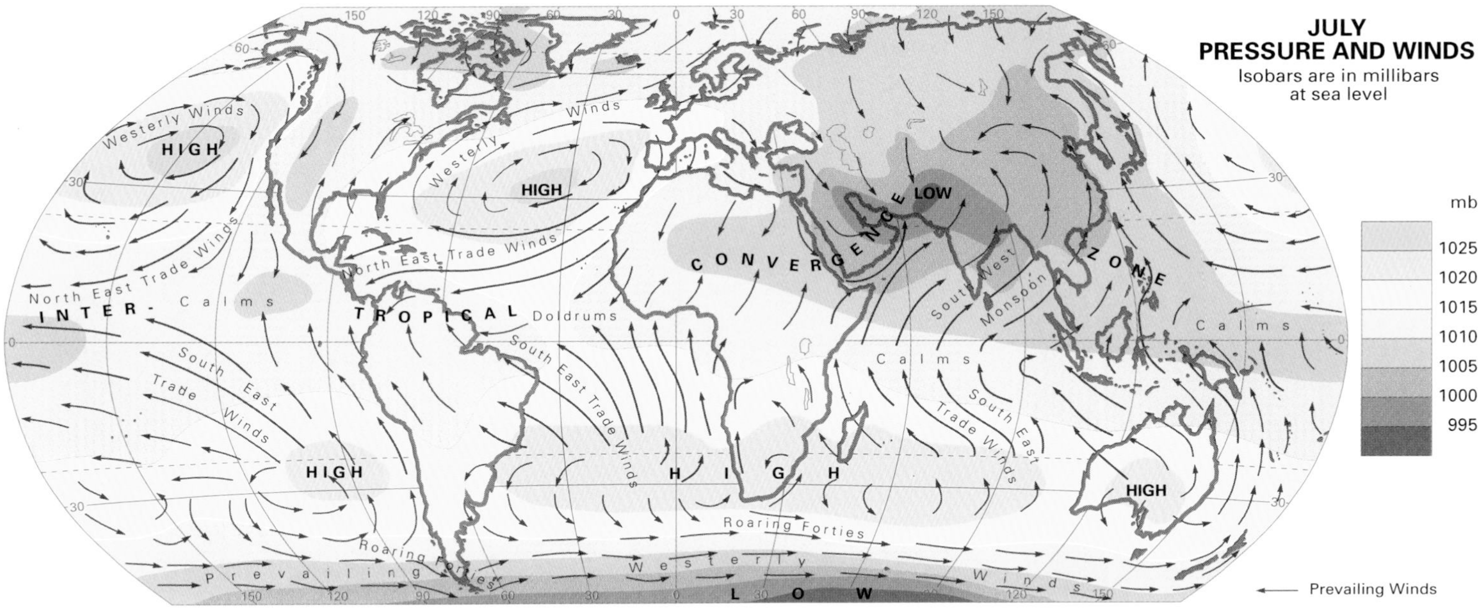

JANUARY PRESSURE AND WINDS

Isobars are in millibars at sea level

mb: 1040, 1035, 1030, 1025, 1020, 1015, 1010, 1005, 1000, 995, 990

← Prevailing Winds

JULY PRESSURE AND WINDS

Isobars are in millibars at sea level

mb: 1025, 1020, 1015, 1010, 1005, 1000, 995

← Prevailing Winds

Climate Records

Pressure and winds

Highest barometric pressure: Agata, Siberia, 1,083.8 mb at altitude 262 m [862 ft], 31 December 1968.

Lowest barometric pressure: Typhoon Tip, 480 km [300 mls] west of Guam, Pacific Ocean, 870 mb, 12 October 1979.

Highest recorded wind speed: Mt Washington, New Hampshire, USA, 371 km/h [231 mph], 12 April 1934. This is three times as strong as hurricane force on the Beaufort Scale.

Windiest place: Commonwealth Bay, George V Coast, Antarctica, where gales frequently reach over 320 km/h [200 mph].

Worst recorded storm: Bangladesh (then East Pakistan) cyclone*, 13 November 1970 – over 300,000 dead or missing. The 1991 cyclone, Bangladesh's and the world's second worst in terms of loss of life, killed an estimated 138,000 people.

Worst recorded tornado: Missouri/Illinois/Indiana, USA, 18 March 1925 – 792 deaths. The tornado was only 275 m [300 yds] wide.

** Tropical cyclones are known as hurricanes in Central and North America, as typhoons in the Far East, and as willy-willies in northern Australia.*

Climate

For more information:

9 Ocean currents
14 Circulation of the air
15 Classification of clouds
Pressure and winds
18 Hydrological cycle
19 Natural vegetation
21 Greenhouse effect
22 Global warming

Weather is the day-to-day or hour-to-hour condition of the air, while climate is weather in the long term, the seasonal pattern of hot and cold, wet and dry, averaged over a long period. Most classifications of climate are based on a system developed by a Russian meteorologist, Vladimir Köppen, in the early 19th century. Using a code based on letters and a classification centred on two main features, temperature and precipitation, he identified five main climatic types: tropical (A), dry (B), warm temperate (C), cold temperate (D), and polar (E). A highland mountain climate (H), was added later to account for the variety of altitudinal climatic zones on high mountains. Each region was then further subdivided.

Latitude is a major factor in determining climate, but other factors add to the complexity. They include the differential heating of land and sea, the distance from the sea, the effect of mountains on winds, and the influence of ocean currents. For example, New York City, Naples and the Gobi Desert share almost the same latitude, but their climates are very different.

Climates are not indefinitely stable. During the last Ice Age, the Earth underwent alternating cold periods, called glacials, separated by warm interglacials. The Milankovich theory suggests such cycles may be caused by variations in the Earth's path around the Sun, changing from almost circular to elliptical every 95,000 years, and variations in the Earth's tilt from 21.5° to 24.5° every 42,000 years. Another factor is that the Earth is now closest to the Sun in the middle of winter in the northern hemisphere and furthest away in summer. But 12,000 years ago, at the height of the last glacial period, the northern winter fell with the Sun at its most distant.

Studies of these cycles suggest we are in an interglacial with a glacial period on the way. But, many scientists believe global warming, largely a result of burning fossil fuels and deforestation, is occurring faster than the slow cycles of the Solar System.

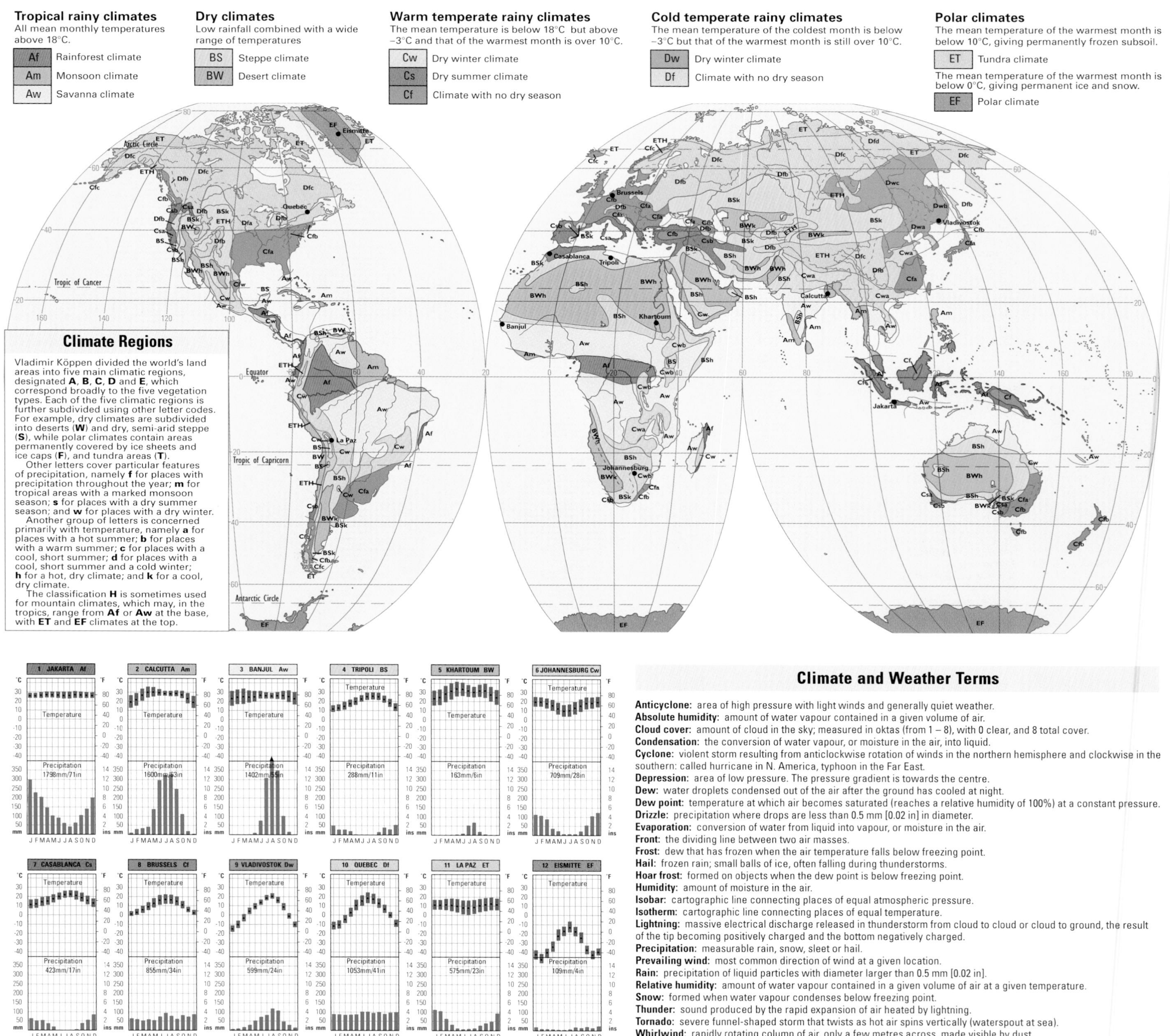

Climate Regions

Vladimir Köppen divided the world's land areas into five main climatic regions, designated **A**, **B**, **C**, **D** and **E**, which correspond broadly to the five vegetation types. Each of the five climatic regions is further subdivided using other letter codes. For example, dry climates are subdivided into deserts (**W**) and dry, semi-arid steppe (**S**), while polar climates contain areas permanently covered by ice sheets and ice caps (**F**), and tundra areas (**T**).

Other letters cover particular features of precipitation, namely **f** for places with precipitation throughout the year; **m** for tropical areas with a marked monsoon season; **s** for places with a dry summer season; and **w** for places with a dry winter.

Another group of letters is concerned primarily with temperature, namely **a** for places with a hot summer; **b** for places with a warm summer; **c** for places with a cool, short summer; **d** for places with a cool, short summer and a cold winter; **h** for a hot, dry climate; and **k** for a cool, dry climate.

The classification **H** is sometimes used for mountain climates, which may, in the tropics, range from **Af** or **Aw** at the base, with **ET** and **EF** climates at the top.

Climate and Weather Terms

Anticyclone: area of high pressure with light winds and generally quiet weather.
Absolute humidity: amount of water vapour contained in a given volume of air.
Cloud cover: amount of cloud in the sky; measured in oktas (from 1 – 8), with 0 clear, and 8 total cover.
Condensation: the conversion of water vapour, or moisture in the air, into liquid.
Cyclone: violent storm resulting from anticlockwise rotation of winds in the northern hemisphere and clockwise in the southern: called hurricane in N. America, typhoon in the Far East.
Depression: area of low pressure. The pressure gradient is towards the centre.
Dew: water droplets condensed out of the air after the ground has cooled at night.
Dew point: temperature at which air becomes saturated (reaches a relative humidity of 100%) at a constant pressure.
Drizzle: precipitation where drops are less than 0.5 mm [0.02 in] in diameter.
Evaporation: conversion of water from liquid into vapour, or moisture in the air.
Front: the dividing line between two air masses.
Frost: dew that has frozen when the air temperature falls below freezing point.
Hail: frozen rain; small balls of ice, often falling during thunderstorms.
Hoar frost: formed on objects when the dew point is below freezing point.
Humidity: amount of moisture in the air.
Isobar: cartographic line connecting places of equal atmospheric pressure.
Isotherm: cartographic line connecting places of equal temperature.
Lightning: massive electrical discharge released in thunderstorm from cloud to cloud or cloud to ground, the result of the tip becoming positively charged and the bottom negatively charged.
Precipitation: measurable rain, snow, sleet or hail.
Prevailing wind: most common direction of wind at a given location.
Rain: precipitation of liquid particles with diameter larger than 0.5 mm [0.02 in].
Relative humidity: amount of water vapour contained in a given volume of air at a given temperature.
Snow: formed when water vapour condenses below freezing point.
Thunder: sound produced by the rapid expansion of air heated by lightning.
Tornado: severe funnel-shaped storm that twists as hot air spins vertically (waterspout at sea).
Whirlwind: rapidly rotating column of air, only a few metres across, made visible by dust.

Climate Change

Human factors, such as the emission of greenhouse gases through the burning of fossil fuels and deforestation, have contributed to global warming. The histogram, below, shows in blue the average global temperatures from 1860 (when sufficient observations became available for global averages to be calculated) to 1996. The red line is a 10-year running average. Overall, there is an upward trend, particularly so since the 1970s, when global warming became a matter of concern in scientific circles. The large year-to-year changes indicate the Earth's natural climatic variability and the influence of such factors as major volcanic eruptions.

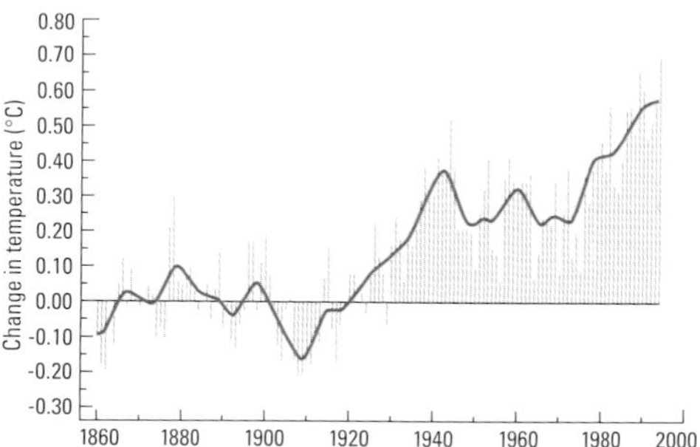

Data from the Hadley Centre for Climate Research and Prediction

Beaufort Wind Scale

Named after the 19th-century British naval officer who devised it, Admiral Beaufort, the Beaufort Scale assesses wind speed according to its effects. It was originally designed as an aid for sailors, but has since been adapted for use on the land. It is used internationally.

Scale	Wind speed km/h	Wind speed mph	Effect
0	0–1	0–1	**Calm** Smoke rises vertically
1	1–5	1–3	**Light air** Wind direction shown only by smoke drift
2	6–11	4–7	**Light breeze** Wind felt on face; leaves rustle; vanes moved by wind
3	12–19	8–12	**Gentle breeze** Leaves and small twigs in constant motion; wind extends small flag
4	20–28	13–18	**Moderate** Raises dust and loose paper; small branches move
5	29–38	19–24	**Fresh** Small trees in leaf sway; crested wavelets on inland waters
6	39–49	25–31	**Strong** Large branches move; difficult to use umbrellas; overhead wires whistle
7	50–61	32–38	**Near gale** Whole trees in motion; difficult to walk against wind
8	62–74	39–46	**Gale** Twigs break from trees; walking very difficult
9	75–88	47–54	**Strong gale** Slight structural damage
10	89–102	55–63	**Storm** Trees uprooted; serious structural damage
11	103–117	64–72	**Violent storm** Widespread damage
12	118+	73+	**Hurricane**

The Monsoon

Monsoon is the term given to the seasonal reversal of wind direction, most noticeably in South-east Asia. It results from a combination of factors: the extreme heating and cooling of large landmasses in relation to the less marked changes in temperature of the adjacent seas; the northwards movement of the Intertropical Convergence Zone (ITCZ); and the effect of the Himalayas on the circulation of the air.

In early March, which normally marks the end of the sub-continent's cool season and the start of the hot season, winds blow outwards from the mainland. But as the overhead Sun and the ITCZ move northwards, the land is intensely heated, and a low-pressure system develops. The south-east trade winds, which are drawn across the Equator, change direction and are sucked into the interior to become south-westerly winds, bringing heavy rain. By November, the overhead Sun and the ITCZ have again moved southwards and the wind directions are again reversed. Cool winds blow from the Asian interior to the sea, losing any moisture on the Himalayas before descending to the coast.

Temperature

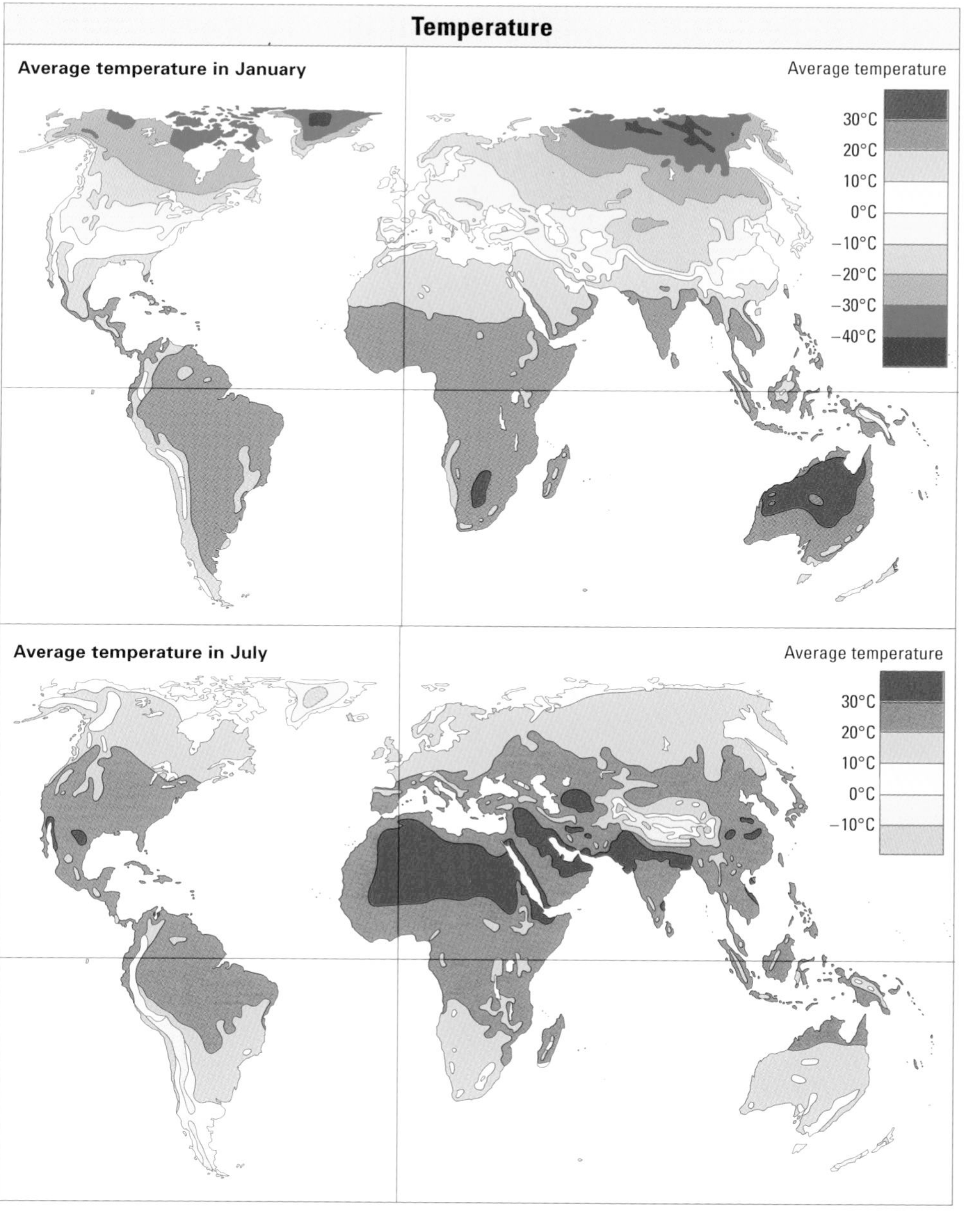

Precipitation

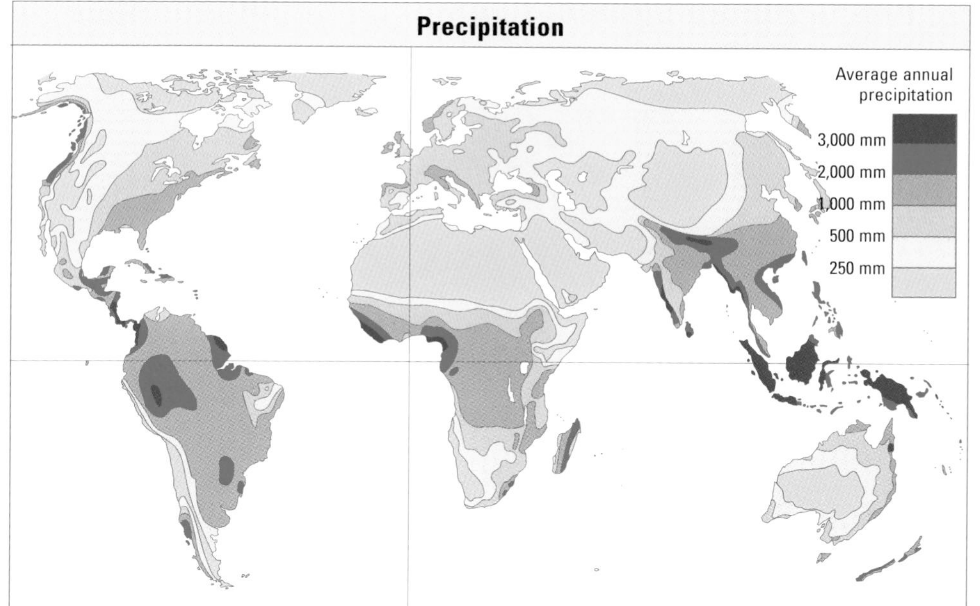

Delhi
Himalayas
Cherrapunji
Bombay (Mumbai)
Bangkok
INDIAN OCEAN
ITCZ

March – Start of the hot, dry season. The ITCZ is over the southern Indian Ocean.

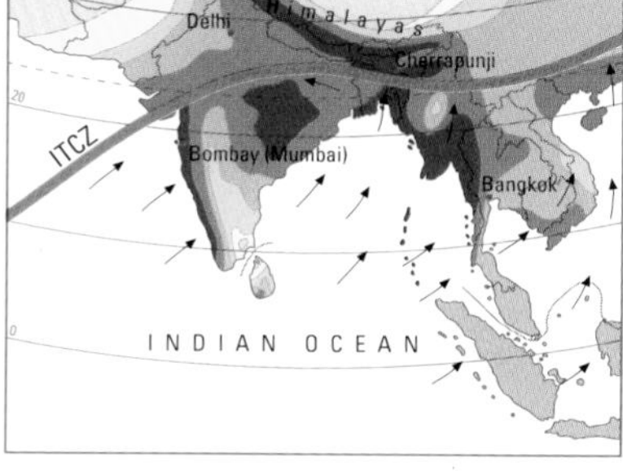

July – The rainy season. The ITCZ has migrated northwards; winds blow onshore.

Delhi
Himalayas
Cherrapunji
Bombay (Mumbai)
Bangkok
INDIAN OCEAN
ITCZ

November – The ITCZ has returned south. The offshore winds are cool and dry.

Monthly rainfall (mm)
>400
200–400
100–200
50–100
25–50
<25
wind direction
ITCZ

Climate Records

Temperature

Highest recorded temperature: Al Aziziyah, Libya, 58°C [136.4°F], 13 September 1922.

Highest mean annual temperature: Dallol, Ethiopia, 34.4°C [94°F], 1960–66.

Longest heatwave: Marble Bar, W. Australia, 162 days over 38°C [100°F], 23 October 1923 to 7 April 1924.

Lowest recorded temperature (outside poles): Verkhoyansk, Siberia, –68°C [–90°F], 6 February 1933. Verkhoyansk also registered the greatest annual range of temperature: –70°C to 37°C [–94°F to 98°F].

Lowest mean annual temperature: Polus Nedostupnosti, Pole of Cold, Antarctica, –57.8°C [–72°F].

Precipitation

Driest place: Calama, N. Chile: no recorded rainfall in 400 years to 1971.

Wettest place (average): Tututendo, Colombia: mean annual rainfall 11,770 mm [463.4 in].

Wettest place (12 months): Cherrapunji, Meghalaya, N.E. India, 26,470 mm [1,040 in], August 1860 to August 1861. Cherrapunji also holds the record for rainfall in one month: 2,930 mm [115 in], July 1861. (See maps below.)

Wettest place (24 hours): Cilaos, Réunion, Indian Ocean, 1,870 mm [73.6 in], 15–16 March 1952.

Heaviest hailstones: Gopalganj, Bangladesh, up to 1.02 kg [2.25 lb], 14 April 1986 (killed 92 people).

Heaviest snowfall (continuous): Bessans, Savoie, France, 1,730 mm [68 in] in 19 hours, 5–6 April 1969.

Heaviest snowfall (season/year): Paradise Ranger Station, Mt Rainier, Washington, USA, 31,102 mm [1,224.5 in], 19 February 1971 to 18 February 1972.

Water and Vegetation

For more information:

12 Rivers and glaciers
14 Types of precipitation
20 Biodiversity

Without the hydrological cycle, whereby water is constantly recycled between the oceans, the atmosphere and the land, the continents would be barren. Precipitation enables plants to grow and soils to form, creating the world's natural vegetation regions and the ecosystems that support animal life. Running water also plays a major role in shaping landforms. Yet in many parts of the world, people do not have safe water to drink and suffer from diseases caused by water-borne organisms or pollution. In addition, the limited water supplies have to be shared with agriculture and industry.

In 1996, UN experts argued that the demand for water is increasing at about twice the rate of population growth. They predict that, by 2025, two-thirds of the world's population will face water shortages. This could lead to conflict and even boundary wars, especially because 300 major rivers cross national frontiers and access to their water is likely to be disputed.

The Hydrological Cycle

The world's water balance is regulated by the constant recycling of water between the oceans, atmosphere and land. The movement of water between these three reservoirs is known as the hydrological cycle. The oceans play a vital role in the hydrological cycle: 74% of the total precipitation falls over the oceans and 84% of the total evaporation comes from the oceans. Water vapour in the atmosphere circulates around the planet, transporting energy as well as the water itself. When the vapour cools, it falls as rain or snow. The whole cycle is driven by the Sun.

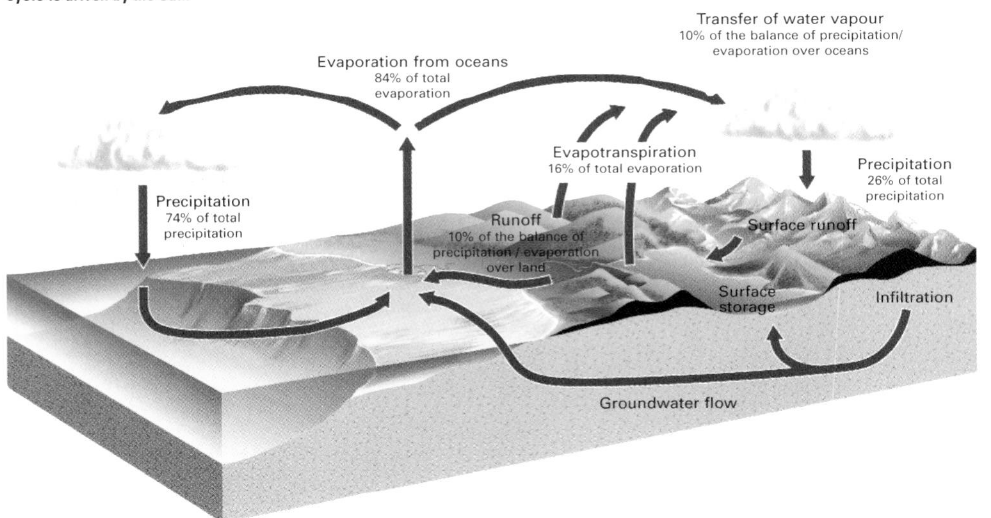

Water Distribution

The distribution of planetary water, by percentage. Oceans and ice caps together account for more than 99% of the total; the breakdown of the remainder is estimated.

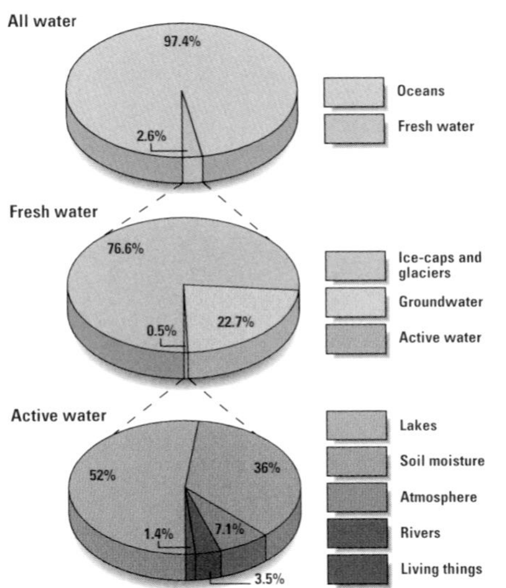

Almost all the world's water is 3,000 million years old, and all of it cycles endlessly through the hydrosphere, though at different rates. Water vapour circulates over days, even hours; deep ocean water circulates over millennia; and ice-cap water remains solid for millions of years.

Water Utilization

The percentage breakdown of water usage by sector, selected countries (1996)

Domestic
Industrial
Agriculture

0 20 40 60 80 100

Algeria
Australia
Egypt
France
Ghana
India
Mexico
Poland
Russian Fed.
Saudi Arabia
UK
USA

Water Runoff

Annual freshwater runoff by continent in cubic kilometres

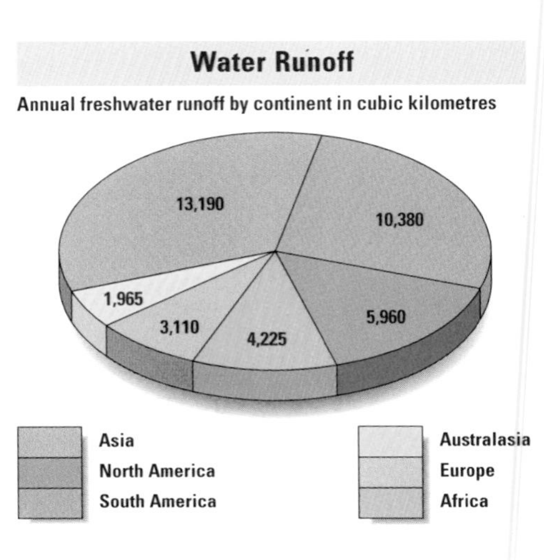

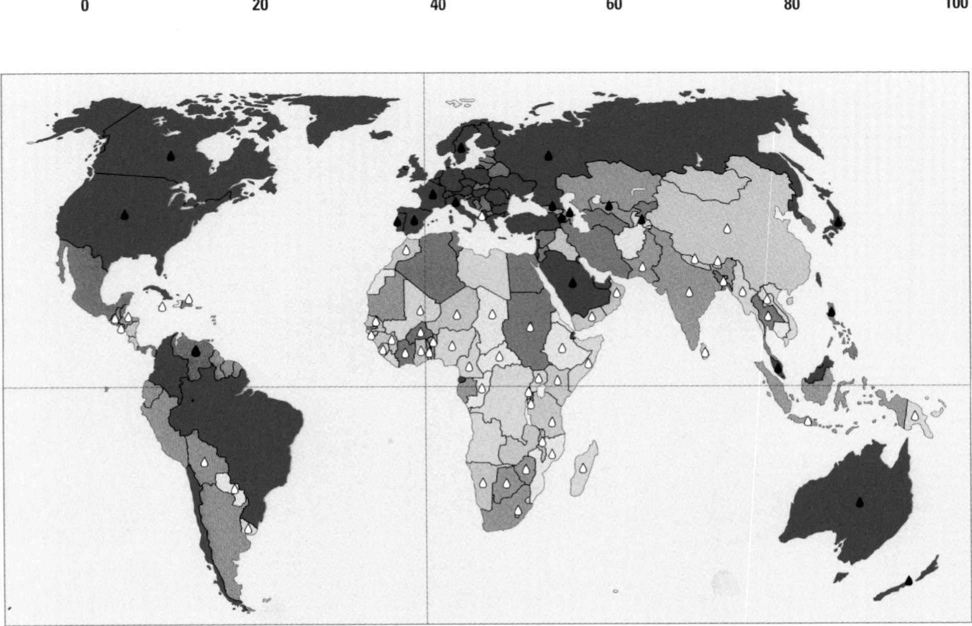

Water Supply

Percentage of total population with access to safe drinking water (1995)

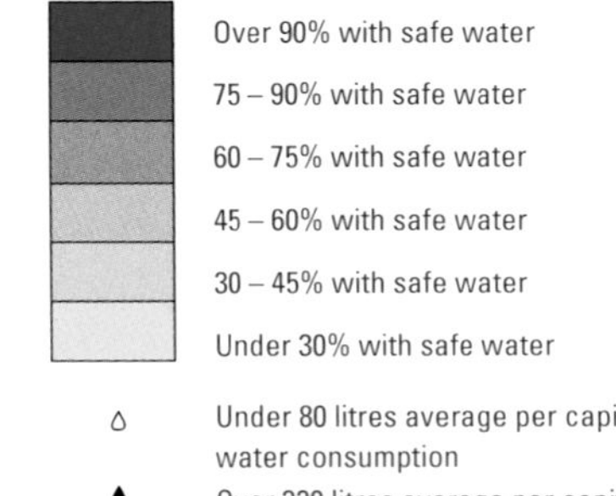

Least well-provided countries

Paraguay	8%	Central Afr. Rep.	18%
Afghanistan	10%	Bhutan	21%
Cambodia	13%	Congo (D. Rep.)	25%

Watersheds

The world's major rivers; the rank of the world's 20 longest is shown in square brackets, led by the Nile and the Amazon.

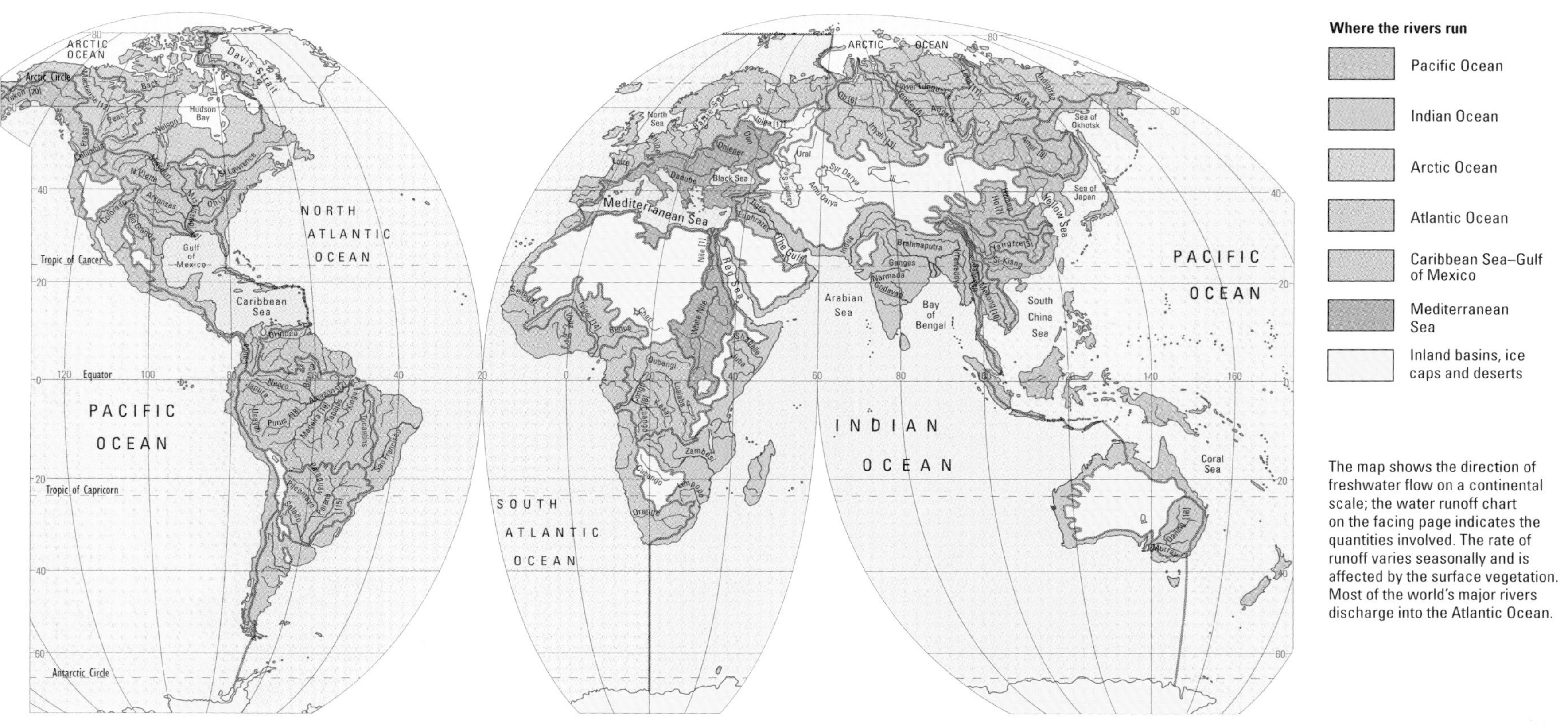

The map shows the direction of freshwater flow on a continental scale; the water runoff chart on the facing page indicates the quantities involved. The rate of runoff varies seasonally and is affected by the surface vegetation. Most of the world's major rivers discharge into the Atlantic Ocean.

Annual Sediment Yield

Around 20% of all land-derived sediment is carried by three Asian rivers: the Brahmaputra, Huang He (Yellow River) and Ganges. Together these three rivers carry 3,206 million tonnes of sediment per year into the oceans. Sediment yield is affected by runoff and vegetation cover and is steadily increasing due to large-scale deforestation, most notably in South-east Asia and the Amazon basin. In these regions, deforesting the slopes allows the heavy tropical rains to wash away whatever thin and fragile soil there is, leading to severe erosion of the land.

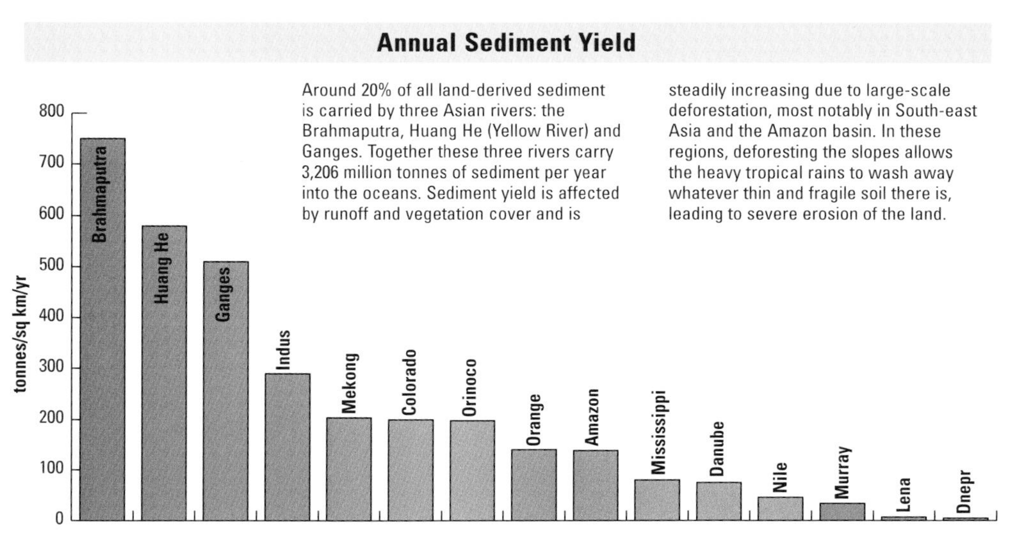

Land Use by Continent

The proportion of productive land has reached its upper limit in Europe, and in Asia more than 80% of potential cropland is already under cultivation.

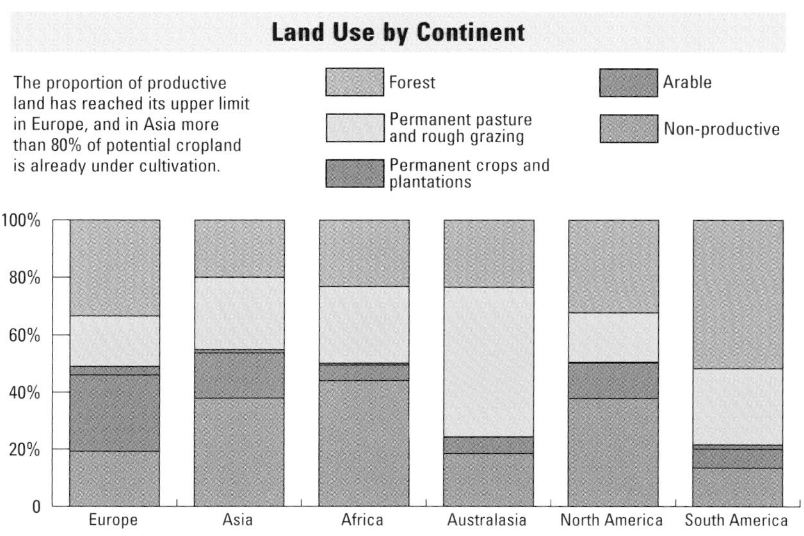

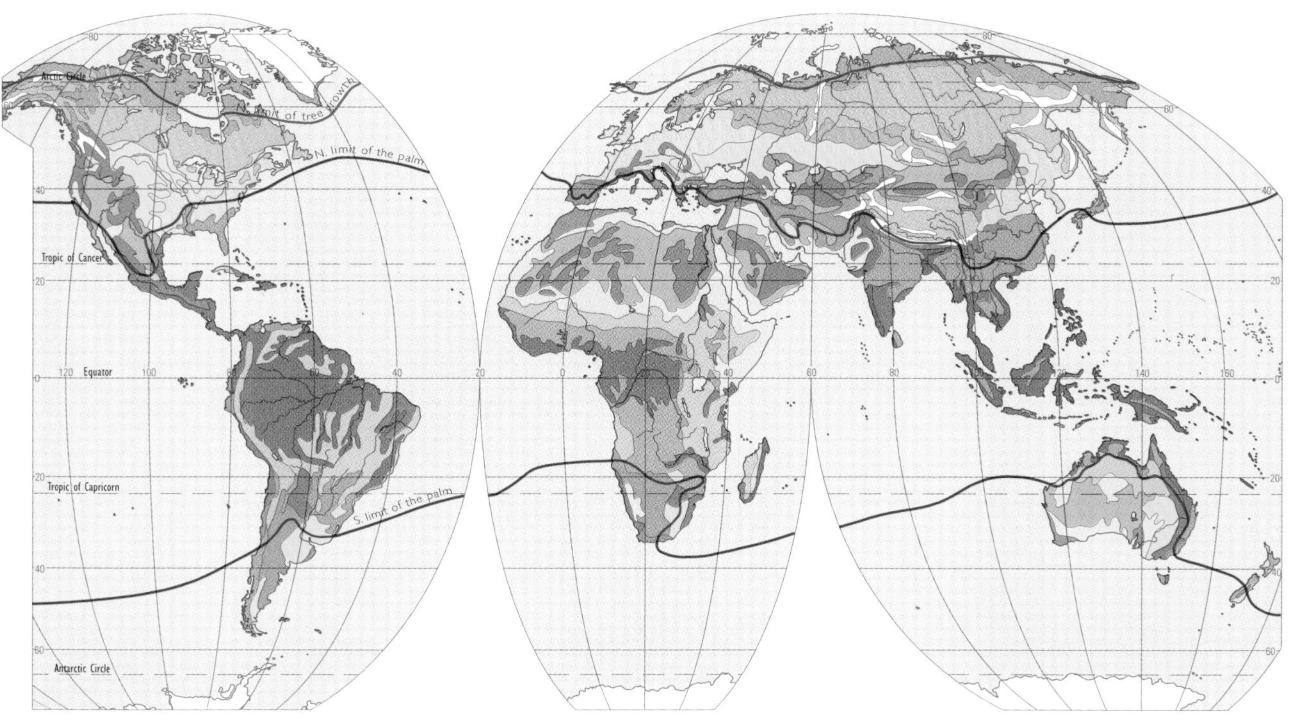

Natural Vegetation

- Tropical rainforest
- Subtropical and temperate rainforest
- Monsoon woodland and open jungle
- Subtropical and temperate woodland, scrub and bush
- Tropical savanna, with low trees and bush
- Tropical savanna and grasslands
- Dry semi-desert, with shrub and grass
- Desert shrub
- Desert
- Dry steppe and shrub
- Temperate grasslands, prairie and steppe
- Mediterranean hardwood forest and scrub
- Temperate deciduous forest and meadow
- Temperate deciduous and coniferous forest
- Northern coniferous forest (taiga)
- Mountainous forest, mainly coniferous
- High plateau steppe and tundra
- Arctic tundra
- Polar and mountainous ice desert

The map illustrates the natural 'climax vegetation' of a region, as dictated by its climate and topography. In most cases, human agricultural activity has drastically altered the vegetation pattern. Western Europe, for example, lost most of its broadleaf forest many centuries ago, while elsewhere irrigation has turned some natural semi-desert into productive land. The various vegetation regions support different kinds of animals and, in an undisturbed state, they are highly developed biological communities, or biomes.

The blue line on the map represents the northern limit of tree growth, and the red lines indicate the northern and southern limits of palm growth.

The Natural Environment

For more information:

8 Oceans
14 Atmosphere
19 Natural vegetation
22 Carbon dioxide
Greenhouse power
Global warming
23 Acid rain
Desertification
Deforestation
Water pollution

Recent discoveries of life forms in some of the world's most hostile environments, such as around the black smokers along the ocean ridges, prepared the way for the announcement by NASA scientists in 1996 that they had found microfossils in a Martian meteorite. But other scientists were sceptical, believing them to be natural mineral structures and not evidence of extraterrestrial life.

Until further evidence is available, the Earth remains the only planet where we know for sure that life exists. According to the fossil record, life on Earth appeared at least 3,500 million years ago. Since then, it has evolved from its primitive beginnings to its modern biodiversity, including millions of plants, animals and micro-organisms. Living organisms have not only adapted to the environment but they have also changed their environment to suit themselves. For example, the Earth's early atmosphere contained little oxygen but the emergence of multi-celled, oxygen-producing algae, around 2,000 million years ago, led to the creation of an oxygen-rich atmosphere. This enabled land animals to populate the ancient continents.

The amount of the greenhouse gas carbon dioxide in the atmosphere would steadily increase from its present 0.03% were it not for plants. Without them, the Earth's atmosphere would, in a few million years, be similar to that of Venus, where surface temperatures reach 475°C. The Earth has evolved into a complex control system, sensing and reacting to changes and tending always to maintain the balance it has achieved.

Much discussion has centred on how that balance changes. Only recently, scientists were suggesting that we may be living in an interglacial stage of the Pleistocene Ice Age. From the 1980s, however, predictions of future climates have concentrated more on global warming, caused by pollution which has led to an increase in greenhouse gases in the atmosphere. Interference in the natural cycles that control the environment may have consequences that are hard to predict.

Furthermore, we are currently experiencing a period of mass extinction of species, causing a rapid reduction in our planet's biodiversity. A report by the World Conservation Union in 1996 stated that, of the 4,327 known mammal species, 1,096 were at risk and 169 'critically endangered'.

Biodiversity in California

The photograph, left, is a false-colour satellite image of central California in the south-western United States. The large inlet of the Pacific Ocean is San Francisco Bay. San Francisco lies just below the entrance to the bay, with Oakland on the far side and San Jose to the south-east. California, nicknamed the Golden State, is the third largest state in the United States and the most populous.

Because of its varied terrain and climate, California has a wide range of diverse habitats within a relatively small area. East of the forested Coast Ranges (the grey and red areas just inland from the bay) lies the fertile Central Valley, which appears as a red and blue chequerboard. The Sierra Nevada is the red area in the top right corner. In the north-west and south-west of the state, not shown here, lie parts of the Basin and Range region, much of which is desert. It includes Death Valley, which contains the country's lowest point on land at 86 m below sea level.

Forests cover about 40% of California and they include bristlecone pines, thought to be the oldest living things on Earth, together with coastal redwoods, the world's tallest trees. Wildlife is still abundant, though some species, such as the rare California condor, are on the endangered list.

The state has achieved much to protect its biodiversity. It contains eight of the 54 national parks in the United States. Two of them, Death Valley and Joshua Tree, were designated national parks as recently as 1994, as part of a conservation measure, including the protection of large areas of wilderness in the deserts.

California has vast resources and, were it a separate nation, it would rank among the world's ten most productive in terms of the total value of its goods and services. This means that, like the United States as a whole, it has resources, which many developing countries lack, to finance conservation measures. For example, the World Conservation Union reported in 1996 that 8% of mammals were threatened in the United States, as compared with 32% in the Philippines and 44% in Madagascar, two countries where habitat destruction has been on a large scale.

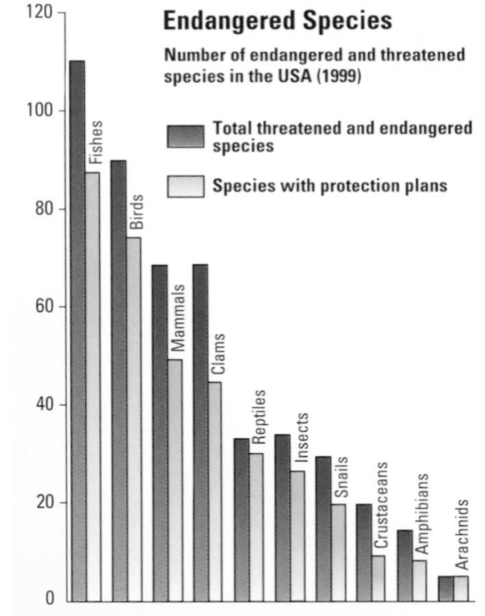

Threatened Mammals

Percentage of mammal species classified as threatened (1996). Many scientists believe we are currently experiencing a period of mass extinction of species rivalling five other periods in the past half a billion years. Among the most threatened mammals are elephants, primates and rhinoceroses.

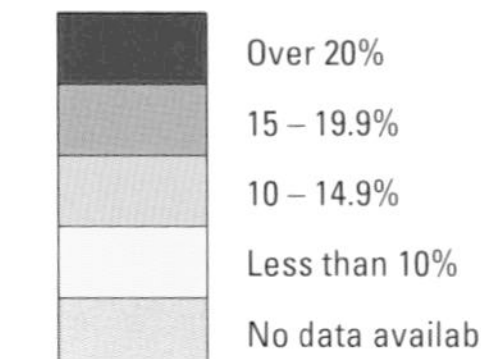

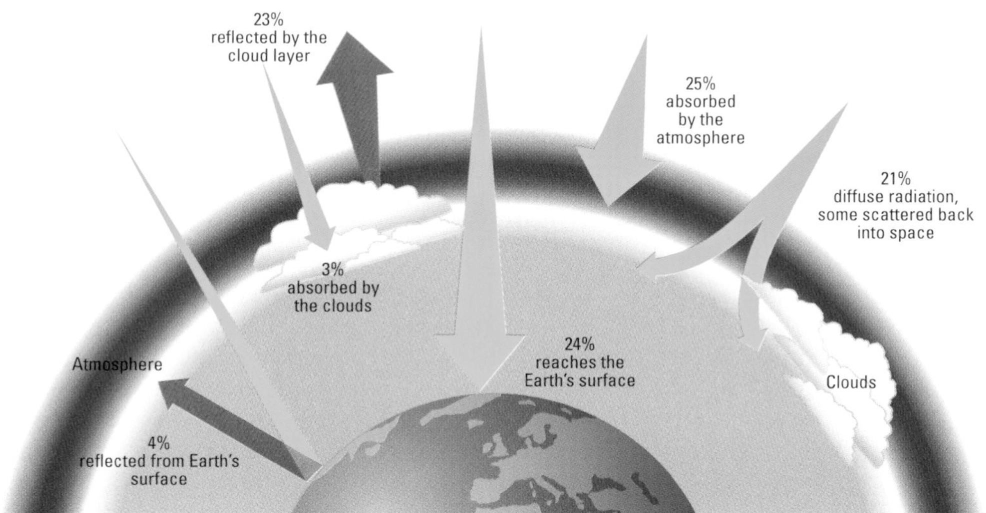

The Earth's Energy Balance

Apart from a modest quantity of internal heat from its molten core, the Earth receives all of its energy from the Sun. If the planet is to remain at a constant temperature, it must reradiate exactly as much energy as it receives. Even a minute surplus would lead to a warmer Earth, a deficit to a cooler one. The temperature at which thermal equilibrium is reached depends on a multitude of interconnected factors. Two of the most important are the relative brightness of the Earth – its index of reflectivity, called the 'albedo' – and the heat-trapping capacity of the atmosphere – the celebrated 'greenhouse effect' (see below).

Because the Sun is very hot, most of its energy arrives in the form of relatively short-wave radiation: the shorter the waves, the more energy they carry. Some of the incoming energy is reflected straight back into space, exactly as it arrived; some is absorbed by the atmosphere on its way towards the surface; some is absorbed by the Earth itself. Absorbed energy heats the Earth and its atmosphere alike. But since its temperature is very much lower than that of the Sun, the outgoing energy is emitted at much longer infra-red wavelengths. Some of the outgoing radiation escapes directly into outer space; some of it is reabsorbed by the atmosphere. Atmospheric energy eventually finds its way back into space, too, after a complex series of interactions. These include the air movements we call the weather and, almost incidentally, the maintenance of life on Earth.

This diagram does not attempt to illustrate the actual mechanisms of heat exchange, but gives a reasonable account (in percentages) of what happens to 100 energy 'units'. Short-wave radiation is shown in yellow, long-wave in orange.

The Carbon Cycle

Most of the constituents of the atmosphere are kept in constant balance by complex cycles in which life plays an essential and indeed a dominant part. The control of carbon dioxide, which if left to its own devices would be the dominant atmospheric gas, is possibly the most important, although since all the Earth's biological and geophysical cycles interact and interlock, it is hard to separate them even in theory and quite impossible in practice.

The Earth has a huge supply of carbon, only a small quantity of which is in the form of carbon dioxide. Of that, around 98% is dissolved in the sea; the fraction circulating in the air amounts to only 340 parts per million of the atmosphere, where its capacity as a greenhouse gas is the key regulator of the planetary temperature. In turn, life regulates the regulator, keeping carbon dioxide concentrations below danger level.

If all life were to vanish from the Earth tomorrow, the atmosphere would begin the process of change immediately, although it might take several million years to achieve a new, inorganic stability. First, the oxygen content would begin to fall away; with no more assistance than a little solar radiation, a few electrical storms and its own high chemical potential, oxygen would steadily combine with atmospheric nitrogen and volcanic outgassing. In doing so, it would yield sufficient acid to react with carbonaceous rocks such as limestone, releasing carbon dioxide. Once carbon dioxide levels exceeded about 1%, its greenhouse power would increase disproportionately. Rising temperatures – well above the boiling point of water – would speed chemical reactions; in time, the Earth's atmosphere would consist of little more than carbon dioxide and superheated water vapour.

Living things, however, circulate carbon. They do so first by simply existing: after all, the carbon atom is the basic building block of living matter. During life, plants absorb carbon dioxide from the atmosphere and, along with various chemicals, as soluble salts from the soil, incorporating the carbon into their structure – leaves and trunks in the case of land plants, shells in the case of plankton and the tiny creatures that feed on it. The oxygen thereby freed is added to the atmosphere, at least for a time. The carbon is returned to circulation when the plants die or is passed up the food chain to the herbivores and then the carnivores that feed on them. As organisms at each of these trophic levels die, they decay, releasing the carbon which then combines once more with the oxygen released during life. However, a small proportion of carbon, about one part in 1,000, is removed almost permanently, buried beneath mud on land or at sea, sinking as dead matter to the ocean floor. In time, it is slowly compressed into sedimentary rocks such as limestone and chalk.

But in the evolution of the Earth, nothing is quite permanent. On an even longer timescale, the planet's crustal movements force new rock upwards in mid-ocean ridges. Limestone deposits are moved, and sea levels change; ancient carboniferous rocks are exposed to weathering, and a little of their carbon is released to be fixed in turn by the current generation of plants.

The carbon cycle has continued quietly for an immensely long time, and without gross disturbance there is no reason why it would not continue almost indefinitely in the future. However, human beings have found a way to release fixed carbon at a rate far faster than existing global systems can recirculate it. The fossil fuels, coal, oil, gas and peat deposits, represent the work of millions of years of carbon accumulation; but it has taken only a few human generations of high-energy scavenging to endanger the entire complex regulatory cycle.

The Greenhouse Effect

Constituting less than 1% of the atmosphere, the natural greenhouse gases (water vapour, carbon dioxide, methane, nitrous oxide and ozone) have a hugely disproportionate effect on the Earth's climate and even its habitability. Like the glass panes in a greenhouse, the gases are transparent to most incoming short-wave radiation, which passes freely to heat the planet beneath. But when the warmed Earth retransmits that energy, in the form of longer-wave infra-red radiation, the gases function as an opaque shield preventing some of it from escaping, so that the planetary surface (like the interior of a greenhouse) stays relatively hot.

Over the last 150 years, there has been a gradual increase in the levels of greenhouse gases (with the exception of water vapour which remains a constant in the system). These increases are causing alarm – global warming associated with a runaway greenhouse effect could bring disaster – and what is more, predictions suggest that there could be a further rise of 1.5–4.5°C by the year 2100. A serious reduction in the greenhouse gases would be just as damaging; a total absence of CO_2, for example, would leave the planet with a temperature roughly 33°C colder than at present.

N.B. The thickness of the Earth's atmosphere is proportionately much thinner than the peel of an apple.

People and the Environment

For more information:

8 Oceans
14 Atmosphere
16 Climate
21 Greenhouse effect
27 Urban pollution

In 1996, the Intergovernmental Panel on Climate Change issued a report stating that 'The balance of evidence suggests a discernible human influence on global climate through emissions of carbon dioxide and other greenhouse gases.' The report acknowledged that average global temperatures have risen by about 0.5°C since the mid-19th century, but there were still reasons for caution, such as discrepancies between measurements of temperatures around the world. Furthermore, our knowledge about how climates change of their own accord is incomplete, as is our understanding of human interference, how this varies in different parts of the world and how it differs from natural climatic variability.

Human interference with nature is nothing new, at least since people turned to agriculture over 10,000 years ago. At first, human actions seemed to have no ill effects because the systems that regulate the global environment absorbed the damage. But from the late 18th century, the Industrial Revolution and population explosion have caused pollution on a scale that threatens to overwhelm the Earth's ability to cope.

The 20th century experienced many disasters, including the dumping of industrial wastes in rivers and seas, accidents at nuclear power stations, and the creation of acid rain through the release of sulphur dioxides and nitrous oxides by the burning of fossil fuels. The release of greenhouse gases are held to be the main reason for global warming, while CFCs (chlorofluorocarbons) have damaged the ozone layer in the stratosphere, the planet's screen against ultraviolet radiation.

Global warming will lead to melting ice sheets and the flooding of fertile coastal plains. Computer models suggest that it might affect ocean currents so that north-western Europe, which owes its mild climate to the Gulf Stream, could expect bitterly cold winters. Some models have suggested that cloud cover could increase, reflecting more solar energy back into space and so start a new Ice Age.

In many tropical areas, deforestation is making productive land barren, while in the dry grasslands bordering deserts, the removal of plant cover is causing desertification. But human ingenuity can respond to this crisis in planet management.

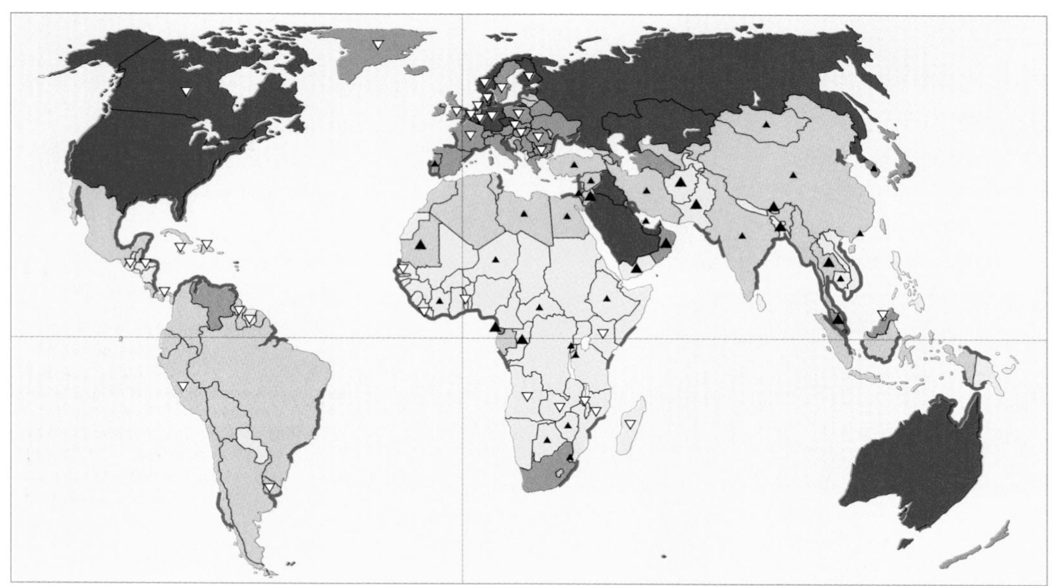

Global Warming

Carbon dioxide emissions in tonnes per person per year (1995)

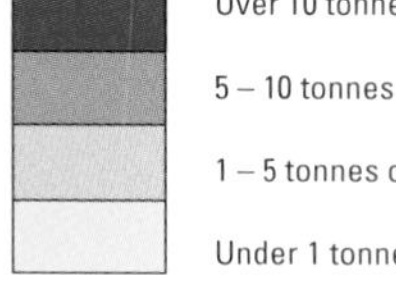

Over 10 tonnes of CO_2
5 – 10 tonnes of CO_2
1 – 5 tonnes of CO_2
Under 1 tonne of CO_2

Changes in CO_2 emissions 1980–90

▲ Over 100% increase
▲ 50–100% increase
▽ Reduction
Coasts in danger of flooding from rising sea levels

Records of global mean surface temperatures from 1860 to the present show that 1995 was the warmest year and that nine of the ten warmest years have occurred since 1983.
This evidence of global warming is attributed mainly to the Greenhouse Effect, caused by the emission of certain gases, notably carbon dioxide (CO_2), into the atmosphere since the start of the Industrial Revolution. At first, much of the CO_2 was absorbed by the oceans. However, the vast increase in fuel combustion since 1950 has led CO_2 content in the atmosphere to increase gradually from 280 parts per million to more than 350 parts per million. Despite international action to control the emissions of some greenhouse gases, CO_2 levels are still rising.

Greenhouse Power

Relative contributions to the Greenhouse Effect by the major heat-absorbing gases in the atmosphere

The chart combines greenhouse potency and volume. Carbon dioxide has a greenhouse potential of only 1, but its concentration of 350 parts per million makes it predominate. CFC 12, with 25,000 times the absorption capacity of CO_2, is present only as 0.00044 ppm.

Carbon dioxide
Ozone
Methane
Nitrous oxide
CFC 12
CFC 11

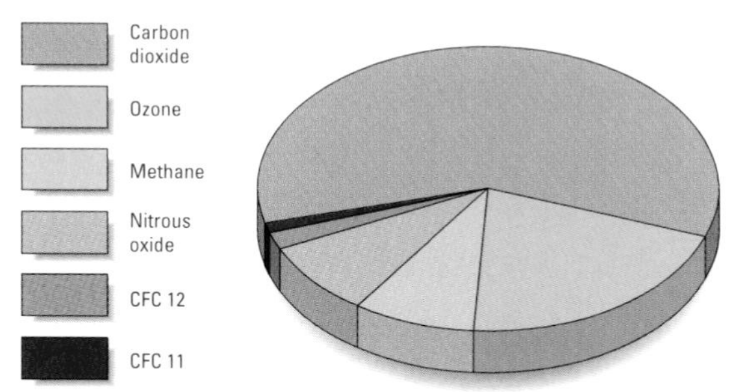

Carbon Dioxide

Carbon dioxide released in millions of tonnes (latest available year)

USA 4,932
Former USSR 3,581
China 2,543
Japan
Germany
India
UK
Iraq
Canada
Italy
France
Mexico

1,000
800
600
400
200

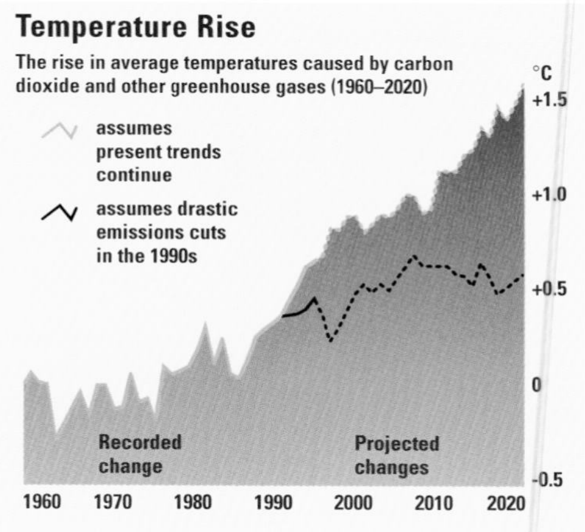

The Thinning Ozone Layer

Total atmospheric ozone concentration in the southern and northern hemispheres (Dobson units, 1995)

In 1985, scientists working in Antarctica discovered a thinning of the ozone layer, commonly known as an 'ozone hole'. This caused immediate alarm because the ozone layer absorbs most of the Sun's dangerous ultraviolet radiation, which is believed to cause an increase in skin cancer, cataracts and damage to the immune system. Since 1985, ozone depletion has increased and, by 1996, the ozone hole over the South Pole was estimated to be as large as North America. The false colour images, right, show the total atmospheric ozone concentration in the southern hemisphere (in October 1995) and the northern hemisphere (in March 1995) with the ozone hole clearly identifiable at the centre. The data are from the Tiros Ozone Vertical Sounder, an instrument on the American TIROS weather satellite. The colours represent the ozone concentration in Dobson Units (DU). Normal healthy values are around 280 DU but the lowest value in the northern hemisphere reached 98 DU. Scientists agree that ozone depletion is caused by CFCs, a group of manufactured chemicals used in air conditioning systems and refrigerators. In a 1987 treaty most industrial nations agreed to phase out CFCs and a complete ban on most CFCs was agreed after the end of 1995. However, scientists believe that the chemicals will remain in the atmosphere for 50 to 100 years. As a result, ozone depletion will continue for many years.

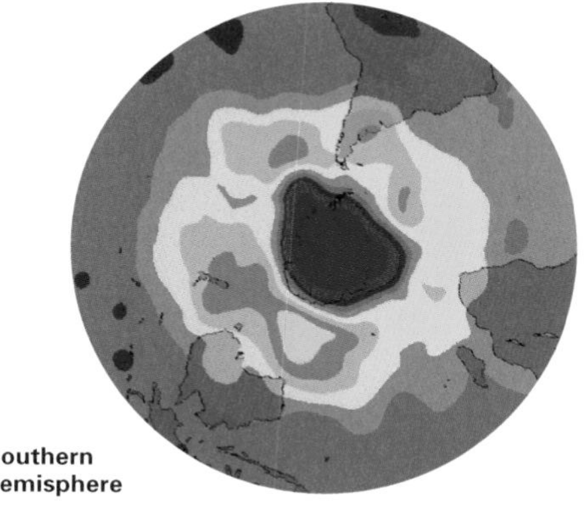

Southern hemisphere

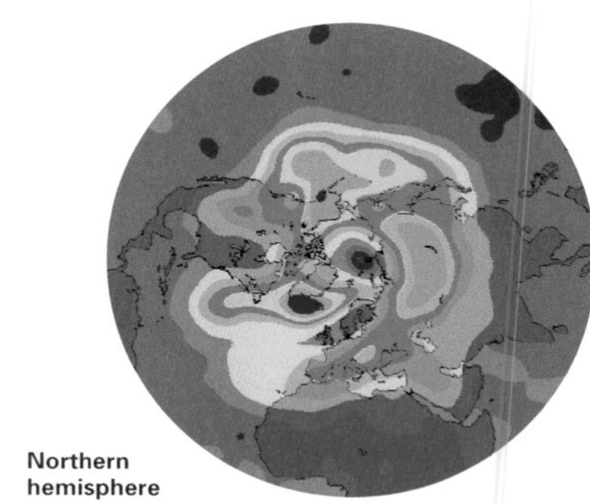

Northern hemisphere

World Pollution

Acid rain and sources of acidic emissions (latest available year)

Acid rain is caused by high levels of sulphur and nitrogen in the atmosphere. They combine with water vapour and oxygen to form acids (H_2SO_4 and HNO_3) which fall as precipitation.

Regions where sulphur and nitrogen oxides are released in high concentrations, mainly from fossil fuel combustion

Major cities with high levels of air pollution (including nitrogen and sulphur emissions)

Areas of heavy acid deposition

pH numbers indicate acidity, decreasing from a neutral 7. Normal rain, slightly acid from dissolved carbon dioxide, never exceeds a pH of 5.6.

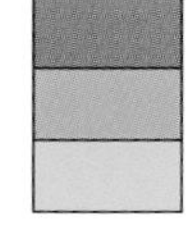
pH less than 4.0 (most acidic)

pH 4.0 to 4.5

pH 4.5 to 5.0

Areas where acid rain is a potential problem

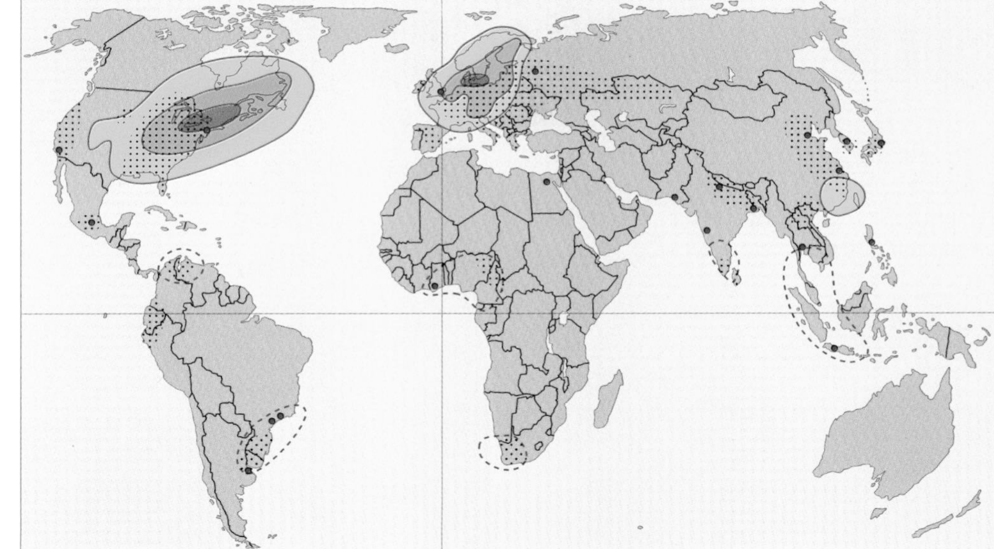

Desertification

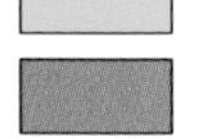
Existing deserts

Areas with a high risk of desertification

Areas with a moderate risk of desertification

Former areas of rainforest

Existing rainforest

Deforestation

Thousands of hectares of forest cleared annually, tropical countries surveyed 1981–85 and 1987–90. Loss as a percentage of remaining stocks is shown in figures on each column.

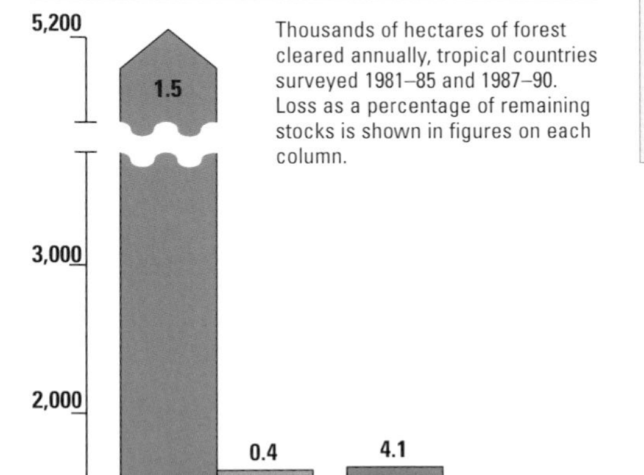

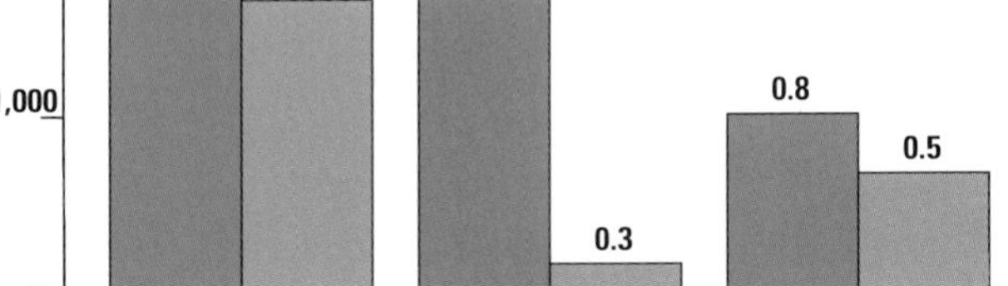

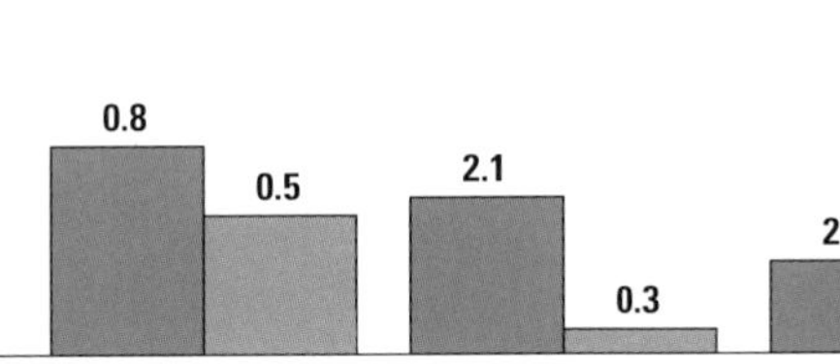

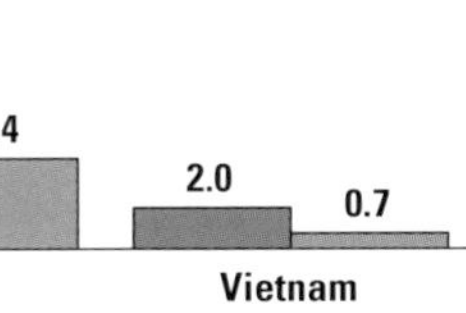

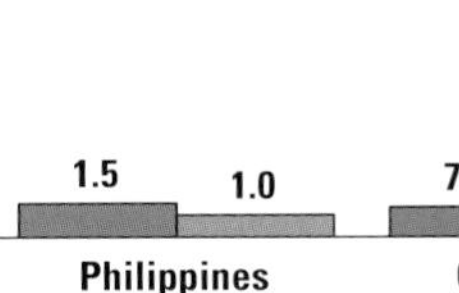

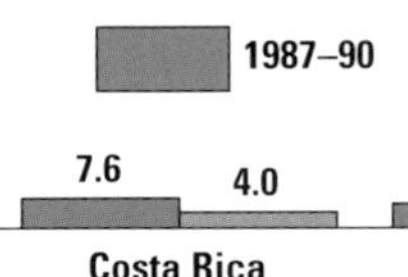

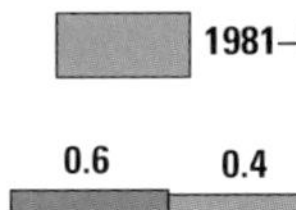

Antarctica

The vast Antarctic ice sheet, containing some 70% of the Earth's fresh water, plays a crucial role in the circulation of the atmosphere and oceans, and hence in determining the planetary climate. The frozen southern continent is also the last remaining wilderness – the largest area to remain free from human colonization.

Ever since Amundsen and Scott raced for the South Pole in 1911, various countries have pressed territorial claims over sections of Antarctica, spurred in recent years by its known and suspected mineral wealth: enough iron ore to supply the world at present levels for 200 years, large oil reserves and, probably, the biggest coal deposits on Earth.

However, the 1961 Antarctic Treaty set aside the area for peaceful uses only, guaranteeing freedom of scientific investigation, banning waste disposal and nuclear testing, and suspending the issue of territorial rights. By 1990, the original 12 signatories had grown to 25, with a further 15 nations granted observer status in subsequent deliberations. However, the Treaty itself was threatened by wrangles between different countries, government agencies and international pressure groups.

Finally, in July 1991, the belated agreement of the UK and the USA assured unanimity on a new accord to ban all mineral exploration for a further 50 years. The ban can only be rescinded if all the present signatories, plus a majority of any future adherents, agree. While the treaty has always lacked a formal mechanism for enforcement, it is firmly underwritten by public concern generated by the efforts of environmental pressure groups such as Greenpeace, which has been foremost in the campaign to have Antarctica declared a 'World Park'.

However, from the mid-1990s, the continent appeared to be under threat from global warming, which some scientists believe was the cause of the break-up of ice shelves along the Antarctic peninsula. Rising temperatures have also disturbed the breeding patterns of Adelie penguins.

Water Pollution

Severely polluted sea areas and lakes

Polluted sea areas and lakes

Areas of frequent oil pollution by shipping

Major oil tanker spills

Major oil rig blow-outs

Offshore dumpsites for industrial and municipal waste

Severely polluted rivers and estuaries

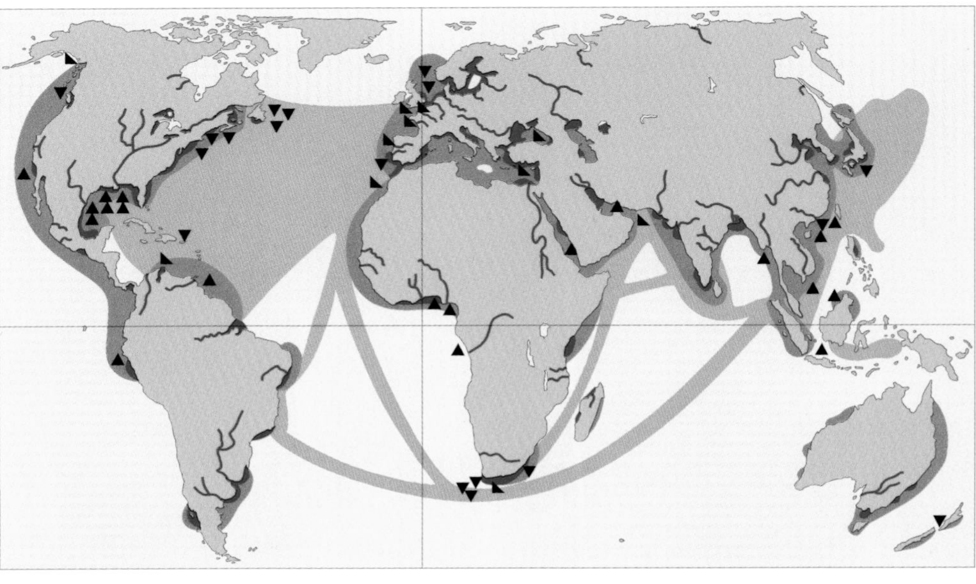

Poisoned rivers, domestic sewage and oil spillage have combined in recent years to reduce the world's oceans to a sorry state of contamination, notably near the crowded coasts of industrialized nations. Shipping routes, too, are constantly affected by tanker discharges. Oil spills of all kinds, however, declined significantly during the 1980s, from a peak of 750,000 tonnes in 1979 to under 50,000 tonnes in 1990. The most notorious tanker spill of that period – when the *Exxon Valdez* (94,999 grt) ran aground in Prince William Sound, Alaska, in March 1989 – released only 267,000 barrels, a relatively small amount compared to the results of blow-outs and war damage. Over 2,500,000 barrels were spilled during the Gulf War of 1991. The worst tanker accident in history occurred in July 1979, when the *Atlantic Empress* and the Aegean Captain collided off Trinidad, polluting the Caribbean with 1,890,000 barrels of crude oil.

Population

For more information:

26 Urbanization of the Earth
Urban population
27 Largest cities
33 Food and population
44 Wealth and population

In 8000 BC, following the development of agriculture, the world had an estimated population of 8 million and by AD 1000 it was about 300 million. The onset of the Industrial Revolution in the late 18th century led to a population explosion. The 1,000 million mark was passed by 1850, it doubled by the 1920s and doubled again to 4,000 million by 1975.

Most demographers agree that the world's population, which passed the 6 billion mark in October 1999, will reach 8.9 billion by 2050. It is not expected to level out until 2200, when it will peak at around 11 billion. After 2200, it is expected to level out or even decline a little. Rapid population growth is concentrated in the developing world; the populations of some developed countries, such as Belgium and Germany, are static or have started to decline.

The developing world includes what the World Bank describes as low-income economies, with an average per capita GNP of US $380, and middle-income economies, with a per capita GNP of $2,520. Most developing countries are in Africa, Asia and Latin America. The developed world, made up of high-income, industrialized economies with an average per capita GNP of $23,420, contains Australasia, most of Europe and North America, and Japan in Asia.

In poorer developing countries, a high proportion of the population is young. They face high levels of expenditure on education and health until population growth rates start to decline. In developed countries, where the population pyramids are becoming increasingly top-heavy, expenditure on pensions and healthcare for the elderly is becoming a social problem.

Crowded Nations

Population per square kilometre (1998), excluding nations of less than 1 million

1.	Monaco	32,894
2.	Macau	25,501
3.	Hong Kong	6,373
4.	Singapore	5,624
5.	Gibraltar	4,239
6.	Bermuda	1,199
7.	Malta	1,214
8.	Vatican City	1,090
9.	Maldives	909
10.	Bahrain	877
11.	Bangladesh	866
12.	Barbados	624
13.	Mauritius	559
14.	Nauru	529
15.	Armenia	487
16.	South Korea	466
17.	Puerto Rico	428
18.	Tuvalu	428
19.	San Marino	424
20.	Netherlands	384

Largest Nations

The world's most populous nations, in millions (2000 est.)

1.	China	1,299
2.	India	1,041
3.	USA	266
4.	Indonesia	218
5.	Brazil	179
6.	Pakistan	162
7.	Russia	155
8.	Bangladesh	150
9.	Japan	128
10.	Mexico	107
11.	Nigeria	105
12.	Vietnam	82
13.	Philippines	77
14.	Germany	76
15.	Iran	68
16.	Turkey	66
17.	Egypt	64
18.	Thailand	63
19.	Ethiopia	61
20.	France	58
21.	UK	58
22.	Italy	57
23.	Ukraine	52
24.	Burma (Myanmar)	51

Population Density

Inhabitants per square kilometre

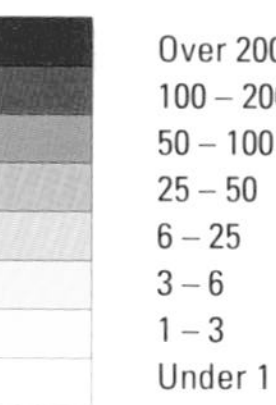

Over 200
100 – 200
50 – 100
25 – 50
6 – 25
3 – 6
1 – 3
Under 1

Urban population

■ Over 10,000,000
● 5,000,000 – 10,000,000
• 1,000,000 – 5,000,000

Places marked are conurbations, not city limits; San Francisco itself, for example, has an official population of less than a million.

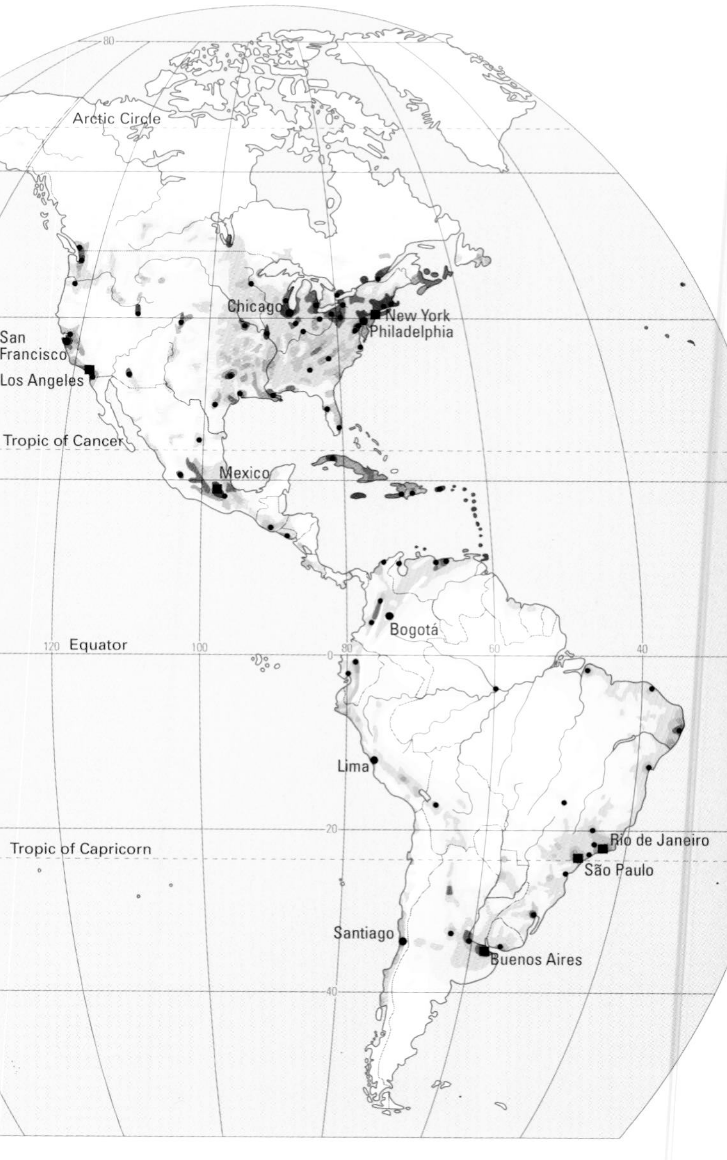

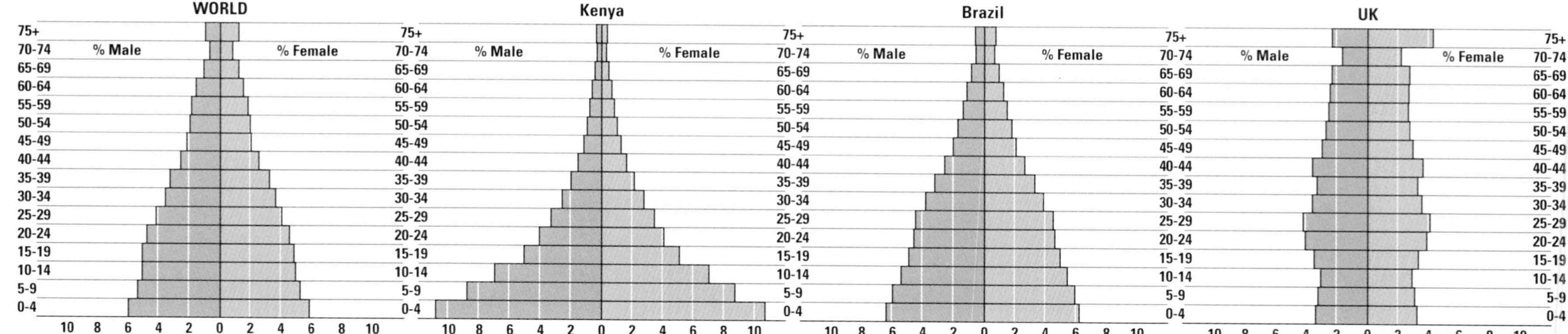

Rates of Growth

The world population doubled between 1950 and 1990. Small rates of population growth led to dramatic increases over two or three generations. The table below translates annual percentage growth into the number of years required to double a population.

% change	Doubling time
0.5	139.0
1.0	69.7
1.5	46.6
2.0	35.0
2.5	28.1
3.0	23.4
3.5	20.1
4.0	17.7

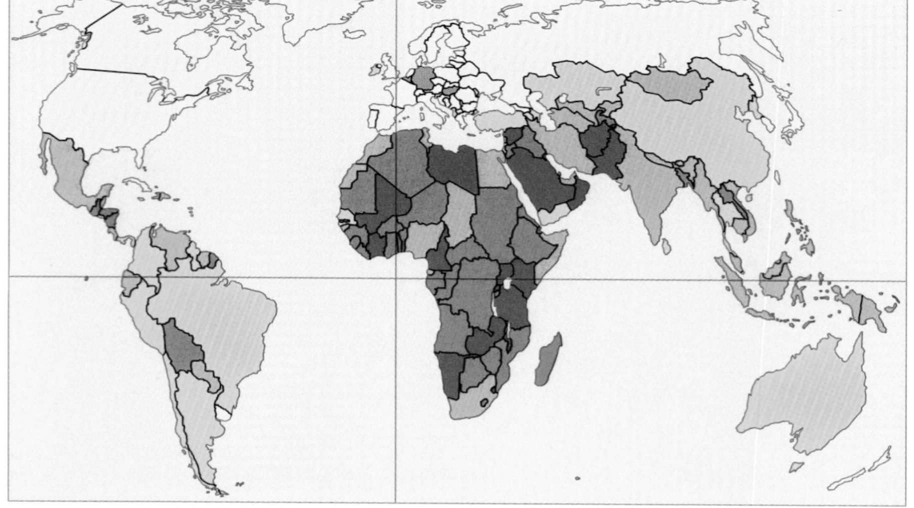

Population Change 1990–2000

The predicted population change for the years 1990–2000

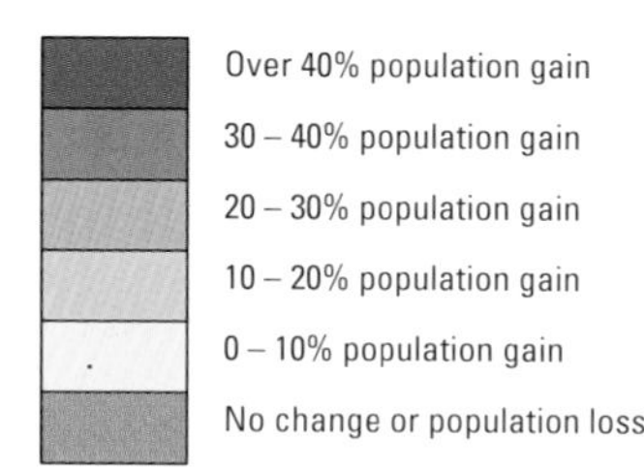

Over 40% population gain
30 – 40% population gain
20 – 30% population gain
10 – 20% population gain
0 – 10% population gain
No change or population loss

Top 5 countries

Kuwait	+75.9%
Namibia	+62.5%
Afghanistan	+60.1%
Mali	+55.5%
Tanzania	+54.6%

Bottom 5 countries

Belgium	–0.1%
Hungary	–0.2%
Grenada	–2.4%
Germany	–3.2%
Tonga	–3.2%

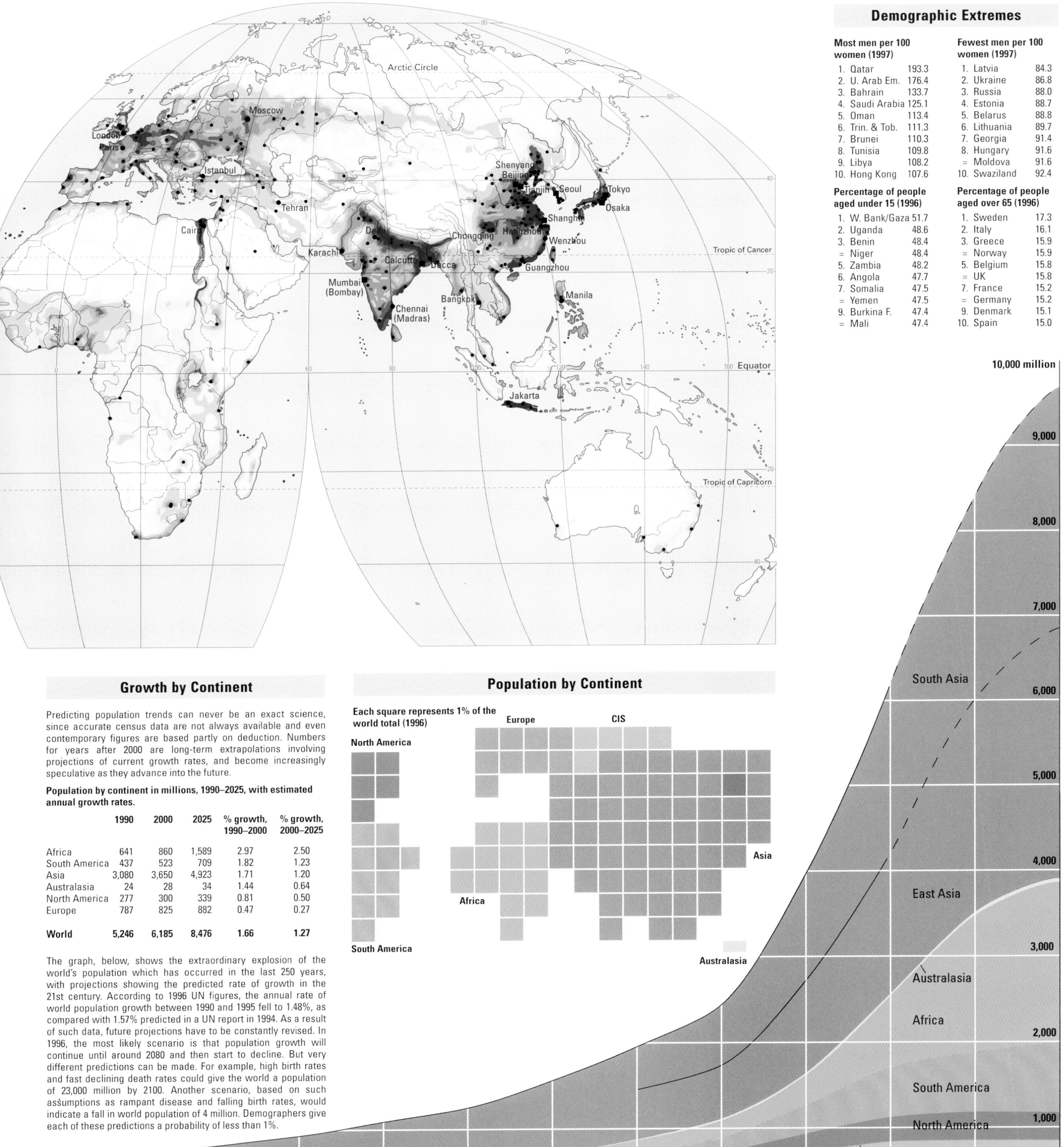

Demographic Extremes

Most men per 100 women (1997)

1.	Qatar	193.3
2.	U. Arab Em.	176.4
3.	Bahrain	133.7
4.	Saudi Arabia	125.1
5.	Oman	113.4
6.	Trin. & Tob.	111.3
7.	Brunei	110.3
8.	Tunisia	109.8
9.	Libya	108.2
10.	Hong Kong	107.6

Fewest men per 100 women (1997)

1.	Latvia	84.3
2.	Ukraine	86.8
3.	Russia	88.0
4.	Estonia	88.7
5.	Belarus	88.8
6.	Lithuania	89.7
7.	Georgia	91.4
8.	Hungary	91.6
=	Moldova	91.6
10.	Swaziland	92.4

Percentage of people aged under 15 (1996)

1.	W. Bank/Gaza	51.7
2.	Uganda	48.6
3.	Benin	48.4
=	Niger	48.4
5.	Zambia	48.2
6.	Angola	47.7
7.	Somalia	47.5
=	Yemen	47.5
9.	Burkina F.	47.4
=	Mali	47.4

Percentage of people aged over 65 (1996)

1.	Sweden	17.3
2.	Italy	16.1
3.	Greece	15.9
=	Norway	15.9
5.	Belgium	15.8
=	UK	15.8
7.	France	15.2
=	Germany	15.2
9.	Denmark	15.1
10.	Spain	15.0

Growth by Continent

Predicting population trends can never be an exact science, since accurate census data are not always available and even contemporary figures are based partly on deduction. Numbers for years after 2000 are long-term extrapolations involving projections of current growth rates, and become increasingly speculative as they advance into the future.

Population by continent in millions, 1990–2025, with estimated annual growth rates.

	1990	2000	2025	% growth, 1990–2000	% growth, 2000–2025
Africa	641	860	1,589	2.97	2.50
South America	437	523	709	1.82	1.23
Asia	3,080	3,650	4,923	1.71	1.20
Australasia	24	28	34	1.44	0.64
North America	277	300	339	0.81	0.50
Europe	787	825	882	0.47	0.27
World	**5,246**	**6,185**	**8,476**	**1.66**	**1.27**

The graph, below, shows the extraordinary explosion of the world's population which has occurred in the last 250 years, with projections showing the predicted rate of growth in the 21st century. According to 1996 UN figures, the annual rate of world population growth between 1990 and 1995 fell to 1.48%, as compared with 1.57% predicted in a UN report in 1994. As a result of such data, future projections have to be constantly revised. In 1996, the most likely scenario is that population growth will continue until around 2080 and then start to decline. But very different predictions can be made. For example, high birth rates and fast declining death rates could give the world a population of 23,000 million by 2100. Another scenario, based on such assumptions as rampant disease and falling birth rates, would indicate a fall in world population of 4 million. Demographers give each of these predictions a probability of less than 1%.

Population by Continent

Each square represents 1% of the world total (1996)

Cities

For more information:
18 Water supply
24 Population density
48 The great ports

Following the development of agriculture more than 10,000 years ago, people began to live in farming villages. Around 5,500 years ago, the world's first cities appeared in the lower Tigris and Euphrates valleys in Mesopotamia. Cities were founded in Ancient Egypt around 5,000 years ago and in China around 3,600 years ago. By contrast with the villages, most people in the early cities were not engaged in farming. Instead, they worked in craft industries, in government services, in religion and trade. Cities became centres of early civilizations and, through trade, their influence spread far and wide. However, they were dependent on the surrounding farming communities for their food and other materials.

In 1750, prior to the start of the Industrial Revolution, barely 3% of the world's population lived in urban areas. By 1850, London and Paris had more than a million people, and, by 1900, 14% of the world's population lived in cities. By 1950, the world had 83 cities with over a million people, and by 1996, there were 280. By 2015, experts predict that there will be more than 500. New York City was the only city with a population of over 10 million in 1950; by 2015 experts predict 27 such cities worldwide, the majority located in the developing world.

By the end of the 20th century, more than half of the world's population was living in urban areas. Despite the rapid growth of cities in developing countries, urbanization is highest in industrialized countries. For example, 78% of the people in the United States live in urban areas, with the European Union not far behind with 77%. But in countries with low-income economies, which contained nearly 60% of the world's total population in 1996, only 28% lived in urban areas.

The rapid rate of urbanization has created problems, especially in cities which have not been able to provide enough jobs and services for the expanding population. Most new city dwellers are people from rural areas and since many of them are young there is a consequent acceleration in the rate of city population growth. In developed countries, with highly mechanized agriculture, it is population pressure that drives many people into urban areas. In developing countries, the grinding poverty of rural life and the lack of services leads to migration to urban areas.

A typical city in a developing country contains millions of people living in shanty towns (or 'informal settlements' in politically correct parlance), while thousands live on the streets. Yet many shanty towns are healthier than the industrial cities of 19th-century Europe and North America. Indeed, surveys have shown that the migrants to the cities in developing countries are less likely to face poverty than they are in rural areas, while benefiting from greater access to healthcare services and education.

Modern cities face many problems, including pollution, crime and unemployment. Yet, given competent central and local government, they are capable of generating the wealth they need to solve them, as well as making a major contribution to the economy.

The Urbanization of the Earth

City-building, 1850–2000; each white spot represents a city of at least 1 million inhabitants.

1850

1900

1925

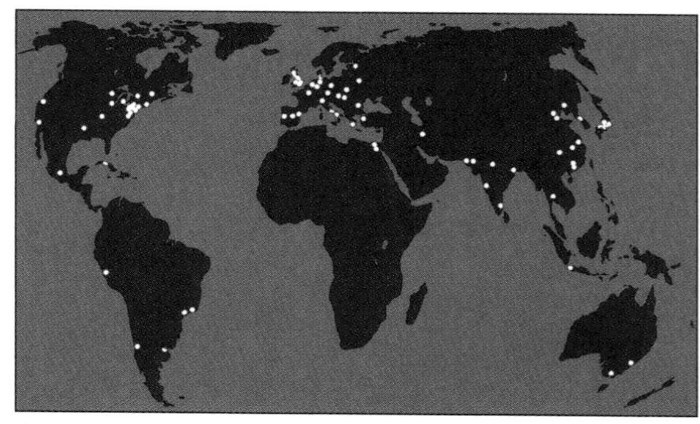

1950

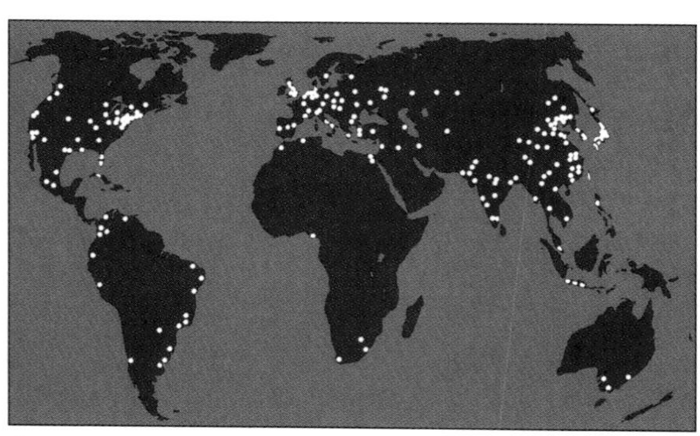

1975

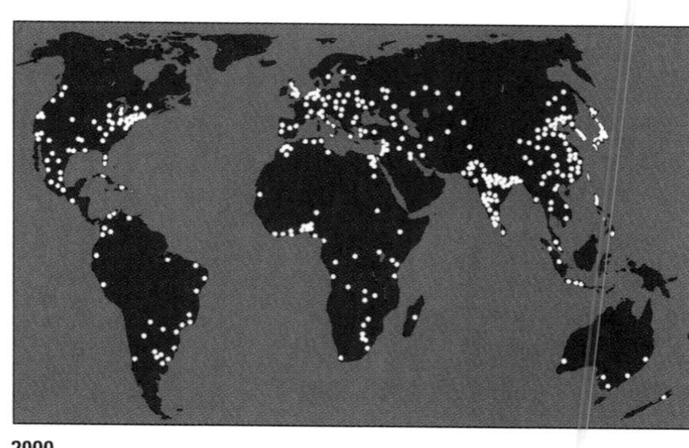

2000

Urban Population

Percentage of total population living in towns and cities (1997)

Most urbanized	
Singapore	100%
Belgium	97%
Israel	91%
Uruguay	91%
Netherlands	89%
[UK 89%]	

Least urbanized	
Rwanda	6%
Bhutan	8%
Burundi	8%
Nepal	11%
Swaziland	12%

Over 75%
50 – 75%
25 – 50%
10 – 25%
Under 10%

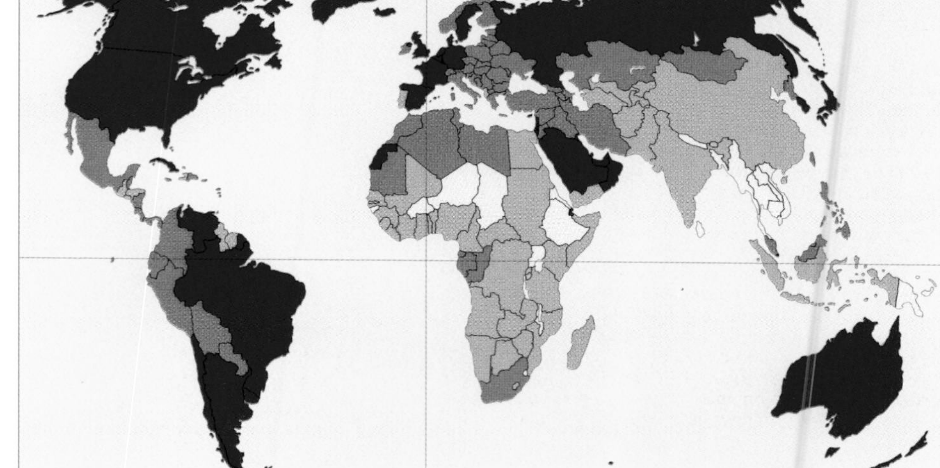

Expanding Cities

The growth of some of the world's largest cities in millions, 1950–2015.

Comparisons of city populations over time are problematic due to changes in the definition of the city limits. These figures attempt to take such changes into consideration. The figure for London is the metropolitan region.

1950 | 2015

New York City | London | Tokyo | Buenos Aires | Calcutta

Shanghai | Mexico City | Rio de Janeiro | São Paulo | Seoul

The graphs show the projected growth of megacities between 1950 and 2015. New York City, the world's largest city in 1950, reached a peak in 1970, but it has experienced periods of negative growth. London's population also declined between 1970 and 1985, before resuming a modest rate of increase. In both cases, the divergence from world trends is explained in part by counting methods. Each lies at the centre of a great agglomeration, and definitions of the 'city limits' may vary over time. Also, in developing countries, many areas around the megacities which are counted as urban, are rural in character. The rates of city population growth in developing countries have also often been over-estimated. For example, it was once predicted that Calcutta would have a population of 40 million by the late 1990s. The reason why many estimates have proven incorrect is partly explained by a new trend, namely that rapid urban growth is now greatest, in some regions, in the smaller cities. For example, the main expansion in West Bengal is no longer in Calcutta, but in a rash of small cities across the state.

Cities in Danger

As the decade of the 1980s advanced, most industrial countries, alarmed by acid rain and urban smog, took significant steps to limit air pollution. Well into the 1990s, however, these controls proved expensive to install and difficult to enforce, and clean air remains a luxury most developed as well as developing cities must live without.

Those taking part in the United Nations' Global Environment Monitoring System (see right) frequently show dangerous levels of pollutants ranging from soot to sulphur dioxide and photochemical smog; air in the majority of cities without such sampling equipment is likely to be at least as bad. Traffic, a major source of air pollution worldwide, loses Thailand's workforce 44 working days each year.

Urban Air Pollution

The world's most polluted cities: number of days each year when sulphur dioxide levels exceeded the WHO threshold of 150 micrograms per cubic metre (averaged over 4 to 15 years, 1970s – 1980s)

Sulphur dioxide is the main pollutant associated with industrial cities. According to the World Health Organization, more than seven days in a year above 150 µg per cubic metre bring a serious risk of respiratory disease: at least 600 million people live in urban areas where SO_2 concentrations regularly reach damaging levels.

Calcutta, India
Milan, Italy
Zagreb, Croatia
Guangzhou, China
Madrid, Spain
Beijing, China
Xian, China
Seoul, South Korea
Tehran, Iran
Shenyang, China

120 | 90 | 60 | 30

Urban Housing Needs

Proportion of the population living in squatter settlements and the number of homeless per thousand, for selected cities (1993)

Urbanization in most developing countries has been proceeding so rapidly that local governments have been unable to provide the necessary services and housing. In some cities, many people find their homes in squatter settlements, frequently without power, water and sanitation. Yet these communities are often a dynamic part of the city's economy, while their inhabitants sometimes take all kinds of initiatives, including the setting up of their own local government and self-help associations. Some of the world's richest cities also have a homeless underclass, although calculating the numbers of people involved is problematic. Yet it is the case that homelessness and unemployment are currently affecting an increasing number of people in the developed world.

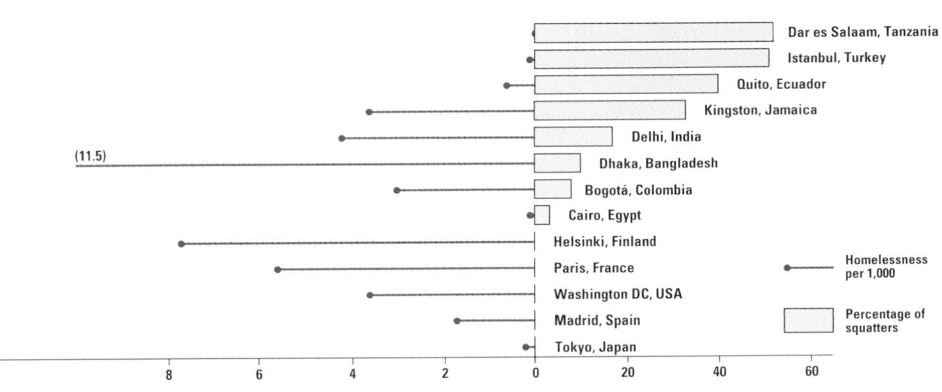

Urban Advantages

Despite overcrowding and poor housing, living standards in the developing world's cities are almost invariably better than in the surrounding countryside. Resources – financial, material and administrative – are concentrated in the towns, which are usually also the centres of political activity and pressure. Governments – frequently unstable, and rarely established on a solid democratic base – are usually more responsive to urban discontent than rural misery.

In many countries, especially in Africa, food prices are kept artificially low, appeasing underemployed urban masses at the expense of agricultural development. The imbalance encourages further cityward migration, helping to account for the astonishing rate of post-1950 urbanization and putting great strain on the ability of many nations to provide even modest improvements for their people.

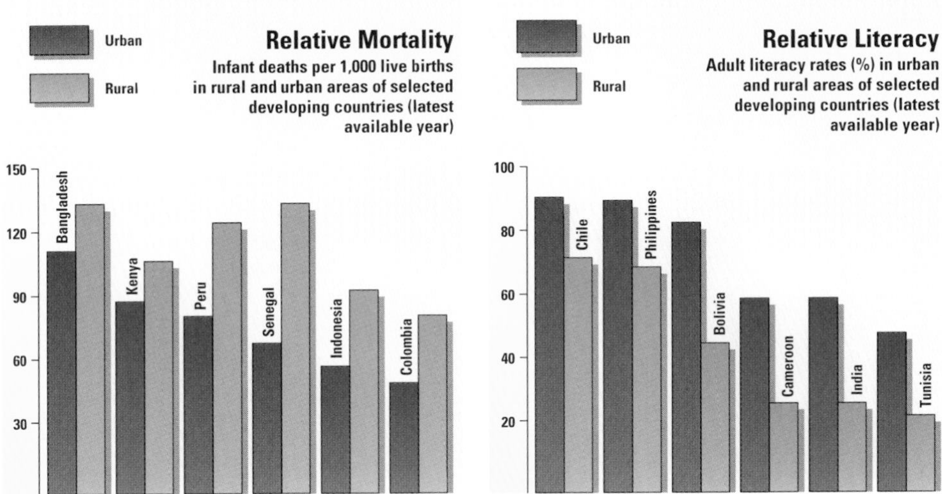

Largest Cities

Early in the 21st century, for the first time in history, the majority of the world's population will live in cities. Below is a list of all the cities with more than 10 million inhabitants, based on estimates for the year 2015.*

	City	Population (millions)
1.	Tokyo–Yokohama	28.7
2.	Bombay	27.4
3.	Lagos	24.1
4.	Shanghai	23.2
5.	Jakarta	21.5
6.	São Paulo	21.0
7.	Karachi	20.6
8.	Beijing	19.6
9.	Dhaka	19.2
10.	Mexico City	19.1
11.	Calcutta	17.6
12.	Delhi	17.5
13.	New York City	17.4
14.	Tianjin	17.1
15.	Manila	14.9
16.	Cairo	14.7
17.	Los Angeles	14.5
18.	Seoul	13.1
19.	Buenos Aires	12.5
20.	Istanbul	12.1
21.	Rio de Janeiro	11.3
22.	Lahore	10.9
23.	Hyderabad	10.6
24.	Bangkok	10.4
25.	Osaka	10.2
26.	Lima	10.1
27.	Tehran	10.0

City populations are based on urban agglomerations rather than legal city limits. In some cases where two adjacent cities have merged into one concentration, such as Tokyo–Yokohama, they have been regarded as a single unit.

* For a list of current city estimates, see page XI.

The Human Family

For more information:

24 Population density
30 The world's refugees
War since 1945
31 United Nations
International organizations

Racial, language and religious differences have led to appalling acts of inhumanity throughout history. Yet strictly speaking, all human beings belong to one species, *Homo sapiens*, which has no subspecies. The differences between the three racial types which most people identify – namely Caucasoid, Mongoloid and Negroid – reflect not so much evolutionary differences as long periods of separation.

Migration has recently mingled the various groups to an unprecedented extent, and most nations now have some degree of racial mixing. For example, the United States has often been called a melting pot, because of the large numbers of people from various geographical locations which make up the population. The country has no official language but, until recently, English was spoken by the vast majority of the people. But in recent years, some of the immigrants from Mexico, Cuba and other parts of Latin America have not learned English and speak only Spanish. This development disturbs those Americans who believe that the use of English binds the nation together, and several states have passed laws stating that English is their only official language.

Language is fundamental to human culture and any particular language is almost the definition of that particular culture. Because definitions of languages vary, estimates of the total number range from 3,000 to 6,000, although most are spoken by only a few people. The world's languages are grouped into families, the largest of which are the Indo-European and Sino-Tibetan. Chinese, a Sino-Tibetan language, is spoken by more people as a first language than any other. English, an Indo-European tongue, ranks second, but it is the leading international language, because so many people speak it as their second tongue.

Like language, religion encourages cohesion in single human groups and it satisfies a deep human need by assigning people a place in a divinely ordered world. Religion is a way in which a culture can express its individuality. For example, the rise of Islamic fundamentalism in the late 20th century was partly an expression of resentment that secular Western values are being imposed on Muslims.

World Migration

The greatest voluntary migration was the colonization of North America by 30–35 million European settlers during the 19th century. The greatest forced migration involved 9–11 million Africans taken as slaves to America between 1550 and 1860. The migrations shown on the map below are mostly international, as population movements within borders are not usually recorded. Many of the statistics are necessarily estimates as so many refugees and migrant workers enter countries illegally and unrecorded. Emigrants may have a variety of motives for leaving, thus making it difficult to distinguish between voluntary and involuntary migrations.

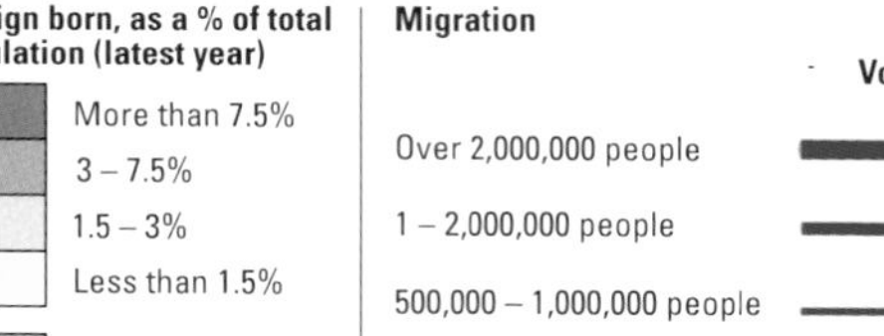

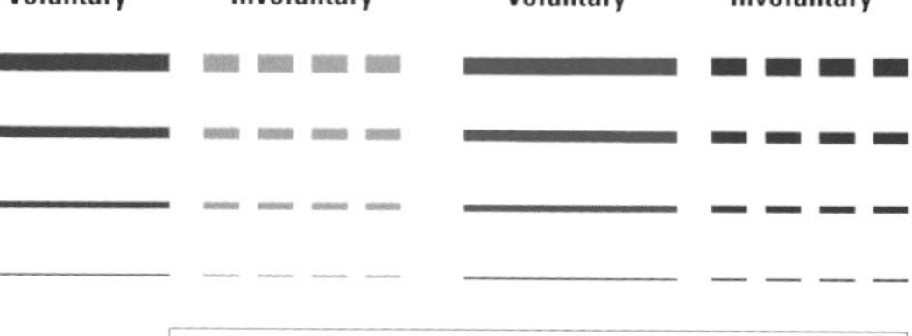

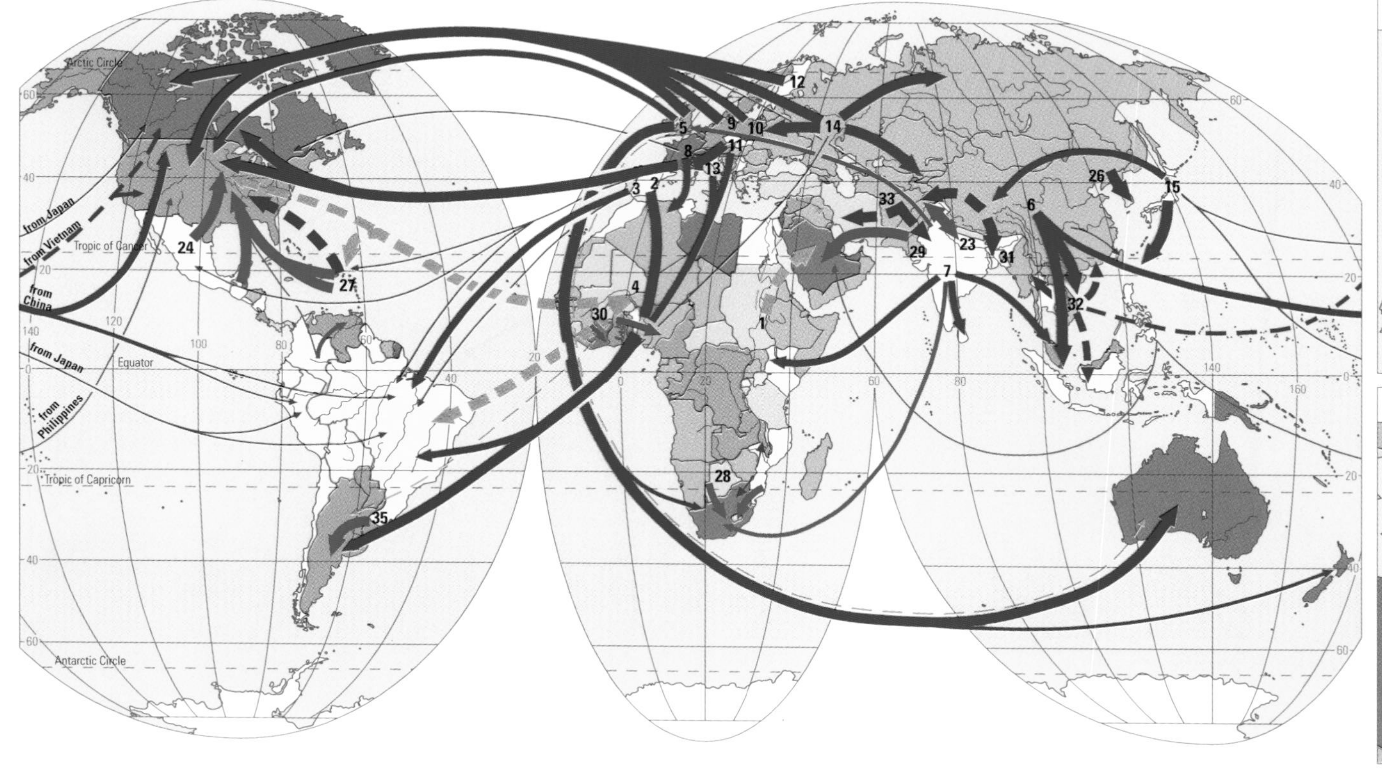

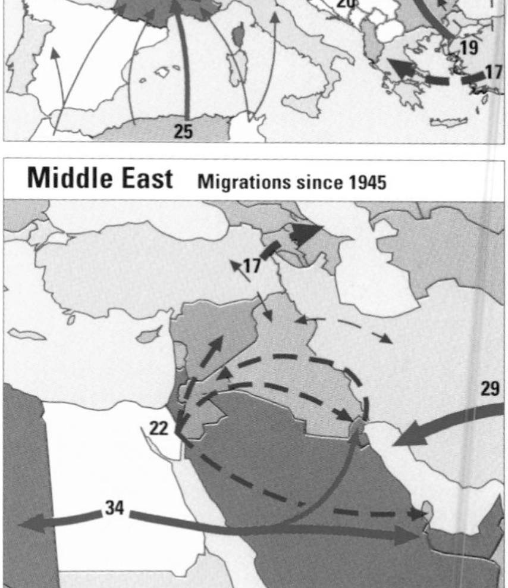

Building the USA

US Immigration 1820–1990

'Give me your tired, your poor / Your huddled masses yearning to breathe free....'

So starts Emma Lazarus's poem 'The New Colossus', inscribed on the Statue of Liberty. For decades the USA was the magnet that attracted millions of immigrants, notably from Central and Eastern Europe, the flow peaking in the early years of the 20th century. By the mid-1990s the proportion of immigrants had increased again to pre-World War II rates. In 1993/4, net immigration accounted for 30% of US population growth. Of the 904,000 immigrants, 40% were from Asia and 31% from Central America and the Caribbean.

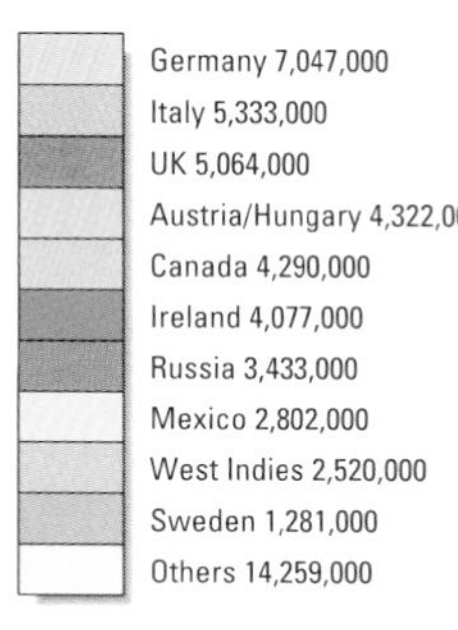

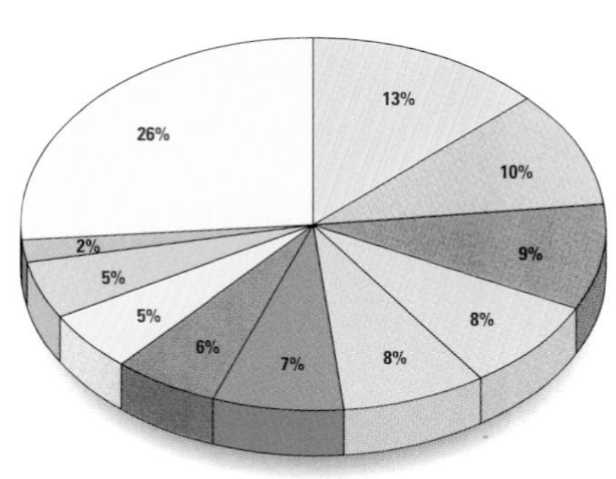

Major world migrations since 1500 (over 1,000,000 people)

1. North and East African slaves to Arabia (4.3m) 1500–1900
2. Spanish to South and Central America (2.3m) 1530–1914
3. Portuguese to Brazil (1.4m) 1530–1914
4. West African slaves... to South America (4.6m) 1550–1860
   to Caribbean (4m) 1580–1860
   to North/Central America (1m) 1650–1820
5. British and Irish .... to North America (13.5m) 1620–1914
   to Australasia and South Africa (3m) 1790–1914
6. Chinese .... to South-east Asia (22m) 1820–1914
   to North America (1m) 1880–1914
7. Indian migrant workers (3m) 1850–1914
8. French to North Africa (1.5m) 1850–1914
9. Germans to North America (5m) 1850–1914
10. Poles to North America (3.6m) 1850–1914
11. Austro-Hungarians.... to North America (3.2m) 1850–1914
    to Western Europe (3.4m) 1850–1914
    to South America (1.8m) 1850–1914
12. Scandinavians to North America (2.7m) 1850–1914
13. Italians .... to North America (5m) 1860–1914
    to South America (3.7m) 1860–1914
14. Russians .... to North America (2.2m) 1880–1914
    to Western Europe (2.2m) 1880–1914
    to Siberia (6m) 1880–1914
    to Central Asia (4m) 1880–1914
15. Japanese to Eastern Asia, South-east Asia and America (8m) 1900–1914
16. Poles to Western Europe (1m) 1920–1940
17. Greeks and Armenians from Turkey (1.6m) 1922–1923
18. European Jews to extermination camps (5m) 1940–1944
19. Turks to Western Europe (1.9m) 1940–
20. Yugoslavs to Western Europe (2m) 1940–
21. Germans to Western Europe (9.8m) 1945–1947
22. Palestinian refugees (2m) 1947–
23. Indian and Pakistani refugees (15m) 1947
24. Mexicans to North America (9m) 1950–
25. North Africans to Western Europe (1.1m) 1950–
26. Korean refugees (5m) 1950–1954
27. Latin Americans and West Indians to North America (4.7m) 1960–
28. Migrant workers to South Africa (1.5m) 1960–
29. Indians and Pakistanis to The Gulf (2.4m) 1970–
30. Migrant workers to Nigeria and Ivory Coast (3m) 1970–
31. Bangladeshi and Pakistani refugees (2m) 1972
32. Vietnamese and Cambodian refugees (1.5m) 1975–
33. Afghan refugees (6.1m) 1979–
34. Egyptians to The Gulf and Libya (2.9m) 1980–
35. Migrant workers to Argentina (2m) 1980–
36. Mozambique refugees (1.7m) 1985–
37. Yugoslav/Balkan refugees (1.7m) 1992–
38. Rwanda/Burundi refugees (2.6m) 1994–

Predominant Languages

INDO-EUROPEAN FAMILY

- 1 Balto-Slavic group (incl. Russian, Ukrainian)
- 2 Germanic group (incl. English, German)
- 3 Celtic group
- 4 Greek
- 5 Albanian
- 6 Iranian group
- 7 Armenian
- 8 Romance group (incl. Spanish, Portuguese, French, Italian)
- 9 Indo-Aryan group (incl. Hindi, Bengali, Urdu, Punjabi, Marathi)

- 10 **CAUCASIAN FAMILY**

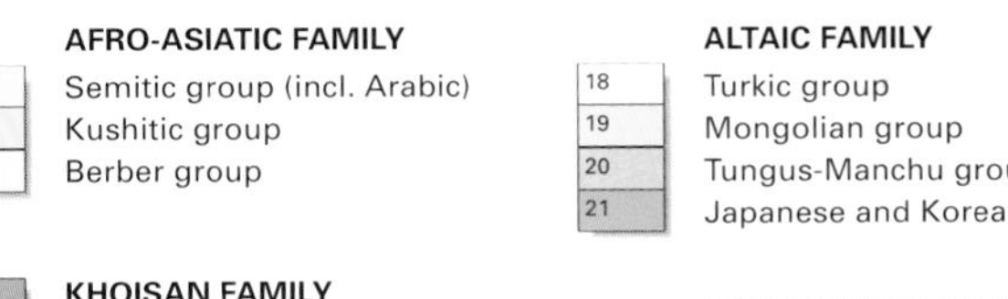

AFRO-ASIATIC FAMILY

- 11 Semitic group (incl. Arabic)
- 12 Kushitic group
- 13 Berber group

- 14 **KHOISAN FAMILY**
- 15 **NIGER-CONGO FAMILY**
- 16 **NILO-SAHARAN FAMILY**
- 17 **URALIC FAMILY**

ALTAIC FAMILY

- 18 Turkic group
- 19 Mongolian group
- 20 Tungus-Manchu group
- 21 Japanese and Korean

SINO-TIBETAN FAMILY

- 22 Sinitic (Chinese) languages
- 23 Tibetic-Burmic languages

- 24 **TAI FAMILY**

AUSTRO-ASIATIC FAMILY

- 25 Mon-Khmer group
- 26 Munda group
- 27 Vietnamese

- 28 **DRAVIDIAN FAMILY** (incl. Telugu, Tamil)
- 29 **AUSTRONESIAN FAMILY** (incl. Malay-Indonesian)
- 30 **OTHER LANGUAGES**

Official Languages

Language	Total population	World %
English	1,400m	27.0%
Chinese	1,070m	19.1%
Hindi	700m	13.5%
Spanish	280m	5.4%
Russian	270m	5.2%
French	220m	4.2%
Arabic	170m	3.3%
Portuguese	160m	3.0%
Malay	160m	3.0%
Bengali	150m	2.9%
Japanese	120m	2.3%

Languages form a kind of tree of development, splitting from a few ancient proto-tongues into branches that have grown apart and further divided with the passage of time. English and Hindi, for example, both belong to the great Indo-European family, although the relationship is only apparent after much analysis and comparison with non-Indo-European languages such as Chinese or Arabic; Hindi is part of the Indo-Aryan subgroup, whereas English is a member of Indo-European's Germanic branch; French, another Indo-European tongue, traces its descent through the Latin, or Romance, branch. A few languages – Basque is one example – have no apparent links with any other, living or dead. Most modern languages, of course, have acquired enormous quantities of vocabulary from each other.

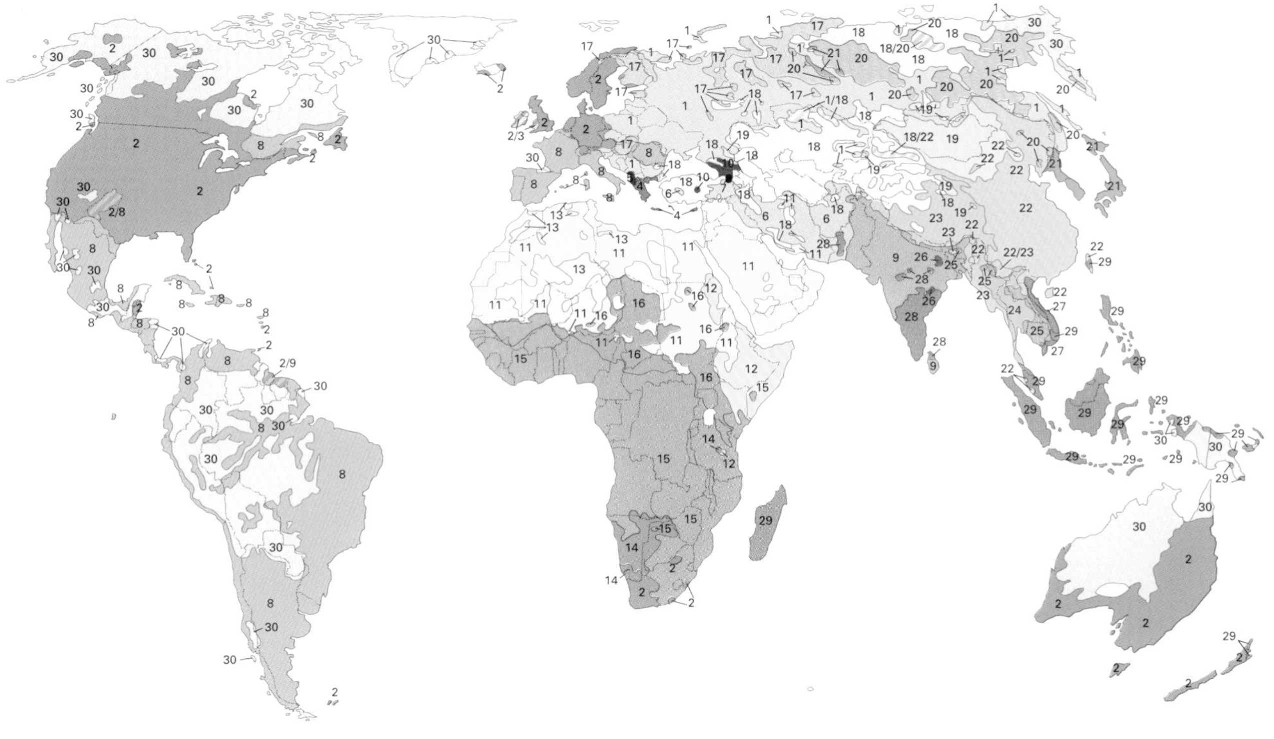

Distribution of Living Languages

The figures refer to the number of languages currently in use in the regions shown.

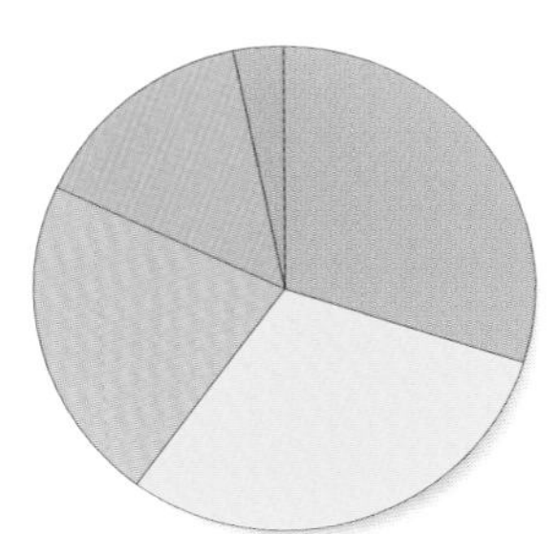

Predominant Religions

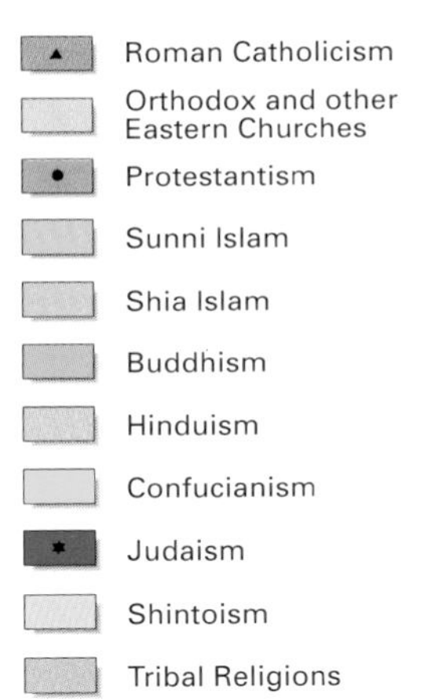

Religions are not as easily mapped as the physical contours of the land. Divisions are often blurred and frequently overlapping: most nations include people of many different faiths – or no faith at all. Some religions, like Islam and Christianity, have proselytes worldwide; others, like Hinduism and Confucianism, are restricted to a particular area, though modern migrations have taken some Indians and Chinese very far from their cultural origins. It is also difficult to show the degree to which religion controls daily life: Christian Western Europe, for example, is now far less dominated by its religion than are the Islamic nations of the Middle East. Similarly, figures for the major faiths' adherents make no distinction between nominal believers enrolled at birth and those for whom religion is a vital part of existence.

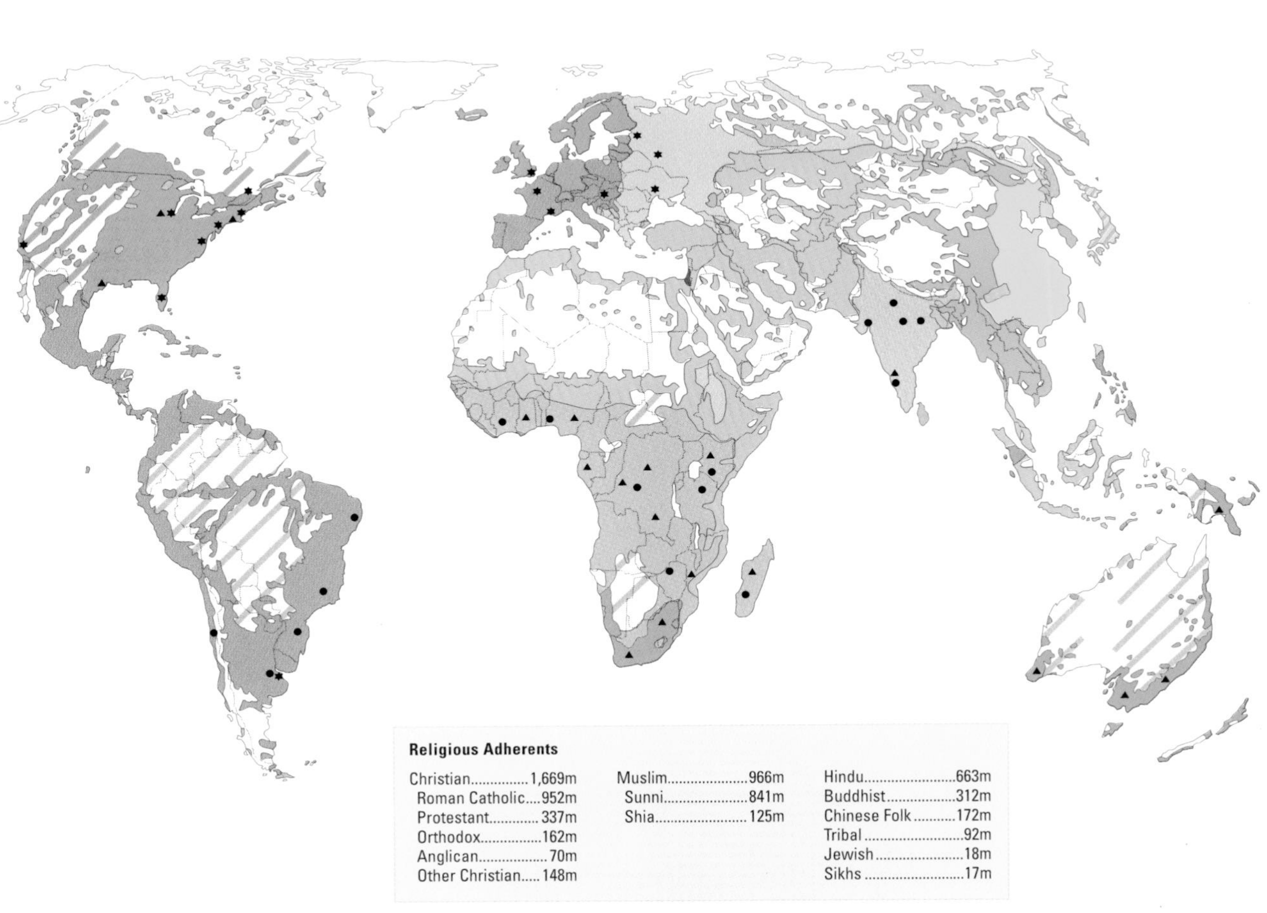

Religious Adherents

Christian	1,669m
Roman Catholic	952m
Protestant	337m
Orthodox	162m
Anglican	70m
Other Christian	148m
Muslim	966m
Sunni	841m
Shia	125m
Hindu	663m
Buddhist	312m
Chinese Folk	172m
Tribal	92m
Jewish	18m
Sikhs	17m

Conflict and Co-operation

For more information:
28 Migration
29 Religion

The 20th century witnessed two world wars, followed by a Cold War which several times threatened to erupt into a third world war, fought with nuclear weapons. The Cold War was marked by a great number of conflicts. Some were colonial wars, as the empires of the first half of the century fell apart, some were border wars, and some were civil wars. All wars have caused great suffering among civilians, many of whom were forced to become refugees.

In the late 1980s, many people hoped that the end of the Cold War, following the collapse of Communist regimes in the former Soviet Union and Eastern Europe, would herald a new era of international stability. Instead, old ethnic and religious antagonisms surfaced in many areas, leading to civil war in such places as Chechenia, in Russia, and the former Yugoslavia. Nationalist rivalries, suppressed under Communist rule, replaced ideological factors as the major cause of conflict.

War is a very human activity, with no real equivalent in other species. Yet humans also function well when they co-operate. Evolution has made this so. Hunter-gatherers in co-operative bands were more effective than animals that prowled. Agriculture, urbanization and industrialization all depend on the ability of humans to co-operate.

The creation of the United Nations in 1945 held out hope that the world's nations, tired of war, would have the means to control humanity's aggressive instincts. Though the UN lacks the power to halt conflicts, it has often helped to achieve negotiation. Economic pressures have led to another kind of co-operation, the creation of common markets and economic unions, such as ASEAN in South-east Asia, the European Union and NAFTA in North America.

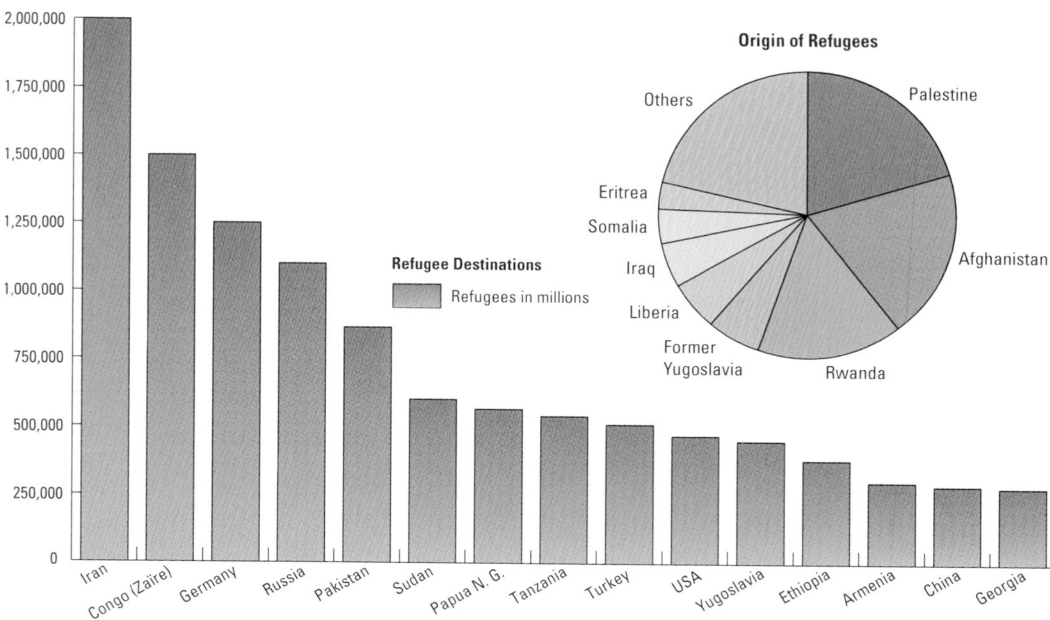

The World's Refugees

Refugees by host nation (bar-chart, left) and by nation of origin (pie-chart, left) (1995). The source is the United Nations High Commission for Refugees (UNHCR). The 3.2 million Palestinian refugees living in Jordan, Syria, Lebanon, Gaza and the West Bank fall under the mandate of United Nations Relief and Works Agency (UNRWA) and are not included on the bar-chart.

The pie-chart shows the origins of the world's refugees, while the bar-chart below shows their destinations. According to the United Nations High Commission for Refugees (UNHCR) in 1995 there were 14.5 million refugees. However, the UNHCR definition of a refugee, 'a person who has left or remains outside their own country because they have a well-founded fear of persecution, or because their safety is threatened by events seriously disturbing public order', does not include people who are in a refugee-like situation but who have not been formally recognized. In 1995, there were a further 3.5 million of these people worldwide and a further 4.5 million people who were internally displaced.

All but a few who cross international boundaries seek asylum in neighbouring countries, which are often the least equipped to deal with them. Lacking any rights or power, they frequently become an unwelcome burden to their hosts. Usually, the best any refugee can hope for is rudimentary food and shelter in temporary camps. Many Palestinians have been forced to live in camps since 1948.

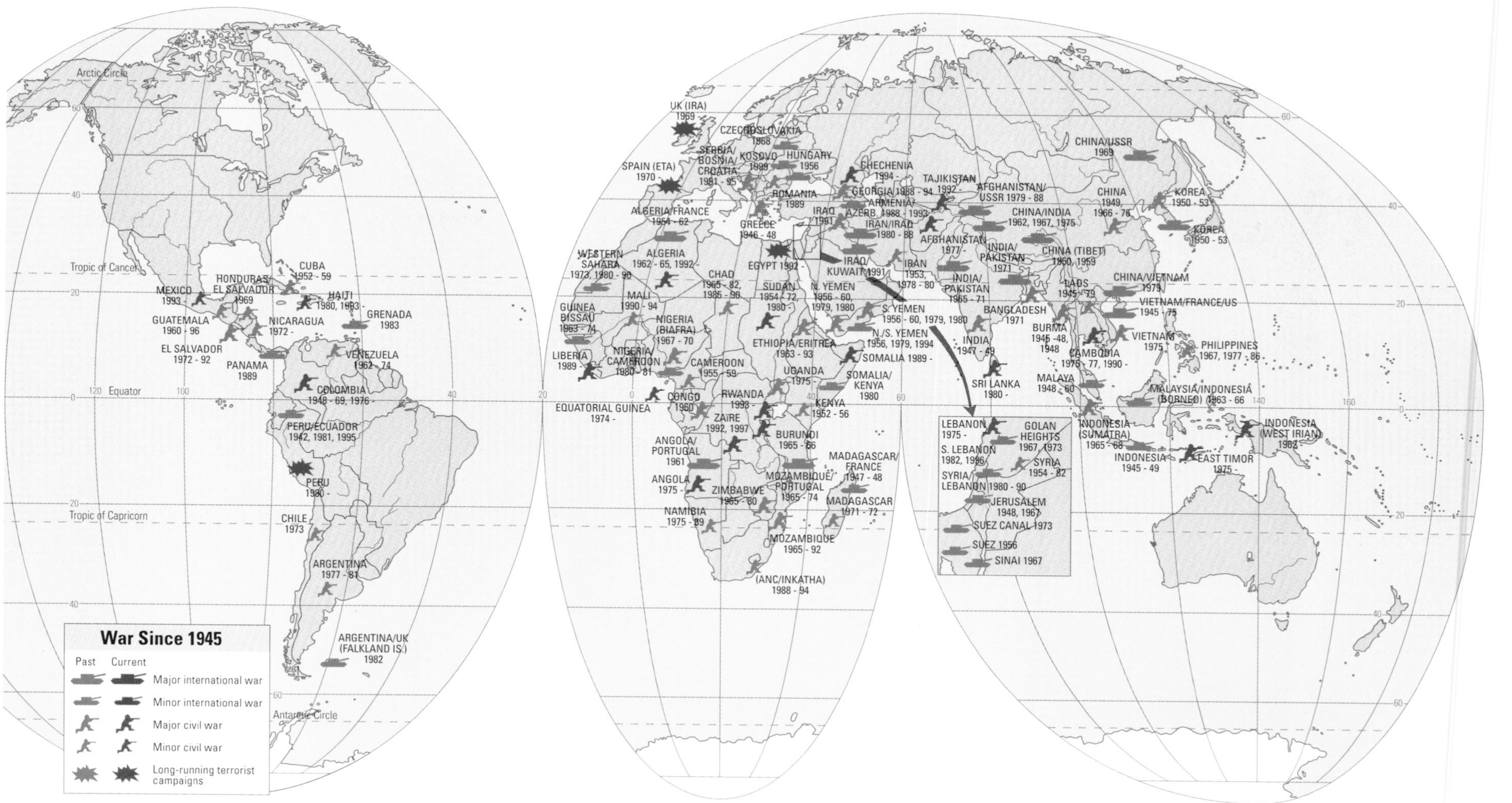

War Since 1945

Past Current
- Major international war
- Minor international war
- Major civil war
- Minor civil war
- Long-running terrorist campaigns

United Nations

The United Nations Organization was born as World War II drew to its conclusion. Six years of strife had strengthened the world's desire for peace, but an effective international organization was needed to help achieve it. That body would replace the League of Nations which, since its inception in 1920, had failed to curb the aggression of at least some of its member nations. At the United Nations Conference on International Organization held in San Francisco, the United Nations Charter was drawn up. Ratified by the Security Council and signed by the 51 original members, it came into effect on 24 October 1945.

The Charter set out the aims of the organization: to maintain peace and security, and develop friendly relations between nations; to achieve international co-operation in solving economic, cultural and humanitarian problems; to promote respect for human rights and fundamental freedoms; and to harmonize the activities of nations in order to achieve these common goals.

The United Nations has five principal organs :

The General Assembly
The forum at which member nations discuss moral and political issues affecting world development, peace and security meets annually in September, under a newly-elected President whose tenure lasts one year. Any member can bring business to the agenda, and each member nation has one vote.

The Security Council
A legislative and executive body, the Security Council is the primary instrument for establishing and maintaining international peace by attempting to settle disputes between nations. It has the power to dispatch UN forces, and member nations undertake to provide armed forces, assistance and facilities. The Security Council has ten temporary members elected by the General Assembly for two-year terms, and five permanent members – China, France, Russia, UK and USA.

The Economic and Social Council
By far the largest United Nations executive, the Council operates as a conduit between the General Assembly and the many United Nations agencies it instructs to implement Assembly decisions, and whose work it co-ordinates. The Council also commissions studies on economic conditions, collects data and makes recommendations to the Assembly.

The Secretariat
This is the staff of the United Nations, and its task is to administer the policies and programmes of the UN and its organs, and assist and advise the Head of the Secretariat, the Secretary-General – a full-time, non-political appointment made by the General Assembly.

The Trusteeship Council
This no longer administers any of the original 11 trust territories as they are all now independent.

The International Court of Justice (the World Court)
The World Court is the judicial organ of the United Nations. It deals only with United Nations disputes and all members are subject to its jurisdiction. There are 15 judges, elected for nine-year terms by the General Assembly and the Security Council.

The social and humanitarian operations of the UN include:
United Nations Development Programme (UNDP) Plans and funds projects to help developing countries make better use of their resources.
United Nations International Childrens' Fund (UNICEF) Created at the General Assembly's first session in 1945 to help children in the aftermath of World War II, it now provides basic health care and aid worldwide.
Food and Agriculture Organization (FAO) Aims to raise living standards and nutrition levels in rural areas by improving food production and distribution.
United Nations Educational, Scientific and Cultural Organization (UNESCO) Promotes international co-operation through broader and better education.
World Health Organization (WHO) Promotes and provides for better health care, public and environmental health and medical research.

United Nations agencies are involved in many aspects of international trade, safety and security:
International Maritime Organization (IMO) Promotes unity amongst merchant shipping, especially in regard to safety, marine pollution and standardization.
International Labour Organization (ILO) Seeks to improve labour conditions and promote productive employment to raise living standards.
World Meteorological Organization (WMO) Promotes co-operation in weather observation, reporting and forecasting.
World Trade Organization (WTO) On 1 January 1995 the WTO replaced GATT. It advocates a common code of conduct and its aim is the liberalization of world trade.
Disarmament Commission Considers and makes recommendations to the General Assembly on disarmament issues.
International Atomic Energy Agency (IAEA) Fosters development of peaceful uses for nuclear energy and establishes safety standards.

The World Bank comprises three United Nations agencies:
International Monetary Fund (IMF) Cultivates international monetary co-operation and expansion of trade.
International Bank for Reconstruction and Development (IBRD) Provides funds and technical assistance to developing countries.
International Finance Corporation (IFC) Encourages the growth of productive private enterprise in less developed countries.

Membership There are four independent states which are not members of the UN – Switzerland, Taiwan, Tuvalu and Vatican City. Official languages are Chinese, English, French, Russian, Spanish and Arabic.
Funding The UN budget for 1996–97 was US $2.6 billion. Contributions are assessed by the members' ability to pay, with the maximum 25% of the total, the minimum 0.01%.
Peacekeeping The UN has been involved in 43 peacekeeping operations worldwide since 1948. At the end of 1996 there were 16 areas of UN patrol and 25,649 'blue berets'.

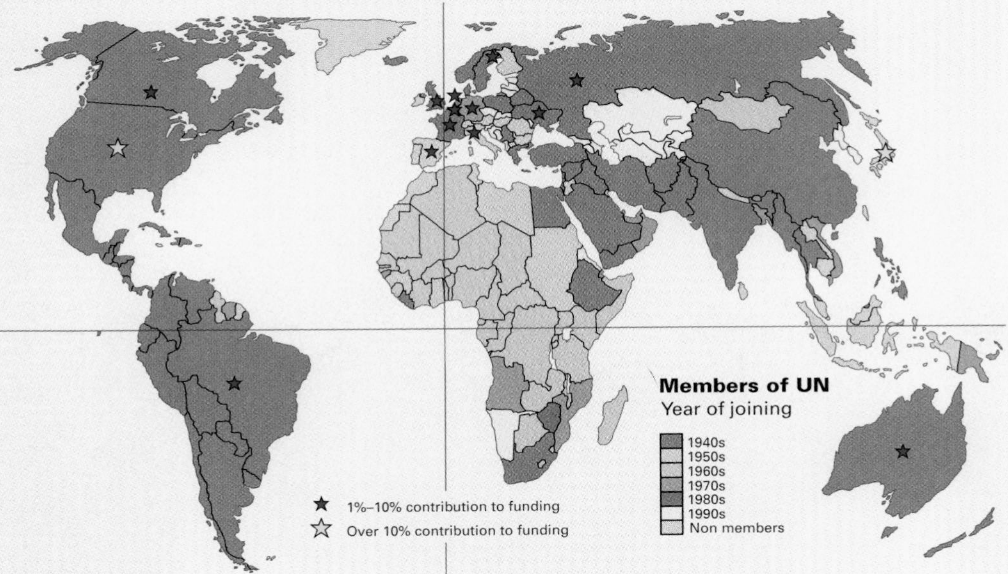

International Organizations

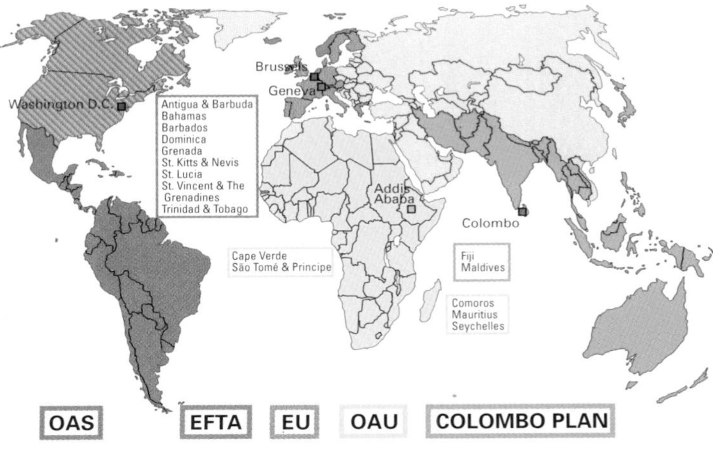

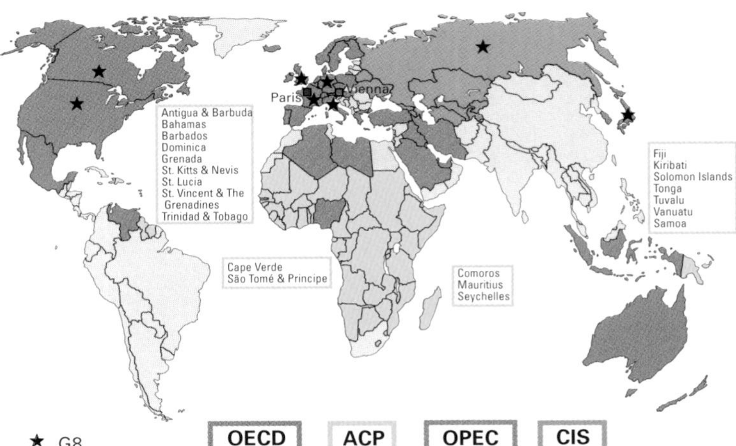

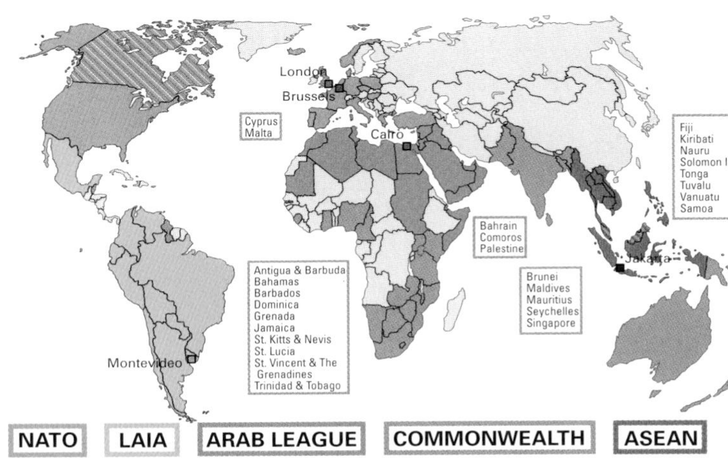

EU The European Union evolved from the European Community (EC) in 1993. The original body, the European Coal and Steel Community (ECSC), was created in 1951 following the signing of the Treaty of Paris. The 15 members of the EU – Austria, Belgium, Denmark, Finland, France, Germany, Greece, Ireland, Italy, Luxembourg, Netherlands, Portugal, Spain, Sweden and the UK – aim to integrate economies, co-ordinate social developments and bring about political union. These members, of what is now the world's biggest market, share agricultural and industrial policies and tariffs on trade.
EFTA European Free Trade Association (formed in 1960). Portugal left the original 'Seven' in 1989 to join what was then the EC, followed by Austria, Finland and Sweden in 1995. There are now only four members: Iceland, Liechtenstein, Norway and Switzerland.
ACP African-Caribbean-Pacific (formed in 1963). Members enjoy economic ties with the EU.
NATO North Atlantic Treaty Organization (formed in 1949). It continues despite the winding up of the Warsaw Pact in 1991. The Czech Rep., Hungary and Poland were the latest to join in 1999.
OAS Organization of American States (formed in 1948). It aims to promote social and economic co-operation between countries in the developed North America and developing Latin America.
ASEAN Association of South-east Asian Nations (formed in 1967). Cambodia joined in 1999.
OAU Organization of African Unity (1963). Its 53 members represent over 94% of Africa's population. Arabic, English, French and Portuguese are recognized as working languages.
LAIA The Latin American Integration Association (formed in 1980) superceded the Latin American Free Trade Association formed in 1961. Its aim is to promote freer regional trade.
OECD Organization for Economic Co-operation and Development (formed in 1961). It comprises 29 major free-market economies. The 'G8' is its 'inner group' of leading industrial nations, comprising Canada, France, Germany, Italy, Japan, Russia, UK and the USA.
COMMONWEALTH The Commonwealth of Nations evolved from the British Empire; it comprises 16 nations recognizing the British monarch as head of state, 32 republics and 5 indigenous monarchies, giving a total of 53. Nigeria was suspended in 1995.
CIS The Commonwealth of Independent States (formed in 1991) comprises the countries of the former Soviet Union except for Estonia, Latvia and Lithuania.
OPEC Organization of Petroleum Exporting Countries (formed in 1960). It controls about three-quarters of the world's oil supply. Gabon formally withdrew from OPEC in August 1996.
ARAB LEAGUE (1945) Aims to promote economic, social, political and military co-operation.
COLOMBO PLAN (formed in 1951) Its 26 members aim to promote economic and social development in Asia and the Pacific.

Military Spending

Military expenditure as a % of GNP or GDP, ranked selection of countries (1994)

Rank	Country	%	Rank	Country	%
1.	Iraq	74.9%	14.	Jordan	7.5%
2.	North Korea	26.3%	15.	Laos	7.4%
3.	Angola	23.9%	16.	Pakistan	6.0%
4.	Oman	18.1%	17.	UAE	5.7%
5.	Syria	17.9%	18.	Seychelles	5.6%
6.	Sudan	17.1%	19.	Sierra Leone	4.9%
7.	Saudi Arabia	14.2%	20.	Taiwan	4.8%
8.	Yemen	14.1%	21.	Liberia	4.8%
9.	Russia	12.4%	22.	Singapore	4.5%
10.	Kuwait	11.1%	23.	Sri Lanka	4.5%
11.	Mozambique	8.7%	24.	USA	4.3%
12.	Israel	8.6%	25.	Malaysia	4.2%
13.	Rwanda	7.6%			

It is worth noting that the total amount of expenditure varies considerably depending on the size of the economy, so that although the percentages show the importance given to military spending within each country, they give no idea as to the total expenditure. In 1997, for example, the USA spent a total of US $271 billion, Russia US $70 billion, and the UK US $36 billion. In 1993, the USA also provided the most military assistance worldwide, providing US $3.4 billion, compared to a total of US $0.9 billion from Western Europe.

The period 1987–94 saw a decline in global military spending which generated what the United Nations Development Programme term a 'peace dividend' of US $935 billion. Unfortunately, there is no clear link between reduced military spending and enhanced expenditure on human development. Moreover, the poorest regions of the world (notably sub-Saharan Africa) failed to contain their military spending and, in some cases, it increased.

Agriculture

For more information:
14 Temperature and precipitation
16 Climate regions
18 Water utilization
19 Natural vegetation
Land use by continent
38 Division of employment

Bad harvests in 1995 caused a drop in world grain reserves to a 20-year low. This revived the ongoing debate as to whether the population explosion will cause major food crises in the 21st century.

Experts estimate that 3 billion tonnes of cereals will be needed to feed the world's population in 25 years' time, as compared with 1.9 billion tonnes at present. To expand food production to this extent, some argue, will place a strain on the environment. One suggestion to alleviate the situation is that people in developed countries should eat less meat. This would release more grain, which is used as cattle fodder, to feed people.

Other experts argue that there should be no food crises. World grain production tripled between 1950 and 1990, largely as a result of the Green Revolution, during which genetically improved, high-yield varieties of maize, rice and wheat, the world's three leading staple crops, were developed. These new varieties have helped many developing countries to achieve food surpluses and prevent widespread starvation.

The only region of the world which seems likely to suffer food shortages in the 21st century is sub-Saharan Africa, where in the late 1990s the average daily calorie intake was 6% less than what was needed and where the population is expected to double in 20 years. Improved land management and a huge increase in global trade, especially in food distribution, is necessary if sub-Saharan Africans are not to go hungry.

The development of agriculture more than 10,000 years ago transformed human existence more than any other major advance. By supporting larger populations, it led to the growth of early civilizations and later it sustained people in the industrial cities which sprang up in the 19th century.

Today, agricultural production greatly varies between the developed world, where it is highly mechanized and employs few people, such as 3% of the workforce in the United States, and the developing world, such as sub-Saharan Africa, where it employs 66% of the workforce. Many Africans are engaged in subsistence farming, providing the basic needs of their families but not contributing to the economy. Much of Africa also suffers from economic mismanagement, as well as civil war.

Political problems have also affected food production in other parts of the world. The former USSR had much excellent farmland, but the failure of the collectives and state farms to maintain sufficiently high levels of production helped to bring about the collapse of Communism.

Farmers are under great pressure not only to maintain high levels of production but to increase them. However, the cultivation of marginal areas is one of the prime causes of soil erosion and desertification.

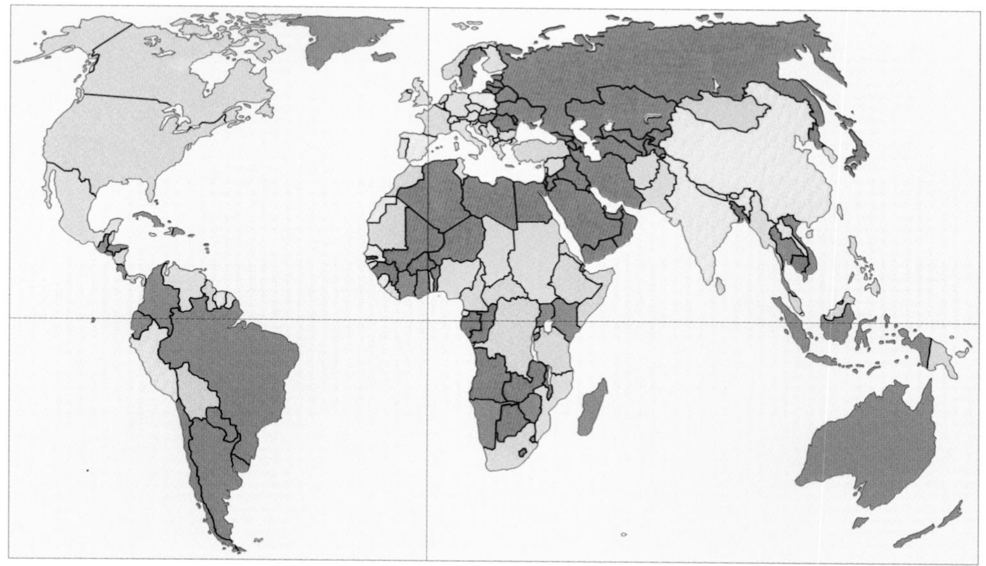

Self-sufficiency in Food

Balance of trade in food products as a percentage of total trade in food products – S.I.T.C. Classes 0, 1 and 4 (latest available year)

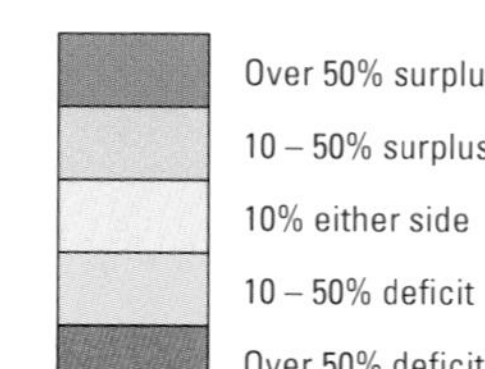

Most self-sufficient		Least self-sufficient	
Argentina	95%	Algeria	–98%
Zimbabwe	87%	Djibouti	–97%
Honduras	81%	Yemen	–95%
Malawi	81%	Zambia	–95%
Costa Rica	79%	Japan	–91%
Iceland	78%	Gabon	–90%
Chile	75%	Kuwait	–90%
Uruguay	75%	Brunei	–89%
Ecuador	74%	Burkina Faso	–82%

Staple Crops

Wheat: Grown in a range of climates, with most varieties – including the highest-quality bread wheats – requiring temperate conditions. Mainly used in baking, it is also used for pasta and breakfast cereals.

China 18.9% India 12.2% USA 11.0% France 5.7% Russia 5.6% Canada 4.6%

World total (1996): 584,874,000 tonnes

Maize: Originating in the New World and still an important human food in Africa and Latin America, in the developed world it is processed into breakfast cereals, oil, starches and adhesives. It is also used for animal feed.

USA 36.4% China 21.8% Brazil 7.0%

World total (1996): 576,821,000 tonnes

Oats: Most widely used to feed livestock, but eaten by humans as oatmeal or porridge. Oats have a beneficial effect on the cardiovascular system, and human consumption is likely to increase.

Russia 29.7% Canada 9.9% USA 8.2% Australia 6.7% Germany 5.6%

World total (1996): 28,794,000 tonnes

Millet: The name covers a number of small-grained cereals, members of the grass family with a short growing season. Used to produce flour, meal and animal feed, and fermented to make beer, especially in Africa.

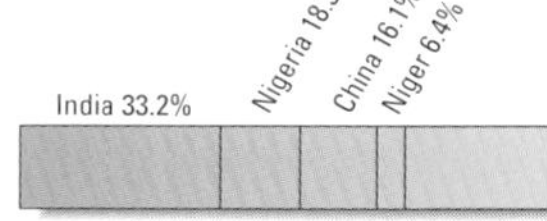

World total (1996): 29,563,000 tonnes

Rice: Thrives on the high humidity and temperatures of the Far East, where it is the traditional staple food of half the human race. Usually grown standing in water, rice responds well to continuous cultivation, with three or four crops annually.

China 34.0% India 21.7% Indonesia 9.0% Bangladesh 4.8% Vietnam 4.4% Thailand 3.8%

World total (1996): 562,259,000 tonnes

Potatoes: The most important of the edible tubers, potatoes grow in well-watered, temperate areas. Weight for weight less nutritious than grain, they are a human staple as well as an important animal feed.

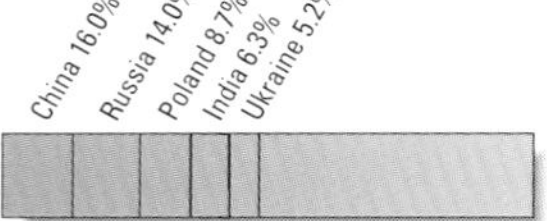

World total (1996): 294,834,000 tonnes

Soya: Beans from soya bushes are very high (30–40%) in protein. Most are processed into oil and proprietary protein foods. Consumption since 1950 has tripled, mainly due to the health-conscious developed world.

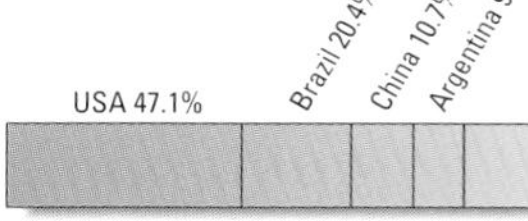

World total (1996): 130,302,000 tonnes

Cassava: A tropical shrub that needs high rainfall (over 1,000 mm annually) and a 10–30 month growing season to produce its large, edible tubers. Used as flour by humans, as cattle feed and in industrial starches.

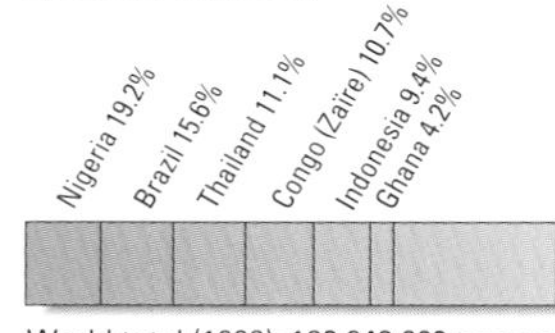

World total (1996): 162,942,000 tonnes

Sugars

Sugar cane: Confined to tropical regions, cane sugar accounts for the bulk of international trade in sugar. Most is produced as a foodstuff, but some countries, notably Brazil and South Africa, distill sugar cane to make motor fuels.

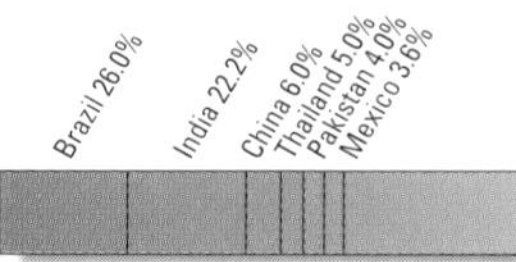

World total (1996): 1,192,555,000 tonnes

Sugar beet: Closely related to the beetroot, sugar beet's yield after processing is indistinguishable from cane sugar. It is replacing sugar-cane imports in Europe, to the detriment of the developing countries that rely on it as a major cash crop.

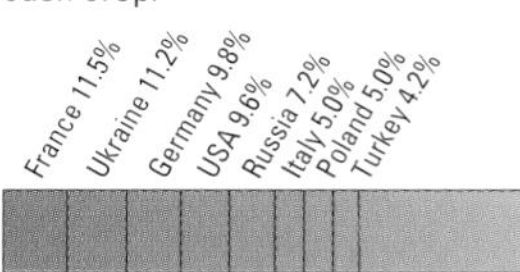

World total (1996): 255,500,000 tonnes

Cereals are grasses with starchy, edible seeds; every important civilization has depended on them as a source of food. The major cereal grains contain about 10% protein and 75% carbohydrate.
Grain contributes more than any other group of foods to the energy and protein content of human diet.
Starchy tuber crops or root crops are second in importance after cereals as staple foods; easily cultivated, they provide high yields for little effort.

Food and Population

Comparison of food production and population by continent.

The left column indicates the % of world food production and the right shows population in proportion.

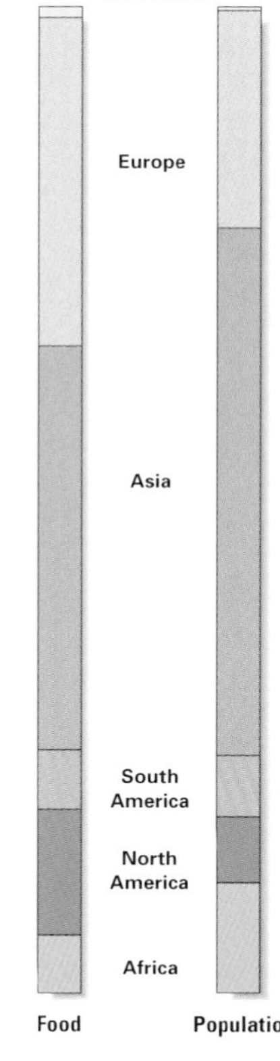

Agricultural Population

Percentage of the total population dependent on agriculture for their livelihood (1997)

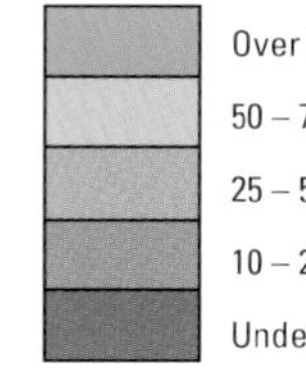

Top 5 countries (1997)

Country	%
Bhutan	94%
Nepal	93%
Burkina Faso	92%
Rwanda	91%
Burundi	91%

Bottom 5 countries (1997)

Country	%
Singapore	0.2%
Kuwait	1.0%
Brunei	1.0%
Bahrain	1.3%
Qatar	1.7%

Animal Products

Traditionally, food animals subsisted on land unsuitable for cultivation, supporting agricultural production with their fertilizing dung. But free-ranging animals grow slowly and yield less meat than those more intensively reared; the demands of urban markets in the developed world have encouraged the growth of factory-like production methods. A large proportion of staple crops, especially cereals, are fed to animals, an inefficient way to produce protein but one likely to continue as long as people value meat and dairy products in their diet.

Cheese: Least perishable of all dairy products, cheese is milk fermented with selected bacterial strains to produce a foodstuff with a potentially immense range of flavours and textures. The vast majority of cheeses are made from cow's milk, although sheep and goat cheeses are highly prized.

USA 23.5% France 10.8% Germany 9.6% Italy 6.0% Netherlands 4.6%

World total (1995): 14,754,000 tonnes

Beef and Veal: Most beef and veal is reared for home markets, and the top five producers are also the biggest consumers. The USA produces nearly a quarter of the world's beef and eats even more.

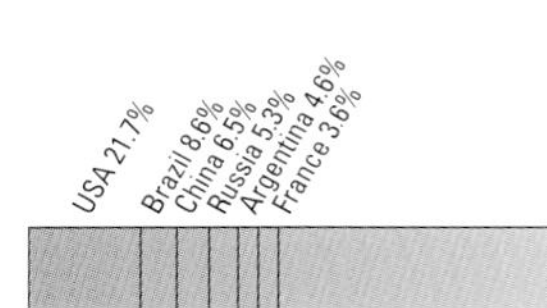

World total (1996): 53,965,000 tonnes

Milk: Many human groups, including most Asians, find raw milk indigestible after infancy, and it is often only the starting point for other dairy products such as butter, cheese and yoghurt. Most world production comes from cows, but sheep's milk and goats' milk are also important.

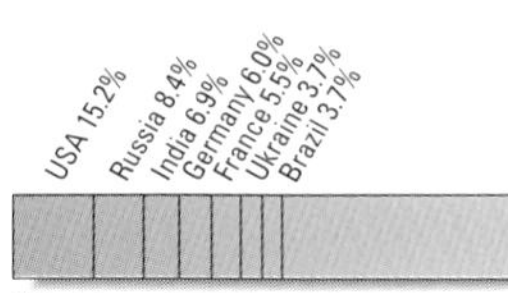

World total (1996): 466,317,000 tonnes

Butter: A traditional source of vitamin A as well as calories, butter has lost much popularity in the developed world for health reasons, although it remains a valuable food. Most butter from India, the world's largest producer, is clarified into ghee, which has religious as well as nutritional importance.

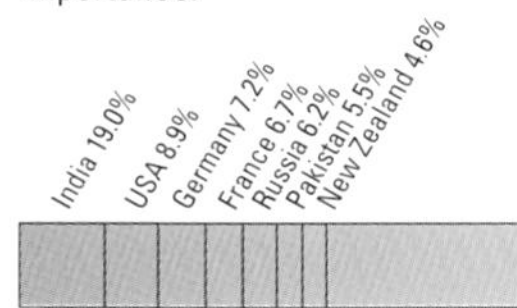

World total (1996): 6,565,000 tonnes

Pork: Although pork is forbidden to many millions, notably Muslims, on religious grounds, more is produced than any other meat in the world, mainly because it is the cheapest. It accounts for about 90% of China's meat output, although per capita meat consumption is relatively low.

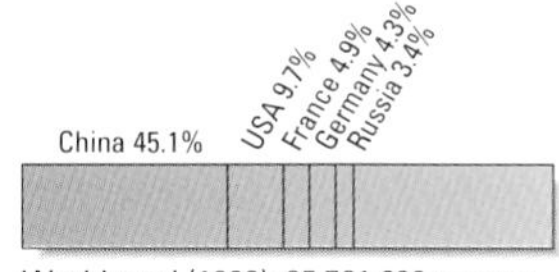

World total (1996): 85,761,000 tonnes

Crisis in Africa

Each year 40 million people, almost half of whom are children, die from starvation and related diseases. In 2000, 600 million people worldwide were estimated to be suffering from malnutrition. Africa suffers from more natural disasters than any other continent; pests such as locusts destroy crops, and tropical storms and flooding ruin harvests. Famines periodically affect parts of Africa causing widespread hardship, even though enough food is produced worldwide to feed everyone.

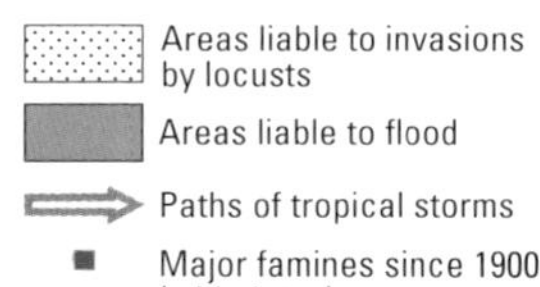

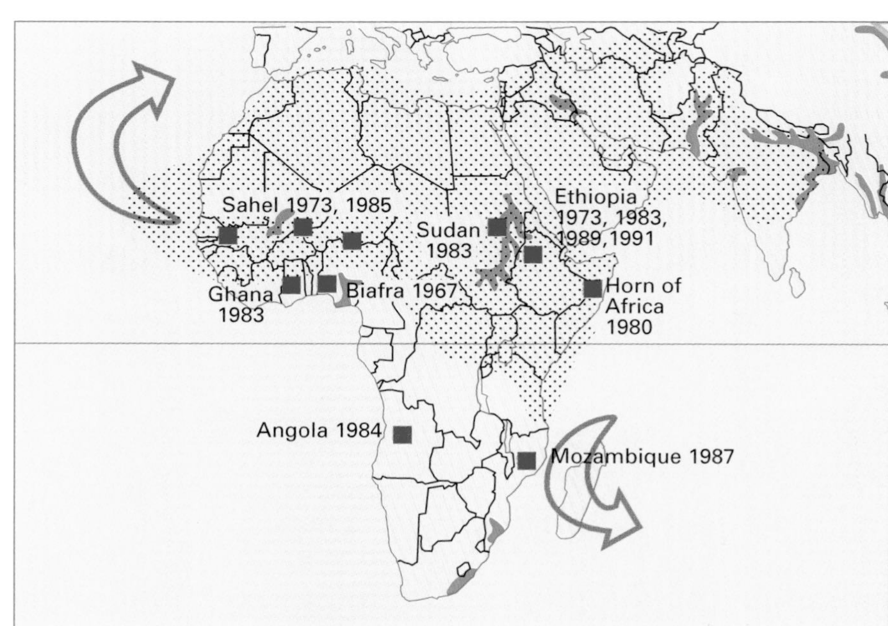

Energy

For more information:

22 Carbon dioxide
Greenhouse power
CO_2 producers
Global warming
23 Water pollution
39 World shipping

Every year, the world's energy consumption is about the equivalent of what would come from burning 8,000 million tonnes of oil (8,000 MtOe) – a twenty-fold increase since 1850. Two-fifths of this total actually comes from burning oil and most of the rest comes from coal and natural gas.

The oil crises in the 1970s precipitated concern over dependence on finite fossil fuels as the primary source of energy, and growing environmental awareness has added impetus to the search for alternative energy resources. Fossil fuel combustion damages the environment through the release of gases and particulate matter but two other major sources of energy, hydroelectricity and nuclear power, are also controversial. For example, hydro electricity production involves flooding large areas to create reservoirs, while nuclear power stations, which are costly to build, generate dangerous radioactive wastes, and can lead to disasters on an international scale.

Alternative energy resources may soon provide a much larger proportion of the world's energy consumption, especially in developing countries where millions of people currently have no access to electricity. Experts have predicted that solar and wind energy may have an important future in such countries as China and India, while other areas under development, such as tidal, wave and geothermal power, all have potential in appropriate areas. World Bank experts have calculated that solar power could, in theory, supply between five and ten times the present electricity supply of developing countries.

Conversions

For historical reasons, oil is still traded in barrels. The weight and volume equivalents shown below are all based on average density 'Arabian light' crude oil, and should be considered approximate.

The energy equivalents given for a tonne of oil are also somewhat imprecise: oil and coal of different qualities will have varying energy contents, a fact usually reflected in their price on world markets.

1 barrel:
0.136 tonnes
159 litres
35 Imperial gallons
42 US gallons

1 tonne:
7.33 barrels
1185 litres
256 Imperial gallons
261 US gallons

1 tonne oil:
1.5 tonnes hard coal
3.0 tonnes lignite
12,000 kWh

1 gallon (Imperial):
227,42 inches
1.201 US gallons
4,546 litres

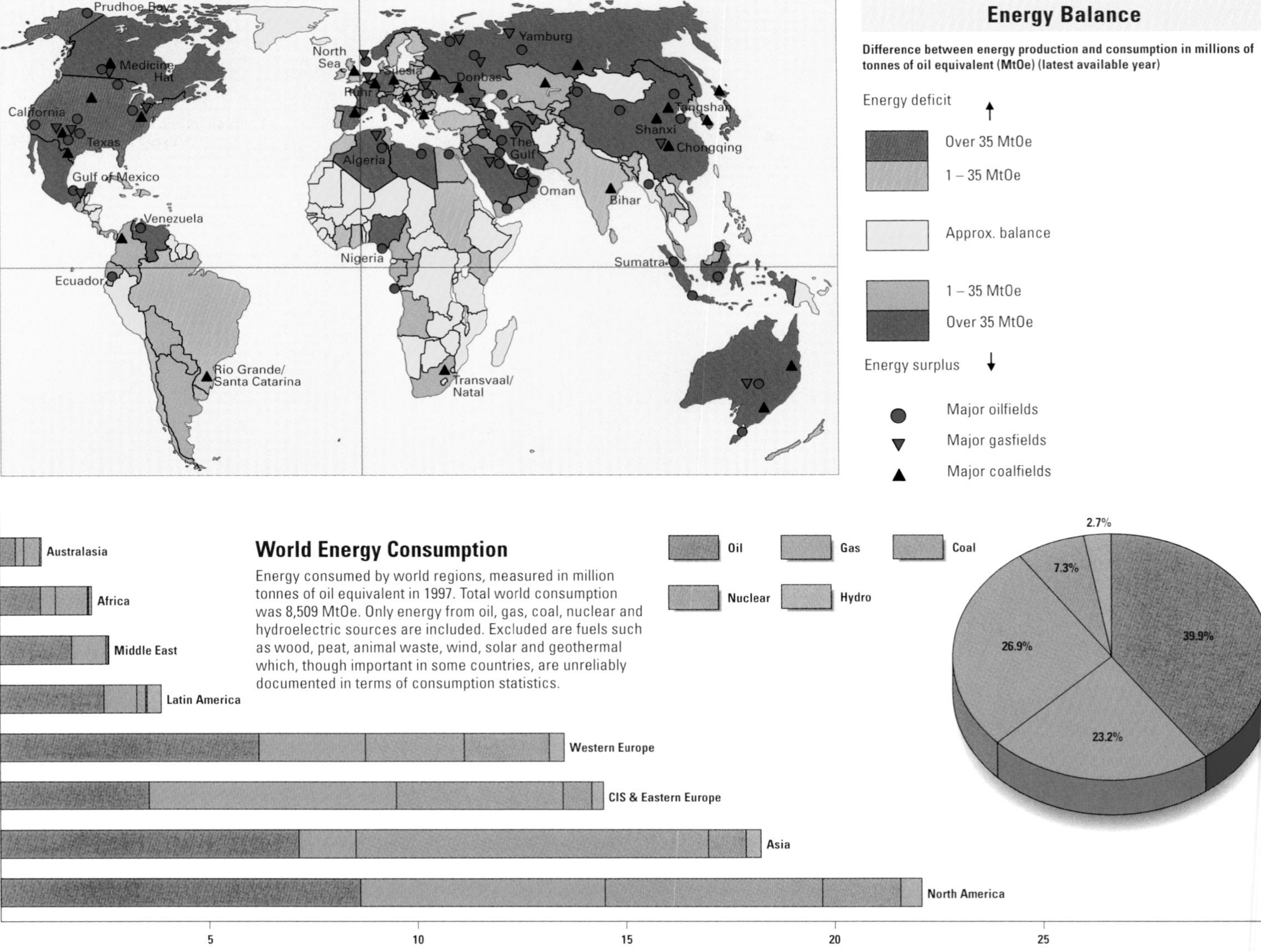

Energy Balance

Difference between energy production and consumption in millions of tonnes of oil equivalent (MtOe) (latest available year)

World Energy Consumption

Energy consumed by world regions, measured in million tonnes of oil equivalent in 1997. Total world consumption was 8,509 MtOe. Only energy from oil, gas, coal, nuclear and hydroelectric sources are included. Excluded are fuels such as wood, peat, animal waste, wind, solar and geothermal which, though important in some countries, are unreliably documented in terms of consumption statistics.

Energy Production

Primary energy production expressed in kilograms of coal equivalent per person (1994)

In developing countries traditional fuels are still very important. These so-called biomass fuels include wood, charcoal and dried dung. The pie-chart highlights the importance of biomass in terms of energy consumption in Nigeria. Collecting fuelwood can be a time-consuming task, sometimes taking all day.

Over 10,000 kg per person
1,000 – 10,000 kg per person
100 – 1,000 kg per person
10 – 100 kg per person
Under 10 kg per person

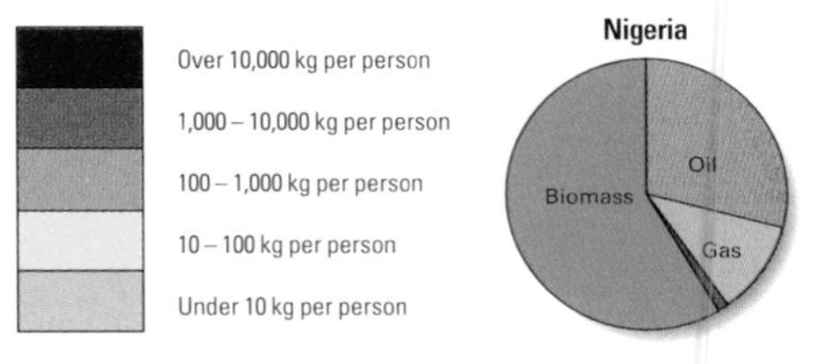

Oil Movements

Major world movements of oil in millions of tonnes (1997)

Middle East to Asia (not Japan)	294.4
Middle East to Japan	218.1
Middle East to Western Europe	187.9
South and Central America to USA	132.1
North Africa to Western Europe	97.9
CIS to Western Europe	90.8
Middle East to USA	86.9
Canada to USA	72.7
West Africa to USA	68.3
Mexico to USA	68.0
West Africa to Western Europe	40.1
Western Europe to USA	32.9
Middle East to Africa	32.0
CIS to Central Europe	31.8
Middle East to South and Central America	27.8
Middle East to Central Europe	19.3

Total world imports ....**1,978,900,000 million tonnes**

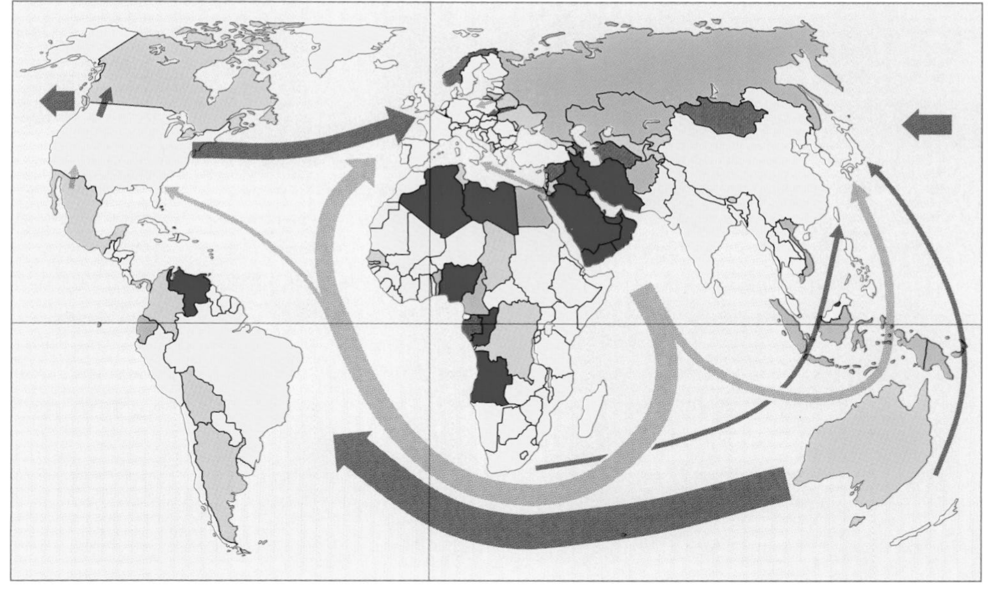

Fuel Exports

Fuels as a percentage of total value of exports (1996)

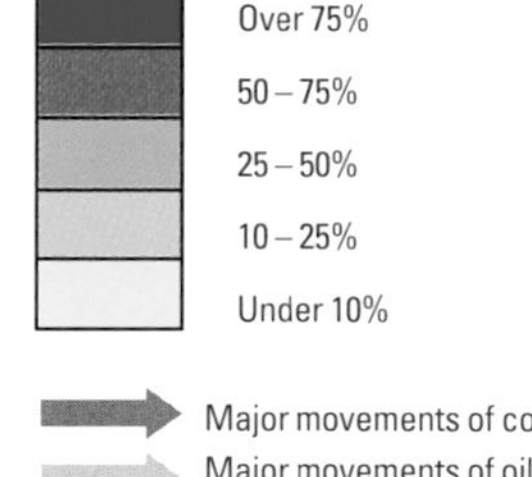

Major movements of coal
Major movements of oil

In the 1970s, oil exports became a political issue when OPEC sought to increase the influence of developing countries in world affairs by raising oil prices and restricting production. But its power was short-lived, following a fall in demand for oil in the 1980s, due to an increase in energy efficiency and development of alternative resources.

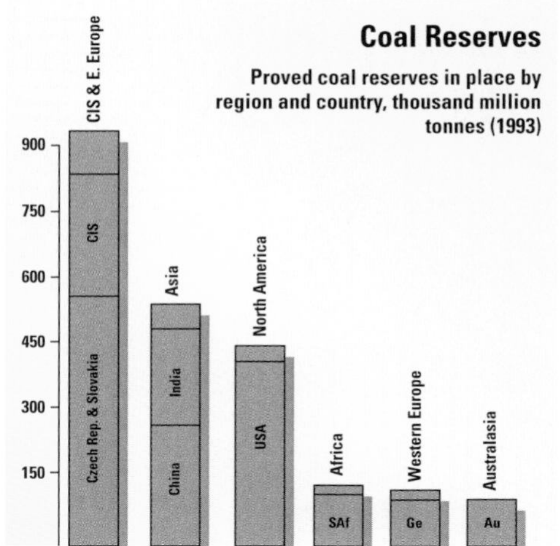

Coal Reserves

Proved coal reserves in place by region and country, thousand million tonnes (1993)

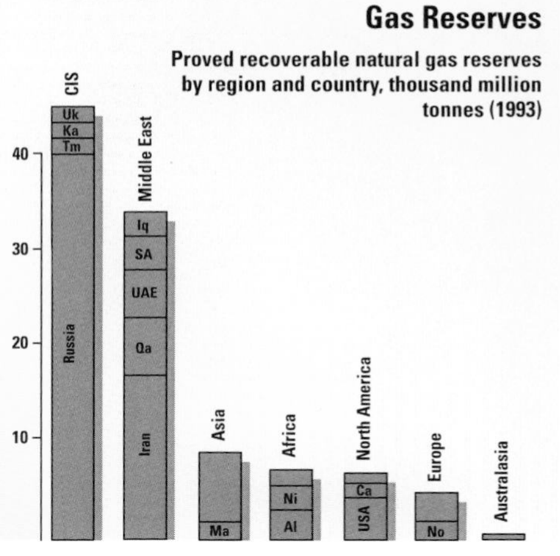

Gas Reserves

Proved recoverable natural gas reserves by region and country, thousand million tonnes (1993)

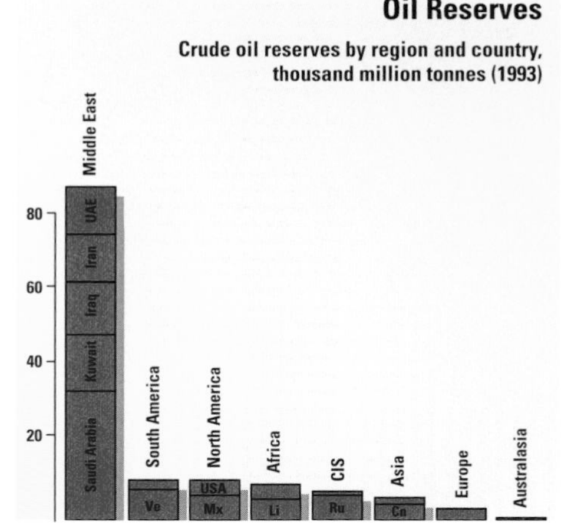

Oil Reserves

Crude oil reserves by region and country, thousand million tonnes (1993)

Al: Algeria
Au: Australia
Ca: Canada
Cn: China
Ge: Germany
Iq: Iraq
Ka: Kazakstan
Li: Libya
Ma: Malaysia
Mx: Mexico
Ni: Nigeria
No: Norway
Qa: Qatar
Ru: Russia
SA: Saudi Arabia
SAf: South Africa
Tm: Turkmenistan
Uk: Ukraine
Ve: Venezuela

Nuclear Power

Percentage of electricity generated by nuclear power stations, leading nations (1995)

1. Lithuania	85%	11. Spain	33%
2. France	77%	12. Finland	30%
3. Belgium	56%	13. Germany	29%
4. Slovak Rep.	49%	14. Japan	29%
5. Sweden	48%	15. UK	27%
6. Bulgaria	41%	16. Ukraine	27%
7. Hungary	41%	17. Czech Rep.	22%
8. Switzerland	39%	18. Canada	19%
9. Slovenia	38%	19. USA	18%
10. South Korea	33%	20. Russia	12%

Although the 1980s were a bad time for the nuclear power industry (major projects ran over budget and fears of long-term environmental damage were heavily reinforced by the 1986 disaster at Chernobyl), the industry picked up in the early 1990s. Whilst the number of reactors is still increasing, however, orders for new plants have shrunk. In 1997, the Swedish government began to decommission the country's 12 nuclear power plants; a bold environmental decision that could cost US $50 billion.

Renewable Energy

Average annual solar irradiance in kWh/m², with selected major hydroelectric and geothermal power stations

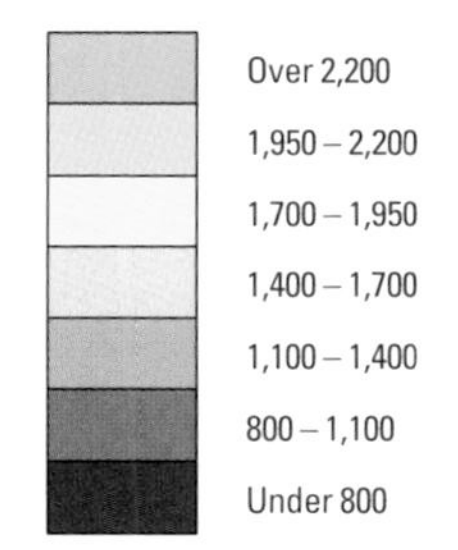

Hydroelectric plants
Geothermal plants

Hydroelectricity

Percentage of electricity generated by hydroelectric power stations, leading nations (1995)

1. Paraguay	99.9%	11. Rwanda	97.6%
2. Congo (D. Rep.)	99.7%	12. Malawi	97.6%
3. Bhutan	99.6%	13. Cameroon	96.9%
4. Zambia	99.5%	14. Nepal	96.7%
5. Norway	99.4%	15. Laos	95.3%
6. Ghana	99.3%	16. Albania	95.2%
7. Congo	99.3%	17. Iceland	94.0%
8. Uganda	99.1%	18. Brazil	92.2%
9. Burundi	98.3%	19. Honduras	87.6%
10. Uruguay	98.0%	20. Tanzania	87.1%

The countries that are heavily reliant on hydroelectricity are usually small and non-industrial: a high proportion of hydroelectric power more often reflects a modest energy budget than vast hydroelectric resources. The USA, for instance, produces only 9% of power requirements from hydroelectricity; yet that 9% amounts to more than three times the hydropower generated by the whole of Africa.

Alternative Energy Resources

Solar: Each year the Sun bestows upon the Earth almost a million times as much energy as is locked up in all the planet's oil reserves, but only an insignificant fraction is trapped and used commercially. In a few installations around the world, mirrors focus the Sun's rays on to boilers, whose steam generates electricity by spinning turbines.

Wind: Caused by uneven heating of the Earth, winds are themselves a form of solar energy. Windmills have been used for centuries to turn wind power into mechanical work; recent models, often arranged in banks on wind-swept high ground, usually generate electricity. Figures for wind power worldwide are given in the table, right.

Tidal: The energy from tides is potentially enormous, although only a few installations have so far been built to exploit it. In theory at least, waves and currents could also provide almost unimaginable power, and the thermal differences in the ocean depths are another huge well of potential energy. But work on extracting it is still in the experimental stage.

Geothermal: The Earth's temperature rises by 1°C for every 30 metres descent, with much steeper temperature gradients in geologically active areas. El Salvador, for example, produces 39% of its electricity from geothermal power stations, whilst the USA, the world leader, produced 3,331 megawatts in 1993. Some of the oldest and most successful applications are in Iceland, where 86% of all households are heated by geothermal energy.

Biomass: The oldest of human fuels ranges from animal dung, still burned in cooking fires in much of North Africa and elsewhere, to sugar cane plantations feeding high-technology distilleries to produce ethanol for motor vehicle engines. In Brazil and South Africa, plant ethanol provides up to 25% of motor fuel. Throughout the developing world, most biomass energy comes from firewood: although accurate figures are impossible to obtain, it may yield as much as 10% of the world's total energy consumption.

Wind Power

World wind energy generating capacity, in megawatts

1980	10
1981	25
1982	90
1983	210
1984	600
1985	1,020
1986	1,270
1987	1,450
1988	1,580
1989	1,730
1990	1,930
1991	2,170
1992	2,510
1993	3,050
1994	3,710

Wind power is the fastest growing source of energy worldwide but still provides only 1% of the world's energy. Output grew by 33% in 1995.

Minerals

For more information:
10 Geology
39 Patterns of production
41 World shipping

The use of metals played a vital part in the evolving technologies of early peoples. Copper first came into use around 10,000 years ago, bronze about 5,000 years ago, and iron 3,300 years ago. In the early stages of the Industrial Revolution, the location of coal, iron ore and water power usually determined the location of new industries. But due to continuing improvements in transport, including oil pipelines, industries can now be located almost anywhere.

Minerals are distributed unevenly and some industrial countries, lacking their own mineral resources, import most of the raw materials they need. Some imports come from mineral-rich countries, such as Australia but others come from developing countries, especially in Africa and South America. Most of the developing countries export unprocessed ores, losing out on the much higher revenues gained from exporting metals.

Most minerals come from land deposits, because undersea deposits, with the exception of oil reserves under the continental shelves, have been regarded as inaccessible. But shortages of terrestrial minerals may one day encourage exploitation of the ocean floor.

Mineral Exports

Minerals and metals as a percentage of total exports (latest available year)

Uranium

In its pure state, uranium is an immensely heavy, white metal; but although spent uranium is employed as projectiles in anti-missile cannons, where its mass ensures a lethal punch, its main use is as a fuel in nuclear reactors, and in nuclear weaponry. Uranium is very scarce: the main source is the rare ore pitchblende, which itself contains only 0.2% uranium oxide. Only a minute fraction of that is the radioactive U^{235} isotope, though so-called breeder reactors can transmute the more common U^{238} into highly radioactive plutonium.

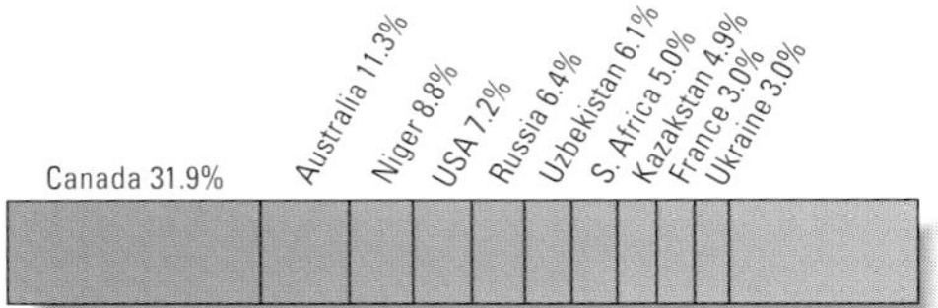

World total (1995): 32,976 tonnes

Metals

*** Figures for aluminium are for refined metal; all other figures refer to ore production.**

The world's leading producers of aluminium ore (bauxite) in 1995 were as follows:

1. Australia 41.9%
2. Papua New Guinea 14.3%
3. Jamaica 10.8%
4. Brazil 10.1%
5. Russia 6.7%
6. China 5.7%
7. India 5.0%
8. Surinam 2.8%
9. Venezuela 2.6%
10. Greece 1.9%

The figures shown above are in stark contrast to the figures showing aluminium production on the right. Australia, for example, produces 41.9% of the world's bauxite but only 5.9% of the aluminium metal. Papua New Guinea and Jamaica account for 25% of the bauxite mined but have no smelters and export virtually all of it to countries like the USA and Canada.

Diamond

Most of the world's diamond is found in kimberlite, or 'blue ground', a basic peridotite rock; erosion may wash the diamond from its kimberlite matrix and deposit it with sand or gravel on river beds. Only a small proportion of the world's diamond, the most flawless, is cut into gemstones – 'diamonds'; most is used in industry, where the material's remarkable hardness and abrasion resistance finds a use in cutting tools, drills and dies, as well as in styluses. Australia, not among the top 12 producers at the beginning of the 1980s, had by 1986 become world leader and by 1993 was the source of 40.6% of world production. The other main producers were Congo (then Zaire) (16.3%), Botswana (14.6%), Russia (11.4%) and South Africa (9.7%). Between them, these five nations accounted for over 82% of the world total of 100,850,000 carats.

Aluminium: Produced mainly from its oxide, bauxite, which yields 25% of its weight in aluminium. The cost of refining and production is often too high for producer-countries to bear, so bauxite is largely exported. Lightweight and corrosion resistant, aluminium alloys are widely used in aircraft, vehicles, cans and packaging.

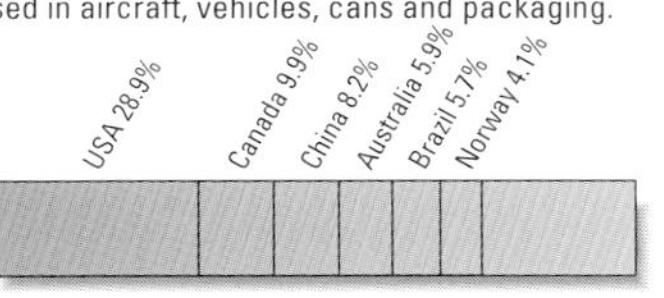

World total (1995): 22,706,000 tonnes *

Lead: A soft metal, obtained mainly from galena (lead sulphide), which occurs in veins associated with iron, zinc and silver sulphides. Its use in vehicle batteries accounts for the USA's prime consumer status; lead is also made into sheeting and piping. Its use as an additive to paints and petrol is decreasing.

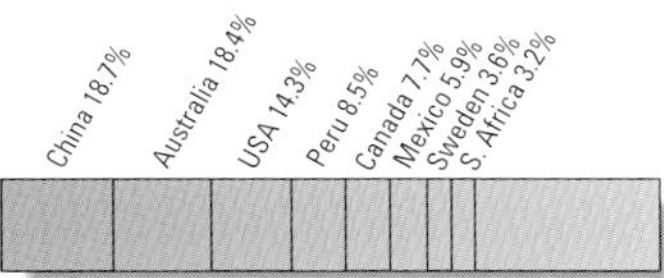

World total (1995): 2,751,000 tonnes *

Tin: Soft, pliable and non-toxic, used to coat 'tin' (tin-plated steel) cans, in the manufacture of foils and in alloys. The principal tin-bearing mineral is cassiterite (SnO_2), found in ore formed from molten rock. Producers and refiners were hit by a price collapse in 1991.

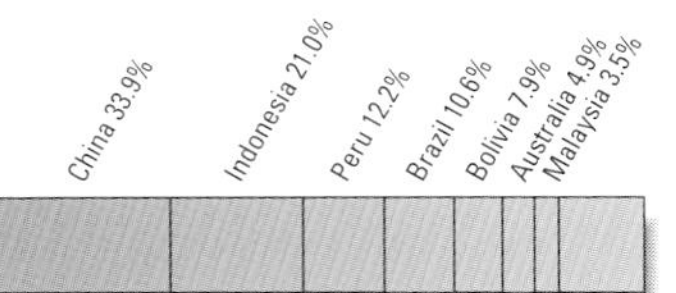

World total (1995): 182,518 tonnes *

Gold: Regarded for centuries as the most valuable metal in the world and used to make coins, gold is still recognized as the monetary standard. A soft metal, it is alloyed to make jewellery; the electronics industry values its corrosion resistance and conductivity.

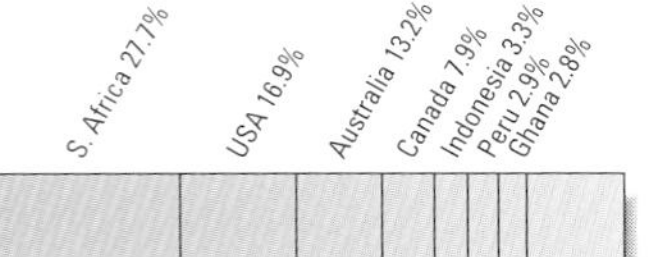

World total (1995): 1,889 tonnes *

Copper: Derived from low-yielding sulphide ores, copper is an important export for several developing countries. An excellent conductor of heat and electricity, it forms part of most electrical items, and is used in the manufacture of brass and bronze. Major importers include Japan and Germany.

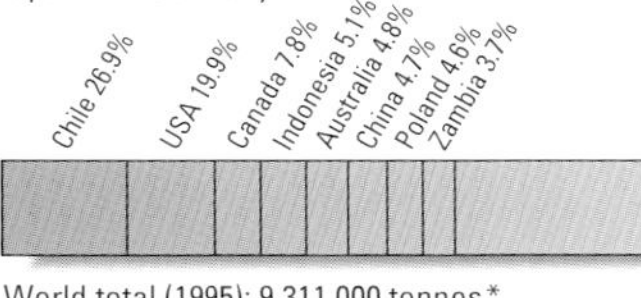

World total (1995): 9,311,000 tonnes *

Mercury: The only metal that is liquid at normal temperatures, most is derived from its sulphide, cinnabar, found only in small quantities in volcanic areas. Apart from its value in thermometers and other instruments, most mercury production is used in anti-fungal and anti-fouling preparations, and to make detonators.

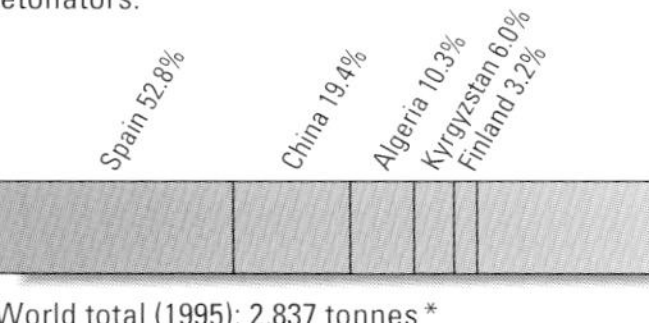

World total (1995): 2,837 tonnes *

Zinc: Often found in association with lead ores, zinc is highly resistant to corrosion, and about 40% of the refined metal is used to plate sheet steel, particularly vehicle bodies – a process known as galvanizing. Zinc is also used in dry batteries, paints and dyes.

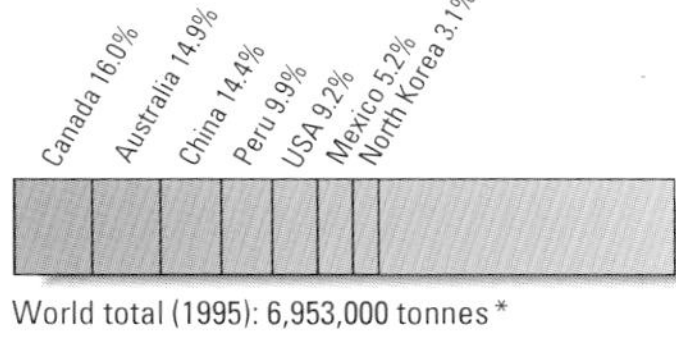

World total (1995): 6,953,000 tonnes *

Silver: Most silver comes from ores mined and processed for other metals (including lead and copper). Pure or alloyed with harder metals, it is used for jewellery and ornaments. Industrial use includes dentistry, electronics, photography and as a chemical catalyst.

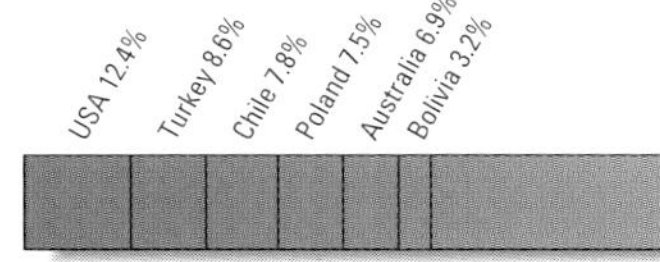

World total (1995): 13,266 tonnes *

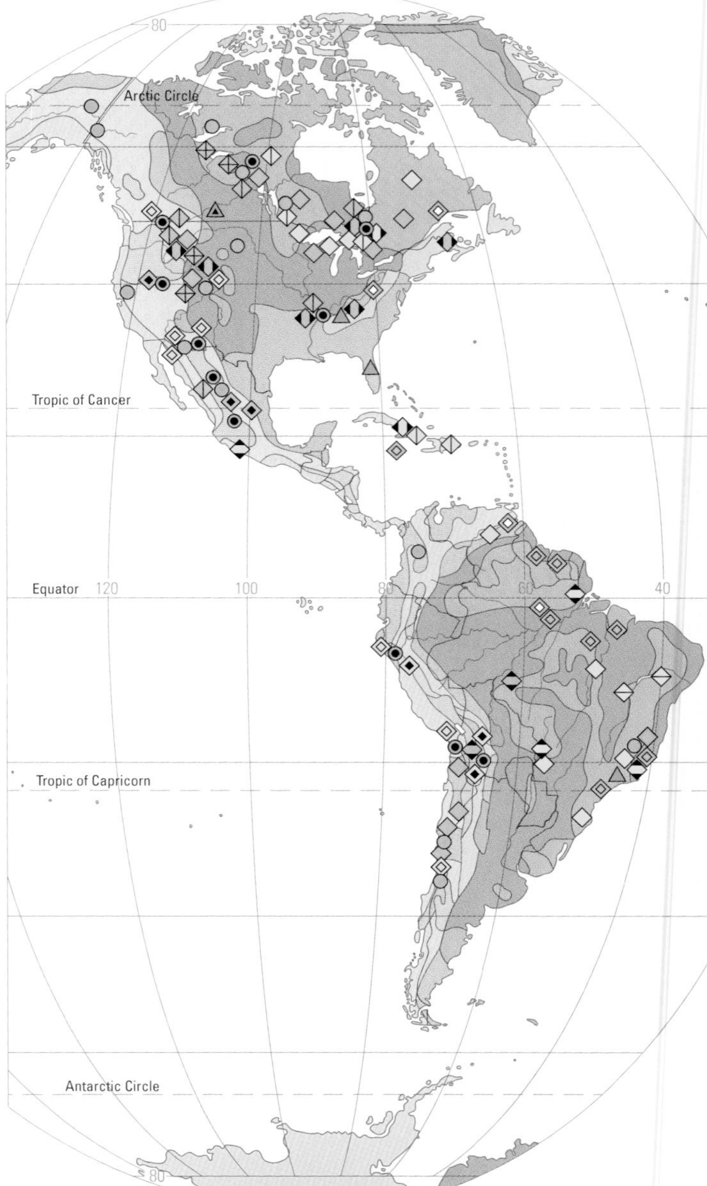

Strategic Minerals

Ever since the art of high-temperature smelting was discovered, some time in the second millennium BC, iron has been by far the most important metal known to man. The earliest iron ploughs transformed primitive agriculture and led to the first human population explosion, while iron weapons – or the lack of them – ensured the rise or fall of entire cultures.

Widely distributed around the world, iron ores usually contain 25–60% iron; blast furnaces process the raw product into pig-iron, which is then alloyed with carbon and other minerals to produce steels of various qualities. From the time of the Industrial Revolution, steel has been almost literally the backbone of modern civilization, the prime structural material on which all else is built.

Iron smelting usually developed close to the sources of ore and, later, to the coalfields that fuelled the furnaces. Today, most ore comes from a few richly-endowed locations where large-scale mining is possible. Iron and steel plants are generally built at coastal sites so that giant ore carriers, which account for a sizeable proportion of the world's merchant fleet, can easily discharge their cargoes.

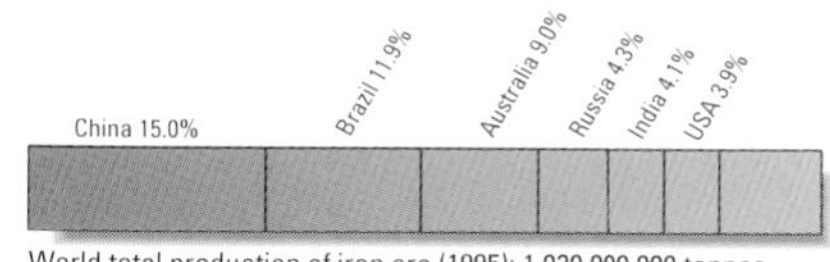

World total production of iron ore (1995): 1,020,000,000 tonnes

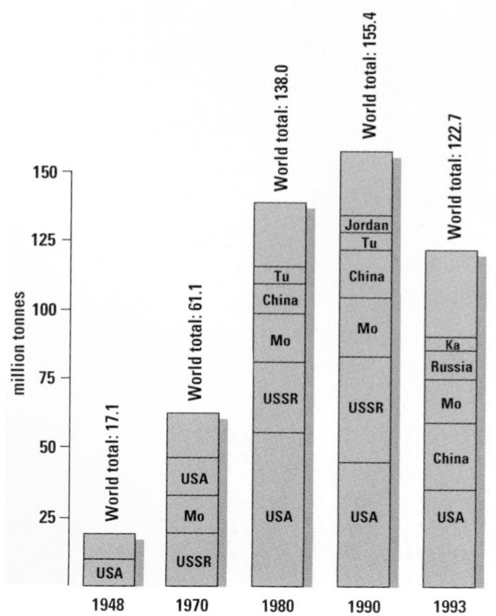

World production of phosphates in millions of tonnes (1993). Phosphate production is vital to the economies of several small countries. Nauru, for example, is heavily dependent on phosphate exports – the island has one of the world's richest deposits. In 1994, 613,000 tonnes were mined, employing 1,000 people. In Togo, earnings from phosphate exports have superseded all agricultural exports.

Percentage of total world phosphate production (1994)

1. USA	32.4%	7. Israel	3.1%
2. China	20.2%	8. Brazil	2.6%
3. Morocco	15.4%	9. South Africa	2.0%
4. Russia	6.2%	10. Togo	1.7%
5. Tunisia	4.4%	11. Kazakstan	1.6%
6. Jordan	3.3%	12. Senegal	1.4%

World production of pig-iron and ferro-alloys (1995).
All countries with an annual output of more than 1 million tonnes are shown

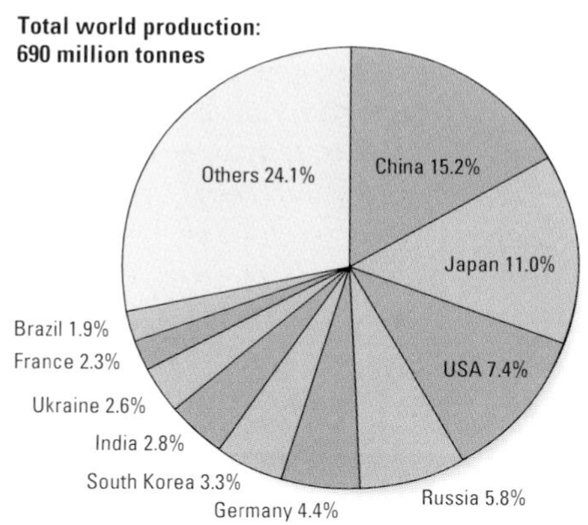

Manganese: In its pure state, manganese is a hard, brittle metal. Alloyed with chrome, iron and nickel, it produces abrasion-resistant steels; manganese-aluminium alloys are light but tough. Found in batteries and inks, manganese is also used in glass production. Manganese ores are frequently found in the same location as sedimentary iron ores. Pyrolusite (MnO_2) and psilomelane are the main economically-exploitable sources.

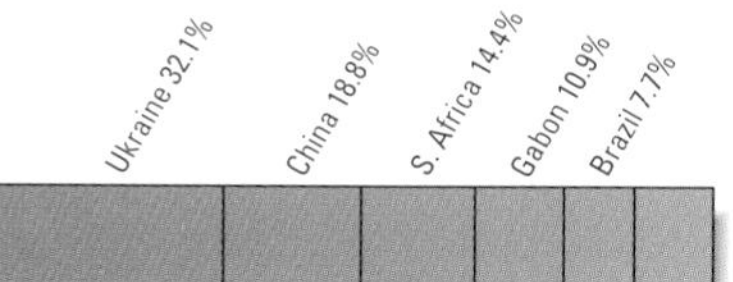

World total (1994): 22,180,000 tonnes

Chromium: Most of the world's chromium production is alloyed with iron and other metals to produce steels with various different properties. Combined with iron, nickel, cobalt and tungsten, chromium produces an exceptionally hard steel, resistant to heat; chrome steels are used for many household items where utility must be matched with appearance – cutlery, for example. Chromium is also used in production of refractory bricks, and its salts for tanning and dyeing leather and cloth.

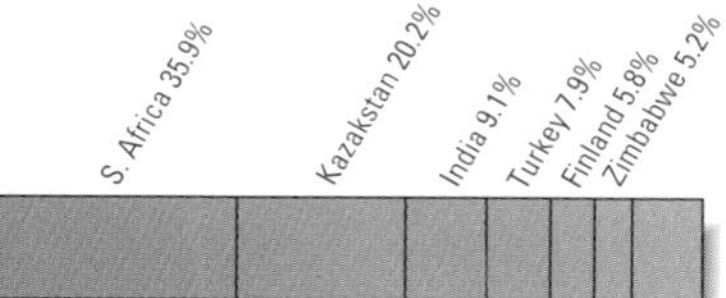

World total (1994): 10,000,000 tonnes

Nickel: Combined with chrome and iron, nickel produces stainless and high-strength steels; similar alloys go to make magnets and electrical heating elements. Nickel combined with copper is widely used to make coins; cupro-nickel alloy is very resistant to corrosion. Its ores yield only modest quantities of nickel – 0.5% to 3.0% – but also contain copper, iron and small amounts of precious metals. Japan, USA, UK, Germany and France are the principal importers.

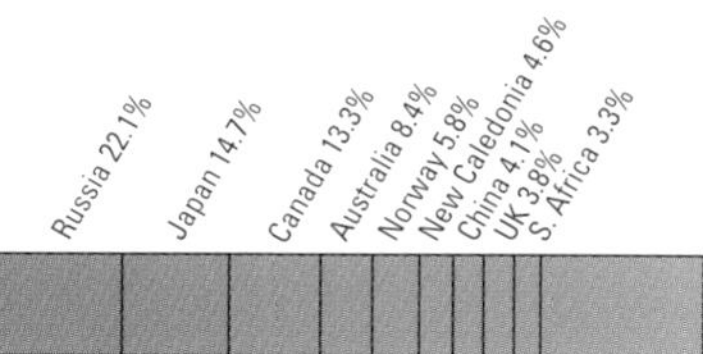

World total (1995): 920,000 tonnes

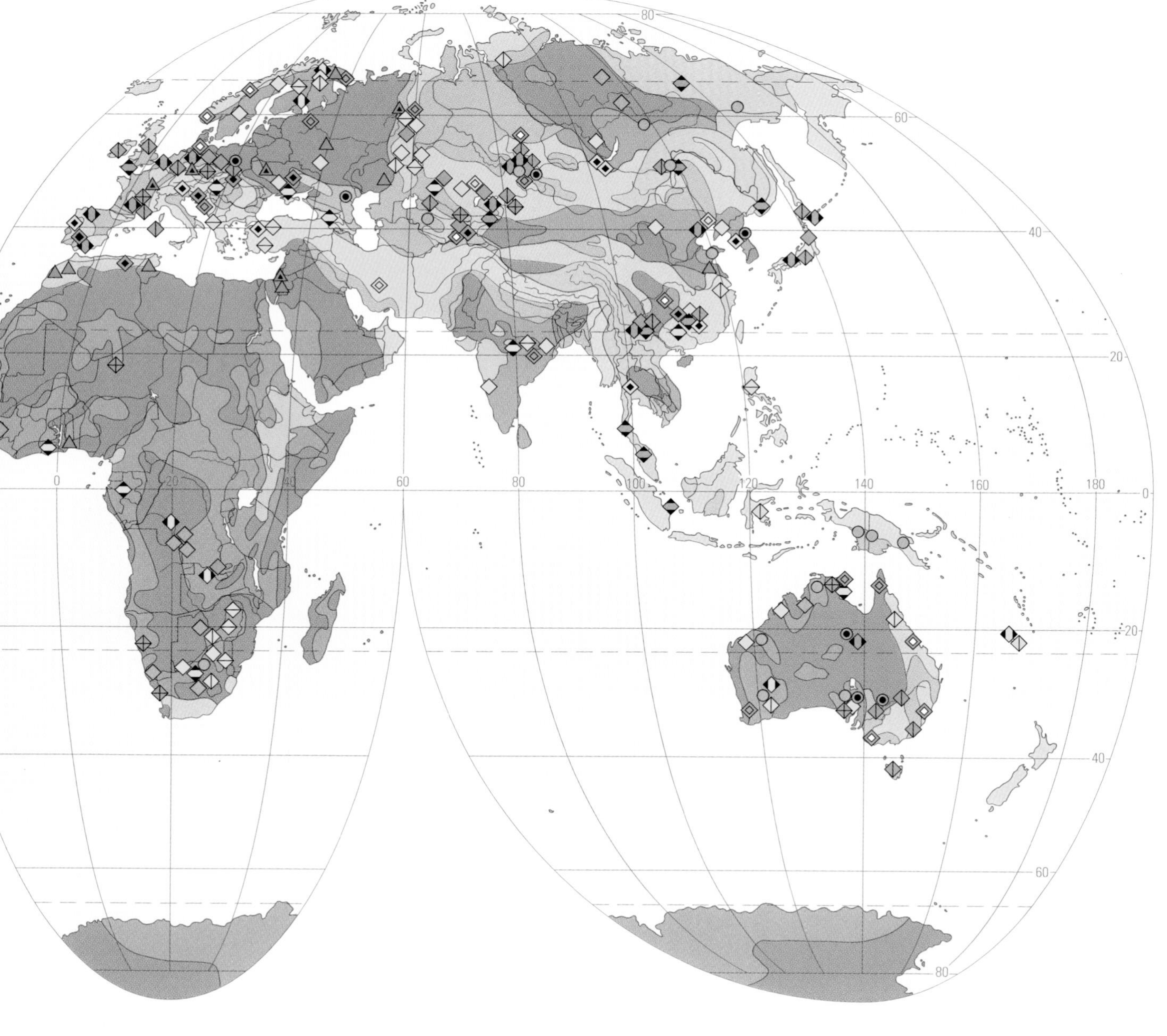

Distribution of Minerals

Structural Regions

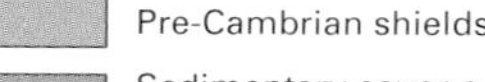

- Pre-Cambrian shields
- Sedimentary cover on Pre-Cambrian shields
- Paleozoic (Caledonian and Hercynian) folding
- Sedimentary cover on Paleozoic folding
- Mesozoic folding
- Sedimentary cover on Mesozoic folding
- Cenozoic (Alpine) folding
- Sedimentary cover on Cenozoic folding
- Intensive Mesozoic and Cenozoic vulcanism

Distribution

Iron and ferro-alloys

- Chrome
- Cobalt
- Iron Ore
- Manganese
- Molybdenum
- Nickel Ore
- Tungsten

Non-ferrous metals

- Bauxite (Aluminium)
- Copper
- Lead
- Mercury
- Tin
- Zinc
- Uranium

Precious metals and stones

- Diamonds
- Gold
- Silver

Fertilizers

- Phosphates
- Potash

Manufacturing

For more information:

18 Water utilization
32 Land use and economy
36 Mineral production
37 Iron and ferro-alloys
40 Trading nations
Major exports
Traded products

The Industrial Revolution which began in Britain in the late 18th century, represented a major technological advance in the evolution of human society. It enabled a group of countries to become prosperous by replacing expensive human labour with increasingly sophisticated machinery. In economic terms, manufacturing is the transformation of raw materials, energy, labour and machines into finished goods, which have a higher value than the various elements used in production.

The economies of countries can be compared by reference to their per capita Gross National Products (or per capita GNPs), namely, the total value of goods and services produced in a country in a year, divided by the population.

The industrialized, or developed, countries accounted for 16% of the world's population in 1997 with an average per capita GNP of US $25,700. On the other hand, developing countries, with comparatively small industrial sectors and low-income economies, accounted for 35% of the world's population, with an average per capita GNP of just $350.

Kenya, with its low-income economy, had a per capita GNP in 1998 of $330. Agriculture employs 77% of the people, industry 8% and services 15%. The major industries are the processing of agricultural products and import substitution (the manufacture of such necessities as cement, footwear and textiles). Heavy industry plays a comparatively small part in the economy. By contrast, Germany, a major industrialized nation, had a per capita GNP in 1998 of $25,850. Agriculture employs only 1% of the population, with 32% in industry, and 67% in services. Germany's industrial sector differs greatly from Kenya's, with an emphasis on the manufacture of vehicles, machinery and chemicals.

Since the 1970s, some former developing countries in Asia have been transformed by rapid industrialization. These 'economic tigers', including China, Malaysia, South Korea, Singapore, Taiwan and Thailand, owe their success to low labour costs and substantial investment in education, together with advances in telecommunications, transport and computers, which have made technology more readily transferable around the world than ever before. They have also benefited from economic freedom and trade liberalization.

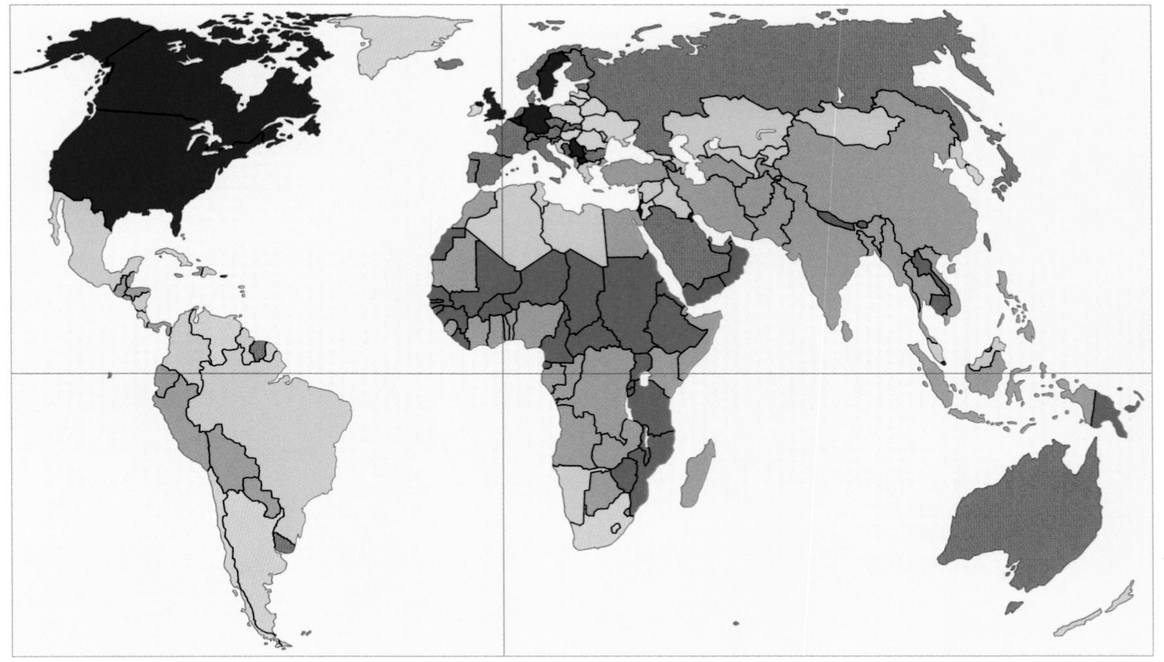

Employment

The number of workers employed in manufacturing for every 100 workers engaged in agriculture (latest available year)

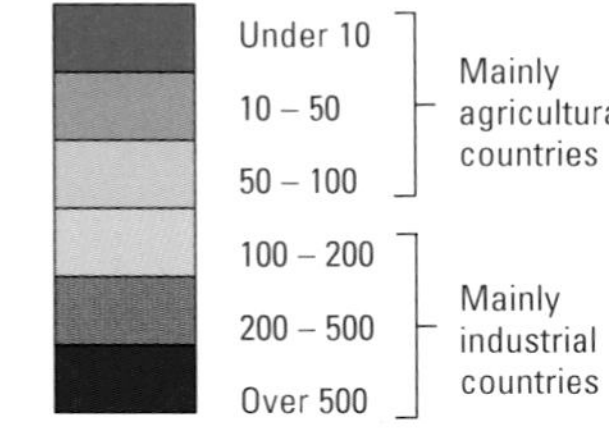

Selected countries (latest available year)

Country	
Singapore	8,860
UK	1,270
Belgium	820
Germany	800
Kuwait	767
Bahrain	660
USA	657
Israel	633

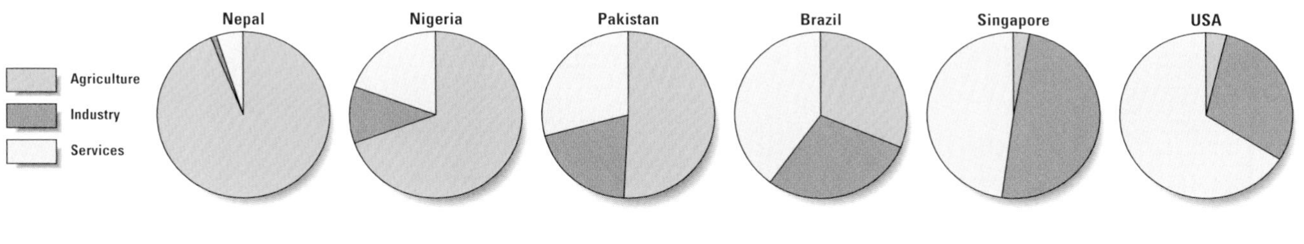

Division of Employment

Distribution of workers between agriculture, industry and services, selected countries (latest available year)

The six countries selected illustrate the usual stages of economic development, from dependence on agriculture through industrial growth to the expansion of the service sector.

The Workforce

Percentages of men and women between 15 and 64 in employment, selected countries (latest available year)

The figures include employees and the self-employed, who in developing countries are often subsistence farmers. People in full-time education are excluded. Because of the population age structure in developing countries, the employed population has to support a far larger number of non-workers than its industrial equivalent. For example, more than 52% of Kenya's people are under 15, an age group that makes up less than a tenth of the UK population.

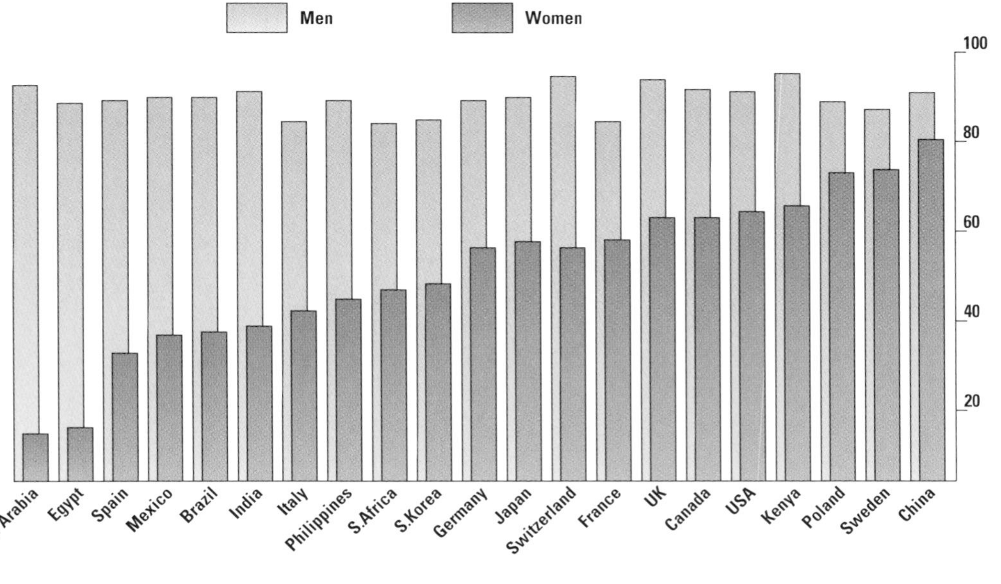

Wealth Creation

The Gross National Product (GNP) of the world's largest economies, US $ million (1998)

1.	USA	7,922,651	21.	Austria	217,163
2.	Japan	4,089,910	22.	Turkey	200,505
3.	Germany	2,122,673	23.	Saudi Arabia	186,000
4.	Italy	1,666,178	24.	Denmark	176,374
5.	France	1,466,014	25.	Hong Kong	158,286
6.	UK	1,263,777	26.	Norway	152,082
7.	China	928,950	27.	Poland	150,798
8.	Botswana	758,043	28.	Indonesia	138,501
9.	Canada	612,332	29.	Thailand	134,433
10.	Spain	553,690	30.	Finland	124,293
11.	India	421,259	31.	Greece	122,880
12.	Netherlands	388,682	32.	South Africa	119,001
13.	Mexico	380,917	33.	Iran	109,645
14.	Australia	380,625	34.	Portugal	106,376
15.	South Korea	369,890	35.	Colombia	106,090
16.	Russia	337,914	36.	Israel	95,179
17.	Argentina	324,084	37.	Singapore	95,095
18.	Switzerland	284,808	38.	Venezuela	81,347
19.	Belgium	259,045	39.	Malaysia	79,848
20.	Sweden	226,861	40.	Egypt	79,208

Patterns of Production

Breakdown of industrial output by value, selected countries (latest available year)

	Food & agric. products	Textiles & clothing	Machinery & transport	Chemicals	Other
Algeria	26%	20%	11%	1%	41%
Argentina	24%	10%	16%	12%	37%
Australia	18%	7%	21%	8%	45%
Austria	17%	8%	25%	6%	43%
Belgium	19%	8%	23%	13%	36%
Brazil	15%	12%	24%	9%	40%
Burkina Faso	62%	18%	2%	1%	17%
Canada	15%	7%	25%	9%	44%
Denmark	22%	6%	23%	10%	39%
Egypt	20%	27%	13%	10%	31%
Finland	13%	6%	24%	7%	50%
France	18%	7%	33%	9%	33%
Germany	12%	5%	38%	10%	36%
Greece	20%	22%	14%	7%	38%
Hungary	6%	11%	37%	11%	35%
India	11%	16%	26%	15%	32%
Indonesia	23%	11%	10%	10%	47%
Iran	13%	22%	22%	7%	36%
Ireland	28%	7%	20%	15%	28%
Israel	13%	10%	28%	8%	42%
Italy	7%	13%	32%	10%	38%
Japan	10%	6%	38%	10%	37%
Kenya	35%	12%	14%	9%	29%
Malaysia	21%	5%	23%	14%	37%
Mexico	24%	12%	14%	12%	39%
Netherlands	19%	4%	28%	11%	38%
New Zealand	26%	10%	16%	6%	43%
Norway	21%	3%	26%	7%	44%
Pakistan	34%	21%	8%	12%	25%
Philippines	40%	7%	7%	10%	35%
Poland	15%	16%	30%	6%	33%
Portugal	17%	22%	16%	8%	38%
Singapore	6%	5%	46%	8%	36%
South Africa	14%	8%	17%	11%	49%
South Korea	15%	17%	24%	9%	35%
Spain	17%	9%	22%	9%	43%
Sweden	10%	2%	35%	8%	44%
Thailand	30%	17%	14%	6%	33%
Turkey	20%	14%	15%	8%	43%
UK	14%	6%	32%	11%	36%
USA	12%	5%	35%	10%	38%
Venezuela	23%	8%	9%	11%	49%

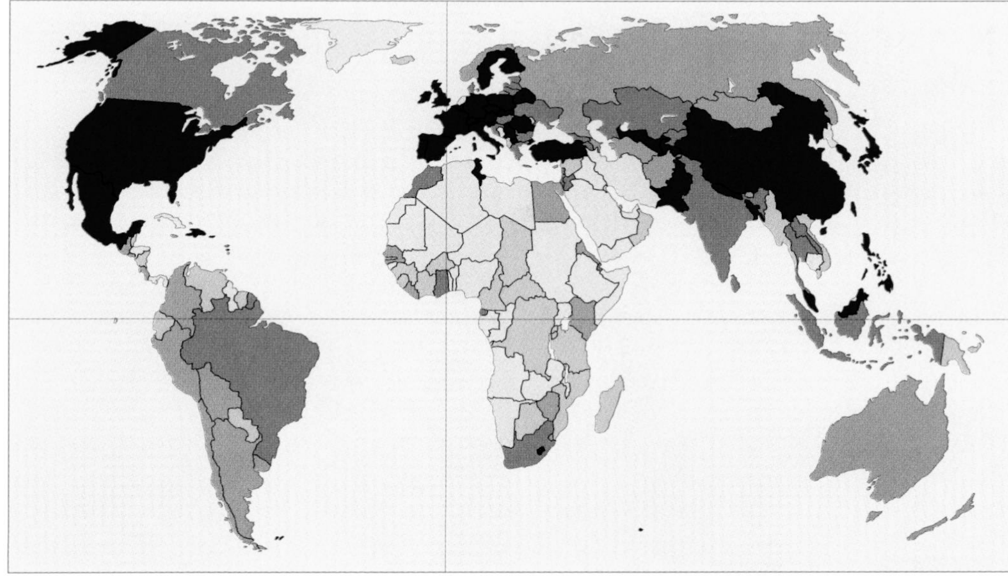

Industry and Trade

Manufactured goods (including machinery and transport) as a percentage of total exports (1996)

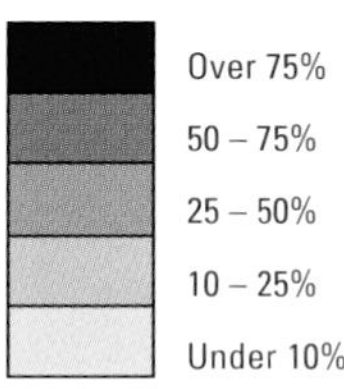

The Far East and South-east Asia (Japan 98%, Macau 96%, Taiwan 95%, Hong Kong [now part of China] 94%, South Korea 94%) are most dominant, but many countries in Europe (e.g. Slovenia 93%) are also heavily dependent on manufactured goods.

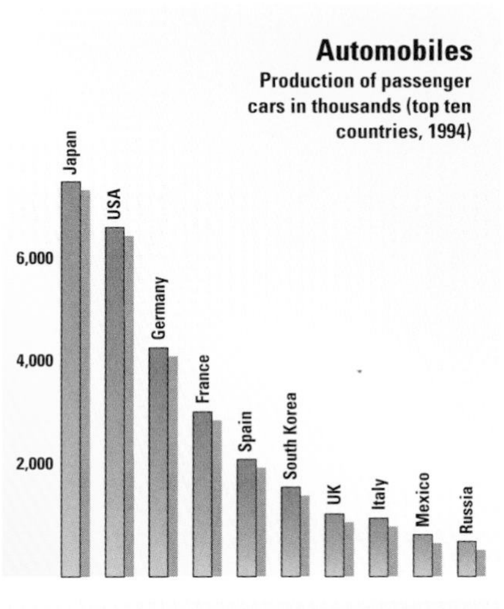

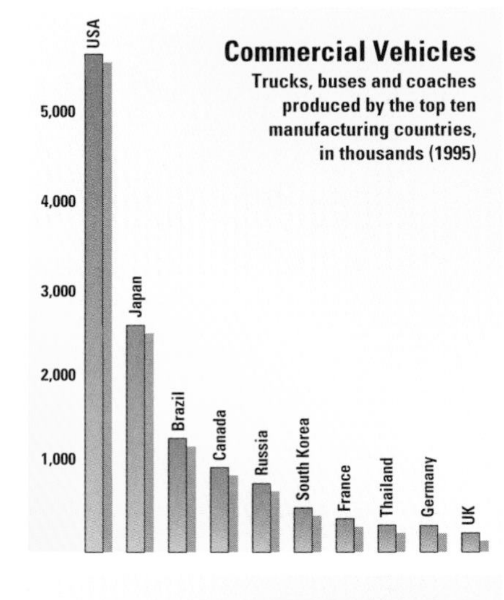

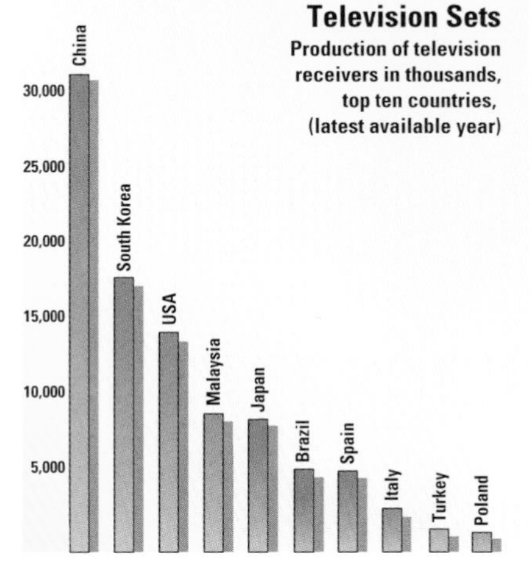

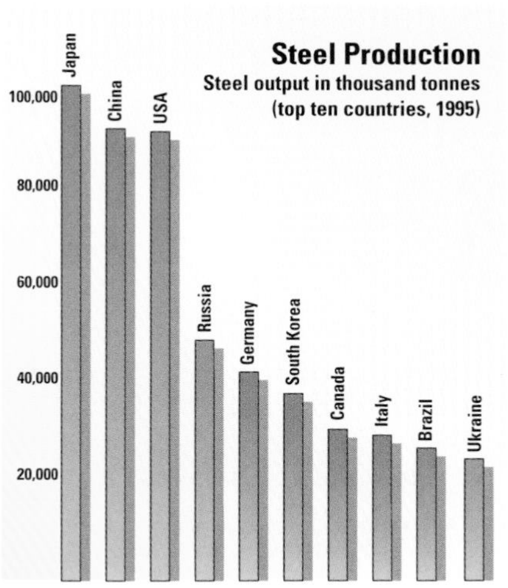

Steel Production

Steel output in thousand tonnes (top ten countries, 1995)

Japan	China	USA	Russia	Germany	South Korea	Canada	Italy	Brazil	Ukraine

(scale: 100,000; 80,000; 60,000; 40,000; 20,000)

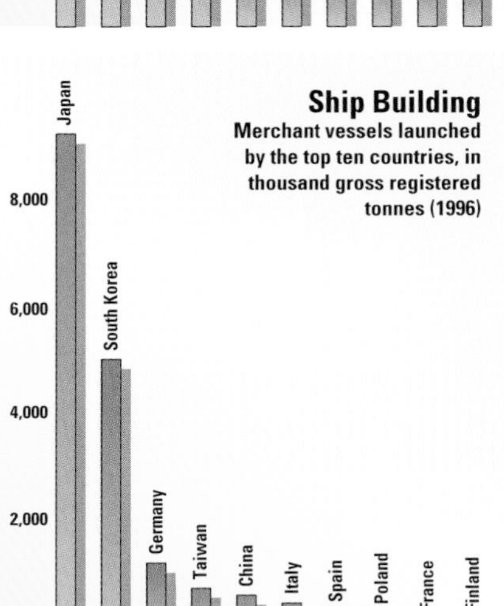

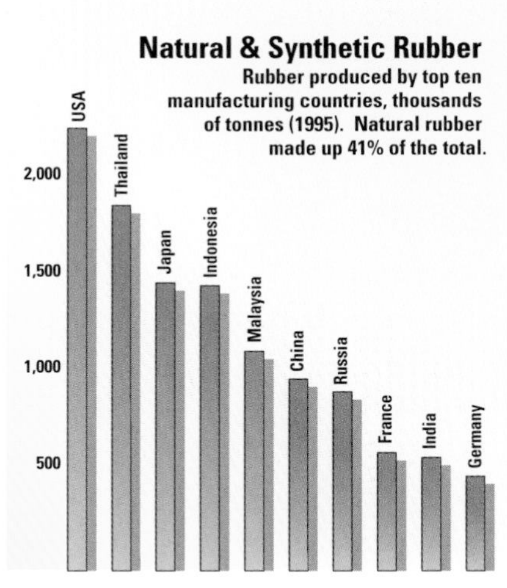

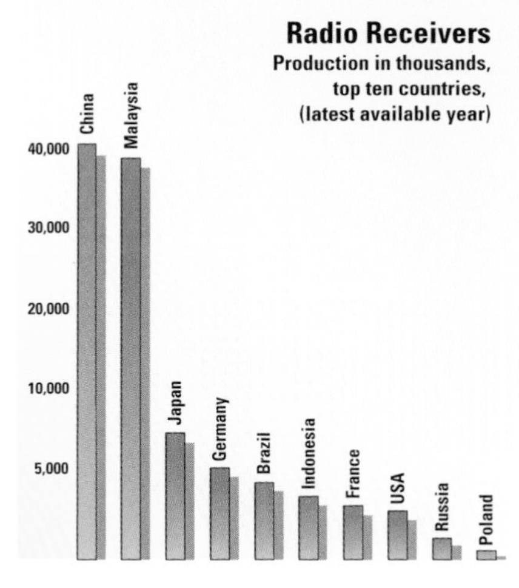

Industrial Output

Industrial output (mining, manufacturing, construction, energy and water production), US $ billion (1995)

1.	Japan	1,941
2.	USA	1,808
3.	Germany	780
4.	France	415
5.	UK	354
6.	Italy	337
7.	China	335
8.	Brazil	255
9.	South Korea	196
10.	Spain	187
11.	Canada	174
12.	Russia	131
13.	Netherlands	107
14.	Australia	98
15.	Switzerland	96
16.	India	94
17.	Argentina	87
18.	Belgium	83
=	Indonesia	83
20.	Austria	79
21.	Sweden	73
22.	Saudi Arabia	67
=	Thailand	67
24.	Mexico	65
25.	Turkey	51
26.	Denmark	50
27.	Finland	46
=	Poland	46
29.	Norway	44
30.	Malaysia	37
=	Portugal	37
32.	Ukraine	34
33.	Greece	33
34.	Singapore	30
35.	Venezuela	29
=	Israel	29
37.	Chile	24
=	Colombia	24
=	Hong Kong	24
=	Philippines	24

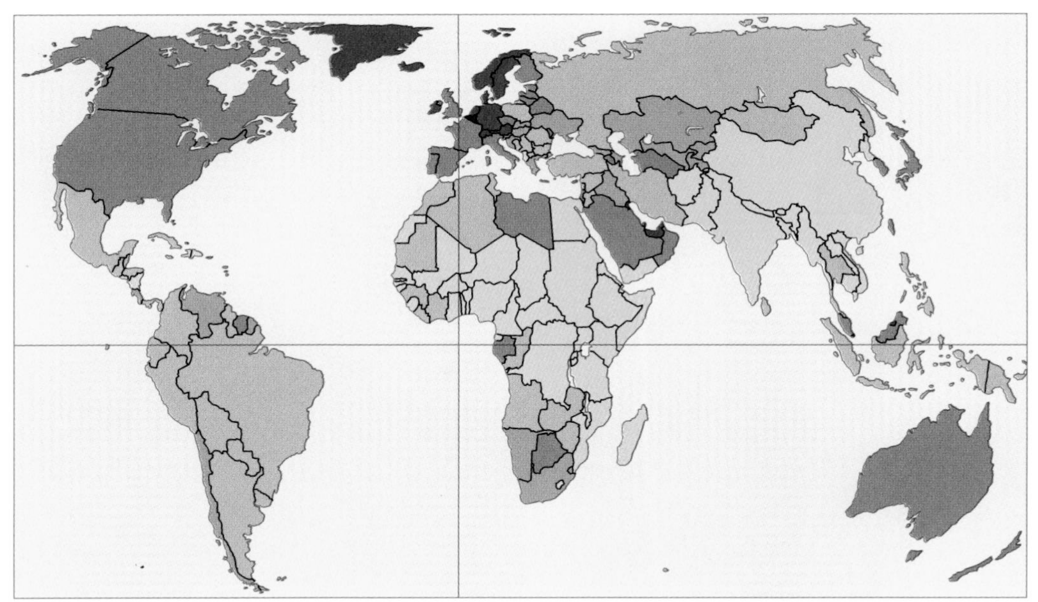

Exports Per Capita

Value of exports in US $, divided by total population (latest available year)

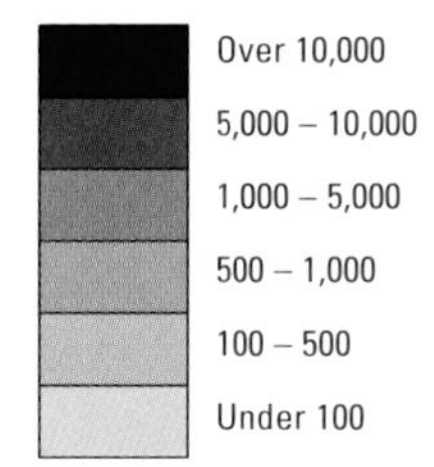

[UK 3,135] [USA 1,967]

Highest per capita exports (1993)

Singapore	25,787
Hong Kong	22,339
Benelux	12,295
Brunei	8,778
Netherlands	8,578
Switzerland	8,457

Trade

For more information:
31 International organizations
35 Fuel exports
Movements of oil
36 Mineral exports
39 Industry and trade
Exports per capita
46 Tourism

Trade played a vital role in the growth of early civilizations and it was later a spur to European exploration and colonization. The colonial powers grew rich by exporting cheap manufactures, such as clothing and footwear, while obtaining primary products from their colonies.

From the late 19th century to the early 1950s, as transport technology improved, primary products, especially oil in the later stages of this period, dominated world trade. However, since that time, manufactures have become the chief commodities in world trade, which is dominated by the industrialized countries. Nearly half of all world trade flows between the developed market economies of the European Union, the United States and Japan, although the Asian 'tiger economies', notably Singapore, South Korea, Taiwan, Malaysia and Thailand, have increased their share in recent years. Recent predictions suggest that the next 'tigers' might include Argentina and Chile in South America, Indonesia, the Philippines and Vietnam in Asia, and the Czech Republic and Poland in Europe.

There is little trade between developing countries, although some mineral- and oil-rich nations obtain a high proportion of their GNP from export sales. Growth in world trade is regarded as a sign of economic health, as is a favourable balance of trade (or trade surplus) in any country.

World Trade

Percentage share of total world exports by value (1996)

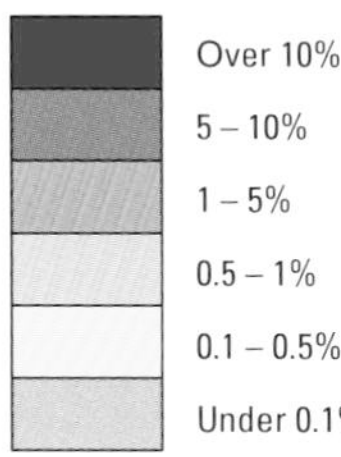

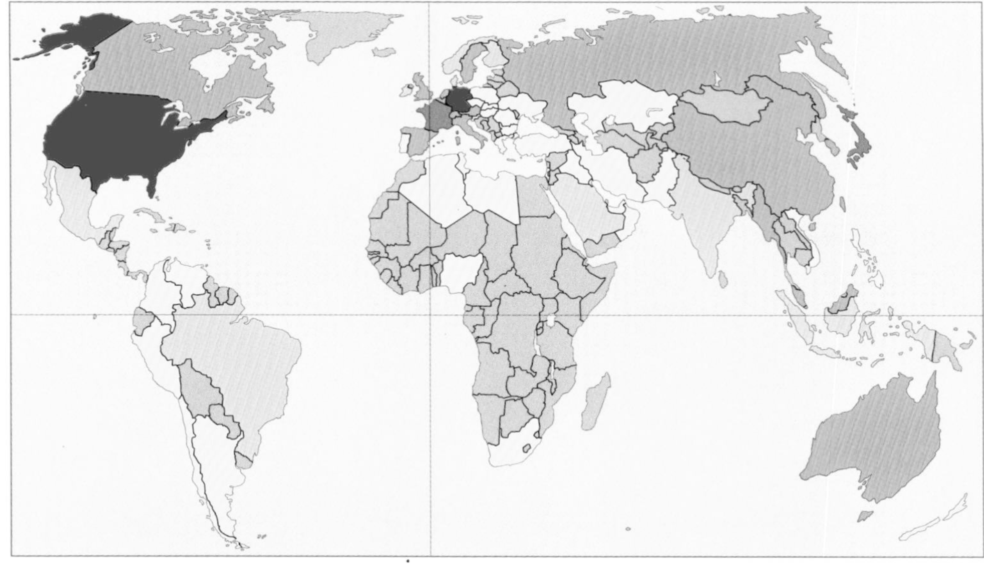

The Main Trading Nations

The imports and exports of the top ten trading nations as a percentage of world trade (1994). Each country's trade in manufactured goods is shown in dark blue. The graph shows that, in 1994, virtually all of Japan's imports and exports were manufactured goods.

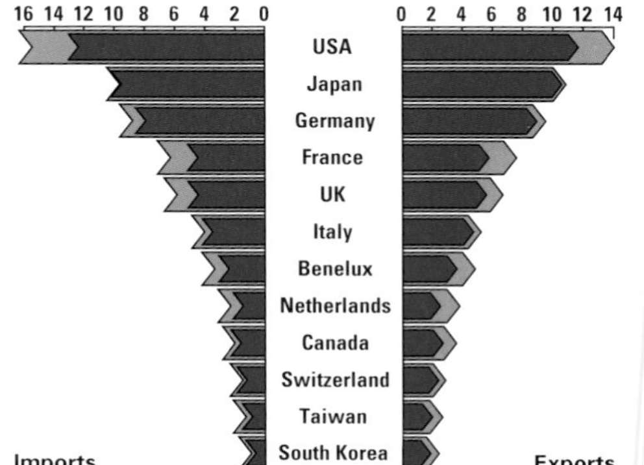

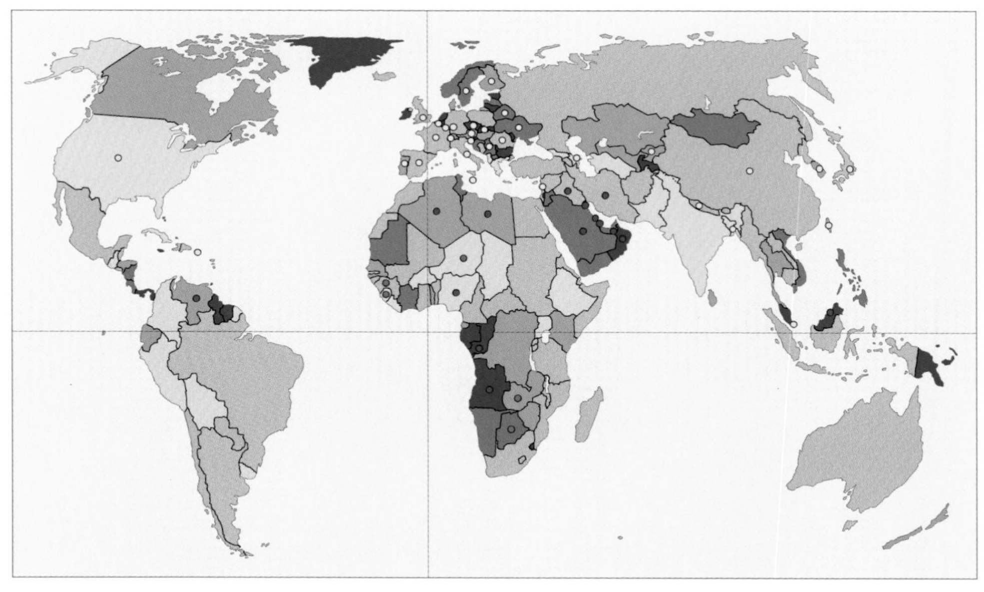

Dependence on Trade

Value of exports as a percentage of Gross Domestic Product (1997)

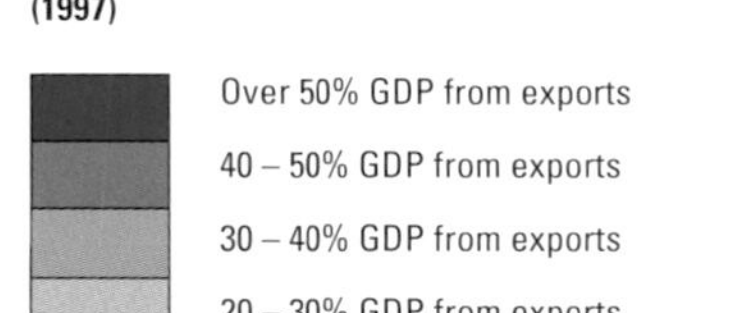

Most dependent on industrial exports (over 75% of total exports)

Most dependent on fuel exports (over 75% of total exports)

Most dependent on metal and mineral exports (over 75% of total exports)

Major Exports

Leading manufactured items and their exporters, by percentage of world total in US $ (latest available year)

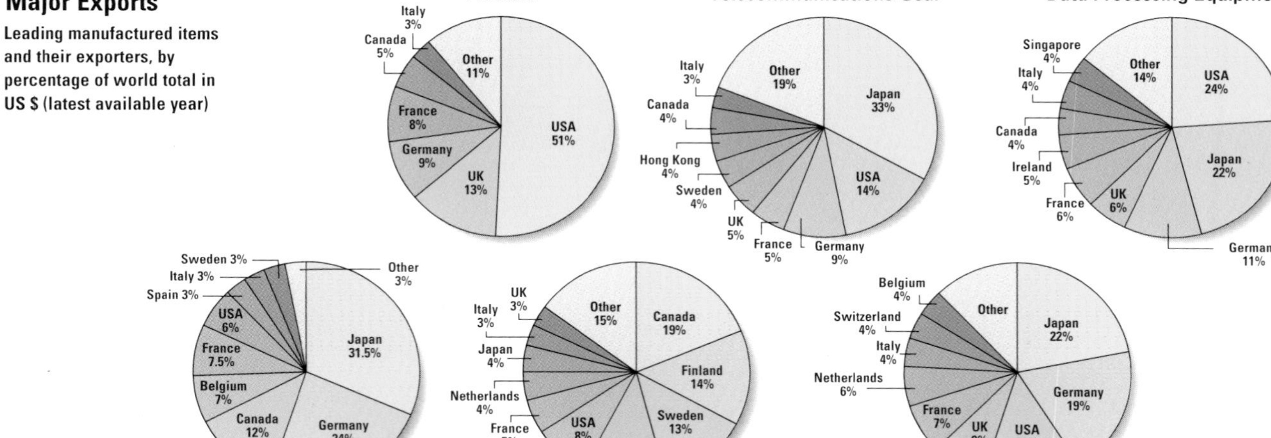

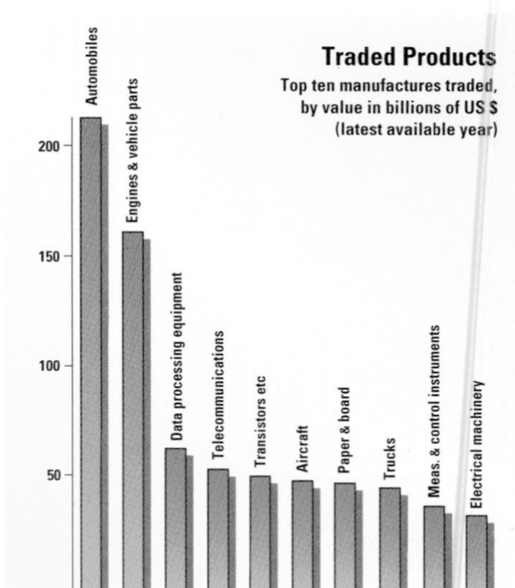

World Shipping

While ocean passenger traffic is nowadays relatively modest, sea transport still carries most of the world's trade. Oil and bulk carriers make up the majority of the world fleet, although the general cargo category is the fastest growing. Two innovations have revolutionized sea transport. The first is the development of the roll-on/roll-off (Ro-Ro) method where lorries or even trains loaded with freight are driven straight on to the ship, thus saving time. The second is containerization in which goods are packed into containers (the dimensions of which are fixed) at the factory, driven to the port and loaded on board by specialist machinery.

Almost 30% of world shipping sails under a 'flag of convenience', whereby owners take advantage of low taxes by registering their vessels in a foreign country the ships will never see, notably Panama and Liberia.

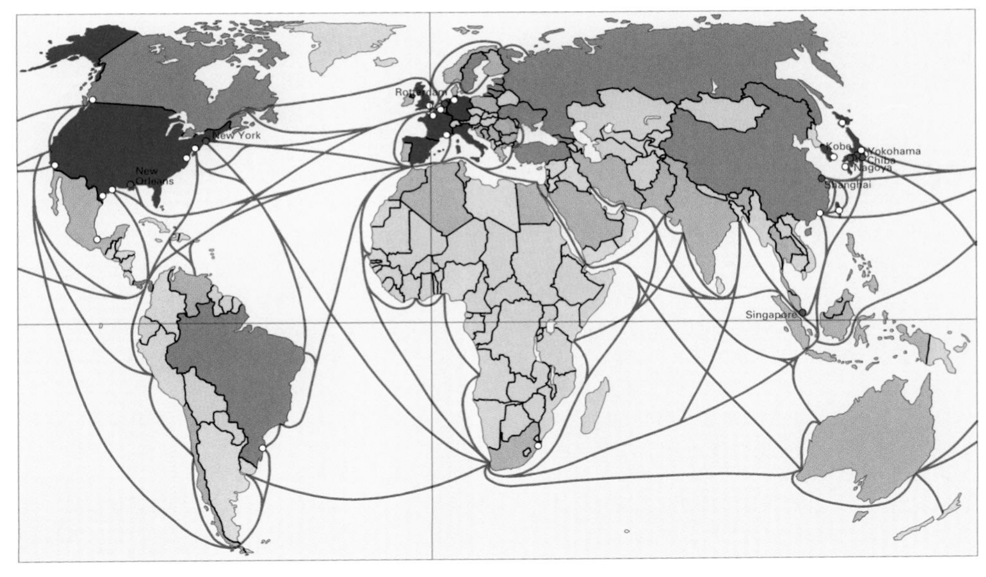

Freight

Freight unloaded in millions of tonnes (latest available year)

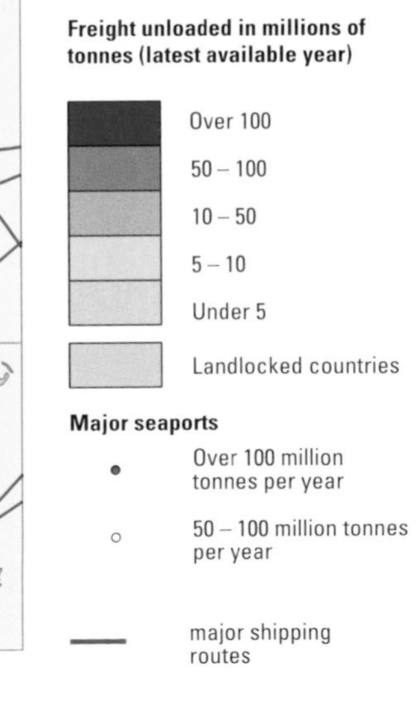

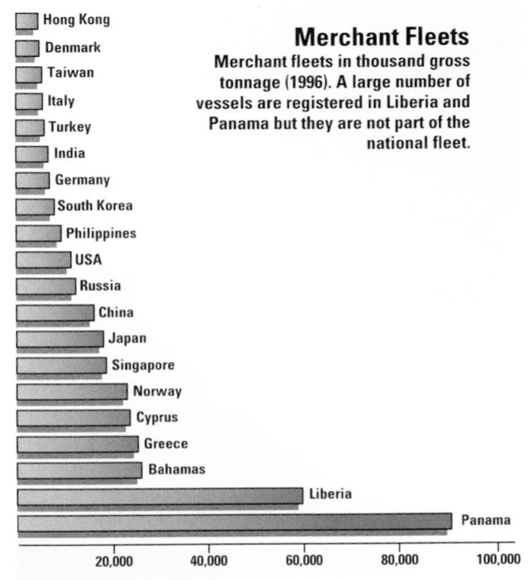

Merchant Fleets

Merchant fleets in thousand gross tonnage (1996). A large number of vessels are registered in Liberia and Panama but they are not part of the national fleet.

Types of Vessels

Oil tankers 38.4%
Ore & bulk carriers 29.9%
General cargo 16.1%
Others 9.7%
Ferries & passenger ships 0.5%
Liquid gas carriers 1.6%
Container ships 3.8%

The Great Ports

Total Cargo Traffic (1995) '000 tonnes

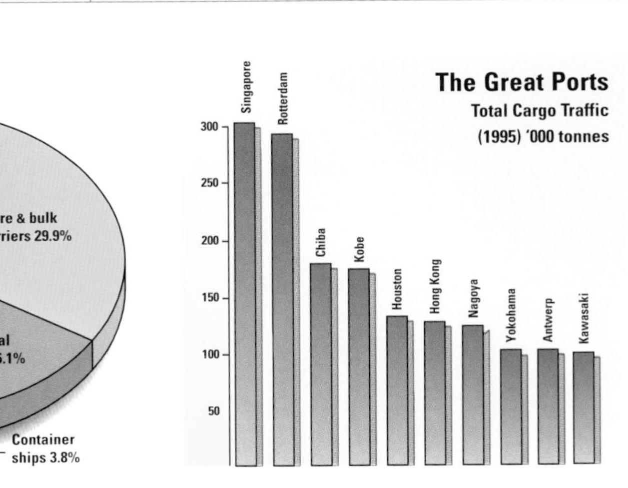

Trade in Primary Products

Primary products (excluding fuels, minerals and metals) as a percentage of total export value (latest available year)

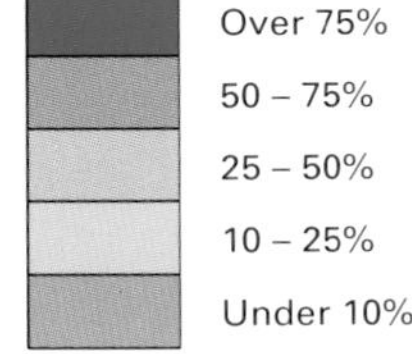

Primary products are raw materials or partly processed products which form the basis for manufacturing. They are the necessary requirements of industries and include agricultural products, minerals and timber, as well as semi-manufactured goods such as cotton, which has been spun but not woven, wood pulp or flour. Many developed countries have few natural resources and rely on imports for the majority of their primary products. The countries of South-east Asia export hardwoods to the rest of the world, whilst many South American countries are heavily dependent on coffee exports.

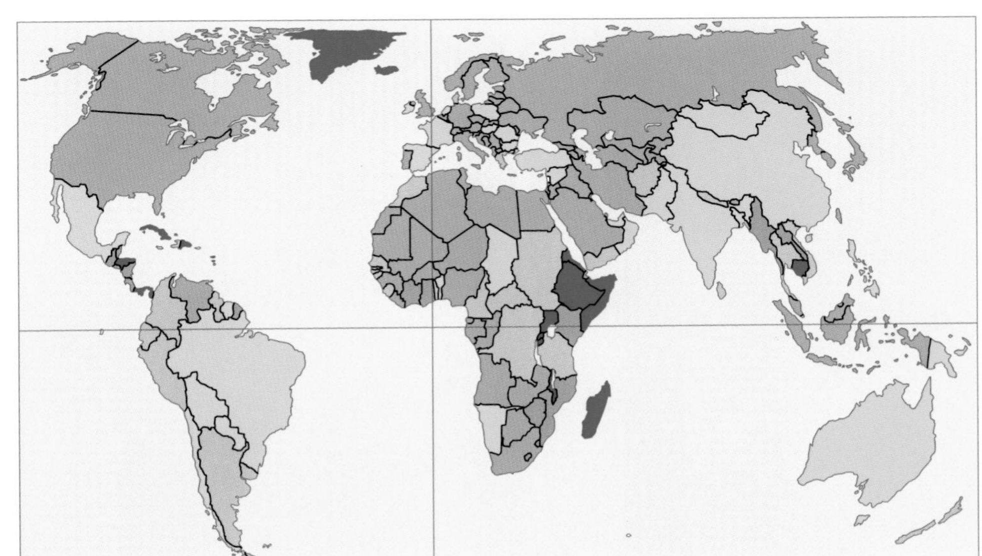

Air Freight

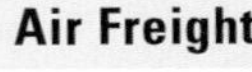

Trends in air freight in million tonne-km*, selected countries (1988–92)

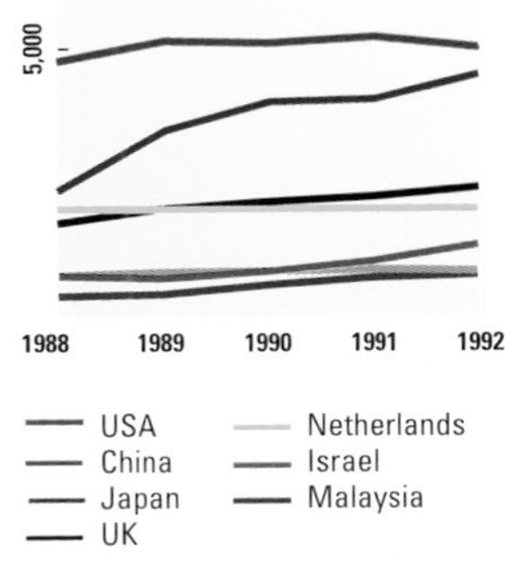

— USA — Netherlands
— China — Israel
— Japan — Malaysia
— UK

* Equivalent to million tonnes of air freight flown over 1 million kilometres per year.

Air transport is important to countries of considerable size; where ground terrain is difficult; when crossing short stretches of sea; and where goods are of high value, light in weight or perishable. Recent deregulation of airlines (in the USA since 1978 and the EU in 1993) has led to increased competition and lower fares.

Balance of Trade

Value of exports in proportion to the value of imports (1995)

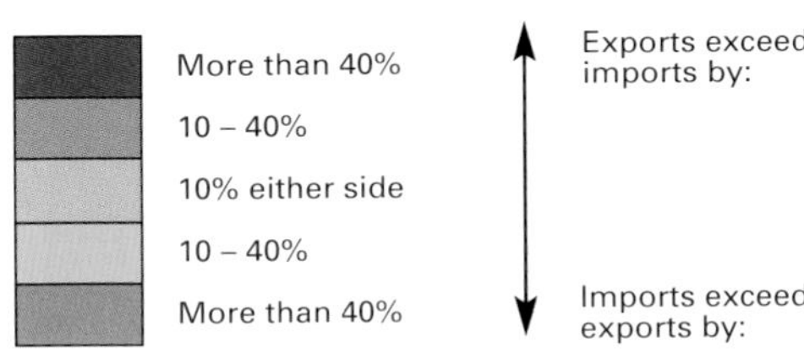

The total world trade balance should amount to zero, since exports must equal imports on a global scale. In practice, at least $100 billion in exports go unrecorded, leaving the world with an apparent deficit and many countries in a better position than public accounting reveals. However, a favourable trade balance is not necessarily a sign of prosperity: many poorer countries must maintain a high surplus in order to service debts, and do so by restricting imports below the levels needed to sustain successful economies.

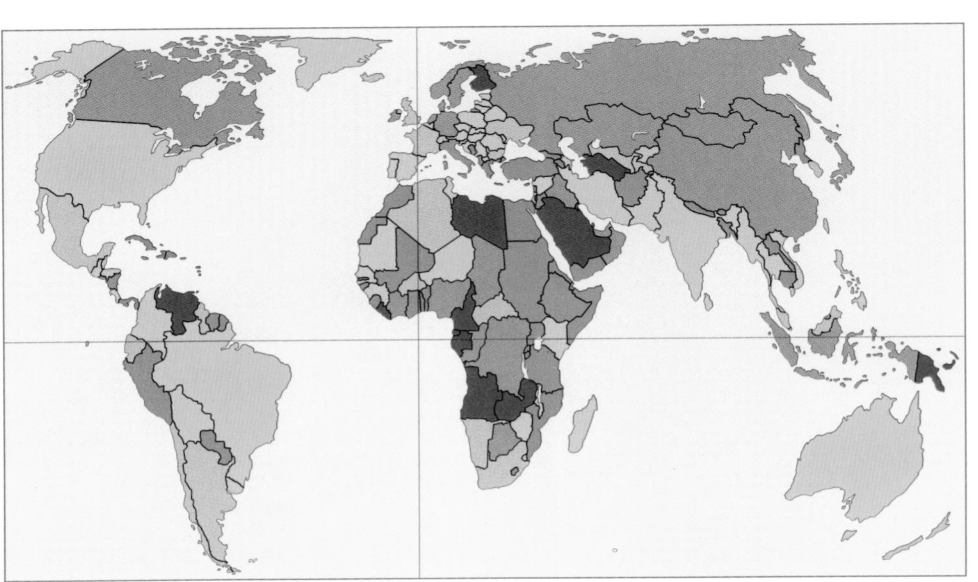

Health

For more information:

18 Water supply

27 Urban pollution

Urban advantages

33 Crisis in Africa

Food and population

47 Distribution of spending

Average life expectancies all over the world have never been higher. They range from an average of 77 years in high-income economies, to 67 years in middle-income economies and 63 in low-income economies. Even in poverty-stricken and strife-torn Burundi and Ethiopia, average life expectancies are around 50 years, as compared with less than 30 years for a citizen of Berlin in 1880.

In global terms, the radical improvements in health have much to do with improvements in agriculture and, hence, nutrition, as well as health education, an increase in sanitation and the quality of drinking water, together with advances in medicine. These radical changes have been responsible for falling death rates and rapid population growth, together with the expectation by most people that improvements in health will continue.

Health standards, life expectancies and causes of death vary greatly between the developed and developing world. The map below shows that in most of Africa, Asia and Latin America, the average daily calorie supply per person is so low as to cause malnutrition. (The daily requirement rated adequate by the World Health Organization is from 2,300 and 2,500 calories per person per day.) Malnutrition is a serious condition. For example, in pregnant women it causes high rates of child mortality.

Deficiency diseases occur when people do not have a balanced diet. Protein deficiency causes stunting and kwashiorkor, which can be fatal, especially among young children, while vitamin deficiencies cause such illnesses as beri beri, pellagra, scurvy and rickets. Iron deficiency causes anaemia, while a lack of iodine causes mental retardation. A UN report in the early 1990s reported that iodine deficiency affected 458 million women worldwide, as compared with 238 million men. Women's nutritional problems are especially acute in southern Asia. For example, the UN report stated that 88% of pregnant women in India were anaemic, as compared with 15% in developed countries.

Infectious diseases in association, directly or indirectly, with deficient diets, continue to affect people in developing countries, especially the 48 countries in the low human development category, where, in 1990–95, only 32% of the people had access to sanitation and 68% to safe water supplies.

A World Health report in 1996 stated that infectious diseases cause 17 million deaths per year. Most of the victims are young and otherwise fit people in developing countries. The major killers in 1995 were respiratory infections, including pneumonia (which caused 4.4 million deaths), cholera, typhoid, dysentery (3.1 million together), tuberculosis (almost 3 million), malaria (2.1 million), hepatitis B (1.1 million), AIDS and measles (more than 1 million each). Many of these diseases are preventable and, according to the United Nations Children's Fund, an investment of US $25,000 million per year, about half the money spent annually on cigarettes in Europe alone, would save the lives of all the children who currently die from avoidable diseases.

Infectious diseases are much less important as causes of death in developed countries, where cancer and circulatory diseases, such as atherosclerosis and hypertension, which cause strokes and heart attacks, are the most common causes of fatality. Because these diseases tend to kill older people, they are relatively less important in developing countries where people have shorter lifespans.

Harmful habits are also generally practised more by the rich than the poor. For example, smoking is an important cause of death in developed countries, though, curiously, the Japanese, with an average life expectancy of 79 years in 1996, are among the highest tobacco consumers. Similarly, high alcohol consumption, although it has bad effects on health, does not seem to affect longevity. The leading consumers, the French, had a life expectancy of 78 in 1996.

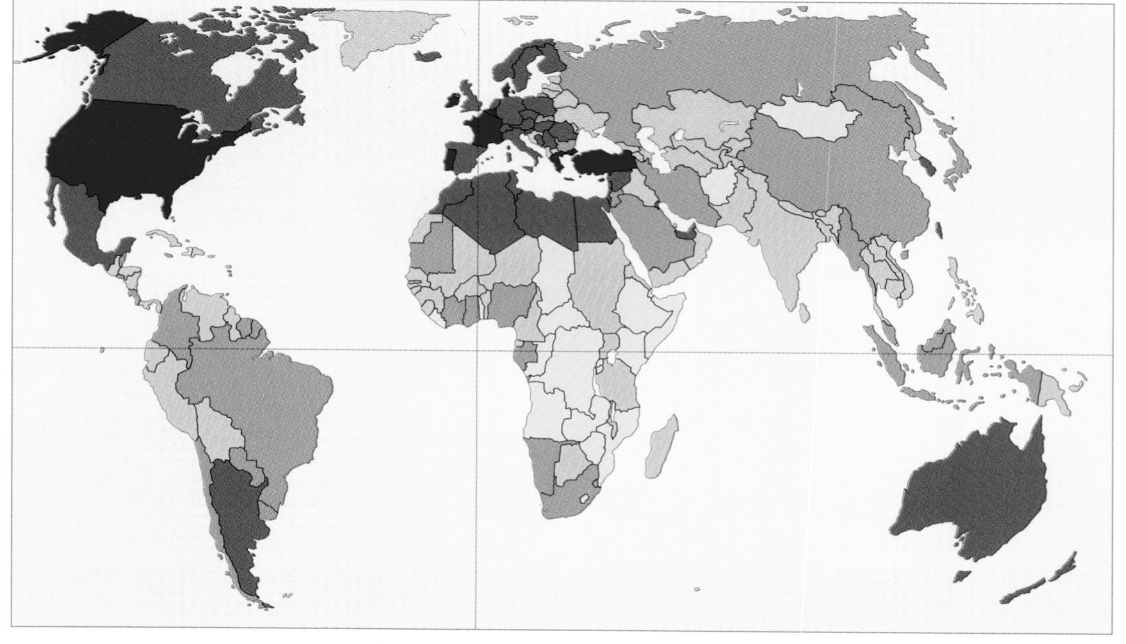

Food Consumption

Average daily food intake in calories per person (1995)

- Over 3,500 calories
- 3,000 – 3,500 calories
- 2,500 – 3,000 calories
- 2,000 – 2,500 calories
- Under 2,000 calories
- No available data

Top 5 countries

Cyprus	3,708 calories
Denmark	3,704 calories
Portugal	3,639 calories
Ireland	3,638 calories
USA	3,603 calories

Bottom 5 countries

Congo (D. Rep.)	1,879 calories
Djibouti	1,831 calories
Togo	1,754 calories
Burundi	1,749 calories
Mozambique	1,678 calories

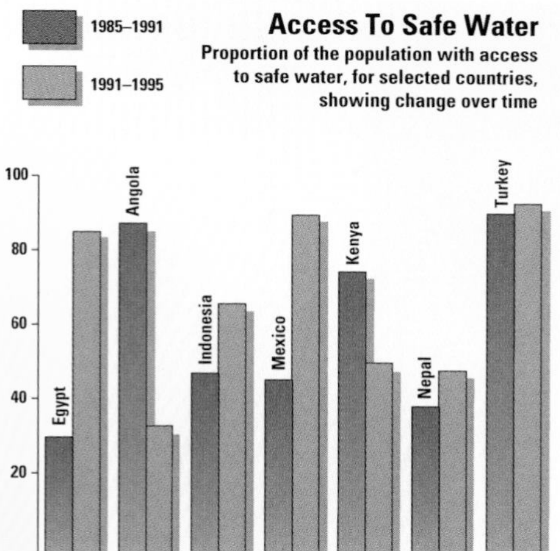

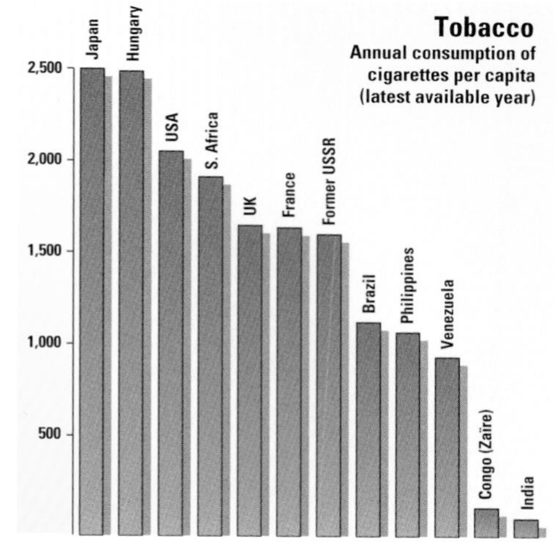

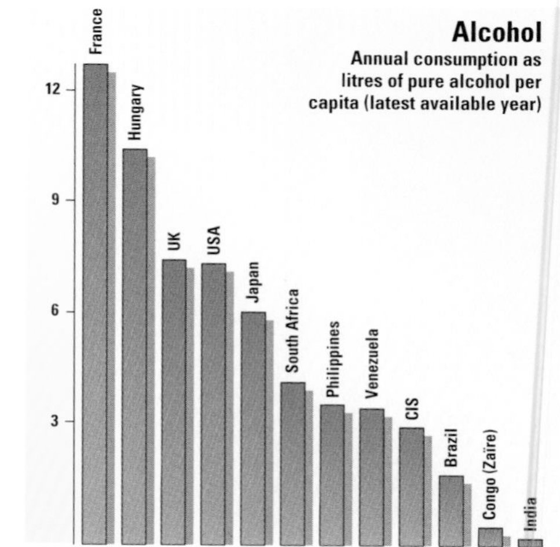

Life Expectancy

Years of life expectancy at birth, selected countries (1997)

The chart shows combined data for both sexes. On average, women live longer than men worldwide, even in developing countries with high maternal mortality rates. Overall, life expectancy is steadily rising, though the difference between rich and poor nations remains dramatic.

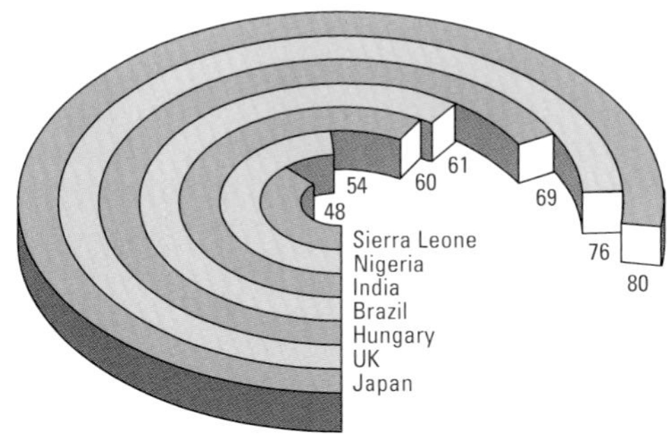

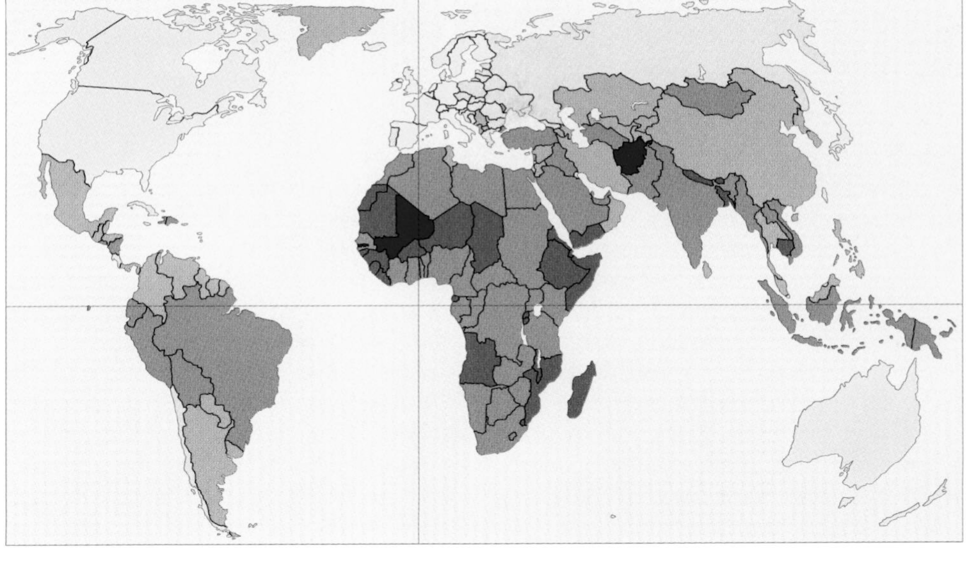

Child Mortality

Number of babies who will die under the age of one, per 1,000 births (average 1990–95)

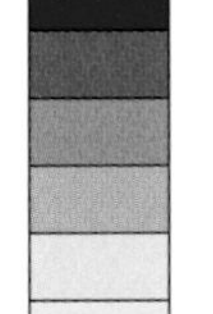

Over 150 deaths
100 – 150 deaths
50 – 100 deaths
20 – 50 deaths
10 – 20 deaths
Under 10 deaths

Highest child mortality

Afghanistan	162 deaths
Mali	159 deaths

Lowest child mortality

Iceland	5 deaths
Finland	5 deaths

[UK 8 deaths] [USA 8 deaths]

Expenditure on Health

Public expenditure on health as a percentage of GDP (1996)

Countries with the highest spending		Countries with the lowest spending	
USA	14.2	Sudan	0.3
Argentina	10.6	Cameroon	1.4
Germany	10.4	Ghana	1.4
Croatia	10.1	Nigeria	1.4
Switzerland	10.0	Indonesia	1.8
France	9.9	Sri Lanka	1.9
Canada	9.6	Eritrea	2.0
Czech Rep.	9.6	Bangladesh	2.4
Australia	8.9	Kenya	2.5

The allocation of limited funds for health care in developing countries is rarely evenly spread – the quality of treatment can vary enormously from place to place within the same country. Urban dwellers tend to have much better access to health provisions than those living in rural areas.

Medical Provision

Doctors per 100,000 population, selected countries (latest available year, 1996)

Although the ratio of people to doctors gives a good approximation of a country's health provision, it is not an absolute indicator. Raw numbers may mask inefficiency and other weaknesses: the high proportion of physicians in Hungary, for example, has not prevented infant mortality rates more than twice as high as in the United Kingdom.

The definition of a doctor also varies from nation to nation. As well as registered medical practitioners, it may include trained medical assistants – an especially important category in developing countries, where they provide many of the same services as fully qualified physicians, including simple operations.

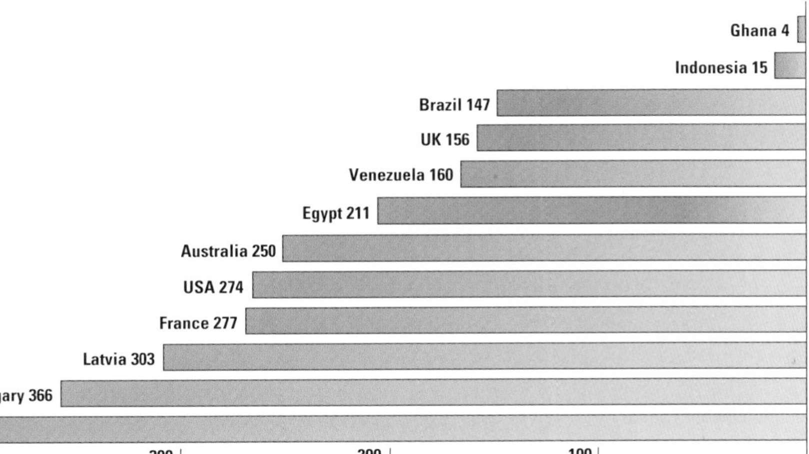

The Aids Crisis

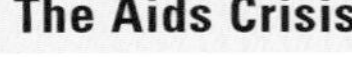

The Acquired Immune Deficiency Syndrome (AIDS) was first identified in 1981 when American doctors found otherwise healthy young men succumbing to rare infections. By 1984 the cause had been traced to the Human Immunodeficiency Virus (HIV) which can remain dormant for many years and perhaps indefinitely: only half of those known to carry the virus in 1981 had developed AIDS ten years later.

In Western countries in the mid-1990s, most AIDS deaths were among male homosexuals or needle-sharing drug-users. However, the disease is spreading fastest among heterosexual men and women, which is its usual vector in the developing world where most of its victims live.

The World Health Organization estimated that 1.3 million people died of AIDS in 1995 and that by the end of the same year 22 million people were HIV-positive. India has the largest number of HIV infections totalling more than 3 million, but two-thirds of all infections are in sub-Saharan Africa (where, unlike the rest of the world, more women are infected than men). It was estimated that two million African children would die of AIDS by the year 2000, and some 10 million would be orphaned.

Causes of Death

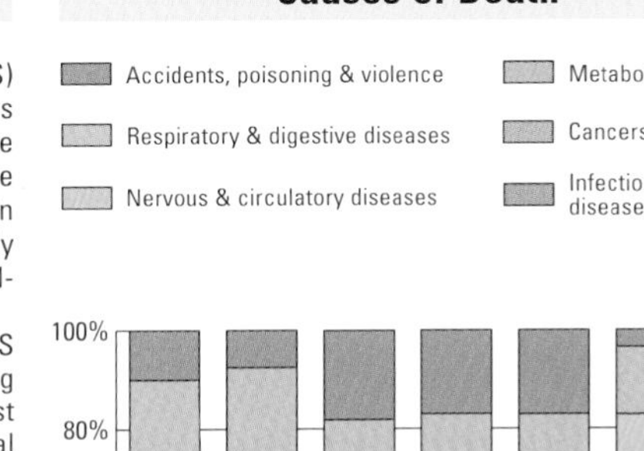

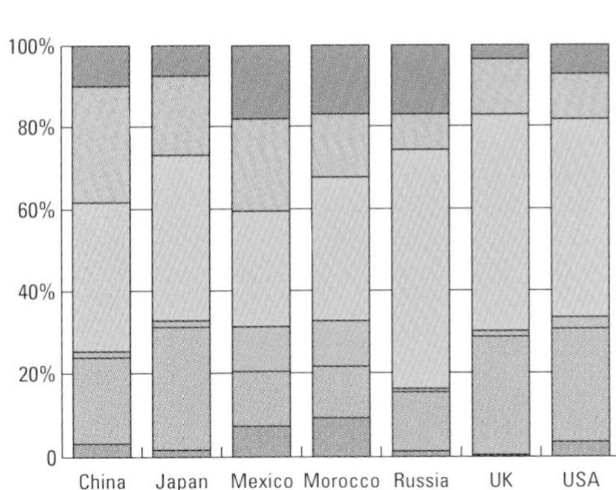

Circulatory Disease in Europe

Diseases of the circulatory system per 100,000 people (latest available year 1992–95)

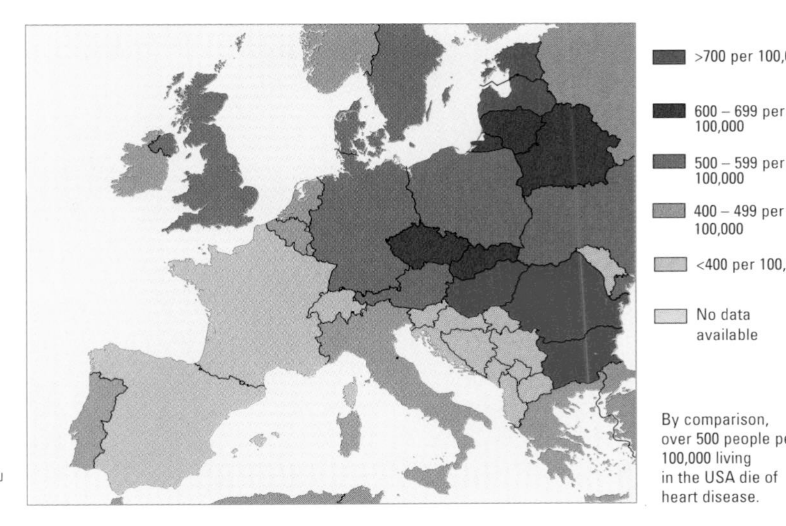

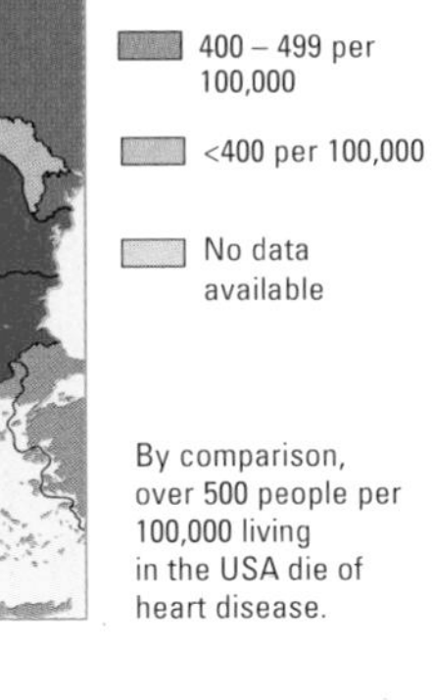

By comparison, over 500 people per 100,000 living in the USA die of heart disease.

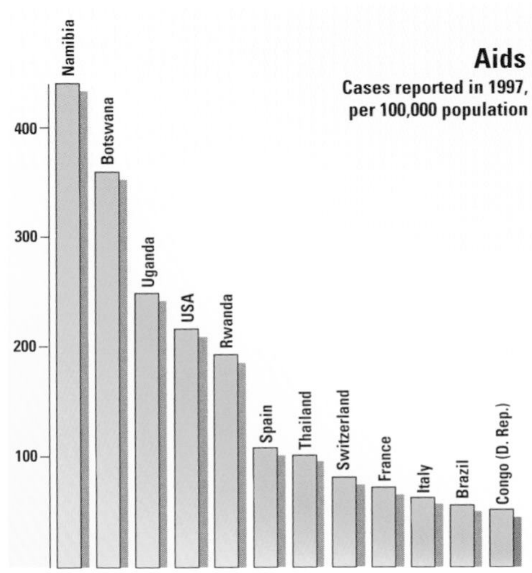

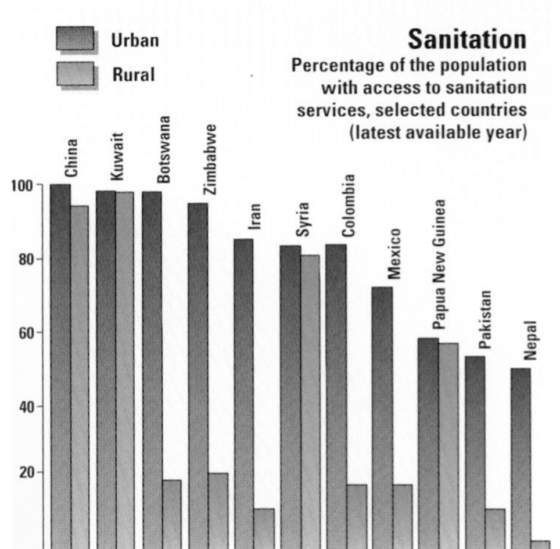

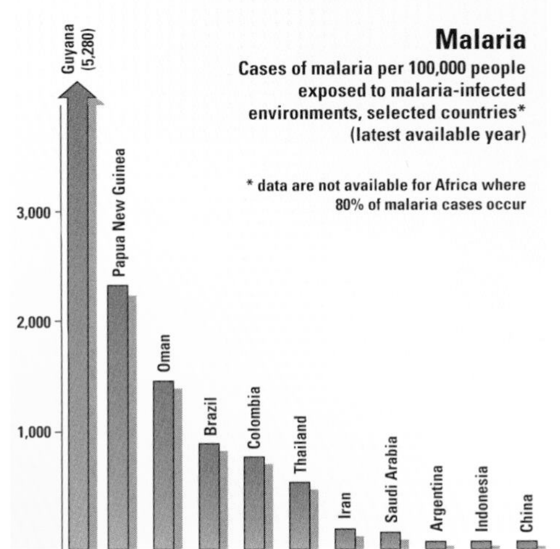

Infectious and parasitic diseases, such as malaria, which claimed 2.1 million lives in 1995, remain a scourge in the developing countries. Respiratory infections and injury also claim more lives in developing countries, which lack the drugs and the medical personnel to deal with them. Developing countries lack the basic services taken for granted in developed nations.
For example, in sub-Saharan Africa in 1990–95, only 31% of the population had access to sanitation and 45% to safe water, with the situation being worse in rural areas. By contrast, circulatory diseases and cancer are the main causes of death in the rich, industrialized countries.
For example, in the UK in the mid-1990s, circulatory diseases, which cause heart attacks and strokes, accounted for nearly half the deaths, with cancer accounting for nearly a quarter.

Wealth

For more information:
38 Wealth creation
39 Industrial power
Exports per capita
40 World trade
Major exports
41 Balance of trade
47 Distribution of spending
Distribution of income

Perhaps the most glaring differences in the world today are those between the rich and the poor. The World Bank divides countries into three main groups based on average economic production expressed in terms of per capita GNP (Gross National Product). They are the low-income economies, including most African countries and much of Asia; the middle-income economies, including most of Latin America and the former USSR; and the high-income economies of Canada, the United States, Western Europe, Japan and Australia.

Per capita GNPs are a measure of the total goods and services produced by a country divided by the population, and converted into US dollars at official exchange rates. They are useful indicators of a country's prosperity, but, like all statistics, must be treated with care. For example, prices for goods and services in China are far cheaper than in the United States. China's per capita GNP in 1998 was $750 (as compared with $29,340 in the USA) but the PPP (Purchasing-Power Parity) estimate of China's per capita GNP was considerably higher at $3,570. Another problem with per capita GNPs is that they are averages, which often conceal wide internal variations.

The pattern of poverty varies from region to region. In Latin America, much progress has been made through industrialization, though startling inequalities still exist between rich and poor. In Asia, the 'tiger economies' have followed Japan's example in pursuing export-led industrial policies, while the success of China's Special Economic Zones, where foreign investment is encouraged, has led to a huge rise in China's per capita GNP, as shown on the map on page 45, bottom right.

Solutions to poverty in Africa are much harder to find because of its high population growth, civil wars, natural disasters and high inflation rates. Although Africa receives more aid than any other continent, aid is only a partial solution. Much aid has been wasted on overambitious projects, in the servicing of huge national debts, or lost by inexperienced or corrupt governments. One initiative in some African countries has been to improve the infrastructure and develop tourism, creating employment and providing much-needed foreign currency. But tourism alone cannot solve the problems of under-development.

The International Monetary Fund and the World Bank argue that real economic progress in Africa will be achieved only when African countries create market-friendly economies that encourage trade through export-led manufacturing, while at the same time strictly controlling public spending on welfare, the civil service and other areas.

Continental Shares

Shares of population and of wealth (GNP) by continent

These generalized continental figures show the startling difference between rich and poor but mask the successes or failures of individual countries. Japan, for example, with less than 4% of Asia's population, produces almost 70% of the continent's output. Within countries, the difference between rich and poor can also be startling. In Brazil, for example, the richest 20% of the population own 60% of the wealth.

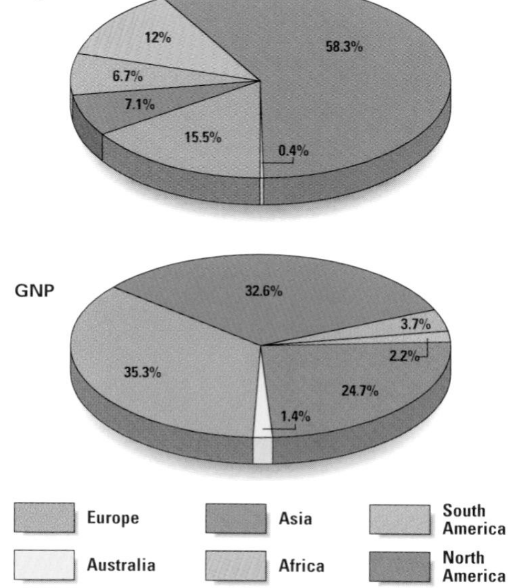

Currencies

Currency units of the world's most powerful economies

1. USA: US dollar ($, US $) = 100 cents
2. Japan: Yen (Y, ¥) = 100 sen
3. Germany: Euro; Deutsche Mark (DM)= 100 Pfennig
4. France: Euro; French franc (Fr) = 100 centimes
5. Italy: Euro; Italian lira (L, £, Lit)
6. UK: Pound sterling (£) = 100 pence
7. Canada: Canadian dollar (C$, Can$) = 100 cents
8. China: Renminbi yuan (RMBY, $, Y) = 10 jiao = 100 fen
9. Brazil: Cruzeiro real (BRC) = 100 centavos
10. Spain: Euro; Peseta (Pta, Pa) = 100 céntimos
11. India: Indian rupee (Re, Rs) = 100 paisa
12. Australia: Australian dollar ($A) = 100 cents
13. Netherlands: Euro; Guilder, florin (Gld, f) = 100 centimes
14. Switzerland: Swiss franc (SFr, SwF) = 100 centimes
15. South Korea: Won (W) = 100 chon
16. Sweden: Swedish krona (SKr) = 100 ore
17. Mexico: Mexican peso (Mex$) = 100 centavos
18. Belgium: Euro; Belgian franc (BFr) = 100 centimes
19. Austria: Euro; Schilling (S, Sch) = 100 Groschen
20. Finland: Euro; Markka (FMk) = 100 penniä
21. Denmark: Danish krone (DKr) = 100 øre
22. Norway: Norwegian krone (NKr) = 100 øre
23. Saudi Arabia: Riyal (SAR, SRI$) = 100 halalah
24. Indonesia: Rupiah (Rp) = 100 sen
25. South Africa: Rand (R) = 100 cents

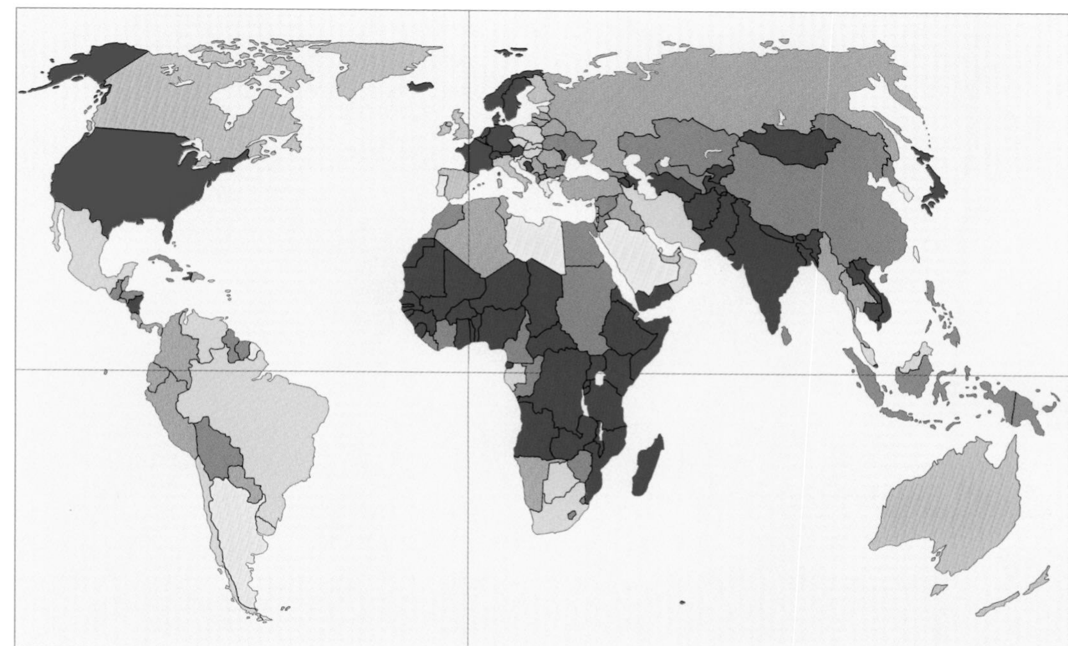

Levels of Income

Gross National Product per capita: the value of total production divided by the population (1997)

Over 400% of world average
200 – 400%
100 – 200%
50 – 100%
25 – 50%
10 – 25%
Under 10%

Top 5 countries

Luxembourg	$45,360
Switzerland	$44,220
Japan	$37,850
Norway	$36,090
Liechtenstein	$33,000

Bottom 5 countries

Mozambique	$90
Ethiopia	$110
Congo (Dem. Rep.)	$110
Burundi	$180
Sierra Leone	$200

The gap between the world's rich and poor is now so great that it is difficult to illustrate on a single graph. Within each income group (as defined by the World Bank), however, comparisons have some meaning; the Chinese, perhaps because of propaganda value, have more TV sets than Indians, whereas Nigerians prefer to spend their money on radios. However, the wealth gap in many developing countries is wide, with a small, rich class and a large, impoverished majority, while many high-income countries contain an underclass of unemployed and homeless people.

High Income

Number of radios, televisions and mobile 'phones for each 10,000 people, selected high income countries (1996)

Radios
Televisions
Mobile 'phones
20,000
15,000
10,000
5,000
USA
Japan
Australia
Germany
UK

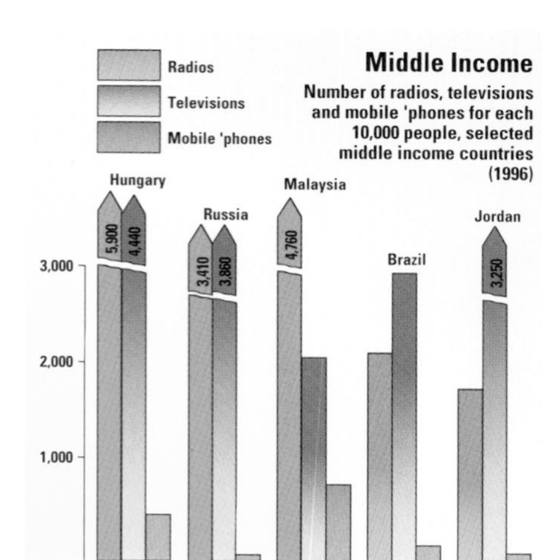

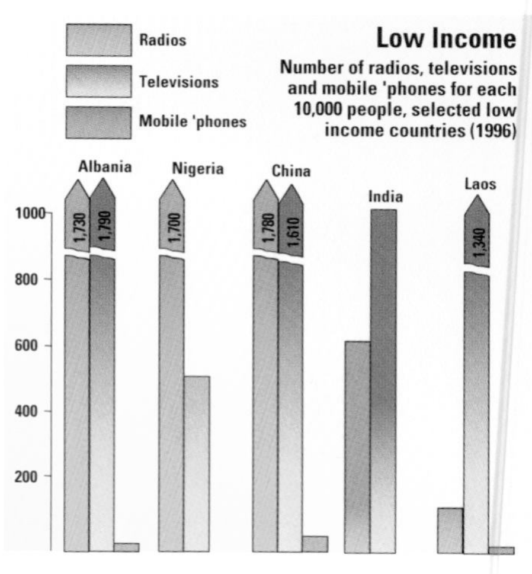

World Tourism

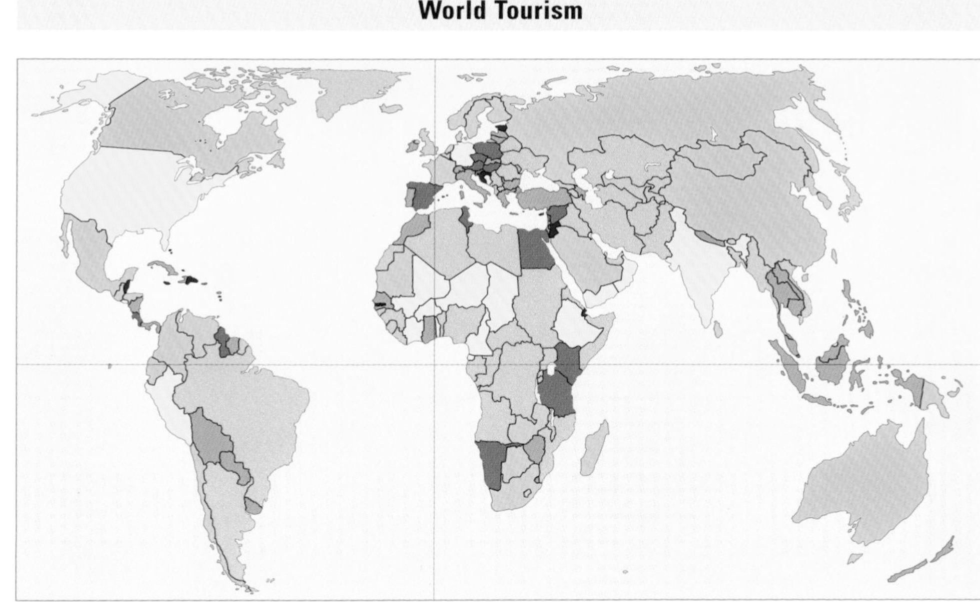

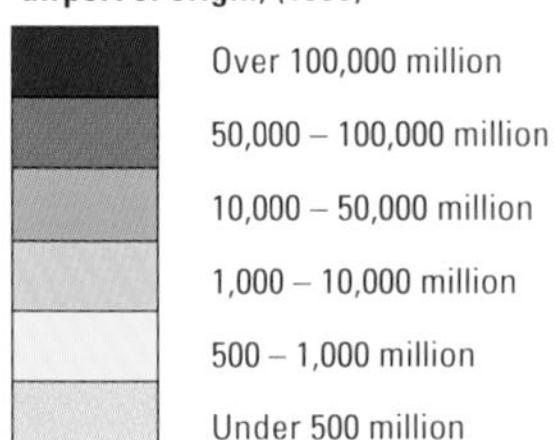

Leisure and tourism is the world's second largest industry in terms of revenue generated. Small economies in attractive areas are often completely dominated by tourism: in some Caribbean islands, tourist spending provides over 90% of the total income and is the biggest foreign exchange earner. In cash terms the USA is the world leader: its 1996 earnings exceeded US $75 billion, though that sum amounted to approximately 0.9% of its total GDP. Of the 49 million visitors to the USA, 34% came from Canada and 25% from Mexico. Germany spends the most on overseas tourism; in 1996 Germany spent over US $50,000 million abroad. The next biggest spenders were the USA, Japan and the UK.

The world's busiest airport in terms of total number of passengers is Chicago's O'Hare Airport (67.3 million passengers in 1996); the busiest international airport is Heathrow, the largest of London's airports.

Aid Donors

Development aid by donor country, in millions of US $ and as a percentage of donor's GNP (latest available year)

Not all aid is given in cash grants: much is delivered in the form of cheap loans or technical assistance. Since the 1970s, OECD countries belonging to the Development Assistance Committee (DAC) have agreed in principle to give 0.7% of their GNP. Most have failed to meet their commitment. In 1994, three countries exceeded this level. They were Norway (1.05%), the Netherlands (1.03%) and Sweden (0.96%). The countries with the largest aid budgets were Japan (US $13,239 million or 0.29% of GNP) and the United States (US $9,927 million or 0.15% of GNP).

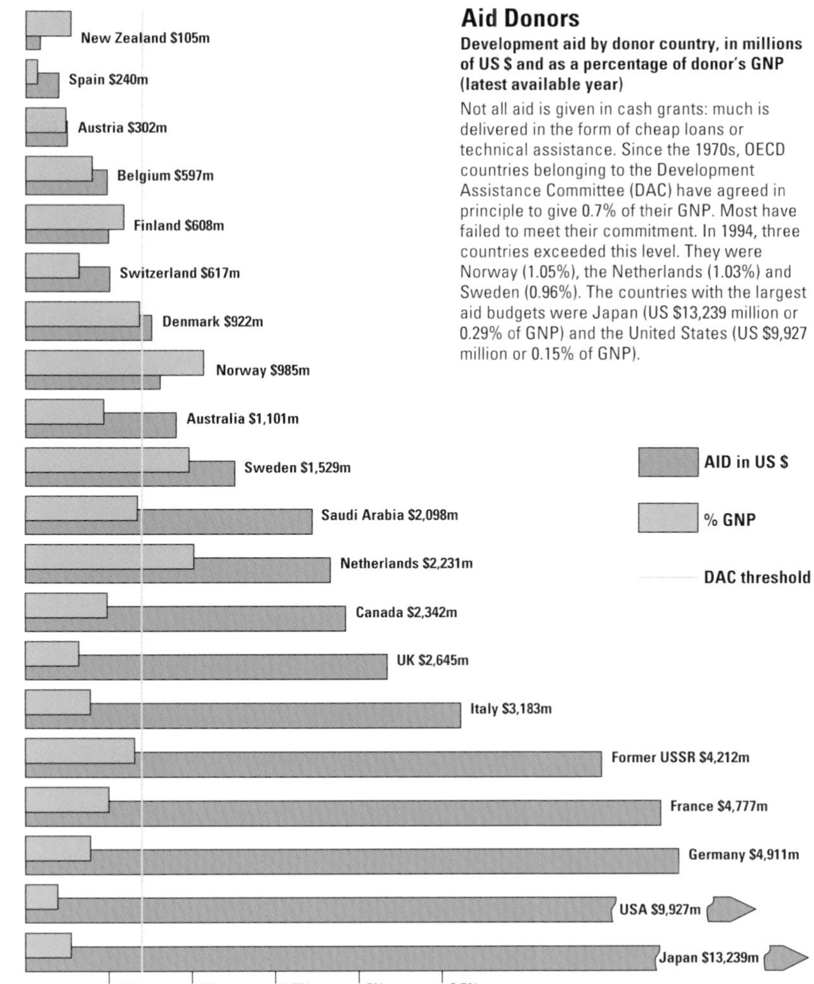

State Finance

Inflation rates, shown on the map, right, are an index of a country's financial stability and usually of its prosperity. Annual inflation rates above 20% are usually marked by slow or even negative growth of the GNP. Above 50%, it becomes hyperinflation and an economy is reeling. In the late 1980s and early 1990s, many high-income countries had to contend with annual inflation rates of 10% or more, while Japan, the growth leader, had an average inflation rate of 1.3% between 1985 and 1994.

The per capita GNP figures listed below are useful indicators of economic success or failure, but they do not account for living costs. Nor do they reveal the gaps between the rich and poor within countries.

Market-friendly policies, including low taxes and state spending, liberal trade policies and a welcome for foreign investors, are major factors in countries which have enjoyed rapid economic growth since 1980. For example, the setting up of Special Economic Zones in eastern China has led to a spectacular rise in the per capita GNP. Other successful countries include the 'tiger economies' of South Korea, Thailand and Singapore, although an Asian market crash in 1997 temporarily halted the dramatic economic expansion in these countries.

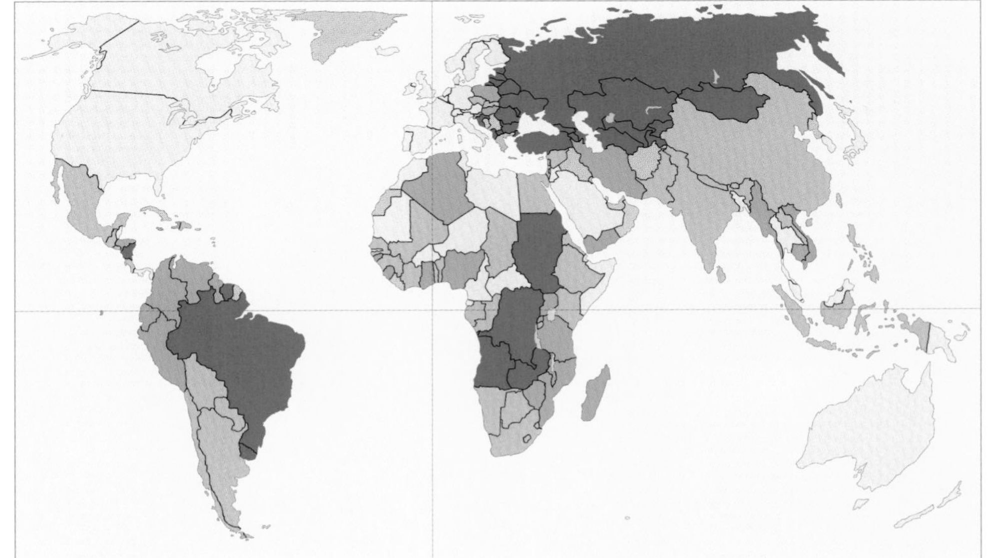

Inflation

Average annual rate of inflation (1990–96)

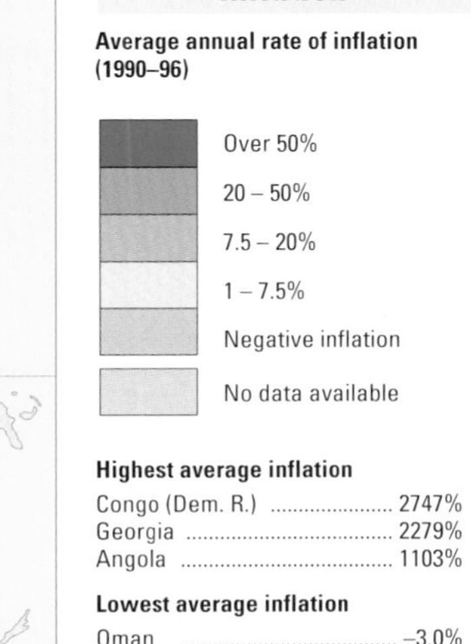

Highest average inflation

Congo (Dem. R.)	2747%
Georgia	2279%
Angola	1103%

Lowest average inflation

Oman	–3.0%
Bahrain	–0.5%
Brunei	–0.0%

The Wealth Gap

The world's richest and poorest countries, by Gross National Product per capita in US $ (1998)

Richest	US $	Poorest	US $
1. Liechtenstein	50,000	1. Ethiopia	100
2. Luxembourg	43,570	2. Congo (D. Rep.)	110
3. Switzerland	40,080	3. Burundi	140
4. Norway	34,330	4. Sierra Leone	140
5. Bermuda	34,000	5. Guinea-Bissau	160
6. Denmark	33,260	6. Niger	190
7. Japan	32,380	7. Eritrea	200
8. Singapore	30,060	8. Malawi	200
9. USA	29,340	9. Mozambique	210
10. Iceland	28,010	10. Nepal	210
11. Austria	26,850	11. Tanzania	210
12. Germany	25,850	12. Chad	230
13. Sweden	25,620	13. Rwanda	230
14. Belgium	25,380	14. Burkina Faso	240
15. Monaco	25,000	15. Mali	250
16. France	24,940	16. Madagascar	260
17. Netherlands	24,760	17. Cambodia	280
18. Finland	24,110	18. São Tomé & Princ.	280
19. Brunei	24,000	19. Sudan	290
20. Hong Kong	23,670	20. Central African Rep.	300

GNP per capita is calculated by dividing a country's Gross National Product by its total population.

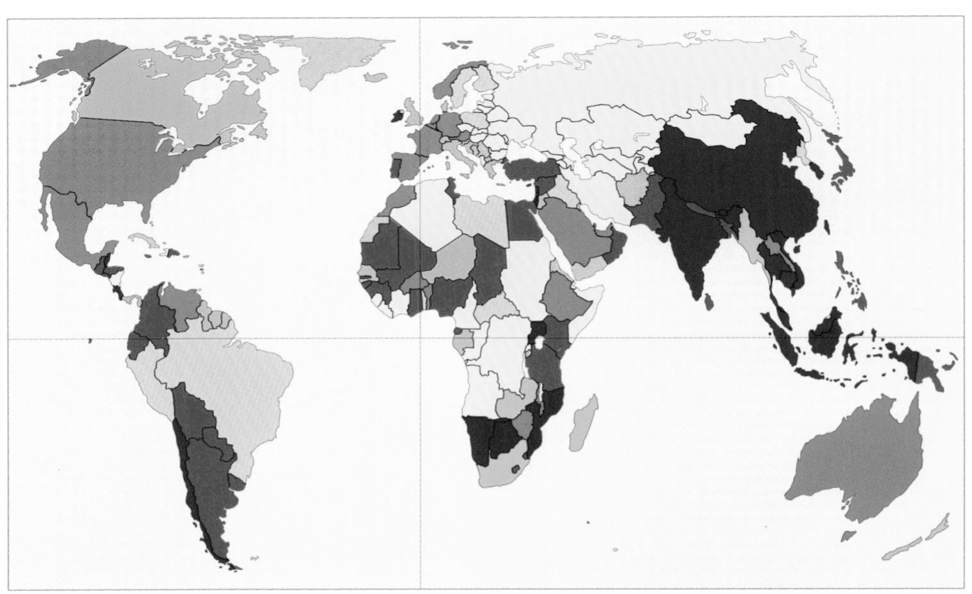

Growth in GNP

GNP per capita annual growth rate (1985–95)

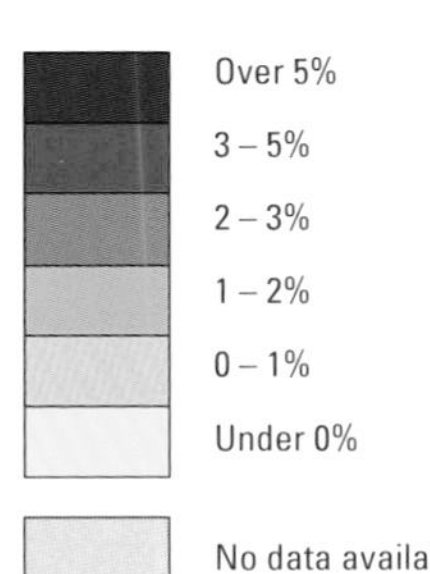

Countries with highest growth rates

Maldives	9.9%
Thailand	9.7%
China	9.3%
Botswana	9.0%
South Korea	8.5%

Standards of Living

For more information:
18 Water supply
24 Population density
27 Urban pollution
Squatter settlements
Urban advantages
30 World's refugees
War since 1945
38 Employment
The workforce
46 The wealth gap
Aid donors
45 Life expectancy
Child mortality

Wealth is a basic factor in determining standards of living. Everywhere, the rich have more of everything, including higher average life expectancies, while the poor spend most of their income on basic human needs, such as food and clothing. Yet poverty and wealth are relative terms. Slum dwellers living on social security in an industrial society feel their poverty acutely, but they have far more resources than an average African living in a rural area.

In 1990 the United Nations Development Programme published its first Human Development Index (HDI), an attempt to construct a comparative scale by which a simplified form of well-being may be measured. The HDI, expressed as a value between 0 and 0.999, combines figures for life expectancy and literacy with a wealth scale, based on Purchasing-Power Parity. The world's countries are divided into three groups, those with a high HDI (0.800 and above); those with a medium HDI (0.500 to 0.799); and those with a low HDI (below 0.500).

National scores for 1993 ranged from 0.951 for Canada to a low of 0.204 in Niger. In fact, of the 48 countries with a low HDI, 37 were from Africa, 10 from Asia, plus Haiti from the Caribbean. Besides having low per capita GNPs, the average life expectancy in these countries was 56 years, while the adult literacy rate was 49%. By comparison, the average life expectancy at birth in countries in the high HDI group was 74 years, while the literacy rate was 97%.

Comparisons between countries with similar per capita GNPs reveal effects of government actions. For example, the World Bank classifies India and China as low income economies, but India's HDI at 0.436 is lower than that of China, at 0.609. This reflects not only China's economic progress in the 1980s and 1990s, but also differences in average life expectancies (61 years in India and 69 years in China), and adult literacy rates (51% in India and 80% in China).

Disparities in standards of living exist not only between countries but also between individuals, groups and regions within countries. For example, income distribution figures for 1995 show that, in the United States, the poorest 20% of households received less than 4% of the income.

Other contrasts exist in developing countries between rural communities, where incomes are low and basic services are often in short supply, and urban areas, where even those living in slums are generally better off than their rural neighbours. Other striking differences exist between men and women. For example, while adult literacy rates for men and women living in developed countries are more or less the same, large differences exist in many developing countries. In 1995, in countries in the lowest HDI category, only 37% of women were literate, as compared with 62% of men.

Female education is a factor in population control, especially as women's fertility rates appear to fall in direct proportion to the amount of secondary education they receive. This point was acknowledged in 1994 by the UN Population Fund, which defined four main objectives relating to women and population control. They were: the reduction of maternal, infant and child mortality; better education, especially for girls; universal access to reproductive health services; and gender equality.

Statistical analysis presents many problems of interpretation, especially when trying to define such intangible factors as a sense of well-being. For example, education helps create wealth; but are rich countries wealthy because their people are well-educated, or are they well-educated because they are rich?

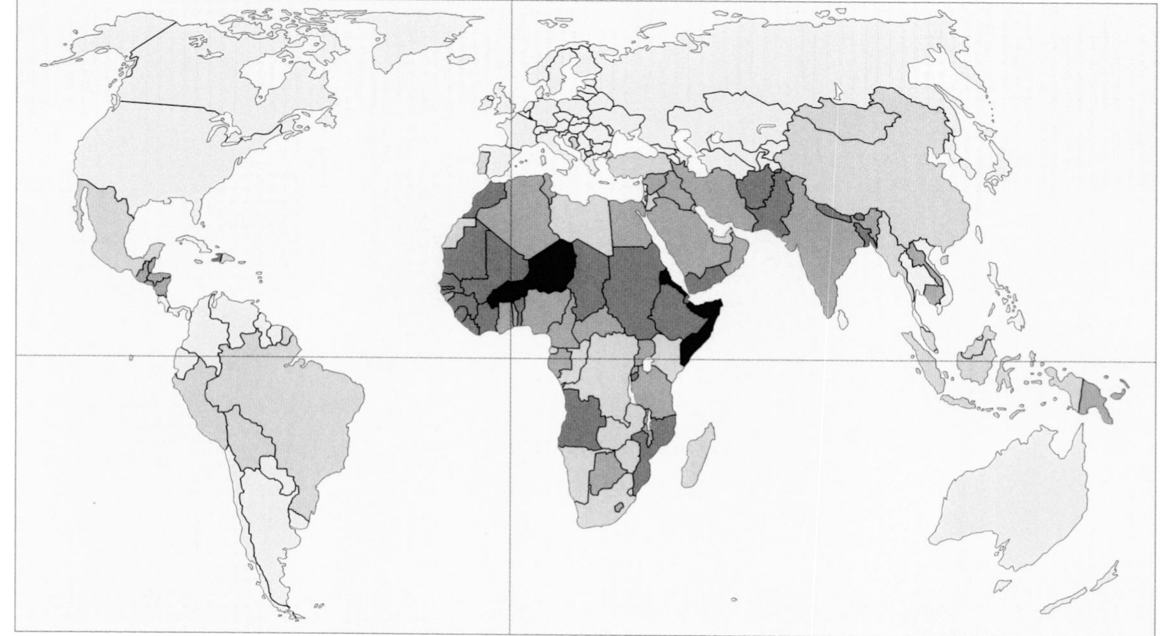

Illiteracy

% of the total population unable to read or write (1996)

- Over 75% illiterate
- 50 – 75% illiterate
- 25 – 50% illiterate
- 10 – 25% illiterate
- Under 10% illiterate

Educational expenditure per person (latest available year)

Top 5 countries

Sweden	$997
Qatar	$989
Canada	$983
Norway	$971
Switzerland	$796

Bottom 5 countries

Chad	$2
Bangladesh	$3
Ethiopia	$3
Nepal	$4
Somalia	$4

Education

The developing countries made great efforts in the 1970s and 1980s to bring at least a basic education to their people. Primary school enrolments rose above 60% in all but the poorest nations. Figures often include teenagers or young adults, however, and there are still an estimated 300 million children worldwide who receive no schooling at all. A lack of resources has restricted the development of secondary and higher education. Most primary education is free in the poorer countries, but fees are often paid for secondary and higher education, thus heightening the differences between rich and poor.

Primary

Percentage of age group in primary school, selected countries (latest available year)

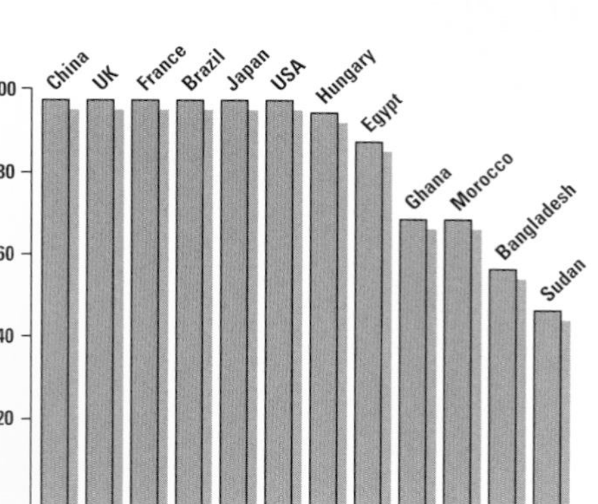

Secondary

Percentage of age group in secondary school, selected countries (latest available year)

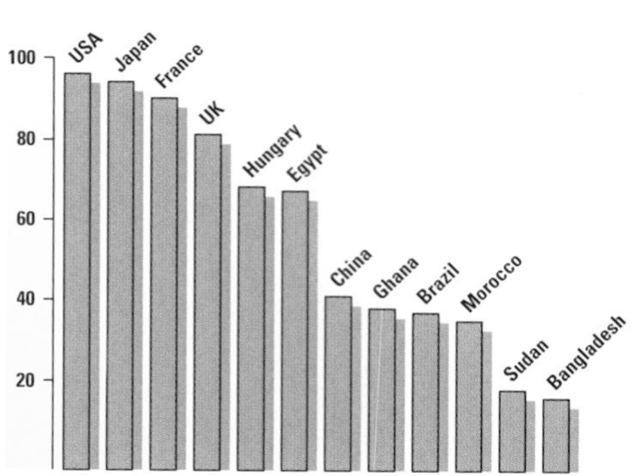

Higher

Percentage of age group in higher education, selected countries (latest available year)

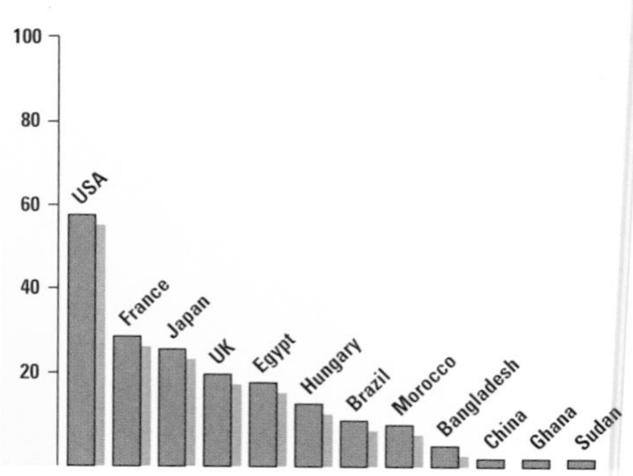

Distribution of Spending

Percentage share of household spending (latest available year)

A high proportion of the average income of households in developing nations is spent on basic needs such as food and clothing. In most Western countries food and clothing account for less than 25% of expenditure.

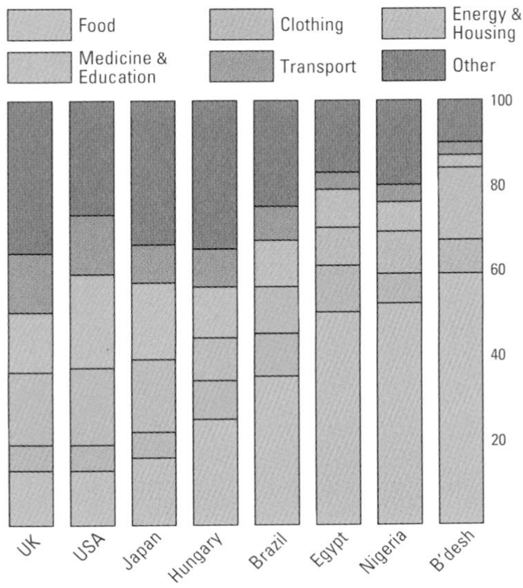

Distribution of Income

Percentage share of household income from poorest fifth to richest fifth, selected countries (latest available year)

The graph below shows that wealth is not distributed evenly throughout the population of the six countries. In every country worldwide the richest 20% of the population have a disproportionately high percentage of the income. This disparity between rich and poor is nowhere more pronounced than in Brazil, where the richest 20% of the population have over 60% of the income. The poorest 20%, on the other hand, have less than 5%.

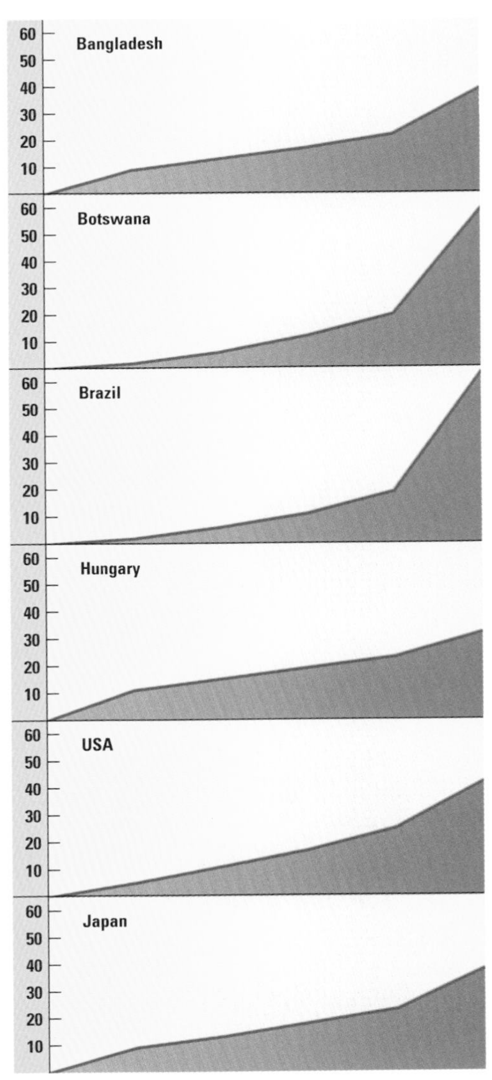

Fertility and Education

Fertility rates compared with female education, selected countries (1992–95)

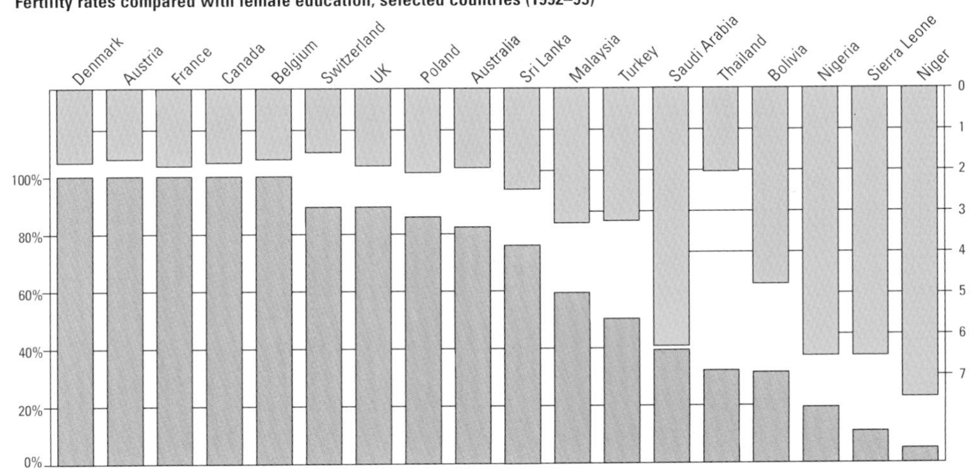
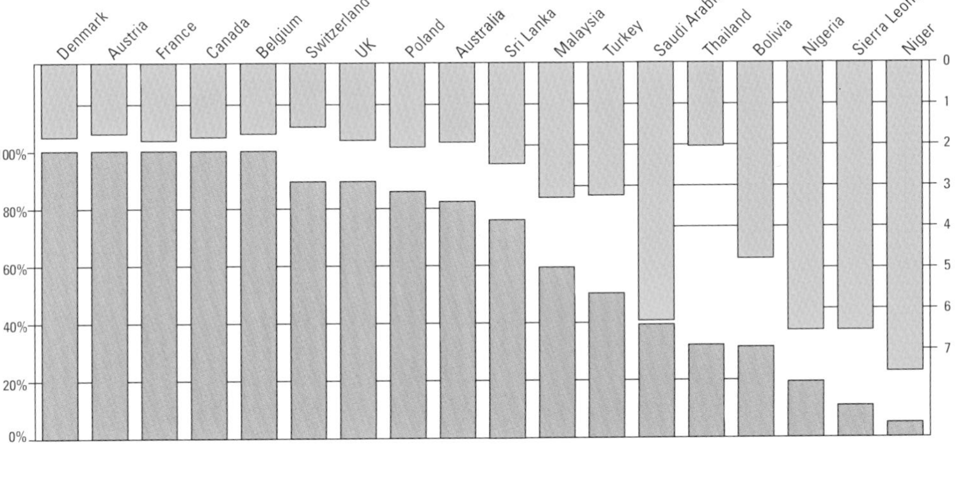

Percentage of females aged 12–17 in secondary education

Fertility rate: average number of children borne per woman

Access to secondary education is closely linked to low fertility rates in developed countries. By contrast, in many developing countries, women's lives are dominated by agriculture, or they lack access to secondary and higher education for cultural reasons, as in Muslim countries. Such disparities are reflected in women's parliamentary representation which is only one-seventh that of men, despite the emergence of such figures as Mrs Indira Gandhi, India's former prime minister. Female wages are also, on average, only two-thirds of those of men.

Women at Work

Women in paid employment as a percentage of the total workforce (1996)

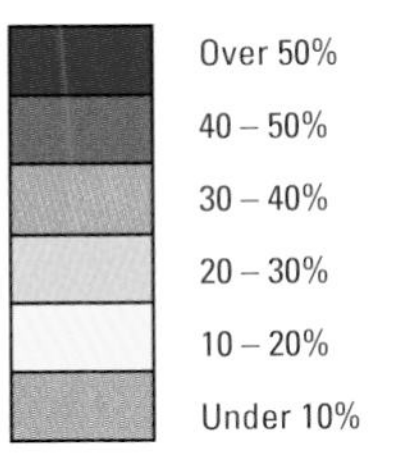

Most women in work

Cambodia	53%
Ghana	51%
Latvia	50%

Fewest women in work

Iraq	18%
Oman	15%
Saudi Arabia	14%

Car Ownership

Proportion of the world's vehicles, by region (1996)

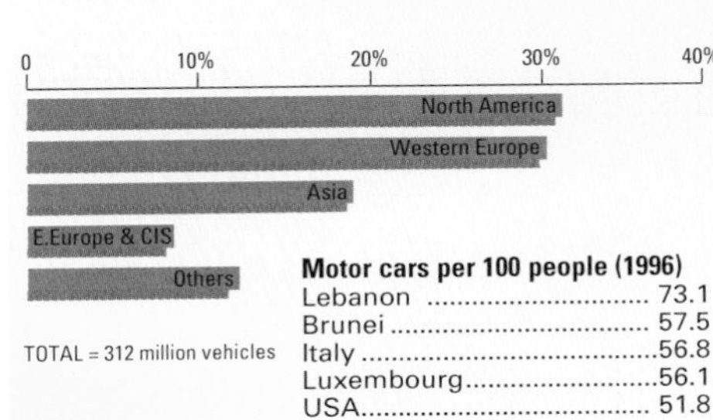

Motor cars per 100 people (1996)

Lebanon	73.1
Brunei	57.5
Italy	56.8
Luxembourg	56.1
USA	51.8

Standards of Living in the USA by Race, Age and Region

A comparison of measures of income and education, by selected characteristics (1995)

Median income per household (US $), by age and region

15–24 years	20,979
25–34 years	34,701
35–44 years	43,465
45–54 years	48,058
55–64 years	38.077
65 years and over	19,096
North-east	36,111
Mid-west	35,839
South	30,942
West	35,979

Per capita income (US $), by race and Hispanic origin of householder

ALL RACES	17,227
White	18,304
Black	10,982
Asian & Pacific Is.	16,567
Hispanic (any race)	9,300

The poorest 20% of households received just 3.6% of the income, whereas the richest 20% received 48.2%.

Percentage of persons aged 25 and over who have completed High School, by race or origin

ALL RACES	1975	62.5
	1995	81.7
White	1975	64.5
	1995	83.0
Black	1975	42.5
	1995	73.8
Hispanic	1975	37.9
	1995	53.4

Regional Inequality in Italy

Gross Domestic Product (GDP) per capita in Italy, by region (1993)

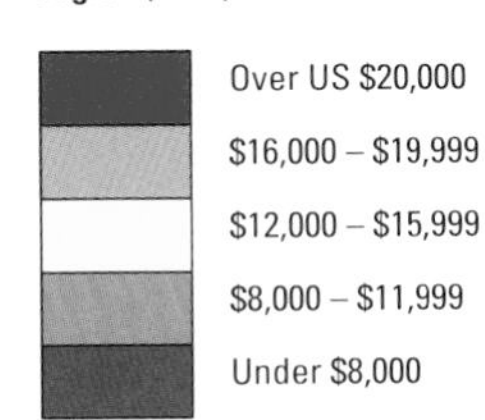

Average GDP per capita for Italy was $18,878. The per capita GDP, by comparison, for the UK was $17,920; for the USA $25,650; and for the EU $25,900.

The number of inhabitants per doctor, another social indicator, varies from less than 500 in the north-west of Italy to over 800 in the far south, with a national average of 607.

The southern part of Italy, known as the *Mezzogiorno* (or 'Land of the midday sun'), has been described as the poorest part of the European Union. It is identifiable on the map, left, as all the regions with a GDP per capita of less than $12,000 (including the two islands of Sicily and Sardinia), plus Abruzzi whose capital is L'Aquila.

The *Mezzogiorno* region suffers from a lack of mineral and energy resources, industry, commerce, services and skilled labour. As a result, standards of living in the region are well below the rest of Italy and Europe. Employment is predominantly agricultural and small-scale.

The north of Italy accounts for 60% of the population but 80% of the GDP, whereas the *Mezzogiorno* accounts for 40% of the population and only 20% of the GDP. Manpower surpluses in the south led to emigration to other parts of Europe and the Americas. It has also led, especially in the last 50 years, to inter-regional migration from the islands and the southern mainland to the north. The main regions attracting migrants were the north-west – the prosperous Liguria–Piedmont–Lombardy triangle with its great industrial cities of Genoa, Milan and Turin – and the Venetia region in the north-east. As a result, the north has experienced much higher population growth rates than the rest of Italy.

In 1996 the Northern League, one of Italy's political parties, exploited the regional differences by declaring the north to be the independent 'Republic of Padania'. However, only a small minority of northerners supports secession.

Tehran, Iran

WORLD MAPS

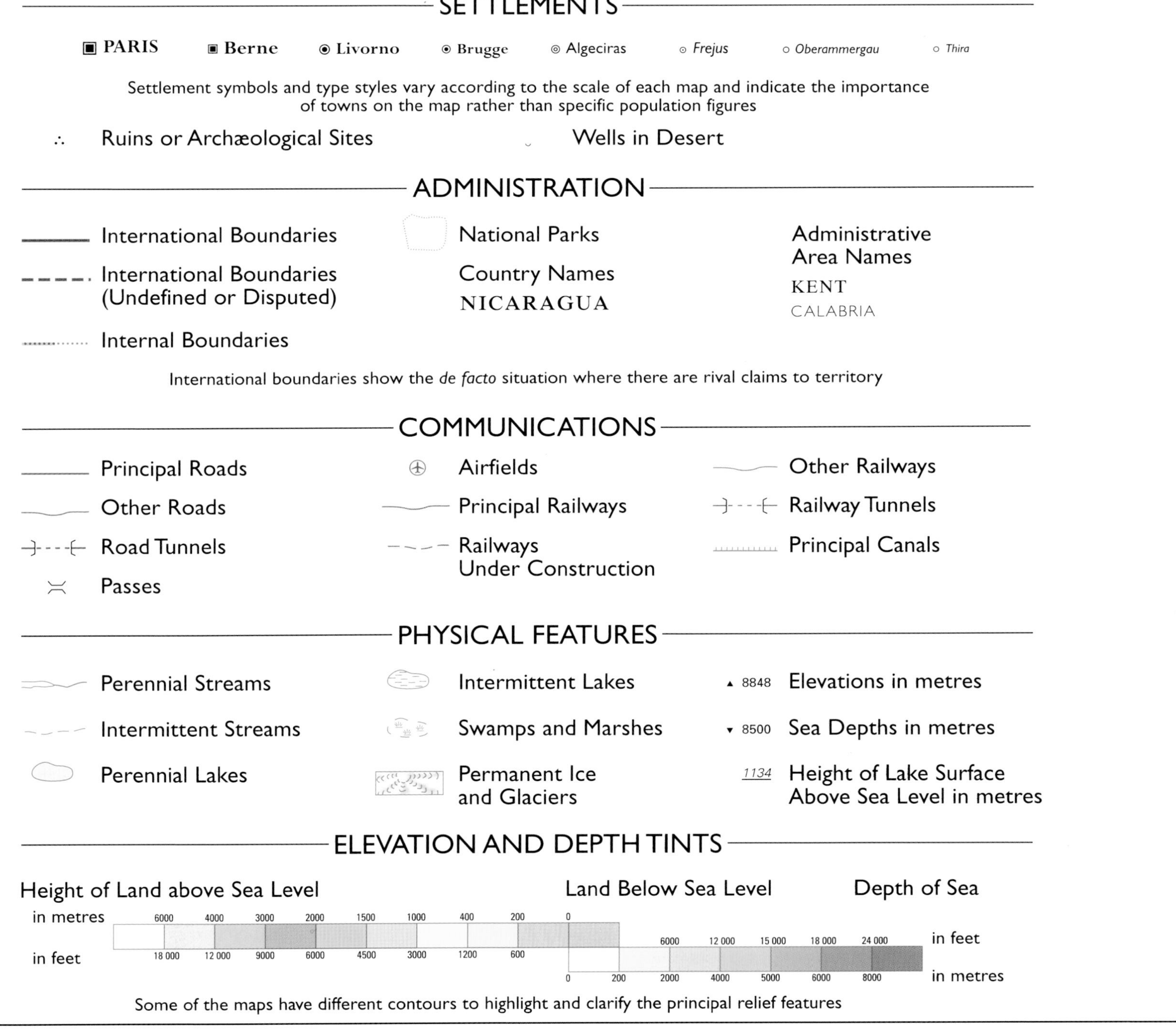

SETTLEMENTS
PARIS
Berne
Livorno
Brugge
Algeciras
Frejus
Oberammergau
Thira
Settlement symbols and type styles vary according to the scale of each map and indicate the importance of towns on the map rather than specific population figures
Ruins or Archæological Sites
Wells in Desert
ADMINISTRATION
International Boundaries
International Boundaries (Undefined or Disputed)
Internal Boundaries
National Parks
Country Names
NICARAGUA
Administrative Area Names
KENT
CALABRIA
International boundaries show the de facto situation where there are rival claims to territory
COMMUNICATIONS
Principal Roads
Other Roads
Road Tunnels
Passes
Airfields
Principal Railways
Railways Under Construction
Other Railways
Railway Tunnels
Principal Canals
PHYSICAL FEATURES
Perennial Streams
Intermittent Streams
Perennial Lakes
Intermittent Lakes
Swamps and Marshes
Permanent Ice and Glaciers
8848 Elevations in metres
8500 Sea Depths in metres
1134 Height of Lake Surface Above Sea Level in metres
ELEVATION AND DEPTH TINTS
Height of Land above Sea Level
Land Below Sea Level
Depth of Sea
in metres
6000 4000 3000 2000 1500 1000 400 200 0
in feet
18 000 12 000 9000 6000 4500 3000 1200 600
6000 12 000 15 000 18 000 24 000
in feet
0 200 2000 4000 5000 6000 8000
in metres
Some of the maps have different contours to highlight and clarify the principal relief features

Projection: *Hammer Equal Area*

Hanoi ◉ Capital Cities

ARCTIC OCEAN 1:29 400 000

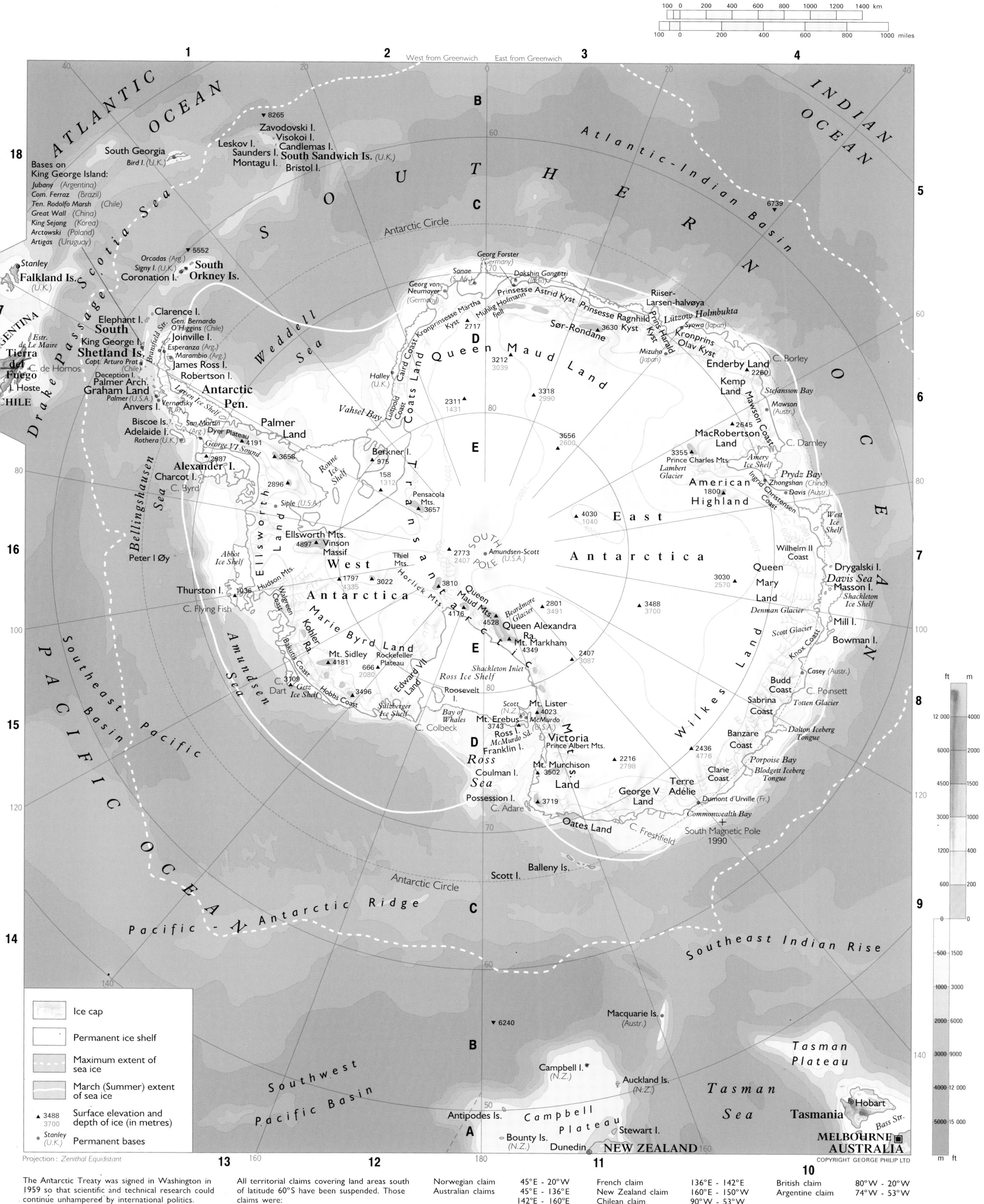

The Antarctic Treaty was signed in Washington in 1959 so that scientific and technical research could continue unhampered by international politics.

All territorial claims covering land areas south of latitude 60°S have been suspended. Those claims were:

Norwegian claim	45°E - 20°W	French claim	136°E - 142°E	British claim	80°W - 20°W
Australian claims	45°E - 136°E	New Zealand claim	160°E - 150°W	Argentine claim	74°W - 53°W
	142°E - 160°E	Chilean claim	90°W - 53°W		

EUROPE : Physical 1:16 800 000

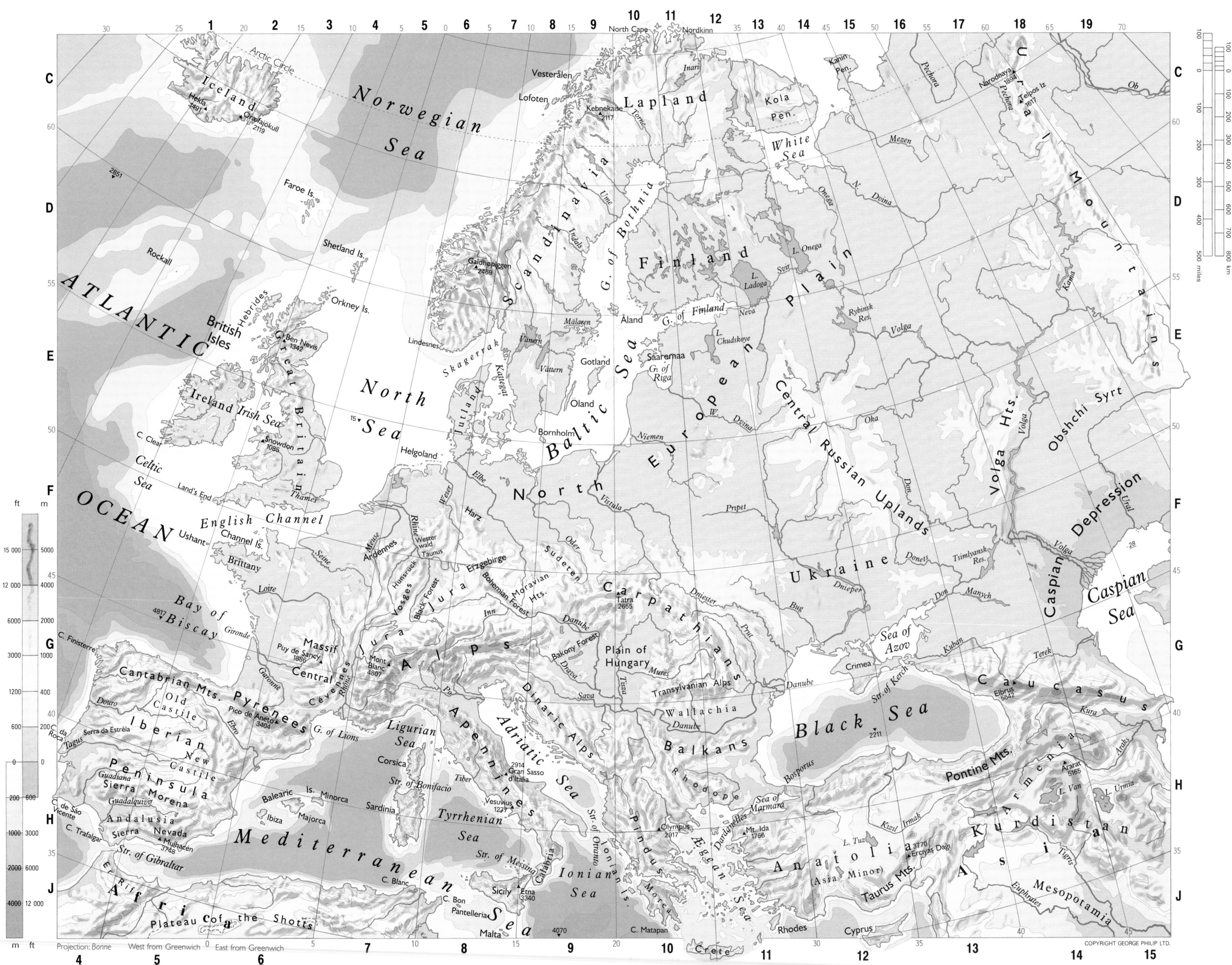

Norwegian Sea
North Sea
ATLANTIC OCEAN
Baltic Sea
Black Sea
Caspian Sea
Mediterranean Sea
Adriatic Sea
Ionian Sea
Tyrrhenian Sea
Ægean Sea
Bay of Biscay
English Channel
White Sea
G. of Bothnia
ICELAND
UNITED KINGDOM
IRELAND
NORWAY
SWEDEN
FINLAND
DENMARK
ESTONIA
LATVIA
LITHUANIA
BELARUS
RUSSIA
UKRAINE
POLAND
GERMANY
NETHER-LANDS
BELGIUM
LUX.
FRANCE
SWITZERLAND
AUSTRIA
CZECH REP.
SLOVAK REP.
HUNGARY
ROMANIA
MOLDOVA
BULGARIA
SLOVENIA
CROATIA
BOSNIA-HERZ.
YUGOSLAVIA
MACEDONIA
ALBANIA
GREECE
ITALY
SPAIN
PORTUGAL
TURKEY
CYPRUS
SYRIA
IRAQ
IRAN
GEORGIA
ARMENIA
AZERBAIJAN
KAZAKSTAN
MOROCCO
ALGERIA
TUNISIA
MALTA
Africa
LONDON
PARIS
MOSCOW
ST. PETERSBURG
ISTANBUL
■ LONDON Capital Cities
Projection: Bonne
West from Greenwich
East from Greenwich
COPYRIGHT GEORGE PHILIP LTD.

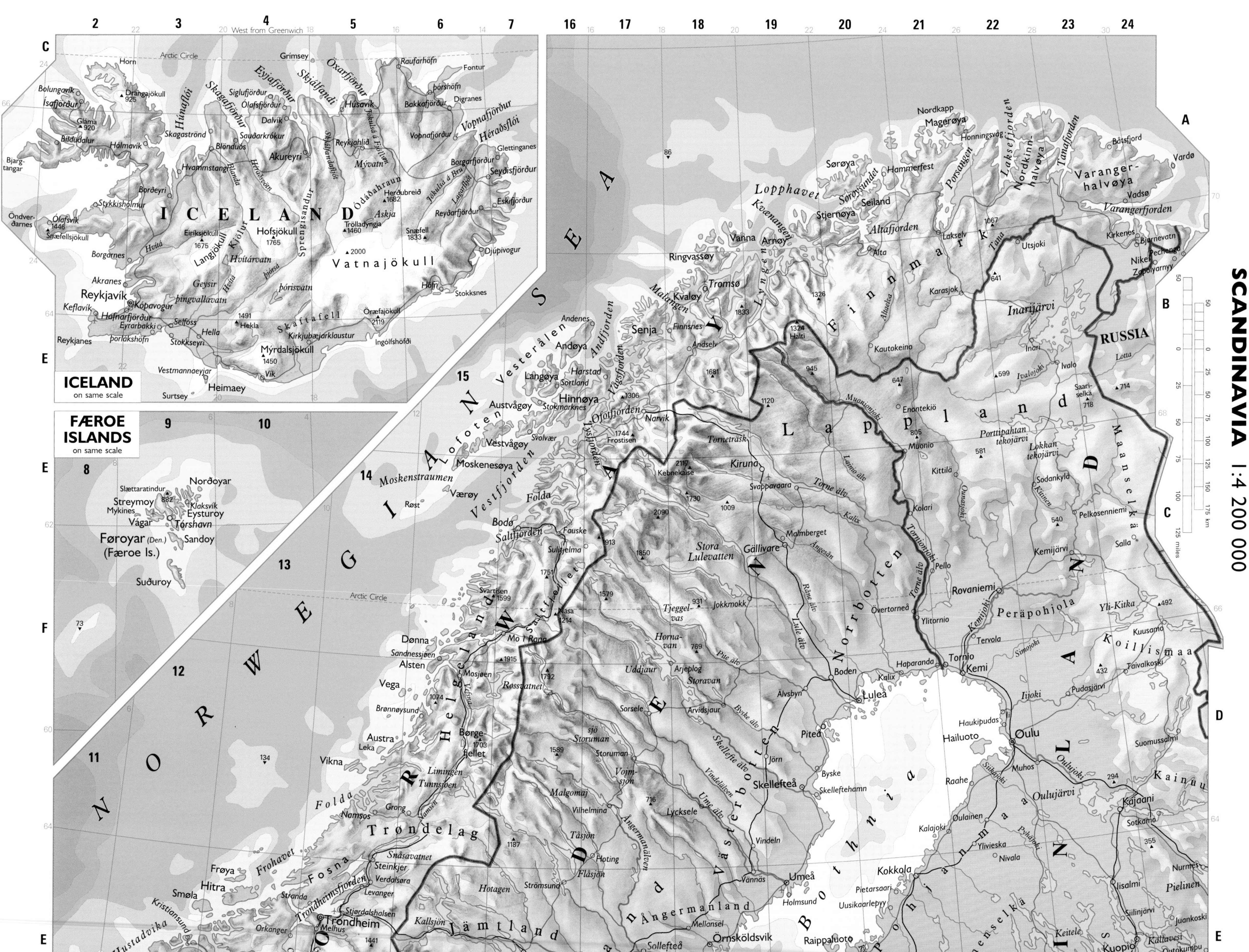

50 0 25 50 75 100 125 150 175 km
50 0 25 50 75 100 125 miles
RUSSIA
Lapland
Finnmark
Norrbotten
Västerbotten
Ångermanland
Jämtland
Trøndelag
Helgeland
Lofoten
Vesterålen
NORWEGIAN SEA
Gulf of Bothnia
FINLAND
Maanselkä
Koillismaa
Kainuu
Pohjanmaa
Peräpohjola
Oulu
Kemi
Tornio
Rovaniemi
Luleå
Umeå
Skellefteå
Kiruna
Gällivare
Narvik
Tromsø
Hammerfest
Nordkapp
Vardø
Vadsø
Kirkenes
Bodø
Trondheim
Varangerfjorden
Porsangen
Laksefjorden
Lopphavet
Vestfjorden
Arctic Circle
ICELAND
Vatnajökull
Hofsjökull
Langjökull
Reykjavík
Akureyri
Heimaey
ICELAND on same scale
FÆROE ISLANDS on same scale
Føroyar (Den.) (Færoe Is.)
Streymoy
Eysturoy
Sandoy
Suðuroy
Vágar
Tórshavn

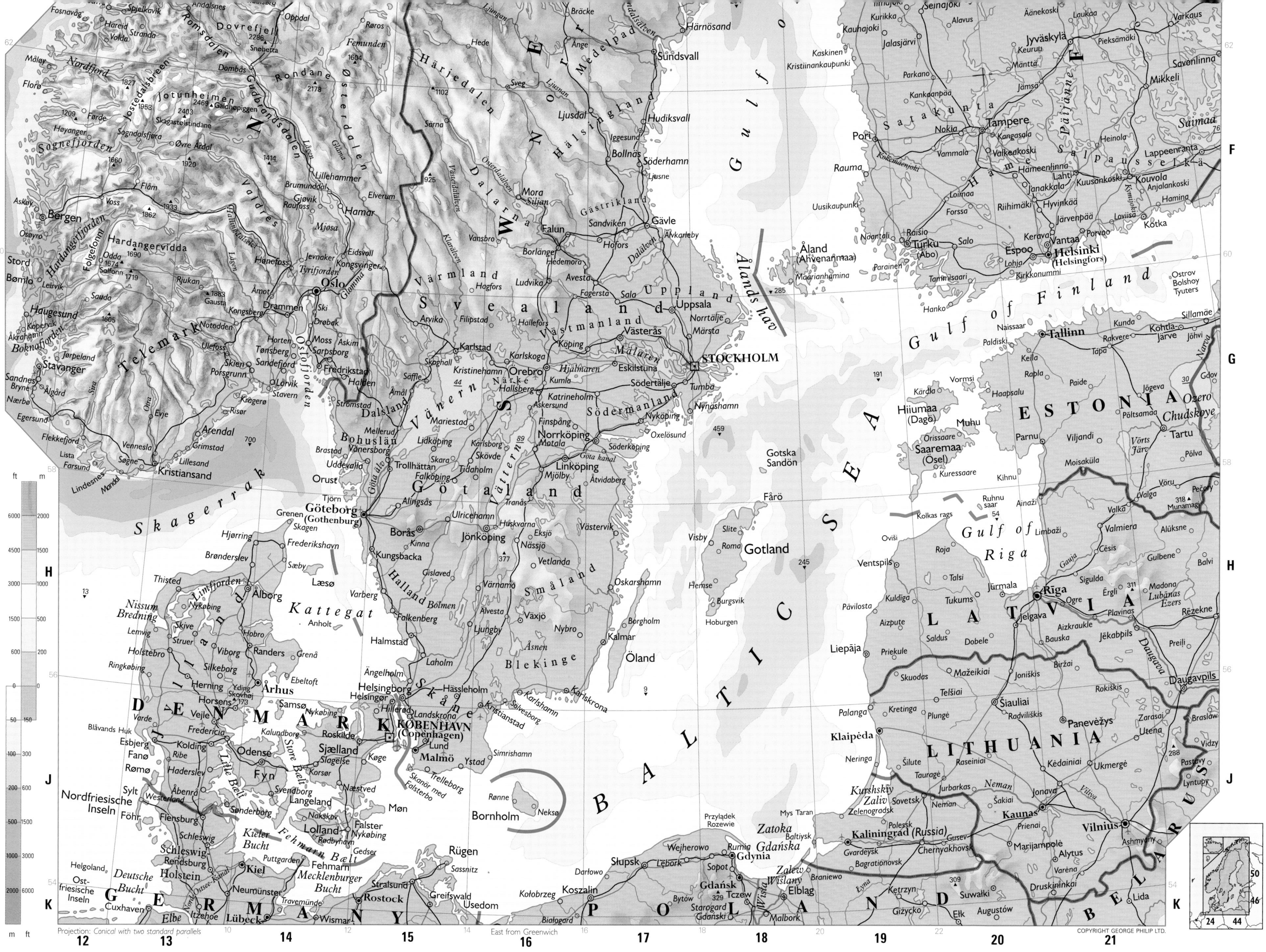

NORWAY
SWEDEN
FINLAND
ESTONIA
LATVIA
LITHUANIA
BELARUS
POLAND
GERMANY
DENMARK

BALTIC SEA
Gulf of Finland
Gulf of Bothnia
Gulf of Riga
Ålands hav
Skagerrak
Kattegat
Oslofjorden
Zatoka Gdańska
Kurshskiy Zaliv
Zalew Wiślany
Kieler Bucht
Mecklenburger Bucht
Deutsche Bucht
Fehmarn Bælt
Store Bælt
Lille Bælt

Svealand
Götaland
Norrland
Dalarna
Värmland
Härjedalen
Hälsingland
Medelpad
Gästrikland
Uppland
Västmanland
Södermanland
Närke
Dalsland
Bohuslän
Halland
Småland
Blekinge
Skåne
Jylland
Sjælland
Fyn
Telemark
Jotunheimen
Hardangervidda
Satakunta
Häme
Salpausselkä
Päijänne
Saimaa

STOCKHOLM
Oslo
Helsinki (Helsingfors)
Tallinn
Riga
Vilnius
KØBENHAVN (Copenhagen)
Göteborg (Gothenburg)
Bergen
Stavanger
Kristiansand
Malmö
Uppsala
Västerås
Örebro
Norrköping
Linköping
Jönköping
Gävle
Sundsvall
Turku (Åbo)
Tampere
Åland (Ahvenanmaa)
Gotland
Öland
Bornholm
Hiiumaa (Dagö)
Saaremaa (Ösel)
Tartu
Pärnu
Liepāja
Ventspils
Daugavpils
Šiauliai
Kaunas
Klaipėda
Kaliningrad (Russia)
Gdańsk
Gdynia
Rostock
Kiel
Lübeck
Århus
Ålborg
Odense
Rügen

Projection: *Conical with two standard parallels*

East from Greenwich

12 13 14 15 16 17 18 19 20 21

COPYRIGHT GEORGE PHILIP LTD.

DENMARK AND SOUTHERN SWEDEN 1:2 100 000

10 0 10 20 30 40 50 60 70 80 90 km

10 0 10 20 30 40 50 60 miles

m: 2000 1500 1000 500 200 0 50 100 200 500 1500

ft: 6000 4500 3000 1500 600 0 150 300 600 1500 4500

Skagerrak
Kattegat
BALTIC SEA
DENMARK
GERMANY
POLAND
Götaland
Småland
Skåne
Jylland
Sjælland
Fyn
Lolland
Falster
Bornholm (Denmark)
Öland (Sweden)
Gotland (Sweden)
Læsø (Denmark)
Anholt (Denmark)
Samsø
Langeland
Ærø
Als
Møn
Fehmarn
Sylt
Föhr
Amrum
Vänern
Vättern
Göteborg
Malmö
København
Helsingborg
Helsingør
Jönköping
Linköping
Norrköping
Nyköping
Kalmar
Karlskrona
Växjö
Halmstad
Borås
Trollhättan
Uddevalla
Västervik
Visby
Ålborg
Århus
Odense
Esbjerg
Randers
Vejle
Kolding
Horsens
Herning
Silkeborg
Viborg
Frederikshavn
Hjørring
Roskilde
Næstved
Slagelse
Flensburg
Schleswig
Eckernförde
Słupsk
Lębork
Arendal
Kristianstad
Lund
Trelleborg
Ystad
Hanöbukten
Bornholmsgattet
Fehmarn Belt
Store Bælt
Lille Bælt
Øresund
Ålborg Bugt
Jammerbugt
ÖSTERGÖTLANDS LÄN
VÄSTRA GÖTALANDS LÄN
JÖNKÖPINGS LÄN
KALMAR LÄN
KRONOBERGS LÄN
HALLANDS LÄN
BLEKINGE LÄN
SKÅNE LÄN
GOTLANDS LÄN
NORDJYLLANDS AMT.
VIBORG AMT.
ÅRHUS AMT.
RINGKØBING AMT.
VEJLE AMT.
RIBE AMT.
SØNDERJYLLANDS AMT.
FYNS AMT.
VESTSJÆLLANDS AMT.
STORSTRØMS AMT.
FREDERIKSBORG AMT.
KØBENHAVNS AMT.
ROSKILDE AMT.
BORNHOLMS AMT.

Projection : Lambert's Conformal Conic
East from Greenwich

10 0 10 20 30 40 50 60 70 80 km
10 0 10 20 30 40 50 miles
Key to English unitary authorities on map.
25. HARTLEPOOL
26. DARLINGTON
27. STOCKTON-ON-TEES
28. MIDDLESBROUGH
29. REDCAR AND CLEVELAND
30. BLACKPOOL
31. BLACKBURN WITH DARWEN
32. HALTON
33. WARRINGTON
34. KINGSTON UPON HULL
35. NORTH EAST LINCOLNSHIRE
36. STOKE-ON-TRENT
37. TELFORD AND WREKIN
38. DERBY CITY
39. CITY OF NOTTINGHAM
40. LEICESTER CITY
41. RUTLAND
42. PETERBOROUGH
43. MILTON KEYNES
44. LUTON
45. NORTH SOMERSET
46. CITY OF BRISTOL
47. BATH AND NORTH EAST SOMERSET
48. SWINDON
49. READING
50. WOKINGHAM
51. WINDSOR AND MAIDENHEAD
52. SLOUGH
53. BRACKNELL FOREST
54. THURROCK
55. SOUTHEND-ON-SEA
56. MEDWAY
57. PLYMOUTH
58. TORBAY
59. POOLE
60. BOURNEMOUTH
61. SOUTHAMPTON
62. PORTSMOUTH
63. BRIGHTON AND HOVE
Key to Welsh unitary authorities on map.
15. SWANSEA
16. NEATH PORT TALBOT
17. BRIDGEND
18. RHONDDA CYNON TAFF
19. MERTHYR TYDFIL
20. CAERPHILLY
21. BLAENAU GWENT
22. TORFAEN
23. CARDIFF
24. NEWPORT
NORTH SEA
IRISH SEA
North Channel
SCOTLAND
NORTHERN IRELAND
ISLE OF MAN
SCOTTISH BORDERS
NORTHUMBERLAND
CUMBRIA
DURHAM
LANCASHIRE
NORTH YORKSHIRE
LINCOLNSHIRE
Edinburgh
Glasgow
Newcastle-upon-Tyne
Sunderland
Middlesbrough
Leeds
Bradford
Manchester
Liverpool
Sheffield
Kingston upon Hull
Nottingham
Derby
Stoke-on-Trent

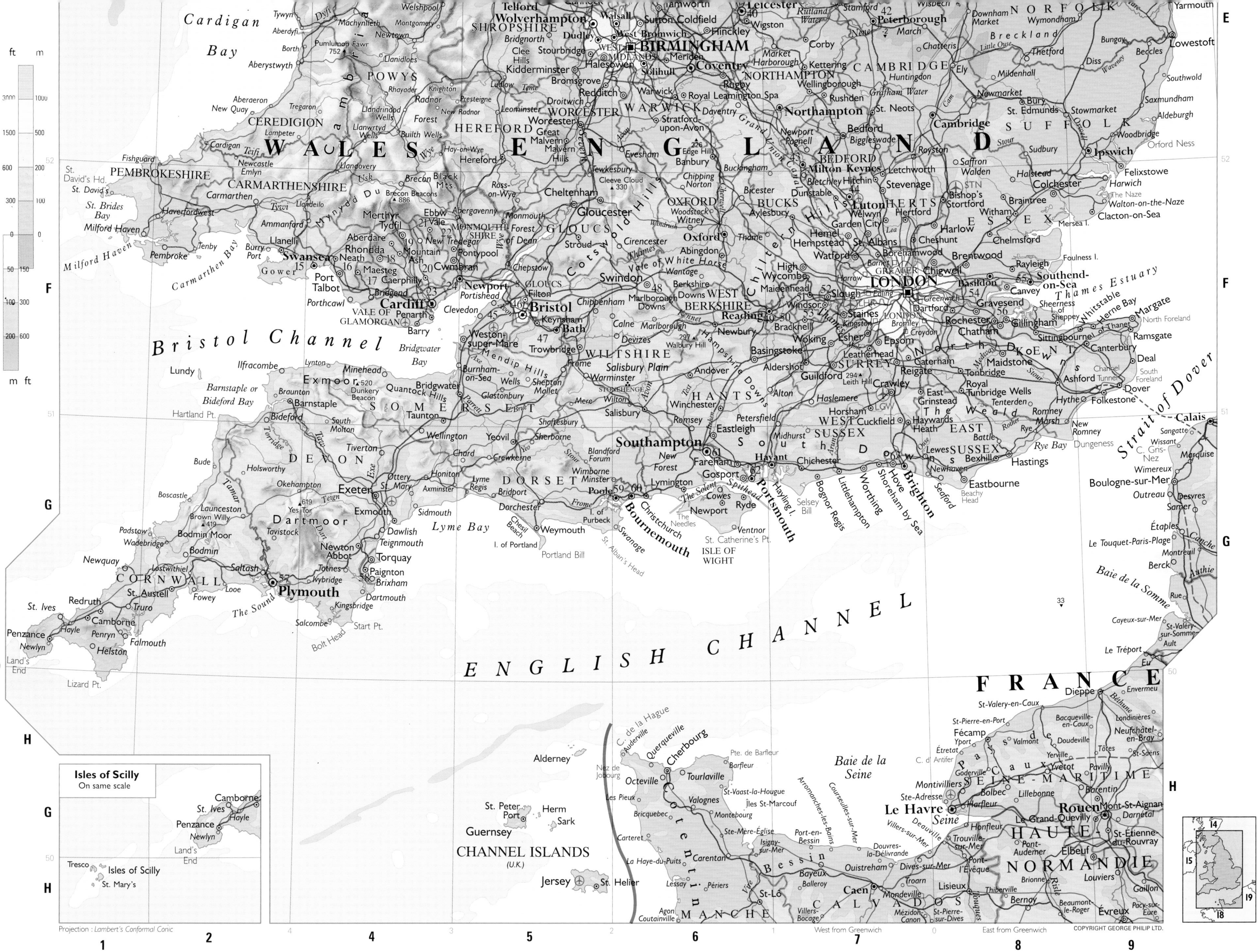

WALES

ENGLAND

FRANCE

ENGLISH CHANNEL

Bristol Channel

Cardigan Bay

Strait of Dover

Baie de la Seine

Baie de la Somme

Lyme Bay

Thames Estuary

CHANNEL ISLANDS (U.K.)

Alderney

Guernsey

Jersey

Sark

Herm

St. Peter Port

St. Helier

BIRMINGHAM

LONDON

Bristol

Cardiff

Swansea

Newport

Plymouth

Exeter

Southampton

Portsmouth

Bournemouth

Brighton

Gloucester

Oxford

Reading

Cambridge

Ipswich

Northampton

Coventry

Wolverhampton

Leicester

Peterborough

Le Havre

Rouen

Caen

Cherbourg

Dieppe

Calais

Boulogne-sur-Mer

PEMBROKESHIRE

CARMARTHENSHIRE

CEREDIGION

POWYS

SHROPSHIRE

HEREFORD

WORCESTER

WARWICK

NORTHAMPTON

CAMBRIDGE

NORFOLK

SUFFOLK

ESSEX

HERTS

BEDFORD

BUCKS

OXFORD

GLOUCS

WILTSHIRE

SOMERSET

DEVON

CORNWALL

DORSET

HANTS

WEST SUSSEX

EAST SUSSEX

SURREY

KENT

BERKSHIRE

WEST BERKSHIRE

ISLE OF WIGHT

VALE OF GLAMORGAN

MONMOUTHSHIRE

SEINE-MARITIME

HAUTE-NORMANDIE

CALVADOS

MANCHE

Cotentin

Pays de Caux

Bessin

Dartmoor

Exmoor

Cotswold Hills

Chiltern Hills

Mendip Hills

Quantock Hills

North Downs

South Downs

The Weald

Hampshire Downs

Salisbury Plain

Brecon Beacons

Isles of Scilly
On same scale

Camborne

St. Ives

Hayle

Penzance

Newlyn

Land's End

Tresco

Isles of Scilly

St. Mary's

ft	m
3000	1000
1500	500
600	200
300	100
0	0
150	50
300	100
600	200
ft	m

Projection : Lambert's Conformal Conic

West from Greenwich

East from Greenwich

1 2 4 5 6 7 8 9

E F G H

Key to Scottish unitary authorities on map
1. CITY OF ABERDEEN
2. DUNDEE CITY
3. WEST DUNBARTONSHIRE
4. EAST DUNBARTONSHIRE
5. CITY OF GLASGOW
6. INVERCLYDE
7. RENFREWSHIRE
8. EAST RENFREWSHIRE
9. NORTH LANARKSHIRE
10. FALKIRK
11. CLACKMANNANSHIRE
12. WEST LOTHIAN
13. CITY OF EDINBURGH
14. MIDLOTHIAN
ORKNEY IS.
On same scale
SHETLAND IS.
On same scale
SCOTLAND
ATLANTIC OCEAN
NORTH SEA
ENGLAND
NORTHERN IRELAND
Projection : Lambert's Conformal Conic
West from Greenwich
COPYRIGHT GEORGE PHILIP LTD.

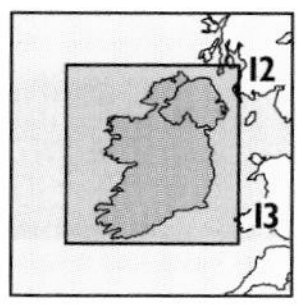

10 0 10 20 30 40 50 60 70 80 km

10 0 10 20 30 40 50 miles

1 2 3 4 5 6

A B C D E

ATLANTIC OCEAN

North Channel

IRISH SEA

St. George's Channel

CELTIC SEA

IRELAND

NORTHERN IRELAND

Ulster

Connacht

Leinster

Munster

Kintyre
Campbeltown
Arran
Brodick
Firth of Clyde
Mull of Oa
Mull of Kintyre
Ailsa Craig
Cairnryan
Stranraer
Portpatrick
Rathlin I.
Fair Hd.
Ballycastle
Giants Causeway
Portrush
Portstewart
Coleraine
Malin Hd.
Malin Pen.
Carndonagh
Inishowen Pen.
Moville
Buncrana
L. Foyle
Lough Swilly
Fanad Hd.
Mulroy B.
Sheep Haven
Horn Hd.
Tory I.
Bloody Foreland
Inishfree B.
Aran I.
Errigal 752
Gweedore
The Rosses
Derryveagh Mts.
683
Rathmelton
Letterkenny
Crohy Hd.
Gweebarra B.
Dawros Hd.
DONEGAL
Loughros More B.
Glenties
Lavagh More 676
Rossan Pt.
Killybegs
Donegal
St. John's Pt.
Donegal Bay
Ballyshannon
Bundoran
Lifford
Strabane
Sion Mills
Newtownstewart
Finn
Mourne
Derg
LONDONDERRY
Londonderry
Limavady
Roe
Sawel Mt. 683
Sperrin Mts.
Bann
Mts. of Antrim
ANTRIM
Ballymoney
554 Trostan
Garron Pt.
Ballymena
Main
Larne
Magherafelt
Randalstown
Ballyclare
Antrim
Carrickfergus
269
Belfast L.
Bangor
Donaghadee
Newtownards
Newtownabbey
Lough Neagh
Belfast
Comber
Strangford L.
Ards Pen.
Lisburn
Saintfield
Portaferry
Ballyquintin Pt.
Castlederg
TYRONE
Omagh
Moneymore
Cookstown
Coalisland
Dungannon
Aughnacloy
Craigavon
Lurgan
DOWN
Lagan
Portadown
Banbridge
Ballynahinch
Tandragee
Armagh
ARMAGH
Blackwater
Downpatrick
Middletown
Dundrum
St. John's Pt.
Dundrum B.
Keady
Newcastle
Newry
Mourne Mts.
852 Slieve Donard
Warrenpoint
Kilkeel
577 Slieve Gullion
Dromore
Irvinestown
Lower L. Erne
Enniskillen
FERMANAGH
Upper L. Erne
Monaghan
Clones
MONAGHAN
Castleblaney
Carrickmacross
Dundalk
Greenore
Carlingford L.
Dundalk Bay
Louth
LOUTH
Ardee
Dunleer
Clogher Hd.
Drogheda
Downpatrick Hd.
Broad Haven
Erris Hd.
Belmullet
Killala B.
Killala
Mullet Pen.
Inishkea North
Inishkea South
Ballina
Blacksod Bay
L. Conn
806 Nephin
Moy
Achill Hd.
Achill I.
Corraun Pen.
MAYO
Newport
Clare I.
Clew Bay
Westport
Castlebar
Inishturk
Croagh Patrick 765
Killary Harbour
Mweelrea 819
Inishbofin
Inishshark
Connemara
Clifden
Slyne Hd.
Sligo Bay
Sligo
Dromore West
544
Ox Mts.
SLIGO
Collooney
Ballymote
L. Arrow
Charlestown
Swinford
Boyle
Ballaghaderreen
Knock
ROSCOMMON
Ballyhaunis
Castlerea
Claremorris
Ballinrobe
Glennamaddy
Lough Mask
Tuam
Roscommon
L. Allen
LEITRIM
Leitrim
Carrick-on-Shannon
Belturbet
Annalee
Cootehill
Cavan
CAVAN
L. Gowna
L. Sheelin
Kingscourt
Granard
LONGFORD
Longford
Castlepollard
Oldcastle
Ceanannus Mor (Kells)
Blackwater
MEATH
An Uaimh (Navan)
Athboy
Boyne
Trim
Inny
Mullingar
Lough Ree
Athlone
WESTMEATH
Royal Canal
Balbriggan
Rush
Lambay I.
Malahide
Swords
DUB
Maynooth
Howth Hd.
Dublin
Dun Laoghaire
Clondalkin
DUBLIN
Bray
Kippure 754
Greystones
123
Lough Corrib
Oughterard
GALWAY
Clare
Suck
Moate
Bertraghboy B.
Kilkieran B.
Galway
Athenry
Ballinasloe
Clara
Brosna
Grand Canal
Bog of Allen
Edenderry
Liffey
KILDARE
Galway Bay
Black Hd.
Aran Is.
Inishmore
Inishmaan
Inisheer
Loughrea
Tullamore
OFFALY
Daingean
Droichead Nua
Naas
Kildare
Portarlington
Monasterevin
Poulaphouca Res.
WICKLOW
368
Slieve Aughty
Portumna
Shannon
Gort
Birr
Mountmellick
Slieve Bloom 528 Arderin
Port Laoise
Athy
Wicklow Mts.
Wicklow
Wicklow Hd.
Lugnaquilla 926
Rathdrum
Avoca
Hags Hd.
Ennistimon
Liscannor Bay
Mal Bay
Milltown Malbay
Mutton I.
Tulla
Lough Derg
Roscrea
Mountrath
LAOIS
Ennis
CLARE
Killaloe
Nenagh
Durrow
Templemore
Carlow
Tullow
Mizen Hd.
Arklow
Shillelagh
Kilkee
Shannon Airport
Sixmilebridge
694 Keeper Hill
Thurles
CARLOW
Muine Bheag
Kilrush
Limerick
TIPPERARY
Kilkenny
Bunclody
Gorey
Loop Hd.
Foynes
LIMERICK
Rathkeale
Golden Vale
KILKENNY
796 Mt. Leinster
Slaney
Cahore Pt.
Callan
Barrow
Mouth of the Shannon
Kerry Hd.
Listowel
Feale
Newcastle West
Tipperary
Cashel
Nore
Enniscorthy
WEXFORD
Slievenamon 722
Carrick-on-Suir
New Ross
Brandon B.
Tralee B.
Smerwick Harbour
Kilfinnane
Galtymore 920
Galty Mts.
Cahir
Suir
Clonmel
Wexford
Wexford Harbour
Rosslare
Greenore Pt.
Tralee
Rath Luirc
Mitchelstown
Knockmealdown Mts. 795
Comeragh Mts. 792
Waterford
Tramore
953 Brandon Mt.
Slieve Mish 853
Dingle
Maine
Newmarket
Buttevant
Kanturk
Fermoy
Carnsore Pt.
Great Blasket I.
KERRY
Laune
Killorglin
Killarney
Mallow
Blackwater
Lismore
WATERFORD
Hook Hd.
Saltee Is.
Dunmore Hd.
Dingle Bay
Inishvickillane
L. Leane
Carrauntoohill 1041
Boggeragh Mts.
646
Dungarvan
Tramore B.
Waterford Harbour
Dungarvan Harbour
Valencia I.
Caherciveen
Macgillycuddy's Reeks
CORK
Youghal
Youghal B.
St. David's Hd.
St. David's
St. Brides Bay
Puffin I.
Kenmare
Macroom
Blarney
Cork
Midleton
Great Skellig
Ballinskelligs B.
Lee
Passage West
Cobh
Crosshaven
Cork Harbour
115
Scariff I.
Kenmare River
Caha Mts.
686
Glengarriff
Dunmanway
Bandon
Bandon
Kinsale
Old Head of Kinsale
Dursey I.
Castletown Bearhaven
Bear I.
Bantry
Clonakilty
Crow Hd.
Bantry Bay
Skibbereen
Clonakilty B.
Dunmanus B.
Skull
Galley Hd.
Long I.
Baltimore
Sherkin I.
Mizen Hd.
C. Clear
Clear I.

ft m
1500 500
600 200
300 100
0 0
50 150
100 300
200 600
500 1500
1000 3000
2000 6000
m ft

Projection : *Lambert's Conformal Conic*

West from Greenwich

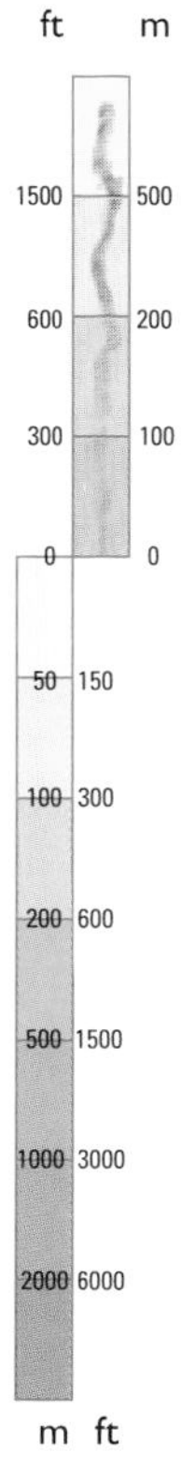

BRITISH ISLES 1:4 200 000

50 0 25 50 75 100 125 150 175 km

50 0 25 50 75 100 125 miles

1 2 3 4 5 6 7 8 9

A B C D E F G

ft m
3000 1000
1500 500
600 200
0 0
50 150
100 300
200 600
500 1500
1000 3000
2000 6000
m ft

ATLANTIC OCEAN

NORTH SEA

CELTIC SEA

IRISH SEA

English Channel

UNITED KINGDOM

SCOTLAND

ENGLAND

WALES

IRELAND

NORTHERN IRELAND

NORWAY

NETHERLANDS

BELGIUM

FRANCE

Shetland Is. Yell Unst Fetlar Mainland Lerwick Foula Fair Isle

Orkney Is. Westray Sanday Stronsay Mainland Kirkwall Hoy South Ronaldsay

Pentland Firth Moray Firth North Minch

Outer Hebrides Lewis Stornoway Harris St. Kilda North Uist Benbecula South Uist Barra

Inner Hebrides Skye Rhum Eigg Coll Tiree Mull Colonsay Jura Islay

C. Wrath Thurso Wick Helmsdale Lairg Golspie Tain Invergordon Dingwall Ullapool Inverness Nairn Elgin Buckie Banff Fraserburgh Peterhead Huntly Inverurie Aberdeen Stonehaven Aviemore Ballater Portree Mallaig Fort William Tobermory Oban Ben Nevis 1342 Montrose Arbroath Forfar Dundee St. Andrews Perth Glenrothes Kirkcaldy Stirling Dunfermline Dunbar Edinburgh Glasgow Greenock Paisley East Kilbride Hamilton Irvine Kilmarnock Ayr Arran Campbeltown Girvan Stranraer Kirkcudbright Dumfries Jedburgh Hawick Galashiels Berwick-upon-Tweed Alnwick

North West Highlands Grampian Mts. Southern Uplands Cheviot Hills North Channel Firth of Clyde L. Ness L. Lomond

Malin Hd. Buncrana Letterkenny Aran I. Coleraine Londonderry Ballymena Larne Lifford Donegal Antrim Bangor Belfast Lough Neagh Omagh Lisburn Lurgan Portadown Armagh Newry Bundoran Lower L. Erne Enniskillen Clones Sligo Ballina Achill I. L. Conn Castlebar Westport Leitrim Cavan Castleblaney Dundalk Drogheda Roscommon Longford Lough Ree Ceanannus Mor Mullingar Boyne Lough Mask Lough Corrib Connemara Athlone Galway Galway B. Aran Is. Ballinasloe Tullamore Dublin Dun Laoghaire Bray Birr Lough Derg Port Laoise Athy Ennis Limerick Thurles Carlow Kilkenny Arklow Wicklow Mts. Kilrush Shannon Listowel Tipperary Tralee Clonmel Carrick-on-Suir Wexford Rosslare Dingle Killarney Mallow Waterford Carrauntoohill 1041 Macgillycuddy's Reeks Valencia I. Cork Cobh Dungarvan Youghal Bantry Bandon Kinsale C. Clear

Connacht Ulster Leinster Munster

Newcastle-upon-Tyne South Shields Sunderland Gateshead Hexham Carlisle Durham Hartlepool Redcar Middlesbrough Darlington Stockton-on-Tees Scarborough Workington Whitehaven Cumbrian Mts. Barrow-in-Furness Lancaster Pennines Mull of Galloway I. of Man Douglas Harrogate York Bridlington Beverley Kingston upon Hull Blackpool Preston Keighley Leeds Bradford Burnley Blackburn Halifax Huddersfield Bolton Oldham Barnsley Doncaster Scunthorpe Grimsby Manchester Liverpool Warrington Stockport Sheffield Rotherham Lincoln Louth Skegness Chester Crewe Chesterfield Mansfield Nottingham Boston The Wash Cromer King's Lynn Norwich Great Yarmouth Lowestoft Stoke on Trent Derby Stafford Grantham Leicester Peterborough Shrewsbury Telford Nuneaton Wolverhampton BIRMINGHAM Coventry Corby Thetford Bury St. Edmunds Ipswich Felixstowe Harwich Colchester Redditch Rugby Northampton Bedford Cambridge Ely Worcester Royal Leamington Spa Milton Keynes Stevenage Hereford Cheltenham Cotswold Hills Gloucester Oxford Hemel Hempstead Luton Harlow Chelmsford High Wycombe Watford Basildon Southend-on-Sea LONDON Slough Reading Swindon Newbury Basingstoke Guildford Reigate Crawley Maidstone Chatham Margate Canterbury Dover Folkestone Ashford Hastings Eastbourne Brighton Worthing Havant Portsmouth Fareham Winchester Southampton Salisbury Isle of Wight Bournemouth Poole Weymouth Newport Yeovil Taunton Weston-super-Mare Bath Bristol Exmoor Barnstaple Bude Exeter Dartmoor 618 Exmouth Torbay Plymouth St. Austell Newquay Truro Falmouth Penzance Land's End Isles of Scilly

Holyhead Anglesey Bangor Colwyn Bay Snowdon 1085 Wrexham Pwllheli Cardigan Bay Aberystwyth Welshpool Cambrian Mts. Brecon 886 Carmarthen Haverfordwest Milford Haven Pembroke Fishguard Llanelli Swansea Neath Merthyr Tydfil Port Talbot Rhondda Cwmbran Newport Cardiff Barry St. George's Channel Bristol Channel

Alderney C. de la Hague Guernsey St. Peter Port Sark Jersey St. Helier Channel Is. (U.K.) Pte. de Barfleur Cherbourg Valognes Cotentin Bayeux Caen Lisieux Trouville-sur-Mer Le Havre Bolbec Fécamp Pays de Caux Rouen Elbeuf Seine Dieppe Le Tréport Abbeville Amiens Somme Picardie Le Touquet-Paris-Plage Boulogne-sur-Mer C. Gris-Nez Calais Str. of Dover Dunkerque St-Omer Béthune Bruay-la-Buissière Lens Lille Villeneuve-d'Ascq Tourcoing Roubaix Valenciennes Cambrai St-Quentin Flandre

Oostende Zeebrugge Brugge Gent Antwerpen Mechelen BRUSSEL (Bruxelles) Tournai Vlissingen Rotterdam Dordrecht Hoek van Holland 's-Gravenhage (Den Haag) Haarlem Alkmaar Den Helder Texel

Askøy Bergen Osøyro Stord Bømlo Leirvik Haugesund Kopervik Åkrahamn Boknafjord Stavanger Sandnes Bryne Nærbø

1224 316 789 1182 1311 1214 973 840 816 893 978 636 926 953 238 16 36 33 99

Projection: Conical with two standard parallels

East from Greenwich

West from Greenwich

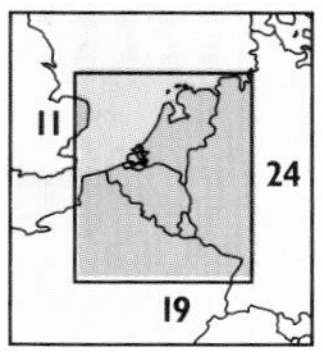

10 0 10 20 30 40 50 60 70 80 90 km

10 0 10 20 30 40 50 60 miles

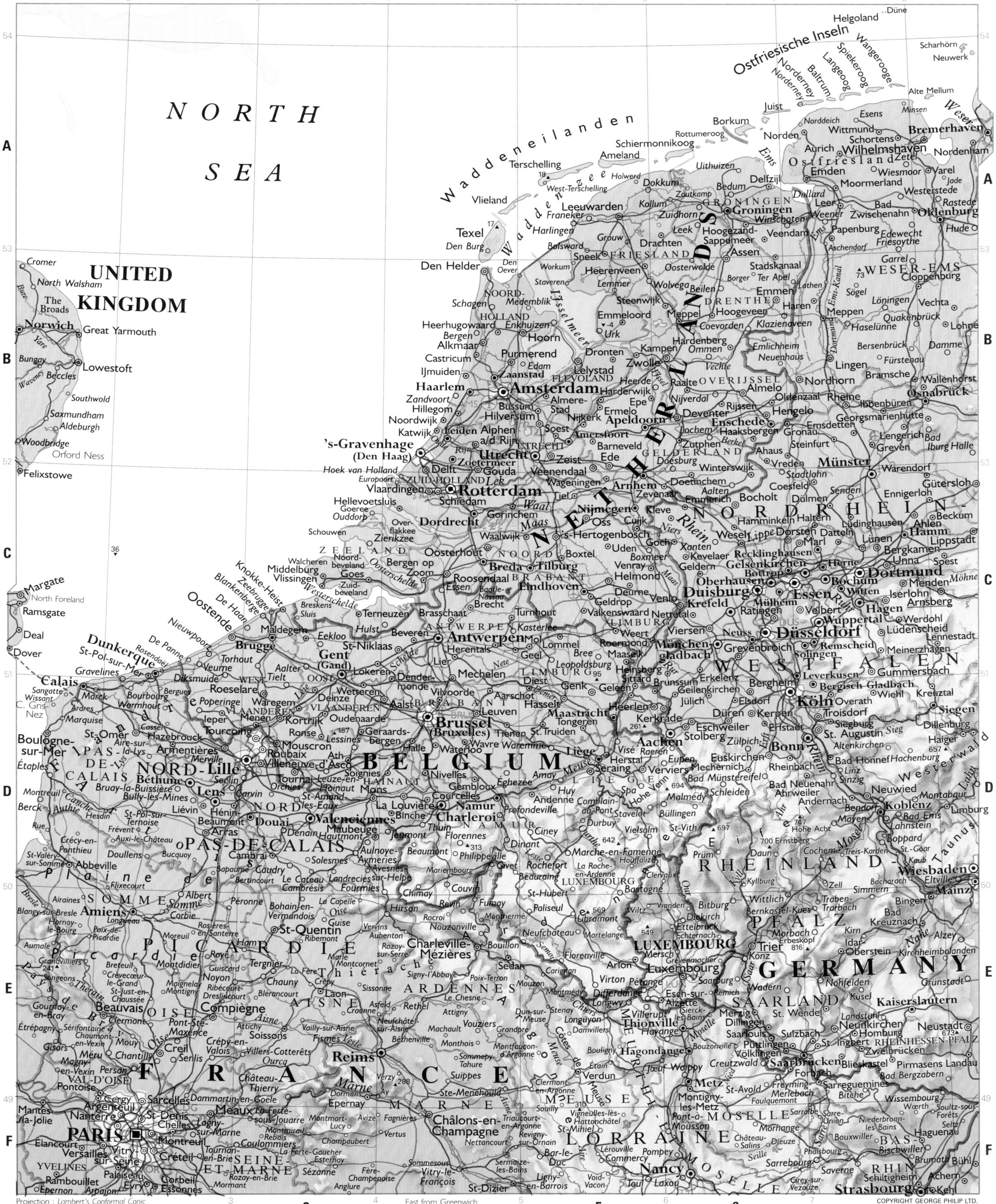

Projection : Lambert's Conformal Conic

East from Greenwich

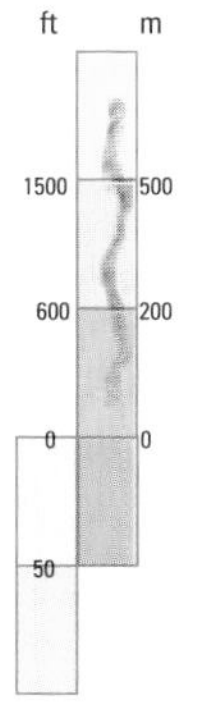

ft m

1500 500

600 200

0 0

50

m ft

Underlined towns give their name to the administrative area in which they stand.

NORTHERN FRANCE 1:2 100 000

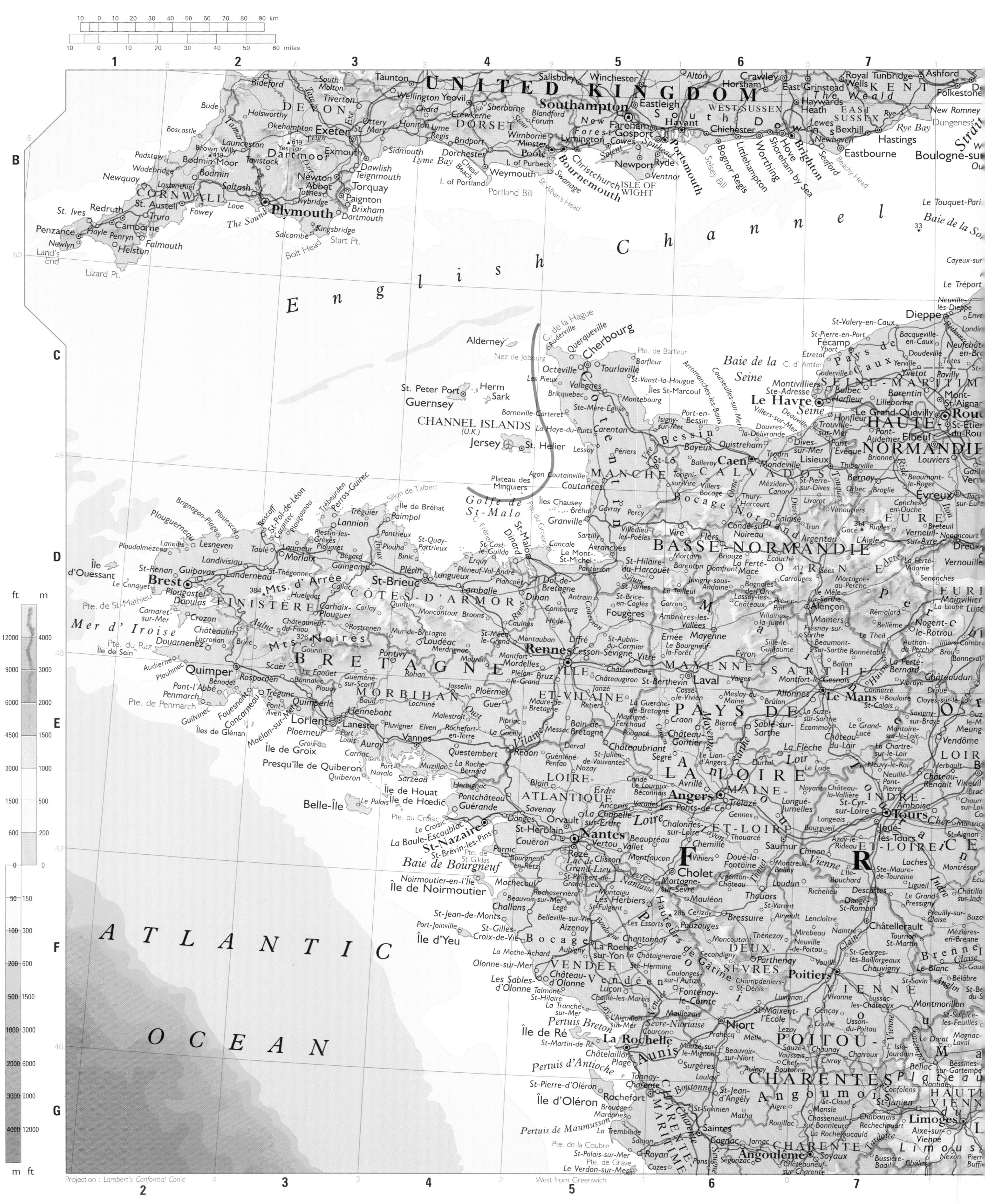

DÉPARTEMENTS IN THE PARIS AREA

1. Ville de Paris
2. Seine-St-Denis
3. Val-de-Marne
4. Hauts-de-Seine

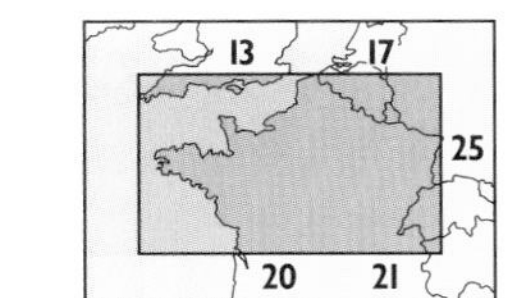

East from Greenwich

Underlined towns give their name to the administrative area in which they stand.

10 0 10 20 30 40 50 60 70 80 90 km
10 0 10 20 30 40 50 60 miles
ATLANTIC OCEAN
Golfe de Gascogne
FRANCE
SPAIN
ANDORRA
Andorra La Vella
POITOU-CHARENTES
LIMOUSIN
AQUITAINE
MIDI-PYRÉNÉES
LANGUEDOC
ROUSSILLON
AUVERGNE
CATALUÑA
NAVARRA
HUESCA
LLEIDA
GIRONA
BARCELONA
ZARAGOZA
PYRÉNÉES-ATLANTIQUES
HAUTES-PYRÉNÉES
PYRÉNÉES-ORIENTALES
CHARENTE-MARITIME
DEUX-SÈVRES
VENDÉE
VIENNE
HAUTE-VIENNE
CHARENTE
DORDOGNE
GIRONDE
LANDES
LOT-ET-GARONNE
LOT
GERS
TARN-ET-GARONNE
HAUTE-GARONNE
ARIÈGE
AUDE
TARN
AVEYRON
CANTAL
CORRÈZE
CREUSE
INDRE
CHER
ALLIER
PUY-DE-DÔME
HÉRAULT
Massif Central
Bordeaux
Toulouse
Limoges
Poitiers
Clermont-Ferrand
Montpellier
Perpignan
Pau
Bayonne
Biarritz
Pamplona
Zaragoza
Lleida
Barcelona
La Rochelle
Rochefort
Niort
Angoulême
Périgueux
Agen
Montauban
Albi
Carcassonne
Béziers
Narbonne
Tarbes
Lourdes
Auch
Cahors
Rodez
Aurillac
Tulle
Brive-la-Gaillarde
Châteauroux
Bourges
Nevers
Moulins
Vichy
Montluçon
Mont-de-Marsan
Dax
Donostia-San Sebastián
Irún
Île d'Yeu
Île de Ré
Île d'Oléron
Gironde
Garonne
Dordogne
Bassin d'Arcachon
Étang de Lacanau
Étang d'Hourtin-Carcans
Étang de Cazaux et de Sanguinet
Étang de Biscarrosse et de Parentis
Pertuis Breton
Pertuis d'Antioche
Pertuis de Maumusson
Étang de Leucate
C. de Creus
G. de Roses
Costa Brava
Pic d'Aneto 3408
Maladeta 3304
Mte. Perdido 3355
Vignemale 3298
Pic de Montcalm 3078
Pic du Midi d'Ossau
Puy de Sancy 1885
Puy-de-Dôme 1464
Sierra de Guara
Serra del Montsec
Sierra del Cadí
Los Monegros
Ebro
ft m
12000 4000
9000 3000
6000 2000
4500 1500
3000 1000
1500 500
600 200
0 0
50 150
100 300
200 600
500 1500
1000 3000
2000 6000
m ft
Projection : Lambert's Conformal Conic
West from Greenwich
East from Greenwich

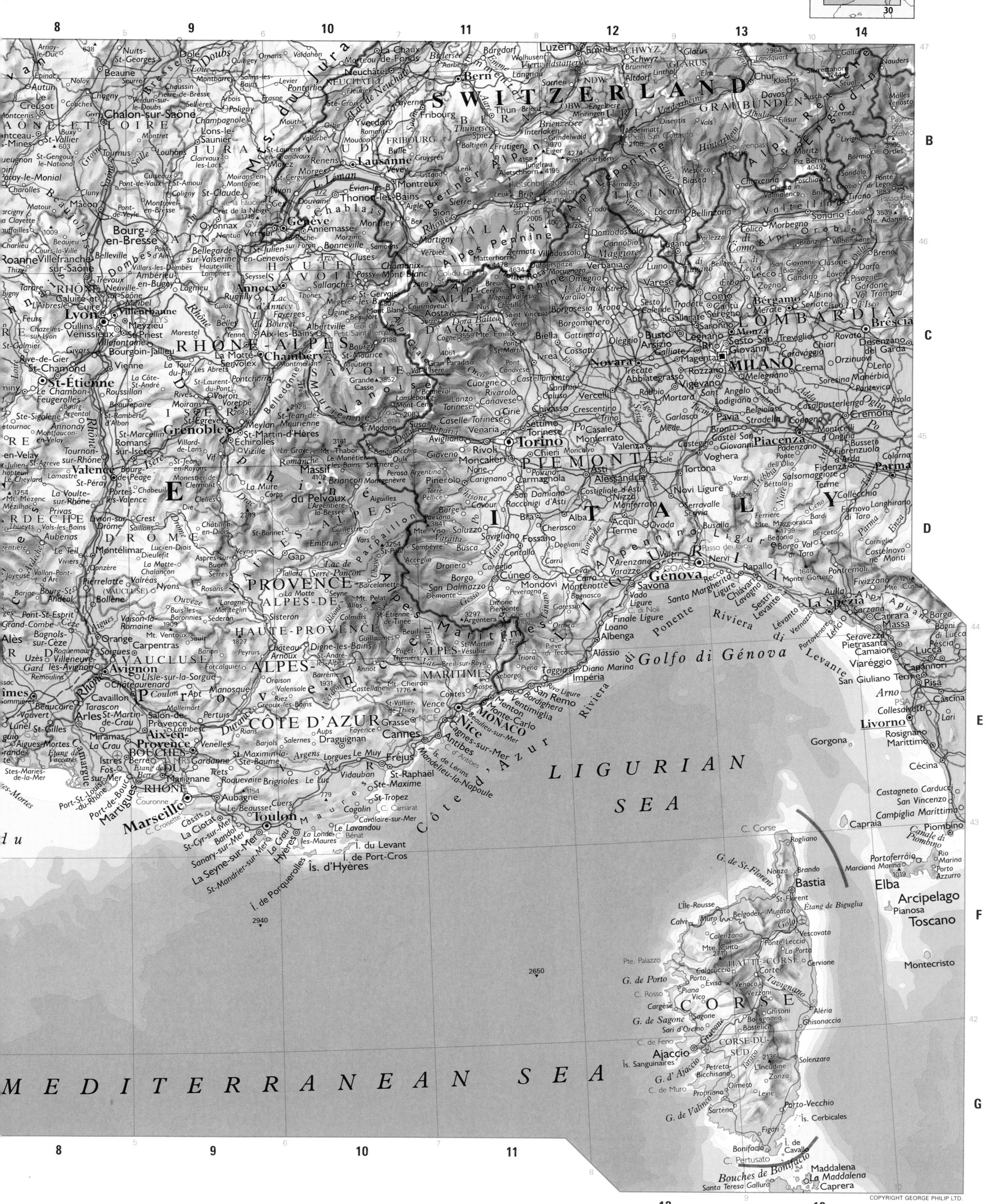
SWITZERLAND
ITALY
FRANCE
LIGURIAN SEA
MEDITERRANEAN SEA
Golfo di Génova
Riviera di Ponente
Riviera di Levante
Côte d'Azur
CÔTE D'AZUR
PROVENCE
RHÔNE-ALPES
PIEMONTE
LOMBARDIA
VALLE D'AOSTA
LIGURIA
CORSE
HAUTE-CORSE
CORSE-DU-SUD
Arcipelago Toscano
Bouches de Bonifacio
Alpi Pennine
Alpes Maritimes
Berner Alpen
Alpi Lepontine
L. Léman
Genève
Lausanne
Bern
Lyon
Grenoble
Chambéry
Annecy
Avignon
Marseille
Toulon
Nice
MONACO
Cannes
Torino
MILANO
Génova
Savona
La Spezia
Livorno
Pisa
Bastia
Ajaccio
Corse
Elba
Bonifacio
Chalon-sur-Saône
St-Étienne
Valence
Aix-en-Provence
Arles
Novara
Alessandria
Asti
Cúneo
Piacenza
Parma
Brescia
Bérgamo
Como
Lugano
Sion
Massif du Pelvoux
Mt. Blanc
Matterhorn
Gran Paradiso
Mte. Viso
Montecristo
Capraia
Gorgona
Pianosa
Maddalena
Caprera
B
C
D
E
F
G
8
9
10
11
12
13
14

50 0 25 50 75 100 125 150 175 km
50 0 25 50 75 100 125 miles
NORTH SEA
BALTIC SEA
UNITED KINGDOM
DENMARK
NETHERLANDS
BELGIUM
LUXEMBOURG
GERMANY
FRANCE
SWITZERLAND
LIECHTENSTEIN
AUSTRIA
CZECH R
SLOVENIA
ITALY
MONACO
SAN MARINO
ADRIATIC SEA
Golfo di Génova
Golfo di Venézia
AMSTERDAM
's-Gravenhage (Den Haag)
ROTTERDAM
BRUSSEL (Bruxelles)
LUXEMBOURG
PARIS
BERLIN
HAMBURG
MÜNCHEN (Munich)
PRAHA (Prague)
MILANO
TORINO (Turin)
LYON
MARSEILLE
Ljubljana
Zagreb
Nordfriesische Inseln
Ostfriesische Inseln
Deutsche Bucht
Kieler Bucht
Mecklenburger Bucht
Fehmarn Bælt
Niedersachsen
Nordrhein-Westfalen
Sachsen-Anhalt
Brandenburg
Mecklenburg
Hessen
Thüringer Wald
Sachsen
Rheinland-Pfalz
Bayern
Baden-Württemberg
Schwäbische Alb
Schwarzwald
Erzgebirge
Böhmerwald
Harz
Ardennes
Picardie
Île-de-France
Champagne
Lorraine
Alsace
Bourgogne
Franche-Comté
Massif Central
Provence
Dauphiné
Alpes Maritimes
Tirol
Tauern
Steiermark
Kärnten
Karawanken
Dolomiti
Lombardia
Piemonte
Liguria
Istra
Karnische Alpen
ft m
12000 4000
9000 3000
6000 2000
4500 1500
3000 1000
1500 500
600 200
0 0
50 150
100 300
200 600
500 1500
1000 3000
2000 6000
m ft
Projection: Conical with two standard parallels

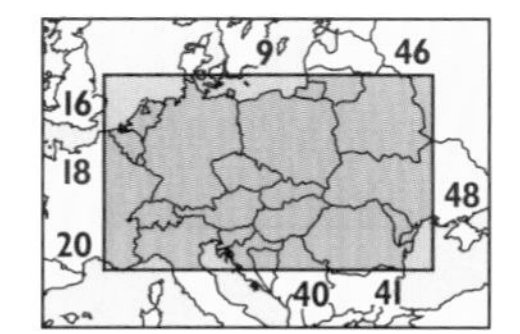

East from Greenwich

GERMANY AND SWITZERLAND 1:2 100 000

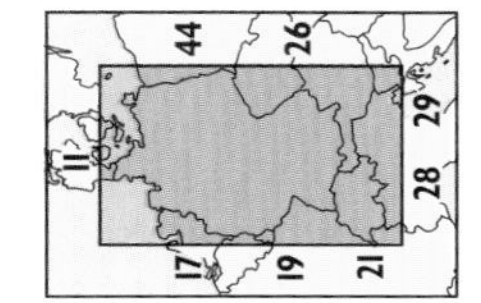

Underlined towns give their name to the administrative area in which they stand.

Projection : Lambert's Conformal Conic

East from Greenwich

GERMANY
CZECH REP.
AUSTRIA
ITALY
SWITZERLAND
SLOVENIA
THÜRINGEN
BAYERN
OBERFRANKEN
UNTERFRANKEN
MITTELFRANKEN
OBERPFALZ
NIEDERBAYERN
OBERBAYERN
SCHWABEN
ZÁPADOČESKÝ
STŘEDOČESKÝ
SEVEROČESKÝ
JIHOČESKÝ
NIEDERÖSTERR
OBERÖSTERREICH
SALZBURG
STEIERMARK
KÄRNTEN
OST-TIROL
VORARLBERG
TRENTINO-ALTO ADIGE
FRIULI-VENEZIA GIULIA
VENETO
LOMBARDIA
Dresden
Chemnitz
Erfurt
Praha
Plzeň
Nürnberg
Regensburg
Stuttgart
Augsburg
München
Salzburg
Linz
Innsbruck
Graz
Klagenfurt
Ljubljana
Trieste
Venézia
Bolzano
Trento
Brescia
Vicenza
Ulm
Würzburg
Hohe Tauern
Zillertaler Alpen
Lechtaler Alpen
Karnische Alpen
Golfo di Venézia
Projection : Lambert's Conformal Conic

Underlined towns give their name to the administrative area in which they stand.

Underlined towns give their name to th
administrative area in which they stand

ministrative divisions in Croatia:

Brodsko-Posavska
Koprivničko-Križevačka
Krapinsko-Zagorska
4. Medimurska
6. Požeško-Slavonska
7. Varaždinska
8. Virovitičko-Podravska
10. Zagrebačka

Inter-entity boundaries as agreed at the 1995 Dayton Peace Agreement.

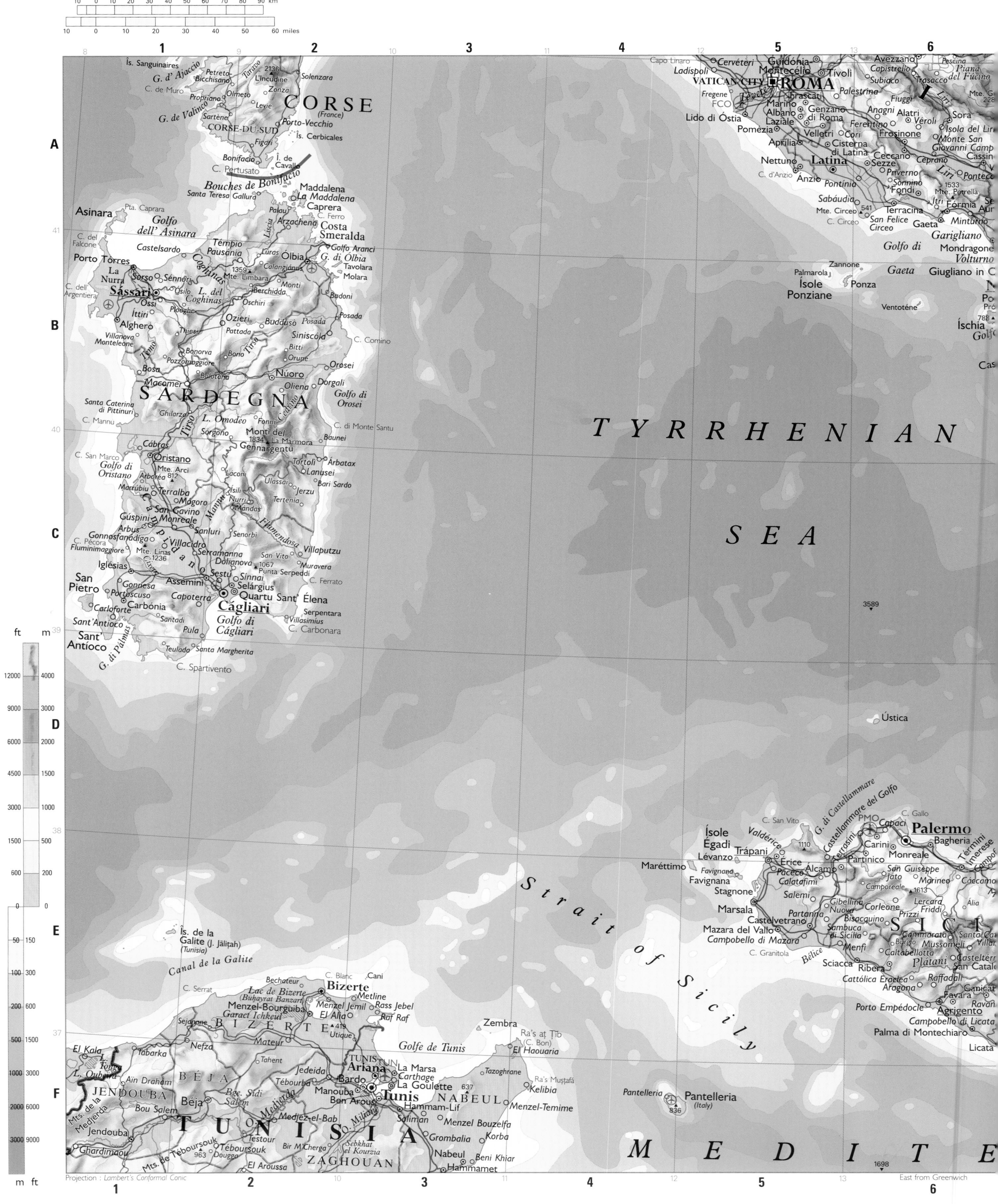
CORSE
(France)
CORSE-DU-SUD
Bouches de Bonifacio
SARDEGNA
Cágliari
Sássari
Nuoro
Oristano
TYRRHENIAN SEA
Strait of Sicily
ROMA
VATICAN CITY
Latina
Ísole Ponziane
Palermo
Trápani
Ísole Égadi
Ústica
Pantelleria
(Italy)
Bizerte
Tunis
Ariana
BIZERTE
BÉJA
JENDOUBA
NABEUL
ZAGHOUAN
TUNISIA
Golfe de Tunis
Canal de la Galite
Ís. de la Galite (J. Jálitah)
(Tunisia)
MEDITE
Projection : Lambert's Conformal Conic
East from Greenwich

COPYRIGHT GEORGE PHILIP LTD.

Underlined towns give their name to the administrative area in which they stand.

10 0 10 20 30 40 50 60 70 80 90 km

10 0 10 20 30 40 50 60 miles

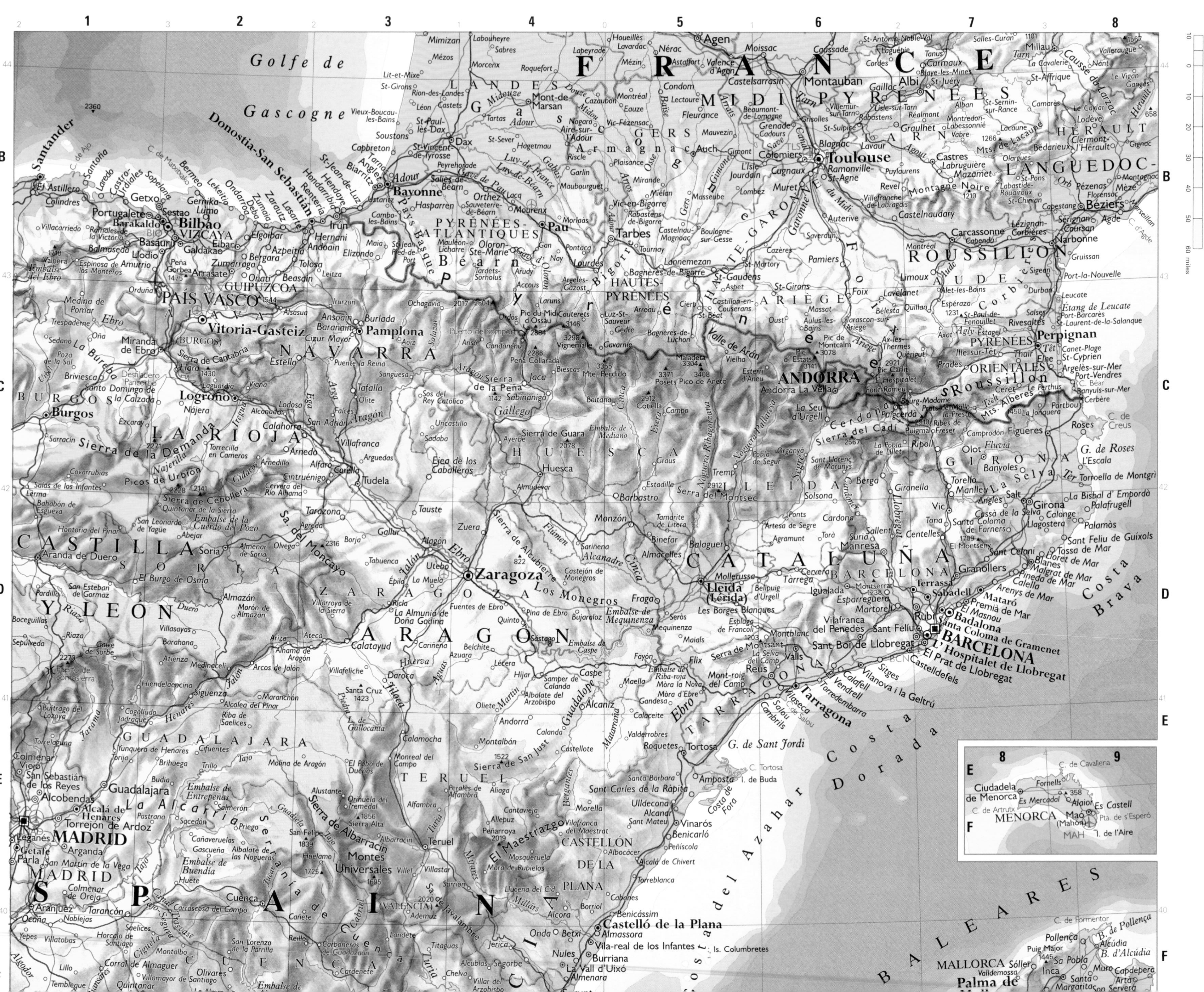

MEDITERRANEAN SEA
ALGERIA
ISLAS BALEARES
Golfo de Valencia
Costa Blanca
Costa del Sol
CASTILLA-LA MANCHA
MURCIA
ALBACETE
CIUDAD REAL
ALICANTE
VALENCIA
GRANADA
ALMERÍA
JAÉN
Valencia
Alicante
Murcia
Cartagena
Albacete
Granada
Almería
Elche
Lorca
Linares
Úbeda
Guadix
Motril
Adra
Águilas
Benidorm
Denia
Gandia
Torrevieja
Mar Menor
G. de Almería
G. de Mazarrón
Sierra de Segura
Sierra de Alcaraz
Sierra Nevada
EIVISSA (IBIZA)
Eivissa (Ibiza)
Formentera
Cabrera
Palma
B. de Palma
Alborán (Sp.)
Melilla (Sp.)
Islas Chafarinas (Sp.)
Nador
ALGER (Algiers)
Blida
Médéa
Tipasa
Cherchell
Ténès
Ech Cheliff
Mostaganem
Oran (Ouahran)
Arzew
Golfe d'Arzew
Relizane
Mascara
Sidi-bel-Abbès
Aïn Témouchent
Tiaret
Tissemsilt
Miliana
Khemis Miliana
Ghazaouet
Beni Saf
AÏN DEFLA
TISSEMSILT
RELIZANE
MASCARA
TIARET
DJELFA
MÉDÉA
MOSTAGANEM
ORAN
AÏN TÉMOUCHENT
Projection : Lambert's Conformal Conic
West from Greenwich
East from Greenwich
COPYRIGHT GEORGE PHILIP LTD.

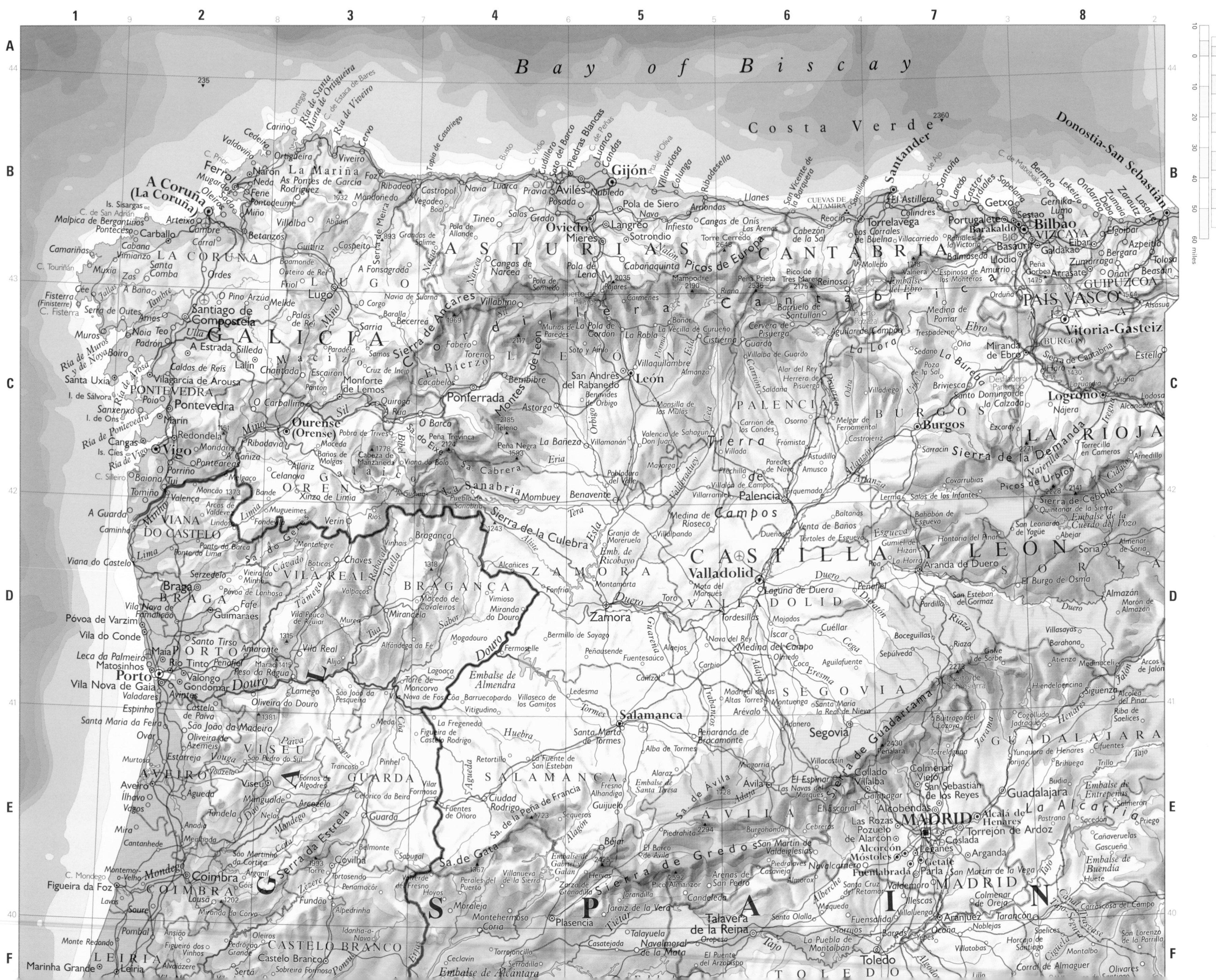
10 0 10 20 30 40 50 60 70 80 90 km
10 0 10 20 30 40 50 60 miles
A
B
C
D
E
F
1
2
3
4
5
6
7
8
Bay of Biscay
Costa Verde
Donostia-San Sebastián
Bilbao
Vitoria-Gasteiz
PAÍS VASCO
GUIPÚZCOA
VIZCAYA
Santander
CANTABRIA
LA RIOJA
Logroño
Burgos
Gijón
Oviedo
Avilés
ASTURIAS
León
Palencia
Valladolid
CASTILLA Y LEÓN
Salamanca
Zamora
Segovia
Ávila
MADRID
Guadalajara
Toledo
A Coruña (La Coruña)
Ferrol
Santiago de Compostela
GALICIA
Lugo
Ourense (Orense)
Pontevedra
Vigo
Ponferrada
Porto
Braga
Coimbra
Viseu
Guarda
Aveiro
Castelo Branco
Plasencia
Talavera de la Reina
Picos de Europa
Sierra de Gredos
Sierra de Guadarrama
Serra da Estrela
Douro
Duero
Tajo
Ebro
Miño
SPAIN

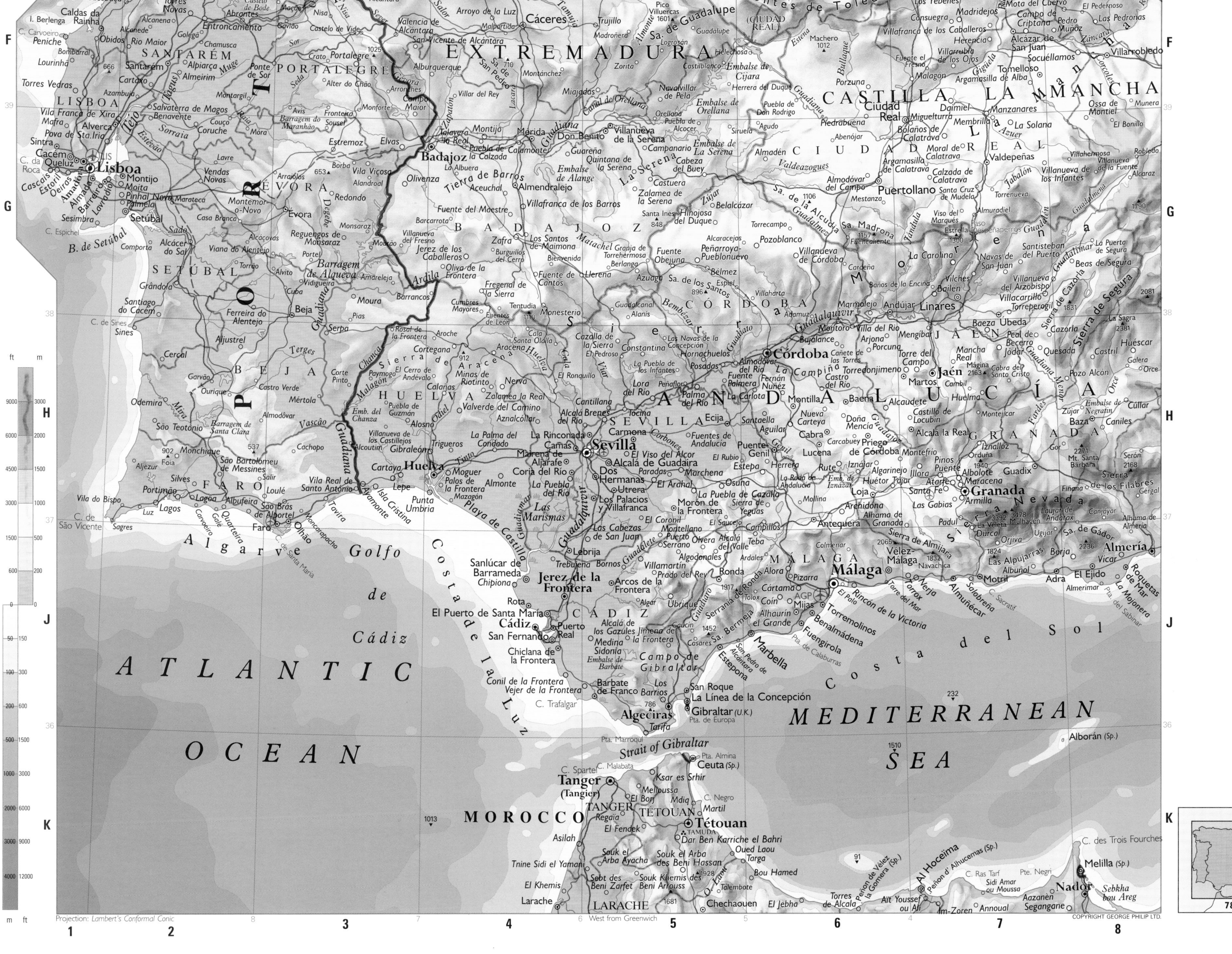
ATLANTIC OCEAN
MEDITERRANEAN SEA
Golfo de Cádiz
Costa de la Luz
Costa del Sol
Strait of Gibraltar
Algarve
PORTUGAL
EXTREMADURA
CASTILLA LA MANCHA
ANDALUCÍA
MOROCCO
SANTARÉM
LISBOA
PORTALEGRE
ÉVORA
SETÚBAL
BEJA
FARO
BADAJOZ
CÁCERES
CIUDAD REAL
CÓRDOBA
JAÉN
GRANADA
SEVILLA
HUELVA
MÁLAGA
CÁDIZ
TANGER
TETOUAN
LARACHE
Sierra Morena
Sierra Nevada
Sierra de Segura
Montes de Toledo
Lisboa
Setúbal
Évora
Beja
Faro
Badajoz
Cáceres
Mérida
Huelva
Sevilla
Córdoba
Jaén
Granada
Almería
Málaga
Marbella
Cádiz
Jerez de la Frontera
Algeciras
Gibraltar (U.K.)
La Línea de la Concepción
Tarifa
Ceuta (Sp.)
Tanger (Tangier)
Tétouan
Larache
Melilla (Sp.)
Nador
Al Hoceima
Chechaouen
Puertollano
Ciudad Real
Linares
Lagos
Sines
Guadiana
Guadalquivir
Tejo
Alborán (Sp.)
Projection: Lambert's Conformal Conic
West from Greenwich
COPYRIGHT GEORGE PHILIP LTD.
F
G
H
J
K
1
2
3
4
5
6
7
8
32
33
78
m
ft

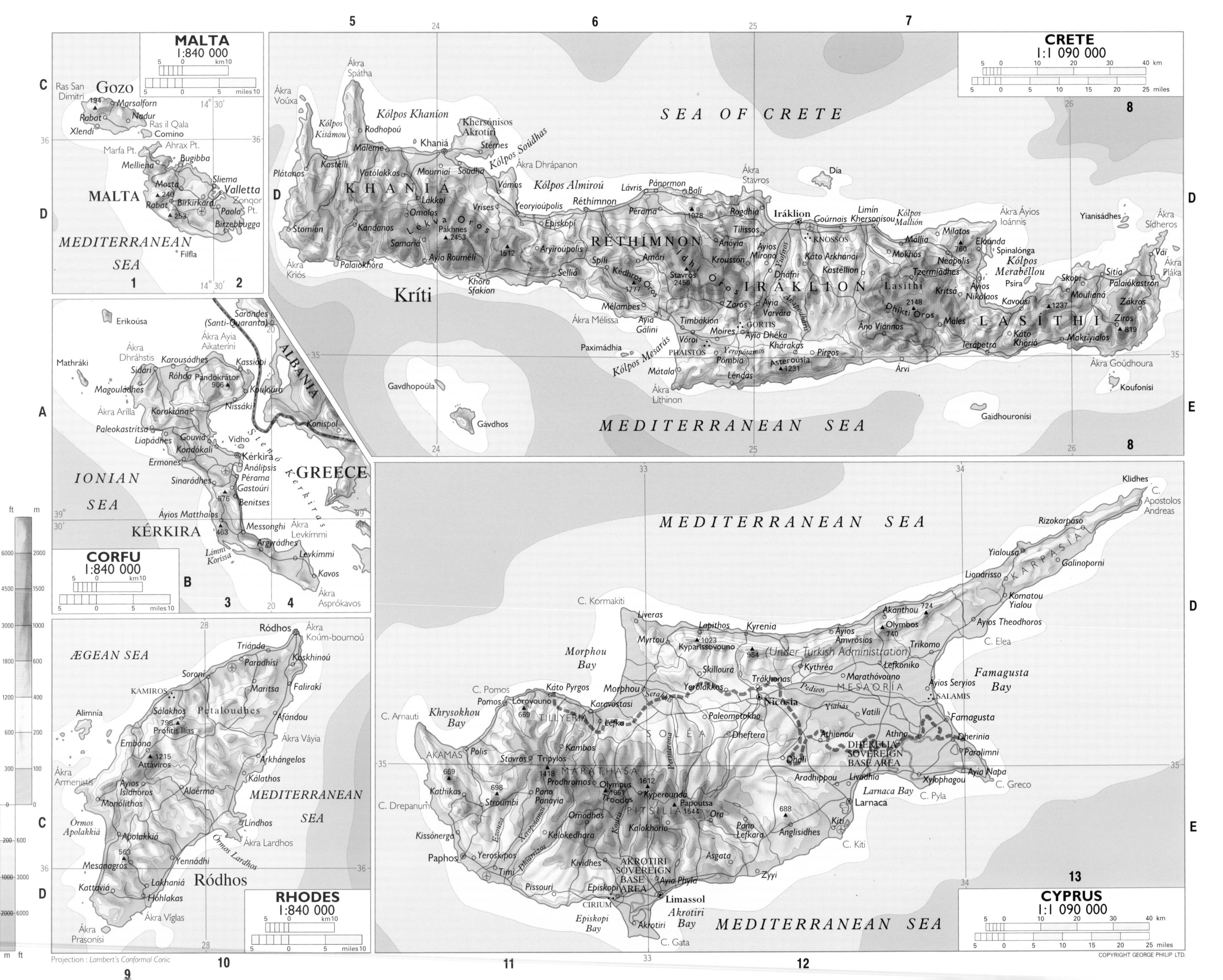

MALTA
1:840 000
Gozo
MALTA
Valletta
MEDITERRANEAN SEA
CRETE
1:1 090 000
SEA OF CRETE
KHANIÁ
RÉTHIMNON
IRÁKLION
LASÍTHI
Kríti
Iráklion
Khaniá
Réthimnon
MEDITERRANEAN SEA
CORFU
1:840 000
IONIAN SEA
KÉRKIRA
Kérkira
ALBANIA
GREECE
RHODES
1:840 000
ÆGEAN SEA
MEDITERRANEAN SEA
Ródhos
CYPRUS
1:1 090 000
MEDITERRANEAN SEA
Morphou Bay
Famagusta Bay
Nicosia
Famagusta
Larnaca
Limassol
Paphos
Kyrenia
(Under Turkish Administration)
AKROTIRI SOVEREIGN BASE AREA
DHEKELIA SOVEREIGN BASE AREA
Projection : Lambert's Conformal Conic
COPYRIGHT GEORGE PHILIP LTD.

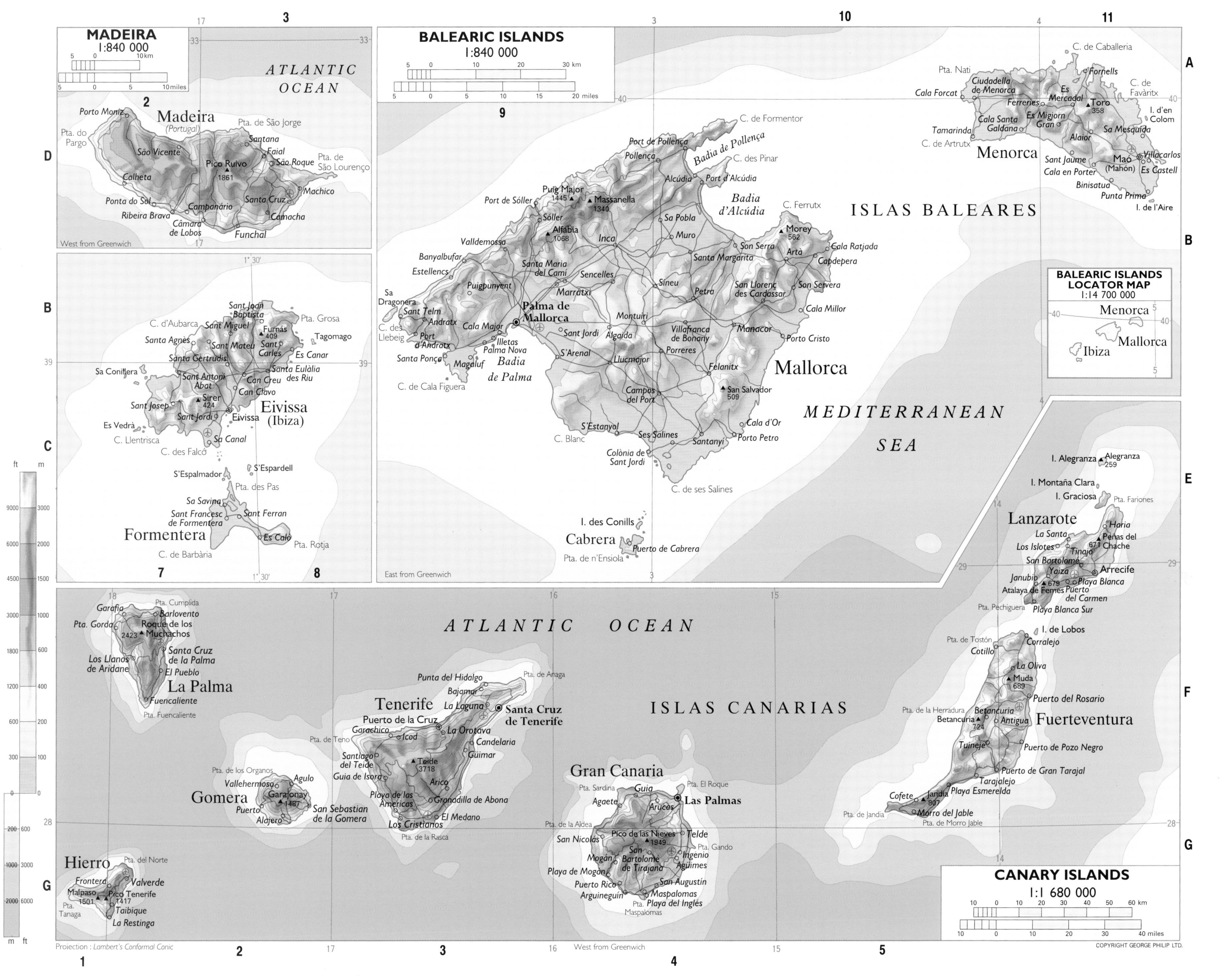
MADEIRA
1:840 000
ATLANTIC OCEAN
Madeira (Portugal)
Porto Moniz
Pta. do Pargo
Pta. de São Jorge
Santana
Faial
São Roque
Pta. de São Lourenço
São Vicente
Pico Ruivo 1861
Calheta
Machico
Santa Cruz
Camacha
Ponta do Sol
Campanário
Ribeira Brava
Câmara de Lobos
Funchal
West from Greenwich
BALEARIC ISLANDS
1:840 000
ISLAS BALEARES
MEDITERRANEAN SEA
Mallorca
C. de Formentor
Badia de Pollença
C. des Pinar
Port de Pollença
Pollença
Alcúdia
Port d'Alcúdia
Badia d'Alcúdia
C. Ferrutx
Port de Sóller
Puig Major 1445
Massanella 1340
Sóller
Alfàbia 1068
Inca
Sa Pobla
Muro
Morey 562
Cala Ratjada
Capdepera
Artà
Son Serra
Santa Margarita
Valldemossa
Banyalbufar
Estellencs
Santa Maria del Camí
Sencelles
Sineu
Petra
Sant Llorenç des Cardassar
Son Servera
Cala Millor
Sa Dragonera
Sant Telm
Andratx
Puigpunyent
Marratxí
Palma de Mallorca
Montuïri
Villafranca de Bonany
Manacor
Porto Cristo
C. des Llebeig
Port d'Andratx
Cala Major
Sant Jordi
Algaida
Porreres
Illetas
Palma Nova
Badia de Palma
Santa Ponça
Magaluf
S'Arenal
Llucmajor
Felanitx
C. de Cala Figuera
Campos del Port
San Salvador 509
S'Estanyol
Ses Salines
Santanyí
Cala d'Or
Porto Petro
C. Blanc
Colònia de Sant Jordi
C. de ses Salines
I. des Conills
Cabrera
Puerto de Cabrera
Pta. de n'Ensiola
East from Greenwich
Menorca
C. de Caballeria
Pta. Nati
Fornells
Ciudadella de Menorca
Cala Forcat
Es Mercadal
Toro 358
C. de Favàritx
Ferreries
Es Migjorn Gran
I. d'en Colom
Cala Santa Galdana
Tamarinda
C. de Artrutx
Alaior
Sa Mesquida
Villacarlos
Sant Jaume
Mao (Mahón)
Es Castell
Cala en Porter
Binisatua
Punta Prima
I. de l'Aire
BALEARIC ISLANDS LOCATOR MAP
1:14 700 000
Menorca
Mallorca
Ibiza
Sant Joan Baptista
Pta. Grosa
C. d'Aubarca
Sant Miquel
Furnás 409
Tagomago
Santa Agnès
Sant Mateu
Sant Carles
Es Canar
Santa Gertrudis
Santa Eulàlia des Riu
Sa Conillera
Sant Antoni Abat
Can Creu
Can Clavo
Sirer 424
Sant Josep
Sant Jordi
Eivissa
Eivissa (Ibiza)
Es Vedrà
C. Llentrisca
Sa Canal
C. des Falcó
S'Espardell
S'Espalmador
Pta. des Pas
Sa Savina
Sant Francesc de Formentera
Sant Ferran
Formentera
Es Caló
Pta. Rotja
C. de Barbària
CANARY ISLANDS
1:1 680 000
ATLANTIC OCEAN
ISLAS CANARIAS
I. Alegranza
Alegranza 259
I. Montaña Clara
I. Graciosa
Pta. Fariones
Lanzarote
La Santa
Haria
Peñas del Chache 671
Los Islotes
Tinajo
San Bartolomé
Yaiza
Arrecife
Janubio
Playa Blanca
Atalaya de Femes
Puerto del Carmen
Pta. Pechiguera
Playa Blanca Sur
I. de Lobos
Pta. de Tostón
Corralejo
Cotillo
La Oliva
Muda 689
Puerto del Rosario
Pta. de la Herradura
Betancuria 724
Antigua
Fuerteventura
Tuineje
Puerto de Pozo Negro
Puerto de Gran Tarajal
Tarajalejo
Cofete
Jandía 807
Playa Esmerelda
Pta. de Jandía
Morro del Jable
Pta. de Morro Jable
Garafía
Pta. Cumplida
Pta. Gorda
Barlovento
Roque de los Muchachos 2423
Los Llanos de Aridane
Santa Cruz de la Palma
El Pueblo
La Palma
Fuencaliente
Pta. Fuencaliente
Punta del Hidalgo
Pta. de Anaga
Bajamar
Tenerife
La Laguna
Santa Cruz de Tenerife
Puerto de la Cruz
Garachico
Icod
La Orotava
Candelaria
Pta. de Teno
Güimar
Santiago del Teide
Teide 3718
Guia de Isora
Arico
Playa de las Americas
Granadilla de Abona
El Medano
Los Cristianos
Pta. de la Rasca
Pta. de los Organos
Vallehermoso
Agulo
Gomera
Garajonay 1487
Puerto
San Sebastian de la Gomera
Alajeró
Gran Canaria
Pta. Sardina
Guía
Pta. El Roque
Agaete
Arucas
Las Palmas
Pta. de la Aldea
Pico de las Nieves 1949
Telde
San Nicolás
Pta. Gando
Mogán
San Bartolomé de Tirajana
Ingenio
Agüimes
Playa de Mogán
Puerto Rico
San Augustín
Arguineguín
Maspalomas
Playa del Inglés
Pta. Maspalomas
Hierro
Pta. del Norte
Frontera
Valverde
Malpaso 1501
Pico Tenerife 1417
Pta. Tanaga
Taibique
La Restinga
Projection : Lambert's Conformal Conic
West from Greenwich
COPYRIGHT GEORGE PHILIP LTD.

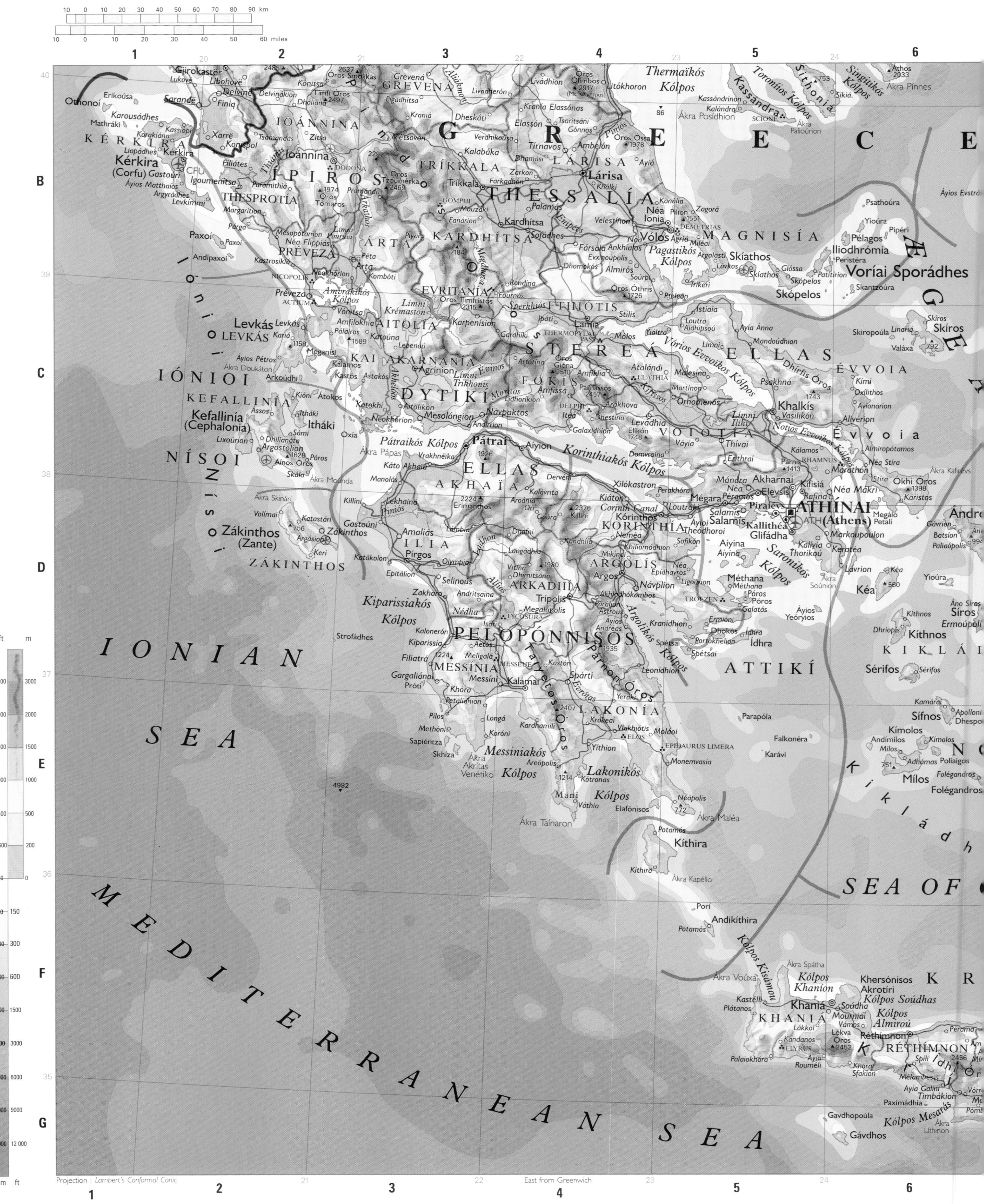
IONIAN SEA
MEDITERRANEAN SEA
GREECE
ATHÍNAI (Athens)
PELOPÓNNISOS
Kérkira (Corfu)
Kefallinía (Cephalonia)
Zákinthos (Zante)
Itháki
Levkás
Pátrai
Lárisa
Vólos
Kíthira
Khaniá
Projection : Lambert's Conformal Conic
East from Greenwich

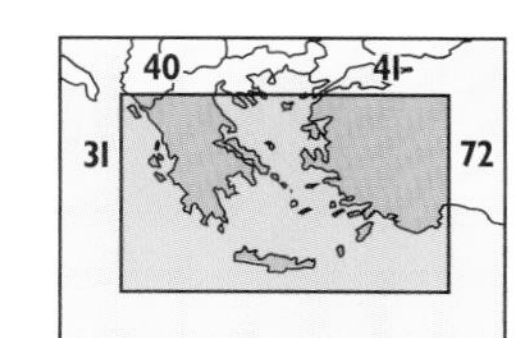

7 8 9 10 11 12

B
C
D
E
F
G

TURKEY

LÉSVOS
VÓRIOS AIYAÍON
KHÍOS
SÁMOS
DHODHEKÁNISOS
NÓTIOS AIYAÍON
LASÍTHI
ÇANAKKALE
BALIKESİR
KÜTAHYA
ESKİŞEHİR
MANİSA
İZMİR
UŞAK
AFYON
AYDIN
DENİZLİ
BURDUR
ISPARTA
MUĞLA
ANTALYA

Mysia
Lydia
Caria
Lycia

Çanakkale
Gökçeada
Bozcaada
Límnos
Ayios Evstrátios
Balıkesir
Edremit
Ayvalık
Bergama
Soma
Akhisar
Manisa
İZMİR (Smyrna)
Çeşme
Khíos
Psará
Sámos
Kuşadası
Aydın
Nazilli
Denizli
Uşak
Kütahya
Eskişehir
Afyon (Afyonkarahisar)
İsparta
Burdur
Muğla
Milas
Bodrum
Marmaris
Fethiye
Kos
Kálimnos
Léros
Pátmos
Ikaría
Fournoi
Mikonos
Náxos
Amorgós
Astipálaia
Thíra (Santorini)
Anáfi
Tilos
Nísiros
Sími
Khálki
Ródhos (Rhodes)
Kárpathos
Kásos
Iráklion
Ierápetra
Sitía
Megiste (Kastellórizon)

Kólpos Kallonis
Çandarlı Körfezi
İzmir Körfezi
Kuşadası Körfezi
Güllük Körfezi
Gökova Körfezi
Fethiye Körfezi
Finike Körfezi
Edremit Körfezi
Kólpos Merabéllou
Stenón Kárpathos
Stenón Kásos

Madra Dağı
Kaz Dağı
Alaçam Dağları
Simav Dağları
Murat Dağı
Boz Dağları
Aydın Dağları
Gölgeli Dağları
Ak Dağlar
Bey Dağları
Barla Dağı
Sultan Dağları

Büyük Menderes
Küçükmenderes
Gediz

MEDITERRANEAN SEA

Inter-entity boundaries as agreed at the 1995 Dayton Peace Agreement.

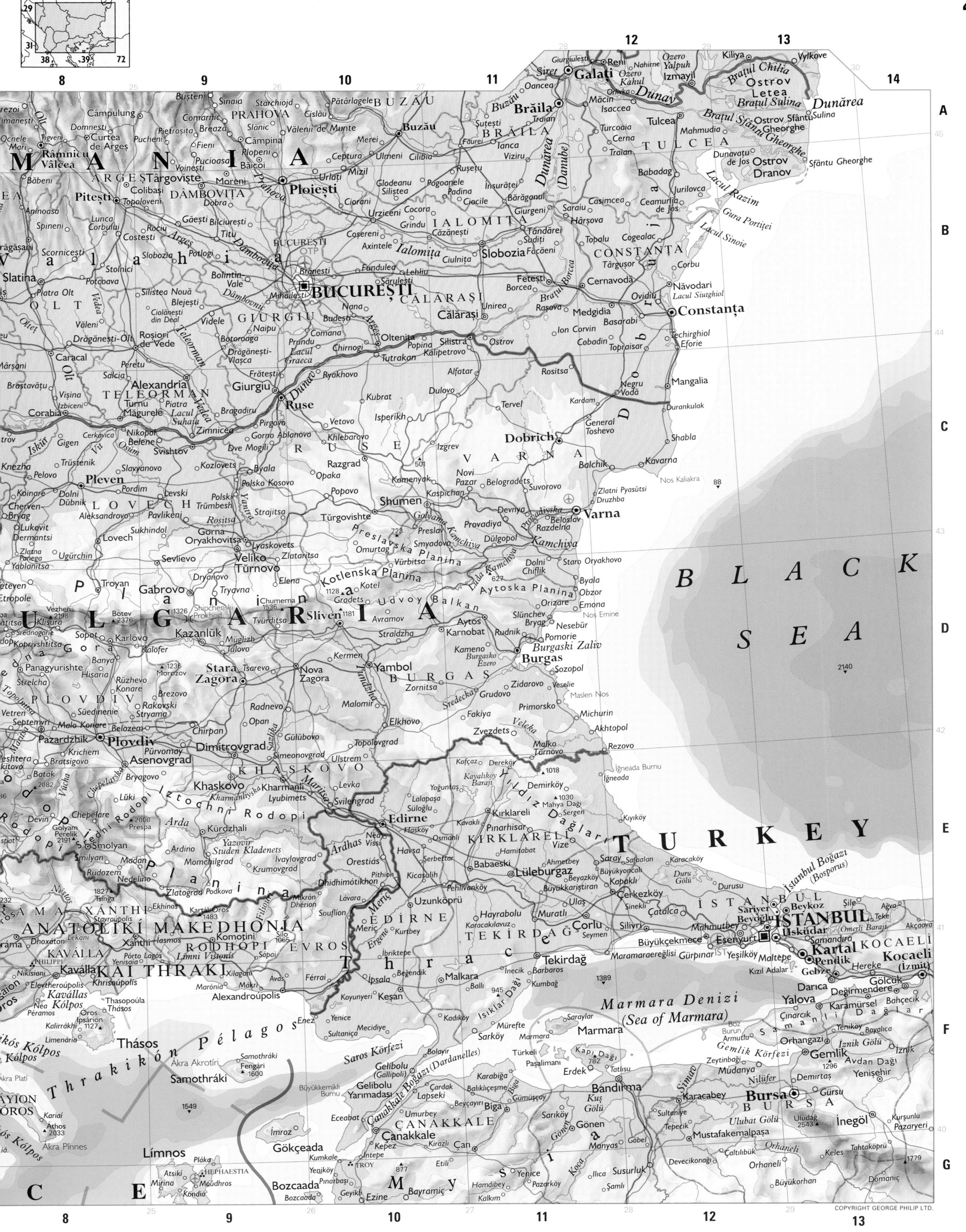

Underlined towns give their name to the administrative area in which they stand.

Administrative divisions in Croatia:
1. Brodsko-Posavska
2. Koprivničko-Križevačka
4. Medimurska
5. Osječko-Baranjska
6. Požeško-Slavonska
8. Virovitičko-Podravska
9. Vukovarsko-Srijemska

Inter-entity boundaries as agreed at the 1995 Dayton Peace Agreement.

Underlined towns give their name to the administrative area in which they stand.

BALTIC SEA
Gulf of Riga
Irbes šaurums (Kura kurk)
Zatoka Gdańska
Kurshskiy Zaliv
Zalew Wiślany
Hanöbukten
Bornholmsgattet
Kalmarsund
LATVIA
LITHUANIA
KALININGRAD (Russia)
SWEDEN
Gotland (Sweden)
Öland (Sweden)
Bornholm (Denmark)
POMORSKIE
WARMIŃSKO-MAZURSKIE
ZACHODNIO-POMORSKIE
Riga
Jelgava
Jūrmala
Ventspils
Liepāja
Klaipėda
Šiauliai
Kaunas
Kaliningrad
Gdańsk
Gdynia
Elbląg
Olsztyn
Szczecin
Koszalin
Słupsk
Kołobrzeg
Visby
Kalmar
Karlskrona
Växjö
Jönköping
Västervik
Rønne
Hrodna
Suwałki
Ełk
Grudziądz
Marijampolė
Alytus

Underlined towns give their name to the administrative area in which they stand.

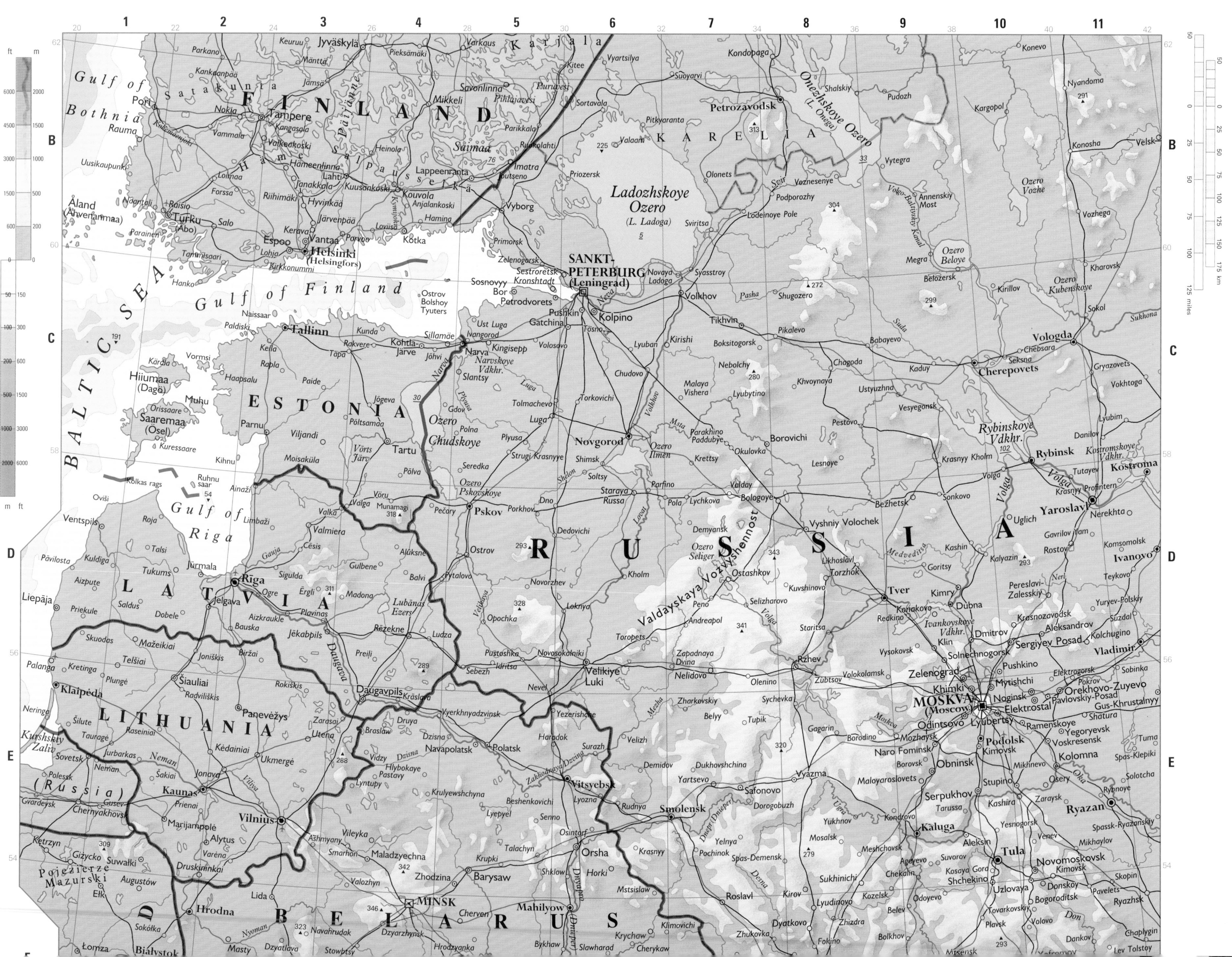
50 0 25 50 75 100 125 150 175 km
50 0 25 50 75 100 125 miles
FINLAND
ESTONIA
LATVIA
LITHUANIA
BELARUS
RUSSIA
KARELIA
BALTIC SEA
Gulf of Finland
Gulf of Riga
Gulf of Bothnia
Ladozhskoye Ozero (L. Ladoga)
Onezhskoye Ozero (L. Onega)
Ozero Chudskoye
SANKT-PETERBURG (Leningrad)
MOSKVA (Moscow)
MINSK
Helsinki (Helsingfors)
Tallinn
Rīga
Vilnius
Kaunas
Tartu
Pskov
Novgorod
Tver
Smolensk
Vitsyebsk
Mahilyow
Daugavpils
Petrozavodsk
Vologda
Cherepovets
Yaroslavl
Tula
Kaluga
Ryazan
Valdayskaya Vozvyshennost
Daugava
Volga
Dnyapro (Dnieper)

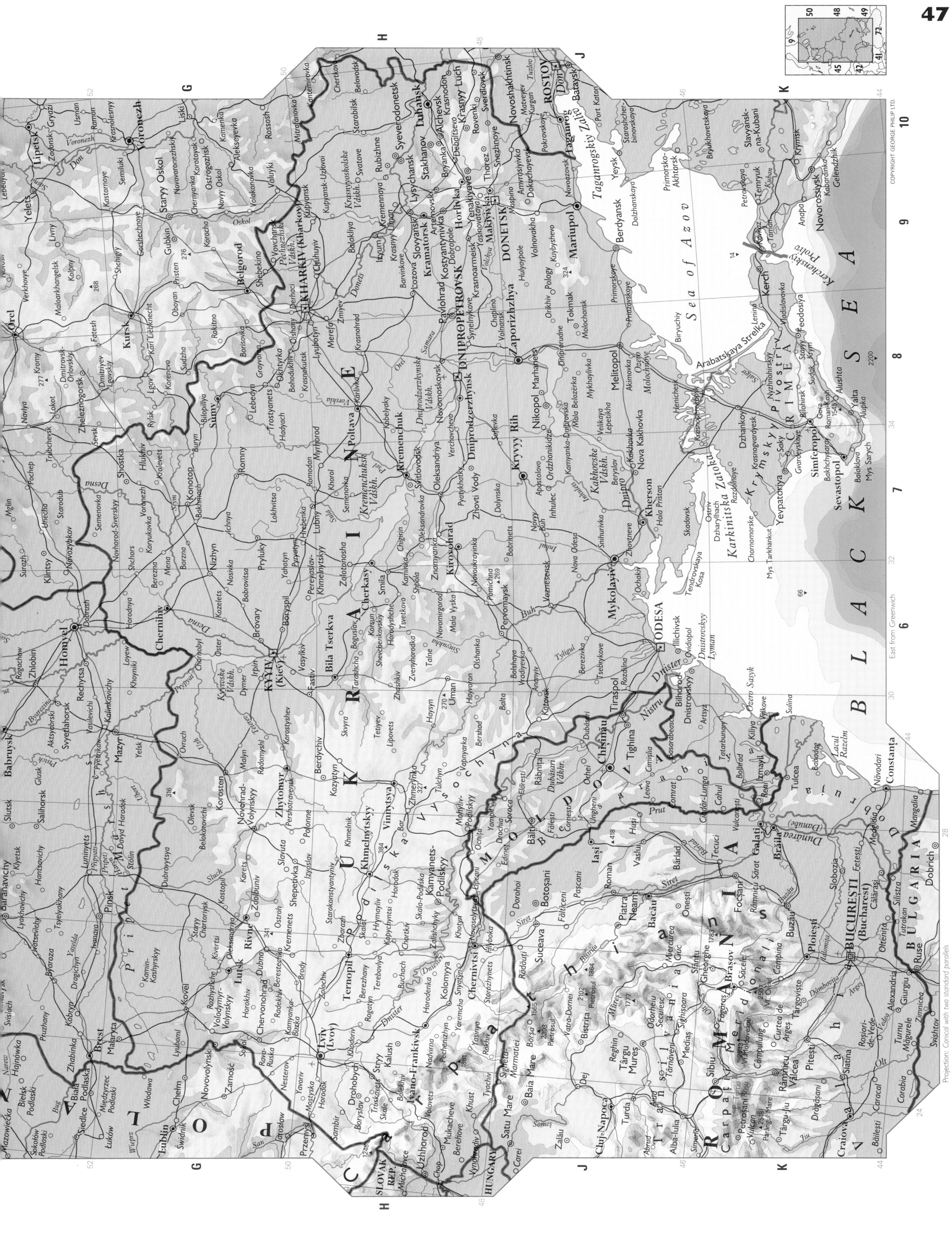
UKRAINE
MOLDOVA
ROMANIA
BULGARIA
B L A C K   S E A
Sea of Azov
CRIMEA
KYIV (Kiev)
KHARKIV (Kharkov)
DNIPROPETROVSK
DONETSK
ODESA
Zaporizhzhya
Kryvyy Rih
Mykolayiv
Kherson
Sevastopol
Simferopol
Lviv (Lvov)
Chişinău
BUCUREŞTI (Bucharest)
Constanţa
Brest
Homyel
Voronezh
Kursk
Belgorod
Rostov
Luhansk
Mariupol
Poltava
Vinnytsya
Zhytomyr
Chernihiv
Cherkasy
Kirovohrad
Sumy
Rivne
Lutsk
Ternopil
Chernivtsi
Khmelnytskyy
Uzhhorod
Ivano-Frankivsk
Iaşi
Galaţi
Brăila
Ploieşti
Braşov
Cluj-Napoca
Craiova
Ruse
Tiraspol
Pripet Marshes
SLOVAK REP.
HUNGARY
Projection: Conical with two standard parallels
East from Greenwich
COPYRIGHT GEORGE PHILIP LTD.

THE VOLGA BASIN AND THE CAUCASUS 1:4 200 000

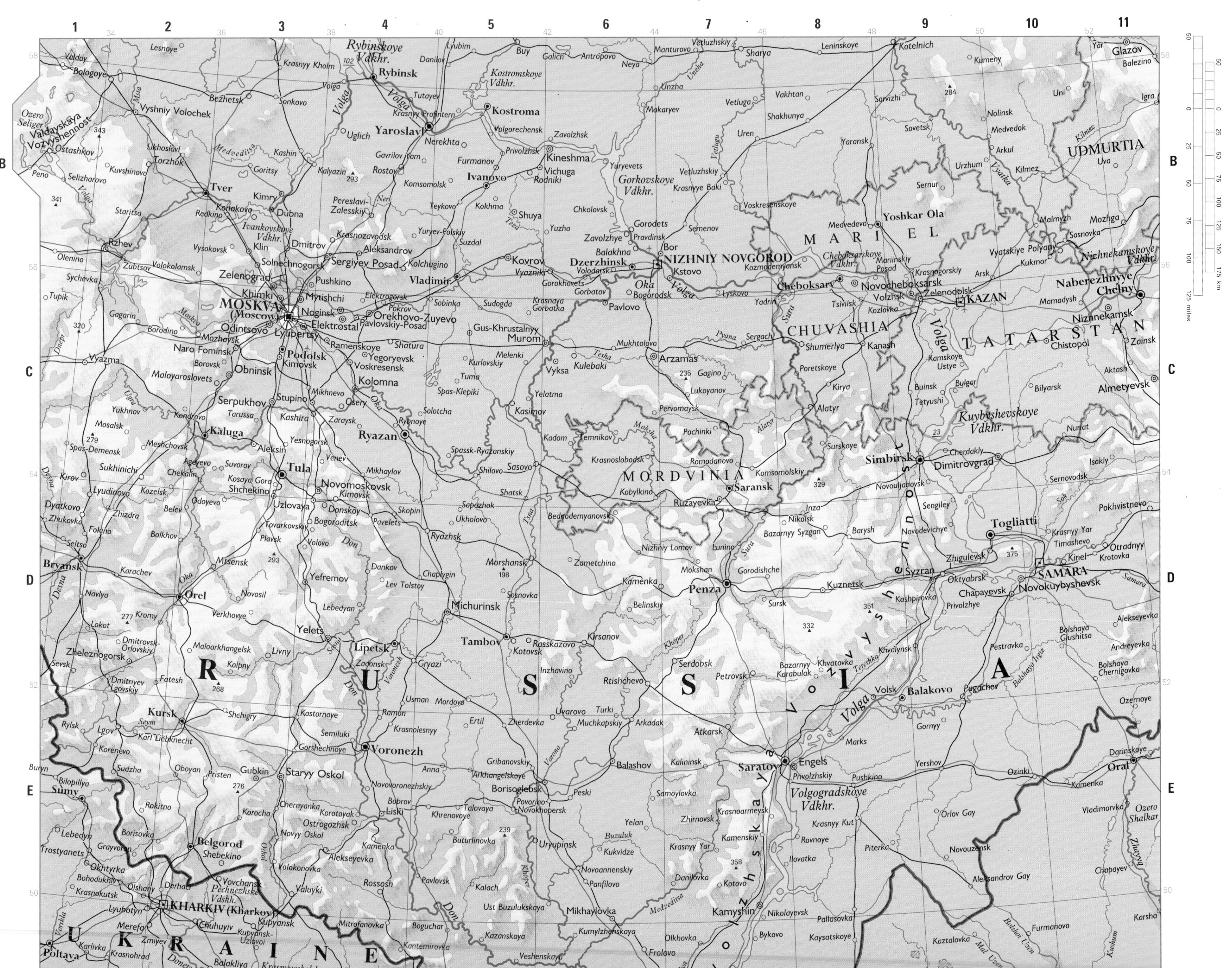

KAZAKSTAN
CASPIAN SEA
BLACK SEA
Sea of Azov
Caspian Depression
Ryn Peski
KALMYKIA
Chernyye Zemli
DAGESTAN
CHECHENIA
INGUSHETIA
NORTH OSSETIA
KABARDINO-BALKARIA
KARACHEY-CHERKESSIA
ADYGEA
ABKHAZIA
AJARIA
GEORGIA
ARMENIA
AZERBAIJAN
TURKEY
CRIMEA
Caucasus Mountains
Kuzey Anadolu Dağları
VOLGOGRAD
Astrakhan
ROSTOV
DONETSK
DNIPROPETROVSK
TBILISI
YEREVAN
BAKI
Krasnodar
Stavropol
Makhachkala
Groznyy
Vladikavkaz
Nalchik
Sochi
Sokhumi
Batumi
Kutaisi
Samsun
Trabzon
Zaporizhzhya
Mariupol
Luhansk
Taganrog
Novorossiysk
Kerch
Volga
Kuban
Manych
Terek
Kür
Projection: Conical with two standard parallels
East from Greenwich
COPYRIGHT GEORGE PHILIP LTD.

100 0 100 200 300 400 500 600 700 800 km
100 0 100 200 300 400 500 miles
RUSSIA
1 Adygea
2 Karachey-Cherkessia
3 Kabardino-Balkaria
4 North Ossetia
5 Ingushetia
6 Chechenia
7 Dagestan
8 Mordvinia
9 Chuvashia
10 Mari El
11 Tatarstan
12 Udmurtia
13 Khakassia
AZERBAIJAN
14 Naxçıvan
GEORGIA
15 Ajaria
16 Abkhazia
UKRAINE
17 Crimea
ft m
12 000 4000
9000 3000
6000 2000
3000 1000
1200 400
600 200
0 0
200 600
2000 6000
4000 12 000
m ft
Projection: Conical Orthomorphic with two standard parallels
East from Greenwich
NORWAY
SWEDEN
FINLAND
ESTONIA
LATVIA
LITHUANIA
POLAND
BELARUS
UKRAINE
MOLDOVA
RUSSIA
KAZAKSTAN
UZBEKISTAN
TURKMENISTAN
KYRGYZSTAN
TAJIKISTAN
AFGHANISTAN
IRAN
IRAQ
TURKEY
GEORGIA
ARMENIA
AZERBAIJAN
DENMARK
GERMANY

ASIA : Physical 1:42 000 000

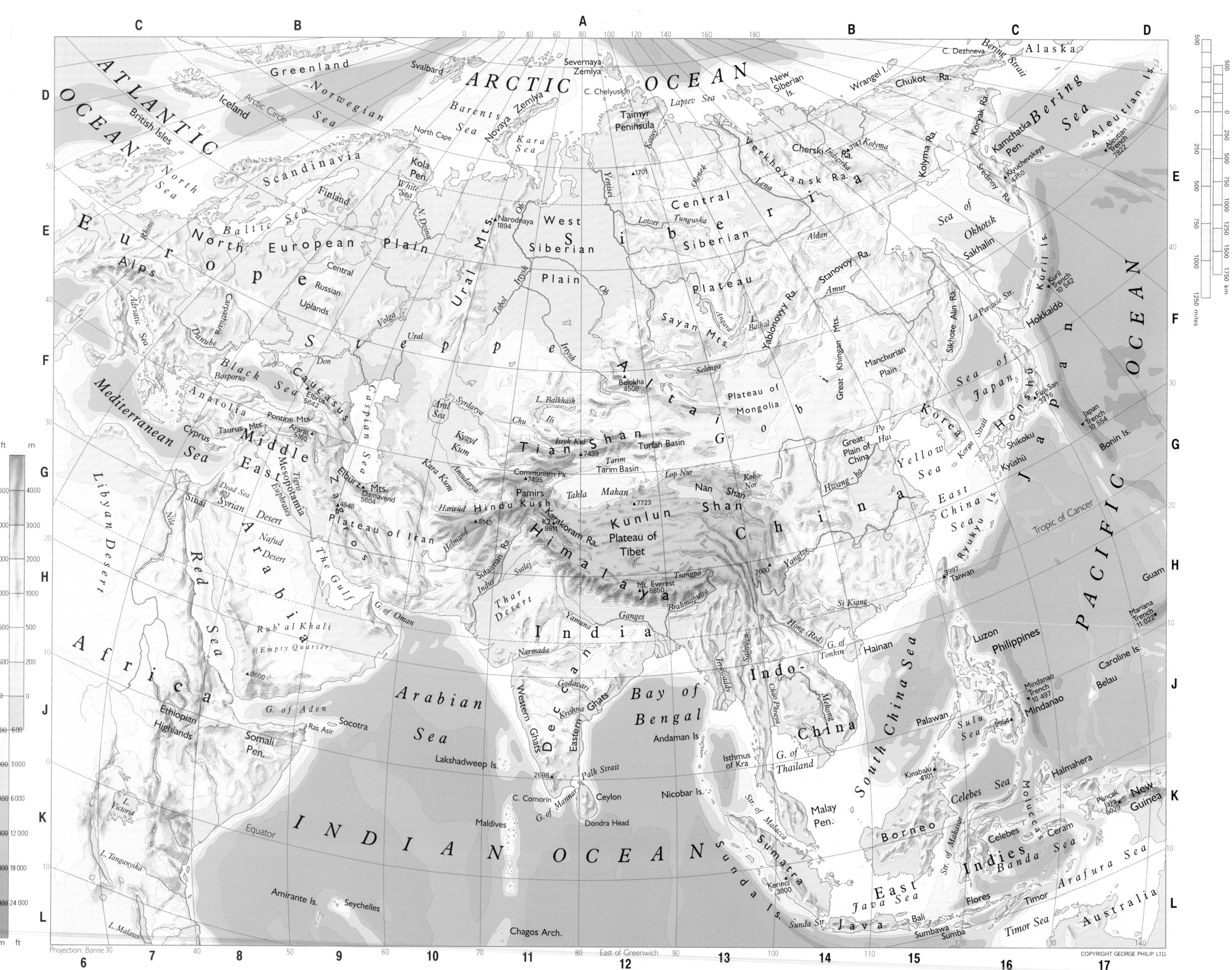

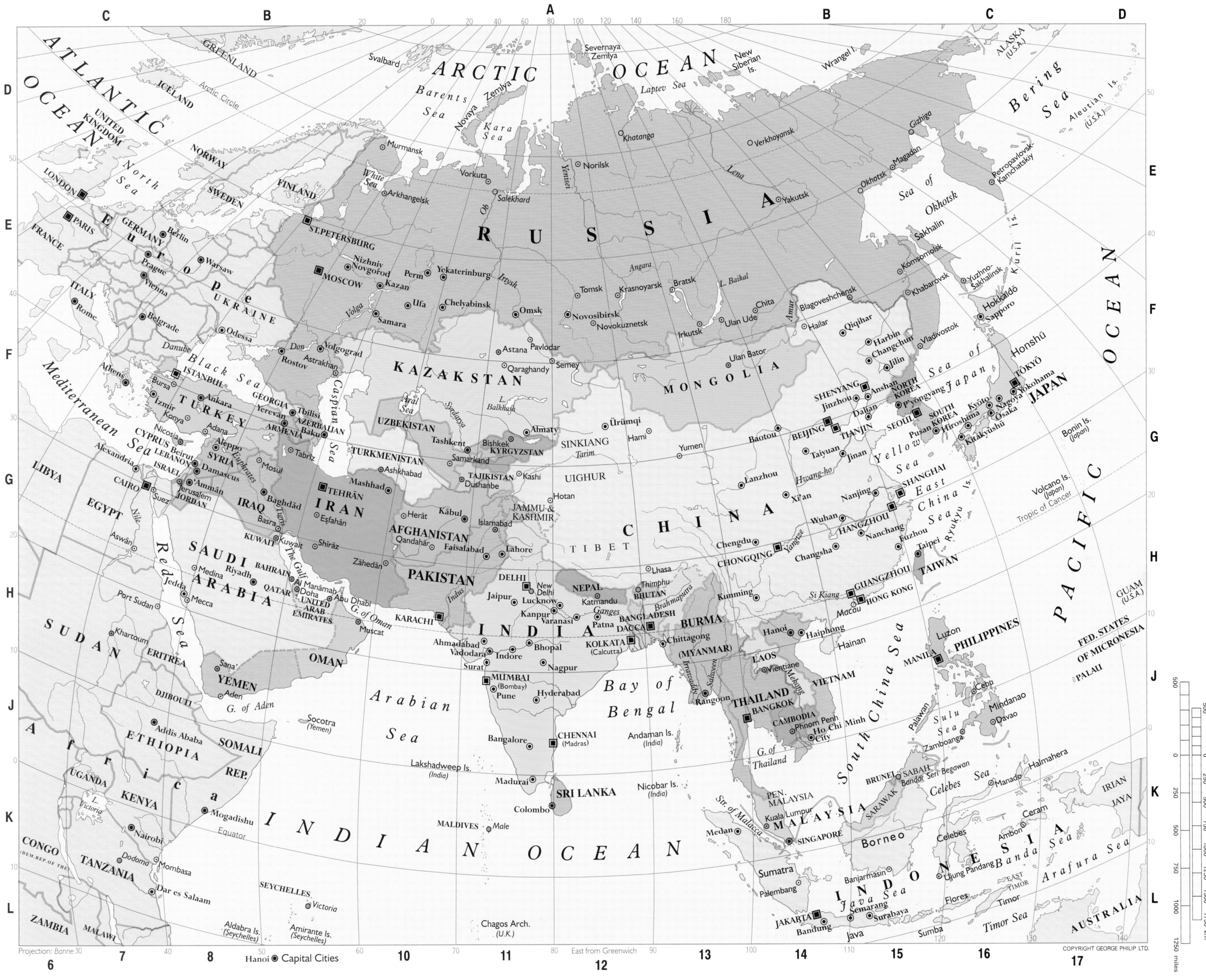
ARCTIC
OCEAN
PACIFIC
OCEAN
INDIAN
OCEAN
ATLANTIC
OCEAN
RUSSIA
KAZAKSTAN
MONGOLIA
CHINA
INDIA
TIBET
SINKIANG
UIGHUR
JAPAN
NORTH KOREA
SOUTH KOREA
TAIWAN
PHILIPPINES
VIETNAM
LAOS
THAILAND
CAMBODIA
BURMA
(MYANMAR)
BANGLADESH
BHUTAN
NEPAL
SRI LANKA
MALDIVES
PAKISTAN
AFGHANISTAN
IRAN
IRAQ
SYRIA
TURKEY
JORDAN
ISRAEL
LEBANON
CYPRUS
SAUDI
ARABIA
YEMEN
OMAN
UNITED
ARAB
EMIRATES
QATAR
BAHRAIN
KUWAIT
GEORGIA
ARMENIA
AZERBAIJAN
TURKMENISTAN
UZBEKISTAN
TAJIKISTAN
KYRGYZSTAN
JAMMU &
KASHMIR
MALAYSIA
SINGAPORE
BRUNEI
INDONESIA
FED. STATES
OF MICRONESIA
PALAU
GUAM
(U.S.A.)
AUSTRALIA
EGYPT
LIBYA
SUDAN
ERITREA
DJIBOUTI
ETHIOPIA
SOMALI
REP.
KENYA
UGANDA
TANZANIA
MALAWI
ZAMBIA
CONGO
(DEM. REP. OF THE)
SEYCHELLES
Africa
Europe
FRANCE
UNITED
KINGDOM
GERMANY
ITALY
UKRAINE
FINLAND
SWEDEN
NORWAY
ICELAND
GREENLAND
Bering Sea
Sea of Okhotsk
Sea of Japan
Yellow Sea
East China Sea
South China Sea
Sulu Sea
Celebes Sea
Java Sea
Banda Sea
Arafura Sea
Timor Sea
Bay of Bengal
Arabian Sea
G. of Aden
G. of Oman
The Gulf
Red Sea
Mediterranean Sea
Black Sea
Caspian Sea
Aral Sea
Kara Sea
Barents Sea
Laptev Sea
North Sea
White Sea
G. of Thailand
Str. of Malacca
TOKYO
BEIJING
SEOUL
SHANGHAI
HONG KONG
MANILA
BANGKOK
DELHI
MUMBAI
(Bombay)
KOLKATA
(Calcutta)
CHENNAI
(Madras)
DACCA
KARACHI
TEHRĀN
MOSCOW
ST. PETERSBURG
ISTANBUL
CAIRO
JAKARTA
LONDON
PARIS
Hanoi
Capital Cities
Projection: Bonne
East from Greenwich
Tropic of Cancer
Equator
Arctic Circle
COPYRIGHT GEORGE PHILIP LTD.
500 0 250 500 750 1000 1250 1500 1750 km
500 0 250 500 750 1000 1250 miles

JAPAN 1:4 200 000

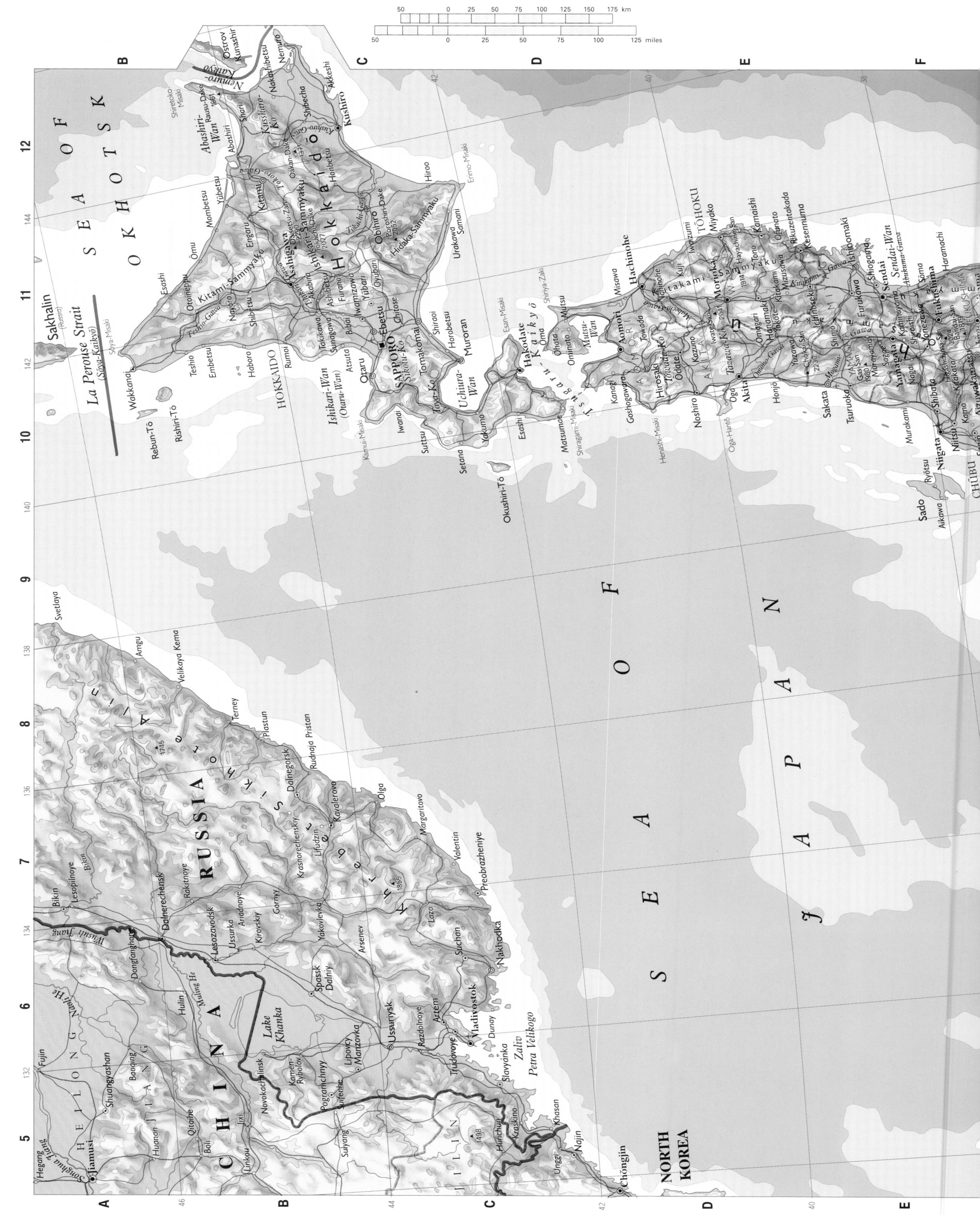

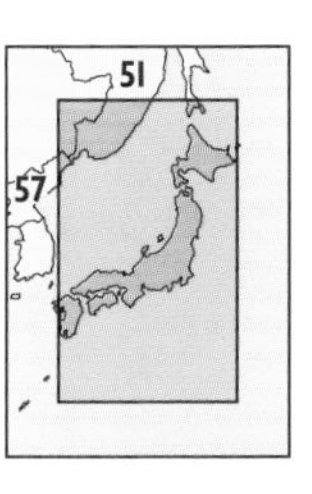

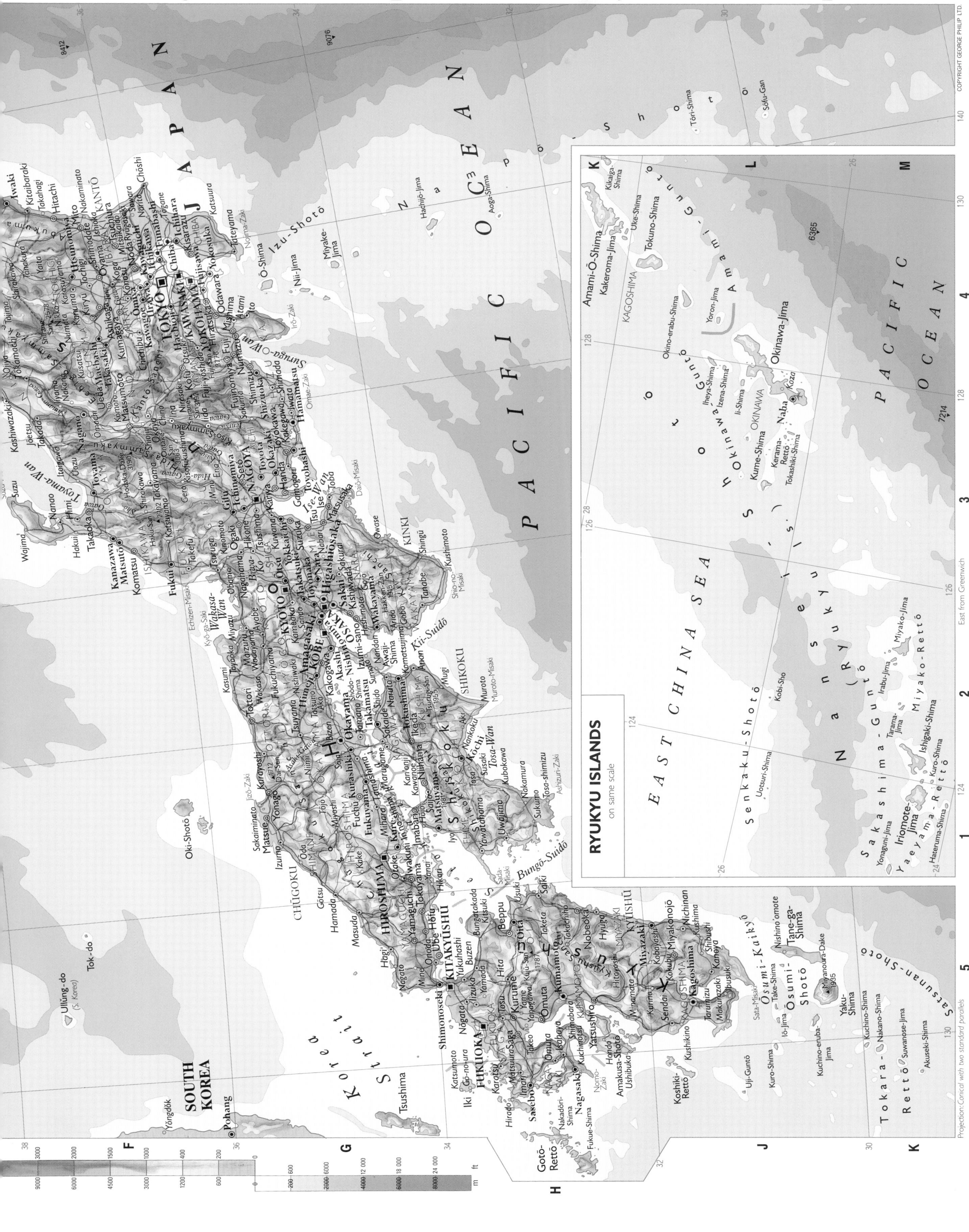

JAPAN
PACIFIC OCEAN
SOUTH KOREA
Korea Strait
TOKYO
KYOTO
OSAKA
KOBE
NAGOYA
YOKOHAMA
KAWASAKI
HIROSHIMA
FUKUOKA
KITAKYUSHU
Kagoshima
Kumamoto
Nagasaki
Miyazaki
Oita
Okayama
Matsuyama
Kochi
Tokushima
Takamatsu
Shikoku
Kyushu
Chugoku
Kinki
Izu-Shotō
Ōsumi-Shotō
Tokara-Rettō
Gotō-Rettō
Tsushima
Oki-Shotō
Ulŭng-do
Tok-do
RYUKYU ISLANDS
on same scale
EAST CHINA SEA
Nansei-Shotō (Ryukyu Is.)
Amami-Guntō
Okinawa-Guntō
Sakashima-Guntō
Miyako-Rettō
Yaeyama-Rettō
Senkaku-Shotō
Okinawa-Jima
Naha
Amami-Ō-Shima
Iriomote-Jima
Ishigaki-Shima
Projection: Conical with two standard parallels
East from Greenwich
COPYRIGHT GEORGE PHILIP LTD.
m ft
0 0
200 600
2000 6000
4000 12 000
6000 18 000
8000 24 000
200 600
400 1200
1000 3000
1500 4500
2000 6000
3000 9000

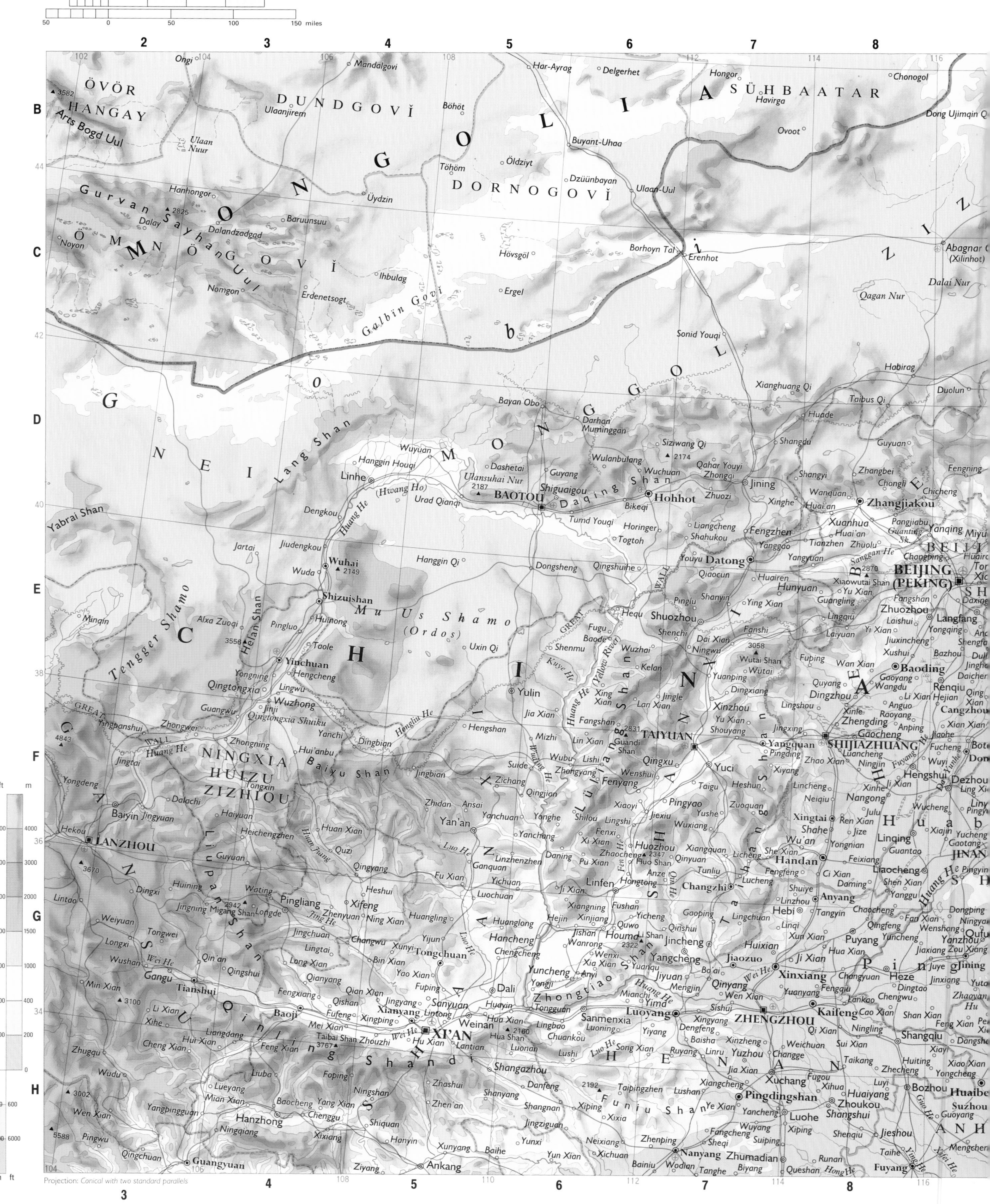
MONGOLIA
ÖVÖR HANGAY
DUNDGOVĬ
DORNOGOVĬ
SÜHBAATAR
ÖMNÖGOVĬ
Gurvan Sayhan Uul
Galbin Govi
Gobi
NEI MONGOL
CHINA
NINGXIA HUIZU ZIZHIQU
GANSU
SHAANXI
SHANXI
HENAN
HEBEI
Mu Us Shamo (Ordos)
Tengger Shamo
Helan Shan
Lang Shan
Daqing Shan
Lüliang Shan
Taihang Shan
Liupan Shan
Qinling Shandi
Funiu Shan
Zhongtiao Shan
Baiyu Shan
Huang He (Hwang Ho)
Yellow River
Wei He
GREAT WALL
Mandalgovi
Ulaanjirem
Dalandzadgad
Erenhot
Sonid Youqi
Abagnar Qi (Xilinhot)
BAOTOU
Hohhot
Jining
Zhangjiakou
Datong
BEIJING (PEKING)
Baoding
SHIJIAZHUANG
TAIYUAN
Yinchuan
Wuhai
Shizuishan
Wuzhong
Yulin
Yan'an
LANZHOU
Tianshui
Baoji
XI'AN
Xianyang
Weinan
Luoyang
ZHENGZHOU
Kaifeng
Xinxiang
Handan
Anyang
Changzhi
Linfen
Yuncheng
Sanmenxia
Pingdingshan
Nanyang
Xuchang
Zhoukou
Luohe
Hanzhong
Ankang
Guangyuan
Fuyang
Projection: Conical with two standard parallels

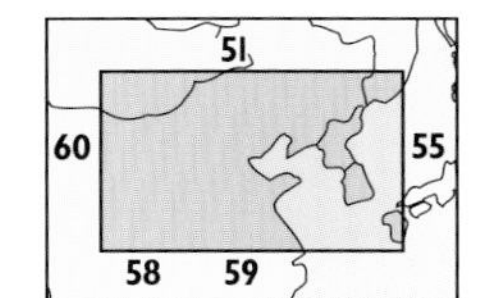

9 10 11 12 13 14 15 16

B C D E F G H

HARBIN
Bin Xian
Acheng
Shuangcheng
Zhaoyuan
Maoxing
Da'an
Zhenlai
Baicheng
Taonan
Horqin Youyi Qianqi (Ullanhot)
Hulingol
Tuquan
Anguang
Qagan Nur
Qian Gorlos
Fuyu
Changchunling
Beitaolaizhao
Sanchahe
Yushu
Wuchang
Shanhetun
Lalin
Yanshou
Shangzhi
Yimianpo
Hengdaohezi
Mudanjiang
Hailin
Ning'an
Linkou
Jixi
Turiy Rog
Ozero Khanka
Muling
Maqiaohe
Xiachengzi
Pogranichnyy
Suifenhe
Suiyang
Golenki
Dongning
Ussuriysk
Razdolnoye
Artem
Tavrichanka
Vladivostok
Slavyanka
Hunchun
Kraskino
Posyet
RUSSIA
HEILONGJIANG
JILIN
LIAONING
Zhangguangcai Ling
Qian an
Shenjingzi
Kaoshan
Nong'an
Dehui
Tongyu
Zhanyu
Beizhengzhen
Fulongquan
Changling
Horqin Zuoyi Zhongqi
Maolin
Huaidezhen
CHANGCHUN
Jiutai
JILIN
Gangyao
Wulajie
Jiaohe
Xinzhan
Emu
Huangsongdian
Jingpo Hu
Chunyang
Dongjingcheng
Luozigou
Dunhua
Daxinggou
Wangqing
Shixian
Tumen
Yanji
Longjing
Helong
Namyang
Mingyuegue
Songhua Hu
Fanjiatun
Gongzhuling
Shuangyang
Yitong
Siping
Lishu
Bamiancheng
Jargalang
Shuangliao
Kailu
Tongliao
Dongliao He
Xinkai He
Xiliao He
Jarud Qi
Bairin Zuoqi
Bairin Youqi
Linxi
Xar Moron He
Ongniud Qi
Wutonghaolai
Laoha He
Hure Qi
Xiawa
Chifeng
Heishui
Beipiao
Qinghemen
Weichang
Ningcheng
Chaoyang
Daling He
Yi Xian
Fuxin
Zhangwu
Xinlitun
Xinmin
SHENYANG
FUSHUN
Kangping
Zhangwu
Faku
Tiefa
Kaiyuan
Tieling
Qingyuan
Xifeng
Liaoyuan
Dongfeng
Meihekou
Shanchengzhen
Huinan
Huadian
Panshi
Baishan
Jingyu
Fusong
Antu
Baihe
Liuhe
Hunjiang
Tonghua
Linjiang
Chunggang-up
Changbai
Hyesan
Paektu-san
Yupyongdong
Changbai Shan
Manchuria
Hoeamdong
Hoeryong
Musan
Puryong
Unggi
Sosura
Najin
Pugodong
Chongjin
Kyongsong
Chuuronjang
Nanam
Hachon
Irhyangdong
Ondaejin
Simpungdong
Kilchu
Musudan
Hapsu
Kapsan
Kimch'aek (Songjin)
Kosongni
Tanch'on
Pukch'ong
Sinch'ang
Sohori
Sinp'o
Hongwon
Hamhung
Hungnam
Tongchon-ni
Tongjoson Man
SEA OF JAPAN
NORTH KOREA
Huch'ang
Kasan-dong
Inpundong
Manp'o
Kanggye
Ji'an
Pujon-chosuji
Chail-bong
Kwangdaeri
Changjin-chosuji
Changjin
Kuup-tong
Ch'osan
Pyoktong
Koin-dong
Sinhung
Huanren
Qinghecheng
Xinbin
Benxi
Liaoyang
Anping
Tianshifu
ANSHAN
Lianshanguan
Haicheng
Niuzhuang
Panjin
Jinzhou
Jinxi
Huludao
Lingyuan
Chengde
Luanne
Luanping
Pingquan
Liugou
Shangbancheng
Kuancheng
Xinglong
Shuangshanzi
Jianchangying
Xingcheng
Suizhong
Yingkou
Dashiqiao
Gaizhou
Xiuyan
Fengcheng
Kuandian
Supung Shuiku
Sakchu
Dandong
Sinuiju
Uiju
Taegwan
Pukchin
Kujang
Yongamp'o
Kusong
Chongju
Anju
Sunch'on
Sinchang-ni
Yonghung
Kowon
Munch'on
Wonsan
Anbyon
Kojo
Tongyang
Kangdong
Songch'on
Sukch'on
Sunan
P'YONGYANG
Chunghwa
Songnim
Namp'o
Koksan
Singosan
Sepo-ri
Hoeyang
Kosong
Chihari
Pyonggang
Kumhwa
Sariwon
Chaeryong
Sinmak
Nam-ch'on
Ch'orwon
Hwachon-chosuji
Sinch'on
Kumch'on
Haeju
Kaesong
Panmunjom
Uijongbu
Ch'unch'on
Hongch'on
Yonan
Ongjin
Munsan
Kanghwa
Puch'on
SOUL
Songnam
INCH'ON
Anyang
Suwon
Ansan
Ich'on
Osan
Yoju
Wonju
Hoengsong
Chongson
Yongwol
Chech'on
Yongju
Samch'ok
Kangnung
Chumunjin
Kansong
Sokch'o
Yangyang
Ullung-do
Ulchin
Yongdok
Andong
Uisong
Chongha
P'ohang
Changgi-Ap
SOUTH KOREA
P'yongt'aek
Ch'onan
Ch'ungju
Chongju
Yech'on
Sosan
Hongsong
Yesan
Kongju
TAEJON
Sangju
Sonsan
Kimch'on
Kumi
Yongch'on
Kyongju
Anmyon-do
Taechon-ni
Nonsan
Kanggyong
Yongdong
Kunsan
Iri
Chonju
Waegwan
TAEGU
Chongdo
Miryang
Ulsan
Kimje
Puan
Chongup
Kochang
Koryong
Hamyang
Namwon
Chiri-san
Chinju
Masan
Kimhae
Tongnae
PUSAN
Sago-ri
Tamyang
Songjong-ni
KWANGJU
Hadong
Ch'angwon
Samch'onp'o
Ch'ungmu
Naju
Sunch'on
Mokp'o
Posong
Polgyo-ri
Yosu
Changhung
Haenam
Huksan-chedo
Chindo
Korea Strait
Sasuna
Saka
Tsushima
Izuhara
Cheju
Cheju-do
Onpyong-ni
Hallim
Taejong
Halla-san
Mosulpo
Sogwipo
Iki
Karatsu
Imari
JAPAN
Sasebo
Kashima
Omura
Isahaya
Nakadori-Shima
Nagasaki
Kuchinotsu
Fukue-Shima
Paengnyong-do
Changyon
Cho-do
Korea Bay
Lushun
DALIAN
Jin Xian
Pikou
Pulandian
Wafangdian
Zhuanghe
Liaodong Bandao
Wanfu
Buyun Shan
Gushan
Donggou
Yalu Jiang
Xiongyuecheng
Liaodong Wan
Qinhuangdao
Funing
Changli
Leting
Luan He
Zunhua
Fengrun
Lulong
Luan Xian
Yutian
Baodi
TANGSHAN
TIANJIN SHI
Hangu
Wuqing
TIANJIN
Tanggu
Dagu
Bo Hai
Oikou
Huanghua
Miaodao Qundao
Yanshan
Qingyun
Wudi
Zhanhua
Huang He
Huimin
Kenli
Binzhou
Dongying
Laizhou Wan
Penglai
Longkou
Daxindian
Yantai
Huang Xian
Fushan
Muping
Weihai
Chengshan Jiao
Qixia
Wendeng
Rongcheng
Zhaoyuan
Laizhou
Shandong Bandao
Laiyang
Rushan
Nanhuang
Shidao
Haiyang
Laixi
Pingdu
Changyi
Guangrao
Shouguang
Huantai
Linzi
Zhoucun
ZIBO
Yidu
Weifang
Fangzi
Anqiu
Gaomi
Jimo
Lancun
Chengyang
Jiaozhou
QINGDAO
Jiaozhou Wan
Boshan
Linqu
SHANDONG
Laiwu
Tai'an
Zhucheng
Xintai
Mengyin
Yishui
Wulian
Ju Xian
Rizhao
Liangcheng
Shijiusuo
Andongwei
Tangtou
Fei Xian
Tengzhou
Linyi
Teng Xian
Ganyu
Haizhou Wan
Lianyungang
Zaozhuang
Tancheng
Haizhou
Lianyungang
Jiawang
Pizhou
Xinyi
Guanyun
Chenjiagang
Xiangshui
Xuzhou
Yaowan
Guannan
Binhai
Suqian
Shuyang
Funing
Sheyang
Shuanggou
Suining
Lianshui
Da Yunhe
JIANGSU
Lingbi
Huaiyin
Huai'an
Hongze Hu
Yancheng
Suzhou
Baoying
Liuzhuang
Guzhen
Wuhe
Xinghua
Bengbu
Fengyang
Gaoyou Hu
Dongtai
HUANG HAI (Yellow Sea)
Great Wall
Willow Wall
1949
2029
2020
1885
1690
1677
2744
2541
1846
2522
1131
1638
1578
923
1108
1915
1950
118 120 122 124 126 128 130 132
44 42 40 38 36 34

9 10 11 12 13 14 15
East from Greenwich

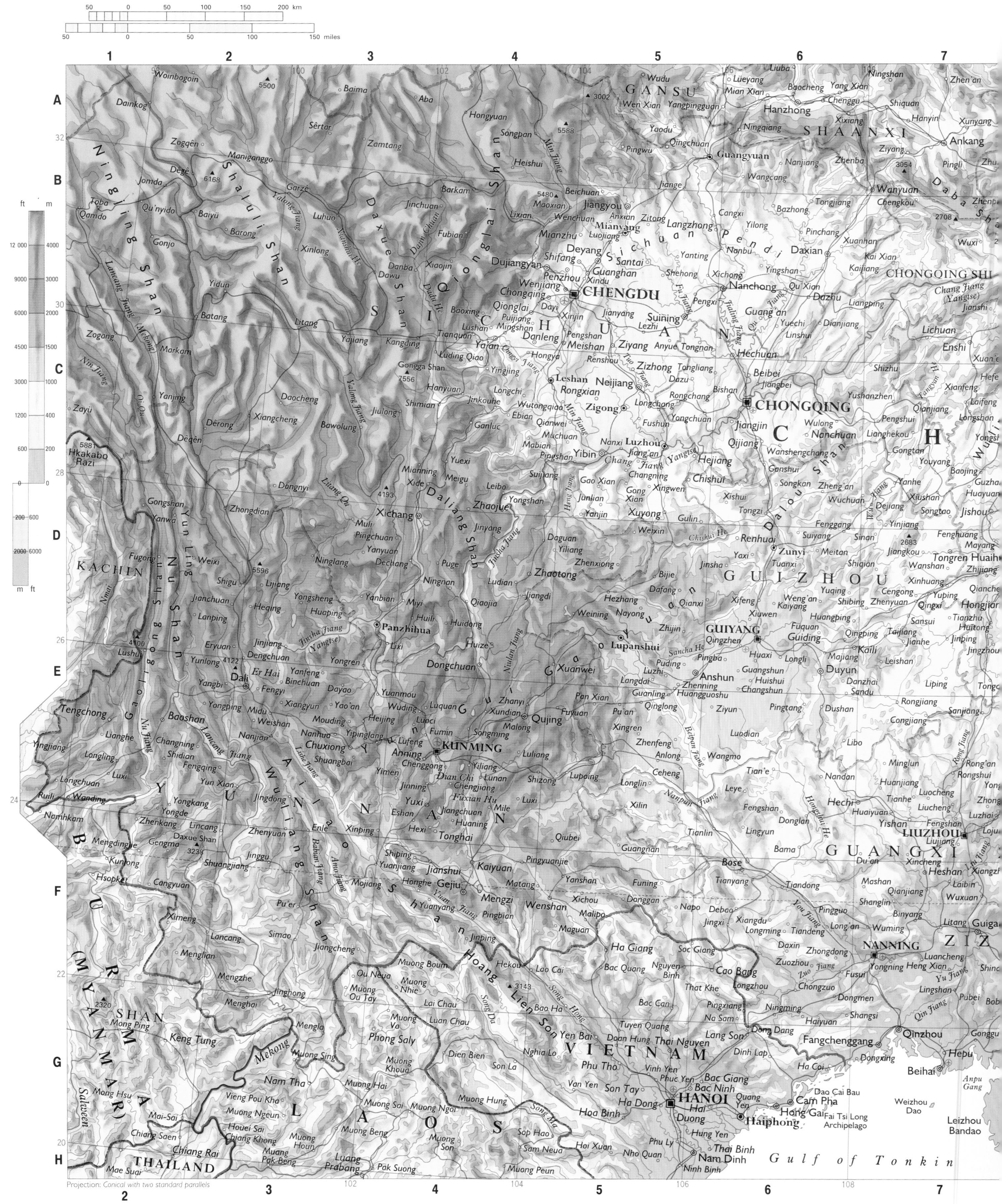

50 0 50 100 150 200 km
50 0 50 100 150 miles
ft m
12 000 4000
9000 3000
6000 2000
4500 1500
3000 1000
1200 400
600 200
0 0
200 600
2000 6000
GANSU
SHAANXI
CHONGQING SHI
SICHUAN
GUIZHOU
YUNNAN
GUANGXI
VIETNAM
LAOS
THAILAND
BURMA (MYANMAR)
KACHIN
SHAN
CHENGDU
CHONGQING
KUNMING
GUIYANG
NANNING
HANOI
LIUZHOU
Haiphong
Hanzhong
Ankang
Guangyuan
Mianyang
Deyang
Jiangyou
Nanchong
Suining
Dazhou
Daxian
Leshan
Zigong
Yibin
Luzhou
Neijiang
Xichang
Panzhihua
Dali
Qujing
Zhaotong
Zunyi
Anshun
Duyun
Kaili
Lupanshui
Gejiu
Kaiyuan
Mengzi
Wenshan
Bose
Baoshan
Tengchong
Ruili
Wanding
Lincang
Jinghong
Lao Cai
Yen Bai
Thai Nguyen
Lang Son
Cao Bang
Ha Giang
Nam Dinh
Thai Binh
Hong Gai
Cam Pha
Qinzhou
Beihai
Hepu
Fangchenggang
Keng Tung
Chiang Rai
Gulf of Tonkin
Leizhou Bandao
Sichuan Pendi
Daba Shan
Dalou Shan
Daxue Shan
Qionglai Shan
Shaluli Shan
Ningjing Shan
Nu Shan
Yun Ling
Gaoligong Shan
Daliang Shan
Wuliang Shan
Ailao Shan
Hoang Lien Son
Jinsha Jiang (Yangtse)
Chang Jiang (Yangtse)
Lancang Jiang (Mekong)
Nu Jiang
Yalong Jiang
Dadu He
Min Jiang
Jialing Jiang
Nanpan Jiang
Hongshui He
Song Hong
Song Da
Er Hai
Dian Chi
Fuxian Hu
Mekong
Salween
Gongga Shan 7556
Hkakabo Razi 5881
Projection: Conical with two standard parallels

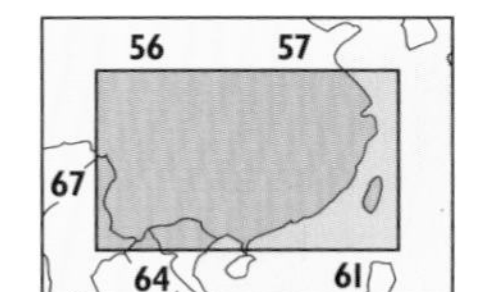

8 9 10 11 12 13 14

A B C D E F G H

HENAN

ANHUI

JIANGSU

HUBEI

HUNAN

JIANGXI

ZHEJIANG

FUJIAN

GUANGDONG

GUANGXI ZHUANGZU

SHANGHAI SHI

TAIWAN

NANJING

SHANGHAI

WUHAN

CHANGSHA

NANCHANG

HANGZHOU

FUZHOU

GUANGZHOU

HONG KONG (XIANGGANG)

T'AIPEI

KAOHSIUNG

Hefei

Huainan

Bengbu

Wuxi

Suzhou

Changzhou

Zhenjiang

Yangzhou

Nantong

Ningbo

Wenzhou

Jinhua

Quzhou

Shaoxing

Jingdezhen

Jiujiang

Yichang

Shashi

Jingmen

Xiangfan

Laohekou

Shiyan

Danjiangkou

Nanyang

Zhumadian

Xinyang

Anqing

Tongling

Wuhu

Ma'anshan

Huangshan

Tunxi

Yueyang

Changde

Yiyang

Xiangtan

Zhuzhou

Hengyang

Shaoyang

Lengshuijiang

Loudi

Chenzhou

Pingxiang

Ji'an

Ganzhou

Yingtan

Shangrao

Fengcheng

Nanping

Sanming

Quanzhou

Xiamen

Zhangzhou

Putian

Longyan

Shantou

Chaozhou

Meizhou

Shaoguan

Huizhou

Shenzhen

Kowloon

Zhuhai

Macau

Foshan

Jiangmen

Zhaoqing

Wuzhou

Maoming

Zhanjiang

Yangjiang

Chilung

Hsinchu

T'aichung

Chunghua

Chiai

T'ainan

Hualien

T'aitung

P'ingtung

Dongting Hu

Poyang Hu

Tai Hu

Hongze Hu

Chang Jiang (Yangtse)

Han Shui

Huai He

Gan Jiang

Xiang Jiang

Min Jiang

Xi Jiang

Bei Jiang

Dong Jiang

Dabie Shan

Jiuling Shan

Wuyi Shan

Nan Ling

Luoxiao Shan

Wugong Shan

Daxue Shan

Chungyang Shanmo

Yunkai Dashan

Three Gorges Dam

Taiwan Strait

Luzon Strait

SOUTH CHINA SEA

Hangzhou Wan

Zhoushan Dao

Chongming Dao

Matsu Tao

Haitan Dao

Chinmen Tao

Penghu

Dangan Liedao

Shangchuan Dao

Xiachuan Dao

Hailing Dao

Donghai Dao

Naozhou Dao

Leizhou Wan

Tungsha Tao

Lü-Tao

Hungt'ou Hsü

Tropic of Cancer

1474

1596

1636

1725

1794

1810

1834

2120

2164

1510

1629

1703

1963

3931

3997

32 30 28 26 24 22 20

112 114 116 118 120 122

East from Greenwich

100 0 100 200 300 400 500 600 700 800 km
100 0 100 200 300 400 500 miles
RUSSIA
MONGOLIA
CHINA
KAZAKSTAN
KYRGYZSTAN
JAMMU & KASHMIR
NEPAL
BHUTAN
BANGLADESH
INDIA
BURMA (MYANMAR)
THAILAND (SIAM)
LAOS
VIETNAM
PHILIPPINES
NORTH KOREA
SOUTH KOREA
JAPAN
TAIWAN (FORMOSA)
HONG KONG
HAINAN
XIZANG ZIZHIQU (TIBET)
XINJIANG UYGUR ZIZHIQU
NEI MONGGOL ZIZHIQU
QINGHAI
SICHUAN
YUNNAN
YELLOW SEA
EAST CHINA SEA
SOUTH CHINA SEA
BAY OF BENGAL
BEIJING (PEKING)
SHANGHAI
TIANJIN
CHONGQING
CHENGDU
WUHAN
NANJING
XI'AN
LANZHOU
ÜRÜMQI
Ulaanbaatar
HARBIN
SHENYANG
GUANGZHOU (CANTON)
KUNMING
DHAKA
KOLKATA (CALCUTTA)
Tarim Pendi
Kunlun Shan
Tropic of Cancer
East from Greenwich
Projection: Bonne

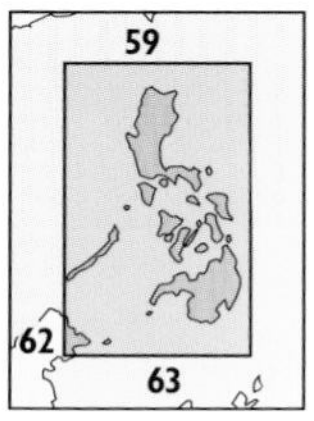

PHILIPPINES

SOUTH CHINA SEA

PACIFIC OCEAN

SULU SEA

CELEBES SEA

Luzon

Mindoro

Panay

Negros

Samar

Leyte

Palawan

Mindanao

MANILA

Quezon City

Caloocan

Cebu

Davao

Zamboanga

Iloilo

Bacolod

Cagayan de Oro

General Santos

Puerto Princesa

Legazpi

Tacloban

Baguio

Batanes Is.

Babuyan Islands

Balintang Channel

Babuyan Channel

Mindanao Trench

Sulu Archipelago

MALAYSIA

SABAH

Borneo

INDONESIA

Projection: Lambert's Conformal Conic

East from Greenwich

BURMA
RANGOON (YANGON)
(MYANMAR)
G. of Martaban
THAILAND
BANGKOK
LAOS
VIETNAM
CAMBODIA
Phnom Penh (Phnum Penh)
THANH PHO HO CHI MINH
Gulf of Thailand
ANDAMAN SEA
SOUTH CHINA SEA
Spratly Is.
Paracel Is.
MALAYSIA
PENINSULAR MALAYSIA
KUALA LUMPUR
SINGAPORE
Strait of Malacca
BRUNEI
SARAWAK
SABAH
Borneo
KALIMANTAN
INDONESIA
Sumatera
MEDAN
PALEMBANG
JAKARTA
BANDUNG
SEMARANG
SURABAYA
Greater Sunda Islands
JAVA SEA
Jawa (Java)
INDIAN OCEAN
Java Trench
Selat Karimata
Kepulauan Riau
Bangka
Belitung
Kepulauan Natuna
Kepulauan Anambas
Kepulauan Mentawai
Pontianak
Banjarmasin
Kuching
Kota Kinabalu
Bandar Seri Begawan
Da Nang
Hue
Vientiane (Viangchan)
Projection: Mercator
East from Greenwich

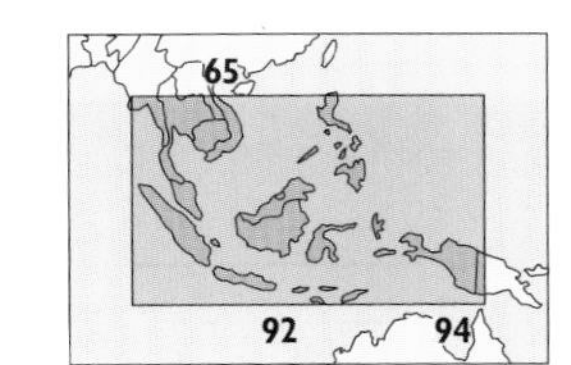

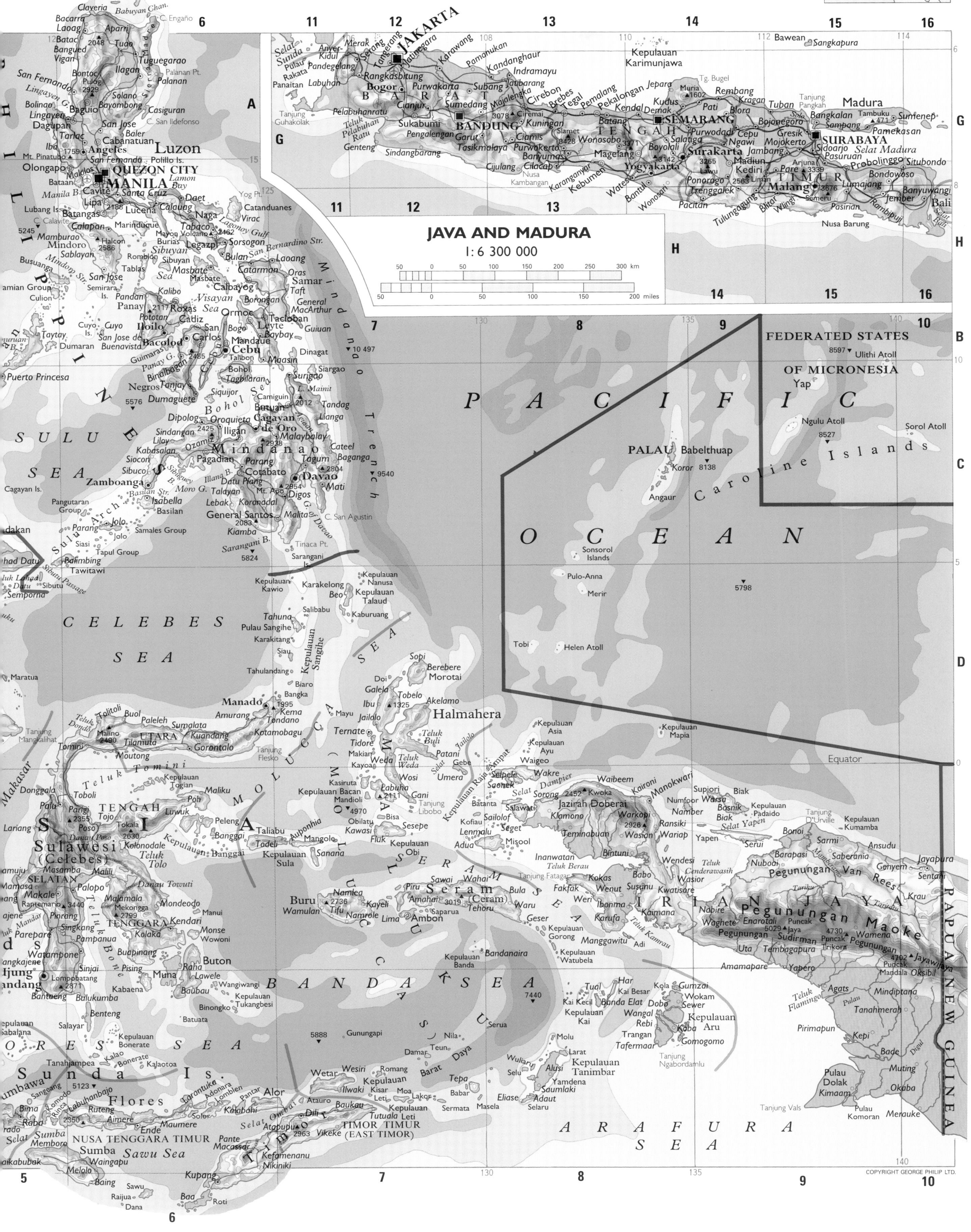

JAVA AND MADURA

1: 6 300 000

50 0 50 100 150 200 km
50 0 50 100 150 miles
CHINA
YUNNAN
GUANGXI ZHUANGZU ZIZHIQU
GUANGDONG
HAINAN
G. of Tonkin
Leizhou Bandao
Qiongzhou Haixia
Haikou
Zhanjiang
Nanning
HANOI
Haiphong
Hue
Da Nang
Vientiane
BANGKOK
Thon Buri
RANGOON
Mandalay
Moulmein
Chiang Mai
THAILAND
LAOS
VIETNAM
CAMBODIA
BURMA
(MYANMAR)
SHAN
KAYAH
KAWTHULE
TENASSERIM
Trung-Phan (Annam)
Bac Phan
Cao Nguyen Khorat
Phnom Dangrek
Chao Phraya Lowlands
Mekong
Tran Ninh
Boloven
Moscos Islands
G. of Martaban

SOUTH CHINA SEA
Gulf of Thailand
MALAYSIA
PENINSULAR MALAYSIA
INDONESIA
Strait of Malacca
Strait of Singapore
Sumatera
Semenanjung Malaysia
Myeik Kyunzu
Nam Phan (Cochin China)
Borneo
SARAWAK (Malaysia)
Mekong
THANH PHO HO CHI MINH (SAIGON)
Phnom Penh
Kuala Lumpur
SINGAPORE
Medan
Pematangsiantar
George Town
Pinang
Butterworth
Ipoh
Cameron Highlands
Kuala Terengganu
Kota Baharu
Kuantan
Johor Baharu
Melaka
Seremban
Port Dickson
Klang
Hat Yai
Songkhla
Pattani
Yala
Narathiwat
Nakhon Si Thammarat
Surat Thani
Chumphon
Ranong
Kho Khot Kra
Phuket
Ko Phuket
Krabi
Trang
Satun
P. Langkawi
Alor Setar
Ko Samui
Ko Phangan
Ko Tao
Ko Chang
Ko Kut
Koh Kong
Koh Rong
Dao Phu Quoc
Hon Panjang
Tenasserim
Kui Buri
Prachuap Khiri Khan
Bang Saphan
Kampot
Kep
Ha Tien
Rach Gia
Long Xuyen
Can Tho
Soc Trang
Bac Lieu
Ca Mau
Mui Ca Mau
Hon Khoai
Con Son
Vung Tau
Bien Hoa
Phan Thiet
Phan Rang
Cam Ranh
Da Lat
Cu Lao Hon
Catwick Is.
Kepulauan Anambas (Indonesia)
P. Matak
Jemaja
Kepulauan Natuna Besar (Indonesia)
Telukbutun
Kepulauan Natuna Selatan
Subi
Serasan
P. Midai
Laut
P. Tenggol
Pulau Tioman
P. Aur
Tanjung Datu
Kucing
Batam
Bintan
Tanjungpinang
Rupat
Dumai
Bengkalis
Tanjungbalai
Tebingtinggi
Sibolga
Musala
Langsa
Kualasimpang
Belawan
Projection: Conical with two standard parallels
East from Greenwich
COPYRIGHT GEORGE PHILIP LTD.
ft 9000 6000 4500 3000 1200 600 0
m 3000 2000 1500 1000 400 200 0
200 600 2000 6000
m ft
G H J K L M
1 2 3 4 5 6 7 8
58 62 67

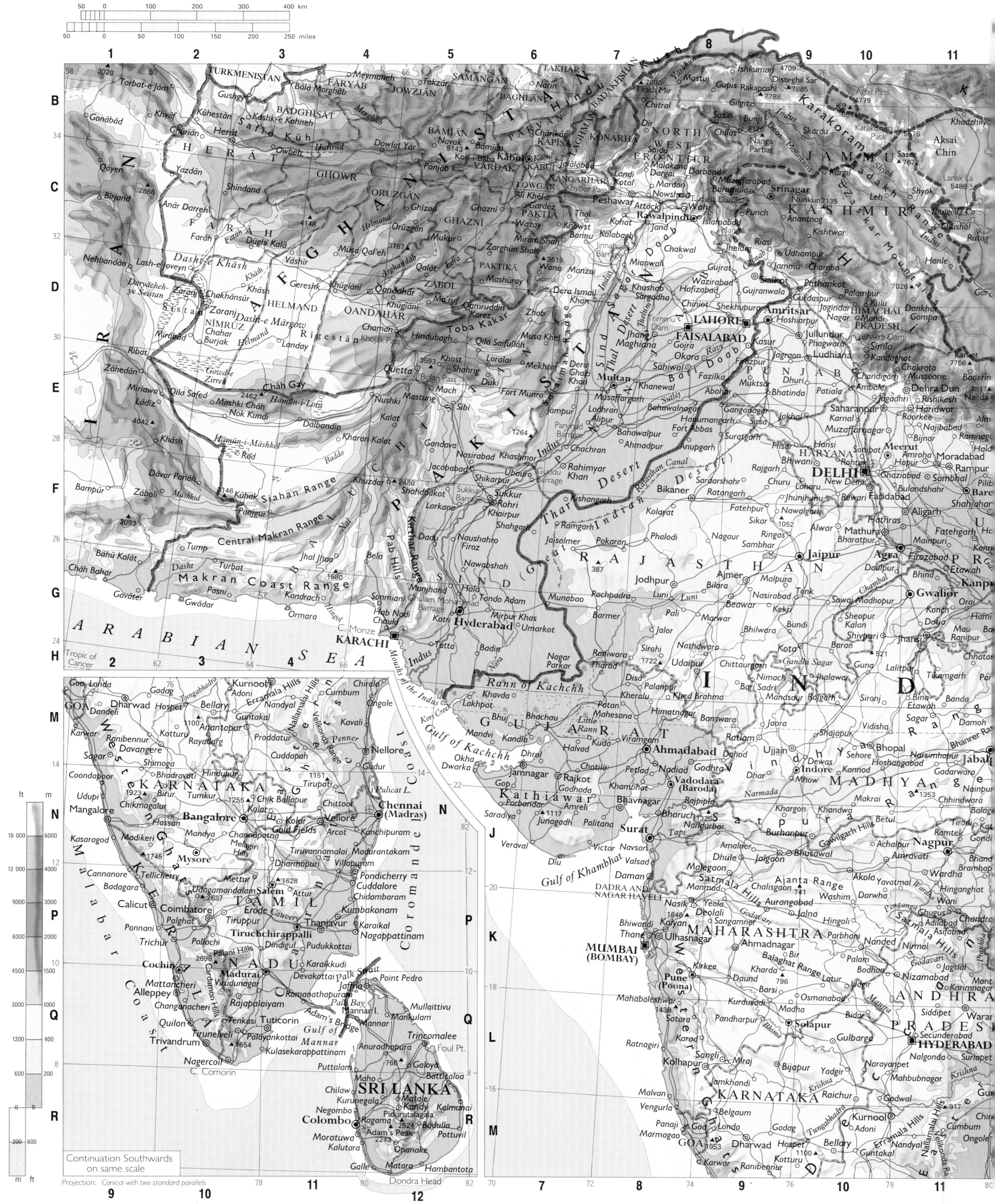
TURKMENISTAN
AFGHANISTAN
PAKISTAN
IRAN
INDIA
SRI LANKA
ARABIAN SEA
Hindu Kush
Karakoram
JAMMU & KASHMIR
Aksai Chin
HERAT
Safid Kūh
GHOWR
ORUZGĀN
GHAZNĪ
FARĀH
HELMAND
NĪMRŪZ
QANDAHĀR
ZĀBOL
PAKTĪKĀ
PAKTĪA
LOWGAR
NANGARHĀR
KONARHA
KĀBUL
KAPISA
PARVĀN
BĀMĪĀN
BADGHĪSAT
JOWZJĀN
FĀRYĀB
SAMANGĀN
BAGHLĀN
TAKHĀR
BADAKHSHĀN
NORTH WEST FRONTIER
Kābul
Herāt
Qandahār
Ghaznī
Jalālābād
Peshawar
Rawalpindi
Islamabad
Srinagar
Leh
Kargil
Gilgit
Quetta
Multan
LAHORE
FAISALABAD
Amritsar
Sialkot
Gujranwala
Bahawalpur
Sukkur
Hyderabad
KARACHI
Gwādar
Makran Coast Range
Central Makran Range
Siahan Range
Rigestān
Dasht-e Mārgow
Dasht-e Khāsh
Toba Kakar
Sulaiman Range
Kirthar Range
Thar Desert
Great Indian Desert
Rajasthan Canal
RAJASTHAN
SIND
PUNJAB
HARYANA
HIMACHAL PRADESH
DELHI
New Delhi
Agra
Jaipur
Jodhpur
Bikaner
Ajmer
Udaipur
Gwalior
Jhansi
Indus
Mouths of the Indus
Rann of Kachchh
Gulf of Kachchh
GUJARAT
Kathiawar
Ahmadabad
Vadodara (Baroda)
Rajkot
Jamnagar
Surat
Gulf of Khambhat
Diu
Daman
DADRA AND NAGAR HAVELI
MUMBAI (BOMBAY)
Pune (Poona)
Nasik
MAHARASHTRA
Aurangabad
Ajanta Range
Satmala Hills
Western Ghats
Nagpur
Indore
Bhopal
Vindhya Range
Satpura Range
MADHYA PRADESH
ANDHRA PRADESH
HYDERABAD
Solapur
Kolhapur
KARNATAKA
GOA
Belgaum
Dharwad
Bellary
Kurnool
Nellore
Chennai (Madras)
Bangalore
Mysore
Vellore
Pondicherry
Coromandel Coast
Malabar Coast
KERALA
TAMIL NADU
Calicut
Coimbatore
Cochin
Madurai
Tiruchchirappalli
Thanjavur
Trivandrum
Nagercoil
C. Comorin
Palk Strait
Adam's Bridge
Gulf of Mannar
Jaffna
Trincomalee
Anuradhapura
Kandy
Colombo
Galle
Dondra Head
Adam's Peak
Tropic of Cancer
Continuation Southwards on same scale
Projection: Conical with two standard parallels

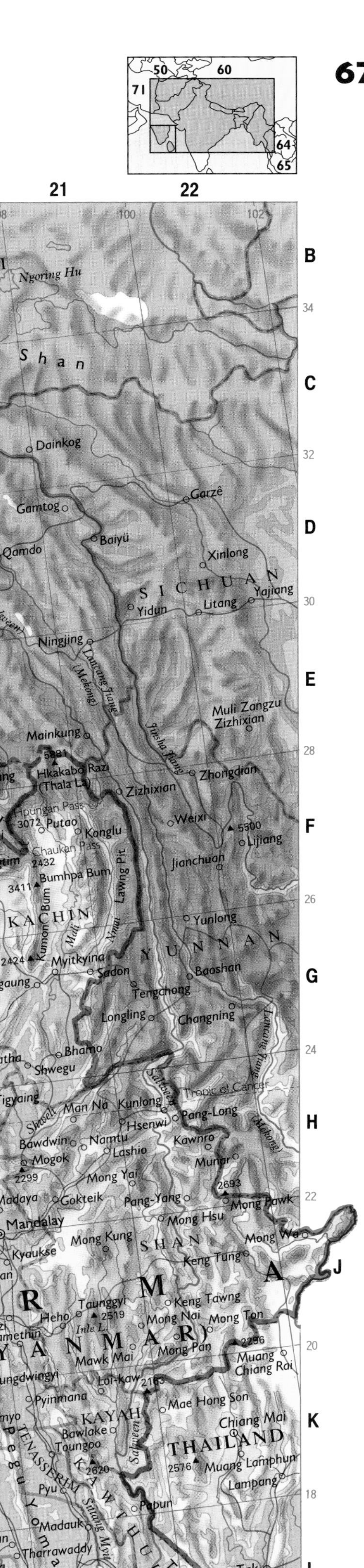

CHINA
XIZANG ZIZHIQU (TIBET)
QINGHAI
SICHUAN
YUNNAN
Huh Xil Shan
Bayan Har Shan
Tanggula (Dangla) Shan
Nyainqentanglha Shan
NEPAL
BHUTAN
SIKKIM
ARUNACHAL PRADESH
ASSAM
MEGHALAYA
NAGALAND
MANIPUR
MIZORAM
TRIPURA
BANGLADESH
WEST BENGAL
BIHAR
ORISSA
BURMA (MYANMAR)
THAILAND
KACHIN
SAGAING
CHIN
MAGWE
ARAKAN
PEGU
IRRAWADDY
KAYAH
SHAN
Lhasa
Mt. Everest 8850
Kanchenjunga 8598
Katmandu
Thimphu
Gangtok
DHAKA
KOLKATA (CALCUTTA)
Chittagong
Patna
Varanasi
Lucknow
Allahabad
Cuttack
Mandalay
RANGOON
Moulmein
Mouths of the Ganges
Mouths of the Irrawaddy
G. of Martaban
BAY OF BENGAL
INDIAN OCEAN
Preparis North Channel
Preparis South Channel
Cox's Bazar
Sittwe (Akyab)
Brahmaputra
Ganga
Irrawaddy
East from Greenwich

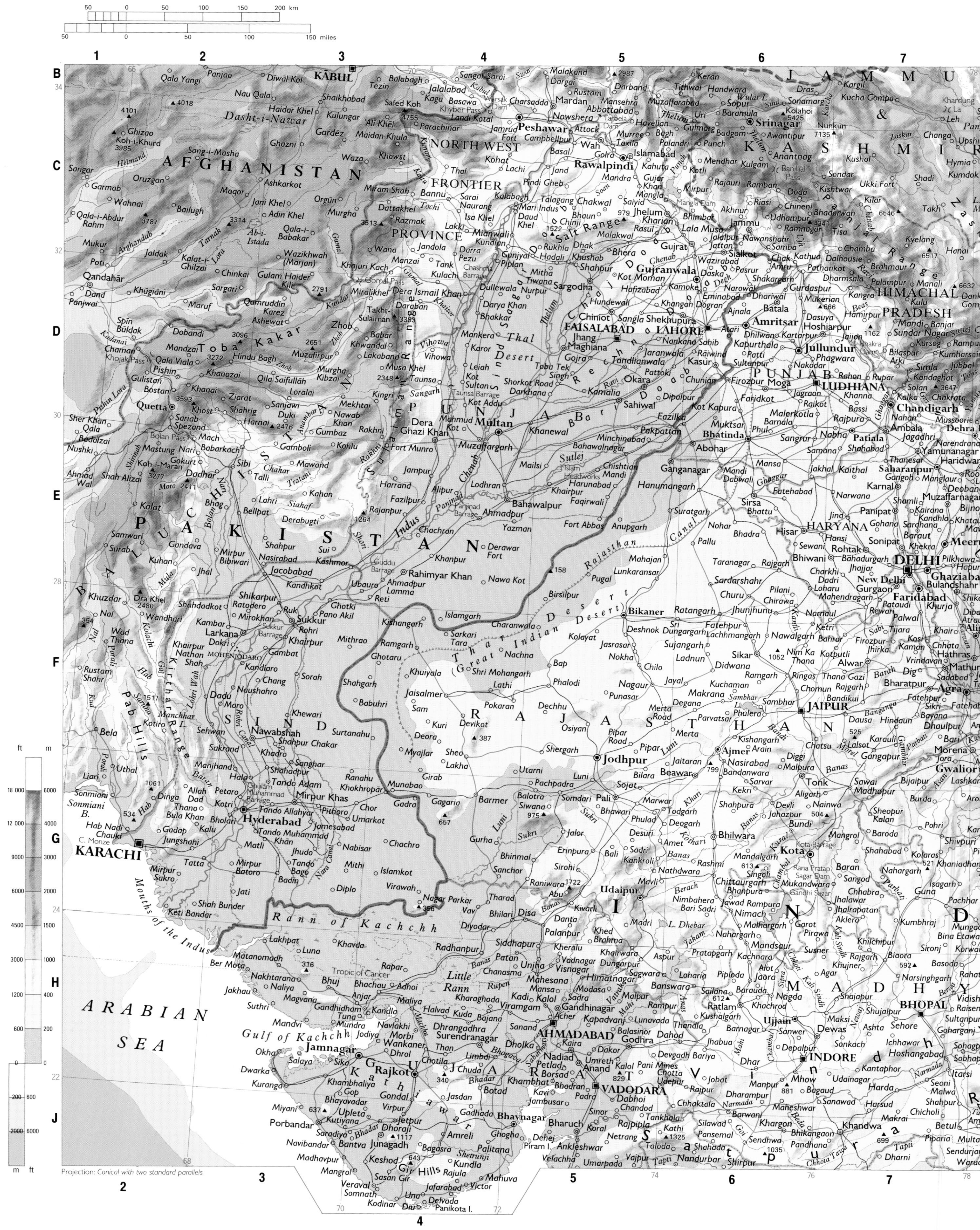

50 0 50 100 150 200 km
50 0 50 100 150 miles
AFGHANISTAN
PAKISTAN
BALUCHISTAN
SIND
PUNJAB
NORTH WEST FRONTIER PROVINCE
JAMMU & KASHMIR
HIMACHAL PRADESH
HARYANA
RAJASTHAN
GUJARAT
MADHYA PRADESH
INDIA
KABUL
Peshawar
Rawalpindi
Islamabad
Srinagar
Qandahar
Quetta
Multan
Sukkur
Hyderabad
KARACHI
FAISALABAD
LAHORE
Gujranwala
Sialkot
Amritsar
Jullundur
LUDHIANA
Chandigarh
DELHI
New Delhi
Agra
JAIPUR
Jodhpur
Bikaner
Ajmer
Udaipur
Kota
Gwalior
AHMADABAD
VADODARA
INDORE
BHOPAL
Ujjain
Rajkot
Jamnagar
Bhavnagar
Surat
Dasht-i-Nawar
Toba Kakar
Salt Range
Thal Desert
Thar (Great Indian) Desert
Rann of Kachchh
Little Rann
Gulf of Kachchh
Mouths of the Indus
ARABIAN SEA
Tropic of Cancer
Kirthar Range
Pab Hills
Sulaiman Range
Gir Hills
Kathiawar
Satpura Range
Vindhya Range
Indus
Chenab
Jhelum
Ravi
Sutlej
Beas
Narmada
Mahi
Luni
Banas
Chambal
Rajasthan Canal
Projection: Conical with two standard parallels

60
66
67
66

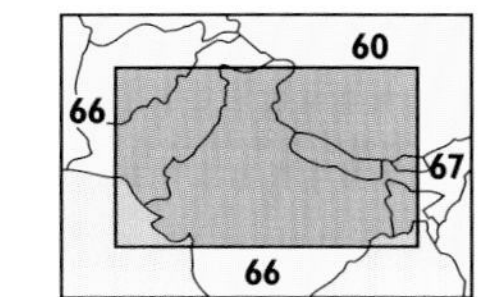

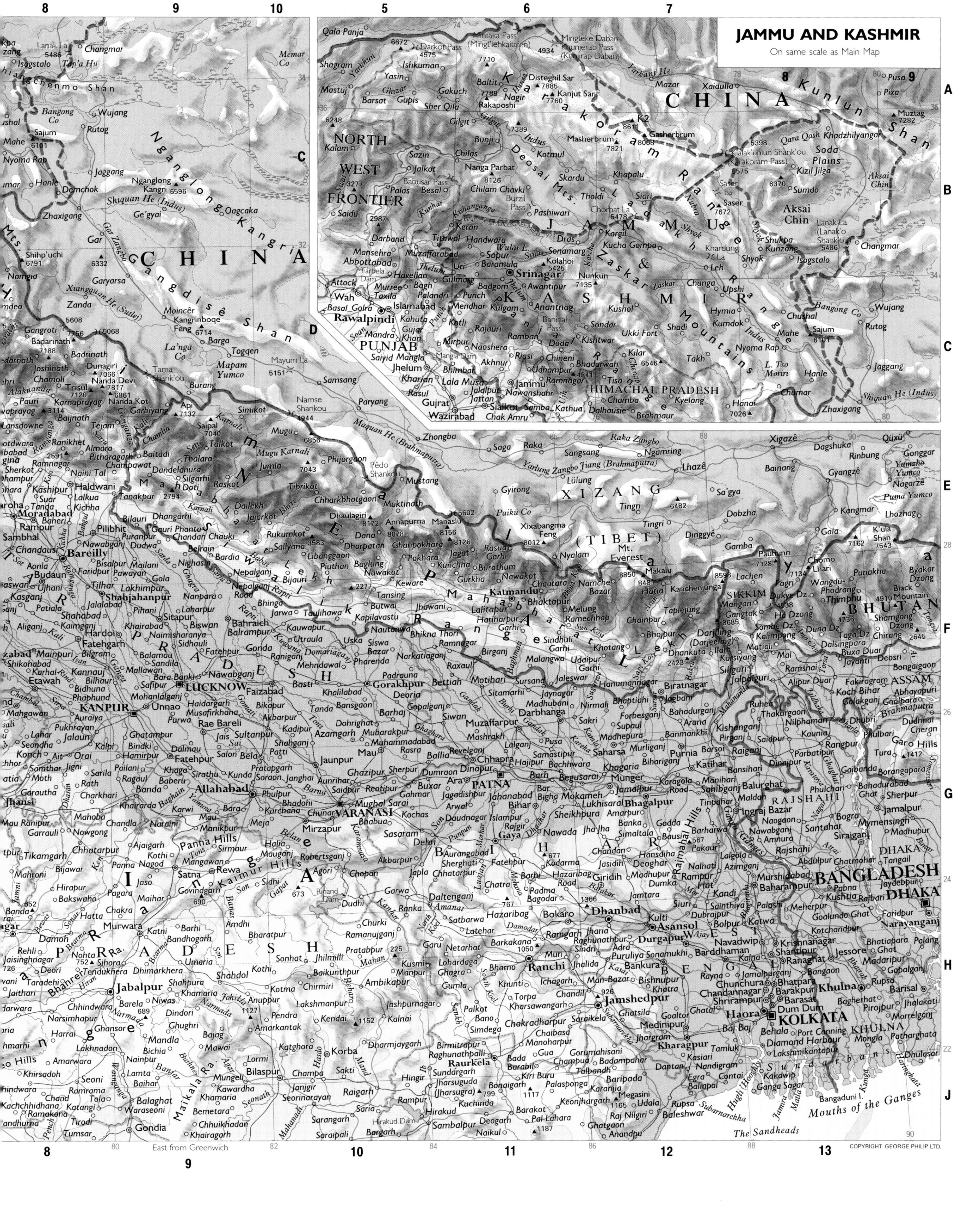

JAMMU AND KASHMIR
On same scale as Main Map
CHINA
KASHMIR
NORTH WEST FRONTIER
PUNJAB
HIMACHAL PRADESH
Karakoram Range
Kunlun Shan
Zaskar Mountains
Ladakh Range
Srinagar
Rawalpindi
Islamabad
Jammu
Aksai Chin
XIZANG
(TIBET)
NEPAL
Katmandu
Mt. Everest
SIKKIM
BHUTAN
Thimphu
BANGLADESH
DHAKA
UTTAR PRADESH
BIHAR
MADHYA PRADESH
WEST BENGAL
LUCKNOW
KANPUR
PATNA
VARANASI
Allahabad
KOLKATA
Haora
Jabalpur
Ranchi
Jamshedpur
Mouths of the Ganges
The Sandheads
East from Greenwich

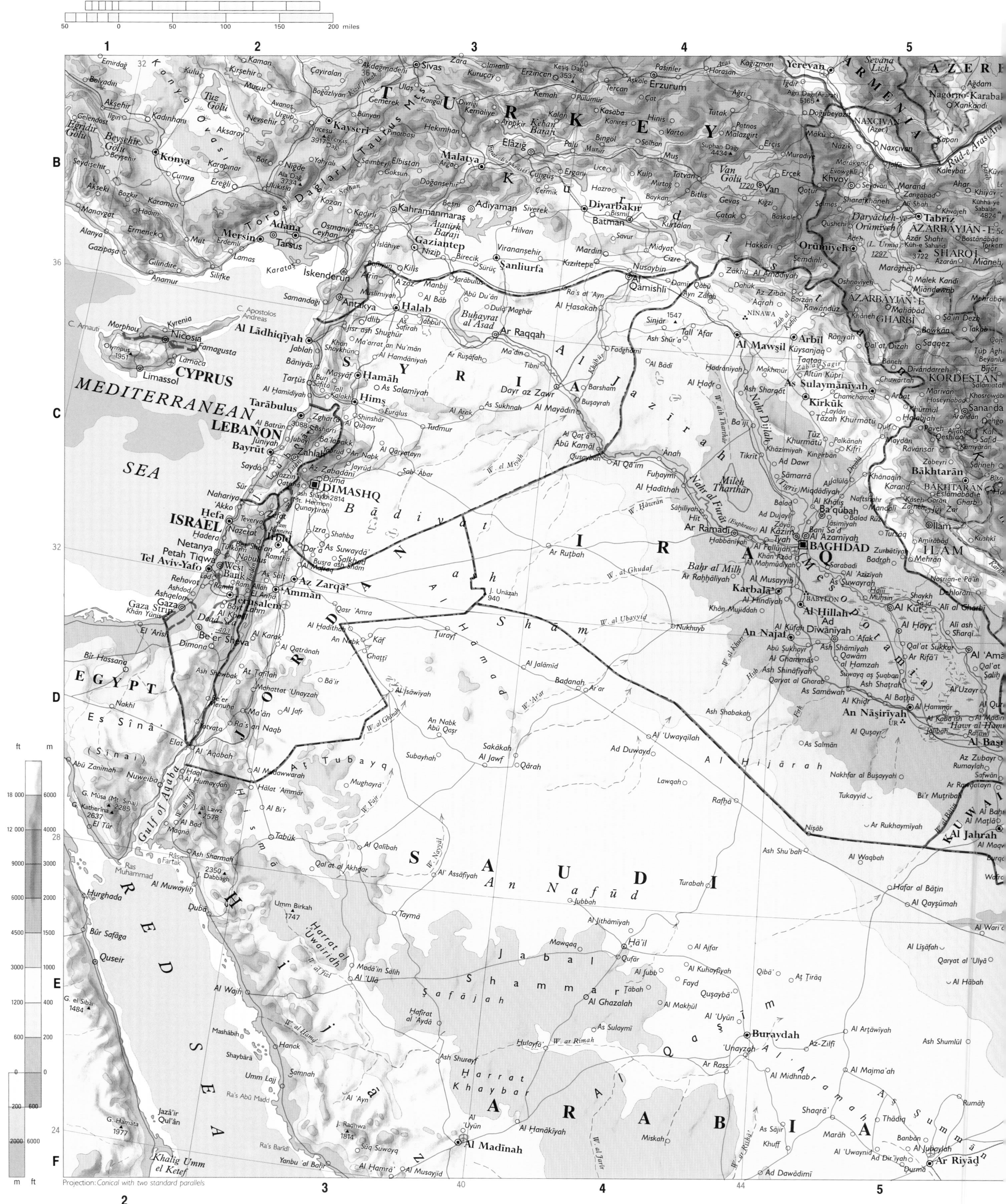

50 0 50 100 150 200 250 300 km
50 0 50 100 150 200 miles
1 2 3 4 5
B C D E F
T U R K E Y
K u r d i s t a n
ARMENIA
AZERBAIJAN
CYPRUS
MEDITERRANEAN SEA
LEBANON
SYRIA
ISRAEL
JORDAN
IRAQ
EGYPT
SAUDI ARABIA
KUWAIT
RED SEA
Gulf of Aqaba
Es Sînâ' (Sinai)
Bādiyat ash Shām
Al Ḥamad
Al Jazīrah
Mesopotamia
An Nafūd
Al Ḥijārah
Jabal Shammar
Ḥarrat Khaybar
Al Qaṣīm
Ad Dahnā'
Nicosia
Limassol
Famagusta
Bayrūt
Ḥalab
Ḥimṣ
Ḥamāh
DIMASHQ
'Ammān
Tel Aviv-Yafo
Jerusalem
Gaza
Al Mawṣil
Arbīl
Kirkūk
BAGHDĀD
Karbalā'
An Najaf
An Nāṣirīyah
Al Baṣrah
Al Madīnah
Ar Riyāḍ
Burayday
Ḥā'il
Tabūk
Mersin
Adana
Konya
Kayseri
Malatya
Diyarbakır
Erzurum
Yerevan
Tabrīz
Orūmīyeh
Van Gölü
Daryācheh-ye Orūmīyeh
Projection: Conical with two standard parallels
ft m
18 000 6000
12 000 4000
9000 3000
6000 2000
4500 1500
3000 1000
1200 400
600 200
0 0
200 600
2000 6000
m ft

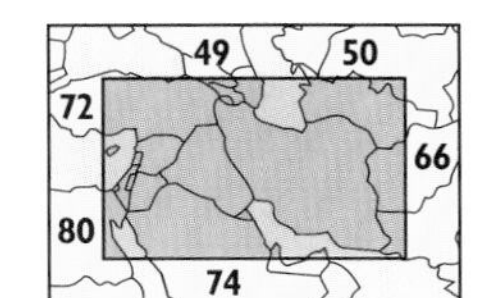

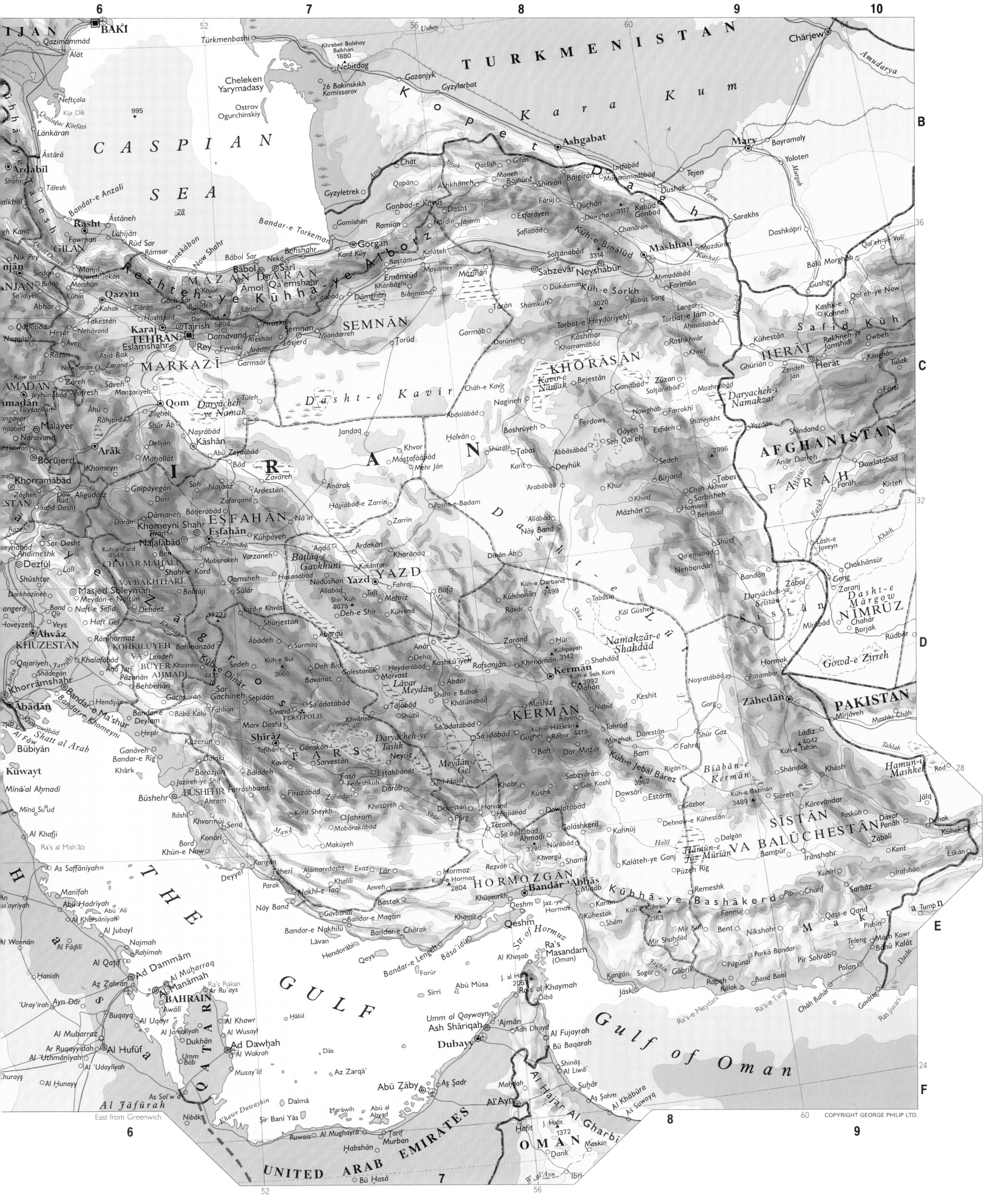

6 7 8 9 10

B

C

D

E

F

East from Greenwich

6 7 8 9

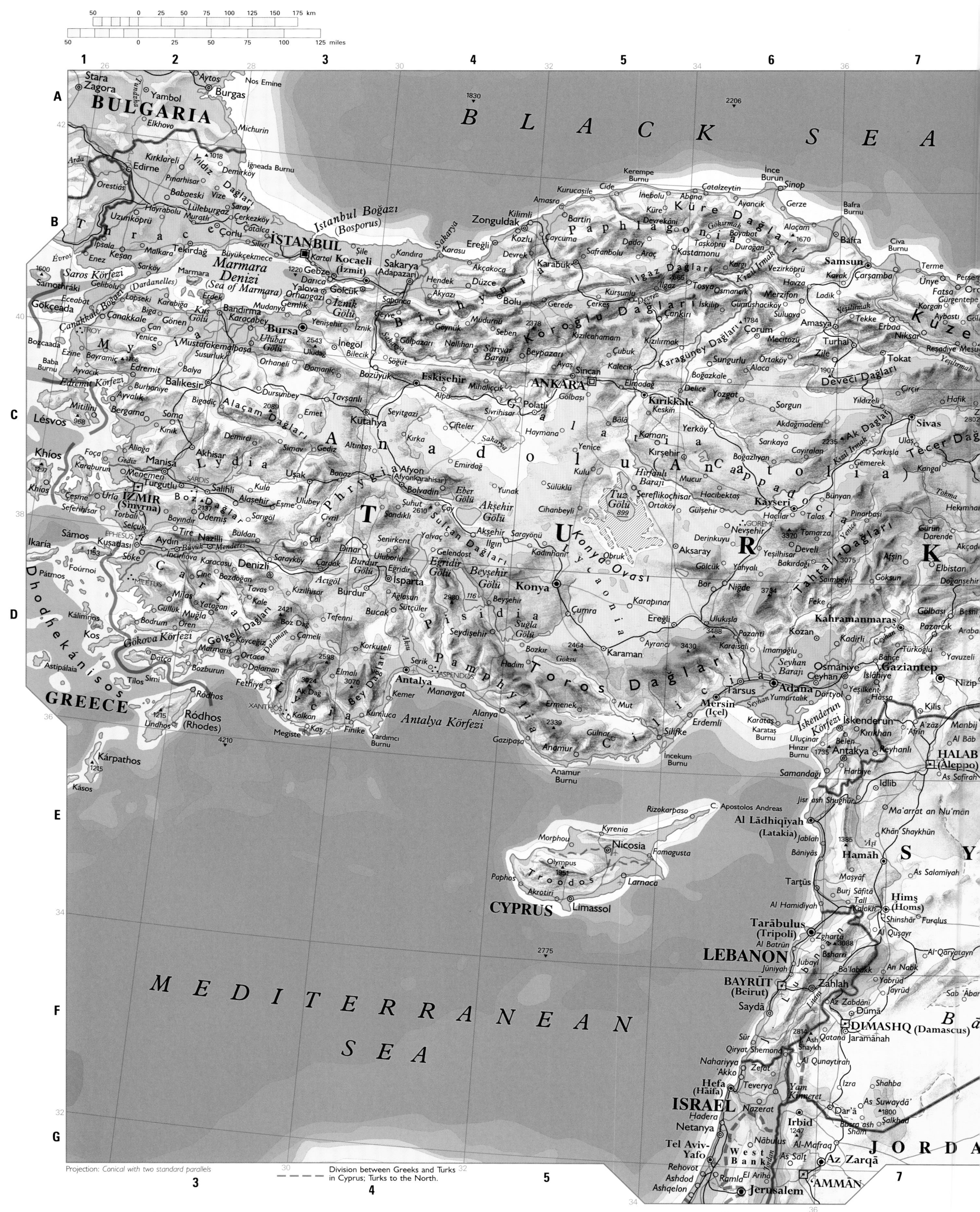
50 0 25 50 75 100 125 150 175 km
50 0 25 50 75 100 125 miles
1 2 3 4 5 6 7
A B C D E F G
BLACK SEA
MEDITERRANEAN SEA
BULGARIA
GREECE
CYPRUS
LEBANON
ISRAEL
JORDA
TURKEY
SY
Stara Zagora
Yambol
Aytos
Burgas
Nos Emine
Elkhovo
Michurin
Kırklareli
Edirne
Orestiás
İğneada Burnu
Demirköy
Yıldız Dağları
Pınarhisar
Babaeski
Vize
Lüleburgaz
Saray
Uzunköprü
Hayrabolu
Muratlı
Çerkezköy
Çatalca
Çorlu
Silivri
Büyükçekmece
Tekirdağ
Malkara
Keşan
İpsala
Enez
Évros
Thrace
Saros Körfezi
Samothráki
Gelibolu
Gökçeada
Eceabat
Çanakkale Boğazı (Dardanelles)
Çanakkale
Lâpseki
Marmara
Marmara Denizi (Sea of Marmara)
Erdek
Kapıdağ
Bandırma
Karacabey
Mudanya
Gemlik
Bursa
Uludağ
Bozcaada
TROY
Ezine
Bayramiç
Biga
Çan
Gönen
Yenice
Mustafakemalpaşa
Ulubat Gölü
Susurluk
Mysia
Baba Burnu
Ayvacık
Edremit
Edremit Körfezi
Burhaniye
Ayvalık
Balıkesir
Balya
Bigadiç
Dursunbey
Mitilíni
Lésvos
Bergama
Soma
Kınık
Alaçam Dağları
Khíos
Foça
Karaburun
Aliağa
Gediz
Manisa
Menemen
Akhisar
Demirci
Lydia
SARDIS
Salihli
Turgutlu
İZMİR (Smyrna)
Urla
Çeşme
Seferihisar
Torbalı
Boz Dağlar
Ödemiş
Bayındır
Tire
Selçuk
EPHESUS
Kuşadası
Sámos
Ikaría
Pátmos
Foúrnoi
Söke
Aydın
Nazilli
Büyük Menderes
Denizli
Çine
Karacasu
Bozdoğan
MILETUS
Milas
Muğla
Yatağan
Kalímnos
Kos
Bodrum
Ören
Gökova Körfezi
Marmaris
Datça
Bozburun
Dhodhekánisos
Astipálaia
Tílos
Sími
Ródhos
Ródhos (Rhodes)
Líndhos
Kárpathos
Kásos
Köyceğiz
Ortaca
Dalaman
Gölgeli Dağları
Fethiye
XANTHOS
Kalkan
Kaş
Megiste
Lycia
Elmalı
Bey Dağları
Finike
Kumluca
Kemer
Antalya
Antalya Körfezi
Yardımcı Burnu
Serik
ASPENDOS
Manavgat
Alanya
Gazipaşa
Anamur
Anamur Burnu
Pamphylia
İSTANBUL
İstanbul Boğazı (Bosporus)
Şile
Kocaeli (İzmit)
Kartal
Gebze
Darıca
Yalova
Gölcük
Orhangazi
İznik Gölü
İznik
Yenişehir
İnegöl
Bilecik
Söğüt
Bozüyük
Domaniç
Orhaneli
Kandıra
Sakarya (Adapazarı)
Sakarya
Karasu
Hendek
Akyazı
Sapanca
Geyve
Gölpazarı
Göynük
Ereğli
Zonguldak
Akçakoca
Düzce
Bolu
Bithynia
Mudurnu
Nallıhan
Seben
Sarıyar Barajı
Beypazarı
Kilimli
Kozlu
Çaycuma
Devrek
Bartın
Amasra
Karabük
Safranbolu
Gerede
Kurucaşile
Cide
Kerempe Burnu
İnebolu
Küre
Devrekâni
Abana
Çatalzeytin
Paphlagonia
Küre Dağları
Daday
Araç
Kastamonu
Taşköprü
Boyabat
Durağan
Ayancık
İnce Burun
Sinop
Gerze
Bafra Burnu
Bafra
Alaçam
Ilgaz Dağları
Ilgaz
Tosya
Osmancık
Kargı
Kızıl Irmak
Vezirköprü
Samsun
Çarşamba
Kavak
Havza
Merzifon
Gümüşhacıköy
Suluova
Amasya
Ladik
Civa Burnu
Terme
Ünye
Fatsa
Korgan
Tekke
Erbaa
Niksar
Yeşilırmak
Turhal
Zile
Tokat
Reşadiye
Köroğlu Dağları
Kurşunlu
Çerkeş
Çankırı
Eskipazar
Kızılcahamam
Şabanözü
Çorum
Mecitözü
Sungurlu
Ortaköy
Alaca
Boğazkale
Karagüney Dağları
Kızılırmak
Kalecik
Çubuk
Ayaş
Sincan
ANKARA
Elmadağ
Gölbaşı
Kırıkkale
Keskin
Delice
Yozgat
Sorgun
Deveci Dağları
Yıldızeli
Çırçır
Hafik
Sivas
Akdağmadeni
Ak Dağlar
Tecer Dağ
Şarkışla
Gemerek
Kangal
Sarıkaya
Çayıralan
Ulaş
Eskişehir
Alpu
Mihalıççık
Polatlı
Sivrihisar
Çifteler
Seyitgazi
Tavşanlı
Kütahya
Emet
Simav
Gediz
Altıntaş
Kırka
Haymana
Anadolu
Yenice
Emirdağ
Sakarya
Afyon
Afyonkarahisar
Phrygia
Banaz
Uşak
Eşme
Alaşehir
Kula
Sarıgöl
Ulubey
Çivril
Bolvadin
Eber Gölü
Akşehir Gölü
Akşehir
Yunak
Çay
Sandıklı
Suhut
Sultan Dağları
Sarayönü
Ilgın
Kadınhanı
Sülüklü
Cihanbeyli
Kulu
Tuz Gölü
Hirfanlı Barajı
Kaman
Kırşehir
Yerköy
Mucur
Şereflikoçhisar
Hacıbektaş
Ortaköy
Gülşehir
Boğazlıyan
Kayseri
Bünyan
Hacılar
Talas
GÖREME
Nevşehir
Derinkuyu
Aksaray
Kappadokia
Konya Ovası
Lycaonia
Konya
Obruk
Çumra
Karapınar
Ereğli
Karaman
Ayrancı
Toros Dağları
Niğde
Bor
Gölcük
Yahyalı
Yeşilhisar
Bakırdoğan
Develi
Tomarza
Pınarbaşı
Sarız
Tahtalı Dağları
Afşin
Elbistan
Göksun
Saimbeyli
Feke
Kahramanmaraş
Ulukışla
Pozantı
Karaisalı
Kozan
Kadirli
İmamoğlu
Seyhan Barajı
Osmaniye
Ceyhan
Adana
Tarsus
Mersin (İçel)
Erdemli
Silifke
İncekum Burnu
Mut
Ermenek
Gülnar
Cilicia
Bozkır
Hadım
Seydişehir
Suğla Gölü
Beyşehir
Beyşehir Gölü
Pisidia
Eğirdir Gölü
Eğirdir
Gelendost
Yalvaç
Senirkent
Uluborlu
Isparta
Ağlasun
Sütçüler
Burdur
Burdur Gölü
Dinar
Acıgöl
Çardak
Sarayköy
Çal
Buldan
Tavas
Kale
Tefenni
Bucak
Çameli
Korkuteli
Kızılhisar
Boz Dağ
Karataş
Karataş Burnu
Yumurtalık
Dörtyol
İskenderun Körfezi
İskenderun
Belen
Kırıkhan
Antakya
Reyhanlı
Samandağı
Uluçınar
Hınzır Burnu
Bahçe
Türkoğlu
Gaziantep
Nizip
İslâhiye
Yeşilkent
Hassa
Kilis
A'zāz
Afrīn
Manbij
Al Bāb
Pazarcık
Gölbaşı
Besni
Araban
Yavuzeli
Doğanşehir
HALAB (Aleppo)
As Safīrah
Idlib
Harbiye
Jisr ash Shughūr
Ma'arrat an Nu'mān
Khān Shaykhūn
Al Lādhiqīyah (Latakia)
Jablah
Bāniyās
Hamāh
As Salamīyah
Maşyāf
Tartūs
Burj Şāfītā
Tall Kalakh
Al Hamīdīyah
Ḩimş (Homs)
Shinshār
Furqlus
Al Quşayr
Ţarābulus (Tripoli)
Zghartā
Bsharrī
Al Batrūn
Jūnīyah
Jubayl
Ba'labakk
An Nabk
Al Qaryatayn
Yabrūd
Jayrūd
BAYRŪT (Beirut)
Zahlah
Az Zabdānī
Dūmā
DIMASHQ (Damascus)
Jaramānah
Qaţanā
Saydā
Sūr
Qiryat Shemona
Nahariyya
'Akko
Zefat
Hefa (Haifa)
Teverya
Yam Kinneret
Nazerat
Hadera
Netanya
Tel Aviv-Yafo
Rehovot
Ashdod
Ashqelon
Ramla
Jerusalem
Nāblus
El Arīḥā
West Bank
Irbid
Al-Mafraq
As Salţ
Az Zarqā
'AMMĀN
Dar'ā
Izra
Shahba
As Suwaydā'
Şalkhad
Busra ash Sham
Rizokarpaso
C. Apostolos Andreas
Kyrenia
Morphou
Nicosia
Famagusta
Olympus
Troodos
Paphos
Akrotiri
Limassol
Larnaca
Projection: Conical with two standard parallels
Division between Greeks and Turks in Cyprus; Turks to the North.

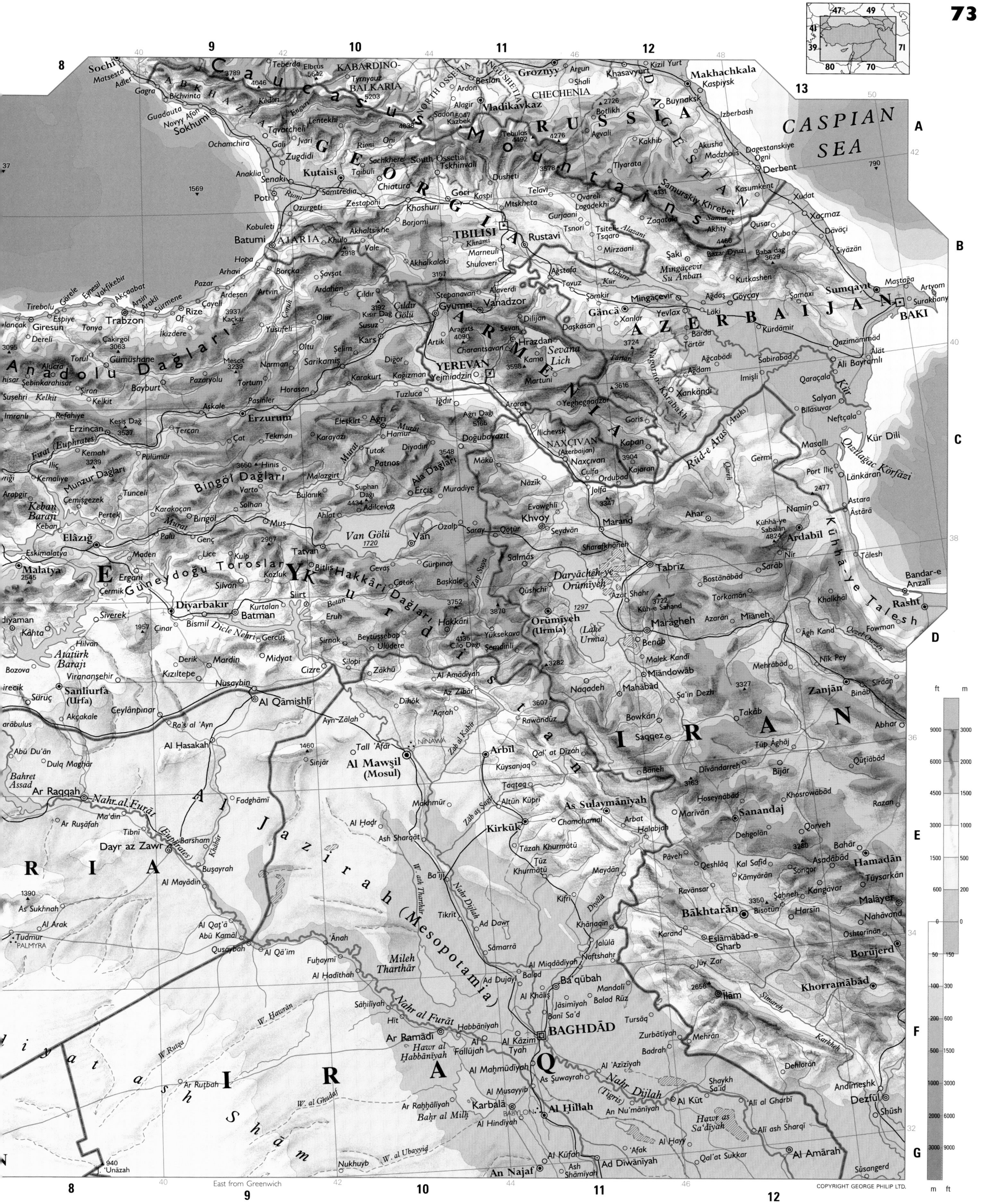

47 49 41 39 71 80 70

8 9 10 11 12 13

40 42 44 46 48 50

Caucasus Mountains
RUSSIA
GEORGIA
ARMENIA
AZERBAIJAN
DAGESTAN
CHECHENIA
INGUSHETIA
NORTH OSSETIA
KABARDINO-BALKARIA
ABKHAZIA
AJARIA
South Ossetia
NAXÇIVAN (Azerbaijan)
CASPIAN SEA
Anadolu Dağları
Güneydoğu Toroslar
Hakkâri Dağları
KURDISTAN
IRAN
IRAQ
SYRIA
TURKEY
Al Jazīrah (Mesopotamia)
Bādiyat ash Shām

Sochi, Matsesta, Adler, Gagra, Bichvinta, Guadauta, Novyy Afon, Sukhumi, Ochamchira, Anaklia, Poti, Kobuleti, Batumi, Hopa, Arhavi, Pazar, Rize, Of, Sürmene, Araklı, Akçaabat, Trabzon, Vakfıkebir, Eynesil, Görele, Tirebolu, Espiye, Giresun, Tonya, Dereli
Teberda, Elbrus 5642, Tyrnyauz, 5203, 3789, 4046, Kodori, Enguri, Lentekhi, Tqvarcheli, Gali, Jvari, Zugdidi, Senaki, Samtredia, Kutaisi, Tqibuli, Chiatura, Sachkhere, Zestaponi, Ozurgeti, Rioni, Oni, 4638
Beslan, Ardon, Alagir, Vladikavkaz, Sadon, Kazbek 5047, Tskhinvali, Tebulos 4492, 4276, Dusheti, Mtskheta, Gori, Kaspi, Khashuri, Borjomi, Akhaltsikhe, Khulo, Vale, Akhalkalaki, TBILISI, Marneuli, Shuloveri, Khrami, Rustavi
Groznyy, Argun, Shali, Khasavyurt, Kizil Yurt, Makhachkala, Kaspiysk, Buynaksk, Botlikh 2726, Agvali, Kakhib, Izberbash, Akusha, Madzhalis, Dagestanskiye Ogni, Derbent, Tlyarata, 3578, Telavi, Qvareli, Lagodekhi, Gurjaani, Tsnori, Tsiteli-Tsqaro, Alazani, Mirzaani, Zaqatala, Samursky Khrebet, Samur, Akhty, 4466, 4131, Kasumkent, Xudat, Xaçmaz, Dəvəçi, Qusar, Quba, Siyəzən, Bazar Dyuzi, Baba dag 3629, Şəki, Mingəçevir Su Anbarı, Qabırri, Kür, Kutkashen, Sumqayıt, Maştağa, Artyom, Surakhany, BAKI
Ağstafa, Tovuz, Şəmkir, Mingəçevir, Yevlax, Ağdaş, Göyçay, Şamaxi, Gəncə, Xanlar, Daşkəsən, Ləki, Bərdə, Tərtər, Kürdəmir, Qazimämmäd, Ağcabədi, Ağdam, Sabirabad, Imişli, Ələt, Əli Bayramlı, Qaraçala, Salyan, Biləsuvar, Neftçala, Kür Dili, Qızılağac Körfəzi, Masallı, Germi, Port Ilıç, Lənkəran, 2477, Astara, Āstārā
Şavşat, Borçka, Ardahan, Çıldır, Çıldır Gölü, 3192, Kısır Dağ, Artvin, Ardeşen, Çayeli, 3937 Kaçkar, İkizdere, Yusufeli, Çoruh, Olur, Susuz, Kars, Gyumri, Stepanavan, Alaverdi, Vanadzor, Dilijan, 3157, Aragats 4090, Artik, Charantsavan, Sevan, Hrazdan, Kamo, Sevana Lich, YEREVAN, Yejmiadzin, 3598, Martuni, 3724, Tärtär, Nagorno Karabakh, Xankändi, 3616, Yeghegnadzor, Goris, Kapan, 3904, Kajaran, Ordubad, Naxçıvan, Culfa, Ilichevsk, Ararat
Çakırgöl 3063, Gümüşhane, Torul, Alucra, Mescit 3239, Narman, Oltu, Sarıkamış, Şelim, Digor, Kağızman, Karakurt, Tuzluca, Iğdır, Ağrı Dağı 5165, Doğubayazıt, Bayburt, Pazaryolu, Tortum, Horasan, Pasinler, Aşkale, Erzurum, Şebinkarahisar, Şiran, Kelkit, Suşehri, Refahiye, İmranlı, Keşiş Dağ 3537, Erzincan, Tercan, Çat, Tekman, Karayazı, Eleşkirt, Ağrı, Murat, Hamur, Tutak, Diyadin, Patnos, Ala Dağları 3548, Malazgirt, Suphan Dağı 4434, Adilcevaz, Erciş, Muradiye, Maku, Nāzīk, Kemah, 3239, İliç, Munzur Dağları, Kemaliye, Pülümür, Hinis 3660, Bingöl Dağları, Varto, Solhan, Tunceli, Çemişgezek, Arapgir, Keban Barajı, Keban, Pertek, Karakoçan, Bingöl, Muş, Bulanık, Ahlat, Fırat (Euphrates)
Elâzığ, Palu, Genç, 2967, Van Gölü 1720, Van, Özalp, Saray, Qotūr, Khvoy, Evowghlī, Seydvān, Jolfa, 3347, Marand, Ahar, Kühhā-ye Sabalān 4824, Ardabīl, Namīn, Nīr, Kühhā-ye Tālesh, Tālesh, Sarāb, Tabrīz, Sharafkhāneh, Salmās, Rūd-e Aras (Araks), Qareh
Eskimalatya, Malatya 2545, Maden, Lice, Kulp, Tatvan, Bitlis, Kozluk, Ergani, Çermik, Silvan, Geva, Gürpınar, Çatak, Başkale, Zap Suyu, Qüshchī, Daryācheh-ye Orūmīyeh, Shahr, Āzar, 3722 Kūh-e Sahand, Bostānābād, Torkamān, Bandar-e Anzalī, Rasht, Khalkhāl
Adıyaman, Kâhta, Siverek, Diyarbakır, Kurtalan, Batman, Siirt, Botan, Eruh, 3752, Hakkâri, 3870, Orūmīyeh (Urmia), 1297, (Lake Urmia), Marāgheh, Azarān, Mīāneh, Āgh Kand, Qezel Owzan, Fowman, Bismil, Dicle Nehri, Gercüş, Çınar, 1957, Hilvan, Şırnak, Beytüşşebap, Uludere, Cilo Dağı 4135, Yüksekova, Şemdinli, Benāb, Malek Kandī, Mīāndowāb, Mehrābād, Nīk Pey
Atatürk Barajı, Bozova, Viranşehir, Birecik, Şanlıurfa (Urfa), Suruç, Akçakale, Ceylânpınar, Derik, Mardin, Midyat, Kızıltepe, Nusaybin, Cizre, Silopi, Zākhū, Al Qāmishlī, Al Amādīyah, Az Zibār, 3282, Naqadeh, Mahābād, Sa'īn Dezh, 3327, Zanjān, Sīrdān, Bīnāb, Abhar
Jarābulus, Abū Du'ān, Dulq Maghār, Bahret Assad, Ar Raqqah, Ra's al 'Ayn, Al Hasakah, Ayn Zālah, Dihōk, 'Aqrah, 3607, Rawāndūz, Bowkān, Saqqez, Takāb, Tūp Āghāj, Qūtīābād, 1460, Sinjār, Tall 'Afar, NINAWA, Al Mawşil (Mosul), Zab al Kabir, Arbīl, Qal' at Dīzah, Kūysanjaq, Bāneh, Dīvāndarreh, Bījār, 3163
Nahr al Furāt, Ma'dīn, Ar Ruşāfah, Fadghāmī, Tibnī, Barsham, Khābūr, Dayr az Zawr, Buşayrah, Al Mayādīn, Makhmūr, Al Ḩaḑr, Ash Sharqāţ, Ţaqţaq, Altūn Kūprī, Zab aş Şaghīr, As Sulaymānīyah, Chamchamal, Arbat, Ḩalabjah, Marīvān, Hoseynābād, Khosrowābād, Sanandaj, Razan, Kirkūk, Ţāzah Khurmātū, Ţūz Khurmātū, Dehgolān, Qorveh, Bahār, Hamadān, Pāveh, Qeshlāq, Kal Safīd, Kāmyārān, Songor, Asadābād, Tūysarkān, 3260
1390, As Sukhnah, Al Arak, Tudmur, PALMYRA, Al Qaţ'ā, Abū Kamāl, Qusaybah, Al Qā'im, 'Ānah, Fuḩaymī, Al Ḩadīthah, Mileh Tharthār, W. ath Tharthār, Ba'ījī, Nahr Dijlah, Tikrīt, Ad Dawr, Sāmarrā, Maydān, Kifrī, Diyālā, Khānaqīn, Jalūlā, Naftshahr, Ravānsar, Kangāvar, Şahneh, 3350, Bīsotūn, Harsīn, Malāyer, Nahāvand, Bākhtarān, Karand, Eslāmābād-e Gharb, Oshtorīnān, Borūjerd
Al Miqdādīyah, Ad Dujayl, Balad, Ba'qūbah, Al Khāliş, Mandalī, Jāsimīyah, Balad Rūz, Banī Sa'd, Jūy Zar, 2656, Īlām, Khorramābād, Sīmareh, Şāḩilīyah, Hīt, Nahr al Furāt, Ḩabbānīyah, Ar Ramādī, Hawr al Ḩabbānīyah, Al Fallūjah, Al Kāzim, Tyah, BAGHDĀD, Tursāq, Zurbāţīyah, Badrah, Mehrān, Karkheh, Dehlorān
W. Ḩawrān, W. Rutqa, Ar Ruţbah, W. al Ghadaf, Al Maḩmūdīyah, As Şuwayrah, Al 'Azīzīyah, Nahr Dijlah (Tigris), Shaykh Sa'd, Al Kūt, 'Alī al Gharbī, Andīmeshk, Dezfūl, Shūsh, Ar Raḩḩālīyah, Baḩr al Milḩ, Karbalā, Al Musayyib, BABYLON, Al Ḩillah, Al Hindīyah, An Nu'mānīyah, Hawr as Sa'dīyah, 'Alī ash Sharqī, Al Ḩayy, W. al Ubayyiḑ, 'Afak, Qal'at Sukkar, Al 'Amārah, Al Kūfah, Ash Shāmīyah, Ad Dīwānīyah, An Najaf, Nukhuyb, 940 'Unāzah, Sūsangerd
37, 1569, 790, 36, 34, 32, 38, 40, 42

A B C D E F G

ft m
9000 3000
6000 2000
4500 1500
3000 1000
1500 500
600 200
0 0
50 150
100 300
200 600
500 1500
1000 3000
2000 6000
3000 9000
m ft

40 East from Greenwich 42 44 46

8 9 10 11 12

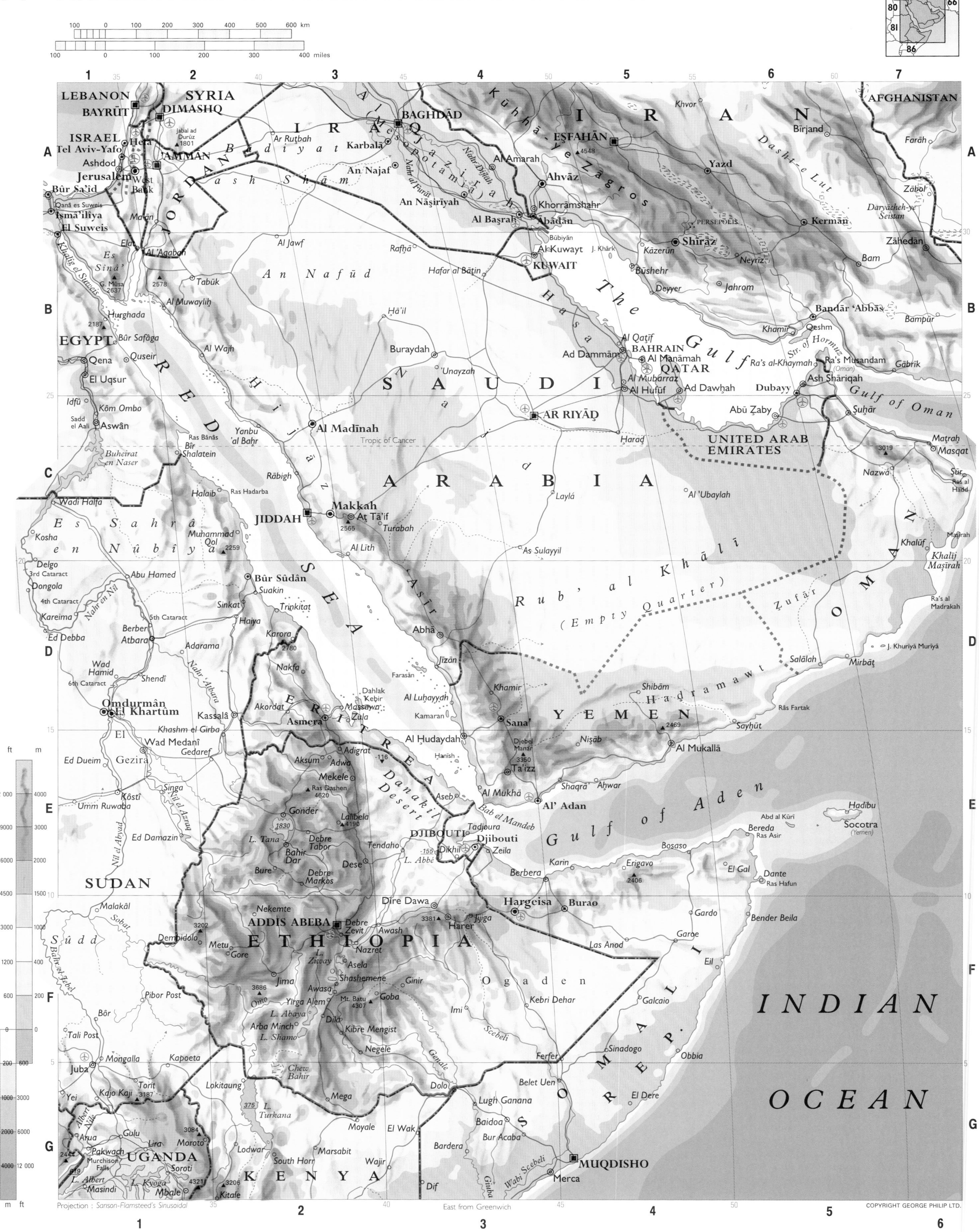
100 0 100 200 300 400 500 600 km
100 0 100 200 300 400 miles
LEBANON
BAYRŪT
SYRIA
DIMASHQ
ISRAEL
Tel Aviv-Yafo
Ashdod
Jerusalem
West Bank
'AMMĀN
JORDAN
BAGHDĀD
IRAQ
Karbalā'
An Najaf
An Nāşirīyah
Al Başrah
Ar Ruţbah
Bādiyat ash Shām
Al Jawf
Rafhā'
Hafar al Bāţin
KUWAIT
Al Kuwayt
IRAN
EŞFAHĀN
Kūhhā-ye Zāgros
Ahvāz
Khorrāmshahr
Ābādān
Al 'Amārah
Yazd
Dasht-e Lut
Bīrjand
Khvor
Kermān
Shīrāz
Kāzerūn
Būshehr
Jahrom
Bandar 'Abbās
Qeshm
Bampūr
Zāhedān
Bam
Farāh
Zābol
Daryācheh-ye Seistan
AFGHANISTAN
Bûr Sa'îd
Isma'iliya
El Suweis
EGYPT
Hurghada
Bûr Safâga
Qena
El Uqsur
Idfû
Kôm Ombo
Aswân
Buheirat en Naser
Wadi Halfa
Es Sînâ'
Elat
Al 'Aqabah
Tabūk
Al Muwaylih
Al Wajh
An Nafūd
Hā'il
Buraydah
'Unayzah
Al Madīnah
Yanbu 'al Bahr
Tropic of Cancer
Rābigh
Makkah
JIDDAH
Aţ Ţā'if
Turabah
Al Līth
SAUDI ARABIA
AR RIYĀD
Ad Dammām
Al Qaţīf
BAHRAIN
Al Manāmah
QATAR
Ad Dawhah
Al Mubarraz
Al Hufūf
Haraḑ
Laylá
As Sulayyil
Al 'Ubaylah
The Gulf
Ra's al-Khaymah
Ash Shāriqah
Dubayy
Abū Zaby
UNITED ARAB EMIRATES
Str. of Hormuz
Ra's Musandam
Gulf of Oman
Şuhār
Maţraḩ
Masqaţ
Nazwá
Şūr
Ra's al Hadd
Maşīrah
Khalīj Maşīrah
Khalūf
Ra's al Madrakah
OMAN
Z̧ufār
Şalālah
Mirbāţ
J. Khuriyā Murīyā
Rub' al Khālī (Empty Quarter)
'Asīr
Abhā
Jīzān
Farasān
Khamir
Al Luhayyah
Kamaran
Sana'
Al Hudaydah
Hanish
Djebel Manar 3350
Ta'izz
Al Mukhā
Al' Adan
YEMEN
Hadramawt
Shibām
Nişāb
Shaqra'
Ahwar
Al Mukallā
Sayhūt
Rās Fartak
Bab el Mandeb
Gulf of Aden
Hadibu
Socotra (Yemen)
Abd al Kūrī
RED SEA
SUDAN
Es Sahrâ en Nûbîya
Kosha
Delgo
3rd Cataract
Dongola
4th Cataract
Kareima
Ed Debba
Abu Hamed
Nahr en Nil
5th Cataract
Berber
Atbara
Adarama
Nahr 'Atbara
Wad Hamid
6th Cataract
Shendi
Omdurmân
El Khartûm
Kassalâ
Khashm el Girba
Wad Medanî
El Gezira
Gedaref
Ed Dueim
Kôstî
Umm Ruwaba
Singa
Nîl el Azraq
Ed Damazin
Nîl el Abyad
Halaib
Ras Hadarba
Muhammad Qol
Bûr Sûdân
Suakin
Sinkat
Trinkitat
Haiya
Karora
Nakfa
Akordat
Asmera
ERITREA
Massawa
Zula
Adigrat
Aksum
Adwa
Mekele
Ras Dashen 4620
Gonder
Lalibela
L. Tana
Bahir Dar
Debre Tabor
Dese
Debre Markos
Bure
Tendaho
Danakil Desert
Aseb
DJIBOUTI
Djibouti
Tadjoura
Dikhil
Zeila
L. Abbé
Berbera
Karin
Bosaso
Erigavo
El Gal
Dante
Ras Hafun
Hargeisa
Burao
Dire Dawa
Harer
Jijiga
ADDIS ABEBA
Debre Zeyit
Awash
Nazret
ETHIOPIA
Nekemte
Dembidolo
Metu
Gore
Jima
L. Ziway
Asela
Shashemene
Awasa
Ginir
Goba
Mt. Batu 4307
Yirga Alem
L. Abaya
Dila
Arba Minch
L. Shamo
Kibre Mengist
Negele
Chew Bahir
Mega
Moyale
Ogaden
Kebri Dehar
Imi
Scebeli
Genale
Dolo
Gardo
Bender Beila
Garoe
Las Anod
Eil
Galcaio
Obbia
Ferfer
Sinadogo
SOMALI REP.
Belet Uen
El Dere
Lugh Ganana
Baidoa
Bur Acaba
Bardera
MUQDISHO
Merca
Wabi Scebeli
Giuba
Dif
El Wak
Wajir
KENYA
Marsabit
South Horr
Lodwar
L. Turkana
Lokitaung
Kapoeta
Torit
Juba
Mongalla
Kajo Kaji
Yei
Bôr
Tali Post
Pibor Post
Malakâl
Sobat
Sûdd
Bahr el Jebel
UGANDA
Gulu
Lira
Moroto
Arua
Pakwach
Murchison Falls
Soroti
L. Kyoga
L. Albert
Masindi
Mbale
Kitale
INDIAN OCEAN
Projection : Sanson-Flamsteed's Sinusoidal
East from Greenwich
COPYRIGHT GEORGE PHILIP LTD.

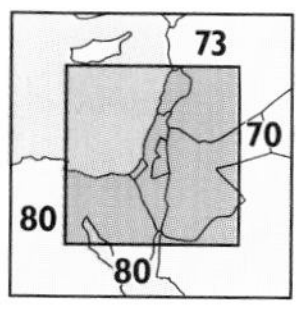

73
70
80
80

10 0 10 20 30 40 50 60 70 80 100 km
10 0 10 20 30 40 50 60 miles

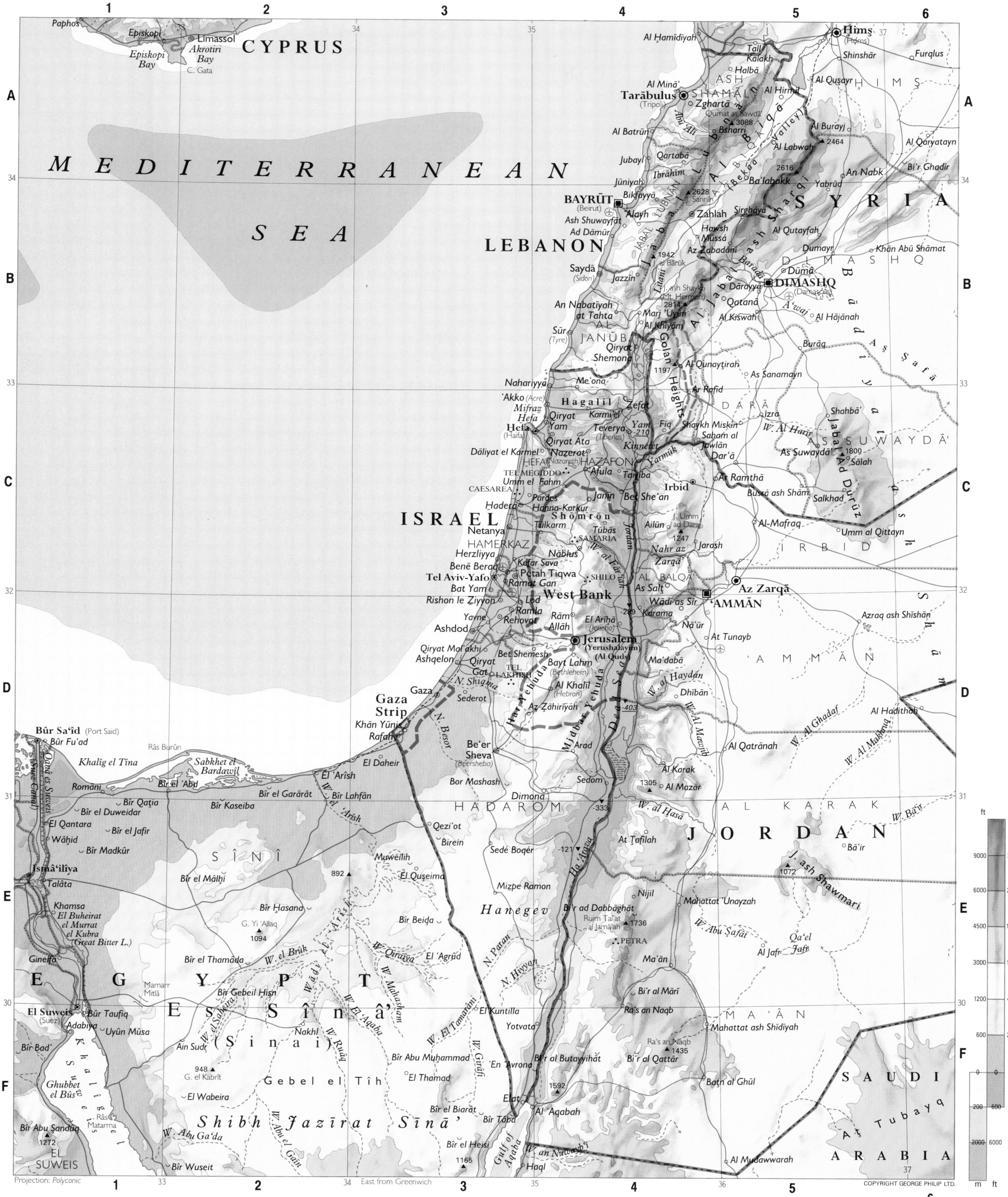

1 2 3 4 5 6

A B C D E F

Paphos
Episkopi
Limassol
Akrotiri Bay
Episkopi Bay
C. Gata
CYPRUS

MEDITERRANEAN
SEA

LEBANON
Al Ḥamīdīyah
Tall Kalakh
Ḥalbā
Al Minā'
Tarābulus (Tripoli)
Zghartā
ASH SHAMĀL
Qumat as Sawdā' 3088
Bsharri
Al Batrūn
Jubayl
Qartabā
Ibrāhīm
Jūniyah
Bikfayyā
2628 Sannin
BAYRŪT (Beirut)
Ash Shuwayfāt
Ad Dāmūr
Alayh
Zaḥlah
Ḥawsh Mūsá
Az Zabadānī
1942 Al Bārūk
Jazzīn
Ṣaydā (Sidon)
An Nabaṭīyah at Taḥta
AL JANŪB
Ṣūr (Tyre)
Marj 'Uyūn
Al Khiyām
Jabal Lubnān
Liṭānī
Jabal ash Sharqī
Al Biqā' (Bekaa Valley)
Ba'labakk
2616

SYRIA
Ḥimṣ (Homs)
Shinshār
Furqlus
Al Quṣayr
ḤIMṢ
Al Hirmil
Al Burayj
Al Labwah
2464
Al Qaryatayn
An Nabk
Bi'r Ghadīr
Yabrūd
Sirghāyā
Al Quṭayfah
Dumayr
Khān Abū Shāmat
DIMASHQ
Dūmā
Baradá
DIMASHQ (Damascus)
Dārayyā
Qaṭanā
A'waj
Al Kiswah
Al Hājānah
J. ash Shaykh (Mt. Hermon) 2814
Al Jabal ash Shaykh
Burāq
Aṣ Ṣafā
Bādiyat ash Shām
Golan Heights
1197
Al Qunayṭirah
As Sanamayn
Ar Rafid
DAR'Ā
Shahbā
Izra
Shaykh Miskīn
W. Al Harīr
Saḥam al Jawlān
ASSUWAYDĀ'
As Suwaydā'
1800
Ṣalāḥ
Jabal Ad Durūz
Dar'ā
Ar Ramthā
Buṣrá ash Shām
Ṣalkhad

ISRAEL
Qiryat Shemona
Nahariyya
Me'ona
'Akko (Acre)
Hagalil
Zefat
Karmi'el
Mifraz Hefa
Hefa (Haifa)
Qiryat Yam
Qiryat Ata
Teverya (Tiberias)
Yam Kinneret -210
Fiq
Dāliyat el Karmel
Nazerat (Nazareth)
HEFA
HAZAFON
Afula
Kinneret
Yarmūk
TEL MEGIDDO
Umm el Fahm
CAESAREA
Tayiba
Bet She'an
Ḥadera
Pardes Ḥanna-Karkur
Janīn
Shomron
Netanya
Ṭulkarm
Ṭūbās
SAMARIA
HAMERKAZ
Herzliyya
Bené Beraq
Kefar Sava
Nāblus
Petah Tiqwa
Ramat Gan
Tel Aviv-Yafo
SHILO
W. al Fāri'ah
Bat Yam
Rishon le Ziyyon
Lod
West Bank
Ramla
Yavne
Reḥovot
Rām Allāh
Ashdod
El Arīhā (Jericho)
Qiryat Mal'akhi
Bet Shemesh
Jerusalem (Yerushalayim) (Al Quds)
Ashqelon
Qiryat Gat
TEL LAKHISH
Bayt Laḥm (Bethlehem)
Al Khalīl (Hebron)
Har Yehuda
Midbar Yehuda
Az Ẓāhirīyah
N. Shiqma
Sederot
Gaza
Gaza Strip
Khān Yūnis
Rafah
N. Besor
Be'er Sheva (Beersheba)
Arad
Dead Sea
-403
Sedom
Bor Mashash
Dimona
HADAROM
-333
Qezi'ot
Birein
Sedé Boqér
-121
Ha 'Arava
Mizpe Ramon
Hanegev
N. Paran
N. Hiyyon
Yotvata
'En Avrona
Elat
Gulf of Aqaba

JORDAN
Irbid
J. Umm ad Daraj
1247
'Ajlūn
Al-Mafraq
Umm al Qittayn
IRBID
Jarash
Nahr az Zarqā'
Jordan
AL BALQĀ'
Az Zarqā'
As Salṭ
Wādī as Sīr
'AMMĀN
-289
Karāma
Nā'ūr
Azraq ash Shīshān
At Tunayb
'AMMĀN
Ma'dabā
W. al Haydān
Dhībān
W. Al Mawjib
Al Qaṭrānah
W. Al Ghadaf
Al Ḥadīthah
W. Al Makmal
Al Karak
1305
Al Mazār
W. al Hasā
AL KARAK
W. Bā'ir
Aṭ Ṭafīlah
Bā'ir
J. ash Shawmari
1072
Nijil
Maḥaṭṭat 'Unayzah
Bi'r ad Dabbāghāt
Ruim Tal'at al Jamā'ah
1736
PETRA
W. Abū Ṣafāt
Qa'el Jafr
Al Jafr
Ma'ān
Bi'r al Mārī
Ra's an Naqb
MA'ĀN
Maḥaṭṭat ash Shīdīyah
Ra's an Naqb 1435
Bi'r al Qaṭṭār
Bir al Butayyihāt
1592
Baṭn al Ghūl
Al 'Aqabah
W. an Nuwayb
Ḥaql
Al Mudawwarah

SAUDI ARABIA
At Tubayq

EGYPT
Bûr Sa'îd (Port Said)
Bûr Fu'ad
Râs Burûn
Qanâ es Suweis (Suez Canal)
Khalîg el Tîna
Sabkhet el Bardawîl
Romani
Bir el 'Abd
Bîr el Garârât
El 'Arîsh
Bîr Lahfân
El Daheir
W. el 'Arîsh
Bîr Qaṭia
Bîr el Duweidar
Bîr Kaseiba
El Qantara
Bîr el Jafir
Wâḥid
Bîr Madkûr
SÎNÎ
Ismâ'iliya
Talâta
Bîr el Mâlḥi
892
Muweilih
El Quseima
Khamsa
El Buheirat el Murrat el Kubra (Great Bitter L.)
Bîr Ḥasana
G. Yi'Allaq 1094
Bîr Beiḍa
Geneifa
Bîr el Thamâda
W. el Brûk
Wâdi el 'Arîsh
W. Qiraiya
Bîr el 'Agrûd
W. Mahashsham
Mamarr Mitlâ
Bîr Gebeil Ḥisn
Sînâ' (Sinai)
El Suweis (Suez)
Bîr Taufîq
Adabiya
'Uyûn Mûsa
W. el Sahēira
W. El 'Aqaba
Nakhl
W. Ruâq
W. El Tamatani
W. Girâfi
El Kuntilla
Ain Sudr
Bîr Abu Muḥammad
948 G. el Kabrît
El Thamad
Bîr Bad'
Gebel el Tîh
Khalîg el Suweis
Ghubbet el Bûs
El Wabeira
Shibh Jazīrat Sīnā'
Bîr el Biarât
Bîr Taba
Râs Matarma
Bîr Abu Sandûq
1272
W. Abu Ga'da
W. Abu el Gain
Bîr el Heisi
1165
EL SUWEIS
Bîr Wuseit

Projection: Polyconic
33 34 East from Greenwich 35 36 37

ft m
9000 3000
6000 2000
4500 1500
3000 1000
1200 400
600 200
0 0
200 600
2000 6000
m ft

1974 Cease Fire Lines

AFRICA : Physical 1:33 600 000

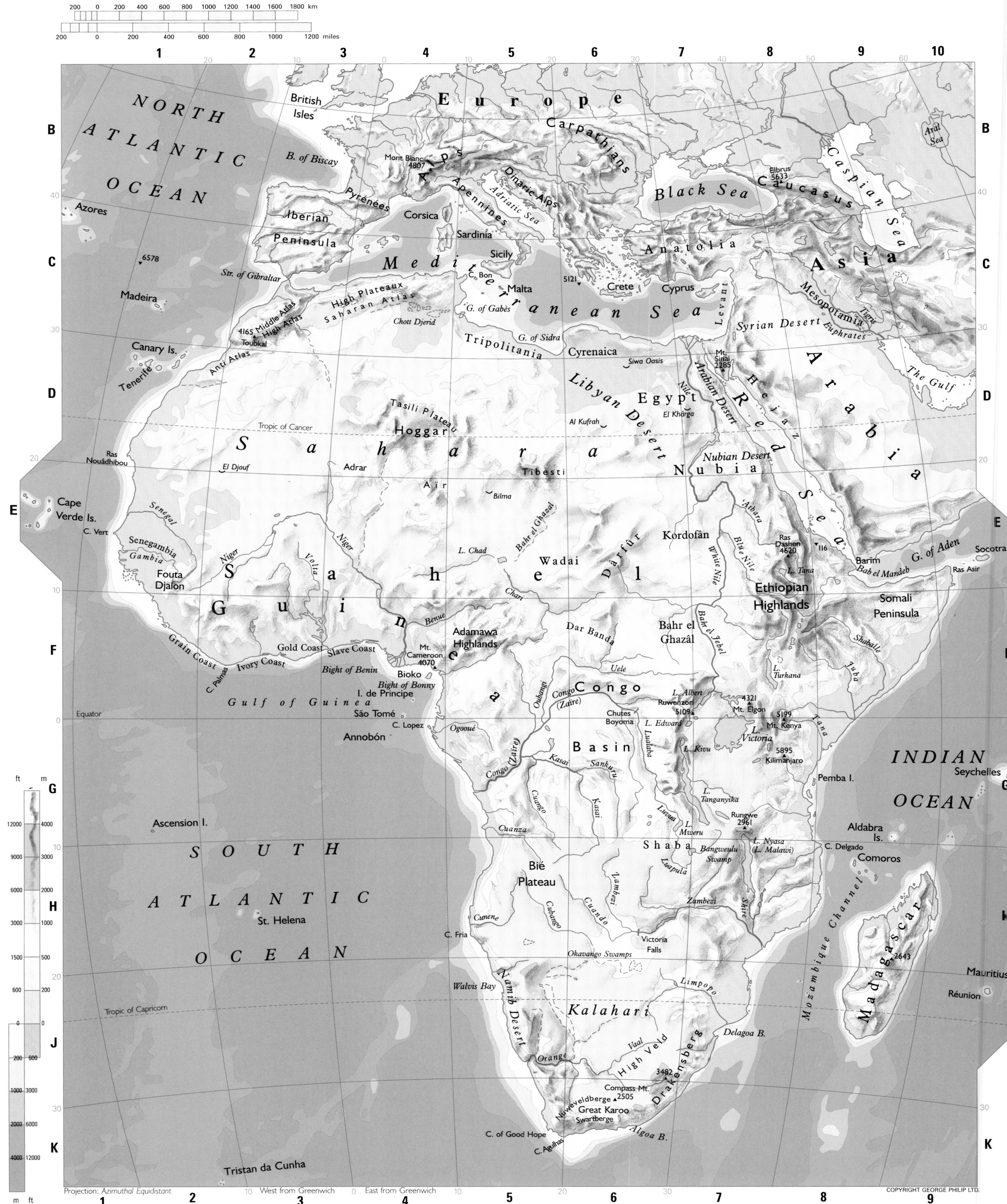

NORTH ATLANTIC OCEAN
SOUTH ATLANTIC OCEAN
INDIAN OCEAN
Mediterranean Sea
Sahara
ALGERIA
LIBYA
EGYPT
MOROCCO
WESTERN SAHARA
MAURITANIA
MALI
NIGER
CHAD
SUDAN
ETHIOPIA
SOMALI REP.
KENYA
TANZANIA
CONGO (DEM. REP. OF THE)
ANGOLA
ZAMBIA
ZIMBABWE
MOZAMBIQUE
NAMIBIA
BOTSWANA
SOUTH AFRICA
MADAGASCAR
NIGERIA
CAMEROON
CENTRAL AFRICAN REP.
GABON
CONGO
SENEGAL
GUINEA
IVORY COAST
GHANA
BURKINA FASO
SAUDI ARABIA
YEMEN
TURKEY
SPAIN
FRANCE
ITALY
Projection: Azimuthal Equidistant
Dakar Capital Cities
COPYRIGHT GEORGE PHILIP LTD.

100 0 100 200 300 400 500 600 km
100 0 100 200 300 400 miles
ATLANTIC
OCEAN
Azores (Port.)
Madeira (Port.)
Porto Santo
Funchal
Islas Canarias (Sp.)
La Palma
Santa Cruz de Tenerife
Tenerife
Gomera
Hierro
Las Palmas
Gran Canaria
Lanzarote
Arrecife
Fuerteventura
SPAIN
Cádiz
Málaga
Almería
Str. of Gibraltar
Gibraltar (U.K.)
Ceuta (Sp.)
Melilla (Sp.)
Tanger
Tétouan
Al Hoceïma
Nador
Oujda
ALGER
Oran
Mostaganem
Ech Cheliff
Médéa
Blida
Tizi-Ouzou
Bejaia
Sétif
Batna
Biskra
Tlemcen
Sidi-bel-Abbès
Mascara
Tiaret
Djelfa
M'sila
Chott el Hodna
Ksar el Kebir
Ouezzane
Kenitra
Salé
Rabat
Fès
Taza
Meknès
Khemisset
Mohammedia
CASABLANCA
El Jadida
Khouribga
Settat
Beni Mellal
Safi
Ras Beddouza
Marrakech
Essaouira
MOROCCO
Moyen Atlas
Haut Atlas
Anti Atlas
Dj. Toubkal 4165
Ouarzazate
Taroudannt
C. Rhir
Agadir
Ifni
Goulimine
Tan-tan
C. Juby
Tarfaya
El Aaiún
Smara
Bu Craa
C. Bojador
WESTERN SAHARA
Dakhla
Bir Mogreïn
Ain Ben Tili
Tindouf
Figuig
Béchar
Abadla
Ar Rachidiya
Er Rif
Mecheria
Aïn-Sefra
El Bayadh
Aflou
Laghouat
Messad
Ghardaïa
Berriane
Touggourt
El Oued
Ouargla
Hassi Messaoud
El Goléa
Kerzaz
Timimoun
Grand Erg Occidental
Grand Erg Oriental
Maghreb
ALGERIA
Plateau du Tademaït
In Salah
Bordj Omar Driss
Bordj Fly Ste. Marie
Zaouiet Reggane
Ohanet
Illizi
Arak
Tassili n Ajjer
Djanet
Ahaggar
Tahat 2918
Tamanrasset
Bordj-in-Eker
Ouallene
Chegga
Erg Iguidi
Erg Chech
Tropic of Cancer
Taoudenni
Tanezrouft
El Djouf
Sahara
Zouîrât
Fdérik
Nouâdhibou
Râs Nouâdhibou
Atâr
Chinguetti
Adrar
Akjoujt
Râs Timirist
MAURITANIA
Rachid
Tidjikja
Nouakchott
Aoukâr
Aleg
Kaédi
Kiffa
'Ayoûn el 'Atroûs
Néma
Rosso
St. Louis
Dagana
Matam
Louga
Linguère
Mboro
Thiès
Tivaouane
C. Vert
DAKAR
SENEGAL
Kaolack
Banjul
GAMBIA
Tambacounda
Georgetown
Sédhiou
Ziguinchor
GUINEA-BISSAU
Bissau
Arq. dos Bijagós
Fouta Djalon
Labé
Gaoual
GUINEA
Dalaba
Dabola
Kindia
Mamou
Faranah
Kankan
C. Verga
Dubréka
Conakry
Kabala
SIERRA LEONE
Port Loko
Freetown
Yonibana
Bo
Kenema
Sherbro I.
Bonthe
Sulima
Monrovia
LIBERIA
Buchanan
River Cess
Harper
C. Palmas
Grain Coast
Kayes
Bakel
Sélibabi
Nioro du Sahel
Nara
Kita
Bafoulabé
Siguiri
Bamako
Ségou
Bougouni
Sikasso
MALI
Tombouctou
Niger
Bourem
Gao
Ansongo
Ménaka
Hombori
Mopti
Diafarabé
Djénné
San
Kidal
Tessalit
Adrar des Iforas
598
Douentza
BURKINA FASO
Ouagadougou
Koudougou
Tougan
Kaya
Dori
Fada-n-Gourma
Bobo-Dioulasso
Gaoua
Niamey
Dosso
Filingué
Tahoua
Birni Nkonni
Maradi
Zinder
NIGER
Arlit
Agadez
Aïr
Iférouane
In-Gall
Tanout
Tumu
Bawku
Dapaong
Mango
Natitingou
Kandi
Bembèrèkè
Parakou
BENIN
TOGO
Sokodé
GHANA
Tamale
Savelugu
Black Volta
Salaga
Wenchi
Kumasi
Obuasi
Lake Volta
Kete Krachi
Koforidua
Accra
Tema
Cape Coast
Sekondi-Takoradi
C. Three Points
Gold Coast
Axim
Tarkwa
Asamankese
IVORY COAST
Odienné
Korhogo
Ferkéssédougou
Boundiali
Kong
Bouna
Bondoukou
Séguéla
Katiola
Bouaké
Man
Danané
Daloa
Yamoussoukro
Abengourou
Gagnoa
Divo
Agboville
Adzope
Lakota
ABIDJAN
Grand Bassam
Sassandra
San Pédro
Tabou
Ivory Coast
Nzérékoré
Lomé
Cotonou
Porto-Novo
LAGOS
Slave Coast
Bight of Benin
Ijebu-Ode
Abeokuta
IBADAN
Ogbomosho
Oyo
Iwo
Ilorin
Offa
Oshogbo
Ilesha
Ife
Owo
Akure
Benin City
Sapele
Warri
Port Harcourt
Aba
Calabar
Onitsha
Enugu
Makurdi
Lafia
Abuja
Minna
Kaduna
Zaria
Kano
Katsina
Gusau
Sokoto
Birnin Kebbi
Jega
Bena
Funtua
Kontagora
Kainji Res.
Shaki
Shanga
Gaya
Botou
NIGERIA
Bauchi
Jos
Kafanchan
Keffi
Bida
Baro
Lokoja
Wukari
Otukpo
Benue
Bamenda
Bafoussam
Kumba
Mt. Cameroun 4070
Limbe
Rey Malabo
Bioko
Projection: Sanson-Flamsteed's Sinusoidal
West from Greenwich
East from Greenwich

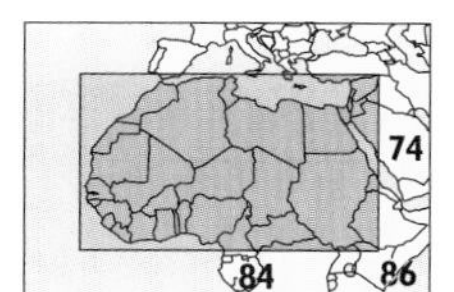

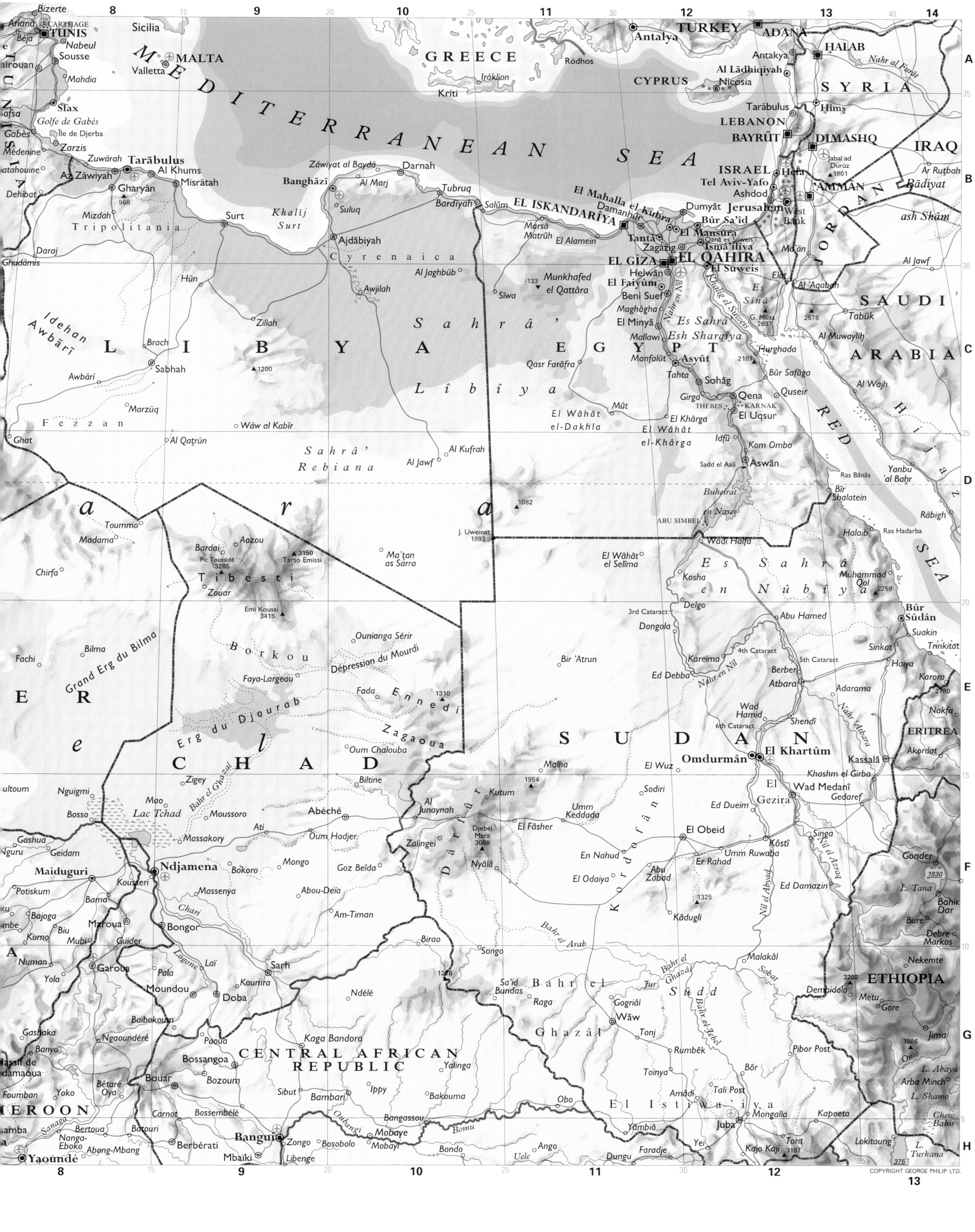

8 9 10 11 12 13 14

A B C D E F G H

MEDITERRANEAN SEA
Sicilia
MALTA
Valletta
GREECE
Kriti
Iráklion
Ródhos
TURKEY
Antalya
ADANA
CYPRUS
Nicosia
HALAB
Antakya
Al Lādhiqiyah
SYRIA
Nahr al Furāt
Ḥimş
Tarābulus
LEBANON
BAYRŪT
DIMASHQ
IRAQ
ISRAEL
Tel Aviv-Yafo
Ashdod
Jerusalem
West Bank
'AMMĀN
JORDAN
Jabal ad Durūz
1801
Ar Ruṭbah
Bādiyat ash Shām
Bizerte
Ariana
CARTHAGE
TUNIS
Béja
Nabeul
Sousse
Kairouan
Mahdia
TUNISIA
Sfax
Golfe de Gabès
Île de Djerba
Gabès
Zarzis
Médenine
Tataouine
Dehibat
Zuwārah
Tarābulus
Az Zāwiyah
Al Khums
Misrātah
Gharyān
968
Mizdah
Tripolitania
Daraj
Ghudāmis
Surt
Khalij Surt
Zāwiyat al Baydā
Darnah
Banghāzī
Al Marj
Tubruq
Bardīyah
Suluq
Ajdābiyah
Cyrenaica
Al Jaghbūb
Awjilah
Hūn
Zillah
Idehan Awbārī
LIBYA
Brach
Sabhah
Awbārī
1200
Marzūq
Fezzan
Wāw al Kabīr
Al Qaṭrūn
Ghat
Ṣaḥrā' Lībīya
Ṣaḥrā' Rebiana
Al Kufrah
Al Jawf
Salûm
EL ISKANDARÎYA
Marsâ Matrûh
El Alamein
El Mahalla el Kubra
Damanhûr
Tanta
Dumyât
Bûr Sa'îd
El Mansûra
Qanâ es Suweis
Ismâ'ilîya
Zagazig
EL QÂHIRA
EL GÎZA
Helwân
El Suweis
El Faiyûm
Beni Suef
Maghâgha
El Minyâ
Mallawi
Manfalût
Asyût
Nahr en Nîl
Khalîg el Suweis
Es Sînâ'
G. Mûsa
2637
Elat
Al 'Aqabah
-133
Munkhafed el Qattâra
Sîwa
Es Sahrâ Esh Sharqîya
EGYPT
Qasr Farâfra
Tahta
Sohâg
Girga
Qena
THEBES
KARNAK
El Uqsur
Hurghada
2187
Bûr Safâga
Quseir
El Wâhât el-Dakhla
Mût
El Khârga
El Wâhât el-Khârga
Idfû
Kom Ombo
Sadd el Aali
Aswân
RED SEA
Buheirat en Naser
ABU SIMBEL
Wadi Halfa
1082
J. Uweinat
1893
SAUDI ARABIA
Tabūk
2578
Al Muwaylih
Al Wajh
Hijaz
Yanbu 'al Bahr
Ras Bānās
Bîr Shalatein
Rābigh
Halaib
Ras Hadarba
Al Jawf
Sahara
Toummo
Madama
Chirfa
Bardai
Aozou
Pic Toussidé
3265
3150
Tarso Emissi
Tibesti
Zouar
Emi Koussi
3415
Ma'tan as Sarra
El Wâhât el Selîma
Es Sahrâ en Nûbîya
Kosha
Delgo
Muhammad Qol
2259
Bûr Sûdân
Suakin
Trinkitat
3rd Cataract
Dongola
Abu Hamed
Bilma
Grand Erg du Bilma
Fachi
Borkou
Ounianga Sérir
Dépression du Mourdi
Faya-Largeau
Fada
Ennedi
1310
Erg du Djourab
Zagaoua
Oum Chalouba
Bir 'Atrun
Kareima
4th Cataract
5th Cataract
Sinkat
Haiya
Ed Debba
Berber
Atbara
Karora
2780
Adarama
Nakfa
ERITREA
Akordat
Wad Hamid
Shendî
6th Cataract
Nahr 'Atbara
Kassalâ
El Khartûm
Omdurmân
El Wuz
SUDAN
CHAD
NIGER
Malha
1954
Kutum
Zigey
Biltine
Nguigmi
Mao
Lac Tchad
Bahr el Ghazal
Bosso
Moussoro
Abéché
Al Junaynah
Umm Keddada
Sodiri
Ed Dueim
Wad Medanî
El Gezira
Khashm el Girba
Gedaref
Gashua
Geidam
Massakory
Ati
Oum Hadjer
Zalingei
Djebel Mara
3088
Dârfûr
El Fâsher
El Obeid
Kordofân
Kôstî
Umm Ruwaba
Singa
Nil el Azraq
Maiduguri
Ndjamena
Bokoro
Mongo
Goz Beïda
Nyâlâ
En Nahud
Er Rahad
Abu Zabad
El Odaiya
Gonder
1830
L. Tana
Bahir Dar
Potiskum
Kousseri
Massenya
Abou-Deïa
Am-Timan
Chari
1325
Kâdugli
Nil el Abyad
Ed Damazin
Bure
Debre Markos
Bajoga
Biu
Maroua
Mubi
Guider
Bongor
Bahr el Arab
Birao
Songo
Malakâl
Sobat
Nekemte
Kumo
Numan
Garoua
Yola
Logone
Laï
Pala
Sarh
Koumra
Moundou
Doba
1275
Ndélé
Sa'id Bundas
Bahr el Ghazâl
Raga
Bahr el Jur
Gogriâl
Wâw
Sudd
Bahr el Jebel
Dembidolo
3202
ETHIOPIA
Metu
Gore
Jima
3686
Omo
Gashaka
Banyo
Ngaoundéré
Baïbokoum
Paoua
Kaga Bandoro
CENTRAL AFRICAN REPUBLIC
Tonj
Rumbêk
Pibor Post
Bôr
Tali Post
Amadi
L. Abaya
Arba Minch
L. Shamo
Massif de l'Adamaoua
Bossangoa
Bozoum
Bétaré Oya
Bouar
Yalinga
Ippy
Sibut
Bambari
Bakouma
Obo
El Istiwa'iya
Toinya
Foumban
Yoko
CAMEROON
Carnot
Bossembélé
Sanaga
Bertoua
Batouri
Nanga-Eboko
Abong-Mbang
Berbérati
Bangui
Zongo
Bosobolo
Mobaye
Mobayi
Bangassou
Oubangi
Bomu
Yambio
Juba
Mongalla
Kapoeta
Chew Bahir
Yaoundé
Mbaïki
Libenge
Bondo
Uele
Ango
Dungu
Faradje
Yei
Kajo Kaji
Torit
3187
Lokitaung
L. Turkana
375

8 9 10 11 12 13

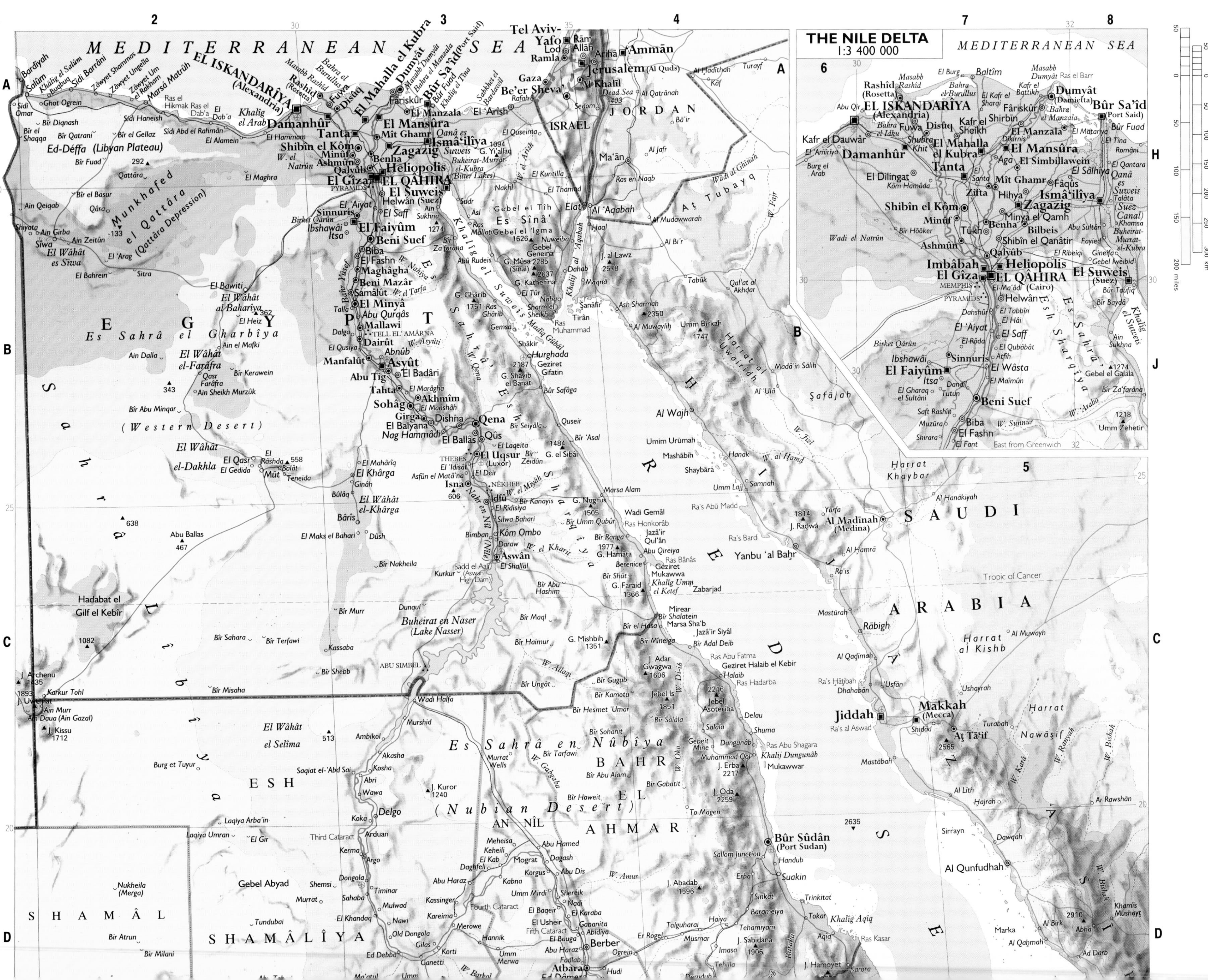
THE NILE DELTA
1:3 400 000
MEDITERRANEAN SEA
EL ISKANDARÎYA (Alexandria)
EL QÂHIRA
Bûr Sa'îd (Port Said)
El Suweis (Suez)
Heliopolis
El Giza
Tanta
Zagazig
El Mansûra
Dumyât
Ismâ'ilîya
Beni Suef
El Faiyûm
Es Sahrâ' esh Sharqîya
SAUDI ARABIA
Al Madînah (Medina)
Makkah (Mecca)
Jiddah
Yanbu 'al Bahr
Aţ Ţâ'if
JORDAN
ISRAEL
Jerusalem
'Ammân
Tel Aviv-Yafo
Gaza
Es Sînâ'
Khalîg el Suweis
RED SEA
Aswân
Qena
Asyût
Sohâg
El Minya
Buheirat en Naser (Lake Nasser)
Bûr Sûdân (Port Sudan)
Atbara
Berber
ESH SHAMÂLÎYA
Sahrâ Lîbîya
Es Sahrâ el Gharbîya (Western Desert)
Es Sahrâ en Nûbîya (Nubian Desert)
El Wâhât el Khârga
El Wâhât el-Dakhla
El Wâhât el-Farâfra
El Wâhât al Bahariya
El Wâhât es Siwa
Munkhafed el Qattâra (Qattara Depression)
Tropic of Cancer

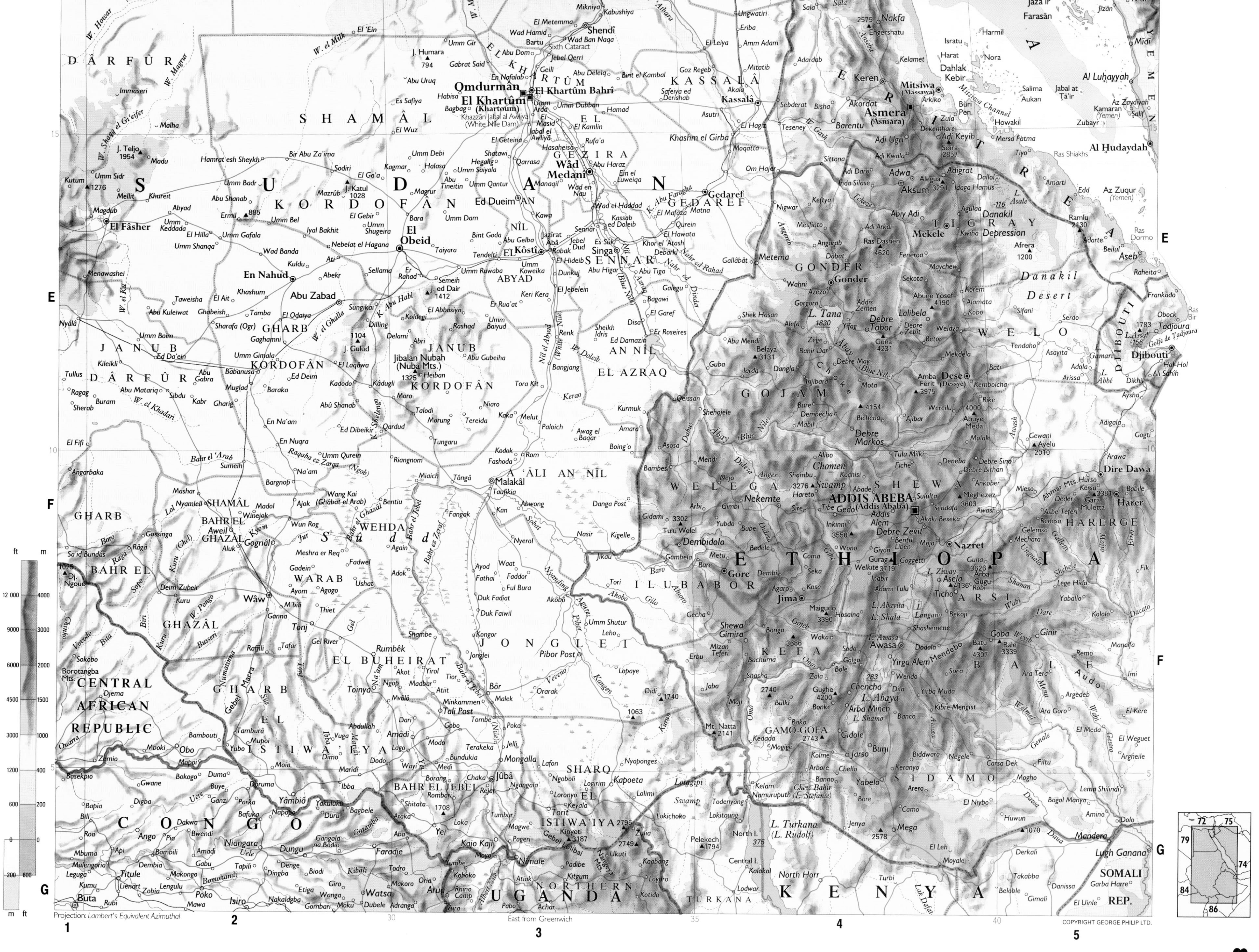

SUDAN
ETHIOPIA
ERITREA
DJIBOUTI
YEMEN
KENYA
UGANDA
CONGO
CENTRAL AFRICAN REPUBLIC
SOMALI REP.
DÂRFÛR
SHAMÂL
KORDOFÂN
JANUB KORDOFÂN
GHARB KORDOFÂN
KASSALÂ
GEDAREF
SENNAR
GEZIRA
EL KHARTÛM
A'ÂLI AN NÎL
AN NÎL EL AZRAQ
JONGLEI
EL BUHEIRAT
WARAB
WEHDA
BAHR EL JEBEL
SHARQ EL ISTIWA'IYA
GHARB EL ISTIWA'IYA
GHARB BAHR EL GHAZÂL
SHAMÂL BAHR EL GHAZÂL
GONDER
GOJAM
WELO
TIGRAY
SHEWA
WELEGA
ILUBABOR
KEFA
GAMO-GOFA
SIDAMO
BALE
ARSI
HARERGE
TURKANA
Danakil Desert
Danakil Depression
Sudd
Omdurmân
El Khartûm (Khartoum)
El Khartûm Bahrî
Wad Medanî
El Obeid
Kôstî
Malakâl
Jûbâ
Wâw
El Fâsher
En Nahud
Kassalâ
Gedaref
Asmera (Asmara)
Mitsiwa (Massawa)
Addis Abeba (Addis Ababa)
Gonder
Dese (Dessye)
Dire Dawa
Harer
Djibouti
Aseb
Al Hudaydah
L. Tana
L. Turkana (L. Rudolf)
Projection: Lambert's Equivalent Azimuthal
East from Greenwich
COPYRIGHT GEORGE PHILIP LTD.

50 0 50 100 150 200 250 300 km
50 0 50 100 150 200 miles
M A U R I T A N I A
S E N E G A L
GAMBIA
GUINEA-BISSAU
G U I N E A
SIERRA LEONE
L I B E R I A
I V O R Y C O A S T
ATLANTIC OCEAN
G U L F
Grain Coast
Ivory Coast
Nouakchott
Dakar
Banjul
Bissau
Conakry
Freetown
Monrovia
Bamako
Abidjan
Yamoussoukro
St. Louis
Thiès
Kaolack
Ziguinchor
Tambacounda
Kayes
Ségou
Mopti
Tombouctou (Timbuktu)
Bobo-Dioulasso
Sikasso
Korhogo
Bouaké
Daloa
Man
Kankan
Labé
Kindia
Bo
Kenema
Buchanan
Harper
San Pédro
Kiffa
Kaédi
Néma
Tidjikja
Akjoujt
Aoukâr
Tagânt
El Mreyyé
Macina
Fouta Djalon
Projection : Lambert's Equivalent Azimuthal
West from Greenwich

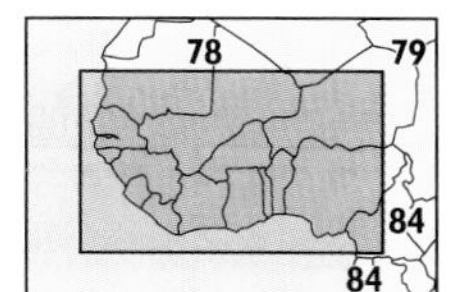

4 5 6 7

A B C D E

ALGERIA
Adrar des Iforas
Talak (Azbine)
Aïr
Ténéré
Agadez
NIGER
Tahoua
Tillabéri
Manga
Nguigmi
Tessalit
Kidal
Gao
Bourem
Ansongo
Tahoua
Agadez (Agadès)
Tanout
Zinder
Maradi
Niamey
Dosso
Birni Nkonni
Dogondoutchi
Ouagadougou
Fada-n-Gourma
Tenkodogo
Bolgatanga
Tamale
Dapaong
Mango
Sokodé
Kara
Atakpamé
Djougou
Parakou
Abomey
Kandi
Natitingou
Sokoto
Gusau
Katsina
Kano
Zaria
Kaduna
Bauchi
Jos
Gombe
Potiskum
Nguru
Gashua
Hadejia
Birnin Kebbi
Kontagora
Minna
Bida
Ilorin
Ogbomosho
Oshogbo
Ibadan
Abeokuta
Ijebu-Ode
Ado-Ekiti
Akure
Ondo
Lagos
Porto-Novo
Cotonou
Lomé
Accra
Tema
Koforidua
Lake Volta
Benin City
Warri
Sapele
Onitsha
Enugu
Abakaliki
Owerri
Aba
Umuahia
Port Harcourt
Calabar
Makurdi
Lafia
Lokoja
Wukari
Jalingo
Numan
Yola
Bamenda
Foumban
Kumba
Buea
Douala
Édéa
Yaoundé
Malabo
Bioko
NIGERIA
GHANA
TOGO
BENIN
CAMEROON
EQUATORIAL GUINEA
Slave Coast
Bight of Benin
Niger Delta
Bight of Bonny
GULF OF GUINEA

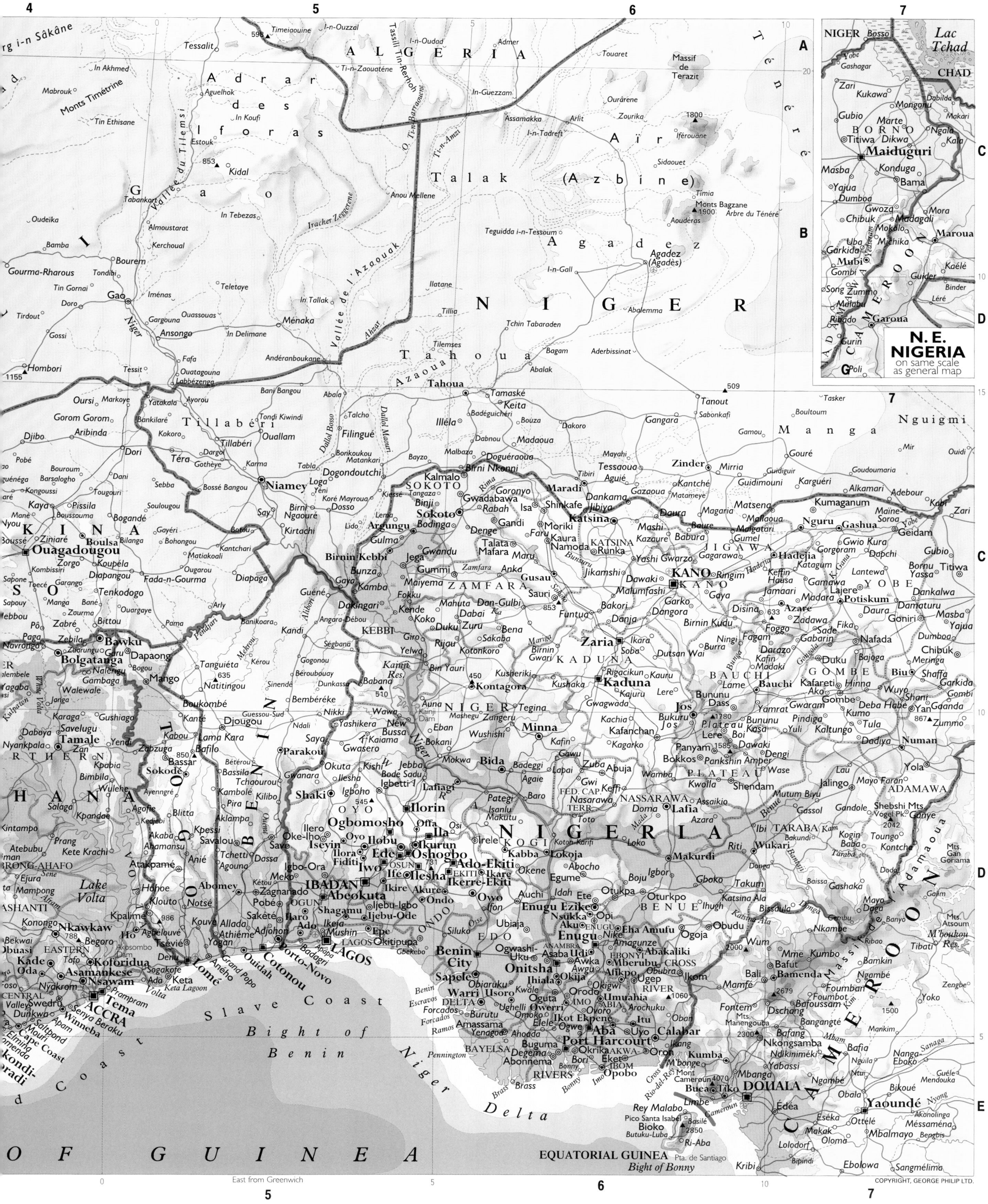

N.E. NIGERIA
on same scale as general map

NIGER
CHAD
Lac Tchad
BORNO
Maiduguri
Bama
Dikwa
Gubio
Marte
Ngala
Kala
Gwoza
Madagali
Mubi
Maroua
Garoua
CAMEROON
ADAMAWA

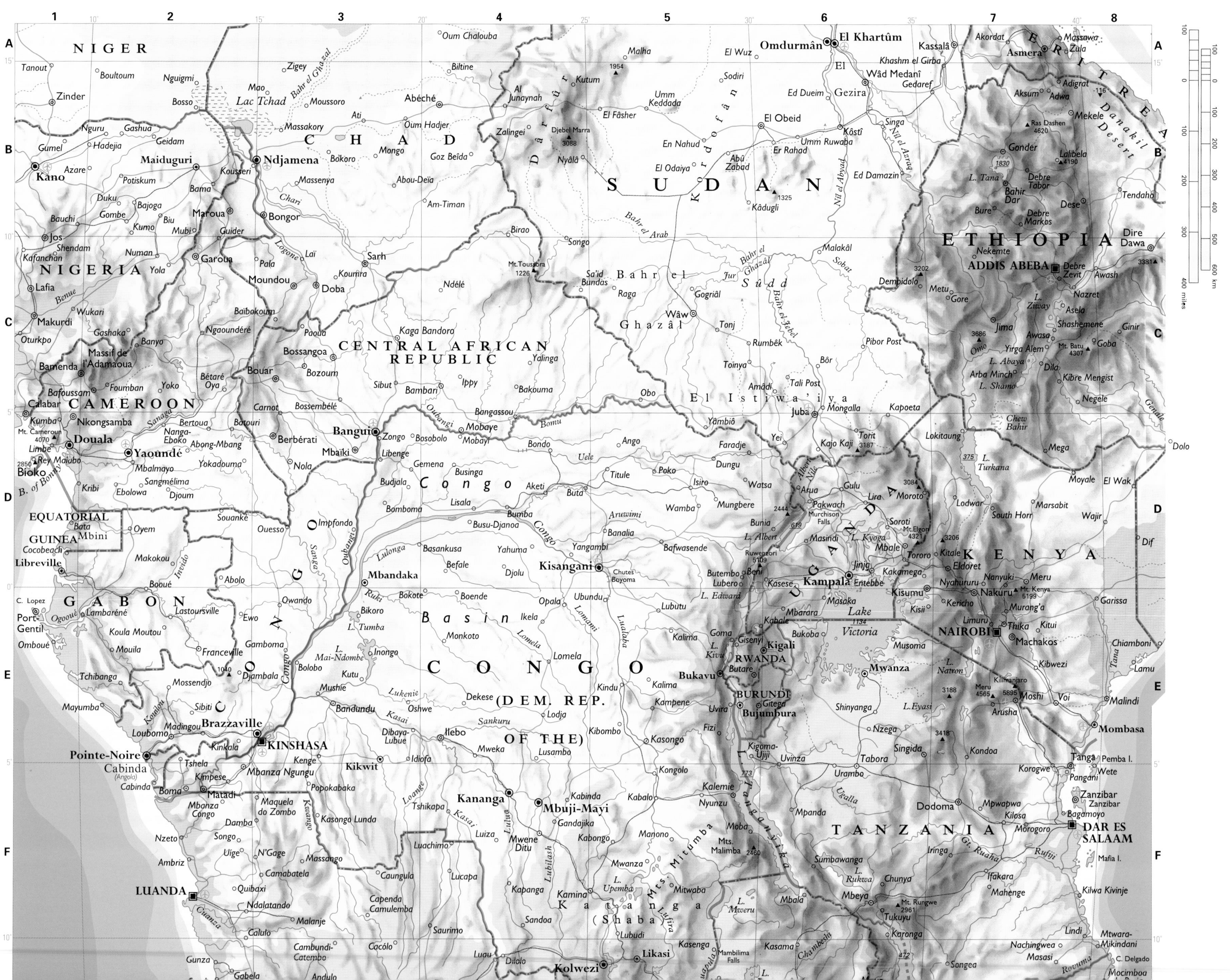
100 0 100 200 300 400 500 600 km
100 0 100 200 300 400 miles
NIGER
NIGERIA
CHAD
SUDAN
ETHIOPIA
ERITREA
KENYA
UGANDA
TANZANIA
RWANDA
BURUNDI
CENTRAL AFRICAN REPUBLIC
CAMEROON
GABON
CONGO
CONGO (DEM. REP. OF THE)
EQUATORIAL GUINEA
Cabinda (Angola)
El Khartûm
Omdurmân
ADDIS ABEBA
NAIROBI
Kampala
DAR ES SALAAM
Kigali
Bujumbura
Bangui
Ndjamena
Yaoundé
Douala
Libreville
Brazzaville
KINSHASA
LUANDA
Kisangani
Mombasa
Kano
Maiduguri
Mbandaka
Kananga
Mbuji-Mayi
Kolwezi
Likasi
Pointe-Noire
Lac Tchad
Lake Victoria
L. Turkana
L. Tana
Congo Basin
Danakil Desert
Bahr el Ghazâl
Dârfûr
Kordofân
Massif de l'Adamaoua
Bioko
Mt. Kenya 5199
Kilimanjaro 5895
Ras Dashen 4620
Djebel Marra 3088
Mt. Cameroun 4070

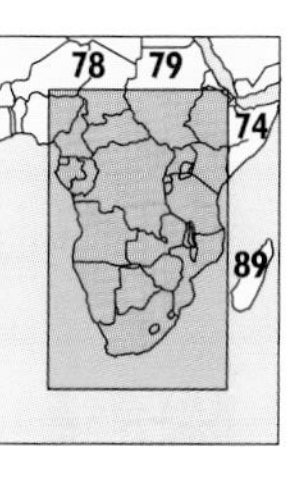

ATLANTIC OCEAN

INDIAN OCEAN

ANGOLA

ZAMBIA

MALAWI

MOZAMBIQUE

ZIMBABWE

NAMIBIA

BOTSWANA

SOUTH AFRICA

LESOTHO

SWAZILAND

Kalahari

Namib Desert

Namaland

Damaraland

Ovamboland

Barotseland

Mashonaland

Matabeleland

Transvaal

Natal

Free State

Cape Province

Caprivi Strip

Tropic of Capricorn

Lusaka
HARARE
Bulawayo
Lilongwe
Windhoek
Gaborone
PRETORIA
JOHANNESBURG
MAPUTO
Maseru
Bloemfontein
DURBAN
CAPE TOWN
Port Elizabeth
East London
Beira
Nampula
Ndola
Kitwe
Livingstone
Francistown
Kimberley
Lüderitz
Walvis Bay
Swakopmund

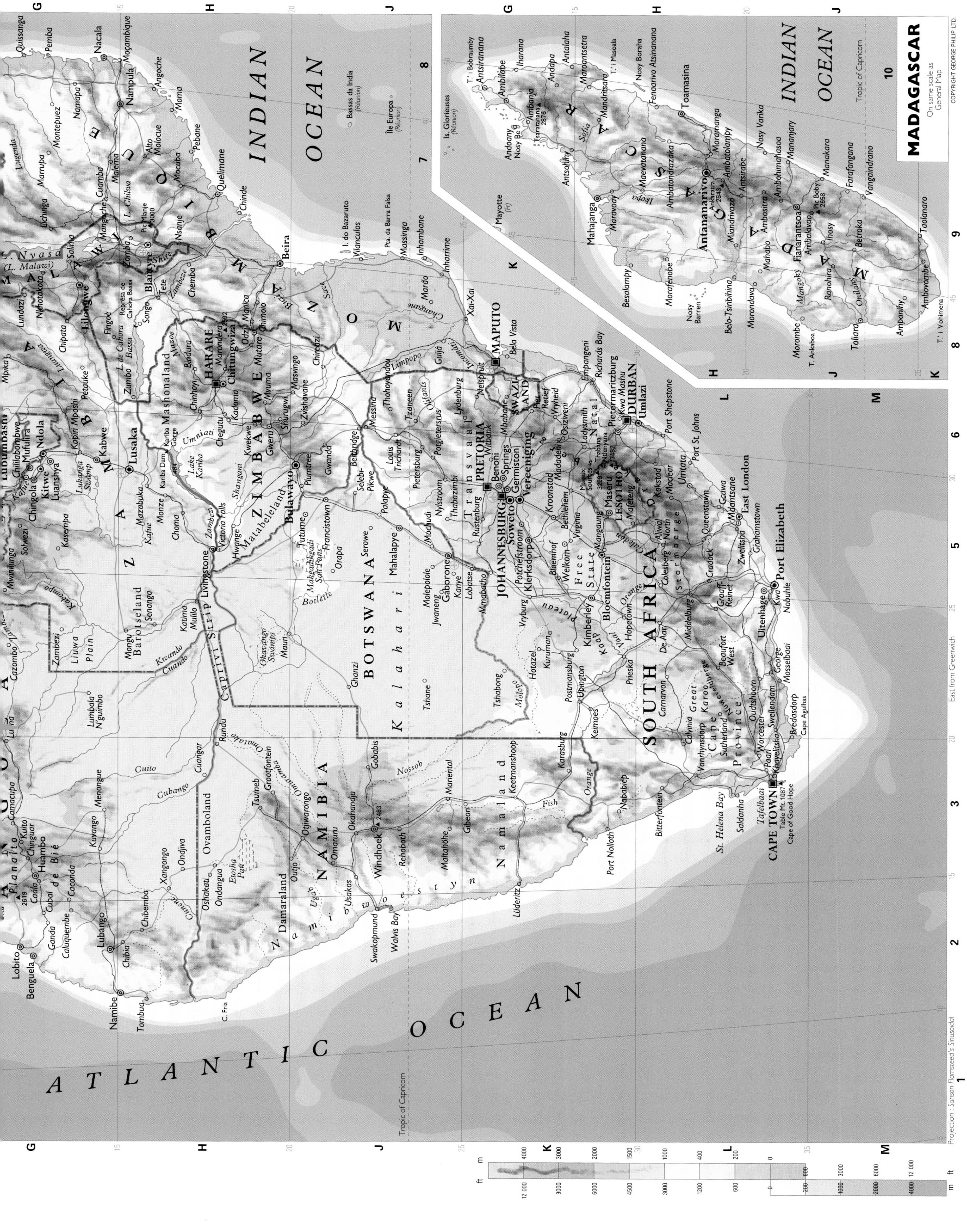

MADAGASCAR

On same scale as General Map

INDIAN OCEAN

Antananarivo
Toamasina
Mahajanga
Fianarantsoa
Toliara
Antsiranana

Projection : Sanson-Flamsteed's Sinusoidal

East from Greenwich

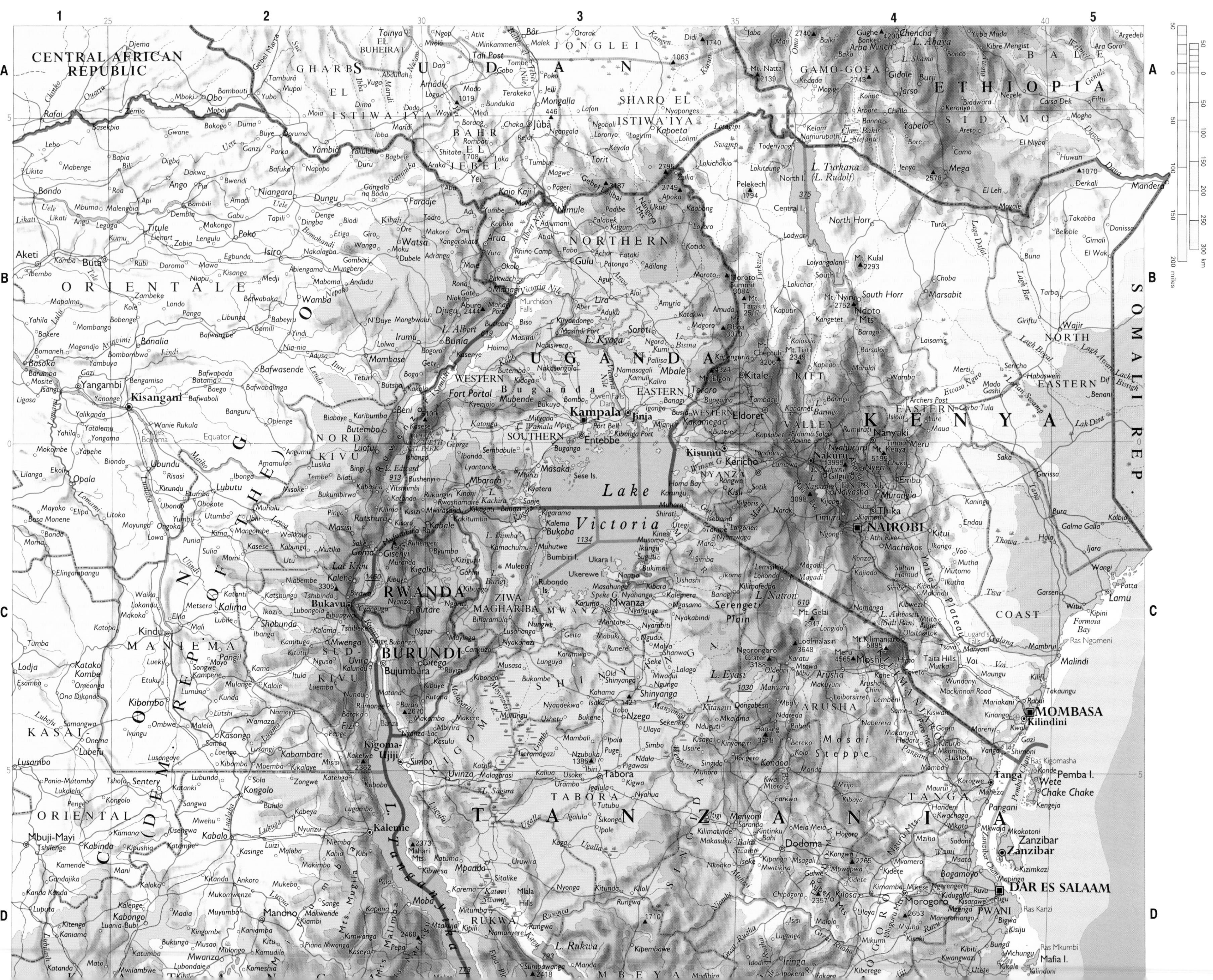
50 0 50 100 150 200 250 300 km
50 0 50 100 150 200 miles
CENTRAL AFRICAN REPUBLIC
SUDAN
ETHIOPIA
SOMALI REP.
KENYA
UGANDA
RWANDA
BURUNDI
TANZANIA
DEM. REP. OF THE CONGO
NAIROBI
MOMBASA
DAR ES SALAAM
Kampala
Kisangani
Lake Victoria
L. Turkana (L. Rudolf)
L. Tanganyika
L. Albert
L. Rukwa
Zanzibar
Dodoma
Tabora

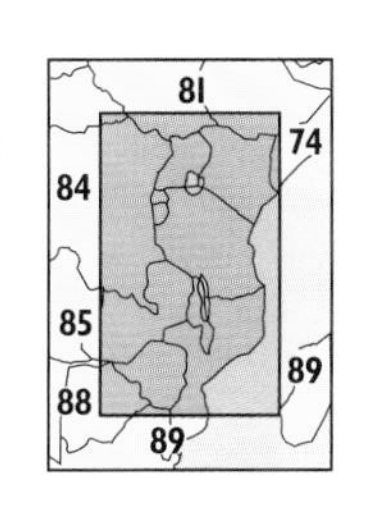

74
81
84
85
88
89

INDIAN OCEAN
BOTSWANA
SOUTH AFRICA
ANGOLA
NAMIBIA
ZIMBABWE
MOZAMBIQUE
ZAMBIA
MALAWI
L. Nyasa
Lusaka
HARARE
BULAWAYO
Lilongwe
Blantyre
Beira
Moçambique
Projection: Lambert's Equivalent Azimuthal
East from Greenwich
COPYRIGHT GEORGE PHILIP LTD.

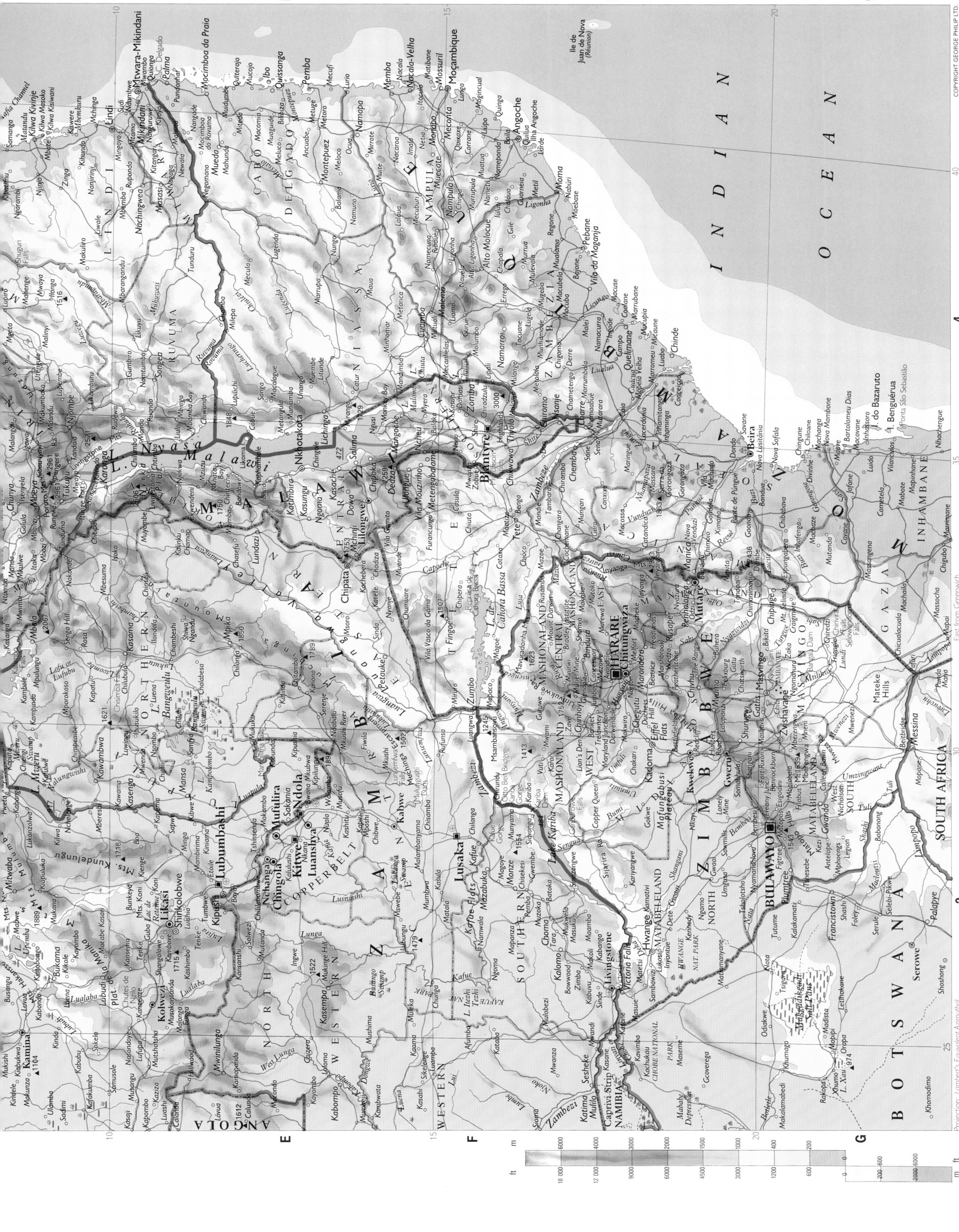

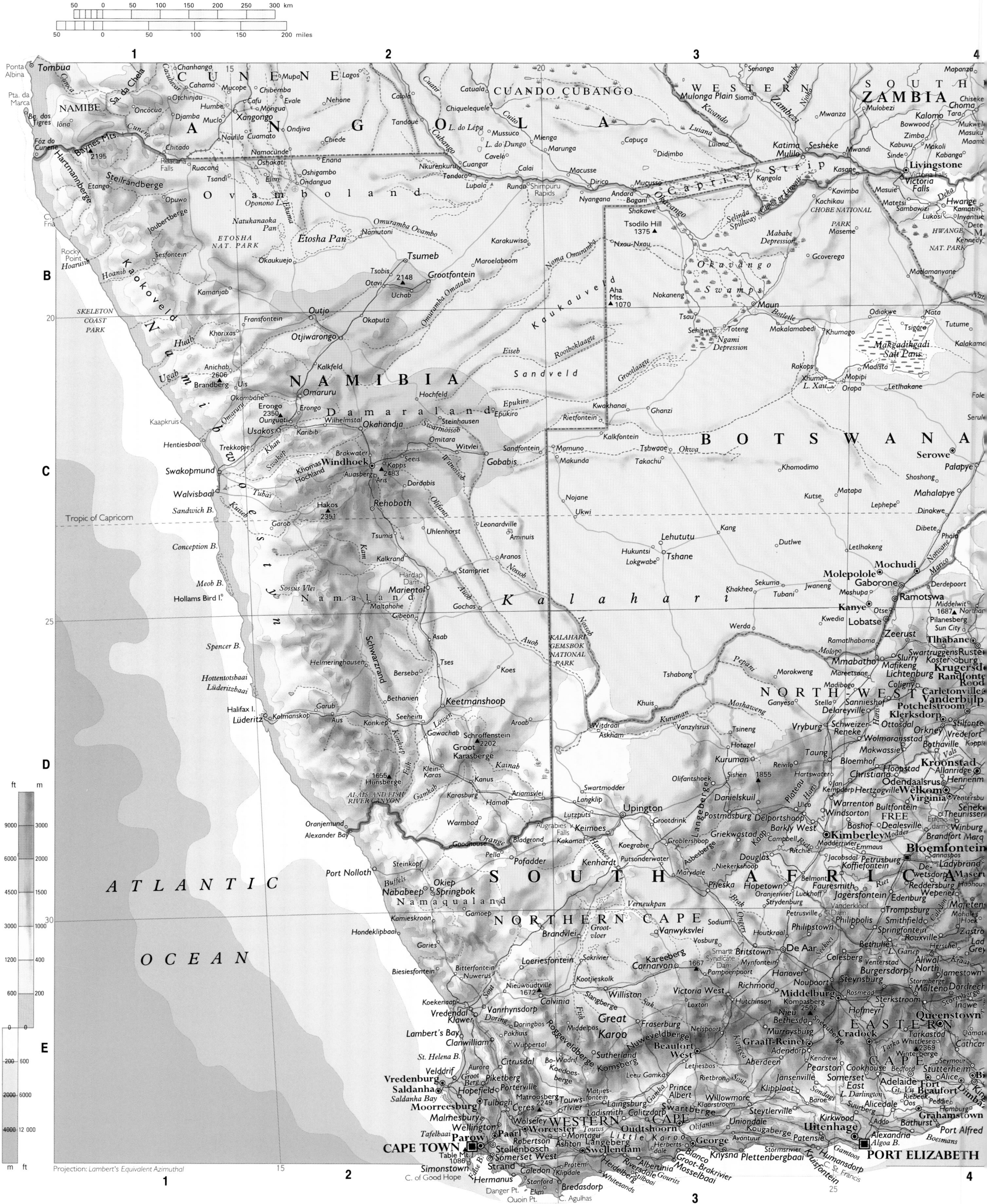
50 0 50 100 150 200 250 300 km
50 0 50 100 150 200 miles
ANGOLA
CUNENE
CUANDO CUBANGO
WESTERN
SOUTH
ZAMBIA
NAMIBE
Ovamboland
Etosha Pan
ETOSHA NAT. PARK
SKELETON COAST PARK
Kaokoveld
NAMIBIA
Damaraland
Namaland
Kaukauveld
Sandveld
Kalahari
BOTSWANA
Caprivi Strip
Okavango Swamps
Makgadikgadi Salt Pans
Ngami Depression
KALAHARI GEMSBOK NATIONAL PARK
Namib Desert
Tropic of Capricorn
ATLANTIC
OCEAN
NORTH-WEST
SOUTH AFRICA
NORTHERN CAPE
Namaqualand
Great Karoo
Little Karoo
WESTERN CAPE
EASTERN CAPE
Windhoek
Swakopmund
Walvisbaai
Lüderitz
Keetmanshoop
Rehoboth
Tsumeb
Grootfontein
Otjiwarongo
Okahandja
Gaborone
Lobatse
Mochudi
Molepolole
Maun
Livingstone
Kimberley
Bloemfontein
Upington
De Aar
Springbok
CAPE TOWN
PORT ELIZABETH
George
Oudtshoorn
Worcester
Paarl
Stellenbosch
Uitenhage
Grahamstown
Queenstown
Cradock
Graaff-Reinet
Beaufort West
Calvinia
Vredenburg
Saldanha
C. of Good Hope
C. Agulhas
Projection: Lambert's Equivalent Azimuthal

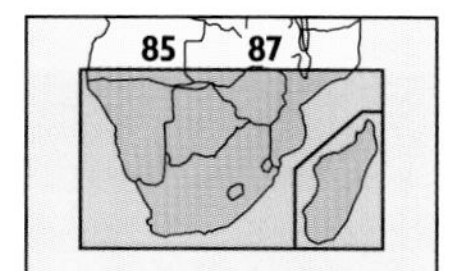

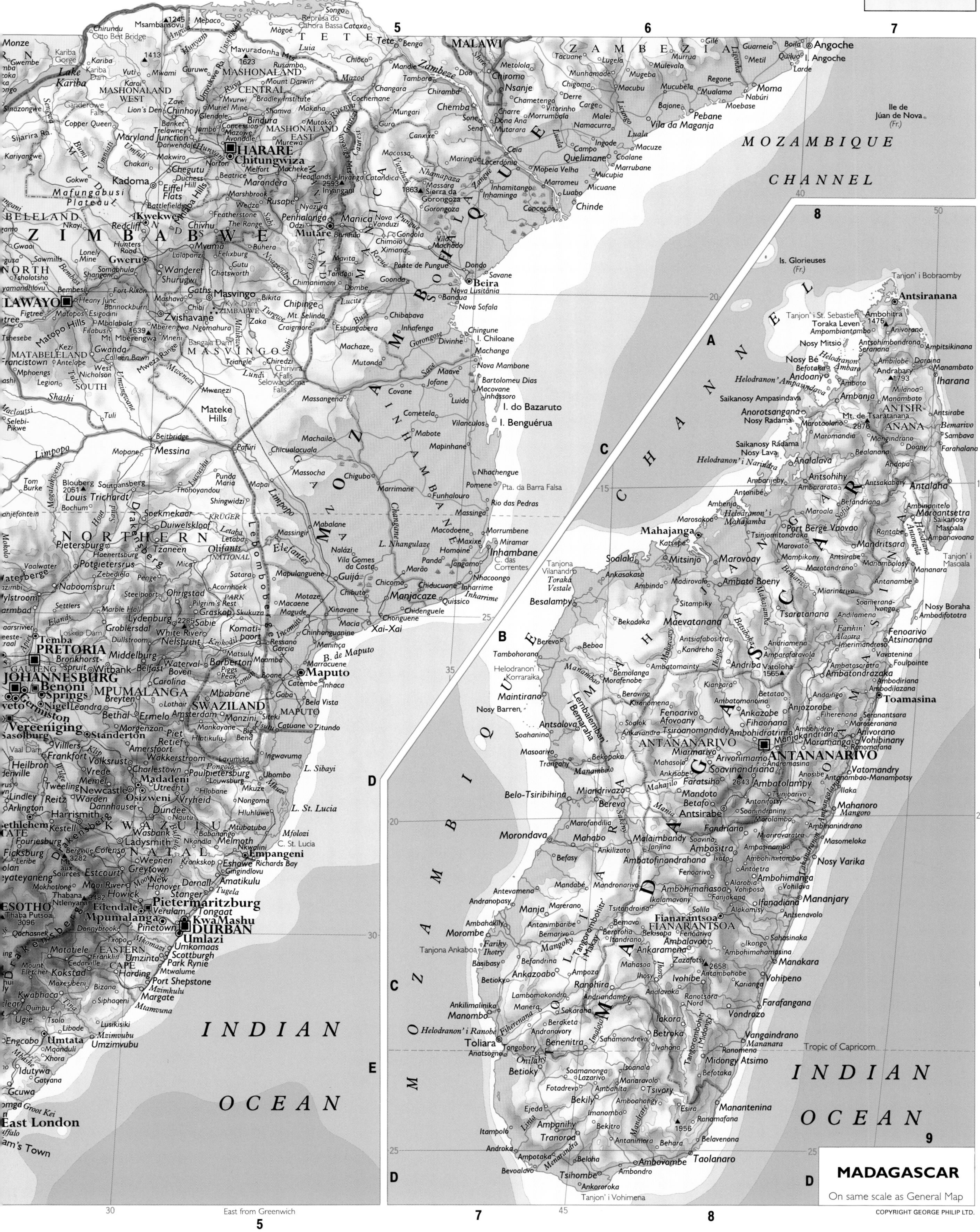

85
87

MADAGASCAR
On same scale as General Map
MOZAMBIQUE CHANNEL
INDIAN OCEAN
INDIAN OCEAN
ZIMBABWE
MOZAMBIQUE
MADAGASCAR
MALAWI
SWAZILAND
ZAMBEZIA
TETE
MANICA
SOFALA
INHAMBANE
GAZA
MAPUTO
MASHONALAND CENTRAL
MASHONALAND WEST
MASHONALAND EAST
MATABELELAND SOUTH
MASVINGO
NORTHERN
MPUMALANGA
GAUTENG
KWAZULU NATAL
EASTERN CAPE
LESOTHO
ANTANANARIVO
FIANARANTSOA
TOLIARA
MAHAJANGA
TOAMASINA
ANTSIRANANA
HARARE
Chitungwiza
Mutare
Beira
Maputo
PRETORIA
JOHANNESBURG
Pietermaritzburg
DURBAN
East London
Antsiranana
Mahajanga
Toamasina
Antsirabe
Fianarantsoa
Toliara
Taolanaro
Morondava
Inhambane
Quelimane
Chinde
Angoche
Ile de Júan de Nova (Fr.)
Is. Glorieuses (Fr.)
Tropic of Capricorn
East from Greenwich
5
6
7
8
9
A
B
C
D
E

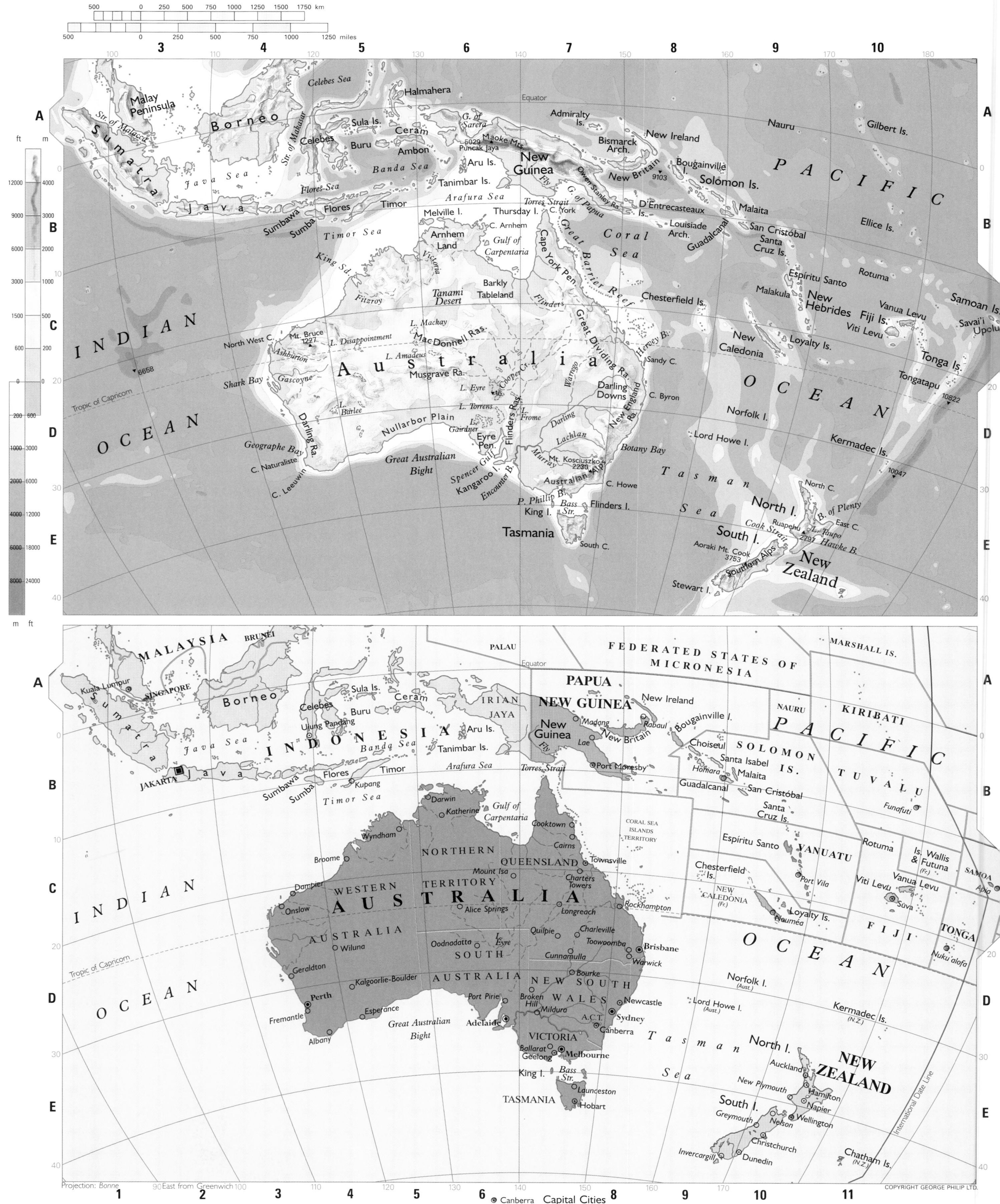

500 0 250 500 750 1000 1250 1500 1750 km
500 0 250 500 750 1000 1250 miles
ft m
12000 4000
9000 3000
6000 2000
3000 1000
1500 500
600 200
0 0
200 600
1000 3000
2000 6000
4000 12000
6000 18000
8000 24000
m ft
Malay Peninsula
Str. of Malacca
Sumatra
Borneo
Celebes Sea
Str. of Makasar
Celebes
Halmahera
Sula Is.
Buru
Ceram
Ambon
Banda Sea
Java Sea
Java
Flores Sea
Sumbawa
Sumba
Flores
Timor
Timor Sea
Equator
G. of Sarera
Maoke Mts.
6029 Puncak Jaya
Aru Is.
Tanimbar Is.
New Guinea
Fly
Owen Stanley Ra.
G. of Papua
Torres Strait
Arafura Sea
Admiralty Is.
Bismarck Arch.
New Ireland
New Britain
9103
Bougainville I.
Solomon Is.
D'Entrecasteaux Is.
Louisiade Arch.
Guadalcanal
Malaita
San Cristóbal
Santa Cruz Is.
Nauru
Gilbert Is.
Ellice Is.
PACIFIC
Rotuma
Espíritu Santo
Malakula
New Hebrides
Fiji Is.
Vanua Levu
Viti Levu
Samoan Is.
Savai'i
Upolu
Tonga Is.
Tongatapu
10822
Loyalty Is.
New Caledonia
Chesterfield Is.
Melville I.
Thursday I.
C. York
C. Arnhem
Arnhem Land
Gulf of Carpentaria
Cape York Pen.
Great Barrier Reef
Coral Sea
King Sd.
Victoria
Fitzroy
Tanami Desert
Barkly Tableland
Flinders
Great Dividing Ra.
Hervey B.
Sandy C.
North West C.
Mt. Bruce 1227
L. Disappointment
L. Mackay
MacDonnell Ras.
L. Amadeus
Ashburton
Gascoyne
Shark Bay
Australia
Musgrave Ra.
L. Eyre -16
Cooper Cr.
Warrego
Darling Downs
C. Byron
L. Barlee
L. Torrens
L. Frome
L. Gairdner
Flinders Ras.
Darling
Nullarbor Plain
Darling Ra.
Eyre Pen.
Lachlan
Murray
New England Ra.
Mt. Kosciuszko 2230
Australian Alps
Botany Bay
C. Howe
Geographe Bay
C. Naturaliste
C. Leeuwin
Great Australian Bight
Spencer Gulf
Kangaroo I.
Encounter B.
P. Phillip B.
King I.
Bass Str.
Flinders I.
Tasmania
South C.
INDIAN OCEAN
6658
Tropic of Capricorn
OCEAN
Norfolk I.
Lord Howe I.
Kermadec Is.
10047
Tasman Sea
North C.
North I.
B. of Plenty
East C.
Ruapehu 2797
L. Taupo
Cook Strait
Hawke B.
South I.
Aoraki Mt. Cook 3753
Southern Alps
New Zealand
Stewart I.
MALAYSIA
BRUNEI
Kuala Lumpur
SINGAPORE
Ujung Pandang
INDONESIA
JAKARTA
Kupang
IRIAN JAYA
PALAU
FEDERATED STATES OF MICRONESIA
MARSHALL IS.
PAPUA NEW GUINEA
Madang
Lae
Rabaul
Port Moresby
Choiseul
Santa Isabel
Honiara
SOLOMON IS.
NAURU
KIRIBATI
TUVALU
Funafuti
VANUATU
Port Vila
Is. Wallis & Futuna (Fr.)
SAMOA
Apia
Suva
FIJI
TONGA
Nuku'alofa
NEW CALEDONIA (Fr.)
Nouméa
CORAL SEA ISLANDS TERRITORY
Darwin
Katherine
Wyndham
Broome
Dampier
Onslow
WESTERN AUSTRALIA
Wiluna
Geraldton
Kalgoorlie-Boulder
Perth
Fremantle
Esperance
Albany
NORTHERN TERRITORY
Alice Springs
Mount Isa
QUEENSLAND
Cooktown
Cairns
Townsville
Charters Towers
Longreach
Rockhampton
Charleville
Quilpie
Toowoomba
Brisbane
Warwick
Cunnamulla
Oodnadatta
L. Eyre
SOUTH AUSTRALIA
Port Pirie
Adelaide
NEW SOUTH WALES
Bourke
Broken Hill
Mildura
Newcastle
Sydney
A.C.T.
Canberra
VICTORIA
Ballarat
Geelong
Melbourne
Launceston
Hobart
TASMANIA
Norfolk I. (Aust.)
Lord Howe I. (Aust.)
Kermadec Is. (N.Z.)
NEW ZEALAND
Auckland
New Plymouth
Hamilton
Napier
Wellington
Nelson
Greymouth
Christchurch
Dunedin
Invercargill
Chatham Is. (N.Z.)
International Date Line
Projection: Bonne
East from Greenwich
Canberra Capital Cities
COPYRIGHT GEORGE PHILIP LTD.

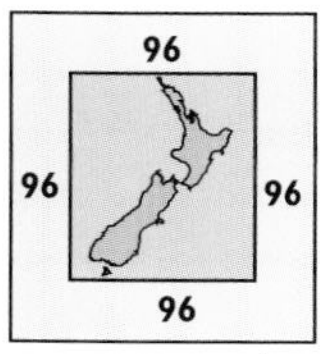

50 0 50 100 150 200 km

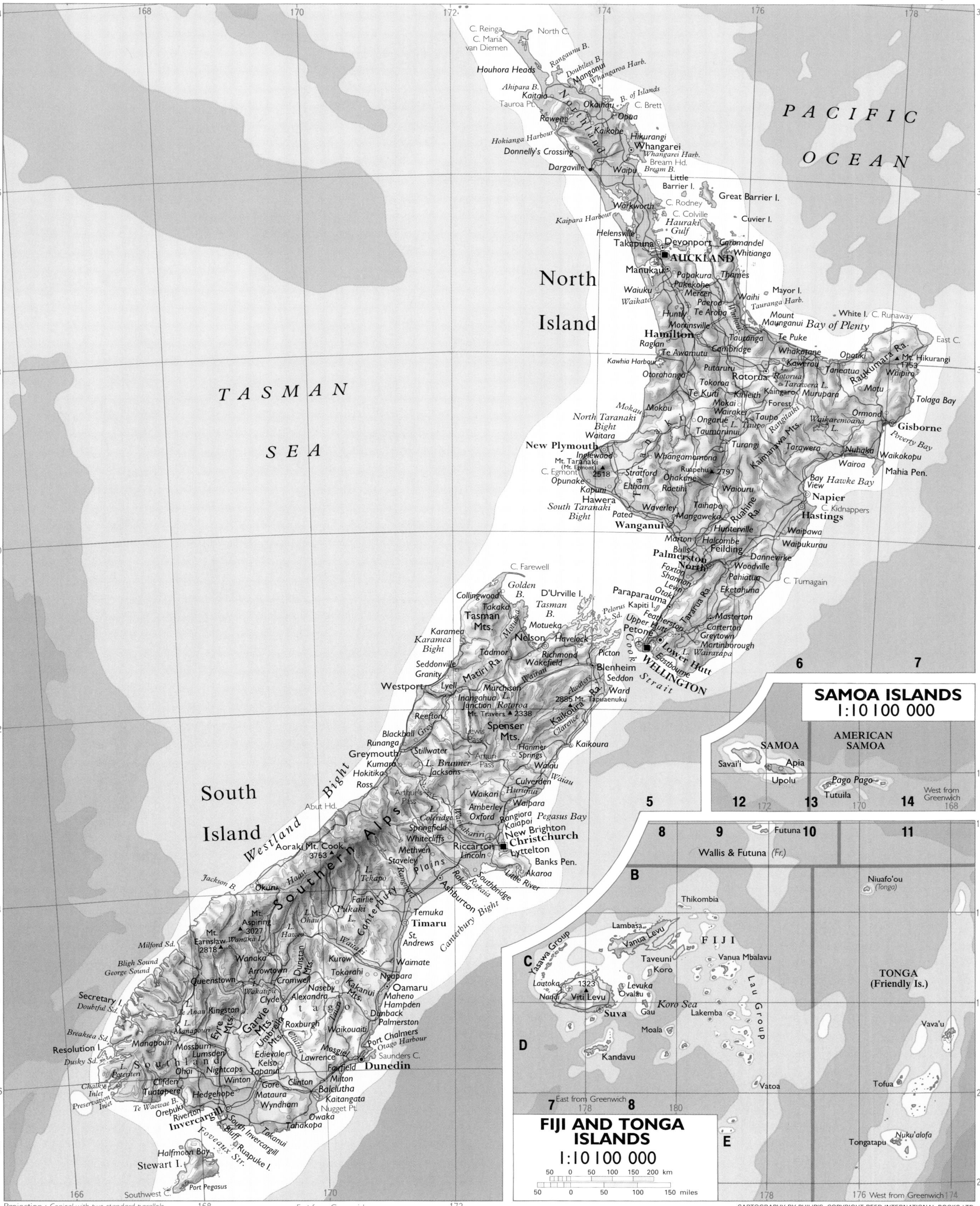

50 0 50 100 150 miles

NEW ZEALAND

1:5 000 000

North Island

South Island

TASMAN SEA

PACIFIC OCEAN

AUCKLAND

WELLINGTON

Christchurch

Dunedin

Southern Alps

Aoraki Mt. Cook 3753

Ruapehu 2797

Mt. Taranaki (Mt. Egmont) 2518

Cook Strait

Foveaux Str.

Stewart I.

SAMOA ISLANDS

1:10 100 000

SAMOA

AMERICAN SAMOA

Savai'i

Upolu

Apia

Pago Pago

Tutuila

West from Greenwich

FIJI AND TONGA ISLANDS

1:10 100 000

50 0 50 100 150 200 km

50 0 50 100 150 miles

FIJI

Viti Levu

Vanua Levu

Suva

Koro Sea

Lau Group

TONGA (Friendly Is.)

Nuku'alofa

Tongatapu

Wallis & Futuna (Fr.)

East from Greenwich

Projection : *Conical with two standard parallels*

East from Greenwich

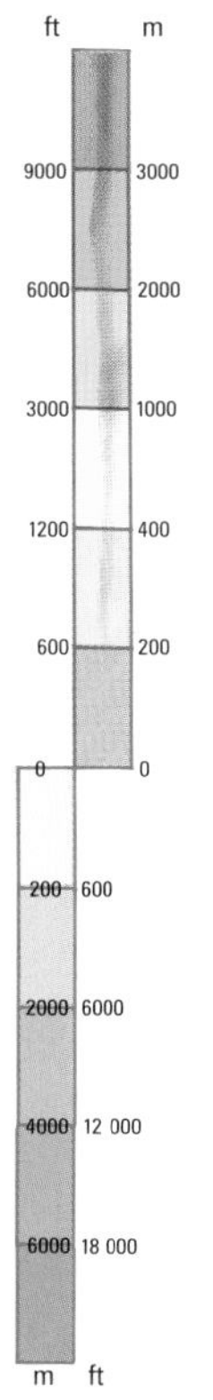

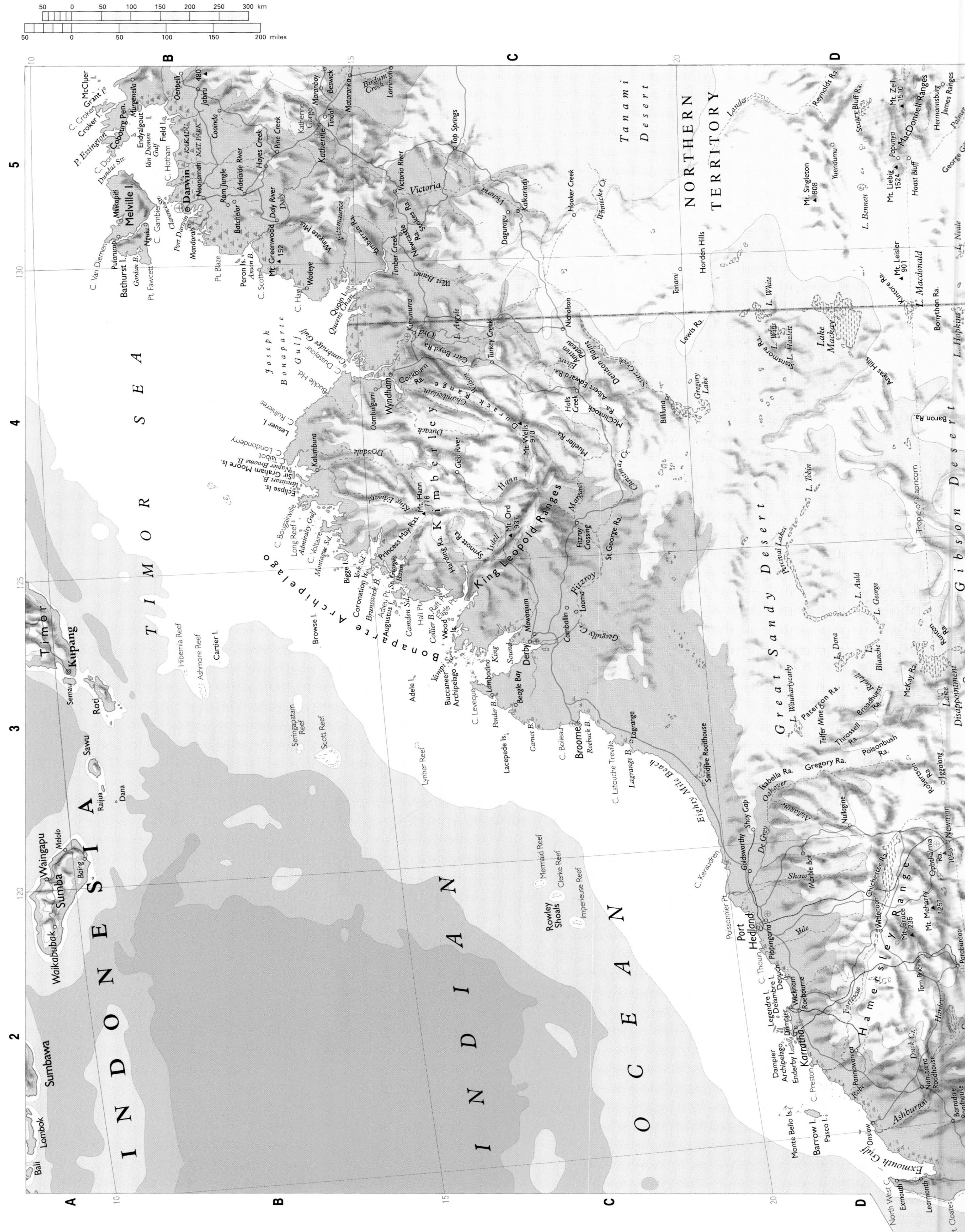
50 0 50 100 150 200 250 300 km
50 0 50 100 150 200 miles
A
B
C
D
INDONESIA
TIMOR SEA
INDIAN OCEAN
NORTHERN TERRITORY
Tanami Desert
Great Sandy Desert
Gibson Desert
Joseph Bonaparte Gulf
Bonaparte Archipelago
Kimberley
King Leopold Ranges
Hamersley Range
Darwin
Katherine
Wyndham
Kununurra
Derby
Broome
Port Hedland
Karratha
Kupang
Timor
Sumba
Sawu
Roti
Melville I.
Bathurst I.
Rowley Shoals
Eighty Mile Beach
Exmouth Gulf
Lake Mackay
Lake Disappointment
Tropic of Capricorn

WESTERN AUSTRALIA
SOUTH AUSTRALIA
INDIAN OCEAN
SOUTHERN OCEAN
Great Australian Bight
Great Victoria Desert
Nullarbor Plain
Hampton Tableland
PERTH
Fremantle
Kwinana
Rockingham
Mandurah
Bunbury
Busselton
Albany
Geraldton
Carnarvon
Kalgoorlie-Boulder
Esperance
Norseman
Merredin
Northam
Katanning
Collie
Ayers Rock
868
Mt. Olga
1069
ULURU NAT. PARK
Yulara
Petermann Ranges
Musgrave Ranges
Mt. Woodroffe
1440
Everard Ranges
Mt. Augustus
1105
Mt. Essendon
906
Mt. Fraser
799
Mt. Eureka
499
Mt. Redcliffe
576
Mt. Ragged
585
Bluff Knoll
1073
Shark Bay
Dirk Hartog I.
Houtman Abrolhos
Archipelago of the Recherche
Eucla
Forrest
Cook
Ooldea
L. Carey
L. Barlee
L. Ballard
L. Moore
L. Cowan
L. Dundas
L. Carnegie
L. Wells
5632
E
F
G
1
2
3
4
5
25
30
35
115
120
125
130
East from Greenwich
Projection: Bonne
COPYRIGHT GEORGE PHILIP LTD.
m
ft
1000
400
200
0
3000
1200
600
200
600
2000
6000
4000
12 000
62
94
95

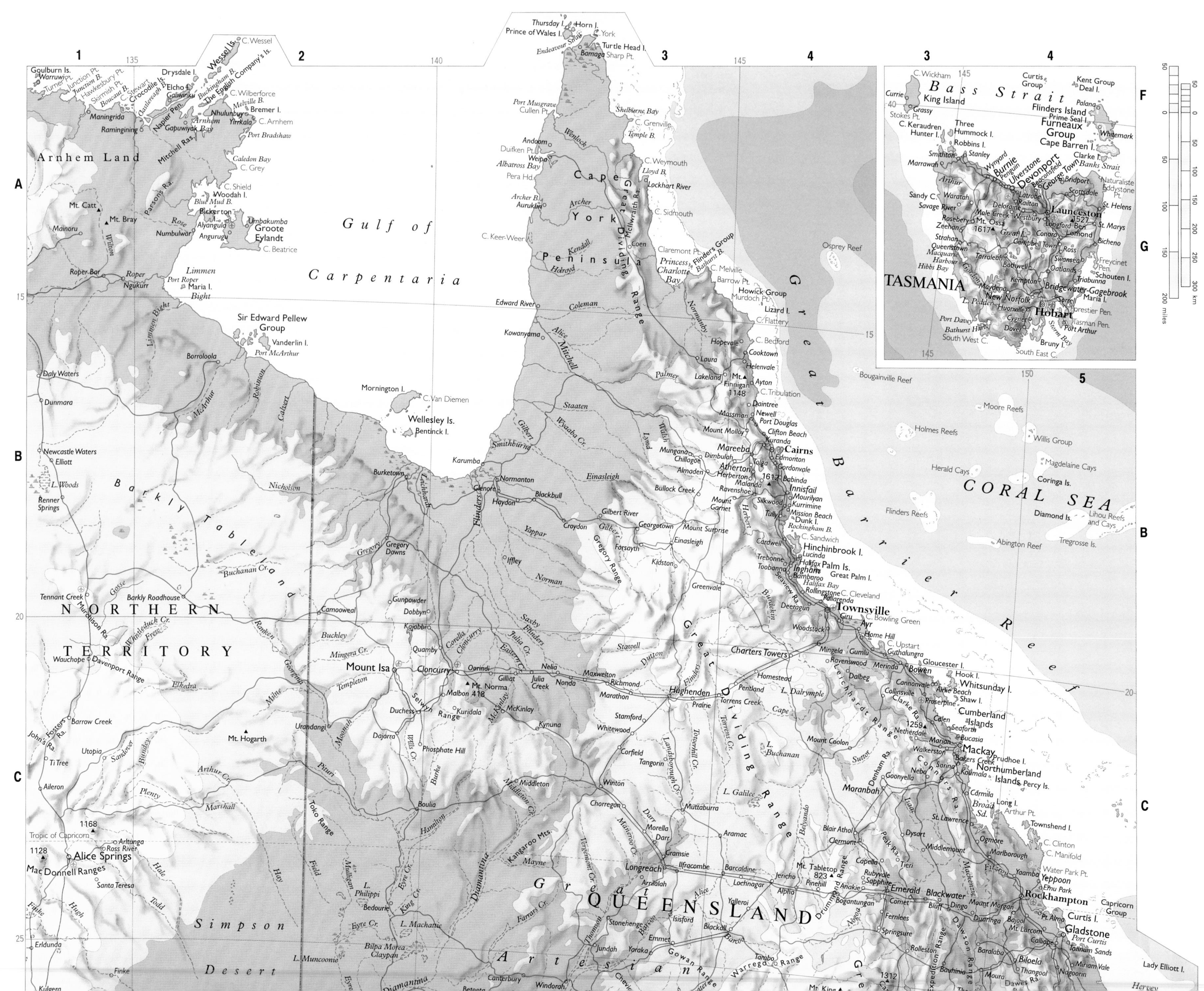

50 0 50 100 150 200 250 300 km
50 0 50 100 150 200 miles
TASMANIA
Bass Strait
King Island
Flinders Island
Furneaux Group
Cape Barren I.
Launceston
Devonport
Burnie
Hobart
CORAL SEA
Great Barrier Reef
Gulf of Carpentaria
Cape York Peninsula
Great Dividing Range
QUEENSLAND
NORTHERN TERRITORY
Barkly Tableland
Simpson Desert
Arnhem Land
Townsville
Cairns
Mackay
Rockhampton
Gladstone
Charters Towers
Mount Isa
Cloncurry
Longreach
Alice Springs
MacDonnell Ranges
Tropic of Capricorn
Wellesley Is.
Mornington I.
Groote Eylandt
Sir Edward Pellew Group
Whitsunday I.
Hinchinbrook I.
Cooktown
Normanton
Hughenden
Winton
Emerald
Tennant Creek

SOUTH AUSTRALIA
NEW SOUTH WALES
VICTORIA
TASMAN SEA
SOUTHERN OCEAN
Bass Strait
SYDNEY
MELBOURNE
ADELAIDE
BRISBANE
Canberra
Newcastle
Wollongong
Gold Coast
Tweed Heads
Broken Hill
Mildura
Kangaroo I.
King Island
Flinders Island
Furneaux Group
Lake Eyre (North)
Lake Eyre (South)
Lake Torrens
Lake Gairdner
Lake Frome
Gippsland
Darling Downs
Grey Range
Projection: Bonne
East from Greenwich
COPYRIGHT, GEORGE PHILIP LTD.

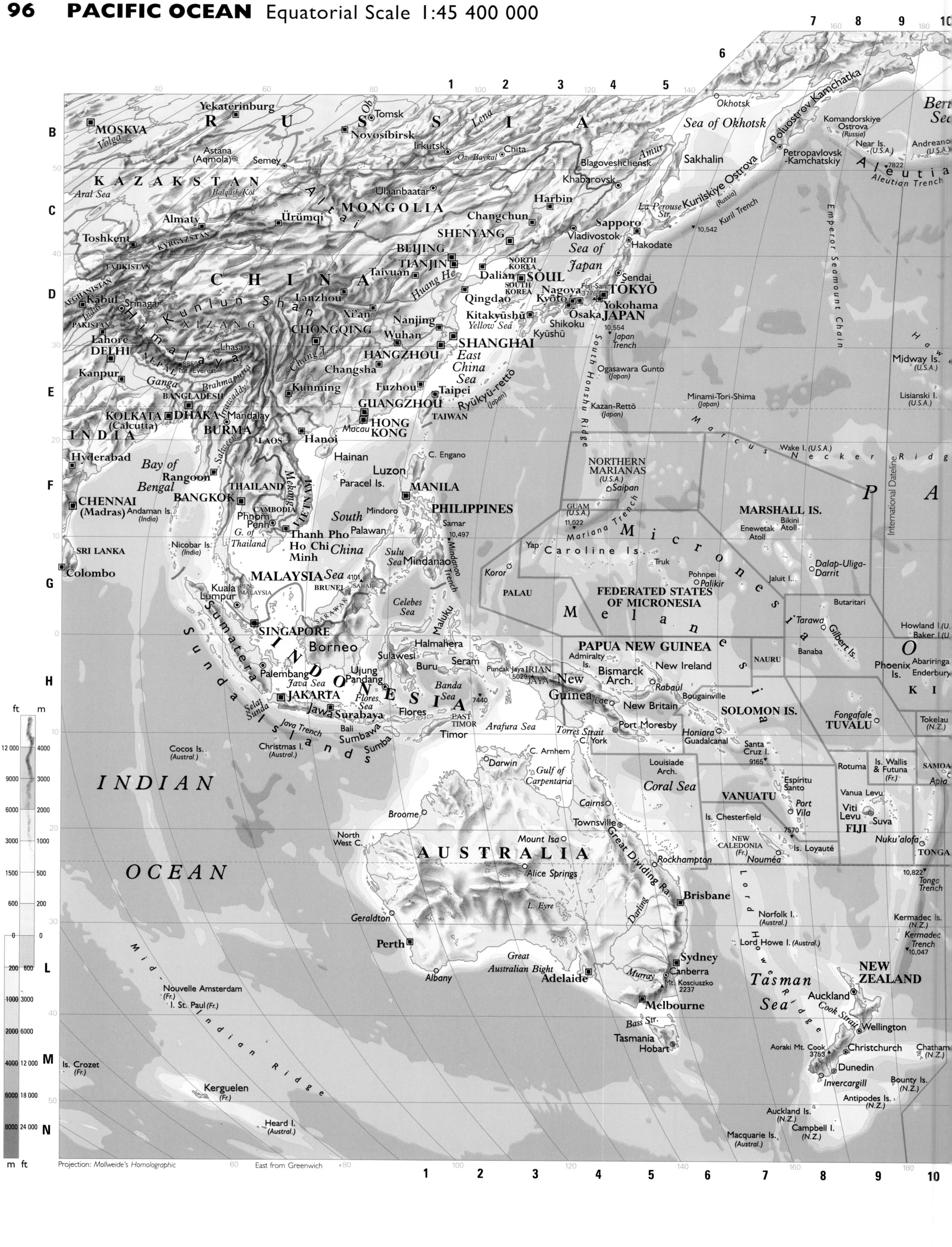

MOSKVA
Volga
Yekaterinburg
R U S S I A
Ob
Tomsk
Novosibirsk
Lena
Irkutsk
Oz. Baykal
Chita
Astana (Aqmola)
Semey
Amur
Blagoveshchensk
Khabarovsk
Okhotsk
Sea of Okhotsk
Poluostrov Kamchatka
Sakhalin
Petropavlovsk -Kamchatskiy
Komandorskiye Ostrova (Russia)
Near Is. (U.S.A.)
Andreanof Is. (U.S.A.)
Bering Sea
7822
Aleutian
Aleutian Trench
K A Z A K S T A N
Aral Sea
Balqash Köl
Altai
MONGOLIA
Ulaanbaatar
Harbin
Changchun
SHENYANG
La Perouse Str.
Kurilskiye Ostrova (Russia)
Kuril Trench
10,542
Sapporo
Vladivostok
Hakodate
Sea of Japan
Sendai
Emperor Seamount Chain
Almaty
KYRGYZSTAN
Ürümqi
Toshkent
TAJIKISTAN
BEIJING
TIANJIN
Taiyuan
Huang He
NORTH KOREA
SOUTH KOREA
Dalian
SÖUL
Qingdao
Nagoya
Fuji-San 3776
TŌKYŌ
Yokohama
Kyōto
Osaka
JAPAN
Kitakyūshū
Shikoku
Kyūshū
Yellow Sea
AFGHANISTAN
Kābul
Srinagar
Indus
C H I N A
Kunlun Shan
XIZANG
Lanzhou
Xi'an
Nanjing
Wuhan
CHONGQING
SHANGHAI
PAKISTAN
Lahore
DELHI
Himalaya
Lhasa
NEPAL
8850 Mt. Everest
Chang Jiang
HANGZHOU
East China Sea
Changsha
10,554 Japan Trench
South Honshu Ridge
Ogasawara Gunto (Japan)
Kanpur
Ganga
Brahmaputra
BANGLADESH
Kunming
Fuzhou
Taipei
Ryūkyū-rettō (Japan)
Kazan-Rettō (Japan)
Minami-Tori-Shima (Japan)
Midway Is. (U.S.A.)
Lisianski I. (U.S.A.)
Hawaiian
KOLKATA (Calcutta)
DHAKA
Irrawaddy
Mandalay
GUANGZHOU
HONG KONG
Macau
TAIWAN
INDIA
BURMA
Salween
LAOS
Hanoi
Marcus Necker Ridge
Wake I. (U.S.A.)
Hyderabad
Bay of Bengal
Rangoon
Mekong
THAILAND
VIETNAM
Hainan
C. Engano
Luzon
Paracel Is.
NORTHERN MARIANAS (U.S.A.)
Saipan
International Dateline
P A
CHENNAI (Madras)
Andaman Is. (India)
BANGKOK
CAMBODIA
Phnom Penh
MANILA
Mindoro
PHILIPPINES
GUAM (U.S.A.)
11,022
Mariana Trench
MARSHALL IS.
Bikini Atoll
Enewetak Atoll
G. of Thailand
Thanh Pho Ho Chi Minh
South China Sea
Palawan
Samar
10,497
Micronesia
SRI LANKA
Colombo
Nicobar Is. (India)
Sulu Sea
Mindanao
Mindanao Trench
Yap
Caroline Is.
Truk
Dalap-Uliga-Darrit
Koror
PALAU
Pohnpei
Palikir
Jaluit I.
MALAYSIA
Kuala Lumpur
PEN. MALAYSIA
BRUNEI
SABAH
4101
SARAWAK
Celebes Sea
FEDERATED STATES OF MICRONESIA
Butaritari
Tarawa
Gilbert Is.
Howland I. (U.S.A.)
Baker I. (U.S.A.)
SINGAPORE
Borneo
Maluku
Halmahera
Melanesia
PAPUA NEW GUINEA
Admiralty Is.
New Ireland
NAURU
Banaba
O
Phoenix Is.
Abariringa
Enderbury
Sumatera
INDONESIA
Sulawesi
Buru
Seram
Puncak Jaya 5029
IRIAN JAYA
New Guinea
Bismarck Arch.
Rabaul
Palembang
Ujung Pandang
Java Sea
Banda Sea
7440
Lae
New Britain
Bougainville
JAKARTA
Surabaya
Jawa
Flores Sea
Flores
Sunda Islands
Selat Sunda
EAST TIMOR
Timor
Arafura Sea
Torres Strait
C. York
Port Moresby
SOLOMON IS.
Honiara
Guadalcanal
Fongafale
TUVALU
Tokelau (N.Z.)
K I
Java Trench
Bali
Sumbawa
Sumba
Christmas I. (Austral.)
Cocos Is. (Austral.)
Darwin
C. Arnhem
Gulf of Carpentaria
Santa Cruz I.
9165
Rotuma
Is. Wallis & Futuna (Fr.)
SAMOA
Apia
INDIAN OCEAN
Louisiade Arch.
Coral Sea
VANUATU
Espíritu Santo
Port Vila
Vanua Levu
Viti Levu
Suva
FIJI
Broome
Cairns
Townsville
Is. Chesterfield
7570
North West C.
Mount Isa
Great Dividing Ra.
NEW CALEDONIA (Fr.)
Nouméa
Is. Loyauté
Nuku'alofa
TONGA
AUSTRALIA
Alice Springs
Rockhampton
10,822
Tonga Trench
Lord Howe Rise
Brisbane
Darling
L. Eyre
Norfolk I. (Austral.)
Kermadec Is. (N.Z.)
Kermadec Trench
10,047
Geraldton
Lord Howe I. (Austral.)
Perth
Great Australian Bight
Sydney
Canberra
Mt. Kosciuszko 2237
Murray
Adelaide
Albany
Mid-Indian Ridge
Nouvelle Amsterdam (Fr.)
I. St. Paul (Fr.)
Tasman Sea
NEW ZEALAND
Auckland
Cook Strait
Wellington
Melbourne
Bass Str.
Tasmania
Hobart
Christchurch
Aoraki Mt. Cook 3753
Chatham Is. (N.Z.)
Dunedin
Invercargill
Bounty Is. (N.Z.)
Antipodes Is. (N.Z.)
Is. Crozet (Fr.)
Kerguelen (Fr.)
Heard I. (Austral.)
Auckland Is. (N.Z.)
Campbell I. (N.Z.)
Macquarie Is. (Austral.)

ft	m
12 000	4000
9000	3000
6000	2000
3000	1000
1500	500
600	200
0	0
200	600
1000	3000
2000	6000
4000	12 000
6000	18 000
8000	24 000
m	ft

Projection: *Mollweide's Homolographic*   East from Greenwich

ALASKA
(U.S.A.)
Anchorage
Gulf of Alaska
Bristol Bay
Juneau
Prince of Wales I.
(U.S.A.) Prince Rupert
Queen Charlotte Is.
(Canada)
C A N A D A
Edmonton
Calgary
Regina
Winnipeg
L. Winnipeg
Vancouver
Victoria
Vancouver I.
Seattle
Portland
Boise
Salt Lake City
Denver
C. Mendocino
Sacramento
SAN FRANCISCO
LOS ANGELES
San Diego
Phoenix
Minneapolis
CHICAGO
Detroit
Toronto
Ottawa
Montréal
Québec
Buffalo
Boston
NEW YORK CITY
PHILADELPHIA
Baltimore
Washington D.C.
Pittsburgh
Cincinnati
St. Louis
Kansas City
Oklahoma City
Memphis
Atlanta
Dallas
Houston
San Antonio
New Orleans
Jacksonville
Miami
UNITED STATES
Newfoundland
St. John's
NORTH ATLANTIC OCEAN
C. Hatteras
Bermuda
(U.K.)
Sargasso Sea
Gulf of Mexico
Monterrey
Ciudad Juárez
Guadalupe
(Mex.)
Golfo de California
Baja California
C. San Lucas
Tropic of Cancer
Honolulu
Oahu
HAWAIIAN IS.
(U.S.A.)
Hawaii
MEXICO
Guadalajara
Puebla
Acapulco
Mérida
Is. Revilla Gigedo
(Mex.)
La Habana
CUBA
BAHAMAS
West Indies
HAITI
DOMINICAN REP.
JAMAICA
Kingston
PUERTO RICO
(U.S.A.)
Leeward Is.
BELIZE
HONDURAS
GUATEMALA
Guatemala
San Salvador
EL SALVADOR
NICARAGUA
Managua
COSTA RICA
San José
Colón
Panamá
PANAMA
Caribbean Sea
BARBADOS
Windward Is.
Barranquilla
Maracaibo
Caracas
VENEZUELA
I. Clipperton
(Fr.)
Palmyra Is.
(U.S.A.)
Teraina
Tabuaeran
Kiritimati
Jarvis I.
(U.S.A.)
Equator
PACIFIC OCEAN
Malden I.
Starbuck I.
KIRIBATI
Medellín
Bogotá
Cali
COLOMBIA
I. del Coco
(Costa Rica)
I. de Malpelo
(Colombia)
Galápagos
(Ecuador)
Quito
ECUADOR
Guayaquil
C. Paliñas
Iquitos
BRAZIL
Trujillo
PERU
LIMA
Cuzco
L. Titicaca
Arequipa
La Paz
BOLIVIA
Nevada Ancohuma
Arica
Iquique
Antofagasta
PARAGUAY
Asunción
San Miguel de Tucumán
Tongareva
Pukapuka
Manihiki
Caroline I.
Vostok I.
Flint I.
Is. Marquises
Suwarrow Is.
Is. de la Société
Tahiti
Papeete
Is. Tuamotu
Cook Is.
(N.Z.)
FRENCH POLYNESIA
Mururoa
Rarotonga
Is. Tubuai
Rapa
Ducie I.
Pitcairn I.
(U.K.)
Austral Seamount Chain
Tuamotu Ridge
East Pacific Ridge
Tropic of Capricorn
Sala-y-Gómez
(Chile)
I. de Pascua
(Chile)
San Felix
(Chile)
San Ambrosio
(Chile)
Chile Trench
Arch. de Juan Fernández
(Chile)
Córdoba
Aconcagua
Rosario
Valparaiso
SANTIAGO
BUENOS AIRES
URUGUAY
Montevideo
Río de la Plata
Porto Alegre
Concepción
ARGENTINA
Chile Rise
Patagonia
SOUTH ATLANTIC OCEAN
Pacific-Antarctic Ridge
Falkland Is.
(U.K.)
Punta Arenas
Est. de Magallanes
Tierra del Fuego
C. de Hornos
South Georgia
(U.K.)
West from Greenwich

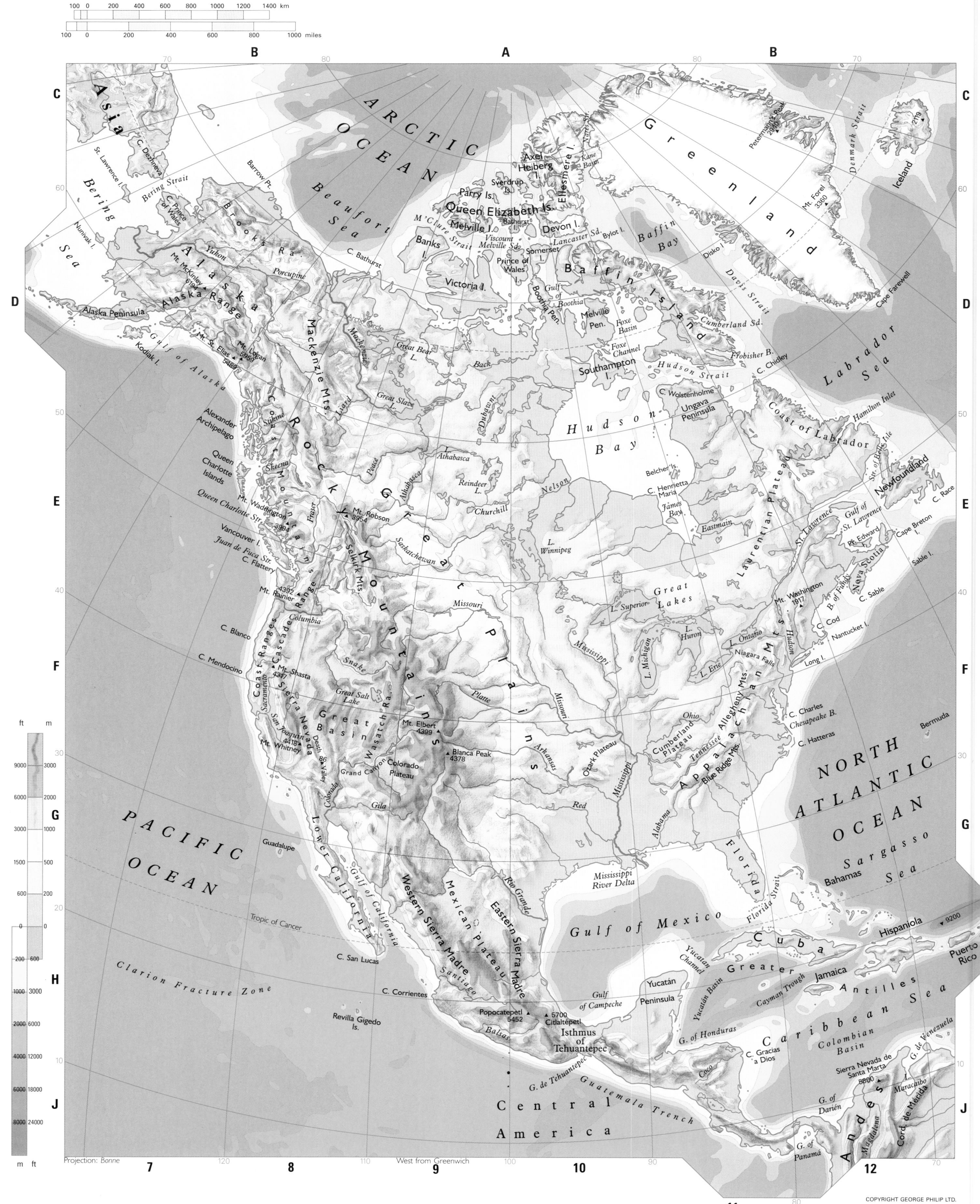

ARCTIC OCEAN
Beaufort Sea
Asia
Bering Sea
Bering Strait
Alaska
Alaska Range
Alaska Peninsula
Brooks Ra.
Gulf of Alaska
Mt. McKinley 6194
Mt. St. Elias 5489
Mt. Logan 5959
Kodiak I.
Yukon
Porcupine
Mackenzie Mts.
Mackenzie
Great Bear L.
Great Slave L.
Rocky Mountains
Coast Mountains
Alexander Archipelago
Queen Charlotte Islands
Queen Charlotte Str.
Mt. Waddington 3994
Vancouver I.
Juan de Fuca Str.
C. Flattery
Mt. Robson 3954
Selkirk Mts.
Great Plains
Mt. Rainier 4392
Cascade Range
Columbia
C. Blanco
C. Mendocino
Mt. Shasta 4317
Sierra Nevada
Coast Ranges
Mt. Whitney 4418
Great Basin
Great Salt Lake
Wasatch Ra.
Mt. Elbert 4399
Blanca Peak 4378
Colorado Plateau
Grand Canyon
Death Valley -86
Snake
Platte
Missouri
Arkansas
Red
Gila
Lower California
Gulf of California
Guadalupe
PACIFIC OCEAN
Tropic of Cancer
C. San Lucas
C. Corrientes
Revilla Gigedo Is.
Clarion Fracture Zone
Western Sierra Madre
Mexican plateau
Eastern Sierra Madre
Rio Grande
Popocatepetl 5452
Citlaltépetl 5700
Isthmus of Tehuantepec
G. de Tehuantepec
Guatemala Trench
Central America
Balsas
Banks I.
Victoria I.
Melville I.
Queen Elizabeth Is.
Parry Is.
Sverdrup Is.
Axel Heiberg I.
Ellesmere I.
Devon I.
Lancaster Sd.
Bylot I.
Baffin Bay
Baffin Island
Somerset I.
Prince of Wales I.
Boothia Pen.
Gulf of Boothia
Melville Pen.
Foxe Basin
Foxe Channel
Southampton I.
Hudson Strait
Hudson Bay
James Bay
Belcher Is.
C. Henrietta Maria
Ungava Peninsula
C. Wolstenholme
C. Chidley
Frobisher B.
Cumberland Sd.
Davis Strait
Greenland
Iceland
Denmark Strait
Cape Farewell
Labrador Sea
Coast of Labrador
Hamilton Inlet
Newfoundland
Gulf of St. Lawrence
Cape Breton I.
Nova Scotia
Sable I.
C. Race
Laurentian Plateau
Great Lakes
L. Superior
L. Michigan
L. Huron
L. Erie
L. Ontario
Niagara Falls
L. Winnipeg
Nelson
Churchill
Reindeer L.
L. Athabasca
Athabasca
Peace
Saskatchewan
Dubawnt
Back
Eastmain
Mt. Washington 1917
C. Cod
Nantucket I.
Long I.
Hudson
Appalachian Mts.
Allegheny Mts.
Blue Ridge Mts.
Cumberland Plateau
Ohio
Tennessee
Mississippi
Ozark Plateau
Alabama
Chesapeake B.
C. Charles
C. Hatteras
Bermuda
NORTH ATLANTIC OCEAN
Sargasso Sea
Bahamas
Florida
Florida Strait
Mississippi River Delta
Gulf of Mexico
Gulf of Campeche
Yucatán Peninsula
Yucatan Channel
Yucatán Basin
Cuba
Greater Antilles
Cayman Trough
Jamaica
Hispaniola
Puerto Rico
Caribbean Sea
Colombian Basin
G. of Honduras
C. Gracias a Dios
Coco
G. of Darién
G. of Panamá
Sierra Nevada de Santa Marta 5800
L. Maracaibo
G. de Venezuela
Andes
Magdalena
Cord. de Mérida
Projection: Bonne
West from Greenwich

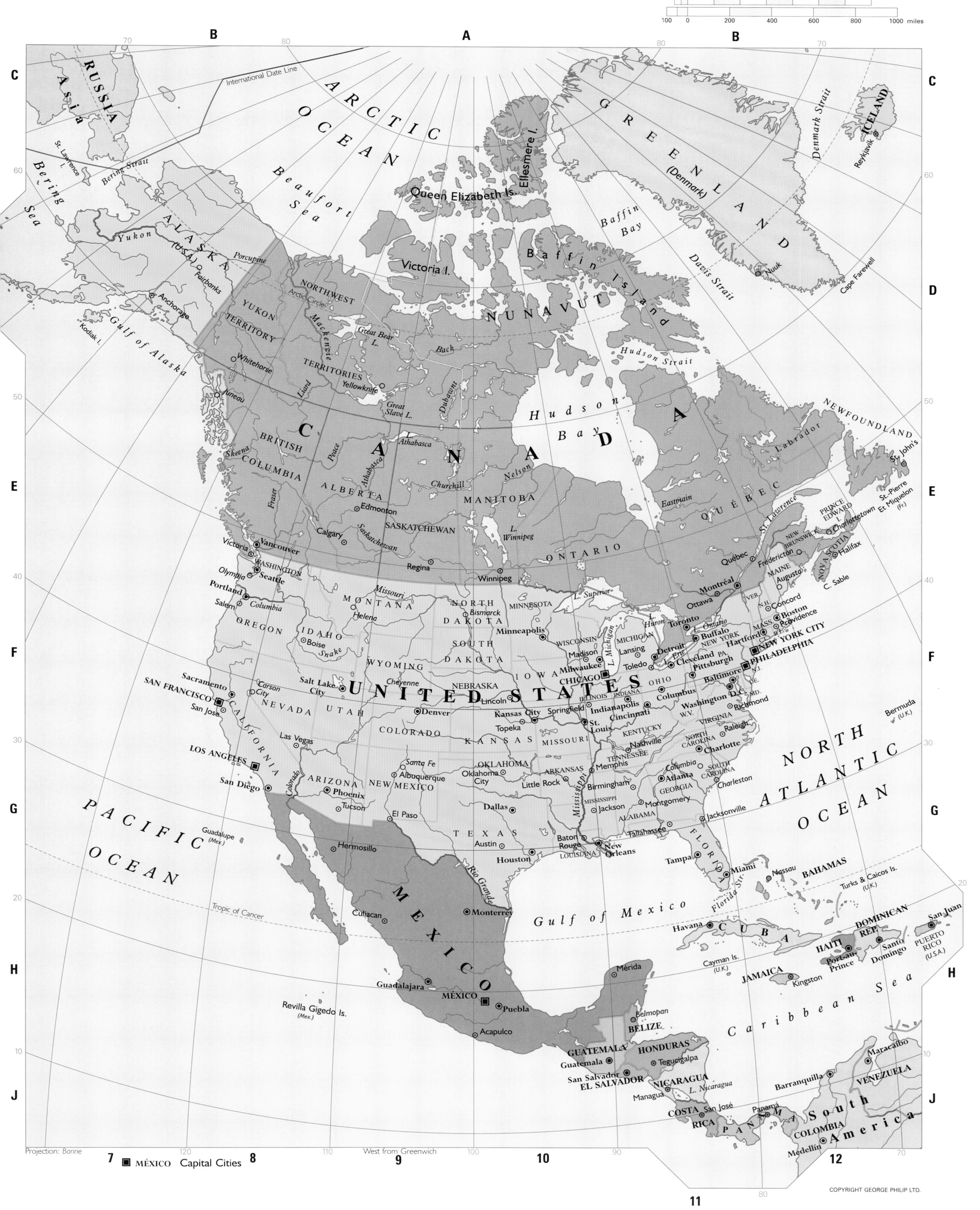
100 0 200 400 600 800 1000 1200 1400 km
100 0 200 400 600 800 1000 miles
ARCTIC OCEAN
Beaufort Sea
RUSSIA
Asia
International Date Line
St. Lawrence I.
Bering Strait
Bering Sea
GREENLAND (Denmark)
ICELAND
Reykjavik
Denmark Strait
Queen Elizabeth Is.
Ellesmere I.
Baffin Bay
Baffin Island
Victoria I.
Davis Strait
Nuuk
Cape Farewell
ALASKA (U.S.A.)
Yukon
Porcupine
Fairbanks
Anchorage
Kodiak I.
Gulf of Alaska
NORTHWEST TERRITORIES
Arctic Circle
YUKON TERRITORY
Mackenzie
Great Bear L.
Back
NUNAVUT
Hudson Strait
Whitehorse
Juneau
Liard
Yellowknife
Great Slave L.
Dubawnt
Hudson Bay
CANADA
NEWFOUNDLAND
Labrador
St John's
BRITISH COLUMBIA
Skeena
Peace
L. Athabasca
Athabasca
Churchill
Nelson
ALBERTA
Fraser
Edmonton
MANITOBA
Eastmain
QUÉBEC
St. Lawrence
PRINCE EDWARD I.
Charlottetown
St.-Pierre Et Miquelon (Fr.)
SASKATCHEWAN
Saskatchewan
Calgary
L. Winnipeg
Victoria
Vancouver
NEW BRUNSWICK
NOVA SCOTIA
Halifax
ONTARIO
Québec
Fredericton
Regina
WASHINGTON
Olympia
Seattle
Winnipeg
MAINE
Augusta
C. Sable
L. Superior
Montréal
Portland
Missouri
Salem
Columbia
MONTANA
Helena
NORTH DAKOTA
Bismarck
MINNESOTA
Ottawa
N.H.
Concord
Boston
Providence
OREGON
IDAHO
Boise
Snake
Minneapolis
SOUTH DAKOTA
WISCONSIN
L. Michigan
MICHIGAN
L. Huron
Toronto
L. Ontario
Buffalo
NEW YORK
MASS.
Hartford
NEW YORK CITY
PHILADELPHIA
WYOMING
Madison
Lansing
Detroit
L. Erie
Cleveland
PA.
Pittsburgh
Milwaukee
Toledo
Sacramento
SAN FRANCISCO
Carson City
Salt Lake City
Cheyenne
UNITED STATES
NEBRASKA
IOWA
CHICAGO
OHIO
Baltimore
N.J.
DE.
MD.
San Jose
NEVADA
UTAH
Denver
Lincoln
ILLINOIS
INDIANA
Indianapolis
Columbus
Washington D.C.
Richmond
Bermuda (U.K.)
CALIFORNIA
Kansas City
Springfield
Cincinnati
W.V.
VIRGINIA
COLORADO
Topeka
St. Louis
KENTUCKY
Raleigh
KANSAS
MISSOURI
NORTH CAROLINA
Charlotte
Las Vegas
Nashville
TENNESSEE
NORTH ATLANTIC OCEAN
LOS ANGELES
Santa Fe
OKLAHOMA
ARKANSAS
Memphis
Columbia
SOUTH CAROLINA
Albuquerque
Oklahoma City
Little Rock
Atlanta
GEORGIA
Charleston
San Diego
Colorado
ARIZONA
NEW MEXICO
Birmingham
Phoenix
MISSISSIPPI
Mississippi
Montgomery
Tucson
El Paso
Dallas
Jackson
ALABAMA
Jacksonville
PACIFIC OCEAN
Guadalupe (Mex.)
TEXAS
Baton Rouge
LOUISIANA
New Orleans
Tallahassee
FLORIDA
Austin
Houston
Hermosillo
Tampa
Miami
Nassau
BAHAMAS
Florida Str.
Rio Grande
Turks & Caicos Is. (U.K.)
MEXICO
Tropic of Cancer
Monterrey
Gulf of Mexico
Culiacan
Havana
CUBA
DOMINICAN REP.
San Juan
HAITI
Port-au-Prince
Santo Domingo
PUERTO RICO (U.S.A.)
Cayman Is. (U.K.)
JAMAICA
Kingston
Mérida
Guadalajara
MÉXICO
Puebla
Revilla Gigedo Is. (Mex.)
Belmopan
BELIZE
Caribbean Sea
Acapulco
GUATEMALA
Guatemala
HONDURAS
Tegucigalpa
Maracaibo
San Salvador
EL SALVADOR
NICARAGUA
L. Nicaragua
Managua
Barranquilla
VENEZUELA
COSTA RICA
San José
Panamá
PANAMA
South America
COLOMBIA
Medellín
Projection: Bonne
West from Greenwich
MÉXICO Capital Cities

ALASKA
1:25 200 000
PACIFIC OCEAN
BRITISH COLUMBIA
ALBERTA
SASKATCHEWAN
MANITOBA
NORTHWEST TERRITORIES
YUKON TERRITORY
Projection : Bonne
West from Greenwich

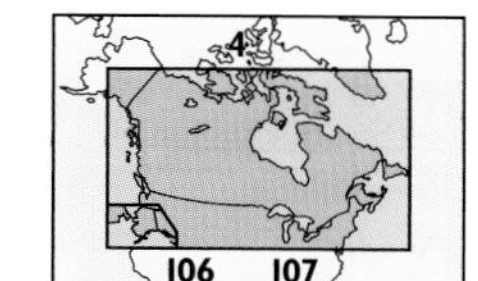

11 12 13 14 15 16

B

Devon I.
Lancaster Sound
Baffin Bay
Nunavik
Uummannaq
Ammassalik
1890
Bylot I.
Arctic Bay
Borden Pen.
Eclipse Sd.
Pond Inlet
Brodeur Peninsula
C. Adair
Qeqertarsuaq
Ilulissat
Qasigiannguit
GREENLAND
(KALAALLIT NUNAAT)
(Denmark)
Clyde River
C. Raper
Kangerlussuaq
Sisimiut
Maniitsoq
Nuuk
2850
Kong Frederik VI's Kyst
Baffin Island
Davis Strait
Home B.
Qikiqtarjuaq
C. Dyer
Fury and Hecla Str.
Igloolik
Sanirajak
Simpson Pen.
Pelly Bay
Committee B.
Melville Peninsula
Foxe Basin
Prince Charles I.
Air Force I.
2591
Cumberland Peninsula
Pangnirtung
Hoare B.
Mercy C.
Cumberland Sd.
Qeqertarsuatsiaat
Paamiut
Arsuk
Qaqortoq
Nanortalik
Alluitsup Paa
Uummannarsuaq
Rae Isthmus
Repulse Bay
Nettilling L.
NUNAVUT
C. Dorchester
Amadjuak L.
Foxe Pen.
Iqaluit
Hall Peninsula
Wager B.
Roes Welcome Sd.
Foxe Channel
Cape Dorset
Meta Incognita Peninsula
Kimmirut
Frobisher Bay
Resolution I.
Southampton I.
Salliq
Bell Pen.
Salisbury I.
Nottingham I.
Hudson Strait
ATLANTIC OCEAN
Labrador Sea
3809

C

Coats I.
Mansel I.
Ivujivik
Salluit
Kangiqsujuaq
Quaqtaq
Akpatok I.
C. Chidley
Péninsule d'Ungava
Kangirsuk
Ungava Bay
1652
Kangiqsualujjuaq
Hebron
Puvirnituq
L. Payne
Arnaud
Hudson Bay
Ottawa Is.
257
Feuilles
Koksoak
Kuujjuaq
Baleine
George
Nain
NEWFOUNDLAND
Hopedale
C. Harrison
Inukjuak
Mélèzes
Caniapiscau
L. Minto
Rigolet
Cartwright
Port Hope Simpson
Belle Isle
Sleeper Is.
King George Is.
Baker's Dozen Is.
Tatnam
Schefferville
Smallwood Res.
Labrador
North West River
Happy Valley-Goose Bay
Churchill Falls
Churchill
Petitsikapau
Esker
L. à l'Eau Claire
L. Bienville
Belcher Is.
Kuujjuarapik
Grande Baleine
C. Bauld
St. Anthony
Notre Dame B.
Str. of Belle Isle
Rés. de Caniapiscau
Kanaaupscow
La Grande
C. Henrietta Maria
Pte. Louis XIV
Peawanuck
Winisk
Severn
Labrador City
Fermont
Ashuanipi
Natashquan
St-Augustin
Romaine
Moisie
Chisasibi
QUÉBEC
1135
Gagnon
Rés. Manicouagan
Manicouagan
Havre-St-Pierre
Natashquan
Î. d'Anticosti
Baie Verte
Lewisporte
Gander
Bonavista
Trinity B.
Carbonear
St. John's
Deer Lake
Grand Falls
Corner Brook
Newfoundland
814
Stephenville
Marystown
Placentia B.
Placentia
C. Race
James Bay
Big Trout L.
Attawapiskat
Akimiski I.
Wemindji
Eastmain
Sept-Îles
Port-Cartier

D

Fort Albany
Charlton I.
Eastmain
Waskaganish
Rupert
L. Mistassini
L. Albanel
Péribonca
Baie Comeau
St. Lawrence
Gulf of St. Lawrence
Cabot Str.
Channel-Port aux Basques
ST-PIERRE et MIQUELON (Fr.)
C. Ray
ONTARIO
Albany
Moosonee
Nottaway
Harricana
Missinaibi
Chibougamau
Matane
Gaspé
Pén. de Gaspé
Îs. de la Madeleine
North C.
Cape Breton I.
Glace Bay
St. Joseph
Nakina
Kenogami
Matagami
L. Matagami
Dolbeau
St-Jean
Chicoutimi
Rimouski
Campbellton
Bathurst
Miramichi
PR. EDWARD I.
Summerside
Charlottetown
Sydney
Port Hawkesbury
Antigonish
Nipigon
L. Nipigon
Geraldton
Hearst
Mattagami
Kapuskasing
Cochrane
Abitibi L.
Amos
Rés. Gouin
Roberval
Jonquière
Rivière-du-Loup
Edmundston
Northumberland Str.
NEW BRUNSWICK
NOVA SCOTIA
New Glasgow
Marathon
Oba
Timmins
1190
Québec
Grand Falls
Moncton
Amherst
Truro
Sable I. (Nova Scotia)
Kirkland Lake
Rouyn-Noranda
Val-d'Or
La Tuque
Lévis
Woodstock
Fredericton
Kentville
Dartmouth
Halifax
Thunder Bay
Chapleau
New Liskeard
Rés. Cabonga
Mont-Laurier
Shawinigan
Trois-Rivières
Thetford Mines
Saint John
Digby
Bridgewater
Liverpool
Lake Superior
Wawa
Joliette
St-Hyacinthe
MAINE
B. of Fundy
Houghton
183
Sault Ste. Marie
Elliot Lake
Sudbury
Outaouais
MONTRÉAL
Sherbrooke
Bangor
Yarmouth
C. Sable
Ironwood
Marquette
L. Nipissing
North Bay
Granby
Augusta
Lewiston
6309
MICHIGAN
Sault Ste. Marie
Manitoulin I.
Parry Sound
Pembroke
Hull
Ottawa
Cornwall
L. Champlain
Montpelier
Portland
Manistique
Georgian Bay
Huntsville
Burlington
VERMONT
NEW HAMPSHIRE
Escanaba
Menominee
Lake Huron
Petoskey
Traverse City
Barrie
Peterborough
Kingston
Concord
Manchester
Green Bay
Owen Sound
Oshawa
Belleville
L. Ontario
WISCONSIN
Wausau
Cadillac
TORONTO
Kitchener
Hamilton
Syracuse
MASS.
BOSTON
C. Cod
Appleton
Sheboygan
L. Michigan
Saginaw
Flint
London
Niagara Falls
Rochester
NEW YORK
Albany
Springfield
Providence
MILWAUKEE
Grand Rapids
Sarnia
BUFFALO
HARTFORD
CONN.
R.I.
Madison
Racine
Kenosha
Lansing
174
L. Erie
Elmira
Binghamton
New Haven
Rockford
Jamestown
Scranton
Bridgeport
CHICAGO
DETROIT
Windsor
Erie
Newark
NEW YORK
Gary
South Bend
Toledo
CLEVELAND
ILLINOIS
INDIANA
OHIO
PENNSYLVANIA
N.J.
Allentown
Trenton

E

11 12 13 14

West from Greenwich

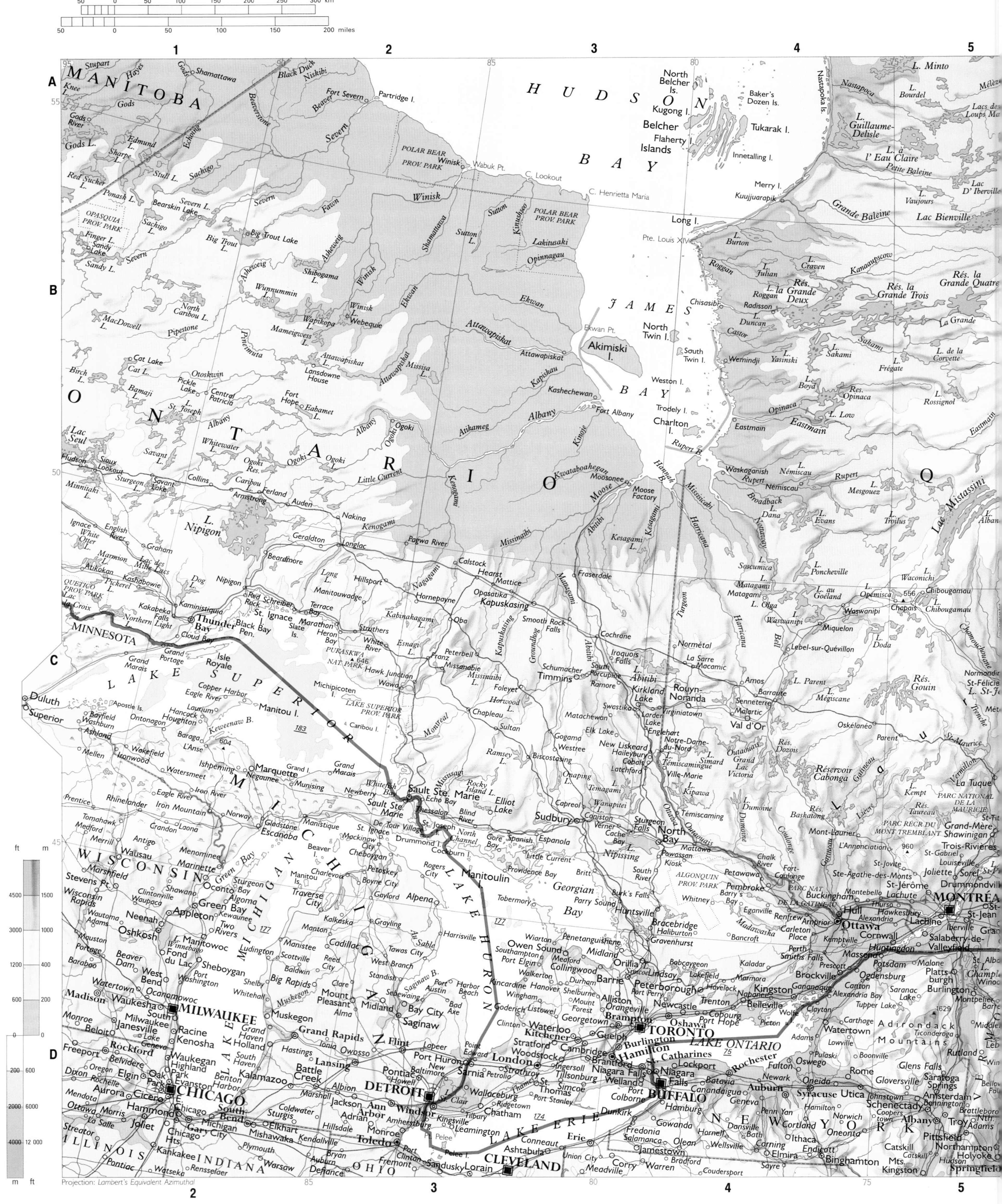

50 0 50 100 150 200 250 300 km
50 0 50 100 150 200 miles
1
2
3
4
5
A
B
C
D
MANITOBA
ONTARIO
HUDSON BAY
JAMES BAY
LAKE SUPERIOR
LAKE HURON
LAKE MICHIGAN
LAKE ERIE
LAKE ONTARIO
MINNESOTA
WISCONSIN
MICHIGAN
ILLINOIS
INDIANA
OHIO
NEW YORK
Belcher Islands
Akimiski I.
Georgian Bay
Manitoulin
Isle Royale
L. Nipigon
Thunder Bay
Sault Ste. Marie
Sudbury
Timmins
North Bay
Ottawa
Hull
MONTRÉAL
TORONTO
Hamilton
London
Kitchener
Windsor
DETROIT
CLEVELAND
BUFFALO
MILWAUKEE
CHICAGO
Duluth
Rochester
Kingston
Lac Seul
Lac Mistassini
Rés. Gouin
POLAR BEAR PROV. PARK
QUETICO PROV. PARK
PUKASKWA NAT. PARK
LAKE SUPERIOR PROV. PARK
ALGONQUIN PROV. PARK
ft m
4500 1500
3000 1000
1200 400
600 200
0 0
200 600
2000 6000
4000 12 000
m ft
Projection: Lambert's Equivalent Azimuthal

LABRADOR SEA
NEWFOUNDLAND
Labrador
Newfoundland
Labrador City
Smallwood Reservoir
Churchill Falls
Happy Valley-Goose Bay
North West River
Nain
Hopedale
Makkovik
Postville
Cartwright
Black Tickle
Mealy Mts.
Mary's Harbour
Battle Harbour
Red Bay
L'Anse au Loup
L'Anse aux Meadows
St. Anthony
Str. of Belle Isle
Belle Isle
Roddickton
Long Range Mts.
GROS MORNE NAT. PARK
Deer Lake
Corner Brook
Stephenville
Port au Port
Channel-Port aux Basques
Cabot Strait
Grand Falls-Windsor
Gander
Lewisporte
Twillingate
Fogo I.
Bonavista
TERRA NOVA NAT. PARK
Clarenville
Carbonear
Harbour Grace
St. John's
Mt. Pearl
Avalon Peninsula
Placentia
Marystown
Burin
Grand Bank
Fortune
ST-PIERRE ET MIQUELON (France)
Miquelon
St-Pierre
C. Race
Schefferville
Fermont
Wabush
Sept-Îles
Port-Cartier
Havre-St-Pierre
Natashquan
Kegaska
Romaine
St-Augustin
Blanc-Sablon
Rés. Manicouagan
Rés. de Caniapiscau
Baie Comeau
Î. d'Anticosti
Dét. de Jacques-Cartier
Dét. d'Honguedo
GULF OF ST. LAWRENCE
St. Lawrence
Pen. de Gaspé
Mts. Chic-Chocs
Gaspé
Percé
Matane
Rimouski
Rivière-du-Loup
Chicoutimi
Jonquière
Alma
La Baie
Québec
Lévis
Montmagny
Sherbrooke
Thetford Mines
St-Georges
Îs. de la Madeleine (Québec)
Î. Brion
Chaleur Bay
Campbellton
Bathurst
Edmundston
NEW BRUNSWICK
Miramichi
Moncton
Fredericton
Saint John
St. Stephen
Shediac
Sackville
Amherst
PRINCE EDWARD ISLAND
Charlottetown
Summerside
Northumberland Str.
NOVA SCOTIA
Halifax
Dartmouth
Truro
New Glasgow
Antigonish
Kentville
Windsor
Digby
Yarmouth
Lunenburg
Bridgewater
Liverpool
Shelburne
C. Sable
KEJIMKUJIK NAT. PARK
Bay of Fundy
Cape Breton Island
CAPE BRETON HIGHLANDS NAT. PARK
Sydney
Glace Bay
Louisbourg
Port Hawkesbury
Bras d'Or L.
Sable I. (Nova Scotia)
ATLANTIC OCEAN
MAINE
Bangor
Augusta
Lewiston
Portland
Waterville
Bar Harbor
Calais
Machias
NEW HAMPSHIRE
Manchester
Nashua
Concord
Portsmouth
Dover
Lowell
Lawrence
Haverhill
Newton
BOSTON
Quincy
Brockton
Gloucester
Lynn
UNITED STATES
A
B
C
D
6
7
8
9
West from Greenwich

km
miles
YUKON TERRITORY
NORTHWEST TERRITORIES
BRITISH COLUMBIA
ALBERTA
ALASKA (U.S.A.)
WASHINGTON
IDAHO
UNITED STATES
PACIFIC OCEAN
GREAT SLAVE LAKE
Queen Charlotte Islands
Queen Charlotte Sound
Vancouver Island
Coast Mountains
Rocky Mountains
Skeena Mountains
Cassiar Mountains
Cariboo Mts.
Columbia Mts.
Monashee Mts.
Purcell Mts.
Birch Mountains
Caribou Mts.
Clear Hills
Swan Hills
Alexander Arch.
Whitehorse
Yellowknife
Juneau
Prince Rupert
Prince George
Fort St. John
Dawson Creek
Grande Prairie
Edmonton
Red Deer
Calgary
Lethbridge
Kamloops
Kelowna
VANCOUVER
Victoria
SEATTLE
Nanaimo
Fort Nelson
Fort McMurray
Mt. Robson 3954
Mt. Waddington 3994
WOOD BUFFALO NATIONAL PARK
JASPER NATIONAL PARK
TWEEDSMUIR PROV. PARK
Dixon Entrance
Hecate Strait
Queen Charlotte Str.
Str. of Georgia
Strait of Juan de Fuca
Projection: Lambert's Equivalent Azimuthal
West from Greenwich

100
102
114
112

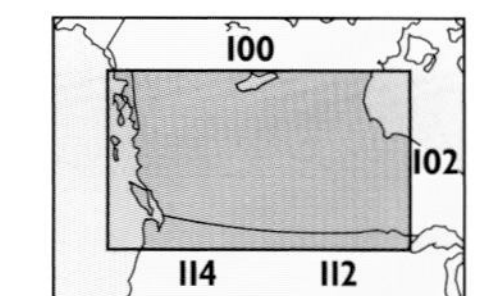

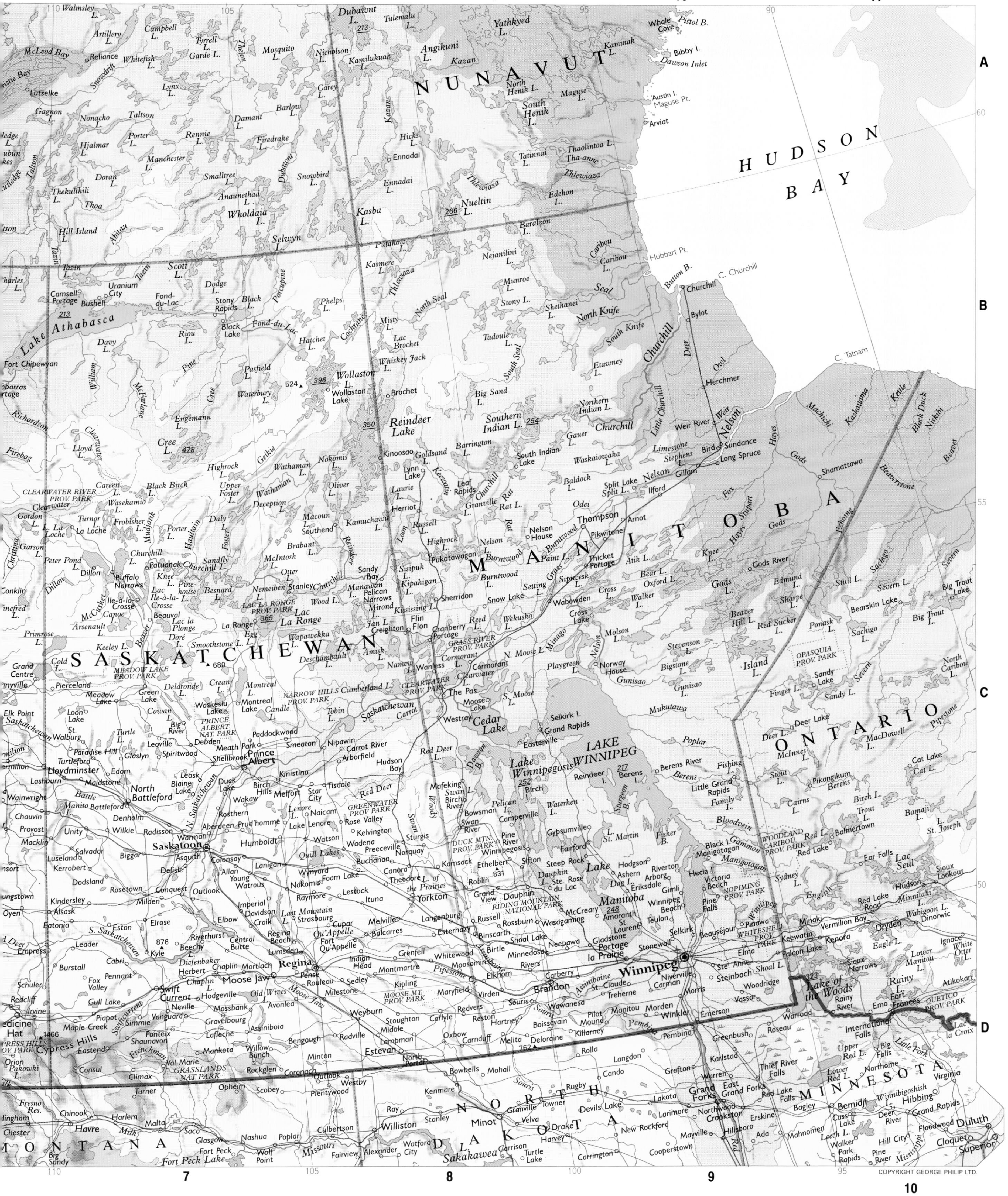

7
8
9
10
11
A
B
C
D
NUNAVUT
HUDSON BAY
MANITOBA
SASKATCHEWAN
ONTARIO
NORTH DAKOTA
MINNESOTA
MONTANA
LAKE WINNIPEG
Lake Winnipegosis
Lake Manitoba
Lake Athabasca
Reindeer Lake
Wollaston Lake
Southern Indian L.
Cedar Lake
Lake of the Woods
Nueltin L.
Dubawnt L.
Yathkyed L.
Churchill
C. Churchill
C. Tatnam
Arviat
Whale Cove
Dawson Inlet
Thompson
Gillam
The Pas
Flin Flon
Lac La Ronge
Prince Albert
Saskatoon
North Battleford
Lloydminster
Regina
Moose Jaw
Swift Current
Medicine Hat
Cypress Hills
Yorkton
Melville
Dauphin
Brandon
Portage la Prairie
Winnipeg
Selkirk
Steinbach
Kenora
Dryden
Fort Frances
International Falls
Estevan
Weyburn
Minot
Williston
Grand Forks
Duluth
Superior
Bemidji
Hibbing
Havre
Sakakawea
Fort Peck Lake
Fond-du-Lac
Uranium City
Fort Chipewyan
La Loche
Buffalo Narrows
Cumberland L.
Grand Rapids
Norway House
Island L.
Gods L.
Lac Seul
Red Lake
Big Trout Lake
Churchill
Nelson
Saskatchewan
Assiniboine
Souris
Red
Missouri
Milk
Winnipeg
Hayes
Seal
South Knife
North Knife
Kazan
Thelon
GRASSLANDS NAT. PARK
PRINCE ALBERT NAT. PARK
RIDING MOUNTAIN NATIONAL PARK
WHITESHELL PROV. PARK
NOPIMING PROV. PARK
WOODLAND CARIBOU PROV. PARK
OPASQUIA PROV. PARK
QUETICO PROV. PARK
MEADOW LAKE PROV. PARK
CLEARWATER RIVER PROV. PARK
LAC LA RONGE PROV. PARK
NARROW HILLS PROV. PARK
GRASS RIVER PROV. PARK
DUCK MTN. PROV. PARK
GREENWATER PROV. PARK
MOOSE MT. PROV. PARK
110
105
100
95
90
60
55
50
COPYRIGHT GEORGE PHILIP LTD.

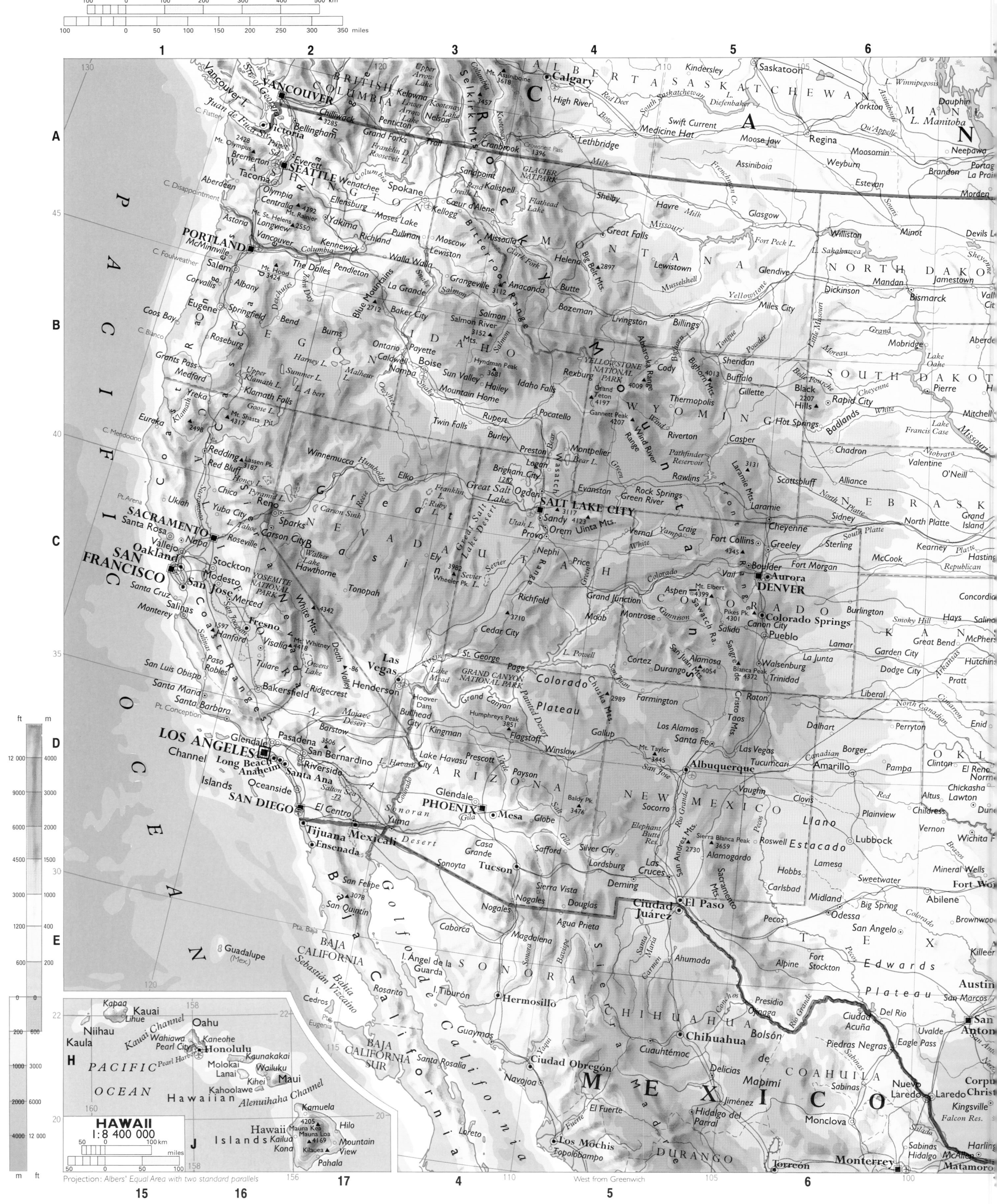
100 0 100 200 300 400 500 km
100 0 50 100 150 200 250 300 350 miles
1
2
3
4
5
6
A
B
C
D
E
H
J
15
16
17
4
5
6
PACIFIC OCEAN
CANADA
BRITISH COLUMBIA
ALBERTA
SASKATCHEWAN
MANITOBA
WASHINGTON
OREGON
IDAHO
MONTANA
WYOMING
NORTH DAKOTA
SOUTH DAKOTA
NEBRASKA
NEVADA
UTAH
COLORADO
KANSAS
CALIFORNIA
ARIZONA
NEW MEXICO
TEXAS
OKLAHOMA
MEXICO
BAJA CALIFORNIA
BAJA CALIFORNIA SUR
SONORA
CHIHUAHUA
COAHUILA
DURANGO
Rocky Mountains
Great Basin
Sierra Nevada
Coast Ranges
Cascade Range
Colorado Plateau
Llano Estacado
Edwards Plateau
Sierra Madre
Golfo de California
Mojave Desert
Sonoran Desert
Great Salt Lake Desert
YELLOWSTONE NATIONAL PARK
GLACIER NAT.PARK
GRAND CANYON NATIONAL PARK
YOSEMITE NATIONAL PARK
VANCOUVER
Victoria
Vancouver I.
Juan de Fuca Str.
Str. of Georgia
Seattle
SEATTLE
Tacoma
Olympia
Everett
Bellingham
Bremerton
Aberdeen
Centralia
Mt. Olympus 2428
Mt. Rainier 4392
Mt. St. Helens 2550
Mt. Hood 3424
Longview
Astoria
Vancouver
PORTLAND
McMinnville
Salem
Corvallis
Albany
Eugene
Springfield
Coos Bay
Roseburg
Grants Pass
Medford
Bend
The Dalles
Pendleton
La Grande
Baker City
Burns
Ontario
Klamath Falls
Upper Klamath L.
Harney L.
Malheur L.
Summer L.
L. Abert
Goose L.
Yreka
Eureka
Mt. Shasta 4317
Redding
Lassen Pk. 3187
Red Bluff
Chico
Ukiah
Yuba City
Reno
Carson City
Sparks
L. Tahoe
SACRAMENTO
Santa Rosa
Vallejo
Napa
Oakland
SAN FRANCISCO
Stockton
Modesto
San Jose
Santa Cruz
Monterey
Salinas
Merced
Fresno
Visalia
Hanford
Tulare
Mt. Whitney 4418
Bakersfield
Ridgecrest
San Luis Obispo
Paso Robles
Santa Maria
Santa Barbara
Pt. Conception
LOS ANGELES
Glendale
Pasadena
San Bernardino
Riverside
Long Beach
Anaheim
Santa Ana
Oceanside
SAN DIEGO
Channel Islands
Salton Sea
El Centro
Tijuana
Mexicali
Ensenada
Barstow
Death Valley
Owens Lake
Las Vegas
Henderson
Hoover Dam
Lake Mead
Bullhead City
Kingman
Lake Havasu City
Yuma
Calgary
High River
Red Deer
Lethbridge
Medicine Hat
Swift Current
Moose Jaw
Regina
Saskatoon
Kindersley
Yorkton
Assiniboia
Weyburn
Estevan
Moosomin
Brandon
Dauphin
Kelowna
Penticton
Nelson
Trail
Chilliwack
Grand Forks
Cranbrook
Spokane
Wenatchee
Ellensburg
Yakima
Moses Lake
Richland
Kennewick
Walla Walla
Pullman
Moscow
Lewiston
Coeur d'Alene
Sandpoint
Kalispell
Missoula
Helena
Great Falls
Butte
Anaconda
Bozeman
Livingston
Billings
Lewistown
Havre
Shelby
Glasgow
Miles City
Glendive
Williston
Minot
Bismarck
Mandan
Dickinson
Jamestown
Grangeville
Boise
Nampa
Caldwell
Payette
Sun Valley
Hailey
Mountain Home
Twin Falls
Idaho Falls
Rexburg
Pocatello
Rupert
Burley
Salmon
Cody
Sheridan
Buffalo
Gillette
Thermopolis
Riverton
Casper
Rawlins
Rock Springs
Green River
Evanston
Laramie
Cheyenne
Scottsbluff
Alliance
Chadron
Rapid City
Black Hills
Pierre
Mobridge
Valentine
O'Neill
North Platte
Sidney
Kearney
Grand Island
McCook
Winnemucca
Elko
Tonopah
Hawthorne
Ely
Logan
Ogden
Brigham City
Great Salt Lake
SALT LAKE CITY
Sandy
Orem
Provo
Uinta Mts.
Nephi
Price
Vernal
Richfield
Moab
Cedar City
St. George
Page
Flagstaff
Winslow
Prescott
Payson
Glendale
PHOENIX
Mesa
Globe
Casa Grande
Tucson
Nogales
Sierra Vista
Douglas
Safford
Gallup
Farmington
Durango
Cortez
Grand Junction
Montrose
Aspen
Vail
Boulder
DENVER
Aurora
Fort Collins
Greeley
Fort Morgan
Colorado Springs
Pueblo
Cañon City
Salida
Alamosa
Walsenburg
Trinidad
Raton
La Junta
Lamar
Los Alamos
Santa Fe
Taos
Las Vegas
Albuquerque
Tucumcari
Socorro
Las Cruces
Alamogordo
Roswell
Carlsbad
Hobbs
Clovis
Lordsburg
Deming
Silver City
El Paso
Ciudad Juárez
Amarillo
Lubbock
Odessa
Midland
Big Spring
San Angelo
Abilene
Dalhart
Borger
Pampa
Perryton
Plainview
Childress
Vernon
Lamesa
Pecos
Alpine
Fort Stockton
Del Rio
Uvalde
Eagle Pass
Piedras Negras
Nuevo Laredo
Laredo
Monterrey
Monclova
Sabinas
Ciudad Acuña
Torreón
Chihuahua
Cuauhtémoc
Delicias
Jiménez
Hidalgo del Parral
Ojinaga
Presidio
Ahumada
Hermosillo
Guaymas
Ciudad Obregón
Navojoa
Los Mochis
Topolobampo
El Fuerte
Caborca
Magdalena
Agua Prieta
Sonoyta
San Felipe
San Quintín
Guadalupe (Mex.)
I. Cedros
Santa Rosalía
I. Tiburón
I. Ángel de la Guarda
Liberal
Dodge City
Garden City
Great Bend
Hays
Pratt
Hutchinson
Projection: Albers' Equal Area with two standard parallels
West from Greenwich
HAWAII 1:8 400 000
Kauai
Kapaa
Lihue
Niihau
Kaula
Kauai Channel
Oahu
Wahiawa
Pearl City
Pearl Harbor
Kaneohe
Honolulu
Molokai
Kaunakakai
Lanai
Wailuku
Maui
Kahoolawe
Kihei
Hawaiian Islands
Alenuihaha Channel
Hawaii
Kamuela
Hilo
Mauna Kea 4205
Mauna Loa 4169
Kailua Kona
Kilauea
Mountain View
Pahala
PACIFIC OCEAN

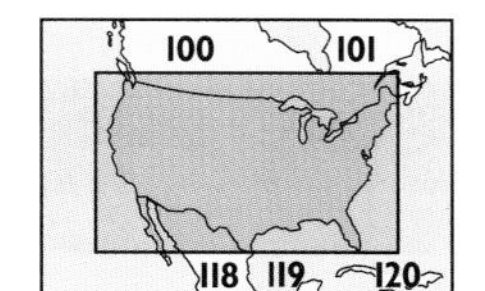
100
101
118
119
120

8
9
10
11
12
13
A
B
C
D
E
F
C A N A D A
Lake Winnipeg
Lake Superior
Lake Michigan
Lake Huron
Lake Ontario
Lake Erie
MINNESOTA
WISCONSIN
MICHIGAN
IOWA
ILLINOIS
INDIANA
OHIO
PENNSYLVANIA
NEW YORK
VERMONT
NEW HAMPSHIRE
MAINE
NEW BRUNSWICK
MISSOURI
KENTUCKY
WEST VIRGINIA
VIRGINIA
TENNESSEE
NORTH CAROLINA
SOUTH CAROLINA
ARKANSAS
MISSISSIPPI
ALABAMA
GEORGIA
LOUISIANA
FLORIDA
Midwest
Ozark Plateau
Appalachian Mountains
Cumberland Plateau
MINNEAPOLIS
ST. PAUL
MILWAUKEE
CHICAGO
DETROIT
TORONTO
MONTRÉAL
Ottawa
Québec
CLEVELAND
BUFFALO
PITTSBURGH
PHILADELPHIA
NEW YORK
BOSTON
HARTFORD
BALTIMORE
WASHINGTON D.C.
COLUMBUS
INDIANAPOLIS
CINCINNATI
ST. LOUIS
KANSAS CITY
Louisville
Nashville
Memphis
CHARLOTTE
ATLANTA
Birmingham
DALLAS
Arlington
HOUSTON
NEW ORLEANS
Jacksonville
TAMPA
MIAMI
BAHAMAS
ATLANTIC OCEAN
GULF OF MEXICO
Straits of Florida
Mississippi River Delta
95
90
85
80
75
70
65
45
40
35
30
25

8 9 10 11 12

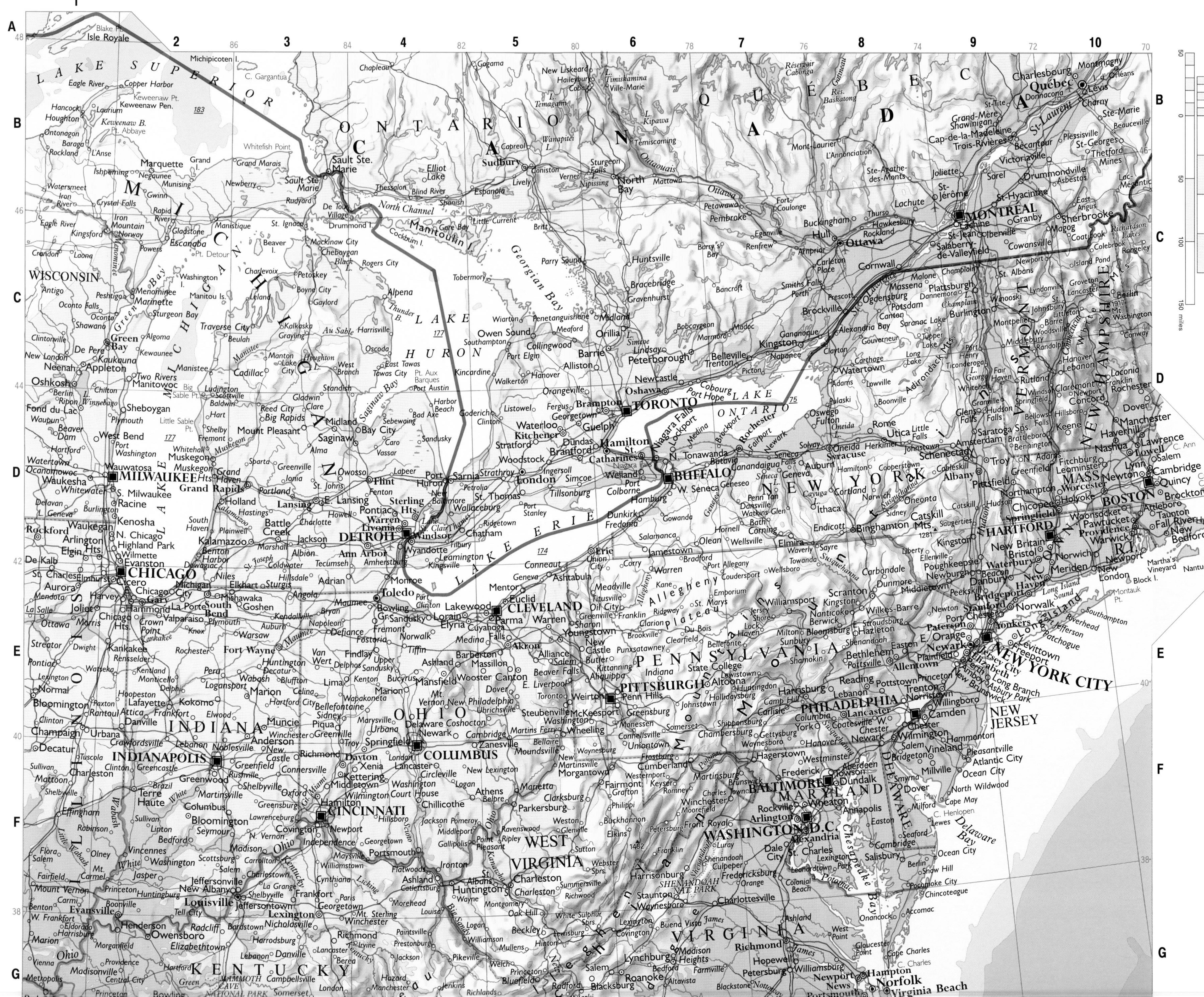
50 0 50 100 150 200 km
50 0 50 100 150 miles
LAKE SUPERIOR
LAKE HURON
LAKE ERIE
LAKE ONTARIO
Georgian Bay
ONTARIO
QUÉBEC
CANADA
MICHIGAN
WISCONSIN
NEW YORK
PENNSYLVANIA
OHIO
INDIANA
MARYLAND
DELAWARE
NEW JERSEY
WEST VIRGINIA
VIRGINIA
KENTUCKY
VERMONT
NEW HAMPSHIRE
MASS.
CONN.
R.I.
NEW YORK CITY
PHILADELPHIA
BOSTON
MONTREAL
TORONTO
BUFFALO
CLEVELAND
PITTSBURGH
DETROIT
CHICAGO
MILWAUKEE
INDIANAPOLIS
COLUMBUS
CINCINNATI
BALTIMORE
WASHINGTON D.C.
HARTFORD

TENNESSEE
NORTH CAROLINA
SOUTH CAROLINA
GEORGIA
ALABAMA
MISSISSIPPI
FLORIDA
MAINE
NEW HAMPSHIRE
CANADA
BAHAMAS
ATLANTIC OCEAN
GULF OF MEXICO
Nashville
CHARLOTTE
ATLANTA
Jacksonville
TAMPA
MIAMI
Birmingham
Montgomery
Mobile
Pensacola
Tallahassee
Savannah
Charleston
Columbia
Raleigh
Wilmington
Macon
Columbus
Orlando
Gainesville
Daytona Beach
St. Petersburg
Clearwater
Fort Lauderdale
West Palm Beach
Chattanooga
Knoxville
Greenville
Huntsville
Portland
Bangor
Augusta
Continuation Eastwards On same scale.
Projection: Albers' Equal Area with two standard parallels
West from Greenwich
COPYRIGHT.GEORGE PHILIP LTD.

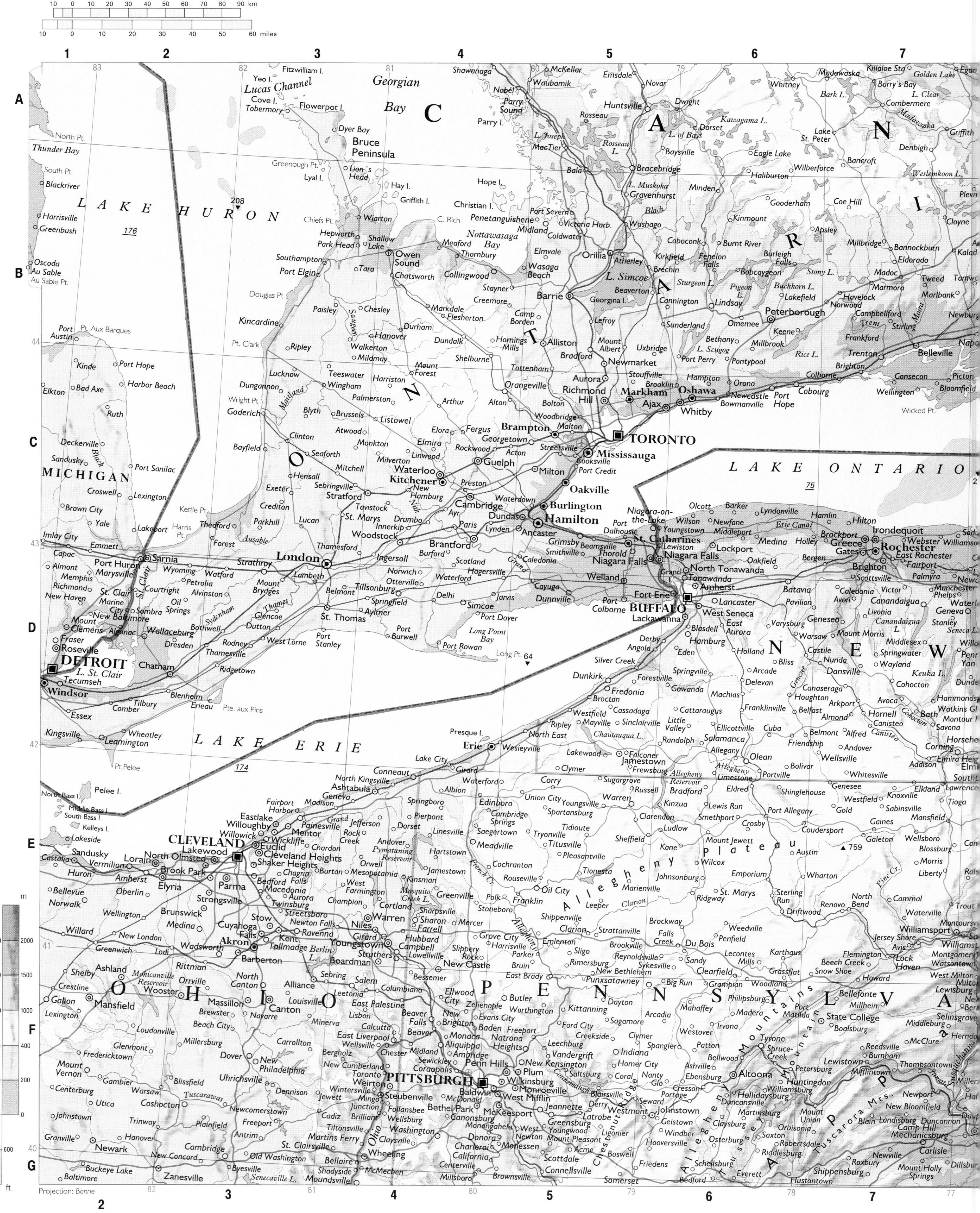
10 0 10 20 30 40 50 60 70 80 90 km
10 0 10 20 30 40 50 60 miles
Georgian Bay
Bruce Peninsula
LAKE HURON
ONTARIO
CANADA
LAKE ONTARIO
LAKE ERIE
MICHIGAN
OHIO
PENNSYLVANIA
NEW
Allegheny Plateau
Allegheny Mountains
Tuscarora Mts.
L. Simcoe
TORONTO
Mississauga
Hamilton
Burlington
Oakville
Kitchener
Waterloo
Guelph
Brampton
Markham
Oshawa
Peterborough
Barrie
London
St. Catharines
Niagara Falls
BUFFALO
Rochester
DETROIT
Windsor
Sarnia
Port Huron
CLEVELAND
Akron
Canton
Youngstown
Erie
PITTSBURGH
Altoona
State College
Williamsport
ft m
6000 2000
4500 1500
3000 1000
1200 400
600 200
0 0
200 600
m ft
Projection: Bonne

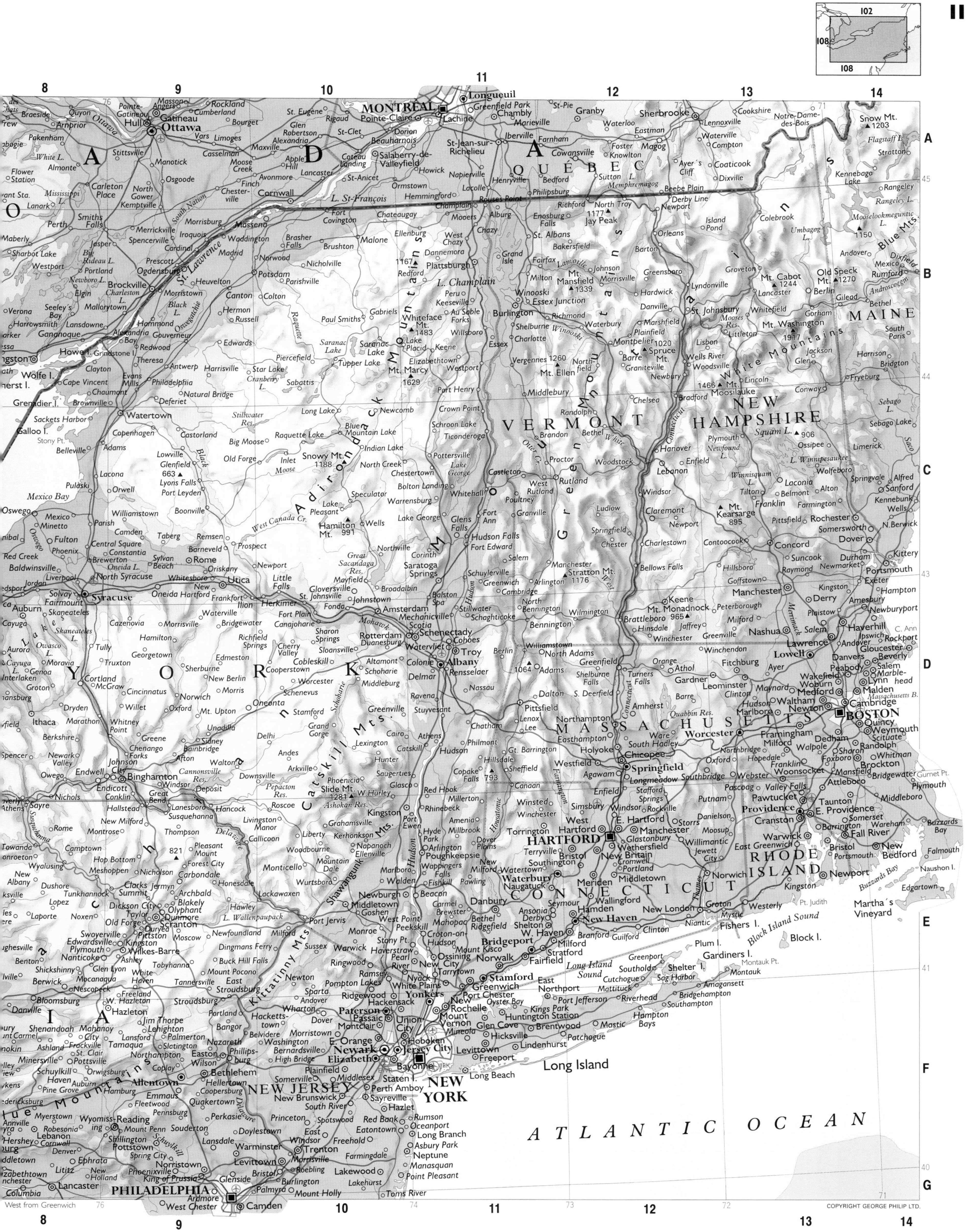

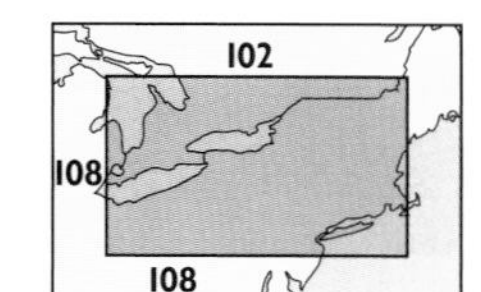

8 9 10 11 12 13 14

A B C D E F G

CANADA
QUÉBEC
MONTREAL
Ottawa
L. St-François
L. Champlain
Adirondack Mountains
Green Mountains
White Mountains
Catskill Mts.
Kittatinny Mts.
Shawangunk Mts.
Blue Mountains
VERMONT
NEW HAMPSHIRE
MAINE
MASSACHUSETTS
BOSTON
CONNECTICUT
HARTFORD
RHODE ISLAND
NEW YORK
NEW JERSEY
PHILADELPHIA
Long Island
Long Island Sound
Block Island Sound
Martha's Vineyard
ATLANTIC OCEAN

West from Greenwich

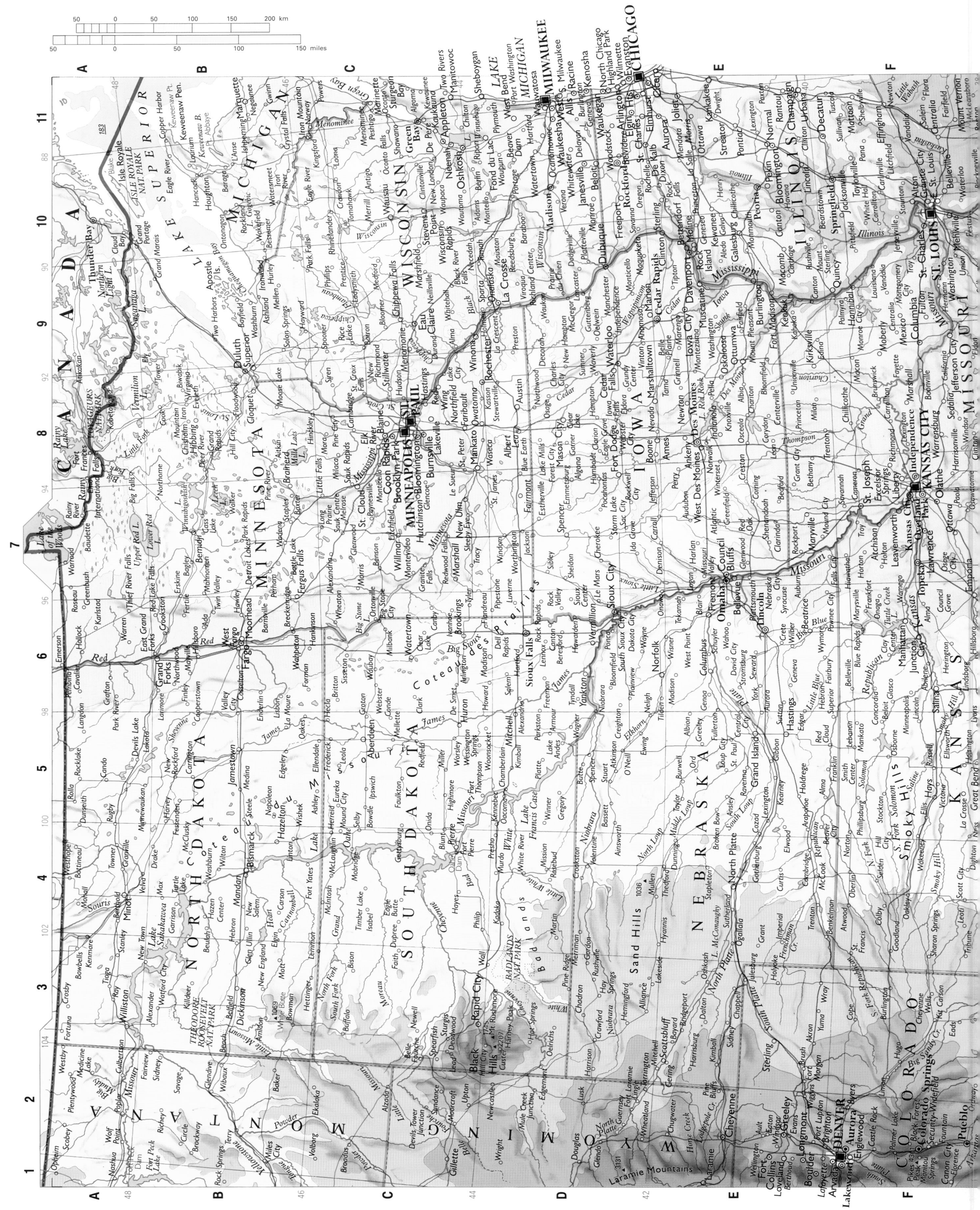
50 0 50 100 150 200 km
50 0 50 100 150 miles
C A N A D A
LAKE SUPERIOR
LAKE MICHIGAN
NORTH DAKOTA
SOUTH DAKOTA
MINNESOTA
WISCONSIN
IOWA
ILLINOIS
MISSOURI
NEBRASKA
KANSAS
COLORADO
WYOMING
MONTANA
MILWAUKEE
CHICAGO
MINNEAPOLIS
ST. PAUL
ST. LOUIS
KANSAS CITY
DENVER
Omaha
Des Moines
Sioux Falls
Bismarck
Duluth
Madison
Lincoln
Topeka
Cheyenne
Rapid City
Fargo
Sand Hills
Black Hills
Laramie Mountains
Mississippi
Missouri
ISLE ROYALE NAT. PARK
THEODORE ROOSEVELT NAT. PARK
BADLANDS NAT. PARK
VOYAGEURS NAT. PARK

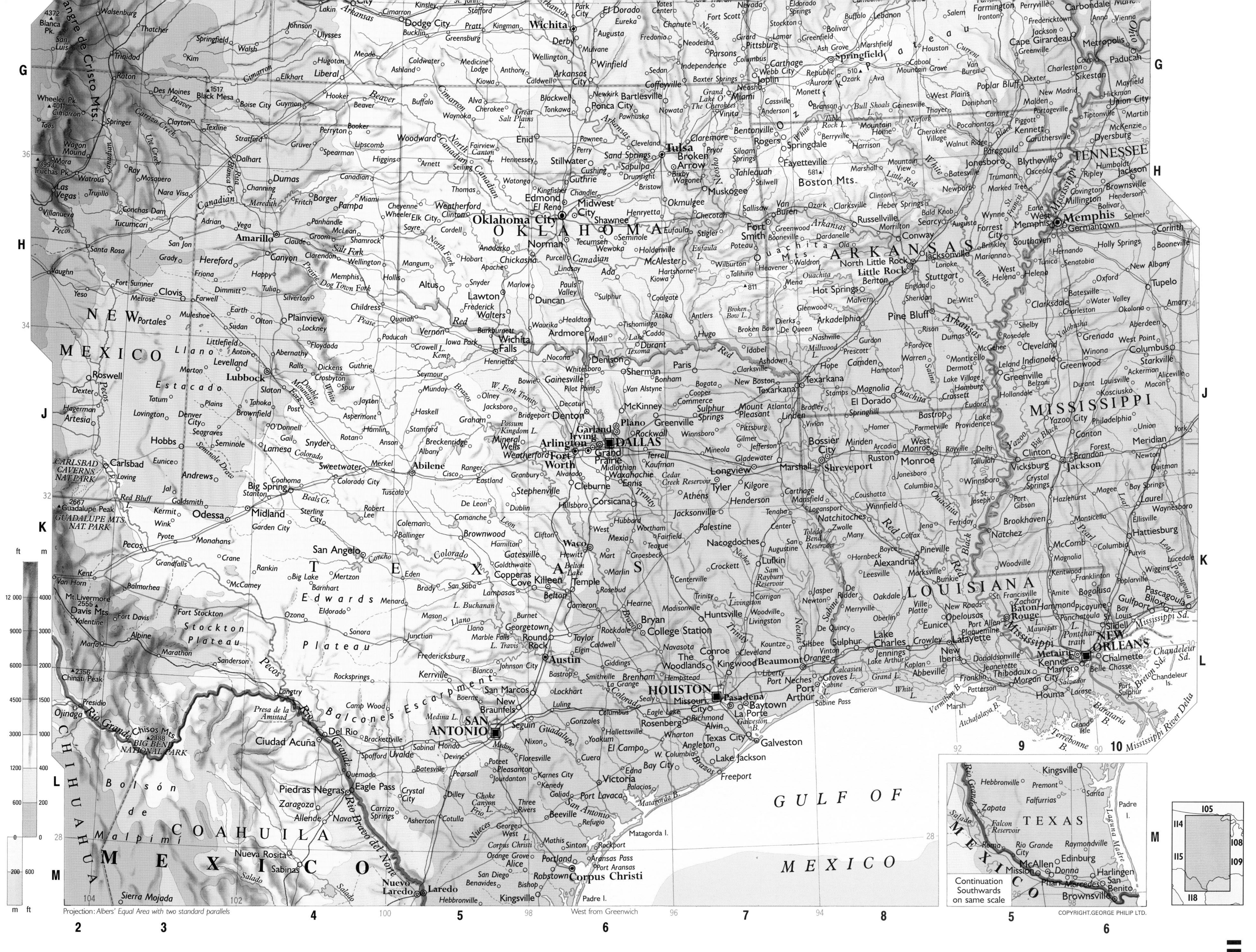

OKLAHOMA
ARKANSAS
MISSISSIPPI
LOUISIANA
TEXAS
NEW MEXICO
TENNESSEE
MEXICO
COAHUILA
CHIHUAHUA
GULF OF MEXICO
Oklahoma City
Tulsa
Dallas
Fort Worth
Houston
San Antonio
Austin
Memphis
New Orleans
Little Rock
Shreveport
Jackson
Amarillo
Lubbock
Wichita
Corpus Christi
Galveston
Laredo
Edwards Plateau
Llano Estacado
Sangre de Cristo Mts.
Boston Mts.
Ouachita Mts.
Stockton Plateau
Bolsón de Mapimí
Balcones Escarpment
CARLSBAD CAVERNS NAT. PARK
GUADALUPE MTS. NAT. PARK
BIG BEND NATIONAL PARK
Continuation Southwards on same scale
West from Greenwich
Projection: Albers' Equal Area with two standard parallels
COPYRIGHT.GEORGE PHILIP LTD.

50 0 50 100 150 200 km

50 0 50 100 150 miles

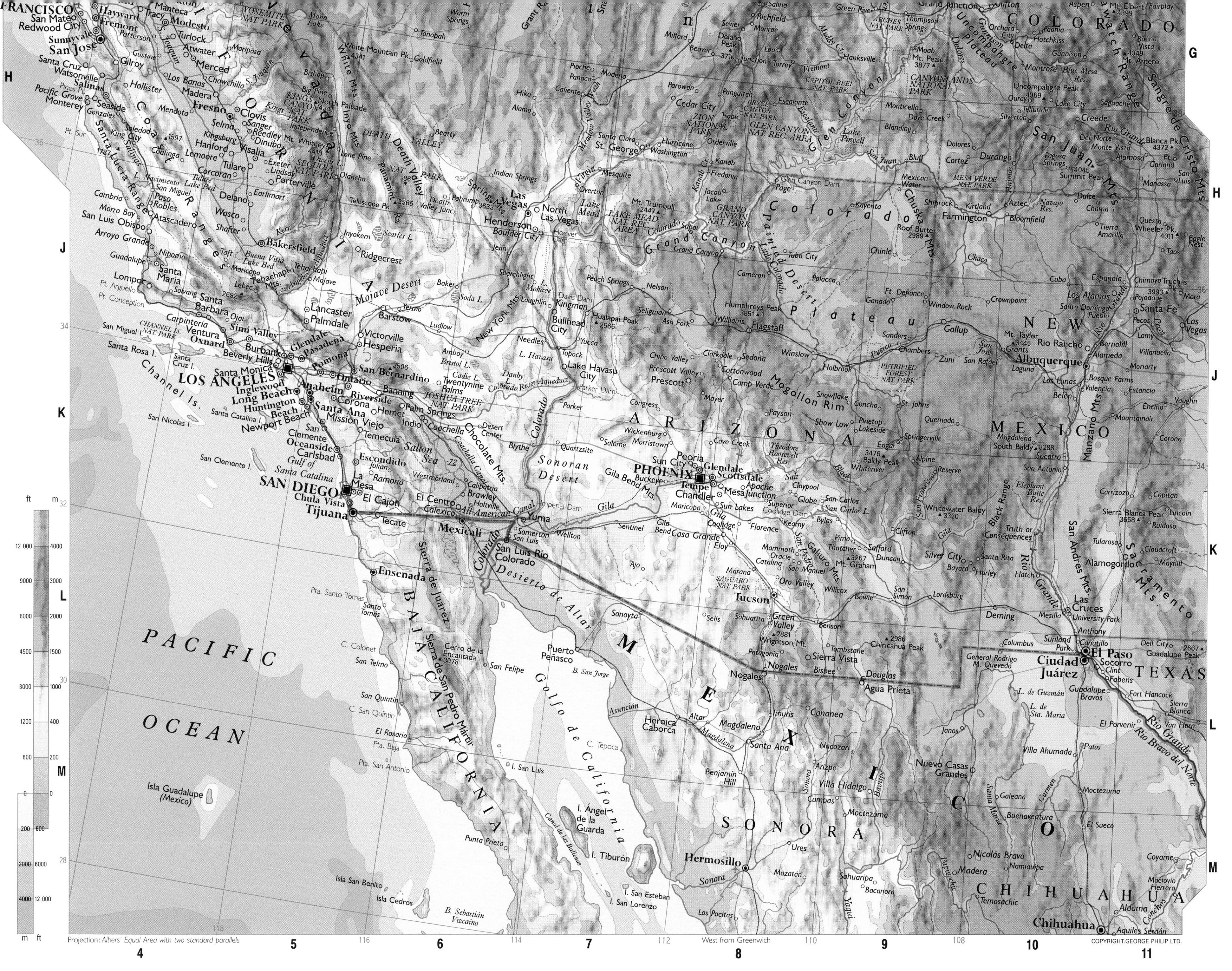
COLORADO
NEW MEXICO
ARIZONA
TEXAS
CHIHUAHUA
SONORA
BAJA CALIFORNIA
MEXICO
PACIFIC OCEAN
Golfo de California
Colorado Plateau
Painted Desert
Sonoran Desert
Mojave Desert
Death Valley
Grand Canyon
Sangre de Cristo Mts.
San Juan Mts.
Sacramento Mts.
Chuska Mts.
Mogollon Rim
Rio Grande
Rio Bravo del Norte
Channel Is.
Sierra de Juárez
Desierto de Altar
LOS ANGELES
SAN DIEGO
PHOENIX
Tijuana
Mexicali
Tucson
Albuquerque
Santa Fe
El Paso
Ciudad Juárez
Chihuahua
Hermosillo
Las Vegas
Flagstaff
Yuma
Ensenada
Bakersfield
Fresno
San Jose
Santa Barbara
Las Cruces
Nogales
Heroica Caborca
Puerto Peñasco
Isla Guadalupe (Mexico)
I. Tiburón
I. Ángel de la Guarda
Projection: Albers' Equal Area with two standard parallels
West from Greenwich
COPYRIGHT.GEORGE PHILIP LTD.
ft
m
12 000
9000
6000
4500
3000
1200
600
0
200
2000
4000
4000
3000
2000
1500
1000
400
200
0
600
6000
12 000
m
ft

CENTRAL AND SOUTHERN CALIFORNIA AND WESTERN WASHINGTON 1:2 100 000

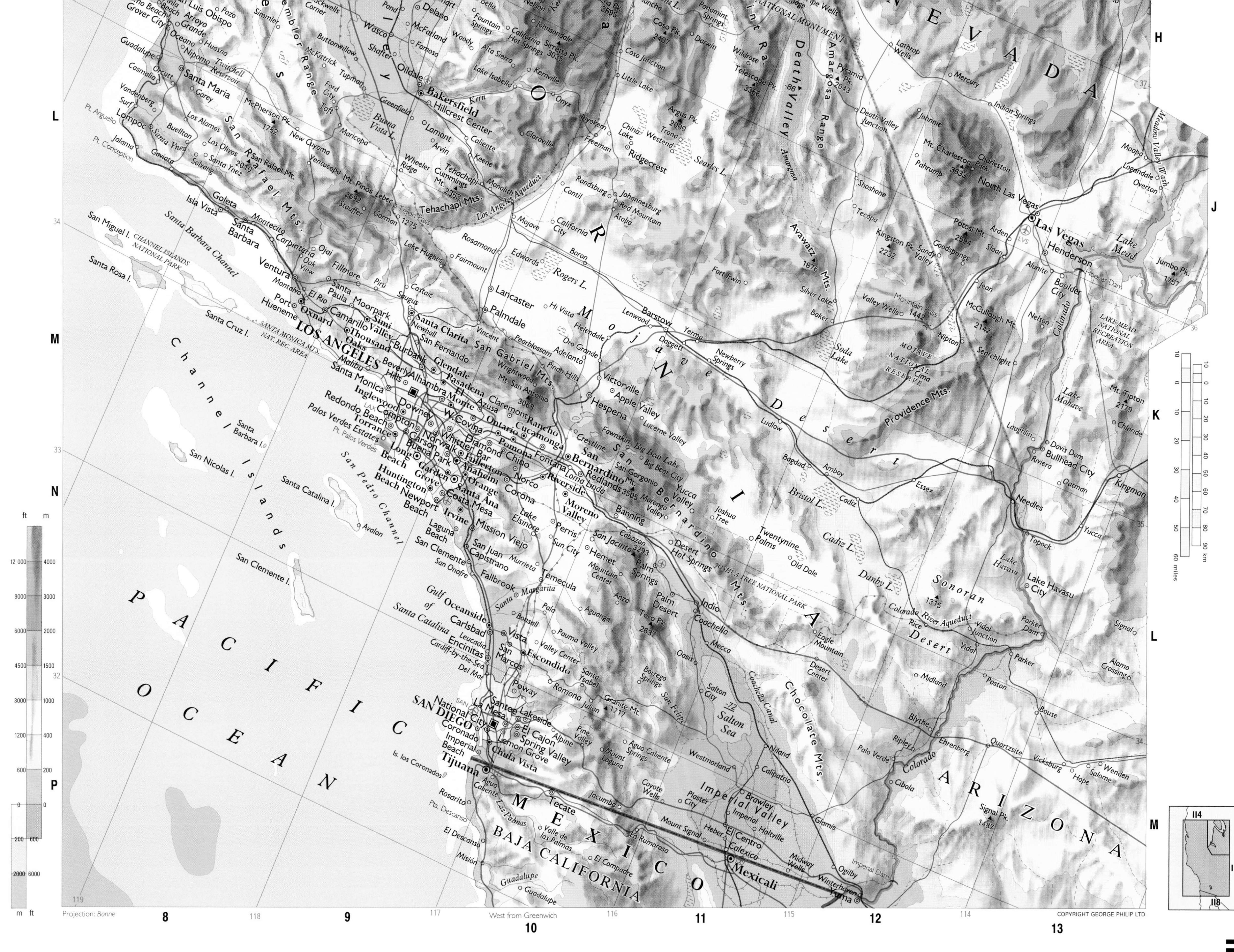
NEVADA
ARIZONA
CALIFORNIA
MEXICO
BAJA CALIFORNIA
PACIFIC OCEAN
Mojave Desert
Sonoran Desert
Death Valley
Amargosa Range
Chocolate Mts.
Salton Sea
Imperial Valley
Channel Islands
San Pedro Channel
Santa Barbara Channel
Gulf of Santa Catalina
LOS ANGELES
SAN DIEGO
Las Vegas
Bakersfield
Tijuana
Mexicali
Santa Barbara
Lake Mead
Colorado
COPYRIGHT GEORGE PHILIP LTD.
Projection: Bonne
West from Greenwich
km
miles
m
ft

REFERENCE TO NUMBERS

1 Distrito Federal
2 Aguascalientes
3 Guanajuato
4 Hidalgo
5 México
6 Morelos
7 Querétaro
8 Tlaxcala

2 3 4

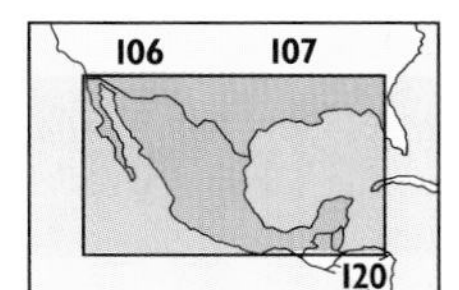

5 6 7 8

A B C D E

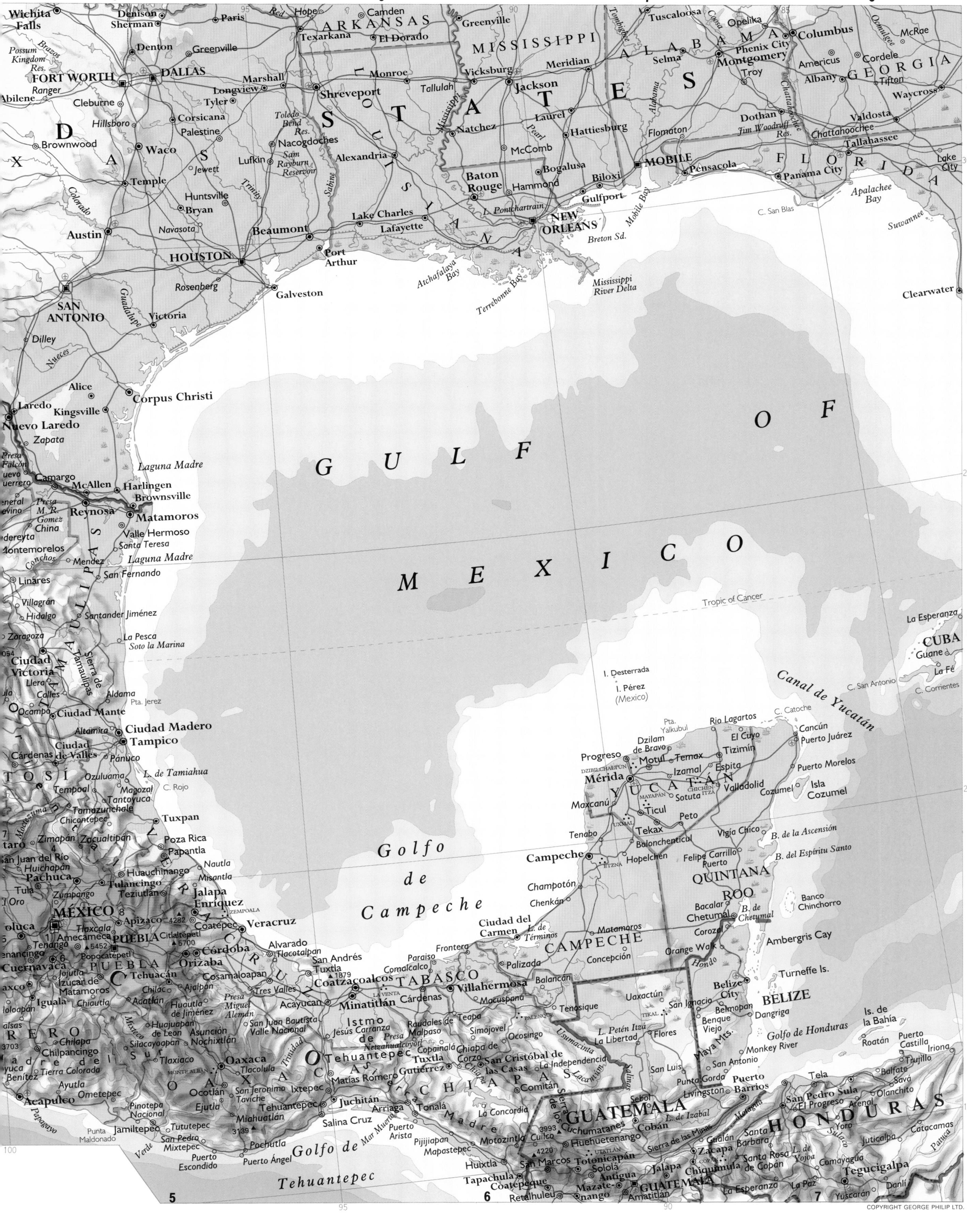

ARKANSAS
MISSISSIPPI
ALABAMA
GEORGIA
LOUISIANA
FLORIDA
UNITED STATES
TEXAS

GULF OF MEXICO

Golfo de Campeche

Canal de Yucatán

Tropic of Cancer

CUBA

YUCATÁN
CAMPECHE
QUINTANA ROO
TABASCO
VERACRUZ
PUEBLA
OAXACA
CHIAPAS
TAMAULIPAS
MÉXICO
GUATEMALA
BELIZE
HONDURAS

Golfo de Honduras
Golfo de Tehuantepec

Wichita Falls, Denison, Sherman, Paris, Hope, Camden, Greenville, Tuscaloosa, Opelika, Columbus, McRae, Denton, Greenville, Texarkana, El Dorado, Meridian, Selma, Phenix City, Montgomery, Americus, Cordele, FORT WORTH, DALLAS, Marshall, Monroe, Vicksburg, Jackson, Troy, Albany, Tifton, Waycross, Ranger, Cleburne, Longview, Tyler, Shreveport, Tallulah, Laurel, Dothan, Valdosta, Hillsboro, Corsicana, Palestine, Nacogdoches, Natchez, Hattiesburg, Flomaton, Chattahoochee, Tallahassee, Brownwood, Waco, Lufkin, Alexandria, McComb, Bogalusa, MOBILE, Pensacola, Panama City, Lake City, Temple, Jewett, Baton Rouge, Hammond, Biloxi, Gulfport, Huntsville, Bryan, Lake Charles, Lafayette, NEW ORLEANS, Austin, Navasota, Beaumont, Port Arthur, HOUSTON, Rosenberg, Galveston, SAN ANTONIO, Victoria, Clearwater, Dilley, Alice, Corpus Christi, Laredo, Kingsville, Nuevo Laredo, Zapata, Camargo, McAllen, Harlingen, Brownsville, Reynosa, Matamoros, Valle Hermoso, Santa Teresa, Mendez, San Fernando, Linares, Villagrán, Hidalgo, Santander Jiménez, La Pesca, Soto la Marina, Zaragoza, Ciudad Victoria, Llera, Aldama, Ocampo, Ciudad Mante, Altamira, Ciudad Madero, Tampico, Ciudad de Valles, Pánuco, Ozuluama, Tempoal, Tantoyuca, Tamazunchale, Tuxpan, Poza Rica, Papantla, Nautla, Misantla, Huauchinango, Tulancingo, Teziutlán, Jalapa Enríquez, Pachuca, Veracruz, Apizaco, Tlaxcala, Puebla, Córdoba, Orizaba, Cuernavaca, Tehuacán, Alvarado, Tlacotalpan, San Andrés Tuxtla, Coatzacoalcos, Minatitlán, Acayucan, Villahermosa, Cárdenas, Frontera, Ciudad del Carmen, Champotón, Campeche, Mérida, Progreso, Motul, Izamal, Tizimín, Valladolid, Cancún, Puerto Juárez, Puerto Morelos, Cozumel, Isla Cozumel, Ticul, Tekax, Peto, Felipe Carrillo Puerto, Bacalar, Chetumal, Corozal, Orange Walk, Ambergris Cay, Belize City, Belmopan, Dangriga, Turneffe Is., Flores, La Libertad, San Luis, Puerto Barrios, Livingston, Tela, San Pedro Sula, El Progreso, La Ceiba, Trujillo, Roatán, Is. de la Bahía, Puerto Castilla, Oaxaca, Tlaxiaco, Chilpancingo, Acapulco, Iguala, Juchitán, Tehuantepec, Salina Cruz, Tuxtla Gutiérrez, San Cristóbal de las Casas, Comitán, Tonalá, Arriaga, Tapachula, Huixtla, Huehuetenango, Quetzaltenango, Cobán, Antigua, GUATEMALA, Zacapa, Chiquimula, Santa Bárbara, Comayagua, Tegucigalpa, Juticalpa, Catacamas, Danlí, Puerto Escondido, Puerto Ángel, Pochutla, Jamiltepec, Pinotepa Nacional

Mississippi River Delta, Atchafalaya Bay, Terrebonne Bay, Breton Sd., Mobile Bay, Apalachee Bay, Laguna Madre, L. de Tamiahua, L. de Términos, B. de la Ascensión, B. del Espíritu Santo, B. de Chetumal, Banco Chinchorro, C. San Blas, C. Catoche, C. San Antonio, C. Corrientes, I. Desterrada, I. Pérez (Mexico), Isla Cozumel

1:6 700 000

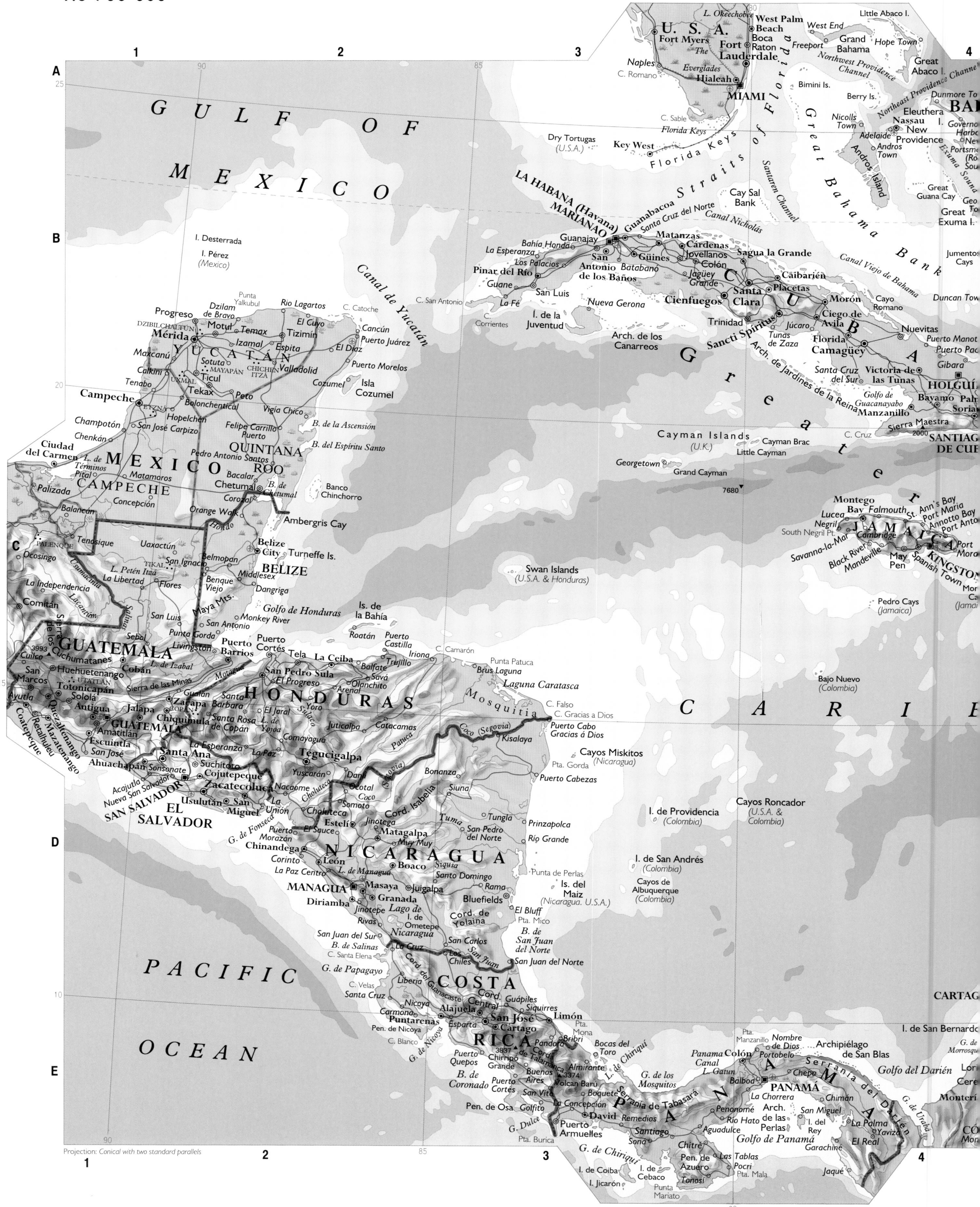

GULF OF MEXICO

PACIFIC OCEAN

CARIB

MEXICO
YUCATÁN
CAMPECHE
QUINTANA ROO
BELIZE
GUATEMALA
HONDURAS
EL SALVADOR
NICARAGUA
COSTA RICA
PANAMA
CUBA
JAMAICA
U. S. A.

Straits of Florida
Florida Keys
Great Bahama Bank
Northwest Providence Channel
Northeast Providence Channel
Santaren Channel
Canal Nicholás
Canal Viejo de Bahama
Canal de Yucatán
Golfo de Honduras
Mosquitia
Greater
Cayman Islands (U.K.)
Swan Islands (U.S.A. & Honduras)
Pedro Cays (Jamaica)
Bajo Nuevo (Colombia)
Cayos Miskitos (Nicaragua)
I. de Providencia (Colombia)
Cayos Roncador (U.S.A. & Colombia)
I. de San Andrés (Colombia)
Cayos de Albuquerque (Colombia)
Is. del Maiz (Nicaragua. U.S.A.)
Dry Tortugas (U.S.A.)
I. Desterrada
I. Pérez (Mexico)
Cay Sal Bank
Banco Chinchorro
Arch. de los Canarreos
Arch. de Jardines de la Reina
I. de la Juventud
Golfo de Guacanayabo
Golfo de Panamá
Golfo del Darién
G. de Chiriquí
G. de Papagayo
G. de Nicoya
G. de Fonseca
G. Dulce
Archipiélago de San Blas
Arch. de las Perlas

L. Okeechobee
West Palm Beach
Fort Myers
Boca Raton
Fort Lauderdale
Naples
C. Romano
The Everglades
Hialeah
MIAMI
C. Sable
Florida Keys
Key West
West End
Freeport
Grand Bahama
Little Abaco I.
Hope Town
Great Abaco I.
Bimini Is.
Berry Is.
Nicolls Town
Nassau
New Providence
Eleuthera I.
Adelaide
Andros Town
Andros Island
Great Guana Cay
Great Exuma I.
Exuma Sound
Jumentos Cays
Duncan Town

LA HABANA (Havana)
MARIANAO
Guanabacoa
Santa Cruz del Norte
Matanzas
Cárdenas
Jovellanos
Colón
Jagüey Grande
Sagua la Grande
Caibarién
Placetas
Santa Clara
Cienfuegos
Trinidad
Sancti Spíritus
Tunas de Zaza
Júcaro
Morón
Cayo Romano
Ciego de Avila
Florida
Camagüey
Nuevitas
Puerto Manatí
Puerto Padre
Gibara
HOLGUÍN
Victoria de las Tunas
Santa Cruz del Sur
Bayamo
Manzanillo
Sierra Maestra
2000
SANTIAGO DE CUBA
C. Cruz
Bahía Honda
Guanajay
La Esperanza
Los Palacios
San Antonio de los Baños
Batabanó
Güines
Pinar del Río
Guane
San Luis
La Fé
C. San Antonio
C. Corrientes
Nueva Gerona

Cayman Brac
Little Cayman
Georgetown
Grand Cayman
7680

Montego Bay
Falmouth
St. Ann's Bay
Port Maria
Annotto Bay
Port Antonio
Lucea
Negril
South Negril Pt.
Savanna-la-Mar
Cambridge
Black River
Mandeville
May Pen
Spanish Town
KINGSTON
Port Morant

Punta Yalkubul
Dzilam de Bravo
Rio Lagartos
C. Catoche
Progreso
DZIBILCHALTÚN
Motul
Temax
El Cuyo
Tizimín
Cancún
Puerto Juárez
Mérida
Izamal
Espita
El Diaz
Maxcanú
Sotuta
MAYAPÁN
CHICHÉN ITZÁ
Valladolid
Puerto Morelos
Calkiní
UXMAL
Ticul
Tenabo
Tekax
Cozumel
Isla Cozumel
Campeche
EDZNÁ
Bolonchentical
Peto
Vigía Chico
Hopelchén
Champotón
San José Carpizo
Felipe Carrillo Puerto
B. de la Ascensión
Chenkán
B. del Espíritu Santo
Ciudad del Carmen
L. de Términos
Pedro Antonio Santos
Pital
Matamoros
Bacalar
Chetumal
B. de Chetumal
Palizada
Concepción
Corozal
Balancán
Orange Walk
Hondo
Ambergris Cay
PALENQUE
Tenosique
Uaxactún
Belize City
Turneffe Is.
Ocosingo
TIKAL
San Ignacio
Belmopan
Usumacinta
L. Petén Itzá
La Libertad
Flores
Middlesex
Benque Viejo
Dangriga
La Independencia
Lacantún
Comitán
Maya Mts.
San Luis
Monkey River
San Antonio
Sierra de los Cuchumatanes
Sebol
Punta Gorda
Is. de la Bahía
Roatán
3993
Livingston
Puerto Barrios
Puerto Cortés
Tela
La Ceiba
Puerto Castilla
Iriona
C. Camarón
Cuilco
Cobán
L. de Izabal
Balfate
Trujillo
Punta Patuca
Brus Laguna
Laguna Caratasca
San Marcos
Huehuetenango
UTATLÁN
San Pedro Sula
El Progreso
Savá
Olanchito
Arenal
Totonicapán
Sierra de las Minas
Motagua
Sololá
Gualán
COPÁN
Quezaltenango
Ayutla
Antigua
Jalapa
Zacapa
Santa Bárbara
El Jaral
Yoro
Sulaco
C. Falso
C. Gracias a Dios
Puerto Cabo Gracias á Dios
Coatepeque
Retalhuleu
Mazatenango
GUATEMALA
Amatitlán
Escuintla
San José
Chiquimula
Santa Rosa de Copán
L. de Yojoa
Juticalpa
Catacamas
Comayagua
Patuca
Coco (Segovia)
Kisalaya
Ahuachapán
Sonsonate
Santa Ana
La Esperanza
La Paz
Tegucigalpa
Pta. Gorda
Puerto Cabezas
Acajutla
Nueva San Salvador
SAN SALVADOR
Suchitoto
Cojutepeque
Zacatecoluca
Yuscarán
Danlí
Bonanza
Siuna
Nacaome
Choluteca
Ocotal
Usulután
San Miguel
La Unión
Somoto
Tungla
Prinzapolca
Estelí
Jinotega
Cord. Isabelia
Tuma
Puerto Morazán
El Sauce
Matagalpa
Muy Muy
San Pedro del Norte
Río Grande
Chinandega
Corinto
León
La Paz Centro
L. de Managua
Boaco
Siquia
Santo Domingo
Punta de Perlas
MANAGUA
Masaya
Juigalpa
Rama
Diriamba
Granada
Bluefields
El Bluff
Jinotepe
Lago de Nicaragua
I. de Ometepe
Cord. de Yolaina
Pta. Mico
Rivas
San Juan del Sur
B. de Salinas
C. Santa Elena
La Cruz
San Carlos
Los Chiles
San Juan
B. de San Juan del Norte
San Juan del Norte
C. Velas
Liberia
Cord. de Guanacaste
Santa Cruz
Nicoya
Cord. Central
Guápiles
Siquirres
Carmona
Alajuela
Limón
Puntarenas
Esparta
San José
Cartago
Pta. Mona
Pen. de Nicoya
C. Blanco
Pandora
Bribri
Bocas del Toro
3837
Chirripó Grande
Cord. de Talamanca
Almirante
L. de Chiriquí
Puerto Quepos
Buenos Aires
3374
Volcán Barú
B. de Coronado
Puerto Cortés
San Vito
Boquete
Pen. de Osa
Golfito
La Concepción
David
Puerto Armuelles
Pta. Burica
Serranía de Tabasará
Remedios
G. de los Mosquitos
Santiago
Soná
Chitré
Pen. de Azuero
Las Tablas
Pocrí
Tonosí
Pta. Mala
Punta Mariato
I. de Coiba
I. de Cebaco
I. Jicarón
Pta. Manzanillo
Nombre de Dios
Portobelo
Panama Canal
Colón
L. Gatún
Balboa
PANAMÁ
Chepo
Serranía del Darién
La Chorrera
Chimán
Penonomé
Río Hato
Aguadulce
San Miguel
I. del Rey
La Palma
Yaviza
El Real
Garachiné
Jaqué
G. de Urabá
CARTAGENA
I. de San Bernardo
Montería

1 2 3 4
A B C D E
25 20 15 10
90 85 80

Projection: Conical with two standard parallels

ATLANTIC OCEAN
Puerto Rico Trench
Tropic of Cancer
HAITI
DOMINICAN REP.
PORT-AU-PRINCE
SANTO DOMINGO
Hispaniola
Antilles
PUERTO RICO (U.S.A.)
SAN JUAN
Lesser Antilles
Leeward Islands
Windward Islands
GUADELOUPE (Fr.)
DOMINICA
MARTINIQUE (Fr.)
ST. LUCIA
ST. VINCENT & THE GRENADINES
BARBADOS
GRENADA
ANTIGUA & BARBUDA
ST. KITTS & NEVIS
TRINIDAD & TOBAGO
NETH. ANTILLES
CARIBBEAN SEA
VENEZUELA
CARACAS
MARACAIBO
BARQUISIMETO
Turks & Caicos (U.K.)
Milwaukee Deep 9200
COPYRIGHT GEORGE PHILIP LTD
West from Greenwich

Caribbean Sea
NORTH ATLANTIC OCEAN
PACIFIC OCEAN
SOUTH ATLANTIC OCEAN
Guiana Highlands
Brazilian Highlands
Plateau of Mato Grosso
Bolivian Plateau
Andes
Selvas
Llanos
Gran Chaco
Pampas
Patagonia
Amazon
Tierra del Fuego
Falkland Is.
Galapagos Is.
Projection: Lambert's Azimuthal Equal Area
COPYRIGHT GEORGE PHILIP LTD.

NORTH ATLANTIC OCEAN

Caribbean Sea

PACIFIC OCEAN

SOUTH ATLANTIC OCEAN

MEXICO, BELIZE, GUATEMALA, HONDURAS, EL SALVADOR, NICARAGUA, COSTA RICA, PANAMA, CUBA, BAHAMAS, JAMAICA, HAITI, DOMINICAN REP., PUERTO RICO (U.S.A.), ST. KITTS & NEVIS, ANTIGUA & BARBUDA, GUADELOUPE (Fr.), DOMINICA, MARTINIQUE (Fr.), ST. LUCIA, ST. VINCENT, BARBADOS, GRENADA, TRINIDAD & TOBAGO, Turks & Caicos Is. (U.K.), Virgin Is. (U.K.)

COLOMBIA, VENEZUELA, GUYANA, SURINAM, FRENCH GUIANA, ECUADOR, PERU, BOLIVIA, BRAZIL, PARAGUAY, URUGUAY, CHILE, ARGENTINA

FALKLAND IS. (U.K.), South Georgia (U.K.), Galapagos Is. (Ecuador), San Félix (Chile), San Ambrosio (Chile), Arch. de Juan Fernández (Chile)

Brazilian states: RORAIMA, AMAPÁ, AMAZONAS, PARÁ, MARANHÃO, CEARÁ, RIO G. DO NORTE, PARAÍBA, PIAUÍ, PERNAMBUCO, ALAGOAS, SERGIPE, ACRE, RONDÔNIA, TOCANTINS, MATO GROSSO, BAHÍA, GOIÁS, DIS. FED., MINAS GERAIS, ESPÍRITO SANTO, MATO GROSSO DO SUL, SÃO PAULO, RIO DE J., PARANÁ, SANTA CATARINA, RIO GRANDE DO SUL

Cities: Havana, Kingston, Port-au-Prince, San Juan, Basse-Terre, Fort-de-France, Castries, Kingstown, Bridgetown, St. George's, Port of Spain, Guatemala, San Salvador, Tegucigalpa, Managua, San José, Panamá, Barranquilla, Cartagena, Maracaibo, Barquisimeto, Valencia, Caracas, Aruba, Curaçao, C. de la Aguja, Cúcuta, San Cristóbal, Ciudad Guayana, Georgetown, Paramaribo, Cayenne, C. Orange, Medellín, Bucaramanga, Bogotá, Cali, Quito, Guayaquil, Iquitos, Manaus, Santarém, Belém, Marajó I., São Luís, Fortaleza, Teresina, C. de São Roque, Natal, Campina Grande, Recife, Maceió, Aracaju, Salvador, Chiclayo, Trujillo, Chimbote, Callao, LIMA, Cuzco, Arequipa, La Paz, Cochabamba, Santa Cruz, Sucre, Pôrto Velho, Cuiabá, Goiânia, Brasília, Belo Horizonte, Ribeirão Prêto, Juiz de Fora, Vitória, Campos, Campinas, SÃO PAULO, RIO DE JANEIRO, Niterói, Curitiba, Asunción, Corrientes, Resistencia, Pôrto Alegre, Pelotas, Montevideo, BUENOS AIRES, La Plata, Mar del Plata, Bahía Blanca, Viedma, Rosario, Paraná, Santa Fe, Córdoba, San Juan, Mendoza, Salta, San Miguel de Tucumán, Iquique, Antofagasta, Viña del Mar, Valparaíso, SANTIAGO, Talca, Concepción, Valdivia, Puerto Montt, Comodoro Rivadavia, Punta Arenas, Stanley, West Falkland, East Falkland, Tierra del Fuego, C. Horn

Physical features: G. of Darién, Gulf of Panamá, G. of Guayaquil, Gulf of San Jorge, Gulf of Penas, Magellan's Str., Río de la Plata, L. Titicaca, Orinoco, Magdalena, Branco, Essequibo, Japurá, Putumayo, Napo, Marañón, Amazon, Ucayali, Juruá, Purus, Madeira, Tapajós, Xingu, Tocantins, Araguaia, Parnaíba, São Francisco, Madre de Dios, Mamoré, Paraguay, Paraná, Pilcomayo, Uruguay, Salado, Colorado, Negro, Chubut

Tropic of Cancer

Equator

Tropic of Capricorn

Scale: 100 0 200 400 600 800 1000 1200 1400 km; 100 0 200 400 600 800 1000 miles

Projection: Lambert's Azimuthal Equal Area

West from Greenwich

■ LIMA Capital Cities

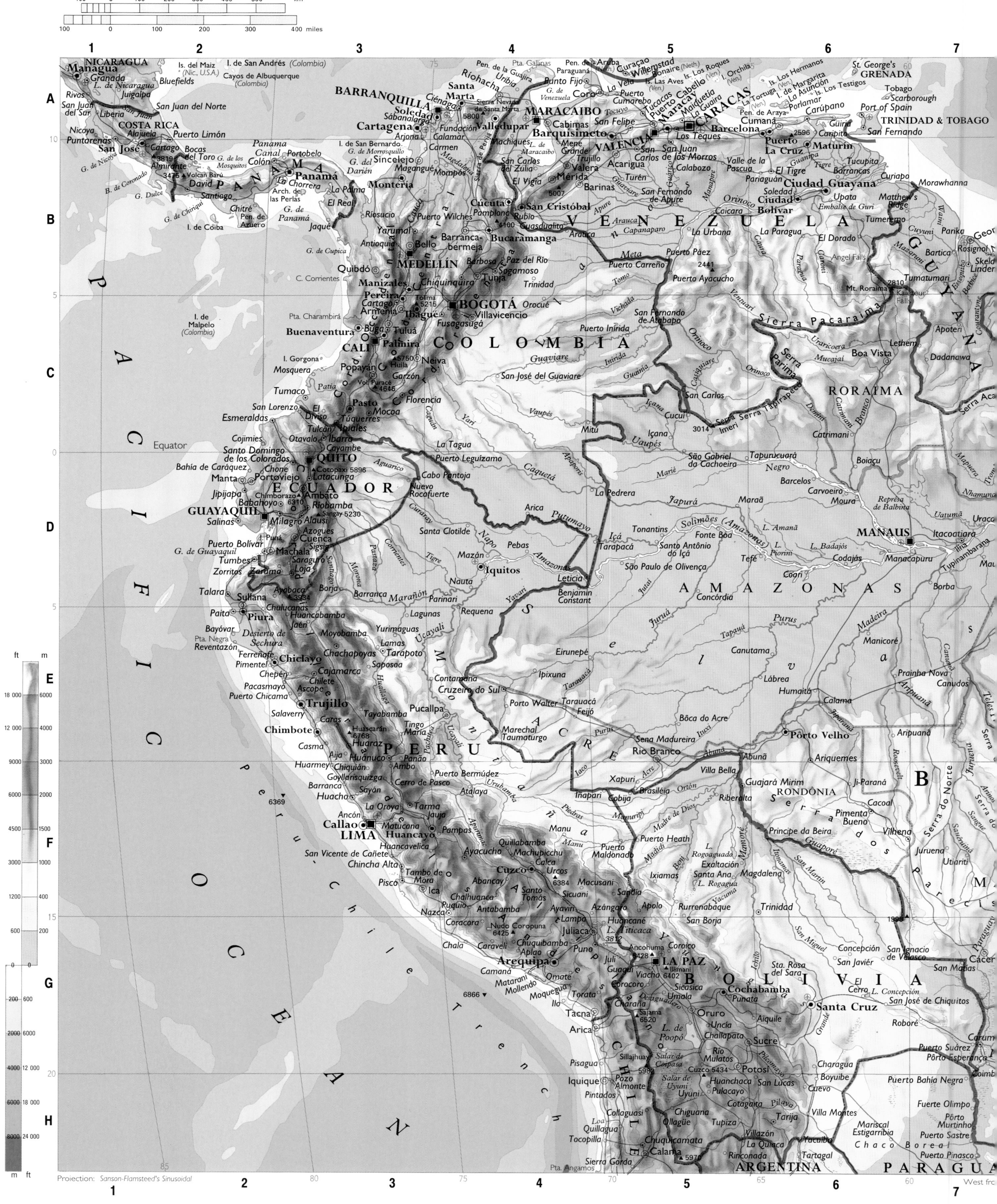
km
miles
PACIFIC OCEAN
Peru-Chile Trench
Equator
NICARAGUA
Managua
Granada
L. de Nicaragua
Bluefields
San Juan del Norte
COSTA RICA
Puerto Limón
San José
PANAMA
Panamá
Colón
I. de Coiba
Is. del Maiz (Nic., U.S.A.)
I. de San Andrés (Colombia)
Cayos de Albuquerque (Colombia)
BARRANQUILLA
Santa Marta
Cartagena
Sincelejo
Montería
Valledupar
MARACAIBO
Barquisimeto
VALENCIA
CARACAS
Barcelona
Cumaná
Maturín
Ciudad Guayana
Ciudad Bolívar
TRINIDAD & TOBAGO
Port of Spain
San Fernando
GRENADA
St. George's
Tobago
Scarborough
Curaçao
Willemstad
Aruba
Bonaire (Neth)
Punto Fijo
Coro
VENEZUELA
Cúcuta
San Cristóbal
Mérida
Barinas
Bucaramanga
MEDELLÍN
Manizales
Pereira
Armenia
Ibagué
BOGOTÁ
Villavicencio
Buenaventura
CALI
Palmira
Popayán
Neiva
Pasto
Florencia
Quibdó
COLOMBIA
I. de Malpelo (Colombia)
I. Gorgona
Tumaco
Esmeraldas
QUITO
Santo Domingo de los Colorados
Manta
Portoviejo
Latacunga
Ambato
Riobamba
Cotopaxi 5896
Chimborazo 6310
Sangay 5230
ECUADOR
GUAYAQUIL
Salinas
Machala
Cuenca
Loja
Tumbes
Talara
Sullana
Piura
Paita
Chiclayo
Cajamarca
Trujillo
Chimbote
Huascarán 6768
Huaraz
Huánuco
Cerro de Pasco
Callao
LIMA
Huancayo
Huancavelica
Ayacucho
Cuzco
Pisco
Ica
Nazca
Arequipa
Juliaca
Puno
L. Titicaca
Tacna
Arica
PERU
Iquitos
Pucallpa
Moyobamba
Tarapoto
Yurimaguas
Marañón
Ucayali
Amazonas
Putumayo
Caquetá
Leticia
Benjamin Constant
Tabatinga
Tefé
Coari
MANAUS
Manacapuru
Itacoatiara
Borba
AMAZONAS
Solimões (Amazonas)
Japurá
Negro
Juruá
Purus
Madeira
Humaitá
Pôrto Velho
Rio Branco
ACRE
Cruzeiro do Sul
RONDÔNIA
Guajará Mirim
Ji-Paraná
Vilhena
Boa Vista
RORAIMA
Lethem
GUYANA
Mt. Roraima 2810
Sierra Pacaraima
Serra Parima
Puerto Ayacucho
Puerto Carreño
San Fernando de Atabapo
Puerto Inírida
Mitú
San Carlos
Cucuí
Tapurucuará
São Gabriel da Cachoeira
Barcelos
BOLIVIA
LA PAZ
Illimani 6402
Oruro
Cochabamba
Santa Cruz
Sucre
Potosí
Tarija
Trinidad
Riberalta
Cobija
Uyuni
Salar de Uyuni
Sajama 6520
CHILE
Iquique
Calama
Chuquicamata
Tocopilla
Pisagua
ARGENTINA
PARAGUAY
Chaco Boreal
Puerto Bahía Negra
Nudo Coropuna 6425
Ancohuma 6428
Ojos del Salado
Projection: Sanson-Flamsteed's Sinusoidal
West from Greenwich

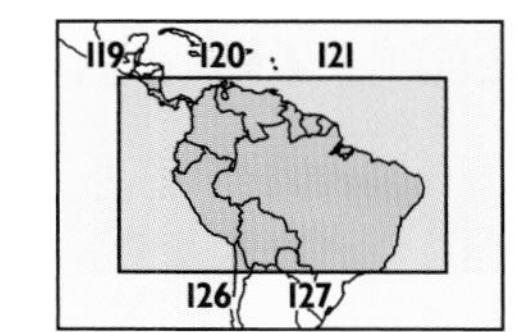

8 9 10 11 12 13

A B C D E F G H

ATLANTIC OCEAN

Equator

São Paulo (Braz.)
Rocas
Fernando de Noronha (Braz.)
Trindade (Braz.)
6059

SURINAM
FRENCH GUIANA
Paramaribo
Nieuw Amsterdam
Nieuw Nickerie
Totness
Moengo
St-Laurent
Kwakoegron
Albina
Iracoubo
Sinnamary
Kourou
Cayenne
Prof. Van Blommestein-meer
Kaw
Approuague
C. Orange
St-Georges
Oiapoque
Tapanahoni
Maroni
Mana
1230
Camopi
Serra Tumucumaque
Amapá
I. de Maracá
AMAPÁ
Araguari
Merirumã
Serra do Navio
Jari
Macapá
I. Caviana
I. Mexiana
Mazagão
Chaves
C. Maguarinho
Afuá
Soure
Curuçá
Salinópolis
I. Grande de Gurupá
I. de Marajó
Vigia
Bragança
Almeirim
BELÉM
Viseu
Gurupá
Breves
Castanhal
Turiaçu
Gururupu
Óbidos
Monte Alegre
Prainha
Pôrto de Móz
Curralinho
Abaetetuba
B. de São Marcos
Alenquer
Amazonas (Amazon)
Cametá
Alcântara
São Luís
Barreirinhas
Juruti
Santarém
Baião
Pinheiro
Tutóia
Luís Correia
Camocim
Parintins
Belterra
Altamira
Rosário
Parnaíba
Granja
Itapipoca
Caucaia
Aveiro
PARÁ
Tucuruí
Itapecuru-Mirim
Santa Inês
FORTALEZA
Brasília Legal
Represa de Tucuruí
Brejo
Piracuruca
Sobral
Maranguape
Cascavel
Itaituba
Iriri
Bacabal
Coroatá
Piripiri
Baturité
Aracati
Codó
Caxias
Ipu
Quixadá
Russas
Areia Branca
Açailândia
Pedreiras
Campo Maior
Oiticica
Macau
Marabá
Tocantins
MARANHÃO
Teresina
Crateús
CEARÁ
Mossoró
RIO GRANDE DO NORTE
Ceará Mirim
C. de São Roque
São João do Araguaia
Imperatriz
Barra do Corda
Senador Pompeu
Natal
Serra dos Carajás
Carajás
Grajaú
Amarante
Valença do Piauí
Caraúbas
Pôrto Franco
Colinas
Iguatu
Caicó
Currais Novos
Canguaretama
Tocantinópolis
Floriano
Oeiras
Picos
Cedro
Sousa
Patos
Alagoa Grande
Mamanguape
Estreito
Loreto
Nova Iorque
Crato
Cajàzeiras
PARAÍBA
Cabedelo
Carolina
Uruçuí
PIAUÍ
Ouricuri
Chapada do Araripe
Juàzeiro do Norte
Campina Grande
João Pessoa
Olinda
Araguaína
Riachão
Paulistana
Salgueiro
Caruaru
RECIFE
Conceição do Araguaia
Serra do Penitente
PERNAMBUCO
Pesqueira
Jaboatão
Araguacema
Serra do Estrondo
Pedro Afonso
São João do Piauí
Garanhuns
Palmares
Vitória de Santo Antão
Santa Filomena
Sa. Dois Irmãos
Petrolina
Petrolândia
Palmeira dos Índios
Rio Largo
Maceió
Serra do Cachimbo
Caracol
Nova Casa Nova
Juàzeiro
Paulo Afonso
Arapiraca
Chapada das Mangabeiras
Novo Remanso
Represa de Sobradinho
São Francisco
ALAGOAS
Penedo
Palmas
Parnaguá
Serra da Tabatinga
Senhor-do-Bonfim
Propriá
SERGIPE
BRAZIL
Pôrto Nacional
Barra
Xique-Xique
Jacobina
Capela
Aracaju
TOCANTINS
Sertão
Itapicuru
São Cristóvão
Santa Isabel do Morro
I. do Bananal
Mundo Novo
Queimadas
Serrinha
Estância
Gurupi
Peixe
Manuel Alves
Taguatinga
BAHIA
Feira de Santana
Alagoinhas
Serra Formosa
Serra do Roncador
Paranã
Barreiras
Ibotirama
Itaberaba
Cachoeira
Santo Amaro
Campos Belos
Serra Geral de Goiás
Bom Jesus da Lapa
Paraguaçu
Castro Alves
SALVADOR
São Domingos
Santa Maria da Vitória
Serra do Sincorá
Valença
B. de Todos os Santos
Serra Dourada
Nazaré
Posse
Carinhanha
Caetité
Jequié
Contas
MATO GROSSO
Planalto do Mato Grosso
Niquelândia
1678
Brumado
Ubaitaba
Uruaçu
Vitória da Conquista
Itabuna
Aruanã
Condeúba
Ilhéus
Monte Azul
Januária
Pardo
Canavieiras
DIST. FED.
Formosa
Cuiabá
Santo Antonio
Barra do Garças
Goiás
Taguatinga
BRASÍLIA
São Francisco
Pedra Azul
Belmonte
Anápolis
Luziânia
Janaúba
Rondonópolis
São Lourenço
Montes Claros
Salinas
Jequitinhonha
Pôrto Seguro
Goiânia
GOIÁS
Vianópolis
Serra do Espinhaço
Itamaraju
Alto Araguaia
Morrinhos
Paracatu
Araçuaí
Teófilo Otoni
Prado
MATO GROSSO DO SUL
Jataí
Rio Verde
Ipameri
Pirapora
Nanuque
Caravelas
Taquari
Coxim
Catalão
Patos de Minas
Diamantina
Mucuri
Quirinópolis
Itumbiara
Araguari
Corinto
1340
Governador Valadares
Conceição da Barra
MINAS GERAIS
Uberlândia
Patrocínio
Curvelo
Ipatinga
Nova Venécia
São Mateus
Pantanal
Paranaíba
Ituiutaba
Prata
Araxá
Ibiá
Sete Lagoas
Itabira
Colatina
Linhares
ESPÍRITO SANTO
Campo Grande
Uberaba
Frutal
BELO HORIZONTE
Sabará
Caratinga
Cariacica
Miranda
Santa Fé do Sul
Água Clara
São José do Barretos
Igarapava
Divinópolis
Nova Lima
Ponte Nova
Vitória
Aquidauana
Ribas do Rio Pardo
Três Lagoas
Rio Prêto
Franca
Ouro Prêto
2890
Vila Velha
Andradina
Passos
Conselheiro Lafaiete
Ubá
Cachoeiro de Itapemirim
Panorama
Araçatuba
Ribeirão Prêto
Guaxupé
São João del Rei
Barbacena
Itaperuna
Presidente Epitácio
Catanduva
Lins
SÃO PAULO
Araraquara
Poços de Caldas
Juiz de Fora
Dourados
Penápolis
São Lourenço
Três Rios
Campos
Presidente Prudente
Marília
São Carlos
Moji-Mirim
2787
Nova Friburgo
Ponta Porã
Bauru
Jaú
Limeira
Volta Redonda
Petrópolis
Pedro Juan Caballero
Paranapanema
Piracicaba
Botucatu
Campinas
Niterói
Cabo Frio
RIO DE JANEIRO

55 50 45 40 35 30
10 5 0 5 10 15 20

Greenwich

8 9 10 11 12 13

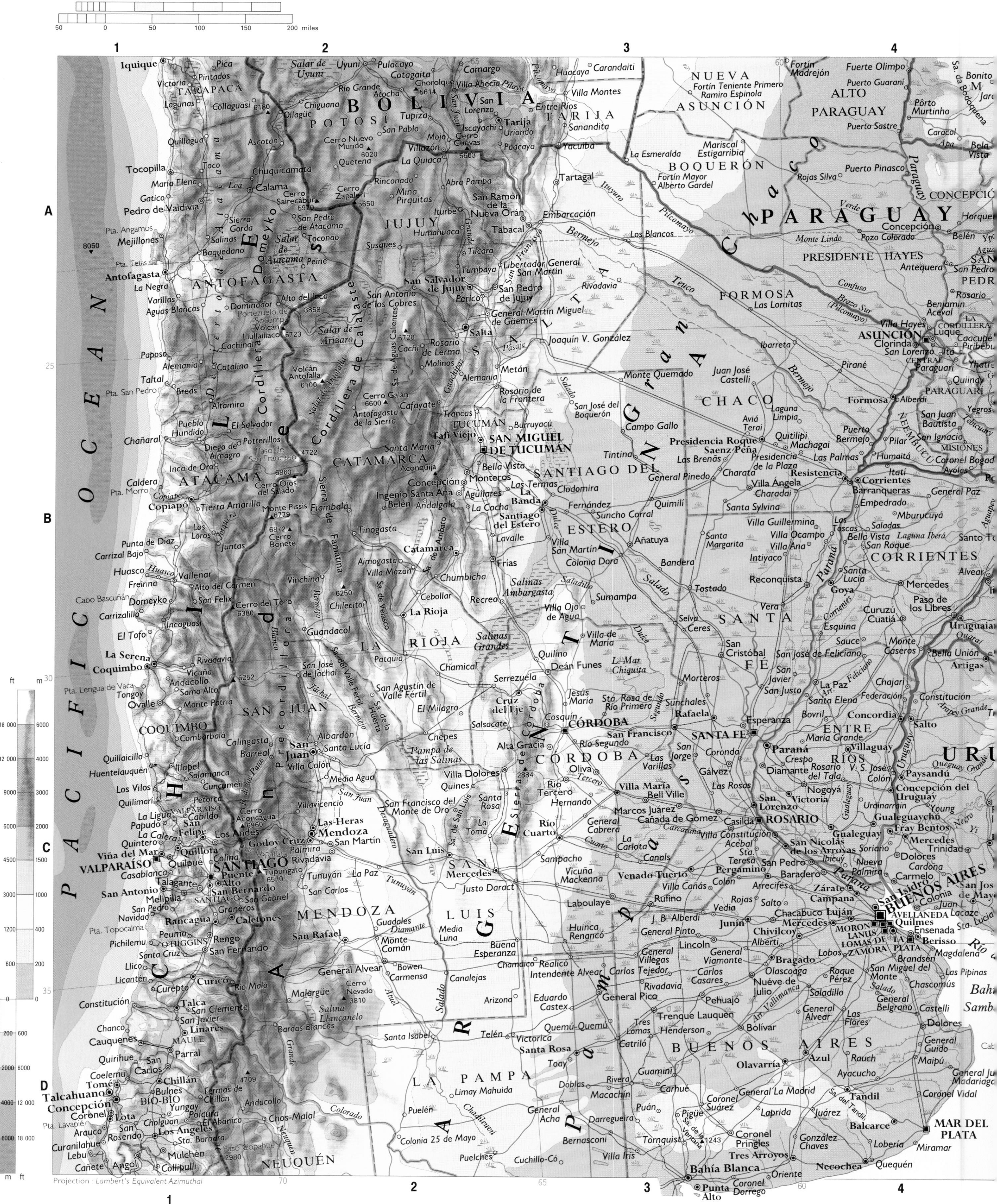
PACIFIC OCEAN
BOLIVIA
PARAGUAY
ARGENTINA
CHILE
Gran Chaco
Pampa
Iquique
Antofagasta
Copiapó
La Serena
Coquimbo
Valparaíso
Santiago
Concepción
Talcahuano
Salta
San Miguel de Tucumán
Córdoba
Mendoza
San Juan
Rosario
Santa Fe
Asunción
Corrientes
Buenos Aires
La Plata
Mar del Plata
Bahía Blanca
Santa Rosa
Projection : Lambert's Equivalent Azimuthal

BELO HORIZONTE
Nova Lima
Itabirito
Vitória
Vila Velha
Guarapari
Cachoeiro de Itapemirim
CAMPOS
Cabo de São Tomé
RIO DE JANEIRO
NITERÓI
DUQUE DE CAXIAS
NOVA IGUAÇU
SÃO GONÇALO
Cabo Frio
Macaé
Nova Friburgo
Petrópolis
Juiz de Fora
Volta Redonda
Tropic of Capricorn
SÃO PAULO
SANTO ANDRÉ
SANTOS
São Bernardo do Campo
São Vicente
Guarujá
Campinas
Jundiaí
Sorocaba
Moji das Cruzes
Ilha de São Sebastião
Ribeirão Prêto
Araraquara
Bauru
Marília
Presidente Prudente
Londrina
Maringá
Três Lagoas
Araçatuba
S Ã O P A U L O
P A R A N Á
B R A Z I L
CURITIBA
Ponta Grossa
Paranaguá
Guarapuava
Cascavel
Foz do Iguaçu
Ciudad del Este
Joinville
São Francisco do Sul
Blumenau
Itajaí
Florianópolis
Ilha de Santa Catarina
SANTA CATARINA
Lajes
Tubarão
Laguna
Cabo Santa Marta Grande
Criciúma
Araranguá
Torres
Caxias do Sul
Novo Hamburgo
São Leopoldo
Canoas
PÔRTO ALEGRE
R I O G R A N D E D O S U L
Passo Fundo
Santa Maria
Santo Ângelo
Uruguaiana
Alegrete
Santana do Livramento
Rivera
Bagé
Pelotas
Rio Grande
Lagoa dos Patos
Lagoa Mirim
Lagoa Mangueira
Jaguarão
Santa Vitória do Palmar
Chuy
MISIONES
Posadas
Encarnación
Tacuarembó
Melo
Treinta y Tres
Minas
Rocha
Maldonado
San Carlos
MONTEVIDEO
A T L A N T I C
O C E A N
5304
West from Greenwich
COPYRIGHT GEORGE PHILIP LTD

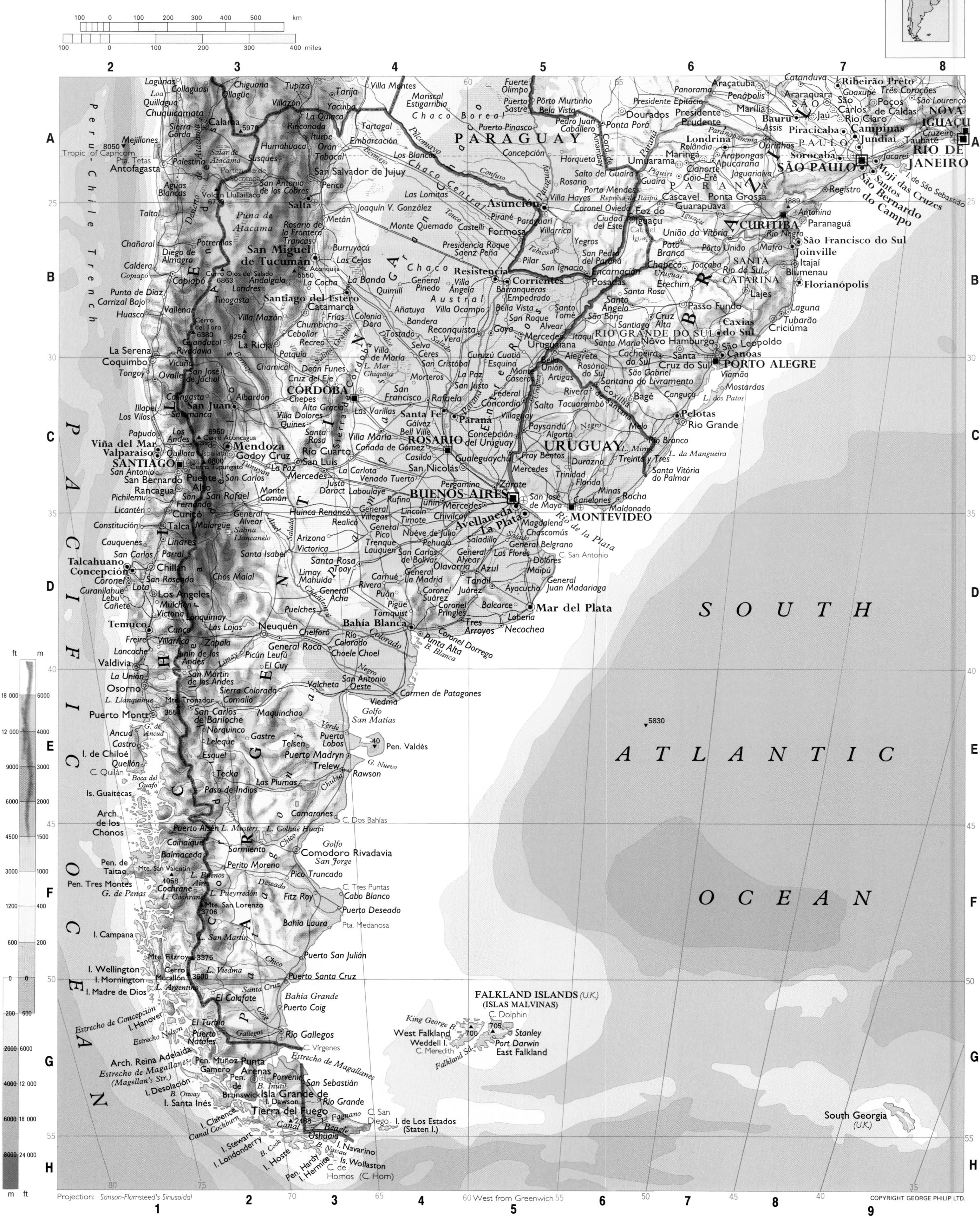

km
miles
PACIFIC OCEAN
SOUTH ATLANTIC OCEAN
Peru-Chile Trench
Tropic of Capricorn
PARAGUAY
URUGUAY
BRAZIL
ARGENTINA
CHILE
Chaco Boreal
Chaco Central
Chaco Austral
Gran Chaco
Puna de Atacama
Desierto de Atacama
Patagonia
Asunción
Encarnación
Resistencia
Corrientes
Posadas
Formosa
Salta
San Salvador de Jujuy
San Miguel de Tucumán
Santiago del Estero
Catamarca
La Rioja
CORDOBA
San Juan
Mendoza
San Luis
Río Cuarto
Santa Fe
Paraná
ROSARIO
BUENOS AIRES
La Plata
Avellaneda
MONTEVIDEO
Mar del Plata
Bahía Blanca
Neuquén
Santa Rosa
Viedma
Carmen de Patagones
Puerto Madryn
Trelew
Rawson
Comodoro Rivadavia
Puerto Deseado
Puerto San Julián
Puerto Santa Cruz
Río Gallegos
Ushuaia
Tierra del Fuego
Isla Grande de Tierra del Fuego
Estrecho de Magallanes
Punta Arenas
Puerto Natales
C. de Hornos (C. Horn)
I. de Los Estados (Staten I.)
Antofagasta
Calama
Copiapó
La Serena
Coquimbo
Valparaíso
SANTIAGO
Viña del Mar
Rancagua
Talca
Chillán
Concepción
Talcahuano
Temuco
Valdivia
Osorno
Puerto Montt
I. de Chiloé
Arch. de los Chonos
Puerto Aisén
Coihaique
Cerro Aconcagua 6960
Ojos del Salado 6863
Rio Grande do Sul
Porto Alegre
Pelotas
Rio Grande
Curitiba
São Paulo
RIO DE JANEIRO
Campinas
Florianópolis
Santa Catarina
Paraná
FALKLAND ISLANDS (U.K.)
(ISLAS MALVINAS)
West Falkland
East Falkland
Stanley
South Georgia (U.K.)
5830
Projection: Sanson-Flamsteed's Sinusoidal
West from Greenwich
COPYRIGHT GEORGE PHILIP LTD.

INDEX TO WORLD MAPS

How to use the index

The index contains the names of all the principal places and features shown on the World Maps. Each name is followed by an additional entry in italics giving the country or region within which it is located. The alphabetical order of names composed of two or more words is governed primarily by the first word and then by the second. This is an example of the rule:

Mīr Kūh, *Iran*	**71 E8**	26 22N 58 55 E
Mīr Shahdād, *Iran*	**71 E8**	26 15N 58 29 E
Mira, *Italy*	**29 B5**	45 26N 12 8 E
Mira por vos Cay, *Bahamas* ..	**121 B5**	22 9N 74 30W
Miraj, *India*	**66 L9**	16 50N 74 45 E

Physical features composed of a proper name (Erie) and a description (Lake) are positioned alphabetically by the proper name. The description is positioned after the proper name and is usually abbreviated:

Erie, L., *N. Amer.* **110 D4** 42 15N 81 0W

Where a description forms part of a settlement or administrative name however, it is always written in full and put in its true alphabetic position:

Mount Morris, *U.S.A.* **110 D7** 42 44N 77 52W

Names beginning with M' and Mc are indexed as if they were spelled Mac. Names beginning St. are alphabetised under Saint, but Sankt, Sint, Sant', Santa and San are all spelt in full and are alphabetised accordingly. If the same place name occurs two or more times in the index and all are in the same country, each is followed by the name of the administrative subdivision in which it is located.

The number in bold type which follows each name in the index refers to the number of the map page where that feature or place will be found. This is usually the largest scale at which the place or feature appears.

The letter and figure which are in bold type immediately after the page number give the grid square on the map page, within which the feature is situated. The letter represents the latitude and the figure the longitude.

In some cases the feature itself may fall within the specified square, while the name is outside. This is usually the case only with features which are larger than a grid square.

The geographical co-ordinates which follow the letter-figure references give the latitude and longitude of each place. The first co-ordinate indicates latitude – the distance north of the Equator. The second co-ordinate indicates longitude – the distance east or west of the Greenwich Meridian. Both latitude and longitude are measured in degrees and minutes (there are 60 minutes in a degree).

The latitude is followed by N(orth) or S(outh) and the longitude by E(ast) or W(est).

Rivers are indexed to their mouths or confluences, and carry the symbol → after their names. A solid square ■ follows the name of a country, while an open square □ refers to a first order administrative area.

How to pronounce place names

English-speaking people usually have no difficulty in reading and pronouncing correctly English place names. However, foreign place name pronunciations may present many problems. Such problems can be minimised by following some simple rules. However, these rules cannot be applied to all situations, and there will be many exceptions.

1. In general, stress each syllable equally, unless your experience suggests otherwise.
2. Pronounce the letter 'a' as a broad 'a' as in 'arm'.
3. Pronounce the letter 'e' as a short 'e' as in 'elm'.
4. Pronounce the letter 'i' as a cross between a short 'i' and long 'e', as the two 'i's in 'California'.
5. Pronounce the letter 'o' as an intermediate 'o' as in 'soft'.
6. Pronounce the letter 'u' as an intermediate 'u' as in 'sure'.
7. Pronounce consonants hard, except in the Romance-language areas where 'g's are likely to be pronounced softly like 'j' in 'jam'; 'j' itself may be pronounced as 'y'; and 'x's may be pronounced as 'h'.
8. For names in mainland China, pronounce 'q' like the 'ch' in 'chin', 'x' like the 'sh' in 'she', 'zh' like the 'j' in 'jam', and 'z' as if it were spelled 'dz'. In general pronounce 'a' as in 'father', 'e' as in 'but', 'i' as in 'keep', 'o' as in 'or', and 'u' as in 'rule'.

Moreover, English has no diacritical marks (accent and pronunciation signs), although some languages do. The following is a brief and general guide to the pronunciation of those most frequently used in the principal Western European languages.

		Pronunciation as in
French	é	day and shows that the e is to be pronounced; e.g. Orléans.
	è	mare
	î	used over any vowel and does not affect pronunciation; shows contraction of the name, usually omission of 's' following a vowel.
	ç	's' before 'a', 'o' and 'u'.
	ë, ï, ü	over 'e', 'i' and 'u' when they are used with another vowel and shows that each is to be pronounced.
German	ä	fate
	ö	fur
	ü	no English equivalent; like French 'tu'
Italian	à, é	over vowels and indicates stress.
Portuguese	ã, õ	vowels pronounced nasally.
	ç	boss
	á	shows stress
	ô	shows that a vowel has an 'i' or 'u' sound combined with it.
Spanish	ñ	canyon
	ü	pronounced as w and separately from adjoining vowels.
	á	usually indicates that this is a stressed vowel.

Abbreviations

A.C.T. – Australian Capital Territory
A.R. – Autonomous Region
Afghan. – Afghanistan
Ala. – Alabama
Alta. – Alberta
Amer. – America(n)
Arch. – Archipelago
Ariz. – Arizona
Ark. – Arkansas
Atl. Oc. – Atlantic Ocean
B. – Baie, Bahía, Bay, Bucht, Bugt
B.C. – British Columbia
Bangla. – Bangladesh
Barr. – Barrage
Bos.-H. – Bosnia-Herzegovina
C. – Cabo, Cap, Cape, Coast
C.A.R. – Central African Republic
C. Prov. – Cape Province
Calif. – California
Cat. – Catarata
Cent. – Central
Chan. – Channel
Colo. – Colorado
Conn. – Connecticut
Cord. – Cordillera
Cr. – Creek
Czech. – Czech Republic
D.C. – District of Columbia
Del. – Delaware
Dem. – Democratic
Dep. – Dependency
Des. – Desert
Dét. – Détroit
Dist. – District
Dj. – Djebel
Domin. – Dominica
Dom. Rep. – Dominican Republic
E. – East
E. Salv. – El Salvador
Eq. Guin. – Equatorial Guinea
Est. – Estrecho
Falk. Is. – Falkland Is.
Fd. – Fjord
Fla. – Florida
Fr. – French
G. – Golfe, Golfo, Gulf, Guba, Gebel
Ga. – Georgia
Gt. – Great, Greater
Guinea-Biss. – Guinea-Bissau
H.K. – Hong Kong
H.P. – Himachal Pradesh
Hants. – Hampshire
Harb. – Harbor, Harbour
Hd. – Head
Hts. – Heights
I.(s). – Île, Ilha, Insel, Isla, Island, Isle
Ill. – Illinois
Ind. – Indiana
Ind. Oc. – Indian Ocean
Ivory C. – Ivory Coast
J. – Jabal, Jebel
Jaz. – Jazīrah
Junc. – Junction
K. – Kap, Kapp
Kans. – Kansas
Kep. – Kepulauan
Ky. – Kentucky
L. – Lac, Lacul, Lago, Lagoa, Lake, Limni, Loch, Lough
La. – Louisiana
Ld. – Land
Liech. – Liechtenstein
Lux. – Luxembourg
Mad. P. – Madhya Pradesh
Madag. – Madagascar
Man. – Manitoba
Mass. – Massachusetts
Md. – Maryland
Me. – Maine
Medit. S. – Mediterranean Sea
Mich. – Michigan
Minn. – Minnesota
Miss. – Mississippi
Mo. – Missouri
Mont. – Montana
Mozam. – Mozambique
Mt.(s) – Mont, Montaña, Mountain
Mte. – Monte
Mti. – Monti
N. – Nord, Norte, North, Northern, Nouveau
N.B. – New Brunswick
N.C. – North Carolina
N. Cal. – New Caledonia
N. Dak. – North Dakota
N.H. – New Hampshire
N.I. – North Island
N.J. – New Jersey
N. Mex. – New Mexico
N.S. – Nova Scotia
N.S.W. – New South Wales
N.W.T. – North West Territory
N.Y. – New York
N.Z. – New Zealand
Nat. – National
Nebr. – Nebraska
Neths. – Netherlands
Nev. – Nevada
Nfld. – Newfoundland
Nic. – Nicaragua
O. – Oued, Ouadi
Occ. – Occidentale
Okla. – Oklahoma
Ont. – Ontario
Or. – Orientale
Oreg. – Oregon
Os. – Ostrov
Oz. – Ozero
P. – Pass, Passo, Pasul, Pulau
P.E.I. – Prince Edward Island
Pa. – Pennsylvania
Pac. Oc. – Pacific Ocean
Papua N.G. – Papua New Guinea
Pass. – Passage
Pen. – Peninsula, Péninsule
Phil. – Philippines
Pk. – Peak
Plat. – Plateau
Prov. – Province, Provincial
Pt. – Point
Pta. – Ponta, Punta
Pte. – Pointe
Qué. – Québec
Queens. – Queensland
R. – Rio, River
R.I. – Rhode Island
Ra. – Range
Raj. – Rajasthan
Récr. – Récréatif
Reg. – Region
Rep. – Republic
Res. – Reserve, Reservoir
Rhld-Pfz. – Rheinland-Pfalz
S. – South, Southern, Sur
Si. Arabia – Saudi Arabia
S.C. – South Carolina
S. Dak. – South Dakota
S.I. – South Island
S. Leone – Sierra Leone
Sa. – Serra, Sierra
Sask. – Saskatchewan
Scot. – Scotland
Sd. – Sound
Sev. – Severnaya
Sib. – Siberia
Sprs. – Springs
St. – Saint
Sta. – Santa
Ste. – Sainte
Sto. – Santo
Str. – Strait, Stretto
Switz. – Switzerland
Tas. – Tasmania
Tenn. – Tennessee
Terr. – Territory, Territoire
Tex. – Texas
Tg. – Tanjung
Trin. & Tob. – Trinidad & Tobago
U.A.E. – United Arab Emirates
U.K. – United Kingdom
U.S.A. – United States of America
Ut. P. – Uttar Pradesh
Va. – Virginia
Vdkhr. – Vodokhranilishche
Vdskh. – Vodoskhovyshche
Vf. – Vírful
Vic. – Victoria
Vol. – Volcano
Vt. – Vermont
W. – Wadi, West
W. Va. – West Virginia
Wall. & F. Is. – Wallis and Futuna Is.
Wash. – Washington
Wis. – Wisconsin
Wlkp. – Wielkopolski
Wyo. – Wyoming
Yorks. – Yorkshire
Yug. – Yugoslavia

A

A Baña, *Spain* **34 C2** 42 58N 8 46W
A Cañiza, *Spain* **34 C2** 42 13N 8 16W
A Coruña, *Spain* **34 B2** 43 20N 8 25W
A Estrada, *Spain* **34 C2** 42 43N 8 27W
A Fonsagrada, *Spain* **34 B3** 43 8N 7 4W
A Guarda, *Spain* **34 D2** 41 56N 8 52W
A Gudiña, *Spain* **34 C3** 42 4N 7 8W
A Rúa, *Spain* **34 C3** 42 24N 7 6W
Aachen, *Germany* **24 E2** 50 45N 6 6 E
Aalborg = Ålborg, *Denmark* **11 G3** 57 2N 9 54 E
Aalen, *Germany* **25 G6** 48 51N 10 6 E
A'âli an Nîl □, *Sudan* **81 F3** 9 30N 33 0 E
Aalst, *Belgium* **17 D4** 50 56N 4 2 E
Aalten, *Neths.* **17 C6** 51 56N 6 35 E
Aalter, *Belgium* **17 C3** 51 5N 3 28 E
Äänekoski, *Finland* **9 E21** 62 36N 25 44 E
Aarau, *Switz.* **25 H4** 47 23N 8 4 E
Aarberg, *Switz.* **25 H3** 47 2N 7 16 E
Aare →, *Switz.* **25 H4** 47 33N 8 14 E
Aargau □, *Switz.* **25 H4** 47 26N 8 10 E
Aarhus = Århus, *Denmark* **11 H4** 56 8N 10 11 E
Aarschot, *Belgium* **17 D4** 50 59N 4 49 E
Aba, *China* **58 A3** 32 59N 101 42 E
Aba, *Dem. Rep. of the Congo* **86 B3** 3 58N 30 17 E
Aba, *Nigeria* **83 D6** 5 10N 7 19 E
Âbâ, Jazîrat, *Sudan* **81 E3** 13 30N 32 31 E
Abadab, J., *Sudan* **80 D4** 18 54N 35 56 E
Ābādān, *Iran* **71 D6** 30 22N 48 20 E
Abade, *Ethiopia* **81 F4** 9 22N 38 3 E
Ābādeh, *Iran* **71 D7** 31 8N 52 40 E
Abadin, *Spain* **34 B3** 43 21N 7 29W
Abadla, *Algeria* **78 B5** 31 2N 2 45W
Abaetetuba, *Brazil* **125 D9** 1 40 S 48 50W
Abagnar Qi, *China* **56 C9** 43 52N 116 2 E
Abai, *Paraguay* **127 B4** 25 58 S 55 54W
Abak, *Nigeria* **83 E6** 4 58N 7 50 E
Abakaliki, *Nigeria* **83 D6** 6 22N 8 2 E
Abakan, *Russia* **51 D10** 53 40N 91 10 E
Abala, *Niger* **83 C5** 14 56N 3 22 E
Abalak, *Niger* **83 B6** 15 22N 6 21 E
Abalemma, *Niger* **83 B6** 16 12N 7 50 E
Abana, *Turkey* **72 B6** 41 59N 34 1 E
Abancay, *Peru* **124 F4** 13 35 S 72 55W
Abano Terme, *Italy* **29 C8** 45 22N 11 46 E
Abarán, *Spain* **33 G3** 38 12N 1 23W
Abariringa, *Kiribati* **96 H10** 2 50 S 171 40W
Abarqū, *Iran* **71 D7** 31 10N 53 20 E
Abashiri, *Japan* **54 B12** 44 0N 144 15 E
Abashiri-Wan, *Japan* **54 C12** 44 0N 144 30 E
Abaújszántó, *Hungary* **42 B6** 48 16N 21 12 E
Abava →, *Latvia* **44 A8** 57 6N 21 54 E
Ābay = Nîl el Azraq →, *Sudan* **81 D3** 15 38N 32 31 E
Abay, *Kazakstan* **50 E8** 49 38N 72 53 E
Abaya, L., *Ethiopia* **81 F4** 6 30N 37 50 E
Abaza, *Russia* **50 D9** 52 39N 90 6 E
Abbadia San Salvatore, *Italy* **29 F8** 42 53N 11 41 E
'Abbāsābād, *Iran* **71 C8** 33 34N 58 23 E
Abbay = Nîl el Azraq →, *Sudan* **81 D3** 15 38N 32 31 E
Abbaye, Pt., *U.S.A.* **108 B1** 46 58N 88 8W
Abbé, L., *Ethiopia* **81 E5** 11 8N 41 47 E
Abbeville, *France* **19 B8** 50 6N 1 49 E
Abbeville, *Ala., U.S.A.* **109 K3** 31 34N 85 15W
Abbeville, *La., U.S.A.* **113 L8** 29 58N 92 8W
Abbeville, *S.C., U.S.A.* **109 H4** 34 11N 82 23W
Abbiategrasso, *Italy* **28 C5** 45 24N 8 54 E
Abbot Ice Shelf, *Antarctica* **5 D16** 73 0 S 92 0W
Abbottabad, *Pakistan* **68 B5** 34 10N 73 15 E
Abd al Kūrī, *Ind. Oc.* **74 E5** 12 5N 52 20 E
Ābdar, *Iran* **71 D7** 30 16N 55 19 E
'Abdolābād, *Iran* **71 C8** 34 12N 56 30 E
Abdulpur, *Bangla.* **69 G13** 24 15N 88 59 E
Abéché, *Chad* **79 F10** 13 50N 20 35 E
Abejar, *Spain* **32 D2** 41 48N 2 47W
Abekr, *Sudan* **81 E2** 12 45N 28 50 E
Abengourou, *Ivory C.* **82 D4** 6 42N 3 27W
Abenójar, *Spain* **35 G6** 38 53N 4 21W
Åbenrå, *Denmark* **11 J3** 55 3N 9 25 E
Abensberg, *Germany* **25 G7** 48 48N 11 51 E
Abeokuta, *Nigeria* **83 D5** 7 3N 3 19 E
Aber, *Uganda* **86 B3** 2 12N 32 25 E
Aberaeron, *U.K.* **13 E3** 52 15N 4 15W
Aberayron = Aberaeron, *U.K.* **13 E3** 52 15N 4 15W
Aberchirder, *U.K.* **14 D6** 57 34N 2 37W
Abercorn = Mbala, *Zambia* **87 D3** 8 46 S 31 24 E
Abercorn, *Australia* **95 D5** 25 12 S 151 5 E
Aberdare, *U.K.* **13 F4** 51 43N 3 27W
Aberdare Ra., *Kenya* **86 C4** 0 15 S 36 50 E
Aberdeen, *Australia* **95 E5** 32 9 S 150 56 E
Aberdeen, *Canada* **105 C7** 52 20N 106 8W
Aberdeen, *S. Africa* **88 E3** 32 28 S 24 2 E
Aberdeen, *U.K.* **14 D6** 57 9N 2 5W
Aberdeen, *Ala., U.S.A.* **109 J1** 33 49N 88 33W
Aberdeen, *Idaho, U.S.A.* **114 E7** 42 57N 112 50W
Aberdeen, *Md., U.S.A.* **108 F7** 39 31N 76 10W
Aberdeen, *S. Dak., U.S.A.* **112 C5** 45 28N 98 29W
Aberdeen, *Wash., U.S.A.* **116 D3** 46 59N 123 50W
Aberdeen, City of □, *U.K.* **14 D6** 57 10N 2 10W
Aberdeenshire □, *U.K.* **14 D6** 57 17N 2 36W
Aberdovey = Aberdyfi, *U.K.* **13 E3** 52 33N 4 3W
Aberdyfi, *U.K.* **13 E3** 52 33N 4 3W
Aberfeldy, *U.K.* **14 E5** 56 37N 3 51W
Abergavenny, *U.K.* **13 F4** 51 49N 3 1W
Abergele, *U.K.* **12 D4** 53 17N 3 35W
Abernathy, *U.S.A.* **113 J4** 33 50N 101 51W
Abert, L., *U.S.A.* **114 E3** 42 38N 120 14W
Aberystwyth, *U.K.* **13 E3** 52 25N 4 5W
Abhā, *Si. Arabia* **74 D3** 18 0N 42 34 E
Abhar, *Iran* **71 B6** 36 9N 49 13 E
Abhayapuri, *India* **69 F14** 26 24N 90 38 E
Abia □, *Nigeria* **83 D6** 5 30N 7 35 E
Abide, *Turkey* **39 C11** 38 55N 29 20 E
Abidiya, *Sudan* **80 D3** 18 18N 34 3 E
Abidjan, *Ivory C.* **82 D4** 5 26N 3 58W
Abilene, *Kans., U.S.A.* **112 F6** 38 55N 97 13W
Abilene, *Tex., U.S.A.* **113 J5** 32 28N 99 43W
Abingdon, *U.K.* **13 F6** 51 40N 1 17W
Abingdon, *U.S.A.* **109 G5** 36 43N 81 59W
Abington Reef, *Australia* **94 B4** 18 0 S 149 35 E
Abitau →, *Canada* **105 B7** 59 53N 109 3W
Abitibi →, *Canada* **102 B3** 51 3N 80 55W
Abitibi, L., *Canada* **102 C4** 48 40N 79 40W
Abiy Adi, *Ethiopia* **81 E4** 13 39N 39 3 E
Abkhaz Republic = Abkhazia □, *Georgia* **49 J5** 43 12N 41 5 E
Abkhazia □, *Georgia* **49 J5** 43 12N 41 5 E
Abminga, *Australia* **95 D1** 26 8 S 134 51 E
Abnûb, *Egypt* **80 B3** 27 18N 31 4 E
Åbo = Turku, *Finland* **9 F20** 60 30N 22 19 E
Abocho, *Nigeria* **83 D6** 7 35N 6 56 E
Abohar, *India* **68 D6** 30 10N 74 10 E
Aboisso, *Ivory C.* **82 D4** 5 30N 3 5W
Abomey, *Benin* **83 D5** 7 10N 2 5 E
Abong-Mbang, *Cameroon* **84 D2** 4 0N 13 8 E
Abonnema, *Nigeria* **83 E6** 4 41N 6 49 E
Abony, *Hungary* **42 C5** 47 12N 20 3 E
Aboso, *Ghana* **82 D4** 5 23N 1 57W
Abou-Deïa, *Chad* **79 F9** 11 20N 19 20 E
Aboyne, *U.K.* **14 D6** 57 4N 2 47W
Abra Pampa, *Argentina* **126 A2** 22 43 S 65 42W
Abraham L., *Canada* **104 C5** 52 15N 116 35W
Abrantes, *Portugal* **35 F2** 39 24N 8 7W
Abreojos, Pta., *Mexico* **118 B2** 26 50N 113 40W
Abri, *Esh Shamâliya, Sudan* **80 C3** 20 50N 30 27 E
Abri, *Janub Kordofân, Sudan* **81 E3** 11 40N 30 21 E
Abrud, *Romania* **42 D8** 46 19N 23 5 E
Abruzzo □, *Italy* **29 F10** 42 15N 14 0 E
Absaroka Range, *U.S.A.* **114 D9** 44 45N 109 50W
Abtenau, *Austria* **26 D6** 47 33N 13 21 E
Abu, *India* **68 G5** 24 41N 72 50 E
Abū al Abyad, *U.A.E.* **71 E7** 24 11N 53 50 E
Abū al Khaşīb, *Iraq* **71 D6** 30 25N 48 0 E
Abū 'Alī, *Si. Arabia* **71 E6** 27 20N 49 27 E
Abū 'Alī →, *Lebanon* **75 A4** 34 25N 35 50 E
Abu Ballas, *Egypt* **80 C2** 24 26N 27 36 E
Abu Deleiq, *Sudan* **81 D3** 15 57N 33 48 E
Abu Dhabi = Abū Ẓāby, *U.A.E.* **71 E7** 24 28N 54 22 E
Abu Dis, *Sudan* **80 D3** 19 12N 33 38 E
Abu Dom, *Sudan* **81 D3** 16 18N 32 25 E
Abū Du'ān, *Syria* **70 B3** 36 25N 38 15 E
Abu el Gairi, W. →, *Egypt* **75 F2** 29 35N 33 30 E
Abu Fatma, Ras, *Sudan* **80 C4** 22 25N 36 25 E
Abu Gabra, *Sudan* **81 E2** 11 2N 26 50 E
Abu Ga'da, W. →, *Egypt* **75 F1** 29 15N 32 53 E
Abu Gelba, *Sudan* **81 E3** 13 11N 31 52 E
Abu Gubeiha, *Sudan* **81 E3** 11 30N 31 15 E
Abu Habl, Khawr →, *Sudan* **81 E3** 12 37N 31 0 E
Abū Ḥadrīyah, *Si. Arabia* **71 E6** 27 20N 48 58 E
Abu Hamed, *Sudan* **80 D3** 19 32N 33 13 E
Abu Haraz, *An Nîl el Azraq, Sudan* **80 D3** 18 1N 33 58 E
Abu Haraz, *El Gezira, Sudan* **81 E3** 14 35N 33 30 E
Abu Haraz, *Esh Shamâliya, Sudan* **80 D3** 19 8N 32 18 E
Abu Higar, *Sudan* **81 E3** 12 50N 33 59 E
Abū Kamāl, *Syria* **70 C4** 34 30N 41 0 E
Abu Kuleiwat, *Sudan* **81 E2** 12 20N 26 0 E
Abū Madd, Ra's, *Si. Arabia* **70 E3** 24 50N 37 7 E
Abu Matariq, *Sudan* **81 E2** 10 59N 26 9 E
Abu Mendi, *Ethiopia* **81 E4** 11 48N 35 42 E
Abū Mūsā, *U.A.E.* **71 E7** 25 52N 55 3 E
Abū Qaşr, *Si. Arabia* **70 D3** 30 21N 38 34 E
Abu Qir, *Egypt* **80 H7** 31 18N 30 0 E
Abu Qireiya, *Egypt* **80 C4** 24 5N 35 28 E
Abu Qurqâs, *Egypt* **80 B3** 28 1N 30 44 E
Abu Şafāt, W. →, *Jordan* **75 E5** 30 24N 36 7 E
Abu Shagara, Ras, *Sudan* **80 C4** 21 4N 37 19 E
Abu Shanab, *Sudan* **81 E2** 13 58N 27 49 E
Abu Simbel, *Egypt* **80 C3** 22 18N 31 40 E
Abū Şukhayr, *Iraq* **70 D5** 31 54N 44 30 E
Abu Sultân, *Egypt* **80 H8** 30 24N 32 21 E
Abu Tabari, *Sudan* **80 D2** 17 32N 28 32 E
Abu Tig, *Egypt* **80 B3** 27 4N 31 15 E
Abu Tiga, *Sudan* **81 E3** 12 47N 34 12 E
Abu Tineitin, *Sudan* **81 E3** 14 24N 31 1 E
Abu Uruq, *Sudan* **81 D3** 15 52N 30 25 E
Abu Zabad, *Sudan* **81 E2** 12 25N 29 10 E
Abū Ẓāby, *U.A.E.* **71 E7** 24 28N 54 22 E
Abū Zeydābād, *Iran* **71 C6** 33 54N 51 45 E
Abuja, *Nigeria* **83 D6** 9 16N 7 2 E
Abukuma-Gawa →, *Japan* **54 E10** 38 6N 140 52 E
Abukuma-Sammyaku, *Japan* **54 F10** 37 30N 140 45 E
Abunã, *Brazil* **124 E5** 9 40 S 65 20W
Abunã →, *Brazil* **124 E5** 9 41 S 65 20W
Abune Yosef, *Ethiopia* **81 E4** 12 5N 39 12 E
Aburo, *Dem. Rep. of the Congo* **86 B3** 2 4N 30 53 E
Abut Hd., *N.Z.* **91 K3** 43 7 S 170 15 E
Abuye Meda, *Ethiopia* **81 E4** 10 30N 39 49 E
Abwong, *Sudan* **81 F3** 9 2N 32 14 E
Åby, *Sweden* **11 F10** 58 40N 16 10 E
Aby, Lagune, *Ivory C.* **82 D4** 5 15N 3 14W
Abyad, *Sudan* **81 E2** 13 47N 26 24 E
Åbybro, *Denmark* **11 G3** 57 10N 9 44 E
Acadia National Park, *U.S.A.* **109 C11** 44 20N 68 13W
Açailândia, *Brazil* **125 D9** 4 57 S 47 0W
Acajutla, *El Salv.* **120 D2** 13 36N 89 50W
Acámbaro, *Mexico* **118 D4** 20 0N 100 40W
Acanthus, *Greece* **40 F7** 40 27N 23 47 E
Acaponeta, *Mexico* **118 C3** 22 30N 105 20W
Acapulco, *Mexico* **119 D5** 16 51N 99 56W
Acarai, Serra, *Brazil* **124 C7** 1 50N 57 50W
Acarigua, *Venezuela* **124 B5** 9 33N 69 12W
Acatlán, *Mexico* **119 D5** 18 10N 98 3W
Acayucan, *Mexico* **119 D6** 17 59N 94 58W
Accéglio, *Italy* **28 D4** 44 28N 7 0 E
Accomac, *U.S.A.* **108 G8** 37 43N 75 40W
Accous, *France* **20 E3** 43 0N 0 36W
Accra, *Ghana* **83 D4** 5 35N 0 6W
Accrington, *U.K.* **12 D5** 53 45N 2 22W
Acebal, *Argentina* **126 C3** 33 20 S 60 50W
Aceh □, *Indonesia* **62 D1** 4 15N 97 30 E
Acerra, *Italy* **31 B7** 40 57N 14 22 E
Aceuchal, *Spain* **35 G4** 38 39N 6 30W
Achalpur, *India* **66 J10** 21 22N 77 32 E
Acheng, *China* **57 B14** 45 30N 126 58 E
Achenkirch, *Austria* **26 D4** 47 32N 11 45 E
Achensee, *Austria* **26 D4** 47 26N 11 45 E
Acher, *India* **68 H5** 23 10N 72 32 E
Achern, *Germany* **25 G4** 48 37N 8 4 E
Achill Hd., *Ireland* **15 C1** 53 58N 10 15W
Achill I., *Ireland* **15 C1** 53 58N 10 1W
Achim, *Germany* **24 B5** 53 1N 9 3 E
Achinsk, *Russia* **51 D10** 56 20N 90 20 E
Acıgöl, *Turkey* **39 D11** 37 50N 29 50 E
Acıpayam, *Turkey* **39 D11** 37 26N 29 22 E
Acireale, *Italy* **31 E8** 37 37N 15 10 E
Ackerman, *U.S.A.* **113 J10** 33 19N 89 11W
Acklins I., *Bahamas* **121 B5** 22 30N 74 0W
Acme, *Canada* **104 C6** 51 33N 113 30W
Acme, *U.S.A.* **110 F5** 40 8N 79 26W
Aconcagua, Cerro, *Argentina* **126 C2** 32 39 S 70 0W
Aconquija, Mt., *Argentina* **126 B2** 27 0 S 66 0W
Açores, Is. dos = Azores, *Atl. Oc.* **78 A1** 38 44N 29 0W
Acornhoek, *S. Africa* **89 C5** 24 37 S 31 2 E
Acquapendente, *Italy* **29 F8** 42 44N 11 52 E
Acquasanta Terme, *Italy* **29 F10** 42 46N 13 24 E
Acquasparta, *Italy* **29 F9** 42 41N 12 33 E
Acquaviva delle Fonti, *Italy* **31 B9** 40 54N 16 50 E
Ácqui Terme, *Italy* **28 D5** 44 41N 8 28 E
Acraman, L., *Australia* **95 E2** 32 2 S 135 23 E
Acre = 'Akko, *Israel* **75 C4** 32 55N 35 4 E
Acre □, *Brazil* **124 E4** 9 1 S 71 0W
Acre →, *Brazil* **124 E5** 8 45 S 67 22W
Acri, *Italy* **31 C9** 39 29N 16 23 E
Acs, *Hungary* **42 C3** 47 42N 18 2 E
Actium, *Greece* **38 C2** 38 57N 20 45 E
Acton, *Canada* **110 C4** 43 38N 80 3W
Acuña, *Mexico* **118 B4** 29 18N 100 55W
Ad Dammām, *Si. Arabia* **71 E6** 26 20N 50 5 E
Ad Dāmūr, *Lebanon* **75 B4** 33 44N 35 27 E
Ad Dawādimī, *Si. Arabia* **70 E5** 24 35N 44 15 E
Ad Dawḩah, *Qatar* **71 E6** 25 15N 51 35 E
Ad Dawr, *Iraq* **70 C4** 34 27N 43 47 E
Ad Dir'īyah, *Si. Arabia* **70 E5** 24 44N 46 35 E
Ad Dīwānīyah, *Iraq* **70 D5** 32 0N 45 0 E
Ad Dujayl, *Iraq* **70 C5** 33 51N 44 14 E
Ad Duwayd, *Si. Arabia* **70 D4** 30 15N 42 17 E
Ada, *Ghana* **83 D5** 5 44N 0 40 E
Ada, *Serbia, Yug.* **42 E5** 45 49N 20 9 E
Ada, *Minn., U.S.A.* **112 B6** 47 18N 96 31W
Ada, *Okla., U.S.A.* **113 H6** 34 46N 96 41W
Adabiya, *Egypt* **75 F1** 29 53N 32 28 E
Adair, C., *Canada* **101 A12** 71 31N 71 24W
Adaja →, *Spain* **34 D6** 41 32N 4 52W
Adak I., *U.S.A.* **100 C2** 51 45N 176 45W
Adamaoua, Massif de l', *Cameroon* **83 D7** 7 20N 12 20 E
Adamawa □, *Nigeria* **83 D7** 9 20N 12 30 E
Adamawa Highlands = Adamaoua, Massif de l', *Cameroon* **83 D7** 7 20N 12 20 E
Adamello, Mte., *Italy* **28 B7** 46 9N 10 30 E
Adami Tulu, *Ethiopia* **81 F4** 7 53N 38 41 E
Adaminaby, *Australia* **95 F4** 36 0 S 148 45 E
Adams, *Mass., U.S.A.* **111 D11** 42 38N 73 7W
Adams, *N.Y., U.S.A.* **111 C8** 43 49N 76 1W
Adams, *Wis., U.S.A.* **112 D10** 43 57N 89 49W
Adam's Bridge, *Sri Lanka* **66 Q11** 9 15N 79 40 E
Adams L., *Canada* **104 C5** 51 10N 119 40W
Adams Mt., *U.S.A.* **116 D5** 46 12N 121 30W
Adam's Peak, *Sri Lanka* **66 R12** 6 48N 80 30 E
Adamuz, *Spain* **35 G6** 38 2N 4 32W
Adana, *Turkey* **70 B2** 37 0N 35 16 E
Adanero, *Spain* **34 E6** 40 56N 4 36W
Adapazarı = Sakarya, *Turkey* **72 B4** 40 48N 30 25 E
Adar Gwagwa, J., *Sudan* **80 C4** 22 15N 35 20 E
Adarama, *Sudan* **81 D3** 17 10N 34 52 E
Adare, C., *Antarctica* **5 D11** 71 0 S 171 0 E
Adarte, *Eritrea* **81 E5** 13 18N 42 8 E
Adaut, *Indonesia* **63 F8** 8 8 S 131 7 E
Adavale, *Australia* **95 D3** 25 52 S 144 32 E
Adda →, *Italy* **28 C6** 45 8N 9 53 E
Addis Ababa = Addis Abeba, *Ethiopia* **81 F4** 9 2N 38 42 E
Addis Abeba, *Ethiopia* **81 F4** 9 2N 38 42 E
Addis Alem, *Ethiopia* **81 F4** 9 0N 38 17 E
Addis Zemen, *Ethiopia* **81 E4** 12 7N 37 47 E
Addison, *U.S.A.* **110 D7** 42 1N 77 14W
Addo, *S. Africa* **88 E4** 33 32 S 25 45 E
Adebour, *Niger* **83 C7** 13 17N 11 50 E
Ādeh, *Iran* **70 B5** 37 42N 45 11 E
Adel, *U.S.A.* **109 K4** 31 8N 83 25W
Adelaide, *Australia* **95 E2** 34 52 S 138 30 E
Adelaide, *Bahamas* **120 A4** 25 4N 77 31W
Adelaide, *S. Africa* **88 E4** 32 42 S 26 20 E
Adelaide I., *Antarctica* **5 C17** 67 15 S 68 30W
Adelaide Pen., *Canada* **100 B10** 68 15N 97 30W
Adelaide River, *Australia* **92 B5** 13 15 S 131 7 E
Adelanto, *U.S.A.* **117 L9** 34 35N 117 22W
Adele I., *Australia* **92 C3** 15 32 S 123 9 E
Adélie, Terre, *Antarctica* **5 C10** 68 0 S 140 0 E
Adélie Land = Adélie, Terre, *Antarctica* **5 C10** 68 0 S 140 0 E
Ademuz, *Spain* **32 E3** 40 5N 1 13W
Aden = Al 'Adan, *Yemen* **74 E4** 12 45N 45 0 E
Aden, G. of, *Asia* **74 E4** 12 30N 47 30 E
Adendorp, *S. Africa* **88 E3** 32 15 S 24 30 E
Aderbissinat, *Niger* **83 B6** 15 34N 7 54 E
Adh Dhayd, *U.A.E.* **71 E7** 25 17N 55 53 E
Adhoi, *India* **68 H4** 23 26N 70 32 E
Adi, *Indonesia* **63 E8** 4 15 S 133 30 E
Adi Arkai, *Ethiopia* **81 E4** 13 35N 37 57 E
Adi Daro, *Ethiopia* **81 E4** 14 20N 38 14 E
Adi Keyih, *Eritrea* **81 E4** 14 51N 39 22 E
Adi Kwala, *Eritrea* **81 E4** 14 38N 38 48 E
Adi Ugri, *Eritrea* **81 E4** 14 58N 38 48 E
Adieu, C., *Australia* **93 F5** 32 0 S 132 10 E
Adieu Pt., *Australia* **92 C3** 15 14 S 124 35 E
Adigala, *Ethiopia* **81 E5** 10 24N 42 15 E
Adige →, *Italy* **29 C9** 45 9N 12 20 E
Adigrat, *Ethiopia* **81 E4** 14 20N 39 26 E
Adıgüzel Barajı, *Turkey* **39 C11** 38 13N 29 14 E
Adilabad, *India* **66 K11** 19 33N 78 20 E
Adilcevaz, *Turkey* **73 C10** 38 47N 42 43 E
Adin Khel, *Afghan.* **66 C6** 32 45N 68 5 E
Adirondack Mts., *U.S.A.* **111 C10** 44 0N 74 0W
Adıyaman, *Turkey* **73 D8** 37 45N 38 16 E
Adjohon, *Benin* **83 D5** 6 41N 2 32 E
Adjud, *Romania* **43 D12** 46 7N 27 10 E
Adjumani, *Uganda* **86 B3** 3 20N 31 50 E
Adlavik Is., *Canada* **103 A8** 55 0N 58 40W
Adler, *Russia* **49 J4** 43 28N 39 52 E
Admer, *Algeria* **83 A6** 20 21N 5 27 E
Admiralty G., *Australia* **92 B4** 14 20 S 125 55 E
Admiralty I., *U.S.A.* **104 B2** 57 30N 134 30W
Admiralty Is., *Papua N. G.* **96 H6** 2 0 S 147 0 E
Ado, *Nigeria* **83 D5** 6 36N 2 56 E
Ado-Ekiti, *Nigeria* **83 D6** 7 38N 5 12 E
Adok, *Sudan* **81 F3** 8 10N 30 20 E
Adola, *Ethiopia* **81 E5** 11 14N 41 44 E
Adonara, *Indonesia* **63 F6** 8 15 S 123 5 E
Adoni, *India* **66 M10** 15 33N 77 18 E
Adony, *Hungary* **42 C3** 47 6N 18 52 E
Adour →, *France* **20 E2** 43 32N 1 32W
Adra, *India* **69 H12** 23 30N 86 42 E
Adra, *Spain* **35 J7** 36 43N 3 3W
Adrano, *Italy* **31 E7** 37 40N 14 50 E
Adrar, *Mauritania* **78 D3** 20 30N 7 30 E
Adrar des Iforas, *Algeria* **76 D4** 27 51N 0 11 E
Ádria, *Italy* **29 C9** 45 3N 12 3 E
Adrian, *Mich., U.S.A.* **108 E3** 41 54N 84 2W
Adrian, *Tex., U.S.A.* **113 H3** 35 16N 102 40W
Adriatic Sea, *Medit. S.* **6 G9** 43 0N 16 0 E
Adua, *Indonesia* **63 E7** 1 45 S 129 50 E
Adwa, *Ethiopia* **81 E4** 14 15N 38 52 E
Adyge □, *Russia* **49 H5** 45 0N 40 0 E
Adzhar Republic = Ajaria □, *Georgia* **49 K6** 41 30N 42 0 E
Adzopé, *Ivory C.* **82 D4** 6 7N 3 49W
Ægean Sea, *Medit. S.* **39 C7** 38 30N 25 0 E
Aerhtai Shan, *Mongolia* **60 B4** 46 40N 92 45 E
Ærø, *Denmark* **11 K4** 54 52N 10 25 E
Ærøskøbing, *Denmark* **11 K4** 54 53N 10 24 E
Aëtós, *Greece* **38 D3** 37 15N 21 50 E
'Afak, *Iraq* **70 C5** 32 4N 45 15 E
Afándou, *Greece* **36 C10** 36 18N 28 12 E
Afghanistan ■, *Asia* **66 C4** 33 0N 65 0 E
Afikpo, *Nigeria* **83 D6** 5 53N 7 54 E
Aflou, *Algeria* **78 B6** 34 7N 2 3 E
Afragóla, *Italy* **31 B7** 40 55N 14 18 E
Afram →, *Ghana* **83 D4** 7 0N 0 52W
Afrera, *Ethiopia* **81 E5** 13 16N 41 5 E
Africa **76 E6** 10 0N 20 0 E
'Afrīn, *Syria* **70 B3** 36 32N 36 50 E
Afşin, *Turkey* **72 C7** 38 14N 36 55 E
Afton, *N.Y., U.S.A.* **111 D9** 42 14N 75 32W
Afton, *Wyo., U.S.A.* **114 E8** 42 44N 110 56W
Afuá, *Brazil* **125 D8** 0 15 S 50 20W
'Afula, *Israel* **75 C4** 32 37N 35 17 E
Afyon, *Turkey* **39 C12** 38 45N 30 33 E
Afyon □, *Turkey* **39 C12** 38 25N 30 30 E
Afyonkarahisar = Afyon, *Turkey* **39 C12** 38 45N 30 33 E
Aga, *Egypt* **80 H7** 30 55N 31 10 E
Agadès = Agadez, *Niger* **83 B6** 16 58N 7 59 E
Agadez, *Niger* **83 B6** 16 58N 7 59 E
Agadir, *Morocco* **78 B4** 30 28N 9 55W
Agaete, *Canary Is.* **37 F4** 28 6N 15 43W
Agaie, *Nigeria* **83 D6** 9 1N 6 18 E
Agam, *Sudan* **81 F2** 8 28N 29 55 E
Ağapınar, *Turkey* **39 B12** 39 48N 30 47 E
Agar, *India* **68 H7** 23 40N 76 2 E
Agaro, *Ethiopia* **81 F4** 7 50N 36 38 E
Agartala, *India* **67 H17** 23 50N 91 23 E
Agăş, *Romania* **43 D11** 46 28N 26 15 E
Agassiz, *Canada* **104 D4** 49 14N 121 46W
Agats, *Indonesia* **63 F9** 5 33 S 138 0 E
Agawam, *U.S.A.* **111 D12** 42 5N 72 37W
Agbélouvé, *Togo* **83 D5** 6 35N 1 14 E
Agboville, *Ivory C.* **82 D4** 5 55N 4 15W
Ağcabädi, *Azerbaijan* **49 K8** 40 5N 47 27 E
Ağdam, *Azerbaijan* **49 L8** 40 0N 46 58 E
Ağdaş, *Azerbaijan* **49 K8** 40 44N 47 22 E
Agde, *France* **20 E7** 43 19N 3 28 E
Agde, C. d', *France* **20 E7** 43 16N 3 28 E
Agdzhabedi = Ağcabädi, *Azerbaijan* **49 K8** 40 5N 47 27 E
Agen, *France* **20 D4** 44 12N 0 38 E
Agerbæk, *Denmark* **11 J2** 55 36N 8 48 E
Agersø, *Denmark* **11 J5** 55 13N 11 12 E
Ageyevo, *Russia* **46 E9** 54 10N 36 27 E
Āgh Kand, *Iran* **71 B6** 37 15N 48 4 E
Aghiresu, *Romania* **43 D8** 46 53N 23 15 E
Aginskoye, *Russia* **51 D12** 51 6N 114 32 E
Ağlasun, *Turkey* **39 D12** 37 39N 30 31 E
Agly →, *France* **20 F7** 42 46N 3 3 E
Agnew, *Australia* **93 E3** 28 1 S 120 31 E
Agnibilékrou, *Ivory C.* **82 D4** 7 10N 3 11W
Agnita, *Romania* **43 E9** 45 59N 24 40 E
Agnone, *Italy* **29 G11** 41 48N 14 22 E
Agofie, *Ghana* **83 D5** 8 27N 0 15 E
Agogna →, *Italy* **28 C5** 45 4N 8 54 E
Agogo, *Sudan* **81 F2** 7 50N 28 45 E
Agön, *Sweden* **10 C11** 61 34N 17 23 E
Agon Coutainville, *France* **18 C5** 49 2N 1 34W
Ágordo, *Italy* **29 B9** 46 18N 12 2 E
Agori, *India* **69 G10** 24 33N 82 57 E
Agouna, *Benin* **83 D5** 7 39N 1 47 E
Agout →, *France* **20 E5** 43 47N 1 41 E
Agra, *India* **68 F7** 27 17N 77 58 E
Agrakhanskiy Poluostrov, *Russia* **49 J8** 43 42N 47 36 E
Agramunt, *Spain* **32 D6** 41 48N 1 6 E
Agreda, *Spain* **32 D3** 41 51N 1 55W
Ağri, *Turkey* **73 C10** 39 44N 43 3 E
Agri →, *Italy* **31 B9** 40 13N 16 44 E
Ağri Dağı, *Turkey* **70 B5** 39 50N 44 15 E
Ağri Karakose = Ağri, *Turkey* **73 C10** 39 44N 43 3 E
Agriá, *Greece* **38 B5** 39 20N 23 1 E
Agrigento, *Italy* **30 E6** 37 19N 13 34 E
Agrínion, *Greece* **38 C3** 38 37N 21 27 E
Agrópoli, *Italy* **31 B7** 40 21N 14 59 E
Ağstafa, *Azerbaijan* **49 K7** 41 7N 45 27 E
Agua Caliente, *Baja Calif., Mexico* **117 N10** 32 29N 116 59W
Agua Caliente, *Sinaloa, Mexico* **118 B3** 26 30N 108 20W
Agua Caliente Springs, *U.S.A.* **117 N10** 32 56N 116 19W
Água Clara, *Brazil* **125 H8** 20 25 S 52 45W
Agua Hechicero, *Mexico* **117 N10** 32 26N 116 14W
Agua Prieta, *Mexico* **118 A3** 31 20N 109 32W
Aguadilla, *Puerto Rico* **121 C6** 18 26N 67 10W
Aguadulce, *Panama* **120 E3** 8 15N 80 32W
Aguanga, *U.S.A.* **117 M10** 33 27N 116 51W
Aguanish, *Canada* **103 B7** 50 14N 62 2W
Aguanus →, *Canada* **103 B7** 50 13N 62 5W
Aguapey →, *Argentina* **126 B4** 29 7 S 56 36W
Aguaray Guazú →, *Paraguay* **126 A4** 24 47 S 57 19W
Aguarico →, *Ecuador* **124 D3** 0 59 S 75 11W
Aguas →, *Spain* **32 D4** 41 20N 0 30W
Aguas Blancas, *Chile* **126 A2** 24 15 S 69 55W
Aguas Calientes, Sierra de, *Argentina* **126 B2** 25 26 S 66 40W
Aguascalientes, *Mexico* **118 C4** 21 53N 102 12W
Aguascalientes □, *Mexico* **118 C4** 22 0N 102 20W
Agudo, *Spain* **35 G6** 38 59N 4 52W
Águeda, *Portugal* **34 E2** 40 34N 8 27W
Agueda →, *Spain* **34 D4** 41 2N 6 56W
Aguelhok, *Mali* **83 B5** 19 29N 0 52 E
Aguié, *Niger* **83 C6** 13 31N 7 46 E
Aguilafuente, *Spain* **34 D6** 41 13N 4 7W
Aguilar, *Spain* **35 H6** 37 31N 4 40W
Aguilar de Campóo, *Spain* **34 C6** 42 47N 4 15W
Aguilares, *Argentina* **126 B2** 27 26 S 65 35W
Águilas, *Spain* **33 H3** 37 23N 1 35W
Agüimes, *Canary Is.* **37 G4** 27 58N 15 27W
Aguja, C. de la, *Colombia* **122 B3** 11 18N 74 12W
Agulaa, *Ethiopia* **81 E4** 13 40N 39 40 E
Agulhas, C., *S. Africa* **88 E3** 34 52 S 20 0 E
Agulo, *Canary Is.* **37 F2** 28 11N 17 12W
Agung, *Indonesia* **62 F5** 8 20 S 115 28 E
Agur, *Uganda* **86 B3** 2 28N 32 55 E
Agusan →, *Phil.* **61 G6** 9 0N 125 30 E
Ağva, *Turkey* **41 E13** 41 8N 29 51 E
Agvali, *Russia* **49 J8** 42 36N 46 8 E
Aha Mts., *Botswana* **88 B3** 19 45 S 21 0 E
Ahaggar, *Algeria* **78 D7** 23 0N 6 30 E
Ahamansu, *Ghana* **83 D5** 7 38N 0 35 E
Ahar, *Iran* **70 B5** 38 35N 47 0 E
Ahat, *Turkey* **39 C11** 38 39N 29 47 E
Ahaus, *Germany* **24 C2** 52 4N 7 0 E
Ahipara B., *N.Z.* **91 F4** 35 5 S 173 5 E
Ahir Dağı, *Turkey* **39 C12** 38 45N 30 10 E
Ahiri, *India* **66 K12** 19 30N 80 0 E
Ahlat, *Turkey* **73 C10** 38 45N 42 29 E
Ahlen, *Germany* **24 D3** 51 45N 7 53 E
Ahmad Wal, *Pakistan* **68 E1** 29 18N 65 58 E
Ahmadabad, *India* **68 H5** 23 0N 72 40 E
Aḥmadābād, *Khorāsān, Iran* **71 C9** 35 3N 60 50 E
Aḥmadābād, *Khorāsān, Iran* **71 C8** 35 49N 59 42 E
Aḥmadī, *Iran* **71 E8** 27 56N 56 42 E
Ahmadnagar, *India* **66 K9** 19 7N 74 46 E
Ahmadpur, *Pakistan* **68 E4** 29 12N 71 10 E
Ahmadpur Lamma, *Pakistan* **68 E4** 28 19N 70 3 E
Ahmar, *Ethiopia* **81 F5** 9 20N 41 15 E
Ahmedabad = Ahmadabad, *India* **68 H5** 23 0N 72 40 E
Ahmednagar = Ahmadnagar, *India* **66 K9** 19 7N 74 46 E
Ahmetbey, *Turkey* **41 E11** 41 26N 27 34 E
Ahmetler, *Turkey* **39 C11** 38 28N 29 5 E
Ahmetli, *Turkey* **39 C9** 38 32N 27 57 E
Ahoada, *Nigeria* **83 D6** 5 8N 6 36 E
Ahome, *Mexico* **118 B3** 25 55N 109 11W
Ahoskie, *U.S.A.* **109 G7** 36 17N 76 59W
Ahr →, *Germany* **24 E3** 50 32N 7 16 E
Ahram, *Iran* **71 D6** 28 52N 51 16 E
Ahrax Pt., *Malta* **36 D1** 35 59N 14 22 E
Ahrensbök, *Germany* **24 A6** 54 2N 10 35 E
Ahrensburg, *Germany* **24 B6** 53 40N 10 13 E
Āhū, *Iran* **71 C6** 34 33N 50 2 E
Ahuachapán, *El Salv.* **120 D2** 13 54N 89 52W
Ahun, *France* **19 F9** 46 4N 2 5 E
Åhus, *Sweden* **11 J8** 55 56N 14 18 E
Ahvāz, *Iran* **71 D6** 31 20N 48 40 E
Ahvenanmaa = Åland, *Finland* **9 F19** 60 15N 20 0 E
Aḥwar, *Yemen* **74 E4** 13 30N 46 40 E
Ahzar →, *Mali* **83 B5** 15 30N 3 20 E
Ai →, *India* **69 F14** 26 26N 90 44 E
Ai-Ais, *Namibia* **88 D2** 27 54 S 17 59 E
Aichach, *Germany* **25 G7** 48 27N 11 8 E
Aichi □, *Japan* **55 G8** 35 0N 137 15 E
Aigle, *Switz.* **25 J2** 46 18N 6 58 E
Aignay-le-Duc, *France* **19 E11** 47 40N 4 43 E
Aigoual, Mt., *France* **20 D7** 44 8N 3 35 E
Aigre, *France* **20 C4** 45 54N 0 1 E
Aigua, *Uruguay* **127 C5** 34 13 S 54 46W
Aigueperse, *France* **19 F10** 46 3N 3 13 E
Aigues →, *France* **21 D8** 44 7N 4 43 E
Aigues-Mortes, *France* **21 E8** 43 35N 4 12 E
Aigues-Mortes, G. d', *France* **21 E8** 43 31N 4 3 E
Aiguilles, *France* **21 D10** 44 47N 6 51 E
Aiguillon, *France* **20 D4** 44 18N 0 21 E
Aigurande, *France* **19 F8** 46 27N 1 49 E
Aihui, *China* **60 A7** 50 10N 127 30 E
Aija, *Peru* **124 E3** 9 50 S 77 45W
Aikawa, *Japan* **54 E9** 38 2N 138 15 E
Aiken, *U.S.A.* **109 J5** 33 34N 81 43W
Ailao Shan, *China* **58 F3** 24 0N 101 20 E
Aileron, *Australia* **94 C1** 22 39 S 133 20 E
Aillant-sur-Tholon, *France* **19 E10** 47 52N 3 20 E
Aillik, *Canada* **103 A8** 55 11N 59 18W
Ailsa Craig, *U.K.* **14 F3** 55 15N 5 6W
'Ailūn, *Jordan* **75 C4** 32 18N 35 47 E
Aim, *Russia* **51 D14** 59 0N 133 55 E
Aimere, *Indonesia* **63 F6** 8 45 S 121 3 E
Aimogasta, *Argentina* **126 B2** 28 33 S 66 50W
Ain □, *France* **19 F12** 46 5N 5 20 E
Ain →, *France* **21 C9** 45 45N 5 11 E
Aïn Ben Tili, *Mauritania* **78 C4** 25 59N 9 27W
Ain Dalla, *Egypt* **80 B2** 27 20N 27 23 E
Ain el Mafki, *Egypt* **80 B2** 27 30N 28 15 E
Ain Girba, *Egypt* **80 B2** 29 20N 25 14 E
Ain Murr, *Sudan* **80 C2** 21 25N 25 9 E
Ain Qeiqab, *Egypt* **80 B1** 29 42N 24 55 E
Aïn-Sefra, *Algeria* **78 B5** 32 47N 0 37W
Ain Sheikh Murzûk, *Egypt* **80 B2** 26 47N 27 45 E
'Ain Sudr, *Egypt* **75 F2** 29 50N 33 6 E
Ain Sukhna, *Egypt* **80 J8** 29 32N 32 20 E
Ain Zeitûn, *Egypt* **80 B2** 29 10N 25 48 E

Ainaži, Latvia 9 H21 57 50N 24 24 E
Aínos Óros, Greece 38 C2 38 10N 20 35 E
Ainsworth, U.S.A. 112 D5 42 33N 99 52W
Aiquile, Bolivia 124 G5 18 10 S 65 10W
Aïr, Niger 83 B6 18 30N 8 0 E
Air Force I., Canada 101 B12 67 58N 74 5W
Air Hitam, Malaysia 65 M4 1 55N 103 11 E
Airaines, France 19 C8 49 58N 1 55 E
Airdrie, Canada 104 C6 51 18N 114 2W
Airdrie, U.K. 14 F5 55 52N 3 57W
Aire →, France 19 C11 49 18N 4 49 E
Aire →, U.K. 12 D7 53 43N 0 55W
Aire, I. de l', Spain 37 B11 39 48N 4 16 E
Aire-sur-la-Lys, France 19 B9 50 37N 2 22 E
Aire-sur-l'Adour, France 20 E3 43 42N 0 15W
Airlie Beach, Australia 94 C4 20 16 S 148 43 E
Airvault, France 18 F6 46 50N 0 8W
Aisch →, Germany 25 F6 49 49N 10 58 E
Aisne □, France 19 C10 49 42N 3 40 E
Aisne →, France 19 C9 49 26N 2 50 E
Ait, India 69 G8 25 54N 79 14 E
Aitana, Sierra de, Spain 33 G4 38 35N 0 24W
Aitkin, U.S.A. 112 B8 46 32N 93 42W
Aitolía Kai Akarnanía □, Greece 38 C3 38 45N 21 18 E
Aitolikón, Greece 38 C3 38 26N 21 21 E
Aiud, Romania 43 D8 46 19N 23 44 E
Aix-en-Provence, France 21 E9 43 32N 5 27 E
Aix-la-Chapelle = Aachen, Germany 24 E2 50 45N 6 6 E
Aix-les-Bains, France 21 C9 45 41N 5 53 E
Aixe-sur-Vienne, France 20 C5 45 47N 1 9 E
Aíyina, Greece 38 D5 37 45N 23 26 E
Aiyínion, Greece 40 F6 40 28N 22 28 E
Aíyion, Greece 38 C4 38 15N 22 5 E
Aizawl, India 67 H18 23 40N 92 44 E
Aizenay, France 18 F5 46 44N 1 38W
Aizkraukle, Latvia 9 H21 56 36N 25 11 E
Aizpute, Latvia 9 H19 56 43N 21 40 E
Aizuwakamatsu, Japan 54 F9 37 30N 139 56 E
Ajaccio, France 21 G12 41 55N 8 40 E
Ajaccio, G. d', France 21 G12 41 52N 8 40 E
Ajaigarh, India 69 G9 24 52N 80 16 E
Ajalpan, Mexico 119 D5 18 22N 97 15W
Ajanta Ra., India 66 J9 20 28N 75 50 E
Ajari Rep. = Ajaria □, Georgia 49 K6 41 30N 42 0 E
Ajaria □, Georgia 49 K6 41 30N 42 0 E
Ajax, Canada 110 C5 43 50N 79 1W
Ajdâbiyah, Libya 79 B10 30 54N 20 4 E
Ajdovščina, Slovenia 29 C10 45 54N 13 54 E
Ajibar, Ethiopia 81 E4 10 35N 38 36 E
Ajka, Hungary 42 C2 47 4N 17 31 E
'Ajmān, U.A.E. 71 E7 25 25N 55 30 E
Ajmer, India 68 F6 26 28N 74 37 E
Ajnala, India 68 D6 31 50N 74 48 E
Ajo, U.S.A. 115 K7 32 22N 112 52W
Ajo, C. de, Spain 34 B7 43 31N 3 35W
Ajok, Sudan 81 F2 9 15N 28 28 E
Ajuy, Phil. 61 F5 11 10N 123 1 E
Ak Dağ, Turkey 39 E11 36 30N 29 32 E
Ak Dağları, Muğla, Turkey 39 E11 36 30N 29 30 E
Ak Dağları, Sivas, Turkey 72 C7 39 32N 36 12 E
Akaba, Togo 83 D5 8 10N 1 2 E
Akabira, Japan 54 C11 43 33N 142 5 E
Akaki Beseka, Ethiopia 81 F4 8 55N 38 45 E
Akala, Sudan 81 D4 15 39N 36 13 E
Akamas □, Cyprus 36 D11 35 3N 32 18 E
Akanthou, Cyprus 36 D12 35 22N 33 45 E
Akarca, Turkey 39 C11 38 35N 29 35 E
Akaroa, N.Z. 91 K4 43 49 S 172 59 E
Akasha, Sudan 80 C3 21 10N 30 32 E
Akashi, Japan 55 G7 34 45N 134 58 E
Akbarpur, Bihar, India 69 G10 24 39N 83 58 E
Akbarpur, Ut. P., India 69 F10 26 25N 82 32 E
Akçaabat, Turkey 73 B8 41 1N 39 34 E
Akçadağ, Turkey 72 C7 38 27N 37 43 E
Akçakale, Turkey 73 D8 36 41N 38 56 E
Akçakoca, Turkey 72 B4 41 5N 31 8 E
Akçaova, Turkey 41 E13 41 2N 29 57 E
Akçay, Turkey 39 E11 36 36N 29 45 E
Akçay →, Turkey 39 D10 37 50N 28 15 E
Akdağ, Turkey 39 C8 38 33N 26 30 E
Akdağmadeni, Turkey 72 C6 39 39N 35 53 E
Akelamo, Indonesia 63 D7 1 35N 129 40 E
Åkers styckebruk, Sweden 10 E11 59 15N 17 5 E
Åkersberga, Sweden 10 E12 59 29N 18 18 E
Aketi, Dem. Rep. of the Congo 84 D4 2 38N 23 47 E
Akhaïa □, Greece 38 C3 38 5N 21 45 E
Akhalkalaki, Georgia 49 K6 41 27N 43 25 E
Akhaltsikhe, Georgia 49 K6 41 40N 43 0 E
Akharnaí, Greece 38 C5 38 5N 23 44 E
Akhelóös →, Greece 38 C3 38 19N 21 7 E
Akhendriá, Greece 39 G7 34 59N 25 16 E
Akhisar, Turkey 39 C9 38 56N 27 48 E
Akhladhókambos, Greece 38 D4 37 31N 22 35 E
Akhmîm, Egypt 80 B3 26 31N 31 47 E
Akhnur, India 69 C6 32 52N 74 45 E
Akhtopol, Bulgaria 41 D11 42 6N 27 56 E
Akhtuba →, Russia 49 G8 47 41N 46 55 E
Akhtubinsk, Russia 49 F8 48 13N 46 7 E
Akhty, Russia 49 K8 41 30N 47 45 E
Akhtyrka = Okhtyrka, Ukraine 47 G8 50 25N 35 0 E
Aki, Japan 55 H6 33 30N 133 54 E
Akimiski I., Canada 102 B3 52 50N 81 30W
Akimovka, Ukraine 47 J8 46 44N 35 0 E
Åkirkeby, Denmark 11 J8 55 4N 14 55 E
Akita, Japan 54 E10 39 45N 140 7 E
Akita □, Japan 54 E10 39 40N 140 30 E
Akjoujt, Mauritania 82 B2 19 45N 14 15W
Akka, Mali 82 B4 15 24N 4 11W
Akkaya Tepesi, Turkey 39 D11 37 25N 29 38 E
Akkeshi, Japan 54 C12 43 2N 144 51 E
'Akko, Israel 75 C4 32 55N 35 4 E
Akköy, Turkey 39 D9 37 29N 27 15 E
Aklampa, Benin 83 D5 8 15N 2 10 E
Aklavik, Canada 100 B6 68 12N 135 0W
Aklera, India 68 G7 24 26N 76 32 E
Akmenė, Lithuania 44 B9 56 15N 22 45 E
Akmenrags, Latvia 44 B8 56 50N 21 4 E
Akmolinsk = Astana, Kazakstan 50 D8 51 10N 71 30 E
Akmonte = Almonte, Spain 35 H4 37 13N 6 38W
Akō, Japan 55 G7 34 45N 134 24 E
Ako, Nigeria 83 C7 10 19N 10 48 E
Akôbô, Sudan 81 F3 7 47N 33 1 E
Akobo →, Ethiopia 81 F3 7 48N 33 3 E
Akola, India 66 J10 20 42N 77 2 E
Akonolinga, Cameroon 83 E7 3 50N 12 18 E
Akor, Mali 82 C3 14 59N 6 58W
Akordat, Eritrea 81 D4 15 30N 37 40 E
Akosombo Dam, Ghana 83 D5 6 20N 0 5 E
Akot, Sudan 81 F3 6 31N 30 9 E
Akoupé, Ivory C. 82 D4 6 23N 3 54W
Akpatok I., Canada 101 B13 60 25N 68 8W
Åkrahamn, Norway 9 G11 59 15N 5 10 E
Akranes, Iceland 8 D2 64 19N 22 5W
Akreïjit, Mauritania 82 B3 18 19N 9 11W
Akrítas Venétiko, Ákra, Greece 38 E3 36 43N 21 54 E
Akron, Colo., U.S.A. 112 E3 40 10N 103 13W
Akron, Ohio, U.S.A. 110 E3 41 5N 81 31W
Akrotiri, Cyprus 36 E11 34 36N 32 57 E
Akrotíri, Ákra, Greece 41 F9 40 26N 25 27 E
Akrotiri Bay, Cyprus 36 E12 34 35N 33 10 E
Aksai Chin, India 69 B8 35 15N 79 55 E
Aksaray, Turkey 70 B2 38 25N 34 2 E
Aksay, Kazakstan 50 D6 51 11N 53 0 E
Akşehir, Turkey 70 B1 38 18N 31 30 E
Akşehir Gölü, Turkey 72 C4 38 30N 31 25 E
Akstafa = Ağstafa, Azerbaijan 49 K7 41 7N 45 27 E
Aksu, China 60 B3 41 5N 80 10 E
Aksu →, Turkey 72 D4 36 52N 30 57 E
Aksum, Ethiopia 81 E4 14 5N 38 40 E
Aktash, Russia 48 C11 55 2N 52 0 E
Aktogay, Kazakstan 50 E8 46 57N 79 40 E
Aktsyabrski, Belarus 47 F5 52 38N 28 53 E
Aktyubinsk = Aqtöbe, Kazakstan 50 D6 50 17N 57 10 E
Aku, Nigeria 83 D6 6 40N 7 18 E
Akure, Nigeria 83 D6 7 15N 5 5 E
Akureyri, Iceland 8 D4 65 40N 18 6W
Akuseki-Shima, Japan 55 K4 29 27N 129 37 E
Akusha, Russia 49 J8 42 18N 47 30 E
Akwa-Ibom □, Nigeria 83 E6 4 30N 7 30 E
Akyab = Sittwe, Burma 67 J18 20 18N 92 45 E
Akyazı, Turkey 72 B4 40 40N 30 38 E
Al 'Adan, Yemen 74 E4 12 45N 45 0 E
Al Aḩsā = Hasa □, Si. Arabia 71 E6 25 50N 49 0 E
Al Ajfar, Si. Arabia 70 E4 27 26N 43 0 E
Al Amādīyah, Iraq 70 B4 37 5N 43 30 E
Al 'Amārah, Iraq 70 D5 31 55N 47 15 E
Al 'Aqabah, Jordan 75 F4 29 31N 35 0 E
Al Arak, Syria 70 C3 34 38N 38 35 E
Al 'Aramah, Si. Arabia 70 E5 25 30N 46 0 E
Al Arţāwīyah, Si. Arabia 70 E5 26 31N 45 20 E
Al 'Āşimah = 'Ammān □, Jordan 75 D5 31 40N 36 30 E
Al 'Assāfīyah, Si. Arabia 70 D3 28 17N 38 59 E
Al 'Ayn, Oman 71 E7 24 15N 55 45 E
Al 'Ayn, Si. Arabia 70 E3 25 4N 38 6 E
Al 'Azamīyah, Iraq 70 C5 33 22N 44 22 E
Al 'Azīzīyah, Iraq 70 C5 32 54N 45 4 E
Al Bāb, Syria 70 B3 36 23N 37 29 E
Al Bad', Si. Arabia 70 D2 28 28N 35 1 E
Al Bādī, Iraq 70 C4 35 56N 41 32 E
Al Baḩrah, Kuwait 70 D5 29 40N 47 52 E
Al Baḩral Mayyit = Dead Sea, Asia 75 D4 31 30N 35 30 E
Al Balqā' □, Jordan 75 C4 32 5N 35 45 E
Al Bārūk, J., Lebanon 75 B4 33 39N 35 40 E
Al Başrah, Iraq 70 D5 30 30N 47 50 E
Al Baţḩā, Iraq 70 D5 31 6N 45 53 E
Al Batrūn, Lebanon 75 A4 34 15N 35 40 E
Al Bayḑā, Libya 79 B10 32 50N 21 44 E
Al Biqā, Lebanon 75 A5 34 10N 36 10 E
Al Bi'r, Si. Arabia 70 D3 28 51N 36 16 E
Al Burayj, Syria 75 A5 34 15N 36 46 E
Al Faḑilī, Si. Arabia 71 E6 26 58N 49 10 E
Al Fallūjah, Iraq 70 C4 33 20N 43 55 E
Al Fāw, Iraq 71 D6 30 0N 48 30 E
Al Fujayrah, U.A.E. 71 E8 25 7N 56 18 E
Al Ghadaf, W. →, Jordan 75 D5 31 26N 36 43 E
Al Ghammās, Iraq 70 D5 31 45N 44 37 E
Al Ghazālah, Si. Arabia 70 E4 26 48N 41 19 E
Al Ḩābah, Si. Arabia 70 E5 27 10N 47 0 E
Al Ḩadīthah, Iraq 70 C4 34 0N 41 13 E
Al Ḩadīthah, Si. Arabia 75 D6 31 28N 37 8 E
Al Ḩaḑr, Iraq 70 C4 35 35N 42 44 E
Al Ḩājānah, Syria 75 B5 33 20N 36 33 E
Al Hajar al Gharbi, Oman 71 E8 24 10N 56 15 E
Al Ḩāmad, Si. Arabia 70 D3 31 30N 39 30 E
Al Hamdānīyah, Syria 70 C3 35 25N 36 50 E
Al Ḩamīdīyah, Syria 75 A4 34 42N 35 57 E
Al Ḩammār, Iraq 70 D5 30 57N 46 51 E
Al Ḩamrā', Si. Arabia 70 E3 24 2N 38 55 E
Al Ḩanākīyah, Si. Arabia 70 E4 24 51N 40 31 E
Al Harīr, W. →, Syria 75 C4 32 44N 35 59 E
Al Ḩasā, W. →, Jordan 75 D4 31 4N 35 29 E
Al Ḩasakah, Syria 70 B4 36 35N 40 45 E
Al Haydān, W. →, Jordan 75 D4 31 29N 35 34 E
Al Ḩayy, Iraq 70 C5 32 5N 46 5 E
Al Ḩijārah, Asia 70 D4 30 25N 44 30 E
Al Ḩillah, Iraq 70 C5 32 30N 44 25 E
Al Hindīyah, Iraq 70 C5 32 30N 44 10 E
Al Hirmil, Lebanon 75 A5 34 26N 36 24 E
Al Hoceïma, Morocco 78 A5 35 8N 3 58W
Al Ḩudaydah, Yemen 74 E3 14 50N 43 0 E
Al Hufūf, Si. Arabia 71 E6 25 25N 49 45 E
Al Ḩumayḑah, Si. Arabia 70 D2 29 14N 34 56 E
Al Ḩunayy, Si. Arabia 71 E6 25 58N 48 45 E
Al Īsāwīyah, Si. Arabia 70 D3 30 43N 37 59 E
Al Jafr, Jordan 75 E5 30 18N 36 14 E
Al Jāfūrah, Si. Arabia 71 E7 25 0N 50 15 E
Al Jaghbūb, Libya 79 C10 29 42N 24 38 E
Al Jahrah, Kuwait 70 D5 29 25N 47 40 E
Al Jalāmīd, Si. Arabia 70 D3 31 20N 40 6 E
Al Jamalīyah, Qatar 71 E6 25 37N 51 5 E
Al Janūb □, Lebanon 75 B4 33 20N 35 20 E
Al Jawf, Libya 79 D10 24 10N 23 24 E
Al Jawf, Si. Arabia 70 D3 29 55N 39 40 E
Al Jazirah, Iraq 70 C5 33 30N 44 0 E
Al Jithāmīyah, Si. Arabia 70 E4 27 41N 41 43 E
Al Jubayl, Si. Arabia 71 E6 27 0N 49 50 E
Al Jubaylah, Si. Arabia 70 E5 24 55N 46 25 E
Al Jubb, Si. Arabia 70 E4 27 11N 42 17 E
Al Junaynah, Sudan 79 F10 13 27N 22 45 E
Al Kabā'ish, Iraq 70 D5 30 58N 47 0 E
Al Karak, Jordan 75 D4 31 11N 35 42 E
Al Karak □, Jordan 75 E5 31 0N 36 0 E
Al Kāzim Tyah, Iraq 70 C5 33 22N 44 12 E
Al Khābūra, Oman 71 F8 23 57N 57 5 E
Al Khafji, Si. Arabia 71 E6 28 24N 48 29 E
Al Khalīl, West Bank 75 D4 31 32N 35 6 E
Al Khāliş, Iraq 70 C5 33 49N 44 32 E
Al Kharsānīyah, Si. Arabia 71 E6 27 13N 49 18 E
Al Khaşab, Oman 71 E8 26 14N 56 15 E
Al Khawr, Qatar 71 E6 25 41N 51 30 E
Al Khiḑr, Iraq 70 D5 31 12N 45 33 E
Al Khiyām, Lebanon 75 B4 33 20N 35 36 E
Al Khums, Libya 79 B8 32 40N 14 17 E
Al Kiswah, Syria 75 B5 33 23N 36 14 E
Al Kūfah, Iraq 70 C5 32 2N 44 24 E
Al Kufrah, Libya 79 D10 24 17N 23 15 E
Al Kuhayfīyah, Si. Arabia 70 E4 27 12N 43 3 E
Al Kūt, Iraq 70 C5 32 30N 46 0 E
Al Kuwayt, Kuwait 70 D5 29 30N 48 0 E
Al Labwah, Lebanon 75 A5 34 11N 36 20 E
Al Lādhiqīyah, Syria 70 C2 35 30N 35 45 E
Al Līth, Si. Arabia 74 C3 20 9N 40 15 E
Al Liwā', Oman 71 E8 24 31N 56 36 E
Al Luḩayyah, Yemen 74 D3 15 45N 42 40 E
Al Madīnah, Iraq 70 D5 30 57N 47 16 E
Al Madīnah, Si. Arabia 70 E3 24 35N 39 52 E
Al Mafraq, Jordan 75 C5 32 17N 36 14 E
Al Maḩmūdīyah, Iraq 70 C5 33 3N 44 21 E
Al Majma'ah, Si. Arabia 70 E5 25 57N 45 22 E
Al Makhruq, W. →, Jordan 75 D6 31 28N 37 0 E
Al Makḩūl, Si. Arabia 70 E4 26 37N 42 39 E
Al Manāmah, Bahrain 71 E6 26 10N 50 30 E
Al Maqwa', Kuwait 70 D5 29 10N 47 59 E
Al Marj, Libya 79 B10 32 25N 20 30 E
Al Maţlā, Kuwait 70 D5 29 24N 47 40 E
Al Mawjib, W. →, Jordan 75 D4 31 28N 35 36 E
Al Mawşil, Iraq 70 B4 36 15N 43 5 E
Al Mayādin, Syria 70 C4 35 1N 40 27 E
Al Mazār, Jordan 75 D4 31 4N 35 41 E
Al Midhnab, Si. Arabia 70 E5 25 50N 44 18 E
Al Minā', Lebanon 75 A4 34 24N 35 49 E
Al Miqdādīyah, Iraq 70 C5 34 0N 45 0 E
Al Mubarraz, Si. Arabia 71 E6 25 30N 49 40 E
Al Mudawwarah, Jordan 75 F5 29 19N 36 0 E
Al Mughayrā', U.A.E. 71 E7 24 5N 53 32 E
Al Muḩarraq, Bahrain 71 E6 26 15N 50 40 E
Al Mukallā, Yemen 74 E4 14 33N 49 2 E
Al Mukhā, Yemen 74 E3 13 18N 43 15 E
Al Musayjīd, Si. Arabia 70 E3 24 5N 39 5 E
Al Musayyib, Iraq 70 C5 32 49N 44 20 E
Al Muwayh, Si. Arabia 80 C5 22 41N 41 37 E
Al Muwayliḩ, Si. Arabia 70 E2 27 40N 35 30 E
Al Owuho = Otukpa, Nigeria 83 D6 7 9N 7 41 E
Al Qā'im, Iraq 70 C4 34 21N 41 7 E
Al Qalībah, Si. Arabia 70 D3 28 24N 37 42 E
Al Qāmishlī, Syria 70 B4 37 2N 41 14 E
Al Qaryatayn, Syria 75 A6 34 12N 37 13 E
Al Qaşīm, Si. Arabia 70 E4 26 0N 43 0 E
Al Qaţ'ā, Syria 70 C4 34 40N 40 48 E
Al Qaţīf, Si. Arabia 71 E6 26 35N 50 0 E
Al Qatrānah, Jordan 75 D5 31 12N 36 6 E
Al Qaţrūn, Libya 79 D9 24 56N 15 3 E
Al Qayşūmah, Si. Arabia 70 D5 28 20N 46 7 E
Al Quds = Jerusalem, Israel 75 D4 31 47N 35 10 E
Al Qunayţirah, Syria 75 C4 32 55N 35 45 E
Al Qunfudhah, Si. Arabia 80 D5 19 3N 41 4 E
Al Qurnah, Iraq 70 D5 31 1N 47 25 E
Al Quşayr, Iraq 70 D5 30 39N 45 50 E
Al Quşayr, Syria 75 A5 34 31N 36 34 E
Al Qutayfah, Syria 75 B5 33 44N 36 36 E
Al 'Ubaylah, Si. Arabia 74 C5 21 59N 50 57 E
Al 'Uḑayliyah, Si. Arabia 71 E6 25 8N 49 18 E
Al 'Ulā, Si. Arabia 70 E3 26 35N 38 0 E
Al 'Uqayr, Si. Arabia 71 E6 25 40N 50 15 E
Al 'Uthmānīyah, Si. Arabia 71 E6 25 5N 49 22 E
Al 'Uwaynid, Si. Arabia 70 E5 24 50N 46 0 E
Al 'Uwayqīlah, Si. Arabia 70 D4 30 30N 42 10 E
Al 'Uyūn, Ḩijāz, Si. Arabia 70 E3 24 33N 39 35 E
Al 'Uyūn, Najd, Si. Arabia 70 E4 26 30N 43 50 E
Al 'Uzayr, Iraq 70 D5 31 19N 47 25 E
Al Wajh, Si. Arabia 70 E3 26 10N 36 30 E
Al Wakrah, Qatar 71 E6 25 10N 51 40 E
Al Wannān, Si. Arabia 71 E6 26 55N 48 24 E
Al Waqbah, Si. Arabia 70 D5 28 48N 45 33 E
Al Wari'āh, Si. Arabia 70 E5 27 51N 47 25 E
Al Wusayl, Qatar 71 E6 25 29N 51 29 E
Ala, Italy 28 C8 45 45N 11 0 E
Ala Dağ, Turkey 70 B2 37 44N 35 9 E
Ala Dağları, Turkey 73 C10 39 15N 43 33 E
Alabama □, U.S.A. 109 J2 33 0N 87 0W
Alabama →, U.S.A. 109 K2 31 8N 87 57W
Alabaster, U.S.A. 109 J2 33 15N 86 49W
Alaca, Turkey 72 B6 40 10N 34 51 E
Alacaatlı, Turkey 39 B10 39 15N 28 3 E
Alaçam, Turkey 72 B6 41 36N 35 36 E
Alaçam Dağları, Turkey 39 B10 39 18N 28 49 E
Alaçatı, Turkey 39 C8 38 15N 26 22 E
Alachua, U.S.A. 109 L4 29 47N 82 30W
Alaejos, Spain 34 D5 41 18N 5 13W
Alaérma, Greece 36 C9 36 9N 27 57 E
Alagir, Russia 49 J7 43 3N 44 14 E
Alagna Valsésia, Italy 28 C4 45 51N 7 56 E
Alagoa Grande, Brazil 125 E11 7 3 S 35 35W
Alagoas □, Brazil 125 E11 9 0 S 36 0W
Alagoinhas, Brazil 125 F11 12 7 S 38 20W
Alagón, Spain 32 D3 41 46N 1 12W
Alagón →, Spain 34 F4 39 44N 6 53W
Alaior, Spain 37 B11 39 57N 4 8 E
Alajero, Canary Is. 37 F2 28 3N 17 13W
Alajuela, Costa Rica 120 D3 10 2N 84 8W
Alakamisy, Madag. 89 C8 21 19 S 47 14 E
Alaknanda →, India 69 D8 30 8N 78 36 E
Alamarvdasht, Iran 71 E7 27 37N 52 59 E
Alamata, Ethiopia 81 E4 12 25N 39 33 E
Alameda, Calif., U.S.A. 116 H4 37 46N 122 15W
Alameda, N. Mex., U.S.A. 115 J10 35 11N 106 37W
Alaminos, Phil. 61 C3 16 10N 119 59 E
Alamo, U.S.A. 117 J11 37 22N 115 10W
Alamo Crossing, U.S.A. 117 L13 34 16N 113 33W
Alamogordo, U.S.A. 115 K11 32 54N 105 57W
Alamos, Mexico 118 B3 27 0N 109 0W
Alamosa, U.S.A. 115 H11 37 28N 105 52W
Åland, Finland 9 F19 60 15N 20 0 E
Alandroal, Portugal 35 G3 38 41N 7 24W
Ålands hav, Sweden 9 F18 60 0N 19 30 E
Alandur, India 66 N12 13 0N 80 15 E
Alange, Presa de, Spain 35 G4 38 45N 6 18W
Alania = North Ossetia □, Russia 49 J7 43 30N 44 30 E
Alanís, Spain 35 G5 38 3N 5 43W
Alanya, Turkey 70 B1 36 38N 32 0 E
Alaotra, Farihin', Madag. 89 B8 17 30 S 48 30 E
Alapayevsk, Russia 50 D7 57 52N 61 42 E
Alar del Rey, Spain 34 C6 42 38N 4 20W
Alaraz, Spain 34 E5 40 45N 5 17W
Alarcón, Embalse de, Spain 32 F2 39 36N 2 10W
Alarobia-Vohiposa, Madag. 89 C8 20 59 S 47 9 E
Alaşehir, Turkey 39 C10 38 23N 28 30 E
Alaska □, U.S.A. 100 B5 64 0N 154 0W
Alaska, G. of, Pac. Oc. 100 C5 58 0N 145 0W
Alaska Peninsula, U.S.A. 100 C4 56 0N 159 0W
Alaska Range, U.S.A. 100 B4 62 50N 151 0W
Alássio, Italy 28 E5 44 0N 8 10 E
Älät, Azerbaijan 49 L9 39 58N 49 25 E
Alatri, Italy 29 G10 41 43N 13 21 E
Alatyr, Russia 48 C8 54 55N 46 35 E
Alatyr →, Russia 48 C8 54 52N 46 36 E
Alausi, Ecuador 124 D3 2 0 S 78 50W
Álava □, Spain 32 C2 42 48N 2 28W
Alava, C., U.S.A. 114 B1 48 10N 124 44W
Alaverdi, Armenia 49 K7 41 15N 44 37 E
Alavus, Finland 9 E20 62 35N 23 36 E
Alawoona, Australia 95 E3 34 45 S 140 30 E
'Alayh, Lebanon 75 B4 33 46N 35 33 E
Alazani →, Azerbaijan 49 K8 41 5N 46 40 E
Alba, Italy 28 D5 44 42N 8 2 E
Alba □, Romania 43 D8 46 10N 23 30 E
Alba Adriática, Italy 29 F10 42 50N 13 56 E
Alba de Tormes, Spain 34 E5 40 50N 5 30W
Alba-Iulia, Romania 43 D8 46 8N 23 39 E
Albac, Romania 42 D7 46 28N 22 58 E
Albacete, Spain 33 F3 39 0N 1 50W
Albacete □, Spain 33 G3 38 50N 2 0W
Albacutya, L., Australia 95 F3 35 45 S 141 58 E
Ålbæk, Denmark 11 G4 57 36N 10 25 E
Ålbæk Bugt, Denmark 11 G4 57 35N 10 40 E
Albaida, Spain 33 G4 38 51N 0 31W
Albalate de las Nogueras, Spain 32 E2 40 22N 2 18W
Albalate del Arzobispo, Spain 32 D4 41 6N 0 31W
Alban, France 20 E6 43 53N 2 28 E
Albanel, L., Canada 102 B5 50 55N 73 12W
Albania ■, Europe 40 E4 41 0N 20 0 E
Albano Laziale, Italy 29 G9 41 44N 12 39 E
Albany, Australia 93 G2 35 1 S 117 58 E
Albany, Ga., U.S.A. 109 K3 31 35N 84 10W
Albany, N.Y., U.S.A. 111 D11 42 39N 73 45W
Albany, Oreg., U.S.A. 114 D2 44 38N 123 6W
Albany, Tex., U.S.A. 113 J5 32 44N 99 18W
Albany →, Canada 102 B3 52 17N 81 31W
Albardón, Argentina 126 C2 31 20 S 68 30W
Albarracín, Spain 32 E3 40 25N 1 26W
Albarracín, Sierra de, Spain 32 E3 40 30N 1 30W
Albatera, Spain 33 G4 38 11N 0 52W
Albatross B., Australia 94 A3 12 45 S 141 30 E
Albegna →, Italy 29 F8 42 30N 11 11 E
Albemarle, U.S.A. 109 H5 35 21N 80 11W
Albemarle Sd., U.S.A. 109 H7 36 5N 76 0W
Albenga, Italy 28 D5 44 3N 8 13 E
Alberche →, Spain 34 F6 39 58N 4 46W
Alberdi, Paraguay 126 B4 26 14 S 58 20W
Alberes, Mts., France 20 F6 42 28N 2 56 E
Ålberga, Sweden 11 F10 58 44N 16 35 E
Albersdorf, Germany 24 A5 54 8N 9 17 E
Albert, France 19 C9 50 0N 2 38 E
Albert, L., Australia 95 F2 35 30 S 139 10 E
Albert Edward Ra., Australia 92 C4 18 17 S 127 57 E
Albert L., Africa 86 B3 1 30N 31 0 E
Albert Lea, U.S.A. 112 D8 43 39N 93 22W
Albert Nile →, Uganda 86 B3 3 36N 32 2 E
Albert Town, Bahamas 121 B5 22 37N 74 33W
Alberta □, Canada 104 C6 54 40N 115 0W
Alberti, Argentina 126 D3 35 1 S 60 16W
Albertinia, S. Africa 88 E3 34 11 S 21 34 E
Albertirsa, Hungary 42 C4 47 14N 19 37 E
Alberton, Canada 103 C7 46 50N 64 0W
Albertville = Kalemie, Dem. Rep. of the Congo 86 D2 5 55 S 29 9 E
Albertville, France 21 C10 45 40N 6 22 E
Albertville, U.S.A. 109 H2 34 16N 86 13W
Albi, France 20 E6 43 56N 2 9 E
Albia, U.S.A. 112 E8 41 2N 92 48W
Albina, Surinam 125 B8 5 37N 54 15W
Albina, Ponta, Angola 88 B1 15 52 S 11 44 E
Albino, Italy 28 C6 45 46N 9 47 E
Albion, Mich., U.S.A. 108 D3 42 15N 84 45W
Albion, Nebr., U.S.A. 112 E6 41 42N 98 0W
Albion, Pa., U.S.A. 110 E4 41 53N 80 22W
Albocácer, Spain 32 E5 40 21N 0 1 E
Albolote, Spain 35 H7 37 14N 3 39W
Alborán, Medit. S. 35 K7 35 57N 3 0W
Alborea, Spain 33 F3 39 17N 1 24W
Ålborg, Denmark 11 G3 57 2N 9 54 E
Ålborg Bugt, Denmark 11 H4 56 50N 10 35 E
Alborz, Reshteh-ye Kūhhā-ye, Iran 71 C7 36 0N 52 0 E
Albox, Spain 33 H2 37 23N 2 8W
Albufeira, Portugal 35 H2 37 5N 8 15W
Albula →, Switz. 25 J5 46 38N 9 28 E
Albuñol, Spain 35 J7 36 48N 3 11W
Albuquerque, U.S.A. 115 J10 35 5N 106 39W
Albuquerque, Cayos de, Caribbean 120 D3 12 10N 81 50W
Alburg, U.S.A. 111 B11 44 59N 73 18W
Alburno, Mte., Italy 31 B8 40 33N 15 17 E
Alburquerque, Spain 35 F4 39 15N 6 59W
Albury-Wodonga, Australia 95 F4 36 3 S 146 56 E
Alcácer do Sal, Portugal 35 G2 38 22N 8 33W
Alcáçovas, Portugal 35 G2 38 23N 8 9W
Alcalá de Chivert, Spain 32 E5 40 19N 0 13 E
Alcalá de Guadaira, Spain 35 H5 37 20N 5 50W
Alcalá de Henares, Spain 34 E7 40 28N 3 22W
Alcalá de los Gazules, Spain 35 J5 36 29N 5 43W
Alcalá del Júcar, Spain 33 F3 39 12N 1 26W
Alcalá del Río, Spain 35 H5 37 31N 5 59W
Alcalá del Valle, Spain 35 J5 36 54N 5 10W
Alcalá la Real, Spain 35 H7 37 27N 3 57W
Álcamo, Italy 30 E5 37 59N 12 55 E
Alcanadre, Spain 32 C2 42 24N 2 7W
Alcanadre →, Spain 32 D4 41 43N 0 12W
Alcanar, Spain 32 E5 40 33N 0 28 E
Alcanede, Portugal 35 F2 39 25N 8 49W
Alcanena, Portugal 35 F2 39 27N 8 40W
Alcañices, Spain 34 D4 41 41N 6 21W
Alcañiz, Spain 32 D4 41 2N 0 8W
Alcântara, Brazil 125 D10 2 20 S 44 30W
Alcántara, Spain 34 F4 39 41N 6 57W
Alcántara, Embalse de, Spain 34 F4 39 44N 6 50W
Alcantarilla, Spain 33 H3 37 59N 1 12W
Alcaracejos, Spain 35 G6 38 24N 4 58W
Alcaraz, Spain 33 G2 38 40N 2 29W
Alcaraz, Sierra de, Spain 33 G2 38 40N 2 20W
Alcaudete, Spain 35 H6 37 35N 4 5W
Alcázar de San Juan, Spain 35 F7 39 24N 3 12W
Alchevsk, Ukraine 47 H10 48 30N 38 45 E
Alcira = Alzira, Spain 33 F4 39 9N 0 30W
Alcobaça, Portugal 35 F2 39 32N 8 58W
Alcobendas, Spain 34 E7 40 32N 3 38W
Alcolea del Pinar, Spain 32 D2 41 2N 2 28W
Alcora, Spain 32 E4 40 5N 0 14W
Alcorcón, Spain 34 E7 40 20N 3 50W
Alcoutim, Portugal 35 H3 37 25N 7 28W
Alcova, U.S.A. 114 E10 42 34N 106 43W
Alcoy, Spain 33 G4 38 43N 0 30W
Alcubierre, Sierra de, Spain 32 D4 41 45N 0 22W
Alcublas, Spain 32 F4 39 48N 0 43W
Alcúdia, Spain 37 B10 39 51N 3 7 E
Alcúdia, B. d', Spain 37 B10 39 47N 3 15 E
Alcudia, Sierra de la, Spain 35 G6 38 34N 4 30W
Aldabra Is., Seychelles 77 G8 9 22 S 46 28 E
Aldama, Mexico 119 C5 23 0N 98 4W
Aldan, Russia 51 D13 58 40N 125 30 E
Aldan →, Russia 51 C13 63 28N 129 35 E
Aldea, Pta. de la, Canary Is. 37 G4 28 0N 15 50W
Aldeburgh, U.K. 13 E9 52 10N 1 37 E
Alder Pk., U.S.A. 116 K5 35 53N 121 22W
Alderney, U.K. 13 H5 49 42N 2 11W
Aldershot, U.K. 13 F7 51 15N 0 44W
Åled, Sweden 11 H6 56 44N 12 57 E
Aledo, U.S.A. 112 E9 41 12N 90 45W
Alefa, Ethiopia 81 E4 11 55N 36 55 E
Aleg, Mauritania 82 B2 17 3N 13 55W
Alegranza, Canary Is. 37 E6 29 23N 13 32W
Alegranza, I., Canary Is. 37 E6 29 23N 13 32W
Alegre, Brazil 127 A7 20 50 S 41 30W
Alegrete, Brazil 127 B4 29 40 S 56 0W
Aleisk, Russia 50 D9 52 40N 83 0 E
Aleksandriya = Oleksandriya, Kirovohrad, Ukraine 47 H7 48 42N 33 3 E
Aleksandriya = Oleksandriya, Rivne, Ukraine 47 G4 50 37N 26 19 E
Aleksandriyskaya, Russia 49 J8 43 58N 47 14 E
Aleksandrov, Russia 46 D10 56 23N 38 44 E
Aleksandrov Gay, Russia 48 E9 50 9N 48 34 E
Aleksandrovac, Serbia, Yug. 40 C5 43 28N 21 3 E
Aleksandrovac, Serbia, Yug. 40 B5 44 28N 21 13 E
Aleksandrovka = Oleksandrovka, Ukraine 47 H7 48 55N 32 20 E
Aleksandrovo, Bulgaria 41 C8 43 14N 24 51 E
Aleksandrovsk-Sakhalinskiy, Russia 51 D15 50 50N 142 20 E
Aleksandrów Kujawski, Poland 45 F5 52 53N 18 43 E
Aleksandrów Łódźki, Poland 45 G6 51 49N 19 17 E
Alekseyevka, Samara, Russia 48 D10 52 35N 51 17 E
Alekseyevka, Voronezh, Russia 47 G10 50 43N 38 40 E
Aleksin, Russia 46 E9 54 31N 37 9 E
Aleksinac, Serbia, Yug. 40 C5 43 31N 21 42 E
Além Paraíba, Brazil 127 A7 21 52 S 42 41W
Alemania, Argentina 126 B2 25 40 S 65 30W
Alemania, Chile 126 B2 25 10 S 69 55W
Alençon, France 18 D7 48 27N 0 4 E
Alenquer, Brazil 125 D8 1 56 S 54 46W
Alenuihaha Channel, U.S.A. 106 H17 20 30N 156 0W
Alépé, Ivory C. 82 D4 5 29N 3 40W
Aleppo = Ḩalab, Syria 70 B3 36 10N 37 15 E
Aléria, France 21 F13 42 5N 9 26 E
Alès, France 21 D8 44 9N 4 5 E
Aleşd, Romania 42 C7 47 3N 22 22 E
Alessándria, Italy 28 D5 44 54N 8 37 E
Ålestrup, Denmark 11 H3 56 42N 9 29 E
Ålesund, Norway 9 E12 62 28N 6 12 E
Alet-les-Bains, France 20 F6 42 59N 2 14 E
Aletschhorn, Switz. 25 J4 46 28N 8 0 E
Aleutian Is., Pac. Oc. 100 C2 52 0N 175 0W
Aleutian Trench, Pac. Oc. 96 C10 48 0N 180 0 E
Alexander, U.S.A. 112 B3 47 51N 103 39W
Alexander, Mt., Australia 93 E3 28 58 S 120 16 E
Alexander Arch., U.S.A. 100 C6 56 0N 136 0W
Alexander Bay, S. Africa 88 D2 28 40 S 16 30 E
Alexander City, U.S.A. 109 J3 32 56N 85 58W
Alexander I., Antarctica 5 C17 69 0 S 70 0W
Alexandra, Australia 95 F4 37 8 S 145 40 E
Alexandra, N.Z. 91 L2 45 14 S 169 25 E
Alexandra Falls, Canada 104 A5 60 29N 116 18W
Alexandria = El Iskandarîya, Egypt 80 H7 31 13N 29 58 E

Alexandria, *B.C., Canada* **104 C4** 52 35N 122 27W
Alexandria, *Ont., Canada* **102 C5** 45 19N 74 38W
Alexandria, *Romania* **43 G10** 43 57N 25 24 E
Alexandria, *S. Africa* **88 E4** 33 38 S 26 28 E
Alexandria, *U.K.* **14 F4** 55 59N 4 35W
Alexandria, *La., U.S.A.* **113 K8** 31 18N 92 27W
Alexandria, *Minn., U.S.A.* **112 C7** 45 53N 95 22W
Alexandria, *S. Dak., U.S.A.* **112 D6** 43 39N 97 47W
Alexandria, *Va., U.S.A.* **108 F7** 38 48N 77 3W
Alexandria Bay, *U.S.A.* **111 B9** 44 20N 75 55W
Alexandrina, L., *Australia* **95 F2** 35 25 S 139 10 E
Alexandroúpolis, *Greece* **41 F9** 40 50N 25 54 E
Alexis →, *Canada* **103 B8** 52 33N 56 8W
Alexis Creek, *Canada* **104 C4** 52 10N 123 20W
Alfabia, *Spain* **37 B9** 39 44N 2 44 E
Alfambra, *Spain* **32 E3** 40 33N 1 5W
Alfândega da Fé, *Portugal* **34 D4** 41 20N 6 59W
Alfaro, *Spain* **32 C3** 42 10N 1 50W
Alfatar, *Bulgaria* **41 C11** 43 59N 27 13 E
Alfaz del Pi, *Spain* **33 G4** 38 35N 0 5W
Alfeld, *Germany* **24 D5** 51 59N 9 50 E
Alfenas, *Brazil* **127 A6** 21 20 S 46 10W
Alfiós →, *Greece* **38 D3** 37 40N 21 33 E
Alföld, *Hungary* **42 D5** 46 30N 20 0 E
Alfonsine, *Italy* **29 D9** 44 30N 12 3 E
Alford, *Aberds., U.K.* **14 D6** 57 14N 2 41W
Alford, *Lincs., U.K.* **12 D8** 53 15N 0 10 E
Alfred, *Maine, U.S.A.* **111 C14** 43 29N 70 43W
Alfred, *N.Y., U.S.A.* **110 D7** 42 16N 77 48W
Alfreton, *U.K.* **12 D6** 53 6N 1 24W
Alfta, *Sweden* **10 C10** 61 21N 16 4 E
Alga, *Kazakstan* **50 E6** 49 53N 57 20 E
Algaida, *Spain* **37 B9** 39 33N 2 53 E
Algar, *Spain* **35 J5** 36 40N 5 39W
Ålgård, *Norway* **9 G11** 58 46N 5 53 E
Algarinejo, *Spain* **35 H6** 37 19N 4 9W
Algarve, *Portugal* **35 J2** 36 58N 8 20W
Algeciras, *Spain* **35 J5** 36 9N 5 28W
Algemesí, *Spain* **33 F4** 39 11N 0 27W
Alger, *Algeria* **78 A6** 36 42N 3 8 E
Algeria ■, *Africa* **78 C6** 28 30N 2 0 E
Alghero, *Italy* **30 B1** 40 33N 8 19 E
Älghult, *Sweden* **11 G9** 57 0N 15 35 E
Algiers = Alger, *Algeria* **78 A6** 36 42N 3 8 E
Algoa B., *S. Africa* **88 E4** 33 50 S 25 45 E
Algodonales, *Spain* **35 J5** 36 54N 5 24W
Algodor →, *Spain* **34 F7** 39 55N 3 53W
Algoma, *U.S.A.* **108 C2** 44 36N 87 26W
Algona, *U.S.A.* **112 D7** 43 4N 94 14W
Algonac, *U.S.A.* **110 D2** 42 37N 82 32W
Algonquin Prov. Park, *Canada* **102 C4** 45 50N 78 30W
Algorta, *Uruguay* **128 C5** 32 25 S 57 23W
Alhama de Almería, *Spain* **35 J8** 36 57N 2 34W
Alhama de Aragón, *Spain* **32 D3** 41 18N 1 54W
Alhama de Granada, *Spain* **35 H7** 37 0N 3 59W
Alhama de Murcia, *Spain* **33 H3** 37 51N 1 25W
Alhambra, *U.S.A.* **117 L8** 34 8N 118 6W
Alhaurín el Grande, *Spain* **35 J6** 36 39N 4 41W
Alhucemas = Al Hoceïma, *Morocco* **78 A5** 35 8N 3 58W
'Alī al Gharbī, *Iraq* **70 C5** 32 30N 46 45 E
'Alī ash Sharqī, *Iraq* **70 C5** 32 7N 46 44 E
Äli Bayramlı, *Azerbaijan* **49 L9** 39 59N 48 52 E
'Alī Khēl, *Afghan.* **68 C3** 33 57N 69 43 E
Ali Sahîh, *Djibouti* **81 E5** 11 10N 42 44 E
Alī Shāh, *Iran* **70 B5** 38 9N 45 50 E
Ália, *Italy* **30 E6** 37 47N 13 43 E
'Alīābād, *Khorāsān, Iran* **71 C8** 32 30N 57 30 E
'Alīābād, *Kordestān, Iran* **70 C5** 35 4N 46 58 E
'Alīābād, *Yazd, Iran* **71 D7** 31 41N 53 49 E
Aliaga, *Spain* **32 E4** 40 40N 0 42W
Aliağa, *Turkey* **39 C8** 38 47N 26 59 E
Aliákmon →, *Greece* **40 F6** 40 30N 22 36 E
Alibo, *Ethiopia* **81 F4** 9 52N 37 5 E
Alibori →, *Benin* **83 C5** 11 56N 3 17 E
Alibunar, *Serbia, Yug.* **42 E5** 45 5N 20 57 E
Alicante, *Spain* **33 G4** 38 23N 0 30W
Alicante □, *Spain* **33 G4** 38 30N 0 37W
Alice, *S. Africa* **88 E4** 32 48 S 26 55 E
Alice, *U.S.A.* **113 M5** 27 45N 98 5W
Alice →, *Queens., Australia* **94 C3** 24 2 S 144 50 E
Alice →, *Queens., Australia* **94 B3** 15 35 S 142 20 E
Alice, Punta, *Italy* **31 C10** 39 24N 17 9 E
Alice Arm, *Canada* **104 B3** 55 29N 129 31W
Alice Springs, *Australia* **94 C1** 23 40 S 133 50 E
Alicedale, *S. Africa* **88 E4** 33 15 S 26 4 E
Aliceville, *U.S.A.* **109 J1** 33 8N 88 9W
Alicudi, *Italy* **31 D7** 38 33N 14 20 E
Aliganj, *India* **69 F8** 27 30N 79 10 E
Aligarh, *Raj., India* **68 G7** 25 55N 76 15 E
Aligarh, *Ut. P., India* **68 F8** 27 55N 78 10 E
Aligūdarz, *Iran* **71 C6** 33 25N 49 45 E
Alijó, *Portugal* **34 D3** 41 16N 7 27W
Alimnía, *Greece* **36 C9** 36 16N 27 43 E
Alingsås, *Sweden* **11 G6** 57 56N 12 31 E
Alipur, *Pakistan* **68 E4** 29 25N 70 55 E
Alipur Duar, *India* **67 F16** 26 30N 89 35 E
Aliquippa, *U.S.A.* **110 F4** 40 37N 80 15W
Alishan, *Taiwan* **59 F13** 23 31N 120 48 E
Aliste →, *Spain* **34 D5** 41 34N 5 58W
Alitus = Alytus, *Lithuania* **9 J21** 54 24N 24 3 E
Alivérion, *Greece* **38 C6** 38 24N 24 2 E
Aliwal North, *S. Africa* **88 E4** 30 45 S 26 45 E
Alix, *Canada* **104 C6** 52 24N 113 11W
Aljezur, *Portugal* **35 H2** 37 18N 8 49W
Aljustrel, *Portugal* **35 H2** 37 55N 8 10W
Alkamari, *Niger* **83 C7** 13 27N 11 10 E
Alkmaar, *Neths.* **17 B4** 52 37N 4 45 E
All American Canal, *U.S.A.* **115 K6** 32 45N 115 15W
Allada, *Benin* **83 D5** 6 41N 2 9 E
Allagash →, *U.S.A.* **109 B11** 47 5N 69 3W
Allah Dad, *Pakistan* **68 G2** 25 38N 67 34 E
Allahabad, *India* **69 G9** 25 25N 81 58 E
Allan, *Canada* **105 C7** 51 53N 106 4W
Allanche, *France* **20 C6** 45 14N 2 57 E
Allanmyo, *Burma* **67 K19** 19 30N 95 17 E
Allanridge, *S. Africa* **88 D4** 27 45 S 26 40 E
Allaqi, Wadi →, *Egypt* **80 C3** 23 7N 32 47 E
Allariz, *Spain* **34 C3** 42 11N 7 50W
Allassac, *France* **20 C5** 45 15N 1 29 E
Ålleberg, *Sweden* **11 F7** 58 8N 13 36 E
Allegany, *U.S.A.* **110 D6** 42 6N 78 30W
Allegheny →, *U.S.A.* **110 F5** 40 27N 80 1W
Allegheny Mts., *U.S.A.* **108 G6** 38 15N 80 10W
Allegheny Reservoir, *U.S.A.* **110 E6** 41 50N 79 0W
Allègre, *France* **20 C7** 45 12N 3 41 E
Allen, Bog of, *Ireland* **15 C5** 53 15N 7 0W
Allen, L., *Ireland* **15 B3** 54 8N 8 4W
Allendale, *U.S.A.* **109 J5** 33 1N 81 18W
Allende, *Mexico* **118 B4** 28 20N 100 50W
Allentown, *U.S.A.* **111 F9** 40 37N 75 29W
Allentsteig, *Austria* **26 C8** 48 41N 15 20 E
Alleppey, *India* **66 Q10** 9 30N 76 28 E
Allepuz, *Spain* **32 E4** 40 29N 0 44W
Aller →, *Germany* **24 C5** 52 56N 9 12 E
Alliance, *Nebr., U.S.A.* **112 D3** 42 6N 102 52W
Alliance, *Ohio, U.S.A.* **110 F3** 40 55N 81 6W
Allier □, *France* **19 F9** 46 25N 2 40 E
Allier →, *France* **19 F10** 46 57N 3 4 E
Alliford Bay, *Canada* **104 C2** 53 12N 131 58W
Allinge, *Denmark* **11 J8** 55 17N 14 50 E
Alliston, *Canada* **102 D4** 44 9N 79 52W
Alloa, *U.K.* **14 E5** 56 7N 3 47W
Allones, *France* **18 D8** 48 20N 1 40 E
Allora, *Australia* **95 D5** 28 2 S 152 0 E
Allos, *France* **21 D10** 44 15N 6 38 E
Alluitsup Paa, *Greenland* **4 C5** 60 30N 45 35W
Alma, *Canada* **103 C5** 48 35N 71 40W
Alma, *Ga., U.S.A.* **109 K4** 31 33N 82 28W
Alma, *Kans., U.S.A.* **112 F6** 39 1N 96 17W
Alma, *Mich., U.S.A.* **108 D3** 43 23N 84 39W
Alma, *Nebr., U.S.A.* **112 E5** 40 6N 99 22W
Alma Ata = Almaty, *Kazakstan* **50 E8** 43 15N 76 57 E
Almacelles, *Spain* **32 D5** 41 43N 0 27 E
Almada, *Portugal* **35 G1** 38 40N 9 9W
Almaden, *Australia* **94 B3** 17 22 S 144 40 E
Almadén, *Spain* **35 G6** 38 49N 4 52W
Almanor, L., *U.S.A.* **114 F3** 40 14N 121 9W
Almansa, *Spain* **33 G3** 38 51N 1 5W
Almanza, *Spain* **34 C5** 42 39N 5 3W
Almanzor, Pico, *Spain* **34 E5** 40 15N 5 18W
Almanzora →, *Spain* **33 H3** 37 14N 1 46W
Almaş, Muntii, *Romania* **42 F7** 44 49N 22 12 E
Almassora, *Spain* **32 F4** 39 57N 0 3W
Almaty, *Kazakstan* **50 E8** 43 15N 76 57 E
Almazán, *Spain* **32 D2** 41 30N 2 30W
Almeirim, *Brazil* **125 D8** 1 30 S 52 34W
Almeirim, *Portugal* **35 F2** 39 12N 8 37W
Almelo, *Neths.* **17 B6** 52 22N 6 42 E
Almenar de Soria, *Spain* **32 D2** 41 43N 2 12W
Almenara, *Spain* **32 F4** 39 46N 0 14W
Almenara, Sierra de la, *Spain* **33 H3** 37 34N 1 32W
Almendra, Embalse de, *Spain* **34 D4** 41 10N 6 5W
Almendralejo, *Spain* **35 G4** 38 41N 6 26W
Almere-Stad, *Neths.* **17 B5** 52 20N 5 15 E
Almería, *Spain* **35 J8** 36 52N 2 27W
Almería □, *Spain* **33 H2** 37 20N 2 20W
Almería, G. de, *Spain* **33 J2** 36 41N 2 28W
Almetyevsk, *Russia* **48 C11** 54 53N 52 20 E
Älmhult, *Sweden* **11 H8** 56 33N 14 8 E
Almirante, *Panama* **120 E3** 9 10N 82 30W
Almiropótamos, *Greece* **38 C6** 38 16N 24 11 E
Almirós, *Greece* **38 B4** 39 11N 22 45 E
Almiroú, Kólpos, *Greece* **36 D6** 35 23N 24 20 E
Almodôvar, *Portugal* **35 H2** 37 31N 8 2W
Almodóvar del Campo, *Spain* **35 G6** 38 43N 4 10W
Almodóvar del Río, *Spain* **35 H5** 37 48N 5 1W
Almond, *U.S.A.* **110 D7** 42 19N 77 44W
Almont, *U.S.A.* **110 D1** 42 55N 83 3W
Almonte, *Canada* **111 A8** 45 14N 76 12W
Almonte, *Spain* **35 H4** 37 13N 6 38W
Almora, *India* **69 E8** 29 38N 79 40 E
Almoradí, *Spain* **33 G4** 38 7N 0 46W
Almorox, *Spain* **34 E6** 40 14N 4 24W
Almoustarat, *Mali* **83 B5** 17 35N 0 8 E
Älmsta, *Sweden* **10 E12** 59 58N 18 50 E
Almudévar, *Spain* **32 C4** 42 3N 0 35W
Almuñécar, *Spain* **35 J7** 36 43N 3 41W
Almunge, *Sweden* **10 E12** 59 53N 18 3 E
Almuradiel, *Spain* **35 G7** 38 32N 3 28W
Alness, *U.K.* **14 D4** 57 41N 4 16W
Alnmouth, *U.K.* **12 B6** 55 24N 1 37W
Alnwick, *U.K.* **12 B6** 55 24N 1 42W
Aloi, *Uganda* **86 B3** 2 16N 33 10 E
Alon, *Burma* **67 H19** 22 12N 95 5 E
Alor, *Indonesia* **63 F6** 8 15 S 124 30 E
Alor Setar, *Malaysia* **65 J3** 6 7N 100 22 E
Álora, *Spain* **35 J6** 36 49N 4 46W
Alosno, *Spain* **35 H3** 37 33N 7 7W
Alot, *India* **68 H6** 23 56N 75 40 E
Aloysius, Mt., *Australia* **93 E4** 26 0 S 128 38 E
Alpaugh, *U.S.A.* **116 K7** 35 53N 119 29W
Alpedrinha, *Portugal* **34 E3** 40 6N 7 27W
Alpena, *U.S.A.* **108 C4** 45 4N 83 27W
Alpes-de-Haute-Provence □, *France* **21 D10** 44 8N 6 10 E
Alpes-Maritimes □, *France* **21 E11** 43 55N 7 10 E
Alpha, *Australia* **94 C4** 23 39 S 146 37 E
Alphen aan den Rijn, *Neths.* **17 B4** 52 7N 4 40 E
Alpiarça, *Portugal* **35 F2** 39 15N 8 35W
Alpine, *Ariz., U.S.A.* **115 K9** 33 51N 109 9W
Alpine, *Calif., U.S.A.* **117 N10** 32 50N 116 46W
Alpine, *Tex., U.S.A.* **113 K3** 30 22N 103 40W
Alps, *Europe* **6 F7** 46 30N 9 30 E
Alpu, *Turkey* **72 C4** 39 46N 30 58 E
Alqueta, Barragem do, *Portugal* **35 G3** 38 20N 7 25W
Alrø, *Denmark* **11 J4** 55 52N 10 5 E
Als, *Denmark* **11 K3** 54 59N 9 55 E
Alsace, *France* **19 D14** 48 15N 7 25 E
Alsask, *Canada* **105 C7** 51 21N 109 59W
Alsasua, *Spain* **32 C2** 42 54N 2 10W
Alsek →, *U.S.A.* **104 B1** 59 10N 138 12W
Alsfeld, *Germany* **24 E5** 50 44N 9 16 E
Alsten, *Norway* **8 D15** 65 58N 12 40 E
Alstermo, *Sweden* **11 H9** 56 58N 15 38 E
Alston, *U.K.* **12 C5** 54 49N 2 25W
Alta, *Norway* **8 B20** 69 57N 23 10 E
Alta, Sierra, *Spain* **32 E3** 40 31N 1 30W
Alta Gracia, *Argentina* **126 C3** 31 40 S 64 30W
Alta Sierra, *U.S.A.* **117 K8** 35 42N 118 33W
Altaelva →, *Norway* **8 B20** 69 54N 23 17 E
Altafjorden, *Norway* **8 A20** 70 5N 23 5 E
Altai = Aerhtai Shan, *Mongolia* **60 B4** 46 40N 92 45 E
Altamaha →, *U.S.A.* **109 K5** 31 20N 81 20W
Altamira, *Brazil* **125 D8** 3 12 S 52 10W
Altamira, *Chile* **126 B2** 25 47 S 69 51W
Altamira, *Mexico* **119 C5** 22 24N 97 55W
Altamira, Cuevas de, *Spain* **34 B6** 43 20N 4 5W
Altamont, *U.S.A.* **111 D10** 42 43N 74 3W
Altamura, *Italy* **31 B9** 40 49N 16 33 E
Altanbulag, *Mongolia* **60 A5** 50 16N 106 30 E
Altar, *Mexico* **118 A2** 30 40N 111 50W
Altar, Desierto de, *Mexico* **118 B2** 30 10N 112 0W
Altata, *Mexico* **118 C3** 24 30N 108 0W
Altavista, *U.S.A.* **108 G6** 37 6N 79 17W
Altay, *China* **60 B3** 47 48N 88 10 E
Altdorf, *Switz.* **25 J4** 46 52N 8 36 E
Alte Mellum, *Germany* **24 B4** 53 43N 8 10 E
Altea, *Spain* **33 G4** 38 38N 0 2W
Altenberg, *Germany* **24 E9** 50 45N 13 45 E
Altenbruch, *Germany* **24 B4** 53 49N 8 46 E
Altenburg, *Germany* **24 E8** 50 59N 12 25 E
Altenkirchen, *Mecklenburg-Vorpommern, Germany* **24 A9** 54 38N 13 22 E
Altenkirchen, *Rhld-Pfz., Germany* **24 E3** 50 41N 7 39 E
Altenmarkt, *Austria* **26 D7** 47 43N 14 39 E
Alter do Chão, *Portugal* **35 F3** 39 12N 7 40W
Altınoluk, *Turkey* **39 B8** 39 34N 26 45 E
Altınova, *Turkey* **39 B8** 39 12N 26 47 E
Altıntaş, *Turkey* **39 B12** 39 4N 30 7 E
Altınyaka, *Turkey* **39 E12** 36 33N 30 20 E
Altınyayla, *Turkey* **39 D11** 37 0N 29 33 E
Altiplano = Bolivian Plateau, *S. Amer.* **122 E4** 20 0 S 67 30W
Altkirch, *France* **19 E14** 47 37N 7 15 E
Altmark, *Germany* **24 C7** 52 45N 11 30 E
Altmühl →, *Germany* **25 G7** 48 54N 11 52 E
Altmunster, *Austria* **26 D6** 47 54N 13 45 E
Alto Adige = Trentino-Alto Adige □, *Italy* **29 B8** 46 30N 11 20 E
Alto Araguaia, *Brazil* **125 G8** 17 15 S 53 20W
Alto Cuchumatanes = Cuchumatanes, Sierra de los, *Guatemala* **120 C1** 15 35N 91 25W
Alto del Carmen, *Chile* **126 B1** 28 46 S 70 30W
Alto del Inca, *Chile* **126 A2** 24 10 S 68 10W
Alto Ligonha, *Mozam.* **87 F4** 15 30 S 38 11 E
Alto Molocue, *Mozam.* **87 F4** 15 50 S 37 35 E
Alto Paraguay □, *Paraguay* **126 A4** 21 0 S 58 30W
Alto Paraná □, *Paraguay* **127 B5** 25 30 S 54 50W
Alton, *Canada* **110 C4** 43 54N 80 5W
Alton, *U.K.* **13 F7** 51 9N 0 59W
Alton, *Ill., U.S.A.* **112 F9** 38 53N 90 11W
Alton, *N.H., U.S.A.* **111 C13** 43 27N 71 13W
Altoona, *U.S.A.* **110 F6** 40 31N 78 24W
Altötting, *Germany* **25 G8** 48 12N 12 39 E
Altstätten, *Switz.* **25 H5** 47 22N 9 33 E
Altūn Kūprī, *Iraq* **70 C5** 35 45N 44 9 E
Altun Shan, *China* **60 C3** 38 30N 88 0 E
Alturas, *U.S.A.* **114 F3** 41 29N 120 32W
Altus, *U.S.A.* **113 H5** 34 38N 99 20W
Alubijid, *Phil.* **61 G6** 8 35N 124 29 E
Alucra, *Turkey* **73 B8** 40 22N 38 47 E
Aluk, *Sudan* **81 F2** 8 25N 27 30 E
Alūksne, *Latvia* **9 H22** 57 24N 27 3 E
Alunda, *Sweden* **10 D12** 60 4N 18 5 E
Alunite, *U.S.A.* **117 K12** 35 59N 114 55W
Aluoro →, *Ethiopia* **81 F3** 8 26N 33 24 E
Alupka, *Ukraine* **47 K8** 44 23N 34 2 E
Alushta, *Ukraine* **47 K8** 44 40N 34 25 E
Alusi, *Indonesia* **63 F8** 7 35 S 131 40 E
Alustante, *Spain* **32 E3** 40 36N 1 40W
Alva, *U.S.A.* **113 G5** 36 48N 98 40W
Alvaiázere, *Portugal* **34 F2** 39 49N 8 23W
Alvängen, *Sweden* **11 G6** 57 58N 12 8 E
Alvarado, *Mexico* **119 D5** 18 40N 95 50W
Alvarado, *U.S.A.* **113 J6** 32 24N 97 13W
Alvaro Obregón, Presa, *Mexico* **118 B3** 27 55N 109 52W
Älvdalen, *Sweden* **10 C8** 61 13N 14 4 E
Alvear, *Argentina* **126 B4** 29 5 S 56 30W
Alverca, *Portugal* **35 G1** 38 56N 9 1W
Alvesta, *Sweden* **11 H8** 56 54N 14 35 E
Alvin, *U.S.A.* **113 L7** 29 26N 95 15W
Alvinston, *Canada* **110 D3** 42 49N 81 52W
Alvito, *Portugal* **35 G3** 38 15N 7 58W
Älvkarleby, *Sweden* **10 D11** 60 34N 17 26 E
Alvord Desert, *U.S.A.* **114 E4** 42 30N 118 25W
Älvros, *Sweden* **10 B8** 62 3N 14 38 E
Älvsbyn, *Sweden* **8 D19** 65 40N 21 0 E
Alwar, *India* **68 F7** 27 38N 76 34 E
Alxa Zuoqi, *China* **56 E3** 38 50N 105 40 E
Alyangula, *Australia* **94 A2** 13 55 S 136 30 E
Alyata = Älät, *Azerbaijan* **49 L9** 39 58N 49 25 E
Alyth, *U.K.* **14 E5** 56 38N 3 13W
Alytus, *Lithuania* **9 J21** 54 24N 24 3 E
Alzada, *U.S.A.* **112 C2** 45 2N 104 25W
Alzey, *Germany* **25 F4** 49 45N 8 7 E
Alzira, *Spain* **33 F4** 39 9N 0 30W
Am-Timan, *Chad* **79 F10** 11 0N 20 10 E
Amadeus, L., *Australia* **93 D5** 24 54 S 131 0 E
Amadi, *Dem. Rep. of the Congo* **86 B2** 3 40N 26 40 E
Amâdi, *Sudan* **81 F3** 5 29N 30 25 E
Amadjuak L., *Canada* **101 B12** 65 0N 71 8W
Amadora, *Portugal* **35 G1** 38 45N 9 13W
Amagansett, *U.S.A.* **111 F12** 40 59N 72 9W
Amagasaki, *Japan* **55 G7** 34 42N 135 20 E
Amager, *Denmark* **11 J6** 55 37N 12 35 E
Amagunze, *Nigeria* **83 D6** 6 20N 7 40 E
Amahai, *Indonesia* **63 E7** 3 20 S 128 55 E
Amakusa-Shotō, *Japan* **55 H5** 32 15N 130 10 E
Åmål, *Sweden* **10 E6** 59 3N 12 42 E
Amalfi, *Italy* **31 B7** 40 38N 14 36 E
Amaliás, *Greece* **38 D3** 37 47N 21 22 E
Amalner, *India* **66 J9** 21 5N 75 5 E
Amamapare, *Indonesia* **63 E9** 4 53 S 136 38 E
Amambaí, *Brazil* **127 A4** 23 5 S 55 13W
Amambaí →, *Brazil* **127 A5** 23 22 S 53 56W
Amambay □, *Paraguay* **127 A4** 23 0 S 56 0W
Amambay, Cordillera de, *S. Amer.* **127 A4** 23 0 S 55 45W
Amami-Guntō, *Japan* **55 L4** 27 16N 129 21 E
Amami-Ō-Shima, *Japan* **55 L4** 28 0N 129 0 E
Amaná, L., *Brazil* **124 D6** 2 35 S 64 40W
Amanat →, *India* **69 G11** 24 7N 84 4 E
Amanda Park, *U.S.A.* **116 C3** 47 28N 123 55W
Amangeldy, *Kazakstan* **50 D7** 50 10N 65 10 E
Amantea, *Italy* **31 C9** 39 8N 16 4 E
Amapá, *Brazil* **125 C8** 2 5N 50 50W
Amapá □, *Brazil* **125 C8** 1 40N 52 0W
Amara, *Sudan* **81 E3** 10 25N 34 10 E
Amarante, *Brazil* **125 E10** 6 14 S 42 50W
Amarante, *Portugal* **34 D2** 41 16N 8 5W
Amaranth, *Canada* **105 C9** 50 36N 98 43W
Amareleja, *Portugal* **35 G3** 38 12N 7 13W
Amargosa →, *U.S.A.* **117 J10** 36 14N 116 51W
Amargosa Range, *U.S.A.* **117 J10** 36 20N 116 45W
Amári, *Greece* **36 D6** 35 13N 24 40 E
Amarillo, *U.S.A.* **113 H4** 35 13N 101 50W
Amarkantak, *India* **69 H9** 22 40N 81 45 E
Amârna, Tell el', *Sudan* **80 B3** 27 38N 30 52 E
Amaro, Mte., *Italy* **29 F11** 42 5N 14 5 E
Amarpur, *India* **69 G12** 25 5N 87 0 E
Amarti, *Eritrea* **81 E5** 14 17N 41 6 E
Amarwara, *India* **69 H8** 22 18N 79 10 E
Amasra, *Turkey* **72 B5** 41 45N 32 23 E
Amassama, *Nigeria* **83 D6** 5 1N 6 2 E
Amasya, *Turkey* **72 B6** 40 40N 35 50 E
Amata, *Australia* **93 E5** 26 9 S 131 9 E
Amatikulu, *S. Africa* **89 D5** 29 3 S 31 33 E
Amatitlán, *Guatemala* **120 D1** 14 29N 90 38W
Amatrice, *Italy* **29 F10** 42 38N 13 17 E
Amay, *Belgium* **17 D5** 50 33N 5 19 E
Amazon = Amazonas →, *S. Amer.* **122 D5** 0 5 S 50 0W
Amazonas □, *Brazil* **124 E6** 5 0 S 65 0W
Amazonas →, *S. Amer.* **122 D5** 0 5 S 50 0W
Amba Ferit, *Ethiopia* **81 E4** 10 55N 38 50 E
Ambah, *India* **68 F8** 26 43N 78 13 E
Ambahakily, *Madag.* **89 C7** 21 36 S 43 41 E
Ambahita, *Madag.* **89 C8** 24 1 S 45 16 E
Ambala, *India* **68 D7** 30 23N 76 56 E
Ambalavao, *Madag.* **89 C8** 21 50 S 46 56 E
Ambanja, *Madag.* **89 A8** 13 40 S 48 27 E
Ambararata, *Madag.* **89 B8** 15 3 S 48 33 E
Ambarchik, *Russia* **51 C17** 69 40N 162 20 E
Ambarijeby, *Madag.* **89 A8** 14 56 S 47 41 E
Ambaro, Helodranon', *Madag.* **89 A8** 13 23 S 48 38 E
Ambato, *Ecuador* **124 D3** 1 5 S 78 42W
Ambato, *Madag.* **89 A8** 13 24 S 48 29 E
Ambato, Sierra de, *Argentina* **126 B2** 28 25 S 66 10W
Ambato Boeny, *Madag.* **89 B8** 16 28 S 46 43 E
Ambatofinandrahana, *Madag.* **89 C8** 20 33 S 46 48 E
Ambatolampy, *Madag.* **89 B8** 19 20 S 47 35 E
Ambatomainty, *Madag.* **89 B8** 17 41 S 45 40 E
Ambatomanoina, *Madag.* **89 B8** 18 18 S 47 37 E
Ambatondrazaka, *Madag.* **89 B8** 17 55 S 48 28 E
Ambatosoratra, *Madag.* **89 B8** 17 37 S 48 31 E
Ambelón, *Greece* **38 B4** 39 45N 22 22 E
Ambenja, *Madag.* **89 B8** 15 17 S 46 58 E
Amberg, *Germany* **25 F7** 49 26N 11 52 E
Ambergris Cay, *Belize* **119 D7** 18 0N 88 0W
Ambérieu-en-Bugey, *France* **21 C9** 45 57N 5 20 E
Amberley, *N.Z.* **91 K4** 43 9 S 172 44 E
Ambert, *France* **20 C7** 45 33N 3 44 E
Ambidédi, *Mali* **82 C2** 14 35N 11 47W
Ambikapur, *India* **69 H10** 23 15N 83 15 E
Ambikol, *Sudan* **80 C3** 21 20N 30 50 E
Ambilobé, *Madag.* **89 A8** 13 10 S 49 3 E
Ambinanindrano, *Madag.* **89 C8** 20 5 S 48 23 E
Ambinanitelo, *Madag.* **89 B8** 15 21 S 49 35 E
Ambinda, *Madag.* **89 B8** 16 25 S 45 52 E
Amble, *U.K.* **12 B6** 55 20N 1 36W
Ambleside, *U.K.* **12 C5** 54 26N 2 58W
Ambo, *Peru* **124 F3** 10 5 S 76 10W
Amboahangy, *Madag.* **89 C8** 24 15 S 46 22 E
Ambodifototra, *Madag.* **89 B8** 16 59 S 49 52 E
Ambodilazana, *Madag.* **89 B8** 18 6 S 49 10 E
Ambodiriana, *Madag.* **89 B8** 17 55 S 49 18 E
Ambohidratrimo, *Madag.* **89 B8** 18 50 S 47 26 E
Ambohidray, *Madag.* **89 B8** 18 36 S 48 18 E
Ambohimahamasina, *Madag.* **89 C8** 21 56 S 47 11 E
Ambohimahasoa, *Madag.* **89 C8** 21 7 S 47 13 E
Ambohimanga, *Madag.* **89 C8** 20 52 S 47 36 E
Ambohimitombo, *Madag.* **89 C8** 20 43 S 47 26 E
Ambohitra, *Madag.* **89 A8** 12 30 S 49 10 E
Amboise, *France* **18 E8** 47 24N 1 2 E
Ambon, *Indonesia* **63 E7** 3 43 S 128 12 E
Ambondro, *Madag.* **89 D8** 25 13 S 45 44 E
Amboseli, L., *Kenya* **86 C4** 2 40 S 37 10 E
Ambositra, *Madag.* **89 C8** 20 31 S 47 25 E
Ambovombe, *Madag.* **89 D8** 25 11 S 46 5 E
Amboy, *U.S.A.* **117 L11** 34 33N 115 45W
Amboyna Cay, *S. China Sea* **62 C4** 7 50N 112 50 E
Ambridge, *U.S.A.* **110 F4** 40 36N 80 14W
Ambriz, *Angola* **84 F2** 7 48 S 13 8 E
Amchitka I., *U.S.A.* **100 C1** 51 32N 179 0 E
Amderma, *Russia* **50 C7** 69 45N 61 30 E
Amdhi, *India* **69 H9** 23 51N 81 27 E
Ameca, *Mexico* **118 C4** 20 30N 104 0W
Ameca →, *Mexico* **118 C3** 20 40N 105 15W
Amecameca, *Mexico* **119 D5** 19 7N 98 46W
Ameland, *Neths.* **17 A5** 53 27N 5 45 E
Amélia, *Italy* **29 F9** 42 33N 12 25 E
Amendolara, *Italy* **31 C9** 39 57N 16 35 E
Amenia, *U.S.A.* **111 E11** 41 51N 73 33W
American Falls, *U.S.A.* **114 E7** 42 47N 112 51W
American Falls Reservoir, *U.S.A.* **114 E7** 42 47N 112 52W
American Fork, *U.S.A.* **114 F8** 40 23N 111 48W
American Highland, *Antarctica* **5 D6** 73 0 S 75 0 E
American Samoa ■, *Pac. Oc.* **91 B13** 14 20 S 170 40W
Americana, *Brazil* **127 A6** 22 45 S 47 20W
Americus, *U.S.A.* **109 K3** 32 4N 84 14W
Amersfoort, *Neths.* **17 B5** 52 9N 5 23 E
Amersfoort, *S. Africa* **89 D4** 26 59 S 29 53 E
Amery Ice Shelf, *Antarctica* **5 C6** 69 30 S 72 0 E
Ames, *Spain* **34 C2** 42 54N 8 38W
Ames, *U.S.A.* **112 E8** 42 2N 93 37W
Amesbury, *U.S.A.* **111 D14** 42 51N 70 56W
Amet, *India* **68 G5** 25 18N 73 56 E
Amfíklia, *Greece* **38 C4** 38 38N 22 35 E
Amfilokhía, *Greece* **38 C3** 38 52N 21 9 E
Amfípolis, *Greece* **40 F7** 40 48N 23 52 E
Ámfissa, *Greece* **38 C4** 38 32N 22 22 E
Amga, *Russia* **51 C14** 60 50N 132 0 E
Amga →, *Russia* **51 C14** 62 38N 134 32 E
Amgu, *Russia* **51 E14** 45 45N 137 15 E
Amgun →, *Russia* **51 D14** 52 56N 139 38 E
Amherst, *Burma* **67 L20** 16 2N 97 20 E
Amherst, *Canada* **103 C7** 45 48N 64 8W
Amherst, *Mass., U.S.A.* **111 D12** 42 23N 72 31W
Amherst, *N.Y., U.S.A.* **110 D6** 42 59N 78 48W
Amherst, *Ohio, U.S.A.* **110 E2** 41 24N 82 14W
Amherst I., *Canada* **111 B8** 44 8N 76 43W
Amherstburg, *Canada* **102 D3** 42 6N 83 6W
Amiata, Mte., *Italy* **29 F8** 42 53N 11 37 E
Amidon, *U.S.A.* **112 B3** 46 29N 103 19W
Amiens, *France* **19 C9** 49 54N 2 16 E
Amindaion, *Greece* **40 F5** 40 42N 21 42 E
Åminne, *Sweden* **11 G7** 57 7N 14 0 E
Amino, *Ethiopia* **81 G5** 4 25N 41 52 E
Aminuis, *Namibia* **88 C2** 23 43 S 19 21 E
Amīrābād, *Iran* **70 C5** 33 20N 46 16 E
Amirante Is., *Seychelles* **52 K9** 6 0 S 53 0 E
Amisk L., *Canada* **105 C8** 54 35N 102 15W
Amistad, Presa de la, *Mexico* **118 B4** 29 24N 101 0W
Amite, *U.S.A.* **113 K9** 30 44N 90 30W
Amla, *India* **68 J8** 21 56N 78 7 E
Amlia I., *U.S.A.* **100 C2** 52 4N 173 30W
Amlwch, *U.K.* **12 D3** 53 24N 4 20W
Amm Adam, *Sudan* **81 D4** 16 20N 36 1 E
'Ammān, *Jordan* **75 D4** 31 57N 35 52 E
'Ammān □, *Jordan* **75 D5** 31 40N 36 30 E
Ammanford, *U.K.* **13 F4** 51 48N 3 59W
Ammassalik = Tasiilaq, *Greenland* **4 C6** 65 40N 37 20W
Ammerån →, *Sweden* **10 A10** 63 9N 16 13 E
Ammersee, *Germany* **25 G7** 48 0N 11 7 E
Ammon, *U.S.A.* **114 E8** 43 28N 111 58W
Amnat Charoen, *Thailand* **64 E5** 15 51N 104 38 E
Amnura, *Bangla.* **69 G13** 24 37N 88 25 E
Amo Jiang →, *China* **58 F3** 23 0N 101 50 E
Āmol, *Iran* **71 B7** 36 23N 52 20 E
Amorgós, *Greece* **39 E7** 36 50N 25 57 E
Amory, *U.S.A.* **109 J1** 33 59N 88 29W
Amos, *Canada* **102 C4** 48 35N 78 5W
Åmot, *Norway* **9 G13** 59 57N 9 54 E
Åmotfors, *Sweden* **10 E6** 59 47N 12 22 E
Amoy = Xiamen, *China* **59 E12** 24 25N 118 4 E
Ampanavoana, *Madag.* **89 B9** 15 41 S 50 22 E
Ampang, *Malaysia* **65 L3** 3 8N 101 45 E
Ampangalana, Lakandranon', *Madag.* **89 C8** 22 48 S 47 50 E
Ampanihy, *Madag.* **89 C7** 24 40 S 44 45 E
Amparafaravola, *Madag.* **89 B8** 17 35 S 48 13 E
Ampasinambo, *Madag.* **89 C8** 20 31 S 48 0 E
Ampasindava, Helodranon', *Madag.* **89 A8** 13 40 S 48 15 E
Ampasindava, Saikanosy, *Madag.* **89 A8** 13 42 S 47 55 E
Ampenan, *Indonesia* **62 F5** 8 35 S 116 13 E
Amper, *Nigeria* **83 D6** 9 25N 9 40 E
Amper →, *Germany* **25 G7** 48 29N 11 55 E
Ampezzo, *Italy* **29 B9** 46 25N 12 48 E
Ampitsikinana, *Réunion* **89 A8** 12 57 S 49 49 E
Ampombiantambo, *Madag.* **89 A8** 12 42 S 48 57 E
Amposta, *Spain* **32 E5** 40 43N 0 34 E
Ampotaka, *Madag.* **89 D7** 25 3 S 44 41 E
Ampoza, *Madag.* **89 C7** 22 20 S 44 44 E
Amqui, *Canada* **103 C6** 48 28N 67 27W
Amravati, *India* **66 J10** 20 55N 77 45 E
Amreli, *India* **68 J4** 21 35N 71 17 E
Amritsar, *India* **68 D6** 31 35N 74 57 E
Amroha, *India* **69 E8** 28 53N 78 30 E
Amrum, *Germany* **24 A4** 54 38N 8 22 E
Amsterdam, *Neths.* **17 B4** 52 23N 4 54 E
Amsterdam, *U.S.A.* **111 D10** 42 56N 74 11W
Amsterdam, I. = Nouvelle-Amsterdam, I., *Ind. Oc.* **3 F13** 38 30 S 77 30 E
Amstetten, *Austria* **26 C7** 48 7N 14 51 E
Amudarya →, *Uzbekistan* **50 E6** 43 58N 59 34 E
Amundsen Gulf, *Canada* **100 A7** 71 0N 124 0W
Amundsen Sea, *Antarctica* **5 D15** 72 0 S 115 0W
Amungen, *Sweden* **10 C9** 61 10N 15 40 E
Amuntai, *Indonesia* **62 E5** 2 28 S 115 25 E
Amur →, *Russia* **51 D15** 52 56N 141 10 E
Amur, W. →, *Sudan* **80 D3** 18 56N 33 34 E
Amurang, *Indonesia* **63 D6** 1 5N 124 40 E
Amuri Pass, *N.Z.* **91 K4** 42 31 S 172 11 E
Amurrio, *Spain* **32 B1** 43 3N 3 0W
Amursk, *Russia* **51 D14** 50 14N 136 54 E
Amusco, *Spain* **34 C6** 42 10N 4 28W
Amvrakikós Kólpos, *Greece* **38 C2** 39 0N 20 55 E
Amvrosiyivka, *Ukraine* **47 J10** 47 43N 38 30 E
Amyderya = Amudarya →, *Uzbekistan* **50 E6** 43 58N 59 34 E
An Bien, *Vietnam* **65 H5** 9 45N 105 0 E
An Hoa, *Vietnam* **64 E7** 15 40N 108 5 E
An Nabatīyah at Tahta, *Lebanon* **75 B4** 33 23N 35 27 E
An Nabk, *Si. Arabia* **70 D3** 31 20N 37 20 E
An Nabk, *Syria* **75 A5** 34 2N 36 44 E
An Nafūd, *Si. Arabia* **70 D4** 28 15N 41 0 E
An Najaf, *Iraq* **70 C5** 32 3N 44 15 E
An Nāṣirīyah, *Iraq* **70 D5** 31 0N 46 15 E
An Nhon, *Vietnam* **64 F7** 13 55N 109 7 E
An Nīl □, *Sudan* **80 D3** 19 30N 33 0 E
An Nîl el Abyad □, *Sudan* **81 E3** 14 0N 32 15 E
An Nîl el Azraq □, *Sudan* **81 E3** 11 30N 34 30 E
An Nu'ayrīyah, *Si. Arabia* **71 E6** 27 30N 48 30 E
An Nu'mānīyah, *Iraq* **73 F11** 32 32N 45 25 E

An Nuwaybʻī, W. →, Si. Arabia 75 F3 29 18N 34 57 E
An Thoi, Dao, Vietnam 65 H4 9 58N 104 0 E
An Uaimh, Ireland 15 C5 53 39N 6 41W
Anabar →, Russia 51 B12 73 8N 113 36 E
ʻAnabtā, West Bank 75 C4 32 19N 35 7 E
Anaconda, U.S.A. 114 C7 46 8N 112 57W
Anacortes, U.S.A. 116 B4 48 30N 122 37W
Anacuao, Mt., Phil. 61 C4 16 16N 121 53 E
Anadarko, U.S.A. 113 H5 35 4N 98 15W
Anadia, Portugal 34 E2 40 26N 8 27W
Anadolu, Turkey 72 C5 39 0N 30 0 E
Anadyr, Russia 51 C18 64 35N 177 20 E
Anadyr →, Russia 51 C18 64 55N 176 5 E
Anadyrskiy Zaliv, Russia 51 C19 64 0N 180 0 E
Anáfi, Greece 39 E7 36 22N 25 48 E
Anafópoulo, Greece 39 E7 36 17N 25 50 E
Anaga, Pta. de, Canary Is. 37 F3 28 34N 16 9W
Anagni, Italy 29 G10 41 44N 13 9 E
ʻĀnah, Iraq 70 C4 34 25N 42 0 E
Anaheim, U.S.A. 117 M9 33 50N 117 55W
Anahim Lake, Canada 104 C3 52 28N 125 18W
Anáhuac, Mexico 118 B4 27 14N 100 9W
Anakapalle, India 67 L13 17 42N 83 6 E
Anakie, Australia 94 C4 23 32 S 147 45 E
Anaklia, Georgia 49 J5 42 22N 41 35 E
Analalava, Madag. 89 A8 14 35 S 48 0 E
Analavoka, Madag. 89 C8 22 23 S 46 30 E
Análipsis, Greece 36 A3 39 36N 19 55 E
Anambar →, Pakistan 68 D3 30 15N 68 50 E
Anambas, Kepulauan, Indonesia 65 L6 3 20N 106 30 E
Anambas Is. = Anambas, Kepulauan, Indonesia 65 L6 3 20N 106 30 E
Anambra □, Nigeria 83 D6 6 20N 7 0 E
Anamosa, U.S.A. 112 D9 42 7N 91 17W
Anamur, Turkey 70 B2 36 8N 32 58 E
Anamur Burnu, Turkey 72 D5 36 2N 32 47 E
Anan, Japan 55 H7 33 54N 134 40 E
Anand, India 68 H5 22 32N 72 59 E
Anánes, Greece 38 E6 36 33N 24 9 E
Anantnag, India 69 C6 33 45N 75 10 E
Ananyiv, Ukraine 47 J5 47 44N 29 58 E
Anapa, Russia 47 K9 44 55N 37 25 E
Anapodháris →, Greece 36 E7 34 59N 25 20 E
Anápolis, Brazil 125 G9 16 15 S 48 50W
Anapu →, Brazil 125 D8 1 53 S 50 53W
Anār, Iran 71 D7 30 55N 55 13 E
Anārak, Iran 71 C7 33 25N 53 40 E
Anarisfjällen, Sweden 10 A7 63 6N 13 10 E
Anas →, India 68 H5 23 26N 74 0 E
Anatolia = Anadolu, Turkey 72 C5 39 0N 30 0 E
Anatsogno, Madag. 89 C7 23 33 S 43 46 E
Añatuya, Argentina 126 B3 28 20 S 62 50W
Anaunethad L., Canada 105 A8 60 55N 104 25W
Anbyŏn, N. Korea 57 E14 39 1N 127 35 E
Ancares, Sierra de, Spain 34 C4 42 51N 6 52W
Ancaster, Canada 110 C5 43 13N 79 59W
Ancenis, France 18 E5 47 21N 1 10W
Anchor Bay, U.S.A. 116 G3 38 48N 123 34W
Anchorage, U.S.A. 100 B5 61 13N 149 54W
Anci, China 56 E9 39 20N 116 40 E
Ancohuma, Nevada, Bolivia 122 E4 16 0 S 68 50W
Ancón, Peru 124 F3 11 50 S 77 10W
Ancona, Italy 29 E10 43 38N 13 30 E
Ancud, Chile 128 E2 42 0 S 73 50W
Ancud, G. de, Chile 128 E2 42 0 S 73 0W
Ancy-le-Franc, France 19 E11 47 46N 4 10 E
Andacollo, Argentina 126 D1 37 10 S 70 42W
Andacollo, Chile 126 C1 30 14 S 71 6W
Andaingo, Madag. 89 B8 18 12 S 48 17 E
Andalgalá, Argentina 126 B2 27 40 S 66 30W
Åndalsnes, Norway 9 E12 62 35N 7 43 E
Andalucía □, Spain 35 H6 37 35N 5 0W
Andalusia = Andalucía □, Spain 35 H6 37 35N 5 0W
Andalusia, U.S.A. 109 K2 31 18N 86 29W
Andaman Is., Ind. Oc. 52 H13 12 30N 92 30 E
Andaman Sea, Ind. Oc. 62 B1 13 0N 96 0 E
Andamooka Opal Fields, Australia 95 E2 30 27 S 137 9 E
Andapa, Madag. 89 A8 14 39 S 49 39 E
Andara, Namibia 88 B3 18 2 S 21 9 E
Andelot-Blancheville, France 19 D12 48 15N 5 18 E
Andenes, Norway 8 B17 69 19N 16 18 E
Andenne, Belgium 17 D5 50 28N 5 5 E
Andéranboukane, Mali 83 B5 15 26N 3 2 E
Andermatt, Switz. 25 J4 46 38N 8 35 E
Andernach, Germany 24 E3 50 26N 7 24 E
Andernos-les-Bains, France 20 D2 44 44N 1 6W
Anderslöv, Sweden 11 J7 55 26N 13 19 E
Anderson, Alaska, U.S.A. 100 B5 64 25N 149 15W
Anderson, Calif., U.S.A. 114 F2 40 27N 122 18W
Anderson, Ind., U.S.A. 108 E3 40 10N 85 41W
Anderson, Mo., U.S.A. 113 G7 36 39N 94 27W
Anderson, S.C., U.S.A. 109 H4 34 31N 82 39W
Anderson →, Canada 100 B7 69 42N 129 0W
Anderstorp, Sweden 11 G7 57 19N 13 39 E
Andes, U.S.A. 111 D10 42 12N 74 47W
Andes, Cord. de los, S. Amer. 122 F4 20 0 S 68 0W
Andfjorden, Norway 8 B17 69 10N 16 20 E
Andhra Pradesh □, India 66 L11 18 0N 79 0 E
Andijon, Uzbekistan 50 E8 41 10N 72 15 E
Andikíthira, Greece 38 F5 35 52N 23 15 E
Andilamena, Madag. 89 B8 17 1 S 48 35 E
Andīmeshk, Iran 71 C6 32 27N 48 21 E
Andímilos, Greece 38 E6 36 47N 24 12 E
Andíparos, Greece 39 D7 37 0N 25 3 E
Andípaxoi, Greece 38 B2 39 9N 20 13 E
Andípsara, Greece 39 C7 38 30N 25 29 E
Andírrion, Greece 38 C3 38 20N 21 46 E
Andizhan = Andijon, Uzbekistan 50 E8 41 10N 72 15 E
Andoain, Spain 32 B2 43 13N 2 1W
Andoany, Madag. 89 A8 13 25 S 48 16 E
Andong, S. Korea 57 F15 36 40N 128 43 E
Andongwei, China 57 G10 35 6N 119 20 E
Andoom, Australia 94 A3 12 25 S 141 53 E
Andorra, Spain 32 E4 40 59N 0 28W
Andorra ■, Europe 20 F5 42 30N 1 30 E
Andorra La Vella, Andorra 20 F5 42 31N 1 32 E
Andover, U.K. 13 F6 51 12N 1 29W
Andover, Maine, U.S.A. 111 B14 44 38N 70 45W
Andover, Mass., U.S.A. 111 D13 42 40N 71 8W
Andover, N.J., U.S.A. 111 F10 40 59N 74 45W
Andover, N.Y., U.S.A. 110 D7 42 10N 77 48W
Andover, Ohio, U.S.A. 110 E4 41 36N 80 34W
Andøya, Norway 8 B16 69 10N 15 50 E
Andradina, Brazil 125 H8 20 54 S 51 23W
Andrahary, Mt., Madag. 89 A8 13 37 S 49 17 E
Andramasina, Madag. 89 B8 19 11 S 47 35 E
Andranopasy, Madag. 89 C7 21 17 S 43 44 E
Andranovory, Madag. 89 C7 23 8 S 44 10 E
Andratx, Spain 37 B9 39 39N 2 25 E
Andreanof Is., U.S.A. 100 C2 51 30N 176 0W
Andreapol, Russia 46 D7 56 40N 32 17 E
Andrews, S.C., U.S.A. 109 J6 33 27N 79 34W
Andrews, Tex., U.S.A. 113 J3 32 19N 102 33W
Andreyevka, Russia 48 D10 52 19N 51 55 E
Ándria, Italy 31 A9 41 13N 16 17 E
Andriamena, Madag. 89 B8 17 26 S 47 30 E
Andriandampy, Madag. 89 C8 22 45 S 45 41 E
Andriba, Madag. 89 B8 17 30 S 46 58 E
Andrijevica, Montenegro, Yug. 40 D3 42 45N 19 48 E
Andrítsaina, Greece 38 D3 37 29N 21 52 E
Androka, Madag. 89 C7 24 58 S 44 2 E
Andropov = Rybinsk, Russia 46 C10 58 5N 38 50 E
Ándros, Greece 38 D6 37 50N 24 57 E
Andros I., Bahamas 120 B4 24 30N 78 0W
Andros Town, Bahamas 120 B4 24 43N 77 47W
Androscoggin →, U.S.A. 111 C14 43 58N 70 0W
Andrychów, Poland 45 J6 49 51N 19 18 E
Andselv, Norway 8 B18 69 4N 18 34 E
Andújar, Spain 35 G6 38 3N 4 5W
Andulo, Angola 84 G3 11 25 S 16 45 E
Aneby, Sweden 11 G8 57 48N 14 49 E
Anegada I., Virgin Is. 121 C7 18 45N 64 20W
Anegada Passage, W. Indies 121 C7 18 15N 63 45W
Anécho, Togo 83 D5 6 12N 1 34 E
Anenni-Noi, Moldova 43 D14 46 53N 29 15 E
Aneto, Pico de, Spain 32 C5 42 37N 0 40 E
Anfu, China 59 D10 27 21N 114 40 E
Ang Thong, Thailand 64 E3 14 35N 100 31 E
Angamos, Punta, Chile 126 A1 23 1 S 70 32W
Angara →, Russia 51 D10 58 5N 94 20 E
Angara-Débou, Benin 83 C5 11 19N 3 3 E
Angarab, Ethiopia 81 E4 13 11N 37 7 E
Angarbaka, Sudan 81 F1 9 44N 24 44 E
Angarsk, Russia 51 D11 52 30N 104 0 E
Angas Hills, Australia 92 D4 23 0 S 127 50 E
Angaston, Australia 95 E2 34 30 S 139 8 E
Angaur I., Pac. Oc. 63 C8 6 54N 134 9 E
Ånge, Sweden 10 B9 62 31N 15 35 E
Ángel, Salto = Angel Falls, Venezuela 124 B6 5 57N 62 30W
Ángel de la Guarda, I., Mexico 118 B2 29 30N 113 30W
Angel Falls, Venezuela 124 B6 5 57N 62 30W
Angeles, Phil. 61 D4 15 9N 120 33 E
Ängelholm, Sweden 11 H6 56 15N 12 58 E
Angels Camp, U.S.A. 116 G6 38 4N 120 32W
Ängelsberg, Sweden 10 E10 59 58N 16 0 E
Anger →, Ethiopia 81 F4 9 37N 36 6 E
Angereb →, Ethiopia 81 E4 13 45N 36 40 E
Ångermanälven →, Sweden 10 B11 62 40N 18 0 E
Ångermanland, Sweden 8 E18 63 36N 17 45 E
Angermünde, Germany 24 B9 53 0N 14 0 E
Angers, Canada 111 A9 45 31N 75 29W
Angers, France 18 E6 47 30N 0 35W
Angerville, France 19 D9 48 19N 2 0 E
Ängesån →, Sweden 8 C20 66 16N 22 47 E
Angikuni L., Canada 105 A9 62 0N 100 0W
Angkor, Cambodia 64 F4 13 22N 103 50 E
Anglès, Spain 32 D7 41 57N 2 38 E
Anglesey, Isle of □, U.K. 12 D3 53 16N 4 18W
Anglet, France 20 E2 43 29N 1 31W
Angleton, U.S.A. 113 L7 29 10N 95 26W
Anglin →, France 20 B4 46 42N 0 52 E
Anglisidhes, Cyprus 36 E12 34 51N 33 27 E
Anglure, France 19 D10 48 35N 3 50 E
Angmagssalik = Tasiilaq, Greenland 4 C6 65 40N 37 20W
Ango, Dem. Rep. of the Congo 86 B2 4 10N 26 5 E
Angoche, Mozam. 87 F4 16 8 S 39 55 E
Angoche, I., Mozam. 87 F4 16 20 S 39 50 E
Angol, Chile 126 D1 37 56 S 72 45W
Angola, Ind., U.S.A. 108 E3 41 38N 85 0W
Angola, N.Y., U.S.A. 110 D5 42 38N 79 2W
Angola ■, Africa 85 G3 12 0 S 18 0 E
Angoulême, France 20 C4 45 39N 0 10 E
Angoumois, France 20 C4 45 50N 0 25 E
Angra dos Reis, Brazil 127 A7 23 0 S 44 10W
Angren, Uzbekistan 50 E8 41 1N 70 12 E
Angtassom, Cambodia 65 G5 11 1N 104 41 E
Angu, Dem. Rep. of the Congo 86 B1 3 23N 24 30 E
Anguang, China 57 B12 45 15N 123 45 E
Anguilla ■, W. Indies 121 C7 18 14N 63 5W
Anguo, China 56 E8 38 28N 115 15 E
Angurugu, Australia 94 A2 14 0 S 136 25 E
Angus □, U.K. 14 E6 56 46N 2 56W
Angwa →, Zimbabwe 89 B5 16 0 S 30 23 E
Anhanduí →, Brazil 127 A5 21 46 S 52 9W
Anholt, Denmark 11 H5 56 42N 11 33 E
Anhua, China 59 C8 28 23N 111 12 E
Anhui □, China 59 B11 32 0N 117 0 E
Anhwei = Anhui □, China 59 B11 32 0N 117 0 E
Anichab, Namibia 88 C1 21 0 S 14 46 E
Anidhros, Greece 39 E7 36 38N 25 43 E
Anié, Togo 83 D5 7 42N 1 8 E
Animas →, U.S.A. 115 H9 36 43N 108 13W
Anina, Romania 42 E6 45 6N 21 51 E
Aninoasa, Romania 43 F9 44 47N 24 10 E
Anivorano, Madag. 89 B8 18 44 S 48 58 E
Anjalankoski, Finland 9 F22 60 45N 26 51 E
Anjar, India 68 H4 23 6N 70 10 E
Anji, China 59 B12 30 46N 119 40 E
Anjidiv I., India 66 M9 14 40N 74 10 E
Anjou, France 18 E6 47 20N 0 15W
Anjozorobe, Madag. 89 B8 18 22 S 47 52 E
Anju, N. Korea 57 E13 39 36N 125 40 E
Anka, Nigeria 83 C6 12 13N 5 58 E
Ankaboa, Tanjona, Madag. 89 C7 21 58 S 43 20 E
Ankang, China 56 H5 32 40N 109 1 E
Ankara, Turkey 72 C5 39 57N 32 54 E
Ankaramena, Madag. 89 C8 21 57 S 46 39 E
Ankaratra, Madag. 85 H9 19 25 S 47 12 E
Ankarsrum, Sweden 11 G10 57 41N 16 20 E
Ankasakasa, Madag. 89 B7 16 21 S 44 52 E
Ankavandra, Madag. 89 B8 18 46 S 45 18 E
Ankazoabo, Madag. 89 C7 22 18 S 44 31 E
Ankazobe, Madag. 89 B8 18 20 S 47 10 E
Ankeny, U.S.A. 112 E8 41 44N 93 36W
Ankilimalinika, Madag. 89 C7 22 58 S 43 45 E
Ankilizato, Madag. 89 C8 20 25 S 45 1 E
Ankisabe, Madag. 89 B8 19 17 S 46 29 E
Anklam, Germany 24 B9 53 51N 13 41 E
Ankober, Ethiopia 81 F4 9 35N 39 40 E
Ankoro, Dem. Rep. of the Congo 86 D2 6 45 S 26 55 E
Ankororoka, Madag. 89 D8 25 30 S 45 11 E
Anlong, China 58 E5 25 2N 105 27 E
Anlu, China 59 B9 31 15N 113 45 E
Anmyŏn-do, S. Korea 57 F14 36 25N 126 25 E
Ånn, Sweden 10 A6 63 16N 12 34 E
Ann, C., U.S.A. 111 D14 42 38N 70 35W
Ann Arbor, U.S.A. 108 D4 42 17N 83 45W
Anna, Russia 48 E5 51 28N 40 23 E
Anna, U.S.A. 113 G10 37 28N 89 15W
Annaba, Algeria 78 A7 36 50N 7 46 E
Annaberg-Buchholz, Germany 24 E9 50 34N 13 0 E
Annalee →, Ireland 15 B4 54 2N 7 24W
Annam, Vietnam 64 E7 16 0N 108 0 E
Annamitique, Chaîne, Asia 64 D6 17 0N 106 0 E
Annan, U.K. 14 G5 54 59N 3 16W
Annan →, U.K. 14 G5 54 58N 3 16W
Annapolis, U.S.A. 108 F7 38 59N 76 30W
Annapolis Royal, Canada 103 D6 44 44N 65 32W
Annapurna, Nepal 69 E10 28 34N 83 50 E
Annean, L., Australia 93 E2 26 54 S 118 14 E
Anneberg, Sweden 11 G8 57 44N 14 49 E
Annecy, France 21 C10 45 55N 6 8 E
Annecy, Lac d', France 21 C10 45 52N 6 10 E
Annemasse, France 19 F13 46 12N 6 16 E
Annenskiy Most, Russia 46 B9 60 45N 37 10 E
Anning, China 58 E4 24 55N 102 26 E
Anniston, U.S.A. 109 J3 33 39N 85 50W
Annobón, Atl. Oc. 77 G4 1 25 S 5 36 E
Annonay, France 21 C8 45 15N 4 40 E
Annot, France 21 E10 43 58N 6 38 E
Annotto Bay, Jamaica 120 C4 18 17N 76 45W
Ånnsjön, Sweden 10 A6 63 19N 12 34 E
Annville, U.S.A. 111 F8 40 20N 76 31W
Annweiler, Germany 25 F3 49 12N 7 57 E
Áno Arkhánai, Greece 39 F7 35 16N 25 11 E
Áno Porróia, Greece 40 E7 41 17N 23 2 E
Áno Síros, Greece 38 D6 37 29N 24 56 E
Áno Viánnos, Greece 36 D7 35 2N 25 21 E
Anorotsangana, Madag. 89 A8 13 56 S 47 55 E
Anosibe, Madag. 89 B8 19 26 S 48 13 E
Anou Mellene, Mali 83 B5 17 29N 0 33 E
Anoumaba, Ivory C. 82 D4 6 23N 4 38W
Anóyia, Greece 36 D6 35 16N 24 52 E
Anping, Hebei, China 56 E8 38 15N 115 30 E
Anping, Liaoning, China 57 D12 41 5N 123 30 E
Anpu Gang, China 58 G7 21 25N 109 50 E
Anqing, China 59 B11 30 30N 117 3 E
Anqiu, China 57 F10 36 25N 119 10 E
Anren, China 59 D9 26 43N 113 18 E
Ansager, Denmark 11 J2 55 43N 8 45 E
Ansai, China 56 F5 36 50N 109 20 E
Ansbach, Germany 25 F6 49 28N 10 34 E
Anseba →, Eritrea 81 D4 16 0N 38 30 E
Ansfelden, Austria 26 C7 48 12N 14 17 E
Anshan, China 57 D12 41 5N 122 58 E
Anshun, China 58 D5 26 18N 105 57 E
Ansião, Portugal 34 F2 39 56N 8 27W
Ansley, U.S.A. 112 E5 41 18N 99 23W
Ansó, Spain 32 C4 42 51N 0 48W
Ansoain, Spain 32 C3 42 50N 1 38W
Anson, U.S.A. 113 J5 32 45N 99 54W
Anson B., Australia 92 B5 13 20 S 130 6 E
Ansongo, Mali 83 B5 15 25N 0 35 E
Ansonia, U.S.A. 111 E11 41 21N 73 5W
Anstruther, U.K. 14 E6 56 14N 2 41W
Ansudu, Indonesia 63 E9 2 11 S 139 22 E
Antabamba, Peru 124 F4 14 40 S 73 0W
Antakya, Turkey 70 B3 36 14N 36 10 E
Antalaha, Madag. 89 A9 14 57 S 50 20 E
Antalya, Turkey 72 D4 36 52N 30 45 E
Antalya □, Turkey 39 E12 36 30N 30 0 E
Antalya Körfezi, Turkey 72 D4 36 15N 31 30 E
Antambohobe, Madag. 89 C8 22 20 S 46 47 E
Antanambao-Manampotsy, Madag. 89 B8 19 29 S 48 34 E
Antanambe, Madag. 89 B8 16 26 S 49 52 E
Antananarivo, Madag. 89 B8 18 55 S 47 31 E
Antananarivo □, Madag. 89 B8 19 0 S 47 0 E
Antanifotsy, Madag. 89 B8 19 39 S 47 19 E
Antanimbaribe, Madag. 89 C7 21 30 S 44 48 E
Antanimora, Madag. 89 C8 24 49 S 45 40 E
Antarctic Pen., Antarctica 5 C18 67 0 S 60 0W
Antarctica 5 E3 90 0 S 0 0W
Antelope, Zimbabwe 87 G2 21 2 S 28 31 E
Antequera, Paraguay 126 A4 24 8 S 57 7W
Antequera, Spain 35 H6 37 5N 4 33W
Antero, Mt., U.S.A. 115 G10 38 41N 106 15W
Antevamena, Madag. 89 C7 21 2 S 44 8 E
Anthemoús, Greece 40 F7 40 31N 23 15 E
Anthony, Kans., U.S.A. 113 G5 37 9N 98 2W
Anthony, N. Mex., U.S.A. 115 K10 32 0N 106 36W
Anti Atlas, Morocco 78 C4 30 0N 8 30W
Anti-Lebanon = Ash Sharqi, Al Jabal, Lebanon 75 B5 33 40N 36 10 E
Antibes, France 21 E11 43 34N 7 6 E
Antibes, C. d', France 21 E11 43 31N 7 7 E
Anticosti, Î. d', Canada 103 C7 49 30N 63 0W
Antifer, C. d', France 18 C7 49 41N 0 10 E
Antigo, U.S.A. 112 C10 45 9N 89 9W
Antigonish, Canada 103 C7 45 38N 61 58W
Antigua, Canary Is. 37 F5 28 24N 14 1W
Antigua, W. Indies 121 C7 17 0N 61 50W
Antigua & Barbuda ■, W. Indies 121 C7 17 20N 61 48W
Antigua Guatemala, Guatemala 120 D1 14 34N 90 41W
Antilla, Cuba 120 B4 20 40N 75 50W
Antilles = West Indies, Cent. Amer. 121 D7 15 0N 65 0W
Antioch, U.S.A. 116 G5 38 1N 121 48W
Antioche, Pertuis d', France 20 B2 46 6N 1 20W
Antioquia, Colombia 124 B3 6 40N 75 55W
Antipodes Is., Pac. Oc. 96 M9 49 45 S 178 40 E
Antlers, U.S.A. 113 H7 34 14N 95 37W
Antoetra, Madag. 89 C8 20 46 S 47 20 E
Antofagasta, Chile 126 A1 23 50 S 70 30W
Antofagasta □, Chile 126 A2 24 0 S 69 0W
Antofagasta de la Sierra, Argentina 126 B2 26 5 S 67 20W
Antofalla, Argentina 126 B2 25 30 S 68 5W
Antofalla, Salar de, Argentina 126 B2 25 40 S 67 45W
Anton, U.S.A. 113 J3 33 49N 102 10W
Antongila, Helodrano, Madag. 89 B8 15 30 S 49 50 E
Antonibé, Madag. 89 B8 15 7 S 47 24 E
Antonibé, Presqu'île d', Madag. 89 A8 14 55 S 47 20 E
Antonina, Brazil 127 B6 25 26 S 48 42W
Antrain, France 18 D5 48 28N 1 30W
Antrim, U.K. 15 B5 54 43N 6 14W
Antrim, U.S.A. 110 F3 40 7N 81 21W
Antrim □, U.K. 15 B5 54 56N 6 25W
Antrim, Mts. of, U.K. 15 A5 55 3N 6 14W
Antrim Plateau, Australia 92 C4 18 8 S 128 20 E
Antrodoco, Italy 29 F10 42 25N 13 5 E
Antropovo, Russia 48 A6 58 24N 43 6 E
Antsakabary, Madag. 89 B8 15 3 S 48 56 E
Antsalova, Madag. 89 B7 18 40 S 44 37 E
Antsenavolo, Madag. 89 C8 21 24 S 48 3 E
Antsiafabositra, Madag. 89 B8 17 18 S 46 57 E
Antsirabe, Antananarivo, Madag. 89 B8 19 55 S 47 2 E
Antsirabe, Antsiranana, Madag. 89 A8 14 0 S 49 59 E
Antsirabe, Mahajanga, Madag. 89 B8 15 57 S 48 58 E
Antsiranana, Madag. 89 A8 12 25 S 49 20 E
Antsiranana □, Madag. 89 A8 12 16 S 49 17 E
Antsohihy, Madag. 89 A8 14 50 S 47 59 E
Antsohimbondrona Seranana, Madag. 89 A8 13 7 S 48 48 E
Antu, China 57 C15 42 30N 128 20 E
Antwerp = Antwerpen, Belgium 17 C4 51 13N 4 25 E
Antwerp, U.S.A. 111 B9 44 12N 75 37W
Antwerpen, Belgium 17 C4 51 13N 4 25 E
Antwerpen □, Belgium 17 C4 51 15N 4 40 E
Anupgarh, India 68 E5 29 10N 73 10 E
Anuppur, India 69 H9 23 6N 81 41 E
Anuradhapura, Sri Lanka 66 Q12 8 22N 80 28 E
Anveh, Iran 71 E7 27 23N 54 11 E
Anvers = Antwerpen, Belgium 17 C4 51 13N 4 25 E
Anvers I., Antarctica 5 C17 64 30 S 63 40W
Anwen, China 59 C13 29 4N 120 26 E
Anxi, Fujian, China 59 E12 25 2N 118 12 E
Anxi, Gansu, China 60 B4 40 30N 95 43 E
Anxian, China 58 B5 31 40N 104 25 E
Anxiang, China 59 C9 29 27N 112 11 E
Anxious B., Australia 95 E1 33 24 S 134 45 E
Anyama, Ivory C. 82 D4 5 30N 4 3W
Anyang, China 56 F8 36 5N 114 21 E
Anyer-Kidul, Indonesia 63 G11 6 4 S 105 53 E
Anyi, Jiangxi, China 59 C10 28 49N 115 25 E
Anyi, Shanxi, China 56 G6 35 2N 111 2 E
Anyuan, China 59 E10 25 9N 115 21 E
Anyue, China 58 B5 30 9N 105 50 E
Anza, U.S.A. 117 M10 33 35N 116 39W
Anze, China 56 F7 36 10N 112 12 E
Anzhero-Sudzhensk, Russia 50 D9 56 10N 86 0 E
Ánzio, Italy 30 A5 41 27N 12 37 E
Aoga-Shima, Japan 55 H9 32 28N 139 46 E
Aoiz, Spain 32 C3 42 46N 1 22W
Aomen = Macau □, China 59 F9 22 16N 113 35 E
Aomori, Japan 54 D10 40 45N 140 45 E
Aomori □, Japan 54 D10 40 45N 140 40 E
Aonla, India 69 E8 28 16N 79 11 E
Aoraki Mount Cook, N.Z. 91 K3 43 36 S 170 9 E
Aosta, Italy 28 C4 45 45N 7 20 E
Aoudéras, Niger 83 B6 17 45N 8 20 E
Aoukâr, Mauritania 82 B3 17 40N 10 0W
Aozou, Chad 79 D9 21 45N 17 28 E
Apa →, S. Amer. 126 A4 22 6 S 58 2W
Apache, U.S.A. 113 H5 34 54N 98 22W
Apache Junction, U.S.A. 115 K8 33 25N 111 33W
Apalachee B., U.S.A. 109 L4 30 0N 84 0W
Apalachicola, U.S.A. 109 L3 29 43N 84 59W
Apalachicola →, U.S.A. 109 L3 29 43N 84 58W
Apam, Ghana 83 D4 5 19N 0 42W
Apapa, Nigeria 83 D5 6 25N 3 25 E
Apaporis →, Colombia 124 D5 1 23 S 69 25W
Aparri, Phil. 61 B4 18 22N 121 38 E
Apateu, Romania 42 D6 46 36N 21 47 E
Apatin, Serbia, Yug. 42 E4 45 40N 19 0 E
Apatity, Russia 50 C4 67 34N 33 22 E
Apatzingán, Mexico 118 D4 19 0N 102 20W
Apeldoorn, Neths. 17 B5 52 13N 5 57 E
Apen, Germany 24 B3 53 13N 7 48 E
Apennines = Appennini, Italy 28 E7 44 0N 10 0 E
Aphrodisias, Turkey 39 D10 37 42N 28 46 E
Apia, Samoa 91 A13 13 50 S 171 50W
Apiacás, Serra dos, Brazil 124 E7 9 50 S 57 0W
Apies →, S. Africa 89 D4 25 15 S 28 8 E
Apizaco, Mexico 119 D5 19 26N 98 9W
Aplao, Peru 124 G4 16 0 S 72 40W
Apo, Mt., Phil. 63 C7 6 53N 125 14 E
Apolakkiá, Greece 36 C9 36 5N 27 48 E
Apolakkiá, Órmos, Greece 36 C9 36 5N 27 45 E
Apolda, Germany 24 D7 51 2N 11 32 E
Apollo Bay, Australia 95 F3 38 45 S 143 40 E
Apollonia, Greece 38 E6 36 58N 24 43 E
Apolo, Bolivia 124 F5 14 30 S 68 30W
Aporé →, Brazil 125 G8 19 27 S 50 57W
Apostle Is., U.S.A. 112 B9 47 0N 90 40W
Apóstoles, Argentina 127 B4 28 0 S 56 0W
Apostolos Andreas, C., Cyprus 36 D13 35 42N 34 35 E
Apostolovo, Ukraine 47 J7 47 39N 33 39 E
Apoteri, Guyana 124 C7 4 2N 58 32W
Appalachian Mts., U.S.A. 108 G6 38 0N 80 0W
Äppelbo, Sweden 10 D8 60 29N 14 1 E
Appennini, Italy 28 E7 44 0N 10 0 E
Appennino Ligure, Italy 28 D6 44 30N 9 0 E
Appenzell-Ausser Rhoden □, Switz. 25 H5 47 23N 9 23 E
Appenzell-Inner Rhoden □, Switz. 25 H5 47 20N 9 25 E
Appiano, Italy 29 B8 46 28N 11 15 E
Apple Hill, Canada 111 A10 45 13N 74 46W
Apple Valley, U.S.A. 117 L9 34 32N 117 14W
Appleby-in-Westmorland, U.K. 12 C5 54 35N 2 29W
Appleton, U.S.A. 108 C1 44 16N 88 25W
Approuague →, Fr. Guiana 125 C8 4 30N 51 57W
Apricena, Italy 29 G12 41 47N 15 27 E
Aprília, Italy 30 A5 41 36N 12 39 E
Apsheronsk, Russia 49 H4 44 28N 39 42 E
Apsley, Canada 110 B6 44 45N 78 6W
Apt, France 21 E9 43 53N 5 24 E
Apuane, Alpi, Italy 28 D7 44 7N 10 14 E
Apucarana, Brazil 127 A5 23 55 S 51 33W
Apulia = Púglia □, Italy 31 A9 41 15N 16 15 E
Apure →, Venezuela 124 B5 7 37N 66 25W
Apurimac →, Peru 124 F4 12 17 S 73 56W
Apuseni, Munții, Romania 42 D7 46 30N 22 45 E
Āqā Jarī, Iran 71 D6 30 42N 49 50 E
Aqaba = Al ʻAqabah, Jordan 75 F4 29 31N 35 0 E
Aqaba, G. of, Red Sea 70 D2 28 15N 33 20 E
ʻAqabah, Khalīj al = Aqaba, G. of, Red Sea 70 D2 28 15N 33 20 E
ʻAqdā, Iran 71 C7 32 26N 53 37 E
Aqîq, Sudan 80 D4 18 14N 38 12 E
Aqîq, Khalîg, Sudan 80 D4 18 20N 38 10 E
Aqmola = Astana, Kazakstan 50 D8 51 10N 71 30 E
ʻAqrah, Iraq 70 B4 36 46N 43 45 E
Aqtaū, Kazakstan 50 E6 43 39N 51 12 E
Aqtöbe, Kazakstan 50 D6 50 17N 57 10 E
Aquidauana, Brazil 125 H7 20 30 S 55 50W
Aquiles Serdán, Mexico 118 B3 28 37N 105 54W
Aquin, Haiti 121 C5 18 16N 73 24W
Aquitaine □, France 20 D3 44 25N 0 30W
Ar Rachidiya, Morocco 78 B5 31 58N 4 20W
Ar Rafīd, Syria 75 C4 32 57N 35 52 E
Ar Raḩḩālīyah, Iraq 70 C4 32 44N 43 23 E
Ar Ramādī, Iraq 70 C4 33 25N 43 20 E
Ar Ramthā, Jordan 75 C5 32 34N 36 0 E
Ar Raqqah, Syria 70 C3 35 59N 39 8 E
Ar Rass, Si. Arabia 70 E4 25 50N 43 40 E
Ar Rawshān, Si. Arabia 80 C5 20 2N 42 36 E
Ar Rifāʻī, Iraq 70 D5 31 50N 46 10 E
Ar Riyāḍ, Si. Arabia 70 E5 24 41N 46 42 E
Ar Ruʻays, Qatar 71 E6 26 8N 51 12 E
Ar Rukhaymīyah, Iraq 70 D5 29 22N 45 38 E
Ar Ruqayyidah, Si. Arabia 71 E6 25 21N 49 34 E
Ar Ruṣāfah, Syria 70 C3 35 45N 38 49 E
Ar Ruṭbah, Iraq 70 C4 33 0N 40 15 E
Ara, India 69 G11 25 35N 84 32 E
Ara Goro, Ethiopia 81 F5 5 48N 41 18 E
Ara Tera, Ethiopia 81 F5 6 38N 40 57 E
Arab, U.S.A. 109 H2 34 19N 86 30W
ʻArab, Bahr el →, Sudan 81 F2 9 0N 29 30 E
Arab, Khalîg el, Egypt 80 A2 30 55N 29 0 E
Arab, Shatt al →, Asia 71 D6 30 0N 48 31 E
ʻAraba, W. →, Egypt 80 J8 28 19N 33 31 E
ʻArabābād, Iran 71 C8 33 2N 57 41 E
Araban, Turkey 72 D7 37 28N 37 44 E
Arabatskaya Strelka, Ukraine 47 K8 45 40N 35 0 E
Arabba, Italy 29 B8 46 30N 11 52 E
Arabia, Asia 52 G8 25 0N 45 0 E
Arabian Desert = Es Sahrâʼ Esh Sharqîya, Egypt 80 B3 27 30N 32 30 E
Arabian Gulf = Gulf, The, Asia 71 E6 27 0N 50 0 E
Arabian Sea, Ind. Oc. 52 H10 16 0N 65 0 E
Araç, Turkey 72 B5 41 15N 33 21 E
Aracaju, Brazil 125 F11 10 55 S 37 4W
Aracati, Brazil 125 D11 4 30 S 37 44W
Araçatuba, Brazil 127 A5 21 10 S 50 30W
Aracena, Spain 35 H4 37 53N 6 38W
Aracena, Sierra de, Spain 35 H4 37 50N 6 50W
Aračinovo, Macedonia 40 D5 42 1N 21 34 E
Araçuaí, Brazil 125 G10 16 52 S 42 4W
ʻArad, Israel 75 D4 31 15N 35 12 E
Arad, Romania 42 D6 46 10N 21 20 E
Arad □, Romania 42 D6 46 20N 22 0 E
Arādān, Iran 71 C7 35 21N 52 30 E
Aradhippou, Cyprus 36 E12 34 57N 33 36 E
Arafura Sea, E. Indies 52 K17 9 0 S 135 0 E
Aragats, Armenia 49 K7 40 30N 44 15 E
Aragón □, Spain 32 D4 41 25N 0 40W
Aragón →, Spain 32 C3 42 13N 1 44W
Aragona, Italy 30 E6 37 24N 13 27 E
Araguacema, Brazil 125 E9 8 50 S 49 20W
Araguaia →, Brazil 122 D6 5 21 S 48 41W
Araguaína, Brazil 125 E9 7 12 S 48 12W
Araguari, Brazil 125 G9 18 38 S 48 11W
Araguari →, Brazil 125 C9 1 15N 49 55W
Arain, India 68 F6 26 27N 75 2 E
Arak, Algeria 78 C6 25 20N 3 45 E
Arāk, Iran 71 C6 34 0N 49 40 E
Araka, Sudan 81 G3 4 20N 30 23 E
Arakan Coast, Burma 67 K19 19 0N 94 0 E
Arakan Yoma, Burma 67 K19 20 0N 94 40 E
Arákhova, Greece 38 C4 38 28N 22 35 E
Arakli, Turkey 73 B8 41 6N 40 2 E
Araks = Aras, Rūd-e →, Asia 49 K9 40 5N 48 29 E
Aral, Kazakstan 50 E7 46 41N 61 45 E
Aral Sea, Asia 50 E7 44 30N 60 0 E
Aral Tengizi = Aral Sea, Asia 50 E7 44 30N 60 0 E
Aralsk = Aral, Kazakstan 50 E7 46 41N 61 45 E
Aralskoye More = Aral Sea, Asia 50 E7 44 30N 60 0 E
Aralsor, Ozero, Kazakstan 49 F9 49 5N 48 12 E
Aramac, Australia 94 C4 22 58 S 145 14 E
Aran I., Ireland 15 A3 55 0N 8 30W
Aran Is., Ireland 15 C2 53 6N 9 38W
Aranda de Duero, Spain 34 D7 41 39N 3 42W
Arandān, Iran 70 C5 35 23N 46 55 E
Aran[d-]elovac, Serbia, Yug. 40 B4 44 18N 20 34 E
Aranjuez, Spain 34 E7 40 1N 3 40W

Aranos, Namibia 88 C2 24 9S 19 7E
Aransas Pass, U.S.A. 113 M6 27 55N 97 9W
Aranyaprathet, Thailand 64 F4 13 41N 102 30 E
Araouane, Mali 82 B4 18 55N 3 30W
Arapahoe, U.S.A. 112 E5 40 18N 99 54W
Arapey Grande →, Uruguay 126 C4 30 55S 57 49W
Arapgir, Turkey 70 B3 39 5N 38 30 E
Arapiraca, Brazil 125 E11 9 45S 36 39W
Arapongas, Brazil 127 A5 23 29S 51 28W
Ar'ar, Si. Arabia 70 D4 30 59N 41 2 E
Araranguá, Brazil 127 B6 29 0S 49 30W
Araraquara, Brazil 125 H9 21 50S 48 0W
Ararás, Serra das, Brazil 127 B5 25 0S 53 10W
Ararat, Armenia 73 C11 39 48N 44 50 E
Ararat, Australia 95 F3 37 16S 143 0 E
Ararat, Mt. = Ağrı Dağı, Turkey 70 B5 39 50N 44 15 E
Araria, India 69 F12 26 9N 87 33 E
Araripe, Chapada do, Brazil 125 E11 7 20S 40 0W
Araruama, L. de, Brazil 127 A7 22 53S 42 12W
Aras, Rūd-e →, Asia 49 K9 40 5N 48 29 E
Aratāne, Mauritania 82 B3 18 24N 8 32W
Arauca, Colombia 124 B4 7 0N 70 40W
Arauca →, Venezuela 124 B5 7 24N 66 35W
Arauco, Chile 126 D1 37 16S 73 25W
Arawa, Ethiopia 81 F5 9 57N 41 58 E
Araxá, Brazil 125 G9 19 35S 46 55W
Araya, Pen. de, Venezuela 124 A6 10 40N 64 0W
Arba Gugu, Ethiopia 81 F5 8 40N 40 15 E
Arba Minch, Ethiopia 81 F4 6 0N 37 30 E
Arbat, Iraq 70 C5 35 25N 45 35 E
Árbatax, Italy 30 C2 39 56N 9 42 E
Arbi, Ethiopia 81 F4 9 4N 35 7 E
Arbīl, Iraq 70 B5 36 15N 44 5 E
Arboga, Sweden 10 E9 59 24N 15 52 E
Arbois, France 19 F12 46 55N 5 46 E
Arbore, Ethiopia 81 F4 5 3N 36 50 E
Arboréa, Italy 30 C1 39 46N 8 35 E
Arborfield, Canada 105 C8 53 6N 103 39W
Arborg, Canada 105 C9 50 54N 97 13W
Arbre du Ténéré, Niger 83 B7 17 50N 10 4 E
Arbroath, U.K. 14 E6 56 34N 2 35W
Arbuckle, U.S.A. 116 F4 39 1N 122 3W
Arbus, Italy 30 C1 39 30N 8 33 E
Arc →, France 21 C10 45 34N 6 12 E
Arc-lès-Gray, France 19 E12 47 28N 5 34 E
Arcachon, France 20 D2 44 40N 1 10W
Arcachon, Bassin d', France 20 D2 44 42N 1 10W
Arcade, Calif., U.S.A. 117 L8 34 2N 118 15W
Arcade, N.Y., U.S.A. 110 D6 42 32N 78 25W
Arcadia, Fla., U.S.A. 109 M5 27 13N 81 52W
Arcadia, La., U.S.A. 113 J8 32 33N 92 55W
Arcadia, Pa., U.S.A. 110 F6 40 47N 78 51W
Arcata, U.S.A. 114 F1 40 52N 124 5W
Arcévia, Italy 29 E9 43 30N 12 56 E
Archangel = Arkhangelsk, Russia 50 C5 64 38N 40 36 E
Archar, Bulgaria 40 C6 43 50N 22 54 E
Archbald, U.S.A. 111 E9 41 30N 75 32W
Archena, Spain 33 G3 38 9N 1 16W
Archer →, Australia 94 A3 13 28S 141 41 E
Archer B., Australia 94 A3 13 20S 141 30 E
Archers Post, Kenya 86 B4 0 35N 37 35 E
Arches National Park, U.S.A. 115 G9 38 45N 109 25W
Archidona, Spain 35 H6 37 6N 4 22W
Arci, Mte., Italy 30 C1 39 47N 8 45 E
Arcidosso, Italy 29 F8 42 52N 11 33 E
Arcis-sur-Aube, France 19 D11 48 32N 4 10 E
Arckaringa Cr. →, Australia 95 D2 28 10S 135 22 E
Arco, Italy 28 C7 45 55N 10 53 E
Arco, U.S.A. 114 E7 43 38N 113 18W
Arcos = Arcos de Jalón, Spain 32 D2 41 12N 2 16W
Arcos de Jalón, Spain 32 D2 41 12N 2 16W
Arcos de la Frontera, Spain 35 J5 36 45N 5 49W
Arcos de Valdevez, Portugal 34 D2 41 55N 8 22W
Arcot, India 66 N11 12 53N 79 20 E
Arcozelo, Portugal 34 E3 40 32N 7 47W
Arctic Bay, Canada 101 A11 73 1N 85 7W
Arctic Ocean, Arctic 4 B18 78 0N 160 0W
Arctic Red River = Tsiigehtchic, Canada 100 B6 67 15N 134 0W
Arda →, Bulgaria 41 E10 41 40N 26 30 E
Arda →, Italy 28 C7 45 2N 10 2 E
Ardabīl, Iran 71 B6 38 15N 48 18 E
Ardahan, Turkey 73 B10 41 7N 42 41 E
Ardakān = Sepīdān, Iran 71 D7 30 20N 52 5 E
Ardakān, Iran 71 C7 32 19N 53 59 E
Ardala, Sweden 11 F7 58 22N 13 19 E
Ardales, Spain 35 J6 36 53N 4 51W
Ardèche □, France 21 D8 44 42N 4 16 E
Ardèche →, France 21 D8 44 16N 4 39 E
Ardee, Ireland 15 C5 53 52N 6 33W
Arden, Canada 110 B8 44 43N 76 56W
Arden, Denmark 11 H3 56 46N 9 52 E
Arden, Calif., U.S.A. 116 G5 38 36N 121 33W
Arden, Nev., U.S.A. 117 J11 36 1N 115 14W
Ardenne, Belgium 6 F7 49 50N 5 5 E
Ardennes = Ardenne, Belgium 6 F7 49 50N 5 5 E
Ardennes □, France 19 C11 49 35N 4 40 E
Ardentes, France 19 F8 46 45N 1 50 E
Arderin, Ireland 15 C4 53 2N 7 39W
Ardeşen, Turkey 73 B9 41 12N 41 2 E
Ardestān, Iran 71 C7 33 20N 52 25 E
Ardhas →, Greece 41 E10 41 40N 26 30 E
Ardhéa, Greece 40 F6 40 58N 22 3 E
Ardila →, Portugal 35 G3 38 12N 7 28W
Ardino, Bulgaria 41 E9 41 34N 25 9 E
Ardivachar Pt., U.K. 14 D1 57 23N 7 26W
Ardlethan, Australia 95 E4 34 22S 146 53 E
Ardmore, Okla., U.S.A. 113 H6 34 10N 97 8W
Ardmore, Pa., U.S.A. 111 G9 39 58N 75 18W
Ardnamurchan, Pt. of, U.K. 14 E2 56 43N 6 14W
Ardnave Pt., U.K. 14 F2 55 53N 6 20W
Ardon, Russia 49 J7 43 10N 44 18 E
Ardore, Italy 31 D9 38 11N 16 10 E
Ardres, France 19 B8 50 50N 1 59 E
Ardrossan, Australia 95 E2 34 26S 137 53 E
Ardrossan, U.K. 14 F4 55 39N 4 49W
Ards Pen., U.K. 15 B6 54 33N 5 34W
Arduan, Sudan 80 D3 19 54N 30 20 E
Ardud, Romania 42 C7 47 37N 22 52 E
Åre, Sweden 10 A7 63 22N 13 15 E
Arecibo, Puerto Rico 121 C6 18 29N 66 43W
Areia Branca, Brazil 125 E11 5 0S 37 0W
Arena, Pt., U.S.A. 116 G3 38 57N 123 44W
Arenal, Honduras 120 C2 15 21N 86 50W
Arenas = Las Arenas, Spain 34 B6 43 17N 4 50W
Arenas de San Pedro, Spain 34 E5 40 12N 5 5W
Arendal, Norway 9 G13 58 28N 8 46 E
Arendsee, Germany 24 C7 52 52N 11 27 E
Arenys de Mar, Spain 32 D7 41 35N 2 33 E
Arenzano, Italy 28 D5 44 24N 8 41 E
Areópolis, Greece 38 E4 36 40N 22 22 E
Arequipa, Peru 124 G4 16 20S 71 30W
Arero, Ethiopia 81 G4 4 41N 38 50 E
Arès, France 20 D2 44 47N 1 8W
Arévalo, Spain 34 D6 41 3N 4 43W
Arezzo, Italy 29 E8 43 25N 11 53 E
Arga, Turkey 70 B3 38 21N 37 59 E
Arga →, Spain 32 C3 42 18N 1 47W
Argalastí, Greece 38 B5 39 13N 23 13 E
Argamasilla de Alba, Spain 35 F7 39 8N 3 5W
Argamasilla de Calatrava, Spain 35 G6 38 44N 4 4W
Arganda, Spain 34 E7 40 19N 3 26W
Arganil, Portugal 34 E2 40 13N 8 3W
Argedeb, Ethiopia 81 F5 6 11N 41 13 E
Argelès-Gazost, France 20 E3 43 0N 0 6W
Argelès-sur-Mer, France 20 F7 42 34N 3 1 E
Argens →, France 21 E10 43 24N 6 44 E
Argent-sur-Sauldre, France 19 E9 47 33N 2 25 E
Argenta, Canada 104 C5 50 11N 116 56W
Argenta, Italy 29 D8 44 37N 11 50 E
Argentan, France 18 D6 48 45N 0 1W
Argentário, Mte., Italy 29 F8 42 24N 11 9 E
Argentat, France 20 C5 45 6N 1 56 E
Argentera, Italy 28 D4 44 12N 7 5 E
Argenteuil, France 19 D9 48 57N 2 14 E
Argentia, Canada 103 C9 47 18N 53 58W
Argentiera, C. dell', Italy 30 B1 40 44N 8 8 E
Argentina ■, S. Amer. 128 D3 35 0S 66 0W
Argentina Is., Antarctica 5 C17 66 0S 64 0W
Argentino, L., Argentina 128 G2 50 10S 73 0W
Argenton-Château, France 18 F6 46 59N 0 27W
Argenton-sur-Creuse, France 19 F8 46 36N 1 30 E
Arges □, Romania 43 F9 45 0N 24 45 E
Arges →, Romania 43 F11 44 5N 26 38 E
Arghandab →, Afghan. 68 D1 31 30N 64 15 E
Argheile, Ethiopia 81 F5 5 19N 42 4 E
Argo, Sudan 80 D3 19 28N 30 30 E
Argolikós Kólpos, Greece 38 D4 37 20N 22 52 E
Argolís □, Greece 38 D4 37 38N 22 50 E
Argonne, France 19 C12 49 10N 5 0 E
Árgos, Greece 38 D4 37 40N 22 43 E
Árgos Orestikón, Greece 40 F5 40 27N 21 18 E
Argostólion, Greece 38 C2 38 12N 20 33 E
Arguedas, Spain 32 C3 42 11N 1 36W
Arguello, Pt., U.S.A. 117 L6 34 35N 120 39W
Arguineguín, Canary Is. 37 G4 27 46N 15 41W
Argun, Russia 49 J7 43 22N 45 55 E
Argun →, Russia 51 D13 53 20N 121 28 E
Argungu, Nigeria 83 C5 12 40N 4 31 E
Argus Pk., U.S.A. 117 K9 35 52N 117 26W
Argyle, L., Australia 92 C4 16 20S 128 40 E
Argyll & Bute □, U.K. 14 E3 56 13N 5 28W
Arhavi, Turkey 73 B9 41 21N 41 18 E
Århus, Denmark 11 H4 56 8N 10 11 E
Århus Amtskommune □, Denmark 11 H4 56 15N 10 15 E
Ariadnoye, Russia 54 B7 45 8N 134 25 E
Ariamsvlei, Namibia 88 D2 28 9S 19 51 E
Ariana, Tunisia 79 A7 36 52N 10 12 E
Ariano Irpino, Italy 31 A8 41 9N 15 5 E
Aribinda, Burkina Faso 83 C4 14 17N 0 52W
Arica, Chile 124 G4 18 32S 70 20W
Arica, Colombia 124 D4 2 0S 71 50W
Arico, Canary Is. 37 F3 28 9N 16 29W
Arid, C., Australia 93 F3 34 1S 123 10 E
Arida, Japan 55 G7 34 5N 135 8 E
Ariège □, France 20 F5 42 56N 1 30 E
Ariège →, France 20 E5 43 30N 1 25 E
Aries →, Romania 43 D8 46 24N 23 20 E
Arihā, Israel 80 A4 31 51N 35 27 E
Arilje, Serbia, Yug. 40 C4 43 44N 20 7 E
Arílla, Ákra, Greece 36 A3 39 43N 19 39 E
Arima, Trin. & Tob. 121 D7 10 38N 61 17W
Arinos →, Brazil 122 E5 10 25S 58 20W
Ario de Rosales, Mexico 118 D4 19 12N 102 0W
Ariogala, Lithuania 44 C10 55 16N 23 28 E
Aripuanã, Brazil 124 E6 9 25S 60 30W
Aripuanã →, Brazil 122 D4 5 7S 60 25W
Ariquemes, Brazil 124 E6 9 55S 63 6W
Arisaig, U.K. 14 E3 56 55N 5 51W
Arîsh, W. el →, Egypt 80 A3 31 9N 33 49 E
Arissa, Ethiopia 81 E5 11 10N 41 35 E
Aristazabal I., Canada 104 C3 52 40N 129 10W
Arivonimamo, Madag. 89 B8 19 1S 47 11 E
Ariza, Spain 32 D2 41 19N 2 3W
Arizaro, Salar de, Argentina 126 A2 24 40S 67 50W
Arizona, Argentina 126 D2 35 45S 65 25W
Arizona □, U.S.A. 115 J8 34 0N 112 0W
Arizpe, Mexico 118 A2 30 20N 110 11W
Årjäng, Sweden 10 E6 59 24N 12 8 E
Arjeplog, Sweden 8 D18 66 3N 18 2 E
Arjona, Colombia 124 A3 10 14N 75 22W
Arjona, Spain 35 H6 37 56N 4 4W
Arjuna, Indonesia 63 G15 7 49S 112 34 E
Arka, Russia 51 C15 60 15N 142 0 E
Arkadak, Russia 48 E6 51 58N 43 30 E
Arkadelphia, U.S.A. 113 H8 34 7N 93 4W
Arkadhía □, Greece 38 D4 37 30N 22 20 E
Arkaig, L., U.K. 14 E3 56 59N 5 10W
Arkalyk = Arqalyk, Kazakstan 50 D7 50 13N 66 50 E
Arkansas □, U.S.A. 113 H8 35 0N 92 30W
Arkansas →, U.S.A. 113 J9 33 47N 91 4W
Arkansas City, U.S.A. 113 G6 37 4N 97 2W
Arkaroola, Australia 95 E2 30 20S 139 22 E
Árkathos →, Greece 38 B3 39 20N 21 4 E
Arkhángelos, Greece 36 C10 36 13N 28 7 E
Arkhangelsk, Russia 50 C5 64 38N 40 36 E
Arkhangelskoye, Russia 48 E5 51 32N 40 58 E
Arki, India 68 D7 31 9N 76 58 E
Arkiko, Eritrea 81 D4 15 33N 39 30 E
Arklow, Ireland 15 D5 52 48N 6 10W
Árkoi, Greece 39 D8 37 24N 26 44 E
Arkona, Kap, Germany 24 A9 54 42N 13 26 E
Arkösund, Sweden 11 F10 58 29N 16 56 E
Arkoúdhi, Greece 38 C2 38 33N 20 43 E
Arkport, U.S.A. 110 D7 42 24N 77 42W
Arkticheskiy, Mys, Russia 51 A10 81 10N 95 0 E
Arkul, Russia 48 B10 57 17N 50 3 E
Arkville, U.S.A. 111 D10 42 9N 74 37W
Årla, Sweden 10 E10 59 17N 16 40 E
Arlanza →, Spain 34 C6 42 6N 4 9W
Arlanzón →, Spain 34 C6 42 3N 4 17W
Arlbergpass, Austria 26 D3 47 9N 10 12 E
Arles, France 21 E8 43 41N 4 40 E
Arlington, S. Africa 89 D4 28 1S 27 53 E
Arlington, N.Y., U.S.A. 111 E11 41 42N 73 54W
Arlington, Oreg., U.S.A. 114 D3 45 43N 120 12W
Arlington, S. Dak., U.S.A. 112 C6 44 22N 97 8W
Arlington, Tex., U.S.A. 113 J6 32 44N 97 7W
Arlington, Va., U.S.A. 108 F7 38 53N 77 7W
Arlington, Vt., U.S.A. 111 C11 43 5N 73 9W
Arlington, Wash., U.S.A. 116 B4 48 12N 122 8W
Arlington Heights, U.S.A. 108 D2 42 5N 87 59W
Arlit, Niger 78 E7 19 0N 7 38 E
Arlon, Belgium 17 E5 49 42N 5 49 E
Arltunga, Australia 94 C1 23 26S 134 41 E
Arly, Burkina Faso 83 C5 11 35N 1 28 E
Armagh, U.K. 15 B5 54 21N 6 39W
Armagh □, U.K. 15 B5 54 18N 6 37W
Armagnac, France 20 E4 43 50N 0 10 E
Armançon →, France 19 E10 47 59N 3 30 E
Armavir, Russia 49 H5 45 2N 41 7 E
Armenia, Colombia 124 C3 4 35N 75 45W
Armenia ■, Asia 49 K7 40 20N 45 0 E
Armenis, Romania 42 E7 45 13N 22 17 E
Armenistís, Ákra, Greece 36 C9 36 8N 27 42 E
Armentières, France 19 B9 50 40N 2 50 E
Armidale, Australia 95 E5 30 30S 151 40 E
Armilla, Spain 35 H7 37 9N 3 37W
Armour, U.S.A. 112 D5 43 19N 98 21W
Armstrong, B.C., Canada 104 C5 50 25N 119 10W
Armstrong, Ont., Canada 102 B2 50 18N 89 4W
Armutlu, Bursa, Turkey 41 F12 40 31N 28 50 E
Armutlu, Izmir, Turkey 39 C9 38 24N 27 34 E
Arnaía, Greece 40 F7 40 30N 23 38 E
Arnarfjörður, Iceland 8 D2 65 48N 23 40W
Arnaud →, Canada 101 B12 60 0N 70 0W
Arnauti, C., Cyprus 36 D11 35 6N 32 17 E
Arnay-le-Duc, France 19 E11 47 10N 4 27 E
Arnedillo, Spain 32 C2 42 13N 2 14W
Arnedo, Spain 32 C2 42 12N 2 5W
Arnett, U.S.A. 113 G5 36 8N 99 46W
Arnhem, Neths. 17 C5 51 58N 5 55 E
Arnhem, C., Australia 94 A2 12 20S 137 30 E
Arnhem B., Australia 94 A2 12 20S 136 10 E
Arnhem Land, Australia 94 A1 13 10S 134 30 E
Árnissa, Greece 40 F5 40 47N 21 49 E
Arno →, Italy 28 E7 43 41N 10 17 E
Arno Bay, Australia 95 E2 33 54S 136 34 E
Arnold, U.K. 12 D6 53 1N 1 7W
Arnold, U.S.A. 116 G6 38 15N 120 20W
Arnoldstein, Austria 26 E6 46 33N 13 43 E
Arnon →, France 19 E9 47 13N 2 1 E
Arnot, Canada 105 B9 55 56N 96 41W
Arnøy, Norway 8 A19 70 9N 20 40 E
Arnprior, Canada 102 C4 45 26N 76 21W
Arnsberg, Germany 24 D4 51 24N 8 5 E
Arnstadt, Germany 24 E6 50 50N 10 56 E
Aroab, Namibia 88 D2 26 41S 19 39 E
Aroánia Óri, Greece 38 D4 37 56N 22 12 E
Aroche, Spain 35 H4 37 56N 6 57W
Arochuku, Nigeria 83 D6 5 21N 7 54 E
Arolsen, Germany 24 D5 51 23N 9 2 E
Aron, India 68 G6 25 57N 77 56 E
Aron →, France 19 F10 46 50N 3 28 E
Arona, Italy 28 C5 45 46N 8 34 E
Aroroy, Phil. 61 E5 12 31N 123 24 E
Arosa, Ría de, Spain 34 C2 42 28N 8 57W
Arpajon, France 19 D9 48 36N 2 15 E
Arpajon-sur-Cère, France 20 D6 44 53N 2 28 E
Arpaşu de Jos, Romania 43 E9 45 47N 24 37 E
Arqalyk, Kazakstan 50 D7 50 13N 66 50 E
Arrah = Ara, India 69 G11 25 35N 84 32 E
Arrah, Ivory C. 82 D4 6 40N 3 58W
Arraiolos, Portugal 35 G3 38 44N 7 59W
Arran, U.K. 14 F3 55 34N 5 12W
Arras, France 19 B9 50 17N 2 46 E
Arrasate, Spain 32 B2 43 4N 2 30W
Arrats →, France 20 D4 44 6N 0 52 E
Arreau, France 20 F4 42 54N 0 22 E
Arrecife, Canary Is. 37 F6 28 57N 13 37W
Arrecifes, Argentina 126 C3 34 6S 60 9W
Arrée, Mts. d', France 18 D3 48 26N 3 55W
Arresø, Denmark 11 J6 55 58N 12 6 E
Arriaga, Chiapas, Mexico 119 D6 16 15N 93 52W
Arriaga, San Luis Potosí, Mexico 118 C4 21 55N 101 23W
Arrilalah, Australia 94 C3 23 43S 143 54 E
Arrino, Australia 93 E2 29 30S 115 40 E
Arriondas, Spain 34 B5 43 23N 5 11W
Arromanches-les-Bains, France 18 C6 49 20N 0 38W
Arronches, Portugal 35 F3 39 8N 7 16W
Arros →, France 20 E3 43 40N 0 2W
Arrow, L., Ireland 15 B3 54 3N 8 19W
Arrowhead, L., U.S.A. 117 L9 34 16N 117 10W
Arrowtown, N.Z. 91 L2 44 57S 168 50 E
Arroyo de la Luz, Spain 35 F4 39 30N 6 38W
Arroyo Grande, U.S.A. 117 K6 35 7N 120 35W
Ärs, Denmark 11 H3 56 48N 9 30 E
Ars, Iran 70 B5 37 9N 47 46 E
Ars-sur-Moselle, France 19 C13 49 5N 6 4 E
Arsenault L., Canada 105 B7 55 6N 108 32W
Arsenev, Russia 54 B6 44 10N 133 15 E
Arsi □, Ethiopia 81 F4 7 45N 39 0 E
Arsiero, Italy 29 C8 45 48N 11 21 E
Arsin, Turkey 73 B8 41 8N 39 55 E
Arsk, Russia 48 B9 56 10N 49 50 E
Årsunda, Sweden 10 D10 60 31N 16 45 E
Árta, Greece 38 B3 39 8N 21 2 E
Artà, Spain 37 B10 39 41N 3 21 E
Árta □, Greece 38 B3 39 15N 21 5 E
Arteaga, Mexico 118 D4 18 50N 102 20W
Arteche, Phil. 61 E6 12 17N 125 22 E
Arteijo = Arteixo, Spain 34 B2 43 19N 8 29W
Arteixo, Spain 34 B2 43 19N 8 29W
Artem = Artyom, Azerbaijan 49 K10 40 28N 50 20 E
Artem, Russia 54 C6 43 22N 132 13 E
Artemovsk, Russia 51 D10 54 45N 93 35 E
Artemovsk, Ukraine 47 H9 48 35N 38 0 E
Artemovskiy, Russia 49 G5 47 45N 40 16 E
Artenay, France 19 D8 48 5N 1 50 E
Artern, Germany 24 D7 51 22N 11 18 E
Artesa de Segre, Spain 32 D6 41 54N 1 3 E
Artesia = Mosomane, Botswana 88 C4 24 2S 26 19 E
Artesia, U.S.A. 113 J2 32 51N 104 24W
Arthington, Liberia 82 D2 6 35N 10 45W
Arthur, Canada 110 C4 43 50N 80 32W
Arthur →, Australia 94 G3 41 2S 144 40 E
Arthur Cr. →, Australia 94 C2 22 30S 136 25 E
Arthur Pt., Australia 94 C5 22 7S 150 3 E
Arthur River, Australia 93 F2 33 20S 117 2 E
Arthur's Pass, N.Z. 91 K3 42 54S 171 35 E
Arthur's Town, Bahamas 121 B4 24 38N 75 42W
Artigas, Uruguay 126 C4 30 20S 56 30W
Artik, Armenia 49 K6 40 38N 43 58 E
Artillery L., Canada 105 A7 63 9N 107 52W
Artois, France 19 B9 50 20N 2 30 E
Artotína, Greece 38 C4 38 42N 22 2 E
Artrutx, C. de, Spain 37 B10 39 55N 3 49 E
Artsyz, Ukraine 47 J5 46 4N 29 26 E
Artvin, Turkey 73 B9 41 14N 41 44 E
Artyom, Azerbaijan 49 K10 40 28N 50 20 E
Aru, Kepulauan, Indonesia 63 F8 6 0S 134 30 E
Aru Is. = Aru, Kepulauan, Indonesia 63 F8 6 0S 134 30 E
Arua, Uganda 86 B3 3 1N 30 58 E
Aruanã, Brazil 125 F8 14 54S 51 10W
Aruba ■, W. Indies 121 D6 12 30N 70 0W
Arucas, Canary Is. 37 F4 28 7N 15 32W
Arudy, France 20 E3 43 7N 0 28W
Arun →, Nepal 69 F12 26 55N 87 10 E
Arun →, U.K. 13 G7 50 49N 0 33W
Arunachal Pradesh □, India 67 F19 28 0N 95 0 E
Arusha, Tanzania 86 C4 3 20S 36 40 E
Arusha □, Tanzania 86 C4 4 0S 36 30 E
Arusha Chini, Tanzania 86 C4 3 32S 37 20 E
Aruwimi →, Dem. Rep. of the Congo 86 B1 1 13N 23 36 E
Arvada, Colo., U.S.A. 112 F2 39 48N 105 5W
Arvada, Wyo., U.S.A. 114 D10 44 39N 106 8W
Arve →, France 19 F13 46 11N 6 8 E
Árvi, Greece 36 E7 34 59N 25 28 E
Arviat, Canada 105 A10 61 6N 93 59W
Arvidsjaur, Sweden 8 D18 65 35N 19 10 E
Arvika, Sweden 10 E6 59 40N 12 36 E
Arvin, U.S.A. 117 K8 35 12N 118 50W
Arwal, India 69 G11 25 15N 84 41 E
Arxan, China 60 B6 47 11N 119 57 E
Åryd, Sweden 11 H8 56 49N 14 59 E
Aryirádhes, Greece 36 B3 39 27N 19 58 E
Aryiroúpolis, Greece 36 D6 35 17N 24 20 E
Arys, Kazakstan 50 E7 42 26N 68 48 E
Arzachena, Italy 30 A2 41 5N 9 23 E
Arzamas, Russia 48 C6 55 27N 43 55 E
Arzgir, Russia 49 H7 45 18N 44 23 E
Arzignano, Italy 29 C8 45 31N 11 20 E
Arzúa, Spain 34 C2 42 56N 8 9W
Aš, Czech Rep. 26 A5 50 13N 12 12 E
Ås, Sweden 10 A8 63 15N 14 34 E
As Pontes de García Rodríguez, Spain 34 B3 43 27N 7 50W
Aş Şadr, U.A.E. 71 E7 24 40N 54 41 E
Aş Şafā, Syria 75 B6 33 10N 37 0 E
As Saffānīyah, Si. Arabia 71 E6 27 55N 48 50 E
As Safīrah, Syria 70 B3 36 5N 37 21 E
Aş Şahm, Oman 71 E8 24 10N 56 53 E
As Sājir, Si. Arabia 70 E5 25 11N 44 36 E
As Salamīyah, Syria 70 C3 35 1N 37 2 E
As Salmān, Iraq 70 D5 30 30N 44 32 E
As Salt, Jordan 75 C4 32 2N 35 43 E
As Sal'w'a, Qatar 71 E6 24 23N 50 50 E
As Samāwah, Iraq 70 D5 31 15N 45 15 E
As Sanamayn, Syria 75 B5 33 3N 36 10 E
As Sohar = Şuḩār, Oman 71 E8 24 20N 56 40 E
As Sukhnah, Syria 70 C3 34 52N 38 52 E
As Sulaymānīyah, Iraq 70 C5 35 35N 45 29 E
As Sulaymī, Si. Arabia 70 E4 26 17N 41 21 E
As Sulayyil, Si. Arabia 74 C4 20 27N 45 34 E
As Summān, Si. Arabia 70 E5 25 0N 47 0 E
As Suwaydā', Syria 75 C5 32 40N 36 30 E
As Suwaydā' □, Syria 75 C5 32 45N 36 45 E
As Suwayq, Oman 71 F8 23 51N 57 26 E
Aş Şuwayrah, Iraq 70 C5 32 55N 45 0 E
Åsa, Sweden 11 G6 57 21N 12 8 E
Asab, Namibia 88 D2 25 30S 18 0 E
Asaba, Nigeria 83 D6 6 12N 6 38 E
Asad, Buḩayrat al, Syria 70 C3 36 0N 38 15 E
Asadābād, Iran 73 E13 34 47N 48 7 E
Asafo, Ghana 82 D4 6 20N 2 40W
Asahi-Gawa →, Japan 55 G6 34 36N 133 58 E
Asahigawa, Japan 54 C11 43 46N 142 22 E
Asale, L., Ethiopia 81 E5 14 0N 40 20 E
Asamankese, Ghana 83 D4 5 50N 0 40W
Asan →, India 69 F8 26 37N 78 24 E
Asansol, India 69 H12 23 40N 87 1 E
Åsarna, Sweden 10 B8 62 39N 14 22 E
Asayita, Ethiopia 81 E5 11 35N 41 23 E
Asbe Teferi, Ethiopia 81 F5 9 4N 40 49 E
Asbesberge, S. Africa 88 D3 29 0S 23 0 E
Asbestos, Canada 103 C5 45 47N 71 58W
Asbury Park, U.S.A. 111 F10 40 13N 74 1W
Ascea, Italy 31 B8 40 8N 15 11 E
Ascensión, Mexico 118 A3 31 6N 107 59W
Ascensión, B. de la, Mexico 119 D7 19 50N 87 20W
Ascension I., Atl. Oc. 77 G2 8 0S 14 15W
Aschach an der Donau, Austria 26 C7 48 22N 14 2 E
Aschaffenburg, Germany 25 F5 49 58N 9 6 E
Aschendorf, Germany 24 B3 53 3N 7 19 E
Aschersleben, Germany 24 D7 51 45N 11 29 E
Asciano, Italy 29 E8 43 14N 11 33 E
Áscoli Piceno, Italy 29 F10 42 51N 13 34 E
Áscoli Satriano, Italy 31 A8 41 11N 15 32 E
Ascope, Peru 124 E3 7 46S 79 8W
Ascotán, Chile 126 A2 21 45S 68 17W
Aseb, Eritrea 81 E5 13 0N 42 40 E
Åseda, Sweden 11 G9 57 10N 15 20 E
Asela, Ethiopia 81 F4 8 0N 39 0 E
Åsen, Sweden 10 C7 61 17N 13 50 E
Asenovgrad, Bulgaria 41 D8 42 1N 24 51 E
Aserradero, Mexico 118 C3 23 40N 105 43W
Asfeld, France 19 C11 49 27N 4 5 E
Asfûn el Matâ'na, Egypt 80 B3 25 26N 32 30 E
Asgata, Cyprus 36 E12 34 46N 33 15 E
Ash Fork, U.S.A. 115 J7 35 13N 112 29W
Ash Grove, U.S.A. 113 G8 37 19N 93 35W
Ash Shabakah, Iraq 70 D4 30 49N 43 39 E
Ash Shamāl □, Lebanon 75 A5 34 25N 36 0 E
Ash Shāmīyah, Iraq 70 D5 31 55N 44 35 E
Ash Shāriqah, U.A.E. 71 E7 25 23N 55 26 E
Ash Sharmah, Si. Arabia 70 D2 28 1N 35 16 E
Ash Sharqāt, Iraq 70 C4 35 27N 43 16 E
Ash Sharqi, Al Jabal, Lebanon 75 B5 33 40N 36 10 E
Ash Shaṭrah, Iraq 70 D5 31 30N 46 10 E
Ash Shawbak, Jordan 70 D2 30 32N 35 34 E
Ash Shawmari, J., Jordan 75 E5 30 35N 36 35 E
Ash Shināfīyah, Iraq 70 D5 31 35N 44 39 E
Ash Shu'bah, Si. Arabia 70 D5 28 54N 44 44 E
Ash Shumlūl, Si. Arabia 70 E5 26 31N 47 20 E
Ash Shūr'a, Iraq 70 C4 35 58N 43 13 E
Ash Shurayf, Si. Arabia 70 E3 25 43N 39 14 E
Ash Shuwayfāt, Lebanon 75 B4 33 45N 35 30 E
Ashanti □, Ghana 83 D4 7 30N 1 30W
Ashau, Vietnam 64 D6 16 6N 107 22 E
Ashbourne, U.K. 12 D6 53 2N 1 43W
Ashburn, U.S.A. 109 K4 31 43N 83 39W
Ashburton, N.Z. 91 K3 43 53S 171 48 E
Ashburton →, Australia 92 D1 21 40S 114 56 E
Ashcroft, Canada 104 C4 50 40N 121 20W
Ashdod, Israel 75 D3 31 49N 34 35 E
Ashdown, U.S.A. 113 J7 33 40N 94 8W
Asheboro, U.S.A. 109 H6 35 43N 79 49W
Ashern, Canada 105 C9 51 11N 98 21W
Asherton, U.S.A. 113 L5 28 27N 99 46W
Asheville, U.S.A. 109 H4 35 36N 82 33W
Ashewat, Pakistan 68 D3 31 22N 68 32 E
Asheweig →, Canada 102 B2 54 17N 87 12W
Ashford, Australia 95 D5 29 15S 151 3 E
Ashford, U.K. 13 F8 51 8N 0 53 E
Ashgabat, Turkmenistan 50 F6 38 0N 57 50 E
Ashibetsu, Japan 54 C11 43 31N 142 11 E
Ashikaga, Japan 55 F9 36 28N 139 29 E
Ashington, U.K. 12 B6 55 11N 1 33W
Ashizuri-Zaki, Japan 55 H6 32 44N 133 0 E
Ashkarkot, Afghan. 68 C2 33 3N 67 58 E
Ashkhabad = Ashgabat, Turkmenistan 50 F6 38 0N 57 50 E
Āshkhāneh, Iran 71 B8 37 26N 56 55 E
Ashland, Kans., U.S.A. 113 G5 37 11N 99 46W
Ashland, Ky., U.S.A. 108 F4 38 28N 82 38W
Ashland, Mont., U.S.A. 114 D10 45 36N 106 16W
Ashland, Ohio, U.S.A. 110 F2 40 52N 82 19W
Ashland, Oreg., U.S.A. 114 E2 42 12N 122 43W
Ashland, Pa., U.S.A. 111 F8 40 45N 76 22W
Ashland, Va., U.S.A. 108 G7 37 46N 77 29W
Ashland, Wis., U.S.A. 112 B9 46 35N 90 53W
Ashley, N. Dak., U.S.A. 112 B5 46 2N 99 22W
Ashley, Pa., U.S.A. 111 E9 41 12N 75 55W
Ashmore Reef, Australia 92 B3 12 14S 123 5 E
Ashmûn, Egypt 80 H7 30 18N 30 55 E
Ashmyany, Belarus 9 J21 54 26N 25 52 E
Ashokan Reservoir, U.S.A. 111 E10 41 56N 74 13W
Ashqelon, Israel 75 D3 31 42N 34 35 E
Ashta, India 68 H7 23 1N 76 43 E
Ashtabula, U.S.A. 110 E4 41 52N 80 47W
Ashton, S. Africa 88 E3 33 50S 20 5 E
Ashton, U.S.A. 114 D8 44 4N 111 27W
Ashuanipi, L., Canada 103 B6 52 45N 66 15W
Ashville, U.S.A. 110 F6 40 34N 78 33W
'Āṣī →, Asia 72 D6 36 1N 35 59 E
Asia 52 E11 45 0N 75 0 E
Asia, Kepulauan, Indonesia 63 D8 1 0N 131 13 E
Āsīā Bak, Iran 71 C6 35 19N 50 30 E
Asiago, Italy 29 C8 45 52N 11 30 E
Asifabad, India 66 K11 19 20N 79 24 E
Asinara, Italy 30 A1 41 4N 8 16 E
Asinara, G. dell', Italy 30 A1 41 0N 8 30 E
Asino, Russia 50 D9 57 0N 86 0 E
Asipovichy, Belarus 46 F5 53 19N 28 33 E
'Asīr □, Si. Arabia 74 D3 18 40N 42 30 E
Asir, Ras, Somali Rep. 74 E5 11 55N 51 10 E
Aşkale, Turkey 73 C9 39 55N 40 41 E
Askersund, Sweden 11 F8 58 53N 14 55 E
Askham, S. Africa 88 D3 26 59S 20 47 E
Askim, Norway 9 G14 59 35N 11 10 E
Askja, Iceland 8 D5 65 3N 16 48W
Askøy, Norway 9 F11 60 29N 5 10 E
Asl, Egypt 80 B3 29 33N 32 44 E
Aslan Burnu, Turkey 39 C8 38 44N 26 45 E
Aslanapa, Turkey 39 B11 39 13N 29 52 E
Asmara = Asmera, Eritrea 81 D4 15 19N 38 55 E
Asmera, Eritrea 81 D4 15 19N 38 55 E
Asnæs, Denmark 11 J4 55 40N 11 0 E
Åsnen, Sweden 11 H8 56 37N 14 45 E
Ásola, Italy 28 C7 45 13N 10 24 E
Asosa, Ethiopia 81 E3 10 3N 34 32 E
Asoteriba, Jebel, Sudan 80 C4 21 51N 36 30 E
Aspe, Spain 33 G4 38 20N 0 40W
Aspen, U.S.A. 115 G10 39 11N 106 49W
Aspendos, Turkey 72 D4 36 54N 31 7 E
Aspermont, U.S.A. 113 J4 33 8N 100 14W
Aspet, France 20 E4 43 1N 0 48 E
Aspiring, Mt., N.Z. 91 L2 44 23S 168 46 E
Aspres-sur-Buëch, France 21 D9 44 32N 5 44 E
Asprókavos, Ákra, Greece 36 B4 39 21N 20 6 E
Aspromonte, Italy 31 D9 38 10N 16 0 E
Aspur, India 68 H6 23 58N 74 7 E
Asquith, Canada 105 C7 52 8N 107 13W

Assâba, Massif de l', Mauritania 82 B2 16 10N 11 45W
Assaikio, Nigeria 83 D6 8 34N 8 55 E
Assal, L., Djibouti 81 E5 11 40N 42 26 E
Assam □, India 67 G18 26 0N 93 0 E
Assamakka, Niger 83 B6 19 21N 5 38 E
Asse, Belgium 17 D4 50 24N 4 10 E
Assémini, Italy 30 C1 39 17N 9 0 E
Assen, Neths. 17 A6 53 0N 6 35 E
Assens, Denmark 11 J3 55 16N 9 55 E
Assini, Ivory C. 82 D4 5 9N 3 17W
Assiniboia, Canada 105 D7 49 40N 105 59W
Assiniboine →, Canada 105 D9 49 53N 97 8W
Assiniboine, Mt., Canada 104 C5 50 52N 115 39W
Assis, Brazil 127 A5 22 40 S 50 20W
Assisi, Italy 29 E9 43 4N 12 37 E
Ássos, Greece 38 C2 38 22N 20 33 E
Assynt, L., U.K. 14 C3 58 10N 5 3W
Astaffort, France 20 D4 44 4N 0 40 E
Astakidha, Greece 39 F8 35 53N 26 50 E
Astakós, Greece 38 C3 38 32N 21 5 E
Astana, Kazakstan 50 D8 51 10N 71 30 E
Āstāneh, Iran 71 B6 37 17N 49 59 E
Astara, Azerbaijan 71 B6 38 30N 48 50 E
Āstārā, Iran 73 C13 38 20N 48 52 E
Asteroúsia, Greece 36 E7 34 59N 25 3 E
Asti, Italy 28 D5 44 54N 8 12 E
Astipálaia, Greece 39 E8 36 32N 26 22 E
Astorga, Spain 34 C4 42 29N 6 8W
Astoria, U.S.A. 116 D3 46 11N 123 50W
Åstorp, Sweden 11 H6 56 6N 12 55 E
Astrakhan, Russia 49 G9 46 25N 48 5 E
Astudillo, Spain 34 C6 42 12N 4 22W
Asturias □, Spain 34 B5 43 15N 6 0W
Asunción, Paraguay 126 B4 25 10 S 57 30W
Asunción Nochixtlán, Mexico 119 D5 17 28N 97 14W
Åsunden, Sweden 11 F9 58 0N 15 51 E
Asutri, Sudan 81 D4 15 25N 35 45 E
Aswa →, Uganda 86 B3 3 43N 31 55 E
Aswad, Ra's al, Si. Arabia 80 C4 21 20N 39 0 E
Aswân, Egypt 80 C3 24 4N 32 57 E
Aswân High Dam = Sadd el Aali, Egypt 80 C3 23 54N 32 54 E
Asyût, Egypt 80 B3 27 11N 31 4 E
Asyûti, Wadi →, Egypt 80 B3 27 11N 31 16 E
Aszód, Hungary 42 C4 47 39N 19 28 E
At Ţafīlah, Jordan 75 E4 30 45N 35 30 E
Aţ Tā'if, Si. Arabia 74 C3 21 5N 40 27 E
Aţ Ţirāq, Si. Arabia 70 E5 27 19N 44 33 E
Aţ Ţubayq, Si. Arabia 70 D3 29 30N 37 0 E
Atabey, Turkey 39 D12 37 57N 30 39 E
Atacama □, Chile 126 B2 27 30 S 70 0W
Atacama, Desierto de, Chile 126 A2 24 0 S 69 20W
Atacama, Salar de, Chile 126 A2 23 30 S 68 20W
Atakpamé, Togo 83 D5 7 31N 1 13 E
Atalándi, Greece 38 C4 38 39N 22 58 E
Atalaya, Peru 124 F4 10 45 S 73 50W
Atalaya de Femes, Canary Is. 37 F6 28 56N 13 47W
Atami, Japan 55 G9 35 5N 139 4 E
Atapupu, Indonesia 63 F6 9 0 S 124 51 E
Atâr, Mauritania 78 D3 20 30N 13 5W
Atarfe, Spain 35 H7 37 13N 3 40W
Atari, Pakistan 68 D6 30 56N 74 2 E
Atascadero, U.S.A. 116 K6 35 29N 120 40W
Atasu, Kazakstan 50 E8 48 30N 71 0 E
Atatürk Barajı, Turkey 73 D8 37 28N 38 30 E
Atauro, Indonesia 63 F7 8 10 S 125 30 E
'Atbara, Sudan 80 D3 17 42N 33 59 E
'Atbara, Nahr →, Sudan 80 D3 17 40N 33 56 E
Atbasar, Kazakstan 50 D7 51 48N 68 20 E
Atça, Turkey 39 D10 37 53N 28 13 E
Atchafalaya B., U.S.A. 113 L9 29 25N 91 25W
Atchison, U.S.A. 112 F7 39 34N 95 7W
Atebubu, Ghana 83 D4 7 47N 1 0W
Ateca, Spain 32 D3 41 20N 1 49W
Aterno →, Italy 29 F10 42 11N 13 51 E
Āteshān, Iran 71 C7 35 35N 52 37 E
Atesine, Alpi, Italy 29 B8 46 55N 11 30 E
Atessa, Italy 29 F11 42 4N 14 27 E
Atfîh, Egypt 80 J7 29 25N 31 15 E
Ath, Belgium 17 D3 50 38N 3 47 E
Athabasca, Canada 104 C6 54 45N 113 20W
Athabasca →, Canada 105 B6 58 40N 110 50W
Athabasca, L., Canada 105 B7 59 15N 109 15W
Athboy, Ireland 15 C5 53 37N 6 56W
Athenry, Ireland 15 C3 53 18N 8 44W
Athens = Athínai, Greece 38 D5 37 58N 23 46 E
Athens, Ala., U.S.A. 109 H2 34 48N 86 58W
Athens, Ga., U.S.A. 109 J4 33 57N 83 23W
Athens, N.Y., U.S.A. 111 D11 42 16N 73 49W
Athens, Ohio, U.S.A. 108 F4 39 20N 82 6W
Athens, Pa., U.S.A. 111 E8 41 57N 76 31W
Athens, Tenn., U.S.A. 109 H3 35 27N 84 36W
Athens, Tex., U.S.A. 113 J7 32 12N 95 51W
Atherley, Canada 110 B5 44 37N 79 20W
Atherton, Australia 94 B4 17 17 S 145 30 E
Athiéme, Benin 83 D5 6 37N 1 40 E
Athienou, Cyprus 36 D12 35 3N 33 32 E
Athínai, Greece 38 D5 37 58N 23 46 E
Athlone, Ireland 15 C4 53 25N 7 56W
Athna, Cyprus 36 D12 35 3N 33 47 E
Athol, U.S.A. 111 D12 42 36N 72 14W
Atholl, Forest of, U.K. 14 E5 56 51N 3 50W
Atholville, Canada 103 C6 47 59N 66 43W
Áthos, Greece 41 F8 40 9N 24 22 E
Athy, Ireland 15 C5 53 0N 7 0W
Ati, Chad 79 F9 13 13N 18 20 E
Ati, Sudan 81 E2 13 5N 29 2 E
Atiak, Uganda 86 B3 3 12N 32 2 E
Atienza, Spain 32 D2 41 12N 2 52W
Atiit, Sudan 81 F3 6 10N 30 35 E
Atik L., Canada 105 B9 55 15N 96 0W
Atikameg →, Canada 102 B3 52 30N 82 46W
Atikokan, Canada 102 C1 48 45N 91 37W
Atikonak L., Canada 103 B7 52 40N 64 32W
Atimonan, Phil. 61 E4 14 0N 121 55 E
Atka, Russia 51 C16 60 50N 151 48 E
Atka I., U.S.A. 100 C2 52 7N 174 30W
Atkarsk, Russia 48 E7 51 55N 45 2 E
Atkinson, U.S.A. 112 D5 42 32N 98 59W
Atlanta, Ga., U.S.A. 109 J3 33 45N 84 23W
Atlanta, Tex., U.S.A. 113 J7 33 7N 94 10W
Atlantic, U.S.A. 112 E7 41 24N 95 1W
Atlantic City, U.S.A. 108 F8 39 21N 74 27W
Atlantic Ocean 2 E9 0 0
Atlas Mts. = Haut Atlas, Morocco 78 B4 32 30N 5 0W
Atlin, Canada 104 B2 59 31N 133 41W
Atlin, L., Canada 104 B2 59 26N 133 45W
Atlin Prov. Park, Canada 104 B2 59 10N 134 30W
Atmore, U.S.A. 109 K2 31 2N 87 29W
Atoka, U.S.A. 113 H6 34 23N 96 8W
Átokos, Greece 38 C2 38 28N 20 49 E
Atolia, U.S.A. 117 K9 35 19N 117 37W
Atrai →, Bangla. 69 G13 24 7N 89 22 E
Atrak = Atrek →, Turkmenistan 71 B8 37 35N 53 58 E
Ätran, Sweden 11 G6 57 7N 12 57 E
Ätran →, Sweden 11 H6 56 53N 12 30 E
Atrauli, India 68 E8 28 2N 78 20 E
Atrek →, Turkmenistan 71 B8 37 35N 53 58 E
Atri, Italy 29 F10 42 35N 13 58 E
Atsikí, Greece 39 B7 39 56N 25 13 E
Atsoum, Mts., Cameroon 83 D7 6 41N 12 57 E
Atsuta, Japan 54 C10 43 24N 141 26 E
Attalla, U.S.A. 109 H2 34 1N 86 6W
Attapu, Laos 64 E6 14 48N 106 50 E
Attáviros, Greece 36 C9 36 12N 27 50 E
Attawapiskat, Canada 102 B3 52 56N 82 24W
Attawapiskat →, Canada 102 B3 52 57N 82 18W
Attawapiskat L., Canada 102 B2 52 18N 87 54W
Attersee, Austria 26 D6 47 55N 13 32 E
Attica, Ind., U.S.A. 108 E2 40 18N 87 15W
Attica, Ohio, U.S.A. 110 E2 41 4N 82 53W
Attichy, France 19 C10 49 25N 3 3 E
Attigny, France 19 C11 49 28N 4 35 E
Attikamagen L., Canada 103 B6 55 0N 66 30W
Attikí □, Greece 38 D5 37 10N 23 40 E
Attleboro, U.S.A. 111 E13 41 57N 71 17W
Attock, Pakistan 68 C5 33 52N 72 20 E
Attopeu = Attapu, Laos 64 E6 14 48N 106 50 E
Attu I., U.S.A. 100 C1 52 55N 172 55 E
Attur, India 66 P11 11 35N 78 30 E
Atuel →, Argentina 126 D2 36 17 S 66 50W
Åtvidaberg, Sweden 11 F10 58 12N 16 0 E
Atwater, U.S.A. 116 H6 37 21N 120 37W
Atwood, Canada 110 C3 43 40N 81 1W
Atwood, U.S.A. 112 F4 39 48N 101 3W
Atyraū, Kazakstan 50 E6 47 5N 52 0 E
Au Sable, U.S.A. 110 B1 44 25N 83 20W
Au Sable →, U.S.A. 108 C4 44 25N 83 20W
Au Sable Forks, U.S.A. 111 B11 44 27N 73 41W
Au Sable Pt., U.S.A. 110 B1 44 20N 83 20W
Aubagne, France 21 E9 43 17N 5 37 E
Aubarca, C. d', Spain 37 B7 39 4N 1 22 E
Aube □, France 19 D11 48 15N 4 10 E
Aube →, France 19 D10 48 34N 3 43 E
Aubenas, France 21 D8 44 37N 4 24 E
Aubenton, France 19 C11 49 50N 4 12 E
Auberry, U.S.A. 116 H7 37 7N 119 29W
Aubigny-sur-Nère, France 19 E9 47 30N 2 24 E
Aubin, France 20 D6 44 33N 2 15 E
Aubrac, Mts. d', France 20 D7 44 40N 3 2 E
Auburn, Ala., U.S.A. 109 J3 32 36N 85 29W
Auburn, Calif., U.S.A. 116 G5 38 54N 121 4W
Auburn, Ind., U.S.A. 108 E3 41 22N 85 4W
Auburn, Maine, U.S.A. 109 C10 44 6N 70 14W
Auburn, N.Y., U.S.A. 111 D8 42 56N 76 34W
Auburn, Nebr., U.S.A. 112 E7 40 23N 95 51W
Auburn, Pa., U.S.A. 111 F8 40 36N 76 6W
Auburn, Wash., U.S.A. 116 C4 47 18N 122 14W
Auburn Ra., Australia 95 D5 25 15 S 150 30 E
Auburndale, U.S.A. 109 L5 28 4N 81 48W
Aubusson, France 20 C6 45 57N 2 11 E
Auce, Latvia 44 B9 56 28N 22 53 E
Auch, France 20 E4 43 39N 0 36 E
Auchi, Nigeria 83 D6 7 6N 6 13 E
Auckland, N.Z. 91 G5 36 52 S 174 46 E
Auckland Is., Pac. Oc. 96 N8 50 40 S 166 5 E
Aude □, France 20 E6 43 8N 2 28 E
Aude →, France 20 E7 43 13N 3 14 E
Auden, Canada 102 B2 50 14N 87 53W
Auderville, France 18 C5 49 43N 1 57W
Audierne, France 18 D2 48 1N 4 34W
Audincourt, France 19 E13 47 30N 6 50 E
Audo, Ethiopia 81 F5 6 20N 41 50 E
Audubon, U.S.A. 112 E7 41 43N 94 56W
Aue, Germany 24 E8 50 35N 12 41 E
Auerbach, Germany 24 E8 50 30N 12 24 E
Augathella, Australia 95 D4 25 48 S 146 35 E
Aughnacloy, U.K. 15 B5 54 25N 6 59W
Augrabies Falls, S. Africa 88 D3 28 35 S 20 20 E
Augsburg, Germany 25 G6 48 25N 10 52 E
Augusta, Australia 93 F2 34 19 S 115 9 E
Augusta, Italy 31 E8 37 13N 15 13 E
Augusta, Ark., U.S.A. 113 H9 35 17N 91 22W
Augusta, Ga., U.S.A. 109 J5 33 28N 81 58W
Augusta, Kans., U.S.A. 113 G6 37 41N 96 59W
Augusta, Maine, U.S.A. 101 D13 44 19N 69 47W
Augusta, Mont., U.S.A. 114 C7 47 30N 112 24W
Augustenborg, Denmark 11 K3 54 57N 9 53 E
Augustów, Poland 44 E9 53 51N 23 0 E
Augustus, Mt., Australia 93 D2 24 20 S 116 50 E
Augustus I., Australia 92 C3 15 20 S 124 30 E
Aukan, Eritrea 81 D5 15 29N 40 50 E
Aukum, U.S.A. 116 G6 38 34N 120 43W
Auld, L., Australia 92 D3 22 25 S 123 50 E
Aulla, Italy 28 D6 44 12N 9 58 E
Aulnay, France 20 B3 46 2N 0 22W
Aulne →, France 18 D2 48 17N 4 16W
Aulnoye-Aymeries, France 19 B10 50 12N 3 50 E
Ault, France 18 B8 50 8N 1 26 E
Ault, U.S.A. 112 E2 40 35N 104 44W
Aulus-les-Bains, France 20 F5 42 49N 1 19 E
Aumale, France 19 C8 49 46N 1 46 E
Aumont-Aubrac, France 20 D7 44 43N 3 17 E
Auna, Nigeria 83 C5 10 9N 4 42 E
Auning, Denmark 11 H4 56 26N 10 22 E
Aunis, France 20 B3 46 5N 0 50W
Auponhia, Indonesia 63 E7 1 58 S 125 27 E
Aups, France 21 E10 43 37N 6 15 E
Aur, Pulau, Malaysia 65 L5 2 35N 104 10 E
Auraiya, India 69 F8 26 28N 79 33 E
Aurangabad, Bihar, India 69 G11 24 45N 84 18 E
Aurangabad, Maharashtra, India 66 K9 19 50N 75 23 E
Auray, France 18 E4 47 40N 2 59W
Aurich, Germany 24 B3 53 28N 7 28 E
Aurillac, France 20 D6 44 55N 2 26 E
Auronzo di Cadore, Italy 29 B9 46 33N 12 26 E
Aurora, Canada 110 C5 44 0N 79 28W
Aurora, S. Africa 88 E2 32 40 S 18 29 E
Aurora, Colo., U.S.A. 112 F2 39 44N 104 52W
Aurora, Ill., U.S.A. 108 E1 41 45N 88 19W
Aurora, Mo., U.S.A. 113 G8 36 58N 93 43W
Aurora, N.Y., U.S.A. 111 D8 42 45N 76 42W
Aurora, Nebr., U.S.A. 112 E6 40 52N 98 0W
Aurora, Ohio, U.S.A. 110 E3 41 21N 81 20W
Aurukun, Australia 94 A3 13 20 S 141 45 E
Aus, Namibia 88 D2 26 35 S 16 12 E
Ausable →, Canada 110 C3 43 19N 81 46W
Auschwitz = Oświęcim, Poland 45 H6 50 2N 19 11 E
Austerlitz = Slavkov u Brna, Czech Rep. 27 B9 49 10N 16 52 E
Austin, Minn., U.S.A. 112 D8 43 40N 92 58W
Austin, Nev., U.S.A. 114 G5 39 30N 117 4W
Austin, Pa., U.S.A. 110 E6 41 38N 78 6W
Austin, Tex., U.S.A. 113 K6 30 17N 97 45W
Austin, L., Australia 93 E2 27 40 S 118 0 E
Austin I., Canada 105 A10 61 10N 94 0W
Austra, Norway 8 D14 65 8N 11 55 E
Austral Is. = Tubuai Is., Pac. Oc. 97 K13 25 0 S 150 0W
Austral Seamount Chain, Pac. Oc. 97 K13 24 0 S 150 0W
Australia ■, Oceania 96 K5 23 0 S 135 0 E
Australian Capital Territory □, Australia 95 F4 35 30 S 149 0 E
Australind, Australia 93 F2 33 17 S 115 42 E
Austria ■, Europe 26 E7 47 0N 14 0 E
Austvågøy, Norway 8 B16 68 20N 14 40 E
Auterive, France 20 E5 43 21N 1 29 E
Authie →, France 19 B8 50 22N 1 38 E
Authon-du-Perche, France 18 D7 48 12N 0 54 E
Autlán, Mexico 118 D4 19 40N 104 30W
Autun, France 19 F11 46 58N 4 17 E
Auvergne, France 20 C7 45 20N 3 15 E
Auvergne, Mts. d', France 20 C6 45 20N 2 55 E
Auvézère →, France 20 C4 45 12N 0 50 E
Auxerre, France 19 E10 47 48N 3 32 E
Auxi-le-Château, France 19 B9 50 15N 2 8 E
Auxonne, France 19 E12 47 10N 5 20 E
Auzances, France 19 F9 46 2N 2 30 E
Ava, U.S.A. 113 G8 36 57N 92 40W
Avallon, France 19 E10 47 30N 3 53 E
Avalon, U.S.A. 117 M8 33 21N 118 20W
Avalon Pen., Canada 103 C9 47 30N 53 20W
Avanos, Turkey 70 B2 38 43N 34 51 E
Avaré, Brazil 127 A6 23 4 S 48 58W
Ávas, Greece 41 F9 40 57N 25 56 E
Avawatz Mts., U.S.A. 117 K10 35 40N 116 30W
Avdan Daği, Turkey 41 F13 40 23N 29 46 E
Aveiro, Brazil 125 D7 3 10 S 55 5W
Aveiro, Portugal 34 E2 40 37N 8 38W
Aveiro □, Portugal 34 E2 40 40N 8 35W
Āvej, Iran 71 C6 35 40N 49 15 E
Avellaneda, Argentina 126 C4 34 50 S 58 10W
Avellino, Italy 31 B7 40 54N 14 47 E
Avenal, U.S.A. 116 K6 36 0N 120 8W
Aversa, Italy 31 B7 40 58N 14 12 E
Avery, U.S.A. 114 C6 47 15N 115 49W
Aves, Is. las, Venezuela 121 D6 12 0N 67 30W
Avesnes-sur-Helpe, France 19 B10 50 8N 3 55 E
Avesta, Sweden 10 D10 60 9N 16 10 E
Aveyron □, France 20 D6 44 22N 2 45 E
Aveyron →, France 20 D5 44 5N 1 16 E
Avezzano, Italy 29 F10 42 2N 13 25 E
Avgó, Greece 39 F7 35 33N 25 37 E
Aviá Terai, Argentina 126 B3 26 45 S 60 50W
Aviano, Italy 29 B9 46 4N 12 36 E
Aviemore, U.K. 14 D5 57 12N 3 50W
Avigliana, Italy 28 C4 45 5N 7 23 E
Avigliano, Italy 31 B8 40 44N 15 43 E
Avignon, France 21 E8 43 57N 4 50 E
Ávila, Spain 34 E6 40 39N 4 43W
Ávila □, Spain 34 E6 40 30N 5 0W
Ávila, Sierra de, Spain 34 E5 40 40N 5 15W
Avila Beach, U.S.A. 117 K6 35 11N 120 44W
Avilés, Spain 34 B5 43 35N 5 57W
Avintes, Portugal 34 D2 41 7N 8 33W
Avionárion, Greece 38 C6 38 31N 24 8 E
Avis, Portugal 35 F3 39 4N 7 53W
Avis, U.S.A. 110 E7 41 11N 77 19W
Avísio →, Italy 28 B8 46 7N 11 5 E
Aviz = Avis, Portugal 35 F3 39 4N 7 53W
Avize, France 19 D11 48 59N 4 1 E
Avlum, Denmark 11 H2 56 16N 8 47 E
Avoca, U.S.A. 110 D7 42 25N 77 25W
Avoca →, Australia 95 F3 35 40 S 143 43 E
Avoca →, Ireland 15 D5 52 48N 6 10W
Avola, Canada 104 C5 51 45N 119 19W
Avola, Italy 31 F8 36 56N 15 7 E
Avon, U.S.A. 110 D7 42 55N 77 45W
Avon →, Australia 93 F2 31 40 S 116 7 E
Avon →, Bristol, U.K. 13 F5 51 29N 2 41W
Avon →, Dorset, U.K. 13 G6 50 44N 1 46W
Avon →, Warks., U.K. 13 E5 52 0N 2 8W
Avon Park, U.S.A. 109 M5 27 36N 81 31W
Avondale, Zimbabwe 87 F3 17 43 S 30 58 E
Avonlea, Canada 105 D8 50 0N 105 0W
Avramov, Bulgaria 41 D10 42 45N 26 38 E
Avranches, France 18 D5 48 40N 1 20W
Avre →, France 18 D8 48 47N 1 22 E
Avrig, Romania 43 E9 45 43N 24 21 E
Avrillé, France 18 E6 47 30N 0 35W
Avtovac, Bos.-H. 40 C2 43 9N 18 35 E
Awag el Baqar, Sudan 81 E3 10 10N 33 40 E
A'waj →, Syria 75 B5 33 23N 36 20 E
Awaji-Shima, Japan 55 G7 34 30N 134 50 E
'Awālī, Bahrain 71 E6 26 0N 50 30 E
Awantipur, India 69 C6 33 55N 75 3 E
Awasa, Ethiopia 81 F4 7 2N 38 28 E
Awasa, L., Ethiopia 81 F4 7 0N 38 30 E
Awash, Ethiopia 81 F5 9 1N 40 10 E
Awash →, Ethiopia 81 E5 11 45N 41 5 E
Awaso, Ghana 82 D4 6 15N 2 22W
Awatere →, N.Z. 91 J5 41 37 S 174 10 E
Awbārī, Libya 79 C8 26 46N 12 57 E
Awe, L., U.K. 14 E3 56 17N 5 16W
Aweil, Sudan 81 F2 8 42N 27 20 E
Awgu, Nigeria 83 D6 6 4N 7 24 E
Awjilah, Libya 79 C10 29 8N 21 7 E
Awka, Nigeria 83 D6 6 12N 7 5 E
Ax-les-Thermes, France 20 F5 42 44N 1 50 E
Axat, France 20 F6 42 48N 2 13 E
Axe →, U.K. 13 F5 50 42N 3 4W
Axel Heiberg I., Canada 4 B3 80 0N 90 0W
Axim, Ghana 82 E4 4 51N 2 15W
Axintele, Romania 43 F11 44 37N 26 47 E
Axiós →, Greece 40 F6 40 57N 22 35 E
Axminster, U.K. 13 G4 50 46N 3 0W
Axvall, Sweden 11 F7 58 23N 13 34 E
Ay, France 19 C11 49 3N 4 1 E
Ayabaca, Peru 124 D3 4 40 S 79 53W
Ayabe, Japan 55 G7 35 20N 135 20 E
Ayacucho, Argentina 126 D4 37 5 S 58 20W
Ayacucho, Peru 124 F4 13 0 S 74 0W
Ayaguz, Kazakstan 50 E9 48 10N 80 10 E
Ayamé, Ivory C. 82 D4 5 35N 3 9W
Ayamonte, Spain 35 H3 37 12N 7 24W
Ayan, Russia 51 D14 56 30N 138 16 E
Ayancık, Turkey 72 B6 41 57N 34 35 E
Ayas, Turkey 72 B5 40 2N 32 21 E
Ayaviri, Peru 124 F4 14 50 S 70 35W
Aybastı, Turkey 72 B7 40 41N 37 23 E
Aydın, Turkey 72 D2 37 51N 27 51 E
Aydin □, Turkey 39 D9 37 50N 28 0 E
Aydin Dağları, Turkey 39 D10 38 0N 28 0 E
Ayelu, Ethiopia 81 E5 10 5N 40 42 E
Ayenngré, Togo 83 D5 8 40N 1 1 E
Ayer, U.S.A. 111 D13 42 34N 71 35W
Ayerbe, Spain 32 C4 42 17N 0 41W
Ayer's Cliff, Canada 111 A12 45 10N 72 3W
Ayers Rock, Australia 93 E5 25 23 S 131 5 E
Ayiá, Greece 38 B4 39 43N 22 45 E
Ayia Aikateríni, Ákra, Greece 36 A3 39 50N 19 50 E
Ayía Ánna, Greece 38 C5 38 52N 23 24 E
Ayía Dhéka, Greece 36 D6 35 3N 24 58 E
Ayía Gálini, Greece 36 D6 35 6N 24 41 E
Ayía Marína, Kásos, Greece 39 F8 35 27N 26 53 E
Ayía Marína, Léros, Greece 39 D8 37 11N 26 48 E
Ayia Napa, Cyprus 36 E13 34 59N 34 0 E
Ayía Paraskeví, Greece 39 B8 39 14N 26 21 E
Ayia Phyla, Cyprus 36 E12 34 43N 33 1 E
Ayía Rouméli, Greece 38 F5 35 14N 23 58 E
Ayía Varvára, Greece 36 D7 35 8N 25 1 E
Ayiássos, Greece 39 B8 39 5N 26 23 E
Áyioi Theódhoroi, Greece 38 D5 37 55N 23 9 E
Áyion Óros □, Greece 41 F8 40 25N 24 6 E
Áyios Amvrósios, Cyprus 36 D12 35 20N 33 35 E
Áyios Andréas, Greece 38 D4 37 21N 22 45 E
Áyios Evstrátios, Greece 38 B6 39 34N 24 58 E
Áyios Ioánnis, Ákra, Greece 36 D7 35 20N 25 40 E
Áyios Isídhoros, Greece 36 C9 36 9N 27 51 E
Áyios Kiríkos, Greece 39 D8 37 34N 26 17 E
Áyios Matthaíos, Greece 36 B3 39 30N 19 47 E
Áyios Mírono, Greece 39 F7 35 15N 25 1 E
Áyios Nikólaos, Greece 36 D7 35 11N 25 41 E
Áyios Pétros, Greece 38 C2 38 38N 20 33 E
Áyios Seryios, Cyprus 36 D12 35 12N 33 53 E
Ayios Theodhoros, Cyprus 36 D13 35 22N 34 1 E
Áyios Yeóryios, Greece 38 D5 37 28N 23 57 E
Aykathonisi, Greece 39 D8 37 28N 27 0 E
Aykirikçi, Turkey 39 B12 39 8N 30 9 E
Aylesbury, U.K. 13 F7 51 49N 0 49W
Aylmer, Canada 110 D4 42 46N 80 59W
Aylmer, L., Canada 100 B8 64 0N 110 8W
'Ayn, Wādī al, Oman 71 F7 22 15N 55 28 E
Ayn Dār, Si. Arabia 71 E7 25 55N 49 10 E
Ayn Zālah, Iraq 70 B4 36 45N 42 35 E
Ayna, Spain 33 G2 38 34N 2 3W
Ayod, Sudan 81 F3 8 7N 31 26 E
Ayolas, Paraguay 126 B4 27 10 S 56 59W
Ayom, Sudan 81 F2 7 49N 28 23 E
Ayon, Ostrov, Russia 51 C17 69 50N 169 0 E
Ayora, Spain 33 F3 39 3N 1 3W
Ayorou, Niger 83 C5 14 53N 1 0 E
'Ayoûn el 'Atroûs, Mauritania 82 B3 16 38N 9 37W
Ayr, Australia 94 B4 19 35 S 147 25 E
Ayr, Canada 110 C4 43 17N 80 27W
Ayr, U.K. 14 F4 55 28N 4 38W
Ayr →, U.K. 14 F4 55 28N 4 38W
Ayrancı, Turkey 72 D5 37 21N 33 41 E
Ayrancılar, Turkey 39 C9 38 15N 27 18 E
Ayre, Pt. of, U.K. 12 C3 54 25N 4 21W
Aysha, Ethiopia 81 E5 10 50N 42 23 E
Ayton, Australia 94 B4 15 56 S 145 22 E
Aytos, Bulgaria 41 D11 42 42N 27 16 E
Aytoska Planina, Bulgaria 41 D11 42 45N 27 30 E
Ayu, Kepulauan, Indonesia 63 D8 0 35N 131 5 E
Ayutla, Guatemala 120 D1 14 40N 92 10W
Ayutla, Mexico 119 D5 16 58N 99 17W
Ayvacık, Turkey 72 C2 39 36N 26 24 E
Ayvalık, Turkey 39 B8 39 20N 26 46 E
Az Zabadānī, Syria 75 B5 33 43N 36 5 E
Az Zāhirīyah, West Bank 75 D3 31 25N 34 58 E
Az Zahrān, Si. Arabia 71 E6 26 10N 50 7 E
Az Zarqā, Jordan 75 C5 32 5N 36 4 E
Az Zarqā', U.A.E. 71 E7 24 53N 53 4 E
Az Zāwiyah, Libya 79 B8 32 52N 12 56 E
Az Zībār, Iraq 70 B5 36 52N 44 4 E
Az Zilfī, Si. Arabia 70 E5 26 12N 44 52 E
Az Zubayr, Iraq 70 D5 30 26N 47 40 E
Az Zuqur, Yemen 81 E5 14 0N 42 45 E
Azambuja, Portugal 35 F2 39 4N 8 51W
Azamgarh, India 69 F10 26 5N 83 13 E
Azangaro, Peru 124 F4 14 55 S 70 13W
Azaoua, Niger 83 B5 15 50N 4 0 E
Azaouad, Mali 82 B4 18 0N 3 20W
Azaouak, Vallée de l', Mali 83 B5 15 50N 3 20 E
Āzār Shahr, Iran 70 B5 37 45N 45 59 E
Azara, Nigeria 83 D6 8 22N 9 12 E
Azarān, Iran 70 B5 37 25N 47 16 E
Azārbayjan = Azerbaijan ■, Asia 49 K9 40 20N 48 0 E
Āzarbāyjān-e Gharbī □, Iran 70 B5 37 0N 44 30 E
Āzarbāyjān-e Sharqī □, Iran 70 B5 37 20N 47 0 E
Azare, Nigeria 83 C7 11 55N 10 10 E
Azay-le-Rideau, France 18 E7 47 16N 0 30 E
A'zāz, Syria 70 B3 36 36N 37 4 E
Azbine = Aïr, Niger 83 B6 18 30N 8 0 E
Azerbaijan ■, Asia 49 K9 40 20N 48 0 E
Azerbaijchan = Azerbaijan ■, Asia 49 K9 40 20N 48 0 E
Azezo, Ethiopia 81 E4 12 28N 37 15 E
Azimganj, India 69 G13 24 14N 88 16 E
Aznalcóllar, Spain 35 H4 37 32N 6 17W
Azogues, Ecuador 124 D3 2 35 S 78 0W
Azores, Atl. Oc. 78 A1 38 44N 29 0W
Azov, Russia 47 J10 47 3N 39 25 E
Azov, Sea of, Europe 47 J9 46 0N 36 30 E
Azovskoye More = Azov, Sea of, Europe 47 J9 46 0N 36 30 E
Azpeitia, Spain 32 B2 43 12N 2 19W
Azraq ash Shīshān, Jordan 75 D5 31 50N 36 49 E
Aztec, U.S.A. 115 H10 36 49N 107 59W
Azúa de Compostela, Dom. Rep. 121 C5 18 25N 70 44W
Azuaga, Spain 35 G5 38 16N 5 39W
Azuara, Spain 32 D4 41 15N 0 53W
Azuer →, Spain 35 F7 39 8N 3 36W
Azuero, Pen. de, Panama 120 E3 7 30N 80 30W
Azuga, Romania 43 E10 45 27N 25 33 E
Azul, Argentina 126 D4 36 42 S 59 43W
Azusa, U.S.A. 117 L9 34 8N 117 52W
Azzano Décimo, Italy 29 C9 45 52N 12 56 E

B

Ba Don, Vietnam 64 D6 17 45N 106 26 E
Ba Dong, Vietnam 65 H6 9 40N 106 33 E
Ba Ngoi = Cam Lam, Vietnam 65 G7 11 54N 109 10 E
Ba Tri, Vietnam 65 G6 10 2N 106 36 E
Ba Xian = Bazhou, China 56 E9 39 8N 116 22 E
Baa, Indonesia 63 F6 10 50 S 123 0 E
Baamonde, Spain 34 B3 43 7N 7 44W
Baarle-Nassau, Belgium 17 C4 51 27N 4 56 E
Bab el Mandeb, Red Sea 74 E3 12 35N 43 25 E
Baba, Bulgaria 40 D7 42 44N 23 59 E
Baba Burnu, Turkey 39 B8 39 29N 26 2 E
Baba dag, Azerbaijan 49 K9 41 0N 48 19 E
Bābā Kalū, Iran 71 D6 30 7N 50 49 E
Babadag, Romania 43 F13 44 53N 28 44 E
Babadağ, Turkey 39 D10 37 49N 28 52 E
Babadayhan, Turkmenistan 50 F7 37 42N 60 23 E
Babaeski, Turkey 41 E11 41 26N 27 6 E
Babahoyo, Ecuador 124 D3 1 40 S 79 30W
Babai = Sarju →, India 69 F9 27 21N 81 23 E
Babana, Nigeria 83 C5 10 31N 3 46 E
Babanusa, Sudan 81 E2 11 20N 27 48 E
Babar, Indonesia 63 F7 8 0 S 129 30 E
Babar, Pakistan 68 D3 31 7N 69 32 E
Babarkach, Pakistan 68 E3 29 45N 68 0 E
Babayevo, Russia 46 C8 59 24N 35 55 E
Babb, U.S.A. 114 B7 48 51N 113 27W
Babelthuap, Pac. Oc. 63 C8 7 30N 134 30 E
Babenhausen, Germany 25 F4 49 57N 8 57 E
Băbeni, Romania 43 F9 44 59N 24 11 E
Baberu, India 69 G9 25 33N 80 43 E
Babi Besar, Pulau, Malaysia 65 L4 2 25N 103 59 E
Babia Gora, Europe 45 J6 49 38N 19 38 E
Babian Jiang →, China 58 F3 22 55N 101 47 E
Babile, Ethiopia 81 F5 9 16N 42 11 E
Babimost, Poland 45 F2 52 10N 15 49 E
Babinda, Australia 94 B4 17 20 S 145 56 E
Babine, Canada 104 B3 55 22N 126 37W
Babine →, Canada 104 B3 55 45N 127 44W
Babine L., Canada 104 C3 54 48N 126 0W
Babo, Indonesia 63 E8 2 30 S 133 30 E
Babócsa, Hungary 42 D2 46 2N 17 21 E
Bābol, Iran 71 B7 36 40N 52 50 E
Bābol Sar, Iran 71 B7 36 45N 52 45 E
Baborów, Poland 45 H5 50 7N 18 1 E
Babruysk, Belarus 47 F5 53 10N 29 15 E
Babuhri, India 68 F3 26 49N 69 43 E
Babuna, Macedonia 40 E5 41 30N 21 40 E
Babura, Nigeria 83 C6 12 51N 8 59 E
Babusar Pass, Pakistan 69 B5 35 12N 73 59 E
Babušnica, Serbia, Yug. 40 C6 43 7N 22 27 E
Babuyan Chan., Phil. 61 B4 18 40N 121 30 E
Babylon, Iraq 70 C5 32 34N 44 22 E
Bač, Serbia, Yug. 42 E4 45 29N 19 17 E
Bâc →, Moldova 43 D14 46 55N 29 26 E
Bac Can, Vietnam 58 F5 22 8N 105 49 E
Bac Giang, Vietnam 58 G6 21 16N 106 11 E
Bac Lieu, Vietnam 65 H5 9 17N 105 43 E
Bac Ninh, Vietnam 58 G6 21 13N 106 4 E
Bac Phan, Vietnam 64 B5 22 0N 105 0 E
Bac Quang, Vietnam 58 F5 22 30N 104 48 E
Bacabal, Brazil 125 D10 4 15 S 44 45W
Bacalar, Mexico 119 D7 18 50N 87 27W
Bacan, Kepulauan, Indonesia 63 E7 0 35 S 127 30 E
Bacarra, Phil. 61 B4 18 15N 120 37 E
Bacău, Romania 43 D11 46 35N 26 55 E
Bacău □, Romania 43 D11 46 30N 26 45 E
Baccarat, France 19 D13 48 28N 6 42 E
Bacerac, Mexico 118 A3 30 18N 108 50W
Băceşti, Romania 43 D12 46 50N 27 11 E
Bach Long Vi, Dao, Vietnam 64 B6 20 10N 107 40 E
Bacharach, Germany 25 E3 50 3N 7 44 E
Bachelina, Russia 50 D7 57 45N 67 20 E
Bachhwara, India 69 G11 25 35N 85 54 E
Bachuma, Ethiopia 81 F4 6 48N 35 53 E
Bačina, Serbia, Yug. 40 C5 43 42N 21 23 E
Back →, Canada 100 B9 65 10N 104 0W
Bačka Palanka, Serbia, Yug. 42 E4 45 17N 19 27 E
Bačka Topola, Serbia, Yug. 42 E4 45 49N 19 39 E
Bäckebo, Sweden 11 H10 56 53N 16 4 E
Bäckefors, Sweden 11 F6 58 48N 12 9 E
Bäckhammar, Sweden 10 E8 59 10N 14 11 E
Bački Petrovac, Serbia, Yug. 42 E4 45 29N 19 32 E
Backnang, Germany 25 G5 48 56N 9 26 E
Baco, Mt., Phil. 61 E4 12 49N 121 10 E
Bacolod, Phil. 61 F5 10 40N 122 57 E
Bacqueville-en-Caux, France 18 C8 49 47N 1 0 E
Bács-Kiskun □, Hungary 42 D4 46 43N 19 30 E
Bácsalmás, Hungary 42 D4 46 8N 19 17 E
Bacuag = Placer, Phil. 61 G6 9 36N 125 38 E

Bacuk, *Malaysia* **65 J4** 6 4N 102 25 E
Bād, *Iran* **71 C7** 33 41N 52 1 E
Bad →, *U.S.A.* **112 C4** 44 21N 100 22W
Bad Aussee, *Austria* **26 D6** 47 43N 13 45 E
Bad Axe, *U.S.A.* **110 C2** 43 48N 83 0W
Bad Bergzabern, *Germany* **25 F3** 49 6N 7 59 E
Bad Berleburg, *Germany* **24 D4** 51 2N 8 26 E
Bad Bevensen, *Germany* **24 B6** 53 5N 10 35 E
Bad Bramstedt, *Germany* **24 B5** 53 55N 9 53 E
Bad Brückenau, *Germany* **25 E5** 50 18N 9 47 E
Bad Doberan, *Germany* **24 A7** 54 6N 11 53 E
Bad Driburg, *Germany* **24 D5** 51 43N 9 1 E
Bad Ems, *Germany* **25 E3** 50 20N 7 43 E
Bad Frankenhausen, *Germany* **24 D7** 51 21N 11 5 E
Bad Freienwalde, *Germany* **24 C10** 52 46N 14 1 E
Bad Goisern, *Austria* **26 D6** 47 38N 13 38 E
Bad Harzburg, *Germany* **24 D6** 51 52N 10 34 E
Bad Hersfeld, *Germany* **24 E5** 50 52N 9 42 E
Bad Hofgastein, *Austria* **26 D6** 47 17N 13 6 E
Bad Homburg, *Germany* **25 E4** 50 13N 8 38 E
Bad Honnef, *Germany* **24 E3** 50 38N 7 13 E
Bad Iburg, *Germany* **24 C4** 52 10N 8 3 E
Bad Ischl, *Austria* **26 D6** 47 44N 13 38 E
Bad Kissingen, *Germany* **25 E6** 50 11N 10 4 E
Bad Königshofen, *Germany* **25 E6** 50 17N 10 28 E
Bad Kreuznach, *Germany* **25 F3** 49 50N 7 51 E
Bad Krozingen, *Germany* **25 H3** 47 54N 7 42 E
Bad Laasphe, *Germany* **24 E4** 50 56N 8 25 E
Bad Lands, *U.S.A.* **112 D3** 43 40N 102 10W
Bad Langensalza, *Germany* **24 D6** 51 5N 10 38 E
Bad Lauterberg, *Germany* **24 D6** 51 38N 10 28 E
Bad Leonfelden, *Austria* **26 C7** 48 31N 14 18 E
Bad Liebenwerda, *Germany* **24 D9** 51 31N 13 24 E
Bad Mergentheim, *Germany* **25 F5** 49 28N 9 42 E
Bad Münstereifel, *Germany* **24 E2** 50 33N 6 46 E
Bad Nauheim, *Germany* **25 E4** 50 21N 8 43 E
Bad Neuenahr-Ahrweiler, *Germany* **24 E3** 50 32N 7 5 E
Bad Neustadt, *Germany* **25 E6** 50 18N 10 13 E
Bad Oeynhausen, *Germany* **24 C4** 52 12N 8 46 E
Bad Oldesloe, *Germany* **24 B6** 53 48N 10 22 E
Bad Orb, *Germany* **25 E5** 50 12N 9 22 E
Bad Pyrmont, *Germany* **24 D5** 51 59N 9 16 E
Bad Reichenhall, *Germany* **25 H8** 47 43N 12 54 E
Bad Säckingen, *Germany* **25 H3** 47 33N 7 56 E
Bad Salzuflen, *Germany* **24 C4** 52 5N 8 45 E
Bad Salzungen, *Germany* **24 E6** 50 48N 10 14 E
Bad Schwartau, *Germany* **24 B6** 53 55N 10 41 E
Bad Segeberg, *Germany* **24 B6** 53 56N 10 17 E
Bad St. Leonhard, *Austria* **26 E7** 46 58N 14 47 E
Bad Tölz, *Germany* **25 H7** 47 45N 11 34 E
Bad Urach, *Germany* **25 G5** 48 29N 9 23 E
Bad Vöslau, *Austria* **27 D9** 47 58N 16 12 E
Bad Waldsee, *Germany* **25 H5** 47 55N 9 45 E
Bad Wildungen, *Germany* **24 D5** 51 6N 9 7 E
Bad Wimpfen, *Germany* **25 F5** 49 13N 9 11 E
Bad Windsheim, *Germany* **25 F6** 49 36N 10 25 E
Bad Zwischenahn, *Germany* **24 B4** 53 12N 8 1 E
Bada Barabil, *India* **69 H11** 22 7N 85 24 E
Badagara, *India* **66 P9** 11 35N 75 40 E
Badagri, *Nigeria* **83 D5** 6 25N 2 55 E
Badajós, L., *Brazil* **124 D6** 3 15 S 62 50W
Badajoz, *Spain* **35 G4** 38 50N 6 59W
Badajoz □, *Spain* **35 G4** 38 40N 6 30W
Badalona, *Spain* **32 D7** 41 26N 2 15 E
Badalzai, *Afghan.* **68 E1** 29 50N 65 35 E
Badampahar, *India* **67 H15** 22 10N 86 10 E
Badanah, *Si. Arabia* **70 D4** 30 58N 41 30 E
Badarinath, *India* **69 D8** 30 45N 79 30 E
Badas, Kepulauan, *Indonesia* **62 D3** 0 45N 107 5 E
Baddo →, *Pakistan* **66 F4** 28 0N 64 20 E
Bade, *Indonesia* **63 F9** 7 10 S 139 35 E
Badeggi, *Nigeria* **83 D6** 9 1N 6 8 E
Badéguichéri, *Niger* **83 C6** 14 30N 5 22 E
Baden, *Austria* **27 C9** 48 1N 16 13 E
Baden, *Switz.* **25 H4** 47 28N 8 18 E
Baden, *U.S.A.* **110 F4** 40 38N 80 14W
Baden-Baden, *Germany* **25 G4** 48 44N 8 13 E
Baden-Württemberg □, *Germany* **25 G4** 48 20N 8 40 E
Badgastein, *Austria* **26 D6** 47 7N 13 9 E
Badger, *Canada* **103 C8** 49 0N 56 4W
Badger, *U.S.A.* **116 J7** 36 38N 119 1W
Bādghīsāt □, *Afghan.* **66 B3** 35 0N 63 0 E
Badgom, *India* **69 B6** 34 1N 74 45 E
Badia Polésine, *Italy* **29 C8** 45 5N 11 29 E
Badin, *Pakistan* **68 G3** 24 38N 68 54 E
Badlands National Park, *U.S.A.* **112 D3** 43 38N 102 56W
Badogo, *Mali* **82 C3** 11 2N 8 13W
Badoumbé, *Mali* **82 C2** 13 42N 10 15W
Badrah, *Iraq* **70 C5** 33 6N 45 58 E
Badrinath, *India* **69 D8** 30 44N 79 29 E
Badulla, *Sri Lanka* **66 R12** 7 1N 81 7 E
Baena, *Spain* **35 H6** 37 37N 4 20W
Baeza, *Spain* **35 H7** 37 57N 3 25W
Bafang, *Cameroon* **83 D7** 5 9N 10 11 E
Bafatá, *Guinea-Biss.* **82 C2** 12 8N 14 40W
Baffin B., *Canada* **4 B4** 72 0N 64 0W
Baffin I., *Canada* **101 B12** 68 0N 75 0W
Bafia, *Cameroon* **83 E7** 4 40N 11 10 E
Bafilo, *Togo* **83 D5** 9 22N 1 22 E
Bafing →, *Mali* **82 C2** 13 49N 10 50W
Bafliyūn, *Syria* **70 B3** 36 37N 36 59 E
Bafoulabé, *Mali* **82 C2** 13 50N 10 55W
Bafoussam, *Cameroon* **83 D7** 5 28N 10 25 E
Bāfq, *Iran* **71 D7** 31 40N 55 25 E
Bafra, *Turkey* **72 B6** 41 34N 35 54 E
Bafra Burnu, *Turkey* **72 B7** 41 45N 36 2 E
Bāft, *Iran* **71 D8** 29 15N 56 38 E
Bafut, *Cameroon* **83 D7** 6 6N 10 2 E
Bafwasende, *Dem. Rep. of the Congo* **86 B2** 1 3N 27 5 E
Bagam, *Niger* **83 B6** 15 43N 6 35 E
Bagamoyo, *Tanzania* **86 D4** 6 28 S 38 55 E
Bagan Datoh, *Malaysia* **65 L3** 3 59N 100 47 E
Bagan Serai, *Malaysia* **65 K3** 5 1N 100 32 E
Baganga, *Phil.* **61 H7** 7 34N 126 33 E
Bagani, *Namibia* **88 B3** 18 7 S 21 41 E
Bagansiapiapi, *Indonesia* **62 D2** 2 12N 100 50 E
Bagasra, *India* **68 J4** 21 30N 71 0 E
Bagaud, *India* **68 H6** 22 19N 75 53 E
Bagawi, *Sudan* **81 E3** 12 20N 34 18 E
Bagbag, *Sudan* **81 D3** 15 23N 31 30 E
Bagdad, *U.S.A.* **117 L11** 34 35N 115 53W
Bagdarin, *Russia* **51 D12** 54 26N 113 36 E
Bagé, *Brazil* **127 C5** 31 20 S 54 15W
Bagenalstown = Muine Bheag, *Ireland* **15 D5** 52 42N 6 58W
Baggs, *U.S.A.* **114 F10** 41 2N 107 39W
Bagh, *Pakistan* **69 C5** 33 59N 73 45 E
Baghain →, *India* **69 G9** 25 32N 81 1 E
Baghdād, *Iraq* **70 C5** 33 20N 44 30 E
Bagheria, *Italy* **30 D6** 38 5N 13 30 E
Baghlān, *Afghan.* **66 A6** 36 12N 69 0 E
Bagley, *U.S.A.* **112 B7** 47 32N 95 24W
Bagnara Cálabra, *Italy* **31 D8** 38 17N 15 48 E
Bagnasco, *Italy* **28 D5** 44 18N 8 2 E
Bagnères-de-Bigorre, *France* **20 E4** 43 5N 0 9 E
Bagnères-de-Luchon, *France* **20 F4** 42 47N 0 38 E
Bagni di Lucca, *Italy* **28 D7** 44 1N 10 35 E
Bagno di Romagna, *Italy* **29 E8** 43 50N 11 57 E
Bagnoles-de-l'Orne, *France* **18 D6** 48 32N 0 25W
Bagnols-sur-Cèze, *France* **21 D8** 44 10N 4 36 E
Bagnorégio, *Italy* **29 F9** 42 37N 12 5 E
Bago = Pegu, *Burma* **67 L20** 17 20N 96 29 E
Bagodar, *India* **69 G11** 24 5N 85 52 E
Bagrationovsk, *Russia* **9 J19** 54 23N 20 39 E
Bagrdan, *Serbia, Yug.* **40 B5** 44 5N 21 11 E
Baguio, *Phil.* **61 C4** 16 26N 120 34 E
Bağyurdu, *Turkey* **39 C9** 38 25N 27 41 E
Bagzane, Monts, *Niger* **83 B6** 17 43N 8 45 E
Bah, *India* **69 F8** 26 53N 78 36 E
Bahabón de Esgueva, *Spain* **34 D7** 41 52N 3 43W
Bahadurganj, *India* **69 F12** 26 16N 87 49 E
Bahadurgarh, *India* **68 E7** 28 40N 76 57 E
Bahama, Canal Viejo de, *W. Indies* **120 B4** 22 10N 77 30W
Bahamas ■, *N. Amer.* **121 B5** 24 0N 75 0W
Bahār, *Iran* **73 E13** 34 54N 48 26 E
Baharampur, *India* **69 G13** 24 2N 88 27 E
Baharîya, El Wâhât al, *Egypt* **80 B2** 28 0N 28 50 E
Bahawalnagar, *Pakistan* **68 E5** 30 0N 73 15 E
Bahawalpur, *Pakistan* **68 E4** 29 24N 71 40 E
Bahçe, *Turkey* **72 D7** 37 13N 36 34 E
Bahçecik, *Turkey* **41 F13** 40 41N 29 44 E
Baheri, *India* **69 E8** 28 45N 79 34 E
Bahgul →, *India* **69 F8** 27 45N 79 36 E
Bahi, *Tanzania* **86 D4** 5 58 S 35 21 E
Bahi Swamp, *Tanzania* **86 D4** 6 10 S 35 0 E
Bahía = Salvador, *Brazil* **125 F11** 13 0 S 38 30W
Bahía □, *Brazil* **125 F10** 12 0 S 42 0W
Bahía, Is. de la, *Honduras* **120 C2** 16 45N 86 15W
Bahía Blanca, *Argentina* **126 D3** 38 35 S 62 13W
Bahía de Caráquez, *Ecuador* **124 D2** 0 40 S 80 27W
Bahía Honda, *Cuba* **120 B3** 22 54N 83 10W
Bahía Laura, *Argentina* **128 F3** 48 10 S 66 30W
Bahía Negra, *Paraguay* **124 H7** 20 5 S 58 5W
Bahir Dar, *Ethiopia* **81 E4** 11 37N 37 10 E
Bahmanzād, *Iran* **71 D6** 31 15N 51 47 E
Bahr el Ahmar □, *Sudan* **80 D4** 20 0N 35 0 E
Bahr el Ghazâl □, *Sudan* **81 F2** 7 0N 28 0 E
Bahr el Jabal □, *Sudan* **81 G3** 4 0N 31 0 E
Bahr Yûsef →, *Egypt* **80 B3** 28 25N 30 35 E
Bahraich, *India* **69 F9** 27 38N 81 37 E
Bahrain ■, *Asia* **71 E6** 26 0N 50 35 E
Bahror, *India* **68 F7** 27 51N 76 20 E
Bāhū Kalāt, *Iran* **71 E9** 25 43N 61 25 E
Bai, *Mali* **82 C4** 13 35N 3 28W
Bai Bung, Mui = Ca Mau, Mui, *Vietnam* **65 H5** 8 38N 104 44 E
Bai Duc, *Vietnam* **64 C5** 18 3N 105 49 E
Bai Thuong, *Vietnam* **64 C5** 19 54N 105 23 E
Baia de Aramă, *Romania* **42 E7** 45 0N 22 50 E
Baia Mare, *Romania* **43 C8** 47 40N 23 35 E
Baia-Sprie, *Romania* **43 C8** 47 41N 23 43 E
Baião, *Brazil* **125 D9** 2 40 S 49 40W
Baïbokoum, *Chad* **79 G9** 7 46N 15 43 E
Baicheng, *China* **57 B12** 45 38N 122 42 E
Băicoi, *Romania* **43 E10** 45 3N 25 52 E
Baidoa, *Somali Rep.* **74 G3** 3 8N 43 30 E
Baie Comeau, *Canada* **103 C6** 49 12N 68 10W
Baie-St-Paul, *Canada* **103 C5** 47 28N 70 32W
Baie Trinité, *Canada* **103 C6** 49 25N 67 20W
Baie Verte, *Canada* **103 C8** 49 55N 56 12W
Baignes-Ste-Radegonde, *France* **20 C3** 45 23N 0 25W
Baigneux-les-Juifs, *France* **19 E11** 47 31N 4 39 E
Baihar, *India* **69 H9** 22 6N 80 33 E
Baihe, *China* **56 H6** 32 50N 110 5 E
Ba'ījī, *Iraq* **70 C4** 35 0N 43 30 E
Baijnath, *India* **69 E8** 29 55N 79 37 E
Baikal, L. = Baykal, Oz., *Russia* **51 D11** 53 0N 108 0 E
Baikunthpur, *India* **69 H10** 23 15N 82 33 E
Baile Atha Cliath = Dublin, *Ireland* **15 C5** 53 21N 6 15W
Băile Govora, *Romania* **43 E9** 45 5N 24 11 E
Băile Herculane, *Romania* **42 F7** 44 53N 22 26 E
Băile Olănești, *Romania* **43 E9** 45 12N 24 14 E
Băile Tușnad, *Romania* **43 D10** 46 9N 25 51 E
Bailén, *Spain* **35 G7** 38 8N 3 48W
Băilești, *Romania* **43 F8** 44 1N 23 20 E
Baima, *China* **58 A3** 33 0N 100 26 E
Bain-de-Bretagne, *France* **18 E5** 47 50N 1 40W
Bainbridge, *Ga., U.S.A.* **109 K3** 30 55N 84 35W
Bainbridge, *N.Y., U.S.A.* **111 D9** 42 18N 75 29W
Baing, *Indonesia* **63 F6** 10 14 S 120 34 E
Bainiu, *China* **56 H7** 32 50N 112 15 E
Baiona, *Spain* **34 C2** 42 6N 8 52W
Bā'ir, *Jordan* **75 E5** 30 45N 36 55 E
Bairin Youqi, *China* **57 C10** 43 30N 118 35 E
Bairin Zuoqi, *China* **57 C10** 43 58N 119 15 E
Bairnsdale, *Australia* **95 F4** 37 48 S 147 36 E
Bais, *Phil.* **61 G5** 9 35N 123 7 E
Baisha, *China* **56 G7** 34 20N 112 32 E
Baissa, *Nigeria* **83 D7** 7 14N 10 38 E
Baitadi, *Nepal* **69 E9** 29 35N 80 25 E
Baiyin, *China* **56 F3** 36 45N 104 14 E
Baiyü, *China* **58 B2** 31 16N 98 50 E
Baiyu Shan, *China* **56 F4** 37 15N 107 30 E
Baiyuda, *Sudan* **80 D3** 17 35N 32 7 E
Baj Baj, *India* **69 H13** 22 30N 88 5 E
Baja, *Hungary* **42 D3** 46 12N 18 59 E
Baja, Pta., *Mexico* **118 B1** 29 50N 116 0W
Baja California, *Mexico* **118 A1** 31 10N 115 12W
Baja California □, *Mexico* **118 B2** 30 0N 115 0W
Baja California Sur □, *Mexico* **118 B2** 25 50N 111 50W
Bajag, *India* **69 H9** 22 40N 81 21 E
Bajamar, *Canary Is.* **37 F3** 28 33N 16 20W
Bajana, *India* **68 H4** 23 7N 71 49 E
Bājgīrān, *Iran* **71 B8** 37 36N 58 24 E
Bajimba, Mt., *Australia* **95 D5** 29 17 S 152 6 E
Bajina Bašta, *Serbia, Yug.* **40 C3** 43 58N 19 35 E
Bajmok, *Serbia, Yug.* **42 E4** 45 57N 19 24 E
Bajo Nuevo, *Caribbean* **120 C4** 15 40N 78 50W
Bajoga, *Nigeria* **83 C7** 10 57N 11 20 E
Bajool, *Australia* **94 C5** 23 40 S 150 35 E
Bak, *Hungary* **42 D1** 46 43N 16 51 E
Bakar, *Croatia* **29 C11** 45 18N 14 32 E
Bakel, *Senegal* **82 C2** 14 56N 12 20W
Baker, *Calif., U.S.A.* **117 K10** 35 16N 116 4W
Baker, *Mont., U.S.A.* **112 B2** 46 22N 104 17W
Baker, L., *Canada* **100 B10** 64 0N 96 0W
Baker City, *U.S.A.* **114 D5** 44 47N 117 50W
Baker I., *Pac. Oc.* **96 G10** 0 10N 176 35W
Baker I., *U.S.A.* **104 B2** 55 20N 133 40W
Baker L., *Australia* **93 E4** 26 54 S 126 5 E
Baker Lake, *Canada* **100 B10** 64 20N 96 3W
Baker Mt., *U.S.A.* **114 B3** 48 50N 121 49W
Bakers Creek, *Australia* **94 C4** 21 13 S 149 7 E
Baker's Dozen Is., *Canada* **102 A4** 56 45N 78 45W
Bakersfield, *Calif., U.S.A.* **117 K8** 35 23N 119 1W
Bakersfield, *Vt., U.S.A.* **111 B12** 44 45N 72 48W
Bakhchysaray, *Ukraine* **47 K7** 44 40N 33 45 E
Bakhmach, *Ukraine* **47 G7** 51 10N 32 45 E
Bākhtarān, *Iran* **70 C5** 34 23N 47 0 E
Bākhtarān □, *Iran* **70 C5** 34 0N 46 30 E
Bakı, *Azerbaijan* **49 K9** 40 29N 49 56 E
Bakır →, *Turkey* **39 C9** 38 55N 27 0 E
Bakırdağı, *Turkey* **72 C6** 38 13N 35 46 E
Bakkafjörður, *Iceland* **8 C6** 66 2N 14 48W
Baklan, *Turkey* **39 C11** 38 0N 29 36 E
Bako, *Ethiopia* **81 F4** 5 51N 36 23 E
Bako, *Ivory C.* **82 D3** 9 8N 7 40W
Bakony, *Hungary* **42 C2** 47 10N 17 30 E
Bakony Forest = Bakony, *Hungary* **42 C2** 47 10N 17 30 E
Bakori, *Nigeria* **83 C6** 11 34N 7 25 E
Bakouma, *C.A.R.* **84 C4** 5 40N 22 56 E
Baksan, *Russia* **49 J6** 43 42N 43 32 E
Bakswaho, *India* **69 G8** 24 15N 79 18 E
Baku = Bakı, *Azerbaijan* **49 K9** 40 29N 49 56 E
Bakundi, *Nigeria* **83 D7** 8 2N 10 45 E
Bakutis Coast, *Antarctica* **5 D15** 74 0 S 120 0W
Baky = Bakı, *Azerbaijan* **49 K9** 40 29N 49 56 E
Bala, *Canada* **110 A5** 45 1N 79 37W
Bala, *Senegal* **82 C2** 14 1N 13 8W
Bâlâ, *Turkey* **72 C5** 39 32N 33 6 E
Bala, *U.K.* **12 E4** 52 54N 3 36W
Bala, L., *U.K.* **12 E4** 52 53N 3 37W
Balabac I., *Phil.* **62 C5** 8 0N 117 0 E
Balabac Str., *E. Indies* **62 C5** 7 53N 117 5 E
Balabagh, *Afghan.* **68 B4** 34 25N 70 12 E
Ba'labakk, *Lebanon* **75 B5** 34 0N 36 10 E
Balabalangan, Kepulauan, *Indonesia* **62 E5** 2 20 S 117 30 E
Bălăcița, *Romania* **43 F8** 44 23N 23 8 E
Balad, *Iraq* **70 C5** 34 1N 44 9 E
Balad Rūz, *Iraq* **70 C5** 33 42N 45 5 E
Bālādeh, *Fārs, Iran* **71 D6** 29 17N 51 56 E
Bālādeh, *Māzandaran, Iran* **71 B6** 36 12N 51 48 E
Balaghat, *India* **66 J12** 21 49N 80 12 E
Balaghat Ra., *India* **66 K10** 18 50N 76 30 E
Balaguer, *Spain* **32 D5** 41 50N 0 50 E
Balakhna, *Russia* **48 B6** 56 25N 43 32 E
Balaklava, *Ukraine* **47 K7** 44 30N 33 30 E
Balakliya, *Ukraine* **47 H9** 49 28N 36 55 E
Balakovo, *Russia* **48 D8** 52 4N 47 55 E
Balamau, *India* **69 F9** 27 10N 80 21 E
Bălan, *Romania* **43 D10** 46 39N 25 49 E
Balancán, *Mexico* **119 D6** 17 48N 91 32W
Balashov, *Russia* **48 E6** 51 30N 43 10 E
Balasinor, *India* **68 H5** 22 57N 73 23 E
Balasore = Baleshwar, *India* **67 J15** 21 35N 87 3 E
Balassagyarmat, *Hungary* **42 B4** 48 4N 19 15 E
Balât, *Egypt* **80 B2** 25 36N 29 19 E
Balaton, *Hungary* **42 D2** 46 50N 17 40 E
Balatonboglár, *Hungary* **42 D2** 46 46N 17 40 E
Balatonfüred, *Hungary* **42 D2** 46 58N 17 54 E
Balatonszentgyörgy, *Hungary* **42 D2** 46 41N 17 19 E
Balayan, *Phil.* **61 E4** 13 57N 120 44 E
Balazote, *Spain* **33 G2** 38 54N 2 9W
Balbieriškis, *Lithuania* **44 D10** 54 32N 23 53 E
Balbigny, *France* **21 C8** 45 49N 4 11 E
Balbina, Reprêsa de, *Brazil* **124 D7** 2 0 S 59 30W
Balboa, *Panama* **120 E4** 8 57N 79 34W
Balbriggan, *Ireland* **15 C5** 53 37N 6 11W
Balcarce, *Argentina* **126 D4** 38 0 S 58 10W
Balcarres, *Canada* **105 C8** 50 50N 103 35W
Bălcești, *Romania* **43 F8** 44 37N 23 57 E
Balchik, *Bulgaria* **41 C12** 43 28N 28 11 E
Balclutha, *N.Z.* **91 M2** 46 15 S 169 45 E
Balcones Escarpment, *U.S.A.* **113 L5** 29 30N 99 15W
Balçova, *Turkey* **39 C9** 38 22N 27 4 E
Bald Hd., *Australia* **93 G2** 35 6 S 118 1 E
Bald I., *Australia* **93 F2** 34 57 S 118 27 E
Bald Knob, *U.S.A.* **113 H9** 35 19N 91 34W
Baldock L., *Canada* **105 B9** 56 33N 97 57W
Baldwin, *Mich., U.S.A.* **108 D3** 43 54N 85 51W
Baldwin, *Pa., U.S.A.* **110 F5** 40 23N 79 59W
Baldwinsville, *U.S.A.* **111 C8** 43 10N 76 20W
Baldy Mt., *U.S.A.* **114 B9** 48 9N 109 39W
Baldy Peak, *U.S.A.* **115 K9** 33 54N 109 34W
Bale, *Croatia* **29 C10** 45 4N 13 46 E
Bale, *Ethiopia* **81 F5** 6 57N 40 8 E
Bale □, *Ethiopia* **81 F5** 6 20N 41 30 E
Baleares, Is., *Spain* **37 B10** 39 30N 3 0 E
Balearic Is. = Baleares, Is., *Spain* **37 B10** 39 30N 3 0 E
Baleine = Whale →, *Canada* **103 A6** 58 15N 67 40W
Băleni, *Romania* **43 E12** 45 48N 27 51 E
Baler, *Phil.* **61 D4** 15 46N 121 34 E
Baler Bay, *Phil.* **61 D4** 15 50N 121 35 E
Baleshare, *U.K.* **14 D1** 57 31N 7 22W
Baleshwar, *India* **67 J15** 21 35N 87 3 E
Balezino, *Russia* **48 B11** 58 2N 53 6 E
Balfate, *Honduras* **120 C2** 15 48N 86 25W
Bali, *Cameroon* **83 D7** 5 54N 10 0 E
Balí, *Greece* **36 D6** 35 25N 24 47 E
Bali, *India* **68 G5** 25 11N 73 17 E
Bali □, *Indonesia* **62 F5** 8 20 S 115 0 E
Bali, Selat, *Indonesia* **63 H16** 8 18 S 114 25 E
Balia, *S. Leone* **82 D2** 9 22N 11 1W
Baliapal, *India* **69 J12** 21 40N 87 17 E
Baligród, *Poland* **45 J9** 49 20N 22 17 E
Balıkesir, *Turkey* **39 B9** 39 39N 27 53 E
Balıkesir □, *Turkey* **39 B9** 39 45N 28 0 E
Balıklıçeşme, *Turkey* **41 F11** 40 18N 27 5 E
Balikpapan, *Indonesia* **62 E5** 1 10 S 116 55 E
Balimbing, *Phil.* **63 C5** 5 5N 119 58 E
Baling, *Malaysia* **65 K3** 5 41N 100 55 E
Balingen, *Germany* **25 G4** 48 16N 8 51 E
Balint, *Romania* **42 E6** 45 48N 21 54 E
Balintang Channel, *Phil.* **61 B4** 19 49N 121 40 E
Balipara, *India* **67 F18** 26 50N 92 45 E
Balkan Mts. = Stara Planina, *Bulgaria* **40 C7** 43 15N 23 0 E
Balkhash = Balqash, *Kazakstan* **50 E8** 46 50N 74 50 E
Balkhash, Ozero = Balqash Köl, *Kazakstan* **50 E8** 46 0N 74 50 E
Balla, *Bangla.* **67 G17** 24 10N 91 35 E
Ballachulish, *U.K.* **14 E3** 56 41N 5 8W
Balladonia, *Australia* **93 F3** 32 27 S 123 51 E
Ballaghaderreen, *Ireland* **15 C3** 53 55N 8 34W
Ballarat, *Australia* **95 F3** 37 33 S 143 50 E
Ballard, L., *Australia* **93 E3** 29 20 S 120 40 E
Ballater, *U.K.* **14 D5** 57 3N 3 3W
Ballé, *Mali* **82 B3** 15 18N 8 33W
Ballenas, Canal de, *Mexico* **118 B2** 29 10N 113 45W
Balleny Is., *Antarctica* **5 C11** 66 30 S 163 0 E
Balleroy, *France* **18 C6** 49 11N 0 50W
Ballerup, *Denmark* **11 J6** 55 44N 12 21 E
Ballı, *Turkey* **41 F11** 40 50N 27 3 E
Ballia, *India* **69 G11** 25 46N 84 12 E
Ballina, *Australia* **95 D5** 28 50 S 153 31 E
Ballina, *Ireland* **15 B2** 54 7N 9 9W
Ballinasloe, *Ireland* **15 C3** 53 20N 8 13W
Ballinger, *U.S.A.* **113 K5** 31 45N 99 57W
Ballinrobe, *Ireland* **15 C2** 53 38N 9 13W
Ballinskelligs B., *Ireland* **15 E1** 51 48N 10 13W
Ballon, *France* **18 D7** 48 10N 0 14 E
Ballsh, *Albania* **40 F3** 40 36N 19 44 E
Ballston Spa, *U.S.A.* **111 D11** 43 0N 73 51W
Ballycastle, *U.K.* **15 A5** 55 12N 6 15W
Ballyclare, *U.K.* **15 B5** 54 46N 6 0W
Ballyhaunis, *Ireland* **15 C3** 53 46N 8 46W
Ballymena, *U.K.* **15 B5** 54 52N 6 17W
Ballymoney, *U.K.* **15 A5** 55 5N 6 31W
Ballymote, *Ireland* **15 B3** 54 5N 8 31W
Ballynahinch, *U.K.* **15 B6** 54 24N 5 54W
Ballyquintin Pt., *U.K.* **15 B6** 54 20N 5 30W
Ballyshannon, *Ireland* **15 B3** 54 30N 8 11W
Balmaceda, *Chile* **128 F2** 46 0 S 71 50W
Balmaseda, *Spain* **32 B1** 43 11N 3 12W
Balmazújváros, *Hungary* **42 C6** 47 37N 21 21 E
Balmertown, *Canada* **105 C10** 51 4N 93 41W
Balmoral, *Australia* **95 F3** 37 15 S 141 48 E
Balmorhea, *U.S.A.* **113 K3** 30 59N 103 45W
Balonne →, *Australia* **95 D4** 28 47 S 147 56 E
Balotra, *India* **68 G5** 25 50N 72 14 E
Balqash, *Kazakstan* **50 E8** 46 50N 74 50 E
Balqash Köl, *Kazakstan* **50 E8** 46 0N 74 50 E
Balrampur, *India* **69 F10** 27 30N 82 20 E
Balranald, *Australia* **95 E3** 34 38 S 143 33 E
Balș, *Romania* **43 F9** 44 22N 24 5 E
Balsas, *Mexico* **119 D5** 18 0N 99 40W
Balsas →, *Brazil* **125 E9** 7 15 S 44 35W
Balsas →, *Mexico* **118 D4** 17 55N 102 10W
Bålsta, *Sweden* **10 E11** 59 35N 17 30 E
Balston Spa, *U.S.A.* **111 D11** 43 0N 73 52W
Balta, *Romania* **42 F7** 44 54N 22 38 E
Balta, *Ukraine* **47 H5** 48 2N 29 45 E
Baltanás, *Spain* **34 D6** 41 56N 4 15W
Bălți, *Moldova* **43 C12** 47 48N 27 58 E
Baltic Sea, *Europe* **9 H18** 57 0N 19 0 E
Baltîm, *Egypt* **80 H7** 31 35N 31 10 E
Baltimore, *Ireland* **15 E2** 51 29N 9 22W
Baltimore, *Md., U.S.A.* **108 F7** 39 17N 76 37W
Baltimore, *Ohio, U.S.A.* **110 G2** 39 51N 82 36W
Baltit, *Pakistan* **69 A6** 36 15N 74 40 E
Baltiysk, *Russia* **9 J18** 54 41N 19 58 E
Baltrum, *Germany* **24 B3** 53 43N 7 24 E
Baluchistan □, *Pakistan* **66 F4** 27 30N 65 0 E
Balurghat, *India* **69 G13** 25 15N 88 44 E
Balvi, *Latvia* **9 H22** 57 8N 27 15 E
Balya, *Turkey* **39 B9** 39 44N 27 35 E
Bam, *Iran* **71 D8** 29 7N 58 14 E
Bama, *China* **58 E6** 24 8N 107 12 E
Bama, *Nigeria* **83 C7** 11 33N 13 41 E
Bamaga, *Australia* **94 A3** 10 50 S 142 25 E
Bamaji L., *Canada* **102 B1** 51 9N 91 25W
Bamako, *Mali* **82 C3** 12 34N 7 55W
Bamba, *Mali* **83 B4** 17 5N 1 24W
Bambara Maoundé, *Mali* **82 B4** 15 26N 4 3W
Bambari, *C.A.R.* **84 C4** 5 40N 20 35 E
Bambaroo, *Australia* **94 B4** 18 50 S 146 10 E
Bambaya, *Guinea* **82 D2** 10 55N 13 38W
Bamberg, *Germany* **25 F6** 49 54N 10 54 E
Bamberg, *U.S.A.* **109 J5** 33 18N 81 2W
Bambesi, *Ethiopia* **81 F3** 9 45N 34 40 E
Bambey, *Senegal* **82 C1** 14 42N 16 28W
Bambili, *Dem. Rep. of the Congo* **86 B2** 3 40N 26 0 E
Bamboi, *Ghana* **82 D4** 8 13N 2 1W
Bamenda, *Cameroon* **83 D7** 5 57N 10 11 E
Bamfield, *Canada* **104 D3** 48 45N 125 10W
Bāmīān □, *Afghan.* **66 B5** 35 0N 67 0 E
Bamiancheng, *China* **57 C13** 43 15N 124 2 E
Bamkin, *Cameroon* **83 D7** 6 3N 11 27 E
Bampūr, *Iran* **71 E9** 27 15N 60 21 E
Ban, *Burkina Faso* **82 C4** 14 5N 2 27W
Ban Ban, *Laos* **64 C4** 19 31N 103 30 E
Ban Bang Hin, *Thailand* **65 H2** 9 32N 98 35 E
Ban Chiang Klang, *Thailand* **64 C3** 19 25N 100 55 E
Ban Chik, *Laos* **64 D4** 17 15N 102 22 E
Ban Choho, *Thailand* **64 E4** 15 2N 102 9 E
Ban Dan Lan Hoi, *Thailand* **64 D2** 17 0N 99 35 E
Ban Don = Surat Thani, *Thailand* **65 H2** 9 6N 99 20 E
Ban Don, *Vietnam* **64 F6** 12 53N 107 48 E
Ban Don, Ao →, *Thailand* **65 H2** 9 20N 99 25 E
Ban Dong, *Thailand* **64 C3** 19 30N 100 59 E
Ban Hong, *Thailand* **64 C2** 18 18N 98 50 E
Ban Kaeng, *Thailand* **64 D3** 17 29N 100 7 E
Ban Kantang, *Thailand* **65 J2** 7 25N 99 31 E
Ban Keun, *Laos* **64 C4** 18 22N 102 35 E
Ban Khai, *Thailand* **64 F3** 12 46N 101 18 E
Ban Kheun, *Laos* **64 B3** 20 13N 101 7 E
Ban Khlong Kua, *Thailand* **65 J3** 6 57N 100 8 E
Ban Khuan Mao, *Thailand* **65 J2** 7 50N 99 37 E
Ban Ko Yai Chim, *Thailand* **65 G2** 11 17N 99 26 E
Ban Kok, *Thailand* **64 D4** 16 40N 103 40 E
Ban Laem, *Thailand* **64 F2** 13 13N 99 59 E
Ban Lao Ngam, *Laos* **64 E6** 15 28N 106 10 E
Ban Le Kathe, *Thailand* **64 E2** 15 49N 98 53 E
Ban Mae Chedi, *Thailand* **64 C2** 19 11N 99 31 E
Ban Mae Laeng, *Thailand* **64 B2** 20 1N 99 17 E
Ban Mae Sariang, *Thailand* **64 C1** 18 10N 97 56 E
Ban Mê Thuôt = Buon Ma Thuot, *Vietnam* **64 F7** 12 40N 108 3 E
Ban Mi, *Thailand* **64 E3** 15 3N 100 32 E
Ban Muong Mo, *Laos* **64 C4** 19 4N 103 58 E
Ban Na Mo, *Laos* **64 D5** 17 7N 105 40 E
Ban Na San, *Thailand* **65 H2** 8 53N 99 52 E
Ban Na Tong, *Laos* **64 B3** 20 56N 101 47 E
Ban Nam Bac, *Laos* **64 B4** 20 38N 102 20 E
Ban Nam Ma, *Laos* **64 A3** 22 2N 101 37 E
Ban Ngang, *Laos* **64 E6** 15 59N 106 11 E
Ban Nong Bok, *Laos* **64 D5** 17 5N 104 48 E
Ban Nong Boua, *Laos* **64 E6** 15 40N 106 33 E
Ban Nong Pling, *Thailand* **64 E3** 15 40N 100 10 E
Ban Pak Chan, *Thailand* **65 G2** 10 32N 98 51 E
Ban Phai, *Thailand* **64 D4** 16 4N 102 44 E
Ban Pong, *Thailand* **64 F2** 13 50N 99 55 E
Ban Ron Phibun, *Thailand* **65 H2** 8 9N 99 51 E
Ban Sanam Chai, *Thailand* **65 J3** 7 33N 100 25 E
Ban Sangkha, *Thailand* **64 E4** 14 37N 103 52 E
Ban Tak, *Thailand* **64 D2** 17 2N 99 4 E
Ban Tako, *Thailand* **64 E4** 14 5N 102 40 E
Ban Tha Dua, *Thailand* **64 D2** 17 59N 98 39 E
Ban Tha Li, *Thailand* **64 D3** 17 37N 101 25 E
Ban Tha Nun, *Thailand* **65 H2** 8 12N 98 18 E
Ban Thahine, *Laos* **64 E5** 14 12N 105 33 E
Ban Xien Kok, *Laos* **64 B3** 20 54N 100 39 E
Ban Yen Nhan, *Vietnam* **64 B6** 20 57N 106 2 E
Banaba, *Kiribati* **96 H8** 0 45 S 169 50 E
Banalia, *Dem. Rep. of the Congo* **86 B2** 1 32N 25 5 E
Banam, *Cambodia* **65 G5** 11 20N 105 17 E
Banamba, *Mali* **82 C3** 13 29N 7 22W
Banana Is., *S. Leone* **82 D2** 8 7N 13 15W
Bananal, I. do, *Brazil* **125 F8** 11 30 S 50 30W
Banaras = Varanasi, *India* **69 G10** 25 22N 83 0 E
Banas →, *Gujarat, India* **68 H4** 23 45N 71 25 E
Banas →, *Mad. P., India* **69 G9** 24 15N 81 30 E
Bânâs, Ras, *Egypt* **80 C4** 23 57N 35 59 E
Banaz, *Turkey* **39 C11** 38 46N 29 46 E
Banaz →, *Turkey* **39 C11** 38 12N 29 14 E
Banbān, *Si. Arabia* **70 E5** 25 1N 46 35 E
Banbridge, *U.K.* **15 B5** 54 22N 6 16W
Banbury, *U.K.* **13 E6** 52 4N 1 20W
Banchory, *U.K.* **14 D6** 57 3N 2 29W
Banco, *Ethiopia* **81 F4** 6 12N 38 13 E
Bancroft, *Canada* **102 C4** 45 3N 77 51W
Band, *Romania* **43 D9** 46 30N 24 25 E
Band Bonī, *Iran* **71 E8** 25 30N 59 33 E
Band Qīr, *Iran* **71 D6** 31 39N 48 53 E
Banda, *Mad. P., India* **69 G8** 24 3N 78 57 E
Banda, *Ut. P., India* **69 G9** 25 30N 80 26 E
Banda, Kepulauan, *Indonesia* **63 E7** 4 37 S 129 50 E
Banda Aceh, *Indonesia* **62 C1** 5 35N 95 20 E
Banda Banda, Mt., *Australia* **95 E5** 31 10 S 152 28 E
Banda Elat, *Indonesia* **63 F8** 5 40 S 133 5 E
Banda Is. = Banda, Kepulauan, *Indonesia* **63 E7** 4 37 S 129 50 E
Banda Sea, *Indonesia* **63 F7** 6 0 S 130 0 E
Bandai-San, *Japan* **54 F10** 37 36N 140 4 E
Bandama →, *Ivory C.* **82 D3** 6 32N 4 30W
Bandama Blanc →, *Ivory C.* **82 D3** 6 55N 5 30W

Bandama Rouge →, Ivory C. 82 D4 6 55N 5 30W
Bandān, Iran 71 D9 31 23N 60 44 E
Bandanaira, Indonesia 63 E7 4 32 S 129 54 E
Bandanwara, India 68 F6 26 9N 74 38 E
Bandar = Machilipatnam, India 67 L12 16 12N 81 8 E
Bandār 'Abbās, Iran 71 E8 27 15N 56 15 E
Bandar-e Anzalī, Iran 71 B6 37 30N 49 30 E
Bandar-e Bushehr = Būshehr, Iran 71 D6 28 55N 50 55 E
Bandar-e Chārak, Iran 71 E7 26 45N 54 20 E
Bandar-e Deylam, Iran 71 D6 30 5N 50 10 E
Bandar-e Khomeynı, Iran 71 D6 30 30N 49 5 E
Bandar-e Lengeh, Iran 71 E7 26 35N 54 58 E
Bandar-e Maqām, Iran 71 E7 26 56N 53 29 E
Bandar-e Ma'shur, Iran 71 D6 30 35N 49 10 E
Bandar-e Nakhīlū, Iran 71 E7 26 58N 53 30 E
Bandar-e Rīg, Iran 71 D6 29 29N 50 38 E
Bandar-e Torkeman, Iran 71 B7 37 0N 54 10 E
Bandar Maharani = Muar, Malaysia 65 L4 2 3N 102 34 E
Bandar Penggaram = Batu Pahat, Malaysia 65 M4 1 50N 102 56 E
Bandar Seri Begawan, Brunei 62 C4 4 52N 115 0 E
Bandar Sri Aman, Malaysia 62 D4 1 15N 111 32 E
Bandawe, Malawi 87 E3 11 58 S 34 5 E
Bande, Spain 34 C3 42 3N 7 58W
Bandeira, Pico da, Brazil 127 A7 20 26 S 41 47W
Bandera, Argentina 126 B3 28 55 S 62 20W
Banderas, B. de, Mexico 118 C3 20 40N 105 30W
Bandhogarh, India 69 H9 23 40N 81 2 E
Bandi →, India 68 F6 26 12N 75 47 E
Bandiagara, Mali 82 C4 14 12N 3 29W
Bandikui, India 68 F7 27 3N 76 34 E
Bandırma, Turkey 41 F11 40 20N 28 0 E
Bandol, France 21 E9 43 8N 5 46 E
Bandon, Ireland 15 E3 51 44N 8 44W
Bandon →, Ireland 15 E3 51 43N 8 37W
Bandula, Mozam. 87 F3 19 0 S 33 7 E
Bandundu, Dem. Rep. of the Congo 84 E3 3 15 S 17 22 E
Bandung, Indonesia 63 G12 6 54 S 107 36 E
Bané, Burkina Faso 83 C4 11 42N 0 15W
Băneasa, Romania 43 E12 45 56N 27 55 E
Bāneh, Iran 70 C5 35 59N 45 53 E
Bañeres, Spain 33 G4 38 44N 0 38W
Banes, Cuba 121 B4 21 0N 75 42W
Banff, Canada 104 C5 51 10N 115 34W
Banff, U.K. 14 D6 57 40N 2 33W
Banff Nat. Park, Canada 104 C5 51 30N 116 15W
Banfora, Burkina Faso 82 C4 10 40N 4 40W
Bang Fai →, Laos 64 D5 16 57N 104 45 E
Bang Hieng →, Laos 64 D5 16 10N 105 10 E
Bang Krathum, Thailand 64 D3 16 34N 100 18 E
Bang Lamung, Thailand 64 F3 13 3N 100 56 E
Bang Mun Nak, Thailand 64 D3 16 2N 100 23 E
Bang Pa In, Thailand 64 E3 14 14N 100 35 E
Bang Rakam, Thailand 64 D3 16 45N 100 7 E
Bang Saphan, Thailand 65 G2 11 14N 99 28 E
Bangaduni I., India 69 J13 21 34N 88 52 E
Bangala Dam, Zimbabwe 87 G3 21 7 S 31 25 E
Bangalore, India 66 N10 12 59N 77 40 E
Banganga →, India 68 F6 27 6N 77 25 E
Bangangté, Cameroon 83 D7 5 8N 10 32 E
Bangaon, India 69 H13 23 0N 88 47 E
Bangassou, C.A.R. 84 D4 4 55N 23 7 E
Banggai, Indonesia 63 E6 1 34 S 123 30 E
Banggai, Kepulauan, Indonesia 63 E6 1 40 S 123 30 E
Banggai Arch. = Banggai, Kepulauan, Indonesia 63 E6 1 40 S 123 30 E
Banggi, Malaysia 62 C5 7 17N 117 12 E
Banghāzī, Libya 79 B10 32 11N 20 3 E
Bangjang, Sudan 81 E3 11 23N 32 41 E
Bangka, Sulawesi, Indonesia 63 D7 1 50N 125 5 E
Bangka, Sumatera, Indonesia 62 E3 2 0 S 105 50 E
Bangka, Selat, Indonesia 62 E3 2 30 S 105 30 E
Bangkalan, Indonesia 63 G15 7 2 S 112 46 E
Bangkinang, Indonesia 62 D2 0 18N 101 5 E
Bangko, Indonesia 62 E2 2 5 S 102 9 E
Bangkok, Thailand 64 F3 13 45N 100 35 E
Bangladesh ■, Asia 67 H17 24 0N 90 0 E
Bangolo, Ivory C. 82 D3 7 1N 7 29W
Bangong Co, India 69 B8 35 50N 79 20 E
Bangor, Down, U.K. 15 B6 54 40N 5 40W
Bangor, Gwynedd, U.K. 12 D3 53 14N 4 8W
Bangor, Maine, U.S.A. 101 D13 44 48N 68 46W
Bangor, Pa., U.S.A. 111 F9 40 52N 75 13W
Bangued, Phil. 61 C4 17 40N 120 37 E
Bangui, C.A.R. 84 D3 4 23N 18 35 E
Bangui, Phil. 61 B4 18 32N 120 46 E
Banguru, Dem. Rep. of the Congo 86 B2 0 30N 27 10 E
Bangweulu, L., Zambia 87 E3 11 0S 30 0 E
Bangweulu Swamp, Zambia 87 E3 11 20 S 30 15 E
Bani, Dom. Rep. 121 C5 18 16N 70 22W
Bani →, Mali 82 C4 14 30N 4 12W
Bani Bangou, Niger 83 B5 15 3N 2 42 E
Banī Sa'd, Iraq 70 C5 33 34N 44 32 E
Bania, Ivory C. 82 D4 9 4N 3 6W
Banihal Pass, India 69 C6 33 30N 75 12 E
Banikoara, Benin 83 C5 11 18N 2 26 E
Bāniyās, Syria 70 C3 35 10N 36 0 E
Banja Luka, Bos.-H. 42 F2 44 49N 17 11 E
Banjar, India 68 D7 31 38N 77 21 E
Banjar →, India 69 H9 22 36N 80 22 E
Banjarmasin, Indonesia 62 E4 3 20 S 114 35 E
Banjul, Gambia 82 C1 13 28N 16 40W
Banka, India 69 G12 24 53N 86 55 E
Bankas, Mali 82 C4 14 4N 3 31W
Bankeryd, Sweden 11 G8 57 53N 14 6 E
Banket, Zimbabwe 87 F3 17 27 S 30 19 E
Bankilaré, Niger 83 C5 14 35N 0 44 E
Bankipore, India 67 G14 25 35N 85 10 E
Banks I., B.C., Canada 104 C3 53 20N 130 0W
Banks I., N.W.T., Canada 100 A7 73 15N 121 30W
Banks Pen., N.Z. 91 K4 43 45 S 173 15 E
Banks Str., Australia 94 G4 40 40 S 148 10 E
Bankura, India 69 H12 23 11N 87 18 E
Bankya, Bulgaria 40 D7 42 43N 23 8 E
Banmankhi, India 69 G12 25 53N 87 11 E
Bann →, Arm., U.K. 15 B5 54 30N 6 31W
Bann →, L'derry., U.K. 15 A5 55 8N 6 41W
Bannalec, France 18 E3 47 57N 3 42W
Bannang Sata, Thailand 65 J3 6 16N 101 16 E
Banning, U.S.A. 117 M10 33 56N 116 53W
Banningville = Bandundu, Dem. Rep. of the Congo 84 E3 3 15 S 17 22 E
Banno, Ethiopia 81 G4 4 51N 37 24 E
Bannockburn, Canada 110 B7 44 39N 77 33W
Bannockburn, U.K. 14 E5 56 5N 3 55W
Bannockburn, Zimbabwe 87 G2 20 17 S 29 48 E
Bannu, Pakistan 66 C7 33 0N 70 18 E
Bano, India 69 H11 22 40N 84 55 E
Bañolas = Banyoles, Spain 32 C7 42 16N 2 44 E
Banon, France 21 D9 44 2N 5 38 E
Baños de la Encina, Spain 35 G7 38 10N 3 46W
Baños de Molgas, Spain 34 C3 42 15N 7 40W
Bánovce nad Bebravou, Slovak Rep. 27 C11 48 44N 18 16 E
Banovići, Bos.-H. 42 F3 44 25N 18 32 E
Bansgaon, India 69 F10 26 33N 83 21 E
Banská Bystrica, Slovak Rep. 27 C12 48 46N 19 14 E
Banská Štiavnica, Slovak Rep. 27 C11 48 25N 18 55 E
Bansko, Bulgaria 40 E7 41 52N 23 28 E
Banskobystrický ☐, Slovak Rep. 27 C12 48 20N 19 0 E
Banswara, India 68 H6 23 32N 74 24 E
Bantaeng, Indonesia 63 F5 5 32 S 119 56 E
Bantaji, Nigeria 83 D7 8 6N 10 5 E
Bantayan, Phil. 61 F5 11 10N 123 43 E
Bantry, Ireland 15 E2 51 41N 9 27W
Bantry B., Ireland 15 E2 51 37N 9 44W
Bantul, Indonesia 63 G14 7 55 S 110 19 E
Bantva, India 68 J4 21 29N 70 12 E
Banu, Afghan. 66 B6 35 35N 69 5 E
Banya, Bulgaria 41 D8 42 33N 24 50 E
Banyak, Kepulauan, Indonesia 62 D1 2 10N 97 10 E
Banyalbufar, Spain 37 B9 39 42N 2 31 E
Banyo, Cameroon 83 D7 6 52N 11 45 E
Banyoles, Spain 32 C7 42 16N 2 44 E
Banyuls-sur-Mer, France 20 F7 42 28N 3 8 E
Banyumas, Indonesia 63 G13 7 32 S 109 18 E
Banyuwangi, Indonesia 63 H16 8 13 S 114 21 E
Banzare Coast, Antarctica 5 C9 68 0 S 125 0 E
Banzyville = Mobayi, Dem. Rep. of the Congo 84 D4 4 15N 21 8 E
Bao Ha, Vietnam 58 F5 22 11N 104 21 E
Bao Lac, Vietnam 64 A5 22 57N 105 40 E
Bao Loc, Vietnam 65 G6 11 32N 107 48 E
Bao'an = Shenzhen, China 59 F10 22 27N 114 10 E
Baocheng, China 56 H4 33 12N 106 56 E
Baode, China 56 E6 39 1N 111 5 E
Baodi, China 57 E9 39 38N 117 20 E
Baoding, China 56 E8 38 50N 115 28 E
Baoji, China 56 G4 34 20N 107 5 E
Baojing, China 58 C7 28 45N 109 41 E
Baokang, China 59 B8 31 54N 111 12 E
Baoshan, Shanghai, China 59 B13 31 27N 121 26 E
Baoshan, Yunnan, China 58 E2 25 10N 99 5 E
Baotou, China 56 D6 40 32N 110 2 E
Baoxing, China 58 B4 30 24N 102 50 E
Baoying, China 57 H10 33 17N 119 20 E
Bap, India 68 F5 27 23N 72 18 E
Bapatla, India 67 M12 15 55N 80 30 E
Bapaume, France 19 B9 50 7N 2 50 E
Bāqerābād, Iran 71 C6 33 2N 51 58 E
Ba'qūbah, Iraq 70 C5 33 45N 44 50 E
Baquedano, Chile 126 A2 23 20 S 69 52W
Bar, Montenegro, Yug. 40 D3 42 8N 19 6 E
Bar, Ukraine 47 H4 49 4N 27 40 E
Bar Bigha, India 69 G11 25 21N 85 47 E
Bar Harbor, U.S.A. 109 C11 44 23N 68 13W
Bar-le-Duc, France 19 D12 48 47N 5 10 E
Bar-sur-Aube, France 19 D11 48 14N 4 40 E
Bar-sur-Seine, France 19 D11 48 7N 4 20 E
Bara, India 69 G9 25 16N 81 43 E
Bâra, Romania 43 C12 47 2N 27 3 E
Bara Banki, India 69 F9 26 55N 81 12 E
Barabai, Indonesia 62 E5 2 32 S 115 34 E
Baraboo, U.S.A. 112 D10 43 28N 89 45W
Baracoa, Cuba 121 B5 20 20N 74 30W
Baradā →, Syria 75 B5 33 33N 36 34 E
Baradero, Argentina 126 C4 33 52 S 59 29W
Baradine, Australia 95 E4 30 56 S 149 4 E
Baraga, U.S.A. 112 B10 46 47N 88 30W
Bărăganul, Romania 43 F12 44 49N 27 31 E
Barah →, India 68 F6 27 42N 77 5 E
Barahona, Dom. Rep. 121 C5 18 13N 71 7W
Barahona, Spain 32 D2 41 17N 2 39W
Barail Range, India 67 G18 25 15N 93 20 E
Baraka, Sudan 81 E2 10 59N 27 59 E
Baraka →, Sudan 80 D4 18 13N 37 35 E
Barakaldo, Spain 32 B2 43 18N 2 59W
Barakar →, India 69 G12 24 7N 86 14 E
Barakhola, India 67 G18 25 0N 92 45 E
Barakot, India 69 J11 21 33N 84 59 E
Barakpur, India 69 H13 22 44N 88 30 E
Baralaba, Australia 94 C4 24 13 S 149 50 E
Baralla, Spain 34 C3 42 53N 7 15W
Baralzon L., Canada 105 B9 60 0N 98 3W
Barameiya, Sudan 80 D4 18 32N 36 38 E
Baramula, India 69 B6 34 15N 74 20 E
Baran, India 68 G7 25 9N 76 40 E
Baran →, Pakistan 68 G3 25 13N 68 17 E
Barañain, Spain 32 C3 42 48N 1 40W
Baranavichy, Belarus 47 F4 53 10N 26 0 E
Barani, Burkina Faso 82 C4 13 9N 3 51W
Baranof, U.S.A. 104 B2 57 5N 134 50W
Baranof I., U.S.A. 100 C6 57 0N 135 0W
Baranów Sandomierski, Poland 45 H8 50 29N 21 30 E
Baranya ☐, Hungary 42 E3 46 0N 18 15 E
Baraolt, Romania 43 D10 46 5N 25 34 E
Barapasi, Indonesia 63 E9 2 15 S 137 5 E
Barasat, India 69 H13 22 46N 88 31 E
Barat Daya, Kepulauan, Indonesia 63 F7 7 30 S 128 0 E
Barataria B., U.S.A. 113 L10 29 20N 89 55W
Barauda, India 68 H6 23 33N 75 15 E
Baraut, India 68 E7 29 13N 77 7 E
Barbacena, Brazil 127 A7 21 15 S 43 56W
Barbados ■, W. Indies 121 D8 13 10N 59 30W
Barban, Croatia 29 C11 45 5N 14 2 E
Barbària, C. de, Spain 37 C7 38 39N 1 24 E
Barbaros, Turkey 41 F11 40 54N 27 27 E
Barbastro, Spain 32 C5 42 2N 0 5 E
Barbate = Barbate de Franco, Spain 35 J5 36 13N 5 56W
Barbate de Franco, Spain 35 J5 36 13N 5 56W
Barberino di Mugello, Italy 29 E8 44 0N 11 15 E
Barberton, S. Africa 89 D5 25 42 S 31 2 E
Barberton, U.S.A. 110 E3 41 0N 81 39W
Barbezieux-St-Hilaire, France 20 C3 45 28N 0 9W
Barbosa, Colombia 124 B4 5 57N 73 37W
Barbourville, U.S.A. 109 G4 36 52N 83 53W
Barbuda, W. Indies 121 C7 17 30N 61 40W
Bârca, Romania 43 G8 43 59N 23 36 E
Barcaldine, Australia 94 C4 23 43 S 145 6 E
Barcarrota, Spain 35 G4 38 31N 6 51W
Barcellona Pozzo di Gotto, Italy 31 D8 38 9N 15 13 E
Barcelona, Spain 32 D7 41 21N 2 10 E
Barcelona, Venezuela 124 A6 10 10N 64 40W
Barcelona ☐, Spain 32 D7 41 30N 2 0 E
Barcelonette, France 21 D10 44 23N 6 40 E
Barcelos, Brazil 124 D6 1 0 S 63 0W
Barcin, Poland 45 F4 52 52N 17 55 E
Barclayville, Liberia 82 E3 4 48N 8 10W
Barcoo →, Australia 94 D3 25 30 S 142 50 E
Barcs, Hungary 42 E2 45 58N 17 28 E
Barczewo, Poland 44 E7 53 50N 20 42 E
Bärdä, Azerbaijan 49 K8 40 25N 47 10 E
Bardaï, Chad 79 D9 21 25N 17 0 E
Bardas Blancas, Argentina 126 D2 35 49 S 69 45W
Barddhaman, India 69 H12 23 14N 87 39 E
Bardejov, Slovak Rep. 27 B14 49 18N 21 15 E
Bardera, Somali Rep. 74 G3 2 20N 42 27 E
Bardi, Italy 28 D6 44 38N 9 44 E
Bardīyah, Libya 79 B10 31 45N 25 5 E
Bardolino, Italy 28 C7 45 33N 10 43 E
Bardonécchia, Italy 28 C3 45 5N 6 42 E
Bardsey I., U.K. 12 E3 52 45N 4 47W
Bardstown, U.S.A. 108 G3 37 49N 85 28W
Bareilly, India 69 E8 28 22N 79 27 E
Barela, India 69 H9 23 6N 80 3 E
Barentin, France 18 C7 49 33N 0 58 E
Barenton, France 18 D6 48 38N 0 50W
Barents Sea, Arctic 4 B9 73 0N 39 0 E
Barentu, Eritrea 81 D4 15 2N 37 35 E
Barfleur, France 18 C5 49 40N 1 17W
Barfleur, Pte. de, France 18 C5 49 42N 1 16W
Barga, Italy 28 D7 44 4N 10 29 E
Bargara, Australia 94 C5 24 50 S 152 25 E
Bargas, Spain 34 F6 39 56N 4 3W
Bârgăului Bistrița, Romania 43 C9 47 13N 24 46 E
Barge, Italy 28 D4 44 43N 7 20 E
Bargnop, Sudan 81 F2 9 32N 28 25 E
Bargteheide, Germany 24 B6 53 44N 10 14 E
Barguzin, Russia 51 D11 53 37N 109 37 E
Barh, India 69 G11 25 29N 85 46 E
Barhaj, India 69 F10 26 18N 83 44 E
Barham, Australia 95 F3 35 36 S 144 8 E
Barharwa, India 69 G12 24 52N 87 47 E
Barhi, India 69 G11 24 15N 85 25 E
Bari, India 68 F7 26 39N 77 39 E
Bari, Italy 31 A9 41 8N 16 51 E
Bari Doab, Pakistan 68 D5 30 20N 73 0 E
Bari Sadri, India 68 G6 24 28N 74 30 E
Bari Sardo, Italy 30 C2 39 50N 9 38 E
Barīdī, Ra's, Si. Arabia 70 E3 24 17N 37 31 E
Barīm, Yemen 76 E8 12 39N 43 25 E
Barinas, Venezuela 124 B4 8 36N 70 15W
Baring, C., Canada 100 B8 70 0N 117 30W
Baringo, Kenya 86 B4 0 47N 36 16 E
Baringo, L., Kenya 86 B4 0 47N 36 16 E
Bârîs, Egypt 80 C3 24 42N 30 31 E
Barisal, Bangla. 67 H17 22 45N 90 20 E
Barisan, Bukit, Indonesia 62 E2 3 30 S 102 15 E
Barito →, Indonesia 62 E4 4 0 S 114 50 E
Barjac, France 21 D8 44 20N 4 22 E
Barjols, France 21 E10 43 34N 6 2 E
Bark L., Canada 110 A7 45 27N 77 51W
Barka = Baraka →, Sudan 80 D4 18 13N 37 35 E
Barkakana, India 69 H11 23 37N 85 29 E
Barkam, China 58 B4 31 51N 102 28 E
Barker, U.S.A. 110 C6 43 20N 78 33W
Barkley, L., U.S.A. 109 G2 37 1N 88 14W
Barkley Sound, Canada 104 D3 48 50N 125 10W
Barkly East, S. Africa 88 E4 30 58 S 27 33 E
Barkly Roadhouse, Australia 94 B2 19 52 S 135 50 E
Barkly Tableland, Australia 94 B2 17 50 S 136 40 E
Barkly West, S. Africa 88 D3 28 5 S 24 31 E
Barkol, Wadi →, Sudan 80 D3 17 40N 32 0 E
Barla Dağı, Turkey 39 C12 38 5N 30 40 E
Bârlad, Romania 43 D12 46 15N 27 38 E
Bârlad →, Romania 43 E12 45 38N 27 32 E
Barlee, L., Australia 93 E2 29 15 S 119 30 E
Barlee, Mt., Australia 93 D4 24 38 S 128 13 E
Barletta, Italy 31 A9 41 19N 16 17 E
Barlinek, Poland 45 F2 53 0N 15 15 E
Barlovento, Canary Is. 37 F2 28 48N 17 48W
Barlow L., Canada 105 A8 62 0N 103 0W
Barmedman, Australia 95 E4 34 9 S 147 21 E
Barmer, India 68 G4 25 45N 71 20 E
Barmera, Australia 95 E3 34 15 S 140 28 E
Barmouth, U.K. 12 E3 52 44N 4 4W
Barmstedt, Germany 24 B5 53 47N 9 46 E
Barna →, India 69 G10 25 21N 83 3 E
Barnagar, India 68 H6 23 7N 75 19 E
Barnala, India 68 D6 30 23N 75 33 E
Barnard Castle, U.K. 12 C6 54 33N 1 55W
Barnaul, Russia 50 D9 53 20N 83 40 E
Barnesville, U.S.A. 109 J3 33 3N 84 9W
Barnet, U.K. 13 F7 51 38N 0 9W
Barneveld, Neths. 17 B5 52 7N 5 36 E
Barneveld, U.S.A. 111 C9 43 16N 75 14W
Barneville-Cartevert, France 18 C5 49 23N 1 46W
Barnhart, U.S.A. 113 K4 31 8N 101 10W
Barnsley, U.K. 12 D6 53 34N 1 27W
Barnstaple, U.K. 13 F3 51 5N 4 4W
Barnstaple Bay = Bideford Bay, U.K. 13 F3 51 5N 4 20W
Barnsville, U.S.A. 112 B6 46 43N 96 28W
Barnwell, U.S.A. 109 J5 33 15N 81 23W
Baro, Nigeria 83 D6 8 35N 6 18 E
Baro →, Ethiopia 81 F3 8 26N 33 13 E
Baroda = Vadodara, India 68 H5 22 20N 73 10 E
Baroda, India 68 G7 25 29N 76 35 E
Baroe, S. Africa 88 E3 33 13 S 24 33 E
Baron Ra., Australia 92 D4 23 30 S 127 45 E
Barong, China 58 B2 31 3N 99 20 E
Barotseland, Zambia 85 H4 15 0 S 24 0 E
Barouéli, Mali 82 C3 13 4N 6 50W
Barpeta, India 67 F17 26 20N 91 10 E
Barques, Pt. Aux, U.S.A. 110 B2 44 4N 82 58W
Barquísimeto, Venezuela 124 A5 10 4N 69 19W
Barr, Ras el, Egypt 80 H7 31 32N 31 50 E
Barr Smith Range, Australia 93 E3 27 4 S 120 20 E
Barra, Brazil 125 F10 11 5 S 43 10W
Barra, U.K. 14 E1 57 0N 7 29W
Barra, Sd. of, U.K. 14 D1 57 4N 7 25W
Barra de Navidad, Mexico 118 D4 19 12N 104 41W
Barra do Corda, Brazil 125 E9 5 30 S 45 10W
Barra do Piraí, Brazil 127 A7 22 30 S 43 50W
Barra Falsa, Pta. da, Mozam. 89 C6 22 58 S 35 37 E
Barra Hd., U.K. 14 E1 56 47N 7 40W
Barra Mansa, Brazil 127 A7 22 35 S 44 12W
Barraba, Australia 95 E5 30 21 S 150 35 E
Barrackpur = Barakpur, India 69 H13 22 44N 88 30 E
Barradale Roadhouse, Australia 92 D1 22 42 S 114 58 E
Barrafranca, Italy 31 E7 37 22N 14 12 E
Barraigh = Barra, U.K. 14 E1 57 0N 7 29W
Barranca, Lima, Peru 124 F3 10 45 S 77 50W
Barranca, Loreto, Peru 124 D3 4 50 S 76 50W
Barrancabermeja, Colombia 124 B4 7 0N 73 50W
Barrancas, Venezuela 124 B6 8 55N 62 5W
Barrancos, Portugal 35 G4 38 10N 6 58W
Barranqueras, Argentina 126 B4 27 30 S 59 0W
Barranquilla, Colombia 124 A4 11 0N 74 50W
Barraute, Canada 102 C4 48 26N 77 38W
Barre, Mass., U.S.A. 111 D12 42 25N 72 6W
Barre, Vt., U.S.A. 111 B12 44 12N 72 30W
Barreal, Argentina 126 C2 31 33 S 69 28W
Barreiras, Brazil 125 F10 12 8 S 45 0W
Barreirinhas, Brazil 125 D10 2 30 S 42 50W
Barreiro, Portugal 35 G1 38 40N 9 6W
Barrême, France 21 E10 43 57N 6 23 E
Barren, Nosy, Madag. 89 B7 18 25 S 43 40 E
Barretos, Brazil 125 H9 20 30 S 48 35W
Barrhead, Canada 104 C6 54 10N 114 24W
Barrie, Canada 102 D4 44 24N 79 40W
Barrier Ra., Australia 95 E3 31 0 S 141 30 E
Barrière, Canada 104 C4 51 12N 120 7W
Barrington, U.S.A. 111 E13 41 44N 71 18W
Barrington L., Canada 105 B8 56 55N 100 15W
Barrington Tops, Australia 95 E5 32 6 S 151 28 E
Barringun, Australia 95 D4 29 1 S 145 41 E
Barro do Garças, Brazil 125 G8 15 54 S 52 16W
Barron, U.S.A. 112 C9 45 24N 91 51W
Barrow, U.S.A. 100 A4 71 18N 156 47W
Barrow →, Ireland 15 D5 52 25N 6 58W
Barrow Creek, Australia 94 C1 21 30 S 133 55 E
Barrow I., Australia 92 D2 20 45 S 115 20 E
Barrow-in-Furness, U.K. 12 C4 54 7N 3 14W
Barrow Pt., Australia 94 A3 14 20 S 144 40 E
Barrow Pt., U.S.A. 98 B4 71 24N 156 29W
Barrow Ra., Australia 93 E4 26 0 S 127 40 E
Barrow Str., Canada 4 B3 74 20N 95 0W
Barruecopardo, Spain 34 D4 41 4N 6 40W
Barruelo de Santullán, Spain 34 C6 42 54N 4 17W
Barry, U.K. 13 F4 51 24N 3 16W
Barry's Bay, Canada 102 C4 45 29N 77 41W
Barsalogho, Burkina Faso 83 C4 13 25N 1 3W
Barsat, Pakistan 69 A5 36 10N 72 45 E
Barsham, Syria 70 C4 35 21N 40 33 E
Barsi, India 66 K9 18 10N 75 50 E
Barsinghausen, Germany 24 C5 52 18N 9 28 E
Barsoi, India 67 G15 25 48N 87 57 E
Barstow, U.S.A. 117 L9 34 54N 117 1W
Barth, Germany 24 A8 54 22N 12 42 E
Barthélemy, Col, Vietnam 64 C5 19 26N 104 6 E
Bartica, Guyana 124 B7 6 25N 58 40W
Bartin, Turkey 72 B5 41 38N 32 21 E
Bartlesville, U.S.A. 113 G7 36 45N 95 59W
Bartlett, U.S.A. 116 J8 36 29N 118 2W
Bartlett, L., Canada 104 A5 63 5N 118 20W
Bartolomeu Dias, Mozam. 87 G4 21 10 S 35 8 E
Barton, U.S.A. 111 B12 44 45N 72 11W
Barton upon Humber, U.K. 12 D7 53 41N 0 25W
Bartoszyce, Poland 44 D7 54 15N 20 55 E
Bartow, U.S.A. 109 M5 27 54N 81 50W
Barú, Volcan, Panama 120 E3 8 55N 82 35W
Barumba, Dem. Rep. of the Congo 86 B1 1 3N 23 37 E
Baruth, Germany 24 C9 52 4N 13 30 E
Baruunsuu, Mongolia 56 C3 43 43N 105 35 E
Barvinkove, Ukraine 47 H9 48 57N 37 0 E
Barwani, India 68 H6 22 2N 74 57 E
Barwice, Poland 44 E3 53 44N 16 21 E
Barycz →, Poland 45 G3 51 42N 16 15 E
Barysaw, Belarus 46 E5 54 17N 28 28 E
Barysh, Russia 48 D8 53 39N 47 8 E
Barzān, Iraq 70 B5 36 55N 44 3 E
Bârzava, Romania 42 D6 46 7N 21 59 E
Bas-Rhin ☐, France 19 D14 48 40N 7 30 E
Bašaid, Serbia, Yug. 42 E5 45 38N 20 25 E
Bāsa'idū, Iran 71 E7 26 35N 55 20 E
Basal, Pakistan 68 C5 33 33N 72 13 E
Basankusa, Dem. Rep. of the Congo 84 D3 1 5N 19 50 E
Basarabeasca, Moldova 43 D13 46 21N 28 58 E
Basarabi, Romania 43 F13 44 10N 28 26 E
Basauri, Spain 32 B2 43 13N 2 53W
Basawa, Afghan. 68 B4 34 15N 70 50 E
Bascuñán, C., Chile 126 B1 28 52 S 71 35W
Basel, Switz. 25 H3 47 35N 7 35 E
Basel-Landschaft ☐, Switz. 25 H3 47 26N 7 45 E
Basento →, Italy 31 B9 40 20N 16 49 E
Bashākerd, Kūhhā-ye, Iran 71 E8 26 42N 58 35 E
Bashaw, Canada 104 C6 52 35N 112 58W
Bāshī, Iran 71 D6 28 41N 51 4 E
Bashkir Republic = Bashkortostan ☐, Russia 50 D6 54 0N 57 0 E
Bashkortostan ☐, Russia 50 D6 54 0N 57 0 E
Basibasy, Madag. 89 C7 22 10 S 43 40 E
Basilan I., Phil. 61 H5 6 35N 122 0 E
Basilan Str., Phil. 61 H5 6 50N 122 0 E
Basildon, U.K. 13 F8 51 34N 0 28 E
Basile, Eq. Guin. 83 E6 3 42N 8 48 E
Basilicata ☐, Italy 31 B9 40 30N 16 30 E
Basim = Washim, India 66 J10 20 3N 77 0 E
Basin, U.S.A. 114 D9 44 23N 108 2W
Basingstoke, U.K. 13 F6 51 15N 1 5W
Baška, Croatia 29 D11 44 58N 14 45 E
Başkale, Turkey 73 C10 38 2N 43 59 E
Baskatong, Rés., Canada 102 C4 46 46N 75 50W
Basle = Basel, Switz. 25 H3 47 35N 7 35 E
Başmakçı, Turkey 39 D12 37 54N 30 1 E
Basoda, India 68 H7 23 52N 77 54 E
Basoka, Dem. Rep. of the Congo 86 B1 1 16N 23 40 E
Basque, Pays, France 20 E2 43 15N 1 20W
Basque Provinces = País Vasco ☐, Spain 32 C2 42 50N 2 45W
Basra = Al Başrah, Iraq 70 D5 30 30N 47 50 E
Bass Str., Australia 94 F4 39 15 S 146 30 E
Bassano, Canada 104 C6 50 48N 112 20W
Bassano del Grappa, Italy 29 C8 45 46N 11 44 E
Bassar, Togo 83 D5 9 19N 0 57 E
Bassas da India, Ind. Oc. 85 J7 22 0 S 39 0 E
Basse-Normandie ☐, France 18 D6 48 45N 0 30W
Basse Santa-Su, Gambia 82 C2 13 13N 14 15W
Basse-Terre, Guadeloupe 121 C7 16 0N 61 44W
Bassein, Burma 67 L19 16 45N 94 30 E
Basseterre, St. Kitts & Nevis 121 C7 17 17N 62 43W
Bassett, U.S.A. 112 D5 42 35N 99 32W
Bassi, India 68 D7 30 44N 76 21 E
Bassigny, France 19 E12 48 0N 5 30 E
Bassikounou, Mauritania 82 B3 15 55N 6 1W
Bassila, Benin 83 D5 9 1N 1 46 E
Bassum, Germany 24 C4 52 50N 8 40 E
Båstad, Sweden 11 H6 56 25N 12 51 E
Bastak, Iran 71 E7 27 15N 54 25 E
Baştām, Iran 71 B7 36 29N 55 4 E
Bastar, India 67 K12 19 15N 81 40 E
Bastelica, France 21 F13 42 1N 9 3 E
Basti, India 69 F10 26 52N 82 55 E
Bastia, France 21 F13 42 40N 9 30 E
Bastogne, Belgium 17 D5 50 1N 5 43 E
Bastrop, La., U.S.A. 113 J9 32 47N 91 55W
Bastrop, Tex., U.S.A. 113 K6 30 7N 97 19W
Bat Yam, Israel 75 C3 32 2N 34 44 E
Bata, Eq. Guin. 84 D1 1 57N 9 50 E
Bata, Romania 42 D7 46 1N 22 4 E
Bataan ☐, Phil. 61 D4 14 40N 120 25 E
Batabanó, Cuba 120 B3 22 40N 82 20W
Batabanó, G. de, Cuba 120 B3 22 30N 82 30W
Batac, Phil. 61 B4 18 3N 120 34 E
Batagai, Russia 51 C14 67 38N 134 38 E
Batajnica, Serbia, Yug. 40 B4 44 54N 20 17 E
Batak, Bulgaria 41 E8 41 57N 24 12 E
Batala, India 68 D6 31 48N 75 12 E
Batalha, Portugal 34 F2 39 40N 8 50W
Batama, Dem. Rep. of the Congo 86 B2 0 58N 26 33 E
Batamay, Russia 51 C13 63 30N 129 15 E
Batang, China 58 B2 30 1N 99 0 E
Batang, Indonesia 63 G13 6 55 S 109 45 E
Batangas, Phil. 61 E4 13 35N 121 10 E
Batanta, Indonesia 63 E8 0 55 S 130 40 E
Batatais, Brazil 127 A6 20 54 S 47 37W
Batavia, U.S.A. 110 D6 43 0N 78 11W
Bataysk, Russia 47 J10 47 3N 39 45 E
Batchelor, Australia 92 B5 13 4 S 131 1 E
Batdambang, Cambodia 64 F4 13 7N 103 12 E
Bateman's B., Australia 95 F5 35 40 S 150 12 E
Batemans Bay, Australia 95 F5 35 44 S 150 11 E
Bates Ra., Australia 93 E3 27 27 S 121 5 E
Batesburg-Leesville, U.S.A. 109 J5 33 54N 81 33W
Batesville, Ark., U.S.A. 113 H9 35 46N 91 39W
Batesville, Miss., U.S.A. 113 H10 34 18N 89 57W
Batesville, Tex., U.S.A. 113 L5 28 58N 99 37W
Bath, Canada 111 B8 44 11N 76 47W
Bath, U.K. 13 F5 51 23N 2 22W
Bath, Maine, U.S.A. 109 D11 43 55N 69 49W
Bath, N.Y., U.S.A. 110 D7 42 20N 77 19W
Bath & North East Somerset ☐, U.K. 13 F5 51 21N 2 27W
Batheay, Cambodia 65 G5 11 59N 104 57 E
Bathurst = Banjul, Gambia 82 C1 13 28N 16 40W
Bathurst, Australia 95 E4 33 25 S 149 31 E
Bathurst, Canada 103 C6 47 37N 65 43W
Bathurst, S. Africa 88 E4 33 30 S 26 50 E
Bathurst, C., Canada 100 A7 70 34N 128 0W
Bathurst B., Australia 94 A3 14 16 S 144 25 E
Bathurst Harb., Australia 94 G4 43 15 S 146 10 E
Bathurst I., Australia 92 B5 11 30 S 130 10 E
Bathurst I., Canada 4 B2 76 0N 100 30W
Bathurst Inlet, Canada 100 B9 66 50N 108 1W
Bati, Ethiopia 81 E5 11 10N 40 0 E
Batie, Burkina Faso 82 D4 9 53N 2 53W
Batlow, Australia 95 F4 35 31 S 148 9 E
Batman, Turkey 70 B4 37 55N 41 5 E
Baṭn al Ghūl, Jordan 75 F4 29 36N 35 56 E
Batna, Algeria 78 A7 35 34N 6 15 E
Batobato = San Isidro, Phil. 61 H7 6 50N 126 5 E
Batočina, Serbia, Yug. 40 B5 44 7N 21 5 E
Batoka, Zambia 87 F2 16 45 S 27 15 E
Baton Rouge, U.S.A. 113 K9 30 27N 91 11W
Batong, Ko, Thailand 65 J2 6 32N 99 12 E
Bátonyterenye, Hungary 42 C4 47 59N 19 50 E

Batopilas, Mexico 118 B3 27 0N 107 45W
Batouri, Cameroon 84 D2 4 30N 14 25 E
Båtsfjord, Norway 8 A23 70 38N 29 39 E
Battambang = Batdambang, Cambodia 64 F4 13 7N 103 12 E
Batticaloa, Sri Lanka 66 R12 7 43N 81 45 E
Battipáglia, Italy 31 B7 40 37N 14 58 E
Battle, U.K. 13 G8 50 55N 0 30 E
Battle →, Canada 105 C7 52 43N 108 15W
Battle Creek, U.S.A. 108 D3 42 19N 85 11W
Battle Ground, U.S.A. 116 E4 45 47N 122 32W
Battle Harbour, Canada 103 B8 52 16N 55 35W
Battle Lake, U.S.A. 112 B7 46 17N 95 43W
Battle Mountain, U.S.A. 114 F5 40 38N 116 56W
Battlefields, Zimbabwe 87 F2 18 37 S 29 47 E
Battleford, Canada 105 C7 52 45N 108 15W
Battonya, Hungary 42 D6 46 16N 21 3 E
Batu, Ethiopia 81 F4 6 55N 39 45 E
Batu, Kepulauan, Indonesia 62 E1 0 30 S 98 25 E
Batu Caves, Malaysia 65 L3 3 15N 101 40 E
Batu Gajah, Malaysia 65 K3 4 28N 101 3 E
Batu Is. = Batu, Kepulauan, Indonesia 62 E1 0 30 S 98 25 E
Batu Pahat, Malaysia 65 M4 1 50N 102 56 E
Batuata, Indonesia 63 F6 6 12 S 122 42 E
Batumi, Georgia 49 K5 41 39N 41 44 E
Baturaja, Indonesia 62 E2 4 11 S 104 15 E
Baturité, Brazil 125 D11 4 28 S 38 45W
Bau, Malaysia 62 D4 1 25N 110 9 E
Baubau, Indonesia 63 F6 5 25 S 122 38 E
Bauchi, Nigeria 83 C6 10 22N 9 48 E
Bauchi □, Nigeria 83 C7 10 30N 10 0 E
Baud, France 18 E3 47 52N 3 1W
Baudette, U.S.A. 112 A7 48 43N 94 36W
Bauer, C., Australia 95 E1 32 44 S 134 4 E
Bauhinia, Australia 94 C4 24 35 S 149 18 E
Baukau, Indonesia 63 F7 8 27 S 126 27 E
Bauld, C., Canada 101 C14 51 38N 55 26W
Baume-les-Dames, France 19 E13 47 22N 6 22 E
Baunatal, Germany 24 D5 51 14N 9 24 E
Baunei, Italy 30 B2 40 2N 9 40 E
Baure, Nigeria 83 C6 12 52N 8 50 E
Bauru, Brazil 127 A6 22 10 S 49 0W
Bausi, India 69 G12 24 48N 87 1 E
Bauska, Latvia 9 H21 56 24N 24 15 E
Bautino, Kazakstan 49 H10 44 35N 50 14 E
Bautzen, Germany 24 D10 51 10N 14 26 E
Bauya, S. Leone 82 D2 8 12N 12 38W
Bavānāt, Iran 71 D7 30 28N 53 27 E
Bavanište, Serbia, Yug. 42 F5 44 49N 20 55 E
Bavaria = Bayern □, Germany 25 G7 48 50N 12 0 E
Båven, Sweden 10 E10 59 0N 16 56 E
Bavispe →, Mexico 118 B3 29 30N 109 11W
Bawdwin, Burma 67 H20 23 5N 97 20 E
Bawean, Indonesia 62 F4 5 46 S 112 35 E
Bawku, Ghana 83 C4 11 3N 0 19W
Bawlake, Burma 67 K20 19 11N 97 21 E
Bawolung, China 58 C3 28 50N 101 16 E
Baxley, U.S.A. 109 K4 31 47N 82 21W
Baxoi, China 58 B1 30 1N 96 50 E
Baxter, U.S.A. 112 B7 46 21N 94 17W
Baxter Springs, U.S.A. 113 G7 37 2N 94 44W
Bay, L. de, Phil. 61 D4 14 20N 121 11 E
Bay City, Mich., U.S.A. 108 D4 43 36N 83 54W
Bay City, Tex., U.S.A. 113 L7 28 59N 95 58W
Bay Minette, U.S.A. 109 K2 30 53N 87 46W
Bay Roberts, Canada 103 C9 47 36N 53 16W
Bay St. Louis, U.S.A. 113 K10 30 19N 89 20W
Bay Springs, U.S.A. 113 K10 31 59N 89 17W
Bay View, N.Z. 91 H6 39 25 S 176 50 E
Baya, Dem. Rep. of the Congo 87 E2 11 53 S 27 25 E
Bayamo, Cuba 120 B4 20 20N 76 40W
Bayamón, Puerto Rico 121 C6 18 24N 66 10W
Bayan Har Shan, China 60 C4 34 0N 98 0 E
Bayan Hot = Alxa Zuoqi, China 56 E3 38 50N 105 40 E
Bayan Obo, China 56 D5 41 52N 109 59 E
Bayan-Ovoo = Erdenetsogt, Mongolia 56 C4 42 55N 106 5 E
Bayana, India 68 F7 26 55N 77 18 E
Bayanaŭyl, Kazakstan 50 D8 50 45N 75 45 E
Bayandalay, Mongolia 56 C2 43 30N 103 29 E
Bayanhongor, Mongolia 60 B5 46 8N 102 43 E
Bayard, N. Mex., U.S.A. 115 K9 32 46N 108 8W
Bayard, Nebr., U.S.A. 112 E3 41 45N 103 20W
Bayawan, Phil. 61 G5 9 46N 122 45 E
Baybay, Phil. 61 F6 10 40N 124 55 E
Bayburt, Turkey 73 B9 40 15N 40 20 E
Bayelsa □, Nigeria 83 E6 4 30N 6 0 E
Bayerische Alpen, Germany 25 H7 47 35N 11 30 E
Bayerischer Wald, Germany 25 G8 48 56N 12 50 E
Bayern □, Germany 25 G7 48 50N 12 0 E
Bayeux, France 18 C6 49 17N 0 42W
Bayfield, Canada 110 C3 43 34N 81 42W
Bayfield, U.S.A. 112 B9 46 49N 90 49W
Bayındır, Turkey 39 C9 38 13N 27 39 E
Baykal, Oz., Russia 51 D11 53 0N 108 0 E
Baykan, Turkey 70 B4 38 7N 41 44 E
Baykonur = Bayqongyr, Kazakstan 50 E7 47 48N 65 50 E
Baynes Mts., Namibia 88 B1 17 15 S 13 0 E
Bayombong, Phil. 61 C4 16 30N 121 10 E
Bayon, France 19 D13 48 30N 6 20 E
Bayona = Baiona, Spain 34 C2 42 6N 8 52W
Bayonne, France 20 E2 43 30N 1 28W
Bayonne, U.S.A. 111 F10 40 40N 74 7W
Bayovar, Peru 124 E2 5 50 S 81 0W
Bayqongyr, Kazakstan 50 E7 47 48N 65 50 E
Bayram-Ali = Bayramaly, Turkmenistan 50 F7 37 37N 62 10 E
Bayramaly, Turkmenistan 50 F7 37 37N 62 10 E
Bayramiç, Turkey 39 B8 39 48N 26 36 E
Bayreuth, Germany 25 F7 49 56N 11 35 E
Bayrischzell, Germany 25 H8 47 41N 12 0 E
Bayrūt, Lebanon 75 B4 33 53N 35 31 E
Bays, L. of, Canada 110 A5 45 15N 79 4W
Baysville, Canada 110 A5 45 9N 79 7W
Bayt Lahm, West Bank 75 D4 31 43N 35 12 E
Baytown, U.S.A. 113 L7 29 43N 94 59W
Bayzo, Niger 83 C5 13 52N 4 35 E
Baza, Spain 35 H8 37 30N 2 47W
Bazar Dyuzi, Russia 49 K8 41 12N 47 50 E
Bazardüzü = Bazar Dyuzi, Russia 49 K8 41 12N 47 50 E
Bazarny Karabulak, Russia 48 D8 52 20N 46 29 E
Bazarnyy Syzgan, Russia 48 D8 53 45N 46 40 E
Bazaruto, I. do, Mozam. 89 C6 21 40 S 35 28 E
Bazas, France 20 D3 44 27N 0 13W
Bazhong, China 58 B6 31 52N 106 46 E
Bazhou, China 56 E9 39 8N 116 22 E
Bazmān, Kūh-e, Iran 71 D9 28 4N 60 1 E
Beach, U.S.A. 112 B3 46 58N 104 0W
Beach City, U.S.A. 110 F3 40 39N 81 35W
Beachport, Australia 95 F3 37 29 S 140 0 E
Beachy Hd., U.K. 13 G8 50 44N 0 15 E
Beacon, Australia 93 F2 30 26 S 117 52 E
Beacon, U.S.A. 111 E11 41 30N 73 58W
Beaconsfield, Australia 94 G4 41 11 S 146 48 E
Beagle, Canal, S. Amer. 122 J4 55 0 S 68 30W
Beagle Bay, Australia 92 C3 16 58 S 122 40 E
Bealanana, Madag. 89 A8 14 33 S 48 44 E
Beals Cr. →, U.S.A. 113 J4 32 10N 100 51W
Beamsville, Canada 110 C5 43 12N 79 28W
Bear →, Calif., U.S.A. 116 G5 38 56N 121 36W
Bear →, Utah, U.S.A. 106 B4 41 30N 112 8W
Béar, C., France 20 F7 42 31N 3 8 E
Bear I., Ireland 15 E2 51 38N 9 50W
Bear L., Canada 105 B9 55 8N 96 0W
Bear L., U.S.A. 114 F8 41 59N 111 21W
Beardmore, Canada 102 C2 49 36N 87 57W
Beardmore Glacier, Antarctica 5 E11 84 30 S 170 0 E
Beardstown, U.S.A. 112 F9 40 1N 90 26W
Bearma →, India 69 G8 24 20N 79 51 E
Béarn, France 20 E3 43 20N 0 30W
Bearpaw Mts., U.S.A. 114 B9 48 12N 109 30W
Bearskin Lake, Canada 102 B1 53 58N 91 2W
Beas →, India 68 D6 31 10N 74 59 E
Beas de Segura, Spain 35 G8 38 15N 2 53W
Beasain, Spain 32 B2 43 3N 2 11W
Beata, C., Dom. Rep. 121 C5 17 40N 71 30W
Beata, I., Dom. Rep. 121 C5 17 34N 71 31W
Beatrice, U.S.A. 112 E6 40 16N 96 45W
Beatrice, Zimbabwe 87 F3 18 15 S 30 55 E
Beatrice, C., Australia 94 A2 14 20 S 136 55 E
Beatton →, Canada 104 B4 56 15N 120 45W
Beatton River, Canada 104 B4 57 26N 121 20W
Beatty, U.S.A. 116 J10 36 54N 116 46W
Beaucaire, France 21 E8 43 48N 4 39 E
Beauce, Plaine de la, France 19 D8 48 10N 1 45 E
Beauceville, Canada 103 C5 46 13N 70 46W
Beaudesert, Australia 95 D5 27 59 S 153 0 E
Beaufort, France 21 C10 45 44N 6 34 E
Beaufort, Malaysia 62 C5 5 30N 115 40 E
Beaufort, N.C., U.S.A. 109 H7 34 43N 76 40W
Beaufort, S.C., U.S.A. 109 J5 32 26N 80 40W
Beaufort Sea, Arctic 4 B1 72 0N 140 0W
Beaufort West, S. Africa 88 E3 32 18 S 22 36 E
Beaugency, France 19 E8 47 47N 1 38 E
Beauharnois, Canada 111 A11 45 20N 73 52W
Beaujeu, France 19 F11 46 10N 4 35 E
Beaujolais, France 19 F11 46 0N 4 22 E
Beaulieu →, Canada 104 A6 62 3N 113 11W
Beaulieu-sur-Dordogne, France 20 D5 44 58N 1 50 E
Beaulieu-sur-Mer, France 21 E11 43 42N 7 20 E
Beauly, U.K. 14 D4 57 30N 4 28W
Beauly →, U.K. 14 D4 57 29N 4 27W
Beaumaris, U.K. 12 D3 53 16N 4 6W
Beaumont, Belgium 17 D4 50 15N 4 14 E
Beaumont, France 20 D4 44 45N 0 46 E
Beaumont, U.S.A. 113 K7 30 5N 94 6W
Beaumont-de-Lomagne, France 20 E5 43 53N 1 0 E
Beaumont-le-Roger, France 18 C7 49 4N 0 47 E
Beaumont-sur-Sarthe, France 18 D7 48 13N 0 8 E
Beaune, France 19 E11 47 2N 4 50 E
Beaune-la-Rolande, France 19 D9 48 4N 2 25 E
Beaupré, Canada 103 C5 47 3N 70 54W
Beaupréau, France 18 E6 47 12N 1 0W
Beauraing, Belgium 17 D4 50 7N 4 57 E
Beaurepaire, France 21 C9 45 22N 5 1 E
Beauséjour, Canada 105 C9 50 5N 96 35W
Beauvais, France 19 C9 49 25N 2 8 E
Beauval, Canada 105 B7 55 9N 107 37W
Beauvoir-sur-Mer, France 18 F4 46 55N 2 2W
Beauvoir-sur-Niort, France 20 B3 46 12N 0 30W
Beaver, Okla., U.S.A. 113 G4 36 49N 100 31W
Beaver, Pa., U.S.A. 110 F4 40 42N 80 19W
Beaver, Utah, U.S.A. 115 G7 38 17N 112 38W
Beaver →, B.C., Canada 104 B4 59 52N 124 20W
Beaver →, Ont., Canada 102 A2 55 55N 87 48W
Beaver →, Sask., Canada 105 B7 55 26N 107 45W
Beaver →, U.S.A. 113 G5 36 35N 99 30W
Beaver City, U.S.A. 112 E5 40 8N 99 50W
Beaver Creek, Canada 100 B5 63 0N 141 0W
Beaver Dam, U.S.A. 112 D10 43 28N 88 50W
Beaver Falls, U.S.A. 110 F4 40 46N 80 20W
Beaver Hill L., Canada 105 C10 54 5N 94 50W
Beaver I., U.S.A. 108 C3 45 40N 85 33W
Beaverhill L., Canada 104 C6 53 27N 112 32W
Beaverlodge, Canada 104 B5 55 11N 119 29W
Beaverstone →, Canada 102 B2 54 59N 89 25W
Beaverton, Canada 110 B5 44 26N 79 9W
Beaverton, U.S.A. 116 E4 45 29N 122 48W
Beawar, India 68 F6 26 3N 74 18 E
Bebedouro, Brazil 127 A6 21 0 S 48 25W
Beboa, Madag. 89 B7 17 22 S 44 33 E
Bebra, Germany 24 E5 50 58N 9 48 E
Beccles, U.K. 13 E9 52 27N 1 35 E
Bečej, Serbia, Yug. 42 E5 45 36N 20 3 E
Beceni, Romania 43 E11 45 23N 26 48 E
Becerreá, Spain 34 C3 42 51N 7 10W
Béchar, Algeria 78 B5 31 38N 2 18W
Bechyně, Czech Rep. 26 B7 49 17N 14 29 E
Beckley, U.S.A. 108 G5 37 47N 81 11W
Beckum, Germany 24 D4 51 45N 8 3 E
Beclean, Romania 43 C9 47 11N 24 11 E
Bečov nad Teplou, Czech Rep. 26 A5 50 5N 12 49 E
Bečva →, Czech Rep. 27 B10 49 31N 17 20 E
Bédar, Spain 33 H3 37 11N 1 59W
Bédarieux, France 20 E7 43 37N 3 10 E
Beddouza, Ras, Morocco 78 B4 32 33N 9 9W
Bedele, Ethiopia 81 F4 8 31N 36 23 E
Bederkesa, Germany 24 B4 53 37N 8 50 E
Bedeso, Ethiopia 81 F5 9 58N 40 52 E
Bedford, Canada 111 A12 45 7N 72 59W
Bedford, S. Africa 88 E4 32 40 S 26 10 E
Bedford, U.K. 13 E7 52 8N 0 28W
Bedford, Ind., U.S.A. 108 F2 38 52N 86 29W
Bedford, Iowa, U.S.A. 112 E7 40 40N 94 44W
Bedford, Ohio, U.S.A. 110 E3 41 23N 81 32W
Bedford, Pa., U.S.A. 110 F6 40 1N 78 30W
Bedford, Va., U.S.A. 108 G6 37 20N 79 31W
Bedford, C., Australia 94 B4 15 14 S 145 21 E
Bedfordshire □, U.K. 13 E7 52 4N 0 28W
Będków, Poland 45 G6 51 36N 19 44 E
Bednja →, Croatia 29 B13 46 20N 16 52 E
Bednodemyanovsk, Russia 48 D6 53 55N 43 15 E
Bedónia, Italy 28 D6 44 30N 9 38 E
Bedourie, Australia 94 C2 24 30 S 139 30 E
Bedum, Neths. 17 A6 53 18N 6 36 E
Będzin, Poland 45 H6 50 19N 19 7 E
Beebe Plain, Canada 111 A12 45 1N 72 9W
Beech Creek, U.S.A. 110 E7 41 5N 77 36W
Beelitz, Germany 24 C8 52 14N 12 58 E
Beenleigh, Australia 95 D5 27 43 S 153 10 E
Be'er Menuha, Israel 70 D2 30 19N 35 8 E
Be'er Sheva, Israel 75 D3 31 15N 34 48 E
Beersheba = Be'er Sheva, Israel 75 D3 31 15N 34 48 E
Beeskow, Germany 24 C10 52 10N 14 15 E
Beestekraal, S. Africa 89 D4 25 23 S 27 38 E
Beeston, U.K. 12 E6 52 56N 1 14W
Beetzendorf, Germany 24 C7 52 42N 11 6 E
Beeville, U.S.A. 113 L6 28 24N 97 45W
Befale, Dem. Rep. of the Congo 84 D4 0 25N 20 45 E
Befandriana, Mahajanga, Madag. 89 B8 15 16 S 48 32 E
Befandriana, Toliara, Madag. 89 C7 21 55 S 44 0 E
Befasy, Madag. 89 C7 20 33 S 44 23 E
Befotaka, Antsiranana, Madag. 89 A8 13 15 S 48 16 E
Befotaka, Fianarantsoa, Madag. 89 C8 23 49 S 47 0 E
Bega, Australia 95 F4 36 41 S 149 51 E
Bega, Canalul, Romania 42 E5 45 37N 20 46 E
Bégard, France 18 D3 48 38N 3 18W
Beğendik, Turkey 41 F10 40 55N 26 34 E
Begoro, Ghana 83 D4 6 23N 0 23W
Begusarai, India 69 G12 25 24N 86 9 E
Behābād, Iran 71 C8 32 24N 59 47 E
Behala, India 69 H13 22 30N 88 20 E
Behara, Madag. 89 C8 24 55 S 46 20 E
Behbehān, Iran 71 D6 30 30N 50 15 E
Behm Canal, U.S.A. 104 B2 55 10N 131 0W
Behshahr, Iran 71 B7 36 45N 53 35 E
Bei Jiang →, China 59 F9 23 2N 112 58 E
Bei'an, China 60 B7 48 10N 126 20 E
Beibei, China 58 C6 29 47N 106 22 E
Beichuan, China 58 B5 31 55N 104 39 E
Beihai, China 58 G7 21 28N 109 6 E
Beijing, China 56 E9 39 55N 116 20 E
Beijing □, China 56 E9 39 55N 116 20 E
Beilen, Neths. 17 B6 52 52N 6 27 E
Beiliu, China 59 F8 22 41N 110 21 E
Beilngries, Germany 25 F7 49 2N 11 28 E
Beilpajah, Australia 95 E3 32 54 S 143 52 E
Beilul, Eritrea 81 E5 13 2N 42 20 E
Beinn na Faoghla = Benbecula, U.K. 14 D1 57 26N 7 21W
Beipan Jiang, China 58 E5 25 7N 106 1 E
Beipiao, China 57 D11 41 52N 120 32 E
Beira, Mozam. 87 F3 19 50 S 34 52 E
Beirut = Bayrūt, Lebanon 75 B4 33 53N 35 31 E
Beiseker, Canada 104 C6 51 23N 113 32W
Beitaolaizhao, China 57 B13 44 58N 125 58 E
Beitbridge, Zimbabwe 87 G3 22 12 S 30 0 E
Beiuş, Romania 42 D7 46 40N 22 21 E
Beizhen = Binzhou, China 57 F10 37 20N 118 2 E
Beizhen, China 57 D11 41 38N 121 54 E
Beizhengzhen, China 57 B12 44 31N 123 30 E
Beja, Portugal 35 G3 38 2N 7 53W
Béja, Tunisia 79 A7 36 43N 9 12 E
Beja □, Portugal 35 H3 37 55N 7 55W
Bejaia, Algeria 78 A7 36 42N 5 2 E
Béjar, Spain 34 E5 40 23N 5 46W
Bejestān, Iran 71 C8 34 30N 58 5 E
Bekçiler, Turkey 39 E11 36 56N 29 44 E
Békés, Hungary 42 D6 46 47N 21 9 E
Békés □, Hungary 42 D6 46 45N 21 0 E
Békéscsaba, Hungary 42 D6 46 40N 21 5 E
Bekilli, Turkey 39 C11 38 17N 29 27 E
Bekily, Madag. 89 C8 24 13 S 45 19 E
Bekisopa, Madag. 89 C8 21 40 S 45 54 E
Bekitro, Madag. 89 C8 24 33 S 45 18 E
Bekodoka, Madag. 89 B8 16 58 S 45 7 E
Bekoji, Ethiopia 81 F4 7 40N 39 17 E
Bekok, Malaysia 65 L4 2 20N 103 7 E
Bekopaka, Madag. 89 B7 19 9 S 44 48 E
Bekwai, Ghana 83 D4 6 30N 1 34W
Bela, India 69 G10 25 50N 82 0 E
Bela, Pakistan 68 F2 26 12N 66 20 E
Bela Crkva, Serbia, Yug. 42 F6 44 55N 21 27 E
Bela Palanka, Serbia, Yug. 40 C6 43 13N 22 17 E
Bela Vista, Brazil 126 A4 22 12 S 56 20W
Bela Vista, Mozam. 89 D5 26 10 S 32 44 E
Bélâbre, France 20 B5 46 34N 1 8 E
Belalcázar, Spain 35 G5 38 35N 5 10W
Belan →, India 69 G9 24 2N 81 45 E
Belanovica, Serbia, Yug. 40 B4 44 15N 20 23 E
Belarus ■, Europe 46 F4 53 30N 27 0 E
Belau = Palau ■, Pac. Oc. 52 J17 7 30N 134 30 E
Belavenona, Madag. 89 C8 24 50 S 47 4 E
Belawan, Indonesia 62 D1 3 33N 98 32 E
Belaya, Ethiopia 81 E4 11 25N 36 8 E
Belaya Glina, Russia 49 G5 46 5N 40 48 E
Belaya Kalitva, Russia 49 F5 48 13N 40 50 E
Belaya Tserkov = Bila Tserkva, Ukraine 47 H6 49 45N 30 10 E
Belceşti, Romania 43 C12 47 19N 27 7 E
Bełchatów, Poland 45 G6 51 21N 19 22 E
Belcher Is., Canada 102 A3 56 15N 78 45W
Belchite, Spain 32 D4 41 18N 0 43W
Belden, U.S.A. 116 E5 40 2N 121 17W
Belém, Brazil 125 D9 1 20 S 48 30W
Belén, Argentina 126 B2 27 40 S 67 5W
Belén, Paraguay 126 A4 23 30 S 57 6W
Belen, U.S.A. 115 J10 34 40N 106 46W
Belene, Bulgaria 41 C9 43 39N 25 10 E
Beleni, Turkey 72 D7 36 31N 36 10 E
Bélesta, France 20 F5 42 55N 1 56 E
Belet Uen, Somali Rep. 74 G4 4 30N 45 5 E
Belev, Russia 46 F9 53 50N 36 5 E
Belevi, Turkey 39 C9 38 0N 27 28 E
Belfair, U.S.A. 116 C4 47 27N 122 50W
Belfast, S. Africa 89 D5 25 42 S 30 2 E
Belfast, U.K. 15 B6 54 37N 5 56W
Belfast, Maine, U.S.A. 109 C11 44 26N 69 1W
Belfast, N.Y., U.S.A. 110 D6 42 21N 78 7W
Belfast L., U.K. 15 B6 54 40N 5 50W
Belfield, U.S.A. 112 B3 46 53N 103 12W
Belfort, France 19 E13 47 38N 6 50 E
Belfort, Territoire de □, France 19 E13 47 40N 6 55 E
Belfry, U.S.A. 114 D9 45 9N 109 1W
Belgaum, India 66 M9 15 55N 74 35 E
Belgioioso, Italy 28 C6 45 10N 9 19 E
Belgium ■, Europe 17 D4 50 30N 5 0 E
Belgodère, France 21 F13 42 35N 9 1 E
Belgorod, Russia 47 G9 50 35N 36 35 E
Belgorod-Dnestrovskiy = Bilhorod-Dnistrovskyy, Ukraine 47 J6 46 11N 30 23 E
Belgrade = Beograd, Serbia, Yug. 40 B4 44 50N 20 37 E
Belgrade, U.S.A. 114 D8 45 47N 111 11W
Belhaven, U.S.A. 109 H7 35 33N 76 37W
Beli Drim →, Europe 40 D4 42 6N 20 25 E
Beli Manastir, Croatia 42 E3 45 45N 18 36 E
Beli Timok →, Serbia, Yug. 40 C6 43 53N 22 14 E
Bélice →, Italy 30 E5 37 35N 12 55 E
Belinskiy, Russia 48 D6 53 0N 43 25 E
Belinyu, Indonesia 62 E3 1 35 S 105 50 E
Beliton Is. = Belitung, Indonesia 62 E3 3 10 S 107 50 E
Belitung, Indonesia 62 E3 3 10 S 107 50 E
Beliu, Romania 42 D6 46 30N 22 0 E
Belize ■, Cent. Amer. 119 D7 17 0N 88 30W
Belize City, Belize 119 D7 17 25N 88 0W
Beljakovci, Macedonia 40 D5 42 6N 21 59 E
Beljanica, Serbia, Yug. 40 B5 44 8N 21 43 E
Belkovskiy, Ostrov, Russia 51 B14 75 32N 135 44 E
Bell →, Canada 102 C4 49 48N 77 38W
Bell I., Canada 103 B8 50 46N 55 35W
Bell-Irving →, Canada 104 B3 56 12N 129 5W
Bell Peninsula, Canada 101 B11 63 50N 82 0W
Bell Ville, Argentina 126 C3 32 40 S 62 40W
Bella, Italy 31 B8 40 45N 15 32 E
Bella Bella, Canada 104 C3 52 10N 128 10W
Bella Coola, Canada 104 C3 52 25N 126 40W
Bella Unión, Uruguay 126 C4 30 15 S 57 40W
Bella Vista, Corrientes, Argentina 126 B4 28 33 S 59 0W
Bella Vista, Tucuman, Argentina 126 B2 27 10 S 65 25W
Bellac, France 20 B5 46 7N 1 3 E
Bellágio, Italy 28 C6 45 59N 9 15 E
Bellaire, U.S.A. 110 F4 40 1N 80 45W
Bellária, Italy 29 D9 44 9N 12 28 E
Bellary, India 66 M10 15 10N 76 56 E
Bellata, Australia 95 D4 29 53 S 149 46 E
Belle-Chasse, U.S.A. 113 L10 29 51N 89 59W
Belle Fourche, U.S.A. 112 C3 44 40N 103 51W
Belle Fourche →, U.S.A. 112 C3 44 26N 102 18W
Belle Glade, U.S.A. 109 M5 26 41N 80 40W
Belle-Île, France 18 E3 47 20N 3 10W
Belle Isle, Canada 103 B8 51 57N 55 25W
Belle Isle, Str. of, Canada 103 B8 51 30N 56 30W
Belle Plaine, U.S.A. 112 E8 41 54N 92 17W
Belle Yella, Liberia 82 D3 7 24N 10 0W
Belledonne, France 21 C10 45 20N 6 10 E
Bellefontaine, U.S.A. 108 E4 40 22N 83 46W
Bellefonte, U.S.A. 110 F7 40 55N 77 47W
Bellegarde, France 19 E9 47 59N 2 26 E
Bellegarde-en-Marche, France 20 C6 45 59N 2 18 E
Bellegarde-sur-Valserine, France 19 F12 46 4N 5 50 E
Bellême, France 18 D7 48 22N 0 34 E
Belleoram, Canada 103 C8 47 31N 55 25W
Belleville, Canada 102 D4 44 10N 77 23W
Belleville, France 19 F11 46 7N 4 45 E
Belleville, Ill., U.S.A. 112 F10 38 31N 89 59W
Belleville, Kans., U.S.A. 112 F6 39 50N 97 38W
Belleville, N.Y., U.S.A. 111 C8 43 46N 76 10W
Belleville-sur-Vie, France 18 F5 46 46N 1 25W
Bellevue, Canada 104 D6 49 35N 114 22W
Bellevue, Idaho, U.S.A. 114 E6 43 28N 114 16W
Bellevue, Nebr., U.S.A. 112 E7 41 8N 95 53W
Bellevue, Ohio, U.S.A. 110 E2 41 17N 82 51W
Bellevue, Wash., U.S.A. 116 C4 47 37N 122 12W
Belley, France 21 C9 45 46N 5 41 E
Bellin = Kangirsuk, Canada 101 B13 60 0N 70 0W
Bellinge, Denmark 11 J4 55 20N 10 20 E
Bellingen, Australia 95 E5 30 25 S 152 50 E
Bellingham, U.S.A. 100 D7 48 46N 122 29W
Bellingshausen Sea, Antarctica 5 C17 66 0 S 80 0W
Bellinzona, Switz. 25 J5 46 11N 9 1 E
Bello, Colombia 124 B3 6 20N 75 33W
Bellows Falls, U.S.A. 111 C12 43 8N 72 27W
Bellpat, Pakistan 68 E3 29 0N 68 5 E
Bellpuig d'Urgell, Spain 32 D6 41 37N 1 1 E
Belluno, Italy 29 B9 46 9N 12 13 E
Bellwood, U.S.A. 110 F6 40 36N 78 20W
Bélmez, Spain 35 G5 38 17N 5 17W
Belmont, Canada 110 D3 42 53N 81 5W
Belmont, S. Africa 88 D3 29 28 S 24 22 E
Belmont, U.S.A. 110 D6 42 14N 78 2W
Belmonte, Brazil 125 G11 16 0 S 39 0W
Belmonte, Portugal 34 E3 40 21N 7 20W
Belmonte, Spain 33 F2 39 34N 2 43W
Belmopan, Belize 119 D7 17 18N 88 30W
Belmullet, Ireland 15 B2 54 14N 9 58W
Belo Horizonte, Brazil 125 G10 19 55 S 43 56W
Belo-sur-Mer, Madag. 89 C7 20 42 S 44 0 E
Belo-Tsiribihina, Madag. 89 B7 19 40 S 44 30 E
Belogorsk = Bilohirsk, Ukraine 47 K8 45 3N 34 35 E
Belogorsk, Russia 51 D13 51 0N 128 20 E
Belogradchik, Bulgaria 40 C6 43 53N 22 42 E
Belogradets, Bulgaria 41 C11 43 22N 27 18 E
Beloha, Madag. 89 D8 25 10 S 45 3 E
Beloit, Kans., U.S.A. 112 F5 39 28N 98 6W
Beloit, Wis., U.S.A. 112 D10 42 31N 89 2W
Belokorovichi, Ukraine 47 G5 51 7N 28 2 E
Belomorsk, Russia 50 C4 64 35N 34 54 E
Belonia, India 67 H17 23 15N 91 30 E
Belopolye = Bilopillya, Ukraine 47 G8 51 14N 34 20 E
Belorechensk, Russia 49 H4 44 46N 39 52 E
Belorussia = Belarus ■, Europe 46 F4 53 30N 27 0 E
Beloslav, Bulgaria 41 C11 43 11N 27 42 E
Belovo, Bulgaria 41 D8 42 13N 24 1 E
Belovo, Russia 50 D9 54 30N 86 0 E
Belovodsk, Ukraine 47 H10 49 13N 39 36 E
Beloye, Ozero, Russia 46 B9 60 10N 37 35 E
Beloye More, Russia 50 C4 66 30N 38 0 E
Belozem, Bulgaria 41 D9 42 12N 25 2 E
Belozersk, Russia 46 B9 60 1N 37 45 E
Belpasso, Italy 31 E7 37 35N 14 58 E
Belpre, U.S.A. 108 F5 39 17N 81 34W
Belrain, India 69 E9 28 23N 80 55 E
Belt, U.S.A. 114 C8 47 23N 110 55W
Beltana, Australia 95 E2 30 48 S 138 25 E
Belterra, Brazil 125 D8 2 45 S 55 0W
Beltinci, Slovenia 29 B13 46 37N 16 20 E
Belton, U.S.A. 113 K6 31 3N 97 28W
Belton L., U.S.A. 113 K6 31 8N 97 32W
Beltsy = Bălţi, Moldova 43 C12 47 48N 27 58 E
Belturbet, Ireland 15 B4 54 6N 7 26W
Belukha, Russia 50 E9 49 50N 86 50 E
Beluran, Malaysia 62 C5 5 48N 117 35 E
Beluša, Slovak Rep. 27 B11 49 5N 18 17 E
Belušić, Serbia, Yug. 40 C5 43 50N 21 10 E
Belvedere Marittimo, Italy 31 C8 39 37N 15 52 E
Belvès, France 20 D5 44 46N 1 0 E
Belvidere, Ill., U.S.A. 112 D10 42 15N 88 50W
Belvidere, N.J., U.S.A. 111 F9 40 50N 75 5W
Belvis de la Jara, Spain 34 F6 39 45N 4 57W
Belyando →, Australia 94 C4 21 38 S 146 50 E
Belyy, Russia 46 E7 55 49N 33 3 E
Belyy, Ostrov, Russia 50 B8 73 30N 71 0 E
Belyy Yar, Russia 50 D9 58 26N 84 39 E
Bełżec, Poland 45 H10 50 23N 23 26 E
Belzig, Germany 24 C8 52 8N 12 35 E
Belzoni, U.S.A. 113 J9 33 11N 90 29W
Bełżyce, Poland 45 G9 51 11N 22 17 E
Bemaraha, Lembalemban' i, Madag. 89 B7 18 40 S 44 45 E
Bemarivo, Madag. 89 C7 21 45 S 44 45 E
Bemarivo →, Antsiranana, Madag. 89 A9 14 9 S 50 9 E
Bemarivo →, Mahajanga, Madag. 89 B8 15 27 S 47 40 E
Bemavo, Madag. 89 C8 21 33 S 45 25 E
Bembéréke, Benin 83 C5 10 11N 2 43 E
Bembesi, Zimbabwe 87 G2 20 0 S 28 58 E
Bembesi →, Zimbabwe 87 F2 18 57 S 27 47 E
Bembézar →, Spain 35 H5 37 45N 5 13W
Bembibre, Spain 34 C4 42 37N 6 25W
Bemetara, India 69 J9 21 42N 81 32 E
Bemidji, U.S.A. 112 B7 47 28N 94 53W
Bemolanga, Madag. 89 B8 17 44 S 45 6 E
Ben, Iran 71 C6 32 32N 50 45 E
Ben Cruachan, U.K. 14 E3 56 26N 5 8W
Ben Dearg, U.K. 14 D4 57 47N 4 56W
Ben Hope, U.K. 14 C4 58 25N 4 36W
Ben Lawers, U.K. 14 E4 56 32N 4 14W
Ben Lomond, N.S.W., Australia 95 E5 30 1 S 151 43 E
Ben Lomond, Tas., Australia 94 G4 41 38 S 147 42 E
Ben Lomond, U.K. 14 E4 56 11N 4 38W
Ben Luc, Vietnam 65 G6 10 39N 106 29 E
Ben Macdhui, U.K. 14 D5 57 4N 3 40W
Ben Mhor, U.K. 14 D1 57 15N 7 18W
Ben More, Arg. & Bute, U.K. 14 E2 56 26N 6 1W
Ben More, Stirl., U.K. 14 E4 56 23N 4 32W
Ben More Assynt, U.K. 14 C4 58 8N 4 52W
Ben Nevis, U.K. 14 E3 56 48N 5 1W
Ben Quang, Vietnam 64 D6 17 3N 106 55 E
Ben Vorlich, U.K. 14 E4 56 21N 4 14W
Ben Wyvis, U.K. 14 D4 57 40N 4 35W
Bena, Nigeria 83 C6 11 20N 5 50 E
Benāb, Iran 73 D12 37 20N 46 4 E
Benalla, Australia 95 F4 36 30 S 146 0 E
Benalmádena, Spain 35 J6 36 36N 4 34W
Benares = Varanasi, India 69 G10 25 22N 83 0 E
Bénat, C., France 21 E10 43 5N 6 22 E
Benavente, Portugal 35 G2 38 59N 8 49W
Benavente, Spain 34 C5 42 2N 5 43W
Benavides, U.S.A. 113 M5 27 36N 98 25W
Benavides de Órbigo, Spain 34 C5 42 30N 5 54W
Benbecula, U.K. 14 D1 57 26N 7 21W
Benbonyathe, Australia 95 E2 30 25 S 139 11 E
Bend, U.S.A. 114 D3 44 4N 121 19W
Bendemeer, Australia 95 E5 30 53 S 151 8 E
Bender Beila, Somali Rep. 74 F5 9 30N 50 48 E
Bendery = Tighina, Moldova 43 D14 46 50N 29 30 E
Bendigo, Australia 95 F3 36 40 S 144 15 E
Bendorf, Germany 24 E3 50 25N 7 35 E
Benē Beraq, Israel 75 C3 32 6N 34 51 E
Bénéna, Mali 82 C4 13 9N 4 17W
Benenitra, Madag. 89 C8 23 27 S 45 5 E
Benešov, Czech Rep. 26 B7 49 46N 14 41 E
Benevento, Italy 31 A7 41 8N 14 45 E
Benfeld, France 19 D14 48 22N 7 34 E
Benga, Mozam. 87 F3 16 11 S 33 40 E
Bengal, Bay of, Ind. Oc. 67 M17 15 0N 90 0 E
Bengbis, Cameroon 83 E7 3 27N 12 36 E
Bengbu, China 57 H9 32 58N 117 20 E
Benghazi = Banghāzī, Libya 79 B10 32 11N 20 3 E
Bengkalis, Indonesia 62 D2 1 30N 102 10 E
Bengkulu, Indonesia 62 E2 3 50 S 102 12 E
Bengkulu □, Indonesia 62 E2 3 48 S 102 16 E
Bengough, Canada 105 D7 49 25N 105 10W
Bengtsfors, Sweden 10 E6 59 2N 12 14 E
Benguela, Angola 85 G2 12 37 S 13 25 E
Benguérua, I., Mozam. 89 C6 21 58 S 35 28 E
Benha, Egypt 80 H7 30 26N 31 8 E
Beni, Dem. Rep. of the Congo 86 B2 0 30N 29 27 E
Beni →, Bolivia 124 F5 10 23 S 65 24W
Beni Mazâr, Egypt 80 B3 28 32N 30 44 E

Beni Mellal, Morocco 78 B4 32 21N 6 21W
Beni Suef, Egypt 80 J7 29 5N 31 6 E
Beniah L., Canada 104 A6 63 23N 112 17W
Benicarló, Spain 32 E5 40 23N 0 23 E
Benicássim, Spain 32 E5 40 3N 0 4 E
Benicia, U.S.A. 116 G4 38 3N 122 9W
Benidorm, Spain 33 G4 38 33N 0 9W
Benin ■, Africa 83 D5 10 0N 2 0 E
Benin →, Nigeria 83 D6 5 45N 5 4 E
Benin, Bight of, W. Afr. 83 E5 5 0N 3 0 E
Benin City, Nigeria 83 D6 6 20N 5 31 E
Benisa, Spain 33 G5 38 43N 0 3 E
Benitses, Greece 36 A3 39 32N 19 55 E
Benjamin Aceval, Paraguay 126 A4 24 58 S 57 34W
Benjamin Constant, Brazil 124 D4 4 40 S 70 15W
Benjamin Hill, Mexico 118 A2 30 10N 111 10W
Benkelman, U.S.A. 112 E4 40 3N 101 32W
Benkovac, Croatia 29 D12 44 2N 15 37 E
Bennett, Canada 104 B2 59 56N 134 53W
Bennett, L., Australia 92 D5 22 50 S 131 2 E
Bennetta, Ostrov, Russia 51 B15 76 21N 148 56 E
Bennettsville, U.S.A. 109 H6 34 37N 79 41W
Bennichchāb, Mauritania 82 B1 19 32N 15 12W
Bennington, N.H., U.S.A. 111 D11 43 0N 71 55W
Bennington, Vt., U.S.A. 111 D11 42 53N 73 12W
Bénodet, France 18 E2 47 53N 4 7W
Benoni, S. Africa 89 D4 26 11 S 28 18 E
Benque Viejo, Belize 119 D7 17 5N 89 8W
Bensheim, Germany 25 F4 49 40N 8 38 E
Benson, Ariz., U.S.A. 115 L8 31 58N 110 18W
Benson, Minn., U.S.A. 112 C7 45 19N 95 36W
Bent, Iran 71 E8 26 20N 59 31 E
Benteng, Indonesia 63 F6 6 10 S 120 30 E
Bentinck I., Australia 94 B2 17 3 S 139 35 E
Bentiu, Sudan 81 F2 9 10N 29 55 E
Bento Gonçalves, Brazil 127 B5 29 10 S 51 31W
Benton, Ark., U.S.A. 113 H8 34 34N 92 35W
Benton, Calif., U.S.A. 116 H8 37 48N 118 32W
Benton, Ill., U.S.A. 112 G10 38 0N 88 55W
Benton, Pa., U.S.A. 111 E8 41 12N 76 23W
Benton Harbor, U.S.A. 108 D2 42 6N 86 27W
Bentonville, U.S.A. 113 G7 36 22N 94 13W
Bentu Liben, Ethiopia 81 F4 8 32N 38 21 E
Bentung, Malaysia 65 L3 3 31N 101 55 E
Benue □, Nigeria 83 D6 7 20N 8 45 E
Benue →, Nigeria 83 D6 7 48N 6 46 E
Benxi, China 57 D12 41 20N 123 48 E
Beo, Indonesia 63 D7 4 25N 126 50 E
Beograd, Serbia, Yug. 40 B4 44 50N 20 37 E
Beoumi, Ivory C. 82 D3 7 45N 5 23W
Bepan Jiang →, China 58 E6 24 55N 106 5 E
Beppu, Japan 55 H5 33 15N 131 30 E
Beqaa Valley = Al Biqā, Lebanon 75 A5 34 10N 36 10 E
Ber Mota, India 68 H3 23 27N 68 34 E
Berach →, India 68 G6 25 15N 75 2 E
Beraketa, Madag. 89 C7 23 7 S 44 25 E
Berane, Montenegro, Yug. 40 D3 42 51N 19 52 E
Berat, Albania 40 F3 40 43N 19 59 E
Berati = Berat, Albania 40 F3 40 43N 19 59 E
Berau, Teluk, Indonesia 63 E8 2 30 S 132 30 E
Beravina, Madag. 89 B8 18 10 S 45 14 E
Berber, Sudan 80 D3 18 0N 34 0 E
Berbera, Somali Rep. 74 E4 10 30N 45 2 E
Berbérati, C.A.R. 84 D3 4 15N 15 40 E
Berbice →, Guyana 124 B7 6 20N 57 32W
Berceto, Italy 28 D6 44 31N 9 51 E
Berchidda, Italy 30 B2 40 47N 9 10 E
Berchtesgaden, Germany 25 H8 47 38N 13 0 E
Berck, France 19 B8 50 25N 1 36 E
Berdichev = Berdychiv, Ukraine 47 H5 49 57N 28 30 E
Berdsk, Russia 50 D9 54 47N 83 2 E
Berdyansk, Ukraine 47 J9 46 45N 36 50 E
Berdychiv, Ukraine 47 H5 49 57N 28 30 E
Berea, U.S.A. 108 G3 37 34N 84 17W
Berebere, Indonesia 63 D7 2 25N 128 45 E
Bereda, Somali Rep. 74 E5 11 45N 51 0 E
Berehove, Ukraine 47 H2 48 15N 22 35 E
Berekum, Ghana 82 D4 7 29N 2 34W
Berenice, Egypt 80 C4 24 2N 35 25 E
Berens →, Canada 105 C9 52 25N 97 2W
Berens I., Canada 105 C9 52 18N 97 18W
Berens River, Canada 105 C9 52 25N 97 0W
Beresford, U.S.A. 112 D6 43 5N 96 47W
Berestechko, Ukraine 47 G3 50 22N 25 5 E
Berești, Romania 43 D12 46 6N 27 50 E
Beretău →, Romania 42 C6 47 10N 21 50 E
Berettyó →, Hungary 42 D6 46 59N 21 7 E
Berettyóújfalu, Hungary 42 C6 47 13N 21 33 E
Berevo, Mahajanga, Madag. 89 B7 17 14 S 44 17 E
Berevo, Toliara, Madag. 89 B7 19 44 S 44 58 E
Bereza = Byaroza, Belarus 47 F3 52 31N 24 51 E
Berezhany, Ukraine 47 H3 49 26N 24 58 E
Berezina = Byarezina →, Belarus 47 F6 52 33N 30 14 E
Berezivka, Ukraine 47 J6 47 14N 30 55 E
Berezna, Ukraine 47 G6 51 35N 31 46 E
Berezniki, Russia 50 C5 62 51N 42 40 E
Berezniki, Russia 50 D6 59 24N 56 46 E
Berezovo, Russia 50 C7 64 0N 65 0 E
Berga, Spain 32 C6 42 6N 1 48 E
Berga, Sweden 11 G10 57 14N 16 3 E
Bergama, Turkey 39 B9 39 8N 27 11 E
Bérgamo, Italy 28 C6 45 41N 9 43 E
Bergara, Spain 32 B2 43 9N 2 28W
Bergby, Sweden 10 D11 60 57N 17 2 E
Bergedorf, Germany 24 B6 53 28N 10 6 E
Bergeforsen, Sweden 10 B11 62 32N 17 23 E
Bergen, Mecklenburg-Vorpommern, Germany 24 A9 54 25N 13 25 E
Bergen, Niedersachsen, Germany 24 C5 52 49N 9 57 E
Bergen, Neths. 17 B4 52 40N 4 43 E
Bergen, Norway 9 F11 60 20N 5 20 E
Bergen, U.S.A. 110 C7 43 5N 77 57W
Bergen op Zoom, Neths. 17 C4 51 28N 4 18 E
Bergerac, France 20 D4 44 51N 0 30 E
Bergheim, Germany 24 E2 50 57N 6 38 E
Bergholz, U.S.A. 110 F4 40 31N 80 53W
Bergisch Gladbach, Germany 17 D7 50 59N 7 8 E
Bergkamen, Germany 24 D3 51 37N 7 38 E
Bergkvara, Sweden 11 H10 56 23N 16 5 E
Bergshamra, Sweden 10 E12 59 38N 18 37 E
Bergsjö, Sweden 10 C11 61 59N 17 3 E
Bergues, France 19 B9 50 58N 2 24 E
Bergviken, Sweden 10 C10 61 15N 16 40 E
Bergville, S. Africa 89 D4 28 52 S 29 18 E
Berhala, Selat, Indonesia 62 E2 1 0 S 104 15 E
Berhampore = Baharampur, India 69 G13 24 2N 88 27 E
Berhampur = Brahmapur, India 67 K14 19 15N 84 54 E
Berheci →, Romania 43 E12 45 58N 27 28 E
Bering Sea, Pac. Oc. 100 C1 58 0N 171 0 E
Bering Strait, Pac. Oc. 100 B3 65 30N 169 0W
Beringovskiy, Russia 51 C18 63 3N 179 19 E
Berisso, Argentina 126 C4 34 56 S 57 50W
Berja, Spain 35 J8 36 50N 2 56W
Berkeley, U.S.A. 116 H4 37 52N 122 16W
Berkner I., Antarctica 5 D18 79 30 S 50 0W
Berkovitsa, Bulgaria 40 C7 43 16N 23 8 E
Berkshire, U.S.A. 111 D8 42 19N 76 11W
Berkshire Downs, U.K. 13 F6 51 33N 1 29W
Berlanga, Spain 35 G5 38 17N 5 50W
Berlenga, I., Portugal 35 F1 39 25N 9 30W
Berlin, Germany 24 C9 52 30N 13 25 E
Berlin, Md., U.S.A. 108 F8 38 20N 75 13W
Berlin, N.H., U.S.A. 111 B13 44 28N 71 11W
Berlin, N.Y., U.S.A. 111 D11 42 42N 73 23W
Berlin, Wis., U.S.A. 108 D1 43 58N 88 57W
Berlin □, Germany 24 C9 52 30N 13 20 E
Berlin L., U.S.A. 110 E4 41 3N 81 0W
Bermeja, Sierra, Spain 35 J5 36 30N 5 11W
Bermejo →, Formosa, Argentina 126 B4 26 51 S 58 23W
Bermejo →, San Juan, Argentina 126 C2 32 30 S 67 30W
Bermen, L., Canada 103 B6 53 35N 68 55W
Bermeo, Spain 32 B2 43 25N 2 47W
Bermillo de Sayago, Spain 34 D4 41 22N 6 8W
Bermuda ■, Atl. Oc. 98 F13 32 45N 65 0W
Bern, Switz. 25 J3 46 57N 7 28 E
Bern □, Switz. 25 J3 46 45N 7 40 E
Bernalda, Italy 31 B9 40 24N 16 41 E
Bernalillo, U.S.A. 115 J10 35 18N 106 33W
Bernardo de Irigoyen, Argentina 127 B5 26 15 S 53 40W
Bernardo O'Higgins □, Chile 126 C1 34 15 S 70 45W
Bernardsville, U.S.A. 111 F10 40 43N 74 34W
Bernasconi, Argentina 126 D3 37 55 S 63 44W
Bernau, Bayern, Germany 25 H8 47 47N 12 22 E
Bernau, Brandenburg, Germany 24 C9 52 40N 13 35 E
Bernay, France 18 C7 49 5N 0 35 E
Bernburg, Germany 24 D7 51 47N 11 44 E
Berndorf, Austria 26 D9 47 59N 16 1 E
Berne = Bern, Switz. 25 J3 46 57N 7 28 E
Berne = Bern □, Switz. 25 J3 46 45N 7 40 E
Berner Alpen, Switz. 25 J3 46 27N 7 35 E
Berneray, U.K. 14 D1 57 43N 7 11W
Bernier I., Australia 93 D1 24 50 S 113 12 E
Bernina, Piz, Switz. 25 J5 46 20N 9 54 E
Bernkastel-Kues, Germany 25 F3 49 55N 7 3 E
Beroroha, Madag. 89 C8 21 40 S 45 10 E
Béroubouay, Benin 83 C5 10 34N 2 46 E
Beroun, Czech Rep. 26 B7 49 57N 14 5 E
Berounka →, Czech Rep. 26 B7 50 0N 14 22 E
Berovo, Macedonia 40 E6 41 38N 22 51 E
Berre, Étang de, France 21 E9 43 27N 5 5 E
Berre-l'Étang, France 21 E9 43 27N 5 10 E
Berri, Australia 95 E3 34 14 S 140 35 E
Berriane, Algeria 78 B6 32 50N 3 46 E
Berrigan, Australia 95 F4 35 38 S 145 49 E
Berry, Australia 95 E5 34 46 S 150 43 E
Berry, France 19 F8 46 50N 2 0 E
Berry Is., Bahamas 120 A4 25 40N 77 50W
Berryessa L., U.S.A. 116 G4 38 31N 122 6W
Berryville, U.S.A. 113 G8 36 22N 93 34W
Berseba, Namibia 88 D2 26 0 S 17 46 E
Bersenbrück, Germany 24 C3 52 34N 7 56 E
Bershad, Ukraine 47 H5 48 22N 29 31 E
Berthold, U.S.A. 112 A4 48 19N 101 44W
Berthoud, U.S.A. 112 E2 40 19N 105 5W
Bertincourt, France 19 B9 50 5N 2 58 E
Bertoua, Cameroon 84 D2 4 30N 13 45 E
Bertraghboy B., Ireland 15 C2 53 22N 9 54W
Berwick, U.S.A. 111 E8 41 3N 76 14W
Berwick-upon-Tweed, U.K. 12 B6 55 46N 2 0W
Berwyn Mts., U.K. 12 E4 52 54N 3 26W
Beryslav, Ukraine 47 J7 46 50N 33 30 E
Berzasca, Romania 42 F6 44 39N 21 58 E
Berzence, Hungary 42 D2 46 12N 17 11 E
Besal, Pakistan 69 B5 35 4N 73 56 E
Besalampy, Madag. 89 B7 16 43 S 44 29 E
Besançon, France 19 E13 47 15N 6 2 E
Besar, Indonesia 62 E5 2 40 S 116 0 E
Beshenkovichi, Belarus 46 E5 55 2N 29 29 E
Beška, Serbia, Yug. 42 E5 45 8N 20 6 E
Beslan, Russia 49 J7 43 15N 44 28 E
Besna Kobila, Serbia, Yug. 40 D6 42 31N 22 10 E
Besnard L., Canada 105 B7 55 25N 106 0W
Besni, Turkey 70 B3 37 41N 37 52 E
Besor, N. →, Egypt 75 D3 31 28N 34 22 E
Bessarabiya, Moldova 47 J5 47 0N 28 10 E
Bessarabka = Basarabeasca, Moldova 43 D13 46 21N 28 58 E
Bessèges, France 21 D8 44 18N 4 8 E
Bessemer, Ala., U.S.A. 109 J2 33 24N 86 58W
Bessemer, Mich., U.S.A. 112 B9 46 29N 90 3W
Bessemer, Pa., U.S.A. 110 F4 40 59N 80 30W
Bessin, France 18 C6 49 18N 1 0W
Bessines-sur-Gartempe, France 20 B5 46 6N 1 22 E
Beswick, Australia 92 B5 14 34 S 132 53 E
Bet She'an, Israel 75 C4 32 30N 35 30 E
Bet Shemesh, Israel 75 D4 31 44N 35 0 E
Betafo, Madag. 89 B8 19 50 S 46 51 E
Betancuria, Canary Is. 37 F5 28 25N 14 3W
Betanzos, Spain 34 B2 43 15N 8 12W
Bétaré Oya, Cameroon 84 C2 5 40N 14 5 E
Betatao, Madag. 89 B8 18 11 S 47 52 E
Bétera, Spain 33 F4 39 35N 0 28W
Bétérou, Benin 83 D5 9 12N 2 16 E
Bethal, S. Africa 89 D4 26 27 S 29 28 E
Bethanien, Namibia 88 D2 26 31 S 17 8 E
Bethany, Canada 110 B6 44 11N 78 34W
Bethany, U.S.A. 112 E7 40 16N 94 2W
Bethel, Alaska, U.S.A. 100 B3 60 48N 161 45W
Bethel, Conn., U.S.A. 111 E11 41 22N 73 25W
Bethel, Maine, U.S.A. 111 B14 44 25N 70 47W
Bethel, Vt., U.S.A. 111 C12 43 50N 72 38W
Bethel Park, U.S.A. 110 F4 40 20N 80 1W
Béthenville, France 19 C11 49 18N 4 23 E
Bethlehem = Bayt Lahm, West Bank 75 D4 31 43N 35 12 E
Bethlehem, S. Africa 89 D4 28 14 S 28 18 E
Bethlehem, U.S.A. 111 F9 40 37N 75 23W
Bethulie, S. Africa 88 E4 30 30 S 25 59 E
Béthune, France 19 B9 50 30N 2 38 E
Béthune →, France 18 C8 49 53N 1 4 E
Betioky, Madag. 89 C7 23 48 S 44 20 E
Betong, Thailand 65 K3 5 45N 101 5 E
Betoota, Australia 94 D3 25 45 S 140 42 E
Betor, Ethiopia 81 E4 11 37N 39 2 E
Betroka, Madag. 89 C8 23 16 S 46 0 E
Betsiamites, Canada 103 C6 48 56N 68 40W
Betsiamites →, Canada 103 C6 48 56N 68 38W
Betsiboka →, Madag. 89 B8 16 3 S 46 36 E
Bettendorf, U.S.A. 112 E9 41 32N 90 30W
Bettiah, India 69 F11 26 48N 84 33 E
Bettna, Sweden 11 F10 58 55N 16 38 E
Béttola, Italy 28 D6 44 47N 9 36 E
Betul, India 66 J10 21 58N 77 59 E
Betung, Malaysia 62 D4 1 24N 111 31 E
Betws-y-Coed, U.K. 12 D4 53 5N 3 48W
Betxi, Spain 32 F4 39 56N 0 12W
Betzdorf, Germany 24 E3 50 46N 7 52 E
Beuil, France 21 D10 44 6N 6 59 E
Beulah, Mich., U.S.A. 108 C2 44 38N 86 6W
Beulah, N. Dak., U.S.A. 112 B4 47 16N 101 47W
Beuvron →, France 18 E8 47 29N 1 15 E
Beveren, Belgium 17 C4 51 12N 4 16 E
Beverley, Australia 93 F2 32 9 S 116 56 E
Beverley, U.K. 12 D7 53 51N 0 26W
Beverley Hills, U.S.A. 109 L4 28 56N 82 28W
Beverly, U.S.A. 111 D14 42 33N 70 53W
Beverly Hills, U.S.A. 117 L8 34 4N 118 25W
Beverungen, Germany 24 D5 51 39N 9 22 E
Bevoalavo, Madag. 89 D7 25 13 S 45 26 E
Bewas →, India 69 H8 23 59N 79 21 E
Bex, Switz. 25 J3 46 15N 7 1 E
Bexhill, U.K. 13 G8 50 51N 0 29 E
Bey Dağları, Turkey 39 E12 36 38N 30 29 E
Beyānlū, Iran 70 C5 36 0N 47 51 E
Beyazköy, Turkey 41 E11 41 21N 27 42 E
Beyçayırı, Turkey 41 F10 40 15N 26 55 E
Beydağ, Turkey 39 C10 38 5N 28 13 E
Beyeğaç, Turkey 39 D10 37 14N 28 53 E
Beyin, Ghana 82 D4 5 1N 2 41W
Beykoz, Turkey 41 E13 41 8N 29 7 E
Beyla, Guinea 82 D3 8 30N 8 38W
Beynat, France 20 C5 45 8N 1 44 E
Beyneu, Kazakstan 50 E6 45 18N 55 9 E
Beyoba, Turkey 39 C9 38 48N 27 47 E
Beyoğlu, Turkey 41 E12 41 2N 29 0 E
Beypazarı, Turkey 72 B4 40 10N 31 56 E
Beyşehir, Turkey 72 D4 37 41N 31 43 E
Beyşehir Gölü, Turkey 70 B1 37 41N 31 33 E
Beytüşşebap, Turkey 73 D10 37 35N 43 10 E
Bezdan, Serbia, Yug. 42 E3 45 50N 18 57 E
Bezhetsk, Russia 46 D9 57 47N 36 39 E
Béziers, France 20 E7 43 20N 3 12 E
Bezwada = Vijayawada, India 67 L12 16 31N 80 39 E
Bhabua, India 69 G10 25 3N 83 37 E
Bhachau, India 66 H7 23 20N 70 16 E
Bhadar →, Gujarat, India 68 H5 22 17N 72 20 E
Bhadar →, Gujarat, India 68 J3 21 27N 69 47 E
Bhadarwah, India 69 C6 32 58N 75 46 E
Bhadohi, India 69 G10 25 25N 82 34 E
Bhadra, India 68 E6 29 8N 75 14 E
Bhadrakh, India 67 J15 21 10N 86 30 E
Bhadran, India 68 H5 22 19N 72 6 E
Bhadravati, India 66 N9 13 49N 75 40 E
Bhag, Pakistan 68 E2 29 2N 67 49 E
Bhagalpur, India 69 G12 25 10N 87 0 E
Bhagirathi →, Ut. P., India 69 D8 30 8N 78 35 E
Bhagirathi →, W. Bengal, India 69 H13 23 25N 88 23 E
Bhakkar, Pakistan 68 D4 31 40N 71 5 E
Bhakra Dam, India 68 D7 31 30N 76 45 E
Bhamo, Burma 67 G20 24 15N 97 15 E
Bhandara, India 66 J11 21 5N 79 42 E
Bhanpura, India 68 G6 24 31N 75 44 E
Bhanrer Ra., India 69 H8 23 40N 79 45 E
Bhaptiahi, India 69 F12 26 19N 86 44 E
Bharat = India ■, Asia 66 K11 20 0N 78 0 E
Bharatpur, Mad. P., India 69 H9 23 44N 81 46 E
Bharatpur, Raj., India 68 F7 27 15N 77 30 E
Bharno, India 69 H11 23 14N 84 53 E
Bhatinda, India 68 D6 30 15N 74 57 E
Bhatpara, India 69 H13 22 50N 88 25 E
Bhattu, India 68 E6 29 36N 75 19 E
Bhaun, Pakistan 68 C5 32 55N 72 40 E
Bhaunagar = Bhavnagar, India 66 J8 21 45N 72 10 E
Bhavnagar, India 66 J8 21 45N 72 10 E
Bhawanipatna, India 67 K12 19 55N 80 10 E
Bhawari, India 68 G5 25 42N 73 4 E
Bhayavadar, India 68 J4 21 51N 70 15 E
Bhera, Pakistan 68 C5 32 29N 72 57 E
Bhikangaon, India 68 J6 21 52N 75 57 E
Bhilsa = Vidisha, India 68 H7 23 28N 77 53 E
Bhilwara, India 68 G6 25 25N 74 38 E
Bhima →, India 66 L10 16 25N 77 17 E
Bhimavaram, India 67 L12 16 30N 81 30 E
Bhimbar, Pakistan 69 C6 32 59N 74 3 E
Bhind, India 69 F8 26 30N 78 46 E
Bhinga, India 69 F9 27 43N 81 56 E
Bhinmal, India 68 G5 25 0N 72 15 E
Bhiwandi, India 66 K8 19 20N 73 0 E
Bhiwani, India 68 E7 28 50N 76 9 E
Bhogava →, India 68 H5 22 26N 72 20 E
Bhola, Bangla. 67 H17 22 45N 90 35 E
Bholari, Pakistan 68 G3 25 19N 68 13 E
Bhopal, India 68 H7 23 20N 77 30 E
Bhubaneshwar, India 67 J14 20 15N 85 50 E
Bhuj, India 68 H3 23 15N 69 49 E
Bhusaval, India 66 J9 21 3N 75 46 E
Bhutan ■, Asia 67 F17 27 25N 90 30 E
Biafra, B. of = Bonny, Bight of, Africa 83 E6 3 30N 9 20 E
Biak, Indonesia 63 E9 1 10 S 136 6 E
Biała, Poland 45 H4 50 24N 17 40 E
Biała →, Poland 45 H7 50 3N 20 55 E
Biała Piska, Poland 44 E9 53 37N 22 5 E
Biała Podlaska, Poland 45 F10 52 4N 23 6 E
Biała Rawska, Poland 45 G7 51 48N 20 29 E
Białobrzegi, Poland 45 G7 51 39N 20 57 E
Białogard, Poland 44 D2 54 2N 15 58 E
Białowieża, Poland 45 F10 52 41N 23 49 E
Biały Bór, Poland 44 E3 53 53N 16 51 E
Białystok, Poland 45 E10 53 10N 23 10 E
Biancavilla, Italy 31 E7 37 38N 14 52 E
Bianco, Italy 31 D9 38 5N 16 9 E
Biankouma, Ivory C. 82 D3 7 50N 7 40W
Biaora, India 68 H7 23 56N 76 56 E
Bīārjmand, Iran 71 B7 36 6N 55 53 E
Biaro, Indonesia 63 D7 2 5N 125 26 E
Biarritz, France 20 E2 43 29N 1 33W
Biasca, Switz. 25 J4 46 22N 8 58 E
Biba, Egypt 80 J7 28 55N 31 0 E
Bibai, Japan 54 C10 43 19N 141 52 E
Bibbiena, Italy 29 E8 43 42N 11 49 E
Bibby I., Canada 105 A10 61 55N 93 0W
Bibel →, Spain 34 C3 42 24N 7 13W
Biberach, Germany 25 G5 48 5N 9 47 E
Bibiani, Ghana 82 D4 6 30N 2 8W
Bibungwa, Dem. Rep. of the Congo 86 C2 2 40 S 28 15 E
Bic, Canada 103 C6 48 20N 68 41W
Bicaj, Albania 40 E4 41 58N 20 25 E
Bicaz, Romania 43 D11 46 53N 26 5 E
Bicazu Ardelean, Romania 43 D10 46 51N 25 56 E
Bíccari, Italy 31 A8 41 23N 15 12 E
Bicester, U.K. 13 F6 51 54N 1 9W
Bichena, Ethiopia 81 E4 10 28N 38 10 E
Bicheno, Australia 94 G4 41 52 S 148 18 E
Bichia, India 69 H9 22 27N 80 42 E
Bichvinta, Georgia 49 J5 43 9N 40 21 E
Bickerton I., Australia 94 A2 13 45 S 136 10 E
Bicske, Hungary 42 C3 47 29N 18 38 E
Bida, Nigeria 83 D6 9 3N 5 58 E
Bidar, India 66 L10 17 55N 77 35 E
Biddeford, U.S.A. 109 D10 43 30N 70 28W
Biddwara, Ethiopia 81 F4 5 11N 38 34 E
Bideford, U.K. 13 F3 51 1N 4 13W
Bideford Bay, U.K. 13 F3 51 5N 4 20W
Bidhuna, India 69 F8 26 49N 79 31 E
Bidor, Malaysia 65 K3 4 6N 101 15 E
Bie, Sweden 10 E10 59 5N 16 12 E
Bié, Planalto de, Angola 85 G3 12 0 S 16 0 E
Bieber, U.S.A. 114 F3 41 7N 121 8W
Biebrza →, Poland 45 E9 53 13N 22 25 E
Biecz, Poland 45 J8 49 44N 21 15 E
Biel, Switz. 25 H3 47 8N 7 14 E
Bielawa, Poland 45 H3 50 43N 16 37 E
Bielefeld, Germany 24 C4 52 1N 8 33 E
Bielersee, Switz. 25 H3 47 6N 7 5 E
Biella, Italy 28 C5 45 34N 8 3 E
Bielsk Podlaski, Poland 45 F10 52 47N 23 12 E
Bielsko-Biała, Poland 45 J6 49 50N 19 2 E
Bien Hoa, Vietnam 65 G6 10 57N 106 49 E
Bienne = Biel, Switz. 25 H3 47 8N 7 14 E
Bienvenida, Spain 35 G4 38 18N 6 12W
Bienville, L., Canada 102 A5 55 5N 72 40W
Bierné, France 18 E6 47 48N 0 33W
Bierun, Poland 45 H6 50 6N 19 6 E
Bierutów, Poland 45 G4 51 7N 17 32 E
Biescas, Spain 32 C4 42 37N 0 20W
Biese →, Germany 24 C7 52 53N 11 46 E
Biesiesfontein, S. Africa 88 E2 30 57 S 17 58 E
Bietigheim-Bissingen, Germany 25 G5 48 58N 9 8 E
Bieżuń, Poland 45 F6 52 58N 19 55 E
Biferno →, Italy 29 G12 41 59N 15 2 E
Big →, Canada 103 B8 54 50N 58 55W
Big B., Canada 103 A7 55 43N 60 35W
Big Bear City, U.S.A. 117 L10 34 16N 116 51W
Big Bear Lake, U.S.A. 117 L10 34 15N 116 56W
Big Belt Mts., U.S.A. 114 C8 46 30N 111 25W
Big Bend, Swaziland 89 D5 26 50 S 31 58 E
Big Bend National Park, U.S.A. 113 L3 29 20N 103 5W
Big Black →, U.S.A. 113 K9 32 3N 91 4W
Big Blue →, U.S.A. 112 F6 39 35N 96 34W
Big Creek, U.S.A. 116 H7 37 11N 119 14W
Big Cypress National Preserve, U.S.A. 109 M5 26 0N 81 10W
Big Cypress Swamp, U.S.A. 109 M5 26 12N 81 10W
Big Falls, U.S.A. 112 A8 48 12N 93 48W
Big Fork →, U.S.A. 112 A8 48 31N 93 43W
Big Horn Mts. = Bighorn Mts., U.S.A. 114 D10 44 30N 107 30W
Big I., Canada 104 A5 61 7N 116 45W
Big Lake, U.S.A. 113 K4 31 12N 101 28W
Big Moose, U.S.A. 111 C10 43 49N 74 58W
Big Muddy Cr. →, U.S.A. 112 A2 48 8N 104 36W
Big Pine, U.S.A. 116 H8 37 10N 118 17W
Big Piney, U.S.A. 114 E8 42 32N 110 7W
Big Rapids, U.S.A. 108 D3 43 42N 85 29W
Big Rideau L., Canada 111 B8 44 40N 76 15W
Big River, Canada 105 C7 53 50N 107 0W
Big Run, U.S.A. 110 F6 40 57N 78 55W
Big Sable Pt., U.S.A. 108 C2 44 3N 86 1W
Big Salmon →, Canada 104 A2 61 52N 134 55W
Big Sand L., Canada 105 B9 57 45N 99 45W
Big Sandy, U.S.A. 114 B8 48 11N 110 7W
Big Sandy →, U.S.A. 108 F4 38 25N 82 36W
Big Sandy Cr. →, U.S.A. 112 F3 38 7N 102 29W
Big Sioux →, U.S.A. 112 D6 42 29N 96 27W
Big Spring, U.S.A. 113 J4 32 15N 101 28W
Big Stone City, U.S.A. 112 C6 45 18N 96 28W
Big Stone Gap, U.S.A. 109 G4 36 52N 82 47W
Big Stone L., U.S.A. 112 C6 45 30N 96 35W
Big Sur, U.S.A. 116 J5 36 15N 121 48W
Big Timber, U.S.A. 114 D9 45 50N 109 57W
Big Trout L., Canada 102 B2 53 40N 90 0W
Big Trout Lake, Canada 102 B2 53 45N 90 0W
Biğa, Turkey 41 F11 40 13N 27 14 E
Biga →, Turkey 41 F11 40 20N 27 14 E
Bigadiç, Turkey 39 B10 39 22N 28 7 E
Biganos, France 20 D3 44 39N 0 59W
Biggar, Canada 105 C7 52 4N 108 0W
Biggar, U.K. 14 F5 55 38N 3 32W
Bigge I., Australia 92 B4 14 35 S 125 10 E
Biggenden, Australia 95 D5 25 31 S 152 4 E
Biggleswade, U.K. 13 E7 52 5N 0 14W
Biggs, U.S.A. 116 F5 39 25N 121 43W
Bighorn, U.S.A. 114 C10 46 10N 107 27W
Bighorn →, U.S.A. 114 C10 46 10N 107 28W
Bighorn L., U.S.A. 114 D9 44 55N 108 15W
Bighorn Mts., U.S.A. 114 D10 44 30N 107 30W
Bignona, Senegal 82 C1 12 52N 16 14W
Bigorre, France 20 E4 43 10N 0 5 E
Bigstone L., Canada 105 C9 53 42N 95 44W
Biguglia, Étang de, France 21 F13 42 36N 9 29 E
Bigwa, Tanzania 86 D4 7 10 S 39 10 E
Bihać, Bos.-H. 29 D12 44 49N 15 57 E
Bihar, India 69 G11 25 5N 85 40 E
Bihar □, India 69 G12 25 0N 86 0 E
Biharamulo, Tanzania 86 C3 2 25 S 31 25 E
Bihariganj, India 69 G12 25 44N 86 59 E
Biharkeresztes, Hungary 42 C6 47 8N 21 44 E
Bihor □, Romania 42 D7 47 0N 22 10 E
Bihor, Munții, Romania 42 D7 46 29N 22 47 E
Bijagós, Arquipélago dos, Guinea-Biss. 82 C1 11 15N 16 10W
Bijaipur, India 68 F7 26 2N 77 20 E
Bijapur, Karnataka, India 66 L9 16 50N 75 55 E
Bijapur, Mad. P., India 67 K12 18 50N 80 50 E
Bījār, Iran 70 C5 35 52N 47 35 E
Bijawar, India 69 G8 24 38N 79 30 E
Bijeljina, Bos.-H. 42 F4 44 46N 19 14 E
Bijelo Polje, Montenegro, Yug. 40 C3 43 1N 19 45 E
Bijie, China 58 D5 27 20N 105 16 E
Bijnor, India 68 E8 29 27N 78 11 E
Bikaner, India 68 E5 28 2N 73 18 E
Bikapur, India 69 F10 26 30N 82 7 E
Bikeqi, China 56 D6 40 43N 111 20 E
Bikfayyā, Lebanon 75 B4 33 55N 35 41 E
Bikin, Russia 51 E14 46 50N 134 20 E
Bikin →, Russia 54 A7 46 51N 134 2 E
Bikini Atoll, Marshall Is. 96 F8 12 0N 167 30 E
Bikita, Zimbabwe 89 C5 20 6 S 31 41 E
Bikoué, Cameroon 83 E7 3 55N 11 50 E
Bila Tserkva, Ukraine 47 H6 49 45N 30 10 E
Bilanga, Burkina Faso 83 C4 12 40N 0 1W
Bilara, India 68 F5 26 14N 73 53 E
Bilaspur, Mad. P., India 69 H10 22 2N 82 15 E
Bilaspur, Punjab, India 68 D7 31 19N 76 50 E
Biläsuvar, Azerbaijan 73 C13 39 27N 48 32 E
Bilauk Taungdan, Thailand 64 F2 13 0N 99 0 E
Bilbao, Spain 32 B2 43 16N 2 56W
Bilbeis, Egypt 80 H7 30 25N 31 34 E
Bilbo = Bilbao, Spain 32 B2 43 16N 2 56W
Bilbor, Romania 43 C10 47 6N 25 30 E
Bilciurești, Romania 43 F10 44 44N 25 48 E
Bíldudalur, Iceland 8 D2 65 41N 23 36W
Bílé Karpaty, Europe 27 B11 49 5N 18 0 E
Bileća, Bos.-H. 40 D2 42 53N 18 27 E
Bilecik, Turkey 72 B4 40 5N 30 5 E
Biłgoraj, Poland 45 H9 50 33N 22 42 E
Bilgram, India 69 F9 27 11N 80 2 E
Bilhaur, India 69 F9 26 51N 80 5 E
Bilhorod-Dnistrovskyy, Ukraine 47 J6 46 11N 30 23 E
Bilibino, Russia 51 C17 68 3N 166 20 E
Bilibiza, Mozam. 87 E5 12 30 S 40 20 E
Bilisht, Albania 40 F5 40 37N 21 2 E
Bilishti = Bilisht, Albania 40 F5 40 37N 21 2 E
Billabalong Roadhouse, Australia 93 E2 27 25 S 115 49 E
Billdal, Sweden 11 G5 57 35N 11 57 E
Billiluna, Australia 92 C4 19 37 S 127 41 E
Billings, U.S.A. 114 D9 45 47N 108 30W
Billiton Is. = Belitung, Indonesia 62 E3 3 10 S 107 50 E
Billsta, Sweden 10 A12 63 20N 18 28 E
Billund, Denmark 11 J3 55 44N 9 6 E
Bilma, Niger 79 E8 18 50N 13 30 E
Bilo Gora, Croatia 42 E2 45 53N 17 15 E
Biloela, Australia 94 C5 24 24 S 150 31 E
Bilohirsk, Ukraine 47 K8 45 3N 34 35 E
Bilopillya, Ukraine 47 G8 51 14N 34 20 E
Biloxi, U.S.A. 113 K10 30 24N 88 53W
Bilpa Morea Claypan, Australia 94 D3 25 0 S 140 0 E
Biltine, Chad 79 F10 14 40N 20 50 E
Bilyarsk, Russia 48 C10 54 58N 50 22 E
Bima, Indonesia 63 F5 8 22 S 118 49 E
Bimban, Egypt 80 C3 24 24N 32 54 E
Bimbila, Ghana 83 D5 8 54N 0 5 E
Bimini Is., Bahamas 120 A4 25 42N 79 25W
Bin Xian, Heilongjiang, China 57 B14 45 42N 127 32 E
Bin Xian, Shaanxi, China 56 G5 35 2N 108 4 E
Bin Yauri, Nigeria 83 C5 10 46N 4 45 E
Bina-Etawah, India 68 G8 24 13N 78 14 E
Bināb, Iran 71 B6 36 35N 48 41 E
Binalbagan, Phil. 61 F5 10 12N 122 50 E
Binalong, Australia 95 E4 34 40 S 148 39 E
Bīnālūd, Kūh-e, Iran 71 B8 36 30N 58 30 E
Binatang = Bintangor, Malaysia 62 D4 2 10N 111 40 E
Binche, Belgium 17 D4 50 26N 4 10 E
Binchuan, China 58 E3 25 42N 100 38 E
Binder, Chad 83 D7 9 56N 14 27 E
Bindki, India 69 F9 26 2N 80 36 E
Bindslev, Denmark 11 G4 57 33N 10 11 E
Bindura, Zimbabwe 87 F3 17 18 S 31 18 E
Binefar, Spain 32 D5 41 51N 0 18 E
Bingara, Australia 95 D5 29 52 S 150 36 E
Bingen, Germany 25 F3 49 57N 7 55 E
Bingerville, Ivory C. 82 D4 5 18N 3 49W
Bingham, U.S.A. 109 C11 45 3N 69 53W
Binghamton, U.S.A. 111 D9 42 6N 75 55W
Bingöl, Turkey 70 B4 38 53N 40 29 E
Bingöl Dağları, Turkey 73 C9 39 16N 41 9 E
Bingsjö, Sweden 10 C9 61 1N 15 39 E
Binh Dinh = An Nhon, Vietnam 64 F7 13 55N 109 7 E
Binh Khe, Vietnam 64 F7 13 57N 108 51 E
Binh Son, Vietnam 64 E7 15 20N 108 40 E
Binhai, China 57 G10 34 2N 119 49 E
Binic, France 18 D4 48 46N 2 50W
Binisatua, Spain 37 B11 39 50N 4 11 E
Binjai, Indonesia 62 D3 3 20N 98 30 E
Binji, Nigeria 83 C5 13 10N 4 55 E
Binnaway, Australia 95 E4 31 28 S 149 24 E
Binongko, Indonesia 63 F6 5 55 S 123 55 E
Binscarth, Canada 105 C8 50 37N 101 17W
Bint Goda, Sudan 81 E3 13 17N 31 33 E
Bintan, Indonesia 62 D2 1 0N 104 0 E
Bintangor, Malaysia 62 D4 2 10N 111 40 E
Bintulu, Malaysia 62 D4 3 10N 113 0 E
Bintuni, Indonesia 63 E8 2 7 S 133 32 E

Binyang, China 58 F7 23 12N 108 47 E
Binz, Germany 24 A9 54 24N 13 35 E
Binzert = Bizerte, Tunisia 79 A7 37 15N 9 50 E
Binzhou, China 57 F10 37 20N 118 2 E
Bío Bío □, Chile 126 D1 37 35 S 72 0W
Biograd na Moru, Croatia 29 E12 43 56N 15 29 E
Bioko, Eq. Guin. 83 E6 3 30N 8 40 E
Biokovo, Croatia 29 E14 43 23N 17 0 E
Bipindi, Cameroon 83 E7 3 6N 10 30 E
Bir, India 66 K9 19 0N 75 54 E
Bir, Ras, Djibouti 81 E5 12 0N 43 20 E
Bîr Abu Hashim, Egypt 80 C3 23 42N 34 6 E
Bîr Abu Minqar, Egypt 80 B2 26 33N 27 33 E
Bîr Abu Muḥammad, Egypt 75 F3 29 44N 34 14 E
Bi'r ad Dabbāghāt, Jordan 75 E4 30 26N 35 32 E
Bîr Adal Deib, Sudan 80 C4 22 35N 36 10 E
Bi'r al Butayyihāt, Jordan 75 F4 29 47N 35 20 E
Bi'r al Mārī, Jordan 75 E4 30 4N 35 33 E
Bi'r al Qattār, Jordan 75 F4 29 47N 35 32 E
Bîr 'Asal, Egypt 80 B3 25 55N 34 20 E
Bîr Atrun, Sudan 80 D2 18 15N 26 40 E
Bîr Beiḍa, Egypt 75 E3 30 25N 34 29 E
Bîr Diqnash, Egypt 80 A2 31 3N 25 23 E
Bîr el 'Abd, Egypt 75 D2 31 2N 33 0 E
Bîr el Basur, Egypt 80 B2 29 51N 25 49 E
Bîr el Biarât, Egypt 75 F3 29 30N 34 43 E
Bîr el Duweidar, Egypt 75 E1 30 56N 32 32 E
Bîr el Garârât, Egypt 75 D2 31 3N 33 34 E
Bîr el Gellaz, Egypt 80 A2 30 50N 26 40 E
Bîr el Heisi, Egypt 75 F3 29 22N 34 36 E
Bîr el Jafir, Egypt 75 E1 30 50N 32 41 E
Bîr el Mâlḥi, Egypt 75 E2 30 38N 33 19 E
Bîr el Shaqqa, Egypt 80 A2 30 54N 25 1 E
Bîr el Thamâda, Egypt 75 E2 30 12N 33 27 E
Bîr Fuad, Egypt 80 A2 30 35N 26 28 E
Bîr Gebeil Ḥiṣn, Egypt 75 E2 30 2N 33 18 E
Bi'r Ghadīr, Syria 75 A6 34 6N 37 3 E
Bîr Haimur, Egypt 80 C3 22 45N 33 40 E
Bîr Ḥasana, Egypt 75 E2 30 29N 33 46 E
Bîr Hôôker, Egypt 80 H7 30 22N 30 21 E
Bîr Kanayis, Egypt 80 C3 24 59N 33 15 E
Bîr Kaseiba, Egypt 75 E2 31 0N 33 17 E
Bîr Kerawein, Egypt 80 B2 27 10N 28 25 E
Bîr Lahfân, Egypt 75 E2 31 0N 33 51 E
Bîr Madkûr, Egypt 75 E1 30 44N 32 33 E
Bîr Maql, Egypt 80 C3 23 7N 33 40 E
Bîr Mîneiga, Sudan 80 C4 22 47N 35 12 E
Bîr Misaha, Egypt 80 C2 22 13N 27 59 E
Bir Mogreïn, Mauritania 78 C3 25 10N 11 25W
Bîr Murr, Egypt 80 C3 23 28N 30 10 E
Bi'r Muṭribah, Kuwait 70 D5 29 54N 47 17 E
Bîr Nakheila, Egypt 80 C3 24 1N 30 50 E
Bîr Qaṭia, Egypt 75 E1 30 58N 32 45 E
Bîr Qatrani, Egypt 80 A2 30 55N 26 10 E
Bîr Ranga, Egypt 80 C4 24 25N 35 15 E
Bîr Sahara, Egypt 80 C2 22 54N 28 40 E
Bîr Seiyâla, Egypt 80 B3 26 10N 33 50 E
Bîr Shalatein, Egypt 80 C4 23 5N 35 25 E
Bîr Shebb, Egypt 80 C2 22 25N 29 40 E
Bîr Shût, Egypt 80 C4 23 50N 35 15 E
Bîr Terfawi, Egypt 80 C2 22 57N 28 55 E
Bîr Umm Qubûr, Egypt 80 C3 24 35N 34 2 E
Bîr Ungât, Egypt 80 C3 22 8N 33 48 E
Bîr Za'farâna, Egypt 80 J8 29 10N 32 40 E
Bîr Zeidûn, Egypt 80 B3 25 45N 33 40 E
Biramféro, Guinea 82 C3 11 40N 9 10W
Biratnagar, Nepal 69 F12 26 27N 87 17 E
Birawa, Dem. Rep. of the Congo 86 C2 2 20 S 28 48 E
Birch →, Canada 104 B6 58 28N 112 17W
Birch Hills, Canada 105 C7 52 59N 105 25W
Birch I., Canada 105 C9 52 26N 99 54W
Birch L., N.W.T., Canada 104 A5 62 4N 116 33W
Birch L., Ont., Canada 102 B1 51 23N 92 18W
Birch Mts., Canada 104 B6 57 30N 113 10W
Birch River, Canada 105 C8 52 24N 101 6W
Birchip, Australia 95 F3 35 56 S 142 55 E
Birchiş, Romania 42 E7 45 58N 22 9 E
Bird, Canada 105 B10 56 30N 94 13W
Bird I. = Las Aves, Is., W. Indies 121 C7 15 45N 63 55W
Birdsville, Australia 94 D2 25 51 S 139 20 E
Birdum Cr., Australia 92 C5 15 14 S 133 0 E
Birecik, Turkey 70 B3 37 2N 38 0 E
Birein, Israel 75 E3 30 50N 34 28 E
Bireuen, Indonesia 62 C1 5 14N 96 39 E
Biri →, Sudan 81 F2 7 56N 26 33 E
Birifo, Gambia 82 C2 13 30N 14 0W
Birigui, Brazil 127 A5 21 18 S 50 16W
Birjand, Iran 71 C8 32 53N 59 13 E
Birkenfeld, Germany 25 F3 49 38N 7 9 E
Birkenhead, U.K. 12 D4 53 23N 3 2W
Birkerød, Denmark 11 J6 55 50N 12 25 E
Birket Qârûn, Egypt 80 J7 29 30N 30 40 E
Birkfeld, Austria 26 D8 47 21N 15 45 E
Bîrlad = Bârlad, Romania 43 D12 46 15N 27 38 E
Birmingham, U.K. 13 E6 52 29N 1 52W
Birmingham, U.S.A. 109 J2 33 31N 86 48W
Birmitrapur, India 67 H14 22 24N 84 46 E
Birni Ngaouré, Niger 83 C5 13 5N 2 51 E
Birni Nkonni, Niger 83 C6 13 55N 5 15 E
Birnin Gwari, Nigeria 83 C6 11 0N 6 45 E
Birnin Kebbi, Nigeria 83 C5 12 32N 4 12 E
Birnin Kudu, Nigeria 83 C6 11 30N 9 29 E
Birobidzhan, Russia 51 E14 48 50N 132 50 E
Birr, Ireland 15 C4 53 6N 7 54W
Birrie →, Australia 95 D4 29 43 S 146 37 E
Birsilpur, India 68 E5 28 11N 72 15 E
Birsk, Russia 50 D6 55 25N 55 30 E
Birštonas, Lithuania 44 D11 54 37N 24 2 E
Birtle, Canada 105 C8 50 30N 101 5W
Birur, India 66 N9 13 30N 75 55 E
Biryuchiy, Ukraine 47 J8 46 10N 35 0 E
Biržai, Lithuania 9 H21 56 11N 24 45 E
Birzebbugga, Malta 36 D2 35 49N 14 32 E
Bisa, Indonesia 63 E7 1 15 S 127 28 E
Bisáccia, Italy 31 A8 41 1N 15 22 E
Bisacquino, Italy 30 E6 37 42N 13 15 E
Bisalpur, India 69 E8 28 14N 79 48 E
Bisbee, U.S.A. 115 L9 31 27N 109 55W
Biscarrosse, France 20 D2 44 22N 1 20W
Biscarrosse et de Parentis, Étang de, France 20 D2 44 21N 1 10W
Biscay, B. of, Atl. Oc. 6 F5 45 0N 2 0W
Biscayne B., U.S.A. 109 N5 25 40N 80 12W
Biscéglie, Italy 31 A9 41 14N 16 30 E
Bischheim, France 19 D14 48 37N 7 46 E
Bischofshofen, Austria 26 D6 47 26N 13 14 E
Bischofswerda, Germany 24 D10 51 7N 14 10 E
Bischwiller, France 19 D14 48 46N 7 50 E
Biscoe Bay, Antarctica 5 D13 77 0 S 152 0W
Biscoe Is., Antarctica 5 C17 66 0 S 67 0W
Biscostasing, Canada 102 C3 47 18N 82 9W
Biševo, Croatia 29 F13 42 57N 16 3 E
Bisha, Eritrea 81 D4 15 30N 37 31 E
Bishah, W. →, Si. Arabia 80 C5 21 24N 43 26 E
Bishan, China 58 C6 29 33N 106 12 E
Bishkek, Kyrgyzstan 50 E8 42 54N 74 46 E
Bishnupur, India 69 H12 23 8N 87 20 E
Bisho, S. Africa 89 E4 32 50 S 27 23 E
Bishop, Calif., U.S.A. 116 H8 37 22N 118 24W
Bishop, Tex., U.S.A. 113 M6 27 35N 97 48W
Bishop Auckland, U.K. 12 C6 54 39N 1 40W
Bishop's Falls, Canada 103 C8 49 2N 55 30W
Bishop's Stortford, U.K. 13 F8 51 52N 0 10 E
Bisignano, Italy 31 C9 39 31N 16 17 E
Bisina, L., Uganda 86 B3 1 38N 33 56 E
Biskra, Algeria 78 B7 34 50N 5 44 E
Biskupiec, Poland 44 E7 53 53N 20 58 E
Bismarck, U.S.A. 112 B4 46 48N 100 47W
Bismarck Arch., Papua N. G. 96 H7 2 30 S 150 0 E
Bismark, Germany 24 C7 52 40N 11 33 E
Bismil, Turkey 73 D9 37 51N 40 40 E
Biso, Uganda 86 B3 1 44N 31 26 E
Bison, U.S.A. 112 C3 45 31N 102 28W
Bīsotūn, Iran 70 C5 34 23N 47 26 E
Bispgården, Sweden 10 A10 63 2N 16 40 E
Bissagos = Bijagós, Arquipélago dos, Guinea-Biss. 82 C1 11 15N 16 10W
Bissau, Guinea-Biss. 82 C1 11 45N 15 45W
Bissaula, Nigeria 83 D7 7 0N 10 27 E
Bissikrima, Guinea 82 C2 10 50N 10 58W
Bissorã, Guinea-Biss. 82 C1 12 16N 15 35W
Bistcho L., Canada 104 B5 59 45N 118 50W
Bistret, Romania 43 G8 43 54N 23 23 E
Bistrica = Ilirska-Bistrica, Slovenia 29 C11 45 34N 14 14 E
Bistriţa, Romania 43 C9 47 9N 24 35 E
Bistriţa →, Romania 43 D11 46 30N 26 57 E
Bistriţa Năsăud □, Romania 43 C9 47 15N 24 30 E
Bistriţei, Muntii, Romania 43 C10 47 15N 25 40 E
Biswan, India 69 F9 27 29N 81 2 E
Bisztynek, Poland 44 D7 54 8N 20 53 E
Bitburg, Germany 25 F2 49 58N 6 31 E
Bitche, France 19 C14 49 2N 7 25 E
Bithynia, Turkey 72 B4 40 40N 31 0 E
Bitlis, Turkey 70 B4 38 20N 42 3 E
Bitola, Macedonia 40 E5 41 1N 21 20 E
Bitolj = Bitola, Macedonia 40 E5 41 1N 21 20 E
Bitonto, Italy 31 A9 41 6N 16 41 E
Bitter Creek, U.S.A. 114 F9 41 33N 108 33W
Bitter L. = Buheirat-Murrat-el-Kubra, Egypt 80 H8 30 18N 32 26 E
Bitterfeld, Germany 24 D8 51 37N 12 20 E
Bitterfontein, S. Africa 88 E2 31 1 S 18 32 E
Bitterroot →, U.S.A. 114 C6 46 52N 114 7W
Bitterroot Range, U.S.A. 114 D6 46 0N 114 20W
Bitterwater, U.S.A. 116 J6 36 23N 121 0W
Bitti, Italy 30 B2 40 29N 9 23 E
Bittou, Burkina Faso 83 C4 11 17N 0 18W
Biu, Nigeria 83 C7 10 40N 12 3 E
Bivolari, Romania 43 C12 47 31N 27 27 E
Bivolu, Vf., Romania 43 C10 47 16N 25 58 E
Biwa-Ko, Japan 55 G8 35 15N 136 10 E
Biwabik, U.S.A. 112 B8 47 32N 92 21W
Bixad, Romania 43 C8 47 56N 23 28 E
Bixby, U.S.A. 113 H7 35 57N 95 53W
Biyang, China 56 H7 32 38N 113 21 E
Biysk, Russia 50 D9 52 40N 85 0 E
Bizana, S. Africa 89 E4 30 50 S 29 52 E
Bizen, Japan 55 G7 34 43N 134 8 E
Bizerte, Tunisia 79 A7 37 15N 9 50 E
Bjargtangar, Iceland 8 D1 65 30N 24 30W
Bjärnum, Sweden 11 H7 56 17N 13 43 E
Bjästa, Sweden 10 A12 63 12N 18 29 E
Bjelasica, Montenegro, Yug. 40 D3 42 50N 19 40 E
Bjelašnica, Bos.-H. 42 G3 43 43N 18 9 E
Bjelovar, Croatia 29 C13 45 56N 16 49 E
Bjerringbro, Denmark 11 H3 56 23N 9 39 E
Björbo, Sweden 10 D8 60 27N 14 44 E
Björklinge, Sweden 10 D11 60 2N 17 33 E
Björneborg, Sweden 10 E8 59 14N 14 16 E
Bjørnevatn, Norway 8 B23 69 40N 30 0 E
Bjørnøya, Arctic 4 B8 74 30N 19 0 E
Bjursås, Sweden 10 D9 60 44N 15 29 E
Bjuv, Sweden 11 H6 56 5N 12 55 E
Bla, Mali 82 C3 12 56N 5 47W
Blace, Serbia, Yug. 40 C5 43 18N 21 17 E
Blachownia, Poland 45 H5 50 49N 18 56 E
Black = Da →, Vietnam 58 G5 21 15N 105 20 E
Black →, Canada 110 B5 44 42N 79 19W
Black →, Ariz., U.S.A. 115 K8 33 44N 110 13W
Black →, Ark., U.S.A. 113 H9 35 38N 91 20W
Black →, Mich., U.S.A. 110 D2 42 59N 82 27W
Black →, N.Y., U.S.A. 111 C8 43 59N 76 4W
Black →, Wis., U.S.A. 112 D9 43 57N 91 22W
Black Bay Pen., Canada 102 C2 48 38N 88 21W
Black Birch L., Canada 105 B7 56 53N 107 45W
Black Diamond, Canada 104 C6 50 45N 114 14W
Black Duck →, Canada 102 A2 56 51N 89 2W
Black Forest = Schwarzwald, Germany 25 G4 48 30N 8 20 E
Black Forest, U.S.A. 112 F2 39 0N 104 43W
Black Hd., Ireland 15 C2 53 9N 9 16W
Black Hills, U.S.A. 112 D3 44 0N 103 45W
Black I., Canada 105 C9 51 12N 96 30W
Black L., Canada 105 B7 59 12N 105 15W
Black L., Mich., U.S.A. 108 C3 45 28N 84 16W
Black L., N.Y., U.S.A. 111 B9 44 31N 75 36W
Black Lake, Canada 105 B7 59 11N 105 20W
Black Mesa, U.S.A. 113 G3 36 58N 102 58W
Black Mt. = Mynydd Du, U.K. 13 F4 51 52N 3 50W
Black Mts., U.K. 13 F4 51 55N 3 7W
Black Range, U.S.A. 115 K10 33 15N 107 50W
Black River, Jamaica 120 C4 18 0N 77 50W
Black River Falls, U.S.A. 112 C9 44 18N 90 51W
Black Sea, Eurasia 6 G12 43 30N 35 0 E
Black Tickle, Canada 103 B8 53 28N 55 45W
Black Volta →, Africa 82 D4 8 41N 1 33W
Black Warrior →, U.S.A. 109 J2 32 32N 87 51W
Blackall, Australia 94 C4 24 25 S 145 45 E
Blackball, N.Z. 91 K3 42 22 S 171 26 E
Blackbull, Australia 94 B3 17 55 S 141 45 E
Blackburn, U.K. 12 D5 53 45N 2 29W
Blackburn with Darwen □, U.K. 12 D5 53 45N 2 29W
Blackfoot, U.S.A. 114 E7 43 11N 112 21W
Blackfoot →, U.S.A. 114 C7 46 52N 113 53W
Blackfoot River Reservoir, U.S.A. 114 E8 43 0N 111 43W
Blackie, Canada 104 C6 50 36N 113 37W
Blackpool, U.K. 12 D4 53 49N 3 3W
Blackpool □, U.K. 12 D4 53 49N 3 3W
Blackriver, U.S.A. 110 B1 44 46N 83 17W
Blacks Harbour, Canada 103 C6 45 3N 66 49W
Blacksburg, U.S.A. 108 G5 37 14N 80 25W
Blacksod B., Ireland 15 B1 54 6N 10 0W
Blackstone, U.S.A. 108 G7 37 4N 78 0W
Blackstone Ra., Australia 93 E4 26 0 S 128 30 E
Blackwater, Australia 94 C4 23 35 S 148 53 E
Blackwater →, Meath, Ireland 15 C4 53 39N 6 41W
Blackwater →, Waterford, Ireland 15 D4 52 4N 7 52W
Blackwater →, U.K. 15 B5 54 31N 6 35W
Blackwell, U.S.A. 113 G6 36 48N 97 17W
Blackwells Corner, U.S.A. 117 K7 35 37N 119 47W
Blaenau Ffestiniog, U.K. 12 E4 53 0N 3 56W
Blaenau Gwent □, U.K. 13 F4 51 48N 3 12W
Blagaj, Bos.-H. 40 C1 43 16N 17 55 E
Blagnac, France 20 E5 43 37N 1 23 E
Blagodarnoye = Blagodarnyy, Russia 49 H6 45 7N 43 37 E
Blagodarnyy, Russia 49 H6 45 7N 43 37 E
Blagoevgrad, Bulgaria 40 D7 42 2N 23 5 E
Blagoveshchensk, Russia 51 D13 50 20N 127 30 E
Blain, France 18 E5 47 29N 1 45W
Blain, U.S.A. 110 F7 40 20N 77 31W
Blaine, Minn., U.S.A. 112 C8 45 10N 93 13W
Blaine, Wash., U.S.A. 116 B4 48 59N 122 45W
Blaine Lake, Canada 105 C7 52 51N 106 52W
Blair, U.S.A. 112 E6 41 33N 96 8W
Blair Athol, Australia 94 C4 22 42 S 147 31 E
Blair Atholl, U.K. 14 E5 56 46N 3 50W
Blairgowrie, U.K. 14 E5 56 35N 3 21W
Blairsden, U.S.A. 116 F6 39 47N 120 37W
Blairsville, U.S.A. 110 F5 40 26N 79 16W
Blaj, Romania 43 D8 46 10N 23 57 E
Blake Pt., U.S.A. 112 A10 48 11N 88 25W
Blakely, Ga., U.S.A. 109 K3 31 23N 84 56W
Blakely, Pa., U.S.A. 111 E9 41 28N 75 37W
Blâmont, France 19 D13 48 35N 6 50 E
Blanc, C., Spain 37 B9 39 21N 2 51 E
Blanc, Mont, Alps 21 C10 45 48N 6 50 E
Blanc-Sablon, Canada 103 B8 51 24N 57 12W
Blanca, B., Argentina 122 G4 39 10 S 61 30W
Blanca Peak, U.S.A. 115 H11 37 35N 105 29W
Blanche, C., Australia 95 E1 33 1 S 134 9 E
Blanche, L., S. Austral., Australia 95 D2 29 15 S 139 40 E
Blanche, L., W. Austral., Australia 92 D3 22 25 S 123 17 E
Blanco, S. Africa 88 E3 33 55 S 22 23 E
Blanco, U.S.A. 113 K5 30 6N 98 25W
Blanco →, Argentina 126 C2 30 20 S 68 42W
Blanco, C., Costa Rica 120 E2 9 34N 85 8W
Blanco, C., U.S.A. 114 E1 42 51N 124 34W
Blanda →, Iceland 8 D3 65 37N 20 9W
Blandford Forum, U.K. 13 G5 50 51N 2 9W
Blanding, U.S.A. 115 H9 37 37N 109 29W
Blanes, Spain 32 D7 41 40N 2 48 E
Blangy-sur-Bresle, France 19 C8 49 55N 1 37 E
Blanice →, Czech Rep. 26 B7 49 10N 14 5 E
Blankaholm, Sweden 11 G10 57 36N 16 31 E
Blankenberge, Belgium 17 C3 51 20N 3 9 E
Blankenburg, Germany 24 D6 51 47N 10 57 E
Blanquefort, France 20 D3 44 55N 0 38W
Blanquilla, I., Venezuela 121 D7 11 51N 64 37W
Blanquillo, Uruguay 127 C4 32 53 S 55 37W
Blansko, Czech Rep. 27 B9 49 22N 16 40 E
Blantyre, Malawi 87 F4 15 45 S 35 0 E
Blarney, Ireland 15 E3 51 56N 8 33W
Blasdell, U.S.A. 110 D6 42 48N 78 50W
Błaszki, Poland 45 G5 51 38N 18 30 E
Blatná, Czech Rep. 26 B6 49 25N 13 52 E
Blato, Croatia 29 F13 42 56N 16 48 E
Blaubeuren, Germany 25 G5 48 24N 9 46 E
Blaustein, Germany 25 G5 48 25N 9 53 E
Blåvands Huk, Denmark 11 J2 55 33N 8 4 E
Blaydon, U.K. 12 C6 54 58N 1 42W
Blaye, France 20 C3 45 8N 0 40W
Blaye-les-Mines, France 20 D6 44 1N 2 8 E
Blayney, Australia 95 E4 33 32 S 149 14 E
Blaze, Pt., Australia 92 B5 12 56 S 130 11 E
Błażowa, Poland 45 J9 49 53N 22 7 E
Bleckede, Germany 24 B6 53 17N 10 43 E
Bled, Slovenia 29 B11 46 27N 14 7 E
Bleiburg, Austria 26 E7 46 35N 14 49 E
Blejeşti, Romania 43 F10 44 19N 25 27 E
Blekinge, Sweden 9 H16 56 25N 15 20 E
Blekinge län □, Sweden 11 H9 56 20N 15 20 E
Blenheim, Canada 110 D3 42 20N 82 0W
Blenheim, N.Z. 91 J4 41 38 S 173 57 E
Bléone →, France 21 D10 44 5N 6 0 E
Blérancourt, France 19 C10 49 31N 3 9 E
Bletchley, U.K. 13 F7 51 59N 0 44W
Blida, Algeria 78 A6 36 30N 2 49 E
Blidö, Sweden 10 E12 59 37N 18 53 E
Blidsberg, Sweden 11 G7 57 56N 13 30 E
Blieskastel, Germany 25 F3 49 14N 7 12 E
Bligh Sound, N.Z. 91 L1 44 47 S 167 32 E
Blind River, Canada 102 C3 46 10N 82 58W
Blinisht, Albania 40 E3 41 52N 19 59 E
Blinishti = Blinisht, Albania 40 E3 41 52N 19 59 E
Bliss, Idaho, U.S.A. 114 E6 42 56N 114 57W
Bliss, N.Y., U.S.A. 110 D6 42 34N 78 15W
Blissfield, U.S.A. 110 F3 40 24N 81 58W
Blitar, Indonesia 63 H15 8 5 S 112 11 E
Blitta, Togo 83 D5 8 23N 1 6 E
Block I., U.S.A. 111 E13 41 11N 71 35W
Block Island Sd., U.S.A. 111 E13 41 15N 71 40W
Blodgett Iceberg Tongue, Antarctica 5 C9 66 8 S 130 35 E
Bloemfontein, S. Africa 88 D4 29 6 S 26 7 E
Bloemhof, S. Africa 88 D4 27 38 S 25 32 E
Blois, France 18 E8 47 35N 1 20 E
Blomskog, Sweden 10 E6 59 16N 12 2 E
Blomstermåla, Sweden 11 H10 56 59N 16 21 E
Blönduós, Iceland 8 D3 65 40N 20 12W
Błonie, Poland 45 F7 52 12N 20 37 E
Bloodvein →, Canada 105 C9 51 47N 96 43W
Bloody Foreland, Ireland 15 A3 55 10N 8 17W
Bloomer, U.S.A. 112 C9 45 6N 91 29W
Bloomfield, Canada 110 C7 43 59N 77 14W
Bloomfield, Iowa, U.S.A. 112 E8 40 45N 92 25W
Bloomfield, N. Mex., U.S.A. 115 H10 36 43N 107 59W
Bloomfield, Nebr., U.S.A. 112 D6 42 36N 97 39W
Bloomington, Ill., U.S.A. 112 E10 40 28N 89 0W
Bloomington, Ind., U.S.A. 108 F2 39 10N 86 32W
Bloomington, Minn., U.S.A. 112 C8 44 50N 93 17W
Bloomsburg, U.S.A. 111 F8 41 0N 76 27W
Blora, Indonesia 63 G14 6 57 S 111 25 E
Blossburg, U.S.A. 110 E7 41 41N 77 4W
Blouberg, S. Africa 89 C4 23 8 S 28 59 E
Blountstown, U.S.A. 109 K3 30 27N 85 3W
Bludenz, Austria 26 D2 47 10N 9 50 E
Blue Earth, U.S.A. 112 D8 43 38N 94 6W
Blue Mesa Reservoir, U.S.A. 115 G10 38 28N 107 20W
Blue Mountain Lake, U.S.A. 111 C10 43 52N 74 30W
Blue Mts., Maine, U.S.A. 111 B14 44 50N 70 35W
Blue Mts., Oreg., U.S.A. 114 D4 45 15N 119 0W
Blue Mts., Pa., U.S.A. 111 F8 40 30N 76 30W
Blue Mud B., Australia 94 A2 13 30 S 136 0 E
Blue Nile = Nîl el Azraq →, Sudan 81 D3 15 38N 32 31 E
Blue Rapids, U.S.A. 112 F6 39 41N 96 39W
Blue Ridge Mts., U.S.A. 109 G5 36 30N 80 15W
Blue River, Canada 104 C5 52 6N 119 18W
Bluefield, U.S.A. 108 G5 37 15N 81 17W
Bluefields, Nic. 120 D3 12 20N 83 50W
Bluff, Australia 94 C4 23 35 S 149 4 E
Bluff, N.Z. 91 M2 46 37 S 168 20 E
Bluff, U.S.A. 115 H9 37 17N 109 33W
Bluff Knoll, Australia 93 F2 34 24 S 118 15 E
Bluff Pt., Australia 93 E1 27 50 S 114 5 E
Bluffton, U.S.A. 108 E3 40 44N 85 11W
Blumenau, Brazil 127 B6 27 0 S 49 0W
Blunt, U.S.A. 112 C5 44 31N 99 59W
Bly, U.S.A. 114 E3 42 24N 121 3W
Blyth, Canada 110 C3 43 44N 81 26W
Blyth, U.K. 12 B6 55 8N 1 31W
Blythe, U.S.A. 117 M12 33 37N 114 36W
Blytheville, U.S.A. 113 H10 35 56N 89 55W
Bo, S. Leone 82 D2 7 55N 11 50W
Bo Duc, Vietnam 65 G6 11 58N 106 50 E
Bo Hai, China 57 E10 39 0N 119 0 E
Bo Xian = Bozhou, China 56 H8 33 55N 115 41 E
Boa Vista, Brazil 124 C6 2 48N 60 30W
Boac, Phil. 61 E4 13 27N 121 50 E
Boaco, Nic. 120 D2 12 29N 85 35W
Bo'ai, China 56 G7 35 10N 113 3 E
Boal, Spain 34 B4 43 25N 6 49W
Boalsburg, U.S.A. 110 F7 40 46N 77 47W
Boane, Mozam. 89 D5 26 6 S 32 19 E
Boardman, U.S.A. 110 E4 41 2N 80 40W
Bobadah, Australia 95 E4 32 19 S 146 41 E
Bobai, China 58 F7 22 17N 109 59 E
Bobbili, India 67 K13 18 35N 83 30 E
Bóbbio, Italy 28 D6 44 46N 9 23 E
Bobcaygeon, Canada 102 D4 44 33N 78 33W
Böblingen, Germany 25 G5 48 40N 9 1 E
Bobo-Dioulasso, Burkina Faso 82 C4 11 8N 4 13W
Bobolice, Poland 44 E3 53 58N 16 37 E
Boboshevo, Bulgaria 40 D7 42 9N 23 0 E
Bobov Dol, Bulgaria 40 D6 42 20N 23 0 E
Bóbr →, Poland 45 F2 52 4N 15 4 E
Bobraomby, Tanjon' i, Madag. 89 A8 12 40 S 49 10 E
Bobrinets, Ukraine 47 H7 48 4N 32 5 E
Bobrov, Russia 48 E5 51 5N 40 2 E
Bobrovitsa, Ukraine 47 G6 50 45N 31 23 E
Bobruysk = Babruysk, Belarus 47 F5 53 10N 29 15 E
Boby, Pic, Madag. 85 J9 22 12 S 46 55 E
Bôca do Acre, Brazil 124 E5 8 50 S 67 27W
Boca Raton, U.S.A. 109 M5 26 21N 80 5W
Bocanda, Ivory C. 82 D4 7 5N 4 31W
Bocas del Toro, Panama 120 E3 9 15N 82 20W
Boceguillas, Spain 34 D7 41 20N 3 39W
Bochnia, Poland 45 J7 49 58N 20 27 E
Bocholt, Germany 24 D2 51 50N 6 36 E
Bochum, Germany 24 D3 51 28N 7 13 E
Bockenem, Germany 24 C6 52 1N 10 8 E
Boćki, Poland 45 F10 52 39N 23 3 E
Bocognano, France 21 F13 42 5N 9 4 E
Bocoyna, Mexico 118 B3 27 52N 107 35W
Bocşa, Romania 42 E6 45 21N 21 47 E
Boda, Dalarnas, Sweden 10 C9 61 1N 15 13 E
Böda, Kalmar, Sweden 11 G11 57 15N 17 3 E
Boda, Västernorrland, Sweden 10 B10 62 52N 16 39 E
Bodafors, Sweden 11 G8 57 48N 14 23 E
Bodaybo, Russia 51 D12 57 50N 114 0 E
Boddam, U.K. 14 B7 59 56N 1 17W
Boddington, Australia 93 F2 32 50 S 116 30 E
Bode Sadu, Nigeria 83 D5 9 0N 4 47 E
Bodega Bay, U.S.A. 116 G3 38 20N 123 3W
Boden, Sweden 8 D19 65 50N 21 42 E
Bodensee, Europe 25 H5 47 35N 9 25 E
Bodenteich, Germany 24 C6 52 50N 10 42 E
Bodhan, India 66 K10 18 40N 77 44 E
Bodinga, Nigeria 83 C6 12 58N 5 10 E
Bodmin, U.K. 13 G3 50 28N 4 43W
Bodmin Moor, U.K. 13 G3 50 33N 4 36W
Bodø, Norway 8 C16 67 17N 14 24 E
Bodrog →, Hungary 42 B6 48 11N 21 22 E
Bodrum, Turkey 39 D9 37 3N 27 30 E
Bódva →, Hungary 42 B5 48 19N 20 45 E
Boën, France 21 C8 45 44N 4 1 E
Boende, Dem. Rep. of the Congo 84 E4 0 24 S 21 12 E
Boerne, U.S.A. 113 L5 29 47N 98 44W
Boesmans →, S. Africa 88 E4 33 42 S 26 39 E
Boffa, Guinea 82 C2 10 16N 14 3W
Bogalusa, U.S.A. 113 K10 30 47N 89 52W
Bogan →, Australia 95 D4 29 59 S 146 17 E
Bogan Gate, Australia 95 E4 33 7 S 147 49 E
Bogandé, Burkina Faso 83 C4 13 2N 0 8W
Bogantungan, Australia 94 C4 23 41 S 147 17 E
Bogata, U.S.A. 113 J7 33 28N 95 13W
Bogatić, Serbia, Yug. 40 B3 44 51N 19 30 E
Boğazkale, Turkey 72 B6 40 2N 34 37 E
Boğazlıyan, Turkey 72 C6 39 11N 35 14 E
Bogen, Sweden 10 D6 60 4N 12 33 E
Bogense, Denmark 11 J4 55 34N 10 5 E
Bogetići, Montenegro, Yug. 40 D2 42 41N 18 58 E
Boggabilla, Australia 95 D5 28 36 S 150 24 E
Boggabri, Australia 95 E5 30 45 S 150 5 E
Boggeragh Mts., Ireland 15 D3 52 2N 8 55W
Boglan = Solhan, Turkey 70 B4 38 57N 41 3 E
Bognor Regis, U.K. 13 G7 50 47N 0 40W
Bogo, Phil. 61 F6 11 3N 124 0 E
Bogodukhov = Bohodukhiv, Ukraine 47 G8 50 9N 35 33 E
Bogol Manya, Ethiopia 81 G5 4 34N 41 29 E
Bogong, Mt., Australia 95 F4 36 47 S 147 17 E
Bogor, Indonesia 63 G12 6 36 S 106 48 E
Bogoroditsk, Russia 46 F10 53 47N 38 8 E
Bogorodsk, Russia 48 B6 56 4N 43 30 E
Bogoso, Ghana 82 D4 5 38N 2 3W
Bogotá, Colombia 124 C4 4 34N 74 0W
Bogotol, Russia 50 D9 56 15N 89 50 E
Bogou, Togo 83 C5 10 40N 0 12 E
Bogra, Bangla. 67 G16 24 51N 89 22 E
Boguchany, Russia 51 D10 58 40N 97 30 E
Boguchar, Russia 48 F5 49 55N 40 32 E
Bogué, Mauritania 82 B2 16 45N 14 10W
Boguslav, Ukraine 47 H6 49 33N 30 56 E
Boguszów-Gorce, Poland 45 H3 50 45N 16 12 E
Bohain-en-Vermandois, France 19 C10 49 59N 3 28 E
Bohemian Forest = Böhmerwald, Germany 25 F9 49 8N 13 14 E
Bohinjska Bistrica, Slovenia 29 B11 46 17N 14 1 E
Böhmerwald, Germany 25 F9 49 8N 13 14 E
Bohmte, Germany 24 C4 52 22N 8 19 E
Bohodukhiv, Ukraine 47 G8 50 9N 35 33 E
Bohol □, Phil. 61 G6 9 50N 124 10 E
Bohol Sea, Phil. 63 C6 9 0N 124 0 E
Bohongou, Burkina Faso 83 C5 12 30N 0 40 E
Böhönye, Hungary 42 D2 46 25N 17 28 E
Bohuslän, Sweden 11 F5 58 25N 12 0 E
Boi, Nigeria 83 D6 9 35N 9 27 E
Boi, Pta. de, Brazil 127 A6 23 55 S 45 15W
Boiaçu, Brazil 124 D6 0 27 S 61 46W
Boileau, C., Australia 92 C3 17 40 S 122 7 E
Boing'o, Sudan 81 F3 9 58N 33 44 E
Boiro, Spain 34 C2 42 39N 8 54W
Boise, U.S.A. 114 E5 43 37N 116 13W
Boise City, U.S.A. 113 G3 36 44N 102 31W
Boissevain, Canada 105 D8 49 15N 100 5W
Bóite →, Italy 29 B9 46 5N 12 5 E
Boitzenburg, Germany 24 B9 53 16N 13 35 E
Boizenburg, Germany 24 B6 53 23N 10 43 E
Bojador C., W. Sahara 78 C3 26 0N 14 30W
Bojana →, Albania 40 E3 41 52N 19 22 E
Bojano, Italy 31 A7 41 29N 14 29 E
Bojanowo, Poland 45 G3 51 43N 16 42 E
Bøjden, Denmark 11 J4 55 6N 10 7 E
Bojnūrd, Iran 71 B8 37 30N 57 20 E
Bojonegoro, Indonesia 63 G14 7 11 S 111 54 E
Boju, Nigeria 83 D6 7 22N 7 55 E
Boka, Serbia, Yug. 42 E5 45 22N 20 52 E
Boka Kotorska, Montenegro, Yug. 40 D2 42 23N 18 32 E
Bokala, Ivory C. 82 D4 8 31N 4 33W
Bokani, Nigeria 83 D6 9 28N 5 10 E
Bokaro, India 69 H11 23 46N 85 55 E
Boké, Guinea 82 C2 10 56N 14 17W
Bokhara →, Australia 95 D4 29 55 S 146 42 E
Bokkos, Nigeria 83 D6 9 17N 9 1 E
Boknafjorden, Norway 9 G11 59 14N 5 40 E
Bokoro, Chad 79 F9 12 25N 17 14 E
Bokpyin, Burma 65 G2 11 18N 98 42 E
Boksitogorsk, Russia 46 C7 59 32N 33 50 E
Bol, Croatia 29 E13 43 18N 16 38 E
Bolama, Guinea-Biss. 82 C1 11 30N 15 30W
Bolan →, Pakistan 68 E2 28 38N 67 42 E
Bolan Pass, Pakistan 66 E5 29 50N 67 20 E
Bolaños →, Mexico 118 C4 21 14N 104 8W
Bolaños de Calatrava, Spain 35 G7 38 54N 3 40W
Bolayır, Turkey 41 F10 40 31N 26 45 E
Bolbec, France 18 C7 49 30N 0 30 E
Boldājī, Iran 71 D6 31 56N 51 3 E
Boldeşti-Scăeni, Romania 43 E11 45 3N 26 2 E
Bole, China 60 B3 45 11N 81 37 E
Bole, Ethiopia 81 F4 6 36N 37 20 E
Bole, Ghana 82 D4 9 3N 2 23W
Bolekhiv, Ukraine 47 H2 49 0N 23 57 E
Bolesławiec, Poland 45 G2 51 17N 15 37 E
Bolgatanga, Ghana 83 C4 10 44N 0 53W
Bolgrad = Bolhrad, Ukraine 47 K5 45 40N 28 32 E
Bolhrad, Ukraine 47 K5 45 40N 28 32 E
Bolinao, Phil. 61 C3 16 23N 119 54 E
Bolintin-Vale, Romania 43 F10 44 27N 25 46 E
Bolívar, Argentina 126 D3 36 15 S 60 53W
Bolivar, Mo., U.S.A. 113 G8 37 37N 93 25W
Bolivar, N.Y., U.S.A. 110 D6 42 4N 78 10W
Bolivar, Tenn., U.S.A. 113 H10 35 12N 89 0W
Bolivia ■, S. Amer. 124 G6 17 6 S 64 0W
Bolivian Plateau, S. Amer. 122 E4 20 0 S 67 30W
Boljevac, Serbia, Yug. 40 C5 43 51N 21 58 E
Bolkhov, Russia 46 F9 53 25N 36 0 E
Bolków, Poland 45 H3 50 55N 16 6 E
Bollebygd, Sweden 11 G6 57 40N 12 35 E
Bollène, France 21 D8 44 18N 4 45 E
Bollnäs, Sweden 10 C10 61 21N 16 24 E
Bollon, Australia 95 D4 28 2 S 147 29 E
Bollstabruk, Sweden 10 B11 62 59N 17 40 E
Bolmen, Sweden 11 H7 56 55N 13 40 E
Bolobo, Dem. Rep. of the Congo 84 E3 2 6 S 16 20 E
Bologna, Italy 29 D8 44 29N 11 20 E

Bologoye, Russia 46 D8 57 55N 34 5 E
Bolonchenticul, Mexico 119 D7 20 0N 89 49W
Bolótana, Italy 30 B1 40 20N 8 52 E
Boloven, Cao Nguyen, Laos 64 E6 15 10N 106 30 E
Bolpur, India 69 H12 23 40N 87 45 E
Bolsena, Italy 29 F8 42 39N 11 59 E
Bolsena, L. di, Italy 29 F8 42 36N 11 56 E
Bolshaya Chernigovka, Russia 48 D10 52 6N 50 52 E
Bolshaya Glushitsa, Russia 48 D10 52 28N 50 30 E
Bolshaya Martynovka, Russia 49 G5 47 19N 41 37 E
Bolshaya Vradiyevka, Ukraine 47 J6 47 50N 30 40 E
Bolshevik, Ostrov, Russia 51 B11 78 30N 102 0 E
Bolshoi Kavkas = Caucasus Mountains, Eurasia 49 J7 42 50N 44 0 E
Bolshoy Anyuy →, Russia 51 C17 68 30N 160 49 E
Bolshoy Begichev, Ostrov, Russia 51 B12 74 20N 112 30 E
Bolshoy Lyakhovskiy, Ostrov, Russia 51 B15 73 35N 142 0 E
Bolshoy Tokmak = Tokmak, Ukraine 47 J8 47 16N 35 42 E
Bolshoy Tyuters, Ostrov, Russia 9 G22 59 51N 27 13 E
Bolsward, Neths. 17 A5 53 3N 5 32 E
Bolt Head, U.K. 13 G4 50 12N 3 48W
Boltaña, Spain 32 C5 42 28N 0 4 E
Boltigen, Switz. 25 J3 46 38N 7 24 E
Bolton, Canada 110 C5 43 54N 79 45W
Bolton, U.K. 12 D5 53 35N 2 26W
Bolton Landing, U.S.A. 111 C11 43 32N 73 35W
Bolu, Turkey 72 B4 40 45N 31 35 E
Bolungavík, Iceland 8 C2 66 9N 23 15W
Boluo, China 59 F10 23 3N 114 21 E
Bolvadin, Turkey 70 B1 38 45N 31 4 E
Bolzano, Italy 29 B8 46 31N 11 22 E
Bom Jesus da Lapa, Brazil 125 F10 13 15 S 43 25W
Boma, Dem. Rep. of the Congo 84 F2 5 50 S 13 4 E
Bombala, Australia 95 F4 36 56 S 149 15 E
Bombarral, Portugal 35 F1 39 15N 9 9W
Bombay = Mumbai, India 66 K8 18 55N 72 50 E
Bomboma, Dem. Rep. of the Congo 84 D3 2 25N 18 55 E
Bombombwa, Dem. Rep. of the Congo 86 B2 1 40N 25 40 E
Bomi Hills, Liberia 82 D2 7 1N 10 38W
Bomili, Dem. Rep. of the Congo 86 B2 1 45N 27 5 E
Bømlo, Norway 9 G11 59 37N 5 13 E
Bomokandi →, Dem. Rep. of the Congo 86 B2 3 39N 26 8 E
Bomu →, C.A.R. 84 D4 4 40N 22 30 E
Bon, C., Tunisia 76 C5 37 1N 11 2 E
Bon Sar Pa, Vietnam 64 F6 12 24N 107 35 E
Bonaigarh, India 69 J11 21 50N 84 57 E
Bonaire, Neth. Ant. 121 D6 12 10N 68 15W
Bonang, Australia 95 F4 37 11 S 148 41 E
Bonanza, Nic. 120 D3 13 54N 84 35W
Bonaparte Arch., Australia 92 B3 14 0 S 124 30 E
Boñar, Spain 34 C5 42 52N 5 19W
Bonaventure, Canada 103 C6 48 5N 65 32W
Bonavista, Canada 103 C9 48 40N 53 5W
Bonavista, C., Canada 103 C9 48 42N 53 5W
Bonavista B., Canada 103 C9 48 45N 53 25W
Bondeno, Italy 29 D8 44 53N 11 25 E
Bondo, Dem. Rep. of the Congo 86 B1 3 55N 23 53 E
Bondoukou, Ivory C. 82 D4 8 2N 2 47W
Bondowoso, Indonesia 63 G15 7 55 S 113 49 E
Bone, Teluk, Indonesia 63 E6 4 10 S 120 50 E
Bonerate, Indonesia 63 F6 7 25 S 121 5 E
Bonerate, Kepulauan, Indonesia 63 F6 6 30 S 121 10 E
Bo'ness, U.K. 14 E5 56 1N 3 37W
Bonete, Cerro, Argentina 126 B2 27 55 S 68 40W
Bong Son = Hoai Nhon, Vietnam 64 E7 14 28N 109 1 E
Bonga, Ethiopia 81 F4 7 15N 36 14 E
Bongabong, Phil. 61 E4 12 45N 121 29 E
Bongor, Chad 79 F9 10 35N 15 20 E
Bongouanou, Ivory C. 82 D4 6 42N 4 15W
Bonham, U.S.A. 113 J6 33 35N 96 11W
Boni, Mali 82 B4 15 3N 2 10W
Bonifacio, France 21 G13 41 24N 9 10 E
Bonifacio, Bouches de, Medit. S. 30 A2 41 12N 9 15 E
Bonin Is. = Ogasawara Gunto, Pac. Oc. 52 G18 27 0N 142 0 E
Bonke, Ethiopia 81 F4 6 5N 37 16 E
Bonkoukou, Niger 83 C5 14 0N 3 15 E
Bonn, Germany 24 E3 50 46N 7 6 E
Bonnat, France 19 F8 46 20N 1 54 E
Bonne Terre, U.S.A. 113 G9 37 55N 90 33W
Bonners Ferry, U.S.A. 114 B5 48 42N 116 19W
Bonnétable, France 18 D7 48 11N 0 25 E
Bonneval, Eure-et-Loir, France 18 D8 48 11N 1 24 E
Bonneval, Savoie, France 21 C11 45 22N 7 3 E
Bonneville, France 19 F13 46 4N 6 24 E
Bonney, L., Australia 95 F3 37 50 S 140 20 E
Bonnie Rock, Australia 93 F2 30 29 S 118 22 E
Bonny, Nigeria 83 E6 4 25N 7 13 E
Bonny →, Nigeria 83 E6 4 20N 7 10 E
Bonny, Bight of, Africa 83 E6 3 30N 9 20 E
Bonny-sur-Loire, France 19 E9 47 33N 2 50 E
Bonnyrigg, U.K. 14 F5 55 53N 3 6W
Bonnyville, Canada 105 C6 54 20N 110 45W
Bono, Italy 30 B2 40 25N 9 2 E
Bonoi, Indonesia 63 E9 1 45 S 137 41 E
Bonorva, Italy 30 B1 40 25N 8 46 E
Bonsall, U.S.A. 117 M9 33 16N 117 14W
Bontang, Indonesia 62 D5 0 10N 117 30 E
Bonthe, S. Leone 82 D2 7 30N 12 33W
Bontoc, Phil. 61 C4 17 7N 120 58 E
Bonyeri, Ghana 82 D4 5 1N 2 46W
Bonyhád, Hungary 42 D3 46 18N 18 32 E
Bonython Ra., Australia 92 D4 23 40 S 128 45 E
Bookabie, Australia 93 F5 31 50 S 132 41 E
Booker, U.S.A. 113 G4 36 27N 100 32W
Boola, Guinea 82 D3 8 22N 8 41 E
Booligal, Australia 95 E3 33 58 S 144 53 E
Boonah, Australia 95 D5 27 58 S 152 41 E
Boone, Iowa, U.S.A. 112 D8 42 4N 93 53W
Boone, N.C., U.S.A. 109 G5 36 13N 81 41W
Booneville, Ark., U.S.A. 113 H8 35 8N 93 55W
Booneville, Miss., U.S.A. 109 H1 34 39N 88 34W
Boonville, Calif., U.S.A. 116 F3 39 1N 123 22W
Boonville, Ind., U.S.A. 108 F2 38 3N 87 16W
Boonville, Mo., U.S.A. 112 F8 38 58N 92 44W
Boonville, N.Y., U.S.A. 111 C9 43 29N 75 20W
Boorindal, Australia 95 E4 30 22 S 146 11 E
Boorowa, Australia 95 E4 34 28 S 148 44 E
Boothia, Gulf of, Canada 101 A11 71 0N 90 0W
Boothia Pen., Canada 100 A10 71 0N 94 0W
Bootle, U.K. 12 D4 53 28N 3 1W
Booué, Gabon 84 E2 0 5 S 11 55 E
Boppard, Germany 25 E3 50 13N 7 36 E
Boquete, Panama 120 E3 8 46N 82 27W
Boquilla, Presa de la, Mexico 118 B3 27 40N 105 30W
Boquillas del Carmen, Mexico 118 B4 29 17N 102 53W
Bor, Czech Rep. 26 B5 49 41N 12 45 E
Bor, Russia 48 B7 56 28N 43 59 E
Bor, Serbia, Yug. 40 B6 44 5N 22 7 E
Bôr, Sudan 81 F3 6 10N 31 40 E
Bor, Sweden 11 G8 57 9N 14 10 E
Bor, Turkey 72 D6 37 54N 34 32 E
Bor Mashash, Israel 75 D3 31 7N 34 50 E
Borah Peak, U.S.A. 114 D7 44 8N 113 47W
Borang, Sudan 81 G3 4 50N 30 59 E
Borås, Sweden 11 G6 57 43N 12 56 E
Borāzjān, Iran 71 D6 29 22N 51 10 E
Borba, Brazil 124 D7 4 12 S 59 34W
Borba, Portugal 35 G3 38 50N 7 26W
Borborema, Planalto da, Brazil 122 D7 7 0 S 37 0W
Borcea, Romania 43 F12 44 20N 27 45 E
Borçka, Turkey 73 B9 41 25N 41 41 E
Bord Khūn-e Now, Iran 71 D6 28 3N 51 28 E
Borda, C., Australia 95 F2 35 45 S 136 34 E
Bordeaux, France 20 D3 44 50N 0 36W
Borden, Australia 93 F2 34 3 S 118 12 E
Borden, Canada 103 C7 46 18N 63 47W
Borden I., Canada 4 B2 78 30N 111 30W
Borden Pen., Canada 101 A11 73 0N 83 0W
Borders = Scottish Borders □, U.K. 14 F6 55 35N 2 50W
Bordertown, Australia 95 F3 36 19 S 140 45 E
Borðeyri, Iceland 8 D3 65 12N 21 6W
Bordighera, Italy 28 E4 43 46N 7 39 E
Bordj Fly Ste. Marie, Algeria 78 C5 27 19N 2 32W
Bordj-in-Eker, Algeria 78 D7 24 9N 5 3 E
Bordj Omar Driss, Algeria 78 C7 28 10N 6 40 E
Bore, Ethiopia 81 G4 4 39N 37 39 E
Borehamwood, U.K. 13 F7 51 40N 0 15W
Borek Wielkopolski, Poland 45 G4 51 54N 17 11 E
Borensberg, Sweden 11 F9 58 34N 15 17 E
Borgå = Porvoo, Finland 9 F21 60 24N 25 40 E
Borgarfjörður, Iceland 8 D7 65 31N 13 49W
Borgarnes, Iceland 8 D3 64 32N 21 55W
Børgefjellet, Norway 8 D15 65 20N 13 45 E
Borger, Neths. 17 B6 52 54N 6 44 E
Borger, U.S.A. 113 H4 35 39N 101 24W
Borgholm, Sweden 11 H10 56 52N 16 39 E
Bórgia, Italy 31 D9 38 49N 16 30 E
Borgo San Dalmazzo, Italy 28 D4 44 20N 7 30 E
Borgo San Lorenzo, Italy 29 E8 43 57N 11 23 E
Borgo Val di Taro, Italy 28 D6 44 29N 9 46 E
Borgo Valsugana, Italy 29 B8 46 3N 11 27 E
Borgomanero, Italy 28 C5 45 42N 8 28 E
Borgorose, Italy 29 F10 42 11N 13 13 E
Borgosésia, Italy 28 C5 45 43N 8 16 E
Borhoyn Tal, Mongolia 56 C6 43 50N 111 58 E
Bori, Nigeria 83 E6 4 42N 7 21 E
Borikhane, Laos 64 C4 18 33N 103 43 E
Borisoglebsk, Russia 48 E6 51 27N 42 5 E
Borisov = Barysaw, Belarus 46 E5 54 17N 28 28 E
Borisovka, Russia 47 G9 50 36N 36 1 E
Borja, Peru 124 D3 4 20 S 77 40W
Borja, Spain 32 D3 41 48N 1 34W
Borjas Blancas = Les Borges Blanques, Spain 32 D5 41 31N 0 52 E
Borjomi, Georgia 49 K6 41 48N 43 28 E
Børkop, Denmark 11 J3 55 39N 9 39 E
Borkou, Chad 79 E9 18 15N 18 50 E
Borkum, Germany 24 B2 53 34N 6 40 E
Borlänge, Sweden 10 D9 60 29N 15 26 E
Borley, C., Antarctica 5 C5 66 15 S 52 30 E
Borlu, Turkey 39 C10 38 44N 28 27 E
Bormida →, Italy 28 D5 44 23N 8 13 E
Bórmio, Italy 28 B7 46 28N 10 22 E
Borna, Germany 24 D8 51 7N 12 29 E
Borne Sulinowo, Poland 44 E3 53 32N 16 36 E
Borneo, E. Indies 62 D5 1 0N 115 0 E
Bornholm, Denmark 11 J8 55 10N 15 0 E
Bornholms Amtskommune □, Denmark 11 J8 55 5N 15 0 E
Bornholmsgattet, Europe 11 J8 55 15N 14 20 E
Borno □, Nigeria 83 C7 11 30N 13 0 E
Bornos, Spain 35 J5 36 48N 5 42W
Bornova, Turkey 39 C9 38 27N 27 14 E
Bornu Yassa, Nigeria 83 C7 12 14N 12 25 E
Boro →, Sudan 81 F2 8 52N 26 11 E
Borodino, Russia 46 E8 55 31N 35 40 E
Borogontsy, Russia 51 C14 62 42N 131 8 E
Boromo, Burkina Faso 82 C4 11 45N 2 58W
Boron, U.S.A. 117 L9 35 0N 117 39W
Borongan, Phil. 61 F6 11 37N 125 26 E
Borotangba Mts., C.A.R. 81 F2 6 30N 25 0 E
Borotou, Ivory C. 82 D3 8 46N 7 30W
Borovan, Bulgaria 40 C7 43 27N 23 45 E
Borovichi, Russia 46 C7 58 25N 33 55 E
Borovsk, Russia 46 E9 55 12N 36 24 E
Borrby, Sweden 11 J8 55 27N 14 10 E
Borrego Springs, U.S.A. 117 M10 33 15N 116 23W
Borriol, Spain 32 E4 40 4N 0 4W
Borroloola, Australia 94 B2 16 4 S 136 17 E
Borşa, Cluj, Romania 43 D8 46 56N 23 40 E
Borşa, Maramureş, Romania 43 C9 47 41N 24 50 E
Borsad, India 68 H5 22 25N 72 54 E
Borsec, Romania 43 D10 46 57N 25 34 E
Borsod-Abaúj-Zemplén □, Hungary 42 B6 48 20N 21 0 E
Bort-les-Orgues, France 20 C6 45 24N 2 29 E
Borth, U.K. 13 E3 52 29N 4 2W
Börtnan, Sweden 10 B7 62 45N 13 50 E
Borūjerd, Iran 71 C6 33 55N 48 50 E
Boryslav, Ukraine 47 H2 49 18N 23 28 E
Boryspil, Ukraine 47 G6 50 21N 30 59 E
Borzhomi = Borjomi, Georgia 49 K6 41 48N 43 28 E
Borzna, Ukraine 47 G7 51 18N 32 26 E
Borzya, Russia 51 D12 50 24N 116 31 E
Bosa, Italy 30 B1 40 18N 8 30 E
Bosanska Dubica, Bos.-H. 29 C13 45 10N 16 50 E
Bosanska Gradiška, Bos.-H. 42 E2 45 10N 17 15 E
Bosanska Kostajnica, Bos.-H. 29 C13 45 11N 16 33 E
Bosanska Krupa, Bos.-H. 29 D13 44 53N 16 10 E
Bosanski Brod, Bos.-H. 42 E2 45 10N 18 0 E
Bosanski Novi, Bos.-H. 29 C13 45 2N 16 22 E
Bosanski Petrovac, Bos.-H. 29 D13 44 35N 16 21 E
Bosanski Šamac, Bos.-H. 42 E3 45 3N 18 29 E
Bosansko Grahovo, Bos.-H. 29 D13 44 12N 16 26 E
Bosaso, Somali Rep. 74 E4 11 12N 49 18 E
Boscastle, U.K. 13 G3 50 41N 4 42W
Bose, China 58 F6 23 53N 106 35 E
Boshan, China 57 F9 36 28N 117 49 E
Boshof, S. Africa 88 D4 28 31 S 25 13 E
Boshrūyeh, Iran 71 C8 33 50N 57 30 E
Bosilegrad, Serbia, Yug. 40 D6 42 30N 22 27 E
Boskovice, Czech Rep. 27 B9 49 29N 16 40 E
Bosna →, Bos.-H. 42 E3 45 4N 18 29 E
Bosna i Hercegovina = Bosnia-Herzegovina ■, Europe 42 G2 44 0N 18 0 E
Bosnia-Herzegovina ■, Europe 42 G2 44 0N 18 0 E
Bosnik, Indonesia 63 E9 1 5 S 136 10 E
Bosobolo, Dem. Rep. of the Congo 84 D3 4 15N 19 50 E
Bosporus = İstanbul Boğazı, Turkey 41 E13 41 10N 29 10 E
Bosque Farms, U.S.A. 115 J10 34 53N 106 40W
Bossangoa, C.A.R. 84 C3 6 35N 17 30 E
Bossé Bangou, Niger 83 C5 13 20N 1 18 E
Bossier City, U.S.A. 113 J8 32 31N 93 44W
Bosso, Niger 83 C7 13 43N 13 19 E
Bosso, Dallol →, Niger 83 C5 12 25N 2 50 E
Bostan, Pakistan 68 D2 30 26N 67 2 E
Bostānābād, Iran 70 B5 37 50N 46 50 E
Bosten Hu, China 60 B3 41 55N 87 40 E
Boston, U.K. 12 E7 52 59N 0 2W
Boston, U.S.A. 111 D13 42 22N 71 4W
Boston Bar, Canada 104 D4 49 52N 121 30W
Boston Mts., U.S.A. 113 H8 35 42N 93 15W
Bosut →, Croatia 42 E3 45 20N 18 45 E
Boswell, Canada 104 D5 49 28N 116 45W
Boswell, U.S.A. 110 F5 40 10N 79 2W
Botad, India 68 H4 22 15N 71 40 E
Botan →, Turkey 73 D10 37 57N 42 2 E
Botene, Laos 64 D3 17 35N 101 12 E
Botev, Bulgaria 41 D8 42 44N 24 52 E
Botevgrad, Bulgaria 40 D7 42 55N 23 47 E
Bothaville, S. Africa 88 D4 27 23 S 26 34 E
Bothnia, G. of, Europe 8 E19 63 0N 20 15 E
Bothwell, Australia 94 G4 42 20 S 147 1 E
Bothwell, Canada 110 D3 42 38N 81 52W
Boticas, Portugal 34 D3 41 41N 7 40W
Botletle →, Botswana 88 C3 20 10 S 23 15 E
Botlikh, Russia 49 J8 42 39N 46 11 E
Botna →, Moldova 43 D14 46 45N 29 34 E
Botoroaga, Romania 43 F10 44 8N 25 32 E
Botoşani, Romania 43 C11 47 42N 26 41 E
Botoşani □, Romania 43 C11 47 50N 26 50 E
Botou, Burkina Faso 83 C5 12 42N 1 59 E
Botricello, Italy 31 D9 38 56N 16 51 E
Botro, Ivory C. 82 D3 7 51N 5 19W
Botswana ■, Africa 88 C3 22 0 S 24 0 E
Bottineau, U.S.A. 112 A4 48 50N 100 27W
Bottnaryd, Sweden 11 G7 57 47N 13 50 E
Bottrop, Germany 17 C6 51 31N 6 58 E
Botucatu, Brazil 127 A6 22 55 S 48 30W
Botwood, Canada 103 C8 49 6N 55 23W
Bou Djébéha, Mali 82 B4 18 25N 2 45W
Bou Rjeïmât, Mauritania 82 B1 19 4N 15 3W
Bouaflé, Ivory C. 82 D3 7 1N 5 47W
Bouaké, Ivory C. 82 D3 7 40N 5 2W
Bouar, C.A.R. 84 C3 6 0N 15 40 E
Bouârfa, Morocco 78 B5 32 32N 1 58W
Boucaut B., Australia 94 A1 12 0 S 134 25 E
Bouches-du-Rhône □, France 21 E9 43 37N 5 2 E
Bougainville, C., Australia 92 B4 13 57 S 126 4 E
Bougainville I., Papua N. G. 96 H7 6 0 S 155 0 E
Bougainville Reef, Australia 94 B4 15 30 S 147 5 E
Bougie = Bejaia, Algeria 78 A7 36 42N 5 2 E
Bougouni, Mali 82 C3 11 30N 7 20W
Bouillon, Belgium 17 E5 49 44N 5 3 E
Boukombé, Benin 83 C5 10 13N 1 9 E
Boulal, Mali 82 B3 15 8N 8 21W
Boulazac, France 20 C4 45 10N 0 47 E
Boulder, Colo., U.S.A. 112 E2 40 1N 105 17W
Boulder, Mont., U.S.A. 114 C7 46 14N 112 7W
Boulder City, U.S.A. 117 K12 35 59N 114 50W
Boulder Creek, U.S.A. 116 H4 37 7N 122 7W
Boulder Dam = Hoover Dam, U.S.A. 117 K12 36 1N 114 44W
Bouli, Mauritania 82 B2 15 17N 12 18W
Boulia, Australia 94 C2 22 52 S 139 51 E
Bouligny, France 19 C12 49 17N 5 45 E
Boulogne →, France 18 E5 47 12N 1 47W
Boulogne-sur-Gesse, France 20 E4 43 18N 0 38 E
Boulogne-sur-Mer, France 19 B8 50 42N 1 36 E
Bouloire, France 18 E7 47 59N 0 45 E
Boulouli, Mali 82 B3 15 30N 9 25W
Boulsa, Burkina Faso 83 C4 12 39N 0 34W
Boultoum, Niger 83 C7 14 45N 10 25 E
Boûmdeïd, Mauritania 82 B2 17 25N 9 50W
Boun Neua, Laos 64 B3 21 38N 101 54 E
Boun Tai, Laos 64 B3 21 23N 101 58 E
Bouna, Ivory C. 82 D4 9 10N 3 0W
Boundary Peak, U.S.A. 116 H8 37 51N 118 21W
Boundiali, Ivory C. 82 D3 9 30N 6 20W
Bountiful, U.S.A. 114 F8 40 53N 111 53W
Bounty Is., Pac. Oc. 96 M9 48 0 S 178 30 E
Boura, Mali 82 C4 12 25N 4 33W
Bourbon-Lancy, France 19 F10 46 37N 3 45 E
Bourbon-l'Archambault, France 19 F10 46 36N 3 4 E
Bourbonnais, France 19 F10 46 28N 3 0 E
Bourbonne-les-Bains, France 19 E12 47 54N 5 45 E
Bourbourg, France 19 B9 50 56N 2 12 E
Bourdel L., Canada 102 A5 56 43N 74 10W
Bourem, Mali 83 B4 17 0N 0 24W
Bourg, France 20 C3 45 3N 0 34W
Bourg-Argental, France 21 C8 45 18N 4 32 E
Bourg-de-Péage, France 21 C9 45 2N 5 3 E
Bourg-en-Bresse, France 19 F12 46 13N 5 12 E
Bourg-Lastic, France 20 C6 45 39N 2 35 E
Bourg-Madame, France 20 F5 42 26N 1 55 E
Bourg-St-Andéol, France 21 D8 44 23N 4 39 E
Bourg-St-Maurice, France 21 C10 45 35N 6 46 E
Bourganeuf, France 20 C5 45 57N 1 45 E
Bourges, France 19 E9 47 9N 2 25 E
Bourget, Canada 111 A9 45 26N 75 9W
Bourget, Lac du, France 21 C9 45 44N 5 52 E
Bourgneuf, B. de, France 18 E4 47 3N 2 10W
Bourgneuf-en-Retz, France 18 E5 47 2N 1 58W
Bourgogne, France 19 F11 47 0N 4 50 E
Bourgoin-Jallieu, France 21 C9 45 36N 5 17 E
Bourgueil, France 18 E7 47 17N 0 10 E
Bourke, Australia 95 E4 30 8 S 145 55 E
Bourne, U.K. 12 E7 52 47N 0 22W
Bournemouth, U.K. 13 G6 50 43N 1 52W
Bournemouth □, U.K. 13 G6 50 43N 1 52W
Bouroum, Burkina Faso 83 C4 13 37N 0 39W
Bouse, U.S.A. 117 M13 33 56N 114 0W
Boussac, France 19 F9 46 22N 2 13 E
Boussé, Burkina Faso 83 C4 12 39N 1 53W
Boussouma, Burkina Faso 83 C4 12 52N 1 13W
Boutilimit, Mauritania 82 B2 17 45N 14 40W
Boutonne →, France 20 C3 45 54N 0 50W
Bouvet I. = Bouvetøya, Antarctica 3 G10 54 26 S 3 24 E
Bouvetøya, Antarctica 3 G10 54 26 S 3 24 E
Bouxwiller, France 19 D14 48 49N 7 27 E
Bouza, Niger 83 C6 14 29N 6 2 E
Bouzonville, France 19 C13 49 17N 6 32 E
Bova Marina, Italy 31 E8 37 56N 15 55 E
Bovalino Marina, Italy 31 D9 38 10N 16 10 E
Bovec, Slovenia 29 B10 46 20N 13 33 E
Bovill, U.S.A. 114 C5 46 51N 116 24W
Bovino, Italy 31 A8 41 15N 15 20 E
Bovril, Argentina 126 C4 31 21 S 59 26W
Bow →, Canada 104 C6 49 57N 111 41W
Bow Island, Canada 104 D6 49 50N 111 23W
Bowbells, U.S.A. 112 A3 48 48N 102 15W
Bowdle, U.S.A. 112 C5 45 27N 99 39W
Bowelling, Australia 93 F2 33 25 S 116 30 E
Bowen, Argentina 126 D2 35 0 S 67 31W
Bowen, Australia 94 C4 20 0 S 148 16 E
Bowen Mts., Australia 95 F4 37 0 S 147 50 E
Bowie, Ariz., U.S.A. 115 K9 32 19N 109 29W
Bowie, Tex., U.S.A. 113 J6 33 34N 97 51W
Bowkān, Iran 70 B5 36 31N 46 12 E
Bowland, Forest of, U.K. 12 D5 54 0N 2 30W
Bowling Green, Ky., U.S.A. 108 G2 36 59N 86 27W
Bowling Green, Ohio, U.S.A. 108 E4 41 23N 83 39W
Bowling Green, C., Australia 94 B4 19 19 S 147 25 E
Bowman, U.S.A. 112 B3 46 11N 103 24W
Bowman I., Antarctica 5 C8 65 0 S 104 0 E
Bowmanville, Canada 110 C6 43 55N 78 41W
Bowmore, U.K. 14 F2 55 45N 6 17W
Bowral, Australia 95 E5 34 26 S 150 27 E
Bowraville, Australia 95 E5 30 37 S 152 52 E
Bowron →, Canada 104 C4 54 3N 121 50W
Bowron Lake Prov. Park, Canada 104 C4 53 10N 121 5W
Bowser L., Canada 104 B3 56 30N 129 30W
Bowsman, Canada 105 C8 52 14N 101 12W
Bowwood, Zambia 87 F2 17 5 S 26 20 E
Box Cr. →, Australia 95 E3 34 10 S 143 50 E
Boxholm, Sweden 11 F9 58 12N 15 3 E
Boxmeer, Neths. 17 C5 51 38N 5 56 E
Boxtel, Neths. 17 C5 51 36N 5 20 E
Boyabat, Turkey 72 B6 41 28N 34 47 E
Boyalıca, Turkey 41 F13 40 29N 29 33 E
Boyang, China 59 C11 29 0N 116 38 E
Boyce, U.S.A. 113 K8 31 23N 92 40W
Boyd L., Canada 102 B4 52 46N 76 42W
Boyle, Canada 104 C6 54 35N 112 49W
Boyle, Ireland 15 C3 53 59N 8 18W
Boyne →, Ireland 15 C5 53 43N 6 15W
Boyne City, U.S.A. 108 C3 45 13N 85 1W
Boynitsa, Bulgaria 40 C6 43 58N 22 32 E
Boynton Beach, U.S.A. 109 M5 26 32N 80 4W
Boyolali, Indonesia 63 G14 7 32 S 110 35 E
Boyoma, Chutes, Dem. Rep. of the Congo 86 B2 0 35N 25 23 E
Boysen Reservoir, U.S.A. 114 E9 43 25N 108 11W
Boyuibe, Bolivia 124 G6 20 25 S 63 17W
Boyup Brook, Australia 93 F2 33 50 S 116 23 E
Boz Burun, Turkey 41 F12 40 32N 28 46 E
Boz Dağ, Turkey 39 D11 37 18N 29 11 E
Boz Dağları, Turkey 39 C10 38 20N 28 0 E
Bozburun, Turkey 39 E10 36 43N 28 4 E
Bozcaada, Turkey 72 C2 39 49N 26 3 E
Bozdoğan, Turkey 39 D10 37 40N 28 17 E
Bozeman, U.S.A. 114 D8 45 41N 111 2W
Bozen = Bolzano, Italy 29 B8 46 31N 11 22 E
Boževac, Serbia, Yug. 40 B5 44 32N 21 24 E
Bozhou, China 56 H8 33 55N 115 41 E
Bozkır, Turkey 72 D5 37 11N 32 14 E
Bozkurt, Turkey 39 D11 37 50N 29 37 E
Bozouls, France 20 D6 44 28N 2 43 E
Bozoum, C.A.R. 84 C3 6 25N 16 35 E
Bozova, Antalya, Turkey 39 D12 37 13N 30 18 E
Bozova, Sanliurfa, Turkey 73 D8 37 21N 38 32 E
Bozovici, Romania 42 F7 44 56N 22 0 E
Bozüyük, Turkey 39 B12 39 54N 30 3 E
Bra, Italy 28 D4 44 42N 7 51 E
Braås, Sweden 11 G9 57 4N 15 3 E
Brabant □, Belgium 17 D4 50 46N 4 30 E
Brabant L., Canada 105 B8 55 58N 103 43W
Brabrand, Denmark 11 H4 56 9N 10 7 E
Brač, Croatia 29 E13 43 20N 16 40 E
Bracadale, L., U.K. 14 D2 57 20N 6 30W
Bracciano, Italy 29 F9 42 6N 12 10 E
Bracciano, L. di, Italy 29 F9 42 7N 12 14 E
Bracebridge, Canada 102 C4 45 2N 79 19W
Brach, Libya 79 C8 27 31N 14 20 E
Bracieux, France 18 E8 47 30N 1 30 E
Bräcke, Sweden 10 B9 62 45N 15 26 E
Brackettville, U.S.A. 113 L4 29 19N 100 25W
Brački Kanal, Croatia 29 E13 43 24N 16 40 E
Bracknell, U.K. 13 F7 51 25N 0 43W
Bracknell Forest □, U.K. 13 F7 51 25N 0 44W
Brad, Romania 42 D7 46 10N 22 50 E
Brădano →, Italy 31 B9 40 23N 16 51 E
Bradenton, U.S.A. 109 M4 27 30N 82 34W
Bradford, Canada 110 B5 44 7N 79 34W
Bradford, U.K. 12 D6 53 47N 1 45W
Bradford, Pa., U.S.A. 110 E6 41 58N 78 38W
Bradford, Vt., U.S.A. 111 C12 43 59N 72 9W
Bradley, Ark., U.S.A. 113 J8 33 6N 93 39W
Bradley, Calif., U.S.A. 116 K6 35 52N 120 48W
Bradley Institute, Zimbabwe 87 F3 17 7 S 31 25 E
Brady, U.S.A. 113 K5 31 9N 99 20W
Brædstrup, Denmark 11 J3 55 58N 9 37 E
Braemar, U.K. 14 D5 57 0N 3 23W
Braeside, Canada 111 A8 45 28N 76 24W
Braga, Portugal 34 D2 41 35N 8 25W
Braga □, Portugal 34 D2 41 30N 8 30W
Bragadiru, Romania 43 G10 43 46N 25 31 E
Bragado, Argentina 126 D3 35 2 S 60 27W
Bragança, Brazil 125 D9 1 0 S 47 2W
Bragança, Portugal 34 D4 41 48N 6 50W
Bragança □, Portugal 34 D4 41 30N 6 45W
Bragança Paulista, Brazil 127 A6 22 55 S 46 32W
Brahmanbaria, Bangla. 67 H17 23 58N 91 15 E
Brahmani →, India 67 J15 20 39N 86 46 E
Brahmapur, India 67 K14 19 15N 84 54 E
Brahmaputra →, India 69 H13 23 58N 89 50 E
Braich-y-pwll, U.K. 12 E3 52 47N 4 46W
Braidwood, Australia 95 F4 35 27 S 149 49 E
Brăila, Romania 43 E12 45 19N 27 59 E
Brăila □, Romania 43 E12 45 5N 27 30 E
Brainerd, U.S.A. 112 B7 46 22N 94 12W
Braintree, U.K. 13 F8 51 53N 0 34 E
Braintree, U.S.A. 111 D14 42 13N 71 0W
Brak →, S. Africa 88 D3 29 35 S 22 55 E
Brake, Germany 24 B4 53 20N 8 28 E
Brakel, Germany 24 D5 51 42N 9 11 E
Bräkne-Hoby, Sweden 11 H9 56 14N 15 6 E
Brakwater, Namibia 88 C2 22 28 S 17 3 E
Brålanda, Sweden 11 F6 58 34N 12 21 E
Bramberg, Germany 25 E6 50 6N 10 40 E
Bramdrupdam, Denmark 11 J3 55 31N 9 28 E
Bramming, Denmark 11 J2 55 28N 8 42 E
Brämön, Sweden 10 B11 62 14N 17 40 E
Brampton, Canada 102 D4 43 45N 79 45W
Brampton, U.K. 12 C5 54 57N 2 44W
Bramsche, Germany 24 C3 52 24N 7 59 E
Branco →, Brazil 122 D4 1 20 S 61 50W
Brandberg, Namibia 88 B2 21 10 S 14 33 E
Brande, Denmark 11 J3 55 57N 9 8 E
Brandenburg = Neubrandenburg, Germany 24 B9 53 33N 13 15 E
Brandenburg, Germany 24 C8 52 25N 12 33 E
Brandenburg □, Germany 24 C9 52 50N 13 0 E
Brandfort, S. Africa 88 D4 28 40 S 26 30 E
Brando, France 21 F13 42 47N 9 27 E
Brandon, Canada 105 D9 49 50N 99 57W
Brandon, U.S.A. 111 C11 43 48N 73 4W
Brandon B., Ireland 15 D1 52 17N 10 8W
Brandon Mt., Ireland 15 D1 52 15N 10 15W
Brandsen, Argentina 126 D4 35 10 S 58 15W
Brandvlei, S. Africa 88 E3 30 25 S 20 30 E
Brandýs nad Labem, Czech Rep. 26 A7 50 10N 14 40 E
Brăneşti, Romania 43 F11 44 27N 26 20 E
Branford, U.S.A. 111 E12 41 17N 72 49W
Braniewo, Poland 44 D6 54 25N 19 50 E
Bransfield Str., Antarctica 5 C18 63 0 S 59 0W
Brańsk, Poland 45 F9 52 45N 22 50 E
Branson, U.S.A. 113 G8 36 39N 93 13W
Brantford, Canada 102 D3 43 10N 80 15W
Brantôme, France 20 C4 45 22N 0 39 E
Branzi, Italy 28 B6 46 1N 9 46 E
Bras d'Or L., Canada 103 C7 45 50N 60 50W
Brasher Falls, U.S.A. 111 B10 44 49N 74 47W
Brasil, Planalto, Brazil 122 E6 18 0 S 46 30W
Brasiléia, Brazil 124 F5 11 0 S 68 45W
Brasília, Brazil 125 G9 15 47 S 47 55W
Brasília Legal, Brazil 125 D7 3 49 S 55 36W
Braslaw, Belarus 9 J22 55 38N 27 0 E
Braslovče, Slovenia 29 B12 46 21N 15 3 E
Braşov, Romania 43 E10 45 38N 25 35 E
Braşov □, Romania 43 E10 45 45N 25 15 E
Brass, Nigeria 83 E6 4 35N 6 14 E
Brass →, Nigeria 83 E6 4 15N 6 13 E
Brassac-les-Mines, France 20 C7 45 24N 3 20 E
Brasschaat, Belgium 17 C4 51 19N 4 27 E
Brassey, Banjaran, Malaysia 62 D5 5 0N 117 15 E
Brassey Ra., Australia 93 E3 25 8 S 122 15 E
Brasstown Bald, U.S.A. 109 H4 34 53N 83 49W
Brastad, Sweden 11 F5 58 23N 11 30 E
Brastavățu, Romania 43 G9 43 55N 24 24 E
Bratan = Morozov, Bulgaria 41 D9 42 30N 25 10 E
Brateş, Romania 43 E11 45 50N 26 4 E
Bratislava, Slovak Rep. 27 C10 48 10N 17 7 E
Bratislavský □, Slovak Rep. 27 C10 48 15N 17 20 E
Bratsigovo, Bulgaria 41 D8 42 1N 24 22 E
Bratsk, Russia 51 D11 56 10N 101 30 E
Brattleboro, U.S.A. 111 D12 42 51N 72 34W

Bratunac, Bos.-H. 42 F4 44 13N 19 21 E
Braunau, Austria 26 C6 48 15N 13 3 E
Braunschweig, Germany 24 C6 52 15N 10 31 E
Braunton, U.K. 13 F3 51 7N 4 10W
Bravicea, Moldova 43 C13 47 22N 28 27 E
Bråviken, Sweden 11 F10 58 38N 16 32 E
Bravo del Norte, Rio = Grande, Rio →, U.S.A. 113 N6 25 58N 97 9W
Brawley, U.S.A. 117 N11 32 59N 115 31W
Bray, Ireland 15 C5 53 13N 6 7W
Bray, Mt., Australia 94 A1 14 0 S 134 30 E
Bray-sur-Seine, France 19 D10 48 25N 3 14 E
Brazeau →, Canada 104 C5 52 55N 115 14W
Brazil, U.S.A. 108 F2 39 32N 87 8W
Brazil ■, S. Amer. 125 F9 12 0 S 50 0W
Brazilian Highlands = Brasil, Planalto, Brazil 122 E6 18 0 S 46 30W
Brazo Sur →, S. Amer. 126 B4 25 21 S 57 42W
Brazos →, U.S.A. 113 L7 28 53N 95 23W
Brazzaville, Congo 84 E3 4 9 S 15 12 E
Brčko, Bos.-H. 42 F3 44 54N 18 46 E
Brda →, Poland 45 E5 53 8N 18 8 E
Brdy, Czech Rep. 26 B6 49 43N 13 55 E
Breaden, L., Australia 93 E4 25 51 S 125 28 E
Breaksea Sd., N.Z. 91 L1 45 35 S 166 35 E
Bream B., N.Z. 91 F5 35 56 S 174 28 E
Bream Hd., N.Z. 91 F5 35 51 S 174 36 E
Breas, Chile 126 B1 25 29 S 70 24W
Breaza, Romania 43 E10 45 11N 25 40 E
Brebes, Indonesia 63 G13 6 52 S 109 3 E
Brechin, Canada 110 B5 44 32N 79 10W
Brechin, U.K. 14 E6 56 44N 2 39W
Brecht, Belgium 17 C4 51 21N 4 38 E
Breckenridge, Colo., U.S.A. 114 G10 39 29N 106 3W
Breckenridge, Minn., U.S.A. 112 B6 46 16N 96 35W
Breckenridge, Tex., U.S.A. 113 J5 32 45N 98 54W
Breckland, U.K. 13 E8 52 30N 0 40 E
Břeclav, Czech Rep. 27 C9 48 46N 16 53 E
Brecon, U.K. 13 F4 51 57N 3 23W
Brecon Beacons, U.K. 13 F4 51 53N 3 26W
Breda, Neths. 17 C4 51 35N 4 45 E
Bredaryd, Sweden 11 G7 57 10N 13 45 E
Bredasdorp, S. Africa 88 E3 34 33 S 20 2 E
Bredebro, Denmark 11 J2 55 4N 8 50 E
Bredstedt, Germany 24 A4 54 37N 8 55 E
Bree, Belgium 17 C5 51 8N 5 35 E
Bregalnica →, Macedonia 40 E6 41 43N 22 9 E
Bregenz, Austria 26 D2 47 30N 9 45 E
Bregovo, Bulgaria 40 B6 44 9N 22 39 E
Bréhal, France 18 D5 48 53N 1 30W
Bréhat, Î. de, France 18 D4 48 51N 3 0W
Breiðafjörður, Iceland 8 D2 65 15N 23 15W
Breil-sur-Roya, France 21 E11 43 56N 7 31 E
Breisach, Germany 25 G3 48 1N 7 36 E
Brejo, Brazil 125 D10 3 41 S 42 47W
Bremen, Germany 24 B4 53 4N 8 47 E
Bremen □, Germany 24 B4 53 4N 8 50 E
Bremer Bay, Australia 93 F2 34 21 S 119 20 E
Bremer I., Australia 94 A2 12 5 S 136 45 E
Bremerhaven, Germany 24 B4 53 33N 8 36 E
Bremerton, U.S.A. 116 C4 47 34N 122 38W
Bremervörde, Germany 24 B5 53 29N 9 8 E
Brenes, Spain 35 H5 37 32N 5 54W
Brenham, U.S.A. 113 K6 30 10N 96 24W
Brenne, France 20 B5 46 44N 1 14 E
Brennerpass, Austria 26 D4 47 2N 11 30 E
Breno, Italy 28 C7 45 57N 10 18 E
Brent, U.S.A. 109 J2 32 56N 87 10W
Brenta →, Italy 29 C9 45 11N 12 18 E
Brentwood, U.K. 13 F8 51 37N 0 19 E
Brentwood, Calif., U.S.A. 116 H5 37 56N 121 42W
Brentwood, N.Y., U.S.A. 111 F11 40 47N 73 15W
Bréscia, Italy 28 C7 45 33N 10 15 E
Breskens, Neths. 17 C3 51 23N 3 33 E
Breslau = Wrocław, Poland 45 G4 51 5N 17 5 E
Bresle →, France 18 B8 50 4N 1 22 E
Bressanone, Italy 29 B8 46 43N 11 39 E
Bressay, U.K. 14 A7 60 9N 1 6W
Bresse, France 19 F12 46 50N 5 10 E
Bressuire, France 18 F6 46 51N 0 30W
Brest, Belarus 47 F2 52 10N 23 40 E
Brest, France 18 D2 48 24N 4 31W
Brest-Litovsk = Brest, Belarus 47 F2 52 10N 23 40 E
Bretagne, France 18 D3 48 10N 3 0W
Bretçu, Romania 43 D11 46 7N 26 18 E
Bretenoux, France 20 D5 44 54N 1 51 E
Breteuil, Eure, France 18 D7 48 50N 0 57 E
Breteuil, Oise, France 19 C9 49 38N 2 18 E
Breton, Canada 104 C6 53 7N 114 28W
Breton, Pertuis, France 20 B2 46 17N 1 25W
Breton Sd., U.S.A. 113 L10 29 35N 89 15W
Brett, C., N.Z. 91 F5 35 10 S 174 20 E
Bretten, Germany 25 F4 49 2N 8 42 E
Breuil-Cervínia, Italy 28 C4 45 56N 7 38 E
Brevard, U.S.A. 109 H4 35 14N 82 44W
Breves, Brazil 125 D8 1 40 S 50 29W
Brewarrina, Australia 95 E4 30 0 S 146 51 E
Brewer, U.S.A. 109 C11 44 48N 68 46W
Brewer, Mt., U.S.A. 116 J8 36 44N 118 28W
Brewerville, Liberia 82 D2 6 26N 10 47W
Brewster, N.Y., U.S.A. 111 E11 41 23N 73 37W
Brewster, Ohio, U.S.A. 110 F3 40 43N 81 36W
Brewster, Wash., U.S.A. 114 B4 48 6N 119 47W
Brewster, Kap = Kangikajik, Greenland 4 B6 70 7N 22 0W
Brewton, U.S.A. 109 K2 31 7N 87 4W
Breyten, S. Africa 89 D5 26 16 S 30 0 E
Breza, Bos.-H. 42 F3 44 2N 18 16 E
Brezhnev = Naberezhnyye Chelny, Russia 48 C11 55 42N 52 19 E
Brežice, Slovenia 29 C12 45 54N 15 35 E
Březnice, Czech Rep. 26 B6 49 32N 13 57 E
Breznik, Bulgaria 40 D6 42 44N 22 55 E
Brezno, Slovak Rep. 27 C12 48 50N 19 40 E
Brezoi, Romania 43 E9 45 21N 24 15 E
Brezovica, Kosovo, Yug. 40 D5 42 15N 21 3 E
Brezovo, Bulgaria 41 D9 42 21N 25 5 E
Briançon, France 21 D10 44 54N 6 39 E
Briare, France 19 E9 47 38N 2 45 E
Briático, Italy 31 D9 38 43N 16 2 E
Bribie I., Australia 95 D5 27 0 S 153 10 E
Bribri, Costa Rica 120 E3 9 38N 82 50W
Briceni, Moldova 43 B12 48 22N 27 6 E
Bricquebec, France 18 C5 49 28N 1 38W
Bridgehampton, U.S.A. 111 F12 40 56N 72 19W
Bridgend, U.K. 13 F4 51 30N 3 34W
Bridgend □, U.K. 13 F4 51 36N 3 36W
Bridgeport, Calif., U.S.A. 116 G7 38 15N 119 14W
Bridgeport, Conn., U.S.A. 111 E11 41 11N 73 12W
Bridgeport, Nebr., U.S.A. 112 E3 41 40N 103 6W
Bridgeport, Tex., U.S.A. 113 J6 33 13N 97 45W
Bridger, U.S.A. 114 D9 45 18N 108 55W
Bridgeton, U.S.A. 108 F8 39 26N 75 14W
Bridgetown, Australia 93 F2 33 58 S 116 7 E
Bridgetown, Barbados 121 D8 13 5N 59 30W
Bridgetown, Canada 103 D6 44 55N 65 18W
Bridgewater, Canada 103 D7 44 25N 64 31W
Bridgewater, Mass., U.S.A. 111 E14 41 59N 70 58W
Bridgewater, N.Y., U.S.A. 111 D9 42 53N 75 15W
Bridgewater, C., Australia 95 F3 38 23 S 141 23 E
Bridgewater-Gagebrook, Australia 94 G4 42 44 S 147 14 E
Bridgnorth, U.K. 13 E5 52 32N 2 25W
Bridgton, U.S.A. 111 B14 44 3N 70 42W
Bridgwater, U.K. 13 F5 51 8N 2 59W
Bridgwater B., U.K. 13 F4 51 15N 3 15W
Bridlington, U.K. 12 C7 54 5N 0 12W
Bridlington B., U.K. 12 C7 54 4N 0 10W
Bridport, Australia 94 G4 40 59 S 147 23 E
Bridport, U.K. 13 G5 50 44N 2 45W
Briec, France 18 D2 48 6N 4 0W
Brienne-le-Château, France 19 D11 48 24N 4 30 E
Brienon-sur-Armançon, France 19 E10 47 59N 3 38 E
Brienz, Switz. 25 J4 46 46N 8 2 E
Brienzersee, Switz. 25 J3 46 44N 7 53 E
Brig, Switz. 25 J3 46 18N 7 59 E
Brigg, U.K. 12 D7 53 34N 0 28W
Brigham City, U.S.A. 114 F7 41 31N 112 1W
Bright, Australia 95 F4 36 42 S 146 56 E
Brighton, Australia 95 F2 35 5 S 138 30 E
Brighton, Canada 110 B7 44 2N 77 44W
Brighton, U.K. 13 G7 50 49N 0 7W
Brighton, Colo., U.S.A. 112 F2 39 59N 104 49W
Brighton, N.Y., U.S.A. 110 C7 43 8N 77 34W
Brignogan-Plage, France 18 D2 48 40N 4 20W
Brignoles, France 21 E10 43 25N 6 5 E
Brihuega, Spain 32 E2 40 45N 2 52W
Brikama, Gambia 82 C1 13 15N 16 45W
Brilliant, U.S.A. 110 F4 40 15N 80 39W
Brilon, Germany 24 D4 51 23N 8 35 E
Bríndisi, Italy 31 B10 40 39N 17 55 E
Brinje, Croatia 29 D12 44 59N 15 9 E
Brinkley, U.S.A. 113 H9 34 53N 91 12W
Brinnon, U.S.A. 116 C4 47 41N 122 54W
Brion, I., Canada 103 C7 47 46N 61 26W
Brionne, France 18 C7 49 11N 0 43 E
Brionski, Croatia 29 D10 44 55N 13 45 E
Brioude, France 20 C7 45 18N 3 24 E
Briouze, France 18 D6 48 42N 0 23W
Brisbane, Australia 95 D5 27 25 S 153 2 E
Brisbane →, Australia 95 D5 27 24 S 153 9 E
Brisighella, Italy 29 D8 44 13N 11 46 E
Bristol, U.K. 13 F5 51 26N 2 35W
Bristol, Conn., U.S.A. 111 E12 41 40N 72 57W
Bristol, Pa., U.S.A. 111 F10 40 6N 74 51W
Bristol, R.I., U.S.A. 111 E13 41 40N 71 16W
Bristol, Tenn., U.S.A. 109 G4 36 36N 82 11W
Bristol, City of □, U.K. 13 F5 51 27N 2 36W
Bristol B., U.S.A. 100 C4 58 0N 160 0W
Bristol Channel, U.K. 13 F3 51 18N 4 30W
Bristol I., Antarctica 5 B1 58 45 S 28 0W
Bristol L., U.S.A. 115 J5 34 23N 116 50W
Bristow, U.S.A. 113 H6 35 50N 96 23W
Britain = Great Britain, Europe 6 E5 54 0N 2 15W
British Columbia □, Canada 104 C3 55 0N 125 15W
British Indian Ocean Terr. = Chagos Arch., Ind. Oc. 52 K11 6 0 S 72 0 E
British Isles, Europe 6 E5 54 0N 4 0W
Brits, S. Africa 89 D4 25 37 S 27 48 E
Britstown, S. Africa 88 E3 30 37 S 23 30 E
Britt, Canada 102 C3 45 46N 80 34W
Brittany = Bretagne, France 18 D3 48 10N 3 0W
Britton, U.S.A. 112 C6 45 48N 97 45W
Brive-la-Gaillarde, France 20 C5 45 10N 1 32 E
Briviesca, Spain 34 C7 42 32N 3 19W
Brixen = Bressanone, Italy 29 B8 46 43N 11 39 E
Brixham, U.K. 13 G4 50 23N 3 31W
Brnaze, Croatia 29 E13 43 41N 16 40 E
Brno, Czech Rep. 27 B9 49 10N 16 35 E
Broad →, U.S.A. 109 J5 34 1N 81 4W
Broad Arrow, Australia 93 F3 30 23 S 121 15 E
Broad B., U.K. 14 C2 58 14N 6 18W
Broad Haven, Ireland 15 B2 54 20N 9 55W
Broad Law, U.K. 14 F5 55 30N 3 21W
Broad Sd., Australia 94 C4 22 0 S 149 45 E
Broadalbin, U.S.A. 111 C10 43 4N 74 12W
Broadback →, Canada 102 B4 51 21N 78 52W
Broadford, Australia 95 F4 37 14 S 145 4 E
Broadhurst Ra., Australia 92 D3 22 30 S 122 30 E
Broads, The, U.K. 12 E9 52 45N 1 30 E
Broadus, U.S.A. 112 C2 45 27N 105 25W
Broager, Denmark 11 K3 54 53N 9 40 E
Broby, Sweden 11 H8 56 15N 14 4 E
Brocēni, Latvia 44 B9 56 42N 22 32 E
Brochet, Canada 105 B8 57 53N 101 40W
Brochet, L., Canada 105 B8 58 36N 101 35W
Brocken, Germany 24 D6 51 47N 10 37 E
Brockport, U.S.A. 110 C7 43 13N 77 56W
Brockton, U.S.A. 111 D13 42 5N 71 1W
Brockville, Canada 102 D4 44 35N 75 41W
Brockway, Mont., U.S.A. 112 B2 47 18N 105 45W
Brockway, Pa., U.S.A. 110 E6 41 15N 78 47W
Brocton, U.S.A. 110 D5 42 23N 79 26W
Brod, Macedonia 40 E5 41 32N 21 17 E
Brodarevo, Serbia, Yug. 40 C3 43 14N 19 44 E
Brodeur Pen., Canada 101 A11 72 30N 88 10W
Brodhead, Mt., U.S.A. 110 E7 41 39N 77 47W
Brodick, U.K. 14 F3 55 35N 5 9W
Brodnica, Poland 45 E6 53 15N 19 25 E
Brody, Ukraine 47 G3 50 5N 25 10 E
Brogan, U.S.A. 114 D5 44 15N 117 31W
Broglie, France 18 C7 49 2N 0 30 E
Brok, Poland 45 F8 52 43N 21 52 E
Broken Arrow, U.S.A. 113 G7 36 3N 95 48W
Broken Bow, Nebr., U.S.A. 112 E5 41 24N 99 38W
Broken Bow, Okla., U.S.A. 113 H7 34 2N 94 44W
Broken Bow Lake, U.S.A. 113 H7 34 9N 94 40W
Broken Hill = Kabwe, Zambia 87 E2 14 30 S 28 29 E
Broken Hill, Australia 95 E3 31 58 S 141 29 E
Brokind, Sweden 11 F9 58 13N 15 42 E
Bromley, U.K. 13 F8 51 24N 0 2 E
Bromölla, Sweden 11 H8 56 5N 14 28 E
Bromsgrove, U.K. 13 E5 52 21N 2 2W
Brønderslev, Denmark 11 G3 57 16N 9 57 E
Brong-Ahafo □, Ghana 82 D4 7 50N 2 0W
Broni, Italy 28 C6 45 4N 9 16 E
Bronkhorstspruit, S. Africa 89 D4 25 46 S 28 45 E
Brønnøysund, Norway 8 D15 65 28N 12 14 E
Bronte, Italy 31 E7 37 47N 14 50 E
Brook Park, U.S.A. 110 E4 41 24N 81 51W
Brookhaven, U.S.A. 113 K9 31 35N 90 26W
Brookings, Oreg., U.S.A. 114 E1 42 3N 124 17W
Brookings, S. Dak., U.S.A. 112 C6 44 19N 96 48W
Brooklin, Canada 110 C6 43 55N 78 55W
Brooklyn Park, U.S.A. 112 C8 45 6N 93 23W
Brooks, Canada 104 C6 50 35N 111 55W
Brooks Range, U.S.A. 100 B5 68 0N 152 0W
Brooksville, U.S.A. 109 L4 28 33N 82 23W
Brookton, Australia 93 F2 32 22 S 117 0 E
Brookville, U.S.A. 110 E5 41 10N 79 5W
Broom, L., U.K. 14 D3 57 55N 5 15W
Broome, Australia 92 C3 18 0 S 122 15 E
Broons, France 18 D4 48 20N 2 16W
Brora, U.K. 14 C5 58 0N 3 52W
Brora →, U.K. 14 C5 58 0N 3 51W
Brørup, Denmark 11 J2 55 29N 9 1 E
Brösarp, Sweden 11 J8 55 43N 14 6 E
Brosna →, Ireland 15 C4 53 14N 7 58W
Broşteni, Mehedinţi, Romania 42 F7 44 45N 22 59 E
Broşteni, Suceava, Romania 43 C10 47 14N 25 43 E
Brothers, U.S.A. 114 E3 43 49N 120 36W
Brou, France 18 D8 48 13N 1 11 E
Brouage, France 20 C2 45 52N 1 4W
Brough, U.K. 12 C5 54 32N 2 18W
Brough Hd., U.K. 14 B5 59 8N 3 20W
Broughton Island = Qikiqtarjuaq, Canada 101 B13 67 33N 63 0W
Broumov, Czech Rep. 27 A9 50 35N 16 20 E
Brovary, Ukraine 47 G6 50 34N 30 48 E
Brovst, Denmark 11 G3 57 6N 9 31 E
Brown, L., Australia 95 F2 31 5 S 118 15 E
Brown, Pt., Australia 95 E1 32 32 S 133 50 E
Brown City, U.S.A. 110 C2 43 13N 82 59W
Brown Willy, U.K. 13 G3 50 35N 4 37W
Brownfield, U.S.A. 113 J3 33 11N 102 17W
Browning, U.S.A. 114 B7 48 34N 113 1W
Brownsville, Oreg., U.S.A. 114 D2 44 24N 122 59W
Brownsville, Pa., U.S.A. 110 F5 40 1N 79 53W
Brownsville, Tenn., U.S.A. 113 H10 35 36N 89 16W
Brownsville, Tex., U.S.A. 113 N6 25 54N 97 30W
Brownville, U.S.A. 111 C9 44 0N 75 59W
Brownwood, U.S.A. 113 K5 31 43N 98 59W
Browse I., Australia 92 B3 14 7 S 123 33 E
Bruas, Malaysia 65 K3 4 30N 100 47 E
Bruay-la-Buissière, France 19 B9 50 29N 2 33 E
Bruce, Mt., Australia 92 D2 22 37 S 118 8 E
Bruce Pen., Canada 110 B3 45 0N 81 30W
Bruce Rock, Australia 93 F2 31 52 S 118 8 E
Bruche →, France 19 D14 48 34N 7 43 E
Bruchsal, Germany 25 F4 49 7N 8 35 E
Bruck an der Leitha, Austria 27 C9 48 1N 16 47 E
Bruck an der Mur, Austria 26 D8 47 24N 15 16 E
Brue →, U.K. 13 F5 51 13N 2 59W
Bruges = Brugge, Belgium 17 C3 51 13N 3 13 E
Brugg, Switz. 25 H4 47 29N 8 11 E
Brugge, Belgium 17 C3 51 13N 3 13 E
Bruin, U.S.A. 110 E5 41 3N 79 43W
Brûlé, Canada 104 C5 53 15N 117 58W
Brûlon, France 18 E6 47 58N 0 15W
Brumado, Brazil 125 F10 14 14 S 41 40W
Brumath, France 19 D14 48 43N 7 40 E
Brumunddal, Norway 9 F14 60 53N 10 56 E
Bruneau, U.S.A. 114 E6 42 53N 115 48W
Bruneau →, U.S.A. 114 E6 42 56N 115 57W
Bruneck = Brunico, Italy 29 B8 46 48N 11 56 E
Brunei = Bandar Seri Begawan, Brunei 62 C4 4 52N 115 0 E
Brunei ■, Asia 62 D4 4 50N 115 0 E
Brunflo, Sweden 10 A8 63 5N 14 50 E
Brunico, Italy 29 B8 46 48N 11 56 E
Brunna, Sweden 10 E11 59 52N 17 25 E
Brunnen, Switz. 25 J4 46 59N 8 37 E
Brunner, L., N.Z. 91 K3 42 37 S 171 27 E
Brunsbüttel, Germany 24 B5 53 53N 9 6 E
Brunssum, Neths. 17 D5 50 57N 5 59 E
Brunswick = Braunschweig, Germany 24 C6 52 15N 10 31 E
Brunswick, Ga., U.S.A. 109 K5 31 10N 81 30W
Brunswick, Maine, U.S.A. 109 D11 43 55N 69 58W
Brunswick, Md., U.S.A. 108 F7 39 19N 77 38W
Brunswick, Mo., U.S.A. 112 F8 39 26N 93 8W
Brunswick, Ohio, U.S.A. 110 E3 41 14N 81 51W
Brunswick, Pen. de, Chile 128 G2 53 30 S 71 30W
Brunswick B., Australia 92 C3 15 15 S 124 50 E
Brunswick Junction, Australia 93 F2 33 15 S 115 50 E
Bruntál, Czech Rep. 27 B10 49 59N 17 27 E
Bruny I., Australia 94 G4 43 20 S 147 15 E
Brus Laguna, Honduras 120 C3 15 47N 84 35W
Brusartsi, Bulgaria 40 C7 43 40N 23 5 E
Brush, U.S.A. 112 E3 40 15N 103 37W
Brushton, U.S.A. 111 B10 44 50N 74 31W
Brusio, Switz. 25 J6 46 14N 10 8 E
Brusque, Brazil 127 B6 27 5 S 49 0W
Brussel, Belgium 17 D4 50 51N 4 21 E
Brussels = Brussel, Belgium 17 D4 50 51N 4 21 E
Brussels, Canada 110 C3 43 44N 81 15W
Brusy, Poland 44 E4 53 53N 17 43 E
Bruthen, Australia 95 F4 37 42 S 147 50 E
Bruxelles = Brussel, Belgium 17 D4 50 51N 4 21 E
Bruyères, France 19 D13 48 10N 6 40 E
Bruz, France 18 D5 48 1N 1 46W
Brwinów, Poland 45 F7 52 9N 20 40 E
Bryagovo, Bulgaria 41 E9 41 58N 25 8 E
Bryan, Ohio, U.S.A. 108 E3 41 28N 84 33W
Bryan, Tex., U.S.A. 113 K6 30 40N 96 22W
Bryan, Mt., Australia 95 E2 33 30 S 139 0 E
Bryanka, Ukraine 47 H10 48 32N 38 45 E
Bryansk, Bryansk, Russia 47 F8 53 13N 34 25 E
Bryansk, Dagestan, Russia 49 H8 44 20N 47 10 E
Bryanskoye = Bryansk, Russia 49 H8 44 20N 47 10 E
Bryce Canyon National Park, U.S.A. 115 H7 37 30N 112 10W
Bryne, Norway 9 G11 58 44N 5 38 E
Bryson City, U.S.A. 109 H4 35 26N 83 27W
Bryukhovetskaya, Russia 47 K10 45 48N 39 0 E
Brza Palanka, Serbia, Yug. 40 B6 44 28N 22 27 E
Brzeg, Poland 45 H4 50 52N 17 30 E
Brzeg Dolny, Poland 45 G3 51 16N 16 41 E
Brześć Kujawski, Poland 45 F5 52 36N 18 55 E
Brzesko, Poland 45 J7 49 59N 20 34 E
Brzeziny, Poland 45 G6 51 49N 19 42 E
Brzozów, Poland 45 J9 49 41N 22 3 E
Bsharri, Lebanon 75 A5 34 15N 36 0 E
Bū Baqarah, U.A.E. 71 E8 25 35N 56 25 E
Bu Craa, W. Sahara 78 C3 26 45N 12 50W
Bū Ḥasā, U.A.E. 71 F7 23 30N 53 20 E
Bua, Sweden 11 G6 57 14N 12 7 E
Bua Yai, Thailand 64 E4 15 33N 102 26 E
Buapinang, Indonesia 63 E6 4 40 S 121 30 E
Buba, Guinea-Biss. 82 C2 11 40N 14 59W
Bubanza, Burundi 86 C2 3 6 S 29 23 E
Bubaque, Guinea-Biss. 82 C1 11 16N 15 51W
Bube, Ethiopia 81 F4 8 46N 35 48 E
Būbiyān, Kuwait 71 D6 29 45N 48 15 E
Buca, Turkey 39 C9 38 22N 27 11 E
Bucak, Turkey 39 D12 37 28N 30 36 E
Bucaramanga, Colombia 124 B4 7 0N 73 0W
Bucas Grande I., Phil. 61 G6 9 40N 125 57 E
Bucasia, Australia 94 C4 21 2 S 149 10 E
Buccaneer Arch., Australia 92 C3 16 7 S 123 20 E
Buccino, Italy 31 B8 40 38N 15 22 E
Bucecea, Romania 43 C11 47 47N 26 28 E
Buchach, Ukraine 47 H3 49 5N 25 25 E
Buchan, U.K. 14 D6 57 32N 2 21W
Buchan Ness, U.K. 14 D7 57 29N 1 46W
Buchanan, Canada 105 C8 51 40N 102 45W
Buchanan, Liberia 82 D2 5 57N 10 2W
Buchanan, L., Queens., Australia 94 C4 21 35 S 145 52 E
Buchanan, L., W. Austral., Australia 93 E3 25 33 S 123 2 E
Buchanan, L., U.S.A. 113 K5 30 45N 98 25W
Buchanan Cr. →, Australia 94 B2 19 13 S 136 33 E
Buchans, Canada 103 C8 48 50N 56 52W
Bucharest = Bucureşti, Romania 43 F11 44 27N 26 10 E
Buchen, Germany 25 F5 49 32N 9 20 E
Buchholz, Germany 24 B5 53 19N 9 52 E
Buchloe, Germany 25 G6 48 1N 10 44 E
Buchon, Pt., U.S.A. 116 K6 35 15N 120 54W
Buciumi, Romania 42 C8 47 3N 23 1 E
Buck Hill Falls, U.S.A. 111 E9 41 11N 75 16W
Bückeburg, Germany 24 C5 52 16N 9 7 E
Buckeye, U.S.A. 115 K7 33 22N 112 35W
Buckeye Lake, U.S.A. 110 G2 39 55N 82 29W
Buckhannon, U.S.A. 108 F5 39 0N 80 8W
Buckhaven, U.K. 14 E5 56 11N 3 3W
Buckhorn L., Canada 110 B6 44 29N 78 23W
Buckie, U.K. 14 D6 57 41N 2 58W
Buckingham, Canada 102 C4 45 37N 75 24W
Buckingham, U.K. 13 F7 51 59N 0 57W
Buckingham B., Australia 94 A2 12 10 S 135 40 E
Buckinghamshire □, U.K. 13 F7 51 53N 0 55W
Buckle Hd., Australia 92 B4 14 26 S 127 52 E
Buckleboo, Australia 95 E2 32 54 S 136 12 E
Buckley, U.K. 12 D4 53 10N 3 5W
Buckley →, Australia 94 C2 20 10 S 138 49 E
Bucklin, U.S.A. 113 G5 37 33N 99 38W
Bucks L., U.S.A. 116 F5 39 54N 121 12W
Bucquoy, France 19 B9 50 9N 2 43 E
Buctouche, Canada 103 C7 46 30N 64 45W
Bucureşti, Romania 43 F11 44 27N 26 10 E
Bucyrus, U.S.A. 108 E4 40 48N 82 59W
Budacu, Vf., Romania 43 C10 47 7N 25 41 E
Budalin, Burma 67 H19 22 20N 95 10 E
Budaörs, Hungary 42 C3 47 27N 18 58 E
Budapest, Hungary 42 C4 47 29N 19 5 E
Budapest □, Hungary 42 C4 47 29N 19 5 E
Budaun, India 69 E8 28 5N 79 10 E
Budd Coast, Antarctica 5 C8 68 0 S 112 0 E
Buddusò, Italy 30 B2 40 35N 9 15 E
Bude, U.K. 13 G3 50 49N 4 34W
Budennovsk, Russia 49 H7 44 50N 44 10 E
Budeşti, Romania 43 F11 44 13N 26 30 E
Budge Budge = Baj Baj, India 69 H13 22 30N 88 5 E
Budgewoi, Australia 95 E5 33 13 S 151 34 E
Budia, Spain 32 E2 40 38N 2 46W
Büdingen, Germany 25 E5 50 16N 9 7 E
Budjala, Dem. Rep. of the Congo 84 D3 2 50N 19 40 E
Budoni, Italy 30 B2 40 40N 9 45 E
Búdrio, Italy 29 D8 44 32N 11 32 E
Budva, Montenegro, Yug. 40 D2 42 17N 18 50 E
Budzyń, Poland 45 F3 52 54N 16 59 E
Buea, Cameroon 83 E6 4 10N 9 9 E
Buellton, U.S.A. 117 L6 34 37N 120 12W
Buena Esperanza, Argentina 126 C2 34 45 S 65 15W
Buena Park, U.S.A. 117 M9 33 52N 117 59W
Buena Vista, Colo., U.S.A. 115 G10 38 51N 106 8W
Buena Vista, Va., U.S.A. 108 G6 37 44N 79 21W
Buena Vista Lake Bed, U.S.A. 117 K7 35 12N 119 18W
Buenaventura, Colombia 124 C3 3 53N 77 4W
Buenaventura, Mexico 118 B3 29 50N 107 30W
Buendía, Embalse de, Spain 32 E2 40 25N 2 43W
Buenos Aires, Argentina 126 C4 34 30 S 58 20W
Buenos Aires, Costa Rica 120 E3 9 10N 83 20W
Buenos Aires □, Argentina 126 D4 36 30 S 60 0W
Buenos Aires, L., Chile 128 F2 46 35 S 72 30W
Buffalo, Mo., U.S.A. 113 G8 37 39N 93 6W
Buffalo, N.Y., U.S.A. 110 D6 42 53N 78 53W
Buffalo, Okla., U.S.A. 113 G5 36 50N 99 38W
Buffalo, S. Dak., U.S.A. 112 C3 45 35N 103 33W
Buffalo, Wyo., U.S.A. 114 D10 44 21N 106 42W
Buffalo →, Canada 104 A5 60 5N 115 5W
Buffalo →, S. Africa 89 D5 28 43 S 30 37 E
Buffalo Head Hills, Canada 104 B5 57 25N 115 55W
Buffalo L., Alta., Canada 104 C6 52 27N 112 54W
Buffalo L., N.W.T., Canada 104 A5 60 12N 115 25W
Buffalo Narrows, Canada 105 B7 55 51N 108 29W
Buffels →, S. Africa 88 D2 29 36 S 17 3 E
Buford, U.S.A. 109 H4 34 10N 84 0W
Bug = Buh →, Ukraine 47 J6 46 59N 31 58 E
Bug →, Poland 45 F8 52 31N 21 5 E
Buga, Colombia 124 C3 4 0N 76 15W
Buganda, Uganda 86 C3 0 0 31 30 E
Buganga, Uganda 86 C3 0 3 S 32 0 E
Bugasong, Phil. 61 F5 11 3N 122 4 E
Bugeat, France 20 C5 45 36N 1 55 E
Bugel, Tanjung, Indonesia 63 G14 6 26 S 111 3 E
Bugibba, Malta 36 D1 35 57N 14 25 E
Bugojno, Bos.-H. 42 F2 44 2N 17 25 E
Bugsuk, Phil. 62 C5 8 15N 117 15 E
Buguma, Nigeria 83 E6 4 42N 6 55 E
Bugun Shara, Mongolia 60 B5 49 0N 104 0 E
Buguruslan, Russia 50 D6 53 39N 52 26 E
Buh →, Ukraine 47 J6 46 59N 31 58 E
Buharkent, Turkey 39 D10 37 58N 28 44 E
Buheirat-Murrat-el-Kubra, Egypt 80 H8 30 18N 32 26 E
Buhera, Zimbabwe 89 B5 19 18 S 31 29 E
Bühl, Germany 25 G4 48 40N 8 8 E
Buhl, U.S.A. 114 E6 42 36N 114 46W
Buhuşi, Romania 43 D11 46 41N 26 45 E
Builth Wells, U.K. 13 E4 52 9N 3 25W
Buinsk, Russia 48 C9 55 0N 48 18 E
Buir Nur, Mongolia 60 B6 47 50N 117 42 E
Buis-les-Baronnies, France 21 D9 44 17N 5 16 E
Buitrago = Buitrago del Lozoya, Spain 34 E7 40 58N 3 38W
Buitrago del Lozoya, Spain 34 E7 40 58N 3 38W
Bujalance, Spain 35 H6 37 54N 4 23W
Bujanovac, Serbia, Yug. 40 D5 42 28N 21 44 E
Bujaraloz, Spain 32 D4 41 29N 0 10W
Buje, Croatia 29 C10 45 24N 13 39 E
Bujumbura, Burundi 86 C2 3 16 S 29 18 E
Bük, Hungary 42 C1 47 22N 16 45 E
Buk, Poland 45 F3 52 21N 16 30 E
Bukachacha, Russia 51 D12 52 55N 116 50 E
Bukama, Dem. Rep. of the Congo 87 D2 9 10 S 25 50 E
Bukavu, Dem. Rep. of the Congo 86 C2 2 20 S 28 52 E
Bukene, Tanzania 86 C3 4 15 S 32 48 E
Bukhara = Bukhoro, Uzbekistan 50 F7 39 48N 64 25 E
Bukhoro, Uzbekistan 50 F7 39 48N 64 25 E
Bukima, Tanzania 86 C3 1 50 S 33 25 E
Bukit Mertajam, Malaysia 65 K3 5 22N 100 28 E
Bukittinggi, Indonesia 62 E2 0 20 S 100 20 E
Bükk, Hungary 42 B5 48 0N 20 30 E
Bukoba, Tanzania 86 C3 1 20 S 31 49 E
Bukuru, Nigeria 83 D6 9 42N 8 48 E
Bukuya, Uganda 86 B3 0 40N 31 52 E
Būl, Kuh-e, Iran 71 D7 30 48N 52 45 E
Bula, Guinea-Biss. 82 C1 12 7N 15 43W
Bula, Indonesia 63 E8 3 6 S 130 30 E
Bülach, Switz. 25 H4 47 31N 8 32 E
Bulahdelah, Australia 95 E5 32 23 S 152 13 E
Bulan, Phil. 61 E5 12 40N 123 52 E
Bulancak, Turkey 73 B8 40 56N 38 14 E
Bulandshahr, India 68 E7 28 28N 77 51 E
Bulanık, Turkey 73 C10 39 4N 42 14 E
Bûlâq, Egypt 80 B3 25 10N 30 38 E
Bulawayo, Zimbabwe 87 G2 20 7 S 28 32 E
Buldan, Turkey 39 C10 38 2N 28 50 E
Bulgar, Russia 48 C9 54 57N 49 4 E
Bulgaria ■, Europe 41 D9 42 35N 25 30 E
Bulgheria, Monte, Italy 31 B8 40 4N 15 26 E
Bulgurca, Turkey 39 C9 38 9N 27 9 E
Buli, Teluk, Indonesia 63 D7 1 5N 128 25 E
Buliluyan, C., Phil. 61 G2 8 20N 117 15 E
Bulki, Ethiopia 81 F4 6 11N 36 31 E
Bulkley →, Canada 104 B3 55 15N 127 40W
Bull Shoals L., U.S.A. 113 G8 36 22N 92 35W
Bullaque →, Spain 35 G6 38 59N 4 17W
Bullas, Spain 33 G3 38 2N 1 40W
Bulle, Switz. 25 J3 46 37N 7 3 E
Bullhead City, U.S.A. 117 K12 35 8N 114 32W
Büllingen, Belgium 17 D6 50 25N 6 16 E
Bullock Creek, Australia 94 B3 17 43 S 144 31 E
Bulloo →, Australia 95 D3 28 43 S 142 30 E
Bulloo L., Australia 95 D3 28 43 S 142 25 E
Bulls, N.Z. 91 J5 40 10 S 175 24 E
Bully-les-Mines, France 19 B9 50 27N 2 44 E
Bulnes, Chile 126 D1 36 42 S 72 19W
Bulqiza = Bulqizë, Albania 40 E4 41 30N 20 21 E
Bulqizë, Albania 40 E4 41 30N 20 21 E
Bulsar = Valsad, India 66 J8 20 40N 72 58 E
Bultfontein, S. Africa 88 D4 28 18 S 26 10 E
Bulukumba, Indonesia 63 F6 5 33 S 120 11 E
Bulun, Russia 51 B13 70 37N 127 30 E
Bumba, Dem. Rep. of the Congo 84 D4 2 13N 22 30 E

Bumbeşti-Jiu, *Romania* **43 E8** 45 10N 23 24 E
Bumbiri I., *Tanzania* .. **86 C3** 1 40 S 31 55 E
Bumbuna, *S. Leone* ... **82 D2** 9 2N 11 49W
Bumhpa Bum, *Burma* **67 F20** 26 51N 97 14 E
Bumi →, *Zimbabwe* .. **87 F2** 17 0 S 28 20 E
Buna, *Kenya* .... **86 B4** 2 58N 39 30 E
Bunawan, *Phil.* ...... **61 G6** 8 12N 125 57 E
Bunazi, *Tanzania* .... **86 C3** 1 3 S 31 23 E
Bunbury, *Australia* ... **93 F2** 33 20 S 115 35 E
Bunclody, *Ireland* **15 D5** 52 39N 6 40W
Buncrana, *Ireland* **15 A4** 55 8N 7 27W
Bundaberg, *Australia* . **95 C5** 24 54 S 152 22 E
Bünde, *Germany* ..... **24 C4** 52 11N 8 35 E
Bundey →, *Australia* . **94 C2** 21 46 S 135 37 E
Bundi, *India* .... **68 G6** 25 30N 75 35 E
Bundoran, *Ireland* **15 B3** 54 28N 8 16W
Bundukia, *Sudan* ..... **81 F3** 5 14N 30 55 E
Bung Kan, *Thailand* .. **64 C4** 18 23N 103 37 E
Bunga →, *Nigeria* .... **83 C6** 11 23N 9 56 E
Bungatakada, *Japan* .. **55 H5** 33 35N 131 25 E
Bungay, *U.K.* .... **13 E9** 52 27N 1 28 E
Bungil Cr. →, *Australia* **95 D4** 27 5 S 149 5 E
Bungo-Suidō, *Japan* .. **55 H6** 33 0N 132 15 E
Bungoma, *Kenya* ..... **86 B3** 0 34N 34 34 E
Bungu, *Tanzania* ..... **86 D4** 7 35 S 39 0 E
Bunia, *Dem. Rep. of the Congo* .... **86 B3** 1 35N 30 20 E
Bunji, *Pakistan* ...... **69 B6** 35 45N 74 40 E
Bunkie, *U.S.A.* **113 K8** 30 57N 92 11W
Bunnell, *U.S.A.* **109 L5** 29 28N 81 16W
Buñol, *Spain* **33 F4** 39 25N 0 47W
Bunsuru, *Nigeria* ..... **83 C5** 13 21N 6 23 E
Buntok, *Indonesia* .... **62 E4** 1 40 S 114 58 E
Bununu Dass, *Nigeria* . **83 C6** 10 5N 9 31 E
Bununu Kasa, *Nigeria* **83 D6** 9 51N 9 32 E
Bünyan, *Turkey* ..... **72 C6** 38 51N 35 51 E
Bunyu, *Indonesia* .... **62 D5** 3 35N 117 50 E
Bunza, *Nigeria* .... **83 C5** 12 8N 4 0 E
Buol, *Indonesia* ...... **63 D6** 1 15N 121 32 E
Buon Brieng, *Vietnam* **64 F7** 13 9N 108 12 E
Buon Ma Thuot, *Vietnam* .... **64 F7** 12 40N 108 3 E
Buong Long, *Cambodia* **64 F6** 13 44N 106 59 E
Buorkhaya, Mys, *Russia* **51 B14** 71 50N 132 40 E
Buqayq, *Si. Arabia* ... **71 E6** 26 0N 49 45 E
Buqbuq, *Egypt* ...... **80 A2** 31 29N 25 29 E
Bur Acaba, *Somali Rep.* **74 G3** 3 12N 44 20 E
Bûr Fuad, *Egypt* ..... **80 H8** 31 15N 32 20 E
Bûr Safâga, *Egypt* ... **70 E2** 26 43N 33 57 E
Bûr Sa'îd, *Egypt* ..... **80 H8** 31 16N 32 18 E
Bûr Sûdân, *Sudan* .... **80 D4** 19 32N 37 9 E
Bûr Taufiq, *Egypt* ... **80 J8** 29 54N 32 32 E
Bura, *Kenya* .... **86 C4** 1 4 S 39 58 E
Burakin, *Australia* ... **93 F2** 30 31 S 117 10 E
Buram, *Sudan* .... **81 E2** 10 51N 25 9 E
Burao, *Somali Rep.* ... **74 F4** 9 32N 45 32 E
Burāq, *Syria* .... **75 B5** 33 11N 36 29 E
Buraydah, *Si. Arabia* . **70 E4** 26 20N 43 59 E
Burbank, *U.S.A.* **117 L8** 34 11N 118 19W
Burda, *India* .... **68 G6** 25 50N 77 35 E
Burdekin →, *Australia* **94 B4** 19 38 S 147 25 E
Burdur, *Turkey* ...... **39 D12** 37 45N 30 17 E
Burdur □, *Turkey* .... **39 D12** 37 45N 30 0 E
Burdur Gölü, *Turkey* . **39 D12** 37 44N 30 10 E
Burdwan = Barddhaman, *India* . **69 H12** 23 14N 87 39 E
Bure, *Gojam, Ethiopia* **81 E4** 10 40N 37 4 E
Bure, *Ilubabor, Ethiopia* .... **81 F4** 8 19N 35 8 E
Bure →, *U.K.* .... **12 E9** 52 38N 1 43 E
Büren, *Germany* ..... **24 D4** 51 33N 8 35 E
Bureya →, *Russia* .... **51 E13** 49 27N 129 30 E
Burford, *Canada* **110 C4** 43 7N 80 27W
Burg, *Germany* ...... **24 C7** 52 16N 11 51 E
Burg auf Fehmarn, *Germany* .... **24 A7** 54 28N 11 9 E
Burg el Arab, *Egypt* .. **80 H6** 30 54N 29 32 E
Burg et Tuyur, *Sudan* . **80 C2** 20 55N 27 56 E
Burg Stargard, *Germany* .... **24 B9** 53 29N 13 18 E
Burgas, *Bulgaria* ..... **41 D11** 42 33N 27 29 E
Burgas □, *Bulgaria* ... **41 D10** 42 30N 26 50 E
Burgaski Zaliv, *Bulgaria* .... **41 D11** 42 30N 27 39 E
Burgdorf, *Germany* ... **24 C6** 52 27N 10 1 E
Burgdorf, *Switz.* ..... **25 H3** 47 3N 7 37 E
Burgenland □, *Austria* **27 D9** 47 20N 16 20 E
Burgeo, *Canada* **103 C8** 47 37N 57 38W
Burgersdorp, *S. Africa* **88 E4** 31 0 S 26 20 E
Burges, Mt., *Australia* . **93 F3** 30 50 S 121 5 E
Burghausen, *Germany* **25 G8** 48 9N 12 49 E
Búrgio, *Italy* .... **30 E6** 37 36N 13 17 E
Burglengenfeld, *Germany* .... **25 F8** 49 12N 12 2 E
Burgohondo, *Spain* ... **34 E6** 40 26N 4 47W
Burgos, *Spain* **34 C7** 42 21N 3 41W
Burgos □, *Spain* **34 C7** 42 21N 3 42W
Burgstädt, *Germany* .. **24 E8** 50 54N 12 49 E
Burgsvik, *Sweden* .... **11 G12** 57 3N 18 19 E
Burguillos del Cerro, *Spain* **35 G4** 38 23N 6 35W
Burgundy = Bourgogne, *France* .... **19 F11** 47 0N 4 50 E
Burhaniye, *Turkey* ... **39 B8** 39 30N 26 58 E
Burhanpur, *India* ..... **66 J10** 21 18N 76 14 E
Burhi Gandak →, *India* **69 G12** 25 20N 86 37 E
Burhner →, *India* .... **69 H9** 22 43N 80 31 E
Buri Pen., *Eritrea* .... **81 D4** 15 25N 39 55 E
Burias I., *Phil.* .... **61 E5** 12 55N 123 5 E
Burica, Pta., *Costa Rica* **120 E3** 8 3N 82 51W
Burien, *U.S.A.* **116 C4** 47 28N 122 21W
Burigi, L., *Tanzania* .. **86 C3** 2 2 S 31 22 E
Burin, *Canada* **103 C8** 47 1N 55 14W
Buriram, *Thailand* .... **64 E4** 15 0N 103 0 E
Burj Sāfitā, *Syria* .... **70 C3** 34 48N 36 7 E
Burji, *Ethiopia* ...... **81 F4** 5 29N 37 51 E
Burkburnett, *U.S.A.* .. **113 H5** 34 6N 98 34W
Burke →, *Australia* .. **94 C2** 23 12 S 139 33 E
Burke Chan., *Canada* . **104 C3** 52 10N 127 30W
Burketown, *Australia* . **94 B2** 17 45 S 139 33 E
Burkina Faso ■, *Africa* **82 C4** 12 0N 1 0W
Burk's Falls, *Canada* .. **102 C4** 45 37N 79 24W
Burlada, *Spain* **32 C3** 42 49N 1 36W
Burleigh Falls, *Canada* **110 B6** 44 33N 78 12W
Burley, *U.S.A.* **114 E7** 42 32N 113 48W
Burlingame, *U.S.A.* ... **116 H4** 37 35N 122 21W
Burlington, *Canada* ... **102 D4** 43 18N 79 45W
Burlington, *Colo., U.S.A.* **112 F3** 39 18N 102 16W
Burlington, *Iowa, U.S.A.* **112 E9** 40 49N 91 14W
Burlington, *Kans., U.S.A.* **112 F7** 38 12N 95 45W
Burlington, *N.C., U.S.A.* **109 G6** 36 6N 79 26W
Burlington, *N.J., U.S.A.* **111 F10** 40 4N 74 51W
Burlington, *Vt., U.S.A.* **111 B11** 44 29N 73 12W
Burlington, *Wash., U.S.A.* **116 B4** 48 28N 122 20W
Burlington, *Wis., U.S.A.* **108 D1** 42 41N 88 17W
Burlyu-Tyube, *Kazakstan* .... **50 E8** 46 30N 79 10 E
Burma ■, *Asia* .... **67 J20** 21 0N 96 30 E
Burnaby I., *Canada* ... **104 C2** 52 25N 131 19W
Burnet, *U.S.A.* **113 K5** 30 45N 98 14W
Burney, *U.S.A.* **114 F3** 40 53N 121 40W
Burnham, *U.S.A.* **110 F7** 40 38N 77 34W
Burnham-on-Sea, *U.K.* **13 F5** 51 14N 3 0W
Burnie, *Australia* ..... **94 G4** 41 4 S 145 56 E
Burnley, *U.K.* **12 D5** 53 47N 2 14W
Burns, *U.S.A.* **114 E4** 43 35N 119 3W
Burns Lake, *Canada* .. **104 C3** 54 20N 125 45W
Burnside →, *Canada* . **100 B9** 66 51N 108 4W
Burnside, L., *Australia* **93 E3** 25 22 S 123 0 E
Burnsville, *U.S.A.* **112 C8** 44 47N 93 17W
Burnt L., *Canada* **103 B7** 53 35N 64 4W
Burnt River, *Canada* .. **110 B6** 44 41N 78 42W
Burntwood →, *Canada* **105 B9** 56 8N 96 34W
Burntwood L., *Canada* **105 B8** 55 22N 100 26W
Burqān, *Kuwait* ...... **70 D5** 29 0N 47 57 E
Burra, *Australia* ..... **95 E2** 33 40 S 138 55 E
Burra, *Nigeria* .... **83 C6** 11 0N 8 56 E
Burray, *U.K.* **14 C6** 58 51N 2 54W
Burrel, *Albania* ...... **40 E4** 41 36N 20 1 E
Burreli = Burrel, *Albania* .... **40 E4** 41 36N 20 1 E
Burren Junction, *Australia* .... **95 E4** 30 7 S 148 59 E
Burriana, *Spain* **32 F4** 39 50N 0 4W
Burrinjuck Res., *Australia* .... **95 F4** 35 0 S 148 36 E
Burro, Serranías del, *Mexico* **118 B4** 29 0N 102 0W
Burrow Hd., *U.K.* **14 G4** 54 41N 4 24W
Burruyacú, *Argentina* . **126 B3** 26 30 S 64 40W
Burry Port, *U.K.* **13 F3** 51 41N 4 15W
Bursa, *Turkey* .... **41 F13** 40 15N 29 5 E
Burseryd, *Sweden* .... **11 G7** 57 12N 13 17 E
Burstall, *Canada* **105 C7** 50 39N 109 54W
Burton, *Ohio, U.S.A.* . **110 E3** 41 28N 81 8W
Burton, *S.C., U.S.A.* .. **109 J5** 32 25N 80 45W
Burton, L., *Canada* ... **102 B4** 54 45N 78 20W
Burton upon Trent, *U.K.* **12 E6** 52 48N 1 38W
Buru, *Indonesia* ..... **63 E7** 3 30 S 126 30 E
Burullus, Bahra el, *Egypt* .... **80 H7** 31 25N 31 0 E
Burûn, Râs, *Egypt* ... **75 D2** 31 14N 33 7 E
Burundi ■, *Africa* .... **86 C3** 3 15 S 30 0 E
Bururi, *Burundi* ..... **86 C2** 3 57 S 29 37 E
Burutu, *Nigeria* ...... **83 D6** 5 20N 5 29 E
Burwell, *U.S.A.* **112 E5** 41 47N 99 8W
Burwick, *U.K.* **14 C5** 58 45N 2 58W
Bury, *U.K.* **12 D5** 53 35N 2 17W
Bury St. Edmunds, *U.K.* **13 E8** 52 15N 0 43 E
Buryatia □, *Russia* ... **51 D11** 53 0N 110 0 E
Buryn, *Ukraine* ...... **47 G7** 51 13N 33 50 E
Burzenin, *Poland* ..... **45 G5** 51 28N 18 47 E
Busalla, *Italy* .... **28 D5** 44 34N 8 57 E
Busango Swamp, *Zambia* .... **87 E2** 14 15 S 25 45 E
Buşayrah, *Syria* ...... **70 C4** 35 9N 40 26 E
Busca, *Italy* .... **28 D4** 44 31N 7 29 E
Bushat, *Albania* ...... **40 E3** 41 58N 19 34 E
Bushati = Bushat, *Albania* .... **40 E3** 41 58N 19 34 E
Būshehr, *Iran* .... **71 D6** 28 55N 50 55 E
Būshehr □, *Iran* ..... **71 D6** 28 20N 51 45 E
Bushell, *Canada* **105 B7** 59 31N 108 45W
Bushenyi, *Uganda* .... **86 C3** 0 35 S 30 10 E
Bushire = Būshehr, *Iran* **71 D6** 28 55N 50 55 E
Busie, *Ghana* **82 C4** 10 29N 2 22W
Businga, *Dem. Rep. of the Congo* .... **84 D4** 3 16N 20 59 E
Busko-Zdrój, *Poland* . **45 H7** 50 28N 20 42 E
Busovača, *Bos.-H.* ... **42 F2** 44 6N 17 53 E
Buşra ash Shām, *Syria* **75 C5** 32 30N 36 25 E
Busselton, *Australia* .. **93 F2** 33 42 S 115 15 E
Busseri →, *Sudan* .... **81 F2** 7 41N 28 3 E
Busseto, *Italy* .... **28 D7** 44 59N 10 2 E
Bussière-Badil, *France* **20 C4** 45 39N 0 36 E
Bussolengo, *Italy* .... **28 C7** 45 28N 10 51 E
Bussum, *Neths.* ...... **17 B5** 52 16N 5 10 E
Buşteni, *Romania* .... **43 E10** 45 24N 25 32 E
Busto, C., *Spain* **34 B4** 43 34N 6 28W
Busto Arsízio, *Italy* .. **28 C5** 45 37N 8 51 E
Busu-Djanoa, *Dem. Rep. of the Congo* .... **84 D4** 1 43N 21 23 E
Busuanga I., *Phil.* .... **61 E3** 12 10N 120 0 E
Büsum, *Germany* .... **24 A4** 54 7N 8 51 E
Buta, *Dem. Rep. of the Congo* .... **86 B1** 2 50N 24 53 E
Butare, *Rwanda* ..... **86 C2** 2 31 S 29 52 E
Butaritari, *Kiribati* ... **96 G9** 3 30N 174 0 E
Bute, *U.K.* **14 F3** 55 48N 5 2W
Bute Inlet, *Canada* ... **104 C4** 50 40N 124 53W
Butemba, *Uganda* .... **86 B3** 1 9N 31 37 E
Butembo, *Dem. Rep. of the Congo* .... **86 B2** 0 9N 29 18 E
Buteni, *Romania* ..... **42 D7** 46 19N 22 7 E
Butera, *Italy* .... **31 E7** 37 11N 14 11 E
Butha Qi, *China* ..... **60 B7** 48 0N 122 32 E
Butiaba, *Uganda* ..... **86 B3** 1 50N 31 20 E
Butler, *Mo., U.S.A.* ... **112 F7** 38 16N 94 20W
Butler, *Pa., U.S.A.* ... **110 F5** 40 52N 79 54W
Buton, *Indonesia* ..... **63 E6** 5 0 S 122 45 E
Butte, *Mont., U.S.A.* .. **114 C7** 46 0N 112 32W
Butte, *Nebr., U.S.A.* .. **112 D5** 42 58N 98 51W
Butte Creek →, *U.S.A.* **116 F5** 39 12N 121 56W
Butterworth = Gcuwa, *S. Africa* .... **89 E4** 32 20 S 28 11 E
Butterworth, *Malaysia* **65 K3** 5 24N 100 23 E
Buttevant, *Ireland* **15 D3** 52 14N 8 40W
Buttfield, Mt., *Australia* **93 D4** 24 45 S 128 9 E
Button B., *Canada* **105 B10** 58 45N 94 23W
Buttonwillow, *U.S.A.* . **117 K7** 35 24N 119 28W
Butty Hd., *Australia* .. **93 F3** 33 54 S 121 39 E
Butuan, *Phil.* .... **61 G6** 8 57N 125 33 E
Butuku-Luba, *Eq. Guin.* .... **83 E6** 3 29N 8 33 E
Butung = Buton, *Indonesia* .... **63 E6** 5 0 S 122 45 E
Buturlinovka, *Russia* . **48 E5** 50 50N 40 35 E
Butzbach, *Germany* .. **25 E4** 50 25N 8 40 E
Bützow, *Germany* .... **24 B7** 53 50N 11 58 E
Buxa Duar, *India* .... **69 F13** 27 45N 89 35 E
Buxar, *India* .... **69 G10** 25 34N 83 58 E
Buxtehude, *Germany* . **24 B5** 53 28N 9 39 E
Buxton, *U.K.* **12 D6** 53 16N 1 54W
Buxy, *France* .... **19 F11** 46 44N 4 40 E
Buy, *Russia* .... **48 A5** 58 28N 41 28 E
Buynaksk, *Russia* .... **49 J8** 42 48N 47 7 E
Buyo, *Ivory C.* **82 D3** 6 21N 7 5W
Buyo, L. de, *Ivory C.* . **82 D3** 6 16N 7 10W
Büyük Menderes →, *Turkey* .... **39 D9** 37 28N 27 11 E
Büyükçekmece, *Turkey* **41 E12** 41 2N 28 35 E
Büyükkariştiran, *Turkey* .... **41 E11** 41 18N 27 33 E
Büyükkemikli Burnu, *Turkey* .... **41 F10** 40 18N 26 14 E
Büyükorhan, *Turkey* .. **39 B10** 39 46N 28 56 E
Büyükyoncalı, *Turkey* **41 E11** 41 20N 27 55 E
Buzançais, *France* .... **18 F8** 46 54N 1 25 E
Buzău, *Romania* ..... **43 E11** 45 10N 26 50 E
Buzău □, *Romania* ... **43 E11** 45 20N 26 30 E
Buzău →, *Romania* ... **43 E12** 45 26N 27 44 E
Buzău, Pasul, *Romania* **43 E11** 45 35N 26 12 E
Buzen, *Japan* .... **55 H5** 33 35N 131 5 E
Buzet, *Croatia* ...... **29 C10** 45 24N 13 58 E
Buzi →, *Mozam.* ..... **87 F3** 19 50 S 34 43 E
Buziaş, *Romania* ..... **42 E6** 45 38N 21 36 E
Buzuluk, *Russia* ..... **50 D6** 52 48N 52 12 E
Buzuluk →, *Russia* ... **48 E6** 50 15N 42 7 E
Buzzards B., *U.S.A.* .. **111 E14** 41 45N 70 37W
Buzzards Bay, *U.S.A.* . **111 E14** 41 44N 70 37W
Bwana Mkubwe, *Dem. Rep. of the Congo* .... **87 E2** 13 8 S 28 38 E
Byala, *Ruse, Bulgaria* . **41 C9** 43 28N 25 44 E
Byala, *Varna, Bulgaria* **41 D11** 42 53N 27 55 E
Byala Slatina, *Bulgaria* **40 C7** 43 26N 23 58 E
Byarezina →, *Belarus* **47 F6** 52 33N 30 14 E
Byaroza, *Belarus* ..... **47 F3** 52 31N 24 51 E
Bychawa, *Poland* ..... **45 G9** 51 1N 22 36 E
Byczyna, *Poland* ..... **45 G5** 51 7N 18 12 E
Bydgoszcz, *Poland* ... **45 E5** 53 10N 18 0 E
Byelarus = Belarus ■, *Europe* .... **46 F4** 53 30N 27 0 E
Byelorussia = Belarus ■, *Europe* .. **46 F4** 53 30N 27 0 E
Byers, *U.S.A.* **112 F2** 39 43N 104 14W
Byesville, *U.S.A.* **110 G3** 39 58N 81 32W
Byford, *Australia* .... **93 F2** 32 15 S 116 0 E
Bykhaw, *Belarus* ..... **46 F6** 53 31N 30 14 E
Bykhov = Bykhaw, *Belarus* .... **46 F6** 53 31N 30 14 E
Bykovo, *Russia* ...... **48 F7** 49 50N 45 25 E
Bylas, *U.S.A.* **115 K8** 33 8N 110 7W
Bylot, *Canada* **105 B10** 58 25N 94 8W
Bylot I., *Canada* **101 A12** 73 13N 78 34W
Byrd, C., *Antarctica* .. **5 C17** 69 38 S 76 7W
Byrock, *Australia* .... **95 E4** 30 40 S 146 27 E
Byron Bay, *Australia* . **95 D5** 28 43 S 153 37 E
Byrranga, Gory, *Russia* **51 B11** 75 0N 100 0 E
Byrranga Mts. = Byrranga, Gory, *Russia* .... **51 B11** 75 0N 100 0 E
Byrum, *Denmark* ..... **11 G5** 57 16N 11 0 E
Byske, *Sweden* ...... **8 D19** 64 57N 21 11 E
Byske älv →, *Sweden* . **8 D19** 64 57N 21 13 E
Bystrzyca →, *Dolnośląskie, Poland* **45 G3** 51 12N 16 55 E
Bystrzyca →, *Lubelskie, Poland* .. **45 G9** 51 21N 22 46 E
Bystrzyca Kłodzka, *Poland* .... **45 H3** 50 19N 16 39 E
Bytča, *Slovak Rep.* ... **27 B11** 49 13N 18 34 E
Bytom, *Poland* ...... **45 H5** 50 25N 18 54 E
Bytom Odrzański, *Poland* .... **45 G2** 51 44N 15 48 E
Bytów, *Poland* ...... **44 D4** 54 10N 17 30 E
Byumba, *Rwanda* .... **86 C3** 1 35 S 30 4 E
Bzenec, *Czech Rep.* ... **27 C10** 48 58N 17 18 E
Bzura →, *Poland* .... **45 F7** 52 25N 20 15 E

C

Ca →, *Vietnam* ...... **64 C5** 18 45N 105 45 E
Ca Mau, *Vietnam* .... **65 H5** 9 7N 105 8 E
Ca Mau, Mui, *Vietnam* **65 H5** 8 38N 104 44 E
Ca Na, *Vietnam* ..... **65 G7** 11 20N 108 54 E
Caacupé, *Paraguay* ... **126 B4** 25 23 S 57 5W
Caála, *Angola* .... **85 G3** 12 46 S 15 30 E
Caamano Sd., *Canada* **104 C3** 52 55N 129 25W
Caazapá, *Paraguay* ... **126 B4** 26 8 S 56 19W
Caazapá □, *Paraguay* . **127 B4** 26 10 S 56 0W
Cabadbaran, *Phil.* .... **61 G6** 9 10N 125 38 E
Cabalian = San Juan, *Phil.* .... **61 F6** 10 16N 125 10 E
Cabana, *Spain* **34 B2** 43 13N 8 54W
Cabañaquinta, *Spain* .. **34 B5** 43 10N 5 38W
Cabanatuan, *Phil.* .... **61 D4** 15 30N 120 58 E
Cabanes, *Spain* ...... **32 E5** 40 9N 0 2 E
Cabano, *Canada* **103 C6** 47 40N 68 56W
Čabar, *Croatia* ...... **29 C11** 45 36N 14 39 E
Cabazon, *U.S.A.* **117 M10** 33 55N 116 47W
Cabedelo, *Brazil* ..... **125 E12** 7 0 S 34 50W
Cabeza del Buey, *Spain* **35 G5** 38 44N 5 13W
Cabezón de la Sal, *Spain* **34 B6** 43 18N 4 14W
Cabildo, *Chile* .... **126 C1** 32 30 S 71 5W
Cabimas, *Venezuela* .. **124 A4** 10 23N 71 25W
Cabinda, *Angola* ..... **84 F2** 5 33 S 12 11 E
Cabinda □, *Angola* ... **84 F2** 5 0 S 12 30 E
Cabinet Mts., *U.S.A.* . **114 C6** 48 0N 115 30W
Cabo Blanco, *Argentina* **128 F3** 47 15 S 65 47W
Cabo Frio, *Brazil* .... **127 A7** 22 51 S 42 3W
Cabo Pantoja, *Peru* ... **124 D3** 1 0 S 75 10W
Cabonga, Réservoir, *Canada* **102 C4** 47 20N 76 40W
Cabool, *U.S.A.* **113 G8** 37 7N 92 6W
Caboolture, *Australia* . **95 D5** 27 5 S 152 58 E
Cabora Bassa Dam = Cahora Bassa, Represa de, *Mozam.* **87 F3** 15 20 S 32 50 E
Caborca, *Mexico* **118 A2** 30 40N 112 10W
Cabot, Mt., *U.S.A.* ... **111 B13** 44 30N 71 25W
Cabot Hd., *Canada* ... **110 A3** 45 14N 81 17W
Cabot Str., *Canada* ... **103 C8** 47 15N 59 40W
Cabra, *Spain* **35 H6** 37 30N 4 28W
Cabra del Santo Cristo, *Spain* **35 H7** 37 42N 3 16W
Cábras, *Italy* .... **30 C1** 39 56N 8 32 E
Cabrera, *Spain* ...... **37 B9** 39 8N 2 57 E
Cabrera, Sierra, *Spain* **34 C4** 42 12N 6 40W
Cabri, *Canada* **105 C7** 50 35N 108 25W
Cabriel →, *Spain* **33 F3** 39 14N 1 3W
Cabugao, *Phil.* .... **61 C4** 17 48N 120 27 E
Cacabelos, *Spain* **34 C4** 42 36N 6 44W
Caçador, *Brazil* ...... **127 B5** 26 47 S 51 0W
Čačak, *Serbia, Yug.* ... **40 C4** 43 54N 20 20 E
Caçapava do Sul, *Brazil* **127 C5** 30 30 S 53 30W
Cáccamo, *Italy* ...... **30 E6** 37 56N 13 40 E
Cacém, *Portugal* **35 G1** 38 46N 9 18W
Cáceres, *Brazil* ...... **124 G7** 16 5 S 57 40W
Cáceres, *Spain* **35 F4** 39 26N 6 23W
Cáceres □, *Spain* **34 F5** 39 45N 6 0W
Cache Bay, *Canada* .. **102 C4** 46 22N 80 0W
Cache Cr. →, *U.S.A.* . **116 G5** 38 42N 121 42W
Cache Creek, *Canada* . **104 C4** 50 48N 121 19W
Cacheu, *Guinea-Biss.* . **82 C1** 12 14N 16 8W
Cachi, *Argentina* ..... **126 B2** 25 5 S 66 10W
Cachimbo, Serra do, *Brazil* .... **125 E7** 9 30 S 55 30W
Cachinal de la Sierra, *Chile* .... **126 A2** 24 58 S 69 32W
Cachoeira, *Brazil* .... **125 F11** 12 30 S 39 0W
Cachoeira de Itapemirim, *Brazil* .. **127 A7** 20 51 S 41 7W
Cachoeira do Sul, *Brazil* .... **127 C5** 30 3 S 52 53W
Cachopo, *Portugal* ... **35 H3** 37 20N 7 49W
Cacine, *Guinea-Biss.* .. **82 C1** 11 8N 14 57W
Cacoal, *Brazil* .... **124 F6** 11 32 S 61 18W
Cacólo, *Angola* ...... **84 G3** 10 9 S 19 21 E
Caconda, *Angola* ..... **85 G3** 13 48 S 15 8 E
Čadca, *Slovak Rep.* ... **27 B11** 49 26N 18 45 E
Caddo, *U.S.A.* **113 H6** 34 7N 96 16W
Cader Idris, *U.K.* **13 E4** 52 42N 3 53W
Cadereyta, *Mexico* ... **118 B5** 25 36N 100 0W
Cadí, Sierra del, *Spain* **32 C6** 42 17N 1 42 E
Cadibarrawirracanna, L., *Australia* ...... **95 D2** 28 52 S 135 27 E
Cadillac, *France* **20 D3** 44 38N 0 20W
Cadillac, *U.S.A.* **108 C3** 44 15N 85 24W
Cadiz, *Phil.* .... **61 F5** 10 57N 123 15 E
Cádiz, *Spain* **35 J4** 36 30N 6 20W
Cadiz, *Calif., U.S.A.* .. **117 L11** 34 30N 115 28W
Cadiz, *Ohio, U.S.A.* .. **110 F4** 40 22N 81 0W
Cádiz □, *Spain* **35 J5** 36 36N 5 45W
Cádiz, G. de, *Spain* ... **35 J3** 36 40N 7 0W
Cadiz L., *U.S.A.* **115 J6** 34 18N 115 24W
Cadney Park, *Australia* **95 D1** 27 55 S 134 3 E
Cadomin, *Canada* **104 C5** 53 2N 117 20W
Cadotte Lake, *Canada* **104 B5** 56 26N 116 23W
Cadours, *France* ..... **20 E5** 43 44N 1 2 E
Cadoux, *Australia* ... **93 F2** 30 46 S 117 7 E
Caen, *France* **18 C6** 49 10N 0 22W
Caernarfon, *U.K.* **12 D3** 53 8N 4 16W
Caernarfon B., *U.K.* .. **12 D3** 53 4N 4 40W
Caernarvon = Caernarfon, *U.K.* ... **12 D3** 53 8N 4 16W
Caerphilly, *U.K.* **13 F4** 51 35N 3 13W
Caerphilly □, *U.K.* ... **13 F4** 51 37N 3 12W
Caesarea, *Israel* ..... **75 C3** 32 30N 34 53 E
Caetité, *Brazil* ...... **125 F10** 13 50 S 42 32W
Cafayate, *Argentina* .. **126 B2** 26 2 S 66 0W
Cafu, *Angola* .... **88 B2** 16 30 S 15 8 E
Cagayan →, *Phil.* .... **61 B4** 18 25N 121 42 E
Cagayan de Oro, *Phil.* **61 G6** 8 30N 124 40 E
Cagayan Is., *Phil.* .... **61 G4** 9 40N 121 16 E
Cagayan Sulu I., *Phil.* . **61 H3** 7 1N 118 30 E
Cagli, *Italy* .... **29 E9** 43 33N 12 39 E
Cágliari, *Italy* .... **30 C2** 39 13N 9 7 E
Cágliari, G. di, *Italy* .. **30 C2** 39 8N 9 11 E
Cagnano Varano, *Italy* **29 G12** 41 49N 15 47 E
Cagnes-sur-Mer, *France* **21 E11** 43 40N 7 9 E
Caguán →, *Colombia* . **124 D4** 0 8 S 74 18W
Caguas, *Puerto Rico* .. **121 C6** 18 14N 66 2W
Caha Mts., *Ireland* ... **15 E2** 51 45N 9 40W
Cahama, *Angola* ..... **88 B1** 16 17 S 14 19 E
Caher, *Ireland* **15 D4** 52 22N 7 56W
Caherciveen, *Ireland* . **15 E1** 51 56N 10 14W
Cahora Bassa, Represa de, *Mozam.* .... **87 F3** 15 20 S 32 50 E
Cahore Pt., *Ireland* ... **15 D5** 52 33N 6 12W
Cahors, *France* ...... **20 D5** 44 27N 1 27 E
Cahul, *Moldova* ..... **43 E13** 45 50N 28 15 E
Cai Bau, Dao, *Vietnam* **58 G6** 21 10N 107 27 E
Cai Nuoc, *Vietnam* ... **65 H5** 8 56N 105 1 E
Caia, *Mozam.* .... **87 F4** 17 51 S 35 24 E
Caianda, *Angola* ..... **87 E1** 11 2 S 23 31 E
Caibarién, *Cuba* **120 B4** 22 30N 79 30W
Caibiran, *Phil.* .... **61 F6** 11 34N 124 35 E
Caicara, *Venezuela* ... **124 B5** 7 38N 66 10W
Caicó, *Brazil* .... **125 E11** 6 20 S 37 0W
Caicos Is., *W. Indies* .. **121 B5** 21 40N 71 40W
Caicos Passage, *W. Indies* **121 B5** 22 45N 72 45W
Caidian, *China* ...... **59 B10** 30 35N 114 2 E
Căinari, *Moldova* .... **43 D14** 46 41N 29 3 E
Caird Coast, *Antarctica* **5 D1** 75 0 S 25 0W
Cairn Gorm, *U.K.* **14 D5** 57 7N 3 39W
Cairngorm Mts., *U.K.* . **14 D5** 57 6N 3 42W
Cairnryan, *U.K.* **14 G3** 54 59N 5 1W
Cairns, *Australia* .... **94 B4** 16 57 S 145 45 E
Cairns L., *Canada* **105 C10** 51 42N 94 30W
Cairo = El Qâhira, *Egypt* .... **80 H7** 30 1N 31 14 E
Cairo, *Ga., U.S.A.* ... **109 K3** 30 52N 84 13W
Cairo, *Ill., U.S.A.* ... **113 G10** 37 0N 89 11W
Cairo, *N.Y., U.S.A.* .. **111 D11** 42 18N 74 0W
Cairo Montenotte, *Italy* **28 D5** 44 23N 8 16 E
Caithness, Ord of, *U.K.* **14 C5** 58 8N 3 36W
Cajamarca, *Peru* ..... **124 E3** 7 5 S 78 28W
Cajarc, *France* ...... **20 D5** 44 29N 1 50 E
Cajàzeiras, *Brazil* .... **125 E11** 6 52 S 38 30W
Čajetina, *Serbia, Yug.* . **40 C3** 43 47N 19 42 E
Çakirgol, *Turkey* .... **73 B8** 40 33N 39 40 E
Çakırlar, *Turkey* ..... **39 E12** 36 52N 30 36 E
Čakovec, *Croatia* .... **29 B13** 46 23N 16 26 E
Çal, *Turkey* .... **39 C11** 38 4N 29 23 E
Cala, *Spain* **35 H4** 37 59N 6 21W
Cala →, *Spain* **35 H4** 37 38N 6 5W
Cala Cadolar, Punta de = Rotja, Pta., *Spain* .... **33 G6** 38 38N 1 35 E
Cala d'Or, *Spain* .... **37 B10** 39 23N 3 14 E
Cala en Porter, *Spain* . **37 B11** 39 52N 4 8 E
Cala Figuera, C. de, *Spain* .... **37 B9** 39 27N 2 31 E
Cala Forcat, *Spain* ... **37 B10** 40 0N 3 47 E
Cala Major, *Spain* ... **37 B9** 39 33N 2 37 E
Cala Mezquida = Sa Mesquida, *Spain* ... **37 B11** 39 55N 4 16 E
Cala Millor, *Spain* ... **37 B10** 39 35N 3 22 E
Cala Ratjada, *Spain* .. **37 B10** 39 43N 3 27 E
Cala Santa Galdana, *Spain* .... **37 B10** 39 56N 3 58 E
Calabanga, *Phil.* ..... **61 E5** 13 42N 123 17 E
Calabar, *Nigeria* ..... **83 E6** 4 57N 8 20 E
Calabogie, *Canada* ... **111 A8** 45 18N 76 43W
Calabozo, *Venezuela* .. **124 B5** 9 0N 67 28W
Calábria □, *Italy* .... **31 C9** 39 0N 16 30 E
Calaburras, Pta. de, *Spain* **35 J6** 36 30N 4 38W
Calaceite, *Spain* ..... **32 D5** 41 1N 0 11 E
Calacuccia, *France* ... **21 F13** 42 21N 9 1 E
Calafat, *Romania* .... **42 G7** 43 58N 22 59 E
Calafate, *Argentina* .. **128 G2** 50 19 S 72 15W
Calafell, *Spain* ...... **32 D6** 41 11N 1 34 E
Calahorra, *Spain* **32 C3** 42 18N 1 59W
Calais, *France* ...... **19 B8** 50 57N 1 56 E
Calais, *U.S.A.* **109 C12** 45 11N 67 17W
Calalaste, Cord. de, *Argentina* .... **126 B2** 25 0 S 67 0W
Calama, *Brazil* ...... **124 E6** 8 0 S 62 50W
Calama, *Chile* .... **126 A2** 22 30 S 68 55W
Calamar, *Colombia* ... **124 A4** 10 15N 74 55W
Calamian Group, *Phil.* **61 F3** 11 50N 119 55 E
Calamocha, *Spain* **32 E3** 40 50N 1 17W
Calamonte, *Spain* **35 G4** 38 53N 6 23W
Călan, *Romania* ..... **42 E7** 45 44N 22 59 E
Calañas, *Spain* **35 H4** 37 40N 6 53W
Calanda, *Spain* **32 E4** 40 56N 0 15W
Calang, *Indonesia* ... **62 D1** 4 37N 95 37 E
Calangiánus, *Italy* ... **30 B2** 40 56N 9 11 E
Calapan, *Phil.* .... **61 E4** 13 25N 121 7 E
Călăraşi, *Moldova* ... **43 C13** 47 16N 28 19 E
Călăraşi, *Romania* ... **43 F12** 44 12N 27 20 E
Călăraşi □, *Romania* . **43 F12** 44 10N 27 0 E
Calasparra, *Spain* **33 G3** 38 14N 1 41W
Calatafimi, *Italy* ..... **30 E5** 37 55N 12 52 E
Calatayud, *Spain* **32 D3** 41 20N 1 40W
Călăţele, *Romania* ... **42 D8** 46 46N 23 1 E
Calato = Kálathos, *Greece* .... **39 E10** 36 9N 28 8 E
Calauag, *Phil.* .... **61 E5** 13 55N 122 15 E
Calavà, C., *Italy* ..... **31 D7** 38 11N 14 55 E
Calavite, C., *Phil.* .... **61 E4** 13 26N 120 20 E
Calayan, *Phil.* .... **61 B4** 19 16N 121 28 E
Calbayog, *Phil.* ...... **61 E6** 12 4N 124 38 E
Calca, *Peru* .... **124 F4** 13 22 S 72 0W
Calcasieu L., *U.S.A.* .. **113 L8** 29 55N 93 18W
Calcutta = Kolkata, *India* .... **69 H13** 22 36N 88 24 E
Calcutta, *U.S.A.* **110 F4** 40 40N 80 34W
Caldaro, *Italy* .... **29 B8** 46 25N 11 14 E
Caldas da Rainha, *Portugal* **35 F1** 39 24N 9 8W
Caldas de Reis, *Spain* . **34 C2** 42 36N 8 39W
Calder →, *U.K.* **12 D6** 53 44N 1 22W
Caldera, *Chile* .... **126 B1** 27 5 S 70 55W
Caldwell, *Idaho, U.S.A.* **114 E5** 43 40N 116 41W
Caldwell, *Kans., U.S.A.* **113 G6** 37 2N 97 37W
Caldwell, *Tex., U.S.A.* . **113 K6** 30 32N 96 42W
Caledon, *S. Africa* ... **88 E2** 34 14 S 19 26 E
Caledon →, *S. Africa* . **88 E4** 30 31 S 26 5 E
Caledon B., *Australia* . **94 A2** 12 45 S 137 0 E
Caledonia, *Canada* ... **110 C5** 43 7N 79 58W
Caledonia, *U.S.A.* ... **110 D7** 42 58N 77 51W
Calella, *Spain* .... **32 D7** 41 37N 2 40 E
Calemba, *Angola* .... **88 B2** 16 0 S 15 44 E
Calen, *Australia* ..... **94 C4** 20 56 S 148 48 E
Calenzana, *France* ... **21 F12** 42 31N 8 51 E
Caletones, *Chile* ..... **126 C1** 34 6 S 70 27W
Calexico, *U.S.A.* **117 N11** 32 40N 115 30W
Calf of Man, *U.K.* **12 C3** 54 3N 4 48W
Calgary, *Canada* **104 C6** 51 0N 114 10W
Calheta, *Madeira* **37 D2** 32 44N 17 11W
Calhoun, *U.S.A.* **109 H3** 34 30N 84 57W
Cali, *Colombia* **124 C3** 3 25N 76 35W
Calicut, *India* .... **66 P9** 11 15N 75 43 E
Caliente, *U.S.A.* **115 H6** 37 37N 114 31W
California, *Mo., U.S.A.* **112 F8** 38 38N 92 34W
California, *Pa., U.S.A.* **110 F5** 40 4N 79 54W
California □, *U.S.A.* . **116 H7** 37 30N 119 30W
California, Baja, *Mexico* **118 A1** 32 10N 115 12W
California, Baja, T.N. = Baja California □, *Mexico* **118 B2** 30 0N 115 0W
California, Baja, T.S. = Baja California Sur □, *Mexico* .. **118 B2** 25 50N 111 50W
California, G. de, *Mexico* **118 B2** 27 0N 111 0W
California City, *U.S.A.* **117 K9** 35 10N 117 55W
California Hot Springs, *U.S.A.* **117 K8** 35 51N 118 41W
Călimăneşti, *Romania* **43 E9** 45 14N 24 20 E
Călimani, Muntii, *Romania* .... **43 C10** 47 12N 25 0 E
Calingasta, *Argentina* . **126 C2** 31 15 S 69 30W
Calipatria, *U.S.A.* ... **117 M11** 33 8N 115 31W
Calistoga, *U.S.A.* **116 G4** 38 35N 122 35W
Calitri, *Italy* .... **31 B8** 40 54N 15 26 E
Calitzdorp, *S. Africa* . **88 E3** 33 33 S 21 42 E
Callabonna, L., *Australia* .... **95 D3** 29 40 S 140 5 E
Callac, *France* **18 D3** 48 25N 3 27W
Callan, *Ireland* **15 D4** 52 32N 7 24W
Callander, *U.K.* **14 E4** 56 15N 4 13W
Callao, *Peru* .... **124 F3** 12 0 S 77 0W
Calles, *Mexico* **119 C5** 23 2N 98 42W
Callicoon, *U.S.A.* **111 E9** 41 46N 75 3W
Calling Lake, *Canada* . **104 B6** 55 15N 113 12W
Calliope, *Australia* .. **94 C5** 24 0 S 151 16 E
Callosa de Ensarriá, *Spain* **33 G4** 38 40N 0 8W
Callosa de Segura, *Spain* **33 G4** 38 7N 0 53W
Calne, *U.K.* **13 F6** 51 26N 2 0W
Calola, *Angola* ...... **88 B2** 16 25 S 17 48 E
Calolbon = San Andres, *Phil.* .... **61 E6** 13 36N 124 6 E
Calonge, *Spain* ..... **32 D8** 41 52N 3 5 E
Caloocan, *Phil.* ..... **61 D4** 14 39N 120 58 E
Calore →, *Italy* ..... **31 A7** 41 11N 14 28 E
Caloundra, *Australia* . **95 D5** 26 45 S 153 10 E
Calpe, *Spain* .... **33 G5** 38 39N 0 3 E
Calpella, *U.S.A.* **116 F3** 39 14N 123 12W
Calpine, *U.S.A.* **116 F6** 39 40N 120 27W
Calstock, *Canada* **102 C3** 49 47N 84 9W
Caltabellotta, *Italy* ... **30 E6** 37 34N 13 13 E
Caltagirone, *Italy* .... **31 E7** 37 14N 14 31 E
Caltanissetta, *Italy* ... **31 E7** 37 29N 14 4 E
Çaltılıbük, *Turkey* ... **41 G12** 39 57N 28 36 E
Caluire-et-Cuire, *France* .... **19 G11** 45 48N 4 52 E
Calulo, *Angola* ..... **84 G2** 10 1 S 14 56 E
Caluso, *Italy* .... **28 C4** 45 18N 7 53 E
Calvados □, *France* .. **18 C6** 49 5N 0 15W
Calvert →, *Australia* . **94 B2** 16 17 S 137 44 E
Calvert I., *Canada* ... **104 C3** 51 30N 128 0W
Calvert Ra., *Australia* . **92 D3** 24 0 S 122 30 E

Calvi, France 21 F12 42 34N 8 45 E
Calviá, Spain 33 F7 39 34N 2 31 E
Calvillo, Mexico 118 C4 21 51N 102 43W
Calvinia, S. Africa 88 E2 31 28 S 19 45 E
Calvo = Calvo, Mte., Italy 29 G12 41 44N 15 46 E
Calvo, Mte., Italy 29 G12 41 44N 15 46 E
Calwa, U.S.A. 116 J7 36 42N 119 46W
Calzada Almuradiel = Almuradiel, Spain 35 G7 38 32N 3 28W
Calzada de Calatrava, Spain 35 G7 38 42N 3 46W
Cam →, U.K. 13 E8 52 21N 0 16 E
Cam Lam, Vietnam 65 G7 11 54N 109 10 E
Cam Pha, Vietnam 58 G6 21 7N 107 18 E
Cam Ranh, Vietnam 65 G7 11 54N 109 12 E
Cam Xuyen, Vietnam 64 C6 18 15N 106 0 E
Camabatela, Angola 84 F3 8 20 S 15 26 E
Camacha, Madeira 37 D3 32 41N 16 49W
Camacho, Mexico 118 C4 24 25N 102 18W
Camacupa, Angola 85 G3 11 58 S 17 22 E
Camagüey, Cuba 120 B4 21 20N 78 0W
Camaiore, Italy 28 E7 43 56N 10 18 E
Camaná, Peru 124 G4 16 30 S 72 50W
Camanche Reservoir, U.S.A. 116 G6 38 14N 121 1W
Camaquã, Brazil 127 C5 30 51 S 51 49W
Camaquã →, Brazil 127 C5 31 17 S 51 47W
Câmara de Lobos, Madeira 37 D3 32 39N 16 59W
Camarat, C., France 21 E10 43 12N 6 41 E
Camarès, France 20 E6 43 49N 2 53 E
Camaret-sur-Mer, France 18 D2 48 16N 4 37W
Camargo, Mexico 119 B5 26 19N 98 50W
Camargue, France 21 E8 43 34N 4 34 E
Camarillo, U.S.A. 117 L7 34 13N 119 2W
Camariñas, Spain 34 B1 43 8N 9 12W
Camarón, C., Honduras 120 C2 16 0N 85 5W
Camarones, Argentina 128 E3 44 50 S 65 40W
Camas, Spain 35 H4 37 24N 6 2W
Camas, U.S.A. 116 E4 45 35N 122 24W
Camas Valley, U.S.A. 114 E2 43 2N 123 40W
Camballin, Australia 92 C3 17 59 S 124 12 E
Cambará, Brazil 127 A5 23 2 S 50 5W
Cambay = Khambhat, India 68 H5 22 23N 72 33 E
Cambay, G. of = Khambhat, G. of, India 66 J8 20 45N 72 30 E
Cambil, Spain 35 H7 37 40N 3 33W
Cambo-les-Bains, France 20 E2 43 22N 1 23W
Cambodia ■, Asia 64 F5 12 15N 105 0 E
Camborne, U.K. 13 G2 50 12N 5 19W
Cambrai, France 19 B10 50 11N 3 14 E
Cambre, Spain 34 B2 43 17N 8 20W
Cambria, U.S.A. 116 K5 35 34N 121 5W
Cambrian Mts., U.K. 13 E4 52 3N 3 57W
Cambridge, Canada 102 D3 43 23N 80 15W
Cambridge, Jamaica 120 C4 18 18N 77 54W
Cambridge, N.Z. 91 G5 37 54 S 175 29 E
Cambridge, U.K. 13 E8 52 12N 0 8 E
Cambridge, Mass., U.S.A. 111 D13 42 22N 71 6W
Cambridge, Minn., U.S.A. 112 C8 45 34N 93 13W
Cambridge, N.Y., U.S.A. 111 C11 43 2N 73 22W
Cambridge, Nebr., U.S.A. 112 E4 40 17N 100 10W
Cambridge, Ohio, U.S.A. 110 F3 40 2N 81 35W
Cambridge Bay = Ikaluktutiak, Canada 100 B9 69 10N 105 0W
Cambridge G., Australia 92 B4 14 55 S 128 15 E
Cambridge Springs, U.S.A. 110 E4 41 48N 80 4W
Cambridgeshire □, U.K. 13 E7 52 25N 0 7W
Cambrils, Spain 32 D6 41 8N 1 3 E
Cambuci, Brazil 127 A7 21 35 S 41 55W
Cambundi-Catembo, Angola 84 G3 10 10 S 17 35 E
Camden, Ala., U.S.A. 109 K2 31 59N 87 17W
Camden, Ark., U.S.A. 113 J8 33 35N 92 50W
Camden, Maine, U.S.A. 109 C11 44 13N 69 4W
Camden, N.J., U.S.A. 111 G9 39 56N 75 7W
Camden, N.Y., U.S.A. 111 C9 43 20N 75 45W
Camden, S.C., U.S.A. 109 H5 34 16N 80 36W
Camden Sd., Australia 92 C3 15 27 S 124 25 E
Camdenton, U.S.A. 113 F8 38 1N 92 45W
Çameli, Turkey 39 D11 37 5N 29 24 E
Camenca, Moldova 43 B13 48 3N 28 42 E
Camerino, Italy 29 E10 43 8N 13 4 E
Cameron, Ariz., U.S.A. 115 J8 35 53N 111 25W
Cameron, La., U.S.A. 113 L8 29 48N 93 20W
Cameron, Mo., U.S.A. 112 F7 39 44N 94 14W
Cameron, Tex., U.S.A. 113 K6 30 51N 96 59W
Cameron Highlands, Malaysia 65 K3 4 27N 101 22 E
Cameron Hills, Canada 104 B5 59 48N 118 0W
Cameroon ■, Africa 84 C2 6 0N 12 30 E
Camerota, Italy 31 B8 40 2N 15 22 E
Cameroun →, Cameroon 83 E6 4 0N 9 35 E
Cameroun, Mt., Cameroon 83 E6 4 13N 9 10 E
Cametá, Brazil 125 D9 2 12 S 49 30W
Çamiçi Gölü, Turkey 39 D9 37 29N 27 28 E
Camiguin □, Phil. 61 G6 9 11N 124 42 E
Camiguin I., Phil. 61 B4 18 56N 121 55 E
Camiling, Phil. 61 D4 15 42N 120 24 E
Camilla, U.S.A. 109 K3 31 14N 84 12W
Caminha, Portugal 34 D2 41 50N 8 50W
Camino, U.S.A. 116 G6 38 44N 120 41W
Camira Creek, Australia 95 D5 29 15 S 152 58 E
Cammal, U.S.A. 110 E7 41 24N 77 28W
Cammarata, Italy 30 E6 37 38N 13 38 E
Camocim, Brazil 125 D10 2 55 S 40 50W
Camooweal, Australia 94 B2 19 56 S 138 7 E
Camopi, Fr. Guiana 125 C8 3 12N 52 17W
Camotes Is., Phil. 61 F6 10 40N 124 24 E
Camotes Sea, Phil. 61 F6 10 30N 124 15 E
Camp Borden, Canada 110 B5 44 18N 79 56W
Camp Hill, U.S.A. 110 F8 40 14N 76 55W
Camp Nelson, U.S.A. 117 J8 36 8N 118 39W
Camp Pendleton, U.S.A. 117 M9 33 16N 117 23W
Camp Verde, U.S.A. 115 J8 34 34N 111 51W
Camp Wood, U.S.A. 113 L5 29 40N 100 1W
Campagna, Italy 31 B8 40 40N 15 6 E
Campana, Argentina 126 C4 34 10 S 58 55W
Campana, I., Chile 128 F1 48 20 S 75 20W
Campanário, Madeira 37 D2 32 39N 17 2W
Campanario, Spain 35 G5 38 52N 5 36W
Campánia □, Italy 31 B7 41 0N 14 30 E
Campbell, S. Africa 88 D3 28 48 S 23 44 E
Campbell, Calif., U.S.A. 116 H5 37 17N 121 57W
Campbell, Ohio, U.S.A. 110 E4 41 5N 80 37W
Campbell I., Pac. Oc. 96 N8 52 30 S 169 0 E
Campbell L., Canada 105 A7 63 14N 106 55W
Campbell River, Canada 104 C3 50 5N 125 20W
Campbell Town, Australia 94 G4 41 52 S 147 30 E
Campbellford, Canada 110 B7 44 18N 77 48W
Campbellpur, Pakistan 68 C5 33 46N 72 26 E
Campbellsville, U.S.A. 108 G3 37 21N 85 20W
Campbellton, Canada 103 C6 47 57N 66 43W
Campbelltown, Australia 95 E5 34 4 S 150 49 E
Campbeltown, U.K. 14 F3 55 26N 5 36W
Campeche, Mexico 119 D6 19 50N 90 32W
Campeche □, Mexico 119 D6 19 50N 90 32W
Campeche, Golfo de, Mexico 119 D6 19 30N 93 0W
Campello, Spain 33 G4 38 26N 0 24W
Câmpeni, Romania 42 D8 46 22N 23 3 E
Camperdown, Australia 95 F3 38 14 S 143 9 E
Camperville, Canada 105 C8 51 59N 100 9W
Campi Salentina, Italy 31 B11 40 24N 18 1 E
Câmpia Turzii, Romania 43 D8 46 34N 23 53 E
Campidano, Italy 30 C1 39 30N 8 47 E
Campíglia Maríttima, Italy 28 E7 43 4N 10 37 E
Campillo de Altobuey, Spain 33 F3 39 36N 1 49W
Campillos, Spain 35 H6 37 4N 4 51W
Câmpina, Romania 43 E10 45 10N 25 45 E
Campina Grande, Brazil 125 E11 7 20 S 35 47W
Campinas, Brazil 127 A6 22 50 S 47 0W
Campli, Italy 29 F10 42 43N 13 41 E
Campo, Spain 32 C5 42 25N 0 24 E
Campo de Criptana, Spain 35 F7 39 24N 3 7W
Campo de Gibraltar, Spain 35 J5 36 15N 5 25W
Campo Grande, Brazil 125 H8 20 25 S 54 40W
Campo Maíor, Brazil 125 D10 4 50 S 42 12W
Campo Maior, Portugal 35 F3 39 2N 7 7W
Campo Mourão, Brazil 127 A5 24 3 S 52 22W
Campo Túres, Italy 29 B8 46 53N 11 55 E
Campobasso, Italy 31 A7 41 34N 14 39 E
Campobello di Licata, Italy 30 E6 37 15N 13 55 E
Campobello di Mazara, Italy 30 E5 37 38N 12 45 E
Campofelice di Roccella, Italy 30 E6 37 59N 13 53 E
Campomarino, Italy 29 G12 41 57N 15 2 E
Camporeale, Italy 30 E6 37 54N 13 6 E
Camporrobles, Spain 32 F3 39 39N 1 24W
Campos, Brazil 127 A7 21 50 S 41 20W
Campos Belos, Brazil 125 F9 13 10 S 47 3W
Campos del Puerto, Spain 37 B10 39 26N 3 1 E
Campos Novos, Brazil 127 B5 27 21 S 51 50W
Camprodón, Spain 32 C7 42 19N 2 23 E
Camptonville, U.S.A. 116 F5 39 27N 121 3W
Camptown, U.S.A. 111 E8 41 44N 76 14W
Câmpulung, Argeş, Romania 43 E10 45 17N 25 3 E
Câmpulung, Suceava, Romania 43 C10 47 32N 25 30 E
Câmpuri, Romania 43 D11 46 0N 26 50 E
Camrose, Canada 104 C6 53 0N 112 50W
Camsell Portage, Canada 105 B7 59 37N 109 15W
Çamyuva, Turkey 39 E12 36 30N 30 30 E
Çan, Turkey 41 F11 40 2N 27 3 E
Can Clavo, Spain 37 C7 38 57N 1 27 E
Can Creu, Spain 37 C7 38 58N 1 28 E
Can Gio, Vietnam 65 G6 10 25N 106 58 E
Can Tho, Vietnam 65 G5 10 2N 105 46 E
Canaan, U.S.A. 111 D11 42 2N 73 20W
Canada ■, N. Amer. 100 C10 60 0N 100 0W
Cañada de Gómez, Argentina 126 C3 32 40 S 61 30W
Canadian, U.S.A. 113 H4 35 55N 100 23W
Canadian →, U.S.A. 113 H7 35 28N 95 3W
Canajoharie, U.S.A. 111 D10 42 54N 74 35W
Çanakkale, Turkey 41 F10 40 8N 26 24 E
Çanakkale □, Turkey 41 F10 40 10N 26 25 E
Çanakkale Boğazı, Turkey 41 F10 40 17N 26 32 E
Canal Flats, Canada 104 C5 50 10N 115 48W
Canalejas, Argentina 126 D2 35 15 S 66 34W
Canals, Argentina 126 C3 33 35 S 62 53W
Canals, Spain 33 G4 38 58N 0 35W
Canandaigua, U.S.A. 110 D7 42 54N 77 17W
Canandaigua L., U.S.A. 110 D7 42 47N 77 19W
Cananea, Mexico 118 A2 31 0N 110 20W
Canarias, Is., Atl. Oc. 37 F4 28 30N 16 0W
Canarreos, Arch. de los, Cuba 120 B3 21 35N 81 40W
Canary Is. = Canarias, Is., Atl. Oc. 37 F4 28 30N 16 0W
Canaseraga, U.S.A. 110 D7 42 27N 77 45W
Canatlán, Mexico 118 C4 24 31N 104 47W
Canaveral, C., U.S.A. 109 L5 28 27N 80 32W
Cañaveruelas, Spain 32 E2 40 24N 2 38W
Canavieiras, Brazil 125 G11 15 39 S 39 0W
Canberra, Australia 95 F4 35 15 S 149 8 E
Canby, Calif., U.S.A. 114 F3 41 27N 120 52W
Canby, Minn., U.S.A. 112 C6 44 43N 96 16W
Canby, Oreg., U.S.A. 116 E4 45 16N 122 42W
Cancale, France 18 D5 48 40N 1 50W
Canche →, France 19 B8 50 31N 1 39 E
Cancún, Mexico 119 C7 21 8N 86 44W
Candanchu, Spain 32 C4 42 47N 0 32W
Çandarlı, Turkey 39 C8 38 56N 26 56 E
Çandarlı Körfezi, Turkey 39 C8 38 52N 26 55 E
Candas, Spain 34 B5 43 35N 5 45W
Candé, France 18 E5 47 34N 1 2W
Candela, Italy 31 A8 41 8N 15 31 E
Candelaria, Argentina 127 B4 27 29 S 55 44W
Candelaria, Canary Is. 37 F3 28 22N 16 22W
Candeleda, Spain 34 E5 40 10N 5 14W
Candelo, Australia 95 F4 36 47 S 149 43 E
Candia = Iráklion, Greece 36 D7 35 20N 25 12 E
Candia, Sea of = Crete, Sea of, Greece 39 E7 36 0N 25 0 E
Candle L., Canada 105 C7 53 50N 105 18W
Candlemas I., Antarctica 5 B1 57 3 S 26 40W
Cando, U.S.A. 112 A5 48 32N 99 12W
Candon, Phil. 61 C4 17 12N 120 27 E
Canea = Khaniá, Greece 36 D6 35 30N 24 4 E
Canelli, Italy 28 D5 44 43N 8 17 E
Canelones, Uruguay 127 C4 34 32 S 56 17W
Canet-Plage, France 20 F7 42 41N 3 2 E
Cañete, Chile 126 D1 37 50 S 73 30W
Cañete, Peru 124 F3 13 8 S 76 30W
Cañete, Spain 32 E3 40 3N 1 54W
Cañete de las Torres, Spain 35 H6 37 53N 4 19W
Cangas, Spain 34 C2 42 16N 8 47W
Cangas de Narcea, Spain 34 B4 43 10N 6 32W
Cangas de Onís, Spain 34 B5 43 21N 5 8W
Cangnan, China 59 D13 27 30N 120 23 E
Canguaretama, Brazil 125 E11 6 20 S 35 5W
Canguçu, Brazil 127 C5 31 22 S 52 43W
Canguçu, Serra do, Brazil 127 C5 31 20 S 52 40W
Cangwu, China 59 F8 23 25N 111 17 E
Cangxi, China 58 B5 31 47N 105 59 E
Cangyuan, China 58 F2 23 12N 99 14 E
Cangzhou, China 56 E9 38 19N 116 52 E
Caniapiscau →, Canada 103 A6 56 40N 69 30W
Caniapiscau Rés. de, Canada 103 B6 54 10N 69 55W
Canicattì, Italy 30 E6 37 21N 13 51 E
Canicattini Bagni, Italy 31 E8 37 2N 15 4 E
Caniles, Spain 35 H8 37 26N 2 43W
Canim Lake, Canada 104 C4 51 47N 120 54W
Canindeyu □, Paraguay 127 A5 24 10 S 55 0W
Canino, Italy 29 F8 42 28N 11 45 E
Canisteo, U.S.A. 110 D7 42 16N 77 36W
Canisteo →, U.S.A. 110 D7 42 7N 77 8W
Cañitas, Mexico 118 C4 23 36N 102 43W
Cañizal, Spain 34 D5 41 12N 5 22W
Canjáyar, Spain 35 H8 37 1N 2 44W
Çankırı, Turkey 72 B5 40 40N 33 37 E
Cankuzo, Burundi 86 C3 3 10 S 30 31 E
Canmore, Canada 104 C5 51 7N 115 18W
Cann River, Australia 95 F4 37 35 S 149 7 E
Canna, U.K. 14 D2 57 3N 6 33W
Cannanore, India 66 P9 11 53N 75 27 E
Cannes, France 21 E11 43 32N 7 1 E
Canning Town = Port Canning, India 69 H13 22 23N 88 40 E
Cannington, Canada 110 B5 44 20N 79 2W
Cannóbio, Italy 28 B5 46 4N 8 42 E
Cannock, U.K. 13 E5 52 41N 2 1W
Cannon Ball →, U.S.A. 112 B4 46 20N 100 38W
Cannondale Mt., Australia 94 D4 25 13 S 148 57 E
Cannonsville Reservoir, U.S.A. 111 D9 42 4N 75 22W
Cannonvale, Australia 94 C4 20 17 S 148 43 E
Canoas, Brazil 127 B5 29 56 S 51 11W
Canoe L., Canada 105 B7 55 10N 108 15W
Canon City, U.S.A. 112 F2 38 27N 105 14W
Canora, Canada 105 C8 51 40N 102 30W
Canosa di Púglia, Italy 31 A9 41 13N 16 4 E
Canowindra, Australia 95 E4 33 35 S 148 38 E
Canso, Canada 103 C7 45 20N 61 0W
Cantabria □, Spain 34 B7 43 10N 4 0W
Cantabria, Sierra de, Spain 32 C2 42 40N 2 30W
Cantabrian Mts. = Cantábrica, Cordillera, Spain 34 C5 43 0N 5 10W
Cantábrica, Cordillera, Spain 34 C5 43 0N 5 10W
Cantal □, France 20 C6 45 5N 2 45 E
Cantal, Plomb du, France 20 C6 45 3N 2 45 E
Cantanhede, Portugal 34 E2 40 20N 8 36W
Cantavieja, Spain 32 E4 40 31N 0 25W
Čantavir, Serbia, Yug. 42 E4 45 55N 19 46 E
Cantemir, Moldova 43 D13 46 17N 28 14 E
Canterbury, Australia 94 D3 25 23 S 141 53 E
Canterbury, U.K. 13 F9 51 16N 1 6 E
Canterbury Bight, N.Z. 91 L3 44 16 S 171 55 E
Canterbury Plains, N.Z. 91 K3 43 55 S 171 22 E
Cantil, U.S.A. 117 K9 35 18N 117 58W
Cantillana, Spain 35 H5 37 36N 5 50W
Canton = Guangzhou, China 59 F9 23 5N 113 10 E
Canton, Ga., U.S.A. 109 H3 34 14N 84 29W
Canton, Ill., U.S.A. 112 E9 40 33N 90 2W
Canton, Miss., U.S.A. 113 J9 32 37N 90 2W
Canton, Mo., U.S.A. 112 E9 40 8N 91 32W
Canton, N.Y., U.S.A. 111 B9 44 36N 75 10W
Canton, Ohio, U.S.A. 110 F3 40 48N 81 23W
Canton, Pa., U.S.A. 110 E8 41 39N 76 51W
Canton, S. Dak., U.S.A. 112 D6 43 18N 96 35W
Canton L., U.S.A. 113 G5 36 6N 98 35W
Cantù, Italy 28 C6 45 44N 9 8 E
Canudos, Brazil 124 E7 7 13 S 58 5W
Canumã →, Brazil 124 D7 3 55 S 59 10W
Canutama, Brazil 124 E6 6 30 S 64 20W
Canutillo, U.S.A. 115 L10 31 55N 106 36W
Canvey, U.K. 13 F8 51 31N 0 37 E
Canyon, U.S.A. 113 H4 34 59N 101 55W
Canyonlands National Park, U.S.A. 115 G9 38 15N 110 0W
Canyonville, U.S.A. 114 E2 42 56N 123 17W
Cao Bang, Vietnam 58 F6 22 40N 106 15 E
Cao He →, China 57 D13 40 10N 124 32 E
Cao Lanh, Vietnam 65 G5 10 27N 105 38 E
Cao Xian, China 56 G8 34 50N 115 35 E
Cáorle, Italy 29 C9 45 36N 12 53 E
Cap-aux-Meules, Canada 103 C7 47 23N 61 52W
Cap-Chat, Canada 103 C6 49 6N 66 40W
Cap-de-la-Madeleine, Canada 102 C5 46 22N 72 31W
Cap-Haïtien, Haiti 121 C5 19 40N 72 20W
Capac, U.S.A. 110 C2 43 1N 82 56W
Capáccio, Italy 31 B8 40 25N 15 5 E
Capaci, Italy 30 D6 38 10N 13 14 E
Capanaparo →, Venezuela 124 B5 7 1N 67 7W
Capánnori, Italy 28 E7 43 50N 10 34 E
Capbreton, France 20 E2 43 39N 1 26W
Capdenac, France 20 D6 44 34N 2 5 E
Capdepera, Spain 32 F8 39 42N 3 26 E
Cape →, Australia 94 C4 20 59 S 146 51 E
Cape Barren I., Australia 94 G4 40 25 S 148 15 E
Cape Breton Highlands Nat. Park, Canada 103 C7 46 50N 60 40W
Cape Breton I., Canada 103 C7 46 0N 60 30W
Cape Charles, U.S.A. 108 G8 37 16N 76 1W
Cape Coast, Ghana 83 D4 5 5N 1 15W
Cape Coral, U.S.A. 109 M5 26 33N 81 57W
Cape Dorset, Canada 101 B12 64 14N 76 32W
Cape Fear →, U.S.A. 109 H6 33 53N 78 1W
Cape Girardeau, U.S.A. 113 G10 37 19N 89 32W
Cape May, U.S.A. 108 F8 38 56N 74 56W
Cape May Point, U.S.A. 108 F8 38 56N 74 58W
Cape Province, S. Africa 85 L3 32 0 S 23 0 E
Cape Tormentine, Canada 103 C7 46 8N 63 47W
Cape Town, S. Africa 88 E2 33 55 S 18 22 E
Cape Verde Is. ■, Atl. Oc. 77 E1 17 10N 25 20W
Cape Vincent, U.S.A. 111 B8 44 8N 76 20W
Cape York Peninsula, Australia 94 A3 12 0 S 142 30 E
Capela, Brazil 125 F11 10 30 S 37 0W
Capella, Australia 94 C4 23 2 S 148 1 E
Capendu, France 20 E6 43 11N 2 31 E
Capestang, France 20 E7 43 20N 3 2 E
Capim →, Brazil 125 D9 1 40 S 47 47W
Capistrello, Italy 29 G10 41 57N 13 23 E
Capitan, U.S.A. 115 K11 33 35N 105 35W
Capitol Reef National Park, U.S.A. 115 G8 38 15N 111 10W
Capitola, U.S.A. 116 J5 36 59N 121 57W
Capizzi, Italy 31 E7 37 51N 14 29 E
Capoche →, Mozam. 87 F3 15 35 S 33 0 E
Capoterra, Italy 30 C1 39 11N 8 58 E
Cappadocia, Turkey 72 C6 39 0N 35 0 E
Capraia, Italy 28 E6 43 2N 9 50 E
Caprara, Pta., Italy 30 A1 41 7N 8 19 E
Caprarola, Italy 29 F9 42 19N 12 14 E
Capreol, Canada 102 C3 46 43N 80 56W
Caprera, Italy 30 A2 41 12N 9 28 E
Capri, Italy 31 B7 40 33N 14 14 E
Capricorn Group, Australia 94 C5 23 30 S 151 55 E
Capricorn Ra., Australia 92 D2 23 20 S 116 50 E
Caprino Veronese, Italy 28 C7 45 36N 10 47 E
Caprivi Strip, Namibia 88 B3 18 0 S 23 0 E
Captain's Flat, Australia 95 F4 35 35 S 149 27 E
Captieux, France 20 D3 44 18N 0 16W
Caquetá →, Colombia 122 D4 1 15 S 69 15W
Caracal, Romania 43 F9 44 8N 24 22 E
Caracas, Venezuela 124 A5 10 30N 66 55W
Caracol, Mato Grosso do Sul, Brazil 126 A4 22 18 S 57 1W
Caracol, Piauí, Brazil 125 E10 9 15 S 43 22W
Caráglio, Italy 28 D4 44 25N 7 26 E
Carajas, Brazil 125 E8 6 5 S 50 23W
Carajás, Serra dos, Brazil 125 E8 6 0 S 51 30W
Carangola, Brazil 127 A7 20 44 S 42 5W
Caransebeş, Romania 42 E7 45 28N 22 18 E
Carantec, France 18 D3 48 40N 3 55W
Caraquet, Canada 103 C6 47 48N 64 57W
Caras, Peru 124 E3 9 3 S 77 47W
Caraş Severin □, Romania 42 E7 45 10N 22 10 E
Caraşova, Romania 42 E6 45 11N 21 51 E
Caratasca, L., Honduras 120 C3 15 20N 83 40W
Caratinga, Brazil 125 G10 19 50 S 42 10W
Caraúbas, Brazil 125 E11 5 43 S 37 33W
Caravaca = Caravaca de la Cruz, Spain 33 G3 38 8N 1 52W
Caravaca de la Cruz, Spain 33 G3 38 8N 1 52W
Caravággio, Italy 28 C6 45 30N 9 38 E
Caravela, Guinea-Biss. 82 C1 11 30N 16 30W
Caravelas, Brazil 125 G11 17 45 S 39 15W
Caraveli, Peru 124 G4 15 45 S 73 25W
Caràzinho, Brazil 127 B5 28 16 S 52 46W
Carballino = O Carballiño, Spain 34 C2 42 26N 8 5W
Carballo, Spain 34 B2 43 13N 8 41W
Carberry, Canada 105 D9 49 50N 99 25W
Carbó, Mexico 118 B2 29 42N 110 58W
Carbonara, C., Italy 30 C2 39 6N 9 31 E
Carbondale, Colo., U.S.A. 114 G10 39 24N 107 13W
Carbondale, Ill., U.S.A. 113 G10 37 44N 89 13W
Carbondale, Pa., U.S.A. 111 E9 41 35N 75 30W
Carbonear, Canada 103 C9 47 42N 53 13W
Carboneras, Spain 33 J3 36 59N 1 53W
Carboneras de Guadazaón, Spain 32 F3 39 54N 1 50W
Carbónia, Italy 30 C1 39 10N 8 30 E
Carcabuey, Spain 35 H6 37 27N 4 17W
Carcagente = Carcaixent, Spain 33 F4 39 8N 0 28W
Carcaixent, Spain 33 F4 39 8N 0 28W
Carcajou, Canada 104 B5 57 47N 117 6W
Carcar, Phil. 61 F5 10 6N 123 38 E
Carcarana →, Argentina 126 C3 32 27 S 60 48W
Carcasse, C., Haiti 121 C5 18 30N 74 28W
Carcassonne, France 20 E6 43 13N 2 20 E
Carcross, Canada 104 A2 60 13N 134 45W
Çardak, Çanakkale, Turkey 41 F10 40 22N 26 43 E
Çardak, Denizli, Turkey 39 D11 37 49N 29 39 E
Cardamon Hills, India 66 Q10 9 30N 77 15 E
Cardeña, Spain 35 G6 38 16N 4 20W
Cárdenas, Cuba 120 B3 23 0N 81 30W
Cárdenas, San Luis Potosí, Mexico 119 C5 22 0N 99 41W
Cárdenas, Tabasco, Mexico 119 D6 17 59N 93 21W
Cardenete, Spain 32 F3 39 46N 1 41W
Cardiff, U.K. 13 F4 51 29N 3 10W
Cardiff □, U.K. 13 F4 51 31N 3 12W
Cardiff-by-the-Sea, U.S.A. 117 M9 33 1N 117 17W
Cardigan, U.K. 13 E3 52 5N 4 40W
Cardigan B., U.K. 13 E3 52 30N 4 30W
Cardinal, Canada 111 B9 44 47N 75 23W
Cardona, Spain 32 D6 41 56N 1 40 E
Cardona, Uruguay 126 C4 33 53 S 57 18W
Cardoner →, Spain 32 D6 41 41N 1 51 E
Cardoso, Ilha do, Brazil 127 B5 25 8 S 47 58W
Cardston, Canada 104 D6 49 15N 113 20W
Cardwell, Australia 94 B4 18 14 S 146 2 E
Careen L., Canada 105 B7 57 0N 108 11W
Carei, Romania 42 C7 47 40N 22 29 E
Careme = Ciremai, Indonesia 63 G13 6 55 S 108 27 E
Carentan, France 18 C5 49 19N 1 15W
Carey, U.S.A. 114 E7 43 19N 113 57W
Carey, L., Australia 93 E3 29 0 S 122 15 E
Carey L., Canada 105 A8 62 12N 102 55W
Careysburg, Liberia 82 D2 6 34N 10 30W
Cargèse, France 21 F12 42 7N 8 35 E
Carhaix-Plouguer, France 18 D3 48 18N 3 36W
Carhué, Argentina 126 D3 37 10 S 62 50W
Caria, Turkey 39 D10 37 20N 28 10 E
Cariacica, Brazil 125 H10 20 16 S 40 25W
Cariati, Italy 31 C9 39 30N 16 57 E
Caribbean Sea, W. Indies 121 D5 15 0N 75 0W
Cariboo Mts., Canada 104 C4 53 0N 121 0W
Caribou, U.S.A. 109 B12 46 52N 68 1W
Caribou →, Man., Canada 105 B10 59 20N 94 44W
Caribou →, N.W.T., Canada 104 A3 61 27N 125 45W
Caribou I., Canada 102 C2 47 22N 85 49W
Caribou Is., Canada 104 A6 61 55N 113 15W
Caribou L., Man., Canada 105 B9 59 21N 96 10W
Caribou L., Ont., Canada 102 B2 50 25N 89 5W
Caribou Mts., Canada 104 B5 59 12N 115 40W
Carichic, Mexico 118 B3 27 56N 107 3W
Carigara, Phil. 61 F6 11 18N 124 41 E
Carignan, France 19 C12 49 38N 5 10 E
Carignano, Italy 28 D4 44 55N 7 40 E
Carillo, Mexico 118 B4 26 50N 103 55W
Carinda, Australia 95 E4 30 28 S 147 41 E
Cariñena, Spain 32 D3 41 20N 1 13W
Carinhanha, Brazil 125 F10 14 15 S 44 46W
Carinhanha →, Brazil 125 F10 14 20 S 43 47W
Carini, Italy 30 D6 38 8N 13 11 E
Cariño, Spain 34 B3 43 45N 7 52W
Carínola, Italy 30 A6 41 11N 13 58 E
Carinthia = Kärnten □, Austria 26 E6 46 52N 13 30 E
Caripito, Venezuela 124 A6 10 8N 63 6W
Carlbrod = Dimitrovgrad, Serbia, Yug. 40 C6 43 2N 22 48 E
Carlet, Spain 33 F4 39 14N 0 31W
Carleton, Mt., Canada 103 C6 47 23N 66 53W
Carleton Place, Canada 102 C4 45 8N 76 9W
Carletonville, S. Africa 88 D4 26 23 S 27 22 E
Cârlibaba, Romania 43 C10 47 35N 25 8 E
Carlin, U.S.A. 114 F5 40 43N 116 7W
Carlingford L., U.K. 15 B5 54 3N 6 9W
Carlinville, U.S.A. 112 F10 39 17N 89 53W
Carlisle, U.K. 12 C5 54 54N 2 56W
Carlisle, U.S.A. 110 F7 40 12N 77 12W
Carlit, Pic, France 20 F5 42 35N 1 55 E
Carloforte, Italy 30 C1 39 8N 8 18 E
Carlos Casares, Argentina 126 D3 35 32 S 61 20W
Carlos Tejedor, Argentina 126 D3 35 25 S 62 25W
Carlow, Ireland 15 D5 52 50N 6 56W
Carlow □, Ireland 15 D5 52 43N 6 50W
Carlsbad, Calif., U.S.A. 117 M9 33 10N 117 21W
Carlsbad, N. Mex., U.S.A. 113 J2 32 25N 104 14W
Carlsbad Caverns National Park, U.S.A. 113 J2 32 10N 104 35W
Carluke, U.K. 14 F5 55 45N 3 50W
Carlyle, Canada 105 D8 49 40N 102 20W
Carmacks, Canada 100 B6 62 5N 136 16W
Carmagnola, Italy 28 D4 44 51N 7 43 E
Carman, Canada 105 D9 49 30N 98 0W
Carmarthen, U.K. 13 F3 51 52N 4 19W
Carmarthen B., U.K. 13 F3 51 40N 4 30W
Carmarthenshire □, U.K. 13 F3 51 55N 4 13W
Carmaux, France 20 D6 44 3N 2 10 E
Carmel, U.S.A. 111 E11 41 26N 73 41W
Carmel-by-the-Sea, U.S.A. 116 J5 36 33N 121 55W
Carmel Valley, U.S.A. 116 J5 36 29N 121 43W
Carmelo, Uruguay 126 C4 34 0 S 58 20W
Carmen, Colombia 124 B3 9 43N 75 8W
Carmen, Paraguay 127 B4 27 13 S 56 12W
Carmen →, Mexico 118 A3 30 42N 106 29W
Carmen, I., Mexico 118 B2 26 0N 111 20W
Carmen de Patagones, Argentina 128 E4 40 50 S 63 0W
Cármenes, Spain 34 C5 42 58N 5 34W
Carmensa, Argentina 126 D2 35 15 S 67 40W
Carmi, Canada 104 D5 49 36N 119 8W
Carmi, U.S.A. 108 F1 38 5N 88 10W
Carmichael, U.S.A. 116 G5 38 38N 121 19W
Carmila, Australia 94 C4 21 55 S 149 24 E
Carmona, Costa Rica 120 E2 10 0N 85 15W
Carmona, Spain 35 H5 37 28N 5 42W
Carn Ban, U.K. 14 D4 57 7N 4 15W
Carn Eige, U.K. 14 D3 57 17N 5 8W
Carnamah, Australia 93 E2 29 41 S 115 53 E
Carnarvon, Australia 93 D1 24 51 S 113 42 E
Carnarvon, S. Africa 88 E3 30 56 S 22 8 E
Carnarvon Ra., Queens., Australia 94 D4 25 15 S 148 30 E
Carnarvon Ra., W. Austral., Australia 93 E3 25 20 S 120 45 E
Carnation, U.S.A. 116 C5 47 39N 121 55W
Carndonagh, Ireland 15 A4 55 16N 7 15W
Carnduff, Canada 105 D8 49 10N 101 50W
Carnegie, U.S.A. 110 F4 40 24N 80 5W
Carnegie, L., Australia 93 E3 26 5 S 122 30 E
Carnic Alps = Karnische Alpen, Europe 26 E6 46 36N 13 0 E
Carniche Alpi = Karnische Alpen, Europe 26 E6 46 36N 13 0 E
Carnot, C.A.R. 84 D3 4 59N 15 56 E
Carnot, C., Australia 95 E2 34 57 S 135 38 E
Carnot B., Australia 92 C3 17 20 S 122 15 E
Carnoustie, U.K. 14 E6 56 30N 2 42W
Carnsore Pt., Ireland 15 D5 52 10N 6 22W
Caro, U.S.A. 108 D4 43 29N 83 24W
Carol City, U.S.A. 109 N5 25 56N 80 16W
Carolina, Brazil 125 E9 7 10 S 47 30W
Carolina, Puerto Rico 121 C6 18 23N 65 58W
Carolina, S. Africa 89 D5 26 5 S 30 6 E
Caroline I., Kiribati 97 H12 9 15 S 150 3W
Caroline Is., Micronesia 52 J17 8 0N 150 0 E
Caroni →, Venezuela 124 B6 8 21N 62 43W
Caronie = Nébrodi, Monti, Italy 31 E7 37 54N 14 35 E

Caroona, *Australia* **95 E5** 31 24 S 150 26 E
Carpathians, *Europe* **6 F10** 49 30N 21 0 E
Carpaţii Meridionali, *Romania* **43 E9** 45 30N 25 0 E
Carpentaria, G. of, *Australia* **94 A2** 14 0 S 139 0 E
Carpentras, *France* **21 D9** 44 3N 5 2 E
Carpi, *Italy* **28 D7** 44 47N 10 53 E
Cărpineni, *Moldova* **43 D13** 46 46N 28 22 E
Carpinteria, *U.S.A.* **117 L7** 34 24N 119 31W
Carpio, *Spain* **34 D5** 41 13N 5 7W
Carr Boyd Ra., *Australia* **92 C4** 16 15 S 128 35 E
Carrabelle, *U.S.A.* **109 L3** 29 51N 84 40W
Carral, *Spain* **34 B2** 43 14N 8 21W
Carranza, Presa V., *Mexico* **118 B4** 27 20N 100 50W
Carrara, *Italy* **28 D7** 44 5N 10 6 E
Carrascal, *Phil.* **61 G6** 9 22N 125 56 E
Carrascosa del Campo, *Spain* **32 E2** 40 2N 2 45W
Carrauntoohill, *Ireland* **15 D2** 52 0N 9 45W
Carrick-on-Shannon, *Ireland* **15 C3** 53 57N 8 5W
Carrick-on-Suir, *Ireland* **15 D4** 52 21N 7 24W
Carrickfergus, *U.K.* **15 B6** 54 43N 5 49W
Carrickmacross, *Ireland* **15 C5** 53 59N 6 43W
Carrieton, *Australia* **95 E2** 32 25 S 138 31 E
Carrington, *U.S.A.* **112 B5** 47 27N 99 8W
Carrión →, *Spain* **34 D6** 41 53N 4 32W
Carrión de los Condes, *Spain* **34 C6** 42 20N 4 37W
Carrizal Bajo, *Chile* **126 B1** 28 5 S 71 20W
Carrizalillo, *Chile* **126 B1** 29 5 S 71 30W
Carrizo Cr. →, *U.S.A.* **113 G3** 36 55N 103 55W
Carrizo Springs, *U.S.A.* **113 L5** 28 31N 99 52W
Carrizozo, *U.S.A.* **115 K11** 33 38N 105 53W
Carroll, *U.S.A.* **112 D7** 42 4N 94 52W
Carrollton, *Ga., U.S.A.* **109 J3** 33 35N 85 5W
Carrollton, *Ill., U.S.A.* **112 F9** 39 18N 90 24W
Carrollton, *Ky., U.S.A.* **108 F3** 38 41N 85 11W
Carrollton, *Mo., U.S.A.* **112 F8** 39 22N 93 30W
Carrollton, *Ohio, U.S.A.* **110 F3** 40 34N 81 5W
Carron →, *U.K.* **14 D4** 57 53N 4 22W
Carron, L., *U.K.* **14 D3** 57 22N 5 35W
Carrot →, *Canada* **105 C8** 53 50N 101 17W
Carrot River, *Canada* **105 C8** 53 17N 103 35W
Carrouges, *France* **18 D6** 48 34N 0 10W
Carrù, *Italy* **28 D4** 44 29N 7 52 E
Carruthers, *Canada* **105 C7** 52 52N 109 16W
Carsa Dek, *Ethiopia* **81 F4** 5 13N 39 50 E
Çarşamba, *Turkey* **72 B7** 41 11N 36 44 E
Carsóli, *Italy* **29 F10** 42 6N 13 5 E
Carson, *Calif., U.S.A.* **117 M8** 33 48N 118 17W
Carson, *N. Dak., U.S.A.* **112 B4** 46 25N 101 34W
Carson →, *U.S.A.* **116 F8** 39 45N 118 40W
Carson City, *U.S.A.* **116 F7** 39 10N 119 46W
Carson Sink, *U.S.A.* **114 G4** 39 50N 118 25W
Cartagena, *Colombia* **124 A3** 10 25N 75 33W
Cartagena, *Spain* **33 H4** 37 38N 0 59W
Cartago, *Colombia* **124 C3** 4 45N 75 55W
Cartago, *Costa Rica* **120 E3** 9 50N 83 55W
Cártama, *Spain* **35 J6** 36 43N 4 39W
Cartaxo, *Portugal* **35 F2** 39 10N 8 47W
Cartaya, *Spain* **35 H3** 37 16N 7 9W
Cartersville, *U.S.A.* **109 H3** 34 10N 84 48W
Carterton, *N.Z.* **91 J5** 41 2 S 175 31 E
Carthage, *Tunisia* **30 F3** 36 50N 10 21 E
Carthage, *Ill., U.S.A.* **112 E9** 40 25N 91 8W
Carthage, *Mo., U.S.A.* **113 G7** 37 11N 94 19W
Carthage, *N.Y., U.S.A.* **108 D8** 43 59N 75 37W
Carthage, *Tex., U.S.A.* **113 J7** 32 9N 94 20W
Cartier I., *Australia* **92 B3** 12 31 S 123 29 E
Cartwright, *Canada* **103 B8** 53 41N 56 58W
Caruaru, *Brazil* **125 E11** 8 15 S 35 55W
Carúpano, *Venezuela* **124 A6** 10 39N 63 15W
Caruthersville, *U.S.A.* **113 G10** 36 11N 89 39W
Carvin, *France* **19 B9** 50 30N 2 57 E
Carvoeiro, *Brazil* **124 D6** 1 30 S 61 59W
Carvoeiro, C., *Portugal* **35 F1** 39 21N 9 24W
Cary, *U.S.A.* **109 H6** 35 47N 78 46W
Casa Branca, *Portugal* **35 G2** 38 29N 8 12W
Casa Grande, *U.S.A.* **115 K8** 32 53N 111 45W
Casablanca, *Chile* **126 C1** 33 20 S 71 25W
Casablanca, *Morocco* **78 B4** 33 36N 7 36W
Casacalenda, *Italy* **29 G11** 41 44N 14 51 E
Casalbordino, *Italy* **29 F11** 42 9N 14 35 E
Casale Monferrato, *Italy* **28 C5** 45 8N 8 27 E
Casalmaggiore, *Italy* **28 D7** 44 59N 10 26 E
Casalpusterlengo, *Italy* **28 C6** 45 11N 9 39 E
Casamance →, *Senegal* **82 C1** 12 33N 16 46W
Casarano, *Italy* **31 B11** 40 0N 18 10 E
Casares, *Spain* **35 J5** 36 27N 5 16W
Casas Ibáñez, *Spain* **33 F3** 39 17N 1 30W
Casasimarro, *Spain* **33 F2** 39 22N 2 3W
Casatejada, *Spain* **34 F5** 39 54N 5 40W
Casavieja, *Spain* **34 E6** 40 17N 4 46W
Cascade, *Idaho, U.S.A.* **114 D5** 44 31N 116 2W
Cascade, *Mont., U.S.A.* **114 C8** 47 16N 111 42W
Cascade Locks, *U.S.A.* **116 E5** 45 40N 121 54W
Cascade Ra., *U.S.A.* **116 D5** 47 0N 121 30W
Cascade Reservoir, *U.S.A.* **114 D5** 44 32N 116 3W
Cascais, *Portugal* **35 G1** 38 41N 9 25W
Cascavel, *Brazil* **127 A5** 24 57 S 53 28W
Cáscina, *Italy* **28 E7** 43 41N 10 33 E
Casco B., *U.S.A.* **109 D10** 43 45N 70 0W
Caselle Torinese, *Italy* **28 C4** 45 10N 7 39 E
Caserta, *Italy* **31 A7** 41 4N 14 20 E
Cashel, *Ireland* **15 D4** 52 30N 7 53W
Casiguran, *Phil.* **61 C5** 16 22N 122 7 E
Casilda, *Argentina* **126 C3** 33 10 S 61 10W
Casimcea, *Romania* **43 F13** 44 45N 28 23 E
Casino, *Australia* **95 D5** 28 52 S 153 3 E
Casiquiare →, *Venezuela* **124 C5** 2 1N 67 7W
Čáslav, *Czech Rep.* **26 B8** 49 54N 15 22 E
Casma, *Peru* **124 E3** 9 30 S 78 20W
Casmalia, *U.S.A.* **117 L6** 34 50N 120 32W
Cásola Valsénio, *Italy* **29 D8** 44 12N 11 40 E
Cásoli, *Italy* **29 F11** 42 7N 14 18 E
Caspe, *Spain* **32 D4** 41 14N 0 1W
Casper, *U.S.A.* **114 E10** 42 51N 106 19W
Caspian Depression, *Eurasia* **49 G9** 47 0N 48 0 E
Caspian Sea, *Eurasia* **50 E6** 43 0N 50 0 E
Cass Lake, *U.S.A.* **112 B7** 47 23N 94 37W
Cassà de la Selva, *Spain* **32 D7** 41 53N 2 52 E
Cassadaga, *U.S.A.* **110 D5** 42 20N 79 19W
Cassano allo Iónio, *Italy* **31 C9** 39 47N 16 20 E
Casse, Grande, *France* **21 C10** 45 24N 6 49 E
Cassel, *France* **19 B9** 50 48N 2 30 E
Casselman, *Canada* **111 A9** 45 19N 75 5W
Casselton, *U.S.A.* **112 B6** 46 54N 97 13W
Cassiar, *Canada* **104 B3** 59 16N 129 40W
Cassiar Mts., *Canada* **104 B2** 59 30N 130 30W
Cassino, *Italy* **30 A6** 41 30N 13 49 E
Cassis, *France* **21 E9** 43 14N 5 32 E
Cassville, *U.S.A.* **113 G8** 36 41N 93 52W
Castagneto Carducci, *Italy* **28 E7** 43 9N 10 36 E
Castaic, *U.S.A.* **117 L8** 34 30N 118 38W
Castalia, *U.S.A.* **110 E2** 41 24N 82 49W
Castanhal, *Brazil* **125 D9** 1 18 S 47 55W
Castéggio, *Italy* **28 C6** 45 0N 9 7 E
Castejón de Monegros, *Spain* **32 D4** 41 37N 0 15W
Castèl di Sangro, *Italy* **29 G11** 41 47N 14 6 E
Castèl San Giovanni, *Italy* **28 C6** 45 4N 9 26 E
Castèl San Pietro Terme, *Italy* **29 D8** 44 24N 11 35 E
Castelbuono, *Italy* **31 E7** 37 56N 14 5 E
Castelfidardo, *Italy* **29 E10** 43 28N 13 33 E
Castelfiorentino, *Italy* **28 E7** 43 36N 10 58 E
Castelfranco Emília, *Italy* **28 D8** 44 37N 11 3 E
Castelfranco Véneto, *Italy* **29 C8** 45 40N 11 55 E
Casteljaloux, *France* **20 D4** 44 19N 0 6 E
Castellabate, *Italy* **31 B7** 40 17N 14 57 E
Castellammare, G. di, *Italy* **30 D5** 38 8N 12 54 E
Castellammare del Golfo, *Italy* **30 D5** 38 1N 12 53 E
Castellammare di Stábia, *Italy* **31 B7** 40 42N 14 29 E
Castellamonte, *Italy* **28 C4** 45 23N 7 42 E
Castellane, *France* **21 E10** 43 50N 6 31 E
Castellaneta, *Italy* **31 B9** 40 38N 16 56 E
Castelli, *Argentina* **126 D4** 36 7 S 57 47W
Castelló de la Plana, *Spain* **32 F4** 39 58N 0 3W
Castellón de la Plana □, *Spain* **32 E4** 40 15N 0 5W
Castellote, *Spain* **32 E4** 40 48N 0 15W
Castelmáuro, *Italy* **29 G11** 41 50N 14 43 E
Castelnau-de-Médoc, *France* **20 C3** 45 2N 0 48W
Castelnau-Magnoac, *France* **20 E4** 43 17N 0 31 E
Castelnaudary, *France* **20 E5** 43 20N 1 58 E
Castelnovo ne' Monti, *Italy* **28 D7** 44 26N 10 24 E
Castelnuovo di Val di Cécina, *Italy* **28 E7** 43 12N 10 59 E
Castelo, *Brazil* **127 A7** 20 33 S 41 14W
Castelo Branco, *Portugal* **34 F3** 39 50N 7 31W
Castelo Branco □, *Portugal* **34 F3** 39 52N 7 45W
Castelo de Paiva, *Portugal* **34 D2** 41 2N 8 16W
Castelo de Vide, *Portugal* **35 F3** 39 25N 7 27W
Castelsardo, *Italy* **30 B1** 40 55N 8 43 E
Castelsarrasin, *France* **20 D5** 44 2N 1 7 E
Casteltérmini, *Italy* **30 E6** 37 32N 13 39 E
Castelvetrano, *Italy* **30 E5** 37 41N 12 47 E
Casterton, *Australia* **95 F3** 37 30 S 141 30 E
Castets, *France* **20 E2** 43 52N 1 6W
Castiglion Fiorentino, *Italy* **29 E8** 43 20N 11 55 E
Castiglione del Lago, *Italy* **29 E9** 43 7N 12 3 E
Castiglione della Pescáia, *Italy* **28 F7** 42 46N 10 53 E
Castiglione delle Stiviere, *Italy* **28 C7** 45 23N 10 29 E
Castilblanco, *Spain* **35 F5** 39 17N 5 5W
Castile, *U.S.A.* **110 D6** 42 38N 78 3W
Castilla, Playa de, *Spain* **35 J4** 37 0N 6 33W
Castilla-La Mancha □, *Spain* **6 H5** 39 30N 3 30W
Castilla y Leon □, *Spain* **34 D6** 42 0N 5 0W
Castillo de Locubín, *Spain* **35 H7** 37 32N 3 56W
Castillon-en-Couserans, *France* **20 F5** 42 56N 1 1 E
Castillonès, *France* **20 D4** 44 39N 0 37 E
Castillos, *Uruguay* **127 C5** 34 12 S 53 52W
Castle Dale, *U.S.A.* **114 G8** 39 13N 111 1W
Castle Douglas, *U.K.* **14 G5** 54 56N 3 56W
Castle Rock, *Colo., U.S.A.* **112 F2** 39 22N 104 51W
Castle Rock, *Wash., U.S.A.* **116 D4** 46 17N 122 54W
Castlebar, *Ireland* **15 C2** 53 52N 9 18W
Castleblaney, *Ireland* **15 B5** 54 7N 6 44W
Castlederg, *U.K.* **15 B4** 54 42N 7 35W
Castleford, *U.K.* **12 D6** 53 43N 1 21W
Castlegar, *Canada* **104 D5** 49 20N 117 40W
Castlemaine, *Australia* **95 F3** 37 2 S 144 12 E
Castlepollard, *Ireland* **15 C4** 53 41N 7 19W
Castlerea, *Ireland* **15 C3** 53 46N 8 29W
Castlereagh →, *Australia* **95 E4** 30 12 S 147 32 E
Castlereagh B., *Australia* **94 A2** 12 10 S 135 10 E
Castleton, *U.S.A.* **111 C11** 43 37N 73 11W
Castletown, *U.K.* **12 C3** 54 5N 4 38W
Castletown Bearhaven, *Ireland* **15 E2** 51 39N 9 55W
Castor, *Canada* **104 C6** 52 15N 111 50W
Castor →, *Canada* **102 B4** 53 24N 78 58W
Castorland, *U.S.A.* **111 C9** 43 53N 75 31W
Castres, *France* **20 E6** 43 37N 2 13 E
Castricum, *Neths.* **17 B4** 52 33N 4 40 E
Castries, *St. Lucia* **121 D7** 14 2N 60 58W
Castril, *Spain* **35 H8** 37 48N 2 46W
Castro, *Brazil* **127 A6** 24 45 S 50 0W
Castro, *Chile* **128 E2** 42 30 S 73 50W
Castro Alves, *Brazil* **125 F11** 12 46 S 39 33W
Castro del Río, *Spain* **35 H6** 37 41N 4 29W
Castro-Urdiales, *Spain* **34 B7** 43 23N 3 11W
Castro Verde, *Portugal* **35 H2** 37 41N 8 4W
Castrojeriz, *Spain* **34 C6** 42 17N 4 9W
Castropol, *Spain* **34 B4** 43 32N 7 0W
Castroreale, *Italy* **31 D8** 38 6N 15 12 E
Castrovíllari, *Italy* **31 C9** 39 49N 16 12 E
Castroville, *U.S.A.* **116 J5** 36 46N 121 45W
Castuera, *Spain* **35 G5** 38 43N 5 37W
Çat, *Turkey* **73 C9** 39 40N 41 3 E
Cat Ba, Dao, *Vietnam* **64 B6** 20 50N 107 0 E
Cat I., *Bahamas* **121 B4** 24 30N 75 30W
Cat L., *Canada* **102 B1** 51 40N 91 50W
Cat Lake, *Canada* **102 B1** 51 40N 91 50W
Čata, *Slovak Rep.* **27 D11** 47 58N 18 38 E
Catacamas, *Honduras* **120 D2** 14 54N 85 56W
Cataguases, *Brazil* **127 A7** 21 23 S 42 39W
Çatak, *Turkey* **73 C10** 38 1N 43 8 E
Catalão, *Brazil* **125 G9** 18 10 S 47 57W
Çatalca, *Turkey* **41 E12** 41 8N 28 27 E
Catalina, *Canada* **103 C9** 48 31N 53 4W
Catalina, *Chile* **126 B2** 25 13 S 69 43W
Catalina, *U.S.A.* **115 K8** 32 30N 110 50W
Catalonia = Cataluña □, *Spain* **32 D6** 41 40N 1 15 E
Cataluña □, *Spain* **32 D6** 41 40N 1 15 E
Çatalzeytin, *Turkey* **72 B6** 41 57N 34 12 E
Catamarca, *Argentina* **126 B2** 28 30 S 65 50W
Catamarca □, *Argentina* **126 B2** 27 0 S 65 50W
Catanauan, *Phil.* **61 E5** 13 36N 122 19 E
Catanduanes □, *Phil.* **61 E6** 13 50N 124 20 E
Catanduva, *Brazil* **127 A6** 21 5 S 48 58W
Catánia, *Italy* **31 E8** 37 30N 15 6 E
Catánia, G. di, *Italy* **31 E8** 37 24N 15 9 E
Catanzaro, *Italy* **31 D9** 38 54N 16 35 E
Catarman, *Phil.* **61 E6** 12 28N 124 35 E
Catbalogan, *Phil.* **61 F6** 11 46N 124 53 E
Cateel, *Phil.* **61 H7** 7 47N 126 24 E
Catembe, *Mozam.* **89 D5** 26 0 S 32 33 E
Caterham, *U.K.* **13 F7** 51 15N 0 4W
Cathcart, *S. Africa* **88 E4** 32 18 S 27 10 E
Cathlamet, *U.S.A.* **116 D3** 46 12N 123 23W
Catio, *Guinea-Biss.* **82 C1** 11 17N 15 15W
Catlettsburg, *U.S.A.* **108 F4** 38 25N 82 36W
Çatma Dağı, *Turkey* **39 C11** 38 25N 29 50 E
Catoche, C., *Mexico* **119 C7** 21 40N 87 8W
Cátria, Mte., *Italy* **29 E9** 43 28N 12 42 E
Catriló, *Argentina* **126 D3** 36 26 S 63 24W
Catrimani, *Brazil* **124 C6** 0 27N 61 41W
Catrimani →, *Brazil* **124 C6** 0 28N 61 44W
Catskill, *U.S.A.* **111 D11** 42 14N 73 52W
Catskill Mts., *U.S.A.* **111 D10** 42 10N 74 25W
Catt, Mt., *Australia* **94 A1** 13 49 S 134 23 E
Cattaraugus, *U.S.A.* **110 D6** 42 22N 78 52W
Cattólica, *Italy* **29 E9** 43 58N 12 44 E
Cattólica Eraclea, *Italy* **30 E6** 37 26N 13 24 E
Catuala, *Angola* **88 B2** 16 25 S 19 2 E
Catuane, *Mozam.* **89 D5** 26 48 S 32 18 E
Catur, *Mozam.* **87 E4** 13 45 S 35 30 E
Catwick Is., *Vietnam* **65 G7** 10 0N 109 0 E
Cauca →, *Colombia* **124 B4** 8 54N 74 28W
Caucaia, *Brazil* **125 D11** 3 40 S 38 35W
Caucasus Mountains, *Eurasia* **49 J7** 42 50N 44 0 E
Caudete, *Spain* **33 G3** 38 42N 1 2W
Caudry, *France* **19 B10** 50 7N 3 22 E
Caulnes, *France* **18 D4** 48 18N 2 10W
Caulónia, *Italy* **31 D9** 38 23N 16 24 E
Caungula, *Angola* **84 F3** 8 26 S 18 38 E
Cauquenes, *Chile* **126 D1** 36 0 S 72 22W
Caura →, *Venezuela* **124 B6** 7 38N 64 53W
Cauresi →, *Mozam.* **87 F3** 17 8 S 33 0 E
Căuşani, *Moldova* **43 D14** 46 38N 29 25 E
Causapscal, *Canada* **103 C6** 48 19N 67 12W
Caussade, *France* **20 D5** 44 10N 1 33 E
Causse-Méjean, *France* **20 D7** 44 18N 3 42 E
Cauterets, *France* **20 F3** 42 52N 0 8W
Cauvery →, *India* **66 P11** 11 9N 78 52 E
Caux, Pays de, *France* **18 C7** 49 38N 0 35 E
Cava de' Tirreni, *Italy* **31 B7** 40 42N 14 42 E
Cávado →, *Portugal* **34 D2** 41 32N 8 48W
Cavaillon, *France* **21 E9** 43 50N 5 2 E
Cavalaire-sur-Mer, *France* **21 E10** 43 10N 6 33 E
Cavalese, *Italy* **29 B8** 46 17N 11 27 E
Cavalier, *U.S.A.* **112 A6** 48 48N 97 37W
Cavalla = Cavally →, *Africa* **82 E3** 4 22N 7 32W
Cavalleria, C. de, *Spain* **37 A11** 40 5N 4 5 E
Cavallo, I. de, *France* **21 G13** 41 22N 9 16 E
Cavally →, *Africa* **82 E3** 4 22N 7 32W
Cavan, *Ireland* **15 B4** 54 0N 7 22W
Cavan □, *Ireland* **15 C4** 54 1N 7 16W
Cavárzere, *Italy* **29 C9** 45 8N 12 5 E
Çavdarhisar, *Turkey* **39 B11** 39 12N 29 37 E
Çavdır, *Turkey* **39 D11** 37 10N 29 42 E
Cave Creek, *U.S.A.* **115 K7** 33 50N 111 57W
Cavenagh Ra., *Australia* **93 E4** 26 12 S 127 55 E
Cavendish, *Australia* **95 F3** 37 31 S 142 2 E
Caviana, I., *Brazil* **125 C8** 0 10N 50 10W
Cavite, *Phil.* **61 D4** 14 29N 120 55 E
Cavnic, *Romania* **43 C8** 47 40N 23 52 E
Cavour, *Italy* **28 D4** 44 47N 7 22 E
Cavtat, *Croatia* **40 D2** 42 35N 18 13 E
Cawndilla L., *Australia* **95 E3** 32 30 S 142 15 E
Cawnpore = Kanpur, *India* **69 F9** 26 28N 80 20 E
Caxias, *Brazil* **125 D10** 4 55 S 43 20W
Caxias do Sul, *Brazil* **127 B5** 29 10 S 51 10W
Çay, *Turkey* **72 C4** 38 35N 31 1 E
Cay Sal Bank, *Bahamas* **120 B4** 23 45N 80 0W
Cayambe, *Ecuador* **124 C3** 0 3N 78 8W
Çaycuma, *Turkey* **72 B5** 41 25N 32 4 E
Çayeli, *Turkey* **73 B9** 41 5N 40 45 E
Cayenne, *Fr. Guiana* **125 B8** 5 5N 52 18W
Caygören Barajı, *Turkey* **39 B10** 39 15N 28 12 E
Cayiralan, *Turkey* **72 C6** 39 17N 35 38 E
Caylus, *France* **20 D5** 44 15N 1 47 E
Cayman Brac, *Cayman Is.* **120 C4** 19 43N 79 49W
Cayman Is. ■, *W. Indies* **120 C3** 19 40N 80 30W
Cayo Romano, *Cuba* **120 B4** 22 0N 78 0W
Cayres, *France* **20 D7** 44 55N 3 48 E
Cayuga, *Canada* **110 D5** 42 59N 79 50W
Cayuga, *U.S.A.* **111 D8** 42 54N 76 44W
Cayuga L., *U.S.A.* **111 D8** 42 41N 76 41W
Cazalla de la Sierra, *Spain* **35 H5** 37 56N 5 45W
Căzăneşti, *Romania* **43 F12** 44 36N 27 3 E
Cazaubon, *France* **20 E3** 43 56N 0 3W
Cazaux et de Sanguinet, Étang de, *France* **20 D2** 44 29N 1 10W
Cazenovia, *U.S.A.* **111 D9** 42 56N 75 51W
Cazères, *France* **20 E5** 43 13N 1 5 E
Cazin, *Bos.-H.* **29 D12** 44 57N 15 57 E
Čazma, *Croatia* **29 C13** 45 45N 16 39 E
Cazombo, *Angola* **85 G4** 11 54 S 22 56 E
Cazorla, *Spain* **35 H7** 37 55N 3 2W
Cazorla, Sierra de, *Spain* **35 G8** 38 5N 2 55W
Cea →, *Spain* **34 C5** 42 0N 5 36W
Ceamurlia de Jos, *Romania* **43 F13** 44 43N 28 47 E
Ceanannus Mor, *Ireland* **15 C5** 53 44N 6 53W
Ceará = Fortaleza, *Brazil* **125 D11** 3 45 S 38 35W
Ceará □, *Brazil* **125 E11** 5 0 S 40 0W
Ceará Mirim, *Brazil* **125 E11** 5 38 S 35 25W
Ceauru, L., *Romania* **43 F8** 44 58N 23 11 E
Cebaco, I. de, *Panama* **120 E3** 7 33N 81 9W
Cebollar, *Argentina* **126 B2** 29 10 S 66 35W
Cebollera, Sierra de, *Spain* **32 D2** 42 0N 2 30W
Cebreros, *Spain* **34 E6** 40 27N 4 28W
Cebu, *Phil.* **61 F5** 10 18N 123 54 E
Čečava, *Bos.-H.* **42 F2** 44 42N 17 44 E
Ceccano, *Italy* **30 A6** 41 34N 13 20 E
Cece, *Hungary* **42 D3** 46 46N 18 39 E
Cechi, *Ivory C.* **82 D4** 6 15N 4 25W
Cecil Plains, *Australia* **95 D5** 27 30 S 151 11 E
Cécina, *Italy* **28 E7** 43 19N 10 31 E
Cécina →, *Italy* **28 E7** 43 18N 10 29 E
Ceclavín, *Spain* **34 F4** 39 50N 6 45W
Cedar →, *U.S.A.* **112 E9** 41 17N 91 21W
Cedar City, *U.S.A.* **115 H7** 37 41N 113 4W
Cedar Creek Reservoir, *U.S.A.* **113 J6** 32 11N 96 4W
Cedar Falls, *Iowa, U.S.A.* **112 D8** 42 32N 92 27W
Cedar Falls, *Wash., U.S.A.* **116 C5** 47 25N 121 45W
Cedar Key, *U.S.A.* **109 L4** 29 8N 83 2W
Cedar L., *Canada* **105 C9** 53 10N 100 0W
Cedar Rapids, *U.S.A.* **112 E9** 41 59N 91 40W
Cedartown, *U.S.A.* **109 H3** 34 1N 85 15W
Cedarvale, *Canada* **104 B3** 55 1N 128 22W
Cedarville, *S. Africa* **89 E4** 30 23 S 29 3 E
Cedeira, *Spain* **34 B2** 43 39N 8 2W
Cedral, *Mexico* **118 C4** 23 50N 100 42W
Cedrino →, *Italy* **30 B2** 40 11N 9 24 E
Cedro, *Brazil* **125 E11** 6 34 S 39 3W
Cedros, I. de, *Mexico* **118 B1** 28 10N 115 20W
Ceduna, *Australia* **95 E1** 32 7 S 133 46 E
Cedynia, *Poland* **45 F1** 52 53N 14 12 E
Cée, *Spain* **34 C1** 42 57N 9 10W
Cefalù, *Italy* **31 D7** 38 2N 14 1 E
Cega →, *Spain* **34 D6** 41 33N 4 46W
Cegléd, *Hungary* **42 C4** 47 11N 19 47 E
Céglie Messápico, *Italy* **31 B10** 40 39N 17 31 E
Cehegín, *Spain* **33 G3** 38 6N 1 48W
Ceheng, *China* **58 E5** 24 58N 105 48 E
Cehu-Silvaniei, *Romania* **43 C8** 47 24N 23 9 E
Ceica, *Romania* **42 D7** 46 53N 22 10 E
Ceira →, *Portugal* **34 E2** 40 13N 8 16W
Čelákovice, *Czech Rep.* **26 A7** 50 10N 14 46 E
Celano, *Italy* **29 F10** 42 5N 13 33 E
Celanova, *Spain* **34 C3** 42 9N 7 58W
Celaya, *Mexico* **118 C4** 20 31N 100 37W
Celebes Sea, *Indonesia* **63 D6** 3 0N 123 0 E
Čelić, *Bos.-H.* **42 F3** 44 43N 18 49 E
Celina, *U.S.A.* **108 E3** 40 33N 84 35W
Celinac, *Bos.-H.* **42 F2** 44 44N 17 22 E
Celje, *Slovenia* **29 B12** 46 16N 15 18 E
Celldömölk, *Hungary* **42 C2** 47 16N 17 10 E
Celle, *Germany* **24 C6** 52 37N 10 4 E
Celorico da Beira, *Portugal* **34 E3** 40 38N 7 24W
Çeltikçi, *Turkey* **39 D12** 37 32N 30 29 E
Çemişgezek, *Turkey* **73 C8** 39 3N 38 56 E
Cenderwasih, Teluk, *Indonesia* **63 E9** 3 0 S 135 20 E
Cengong, *China* **58 D7** 27 13N 108 44 E
Ceno →, *Italy* **28 D7** 44 43N 10 5 E
Centallo, *Italy* **28 D4** 44 30N 7 35 E
Centelles, *Spain* **32 D7** 41 50N 2 14 E
Center, *N. Dak., U.S.A.* **112 B4** 47 7N 101 18W
Center, *Tex., U.S.A.* **113 K7** 31 48N 94 11W
Centerburg, *U.S.A.* **110 F2** 40 18N 82 42W
Centerville, *Calif., U.S.A.* **116 J7** 36 44N 119 30W
Centerville, *Iowa, U.S.A.* **112 E8** 40 44N 92 52W
Centerville, *Pa., U.S.A.* **110 F5** 40 3N 79 59W
Centerville, *Tenn., U.S.A.* **109 H2** 35 47N 87 28W
Centerville, *Tex., U.S.A.* **113 K7** 31 16N 95 59W
Cento, *Italy* **29 D8** 44 43N 11 17 E
Central □, *Ghana* **83 D4** 5 30N 1 0W
Central □, *Kenya* **86 C4** 0 30 S 37 30 E
Central □, *Malawi* **87 E3** 13 30 S 33 30 E
Central □, *Zambia* **87 E2** 14 25 S 28 50 E
Central, Cordillera, *Colombia* **122 C3** 5 0N 75 0W
Central, Cordillera, *Costa Rica* **120 D3** 10 10N 84 5W
Central, Cordillera, *Dom. Rep.* **121 C5** 19 15N 71 0W
Central, Cordillera, *Phil.* **61 C4** 17 20N 120 57 E
Central African Rep. ■, *Africa* **84 C4** 7 0N 20 0 E
Central America, *America* **98 H11** 12 0N 85 0W
Central Butte, *Canada* **105 C7** 50 48N 106 31W
Central City, *Colo., U.S.A.* **114 G11** 39 48N 105 31W
Central City, *Ky., U.S.A.* **108 G2** 37 18N 87 7W
Central City, *Nebr., U.S.A.* **112 E6** 41 7N 98 0W
Central I., *Kenya* **86 B4** 3 30N 36 0 E
Central Makran Range, *Pakistan* **66 F4** 26 30N 64 15 E
Central Patricia, *Canada* **102 B1** 51 30N 90 9W
Central Point, *U.S.A.* **114 E2** 42 23N 122 55W
Central Russian Uplands, *Europe* **6 E13** 54 0N 36 0 E
Central Siberian Plateau, *Russia* **52 C14** 65 0N 105 0 E
Central Square, *U.S.A.* **111 C8** 43 17N 76 9W
Centralia, *Ill., U.S.A.* **112 F10** 38 32N 89 8W
Centralia, *Mo., U.S.A.* **112 F8** 39 13N 92 8W
Centralia, *Wash., U.S.A.* **116 D4** 46 43N 122 58W
Cenxi, *China* **59 F8** 22 57N 110 57 E
Čeotina →, *Bos.-H.* **40 C2** 43 36N 18 50 E
Cephalonia = Kefallinía, *Greece* **38 C2** 38 20N 20 30 E
Čepin, *Croatia* **42 E3** 45 32N 18 34 E
Ceprano, *Italy* **30 A6** 41 33N 13 31 E
Ceptura, *Romania* **43 E11** 45 1N 26 21 E
Cepu, *Indonesia* **63 G14** 7 9 S 111 35 E
Ceram = Seram, *Indonesia* **63 E7** 3 10 S 129 0 E
Ceram Sea = Seram Sea, *Indonesia* **63 E7** 2 30 S 128 30 E
Cerbère, *France* **20 F7** 42 26N 3 10 E
Cerbicales, Is., *France* **21 G13** 41 33N 9 22 E
Cercal, *Portugal* **35 H2** 37 48N 8 40W
Cerdaña, *Spain* **32 C6** 42 22N 1 35 E
Cère →, *France* **20 D5** 44 55N 1 49 E
Cerea, *Italy* **29 C8** 45 12N 11 13 E
Ceredigion □, *U.K.* **13 E3** 52 16N 4 15W
Ceres, *Argentina* **126 B3** 29 55 S 61 55W
Ceres, *S. Africa* **88 E2** 33 21 S 19 18 E
Ceres, *U.S.A.* **116 H6** 37 35N 120 57W
Céret, *France* **20 F6** 42 30N 2 42 E
Cergy, *France* **19 C9** 49 2N 2 4 E
Cerignola, *Italy* **31 A8** 41 17N 15 53 E
Cerigo = Kíthira, *Greece* **38 E5** 36 8N 23 0 E
Cérilly, *France* **19 F9** 46 37N 2 50 E
Cerisiers, *France* **19 D10** 48 8N 3 30 E
Cerizay, *France* **18 F6** 46 50N 0 40W
Çerkeş, *Turkey* **72 B5** 40 49N 32 52 E
Çerkezköy, *Turkey* **41 E12** 41 17N 28 0 E
Cerknica, *Slovenia* **29 C11** 45 48N 14 21 E
Cerkovica, *Bulgaria* **41 C8** 43 41N 24 50 E
Cermerno, *Serbia, Yug.* **40 C4** 43 35N 20 25 E
Çermik, *Turkey* **73 C8** 38 8N 39 26 E
Cerna, *Romania* **43 E13** 45 4N 28 17 E
Cerna →, *Romania* **43 F8** 44 38N 23 58 E
Cernavodă, *Romania* **43 F13** 44 22N 28 3 E
Cernay, *France* **19 E14** 47 44N 7 10 E
Cernik, *Croatia* **42 E2** 45 17N 17 22 E
Cerralvo, I., *Mexico* **118 C3** 24 20N 109 45W
Cërrik, *Albania* **40 E3** 41 2N 19 58 E
Cerritos, *Mexico* **118 C4** 22 27N 100 20W
Cerro Chato, *Uruguay* **127 C4** 33 6 S 55 8W
Certaldo, *Italy* **28 E8** 43 33N 11 2 E
Cervaro →, *Italy* **31 A8** 41 30N 15 52 E
Cervati, Monte, *Italy* **31 B8** 40 17N 15 29 E
Cerventes, *Australia* **93 F2** 30 31 S 115 3 E
Cervera, *Spain* **32 D6** 41 40N 1 16 E
Cervera de Pisuerga, *Spain* **34 C6** 42 51N 4 30W
Cervera del Río Alhama, *Spain* **32 C3** 42 2N 1 58W
Cervéteri, *Italy* **29 F9** 42 0N 12 6 E
Cérvia, *Italy* **29 D9** 44 15N 12 22 E
Cervignano del Friuli, *Italy* **29 C10** 45 49N 13 20 E
Cervinara, *Italy* **31 A7** 41 1N 14 37 E
Cervione, *France* **21 F13** 42 20N 9 29 E
Cervo, *Spain* **34 B3** 43 40N 7 24W
Cesarò, *Italy* **31 E7** 37 50N 14 38 E
Cesena, *Italy* **29 D9** 44 8N 12 15 E
Cesenático, *Italy* **29 D9** 44 12N 12 24 E
Cēsis, *Latvia* **9 H21** 57 18N 25 15 E
Česká Lípa, *Czech Rep.* **26 A7** 50 45N 14 30 E
Česká Třebová, *Czech Rep.* **27 B9** 49 54N 16 27 E
České Budějovice, *Czech Rep.* **26 C7** 48 55N 14 25 E
České Velenice, *Czech Rep.* **26 C7** 48 45N 14 57 E
Českomoravská Vrchovina, *Czech Rep.* **26 B8** 49 30N 15 40 E
Český Brod, *Czech Rep.* **26 A7** 50 4N 14 52 E
Český Krumlov, *Czech Rep.* **26 C7** 48 43N 14 21 E
Český Těšín, *Czech Rep.* **27 B11** 49 45N 18 39 E
Česma →, *Croatia* **29 C13** 45 35N 16 29 E
Çeşme, *Turkey* **39 C8** 38 20N 26 23 E
Cessnock, *Australia* **95 E5** 32 50 S 151 21 E
Cesson-Sévigné, *France* **18 D5** 48 7N 1 36W
Cestas, *France* **20 D3** 44 44N 0 41W
Cestos →, *Liberia* **82 D3** 5 40N 9 10W
Cetate, *Romania* **42 F8** 44 7N 23 2 E
Cetin Grad, *Croatia* **29 C12** 45 9N 15 45 E
Cetina →, *Croatia* **29 E13** 43 26N 16 42 E
Cetinje, *Montenegro, Yug.* **40 D2** 42 23N 18 59 E
Cetraro, *Italy* **31 C8** 39 31N 15 55 E
Ceuta, *N. Afr.* **78 A4** 35 52N 5 18W
Ceva, *Italy* **28 D5** 44 23N 8 2 E
Cévennes, *France* **20 D7** 44 10N 3 50 E
Ceyhan, *Turkey* **70 B2** 37 4N 35 47 E
Ceyhan →, *Turkey* **72 D6** 36 38N 35 40 E
Ceylânpınar, *Turkey* **73 D9** 36 50N 40 2 E
Ceylon = Sri Lanka ■, *Asia* **66 R12** 7 30N 80 50 E
Cèze →, *France* **21 D8** 44 6N 4 43 E
Cha-am, *Thailand* **64 F2** 12 48N 99 58 E
Cha Pa, *Vietnam* **64 A4** 22 20N 103 47 E
Chabanais, *France* **20 C4** 45 52N 0 48 E
Chabeuil, *France* **21 D9** 44 54N 5 3 E
Chablais, *France* **19 F13** 46 20N 6 36 E
Chablis, *France* **19 E10** 47 47N 3 48 E
Chacabuco, *Argentina* **126 C3** 34 40 S 60 27W
Chachapoyas, *Peru* **124 E3** 6 15 S 77 50W
Chachoengsao, *Thailand* **64 F3** 13 42N 101 5 E
Chachran, *Pakistan* **66 E7** 28 55N 70 30 E
Chachro, *Pakistan* **68 G4** 25 5N 70 15 E
Chaco □, *Argentina* **126 B3** 26 30 S 61 0W
Chaco □, *Paraguay* **126 B4** 26 0 S 60 0W
Chaco →, *U.S.A.* **115 H9** 36 46N 108 39W
Chaco Austral, *S. Amer.* **128 B4** 27 0 S 61 30W
Chaco Boreal, *S. Amer.* **124 H6** 22 0 S 60 0W
Chaco Central, *S. Amer.* **128 A4** 24 0 S 61 0W
Chacon, C., *U.S.A.* **104 C2** 54 42N 132 0W
Chad ■, *Africa* **79 E9** 15 0N 17 15 E
Chad, L. = Tchad, L., *Chad* **79 F8** 13 30N 14 30 E
Chadan, *Russia* **51 D10** 51 17N 91 35 E
Chadileuvú →, *Argentina* **126 D2** 37 46 S 66 0W
Chadiza, *Zambia* **87 E3** 14 45 S 32 27 E
Chadron, *U.S.A.* **112 D3** 42 50N 103 0W
Chadyr-Lunga = Ciadâr-Lunga, *Moldova* **43 D13** 46 3N 28 51 E
Chae Hom, *Thailand* **64 C2** 18 43N 99 35 E
Chaem →, *Thailand* **64 C2** 18 11N 98 38 E
Chaeryŏng, *N. Korea* **57 E13** 38 24N 125 36 E
Chagai Hills, *Afghan.* **66 E3** 29 30N 63 0 E
Chagda, *Russia* **51 D14** 58 45N 130 38 E
Chagny, *France* **19 F11** 46 57N 4 45 E
Chagoda, *Russia* **46 C8** 59 10N 35 15 E
Chagos Arch., *Ind. Oc.* **52 K11** 6 0 S 72 0 E
Chagrin Falls, *U.S.A.* **110 E3** 41 26N 81 24W
Chāh Ākhvor, *Iran* **71 C8** 32 41N 59 40 E
Chāh Bahar, *Iran* **71 E9** 25 20N 60 40 E
Chāh-e Kavīr, *Iran* **71 C8** 34 29N 56 52 E
Chahar Burjak, *Afghan.* **66 D3** 30 15N 62 0 E

Chahār Mahāll va Bakhtīarī □, *Iran* **71 C6** 32 0N 49 0 E
Chaibasa, *India* **67 H14** 22 42N 85 49 E
Chaillé-les-Marais, *France* **20 B2** 46 25N 1 2W
Chainat, *Thailand* **64 E3** 15 11N 100 8 E
Chaiya, *Thailand* **65 H2** 9 23N 99 14 E
Chaj Doab, *Pakistan* **68 C5** 32 15N 73 0 E
Chajari, *Argentina* **126 C4** 30 42S 58 0W
Chak Amru, *Pakistan* **68 C6** 32 22N 75 11 E
Chaka, *Sudan* **81 G3** 4 49N 31 14 E
Chakar →, *Pakistan* **68 E3** 29 29N 68 2 E
Chakari, *Zimbabwe* **89 B4** 18 5S 29 51 E
Chake Chake, *Tanzania* **86 D4** 5 15S 39 45 E
Chakhānsūr, *Afghan.* **66 D3** 31 10N 62 0 E
Chakonipau, L., *Canada* **103 A6** 56 18N 68 30W
Chakradharpur, *India* **69 H11** 22 45N 85 40 E
Chakrata, *India* **68 D7** 30 42N 77 51 E
Chakwal, *Pakistan* **68 C5** 32 56N 72 53 E
Chala, *Peru* **124 G4** 15 48S 74 20W
Chalais, *France* **20 C4** 45 16N 0 3 E
Chalchihuites, *Mexico* **118 C4** 23 29N 103 53W
Chalcis = Khalkís, *Greece* **38 C5** 38 27N 23 42 E
Châlette-sur-Loing, *France* **19 D9** 48 1N 2 44 E
Chaleur B., *Canada* **103 C6** 47 55N 65 30W
Chalfant, *U.S.A.* **116 H8** 37 32N 118 21W
Chalhuanca, *Peru* **124 F4** 14 15S 73 15W
Chalindrey, *France* **19 E12** 47 43N 5 26 E
Chaling, *China* **59 D9** 26 58N 113 30 E
Chalisgaon, *India* **66 J9** 20 30N 75 10 E
Chalk River, *Canada* **102 C4** 46 1N 77 27W
Chalky Inlet, *N.Z.* **91 M1** 46 3S 166 31 E
Challans, *France* **18 F5** 46 50N 1 52W
Challapata, *Bolivia* **124 G5** 18 53S 66 50W
Challis, *U.S.A.* **114 D6** 44 30N 114 14W
Chalmette, *U.S.A.* **113 L10** 29 56N 89 58W
Chalon-sur-Saône, *France* **19 F11** 46 48N 4 50 E
Chalonnes-sur-Loire, *France* **18 E6** 47 20N 0 45W
Châlons-en-Champagne, *France* **19 D11** 48 58N 4 20 E
Châlus, *France* **20 C4** 45 39N 0 58 E
Chalyaphum, *Thailand* **64 E4** 15 48N 102 2 E
Cham, *Germany* **25 F8** 49 13N 12 39 E
Cham, Cu Lao, *Vietnam* **64 E7** 15 57N 108 30 E
Chama, *U.S.A.* **115 H10** 36 54N 106 35W
Chamaicó, *Argentina* **126 D3** 35 3S 64 58W
Chaman, *Pakistan* **66 D5** 30 58N 66 25 E
Chamba, *India* **68 C7** 32 35N 76 10 E
Chamba, *Tanzania* **87 E4** 11 37S 37 0 E
Chambal →, *India* **69 F8** 26 29N 79 15 E
Chamberlain, *U.S.A.* **112 D5** 43 49N 99 20W
Chamberlain →, *Australia* **92 C4** 15 30S 127 54 E
Chamberlain L., *U.S.A.* **109 B11** 46 14N 69 19W
Chambers, *U.S.A.* **115 J9** 35 11N 109 26W
Chambersburg, *U.S.A.* **108 F7** 39 56N 77 40W
Chambéry, *France* **21 C9** 45 34N 5 55 E
Chambeshi →, *Zambia* **84 G6** 11 53S 29 48 E
Chambly, *Canada* **111 A11** 45 27N 73 17W
Chambord, *Canada* **103 C5** 48 25N 72 6W
Chamboulive, *France* **20 C5** 45 26N 1 42 E
Chamchamal, *Iraq* **70 C5** 35 32N 44 50 E
Chamela, *Mexico* **118 D3** 19 32N 105 5W
Chamical, *Argentina* **126 C2** 30 22S 66 27W
Chamkar Luong, *Cambodia* **65 G4** 11 0N 103 45 E
Chamoli, *India* **69 D8** 30 24N 79 21 E
Chamonix-Mont Blanc, *France* **21 C10** 45 55N 6 51 E
Chamouchouane →, *Canada* **102 C5** 48 37N 72 20W
Champa, *India* **69 H10** 22 2N 82 43 E
Champagne, *Canada* **104 A1** 60 49N 136 30W
Champagne, *France* **19 D11** 48 40N 4 20 E
Champagnole, *France* **19 F12** 46 45N 5 55 E
Champaign, *U.S.A.* **108 E1** 40 7N 88 15W
Champassak, *Laos* **64 E5** 14 53N 105 52 E
Champaubert, *France* **19 D10** 48 50N 3 45 E
Champawat, *India* **69 E9** 29 20N 80 6 E
Champdeniers-St-Denis, *France* **20 B3** 46 29N 0 25W
Champdoré, L., *Canada* **103 A6** 55 55N 65 49W
Champeix, *France* **20 C7** 45 37N 3 8 E
Champion, *U.S.A.* **110 E4** 41 19N 80 51W
Champlain, *U.S.A.* **111 B11** 44 59N 73 27W
Champlain, L., *U.S.A.* **111 B11** 44 40N 73 20W
Champlitte, *France* **19 E12** 47 32N 5 31 E
Champotón, *Mexico* **119 D6** 19 20N 90 50W
Champua, *India* **69 H11** 22 5N 85 40 E
Chamusca, *Portugal* **35 F2** 39 21N 8 29W
Chana, *Thailand* **65 J3** 6 55N 100 44 E
Chañaral, *Chile* **126 B1** 26 23S 70 40W
Chanārān, *Iran* **71 B8** 36 39N 59 6 E
Chanasma, *India* **68 H5** 23 44N 72 5 E
Chanco, *Chile* **126 D1** 35 44S 72 32W
Chand, *India* **69 J8** 21 57N 79 7 E
Chandan, *India* **69 G12** 24 38N 86 40 E
Chandan Chauki, *India* **69 E9** 28 33N 80 47 E
Chandannagar, *India* **69 H13** 22 52N 88 24 E
Chandausi, *India* **69 E8** 28 27N 78 49 E
Chandeleur Is., *U.S.A.* **113 L10** 29 55N 88 57W
Chandeleur Sd., *U.S.A.* **113 L10** 29 55N 89 0W
Chandigarh, *India* **68 D7** 30 43N 76 47 E
Chandil, *India* **69 H12** 22 58N 86 3 E
Chandler, *Australia* **95 D1** 27 0S 133 19 E
Chandler, *Canada* **103 C7** 48 18N 64 46W
Chandler, *Ariz., U.S.A.* **115 K8** 33 18N 111 50W
Chandler, *Okla., U.S.A.* **113 H6** 35 42N 96 53W
Chandod, *India* **68 J5** 21 59N 73 28 E
Chandpur, *Bangla.* **67 H17** 23 8N 90 45 E
Chandrapur, *India* **66 K11** 19 57N 79 25 E
Chānf, *Iran* **71 E9** 26 38N 60 29 E
Chang, *Pakistan* **68 F3** 26 59N 68 30 E
Chang, Ko, *Thailand* **65 F4** 12 0N 102 23 E
Ch'ang Chiang = Chang Jiang →, *China* **59 B13** 31 48N 121 10 E
Chang Jiang →, *China* **59 B13** 31 48N 121 10 E
Changa, *India* **69 C7** 33 53N 77 35 E
Changanacheri, *India* **66 Q10** 9 25N 76 31 E
Changane →, *Mozam.* **89 C5** 24 30S 33 30 E
Changbai, *China* **57 D15** 41 25N 128 5 E
Changbai Shan, *China* **57 C15** 42 20N 129 0 E
Changchiak'ou = Zhangjiakou, *China* **56 D8** 40 48N 114 55 E
Ch'angchou = Changzhou, *China* **59 B12** 31 47N 119 58 E
Changchun, *China* **57 C13** 43 57N 125 17 E
Changchunling, *China* **57 B13** 45 18N 125 27 E
Changde, *China* **59 C8** 29 4N 111 35 E
Changdo-ri, *N. Korea* **57 E14** 38 30N 127 40 E
Changfeng, *China* **59 A11** 32 28N 117 10 E
Changhai = Shanghai, *China* **59 B13** 31 15N 121 26 E
Changhua, *China* **59 B12** 30 12N 119 12 E
Changhua, *Taiwan* **59 E13** 24 2N 120 30 E
Changhŭng, *S. Korea* **57 G14** 34 41N 126 52 E
Changhŭngni, *N. Korea* **57 D15** 40 24N 128 19 E
Changjiang, *China* **64 C7** 19 20N 108 55 E
Changjin, *N. Korea* **57 D14** 40 23N 127 15 E
Changjin-chŏsuji, *N. Korea* **57 D14** 40 30N 127 15 E
Changle, *China* **59 E12** 25 59N 119 27 E
Changli, *China* **57 E10** 39 40N 119 13 E
Changling, *China* **57 B12** 44 20N 123 58 E
Changlun, *Malaysia* **65 J3** 6 25N 100 26 E
Changning, *Hunan, China* **59 D9** 26 28N 112 22 E
Changning, *Sichuan, China* **58 C5** 28 40N 104 56 E
Changning, *Yunnan, China* **58 E2** 24 45N 99 30 E
Changping, *China* **56 D9** 40 14N 116 12 E
Changsha, *China* **59 C9** 28 12N 113 0 E
Changshan, *China* **59 C12** 28 55N 118 27 E
Changshu, *China* **59 B13** 31 38N 120 43 E
Changshun, *China* **58 D6** 26 3N 106 25 E
Changtai, *China* **59 E11** 24 35N 117 42 E
Changting, *China* **59 E11** 25 50N 116 22 E
Changwu, *China* **56 G4** 35 10N 107 45 E
Changxing, *China* **59 B12** 31 0N 119 55 E
Changyang, *China* **59 B8** 30 30N 111 10 E
Changyi, *China* **57 F10** 36 40N 119 30 E
Changyŏn, *N. Korea* **57 E13** 38 15N 125 6 E
Changyuan, *China* **56 G8** 35 15N 114 42 E
Changzhi, *China* **56 F7** 36 10N 113 6 E
Changzhou, *China* **59 B12** 31 47N 119 58 E
Chanhanga, *Angola* **88 B1** 16 0S 14 8 E
Chanlar = Xanlar, *Azerbaijan* **49 K8** 40 37N 46 12 E
Channapatna, *India* **66 N10** 12 40N 77 15 E
Channel Is., *U.K.* **13 H5** 49 19N 2 24W
Channel Is., *U.S.A.* **117 M7** 33 40N 119 15W
Channel Islands National Park, *U.S.A.* **117 M8** 33 30N 119 0W
Channel-Port aux Basques, *Canada* **103 C8** 47 30N 59 9W
Channel Tunnel, *Europe* **13 F9** 51 0N 1 30 E
Channing, *U.S.A.* **113 H3** 35 41N 102 20W
Chantada, *Spain* **34 C3** 42 36N 7 46W
Chanthaburi, *Thailand* **64 F4** 12 38N 102 12 E
Chantilly, *France* **19 C9** 49 12N 2 29 E
Chantonnay, *France* **18 F5** 46 40N 1 3W
Chantrey Inlet, *Canada* **100 B10** 67 48N 96 20W
Chanute, *U.S.A.* **113 G7** 37 41N 95 27W
Chanza →, *Spain* **35 H3** 37 32N 7 30W
Chao Hu, *China* **59 B11** 31 30N 117 30 E
Chao Phraya →, *Thailand* **64 F3** 13 32N 100 36 E
Chao Phraya Lowlands, *Thailand* **64 E3** 15 30N 100 0 E
Chaocheng, *China* **56 F8** 36 4N 115 37 E
Chaohu, *China* **59 B11** 31 38N 117 50 E
Chaoyang, *Guangdong, China* **59 F11** 23 17N 116 30 E
Chaoyang, *Liaoning, China* **57 D11** 41 35N 120 22 E
Chaozhou, *China* **59 F11** 23 42N 116 32 E
Chapais, *Canada* **102 C5** 49 47N 74 51W
Chapala, *Mozam.* **87 F4** 15 50S 37 35 E
Chapala, L. de, *Mexico* **118 C4** 20 10N 103 20W
Chapayev, *Kazakstan* **48 E10** 50 25N 51 10 E
Chapayevsk, *Russia* **48 D9** 53 0N 49 40 E
Chapecó, *Brazil* **127 B5** 27 14S 52 41W
Chapel Hill, *U.S.A.* **109 H6** 35 55N 79 4W
Chapleau, *Canada* **102 C3** 47 50N 83 24W
Chaplin, *Canada* **105 C7** 50 28N 106 40W
Chaplin L., *Canada* **105 C7** 50 22N 106 36W
Chaplino, *Ukraine* **47 H9** 48 8N 36 15 E
Chaplygin, *Russia* **46 F11** 53 15N 40 0 E
Chappell, *U.S.A.* **112 E3** 41 6N 102 28W
Chapra = Chhapra, *India* **69 G11** 25 48N 84 44 E
Chara, *Russia* **51 D12** 56 54N 118 20 E
Charadai, *Argentina* **126 B4** 27 35S 59 55W
Charagua, *Bolivia* **124 G6** 19 45S 63 10W
Charambirá, Punta, *Colombia* **124 C3** 4 16N 77 32W
Charaña, *Bolivia* **124 G5** 17 30S 69 25W
Charantsavan, *Armenia* **49 K7** 40 35N 44 41 E
Charanwala, *India* **68 F5** 27 51N 72 10 E
Charata, *Argentina* **126 B3** 27 13S 61 14W
Charcas, *Mexico* **118 C4** 23 10N 101 20W
Chard, *U.K.* **13 G5** 50 52N 2 58W
Chardon, *U.S.A.* **110 E3** 41 35N 81 12W
Chardzhou = Chärjew, *Turkmenistan* **50 F7** 39 6N 63 34 E
Charente □, *France* **20 C4** 45 50N 0 16 E
Charente →, *France* **20 C2** 45 57N 1 5W
Charente-Maritime □, *France* **20 C3** 45 45N 0 45W
Charenton-du-Cher, *France* **19 F9** 46 44N 2 39 E
Chari →, *Chad* **79 F8** 12 58N 14 31 E
Chārīkār, *Afghan.* **66 B6** 35 0N 69 10 E
Chariton →, *U.S.A.* **112 F8** 39 19N 92 58W
Chärjew, *Turkmenistan* **50 F7** 39 6N 63 34 E
Charkhari, *India* **69 G8** 25 24N 79 45 E
Charkhi Dadri, *India* **68 E7** 28 37N 76 17 E
Charleroi, *Belgium* **17 D4** 50 24N 4 27 E
Charleroi, *U.S.A.* **110 F5** 40 9N 79 57W
Charles, C., *U.S.A.* **108 G8** 37 7N 75 58W
Charles City, *U.S.A.* **112 D8** 43 4N 92 41W
Charles L., *Canada* **105 B6** 59 50N 110 33W
Charles Town, *U.S.A.* **108 F7** 39 17N 77 52W
Charleston, *Ill., U.S.A.* **108 F1** 39 30N 88 10W
Charleston, *Miss., U.S.A.* **113 H9** 34 1N 90 4W
Charleston, *Mo., U.S.A.* **113 G10** 36 55N 89 21W
Charleston, *S.C., U.S.A.* **109 J6** 32 46N 79 56W
Charleston, *W. Va., U.S.A.* **108 F5** 38 21N 81 38W
Charleston L., *Canada* **111 B9** 44 32N 76 0W
Charleston Peak, *U.S.A.* **117 J11** 36 16N 115 42W
Charlestown, *Ireland* **15 C3** 53 58N 8 48W
Charlestown, *S. Africa* **89 D4** 27 26S 29 53 E
Charlestown, *Ind., U.S.A.* **108 F3** 38 27N 85 40W
Charlestown, *N.H., U.S.A.* **111 C12** 43 14N 72 25W
Charleville = Rath Luirc, *Ireland* **15 D3** 52 21N 8 40W
Charleville, *Australia* **95 D4** 26 24S 146 15 E
Charleville-Mézières, *France* **19 C11** 49 44N 4 40 E
Charlevoix, *U.S.A.* **108 C3** 45 19N 85 16W
Charlieu, *France* **19 F11** 46 10N 4 10 E
Charlotte, *Mich., U.S.A.* **108 D3** 42 34N 84 50W
Charlotte, *N.C., U.S.A.* **109 H5** 35 13N 80 51W
Charlotte, *Vt., U.S.A.* **111 B11** 44 19N 73 14W
Charlotte Amalie, *Virgin Is.* **121 C7** 18 21N 64 56W
Charlotte Harbor, *U.S.A.* **109 M4** 26 50N 82 10W
Charlotte L., *Canada* **104 C3** 52 12N 125 19W
Charlottenberg, *Sweden* **10 E6** 59 54N 12 17 E
Charlottesville, *U.S.A.* **108 F6** 38 2N 78 30W
Charlottetown, *Nfld., Canada* **103 B8** 52 46N 56 7W
Charlottetown, *P.E.I., Canada* **103 C7** 46 14N 63 8W
Charlton, *Australia* **95 F3** 36 16S 143 24 E
Charlton, *U.S.A.* **112 E8** 40 59N 93 20W
Charlton I., *Canada* **102 B4** 52 0N 79 20W
Charmes, *France* **19 D13** 48 22N 6 17 E
Charny, *Canada* **103 C5** 46 43N 71 15W
Charolles, *France* **19 F11** 46 27N 4 16 E
Chârost, *France* **19 F9** 47 0N 2 7 E
Charre, *Mozam.* **87 F4** 17 13S 35 10 E
Charroux, *France* **20 B4** 46 9N 0 25 E
Charsadda, *Pakistan* **68 B4** 34 7N 71 45 E
Charters Towers, *Australia* **94 C4** 20 5S 146 13 E
Chartres, *France* **18 D8** 48 29N 1 30 E
Chascomús, *Argentina* **126 D4** 35 30S 58 0W
Chasefu, *Zambia* **87 E3** 11 55S 33 8 E
Chashma Barrage, *Pakistan* **68 C4** 32 27N 71 20 E
Chasseneuil-sur-Bonnieure, *France* **20 C4** 45 52N 0 29 E
Chāt, *Iran* **71 B7** 37 59N 55 16 E
Chatal Balkan = Udvoy Balkan, *Bulgaria* **41 D10** 42 50N 26 50 E
Château-Arnoux, *France* **21 D10** 44 6N 6 0 E
Château-Chinon, *France* **19 E10** 47 4N 3 56 E
Château-d'Olonne, *France* **20 B2** 46 30N 1 44W
Château-du-Loir, *France* **18 E7** 47 40N 0 25 E
Château-Gontier, *France* **18 E6** 47 50N 0 48W
Château-la-Vallière, *France* **18 E7** 47 30N 0 20 E
Château-Landon, *France* **19 D9** 48 8N 2 40 E
Château-Renault, *France* **18 E7** 47 36N 0 56 E
Château-Salins, *France* **19 D13** 48 50N 6 30 E
Château-Thierry, *France* **19 C10** 49 3N 3 20 E
Châteaubourg, *France* **18 D5** 48 7N 1 25W
Châteaubriant, *France* **18 E5** 47 43N 1 23W
Châteaudun, *France* **18 D8** 48 3N 1 20 E
Châteaugay, *U.S.A.* **111 B10** 44 56N 74 5W
Châteaugiron, *France* **18 D5** 48 3N 1 30W
Châteauguay, L., *Canada* **103 A5** 56 26N 70 3W
Châteaulin, *France* **18 D2** 48 11N 4 8W
Châteaumeillant, *France* **19 F9** 46 35N 2 12 E
Châteauneuf-du-Faou, *France* **18 D3** 48 11N 3 50W
Châteauneuf-sur-Charente, *France* **20 C3** 45 36N 0 3W
Châteauneuf-sur-Cher, *France* **19 F9** 46 52N 2 18 E
Châteauneuf-sur-Loire, *France* **19 E9** 47 52N 2 13 E
Châteaurenard, *Bouches-du-Rhône, France* **21 E8** 43 53N 4 51 E
Châteaurenard, *Loiret, France* **19 E9** 47 56N 2 55 E
Châteauroux, *France* **19 F8** 46 50N 1 40 E
Châteauvillain, *France* **19 D11** 48 2N 4 55 E
Châtelaillon-Plage, *France* **20 B2** 46 5N 1 5W
Châtelguyon, *France* **20 C7** 45 55N 3 4 E
Châtellerault, *France* **18 F7** 46 50N 0 30 E
Châtelus-Malvaleix, *France* **19 F9** 46 18N 2 1 E
Chatham = Miramichi, *Canada* **103 C6** 47 2N 65 28W
Chatham, *Canada* **102 D3** 42 24N 82 11W
Chatham, *U.K.* **13 F8** 51 22N 0 32 E
Chatham, *U.S.A.* **111 D11** 42 21N 73 36W
Chatham Is., *Pac. Oc.* **96 M10** 44 0S 176 40W
Châtillon, *Italy* **28 C4** 45 45N 7 37 E
Châtillon-Coligny, *France* **19 E9** 47 50N 2 51 E
Châtillon-en-Diois, *France* **21 D9** 44 41N 5 29 E
Châtillon-sur-Indre, *France* **18 F8** 46 59N 1 10 E
Châtillon-sur-Loire, *France* **19 E9** 47 35N 2 44 E
Châtillon-sur-Seine, *France* **19 E11** 47 50N 4 33 E
Chatmohar, *Bangla.* **69 G13** 24 15N 89 15 E
Chatra, *India* **69 G11** 24 12N 84 56 E
Chatrapur, *India* **67 K14** 19 22N 85 2 E
Chats, L. des, *Canada* **111 A8** 45 30N 76 20W
Chatsu, *India* **68 F6** 26 36N 75 57 E
Chatsworth, *Canada* **110 B4** 44 27N 80 54W
Chatsworth, *Zimbabwe* **87 F3** 19 38S 31 13 E
Chattahoochee, *U.S.A.* **109 K3** 30 42N 84 51W
Chattahoochee →, *U.S.A.* **109 K3** 30 54N 84 57W
Chattanooga, *U.S.A.* **109 H3** 35 3N 85 19W
Chatteris, *U.K.* **13 E8** 52 28N 0 2 E
Chaturat, *Thailand* **64 E3** 15 40N 101 51 E
Chau Doc, *Vietnam* **65 G5** 10 42N 105 7 E
Chaudes-Aigues, *France* **20 D7** 44 51N 3 1 E
Chauffailles, *France* **19 F11** 46 13N 4 20 E
Chauk, *Burma* **67 J19** 20 53N 94 49 E
Chaukan La, *Burma* **67 F20** 27 0N 97 15 E
Chaumont, *France* **19 D12** 48 7N 5 8 E
Chaumont, *U.S.A.* **111 B8** 44 4N 76 8W
Chaumont-en-Vexin, *France* **19 C8** 49 16N 1 53 E
Chaumont-sur-Loire, *France* **18 E8** 47 29N 1 11 E
Chaunay, *France* **20 B4** 46 13N 0 9 E
Chauny, *France* **19 C10** 49 37N 3 12 E
Chausey, Îs., *France* **18 D5** 48 52N 1 49W
Chaussin, *France* **19 F12** 46 59N 5 22 E
Chautauqua L., *U.S.A.* **110 D5** 42 10N 79 24W
Chauvigny, *France* **18 F7** 46 34N 0 39 E
Chauvin, *Canada* **105 C6** 52 45N 110 10W
Chavanges, *France* **19 D11** 48 30N 4 35 E
Chaves, *Brazil* **125 D9** 0 15S 49 55W
Chaves, *Portugal* **34 D3** 41 45N 7 32W
Chawang, *Thailand* **65 H2** 8 25N 99 30 E
Chazelles-sur-Lyon, *France* **21 C8** 45 39N 4 22 E
Chazy, *U.S.A.* **111 B11** 44 53N 73 26W
Cheb, *Czech Rep.* **26 A5** 50 9N 12 28 E
Cheboksarskoye Vdkhr., *Russia* **48 B8** 56 13N 46 58 E
Cheboksary, *Russia* **48 B8** 56 8N 47 12 E
Cheboygan, *U.S.A.* **108 C3** 45 39N 84 29W
Chebsara, *Russia* **46 C10** 59 10N 38 59 E
Chech, Erg, *Africa* **78 D5** 25 0N 2 15W
Chechen, Ostrov, *Russia* **49 H8** 43 59N 47 40 E
Chechenia □, *Russia* **49 J7** 43 30N 45 29 E
Checheno-Ingush Republic = Chechenia □, *Russia* **49 J7** 43 30N 45 29 E
Chechnya = Chechenia □, *Russia* **49 J7** 43 30N 45 29 E
Chech'ŏn, *S. Korea* **57 F15** 37 8N 128 12 E
Chęciny, *Poland* **45 H7** 50 46N 20 28 E
Checotah, *U.S.A.* **113 H7** 35 28N 95 31W
Chedabucto B., *Canada* **103 C7** 45 25N 61 8W
Cheduba I., *Burma* **67 K18** 18 45N 93 40 E
Cheepie, *Australia* **95 D4** 26 33S 145 1 E
Chef-Boutonne, *France* **20 B3** 46 7N 0 4W
Chegdomyn, *Russia* **51 D14** 51 7N 133 1 E
Chegga, *Mauritania* **78 C4** 25 27N 5 40W
Chegutu, *Zimbabwe* **87 F3** 18 10S 30 14 E
Chehalis, *U.S.A.* **116 D4** 46 40N 122 58W
Chehalis →, *U.S.A.* **116 D3** 46 57N 123 50W
Cheiron, Mt., *France* **21 E10** 43 49N 6 58 E
Cheju do, *S. Korea* **57 H14** 33 29N 126 34 E
Chekalin, *Russia* **46 E9** 54 10N 36 10 E
Chekiang = Zhejiang □, *China* **59 C13** 29 0N 120 0 E
Chel = Kuru, Bahr el →, *Sudan* **81 F2** 8 10N 26 50 E
Chela, Sa. da, *Angola* **88 B1** 16 20S 13 20 E
Chelan, *U.S.A.* **114 C4** 47 51N 120 1W
Chelan, L., *U.S.A.* **114 B3** 48 11N 120 30W
Cheleken, *Turkmenistan* **50 F6** 39 34N 53 16 E
Cheleken Yarymadasy, *Turkmenistan* **71 B7** 39 30N 53 15 E
Chelforó, *Argentina* **128 D3** 39 0S 66 33W
Chelkar = Shalqar, *Kazakstan* **50 E6** 47 48N 59 39 E
Chelkar Tengiz, Solonchak, *Kazakstan* **50 E7** 48 5N 63 7 E
Chella, *Ethiopia* **81 F4** 5 0N 37 26 E
Chelles, *France* **19 D9** 48 52N 2 33 E
Chełm, *Poland* **45 G10** 51 8N 23 30 E
Chełmno, *Poland* **45 E5** 53 20N 18 30 E
Chelmsford, *U.K.* **13 F8** 51 44N 0 29 E
Chełmża, *Poland* **45 E5** 53 10N 18 39 E
Chelsea, *U.S.A.* **111 C12** 43 59N 72 27W
Cheltenham, *U.K.* **13 F5** 51 54N 2 4W
Chelva, *Spain* **32 F4** 39 45N 1 0W
Chelyabinsk, *Russia* **50 D7** 55 10N 61 24 E
Chelyuskin, C., *Russia* **52 B14** 77 30N 103 0 E
Chemainus, *Canada* **116 B3** 48 55N 123 42W
Chemba, *Mozam.* **85 H6** 17 9S 34 53 E
Chembar = Belinskiy, *Russia* **48 D6** 53 0N 43 25 E
Chemillé, *France* **18 E6** 47 14N 0 45W
Chemnitz, *Germany* **24 E8** 50 51N 12 54 E
Chemult, *U.S.A.* **114 E3** 43 14N 121 47W
Chen, Gora, *Russia* **51 C15** 65 16N 141 50 E
Chenab →, *Pakistan* **68 D4** 30 23N 71 2 E
Chenango Forks, *U.S.A.* **111 D9** 42 15N 75 51W
Chencha, *Ethiopia* **81 F4** 6 15N 37 32 E
Chenchiang = Zhenjiang, *China* **59 A12** 32 11N 119 26 E
Cheney, *U.S.A.* **114 C5** 47 30N 117 35W
Cheng Xian, *China* **56 H3** 33 43N 105 42 E
Chengbu, *China* **59 D8** 26 18N 110 16 E
Chengcheng, *China* **56 G5** 35 8N 109 56 E
Chengchou = Zhengzhou, *China* **56 G7** 34 45N 113 34 E
Chengde, *China* **57 D9** 40 59N 117 58 E
Chengdong Hu, *China* **59 A11** 32 15N 116 20 E
Chengdu, *China* **58 B5** 30 38N 104 2 E
Chenggong, *China* **58 E4** 24 52N 102 56 E
Chenggu, *China* **56 H4** 33 10N 107 21 E
Chenghai, *China* **59 F11** 23 30N 116 42 E
Chengjiang, *China* **58 E4** 24 39N 103 0 E
Chengkou, *China* **58 B7** 31 54N 108 31 E
Ch'engmai, *China* **64 C7** 19 50N 109 58 E
Ch'engtu = Chengdu, *China* **58 B5** 30 38N 104 2 E
Chengwu, *China* **56 G8** 34 58N 115 50 E
Chengxi Hu, *China* **59 A11** 32 15N 116 10 E
Chengyang, *China* **57 F11** 36 18N 120 21 E
Chenjiagang, *China* **57 G10** 34 23N 119 47 E
Chenkán, *Mexico* **119 D6** 19 8N 90 58W
Chennai, *India* **66 N12** 13 8N 80 19 E
Chenôve, *France* **19 E12** 47 16N 5 1 E
Chenxi, *China* **59 C8** 28 2N 110 12 E
Chenzhou, *China* **59 E9** 25 47N 113 1 E
Cheo Reo, *Vietnam* **62 B3** 13 25N 108 28 E
Cheom Ksan, *Cambodia* **64 E5** 14 13N 104 56 E
Chepelare, *Bulgaria* **41 E8** 41 44N 24 40 E
Chepén, *Peru* **124 E3** 7 15S 79 23W
Chepes, *Argentina* **126 C2** 31 20S 66 35W
Chepo, *Panama* **120 E4** 9 10N 79 6W
Chepstow, *U.K.* **13 F5** 51 38N 2 41W
Cheptulil, Mt., *Kenya* **86 B4** 1 25N 35 35 E
Chequamegon B., *U.S.A.* **112 B9** 46 40N 90 30W
Cher □, *France* **19 E9** 47 10N 2 30 E
Cher →, *France* **18 E7** 47 21N 0 29 E
Chéradi, *Italy* **31 B10** 40 27N 17 10 E
Cherasco, *Italy* **28 D4** 44 39N 7 51 E
Cheraw, *U.S.A.* **109 H6** 34 42N 79 53W
Cherbourg, *France* **18 C5** 49 39N 1 40W
Cherdakly, *Russia* **48 C9** 54 25N 48 50 E
Cherdyn, *Russia* **50 C6** 60 24N 56 29 E
Cheremkhovo, *Russia* **51 D11** 53 8N 103 1 E
Cherepanovo, *Russia* **50 D9** 54 15N 83 30 E
Cherepovets, *Russia* **46 C9** 59 5N 37 55 E
Chergui, Chott ech, *Algeria* **78 B6** 34 21N 0 25 E
Cherikov = Cherykaw, *Belarus* **46 F6** 53 32N 31 20 E
Cherkasy, *Ukraine* **47 H7** 49 27N 32 4 E
Cherkessk, *Russia* **49 H6** 44 15N 42 5 E
Cherlak, *Russia* **50 D8** 54 15N 74 55 E
Chernaya, *Russia* **51 B9** 70 30N 89 10 E
Cherni, *Bulgaria* **40 D7** 42 35N 23 18 E
Chernigov = Chernihiv, *Ukraine* **47 G6** 51 28N 31 20 E
Chernihiv, *Ukraine* **47 G6** 51 28N 31 20 E
Chernivtsi, *Ukraine* **47 H3** 48 15N 25 52 E
Chernobyl = Chornobyl, *Ukraine* **47 G6** 51 20N 30 15 E
Chernogorsk, *Russia* **51 D10** 53 49N 91 18 E
Chernomorskoye = Chornomorske, *Ukraine* **47 K7** 45 31N 32 40 E
Chernovtsy = Chernivtsi, *Ukraine* **47 H3** 48 15N 25 52 E
Chernyakhovsk, *Russia* **9 J19** 54 36N 21 48 E
Chernyanka, *Russia* **47 G9** 50 56N 37 49 E
Chernysheyskiy, *Russia* **51 C12** 63 0N 112 30 E
Chernyye Zemli, *Russia* **49 H8** 46 10N 46 0 E
Cherokee, *Iowa, U.S.A.* **112 D7** 42 45N 95 33W
Cherokee, *Okla., U.S.A.* **113 G5** 36 45N 98 21W
Cherokee Village, *U.S.A.* **113 G9** 36 17N 91 30W
Cherokees, Grand Lake O' The, *U.S.A.* **113 G7** 36 28N 95 2W
Cherrapunji, *India* **67 G17** 25 17N 91 47 E
Cherry Valley, *Calif., U.S.A.* **117 M10** 33 59N 116 57W
Cherry Valley, *N.Y., U.S.A.* **111 D10** 42 48N 74 45W
Cherskiy, *Russia* **51 C17** 68 45N 161 18 E
Cherskogo Khrebet, *Russia* **51 C15** 65 0N 143 0 E
Chertkovo, *Russia* **47 H11** 49 25N 40 19 E
Cherven, *Belarus* **46 F5** 53 45N 28 28 E
Cherven-Bryag, *Bulgaria* **41 C8** 43 17N 24 7 E
Chervonohrad, *Ukraine* **47 G3** 50 25N 24 10 E
Cherwell →, *U.K.* **13 F6** 51 44N 1 14W
Cherykaw, *Belarus* **46 F6** 53 32N 31 20 E
Chesapeake, *U.S.A.* **108 G7** 36 50N 76 17W
Chesapeake B., *U.S.A.* **108 G7** 38 0N 76 10W
Cheshire □, *U.K.* **12 D5** 53 14N 2 30W
Cheshskaya Guba, *Russia* **50 C5** 67 20N 47 0 E
Cheshunt, *U.K.* **13 F7** 51 43N 0 1W
Chesil Beach, *U.K.* **13 G5** 50 37N 2 33W
Chesley, *Canada* **110 B3** 44 17N 81 5W
Cheste, *Spain* **33 F4** 39 30N 0 41W
Chester, *U.K.* **12 D5** 53 12N 2 53W
Chester, *Calif., U.S.A.* **114 F3** 40 19N 121 14W
Chester, *Ill., U.S.A.* **113 G10** 37 55N 89 49W
Chester, *Mont., U.S.A.* **114 B8** 48 31N 110 58W
Chester, *Pa., U.S.A.* **108 F8** 39 51N 75 22W
Chester, *S.C., U.S.A.* **109 H5** 34 43N 81 12W
Chester, *Vt., U.S.A.* **111 C12** 43 16N 72 36W
Chester, *W. Va., U.S.A.* **110 F4** 40 37N 80 34W
Chester-le-Street, *U.K.* **12 C6** 54 51N 1 34W
Chesterfield, *U.K.* **12 D6** 53 15N 1 25W
Chesterfield, Is., *N. Cal.* **96 J7** 19 52S 158 15 E
Chesterfield Inlet, *Canada* **100 B10** 63 30N 90 45W
Chesterton Ra., *Australia* **95 D4** 25 30S 147 27 E
Chestertown, *U.S.A.* **111 C11** 43 40N 73 48W
Chesterville, *Canada* **111 A9** 45 6N 75 14W
Chestnut Ridge, *U.S.A.* **110 F5** 40 20N 79 10W
Chesuncook L., *U.S.A.* **109 C11** 46 0N 69 21W
Chéticamp, *Canada* **103 C7** 46 37N 60 59W
Chetrosu, *Moldova* **43 B12** 48 5N 27 54 E
Chetumal, *Mexico* **119 D7** 18 30N 88 20W
Chetumal, B. de, *Mexico* **119 D7** 18 40N 88 10W
Chetwynd, *Canada* **104 B4** 55 45N 121 36W
Chevanceaux, *France* **20 C3** 45 18N 0 14W
Cheviot, The, *U.K.* **12 B5** 55 29N 2 9W
Cheviot Hills, *U.K.* **12 B5** 55 20N 2 30W
Cheviot Ra., *Australia* **94 D3** 25 20S 143 45 E
Chew Bahir, *Ethiopia* **81 G4** 4 40N 36 50 E
Chewelah, *U.S.A.* **114 B5** 48 17N 117 43W
Cheyenne, *Okla., U.S.A.* **113 H5** 35 37N 99 40W
Cheyenne, *Wyo., U.S.A.* **112 E2** 41 8N 104 49W
Cheyenne →, *U.S.A.* **112 C4** 44 41N 101 18W
Cheyenne Wells, *U.S.A.* **112 F3** 38 49N 102 21W
Cheyne B., *Australia* **93 F2** 34 35S 118 50 E
Chhabra, *India* **68 G7** 24 40N 76 54 E
Chhaktala, *India* **68 H6** 22 6N 74 11 E
Chhapra, *India* **69 G11** 25 48N 84 44 E
Chhata, *India* **68 F7** 27 42N 77 30 E
Chhatarpur, *Bihar, India* **69 G11** 24 23N 84 11 E
Chhatarpur, *Mad. P., India* **69 G8** 24 55N 79 35 E
Chhep, *Cambodia* **64 F5** 13 45N 105 24 E
Chhindwara, *Mad. P., India* **69 H8** 23 3N 79 29 E
Chhindwara, *Mad. P., India* **69 H8** 22 2N 78 59 E
Chhlong, *Cambodia* **65 F5** 12 15N 105 58 E
Chhota Tawa →, *India* **68 H7** 22 14N 76 36 E
Chhoti Kali Sindh →, *India* **68 G6** 24 2N 75 31 E
Chhuikhadan, *India* **69 J9** 21 32N 80 59 E
Chhuk, *Cambodia* **65 G5** 10 46N 104 28 E
Chi →, *Thailand* **64 E5** 15 11N 104 43 E
Chiai, *Taiwan* **59 F13** 23 29N 120 25 E
Chiali, *Taiwan* **59 F13** 23 10N 120 11 E
Chiamboni, *Somali Rep.* **84 E8** 1 39S 41 35 E
Chiamussu = Jiamusi, *China* **60 B8** 46 40N 130 26 E
Chianciano Terme, *Italy* **29 E8** 43 2N 11 49 E
Chiang Dao, *Thailand* **64 C2** 19 22N 98 58 E
Chiang Kham, *Thailand* **64 C3** 19 32N 100 18 E
Chiang Khan, *Thailand* **64 D3** 17 52N 101 36 E
Chiang Khong, *Thailand* **58 G3** 20 17N 100 24 E
Chiang Mai, *Thailand* **64 C2** 18 47N 98 59 E
Chiang Rai, *Thailand* **58 H2** 19 52N 99 50 E
Chiang Saen, *Thailand* **58 G3** 20 16N 100 5 E
Chiapa →, *Mexico* **119 D6** 16 42N 93 0W
Chiapa de Corzo, *Mexico* **119 D6** 16 42N 93 0W
Chiapas □, *Mexico* **119 D6** 17 0N 92 45W
Chiaramonte Gulfi, *Italy* **31 E7** 37 2N 14 42 E
Chiaravalle, *Italy* **29 E10** 43 36N 13 19 E
Chiaravalle Centrale, *Italy* **31 D9** 38 41N 16 25 E
Chiari, *Italy* **28 C6** 45 32N 9 56 E

Chiatura, *Georgia* **49 J6** 42 15N 43 17 E
Chiautla, *Mexico* **119 D5** 18 18N 98 34W
Chiávari, *Italy* **28 D6** 44 19N 9 19 E
Chiavenna, *Italy* **28 B6** 46 19N 9 24 E
Chiba, *Japan* **55 G10** 35 30N 140 7 E
Chiba □, *Japan* **55 G10** 35 30N 140 20 E
Chibabava, *Mozam.* **89 C5** 20 17 S 33 35 E
Chibemba, *Cunene, Angola* **85 H2** 15 48 S 14 8 E
Chibemba, *Huila, Angola* **88 B2** 16 20 S 15 20 E
Chibi, *Zimbabwe* **89 C5** 20 18 S 30 25 E
Chibia, *Angola* **85 H2** 15 10 S 13 42 E
Chibougamau, *Canada* **102 C5** 49 56N 74 24W
Chibougamau, L., *Canada* **102 C5** 49 50N 74 20W
Chibuk, *Nigeria* **83 C7** 10 52N 12 50 E
Chibuto, *Mozam.* **89 C5** 24 40 S 33 33 E
Chic-Chocs, Mts., *Canada* **103 C6** 48 55N 66 0W
Chicacole = Srikakulam, *India* **67 K13** 18 14N 83 58 E
Chicago, *U.S.A.* **108 E2** 41 53N 87 38W
Chicago Heights, *U.S.A.* **108 E2** 41 30N 87 38W
Chichagof I., *U.S.A.* **100 C6** 57 30N 135 30W
Chichén-Itzá, *Mexico* **119 C7** 20 40N 88 36W
Chicheng, *China* **56 D8** 40 55N 115 55 E
Chichester, *U.K.* **13 G7** 50 50N 0 47W
Chichester Ra., *Australia* **92 D2** 22 12 S 119 15 E
Chichibu, *Japan* **55 F9** 35 59N 139 10 E
Ch'ich'ihaerh = Qiqihar, *China* **51 E13** 47 26N 124 0 E
Chicholi, *India* **68 H8** 22 1N 77 40 E
Chickasha, *U.S.A.* **113 H6** 35 3N 97 58W
Chiclana de la Frontera, *Spain* **35 J4** 36 26N 6 9W
Chiclayo, *Peru* **124 E3** 6 42 S 79 50W
Chico, *U.S.A.* **116 F5** 39 44N 121 50W
Chico →, *Chubut, Argentina* **128 E3** 44 0 S 67 0W
Chico →, *Santa Cruz, Argentina* **128 G3** 50 0 S 68 30W
Chicomo, *Mozam.* **89 C5** 24 31 S 34 6 E
Chicontepec, *Mexico* **119 C5** 20 58N 98 10W
Chicopee, *U.S.A.* **111 D12** 42 9N 72 37W
Chicoutimi, *Canada* **103 C5** 48 28N 71 5W
Chicualacuala, *Mozam.* **89 C5** 22 6 S 31 42 E
Chidambaram, *India* **66 P11** 11 20N 79 45 E
Chidenguele, *Mozam.* **89 C5** 24 55 S 34 11 E
Chidley, C., *Canada* **101 B13** 60 23N 64 26W
Chiducuane, *Mozam.* **89 C5** 24 35 S 34 25 E
Chiede, *Angola* **88 B2** 17 15 S 16 22 E
Chiefs Pt., *Canada* **110 B3** 44 41N 81 18W
Chiem Hoa, *Vietnam* **64 A5** 22 12N 105 17 E
Chiemsee, *Germany* **25 H8** 47 53N 12 28 E
Chiengi, *Zambia* **87 D2** 8 45 S 29 10 E
Chiengmai = Chiang Mai, *Thailand* **64 C2** 18 47N 98 59 E
Chienti →, *Italy* **29 E10** 43 18N 13 45 E
Chieri, *Italy* **28 C4** 45 1N 7 49 E
Chiers →, *France* **19 C11** 49 39N 4 59 E
Chiesa in Valmalenco, *Italy* **28 B6** 46 16N 9 51 E
Chiese →, *Italy* **28 C7** 45 8N 10 25 E
Chieti, *Italy* **29 F11** 42 21N 14 10 E
Chifeng, *China* **57 C10** 42 18N 118 58 E
Chigirin, *Ukraine* **47 H7** 49 4N 32 38 E
Chignecto B., *Canada* **103 C7** 45 30N 64 40W
Chiguana, *Bolivia* **126 A2** 21 0 S 67 58W
Chigwell, *U.K.* **13 F8** 51 37N 0 5 E
Chiha-ri, *N. Korea* **57 E14** 38 40N 126 30 E
Chihli, G. of = Bo Hai, *China* **57 E10** 39 0N 119 0 E
Chihuahua, *Mexico* **118 B3** 28 40N 106 3W
Chihuahua □, *Mexico* **118 B3** 28 40N 106 3W
Chili, *Kazakstan* **50 E7** 44 20N 66 15 E
Chik Bollapur, *India* **66 N10** 13 25N 77 45 E
Chikmagalur, *India* **66 N9** 13 15N 75 45 E
Chikwawa, *Malawi* **87 F3** 16 2 S 34 50 E
Chilac, *Mexico* **119 D5** 18 20N 97 24W
Chilam Chavki, *Pakistan* **69 B6** 35 5N 75 5 E
Chilanga, *Zambia* **87 F2** 15 33 S 28 16 E
Chilapa, *Mexico* **119 D5** 17 40N 99 11W
Chilas, *Pakistan* **69 B6** 35 25N 74 5 E
Chilaw, *Sri Lanka* **66 R11** 7 30N 79 50 E
Chilcotin →, *Canada* **104 C4** 51 44N 122 23W
Childers, *Australia* **95 D5** 25 15 S 152 17 E
Childress, *U.S.A.* **113 H4** 34 25N 100 13W
Chile ■, *S. Amer.* **128 D2** 35 0 S 72 0W
Chile Rise, *Pac. Oc.* **97 L18** 38 0 S 92 0W
Chilecito, *Argentina* **126 B2** 29 10 S 67 30W
Chilete, *Peru* **124 E3** 7 10 S 78 50W
Chilia, Bratul →, *Romania* **43 E14** 45 14N 29 42 E
Chililabombwe, *Zambia* **87 E2** 12 18 S 27 43 E
Chilin = Jilin, *China* **57 C14** 43 44N 126 30 E
Chilka L., *India* **67 K14** 19 40N 85 25 E
Chilko →, *Canada* **104 C4** 52 0N 123 40W
Chilko, L., *Canada* **104 C4** 51 20N 124 10W
Chillagoe, *Australia* **94 B3** 17 7 S 144 33 E
Chillán, *Chile* **126 D1** 36 40 S 72 10W
Chillicothe, *Ill., U.S.A.* **112 E10** 40 55N 89 29W
Chillicothe, *Mo., U.S.A.* **112 F8** 39 48N 93 33W
Chillicothe, *Ohio, U.S.A.* **108 F4** 39 20N 82 59W
Chilliwack, *Canada* **104 D4** 49 10N 121 54W
Chilo, *India* **68 F5** 27 25N 73 32 E
Chiloane, I., *Mozam.* **89 C5** 20 40 S 34 55 E
Chiloé, I. de, *Chile* **122 H3** 42 30 S 73 50W
Chilpancingo, *Mexico* **119 D5** 17 30N 99 30W
Chiltern Hills, *U.K.* **13 F7** 51 40N 0 53W
Chilton, *U.S.A.* **108 C1** 44 2N 88 10W
Chilubi, *Zambia* **87 E2** 11 5 S 29 58 E
Chilubula, *Zambia* **87 E3** 10 14 S 30 51 E
Chilumba, *Malawi* **87 E3** 10 28 S 34 12 E
Chilung, *Taiwan* **59 E13** 25 3N 121 45 E
Chilwa, L., *Malawi* **87 F4** 15 15 S 35 40 E
Chimaltitán, *Mexico* **118 C4** 21 46N 103 50W
Chimán, *Panama* **120 E4** 8 45N 78 40W
Chimanimani, *Zimbabwe* **89 B5** 19 48 S 32 52 E
Chimay, *Belgium* **17 D4** 50 3N 4 20 E
Chimayo, *U.S.A.* **115 H11** 36 0N 105 56W
Chimbay, *Uzbekistan* **50 E6** 42 57N 59 47 E
Chimborazo, *Ecuador* **122 D3** 1 29 S 78 55W
Chimbote, *Peru* **124 E3** 9 0 S 78 35W
Chimkent = Shymkent, *Kazakstan* **50 E7** 42 18N 69 36 E
Chimoio, *Mozam.* **87 F3** 19 4 S 33 30 E
Chimpembe, *Zambia* **87 D2** 9 31 S 29 33 E
Chin □, *Burma* **67 J18** 22 0N 93 0 E
Chin Ling Shan = Qinling Shandi, *China* **56 H5** 33 50N 108 10 E
China, *Mexico* **119 B5** 25 40N 99 20W
China ■, *Asia* **60 D6** 30 0N 110 0 E
China Lake, *U.S.A.* **117 K9** 35 44N 117 37W
Chinan = Jinan, *China* **56 F9** 36 38N 117 1 E
Chinandega, *Nic.* **120 D2** 12 35N 87 12W
Chinati Peak, *U.S.A.* **113 L2** 29 57N 104 29W
Chincha Alta, *Peru* **122 E3** 13 25 S 76 7W
Chinchaga →, *Canada* **104 B5** 58 53N 118 20W
Chinchilla, *Australia* **95 D5** 26 45 S 150 38 E
Chinchilla de Monte Aragón, *Spain* **33 G3** 38 53N 1 40W
Chinchorro, Banco, *Mexico* **119 D7** 18 35N 87 20W
Chinchou = Jinzhou, *China* **57 D11** 41 5N 121 3 E
Chincoteague, *U.S.A.* **108 G8** 37 56N 75 23W
Chinde, *Mozam.* **87 F4** 18 35 S 36 30 E
Chindo, *S. Korea* **57 G14** 34 28N 126 15 E
Chindwin →, *Burma* **67 J19** 21 26N 95 15 E
Chineni, *India* **69 C6** 33 2N 75 15 E
Chinga, *Mozam.* **87 F4** 15 13 S 38 35 E
Chingola, *Zambia* **87 E2** 12 31 S 27 53 E
Chingole, *Malawi* **87 E3** 13 4 S 34 17 E
Ch'ingtao = Qingdao, *China* **57 F11** 36 5N 120 20 E
Chinguetti, *Mauritania* **78 D3** 20 25N 12 24W
Chingune, *Mozam.* **89 C5** 20 33 S 34 58 E
Chinhae, *S. Korea* **57 G15** 35 9N 128 47 E
Chinhanguanine, *Mozam.* **89 D5** 25 21 S 32 30 E
Chinhoyi, *Zimbabwe* **87 F3** 17 20 S 30 8 E
Chini, *India* **68 D8** 31 32N 78 15 E
Chiniot, *Pakistan* **68 D5** 31 45N 73 0 E
Chínipas, *Mexico* **118 B3** 27 22N 108 32W
Chinji, *Pakistan* **68 C5** 32 42N 72 22 E
Chinju, *S. Korea* **57 G15** 35 12N 128 2 E
Chinle, *U.S.A.* **115 H9** 36 9N 109 33W
Chinmen, *Taiwan* **59 E13** 24 26N 118 19 E
Chinmen Tao, *Taiwan* **59 E12** 24 27N 118 23 E
Chinnampo = Namp'o, *N. Korea* **57 E13** 38 52N 125 10 E
Chino, *Japan* **55 G9** 35 59N 138 9 E
Chino, *U.S.A.* **117 L9** 34 1N 117 41W
Chino Valley, *U.S.A.* **115 J7** 34 45N 112 27W
Chinon, *France* **18 E7** 47 10N 0 15 E
Chinook, *U.S.A.* **114 B9** 48 35N 109 14W
Chinsali, *Zambia* **87 E3** 10 30 S 32 2 E
Chióggia, *Italy* **29 C9** 45 13N 12 17 E
Chíos = Khíos, *Greece* **39 C8** 38 27N 26 9 E
Chipata, *Zambia* **87 E3** 13 38 S 32 28 E
Chiperceni, *Moldova* **43 C13** 47 31N 28 50 E
Chipinge, *Zimbabwe* **87 G3** 20 13 S 32 28 E
Chipiona, *Spain* **35 J4** 36 44N 6 26W
Chipley, *U.S.A.* **109 K3** 30 47N 85 32W
Chipman, *Canada* **103 C6** 46 6N 65 53W
Chipoka, *Malawi* **87 E3** 13 57 S 34 28 E
Chippenham, *U.K.* **13 F5** 51 27N 2 6W
Chippewa →, *U.S.A.* **112 C8** 44 25N 92 5W
Chippewa Falls, *U.S.A.* **112 C9** 44 56N 91 24W
Chipping Norton, *U.K.* **13 F6** 51 56N 1 32W
Chiprovtsi, *Bulgaria* **40 C6** 43 24N 22 52 E
Chiputneticook Lakes, *U.S.A.* **109 C11** 45 35N 67 35W
Chiquián, *Peru* **124 F3** 10 10 S 77 0W
Chiquimula, *Guatemala* **120 D2** 14 51N 89 37W
Chiquinquira, *Colombia* **124 B4** 5 37N 73 50W
Chir →, *Russia* **49 F6** 48 30N 43 0 E
Chirala, *India* **66 M12** 15 50N 80 26 E
Chiramba, *Mozam.* **87 F3** 16 55 S 34 39 E
Chirawa, *India* **68 E6** 28 14N 75 42 E
Chirchiq, *Uzbekistan* **50 E7** 41 29N 69 35 E
Chiredzi, *Zimbabwe* **89 C5** 21 0 S 31 38 E
Chirfa, *Niger* **79 D8** 20 55N 12 22 E
Chiricahua Peak, *U.S.A.* **115 L9** 31 51N 109 18W
Chiriquí, G. de, *Panama* **120 E3** 8 0N 82 10W
Chiriquí, L. de, *Panama* **120 E3** 9 10N 82 0W
Chirivira Falls, *Zimbabwe* **87 G3** 21 10 S 32 12 E
Chirmiri, *India* **67 H13** 23 15N 82 20 E
Chirnogi, *Romania* **43 F11** 44 7N 26 32 E
Chirpan, *Bulgaria* **41 D9** 42 10N 25 19 E
Chirripó Grande, Cerro, *Costa Rica* **120 E3** 9 29N 83 29W
Chirundu, *Zimbabwe* **89 B4** 16 3 S 28 50 E
Chisamba, *Zambia* **87 E2** 14 55 S 28 20 E
Chisapani Garhi, *Nepal* **67 F14** 27 30N 84 2 E
Chisasibi, *Canada* **102 B4** 53 50N 79 0W
Ch'ishan, *Taiwan* **59 F13** 22 44N 120 31 E
Chisholm, *Canada* **104 C6** 54 55N 114 10W
Chisholm, *U.S.A.* **112 B8** 47 29N 92 53W
Chishtian Mandi, *Pakistan* **68 E5** 29 50N 72 55 E
Chishui, *China* **58 C5** 28 30N 105 42 E
Chishui He →, *China* **58 C5** 28 49N 105 50 E
Chisimaio, *Somali Rep.* **77 G8** 0 22 S 42 32 E
Chisimba Falls, *Zambia* **87 E3** 10 12 S 30 56 E
Chişinău, *Moldova* **43 C13** 47 2N 28 50 E
Chişineu Criş, *Romania* **42 D6** 46 32N 21 37 E
Chisone →, *Italy* **28 D4** 44 49N 7 25 E
Chisos Mts., *U.S.A.* **113 L3** 29 5N 103 15W
Chistopol, *Russia* **48 C10** 55 25N 50 38 E
Chita, *Russia* **51 D12** 52 0N 113 35 E
Chitipa, *Malawi* **87 D3** 9 41 S 33 19 E
Chitose, *Japan* **54 C10** 42 49N 141 39 E
Chitral, *Pakistan* **66 B7** 35 50N 71 56 E
Chitré, *Panama* **120 E3** 7 59N 80 27W
Chittagong, *Bangla.* **67 H17** 22 19N 91 48 E
Chittagong □, *Bangla.* **67 G17** 24 5N 91 0 E
Chittaurgarh, *India* **68 G6** 24 52N 74 38 E
Chittoor, *India* **66 N11** 13 15N 79 5 E
Chitungwiza, *Zimbabwe* **87 F3** 18 0 S 31 6 E
Chiusi, *Italy* **29 E8** 43 1N 11 57 E
Chiva, *Spain* **33 F4** 39 27N 0 41W
Chivasso, *Italy* **28 C4** 45 11N 7 53 E
Chivhu, *Zimbabwe* **87 F3** 19 2 S 30 52 E
Chivilcoy, *Argentina* **126 C4** 34 55 S 60 0W
Chiwanda, *Tanzania* **87 E3** 11 23 S 34 55 E
Chixi, *China* **59 G9** 22 0N 112 58 E
Chizera, *Zambia* **87 E2** 13 10 S 25 0 E
Chkalov = Orenburg, *Russia* **50 D6** 51 45N 55 6 E
Chkolovsk, *Russia* **48 B6** 56 50N 43 10 E
Chloride, *U.S.A.* **117 K12** 35 25N 114 12W
Chlumec nad Cidlinou, *Czech Rep.* **26 A8** 50 9N 15 29 E
Chmielnik, *Poland* **45 H7** 50 37N 20 43 E
Cho Bo, *Vietnam* **58 G5** 20 46N 105 10 E
Cho-do, *N. Korea* **57 E13** 38 30N 124 40 E
Cho Phuoc Hai, *Vietnam* **65 G6** 10 26N 107 18 E
Choba, *Kenya* **86 B4** 2 30N 38 5 E
Chobe National Park, *Botswana* **88 B4** 18 0 S 25 0 E
Choch'iwŏn, *S. Korea* **57 F14** 36 37N 127 18 E
Chocianów, *Poland* **45 G2** 51 27N 15 55 E
Chociwel, *Poland* **44 E2** 53 29N 15 21 E
Chocolate Mts., *U.S.A.* **117 M11** 33 15N 115 15W
Choctawhatchee →, *U.S.A.* **109 K3** 30 25N 86 8W
Chodecz, *Poland* **45 F6** 52 24N 19 2 E
Chodov, *Czech Rep.* **26 A5** 50 15N 12 45 E
Chodziez, *Poland* **45 F3** 52 58N 16 58 E
Choele Choel, *Argentina* **128 D3** 39 11 S 65 40W
Choix, *Mexico* **118 B3** 26 40N 108 23W
Chojna, *Poland* **45 F1** 52 58N 14 25 E
Chojnice, *Poland* **44 E4** 53 42N 17 32 E
Chojnów, *Poland* **45 G2** 51 18N 15 58 E
Chōkai-San, *Japan* **54 E10** 39 6N 140 3 E
Choke, *Ethiopia* **81 E4** 11 18N 37 15 E
Choke Canyon L., *U.S.A.* **113 L5** 28 30N 98 20W
Chokurdakh, *Russia* **51 B15** 70 38N 147 55 E
Cholame, *U.S.A.* **116 K6** 35 44N 120 18W
Cholet, *France* **18 E6** 47 4N 0 52W
Cholguan, *Chile* **126 D1** 37 10 S 72 3W
Choluteca, *Honduras* **120 D2** 13 20N 87 14W
Choluteca →, *Honduras* **120 D2** 13 0N 87 20W
Chom Bung, *Thailand* **64 F2** 13 37N 99 36 E
Chom Thong, *Thailand* **64 C2** 18 25N 98 41 E
Choma, *Zambia* **87 F2** 16 48 S 26 59 E
Chomen Swamp, *Ethiopia* **81 F4** 9 20N 37 10 E
Chomun, *India* **68 F6** 27 15N 75 40 E
Chomutov, *Czech Rep.* **26 A6** 50 28N 13 23 E
Chon Buri, *Thailand* **64 F3** 13 21N 101 1 E
Chon Thanh, *Vietnam* **65 G6** 11 24N 106 36 E
Ch'onan, *S. Korea* **57 F14** 36 48N 127 9 E
Chone, *Ecuador* **124 D3** 0 40 S 80 0W
Chong Kai, *Cambodia* **64 F4** 13 57N 103 35 E
Chong Mek, *Thailand* **64 E5** 15 10N 105 27 E
Chongde, *China* **59 B13** 30 32N 120 26 E
Chŏngdo, *S. Korea* **57 G15** 35 38N 128 42 E
Chŏngha, *S. Korea* **57 F15** 36 12N 129 21 E
Chŏngjin, *N. Korea* **57 D15** 41 47N 129 50 E
Chŏngjiu, *S. Korea* **57 F14** 36 39N 127 27 E
Chŏngju, *N. Korea* **57 E13** 39 40N 125 5 E
Chongli, *China* **56 D8** 40 58N 115 15 E
Chongming, *China* **59 B13** 31 38N 121 23 E
Chongming Dao, *China* **59 B13** 31 40N 121 30 E
Chongqing, *Chongqing, China* **58 C6** 29 35N 106 25 E
Chongqing, *Sichuan, China* **58 B4** 30 38N 103 40 E
Chongqing □, *China* **60 C5** 30 0N 108 0 E
Chongqing Shi □, *China* **58 C6** 30 0N 108 0 E
Chongren, *China* **59 D11** 27 46N 116 3 E
Chonguene, *Mozam.* **89 C5** 25 3 S 33 49 E
Chŏngŭp, *S. Korea* **57 G14** 35 35N 126 50 E
Chongyi, *China* **59 E10** 25 45N 114 29 E
Chongzuo, *China* **58 F6** 22 23N 107 20 E
Chŏnju, *S. Korea* **57 G14** 35 50N 127 4 E
Chonos, Arch. de los, *Chile* **122 H3** 45 0 S 75 0W
Chop, *Ukraine* **47 H2** 48 26N 22 12 E
Chopim →, *Brazil* **127 B5** 25 35 S 53 5W
Chor, *Pakistan* **68 G3** 25 31N 69 46 E
Chorbat La, *India* **69 B7** 34 42N 76 37 E
Chorley, *U.K.* **12 D5** 53 39N 2 38W
Chornobyl, *Ukraine* **47 G6** 51 20N 30 15 E
Chornomorske, *Ukraine* **47 K7** 45 31N 32 40 E
Chorolque, Cerro, *Bolivia* **126 A2** 20 59 S 66 5W
Choroszcz, *Poland* **45 E9** 53 10N 22 59 E
Chorregon, *Australia* **94 C3** 22 40 S 143 32 E
Chortkiv, *Ukraine* **47 H3** 49 2N 25 46 E
Ch'ŏrwon, *S. Korea* **57 E14** 38 15N 127 10 E
Chorzele, *Poland* **45 E7** 53 15N 20 55 E
Chorzów, *Poland* **45 H5** 50 18N 18 57 E
Chos-Malal, *Argentina* **126 D1** 37 20 S 70 15W
Ch'osan, *N. Korea* **57 D13** 40 50N 125 47 E
Choszczno, *Poland* **45 E2** 53 7N 15 25 E
Choteau, *U.S.A.* **114 C7** 47 49N 112 11W
Chotěboř, *Czech Rep.* **26 B8** 49 43N 15 40 E
Chotila, *India* **68 H4** 22 23N 71 15 E
Chotta Udepur, *India* **68 H6** 22 19N 74 1 E
Chowchilla, *U.S.A.* **116 H6** 37 7N 120 16W
Choybalsan, *Mongolia* **60 B6** 48 4N 114 30 E
Christchurch, *N.Z.* **91 K4** 43 33 S 172 47 E
Christchurch, *U.K.* **13 G6** 50 44N 1 47W
Christian I., *Canada* **110 B4** 44 50N 80 12W
Christiana, *S. Africa* **88 D4** 27 52 S 25 8 E
Christiansfeld, *Denmark* **11 J3** 55 21N 9 29 E
Christiansted, *Virgin Is.* **121 C7** 17 45N 64 42W
Christie B., *Canada* **105 A6** 62 32N 111 10W
Christina →, *Canada* **105 B6** 56 40N 111 3W
Christmas Cr. →, *Australia* **92 C4** 18 29 S 125 23 E
Christmas I. = Kiritimati, *Kiribati* **97 G12** 1 58N 157 27W
Christmas I., *Ind. Oc.* **96 J2** 10 30 S 105 40 E
Christopher L., *Australia* **93 D4** 24 49 S 127 42 E
Chrudim, *Czech Rep.* **26 B8** 49 58N 15 43 E
Chrzanów, *Poland* **45 H6** 50 10N 19 21 E
Chtimba, *Malawi* **87 E3** 10 35 S 34 13 E
Chu = Shu, *Kazakstan* **50 E8** 43 36N 73 42 E
Chu = Shu →, *Kazakstan* **52 E10** 45 0N 67 44 E
Chu →, *Vietnam* **64 C5** 19 53N 105 45 E
Chu Lai, *Vietnam* **64 E7** 15 28N 108 45 E
Ch'uanchou = Quanzhou, *China* **59 E12** 24 55N 118 34 E
Chuankou, *China* **56 G6** 34 20N 110 59 E
Chubbuck, *U.S.A.* **114 E7** 42 55N 112 28W
Chūbu □, *Japan* **55 F8** 36 45N 137 30 E
Chubut →, *Argentina* **122 H4** 43 20 S 65 5W
Chuchi L., *Canada* **104 B4** 55 12N 124 30W
Chuda, *India* **68 H4** 22 29N 71 41 E
Chudovo, *Russia* **46 C6** 59 10N 31 41 E
Chudskoye, Ozero, *Russia* **9 G22** 58 13N 27 30 E
Chūgoku □, *Japan* **55 G6** 35 0N 133 0 E
Chūgoku-Sanchi, *Japan* **55 G6** 35 0N 133 0 E
Chuguyev = Chuhuiv, *Ukraine* **47 H9** 49 55N 36 45 E
Chugwater, *U.S.A.* **112 E2** 41 46N 104 50W
Chuhuiv, *Ukraine* **47 H9** 49 55N 36 45 E
Chukchi Sea, *Russia* **51 C19** 68 0N 175 0W
Chukotskoye Nagorye, *Russia* **51 C18** 68 0N 175 0 E
Chula Vista, *U.S.A.* **117 N9** 32 39N 117 5W
Chulucanas, *Peru* **124 E2** 5 8 S 80 10W
Chulym →, *Russia* **50 D9** 57 43N 83 51 E
Chum Phae, *Thailand* **64 D4** 16 40N 102 6 E
Chum Saeng, *Thailand* **64 E3** 15 55N 100 15 E
Chumar, *India* **69 C8** 32 40N 78 35 E
Chumbicha, *Argentina* **126 B2** 29 0 S 66 10W
Chumerna, *Bulgaria* **41 D9** 42 45N 25 55 E
Chumikan, *Russia* **51 D14** 54 40N 135 10 E
Chumphon, *Thailand* **65 G2** 10 35N 99 14 E
Chumuare, *Mozam.* **87 E3** 14 31 S 31 50 E
Chumunjin, *S. Korea* **57 F15** 37 55N 128 54 E
Chuna →, *Russia* **51 D10** 57 47N 94 37 E
Chun'an, *China* **59 C12** 29 35N 119 3 E
Ch'unch'ŏn, *S. Korea* **57 F14** 37 58N 127 44 E
Chunchura, *India* **69 H13** 22 53N 88 27 E
Chunga, *Zambia* **87 F2** 15 0 S 26 2 E
Chunggang-ŭp, *N. Korea* **57 D14** 41 48N 126 48 E
Chunghwa, *N. Korea* **57 E13** 38 52N 125 47 E
Ch'ungju, *S. Korea* **57 F14** 36 58N 127 58 E
Chungking = Chongqing, *China* **58 C6** 29 35N 106 25 E
Chungli, *Taiwan* **59 E13** 24 57N 121 13 E
Ch'ungmu, *S. Korea* **57 G15** 34 50N 128 20 E
Chungt'iaoshan = Zhongtiao Shan, *China* **56 G6** 35 0N 111 10 E
Chungyang Shanmo, *Taiwan* **59 F13** 23 10N 121 0 E
Chunian, *Pakistan* **68 D6** 30 57N 74 0 E
Chunya, *Tanzania* **87 D3** 8 30 S 33 27 E
Chunyang, *China* **57 C15** 43 38N 129 23 E
Chuquibamba, *Peru* **124 G4** 15 47 S 72 44W
Chuquicamata, *Chile* **126 A2** 22 15 S 69 0W
Chur, *Switz.* **25 J5** 46 52N 9 32 E
Churachandpur, *India* **67 G18** 24 20N 93 40 E
Churchill, *Canada* **105 B10** 58 47N 94 11W
Churchill →, *Man., Canada* **105 B10** 58 47N 94 12W
Churchill →, *Nfld., Canada* **103 B7** 53 19N 60 10W
Churchill, C., *Canada* **105 B10** 58 46N 93 12W
Churchill Falls, *Canada* **103 B7** 53 36N 64 19W
Churchill L., *Canada* **105 B7** 55 55N 108 20W
Churchill Pk., *Canada* **104 B3** 58 10N 125 10W
Churki, *India* **69 H10** 23 50N 83 12 E
Churu, *India* **68 E6** 28 20N 74 50 E
Churún Merú = Angel Falls, *Venezuela* **124 B6** 5 57N 62 30W
Chushal, *India* **69 C8** 33 40N 78 40 E
Chuska Mts., *U.S.A.* **115 H9** 36 15N 108 50W
Chusovoy, *Russia* **50 D6** 58 22N 57 50 E
Chute-aux-Outardes, *Canada* **103 C6** 49 7N 68 24W
Chuuronjang, *N. Korea* **57 D15** 41 35N 129 40 E
Chuvash Republic = Chuvashia □, *Russia* **48 C8** 55 30N 47 0 E
Chuvashia □, *Russia* **48 C8** 55 30N 47 0 E
Chuwārtah, *Iraq* **70 C5** 35 43N 45 34 E
Chuxiong, *China* **58 E3** 25 2N 101 28 E
Chuy, *Uruguay* **127 C5** 33 41 S 53 27W
Chuzhou, *China* **59 A12** 32 19N 118 20 E
Ci Xian, *China* **56 F8** 36 20N 114 25 E
Ciacova, *Romania* **42 E6** 45 35N 21 10 E
Ciadâr-Lunga, *Moldova* **43 D13** 46 3N 28 51 E
Ciamis, *Indonesia* **63 G13** 7 20 S 108 21 E
Cianjur, *Indonesia* **63 G12** 6 49 S 107 8 E
Cianorte, *Brazil* **127 A5** 23 37 S 52 37W
Cibola, *U.S.A.* **117 M12** 33 17N 114 42W
Cicero, *U.S.A.* **108 E2** 41 48N 87 48W
Cidacos →, *Spain* **32 C3** 42 21N 1 38W
Cide, *Turkey* **72 B5** 41 53N 33 1 E
Ciechanów, *Poland* **45 F7** 52 52N 20 38 E
Ciechanowiec, *Poland* **45 F9** 52 40N 22 31 E
Ciechocinek, *Poland* **45 F5** 52 53N 18 45 E
Ciego de Avila, *Cuba* **120 B4** 21 50N 78 50W
Ciénaga, *Colombia* **124 A4** 11 1N 74 15W
Cienfuegos, *Cuba* **120 B3** 22 10N 80 30W
Cierp, *France* **20 F4** 42 55N 0 40 E
Cíes, Is., *Spain* **34 C2** 42 12N 8 55W
Cieszanów, *Poland* **45 H10** 50 14N 23 8 E
Cieszyn, *Poland* **45 J5** 49 45N 18 35 E
Cieza, *Spain* **33 G3** 38 17N 1 23W
Çifteler, *Turkey* **72 C4** 39 22N 31 2 E
Cifuentes, *Spain* **32 E2** 40 47N 2 37W
Cihanbeyli, *Turkey* **72 C5** 38 40N 32 55 E
Cihuatlán, *Mexico* **118 D4** 19 14N 104 35W
Cijara, Embalse de, *Spain* **35 F6** 39 18N 4 52W
Cijulang, *Indonesia* **63 G13** 7 42 S 108 27 E
Cilacap, *Indonesia* **63 G13** 7 43 S 109 0 E
Çıldır, *Turkey* **73 B10** 41 7N 43 8 E
Çıldır Gölü, *Turkey* **73 B10** 41 5N 43 15 E
Cili, *China* **59 C8** 29 30N 111 8 E
Cilibia, *Romania* **43 E12** 45 4N 27 4 E
Cilicia, *Turkey* **72 D5** 36 30N 33 40 E
Cill Chainnigh = Kilkenny, *Ireland* **15 D4** 52 39N 7 15W
Cilo Dağı, *Turkey* **73 D10** 37 28N 43 55 E
Cima, *U.S.A.* **117 K11** 35 14N 115 30W
Cimarron, *Kans., U.S.A.* **113 G4** 37 48N 100 21W
Cimarron, *N. Mex., U.S.A.* **113 G2** 36 31N 104 55W
Cimarron →, *U.S.A.* **113 G6** 36 10N 96 17W
Cimişlia, *Moldova* **43 D13** 46 34N 28 44 E
Cimone, Mte., *Italy* **28 D7** 44 12N 10 42 E
Çinar, *Turkey* **73 D9** 37 46N 40 19 E
Çınarcık, *Turkey* **41 F13** 40 38N 29 5 E
Cinca →, *Spain* **32 D5** 41 26N 0 21 E
Cincar, *Bos.-H.* **42 G2** 43 55N 17 5 E
Cincinnati, *U.S.A.* **108 F3** 39 6N 84 31W
Cincinnatus, *U.S.A.* **111 D9** 42 33N 75 54W
Çine, *Turkey* **39 D10** 37 37N 28 2 E
Ciney, *Belgium* **17 D5** 50 18N 5 5 E
Cíngoli, *Italy* **29 E10** 43 23N 13 10 E
Cinigiano, *Italy* **29 F8** 42 53N 11 24 E
Cinto, Mte., *France* **21 F12** 42 24N 8 54 E
Cintruénigo, *Spain* **32 C3** 42 5N 1 49W
Ciocile, *Romania* **43 F12** 44 49N 27 14 E
Ciolănești din Deal, *Romania* **43 F10** 44 19N 25 5 E
Ciorani, *Romania* **43 F11** 44 45N 26 25 E
Čiovo, *Croatia* **29 E13** 43 30N 16 17 E
Circeo, Mte., *Italy* **30 A6** 41 14N 13 3 E
Çırçır, *Turkey* **72 C7** 40 5N 36 47 E
Circle, *Alaska, U.S.A.* **100 B5** 65 50N 144 4W
Circle, *Mont., U.S.A.* **112 B2** 47 25N 105 35W
Circleville, *U.S.A.* **108 F4** 39 36N 82 57W
Cirebon, *Indonesia* **63 G13** 6 45 S 108 32 E
Ciremai, *Indonesia* **63 G13** 6 55 S 108 27 E
Cirencester, *U.K.* **13 F6** 51 43N 1 57W
Cireşu, *Romania* **42 F7** 44 47N 22 31 E
Cirey-sur-Vezouze, *France* **19 D13** 48 35N 6 57 E
Ciriè, *Italy* **28 C4** 45 14N 7 36 E
Cirium, *Cyprus* **36 E11** 34 40N 32 53 E
Cirò, *Italy* **31 C10** 39 23N 17 4 E
Cirò Marina, *Italy* **31 C10** 39 22N 17 8 E
Ciron →, *France* **20 D3** 44 36N 0 18W
Cisco, *U.S.A.* **113 J5** 32 23N 98 59W
Cislău, *Romania* **43 E11** 45 14N 26 20 E
Cisna, *Poland* **45 J9** 49 12N 22 20 E
Cisnădie, *Romania* **43 E9** 45 42N 24 9 E
Cisterna di Latina, *Italy* **30 A5** 41 35N 12 49 E
Cisternino, *Italy* **31 B10** 40 44N 17 25 E
Cistierna, *Spain* **34 C5** 42 48N 5 7W
Citeli-Ckaro = Tsiteli-Tsqaro, *Georgia* **49 K8** 41 33N 46 0 E
Citlaltépetl, *Mexico* **119 D5** 19 0N 97 20W
Citrus Heights, *U.S.A.* **116 G5** 38 42N 121 17W
Citrusdal, *S. Africa* **88 E2** 32 35 S 19 0 E
Città della Pieve, *Italy* **29 F9** 42 57N 12 1 E
Città di Castello, *Italy* **29 E9** 43 27N 12 14 E
Città Sant' Angelo, *Italy* **29 F11** 42 32N 14 5 E
Cittadella, *Italy* **29 C8** 45 39N 11 47 E
Cittaducale, *Italy* **29 F9** 42 23N 12 57 E
Cittanova, *Italy* **31 D9** 38 21N 16 5 E
Ciuc, Munții, *Romania* **43 D11** 46 25N 26 5 E
Ciucaş, Vf., *Romania* **43 E10** 45 31N 25 56 E
Ciucea, *Romania* **42 D7** 46 57N 22 49 E
Ciuciulea, *Moldova* **43 C12** 47 40N 27 29 E
Ciuciuleni, *Moldova* **43 C13** 47 2N 28 25 E
Ciudad Altamirano, *Mexico* **118 D4** 18 20N 100 40W
Ciudad Bolívar, *Venezuela* **124 B6** 8 5N 63 36W
Ciudad Camargo, *Mexico* **118 B3** 27 41N 105 10W
Ciudad de Valles, *Mexico* **119 C5** 22 0N 99 0W
Ciudad del Carmen, *Mexico* **119 D6** 18 38N 91 50W
Ciudad del Este, *Paraguay* **127 B5** 25 30 S 54 50W
Ciudad Delicias = Delicias, *Mexico* **118 B3** 28 10N 105 30W
Ciudad Guayana, *Venezuela* **124 B6** 8 0N 62 30W
Ciudad Guerrero, *Mexico* **118 B3** 28 33N 107 28W
Ciudad Guzmán, *Mexico* **118 D4** 19 40N 103 30W
Ciudad Juárez, *Mexico* **118 A3** 31 40N 106 28W
Ciudad Madero, *Mexico* **119 C5** 22 19N 97 50W
Ciudad Mante, *Mexico* **119 C5** 22 50N 99 0W
Ciudad Obregón, *Mexico* **118 B3** 27 28N 109 59W
Ciudad Real, *Spain* **35 G7** 38 59N 3 55W
Ciudad Real □, *Spain* **35 G7** 38 50N 4 0W
Ciudad Rodrigo, *Spain* **34 E4** 40 35N 6 32W
Ciudad Trujillo = Santo Domingo, *Dom. Rep.* **121 C6** 18 30N 69 59W
Ciudad Victoria, *Mexico* **119 C5** 23 41N 99 9W
Ciudadela, *Spain* **37 B10** 40 0N 3 50 E
Ciulnița, *Romania* **43 F12** 44 26N 27 22 E
Ciumeghiu, *Romania* **42 D6** 46 44N 21 35 E
Ciuperceni, *Romania* **42 F8** 44 54N 23 4 E
Civa Burnu, *Turkey* **72 B7** 41 21N 36 38 E
Cividale del Friuli, *Italy* **29 B10** 46 6N 13 25 E
Cívita Castellana, *Italy* **29 F9** 42 18N 12 24 E
Civitanova Marche, *Italy* **29 E10** 43 18N 13 44 E
Civitavécchia, *Italy* **29 F8** 42 6N 11 48 E
Civray, *France* **20 B4** 46 10N 0 17 E
Çivril, *Turkey* **39 C11** 38 20N 29 43 E
Cixerri →, *Italy* **30 C1** 39 17N 8 59 E
Cixi, *China* **59 B13** 30 17N 121 9 E
Cizre, *Turkey* **70 B4** 37 19N 42 10 E
Cizur Mayor, *Spain* **32 C3** 42 47N 1 41W
Clackmannanshire □, *U.K.* **14 E5** 56 10N 3 43W
Clacton-on-Sea, *U.K.* **13 F9** 51 47N 1 11 E
Clain →, *France* **18 F7** 46 47N 0 33 E
Claire, L., *Canada* **104 B6** 58 35N 112 5W
Clairton, *U.S.A.* **110 F5** 40 18N 79 53W
Clairvaux-les-Lacs, *France* **19 F12** 46 35N 5 45 E
Claise →, *France* **20 B5** 46 56N 0 42 E
Clallam Bay, *U.S.A.* **116 B2** 48 15N 124 16W
Clamecy, *France* **19 E10** 47 28N 3 30 E
Clanton, *U.S.A.* **109 J2** 32 51N 86 38W
Clanwilliam, *S. Africa* **88 E2** 32 11 S 18 52 E
Clara, *Ireland* **15 C4** 53 21N 7 37W
Claraville, *U.S.A.* **117 K8** 35 24N 118 20W
Clare, *Australia* **95 E2** 33 50 S 138 37 E
Clare, *U.S.A.* **108 D3** 43 49N 84 46W
Clare □, *Ireland* **15 D3** 52 45N 9 0W
Clare →, *Ireland* **15 C2** 53 20N 9 2W
Clare I., *Ireland* **15 C1** 53 49N 10 0W
Claremont, *Calif., U.S.A.* **117 L9** 34 6N 117 43W
Claremont, *N.H., U.S.A.* **111 C12** 43 23N 72 20W
Claremont Pt., *Australia* **94 A3** 14 1 S 143 41 E
Claremore, *U.S.A.* **113 G7** 36 19N 95 36W
Claremorris, *Ireland* **15 C3** 53 45N 9 0W
Clarence →, *Australia* **95 D5** 29 25 S 153 22 E
Clarence →, *N.Z.* **91 K4** 42 10 S 173 56 E
Clarence, I., *Chile* **128 G2** 54 0 S 72 0W
Clarence I., *Antarctica* **5 C18** 61 10 S 54 0W
Clarence Str., *Australia* **92 B5** 12 0 S 131 0 E
Clarence Town, *Bahamas* **121 B5** 23 6N 74 59W
Clarendon, *Pa., U.S.A.* **110 E5** 41 47N 79 6W
Clarendon, *Tex., U.S.A.* **113 H4** 34 56N 100 53W
Clarenville, *Canada* **103 C9** 48 10N 54 1W
Claresholm, *Canada* **104 D6** 50 0N 113 33W
Clarie Coast, *Antarctica* **5 C9** 68 0 S 135 0 E
Clarinda, *U.S.A.* **112 E7** 40 44N 95 2W
Clarion, *Iowa, U.S.A.* **112 D8** 42 44N 93 44W
Clarion, *Pa., U.S.A.* **110 E5** 41 13N 79 23W
Clarion →, *U.S.A.* **110 E5** 41 7N 79 41W
Clark, *U.S.A.* **112 C6** 44 53N 97 44W
Clark, Pt., *Canada* **110 B3** 44 4N 81 45W
Clark Fork, *U.S.A.* **114 B5** 48 9N 116 11W
Clark Fork →, *U.S.A.* **114 B5** 48 9N 116 15W
Clarkdale, *U.S.A.* **115 J7** 34 46N 112 3W
Clarke City, *Canada* **103 B6** 50 12N 66 38W
Clarke I., *Australia* **94 G4** 40 32 S 148 10 E
Clarke Ra., *Australia* **94 C4** 20 40 S 148 30 E
Clark's Fork →, *U.S.A.* **114 D9** 45 39N 108 43W
Clark's Harbour, *Canada* **103 D6** 43 25N 65 38W
Clarks Hill L., *U.S.A.* **109 J4** 33 40N 82 12W
Clarks Summit, *U.S.A.* **111 E9** 41 30N 75 42W
Clarksburg, *U.S.A.* **108 F5** 39 17N 80 30W
Clarksdale, *U.S.A.* **113 H9** 34 12N 90 35W

Clarksville, Ark., U.S.A. 113 H8 35 28N 93 28W
Clarksville, Tenn., U.S.A. 109 G2 36 32N 87 21W
Clarksville, Tex., U.S.A. 113 J7 33 37N 95 3W
Clatskanie, U.S.A. 116 D3 46 6N 123 12W
Claude, U.S.A. 113 H4 35 7N 101 22W
Claveria, Phil. 61 B4 18 37N 121 4 E
Clay, U.S.A. 116 G5 38 17N 121 10W
Clay Center, U.S.A. 112 F6 39 23N 97 8W
Claypool, U.S.A. 115 K8 33 25N 110 51W
Claysburg, U.S.A. 110 F6 40 17N 78 27W
Claysville, U.S.A. 110 F4 40 7N 80 25W
Clayton, N. Mex., U.S.A. 113 G3 36 27N 103 11W
Clayton, N.Y., U.S.A. 111 B8 44 14N 76 5W
Clear, C., Ireland 15 E2 51 25N 9 32W
Clear, L., Canada 110 A7 45 26N 77 12W
Clear Hills, Canada 104 B5 56 40N 119 30W
Clear I., Ireland 15 E2 51 26N 9 30W
Clear L., U.S.A. 116 F4 39 2N 122 47W
Clear Lake, Iowa, U.S.A. 112 D8 43 8N 93 23W
Clear Lake, S. Dak., U.S.A. 112 C6 44 45N 96 41W
Clear Lake Reservoir, U.S.A. 114 F3 41 56N 121 5W
Clearfield, Pa., U.S.A. 110 E6 41 2N 78 27W
Clearfield, Utah, U.S.A. 114 F8 41 7N 112 2W
Clearlake, U.S.A. 114 G2 38 57N 122 38W
Clearlake Highlands, U.S.A. 116 G4 38 57N 122 38W
Clearwater, Canada 104 C4 51 38N 120 2W
Clearwater, U.S.A. 109 M4 27 58N 82 48W
Clearwater →, Alta., Canada 104 C6 52 22N 114 57W
Clearwater →, Alta., Canada 105 B6 56 44N 111 23W
Clearwater L., Canada 105 C9 53 34N 99 49W
Clearwater Mts., U.S.A. 114 C6 46 5N 115 20W
Clearwater Prov. Park, Canada 105 C8 54 0N 101 0W
Clearwater River Prov. Park, Canada 105 B7 56 55N 109 10W
Cleburne, U.S.A. 113 J6 32 21N 97 23W
Clee Hills, U.K. 13 E5 52 26N 2 35W
Cleethorpes, U.K. 12 D7 53 33N 0 3W
Cleeve Cloud, U.K. 13 F6 51 56N 2 0W
Clelles, France 21 D9 44 50N 5 38 E
Clemson, U.S.A. 109 H4 34 41N 82 50W
Clerke Reef, Australia 92 C2 17 22 S 119 20 E
Clermont, Australia 94 C4 22 49 S 147 39 E
Clermont, France 19 C9 49 23N 2 24 E
Clermont, U.S.A. 109 L5 28 33N 81 46W
Clermont-en-Argonne, France 19 C12 49 5N 5 4 E
Clermont-Ferrand, France 20 C7 45 46N 3 4 E
Clermont-l'Hérault, France 20 E7 43 38N 3 26 E
Clerval, France 19 E13 47 25N 6 30 E
Clervaux, Lux. 17 D6 50 4N 6 2 E
Cles, Italy 28 B8 46 22N 11 2 E
Cleve, Australia 95 E2 33 43 S 136 30 E
Clevedon, U.K. 13 F5 51 26N 2 52W
Cleveland, Miss., U.S.A. 113 J9 33 45N 90 43W
Cleveland, Ohio, U.S.A. 110 E3 41 30N 81 42W
Cleveland, Okla., U.S.A. 113 G6 36 19N 96 28W
Cleveland, Tenn., U.S.A. 109 H3 35 10N 84 53W
Cleveland, Tex., U.S.A. 113 K7 30 21N 95 5W
Cleveland, C., Australia 94 B4 19 11 S 147 1 E
Cleveland, Mt., U.S.A. 114 B7 48 56N 113 51W
Cleveland Heights, U.S.A. 110 E3 41 30N 81 34W
Clevelândia, Brazil 127 B5 26 24 S 52 23W
Clew B., Ireland 15 C2 53 50N 9 49W
Clewiston, U.S.A. 109 M5 26 45N 80 56W
Clifden, Ireland 15 C1 53 29N 10 1W
Clifden, N.Z. 91 M1 46 1 S 167 42 E
Cliffdell, U.S.A. 116 D5 46 56N 121 5W
Cliffy Hd., Australia 93 G2 35 1 S 116 29 E
Clifton, Australia 95 D5 27 59 S 151 53 E
Clifton, Ariz., U.S.A. 115 K9 33 3N 109 18W
Clifton, Colo., U.S.A. 115 G9 39 7N 108 25W
Clifton, Tex., U.S.A. 113 K6 31 47N 97 35W
Clifton Beach, Australia 94 B4 16 46 S 145 39 E
Climax, Canada 105 D7 49 10N 108 20W
Clinch →, U.S.A. 109 H3 35 53N 84 29W
Clingmans Dome, U.S.A. 109 H4 35 34N 83 30W
Clint, U.S.A. 115 L10 31 35N 106 14W
Clinton, B.C., Canada 104 C4 51 6N 121 35W
Clinton, Ont., Canada 102 D3 43 37N 81 32W
Clinton, N.Z. 91 M2 46 12 S 169 23 E
Clinton, Ark., U.S.A. 113 H8 35 36N 92 28W
Clinton, Conn., U.S.A. 111 E12 41 17N 72 32W
Clinton, Ill., U.S.A. 112 E10 40 9N 88 57W
Clinton, Ind., U.S.A. 108 F2 39 40N 87 24W
Clinton, Iowa, U.S.A. 112 E9 41 51N 90 12W
Clinton, Mass., U.S.A. 111 D13 42 25N 71 41W
Clinton, Miss., U.S.A. 113 J9 32 20N 90 20W
Clinton, Mo., U.S.A. 112 F8 38 22N 93 46W
Clinton, N.C., U.S.A. 109 H6 35 0N 78 22W
Clinton, Okla., U.S.A. 113 H5 35 31N 98 58W
Clinton, S.C., U.S.A. 109 H5 34 29N 81 53W
Clinton, Tenn., U.S.A. 109 G3 36 6N 84 8W
Clinton, Wash., U.S.A. 116 C4 47 59N 122 21W
Clinton C., Australia 94 C5 22 30 S 150 45 E
Clinton Colden L., Canada 100 B9 63 58N 107 27W
Clintonville, U.S.A. 112 C10 44 37N 88 46W
Clipperton, I., Pac. Oc. 97 F17 10 18N 109 13W
Clisham, U.K. 14 D2 57 57N 6 49W
Clisson, France 18 E5 47 5N 1 16W
Clitheroe, U.K. 12 D5 53 53N 2 22W
Clo-oose, Canada 116 B2 48 39N 124 49W
Cloates, Pt., Australia 92 D1 22 43 S 113 40 E
Clocolan, S. Africa 89 D4 28 55 S 27 34 E
Clodomira, Argentina 126 B3 27 35 S 64 14W
Clogher Hd., Ireland 15 C5 53 48N 6 14W
Clonakilty, Ireland 15 E3 51 37N 8 53W
Clonakilty B., Ireland 15 E3 51 35N 8 51W
Cloncurry, Australia 94 C3 20 40 S 140 28 E
Cloncurry →, Australia 94 B3 18 37 S 140 40 E
Clondalkin, Ireland 15 C5 53 19N 6 25W
Clones, Ireland 15 B4 54 11N 7 15W
Clonmel, Ireland 15 D4 52 21N 7 42W
Cloppenburg, Germany 24 C4 52 51N 8 1 E
Cloquet, U.S.A. 112 B8 46 43N 92 28W
Clorinda, Argentina 126 B4 25 16 S 57 45W
Cloud Bay, Canada 102 C2 48 5N 89 26W
Cloud Peak, U.S.A. 114 D10 44 23N 107 11W
Cloudcroft, U.S.A. 115 K11 32 58N 105 45W
Cloverdale, U.S.A. 116 G4 38 48N 123 1W
Clovis, Calif., U.S.A. 116 J7 36 49N 119 42W
Clovis, N. Mex., U.S.A. 113 H3 34 24N 103 12W
Cloyes-sur-le-Loir, France 18 E8 48 0N 1 14 E
Cloyne, Canada 110 B7 44 49N 77 11W
Cluj □, Romania 43 D8 46 45N 23 30 E
Cluj-Napoca, Romania 43 D8 46 47N 23 38 E
Clunes, Australia 95 F3 37 20 S 143 45 E
Cluny, France 19 F11 46 26N 4 38 E
Cluses, France 19 F13 46 5N 6 35 E
Clusone, Italy 28 C6 45 53N 9 57 E
Clutha →, N.Z. 91 M2 46 20 S 169 49 E
Clwyd →, U.K. 12 D4 53 19N 3 31W
Clyde, Canada 104 C6 54 9N 113 39W
Clyde, N.Z. 91 L2 45 12 S 169 20 E
Clyde, U.S.A. 110 C8 43 5N 76 52W
Clyde →, U.K. 14 F4 55 55N 4 30W
Clyde, Firth of, U.K. 14 F3 55 22N 5 1W
Clyde River, Canada 101 A13 70 30N 68 30W
Clydebank, U.K. 14 F4 55 54N 4 23W
Clymer, N.Y., U.S.A. 110 D5 42 1N 79 37W
Clymer, Pa., U.S.A. 110 D5 40 40N 79 1W
Ćmielów, Poland 45 H8 50 53N 21 31 E
Côa →, Portugal 34 D3 41 5N 7 6W
Coachella, U.S.A. 117 M10 33 41N 116 10W
Coachella Canal, U.S.A. 117 N12 32 43N 114 57W
Coahoma, U.S.A. 113 J4 32 18N 101 18W
Coahuayana →, Mexico 118 D4 18 41N 103 45W
Coahuila □, Mexico 118 B4 27 0N 103 0W
Coal →, Canada 104 B3 59 39N 126 57W
Coalane, Mozam. 87 F4 17 48 S 37 2 E
Coalcomán, Mexico 118 D4 18 40N 103 10W
Coaldale, Canada 104 D6 49 45N 112 35W
Coalgate, U.S.A. 113 H6 34 32N 96 13W
Coalinga, U.S.A. 116 J6 36 9N 120 21W
Coalisland, U.K. 15 B5 54 33N 6 42W
Coalville, U.K. 12 E6 52 44N 1 23W
Coalville, U.S.A. 114 F8 40 55N 111 24W
Coari, Brazil 124 D6 4 8 S 63 7W
Coast □, Kenya 86 C4 2 40 S 39 45 E
Coast Mts., Canada 104 C3 55 0N 129 20W
Coast Ranges, U.S.A. 116 G4 39 0N 123 0W
Coatbridge, U.K. 14 F4 55 52N 4 6W
Coatepec, Mexico 119 D5 19 27N 96 58W
Coatepeque, Guatemala 120 D1 14 46N 91 55W
Coatesville, U.S.A. 108 F8 39 59N 75 50W
Coaticook, Canada 103 C5 45 10N 71 46W
Coats I., Canada 101 B11 62 30N 83 0W
Coats Land, Antarctica 5 D1 77 0 S 25 0W
Coatzacoalcos, Mexico 119 D6 18 7N 94 25W
Cobadin, Romania 43 F13 44 5N 28 13 E
Cobalt, Canada 102 C4 47 25N 79 42W
Cobán, Guatemala 120 C1 15 30N 90 21W
Çobanlar, Turkey 39 C12 38 41N 30 47 E
Cobar, Australia 95 E4 31 27 S 145 48 E
Cobargo, Australia 95 F4 36 20 S 149 55 E
Cóbh, Ireland 15 E3 51 51N 8 17W
Cobija, Bolivia 124 F5 11 0 S 68 50W
Cobleskill, U.S.A. 111 D10 42 41N 74 29W
Coboconk, Canada 110 B6 44 39N 78 48W
Cobourg, Canada 102 D4 43 58N 78 10W
Cobourg Pen., Australia 92 B5 11 20 S 132 15 E
Cobram, Australia 95 F4 35 54 S 145 40 E
Cóbué, Mozam. 87 E3 12 0 S 34 58 E
Coburg, Germany 25 E6 50 15N 10 58 E
Coca, Spain 34 D6 41 13N 4 32W
Cocanada = Kakinada, India 67 L13 16 57N 82 11 E
Cocentaina, Spain 33 G4 38 45N 0 27W
Cochabamba, Bolivia 124 G5 17 26 S 66 10W
Cochem, Germany 25 E3 50 9N 7 9 E
Cochemane, Mozam. 87 F3 17 0 S 32 54 E
Cochin, India 66 Q10 9 59N 76 22 E
Cochin China = Nam-Phan, Vietnam 65 G6 10 30N 106 0 E
Cochran, U.S.A. 109 J4 32 23N 83 21W
Cochrane, Alta., Canada 104 C6 51 11N 114 30W
Cochrane, Ont., Canada 102 C3 49 0N 81 0W
Cochrane, Chile 128 F2 47 15 S 72 33W
Cochrane →, Canada 105 B8 59 0N 103 40W
Cochrane, L., Chile 128 F2 47 10 S 72 0W
Cochranton, U.S.A. 110 E4 41 31N 80 3W
Cockburn, Australia 95 E3 32 5 S 141 0 E
Cockburn, Canal, Chile 122 J3 54 30 S 72 0W
Cockburn I., Canada 102 C3 45 55N 83 22W
Cockburn Ra., Australia 92 C4 15 46 S 128 0 E
Cockermouth, U.K. 12 C4 54 40N 3 22W
Cocklebiddy, Australia 93 F4 32 0 S 126 3 E
Coco →, Cent. Amer. 120 D3 15 0N 83 8W
Coco, I. del, Pac. Oc. 97 G19 5 25N 87 55W
Cocoa, U.S.A. 109 L5 28 21N 80 44W
Cocobeach, Gabon 84 D1 0 59N 9 34 E
Cocora, Romania 43 F12 44 45N 27 3 E
Cocos Is., Ind. Oc. 96 J1 12 10 S 96 55 E
Cod, C., U.S.A. 108 D10 42 5N 70 10W
Codajás, Brazil 124 D6 3 55 S 62 0W
Codigoro, Italy 29 D9 44 49N 12 8 E
Codlea, Romania 43 E10 45 42N 25 27 E
Codó, Brazil 125 D10 4 30 S 43 55W
Codogno, Italy 28 C6 45 9N 9 42 E
Codróipo, Italy 29 C10 45 58N 13 0 E
Codru, Muntii, Romania 42 D7 46 30N 22 15 E
Cody, U.S.A. 114 D9 44 32N 109 3W
Coe Hill, Canada 110 B7 44 52N 77 50W
Coelemu, Chile 126 D1 36 30 S 72 48W
Coen, Australia 94 A3 13 52 S 143 12 E
Coesfeld, Germany 24 D3 51 56N 7 10 E
Cœur d'Alene, U.S.A. 114 C5 47 45N 116 51W
Cœur d'Alene L., U.S.A. 114 C5 47 32N 116 48W
Coevorden, Neths. 17 B6 52 40N 6 44 E
Cofete, Canary Is. 37 F5 28 6N 14 23W
Coffeyville, U.S.A. 113 G7 37 2N 95 37W
Coffin B., Australia 95 E2 34 38 S 135 28 E
Coffin Bay, Australia 95 E2 34 37 S 135 29 E
Coffin Bay Peninsula, Australia 95 E2 34 32 S 135 15 E
Coffs Harbour, Australia 95 E5 30 16 S 153 5 E
Cofrentes, Spain 33 F3 39 13N 1 5W
Cogalnic →, Moldova 43 E14 45 49N 29 40 E
Cogealac, Romania 43 F13 44 36N 28 36 E
Coghinas →, Italy 30 B1 40 55N 8 48 E
Coghinas, L. del, Italy 30 B2 40 46N 9 3 E
Cognac, France 20 C3 45 41N 0 20W
Cogne, Italy 28 C4 45 37N 7 21 E
Cogolin, France 21 E10 43 15N 6 32 E
Cogolludo, Spain 32 E1 40 59N 3 10W
Cohocton, U.S.A. 110 D7 42 30N 77 30W
Cohocton →, U.S.A. 110 D7 42 9N 77 6W
Cohoes, U.S.A. 111 D11 42 46N 73 42W
Cohuna, Australia 95 F3 35 45 S 144 15 E
Coiba, I., Panama 120 E3 7 30N 81 40W
Coig →, Argentina 128 G3 51 0 S 69 10W
Coigeach, Rubha, U.K. 14 C3 58 6N 5 26W
Coihaique, Chile 128 F2 45 30 S 71 45W
Coimbatore, India 66 P10 11 2N 76 59 E
Coimbra, Brazil 124 G7 19 55 S 57 48W
Coimbra, Portugal 34 E2 40 15N 8 27W
Coimbra □, Portugal 34 E2 40 12N 8 25W
Coín, Spain 35 J6 36 40N 4 48W
Coipasa, Salar de, Bolivia 124 G5 19 26 S 68 9W
Cojimies, Ecuador 124 C3 0 20N 80 0W
Cojocna, Romania 43 D8 46 45N 23 50 E
Cojutepequé, El Salv. 120 D2 13 41N 88 54W
Čoka, Serbia, Yug. 42 E5 45 57N 20 12 E
Cokeville, U.S.A. 114 E8 42 5N 110 57W
Colac, Australia 95 F3 38 21 S 143 35 E
Colatina, Brazil 125 G10 19 32 S 40 37W
Colbeck, C., Antarctica 5 D13 77 6 S 157 48W
Colborne, Canada 110 C7 44 0N 77 53W
Colby, U.S.A. 112 F4 39 24N 101 3W
Colchester, U.K. 13 F8 51 54N 0 55 E
Cold L., Canada 105 C7 54 33N 110 5W
Coldstream, Canada 104 C5 50 13N 119 11W
Coldstream, U.K. 14 F6 55 39N 2 15W
Coldwater, Canada 110 B5 44 42N 79 40W
Coldwater, Kans., U.S.A. 113 G5 37 16N 99 20W
Coldwater, Mich., U.S.A. 108 E3 41 57N 85 0W
Coleambally, Australia 95 E4 34 49 S 145 52 E
Colebrook, U.S.A. 111 B13 44 54N 71 30W
Coleman, U.S.A. 113 K5 31 50N 99 26W
Coleman →, Australia 94 B3 15 6 S 141 38 E
Colenso, S. Africa 89 D4 28 44 S 29 50 E
Coleraine, Australia 95 F3 37 36 S 141 40 E
Coleraine, U.K. 15 A5 55 8N 6 41W
Coleridge, L., N.Z. 91 K3 43 17 S 171 30 E
Colesberg, S. Africa 88 E4 30 45 S 25 5 E
Coleville, U.S.A. 116 G7 38 34N 119 30W
Colfax, Calif., U.S.A. 116 F6 39 6N 120 57W
Colfax, La., U.S.A. 113 K8 31 31N 92 42W
Colfax, Wash., U.S.A. 114 C5 46 53N 117 22W
Colhué Huapi, L., Argentina 128 F3 45 30 S 69 0W
Colibași, Moldova 43 E13 45 43N 28 11 E
Colibași, Romania 43 F9 44 56N 24 54 E
Cólico, Italy 28 B6 46 8N 9 22 E
Coligny, France 19 F12 46 23N 5 21 E
Coligny, S. Africa 89 D4 26 17 S 26 15 E
Colima, Mexico 118 D4 19 14N 103 43W
Colima □, Mexico 118 D4 19 10N 103 40W
Colima, Nevado de, Mexico 118 D4 19 35N 103 45W
Colina, Chile 126 C1 33 13 S 70 45W
Colina do Norte, Guinea-Biss. 82 C2 12 28N 15 0W
Colinas, Brazil 125 E10 6 0 S 44 10W
Colindres, Spain 34 B7 43 24N 3 27W
Coll, U.K. 14 E2 56 39N 6 34W
Collaguasi, Chile 126 A2 21 5 S 68 45W
Collarada, Peña, Spain 32 C4 42 43N 0 29W
Collarenebri, Australia 95 D4 29 33 S 148 34 E
Colle di Val d'Elsa, Italy 28 E8 43 25N 11 7 E
Collécchio, Italy 28 D7 44 45N 10 13 E
Colleen Bawn, Zimbabwe 87 G2 21 0 S 29 12 E
College Park, U.S.A. 109 J3 33 40N 84 27W
College Station, U.S.A. 113 K6 30 37N 96 21W
Collesalvetti, Italy 28 E7 43 34N 10 29 E
Collie, Australia 93 F2 33 22 S 116 8 E
Collier B., Australia 92 C3 16 10 S 124 15 E
Collier Ra., Australia 93 D2 24 45 S 119 10 E
Collina, Passo di, Italy 28 D7 44 2N 10 56 E
Collingwood, Canada 102 D3 44 29N 80 13W
Collingwood, N.Z. 91 J4 40 41 S 172 40 E
Collins, Canada 102 B2 50 17N 89 27W
Collinsville, Australia 94 C4 20 30 S 147 56 E
Collipulli, Chile 126 D1 37 55 S 72 30W
Collooney, Ireland 15 B3 54 11N 8 29W
Colmar, France 19 D14 48 5N 7 20 E
Colmars, France 21 D10 44 11N 6 39 E
Colmenar, Spain 35 J6 36 54N 4 20W
Colmenar de Oreja, Spain 34 E7 40 6N 3 25W
Colmenar Viejo, Spain 34 E7 40 39N 3 47W
Colo →, Australia 95 E5 33 25 S 150 52 E
Cologne = Köln, Germany 24 E2 50 56N 6 57 E
Colom, I. d'en, Spain 37 B11 39 58N 4 16 E
Coloma, U.S.A. 116 G6 38 48N 120 53W
Colomb-Béchar = Béchar, Algeria 78 B5 31 38N 2 18W
Colombey-les-Belles, France 19 D12 48 32N 5 54 E
Colombey-les-Deux-Églises, France 19 D11 48 13N 4 50 E
Colombia ■, S. Amer. 124 C4 3 45N 73 0W
Colombian Basin, S. Amer. 98 H12 14 0N 76 0W
Colombo, Sri Lanka 66 R11 6 56N 79 58 E
Colomiers, France 20 E5 43 36N 1 21 E
Colón, Buenos Aires, Argentina 126 C3 33 53 S 61 7W
Colón, Entre Ríos, Argentina 126 C4 32 12 S 58 10W
Colón, Cuba 120 B3 22 42N 80 54W
Colón, Panama 120 E4 9 20N 79 54W
Colonia de Sant Jordi, Spain 37 B9 39 19N 2 59 E
Colonia del Sacramento, Uruguay 126 C4 34 25 S 57 50W
Colonia Dora, Argentina 126 B3 28 34 S 62 59W
Colonial Beach, U.S.A. 108 F7 38 15N 76 58W
Colonie, U.S.A. 111 D11 42 43N 73 50W
Colonna, C., Italy 31 C10 39 2N 17 12 E
Colonsay, Canada 105 C7 51 59N 105 52W
Colonsay, U.K. 14 E2 56 5N 6 12W
Colorado □, U.S.A. 115 G10 39 30N 105 30W
Colorado →, Argentina 128 D4 39 50 S 62 8W
Colorado →, N. Amer. 115 L6 31 45N 114 40W
Colorado →, U.S.A. 113 L7 28 36N 95 59W
Colorado City, U.S.A. 113 J4 32 24N 100 52W
Colorado Plateau, U.S.A. 115 H8 37 0N 111 0W
Colorado River Aqueduct, U.S.A. 117 L12 34 17N 114 10W
Colorado Springs, U.S.A. 112 F2 38 50N 104 49W
Colorno, Italy 28 D7 44 56N 10 23 E
Colotlán, Mexico 118 C4 22 6N 103 16W
Colstrip, U.S.A. 114 D10 45 53N 106 38W
Colton, U.S.A. 111 B10 44 33N 74 56W
Columbia, Ky., U.S.A. 108 G3 37 6N 85 18W
Columbia, La., U.S.A. 113 J8 32 6N 92 5W
Columbia, Miss., U.S.A. 113 K10 31 15N 89 50W
Columbia, Mo., U.S.A. 112 F8 38 57N 92 20W
Columbia, Pa., U.S.A. 111 F8 40 2N 76 30W
Columbia, S.C., U.S.A. 109 J5 34 0N 81 2W
Columbia, Tenn., U.S.A. 109 H2 35 37N 87 2W
Columbia →, N. Amer. 116 D2 46 15N 124 5W
Columbia, C., Canada 4 A4 83 0N 70 0W
Columbia, District of □, U.S.A. 108 F7 38 55N 77 0W
Columbia, Mt., Canada 104 C5 52 8N 117 20W
Columbia Basin, U.S.A. 114 C4 46 45N 119 5W
Columbia Falls, U.S.A. 114 B6 48 23N 114 11W
Columbia Mts., Canada 104 C5 52 0N 119 0W
Columbia Plateau, U.S.A. 114 D5 44 0N 117 30W
Columbiana, U.S.A. 110 F4 40 53N 80 42W
Columbretes, Is., Spain 32 F5 39 50N 0 50 E
Columbus, Ga., U.S.A. 109 J3 32 28N 84 59W
Columbus, Ind., U.S.A. 108 F3 39 13N 85 55W
Columbus, Kans., U.S.A. 113 G7 37 10N 94 50W
Columbus, Miss., U.S.A. 109 J1 33 30N 88 25W
Columbus, Mont., U.S.A. 114 D9 45 38N 109 15W
Columbus, N. Mex., U.S.A. 115 L10 31 50N 107 38W
Columbus, Nebr., U.S.A. 112 E6 41 26N 97 22W
Columbus, Ohio, U.S.A. 108 F4 39 58N 83 0W
Columbus, Tex., U.S.A. 113 L6 29 42N 96 33W
Colunga, Spain 34 B5 43 29N 5 16W
Colusa, U.S.A. 116 F4 39 13N 122 1W
Colville, U.S.A. 114 B5 48 33N 117 54W
Colville →, U.S.A. 100 A4 70 25N 150 30W
Colville, C., N.Z. 91 G5 36 29 S 175 21 E
Colwood, Canada 116 B3 48 26N 123 29W
Colwyn Bay, U.K. 12 D4 53 18N 3 44W
Coma, Ethiopia 81 F4 8 29N 36 53 E
Comácchio, Italy 29 D9 44 42N 12 11 E
Comalcalco, Mexico 119 D6 18 16N 93 13W
Comallo, Argentina 128 E2 41 0 S 70 5W
Comana, Romania 43 F11 44 10N 26 10 E
Comanche, U.S.A. 113 K5 31 54N 98 36W
Comănești, Romania 43 D11 46 25N 26 26 E
Comarnic, Romania 43 E10 45 15N 25 38 E
Comayagua, Honduras 120 D2 14 25N 87 37W
Combahee →, U.S.A. 109 J5 32 30N 80 31W
Combarbalá, Chile 126 C1 31 11 S 71 2W
Combeaufontaine, France 19 E12 47 38N 5 54 E
Comber, Canada 110 D2 42 14N 82 33W
Comber, U.K. 15 B6 54 33N 5 45W
Combermere, Canada 110 A7 45 22N 77 37W
Comblain-au-Pont, Belgium 17 D5 50 29N 5 35 E
Combourg, France 18 D5 48 25N 1 46W
Combrailles, France 19 F9 46 8N 2 8 E
Combronde, France 20 C7 45 58N 3 5 E
Comeragh Mts., Ireland 15 D4 52 18N 7 34W
Comet, Australia 94 C4 23 36 S 148 38 E
Comilla, Bangla. 67 H17 23 28N 91 10 E
Comino, Malta 36 C1 36 2N 14 20 E
Comino, C., Italy 30 B2 40 32N 9 49 E
Cómiso, Italy 31 F7 36 56N 14 36 E
Comitán, Mexico 119 D6 16 18N 92 9W
Commentry, France 19 F9 46 20N 2 46 E
Commerce, Ga., U.S.A. 109 H4 34 12N 83 28W
Commerce, Tex., U.S.A. 113 J7 33 15N 95 54W
Commercy, France 19 D12 48 43N 5 34 E
Committee B., Canada 101 B11 68 30N 86 30W
Commonwealth B., Antarctica 5 C10 67 0 S 144 0 E
Commoron Cr. →, Australia 95 D5 28 22 S 150 8 E
Communism Pk. = Kommunizma, Pik, Tajikistan 50 F8 39 0N 72 2 E
Como, Italy 28 C6 45 47N 9 5 E
Como, Lago di, Italy 28 B6 46 0N 9 11 E
Comodoro Rivadavia, Argentina 128 F3 45 50 S 67 40W
Comorâște, Romania 42 E6 45 10N 21 34 E
Comorin, C., India 66 Q10 8 3N 77 40 E
Comoro Is. = Comoros ■, Ind. Oc. 77 H8 12 10 S 44 15 E
Comoros ■, Ind. Oc. 77 H8 12 10 S 44 15 E
Comox, Canada 104 D4 49 42N 124 55W
Compiègne, France 19 C9 49 24N 2 50 E
Comporta, Portugal 35 G2 38 22N 8 46W
Compostela, Mexico 118 C4 21 15N 104 53W
Comprida, I., Brazil 127 A6 24 50 S 47 42W
Compton, Canada 111 A13 45 14N 71 49W
Compton, U.S.A. 117 M8 33 54N 118 13W
Comrat, Moldova 43 D13 46 18N 28 40 E
Con Cuong, Vietnam 64 C5 19 2N 104 54 E
Con Son, Vietnam 65 H6 8 41N 106 37 E
Conakry, Guinea 82 D2 9 29N 13 49W
Conara, Australia 94 G4 41 50 S 147 26 E
Concarneau, France 18 E3 47 52N 3 56W
Conceição, Mozam. 87 F4 18 47 S 36 7 E
Conceição da Barra, Brazil 125 G11 18 35 S 39 45W
Conceição do Araguaia, Brazil 125 E9 8 0 S 49 2W
Concepción, Argentina 126 B2 27 20 S 65 35W
Concepción, Bolivia 124 G6 16 15 S 62 8W
Concepción, Chile 126 D1 36 50 S 73 0W
Concepción, Mexico 119 D6 18 15N 90 5W
Concepción, Paraguay 126 A4 23 22 S 57 26W
Concepción □, Chile 126 D1 37 0 S 72 30W
Concepción →, Mexico 118 A2 30 32N 113 2W
Concepción, Est. de, Chile 128 G2 50 30 S 74 55W
Concepción, L., Bolivia 124 G6 17 20 S 61 20W
Concepción, Punta, Mexico 118 B2 26 55N 111 59W
Concepción del Oro, Mexico 118 C4 24 40N 101 30W
Concepción del Uruguay, Argentina 126 C4 32 35 S 58 20W
Conception, Pt., U.S.A. 117 L6 34 27N 120 28W
Conception B., Canada 103 C9 47 45N 53 0W
Conception B., Namibia 88 C1 23 55 S 14 22 E
Conception I., Bahamas 121 B4 23 52N 75 9W
Concession, Zimbabwe 87 F3 17 27 S 30 56 E
Conchas Dam, U.S.A. 113 H2 35 22N 104 11W
Conches-en-Ouche, France 18 D7 48 58N 0 56 E
Concho, U.S.A. 115 J9 34 28N 109 36W
Concho →, U.S.A. 113 K5 31 34N 99 43W
Conchos →, Chihuahua, Mexico 118 B4 29 32N 105 0W
Conchos →, Tamaulipas, Mexico 119 B5 25 9N 98 35W
Concord, Calif., U.S.A. 116 H4 37 59N 122 2W
Concord, N.C., U.S.A. 109 H5 35 25N 80 35W
Concord, N.H., U.S.A. 111 C13 43 12N 71 32W
Concordia, Argentina 126 C4 31 20 S 58 2W
Concórdia, Brazil 124 D5 4 36 S 66 36W
Concordia, Mexico 118 C3 23 18N 106 2W
Concordia, U.S.A. 112 F6 39 34N 97 40W
Concrete, U.S.A. 114 B3 48 32N 121 45W
Condamine, Australia 95 D5 26 56 S 150 9 E
Condat, France 20 C6 45 21N 2 46 E
Conde, U.S.A. 112 C5 45 9N 98 6W
Condé-sur-Noireau, France 18 D6 48 51N 0 33W
Condeúba, Brazil 125 F10 14 52 S 42 0W
Condobolin, Australia 95 E4 33 4 S 147 6 E
Condom, France 20 E4 43 57N 0 22 E
Condon, U.S.A. 114 D3 45 14N 120 11W
Conegliano, Italy 29 C9 45 53N 12 18 E
Conejera, I. = Conills, I. des, Spain 37 B9 39 11N 2 58 E
Conejos, Mexico 118 B4 26 14N 103 53W
Confolens, France 20 B4 46 2N 0 40 E
Confuso →, Paraguay 126 B4 25 9 S 57 34W
Congaz, Moldova 43 D13 46 7N 28 36 E
Conghua, China 59 F9 23 36N 113 31 E
Congjiang, China 58 E7 25 43N 108 52 E
Congleton, U.K. 12 D5 53 10N 2 13W
Congo (Kinshasa) = Congo, Dem. Rep. of the ■, Africa 84 E4 3 0 S 23 0 E
Congo ■, Africa 84 E3 1 0 S 16 0 E
Congo →, Africa 84 F2 6 4 S 12 24 E
Congo, Dem. Rep. of the ■, Africa 84 E4 3 0 S 23 0 E
Congo Basin, Africa 84 E4 0 10 S 24 30 E
Congonhas, Brazil 127 A7 20 30 S 43 52W
Congress, U.S.A. 115 J7 34 9N 112 51W
Conil = Conil de la Frontera, Spain 35 J4 36 17N 6 10W
Conil de la Frontera, Spain 35 J4 36 17N 6 10W
Conills, I. des, Spain 37 B9 39 11N 2 58 E
Coniston, Canada 102 C3 46 29N 80 51W
Conjeeveram = Kanchipuram, India 66 N11 12 52N 79 45 E
Conklin, Canada 105 B6 55 38N 111 5W
Conklin, U.S.A. 111 D9 42 2N 75 49W
Conn, L., Ireland 15 B2 54 3N 9 15W
Connacht □, Ireland 15 C2 53 43N 9 12W
Conneaut, U.S.A. 110 E4 41 57N 80 34W
Connecticut □, U.S.A. 111 E12 41 30N 72 45W
Connecticut →, U.S.A. 111 E12 41 16N 72 20W
Connell, U.S.A. 114 C4 46 40N 118 52W
Connellsville, U.S.A. 110 F5 40 1N 79 35W
Connemara, Ireland 15 C2 53 29N 9 45W
Connemaugh →, U.S.A. 110 F5 40 28N 79 19W
Connerré, France 18 D7 48 3N 0 30 E
Connersville, U.S.A. 108 F3 39 39N 85 8W
Connors Ra., Australia 94 C4 21 40 S 149 10 E
Conques, France 20 D6 44 36N 2 23 E
Conquest, Canada 105 C7 51 32N 107 14W
Conrad, U.S.A. 114 B8 48 10N 111 57W
Conran, C., Australia 95 F4 37 49 S 148 44 E
Conroe, U.S.A. 113 K7 30 19N 95 27W
Consecon, Canada 110 C7 44 0N 77 31W
Conselheiro Lafaiete, Brazil 127 A7 20 40 S 43 48W
Conselve, Italy 29 C8 45 14N 11 52 E
Consett, U.K. 12 C6 54 51N 1 50W
Consort, Canada 105 C6 52 1N 110 46W
Constance = Konstanz, Germany 25 H5 47 40N 9 10 E
Constance, L. = Bodensee, Europe 25 H5 47 35N 9 25 E
Constanța, Romania 43 F13 44 14N 28 38 E
Constanța □, Romania 43 F13 44 15N 28 15 E
Constantia, U.S.A. 111 C8 43 15N 76 1W
Constantina, Spain 35 H5 37 51N 5 40W
Constantine, Algeria 78 A7 36 25N 6 42 E
Constitución, Chile 126 D1 35 20 S 72 30W
Constitución, Uruguay 126 C4 31 0 S 57 50W
Consuegra, Spain 35 F7 39 28N 3 36W
Consul, Canada 105 D7 49 20N 109 30W
Contact, U.S.A. 114 F6 41 46N 114 45W
Contai, India 69 J12 21 54N 87 46 E
Contamana, Peru 124 E4 7 19 S 74 55W
Contarina, Italy 29 C9 45 1N 12 13 E
Contas →, Brazil 125 F11 14 17 S 39 1W
Contes, France 21 E11 43 49N 7 19 E
Contoocook, U.S.A. 111 C13 43 13N 71 45W
Contra Costa, Mozam. 89 D5 25 9 S 33 30 E
Contres, France 18 E8 47 24N 1 26 E
Contrexéville, France 19 D12 48 10N 5 53 E
Contwoyto L., Canada 100 B8 65 42N 110 50W
Conversano, Italy 31 B10 40 58N 17 7 E
Conway = Conwy, U.K. 12 D4 53 17N 3 50W
Conway = Conwy →, U.K. 12 D4 53 17N 3 50W
Conway, Ark., U.S.A. 113 H8 35 5N 92 26W
Conway, N.H., U.S.A. 111 C13 43 59N 71 7W
Conway, S.C., U.S.A. 109 J6 33 51N 79 3W
Conway, L., Australia 95 D2 28 17 S 135 35 E
Conwy, U.K. 12 D4 53 17N 3 50W
Conwy □, U.K. 12 D4 53 10N 3 44W
Conwy →, U.K. 12 D4 53 17N 3 50W
Coober Pedy, Australia 95 D1 29 1 S 134 43 E
Cooch Behar = Koch Bihar, India 67 F16 26 22N 89 29 E
Cooinda, Australia 92 B5 13 15 S 130 5 E
Cook, Australia 93 F5 30 37 S 130 25 E
Cook, U.S.A. 112 B8 47 49N 92 39W
Cook, B., Chile 128 H3 55 10 S 70 0W
Cook, C., Canada 104 C3 50 8N 127 55W
Cook, Mt. = Aoraki Mount Cook, N.Z. 91 K3 43 36 S 170 9 E
Cook Inlet, U.S.A. 100 C4 60 0N 152 0W
Cook Is., Pac. Oc. 97 J12 17 0 S 160 0W
Cook Strait, N.Z. 91 J5 41 15 S 174 29 E
Cookeville, U.S.A. 109 G3 36 10N 85 30W
Cookhouse, S. Africa 88 E4 32 44 S 25 47 E
Cookshire, Canada 111 A13 45 25N 71 38W
Cookstown, U.K. 15 B5 54 39N 6 45W
Cooksville, Canada 110 C5 43 36N 79 35W
Cooktown, Australia 94 B4 15 30 S 145 16 E
Coolabah, Australia 95 E4 31 1 S 146 43 E
Cooladdi, Australia 95 D4 26 37 S 145 23 E
Coolah, Australia 95 E4 31 48 S 149 41 E
Coolamon, Australia 95 E4 34 46 S 147 8 E

Coolgardie, Australia . 93 F3 30 55 S 121 8 E
Coolidge, U.S.A. 115 K8 32 59N 111 31W
Coolidge Dam, U.S.A. 115 K8 33 0N 110 20W
Cooma, Australia 95 F4 36 12 S 149 8 E
Coon Rapids, U.S.A. 112 C8 45 9N 93 19W
Coonabarabran, Australia 95 E4 31 14 S 149 18 E
Coonalpyn, Australia 95 F2 35 43 S 139 52 E
Coonamble, Australia 95 E4 30 56 S 148 27 E
Coonana, Australia 93 F3 31 0 S 123 0 E
Coondapoor, India 66 N9 13 42N 74 40 E
Cooninie, L., Australia 95 D2 26 4 S 139 59 E
Cooper, U.S.A. 113 J7 33 23N 95 42W
Cooper Cr. →, Australia 95 D2 28 29 S 137 46 E
Cooperstown, N. Dak., U.S.A. 112 B5 47 27N 98 8W
Cooperstown, N.Y., U.S.A. 111 D10 42 42N 74 56W
Coorabie, Australia 93 F5 31 54 S 132 18 E
Coorow, Australia 93 E2 29 53 S 116 2 E
Cooroy, Australia 95 D5 26 22 S 152 54 E
Coos Bay, U.S.A. 114 E1 43 22N 124 13W
Coosa →, U.S.A. 109 J2 32 30N 86 16W
Cootamundra, Australia 95 E4 34 36 S 148 1 E
Cootehill, Ireland 15 B4 54 4N 7 5W
Copahue Paso, Argentina 126 D1 37 49 S 71 8W
Copainalá, Mexico 119 D6 17 8N 93 11W
Copake Falls, U.S.A. 111 D11 42 7N 73 31W
Copalnic Mănăştur, Romania 43 C8 47 30N 23 41 E
Copán, Honduras 120 D2 14 50N 89 9W
Cope, U.S.A. 112 F3 39 40N 102 51W
Cope, C., Spain 33 H3 37 26N 1 28W
Copenhagen = København, Denmark 11 J6 55 41N 12 34 E
Copenhagen, U.S.A. 111 C9 43 54N 75 41W
Copertino, Italy 31 B11 40 16N 18 3 E
Copiapó, Chile 126 B1 27 30 S 70 20W
Copiapó →, Chile 126 B1 27 19 S 70 56W
Coplay, U.S.A. 111 F9 40 44N 75 29W
Copp L., Canada 104 A6 60 14N 114 40W
Copparo, Italy 29 D8 44 54N 11 49 E
Coppename →, Surinam 125 B7 5 48N 55 55W
Copper Harbor, U.S.A. 108 B2 47 28N 87 53W
Copper Queen, Zimbabwe 87 F2 17 29 S 29 18 E
Copperas Cove, U.S.A. 113 K6 31 8N 97 54W
Copperbelt □, Zambia 87 E2 13 15 S 27 30 E
Coppermine = Kugluktuk, Canada 100 B8 67 50N 115 5W
Coppermine →, Canada 100 B8 67 49N 116 4W
Copperopolis, U.S.A. 116 H6 37 58N 120 38W
Copşa Mică, Romania 43 D9 46 7N 24 15 E
Coquet →, U.K. 12 B6 55 20N 1 32W
Coquilhatville = Mbandaka, Dem. Rep. of the Congo 84 D3 0 1N 18 18 E
Coquille, U.S.A. 114 E1 43 11N 124 11W
Coquimbo, Chile 126 C1 30 0 S 71 20W
Coquimbo □, Chile 126 C1 31 0 S 71 0W
Corabia, Romania 43 G9 43 48N 24 30 E
Coracora, Peru 124 G4 15 5 S 73 45W
Coraki, Australia 95 D5 28 59 S 153 17 E
Coral, U.S.A. 110 F5 40 29N 79 10W
Coral Gables, U.S.A. 109 N5 25 45N 80 16W
Coral Harbour = Salliq, Canada 101 B11 64 8N 83 10W
Coral Sea, Pac. Oc. 96 J7 15 0 S 150 0 E
Coral Springs, U.S.A. 109 M5 26 16N 80 13W
Coraopolis, U.S.A. 110 F4 40 31N 80 10W
Corato, Italy 31 A9 41 9N 16 25 E
Corbeil-Essonnes, France 19 D9 48 36N 2 26 E
Corbie, France 19 C9 49 54N 2 30 E
Corbières, France 20 F6 42 55N 2 35 E
Corbigny, France 19 E10 47 16N 3 40 E
Corbin, U.S.A. 108 G3 36 57N 84 6W
Corbones →, Spain 35 H5 37 36N 5 39W
Corbu, Romania 43 F13 44 25N 28 39 E
Corby, U.K. 13 E7 52 30N 0 41W
Corcaigh = Cork, Ireland 15 E3 51 54N 8 29W
Corcoran, U.S.A. 116 J7 36 6N 119 33W
Cordele, U.S.A. 109 K4 31 58N 83 47W
Cordell, U.S.A. 113 H5 35 17N 98 59W
Cordenòns, Italy 29 C9 45 59N 12 42 E
Cordes, France 20 D5 44 5N 1 57 E
Córdoba, Argentina 126 C3 31 20 S 64 10W
Córdoba, Mexico 119 D5 18 50N 97 0W
Córdoba, Spain 35 H6 37 50N 4 50W
Córdoba □, Argentina 126 C3 31 22 S 64 15W
Córdoba □, Spain 35 G6 38 5N 5 0W
Córdoba, Sierra de, Argentina 126 C3 31 10 S 64 25W
Cordon, Phil. 61 C4 16 42N 121 32 E
Cordova, U.S.A. 100 B5 60 33N 145 45W
Corella, Spain 32 C3 42 7N 1 48W
Corella →, Australia 94 B3 19 34 S 140 47 E
Corfield, Australia 94 C3 21 40 S 143 21 E
Corfu = Kérkira, Greece 36 A3 39 38N 19 50 E
Corfu, Str. of, Greece 36 A4 39 34N 20 0 E
Corgo = O Corgo, Spain 34 C3 42 56N 7 25W
Cori, Italy 30 A5 41 39N 12 55 E
Coria, Spain 34 F4 39 58N 6 33W
Coria del Río, Spain 35 H4 37 16N 6 3W
Corigliano Cálabro, Italy 31 C9 39 36N 16 31 E
Coringa Is., Australia 94 B4 16 58 S 149 58 E
Corinth = Kórinthos, Greece 38 D4 37 56N 22 55 E
Corinth, Miss., U.S.A. 109 H1 34 56N 88 31W
Corinth, N.Y., U.S.A. 111 C11 43 15N 73 49W
Corinth, G. of = Korinthiakós Kólpos, Greece 38 C4 38 16N 22 30 E
Corinth Canal, Greece 38 D4 37 58N 23 0 E
Corinto, Brazil 125 G10 18 20 S 44 30W
Corinto, Nic. 120 D2 12 30N 87 10W
Cork, Ireland 15 E3 51 54N 8 29W
Cork □, Ireland 15 E3 51 57N 8 40W
Cork Harbour, Ireland 15 E3 51 47N 8 16W
Corlay, France 18 D3 48 20N 3 5W
Corleone, Italy 30 E6 37 49N 13 18 E
Corleto Perticara, Italy 31 B9 40 23N 16 2 E
Çorlu, Turkey 41 E11 41 11N 27 49 E
Cormack L., Canada 104 A4 60 56N 121 37W
Cormòns, Italy 29 C10 45 58N 13 28 E
Cormorant, Canada 105 C8 54 14N 100 35W
Cormorant L., Canada 105 C8 54 15N 100 50W
Corn Is. = Maíz, Is. del, Nic. 120 D3 12 15N 83 4W
Cornélio Procópio, Brazil 127 A5 23 7 S 50 40W
Corner Brook, Canada 103 C8 48 57N 57 58W
Corneşti, Moldova 43 C13 47 21N 28 1 E
Corníglio, Italy 28 D7 44 29N 10 5 E
Corning, Ark., U.S.A. 113 G9 36 25N 90 35W
Corning, Calif., U.S.A. 114 G2 39 56N 122 11W
Corning, Iowa, U.S.A. 112 E7 40 59N 94 44W
Corning, N.Y., U.S.A. 110 D7 42 9N 77 3W
Corno Grande, Italy 29 F10 42 28N 13 34 E
Cornwall, Canada 102 C5 45 2N 74 44W
Cornwall, U.S.A. 111 F8 40 17N 76 25W
Cornwall □, U.K. 13 G3 50 26N 4 40W
Corny Pt., Australia 95 E2 34 55 S 137 0 E
Coro, Venezuela 124 A5 11 25N 69 41W
Coroatá, Brazil 125 D10 4 8 S 44 0W
Corocoro, Bolivia 124 G5 17 15 S 68 28W
Coroico, Bolivia 124 G5 16 0 S 67 50W
Coromandel, N.Z. 91 G5 36 45 S 175 31 E
Coromandel Coast, India 66 N12 12 30N 81 0 E
Corona, Calif., U.S.A. 117 M9 33 53N 117 34W
Corona, N. Mex., U.S.A. 115 J11 34 15N 105 36W
Coronach, Canada 105 D7 49 7N 105 31W
Coronado, U.S.A. 117 N9 32 41N 117 11W
Coronado, B. de, Costa Rica 120 E3 9 0N 83 40W
Coronados, Is. los, U.S.A. 117 N9 32 25N 117 15W
Coronation, Canada 104 C6 52 5N 111 27W
Coronation Gulf, Canada 100 B8 68 25N 110 0W
Coronation I., Antarctica 5 C18 60 45 S 46 0W
Coronation Is., Australia 92 B3 14 57 S 124 55 E
Coronda, Argentina 126 C3 31 58 S 60 56W
Coronel, Chile 126 D1 37 0 S 73 10W
Coronel Bogado, Paraguay 126 B4 27 11 S 56 18W
Coronel Dorrego, Argentina 126 D3 38 40 S 61 10W
Coronel Oviedo, Paraguay 126 B4 25 24 S 56 30W
Coronel Pringles, Argentina 126 D3 38 0 S 61 30W
Coronel Suárez, Argentina 126 D3 37 30 S 61 52W
Coronel Vidal, Argentina 126 D4 37 28 S 57 45W
Coropuna, Nevado, Peru 124 G4 15 30 S 72 41W
Çorovoda = Çorovodë, Albania 40 F4 40 31N 20 14 E
Çorovodë, Albania 40 F4 40 31N 20 14 E
Corowa, Australia 95 F4 35 58 S 146 21 E
Corozal, Belize 119 D7 18 23N 88 23W
Corps, France 21 D9 44 50N 5 56 E
Corpus, Argentina 127 B4 27 10 S 55 30W
Corpus Christi, U.S.A. 113 M6 27 47N 97 24W
Corpus Christi, L., U.S.A. 113 L6 28 2N 97 52W
Corral de Almaguer, Spain 34 F7 39 45N 3 10W
Corralejo, Canary Is. 37 F6 28 43N 13 53W
Corran Pen., Ireland 15 C2 53 54N 9 54W
Corréggio, Italy 28 D7 44 46N 10 47 E
Correntes, C. das, Mozam. 89 C6 24 6 S 35 34 E
Corrèze □, France 20 C5 45 20N 1 45 E
Corrèze →, France 20 C5 45 10N 1 28 E
Corrib, L., Ireland 15 C2 53 27N 9 16W
Corridónia, Italy 29 E10 43 15N 13 30 E
Corrientes, Argentina 126 B4 27 30 S 58 45W
Corrientes □, Argentina 126 B4 28 0 S 57 0W
Corrientes →, Argentina 126 C4 30 42 S 59 38W
Corrientes →, Peru 124 D4 3 43 S 74 35W
Corrientes, C., Colombia 124 B3 5 30N 77 34W
Corrientes, C., Cuba 120 B3 21 43N 84 30W
Corrientes, C., Mexico 118 C3 20 25N 105 42W
Corrigan, U.S.A. 113 K7 31 0N 94 52W
Corrigin, Australia 93 F2 32 20 S 117 53 E
Corry, U.S.A. 110 E5 41 55N 79 39W
Corryong, Australia 95 F4 36 12 S 147 53 E
Corse, France 21 G13 42 0N 9 0 E
Corse, C., France 21 E13 43 1N 9 25 E
Corse-du-Sud □, France 21 G13 41 45N 9 0 E
Corsica = Corse, France 21 G13 42 0N 9 0 E
Corsicana, U.S.A. 113 J6 32 6N 96 28W
Corte, France 21 F13 42 19N 9 11 E
Corte Pinto, Portugal 35 H3 37 42N 7 29W
Cortegana, Spain 35 H4 37 52N 6 49W
Cortez, U.S.A. 115 H9 37 21N 108 35W
Cortina d'Ampezzo, Italy 29 B9 46 32N 12 8 E
Cortland, N.Y., U.S.A. 111 D8 42 36N 76 11W
Cortland, Ohio, U.S.A. 110 E4 41 20N 80 44W
Cortona, Italy 29 E8 43 16N 11 59 E
Corubal →, Guinea-Biss. 82 C2 11 57N 15 5W
Coruche, Portugal 35 G2 38 57N 8 30W
Çoruh →, Turkey 49 K5 41 38N 41 38 E
Çorum, Turkey 72 B6 40 30N 34 57 E
Corumbá, Brazil 124 G7 19 0 S 57 30W
Corund, Romania 43 D10 46 30N 25 13 E
Corunna = A Coruña, Spain 34 B2 43 20N 8 25W
Corvallis, U.S.A. 114 D2 44 34N 123 16W
Corvette, L. de la, Canada 102 B5 53 25N 74 3W
Corydon, U.S.A. 112 E8 40 46N 93 19W
Cosalá, Mexico 118 C3 24 28N 106 40W
Cosamaloapan, Mexico 119 D5 18 23N 95 50W
Cosenza, Italy 31 C9 39 18N 16 15 E
Coşereni, Romania 43 F11 44 38N 26 35 E
Coshocton, U.S.A. 110 F3 40 16N 81 51W
Cosmo Newberry, Australia 93 E3 28 0 S 122 54 E
Cosne-Cours-sur-Loire, France 19 E9 47 24N 2 54 E
Coso Junction, U.S.A. 117 J9 36 3N 117 57W
Coso Pk., U.S.A. 117 J9 36 13N 117 44W
Cospeito, Spain 34 B3 43 12N 7 34W
Cosquín, Argentina 126 C3 31 15 S 64 30W
Cossato, Italy 28 C5 45 34N 8 10 E
Cossé-le-Vivien, France 18 E6 47 57N 0 54W
Cosson →, France 18 E8 47 30N 1 15 E
Costa Blanca, Spain 33 G4 38 25N 0 10W
Costa Brava, Spain 32 D8 41 30N 3 0 E
Costa del Sol, Spain 35 J6 36 30N 4 30W
Costa Dorada, Spain 32 D6 41 12N 1 15 E
Costa Mesa, U.S.A. 117 M9 33 38N 117 55W
Costa Rica ■, Cent. Amer. 120 E3 10 0N 84 0W
Costa Smeralda, Italy 30 A2 41 5N 9 35 E
Costeşti, Romania 43 F9 44 40N 24 53 E
Costigliole d'Asti, Italy 28 D5 44 47N 8 11 E
Cosumnes →, U.S.A. 116 G5 38 16N 121 26W
Coswig, Sachsen, Germany 24 D9 51 7N 13 34 E
Coswig, Sachsen-Anhalt, Germany 24 D8 51 53N 12 27 E
Cotabato, Phil. 61 H6 7 14N 124 15 E
Cotagaita, Bolivia 126 A2 20 45 S 65 40W
Côte d'Azur, France 21 E11 43 25N 7 10 E
Côte-d'Ivoire = Ivory Coast ■, Africa 82 D4 7 30N 5 0W
Côte d'Or, France 19 E11 47 10N 4 50 E
Côte-d'Or □, France 19 E11 47 30N 4 50 E
Coteau des Prairies, U.S.A. 112 C6 45 20N 97 50W
Coteau du Missouri, U.S.A. 112 B4 47 0N 100 0W
Coteau Landing, Canada 111 A10 45 15N 74 13W
Cotentin, France 18 C5 49 15N 1 30W
Côtes-d'Armor □, France 18 D4 48 25N 2 40W
Côtes de Meuse, France 19 C12 49 15N 5 22 E
Côtes-du-Nord = Côtes-d'Armor □, France 18 D4 48 25N 2 40W
Cotiella, Spain 32 C5 42 31N 0 19 E
Cotillo, Canary Is. 37 F5 28 41N 14 1W
Cotiujeni, Moldova 43 C13 47 51N 28 33 E
Cotonou, Benin 83 D5 6 20N 2 25 E
Cotopaxi, Ecuador 122 D3 0 40 S 78 30W
Cotronei, Italy 31 C9 39 9N 16 47 E
Cotswold Hills, U.K. 13 F5 51 42N 2 10W
Cottage Grove, U.S.A. 114 E2 43 48N 123 3W
Cottbus, Germany 24 D10 51 45N 14 20 E
Cottonwood, U.S.A. 115 J7 34 45N 112 1W
Cotulla, U.S.A. 113 L5 28 26N 99 14W
Coubre, Pte. de la, France 20 C2 45 42N 1 15W
Couches, France 19 F11 46 53N 4 30 E
Couço, Portugal 35 G2 38 59N 8 17W
Coudersport, U.S.A. 110 E6 41 46N 78 1W
Couedic, C. du, Australia 95 F2 36 5 S 136 40 E
Couëron, France 18 E5 47 13N 1 44W
Couesnon →, France 18 D5 48 38N 1 32W
Couhé, France 20 B4 46 17N 0 11 E
Coulanges-sur-Yonne, France 19 E10 47 31N 3 33 E
Coulee City, U.S.A. 114 C4 47 37N 119 17W
Coulman I., Antarctica 5 D11 73 35 S 170 0 E
Coulommiers, France 19 D10 48 50N 3 3 E
Coulon →, France 21 E9 43 51N 5 6 E
Coulonge →, Canada 102 C4 45 52N 76 46W
Coulonges-sur-l'Autize, France 20 B3 46 29N 0 36W
Coulounieix-Chamiers, France 20 C4 45 11N 0 42 E
Coulterville, U.S.A. 116 H6 37 43N 120 12W
Council, U.S.A. 114 D5 44 44N 116 26W
Council Bluffs, U.S.A. 112 E7 41 16N 95 52W
Council Grove, U.S.A. 112 F6 38 40N 96 29W
Coupeville, U.S.A. 116 B4 48 13N 122 41W
Courantyne →, S. Amer. 122 C5 5 55N 57 5W
Courcelles, Belgium 17 D4 50 28N 4 22 E
Courçon, France 20 B3 46 15N 0 50W
Courmayeur, Italy 28 C3 45 47N 6 58 E
Couronne, C., France 21 E9 43 19N 5 3 E
Cours-la-Ville, France 19 F11 46 7N 4 19 E
Coursan, France 20 E7 43 14N 3 4 E
Courseulles-sur-Mer, France 18 C6 49 20N 0 29W
Courtenay, Canada 104 D4 49 45N 125 0W
Courtenay, France 19 D10 48 2N 3 3 E
Courtland, U.S.A. 116 G5 38 20N 121 34W
Courtrai = Kortrijk, Belgium 17 D3 50 50N 3 17 E
Courtright, Canada 110 D2 42 49N 82 28W
Coushatta, U.S.A. 113 J8 32 1N 93 21W
Coutances, France 18 C5 49 3N 1 28W
Coutras, France 20 C3 45 3N 0 8W
Coutts Crossing, Australia 95 D5 29 49 S 152 55 E
Couvin, Belgium 17 D4 50 3N 4 29 E
Covarrubias, Spain 34 C7 42 4N 3 31W
Covasna, Romania 43 E11 45 50N 26 10 E
Covasna □, Romania 43 E10 45 50N 26 0 E
Cove I., Canada 110 A3 45 17N 81 44W
Coventry, U.K. 13 E6 52 25N 1 28W
Covilhã, Portugal 34 E3 40 17N 7 31W
Covington, Ga., U.S.A. 109 J4 33 36N 83 51W
Covington, Ky., U.S.A. 108 F3 39 5N 84 31W
Covington, Okla., U.S.A. 113 G6 36 18N 97 35W
Covington, Tenn., U.S.A. 113 H10 35 34N 89 39W
Covington, Va., U.S.A. 108 G5 37 47N 79 59W
Cowal, L., Australia 95 E4 33 40 S 147 25 E
Cowan, L., Australia 93 F3 31 45 S 121 45 E
Cowan L., Canada 105 C7 54 0N 107 15W
Cowangie, Australia 95 F3 35 12 S 141 26 E
Cowansville, Canada 102 C5 45 14N 72 46W
Coward Springs, Australia 95 D2 29 24 S 136 49 E
Cowcowing Lakes, Australia 93 F2 30 55 S 117 20 E
Cowdenbeath, U.K. 14 E5 56 7N 3 21W
Cowell, Australia 95 E2 33 39 S 136 56 E
Cowes, U.K. 13 G6 50 45N 1 18W
Cowichan L., Canada 116 B2 48 53N 124 17W
Cowlitz →, U.S.A. 116 D4 46 6N 122 55W
Cowra, Australia 95 E4 33 49 S 148 42 E
Cox, Spain 33 G4 38 8N 0 53W
Coxilha Grande, Brazil 127 B5 28 18 S 51 30W
Coxim, Brazil 125 G8 18 30 S 54 55W
Cox's Bazar, Bangla. 67 J17 21 26N 91 59 E
Coyote Wells, U.S.A. 117 N11 32 44N 115 58W
Coyuca de Benítez, Mexico 119 D4 17 1N 100 8W
Coyuca de Catalan, Mexico 118 D4 18 18N 100 41W
Cozad, U.S.A. 112 E5 40 52N 99 59W
Cozes, France 20 C3 45 34N 0 49W
Cozumel, Mexico 119 C7 20 31N 86 55W
Cozumel, Isla, Mexico 119 C7 20 30N 86 40W
Cracow = Kraków, Poland 45 H6 50 4N 19 57 E
Cracow, Australia 95 D5 25 17 S 150 17 E
Cradock, Australia 95 E2 32 6 S 138 31 E
Cradock, S. Africa 88 E4 32 8 S 25 36 E
Craig, U.S.A. 114 F10 40 31N 107 33W
Craigavon, U.K. 15 B5 54 27N 6 23W
Craigmore, Zimbabwe 87 G3 20 28 S 32 50 E
Craik, Canada 105 C7 51 3N 105 49W
Crailsheim, Germany 25 F6 49 8N 10 5 E
Craiova, Romania 43 F8 44 21N 23 48 E
Cramsie, Australia 94 C3 23 20 S 144 15 E
Cranberry L., U.S.A. 111 B10 44 11N 74 50W
Cranberry Portage, Canada 105 C8 54 35N 101 23W
Cranbrook, Australia 93 F2 34 18 S 117 33 E
Cranbrook, Canada 104 D5 49 30N 115 46W
Crandon, U.S.A. 112 C10 45 34N 88 54W
Crane, Oreg., U.S.A. 114 E4 43 25N 118 35W
Crane, Tex., U.S.A. 113 K3 31 24N 102 21W
Cranston, U.S.A. 111 E13 41 47N 71 26W
Craon, France 18 E6 47 50N 0 58W
Craonne, France 19 C10 49 27N 3 46 E
Craponne-sur-Arzon, France 20 C7 45 19N 3 51 E
Crasna, Romania 43 D12 46 32N 27 51 E
Crasna →, Romania 42 C7 47 44N 22 35 E
Crasnei, Muntii, Romania 43 C8 47 0N 23 20 E
Crater L., U.S.A. 114 E2 42 56N 122 6W
Crater Lake National Park, U.S.A. 114 E2 42 55N 122 10W
Crateús, Brazil 125 E10 5 10 S 40 39W
Crati →, Italy 31 C9 39 43N 16 31 E
Crato, Brazil 125 E11 7 10 S 39 25W
Crato, Portugal 35 F3 39 16N 7 39W
Craven, L., Canada 102 B4 54 20N 76 56W
Crawford, U.S.A. 112 D3 42 41N 103 25W
Crawfordsville, U.S.A. 108 E2 40 2N 86 54W
Crawley, U.K. 13 F7 51 7N 0 11W
Crazy Mts., U.S.A. 114 C8 46 12N 110 20W
Crean L., Canada 105 C7 54 5N 106 9W
Crécy-en-Ponthieu, France 19 B8 50 15N 1 53 E
Crediton, Canada 110 C3 43 17N 81 33W
Cree →, Canada 105 B7 58 57N 105 47W
Cree →, U.K. 14 G4 54 55N 4 25W
Cree L., Canada 105 B7 57 30N 106 30W
Creede, U.S.A. 115 H10 37 51N 106 56W
Creekside, U.S.A. 110 F5 40 40N 79 11W
Creel, Mexico 118 B3 27 45N 107 38W
Creemore, Canada 110 B4 44 19N 80 6W
Creighton, Canada 105 C8 54 45N 101 54W
Creighton, U.S.A. 112 D6 42 28N 97 54W
Creil, France 19 C9 49 15N 2 29 E
Crema, Italy 28 C6 45 22N 9 41 E
Cremona, Italy 28 C7 45 7N 10 2 E
Crepaja, Serbia, Yug. 42 E5 45 1N 20 38 E
Crépy, France 19 C10 49 35N 3 32 E
Crépy-en-Valois, France 19 C9 49 14N 2 54 E
Cres, Croatia 29 D11 44 58N 14 25 E
Crescent City, U.S.A. 114 F1 41 45N 124 12W
Crescentino, Italy 28 C5 45 11N 8 6 E
Crespo, Argentina 126 C3 32 2 S 60 19W
Cresson, U.S.A. 110 F6 40 28N 78 36W
Crest, France 21 D9 44 44N 5 2 E
Cresta, Mt., Phil. 61 C5 17 17N 122 6 E
Crestline, Calif., U.S.A. 117 L9 34 14N 117 18W
Crestline, Ohio, U.S.A. 110 F2 40 47N 82 44W
Creston, Canada 104 D5 49 10N 116 31W
Creston, Calif., U.S.A. 116 K6 35 32N 120 33W
Creston, Iowa, U.S.A. 112 E7 41 4N 94 22W
Crestview, Calif., U.S.A. 116 H8 37 46N 118 58W
Crestview, Fla., U.S.A. 109 K2 30 46N 86 34W
Crêt de la Neige, France 19 F12 46 16N 5 58 E
Crete = Kríti, Greece 36 D7 35 15N 25 0 E
Crete, U.S.A. 112 E6 40 38N 96 58W
Crete, Sea of, Greece 39 E7 36 0N 25 0 E
Créteil, France 19 D9 48 47N 2 28 E
Creus, C. de, Spain 32 C8 42 20N 3 19 E
Creuse □, France 19 F9 46 10N 2 0 E
Creuse →, France 20 B4 47 0N 0 34 E
Creutzwald, France 19 C13 49 12N 6 42 E
Creuzburg, Germany 24 D6 51 3N 10 14 E
Crèvecœur-le-Grand, France 19 C9 49 37N 2 5 E
Crevillente, Spain 33 G4 38 12N 0 48W
Crewe, U.K. 12 D5 53 6N 2 26W
Crewkerne, U.K. 13 G5 50 53N 2 48W
Criciúma, Brazil 127 B6 28 40 S 49 23W
Cricova, Moldova 43 C13 47 8N 28 52 E
Crieff, U.K. 14 E5 56 22N 3 50W
Crikvenica, Croatia 29 C11 45 11N 14 40 E
Crimea □, Ukraine 47 K8 45 30N 33 10 E
Crimean Pen. = Krymskyy Pivostriv, Ukraine 47 K8 45 0N 34 0 E
Crimmitschau, Germany 24 E8 50 48N 12 24 E
Cristuru Secuiesc, Romania 43 D10 46 17N 25 2 E
Crişul Alb →, Romania 42 D6 46 42N 21 17 E
Crişul Negru →, Romania 42 D6 46 42N 21 16 E
Crişul Repede →, Romania 42 D5 46 55N 20 59 E
Criuleni, Moldova 43 C14 47 13N 29 10 E
Crivitz, Germany 24 B7 53 34N 11 39 E
Crna →, Macedonia 40 E5 41 33N 21 59 E
Crna Gora = Montenegro □, Yugoslavia 40 D3 42 40N 19 20 E
Crna Gora, Macedonia 40 D5 42 10N 21 30 E
Crna Reka = Crna →, Macedonia 40 E5 41 33N 21 59 E
Crna Trava, Serbia, Yug. 40 D6 42 49N 22 19 E
Crni Drim →, Macedonia 40 E4 41 17N 20 40 E
Crni Timok →, Serbia, Yug. 40 C6 43 53N 22 15 E
Crnoljeva Planina, Kosovo, Yug. 40 D5 42 20N 21 0 E
Črnomelj, Slovenia 29 C12 45 33N 15 10 E
Croagh Patrick, Ireland 15 C2 53 46N 9 40W
Croatia ■, Europe 29 C13 45 20N 16 0 E
Crocker, Banjaran, Malaysia 62 C5 5 40N 116 30 E
Crockett, U.S.A. 113 K7 31 19N 95 27W
Crocodile = Krokodil →, Mozam. 89 D5 25 14 S 32 18 E
Crocodile Is., Australia 94 A1 12 3 S 134 58 E
Crocq, France 20 C6 45 52N 2 21 E
Crodo, Italy 28 B5 46 13N 8 19 E
Crohy Hd., Ireland 15 B3 54 55N 8 26W
Croisette, C., France 21 E9 43 14N 5 22 E
Croisic, Pte. du, France 18 E4 47 19N 2 31W
Croix, L. La, Canada 102 C1 48 20N 92 15W
Croker, C., Australia 92 B5 10 58 S 132 35 E
Croker, C., Canada 110 B4 44 58N 80 59W
Croker I., Australia 92 B5 11 12 S 132 32 E
Cromarty, U.K. 14 D4 57 40N 4 2W
Cromer, U.K. 12 E9 52 56N 1 17 E
Cromwell, N.Z. 91 L2 45 3 S 169 14 E
Cromwell, U.S.A. 111 E12 41 36N 72 39W
Cronat, France 19 F10 46 43N 3 40 E
Crook, U.K. 12 C6 54 43N 1 45W
Crooked →, Canada 104 C4 54 50N 122 54W
Crooked →, U.S.A. 114 D3 44 32N 121 16W
Crooked I., Bahamas 121 B5 22 50N 74 10W
Crooked Island Passage, Bahamas 121 B5 23 0N 74 30W
Crookston, Minn., U.S.A. 112 B6 47 47N 96 37W
Crookston, Nebr., U.S.A. 112 D4 42 56N 100 45W
Crookwell, Australia 95 E4 34 28 S 149 24 E
Crosby, U.K. 12 D4 53 30N 3 3W
Crosby, N. Dak., U.S.A. 112 A3 48 55N 103 18W
Crosby, Pa., U.S.A. 110 E6 41 45N 78 23W
Crosbyton, U.S.A. 113 J4 33 40N 101 14W
Crosía, Italy 31 C9 39 35N 16 45 E
Cross →, Nigeria 83 E6 4 42N 8 21 E
Cross City, U.S.A. 109 L4 29 38N 83 7W
Cross Fell, U.K. 12 C5 54 43N 2 28W
Cross L., Canada 105 C9 54 45N 97 30W
Cross Lake, Canada 105 C9 54 37N 97 47W
Cross River □, Nigeria 83 D6 6 0N 8 0 E
Cross Sound, U.S.A. 100 C6 58 0N 135 0W
Crossett, U.S.A. 113 J9 33 8N 91 58W
Crosshaven, Ireland 15 E3 51 47N 8 17W
Crossville, U.S.A. 109 G3 35 57N 85 2W
Croswell, U.S.A. 110 C2 43 16N 82 37W
Croton-on-Hudson, U.S.A. 111 E11 41 12N 73 55W
Crotone, Italy 31 C10 39 5N 17 8 E
Crow →, Canada 104 B4 59 41N 124 20W
Crow Agency, U.S.A. 114 D10 45 36N 107 28W
Crow Hd., Ireland 15 E1 51 35N 10 9W
Crowell, U.S.A. 113 J5 33 59N 99 43W
Crowley, U.S.A. 113 K8 30 13N 92 22W
Crowley, L., U.S.A. 116 H8 37 35N 118 42W
Crown Point, Ind., U.S.A. 108 E2 41 25N 87 22W
Crown Point, N.Y., U.S.A. 111 C11 43 57N 73 26W
Crownpoint, U.S.A. 115 J9 35 41N 108 9W
Crows Landing, U.S.A. 116 H5 37 23N 121 6W
Crows Nest, Australia 95 D5 27 16 S 152 4 E
Crowsnest Pass, Canada 104 D6 49 40N 114 40W
Croydon, Australia 94 B3 18 13 S 142 14 E
Croydon, U.K. 13 F7 51 22N 0 5W
Crozet, Is., Ind. Oc. 3 G12 46 27 S 52 0 E
Crozon, France 18 D2 48 15N 4 30W
Cruz, C., Cuba 120 C4 19 50N 77 50W
Cruz Alta, Brazil 127 B5 28 45 S 53 40W
Cruz de Incio, Spain 34 C3 42 39N 7 21W
Cruz del Eje, Argentina 126 C3 30 45 S 64 50W
Cruzeiro, Brazil 127 A7 22 33 S 45 0W
Cruzeiro do Oeste, Brazil 127 A5 23 46 S 53 4W
Cruzeiro do Sul, Brazil 124 E4 7 35 S 72 35W
Cry L., Canada 104 B3 58 45N 129 0W
Crystal Bay, U.S.A. 116 F7 39 15N 120 0W
Crystal Brook, Australia 95 E2 33 21 S 138 12 E
Crystal City, U.S.A. 113 L5 28 41N 99 50W
Crystal Falls, U.S.A. 108 B1 46 5N 88 20W
Crystal River, U.S.A. 109 L4 28 54N 82 35W
Crystal Springs, U.S.A. 113 K9 31 59N 90 21W
Csenger, Hungary 42 C7 47 50N 22 41 E
Csongrád, Hungary 42 D5 46 43N 20 12 E
Csongrád □, Hungary 42 D5 46 32N 20 15 E
Csorna, Hungary 42 C2 47 38N 17 18 E
Csurgo, Hungary 42 D2 46 16N 17 9 E
Cu Lao Hon, Vietnam 65 G7 10 54N 108 18 E
Cua Rao, Vietnam 64 C5 19 16N 104 27 E
Cuácua →, Mozam. 87 F4 17 54 S 37 0 E
Cuamato, Angola 88 B2 17 2 S 15 7 E
Cuamba, Mozam. 87 E4 14 45 S 36 22 E
Cuando →, Angola 85 H4 17 30 S 23 15 E
Cuando Cubango □, Angola 88 B3 16 25 S 20 0 E
Cuangar, Angola 88 B2 17 36 S 18 39 E
Cuango = Kwango →, Dem. Rep. of the Congo 77 G5 3 14 S 17 22 E
Cuanza →, Angola 76 G5 9 21 S 13 9 E
Cuarto →, Argentina 126 C3 33 25 S 63 2W
Cuatrociénegas, Mexico 118 B4 26 59N 102 5W
Cuauhtémoc, Mexico 118 B3 28 25N 106 52W
Cuba, Portugal 35 G3 38 10N 7 54W
Cuba, N. Mex., U.S.A. 115 J10 36 1N 107 4W
Cuba, N.Y., U.S.A. 110 D6 42 13N 78 17W
Cuba ■, W. Indies 120 B4 22 0N 79 0W
Cubango →, Africa 88 B3 18 50 S 22 25 E
Çubuk, Turkey 72 B5 40 14N 33 3 E
Cuchumatanes, Sierra de los, Guatemala 120 C1 15 35N 91 25W
Cuckfield, U.K. 13 F7 51 1N 0 8W
Cucuí, Brazil 124 C5 1 12N 66 50W
Cucurpe, Mexico 118 A2 30 20N 110 43W
Cúcuta, Colombia 124 B4 7 54N 72 31W
Cudalbi, Romania 43 E12 45 46N 27 41 E
Cuddalore, India 66 P11 11 46N 79 45 E
Cuddapah, India 66 M11 14 30N 78 47 E
Cuddapan, L., Australia 94 D3 25 45 S 141 26 E
Cudillero, Spain 34 B4 43 33N 6 9W
Cue, Australia 93 E2 27 25 S 117 54 E
Cuéllar, Spain 34 D6 41 23N 4 21W
Cuenca, Ecuador 124 D3 2 50 S 79 9W
Cuenca, Spain 32 E2 40 5N 2 10W
Cuenca □, Spain 32 F3 40 0N 2 0W
Cuenca, Serranía de, Spain 32 F3 39 55N 1 50W
Cuerdo del Pozo, Embalse de la, Spain 32 D2 41 51N 2 44W
Cuernavaca, Mexico 119 D5 18 55N 99 15W
Cuero, U.S.A. 113 L6 29 6N 97 17W
Cuers, France 21 E10 43 14N 6 5 E
Cuevas del Almanzora, Spain 33 H3 37 18N 1 58W
Cuevo, Bolivia 124 H6 20 15 S 63 30W
Cugir, Romania 43 E8 45 48N 23 25 E
Cugnaux, France 20 E5 43 32N 1 20 E
Cuhai-Bakony →, Hungary 42 C2 47 35N 17 54 E

Cuiabá, Brazil 125 G7 15 30 S 56 0W
Cuiabá →, Brazil 125 G7 17 5 S 56 36W
Cuijk, Neths. 17 C5 51 44N 5 50 E
Cuilco, Guatemala 120 C1 15 24N 91 58W
Cuillin Hills, U.K. 14 D2 57 13N 6 15W
Cuillin Sd., U.K. 14 D2 57 4N 6 20W
Cuiseaux, France 19 F12 46 30N 5 22 E
Cuito →, Angola 88 B3 18 1 S 20 48 E
Cuitzeo, L. de, Mexico 118 D4 19 55N 101 5W
Cujmir, Romania 42 F7 44 13N 22 57 E
Cukai, Malaysia 65 K4 4 13N 103 25 E
Culbertson, U.S.A. 112 A2 48 9N 104 31W
Culcairn, Australia 95 F4 35 41 S 147 3 E
Culebra, Sierra de la, Spain 34 D4 41 55N 6 20W
Culfa, Azerbaijan 73 C11 38 57N 45 38 E
Culgoa →, Australia 95 D4 29 56 S 146 20 E
Culiacán, Mexico 118 C3 24 50N 107 23W
Culiacán →, Mexico 118 C3 24 30N 107 42W
Culion, Phil. 61 F4 11 54N 119 58 E
Cúllar, Spain 35 H8 37 35N 2 34W
Cullarin Ra., Australia 95 E4 34 30 S 149 30 E
Cullen, U.K. 14 D6 57 42N 2 49W
Cullen Pt., Australia 94 A3 11 57 S 141 54 E
Cullera, Spain 33 F4 39 9N 0 17W
Cullman, U.S.A. 109 H2 34 11N 86 51W
Culoz, France 21 C9 45 47N 5 46 E
Culpeper, U.S.A. 108 F7 38 30N 78 0W
Culuene →, Brazil 125 F8 12 56 S 52 51W
Culver, Pt., Australia 93 F3 32 54 S 124 43 E
Culverden, N.Z. 91 K4 42 47 S 172 49 E
Cumaná, Venezuela 124 A6 10 30N 64 5W
Cumaovası, Turkey 39 C9 38 15N 27 9 E
Cumberland, B.C., Canada 104 D4 49 40N 125 0W
Cumberland, Ont., Canada 111 A9 45 29N 75 24W
Cumberland, U.S.A. 108 F6 39 39N 78 46W
Cumberland →, U.S.A. 109 G2 36 15N 87 0W
Cumberland, L., U.S.A. 109 G3 36 57N 84 55W
Cumberland I., U.S.A. 109 K5 30 50N 81 25W
Cumberland Is., Australia 94 C4 20 35 S 149 10 E
Cumberland L., Canada 105 C8 54 3N 102 18W
Cumberland Pen., Canada 101 B13 67 0N 64 0W
Cumberland Plateau, U.S.A. 109 H3 36 0N 85 0W
Cumberland Sd., Canada 101 B13 65 30N 66 0W
Cumbernauld, U.K. 14 F5 55 57N 3 58W
Cumborah, Australia 95 D4 29 40 S 147 45 E
Cumbres Mayores, Spain 35 G4 38 4N 6 39W
Cumbria □, U.K. 12 C5 54 42N 2 52W
Cumbrian Mts., U.K. 12 C5 54 30N 3 0W
Cumbum, India 66 M11 15 40N 79 10 E
Cuminá →, Brazil 125 D7 1 30 S 56 0W
Cummings Mt., U.S.A. 117 K8 35 2N 118 34W
Cummins, Australia 95 E2 34 16 S 135 43 E
Cumnock, Australia 95 E4 32 59 S 148 46 E
Cumnock, U.K. 14 F4 55 28N 4 17W
Cumpas, Mexico 118 B3 30 0N 109 48W
Cumplida, Pta., Canary Is. 37 F2 28 50N 17 48W
Çumra, Turkey 72 D5 37 34N 32 45 E
Cunco, Chile 128 D2 38 55 S 72 2W
Cuncumén, Chile 126 C1 31 53 S 70 38W
Cunderdin, Australia 93 F2 31 37 S 117 12 E
Cunene →, Angola 88 B1 17 20 S 11 50 E
Cúneo, Italy 28 D4 44 23N 7 32 E
Çüngüş, Turkey 70 B3 38 13N 39 17 E
Cunillera, I. = Sa Conillera, Spain 37 C7 38 59N 1 13 E
Cunlhat, France 20 C7 45 38N 3 32 E
Cunnamulla, Australia 95 D4 28 2 S 145 38 E
Cuorgnè, Italy 28 C4 45 23N 7 39 E
Cupar, Canada 105 C8 50 57N 104 10W
Cupar, U.K. 14 E5 56 19N 3 1W
Cupcini, Moldova 43 B12 48 6N 27 23 E
Cupica, G. de, Colombia 124 B3 6 25N 77 30W
Ćuprija, Serbia, Yug. 40 C5 43 57N 21 26 E
Curaçao, Neth. Ant. 121 D6 12 10N 69 0W
Curanilahue, Chile 126 D1 37 29 S 73 28W
Curaray →, Peru 124 D4 2 20 S 74 5W
Cure →, France 19 E10 47 40N 3 41 E
Curepto, Chile 126 D1 35 8 S 72 1W
Curiapo, Venezuela 124 B6 8 33N 61 5W
Curicó, Chile 126 C1 34 55 S 71 20W
Curinga, Italy 31 D9 38 49N 16 19 E
Curitiba, Brazil 127 B6 25 20 S 49 10W
Curitibanos, Brazil 127 B5 27 18 S 50 36W
Currabubula, Australia 95 E5 31 16 S 150 44 E
Currais Novos, Brazil 125 E11 6 13 S 36 30W
Curralinho, Brazil 125 D9 1 45 S 49 46W
Currant, U.S.A. 114 G6 38 51N 115 32W
Current →, U.S.A. 113 G9 36 15N 90 55W
Currie, Australia 94 F3 39 56 S 143 53 E
Currie, U.S.A. 114 F6 40 16N 114 45W
Curtea de Argeș, Romania 43 E9 45 12N 24 42 E
Curtici, Romania 42 D6 46 21N 21 18 E
Curtis, U.S.A. 112 E4 40 38N 100 31W
Curtis Group, Australia 94 F4 39 30 S 146 37 E
Curtis I., Australia 94 C5 23 35 S 151 10 E
Curuápanema →, Brazil 125 D7 2 25 S 55 2W
Curuçá, Brazil 125 D9 0 43 S 47 50W
Curuguaty, Paraguay 127 A4 24 31 S 55 42W
Curup, Indonesia 62 E2 4 26 S 102 13 E
Cururupu, Brazil 125 D10 1 50 S 44 50W
Curuzú Cuatiá, Argentina 126 B4 29 50 S 58 5W
Curvelo, Brazil 125 G10 18 45 S 44 27W
Cushing, U.S.A. 113 H6 35 59N 96 46W
Cushing, Mt., Canada 104 B3 57 35N 126 57W
Cusihuiriáchic, Mexico 118 B3 28 10N 106 50W
Cusna, Mte., Italy 28 D7 44 17N 10 23 E
Cusset, France 19 F10 46 8N 3 28 E
Custer, U.S.A. 112 D3 43 46N 103 36W
Cut Bank, U.S.A. 114 B7 48 38N 112 20W
Cutchogue, U.S.A. 111 E12 41 1N 72 30W
Cuthbert, U.S.A. 109 K3 31 46N 84 48W
Cutler, U.S.A. 116 J7 36 31N 119 17W
Cutro, Italy 31 C9 39 2N 16 59 E
Cuttaburra →, Australia 95 D3 29 43 S 144 22 E
Cuttack, India 67 J14 20 25N 85 57 E
Cuvier, C., Australia 93 D1 23 14 S 113 22 E
Cuvier I., N.Z. 91 G5 36 27 S 175 50 E
Cuxhaven, Germany 24 B4 53 51N 8 41 E
Cuyahoga Falls, U.S.A. 110 E3 41 8N 81 29W
Cuyapo, Phil. 61 D4 15 46N 120 40 E
Cuyo, Phil. 61 F4 10 50N 121 5 E
Cuyo East Pass, Phil. 61 F4 11 0N 121 28 E
Cuyo West Pass, Phil. 61 F4 11 0N 120 30 E
Cuyuni →, Guyana 124 B7 6 23N 58 41W
Cuzco, Bolivia 124 H5 20 0 S 66 50W
Cuzco, Peru 124 F4 13 32 S 72 0W
Čvrsnica, Bos.-H. 42 G2 43 36N 17 35 E
Cwmbran, U.K. 13 F4 51 39N 3 2W
Cyangugu, Rwanda 86 C2 2 29 S 28 54 E
Cybinka, Poland 45 F1 52 12N 14 46 E
Cyclades = Kikládhes, Greece 38 E6 37 0N 24 30 E
Cygnet, Australia 94 G4 43 8 S 147 1 E
Cynthiana, U.S.A. 108 F3 38 23N 84 18W
Cypress Hills, Canada 105 D7 49 40N 109 30W
Cypress Hills Prov. Park, Canada 105 D7 49 40N 109 30W
Cyprus ■, Asia 36 E12 35 0N 33 0 E
Cyrenaica, Libya 79 C10 27 0N 23 0 E
Czaplinek, Poland 44 E3 53 34N 16 14 E
Czar, Canada 105 C6 52 27N 110 50W
Czarna →, Łódzkie, Poland 45 G6 51 18N 19 55 E
Czarna →, Świętokrzyskie, Poland 45 H8 50 28N 21 21 E
Czarna Białostocka, Poland 45 E10 53 18N 23 17 E
Czarna Woda, Poland 44 E5 53 51N 18 6 E
Czarne, Poland 44 E3 53 42N 16 58 E
Czarnków, Poland 45 F3 52 55N 16 38 E
Czech Rep. ■, Europe 26 B8 50 0N 15 0 E
Czechowice-Dziedzice, Poland 45 J5 49 54N 18 59 E
Czempiń, Poland 45 F3 52 9N 16 43 E
Czeremcha, Poland 45 F10 52 31N 23 21 E
Czerniejewo, Poland 45 F4 52 26N 17 30 E
Czersk, Poland 44 E4 53 46N 17 58 E
Czerwieńsk, Poland 45 F2 52 1N 15 23 E
Czerwionka-Leszczyny, Poland 45 H5 50 7N 18 37 E
Częstochowa, Poland 45 H6 50 49N 19 7 E
Człopa, Poland 45 E3 53 6N 16 6 E
Człuchów, Poland 44 E4 53 41N 17 22 E
Czyżew-Osada, Poland 45 F9 52 48N 22 19 E

D

Da →, Vietnam 58 G5 21 15N 105 20 E
Da Hinggan Ling, China 60 B7 48 0N 121 0 E
Da Lat, Vietnam 65 G7 11 56N 108 25 E
Da Nang, Vietnam 64 D7 16 4N 108 13 E
Da Qaidam, China 60 C4 37 50N 95 15 E
Da Yunhe →, China 57 G11 34 25N 120 5 E
Da'an, China 57 B13 45 30N 124 7 E
Dab'a, Ras el, Egypt 80 H6 31 3N 28 31 E
Daba Shan, China 58 B7 32 0N 109 0 E
Dabai, Nigeria 83 C6 11 25N 5 15 E
Dabakala, Ivory C. 82 D4 8 15N 4 20W
Dabas, Hungary 42 C4 47 11N 19 19 E
Dabat, Ethiopia 81 E4 12 58N 37 41 E
Dabbagh, Jabal, Si. Arabia 70 E2 27 52N 35 45 E
Dabhoi, India 68 H5 22 10N 73 20 E
Dąbie, Poland 45 F5 52 5N 18 50 E
Dabie Shan, China 59 B10 31 20N 115 20 E
Dabilda, Cameroon 83 C7 12 45N 14 35 E
Dabnou, Niger 83 C6 14 10N 5 22 E
Dabo = Pasirkuning, Indonesia 62 E2 0 30 S 104 33 E
Dabola, Guinea 82 C2 10 50N 11 5W
Dabou, Ivory C. 82 D4 5 20N 4 23W
Daboya, Ghana 83 D4 9 30N 1 20W
Dąbrowa Białostocka, Poland 44 E10 53 40N 23 21 E
Dąbrowa Górnicza, Poland 45 H6 50 15N 19 10 E
Dąbrowa Tarnowska, Poland 45 H7 50 10N 20 59 E
Dabu, China 59 E11 24 22N 116 41 E
Dabung, Malaysia 65 K4 5 23N 102 1 E
Dabus →, Ethiopia 81 E4 10 48N 35 10 E
Dacato →, Ethiopia 81 F5 7 25N 42 40 E
Dacca = Dhaka, Bangla. 69 H14 23 43N 90 26 E
Dacca = Dhaka □, Bangla. 69 G14 24 25N 90 25 E
Dachau, Germany 25 G7 48 15N 11 26 E
Dachstein, Hoher, Austria 26 D6 47 28N 13 35 E
Dačice, Czech Rep. 26 B8 49 5N 15 26 E
Dadanawa, Guyana 124 C7 2 50N 59 30W
Daday, Turkey 72 B5 41 28N 33 27 E
Dade City, U.S.A. 109 L4 28 22N 82 11W
Dadhar, Pakistan 68 E2 29 28N 67 39 E
Dadiya, Nigeria 83 D7 9 35N 11 24 E
Dadra & Nagar Haveli □, India 66 J8 20 5N 73 0 E
Dadri = Charkhi Dadri, India 68 E7 28 37N 76 17 E
Dadu, Pakistan 68 F2 26 45N 67 45 E
Dadu He →, China 58 C4 29 31N 103 46 E
Daet, Phil. 61 D5 14 2N 122 55 E
Dafang, China 58 D5 27 9N 105 39 E
Dağ, Turkey 39 D12 37 12N 30 31 E
Dagana, Senegal 82 B1 16 30N 15 35W
Dagash, Sudan 80 D3 19 19N 33 25 E
Dagestan □, Russia 49 J8 42 30N 47 0 E
Dagestanskiye Ogni, Russia 49 J9 42 6N 48 12 E
Daggett, U.S.A. 117 L10 34 52N 116 52W
Daghestan Republic = Dagestan □, Russia 49 J8 42 30N 47 0 E
Daghfeli, Sudan 80 D3 19 18N 32 40 E
Dağlıq Qarabağ = Nagorno-Karabakh, Azerbaijan 70 B5 39 55N 46 45 E
Dagö = Hiiumaa, Estonia 9 G20 58 50N 22 45 E
Dagu, China 57 E9 38 59N 117 40 E
Daguan, China 58 D4 27 43N 103 56 E
Dagupan, Phil. 61 C4 16 3N 120 20 E
Daguragu, Australia 92 C5 17 33 S 130 30 E
Dahab, Egypt 80 B3 28 31N 34 31 E
Dahlak Kebir, Eritrea 81 D5 15 50N 40 10 E
Dahlenburg, Germany 24 B6 53 11N 10 44 E
Dahlonega, U.S.A. 109 H4 34 32N 83 59W
Dahme, Germany 24 D9 51 52N 13 25 E
Dahod, India 68 H6 22 50N 74 15 E
Dahomey = Benin ■, Africa 83 D5 10 0N 2 0 E
Dahong Shan, China 59 B9 31 25N 113 0 E
Dahra, Senegal 82 B1 15 22N 15 30W
Dahshûr, Egypt 80 J7 29 45N 31 14 E
Dahūk, Iraq 70 B3 36 50N 43 1 E
Dai Hao, Vietnam 64 C6 18 1N 106 25 E
Dai-Sen, Japan 55 G6 35 22N 133 32 E
Dai Shan, China 59 B14 30 25N 122 10 E
Dai Xian, China 56 E7 39 4N 112 58 E
Daicheng, China 56 E9 38 42N 116 38 E
Daimiel, Spain 35 F7 39 5N 3 35W
Daingean, Ireland 15 C4 53 18N 7 17W
Dainkog, China 58 A1 32 30N 97 58 E
Daintree, Australia 94 B4 16 20 S 145 20 E
Daiō-Misaki, Japan 55 G8 34 15N 136 45 E
Dair, J. ed, Sudan 81 E3 12 27N 30 42 E
Dairût, Egypt 80 B3 27 34N 30 43 E
Daisetsu-Zan, Japan 54 C11 43 30N 142 57 E
Dajarra, Australia 94 C2 21 42 S 139 30 E
Dajin Chuan →, China 58 B3 31 16N 101 59 E
Dak Dam, Cambodia 64 F6 12 20N 107 21 E
Dak Nhe, Vietnam 64 E6 15 28N 107 48 E
Dak Pek, Vietnam 64 E6 15 4N 107 44 E
Dak Song, Vietnam 65 F6 12 19N 107 35 E
Dak Sui, Vietnam 64 E6 14 55N 107 43 E
Dakar, Senegal 82 C1 14 34N 17 29W
Dakhla, W. Sahara 78 D2 23 50N 15 53W
Dakhla, El Wâhât el-, Egypt 80 B2 25 30N 28 50 E
Dakingari, Nigeria 83 C5 11 37N 4 1 E
Dakor, India 68 H5 22 45N 73 11 E
Dakoro, Niger 83 C6 14 31N 6 46 E
Dakota City, U.S.A. 112 D6 42 25N 96 25W
Đakovica, Kosovo, Yug. 40 D4 42 22N 20 26 E
Đakovo, Croatia 42 E3 45 19N 18 24 E
Dalaba, Guinea 82 C2 10 47N 12 12W
Dalachi, China 56 F3 36 48N 105 0 E
Dalai Nur, China 56 C9 43 20N 116 45 E
Dālakī, Iran 71 D6 29 26N 51 17 E
Dalälven, Sweden 10 D10 60 12N 16 43 E
Dalaman, Turkey 39 E10 36 48N 28 47 E
Dalaman →, Turkey 39 E10 36 41N 28 43 E
Dalandzadgad, Mongolia 56 C3 43 27N 104 30 E
Dalap-Uliga-Darrit, Marshall Is. 96 G9 7 7N 171 24 E
Dalarna, Sweden 10 D8 61 0N 14 0 E
Dalarnas län □, Sweden 10 C8 61 0N 14 15 E
Dālbandīn, Pakistan 66 E4 29 0N 64 23 E
Dalbeattie, U.K. 14 G5 54 56N 3 50W
Dalbeg, Australia 94 C4 20 16 S 147 18 E
Dalbosjön, Sweden 11 F6 58 40N 12 45 E
Dalby, Australia 95 D5 27 10 S 151 17 E
Dalby, Sweden 11 J7 55 40N 13 22 E
Dale City, U.S.A. 108 F7 38 38N 77 18W
Dale Hollow L., U.S.A. 109 G3 36 32N 85 27W
Dalga, Egypt 80 B3 27 39N 30 41 E
Dalgān, Iran 71 E8 27 31N 59 19 E
Dalhart, U.S.A. 113 G3 36 4N 102 31W
Dalhousie, Canada 103 C6 48 5N 66 26W
Dalhousie, India 68 C6 32 38N 75 58 E
Dali, Shaanxi, China 56 G5 34 48N 109 58 E
Dali, Yunnan, China 58 E3 25 40N 100 10 E
Dalian, China 57 E11 38 50N 121 40 E
Daliang Shan, China 58 D4 28 0N 102 45 E
Daling He →, China 57 D11 40 55N 121 40 E
Dāliyat el Karmel, Israel 75 C4 32 43N 35 2 E
Dalj, Croatia 42 E3 45 29N 18 59 E
Dalkeith, U.K. 14 F5 55 54N 3 4W
Dalkey, Ireland 15 C5 53 16N 6 6W
Dallas, Oreg., U.S.A. 114 D2 44 55N 123 19W
Dallas, Tex., U.S.A. 113 J6 32 47N 96 49W
Dallol, Ethiopia 81 E5 14 14N 40 17 E
Dalmā, U.A.E. 71 E7 24 30N 52 20 E
Dalmacija, Croatia 29 E13 43 20N 17 0 E
Dalmas, L., Canada 103 B5 53 30N 71 50W
Dalmatia = Dalmacija, Croatia 29 E13 43 20N 17 0 E
Dalmau, India 69 F9 26 4N 81 2 E
Dalmellington, U.K. 14 F4 55 19N 4 23W
Dalnegorsk, Russia 51 E14 44 32N 135 33 E
Dalnerechensk, Russia 51 E14 45 50N 133 40 E
Daloa, Ivory C. 82 D3 7 0N 6 30W
Dalou Shan, China 58 C6 28 15N 107 0 E
Dalry, U.K. 14 F4 55 42N 4 43W
Dalrymple, L., Australia 94 C4 20 40 S 147 0 E
Dals Långed, Sweden 11 F6 58 56N 12 18 E
Dalsjöfors, Sweden 11 G7 57 46N 13 5 E
Dalsland, Sweden 11 F6 58 50N 12 15 E
Daltenganj, India 69 H11 24 0N 84 4 E
Dalton, Ga., U.S.A. 109 H3 34 46N 84 58W
Dalton, Mass., U.S.A. 111 D11 42 28N 73 11W
Dalton, Nebr., U.S.A. 112 E3 41 25N 102 58W
Dalton Iceberg Tongue, Antarctica 5 C9 66 15 S 121 30 E
Dalton-in-Furness, U.K. 12 C4 54 10N 3 11W
Dalupiri I., Phil. 61 B4 19 5N 121 12 E
Dalvík, Iceland 8 D4 65 58N 18 32W
Dalwallinu, Australia 93 F2 30 17 S 116 40 E
Daly →, Australia 92 B5 13 35 S 130 19 E
Daly City, U.S.A. 116 H4 37 42N 122 28W
Daly L., Canada 105 B7 56 32N 105 39W
Daly River, Australia 92 B5 13 46 S 130 42 E
Daly Waters, Australia 94 B1 16 15 S 133 24 E
Dalyan, Turkey 39 E10 36 50N 28 39 E
Dam Doi, Vietnam 65 H5 8 50N 105 12 E
Dam Ha, Vietnam 64 B6 21 21N 107 36 E
Daman, India 66 J8 20 25N 72 57 E
Dāmaneh, Iran 71 C6 33 1N 50 29 E
Damanhûr, Egypt 80 H7 31 0N 30 30 E
Damant L., Canada 105 A7 61 45N 105 5W
Damanzhuang, China 56 E9 38 5N 116 35 E
Damar, Indonesia 63 F7 7 7 S 128 40 E
Damaraland, Namibia 88 C2 20 0 S 15 0 E
Damascus = Dimashq, Syria 75 B5 33 30N 36 18 E
Damaturu, Nigeria 83 C7 11 45N 11 55 E
Damāvand, Iran 71 C7 35 47N 52 0 E
Damāvand, Qolleh-ye, Iran 71 C7 35 56N 52 10 E
Damba, Angola 84 F3 6 44 S 15 20 E
Dâmbovița □, Romania 43 F10 45 0N 25 30 E
Dâmbovița →, Romania 43 F11 44 12N 26 26 E
Dâmbovnic →, Romania 43 F10 44 28N 25 18 E
Dame Marie, Haiti 121 C5 18 36N 74 26W
Dāmghān, Iran 71 B7 36 10N 54 17 E
Dămienesti, Romania 43 D11 46 44N 26 59 E
Damietta = Dumyât, Egypt 80 H7 31 24N 31 48 E
Daming, China 56 F8 36 15N 115 6 E
Damīr Qābū, Syria 70 B4 36 58N 41 51 E
Dammam = Ad Dammām, Si. Arabia 71 E6 26 20N 50 5 E
Dammarie-les-Lys, France 19 D9 48 31N 2 39 E
Dammartin-en-Goële, France 19 C9 49 3N 2 41 E
Damme, Germany 24 C4 52 32N 8 11 E
Damodar →, India 69 H12 23 17N 87 35 E
Damoh, India 69 H8 23 50N 79 28 E
Dampier, Australia 92 D2 20 41 S 116 42 E
Dampier, Selat, Indonesia 63 E8 0 40 S 131 0 E
Dampier Arch., Australia 92 D2 20 38 S 116 32 E
Damrei, Chuor Phnum, Cambodia 65 G4 11 30N 103 0 E
Damvillers, France 19 C12 49 20N 5 21 E
Dan-Gulbi, Nigeria 83 C6 11 40N 6 15 E
Dan Xian, China 64 C7 19 31N 109 33 E
Dana, Indonesia 63 F6 11 0 S 122 52 E
Dana, L., Canada 102 B4 50 53N 77 20W
Dana, Mt., U.S.A. 116 H7 37 54N 119 12W
Danakil Desert, Ethiopia 81 E5 12 45N 41 0 E
Danakil Desert, Ethiopia 81 E5 12 30N 41 30 E
Danané, Ivory C. 82 D3 7 16N 8 9W
Danao, Phil. 61 F6 10 31N 124 1 E
Danau Poso, Indonesia 63 E6 1 52 S 120 35 E
Danba, China 58 B3 30 54N 101 48 E
Danbury, U.S.A. 111 E11 41 24N 73 28W
Danby L., U.S.A. 115 J6 34 13N 115 5W
Dand, Afghan. 68 D1 31 28N 65 32 E
Dandeldhura, Nepal 69 E9 29 20N 80 35 E
Dandeli, India 66 M9 15 5N 74 30 E
Dandenong, Australia 95 F4 38 0 S 145 15 E
Dandīl, Egypt 80 J7 29 10N 31 2 E
Dandong, China 57 D13 40 10N 124 20 E
Danfeng, China 56 H6 33 45N 110 25 E
Dangan Liedao, China 59 F10 22 2N 114 8 E
Dangé-St-Romain, France 20 B4 46 56N 0 36 E
Dângeni, Romania 43 C11 47 51N 26 58 E
Danger Is. = Pukapuka, Cook Is. 97 J11 10 53 S 165 49W
Danger Pt., S. Africa 88 E2 34 40 S 19 17 E
Dangla, Ethiopia 81 E4 11 18N 36 56 E
Dangla Shan = Tanggula Shan, China 60 C4 32 40N 92 10 E
Dangora, Nigeria 83 C6 11 30N 8 7 E
Dangouadougou, Burkina Faso 82 D4 10 9N 4 56W
Dangrek, Phnom, Thailand 64 E5 14 15N 105 0 E
Dangriga, Belize 119 D7 17 0N 88 13W
Dangshan, China 56 G9 34 27N 116 22 E
Dangtu, China 59 B12 31 32N 118 25 E
Dangyang, China 59 B8 30 52N 111 44 E
Dani, Burkina Faso 83 C4 13 43N 0 10W
Daniel, U.S.A. 114 E8 42 52N 110 4W
Daniel's Harbour, Canada 103 B8 50 13N 57 35W
Danielskuil, S. Africa 88 D3 28 11 S 23 33 E
Danielson, U.S.A. 111 E13 41 48N 71 53W
Danilov, Russia 46 C11 58 16N 40 13 E
Danilovgrad, Montenegro, Yug. 40 D3 42 38N 19 4 E
Danilovka, Russia 48 E7 50 25N 44 12 E
Daning, China 56 F6 36 28N 110 45 E
Danissa, Kenya 86 B5 3 15N 40 58 E
Danja, Nigeria 83 C6 11 21N 7 30 E
Danjiangkou, China 59 A8 32 31N 111 30 E
Danjiangkou Shuiku, China 59 A8 32 37N 111 30 E
Dank, Oman 71 F8 23 33N 56 16 E
Dankalwa, Nigeria 83 C7 11 52N 12 12 E
Dankama, Nigeria 83 C6 13 20N 7 44 E
Dankhar Gompa, India 66 C11 32 10N 78 10 E
Dankov, Russia 46 F10 53 20N 39 5 E
Danleng, China 58 B4 30 1N 103 31 E
Danlí, Honduras 120 D2 14 4N 86 35W
Dannemora, U.S.A. 111 B11 44 43N 73 44W
Dannenberg, Germany 24 B7 53 6N 11 5 E
Dannevirke, N.Z. 91 J6 40 12 S 176 8 E
Dannhauser, S. Africa 89 D5 28 0 S 30 3 E
Dansville, U.S.A. 110 D7 42 34N 77 42W
Danta, India 68 G5 24 11N 72 46 E
Dantan, India 69 J12 21 57N 87 20 E
Dante, Somali Rep. 74 E5 10 25N 51 16 E
Danube = Dunărea →, Europe 43 E14 45 20N 29 40 E
Danvers, U.S.A. 111 D14 42 34N 70 56W
Danville, Ill., U.S.A. 108 E2 40 8N 87 37W
Danville, Ky., U.S.A. 108 G3 37 39N 84 46W
Danville, Pa., U.S.A. 111 F8 40 58N 76 37W
Danville, Va., U.S.A. 109 G6 36 36N 79 23W
Danville, Vt., U.S.A. 111 B12 44 25N 72 9W
Danyang, China 59 B12 32 0N 119 31 E
Danzhai, China 58 D6 26 11N 107 48 E
Danzig = Gdańsk, Poland 44 D5 54 22N 18 40 E
Dão →, Portugal 34 E2 40 20N 8 11W
Dao Xian, China 59 E8 25 36N 111 31 E
Daocheng, China 58 C3 29 0N 100 10 E
Daoukro, Ivory C. 82 D4 7 10N 3 58W
Dapaong, Togo 83 C5 10 55N 0 16 E
Dapchi, Nigeria 83 C7 12 32N 11 31 E
Dapitan, Phil. 61 G5 8 39N 123 25 E
Daqing Shan, China 56 D6 40 40N 111 0 E
Daqu Shan, China 59 B14 30 25N 122 20 E
Dar Banda, Africa 76 F6 8 0N 23 0 E
Dar el Beida = Casablanca, Morocco 78 B4 33 36N 7 36W
Dar es Salaam, Tanzania 86 D4 6 50 S 39 12 E
Dar Mazār, Iran 71 D8 29 14N 57 20 E
Dar'ā, Syria 75 C5 32 36N 36 7 E
Dar'ā □, Syria 75 C5 32 55N 36 10 E
Dārāb, Iran 71 D7 28 50N 54 30 E
Daraban, Pakistan 68 D4 31 44N 70 20 E
Darabani, Romania 43 B11 48 10N 26 39 E
Daraina, Madag. 89 A8 13 12 S 49 40 E
Daraj, Libya 79 B8 30 10N 10 28 E
Dārān, Iran 71 C6 32 59N 50 24 E
Daravica, Kosovo, Yug. 40 D4 42 32N 20 8 E
Daraw, Egypt 80 C3 24 22N 32 51 E
Dārayyā, Syria 75 B5 33 28N 36 15 E
Darazo, Nigeria 83 C7 11 1N 10 24 E
Darband, Pakistan 68 B5 34 20N 72 50 E
Darband, Kūh-e, Iran 71 D8 31 34N 57 8 E
Darbhanga, India 69 F11 26 15N 85 55 E
D'Arcy, Canada 104 C4 50 27N 122 35W
Darda, Croatia 42 E3 45 40N 18 41 E
Dardanelle, Ark., U.S.A. 113 H8 35 13N 93 9W
Dardanelle, Calif., U.S.A. 116 G7 38 20N 119 50W
Dardanelles = Çanakkale Boğazı, Turkey 41 F10 40 17N 26 32 E
Dare →, Ethiopia 81 F5 7 20N 42 11 E
Darende, Turkey 72 C7 38 31N 37 30 E
Dārestān, Iran 71 D8 29 9N 58 42 E
Darfo, Italy 28 C7 45 53N 10 11 E
Dārfūr, Sudan 79 F10 13 40N 24 0 E
Dargai, Pakistan 68 B4 34 25N 71 55 E
Dargan Ata, Uzbekistan 50 E7 40 29N 62 10 E
Dargaville, N.Z. 91 F4 35 57 S 173 52 E
Dargol, Niger 83 C5 13 54N 1 22 E
Darhan Muminggan Lianheqi, China 56 D6 41 40N 110 28 E
Dari, Sudan 81 F3 5 48N 30 26 E
Darıca, Turkey 72 B3 40 45N 29 23 E
Darién, G. del, Colombia 122 C3 9 0N 77 0W
Dariganga = Ovoot, Mongolia 56 B7 45 21N 113 45 E
Darinskoye, Kazakstan 48 E10 51 20N 51 44 E
Darjeeling = Darjiling, India 69 F13 27 3N 88 18 E
Darjiling, India 69 F13 27 3N 88 18 E
Darkan, Australia 93 F2 33 20 S 116 43 E
Darkhana, Pakistan 68 D5 30 39N 72 11 E
Darkhazīneh, Iran 71 D6 31 54N 48 39 E
Darkot Pass, Pakistan 69 A5 36 45N 73 26 E
Darling →, Australia 95 E3 34 4 S 141 54 E
Darling Downs, Australia 95 D5 27 30 S 150 30 E
Darling Ra., Australia 93 F2 32 30 S 116 0 E
Darlington, U.K. 12 C6 54 32N 1 33W
Darlington, U.S.A. 109 H6 34 18N 79 52W
Darlington □, U.K. 12 C6 54 32N 1 33W
Darlington, L., S. Africa 88 E4 33 10 S 25 9 E
Darlington Point, Australia 95 E4 34 37 S 146 1 E
Darlot, L., Australia 93 E3 27 48 S 121 35 E
Darłowo, Poland 44 D3 54 25N 16 25 E
Dărmănești, Bacău, Romania 43 D11 46 21N 26 33 E
Dărmănești, Suceava, Romania 43 C11 47 44N 26 9 E
Darmstadt, Germany 25 F4 49 51N 8 39 E
Darnah, Libya 79 B10 32 45N 22 45 E
Darnall, S. Africa 89 D5 29 23 S 31 18 E
Darney, France 19 D13 48 5N 6 2 E
Darnley, C., Antarctica 5 C6 68 0 S 69 0 E
Darnley B., Canada 100 B7 69 30N 123 30W
Daroca, Spain 32 D3 41 9N 1 25W
Darou-Mousti, Senegal 82 B1 15 3N 16 3W
Darr →, Australia 94 C3 23 39 S 143 50 E
Darra Pezu, Pakistan 68 C4 32 19N 70 44 E
Darrequeira, Argentina 126 D3 37 42 S 63 10W
Darrington, U.S.A. 114 B3 48 15N 121 36W
Darsser Ort, Germany 24 A8 54 28N 12 32 E
Dart →, U.K. 13 G4 50 24N 3 39W
Dart, C., Antarctica 5 D14 73 6 S 126 20W
Dartford, U.K. 13 F8 51 26N 0 13 E
Dartmoor, U.K. 13 G4 50 38N 3 57W
Dartmouth, Canada 103 D7 44 40N 63 30W
Dartmouth, U.K. 13 G4 50 21N 3 36W
Dartmouth, L., Australia 95 D4 26 4 S 145 18 E
Dartuch, C. = Artrutx, C. de, Spain 37 B10 39 55N 3 49 E
Daruvar, Croatia 42 E2 45 35N 17 14 E
Darvaza, Turkmenistan 50 E6 40 11N 58 24 E
Darvel, Teluk = Lahad Datu, Teluk, Malaysia 63 D5 4 50N 118 20 E
Darwen, U.K. 12 D5 53 42N 2 29W
Darwendale, Zimbabwe 89 B5 17 41 S 30 33 E
Darwha, India 66 J10 20 15N 77 45 E
Darwin, Australia 92 B5 12 25 S 130 51 E
Darwin, U.S.A. 117 J9 36 15N 117 35W
Darya Khan, Pakistan 68 D4 31 48N 71 6 E
Daryoi Amu = Amudarya →, Uzbekistan 50 E6 43 58N 59 34 E
Dās, U.A.E. 71 E7 25 20N 53 30 E
Dashen, Ras, Ethiopia 81 E4 13 8N 38 26 E
Dashetai, China 56 D5 41 0N 109 5 E
Dashhowuz, Turkmenistan 50 E6 41 49N 59 58 E
Dashkesan = Daşkäsän, Azerbaijan 49 K7 40 25N 46 0 E
Dashköpri, Turkmenistan 71 B9 36 16N 62 8 E
Dasht, Iran 71 B8 37 17N 56 7 E
Dasht →, Pakistan 66 G2 25 10N 61 40 E
Daska, Pakistan 68 C6 32 20N 74 20 E
Daşkäsän, Azerbaijan 49 K7 40 25N 46 0 E
Dassa, Benin 83 D5 7 46N 2 14 E
Dasuya, India 68 D6 31 49N 75 38 E
Datça, Turkey 39 E9 36 46N 27 40 E
Datia, India 69 G8 25 39N 78 27 E
Datian, China 59 E11 25 40N 117 50 E
Datong, Anhui, China 59 B11 30 48N 117 44 E
Datong, Shanxi, China 56 D7 40 6N 113 18 E
Dattakhel, Pakistan 68 C3 32 54N 69 46 E
Datteln, Germany 24 D3 51 39N 7 21 E
Datu, Tanjung, Indonesia 62 D3 2 5N 109 39 E
Datu Piang, Phil. 61 H6 7 2N 124 30 E
Datuk, Tanjong = Datu, Tanjung, Indonesia 62 D3 2 5N 109 39 E
Daud Khel, Pakistan 68 C4 32 53N 71 34 E
Daudnagar, India 69 G11 25 2N 84 24 E
Daugava →, Latvia 9 H21 57 4N 24 3 E
Daugavpils, Latvia 9 J22 55 53N 26 32 E
Daulpur, India 68 F7 26 45N 77 59 E
Daun, Germany 25 E2 50 11N 6 49 E
Dauphin, Canada 105 C8 51 9N 100 5W
Dauphin, U.S.A. 110 F8 40 22N 76 56W
Dauphin L., Canada 105 C9 51 20N 99 45W
Dauphiné, France 21 C9 45 15N 5 25 E
Daura, Borno, Nigeria 83 C7 11 31N 11 24 E
Daura, Katsina, Nigeria 83 C6 13 2N 8 21 E
Dausa, India 68 F7 26 52N 76 20 E
Dăvăçi, Azerbaijan 49 K9 41 15N 48 57 E
Davangere, India 66 M9 14 25N 75 55 E
Davao, Phil. 61 H6 7 0N 125 40 E
Davao G., Phil. 61 H6 6 30N 125 48 E
Dāvar Panāh, Iran 71 E9 27 25N 62 15 E
Davenport, Calif., U.S.A. 116 H4 37 1N 122 12W
Davenport, Iowa, U.S.A. 112 E9 41 32N 90 35W
Davenport, Wash., U.S.A. 114 C4 47 39N 118 9W

Davenport Ra., Australia **94 C1** 20 28 S 134 0 E
Daventry, U.K. **13 E6** 52 16N 1 10W
David, Panama **120 E3** 8 30N 82 30W
David City, U.S.A. **112 E6** 41 15N 97 8W
David Gorodok = Davyd Haradok, Belarus **47 F4** 52 4N 27 8 E
Davidson, Canada **105 C7** 51 16N 105 59W
Davis, U.S.A. **116 G5** 38 33N 121 44W
Davis Dam, U.S.A. **117 K12** 35 11N 114 34W
Davis Inlet, Canada **103 A7** 55 50N 60 59W
Davis Mts., U.S.A. **113 K2** 30 50N 103 55W
Davis Sea, Antarctica **5 C7** 66 0 S 92 0 E
Davis Str., N. Amer. **101 B14** 65 0N 58 0W
Davo →, Ivory C. **82 D3** 5 0N 6 10W
Davos, Switz. **25 J5** 46 48N 9 49 E
Davutlar, Turkey **39 D9** 37 43N 27 17 E
Davy L., Canada **105 B7** 58 53N 108 18W
Davyd Haradok, Belarus **47 F4** 52 4N 27 8 E
Dawa →, Ethiopia **81 G5** 4 11N 42 6 E
Dawaki, Bauchi, Nigeria **83 D6** 9 25N 9 33 E
Dawaki, Kano, Nigeria **83 C6** 12 5N 8 23 E
Dawei, Burma **64 E2** 14 2N 98 12 E
Dawes Ra., Australia **94 C5** 24 40 S 150 40 E
Dawlish, U.K. **13 G4** 50 35N 3 28W
Dawros Hd., Ireland **15 B3** 54 50N 8 33W
Dawson, Canada **100 B6** 64 10N 139 30W
Dawson, U.S.A. **109 K3** 31 46N 84 27W
Dawson, I., Chile **128 G2** 53 50 S 70 50W
Dawson B., Canada **105 C8** 52 53N 100 49W
Dawson Creek, Canada **104 B4** 55 45N 120 15W
Dawson Inlet, Canada **105 A10** 61 50N 93 25W
Dawson Ra., Australia **94 C4** 24 30 S 149 48 E
Dawu, Hubei, China **59 B9** 31 34N 114 7 E
Dawu, Sichuan, China **58 B3** 30 55N 101 10 E
Dax, France **20 E2** 43 44N 1 3W
Daxian, China **58 B6** 31 15N 107 23 E
Daxin, China **58 F6** 22 50N 107 11 E
Daxindian, China **57 F11** 37 30N 120 50 E
Daxinggou, China **57 C15** 43 25N 129 40 E
Daxue Shan, Sichuan, China **58 B3** 30 30N 101 30 E
Daxue Shan, Yunnan, China **58 F2** 23 42N 99 48 E
Dayao, China **58 E3** 25 43N 101 20 E
Daye, China **59 B10** 30 6N 114 58 E
Dayet en Naharat, Mali **82 B4** 17 39N 3 10W
Dayi, China **58 B4** 30 41N 103 29 E
Daylesford, Australia **95 F3** 37 21 S 144 9 E
Dayong, China **59 C8** 29 11N 110 30 E
Dayr az Zawr, Syria **70 C4** 35 20N 40 5 E
Daysland, Canada **104 C6** 52 50N 112 20W
Dayton, Nev., U.S.A. **116 F7** 39 14N 119 36W
Dayton, Ohio, U.S.A. **108 F3** 39 45N 84 12W
Dayton, Pa., U.S.A. **110 F5** 40 53N 79 15W
Dayton, Tenn., U.S.A. **109 H3** 35 30N 85 1W
Dayton, Wash., U.S.A. **114 C4** 46 19N 117 59W
Dayton, Wyo., U.S.A. **114 D10** 44 53N 107 16W
Daytona Beach, U.S.A. **109 L5** 29 13N 81 1W
Dayu, China **59 E10** 25 24N 114 22 E
Dayville, U.S.A. **114 D4** 44 28N 119 32W
Dazhu, China **58 B6** 30 41N 107 15 E
Dazkırı, Turkey **39 D11** 37 57N 29 52 E
Dazu, China **58 C5** 29 40N 105 42 E
De Aar, S. Africa **88 E3** 30 39 S 24 0 E
De Funiak Springs, U.S.A. **109 K2** 30 43N 86 7W
De Grey →, Australia **92 D2** 20 12 S 119 13 E
De Haan, Belgium **17 C3** 51 16N 3 2 E
De Kalb, U.S.A. **112 E10** 41 56N 88 46W
De Land, U.S.A. **109 L5** 29 2N 81 18W
De Leon, U.S.A. **113 J5** 32 7N 98 32W
De Panne, Belgium **17 C2** 51 6N 2 34 E
De Pere, U.S.A. **108 C1** 44 27N 88 4W
De Queen, U.S.A. **113 H7** 34 2N 94 21W
De Quincy, U.S.A. **113 K8** 30 27N 93 26W
De Ridder, U.S.A. **113 K8** 30 51N 93 17W
De Smet, U.S.A. **112 C6** 44 23N 97 33W
De Soto, U.S.A. **112 F9** 38 8N 90 34W
De Tour Village, U.S.A. **108 C4** 46 0N 83 56W
De Witt, U.S.A. **113 H9** 34 18N 91 20W
Dead Sea, Asia **75 D4** 31 30N 35 30 E
Deadwood, U.S.A. **112 C3** 44 23N 103 44W
Deadwood L., Canada **104 B3** 59 10N 128 30W
Deal, U.K. **13 F9** 51 13N 1 25 E
Deal I., Australia **94 F4** 39 30 S 147 20 E
Dealesville, S. Africa **88 D4** 28 41 S 25 44 E
De'an, China **59 C10** 29 21N 115 46 E
Dean →, Canada **104 C3** 52 49N 126 58W
Dean, Forest of, U.K. **13 F5** 51 45N 2 33W
Dean Chan., Canada **104 C3** 52 30N 127 15W
Deán Funes, Argentina **126 C3** 30 20 S 64 20W
Dease →, Canada **104 B3** 59 56N 128 32W
Dease L., Canada **104 B2** 58 40N 130 5W
Dease Lake, Canada **104 B2** 58 25N 130 6W
Death Valley, U.S.A. **117 J10** 36 15N 116 50W
Death Valley Junction, U.S.A. **117 J10** 36 20N 116 25W
Death Valley National Park, U.S.A. **117 J10** 36 45N 117 15W
Deauville, France **18 C7** 49 23N 0 2 E
Deba, Spain **32 B2** 43 18N 2 21W
Deba Habe, Nigeria **83 C7** 10 14N 11 20 E
Debaltsevo, Ukraine **47 H10** 48 22N 38 26 E
Debao, China **58 F6** 23 21N 106 46 E
Debar, Macedonia **40 E4** 41 31N 20 30 E
Debden, Canada **105 C7** 53 30N 106 50W
Dębica, Poland **45 H8** 50 2N 21 25 E
Dęblin, Poland **45 G8** 51 34N 21 50 E
Dębno, Poland **45 F1** 52 44N 14 41 E
Débo, L., Mali **82 B4** 15 14N 4 15W
Debolt, Canada **104 B5** 55 12N 118 1W
Deborah East, L., Australia **93 F2** 30 45 S 119 0 E
Deborah West, L., Australia **93 F2** 30 45 S 118 50 E
Debrc, Serbia, Yug. **40 B3** 44 38N 19 53 E
Debre Birhan, Ethiopia **81 F4** 9 41N 39 31 E
Debre Markos, Ethiopia **81 E4** 10 20N 37 40 E
Debre May, Ethiopia **81 E4** 11 20N 37 25 E
Debre Sina, Ethiopia **81 F4** 9 51N 39 50 E
Debre Tabor, Ethiopia **81 E4** 11 50N 38 26 E
Debre Zevit, Ethiopia **81 F4** 8 50N 39 0 E
Debre Zeyit, Ethiopia **81 E4** 11 48N 38 30 E
Debrecen, Hungary **42 C6** 47 33N 21 42 E
Debrzno, Poland **44 E4** 53 31N 17 14 E
Dečani, Kosovo, Yug. **40 D4** 42 30N 20 18 E
Decatur, Ala., U.S.A. **109 H2** 34 36N 86 59W
Decatur, Ga., U.S.A. **109 J3** 33 47N 84 18W
Decatur, Ill., U.S.A. **112 F10** 39 51N 88 57W
Decatur, Ind., U.S.A. **108 E3** 40 50N 84 56W
Decatur, Tex., U.S.A. **113 J6** 33 14N 97 35W
Decazeville, France **20 D6** 44 34N 2 15 E
Deccan, India **66 L11** 18 0N 79 0 E
Deception Bay, Australia **95 D5** 27 10 S 153 5 E
Deception L., Canada **105 B8** 56 33N 104 13W
Dechang, China **58 D4** 27 25N 102 11 E
Dechhu, India **68 F5** 26 46N 72 20 E
Děčín, Czech Rep. **26 A7** 50 47N 14 12 E
Decize, France **19 F10** 46 50N 3 28 E
Deckerville, U.S.A. **110 C2** 43 32N 82 44W
Decollatura, Italy **31 C9** 39 3N 16 21 E
Decorah, U.S.A. **112 D9** 43 18N 91 48W
Deda, Romania **43 D9** 46 56N 24 50 E
Dedéagach = Alexandroúpolis, Greece **41 F9** 40 50N 25 54 E
Deder, Ethiopia **81 F5** 9 19N 41 27 E
Dedham, U.S.A. **111 D13** 42 15N 71 10W
Dédougou, Burkina Faso **82 C4** 12 30N 3 25W
Dedovichi, Russia **46 D5** 57 32N 29 56 E
Dedza, Malawi **87 E3** 14 20 S 34 20 E
Dee →, Aberds., U.K. **14 D6** 57 9N 2 5W
Dee →, Dumf. & Gall., U.K. **14 G4** 54 51N 4 3W
Dee →, Wales, U.K. **12 D4** 53 22N 3 17W
Deep B., Canada **104 A5** 61 15N 116 35W
Deepwater, Australia **95 D5** 29 25 S 151 51 E
Deer →, Canada **105 B10** 58 23N 94 13W
Deer L., Canada **105 C10** 52 40N 94 20W
Deer Lake, Nfld., Canada **103 C8** 49 11N 57 27W
Deer Lake, Ont., Canada **105 C10** 52 36N 94 20W
Deer Lodge, U.S.A. **114 C7** 46 24N 112 44W
Deer Park, U.S.A. **114 C5** 47 57N 117 28W
Deer River, U.S.A. **112 B8** 47 20N 93 48W
Deeragun, Australia **94 B4** 19 16 S 146 33 E
Deerdepoort, S. Africa **88 C4** 24 37 S 26 27 E
Deferiet, U.S.A. **111 B9** 44 2N 75 41W
Defiance, U.S.A. **108 E3** 41 17N 84 22W
Degana, India **68 F6** 26 50N 74 20 E
Dêgê, China **58 B2** 31 44N 98 39 E
Degebe →, Portugal **35 G3** 38 13N 7 29W
Degeberga, Sweden **11 J8** 55 51N 14 5 E
Dégelis, Canada **103 C6** 47 30N 68 35W
Degema, Nigeria **83 E6** 4 50N 6 48 E
Degerfors, Sweden **10 E8** 59 15N 14 27 E
Degerhamn, Sweden **11 H10** 56 20N 16 24 E
Deggendorf, Germany **25 G8** 48 50N 12 57 E
Degh →, Pakistan **68 D5** 31 3N 73 21 E
Değirmendere, Turkey **41 F13** 40 42N 29 47 E
Deh Bīd, Iran **71 D7** 30 39N 53 11 E
Deh-e Shīr, Iran **71 D7** 31 29N 53 45 E
Dehaj, Iran **71 D7** 30 42N 54 53 E
Dehak, Iran **71 E9** 27 11N 62 37 E
Dehdez, Iran **71 D6** 31 43N 50 17 E
Dehej, India **68 J5** 21 44N 72 40 E
Dehestān, Iran **71 D7** 28 30N 55 35 E
Dehgolān, Iran **70 C5** 35 17N 47 25 E
Dehi Titan, Afghan. **66 C3** 33 45N 63 50 E
Dehibat, Tunisia **79 B8** 32 0N 10 47 E
Dehlorān, Iran **70 C5** 32 41N 47 16 E
Dehnow-e Kühestān, Iran **71 E8** 27 58N 58 32 E
Dehra Dun, India **68 D8** 30 20N 78 4 E
Dehri, India **69 G11** 24 50N 84 15 E
Dehua, China **59 E12** 25 26N 118 14 E
Dehui, China **57 B13** 44 30N 125 40 E
Deim Zubeir, Sudan **81 F2** 7 49N 26 16 E
Deinze, Belgium **17 D3** 50 59N 3 32 E
Dej, Romania **43 C8** 47 10N 23 52 E
Deje, Sweden **10 E7** 59 35N 13 29 E
Dejiang, China **58 C7** 28 18N 108 7 E
Deka →, S. Africa **88 B4** 18 4 S 26 42 E
Dekemhare, Eritrea **81 D4** 15 6N 39 0 E
Dekese, Dem. Rep. of the Congo **84 E4** 3 24 S 21 24 E
Del Mar, U.S.A. **117 N9** 32 58N 117 16W
Del Norte, U.S.A. **115 H10** 37 41N 106 21W
Del Rio, U.S.A. **113 L4** 29 22N 100 54W
Delai, Sudan **80 D4** 17 21N 36 6 E
Delambre I., Australia **92 D2** 20 26 S 117 5 E
Delami, Sudan **81 E3** 11 38N 30 28 E
Delano, U.S.A. **117 K7** 35 46N 119 15W
Delano Peak, U.S.A. **115 G7** 38 22N 112 22W
Delareyville, S. Africa **88 D4** 26 41 S 25 26 E
Delaronde L., Canada **105 C7** 54 3N 107 3W
Delavan, U.S.A. **112 D10** 42 38N 88 39W
Delaware, U.S.A. **108 E4** 40 18N 83 4W
Delaware □, U.S.A. **108 F8** 39 0N 75 20W
Delaware →, U.S.A. **111 G9** 39 15N 75 20W
Delaware B., U.S.A. **108 F8** 39 0N 75 10W
Delay →, Canada **103 A5** 56 56N 71 28W
Delbrück, Germany **24 D4** 51 46N 8 34 E
Delčevo, Macedonia **40 E6** 41 58N 22 46 E
Delegate, Australia **95 F4** 37 4 S 148 56 E
Delémont, Switz. **25 H3** 47 22N 7 20 E
Delevan, U.S.A. **110 D6** 42 29N 78 29W
Delft, Neths. **17 B4** 52 1N 4 22 E
Delfzijl, Neths. **17 A6** 53 20N 6 55 E
Delgado, C., Mozam. **87 E5** 10 45 S 40 40 E
Delgerhet, Mongolia **56 B6** 45 50N 110 30 E
Delgo, Sudan **80 C3** 20 6N 30 40 E
Delhi, Canada **110 D4** 42 51N 80 30W
Delhi, India **68 E7** 28 38N 77 17 E
Delhi, La., U.S.A. **113 J9** 32 28N 91 30W
Delhi, N.Y., U.S.A. **111 D10** 42 17N 74 55W
Deli Jovan, Serbia, Yug. **40 B6** 44 13N 22 9 E
Delia, Canada **104 C6** 51 38N 112 23W
Delice, Turkey **72 C6** 39 54N 34 2 E
Delicias, Mexico **118 B3** 28 10N 105 30W
Delījān, Iran **71 C6** 33 59N 50 40 E
Déline, Canada **100 B7** 65 10N 123 30W
Delisle, Canada **105 C7** 51 55N 107 8W
Delitzsch, Germany **24 D8** 51 31N 12 20 E
Dell City, U.S.A. **115 L11** 31 56N 105 12W
Dell Rapids, U.S.A. **112 D6** 43 50N 96 43W
Delle, France **19 E14** 47 30N 7 2 E
Delmar, U.S.A. **111 D11** 42 37N 73 47W
Delmenhorst, Germany **24 B4** 53 3N 8 37 E
Delnice, Croatia **29 C11** 45 23N 14 50 E
Delonga, Ostrova, Russia **51 B15** 76 40N 149 20 E
Deloraine, Australia **94 G4** 41 30 S 146 40 E
Deloraine, Canada **105 D8** 49 15N 100 29W
Delphi, Greece **38 C4** 38 28N 22 30 E
Delphi, U.S.A. **108 E2** 40 36N 86 41W
Delphos, U.S.A. **108 E3** 40 51N 84 21W
Delportshoop, S. Africa **88 D3** 28 22 S 24 20 E
Delray Beach, U.S.A. **109 M5** 26 28N 80 4W
Delsbo, Sweden **10 C10** 61 48N 16 32 E
Delta, Colo., U.S.A. **115 G9** 38 44N 108 4W
Delta, Utah, U.S.A. **114 G7** 39 21N 112 35W
Delta □, Nigeria **83 D6** 5 30N 6 0 E
Delta Junction, U.S.A. **100 B5** 64 2N 145 44W
Deltona, U.S.A. **109 L5** 28 54N 81 16W
Delungra, Australia **95 D5** 29 39 S 150 51 E
Delvada, India **68 J4** 20 46N 71 2 E
Delvinákion, Greece **38 B2** 39 57N 20 32 E
Delvinë, Albania **40 G4** 39 59N 20 6 E
Demak, Indonesia **63 G14** 6 53 S 110 38 E
Demanda, Sierra de la, Spain **32 C2** 42 15N 3 0W
Demavand = Damāvand, Iran **71 C7** 35 47N 52 0 E
Dembecha, Ethiopia **81 E4** 10 32N 37 30 E
Dembi, Ethiopia **81 F4** 8 5N 36 25 E
Dembia, Dem. Rep. of the Congo **86 B2** 3 33N 25 48 E
Dembidolo, Ethiopia **81 F3** 8 34N 34 50 E
Demchok, India **69 C8** 32 42N 79 29 E
Demer →, Belgium **17 D4** 50 57N 4 42 E
Demetrias, Greece **38 B5** 39 22N 23 1 E
Demidov, Russia **46 E6** 55 16N 31 30 E
Deming, N. Mex., U.S.A. **115 K10** 32 16N 107 46W
Deming, Wash., U.S.A. **116 B4** 48 50N 122 13W
Demini →, Brazil **124 D6** 0 46 S 62 56W
Demirci, Turkey **39 B10** 39 2N 28 38 E
Demirköprü Barajı, Turkey **39 C10** 38 42N 28 25 E
Demirköy, Turkey **41 E11** 41 49N 27 45 E
Demmin, Germany **24 B9** 53 54N 13 2 E
Demonte, Italy **28 D4** 44 19N 7 17 E
Demopolis, U.S.A. **109 J2** 32 31N 87 50W
Dempo, Indonesia **62 E2** 4 2 S 103 15 E
Demyansk, Russia **46 D7** 57 40N 32 27 E
Den Burg, Neths. **17 A4** 53 3N 4 47 E
Den Chai, Thailand **64 D3** 17 59N 100 4 E
Den Haag = 's-Gravenhage, Neths. **17 B4** 52 7N 4 17 E
Den Helder, Neths. **17 B4** 52 57N 4 45 E
Den Oever, Neths. **17 B5** 52 56N 5 2 E
Denain, France **19 B10** 50 20N 3 22 E
Denair, U.S.A. **116 H6** 37 32N 120 48W
Denau, Uzbekistan **50 F7** 38 16N 67 54 E
Denbigh, Canada **110 A7** 45 8N 77 15W
Denbigh, U.K. **12 D4** 53 12N 3 25W
Denbighshire □, U.K. **12 D4** 53 8N 3 22W
Dendang, Indonesia **62 E3** 3 7 S 107 56 E
Dendermonde, Belgium **17 C4** 51 2N 4 5 E
Deneba, Ethiopia **81 F4** 9 47N 39 10 E
Dengchuan, China **58 E3** 25 59N 100 3 E
Denge, Nigeria **83 C6** 12 52N 5 21 E
Dengfeng, China **56 G7** 34 25N 113 2 E
Dengi, Nigeria **83 D6** 9 25N 9 55 E
Dengkou, China **56 D4** 40 18N 106 55 E
Dengzhou, China **59 A9** 32 34N 112 4 E
Denham, Australia **93 E1** 25 56 S 113 31 E
Denham Ra., Australia **94 C4** 21 55 S 147 46 E
Denham Sd., Australia **93 E1** 25 45 S 113 15 E
Denholm, Canada **105 C7** 52 39N 108 1W
Denia, Spain **33 G5** 38 49N 0 8 E
Denial B., Australia **95 E1** 32 14 S 133 32 E
Deniliquin, Australia **95 F3** 35 30 S 144 58 E
Denison, Iowa, U.S.A. **112 E7** 42 1N 95 21W
Denison, Tex., U.S.A. **113 J6** 33 45N 96 33W
Denison Plains, Australia **92 C4** 18 35 S 128 0 E
Denizli, Turkey **39 D11** 37 42N 29 2 E
Denizli □, Turkey **39 D11** 37 45N 29 5 E
Denman Glacier, Antarctica **5 C7** 66 45 S 99 25 E
Denmark, Australia **93 F2** 34 59 S 117 25 E
Denmark ■, Europe **11 J3** 55 45N 10 0 E
Denmark Str., Atl. Oc. **4 C6** 66 0N 30 0W
Dennison, U.S.A. **110 F3** 40 24N 81 19W
Denny, U.K. **14 E5** 56 1N 3 55W
Denpasar, Indonesia **62 F5** 8 45 S 115 14 E
Denton, Mont., U.S.A. **114 C9** 47 19N 109 57W
Denton, Tex., U.S.A. **113 J6** 33 13N 97 8W
D'Entrecasteaux, Pt., Australia **93 F2** 34 50 S 115 57 E
Denu, Ghana **83 D5** 6 4N 1 8 E
Denver, Colo., U.S.A. **112 F2** 39 44N 104 59W
Denver, Pa., U.S.A. **111 F8** 40 14N 76 8W
Denver City, U.S.A. **113 J3** 32 58N 102 50W
Deoband, India **68 E7** 29 42N 77 43 E
Deogarh, India **68 G5** 25 32N 73 54 E
Deoghar, India **69 G12** 24 30N 86 42 E
Deolali, India **66 K8** 19 58N 73 50 E
Deoli = Devli, India **68 G6** 25 50N 75 20 E
Déols, France **19 F8** 46 50N 1 43 E
Deora, India **68 F4** 26 22N 70 55 E
Deori, India **69 H8** 23 24N 79 1 E
Deoria, India **69 F10** 26 31N 83 48 E
Deosai Mts., Pakistan **69 B6** 35 40N 75 0 E
Deosri, India **69 F14** 26 46N 90 29 E
Depalpur, India **68 H6** 22 51N 75 33 E
Deping, China **57 F9** 37 25N 116 58 E
Deposit, U.S.A. **111 D9** 42 4N 75 25W
Depuch I., Australia **92 D2** 20 37 S 117 44 E
Deputatskiy, Russia **51 C14** 69 18N 139 54 E
Dêqên, China **58 C2** 28 34N 98 51 E
Deqing, China **59 F8** 23 8N 111 42 E
Dera Ghazi Khan, Pakistan **68 D4** 30 5N 70 43 E
Dera Ismail Khan, Pakistan **68 D4** 31 50N 70 50 E
Derabugti, Pakistan **68 E3** 29 2N 69 9 E
Derawar Fort, Pakistan **68 E4** 28 46N 71 20 E
Derbent, Russia **49 J9** 42 5N 48 15 E
Derbent, Turkey **39 C10** 38 11N 28 33 E
Derby, Australia **92 C3** 17 18 S 123 38 E
Derby, U.K. **12 E6** 52 56N 1 28W
Derby, Conn., U.S.A. **111 E11** 41 19N 73 5W
Derby, Kans., U.S.A. **113 G6** 37 33N 97 16W
Derby, N.Y., U.S.A. **110 D6** 42 41N 78 58W
Derby City □, U.K. **12 E6** 52 56N 1 28W
Derby Line, U.S.A. **111 B12** 45 0N 72 6W
Derbyshire □, U.K. **12 D6** 53 11N 1 38W
Derecske, Hungary **42 C6** 47 20N 21 33 E
Dereköy, Turkey **41 E11** 41 55N 27 21 E
Dereli, Turkey **73 B8** 40 44N 38 26 E
Derg →, U.K. **15 B4** 54 44N 7 26W
Derg, L., Ireland **15 D3** 53 0N 8 20W
Dergachi = Derhaci, Ukraine **47 G9** 50 9N 36 11 E
Dergaon, India **67 F19** 26 45N 94 0 E
Derhaci, Ukraine **47 G9** 50 9N 36 11 E
Derik, Turkey **73 D9** 37 21N 40 18 E
Derinkuyu, Turkey **72 C6** 38 22N 34 45 E
Dermantsi, Bulgaria **41 C8** 43 8N 24 17 E
Dermott, U.S.A. **113 J9** 33 32N 91 26W
Dêrong, China **58 C2** 28 44N 99 9 E
Derry = Londonderry, U.K. **15 B4** 55 0N 7 20W
Derry = Londonderry □, U.K. **15 B4** 55 0N 7 20W
Derry, N.H., U.S.A. **111 D13** 42 53N 71 19W
Derry, Pa., U.S.A. **110 F5** 40 20N 79 18W
Derryveagh Mts., Ireland **15 B3** 54 56N 8 11W
Derudub, Sudan **80 D4** 17 31N 36 7 E
Derval, France **18 E5** 47 40N 1 41W
Dervéni, Greece **38 C4** 38 8N 22 25 E
Derventa, Bos.-H. **42 F2** 44 59N 17 55 E
Derwent →, Cumb., U.K. **12 C4** 54 39N 3 33W
Derwent →, Derby, U.K. **12 E6** 52 57N 1 28W
Derwent →, N. Yorks., U.K. **12 D7** 53 45N 0 58W
Derwent Water, U.K. **12 C4** 54 35N 3 9W
Des Moines, Iowa, U.S.A. **112 E8** 41 35N 93 37W
Des Moines, N. Mex., U.S.A. **113 G3** 36 46N 103 50W
Des Moines →, U.S.A. **112 E9** 40 23N 91 25W
Desa, Romania **42 G8** 43 52N 23 2 E
Desaguadero →, Argentina **126 C2** 34 30 S 66 46W
Desaguadero →, Bolivia **124 G5** 16 35 S 69 5W
Descanso, Pta., Mexico **117 N9** 32 21N 117 3W
Descartes, France **20 B4** 46 59N 0 42 E
Deschaillons, Canada **103 C5** 46 32N 72 7W
Deschambault L., Canada **105 C8** 54 50N 103 30W
Deschutes →, U.S.A. **114 D3** 45 38N 120 55W
Dese, Ethiopia **81 E4** 11 5N 39 40 E
Deseado →, Argentina **128 F3** 47 45 S 65 54W
Desenzano del Garda, Italy **28 C7** 45 28N 10 32 E
Desert Center, U.S.A. **117 M11** 33 43N 115 24W
Desert Hot Springs, U.S.A. **117 M10** 33 58N 116 30W
Deshnok, India **68 F5** 27 48N 73 21 E
Desna →, Ukraine **47 G6** 50 33N 30 32 E
Desnătui →, Romania **43 G8** 43 53N 23 35 E
Desolación, I., Chile **128 G2** 53 0 S 74 0W
Despeñaperros, Paso, Spain **35 G7** 38 24N 3 30W
Despotovac, Serbia, Yug. **40 B5** 44 6N 21 30 E
Dessau, Germany **24 D8** 51 51N 12 14 E
Dessye = Dese, Ethiopia **81 E4** 11 5N 39 40 E
D'Estrees B., Australia **95 F2** 35 55 S 137 45 E
Desuri, India **68 G5** 25 18N 73 35 E
Desvres, France **19 B8** 50 40N 1 48 E
Det Udom, Thailand **64 E5** 14 54N 105 5 E
Deta, Romania **42 E6** 45 24N 21 13 E
Dete, S. Africa **88 B4** 18 38 S 26 50 E
Dete, Zimbabwe **87 F2** 18 38 S 26 50 E
Đetinja →, Serbia, Yug. **40 C4** 43 51N 20 5 E
Detmold, Germany **24 D4** 51 56N 8 52 E
Detour, Pt., U.S.A. **108 C2** 45 40N 86 40W
Detroit, U.S.A. **110 D1** 42 20N 83 3W
Detroit Lakes, U.S.A. **112 B7** 46 49N 95 51W
Detva, Slovak Rep. **27 C12** 48 34N 19 25 E
Deurne, Neths. **17 C5** 51 27N 5 49 E
Deutsche Bucht, Germany **24 A4** 54 15N 8 0 E
Deutschlandsberg, Austria **26 E8** 46 49N 15 14 E
Deux-Sèvres □, France **18 F6** 46 35N 0 20W
Deva, Romania **42 E7** 45 53N 22 55 E
Devakottai, India **66 Q11** 9 55N 78 45 E
Devaprayag, India **69 D8** 30 13N 78 35 E
Dévaványa, Hungary **42 C5** 47 2N 20 59 E
Deveci Dağları, Turkey **72 B7** 40 6N 36 15 E
Devecikonağı, Turkey **41 G12** 39 55N 28 34 E
Devecser, Hungary **42 C2** 47 6N 17 26 E
Develi, Turkey **72 C6** 38 23N 35 29 E
Deventer, Neths. **17 B6** 52 15N 6 10 E
Deveron →, U.K. **14 D6** 57 41N 2 32W
Devesel, Romania **42 F7** 44 28N 22 41 E
Devgadh Bariya, India **68 H5** 22 40N 73 55 E
Devikot, India **68 F4** 26 42N 71 12 E
Devils Den, U.S.A. **116 K7** 35 46N 119 58W
Devils Lake, U.S.A. **112 A5** 48 7N 98 52W
Devils Paw, Canada **104 B2** 58 47N 134 0W
Devils Tower Junction, U.S.A. **112 C2** 44 31N 104 57W
Devin, Bulgaria **41 E8** 41 44N 24 24 E
Devine, U.S.A. **113 L5** 29 8N 98 54W
Devizes, U.K. **13 F6** 51 22N 1 58W
Devli, India **68 G6** 25 50N 75 20 E
Devnya, Bulgaria **41 C11** 43 13N 27 33 E
Devolii → = Devoll →, Albania **40 F4** 40 57N 20 15 E
Devoll →, Albania **40 F4** 40 57N 20 15 E
Devon, Canada **104 C6** 53 24N 113 44W
Devon □, U.K. **13 G4** 50 50N 3 40W
Devon I., Canada **4 B3** 75 10N 85 0W
Devonport, Australia **94 G4** 41 10 S 146 22 E
Devonport, N.Z. **91 G5** 36 49 S 174 49 E
Devrek, Turkey **72 B4** 41 13N 31 57 E
Devrekâni, Turkey **72 B5** 41 36N 33 50 E
Devrez →, Turkey **72 B6** 41 6N 34 25 E
Dewas, India **68 H7** 22 59N 76 3 E
Dewetsdorp, S. Africa **88 D4** 29 33 S 26 39 E
Dexing, China **59 C11** 28 46N 117 30 E
Dexter, Maine, U.S.A. **109 C11** 45 1N 69 18W
Dexter, Mo., U.S.A. **113 G10** 36 48N 89 57W
Dexter, N. Mex., U.S.A. **113 J2** 33 12N 104 22W
Dey-Dey, L., Australia **93 E5** 29 12 S 131 4 E
Deyang, China **58 B5** 31 3N 104 27 E
Deyhūk, Iran **71 C8** 33 15N 57 30 E
Deyyer, Iran **71 E6** 27 55N 51 55 E
Dezadeash L., Canada **104 A1** 60 28N 136 58W
Dezfūl, Iran **71 C6** 32 20N 48 30 E
Dezhneva, Mys, Russia **51 C19** 66 5N 169 40W
Dezhou, China **56 F9** 37 26N 116 18 E
Dhadhar →, India **69 G11** 24 56N 85 24 E
Dháfni, Kríti, Greece **36 D7** 35 13N 25 3 E
Dháfni, Pelóponnisos, Greece **38 D4** 37 48N 22 1 E
Dhahabān, Si. Arabia **80 C4** 21 58N 39 3 E
Dhahiriya = Aẓ Ẓāhirīyah, West Bank **75 D3** 31 25N 34 58 E
Dhahran = Aẓ Ẓahrān, Si. Arabia **71 E6** 26 10N 50 7 E
Dhak, Pakistan **68 C5** 32 25N 72 33 E
Dhaka, Bangla. **69 H14** 23 43N 90 26 E
Dhaka □, Bangla. **69 G14** 24 25N 90 25 E
Dhali, Cyprus **36 D12** 35 1N 33 25 E
Dhamási, Greece **38 B4** 39 43N 22 11 E
Dhampur, India **69 E8** 29 19N 78 33 E
Dhamtari, India **67 J12** 20 42N 81 35 E
Dhanbad, India **69 H12** 23 50N 86 30 E
Dhangarhi, Nepal **67 E12** 28 55N 80 40 E
Dhankuta, Nepal **69 F12** 26 55N 87 40 E
Dhar, India **68 H6** 22 35N 75 26 E
Dharampur, India **68 H6** 22 13N 75 18 E
Dharamsala = Dharmsala, India **68 C7** 32 16N 76 23 E
Dhariwal, India **68 D6** 31 57N 75 19 E
Dharla →, Bangla. **69 G13** 25 46N 89 42 E
Dharmapuri, India **66 N11** 12 10N 78 10 E
Dharmjaygarh, India **69 H10** 22 28N 83 13 E
Dharmsala, India **68 C7** 32 16N 76 23 E
Dharni, India **68 J7** 21 33N 76 53 E
Dhasan →, India **69 G8** 25 48N 79 24 E
Dhaulagiri, Nepal **69 E10** 28 39N 83 28 E
Dhebar, L., India **68 G6** 24 10N 74 0 E
Dheftera, Cyprus **36 D12** 35 5N 33 16 E
Dhenkanal, India **67 J14** 20 45N 85 35 E
Dhenoúsa, Greece **39 D7** 37 8N 25 48 E
Dherinia, Cyprus **36 D12** 35 3N 33 57 E
Dheskáti, Greece **40 G5** 39 55N 21 49 E
Dhespotikó, Greece **38 E6** 36 57N 24 58 E
Dhestina, Greece **38 C4** 38 25N 22 31 E
Dhiarrizos →, Cyprus **36 E11** 34 41N 32 34 E
Dhībān, Jordan **75 D4** 31 30N 35 46 E
Dhidhimótikhon, Greece **41 E10** 41 22N 26 29 E
Dhíkti Óros, Greece **36 D7** 35 8N 25 30 E
Dhilianáta, Greece **38 C2** 38 15N 20 34 E
Dhílos, Greece **39 D7** 37 23N 25 15 E
Dhilwan, India **68 D6** 31 31N 75 21 E
Dhimarkhera, India **69 H9** 23 28N 80 22 E
Dhimitsána, Greece **38 D4** 37 36N 22 3 E
Dhírfis = Dhírfis Óros, Greece **38 C5** 38 40N 23 54 E
Dhírfis Óros, Greece **38 C5** 38 40N 23 54 E
Dhodhekánisos, Greece **39 E8** 36 35N 27 0 E
Dhodhekánisos □, Greece **39 E8** 36 35N 27 0 E
Dhokós, Greece **38 D5** 37 20N 23 20 E
Dholiana, Greece **38 B2** 39 54N 20 32 E
Dholka, India **68 H5** 22 44N 72 29 E
Dhomokós, Greece **38 B4** 39 10N 22 18 E
Dhoraji, India **68 J4** 21 45N 70 37 E
Dhoxáton, Greece **41 E8** 41 9N 24 16 E
Dhragonísi, Greece **39 D7** 37 27N 25 29 E
Dhráhstis, Ákra, Greece **36 A3** 39 48N 19 40 E
Dhrangadhra, India **68 H4** 22 59N 71 31 E
Dhrápanon, Ákra, Greece **36 D6** 35 28N 24 14 E
Dhriopís, Greece **38 D6** 37 25N 24 26 E
Dhrol, India **68 H4** 22 33N 70 25 E
Dhuburi, India **67 F16** 26 2N 89 59 E
Dhule, India **66 J9** 20 58N 74 50 E
Di-ib, W. →, Sudan **80 C4** 22 38N 36 6 E
Di Linh, Vietnam **65 G7** 11 35N 108 4 E
Di Linh, Cao Nguyen, Vietnam **65 G7** 11 30N 108 0 E
Día, Greece **36 D7** 35 28N 25 14 E
Diabakania, Guinea **82 C2** 10 38N 10 58W
Diablo, Mt., U.S.A. **116 H5** 37 53N 121 56W
Diablo Range, U.S.A. **116 J5** 37 20N 121 25W
Diafarabé, Mali **82 C4** 14 9N 4 57W
Diala, Mali **82 C3** 14 10N 9 58W
Dialakoro, Mali **82 C3** 12 18N 7 54W
Dialakoto, Senegal **82 C2** 13 21N 13 19W
Diallassagou, Mali **82 C4** 13 47N 3 41W
Diamante, Argentina **126 C3** 32 5 S 60 40W
Diamante, Italy **31 C8** 39 41N 15 49 E
Diamante →, Argentina **126 C2** 34 30 S 66 46W
Diamantina, Brazil **125 G10** 18 17 S 43 40W
Diamantina →, Australia **95 D2** 26 45 S 139 10 E
Diamantino, Brazil **125 F7** 14 30 S 56 30W
Diamond Bar, U.S.A. **117 L9** 34 1N 117 48W
Diamond Harbour, India **69 H13** 22 11N 88 14 E
Diamond Is., Australia **94 B5** 17 25 S 151 5 E
Diamond Mts., U.S.A. **114 G6** 39 50N 115 30W
Diamond Springs, U.S.A. **116 G6** 38 42N 120 49W
Dian Chi, China **58 E4** 24 50N 102 43 E
Dianalund, Denmark **11 J5** 55 32N 11 30 E
Dianbai, China **59 G8** 21 33N 111 0 E
Diancheng, China **59 G8** 21 30N 111 4 E
Dianjiang, China **58 B6** 30 24N 107 20 E
Diano Marina, Italy **28 E5** 43 54N 8 5 E
Dianra, Ivory C. **82 D3** 8 45N 6 14W
Diapaga, Burkina Faso **83 C5** 12 5N 1 46 E
Diapangou, Burkina Faso **83 C5** 12 5N 0 10 E
Diariguila, Guinea **82 C2** 10 35N 10 2W
Dībā, Oman **71 E8** 25 45N 56 16 E
Dibai, India **68 E8** 28 13N 78 15 E
Dibaya-Lubue, Dem. Rep. of the Congo **84 E3** 4 12 S 19 54 E
Dibete, Botswana **88 C4** 23 45 S 26 32 E
Dibrugarh, India **67 F19** 27 29N 94 55 E
Dickens, U.S.A. **113 J4** 33 37N 100 50W
Dickinson, U.S.A. **112 B3** 46 53N 102 47W
Dickson = Dikson, Russia **50 B9** 73 40N 80 5 E
Dickson, U.S.A. **109 G2** 36 5N 87 23W
Dickson City, U.S.A. **111 E9** 41 29N 75 40W
Dicle Nehri →, Turkey **73 D9** 37 44N 41 10 E
Dicomano, Italy **29 E8** 43 53N 11 31 E
Didesa, W. →, Ethiopia **81 E4** 10 2N 35 32 E
Didi, Sudan **81 F3** 6 18N 34 29 E
Didiéni, Mali **82 C3** 13 53N 8 6W
Didsbury, Canada **104 C6** 51 35N 114 10W
Didwana, India **68 F6** 27 23N 74 36 E
Die, France **21 D9** 44 47N 5 22 E
Diébougou, Burkina Faso **82 C4** 11 0N 3 15W
Diecke, Guinea **82 D3** 7 27N 8 54W
Diefenbaker, L., Canada **105 C7** 51 0N 106 55W
Diego de Almagro, Chile **126 B1** 26 22 S 70 3W
Diego Garcia, Ind. Oc. **3 E13** 7 50 S 72 50 E
Diekirch, Lux. **17 E6** 49 52N 6 10 E
Diéma, Mali **82 C3** 14 32N 9 12W
Diembéring, Senegal **82 C1** 12 29N 16 47W
Dien Ban, Vietnam **64 E7** 15 53N 108 16 E
Dien Bien, Vietnam **58 G4** 21 20N 103 0 E
Dien Khanh, Vietnam **65 F7** 12 15N 109 6 E
Diepholz, Germany **24 C4** 52 37N 8 22 E
Dieppe, France **18 C8** 49 54N 1 4 E
Dierks, U.S.A. **113 H8** 34 7N 94 1W
Diest, Belgium **17 D5** 50 58N 5 4 E
Dietikon, Switz. **25 H4** 47 24N 8 24 E

Dieulefit, *France* 21 D9 44 32N 5 4 E
Dieuze, *France* 19 D13 48 49N 6 43 E
Dif, *Somali Rep.* 74 G3 0 59N 0 56 E
Differdange, *Lux.* 17 E5 49 31N 5 54 E
Dig, *India* 68 F7 27 28N 77 20 E
Digba, *Dem. Rep. of the Congo* 86 B2 4 25N 25 48 E
Digby, *Canada* 103 D6 44 38N 65 50W
Diggi, *India* 68 F6 26 22N 75 26 E
Dighinala, *Bangla.* 67 H18 23 15N 92 5 E
Dighton, *U.S.A.* 112 F4 38 29N 100 28W
Digna, *Mali* 82 C3 14 48N 8 10W
Digne-les-Bains, *France* 21 D10 44 5N 6 12 E
Digoin, *France* 19 F11 46 29N 4 1 E
Digor, *Turkey* 73 B10 40 22N 43 25 E
Digos, *Phil.* 61 H6 6 45N 125 20 E
Digranes, *Iceland* 8 C6 66 4N 14 44W
Digul →, *Indonesia* 63 F9 7 7 S 138 42 E
Dihang →, *India* 67 F19 27 48N 95 30 E
Dijlah, Nahr →, *Asia* 70 D5 31 0N 47 25 E
Dijon, *France* 19 E12 47 20N 5 3 E
Dikhil, *Djibouti* 81 E5 11 8N 42 20 E
Dikili, *Turkey* 39 B8 39 4N 26 53 E
Dikirnis, *Egypt* 80 H7 31 6N 31 35 E
Dikkil = Dikhil, *Djibouti* 81 E5 11 8N 42 20 E
Dikodougou, *Ivory C.* 82 D3 9 4N 5 45W
Diksmuide, *Belgium* 17 C2 51 2N 2 52 E
Dikson, *Russia* 50 B9 73 40N 80 5 E
Dikwa, *Nigeria* 83 C7 12 4N 13 30 E
Dila, *Ethiopia* 81 F4 6 21N 38 22 E
Dili, *Indonesia* 63 F7 8 39 S 125 34 E
Dilijan, *Armenia* 49 K7 40 46N 44 57 E
Dilizhan = Dilijan, *Armenia* 49 K7 40 46N 44 57 E
Dilj, *Croatia* 42 E3 45 29N 18 1 E
Dillenburg, *Germany* 24 E4 50 43N 8 17 E
Dilley, *U.S.A.* 113 L5 28 40N 99 10W
Dilling, *Sudan* 81 E2 12 3N 29 35 E
Dillingen, *Bayern, Germany* 25 G6 48 36N 10 30 E
Dillingen, *Saarland, Germany* 25 F2 49 22N 6 43 E
Dillingham, *U.S.A.* 100 C4 59 3N 158 28W
Dillon, *Canada* 105 B7 55 56N 108 35W
Dillon, *Mont., U.S.A.* 114 D7 45 13N 112 38W
Dillon, *S.C., U.S.A.* 109 H6 34 25N 79 22W
Dillon →, *Canada* 105 B7 55 56N 108 56W
Dillsburg, *U.S.A.* 110 F7 40 7N 77 2W
Dilly, *Mali* 82 C3 15 1N 7 40W
Dilolo, *Dem. Rep. of the Congo* 84 G4 10 28 S 22 18 E
Dimas, *Mexico* 118 C3 23 43N 106 47W
Dimashq, *Syria* 75 B5 33 30N 36 18 E
Dimashq □, *Syria* 75 B5 33 30N 36 30 E
Dimbaza, *S. Africa* 89 E4 32 50 S 27 14 E
Dimbokro, *Ivory C.* 82 D4 6 45N 4 46W
Dimboola, *Australia* 95 F3 36 28 S 142 7 E
Dâmbovița = Dâmbovița →, *Romania* 43 F11 44 12N 26 26 E
Dimbulah, *Australia* 94 B4 17 8 S 145 4 E
Dimitrovgrad, *Bulgaria* 41 D9 42 5N 25 35 E
Dimitrovgrad, *Russia* 48 C9 54 14N 49 39 E
Dimitrovgrad, *Serbia, Yug.* 40 C6 43 2N 22 48 E
Dimitrovo = Pernik, *Bulgaria* 40 D7 42 35N 23 2 E
Dimmitt, *U.S.A.* 113 H3 34 33N 102 19W
Dimo, *Sudan* 81 F2 5 19N 29 10 E
Dimona, *Israel* 75 D4 31 2N 35 1 E
Dimovo, *Bulgaria* 40 C6 43 43N 22 50 E
Dinagat, *Phil.* 61 F6 10 10N 125 40 E
Dinajpur, *Bangla.* 67 G16 25 33N 88 43 E
Dinan, *France* 18 D4 48 28N 2 2W
Dīnān Āb, *Iran* 71 C8 32 4N 56 49 E
Dinant, *Belgium* 17 D4 50 16N 4 55 E
Dinapur, *India* 69 G11 25 38N 85 5 E
Dinar, *Turkey* 39 C12 38 5N 30 10 E
Dīnār, Kūh-e, *Iran* 71 D6 30 42N 51 46 E
Dinara Planina, *Croatia* 29 D13 44 0N 16 30 E
Dinard, *France* 18 D4 48 38N 2 6W
Dinaric Alps = Dinara Planina, *Croatia* 29 D13 44 0N 16 30 E
Dindanko, *Mali* 82 C3 14 8N 9 30W
Dinder, Nahr ed →, *Sudan* 81 E3 14 6N 33 40 E
Dindigul, *India* 66 P11 10 25N 78 0 E
Dindori, *India* 69 H9 22 57N 81 5 E
Ding Xian = Dingzhou, *China* 56 E8 38 30N 114 59 E
Dinga, *Pakistan* 68 G2 25 26N 67 10 E
Dingalan, *Phil.* 61 D4 15 18N 121 25 E
Dingbian, *China* 56 F4 37 35N 107 32 E
Dingelstädt, *Germany* 24 D6 51 18N 10 19 E
Dingle, *Ireland* 15 D1 52 9N 10 17W
Dingle, *Sweden* 11 F5 58 32N 11 35 E
Dingle B., *Ireland* 15 D1 52 3N 10 20W
Dingmans Ferry, *U.S.A.* 111 E10 41 13N 74 55W
Dingnan, *China* 59 E10 24 45N 115 0 E
Dingo, *Australia* 94 C4 23 38 S 149 19 E
Dingolfing, *Germany* 25 G8 48 37N 12 30 E
Dingtao, *China* 56 G8 35 5N 115 35 E
Dinguira, *Mali* 82 C2 14 11N 11 16W
Dinguiraye, *Guinea* 82 C2 11 18N 10 49W
Dingwall, *U.K.* 14 D4 57 36N 4 26W
Dingxi, *China* 56 G3 35 30N 104 33 E
Dingxiang, *China* 56 E7 38 30N 112 58 E
Dingyuan, *China* 59 A11 32 32N 117 41 E
Dingzhou, *China* 56 E8 38 30N 114 59 E
Dinh, Mui, *Vietnam* 65 G7 11 22N 109 1 E
Dinh Lap, *Vietnam* 58 G6 21 33N 107 6 E
Dinokwe, *Botswana* 88 C4 23 29 S 26 37 E
Dinorwic, *Canada* 105 D10 49 41N 92 30W
Dinosaur National Monument, *U.S.A.* 114 F9 40 30N 108 45W
Dinosaur Prov. Park, *Canada* 104 C6 50 47N 111 30W
Dinuba, *U.S.A.* 116 J7 36 32N 119 23W
Diö, *Sweden* 11 H8 56 37N 14 15 E
Dioïla, *Mali* 82 C3 12 23N 6 50W
Dioka, *Mali* 82 C2 14 57N 10 4W
Diongoï, *Mali* 82 C3 14 38N 8 34W
Diósgyör, *Hungary* 42 B5 48 7N 20 43 E
Diosig, *Romania* 42 C7 47 18N 22 2 E
Diougani, *Mali* 82 C4 14 19N 2 44W
Diouloulou, *Senegal* 82 C1 13 5N 16 38W
Dioura, *Mali* 82 C3 14 59N 5 12W
Diourbel, *Senegal* 82 C1 14 39N 16 12W
Dipalpur, *Pakistan* 68 D5 30 40N 73 39 E
Diplo, *Pakistan* 68 G3 24 35N 69 35 E
Dipolog, *Phil.* 61 G5 8 36N 123 20 E
Dir, *Pakistan* 66 B7 35 8N 71 59 E
Diré, *Mali* 82 B4 16 20N 3 25W
Dire Dawa, *Ethiopia* 81 F5 9 35N 41 45 E
Diriamba, *Nic.* 120 D2 11 51N 86 19W
Dirk Hartog I., *Australia* 93 E1 25 50 S 113 5 E
Dirranbandi, *Australia* 95 D4 28 33 S 148 17 E
Disa, *India* 68 G5 24 18N 72 10 E
Disa, *Sudan* 81 E3 12 5N 34 15 E
Disappointment, C., *U.S.A.* 114 C2 46 18N 124 5W
Disappointment, L., *Australia* 92 D3 23 20 S 122 40 E
Disaster B., *Australia* 95 F4 37 15 S 149 58 E
Discovery B., *Australia* 95 F3 38 10 S 140 40 E
Disentis Muster, *Switz.* 25 J4 46 42N 8 50 E
Dishna, *Egypt* 80 B3 26 9N 32 32 E
Disina, *Nigeria* 83 C6 11 35N 9 50 E
Disko = Qeqertarsuaq, *Greenland* 4 C5 69 45N 53 30W
Disko Bugt, *Greenland* 4 C5 69 10N 52 0W
Disna = Dzisna →, *Belarus* 46 E5 55 34N 28 12 E
Diss, *U.K.* 13 E9 52 23N 1 7 E
Disteghil Sar, *Pakistan* 69 A6 36 20N 75 12 E
Distrito Federal □, *Brazil* 125 G9 15 45 S 47 45W
Distrito Federal □, *Mexico* 119 D5 19 15N 99 10W
Disûq, *Egypt* 80 H7 31 8N 30 35 E
Diu, *India* 68 J4 20 45N 70 58 E
Dīvāndarreh, *Iran* 70 C5 35 55N 47 2 E
Dives →, *France* 18 C6 49 18N 0 7W
Dives-sur-Mer, *France* 18 C6 49 18N 0 8W
Divichi = Däväçi, *Azerbaijan* 49 K9 41 15N 48 57 E
Divide, *U.S.A.* 114 D7 45 45N 112 45W
Dividing Ra., *Australia* 93 E2 27 45 S 116 0 E
Divinópolis, *Brazil* 125 H10 20 10 S 44 54W
Divjake, *Albania* 40 F3 41 0N 19 32 E
Divnoye, *Russia* 49 H6 45 55N 43 21 E
Divo, *Ivory C.* 82 D3 5 48N 5 15W
Divriği, *Turkey* 73 C8 39 22N 38 7 E
Dīwāl Kol, *Afghan.* 68 B2 34 23N 67 52 E
Dixie Mt., *U.S.A.* 116 F6 39 55N 120 16W
Dixon, *Calif., U.S.A.* 116 G5 38 27N 121 49W
Dixon, *Ill., U.S.A.* 112 E10 41 50N 89 29W
Dixon Entrance, *U.S.A.* 100 C6 54 30N 132 0W
Dixville, *Canada* 111 A13 45 4N 71 46W
Diyadin, *Turkey* 73 C10 39 33N 43 40 E
Diyālā →, *Iraq* 70 C5 33 14N 44 31 E
Diyarbakır, *Turkey* 70 B4 37 55N 40 18 E
Diyodar, *India* 68 G4 24 8N 71 50 E
Djakarta = Jakarta, *Indonesia* 63 G12 6 9 S 106 49 E
Djamba, *Angola* 88 B1 16 45 S 13 58 E
Djambala, *Congo* 84 E2 2 32 S 14 30 E
Djanet, *Algeria* 78 D7 24 35N 9 32 E
Djawa = Jawa, *Indonesia* 63 G14 7 0 S 110 0 E
Djelfa, *Algeria* 78 B6 34 40N 3 15 E
Djema, *C.A.R.* 86 A2 6 3N 25 15 E
Djenné, *Mali* 82 C4 14 0N 4 30W
Djerba, I. de, *Tunisia* 79 B8 33 50N 10 48 E
Djerid, Chott, *Tunisia* 78 B7 33 42N 8 30 E
Djibo, *Burkina Faso* 83 C4 14 9N 1 35W
Djibouti, *Djibouti* 81 E5 11 30N 43 5 E
Djibouti ■, *Africa* 81 E5 12 0N 43 0 E
Djolu, *Dem. Rep. of the Congo* 84 D4 0 35N 22 5 E
Djougou, *Benin* 83 D5 9 40N 1 45 E
Djoum, *Cameroon* 84 D2 2 41N 12 35 E
Djourab, Erg du, *Chad* 79 E9 16 40N 18 50 E
Djugu, *Dem. Rep. of the Congo* 86 B3 1 55N 30 35 E
Djúpivogur, *Iceland* 8 D6 64 39N 14 17W
Djurås, *Sweden* 10 D9 60 34N 15 8 E
Djursland, *Denmark* 11 H4 56 27N 10 45 E
Dmitriya Lapteva, Proliv, *Russia* 51 B15 73 0N 140 0 E
Dmitriyev Lgovskiy, *Russia* 47 F8 52 10N 35 0 E
Dmitrov, *Russia* 46 D9 56 25N 37 32 E
Dmitrovsk-Orlovskiy, *Russia* 47 F8 52 29N 35 10 E
Dnepr → = Dnipro →, *Ukraine* 47 J7 46 30N 32 18 E
Dneprodzerzhinsk = Dniprodzerzhynsk, *Ukraine* 47 H8 48 32N 34 37 E
Dneprodzerzhinskoye Vdkhr. = Dniprodzerzhynske Vdskh., *Ukraine* 47 H8 48 49N 34 8 E
Dnepropetrovsk = Dnipropetrovsk, *Ukraine* 47 H8 48 30N 35 0 E
Dneprorudnoye = Dniprorudne, *Ukraine* 47 J8 47 21N 34 58 E
Dnestr → = Dnister →, *Europe* 47 J6 46 18N 30 17 E
Dnestrovski = Belgorod, *Russia* 47 G9 50 35N 36 35 E
Dnieper = Dnipro →, *Ukraine* 47 J7 46 30N 32 18 E
Dniester = Dnister →, *Europe* 47 J6 46 18N 30 17 E
Dnipro →, *Ukraine* 47 J7 46 30N 32 18 E
Dniprodzerzhynsk, *Ukraine* 47 H8 48 32N 34 37 E
Dniprodzerzhynske Vdskh., *Ukraine* 47 H8 48 49N 34 8 E
Dnipropetrovsk, *Ukraine* 47 H8 48 30N 35 0 E
Dniprorudne, *Ukraine* 47 J8 47 21N 34 58 E
Dnister →, *Europe* 47 J6 46 18N 30 17 E
Dnistrovskyy Lyman, *Ukraine* 47 J6 46 15N 30 17 E
Dno, *Russia* 46 D5 57 50N 29 58 E
Dnyapro = Dnipro →, *Ukraine* 47 J7 46 30N 32 18 E
Doaktown, *Canada* 103 C6 46 33N 66 8W
Doan Hung, *Vietnam* 58 G5 21 30N 105 10 E
Doany, *Madag.* 89 A8 14 21 S 49 30 E
Doba, *Chad* 79 G9 8 40N 16 50 E
Dobandi, *Pakistan* 68 D2 31 13N 66 50 E
Dobbiaco, *Italy* 29 B9 46 44N 12 14 E
Dobbyn, *Australia* 94 B3 19 44 S 140 2 E
Dobczyce, *Poland* 45 J7 49 52N 20 25 E
Dobele, *Latvia* 9 H20 56 37N 23 16 E
Dobele □, *Latvia* 44 B10 56 35N 23 5 E
Döbeln, *Germany* 24 D9 51 6N 13 7 E
Doberai, Jazirah, *Indonesia* 63 E8 1 25 S 133 0 E
Dobiegniew, *Poland* 45 F2 52 59N 15 45 E
Doblas, *Argentina* 126 D3 37 5 S 64 0W
Dobo, *Indonesia* 63 F8 5 45 S 134 15 E
Doboj, *Bos.-H.* 42 F3 44 46N 18 4 E
Dobra, *Wielkopolskie, Poland* 45 G5 51 55N 18 37 E
Dobra, *Zachodnio-Pomorskie, Poland* 44 E2 53 34N 15 20 E
Dobra, *Dîmbovita, Romania* 43 F10 44 52N 25 40 E
Dobra, *Hunedoara, Romania* 42 E7 45 54N 22 36 E
Dobre Miasto, *Poland* 44 E7 53 58N 20 26 E
Dobrești, *Romania* 42 D7 46 51N 22 18 E
Dobreta-Turnu Severin, *Romania* 42 F7 44 39N 22 41 E
Dobrich, *Bulgaria* 41 C11 43 37N 27 49 E
Dobrinishta, *Bulgaria* 40 E7 41 49N 23 34 E
Dobříš, *Czech Rep.* 26 B7 49 46N 14 10 E
Dobrodzień, *Poland* 45 H5 50 45N 18 25 E
Dobropole, *Ukraine* 47 H9 48 25N 37 2 E
Dobruja, *Europe* 43 F13 44 30N 28 15 E
Dobrush, *Belarus* 47 F6 52 25N 31 22 E
Dobrzany, *Poland* 44 E2 53 22N 15 25 E
Dobrzyń nad Wisłą, *Poland* 45 F6 52 39N 19 22 E
Doc, Mui, *Vietnam* 64 D6 17 58N 106 30 E
Docker River, *Australia* 93 D4 24 52 S 129 5 E
Docksta, *Sweden* 10 A12 63 3N 18 18 E
Doctor Arroyo, *Mexico* 118 C4 23 40N 100 11W
Doda, *India* 69 C6 33 10N 75 34 E
Doda, L., *Canada* 102 C4 49 25N 75 13W
Dodecanese = Dhodhekánisos, *Greece* 39 E8 36 35N 27 0 E
Dodge City, *U.S.A.* 113 G5 37 45N 100 1W
Dodge L., *Canada* 105 B7 59 50N 105 36W
Dodgeville, *U.S.A.* 112 D9 42 58N 90 8W
Dodo, *Cameroon* 83 D7 7 30N 12 3 E
Dodo, *Sudan* 81 F2 5 10N 29 57 E
Dodola, *Ethiopia* 81 F4 6 59N 39 11 E
Dodoma, *Tanzania* 86 D4 6 8 S 35 45 E
Dodoma □, *Tanzania* 86 D4 6 0 S 36 0 E
Dodona, *Greece* 38 B2 39 40N 20 46 E
Dodsland, *Canada* 105 C7 51 50N 108 45W
Dodson, *U.S.A.* 114 B9 48 24N 108 15W
Dodurga, *Turkey* 39 B11 39 49N 29 57 E
Doesburg, *Neths.* 17 B6 52 1N 6 9 E
Doetinchem, *Neths.* 17 C6 51 59N 6 18 E
Dog Creek, *Canada* 104 C4 51 35N 122 14W
Dog L., *Man., Canada* 105 C9 51 2N 98 31W
Dog L., *Ont., Canada* 102 C2 48 48N 89 30W
Doğanşehir, *Turkey* 72 C7 38 5N 37 53 E
Dogi, *Afghan.* 66 C3 32 20N 62 50 E
Dogliani, *Italy* 28 D4 44 32N 7 56 E
Dogondoutchi, *Niger* 83 C5 13 38N 4 2 E
Dogran, *Pakistan* 68 D5 31 48N 73 35 E
Doğubayazıt, *Turkey* 70 B5 39 31N 44 5 E
Doguéraoua, *Niger* 83 C6 14 0N 5 31 E
Doha = Ad Dawḩah, *Qatar* 71 E6 25 15N 51 35 E
Dohazari, *Bangla.* 67 H18 22 10N 92 5 E
Dohrighat, *India* 69 F10 26 16N 83 31 E
Doi, *Indonesia* 63 D7 2 14N 127 49 E
Doi Luang, *Thailand* 64 C3 18 30N 101 0 E
Doi Saket, *Thailand* 64 C2 18 52N 99 9 E
Dois Irmãos, Sa., *Brazil* 125 E10 9 0 S 42 30W
Dojransko Jezero, *Macedonia* 40 E6 41 13N 22 44 E
Dokkum, *Neths.* 17 A5 53 20N 5 59 E
Dokri, *Pakistan* 68 F3 27 25N 68 7 E
Dokuchayevsk, *Ukraine* 47 J9 47 44N 37 40 E
Dol-de-Bretagne, *France* 18 D5 48 34N 1 47W
Dolac, *Kosovo, Yug.* 40 D4 42 36N 20 36 E
Dolak, Pulau, *Indonesia* 63 F9 8 0 S 138 30 E
Dolbeau, *Canada* 103 C5 48 53N 72 18W
Dole, *France* 19 E12 47 7N 5 31 E
Doleib, Wadi →, *Sudan* 81 E3 12 10N 33 15 E
Dolenji Logatec, *Slovenia* 29 C11 45 56N 14 15 E
Dolgellau, *U.K.* 12 E4 52 45N 3 53W
Dolgelley = Dolgellau, *U.K.* 12 E4 52 45N 3 53W
Dolhasca, *Romania* 43 C11 47 26N 26 36 E
Dolianova, *Italy* 30 C2 39 22N 9 10 E
Dolinskaya = Dolynska, *Ukraine* 47 H7 48 6N 32 46 E
Dolj □, *Romania* 43 F8 44 10N 23 30 E
Dollard, *Neths.* 17 A7 53 20N 7 10 E
Dolna Banya, *Bulgaria* 40 D7 42 18N 23 44 E
Dolni Chiflik, *Bulgaria* 41 D11 42 59N 27 43 E
Dolni Dŭbnik, *Bulgaria* 41 C8 43 24N 24 26 E
Dolnośląskie □, *Poland* 45 G3 51 10N 16 30 E
Dolný Kubín, *Slovak Rep.* 27 B12 49 12N 19 18 E
Dolo, *Ethiopia* 81 G5 4 11N 42 3 E
Dolo, *Italy* 29 C9 45 25N 12 5 E
Dolomites = Dolomiti, *Italy* 29 B8 46 23N 11 51 E
Dolomiti, *Italy* 29 B8 46 23N 11 51 E
Dolores, *Argentina* 126 D4 36 20 S 57 40W
Dolores, *Uruguay* 126 C4 33 34 S 58 15W
Dolores, *U.S.A.* 115 H9 37 28N 108 30W
Dolores →, *U.S.A.* 115 G9 38 49N 109 17W
Dolovo, *Serbia, Yug.* 42 F5 44 55N 20 52 E
Dolphin, C., *Falk. Is.* 128 G5 51 10 S 59 0W
Dolphin and Union Str., *Canada* 100 B8 69 5N 114 45W
Dolsk, *Poland* 45 G4 51 59N 17 3 E
Dolynska, *Ukraine* 47 H7 48 6N 32 46 E
Dolzhanskaya, *Russia* 47 J9 46 37N 37 48 E
Dom Pedrito, *Brazil* 127 C5 31 0 S 54 40W
Doma, *Nigeria* 83 D6 8 25N 8 18 E
Domaniç, *Turkey* 39 B11 39 48N 29 36 E
Domariaganj →, *India* 69 F10 26 17N 83 44 E
Domasi, *Malawi* 87 F4 15 15 S 35 22 E
Domažlice, *Czech Rep.* 26 B5 49 28N 12 58 E
Dombarovskiy, *Russia* 50 D6 50 46N 59 32 E
Dombås, *Norway* 9 E13 62 4N 9 8 E
Dombasle-sur-Meurthe, *France* 19 D13 48 38N 6 21 E
Dombes, *France* 21 C9 45 58N 5 0 E
Dombóvár, *Hungary* 42 D3 46 21N 18 9 E
Dombrád, *Hungary* 42 B6 48 13N 21 54 E
Domel I. = Letsôk-aw Kyun, *Burma* 65 G2 11 30N 98 25 E
Domérat, *France* 19 F9 46 21N 2 32 E
Domeyko, *Chile* 126 B1 29 0 S 71 0W
Domeyko, Cordillera, *Chile* 126 A2 24 30 S 69 0W
Domfront, *France* 18 D6 48 37N 0 40W
Dominador, *Chile* 126 A2 24 21 S 69 20W
Dominica ■, *W. Indies* 121 C7 15 20N 61 20W
Dominica Passage, *W. Indies* 121 C7 15 10N 61 20W
Dominican Rep. ■, *W. Indies* 121 C5 19 0N 70 30W
Dömitz, *Germany* 24 B7 53 8N 11 15 E
Domme, *France* 20 D5 44 48N 1 12 E
Domnești, *Romania* 43 E9 45 12N 24 50 E
Domodóssola, *Italy* 28 B5 46 7N 8 17 E
Dompaire, *France* 19 D13 48 14N 6 14 E
Dompierre-sur-Besbre, *France* 19 F10 46 31N 3 41 E
Dompim, *Ghana* 82 D4 5 10N 2 5W
Domrémy-la-Pucelle, *France* 19 D12 48 26N 5 40 E
Domville, Mt., *Australia* 95 D5 28 1 S 151 15 E
Domvraína, *Greece* 38 C4 38 15N 22 59 E
Domžale, *Slovenia* 29 B11 46 9N 14 35 E
Don →, *Russia* 47 J10 47 4N 39 18 E
Don →, *Aberds., U.K.* 14 D6 57 11N 2 5W
Don →, *S. Yorks., U.K.* 12 D7 53 41N 0 52W
Don, C., *Australia* 92 B5 11 18 S 131 46 E
Don Benito, *Spain* 35 G5 38 53N 5 51W
Dona Ana = Nhamaabué, *Mozam.* 87 F4 17 25 S 35 5 E
Doña Mencía, *Spain* 35 H6 37 33N 4 21W
Donaghadee, *U.K.* 15 B6 54 39N 5 33W
Donald, *Australia* 95 F3 36 23 S 143 0 E
Donaldsonville, *U.S.A.* 113 K9 30 6N 90 59W
Donalsonville, *U.S.A.* 109 K3 31 3N 84 53W
Donau = Dunărea →, *Europe* 43 E14 45 20N 29 40 E
Donau →, *Austria* 17 D3 48 10N 17 0 E
Donaueschingen, *Germany* 25 H4 47 56N 8 29 E
Donauwörth, *Germany* 25 G6 48 43N 10 47 E
Doncaster, *U.K.* 12 D6 53 32N 1 6W
Dondo, *Mozam.* 87 F3 19 33 S 34 46 E
Dondo, Teluk, *Indonesia* 63 D6 0 50N 120 30 E
Dondra Head, *Sri Lanka* 66 S12 5 55N 80 40 E
Donduşeni, *Moldova* 43 B12 48 14N 27 36 E
Donegal, *Ireland* 15 B3 54 39N 8 5W
Donegal □, *Ireland* 15 B4 54 53N 8 0W
Donegal B., *Ireland* 15 B3 54 31N 8 49W
Donets →, *Russia* 49 G5 47 33N 40 55 E
Donetsk, *Ukraine* 47 J9 48 0N 37 45 E
Dong Ba Thin, *Vietnam* 65 F7 12 8N 109 13 E
Dong Dang, *Vietnam* 58 G6 21 54N 106 42 E
Dong Giam, *Vietnam* 64 C5 19 25N 105 31 E
Dong Ha, *Vietnam* 64 D6 16 55N 107 8 E
Dong Hene, *Laos* 64 D5 16 40N 105 18 E
Dong Hoi, *Vietnam* 64 D6 17 29N 106 36 E
Dong Jiang →, *China* 59 F10 23 6N 114 0 E
Dong Khe, *Vietnam* 64 A6 22 26N 106 27 E
Dong Ujimqin Qi, *China* 56 B9 45 32N 116 55 E
Dong Van, *Vietnam* 64 A5 23 16N 105 22 E
Dong Xoai, *Vietnam* 65 G6 11 32N 106 55 E
Donga, *Nigeria* 83 D7 7 45N 10 2 E
Donga →, *Nigeria* 83 D7 8 20N 9 58 E
Dong'an, *China* 59 D8 26 23N 111 12 E
Dongara, *Australia* 93 E1 29 14 S 114 57 E
Dongbei, *China* 57 D13 45 0N 125 0 E
Dongchuan, *China* 58 D4 26 8N 103 1 E
Donges, *France* 18 E4 47 18N 2 4W
Dongfang, *China* 64 C7 18 50N 108 33 E
Dongfeng, *China* 57 C13 42 40N 125 34 E
Donggala, *Indonesia* 63 E5 0 30 S 119 40 E
Donggan, *China* 58 F5 23 22N 105 9 E
Donggou, *China* 57 E13 39 52N 124 10 E
Dongguan, *China* 59 F9 22 58N 113 44 E
Dongguang, *China* 56 F9 37 50N 116 30 E
Donghai Dao, *China* 59 G8 21 0N 110 15 E
Dongjingcheng, *China* 57 B15 44 5N 129 10 E
Dongkou, *China* 59 D8 27 6N 110 35 E
Donglan, *China* 58 E6 24 30N 107 21 E
Dongliu, *China* 59 B11 30 13N 116 55 E
Dongmen, *China* 58 F6 22 20N 107 48 E
Dongning, *China* 57 B16 44 2N 131 5 E
Dongnyi, *China* 58 C3 28 3N 100 15 E
Dongola, *Sudan* 80 D3 19 9N 30 22 E
Dongping, *China* 56 G9 35 55N 116 20 E
Dongshan, *China* 59 F11 23 43N 117 30 E
Dongsheng, *China* 56 E6 39 50N 110 0 E
Dongtai, *China* 57 H11 32 51N 120 21 E
Dongting Hu, *China* 59 C9 29 18N 112 45 E
Dongtou, *China* 59 D13 27 51N 121 10 E
Dongxiang, *China* 59 C11 28 11N 116 34 E
Dongxing, *China* 58 G7 21 34N 108 0 E
Dongyang, *China* 59 C13 29 13N 120 15 E
Dongzhi, *China* 59 B11 30 9N 117 0 E
Donington, C., *Australia* 95 E2 34 45 S 136 0 E
Doniphan, *U.S.A.* 113 G9 36 37N 90 50W
Donja Stubica, *Croatia* 29 C12 45 59N 15 59 E
Donji Dušnik, *Serbia, Yug.* 40 C6 43 12N 22 5 E
Donji Miholjac, *Croatia* 42 E3 45 45N 18 10 E
Donji Milanovac, *Serbia, Yug.* 40 B6 44 28N 22 6 E
Donji Vakuf, *Bos.-H.* 42 F2 44 8N 17 24 E
Dønna, *Norway* 8 C15 66 6N 12 30 E
Donna, *U.S.A.* 113 M5 26 9N 98 4W
Donnaconna, *Canada* 103 C5 46 41N 71 41W
Donnelly's Crossing, *N.Z.* 91 F4 35 42 S 173 38 E
Donnybrook, *Australia* 93 F2 33 34 S 115 48 E
Donnybrook, *S. Africa* 89 D4 29 59 S 29 48 E
Donora, *U.S.A.* 110 F5 40 11N 79 52W
Donostia = Donostia-San Sebastián, *Spain* 32 B3 43 17N 1 58W
Donostia-San Sebastián, *Spain* 32 B3 43 17N 1 58W
Donskoy, *Russia* 46 F10 53 55N 38 15 E
Donsol, *Phil.* 61 E5 12 54N 123 36 E
Donzère, *France* 21 D8 44 28N 4 43 E
Donzy, *France* 19 E10 47 20N 3 6 E
Doon →, *U.K.* 14 F4 55 27N 4 39W
Dora, L., *Australia* 92 D3 22 0 S 123 0 E
Dora Báltea →, *Italy* 28 C5 45 11N 8 3 E
Dora Ripária →, *Italy* 28 C4 45 5N 7 44 E
Doran L., *Canada* 105 A7 61 13N 108 6W
Dorchester, *U.K.* 13 G5 50 42N 2 27W
Dorchester, C., *Canada* 101 B12 65 27N 77 27W
Dordabis, *Namibia* 88 C2 22 52 S 17 38 E
Dordogne □, *France* 20 C4 45 5N 0 40 E
Dordogne →, *France* 20 C3 45 2N 0 36W
Dordrecht, *Neths.* 17 C4 51 48N 4 39 E
Dordrecht, *S. Africa* 88 E4 31 20 S 27 3 E
Dore →, *France* 20 C7 45 50N 3 35 E
Dore, Mts., *France* 20 C6 45 32N 2 50 E
Doré L., *Canada* 105 C7 54 46N 107 17W
Doré Lake, *Canada* 105 C7 54 38N 107 36W
Dorfen, *Germany* 25 G8 48 15N 12 8 E
Dorgali, *Italy* 30 B2 40 17N 9 35 E
Dori, *Burkina Faso* 83 C4 14 3N 0 2W
Doring →, *S. Africa* 88 E2 31 54 S 18 39 E
Doringbos, *S. Africa* 88 E2 31 59 S 19 16 E
Dorion, *Canada* 111 A10 45 23N 74 3W
Dormaa-Ahenkro, *Ghana* 82 D4 7 15N 2 52W
Dormans, *France* 19 C10 49 4N 3 38 E
Dormo, Ras, *Eritrea* 81 E5 13 14N 42 35 E
Dornbirn, *Austria* 26 D2 47 25N 9 45 E
Dornes, *France* 19 F10 46 48N 3 18 E
Dornești, *Romania* 43 C11 47 52N 26 1 E
Dornie, *U.K.* 14 D3 57 17N 5 31W
Dornoch, *U.K.* 14 D4 57 53N 4 2W
Dornoch Firth, *U.K.* 14 D4 57 51N 4 4W
Dornogovĭ □, *Mongolia* 56 C6 44 0N 110 0 E
Doro, *Mali* 83 B4 16 9N 0 51W
Dorog, *Hungary* 42 C3 47 42N 18 45 E
Dorogobuzh, *Russia* 46 E7 54 50N 33 18 E
Dorohoi, *Romania* 43 C11 47 56N 26 23 E
Döröö Nuur, *Mongolia* 60 B4 48 0N 93 0 E
Dorr, *Iran* 71 C6 33 17N 50 38 E
Dorre I., *Australia* 93 E1 25 13 S 113 12 E
Dorrigo, *Australia* 95 E5 30 20 S 152 44 E
Dorris, *U.S.A.* 114 F3 41 58N 121 55W
Dorset, *Canada* 110 A6 45 14N 78 54W
Dorset, *U.S.A.* 110 E4 41 40N 80 40W
Dorset □, *U.K.* 13 G5 50 45N 2 26W
Dorsten, *Germany* 24 D2 51 40N 6 58 E
Dortmund, *Germany* 24 D3 51 30N 7 28 E
Dortmund-Ems-Kanal →, *Germany* 24 D3 51 50N 7 26 E
Dörtyol, *Turkey* 72 D7 36 50N 36 13 E
Dorum, *Germany* 24 B4 53 41N 8 34 E
Doruma, *Dem. Rep. of the Congo* 86 B2 4 42N 27 33 E
Dorūneh, *Iran* 71 C8 35 10N 57 18 E
Dos Bahías, C., *Argentina* 128 E3 44 58 S 65 32W
Dos Hermanas, *Spain* 35 H5 37 16N 5 55W
Dos Palos, *U.S.A.* 116 J6 36 59N 120 37W
Döşemealtı, *Turkey* 39 D12 37 4N 30 36 E
Dosso, *Niger* 83 C5 13 0N 3 13 E
Dothan, *U.S.A.* 109 K3 31 13N 85 24W
Doty, *U.S.A.* 116 D3 46 38N 123 17W
Douai, *France* 19 B10 50 21N 3 4 E
Douako, *Guinea* 82 D2 9 45N 10 8W
Douala, *Cameroon* 83 E6 4 0N 9 45 E
Douarnenez, *France* 18 D2 48 6N 4 21W
Doubabougou, *Mali* 82 C3 14 13N 7 59W
Double Island Pt., *Australia* 95 D5 25 56 S 153 11 E
Double Mountain Fork →, *U.S.A.* 113 J4 33 16N 100 0W
Doubrava →, *Czech Rep.* 26 A8 50 2N 15 20 E
Doubs □, *France* 19 E13 47 10N 6 20 E
Doubs →, *France* 19 F12 46 53N 5 1 E
Doubtful Sd., *N.Z.* 91 L1 45 20 S 166 49 E
Doubtless B., *N.Z.* 91 F4 34 55 S 173 26 E
Doudeville, *France* 18 C7 49 43N 0 47 E
Doué-la-Fontaine, *France* 18 E6 47 11N 0 16W
Douentza, *Mali* 82 C4 14 58N 2 48W
Douglas, *S. Africa* 88 D3 29 4 S 23 46 E
Douglas, *U.K.* 12 C3 54 10N 4 28W
Douglas, *Ariz., U.S.A.* 115 L9 31 21N 109 33W
Douglas, *Ga., U.S.A.* 109 K4 31 31N 82 51W
Douglas, *Wyo., U.S.A.* 112 D2 42 45N 105 24W
Douglas Chan., *Canada* 104 C3 53 40N 129 20W
Douglas Pt., *Canada* 110 B3 44 19N 81 37W
Douglasville, *U.S.A.* 109 J3 33 45N 84 45W
Doukáton, Ákra, *Greece* 38 C2 38 34N 20 30 E
Doulevant-le-Château, *France* 19 D11 48 23N 4 55 E
Doullens, *France* 19 B9 50 10N 2 20 E
Doumen, *China* 59 F9 22 10N 113 18 E
Douna, *Mali* 82 C3 13 13N 6 0W
Douna, *Mali* 83 C4 14 44N 1 38W
Dounreay, *U.K.* 14 C5 58 35N 3 44W
Dourada, Serra, *Brazil* 125 F9 13 10 S 48 45W
Dourados, *Brazil* 127 A5 22 9 S 54 50W
Dourados →, *Brazil* 127 A5 21 58 S 54 18W
Dourados, Serra dos, *Brazil* 127 A5 23 30 S 53 30W
Dourdan, *France* 19 D9 48 30N 2 1 E
Douro →, *Europe* 34 D2 41 8N 8 40W
Douvaine, *France* 19 F13 46 19N 6 16 E
Douvres-la-Délivrande, *France* 18 C6 49 17N 0 23W
Douze →, *France* 20 E3 43 54N 0 30W
Dove →, *U.K.* 12 E6 52 51N 1 36W
Dove Creek, *U.S.A.* 115 H9 37 46N 108 54W
Dover, *Australia* 94 G4 43 18 S 147 2 E
Dover, *U.K.* 13 F9 51 7N 1 19 E
Dover, *Del., U.S.A.* 108 F8 39 10N 75 32W
Dover, *N.H., U.S.A.* 111 C14 43 12N 70 56W
Dover, *N.J., U.S.A.* 111 F10 40 53N 74 34W
Dover, *Ohio, U.S.A.* 110 F3 40 32N 81 29W
Dover, Pt., *Australia* 93 F4 32 32 S 125 32 E
Dover, Str. of, *Europe* 13 G9 51 0N 1 30 E
Dover-Foxcroft, *U.S.A.* 109 C11 45 11N 69 13W
Dover Plains, *U.S.A.* 111 E11 41 43N 73 35W
Dovey = Dyfi →, *U.K.* 13 E3 52 32N 4 3W
Dovrefjell, *Norway* 9 E13 62 15N 9 33 E
Dow Rūd, *Iran* 71 C6 33 28N 49 4 E
Dowa, *Malawi* 87 E3 13 38 S 33 58 E
Dowagiac, *U.S.A.* 108 E2 41 59N 86 6W
Dowerin, *Australia* 93 F2 31 12 S 117 2 E
Dowgha'i, *Iran* 71 B8 36 54N 58 32 E
Dowlatābād, *Iran* 71 D8 28 20N 56 40 E
Down □, *U.K.* 15 B5 54 23N 6 2W
Downey, *Calif., U.S.A.* 117 M8 33 56N 118 7W
Downey, *Idaho, U.S.A.* 114 E7 42 26N 112 7W
Downham Market, *U.K.* 13 E8 52 37N 0 23 E
Downieville, *U.S.A.* 116 F6 39 34N 120 50W
Downpatrick, *U.K.* 15 B6 54 20N 5 43W
Downpatrick Hd., *Ireland* 15 B2 54 20N 9 21W
Downsville, *U.S.A.* 111 D10 42 5N 74 50W
Downton, Mt., *Canada* 104 C4 52 42N 124 52W
Dowsārī, *Iran* 71 D8 28 25N 57 59 E
Doyle, *U.S.A.* 116 E6 40 2N 120 6W
Doylestown, *U.S.A.* 111 F9 40 21N 75 10W
Dozois, Rés., *Canada* 102 C4 47 30N 77 5W
Dra Khel, *Pakistan* 68 F2 27 58N 66 45 E
Drac →, *France* 21 C9 45 12N 5 42 E
Dračevo, *Macedonia* 40 E5 41 56N 21 31 E
Drachten, *Neths.* 17 A6 53 7N 6 5 E
Drăgănești, *Moldova* 43 C13 47 43N 28 15 E

Drăgăneşti-Olt, Romania 43 F9 44 9N 24 32 E
Drăgăneşti-Vlaşca, Romania 43 F10 44 5N 25 33 E
Dragaš, Kosovo, Yug. 40 D4 42 5N 20 41 E
Drăgăşani, Romania 43 F9 44 39N 24 17 E
Dragichyn, Belarus 47 F3 52 15N 25 8 E
Dragocvet, Serbia, Yug. 40 C5 43 58N 21 15 E
Dragovishtitsa, Bulgaria 40 D6 42 22N 22 39 E
Draguignan, France 21 E10 43 32N 6 27 E
Drain, U.S.A. 114 E2 43 40N 123 19W
Drake, U.S.A. 112 B4 47 55N 100 23W
Drake Passage, S. Ocean 5 B17 58 0S 68 0W
Drakensberg, S. Africa 89 D4 31 0S 28 0 E
Dráma, Greece 41 E8 41 9N 24 10 E
Dráma □, Greece 41 E8 41 20N 24 0 E
Drammen, Norway 9 G14 59 42N 10 12 E
Drangajökull, Iceland 8 C2 66 9N 22 15W
Dranov, Ostrov, Romania 43 F14 44 55N 29 30 E
Dras, India 69 B6 34 25N 75 48 E
Drau = Drava →, Croatia 42 E3 45 33N 18 55 E
Drava →, Croatia 42 E3 45 33N 18 55 E
Dravograd, Slovenia 29 B12 46 36N 15 5 E
Drawa →, Poland 45 F2 52 52N 15 59 E
Drawno, Poland 45 E2 53 13N 15 46 E
Drawsko Pomorskie, Poland 44 E2 53 35N 15 50 E
Drayton Valley, Canada 104 C6 53 12N 114 58W
Dreieich, Germany 25 E4 50 1N 8 41 E
Dren, Kosovo, Yug. 40 C4 43 8N 20 46 E
Drenthe □, Neths. 17 B6 52 52N 6 40 E
Drepanum, C., Cyprus 36 E11 34 54N 32 19 E
Dresden, Canada 110 D2 42 35N 82 11W
Dresden, Germany 24 D9 51 3N 13 44 E
Dreux, France 18 D8 48 44N 1 23 E
Drezdenko, Poland 45 F2 52 50N 15 49 E
Driffield, U.K. 12 C7 54 0N 0 26W
Driftwood, U.S.A. 110 E6 41 20N 78 8W
Driggs, U.S.A. 114 E8 43 44N 111 6W
Drin →, Albania 40 D3 42 1N 19 38 E
Drin i Zi →, Albania 40 E4 41 37N 20 28 E
Drina →, Bos.-H. 40 B3 44 53N 19 21 E
Drincea →, Romania 42 F7 44 20N 22 55 E
Drini → = Drin →, Albania 40 D3 42 1N 19 38 E
Drinjača →, Bos.-H. 42 F4 44 15N 19 8 E
Drissa = Vyerkhnyadzvinsk, Belarus 46 E4 55 45N 27 58 E
Drniš, Croatia 29 E13 43 51N 16 10 E
Drøbak, Norway 9 G14 59 39N 10 39 E
Drobin, Poland 45 F6 52 42N 19 58 E
Drochia, Moldova 43 B12 48 2N 27 48 E
Drogheda, Ireland 15 C5 53 43N 6 22W
Drogichin = Dragichyn, Belarus 47 F3 52 15N 25 8 E
Drogobych = Drohobych, Ukraine 47 H2 49 20N 23 30 E
Drohiczyn, Poland 45 F9 52 24N 22 39 E
Drohobych, Ukraine 47 H2 49 20N 23 30 E
Droichead Atha = Drogheda, Ireland 15 C5 53 43N 6 22W
Droichead Nua, Ireland 15 C5 53 11N 6 48W
Droitwich, U.K. 13 E5 52 16N 2 8W
Drôme □, France 21 D9 44 38N 5 15 E
Drôme →, France 21 D8 44 46N 4 46 E
Dromedary, C., Australia 95 F5 36 17S 150 10 E
Dromore, U.K. 15 B4 54 31N 7 28W
Dromore West, Ireland 15 B3 54 15N 8 52W
Dronero, Italy 28 D4 44 28N 7 22 E
Dronfield, U.K. 12 D6 53 19N 1 27W
Dronne →, France 20 C3 45 2N 0 9W
Dronninglund, Denmark 11 G4 57 10N 10 19 E
Dronten, Neths. 17 B5 52 32N 5 43 E
Dropt →, France 20 D3 44 35N 0 6W
Drosendorf, Austria 26 C8 48 52N 15 37 E
Droué, France 18 D8 48 3N 1 6 E
Drumbo, Canada 110 C4 43 16N 80 35W
Drumheller, Canada 104 C6 51 25N 112 40W
Drummond, U.S.A. 114 C7 46 40N 113 9W
Drummond I., U.S.A. 108 C4 46 1N 83 39W
Drummond Pt., Australia 95 E2 34 9S 135 16 E
Drummond Ra., Australia 94 C4 23 45S 147 10 E
Drummondville, Canada 102 C5 45 55N 72 25W
Drumright, U.S.A. 113 H6 35 59N 96 36W
Druskininkai, Lithuania 9 J20 54 3N 23 58 E
Drut →, Belarus 47 F6 53 8N 30 5 E
Druya, Belarus 46 E4 55 45N 27 28 E
Druzhba, Bulgaria 41 C12 43 15N 28 1 E
Druzhina, Russia 51 C15 68 14N 145 18 E
Drvar, Bos.-H. 29 D13 44 21N 16 23 E
Drvenik, Croatia 29 E13 43 27N 16 3 E
Drwęca →, Poland 45 E5 53 0N 18 42 E
Dry Tortugas, U.S.A. 120 B3 24 38N 82 55W
Dryanovo, Bulgaria 41 D9 42 59N 25 28 E
Dryden, Canada 105 D10 49 47N 92 50W
Dryden, U.S.A. 111 D8 42 30N 76 18W
Drygalski I., Antarctica 5 C7 66 0S 92 0 E
Drysdale →, Australia 92 B4 13 59S 126 51 E
Drysdale I., Australia 94 A2 11 41S 136 0 E
Drzewica, Poland 45 G7 51 27N 20 29 E
Drzewiczka →, Poland 45 G7 51 36N 20 36 E
Dschang, Cameroon 83 D7 5 32N 10 3 E
Du Bois, U.S.A. 110 E6 41 8N 78 46W
Du Gué →, Canada 102 A5 57 21N 70 45W
Du He, China 59 A8 32 48N 110 40 E
Du Quoin, U.S.A. 112 G10 38 1N 89 14W
Du'an, China 58 F7 23 59N 108 3 E
Duanesburg, U.S.A. 111 D10 42 45N 74 11W
Duaringa, Australia 94 C4 23 42S 149 42 E
Ḑubā, Si. Arabia 70 E2 27 10N 35 40 E
Dubai = Dubayy, U.A.E. 71 E7 25 18N 55 20 E
Dubăsari, Moldova 43 C14 47 15N 29 10 E
Dubăsari Vdkhr., Moldova 43 C13 47 30N 29 0 E
Dubawnt →, Canada 105 A8 64 33N 100 6W
Dubawnt, L., Canada 105 A8 63 4N 101 42W
Dubayy, U.A.E. 71 E7 25 18N 55 20 E
Dubbo, Australia 95 E4 32 11S 148 35 E
Dubele, Dem. Rep. of the Congo 86 B2 2 56N 29 35 E
Dübendorf, Switz. 25 H4 47 24N 8 37 E
Dubica, Croatia 29 C13 45 11N 16 48 E
Dublin, Ireland 15 C5 53 21N 6 15W
Dublin, Ga., U.S.A. 109 J4 32 32N 82 54W
Dublin, Tex., U.S.A. 113 J5 32 5N 98 21W
Dublin □, Ireland 15 C5 53 24N 6 20W
Dubna, Russia 46 D9 56 44N 37 10 E
Dubnica nad Váhom, Slovak Rep. 27 C11 48 58N 18 11 E
Dubno, Ukraine 47 G3 50 25N 25 45 E
Dubois, U.S.A. 114 D7 44 10N 112 14W
Dubossary = Dubăsari, Moldova 43 C14 47 15N 29 10 E
Dubossary Vdkhr. = Dubăsari Vdkhr., Moldova 43 C13 47 30N 29 0 E
Dubovka, Russia 49 F7 49 5N 44 50 E
Dubovskoye, Russia 49 G6 47 28N 42 46 E
Dubrajpur, India 69 H12 23 48N 87 25 E
Dubréka, Guinea 82 D2 9 46N 13 31W
Dubrovitsa = Dubrovytsya, Ukraine 47 G4 51 31N 26 35 E
Dubrovnik, Croatia 40 D2 42 39N 18 6 E
Dubrovytsya, Ukraine 47 G4 51 31N 26 35 E
Dubuque, U.S.A. 112 D9 42 30N 90 41W
Dubysa →, Lithuania 44 C10 55 5N 23 26 E
Duchang, China 59 C11 29 18N 116 12 E
Duchesne, U.S.A. 114 F8 40 10N 110 24W
Duchess, Australia 94 C2 21 20S 139 50 E
Ducie I., Pac. Oc. 97 K15 24 40S 124 48W
Duck →, U.S.A. 109 G2 36 2N 87 52W
Duck Cr. →, Australia 92 D2 22 37S 116 53 E
Duck Lake, Canada 105 C7 52 50N 106 16W
Duck Mountain Prov. Park, Canada 105 C8 51 45N 101 0W
Duckwall, Mt., U.S.A. 116 H6 37 58N 120 7W
Duderstadt, Germany 24 D6 51 31N 10 15 E
Dudhi, India 67 G13 24 15N 83 10 E
Dudinka, Russia 51 C9 69 30N 86 13 E
Dudley, U.K. 13 E5 52 31N 2 5W
Dudwa, India 69 E9 28 30N 80 41 E
Duékoué, Ivory C. 82 D3 6 40N 7 15W
Dueñas, Spain 34 D6 41 52N 4 33W
Duero = Douro →, Europe 34 D2 41 8N 8 40W
Dufftown, U.K. 14 D5 57 27N 3 8W
Dufourspitz, Switz. 25 K3 45 56N 7 52 E
Dugi Otok, Croatia 29 D11 44 0N 15 3 E
Dugo Selo, Croatia 29 C13 45 51N 16 18 E
Duifken Pt., Australia 94 A3 12 33S 141 38 E
Duisburg, Germany 24 D2 51 26N 6 45 E
Duiwelskloof, S. Africa 89 C5 23 42S 30 10 E
Dujiangyan, China 58 B4 31 2N 103 38 E
Duk Fadiat, Sudan 81 F3 7 45N 31 29 E
Duk Faiwil, Sudan 81 F3 7 30N 31 29 E
Dukat, Albania 40 F3 40 16N 19 32 E
Dukati = Dukat, Albania 40 F3 40 16N 19 32 E
Dūkdamīn, Iran 71 C8 35 59N 57 43 E
Dukelský Průsmyk, Slovak Rep. 27 B14 49 25N 21 42 E
Dukhān, Qatar 71 E6 25 25N 50 50 E
Dukhovshchina, Russia 46 E7 55 15N 32 27 E
Duki, Pakistan 66 D6 30 14N 68 25 E
Dukla, Poland 45 J8 49 30N 21 35 E
Duku, Bauchi, Nigeria 83 C7 10 43N 10 43 E
Duku, Sokoto, Nigeria 83 C5 11 11N 4 55 E
Dulag, Phil. 61 F6 10 57N 125 2 E
Dulce, U.S.A. 115 H10 36 56N 107 0W
Dulce →, Argentina 126 C3 30 32S 62 33W
Dulce, G., Costa Rica 120 E3 8 40N 83 20W
Dulf, Iraq 70 C5 35 7N 45 51 E
Dŭlgopol, Bulgaria 41 C11 43 3N 27 22 E
Dulit, Banjaran, Malaysia 62 D4 3 15N 114 30 E
Duliu, China 56 E9 39 2N 116 55 E
Dullewala, Pakistan 68 D4 31 50N 71 25 E
Dullstroom, S. Africa 89 D5 25 27S 30 7 E
Dülmen, Germany 24 D3 51 49N 7 17 E
Dulovo, Bulgaria 41 C11 43 48N 27 9 E
Dulq Maghār, Syria 70 B3 36 22N 38 39 E
Duluth, U.S.A. 112 B8 46 47N 92 6W
Dum Dum, India 69 H13 22 39N 88 33 E
Dum Duma, India 67 F19 27 40N 95 40 E
Dūmā, Syria 75 B5 33 34N 36 24 E
Dumaguete, Phil. 61 G5 9 17N 123 15 E
Dumai, Indonesia 62 D2 1 35N 101 28 E
Dumaran, Phil. 61 F3 10 33N 119 50 E
Dumas, Ark., U.S.A. 113 J9 33 53N 91 29W
Dumas, Tex., U.S.A. 113 H4 35 52N 101 58W
Ḑumayr, Syria 75 B5 33 39N 36 42 E
Dumbarton, U.K. 14 F4 55 57N 4 33W
Dumbier, Slovak Rep. 27 C12 48 56N 19 38 E
Dumbleyung, Australia 93 F2 33 17S 117 42 E
Dumboa, Nigeria 83 C7 11 15N 12 55 E
Dumbrăveni, Romania 43 D9 46 14N 24 34 E
Dumfries, U.K. 14 F5 55 4N 3 37W
Dumfries & Galloway □, U.K. 14 F5 55 9N 3 58W
Dumitreşti, Romania 43 E11 45 33N 26 55 E
Dumka, India 69 G12 24 12N 87 15 E
Dumlupınar, Turkey 39 C12 38 53N 30 0 E
Dümmer, Germany 24 C4 52 31N 8 20 E
Dumoine →, Canada 102 C4 46 13N 77 51W
Dumoine, L., Canada 102 C4 46 55N 77 55W
Dumraon, India 69 G11 25 33N 84 8 E
Dumyât, Egypt 80 H7 31 24N 31 48 E
Dumyât, Masabb, Egypt 80 H7 31 28N 31 51 E
Dún Dealgan = Dundalk, Ireland 15 B5 54 1N 6 24W
Dun Laoghaire, Ireland 15 C5 53 17N 6 8W
Dun-le-Palestel, France 19 F8 46 18N 1 39 E
Dun-sur-Auron, France 19 F9 46 53N 2 33 E
Dun-sur-Meuse, France 19 C12 49 23N 5 11 E
Duna = Dunărea →, Europe 43 E14 45 20N 29 40 E
Duna →, Hungary 42 E3 45 51N 18 48 E
Duna-völgyi-főcsatorna, Hungary 42 D4 46 40N 19 14 E
Dunaföldvár, Hungary 42 D3 46 50N 18 57 E
Dunagiri, India 69 D8 30 31N 79 52 E
Dunaj = Dunărea →, Europe 43 E14 45 20N 29 40 E
Dunaj →, Slovak Rep. 27 D11 47 50N 18 50 E
Dunajec →, Poland 45 H7 50 15N 20 44 E
Dunajská Streda, Slovak Rep. 27 C10 48 0N 17 37 E
Dunakeszi, Hungary 42 C4 47 37N 19 8 E
Dunapataj, Hungary 42 D4 46 39N 19 4 E
Dunărea →, Europe 43 E14 45 20N 29 40 E
Dunaszekcső, Hungary 42 D3 46 6N 18 45 E
Dunaújváros, Hungary 42 D3 46 58N 18 57 E
Dunav = Dunărea →, Europe 43 E14 45 20N 29 40 E
Dunavaţu de Jos, Romania 43 F14 44 59N 29 13 E
Dunavtsi, Bulgaria 40 C6 43 57N 22 53 E
Dunay, Russia 54 C6 42 52N 132 22 E
Dunback, N.Z. 91 L3 45 23S 170 36 E
Dunbar, U.K. 14 E6 56 0N 2 31W
Dunblane, U.K. 14 E5 56 11N 3 58W
Duncan, Canada 104 D4 48 45N 123 40W
Duncan, Ariz., U.S.A. 115 K9 32 43N 109 6W
Duncan, Okla., U.S.A. 113 H6 34 30N 97 57W
Duncan, L., Canada 102 B4 53 29N 77 58W
Duncan L., Canada 104 A6 62 51N 113 58W
Duncan Town, Bahamas 120 B4 22 15N 75 45W
Duncannon, U.S.A. 110 F7 40 23N 77 2W
Duncansby Head, U.K. 14 C5 58 38N 3 1W
Duncansville, U.S.A. 110 F6 40 25N 78 26W
Dundaga, Latvia 44 A9 57 31N 22 21 E
Dundalk, Canada 110 B4 44 10N 80 24W
Dundalk, Ireland 15 B5 54 1N 6 24W
Dundalk, U.S.A. 108 F7 39 16N 76 32W
Dundalk Bay, Ireland 15 C5 53 55N 6 15W
Dundas, Canada 110 C5 43 17N 79 59W
Dundas, L., Australia 93 F3 32 35S 121 50 E
Dundas I., Canada 104 C2 54 30N 130 50W
Dundas Str., Australia 92 B5 11 15S 131 35 E
Dundee, S. Africa 89 D5 28 11S 30 15 E
Dundee, U.K. 14 E6 56 28N 2 59W
Dundee, U.S.A. 110 D8 42 32N 76 59W
Dundee City □, U.K. 14 E6 56 30N 2 58W
Dundgovĭ □, Mongolia 56 B4 45 10N 106 0 E
Dundrum, U.K. 15 B6 54 16N 5 52W
Dundrum B., U.K. 15 B6 54 13N 5 47W
Dunedin, N.Z. 91 L3 45 50S 170 33 E
Dunedin, U.S.A. 109 L4 28 1N 82 47W
Dunedoo, Australia 95 E4 32 0S 149 25 E
Dunfermline, U.K. 14 E5 56 5N 3 27W
Dungannon, Canada 110 C3 43 51N 81 36W
Dungannon, U.K. 15 B5 54 31N 6 46W
Dungarpur, India 68 H5 23 52N 73 45 E
Dungarvan, Ireland 15 D4 52 5N 7 37W
Dungarvan Harbour, Ireland 15 D4 52 4N 7 35W
Dungeness, U.K. 13 G8 50 54N 0 59 E
Dungo, L. do, Angola 88 B2 17 15S 19 0 E
Dungog, Australia 95 E5 32 22S 151 46 E
Dungu, Dem. Rep. of the Congo 86 B2 3 40N 28 32 E
Dungun, Malaysia 65 K4 4 45N 103 25 E
Dunguna, Sudan 80 C4 21 10N 37 9 E
Dungunâb, Khalij, Sudan 80 C4 21 5N 37 12 E
Dunhua, China 57 C15 43 20N 128 14 E
Dunhuang, China 60 B4 40 8N 94 36 E
Dunk I., Australia 94 B4 17 59S 146 29 E
Dunkassa, Benin 83 C5 10 21N 3 10 E
Dunkeld, Australia 95 E4 33 25S 149 29 E
Dunkeld, U.K. 14 E5 56 34N 3 35W
Dunkerque, France 19 A9 51 2N 2 20 E
Dunkery Beacon, U.K. 13 F4 51 9N 3 36W
Dunkirk = Dunkerque, France 19 A9 51 2N 2 20 E
Dunkirk, U.S.A. 110 D5 42 29N 79 20W
Dunkuj, Sudan 81 E3 12 50N 32 49 E
Dunkwa, Central, Ghana 82 D4 6 0N 1 47W
Dunkwa, Central, Ghana 83 D4 5 30N 1 0W
Dúnleary = Dun Laoghaire, Ireland 15 C5 53 17N 6 8W
Dunleer, Ireland 15 C5 53 50N 6 24W
Dunmanus B., Ireland 15 E2 51 31N 9 50W
Dunmanway, Ireland 15 E2 51 43N 9 6W
Dunmara, Australia 94 B1 16 42S 133 25 E
Dunmore, U.S.A. 111 E9 41 25N 75 38W
Dunmore Hd., Ireland 15 D1 52 10N 10 35W
Dunmore Town, Bahamas 120 A4 25 30N 76 39W
Dunn, U.S.A. 109 H6 35 19N 78 37W
Dunnellon, U.S.A. 109 L4 29 3N 82 28W
Dunnet Hd., U.K. 14 C5 58 40N 3 21W
Dunning, U.S.A. 112 E4 41 50N 100 6W
Dunnville, Canada 110 D5 42 54N 79 36W
Dunolly, Australia 95 F3 36 51S 143 44 E
Dunoon, U.K. 14 F4 55 57N 4 56W
Dunphy, U.S.A. 114 F5 40 42N 116 31W
Dunqul, Egypt 80 C3 23 26N 31 37 E
Duns, U.K. 14 F6 55 47N 2 20W
Dunseith, U.S.A. 112 A4 48 50N 100 3W
Dunsmuir, U.S.A. 114 F2 41 13N 122 16W
Dunstable, U.K. 13 F7 51 53N 0 32W
Dunstan Mts., N.Z. 91 L2 44 53S 169 35 E
Dunster, Canada 104 C5 53 8N 119 50W
Dunvegan L., Canada 105 A7 60 8N 107 10W
Duolun, China 56 C9 42 12N 116 28 E
Duong Dong, Vietnam 65 G4 10 13N 103 58 E
Dupree, U.S.A. 112 C4 45 4N 101 35W
Dupuyer, U.S.A. 114 B7 48 13N 112 30W
Duque de Caxias, Brazil 127 A7 22 45S 43 19W
Durack →, Australia 92 C4 15 33S 127 52 E
Durack Ra., Australia 92 C4 16 50S 127 40 E
Durağan, Turkey 72 B6 41 25N 35 3 E
Durak, Turkey 39 B10 39 42N 28 17 E
Đurakovac, Kosovo, Yug. 40 D4 42 43N 20 29 E
Durance →, France 21 E8 43 55N 4 45 E
Durand, U.S.A. 112 C9 44 38N 91 58W
Durango, Mexico 118 C4 24 3N 104 39W
Durango, U.S.A. 115 H10 37 16N 107 53W
Durango □, Mexico 118 C4 25 0N 105 0W
Durankulak, Bulgaria 41 C12 43 41N 28 32 E
Durant, Miss., U.S.A. 113 J10 33 4N 89 51W
Durant, Okla., U.S.A. 113 J6 33 59N 96 25W
Duratón →, Spain 34 D6 41 37N 4 7W
Durazno, Uruguay 126 C4 33 25S 56 31W
Durazzo = Durrës, Albania 40 E3 41 19N 19 28 E
Durban, France 20 F6 42 59N 2 49 E
Durban, S. Africa 89 D5 29 49S 31 1 E
Durbuy, Belgium 17 D5 50 21N 5 28 E
Dúrcal, Spain 35 J7 36 59N 3 34W
Đur[d-]evac, Croatia 42 D2 46 2N 17 3 E
Düren, Germany 24 E2 50 48N 6 29 E
Durg, India 67 J12 21 15N 81 22 E
Durgapur, India 69 H12 23 30N 87 20 E
Durham, Canada 102 D3 44 10N 80 49W
Durham, U.K. 12 C6 54 47N 1 34W
Durham, Calif., U.S.A. 116 F5 39 39N 121 48W
Durham, N.C., U.S.A. 109 H6 35 59N 78 54W
Durham, N.H., U.S.A. 111 C14 43 8N 70 56W
Durham □, U.K. 12 C6 54 42N 1 45W
Durleşti, Moldova 43 C13 47 1N 28 46 E
Ḑurmā, Si. Arabia 70 E5 24 37N 46 8 E
Durmitor, Montenegro, Yug. 40 C2 43 10N 19 0 E
Durness, U.K. 14 C4 58 34N 4 45W
Durrës, Albania 40 E3 41 19N 19 28 E
Durrësi = Durrës, Albania 40 E3 41 19N 19 28 E
Durrow, Ireland 15 D4 52 51N 7 24W
Dursey I., Ireland 15 E1 51 36N 10 12W
Dursunbey, Turkey 39 B10 39 35N 28 37 E
Durtal, France 18 E6 47 40N 0 18W
Duru, Dem. Rep. of the Congo 86 B2 4 14N 28 50 E
Duru Gölü, Turkey 41 E12 41 20N 28 35 E
Durusu, Turkey 41 E12 41 17N 28 41 E
Durūz, Jabal ad, Jordan 75 C5 32 35N 36 40 E
D'Urville, Tanjung, Indonesia 63 E9 1 28S 137 54 E
D'Urville I., N.Z. 91 J4 40 50S 173 55 E
Duryea, U.S.A. 111 E9 41 20N 75 45W
Dûsh, Egypt 80 C3 24 35N 30 41 E
Dushak, Turkmenistan 50 F7 37 13N 60 1 E
Dushan, China 58 E6 25 48N 107 30 E
Dushanbe, Tajikistan 50 F7 38 33N 68 48 E
Dusheti, Georgia 49 J7 42 10N 44 42 E
Dushore, U.S.A. 111 E8 41 31N 76 24W
Dusky Sd., N.Z. 91 L1 45 47S 166 30 E
Dussejour, C., Australia 92 B4 14 45S 128 13 E
Düsseldorf, Germany 24 D2 51 14N 6 47 E
Duszniki-Zdrój, Poland 45 H3 50 24N 16 24 E
Dutch Harbor, U.S.A. 100 C3 53 53N 166 32W
Dutlwe, Botswana 88 C3 23 58S 23 46 E
Dutsan Wai, Nigeria 83 C6 10 50N 8 10 E
Dutton, Canada 110 D3 42 39N 81 30W
Dutton →, Australia 94 C3 20 44S 143 10 E
Duved, Sweden 10 A6 63 24N 12 55 E
Düvertepe, Turkey 39 B10 39 14N 28 27 E
Duwayhin, Khawr, U.A.E. 71 E6 24 20N 51 25 E
Duyun, China 58 D6 26 18N 107 29 E
Düzağac, Turkey 39 C12 38 48N 30 10 E
Düzce, Turkey 72 B4 40 50N 31 10 E
Duzdab = Zāhedān, Iran 71 D9 29 30N 60 50 E
Dve Mogili, Bulgaria 41 C9 43 35N 25 55 E
Dvina, Severnaya →, Russia 50 C5 64 32N 40 30 E
Dvinsk = Daugavpils, Latvia 9 J22 55 53N 26 32 E
Dvor, Croatia 29 C13 45 4N 16 22 E
Dvůr Králové nad Labem, Czech Rep. 26 A8 50 27N 15 50 E
Dwarka, India 68 H3 22 18N 69 8 E
Dwellingup, Australia 93 F2 32 43S 116 4 E
Dwight, Canada 110 A5 45 20N 79 1W
Dwight, U.S.A. 108 E1 41 5N 88 26W
Dyatkovo, Russia 46 F8 53 40N 34 27 E
Dyatlovo = Dzyatlava, Belarus 46 F3 53 28N 25 28 E
Dyce, U.K. 14 D6 57 13N 2 12W
Dyer, C., Canada 101 B13 66 40N 61 0W
Dyer Bay, Canada 110 A3 45 10N 81 20W
Dyer Plateau, Antarctica 5 D17 70 45S 65 30W
Dyersburg, U.S.A. 113 G10 36 3N 89 23W
Dyfi →, U.K. 13 E3 52 32N 4 3W
Dyje →, Czech Rep. 27 C9 48 37N 16 56 E
Dymer, Ukraine 47 G6 50 47N 30 18 E
Dynów, Poland 45 J9 49 50N 22 11 E
Dysart, Australia 94 C4 22 32S 148 23 E
Dzamin Üüd = Borhoyn Tal, Mongolia 56 C6 43 50N 111 58 E
Dzerzhinsk, Russia 48 B6 56 14N 43 30 E
Dzhalinda, Russia 51 D13 53 26N 124 0 E
Dzhambul = Zhambyl, Kazakstan 50 E8 42 54N 71 22 E
Dzhankoy, Ukraine 47 K8 45 40N 34 20 E
Dzhanybek, Kazakstan 48 F8 49 25N 46 50 E
Dzharylhach, Ostriv, Ukraine 47 J7 46 2N 32 55 E
Dzhezkazgan = Zhezqazghan, Kazakstan 50 E7 47 44N 67 40 E
Dzhizak = Jizzakh, Uzbekistan 50 E7 40 6N 67 50 E
Dzhugdzur, Khrebet, Russia 51 D14 57 30N 138 0 E
Dzhvari = Jvari, Georgia 49 J6 42 42N 42 4 E
Działdowo, Poland 45 E7 53 15N 20 15 E
Działoszyce, Poland 45 H7 50 22N 20 20 E
Działoszyn, Poland 45 G5 51 6N 18 50 E
Dzibilchaltun, Mexico 119 C7 21 5N 89 36W
Dzierzgoń, Poland 44 E6 53 58N 19 20 E
Dzierżoniów, Poland 45 H3 50 45N 16 39 E
Dzilam de Bravo, Mexico 119 C7 21 24N 88 53W
Dzisna, Belarus 46 E5 55 34N 28 12 E
Dzisna →, Belarus 46 E5 55 34N 28 12 E
Dziwnów, Poland 44 D1 54 2N 14 45 E
Dzungaria = Junggar Pendi, China 60 B3 44 30N 86 0 E
Dzuumod, Mongolia 60 B5 47 45N 106 58 E
Dzyarzhynsk, Belarus 46 F4 53 40N 27 1 E
Dzyatlava, Belarus 46 F3 53 28N 25 28 E

E

Eabamet L., Canada 102 B2 51 30N 87 46W
Eads, U.S.A. 112 F3 38 29N 102 47W
Eagar, U.S.A. 115 J9 34 6N 109 17W
Eagle, Alaska, U.S.A. 100 B5 64 47N 141 12W
Eagle, Colo., U.S.A. 114 G10 39 39N 106 50W
Eagle →, Canada 103 B8 53 36N 57 26W
Eagle Butte, U.S.A. 112 C4 45 0N 101 10W
Eagle Grove, U.S.A. 112 D8 42 40N 93 54W
Eagle L., Canada 105 D10 49 42N 93 13W
Eagle L., Calif., U.S.A. 114 F3 40 39N 120 45W
Eagle L., Maine, U.S.A. 109 B11 46 20N 69 22W
Eagle Lake, Canada 110 A6 45 8N 78 29W
Eagle Lake, Maine, U.S.A. 109 B11 47 3N 68 36W
Eagle Lake, Tex., U.S.A. 113 L6 29 35N 96 20W
Eagle Mountain, U.S.A. 117 M11 33 49N 115 27W
Eagle Nest, U.S.A. 115 H11 36 33N 105 16W
Eagle Pass, U.S.A. 113 L4 28 43N 100 30W
Eagle Pk., U.S.A. 116 G7 38 10N 119 25W
Eagle Pt., Australia 92 C3 16 11S 124 23 E
Eagle River, Mich., U.S.A. 108 B1 47 24N 88 18W
Eagle River, Wis., U.S.A. 112 C10 45 55N 89 15W
Eaglehawk, Australia 95 F3 36 44S 144 15 E
Eagles Mere, U.S.A. 111 E8 41 25N 76 33W
Ealing, U.K. 13 F7 51 31N 0 20W
Ear Falls, Canada 105 C10 50 38N 93 13W
Earle, U.S.A. 113 H9 35 16N 90 28W
Earlimart, U.S.A. 117 K7 35 53N 119 16W
Earn →, U.K. 14 E5 56 21N 3 18W
Earn, L., U.K. 14 E4 56 23N 4 13W
Earnslaw, Mt., N.Z. 91 L2 44 32S 168 27 E
Earth, U.S.A. 113 H3 34 14N 102 24W
Easley, U.S.A. 109 H4 34 50N 82 36W
East Anglia, U.K. 12 E9 52 30N 1 0 E
East Angus, Canada 103 C5 45 30N 71 40W
East Aurora, U.S.A. 110 D6 42 46N 78 37W
East Ayrshire □, U.K. 14 F4 55 26N 4 11W
East Bengal, Bangla. 67 H17 24 0N 90 0 E
East Beskids = Vychodné Beskydy, Europe 27 B15 49 20N 22 0 E
East Brady, U.S.A. 110 F5 40 59N 79 36W
East C., N.Z. 91 G7 37 42S 178 35 E
East Chicago, U.S.A. 108 E2 41 38N 87 27W
East China Sea, Asia 60 C7 30 0N 126 0 E
East Coulee, Canada 104 C6 51 23N 112 27W
East Dereham, U.K. 13 E8 52 41N 0 57 E
East Dunbartonshire □, U.K. 14 F4 55 57N 4 13W
East Falkland, Falk. Is. 122 J5 51 30S 58 30W
East Grand Forks, U.S.A. 112 B6 47 56N 97 1W
East Greenwich, U.S.A. 111 E13 41 40N 71 27W
East Grinstead, U.K. 13 F8 51 7N 0 0W
East Hartford, U.S.A. 111 E12 41 46N 72 39W
East Helena, U.S.A. 114 C8 46 35N 111 56W
East Indies, Asia 52 K15 0 0 120 0 E
East Kilbride, U.K. 14 F4 55 47N 4 11W
East Lansing, U.S.A. 108 D3 42 44N 84 29W
East Liverpool, U.S.A. 110 F4 40 37N 80 35W
East London, S. Africa 89 E4 33 0S 27 55 E
East Lothian □, U.K. 14 F6 55 58N 2 44W
East Main = Eastmain, Canada 102 B4 52 10N 78 30W
East Northport, U.S.A. 111 F11 40 53N 73 20W
East Orange, U.S.A. 111 F10 40 46N 74 13W
East Pacific Ridge, Pac. Oc. 97 J17 15 0S 110 0W
East Palestine, U.S.A. 110 F4 40 50N 80 33W
East Pine, Canada 104 B4 55 48N 120 12W
East Point, U.S.A. 109 J3 33 41N 84 27W
East Providence, U.S.A. 111 E13 41 49N 71 23W
East Pt., Canada 103 C7 46 27N 61 58W
East Renfrewshire □, U.K. 14 F4 55 46N 4 21W
East Retford = Retford, U.K. 12 D7 53 19N 0 56W
East Riding of Yorkshire □, U.K. 12 D7 53 55N 0 30W
East Rochester, U.S.A. 110 C7 43 7N 77 29W
East St. Louis, U.S.A. 112 F9 38 37N 90 9W
East Schelde = Oosterschelde →, Neths. 17 C4 51 33N 4 0 E
East Siberian Sea, Russia 51 B17 73 0N 160 0 E
East Stroudsburg, U.S.A. 111 E9 41 1N 75 11W
East Sussex □, U.K. 13 G8 50 56N 0 19 E
East Tawas, U.S.A. 108 C4 44 17N 83 29W
East Timor = Timor Timur □, Indonesia 63 F7 9 0S 125 0 E
East Toorale, Australia 95 E4 30 27S 145 28 E
East Walker →, U.S.A. 116 G7 38 52N 119 10W
East Windsor, U.S.A. 111 F10 40 17N 74 34W
Eastbourne, N.Z. 91 J5 41 19S 174 55 E
Eastbourne, U.K. 13 G8 50 46N 0 18 E
Eastend, Canada 105 D7 49 32N 108 50W
Easter I. = Pascua, I. de, Pac. Oc. 97 K17 27 0S 109 0W
Eastern □, Ghana 83 D4 6 30N 0 30W
Eastern □, Kenya 86 C4 0 0 38 30 E
Eastern □, Uganda 86 B3 1 50N 33 45 E
Eastern Cape □, S. Africa 88 E4 32 0S 26 0 E
Eastern Cr. →, Australia 94 C3 20 40S 141 35 E
Eastern Ghats, India 66 N11 14 0N 78 50 E
Eastern Group = Lau Group, Fiji 91 C9 17 0S 178 30W
Eastern Group, Australia 93 F3 33 30S 124 30 E
Eastern Province □, S. Leone 82 D2 8 15N 11 0W
Eastern Transvaal = Mpumalanga □, S. Africa 89 B5 26 0S 30 0 E
Easterville, Canada 105 C9 53 8N 99 49W
Easthampton, U.S.A. 111 D12 42 16N 72 40W
Eastlake, U.S.A. 110 E3 41 40N 81 26W
Eastland, U.S.A. 113 J5 32 24N 98 49W
Eastleigh, U.K. 13 G6 50 58N 1 21W
Eastmain, Canada 102 B4 52 10N 78 30W
Eastmain →, Canada 102 B4 52 27N 78 26W
Eastman, Canada 111 A12 45 18N 72 19W
Eastman, U.S.A. 109 J4 32 12N 83 11W
Easton, Md., U.S.A. 108 F7 38 47N 76 5W
Easton, Pa., U.S.A. 111 F9 40 41N 75 13W
Easton, Wash., U.S.A. 116 C5 47 14N 121 11W
Eastpointe, U.S.A. 110 D2 42 27N 82 56W
Eastport, U.S.A. 109 C12 44 56N 67 0W
Eastsound, U.S.A. 116 B4 48 42N 122 55W
Eaton, U.S.A. 112 E2 40 32N 104 42W
Eatonia, Canada 105 C7 51 13N 109 25W
Eatonton, U.S.A. 109 J4 33 20N 83 23W
Eatontown, U.S.A. 111 F10 40 19N 74 4W
Eatonville, U.S.A. 116 D4 46 52N 122 16W
Eau Claire, U.S.A. 112 C9 44 49N 91 30W
Eau Claire, L. à l', Canada 102 A5 56 10N 74 25W
Eauze, France 20 E4 43 53N 0 7 E
Eban, Nigeria 83 D5 9 40N 4 50 E
Ebbw Vale, U.K. 13 F4 51 46N 3 12W
Ebeltoft, Denmark 11 H4 56 12N 10 41 E
Ebeltoft Vig, Denmark 11 H4 56 10N 10 35 E
Ebensburg, U.S.A. 110 F6 40 29N 78 44W
Ebensee, Austria 26 D6 47 48N 13 46 E
Eber Gölü, Turkey 72 C4 38 38N 31 11 E
Eberbach, Germany 25 F4 49 28N 8 59 E
Eberswalde-Finow, Germany 24 C9 52 50N 13 49 E
Ebetsu, Japan 54 C10 43 7N 141 34 E
Ebian, China 58 C4 29 11N 103 13 E
Ebingen, Germany 25 G5 48 13N 9 1 E
Éboli, Italy 31 B8 40 39N 15 2 E
Ebolowa, Cameroon 83 E7 2 55N 11 10 E
Ebonyi □, Nigeria 83 D6 6 20N 8 0 E

Ebrach, *Germany* **25 F6** 49 51N 10 29 E
Ébrié, Lagune, *Ivory C.* **82 D4** 5 12N 4 26W
Ebro →, *Spain* **32 E5** 40 43N 0 54 E
Ebro, Embalse del, *Spain* **34 C7** 43 0N 3 58W
Ebstorf, *Germany* **24 B6** 53 2N 10 23 E
Eceabat, *Turkey* **41 F10** 40 11N 26 21 E
Ech Cheliff, *Algeria* **78 A6** 36 10N 1 20 E
Echigo-Sammyaku, *Japan* **55 F9** 36 50N 139 50 E
Échirolles, *France* **21 C9** 45 8N 5 43 E
Echizen-Misaki, *Japan* **55 G7** 35 59N 135 57 E
Echmiadzin = Yejmiadzin, *Armenia* **49 K7** 40 12N 44 19 E
Echo Bay, *N.W.T., Canada* **100 B8** 66 5N 117 55W
Echo Bay, *Ont., Canada* **102 C3** 46 29N 84 4W
Echoing →, *Canada* **102 B1** 55 51N 92 5W
Echternach, *Lux.* **17 E6** 49 49N 6 25 E
Echuca, *Australia* **95 F3** 36 10 S 144 20 E
Ecija, *Spain* **35 H5** 37 30N 5 10W
Eckental, *Germany* **25 F7** 49 35N 11 12 E
Eckernförde, *Germany* **24 A5** 54 28N 9 50 E
Eclipse Is., *Australia* **92 B4** 13 54 S 126 19 E
Eclipse Sd., *Canada* **101 A11** 72 38N 79 0W
Écommoy, *France* **18 E7** 47 50N 0 17 E
Écouché, *France* **18 D6** 48 42N 0 10W
Ecuador ■, *S. Amer.* **124 D3** 2 0 S 78 0W
Écueillé, *France* **18 E8** 47 5N 1 21 E
Ed, *Sweden* **11 F5** 58 55N 11 55 E
Ed Dabbura, *Sudan* **80 D3** 17 40N 34 15 E
Ed Da'ein, *Sudan* **81 E2** 11 26N 26 9 E
Ed Damazin, *Sudan* **79 F12** 11 46N 34 21 E
Ed Dâmer, *Sudan* **80 D3** 17 27N 34 0 E
Ed Debba, *Sudan* **80 D3** 18 0N 30 51 E
Ed-Déffa, *Egypt* **80 A2** 30 40N 26 30 E
Ed Deim, *Sudan* **81 E2** 10 10N 28 20 E
Ed Dueim, *Sudan* **81 E3** 14 0N 32 10 E
Edam, *Canada* **105 C7** 53 11N 108 46W
Edam, *Neths.* **17 B5** 52 31N 5 3 E
Edane, *Sweden* **10 E6** 59 38N 12 49 E
Eday, *U.K.* **14 B6** 59 11N 2 47W
Edd, *Eritrea* **81 E5** 14 0N 41 38 E
Eddrachillis B., *U.K.* **14 C3** 58 17N 5 14W
Eddystone Pt., *Australia* **94 G4** 40 59 S 148 20 E
Ede, *Neths.* **17 B5** 52 4N 5 40 E
Ede, *Nigeria* **83 D5** 7 45N 4 29 E
Edéa, *Cameroon* **83 E7** 3 51N 10 9 E
Edebäck, *Sweden* **10 D7** 60 4N 13 32 E
Edehon L., *Canada* **105 A9** 60 25N 97 15W
Edelény, *Hungary* **42 B5** 48 18N 20 44 E
Eden, *Australia* **95 F4** 37 3 S 149 55 E
Eden, *N.C., U.S.A.* **109 G6** 36 29N 79 53W
Eden, *N.Y., U.S.A.* **110 D6** 42 39N 78 55W
Eden, *Tex., U.S.A.* **113 K5** 31 13N 99 51W
Eden →, *U.K.* **12 C4** 54 57N 3 1W
Edenburg, *S. Africa* **88 D4** 29 43 S 25 58 E
Edendale, *S. Africa* **89 D5** 29 39 S 30 18 E
Edenderry, *Ireland* **15 C4** 53 21N 7 4W
Edenhope, *Australia* **95 F3** 37 4 S 141 19 E
Edenton, *U.S.A.* **109 G7** 36 4N 76 39W
Edenville, *S. Africa* **89 D4** 27 37 S 27 34 E
Eder →, *Germany* **24 D5** 51 12N 9 28 E
Eder-Stausee, *Germany* **24 D4** 51 10N 8 57 E
Edewecht, *Germany* **24 B3** 53 8N 7 58 E
Edgar, *U.S.A.* **112 E6** 40 22N 97 58W
Edgartown, *U.S.A.* **111 E14** 41 23N 70 31W
Edge Hill, *U.K.* **13 E6** 52 8N 1 26W
Edgefield, *U.S.A.* **109 J5** 33 47N 81 56W
Edgeley, *U.S.A.* **112 B5** 46 22N 98 43W
Edgemont, *U.S.A.* **112 D3** 43 18N 103 50W
Edgeøya, *Svalbard* **4 B9** 77 45N 22 30 E
Édhessa, *Greece* **40 F6** 40 48N 22 5 E
Edievale, *N.Z.* **91 L2** 45 49 S 169 22 E
Edina, *Liberia* **82 D2** 6 0N 10 10W
Edina, *U.S.A.* **112 E8** 40 10N 92 11W
Edinboro, *U.S.A.* **110 E4** 41 52N 80 8W
Edinburg, *U.S.A.* **113 M5** 26 18N 98 10W
Edinburgh, *U.K.* **14 F5** 55 57N 3 13W
Edinburgh, City of □, *U.K.* **14 F5** 55 57N 3 17W
Edinet, *Moldova* **43 B12** 48 9N 27 18 E
Edirne, *Turkey* **41 E10** 41 40N 26 34 E
Edirne □, *Turkey* **41 E10** 41 12N 26 30 E
Edison, *U.S.A.* **116 B4** 48 33N 122 27W
Edithburgh, *Australia* **95 F2** 35 5 S 137 43 E
Edmeston, *U.S.A.* **111 D9** 42 42N 75 15W
Edmond, *U.S.A.* **113 H6** 35 39N 97 29W
Edmonds, *U.S.A.* **116 C4** 47 49N 122 23W
Edmonton, *Australia* **94 B4** 17 2 S 145 46 E
Edmonton, *Canada* **104 C6** 53 30N 113 30W
Edmund L., *Canada* **102 B1** 54 45N 93 17W
Edmundston, *Canada* **103 C6** 47 23N 68 20W
Edna, *U.S.A.* **113 L6** 28 59N 96 39W
Edo □, *Nigeria* **83 D6** 6 30N 6 0 E
Edolo, *Italy* **28 B7** 46 10N 10 21 E
Edremit, *Turkey* **39 B9** 39 34N 27 0 E
Edremit Körfezi, *Turkey* **39 B8** 39 30N 26 45 E
Edsbro, *Sweden* **10 E12** 59 54N 18 29 E
Edsbyn, *Sweden* **10 C9** 61 23N 15 49 E
Edson, *Canada* **104 C5** 53 35N 116 28W
Eduardo Castex, *Argentina* **126 D3** 35 50 S 64 18W
Edward →, *Australia* **95 F3** 35 5 S 143 30 E
Edward, L., *Africa* **86 C2** 0 25 S 29 40 E
Edward River, *Australia* **94 A3** 14 59 S 141 26 E
Edward VII Land, *Antarctica* **5 E13** 80 0 S 150 0W
Edwards, *Calif., U.S.A.* **117 L9** 34 55N 117 51W
Edwards, *N.Y., U.S.A.* **111 B9** 44 20N 75 15W
Edwards Air Force Base, *U.S.A.* **117 L9** 34 50N 117 40W
Edwards Plateau, *U.S.A.* **113 K4** 30 45N 101 20W
Edwardsville, *U.S.A.* **111 E9** 41 15N 75 56W
Edzo, *Canada* **104 A5** 62 49N 116 4W
Eeklo, *Belgium* **17 C3** 51 11N 3 33 E
Eferding, *Austria* **26 C7** 48 18N 14 1 E
Effingham, *U.S.A.* **108 F1** 39 7N 88 33W
Eforie, *Romania* **43 F13** 44 1N 28 37 E
Ega →, *Spain* **32 C3** 42 19N 1 55W
Égadi, Ísole, *Italy* **30 E5** 37 55N 12 16 E
Egan Range, *U.S.A.* **114 G6** 39 35N 114 55W
Eganville, *Canada* **102 C4** 45 32N 77 5W
Eger = Cheb, *Czech Rep.* **26 A5** 50 9N 12 28 E
Eger, *Hungary* **42 C5** 47 53N 20 27 E
Eger →, *Hungary* **42 C5** 47 38N 20 50 E
Egersund, *Norway* **9 G12** 58 26N 6 1 E
Egg L., *Canada* **105 B7** 55 5N 105 30W
Eggenburg, *Austria* **26 C8** 48 38N 15 50 E
Eggenfelden, *Germany* **25 G8** 48 23N 12 46 E
Éghezée, *Belgium* **17 D4** 50 35N 4 55 E
Égletons, *France* **20 C6** 45 24N 2 3 E
Egmont, *Canada* **104 D4** 49 45N 123 56W
Egmont, C., *N.Z.* **91 H4** 39 16 S 173 45 E
Egmont, Mt. = Taranaki, Mt., *N.Z.* **91 H5** 39 17 S 174 5 E
Egra, *India* **69 J12** 21 54N 87 32 E
Eğridir, *Turkey* **72 D4** 37 52N 30 51 E
Eğridir Gölü, *Turkey* **70 B1** 37 53N 30 50 E
Egtved, *Denmark* **11 J3** 55 38N 9 18 E
Egume, *Nigeria* **83 D6** 7 30N 7 14 E
Éguzon-Chantôme, *France* **19 F8** 46 27N 1 33 E
Egvekinot, *Russia* **51 C19** 66 19N 179 50W
Egyek, *Hungary* **42 C5** 47 39N 20 52 E
Egypt ■, *Africa* **80 B3** 28 0N 31 0 E
Eha Amufu, *Nigeria* **83 D6** 6 30N 7 46 E
Ehime □, *Japan* **55 H6** 33 30N 132 40 E
Ehingen, *Germany* **25 G5** 48 16N 9 43 E
Ehrenberg, *U.S.A.* **117 M12** 33 36N 114 31W
Ehrwald, *Austria* **26 D3** 47 24N 10 56 E
Eibar, *Spain* **32 B2** 43 11N 2 28W
Eichstätt, *Germany* **25 G7** 48 54N 11 11 E
Eider →, *Germany* **24 A4** 54 19N 8 57 E
Eidsvold, *Australia* **95 D5** 25 25 S 151 12 E
Eidsvold, *Norway* **9 F14** 60 19N 11 14 E
Eifel, *Germany* **25 E2** 50 15N 6 50 E
Eiffel Flats, *Zimbabwe* **87 F3** 18 20 S 30 0 E
Eiger, *Switz.* **28 B5** 46 34N 8 1 E
Eigg, *U.K.* **14 E2** 56 54N 6 10W
Eighty Mile Beach, *Australia* **92 C3** 19 30 S 120 40 E
Eil, *Somali Rep.* **74 F4** 8 0N 49 50 E
Eil, L., *U.K.* **14 E3** 56 51N 5 16W
Eildon, *Australia* **95 F4** 37 14 S 145 55 E
Eildon, L., *Australia* **95 F4** 37 10 S 146 0 E
Eilenburg, *Germany* **24 D8** 51 27N 12 36 E
Ein el Luweiqa, *Sudan* **81 E3** 14 5N 33 50 E
Einasleigh, *Australia* **94 B3** 18 32 S 144 5 E
Einasleigh →, *Australia* **94 B3** 17 30 S 142 17 E
Einbeck, *Germany* **24 D5** 51 49N 9 53 E
Eindhoven, *Neths.* **17 C5** 51 26N 5 28 E
Einsiedeln, *Switz.* **25 H4** 47 7N 8 46 E
Eire = Ireland ■, *Europe* **15 C4** 53 50N 7 52W
Eiríksjökull, *Iceland* **8 D3** 64 46N 20 24W
Eirunepé, *Brazil* **124 E5** 6 35 S 69 53W
Eiseb →, *Namibia* **88 C2** 20 33 S 20 59 E
Eisenach, *Germany* **24 E6** 50 58N 10 19 E
Eisenberg, *Germany* **24 E7** 50 58N 11 54 E
Eisenerz, *Austria* **26 D7** 47 32N 14 54 E
Eisenhüttenstadt, *Germany* **24 C10** 52 9N 14 38 E
Eisenkappel, *Austria* **26 E7** 46 29N 14 36 E
Eisenstadt, *Austria* **27 D9** 47 51N 16 31 E
Eisfeld, *Germany* **25 E6** 50 25N 10 54 E
Eisleben, *Germany* **24 D7** 51 32N 11 32 E
Eislingen, *Germany* **25 G5** 48 41N 9 42 E
Eivissa, *Spain* **37 C7** 38 54N 1 26 E
Eixe, Serra do, *Spain* **34 C4** 42 24N 6 54W
Ejea de los Caballeros, *Spain* **32 C3** 42 7N 1 9W
Ejeda, *Madag.* **89 C7** 24 20 S 44 31 E
Ejura, *Ghana* **83 D4** 7 23N 1 15W
Ejutla, *Mexico* **119 D5** 16 34N 96 44W
Ekalaka, *U.S.A.* **112 C2** 45 53N 104 33W
Ekenässjön, *Sweden* **11 G9** 57 28N 15 1 E
Ekerö, *Sweden* **10 E11** 59 16N 17 45 E
Eket, *Nigeria* **83 E6** 4 38N 7 56 E
Eketahuna, *N.Z.* **91 J5** 40 38 S 175 43 E
Ekhínos, *Greece* **41 E9** 41 16N 25 1 E
Ekibastuz, *Kazakstan* **50 D8** 51 50N 75 10 E
Ekiti □, *Nigeria* **83 D6** 7 25N 5 20 E
Ekoli, *Dem. Rep. of the Congo* **86 C1** 0 23 S 24 13 E
Ekoln, *Sweden* **10 E11** 59 45N 17 37 E
Ekshärad, *Sweden* **10 D7** 60 10N 13 30 E
Eksjö, *Sweden* **11 G8** 57 40N 14 58 E
Ekuma →, *Namibia* **88 B2** 18 40 S 16 2 E
Ekwan →, *Canada* **102 B3** 53 12N 82 15W
Ekwan Pt., *Canada* **102 B3** 53 16N 82 7W
El Aaiún, *W. Sahara* **78 C3** 27 9N 13 12W
El Abanico, *Chile* **126 D1** 37 20 S 71 31W
El Abbasiya, *Sudan* **81 E3** 12 10N 31 18 E
El 'Agrûd, *Egypt* **75 E3** 30 14N 34 24 E
El Ait, *Sudan* **81 E2** 12 22N 27 27 E
El 'Aiyat, *Egypt* **80 J7** 29 36N 31 15 E
El Alamein, *Egypt* **80 A2** 30 48N 28 58 E
El 'Aqaba, W. →, *Egypt* **75 E2** 30 7N 33 54 E
El 'Arag, *Egypt* **80 B2** 28 40N 26 20 E
El Arahal, *Spain* **35 H5** 37 15N 5 33W
El Arīḩā, *West Bank* **75 D4** 31 52N 35 27 E
El 'Arîsh, *Egypt* **75 D2** 31 8N 33 50 E
El 'Arîsh, W. →, *Egypt* **75 D2** 31 8N 33 47 E
El Asnam = Ech Cheliff, *Algeria* **78 A6** 36 10N 1 20 E
El Astillero, *Spain* **34 B7** 43 24N 3 49W
El Badâri, *Egypt* **80 B3** 27 4N 31 25 E
El Bahrein, *Egypt* **80 B2** 28 30N 26 25 E
El Ballâs, *Egypt* **80 B3** 26 2N 32 43 E
El Balyana, *Egypt* **80 B3** 26 10N 32 3 E
El Baqeir, *Sudan* **80 D3** 18 40N 33 40 E
El Barco de Ávila, *Spain* **34 E5** 40 21N 5 31W
El Barco de Valdeorras = O Barco, *Spain* **34 C4** 42 23N 6 58W
El Bauga, *Sudan* **80 D3** 18 18N 33 52 E
El Bawiti, *Egypt* **80 B2** 28 25N 28 45 E
El Bayadh, *Algeria* **78 B6** 33 40N 1 1 E
El Bierzo, *Spain* **34 C4** 42 45N 6 30W
El Bluff, *Nic.* **120 D3** 11 59N 83 40W
El Bonillo, *Spain* **33 G2** 38 57N 2 35W
El Brûk, W. →, *Egypt* **75 E2** 30 15N 33 50 E
El Buheirat □, *Sudan* **81 F3** 7 0N 30 0 E
El Burgo de Osma, *Spain* **32 D1** 41 35N 3 4W
El Cajon, *U.S.A.* **117 N10** 32 48N 116 58W
El Campo, *U.S.A.* **113 L6** 29 12N 96 16W
El Centro, *U.S.A.* **117 N11** 32 48N 115 34W
El Cerro, *Bolivia* **124 G6** 17 30 S 61 40W
El Cerro de Andévalo, *Spain* **35 H4** 37 45N 6 57W
El Compadre, *Mexico* **117 N10** 32 20N 116 14W
El Coronil, *Spain* **35 H5** 37 5N 5 38W
El Cuy, *Argentina* **128 D3** 39 55 S 68 25W
El Cuyo, *Mexico* **119 C7** 21 30N 87 40W
El Dab'a, *Egypt* **80 H6** 31 0N 28 27 E
El Daheir, *Egypt* **75 D3** 31 13N 34 10 E
El Dátil, *Mexico* **118 B2** 30 7N 112 15W
El Deir, *Egypt* **80 B3** 25 25N 32 20 E
El Dere, *Somali Rep.* **74 G4** 3 50N 47 8 E
El Descanso, *Mexico* **117 N10** 32 12N 116 58W
El Desemboque, *Mexico* **118 A2** 30 30N 112 57W
El Dilingat, *Egypt* **80 H7** 30 50N 30 31 E
El Diviso, *Colombia* **124 C3** 1 22N 78 14W
El Djouf, *Mauritania* **78 D4** 20 0N 9 0W
El Dorado, *Ark., U.S.A.* **113 J8** 33 12N 92 40W
El Dorado, *Kans., U.S.A.* **113 G6** 37 49N 96 52W
El Dorado, *Venezuela* **124 B6** 6 55N 61 37W
El 'Ein, *Sudan* **81 D2** 16 35N 29 22 E
El Ejido, *Spain* **35 J8** 36 47N 2 49W
El Escorial, *Spain* **34 E6** 40 35N 4 7W
El Espinar, *Spain* **34 D6** 41 43N 4 15W
El Faiyûm, *Egypt* **80 J7** 29 19N 30 50 E
El Fâsher, *Sudan* **81 E2** 13 33N 25 26 E
El Fashn, *Egypt* **80 J7** 28 50N 30 54 E
El Ferrol = Ferrol, *Spain* **34 B2** 43 29N 8 15W
El Fifi, *Sudan* **81 E2** 10 4N 25 0 E
El Fuerte, *Mexico* **118 B3** 26 30N 108 40W
El Ga'a, *Sudan* **81 E2** 14 16N 29 59 E
El Gal, *Somali Rep.* **74 E5** 10 58N 50 20 E
El Garef, *Sudan* **81 E3** 12 1N 34 19 E
El Gebir, *Sudan* **81 E2** 13 40N 29 40 E
El Gedida, *Egypt* **80 B2** 25 40N 28 30 E
El Geneina = Al Junaynah, *Sudan* **79 F10** 13 27N 22 45 E
El Geteina, *Sudan* **81 E3** 14 50N 32 27 E
El Gezira □, *Sudan* **81 E3** 15 0N 33 0 E
El Gir, *Sudan* **80 D2** 19 50N 28 18 E
El Gîza, *Egypt* **80 J7** 30 0N 31 10 E
El Goléa, *Algeria* **78 B6** 30 30N 2 50 E
El Grau, *Spain* **33 G4** 39 0N 0 7W
El Hagiz, *Sudan* **81 D4** 15 15N 35 50 E
El Hâi, *Egypt* **80 J7** 29 39N 31 18 E
El Hammam, *Egypt* **80 A2** 30 52N 29 25 E
El Hawata, *Sudan* **81 E3** 13 25N 34 42 E
El Heiz, *Egypt* **80 B2** 27 50N 28 40 E
El Hideib, *Sudan* **81 E3** 13 0N 32 50 E
El Hilla, *Sudan* **81 E2** 13 24N 27 2 E
El 'Idisât, *Egypt* **80 B3** 25 30N 32 35 E
El Iskandarîya, *Egypt* **80 H7** 31 13N 29 58 E
El Istiwa'iya, *Sudan* **79 G11** 5 0N 28 0 E
El Jadida, *Morocco* **78 B4** 33 11N 8 17W
El Jardal, *Honduras* **120 D2** 14 54N 88 50W
El Jebelein, *Sudan* **81 E3** 12 40N 32 55 E
El Kab, *Sudan* **80 D3** 19 27N 32 46 E
El Kabrît, G., *Egypt* **75 F2** 29 42N 33 16 E
El Kafr el Sharqi, *Egypt* **80 H7** 31 16N 31 10 E
El Kamlin, *Sudan* **81 D3** 15 3N 33 11 E
El Karaba, *Sudan* **80 D3** 18 32N 33 41 E
El Kere, *Ethiopia* **81 F5** 5 50N 42 5 E
El Khandaq, *Sudan* **80 D3** 18 30N 30 30 E
El Khârga, *Egypt* **80 B3** 25 30N 30 33 E
El Khartûm, *Sudan* **81 D3** 15 31N 32 35 E
El Khartûm □, *Sudan* **81 D3** 16 0N 33 0 E
El Khartûm Bahrî, *Sudan* **81 D3** 15 40N 32 31 E
El Kuntilla, *Egypt* **75 E3** 30 1N 34 45 E
El Laqâwa, *Sudan* **81 E2** 11 25N 29 1 E
El Laqeita, *Egypt* **80 B3** 25 50N 33 15 E
El Leh, *Ethiopia* **81 G4** 3 46N 39 13 E
El Leiya, *Sudan* **81 D4** 16 15N 35 28 E
El Maestrazgo, *Spain* **32 E4** 40 30N 0 25W
El Mafâza, *Sudan* **81 E3** 13 38N 34 30 E
El Maghra, *Egypt* **80 A2** 30 15N 28 55 E
El Mahalla el Kubra, *Egypt* **80 H7** 31 0N 31 0 E
El Mahârîq, *Egypt* **80 B3** 25 35N 30 35 E
El Maîmûn, *Egypt* **80 J7** 29 14N 31 12 E
El Maks el Bahari, *Egypt* **80 C3** 24 30N 30 40 E
El Manshâh, *Egypt* **80 B3** 26 26N 31 50 E
El Mansûra, *Egypt* **80 H7** 31 0N 31 19 E
El Manzala, *Egypt* **80 H7** 31 10N 31 50 E
El Marâgha, *Egypt* **80 B3** 26 35N 31 10 E
El Masid, *Sudan* **81 D3** 15 15N 33 0 E
El Masnou, *Spain* **32 D7** 41 28N 2 20 E
El Matariya, *Egypt* **80 H8** 31 15N 32 0 E
El Meda, *Ethiopia* **81 F5** 5 39N 41 47 E
El Medano, *Canary Is.* **37 F3** 28 3N 16 32W
El Metemma, *Sudan* **81 D3** 16 50N 33 10 E
El Milagro, *Argentina* **126 C2** 30 59 S 65 59W
El Minyâ, *Egypt* **80 B3** 28 7N 30 33 E
El Monte, *U.S.A.* **117 L8** 34 4N 118 1W
El Montseny, *Spain* **32 D7** 41 55N 2 25 E
El Mreyye, *Mauritania* **82 B3** 18 0N 6 0W
El Niybo, *Ethiopia* **81 G4** 4 40N 39 55 E
El Obeid, *Sudan* **81 E3** 13 8N 30 10 E
El Odaiya, *Sudan* **81 E2** 12 8N 28 12 E
El Oro, *Mexico* **119 D4** 19 48N 100 8W
El Oued, *Algeria* **78 B7** 33 20N 6 58 E
El Palmito, Presa, *Mexico* **118 B3** 25 40N 105 30W
El Paso, *U.S.A.* **115 L10** 31 45N 106 29W
El Paso Robles, *U.S.A.* **116 K6** 35 38N 120 41W
El Pedernoso, *Spain* **33 F2** 39 29N 2 45W
El Pedroso, *Spain* **35 H5** 37 51N 5 45W
El Pobo de Dueñas, *Spain* **32 E3** 40 46N 1 39W
El Portal, *U.S.A.* **116 H7** 37 41N 119 47W
El Porvenir, *Mexico* **118 A3** 31 15N 105 51W
El Prat de Llobregat, *Spain* **32 D7** 41 18N 2 3 E
El Progreso, *Honduras* **120 C2** 15 26N 87 51W
El Pueblito, *Mexico* **118 B3** 29 3N 105 4W
El Pueblo, *Canary Is.* **37 F2** 28 36N 17 47W
El Puente del Arzobispo, *Spain* **34 F5** 39 48N 5 10W
El Puerto de Santa María, *Spain* **35 J4** 36 36N 6 13W
El Qâhira, *Egypt* **80 H7** 30 1N 31 14 E
El Qantara, *Egypt* **75 E1** 30 51N 32 20 E
El Qasr, *Egypt* **80 B2** 25 44N 28 42 E
El Qubâbât, *Egypt* **80 J7** 29 28N 31 16 E
El Quseima, *Egypt* **75 E3** 30 40N 34 15 E
El Qusîya, *Egypt* **80 B3** 27 29N 30 44 E
El Râshda, *Egypt* **80 B2** 25 36N 28 57 E
El Real, *Panama* **124 B3** 8 0N 77 40W
El Reno, *U.S.A.* **113 H6** 35 32N 97 57W
El Rîdisiya, *Egypt* **80 C3** 24 56N 32 51 E
El Rio, *U.S.A.* **117 L7** 34 14N 119 10W
El Ronquillo, *Spain* **35 H4** 37 44N 6 10W
El Roque, Pta., *Canary Is.* **37 F4** 28 10N 15 25W
El Rosarito, *Mexico* **118 B2** 28 38N 114 4W
El Rubio, *Spain* **35 H5** 37 22N 5 0W
El Saff, *Egypt* **80 J7** 29 34N 31 16 E
El Saheira, W. →, *Egypt* **75 E2** 30 5N 33 25 E
El Salto, *Mexico* **118 C3** 23 47N 105 22W
El Salvador ■, *Cent. Amer.* **120 D2** 13 50N 89 0W
El Sauce, *Nic.* **120 D2** 13 0N 86 40W
El Saucejo, *Spain* **35 H5** 37 4N 5 6W
El Shallal, *Egypt* **80 C3** 24 0N 32 53 E
El Simbillawein, *Egypt* **80 H7** 30 48N 31 13 E
El Sueco, *Mexico* **118 B3** 29 54N 106 24W
El Suweis, *Egypt* **80 J8** 29 58N 32 31 E
El Tabbîn, *Egypt* **80 J7** 29 47N 31 18 E
El Tamarâni, W. →, *Egypt* **75 E3** 30 7N 34 43 E
El Thamad, *Egypt* **75 F3** 29 40N 34 28 E
El Tigre, *Venezuela* **124 B6** 8 44N 64 15W
El Tîh, Gebal, *Egypt* **75 F2** 29 40N 33 50 E
El Tîna, *Egypt* **80 H8** 31 3N 32 22 E
El Tîna, Khalîg, *Egypt* **75 D1** 31 10N 32 40 E
El Tofo, *Chile* **126 B1** 29 22 S 71 18W
El Tránsito, *Chile* **126 B1** 28 52 S 70 17W
El Tûr, *Egypt* **70 D2** 28 14N 33 36 E
El Turbio, *Argentina* **128 G2** 51 45 S 72 5W
El Uqsur, *Egypt* **80 B3** 25 41N 32 38 E
El Venado, *Mexico* **118 C4** 22 56N 101 10W
El Vendrell, *Spain* **32 D6** 41 10N 1 30 E
El Vergel, *Mexico* **118 B3** 26 28N 106 22W
El Vigía, *Venezuela* **124 B4** 8 38N 71 39W
El Viso del Alcor, *Spain* **35 H5** 37 23N 5 43W
El Wabeira, *Egypt* **75 F2** 29 34N 33 6 E
El Wak, *Kenya* **86 B5** 2 49N 40 56 E
El Waqf, *Egypt* **80 B3** 25 45N 32 15 E
El Weguet, *Ethiopia* **81 F5** 5 28N 42 17 E
El Wuz, *Sudan* **81 D3** 15 5N 30 7 E
Elafónisos, *Greece* **38 E4** 36 29N 22 56 E
Élancourt, *France* **19 D8** 48 47N 1 58 E
Élassa, *Greece* **39 F8** 35 18N 26 21 E
Elassón, *Greece* **38 B4** 39 53N 22 12 E
Elat, *Israel* **75 F3** 29 30N 34 56 E
Eláthia, *Greece* **38 C4** 38 37N 22 46 E
Elâzığ, *Turkey* **70 B3** 38 37N 39 14 E
Elba, *Italy* **28 F7** 42 46N 10 17 E
Elba, *U.S.A.* **109 K2** 31 25N 86 4W
Elbasan, *Albania* **40 E4** 41 9N 20 9 E
Elbasani = Elbasan, *Albania* **40 E4** 41 9N 20 9 E
Elbe, *U.S.A.* **116 D4** 46 45N 122 10W
Elbe →, *Europe* **24 B4** 53 50N 9 0 E
Elbe-Seitenkanal, *Germany* **24 C6** 52 45N 10 32 E
Elbert, Mt., *U.S.A.* **115 G10** 39 7N 106 27W
Elberton, *U.S.A.* **109 H4** 34 7N 82 52W
Elbeuf, *France* **18 C8** 49 17N 1 2 E
Elbidtan, *Turkey* **70 B3** 38 13N 37 12 E
Elbing = Elbląg, *Poland* **44 D6** 54 10N 19 25 E
Elbistan, *Turkey* **72 C7** 38 13N 37 15 E
Elbląg, *Poland* **44 D6** 54 10N 19 25 E
Elbow, *Canada* **105 C7** 51 7N 106 35W
Elbrus, *Asia* **49 J6** 43 21N 42 30 E
Elburz Mts. = Alborz, Reshteh-ye Kūhhā-ye, *Iran* **71 C7** 36 0N 52 0 E
Elche, *Spain* **33 G4** 38 15N 0 42W
Elche de la Sierra, *Spain* **33 G2** 38 27N 2 3W
Elcho I., *Australia* **94 A2** 11 55 S 135 45 E
Elda, *Spain* **33 G4** 38 29N 0 47W
Elde →, *Germany* **24 B7** 53 7N 11 15 E
Eldon, *Mo., U.S.A.* **112 F8** 38 21N 92 35W
Eldon, *Wash., U.S.A.* **116 C3** 47 33N 123 3W
Eldora, *U.S.A.* **112 D8** 42 22N 93 5W
Eldorado, *Argentina* **127 B5** 26 28 S 54 43W
Eldorado, *Canada* **110 B7** 44 35N 77 31W
Eldorado, *Mexico* **118 C3** 24 20N 107 22W
Eldorado, *Ill., U.S.A.* **108 G1** 37 49N 88 26W
Eldorado, *Tex., U.S.A.* **113 K4** 30 52N 100 36W
Eldorado Springs, *U.S.A.* **113 G8** 37 52N 94 1W
Eldoret, *Kenya* **86 B4** 0 30N 35 17 E
Eldred, *U.S.A.* **110 E6** 41 58N 78 23W
Elea, C., *Cyprus* **36 D13** 35 19N 34 4 E
Eleanora, Pk., *Australia* **93 F3** 32 57 S 121 9 E
Elefantes →, *Mozam.* **89 C5** 24 10 S 32 40 E
Elektrogorsk, *Russia* **46 E10** 55 56N 38 50 E
Elektrostal, *Russia* **46 E10** 55 41N 38 32 E
Elele, *Nigeria* **83 D6** 5 5N 6 50 E
Elena, *Bulgaria* **41 D9** 42 55N 25 53 E
Elephant Butte Reservoir, *U.S.A.* **115 K10** 33 9N 107 11W
Elephant I., *Antarctica* **5 C18** 61 0 S 55 0W
Eleshnitsa, *Bulgaria* **40 E7** 41 52N 23 36 E
Eleşkirt, *Turkey* **73 C10** 39 50N 42 50 E
Eleuthera, *Bahamas* **120 B4** 25 0N 76 20W
Elevsís, *Greece* **38 C5** 38 4N 23 26 E
Elevtheroúpolis, *Greece* **41 F8** 40 52N 24 20 E
Elgin, *Canada* **111 B8** 44 36N 76 13W
Elgin, *U.K.* **14 D5** 57 39N 3 19W
Elgin, *Ill., U.S.A.* **108 D1** 42 2N 88 17W
Elgin, *N. Dak., U.S.A.* **112 B4** 46 24N 101 51W
Elgin, *Oreg., U.S.A.* **114 D5** 45 34N 117 55W
Elgin, *Tex., U.S.A.* **113 K6** 30 21N 97 22W
Elgoibar, *Spain* **32 B2** 43 13N 2 24W
Elgon, Mt., *Africa* **86 B3** 1 10N 34 30 E
Eliase, *Indonesia* **63 F8** 8 21 S 130 48 E
Elikón, *Greece* **38 C4** 38 18N 22 45 E
Elim, *Namibia* **88 B2** 17 48 S 15 31 E
Elim, *S. Africa* **88 E2** 34 35 S 19 45 E
Elin Pelin, *Bulgaria* **40 D7** 42 40N 23 36 E
Elisabethville = Lubumbashi, *Dem. Rep. of the Congo* **87 E2** 11 40 S 27 28 E
Elista, *Russia* **49 G7** 46 16N 44 14 E
Elizabeth, *Australia* **95 E2** 34 42 S 138 41 E
Elizabeth, *N.J., U.S.A.* **111 F10** 40 39N 74 13W
Elizabeth, *N.J., U.S.A.* **111 F10** 40 40N 74 13W
Elizabeth City, *U.S.A.* **109 G7** 36 18N 76 14W
Elizabethton, *U.S.A.* **109 G4** 36 21N 82 13W
Elizabethtown, *Ky., U.S.A.* **108 G3** 37 42N 85 52W
Elizabethtown, *N.Y., U.S.A.* **111 B11** 44 13N 73 36W
Elizabethtown, *Pa., U.S.A.* **111 F8** 40 9N 76 36W
Elizondo, *Spain* **32 B3** 43 12N 1 30W
Ełk, *Poland* **44 E9** 53 50N 22 21 E
Elk →, *Canada* **104 C5** 49 11N 115 14W
Ełk →, *Poland* **44 E9** 53 41N 22 28 E
Elk →, *U.S.A.* **109 H2** 34 46N 87 16W
Elk City, *U.S.A.* **113 H5** 35 25N 99 25W
Elk Creek, *U.S.A.* **116 F4** 39 36N 122 32W
Elk Grove, *U.S.A.* **116 G5** 38 25N 121 22W
Elk Island Nat. Park, *Canada* **104 C6** 53 35N 112 59W
Elk Lake, *Canada* **102 C3** 47 40N 80 25W
Elk Point, *Canada* **105 C6** 53 54N 110 55W
Elk River, *Idaho, U.S.A.* **114 C5** 46 47N 116 11W
Elk River, *Minn., U.S.A.* **112 C8** 45 18N 93 35W
Elkedra →, *Australia* **94 C2** 21 8 S 136 22 E
Elkhart, *Ind., U.S.A.* **108 E3** 41 41N 85 58W
Elkhart, *Kans., U.S.A.* **113 G4** 37 0N 101 54W
Elkhorn, *Canada* **105 D8** 49 59N 101 14W
Elkhorn →, *U.S.A.* **112 E6** 41 8N 96 19W
Elkhovo, *Bulgaria* **41 D10** 42 10N 26 35 E
Elkin, *U.S.A.* **109 G5** 36 15N 80 51W
Elkins, *U.S.A.* **108 F6** 38 55N 79 51W
Elkland, *U.S.A.* **110 E7** 41 59N 77 19W
Elko, *Canada* **104 D5** 49 20N 115 10W
Elko, *U.S.A.* **114 F6** 40 50N 115 46W
Elkton, *U.S.A.* **110 C1** 43 49N 83 11W
Ell, L., *Australia* **93 E4** 29 13 S 127 46 E
Ellef Ringnes I., *Canada* **4 B2** 78 30N 102 2W
Ellen, Mt., *U.S.A.* **111 B12** 44 9N 72 56W
Ellenburg, *U.S.A.* **111 B11** 44 54N 73 48W
Ellendale, *U.S.A.* **112 B5** 46 0N 98 32W
Ellensburg, *U.S.A.* **114 C3** 46 59N 120 34W
Ellenville, *U.S.A.* **111 E10** 41 43N 74 24W
Ellery, Mt., *Australia* **95 F4** 37 28 S 148 47 E
Ellesmere, L., *N.Z.* **91 M4** 43 47 S 172 28 E
Ellesmere I., *Canada* **4 B4** 79 30N 80 0W
Ellesmere Port, *U.K.* **12 D5** 53 17N 2 54W
Ellice Is. = Tuvalu ■, *Pac. Oc.* **96 H9** 8 0 S 178 0 E
Ellicottville, *U.S.A.* **110 D6** 42 17N 78 40W
Elliot, *Australia* **94 B1** 17 33 S 133 32 E
Elliot, *S. Africa* **89 E4** 31 22 S 27 48 E
Elliot Lake, *Canada* **102 C3** 46 25N 82 35W
Elliotdale = Xhora, *S. Africa* **89 E4** 31 55 S 28 38 E
Ellis, *U.S.A.* **112 F5** 38 56N 99 34W
Elliston, *Australia* **95 E1** 33 39 S 134 53 E
Ellisville, *U.S.A.* **113 K10** 31 36N 89 12W
Ellon, *U.K.* **14 D6** 57 22N 2 4W
Ellore = Eluru, *India* **67 L12** 16 48N 81 8 E
Ellsworth, *Kans., U.S.A.* **112 F5** 38 44N 98 14W
Ellsworth, *Maine, U.S.A.* **109 C11** 44 33N 68 25W
Ellsworth Land, *Antarctica* **5 D16** 76 0 S 89 0W
Ellsworth Mts., *Antarctica* **5 D16** 78 30 S 85 0W
Ellwangen, *Germany* **25 G6** 48 57N 10 8 E
Ellwood City, *U.S.A.* **110 F4** 40 52N 80 17W
Elm, *Switz.* **25 J5** 46 54N 9 10 E
Elma, *Canada* **105 D9** 49 52N 95 55W
Elma, *U.S.A.* **116 D3** 47 0N 123 25W
Elmadağ, *Turkey* **72 C5** 39 55N 33 14 E
Elmalı, *Turkey* **39 E11** 36 44N 29 56 E
Elmhurst, *U.S.A.* **108 E2** 41 53N 87 56W
Elmina, *Ghana* **83 D4** 5 5N 1 21W
Elmira, *Canada* **110 C4** 43 36N 80 33W
Elmira, *U.S.A.* **110 D8** 42 6N 76 48W
Elmira Heights, *U.S.A.* **110 D8** 42 8N 76 50W
Elmore, *Australia* **95 F3** 36 30 S 144 37 E
Elmore, *U.S.A.* **117 M11** 33 7N 115 49W
Elmshorn, *Germany* **24 B5** 53 43N 9 40 E
Elmvale, *Canada* **110 B5** 44 35N 79 52W
Elne, *France* **20 F6** 42 36N 2 58 E
Elora, *Canada* **110 C4** 43 41N 80 26W
Elos, *Greece* **38 E4** 36 46N 22 43 E
Eloúnda, *Greece* **36 D7** 35 16N 25 42 E
Eloy, *U.S.A.* **115 K8** 32 45N 111 33W
Éloyes, *France* **19 D13** 48 6N 6 36 E
Elrose, *Canada* **105 C7** 51 12N 108 0W
Elsdorf, *Germany* **24 E2** 50 55N 6 34 E
Elsie, *U.S.A.* **116 E3** 45 52N 123 36W
Elsinore = Helsingør, *Denmark* **11 H6** 56 2N 12 35 E
Elster →, *Germany* **24 D7** 51 25N 11 57 E
Elsterwerda, *Germany* **24 D9** 51 27N 13 31 E
Eltham, *N.Z.* **91 H5** 39 26 S 174 19 E
Elton, *Russia* **49 F8** 49 5N 46 52 E
Elton, Ozero, *Russia* **49 F8** 49 5N 46 42 E
Eltville, *Germany* **25 E4** 50 2N 8 7 E
Eluru, *India* **67 L12** 16 48N 81 8 E
Elvas, *Portugal* **35 G3** 38 50N 7 10W
Elven, *France* **18 E4** 47 44N 2 36W
Elverum, *Norway* **9 F14** 60 53N 11 34 E
Elvire →, *Australia* **92 C4** 17 51 S 128 11 E
Elvire, Mt., *Australia* **93 E2** 29 22 S 119 36 E
Elvo →, *Italy* **28 C5** 45 23N 8 21 E
Elwell, L., *U.S.A.* **114 B8** 48 22N 111 17W
Elwood, *Ind., U.S.A.* **108 E3** 40 17N 85 50W
Elwood, *Nebr., U.S.A.* **112 E5** 40 36N 99 52W
Elx = Elche, *Spain* **33 G4** 38 15N 0 42W
Ely, *U.K.* **13 E8** 52 24N 0 16 E
Ely, *Minn., U.S.A.* **112 B9** 47 55N 91 51W
Ely, *Nev., U.S.A.* **114 G6** 39 15N 114 54W
Elyria, *U.S.A.* **110 E2** 41 22N 82 7W
Elyrus, *Greece* **38 F5** 35 15N 23 45 E
Elz →, *Germany* **25 G3** 48 18N 7 44 E
Emådalen, *Sweden* **10 C8** 61 20N 14 44 E
Emāmrūd, *Iran* **71 B7** 36 30N 55 0 E
Emån →, *Sweden* **11 G10** 57 8N 16 30 E
Emba, *Kazakstan* **50 E6** 48 50N 58 8 E
Emba →, *Kazakstan* **50 E6** 46 55N 53 28 E
Embarcación, *Argentina* **126 A3** 23 10 S 64 0W
Embarras Portage, *Canada* **105 B6** 58 27N 111 28W
Embetsu, *Japan* **54 B10** 44 44N 141 47 E
Embi = Emba, *Kazakstan* **50 E6** 48 50N 58 8 E
Embi = Emba →, *Kazakstan* **50 E6** 46 55N 53 28 E
Embóna, *Greece* **36 C9** 36 13N 27 51 E
Embrun, *France* **21 D10** 44 34N 6 30 E
Embu, *Kenya* **86 C4** 0 32 S 37 38 E
Emden, *Germany* **24 B3** 53 21N 7 12 E
Emecik, *Turkey* **39 E9** 36 46N 27 49 E
Emerald, *Australia* **94 C4** 23 32 S 148 10 E
Emerson, *Canada* **105 D9** 49 0N 97 10W
Emet, *Turkey* **39 B11** 39 20N 29 15 E
Emi Koussi, *Chad* **79 E9** 19 45N 18 55 E
Emília-Romagna □, *Italy* **28 D8** 44 45N 11 0 E
Emilius, Mte., *Italy* **28 C4** 45 45N 7 20 E
Eminabad, *Pakistan* **68 C6** 32 2N 74 8 E
Emine, Nos, *Bulgaria* **41 D11** 42 40N 27 56 E
Emirdağ, *Turkey* **72 C4** 39 2N 31 8 E
Emlenton, *U.S.A.* **110 E5** 41 11N 79 43W
Emlichheim, *Germany* **24 C2** 52 37N 6 51 E
Emmaboda, *Sweden* **11 H9** 56 37N 15 32 E
Emmaus, *S. Africa* **88 D4** 29 2 S 25 15 E
Emmaus, *U.S.A.* **111 F9** 40 32N 75 30W
Emme →, *Switz.* **25 H3** 47 14N 7 32 E
Emmeloord, *Neths.* **17 B5** 52 44N 5 46 E
Emmen, *Neths.* **17 B6** 52 48N 6 57 E
Emmen, *Switz.* **25 H4** 47 5N 8 18 E
Emmendingen, *Germany* **25 G3** 48 6N 7 51 E
Emmental, *Switz.* **25 J3** 46 55N 7 40 E

Emmerich, Germany 24 D2 51 50N 6 14 E
Emmet, Australia 94 C3 24 45 S 144 30 E
Emmetsburg, U.S.A. 112 D7 43 7N 94 41W
Emmett, Idaho, U.S.A. 114 E5 43 52N 116 30W
Emmett, Mich., U.S.A. 110 D2 42 59N 82 46W
Emmonak, U.S.A. 100 B3 62 46N 164 30W
Emo, Canada 105 D10 48 38N 93 50W
Emőd, Hungary 42 C5 47 57N 20 47 E
Emona, Bulgaria 41 D11 42 43N 27 53 E
Empalme, Mexico 118 B2 28 1N 110 49W
Empangeni, S. Africa 89 D5 28 50 S 31 52 E
Empedrado, Argentina 126 B4 28 0 S 58 46W
Emperor Seamount Chain, Pac. Oc. 96 D9 40 0N 170 0 E
Empoli, Italy 28 E7 43 43N 10 57 E
Emporia, Kans., U.S.A. 112 F6 38 25N 96 11W
Emporia, Va., U.S.A. 109 G7 36 42N 77 32W
Emporium, U.S.A. 110 E6 41 31N 78 14W
Empress, Canada 105 C7 50 57N 110 0W
Empty Quarter = Rub' al Khālī, Si. Arabia 74 D4 18 0N 48 0 E
Ems →, Germany 24 B3 53 20N 7 12 E
Emsdale, Canada 110 A5 45 32N 79 19W
Emsdetten, Germany 24 C3 52 10N 7 32 E
Emu, China 57 C15 43 40N 128 6 E
Emu Park, Australia 94 C5 23 13 S 150 50 E
'En 'Avrona, Israel 75 F4 29 43N 35 0 E
En Nahud, Sudan 81 E2 12 45N 28 25 E
En Nofalab, Sudan 81 D3 15 52N 32 52 E
Ena, Japan 55 G8 35 25N 137 25 E
Enana, Namibia 88 B2 17 30 S 16 23 E
Enånger, Sweden 10 C11 61 30N 17 9 E
Enaratoli, Indonesia 63 E9 3 55 S 136 21 E
Enard B., U.K. 14 C3 58 5N 5 20W
Enare = Inarijärvi, Finland 8 B22 69 0N 28 0 E
Encampment, U.S.A. 114 F10 41 12N 106 47W
Encantadas, Serra, Brazil 127 C5 30 40 S 53 0W
Encarnación, Paraguay 127 B4 27 15 S 55 50W
Encarnación de Diaz, Mexico 118 C4 21 30N 102 13W
Enchi, Ghana 82 D4 5 53N 2 48W
Encinitas, U.S.A. 117 M9 33 3N 117 17W
Encino, U.S.A. 115 J11 34 39N 105 28W
Encounter B., Australia 95 F2 35 45 S 138 45 E
Encs, Hungary 42 B6 48 20N 21 8 E
Endako, Canada 104 C3 54 6N 125 2W
Ende, Indonesia 63 F6 8 45 S 121 40 E
Endeavour Str., Australia 94 A3 10 45 S 142 0 E
Endelave, Denmark 11 J4 55 46N 10 18 E
Enderbury I., Kiribati 96 H10 3 8 S 171 5W
Enderby, Canada 104 C5 50 35N 119 10W
Enderby I., Australia 92 D2 20 35 S 116 30 E
Enderby Land, Antarctica 5 C5 66 0 S 53 0 E
Enderlin, U.S.A. 112 B6 46 38N 97 36W
Endicott, U.S.A. 111 D8 42 6N 76 4W
Endwell, U.S.A. 111 D8 42 6N 76 2W
Endyalgout I., Australia 92 B5 11 40 S 132 35 E
Eneabba, Australia 93 E2 29 49 S 115 16 E
Enewetak Atoll, Marshall Is. 96 F8 11 30N 162 15 E
Enez, Turkey 41 F10 40 45N 26 5 E
Enfield, Canada 103 D7 44 56N 63 32W
Enfield, Conn., U.S.A. 111 E12 41 58N 72 36W
Enfield, N.H., U.S.A. 111 C12 43 39N 72 9W
Engadin, Switz. 25 J6 46 45N 10 10 E
Engaño, C., Dom. Rep. 121 C6 18 30N 68 20W
Engaño, C., Phil. 63 A6 18 35N 122 23 E
Engaru, Japan 54 B11 44 3N 143 31 E
Engcobo, S. Africa 89 E4 31 37 S 28 0 E
Engelberg, Switz. 25 J4 46 48N 8 26 E
Engels, Russia 48 E8 51 28N 46 6 E
Engemann L., Canada 105 B7 58 0N 106 55W
Engershatu, Eritrea 81 D4 16 7N 38 34 E
Enggano, Indonesia 62 F2 5 20 S 102 40 E
England, U.S.A. 113 H9 34 33N 91 58W
England □, U.K. 12 D7 53 0N 2 0W
Englee, Canada 103 B8 50 45N 56 5W
Englehart, Canada 102 C4 47 49N 79 52W
Englewood, U.S.A. 112 F2 39 39N 104 59W
English →, Canada 105 C10 50 35N 93 30W
English Bazar = Ingraj Bazar, India 69 G13 24 58N 88 10 E
English Channel, Europe 13 G6 50 0N 2 0W
English River, Canada 102 C1 49 14N 91 0W
Engures ezers, Latvia 44 A10 57 16N 23 6 E
Enguri →, Georgia 49 J5 42 27N 41 38 E
Enid, U.S.A. 113 G6 36 24N 97 53W
Enipévs →, Greece 38 B4 39 22N 22 17 E
Enkhuizen, Neths. 17 B5 52 42N 5 17 E
Enköping, Sweden 10 E11 59 37N 17 4 E
Enle, China 58 F3 24 0N 101 9 E
Enna, Italy 31 E7 37 34N 14 16 E
Ennadai, Canada 105 A8 61 8N 100 53W
Ennadai L., Canada 105 A8 61 0N 101 0W
Ennedi, Chad 79 E10 17 15N 22 0 E
Enngonia, Australia 95 D4 29 21 S 145 50 E
Ennigerloh, Germany 24 D4 51 50N 8 2 E
Ennis, Ireland 15 D3 52 51N 8 59W
Ennis, Mont., U.S.A. 114 D8 45 21N 111 44W
Ennis, Tex., U.S.A. 113 J6 32 20N 96 38W
Enniscorthy, Ireland 15 D5 52 30N 6 34W
Enniskillen, U.K. 15 B4 54 21N 7 39W
Ennistimon, Ireland 15 D2 52 57N 9 17W
Enns, Austria 26 C7 48 12N 14 28 E
Enns →, Austria 26 C7 48 14N 14 32 E
Enontekiö, Finland 8 B20 68 23N 23 37 E
Enosburg Falls, U.S.A. 111 B12 44 55N 72 48W
Enping, China 59 F9 22 16N 112 21 E
Enriquillo, L., Dom. Rep. 121 C5 18 20N 72 5W
Enschede, Neths. 17 B6 52 13N 6 53 E
Ensenada, Argentina 126 C4 34 55 S 57 55W
Ensenada, Mexico 118 A1 31 50N 116 50W
Ensenada de los Muertos, Mexico 118 C2 23 59N 109 50W
Enshi, China 58 B7 30 18N 109 29 E
Ensiola, Pta. de n', Spain 37 B9 39 7N 2 55 E
Ensisheim, France 19 E14 47 50N 7 20 E
Entebbe, Uganda 86 B3 0 4N 32 28 E
Enterprise, Canada 104 A5 60 47N 115 45W
Enterprise, Ala., U.S.A. 109 K3 31 19N 85 51W
Enterprise, Oreg., U.S.A. 114 D5 45 25N 117 17W
Entraygues-sur-Truyère, France 20 D6 44 38N 2 35 E
Entre Ríos, Bolivia 126 A3 21 30 S 64 25W
Entre Ríos □, Argentina 126 C4 30 30 S 58 30W
Entrepeñas, Embalse de, Spain 32 E2 40 34N 2 42W
Entroncamento, Portugal 35 F2 39 28N 8 28W
Enugu, Nigeria 83 D6 6 30N 7 30 E
Enugu □, Nigeria 83 D6 6 30N 7 45 E
Enugu Ezike, Nigeria 83 D6 7 0N 7 29 E
Enumclaw, U.S.A. 116 C5 47 12N 121 59W
Envermeu, France 18 C8 49 53N 1 15 E
Enviken, Sweden 10 D9 60 49N 15 46 E
Enying, Hungary 42 D3 46 56N 18 15 E
Enza →, Italy 28 D7 44 54N 10 31 E
Eólie, Ís., Italy 31 D7 38 30N 14 57 E
Epanomí, Greece 40 F6 40 25N 22 59 E
Epe, Neths. 17 B5 52 21N 5 59 E
Epe, Nigeria 83 D5 6 36N 3 59 E
Épernay, France 19 C10 49 3N 3 56 E
Épernon, France 19 D8 48 35N 1 40 E
Ephesus, Turkey 39 D9 37 55N 27 22 E
Ephraim, U.S.A. 114 G8 39 22N 111 35W
Ephrata, Pa., U.S.A. 111 F8 40 11N 76 11W
Ephrata, Wash., U.S.A. 114 C4 47 19N 119 33W
Epidaurus Limera, Greece 38 E5 36 46N 23 0 E
Épila, Spain 32 D3 41 36N 1 17W
Épinac, France 19 F11 46 59N 4 31 E
Épinal, France 19 D13 48 10N 6 27 E
Episkopi, Cyprus 36 E11 34 40N 32 54 E
Episkopí, Greece 36 D6 35 20N 24 20 E
Episkopi Bay, Cyprus 36 E11 34 35N 32 50 E
Epitálion, Greece 38 D3 37 37N 21 30 E
Eppan = Appiano, Italy 29 B8 46 28N 11 15 E
Eppingen, Germany 25 F4 49 8N 8 53 E
Epsom, U.K. 13 F7 51 19N 0 16W
Epukiro, Namibia 88 C2 21 40 S 19 9 E
Equatorial Guinea ■, Africa 84 D1 2 0N 8 0 E
Er Hai, China 58 E3 25 48N 100 11 E
Er Rahad, Sudan 81 E3 12 45N 30 32 E
Er Rif, Morocco 78 A5 35 1N 4 1W
Er Rogel, Sudan 80 D4 18 10N 35 25 E
Er Roseires, Sudan 81 E3 11 55N 34 30 E
Er Rua'at, Sudan 81 E3 12 21N 32 17 E
Eraclea, Italy 29 C9 45 35N 12 40 E
Erāwadī Myit = Irrawaddy →, Burma 67 M19 15 50N 95 6 E
Erba, Italy 28 C6 45 48N 9 15 E
Erba, Sudan 80 D4 19 5N 36 51 E
Erba, J., Sudan 80 C4 20 48N 36 47 E
Erbaa, Turkey 72 B7 40 42N 36 36 E
Erbeskopf, Germany 25 F3 49 44N 7 2 E
Erbil = Arbīl, Iraq 70 B5 36 15N 44 5 E
Erbu, Ethiopia 81 E3 6 44N 34 53 E
Erçek, Turkey 70 B4 38 39N 43 36 E
Erçis, Turkey 73 C10 39 2N 43 21 E
Erciyaş Daği, Turkey 70 B2 38 30N 35 30 E
Érd, Hungary 42 C3 47 22N 18 56 E
Erdao Jiang →, China 57 C14 43 0N 127 0 E
Erdek, Turkey 41 F11 40 23N 27 47 E
Erdemli, Turkey 72 D6 36 36N 34 19 E
Erdene = Ulaan-Uul, Mongolia 56 B6 44 13N 111 10 E
Erdenetsogt, Mongolia 56 C4 42 55N 106 5 E
Erding, Germany 25 G7 48 18N 11 54 E
Erdre →, France 18 E5 47 13N 1 32W
Erebus, Mt., Antarctica 5 D11 77 35 S 167 0 E
Erechim, Brazil 127 B5 27 35 S 52 15W
Ereğli, Konya, Turkey 70 B2 37 31N 34 4 E
Ereğli, Zonguldak, Turkey 72 B4 41 15N 31 24 E
Erei, Monti, Italy 31 E7 37 20N 14 20 E
Erenhot, China 56 C7 43 48N 112 2 E
Eresma →, Spain 34 D6 41 26N 4 45W
Eressós, Greece 39 B7 39 11N 25 57 E
Erewadi Myitwanya, Burma 67 M19 15 30N 95 0 E
Erfenisdam, S. Africa 88 D4 28 30 S 26 50 E
Erfstadt, Germany 24 E2 50 50N 6 50 E
Erft →, Germany 24 D2 51 11N 6 44 E
Erfurt, Germany 24 E7 50 58N 11 2 E
Erg Iguidi, Africa 78 C4 27 0N 7 0 E
Ergani, Turkey 70 B3 38 17N 39 49 E
Ergel, Mongolia 56 C5 43 8N 109 5 E
Ergene →, Turkey 41 E10 41 1N 26 22 E
Ergeni Vozvyshennost, Russia 49 G7 47 0N 44 0 E
Ērgli, Latvia 9 H21 56 54N 25 38 E
Erhlin, Taiwan 59 F13 23 54N 120 22 E
Eria →, Spain 34 C5 42 3N 5 44W
Eriba, Sudan 81 D4 16 40N 36 10 E
Eriboll, L., U.K. 14 C4 58 30N 4 42W
Érice, Italy 30 D5 38 2N 12 35 E
Erie, U.S.A. 110 D4 42 8N 80 5W
Erie, L., N. Amer. 110 D4 42 15N 81 0W
Erie Canal, U.S.A. 110 C7 43 5N 78 43W
Erieau, Canada 110 D3 42 16N 81 57W
Erigavo, Somali Rep. 74 E4 10 35N 47 20 E
Erikoúsa, Greece 36 A3 39 53N 19 34 E
Eriksdale, Canada 105 C9 50 52N 98 7W
Erímanthos, Greece 38 D3 37 57N 21 50 E
Erimo-misaki, Japan 54 D11 41 50N 143 15 E
Erinpura, India 68 G5 25 9N 73 3 E
Eriskay, U.K. 14 D1 57 4N 7 18W
Erithraí, Greece 38 C5 38 13N 23 20 E
Eritrea ■, Africa 81 E4 14 0N 38 30 E
Erjas →, Portugal 34 F3 39 40N 7 1W
Erkelenz, Germany 24 D2 51 4N 6 19 E
Erkner, Germany 24 C9 52 25N 13 44 E
Erlangen, Germany 25 F6 49 36N 11 0 E
Erldunda, Australia 94 D1 25 14 S 133 12 E
Ermelo, Neths. 17 B5 52 18N 5 35 E
Ermelo, S. Africa 89 D4 26 31 S 29 59 E
Ermenek, Turkey 70 B2 36 38N 33 0 E
Ermil, Sudan 81 E2 13 35N 27 40 E
Ermióni, Greece 38 D5 37 23N 23 15 E
Ermones, Greece 36 A3 39 37N 19 46 E
Ermoúpolis = Síros, Greece 38 D6 37 28N 24 57 E
Ernakulam = Cochin, India 66 Q10 9 59N 76 22 E
Erne →, Ireland 15 B3 54 30N 8 16W
Erne, Lower L., U.K. 15 B4 54 28N 7 47W
Erne, Upper L., U.K. 15 B4 54 14N 7 32W
Ernée, France 18 D6 48 18N 0 56W
Ernest Giles Ra., Australia 93 E3 27 0 S 123 45 E
Ernstberg, Germany 25 E2 50 13N 6 47 E
Erode, India 66 P10 11 24N 77 45 E
Eromanga, Australia 95 D3 26 40 S 143 11 E
Erongo, Namibia 88 C2 21 39 S 15 58 E
Erquy, France 18 D4 48 38N 2 29W
Erramala Hills, India 66 M11 15 30N 78 15 E
Errer →, Ethiopia 81 F5 7 32N 42 35 E
Errigal, Ireland 15 A3 55 2N 8 6W
Erris Hd., Ireland 15 B1 54 19N 10 0W
Erseka = Ersekë, Albania 40 F4 40 22N 20 40 E
Ersekë, Albania 40 F4 40 22N 20 40 E
Erskine, U.S.A. 112 B7 47 40N 96 0W
Erstein, France 19 D14 48 25N 7 38 E
Ertholmene, Denmark 11 J9 55 19N 15 11 E
Ertil, Russia 48 E5 51 55N 40 50 E
Ertis = Irtysh →, Russia 50 C7 61 4N 68 52 E
Eruh, Turkey 73 D10 37 46N 42 13 E
Eruwa, Nigeria 83 D5 7 33N 3 26 E
Ervy-le-Châtel, France 19 D10 48 2N 3 55 E
Erwin, U.S.A. 109 G4 36 9N 82 25W
Eryuan, China 58 D2 26 7N 99 57 E
Erzgebirge, Germany 24 E8 50 27N 12 55 E
Erzin, Russia 51 D10 50 15N 95 10 E
Erzincan, Turkey 70 B3 39 46N 39 30 E
Erzurum, Turkey 70 B4 39 57N 41 15 E
Es Caló, Spain 37 C8 38 40N 1 30 E
Es Canar, Spain 37 B8 39 2N 1 36 E
Es Mercadal, Spain 37 B11 39 59N 4 5 E
Es Migjorn Gran, Spain 37 B11 39 57N 4 3 E
Es Safiya, Sudan 81 D3 15 31N 30 7 E
Es Sahrâ' Esh Sharqîya, Egypt 80 B3 27 30N 32 30 E
Es Sînâ', Egypt 75 F3 29 0N 34 0 E
Es Sûkî, Sudan 81 E3 13 20N 33 58 E
Es Vedrà, Spain 37 C7 38 52N 1 12 E
Esambo, Dem. Rep. of the Congo 86 C1 3 48 S 23 30 E
Esan-Misaki, Japan 54 D10 41 40N 141 10 E
Esashi, Hokkaidō, Japan 54 B11 44 56N 142 35 E
Esashi, Hokkaidō, Japan 54 D10 41 52N 140 7 E
Esbjerg, Denmark 11 J2 55 29N 8 29 E
Escalante, U.S.A. 115 H8 37 47N 111 36W
Escalante →, U.S.A. 115 H8 37 24N 110 57W
Escalón, Mexico 118 B4 26 46N 104 20W
Escambia →, U.S.A. 109 K2 30 32N 87 11W
Escanaba, U.S.A. 108 C2 45 45N 87 4W
Esch-sur-Alzette, Lux. 17 E6 49 32N 6 0 E
Eschede, Germany 24 C6 52 44N 10 14 E
Eschwege, Germany 24 D6 51 11N 10 2 E
Eschweiler, Germany 24 E2 50 49N 6 15 E
Escondido, U.S.A. 117 M9 33 7N 117 5W
Escravos →, Nigeria 83 D6 5 35N 5 10 E
Escuinapa, Mexico 118 C3 22 50N 105 50W
Escuintla, Guatemala 120 D1 14 20N 90 48W
Eséka, Cameroon 83 E7 3 41N 10 44 E
Eşen →, Turkey 39 E11 36 27N 29 16 E
Esenguly, Turkmenistan 50 F6 37 37N 53 59 E
Esens, Germany 24 B3 53 38N 7 36 E
Esenyurt, Turkey 41 E12 41 3N 28 48 E
Esera →, Spain 32 C5 42 6N 0 15 E
Eşfahān, Iran 71 C6 32 39N 51 43 E
Eşfahān □, Iran 71 C6 32 50N 51 50 E
Esfarāyen, Iran 71 B8 37 4N 57 30 E
Esfideh, Iran 71 C8 33 39N 59 46 E
Esgueva →, Spain 34 D6 41 40N 4 43W
Esh Sham = Dimashq, Syria 75 B5 33 30N 36 18 E
Esh Shamâlîya □, Sudan 80 D2 19 0N 29 0 E
Esha Ness, U.K. 14 A7 60 29N 1 38W
Eshan, China 58 E4 24 11N 102 24 E
Esher, U.K. 13 F7 51 21N 0 20W
Eshowe, S. Africa 89 D5 28 50 S 31 30 E
Esiama, Ghana 82 E4 4 56N 2 25W
Esigodini, Zimbabwe 89 C4 20 18 S 28 56 E
Esil = Ishim →, Russia 50 D8 57 45N 71 10 E
Esino →, Italy 29 E10 43 39N 13 22 E
Esira, Madag. 89 C8 24 20 S 46 42 E
Esk →, Cumb., U.K. 14 G5 54 58N 3 2W
Esk →, N. Yorks., U.K. 12 C7 54 30N 0 37W
Eskān, Iran 71 E9 26 48N 63 9 E
Esker, Canada 103 B6 53 53N 66 25W
Eskifjörður, Iceland 8 D7 65 3N 13 55W
Eskilsäter, Sweden 11 F7 58 57N 13 10 E
Eskilstuna, Sweden 10 E10 59 22N 16 32 E
Eskimalatya, Turkey 73 C8 38 24N 38 22 E
Eskimo Pt., Canada 100 B10 61 10N 94 15W
Eskişehir, Turkey 39 B12 39 50N 30 30 E
Eskişehir □, Turkey 39 B12 39 40N 31 0 E
Esla →, Spain 34 D4 41 29N 6 3W
Eslāmābād-e Gharb, Iran 70 C5 34 10N 46 30 E
Eslāmshahr, Iran 71 C6 35 40N 51 10 E
Eslöv, Sweden 11 J7 55 50N 13 20 E
Eşme, Turkey 39 C10 38 23N 28 58 E
Esmeraldas, Ecuador 124 C3 1 0N 79 40W
Esnagi L., Canada 102 C3 48 36N 84 33W
Espalion, France 20 D6 44 32N 2 47 E
Espanola, Canada 102 C3 46 15N 81 46W
Espanola, U.S.A. 115 H10 35 59N 106 5W
Esparreguera, Spain 32 D6 41 33N 1 52 E
Esparta, Costa Rica 120 E3 9 59N 84 40W
Espelkamp, Germany 24 C4 52 24N 8 36 E
Esperance, Australia 93 F3 33 45 S 121 55 E
Esperance B., Australia 93 F3 33 48 S 121 55 E
Esperanza, Argentina 126 C3 31 29 S 61 3W
Esperanza, Phil. 61 G6 8 43N 125 36 E
Espéraza, France 20 F6 42 56N 2 14 E
Espichel, C., Portugal 35 G1 38 22N 9 16W
Espiel, Spain 35 G5 38 11N 5 1W
Espigão, Serra do, Brazil 127 B5 26 35 S 50 30W
Espinazo, Sierra del = Espinhaço, Serra do, Brazil 125 G10 17 30 S 43 30W
Espinhaço, Serra do, Brazil 125 G10 17 30 S 43 30W
Espinho, Portugal 34 D2 41 1N 8 38W
Espinilho, Serra do, Brazil 127 B5 28 30 S 55 0W
Espinosa de los Monteros, Spain 34 B7 43 5N 3 34W
Espíritu Santo □, Brazil 125 H10 20 0 S 40 45W
Espíritu Santo, Vanuatu 96 J8 15 15 S 166 50 E
Espíritu Santo, B. del, Mexico 119 D7 19 15N 87 0W
Espíritu Santo, I., Mexico 118 C2 24 30N 110 23W
Espita, Mexico 119 C7 21 1N 88 19W
Espiye, Turkey 73 B8 40 56N 38 43 E
Espluga de Francolí, Spain 32 D6 41 24N 1 7 E
Espoo, Finland 9 F21 60 12N 24 40 E
Espuña, Sierra de, Spain 33 H3 37 51N 1 35W
Espungabera, Mozam. 89 C5 20 29 S 32 45 E
Esquel, Argentina 128 E2 42 55 S 71 20W
Esquimalt, Canada 104 D4 48 26N 123 25W
Esquina, Argentina 126 C4 30 0 S 59 30W
Essaouira, Morocco 78 B4 31 32N 9 42W
Essebie, Dem. Rep. of the Congo 86 B3 2 58N 30 40 E
Essen, Belgium 17 C4 51 28N 4 28 E
Essen, Germany 24 D3 51 28N 7 2 E
Essendon, Mt., Australia 93 E3 25 0 S 120 29 E
Essequibo →, Guyana 122 C5 6 50N 58 30W
Essex, Canada 110 D2 42 10N 82 49W
Essex, Calif., U.S.A. 117 L11 34 44N 115 15W
Essex, N.Y., U.S.A. 111 B11 44 19N 73 21W
Essex □, U.K. 13 F8 51 54N 0 27 E
Essex Junction, U.S.A. 111 B11 44 29N 73 7W
Esslingen, Germany 25 G5 48 44N 9 18 E
Essonne □, France 19 D9 48 30N 2 20 E
Estaca de Bares, C. de, Spain 34 B3 43 46N 7 42W
Estadilla, Spain 32 C5 42 4N 0 16 E
Estados, I. de Los, Argentina 122 J4 54 40 S 64 30W
Estagel, France 20 F6 42 47N 2 40 E
Eşţahbānāt, Iran 71 D7 29 8N 54 4 E
Estância, Brazil 125 F11 11 16 S 37 26W
Estancia, U.S.A. 115 J10 34 46N 106 4W
Estārm, Iran 71 D8 28 21N 58 21 E
Estarreja, Portugal 34 E2 40 45N 8 35W
Estats, Pic d', Spain 32 C6 42 40N 1 24 E
Estcourt, S. Africa 89 D4 29 0 S 29 53 E
Este, Italy 29 C8 45 14N 11 39 E
Estelí, Nic. 120 D2 13 9N 86 22W
Estella, Spain 32 C2 42 40N 2 2W
Estellencs, Spain 37 B9 39 39N 2 29 E
Estena →, Spain 35 F6 39 23N 4 44W
Estepa, Spain 35 H6 37 17N 4 52W
Estepona, Spain 35 J5 36 24N 5 7W
Esterhazy, Canada 105 C8 50 37N 102 5W
Esternay, France 19 D10 48 44N 3 33 E
Esterri d'Aneu, Spain 32 C6 42 38N 1 5 E
Estevan, Canada 105 D8 49 10N 102 59W
Estevan Group, Canada 104 C3 53 3N 129 38W
Estherville, U.S.A. 112 D7 43 24N 94 50W
Estissac, France 19 D10 48 16N 3 48 E
Eston, Canada 105 C7 51 8N 108 40W
Estonia ■, Europe 9 G21 58 30N 25 30 E
Estoril, Portugal 35 G1 38 42N 9 23W
Estouk, Mali 83 B5 18 14N 1 2 E
Estreito, Brazil 125 E9 6 32 S 47 25W
Estrela, Serra da, Portugal 34 E3 40 10N 7 45W
Estrella, Spain 35 G7 38 25N 3 35W
Estremoz, Portugal 35 G3 38 51N 7 39W
Estrondo, Serra do, Brazil 125 E9 7 20 S 48 0W
Esztergom, Hungary 42 C3 47 47N 18 44 E
Et Tîdra, Mauritania 82 B1 19 45N 16 20W
Etah, India 69 F8 27 35N 78 40 E
Étain, France 19 C12 49 13N 5 38 E
Étampes, France 19 D9 48 26N 2 10 E
Etanga, Namibia 88 B1 17 55 S 13 0 E
Étaples, France 19 B8 50 30N 1 39 E
Etawah, India 69 F8 26 48N 79 6 E
Etawney L., Canada 105 B9 57 50N 96 50W
Ete, Nigeria 83 D6 7 2N 7 28 E
Ethel, U.S.A. 116 D4 46 32N 122 46W
Ethelbert, Canada 105 C8 51 32N 100 25W
Ethiopia ■, Africa 74 F3 8 0N 40 0 E
Ethiopian Highlands, Ethiopia 52 J7 10 0N 37 0 E
Etili, Turkey 41 G10 39 59N 26 54 E
Etive, L., U.K. 14 E3 56 29N 5 10W
Etna, Italy 31 E7 37 50N 14 55 E
Etoile, Dem. Rep. of the Congo 87 E2 11 33 S 27 30 E
Etosha Nat. Park, Namibia 88 B2 19 0 S 16 0 E
Etosha Pan, Namibia 88 B2 18 40 S 16 30 E
Etowah, U.S.A. 109 H3 35 20N 84 32W
Étréchy, France 19 D9 48 30N 2 12 E
Étrépagny, France 19 C8 49 18N 1 36 E
Étretat, France 18 C7 49 42N 0 12 E
Etropole, Bulgaria 41 D8 42 50N 24 0 E
Ettelbruck, Lux. 17 E6 49 51N 6 5 E
Ettlingen, Germany 25 G4 48 56N 8 25 E
Ettrick Water →, U.K. 14 F6 55 31N 2 55W
Etuku, Dem. Rep. of the Congo 86 C2 3 42 S 25 45 E
Etulia, Moldova 43 E13 45 32N 28 27 E
Etzatlán, Mexico 118 C4 20 48N 104 5W
Etzná, Mexico 119 D6 19 35N 90 15W
Eu, France 18 B8 50 3N 1 26 E
Euboea = Évvoia, Greece 38 C6 38 30N 24 0 E
Eucla, Australia 93 F4 31 41 S 128 52 E
Euclid, U.S.A. 110 E3 41 34N 81 32W
Eucumbene, L., Australia 95 F4 36 2 S 148 40 E
Eudora, U.S.A. 113 J9 33 7N 91 16W
Eufaula, Ala., U.S.A. 109 K3 31 54N 85 9W
Eufaula, Okla., U.S.A. 113 H7 35 17N 95 35W
Eufaula L., U.S.A. 113 H7 35 18N 95 21W
Eugene, U.S.A. 114 E2 44 5N 123 4W
Eugowra, Australia 95 E4 33 22 S 148 24 E
Eulo, Australia 95 D4 28 10 S 145 3 E
Eunice, La., U.S.A. 113 K8 30 30N 92 25W
Eunice, N. Mex., U.S.A. 113 J3 32 26N 103 10W
Eupen, Belgium 17 D6 50 37N 6 3 E
Euphrates = Furāt, Nahr al →, Asia 70 D5 31 0N 47 25 E
Eure □, France 18 C8 49 10N 1 0 E
Eure →, France 18 C8 49 18N 1 12 E
Eure-et-Loir □, France 18 D8 48 22N 1 30 E
Eureka, Canada 4 B3 80 0N 85 56W
Eureka, Calif., U.S.A. 114 F1 40 47N 124 9W
Eureka, Kans., U.S.A. 113 G6 37 49N 96 17W
Eureka, Mont., U.S.A. 114 B6 48 53N 115 3W
Eureka, Nev., U.S.A. 114 G5 39 31N 115 58W
Eureka, S. Dak., U.S.A. 112 C5 45 46N 99 38W
Eureka, Mt., Australia 93 E3 26 35 S 121 35 E
Euroa, Australia 95 F4 36 44 S 145 35 E
Europa, Île, Ind. Oc. 85 J8 22 20 S 40 22 E
Europa, Picos de, Spain 34 B6 43 10N 4 49W
Europa, Pta. de, Gib. 35 J5 36 3N 5 21W
Europe 6 E10 50 0N 20 0 E
Europoort, Neths. 17 C4 51 57N 4 10 E
Euskirchen, Germany 24 E2 50 39N 6 48 E
Eustis, U.S.A. 109 L5 28 51N 81 41W
Euston, Australia 95 E3 34 30 S 142 46 E
Eutin, Germany 24 A6 54 8N 10 36 E
Eutsuk L., Canada 104 C3 53 20N 126 45W
Evale, Angola 88 B2 16 33 S 15 44 E
Evans, U.S.A. 112 E2 40 23N 104 41W
Evans, L., Canada 102 B4 50 50N 77 0W
Evans City, U.S.A. 110 F4 40 46N 80 4W
Evans Head, Australia 95 D5 29 7 S 153 27 E
Evans Mills, U.S.A. 111 B9 44 6N 75 48W
Evansburg, Canada 104 C5 53 36N 114 59W
Evanston, Ill., U.S.A. 108 E2 42 3N 87 41W
Evanston, Wyo., U.S.A. 114 F8 41 16N 110 58W
Evansville, U.S.A. 108 G2 37 58N 87 35W
Évaux-les-Bains, France 19 F9 46 12N 2 29 E
Evaz, Iran 71 E7 27 46N 53 59 E
Evciler, Afyon, Turkey 39 C11 38 4N 29 54 E
Evciler, Çanakkale, Turkey 39 B8 39 47N 26 44 E
Eveleth, U.S.A. 112 B8 47 28N 92 32W
Evensk, Russia 51 C16 62 12N 159 30 E
Everard, L., Australia 95 E2 31 30 S 135 0 E
Everard Ranges, Australia 93 E5 27 5 S 132 28 E
Everest, Mt., Nepal 69 E12 28 5N 86 58 E
Everett, Pa., U.S.A. 110 F6 40 1N 78 23W
Everett, Wash., U.S.A. 116 C4 47 59N 122 12W
Everglades, The, U.S.A. 109 N5 25 50N 81 0W
Everglades City, U.S.A. 109 N5 25 52N 81 23W
Everglades National Park, U.S.A. 109 N5 25 30N 81 0W
Evergreen, Ala., U.S.A. 109 K2 31 26N 86 57W
Evergreen, Mont., U.S.A. 114 B6 48 9N 114 13W
Everöd, Sweden 11 J8 55 53N 14 5 E
Evertsberg, Sweden 10 C7 61 8N 13 58 E
Evesham, U.K. 13 E6 52 6N 1 56W
Évian-les-Bains, France 19 F13 46 24N 6 35 E
Évinos →, Greece 38 C3 38 27N 21 40 E
Évisa, France 21 F12 42 15N 8 48 E
Evje, Norway 9 G12 58 36N 7 51 E
Évora, Portugal 35 G3 38 33N 7 57W
Évora □, Portugal 35 G3 38 33N 7 50W
Evowghlī, Iran 70 B5 38 43N 45 13 E
Évreux, France 18 C8 49 3N 1 8 E
Evritanía □, Greece 38 B3 39 5N 21 30 E
Évron, France 18 D6 48 10N 0 24W
Évros □, Greece 41 E10 41 10N 26 0 E
Évros →, Bulgaria 72 B2 41 40N 26 34 E
Evrótas →, Greece 38 E4 36 50N 22 40 E
Évry, France 19 D9 48 38N 2 27 E
Évvoia, Greece 38 C6 38 30N 24 0 E
Évvoia □, Greece 38 C5 38 40N 23 40 E
Evxinoúpolis, Greece 38 B4 39 12N 22 42 E
Ewe, L., U.K. 14 D3 57 49N 5 38W
Ewing, U.S.A. 112 D5 42 16N 98 21W
Ewo, Congo 84 E2 0 48 S 14 45 E
Exaltación, Bolivia 124 F5 13 10 S 65 20W
Excelsior Springs, U.S.A. 112 F7 39 20N 94 13W
Excideuil, France 20 C5 45 20N 1 4 E
Exe →, U.K. 13 G4 50 41N 3 29W
Exeter, Canada 110 C3 43 21N 81 29W
Exeter, U.K. 13 G4 50 43N 3 31W
Exeter, Calif., U.S.A. 116 J7 36 18N 119 9W
Exeter, N.H., U.S.A. 111 D14 42 59N 70 57W
Exmoor, U.K. 13 F4 51 12N 3 45W
Exmouth, Australia 92 D1 21 54 S 114 10 E
Exmouth, U.K. 13 G4 50 37N 3 25W
Exmouth G., Australia 92 D1 22 15 S 114 15 E
Expedition Ra., Australia 94 C4 24 30 S 149 12 E
Extremadura □, Spain 35 F4 39 30N 6 5W
Exuma Sound, Bahamas 120 B4 24 30N 76 20W
Eyasi, L., Tanzania 86 C4 3 30 S 35 0 E
Eye Pen., U.K. 14 C2 58 13N 6 10W
Eyemouth, U.K. 14 F6 55 52N 2 5W
Eygurande, France 19 G9 45 40N 2 26 E
Eyjafjörður, Iceland 8 C4 66 15N 18 30W
Eymet, France 20 D4 44 40N 0 25 E
Eymoutiers, France 20 C5 45 40N 1 45 E
Eynesil, Turkey 73 B8 41 4N 39 9 E
Eyre (North), L., Australia 95 D2 28 30 S 137 20 E
Eyre (South), L., Australia 95 D2 29 18 S 137 25 E
Eyre Mts., N.Z. 91 L2 45 25 S 168 25 E
Eyre Pen., Australia 95 E2 33 30 S 136 17 E
Eysturoy, Færoe Is. 8 E9 62 13N 6 54W
Eyvānkī, Iran 71 C6 35 24N 51 56 E
Ez Zeidab, Sudan 80 D3 17 25N 33 55 E
Ezcaray, Spain 32 C1 42 19N 3 0W
Ežerėlis, Lithuania 44 D10 54 53N 23 37 E
Ezhou, China 59 B10 30 23N 114 50 E
Ezine, Turkey 39 B8 39 48N 26 20 E
Ezouza →, Cyprus 36 E11 34 44N 32 27 E

F

F.Y.R.O.M. = Macedonia ■, Europe 40 E5 41 53N 21 40 E
Fabala, Guinea 82 D3 9 44N 9 5W
Fabens, U.S.A. 115 L10 31 30N 106 10W
Fabero, Spain 34 C4 42 46N 6 37W
Fåborg, Denmark 11 J4 55 6N 10 15 E
Fabriano, Italy 29 E9 43 20N 12 54 E
Făcăeni, Romania 43 F12 44 32N 27 53 E
Fachi, Niger 79 E8 18 6N 11 34 E
Fada, Chad 79 E10 17 13N 21 34 E
Fada-n-Gourma, Burkina Faso 83 C5 12 10N 0 30 E
Fadd, Hungary 42 D3 46 28N 18 49 E
Faddeyevskiy, Ostrov, Russia 51 B15 76 0N 144 0 E
Faddor, Sudan 81 F3 8 7N 32 17 E
Fadghāmī, Syria 70 C4 35 53N 40 52 E
Fadlab, Sudan 80 D3 17 42N 34 2 E
Faenza, Italy 29 D8 44 17N 11 53 E
Færoe Is. = Føroyar, Atl. Oc. 8 F9 62 0N 7 0W
Fafa, Mali 83 B5 15 22N 0 48 E
Fafe, Portugal 34 D2 41 27N 8 11W
Fagam, Nigeria 83 C7 11 1N 10 1 E
Făgăras, Romania 43 E9 45 48N 24 58 E
Făgăras, Muntii, Romania 43 E9 45 40N 24 40 E
Fågelmara, Sweden 11 H9 56 16N 15 58 E
Fagerhult, Sweden 11 G9 57 8N 15 40 E
Fagersta, Sweden 10 D9 60 1N 15 46 E
Făget, Romania 42 E7 45 52N 22 10 E
Făget, Muntii, Romania 43 C8 47 40N 23 10 E
Fagnano, L., Argentina 128 G3 54 30 S 68 0W
Fagnières, France 19 D11 48 58N 4 20 E
Faguibine, L., Mali 82 B4 16 45N 4 0W
Fahlīān, Iran 71 D6 30 11N 51 28 E
Fahraj, Kermān, Iran 71 D8 29 0N 59 0 E
Fahraj, Yazd, Iran 71 D7 31 46N 54 36 E
Fai Tsi Long Archipelago, Vietnam 58 G6 21 0N 107 30 E

Faial, *Madeira* **37 D3** 32 47N 16 53W
Fair Haven, *U.S.A.* **108 D9** 43 36N 73 16W
Fair Hd., *U.K.* **15 A5** 55 14N 6 9W
Fair Oaks, *U.S.A.* **116 G5** 38 39N 121 16W
Fairbanks, *U.S.A.* **100 B5** 64 51N 147 43W
Fairbury, *U.S.A.* **112 E6** 40 8N 97 11W
Fairfax, *U.S.A.* **111 B11** 44 40N 73 1W
Fairfield, *Ala., U.S.A.* **109 J2** 33 29N 86 55W
Fairfield, *Calif., U.S.A.* **116 G4** 38 15N 122 3W
Fairfield, *Conn., U.S.A.* **111 E11** 41 9N 73 16W
Fairfield, *Idaho, U.S.A.* **114 E6** 43 21N 114 44W
Fairfield, *Ill., U.S.A.* **108 F1** 38 23N 88 22W
Fairfield, *Iowa, U.S.A.* **112 E9** 40 56N 91 57W
Fairfield, *Tex., U.S.A.* **113 K7** 31 44N 96 10W
Fairford, *Canada* **105 C9** 51 37N 98 38W
Fairhope, *U.S.A.* **109 K2** 30 31N 87 54W
Fairlie, *N.Z.* **91 L3** 44 5S 170 49E
Fairmead, *U.S.A.* **116 H6** 37 5N 120 10W
Fairmont, *Minn., U.S.A.* **112 D7** 43 39N 94 28W
Fairmont, *W. Va., U.S.A.* **108 F5** 39 29N 80 9W
Fairmount, *Calif., U.S.A.* **117 L8** 34 45N 118 26W
Fairmount, *N.Y., U.S.A.* **111 C8** 43 5N 76 12W
Fairplay, *U.S.A.* **115 G11** 39 15N 106 2W
Fairport, *U.S.A.* **110 C7** 43 6N 77 27W
Fairport Harbor, *U.S.A.* **110 E3** 41 45N 81 17W
Fairview, *Canada* **104 B5** 56 5N 118 25W
Fairview, *Mont., U.S.A.* **112 B2** 47 51N 104 3W
Fairview, *Okla., U.S.A.* **113 G5** 36 16N 98 29W
Fairweather, Mt., *U.S.A.* **104 B1** 58 55N 137 32W
Faisalabad, *Pakistan* **68 D5** 31 30N 73 5E
Faith, *U.S.A.* **112 C3** 45 2N 102 2W
Faizabad, *India* **69 F10** 26 45N 82 10E
Fajardo, *Puerto Rico* **121 C6** 18 20N 65 39W
Fajr, W. →, *Si. Arabia* **70 D3** 29 10N 38 10E
Fakenham, *U.K.* **12 E8** 52 51N 0 51E
Fåker, *Sweden* **10 A8** 63 0N 14 34E
Fakfak, *Indonesia* **63 E8** 3 0S 132 15E
Fakiya, *Bulgaria* **41 D11** 42 10N 27 6E
Fakobli, *Ivory C.* **82 D3** 7 23N 7 23W
Fakse, *Denmark* **11 J6** 55 15N 12 8E
Fakse Bugt, *Denmark* **11 J6** 55 11N 12 15E
Fakse Ladeplads, *Denmark* **11 J6** 55 11N 12 9E
Faku, *China* **57 C12** 42 32N 123 21E
Falaba, *S. Leone* **82 D2** 9 54N 11 22W
Falaise, *France* **18 D6** 48 54N 0 12W
Falaise, Mui, *Vietnam* **64 C5** 19 6N 105 45E
Falakrón Óros, *Greece* **40 E7** 41 15N 23 58E
Falam, *Burma* **67 H18** 23 0N 93 45E
Falces, *Spain* **32 C3** 42 24N 1 48W
Fălciu, *Romania* **43 D13** 46 17N 28 7E
Falcó, C. des, *Spain* **37 C7** 38 50N 1 23E
Falcón, Presa, *Mexico* **119 B5** 26 35N 99 10W
Falcon Lake, *Canada* **105 D9** 49 42N 95 15W
Falcon Reservoir, *U.S.A.* **113 M5** 26 34N 99 10W
Falconara Marittima, *Italy* **29 E10** 43 37N 13 24E
Falcone, C. del, *Italy* **30 B1** 40 58N 8 12E
Falconer, *U.S.A.* **110 D5** 42 7N 79 13W
Faléa, *Mali* **82 C2** 12 16N 11 17W
Falémé →, *Senegal* **82 C2** 14 46N 12 14W
Falerum, *Sweden* **11 F10** 58 8N 16 13E
Faleshty = Fălești, *Moldova* **43 C12** 47 32N 27 44E
Fălești, *Moldova* **43 C12** 47 32N 27 44E
Falfurrias, *U.S.A.* **113 M5** 27 14N 98 9W
Falher, *Canada* **104 B5** 55 44N 117 15W
Falirakí, *Greece* **36 C10** 36 22N 28 12E
Falkenberg, *Germany* **24 D9** 51 35N 13 14E
Falkenberg, *Sweden* **11 H6** 56 54N 12 30E
Falkensee, *Germany* **24 C9** 52 34N 13 4E
Falkirk, *U.K.* **14 F5** 56 0N 3 47W
Falkirk □, *U.K.* **14 F5** 55 58N 3 49W
Falkland, *U.K.* **14 E5** 56 16N 3 12W
Falkland Is. □, *Atl. Oc.* **128 G5** 51 30S 59 0W
Falkland Sd., *Falk. Is.* **128 G5** 52 0S 60 0W
Falkonéra, *Greece* **38 E5** 36 50N 23 52E
Falköping, *Sweden* **11 F7** 58 12N 13 33E
Fall River, *U.S.A.* **111 E13** 41 43N 71 10W
Fallbrook, *U.S.A.* **117 M9** 33 23N 117 15W
Fallon, *U.S.A.* **114 G4** 39 28N 118 47W
Falls City, *U.S.A.* **112 E7** 40 3N 95 36W
Falls Creek, *U.S.A.* **110 E6** 41 9N 78 48W
Falmouth, *Jamaica* **120 C4** 18 30N 77 40W
Falmouth, *U.K.* **13 G2** 50 9N 5 5W
Falmouth, *U.S.A.* **111 E14** 41 33N 70 37W
Falsa, Pta., *Mexico* **118 B1** 27 51N 115 3W
False B., *S. Africa* **88 E2** 34 15S 18 40E
Falso, C., *Honduras* **120 C3** 15 12N 83 21W
Falster, *Denmark* **11 K5** 54 45N 11 55E
Falsterbo, *Sweden* **9 J15** 55 23N 12 50E
Fălticeni, *Romania* **43 C11** 47 21N 26 20E
Falun, *Sweden* **10 D9** 60 37N 15 37E
Famagusta, *Cyprus* **36 D12** 35 8N 33 55E
Famagusta Bay, *Cyprus* **36 D13** 35 15N 34 0E
Famalé, *Niger* **78 F6** 14 33N 1 5E
Famatina, Sierra de, *Argentina* **126 B2** 27 30S 68 0W
Family L., *Canada* **105 C9** 51 54N 95 27W
Famoso, *U.S.A.* **117 K7** 35 37N 119 12W
Fan Xian, *China* **56 G8** 35 55N 115 38E
Fana, *Mali* **82 C3** 13 0N 6 56W
Fanad Hd., *Ireland* **15 A4** 55 17N 7 38W
Fanárion, *Greece* **38 B3** 39 24N 21 47E
Fandriana, *Madag.* **89 C8** 20 14S 47 21E
Fang, *Thailand* **58 H2** 19 55N 99 13E
Fang Xian, *China* **59 A8** 32 3N 110 40E
Fangaga, *Sudan* **80 D4** 17 40N 37 50E
Fangak, *Sudan* **81 F3** 9 4N 30 53E
Fangchang, *China* **59 B12** 31 5N 118 4E
Fangcheng, *China* **56 H7** 33 18N 112 59E
Fangchenggang, *China* **58 G7** 21 42N 108 21E
Fangliao, *Taiwan* **59 F13** 22 22N 120 38E
Fangshan, *China* **56 E6** 38 3N 111 25E
Fangzi, *China* **57 F10** 36 33N 119 10E
Fani i Madh →, *Albania* **40 E4** 41 56N 20 16E
Fanjakana, *Madag.* **89 C8** 21 10S 46 53E
Fanjiatun, *China* **57 C13** 43 40N 125 15E
Fannich, L., *U.K.* **14 D4** 57 38N 4 59W
Fannūj, *Iran* **71 E8** 26 35N 59 38E
Fanø, *Denmark* **11 J2** 55 25N 8 25E
Fano, *Italy* **29 E10** 43 50N 13 1E
Fanshi, *China* **56 E7** 39 12N 113 20E
Fao = Al Fāw, *Iraq* **71 D6** 30 0N 48 30E
Faqirwali, *Pakistan* **68 E5** 29 27N 73 0E
Fâqûs, *Egypt* **80 H7** 30 44N 31 47E
Fara in Sabina, *Italy* **29 F9** 42 12N 12 43E
Faradje, *Dem. Rep. of the Congo* **86 B2** 3 50N 29 45E
Farafangana, *Madag.* **89 C8** 22 49S 47 50E
Farâfra, El Wâhât el-, *Egypt* **80 B2** 27 15N 28 20E
Farāh, *Afghan.* **66 C3** 32 20N 62 7E
Farāh □, *Afghan.* **66 C3** 32 25N 62 10E
Farahalana, *Madag.* **89 A9** 14 26S 50 10E
Faraid, Gebel, *Egypt* **80 C4** 23 33N 35 19E
Farako, *Ivory C.* **82 D4** 10 45N 6 50W
Faramana, *Burkina Faso* **82 C4** 11 56N 4 45W
Faranah, *Guinea* **82 C2** 10 3N 10 45W
Farasān, Jazā'ir, *Si. Arabia* **74 D3** 16 45N 41 55E
Farasan Is. = Farasān, Jazā'ir, *Si. Arabia* **74 D3** 16 45N 41 55E
Faratsiho, *Madag.* **89 B8** 19 24S 46 57E
Fardes →, *Spain* **35 H7** 37 35N 3 0W
Fareham, *U.K.* **13 G6** 50 51N 1 11W
Farewell, C., *N.Z.* **91 J4** 40 29S 172 43E
Farewell C. = Nunap Isua, *Greenland* **4 D5** 59 48N 43 55W
Färgelanda, *Sweden* **11 F5** 58 34N 12 0E
Farghona, *Uzbekistan* **50 E8** 40 23N 71 19E
Fargo, *U.S.A.* **112 B6** 46 53N 96 48W
Fār'iah, W. al →, *West Bank* **75 C4** 32 12N 35 27E
Faribault, *U.S.A.* **112 C8** 44 18N 93 16W
Faridabad, *India* **68 E6** 28 26N 77 19E
Faridkot, *India* **68 D6** 30 44N 74 45E
Faridpur, *Bangla.* **69 H13** 23 15N 89 55E
Faridpur, *India* **69 E8** 28 13N 79 33E
Färila, *Sweden* **10 C9** 61 48N 15 50E
Farim, *Guinea-Biss.* **82 C1** 12 27N 15 9W
Farīmān, *Iran* **71 C8** 35 40N 59 49E
Farina, *Australia* **95 E2** 30 3S 138 15E
Fariones, Pta., *Canary Is.* **37 E6** 29 13N 13 28W
Fâriskûr, *Egypt* **80 H7** 31 20N 31 43E
Färjestaden, *Sweden* **11 H10** 56 39N 16 27E
Farkadhón, *Greece* **38 B4** 39 36N 22 4E
Farmakonisi, *Greece* **39 D9** 37 17N 27 5E
Farmerville, *U.S.A.* **113 J8** 32 47N 92 24W
Farmingdale, *U.S.A.* **111 F10** 40 12N 74 10W
Farmington, *Canada* **104 B4** 55 54N 120 30W
Farmington, *Calif., U.S.A.* **116 H6** 37 55N 120 59W
Farmington, *Maine, U.S.A.* **109 C10** 44 40N 70 9W
Farmington, *Mo., U.S.A.* **113 G9** 37 47N 90 25W
Farmington, *N.H., U.S.A.* **111 C13** 43 24N 71 4W
Farmington, *N. Mex., U.S.A.* **115 H9** 36 44N 108 12W
Farmington, *Utah, U.S.A.* **114 F8** 41 0N 111 12W
Farmington →, *U.S.A.* **111 E12** 41 51N 72 38W
Farmville, *U.S.A.* **108 G6** 37 18N 78 24W
Färnäs, *Sweden* **10 D8** 61 0N 14 39E
Farne Is., *U.K.* **12 B6** 55 38N 1 37W
Farnham, *Canada* **111 A12** 45 17N 72 59W
Farnham, Mt., *Canada* **104 C5** 50 29N 116 30W
Faro, *Brazil* **125 D7** 2 10S 56 39W
Faro, *Canada* **100 B6** 62 11N 133 22W
Faro, *Portugal* **35 H3** 37 2N 7 55W
Fårö, *Sweden* **9 H18** 57 55N 19 5E
Faro □, *Portugal* **35 H2** 37 12N 8 10W
Fårösund, *Sweden* **11 G13** 57 52N 19 2E
Farquhar, C., *Australia* **93 D1** 23 50S 113 36E
Farrars Cr. →, *Australia* **94 D3** 25 35S 140 43E
Farrāshband, *Iran* **71 D7** 28 57N 52 5E
Farrell, *U.S.A.* **110 E4** 41 13N 80 30W
Farrokhī, *Iran* **71 C8** 33 50N 59 31E
Farruch, C. = Ferrutx, C., *Spain* **37 B10** 39 47N 3 21E
Farrukhabad-cum-Fatehgarh, *India* **66 F11** 27 30N 79 32E
Fārs □, *Iran* **71 D7** 29 30N 55 0E
Fársala, *Greece* **38 B4** 39 17N 22 23E
Farsø, *Denmark* **11 H3** 56 46N 9 19E
Farson, *U.S.A.* **114 E9** 42 6N 109 27W
Farsund, *Norway* **9 G12** 58 5N 6 55E
Fartak, Râs, *Si. Arabia* **70 D2** 28 5N 34 34E
Fartak, Ra's, *Yemen* **74 D5** 15 38N 52 15E
Fărtănești, *Romania* **43 E12** 45 49N 27 59E
Fartura, Serra da, *Brazil* **127 B5** 26 21S 52 52W
Faru, *Nigeria* **83 C6** 12 48N 6 12E
Fārūj, *Iran* **71 B8** 37 14N 58 14E
Fårup, *Denmark* **11 H3** 56 33N 9 51E
Farvel, Kap = Nunap Isua, *Greenland* **4 D5** 59 48N 43 55W
Farwell, *U.S.A.* **113 H3** 34 23N 103 2W
Fasā, *Iran* **71 D7** 29 0N 53 39E
Fasano, *Italy* **31 B10** 40 50N 17 22E
Fashoda, *Sudan* **81 F3** 9 50N 32 2E
Fassa, *Mali* **82 C3** 13 26N 8 15E
Fastiv, *Ukraine* **47 G5** 50 7N 29 57E
Fastov = Fastiv, *Ukraine* **47 G5** 50 7N 29 57E
Fatagar, Tanjung, *Indonesia* **63 E8** 2 46S 131 57E
Fatehabad, *Haryana, India* **68 E6** 29 31N 75 27E
Fatehabad, *Ut. P., India* **68 F8** 27 1N 78 19E
Fatehgarh, *India* **69 F8** 27 25N 79 35E
Fatehpur, *Bihar, India* **69 G11** 24 38N 85 14E
Fatehpur, *Raj., India* **68 F6** 28 0N 74 40E
Fatehpur, *Ut. P., India* **69 G9** 25 56N 81 13E
Fatehpur, *Ut. P., India* **69 F9** 27 10N 81 13E
Fatehpur Sikri, *India* **68 F6** 27 6N 77 40E
Fatesh, *Russia* **47 F8** 52 8N 35 57E
Fathai, *Sudan* **81 F3** 8 5N 31 48E
Fatick, *Senegal* **82 C1** 14 19N 16 27W
Fatima, *Canada* **103 C7** 47 24N 61 53W
Fátima, *Portugal* **35 F2** 39 37N 8 39W
Fatoya, *Guinea* **82 C3** 11 37N 9 10W
Fatsa, *Turkey* **72 B7** 41 2N 37 31E
Faucille, Col de la, *France* **19 F13** 46 22N 6 2E
Faulkton, *U.S.A.* **112 C5** 45 2N 99 8W
Faulquemont, *France* **19 C13** 49 3N 6 36E
Faure I., *Australia* **93 E1** 25 52S 113 50E
Făurei, *Romania* **43 E12** 45 6N 27 19E
Fauresmith, *S. Africa* **88 D4** 29 44S 25 17E
Fauske, *Norway* **8 C16** 67 17N 15 25E
Favara, *Italy* **30 E6** 37 19N 13 39E
Favàritx, C. de, *Spain* **37 B11** 40 0N 4 15E
Faverges, *France* **21 C10** 45 45N 6 17E
Favignana, *Italy* **30 E5** 37 56N 12 20E
Favignana, I., *Italy* **30 E5** 37 56N 12 19E
Fawcett, Pt., *Australia* **92 B5** 11 46S 130 2E
Fawn →, *Canada* **102 A2** 55 20N 87 35W
Fawnskin, *U.S.A.* **117 L10** 34 16N 116 56W
Faxaflói, *Iceland* **8 D2** 64 29N 23 0W
Faxälven →, *Sweden* **10 A10** 63 13N 17 13E
Faya-Largeau, *Chad* **79 E9** 17 58N 19 6E
Fayd, *Si. Arabia* **70 E4** 27 1N 42 52E
Fayence, *France* **21 E10** 43 38N 6 42E
Fayette, *Ala., U.S.A.* **109 J2** 33 41N 87 50W
Fayette, *Mo., U.S.A.* **112 F8** 39 9N 92 41W
Fayetteville, *Ark., U.S.A.* **113 G7** 36 4N 94 10W
Fayetteville, *N.C., U.S.A.* **109 H6** 35 3N 78 53W
Fayetteville, *Tenn., U.S.A.* **109 H2** 35 9N 86 34W
Fayied, *Egypt* **80 H8** 30 18N 32 16E
Fayón, *Spain* **32 D5** 41 15N 0 20E
Fazilka, *India* **68 D6** 30 27N 74 2E
Fazilpur, *Pakistan* **68 E4** 29 18N 70 29E
Fdérik, *Mauritania* **78 D3** 22 40N 12 45W
Feale →, *Ireland* **15 D2** 52 27N 9 37W
Fear, C., *U.S.A.* **109 J7** 33 50N 77 58W
Feather →, *U.S.A.* **114 G3** 38 47N 121 36W
Feather Falls, *U.S.A.* **116 F5** 39 36N 121 16W
Featherston, *N.Z.* **91 J5** 41 6S 175 20E
Featherstone, *Zimbabwe* **87 F3** 18 42S 30 55E
Fécamp, *France* **18 C7** 49 45N 0 22E
Fedala = Mohammedia, *Morocco* **78 B4** 33 44N 7 21W
Federación, *Argentina* **126 C4** 31 0S 57 55W
Féderal, *Argentina* **128 C5** 30 57S 58 48W
Federal Capital Terr. □, *Nigeria* **83 D6** 9 0N 7 10E
Federal Way, *U.S.A.* **116 C4** 47 18N 122 19W
Fedeshkūh, *Iran* **71 D7** 28 49N 53 50E
Fehérgyarmat, *Hungary* **42 C7** 47 58N 22 30E
Fehmarn, *Germany* **24 A7** 54 27N 11 7E
Fehmarn Bælt, *Europe* **11 K5** 54 35N 11 20E
Fehmarn Belt = Fehmarn Bælt, *Europe* **11 K5** 54 35N 11 20E
Fei Xian, *China* **57 G9** 35 18N 117 59E
Feijó, *Brazil* **124 E4** 8 9S 70 21W
Feilding, *N.Z.* **91 J5** 40 13S 175 35E
Feira de Santana, *Brazil* **125 F11** 12 15S 38 57W
Feixi, *China* **59 B11** 31 43N 117 59E
Feixiang, *China* **56 F8** 36 30N 114 45E
Fejér □, *Hungary* **42 C3** 47 9N 18 30E
Fejø, *Denmark* **11 K5** 54 55N 11 30E
Feke, *Turkey* **72 D6** 37 48N 35 56E
Fekete →, *Hungary* **42 E3** 45 47N 18 15E
Felanitx, *Spain* **37 B10** 39 28N 3 9E
Feldbach, *Austria* **26 E8** 46 57N 15 52E
Feldberg, *Baden-W., Germany* **25 H3** 47 52N 8 0E
Feldberg, *Mecklenburg-Vorpommern, Germany* **24 B9** 53 20N 13 25E
Feldkirch, *Austria* **26 D2** 47 15N 9 37E
Feldkirchen, *Austria* **26 E7** 46 44N 14 6E
Felipe Carrillo Puerto, *Mexico* **119 D7** 19 38N 88 3W
Felixburg, *Zimbabwe* **89 B5** 19 29S 30 51E
Felixstowe, *U.K.* **13 F9** 51 58N 1 23E
Felletin, *France* **20 C6** 45 53N 2 11E
Fellingsbro, *Sweden* **10 E9** 59 26N 15 37E
Felton, *U.S.A.* **116 H4** 37 3N 122 4W
Feltre, *Italy* **29 B8** 46 1N 11 54E
Femer Bælt = Fehmarn Bælt, *Europe* **11 K5** 54 35N 11 20E
Femø, *Denmark* **11 K5** 54 58N 11 35E
Femunden, *Norway* **9 E14** 62 10N 11 53E
Fen He →, *China* **56 G6** 35 36N 110 42E
Fene, *Spain* **34 B2** 43 27N 8 9W
Fenelon Falls, *Canada* **110 B6** 44 32N 78 45W
Fener Burnu, *Turkey* **39 E9** 36 58N 27 18E
Feneroa, *Ethiopia* **81 E4** 13 5N 39 3E
Feng Xian, *Jiangsu, China* **56 G9** 34 43N 116 35E
Feng Xian, *Shaanxi, China* **56 H4** 33 54N 106 40E
Fengári, *Greece* **41 F9** 40 25N 25 32E
Fengcheng, *Jiangxi, China* **59 C10** 28 12N 115 48E
Fengcheng, *Liaoning, China* **57 D13** 40 28N 124 5E
Fengfeng, *China* **56 F8** 36 28N 114 8E
Fenggang, *China* **58 D6** 27 57N 107 47E
Fenghua, *China* **59 C13** 29 40N 121 25E
Fenghuang, *China* **58 D7** 27 57N 109 29E
Fengkai, *China* **59 F8** 23 24N 111 30E
Fengkang, *Taiwan* **59 F13** 22 12N 120 41E
Fengle, *China* **59 B9** 31 29N 112 29E
Fenglin, *Taiwan* **59 F13** 23 45N 121 26E
Fengning, *China* **56 D9** 41 10N 116 33E
Fengqing, *China* **58 E2** 24 38N 99 55E
Fengqiu, *China* **56 G8** 35 2N 114 25E
Fengrun, *China* **57 E10** 39 48N 118 8E
Fengshan, *Guangxi Zhuangzu, China* **58 E7** 24 39N 109 15E
Fengshan, *Guangxi Zhuangzu, China* **58 E6** 24 31N 107 3E
Fengshan, *Taiwan* **59 F13** 22 38N 120 21E
Fengshun, *China* **59 F11** 23 46N 116 10E
Fengtai, *Anhui, China* **59 A11** 32 50N 116 40E
Fengtai, *Beijing, China* **56 E9** 39 50N 116 18E
Fengxian, *China* **59 B13** 30 55N 121 26E
Fengxiang, *China* **56 G4** 34 29N 107 25E
Fengxin, *China* **59 C10** 28 41N 115 18E
Fengyang, *China* **57 H9** 32 51N 117 29E
Fengyi, *China* **58 E3** 25 37N 100 20E
Fengyüan, *Taiwan* **59 E13** 24 15N 120 35E
Fengzhen, *China* **56 D7** 40 25N 113 2E
Feno, C. de, *France* **21 G12** 41 58N 8 33E
Fenoarivo, *Fianarantsoa, Madag.* **89 C8** 21 43S 46 24E
Fenoarivo, *Fianarantsoa, Madag.* **89 C8** 20 52S 46 53E
Fenoarivo Afovoany, *Madag.* **89 B8** 18 26S 46 34E
Fenoarivo Atsinanana, *Madag.* **89 B8** 17 22S 49 25E
Fens, The, *U.K.* **12 E7** 52 38N 0 2W
Fensmark, *Denmark* **11 J5** 55 17N 11 48E
Fenton, *U.S.A.* **108 D4** 42 48N 83 42W
Fenxi, *China* **56 F6** 36 40N 111 31E
Fenyang, *China* **56 F6** 37 18N 111 48E
Fenyi, *China* **59 D10** 27 45N 114 47E
Feodosiya, *Ukraine* **47 K8** 45 2N 35 16E
Ferdows, *Iran* **71 C8** 33 58N 58 2E
Fère-Champenoise, *France* **19 D10** 48 45N 3 59E
Fère-en-Tardenois, *France* **19 C10** 49 10N 3 30E
Ferentino, *Italy* **29 G10** 41 42N 13 15E
Ferfer, *Somali Rep.* **74 F4** 5 4N 45 9E
Fergana = Farghona, *Uzbekistan* **50 E8** 40 23N 71 19E
Fergus, *Canada* **110 C4** 43 43N 80 24W
Fergus Falls, *U.S.A.* **112 B6** 46 17N 96 4W
Feričanci, *Croatia* **42 E2** 45 32N 18 0E
Ferkéssédougou, *Ivory C.* **82 D3** 9 35N 5 6W
Ferlach, *Austria* **26 E7** 46 32N 14 18E
Ferland, *Canada* **102 B2** 50 19N 88 27W
Ferlo, Vallée du, *Senegal* **82 B2** 15 15N 14 15W
Fermanagh □, *U.K.* **15 B4** 54 21N 7 40W
Fermo, *Italy* **29 E10** 43 9N 13 43E
Fermont, *Canada* **103 B6** 52 47N 67 5W
Fermoselle, *Spain* **34 D4** 41 19N 6 27W
Fermoy, *Ireland* **15 D3** 52 9N 8 16W
Fernán Nuñéz, *Spain* **35 H6** 37 40N 4 44W
Fernández, *Argentina* **126 B3** 27 55S 63 50W
Fernandina Beach, *U.S.A.* **109 K5** 30 40N 81 27W
Fernando de Noronha, *Brazil* **125 D12** 4 0S 33 10W
Fernando Póo = Bioko, *Eq. Guin.* **83 E6** 3 30N 8 40E
Ferndale, *U.S.A.* **116 B4** 48 51N 122 36W
Fernie, *Canada* **104 D5** 49 30N 115 5W
Fernlees, *Australia* **94 C4** 23 51S 148 7E
Fernley, *U.S.A.* **114 G4** 39 36N 119 15W
Ferozepore = Firozpur, *India* **68 D6** 30 55N 74 40E
Férrai, *Greece* **41 F10** 40 53N 26 10E
Ferrandina, *Italy* **31 B9** 40 29N 16 27E
Ferrara, *Italy* **29 D8** 44 50N 11 35E
Ferrato, C., *Italy* **30 C2** 39 18N 9 38E
Ferreira do Alentejo, *Portugal* **35 G2** 38 4N 8 6W
Ferreñafe, *Peru* **124 E3** 6 42S 79 50W
Ferrerías, *Spain* **37 B11** 39 59N 4 1E
Ferret, C., *France* **20 D2** 44 38N 1 15W
Ferrette, *France* **19 E14** 47 30N 7 20E
Ferriday, *U.S.A.* **113 K9** 31 38N 91 33W
Ferriere, *Italy* **28 D6** 44 40N 9 30E
Ferrières, *France* **19 D9** 48 5N 2 48E
Ferro, Capo, *Italy* **30 A2** 41 9N 9 31E
Ferrol, *Spain* **34 B2** 43 29N 8 15W
Ferron, *U.S.A.* **115 G8** 39 5N 111 8W
Ferrutx, C., *Spain* **37 B10** 39 47N 3 21E
Ferryland, *Canada* **103 C9** 47 2N 52 53W
Fertile, *U.S.A.* **112 B6** 47 32N 96 17W
Fertőszentmiklós, *Hungary* **42 C1** 47 35N 16 53E
Fès, *Morocco* **78 B5** 34 0N 5 0W
Fessenden, *U.S.A.* **112 B5** 47 39N 99 38W
Festus, *U.S.A.* **112 F9** 38 13N 90 24W
Feté Bowé, *Senegal* **82 C2** 14 56N 13 30W
Fetești, *Romania* **43 F12** 44 22N 27 51E
Fethiye, *Turkey* **39 E11** 36 36N 29 6E
Fethiye Körfezi, *Turkey* **39 E10** 36 40N 28 50E
Fetlar, *U.K.* **14 A8** 60 36N 0 52W
Feuilles →, *Canada* **101 C12** 58 47N 70 4W
Feurs, *France* **21 C8** 45 45N 4 13E
Fez = Fès, *Morocco* **78 B5** 34 0N 5 0W
Fezzan, *Libya* **79 C8** 27 0N 13 0E
Fiambalá, *Argentina* **126 B2** 27 45S 67 37W
Fianarantsoa, *Madag.* **89 C8** 21 26S 47 5E
Fianarantsoa □, *Madag.* **89 B8** 19 30S 47 0E
Fiche, *Ethiopia* **81 F4** 9 50N 38 46E
Fichtelgebirge, *Germany* **25 E7** 50 2N 11 55E
Ficksburg, *S. Africa* **89 D4** 28 51S 27 53E
Fidenza, *Italy* **28 D7** 44 52N 10 3E
Fiditi, *Nigeria* **83 D5** 7 45N 3 53E
Field →, *Australia* **94 C2** 23 48S 138 0E
Field I., *Australia* **92 B5** 12 5S 132 23E
Fieni, *Romania* **43 E10** 45 8N 25 25E
Fier, *Albania* **40 F3** 40 43N 19 33E
Fieri = Fier, *Albania* **40 F3** 40 43N 19 33E
Fierzë, *Albania* **40 D4** 42 15N 20 1E
Fife □, *U.K.* **14 E5** 56 16N 3 1W
Fife Ness, *U.K.* **14 E6** 56 17N 2 35W
Fifth Cataract, *Sudan* **80 D3** 18 22N 33 50E
Figari, *France* **21 G13** 41 29N 9 7E
Figeac, *France* **20 D6** 44 37N 2 2E
Figeholm, *Sweden* **11 G10** 57 22N 16 33E
Figline Valdarno, *Italy* **29 E8** 43 37N 11 28E
Figtree, *Zimbabwe* **87 G2** 20 22S 28 20E
Figueira Castelo Rodrigo, *Portugal* **34 E4** 40 57N 6 58W
Figueira da Foz, *Portugal* **34 E2** 40 7N 8 54W
Figueiró dos Vinhos, *Portugal* **34 F2** 39 55N 8 16W
Figueres, *Spain* **32 C7** 42 18N 2 58E
Figuig, *Morocco* **78 B5** 32 5N 1 11W
Fihaonana, *Madag.* **89 B8** 18 36S 47 12E
Fiherenana, *Madag.* **89 B8** 18 29S 48 24E
Fiherenana →, *Madag.* **89 C7** 23 19S 43 37E
Fiji ■, *Pac. Oc.* **91 C8** 17 20S 179 0E
Fik, *Ethiopia* **81 F5** 8 10N 42 19E
Fika, *Nigeria* **83 C7** 11 15N 11 13E
Filabres, Sierra de los, *Spain* **35 H8** 37 13N 2 20W
Filabusi, *Zimbabwe* **89 C4** 20 34S 29 20E
Filadélfia, *Italy* **31 D9** 38 47N 16 17E
Fil'akovo, *Slovak Rep.* **27 C12** 48 17N 19 50E
Filey, *U.K.* **12 C7** 54 12N 0 18W
Filey B., *U.K.* **12 C7** 54 12N 0 15W
Filfla, *Malta* **36 D1** 35 47N 14 24E
Filiași, *Romania* **43 F8** 44 32N 23 31E
Filiátes, *Greece* **38 B2** 39 38N 20 16E
Filiatrá, *Greece* **38 D3** 37 9N 21 35E
Filicudi, *Italy* **31 D7** 38 35N 14 33E
Filingué, *Niger* **83 C5** 14 21N 3 22E
Filiourí →, *Greece* **41 E9** 41 15N 25 40E
Filipstad, *Sweden* **10 E8** 59 43N 14 9E
Filisur, *Switz.* **25 J5** 46 41N 9 40E
Fillmore, *Calif., U.S.A.* **117 L8** 34 24N 118 55W
Fillmore, *Utah, U.S.A.* **115 G7** 38 58N 112 20W
Filótion, *Greece* **39 D7** 37 3N 25 30E
Filottrano, *Italy* **29 E10** 43 26N 13 21E
Filtu, *Ethiopia* **81 F5** 5 8N 40 35E
Finale Emília, *Italy* **29 D8** 44 50N 11 17E
Finale Lígure, *Italy* **28 D5** 44 10N 8 20E
Fiñana, *Spain* **35 H8** 37 10N 2 50W
Finch, *Canada* **111 A9** 45 11N 75 7W
Findhorn →, *U.K.* **14 D5** 57 38N 3 38W
Findlay, *U.S.A.* **108 E4** 41 2N 83 39W
Finger L., *Canada* **102 B1** 53 33N 93 30W
Finger Lakes, *U.S.A.* **111 D8** 42 40N 76 30W
Fingoè, *Mozam.* **87 E3** 14 55S 31 50E
Finike, *Turkey* **39 E12** 36 21N 30 10E
Finike Körfezi, *Turkey* **39 E12** 36 17N 30 16E
Finiq, *Albania* **40 G4** 39 54N 20 3E
Finistère □, *France* **18 D3** 48 20N 4 0W
Finisterre = Fisterra, *Spain* **34 C1** 42 54N 9 16W
Finisterre, C. = Fisterra, C., *Spain* **34 C1** 42 50N 9 19W
Finke, *Australia* **94 D1** 25 34S 134 35E
Finland ■, *Europe* **8 E22** 63 0N 27 0E
Finland, G. of, *Europe* **9 G21** 60 0N 26 0E
Finlay →, *Canada* **104 B3** 57 0N 125 10W
Finley, *Australia* **95 F4** 35 38S 145 35E
Finley, *U.S.A.* **112 B6** 47 31N 97 50W
Finn →, *Ireland* **15 B4** 54 51N 7 28W
Finnerödja, *Sweden* **11 F8** 58 57N 14 24E
Finnigan, Mt., *Australia* **94 B4** 15 49S 145 17E
Finniss, C., *Australia* **95 E1** 33 8S 134 51E
Finnmark, *Norway* **8 B20** 69 37N 23 57E
Finnsnes, *Norway* **8 B18** 69 14N 18 0E
Finspång, *Sweden* **11 F9** 58 43N 15 47E
Finsteraarhorn, *Switz.* **25 J4** 46 31N 8 10E
Finsterwalde, *Germany* **24 D9** 51 37N 13 42E
Fiora →, *Italy* **29 F8** 42 20N 11 34E
Fiorenzuola d'Arda, *Italy* **28 D6** 44 56N 9 55E
Fīq, *Syria* **75 C4** 32 46N 35 41E
Firat = Furāt, Nahr al →, *Asia* **70 D5** 31 0N 47 25E
Firebag →, *Canada* **105 B6** 57 45N 111 21W
Firebaugh, *U.S.A.* **116 J6** 36 52N 120 27W
Firedrake L., *Canada* **105 A8** 61 25N 104 30W
Firenze, *Italy* **29 E8** 43 46N 11 15E
Firenzuola, *Italy* **29 D8** 44 7N 11 23E
Firk →, *Iraq* **70 D5** 30 59N 44 34E
Firmi, *France* **20 D6** 44 33N 2 19E
Firminy, *France* **21 C8** 45 23N 4 18E
Firozabad, *India* **69 F8** 27 10N 78 25E
Firozpur, *India* **68 D6** 30 55N 74 40E
Firozpur-Jhirka, *India* **68 F7** 27 48N 76 57E
Fīrūzābād, *Iran* **71 D7** 28 52N 52 35E
Fīrūzkūh, *Iran* **71 C7** 35 50N 52 50E
Firvale, *Canada* **104 C3** 52 27N 126 13W
Fish →, *Namibia* **88 D2** 28 7S 17 10E
Fish →, *S. Africa* **88 E3** 31 30S 20 16E
Fish River Canyon, *Namibia* **88 D2** 27 40S 17 35E
Fisher, *Australia* **93 F5** 30 30S 131 0E
Fisher B., *Canada* **105 C9** 51 35N 97 13W
Fishers I., *U.S.A.* **111 E13** 41 15N 72 0W
Fishguard, *U.K.* **13 E3** 52 0N 4 58W
Fishing L., *Canada* **105 C9** 52 10N 95 24W
Fishkill, *U.S.A.* **111 E11** 41 32N 73 53W
Fismes, *France* **19 C10** 49 20N 3 40E
Fisterra, *Spain* **34 C1** 42 54N 9 16W
Fisterra, C., *Spain* **34 C1** 42 50N 9 19W
Fitchburg, *U.S.A.* **111 D13** 42 35N 71 48W
Fitz Roy, *Argentina* **128 F3** 47 0S 67 0W
Fitzgerald, *Canada* **104 B6** 59 51N 111 36W
Fitzgerald, *U.S.A.* **109 K4** 31 43N 83 15W
Fitzmaurice →, *Australia* **92 B5** 14 45S 130 5E
Fitzroy →, *Queens., Australia* **94 C5** 23 32S 150 52E
Fitzroy →, *W. Austral., Australia* **92 C3** 17 31S 123 35E
Fitzroy, Mte., *Argentina* **128 F2** 49 17S 73 5W
Fitzroy Crossing, *Australia* **92 C4** 18 9S 125 38E
Fitzwilliam I., *Canada* **110 A3** 45 30N 81 45W
Fiuggi, *Italy* **29 G10** 41 48N 13 13E
Fiume = Rijeka, *Croatia* **29 C11** 45 20N 14 21E
Five Points, *U.S.A.* **116 J6** 36 26N 120 6W
Fivizzano, *Italy* **28 D7** 44 14N 10 8E
Fizi, *Dem. Rep. of the Congo* **86 C2** 4 17S 28 55E
Fjällbacka, *Sweden* **11 F5** 58 36N 11 17E
Fjärdhundra, *Sweden* **10 E10** 59 47N 16 56E
Fjellerup, *Denmark* **11 H4** 56 29N 10 34E
Fjerritslev, *Denmark* **11 G3** 57 5N 9 15E
Fjugesta, *Sweden* **10 E8** 59 11N 14 52E
Flagstaff, *U.S.A.* **115 J8** 35 12N 111 39W
Flagstaff L., *U.S.A.* **109 C10** 45 12N 70 18W
Flaherty I., *Canada* **102 A4** 56 15N 79 15W
Flåm, *Norway* **9 F12** 60 50N 7 7E
Flambeau →, *U.S.A.* **112 C9** 45 18N 91 14W
Flamborough Hd., *U.K.* **12 C7** 54 7N 0 5W
Fläming, *Germany* **24 C8** 52 6N 12 23E
Flaming Gorge Reservoir, *U.S.A.* **114 F9** 41 10N 109 25W
Flamingo, Teluk, *Indonesia* **63 F9** 5 30S 138 0E
Flanders = Flandre, *Europe* **19 B9** 50 50N 2 30E
Flandre, *Europe* **19 B9** 50 50N 2 30E
Flandre Occidentale = West-Vlaanderen □, *Belgium* **17 D2** 51 0N 3 0E
Flandre Orientale = Oost-Vlaanderen □, *Belgium* **17 C3** 51 5N 3 50E
Flandreau, *U.S.A.* **112 C6** 44 3N 96 36W
Flanigan, *U.S.A.* **116 E7** 40 10N 119 53W
Flannan Is., *U.K.* **14 C1** 58 9N 7 52W
Flåsjön, *Sweden* **8 D16** 64 5N 15 40E
Flat →, *Canada* **104 A3** 61 33N 125 18W
Flathead L., *U.S.A.* **114 C7** 47 51N 114 8W
Flattery, C., *Australia* **94 A4** 14 58S 145 21E
Flattery, C., *U.S.A.* **116 B2** 48 23N 124 29W
Flatwoods, *U.S.A.* **108 F4** 38 31N 82 43W
Fleetwood, *U.K.* **12 D4** 53 55N 3 1W
Fleetwood, *U.S.A.* **111 F9** 40 27N 75 49W
Flekkefjord, *Norway* **9 G12** 58 18N 6 39E
Flemington, *U.S.A.* **110 E7** 41 7N 77 28W
Flen, *Sweden* **10 E10** 59 4N 16 35E
Flensburg, *Germany* **24 A5** 54 47N 9 27E
Flers, *France* **18 D6** 48 47N 0 33W
Flesherton, *Canada* **110 B4** 44 16N 80 33W
Flesko, Tanjung, *Indonesia* **63 D6** 0 29N 124 30E
Fleurance, *France* **20 E4** 43 52N 0 40E
Fleurier, *Switz.* **25 J2** 46 54N 6 35E
Fleurieu Pen., *Australia* **95 F2** 35 40S 138 5E
Flevoland □, *Neths.* **17 B5** 52 30N 5 30E
Flin Flon, *Canada* **105 C8** 54 46N 101 53W
Flinders →, *Australia* **94 B3** 17 36S 140 36E
Flinders B., *Australia* **93 F2** 34 19S 115 19E
Flinders Group, *Australia* **94 A3** 14 11S 144 15E
Flinders I., *S. Austral., Australia* **95 E1** 33 44S 134 41E
Flinders I., *Tas., Australia* **94 G4** 40 0S 148 0E

Flinders Ranges, Australia **95 E2** 31 30 S 138 30 E
Flinders Reefs, Australia **94 B4** 17 37 S 148 31 E
Flint, U.K. **12 D4** 53 15N 3 8W
Flint, U.S.A. **108 D4** 43 1N 83 41W
Flint →, U.S.A. **109 K3** 30 57N 84 34W
Flint I., Kiribati **97 J12** 11 26 S 151 48W
Flintshire □, U.K. **12 D4** 53 17N 3 17W
Fliseryd, Sweden **11 G10** 57 6N 16 15 E
Flix, Spain **32 D5** 41 14N 0 32 E
Flixecourt, France **19 B9** 50 1N 2 5 E
Floby, Sweden **11 F7** 58 8N 13 20 E
Floda, Sweden **11 G6** 57 49N 12 22 E
Flodden, U.K. **12 B5** 55 37N 2 8W
Flogny-la-Chapelle, France **19 E10** 47 57N 3 57 E
Floodwood, U.S.A. **112 B8** 46 55N 92 55W
Flora, U.S.A. **108 F1** 38 40N 88 29W
Florac, France **20 D7** 44 20N 3 37 E
Florala, U.S.A. **109 K2** 31 0N 86 20W
Florence = Firenze, Italy **29 E8** 43 46N 11 15 E
Florence, Ala., U.S.A. **109 H2** 34 48N 87 41W
Florence, Ariz., U.S.A. **115 K8** 33 2N 111 23W
Florence, Colo., U.S.A. **112 F2** 38 23N 105 8W
Florence, Oreg., U.S.A. **114 E1** 43 58N 124 7W
Florence, S.C., U.S.A. **109 H6** 34 12N 79 46W
Florence, L., Australia **95 D2** 28 53 S 138 9 E
Florencia, Colombia **124 C3** 1 36N 75 36W
Florennes, Belgium **17 D4** 50 15N 4 35 E
Florensac, France **20 E7** 43 23N 3 28 E
Florenville, Belgium **17 E5** 49 40N 5 19 E
Flores, Guatemala **120 C2** 16 59N 89 50W
Flores, Indonesia **63 F6** 8 35 S 121 0 E
Flores I., Canada **104 D3** 49 20N 126 10W
Flores Sea, Indonesia **63 F6** 6 30 S 120 0 E
Floreşti, Moldova **43 C13** 47 53N 28 17 E
Floresville, U.S.A. **113 L5** 29 8N 98 10W
Floriano, Brazil **125 E10** 6 50 S 43 0W
Florianópolis, Brazil **127 B6** 27 30 S 48 30W
Florida, Cuba **120 B4** 21 32N 78 14W
Florida, Uruguay **127 C4** 34 7 S 56 10W
Florida □, U.S.A. **109 L5** 28 0N 82 0W
Florida, Straits of, U.S.A. **120 B4** 25 0N 80 0W
Florida B., U.S.A. **120 B3** 25 0N 80 45W
Florida Keys, U.S.A. **109 N5** 24 40N 81 0W
Florídia, Italy **31 E8** 37 5N 15 9 E
Flórina, Greece **40 F5** 40 48N 21 26 E
Flórina □, Greece **40 F5** 40 45N 21 20 E
Florø, Norway **9 F11** 61 35N 5 1 E
Flower Station, Canada **111 A8** 45 10N 76 41W
Flowerpot I., Canada **110 A3** 45 18N 81 38W
Floydada, U.S.A. **113 J4** 33 59N 101 20W
Fluk, Indonesia **63 E7** 1 42 S 127 44 E
Flúmen →, Spain **32 D4** 41 43N 0 9W
Flumendosa →, Italy **30 C2** 39 26N 9 37 E
Fluminimaggiore, Italy **30 C1** 39 26N 8 30 E
Flushing = Vlissingen, Neths. **17 C3** 51 26N 3 34 E
Fluviá →, Spain **32 C8** 42 12N 3 7 E
Flying Fish, C., Antarctica **5 D15** 72 6 S 102 29W
Foam Lake, Canada **105 C8** 51 40N 103 32W
Foča, Bos.-H. **40 C2** 43 31N 18 47 E
Foça, Turkey **39 C8** 38 39N 26 46 E
Focşani, Romania **43 E12** 45 41N 27 15 E
Fodécontéa, Guinea **82 C2** 10 50N 14 22W
Fogang, China **59 F9** 23 52N 113 30 E
Fóggia, Italy **31 A8** 41 27N 15 34 E
Foggo, Nigeria **83 C6** 11 21N 9 57 E
Foglia →, Italy **29 E9** 43 55N 12 54 E
Fogo, Canada **103 C9** 49 43N 54 17W
Fogo I., Canada **103 C9** 49 40N 54 5W
Fohnsdorf, Austria **26 D7** 47 12N 14 40 E
Föhr, Germany **24 A4** 54 43N 8 30 E
Foia, Portugal **35 H2** 37 19N 8 37W
Foix, France **20 E5** 42 58N 1 38 E
Fojnica, Bos.-H. **42 G2** 43 59N 17 51 E
Fokino, Russia **46 F8** 53 30N 34 22 E
Fokís □, Greece **38 C4** 38 30N 22 15 E
Fokku, Nigeria **83 C5** 11 36N 4 32 E
Folda, Nord-Trøndelag, Norway **8 D14** 64 32N 10 30 E
Folda, Nordland, Norway **8 C16** 67 38N 14 50 E
Földeák, Hungary **42 D5** 46 19N 20 30 E
Folégandros, Greece **38 E6** 36 40N 24 55 E
Foley, Botswana **88 C4** 21 34 S 27 21 E
Foley, U.S.A. **109 K2** 30 24N 87 41W
Foleyet, Canada **102 C3** 48 15N 82 25W
Folgefonni, Norway **9 F12** 60 3N 6 23 E
Foligno, Italy **29 F9** 42 57N 12 42 E
Folkestone, U.K. **13 F9** 51 5N 1 12 E
Folkston, U.S.A. **109 K5** 30 50N 82 0W
Follansbee, U.S.A. **110 F4** 40 19N 80 35W
Follónica, Italy **28 F7** 42 55N 10 45 E
Follónica, G. di, Italy **28 F7** 42 54N 10 43 E
Folsom L., U.S.A. **116 G5** 38 42N 121 9W
Folteşti, Romania **43 E13** 45 45N 28 3 E
Fond-du-Lac, Canada **105 B7** 59 19N 107 12W
Fond du Lac, U.S.A. **112 D10** 43 47N 88 27W
Fond-du-Lac →, Canada **105 B7** 59 17N 106 0W
Fonda, U.S.A. **111 D10** 42 57N 74 22W
Fondi, Italy **30 A6** 41 21N 13 25 E
Fonfría, Spain **34 D4** 41 37N 6 9W
Fongafale, Tuvalu **96 H9** 8 31 S 179 13 E
Fonni, Italy **30 B2** 40 7N 9 15 E
Fonsagrada = A Fonsagrada, Spain **34 B3** 43 8N 7 4W
Fonseca, G. de, Cent. Amer. **120 D2** 13 10N 87 40W
Font-Romeu, France **20 F5** 42 31N 2 3 E
Fontaine-Française, France **19 E12** 47 32N 5 21 E
Fontainebleau, France **19 D9** 48 24N 2 40 E
Fontana, U.S.A. **117 L9** 34 6N 117 26W
Fontas →, Canada **104 B4** 58 14N 121 48W
Fonte Boa, Brazil **124 D5** 2 33 S 66 0W
Fontem, Cameroon **83 D6** 5 32N 9 52 E
Fontenay-le-Comte, France **20 B3** 46 28N 0 48W
Fontenelle Reservoir, U.S.A. **114 E8** 42 1N 110 3W
Fontur, Iceland **8 C6** 66 23N 14 32W
Fonyód, Hungary **42 D2** 46 44N 17 33 E
Foochow = Fuzhou, China **59 D12** 26 5N 119 16 E
Foping, China **56 H5** 33 41N 108 0 E
Forbach, France **19 C13** 49 10N 6 52 E
Forbes, Australia **95 E4** 33 22 S 148 0 E
Forbesganj, India **69 F12** 26 17N 87 18 E
Forcados, Nigeria **83 D6** 5 26N 5 26 E
Forcados →, Nigeria **83 D6** 5 25N 5 19 E
Forcalquier, France **21 E9** 43 58N 5 47 E
Forchheim, Germany **25 F7** 49 43N 11 2 E
Ford City, Calif., U.S.A. **117 K7** 35 9N 119 27W
Ford City, Pa., U.S.A. **110 F5** 40 46N 79 32W
Førde, Norway **9 F11** 61 27N 5 53 E
Ford's Bridge, Australia **95 D4** 29 41 S 145 29 E
Fordyce, U.S.A. **113 J8** 33 49N 92 25W
Forécariah, Guinea **82 D2** 9 28N 13 10W
Forel, Mt., Greenland **4 C6** 66 52N 36 55W
Foremost, Canada **104 D6** 49 26N 111 34W
Forest, Canada **110 C3** 43 6N 82 0W
Forest, U.S.A. **113 J10** 32 22N 89 29W
Forest City, Iowa, U.S.A. **112 D8** 43 16N 93 39W
Forest City, N.C., U.S.A. **109 H5** 35 20N 81 52W
Forest City, Pa., U.S.A. **111 E9** 41 39N 75 28W
Forest Grove, U.S.A. **116 E3** 45 31N 123 7W
Forestburg, Canada **104 C6** 52 35N 112 1W
Foresthill, U.S.A. **116 F6** 39 1N 120 49W
Forestier Pen., Australia **94 G4** 43 0 S 148 0 E
Forestville, Canada **103 C6** 48 48N 69 2W
Forestville, Calif., U.S.A. **116 G4** 38 28N 122 54W
Forestville, N.Y., U.S.A. **110 D5** 42 28N 79 10W
Forez, Mts. du, France **20 C7** 45 40N 3 50 E
Forfar, U.K. **14 E6** 56 39N 2 53W
Forks, U.S.A. **116 C2** 47 57N 124 23W
Forksville, U.S.A. **111 E8** 41 29N 76 35W
Forlì, Italy **29 D9** 44 13N 12 3 E
Forman, U.S.A. **112 B6** 46 7N 97 38W
Formazza, Italy **28 B5** 46 22N 8 26 E
Formby Pt., U.K. **12 D4** 53 33N 3 6W
Formentera, Spain **37 C7** 38 43N 1 27 E
Formentor, C. de, Spain **37 B10** 39 58N 3 13 E
Former Yugoslav Republic of Macedonia = Macedonia ■, Europe **40 E5** 41 53N 21 40 E
Fórmia, Italy **30 A6** 41 15N 13 37 E
Formígine, Italy **28 D7** 44 37N 10 51 E
Formosa = Taiwan ■, Asia **59 F13** 23 30N 121 0 E
Formosa, Argentina **126 B4** 26 15 S 58 10W
Formosa, Brazil **125 G9** 15 32 S 47 20W
Formosa □, Argentina **126 B4** 25 0 S 60 0W
Formosa, Serra, Brazil **125 F8** 12 0 S 55 0W
Formosa Bay, Kenya **86 C5** 2 40 S 40 20 E
Formosa Strait = Taiwan Strait, Asia **59 E12** 24 40N 120 0 E
Fornells, Spain **37 A11** 40 3N 4 7 E
Fornos de Algodres, Portugal **34 E3** 40 38N 7 32W
Fornovo di Taro, Italy **28 D7** 44 42N 10 6 E
Føroyar, Atl. Oc. **8 F9** 62 0N 7 0W
Forres, U.K. **14 D5** 57 37N 3 37W
Forrest, Australia **93 F4** 30 51 S 128 6 E
Forrest, Mt., Australia **93 D4** 24 48 S 127 45 E
Forrest City, U.S.A. **113 H9** 35 1N 90 47W
Fors, Sweden **10 D10** 60 14N 16 20 E
Forsayth, Australia **94 B3** 18 33 S 143 34 E
Forshaga, Sweden **10 E7** 59 33N 13 29 E
Förslöv, Sweden **11 H6** 56 21N 12 48 E
Forsmo, Sweden **10 A11** 63 16N 17 11 E
Forssa, Finland **9 F20** 60 49N 23 38 E
Forst, Germany **24 D10** 51 45N 14 37 E
Forsvik, Sweden **11 F8** 58 35N 14 26 E
Forsyth, U.S.A. **114 C10** 46 16N 106 41W
Fort Abbas, Pakistan **68 E5** 29 12N 72 52 E
Fort Albany, Canada **102 B3** 52 15N 81 35W
Fort Ann, U.S.A. **111 C11** 43 25N 73 30W
Fort Assiniboine, Canada **104 C6** 54 20N 114 45W
Fort Augustus, U.K. **14 D4** 57 9N 4 42W
Fort Beaufort, S. Africa **88 E4** 32 46 S 26 40 E
Fort Benton, U.S.A. **114 C8** 47 49N 110 40W
Fort Bragg, U.S.A. **114 G2** 39 26N 123 48W
Fort Bridger, U.S.A. **114 F8** 41 19N 110 23W
Fort Chipewyan, Canada **105 B6** 58 42N 111 8W
Fort Collins, U.S.A. **112 E2** 40 35N 105 5W
Fort-Coulonge, Canada **102 C4** 45 50N 76 45W
Fort Covington, U.S.A. **111 B10** 44 59N 74 29W
Fort Davis, U.S.A. **113 K3** 30 35N 103 54W
Fort-de-France, Martinique **121 D7** 14 36N 61 2W
Fort Defiance, U.S.A. **115 J9** 35 45N 109 5W
Fort Dodge, U.S.A. **112 D7** 42 30N 94 11W
Fort Edward, U.S.A. **111 C11** 43 16N 73 35W
Fort Erie, Canada **110 D6** 42 54N 78 56W
Fort Fairfield, U.S.A. **109 B12** 46 46N 67 50W
Fort Frances, Canada **105 D10** 48 36N 93 24W
Fort Garland, U.S.A. **115 H11** 37 26N 105 26W
Fort George = Chisasibi, Canada **102 B4** 53 50N 79 0W
Fort Good-Hope, Canada **100 B7** 66 14N 128 40W
Fort Hancock, U.S.A. **115 L11** 31 18N 105 51W
Fort Hertz = Putao, Burma **67 F20** 27 28N 97 30 E
Fort Hope, Canada **102 B2** 51 30N 88 0W
Fort Irwin, U.S.A. **117 K10** 35 16N 116 34W
Fort Jameson = Chipata, Zambia **87 E3** 13 38 S 32 28 E
Fort Kent, U.S.A. **109 B11** 47 15N 68 36W
Fort Klamath, U.S.A. **114 E3** 42 42N 122 0W
Fort-Lamy = Ndjamena, Chad **79 F8** 12 10N 14 59 E
Fort Laramie, U.S.A. **112 D2** 42 13N 104 31W
Fort Lauderdale, U.S.A. **109 M5** 26 7N 80 8W
Fort Liard, Canada **104 A4** 60 14N 123 30W
Fort Liberté, Haiti **121 C5** 19 42N 71 51W
Fort Lupton, U.S.A. **112 E2** 40 5N 104 49W
Fort Mackay, Canada **104 B6** 57 12N 111 41W
Fort Macleod, Canada **104 D6** 49 45N 113 30W
Fort McMurray, Canada **104 B6** 56 44N 111 7W
Fort McPherson, Canada **100 B6** 67 30N 134 55W
Fort Madison, U.S.A. **112 E9** 40 38N 91 27W
Fort Meade, U.S.A. **109 M5** 27 45N 81 48W
Fort Morgan, U.S.A. **112 E3** 40 15N 103 48W
Fort Munro, Pakistan **68 E3** 29 54N 69 58 E
Fort Myers, U.S.A. **109 M5** 26 39N 81 52W
Fort Nelson, Canada **104 B4** 58 50N 122 44W
Fort Nelson →, Canada **104 B4** 59 32N 124 0W
Fort Norman = Tulita, Canada **100 B7** 64 57N 125 30W
Fort Payne, U.S.A. **109 H3** 34 26N 85 43W
Fort Peck, U.S.A. **114 B10** 48 1N 106 27W
Fort Peck Dam, U.S.A. **114 C10** 48 0N 106 26W
Fort Peck L., U.S.A. **114 C10** 48 0N 106 26W
Fort Pierce, U.S.A. **109 M5** 27 27N 80 20W
Fort Pierre, U.S.A. **112 C4** 44 21N 100 22W
Fort Pierre Bordes = Ti-n-Zaouatène, Algeria **83 B5** 19 55N 2 55 E
Fort Plain, U.S.A. **111 D10** 42 56N 74 37W
Fort Portal, Uganda **86 B3** 0 40N 30 20 E
Fort Providence, Canada **104 A5** 61 3N 117 40W
Fort Qu'Appelle, Canada **105 C8** 50 45N 103 50W
Fort Resolution, Canada **104 A6** 61 10N 113 40W
Fort Rixon, Zimbabwe **87 G2** 20 2 S 29 17 E
Fort Rosebery = Mansa, Zambia **87 E2** 11 13 S 28 55 E
Fort Ross, U.S.A. **116 G3** 38 32N 123 13W
Fort Rupert = Waskaganish, Canada **102 B4** 51 30N 78 40W
Fort St. James, Canada **104 C4** 54 30N 124 10W
Fort St. John, Canada **104 B4** 56 15N 120 50W
Fort Sandeman = Zhob, Pakistan **68 D3** 31 20N 69 31 E
Fort Saskatchewan, Canada **104 C6** 53 40N 113 15W
Fort Scott, U.S.A. **113 G7** 37 50N 94 42W
Fort Severn, Canada **102 A2** 56 0N 87 40W
Fort Shevchenko, Kazakstan **49 H10** 44 35N 50 23 E
Fort Simpson, Canada **104 A4** 61 45N 121 15W
Fort Smith, Canada **104 B6** 60 0N 111 51W
Fort Smith, U.S.A. **113 H7** 35 23N 94 25W
Fort Stockton, U.S.A. **113 K3** 30 53N 102 53W
Fort Sumner, U.S.A. **113 H2** 34 28N 104 15W
Fort Thompson, U.S.A. **112 C5** 44 3N 99 26W
Fort Trinquet = Bir Mogreïn, Mauritania **78 C3** 25 10N 11 25W
Fort Valley, U.S.A. **109 J4** 32 33N 83 53W
Fort Vermilion, Canada **104 B5** 58 24N 116 0W
Fort Walton Beach, U.S.A. **109 K2** 30 25N 86 36W
Fort Wayne, U.S.A. **108 E3** 41 4N 85 9W
Fort William, U.K. **14 E3** 56 49N 5 7W
Fort Worth, U.S.A. **113 J6** 32 45N 97 18W
Fort Yates, U.S.A. **112 B4** 46 5N 100 38W
Fort Yukon, U.S.A. **100 B5** 66 34N 145 16W
Fortaleza, Brazil **125 D11** 3 45 S 38 35W
Forteau, Canada **103 B8** 51 28N 56 58W
Fortescue →, Australia **92 D2** 21 0 S 116 4 E
Forth →, U.K. **14 E5** 56 9N 3 50W
Forth, Firth of, U.K. **14 E6** 56 5N 2 55W
Fortore →, Italy **29 G12** 41 55N 15 17 E
Fortrose, U.K. **14 D4** 57 35N 4 9W
Fortuna, Spain **33 G3** 38 11N 1 7W
Fortuna, Calif., U.S.A. **114 F1** 40 36N 124 9W
Fortuna, N. Dak., U.S.A. **112 A3** 48 55N 103 47W
Fortune, Canada **103 C8** 47 4N 55 50W
Fortune B., Canada **103 C8** 47 30N 55 22W
Forūr, Iran **71 E7** 26 17N 54 32 E
Fos-sur-Mer, France **21 E8** 43 26N 4 56 E
Foshan, China **59 F9** 23 4N 113 5 E
Fosna, Norway **8 E14** 63 50N 10 20 E
Fosnavåg, Norway **9 E11** 62 22N 5 38 E
Foso, Ghana **83 D4** 5 43N 1 17W
Fossano, Italy **28 D4** 44 33N 7 43 E
Fossil, U.S.A. **114 D3** 45 0N 120 9W
Fossombrone, Italy **29 E9** 43 41N 12 48 E
Foster, Australia **95 F4** 38 40 S 146 15 E
Foster, Canada **111 A12** 45 17N 72 30W
Foster →, Canada **105 B7** 55 47N 105 49W
Fosters Ra., Australia **94 C1** 21 35 S 133 48 E
Fostoria, U.S.A. **108 E4** 41 10N 83 25W
Fotadrevo, Madag. **89 C8** 24 3 S 45 1 E
Fouesnant, France **18 E2** 47 53N 4 1W
Fougères, France **18 D5** 48 21N 1 14W
Foul Pt., Sri Lanka **66 Q12** 8 35N 81 18 E
Foula, U.K. **14 A6** 60 10N 2 5W
Foulalaba, Mali **82 C3** 10 40N 7 20W
Foulness I., U.K. **13 F8** 51 36N 0 55 E
Foulpointe, Madag. **89 B8** 17 41 S 49 31 E
Foulweather, C., U.S.A. **106 B2** 44 50N 124 5W
Foumban, Cameroon **83 D7** 5 45N 10 50 E
Foumbot, Cameroon **83 D7** 5 31N 10 28 E
Foundiougne, Senegal **82 C1** 14 5N 16 32W
Fountain, U.S.A. **112 F2** 38 41N 104 42W
Fountain Springs, U.S.A. **117 K8** 35 54N 118 51W
Fourchambault, France **19 E10** 47 2N 3 3 E
Fouriesburg, S. Africa **88 D4** 28 38 S 28 14 E
Fourmies, France **19 B11** 50 1N 4 2 E
Fournás, Greece **38 B3** 39 3N 21 52 E
Foúrnoi, Greece **39 D8** 37 36N 26 32 E
Fours, France **19 F10** 46 50N 3 42 E
Fourth Cataract, Sudan **80 D3** 18 47N 32 3 E
Fouta Djalon, Guinea **82 C2** 11 20N 12 10W
Foux, Cap-à-, Haiti **121 C5** 19 43N 73 27W
Foveaux Str., N.Z. **91 M2** 46 42 S 168 10 E
Fowey, U.K. **13 G3** 50 20N 4 39W
Fowler, Calif., U.S.A. **116 J7** 36 38N 119 41W
Fowler, Colo., U.S.A. **112 F3** 38 8N 104 2W
Fowlers B., Australia **93 F5** 31 59 S 132 34 E
Fowman, Iran **71 B6** 37 13N 49 19 E
Fox →, Canada **105 B10** 56 3N 93 18W
Fox Creek, Canada **104 C5** 54 24N 116 48W
Fox Lake, Canada **104 B6** 58 28N 114 31W
Fox Valley, Canada **105 C7** 50 30N 109 25W
Foxboro, U.S.A. **111 D13** 42 4N 71 16W
Foxe Basin, Canada **101 B12** 66 0N 77 0W
Foxe Chan., Canada **101 B11** 65 0N 80 0W
Foxe Pen., Canada **101 B12** 65 0N 76 0W
Foxen, Sweden **10 E5** 59 25N 11 55 E
Foxton, N.Z. **91 J5** 40 29 S 175 18 E
Foyle, Lough, U.K. **15 A4** 55 7N 7 4W
Foynes, Ireland **15 D2** 52 37N 9 7W
Foz, Spain **34 B3** 43 33N 7 20W
Fóz do Cunene, Angola **88 B1** 17 15 S 11 48 E
Foz do Iguaçu, Brazil **127 B5** 25 30 S 54 30W
Frackville, U.S.A. **111 F8** 40 47N 76 14W
Fraga, Spain **32 D5** 41 32N 0 21 E
Fraile Muerto, Uruguay **127 C5** 32 31 S 54 32W
Framingham, U.S.A. **111 D13** 42 17N 71 25W
Frampol, Poland **45 H9** 50 41N 22 40 E
Franca, Brazil **125 H9** 20 33 S 47 30W
Francavilla al Mare, Italy **29 F11** 42 25N 14 17 E
Francavilla Fontana, Italy **31 B10** 40 32N 17 35 E
France ■, Europe **7 F6** 47 0N 3 0 E
Frances, Australia **95 F3** 36 41 S 140 55 E
Frances →, Canada **104 A3** 60 16N 129 10W
Frances L., Canada **104 A3** 61 23N 129 30W
Franceville, Gabon **84 E2** 1 40 S 13 32 E
Franche-Comté, France **19 F12** 46 50N 5 55 E
Francis Case, L., U.S.A. **112 D5** 43 4N 98 34W
Francisco Beltrão, Brazil **127 B5** 26 5 S 53 4W
Francisco I. Madero, Coahuila, Mexico **118 B4** 25 48N 103 18W
Francisco I. Madero, Durango, Mexico **118 C4** 24 32N 104 22W
Francistown, Botswana **89 C4** 21 7 S 27 33 E
Francofonte, Italy **31 E7** 37 14N 14 53 E
François, Canada **103 C8** 47 35N 56 45W
François L., Canada **104 C3** 54 0N 125 30W
Franeker, Neths. **17 A5** 53 12N 5 33 E
Frankado, Djibouti **81 E5** 12 30N 43 12 E
Frankenberg, Germany **24 D4** 51 3N 8 48 E
Frankenwald, Germany **25 E7** 50 20N 11 30 E
Frankford, Canada **110 B7** 44 12N 77 36W
Frankfort, S. Africa **89 D4** 27 17 S 28 30 E
Frankfort, Ind., U.S.A. **108 E2** 40 17N 86 31W
Frankfort, Kans., U.S.A. **112 F6** 39 42N 96 25W
Frankfort, Ky., U.S.A. **108 F3** 38 12N 84 52W
Frankfort, N.Y., U.S.A. **111 C9** 43 2N 75 4W
Frankfurt, Brandenburg, Germany **24 C10** 52 20N 14 32 E
Frankfurt, Hessen, Germany **25 E4** 50 7N 8 41 E
Fränkische Alb, Germany **25 F7** 49 10N 11 23 E
Fränkische Rezat →, Germany **25 F7** 49 11N 11 1 E
Fränkische Saale →, Germany **25 E5** 50 3N 9 42 E
Fränkische Schweiz, Germany **25 F7** 49 50N 11 16 E
Frankland →, Australia **93 G2** 35 0 S 116 48 E
Franklin, Ky., U.S.A. **109 G2** 36 43N 86 35W
Franklin, La., U.S.A. **113 L9** 29 48N 91 30W
Franklin, Mass., U.S.A. **111 D13** 42 5N 71 24W
Franklin, N.H., U.S.A. **111 C13** 43 27N 71 39W
Franklin, Nebr., U.S.A. **112 E5** 40 6N 98 57W
Franklin, Pa., U.S.A. **110 E5** 41 24N 79 50W
Franklin, Va., U.S.A. **109 G7** 36 41N 76 56W
Franklin, W. Va., U.S.A. **108 F6** 38 39N 79 20W
Franklin B., Canada **100 B7** 69 45N 126 0W
Franklin D. Roosevelt L., U.S.A. **114 B4** 48 18N 118 9W
Franklin I., Antarctica **5 D11** 76 10 S 168 30 E
Franklin L., U.S.A. **114 F6** 40 25N 115 22W
Franklin Mts., Canada **100 B7** 65 0N 125 0W
Franklin Str., Canada **100 A10** 72 0N 96 0W
Franklinton, U.S.A. **113 K9** 30 51N 90 9W
Franklinville, U.S.A. **110 D6** 42 20N 78 27W
Franks Pk., U.S.A. **114 E9** 43 58N 109 18W
Frankston, Australia **95 F4** 38 8 S 145 8 E
Fränö, Sweden **10 B11** 62 55N 17 50 E
Fransfontein, Namibia **88 C2** 20 12 S 15 1 E
Fränsta, Sweden **10 B10** 62 30N 16 11 E
Frantsa Iosifa, Zemlya, Russia **50 A6** 82 0N 55 0 E
Franz, Canada **102 C3** 48 25N 84 30W
Franz Josef Land = Frantsa Iosifa, Zemlya, Russia **50 A6** 82 0N 55 0 E
Franzburg, Germany **24 A8** 54 11N 12 51 E
Frascati, Italy **29 G9** 41 48N 12 41 E
Fraser, U.S.A. **110 D2** 42 32N 82 57W
Fraser →, B.C., Canada **104 D4** 49 7N 123 11W
Fraser →, Nfld., Canada **103 A7** 56 39N 62 10W
Fraser, Mt., Australia **93 E2** 25 35 S 118 20 E
Fraser I., Australia **95 D5** 25 15 S 153 10 E
Fraser Lake, Canada **104 C4** 54 0N 124 50W
Fraserburg, S. Africa **88 E3** 31 55 S 21 30 E
Fraserburgh, U.K. **14 D6** 57 42N 2 1W
Fraserdale, Canada **102 C3** 49 55N 81 37W
Frashër, Albania **40 F4** 40 23N 20 26 E
Frashëri = Frashër, Albania **40 F4** 40 23N 20 30 E
Frasne, France **19 F13** 46 50N 6 10 E
Frătești, Romania **43 G10** 43 58N 25 58 E
Frauenfeld, Switz. **25 H4** 47 34N 8 54 E
Fray Bentos, Uruguay **126 C4** 33 10 S 58 15W
Frechilla, Spain **34 C6** 42 8N 4 50W
Fredericia, Denmark **11 J3** 55 34N 9 45 E
Frederick, Md., U.S.A. **108 F7** 39 25N 77 25W
Frederick, Okla., U.S.A. **113 H5** 34 23N 99 1W
Frederick, S. Dak., U.S.A. **112 C5** 45 50N 98 31W
Fredericksburg, Pa., U.S.A. **111 F8** 40 27N 76 26W
Fredericksburg, Tex., U.S.A. **113 K5** 30 16N 98 52W
Fredericksburg, Va., U.S.A. **108 F7** 38 18N 77 28W
Fredericktown, Mo., U.S.A. **113 G9** 37 34N 90 18W
Fredericktown, Ohio, U.S.A. **110 F2** 40 29N 82 33W
Frederico I. Madero, Presa, Mexico **118 B3** 28 7N 105 40W
Frederico Westphalen, Brazil **127 B5** 27 22 S 53 24W
Fredericton, Canada **103 C6** 45 57N 66 40W
Fredericton Junction, Canada **103 C6** 45 41N 66 40W
Frederiksborg Amtskommune □, Denmark **11 J6** 55 50N 12 10 E
Frederikshåb = Paamiut, Greenland **4 C5** 62 0N 49 43W
Frederikshavn, Denmark **11 G4** 57 28N 10 31 E
Frederikssund, Denmark **11 J6** 55 50N 12 3 E
Frederiksted, Virgin Is. **121 C7** 17 43N 64 53W
Frederiksværk, Denmark **11 J6** 55 58N 12 4 E
Fredonia, Ariz., U.S.A. **115 H7** 36 57N 112 32W
Fredonia, Kans., U.S.A. **113 G7** 37 32N 95 49W
Fredonia, N.Y., U.S.A. **110 D5** 42 26N 79 20W
Fredriksberg, Sweden **10 D8** 60 8N 14 23 E
Fredrikstad, Norway **9 G14** 59 13N 10 57 E
Free State □, S. Africa **88 D4** 28 30 S 27 0 E
Freehold, U.S.A. **111 F10** 40 16N 74 17W
Freel Peak, U.S.A. **116 G7** 38 52N 119 54W
Freeland, U.S.A. **111 E9** 41 1N 75 54W
Freels, C., Canada **103 C9** 49 15N 53 30W
Freeman, Calif., U.S.A. **117 K9** 35 35N 117 53W
Freeman, S. Dak., U.S.A. **112 D6** 43 21N 97 26W
Freeport, Bahamas **120 A4** 26 30N 78 47W
Freeport, Ill., U.S.A. **112 D10** 42 17N 89 36W
Freeport, N.Y., U.S.A. **111 F11** 40 39N 73 35W
Freeport, Ohio, U.S.A. **110 F3** 40 12N 81 15W
Freeport, Pa., U.S.A. **110 F5** 40 41N 79 41W
Freeport, Tex., U.S.A. **113 L7** 28 57N 95 21W
Freetown, S. Leone **82 D2** 8 30N 13 17W
Frégate, L., Canada **102 B5** 53 15N 74 45W
Fregenal de la Sierra, Spain **35 G4** 38 10N 6 39W
Fregene, Italy **29 G9** 41 51N 12 12 E
Fréhel, C., France **18 D4** 48 40N 2 20W
Freiberg, Germany **24 E9** 50 55N 13 20 E
Freibourg = Fribourg, Switz. **25 J3** 46 49N 7 9 E
Freiburg, Baden-W., Germany **25 H3** 47 59N 7 51 E
Freiburg, Niedersachsen, Germany **24 B5** 53 49N 9 16 E
Freilassing, Germany **25 H8** 47 50N 12 58 E
Freire, Chile **128 D2** 38 54 S 72 38W
Freirina, Chile **126 B1** 28 30 S 71 10W
Freising, Germany **25 G7** 48 24N 11 45 E
Freistadt, Austria **26 C7** 48 30N 14 30 E
Freital, Germany **24 D9** 51 1N 13 39 E
Fréjus, France **21 E10** 43 25N 6 44 E
Fremantle, Australia **93 F2** 32 7 S 115 47 E
Fremont, Calif., U.S.A. **116 H4** 37 32N 121 57W
Fremont, Mich., U.S.A. **108 D3** 43 28N 85 57W
Fremont, Nebr., U.S.A. **112 E6** 41 26N 96 30W
Fremont, Ohio, U.S.A. **108 E4** 41 21N 83 7W
Fremont →, U.S.A. **115 G8** 38 24N 110 42W
French Camp, U.S.A. **116 H5** 37 53N 121 16W
French Creek →, U.S.A. **110 E5** 41 24N 79 50W
French Guiana ■, S. Amer. **125 C8** 4 0N 53 0W
French Polynesia ■, Pac. Oc. **97 K13** 20 0 S 145 0W
Frenchman Cr. →, N. Amer. **114 B10** 48 31N 107 10W
Frenchman Cr. →, U.S.A. **112 E4** 40 14N 100 50W
Frenštát pod Radhoštěm, Czech Rep. **27 B11** 49 33N 18 13 E
Fresco, Ivory C. **82 D3** 5 3N 5 31W
Fresco →, Brazil **125 E8** 7 15 S 51 30W
Freshfield, C., Antarctica **5 C10** 68 25 S 151 10 E
Fresnay-sur-Sarthe, France **18 D7** 48 17N 0 1 E
Fresnillo, Mexico **118 C4** 23 10N 103 0W
Fresno, U.S.A. **116 J7** 36 44N 119 47W
Fresno Alhandiga, Spain **34 E5** 40 42N 5 37W
Fresno Reservoir, U.S.A. **114 B9** 48 36N 109 57W
Freudenstadt, Germany **25 G4** 48 27N 8 24 E
Frévent, France **19 B9** 50 15N 2 17 E
Frew →, Australia **94 C2** 20 0 S 135 38 E
Frewsburg, U.S.A. **110 D5** 42 3N 79 10W
Freycinet Pen., Australia **94 G4** 42 10 S 148 25 E
Freyming-Merlebach, France **19 C13** 49 8N 6 48 E
Freyung, Germany **25 G9** 48 48N 13 31 E
Fria, Guinea **82 C2** 10 27N 13 38W
Fria, C., Namibia **88 B1** 18 0 S 12 0 E
Friant, U.S.A. **116 J7** 36 59N 119 43W
Frías, Argentina **126 B2** 28 40 S 65 5W
Fribourg, Switz. **25 J3** 46 49N 7 9 E
Fribourg □, Switz. **25 J3** 46 40N 7 0 E
Fridafors, Sweden **11 H8** 56 25N 14 39 E
Friday Harbor, U.S.A. **116 B3** 48 32N 123 1W
Friedberg, Bayern, Germany **25 G6** 48 21N 10 59 E
Friedberg, Hessen, Germany **25 E4** 50 19N 8 45 E
Friedens, U.S.A. **110 F6** 40 3N 78 59W
Friedland, Germany **24 B9** 53 40N 13 33 E
Friedrichshafen, Germany **25 H5** 47 39N 9 30 E
Friedrichskoog, Germany **24 A4** 54 1N 8 53 E
Friedrichstadt, Germany **24 A5** 54 23N 9 6 E
Friendly Is. = Tonga ■, Pac. Oc. **91 D11** 19 50 S 174 30W
Friendship, U.S.A. **110 D6** 42 12N 78 8W
Friesach, Austria **26 E7** 46 57N 14 24 E
Friesack, Germany **24 C8** 52 44N 12 34 E
Friesland □, Neths. **17 A5** 53 5N 5 50 E
Friesoythe, Germany **24 B3** 53 1N 7 51 E
Friggesund, Sweden **10 C10** 61 54N 16 33 E
Frillesås, Sweden **11 G6** 57 20N 12 12 E
Frinnaryd, Sweden **11 G8** 57 55N 14 50 E
Frio →, U.S.A. **113 L5** 28 26N 98 11W
Frio, C., Brazil **122 F6** 22 50 S 41 50W
Friol, Spain **34 B3** 43 2N 7 47W
Friona, U.S.A. **113 H3** 34 38N 102 43W
Fristad, Sweden **11 G6** 57 50N 13 0 E
Fritch, U.S.A. **113 H4** 35 38N 101 36W
Fritsla, Sweden **11 G6** 57 33N 12 47 E
Fritzlar, Germany **24 D5** 51 7N 9 16 E
Friuli-Venézia Giulia □, Italy **29 B9** 46 0N 13 0 E
Frobisher B., Canada **101 B13** 62 30N 66 0W
Frobisher Bay = Iqaluit, Canada **101 B13** 63 44N 68 31W
Frobisher L., Canada **105 B7** 56 20N 108 15W
Frohavet, Norway **8 E13** 64 0N 9 30 E
Frohnleiten, Austria **26 D8** 47 16N 15 19 E
Frolovo, Russia **48 F6** 49 45N 43 40 E
Frombork, Poland **44 D6** 54 21N 19 41 E
Frome, U.K. **13 F5** 51 14N 2 19W
Frome →, U.K. **13 G5** 50 41N 2 6W
Frome, L., Australia **95 E2** 30 45 S 139 45 E
Frómista, Spain **34 C6** 42 16N 4 25W
Front Range, U.S.A. **106 C5** 40 25N 105 45W
Front Royal, U.S.A. **108 F6** 38 55N 78 12W
Fronteira, Portugal **35 F3** 39 3N 7 39W
Frontera, Canary Is. **37 G2** 27 47N 17 59W
Frontera, Mexico **119 D6** 18 30N 92 40W
Fronteras, Mexico **118 A3** 30 56N 109 31W
Frontignan, France **20 E7** 43 27N 3 45 E
Frosinone, Italy **30 A6** 41 38N 13 19 E
Frostburg, U.S.A. **108 F6** 39 39N 78 56W
Frostisen, Norway **8 B17** 68 14N 17 10 E
Frouard, France **19 D13** 48 47N 6 8 E
Frövi, Sweden **10 E9** 59 28N 15 24 E
Frøya, Norway **8 E13** 63 43N 8 40 E
Frumoasa, Romania **43 D10** 46 28N 25 48 E
Frunze = Bishkek, Kyrgyzstan **50 E8** 42 54N 74 46 E
Fruška Gora, Serbia, Yug. **42 E4** 45 7N 19 30 E

Frutal, *Brazil* 125 H9 20 0 S 49 0W
Frutigen, *Switz.* 25 J3 46 35N 7 38 E
Frýdek-Místek, *Czech Rep.* 27 B11 49 40N 18 20 E
Frýdlant, *Czech Rep.* 26 A8 50 56N 15 9 E
Fryeburg, *U.S.A.* 111 B14 44 1N 70 59W
Fryvaldov = Jeseník, *Czech Rep.* 27 A10 50 14N 17 8 E
Fthiótis □, *Greece* 38 C4 38 50N 22 25 E
Fu Jiang →, *China* 58 C6 30 0N 106 16 E
Fu Xian = Wafangdian, *China* 57 E11 39 38N 121 58 E
Fu Xian, *China* 56 G5 36 0N 109 20 E
Fu'an, *China* 59 D12 27 11N 119 36 E
Fubian, *China* 58 B4 31 17N 102 22 E
Fucécchio, *Italy* 28 E7 43 44N 10 48 E
Fucheng, *China* 56 F9 37 50N 116 10 E
Fuchou = Fuzhou, *China* 59 D12 26 5N 119 16 E
Fuchū, *Japan* 55 G6 34 34N 133 14 E
Fuchuan, *China* 59 E8 24 50N 111 5 E
Fuchun Jiang →, *China* 59 B13 30 5N 120 5 E
Fúcino, Piana del, *Italy* 29 F10 42 1N 13 31 E
Fuding, *China* 59 D13 27 20N 120 12 E
Fuencaliente, *Canary Is.* 37 F2 28 28N 17 50W
Fuencaliente, *Spain* 35 G6 38 25N 4 18W
Fuencaliente, Pta., *Canary Is.* 37 F2 28 27N 17 51W
Fuengirola, *Spain* 35 J6 36 32N 4 41W
Fuenlabrada, *Spain* 34 E7 40 17N 3 48W
Fuensalida, *Spain* 34 E6 40 3N 4 12W
Fuente-Alamo, *Spain* 33 G3 38 44N 1 24W
Fuente-Álamo de Murcia, *Spain* 33 H3 37 42N 1 6W
Fuente de Cantos, *Spain* 35 G4 38 15N 6 18W
Fuente del Maestre, *Spain* 35 G4 38 31N 6 28W
Fuente el Fresno, *Spain* 35 F7 39 14N 3 46W
Fuente Obejuna, *Spain* 35 G5 38 15N 5 25W
Fuente Palmera, *Spain* 35 H5 37 42N 5 6W
Fuentes de Andalucía, *Spain* 35 H5 37 28N 5 20W
Fuentes de Ebro, *Spain* 32 D4 41 31N 0 38W
Fuentes de León, *Spain* 35 G4 38 5N 6 32W
Fuentes de Oñoro, *Spain* 34 E4 40 33N 6 52W
Fuentesaúco, *Spain* 34 D5 41 15N 5 30W
Fuerte →, *Mexico* 118 B3 25 50N 109 25W
Fuerte Olimpo, *Paraguay* 126 A4 21 0 S 57 51W
Fuerteventura, *Canary Is.* 37 F6 28 30N 14 0W
Fufeng, *China* 56 G5 34 22N 108 0 E
Fuga I., *Phil.* 61 B4 18 52N 121 20 E
Fugong, *China* 58 D2 27 5N 98 47 E
Fugou, *China* 56 G8 34 3N 114 25 E
Fugu, *China* 56 E6 39 2N 111 3 E
Fuhai, *China* 60 B3 47 2N 87 25 E
Fuḥaymī, *Iraq* 70 C4 34 16N 42 10 E
Fuji, *Japan* 55 G9 35 9N 138 39 E
Fuji-San, *Japan* 55 G9 35 22N 138 44 E
Fuji-Yoshida, *Japan* 55 G9 35 30N 138 46 E
Fujian □, *China* 59 E12 26 0N 118 0 E
Fujinomiya, *Japan* 55 G9 35 10N 138 40 E
Fujisawa, *Japan* 55 G9 35 22N 139 29 E
Fujiyama, Mt. = Fuji-San, *Japan* 55 G9 35 22N 138 44 E
Fukien = Fujian □, *China* 59 E12 26 0N 118 0 E
Fukuchiyama, *Japan* 55 G7 35 19N 135 9 E
Fukue-Shima, *Japan* 55 H4 32 40N 128 45 E
Fukui, *Japan* 55 F8 36 5N 136 10 E
Fukui □, *Japan* 55 G8 36 0N 136 12 E
Fukuoka, *Japan* 55 H5 33 39N 130 21 E
Fukuoka □, *Japan* 55 H5 33 30N 131 0 E
Fukushima, *Japan* 54 F10 37 44N 140 28 E
Fukushima □, *Japan* 54 F10 37 30N 140 15 E
Fukuyama, *Japan* 55 G6 34 35N 133 20 E
Fulacunda, *Guinea-Biss.* 82 C1 11 44N 15 3W
Fulda, *Germany* 24 E5 50 32N 9 40 E
Fulda →, *Germany* 24 D5 51 25N 9 39 E
Fulford Harbour, *Canada* 116 B3 48 47N 123 27W
Fuliang, *China* 59 C11 29 23N 117 14 E
Fullerton, *Calif., U.S.A.* 117 M9 33 53N 117 56W
Fullerton, *Nebr., U.S.A.* 112 E6 41 22N 97 58W
Fulongquan, *China* 57 B13 44 20N 124 42 E
Fülöpszállás, *Hungary* 42 D4 46 49N 19 15 E
Fulton, *Mo., U.S.A.* 112 F9 38 52N 91 57W
Fulton, *N.Y., U.S.A.* 111 C8 43 19N 76 25W
Fuluälven →, *Sweden* 10 C7 61 18N 13 4 E
Fulufjället, *Sweden* 10 C6 61 32N 12 41 E
Fumay, *France* 19 C11 49 58N 4 40 E
Fumel, *France* 20 D4 44 30N 0 58 E
Fumin, *China* 58 E4 25 10N 102 20 E
Funabashi, *Japan* 55 G10 35 45N 140 0 E
Funäsdalen, *Sweden* 10 B6 62 33N 12 32 E
Funchal, *Madeira* 37 D3 32 38N 16 54W
Fundación, *Colombia* 124 A4 10 31N 74 11W
Fundão, *Portugal* 34 E3 40 8N 7 30W
Fundu Moldovei, *Romania* 43 C10 47 32N 25 24 E
Fundulea, *Romania* 43 F11 44 28N 26 31 E
Fundy, B. of, *Canada* 103 D6 45 0N 66 0W
Funhalouro, *Mozam.* 89 C5 23 3 S 34 25 E
Funing, *Hebei, China* 57 E10 39 53N 119 12 E
Funing, *Jiangsu, China* 57 H10 33 45N 119 50 E
Funing, *Yunnan, China* 58 F5 23 35N 105 45 E
Funiu Shan, *China* 56 H7 33 30N 112 20 E
Funsi, *Ghana* 82 C4 10 21N 1 54W
Funtua, *Nigeria* 83 C6 11 30N 7 18 E
Fuping, *Hebei, China* 56 E8 38 48N 114 12 E
Fuping, *Shaanxi, China* 56 G5 34 42N 109 10 E
Fuqing, *China* 59 E12 25 41N 119 21 E
Fuquan, *China* 58 D6 26 40N 107 27 E
Furano, *Japan* 54 C11 43 21N 142 23 E
Furāt, Nahr al →, *Asia* 70 D5 31 0N 47 25 E
Fürg, *Iran* 71 D7 28 18N 55 13 E
Furmanov, *Russia* 48 B5 57 10N 41 9 E
Furmanovo, *Kazakstan* 48 F9 49 42N 49 25 E
Furnás, *Spain* 37 B8 39 3N 1 32 E
Furnas, Represa de, *Brazil* 127 A6 20 50 S 45 30W
Furneaux Group, *Australia* 94 G4 40 10 S 147 50 E
Furqlus, *Syria* 75 A6 34 36N 37 8 E
Fürstenau, *Germany* 24 C3 52 31N 7 40 E
Fürstenberg, *Germany* 24 B9 53 10N 13 8 E
Fürstenfeld, *Austria* 26 D9 47 3N 16 3 E
Fürstenfeldbruck, *Germany* 25 G7 48 11N 11 15 E
Fürstenwalde, *Germany* 24 C10 52 22N 14 3 E
Fürth, *Germany* 25 F6 49 28N 10 59 E
Furth im Wald, *Germany* 25 F8 49 18N 12 50 E
Furtwangen, *Germany* 25 G4 48 2N 8 12 E
Furudal, *Sweden* 10 C9 61 10N 15 11 E
Furukawa, *Japan* 54 E10 38 34N 140 58 E
Furulund, *Sweden* 11 J7 55 46N 13 6 E
Fury and Hecla Str., *Canada* 101 B11 69 56N 84 0W
Fusagasuga, *Colombia* 124 C4 4 21N 74 22W
Fuscaldo, *Italy* 31 C9 39 25N 16 2 E
Fushan, *Shandong, China* 57 F11 37 30N 121 15 E
Fushan, *Shanxi, China* 56 G6 35 58N 111 51 E
Fushë Arrëz, *Albania* 40 D4 42 4N 20 2 E
Fushë Arrëzi = Fushë Arrëz, *Albania* 40 D4 42 4N 20 2 E
Fushë-Krujë, *Albania* 40 E3 41 29N 19 43 E
Fushun, *Liaoning, China* 57 D12 41 50N 123 56 E
Fushun, *Sichuan, China* 58 C5 29 13N 104 52 E
Fusong, *China* 57 C14 42 20N 127 15 E
Füssen, *Germany* 25 H6 47 34N 10 42 E
Fusui, *China* 58 F6 22 40N 107 56 E
Futog, *Yugoslavia* 42 E4 45 15N 19 42 E
Futuna, *Wall. & F. Is.* 91 B8 14 25 S 178 20W
Fuwa, *Egypt* 80 H7 31 12N 30 33 E
Fuxian Hu, *China* 58 E4 24 30N 102 53 E
Fuxin, *China* 57 C11 42 5N 121 48 E
Fuyang, *Anhui, China* 56 H8 33 0N 115 48 E
Fuyang, *Zhejiang, China* 59 B12 30 5N 119 57 E
Fuyang He →, *China* 56 E9 38 12N 117 0 E
Fuying Dao, *China* 59 D13 26 34N 120 9 E
Fuyu, *China* 57 B13 45 12N 124 43 E
Fuyuan, *China* 58 E5 25 40N 104 16 E
Füzesgyarmat, *Hungary* 42 C6 47 6N 21 14 E
Fuzhou, *China* 59 D12 26 5N 119 16 E
Fylde, *U.K.* 12 D5 53 50N 2 58W
Fyn, *Denmark* 11 J4 55 20N 10 30 E
Fyne, L., *U.K.* 14 F3 55 59N 5 23W
Fyns Amtskommune □, *Denmark* 11 J4 55 15N 10 30 E
Fynshav, *Denmark* 11 K3 54 59N 9 59 E

G

Ga, *Ghana* 82 D4 9 47N 2 30W
Gaanda, *Nigeria* 83 C7 10 10N 12 27 E
Gabarin, *Nigeria* 83 C7 11 8N 10 27 E
Gabas →, *France* 20 E3 43 46N 0 42W
Gabela, *Angola* 84 G2 11 0 S 14 24 E
Gabès, *Tunisia* 79 B8 33 53N 10 2 E
Gabès, G. de, *Tunisia* 79 B8 34 0N 10 30 E
Gabgaba, W. →, *Egypt* 80 C3 22 10N 33 5 E
Gąbin, *Poland* 45 F6 52 23N 19 41 E
Gabon ■, *Africa* 84 E2 0 10 S 10 0 E
Gaborone, *Botswana* 88 C4 24 45 S 25 57 E
Gabriels, *U.S.A.* 111 B10 44 26N 74 12W
Gābrīk, *Iran* 71 E8 25 44N 58 28 E
Gabrovo, *Bulgaria* 41 D9 42 52N 25 19 E
Gacé, *France* 18 D7 48 49N 0 20 E
Gāch Sār, *Iran* 71 B6 36 7N 51 19 E
Gachsārān, *Iran* 71 D6 30 15N 50 45 E
Gacko, *Bos.-H.* 40 C2 43 10N 18 33 E
Gadag, *India* 66 M9 15 30N 75 45 E
Gadamai, *Sudan* 81 D4 17 11N 36 10 E
Gadap, *Pakistan* 68 G2 25 5N 67 28 E
Gadarwara, *India* 69 H8 22 50N 78 50 E
Gadebusch, *Germany* 24 B7 53 42N 11 7 E
Gadein, *Sudan* 81 F2 8 10N 28 45 E
Gadhada, *India* 68 J4 22 0N 71 35 E
Gádor, Sierra de, *Spain* 35 J8 36 57N 2 45W
Gadra, *Pakistan* 68 G4 25 40N 70 38 E
Gadsden, *U.S.A.* 109 H3 34 1N 86 1W
Gadwal, *India* 66 L10 16 10N 77 50 E
Gadyach = Hadyach, *Ukraine* 47 G8 50 21N 34 0 E
Găeşti, *Romania* 43 F10 44 48N 25 19 E
Gaeta, *Italy* 30 A6 41 12N 13 35 E
Gaeta, G. di, *Italy* 30 A6 41 6N 13 30 E
Gaffney, *U.S.A.* 109 H5 35 5N 81 39W
Gafsa, *Tunisia* 78 B7 34 24N 8 43 E
Gagarawa, *Nigeria* 83 C6 12 25N 9 32 E
Gagaria, *India* 68 G4 25 43N 70 46 E
Gagarin, *Russia* 46 E8 55 38N 35 0 E
Gaggenau, *Germany* 25 G4 48 48N 8 18 E
Gaghamni, *Sudan* 81 E2 11 41N 28 19 E
Gagino, *Russia* 48 C7 55 15N 45 1 E
Gagliano del Capo, *Italy* 31 C11 39 50N 18 22 E
Gagnef, *Sweden* 10 D9 60 36N 15 5 E
Gagnoa, *Ivory C.* 82 D3 6 56N 5 16W
Gagnon, *Canada* 103 B6 51 50N 68 5W
Gagnon, L., *Canada* 105 A6 62 3N 110 27W
Gagra, *Georgia* 49 J5 43 20N 40 10 E
Gahini, *Rwanda* 86 C3 1 50 S 30 30 E
Gahmar, *India* 69 G10 25 27N 83 49 E
Gai Xian = Gaizhou, *China* 57 D12 40 22N 122 20 E
Gaïdhouronísi, *Greece* 36 E7 34 53N 25 41 E
Gail, *U.S.A.* 113 J4 32 46N 101 27W
Gail →, *Austria* 26 E6 46 36N 13 53 E
Gaillac, *France* 20 E5 43 54N 1 54 E
Gaillimh = Galway, *Ireland* 15 C2 53 17N 9 3W
Gaillon, *France* 18 C8 49 10N 1 20 E
Gaines, *U.S.A.* 110 E7 41 46N 77 35W
Gainesville, *Fla., U.S.A.* 109 L4 29 40N 82 20W
Gainesville, *Ga., U.S.A.* 109 H4 34 18N 83 50W
Gainesville, *Mo., U.S.A.* 113 G8 36 36N 92 26W
Gainesville, *Tex., U.S.A.* 113 J6 33 38N 97 8W
Gainsborough, *U.K.* 12 D7 53 24N 0 46W
Gairdner, L., *Australia* 95 E2 31 30 S 136 0 E
Gairloch, L., *U.K.* 14 D3 57 43N 5 45W
Gaizhou, *China* 57 D12 40 22N 122 20 E
Gaj, *Croatia* 42 E2 45 28N 17 3 E
Gaj →, *Pakistan* 68 F2 26 26N 67 21 E
Gakuch, *Pakistan* 69 A5 36 7N 73 45 E
Galach, Gebel el, *Egypt* 80 J8 29 21N 32 22 E
Galán, Cerro, *Argentina* 126 B2 25 55 S 66 52W
Galana →, *Kenya* 86 C5 3 9 S 40 8 E
Galanta, *Slovak Rep.* 27 C10 48 11N 17 45 E
Galapagar, *Spain* 34 E7 40 36N 3 58W
Galápagos, *Pac. Oc.* 122 D1 0 0 91 0W
Galashiels, *U.K.* 14 F6 55 37N 2 49W
Galatás, *Greece* 38 D5 37 30N 23 26 E
Galați, *Romania* 43 E13 45 27N 28 2 E
Galați □, *Romania* 43 E12 45 45N 27 30 E
Galatia, *Turkey* 72 C5 39 30N 33 0 E
Galatina, *Italy* 31 B11 40 10N 18 10 E
Galátone, *Italy* 31 B11 40 9N 18 4 E
Galax, *U.S.A.* 109 G5 36 40N 80 56W
Galaxídhion, *Greece* 38 C4 38 22N 22 23 E
Galcaio, *Somali Rep.* 74 F4 6 30N 47 30 E
Galdhøpiggen, *Norway* 9 F12 61 38N 8 18 E
Galeana, *Chihuahua, Mexico* 118 A3 30 7N 107 38W
Galeana, *Nuevo León, Mexico* 118 A3 24 50N 100 4W
Galegu, *Sudan* 81 E4 12 36N 35 2 E
Galela, *Indonesia* 63 D7 1 50N 127 49 E
Galena, *U.S.A.* 100 B4 64 44N 156 56W
Galera, *Spain* 33 H2 37 45N 2 33W
Galera Point, *Trin. & Tob.* 121 D7 10 8N 61 0W
Galesburg, *U.S.A.* 112 E9 40 57N 90 22W
Galeton, *U.S.A.* 110 E7 41 44N 77 39W
Galga, *Ethiopia* 81 F4 6 39N 37 47 E
Gali, *Georgia* 49 J5 42 37N 41 46 E
Galicea Mare, *Romania* 43 F8 44 4N 23 19 E
Galich, *Russia* 48 A6 58 22N 42 24 E
Galiche, *Bulgaria* 40 C7 43 34N 23 53 E
Galicia □, *Spain* 34 C3 42 43N 7 45W
Galilee = Hagalil, *Israel* 75 C4 32 53N 35 18 E
Galilee, L., *Australia* 94 C4 22 20 S 145 50 E
Galilee, Sea of = Yam Kinneret, *Israel* 75 C4 32 45N 35 35 E
Galim, *Cameroon* 83 D7 7 6N 12 25 E
Galinoporni, *Cyprus* 36 D13 35 31N 34 18 E
Galion, *U.S.A.* 110 F2 40 44N 82 47W
Galiuro Mts., *U.S.A.* 115 K8 32 30N 110 20W
Galiwinku, *Australia* 94 A2 12 2 S 135 34 E
Gallabat, *Sudan* 81 E4 12 58N 36 11 E
Gallan Hd., *U.K.* 14 C1 58 15N 7 2W
Gallarate, *Italy* 28 C5 45 40N 8 48 E
Gallatin, *U.S.A.* 109 G2 36 24N 86 27W
Galle, *Sri Lanka* 66 R12 6 5N 80 10 E
Gállego →, *Spain* 32 D4 41 39N 0 51W
Gallegos →, *Argentina* 128 G3 51 35 S 69 0W
Galletti →, *Ethiopia* 81 F5 8 46N 41 10 E
Galley Hd., *Ireland* 15 E3 51 32N 8 55W
Galliate, *Italy* 28 C5 45 29N 8 42 E
Gallinas, Pta., *Colombia* 124 A4 12 28N 71 40W
Gallipoli = Gelibolu, *Turkey* 41 F10 40 28N 26 43 E
Gallípoli, *Italy* 31 B10 40 3N 17 58 E
Gallipolis, *U.S.A.* 108 F4 38 49N 82 12W
Gällivare, *Sweden* 8 C19 67 9N 20 40 E
Gallneukirchen, *Austria* 26 C7 48 21N 14 25 E
Gällö, *Sweden* 10 B9 62 55N 15 13 E
Gallo, C., *Italy* 30 D6 38 13N 13 19 E
Gallocanta, L. de, *Spain* 32 E3 40 58N 1 30W
Galloo I., *U.S.A.* 111 C8 43 55N 76 25W
Galloway, *U.K.* 14 F4 55 1N 4 29W
Galloway, Mull of, *U.K.* 14 G4 54 39N 4 52W
Gallup, *U.S.A.* 115 J9 35 32N 108 45W
Gallur, *Spain* 32 D3 41 52N 1 19W
Galoya, *Sri Lanka* 66 Q12 8 10N 80 55 E
Galt, *U.S.A.* 116 G5 38 15N 121 18W
Galten, *Denmark* 11 H3 56 9N 9 54 E
Galtür, *Austria* 26 E3 46 58N 10 11 E
Galty Mts., *Ireland* 15 D3 52 22N 8 10W
Galtymore, *Ireland* 15 D3 52 21N 8 11W
Galva, *U.S.A.* 112 E9 41 10N 90 3W
Galve de Sorbe, *Spain* 32 D1 41 13N 3 10W
Galveston, *U.S.A.* 113 L7 29 18N 94 48W
Galveston B., *U.S.A.* 113 L7 29 36N 94 50W
Gálvez, *Argentina* 126 C3 32 0 S 61 14W
Galway, *Ireland* 15 C2 53 17N 9 3W
Galway □, *Ireland* 15 C2 53 22N 9 1W
Galway B., *Ireland* 15 C2 53 13N 9 10W
Gam →, *Vietnam* 64 B5 21 55N 105 12 E
Gamagori, *Japan* 55 G8 34 50N 137 14 E
Gamari, L., *Ethiopia* 81 E5 11 32N 41 40 E
Gamawa, *Nigeria* 83 C7 12 10N 10 31 E
Gamay, *Phil.* 61 E6 12 23N 125 18 E
Gambaga, *Ghana* 83 C4 10 30N 0 28W
Gambat, *Pakistan* 68 F3 27 17N 68 26 E
Gambela, *Ethiopia* 81 F3 8 14N 34 38 E
Gambhir →, *India* 68 F6 26 58N 77 27 E
Gambia ■, *W. Afr.* 82 C1 13 25N 16 0W
Gambia →, *W. Afr.* 82 C1 13 28N 16 34W
Gambier, *U.S.A.* 110 F2 40 22N 82 23W
Gambier, C., *Australia* 92 B5 11 56 S 130 57 E
Gambier Is., *Australia* 95 F2 35 3 S 136 30 E
Gambo, *Canada* 103 C9 48 47N 54 13W
Gamboli, *Pakistan* 68 E3 29 53N 68 24 E
Gamboma, *Congo* 84 E3 1 55 S 15 52 E
Gamka →, *S. Africa* 88 E3 33 18 S 21 39 E
Gamkab →, *Namibia* 88 D2 28 4 S 17 54 E
Gamla Uppsala, *Sweden* 10 E11 59 54N 17 40 E
Gamlakarleby = Kokkola, *Finland* 8 E20 63 50N 23 8 E
Gamleby, *Sweden* 11 G10 57 54N 16 24 E
Gammon →, *Canada* 105 C9 51 24N 95 44W
Gamo-Gofa □, *Ethiopia* 81 F4 5 40N 36 40 E
Gamou, *Niger* 83 C6 14 20N 9 55 E
Gamtoos →, *S. Africa* 88 E4 33 58 S 25 1 E
Gan, *France* 20 E3 43 12N 0 27W
Gan Goriama, Mts., *Cameroon* 83 D7 7 44N 12 45 E
Gan Jiang →, *China* 59 C11 29 15N 116 0 E
Ganado, *U.S.A.* 115 J9 35 43N 109 33W
Gananita, *Sudan* 80 D3 18 22N 33 50 E
Gananoque, *Canada* 102 D4 44 20N 76 10W
Ganāveh, *Iran* 71 D6 29 35N 50 35 E
Gäncä, *Azerbaijan* 49 K8 40 45N 46 20 E
Gancheng, *China* 64 C7 18 51N 108 37 E
Gand = Gent, *Belgium* 17 C3 51 2N 3 42 E
Ganda, *Angola* 85 G2 13 3 S 14 35 E
Gandajika, *Dem. Rep. of the Congo* 84 F4 6 46 S 23 57 E
Gandak →, *India* 69 G11 25 39N 85 13 E
Gandava, *Pakistan* 68 E2 28 32N 67 32 E
Gander, *Canada* 103 C9 48 58N 54 35W
Gander L., *Canada* 103 C9 48 58N 54 35W
Ganderkesee, *Germany* 24 B4 53 2N 8 32 E
Ganderowe Falls, *Zimbabwe* 87 F2 17 20 S 29 10 E
Gandesa, *Spain* 32 D5 41 3N 0 26 E
Gandhi Sagar, *India* 68 G6 24 40N 75 40 E
Gandhinagar, *India* 68 H5 23 15N 72 45 E
Gandi, *Nigeria* 83 C6 12 55N 5 49 E
Gandía, *Spain* 33 G4 38 58N 0 9W
Gandino, *Italy* 28 C6 45 49N 9 54 E
Gando, Pta., *Canary Is.* 37 G4 27 55N 15 22W
Gandole, *Nigeria* 83 D7 8 28N 11 35 E
Gâneb, *Mauritania* 82 B2 18 29N 10 8W
Ganedidalem = Gani, *Indonesia* 63 E7 0 48 S 128 14 E
Ganetti, *Sudan* 80 D3 18 0N 31 10 E
Ganga →, *India* 69 H14 23 20N 90 30 E
Ganga Sagar, *India* 69 J13 21 38N 88 5 E
Gangafani, *Mali* 82 C4 14 20N 2 20W
Gangan →, *India* 69 E8 28 38N 78 58 E
Ganganagar, *India* 68 E5 29 56N 73 56 E
Gangapur, *India* 68 F7 26 32N 76 49 E
Gangara, *Niger* 83 C6 14 35N 8 29 E
Gangaw, *Burma* 67 H19 22 5N 94 5 E
Gangdisê Shan, *China* 67 D12 31 20N 81 0 E
Ganges = Ganga →, *India* 69 H14 23 20N 90 30 E
Ganges, *Canada* 104 D4 48 51N 123 31W
Ganges, *France* 20 E7 43 56N 3 42 E
Ganges, Mouths of the, *India* 69 J14 21 30N 90 0 E
Gånghester, *Sweden* 11 G7 57 42N 13 1 E
Gangi, *Italy* 31 E7 37 48N 14 12 E
Gângiova, *Romania* 43 G8 43 54N 23 50 E
Gangoh, *India* 68 E7 29 46N 77 18 E
Gangroti, *India* 69 D8 30 50N 79 10 E
Gangtok, *India* 67 F16 27 20N 88 37 E
Gangu, *China* 56 G3 34 40N 105 15 E
Gangyao, *China* 57 B14 44 12N 126 37 E
Gani, *Indonesia* 63 E7 0 48 S 128 14 E
Ganj, *India* 69 F8 27 45N 78 57 E
Ganluc, *China* 58 C4 28 58N 102 59 E
Gannat, *France* 19 F10 46 7N 3 11 E
Gannett Peak, *U.S.A.* 114 E9 43 11N 109 39W
Ganquan, *China* 56 F5 36 20N 109 20 E
Gänserdorf, *Austria* 27 C9 48 20N 16 43 E
Ganshui, *China* 58 C6 28 40N 106 40 E
Gansu □, *China* 56 G3 36 0N 104 0 E
Ganta, *Liberia* 82 D3 7 15N 8 59W
Gantheaume, C., *Australia* 95 F2 36 4 S 137 32 E
Gantheaume B., *Australia* 93 E1 27 40 S 114 10 E
Gantsevichi = Hantsavichy, *Belarus* 47 F4 52 49N 26 30 E
Ganye, *Nigeria* 83 D7 8 25N 12 4 E
Ganyem = Genyem, *Indonesia* 63 E10 2 46 S 140 12 E
Ganyu, *China* 57 G10 34 50N 119 8 E
Ganyushkino, *Kazakstan* 49 G9 46 35N 49 20 E
Ganzhou, *China* 59 E10 25 51N 114 56 E
Gao, *Mali* 83 B4 16 15N 0 5W
Gao Xian, *China* 58 C5 28 21N 104 32 E
Gao'an, *China* 59 C10 28 26N 115 17 E
Gaochun, *China* 59 B12 31 20N 118 49 E
Gaohe, *China* 59 F9 22 46N 112 57 E
Gaohebu, *China* 59 B11 30 43N 116 49 E
Gaokeng, *China* 59 D9 27 40N 113 58 E
Gaolan Dao, *China* 59 G9 21 55N 113 10 E
Gaoligong Shan, *China* 58 E2 24 45N 98 45 E
Gaomi, *China* 57 F10 36 20N 119 42 E
Gaoming, *China* 59 F9 36 9N 113 1 E
Gaoping, *China* 56 G7 35 45N 112 55 E
Gaotang, *China* 56 F9 36 50N 116 15 E
Gaoua, *Burkina Faso* 82 C4 10 20N 3 8W
Gaoual, *Guinea* 82 C2 11 45N 13 25W
Gaoxiong = Kaohsiung, *Taiwan* 59 F13 22 35N 120 16 E
Gaoyang, *China* 56 E8 38 40N 115 45 E
Gaoyao, *China* 59 F9 23 3N 112 27 E
Gaoyou, *China* 59 A12 32 47N 119 26 E
Gaoyou Hu, *China* 57 H10 32 45N 119 20 E
Gaoyuan, *China* 57 F9 37 8N 117 58 E
Gaozhou, *China* 59 G8 21 58N 110 50 E
Gap, *France* 21 D10 44 33N 6 5 E
Gapan, *Phil.* 61 D4 15 19N 120 57 E
Gapat →, *India* 69 G10 24 30N 82 28 E
Gapuwiyak, *Australia* 94 A2 12 25 S 135 43 E
Gar, *China* 60 C2 32 10N 79 58 E
Garabogazköl Aylagy, *Turkmenistan* 50 E6 41 0N 53 30 E
Garachico, *Canary Is.* 37 F3 28 22N 16 46W
Garachiné, *Panama* 120 E4 8 0N 78 12W
Garafia, *Canary Is.* 37 F2 28 48N 17 57W
Garah, *Australia* 95 D4 29 5 S 149 38 E
Garajonay, *Canary Is.* 37 F2 28 7N 17 14W
Garango, *Burkina Faso* 83 C4 11 48N 0 34W
Garanhuns, *Brazil* 125 E11 8 50 S 36 30W
Garautha, *India* 69 G8 25 34N 79 18 E
Garawe, *Liberia* 82 E3 4 35N 8 0W
Garba Tula, *Kenya* 86 B4 0 30N 38 32 E
Garberville, *U.S.A.* 114 F2 40 6N 123 48W
Garbiyang, *India* 69 D9 30 8N 80 54 E
Garbsen, *Germany* 24 C5 52 26N 9 31 E
Gard □, *France* 21 D8 44 2N 4 10 E
Gard →, *France* 21 E8 43 51N 4 37 E
Garda, L. di, *Italy* 28 C7 45 40N 10 41 E
Gardanne, *France* 21 E9 43 27N 5 27 E
Gårdby, *Sweden* 11 H10 56 36N 16 38 E
Garde L., *Canada* 105 A7 62 50N 106 13W
Gardelegen, *Germany* 24 C7 52 32N 11 24 E
Garden City, *Ga., U.S.A.* 109 J5 32 6N 81 9W
Garden City, *Kans., U.S.A.* 113 G4 37 58N 100 53W
Garden City, *Tex., U.S.A.* 113 K4 31 52N 101 29W
Garden Grove, *U.S.A.* 117 M9 33 47N 117 55W
Gardēz, *Afghan.* 68 C3 33 37N 69 9 E
Gardhíki, *Greece* 38 C3 38 50N 21 55 E
Gardiner, *Maine, U.S.A.* 109 C11 44 14N 69 47W
Gardiner, *Mont., U.S.A.* 114 D8 45 2N 110 22W
Gardiners I., *U.S.A.* 111 E12 41 6N 72 6W
Gardner, *U.S.A.* 111 D13 42 34N 71 59W
Gardner Canal, *Canada* 104 C3 53 27N 128 8W
Gardnerville, *U.S.A.* 116 G7 38 56N 119 45W
Gardno, Jezioro, *Poland* 44 D4 54 40N 17 7 E
Gardo, *Somali Rep.* 74 F4 9 30N 49 6 E
Gardone Val Trómpia, *Italy* 28 C7 45 41N 10 11 E
Gárdony, *Hungary* 42 C3 47 12N 18 39 E
Garešnica, *Croatia* 29 C13 45 36N 16 56 E
Garéssio, *Italy* 28 D5 44 12N 8 2 E
Garey, *U.S.A.* 117 L6 34 53N 120 19W
Garfield, *U.S.A.* 114 C5 47 1N 117 9W
Garforth, *U.K.* 12 D6 53 47N 1 24W
Gargaliánoi, *Greece* 38 D3 37 4N 21 38 E
Gargan, Mt., *France* 20 C5 45 37N 1 39 E
Gargouna, *Mali* 83 B5 15 56N 0 13 E
Gargždai, *Lithuania* 44 C8 55 43N 21 24 E
Garibaldi Prov. Park, *Canada* 104 D4 49 50N 122 40W
Gariep, L., *S. Africa* 88 E4 30 40 S 25 40 E
Garies, *S. Africa* 88 E2 30 32 S 17 59 E
Garigliano →, *Italy* 30 A6 41 13N 13 45 E
Garissa, *Kenya* 86 C4 0 25 S 39 40 E
Garkida, *Nigeria* 83 C7 10 27N 12 36 E
Garko, *Nigeria* 83 C6 11 45N 8 35 E
Garland, *Tex., U.S.A.* 113 J6 32 55N 96 38W
Garland, *Utah, U.S.A.* 114 F7 41 47N 112 10W
Garlasco, *Italy* 28 C5 45 12N 8 55 E
Garliava, *Lithuania* 44 D10 54 49N 23 52 E
Garlin, *France* 20 E3 43 33N 0 16W
Garm, *Tajikistan* 50 F8 39 0N 70 20 E
Garmāb, *Iran* 71 C8 35 25N 56 45 E
Garmisch-Partenkirchen, *Germany* 25 H7 47 30N 11 6 E
Garmsār, *Iran* 71 C7 35 20N 52 25 E
Garner, *U.S.A.* 112 D8 43 6N 93 36W
Garnett, *U.S.A.* 112 F7 38 17N 95 14W
Garo Hills, *India* 69 G14 25 30N 90 30 E
Garoe, *Somali Rep.* 74 F4 8 25N 48 33 E
Garonne →, *France* 20 C3 45 2N 0 36W
Garonne, Canal Latéral à la, *France* 20 D4 44 15N 0 18 E
Garot, *India* 68 G6 24 19N 75 41 E
Garoua, *Cameroon* 83 D7 9 19N 13 21 E
Garpenberg, *Sweden* 10 D10 60 19N 16 12 E
Garphyttan, *Sweden* 10 E8 59 18N 14 56 E
Garrauli, *India* 69 G8 25 5N 79 22 E
Garrel, *Germany* 24 C4 52 57N 8 1 E
Garrigue = Garrigues, *France* 20 E7 43 40N 3 55 E
Garrigues, *France* 20 E7 43 40N 3 55 E
Garrison, *Mont., U.S.A.* 114 C7 46 31N 112 49W
Garrison, *N. Dak., U.S.A.* 112 B4 47 40N 101 25W
Garrison Res. = Sakakawea, L., *U.S.A.* 112 B4 47 30N 101 25W
Garron Pt., *U.K.* 15 A6 55 3N 5 59W
Garrovillas, *Spain* 35 F4 39 40N 6 33W
Garrucha, *Spain* 33 H3 37 11N 1 49W
Garry →, *U.K.* 14 E5 56 44N 3 47W
Garry, L., *Canada* 100 B9 65 58N 100 18W
Garsen, *Kenya* 86 C5 2 20 S 40 5 E
Gärsnäs, *Sweden* 11 J8 55 32N 14 10 E
Garson L., *Canada* 105 B6 56 19N 110 2W
Gartempe →, *France* 20 B4 46 47N 0 49 E
Gartz, *Germany* 24 B10 53 13N 14 22 E
Garu, *Ghana* 83 C4 10 55N 0 11W
Garu, *India* 69 H11 23 40N 84 14 E
Garub, *Namibia* 88 D2 26 37 S 16 0 E
Garut, *Indonesia* 63 G12 7 14 S 107 53 E
Garvão, *Portugal* 35 H2 37 42N 8 21W
Garvie Mts., *N.Z.* 91 L2 45 30 S 168 50 E
Garwa = Garoua, *Cameroon* 83 D7 9 19N 13 21 E
Garwa, *India* 69 G10 24 11N 83 47 E
Garwolin, *Poland* 45 G8 51 55N 21 38 E
Gary, *U.S.A.* 108 E2 41 36N 87 20W
Garz, *Germany* 24 A9 54 19N 13 20 E
Garzê, *China* 58 B3 31 38N 100 1 E
Garzón, *Colombia* 124 C3 2 10N 75 40W
Gas-San, *Japan* 54 E10 38 32N 140 1 E
Gasan Kuli = Esenguly, *Turkmenistan* 50 F6 37 37N 53 59 E
Gascogne, *France* 20 E4 43 45N 0 20 E
Gascogne, G. de, *Europe* 20 E2 44 0N 2 0W
Gascony = Gascogne, *France* 20 E4 43 45N 0 20 E
Gascoyne →, *Australia* 93 D1 24 52 S 113 37 E
Gascoyne Junction, *Australia* 93 E2 25 2 S 115 17 E
Gascueña, *Spain* 32 E2 40 18N 2 31W
Gash, Wadi →, *Ethiopia* 81 D4 16 48N 35 51 E
Gashagar, *Nigeria* 83 C7 13 22N 12 47 E
Gashaka, *Nigeria* 83 D7 7 20N 11 29 E
Gasherbrum, *Pakistan* 69 B7 35 40N 76 40 E
Gashua, *Nigeria* 83 C7 12 54N 11 0 E
Gaspé, *Canada* 103 C7 48 52N 64 30W
Gaspé, C. de, *Canada* 103 C7 48 48N 64 7W
Gaspé, Pén. de, *Canada* 103 C6 48 45N 65 40W
Gaspésie, Parc de Conservation de la, *Canada* 103 C6 48 55N 65 50W
Gassan, *Burkina Faso* 82 C4 12 49N 3 12W
Gassol, *Nigeria* 83 D7 8 34N 10 25 E
Gasteiz = Vitoria-Gasteiz, *Spain* 32 C2 42 50N 2 41W
Gastonia, *U.S.A.* 109 H5 35 16N 81 11W
Gastoúni, *Greece* 38 D3 37 51N 21 15 E
Gastoúri, *Greece* 38 B1 39 34N 19 54 E
Gastre, *Argentina* 128 E3 42 20 S 69 15W
Gästrikland, *Sweden* 10 D10 60 45N 16 40 E
Gata, C., *Cyprus* 36 E12 34 34N 33 2 E
Gata, C. de, *Spain* 33 J2 36 41N 2 13W
Gata, Sierra de, *Spain* 34 E4 40 20N 6 45W
Gataga →, *Canada* 104 B3 58 35N 126 59W
Gătaia, *Romania* 42 E6 45 26N 21 30 E
Gatchina, *Russia* 46 C6 59 35N 30 9 E
Gatehouse of Fleet, *U.K.* 14 G4 54 53N 4 12W
Gates, *U.S.A.* 110 C7 43 9N 77 42W
Gateshead, *U.K.* 12 C6 54 57N 1 35W
Gatesville, *U.S.A.* 113 K6 31 26N 97 45W
Gaths, *Zimbabwe* 87 G3 20 2 S 30 32 E
Gatico, *Chile* 126 A1 22 29 S 70 20W
Gâtinais, *France* 19 D9 48 5N 2 40 E
Gâtine, Hauteurs de, *France* 20 B3 46 35N 0 45W
Gatineau, *Canada* 111 A9 45 29N 75 38W
Gatineau →, *Canada* 102 C4 45 27N 75 42W
Gatineau, Parc Nat. de la, *Canada* 102 C4 45 40N 76 0W
Gattaran, *Phil.* 61 B4 18 4N 121 38 E
Gattinara, *Italy* 28 C5 45 37N 8 22 E
Gatton, *Australia* 95 D5 27 32 S 152 17 E
Gatun, L., *Panama* 120 E4 9 7N 79 56W
Gatyana, *S. Africa* 89 E4 32 16 S 28 31 E
Gau, *Fiji* 91 D8 18 2 S 179 18 E
Gaucín, *Spain* 35 J5 36 31N 5 19W
Gauer L., *Canada* 105 B9 57 0N 97 50W
Gauhati, *India* 67 F17 26 10N 91 45 E
Gauja →, *Latvia* 9 H21 57 10N 24 16 E
Gaula →, *Norway* 8 E14 63 21N 10 14 E
Gauri Phanta, *India* 69 E9 28 41N 80 36 E
Gausta, *Norway* 9 G13 59 48N 8 40 E
Gauteng □, *S. Africa* 89 D4 26 0 S 28 0 E
Gāv Koshī, *Iran* 71 D8 28 38N 57 12 E
Gāvakān, *Iran* 71 D7 29 37N 53 10 E
Gavarnie, *France* 20 F3 42 44N 0 1W
Gavāter, *Iran* 71 E9 25 10N 61 31 E
Gāvbandī, *Iran* 71 E7 27 12N 53 4 E
Gavdhopoúla, *Greece* 36 E6 34 56N 24 0 E
Gávdhos, *Greece* 36 E6 34 50N 24 5 E
Gavi, *Italy* 28 D5 44 41N 8 49 E
Gavião, *Portugal* 35 F3 39 28N 7 56W

Gaviota, U.S.A. 117 L6 34 29N 120 13W
Gāvkhūnī, Bāţlāq-e, Iran 71 C7 32 6N 52 52 E
Gävle, Sweden 10 D11 60 40N 17 9 E
Gävleborgs län □, Sweden 10 C10 61 30N 16 15 E
Gävlebukten, Sweden 10 D11 60 40N 17 20 E
Gavorrano, Italy 28 F7 42 55N 10 54 E
Gavray, France 18 D5 48 55N 1 20W
Gavrilov Yam, Russia 46 D10 57 18N 39 49 E
Gávrion, Greece 38 D6 37 54N 24 44 E
Gawachab, Namibia 88 D2 27 4 S 17 55 E
Gawilgarh Hills, India 66 J10 21 15N 76 45 E
Gawler, Australia 95 E2 34 30 S 138 42 E
Gawu, Nigeria 83 D6 9 14N 6 52 E
Gaxun Nur, China 60 B5 42 22N 100 30 E
Gaya, India 69 G11 24 47N 85 4 E
Gaya, Niger 83 C5 11 52N 3 28 E
Gaya, Nigeria 83 C6 11 57N 9 0 E
Gayéri, Burkina Faso 83 C5 12 39N 0 29 E
Gaylord, U.S.A. 108 C3 45 2N 84 41W
Gayndah, Australia 95 D5 25 35 S 151 32 E
Gaysin = Haysyn, Ukraine 47 H5 48 57N 29 25 E
Gayvoron = Hayvoron, Ukraine 47 H5 48 22N 29 52 E
Gaza, Gaza Strip 75 D3 31 30N 34 28 E
Gaza □, Mozam. 89 C5 23 10 S 32 45 E
Gaza Strip □, Asia 75 D3 31 29N 34 25 E
Gazanjyk, Turkmenistan 71 B7 39 16N 55 32 E
Gazaoua, Niger 83 C6 13 32N 7 55 E
Gāzbor, Iran 71 D8 28 5N 58 51 E
Gazi, Dem. Rep. of the Congo 86 B1 1 3N 24 30 E
Gaziantep, Turkey 70 B3 37 6N 37 23 E
Gazipaşa, Turkey 72 D5 36 16N 32 18 E
Gbarnga, Liberia 82 D3 7 19N 9 13W
Gbekebo, Nigeria 83 D5 6 20N 4 56 E
Gboko, Nigeria 83 D6 7 17N 9 4 E
Gbongan, Nigeria 83 D5 7 28N 4 20 E
Gcoverega, Botswana 88 B3 19 8 S 24 18 E
Gcuwa, S. Africa 89 E4 32 20 S 28 11 E
Gdańsk, Poland 44 D5 54 22N 18 40 E
Gdańska, Zatoka, Poland 44 D6 54 30N 19 20 E
Gdov, Russia 9 G22 58 48N 27 55 E
Gdynia, Poland 44 D5 54 35N 18 33 E
Geba →, Guinea-Biss. 82 C1 11 46N 15 36W
Gebe, Indonesia 63 D7 0 5N 129 25 E
Gebeciler, Turkey 39 C12 38 46N 30 46 E
Gebeit Mine, Sudan 80 C4 21 3N 36 29 E
Gebel Abyad, Sudan 80 D2 19 0N 28 0 E
Gebel Iweibid, Egypt 80 H8 30 8N 32 13 E
Gebze, Turkey 41 F13 40 47N 29 25 E
Gecha, Ethiopia 81 F4 7 30N 35 18 E
Gedaref, Sudan 81 E4 14 2N 35 28 E
Gedaref □, Sudan 81 E4 14 0N 35 0 E
Gediz, Turkey 39 B11 39 1N 29 24 E
Gediz →, Turkey 39 C8 38 35N 26 48 E
Gedo, Ethiopia 81 F4 9 2N 37 25 E
Gèdre, France 20 F4 42 47N 0 2 E
Gedser, Denmark 11 K5 54 35N 11 55 E
Geegully Cr. →, Australia 92 C3 18 32 S 123 41 E
Geel, Belgium 17 C4 51 10N 4 59 E
Geelong, Australia 95 F3 38 10 S 144 22 E
Geelvink B. = Cenderwasih, Teluk, Indonesia 63 E9 3 0 S 135 20 E
Geelvink Chan., Australia 93 E1 28 30 S 114 0 E
Geesthacht, Germany 24 B6 53 26N 10 22 E
Geidam, Nigeria 83 C7 12 57N 11 57 E
Geikie →, Canada 105 B8 57 45N 103 52W
Geilenkirchen, Germany 24 E2 50 57N 6 8 E
Geili, Sudan 81 D3 16 1N 32 37 E
Geisingen, Germany 25 H4 47 54N 8 38 E
Geislingen, Germany 25 G5 48 37N 9 50 E
Geistown, U.S.A. 110 F6 40 18N 78 52W
Geita, Tanzania 86 C3 2 48 S 32 12 E
Gejiu, China 58 F4 23 20N 103 10 E
Gel →, Sudan 81 F2 7 5N 29 10 E
Gel, Meydān-e, Iran 71 D7 29 4N 54 50 E
Gel River, Sudan 81 F2 7 5N 29 10 E
Gela, Italy 31 E7 37 4N 14 15 E
Gela, G. di, Italy 31 F7 37 0N 14 20 E
Gelahun, Liberia 82 D2 7 55N 10 28W
Gelderland □, Neths. 17 B6 52 5N 6 10 E
Geldern, Germany 24 D2 51 31N 6 20 E
Geldrop, Neths. 17 C5 51 25N 5 32 E
Geleen, Neths. 17 D5 50 57N 5 49 E
Gelehun, S. Leone 82 D2 8 20N 11 40W
Gelembe, Turkey 39 B9 39 10N 27 50 E
Gelemso, Ethiopia 81 F5 8 49N 40 31 E
Gelendost, Turkey 72 C4 38 7N 31 1 E
Gelendzhik, Russia 47 K10 44 33N 38 10 E
Gelibolu, Turkey 41 F10 40 28N 26 43 E
Gelibolu Yarımadası, Turkey 41 F10 40 20N 26 30 E
Gelidonya Burnu, Turkey 72 D4 36 12N 30 24 E
Gelnhausen, Germany 25 E5 50 11N 9 11 E
Gelnica, Slovak Rep. 27 C13 48 51N 20 55 E
Gelsenkirchen, Germany 24 D3 51 32N 7 6 E
Gelting, Germany 24 A5 54 45N 9 53 E
Gemas, Malaysia 65 L4 2 37N 102 36 E
Gembloux, Belgium 17 D4 50 34N 4 43 E
Gembu, Nigeria 83 D7 6 42N 11 10 E
Gemena, Dem. Rep. of the Congo 84 D3 3 13N 19 48 E
Gemerek, Turkey 70 B3 39 15N 36 10 E
Gemla, Sweden 11 H8 56 52N 14 39 E
Gemlik, Turkey 41 F13 40 26N 29 9 E
Gemlik Körfezi, Turkey 41 F12 40 25N 28 55 E
Gemona del Friuli, Italy 29 B10 46 16N 13 9 E
Gemsa, Egypt 80 B3 27 39N 33 35 E
Gemünden, Germany 25 E5 50 3N 9 42 E
Genale →, Ethiopia 81 F4 6 2N 39 1 E
Genç, Turkey 73 C9 38 44N 40 34 E
Gençay, France 20 B4 46 23N 0 23 E
Geneina, Gebel, Egypt 80 B3 29 2N 33 55 E
General Acha, Argentina 126 D3 37 20 S 64 38W
General Alvear, Buenos Aires, Argentina 126 D4 36 0 S 60 0W
General Alvear, Mendoza, Argentina 126 D2 35 0 S 67 40W
General Artigas, Paraguay 126 B4 26 52 S 56 16W
General Belgrano, Argentina 126 D4 36 35 S 58 47W
General Cabrera, Argentina 126 C3 32 53 S 63 52W
General Cepeda, Mexico 118 B4 25 23N 101 27W
General Guido, Argentina 126 D4 36 40 S 57 50W
General Juan Madariaga, Argentina 126 D4 37 0 S 57 0W
General La Madrid, Argentina 126 D3 37 17 S 61 20W
General MacArthur, Phil. 61 F6 11 18N 125 28 E
General Martin Miguel de Güemes, Argentina 126 A3 24 50 S 65 0W
General Paz, Argentina 126 B4 27 45 S 57 36W
General Pico, Argentina 126 D3 35 45 S 63 50W
General Pinedo, Argentina 126 B3 27 15 S 61 20W
General Pinto, Argentina 126 C3 34 45 S 61 50W
General Roca, Argentina 128 D3 39 2 S 67 35W
General Santos, Phil. 61 H6 6 5N 125 14 E
General Toshevo, Bulgaria 41 C12 43 42N 28 6 E
General Trevino, Mexico 119 B5 26 14N 99 29W
General Trías, Mexico 118 B3 28 21N 106 22W
General Viamonte, Argentina 126 D3 35 1 S 61 3W
General Villegas, Argentina 126 D3 35 5 S 63 0W
Genesee, Idaho, U.S.A. 114 C5 46 33N 116 56W
Genesee, Pa., U.S.A. 110 E7 41 59N 77 54W
Genesee →, U.S.A. 110 C7 43 16N 77 36W
Geneseo, Ill., U.S.A. 112 E9 41 27N 90 9W
Geneseo, N.Y., U.S.A. 110 D7 42 48N 77 49W
Geneva = Genève, Switz. 25 J2 46 12N 6 9 E
Geneva, Ala., U.S.A. 109 K3 31 2N 85 52W
Geneva, N.Y., U.S.A. 110 D8 42 52N 76 59W
Geneva, Nebr., U.S.A. 112 E6 40 32N 97 36W
Geneva, Ohio, U.S.A. 110 E4 41 48N 80 57W
Geneva, L. = Léman, L., Europe 19 F13 46 26N 6 30 E
Geneva, L., U.S.A. 108 D1 42 38N 88 30W
Genève, Switz. 25 J2 46 12N 6 9 E
Gengenbach, Germany 25 G4 48 24N 8 1 E
Gengma, China 58 F2 23 32N 99 20 E
Genichesk = Henichesk, Ukraine 47 J8 46 12N 34 50 E
Genil →, Spain 35 H5 37 42N 5 19W
Genk, Belgium 17 D5 50 58N 5 32 E
Genlis, France 19 E12 47 11N 5 12 E
Gennargentu, Mti. del, Italy 30 B2 40 1N 9 19 E
Gennes, France 18 E6 47 20N 0 17W
Genoa = Génova, Italy 28 D5 44 25N 8 57 E
Genoa, Australia 95 F4 37 29 S 149 35 E
Genoa, N.Y., U.S.A. 111 D8 42 40N 76 32W
Genoa, Nebr., U.S.A. 112 E6 41 27N 97 44W
Genoa, Nev., U.S.A. 116 F7 39 2N 119 50W
Génova, Italy 28 D5 44 25N 8 57 E
Génova, G. di, Italy 28 E6 44 0N 9 0 E
Genriyetty, Ostrov, Russia 51 B16 77 6N 156 30 E
Gent, Belgium 17 C3 51 2N 3 42 E
Genteng, Indonesia 63 G12 7 22 S 106 24 E
Genthin, Germany 24 C8 52 25N 12 9 E
Genyem, Indonesia 63 E10 2 46 S 140 12 E
Genzano di Lucánia, Italy 31 B9 40 51N 16 2 E
Genzano di Roma, Italy 29 G9 41 42N 12 41 E
Geoagiu, Romania 43 E8 45 55N 23 12 E
Geographe B., Australia 93 F2 33 30 S 115 15 E
Geographe Chan., Australia 93 D1 24 30 S 113 0 E
Geokchay = Göyçay, Azerbaijan 49 K8 40 42N 47 43 E
Georga, Zemlya, Russia 50 A5 80 30N 49 0 E
George, S. Africa 88 E3 33 58 S 22 29 E
George →, Canada 103 A6 58 49N 66 10W
George, L., N.S.W., Australia 95 F4 35 10 S 149 25 E
George, L., S. Austral., Australia 95 F3 37 25 S 140 0 E
George, L., W. Austral., Australia 92 D3 22 45 S 123 40 E
George, L., Uganda 86 B3 0 5N 30 10 E
George, L., Fla., U.S.A. 109 L5 29 17N 81 36W
George, L., N.Y., U.S.A. 111 C11 43 37N 73 33W
George Gill Ra., Australia 92 D5 24 22 S 131 45 E
George River = Kangiqsualujjuaq, Canada 101 C13 58 30N 65 59W
George Sound, N.Z. 91 L1 44 52 S 167 25 E
George Town, Australia 94 G4 41 6 S 146 49 E
George Town, Bahamas 120 B4 23 33N 75 47W
George Town, Malaysia 65 K3 5 25N 100 15 E
George V Land, Antarctica 5 C10 69 0 S 148 0 E
George VI Sound, Antarctica 5 D17 71 0 S 68 0W
George West, U.S.A. 113 L5 28 20N 98 7W
Georgetown, Australia 94 B3 18 17 S 143 33 E
Georgetown, Ont., Canada 102 D4 43 40N 79 56W
Georgetown, P.E.I., Canada 103 C7 46 13N 62 24W
Georgetown, Cayman Is. 120 C3 19 20N 81 24W
Georgetown, Gambia 82 C2 13 30N 14 47W
Georgetown, Guyana 124 B7 6 50N 58 12W
Georgetown, Calif., U.S.A. 116 G6 38 54N 120 50W
Georgetown, Colo., U.S.A. 114 G11 39 42N 105 42W
Georgetown, Ky., U.S.A. 108 F3 38 13N 84 33W
Georgetown, N.Y., U.S.A. 111 D9 42 46N 75 44W
Georgetown, Ohio, U.S.A. 108 F4 38 52N 83 54W
Georgetown, S.C., U.S.A. 109 J6 33 23N 79 17W
Georgetown, Tex., U.S.A. 113 K6 30 38N 97 41W
Georgia □, U.S.A. 109 K5 32 50N 83 15W
Georgia ■, Asia 49 J6 42 0N 43 0 E
Georgia, Str. of, Canada 104 D4 49 25N 124 0W
Georgian B., Canada 102 C3 45 15N 81 0W
Georgina →, Australia 94 C2 23 30 S 139 47 E
Georgina I., Canada 110 B5 44 22N 79 17W
Georgiu-Dezh = Liski, Russia 47 G10 51 3N 39 30 E
Georgiyevsk, Russia 49 H6 44 12N 43 28 E
Georgsmarienhütte, Germany 24 C4 52 13N 8 3 E
Gera, Germany 24 E8 50 53N 12 4 E
Geraardsbergen, Belgium 17 D3 50 45N 3 53 E
Geral, Serra, Brazil 127 B6 26 25 S 50 0W
Geral de Goiás, Serra, Brazil 125 F9 12 0 S 46 0W
Geraldine, U.S.A. 114 C8 47 36N 110 16W
Geraldton, Australia 93 E1 28 48 S 114 32 E
Geraldton, Canada 102 C2 49 44N 86 59W
Gérardmer, France 19 D13 48 3N 6 50 E
Gercüş, Turkey 73 D9 37 34N 41 23 E
Gerede, Turkey 72 B5 40 45N 32 10 E
Gerês, Sierra do, Portugal 34 D3 41 48N 8 0W
Gereshk, Afghan. 66 D4 31 47N 64 35 E
Geretsried, Germany 25 H7 47 51N 11 28 E
Gérgal, Spain 33 H2 37 7N 2 31W
Gerik, Malaysia 65 K3 5 50N 101 15 E
Gering, U.S.A. 112 E3 41 50N 103 40W
Gerlach, U.S.A. 114 F4 40 39N 119 21W
Gerlachovský štit, Slovak Rep. 27 B13 49 11N 20 7 E
German Planina, Macedonia 40 D6 42 20N 22 0 E
Germansen Landing, Canada 104 B4 55 43N 124 40W
Germantown, U.S.A. 113 M10 35 5N 89 49W
Germany ■, Europe 24 E6 51 0N 10 0 E
Germencik, Turkey 39 D9 37 52N 27 37 E
Germering, Germany 25 G7 48 8N 11 22 E
Germersheim, Germany 25 F4 49 12N 8 22 E
Germī, Iran 71 B6 39 1N 48 3 E
Germiston, S. Africa 89 D4 26 15 S 28 10 E
Gernika-Lumo, Spain 32 B2 43 19N 2 40W
Gernsheim, Germany 25 F4 49 45N 8 30 E
Gero, Japan 55 G8 35 48N 137 14 E
Gerolzhofen, Germany 25 F6 49 54N 10 21 E
Gerona = Girona, Spain 32 D7 41 58N 2 46 E
Gerrard, Canada 104 C5 50 30N 117 17W
Gers □, France 20 E4 43 35N 0 30 E
Gers →, France 20 D4 44 9N 0 39 E
Gersfeld, Germany 24 E5 50 27N 9 56 E
Gersthofen, Germany 25 G6 48 25N 10 53 E
Gerzat, France 20 C7 45 48N 3 8 E
Gerze, Turkey 72 B6 41 48N 35 12 E
Geseke, Germany 24 D4 51 38N 8 31 E
Geser, Indonesia 63 E8 3 50 S 130 54 E
Gesso →, Italy 28 D4 44 24N 7 33 E
Gestro, Wabi →, Ethiopia 81 G5 4 12N 42 2 E
Getafe, Spain 34 E7 40 18N 3 44W
Getinge, Sweden 11 H6 56 49N 12 44 E
Gettysburg, Pa., U.S.A. 108 F7 39 50N 77 14W
Gettysburg, S. Dak., U.S.A. 112 C5 45 1N 99 57W
Getxo, Spain 32 B2 43 21N 2 59W
Getz Ice Shelf, Antarctica 5 D14 75 0 S 130 0W
Gevaş, Turkey 73 C10 38 15N 43 6 E
Gévaudan, France 20 D7 44 40N 3 40 E
Gevgelija, Macedonia 40 E6 41 9N 22 30 E
Gévora →, Spain 35 G4 38 53N 6 57W
Gewani, Ethiopia 81 E5 10 12N 40 40 E
Gex, France 19 F13 46 21N 6 3 E
Geyikli, Turkey 39 B8 39 48N 26 12 E
Geyser, U.S.A. 114 C8 47 16N 110 30W
Geyserville, U.S.A. 116 G4 38 42N 122 54W
Geyve, Turkey 72 B4 40 30N 30 18 E
Ghâbat el Arab = Wang Kai, Sudan 81 F2 9 3N 29 23 E
Ghabeish, Sudan 81 E2 12 9N 27 21 E
Ghaggar →, India 68 E6 29 30N 74 53 E
Ghaghara →, India 69 G11 25 45N 84 40 E
Ghaghat →, Bangla. 69 G13 25 19N 89 38 E
Ghagra, India 69 H11 23 17N 84 33 E
Ghagra →, India 69 F9 27 29N 81 9 E
Ghalla, Wadi el →, Sudan 81 E2 10 25N 27 32 E
Ghana ■, W. Afr. 83 D4 8 0N 1 0W
Ghansor, India 69 H9 22 39N 80 1 E
Ghanzi, Botswana 88 C3 21 50 S 21 34 E
Gharb el Istiwa'iya □, Sudan 81 G3 5 0N 30 0 E
Gharb Kordofân, Sudan 81 E2 12 0N 28 0 E
Gharbîya, Es Sahrâ el, Egypt 80 B2 27 40N 26 30 E
Ghardaïa, Algeria 78 B6 32 20N 3 37 E
Ghârib, G., Egypt 80 B3 28 6N 32 54 E
Gharig, Sudan 81 E2 10 47N 27 33 E
Gharyān, Libya 79 B8 32 10N 13 0 E
Ghat, Libya 79 D8 24 59N 10 11 E
Ghatal, India 69 H12 22 40N 87 46 E
Ghatampur, India 69 F9 26 8N 80 13 E
Ghatsila, India 69 H12 22 36N 86 29 E
Ghaţţī, Si. Arabia 70 D3 31 16N 37 31 E
Ghawdex = Gozo, Malta 36 C1 36 3N 14 13 E
Ghazal, Bahr el →, Chad 79 F9 13 0N 15 47 E
Ghazâl, Bahr el →, Sudan 81 F3 9 31N 30 25 E
Ghaziabad, India 68 E7 28 42N 77 26 E
Ghazipur, India 69 G10 25 38N 83 35 E
Ghaznī, Afghan. 68 C3 33 30N 68 28 E
Ghaznī □, Afghan. 66 C6 32 10N 68 20 E
Ghedi, Italy 28 C7 45 24N 10 16 E
Ghelari, Romania 42 E7 45 38N 22 45 E
Ghent = Gent, Belgium 17 C3 51 2N 3 42 E
Gheorghe Gheorghiu-Dej = Oneşti, Romania 43 D11 46 17N 26 47 E
Gheorgheni, Romania 43 D10 46 43N 25 41 E
Gherla, Romania 43 C8 47 2N 23 57 E
Ghidigeni, Romania 43 D12 46 3N 27 30 E
Ghilarza, Italy 30 B1 40 7N 8 50 E
Ghimeş-Făget, Romania 43 D11 46 35N 26 2 E
Ghīnah, Wādī al →, Si. Arabia 70 D3 30 27N 38 14 E
Ghisonaccia, France 21 F13 42 1N 9 26 E
Ghisoni, France 21 F13 42 7N 9 12 E
Ghizao, Afghan. 68 C1 33 20N 65 44 E
Ghizar →, Pakistan 69 A5 36 15N 73 43 E
Ghot Ogrein, Egypt 80 A2 31 10N 25 20 E
Ghotaru, India 68 F4 27 20N 70 1 E
Ghotki, Pakistan 68 E3 28 5N 69 21 E
Ghowr □, Afghan. 66 C4 34 0N 64 20 E
Ghudaf, W. al →, Iraq 70 C4 32 56N 43 30 E
Ghudāmis, Libya 79 B7 30 11N 9 29 E
Ghughri, India 69 H9 22 39N 80 41 E
Ghugus, India 66 K11 19 58N 79 12 E
Ghulam Mohammad Barrage, Pakistan 68 G3 25 30N 68 20 E
Ghūrīān, Afghan. 66 B2 34 17N 61 25 E
Gia Dinh, Vietnam 65 G6 10 49N 106 42 E
Gia Lai = Plei Ku, Vietnam 64 F7 13 57N 108 0 E
Gia Nghia, Vietnam 65 G6 11 58N 107 42 E
Gia Ngoc, Vietnam 64 E7 14 50N 108 58 E
Gia Vuc, Vietnam 64 E7 14 42N 108 34 E
Giannutri, Italy 28 F8 42 15N 11 6 E
Giant Forest, U.S.A. 116 J8 36 36N 118 43W
Giant Mts. = Krkonoše, Czech Rep. 26 A8 50 50N 15 35 E
Giants Causeway, U.K. 15 A5 55 16N 6 29W
Giarabub = Al Jaghbūb, Libya 79 C10 29 42N 24 38 E
Giarre, Italy 31 E8 37 43N 15 11 E
Giaveno, Italy 28 C4 45 2N 7 21 E
Gibara, Cuba 120 B4 21 9N 76 11W
Gibb River, Australia 92 C4 16 26 S 126 26 E
Gibbon, U.S.A. 112 E5 40 45N 98 51W
Gibe →, Ethiopia 81 F4 7 20N 37 36 E
Gibellina Nuova, Italy 30 E5 37 47N 12 58 E
Gibeon, Namibia 88 D2 25 9 S 17 43 E
Gibraleón, Spain 35 H4 37 23N 6 58W
Gibraltar ■, Europe 35 J5 36 7N 5 22W
Gibraltar, Str. of, Medit. S. 35 K5 35 55N 5 40W
Gibson Desert, Australia 92 D4 24 0 S 126 0 E
Gibsons, Canada 104 D4 49 24N 123 32W
Gibsonville, U.S.A. 116 F6 39 46N 120 54W
Giddings, U.S.A. 113 K6 30 11N 96 56W
Gidole, Ethiopia 81 F4 5 40N 37 25 E
Gien, France 19 E9 47 40N 2 36 E
Giengen, Germany 25 G6 48 37N 10 14 E
Giessen, Germany 24 E4 50 34N 8 41 E
Gīfān, Iran 71 B8 37 54N 57 28 E
Gifatin, Geziret, Egypt 80 B3 27 10N 33 50 E
Gifhorn, Germany 24 C6 52 30N 10 33 E
Gift Lake, Canada 104 B5 55 53N 115 49W
Gifu, Japan 55 G8 35 30N 136 45 E
Gifu □, Japan 55 G8 35 40N 137 0 E
Gigant, Russia 49 G5 46 28N 41 20 E
Giganta, Sa. de la, Mexico 118 B2 25 30N 111 30W
Gigen, Bulgaria 41 C8 43 40N 24 28 E
Gigha, U.K. 14 F3 55 42N 5 44W
Gíglio, Italy 28 F7 42 20N 10 52 E
Gignac, France 20 E7 43 39N 3 32 E
Gigüela →, Spain 35 F7 39 8N 3 44W
Gijón, Spain 34 B5 43 32N 5 42W
Gil I., Canada 104 C3 53 12N 129 15W
Gila →, U.S.A. 115 K6 32 43N 114 33W
Gila Bend, U.S.A. 115 K7 32 57N 112 43W
Gila Bend Mts., U.S.A. 115 K7 33 10N 113 0W
Gīlān □, Iran 71 B6 37 0N 50 0 E
Gilău, Romania 43 D8 46 45N 23 23 E
Gilbert →, Australia 94 B3 16 35 S 141 15 E
Gilbert Is., Kiribati 96 G9 1 0N 172 0 E
Gilbert River, Australia 94 B3 18 9 S 142 52 E
Gilead, U.S.A. 111 B14 44 24N 70 59W
Gilf el Kebîr, Hadabat el, Egypt 80 C2 23 50N 25 50 E
Gilford I., Canada 104 C3 50 40N 126 30W
Gilgandra, Australia 95 E4 31 43 S 148 39 E
Gilgil, Kenya 86 C4 0 30 S 36 20 E
Gilgit, India 69 B6 35 50N 74 15 E
Gilgit →, Pakistan 69 B6 35 44N 74 37 E
Gilgunnia, Australia 95 E4 32 26 S 146 2 E
Giljeva Planina, Serbia, Yug. 40 C3 43 9N 20 0 E
Gillam, Canada 105 B10 56 20N 94 40W
Gilleleje, Denmark 11 H6 56 8N 12 19 E
Gillen, L., Australia 93 E3 26 11 S 124 38 E
Gilles, L., Australia 95 E2 32 50 S 136 45 E
Gillette, U.S.A. 112 C2 44 18N 105 30W
Gilliat, Australia 94 C3 20 40 S 141 28 E
Gillingham, U.K. 13 F8 51 23N 0 33 E
Gilmer, U.S.A. 113 J7 32 44N 94 57W
Gilmore, L., Australia 93 F3 32 29 S 121 37 E
Gilo →, Ethiopia 81 F3 8 10N 33 15 E
Gilort →, Romania 43 F8 44 38N 23 32 E
Gilroy, U.S.A. 116 H5 37 1N 121 34W
Gimbi, Ethiopia 81 F4 9 3N 35 42 E
Gimli, Canada 105 C9 50 40N 97 0W
Gimo, Sweden 10 D12 60 11N 18 12 E
Gimone →, France 20 E5 44 0N 1 6 E
Gimont, France 20 E4 43 38N 0 52 E
Gin Gin, Australia 95 D5 25 0 S 151 58 E
Ginâh, Egypt 80 B3 25 21N 30 30 E
Gineifa, Egypt 80 H8 30 12N 32 25 E
Gingin, Australia 93 F2 31 22 S 115 54 E
Gingindlovu, S. Africa 89 D5 29 2 S 31 30 E
Ginir, Ethiopia 81 F5 7 6N 40 40 E
Ginosa, Italy 31 B9 40 35N 16 45 E
Ginzo de Limia = Xinzo de Limia, Spain 34 C3 42 3N 7 47W
Gióia, G. di, Italy 31 D8 38 30N 15 45 E
Gióia del Colle, Italy 31 B9 40 48N 16 55 E
Gióia Táuro, Italy 31 D8 38 25N 15 54 E
Gioiosa Iónica, Italy 31 D9 38 20N 16 18 E
Gioiosa Marea, Italy 31 D7 38 10N 14 54 E
Gióna, Óros, Greece 38 C4 38 38N 22 14 E
Giovi, Passo dei, Italy 28 D5 44 33N 8 57 E
Giovinazzo, Italy 31 A9 41 11N 16 40 E
Gippsland, Australia 95 F4 37 52 S 147 0 E
Gir Hills, India 68 J4 21 0N 71 0 E
Girab, India 68 F4 26 2N 70 38 E
Girâfi, W. →, Egypt 75 F3 29 58N 34 39 E
Giraltovce, Slovak Rep. 27 B14 49 7N 21 32 E
Girard, Kans., U.S.A. 113 G7 37 31N 94 51W
Girard, Ohio, U.S.A. 110 E4 41 9N 80 42W
Girard, Pa., U.S.A. 110 D4 42 0N 80 19W
Girard, Pa., U.S.A. 110 E4 42 0N 80 19W
Girdle Ness, U.K. 14 D6 57 9N 2 3W
Giresun, Turkey 73 B8 40 55N 38 30 E
Girga, Egypt 80 B3 26 17N 31 55 E
Giri →, India 68 D7 30 28N 77 41 E
Giridih, India 69 G12 24 10N 86 21 E
Girifalco, Italy 31 D9 38 49N 16 25 E
Girne = Kyrenia, Cyprus 36 D12 35 20N 33 20 E
Giro, Nigeria 83 C5 11 7N 4 42 E
Giromagny, France 19 E13 47 45N 6 50 E
Girona, Spain 32 D7 41 58N 2 46 E
Girona □, Spain 32 C7 42 11N 2 30 E
Gironde □, France 20 D3 44 45N 0 30W
Gironde →, France 20 C2 45 32N 1 7W
Gironella, Spain 32 C6 42 2N 1 53 E
Giru, Australia 94 B4 19 30 S 147 5 E
Girvan, U.K. 14 F4 55 14N 4 51W
Gisborne, N.Z. 91 H7 38 39 S 178 5 E
Gisenyi, Rwanda 86 C2 1 41 S 29 15 E
Gislaved, Sweden 11 G7 57 19N 13 32 E
Gisors, France 19 C8 49 15N 1 47 E
Gitega, Burundi 86 C2 3 26 S 29 56 E
Giuba →, Somali Rep. 74 G3 1 30N 42 35 E
Giugliano in Campania, Italy 31 B7 40 56N 14 12 E
Giulianova, Italy 29 F10 42 45N 13 57 E
Giurgeni, Romania 43 F12 44 45N 27 48 E
Giurgiu, Romania 43 G10 43 52N 25 57 E
Giurgiu □, Romania 43 F10 44 20N 26 0 E
Giurgiuleşti, Moldova 43 E13 45 29N 28 12 E
Give, Denmark 11 J3 55 51N 9 13 E
Givet, France 19 B11 50 8N 4 49 E
Givors, France 21 C8 45 35N 4 45 E
Givry, France 19 F11 46 41N 4 46 E
Giyon, Ethiopia 81 F4 8 33N 38 1 E
Giza = El Gîza, Egypt 80 J7 30 0N 31 10 E
Gizhiga, Russia 51 C17 62 3N 160 30 E
Gizhiginskaya Guba, Russia 51 C16 61 0N 158 0 E
Giżycko, Poland 44 D8 54 2N 21 48 E
Gizzeria, Italy 31 D9 38 59N 16 12 E
Gjalicë e Lumës, Mal., Albania 40 D4 42 2N 20 25 E
Gjalicës së Lumës, Mal i = Gjalicë e Lumës, Mal., Albania 40 D4 42 2N 20 25 E
Gjegjan, Albania 40 E4 41 58N 20 3 E
Gjegjani = Gjegjan, Albania 40 E4 41 58N 20 3 E
Gjirokastër, Albania 40 F4 40 7N 20 10 E
Gjirokastra = Gjirokastër, Albania 40 F4 40 7N 20 10 E
Gjoa Haven, Canada 100 B10 68 20N 96 8W
Gjøvik, Norway 9 F14 60 47N 10 43 E
Gjuhës, Kep i, Albania 40 F3 40 28N 19 15 E
Glace Bay, Canada 103 C8 46 11N 59 58W
Glacier Bay National Park and Preserve, U.S.A. 104 B1 58 45N 136 30W
Glacier National Park, Canada 104 C5 51 15N 117 30W
Glacier National Park, U.S.A. 114 B7 48 30N 113 18W
Glacier Peak, U.S.A. 114 B3 48 7N 121 7W
Gladewater, U.S.A. 113 J7 32 33N 94 56W
Gladstone, Queens., Australia 94 C5 23 52 S 151 16 E
Gladstone, S. Austral., Australia 95 E2 33 15 S 138 22 E
Gladstone, Canada 105 C9 50 13N 98 57W
Gladstone, U.S.A. 108 C2 45 51N 87 1W
Gladwin, U.S.A. 108 D3 43 59N 84 29W
Glafsfjorden, Sweden 10 E6 59 30N 12 37 E
Głagów Małapolski, Poland 45 H8 50 10N 21 56 E
Glåma = Glomma →, Norway 9 G14 59 12N 10 57 E
Gláma, Iceland 8 D2 65 48N 23 0W
Glamis, U.S.A. 117 N11 32 55N 115 5W
Glamoč, Bos.-H. 29 D13 44 3N 16 51 E
Glamsbjerg, Denmark 11 J4 55 17N 10 6 E
Glarus, Switz. 25 H5 47 3N 9 4 E
Glarus □, Switz. 25 J5 47 0N 9 5 E
Glasco, Kans., U.S.A. 112 F6 39 22N 97 50W
Glasco, N.Y., U.S.A. 111 D11 42 3N 73 57W
Glasgow, U.K. 14 F4 55 51N 4 15W
Glasgow, Ky., U.S.A. 108 G3 37 0N 85 55W
Glasgow, Mont., U.S.A. 114 B10 48 12N 106 38W
Glasgow, City of □, U.K. 14 F4 55 51N 4 12W
Glaslyn, Canada 105 C7 53 22N 108 21W
Glastonbury, U.K. 13 F5 51 9N 2 43W
Glastonbury, U.S.A. 111 E12 41 43N 72 37W
Glauchau, Germany 24 E8 50 49N 12 31 E
Glava, Sweden 10 E6 59 33N 12 35 E
Glavice, Croatia 29 E13 43 43N 16 41 E
Glazov, Russia 48 A11 58 9N 52 40 E
Gleichen, Canada 104 C6 50 52N 113 3W
Gleisdorf, Austria 26 D8 47 6N 15 44 E
Gleiwitz = Gliwice, Poland 45 H5 50 22N 18 41 E
Glen, U.S.A. 111 B13 44 7N 71 11W
Glen Affric, U.K. 14 D3 57 17N 5 1W
Glen Canyon, U.S.A. 115 H8 37 30N 110 40W
Glen Canyon Dam, U.S.A. 115 H8 36 57N 111 29W
Glen Canyon National Recreation Area, U.S.A. 115 H8 37 15N 111 0W
Glen Coe, U.K. 14 E3 56 40N 5 0W
Glen Cove, U.S.A. 111 F11 40 52N 73 38W
Glen Garry, U.K. 14 D3 57 3N 5 7W
Glen Innes, Australia 95 D5 29 44 S 151 44 E
Glen Lyon, U.S.A. 111 E8 41 10N 76 5W
Glen Mor, U.K. 14 D4 57 9N 4 37W
Glen Moriston, U.K. 14 D4 57 11N 4 52W
Glen Robertson, Canada 111 A10 45 22N 74 30W
Glen Spean, U.K. 14 E4 56 53N 4 40W
Glen Ullin, U.S.A. 112 B4 46 49N 101 50W
Glénan, Îs. de, France 18 E3 47 42N 4 0W
Glencoe, Canada 110 D3 42 45N 81 43W
Glencoe, S. Africa 89 D5 28 11 S 30 11 E
Glencoe, U.S.A. 112 C7 44 46N 94 9W
Glendale, Ariz., U.S.A. 115 K7 33 32N 112 11W
Glendale, Calif., U.S.A. 117 L8 34 9N 118 15W
Glendale, Zimbabwe 87 F3 17 22 S 31 5 E
Glendive, U.S.A. 112 B2 47 7N 104 43W
Glendo, U.S.A. 112 D2 42 30N 105 2W
Glenelg →, Australia 95 F3 38 4 S 140 59 E
Glenfield, U.S.A. 111 C9 43 43N 75 24W
Glengarriff, Ireland 15 E2 51 45N 9 34W
Glenmont, U.S.A. 110 F2 40 31N 82 6W
Glenmorgan, Australia 95 D4 27 14 S 149 42 E
Glenn, U.S.A. 116 F4 39 31N 122 1W
Glennallen, U.S.A. 100 B5 62 7N 145 33W
Glennamaddy, Ireland 15 C3 53 37N 8 33W
Glenns Ferry, U.S.A. 114 E6 42 57N 115 18W
Glenore, Australia 94 B3 17 50 S 141 12 E
Glenreagh, Australia 95 E5 30 2 S 153 1 E
Glenrock, U.S.A. 114 E11 42 52N 105 52W
Glenrothes, U.K. 14 E5 56 12N 3 10W
Glens Falls, U.S.A. 111 C11 43 19N 73 39W
Glenside, U.S.A. 111 F9 40 6N 75 9W
Glenties, Ireland 15 B3 54 49N 8 16W
Glenville, U.S.A. 108 F5 38 56N 80 50W
Glenwood, Canada 103 C9 49 0N 54 58W
Glenwood, Ark., U.S.A. 113 H8 34 20N 93 33W

Glenwood, Hawaii, U.S.A. **106 J17** 19 29N 155 9W
Glenwood, Iowa, U.S.A. **112 E7** 41 3N 95 45W
Glenwood, Minn., U.S.A. **112 C7** 45 39N 95 23W
Glenwood, Wash., U.S.A. **116 D5** 46 1N 121 17W
Glenwood Springs, U.S.A. **114 G10** 39 33N 107 19W
Glettinganes, Iceland **8 D7** 65 30N 13 37W
Glifádha, Greece **38 D5** 37 52N 23 45 E
Glimåkra, Sweden **11 H8** 56 19N 14 7 E
Glina, Croatia **29 C13** 45 20N 16 6 E
Glinojeck, Poland **45 F7** 52 49N 20 21 E
Gliwice, Poland **45 H5** 50 22N 18 41 E
Globe, U.S.A. **115 K8** 33 24N 110 47W
Glodeanu Siliştea, Romania **43 F11** 44 50N 26 48 E
Glodeni, Moldova **43 C12** 47 45N 27 31 E
Glödnitz, Austria **26 E7** 46 53N 14 7 E
Gloggnitz, Austria **26 D8** 47 41N 15 56 E
Głogów, Poland **45 G3** 51 37N 16 5 E
Głogówek, Poland **45 H4** 50 21N 17 53 E
Glomma →, Norway **9 G14** 59 12N 10 57 E
Glorieuses, Is., Ind. Oc. **89 A8** 11 30 S 47 20 E
Glóssa, Greece **38 B5** 39 10N 23 45 E
Glossop, U.K. **12 D6** 53 27N 1 56W
Gloucester, Australia **95 E5** 32 0 S 151 59 E
Gloucester, U.K. **13 F5** 51 53N 2 15W
Gloucester, U.S.A. **111 D14** 42 37N 70 40W
Gloucester I., Australia **94 C4** 20 0 S 148 30 E
Gloucester Point, U.S.A. **108 G7** 37 15N 76 29W
Gloucestershire □, U.K. **13 F5** 51 46N 2 15W
Gloversville, U.S.A. **111 C10** 43 3N 74 21W
Glovertown, Canada **103 C9** 48 40N 54 3W
Głowno, Poland **45 G6** 51 59N 19 42 E
Głubczyce, Poland **45 H4** 50 13N 17 52 E
Glubokiy, Russia **49 F5** 48 35N 40 25 E
Glubokoye = Hlybokaye, Belarus **46 E4** 55 10N 27 45 E
Głuchołazy, Poland **45 H4** 50 19N 17 24 E
Glücksburg, Germany **24 A5** 54 50N 9 33 E
Glückstadt, Germany **24 B5** 53 45N 9 25 E
Glukhov = Hlukhiv, Ukraine **47 G7** 51 40N 33 58 E
Glusk, Belarus **47 F5** 52 53N 28 41 E
Głuszyca, Poland **45 H3** 50 41N 16 23 E
Glyngøre, Denmark **11 H2** 56 46N 8 52 E
Gmünd, Kärnten, Austria **26 E6** 46 54N 13 31 E
Gmünd, Niederösterreich, Austria **26 C8** 48 45N 15 0 E
Gmunden, Austria **26 D6** 47 55N 13 48 E
Gnarp, Sweden **10 B11** 62 3N 17 16 E
Gnesta, Sweden **10 E11** 59 3N 17 17 E
Gniew, Poland **44 E5** 53 50N 18 50 E
Gniewkowo, Poland **45 F5** 52 54N 18 25 E
Gniezno, Poland **45 F4** 52 30N 17 35 E
Gnjilane, Kosovo, Yug. **40 D5** 42 28N 21 29 E
Gnoien, Germany **24 B8** 53 58N 12 41 E
Gnosjö, Sweden **11 G7** 57 22N 13 43 E
Gnowangerup, Australia **93 F2** 33 58 S 117 59 E
Go Cong, Vietnam **65 G6** 10 22N 106 40 E
Gō-no-ura, Japan **55 H4** 33 44N 129 40 E
Goa, India **66 M8** 15 33N 73 59 E
Goa □, India **66 M8** 15 33N 73 59 E
Goalen Hd., Australia **95 F5** 36 33 S 150 4 E
Goalpara, India **67 F17** 26 10N 90 40 E
Goaltor, India **69 H12** 22 43N 87 10 E
Goalundo Ghat, Bangla. **69 H13** 23 50N 89 47 E
Goaso, Ghana **82 D4** 6 48N 2 30W
Goat Fell, U.K. **14 F3** 55 38N 5 11W
Goba, Ethiopia **81 F4** 7 1N 39 59 E
Goba, Mozam. **89 D5** 26 15 S 32 13 E
Gobabis, Namibia **88 C2** 22 30 S 19 0 E
Göbel, Turkey **41 F12** 40 0N 28 9 E
Gobi, Asia **56 C6** 44 0N 110 0 E
Gobō, Japan **55 H7** 33 53N 135 10 E
Gobo, Sudan **81 F3** 5 40N 31 10 E
Göçbeyli, Turkey **39 B9** 39 13N 27 25 E
Goch, Germany **24 D2** 51 41N 6 9 E
Gochas, Namibia **88 C2** 24 59 S 18 55 E
Godavari →, India **67 L13** 16 25N 82 18 E
Godavari Pt., India **67 L13** 17 0N 82 20 E
Godbout, Canada **103 C6** 49 20N 67 38W
Godda, India **69 G12** 24 50N 87 13 E
Godech, Bulgaria **40 C7** 43 1N 23 4 E
Goderich, Canada **102 D3** 43 45N 81 41W
Goderville, France **18 C7** 49 38N 0 22 E
Godfrey Ra., Australia **93 D2** 24 0 S 117 0 E
Godhavn = Qeqertarsuaq, Greenland **4 C5** 69 15N 53 38W
Godhra, India **68 H5** 22 49N 73 40 E
Gödöllő, Hungary **42 C4** 47 38N 19 25 E
Godoy Cruz, Argentina **126 C2** 32 56 S 68 52W
Gods →, Canada **102 A1** 56 22N 92 51W
Gods L., Canada **102 B1** 54 40N 94 15W
Gods River, Canada **105 C10** 54 50N 94 5W
Godthåb = Nuuk, Greenland **101 B14** 64 10N 51 35W
Godwin Austen = K2, Pakistan **69 B7** 35 58N 76 32 E
Goeie Hoop, Kaap die = Good Hope, C. of, S. Africa **88 E2** 34 24 S 18 30 E
Goéland, L. au, Canada **102 C4** 49 50N 76 48W
Goeree, Neths. **17 C3** 51 50N 4 0 E
Goes, Neths. **17 C3** 51 30N 3 55 E
Goffstown, U.S.A. **111 C13** 43 1N 71 36W
Gogama, Canada **102 C3** 47 35N 81 43W
Gogebic, L., U.S.A. **112 B10** 46 30N 89 35W
Goggetti, Ethiopia **81 F4** 8 11N 38 35 E
Gogolin, Poland **45 H5** 50 30N 18 0 E
Gogonou, Benin **83 C5** 10 50N 2 50 E
Gogra = Ghaghara →, India **69 G11** 25 45N 84 40 E
Gogriâl, Sudan **81 F2** 8 30N 28 8 E
Gogti, Ethiopia **81 E5** 10 7N 42 51 E
Gohana, India **68 E7** 29 8N 76 42 E
Goharganj, India **68 H7** 23 1N 77 41 E
Goi →, India **68 H6** 22 4N 74 46 E
Goiânia, Brazil **125 G9** 16 43 S 49 20W
Goiás, Brazil **125 G8** 15 55 S 50 10W
Goiás □, Brazil **125 F9** 12 10 S 48 0W
Goio-Ere, Brazil **127 A5** 24 12 S 53 1W
Góis, Portugal **34 E2** 40 10N 8 6W
Gojam □, Ethiopia **81 E4** 10 55N 36 30 E
Gojeb, Wabi →, Ethiopia **81 F4** 7 12N 36 40 E
Gojō, Japan **55 G7** 34 21N 135 42 E
Gojra, Pakistan **68 D5** 31 10N 72 40 E
Gökçeada, Turkey **41 F9** 40 10N 25 50 E
Gökçedağ, Turkey **39 B10** 39 33N 28 56 E
Gökçen, Turkey **39 C9** 38 7N 27 53 E
Gökçeören, Turkey **39 C10** 38 37N 28 35 E
Gökçeyazı, Turkey **39 B9** 39 40N 27 40 E
Gökırmak →, Turkey **72 B6** 41 25N 35 8 E
Gökova, Turkey **39 D10** 37 1N 28 17 E
Gökova Körfezi, Turkey **39 E9** 36 55N 27 50 E
Göksu →, Turkey **72 D6** 36 19N 34 5 E
Göksun, Turkey **72 C7** 38 2N 36 30 E
Gokteik, Burma **67 H20** 22 26N 97 0 E
Göktepe, Turkey **39 D10** 37 25N 28 34 E
Gokurt, Pakistan **68 E2** 29 40N 67 26 E
Gokwe, Zimbabwe **89 B4** 18 7 S 28 58 E
Gol Gol, Australia **95 E3** 34 12 S 142 14 E
Gola, India **69 E9** 28 3N 80 32 E
Golakganj, India **69 F13** 26 8N 89 52 E
Golan Heights = Hagolan, Syria **75 C4** 33 0N 35 45 E
Gołańcz, Poland **45 F4** 52 57N 17 18 E
Golāshkerd, Iran **71 E8** 27 59N 57 16 E
Golaya Pristen = Hola Pristan, Ukraine **47 J7** 46 29N 32 32 E
Gölbaşı, Adiyaman, Turkey **72 D7** 37 43N 37 25 E
Gölbaşı, Ankara, Turkey **72 C5** 39 47N 32 49 E
Golchikha, Russia **4 B12** 71 45N 83 30 E
Golconda, U.S.A. **114 F5** 40 58N 117 30W
Gölcük, Kocaeli, Turkey **41 F13** 40 42N 29 48 E
Gölcük, Niğde, Turkey **72 C6** 38 14N 34 47 E
Gold, U.S.A. **110 E7** 41 52N 77 50W
Gold Beach, U.S.A. **114 E1** 42 25N 124 25W
Gold Coast, W. Afr. **83 E4** 4 0N 1 40W
Gold Hill, U.S.A. **114 E2** 42 26N 123 3W
Gold River, Canada **104 D3** 49 46N 126 3W
Gołdap, Poland **44 D9** 54 19N 22 18 E
Goldberg, Germany **24 B8** 53 35N 12 4 E
Golden, Canada **104 C5** 51 20N 116 59W
Golden B., N.Z. **91 J4** 40 40 S 172 50 E
Golden Gate, U.S.A. **114 H2** 37 54N 122 30W
Golden Hinde, Canada **104 D3** 49 40N 125 44W
Golden Lake, Canada **110 A7** 45 34N 77 21W
Golden Vale, Ireland **15 D3** 52 33N 8 17W
Goldendale, U.S.A. **114 D3** 45 49N 120 50W
Goldfield, U.S.A. **115 H5** 37 42N 117 14W
Goldsand L., Canada **105 B8** 57 2N 101 8W
Goldsboro, U.S.A. **109 H7** 35 23N 77 59W
Goldsmith, U.S.A. **113 K3** 31 59N 102 37W
Goldsworthy, Australia **92 D2** 20 21 S 119 30 E
Goldthwaite, U.S.A. **113 K5** 31 27N 98 34W
Golegã, Portugal **35 F2** 39 24N 8 29W
Goleniów, Poland **44 E1** 53 35N 14 50 E
Golestānak, Iran **71 D7** 30 36N 54 14 E
Goleta, U.S.A. **117 L7** 34 27N 119 50W
Golfito, Costa Rica **120 E3** 8 41N 83 5W
Golfo Aranci, Italy **30 B2** 40 59N 9 38 E
Gölgeli Dağları, Turkey **39 D10** 37 10N 28 55 E
Gölhisar, Turkey **39 D11** 37 8N 29 31 E
Goliad, U.S.A. **113 L6** 28 40N 97 23W
Golija, Montenegro, Yug. **40 C2** 43 5N 18 45 E
Golija, Serbia, Yug. **40 C4** 43 22N 20 15 E
Golina, Poland **45 F5** 52 15N 18 4 E
Gölköy, Turkey **72 B7** 40 41N 37 37 E
Göllersdorf, Austria **26 C9** 48 29N 16 7 E
Gölmarmara, Turkey **39 C9** 38 42N 27 55 E
Golo →, France **21 F13** 42 31N 9 32 E
Gölova, Turkey **39 E12** 36 48N 30 5 E
Golpāyegān, Iran **71 C6** 33 27N 50 18 E
Gölpazarı, Turkey **72 B4** 40 16N 30 18 E
Golra, Pakistan **68 C5** 33 37N 72 56 E
Golspie, U.K. **14 D5** 57 58N 3 59W
Golub-Dobrzyń, Poland **45 E6** 53 7N 19 2 E
Golubac, Serbia, Yug. **40 B5** 44 38N 21 38 E
Golyam Perelik, Bulgaria **41 E8** 41 36N 24 33 E
Golyama Kamchiya →, Bulgaria **41 C11** 43 10N 27 55 E
Goma, Dem. Rep. of the Congo **86 C2** 1 37 S 29 10 E
Gomal Pass, Pakistan **68 D3** 31 56N 69 20 E
Gomati →, India **69 G10** 25 32N 83 11 E
Gombari, Dem. Rep. of the Congo **86 B2** 2 45N 29 3 E
Gombe, Nigeria **83 C7** 10 19N 11 2 E
Gömbe, Turkey **39 E11** 36 33N 29 38 E
Gombe □, Nigeria **83 C7** 10 0N 11 10 E
Gombe →, Tanzania **86 C3** 4 38 S 31 40 E
Gombi, Nigeria **83 C7** 10 12N 12 30 E
Gomel = Homyel, Belarus **47 F6** 52 28N 31 0 E
Gomera, Canary Is. **37 F2** 28 7N 17 14W
Gómez Palacio, Mexico **118 B4** 25 40N 104 0W
Gomīshān, Iran **71 B7** 37 4N 54 6 E
Gommern, Germany **24 C7** 52 4N 11 50 E
Gomogomo, Indonesia **63 F8** 6 39 S 134 43 E
Gomoh, India **67 H15** 23 52N 86 10 E
Gomotartsi, Bulgaria **40 B6** 44 6N 22 57 E
Gompa = Ganta, Liberia **82 D3** 7 15N 8 59W
Gomphi, Greece **38 B3** 39 26N 21 36 E
Gonābād, Iran **71 C8** 34 15N 58 45 E
Gonaïves, Haiti **121 C5** 19 20N 72 42W
Gonâve, G. de la, Haiti **121 C5** 19 29N 72 42W
Gonâve, I. de la, Haiti **121 C5** 18 45N 73 0W
Gonbad-e Kāvūs, Iran **71 B7** 37 20N 55 25 E
Gönc, Hungary **42 B6** 48 28N 21 14 E
Gonda, India **69 F9** 27 9N 81 58 E
Gondal, India **68 J4** 21 58N 70 52 E
Gonder, Ethiopia **81 E4** 12 39N 37 30 E
Gonder □, Ethiopia **81 E4** 12 55N 37 30 E
Gondia, India **66 J12** 21 23N 80 10 E
Gondola, Mozam. **87 F3** 19 10 S 33 37 E
Gondomar, Portugal **34 D2** 41 10N 8 35W
Gondrecourt-le-Château, France **19 D12** 48 31N 5 30 E
Gönen, Balıkesir, Turkey **41 F11** 40 6N 27 39 E
Gönen, Isparta, Turkey **39 D12** 37 57N 30 31 E
Gönen →, Turkey **41 F11** 40 6N 27 39 E
Gong Xian, China **58 C5** 28 23N 104 47 E
Gong'an, China **59 B9** 30 7N 112 12 E
Gongcheng, China **59 E8** 24 50N 110 49 E
Gongga Shan, China **58 C3** 29 40N 101 55 E
Gongguan, China **58 G7** 21 48N 109 36 E
Gonghe, China **60 C5** 36 18N 100 32 E
Gongola →, Nigeria **83 D7** 9 30N 12 4 E
Gongolgon, Australia **95 E4** 30 21 S 146 54 E
Gongshan, China **58 D2** 27 43N 98 29 E
Gongtan, China **58 C7** 28 55N 108 20 E
Gongzhuling, China **57 C13** 43 30N 124 40 E
Goniadz, Poland **44 E9** 53 30N 22 44 E
Goniri, Nigeria **83 C7** 11 30N 12 15 E
Gonjo, China **58 B2** 30 52N 98 17 E
Gonnesa, Italy **30 C1** 39 16N 8 28 E
Gónnos, Greece **38 B4** 39 52N 22 29 E
Gonnosfanàdiga, Italy **30 C1** 39 29N 8 39 E
Gonzaga, Phil. **61 B5** 18 16N 122 0 E
Gonzales, Calif., U.S.A. **116 J5** 36 30N 121 26W
Gonzales, Tex., U.S.A. **113 L6** 29 30N 97 27W
González Chaves, Argentina **126 D3** 38 2 S 60 5W
Good Hope, C. of, S. Africa **88 E2** 34 24 S 18 30 E
Gooderham, Canada **110 B6** 44 54N 78 21W
Goodhouse, S. Africa **88 D2** 28 57 S 18 13 E
Gooding, U.S.A. **114 E6** 42 56N 114 43W
Goodland, U.S.A. **112 F4** 39 21N 101 43W
Goodlow, Canada **104 B4** 56 20N 120 8W
Goodooga, Australia **95 D4** 29 3 S 147 28 E
Goodsprings, U.S.A. **117 K11** 35 49N 115 27W
Goole, U.K. **12 D7** 53 42N 0 53W
Goolgowi, Australia **95 E4** 33 58 S 145 41 E
Goolwa, Australia **95 F2** 35 30 S 138 47 E
Goomalling, Australia **93 F2** 31 15 S 116 49 E
Goomeri, Australia **95 D5** 26 12 S 152 6 E
Goonda, Mozam. **87 F3** 19 48 S 33 57 E
Goondiwindi, Australia **95 D5** 28 30 S 150 21 E
Goongarrie, L., Australia **93 F3** 30 3 S 121 9 E
Goonyella, Australia **94 C4** 21 47 S 147 58 E
Goose →, Canada **103 B7** 53 20N 60 35W
Goose Creek, U.S.A. **109 J5** 32 59N 80 2W
Goose L., U.S.A. **114 F3** 41 56N 120 26W
Gop, India **66 H6** 22 5N 69 50 E
Gopalganj, India **69 F11** 26 28N 84 30 E
Göppingen, Germany **25 G5** 48 42N 9 39 E
Gor, Spain **35 H8** 37 23N 2 58W
Góra, Dolnośląskie, Poland **45 G3** 51 40N 16 31 E
Góra, Mazowieckie, Poland **45 F7** 52 39N 20 6 E
Góra Kalwaria, Poland **45 G8** 51 59N 21 14 E
Gorakhpur, India **69 F10** 26 47N 83 23 E
Goražde, Bos.-H. **42 G3** 43 38N 18 58 E
Gorbatov, Russia **48 B6** 56 12N 43 2 E
Gorbea, Peña, Spain **32 B2** 43 1N 2 50W
Gorda, U.S.A. **116 K5** 35 53N 121 26W
Gorda, Pta., Canary Is. **37 F2** 28 45N 18 0W
Gorda, Pta., Nic. **120 D3** 14 20N 83 10W
Gordan B., Australia **92 B5** 11 35 S 130 10 E
Gördes, Turkey **39 C10** 38 54N 28 17 E
Gordon, U.S.A. **112 D3** 42 48N 102 12W
Gordon →, Australia **94 G4** 42 27 S 145 30 E
Gordon L., Alta., Canada **105 B6** 56 30N 110 25W
Gordon L., N.W.T., Canada **104 A6** 63 5N 113 11W
Gordonvale, Australia **94 B4** 17 5 S 145 50 E
Gore, Ethiopia **81 F4** 8 12N 35 32 E
Gore, N.Z. **91 M2** 46 5 S 168 58 E
Gore Bay, Canada **102 C3** 45 57N 82 28W
Görele, Turkey **73 B8** 41 2N 39 0 E
Goreme, Turkey **72 C6** 38 35N 34 52 E
Gorey, Ireland **15 D5** 52 41N 6 18W
Gorg, Iran **71 D8** 29 29N 59 43 E
Gorgān, Iran **71 B7** 36 50N 54 29 E
Gorgona, Italy **28 E6** 43 26N 9 54 E
Gorgona, I., Colombia **124 C3** 3 0N 78 10W
Gorgora, Ethiopia **81 E4** 12 15N 37 17 E
Gorgoram, Nigeria **83 C7** 12 40N 10 45 E
Gorham, U.S.A. **111 B13** 44 23N 71 10W
Gori, Georgia **49 J7** 42 0N 44 7 E
Goriganga →, India **69 E9** 29 45N 80 23 E
Gorinchem, Neths. **17 C4** 51 50N 4 59 E
Goris, Armenia **73 C12** 39 31N 46 22 E
Goritsy, Russia **46 D9** 57 4N 36 43 E
Gorizia, Italy **29 C10** 45 56N 13 37 E
Gorj □, Romania **43 E8** 45 5N 23 25 E
Gorki = Horki, Belarus **46 E6** 54 17N 30 59 E
Gorki = Nizhniy Novgorod, Russia **48 B7** 56 20N 44 0 E
Gorkiy = Nizhniy Novgorod, Russia **48 B7** 56 20N 44 0 E
Gorkovskoye Vdkhr., Russia **48 B6** 57 2N 43 4 E
Gorlice, Poland **45 J8** 49 35N 21 11 E
Görlitz, Germany **24 D10** 51 9N 14 58 E
Gorlovka = Horlivka, Ukraine **47 H10** 48 19N 38 5 E
Gorman, U.S.A. **117 L8** 34 47N 118 51W
Gorna Dzhumayo = Blagoevgrad, Bulgaria **40 D7** 42 2N 23 5 E
Gorna Oryakhovitsa, Bulgaria **41 C9** 43 7N 25 40 E
Gornja Radgona, Slovenia **29 B13** 46 40N 16 2 E
Gornja Tuzla, Bos.-H. **42 F3** 44 35N 18 46 E
Gornji Grad, Slovenia **29 B11** 46 20N 14 52 E
Gornji Milanovac, Serbia, Yug. **40 B4** 44 3N 20 29 E
Gornji Vakuf, Bos.-H. **42 G2** 43 57N 17 34 E
Gorno Ablanovo, Bulgaria **41 C9** 43 37N 25 43 E
Gorno-Altay □, Russia **50 D9** 51 0N 86 0 E
Gorno-Altaysk, Russia **50 D9** 51 50N 86 5 E
Gornyatskiy, Russia **49 F5** 48 18N 40 56 E
Gornyy, Saratov, Russia **48 E9** 51 50N 48 30 E
Gornyy, Sib., Russia **54 B6** 44 57N 133 59 E
Gorodenka = Horodenka, Ukraine **47 H3** 48 41N 25 29 E
Gorodets, Russia **48 B6** 56 38N 43 28 E
Gorodishche = Horodyshche, Ukraine **47 H6** 49 17N 31 27 E
Gorodishche, Russia **48 D7** 53 13N 45 40 E
Gorodnya = Horodnya, Ukraine **47 G6** 51 55N 31 33 E
Gorodok = Haradok, Belarus **46 E6** 55 30N 30 3 E
Gorodok = Horodok, Ukraine **47 H2** 49 46N 23 32 E
Gorodovikovsk, Russia **49 G5** 46 8N 41 58 E
Gorokhov = Horokhiv, Ukraine **47 G3** 50 30N 24 45 E
Gorokhovets, Russia **48 B6** 56 13N 42 39 E
Gorom Gorom, Burkina Faso **83 C4** 14 26N 0 14W
Goromonzi, Zimbabwe **87 F3** 17 52 S 31 22 E
Gorong, Kepulauan, Indonesia **63 E8** 3 59 S 131 25 E
Gorongose →, Mozam. **89 C5** 20 30 S 34 40 E
Gorongoza, Mozam. **87 F3** 18 44 S 34 2 E
Gorongoza, Sa. da, Mozam. **87 F3** 18 27 S 34 2 E
Gorontalo, Indonesia **63 D6** 0 35N 123 5 E
Goronyo, Nigeria **83 C6** 13 29N 5 39 E
Górowo Iławeckie, Poland **44 D7** 54 17N 20 30 E
Gorron, France **18 D6** 48 25N 0 50W
Gorshechnoye, Russia **47 G10** 51 31N 38 2 E
Gort, Ireland **15 C3** 53 3N 8 49W
Gortis, Greece **36 D6** 35 4N 24 58 E
Góry Bystrzyckie, Poland **45 H3** 50 16N 16 33 E
Goryachiy Klyuch, Russia **49 H4** 44 38N 39 8 E
Gorzkowice, Poland **45 G6** 51 13N 19 36 E
Górzno, Poland **45 E6** 53 12N 19 38 E
Gorzów Śląski, Poland **45 G5** 51 3N 18 22 E
Gorzów Wielkopolski, Poland **45 F2** 52 43N 15 15 E
Gosford, Australia **95 E5** 33 23 S 151 18 E
Goshen, Calif., U.S.A. **116 J7** 36 21N 119 25W
Goshen, Ind., U.S.A. **108 E3** 41 35N 85 50W
Goshen, N.Y., U.S.A. **111 E10** 41 24N 74 20W
Goshogawara, Japan **54 D10** 40 48N 140 27 E
Goslar, Germany **24 D6** 51 54N 10 25 E
Gospič, Croatia **29 D12** 44 35N 15 23 E
Gosport, U.K. **13 G6** 50 48N 1 9W
Gossas, Senegal **82 C1** 14 28N 16 0W
Gosse →, Australia **94 B1** 19 32 S 134 37 E
Gossi, Mali **83 B4** 15 48N 1 20W
Gossinga, Sudan **81 F2** 8 36N 25 59 E
Gostivar, Macedonia **40 E4** 41 48N 20 57 E
Gostyń, Poland **45 G4** 51 50N 17 3 E
Gostynin, Poland **45 F6** 52 26N 19 29 E
Göta älv →, Sweden **11 G5** 57 42N 11 54 E
Göta kanal, Sweden **11 F9** 58 30N 15 58 E
Götaland, Sweden **11 G8** 57 30N 14 30 E
Göteborg, Sweden **11 G5** 57 43N 11 59 E
Götene, Sweden **11 F7** 58 32N 13 30 E
Goteşti, Moldova **43 D13** 46 9N 28 10 E
Gotha, Germany **24 E6** 50 56N 10 42 E
Gothenburg = Göteborg, Sweden **11 G5** 57 43N 11 59 E
Gothenburg, U.S.A. **112 E4** 40 56N 100 10W
Gothèye, Niger **83 C5** 13 52N 1 34 E
Gotland, Sweden **11 G12** 57 30N 18 33 E
Gotlands län □, Sweden **11 G12** 57 15N 18 30 E
Gotō-Rettō, Japan **55 H4** 32 55N 129 5 E
Gotse Delchev, Bulgaria **40 E7** 41 36N 23 46 E
Gotska Sandön, Sweden **9 G18** 58 24N 19 15 E
Gōtsu, Japan **55 G6** 35 0N 132 14 E
Gott Pk., Canada **104 C4** 50 18N 122 16W
Gòttero, Monte, Italy **28 D6** 44 22N 9 42 E
Göttingen, Germany **24 D5** 51 31N 9 55 E
Gottwald = Zmiyev, Ukraine **47 H9** 49 39N 36 27 E
Gottwaldov = Zlín, Czech Rep. **27 B10** 49 14N 17 40 E
Goubangzi, China **57 D11** 41 20N 121 52 E
Gouda, Neths. **17 B4** 52 1N 4 42 E
Goúdhoura, Ákra, Greece **36 E8** 34 59N 26 6 E
Goudiry, Senegal **82 C2** 14 15N 12 45W
Goudoumaria, Niger **83 C7** 13 40N 11 10 E
Gouéké, Guinea **82 D3** 8 2N 8 43W
Gough I., Atl. Oc. **2 G9** 40 10 S 9 45W
Gouin, Rés., Canada **102 C5** 48 35N 74 40W
Gouitafla, Ivory C. **82 D3** 7 30N 5 53W
Goulburn, Australia **95 E4** 34 44 S 149 44 E
Goulburn Is., Australia **94 A1** 11 40 S 133 20 E
Goulia, Ivory C. **82 C3** 10 1N 7 11W
Goulimine, Morocco **78 C3** 28 56N 10 0W
Goumbou, Mali **82 B3** 15 2N 7 25W
Gouménissa, Greece **40 F6** 40 56N 22 37 E
Goundam, Mali **82 B4** 16 27N 3 40W
Goúra, Greece **38 D4** 37 56N 22 20 E
Gourbassi, Mali **82 C2** 13 24N 11 38W
Gourdon, France **20 D5** 44 44N 1 23 E
Gouré, Niger **83 C7** 14 0N 10 10 E
Gourin, France **18 D3** 48 8N 3 37W
Gourits →, S. Africa **88 E3** 34 21 S 21 52 E
Gourma-Rharous, Mali **83 B4** 16 55N 1 50W
Goúrnais, Greece **36 D7** 35 19N 25 16 E
Gournay-en-Bray, France **19 C8** 49 29N 1 44 E
Goursi, Burkina Faso **82 C4** 12 42N 2 37W
Gouverneur, U.S.A. **111 B9** 44 20N 75 28W
Gouviá, Greece **36 A3** 39 39N 19 50 E
Gouzon, France **19 F9** 46 12N 2 14 E
Governador Valadares, Brazil **125 G10** 18 15 S 41 57W
Governor's Harbour, Bahamas **120 A4** 25 10N 76 14W
Govindgarh, India **69 G9** 24 23N 81 18 E
Gowan Ra., Australia **94 D4** 25 0 S 145 0 E
Gowanda, U.S.A. **110 D6** 42 28N 78 56W
Gowd-e Zirreh, Afghan. **66 E3** 29 45N 62 0 E
Gower, U.K. **13 F3** 51 35N 4 10W
Gowna, L., Ireland **15 C4** 53 51N 7 34W
Goya, Argentina **126 B4** 29 10 S 59 10W
Göyçay, Azerbaijan **49 K8** 40 42N 47 43 E
Goyder Lagoon, Australia **95 D2** 27 3 S 138 58 E
Goyllarisquisga, Peru **124 F3** 10 31 S 76 24W
Göynük, Antalya, Turkey **39 E12** 36 41N 30 33 E
Göynük, Bolu, Turkey **72 B4** 40 24N 30 48 E
Goz Beîda, Chad **79 F10** 12 10N 21 20 E
Goz Regeb, Sudan **81 D4** 16 3N 35 33 E
Gozdnica, Poland **45 G2** 51 28N 15 4 E
Gozo, Malta **36 C1** 36 3N 14 13 E
Graaff-Reinet, S. Africa **88 E3** 32 13 S 24 32 E
Grabo, Ivory C. **82 D3** 4 57N 7 30W
Grabow, Germany **24 B7** 53 17N 11 34 E
Grabów nad Prosną, Poland **45 G5** 51 31N 18 7 E
Gračac, Croatia **29 D12** 44 18N 15 57 E
Gračanica, Bos.-H. **42 F3** 44 43N 18 18 E
Graçay, France **19 E8** 47 10N 1 50 E
Gracias a Dios, C., Honduras **120 D3** 15 0N 83 10W
Graciosa, I., Canary Is. **37 E6** 29 15N 13 32W
Grad Sofiya □, Bulgaria **40 D7** 42 35N 23 20 E
Gradac, Montenegro, Yug. **40 C3** 43 23N 19 9 E
Gradačac, Bos.-H. **42 F3** 44 52N 18 26 E
Gradeška Planina, Macedonia **40 E6** 41 30N 22 15 E
Gradets, Bulgaria **41 D10** 42 46N 26 30 E
Gradišče, Slovenia **29 B12** 46 37N 15 50 E
Grădiştea de Munte, Romania **43 E8** 45 37N 23 13 E
Grado, Italy **29 C10** 45 40N 13 23 E
Grado, Spain **34 B4** 43 23N 6 4W
Grady, U.S.A. **113 H3** 34 49N 103 19W
Graeca, Lacul, Romania **43 F11** 44 5N 26 10 E
Grafenau, Germany **25 G9** 48 51N 13 22 E
Gräfenberg, Germany **25 F7** 49 39N 11 14 E
Grafham Water, U.K. **13 E7** 52 19N 0 18W
Grafton, Australia **95 D5** 29 38 S 152 58 E
Grafton, N. Dak., U.S.A. **112 A6** 48 25N 97 25W
Grafton, W. Va., U.S.A. **108 F5** 39 21N 80 2W
Graham, Canada **102 C1** 49 20N 90 30W
Graham, U.S.A. **113 J5** 33 6N 98 35W
Graham, Mt., U.S.A. **115 K9** 32 42N 109 52W
Graham Bell, Ostrov = Greem-Bell, Ostrov, Russia **50 A7** 81 0N 62 0 E
Graham I., B.C., Canada **104 C2** 53 40N 132 30W
Graham I., N.W.T., Canada **100 C6** 77 25N 90 30W
Graham Land, Antarctica **5 C17** 65 0 S 64 0W
Grahamstown, S. Africa **88 E4** 33 19 S 26 31 E
Grahamsville, U.S.A. **111 E10** 41 51N 74 33W
Grahovo, Montenegro, Yug. **40 D2** 42 40N 18 40 E
Graie, Alpi, Europe **21 C11** 45 30N 7 10 E
Grain Coast, W. Afr. **82 E3** 4 20N 10 0W
Grajaú, Brazil **125 E9** 5 50 S 46 4W
Grajaú →, Brazil **125 D10** 3 41 S 44 48W
Grajewo, Poland **44 E9** 53 39N 22 30 E
Gramada, Bulgaria **40 C6** 43 49N 22 39 E
Gramat, France **20 D5** 44 48N 1 43 E
Grammichele, Italy **31 E7** 37 13N 14 38 E
Grámmos, Óros, Greece **40 F4** 40 18N 20 47 E
Grampian, U.S.A. **110 F6** 40 58N 78 37W
Grampian Highlands = Grampian Mts., U.K. **14 E5** 56 50N 4 0W
Grampian Mts., U.K. **14 E5** 56 50N 4 0W
Grampians, The, Australia **95 F3** 37 0 S 142 20 E
Gramsh, Albania **40 F4** 40 52N 20 12 E
Gran Canaria, Canary Is. **37 G4** 27 55N 15 35W
Gran Chaco, S. Amer. **126 B3** 25 0 S 61 0W
Gran Paradiso, Italy **28 C4** 45 33N 7 17 E
Gran Sasso d'Itália, Italy **29 F10** 42 27N 13 42 E
Granada, Nic. **120 D2** 11 58N 86 0W
Granada, Spain **35 H7** 37 10N 3 35W
Granada, U.S.A. **113 F3** 38 4N 102 19W
Granada □, Spain **35 H7** 37 18N 3 0W
Granadilla de Abona, Canary Is. **37 F3** 28 7N 16 33W
Granard, Ireland **15 C4** 53 47N 7 30W
Granbury, U.S.A. **113 J6** 32 27N 97 47W
Granby, Canada **102 C5** 45 25N 72 45W
Granby, U.S.A. **114 F11** 40 5N 105 56W
Grand →, Canada **110 D5** 42 51N 79 34W
Grand →, Mo., U.S.A. **112 F8** 39 23N 93 7W
Grand →, S. Dak., U.S.A. **112 C4** 45 40N 100 45W
Grand Bahama, Bahamas **120 A4** 26 40N 78 30W
Grand Bank, Canada **103 C8** 47 6N 55 48W
Grand Bassam, Ivory C. **82 D4** 5 10N 3 49W
Grand Béréby, Ivory C. **82 E3** 4 38N 6 55W
Grand-Bourg, Guadeloupe **121 C7** 15 53N 61 19W
Grand Canal = Yun Ho →, China **57 E9** 39 10N 117 10 E
Grand Canyon, U.S.A. **115 H7** 36 3N 112 9W
Grand Canyon National Park, U.S.A. **115 H7** 36 15N 112 30W
Grand Cayman, Cayman Is. **120 C3** 19 20N 81 20W
Grand Centre, Canada **105 C6** 54 25N 110 13W
Grand Cess, Liberia **82 E3** 4 40N 8 12W
Grand Coulee, U.S.A. **114 C4** 47 57N 119 0W
Grand Coulee Dam, U.S.A. **114 C4** 47 57N 118 59W
Grand Erg du Bilma, Niger **79 E8** 18 30N 14 0 E
Grand Erg Occidental, Algeria **78 B6** 30 20N 1 0 E
Grand Erg Oriental, Algeria **78 B7** 30 0N 6 30 E
Grand Falls, Canada **103 C6** 47 3N 67 44W
Grand Falls-Windsor, Canada **103 C8** 48 56N 55 40W
Grand Forks, Canada **104 D5** 49 0N 118 30W
Grand Forks, U.S.A. **112 B6** 47 55N 97 3W
Grand Gorge, U.S.A. **111 D10** 42 21N 74 29W
Grand Haven, U.S.A. **108 D2** 43 4N 86 13W
Grand I., Mich., U.S.A. **108 B2** 46 31N 86 40W
Grand I., N.Y., U.S.A. **110 D6** 43 0N 78 58W
Grand Island, U.S.A. **112 E5** 40 55N 98 21W
Grand Isle, La., U.S.A. **113 L9** 29 14N 90 0W
Grand Isle, Vt., U.S.A. **111 B11** 44 43N 73 18W
Grand Junction, U.S.A. **115 G9** 39 4N 108 33W
Grand L., N.B., Canada **103 C6** 45 57N 66 7W
Grand L., Nfld., Canada **103 C8** 49 0N 57 30W
Grand L., Nfld., Canada **103 B7** 53 40N 60 30W
Grand L., U.S.A. **113 L8** 29 55N 92 47W
Grand Lahou, Ivory C. **82 D3** 5 10N 5 5W
Grand Lake, U.S.A. **114 F11** 40 15N 105 49W
Grand-Lieu, L. de, France **18 E5** 47 6N 1 40W
Grand Manan I., Canada **103 D6** 44 45N 66 52W
Grand Marais, Canada **112 B9** 47 45N 90 25W
Grand Marais, U.S.A. **108 B3** 46 40N 85 59W
Grand-Mère, Canada **102 C5** 46 36N 72 40W
Grand Popo, Benin **83 D5** 6 15N 1 57 E
Grand Portage, U.S.A. **112 B10** 47 58N 89 41W
Grand Prairie, U.S.A. **113 J6** 32 47N 97 0W
Grand Rapids, Canada **105 C9** 53 12N 99 19W
Grand Rapids, Mich., U.S.A. **108 D2** 42 58N 85 40W
Grand Rapids, Minn., U.S.A. **112 B8** 47 14N 93 31W
Grand St-Bernard, Col du, Europe **25 K3** 45 50N 7 10 E
Grand Teton, U.S.A. **114 E8** 43 54N 111 50W
Grand Teton National Park, U.S.A. **114 D8** 43 50N 110 50W
Grand Union Canal, U.K. **13 E7** 52 7N 0 53W
Grand View, Canada **105 C8** 51 10N 100 42W

Grandas de Salime, *Spain* **34 B4** 43 13N 6 53W
Grande →, *Jujuy, Argentina* **126 A2** 24 20S 65 2W
Grande →, *Mendoza, Argentina* **126 D2** 36 52S 69 45W
Grande →, *Bolivia* **124 G6** 15 51S 64 39W
Grande →, *Bahia, Brazil* **125 F10** 11 30S 44 30W
Grande →, *Minas Gerais, Brazil* **125 H8** 20 6S 51 4W
Grande, B., *Argentina* **128 G3** 50 30S 68 20W
Grande, Rio →, *U.S.A.* **113 N6** 25 58N 97 9W
Grande Baleine, R. de la →, *Canada* **102 A4** 55 16N 77 47W
Grande Cache, *Canada* **104 C5** 53 53N 119 8W
Grande-Entrée, *Canada* **103 C7** 47 30N 61 40W
Grande Prairie, *Canada* **104 B5** 55 10N 118 50W
Grande-Rivière, *Canada* **103 C7** 48 26N 64 30W
Grande-Vallée, *Canada* **103 C6** 49 14N 65 8W
Grandfalls, *U.S.A.* **113 K3** 31 20N 102 51W
Grândola, *Portugal* **35 G2** 38 12N 8 35W
Grandpré, *France* **19 C11** 49 20N 4 50 E
Grandview, *U.S.A.* **114 C4** 46 15N 119 54W
Grandvilliers, *France* **19 C8** 49 40N 1 57 E
Graneros, *Chile* **126 C1** 34 5S 70 45W
Grangemouth, *U.K.* **14 E5** 56 1N 3 42W
Granger, *U.S.A.* **114 F9** 41 35N 109 58W
Grängesberg, *Sweden* **10 D9** 60 6N 15 1 E
Grangeville, *U.S.A.* **114 D5** 45 56N 116 7W
Granisle, *Canada* **104 C3** 54 53N 126 13W
Granite City, *U.S.A.* **112 F9** 38 42N 90 9W
Granite Falls, *U.S.A.* **112 C7** 44 49N 95 33W
Granite L., *Canada* **103 C8** 48 8N 57 5W
Granite Mt., *U.S.A.* **117 M10** 33 5N 116 28W
Granite Pk., *U.S.A.* **114 D9** 45 10N 109 48W
Graniteville, *U.S.A.* **111 B12** 44 8N 72 29W
Granitola, C., *Italy* **30 E5** 37 34N 12 39 E
Granity, *N.Z.* **91 J3** 41 39S 171 51 E
Granja, *Brazil* **125 D10** 3 7S 40 50W
Granja de Moreruela, *Spain* **34 D5** 41 48N 5 44W
Granja de Torrehermosa, *Spain* **35 G5** 38 19N 5 35W
Gränna, *Sweden* **11 F8** 58 1N 14 28 E
Granollers, *Spain* **32 D7** 41 39N 2 18 E
Gransee, *Germany* **24 B9** 53 1N 13 8 E
Grant, *U.S.A.* **112 E4** 40 53N 101 42W
Grant, Mt., *U.S.A.* **114 G4** 38 34N 118 48W
Grant City, *U.S.A.* **112 E7** 40 29N 94 25W
Grant I., *Australia* **92 B5** 11 10S 132 52 E
Grant Range, *U.S.A.* **115 G6** 38 30N 115 25W
Grantham, *U.K.* **12 E7** 52 55N 0 38W
Grantown-on-Spey, *U.K.* **14 D5** 57 20N 3 36W
Grants, *U.S.A.* **115 J10** 35 9N 107 52W
Grants Pass, *U.S.A.* **114 E2** 42 26N 123 19W
Grantsville, *U.S.A.* **114 F7** 40 36N 112 28W
Granville, *France* **18 D5** 48 50N 1 35W
Granville, *N. Dak., U.S.A.* **112 A4** 48 16N 100 47W
Granville, *N.Y., U.S.A.* **111 C11** 43 24N 73 16W
Granville, *Ohio, U.S.A.* **110 F2** 40 4N 82 31W
Granville L., *Canada* **105 B8** 56 18N 100 30W
Graskop, *S. Africa* **89 C5** 24 56S 30 49 E
Gräsö, *Sweden* **10 D12** 60 28N 18 35 E
Grass →, *Canada* **105 B9** 56 3N 96 33W
Grass Range, *U.S.A.* **114 C9** 47 0N 109 0W
Grass River Prov. Park, *Canada* **105 C8** 54 40N 100 50W
Grass Valley, *Calif., U.S.A.* **116 F6** 39 13N 121 4W
Grass Valley, *Oreg., U.S.A.* **114 D3** 45 22N 120 47W
Grassano, *Italy* **31 B9** 40 38N 16 17 E
Grasse, *France* **21 E10** 43 38N 6 56 E
Grassflat, *U.S.A.* **110 F6** 41 0N 78 6W
Grasslands Nat. Park, *Canada* **105 D7** 49 11N 107 38W
Grassy, *Australia* **94 G3** 40 3S 144 5 E
Gråsten, *Denmark* **11 K3** 54 55N 9 35 E
Grästorp, *Sweden* **11 F6** 58 20N 12 40 E
Gratkorn, *Austria* **26 D8** 47 8N 15 21 E
Graubünden □, *Switz.* **25 J5** 46 45N 9 30 E
Graulhet, *France* **20 E5** 43 45N 1 59 E
Graus, *Spain* **32 C5** 42 11N 0 20 E
Grave, Pte. de, *France* **20 C2** 45 34N 1 4W
Gravelbourg, *Canada* **105 D7** 49 50N 106 35W
Gravelines, *France* **19 A9** 51 1N 2 10 E
's-Gravenhage, *Neths.* **17 B4** 52 7N 4 17 E
Gravenhurst, *Canada* **102 D4** 44 52N 79 20W
Gravesend, *Australia* **95 D5** 29 35S 150 20 E
Gravesend, *U.K.* **13 F8** 51 26N 0 22 E
Gravina in Púglia, *Italy* **31 B9** 40 49N 16 25 E
Gravois, Pointe-à-, *Haiti* **121 C5** 18 15N 73 56W
Gravone →, *France* **21 G12** 41 58N 8 45 E
Gray, *France* **19 E12** 47 22N 5 35 E
Grayling, *U.S.A.* **108 C3** 44 40N 84 43W
Grays Harbor, *U.S.A.* **114 C1** 46 59N 124 1W
Grays L., *U.S.A.* **114 E8** 43 4N 111 26W
Grays River, *U.S.A.* **116 D3** 46 21N 123 37W
Grayvoron, *Russia* **47 G8** 50 29N 35 41 E
Graz, *Austria* **26 D8** 47 4N 15 27 E
Grdelica, *Serbia, Yug.* **40 D6** 42 55N 22 3 E
Greasy L., *Canada* **104 A4** 62 55N 122 12W
Great Abaco I., *Bahamas* **120 A4** 26 25N 77 10W
Great Artesian Basin, *Australia* **94 C3** 23 0S 144 0 E
Great Australian Bight, *Australia* **93 F5** 33 30S 130 0 E
Great Bahama Bank, *Bahamas* **120 B4** 23 15N 78 0W
Great Barrier I., *N.Z.* **91 G5** 36 11S 175 25 E
Great Barrier Reef, *Australia* **94 B4** 18 0S 146 50 E
Great Barrington, *U.S.A.* **111 D11** 42 12N 73 22W
Great Basin, *U.S.A.* **114 G5** 40 0N 117 0W
Great Basin Nat. Park, *U.S.A.* **114 G6** 38 55N 114 14W
Great Bear →, *Canada* **100 B7** 65 0N 124 0W
Great Bear L., *Canada* **100 B7** 65 30N 120 0W
Great Belt = Store Bælt, *Denmark* **11 J4** 55 20N 11 0 E
Great Bend, *Kans., U.S.A.* **112 F5** 38 22N 98 46W
Great Bend, *Pa., U.S.A.* **111 E9** 41 58N 75 45W
Great Blasket I., *Ireland* **15 D1** 52 6N 10 32W
Great Britain, *Europe* **6 E5** 54 0N 2 15W
Great Codroy, *Canada* **103 C8** 47 51N 59 16W
Great Dividing Ra., *Australia* **94 C4** 23 0S 146 0 E
Great Driffield = Driffield, *U.K.* **12 C7** 54 0N 0 26W
Great Exuma I., *Bahamas* **120 B4** 23 30N 75 50W
Great Falls, *U.S.A.* **114 C8** 47 30N 111 17W
Great Fish = Groot Vis →, *S. Africa* **88 E4** 33 28S 27 5 E
Great Guana Cay, *Bahamas* **120 B4** 24 0N 76 20W
Great Inagua I., *Bahamas* **121 B5** 21 0N 73 20W
Great Indian Desert = Thar Desert, *India* **68 F5** 28 0N 72 0 E
Great Karoo, *S. Africa* **88 E3** 31 55S 21 0 E
Great Lake, *Australia* **94 G4** 41 50S 146 40 E
Great Lakes, *N. Amer.* **98 E11** 46 0N 84 0W
Great Malvern, *U.K.* **13 E5** 52 7N 2 18W
Great Miami →, *U.S.A.* **108 F3** 39 20N 84 40W
Great Ormes Head, *U.K.* **12 D4** 53 20N 3 52W
Great Ouse →, *U.K.* **12 E8** 52 48N 0 21 E
Great Palm I., *Australia* **94 B4** 18 45S 146 40 E
Great Plains, *N. Amer.* **106 A6** 47 0N 105 0W
Great Ruaha →, *Tanzania* **86 D4** 7 56S 37 52 E
Great Sacandaga Res., *U.S.A.* **111 C10** 43 6N 74 16W
Great Saint Bernard Pass = Grand St-Bernard, Col du, *Europe* **25 K3** 45 50N 7 10 E
Great Salt L., *U.S.A.* **114 F7** 41 15N 112 40W
Great Salt Lake Desert, *U.S.A.* **114 F7** 40 50N 113 30W
Great Salt Plains L., *U.S.A.* **113 G5** 36 45N 98 8W
Great Sandy Desert, *Australia* **92 D3** 21 0S 124 0 E
Great Sangi = Sangihe, Pulau, *Indonesia* **63 D7** 3 45N 125 30 E
Great Scarcies →, *S. Leone* **82 D2** 9 0N 13 0W
Great Skellig, *Ireland* **15 E1** 51 47N 10 33W
Great Slave L., *Canada* **104 A5** 61 23N 115 38W
Great Smoky Mts. Nat. Park, *U.S.A.* **109 H4** 35 40N 83 40W
Great Snow Mt., *Canada* **104 B4** 57 26N 124 0W
Great Stour = Stour →, *U.K.* **13 F9** 51 18N 1 22 E
Great Victoria Desert, *Australia* **93 E4** 29 30S 126 30 E
Great Wall, *China* **56 E5** 38 30N 109 30 E
Great Whernside, *U.K.* **12 C6** 54 10N 1 58W
Great Yarmouth, *U.K.* **13 E9** 52 37N 1 44 E
Greater Antilles, *W. Indies* **121 C5** 17 40N 74 0W
Greater London □, *U.K.* **13 F7** 51 31N 0 6W
Greater Manchester □, *U.K.* **12 D5** 53 30N 2 15W
Greater Sunda Is., *Indonesia* **62 F4** 7 0S 112 0 E
Grebbestad, *Sweden* **11 F5** 58 42N 11 15 E
Grebenka = Hrebenka, *Ukraine* **47 G7** 50 9N 32 22 E
Greco, C., *Cyprus* **36 E13** 34 57N 34 5 E
Greco, Mte., *Italy* **29 G10** 41 48N 13 58 E
Gredos, Sierra de, *Spain* **34 E6** 40 20N 5 0W
Greece, *U.S.A.* **110 C7** 43 13N 77 41W
Greece ■, *Europe* **38 B3** 40 0N 23 0 E
Greeley, *Colo., U.S.A.* **112 E2** 40 25N 104 42W
Greeley, *Nebr., U.S.A.* **112 E5** 41 33N 98 32W
Greem-Bell, Ostrov, *Russia* **50 A7** 81 0N 62 0 E
Green, *U.S.A.* **114 E2** 43 9N 123 22W
Green →, *Ky., U.S.A.* **108 G2** 37 54N 87 30W
Green →, *Utah, U.S.A.* **115 G9** 38 11N 109 53W
Green B., *U.S.A.* **108 C2** 45 0N 87 30W
Green Bay, *U.S.A.* **108 C2** 44 31N 88 0W
Green C., *Australia* **95 F5** 37 13S 150 1 E
Green Cove Springs, *U.S.A.* **109 L5** 29 59N 81 42W
Green Lake, *Canada* **105 C7** 54 17N 107 47W
Green Mts., *U.S.A.* **111 C12** 43 45N 72 45W
Green River, *Utah, U.S.A.* **115 G8** 38 59N 110 10W
Green River, *Wyo., U.S.A.* **114 F9** 41 32N 109 28W
Green Valley, *U.S.A.* **115 L8** 31 52N 110 56W
Greenbank, *U.S.A.* **116 B4** 48 6N 122 34W
Greenbush, *Mich., U.S.A.* **110 B1** 44 35N 83 19W
Greenbush, *Minn., U.S.A.* **112 A6** 48 42N 96 11W
Greencastle, *U.S.A.* **108 F2** 39 38N 86 52W
Greene, *U.S.A.* **111 D9** 42 20N 75 46W
Greenfield, *Calif., U.S.A.* **116 J5** 36 19N 121 15W
Greenfield, *Calif., U.S.A.* **117 K8** 35 15N 119 0W
Greenfield, *Ind., U.S.A.* **108 F3** 39 47N 85 46W
Greenfield, *Iowa, U.S.A.* **112 E7** 41 18N 94 28W
Greenfield, *Mass., U.S.A.* **111 D12** 42 35N 72 36W
Greenfield, *Mo., U.S.A.* **113 G8** 37 25N 93 51W
Greenfield Park, *Canada* **111 A11** 45 29N 73 29W
Greenland ■, *N. Amer.* **4 C5** 66 0N 45 0W
Greenland Sea, *Arctic* **4 B7** 73 0N 10 0W
Greenock, *U.K.* **14 F4** 55 57N 4 46W
Greenore, *Ireland* **15 B5** 54 2N 6 8W
Greenore Pt., *Ireland* **15 D5** 52 14N 6 19W
Greenough, *Australia* **93 E1** 28 58S 114 43 E
Greenough →, *Australia* **93 E1** 28 51S 114 38 E
Greenough Pt., *Canada* **110 B3** 44 58N 81 26W
Greenport, *U.S.A.* **111 E12** 41 6N 72 22W
Greensboro, *Ga., U.S.A.* **109 J4** 33 35N 83 11W
Greensboro, *N.C., U.S.A.* **109 G6** 36 4N 79 48W
Greensboro, *Vt., U.S.A.* **111 B12** 44 36N 72 18W
Greensburg, *Ind., U.S.A.* **108 F3** 39 20N 85 29W
Greensburg, *Kans., U.S.A.* **113 G5** 37 36N 99 18W
Greensburg, *Pa., U.S.A.* **110 F5** 40 18N 79 33W
Greenstone Pt., *U.K.* **14 D3** 57 55N 5 37W
Greenvale, *Australia* **94 B4** 18 59S 145 7 E
Greenville, *Liberia* **82 D3** 5 1N 9 6W
Greenville, *Ala., U.S.A.* **109 K2** 31 50N 86 38W
Greenville, *Calif., U.S.A.* **116 E6** 40 8N 120 57W
Greenville, *Maine, U.S.A.* **109 C11** 45 28N 69 35W
Greenville, *Mich., U.S.A.* **108 D3** 43 11N 85 15W
Greenville, *Miss., U.S.A.* **113 J9** 33 24N 91 4W
Greenville, *Mo., U.S.A.* **113 G9** 37 8N 90 27W
Greenville, *N.C., U.S.A.* **109 H7** 35 37N 77 23W
Greenville, *N.H., U.S.A.* **111 D13** 42 46N 71 49W
Greenville, *N.Y., U.S.A.* **111 D10** 42 25N 74 1W
Greenville, *Ohio, U.S.A.* **108 E3** 40 6N 84 38W
Greenville, *Pa., U.S.A.* **110 E4** 41 24N 80 23W
Greenville, *S.C., U.S.A.* **109 H4** 34 51N 82 24W
Greenville, *Tenn., U.S.A.* **109 G4** 36 13N 82 51W
Greenville, *Tex., U.S.A.* **113 J6** 33 8N 96 7W
Greenwater Lake Prov. Park, *Canada* **105 C8** 52 32N 103 30W
Greenwich, *U.K.* **13 F8** 51 29N 0 1 E
Greenwich, *Conn., U.S.A.* **111 E11** 41 2N 73 38W
Greenwich, *N.Y., U.S.A.* **111 C11** 43 5N 73 30W
Greenwich, *Ohio, U.S.A.* **110 E2** 41 2N 82 31W
Greenwood, *Canada* **104 D5** 49 10N 118 40W
Greenwood, *Ark., U.S.A.* **113 H7** 35 13N 94 16W
Greenwood, *Ind., U.S.A.* **108 F2** 39 37N 86 7W
Greenwood, *Miss., U.S.A.* **113 J9** 33 31N 90 11W
Greenwood, *S.C., U.S.A.* **109 H4** 34 12N 82 10W
Greenwood, Mt., *Australia* **92 B5** 13 48S 130 4 E
Gregbe, *Ivory C.* **82 D3** 6 48N 6 43W
Gregory, *U.S.A.* **112 D5** 43 14N 99 20W
Gregory →, *Australia* **94 B2** 17 53S 139 17 E
Gregory, L., *S. Austral., Australia* **95 D2** 28 55S 139 0 E
Gregory, L., *W. Austral., Australia* **93 E2** 25 38S 119 58 E
Gregory Downs, *Australia* **94 B2** 18 35S 138 45 E
Gregory L., *Australia* **92 D4** 20 0S 127 40 E
Gregory Ra., *Queens., Australia* **94 B3** 19 30S 143 40 E
Gregory Ra., *W. Austral., Australia* **92 D3** 21 20S 121 12 E
Greiffenberg, *Germany* **24 B9** 53 5N 13 57 E
Greifswald, *Germany* **24 A9** 54 5N 13 23 E
Greifswalder Bodden, *Germany* **24 A9** 54 12N 13 35 E
Grein, *Austria* **26 C7** 48 14N 14 51 E
Greiz, *Germany* **24 E8** 50 39N 12 10 E
Gremikha, *Russia* **50 C4** 67 59N 39 47 E
Grenå, *Denmark* **11 H4** 56 25N 10 53 E
Grenada, *U.S.A.* **113 J10** 33 47N 89 49W
Grenada ■, *W. Indies* **121 D7** 12 10N 61 40W
Grenade, *France* **20 E5** 43 47N 1 17 E
Grenadier I., *U.S.A.* **111 B8** 44 3N 76 22W
Grenadines, *W. Indies* **121 D7** 12 40N 61 20W
Grenchen, *Switz.* **25 H3** 47 12N 7 24 E
Grenen, *Denmark* **11 G4** 57 44N 10 40 E
Grenfell, *Australia* **95 E4** 33 52S 148 8 E
Grenfell, *Canada* **105 C8** 50 30N 102 56W
Grenoble, *France* **21 C9** 45 12N 5 42 E
Grenville, C., *Australia* **94 A3** 12 0S 143 13 E
Grenville Chan., *Canada* **104 C3** 53 40N 129 46W
Gréoux-les-Bains, *France* **21 E9** 43 45N 5 52 E
Gresham, *U.S.A.* **116 E4** 45 30N 122 26W
Gresik, *Indonesia* **63 G15** 7 13S 112 38 E
Gretna, *U.K.* **14 F5** 55 0N 3 3W
Greven, *Germany* **24 C3** 52 6N 7 37 E
Grevená, *Greece* **40 F5** 40 4N 21 25 E
Grevená □, *Greece* **40 F5** 40 2N 21 25 E
Grevenbroich, *Germany* **24 D2** 51 5N 6 35 E
Grevenmacher, *Lux.* **17 E6** 49 41N 6 26 E
Grevesmühlen, *Germany* **24 B7** 53 52N 11 12 E
Grevestrand, *Denmark* **11 J6** 55 36N 12 19 E
Grey →, *Canada* **103 C8** 47 34N 57 6W
Grey →, *N.Z.* **91 K3** 42 27S 171 12 E
Grey, C., *Australia* **94 A2** 13 0S 136 35 E
Grey Ra., *Australia* **95 D3** 27 0S 143 30 E
Greybull, *U.S.A.* **114 D9** 44 30N 108 3W
Greymouth, *N.Z.* **91 K3** 42 29S 171 13 E
Greystones, *Ireland* **15 C5** 53 9N 6 5W
Greytown, *N.Z.* **91 J5** 41 5S 175 29 E
Greytown, *S. Africa* **89 D5** 29 1S 30 36 E
Gribanovskiy, *Russia* **48 E5** 51 28N 41 50 E
Gribbell I., *Canada* **104 C3** 53 23N 129 0W
Gribës, Mal i, *Albania* **40 F3** 40 17N 19 45 E
Gridley, *U.S.A.* **116 F5** 39 22N 121 42W
Griekwastad, *S. Africa* **88 D3** 28 49S 23 15 E
Griesheim, *Germany* **25 F4** 49 51N 8 33 E
Grieskirchen, *Austria* **26 C6** 48 16N 13 48 E
Griffin, *U.S.A.* **109 J3** 33 15N 84 16W
Griffith, *Australia* **95 E4** 34 18S 146 2 E
Griffith, *Canada* **110 A7** 45 15N 77 10W
Griffith I., *Canada* **110 B4** 44 50N 80 55W
Grignols, *France* **20 D3** 44 23N 0 2W
Grigoriopol, *Moldova* **43 C14** 47 9N 29 18 E
Grimaylov = Hrymayliv, *Ukraine* **47 H4** 49 20N 26 5 E
Grimes, *U.S.A.* **116 F5** 39 4N 121 54W
Grimma, *Germany* **24 D8** 51 14N 12 43 E
Grimmen, *Germany* **24 A9** 54 7N 13 3 E
Grimsay, *U.K.* **14 D1** 57 29N 7 14W
Grimsby, *Canada* **110 C5** 43 12N 79 34W
Grimsby, *U.K.* **12 D7** 53 34N 0 5W
Grímsey, *Iceland* **8 C5** 66 33N 17 58W
Grimshaw, *Canada* **104 B5** 56 10N 117 40W
Grimslöv, *Sweden* **11 H8** 56 44N 14 34 E
Grimstad, *Norway* **9 G13** 58 20N 8 35 E
Grindelwald, *Switz.* **25 J4** 46 38N 8 2 E
Grindsted, *Denmark* **11 J2** 55 46N 8 55 E
Grindstone I., *Canada* **111 B8** 44 43N 76 14W
Grindu, *Romania* **43 F11** 44 44N 26 50 E
Grinnell, *U.S.A.* **112 E8** 41 45N 92 43W
Grintavec, *Slovenia* **29 B11** 46 22N 14 32 E
Gris-Nez, C., *France* **19 B8** 50 52N 1 35 E
Grisolles, *France* **20 E5** 43 49N 1 19 E
Grisons = Graubünden □, *Switz.* **25 J5** 46 45N 9 30 E
Grisslehamn, *Sweden* **10 D12** 60 5N 18 49 E
Grmeč Planina, *Bos.-H.* **29 D13** 44 43N 16 16 E
Groais I., *Canada* **103 B8** 50 55N 55 35W
Grobiņa, *Latvia* **44 B8** 56 33N 21 10 E
Groblersdal, *S. Africa* **89 D4** 25 15S 29 25 E
Grobming, *Austria* **26 D6** 47 27N 13 54 E
Grocka, *Serbia, Yug.* **40 B4** 44 40N 20 42 E
Gródek, *Poland* **45 E10** 53 6N 23 40 E
Grodków, *Poland* **45 H4** 50 43N 17 21 E
Grodno = Hrodna, *Belarus* **46 F2** 53 42N 23 52 E
Grodzisk Mazowiecki, *Poland* **45 F7** 52 7N 20 37 E
Grodzisk Wielkopolski, *Poland* **45 F3** 52 15N 16 22 E
Grodzyanka = Hrodzyanka, *Belarus* **46 F5** 53 31N 28 42 E
Groesbeck, *U.S.A.* **113 K6** 30 48N 96 31W
Groix, *France* **18 E3** 47 38N 3 29W
Groix, Î. de, *France* **18 E3** 47 38N 3 28W
Grójec, *Poland* **45 G7** 51 50N 20 58 E
Gronau, *Niedersachsen, Germany* **24 C5** 52 5N 9 47 E
Gronau, *Nordrhein-Westfalen, Germany* **24 C3** 52 12N 7 2 E
Grong, *Norway* **8 D15** 64 25N 12 8 E
Grönhögen, *Sweden* **11 H10** 56 16N 16 24 E
Groningen, *Neths.* **17 A6** 53 15N 6 35 E
Groningen □, *Neths.* **17 A6** 53 16N 6 40 E
Groom, *U.S.A.* **113 H4** 35 12N 101 6W
Groot →, *S. Africa* **88 E3** 33 45S 24 36 E
Groot Berg →, *S. Africa* **88 E2** 32 47S 18 8 E
Groot-Brakrivier, *S. Africa* **88 E3** 34 2S 22 18 E
Groot Karasberge, *Namibia* **88 D2** 27 20S 18 40 E
Groot-Kei →, *S. Africa* **89 E4** 32 41S 28 22 E
Groot Vis →, *S. Africa* **88 E4** 33 28S 27 5 E
Grootdrink, *S. Africa* **88 D3** 28 33S 21 42 E
Groote Eylandt, *Australia* **94 A2** 14 0S 136 40 E
Grootfontein, *Namibia* **88 B2** 19 31S 18 6 E
Grootlaagte →, *Africa* **88 C3** 20 55S 21 27 E
Grootvloer →, *S. Africa* **88 E3** 30 0S 20 40 E
Gros C., *Canada* **104 A6** 61 59N 113 32W
Gros Morne Nat. Park, *Canada* **103 C8** 49 40N 57 50W
Grósio, *Italy* **28 B7** 46 18N 10 16 E
Grosne →, *France* **19 F11** 46 42N 4 56 E
Grossa, Pta., *Spain* **37 B8** 39 6N 1 36 E
Grossenbrode, *Germany* **24 A7** 54 21N 11 4 E
Grossenhain, *Germany* **24 D9** 51 17N 13 32 E
Grosser Arber, *Germany* **25 F9** 49 6N 13 8 E
Grosser Plöner See, *Germany* **24 A6** 54 10N 10 22 E
Grosseto, *Italy* **29 F8** 42 46N 11 8 E
Grossgerungs, *Austria* **26 C7** 48 34N 14 57 E
Grossglockner, *Austria* **26 D5** 47 5N 12 40 E
Groswater B., *Canada* **103 B8** 54 20N 57 40W
Groton, *Conn., U.S.A.* **111 E12** 41 21N 72 5W
Groton, *N.Y., U.S.A.* **111 D8** 42 36N 76 22W
Groton, *S. Dak., U.S.A.* **112 C5** 45 27N 98 6W
Grottáglie, *Italy* **31 B10** 40 32N 17 26 E
Grottaminarda, *Italy* **31 A8** 41 4N 15 2 E
Grottammare, *Italy* **29 F10** 42 59N 13 52 E
Grouard Mission, *Canada* **104 B5** 55 33N 116 9W
Grouin, Pte. du, *France* **18 D5** 48 43N 1 51W
Groundhog →, *Canada* **102 C3** 48 45N 82 58W
Grouw, *Neths.* **17 A5** 53 5N 5 51 E
Grove City, *U.S.A.* **110 E4** 41 10N 80 5W
Grove Hill, *U.S.A.* **109 K2** 31 42N 87 47W
Groveland, *U.S.A.* **116 H6** 37 50N 120 14W
Grover City, *U.S.A.* **117 K6** 35 7N 120 37W
Groves, *U.S.A.* **113 L8** 29 57N 93 54W
Groveton, *U.S.A.* **111 B13** 44 36N 71 31W
Grožnjan, *Croatia* **29 C10** 45 22N 13 43 E
Groznyy, *Russia* **49 J7** 43 20N 45 45 E
Grubišno Polje, *Croatia* **42 E2** 45 44N 17 12 E
Grudovo, *Bulgaria* **41 D11** 42 21N 27 10 E
Grudusk, *Poland* **45 E7** 53 3N 20 38 E
Grudziądz, *Poland* **44 E5** 53 30N 18 47 E
Gruinard B., *U.K.* **14 D3** 57 56N 5 35W
Gruissan, *France* **20 E7** 43 8N 3 7 E
Grumo Áppula, *Italy* **31 A9** 41 1N 16 42 E
Grums, *Sweden* **10 E7** 59 22N 13 5 E
Grünberg, *Germany* **24 E4** 50 35N 8 58 E
Gründau, *Germany* **25 E5** 50 10N 9 9 E
Grundy Center, *U.S.A.* **112 D8** 42 22N 92 47W
Grünstadt, *Germany* **25 F4** 49 34N 8 9 E
Gruvberget, *Sweden* **10 C10** 61 6N 16 10 E
Gruver, *U.S.A.* **113 G4** 36 16N 101 24W
Gruyères, *Switz.* **25 J3** 46 35N 7 4 E
Gruža, *Serbia, Yug.* **40 C4** 43 54N 20 46 E
Gryazi, *Russia* **47 F10** 52 30N 39 58 E
Gryazovets, *Russia* **46 C11** 58 50N 40 10 E
Grybów, *Poland* **45 J7** 49 36N 20 55 E
Gryckbo, *Sweden* **10 D9** 60 40N 15 29 E
Gryfice, *Poland* **44 E2** 53 55N 15 13 E
Gryfino, *Poland* **45 E1** 53 16N 14 29 E
Gryfów Śląski, *Poland* **45 G2** 51 2N 15 24 E
Grythyttan, *Sweden* **10 E8** 59 41N 14 32 E
Gstaad, *Switz.* **25 J3** 46 28N 7 18 E
Gua, *India* **67 H14** 22 18N 85 20 E
Gua Musang, *Malaysia* **65 K3** 4 53N 101 58 E
Guacanayabo, G. de, *Cuba* **120 B4** 20 40N 77 20W
Guachípas →, *Argentina* **126 B2** 25 40S 65 30W
Guadajoz →, *Spain* **35 H6** 37 50N 4 51W
Guadalajara, *Mexico* **118 C4** 20 40N 103 20W
Guadalajara, *Spain* **32 E1** 40 37N 3 12W
Guadalajara □, *Spain* **32 E2** 40 47N 2 30W
Guadalcanal, *Solomon Is.* **96 H8** 9 32S 160 12 E
Guadalcanal, *Spain* **35 G5** 38 5N 5 52W
Guadalén →, *Spain* **35 G7** 38 5N 3 32W
Guadales, *Argentina* **126 C2** 34 30S 67 55W
Guadalete →, *Spain* **35 J4** 36 35N 6 13W
Guadalimar →, *Spain* **35 G7** 38 5N 3 28W
Guadalmena →, *Spain* **35 G8** 38 19N 2 56W
Guadalmez →, *Spain* **35 G5** 38 46N 5 4W
Guadalope →, *Spain* **32 D4** 41 15N 0 3W
Guadalquivir →, *Spain* **35 J4** 36 47N 6 22W
Guadalupe = Guadeloupe ■, *W. Indies* **121 C7** 16 20N 61 40W
Guadalupe, *Mexico* **117 N10** 32 4N 116 32W
Guadalupe, *Spain* **35 F5** 39 27N 5 17W
Guadalupe, *U.S.A.* **117 L6** 34 59N 120 33W
Guadalupe →, *Mexico* **117 N10** 32 6N 116 51W
Guadalupe →, *U.S.A.* **113 L6** 28 27N 96 47W
Guadalupe, Sierra de, *Spain* **35 F5** 39 28N 5 30W
Guadalupe Bravos, *Mexico* **118 A3** 31 20N 106 10W
Guadalupe I., *Pac. Oc.* **98 G8** 29 0N 118 50W
Guadalupe Mts. Nat. Park, *U.S.A.* **113 K2** 32 0N 104 30W
Guadalupe Peak, *U.S.A.* **113 K2** 31 50N 104 52W
Guadalupe y Calvo, *Mexico* **118 B3** 26 6N 106 58W
Guadarrama, Sierra de, *Spain* **34 E7** 41 0N 4 0W
Guadauta, *Georgia* **49 J5** 43 7N 40 32 E
Guadeloupe ■, *W. Indies* **121 C7** 16 20N 61 40W
Guadeloupe Passage, *W. Indies* **121 C7** 16 50N 62 15W
Guadiamar →, *Spain* **35 J4** 36 55N 6 24W
Guadiana →, *Portugal* **35 H3** 37 14N 7 22W
Guadiana Menor →, *Spain* **35 H7** 37 56N 3 15W
Guadiaro →, *Spain* **35 J5** 36 17N 5 17W
Guadiato →, *Spain* **35 H5** 37 48N 5 5W
Guadiela →, *Spain* **32 E2** 40 22N 2 49W
Guadix, *Spain* **35 H7** 37 18N 3 11W
Guafo, Boca del, *Chile* **128 E2** 43 35S 74 0W
Guainía →, *Colombia* **124 C5** 2 1N 67 7W
Guaíra, *Brazil* **127 A5** 24 5S 54 10W
Guaíra □, *Paraguay* **126 B4** 25 45S 56 30W
Guaitecas, Is., *Chile* **128 E2** 44 0S 74 30W
Guajará-Mirim, *Brazil* **124 F5** 10 50S 65 20W
Guajira, Pen. de la, *Colombia* **124 A4** 12 0N 72 0W
Gualán, *Guatemala* **120 C2** 15 8N 89 22W
Gualdo Tadino, *Italy* **29 E9** 43 14N 12 47 E
Gualeguay, *Argentina* **126 C4** 33 10S 59 14W
Gualeguaychú, *Argentina* **126 C4** 33 3S 59 31W
Gualequay →, *Argentina* **126 C4** 33 19S 59 39W
Guam ■, *Pac. Oc.* **96 F6** 13 27N 144 45 E
Guaminí, *Argentina* **126 D3** 37 1S 62 28W
Guamúchil, *Mexico* **118 B3** 25 25N 108 3W
Guanabacoa, *Cuba* **120 B3** 23 8N 82 18W
Guanacaste, Cordillera del, *Costa Rica* **120 D2** 10 40N 85 4W
Guanaceví, *Mexico* **118 B3** 25 40N 106 0W
Guanahani = San Salvador I., *Bahamas* **121 B5** 24 0N 74 40W
Guanajay, *Cuba* **120 B3** 22 56N 82 42W
Guanajuato, *Mexico* **118 C4** 21 0N 101 20W
Guanajuato □, *Mexico* **118 C4** 20 40N 101 20W
Guandacol, *Argentina* **126 B2** 29 30S 68 40W
Guane, *Cuba* **120 B3** 22 10N 84 7W
Guang'an, *China* **58 B6** 30 28N 106 35 E
Guangchang, *China* **59 D11** 26 50N 116 21 E
Guangde, *China* **59 B12** 30 54N 119 25 E
Guangdong □, *China* **59 F9** 23 0N 113 0 E
Guangfeng, *China* **59 C12** 28 20N 118 15 E
Guanghan, *China* **58 B5** 30 58N 104 17 E
Guangling, *China* **56 E8** 39 47N 114 22 E
Guangnan, *China* **58 E5** 24 5N 105 4 E
Guangning, *China* **59 F9** 23 40N 112 22 E
Guangrao, *China* **57 F10** 37 5N 118 25 E
Guangshui, *China* **59 B9** 31 37N 114 0 E
Guangshun, *China* **58 D6** 26 8N 106 21 E
Guangwu, *China* **56 F3** 37 48N 105 57 E
Guangxi Zhuangzu Zizhiqu □, *China* **58 F7** 24 0N 109 0 E
Guangyuan, *China* **58 A5** 32 26N 105 51 E
Guangze, *China* **59 D11** 27 30N 117 12 E
Guangzhou, *China* **59 F9** 23 5N 113 10 E
Guanipa →, *Venezuela* **124 B6** 9 56N 62 26W
Guanling, *China* **58 E5** 25 56N 105 35 E
Guannan, *China* **57 G10** 34 8N 119 21 E
Guantánamo, *Cuba* **121 B4** 20 10N 75 14W
Guantao, *China* **56 F8** 36 42N 115 25 E
Guanyang, *China* **59 E8** 25 30N 111 8 E
Guanyun, *China* **57 G10** 34 20N 119 18 E
Guápiles, *Costa Rica* **120 D3** 10 10N 83 46W
Guaporé, *Brazil* **127 B5** 28 51S 51 54W
Guaporé →, *Brazil* **122 E4** 11 55S 65 4W
Guaqui, *Bolivia* **124 G5** 16 41S 68 54W
Guara, Sierra de, *Spain* **32 C4** 42 19N 0 15W
Guarapari, *Brazil* **127 A7** 20 40S 40 30W
Guarapuava, *Brazil* **127 B5** 25 20S 51 30W
Guaratinguetá, *Brazil* **127 A6** 22 49S 45 9W
Guaratuba, *Brazil* **127 B6** 25 53S 48 38W
Guarda, *Portugal* **34 E3** 40 32N 7 20W
Guarda □, *Portugal* **34 E3** 40 40N 7 20W
Guardafui, C. = Asir, Ras, *Somali Rep.* **74 E5** 11 55N 51 10 E
Guardamar del Segura, *Spain* **33 G4** 38 5N 0 39W
Guardavalle, *Italy* **31 D9** 38 30N 16 30 E
Guárdia Sanframondi, *Italy* **31 A7** 41 15N 14 36 E
Guardiagrele, *Italy* **29 F11** 42 11N 14 13 E
Guardo, *Spain* **34 C6** 42 47N 4 50W
Guareña, *Spain* **35 G4** 38 51N 6 6W
Guareña →, *Spain* **34 D5** 41 29N 5 23W
Guárico □, *Venezuela* **124 B5** 8 40N 66 35W
Guarujá, *Brazil* **127 A6** 24 2S 46 25W
Guarus, *Brazil* **127 A7** 21 44S 41 20W
Guasave, *Mexico* **118 B3** 25 34N 108 27W
Guasdualito, *Venezuela* **124 B4** 7 15N 70 44W
Guastalla, *Italy* **28 D7** 44 55N 10 39 E
Guatemala, *Guatemala* **120 D1** 14 40N 90 22W
Guatemala ■, *Cent. Amer.* **120 C1** 15 40N 90 30W
Guaviare →, *Colombia* **122 C4** 4 3N 67 44W
Guaxupé, *Brazil* **127 A6** 21 10S 47 5W
Guayama, *Puerto Rico* **121 C6** 17 59N 66 7W
Guayaquil, *Ecuador* **124 D3** 2 15S 79 52W
Guayaquil, G. de, *Ecuador* **122 D2** 3 10S 81 0W
Guaymas, *Mexico* **118 B2** 27 59N 110 54W
Guba, *Dem. Rep. of the Congo* **87 E2** 10 38S 26 27 E
Guba, *Ethiopia* **81 E4** 11 17N 35 20 E
Gûbâl, Madîq, *Egypt* **80 B3** 27 30N 34 0 E
Gubat, *Phil.* **61 E6** 12 55N 124 7 E
Gúbbio, *Italy* **29 E9** 43 21N 12 35 E
Guben, *Germany* **24 D10** 51 57N 14 43 E
Gubin, *Poland* **45 G1** 51 57N 14 43 E

Gubio, *Nigeria* **83 C7** 12 30N 12 42 E
Gubkin, *Russia* **47 G9** 51 17N 37 32 E
Guča, *Serbia, Yug.* **40 C4** 43 46N 20 15 E
Gucheng, *China* **59 A8** 32 20N 111 30 E
Gudata = Guadauta, *Georgia* **49 J5** 43 7N 40 32 E
Gudbrandsdalen, *Norway* **9 F14** 61 33N 10 10 E
Guddu Barrage, *Pakistan* **66 E6** 28 30N 69 50 E
Gudenå →, *Denmark* **11 H4** 56 29N 10 13 E
Gudermes, *Russia* **49 J8** 43 24N 46 5 E
Gudhjem, *Denmark* **11 J8** 55 12N 14 58 E
Gudivada, *India* **67 L12** 16 30N 81 3 E
Gudur, *India* **66 M11** 14 12N 79 55 E
Guebwiller, *France* **19 E14** 47 55N 7 12 E
Guecho = Getxo, *Spain* **32 B2** 43 21N 2 59W
Guékédou, *Guinea* **82 D2** 8 40N 10 5W
Guéle Mendouka, *Cameroon* **83 E7** 4 23N 12 55 E
Guelph, *Canada* **102 D3** 43 35N 80 20W
Guéméné-Penfao, *France* **18 E5** 47 38N 1 50W
Guéméné-sur-Scorff, *France* **18 D3** 48 4N 3 13W
Guéné, *Benin* **83 C5** 11 44N 3 16 E
Guer, *France* **18 E4** 47 54N 2 8W
Guérande, *France* **18 E4** 47 20N 2 26W
Guéret, *France* **19 F8** 46 11N 1 51 E
Guérigny, *France* **19 E10** 47 6N 3 10 E
Guerneville, *U.S.A.* **116 G4** 38 30N 123 0W
Guernica = Gernika-Lumo, *Spain* **32 B2** 43 19N 2 40W
Guernsey, *U.K.* **13 H5** 49 26N 2 35W
Guernsey, *U.S.A.* **112 D2** 42 19N 104 45W
Guerrero □, *Mexico* **119 D5** 17 30N 100 0W
Guessou-Sud, *Benin* **83 C5** 10 3N 2 38 E
Gueugnon, *France* **19 F11** 46 36N 4 4 E
Guéyo, *Ivory C.* **82 D3** 5 25N 6 5W
Gughe, *Ethiopia* **81 F4** 6 12N 37 30 E
Gügher, *Iran* **71 D8** 29 28N 56 27 E
Guglionesi, *Italy* **29 G11** 41 55N 14 55 E
Guhakolak, Tanjung, *Indonesia* **63 G11** 6 50 S 105 14 E
Gui Jiang →, *China* **59 F8** 23 30N 111 15 E
Guia, *Canary Is.* **37 F4** 28 8N 15 38W
Guia de Isora, *Canary Is.* **37 F3** 28 12N 16 46W
Guia Lopes da Laguna, *Brazil* **127 A4** 21 26 S 56 7W
Guiana, *S. Amer.* **122 C4** 5 10N 60 40W
Guibéroua, *Ivory C.* **82 D3** 6 14N 6 10W
Guichi, *China* **59 B11** 30 39N 117 27 E
Guider, *Cameroon* **83 D7** 9 56N 13 57 E
Guidiguir, *Niger* **83 C6** 13 40N 9 50 E
Guidimouni, *Niger* **83 C6** 13 42N 9 31 E
Guiding, *China* **58 D6** 26 34N 107 11 E
Guidong, *China* **59 D9** 26 7N 113 57 E
Guidónia-Montecélio, *Italy* **29 F9** 42 1N 12 45 E
Guiers, L. de, *Senegal* **82 B1** 16 10N 15 50W
Guigang, *China* **58 F7** 23 8N 109 35 E
Guiglo, *Ivory C.* **82 D3** 6 45N 7 30W
Guihulñgan, *Phil.* **61 F5** 10 7N 123 16 E
Guijá, *Mozam.* **89 C5** 24 27 S 33 0 E
Guijuelo, *Spain* **34 E5** 40 33N 5 40W
Guildford, *U.K.* **13 F7** 51 14N 0 34W
Guilford, *U.S.A.* **111 E12** 41 17N 72 41W
Guilin, *China* **59 E8** 25 18N 110 15 E
Guillaume-Delisle L., *Canada* **102 A4** 56 15N 76 17W
Guillaumes, *France* **21 D10** 44 5N 6 52 E
Guillestre, *France* **21 D10** 44 39N 6 40 E
Guilvinec, *France* **18 E2** 47 48N 4 17W
Güimar, *Canary Is.* **37 F3** 28 18N 16 24W
Guimarães, *Portugal* **34 D2** 41 28N 8 24W
Guimaras □, *Phil.* **61 F5** 10 35N 122 37 E
Guinda, *U.S.A.* **116 G4** 38 50N 122 12W
Guinea, *Africa* **76 F4** 8 0N 8 0 E
Guinea ■, *W. Afr.* **82 C2** 10 20N 11 30W
Guinea, Gulf of, *Atl. Oc.* **83 E5** 3 0N 2 30 E
Guinea-Bissau ■, *Africa* **82 C2** 12 0N 15 0W
Güines, *Cuba* **120 B3** 22 50N 82 0W
Guingamp, *France* **18 D3** 48 34N 3 10W
Guinguinéo, *Senegal* **82 C1** 14 20N 15 57W
Guipavas, *France* **18 D2** 48 26N 4 29W
Guiping, *China* **59 F8** 23 21N 110 2 E
Guipúzcoa □, *Spain* **32 B2** 43 12N 2 15W
Guir, *Mali* **82 B4** 18 52N 2 52W
Guirel, *Mauritania* **82 B3** 15 30N 7 3W
Güiria, *Venezuela* **124 A6** 10 32N 62 18W
Guiscard, *France* **19 C10** 49 40N 3 1 E
Guise, *France* **19 C10** 49 52N 3 35 E
Guitiriz, *Spain* **34 B3** 43 11N 7 50W
Guitri, *Ivory C.* **82 D3** 5 30N 5 14W
Guiuan, *Phil.* **61 F6** 11 5N 125 55 E
Guixi, *China* **59 C11** 28 16N 117 15 E
Guiyang, *Guizhou, China* **58 D6** 26 32N 106 40 E
Guiyang, *Hunan, China* **59 E9** 25 46N 112 42 E
Guizhou □, *China* **58 D6** 27 0N 107 0 E
Gujan-Mestras, *France* **20 D2** 44 38N 1 4W
Gujar Khan, *Pakistan* **68 C5** 33 16N 73 19 E
Gujarat □, *India* **68 H4** 23 20N 71 0 E
Gujiang, *China* **59 D10** 27 11N 114 47 E
Gujranwala, *Pakistan* **68 C6** 32 10N 74 12 E
Gujrat, *Pakistan* **68 C6** 32 40N 74 2 E
Gukovo, *Russia* **49 F5** 48 1N 39 58 E
Gulargambone, *Australia* **95 E4** 31 20 S 148 30 E
Gulbarga, *India* **66 L10** 17 20N 76 50 E
Gulbene, *Latvia* **9 H22** 57 8N 26 52 E
Gulf, The, *Asia* **71 E6** 27 0N 50 0 E
Gulfport, *U.S.A.* **113 K10** 30 22N 89 6W
Gulgong, *Australia* **95 E4** 32 20 S 149 49 E
Gulin, *China* **58 C5** 28 1N 105 50 E
Gulistan, *Pakistan* **68 D2** 30 30N 66 35 E
Gull Lake, *Canada* **105 C7** 50 10N 108 29W
Gullbrandstorp, *Sweden* **11 H6** 56 42N 12 43 E
Gullspång, *Sweden* **11 F8** 58 59N 14 6 E
Güllük, *Turkey* **39 D9** 37 14N 27 35 E
Güllük Korfezi, *Turkey* **39 D9** 37 12N 27 30 E
Gulma, *Nigeria* **83 C5** 12 40N 4 23 E
Gulmarg, *India* **69 B6** 34 3N 74 25 E
Gülnar, *Turkey* **72 D5** 36 19N 33 24 E
Gülpınar, *Turkey* **39 B8** 39 32N 26 7 E
Gülşehir, *Turkey* **72 C6** 38 44N 34 37 E
Gulshad, *Kazakstan* **50 E8** 46 45N 74 25 E
Gulu, *Uganda* **86 B3** 2 48N 32 17 E
Gülübovo, *Bulgaria* **41 D9** 42 8N 25 55 E
Gulud, J., *Sudan* **81 E2** 11 41N 29 31 E
Gulwe, *Tanzania* **86 D4** 6 30 S 36 25 E
Gulyaypole = Hulyaypole, *Ukraine* **47 J9** 47 45N 36 21 E
Gumal →, *Pakistan* **68 D4** 31 40N 71 50 E
Gumbaz, *Pakistan* **68 D3** 30 2N 69 0 E
Gumel, *Nigeria* **83 C6** 12 39N 9 22 E
Gumiel de Hizán, *Spain* **34 D7** 41 46N 3 41W
Gumla, *India* **69 H11** 23 3N 84 33 E
Gumlu, *Australia* **94 B4** 19 53 S 147 41 E
Gumma □, *Japan* **55 F9** 36 30N 138 20 E
Gummersbach, *Germany* **24 D3** 51 1N 7 34 E
Gummi, *Nigeria* **83 C6** 12 4N 5 9 E
Gümüldür, *Turkey* **39 C9** 38 6N 27 0 E
Gümüşçay, *Turkey* **41 F11** 40 16N 27 17 E
Gümüşhaciköy, *Turkey* **72 B6** 40 50N 35 18 E
Gümüşhane, *Turkey* **73 B8** 40 30N 39 30 E
Gümüşsu, *Turkey* **39 C11** 38 14N 29 1 E
Gumzai, *Indonesia* **63 F8** 5 28 S 134 42 E
Guna, *Ethiopia* **81 F4** 8 18N 39 52 E
Guna, *India* **68 G7** 24 40N 77 19 E
Gundelfingen, *Germany* **25 G6** 48 34N 10 22 E
Güney, *Burdur, Turkey* **39 D11** 37 29N 29 34 E
Güney, *Denizli, Turkey* **39 C11** 38 10N 29 4 E
Güneydoğu Toroslar, *Turkey* **73 C9** 38 20N 40 30 E
Gunisao →, *Canada* **105 C9** 53 56N 97 53W
Gunisao L., *Canada* **105 C9** 53 33N 96 15W
Gunjyal, *Pakistan* **68 C4** 32 20N 71 55 E
Günlüce, *Turkey* **39 E10** 36 50N 28 20 E
Gunnarskog, *Sweden* **10 E6** 59 49N 12 34 E
Gunnbjørn Fjeld, *Greenland* **4 C6** 68 55N 29 47W
Gunnebo, *Sweden* **11 G10** 57 44N 16 32 E
Gunnedah, *Australia* **95 E5** 30 59 S 150 15 E
Gunnewin, *Australia* **95 D4** 25 59 S 148 33 E
Gunningbar Cr. →, *Australia* **95 E4** 31 14 S 147 6 E
Gunnison, *Colo., U.S.A.* **115 G10** 38 33N 106 56W
Gunnison, *Utah, U.S.A.* **114 G8** 39 9N 111 49W
Gunnison →, *U.S.A.* **115 G9** 39 4N 108 35W
Gunpowder, *Australia* **94 B2** 19 42 S 139 22 E
Guntakal, *India* **66 M10** 15 11N 77 27 E
Guntersville, *U.S.A.* **109 H2** 34 21N 86 18W
Guntong, *Malaysia* **65 K3** 4 36N 101 3 E
Guntur, *India* **67 L12** 16 23N 80 30 E
Gunungapi, *Indonesia* **63 F7** 6 45 S 126 30 E
Gunungsitoli, *Indonesia* **62 D1** 1 15N 97 30 E
Günz →, *Germany* **25 G6** 48 27N 10 16 E
Gunza, *Angola* **84 G2** 10 50 S 13 50 E
Günzburg, *Germany* **25 G6** 48 26N 10 17 E
Gunzenhausen, *Germany* **25 F6** 49 7N 10 44 E
Guo He →, *China* **57 H9** 32 59N 117 10 E
Guoyang, *China* **56 H9** 33 32N 116 12 E
Gupis, *Pakistan* **69 A5** 36 15N 73 20 E
Gura Humorului, *Romania* **43 C10** 47 35N 25 53 E
Gura-Teghii, *Romania* **43 E11** 45 30N 26 25 E
Gurag, *Ethiopia* **81 F4** 8 20N 38 20 E
Gurahont, *Romania* **42 D7** 46 16N 22 21 E
Gurdaspur, *India* **68 C6** 32 5N 75 31 E
Gurdon, *U.S.A.* **113 J8** 33 55N 93 9W
Güre, *Balıkesir, Turkey* **39 B8** 39 36N 26 54 E
Güre, *Uşak, Turkey* **39 C11** 38 39N 29 10 E
Gurgaon, *India* **68 E7** 28 27N 77 1 E
Gürgentepe, *Turkey* **72 B7** 40 51N 37 50 E
Gurghiu, Munții, *Romania* **43 D10** 46 41N 25 15 E
Gurgueia →, *Brazil* **125 E10** 6 50 S 43 24W
Gurha, *India* **68 G4** 25 12N 71 39 E
Guri, Embalse de, *Venezuela* **124 B6** 7 50N 62 52W
Gurin, *Nigeria* **83 D7** 9 5N 12 54 E
Gurjaani, *Georgia* **49 K7** 41 43N 45 52 E
Gurk →, *Austria* **26 E7** 46 35N 14 31 E
Gurkha, *Nepal* **69 E11** 28 5N 84 40 E
Gurley, *Australia* **95 D4** 29 45 S 149 48 E
Gurnet Point, *U.S.A.* **111 D14** 42 1N 70 34W
Gürpınar, *İst., Turkey* **41 F12** 40 59N 28 37 E
Gürpınar, *Van, Turkey* **73 C10** 38 18N 43 25 E
Gürsu, *Turkey* **41 F13** 40 13N 29 11 E
Gurué, *Mozam.* **87 F4** 15 25 S 36 58 E
Gurun, *Malaysia* **65 K3** 5 49N 100 27 E
Gürün, *Turkey* **72 C7** 38 43N 37 15 E
Gurupá, *Brazil* **125 D8** 1 25 S 51 35W
Gurupá, I. Grande de, *Brazil* **125 D8** 1 25 S 51 45W
Gurupi, *Brazil* **125 F9** 11 43 S 49 4W
Gurupi →, *Brazil* **125 D9** 1 13 S 46 6W
Guruwe, *Zimbabwe* **89 B5** 16 40 S 30 42 E
Guryev = Atyraū, *Kazakstan* **50 E6** 47 5N 52 0 E
Gus-Khrustalnyy, *Russia* **48 C5** 55 42N 40 44 E
Gusau, *Nigeria* **83 C6** 12 12N 6 40 E
Gusev, *Russia* **9 J20** 54 35N 22 10 E
Gushan, *China* **57 E12** 39 50N 123 35 E
Gushgy, *Turkmenistan* **50 F7** 35 20N 62 18 E
Gushi, *China* **59 A10** 32 11N 115 41 E
Gushiago, *Ghana* **83 D4** 9 55N 0 15W
Gusinje, *Montenegro, Yug.* **40 D3** 42 35N 19 50 E
Gusinoozersk, *Russia* **51 D11** 51 16N 106 27 E
Gúspini, *Italy* **30 C1** 39 32N 8 37 E
Güssing, *Austria* **27 D9** 47 3N 16 20 E
Gustavsberg, *Sweden* **10 E12** 59 19N 18 23 E
Gustavus, *U.S.A.* **104 B1** 58 25N 135 44W
Gustine, *U.S.A.* **116 H6** 37 16N 121 0W
Güstrow, *Germany* **24 B8** 53 47N 12 10 E
Gusum, *Sweden* **11 F10** 58 16N 16 30 E
Guta = Kolárovo, *Slovak Rep.* **27 D10** 47 54N 18 0 E
Gütersloh, *Germany* **24 D4** 51 54N 8 24 E
Gutha, *Australia* **93 E2** 28 58 S 115 55 E
Guthalungra, *Australia* **94 B4** 19 52 S 147 50 E
Guthrie, *Okla., U.S.A.* **113 H6** 35 53N 97 25W
Guthrie, *Tex., U.S.A.* **113 J4** 33 37N 100 19W
Gutian, *China* **59 D12** 26 32N 118 43 E
Guttenberg, *U.S.A.* **112 D9** 42 47N 91 6W
Gutu, *Zimbabwe* **89 B5** 19 41 S 31 9 E
Guyana ■, *S. Amer.* **124 C7** 5 0N 59 0W
Guyane française = French Guiana ■, *S. Amer.* **125 C8** 4 0N 53 0W
Guyang, *China* **56 D6** 41 0N 110 5 E
Guyenne, *France* **20 D4** 44 30N 0 40 E
Guymon, *U.S.A.* **113 G4** 36 41N 101 29W
Guyra, *Australia* **95 E5** 30 15 S 151 40 E
Guyuan, *Hebei, China* **56 D8** 41 37N 115 40 E
Guyuan, *Ningxia Huizu, China* **56 G4** 36 0N 106 20 E
Güzelbahçe, *Turkey* **39 C8** 38 21N 26 54 E
Guzhang, *China* **58 C7** 28 42N 109 58 E
Guzhen, *China* **57 H9** 33 22N 117 18 E
Guzmán, L. de, *Mexico* **118 A3** 31 25N 107 25W
Gvardeysk, *Russia* **9 J19** 54 39N 21 5 E
Gvardeyskoye, *Ukraine* **47 K8** 45 7N 34 1 E
Gwa, *Burma* **67 L19** 17 36N 94 34 E
Gwaai, *Zimbabwe* **87 F2** 19 15 S 27 45 E
Gwabegar, *Australia* **95 E4** 30 31 S 149 0 E
Gwadabawa, *Nigeria* **83 C6** 13 28N 5 15 E
Gwādar, *Pakistan* **66 G3** 25 10N 62 18 E
Gwagwada, *Nigeria* **83 C6** 10 15N 7 15 E
Gwalior, *India* **68 F8** 26 12N 78 10 E
Gwanara, *Nigeria* **83 D5** 8 55N 3 9 E
Gwanda, *Zimbabwe* **87 G2** 20 55 S 29 0 E
Gwandu, *Nigeria* **83 C5** 12 30N 4 41 E
Gwane, *Dem. Rep. of the Congo* **86 B2** 4 45N 25 48 E
Gwaram, *Nigeria* **83 C7** 10 15N 10 25 E
Gwarzo, *Nigeria* **83 C6** 12 20N 8 55 E
Gwasero, *Nigeria* **83 D5** 9 29N 3 30 E
Gwda →, *Poland* **45 E3** 53 3N 16 44 E
Gweebarra B., *Ireland* **15 B3** 54 51N 8 23W
Gweedore, *Ireland* **15 A3** 55 3N 8 13W
Gweru, *Zimbabwe* **87 F2** 19 28 S 29 45 E
Gwi, *Nigeria* **83 D6** 9 0N 7 10 E
Gwinn, *U.S.A.* **108 B2** 46 19N 87 27W
Gwio Kura, *Nigeria* **83 C7** 12 40N 11 2 E
Gwoza, *Nigeria* **83 C7** 11 5N 13 40 E
Gwydir →, *Australia* **95 D4** 29 27 S 149 48 E
Gwynedd □, *U.K.* **12 E3** 52 52N 4 10W
Gyandzha = Gäncä, *Azerbaijan* **49 K8** 40 45N 46 20 E
Gyaring Hu, *China* **60 C4** 34 50N 97 40 E
Gydanskiy Poluostrov, *Russia* **50 C8** 70 0N 78 0 E
Gympie, *Australia* **95 D5** 26 11 S 152 38 E
Gyomaendrőd, *Hungary* **42 D5** 46 56N 20 50 E
Gyöngyös, *Hungary* **42 C4** 47 48N 19 56 E
Győr, *Hungary* **42 C2** 47 41N 17 40 E
Győr-Moson-Sopron □, *Hungary* **42 C2** 47 40N 17 20 E
Gypsum Pt., *Canada* **104 A6** 61 53N 114 35W
Gypsumville, *Canada* **105 C9** 51 45N 98 40W
Gyueshevo, *Bulgaria* **40 D6** 42 14N 22 28 E
Gyula, *Hungary* **42 D6** 46 38N 21 17 E
Gyumri, *Armenia* **49 K6** 40 47N 43 50 E
Gyzylarbat, *Turkmenistan* **50 F6** 39 4N 56 23 E
Gyzyletrek, *Turkmenistan* **71 B7** 37 36N 54 46 E
Gzhatsk = Gagarin, *Russia* **46 E8** 55 38N 35 0 E

H

Ha 'Arava →, *Israel* **75 E4** 30 50N 35 20 E
Ha Coi, *Vietnam* **58 G6** 21 26N 107 46 E
Ha Dong, *Vietnam* **58 G5** 20 58N 105 46 E
Ha Giang, *Vietnam* **58 F5** 22 50N 104 59 E
Ha Tien, *Vietnam* **65 G5** 10 23N 104 29 E
Ha Tinh, *Vietnam* **64 C5** 18 20N 105 54 E
Ha Trung, *Vietnam* **64 C5** 19 58N 105 50 E
Haaksbergen, *Neths.* **17 B6** 52 9N 6 45 E
Haapsalu, *Estonia* **9 G20** 58 56N 23 30 E
Haarlem, *Neths.* **17 B4** 52 23N 4 39 E
Haast →, *N.Z.* **91 K2** 43 50 S 169 2 E
Haast Bluff, *Australia* **92 D5** 23 22 S 132 0 E
Hab →, *Pakistan* **68 G3** 24 53N 66 41 E
Hab Nadi Chauki, *Pakistan* **68 G2** 25 0N 66 50 E
Habaswein, *Kenya* **86 B4** 1 2N 39 30 E
Habay, *Canada* **104 B5** 58 50N 118 44W
Ḩabbānīyah, *Iraq* **70 C4** 33 17N 43 29 E
Ḩabbānīyah, Hawr al, *Iraq* **73 F10** 33 17N 43 29 E
Habo, *Sweden* **11 G8** 57 55N 14 6 E
Haboro, *Japan* **54 B10** 44 22N 141 42 E
Ḩabshān, *U.A.E.* **71 F7** 23 50N 53 37 E
Hachenburg, *Germany* **24 E3** 50 40N 7 49 E
Hachijō-Jima, *Japan* **55 H9** 33 5N 139 45 E
Hachinohe, *Japan* **54 D10** 40 30N 141 29 E
Hachiōji, *Japan* **55 G9** 35 40N 139 20 E
Hachŏn, *N. Korea* **57 D15** 41 29N 129 2 E
Hacıbektaş, *Turkey* **72 C6** 38 56N 34 33 E
Hacılar, *Turkey* **72 C6** 38 38N 35 26 E
Hackås, *Sweden* **10 B8** 62 56N 14 30 E
Hackensack, *U.S.A.* **111 F10** 40 53N 74 3W
Hackettstown, *U.S.A.* **111 F10** 40 51N 74 50W
Hadali, *Pakistan* **68 C5** 32 16N 72 11 E
Hadarba, Ras, *Sudan* **80 C4** 22 4N 36 51 E
Hadarom □, *Israel* **75 E4** 31 0N 35 0 E
Hadd, Ra's al, *Oman* **74 C6** 22 35N 59 50 E
Hadejia, *Nigeria* **83 C7** 12 30N 10 5 E
Hadejia →, *Nigeria* **83 C7** 12 50N 10 51 E
Ḩadera, *Israel* **75 C3** 32 27N 34 55 E
Ḩadera, N. →, *Israel* **75 C3** 32 28N 34 52 E
Haderslev, *Denmark* **11 J3** 55 15N 9 30 E
Hadhramaut = Ḩaḑramawt, *Yemen* **74 D4** 15 30N 49 30 E
Hadibu, *Yemen* **74 E5** 12 39N 54 2 E
Hadım, *Turkey* **72 D5** 36 58N 32 26 E
Hadong, *S. Korea* **57 G14** 35 5N 127 44 E
Ḩaḑramawt, *Yemen* **74 D4** 15 30N 49 30 E
Ḩadrānīyah, *Iraq* **70 C4** 35 38N 43 14 E
Hadrian's Wall, *U.K.* **12 B5** 55 0N 2 30W
Hadsten, *Denmark* **11 H4** 56 19N 10 3 E
Hadsund, *Denmark* **11 H4** 56 44N 10 8 E
Hadyach, *Ukraine* **47 G8** 50 21N 34 0 E
Haeju, *N. Korea* **57 E13** 38 3N 125 45 E
Haenam, *S. Korea* **57 G14** 34 34N 126 35 E
Haenertsburg, *S. Africa* **89 C4** 24 0 S 29 50 E
Haerhpin = Harbin, *China* **57 B14** 45 48N 126 40 E
Hafar al Bāţin, *Si. Arabia* **70 D5** 28 32N 45 52 E
Hafik, *Turkey* **72 C7** 39 51N 37 23 E
Ḩafīrat al 'Aydā, *Si. Arabia* **70 E3** 26 26N 39 12 E
Ḩafit, *Oman* **71 F7** 23 59N 55 49 E
Ḩafit, Jabal, *Oman* **71 E7** 24 3N 55 46 E
Hafizabad, *Pakistan* **68 C5** 32 5N 73 40 E
Haflong, *India* **67 G18** 25 10N 93 5 E
Hafnarfjörður, *Iceland* **8 D3** 64 4N 21 57W
Haft Gel, *Iran* **71 D6** 31 30N 49 32 E
Hafun, Ras, *Somali Rep.* **74 E5** 10 29N 51 30 E
Hagalil, *Israel* **75 C4** 32 53N 35 18 E
Hagby, *Sweden* **11 H10** 56 34N 16 11 E
Hagen, *Germany* **24 D3** 51 21N 7 27 E
Hagenow, *Germany* **24 B7** 53 26N 11 12 E
Hagerman, *U.S.A.* **113 J2** 33 7N 104 20W
Hagerstown, *U.S.A.* **108 F7** 39 39N 77 43W
Hagersville, *Canada* **110 D4** 42 58N 80 3W
Hagetmau, *France* **20 E3** 43 39N 0 37W
Hagfors, *Sweden* **10 D7** 60 3N 13 45 E
Hagi, *Japan* **55 G5** 34 30N 131 22 E
Hagolan, *Syria* **75 C4** 33 0N 35 45 E
Hagondange, *France* **19 C13** 49 16N 6 11 E
Hags Hd., *Ireland* **15 D2** 52 57N 9 28W
Hague, C. de la, *France* **18 C5** 49 44N 1 56W
Hague, The = 's-Gravenhage, *Neths.* **17 B4** 52 7N 4 17 E
Haguenau, *France* **19 D14** 48 49N 7 47 E
Hai Duong, *Vietnam* **58 G6** 20 56N 106 19 E
Hai'an, *Guangdong, China* **59 G8** 20 18N 110 11 E
Hai'an, *Jiangsu, China* **59 A13** 32 37N 120 27 E
Haicheng, *Fujian, China* **59 E11** 24 23N 117 48 E
Haicheng, *Liaoning, China* **57 D12** 40 50N 122 45 E
Haidar Khel, *Afghan.* **68 C3** 33 58N 68 38 E
Haidargarh, *India* **69 F9** 26 37N 81 22 E
Haifa = Ḩefa, *Israel* **75 C4** 32 46N 35 0 E
Haifeng, *China* **59 F10** 22 58N 115 10 E
Haiger, *Germany* **24 E4** 50 43N 8 12 E
Haikou, *China* **60 D6** 20 1N 110 16 E
Ḩā'il, *Si. Arabia* **70 E4** 27 28N 41 45 E
Hailar, *China* **60 B6** 49 10N 119 38 E
Hailey, *U.S.A.* **114 E6** 43 31N 114 19W
Haileybury, *Canada* **102 C4** 47 30N 79 38W
Hailin, *China* **57 B15** 44 37N 129 30 E
Hailing Dao, *China* **59 G8** 21 35N 111 47 E
Hailong, *China* **57 C13** 42 32N 125 40 E
Hailuoto, *Finland* **8 D21** 65 3N 24 45 E
Haimen, *Guangdong, China* **59 F11** 23 15N 116 38 E
Haimen, *Jiangsu, China* **59 B13** 31 52N 121 10 E
Hainan □, *China* **60 E5** 19 0N 109 30 E
Hainaut □, *Belgium* **17 D4** 50 30N 4 0 E
Hainburg, *Austria* **27 C9** 48 9N 16 56 E
Haines, *Alaska, U.S.A.* **104 B1** 59 14N 135 26W
Haines, *Oreg., U.S.A.* **114 D5** 44 55N 117 56W
Haines City, *U.S.A.* **109 L5** 28 7N 81 38W
Haines Junction, *Canada* **104 A1** 60 45N 137 30W
Hainfeld, *Austria* **26 C8** 48 3N 15 48 E
Haining, *China* **59 B13** 30 28N 120 40 E
Haiphong, *Vietnam* **58 G6** 20 47N 106 41 E
Haitan Dao, *China* **59 E12** 25 30N 119 45 E
Haiti ■, *W. Indies* **121 C5** 19 0N 72 30W
Haiya, *Sudan* **80 D4** 18 20N 36 21 E
Haiyan, *China* **59 B13** 30 28N 120 58 E
Haiyang, *China* **57 F11** 36 47N 121 9 E
Haiyuan, *Guangxi Zhuangzu, China* **58 F6** 22 8N 107 35 E
Haiyuan, *Ningxia Huizu, China* **56 F3** 36 35N 105 52 E
Haizhou, *China* **57 G10** 34 37N 119 7 E
Haizhou Wan, *China* **57 G10** 34 50N 119 20 E
Hajdú-Bihar □, *Hungary* **42 C6** 47 30N 21 30 E
Hajdúböszörmény, *Hungary* **42 C6** 47 40N 21 30 E
Hajdúdorog, *Hungary* **42 C6** 47 48N 21 30 E
Hajdúhadház, *Hungary* **42 C6** 47 40N 21 40 E
Hajdúnánás, *Hungary* **42 C6** 47 50N 21 26 E
Hajdúsámson, *Hungary* **42 C6** 47 37N 21 42 E
Hajdúszoboszló, *Hungary* **42 C6** 47 27N 21 22 E
Hajipur, *India* **69 G11** 25 45N 85 13 E
Ḩājjī Muḩsin, *Iraq* **70 C5** 32 35N 45 29 E
Ḩājjīābād, *Iran* **71 D7** 28 19N 55 55 E
Ḩājjīābād-e Zarrīn, *Iran* **71 C7** 33 9N 54 51 E
Hajnówka, *Poland* **45 F10** 52 47N 23 35 E
Hakansson, Mts., *Dem. Rep. of the Congo* **87 D2** 8 40 S 25 45 E
Hakkâri, *Turkey* **70 B4** 37 34N 43 44 E
Hakkâri Dağları, *Turkey* **73 C10** 38 2N 42 58 E
Hakken-Zan, *Japan* **55 G7** 34 10N 135 54 E
Hakodate, *Japan* **54 D10** 41 45N 140 44 E
Hakos, *Namibia* **88 C2** 23 13 S 16 21 E
Håksberg, *Sweden* **10 D9** 60 11N 15 12 E
Haku-San, *Japan* **55 F8** 36 9N 136 46 E
Hakui, *Japan* **55 F8** 36 53N 136 47 E
Hala, *Pakistan* **66 G6** 25 43N 68 20 E
Ḩalab, *Syria* **70 B3** 36 10N 37 15 E
Ḩalabjah, *Iraq* **70 C5** 35 10N 45 58 E
Halaib, *Sudan* **80 C4** 22 12N 36 30 E
Halasa, *Sudan* **81 E3** 14 26N 30 39 E
Hālat 'Ammār, *Si. Arabia* **70 D3** 29 10N 36 4 E
Halbā, *Lebanon* **75 A5** 34 34N 36 6 E
Halberstadt, *Germany* **24 D7** 51 54N 11 3 E
Halcombe, *N.Z.* **91 J5** 40 8 S 175 30 E
Halcon, *Phil.* **63 B6** 13 0N 121 30 E
Halden, *Norway* **9 G14** 59 9N 11 23 E
Haldensleben, *Germany* **24 C7** 52 17N 11 24 E
Haldia, *India* **67 H16** 22 5N 88 3 E
Haldwani, *India* **69 E8** 29 31N 79 30 E
Hale →, *Australia* **94 C2** 24 56 S 135 53 E
Haleakala Crater, *U.S.A.* **106 H16** 20 43N 156 16W
Halesowen, *U.K.* **13 E5** 52 27N 2 3W
Haleyville, *U.S.A.* **109 H2** 34 14N 87 37W
Halfmoon Bay, *N.Z.* **91 M2** 46 50 S 168 5 E
Halfway →, *Canada* **104 B4** 56 12N 121 32W
Halia, *India* **69 G10** 24 50N 82 19 E
Haliburton, *Canada* **102 C4** 45 3N 78 30W
Halifax, *Australia* **94 B4** 18 32 S 146 22 E
Halifax, *Canada* **103 D7** 44 38N 63 35W
Halifax, *U.K.* **12 D6** 53 43N 1 52W
Halifax, *U.S.A.* **110 F8** 40 25N 76 55W
Halifax B., *Australia* **94 B4** 18 50 S 147 0 E
Halifax I., *Namibia* **88 D2** 26 38 S 15 4 E
Halīl →, *Iran* **71 E8** 27 40N 58 30 E
Halkirk, *U.K.* **14 C5** 58 30N 3 29W
Hall Beach = Sanirajak, *Canada* **101 B11** 68 46N 81 12W
Hall in Tirol, *Austria* **26 D4** 47 17N 11 30 E
Hall Pen., *Canada* **101 B13** 63 30N 66 0W
Hall Pt., *Australia* **92 C3** 15 40 S 124 23 E
Hallabro, *Sweden* **11 H9** 56 22N 15 5 E
Halland, *Sweden* **9 H15** 57 8N 12 47 E
Hallands län □, *Sweden* **11 H6** 57 0N 12 40 E
Hallands Väderö, *Sweden* **11 H6** 56 27N 12 34 E
Hallandsås, *Sweden* **11 H7** 56 22N 13 0 E
Hällbybrunn, *Sweden* **10 E10** 59 24N 16 25 E
Halle, *Belgium* **17 D4** 50 44N 4 13 E
Halle, *Nordrhein-Westfalen, Germany* **24 C4** 52 3N 8 22 E
Halle, *Sachsen-Anhalt, Germany* **24 D7** 51 30N 11 56 E
Hällefors, *Sweden* **10 E8** 59 47N 14 31 E
Hälleforsnäs, *Sweden* **10 E10** 59 10N 16 30 E
Hallein, *Austria* **26 D6** 47 40N 13 5 E
Hällekis, *Sweden* **11 F7** 58 38N 13 27 E
Hallen, *Sweden* **10 A8** 63 11N 14 4 E
Hallett, *Australia* **95 E2** 33 25 S 138 55 E
Hallettsville, *U.S.A.* **113 L6** 29 27N 96 57W
Hallim, *S. Korea* **57 H14** 33 24N 126 15 E
Hallingdalselvi →, *Norway* **9 F13** 60 23N 9 35 E
Hallock, *U.S.A.* **112 A6** 48 47N 96 57W
Halls Creek, *Australia* **92 C4** 18 16 S 127 38 E
Hallsberg, *Sweden* **10 E9** 59 5N 15 7 E
Hallstahammar, *Sweden* **10 E10** 59 38N 16 15 E
Hallstatt, *Austria* **26 D6** 47 33N 13 38 E
Hallstavik, *Sweden* **10 D12** 60 5N 18 37 E
Hallstead, *U.S.A.* **111 E9** 41 58N 75 45W
Halmahera, *Indonesia* **63 D7** 0 40N 128 0 E
Halmeu, *Romania* **42 C8** 47 57N 23 2 E
Halmstad, *Sweden* **11 H6** 56 41N 12 52 E
Hals, *Denmark* **11 H4** 57 0N 10 18 E
Hälsingborg = Helsingborg, *Sweden* **11 H6** 56 3N 12 42 E
Hälsingland, *Sweden* **10 C10** 61 40N 16 5 E
Halstead, *U.K.* **13 F8** 51 57N 0 40 E
Haltern, *Germany* **24 D3** 51 44N 7 11 E
Halti, *Finland* **8 B19** 69 17N 21 18 E
Halton □, *U.K.* **12 D5** 53 22N 2 45W
Haltwhistle, *U.K.* **12 C5** 54 58N 2 26W
Ḩalul, *Qatar* **71 E7** 25 40N 52 40 E
Halvad, *India* **68 H4** 23 1N 71 11 E
Ḩalvān, *Iran* **71 C8** 33 57N 56 15 E
Ham, *France* **19 C10** 49 45N 3 4 E
Ham Tan, *Vietnam* **65 G6** 10 40N 107 45 E
Ham Yen, *Vietnam* **64 A5** 22 4N 105 3 E
Hamab, *Namibia* **88 D2** 28 7 S 19 16 E
Hamad, *Sudan* **81 D3** 15 20N 33 32 E
Hamada, *Japan* **55 G6** 34 56N 132 4 E
Hamadān, *Iran* **71 C6** 34 52N 48 32 E
Hamadān □, *Iran* **71 C6** 35 0N 49 0 E
Ḩamāh, *Syria* **70 C3** 35 5N 36 40 E
Hamamatsu, *Japan* **55 G8** 34 45N 137 45 E
Hamar, *Norway* **9 F14** 60 48N 11 7 E
Hamâta, Gebel, *Egypt* **70 E2** 24 17N 35 0 E
Hambantota, *Sri Lanka* **66 R12** 6 10N 81 10 E
Hamber Prov. Park, *Canada* **104 C5** 52 20N 118 0W
Hamburg, *Germany* **24 B5** 53 33N 9 59 E
Hamburg, *Ark., U.S.A.* **113 J9** 33 14N 91 48W
Hamburg, *N.Y., U.S.A.* **110 D6** 42 43N 78 50W
Hamburg, *Pa., U.S.A.* **111 F9** 40 33N 75 59W
Hamburg □, *Germany* **24 B5** 53 30N 10 0 E
Ḩamḑ, W. al →, *Si. Arabia* **70 E3** 24 55N 36 20 E
Hamden, *U.S.A.* **111 E12** 41 23N 72 54W
Hamdibey, *Turkey* **39 B9** 39 50N 27 15 E
Häme, *Finland* **9 F20** 61 38N 25 10 E
Hämeenlinna, *Finland* **9 F21** 61 0N 24 28 E
Hamélé, *Ghana* **82 C4** 10 56N 2 45W
Hamelin Pool, *Australia* **93 E1** 26 22 S 114 20 E
Hameln, *Germany* **24 C5** 52 6N 9 21 E
Hamerkaz □, *Israel* **75 C3** 32 15N 34 55 E
Hamersley Ra., *Australia* **92 D2** 22 0 S 117 45 E
Hamhung, *N. Korea* **57 E14** 39 54N 127 30 E
Hami, *China* **60 B4** 42 55N 93 25 E
Hamilton, *Australia* **95 F3** 37 45 S 142 2 E
Hamilton, *Canada* **102 D4** 43 15N 79 50W
Hamilton, *N.Z.* **91 G5** 37 47 S 175 19 E
Hamilton, *U.K.* **14 F4** 55 46N 4 2W
Hamilton, *Ala., U.S.A.* **109 H1** 34 9N 87 59W
Hamilton, *Mont., U.S.A.* **114 C6** 46 15N 114 10W
Hamilton, *N.Y., U.S.A.* **111 D9** 42 50N 75 33W
Hamilton, *Ohio, U.S.A.* **108 F3** 39 24N 84 34W
Hamilton, *Tex., U.S.A.* **113 K5** 31 42N 98 7W
Hamilton →, *Australia* **94 C2** 23 30 S 139 47 E
Hamilton City, *U.S.A.* **116 F4** 39 45N 122 1W
Hamilton Inlet, *Canada* **103 B8** 54 0N 57 30W
Hamilton Mt., *U.S.A.* **111 C10** 43 25N 74 22W
Hamina, *Finland* **9 F22** 60 34N 27 12 E
Hamirpur, *H.P., India* **68 D7** 31 41N 76 31 E
Hamirpur, *Ut. P., India* **69 G9** 25 57N 80 9 E
Hamitabat, *Turkey* **41 E11** 41 30N 27 17 E
Hamlet, *U.S.A.* **109 H6** 34 53N 79 42W
Hamley Bridge, *Australia* **95 E2** 34 17 S 138 35 E
Hamlin = Hameln, *Germany* **24 C5** 52 6N 9 21 E
Hamlin, *N.Y., U.S.A.* **110 C7** 43 17N 77 55W
Hamlin, *Tex., U.S.A.* **113 J4** 32 53N 100 8W
Hamm, *Germany* **24 D3** 51 40N 7 50 E
Ḩammār, Hawr al, *Iraq* **70 D5** 30 50N 47 10 E
Hammarstrand, *Sweden* **10 A10** 63 7N 16 20 E
Hammelburg, *Germany* **25 E5** 50 6N 9 53 E
Hammeren, *Denmark* **11 J8** 55 18N 14 47 E
Hammerfest, *Norway* **8 A20** 70 39N 23 41 E
Hammerum, *Denmark* **11 H3** 56 8N 9 3 E
Hamminkeln, *Germany* **24 D2** 51 43N 6 35 E
Hammond, *Ind., U.S.A.* **108 E2** 41 38N 87 30W
Hammond, *La., U.S.A.* **113 K9** 30 30N 90 28W
Hammond, *N.Y., U.S.A.* **111 B9** 44 27N 75 42W
Hammondsport, *U.S.A.* **110 D7** 42 25N 77 13W
Hammonton, *U.S.A.* **108 F8** 39 39N 74 48W
Hamneda, *Sweden* **11 H7** 56 41N 13 51 E
Hamoyet, Jebel, *Sudan* **80 D4** 17 33N 38 2 E
Hampden, *N.Z.* **91 L3** 45 18 S 170 50 E
Hampshire □, *U.K.* **13 F6** 51 7N 1 23W
Hampshire Downs, *U.K.* **13 F6** 51 15N 1 10W
Hampton, *N.B., Canada* **103 C6** 45 32N 65 51W
Hampton, *Ont., Canada* **110 C6** 43 58N 78 45W
Hampton, *Ark., U.S.A.* **113 J8** 33 32N 92 28W
Hampton, *Iowa, U.S.A.* **112 D8** 42 45N 93 13W
Hampton, *N.H., U.S.A.* **111 D14** 42 57N 70 50W
Hampton, *S.C., U.S.A.* **109 J5** 32 52N 81 7W
Hampton, *Va., U.S.A.* **108 G7** 37 2N 76 21W
Hampton Bays, *U.S.A.* **111 F12** 40 53N 72 30W
Hampton Tableland, *Australia* **93 F4** 32 0 S 127 0 E
Hamra, *Sweden* **10 C8** 61 39N 14 59 E
Hamrat esh Sheykh, *Sudan* **81 E2** 14 38N 27 55 E
Hamur, *Turkey* **73 C10** 39 37N 43 3 E
Hamyang, *S. Korea* **57 G14** 35 32N 127 42 E
Han Jiang →, *China* **59 F11** 23 25N 116 40 E
Han Shui, *China* **58 A7** 30 34N 114 17 E
Han Shui →, *China* **59 B10** 30 35N 114 18 E
Hana, *U.S.A.* **106 H17** 20 45N 155 59W
Hanak, *Si. Arabia* **70 E3** 25 32N 37 0 E
Hanamaki, *Japan* **54 E10** 39 23N 141 7 E
Hanang, *Tanzania* **86 C4** 4 30 S 35 25 E

Hanau, *Germany* **25 E4** 50 7N 8 56 E
Hanbogd = Ihbulag, *Mongolia* **56 C4** 43 11N 107 10 E
Hançalar, *Turkey* **39 C11** 38 8N 29 24 E
Hâncești, *Moldova* **43 D13** 46 50N 28 36 E
Hancheng, *China* **56 G6** 35 31N 110 25 E
Hanchuan, *China* **59 B9** 30 40N 113 50 E
Hancock, *Mich., U.S.A.* **112 B10** 47 8N 88 35W
Hancock, *N.Y., U.S.A.* **111 E9** 41 57N 75 17W
Handa, *Japan* **55 G8** 34 53N 136 55 E
Handan, *China* **56 F8** 36 35N 114 28 E
Handeni, *Tanzania* **86 D4** 5 25 S 38 2 E
Handlová, *Slovak Rep.* **27 C11** 48 45N 18 35 E
Handub, *Sudan* **80 D4** 19 15N 37 16 E
Handwara, *India* **69 B6** 34 21N 74 20 E
Hanegev, *Israel* **75 E4** 30 50N 35 0 E
Hanford, *U.S.A.* **116 J7** 36 20N 119 39W
Hang Chat, *Thailand* **64 C2** 18 20N 99 21 E
Hang Dong, *Thailand* **64 C2** 18 41N 98 55 E
Hangang →, *S. Korea* **57 F14** 37 50N 126 30 E
Hangayn Nuruu, *Mongolia* **60 B4** 47 30N 99 0 E
Hangchou = Hangzhou, *China* **59 B13** 30 18N 120 11 E
Hanggin Houqi, *China* **56 D4** 40 58N 107 4 E
Hanggin Qi, *China* **56 E5** 39 52N 108 50 E
Hangu, *China* **57 E9** 39 18N 117 53 E
Hangzhou, *China* **59 B13** 30 18N 120 11 E
Hangzhou Wan, *China* **59 B13** 30 15N 120 45 E
Hanhongor, *Mongolia* **56 C3** 43 55N 104 28 E
Hanīdh, *Si. Arabia* **71 E6** 26 35N 48 38 E
Hanīsh, *Yemen* **74 E3** 13 45N 42 46 E
Haniska, *Slovak Rep.* **27 C14** 48 37N 21 15 E
Hanjiang, *China* **59 E12** 25 26N 119 6 E
Hankinson, *U.S.A.* **112 B6** 46 4N 96 54W
Hanko, *Finland* **9 G20** 59 50N 22 57 E
Hankou, *China* **59 B10** 30 35N 114 30 E
Hanksville, *U.S.A.* **115 G8** 38 22N 110 43W
Hanle, *India* **69 C8** 32 42N 79 4 E
Hanmer Springs, *N.Z.* **91 K4** 42 32 S 172 50 E
Hann →, *Australia* **92 C4** 17 26 S 126 17 E
Hann, Mt., *Australia* **92 C4** 15 45 S 126 0 E
Hanna, *Canada* **104 C6** 51 40N 111 54W
Hanna, *U.S.A.* **114 F10** 41 52N 106 34W
Hannah B., *Canada* **102 B4** 51 40N 80 0W
Hannibal, *Mo., U.S.A.* **112 F9** 39 42N 91 22W
Hannibal, *N.Y., U.S.A.* **111 C8** 43 19N 76 35W
Hannik, *Sudan* **80 D3** 18 12N 32 20 E
Hannover, *Germany* **24 C5** 52 22N 9 46 E
Hanö, *Sweden* **11 H8** 56 1N 14 50 E
Hanöbukten, *Sweden* **11 J8** 55 35N 14 30 E
Hanoi, *Vietnam* **58 G5** 21 5N 105 55 E
Hanover = Hannover, *Germany* **24 C5** 52 22N 9 46 E
Hanover, *Canada* **102 D3** 44 9N 81 2W
Hanover, *S. Africa* **88 E3** 31 4 S 24 29 E
Hanover, *N.H., U.S.A.* **111 C12** 43 42N 72 17W
Hanover, *Ohio, U.S.A.* **110 F2** 40 4N 82 16W
Hanover, *Pa., U.S.A.* **108 F7** 39 48N 76 59W
Hanover, I., *Chile* **128 G2** 51 0 S 74 50W
Hansdiha, *India* **69 G12** 24 36N 87 5 E
Hanshou, *China* **59 C8** 28 56N 111 50 E
Hansi, *India* **68 E6** 29 10N 75 57 E
Hanson, L., *Australia* **95 E2** 31 0 S 136 15 E
Hanstholm, *Denmark* **11 G2** 57 7N 8 36 E
Hantsavichy, *Belarus* **47 F4** 52 49N 26 30 E
Hanumangarh, *India* **68 E6** 29 35N 74 19 E
Hanyin, *China* **58 A7** 32 54N 108 28 E
Hanyuan, *China* **58 C4** 29 21N 102 40 E
Hanzhong, *China* **56 H4** 33 10N 107 1 E
Hanzhuang, *China* **57 G9** 34 33N 117 23 E
Haora, *India* **69 H13** 22 37N 88 20 E
Haoxue, *China* **59 B9** 30 3N 112 24 E
Haparanda, *Sweden* **8 D21** 65 52N 24 8 E
Happy, *U.S.A.* **113 H4** 34 45N 101 52W
Happy Camp, *U.S.A.* **114 F2** 41 48N 123 23W
Happy Valley-Goose Bay, *Canada* **103 B7** 53 15N 60 20W
Hapsu, *N. Korea* **57 D15** 41 13N 128 51 E
Hapur, *India* **68 E7** 28 45N 77 45 E
Ḥaql, *Si. Arabia* **75 F3** 29 10N 34 58 E
Har, *Indonesia* **63 F8** 5 16 S 133 14 E
Har-Ayrag, *Mongolia* **56 B5** 45 47N 109 16 E
Har Hu, *China* **60 C4** 38 20N 97 38 E
Har Us Nuur, *Mongolia* **60 B4** 48 0N 92 0 E
Har Yehuda, *Israel* **75 D3** 31 35N 34 57 E
Ḥaraḍ, *Si. Arabia* **74 C4** 24 22N 49 0 E
Haradok, *Belarus* **46 E6** 55 30N 30 3 E
Häradsbäck, *Sweden* **11 H8** 56 32N 14 26 E
Haranomachi, *Japan* **54 F10** 37 38N 140 58 E
Harare, *Zimbabwe* **87 F3** 17 43 S 31 2 E
Harat, *Eritrea* **81 D4** 16 5N 39 26 E
Harbin, *China* **57 B14** 45 48N 126 40 E
Harbiye, *Turkey* **72 D7** 36 10N 36 8 E
Harbo, *Sweden* **10 D11** 60 7N 17 12 E
Harboør, *Denmark* **11 H2** 56 38N 8 10 E
Harbor Beach, *U.S.A.* **110 C2** 43 51N 82 39W
Harbour Breton, *Canada* **103 C8** 47 29N 55 50W
Harbour Deep, *Canada* **103 B8** 50 25N 56 32W
Harburg, *Germany* **24 B5** 53 27N 9 58 E
Hårby, *Denmark* **11 J4** 55 13N 10 7 E
Harda, *India* **68 H7** 22 27N 77 5 E
Hardangerfjorden, *Norway* **9 F12** 60 5N 6 0 E
Hardangervidda, *Norway* **9 F12** 60 7N 7 20 E
Hardap Dam, *Namibia* **88 C2** 24 32 S 17 50 E
Hardenberg, *Neths.* **17 B6** 52 34N 6 37 E
Harderwijk, *Neths.* **17 B5** 52 21N 5 38 E
Hardey →, *Australia* **92 D2** 22 45 S 116 8 E
Hardin, *U.S.A.* **114 D10** 45 44N 107 37W
Harding, *S. Africa* **89 E4** 30 35 S 29 55 E
Harding Ra., *Australia* **92 C3** 16 17 S 124 55 E
Hardisty, *Canada* **104 C6** 52 40N 111 18W
Hardoi, *India* **69 F9** 27 26N 80 6 E
Hardwar = Haridwar, *India* **68 E8** 29 58N 78 9 E
Hardwick, *U.S.A.* **111 B12** 44 30N 72 22W
Hardy, Pen., *Chile* **128 H3** 55 30 S 68 20W
Hare B., *Canada* **103 B8** 51 15N 55 45W
Hareid, *Norway* **9 E12** 62 22N 6 1 E
Haren, *Germany* **24 C3** 52 47N 7 13 E
Harer, *Ethiopia* **81 F5** 9 20N 42 8 E
Harerge □, *Ethiopia* **81 F5** 7 12N 42 0 E
Hareto, *Ethiopia* **81 F4** 9 23N 37 6 E
Harfleur, *France* **18 C7** 49 30N 0 10 E
Hargeisa, *Somali Rep.* **74 F3** 9 30N 44 2 E
Harghita □, *Romania* **43 D10** 46 30N 25 30 E
Harghita, Munţii, *Romania* **43 D10** 46 25N 25 35 E
Hargshamn, *Sweden* **10 D12** 60 12N 18 30 E
Hari →, *Indonesia* **62 E2** 1 16 S 104 5 E
Haria, *Canary Is.* **37 E6** 29 8N 13 32W
Haridwar, *India* **68 E8** 29 58N 78 9 E
Harim, Jabal al, *Oman* **71 E8** 25 58N 56 14 E
Haringhata →, *Bangla.* **67 J16** 22 0N 89 58 E
Harīrūd →, *Asia* **66 A2** 37 24N 60 38 E
Härjedalen, *Sweden* **10 B7** 62 22N 13 5 E
Harlan, *Iowa, U.S.A.* **112 E7** 41 39N 95 19W
Harlan, *Ky., U.S.A.* **109 G4** 36 51N 83 19W
Hârlău, *Romania* **43 C11** 47 23N 26 55 E
Harlech, *U.K.* **12 E3** 52 52N 4 6W
Harlem, *U.S.A.* **114 B9** 48 32N 108 47W
Hårlev, *Denmark* **11 J6** 55 21N 12 14 E
Harlingen, *Neths.* **17 A5** 53 11N 5 25 E
Harlingen, *U.S.A.* **113 M6** 26 12N 97 42W
Harlow, *U.K.* **13 F8** 51 46N 0 8 E
Harlowton, *U.S.A.* **114 C9** 46 26N 109 50W
Harmancık, *Turkey* **39 B11** 39 41N 29 9 E
Harmånger, *Sweden* **10 C11** 61 55N 17 20 E
Harmil, *Eritrea* **81 D5** 16 30N 40 10 E
Harnai, *Pakistan* **68 D2** 30 6N 67 56 E
Harney Basin, *U.S.A.* **114 E4** 43 30N 119 0W
Harney L., *U.S.A.* **114 E4** 43 14N 119 8W
Harney Peak, *U.S.A.* **112 D3** 43 52N 103 32W
Härnön, *Sweden* **10 B12** 62 36N 18 0 E
Härnösand, *Sweden* **10 B11** 62 38N 17 55 E
Haro, *Spain* **32 C2** 42 35N 2 55W
Haroldswick, *U.K.* **14 A8** 60 48N 0 50W
Harp L., *Canada* **103 A7** 55 5N 61 50W
Harper, *Liberia* **82 E3** 4 25N 7 43W
Harplinge, *Sweden* **11 H6** 56 45N 12 45 E
Harr, *Mauritania* **82 B2** 15 20N 12 28W
Harrai, *India* **69 H8** 22 37N 79 13 E
Harrand, *Pakistan* **68 E4** 29 28N 70 3 E
Ḥarrat Khaybar, *Si. Arabia* **80 B5** 25 30N 39 45 E
Ḥarrat Nawāşīf, *Si. Arabia* **80 C5** 21 20N 42 10 E
Harricana →, *Canada* **102 B4** 50 56N 79 32W
Harriman, *U.S.A.* **109 H3** 35 56N 84 33W
Harrington Harbour, *Canada* **103 B8** 50 31N 59 30W
Harris, *U.K.* **14 D2** 57 50N 6 55W
Harris, Sd. of, *U.K.* **14 D1** 57 44N 7 6W
Harris L., *Australia* **95 E2** 31 10 S 135 10 E
Harris Pt., *Canada* **110 C2** 43 6N 82 9W
Harrisburg, *Ill., U.S.A.* **113 G10** 37 44N 88 32W
Harrisburg, *Nebr., U.S.A.* **112 E3** 41 33N 103 44W
Harrisburg, *Pa., U.S.A.* **110 F8** 40 16N 76 53W
Harrismith, *S. Africa* **89 D4** 28 15 S 29 8 E
Harrison, *Ark., U.S.A.* **113 G8** 36 14N 93 7W
Harrison, *Maine, U.S.A.* **111 B14** 44 7N 70 39W
Harrison, *Nebr., U.S.A.* **112 D3** 42 41N 103 53W
Harrison, C., *Canada* **103 B8** 54 55N 57 55W
Harrison L., *Canada* **104 D4** 49 33N 121 50W
Harrisonburg, *U.S.A.* **108 F6** 38 27N 78 52W
Harrisonville, *U.S.A.* **112 F7** 38 39N 94 21W
Harriston, *Canada* **110 C4** 43 57N 80 53W
Harrisville, *Mich., U.S.A.* **110 B1** 44 39N 83 17W
Harrisville, *N.Y., U.S.A.* **111 B9** 44 9N 75 19W
Harrisville, *Pa., U.S.A.* **110 E5** 41 8N 80 0W
Harrodsburg, *U.S.A.* **108 G3** 37 46N 84 51W
Harrogate, *U.K.* **12 C6** 54 0N 1 33W
Harrow, *U.K.* **13 F7** 51 35N 0 21W
Harrowsmith, *Canada* **111 B8** 44 24N 76 40W
Harry S. Truman Reservoir, *U.S.A.* **112 F7** 38 16N 93 24W
Harsefeld, *Germany* **24 B5** 53 27N 9 30 E
Harsewinkel, *Germany* **24 D4** 51 56N 8 14 E
Harsīn, *Iran* **70 C5** 34 18N 47 33 E
Hârşova, *Romania* **43 F12** 44 40N 27 59 E
Harstad, *Norway* **8 B17** 68 48N 16 30 E
Harsud, *India* **68 H7** 22 6N 76 44 E
Hart, *U.S.A.* **108 D2** 43 42N 86 22W
Hart, L., *Australia* **95 E2** 31 10 S 136 25 E
Hartbees →, *S. Africa* **88 D3** 28 45 S 20 32 E
Hartberg, *Austria* **26 D8** 47 17N 15 58 E
Hartford, *Conn., U.S.A.* **111 E12** 41 46N 72 41W
Hartford, *Ky., U.S.A.* **108 G2** 37 27N 86 55W
Hartford, *S. Dak., U.S.A.* **112 D6** 43 38N 96 57W
Hartford, *Wis., U.S.A.* **112 D10** 43 19N 88 22W
Hartford City, *U.S.A.* **108 E3** 40 27N 85 22W
Hartland, *Canada* **103 C6** 46 20N 67 32W
Hartland Pt., *U.K.* **13 F3** 51 1N 4 32W
Hartlepool, *U.K.* **12 C6** 54 42N 1 13W
Hartlepool □, *U.K.* **12 C6** 54 42N 1 17W
Hartley Bay, *Canada* **104 C3** 53 25N 129 15W
Hartmannberge, *Namibia* **88 B1** 17 0 S 13 0 E
Hartney, *Canada* **105 D8** 49 30N 100 35W
Hârtop, *Moldova* **43 D13** 46 39N 28 40 E
Harts →, *S. Africa* **88 D3** 28 24 S 24 17 E
Hartselle, *U.S.A.* **109 H2** 34 27N 86 56W
Hartshorne, *U.S.A.* **113 H7** 34 51N 95 34W
Hartstown, *U.S.A.* **110 E4** 41 33N 80 23W
Hartsville, *U.S.A.* **109 H5** 34 23N 80 4W
Hartswater, *S. Africa* **88 D3** 27 34 S 24 43 E
Hartwell, *U.S.A.* **109 H4** 34 21N 82 56W
Harunabad, *Pakistan* **68 E5** 29 35N 73 8 E
Harvand, *Iran* **71 D7** 28 25N 55 43 E
Harvey, *Australia* **93 F2** 33 5 S 115 54 E
Harvey, *Ill., U.S.A.* **108 E2** 41 36N 87 50W
Harvey, *N. Dak., U.S.A.* **112 B5** 47 47N 99 56W
Harwich, *U.K.* **13 F9** 51 56N 1 17 E
Haryana □, *India* **68 E7** 29 0N 76 10 E
Haryn →, *Belarus* **47 F4** 52 7N 27 17 E
Harz, *Germany* **24 D6** 51 38N 10 44 E
Harzgerode, *Germany* **24 D7** 51 38N 11 8 E
Hasa □, *Si. Arabia* **71 E6** 25 50N 49 0 E
Hasaheisa, *Sudan* **81 E3** 14 44N 33 20 E
Ḥasanābād, *Iran* **71 C7** 32 8N 52 44 E
Hasdo →, *India* **69 J10** 21 44N 82 44 E
Haselünne, *Germany* **24 C3** 52 40N 7 29 E
Hashimoto, *Japan* **55 G7** 34 19N 135 37 E
Hashtjerd, *Iran* **71 C6** 35 52N 50 40 E
Haskell, *U.S.A.* **113 J5** 33 10N 99 44W
Hasköy, *Turkey* **41 E10** 41 38N 26 52 E
Haslach, *Germany* **25 G4** 48 16N 8 5 E
Hasle, *Denmark* **11 J8** 55 11N 14 44 E
Haslemere, *U.K.* **13 F7** 51 5N 0 43W
Haslev, *Denmark* **11 J5** 55 18N 11 57 E
Hasparren, *France* **20 E2** 43 24N 1 18W
Hassa, *Turkey* **72 D7** 36 48N 36 29 E
Hassela, *Sweden* **10 B10** 62 7N 16 42 E
Hasselt, *Belgium* **17 D5** 50 56N 5 21 E
Hassfurt, *Germany* **25 E6** 50 2N 10 30 E
Hassi Messaoud, *Algeria* **78 B7** 31 51N 6 1 E
Hässleholm, *Sweden* **11 H7** 56 10N 13 46 E
Hassloch, *Germany* **25 F4** 49 22N 8 16 E
Hästholmen, *Sweden* **11 F8** 58 17N 14 38 E
Hastings, *N.Z.* **91 H6** 39 39 S 176 52 E
Hastings, *U.K.* **13 G8** 50 51N 0 35 E
Hastings, *Mich., U.S.A.* **108 D3** 42 39N 85 17W
Hastings, *Minn., U.S.A.* **112 C8** 44 44N 92 51W
Hastings, *Nebr., U.S.A.* **112 E5** 40 35N 98 23W
Hastings Ra., *Australia* **95 E5** 31 15 S 152 14 E
Hästveda, *Sweden* **11 H7** 56 17N 13 55 E
Hat Yai, *Thailand* **65 J3** 7 1N 100 27 E
Hatanbulag = Ergel, *Mongolia* **56 C5** 43 8N 109 5 E
Hatay = Antalya, *Turkey* **72 D4** 36 52N 30 45 E
Hatch, *U.S.A.* **115 K10** 32 40N 107 9W
Hatchet L., *Canada* **105 B8** 58 36N 103 40W
Haţeg, *Romania* **42 E7** 45 36N 22 55 E
Hateruma-Shima, *Japan* **55 M1** 24 3N 123 47 E
Hatfield P.O., *Australia* **95 E3** 33 54 S 143 49 E
Hatgal, *Mongolia* **60 A5** 50 26N 100 9 E
Hathras, *India* **68 F8** 27 36N 78 6 E
Hatia, *Bangla.* **67 H17** 22 30N 91 5 E
Ḥāṭibah, Ra's, *Si. Arabia* **80 C4** 21 55N 38 57 E
Hato Mayor, *Dom. Rep.* **121 C6** 18 46N 69 15W
Hatta, *India* **69 G8** 24 7N 79 36 E
Hattah, *Australia* **95 E3** 34 48 S 142 17 E
Hatteras, C., *U.S.A.* **109 H8** 35 14N 75 32W
Hattiesburg, *U.S.A.* **113 K10** 31 20N 89 17W
Hatvan, *Hungary* **42 C4** 47 40N 19 45 E
Hau Bon = Cheo Reo, *Vietnam* **62 B3** 13 25N 108 28 E
Hau Duc, *Vietnam* **64 E7** 15 20N 108 13 E
Haugesund, *Norway* **9 G11** 59 23N 5 13 E
Haukipudas, *Finland* **8 D21** 65 12N 25 20 E
Haultain →, *Canada* **105 B7** 55 51N 106 46W
Hauraki G., *N.Z.* **91 G5** 36 35 S 175 5 E
Hausruck, *Austria* **26 C6** 48 6N 13 30 E
Haut Atlas, *Morocco* **78 B4** 32 30N 5 0W
Haut-Rhin □, *France* **19 E14** 48 0N 7 15 E
Haut-Zaïre = Orientale □, *Dem. Rep. of the Congo* **86 B2** 2 20N 26 0 E
Haute-Corse □, *France* **21 F13** 42 30N 9 30 E
Haute-Garonne □, *France* **20 E5** 43 30N 1 30 E
Haute-Loire □, *France* **20 C7** 45 5N 3 50 E
Haute-Marne □, *France* **19 D12** 48 10N 5 20 E
Haute-Normandie □, *France* **18 C7** 49 20N 1 0 E
Haute-Saône □, *France* **19 E13** 47 45N 6 10 E
Haute-Savoie □, *France* **21 C10** 46 0N 6 20 E
Haute-Vienne □, *France* **20 C5** 45 50N 1 10 E
Hautes-Alpes □, *France* **21 D10** 44 42N 6 20 E
Hautes Fagnes = Hohe Venn, *Belgium* **17 D6** 50 30N 6 5 E
Hautes-Pyrénées □, *France* **20 F4** 43 0N 0 10 E
Hauteville-Lompnès, *France* **21 C9** 45 58N 5 36 E
Hautmont, *France* **19 B10** 50 15N 3 55 E
Hauts-de-Seine □, *France* **19 D9** 48 52N 2 15 E
Hauts Plateaux, *Algeria* **76 C4** 35 0N 1 0 E
Hauzenberg, *Germany* **25 G9** 48 40N 13 37 E
Havana = La Habana, *Cuba* **120 B3** 23 8N 82 22W
Havana, *U.S.A.* **112 E9** 40 18N 90 4W
Havant, *U.K.* **13 G7** 50 51N 0 58W
Havârna, *Romania* **43 B11** 48 4N 26 43 E
Havasu, L., *U.S.A.* **117 L12** 34 18N 114 28W
Havdhem, *Sweden* **11 G12** 57 10N 18 20 E
Havel →, *Germany* **24 C8** 52 50N 12 3 E
Havelian, *Pakistan* **68 B5** 34 2N 73 10 E
Havelock, *Canada* **102 D4** 44 26N 77 53W
Havelock, *N.Z.* **91 J4** 41 17 S 173 48 E
Havelock, *U.S.A.* **109 H7** 34 53N 76 54W
Haverfordwest, *U.K.* **13 F3** 51 48N 4 58W
Haverhill, *U.S.A.* **111 D13** 42 47N 71 5W
Haverstraw, *U.S.A.* **111 E11** 41 12N 73 58W
Håverud, *Sweden* **11 F6** 58 50N 12 28 E
Havirga, *Mongolia* **56 B7** 45 41N 113 5 E
Havířov, *Czech.* **27 B11** 49 46N 18 20 E
Havlíčkův Brod, *Czech Rep.* **26 B8** 49 36N 15 33 E
Havneby, *Denmark* **11 J2** 55 5N 8 34 E
Havran, *Turkey* **39 B9** 39 33N 27 6 E
Havre, *U.S.A.* **114 B9** 48 33N 109 41W
Havre-Aubert, *Canada* **103 C7** 47 12N 61 56W
Havre-St.-Pierre, *Canada* **103 B7** 50 18N 63 33W
Havsa, *Turkey* **41 E10** 41 31N 26 48 E
Havza, *Turkey* **72 B6** 41 0N 35 35 E
Haw →, *U.S.A.* **109 H6** 35 36N 79 3W
Hawaii □, *U.S.A.* **106 H16** 19 30N 156 30W
Hawaii I., *Pac. Oc.* **106 J17** 20 0N 155 0W
Hawaiian Is., *Pac. Oc.* **106 H17** 20 30N 156 0W
Hawaiian Ridge, *Pac. Oc.* **97 E11** 24 0N 165 0W
Hawarden, *U.S.A.* **112 D6** 43 0N 96 29W
Hawea, L., *N.Z.* **91 L2** 44 28 S 169 19 E
Hawera, *N.Z.* **91 H5** 39 35 S 174 19 E
Hawick, *U.K.* **14 F6** 55 26N 2 47W
Hawk Junction, *Canada* **102 C3** 48 5N 84 38W
Hawke B., *N.Z.* **91 H6** 39 25 S 177 20 E
Hawker, *Australia* **95 E2** 31 59 S 138 22 E
Hawkesbury, *Canada* **102 C5** 45 37N 74 37W
Hawkesbury I., *Canada* **104 C3** 53 37N 129 3W
Hawkesbury Pt., *Australia* **94 A1** 11 55 S 134 5 E
Hawkinsville, *U.S.A.* **109 J4** 32 17N 83 28W
Hawley, *Minn., U.S.A.* **112 B6** 46 53N 96 19W
Hawley, *Pa., U.S.A.* **111 E9** 41 28N 75 11W
Ḥawrān, W. →, *Iraq* **70 C4** 33 58N 42 34 E
Hawsh Mūssá, *Lebanon* **75 B4** 33 45N 35 55 E
Hawthorne, *U.S.A.* **114 G4** 38 32N 118 38W
Hay, *Australia* **95 E3** 34 30 S 144 51 E
Hay →, *Australia* **94 C2** 24 50 S 138 0 E
Hay →, *Canada* **104 A5** 60 50N 116 26W
Hay, C., *Australia* **92 B4** 14 5 S 129 29 E
Hay I., *Canada* **110 B4** 44 53N 80 58W
Hay L., *Canada* **104 B5** 58 50N 118 50W
Hay-on-Wye, *U.K.* **13 E4** 52 5N 3 8W
Hay River, *Canada* **104 A5** 60 51N 115 44W
Hay Springs, *U.S.A.* **112 D3** 42 41N 102 41W
Haya = Tehoru, *Indonesia* **63 E7** 3 19 S 129 37 E
Hayachine-San, *Japan* **54 E10** 39 34N 141 29 E
Hayange, *France* **19 C13** 49 20N 6 2 E
Haydarlı, *Turkey* **39 C12** 38 16N 30 23 E
Hayden, *U.S.A.* **114 F10** 40 30N 107 16W
Haydon, *Australia* **94 B3** 18 0 S 141 30 E
Hayes, *U.S.A.* **112 C4** 44 23N 101 1W
Hayes →, *Canada* **102 A1** 57 3N 92 12W
Hayes Creek, *Australia* **92 B5** 13 43 S 131 22 E
Hayle, *U.K.* **13 G2** 50 11N 5 26W
Hayling I., *U.K.* **13 G7** 50 48N 0 59W
Haymana, *Turkey* **72 C5** 39 26N 32 31 E
Hayrabolu, *Turkey* **41 E11** 41 12N 27 5 E
Hays, *Canada* **104 C6** 50 6N 111 48W
Hays, *U.S.A.* **112 F5** 38 53N 99 20W
Haysyn, *Ukraine* **47 H5** 48 57N 29 25 E
Hayvoron, *Ukraine* **47 H5** 48 22N 29 52 E
Hayward, *Calif., U.S.A.* **116 H4** 37 40N 122 5W
Hayward, *Wis., U.S.A.* **112 B9** 46 1N 91 29W
Haywards Heath, *U.K.* **13 G7** 51 0N 0 5W
Hazafon □, *Israel* **75 C4** 32 40N 35 20 E
Hazārān, Kūh-e, *Iran* **71 D8** 29 35N 57 20 E
Hazard, *U.S.A.* **108 G4** 37 15N 83 12W
Hazaribag, *India* **69 H11** 23 58N 85 26 E
Hazaribag Road, *India* **69 G11** 24 12N 85 57 E
Hazebrouck, *France* **19 B9** 50 42N 2 31 E
Hazelton, *Canada* **104 B3** 55 20N 127 42W
Hazelton, *U.S.A.* **112 B4** 46 29N 100 17W
Hazen, *U.S.A.* **112 B4** 47 18N 101 38W
Hazlehurst, *Ga., U.S.A.* **109 K4** 31 52N 82 36W
Hazlehurst, *Miss., U.S.A.* **113 K9** 31 52N 90 24W
Hazlet, *U.S.A.* **111 F10** 40 25N 74 12W
Hazleton, *U.S.A.* **111 F9** 40 57N 75 59W
Hazlett, L., *Australia* **92 D4** 21 30 S 128 48 E
Hazro, *Turkey* **70 B4** 38 15N 40 47 E
He Xian, *Anhui, China* **59 B12** 31 45N 118 20 E
He Xian, *Guangxi Zhuangzu, China* **59 E8** 24 27N 111 30 E
Head of Bight, *Australia* **93 F5** 31 30 S 131 25 E
Headlands, *Zimbabwe* **87 F3** 18 15 S 32 2 E
Healdsburg, *U.S.A.* **116 G4** 38 37N 122 52W
Healdton, *U.S.A.* **113 H6** 34 14N 97 29W
Healesville, *Australia* **95 F4** 37 35 S 145 30 E
Heany Junction, *Zimbabwe* **89 C4** 20 6 S 28 54 E
Heard I., *Ind. Oc.* **3 G13** 53 0 S 74 0 E
Hearne, *U.S.A.* **113 K6** 30 53N 96 36W
Hearst, *Canada* **102 C3** 49 40N 83 41W
Heart →, *U.S.A.* **112 B4** 46 46N 100 50W
Heart's Content, *Canada* **103 C9** 47 54N 53 27W
Heath Pt., *Canada* **103 C7** 49 8N 61 40W
Heavener, *U.S.A.* **113 H7** 34 53N 94 36W
Hebbronville, *U.S.A.* **113 M5** 27 18N 98 41W
Hebei □, *China* **56 E9** 39 0N 116 0 E
Hebel, *Australia* **95 D4** 28 58 S 147 47 E
Heber, *U.S.A.* **117 N11** 32 44N 115 32W
Heber City, *U.S.A.* **114 F8** 40 31N 111 25W
Heber Springs, *U.S.A.* **113 H9** 35 30N 92 2W
Hebert, *Canada* **105 C7** 50 30N 107 10W
Hebgen L., *U.S.A.* **114 D8** 44 52N 111 20W
Hebi, *China* **56 G8** 35 57N 114 7 E
Hebrides, *U.K.* **6 D4** 57 30N 7 0W
Hebron = Al Khalīl, *West Bank* **75 D4** 31 32N 35 6 E
Hebron, *Canada* **101 C13** 58 5N 62 30W
Hebron, *N. Dak., U.S.A.* **112 B3** 46 54N 102 3W
Hebron, *Nebr., U.S.A.* **112 E6** 40 10N 97 35W
Heby, *Sweden* **10 E10** 59 56N 16 53 E
Hecate Str., *Canada* **104 C2** 53 10N 130 30W
Heceta I., *U.S.A.* **104 B2** 55 46N 133 40W
Hechi, *China* **58 E7** 24 40N 108 2 E
Hechingen, *Germany* **25 G4** 48 20N 8 57 E
Hechuan, *China* **58 B6** 30 2N 106 12 E
Hecla, *U.S.A.* **112 C5** 45 53N 98 9W
Hecla I., *Canada* **105 C9** 51 10N 96 43W
Hédé, *France* **18 D5** 48 18N 1 49W
Hede, *Sweden* **10 B7** 62 23N 13 30 E
Hedemora, *Sweden* **10 D9** 60 18N 15 58 E
Hedensted, *Denmark* **11 J3** 55 46N 9 42 E
Hedesunda, *Sweden* **10 D10** 60 24N 17 0 E
Heerde, *Neths.* **17 B6** 52 24N 6 2 E
Heerenveen, *Neths.* **17 B5** 52 57N 5 55 E
Heerhugowaard, *Neths.* **17 B4** 52 40N 4 51 E
Heerlen, *Neths.* **17 D5** 50 55N 5 58 E
Ḥefa, *Israel* **75 C4** 32 46N 35 0 E
Ḥefa □, *Israel* **75 C4** 32 40N 35 0 E
Hefei, *China* **59 B11** 31 52N 117 18 E
Hefeng, *China* **59 C8** 29 55N 109 52 E
Hegalig, *Sudan* **81 E3** 14 36N 31 54 E
Hegang, *China* **60 B8** 47 20N 130 19 E
Heiban, *Sudan* **81 E3** 11 13N 30 31 E
Heichengzhen, *China* **56 F4** 36 24N 106 3 E
Heide, *Germany* **24 A5** 54 11N 9 6 E
Heidelberg, *Germany* **25 F4** 49 24N 8 42 E
Heidelberg, *S. Africa* **88 E3** 34 6 S 20 59 E
Heidenau, *Germany* **24 E9** 50 57N 13 52 E
Heidenheim, *Germany* **25 G6** 48 41N 10 9 E
Heijing, *China* **58 E3** 25 22N 101 44 E
Heilbad Heiligenstadt, *Germany* **24 D6** 51 22N 10 8 E
Heilbron, *S. Africa* **89 D4** 27 16 S 27 59 E
Heilbronn, *Germany* **25 F5** 49 9N 9 13 E
Heiligenblut, *Austria* **26 D5** 47 2N 12 51 E
Heiligenhafen, *Germany* **24 A6** 54 22N 10 59 E
Heilongjiang □, *China* **60 B7** 48 0N 126 0 E
Heilunkiang = Heilongjiang □, *China* **60 B7** 48 0N 126 0 E
Heimaey, *Iceland* **8 E3** 63 26N 20 17W
Heinola, *Finland* **9 F22** 61 13N 26 2 E
Heinsberg, *Germany* **24 D2** 51 3N 6 5 E
Heinze Is., *Burma* **67 M20** 14 25N 97 45 E
Heishan, *China* **57 D12** 41 40N 122 5 E
Heishui, *Liaoning, China* **57 C10** 42 8N 119 30 E
Heishui, *Sichuan, China* **58 A4** 32 4N 103 2 E
Hejaz = Ḥijāz □, *Si. Arabia* **70 E3** 24 0N 40 0 E
Hejian, *China* **56 E9** 38 25N 116 5 E
Hejiang, *China* **58 C5** 28 43N 105 46 E
Hejin, *China* **56 G6** 35 35N 110 42 E
Hekımhan, *Turkey* **70 B3** 38 50N 37 55 E
Hekla, *Iceland* **8 E4** 63 56N 19 35W
Hekou, *Guangdong, China* **59 F9** 23 13N 112 45 E
Hekou, *Yunnan, China* **58 F4** 22 30N 103 59 E
Hel, *Poland* **44 D5** 54 37N 18 47 E
Helagsfjället, *Sweden* **10 B6** 62 54N 12 25 E
Helan Shan, *China* **56 E3** 38 30N 105 55 E
Helechosa, *Spain* **35 F6** 39 22N 4 53W
Helen Atoll, *Pac. Oc.* **63 D8** 2 40N 132 0 E
Helena, *Ark., U.S.A.* **113 H9** 34 32N 90 36W
Helena, *Mont., U.S.A.* **114 C7** 46 36N 112 2W
Helendale, *U.S.A.* **117 L9** 34 44N 117 19W
Helensburgh, *U.K.* **14 E4** 56 1N 4 43W
Helensville, *N.Z.* **91 G5** 36 41 S 174 29 E
Helenvale, *Australia* **94 B4** 15 43 S 145 14 E
Helgasjön, *Sweden* **11 H8** 56 55N 14 50 E
Helgeland, *Norway* **8 C15** 66 7N 13 29 E
Helgoland, *Germany* **24 A3** 54 10N 7 53 E
Heligoland = Helgoland, *Germany* **24 A3** 54 10N 7 53 E
Heligoland B. = Deutsche Bucht, *Germany* **24 A4** 54 15N 8 0 E
Heliopolis, *Egypt* **80 H7** 30 6N 31 17 E
Hella, *Iceland* **8 E3** 63 50N 20 24W
Hellertown, *U.S.A.* **111 F9** 40 35N 75 21W
Hellespont = Çanakkale Boğazı, *Turkey* **41 F10** 40 17N 26 32 E
Hellevoetsluis, *Neths.* **17 C4** 51 50N 4 8 E
Hellín, *Spain* **33 G3** 38 31N 1 40W
Helmand □, *Afghan.* **66 D4** 31 20N 64 0 E
Helmand →, *Afghan.* **66 D2** 31 12N 61 34 E
Helme →, *Germany* **24 D7** 51 20N 11 21 E
Helmeringhausen, *Namibia* **88 D2** 25 54 S 16 57 E
Helmond, *Neths.* **17 C5** 51 29N 5 41 E
Helmsdale, *U.K.* **14 C5** 58 7N 3 39W
Helmsdale →, *U.K.* **14 C5** 58 7N 3 40W
Helmstedt, *Germany* **24 C7** 52 12N 11 0 E
Helong, *China* **57 C15** 42 40N 129 0 E
Helper, *U.S.A.* **114 G8** 39 41N 110 51W
Helsingborg, *Sweden* **11 H6** 56 3N 12 42 E
Helsinge, *Denmark* **11 H6** 56 2N 12 12 E
Helsingfors = Helsinki, *Finland* **9 F21** 60 15N 25 3 E
Helsingør, *Denmark* **11 H6** 56 2N 12 35 E
Helsinki, *Finland* **9 F21** 60 15N 25 3 E
Helska, Mierzeja, *Poland* **44 D5** 54 45N 18 40 E
Helston, *U.K.* **13 G2** 50 6N 5 17W
Helvellyn, *U.K.* **12 C4** 54 32N 3 1W
Helwân, *Egypt* **80 J7** 29 50N 31 20 E
Hemel Hempstead, *U.K.* **13 F7** 51 44N 0 28W
Hemet, *U.S.A.* **117 M10** 33 45N 116 58W
Hemingford, *U.S.A.* **112 D3** 42 19N 103 4W
Hemmingford, *Canada* **111 A11** 45 3N 73 35W
Hempstead, *U.S.A.* **113 K6** 30 6N 96 5W
Hemse, *Sweden* **11 G12** 57 15N 18 22 E
Hemsön, *Sweden* **10 B12** 62 42N 18 5 E
Henån, *Sweden* **11 F5** 58 14N 11 40 E
Henan □, *China* **56 H8** 34 0N 114 0 E
Henares →, *Spain* **34 E7** 40 24N 3 30W
Henashi-Misaki, *Japan* **54 D9** 40 37N 139 51 E
Hendaye, *France* **20 E2** 43 23N 1 47W
Hendek, *Turkey* **72 B4** 40 48N 30 44 E
Henderson, *Argentina* **126 D3** 36 18 S 61 43W
Henderson, *Ky., U.S.A.* **108 G2** 37 50N 87 35W
Henderson, *N.C., U.S.A.* **109 G6** 36 20N 78 25W
Henderson, *Nev., U.S.A.* **117 J12** 36 2N 114 59W
Henderson, *Tenn., U.S.A.* **109 H1** 35 26N 88 38W
Henderson, *Tex., U.S.A.* **113 J7** 32 9N 94 48W
Hendersonville, *N.C., U.S.A.* **109 H4** 35 19N 82 28W
Hendersonville, *Tenn., U.S.A.* **109 G2** 36 18N 86 37W
Hendījān, *Iran* **71 D6** 30 14N 49 43 E
Hendorābī, *Iran* **71 E7** 26 40N 53 37 E
Heng Jiang, *China* **58 C5** 28 40N 104 25 E
Heng Xian, *China* **58 F7** 22 40N 109 17 E
Hengcheng, *China* **56 E4** 38 18N 106 28 E
Hèngchun, *Taiwan* **59 F13** 22 0N 120 44 E
Hengdaohezi, *China* **57 B15** 44 52N 129 0 E
Hengelo, *Neths.* **17 B6** 52 16N 6 48 E
Hengfeng, *China* **59 C10** 28 12N 115 48 E
Hengshan, *Hunan, China* **59 D9** 27 16N 112 45 E
Hengshan, *Shaanxi, China* **56 F5** 37 58N 109 5 E
Hengshui, *China* **56 F8** 37 41N 115 40 E
Hengyang, *China* **59 D9** 26 59N 112 22 E
Henichesk, *Ukraine* **47 J8** 46 12N 34 50 E
Hénin-Beaumont, *France* **19 B9** 50 25N 2 58 E
Henlopen, C., *U.S.A.* **108 F8** 38 48N 75 6W
Hennan, *Sweden* **10 B9** 62 2N 15 54 E
Hennebont, *France* **18 E3** 47 49N 3 19W
Hennenman, *S. Africa* **88 D4** 27 59 S 27 1 E
Hennessey, *U.S.A.* **113 G6** 36 6N 97 54W
Hennigsdorf, *Germany* **24 C9** 52 38N 13 12 E
Henrietta, *U.S.A.* **113 J5** 33 49N 98 12W
Henrietta, Ostrov = Genriyetty, Ostrov, *Russia* **51 B16** 77 6N 156 30 E
Henrietta Maria, C., *Canada* **102 A3** 55 9N 82 20W
Henry, *U.S.A.* **112 E10** 41 7N 89 22W
Henryetta, *U.S.A.* **113 H7** 35 27N 95 59W
Henryville, *Canada* **111 A11** 45 8N 73 11W
Hensall, *Canada* **110 C3** 43 26N 81 30W
Henstedt-Ulzburg, *Germany* **24 B6** 53 47N 10 0 E
Hentiesbaai, *Namibia* **88 C1** 22 8 S 14 18 E
Hentiyn Nuruu, *Mongolia* **60 B5** 48 30N 108 30 E
Henty, *Australia* **95 F4** 35 30 S 147 0 E
Henzada, *Burma* **67 L19** 17 38N 95 26 E
Hephaestia, *Greece* **39 B7** 39 55N 25 14 E
Heping, *China* **59 E10** 24 29N 115 0 E
Heppner, *U.S.A.* **114 D4** 45 21N 119 33W
Hepu, *China* **58 G7** 21 40N 109 12 E
Hepworth, *Canada* **110 B3** 44 37N 81 9W
Heqing, *China* **58 D3** 26 37N 100 11 E
Hequ, *China* **56 E6** 39 20N 111 15 E
Héraðsflói, *Iceland* **8 D6** 65 42N 14 12W
Héraðsvötn →, *Iceland* **8 D4** 65 45N 19 25W
Herald Cays, *Australia* **94 B4** 16 58 S 149 9 E
Herāt, *Afghan.* **66 B3** 34 20N 62 7 E
Herāt □, *Afghan.* **66 B3** 35 0N 62 0 E
Hérault □, *France* **20 E7** 43 34N 3 15 E
Hérault →, *France* **20 E7** 43 17N 3 26 E
Herbault, *France* **18 E8** 47 36N 1 8 E
Herbert →, *Australia* **94 B4** 18 31 S 146 17 E
Herberton, *Australia* **94 B4** 17 20 S 145 25 E
Herbertsdale, *S. Africa* **88 E3** 34 1 S 21 46 E
Herbignac, *France* **18 E4** 47 27N 2 18W
Herborn, *Germany* **24 E4** 50 40N 8 18 E
Herby, *Poland* **45 H5** 50 45N 18 50 E
Herceg-Novi, *Montenegro, Yug.* **40 D2** 42 30N 18 33 E
Herchmer, *Canada* **105 B10** 57 22N 94 10W
Herðubreið, *Iceland* **8 D5** 65 11N 16 21W
Hereford, *U.K.* **13 E5** 52 4N 2 43W
Hereford, *U.S.A.* **113 H3** 34 49N 102 24W
Herefordshire □, *U.K.* **13 E5** 52 8N 2 40W
Hereke, *Turkey* **41 F13** 40 47N 29 38 E
Herencia, *Spain* **35 F7** 39 21N 3 22W

Herentals, *Belgium* **17 C4** 51 12N 4 51 E
Herford, *Germany* **24 C4** 52 7N 8 39 E
Héricourt, *France* **19 E13** 47 32N 6 45 E
Herington, *U.S.A.* **112 F6** 38 40N 96 57W
Herisau, *Switz.* **25 H5** 47 22N 9 17 E
Hérisson, *France* **19 F9** 46 32N 2 42 E
Herkimer, *U.S.A.* **111 D10** 43 0N 74 59W
Herlong, *U.S.A.* **116 E6** 40 8N 120 8W
Herm, *U.K.* **13 H5** 49 30N 2 28W
Hermann, *U.S.A.* **112 F9** 38 42N 91 27W
Hermannsburg, *Australia* **92 D5** 23 57 S 132 45 E
Hermannsburg, *Germany* **24 C6** 52 50N 10 5 E
Hermanus, *S. Africa* **88 E2** 34 27 S 19 12 E
Herment, *France* **20 C6** 45 45N 2 24 E
Hermidale, *Australia* **95 E4** 31 30 S 146 42 E
Hermiston, *U.S.A.* **114 D4** 45 51N 119 17W
Hermite, I., *Chile* **128 H3** 55 50 S 68 0W
Hermon, *U.S.A.* **111 B9** 44 28N 75 14W
Hermon, Mt. = Shaykh, J. ash, *Lebanon* **75 B4** 33 25N 35 50 E
Hermosillo, *Mexico* **118 B2** 29 10N 111 0W
Hernád →, *Hungary* **42 C6** 47 56N 21 8 E
Hernandarias, *Paraguay* **127 B5** 25 20 S 54 40W
Hernandez, *U.S.A.* **116 J6** 36 24N 120 46W
Hernando, *Argentina* **126 C3** 32 28 S 63 40W
Hernando, *U.S.A.* **113 H10** 34 50N 90 0W
Hernani, *Spain* **32 B3** 43 16N 1 58W
Herndon, *U.S.A.* **110 F8** 40 43N 76 51W
Herne, *Germany* **17 C7** 51 32N 7 14 E
Herne Bay, *U.K.* **13 F9** 51 21N 1 8 E
Herning, *Denmark* **11 H2** 56 8N 8 58 E
Heroica = Caborca, *Mexico* **118 A2** 30 40N 112 10W
Heroica Nogales = Nogales, *Mexico* **118 A2** 31 20N 110 56W
Heron Bay, *Canada* **102 C2** 48 40N 86 25W
Herradura, Pta. de la, *Canary Is.* **37 F5** 28 26N 14 8W
Herreid, *U.S.A.* **112 C4** 45 50N 100 4W
Herrenberg, *Germany* **25 G4** 48 35N 8 52 E
Herrera, *Spain* **35 H6** 37 26N 4 55W
Herrera de Alcántara, *Spain* **35 F3** 39 39N 7 25W
Herrera de Pisuerga, *Spain* **34 C6** 42 35N 4 20W
Herrera del Duque, *Spain* **35 F5** 39 10N 5 3W
Herrestad, *Sweden* **11 F5** 58 21N 11 50 E
Herrin, *U.S.A.* **113 G10** 37 48N 89 2W
Herriot, *Canada* **105 B8** 56 22N 101 16W
Herrljunga, *Sweden* **11 F7** 58 5N 13 1 E
Hersbruck, *Germany* **25 F7** 49 30N 11 26 E
Hershey, *U.S.A.* **111 F8** 40 17N 76 39W
Hersonissos, *Greece* **36 D7** 35 18N 25 22 E
Herstal, *Belgium* **17 D5** 50 40N 5 38 E
Hertford, *U.K.* **13 F7** 51 48N 0 4W
Hertfordshire □, *U.K.* **13 F7** 51 51N 0 5W
's-Hertogenbosch, *Neths.* **17 C5** 51 42N 5 17 E
Hertzogville, *S. Africa* **88 D4** 28 9 S 25 30 E
Hervás, *Spain* **34 E5** 40 16N 5 52W
Hervey B., *Australia* **94 C5** 25 0 S 152 52 E
Herzberg, *Brandenburg, Germany* **24 D9** 51 41N 13 14 E
Herzberg, *Niedersachsen, Germany* **24 D6** 51 38N 10 20 E
Herzliyya, *Israel* **75 C3** 32 10N 34 50 E
Herzogenburg, *Austria* **26 C8** 48 17N 15 41 E
Ḥeṣār, *Fārs, Iran* **71 D6** 29 52N 50 16 E
Ḥeṣār, *Markazī, Iran* **71 C6** 35 50N 49 12 E
Hesdin, *France* **19 B9** 50 21N 2 2 E
Heshan, *China* **58 F7** 23 50N 108 53 E
Heshui, *China* **56 G5** 35 48N 108 0 E
Heshun, *China* **56 F7** 37 22N 113 32 E
Hesperia, *U.S.A.* **117 L9** 34 25N 117 18W
Hesse = Hessen □, *Germany* **24 E4** 50 30N 9 0 E
Hessen □, *Germany* **24 E4** 50 30N 9 0 E
Hestra, *Sweden* **11 G7** 57 26N 13 35 E
Hetch Hetchy Aqueduct, *U.S.A.* **116 H5** 37 29N 122 19W
Hettinger, *U.S.A.* **112 C3** 46 0N 102 42W
Hettstedt, *Germany* **24 D7** 51 39N 11 31 E
Heuvelton, *U.S.A.* **111 B9** 44 37N 75 25W
Heves, *Hungary* **42 C5** 47 36N 20 17 E
Heves □, *Hungary* **42 C5** 47 50N 20 0 E
Hewitt, *U.S.A.* **113 K6** 31 27N 97 11W
Hexham, *U.K.* **12 C5** 54 58N 2 4W
Hexi, *Yunnan, China* **58 E4** 24 9N 102 38 E
Hexi, *Zhejiang, China* **59 D12** 27 58N 119 38 E
Hexigten Qi, *China* **57 C9** 43 18N 117 30 E
Ḥeydarābād, *Iran* **71 D7** 30 33N 55 38 E
Heysham, *U.K.* **12 C5** 54 3N 2 53W
Heyuan, *China* **59 F10** 23 39N 114 40 E
Heywood, *Australia* **95 F3** 38 8 S 141 37 E
Heze, *China* **56 G8** 35 14N 115 20 E
Hezhang, *China* **58 D5** 27 8N 104 41 E
Hi Vista, *U.S.A.* **117 L9** 34 45N 117 46W
Hialeah, *U.S.A.* **109 N5** 25 50N 80 17W
Hiawatha, *U.S.A.* **112 F7** 39 51N 95 32W
Hibbing, *U.S.A.* **112 B8** 47 25N 92 56W
Hibbs B., *Australia* **94 G4** 42 35 S 145 15 E
Hibernia Reef, *Australia* **92 B3** 12 0 S 123 23 E
Hickman, *U.S.A.* **113 G10** 36 34N 89 11W
Hickory, *U.S.A.* **109 H5** 35 44N 81 21W
Hicks, Pt., *Australia* **95 F4** 37 49 S 149 17 E
Hicks L., *Canada* **105 A9** 61 25N 100 0W
Hicksville, *U.S.A.* **111 F11** 40 46N 73 32W
Hida, *Romania* **43 C8** 47 10N 23 19 E
Hida-Gawa →, *Japan* **55 G8** 35 26N 137 3 E
Hida-Sammyaku, *Japan* **55 F8** 36 30N 137 40 E
Hidaka-Sammyaku, *Japan* **54 C11** 42 35N 142 45 E
Hidalgo, *Mexico* **119 C5** 24 15N 99 26W
Hidalgo □, *Mexico* **119 C5** 20 30N 99 10W
Hidalgo, Presa M., *Mexico* **118 B3** 26 30N 108 35W
Hidalgo, Pta. del, *Canary Is.* **37 F3** 28 33N 16 19W
Hidalgo del Parral, *Mexico* **118 B3** 26 58N 105 40W
Hiddensee, *Germany* **24 A9** 54 32N 13 6 E
Hieflau, *Austria* **26 D7** 47 36N 14 46 E
Hiendelaencina, *Spain* **32 D2** 41 5N 3 0W
Hierro, *Canary Is.* **37 G1** 27 44N 18 0W
Higashiajima-San, *Japan* **54 F10** 37 40N 140 10 E
Higashiōsaka, *Japan* **55 G7** 34 40N 135 37 E
Higgins, *U.S.A.* **113 G4** 36 7N 100 2W
Higgins Corner, *U.S.A.* **116 F5** 39 2N 121 5W
High Atlas = Haut Atlas, *Morocco* **78 B4** 32 30N 5 0W
High Bridge, *U.S.A.* **111 F10** 40 40N 74 54W
High Level, *Canada* **104 B5** 58 31N 117 8W
High Point, *U.S.A.* **109 H6** 35 57N 80 0W
High Prairie, *Canada* **104 B5** 55 30N 116 30W
High River, *Canada* **104 C6** 50 30N 113 50W
High Tatra = Tatry, *Slovak Rep.* **27 B13** 49 20N 20 0 E
High Veld, *Africa* **76 J6** 27 0 S 27 0 E
High Wycombe, *U.K.* **13 F7** 51 37N 0 45W
Highland □, *U.K.* **14 D4** 57 17N 4 21W
Highland Park, *U.S.A.* **108 D2** 42 11N 87 48W
Highmore, *U.S.A.* **112 C5** 44 31N 99 27W
Highrock L., *Man., Canada* **105 B8** 55 45N 100 30W
Highrock L., *Sask., Canada* **105 B7** 57 5N 105 32W
Higüey, *Dom. Rep.* **121 C6** 18 37N 68 42W
Hihya, *Egypt* **80 H7** 30 40N 31 36 E
Hiiumaa, *Estonia* **9 G20** 58 50N 22 45 E
Híjar, *Spain* **32 D4** 41 10N 0 27W
Ḥijāz □, *Si. Arabia* **70 E3** 24 0N 40 0 E
Hijo = Tagum, *Phil.* **61 H6** 7 33N 125 53 E
Hikari, *Japan* **55 H5** 33 58N 131 58 E
Hikmak, Ras el, *Egypt* **80 A2** 31 15N 27 51 E
Hiko, *U.S.A.* **116 H11** 37 32N 115 14W
Hikone, *Japan* **55 G8** 35 15N 136 10 E
Hikurangi, *N.Z.* **91 F5** 35 36 S 174 17 E
Hikurangi, Mt., *N.Z.* **91 H6** 37 55 S 178 4 E
Hildburghausen, *Germany* **24 E6** 50 25N 10 42 E
Hildesheim, *Germany* **24 C5** 52 9N 9 56 E
Hill →, *Australia* **93 F2** 30 23 S 115 3 E
Hill City, *Idaho, U.S.A.* **114 E6** 43 18N 115 3W
Hill City, *Kans., U.S.A.* **112 F5** 39 22N 99 51W
Hill City, *S. Dak., U.S.A.* **112 D3** 43 56N 103 35W
Hill Island L., *Canada* **105 A7** 60 30N 109 50W
Hillared, *Sweden* **11 G7** 57 37N 13 10 E
Hillcrest Center, *U.S.A.* **117 K8** 35 23N 118 57W
Hillegom, *Neths.* **17 B4** 52 18N 4 35 E
Hillerød, *Denmark* **11 J6** 55 56N 12 19 E
Hillerstorp, *Sweden* **11 G7** 57 20N 13 52 E
Hillsboro, *Kans., U.S.A.* **112 F6** 38 21N 97 12W
Hillsboro, *N. Dak., U.S.A.* **112 B6** 47 26N 97 3W
Hillsboro, *N.H., U.S.A.* **111 C13** 43 7N 71 54W
Hillsboro, *Ohio, U.S.A.* **108 F4** 39 12N 83 37W
Hillsboro, *Oreg., U.S.A.* **116 E4** 45 31N 122 59W
Hillsboro, *Tex., U.S.A.* **113 J6** 32 1N 97 8W
Hillsborough, *Grenada* **121 D7** 12 28N 61 28W
Hillsdale, *Mich., U.S.A.* **108 E3** 41 56N 84 38W
Hillsdale, *N.Y., U.S.A.* **111 D11** 42 11N 73 30W
Hillsport, *Canada* **102 C2** 49 27N 85 34W
Hillston, *Australia* **95 E4** 33 30 S 145 31 E
Hilo, *U.S.A.* **106 J17** 19 44N 155 5W
Hilton, *U.S.A.* **110 C7** 43 17N 77 48W
Hilton Head Island, *U.S.A.* **109 J5** 32 13N 80 45W
Hilvan, *Turkey* **73 D8** 37 34N 38 58 E
Hilversum, *Neths.* **17 B5** 52 14N 5 10 E
Himachal Pradesh □, *India* **68 D7** 31 30N 77 0 E
Himalaya, *Asia* **69 E11** 29 0N 84 0 E
Himamaylan, *Phil.* **61 F5** 10 6N 122 52 E
Himara = Himarë, *Albania* **40 F3** 40 8N 19 43 E
Himarë, *Albania* **40 F3** 40 8N 19 43 E
Himatnagar, *India* **66 H8** 23 37N 72 57 E
Himeji, *Japan* **55 G7** 34 50N 134 40 E
Himi, *Japan* **55 F8** 36 50N 136 55 E
Himmerland, *Denmark* **11 H3** 56 45N 9 30 E
Ḥimṣ, *Syria* **75 A5** 34 40N 36 45 E
Ḥimṣ □, *Syria* **75 A6** 34 30N 37 0 E
Hinche, *Haiti* **121 C5** 19 9N 72 1W
Hinchinbrook I., *Australia* **94 B4** 18 20 S 146 15 E
Hinckley, *U.K.* **13 E6** 52 33N 1 22W
Hinckley, *U.S.A.* **112 B8** 46 1N 92 56W
Hindaun, *India* **68 F7** 26 44N 77 5 E
Hindmarsh, L., *Australia* **95 F3** 36 5 S 141 55 E
Hindsholm, *Denmark* **11 J4** 55 30N 10 40 E
Hindu Bagh, *Pakistan* **68 D2** 30 56N 67 50 E
Hindu Kush, *Asia* **66 B7** 36 0N 71 0 E
Hindubagh, *Pakistan* **66 D5** 30 56N 67 57 E
Hindupur, *India* **66 N10** 13 49N 77 32 E
Hines Creek, *Canada* **104 B5** 56 20N 118 40W
Hinesville, *U.S.A.* **109 K5** 31 51N 81 36W
Hinganghat, *India* **66 J11** 20 30N 78 52 E
Hingham, *U.S.A.* **114 B8** 48 33N 110 25W
Hingir, *India* **69 J10** 21 57N 83 41 E
Hingoli, *India* **66 K10** 19 41N 77 15 E
Hinigaran, *Phil.* **61 F5** 10 16N 122 50 E
Hinis, *Turkey* **73 C9** 39 22N 41 43 E
Hinna = Imi, *Ethiopia* **81 F5** 6 28N 42 10 E
Hinna, *Nigeria* **83 C7** 10 25N 11 35 E
Hinnerup, *Denmark* **11 H4** 56 16N 10 4 E
Hinnøya, *Norway* **8 B16** 68 35N 15 50 E
Hinojosa del Duque, *Spain* **35 G5** 38 30N 5 9W
Hinsdale, *U.S.A.* **111 D12** 42 47N 72 29W
Hinterrhein →, *Switz.* **25 J5** 46 40N 9 25 E
Hinton, *Canada* **104 C5** 53 26N 117 34W
Hinton, *U.S.A.* **108 G5** 37 40N 80 54W
Hınzır Burnu, *Turkey* **72 D6** 36 19N 35 46 E
Hirado, *Japan* **55 H4** 33 22N 129 33 E
Hirakud Dam, *India* **67 J13** 21 32N 83 45 E
Hiran →, *India* **69 H8** 23 6N 79 21 E
Hirapur, *India* **69 G8** 24 22N 79 13 E
Hiratsuka, *Japan* **55 G9** 35 19N 139 21 E
Hirfanlı Baraji, *Turkey* **72 C5** 39 18N 33 31 E
Hiroo, *Japan* **54 C11** 42 17N 143 19 E
Hirosaki, *Japan* **54 D10** 40 34N 140 28 E
Hiroshima, *Japan* **55 G6** 34 24N 132 30 E
Hiroshima □, *Japan* **55 G6** 34 50N 133 0 E
Hirson, *France* **19 C11** 49 55N 4 4 E
Hirtshals, *Denmark* **11 G3** 57 36N 9 57 E
Hisar, *India* **68 E6** 29 12N 75 45 E
Hisarcık, *Turkey* **39 B11** 39 15N 29 14 E
Hisaria, *Bulgaria* **41 D8** 42 30N 24 44 E
Hisb →, *Iraq* **70 D5** 31 45N 44 17 E
Ḥismá, *Si. Arabia* **70 D3** 28 30N 36 0 E
Hispaniola, *W. Indies* **121 C5** 19 0N 71 0W
Hīt, *Iraq* **70 C4** 33 38N 42 49 E
Hita, *Japan* **55 H5** 33 20N 130 58 E
Hitachi, *Japan* **55 F10** 36 36N 140 39 E
Hitchin, *U.K.* **13 F7** 51 58N 0 16W
Hitoyoshi, *Japan* **55 H5** 32 13N 130 45 E
Hitra, *Norway* **8 E13** 63 30N 8 45 E
Hitzacker, *Germany* **24 B7** 53 9N 11 2 E
Hixon, *Canada* **104 C4** 53 25N 122 35W
Ḥiyyon, N. →, *Israel* **75 E4** 30 25N 35 10 E
Hjalmar L., *Canada* **105 A7** 61 33N 109 25W
Hjälmaren, *Sweden* **10 E9** 59 18N 15 40 E
Hjältevad, *Sweden* **11 G9** 57 38N 15 20 E
Hjo, *Sweden* **11 F8** 58 22N 14 17 E
Hjørring, *Denmark* **11 G3** 57 29N 9 59 E
Hjortkvarn, *Sweden* **11 F9** 58 54N 15 26 E
Hlinsko, *Czech Rep.* **26 B8** 49 45N 15 54 E
Hlobane, *S. Africa* **89 D5** 27 42 S 31 0 E
Hlohovec, *Slovak Rep.* **27 C10** 48 26N 17 49 E
Hlučín, *Czech Rep.* **27 B11** 49 54N 18 11 E
Hluhluwe, *S. Africa* **89 D5** 28 1 S 32 15 E
Hlukhiv, *Ukraine* **47 G7** 51 40N 33 58 E
Hlyboka, *Ukraine* **47 H3** 48 5N 25 56 E
Hlybokaye, *Belarus* **46 E4** 55 10N 27 45 E
Hnúšt'a, *Slovak Rep.* **27 C12** 48 35N 19 58 E
Ho, *Ghana* **83 D5** 6 37N 0 27 E
Ho Chi Minh City = Thanh Pho Ho Chi Minh, *Vietnam* **65 G6** 10 58N 106 40 E
Ho Thuong, *Vietnam* **64 C5** 19 32N 105 48 E
Hoa Binh, *Vietnam* **58 G5** 20 50N 105 20 E
Hoa Da, *Vietnam* **65 G7** 11 16N 108 40 E
Hoa Hiep, *Vietnam* **65 G5** 11 34N 105 51 E
Hoai Nhon, *Vietnam* **64 E7** 14 28N 109 1 E
Hoang Lien Son, *Vietnam* **58 F4** 22 0N 104 0 E
Hoanib →, *Namibia* **88 B1** 19 27 S 12 46 E
Hoare B., *Canada* **101 B13** 65 17N 62 30W
Hoarusib →, *Namibia* **88 B2** 19 3 S 12 36 E
Hobart, *Australia* **94 G4** 42 50 S 147 21 E
Hobart, *U.S.A.* **113 H5** 35 1N 99 6W
Hobbs, *U.S.A.* **113 J3** 32 42N 103 8W
Hobbs Coast, *Antarctica* **5 D14** 74 50 S 131 0W
Hobe Sound, *U.S.A.* **109 M5** 27 4N 80 8W
Hoboken, *U.S.A.* **111 F10** 40 45N 74 4W
Hobro, *Denmark* **11 H3** 56 39N 9 46 E
Hoburgen, *Sweden* **11 H12** 56 55N 18 7 E
Hocalar, *Turkey* **39 C11** 38 36N 30 0 E
Hochfeld, *Namibia* **88 C2** 21 28 S 17 58 E
Hochschwab, *Austria* **26 D8** 47 35N 15 0 E
Höchstadt, *Germany* **25 F6** 49 42N 10 47 E
Hockenheim, *Germany* **25 F4** 49 19N 8 32 E
Hodaka-Dake, *Japan* **55 F8** 36 17N 137 39 E
Hodgeville, *Canada* **105 C7** 50 7N 106 58W
Hodgson, *Canada* **105 C9** 51 13N 97 36W
Hódmezővásárhely, *Hungary* **42 D5** 46 28N 20 22 E
Hodna, Chott el, *Algeria* **78 A6** 35 26N 4 43 E
Hodonín, *Czech Rep.* **27 C10** 48 50N 17 10 E
Hoeamdong, *N. Korea* **57 C16** 42 30N 130 16 E
Hœdic, I. de, *France* **18 E4** 47 20N 2 53W
Hoek van Holland, *Neths.* **17 C4** 52 0N 4 7 E
Hoengsŏng, *S. Korea* **57 F14** 37 29N 127 59 E
Hoeryong, *N. Korea* **57 C15** 42 30N 129 45 E
Hoeyang, *N. Korea* **57 E14** 38 43N 127 36 E
Hof, *Germany* **25 E7** 50 19N 11 55 E
Hofgeismar, *Germany* **24 D5** 51 29N 9 23 E
Hofheim, *Germany* **25 E4** 50 5N 8 26 E
Hofmeyr, *S. Africa* **88 E4** 31 39 S 25 50 E
Höfn, *Iceland* **8 D6** 64 15N 15 13W
Hofors, *Sweden* **10 D10** 60 31N 16 15 E
Hofsjökull, *Iceland* **8 D4** 64 49N 18 48W
Hōfu, *Japan* **55 G5** 34 3N 131 34 E
Hogan Group, *Australia* **95 F4** 39 13 S 147 1 E
Höganäs, *Sweden* **11 H6** 56 12N 12 33 E
Hogarth, Mt., *Australia* **94 C2** 21 48 S 136 58 E
Hoggar = Ahaggar, *Algeria* **78 D7** 23 0N 6 30 E
Högsäter, *Sweden* **11 F6** 58 38N 12 5 E
Högsby, *Sweden* **11 G10** 57 10N 16 1 E
Högsjö, *Sweden* **10 E9** 59 4N 15 44 E
Hogsty Reef, *Bahamas* **121 B5** 21 41N 73 48W
Hoh →, *U.S.A.* **116 C2** 47 45N 124 29W
Hohe Acht, *Germany* **25 E3** 50 22N 7 0 E
Hohe Tauern, *Austria* **26 D5** 47 11N 12 40 E
Hohe Venn, *Belgium* **17 D6** 50 30N 6 5 E
Hohenau, *Austria* **27 C9** 48 36N 16 55 E
Hohenems, *Austria* **26 D2** 47 22N 9 42 E
Hohenloher Ebene, *Germany* **25 F5** 49 14N 9 36 E
Hohenwald, *U.S.A.* **109 H2** 35 33N 87 33W
Hohenwestedt, *Germany* **24 A5** 54 5N 9 40 E
Hoher Rhön = Rhön, *Germany* **24 E5** 50 24N 9 58 E
Hohhot, *China* **56 D6** 40 52N 111 40 E
Hóhlakas, *Greece* **36 D9** 35 57N 27 53 E
Hohoe, *Ghana* **83 D5** 7 8N 0 32 E
Hoi An, *Vietnam* **64 E7** 15 30N 108 19 E
Hoi Xuan, *Vietnam* **58 G5** 20 25N 105 9 E
Hoisington, *U.S.A.* **112 F5** 38 31N 98 47W
Højer, *Denmark* **11 K2** 54 58N 8 42 E
Hōjō, *Japan* **55 H6** 33 58N 132 46 E
Hok, *Sweden* **11 G8** 57 31N 14 16 E
Hökensås, *Sweden* **11 G8** 58 0N 14 5 E
Hökerum, *Sweden* **11 G7** 57 51N 13 16 E
Hokianga Harbour, *N.Z.* **91 F4** 35 31 S 173 22 E
Hokitika, *N.Z.* **91 K3** 42 42 S 171 0 E
Hokkaidō □, *Japan* **54 C11** 43 30N 143 0 E
Hol-Hol, *Djibouti* **81 E5** 11 20N 42 50 E
Hola Pristan, *Ukraine* **47 J7** 46 29N 32 32 E
Holbæk, *Denmark* **11 J5** 55 43N 11 43 E
Holbrook, *Australia* **95 F4** 35 42 S 147 18 E
Holbrook, *U.S.A.* **115 J8** 34 54N 110 10W
Holden, *U.S.A.* **114 G7** 39 6N 112 16W
Holdenville, *U.S.A.* **113 H6** 35 5N 96 24W
Holdrege, *U.S.A.* **112 E5** 40 26N 99 23W
Holešov, *Czech Rep.* **27 B10** 49 20N 17 35 E
Holguín, *Cuba* **120 B4** 20 50N 76 20W
Holíč, *Slovak Rep.* **27 C10** 48 49N 17 10 E
Holice, *Czech Rep.* **26 A8** 50 5N 16 0 E
Höljes, *Sweden* **10 D6** 60 50N 12 35 E
Hollabrunn, *Austria* **26 C9** 48 34N 16 5 E
Hollams Bird I., *Namibia* **88 C1** 24 40 S 14 30 E
Holland, *Mich., U.S.A.* **108 D2** 42 47N 86 7W
Holland, *N.Y., U.S.A.* **110 D6** 42 38N 78 32W
Hollandale, *U.S.A.* **113 J9** 33 10N 90 51W
Hollandia = Jayapura, *Indonesia* **63 E10** 2 28 S 140 38 E
Holley, *U.S.A.* **110 C6** 43 14N 78 2W
Hollfeld, *Germany* **25 F7** 49 56N 11 18 E
Hollidaysburg, *U.S.A.* **110 F6** 40 26N 78 24W
Hollis, *U.S.A.* **113 H5** 34 41N 99 55W
Hollister, *Calif., U.S.A.* **116 J5** 36 51N 121 24W
Hollister, *Idaho, U.S.A.* **114 E6** 42 21N 114 35W
Höllviken = Höllviksnäs, *Sweden* **11 J6** 55 26N 12 58 E
Höllviksnäs, *Sweden* **11 J6** 55 26N 12 58 E
Holly Hill, *U.S.A.* **109 L5** 29 16N 81 3W
Holly Springs, *U.S.A.* **113 H10** 34 46N 89 27W
Hollywood, *U.S.A.* **109 N5** 26 1N 80 9W
Holman, *Canada* **100 A8** 70 44N 117 44W
Hólmavík, *Iceland* **8 D3** 65 42N 21 40W
Holmen, *U.S.A.* **112 D9** 43 58N 91 15W
Holmes Reefs, *Australia* **94 B4** 16 27 S 148 0 E
Holmsjö, *Sweden* **11 H9** 56 25N 15 32 E
Holmsjön, *Västernorrland, Sweden* **10 B10** 62 41N 16 33 E
Holmsjön, *Västernorrland, Sweden* **10 B9** 62 26N 15 20 E
Holmsland Klit, *Denmark* **11 J2** 56 0N 8 5 E
Holmsund, *Sweden* **8 E19** 63 41N 20 20 E
Holod, *Romania* **42 D7** 46 49N 22 8 E
Holroyd →, *Australia* **94 A3** 14 10 S 141 36 E
Holstebro, *Denmark* **11 H2** 56 22N 8 37 E
Holsworthy, *U.K.* **13 G3** 50 48N 4 22W
Holton, *Canada* **103 B8** 54 31N 57 12W
Holton, *U.S.A.* **112 F7** 39 28N 95 44W
Holtville, *U.S.A.* **117 N11** 32 49N 115 23W
Holwerd, *Neths.* **17 A5** 53 22N 5 54 E
Holy I., *Angl., U.K.* **12 D3** 53 17N 4 37W
Holy I., *Northumb., U.K.* **12 B6** 55 40N 1 47W
Holyhead, *U.K.* **12 D3** 53 18N 4 38W
Holyoke, *Colo., U.S.A.* **112 E3** 40 35N 102 18W
Holyoke, *Mass., U.S.A.* **111 D12** 42 12N 72 37W
Holyrood, *Canada* **103 C9** 47 27N 53 8W
Holzkirchen, *Germany* **25 H7** 47 52N 11 42 E
Holzminden, *Germany* **24 D5** 51 50N 9 28 E
Homa Bay, *Kenya* **86 C3** 0 36 S 34 30 E
Homalin, *Burma* **67 G19** 24 55N 95 0 E
Homand, *Iran* **71 C8** 32 28N 59 37 E
Homathko →, *Canada* **104 C4** 51 0N 124 56W
Homberg, *Germany* **24 D5** 51 2N 9 25 E
Hombori, *Mali* **83 B4** 15 20N 1 38W
Homburg, *Germany* **25 F3** 49 28N 7 18 E
Home B., *Canada* **101 B13** 68 40N 67 10W
Home Hill, *Australia* **94 B4** 19 43 S 147 25 E
Homedale, *U.S.A.* **114 E5** 43 37N 116 56W
Homer, *Alaska, U.S.A.* **100 C4** 59 39N 151 33W
Homer, *La., U.S.A.* **113 J8** 32 48N 93 4W
Homer City, *U.S.A.* **110 F5** 40 32N 79 10W
Homestead, *Australia* **94 C4** 20 20 S 145 40 E
Homestead, *U.S.A.* **109 N5** 25 28N 80 29W
Homewood, *U.S.A.* **116 F6** 39 4N 120 8W
Homoine, *Mozam.* **89 C6** 23 55 S 35 8 E
Homoljske Planina, *Serbia, Yug.* **40 B5** 44 10N 21 45 E
Homorod, *Romania* **43 D10** 46 5N 25 15 E
Homs = Ḥimṣ, *Syria* **75 A5** 34 40N 36 45 E
Homyel, *Belarus* **47 F6** 52 28N 31 0 E
Hon Chong, *Vietnam* **65 G5** 10 25N 104 30 E
Hon Me, *Vietnam* **64 C5** 19 23N 105 56 E
Honan = Henan □, *China* **56 H8** 34 0N 114 0 E
Honaz, *Turkey* **39 D11** 37 46N 29 18 E
Honbetsu, *Japan* **54 C11** 43 7N 143 37 E
Honcut, *U.S.A.* **116 F5** 39 20N 121 32W
Honda Bay, *Phil.* **61 G3** 9 53N 118 49 E
Hondarribia, *Spain* **32 B3** 43 22N 1 47W
Hondeklipbaai, *S. Africa* **88 E2** 30 19 S 17 17 E
Hondo, *Japan* **55 H5** 32 27N 130 12 E
Hondo, *U.S.A.* **113 L5** 29 21N 99 9W
Hondo →, *Belize* **119 D7** 18 25N 88 21W
Honduras ■, *Cent. Amer.* **120 D2** 14 40N 86 30W
Honduras, G. de, *Caribbean* **120 C2** 16 50N 87 0W
Hønefoss, *Norway* **9 F14** 60 10N 10 18 E
Honesdale, *U.S.A.* **111 E9** 41 34N 75 16W
Honey L., *U.S.A.* **116 E6** 40 15N 120 19W
Honfleur, *France* **18 C7** 49 25N 0 13 E
Høng, *Denmark* **11 J5** 55 31N 11 18 E
Hong →, *Vietnam* **58 F5** 22 0N 104 0 E
Hong Gai, *Vietnam* **58 G6** 20 57N 107 5 E
Hong He →, *China* **56 H8** 32 25N 115 35 E
Hong Hu, *China* **59 C9** 29 54N 113 24 E
Hong Kong □, *China* **59 F10** 22 11N 114 14 E
Hong'an, *China* **59 B10** 31 20N 114 40 E
Hongch'ŏn, *S. Korea* **57 F14** 37 44N 127 53 E
Honghai Wan, *China* **59 F10** 22 40N 115 0 E
Honghe, *China* **58 F4** 23 25N 102 25 E
Honghu, *China* **59 C9** 29 50N 113 30 E
Hongjiang, *China* **58 D7** 27 7N 109 59 E
Hongliu He →, *China* **56 F5** 38 0N 109 50 E
Hongor, *Mongolia* **56 B7** 45 45N 112 50 E
Hongsa, *Laos* **64 C3** 19 43N 101 20 E
Hongshui He →, *China* **58 F7** 23 48N 109 30 E
Hongsŏng, *S. Korea* **57 F14** 36 37N 126 38 E
Hongtong, *China* **56 F6** 36 16N 111 40 E
Honguedo, Détroit d', *Canada* **103 C7** 49 15N 64 0W
Hongwon, *N. Korea* **57 E14** 40 0N 127 56 E
Hongya, *China* **58 C4** 29 57N 103 22 E
Hongyuan, *China* **58 A4** 32 51N 102 40 E
Hongze Hu, *China* **57 H10** 33 15N 118 35 E
Honiara, *Solomon Is.* **96 H7** 9 27 S 159 57 E
Honiton, *U.K.* **13 G4** 50 47N 3 11W
Honjō, *Japan* **54 E10** 39 23N 140 3 E
Honkorâb, Ras, *Egypt* **80 C4** 24 35N 35 10 E
Honningsvåg, *Norway* **8 A21** 70 59N 25 59 E
Hönö, *Sweden* **11 G5** 57 41N 11 39 E
Honolulu, *U.S.A.* **106 H16** 21 19N 157 52W
Hontoria del Pinar, *Spain* **32 D1** 41 50N 3 10W
Hood, Mt., *U.S.A.* **114 D3** 45 23N 121 42W
Hood, Pt., *Australia* **93 F2** 34 23 S 119 34 E
Hood River, *U.S.A.* **114 D3** 45 43N 121 31W
Hoodsport, *U.S.A.* **116 C3** 47 24N 123 9W
Hooge, *Germany* **24 A4** 54 34N 8 33 E
Hoogeveen, *Neths.* **17 B6** 52 44N 6 28 E
Hoogezand-Sappemeer, *Neths.* **17 A6** 53 9N 6 45 E
Hooghly = Hugli →, *India* **69 J13** 21 56N 88 4 E
Hooghly-Chinsura = Chunchura, *India* **69 H13** 22 53N 88 27 E
Hook Hd., *Ireland* **15 D5** 52 7N 6 56W
Hook I., *Australia* **94 C4** 20 4 S 149 0 E
Hook of Holland = Hoek van Holland, *Neths.* **17 C4** 52 0N 4 7 E
Hooker, *U.S.A.* **113 G4** 36 52N 101 13W
Hooker Creek, *Australia* **92 C5** 18 23 S 130 38 E
Hoonah, *U.S.A.* **104 B1** 58 7N 135 27W
Hooper Bay, *U.S.A.* **100 B3** 61 32N 166 6W
Hoopeston, *U.S.A.* **108 E2** 40 28N 87 40W
Hoopstad, *S. Africa* **88 D4** 27 50 S 25 55 E
Höör, *Sweden* **11 J7** 55 56N 13 33 E
Hoorn, *Neths.* **17 B5** 52 38N 5 4 E
Hoover, *U.S.A.* **109 J2** 33 20N 86 11W
Hoover Dam, *U.S.A.* **117 K12** 36 1N 114 44W
Hooversville, *U.S.A.* **110 F6** 40 9N 78 55W
Hop Bottom, *U.S.A.* **111 E9** 41 42N 75 46W
Hopa, *Turkey* **73 B9** 41 28N 41 30 E
Hope, *Canada* **104 D4** 49 25N 121 25W
Hope, *Ariz., U.S.A.* **117 M13** 33 43N 113 42W
Hope, *Ark., U.S.A.* **113 J8** 33 40N 93 36W
Hope, L., *S. Austral., Australia* **95 D2** 28 24 S 139 18 E
Hope, L., *W. Austral., Australia* **93 F3** 32 35 S 120 15 E
Hope I., *Canada* **110 B4** 44 55N 80 11W
Hope Town, *Bahamas* **120 A4** 26 35N 76 57W
Hopedale, *Canada* **103 A7** 55 28N 60 13W
Hopedale, *U.S.A.* **111 D13** 42 8N 71 33W
Hopefield, *S. Africa* **88 E2** 33 3 S 18 22 E
Hopei = Hebei □, *China* **56 E9** 39 0N 116 0 E
Hopelchén, *Mexico* **119 D7** 19 46N 89 50W
Hopetoun, *Vic., Australia* **95 F3** 35 42 S 142 22 E
Hopetoun, *W. Austral., Australia* **93 F3** 33 57 S 120 7 E
Hopetown, *S. Africa* **88 D3** 29 34 S 24 3 E
Hopevale, *Australia* **94 B4** 15 16 S 145 20 E
Hopewell, *U.S.A.* **108 G7** 37 18N 77 17W
Hopfgarten, *Austria* **26 D5** 47 27N 12 10 E
Hopkins, L., *Australia* **92 D4** 24 15 S 128 35 E
Hopkinsville, *U.S.A.* **109 G2** 36 52N 87 29W
Hopland, *U.S.A.* **116 G3** 38 58N 123 7W
Hoquiam, *U.S.A.* **116 D3** 46 59N 123 53W
Horasan, *Turkey* **73 B10** 40 3N 42 11 E
Horažďovice, *Czech Rep.* **26 B6** 49 19N 13 42 E
Horb, *Germany* **25 G4** 48 26N 8 47 E
Hörby, *Sweden* **11 J7** 55 51N 13 40 E
Horcajo de Santiago, *Spain* **32 F1** 39 50N 3 1W
Horden Hills, *Australia* **92 D5** 20 15 S 130 0 E
Horezu, *Romania* **43 E8** 45 6N 24 0 E
Horgen, *Switz.* **25 H4** 47 15N 8 35 E
Horgoš, *Serbia, Yug.* **42 D4** 46 10N 20 0 E
Hořice, *Czech Rep.* **26 A8** 50 21N 15 39 E
Horinger, *China* **56 D6** 40 28N 111 48 E
Horki, *Belarus* **46 E6** 54 17N 30 59 E
Horlick Mts., *Antarctica* **5 E15** 84 0 S 102 0W
Horlivka, *Ukraine* **47 H10** 48 19N 38 5 E
Hormak, *Iran* **71 D9** 29 58N 60 51 E
Hormoz, *Iran* **71 E7** 27 35N 55 0 E
Hormoz, Jaz.-ye, *Iran* **71 E8** 27 8N 56 28 E
Hormozgān □, *Iran* **71 E8** 27 30N 56 0 E
Hormuz, Kūh-e, *Iran* **71 E7** 27 27N 55 10 E
Hormuz, Str. of, *The Gulf* **71 E8** 26 30N 56 30 E
Horn, *Austria* **26 C8** 48 39N 15 40 E
Horn, *Iceland* **8 C2** 66 28N 22 28W
Horn, *Sweden* **11 G9** 57 54N 15 51 E
Horn →, *Canada* **104 A5** 61 30N 118 1W
Horn, Cape = Hornos, C. de, *Chile* **122 J4** 55 50 S 67 30W
Horn Head, *Ireland* **15 A3** 55 14N 8 0W
Horn I., *Australia* **94 A3** 10 37 S 142 17 E
Horn Mts., *Canada* **104 A5** 62 15N 119 15W
Hornachuelos, *Spain* **35 H5** 37 50N 5 14W
Hornavan, *Sweden* **8 C17** 66 15N 17 30 E
Hornbeck, *U.S.A.* **113 K8** 31 20N 93 24W
Hornbrook, *U.S.A.* **114 F2** 41 55N 122 33W
Hornburg, *Germany* **24 C6** 52 2N 10 37 E
Horncastle, *U.K.* **12 D7** 53 13N 0 7W
Horndal, *Sweden* **10 D10** 60 18N 16 23 E
Hornell, *U.S.A.* **110 D7** 42 20N 77 40W
Hornell L., *Canada* **104 A5** 62 20N 119 25W
Hornepayne, *Canada* **102 C3** 49 14N 84 48W
Horní Planá, *Czech Rep.* **26 C7** 48 46N 14 2 E
Hornings Mills, *Canada* **110 B4** 44 9N 80 12W
Hornitos, *U.S.A.* **116 H6** 37 30N 120 14W
Hornos, C. de, *Chile* **122 J4** 55 50 S 67 30W
Hornoy-le-Bourg, *France* **19 C8** 49 50N 1 54 E
Hornsea, *U.K.* **12 D7** 53 55N 0 11W
Hornslandet, *Sweden* **10 C11** 61 35N 17 37 E
Hornum, *Germany* **24 A4** 54 45N 8 17 E
Horobetsu, *Japan* **54 C10** 42 24N 141 6 E
Horodenka, *Ukraine* **47 H3** 48 41N 25 29 E
Horodnya, *Ukraine* **47 G6** 51 55N 31 33 E
Horodok, *Khmelnytskyy, Ukraine* **47 H4** 49 10N 26 34 E
Horodok, *Lviv, Ukraine* **47 H2** 49 46N 23 32 E
Horodyshche, *Ukraine* **47 H6** 49 17N 31 27 E
Horokhiv, *Ukraine* **47 G3** 50 30N 24 45 E
Horovice, *Czech Rep.* **26 B6** 49 48N 13 53 E
Horqin Youyi Qianqi, *China* **57 A12** 46 5N 122 3 E
Horqueta, *Paraguay* **126 A4** 23 15 S 56 55W
Horred, *Sweden* **11 G6** 57 22N 12 28 E
Horse Creek, *U.S.A.* **112 E3** 41 57N 105 10W
Horse Is., *Canada* **103 B8** 50 15N 55 50W
Horsefly L., *Canada* **104 C4** 52 25N 121 0W
Horseheads, *U.S.A.* **110 D8** 42 10N 76 49W
Horsens, *Denmark* **11 J3** 55 52N 9 51 E
Horsham, *Australia* **95 F3** 36 44 S 142 13 E
Horsham, *U.K.* **13 F7** 51 4N 0 20W
Horšovský Týn, *Czech Rep.* **26 B5** 49 31N 12 58 E
Horten, *Norway* **9 G14** 59 25N 10 32 E
Hortobágy →, *Hungary* **42 C6** 47 30N 21 6 E
Horton, *U.S.A.* **112 F7** 39 40N 95 32W
Horton →, *Canada* **100 B7** 69 56N 126 52W
Horwood L., *Canada* **102 C3** 48 5N 82 20W
Hosaina, *Ethiopia* **81 F4** 7 30N 37 47 E
Hose, Gunung-Gunung, *Malaysia* **62 D4** 2 5N 114 6 E
Ḥoseynābād, *Khuzestān, Iran* **71 C6** 32 45N 48 20 E
Ḥoseynābād, *Kordestān, Iran* **70 C5** 35 33N 47 8 E
Hoshangabad, *India* **68 H7** 22 45N 77 45 E
Hoshiarpur, *India* **68 D6** 31 30N 75 58 E
Hospet, *India* **66 M10** 15 15N 76 20 E
Hoste, I., *Chile* **128 H3** 55 0 S 69 0W
Hostens, *France* **20 D3** 44 30N 0 40W
Hot, *Thailand* **64 C2** 18 8N 98 29 E
Hot Creek Range, *U.S.A.* **114 G6** 38 40N 116 20W
Hot Springs, *Ark., U.S.A.* **113 H8** 34 31N 93 3W

Hot Springs, S. Dak., U.S.A. 112 D3 43 26N 103 29W
Hotagen, Sweden 8 E16 63 50N 14 30 E
Hotan, China 60 C2 37 25N 79 55 E
Hotazel, S. Africa 88 D3 27 17 S 22 58 E
Hotchkiss, U.S.A. 115 G10 38 48N 107 43W
Hotham, C., Australia 92 B5 12 2 S 131 18 E
Hoting, Sweden 8 D17 64 8N 16 15 E
Hotolisht, Albania 40 E4 41 10N 20 25 E
Hotolishti = Hotolisht, Albania 40 E4 41 10N 20 25 E
Hotte, Massif de la, Haiti 121 C5 18 30N 73 45W
Hottentotsbaai, Namibia 88 D1 26 8 S 14 59 E
Houat, Î. de, France 18 E4 47 24N 2 58W
Houdan, France 19 D8 48 48N 1 35 E
Houei Sai, Laos 58 G3 20 18N 100 26 E
Houeillès, France 20 D4 44 12N 0 2 E
Houffalize, Belgium 17 D5 50 8N 5 48 E
Houghton, Mich., U.S.A. 112 B10 47 7N 88 34W
Houghton, N.Y., U.S.A. 110 D6 42 25N 78 10W
Houghton L., U.S.A. 108 C3 44 21N 84 44W
Houhora Heads, N.Z. 91 F4 34 49 S 173 9 E
Houlton, U.S.A. 109 B12 46 8N 67 51W
Houma, U.S.A. 113 L9 29 36N 90 43W
Houndé, Burkina Faso 82 C4 11 34N 3 31W
Hourtin, France 20 C2 45 11N 1 4W
Hourtin-Carcans, Étang d', France 20 C2 45 10N 1 6W
Housatonic →, U.S.A. 111 E11 41 10N 73 7W
Houston, Canada 104 C3 54 25N 126 39W
Houston, Mo., U.S.A. 113 G9 37 22N 91 58W
Houston, Tex., U.S.A. 113 L7 29 46N 95 22W
Hout →, S. Africa 89 C4 23 4 S 29 36 E
Houtkraal, S. Africa 88 E3 30 23 S 24 5 E
Houtman Abrolhos, Australia 93 E1 28 43 S 113 48 E
Hovd, Mongolia 60 B4 48 2N 91 37 E
Hove, U.K. 13 G7 50 50N 0 10W
Hoveyzeh, Iran 71 D6 31 27N 48 4 E
Hovmantorp, Sweden 11 H9 56 47N 15 7 E
Hövsgöl, Mongolia 56 C5 43 37N 109 39 E
Hövsgöl Nuur, Mongolia 60 A5 51 0N 100 30 E
Hovsta, Sweden 10 E9 59 22N 15 15 E
Howakil, Eritrea 81 D5 15 10N 40 16 E
Howar, Wadi →, Sudan 81 D2 17 30N 27 8 E
Howard, Australia 95 D5 25 16 S 152 32 E
Howard, Pa., U.S.A. 110 F7 41 1N 77 40W
Howard, S. Dak., U.S.A. 112 C6 44 1N 97 32W
Howe, U.S.A. 114 E7 43 48N 113 0W
Howe, C., Australia 95 F5 37 30 S 150 0 E
Howe I., Canada 111 B8 44 16N 76 17W
Howell, U.S.A. 108 D4 42 36N 83 56W
Howick, Canada 111 A11 45 11N 73 51W
Howick, S. Africa 89 D5 29 28 S 30 14 E
Howick Group, Australia 94 A4 14 20 S 145 30 E
Howitt, L., Australia 95 D2 27 40 S 138 40 E
Howland I., Pac. Oc. 96 G10 0 48N 176 38W
Howrah = Haora, India 69 H13 22 37N 88 20 E
Howth Hd., Ireland 15 C5 53 22N 6 3W
Höxter, Germany 24 D5 51 46N 9 22 E
Hoy, U.K. 14 C5 58 50N 3 15W
Hoya, Germany 24 C5 52 49N 9 8 E
Høyanger, Norway 9 F12 61 13N 6 4 E
Hoyerswerda, Germany 24 D10 51 26N 14 14 E
Hoylake, U.K. 12 D4 53 24N 3 10W
Hoyos, Spain 34 E4 40 9N 6 45W
Hpa-an = Pa-an, Burma 67 L20 16 51N 97 40 E
Hpungan Pass, Burma 67 F20 27 30N 96 55 E
Hradec Králové, Czech Rep. 26 A8 50 15N 15 50 E
Hrádek, Czech Rep. 27 C9 48 46N 16 16 E
Hranice, Czech Rep. 27 B10 49 34N 17 45 E
Hrazdan, Armenia 49 K7 40 30N 44 46 E
Hrebenka, Ukraine 47 G7 50 9N 32 22 E
Hrodna, Belarus 46 F2 53 42N 23 52 E
Hrodzyanka, Belarus 46 F5 53 31N 28 42 E
Hron →, Slovak Rep. 27 D11 47 49N 18 45 E
Hrubieszów, Poland 45 H10 50 49N 23 51 E
Hrubý Jeseník, Czech Rep. 27 A10 50 5N 17 10 E
Hrvatska = Croatia ■, Europe 29 C13 45 20N 16 0 E
Hrymayliv, Ukraine 47 H4 49 20N 26 5 E
Hsenwi, Burma 67 H20 23 22N 97 55 E
Hsiamen = Xiamen, China 59 E12 24 25N 118 4 E
Hsian = Xi'an, China 56 G5 34 15N 109 0 E
Hsinchu, Taiwan 59 E13 24 48N 120 58 E
Hsinhailien = Lianyungang, China 57 G10 34 40N 119 11 E
Hsinying, Taiwan 59 F13 23 18N 120 19 E
Hsopket, Burma 58 F2 23 11N 98 26 E
Hsüchou = Xuzhou, China 57 G9 34 18N 117 10 E
Hu Xian, China 56 G5 34 8N 108 42 E
Hua Hin, Thailand 64 F2 12 34N 99 58 E
Hua Xian, Henan, China 56 G8 35 30N 114 30 E
Hua Xian, Shaanxi, China 56 G5 34 30N 109 48 E
Hua'an, China 59 E11 25 1N 117 32 E
Huab →, Namibia 88 B2 20 52 S 13 25 E
Huacheng, China 59 E10 24 4N 115 37 E
Huachinera, Mexico 118 A3 30 9N 108 55W
Huacho, Peru 124 F3 11 10 S 77 35W
Huade, China 56 D7 41 55N 113 59 E
Huadian, China 57 C14 43 0N 126 40 E
Huadu, China 59 F9 23 22N 113 12 E
Huai He →, China 59 A12 33 0N 118 30 E
Huai Yot, Thailand 65 J2 7 45N 99 37 E
Huai'an, Hebei, China 56 D8 40 30N 114 20 E
Huai'an, Jiangsu, China 57 H10 33 30N 119 10 E
Huaibei, China 56 G9 34 0N 116 48 E
Huaibin, China 59 A10 32 32N 115 27 E
Huaide = Gongzhuling, China 57 C13 43 30N 124 40 E
Huaidezhen, China 57 C13 43 48N 124 50 E
Huaihua, China 58 D7 27 32N 109 57 E
Huaiji, China 59 F9 23 55N 112 12 E
Huainan, China 59 A11 32 38N 116 58 E
Huaining, China 59 B11 30 24N 116 40 E
Huairen, China 56 E7 39 48N 113 20 E
Huairou, China 56 D9 40 20N 116 35 E
Huaiyang, China 56 H8 33 40N 114 52 E
Huaiyin, China 57 H10 33 30N 119 2 E
Huaiyuan, Anhui, China 57 H9 32 55N 117 10 E
Huaiyuan, Guangxi Zhuangzu, China 58 E7 24 31N 108 22 E
Huajianzi, China 57 D13 41 23N 125 20 E
Huajuapan de Leon, Mexico 119 D5 17 50N 97 48W
Hualapai Peak, U.S.A. 115 J7 35 5N 113 54W
Hualien, Taiwan 59 E13 24 0N 121 30 E
Huallaga →, Peru 124 E3 5 15 S 75 30W
Huambo, Angola 85 G3 12 42 S 15 54 E
Huan Jiang →, China 56 G5 34 28N 109 0 E
Huan Xian, China 56 F4 36 33N 107 7 E
Huancabamba, Peru 124 E3 5 10 S 79 15W
Huancane, Peru 124 G5 15 10 S 69 44W
Huancavelica, Peru 124 F3 12 50 S 75 5W
Huancayo, Peru 124 F3 12 5 S 75 12W
Huanchaca, Bolivia 124 H5 20 15 S 66 40W
Huang Hai = Yellow Sea, China 57 G12 35 0N 123 0 E
Huang He →, China 57 F10 37 55N 118 50 E
Huang Xian, China 57 F11 37 38N 120 30 E
Huangchuan, China 59 A10 32 15N 115 10 E
Huanggang, China 59 B10 30 29N 114 52 E
Huangguoshu, China 58 E5 26 0N 105 40 E
Huangling, China 56 G5 35 34N 109 15 E
Huanglong, China 56 G5 35 30N 109 59 E
Huanglongtan, China 59 A8 32 40N 110 33 E
Huangmei, China 59 B10 30 5N 115 56 E
Huangpi, China 59 B10 30 50N 114 22 E
Huangping, China 58 D6 26 52N 107 54 E
Huangshan, China 59 C12 29 42N 118 25 E
Huangshi, China 59 B10 30 10N 115 3 E
Huangsongdian, China 57 C14 43 45N 127 25 E
Huangyan, China 59 C13 28 38N 121 19 E
Huangyangsi, China 59 D8 26 33N 111 39 E
Huaning, China 58 E4 24 17N 102 56 E
Huanjiang, China 58 E7 24 50N 108 18 E
Huantai, China 57 F9 36 58N 117 56 E
Huánuco, Peru 124 E3 9 55 S 76 15W
Huaping, China 58 D3 26 46N 101 25 E
Huaraz, Peru 124 E3 9 30 S 77 32W
Huarmey, Peru 124 F3 10 5 S 78 5W
Huarong, China 59 C9 29 29N 112 30 E
Huascarán, Peru 122 D3 9 8 S 77 36W
Huasco, Chile 126 B1 28 30 S 71 15W
Huasco →, Chile 126 B1 28 27 S 71 13W
Huasna, U.S.A. 117 K6 35 6N 120 24W
Huatabampo, Mexico 118 B3 26 50N 109 50W
Huauchinango, Mexico 119 C5 20 11N 98 3W
Huautla de Jiménez, Mexico 119 D5 18 8N 96 51W
Huaxi, China 58 D6 26 25N 106 40 E
Huay Namota, Mexico 118 C4 21 56N 104 30W
Huayin, China 56 G6 34 35N 110 5 E
Huayuan, China 58 C7 28 37N 109 29 E
Huayun, China 58 B6 30 14N 106 40 E
Huazhou, China 59 G8 21 33N 110 33 E
Hubbard, Ohio, U.S.A. 110 E4 41 9N 80 34W
Hubbard, Tex., U.S.A. 113 K6 31 51N 96 48W
Hubbart Pt., Canada 105 B10 59 21N 94 41W
Hubei □, China 59 B9 31 0N 112 0 E
Hubli, India 66 M9 15 22N 75 15 E
Huch'ang, N. Korea 57 D14 41 25N 127 2 E
Hucknall, U.K. 12 D6 53 3N 1 13W
Huddersfield, U.K. 12 D6 53 39N 1 47W
Hude, Germany 24 B4 53 7N 8 26 E
Hudi, Sudan 80 D3 17 43N 34 18 E
Hudiksvall, Sweden 10 C11 61 43N 17 10 E
Hudson, Canada 102 B1 50 6N 92 9W
Hudson, Mass., U.S.A. 111 D13 42 23N 71 34W
Hudson, N.Y., U.S.A. 111 D11 42 15N 73 46W
Hudson, Wis., U.S.A. 112 C8 44 58N 92 45W
Hudson, Wyo., U.S.A. 114 E9 42 54N 108 35W
Hudson →, U.S.A. 111 F10 40 42N 74 2W
Hudson Bay, N.W.T., Canada 101 C11 60 0N 86 0W
Hudson Bay, Sask., Canada 105 C8 52 51N 102 23W
Hudson Falls, U.S.A. 111 C11 43 18N 73 35W
Hudson Mts., Antarctica 5 D16 74 32 S 99 20W
Hudson Str., Canada 101 B13 62 0N 70 0W
Hudson's Hope, Canada 104 B4 56 0N 121 54W
Hue, Vietnam 64 D6 16 30N 107 35 E
Huebra →, Spain 34 D4 41 2N 6 48W
Huedin, Romania 42 D8 46 52N 23 2 E
Huehuetenango, Guatemala 120 C1 15 20N 91 28W
Huejúcar, Mexico 118 C4 22 21N 103 13W
Huélamo, Spain 32 E3 40 17N 1 48W
Huelgoat, France 18 D3 48 22N 3 46W
Huelma, Spain 35 H7 37 39N 3 28W
Huelva, Spain 35 H4 37 18N 6 57W
Huelva □, Spain 35 H4 37 40N 7 0W
Huelva →, Spain 35 H5 37 27N 6 0W
Huentelauquén, Chile 126 C1 31 38 S 71 33W
Huércal-Overa, Spain 33 H3 37 23N 1 57W
Huerta, Sa. de la, Argentina 126 C2 31 10 S 67 30W
Huertas, C. de las, Spain 33 G4 38 21N 0 24W
Huerva →, Spain 32 D4 41 39N 0 52W
Huesca, Spain 32 C4 42 8N 0 25W
Huesca □, Spain 32 C5 42 20N 0 1 E
Huéscar, Spain 33 H2 37 44N 2 35W
Huetamo, Mexico 118 D4 18 36N 100 54W
Huete, Spain 32 E2 40 10N 2 43W
Hugh →, Australia 94 D1 25 1 S 134 1 E
Hughenden, Australia 94 C3 20 52 S 144 10 E
Hughes, Australia 93 F4 30 42 S 129 31 E
Hughesville, U.S.A. 111 E8 41 14N 76 44W
Hugli →, India 69 J13 21 56N 88 4 E
Hugo, Colo., U.S.A. 112 F3 39 8N 103 28W
Hugo, Okla., U.S.A. 113 H7 34 1N 95 31W
Hugoton, U.S.A. 113 G4 37 11N 101 21W
Hui Xian = Huixian, China 56 G7 35 27N 113 12 E
Hui Xian, China 56 H4 33 50N 106 4 E
Hui'an, China 59 E12 25 1N 118 43 E
Hui'anbu, China 56 F4 37 28N 106 38 E
Huichang, China 59 E10 25 32N 115 45 E
Huichapán, Mexico 119 C5 20 24N 99 40W
Huidong, Guangdong, China 59 F10 22 58N 114 43 E
Huidong, Sichuan, China 58 D4 26 34N 102 35 E
Huifa He →, China 57 C14 43 0N 127 50 E
Huila, Nevado del, Colombia 124 C3 3 0N 76 0W
Huilai, China 59 F11 23 0N 116 18 E
Huili, China 58 D4 26 35N 102 17 E
Huimin, China 57 F9 37 27N 117 28 E
Huinan, China 57 C14 42 40N 126 2 E
Huinca Renancó, Argentina 126 C3 34 51 S 64 22W
Huining, China 56 G3 35 38N 105 0 E
Huinong, China 56 E4 39 5N 106 35 E
Huisache, Mexico 118 C4 22 55N 100 25W
Huishui, China 58 D6 26 7N 106 38 E
Huisne →, France 18 E7 47 59N 0 11 E
Huiting, China 56 G9 34 5N 116 5 E
Huitong, China 58 D7 26 51N 109 45 E
Huixian, China 56 G7 35 27N 113 12 E
Huixtla, Mexico 119 D6 15 9N 92 28W
Huize, China 58 D4 26 24N 103 15 E
Huizhou, China 59 F10 23 0N 114 23 E
Hukawng Valley, Burma 67 F20 26 30N 96 30 E
Hukou, China 59 C11 29 45N 116 21 E
Hukuntsi, Botswana 88 C3 23 58 S 21 45 E
Ḥulayfā', Si. Arabia 70 E4 25 58N 40 45 E
Huld = Ulaanjirem, Mongolia 56 B3 45 5N 105 30 E
Hulin He →, China 57 B12 45 0N 122 10 E
Hull = Kingston upon Hull, U.K. 12 D7 53 45N 0 21W
Hull, Canada 102 C4 45 25N 75 44W
Hull →, U.K. 12 D7 53 44N 0 20W
Hulst, Neths. 17 C4 51 17N 4 2 E
Hultsfred, Sweden 11 G9 57 30N 15 52 E
Hulun Nur, China 60 B6 49 0N 117 30 E
Hulyaypole, Ukraine 47 J9 47 45N 36 21 E
Humahuaca, Argentina 126 A2 23 10 S 65 25W
Humaitá, Brazil 124 E6 7 35 S 63 1W
Humaitá, Paraguay 126 B4 27 2 S 58 31W
Humansdorp, S. Africa 88 E3 34 2 S 24 46 E
Humara, J., Sudan 81 D3 16 16N 30 59 E
Humbe, Angola 88 B1 16 40 S 14 55 E
Humber →, U.K. 12 D7 53 42N 0 27W
Humboldt, Canada 105 C7 52 15N 105 9W
Humboldt, Iowa, U.S.A. 112 D7 42 44N 94 13W
Humboldt, Tenn., U.S.A. 113 H10 35 50N 88 55W
Humboldt →, U.S.A. 114 F4 39 59N 118 36W
Humboldt Gletscher, Greenland 4 B4 79 30N 62 0W
Hume, U.S.A. 116 J8 36 48N 118 54W
Hume, L., Australia 95 F4 36 0 S 147 5 E
Humenné, Slovak Rep. 27 C14 48 55N 21 50 E
Hummelsta, Sweden 10 E10 59 34N 16 58 E
Humphreys, Mt., U.S.A. 116 H8 37 17N 118 40W
Humphreys Peak, U.S.A. 115 J8 35 21N 111 41W
Humpolec, Czech Rep. 26 B8 49 31N 15 20 E
Humptulips, U.S.A. 116 C3 47 14N 123 57W
Hūn, Libya 79 C9 29 2N 16 0 E
Hun Jiang →, China 57 D13 40 50N 125 38 E
Húnaflói, Iceland 8 D3 65 50N 20 50W
Hunan □, China 59 D9 27 30N 112 0 E
Hunchun, China 57 C16 42 52N 130 28 E
Hundested, Denmark 11 J5 55 58N 11 52 E
Hundewali, Pakistan 68 D5 31 55N 72 38 E
Hundred Mile House, Canada 104 C4 51 38N 121 18W
Hunedoara, Romania 42 E7 45 40N 22 50 E
Hunedoara □, Romania 42 E7 45 50N 22 54 E
Hünfeld, Germany 24 E5 50 39N 9 46 E
Hung Yen, Vietnam 58 G6 20 39N 106 4 E
Hungary ■, Europe 27 D12 47 20N 19 20 E
Hungary, Plain of, Europe 6 F10 47 0N 20 0 E
Hungerford, Australia 95 D3 28 58 S 144 24 E
Hŭngnam, N. Korea 57 E14 39 49N 127 45 E
Hungt'ou Hsü, Taiwan 59 F13 22 0N 121 30 E
Huni Valley, Ghana 82 D4 5 33N 1 56W
Hunneberg, Sweden 11 F6 58 18N 12 30 E
Hunnebostrand, Sweden 11 F5 58 27N 11 18 E
Hunsberge, Namibia 88 D2 27 45 S 17 12 E
Hunsrück, Germany 25 F3 49 56N 7 27 E
Hunstanton, U.K. 12 E8 52 56N 0 29 E
Hunte →, Germany 24 B4 53 14N 8 28 E
Hunter, U.S.A. 111 D10 42 13N 74 13W
Hunter I., Australia 94 G3 40 30 S 144 45 E
Hunter I., Canada 104 C3 51 55N 128 0W
Hunter Ra., Australia 95 E5 32 45 S 150 15 E
Hunters Road, Zimbabwe 87 F2 19 9 S 29 49 E
Hunterville, N.Z. 91 H5 39 56 S 175 35 E
Huntingburg, U.S.A. 108 F2 38 18N 86 57W
Huntingdon, Canada 102 C5 45 6N 74 10W
Huntingdon, U.K. 13 E7 52 20N 0 11W
Huntingdon, U.S.A. 110 F6 40 30N 78 1W
Huntington, Ind., U.S.A. 108 E3 40 53N 85 30W
Huntington, Oreg., U.S.A. 114 D5 44 21N 117 16W
Huntington, Utah, U.S.A. 114 G8 39 20N 110 58W
Huntington, W. Va., U.S.A. 108 F4 38 25N 82 27W
Huntington Beach, U.S.A. 117 M9 33 40N 118 5W
Huntington Station, U.S.A. 111 F11 40 52N 73 26W
Huntly, N.Z. 91 G5 37 34 S 175 11 E
Huntly, U.K. 14 D6 57 27N 2 47W
Huntsville, Canada 102 C4 45 20N 79 14W
Huntsville, Ala., U.S.A. 109 H2 34 44N 86 35W
Huntsville, Tex., U.S.A. 113 K7 30 43N 95 33W
Hunyani →, Zimbabwe 87 F3 15 57 S 30 39 E
Hunyuan, China 56 E7 39 42N 113 42 E
Hunza →, India 69 B6 35 54N 74 20 E
Huo Xian = Huozhou, China 56 F6 36 36N 111 42 E
Huong Hoa, Vietnam 64 D6 16 37N 106 45 E
Huong Khe, Vietnam 64 C5 18 13N 105 41 E
Huonville, Australia 94 G4 43 0 S 147 5 E
Huoqiu, China 59 A11 32 20N 116 12 E
Huoshan, Anhui, China 59 A12 32 28N 118 30 E
Huoshan, Anhui, China 59 B11 31 25N 116 20 E
Huoshao Dao = Lü-Tao, Taiwan 59 F13 22 40N 121 30 E
Huozhou, China 56 F6 36 36N 111 42 E
Hupeh = Hubei □, China 59 B9 31 0N 112 0 E
Ḥūr, Iran 71 D8 30 50N 57 7 E
Hurbanovo, Slovak Rep. 27 D11 47 51N 18 11 E
Hurd, C., Canada 110 A3 45 13N 81 44W
Hure Qi, China 57 C11 42 45N 121 45 E
Hurezani, Romania 43 F8 44 49N 23 40 E
Hurghada, Egypt 80 B3 27 15N 33 50 E
Hurley, N. Mex., U.S.A. 115 K9 32 42N 108 8W
Hurley, Wis., U.S.A. 112 B9 46 27N 90 11W
Huron, Calif., U.S.A. 116 J6 36 12N 120 6W
Huron, Ohio, U.S.A. 110 E2 41 24N 82 33W
Huron, S. Dak., U.S.A. 112 C5 44 22N 98 13W
Huron, L., U.S.A. 110 B2 44 30N 82 40W
Hurricane, U.S.A. 115 H7 37 11N 113 17W
Hurso, Ethiopia 81 F5 9 35N 41 33 E
Hurunui →, N.Z. 91 K4 42 54 S 173 18 E
Hurup, Denmark 11 H2 56 46N 8 25 E
Húsavík, Iceland 8 C5 66 3N 17 21W
Huşi, Romania 43 D13 46 41N 28 7 E
Huskvarna, Sweden 11 G8 57 47N 14 15 E
Hustadvika, Norway 8 E12 63 0N 7 0 E
Hustontown, U.S.A. 110 F6 40 3N 78 2W
Hustopeče, Czech Rep. 27 C9 48 57N 16 43 E
Husum, Germany 24 A5 54 28N 9 4 E
Husum, Sweden 10 A13 63 21N 19 12 E
Hutchinson, Kans., U.S.A. 113 F6 38 5N 97 56W
Hutchinson, Minn., U.S.A. 112 C7 44 54N 94 22W
Hutte Sauvage, L. de la, Canada 103 A7 56 15N 64 45W
Hüttenberg, Austria 26 E7 46 56N 14 33 E
Hutton, Mt., Australia 95 D4 25 51 S 148 20 E
Huwun, Ethiopia 81 G5 4 23N 40 6 E
Huy, Belgium 17 D5 50 31N 5 15 E
Huzhou, China 59 B13 30 51N 120 8 E
Hvalpsund, Denmark 11 H3 56 42N 9 11 E
Hvammstangi, Iceland 8 D3 65 24N 20 57W
Hvar, Croatia 29 E13 43 11N 16 28 E
Hvarski Kanal, Croatia 29 E13 43 15N 16 35 E
Hvítá →, Iceland 8 D3 64 30N 21 58W
Hwachŏn-chŏsuji, S. Korea 57 E14 38 5N 127 50 E
Hwang Ho = Huang He →, China 57 F10 37 55N 118 50 E
Hwange, Zimbabwe 87 F2 18 18 S 26 30 E
Hwange Nat. Park, Zimbabwe 88 B4 19 0 S 26 30 E
Hyannis, Mass., U.S.A. 108 E10 41 39N 70 17W
Hyannis, Nebr., U.S.A. 112 E4 42 0N 101 46W
Hyargas Nuur, Mongolia 60 B4 49 0N 93 0 E
Hybo, Sweden 10 C10 61 49N 16 15 E
Hydaburg, U.S.A. 104 B2 55 15N 132 50W
Hyde Park, U.S.A. 111 E11 41 47N 73 56W
Hyden, Australia 93 F2 32 24 S 118 53 E
Hyder, U.S.A. 104 B2 55 55N 130 5W
Hyderabad, India 66 L11 17 22N 78 29 E
Hyderabad, Pakistan 68 G3 25 23N 68 24 E
Hyères, France 21 E10 43 8N 6 9 E
Hyères, Îs. d', France 21 F10 43 0N 6 20 E
Hyesan, N. Korea 57 D15 41 20N 128 10 E
Hyland →, Canada 104 B3 59 52N 128 12W
Hyltebruk, Sweden 11 H7 56 59N 13 15 E
Hymia, India 69 C8 33 40N 78 2 E
Hyndman Peak, U.S.A. 114 E6 43 45N 114 8W
Hyōgo □, Japan 55 G7 35 15N 134 50 E
Hyrum, U.S.A. 114 F8 41 38N 111 51W
Hysham, U.S.A. 114 C10 46 18N 107 14W
Hythe, U.K. 13 F9 51 4N 1 5 E
Hyūga, Japan 55 H5 32 25N 131 35 E
Hyvinge = Hyvinkää, Finland 9 F21 60 38N 24 50 E
Hyvinkää, Finland 9 F21 60 38N 24 50 E

I

I-n-Gall, Niger 83 B6 16 51N 7 1 E
I-n-Oudad, Algeria 83 A5 20 17N 4 38 E
I-n-Ouzzal, Algeria 83 A5 20 40N 2 35 E
I-n-Tadreft, Niger 83 B6 19 5N 6 38 E
Iablaniţa, Romania 42 F7 44 57N 22 19 E
Iaco →, Brazil 124 E5 9 3 S 68 34W
Iacobeni, Romania 43 C10 47 25N 25 20 E
Iakora, Madag. 89 C8 23 6 S 46 40 E
Ialomiţa □, Romania 43 F12 44 30N 27 30 E
Ialomiţa →, Romania 43 F12 44 42N 27 51 E
Ialoveni, Moldova 43 D13 46 56N 28 47 E
Ialpug →, Moldova 43 E13 45 41N 28 15 E
Ianca, Romania 43 E12 45 6N 27 29 E
Iara, Romania 43 D8 46 31N 23 35 E
Iarda, Ethiopia 81 E4 11 9N 35 53 E
Iargara, Moldova 43 D13 46 24N 28 23 E
Iaşi, Romania 43 C12 47 10N 27 40 E
Iaşi □, Romania 43 C12 47 20N 27 0 E
Iássos, Greece 41 E9 41 8N 25 11 E
Ib →, India 69 J10 21 34N 83 48 E
Iba, Phil. 61 D3 15 22N 120 0 E
Ibadan, Nigeria 83 D5 7 22N 3 58 E
Ibagué, Colombia 124 C3 4 20N 75 20W
Iballë, Albania 40 D4 42 12N 20 2 E
Iballja = Iballë, Albania 40 D4 42 12N 20 2 E
Ibăneşti, Botoşani, Romania 43 B11 48 4N 26 22 E
Ibăneşti, Mureş, Romania 43 D9 46 45N 24 57 E
Ibar →, Serbia, Yug. 40 C4 43 43N 20 45 E
Ibaraki □, Japan 55 F10 36 10N 140 10 E
Ibarra, Ecuador 124 C3 0 21N 78 7W
Ibba, Sudan 81 G2 4 49N 29 2 E
Ibba, Bahr el →, Sudan 81 F2 5 30N 28 55 E
Ibbenbüren, Germany 24 C3 52 16N 7 43 E
Ibembo, Dem. Rep. of the Congo 86 B1 2 35N 23 35 E
Ibera, L., Argentina 126 B4 28 30 S 57 9W
Iberian Peninsula, Europe 6 H5 40 0N 5 0W
Iberville, Canada 102 C5 45 19N 73 17W
Iberville, Lac d', Canada 102 A5 55 55N 73 15W
Ibi, Nigeria 83 D6 8 15N 9 44 E
Ibi, Spain 33 G4 38 38N 0 34W
Ibiá, Brazil 125 G9 19 30 S 46 30W
Ibicuí →, Brazil 127 B4 29 25 S 56 47W
Ibicuy, Argentina 126 C4 33 55 S 59 10W
Ibioapaba, Sa. da, Brazil 125 D10 4 0 S 41 30W
Ibiza = Eivissa, Spain 37 C7 38 54N 1 26 E
Íblei, Monti, Italy 31 E7 37 15N 14 45 E
Ibo, Mozam. 87 E5 12 22 S 40 40 E
Ibonma, Indonesia 63 E8 3 29 S 133 31 E
Ibotirama, Brazil 125 F10 12 13 S 43 12W
Ibrāhīm →, Lebanon 75 A4 34 4N 35 38 E
'Ibrī, Oman 71 F8 23 14N 56 30 E
İbriktepe, Turkey 41 E10 41 0N 26 30 E
Ibshawâi, Egypt 80 J7 29 21N 30 40 E
Ibu, Indonesia 63 D7 1 35N 127 33 E
Ibusuki, Japan 55 J5 31 12N 130 40 E
Ica, Peru 124 F3 14 0 S 75 48W
Iça →, Brazil 124 D5 2 55 S 67 58W
Içana, Brazil 124 C5 0 21N 67 19W
Içana →, Brazil 124 C5 0 26N 67 19W
Içel = Mersin, Turkey 70 B2 36 51N 34 36 E
Iceland ■, Europe 8 D4 64 45N 19 0W
Ich'ang = Yichang, China 59 B8 30 40N 111 20 E
Ichchapuram, India 67 K14 19 10N 84 40 E
Ichhawar, India 68 H7 23 1N 77 1 E
Ichihara, Japan 55 G10 35 28N 140 5 E
Ichikawa, Japan 55 G9 35 44N 139 55 E
Ichilo →, Bolivia 124 G6 15 57 S 64 50W
Ichinohe, Japan 54 D10 40 13N 141 17 E
Ichinomiya, Japan 55 G8 35 18N 136 48 E
Ichinoseki, Japan 54 E10 38 55N 141 8 E
Ichnya, Ukraine 47 G7 50 52N 32 24 E
Icod, Canary Is. 37 F3 28 22N 16 43W
Ida Grove, U.S.A. 112 D7 42 21N 95 28W
Idabel, U.S.A. 113 J7 33 54N 94 50W
Idaga Hamus, Ethiopia 81 E4 14 13N 39 48 E
Idah, Nigeria 83 D6 7 5N 6 40 E
Idaho □, U.S.A. 114 D7 45 0N 115 0W
Idaho City, U.S.A. 114 E6 43 50N 115 50W
Idaho Falls, U.S.A. 114 E7 43 30N 112 2W
Idanha-a-Nova, Portugal 34 F3 39 50N 7 15W
Idar-Oberstein, Germany 25 F3 49 43N 7 16 E
Idfû, Egypt 80 C3 24 55N 32 49 E
Ídhi Óros, Greece 36 D6 35 15N 24 45 E
Ídhra, Greece 38 D5 37 20N 23 28 E
Idi, Indonesia 62 C1 5 2N 97 37 E
Idiofa, Dem. Rep. of the Congo 84 E3 4 55 S 19 42 E
Idkerberget, Sweden 10 D9 60 22N 15 15 E
Idku, Bahra el, Egypt 80 H7 31 18N 30 18 E
Idlib, Syria 70 C3 35 55N 36 36 E
Idre, Sweden 10 C6 61 52N 12 42 E
Idria, U.S.A. 116 J6 36 25N 120 41W
Idrija, Slovenia 29 C11 46 0N 14 5 E
Idritsa, Russia 46 D5 56 17N 28 53 E
Idutywa, S. Africa 89 E4 32 8 S 28 18 E
Ieper, Belgium 17 D2 50 51N 2 53 E
Ierápetra, Greece 36 E7 35 1N 25 44 E
Ierissós, Greece 40 F7 40 22N 23 52 E
Ierissóu Kólpos, Greece 40 F7 40 27N 23 57 E
Iernut, Romania 43 D9 46 27N 24 15 E
Iesi, Italy 29 E10 43 31N 13 14 E
Iésolo, Italy 29 C9 45 32N 12 38 E
Ifach, Peñón de, Spain 33 G5 38 38N 0 5 E
Ifakara, Tanzania 84 F7 8 8 S 36 41 E
'Ifāl, W. al →, Si. Arabia 70 D2 28 7N 35 3 E
Ifanadiana, Madag. 89 C8 21 19 S 47 39 E
Ife, Nigeria 83 D5 7 30N 4 31 E
Iférouâne, Niger 83 B6 19 5N 8 24 E
Iffley, Australia 94 B3 18 53 S 141 12 E
Ifni, Morocco 78 C3 29 29N 10 12W
Ifon, Nigeria 83 D6 6 58N 5 40 E
Iforas, Adrar des, Mali 83 B5 19 40N 1 40 E
Ifould, L., Australia 93 F5 30 52 S 132 6 E
Iganga, Uganda 86 B3 0 37N 33 28 E
Igarapava, Brazil 125 H9 20 3 S 47 47W
Igarka, Russia 50 C9 67 30N 86 33 E
Igatimi, Paraguay 127 A4 24 5 S 55 40W
Igbetti, Nigeria 83 D5 8 44N 4 8 E
Igbo-Ora, Nigeria 83 D5 7 29N 3 15 E
Igboho, Nigeria 83 D5 8 53N 3 50 E
Igbor, Nigeria 83 D6 7 27N 8 34 E
Iğdır, Turkey 73 C11 39 55N 44 2 E
Igelfors, Sweden 11 F9 58 52N 15 41 E
Iggesund, Sweden 10 C11 61 39N 17 10 E
Iglésias, Italy 30 C1 39 19N 8 32 E
Igloolik, Canada 101 B11 69 20N 81 49W
Igluligaarjuk, Canada 101 B10 63 21N 90 42W
'Igma, Gebel el, Egypt 80 B3 28 55N 34 0 E
Ignace, Canada 102 C1 49 30N 91 40W
İğneada, Turkey 41 E11 41 52N 27 59 E
İğneada Burnu, Turkey 41 E12 41 53N 28 2 E
Igoumenítsa, Greece 38 B2 39 32N 20 18 E
Igra, Russia 48 B11 57 33N 53 7 E
Iguaçu →, Brazil 127 B5 25 36 S 54 36W
Iguaçu, Cat. del, Brazil 127 B5 25 41 S 54 26W
Iguaçu Falls = Iguaçu, Cat. del, Brazil 127 B5 25 41 S 54 26W
Iguala, Mexico 119 D5 18 20N 99 40W
Igualada, Spain 32 D6 41 37N 1 37 E
Iguassu = Iguaçu →, Brazil 127 B5 25 36 S 54 36W
Iguatu, Brazil 125 E11 6 20 S 39 18W
Iharana, Madag. 89 A9 13 25 S 50 0 E
Ihbulag, Mongolia 56 C4 43 11N 107 10 E
Iheya-Shima, Japan 55 L3 27 4N 127 58 E
Ihiala, Nigeria 83 D6 5 51N 6 55 E
Ihosy, Madag. 89 C8 22 24 S 46 8 E
Ihotry, Farihy, Madag. 89 C7 21 56 S 43 41 E
Ihugh, Nigeria 83 D6 7 2N 9 0 E
Ii, Finland 8 D21 65 19N 25 22 E
Ii-Shima, Japan 55 L3 26 43N 127 47 E
Iida, Japan 55 G8 35 35N 137 50 E
Iijoki →, Finland 8 D21 65 20N 25 20 E
Iisalmi, Finland 8 E22 63 32N 27 10 E
Iiyama, Japan 55 F9 36 51N 138 22 E
Iizuka, Japan 55 H5 33 38N 130 42 E
Ijebu-Igbo, Nigeria 83 D5 6 56N 4 1 E
Ijebu-Ode, Nigeria 83 D5 6 47N 3 58 E
IJmuiden, Neths. 17 B4 52 28N 4 35 E
IJssel →, Neths. 17 B5 52 35N 5 50 E
IJsselmeer, Neths. 17 B5 52 45N 5 20 E
Ijuí, Brazil 127 B5 28 23 S 53 55W
Ijuí →, Brazil 127 B4 27 58 S 55 20W
Ikalamavony, Madag. 89 C8 21 9 S 46 35 E
Ikale, Nigeria 83 D6 7 40N 5 37 E
Ikaluktutiak, Canada 100 B9 69 10N 105 0W
Ikang, Nigeria 83 E6 4 49N 8 30 E
Ikara, Nigeria 83 C6 11 12N 8 15 E
Ikare, Nigeria 83 D6 7 32N 5 40 E
Ikaría, Greece 39 D8 37 35N 26 10 E
Ikast, Denmark 11 H3 56 8N 9 10 E
Ikeda, Japan 55 G6 34 1N 133 48 E
Ikeja, Nigeria 83 D5 6 36N 3 23 E
Ikela, Dem. Rep. of the Congo 84 E4 1 6 S 23 6 E
Ikerre-Ekiti, Nigeria 83 D6 7 25N 5 19 E
Ikhtiman, Bulgaria 40 D7 42 27N 23 48 E
Iki, Japan 55 H4 33 45N 129 42 E
Ikimba L., Tanzania 86 C3 1 30 S 31 20 E
Ikire, Nigeria 83 D5 7 23N 4 15 E
Ikizdere, Turkey 73 B9 40 46N 40 32 E
Ikom, Nigeria 83 D6 6 0N 8 42 E
Ikongo, Madag. 89 C8 21 52 S 47 27 E
Ikopa →, Madag. 89 B8 16 45 S 46 40 E
Ikot Ekpene, Nigeria 83 D6 5 12N 7 40 E
Ikungu, Tanzania 86 C3 1 33 S 33 42 E
Ikurun, Nigeria 83 D5 7 54N 4 40 E
Ila, Nigeria 83 D5 8 0N 4 39 E
Ilagan, Phil. 61 C4 17 7N 121 53 E
Ilaka, Madag. 89 B8 19 33 S 48 52 E

Īlām, Iran **70 C5** 33 36N 46 36 E
Ilam, Nepal **69 F12** 26 58N 87 58 E
Ilam □, Iran **70 C5** 33 0N 47 0 E
Ilan, Taiwan **59 E13** 24 45N 121 44 E
Ilanskiy, Russia **51 D10** 56 14N 96 3 E
Ilaro, Nigeria **83 D5** 6 53N 3 3 E
Ilatane, Niger **83 B5** 16 30N 4 45 E
Iława, Poland **44 E6** 53 36N 19 34 E
Ile-à-la-Crosse, Canada **105 B7** 55 27N 107 53W
Ile-à-la-Crosse, Lac, Canada **105 B7** 55 40N 107 45W
Île-de-France □, France **19 D9** 49 0N 2 20 E
Ileanda, Romania **43 C8** 47 20N 23 38 E
Ilebo, Dem. Rep. of the Congo **84 E4** 4 17 S 20 55 E
Ilek, Russia **50 D6** 51 32N 53 21 E
Ilero, Nigeria **83 D5** 8 0N 3 20 E
Ilesha, Kwara, Nigeria **83 D5** 8 57N 3 28 E
Ilesha, Oyo, Nigeria **83 D5** 7 37N 4 40 E
Ilford, Canada **105 B9** 56 4N 95 35W
Ilfracombe, Australia **94 C3** 23 30 S 144 30 E
Ilfracombe, U.K. **13 F3** 51 12N 4 8W
Ilgaz, Turkey **72 B5** 40 55N 33 37 E
Ilgaz Dağları, Turkey **72 B5** 41 10N 33 50 E
Ilgın, Turkey **72 C4** 38 16N 31 55 E
Ílhavo, Portugal **34 E2** 40 33N 8 43W
Ilhéus, Brazil **125 F11** 14 49 S 39 2W
Ili →, Kazakstan **50 E8** 45 53N 77 10 E
Ilia, Romania **42 E7** 45 57N 22 40 E
Ilia □, Greece **38 D3** 37 45N 21 35 E
Iliamna L., U.S.A. **100 C4** 59 30N 155 0W
Iliç, Turkey **73 C8** 39 27N 38 33 E
Ilıca, Turkey **39 B9** 39 52N 27 46 E
Ilichevsk, Azerbaijan **73 C11** 39 22N 45 5 E
Iligan, Phil. **61 G6** 8 12N 124 13 E
Iligan Bay, Phil. **61 G6** 8 25N 124 5 E
Ilíkí, L., Greece **38 C5** 38 24N 23 15 E
Ilin I., Phil. **61 E4** 12 14N 121 5 E
Iliodhrómia, Greece **38 B5** 39 12N 23 50 E
Ilion, U.S.A. **111 D9** 43 1N 75 2W
Ilirska-Bistrica, Slovenia **29 C11** 45 34N 14 14 E
Ilkeston, U.K. **12 E6** 52 58N 1 19W
Ilkley, U.K. **12 D6** 53 56N 1 48W
Illampu = Ancohuma, Nevada, Bolivia **122 E4** 16 0 S 68 50W
Illana B., Phil. **61 H5** 7 35N 123 45 E
Illapel, Chile **126 C1** 32 0 S 71 10W
Ille-et-Vilaine □, France **18 D5** 48 10N 1 30W
Ille-sur-Têt, France **20 F6** 42 40N 2 38 E
Illéla, Niger **83 C6** 14 32N 5 20 E
Iller →, Germany **25 G5** 48 23N 9 58 E
Illertissen, Germany **25 G6** 48 12N 10 7 E
Illescas, Spain **34 E7** 40 8N 3 51W
Illetas, Spain **37 B9** 39 32N 2 35 E
Illichivsk, Ukraine **47 J6** 46 20N 30 35 E
Illiers-Combray, France **18 D8** 48 18N 1 15 E
Illimani, Nevado, Bolivia **124 G5** 16 30 S 67 50W
Illinois □, U.S.A. **112 E10** 40 15N 89 30W
Illinois →, U.S.A. **107 C8** 38 58N 90 28W
Illium = Troy, Turkey **39 B8** 39 57N 26 12 E
Illizi, Algeria **78 C7** 26 31N 8 32 E
Illkirch-Graffenstaden, France **19 D14** 48 34N 7 42 E
Illoqqortoormiit, Greenland **4 B6** 70 20N 23 0W
Íllora, Spain **35 H7** 37 17N 3 53W
Ilm →, Germany **24 D7** 51 6N 11 40 E
Ilmajoki, Finland **9 E20** 62 44N 22 34 E
Ilmen, Ozero, Russia **46 C6** 58 15N 31 10 E
Ilmenau, Germany **24 E6** 50 41N 10 54 E
Ilo, Peru **124 G4** 17 40 S 71 20W
Ilobu, Nigeria **83 D5** 7 45N 4 25 E
Iloilo, Phil. **61 F5** 10 45N 122 33 E
Ilora, Nigeria **83 D5** 7 45N 3 50 E
Ilorin, Nigeria **83 D5** 8 30N 4 35 E
Ilovatka, Russia **48 E7** 50 30N 45 50 E
Ilovlya, Russia **49 F7** 49 15N 44 2 E
Ilovlya →, Russia **49 F7** 49 14N 44 0 E
Iłowa, Poland **45 G2** 51 30N 15 10 E
Ilubabor □, Ethiopia **81 F4** 7 25N 35 0 E
Ilva Mică, Romania **43 C9** 47 17N 24 40 E
Ilwaco, U.S.A. **116 D2** 46 19N 124 3W
Ilwaki, Indonesia **63 F7** 7 55 S 126 30 E
Ilyichevsk = Illichivsk, Ukraine **47 J6** 46 20N 30 35 E
Iłża, Poland **45 G8** 51 10N 21 15 E
Iłzanka →, Poland **45 G8** 51 14N 21 48 E
Imabari, Japan **55 G6** 34 4N 133 0 E
Imaloto →, Madag. **89 C8** 23 27 S 45 13 E
İmamoğlu, Turkey **72 D6** 37 15N 35 38 E
Imandra, Ozero, Russia **50 C4** 67 30N 33 0 E
Imanombo, Madag. **89 C8** 24 26 S 45 49 E
Imari, Japan **55 H4** 33 15N 129 52 E
Imasa, Sudan **80 D4** 18 0N 36 12 E
Imathía □, Greece **40 F6** 40 30N 22 15 E
Imatra, Finland **46 B5** 61 12N 28 48 E
Imbil, Australia **95 D5** 26 22 S 152 32 E
Iménas, Mali **83 B5** 16 20N 0 40 E
imeni 26 Bakinskikh Komissarov = Neftçala, Azerbaijan **71 B6** 39 19N 49 12 E
imeni 26 Bakinskikh Komissarov, Turkmenistan **71 B7** 39 22N 54 10 E
Imeri, Serra, Brazil **124 C5** 0 50N 65 25W
Imerimandroso, Madag. **89 B8** 17 26 S 48 35 E
Imi, Ethiopia **81 F5** 6 28N 42 10 E
Imishly = Imişli, Azerbaijan **49 L9** 39 55N 48 4 E
Imişli, Azerbaijan **49 L9** 39 55N 48 4 E
Imlay, U.S.A. **114 F4** 40 40N 118 9W
Imlay City, U.S.A. **110 D1** 43 2N 83 5W
Immaseri, Sudan **81 D2** 15 40N 25 31 E
Immenstadt, Germany **25 H6** 47 33N 10 13 E
Immingham, U.K. **12 D7** 53 37N 0 13W
Immokalee, U.S.A. **109 M5** 26 25N 81 25W
Imo □, Nigeria **83 D6** 5 30N 7 10 E
Imo →, Nigeria **83 E6** 4 36N 7 35 E
Ímola, Italy **29 D8** 44 20N 11 42 E
Imotski, Croatia **29 E14** 43 27N 17 12 E
Imperatriz, Brazil **125 E9** 5 30 S 47 29W
Impéria, Italy **28 E5** 43 53N 8 3 E
Imperial, Canada **105 C7** 51 21N 105 28W
Imperial, Calif., U.S.A. **117 N11** 32 51N 115 34W
Imperial, Nebr., U.S.A. **112 E4** 40 31N 101 39W
Imperial Beach, U.S.A. **117 N9** 32 35N 117 8W
Imperial Dam, U.S.A. **117 N12** 32 55N 114 25W
Imperial Reservoir, U.S.A. **117 N12** 32 53N 114 28W
Imperial Valley, U.S.A. **117 N11** 33 0N 115 30W
Imperieuse Reef, Australia **92 C2** 17 36 S 118 50 E
Impfondo, Congo **84 D3** 1 40N 18 0 E
Imphal, India **67 G18** 24 48N 93 56 E
Imphy, France **19 F10** 46 55N 3 16 E
Imranlı, Turkey **73 C8** 39 54N 38 7 E
İmroz = Gökçeada, Turkey **41 F9** 40 10N 25 50 E
İmroz, Turkey **41 F9** 40 10N 25 55 E
Imst, Austria **26 D3** 47 15N 10 44 E
Imuris, Mexico **118 A2** 30 47N 110 52W
Imuruan B., Phil. **63 B5** 10 40N 119 10 E
In Akhmed, Mali **83 B4** 19 49N 0 56W
In-Aleï, Mali **82 B4** 17 42N 2 30W
In Delimane, Mali **83 B5** 15 52N 1 31 E
In-Guezzam, Niger **83 B6** 19 37N 5 52 E
In Koufi, Mali **83 B5** 19 11N 1 25 E
In Salah, Algeria **78 C6** 27 10N 2 32 E
In Tallak, Mali **83 B5** 16 19N 3 15 E
In Tebezas, Mali **83 B5** 17 49N 1 53 E
Ina, Japan **55 G8** 35 50N 137 55 E
Inangahua Junction, N.Z. **91 J3** 41 52 S 171 59 E
Inanwatan, Indonesia **63 E8** 2 10 S 132 14 E
Iñapari, Peru **124 F5** 11 0 S 69 40W
Inari, Finland **8 B22** 68 54N 27 5 E
Inarijärvi, Finland **8 B22** 69 0N 28 0 E
Inawashiro-Ko, Japan **54 F10** 37 29N 140 6 E
Inca, Spain **37 B9** 39 43N 2 54 E
Inca de Oro, Chile **126 B2** 26 45 S 69 54W
Incaguasi, Chile **126 B1** 29 12 S 71 5W
İnce Burun, Turkey **72 A6** 42 7N 34 56 E
İncekum Burnu, Turkey **72 D5** 36 13N 33 57 E
İncesu, Turkey **70 B2** 38 38N 35 11 E
Inch'ŏn, S. Korea **57 F14** 37 27N 126 40 E
Incio = Cruz de Incio, Spain **34 C3** 42 39N 7 21W
İncirliova, Turkey **39 D9** 37 50N 27 41 E
Incline Village, U.S.A. **114 G4** 39 10N 119 58W
Incomáti →, Mozam. **89 D5** 25 46 S 32 43 E
Inda Silase, Ethiopia **81 E4** 14 10N 38 15 E
Indal, Sweden **10 B11** 62 35N 17 5 E
Indalsälven →, Sweden **10 B11** 62 36N 17 30 E
Indaw, Burma **67 G20** 24 15N 96 5 E
Indbir, Ethiopia **81 F4** 8 7N 37 52 E
Independence, Calif., U.S.A. **116 J8** 36 48N 118 12W
Independence, Iowa, U.S.A. **112 D9** 42 28N 91 54W
Independence, Kans., U.S.A. **113 G7** 37 14N 95 42W
Independence, Ky., U.S.A. **108 F3** 38 57N 84 33W
Independence, Mo., U.S.A. **112 F7** 39 6N 94 25W
Independence Fjord, Greenland **4 A6** 82 10N 29 0W
Independence Mts., U.S.A. **114 F5** 41 20N 116 0W
Independenţa, Romania **43 E12** 45 25N 27 42 E
Index, U.S.A. **116 C5** 47 50N 121 33W
India ■, Asia **66 K11** 20 0N 78 0 E
Indian →, U.S.A. **109 M5** 27 59N 80 34W
Indian Cabins, Canada **104 B5** 59 52N 117 40W
Indian Harbour, Canada **103 B8** 54 27N 57 13W
Indian Head, Canada **105 C8** 50 30N 103 41W
Indian Lake, U.S.A. **111 C10** 43 47N 74 16W
Indian Ocean **52 K11** 5 0 S 75 0 E
Indian Springs, U.S.A. **117 J11** 36 35N 115 40W
Indiana, U.S.A. **110 F5** 40 37N 79 9W
Indiana □, U.S.A. **108 F3** 40 0N 86 0W
Indianapolis, U.S.A. **108 F2** 39 46N 86 9W
Indianola, Iowa, U.S.A. **112 E8** 41 22N 93 34W
Indianola, Miss., U.S.A. **113 J9** 33 27N 90 39W
Indigirka →, Russia **51 B15** 70 48N 148 54 E
In{d-}ija, Serbia, Yug. **42 E5** 45 6N 20 7 E
Indio, U.S.A. **117 M10** 33 43N 116 13W
Indo-China, Asia **52 H14** 15 0N 102 0 E
Indonesia ■, Asia **62 F5** 5 0 S 115 0 E
Indore, India **68 H6** 22 42N 75 53 E
Indramayu, Indonesia **63 G13** 6 20 S 108 19 E
Indravati →, India **67 K12** 19 20N 80 20 E
Indre □, France **19 F8** 46 50N 1 39 E
Indre →, France **18 E7** 47 16N 0 11 E
Indre-et-Loire □, France **18 E7** 47 20N 0 40 E
Indulkana, Australia **95 D1** 26 58 S 133 5 E
Indus →, Pakistan **68 G2** 24 20N 67 47 E
Indus, Mouth of the, Pakistan **68 H3** 24 0N 68 0 E
İnebolu, Turkey **72 B5** 41 55N 33 40 E
İnecik, Turkey **41 F11** 40 56N 27 16 E
İnegöl, Turkey **41 F13** 40 5N 29 31 E
Ineu, Romania **42 D6** 46 26N 21 51 E
Infantes = Villanueva de los Infantes, Spain **35 G7** 38 43N 3 1W
Infiernillo, Presa del, Mexico **118 D4** 18 9N 102 0W
Infiesto, Spain **34 B5** 43 21N 5 21W
Ingelstad, Sweden **11 H8** 56 45N 14 56 E
Ingenio, Canary Is. **37 G4** 27 55N 15 26W
Ingenio Santa Ana, Argentina **126 B2** 27 25 S 65 40W
Ingersoll, Canada **102 D3** 43 4N 80 55W
Ingham, Australia **94 B4** 18 43 S 146 10 E
Ingleborough, U.K. **12 C5** 54 10N 2 22W
Inglewood, Queens., Australia **95 D5** 28 25 S 151 2 E
Inglewood, Vic., Australia **95 F3** 36 29 S 143 53 E
Inglewood, N.Z. **91 H5** 39 9 S 174 14 E
Inglewood, U.S.A. **117 M8** 33 58N 118 21W
Ingólfshöfði, Iceland **8 E5** 63 48N 16 39W
Ingolstadt, Germany **25 G7** 48 46N 11 26 E
Ingomar, U.S.A. **114 C10** 46 35N 107 23W
Ingonish, Canada **103 C7** 46 42N 60 18W
Ingore, Guinea-Biss. **82 C1** 12 24N 15 48W
Ingraj Bazar, India **69 G13** 24 58N 88 10 E
Ingrid Christensen Coast, Antarctica **5 C6** 69 30 S 76 0 E
Ingul → = Inhul →, Ukraine **47 J7** 46 50N 32 0 E
Ingulec = Inhulec, Ukraine **47 J7** 47 42N 33 14 E
Ingulets → = Inhulets →, Ukraine **47 J7** 46 46N 32 47 E
Inguri → = Enguri →, Georgia **49 J5** 42 27N 41 38 E
Ingushetia □, Russia **49 J7** 43 20N 44 50 E
Ingwavuma, S. Africa **89 D5** 27 9 S 31 59 E
Inhaca, Mozam. **89 D5** 26 1 S 32 57 E
Inhafenga, Mozam. **89 C5** 20 36 S 33 53 E
Inhambane, Mozam. **89 C6** 23 54 S 35 30 E
Inhambane □, Mozam. **89 C5** 22 30 S 34 20 E
Inhaminga, Mozam. **87 F4** 18 26 S 35 0 E
Inharrime, Mozam. **89 C6** 24 30 S 35 0 E
Inharrime →, Mozam. **89 C6** 24 30 S 35 0 E
Inhisar, Turkey **39 A12** 40 3N 30 23 E
Inhul →, Ukraine **47 J7** 46 50N 32 0 E
Inhulec, Ukraine **47 J7** 47 42N 33 14 E
Inhulets →, Ukraine **47 J7** 46 46N 32 47 E
Iniesta, Spain **33 F3** 39 27N 1 45W
Ining = Yining, China **50 E9** 43 58N 81 10 E
Inírida →, Colombia **124 C5** 3 55N 67 52W
Inishbofin, Ireland **15 C1** 53 37N 10 13W
Inisheer, Ireland **15 C2** 53 3N 9 32W
Inishfree B., Ireland **15 A3** 55 4N 8 23W
Inishkea North, Ireland **15 B1** 54 9N 10 11W
Inishkea South, Ireland **15 B1** 54 7N 10 12W
Inishmaan, Ireland **15 C2** 53 5N 9 35W
Inishmore, Ireland **15 C2** 53 8N 9 45W
Inishowen Pen., Ireland **15 A4** 55 14N 7 15W
Inishshark, Ireland **15 C1** 53 37N 10 16W
Inishturk, Ireland **15 C1** 53 42N 10 7W
Inishvickillane, Ireland **15 D1** 52 3N 10 37W
Injibara, Ethiopia **81 E4** 10 59N 37 0 E
Injune, Australia **95 D4** 25 53 S 148 32 E
Inklin →, Canada **104 B2** 58 50N 133 10W
Inle L., Burma **67 J20** 20 30N 96 58 E
Inlet, U.S.A. **111 C10** 43 45N 74 48W
Inn →, Austria **26 C6** 48 35N 13 28 E
Innamincka, Australia **95 D3** 27 44 S 140 46 E
Inner Hebrides, U.K. **14 E2** 57 0N 6 30W
Inner Mongolia = Nei Monggol Zizhiqu □, China **56 D7** 42 0N 112 0 E
Inner Sound, U.K. **14 D3** 57 30N 5 55W
Innerkip, Canada **110 C4** 43 13N 80 42W
Innetalling I., Canada **102 A4** 56 0N 79 0W
Innisfail, Australia **94 B4** 17 33 S 146 5 E
Innisfail, Canada **104 C6** 52 0N 113 57W
In'noshima, Japan **55 G6** 34 19N 133 10 E
Innsbruck, Austria **26 D4** 47 16N 11 23 E
Innviertel, Austria **26 C6** 48 15N 13 15 E
Inny →, Ireland **15 C4** 53 30N 7 50W
Inongo, Dem. Rep. of the Congo **84 E3** 1 55 S 18 30 E
İnönü, Turkey **39 B12** 39 48N 30 9 E
Inoucdjouac = Inukjuak, Canada **101 C12** 58 25N 78 15W
Inowrocław, Poland **45 F5** 52 50N 18 12 E
Inpundong, N. Korea **57 D14** 41 25N 126 34 E
Inscription, C., Australia **93 E1** 25 29 S 112 59 E
Insein, Burma **67 L20** 16 50N 96 5 E
Insjön, Sweden **10 D9** 60 41N 15 6 E
Ińsko, Poland **44 E2** 53 25N 15 32 E
Însurăţei, Romania **43 F12** 44 50N 27 40 E
Inta, Russia **50 C6** 66 5N 60 8 E
Intendente Alvear, Argentina **126 D3** 35 12 S 63 32W
İntepe, Turkey **39 A8** 40 1N 26 20 E
Interlaken, Switz. **25 J3** 46 41N 7 50 E
Interlaken, U.S.A. **111 D8** 42 37N 76 44W
International Falls, U.S.A. **112 A8** 48 36N 93 25W
Intiyaco, Argentina **126 B3** 28 43 S 60 5W
Întorsura Buzăului, Romania **43 E11** 45 41N 26 2 E
Inukjuak, Canada **101 C12** 58 25N 78 15W
Inútil, B., Chile **128 G2** 53 30 S 70 15W
Inuvik, Canada **100 B6** 68 16N 133 40W
Inveraray, U.K. **14 E3** 56 14N 5 5W
Inverbervie, U.K. **14 E6** 56 51N 2 17W
Invercargill, N.Z. **91 M2** 46 24 S 168 24 E
Inverclyde □, U.K. **14 F4** 55 55N 4 49W
Inverell, Australia **95 D5** 29 45 S 151 8 E
Invergordon, U.K. **14 D4** 57 41N 4 10W
Inverloch, Australia **95 F4** 38 38 S 145 45 E
Invermere, Canada **104 C5** 50 30N 116 2W
Inverness, Canada **103 C7** 46 15N 61 19W
Inverness, U.K. **14 D4** 57 29N 4 13W
Inverness, U.S.A. **109 L4** 28 50N 82 20W
Inverurie, U.K. **14 D6** 57 17N 2 23W
Investigator Group, Australia **95 E1** 34 45 S 134 20 E
Investigator Str., Australia **95 F2** 35 30 S 137 0 E
Inya, Russia **50 D9** 50 28N 86 37 E
Inyanga, Zimbabwe **87 F3** 18 12 S 32 40 E
Inyangani, Zimbabwe **87 F3** 18 5 S 32 50 E
Inyantue, Zimbabwe **88 B4** 18 33 S 26 39 E
Inyo Mts., U.S.A. **116 J9** 36 40N 118 0W
Inyokern, U.S.A. **117 K9** 35 39N 117 49W
Inza, Russia **48 D8** 53 55N 46 25 E
Inzhavino, Russia **48 D6** 52 22N 42 30 E
Iō-Jima, Japan **55 J5** 30 48N 130 18 E
Ioánnina, Greece **38 B2** 39 42N 20 47 E
Ioánnina □, Greece **38 B2** 39 39N 20 57 E
Iola, U.S.A. **113 G7** 37 55N 95 24W
Ion Corvin, Romania **43 F12** 44 7N 27 50 E
Iona, U.K. **14 E2** 56 20N 6 25W
Ione, U.S.A. **116 G6** 38 21N 120 56W
Ionia, U.S.A. **108 D3** 42 59N 85 4W
Ionian Is. = Iónioi Nísoi, Greece **38 C2** 38 40N 20 0 E
Ionian Sea, Medit. S. **6 H9** 37 30N 17 30 E
Iónioi Nísoi, Greece **38 C2** 38 40N 20 0 E
Iónioi Nísoi □, Greece **38 C2** 38 40N 20 0 E
Íos, Greece **39 E7** 36 41N 25 20 E
Iowa □, U.S.A. **112 D8** 42 18N 93 30W
Iowa →, U.S.A. **112 E9** 41 10N 91 1W
Iowa City, U.S.A. **112 E9** 41 40N 91 32W
Iowa Falls, U.S.A. **112 D8** 42 31N 93 16W
Iowa Park, U.S.A. **113 J5** 33 57N 98 40W
Ipala, Tanzania **86 C3** 4 30 S 32 52 E
Ipameri, Brazil **125 G9** 17 44 S 48 9W
Ipáti, Greece **38 C4** 38 52N 22 14 E
Ipatinga, Brazil **125 G10** 19 32 S 42 30W
Ipatovo, Russia **49 H6** 45 45N 42 50 E
Ipel' →, Europe **27 D11** 47 48N 18 53 E
Ipiales, Colombia **124 C3** 0 50N 77 37W
Ipin = Yibin, China **58 C5** 28 45N 104 32 E
Ípiros □, Greece **38 B2** 39 30N 20 30 E
Ipixuna, Brazil **124 E4** 7 0 S 71 40W
Ipoh, Malaysia **65 K3** 4 35N 101 5 E
Ippy, C.A.R. **84 C4** 6 5N 21 7 E
İpsala, Turkey **41 F10** 40 55N 26 23 E
Ipsárion, Óros, Greece **41 F8** 40 40N 24 40 E
Ipswich, Australia **95 D5** 27 35 S 152 40 E
Ipswich, U.K. **13 E9** 52 4N 1 10 E
Ipswich, Mass., U.S.A. **111 D14** 42 41N 70 50W
Ipswich, S. Dak., U.S.A. **112 C5** 45 27N 99 2W
Ipu, Brazil **125 D10** 4 23 S 40 44W
Iqaluit, Canada **101 B13** 63 44N 68 31W
Iquique, Chile **124 H4** 20 19 S 70 5W
Iquitos, Peru **124 D4** 3 45 S 73 10W
Irabu-Jima, Japan **55 M2** 24 50N 125 10 E
Iracoubo, Fr. Guiana **125 B8** 5 30N 53 10W
Īrafshān, Iran **71 E9** 26 42N 61 56 E
Irahuan, Phil. **61 G3** 9 48N 118 41 E
Iráklia, Kikládhes, Greece **39 E7** 36 50N 25 28 E
Iráklia, Sérrai, Greece **40 E7** 41 10N 23 16 E
Iráklion, Greece **36 D7** 35 20N 25 12 E
Iráklion □, Greece **36 D7** 35 10N 25 10 E
Irala, Paraguay **127 B5** 25 55 S 54 35W
Iran ■, Asia **71 C7** 33 0N 53 0 E
Iran, Gunung-Gunung, Malaysia **62 D4** 2 20N 114 50 E
Iran, Plateau of, Asia **52 F9** 32 0N 55 0 E
Iran Ra. = Iran, Gunung-Gunung, Malaysia **62 D4** 2 20N 114 50 E
Īrānshahr, Iran **71 E9** 27 15N 60 40 E
Irapuato, Mexico **118 C4** 20 40N 101 30W
Iraq ■, Asia **70 C5** 33 0N 44 0 E
Irati, Brazil **127 B5** 25 25 S 50 38W
Irbes saurums, Latvia **44 A9** 57 45N 22 5 E
Irbid, Jordan **75 C4** 32 35N 35 48 E
Irbid □, Jordan **75 C5** 32 15N 36 35 E
Iregua →, Spain **32 C7** 42 27N 2 24 E
Ireland ■, Europe **15 C4** 53 50N 7 52W
Irele, Nigeria **83 D6** 7 40N 5 40 E
Irgiz, Bolshaya →, Russia **48 D9** 52 10N 49 10 E
Irhyangdong, N. Korea **57 D15** 41 15N 129 30 E
Iri, S. Korea **57 G14** 35 59N 127 0 E
Irian Jaya □, Indonesia **63 E9** 4 0 S 137 0 E
Irié, Guinea **82 D3** 8 15N 9 10W
Iriga, Phil. **61 E5** 13 25N 123 25 E
Iringa, Tanzania **86 D4** 7 48 S 35 43 E
Iringa □, Tanzania **86 D4** 7 48 S 35 43 E
Iriomote-Jima, Japan **55 M1** 24 19N 123 48 E
Iriona, Honduras **120 C2** 15 57N 85 11W
Iriri →, Brazil **125 D8** 3 52 S 52 37W
Irish Republic ■, Europe **15 C3** 53 0N 8 0W
Irish Sea, U.K. **12 D3** 53 38N 4 48W
Irkutsk, Russia **51 D11** 52 18N 104 20 E
Irlığanlı, Turkey **39 D11** 37 53N 29 12 E
Irma, Canada **105 C6** 52 55N 111 14W
Irō-Zaki, Japan **55 G9** 34 36N 138 51 E
Iroise, Mer d', France **18 D2** 48 15N 4 45W
Iron Baron, Australia **95 E2** 32 58 S 137 11 E
Iron Gate = Portile de Fier, Europe **42 F7** 44 44N 22 30 E
Iron Knob, Australia **95 E2** 32 46 S 137 8 E
Iron Mountain, U.S.A. **108 C1** 45 49N 88 4W
Iron River, U.S.A. **112 B10** 46 6N 88 39W
Irondequoit, U.S.A. **110 C7** 43 13N 77 35W
Ironton, Mo., U.S.A. **113 G9** 37 36N 90 38W
Ironton, Ohio, U.S.A. **108 F4** 38 32N 82 41W
Ironwood, U.S.A. **112 B9** 46 27N 90 9W
Iroquois, Canada **111 B9** 44 51N 75 19W
Iroquois Falls, Canada **102 C3** 48 46N 80 41W
Irosin, Phil. **61 E6** 12 42N 124 2 E
Irpin, Ukraine **47 G6** 50 30N 30 15 E
Irrara Cr. →, Australia **95 D4** 29 35 S 145 31 E
Irrawaddy □, Burma **67 L19** 17 0N 95 0 E
Irrawaddy →, Burma **67 M19** 15 50N 95 6 E
Irricana, Canada **104 C6** 51 19N 113 37W
Irsina, Italy **31 B9** 40 45N 16 14 E
Irtysh →, Russia **50 C7** 61 4N 68 52 E
Irumu, Dem. Rep. of the Congo **86 B2** 1 32N 29 53 E
Irún, Spain **32 B3** 43 20N 1 52W
Irunea = Pamplona, Spain **32 C3** 42 48N 1 38W
Irurzun, Spain **32 C3** 42 55N 1 50W
Irvine, Canada **105 D6** 49 57N 110 16W
Irvine, U.K. **14 F4** 55 37N 4 41W
Irvine, Calif., U.S.A. **117 M9** 33 41N 117 46W
Irvine, Ky., U.S.A. **108 G4** 37 42N 83 58W
Irvinestown, U.K. **15 B4** 54 28N 7 39W
Irving, U.S.A. **113 J6** 32 49N 96 56W
Irvona, U.S.A. **110 F6** 40 46N 78 33W
Irwin →, Australia **93 E1** 29 15 S 114 54 E
Irymple, Australia **95 E3** 34 14 S 142 8 E
Is, Jebel, Sudan **80 C4** 22 3N 35 28 E
Is-sur-Tille, France **19 E12** 47 30N 5 8 E
Isa, Nigeria **83 C6** 13 14N 6 24 E
Isa Khel, Pakistan **68 C4** 32 41N 71 17 E
Isaac →, Australia **94 C4** 22 55 S 149 20 E
Isabel, U.S.A. **112 C4** 45 24N 101 26W
Isabela, Phil. **61 H5** 6 40N 122 10 E
Isabela, I., Mexico **118 C3** 21 51N 105 55W
Isabelia, Cord., Nic. **120 D2** 13 30N 85 25W
Isabella Ra., Australia **92 D3** 21 0 S 121 4 E
Isaccea, Romania **43 E13** 45 16N 28 28 E
Ísafjarðardjúp, Iceland **8 C2** 66 10N 23 0W
Ísafjörður, Iceland **8 C2** 66 5N 23 9W
Isagarh, India **68 G7** 24 48N 77 51 E
Isahaya, Japan **55 H5** 32 52N 130 2 E
Isaka, Tanzania **86 C3** 3 56 S 32 59 E
Isakly, Russia **48 C10** 54 8N 51 32 E
Işalniţa, Romania **43 F8** 44 24N 23 44 E
Isan →, India **69 F9** 26 51N 80 7 E
Isana = Içana →, Brazil **124 C5** 0 26N 67 19W
Isanlu Makutu, Nigeria **83 D6** 8 20N 5 50 E
Isar →, Germany **25 G8** 48 48N 12 57 E
Isarco →, Italy **29 B8** 46 27N 11 18 E
Ísari, Greece **38 D3** 37 22N 22 0 E
Íscar, Spain **34 D6** 41 22N 4 32W
İscehisar, Turkey **39 C12** 38 51N 30 45 E
Íschia, Italy **30 B6** 40 44N 13 57 E
Isdell →, Australia **92 C3** 16 27 S 124 51 E
Ise, Japan **55 G8** 34 25N 136 45 E
Ise-Wan, Japan **55 G8** 34 43N 136 43 E
Isefjord, Denmark **11 J5** 55 53N 11 50 E
Isel →, Austria **26 E5** 46 50N 12 47 E
Iseo, Italy **28 C7** 45 39N 10 3 E
Iseo, L. d', Italy **28 C7** 45 43N 10 4 E
Iseramagazi, Tanzania **86 C3** 4 37 S 32 10 E
Isère □, France **21 C9** 45 15N 5 40 E
Isère →, France **21 D8** 44 59N 4 51 E
Iserlohn, Germany **24 D3** 51 22N 7 41 E
Isérnia, Italy **31 A7** 41 36N 14 14 E
Iseyin, Nigeria **83 D5** 8 0N 3 36 E
Isfahan = Eşfahān, Iran **71 C6** 32 39N 51 43 E
Ishëm, Albania **40 E3** 41 33N 19 34 E
Ishigaki-Shima, Japan **55 M2** 24 20N 124 10 E
Ishikari-Gawa →, Japan **54 C10** 43 15N 141 23 E
Ishikari-Sammyaku, Japan **54 C11** 43 30N 143 0 E
Ishikari-Wan, Japan **54 C10** 43 25N 141 1 E
Ishikawa □, Japan **55 F8** 36 30N 136 30 E
Ishim, Russia **50 D7** 56 10N 69 30 E
Ishim →, Russia **50 D8** 57 45N 71 10 E
Ishinomaki, Japan **54 E10** 38 32N 141 20 E
Ishioka, Japan **55 F10** 36 11N 140 16 E
Ishkuman, Pakistan **69 A5** 36 30N 73 50 E
Ishmi = Ishëm, Albania **40 E3** 41 33N 19 34 E
Ishpeming, U.S.A. **108 B2** 46 29N 87 40W
Isigny-sur-Mer, France **18 C5** 49 19N 1 6W
Isıklar Dağı, Turkey **41 F11** 40 45N 27 15 E
Işıklı, Turkey **39 C11** 38 19N 29 51 E
Isil Kul, Russia **50 D8** 54 55N 71 16 E
Ísili, Italy **30 C2** 39 44N 9 6 E
Isiolo, Kenya **86 B4** 0 24N 37 33 E
Isiro, Dem. Rep. of the Congo **86 B2** 2 53N 27 40 E
Isisford, Australia **94 C3** 24 15 S 144 21 E
İskenderun, Turkey **70 B3** 36 32N 36 10 E
İskenderun Körfezi, Turkey **72 D6** 36 40N 35 50 E
İskilip, Turkey **72 B6** 40 45N 34 29 E
Iskŭr →, Bulgaria **41 C8** 43 45N 24 25 E
Iskŭr, Yazovir, Bulgaria **40 D7** 42 23N 23 30 E
Iskut →, Canada **104 B2** 56 45N 131 49W
Isla →, U.K. **14 E5** 56 32N 3 20W
Isla Cristina, Spain **35 H3** 37 13N 7 17W
Isla Vista, U.S.A. **117 L7** 34 25N 119 53W
İslâhiye, Turkey **72 D7** 37 0N 36 35 E
Islam Headworks, Pakistan **68 E5** 29 49N 72 33 E
Islamabad, Pakistan **68 C5** 33 40N 73 10 E
Islamgarh, Pakistan **68 F4** 27 51N 70 48 E
Islamkot, Pakistan **68 G4** 24 42N 70 13 E
Islampur, India **69 G11** 25 9N 85 12 E
Island L., Canada **105 C10** 53 47N 94 25W
Island Lagoon, Australia **95 E2** 31 30 S 136 40 E
Island Pond, U.S.A. **111 B13** 44 49N 71 53W
Islands, B. of, Canada **103 C8** 49 11N 58 15W
Islands, B. of, N.Z. **91 F5** 35 15 S 174 6 E
Islay, U.K. **14 F2** 55 46N 6 10W
Isle →, France **20 D3** 44 55N 0 15W
Isle aux Morts, Canada **103 C8** 47 35N 59 0W
Isle of Wight □, U.K. **13 G6** 50 41N 1 17W
Isle Royale, U.S.A. **112 B10** 48 0N 88 54W
Isle Royale National Park, U.S.A. **112 B10** 48 0N 88 55W
Isleton, U.S.A. **116 G5** 38 10N 121 37W
Ismail = Izmayil, Ukraine **47 K5** 45 22N 28 46 E
Ismâ'ilîya, Egypt **80 H8** 30 37N 32 18 E
Ismaning, Germany **25 G7** 48 13N 11 40 E
Isna, Egypt **80 B3** 25 17N 32 30 E
Isoanala, Madag. **89 C8** 23 50 S 45 44 E
Isogstalo, India **69 B8** 34 15N 78 46 E
Ísola del Liri, Italy **29 G10** 41 41N 13 34 E
Ísola della Scala, Italy **28 C7** 45 16N 11 0 E
Ísola di Capo Rizzuto, Italy **31 D10** 38 58N 17 6 E
İsparta, Turkey **39 D12** 37 47N 30 30 E
Isperikh, Bulgaria **41 C10** 43 43N 26 50 E
Íspica, Italy **31 F7** 36 47N 14 55 E
Israel ■, Asia **75 D3** 32 0N 34 50 E
Isratu, Eritrea **81 D4** 16 20N 39 53 E
Issia, Ivory C. **82 D3** 6 33N 6 33W
Issoire, France **20 C7** 45 32N 3 15 E
Issoudun, France **19 F8** 46 57N 1 59 E
Issyk-Kul, Ozero = Ysyk-Köl, Ozero, Kyrgyzstan **50 E8** 42 25N 77 15 E
Ist, Croatia **29 D11** 44 17N 14 47 E
Istállós-kő, Hungary **42 B5** 48 4N 20 26 E
İstanbul, Turkey **41 E12** 41 0N 29 0 E
İstanbul □, Turkey **41 E12** 41 0N 29 0 E
İstanbul Boğazı, Turkey **41 E13** 41 10N 29 10 E
Istiaía, Greece **38 C5** 38 57N 23 9 E
Istok, Kosovo, Yug. **40 D4** 42 45N 20 24 E
Istokpoga, L., U.S.A. **109 M5** 27 23N 81 17W
Istra, Croatia **29 C10** 45 10N 14 0 E
Istres, France **21 E8** 43 31N 4 59 E
Istria = Istra, Croatia **29 C10** 45 10N 14 0 E
Itá, Paraguay **126 B4** 25 29 S 57 21W
Itaberaba, Brazil **125 F10** 12 32 S 40 18W
Itabira, Brazil **125 G10** 19 37 S 43 13W
Itabirito, Brazil **127 A7** 20 15 S 43 48W
Itabuna, Brazil **125 F11** 14 48 S 39 16W
Itacaunas →, Brazil **125 E9** 5 21 S 49 8W
Itacoatiara, Brazil **124 D7** 3 8 S 58 25W
Itaipú, Represa de, Brazil **127 B5** 25 30 S 54 30W
Itaituba, Brazil **125 D7** 4 10 S 55 50W
Itajaí, Brazil **127 B6** 27 50 S 48 39W
Itajubá, Brazil **127 A6** 22 24 S 45 30W
Itaka, Tanzania **87 D3** 8 50 S 32 49 E
Italy ■, Europe **7 G8** 42 0N 13 0 E
Itamaraju, Brazil **125 G11** 17 5 S 39 31W
Itampolo, Madag. **89 C7** 24 41 S 43 57 E
Itandrano, Madag. **89 C8** 21 47 S 45 17 E
Itapecuru-Mirim, Brazil **125 D10** 3 24 S 44 20W
Itaperuna, Brazil **127 A7** 21 10 S 41 54W
Itapetininga, Brazil **127 A6** 23 36 S 48 7W
Itapeva, Brazil **127 A6** 23 59 S 48 59W
Itapicuru →, Bahia, Brazil **125 F11** 11 47 S 37 32W
Itapicuru →, Maranhão, Brazil **125 D10** 2 52 S 44 12W
Itapipoca, Brazil **125 D11** 3 30 S 39 35W
Itapuá □, Paraguay **127 B4** 26 40 S 55 40W
Itaquari, Brazil **127 A7** 20 20 S 40 25W
Itaquí, Brazil **126 B4** 29 8 S 56 30W
Itararé, Brazil **127 A6** 24 6 S 49 23W
Itarsi, India **68 H7** 22 36N 77 51 E
Itatí, Argentina **126 B4** 27 16 S 58 15W
Itbayat, Phil. **61 A4** 20 47N 121 51 E
Itchen →, U.K. **13 G6** 50 55N 1 22W
Itéa, Greece **38 C4** 38 25N 22 25 E
Itezhi Tezhi, L., Zambia **87 F2** 15 30 S 25 30 E
Ithaca = Itháki, Greece **38 C2** 38 25N 20 40 E
Ithaca, U.S.A. **111 D8** 42 27N 76 30W
Itháki, Greece **38 C2** 38 25N 20 40 E
Itiquira →, Brazil **125 G7** 17 18 S 56 44W
Ito, Japan **55 G9** 34 58N 139 5 E
Ito Aba I., S. China Sea **62 B4** 10 23N 114 21 E
Itoigawa, Japan **55 F8** 37 2N 137 51 E
Iton →, France **18 C8** 49 9N 1 12 E
Itonamas →, Bolivia **124 F6** 12 28 S 64 24W
Itri, Italy **30 A6** 41 17N 13 32 E
Itsa, Egypt **80 J7** 29 15N 30 47 E
Íttiri, Italy **30 B1** 40 36N 8 34 E
Itu, Brazil **127 A6** 23 17 S 47 15W
Itu, Nigeria **83 D6** 5 10N 7 58 E
Ituiutaba, Brazil **125 G9** 19 0 S 49 25W
Itumbiara, Brazil **125 G9** 18 20 S 49 10W
Ituna, Canada **105 C8** 51 10N 103 24W
Itunge Port, Tanzania **87 D3** 9 40 S 33 55 E
Iturbe, Argentina **126 A2** 23 0 S 65 25W
Ituri →, Dem. Rep. of the Congo **86 B2** 1 40N 27 1 E

Iturup, Ostrov, Russia 51 E15 45 0N 148 0 E
Ituxi →, Brazil 124 E6 7 18 S 64 51W
Ituyuro →, Argentina 126 A3 22 40 S 63 50W
Itzehoe, Germany 24 B5 53 55N 9 31 E
Ivahona, Madag. 89 C8 23 27 S 46 10 E
Ivaí →, Brazil 127 A5 23 18 S 53 42W
Ivalo, Finland 8 B22 68 38N 27 35 E
Ivalojoki →, Finland 8 B22 68 40N 27 40 E
Ivanava, Belarus 47 F3 52 7N 25 29 E
Ivančice, Czech Rep. 27 B9 49 6N 16 23 E
Ivănești, Romania 43 D12 46 39N 27 27 E
Ivangorod, Russia 46 C5 59 27N 28 13 E
Ivanhoe, Australia 95 E3 32 56 S 144 20 E
Ivanhoe, Calif., U.S.A. 116 J7 36 23N 119 13W
Ivanhoe, Minn., U.S.A. 112 C6 44 28N 96 15W
Ivanić Grad, Croatia 29 C13 45 41N 16 25 E
Ivanjica, Serbia, Yug. 40 C4 43 35N 20 12 E
Ivanjska, Bos.-H. 42 F2 44 55N 17 4 E
Ivankoyskoye Vdkhr., Russia 46 D9 56 37N 36 32 E
Ivano-Frankivsk, Ukraine 47 H3 48 40N 24 40 E
Ivano-Frankovsk = Ivano-Frankivsk, Ukraine 47 H3 48 40N 24 40 E
Ivanovo = Ivanava, Belarus 47 F3 52 7N 25 29 E
Ivanovo, Russia 46 D11 57 5N 41 0 E
Ivanšćica, Croatia 29 B13 46 12N 16 13 E
Ivato, Madag. 89 C8 20 37 S 47 10 E
Ivatsevichy, Belarus 47 F3 52 43N 25 21 E
Ivaylovgrad, Bulgaria 41 E10 41 32N 26 8 E
Ivinheima →, Brazil 127 A5 23 14 S 53 42W
Ivinhema, Brazil 127 A5 22 10 S 53 37W
Ivohibe, Madag. 89 C8 22 31 S 46 57 E
Ivory Coast, W. Afr. 82 E4 4 20N 5 0W
Ivory Coast ■, Africa 82 D4 7 30N 5 0W
Ivösjön, Sweden 11 H8 56 8N 14 25 E
Ivrea, Italy 28 C4 45 28N 7 52 E
Ivrindi, Turkey 39 B9 39 34N 27 30 E
Ivujivik, Canada 101 B12 62 24N 77 55W
Ivybridge, U.K. 13 G4 50 23N 3 56W
Iwaizumi, Japan 54 E10 39 50N 141 45 E
Iwaki, Japan 55 F10 37 3N 140 55 E
Iwakuni, Japan 55 G6 34 15N 132 8 E
Iwamizawa, Japan 54 C10 43 12N 141 46 E
Iwanai, Japan 54 C10 42 58N 140 30 E
Iwata, Japan 55 G8 34 42N 137 51 E
Iwate □, Japan 54 E10 39 30N 141 30 E
Iwate-San, Japan 54 E10 39 51N 141 0 E
Iwo, Nigeria 83 D5 7 39N 4 9 E
Iwonicz-Zdrój, Poland 45 J8 49 37N 21 47 E
Ixiamas, Bolivia 124 F5 13 50 S 68 5W
Ixopo, S. Africa 89 E5 30 11 S 30 5 E
Ixtepec, Mexico 119 D5 16 32N 95 10W
Ixtlán del Río, Mexico 118 C4 21 5N 104 21W
Iyal Bakhit, Sudan 81 E2 13 20N 28 39 E
Iyo, Japan 55 H6 33 45N 132 45 E
Izabal, L. de, Guatemala 120 C2 15 30N 89 10W
Izamal, Mexico 119 C7 20 56N 89 1W
Izberbash, Russia 49 J8 42 35N 47 52 E
Izbica, Poland 45 H10 50 53N 23 10 E
Izbica Kujawska, Poland 45 F5 52 25N 18 40 E
Izbiceni, Romania 43 G9 43 45N 24 40 E
Izena-Shima, Japan 55 L3 26 56N 127 56 E
Izgrev, Bulgaria 41 C10 43 36N 26 58 E
Izhevsk, Russia 50 D6 56 51N 53 14 E
Izmayil, Ukraine 47 K5 45 22N 28 46 E
Izmir, Turkey 39 C9 38 25N 27 8 E
Izmir □, Turkey 39 C9 38 15N 27 40 E
Izmir Körfezi, Turkey 39 C8 38 30N 26 50 E
Izmit = Kocaeli, Turkey 41 F13 40 45N 29 50 E
Iznájar, Spain 35 H6 37 15N 4 19W
Iznalloz, Spain 35 H7 37 24N 3 30W
Iznik, Turkey 72 B3 40 23N 29 46 E
Iznik Gölü, Turkey 41 F13 40 27N 29 30 E
Izobil'nyy, Russia 49 H5 45 25N 41 44 E
Izola, Slovenia 29 C10 45 32N 13 39 E
Izra, Syria 75 C5 32 51N 36 15 E
Iztochni Rodopi, Bulgaria 41 E9 41 45N 25 30 E
Izu-Shotō, Japan 55 G10 34 30N 140 0 E
Izúcar de Matamoros, Mexico 119 D5 18 36N 98 28W
Izumi-Sano, Japan 55 G7 34 23N 135 18 E
Izumo, Japan 55 G6 35 20N 132 46 E
Izyaslav, Ukraine 47 G4 50 5N 26 50 E
Izyum, Ukraine 47 H9 49 12N 37 19 E

J

Jaba, Ethiopia 81 F4 6 20N 35 7 E
Jabal at Tā'ir, Red Sea 81 D5 15 35N 41 52 E
Jabalón →, Spain 35 G6 38 53N 4 5W
Jabalpur, India 69 H8 23 9N 79 58 E
Jabbūl, Syria 70 B3 36 4N 37 30 E
Jabiru, Australia 92 B5 12 40 S 132 53 E
Jablah, Syria 70 C3 35 20N 36 0 E
Jablanac, Croatia 29 D11 44 42N 14 56 E
Jablanica, Bos.-H. 42 G2 43 40N 17 45 E
Jablonec nad Nisou, Czech Rep. 26 A8 50 43N 15 10 E
Jablonica, Slovak Rep. 27 C10 48 37N 17 26 E
Jabłonowo Pomorskie, Poland 44 E6 53 23N 19 10 E
Jablunkov, Czech Rep. 27 B11 49 35N 18 46 E
Jaboatão, Brazil 125 E11 8 7 S 35 1W
Jaboticabal, Brazil 127 A6 21 15 S 48 17W
Jabukovac, Serbia, Yug. 40 B6 44 22N 22 21 E
Jaca, Spain 32 C4 42 35N 0 33W
Jacareí, Brazil 127 A6 23 20 S 46 0W
Jacarèzinho, Brazil 127 A6 23 5 S 49 58W
Jackman, U.S.A. 109 C10 45 35N 70 17W
Jacksboro, U.S.A. 113 J5 33 14N 98 15W
Jackson, Ala., U.S.A. 109 K2 31 31N 87 53W
Jackson, Calif., U.S.A. 116 G6 38 21N 120 46W
Jackson, Ky., U.S.A. 108 G4 37 33N 83 23W
Jackson, Mich., U.S.A. 108 D3 42 15N 84 24W
Jackson, Minn., U.S.A. 112 D7 43 37N 95 1W
Jackson, Miss., U.S.A. 113 J9 32 18N 90 12W
Jackson, Mo., U.S.A. 113 G10 37 23N 89 40W
Jackson, N.H., U.S.A. 111 B13 44 10N 71 11W
Jackson, Ohio, U.S.A. 108 F4 39 3N 82 39W
Jackson, Tenn., U.S.A. 109 H1 35 37N 88 49W
Jackson, Wyo., U.S.A. 114 E8 43 29N 110 46W
Jackson B., N.Z. 91 K2 43 58 S 168 42 E
Jackson L., U.S.A. 114 E8 43 52N 110 36W
Jacksons, N.Z. 91 K3 42 46 S 171 32 E
Jackson's Arm, Canada 103 C8 49 52N 56 47W
Jacksonville, Ala., U.S.A. 109 J3 33 49N 85 46W
Jacksonville, Ark., U.S.A. 113 H8 34 52N 92 7W
Jacksonville, Calif., U.S.A. 116 H6 37 52N 120 24W
Jacksonville, Fla., U.S.A. 109 K5 30 20N 81 39W
Jacksonville, Ill., U.S.A. 112 F9 39 44N 90 14W
Jacksonville, N.C., U.S.A. 109 H7 34 45N 77 26W
Jacksonville, Tex., U.S.A. 113 K7 31 58N 95 17W
Jacksonville Beach, U.S.A. 109 K5 30 17N 81 24W
Jacmel, Haiti 121 C5 18 14N 72 32W
Jacob Lake, U.S.A. 115 H7 36 43N 112 13W
Jacobabad, Pakistan 68 E3 28 20N 68 29 E
Jacobina, Brazil 125 F10 11 11 S 40 30W
Jacques Cartier, Dét. de, Canada 103 C7 50 0N 63 30W
Jacques-Cartier, Mt., Canada 103 C6 48 57N 66 0W
Jacques Cartier, Parc Prov., Canada 103 C5 47 15N 71 33W
Jacqueville, Ivory C. 82 D4 5 12N 4 25W
Jacuí →, Brazil 127 C5 30 2 S 51 15W
Jacumba, U.S.A. 117 N10 32 37N 116 11W
Jacundá →, Brazil 125 D8 1 57 S 50 26W
Jade, Germany 24 B4 53 20N 8 14 E
Jadebusen, Germany 24 B4 53 29N 8 12 E
Jadotville = Likasi, Dem. Rep. of the Congo 87 E2 10 55 S 26 48 E
Jadovnik, Serbia, Yug. 40 C3 43 20N 19 45 E
Jadraque, Spain 32 E2 40 55N 2 55W
Jaén, Peru 124 E3 5 25 S 78 40W
Jaén, Spain 35 H7 37 44N 3 43W
Jaén □, Spain 35 H7 37 50N 3 30W
Jafarabad, India 68 J4 20 52N 71 22 E
Jaffa = Tel Aviv-Yafo, Israel 75 C3 32 4N 34 48 E
Jaffa, C., Australia 95 F2 36 58 S 139 40 E
Jaffna, Sri Lanka 66 Q12 9 45N 80 2 E
Jaffrey, U.S.A. 111 D12 42 49N 72 2W
Jagadhri, India 68 D7 30 10N 77 20 E
Jagadishpur, India 69 G11 25 30N 84 21 E
Jagdalpur, India 67 K13 19 3N 82 0 E
Jagersfontein, S. Africa 88 D4 29 44 S 25 27 E
Jaghīn →, Iran 71 E8 27 17N 57 13 E
Jagodina, Serbia, Yug. 40 B5 44 5N 21 15 E
Jagraon, India 66 D9 30 50N 75 25 E
Jagst →, Germany 25 F5 49 14N 9 10 E
Jagtial, India 66 K11 18 50N 79 0 E
Jaguariaíva, Brazil 127 A6 24 10 S 49 50W
Jaguaribe →, Brazil 125 D11 4 25 S 37 45W
Jagüey Grande, Cuba 120 B3 22 35N 81 7W
Jahanabad, India 69 G11 25 13N 84 59 E
Jahazpur, India 68 G6 25 37N 75 17 E
Jahrom, Iran 71 D7 28 30N 53 31 E
Jaijon, India 68 D7 31 21N 76 9 E
Jailolo, Indonesia 63 D7 1 5N 127 30 E
Jailolo, Selat, Indonesia 63 D7 0 5N 129 5 E
Jaipur, India 68 F6 27 0N 75 50 E
Jais, India 69 F9 26 15N 81 32 E
Jaisalmer, India 68 F4 26 55N 70 54 E
Jaisinghnagar, India 69 H8 23 38N 78 34 E
Jaitaran, India 68 F5 26 12N 73 56 E
Jaithari, India 69 H8 23 14N 78 37 E
Jājarm, Iran 71 B8 36 58N 56 27 E
Jajce, Bos.-H. 42 F2 44 19N 17 17 E
Jakam →, India 68 H6 23 54N 74 13 E
Jakarta, Indonesia 63 G12 6 9 S 106 49 E
Jakhal, India 68 E6 29 48N 75 50 E
Jakhau, India 68 H3 23 13N 68 43 E
Jakobstad = Pietarsaari, Finland 8 E20 63 40N 22 43 E
Jakupica, Macedonia 40 E5 41 45N 21 22 E
Jal, U.S.A. 113 J3 32 7N 103 12W
Jalālābād, Afghan. 68 B4 34 30N 70 29 E
Jalalabad, India 69 F8 27 41N 79 42 E
Jalalpur Jattan, Pakistan 68 C6 32 38N 74 11 E
Jalama, U.S.A. 117 L6 34 29N 120 29W
Jalapa, Guatemala 120 D2 14 39N 89 59W
Jalapa Enríquez, Mexico 119 D5 19 32N 96 55W
Jalasjärvi, Finland 9 E20 62 29N 22 47 E
Jalaun, India 69 F8 26 8N 79 25 E
Jaldhaka →, Bangla. 69 F13 26 16N 89 16 E
Jalesar, India 68 F8 27 29N 78 19 E
Jaleswar, Nepal 69 F11 26 38N 85 48 E
Jalgaon, Maharashtra, India 66 J10 21 2N 76 31 E
Jalgaon, Maharashtra, India 66 J9 21 0N 75 42 E
Jalībah, Iraq 70 D5 30 35N 46 32 E
Jalingo, Nigeria 83 D7 8 55N 11 25 E
Jalisco □, Mexico 118 D4 20 0N 104 0W
Jalkot, Pakistan 69 B5 35 14N 73 24 E
Jallas →, Spain 34 C1 42 54N 9 8W
Jalna, India 66 K9 19 48N 75 38 E
Jalón →, Spain 32 D3 41 47N 1 4W
Jalor, India 68 G5 25 21N 72 37 E
Jalpa, Mexico 118 C4 21 38N 102 58W
Jalpaiguri, India 67 F16 26 32N 88 46 E
Jaluit I., Marshall Is. 96 G8 6 0N 169 30 E
Jalūlā, Iraq 70 C5 34 16N 45 10 E
Jamaari, Nigeria 83 C6 11 44N 9 53 E
Jamaica ■, W. Indies 120 C4 18 10N 77 30W
Jamalpur, Bangla. 67 G16 24 52N 89 56 E
Jamalpur, India 69 G12 25 18N 86 28 E
Jamalpurganj, India 69 H13 23 2N 87 59 E
Jamanxim →, Brazil 125 D7 4 43 S 56 18W
Jambi, Indonesia 62 E2 1 38 S 103 30 E
Jambi □, Indonesia 62 E2 1 30 S 102 30 E
Jambusar, India 68 H5 22 3N 72 51 E
James →, S. Dak., U.S.A. 112 D6 42 52N 97 18W
James →, Va., U.S.A. 108 G7 36 56N 76 27W
James B., Canada 102 B3 54 0N 80 0W
James Ranges, Australia 92 D5 24 10 S 132 30 E
James Ross I., Antarctica 5 C18 63 58 S 57 50W
Jamesabad, Pakistan 68 G3 25 17N 69 15 E
Jamestown, Australia 95 E2 33 10 S 138 32 E
Jamestown, S. Africa 88 E4 31 6 S 26 45 E
Jamestown, N. Dak., U.S.A. 112 B5 46 54N 98 42W
Jamestown, N.Y., U.S.A. 110 D5 42 6N 79 14W
Jamestown, Pa., U.S.A. 110 E4 41 29N 80 27W
Jamīlābād, Iran 71 C6 34 24N 48 28 E
Jamiltepec, Mexico 119 D5 16 17N 97 49W
Jamira →, India 69 J13 21 35N 88 28 E
Jämjö, Sweden 11 H9 56 12N 15 49 E
Jamkhandi, India 66 L9 16 30N 75 15 E
Jammerbugt, Denmark 11 G3 57 15N 9 20 E
Jammu, India 68 C6 32 43N 74 54 E
Jammu & Kashmir □, India 69 B7 34 25N 77 0 E
Jamnagar, India 68 H4 22 30N 70 6 E
Jamni →, India 69 G8 25 13N 78 35 E
Jampur, Pakistan 68 E4 29 39N 70 40 E
Jamrud, Pakistan 68 C4 33 59N 71 24 E
Jämsä, Finland 9 F21 61 53N 25 10 E
Jamshedpur, India 69 H12 22 44N 86 12 E
Jamtara, India 69 H12 23 59N 86 49 E
Jämtland, Sweden 8 E15 63 31N 14 0 E
Jämtlands län □, Sweden 10 B7 62 40N 13 50 E
Jan L., Canada 105 C8 54 56N 102 55W
Jan Mayen, Arctic 4 B7 71 0N 9 0W
Janakkala, Finland 9 F21 60 54N 24 36 E
Janaúba, Brazil 125 G10 15 48 S 43 19W
Jand, Pakistan 68 C5 33 30N 72 6 E
Jandaq, Iran 71 C7 34 3N 54 22 E
Jandia, Canary Is. 37 F5 28 6N 14 21W
Jandia, Pta. de, Canary Is. 37 F5 28 3N 14 31W
Jandola, Pakistan 68 C4 32 20N 70 9 E
Jandowae, Australia 95 D5 26 45 S 151 7 E
Jándula →, Spain 35 G6 38 3N 4 6W
Janesville, U.S.A. 112 D10 42 41N 89 1W
Janga, Ghana 83 C4 10 5N 1 0W
Jangamo, Mozam. 89 C6 24 6 S 35 21 E
Janghai, India 69 G10 25 33N 82 19 E
Janikowo, Poland 45 F5 52 45N 18 7 E
Janīn, West Bank 75 C4 32 28N 35 18 E
Janinà = Ioánnina □, Greece 38 B2 39 39N 20 57 E
Janja, Bos.-H. 42 F4 44 40N 19 14 E
Janjevo, Kosovo, Yug. 40 D5 42 35N 21 19 E
Janjgir, India 69 J10 22 1N 82 34 E
Janjina, Croatia 29 F14 42 58N 17 25 E
Janjina, Madag. 89 C8 20 30 S 45 50 E
Janos, Mexico 118 A3 30 45N 108 10W
Jánoshalma, Hungary 42 D4 46 18N 19 21 E
Jánosháza, Hungary 42 C2 47 8N 17 12 E
Jánossomorja, Hungary 42 C2 47 47N 17 11 E
Janów, Poland 45 H6 50 44N 19 27 E
Janów Lubelski, Poland 45 H9 50 48N 22 23 E
Janów Podlaski, Poland 45 F10 52 11N 23 11 E
Janowiec Wielkopolski, Poland 45 F4 52 45N 17 30 E
Januária, Brazil 125 G10 15 25 S 44 25W
Janub Dârfûr □, Sudan 81 E2 11 0N 25 0 E
Janub Kordofân □, Sudan 81 E3 12 0N 30 0 E
Janubio, Canary Is. 37 F6 28 56N 13 50W
Janville, France 19 D8 48 10N 1 50 E
Janzé, France 18 E5 47 55N 1 28W
Jaora, India 68 H6 23 40N 75 10 E
Japan ■, Asia 55 G8 36 0N 136 0 E
Japan, Sea of, Asia 54 E7 40 0N 135 0 E
Japan Trench, Pac. Oc. 52 F18 32 0N 142 0 E
Japen = Yapen, Indonesia 63 E9 1 50 S 136 0 E
Japla, India 69 G11 24 33N 84 1 E
Japurá →, Brazil 122 D4 3 8 S 65 46W
Jaquarão, Brazil 127 C5 32 34 S 53 23W
Jaqué, Panama 120 E4 7 27N 78 8W
Jarābulus, Syria 70 B3 36 49N 38 1 E
Jaraicejo, Spain 35 F5 39 40N 5 49W
Jaraíz de la Vera, Spain 34 E5 40 4N 5 45W
Jarama →, Spain 34 E7 40 24N 3 32W
Jaramānah, Syria 72 F7 33 29N 36 21 E
Jarandilla, Spain 34 E5 40 8N 5 39W
Jaranwala, Pakistan 68 D5 31 15N 73 26 E
Jarash, Jordan 75 C4 32 17N 35 54 E
Järbo, Sweden 10 D10 60 43N 16 36 E
Jardim, Brazil 126 A4 21 28 S 56 2W
Jardín →, Spain 33 G2 38 50N 2 10W
Jardines de la Reina, Arch. de los, Cuba 120 B4 20 50N 78 50W
Jargalang, China 57 C12 43 5N 122 55 E
Jargalant = Hovd, Mongolia 60 B4 48 2N 91 37 E
Jari →, Brazil 125 D8 1 9 S 51 54W
Jarīr, W. al →, Si. Arabia 70 E4 25 38N 42 30 E
Järlåsa, Sweden 10 E11 59 53N 17 12 E
Jarmen, Germany 24 B9 53 54N 13 20 E
Järna, Dalarnas, Sweden 10 D8 60 33N 14 26 E
Järna, Stockholm, Sweden 10 E11 59 6N 17 34 E
Jarnac, France 20 C3 45 40N 0 11W
Jarny, France 19 C12 49 9N 5 53 E
Jarocin, Poland 45 G4 51 59N 17 29 E
Jaroměř, Czech Rep. 26 A8 50 22N 15 52 E
Jarosław, Poland 45 H9 50 2N 22 42 E
Järpås, Sweden 11 F6 58 23N 12 57 E
Järpen, Sweden 10 A7 63 21N 13 26 E
Jarrahdale, Australia 93 F2 32 24 S 116 5 E
Jarrahi →, Iran 71 D6 30 49N 48 48 E
Jarres, Plaine des, Laos 64 C4 19 27N 103 10 E
Jarso, Ethiopia 81 F4 5 15N 37 30 E
Jartai, China 56 E3 39 45N 105 48 E
Jarud Qi, China 57 B11 44 28N 120 50 E
Järvenpää, Finland 9 F21 60 29N 25 5 E
Jarvis, Canada 110 D4 42 53N 80 6W
Jarvis I., Pac. Oc. 97 H12 0 15 S 159 55W
Jarvorník, Czech Rep. 27 A10 50 23N 17 2 E
Järvsö, Sweden 10 C10 61 43N 16 10 E
Jarwa, India 69 F10 27 38N 82 30 E
Jaša Tomić, Serbia, Yug. 42 E5 45 26N 20 50 E
Jasdan, India 68 H4 22 2N 71 12 E
Jashpurnagar, India 69 H11 22 54N 84 9 E
Jasidih, India 69 G12 24 31N 86 39 E
Jasień, Poland 45 G2 51 46N 15 0 E
Jāsimīyah, Iraq 70 C5 33 45N 44 41 E
Jasin, Malaysia 65 L4 2 20N 102 26 E
Jāsk, Iran 71 E8 25 38N 57 45 E
Jasło, Poland 45 J8 49 45N 21 30 E
Jasmund, Germany 24 A9 54 32N 13 35 E
Jaso, India 69 G9 24 30N 80 29 E
Jasper, Alta., Canada 104 C5 52 55N 118 5W
Jasper, Ont., Canada 111 B9 44 52N 75 57W
Jasper, Ala., U.S.A. 109 J2 33 50N 87 17W
Jasper, Fla., U.S.A. 109 K4 30 31N 82 57W
Jasper, Ind., U.S.A. 108 F2 38 24N 86 56W
Jasper, Tex., U.S.A. 113 K8 30 56N 94 1W
Jasper Nat. Park, Canada 104 C5 52 50N 118 8W
Jasrasar, India 68 F5 27 43N 73 49 E
Jastarnia, Poland 44 D5 54 42N 18 40 E
Jastrebarsko, Croatia 29 C12 45 41N 15 39 E
Jastrowie, Poland 44 E3 53 26N 16 49 E
Jastrzębie Zdrój, Poland 45 J5 49 57N 18 35 E
Jász-Nagykun-Szolnok □, Hungary 42 C5 47 15N 20 30 E
Jászapáti, Hungary 42 C5 47 32N 20 10 E
Jászárokszállás, Hungary 42 C4 47 39N 19 58 E
Jászberény, Hungary 42 C4 47 30N 19 55 E
Jászkisér, Hungary 42 C5 47 27N 20 20 E
Jászladány, Hungary 42 C5 47 23N 20 10 E
Jataí, Brazil 125 G8 17 58 S 51 48W
Jati, Pakistan 68 G3 24 20N 68 19 E
Jatibarang, Indonesia 63 G13 6 28 S 108 18 E
Jatinegara, Indonesia 63 G12 6 13 S 106 52 E
Játiva = Xátiva, Spain 33 G4 38 59N 0 32W
Jättendal, Sweden 10 C11 61 58N 17 15 E
Jaú, Brazil 127 A6 22 10 S 48 30W
Jauja, Peru 124 F3 11 45 S 75 15W
Jaunpur, India 69 G10 25 46N 82 44 E
Java = Jawa, Indonesia 63 G14 7 0 S 110 0 E
Java Barat □, Indonesia 63 G12 7 0 S 107 0 E
Java Sea, Indonesia 62 E3 4 35 S 107 15 E
Java Tengah □, Indonesia 63 G14 7 0 S 110 0 E
Java Timur □, Indonesia 63 G15 8 0 S 113 0 E
Java Trench, Ind. Oc. 62 F3 9 0 S 105 0 E
Javalambre, Sa. de, Spain 32 E4 40 6N 1 0W
Jávea, Spain 33 G5 38 48N 0 10 E
Javhlant = Uliastay, Mongolia 60 B4 47 56N 97 28 E
Jawa, Indonesia 63 G14 7 0 S 110 0 E
Jawad, India 68 G6 24 36N 74 51 E
Jawor, Poland 45 G3 51 4N 16 11 E
Jaworzno, Poland 45 H6 50 13N 19 11 E
Jaworzyna Śląska, Poland 45 H3 50 55N 16 28 E
Jay Peak, U.S.A. 111 B12 44 55N 72 32W
Jaya, Puncak, Indonesia 63 E9 3 57 S 137 17 E
Jayanti, India 67 F16 26 45N 89 40 E
Jayapura, Indonesia 63 E10 2 28 S 140 38 E
Jayawijaya, Pegunungan, Indonesia 63 E9 5 0 S 139 0 E
Jaynagar, India 67 F15 26 43N 86 9 E
Jayrūd, Syria 70 C3 33 49N 36 44 E
Jayton, U.S.A. 113 J4 33 15N 100 34W
Jāz Mūrīān, Hāmūn-e, Iran 71 E8 27 20N 58 55 E
Jazīreh-ye Shīf, Iran 71 D6 29 4N 50 54 E
Jazminal, Mexico 118 C4 24 56N 101 25W
Jazzīn, Lebanon 75 B4 33 31N 35 35 E
Jean, U.S.A. 117 K11 35 47N 115 20W
Jean Marie River, Canada 104 A4 61 32N 120 38W
Jean Rabel, Haiti 121 C5 19 50N 73 5W
Jeanerette, U.S.A. 113 L9 29 55N 91 40W
Jeanette, Ostrov = Zhannetty, Ostrov, Russia 51 B16 76 43N 158 0 E
Jeannette, U.S.A. 110 F5 40 20N 79 36W
Jebāl Bārez, Kūh-e, Iran 71 D8 28 30N 58 20 E
Jebba, Nigeria 83 D5 9 9N 4 48 E
Jebel, Bahr el →, Sudan 81 F3 9 30N 30 25 E
Jebel Dud, Sudan 81 E3 13 25N 33 9 E
Jebel Qerri, Sudan 81 D3 16 16N 32 50 E
Jedburgh, U.K. 14 F6 55 29N 2 33W
Jedda = Jiddah, Si. Arabia 74 C2 21 29N 39 10 E
Jeddore L., Canada 103 C8 48 3N 55 55W
Jedlicze, Poland 45 J8 49 43N 21 40 E
Jędrzejów, Poland 45 H7 50 35N 20 15 E
Jedwabne, Poland 45 E9 53 17N 22 18 E
Jeetzel →, Germany 24 B7 53 9N 11 3 E
Jefferson, Iowa, U.S.A. 112 D7 42 1N 94 23W
Jefferson, Ohio, U.S.A. 110 E4 41 44N 80 46W
Jefferson, Tex., U.S.A. 113 J7 32 46N 94 21W
Jefferson, Mt., Nev., U.S.A. 114 G5 38 51N 117 0W
Jefferson, Mt., Oreg., U.S.A. 114 D3 44 41N 121 48W
Jefferson City, Mo., U.S.A. 112 F8 38 34N 92 10W
Jefferson City, Tenn., U.S.A. 109 G4 36 7N 83 30W
Jeffersontown, U.S.A. 108 F3 38 12N 85 35W
Jeffersonville, U.S.A. 108 F3 38 17N 85 44W
Jeffrey City, U.S.A. 114 E10 42 30N 107 49W
Jega, Nigeria 83 C5 12 15N 4 23 E
Jēkabpils, Latvia 9 H21 56 29N 25 57 E
Jekyll I., U.S.A. 109 K5 31 4N 81 25W
Jelcz-Laskowice, Poland 45 G4 51 2N 17 19 E
Jelenia Góra, Poland 45 H2 50 50N 15 45 E
Jelgava, Latvia 9 H20 56 41N 23 49 E
Jelgava □, Latvia 44 B10 56 35N 23 45 E
Jelica, Serbia, Yug. 40 C4 43 50N 20 17 E
Jelli, Sudan 81 F3 5 25N 31 45 E
Jelšava, Slovak Rep. 27 C13 48 37N 20 15 E
Jemaja, Indonesia 65 L5 3 5N 105 45 E
Jemaluang, Malaysia 65 L4 2 16N 103 52 E
Jember, Indonesia 63 H15 8 11 S 113 41 E
Jembongan, Malaysia 62 C5 6 45N 117 20 E
Jena, Germany 24 E7 50 54N 11 35 E
Jena, U.S.A. 113 K8 31 41N 92 8W
Jenbach, Austria 26 D4 47 24N 11 47 E
Jenkins, U.S.A. 108 G4 37 10N 82 38W
Jenner, U.S.A. 116 G3 38 27N 123 7W
Jennings, U.S.A. 113 K8 30 13N 92 40W
Jepara, Indonesia 63 G14 7 40 S 109 14 E
Jeparit, Australia 95 F3 36 8 S 142 1 E
Jequié, Brazil 125 F10 13 51 S 40 5W
Jequitinhonha, Brazil 125 G10 16 30 S 41 0W
Jequitinhonha →, Brazil 125 G11 15 51 S 38 53W
Jerantut, Malaysia 65 L4 3 56N 102 22 E
Jérémie, Haiti 121 C5 18 40N 74 10W
Jerez, Punta, Mexico 119 C5 22 58N 97 40W
Jerez de García Salinas, Mexico 118 C4 22 39N 103 0W
Jerez de la Frontera, Spain 35 J4 36 41N 6 7W
Jerez de los Caballeros, Spain 35 G4 38 20N 6 45W
Jericho = El Arīḥā, West Bank 75 D4 31 52N 35 27 E
Jericho, Australia 94 C4 23 38 S 146 6 E
Jerichow, Germany 24 C8 52 30N 12 1 E
Jerilderie, Australia 95 F4 35 20 S 145 41 E
Jermyn, U.S.A. 111 E9 41 31N 75 31W
Jerome, U.S.A. 114 E6 42 44N 114 31W
Jerramungup, Australia 93 F2 33 55 S 118 55 E
Jersey, U.K. 13 H5 49 11N 2 7W
Jersey City, U.S.A. 111 F10 40 44N 74 4W
Jersey Shore, U.S.A. 110 E7 41 12N 77 15W
Jerseyville, U.S.A. 112 F9 39 7N 90 20W
Jerusalem, Israel 75 D4 31 47N 35 10 E
Jervis B., Australia 95 F5 35 8 S 150 46 E
Jervis Inlet, Canada 104 C4 50 0N 123 57W
Jerzu, Italy 30 C2 39 47N 9 31 E
Jesenice, Slovenia 29 B11 46 28N 14 3 E
Jeseník, Czech Rep. 27 A10 50 14N 17 8 E
Jesenké, Slovak Rep. 27 C13 48 20N 20 10 E
Jesi = Iesi, Italy 29 E10 43 31N 13 14 E
Jesselton = Kota Kinabalu, Malaysia 62 C5 6 0N 116 4 E
Jessnitz, Germany 24 D8 51 40N 12 18 E
Jessore, Bangla. 67 H16 23 10N 89 10 E
Jesup, U.S.A. 109 K5 31 36N 81 53W
Jesús Carranza, Mexico 119 D5 17 28N 95 1W
Jesús María, Argentina 126 C3 30 59 S 64 5W
Jetmore, U.S.A. 113 F5 38 4N 99 54W
Jetpur, India 68 J4 21 45N 70 10 E
Jeumont, France 19 B11 50 18N 4 6 E
Jevnaker, Norway 9 F14 60 15N 10 26 E
Jewett, U.S.A. 110 F3 40 22N 81 2W
Jewett City, U.S.A. 111 E13 41 36N 72 0W
Jeyḥūnābād, Iran 71 C6 34 58N 48 59 E
Jeypore, India 67 K13 18 50N 82 38 E
Jeziorak, Jezioro, Poland 44 E6 53 40N 19 35 E
Jeziorany, Poland 44 E7 53 58N 20 46 E
Jeziorka →, Poland 45 F8 52 8N 21 9 E
Jha Jha, India 69 G12 24 46N 86 22 E
Jhabua, India 68 H6 22 46N 74 36 E
Jhajjar, India 68 E7 28 37N 76 42 E
Jhal, Pakistan 68 E2 28 17N 67 27 E
Jhal Jhao, Pakistan 66 F4 26 20N 65 35 E
Jhalawar, India 68 G7 24 40N 76 10 E
Jhalida, India 69 H11 23 22N 85 58 E
Jhalrapatan, India 68 G7 24 33N 76 10 E
Jhang Maghiana, Pakistan 68 D5 31 15N 72 22 E
Jhansi, India 69 G8 25 30N 78 36 E
Jhargram, India 69 H12 22 27N 86 59 E
Jharia, India 69 H12 23 45N 86 26 E
Jharsuguda, India 67 J14 21 56N 84 5 E
Jhelum, Pakistan 68 C5 33 0N 73 45 E
Jhelum →, Pakistan 68 D5 31 20N 72 10 E
Jhilmilli, India 69 H10 23 24N 82 51 E
Jhudo, Pakistan 68 G3 24 58N 69 18 E
Jhunjhunu, India 68 E6 28 10N 75 30 E
Ji-Paraná, Brazil 124 F6 10 52 S 62 57W
Ji Xian, Hebei, China 56 F8 37 35N 115 30 E
Ji Xian, Henan, China 56 G8 35 22N 114 5 E
Ji Xian, Shanxi, China 56 F6 36 7N 110 40 E
Jia Xian, Henan, China 56 H7 33 59N 113 12 E
Jia Xian, Shaanxi, China 56 E6 38 12N 110 28 E
Jiading, China 59 B13 31 22N 121 15 E
Jiahe, China 59 E9 25 38N 112 19 E
Jialing Jiang →, China 58 C6 29 30N 106 20 E
Jiamusi, China 60 B8 46 40N 130 26 E
Ji'an, Jiangxi, China 59 D10 27 6N 114 59 E
Ji'an, Jilin, China 57 D14 41 5N 126 10 E
Jianchang, China 57 D11 40 55N 120 35 E
Jianchangying, China 57 D10 40 10N 118 50 E
Jianchuan, China 58 D2 26 38N 99 55 E
Jiande, China 59 C12 29 23N 119 15 E
Jiang'an, China 58 C5 28 40N 105 3 E
Jiangbei, China 58 C6 29 40N 106 34 E
Jiangcheng, China 58 F3 22 36N 101 52 E
Jiangchuan, China 58 E4 24 8N 102 39 E
Jiangdi, China 58 D4 26 57N 103 37 E
Jiangdu, China 59 A12 32 27N 119 36 E
Jiange, China 58 A5 32 4N 105 32 E
Jianghua, China 59 E8 25 0N 111 47 E
Jiangjin, China 58 C6 29 14N 106 14 E
Jiangkou, China 58 D7 27 40N 108 49 E
Jiangle, China 59 D11 26 42N 117 23 E
Jiangling, China 59 B9 30 25N 112 12 E
Jiangmen, China 59 F9 22 32N 113 0 E
Jiangning, China 59 B12 31 55N 118 50 E
Jiangshan, China 59 C12 28 40N 118 37 E
Jiangsu □, China 57 H11 33 0N 120 0 E
Jiangxi □, China 59 D11 27 30N 116 0 E
Jiangyan, China 59 A13 32 30N 120 7 E
Jiangyin, China 59 B13 31 54N 120 17 E
Jiangyong, China 59 E8 25 20N 111 22 E
Jiangyou, China 58 B5 31 44N 104 43 E
Jianhe, China 58 D7 26 37N 108 31 E
Jianli, China 59 C9 29 46N 112 56 E
Jianning, China 59 D11 26 50N 116 50 E
Jian'ou, China 59 D12 27 3N 118 17 E
Jianshi, China 58 B7 30 37N 109 38 E
Jianshui, China 58 F4 23 36N 102 43 E
Jianyang, Fujian, China 59 D12 27 20N 118 5 E
Jianyang, Sichuan, China 58 B5 30 24N 104 33 E
Jiao Xian = Jiaozhou, China 57 F11 36 18N 120 1 E
Jiaohe, Hebei, China 56 E9 38 2N 116 20 E
Jiaohe, Jilin, China 57 C14 43 40N 127 22 E
Jiaojiang, China 59 C13 28 40N 121 24 E
Jiaoling, China 59 E11 24 41N 116 12 E
Jiaozhou, China 57 F11 36 18N 120 1 E
Jiaozhou Wan, China 57 F11 36 5N 120 10 E
Jiaozuo, China 56 G7 35 16N 113 12 E
Jiashan, China 59 B13 30 55N 120 55 E
Jiawang, China 57 G9 34 28N 117 26 E
Jiaxiang, China 56 G9 35 25N 116 20 E
Jiaxing, China 59 B13 30 49N 120 45 E
Jiayi = Chiai, Taiwan 59 F13 23 29N 120 25 E
Jiayu, China 59 C9 29 55N 113 55 E
Jibiya, Nigeria 83 C6 13 5N 7 12 E
Jibou, Romania 43 C8 47 15N 23 17 E
Jibuti = Djibouti ■, Africa 81 E5 12 0N 43 0 E
Jicarón, I., Panama 120 E3 7 10N 81 50W
Jičín, Czech Rep. 26 A8 50 25N 15 28 E
Jiddah, Si. Arabia 74 C2 21 29N 39 10 E
Jido, India 67 E19 29 2N 94 58 E
Jieshou, China 56 H8 33 18N 115 22 E
Jiexiu, China 56 F6 37 2N 111 55 E
Jieyang, China 59 F11 23 35N 116 21 E
Jigawa □, Nigeria 83 C6 12 0N 9 45 E
Jiggalong, Australia 92 D3 23 21 S 120 47 E
Jigni, India 69 G8 25 45N 79 25 E
Jihlava, Czech Rep. 26 B8 49 28N 15 35 E
Jihlava →, Czech Rep. 27 C9 48 55N 16 36 E
Jihočeský □, Czech Rep. 26 B7 49 8N 14 35 E
Jihomoravský □, Czech Rep. 27 B9 49 5N 16 30 E
Jijiga, Ethiopia 74 F3 9 20N 42 50 E
Jikamshi, Nigeria 83 C6 12 12N 7 45 E

Jikau, *Sudan* **81 F3** 8 28N 33 47 E
Jilin, *China* **57 C14** 43 44N 126 30 E
Jilin □, *China* **57 C14** 44 0N 127 0 E
Jiloca →, *Spain* **32 D3** 41 21N 1 39W
Jilong = Chilung, *Taiwan* **59 E13** 25 3N 121 45 E
Jim Thorpe, *U.S.A.* **111 F9** 40 52N 75 44W
Jima, *Ethiopia* **81 F4** 7 40N 36 47 E
Jimbolia, *Romania* **42 E5** 45 47N 20 43 E
Jimena de la Frontera, *Spain* **35 J5** 36 27N 5 24W
Jiménez, *Mexico* **118 B4** 27 10N 104 54W
Jimo, *China* **57 F11** 36 23N 120 30 E
Jin Jiang →, *China* **59 C10** 28 24N 115 48 E
Jin Xian = Jinzhou, *China* **56 E8** 38 2N 115 2 E
Jin Xian, *China* **57 E11** 38 55N 121 42 E
Jinan, *China* **56 F9** 36 38N 117 1 E
Jincheng, *China* **56 G7** 35 29N 112 50 E
Jinchuan, *China* **58 B4** 31 30N 102 3 E
Jind, *India* **68 E7** 29 19N 76 22 E
Jindabyne, *Australia* **95 F4** 36 25 S 148 35 E
Jindřichův Hradec, *Czech Rep.* **26 B8** 49 10N 15 2 E
Jing He →, *China* **56 G5** 34 27N 109 4 E
Jing Shan, *China* **59 B8** 31 20N 111 35 E
Jing Xian, *China* **59 B12** 30 38N 118 25 E
Jing'an, *China* **59 C10** 28 50N 115 17 E
Jingbian, *China* **56 F5** 37 20N 108 30 E
Jingchuan, *China* **56 G4** 35 20N 107 20 E
Jingde, *China* **59 B12** 30 15N 118 27 E
Jingdezhen, *China* **59 C11** 29 20N 117 11 E
Jingdong, *China* **58 E3** 24 23N 100 47 E
Jinggangshan, *China* **59 D10** 26 58N 114 15 E
Jinggu, *China* **58 F3** 23 35N 100 41 E
Jinghai, *China* **56 E9** 38 55N 116 55 E
Jinghong, *China* **58 G3** 22 0N 100 45 E
Jingjiang, *China* **59 A13** 32 2N 120 16 E
Jingle, *China* **56 E6** 38 20N 111 55 E
Jingmen, *China* **59 B9** 31 0N 112 10 E
Jingning, *China* **56 G3** 35 30N 105 43 E
Jingpo Hu, *China* **57 C15** 43 55N 128 55 E
Jingshan, *China* **59 B9** 31 1N 113 7 E
Jingtai, *China* **56 F3** 37 10N 104 6 E
Jingxi, *China* **58 F6** 23 8N 106 27 E
Jingxing, *China* **56 E8** 38 2N 114 8 E
Jingyang, *China* **56 G5** 34 30N 108 50 E
Jingyu, *China* **57 C14** 42 25N 126 45 E
Jingyuan, *China* **56 F3** 36 30N 104 40 E
Jingzhou, *China* **58 D7** 26 33N 109 40 E
Jingziguan, *China* **56 H6** 33 15N 111 0 E
Jinhua, *China* **59 C12** 29 8N 119 38 E
Jining, *Nei Monggol Zizhiqu, China* **56 D7** 41 5N 113 0 E
Jining, *Shandong, China* **56 G9** 35 22N 116 34 E
Jinja, *Uganda* **86 B3** 0 25N 33 12 E
Jinjang, *Malaysia* **65 L3** 3 13N 101 39 E
Jinji, *China* **56 F4** 37 58N 106 8 E
Jinjiang, *Fujian, China* **59 E12** 24 43N 118 33 E
Jinjiang, *Yunnan, China* **58 D3** 26 14N 100 34 E
Jinjini, *Ghana* **82 D4** 7 26N 2 42W
Jinkou, *China* **59 B10** 30 20N 114 8 E
Jinkouhe, *China* **58 C4** 29 18N 103 4 E
Jinmen Dao, *China* **59 E12** 24 25N 118 25 E
Jinnah Barrage, *Pakistan* **66 C7** 32 58N 71 33 E
Jinning, *China* **58 E4** 24 38N 102 38 E
Jinotega, *Nic.* **120 D2** 13 6N 85 59W
Jinotepe, *Nic.* **120 D2** 11 50N 86 10W
Jinping, *Guizhou, China* **58 D7** 26 41N 109 10 E
Jinping, *Yunnan, China* **58 F4** 22 45N 103 18 E
Jinsha, *China* **58 D6** 27 29N 106 12 E
Jinsha Jiang →, *China* **58 C5** 28 50N 104 36 E
Jinshan, *China* **59 B13** 30 54N 121 10 E
Jinshi, *China* **59 C8** 29 40N 111 50 E
Jintan, *China* **59 B12** 31 42N 119 36 E
Jinxi, *Jiangxi, China* **59 D11** 27 56N 116 45 E
Jinxi, *Liaoning, China* **57 D11** 40 52N 120 50 E
Jinxian, *China* **59 C11** 28 26N 116 17 E
Jinxiang, *China* **56 G9** 35 5N 116 22 E
Jinyang, *China* **58 D4** 27 28N 103 5 E
Jinyun, *China* **59 C13** 28 35N 120 5 E
Jinzhai, *China* **59 B10** 31 40N 115 53 E
Jinzhou, *Hebei, China* **56 E8** 38 2N 115 2 E
Jinzhou, *Liaoning, China* **57 D11** 41 5N 121 3 E
Jiparaná →, *Brazil* **124 E6** 8 3 S 62 52W
Jipijapa, *Ecuador* **124 D2** 1 0 S 80 40W
Jiquilpan, *Mexico* **118 D4** 19 57N 102 42W
Jishan, *China* **56 G6** 35 34N 110 58 E
Jishou, *China* **58 C7** 28 21N 109 43 E
Jishui, *China* **59 D10** 27 12N 115 8 E
Jisr ash Shughūr, *Syria* **70 C3** 35 49N 36 18 E
Jitarning, *Australia* **93 F2** 32 48 S 117 57 E
Jitra, *Malaysia* **65 J3** 6 16N 100 25 E
Jiu →, *Romania* **43 G8** 43 47N 23 48 E
Jiudengkou, *China* **56 E4** 39 56N 106 40 E
Jiujiang, *Guangdong, China* **59 F9** 22 50N 113 0 E
Jiujiang, *Jiangxi, China* **59 C10** 29 42N 115 58 E
Jiuling Shan, *China* **59 C10** 28 40N 114 40 E
Jiulong, *China* **58 C3** 28 57N 101 31 E
Jiutai, *China* **57 B13** 44 10N 125 50 E
Jiuxincheng, *China* **56 E8** 39 17N 115 59 E
Jiuyuhang, *China* **59 B12** 30 18N 119 56 E
Jixi, *Anhui, China* **59 B12** 30 5N 118 34 E
Jixi, *Heilongjiang, China* **57 B16** 45 20N 130 50 E
Jiyang, *China* **57 F9** 37 0N 117 12 E
Jiyuan, *China* **56 G7** 35 7N 112 57 E
Jīzān, *Si. Arabia* **74 D3** 17 0N 42 20 E
Jize, *China* **56 F8** 36 54N 114 56 E
Jizera →, *Czech Rep.* **26 A7** 50 10N 14 43 E
Jizl, W. →, *Si. Arabia* **80 B4** 25 39N 38 25 E
Jizl, Wādī al, *Si. Arabia* **70 E3** 25 39N 38 25 E
Jizō-Zaki, *Japan* **55 G6** 35 34N 133 20 E
Jizzakh, *Uzbekistan* **50 E7** 40 6N 67 50 E
Joaçaba, *Brazil* **127 B5** 27 5 S 51 31W
Joal Fadiout, *Senegal* **82 C1** 14 9N 16 50W
João Pessoa, *Brazil* **125 E12** 7 10 S 34 52W
Joaquín V. González, *Argentina* **126 B3** 25 10 S 64 0W
Jobat, *India* **68 H6** 22 25N 74 34 E
Jobourg, Nez de, *France* **18 C5** 49 41N 1 57W
Jódar, *Spain* **35 H7** 37 50N 3 21W
Jodhpur, *India* **68 F5** 26 23N 73 8 E
Jodiya, *India* **68 H4** 22 42N 70 18 E
Jōetsu, *Japan* **55 F9** 37 12N 138 10 E
Jœuf, *France* **19 C12** 49 12N 6 0 E
Jofane, *Mozam.* **89 C5** 21 15 S 34 18 E
Jogbani, *India* **69 F12** 26 25N 87 15 E
Jõgeva, *Estonia* **9 G22** 58 45N 26 24 E
Jogjakarta = Yogyakarta, *Indonesia* **63 G14** 7 49 S 110 22 E
Johannesburg, *S. Africa* **89 D4** 26 10 S 28 2 E
Johannesburg, *U.S.A.* **117 K9** 35 22N 117 38W
Johansfors, *Sweden* **11 H9** 56 42N 15 32 E
Johilla →, *India* **69 H9** 23 37N 81 14 E
John Day, *U.S.A.* **114 D4** 44 25N 118 57W
John Day →, *U.S.A.* **114 D3** 45 44N 120 39W
John D'Or Prairie, *Canada* **104 B5** 58 30N 115 8W
John H. Kerr Reservoir, *U.S.A.* **109 G6** 36 36N 78 18W
John o' Groats, *U.K.* **14 C5** 58 38N 3 4W
Johnnie, *U.S.A.* **117 J10** 36 25N 116 5W
John's Ra., *Australia* **94 C1** 21 55 S 133 23 E
Johnson, *Kans., U.S.A.* **113 G4** 37 34N 101 45W
Johnson, *Vt., U.S.A.* **111 B12** 44 38N 72 41W
Johnson City, *N.Y., U.S.A.* **111 D9** 42 7N 75 58W
Johnson City, *Tenn., U.S.A.* **109 G4** 36 19N 82 21W
Johnson City, *Tex., U.S.A.* **113 K5** 30 17N 98 25W
Johnsonburg, *U.S.A.* **110 E6** 41 29N 78 41W
Johnsondale, *U.S.A.* **117 K8** 35 58N 118 32W
Johnson's Crossing, *Canada* **104 A2** 60 29N 133 18W
Johnston, L., *Australia* **93 F3** 32 25 S 120 30 E
Johnston Falls = Mambilima Falls, *Zambia* **87 E2** 10 31 S 28 45 E
Johnston I., *Pac. Oc.* **97 F11** 17 10N 169 8W
Johnstone Str., *Canada* **104 C3** 50 28N 126 0W
Johnstown, *N.Y., U.S.A.* **111 C10** 43 0N 74 22W
Johnstown, *Ohio, U.S.A.* **110 F2** 40 9N 82 41W
Johnstown, *Pa., U.S.A.* **110 F6** 40 20N 78 55W
Johor Baharu, *Malaysia* **65 M4** 1 28N 103 46 E
Jõhvi, *Estonia* **9 G22** 59 22N 27 27 E
Joigny, *France* **19 E10** 47 58N 3 20 E
Joinville, *Brazil* **127 B6** 26 15 S 48 55W
Joinville, *France* **19 D12** 48 27N 5 10 E
Joinville I., *Antarctica* **5 C18** 65 0 S 55 30W
Jojutla, *Mexico* **119 D5** 18 37N 99 11W
Jokkmokk, *Sweden* **8 C18** 66 35N 19 50 E
Jökulsá á Bru →, *Iceland* **8 D6** 65 40N 14 16W
Jökulsá á Fjöllum →, *Iceland* **8 C5** 66 10N 16 30W
Jolfā, *Āzarbājān-e Sharqī, Iran* **70 B5** 38 57N 45 38 E
Jolfā, *Eşfahan, Iran* **71 C6** 32 58N 51 37 E
Joliet, *U.S.A.* **108 E1** 41 32N 88 5W
Joliette, *Canada* **102 C5** 46 3N 73 24W
Jolo, *Phil.* **61 J4** 6 0N 121 0 E
Jolon, *U.S.A.* **116 K5** 35 58N 121 9W
Jomalig I., *Phil.* **61 D5** 14 42N 122 22 E
Jombang, *Indonesia* **63 G15** 7 33 S 112 14 E
Jomda, *China* **58 B2** 31 28N 98 12 E
Jonava, *Lithuania* **9 J21** 55 8N 24 12 E
Jones Sound, *Canada* **4 B3** 76 0N 85 0W
Jonesboro, *Ark., U.S.A.* **113 H9** 35 50N 90 42W
Jonesboro, *La., U.S.A.* **113 J8** 32 15N 92 43W
Jong →, *S. Leone* **82 D2** 7 32N 12 23W
Jonglei, *Sudan* **81 F3** 6 25N 30 50 E
Jonglei □, *Sudan* **81 F3** 7 30N 32 30 E
Joniškis, *Lithuania* **9 H20** 56 13N 23 35 E
Jönköping, *Sweden* **11 G8** 57 45N 14 8 E
Jönköpings län □, *Sweden* **11 G8** 57 30N 14 30 E
Jonquière, *Canada* **103 C5** 48 27N 71 14W
Jonsered, *Sweden* **11 G6** 57 45N 12 10 E
Jonzac, *France* **20 C3** 45 27N 0 28W
Joplin, *U.S.A.* **113 G7** 37 6N 94 31W
Jora, *India* **68 F6** 26 20N 77 49 E
Jordan, *Mont., U.S.A.* **114 C10** 47 19N 106 55W
Jordan, *N.Y., U.S.A.* **111 C8** 43 4N 76 29W
Jordan ■, *Asia* **75 E5** 31 0N 36 0 E
Jordan →, *Asia* **75 D4** 31 48N 35 32 E
Jordan Valley, *U.S.A.* **114 E5** 42 59N 117 3W
Jordanów, *Poland* **45 J6** 49 41N 19 49 E
Jorhat, *India* **67 F19** 26 45N 94 12 E
Jörn, *Sweden* **8 D19** 65 4N 20 1 E
Jorong, *Indonesia* **62 E4** 3 58 S 114 56 E
Jørpeland, *Norway* **9 G11** 59 3N 6 1 E
Jorquera →, *Chile* **126 B2** 28 3 S 69 58W
Jos, *Nigeria* **83 D6** 9 53N 8 51 E
Jos Plateau, *Nigeria* **83 D6** 9 55N 9 0 E
Jošanička Banja, *Serbia, Yug.* **40 C4** 43 24N 20 47 E
José Batlle y Ordóñez, *Uruguay* **127 C4** 33 20 S 55 10W
Joseni, *Romania* **43 D10** 46 42N 25 29 E
Joseph, L., *Nfld., Canada* **103 B6** 52 45N 65 18W
Joseph, L., *Ont., Canada* **110 A5** 45 10N 79 44W
Joseph Bonaparte G., *Australia* **92 B4** 14 35 S 128 50 E
Joshinath, *India* **69 D8** 30 34N 79 34 E
Joshua Tree, *U.S.A.* **117 L10** 34 8N 116 19W
Joshua Tree National Park, *U.S.A.* **117 M10** 33 55N 116 0W
Josselin, *France* **18 E4** 47 57N 2 33W
Jostedalsbreen, *Norway* **9 F12** 61 40N 6 59 E
Jotunheimen, *Norway* **9 F13** 61 35N 8 25 E
Joubertberge, *Namibia* **88 B1** 18 30 S 14 0 E
Joué-lès-Tours, *France* **18 E7** 47 21N 0 40 E
Jourdanton, *U.S.A.* **113 L5** 28 55N 98 33W
Joutseno, *Finland* **46 B5** 61 7N 28 31 E
Jovellanos, *Cuba* **120 B3** 22 40N 81 10W
Joyeuse, *France* **21 D8** 44 29N 4 16 E
Józefów, *Lubelskie, Poland* **45 H10** 50 28N 23 2 E
Józefów, *Mazowieckie, Poland* **45 F8** 52 10N 21 11 E
Ju Xian, *China* **57 F10** 36 35N 118 20 E
Juan Aldama, *Mexico* **118 C4** 24 20N 103 23W
Juan Bautista Alberdi, *Argentina* **126 C3** 34 26 S 61 48W
Juan de Fuca Str., *Canada* **116 B3** 48 15N 124 0W
Juan de Nova, *Ind. Oc.* **89 B7** 17 3 S 43 45 E
Juan Fernández, Arch. de, *Pac. Oc.* **122 G2** 33 50 S 80 0W
Juan José Castelli, *Argentina* **126 B3** 25 27 S 60 57W
Juan L. Lacaze, *Uruguay* **126 C4** 34 26 S 57 25W
Juankoski, *Finland* **8 E23** 63 3N 28 19 E
Juárez, *Argentina* **126 D4** 37 40 S 59 43W
Juárez, *Mexico* **117 N11** 32 20N 115 57W
Juárez, Sierra de, *Mexico* **118 A1** 32 0N 116 0W
Juàzeiro, *Brazil* **125 E10** 9 30 S 40 30W
Juàzeiro do Norte, *Brazil* **125 E11** 7 10 S 39 18W
Juba, *Sudan* **81 G3** 4 50N 31 35 E
Jubayl, *Lebanon* **75 A4** 34 5N 35 39 E
Jubbah, *Si. Arabia* **70 D4** 28 2N 40 56 E
Jubbal, *India* **68 D7** 31 5N 77 40 E
Jubbulpore = Jabalpur, *India* **69 H8** 23 9N 79 58 E
Jübek, *Germany* **24 A5** 54 33N 9 22 E
Jubga, *Russia* **49 H4** 44 19N 38 48 E
Jubilee L., *Australia* **93 E4** 29 0 S 126 50 E
Juby, C., *Morocco* **78 C3** 28 0N 12 59W
Júcar = Xúquer →, *Spain* **33 F4** 39 5N 0 10W
Júcaro, *Cuba* **120 B4** 21 37N 78 51W
Juchitán, *Mexico* **119 D5** 16 27N 95 5W
Judaea = Har Yehuda, *Israel* **75 D3** 31 35N 34 57 E
Judenburg, *Austria* **26 D7** 47 12N 14 38 E
Judith →, *U.S.A.* **114 C9** 47 44N 109 39W
Judith, Pt., *U.S.A.* **111 E13** 41 22N 71 29W
Judith Gap, *U.S.A.* **114 C9** 46 41N 109 45W
Juelsminde, *Denmark* **11 J4** 55 43N 10 1 E
Jugoslavia = Yugoslavia ■, *Europe* **40 C4** 43 20N 20 0 E
Juigalpa, *Nic.* **120 D2** 12 6N 85 26W
Juillac, *France* **20 C5** 45 20N 1 19 E
Juist, *Germany* **24 B2** 53 40N 6 59 E
Juiz de Fora, *Brazil* **127 A7** 21 43 S 43 19W
Jujuy □, *Argentina* **126 A2** 23 20 S 65 40W
Julesburg, *U.S.A.* **112 E3** 40 59N 102 16W
Juli, *Peru* **124 G5** 16 10 S 69 25W
Julia Cr. →, *Australia* **94 C3** 20 0 S 141 11 E
Julia Creek, *Australia* **94 C3** 20 39 S 141 44 E
Juliaca, *Peru* **124 G4** 15 25 S 70 10W
Julian, *U.S.A.* **117 M10** 33 4N 116 38W
Julian Alps = Julijske Alpe, *Slovenia* **29 B11** 46 15N 14 1 E
Julian L., *Canada* **102 B4** 54 25N 77 57W
Julianatop, *Surinam* **125 C7** 3 40N 56 30W
Julianehåb = Qaqortoq, *Greenland* **4 C5** 60 43N 46 0W
Jülich, *Germany* **24 E2** 50 55N 6 22 E
Julijske Alpe, *Slovenia* **29 B11** 46 15N 14 1 E
Julimes, *Mexico* **118 B3** 28 25N 105 27W
Jullundur, *India* **68 D6** 31 20N 75 40 E
Julu, *China* **56 F8** 37 15N 115 2 E
Jumbo, *Zimbabwe* **87 F3** 17 30 S 30 58 E
Jumbo Pk., *U.S.A.* **117 J12** 36 12N 114 11W
Jumentos Cays, *Bahamas* **120 B4** 23 0N 75 40W
Jumilla, *Spain* **33 G3** 38 28N 1 19W
Jumla, *Nepal* **69 E10** 29 15N 82 13 E
Jumna = Yamuna →, *India* **69 G9** 25 30N 81 53 E
Junagadh, *India* **68 J4** 21 30N 70 30 E
Junction, *Tex., U.S.A.* **113 K5** 30 29N 99 46W
Junction, *Utah, U.S.A.* **115 G7** 38 14N 112 13W
Junction B., *Australia* **94 A1** 11 52 S 133 55 E
Junction City, *Kans., U.S.A.* **112 F6** 39 2N 96 50W
Junction City, *Oreg., U.S.A.* **114 D2** 44 13N 123 12W
Junction Pt., *Australia* **94 A1** 11 45 S 133 50 E
Jundah, *Australia* **94 C3** 24 46 S 143 2 E
Jundiaí, *Brazil* **127 A6** 24 30 S 47 0W
Juneau, *U.S.A.* **104 B2** 58 18N 134 25W
Junee, *Australia* **95 E4** 34 53 S 147 35 E
Jungfrau, *Switz.* **25 J3** 46 32N 7 58 E
Junggar Pendi, *China* **60 B3** 44 30N 86 0 E
Jungshahi, *Pakistan* **68 G2** 24 52N 67 44 E
Juniata →, *U.S.A.* **110 F7** 40 30N 77 40W
Junín, *Argentina* **126 C3** 34 33 S 60 57W
Junín de los Andes, *Argentina* **128 D2** 39 45 S 71 0W
Jūniyah, *Lebanon* **75 B4** 33 59N 35 38 E
Junlian, *China* **58 C5** 28 8N 104 29 E
Juntas, *Chile* **126 B2** 28 24 S 69 58W
Juntura, *U.S.A.* **114 E4** 43 45N 118 5W
Jur, Nahr el →, *Sudan* **81 F2** 8 45N 29 15 E
Jura = Jura, Mts. du, *Europe* **19 F13** 46 40N 6 5 E
Jura = Schwäbische Alb, *Germany* **25 G5** 48 20N 9 30 E
Jura, *U.K.* **14 F3** 56 0N 5 50W
Jura □, *France* **19 F12** 46 47N 5 45 E
Jura □, *Switz.* **25 H3** 47 20N 7 20 E
Jūra →, *Lithuania* **44 C9** 55 3N 22 9 E
Jura, Mts. du, *Europe* **19 F13** 46 40N 6 5 E
Jura, Sd. of, *U.K.* **14 F3** 55 57N 5 45W
Jurbarkas, *Lithuania* **9 J20** 55 4N 22 46 E
Jurien, *Australia* **93 F2** 30 18 S 115 2 E
Jurilovca, *Romania* **43 F13** 44 46N 28 52 E
Jūrmala, *Latvia* **9 H20** 56 58N 23 34 E
Jurong, *China* **59 B12** 31 57N 119 9 E
Juruá →, *Brazil* **122 D4** 2 37 S 65 44W
Juruena, *Brazil* **124 F7** 13 0 S 58 10W
Juruena →, *Brazil* **124 E7** 7 20 S 58 3W
Juruti, *Brazil* **125 D7** 2 9 S 56 4W
Jussey, *France* **19 E12** 47 50N 5 55 E
Justo Daract, *Argentina* **126 C2** 33 52 S 65 12W
Jutaí →, *Brazil* **124 D5** 2 43 S 66 57W
Jüterbog, *Germany* **24 D9** 51 59N 13 5 E
Juticalpa, *Honduras* **120 D2** 14 40N 86 12W
Jutland = Jylland, *Denmark* **11 H3** 56 25N 9 30 E
Juventud, I. de la, *Cuba* **120 B3** 21 40N 82 40W
Juvigny-sous-Andaine, *France* **18 D6** 48 32N 0 30W
Juwain, *Afghan.* **66 D2** 31 45N 61 30 E
Jūy Zar, *Iran* **70 C5** 33 50N 46 18 E
Juye, *China* **56 G9** 35 22N 116 5 E
Juzennecourt, *France* **19 D11** 48 10N 4 58 E
Jvari, *Georgia* **49 J6** 42 42N 42 4 E
Jwaneng, *Botswana* **85 J4** 24 45 S 24 50 E
Jyderup, *Denmark* **11 J5** 55 40N 11 26 E
Jylland, *Denmark* **11 H3** 56 25N 9 30 E
Jyväskylä, *Finland* **9 E21** 62 14N 25 50 E

K

K2, *Pakistan* **69 B7** 35 58N 76 32 E
Ka →, *Nigeria* **83 C5** 11 40N 4 10 E
Kaap Plateau, *S. Africa* **88 D3** 28 30 S 24 0 E
Kaapkruis, *Namibia* **88 C1** 21 55 S 13 57 E
Kaapstad = Cape Town, *S. Africa* **88 E2** 33 55 S 18 22 E
Kaba, *Guinea* **82 C2** 10 9N 11 40W
Kabaena, *Indonesia* **63 F6** 5 15 S 122 0 E
Kabala, *S. Leone* **82 D2** 9 38N 11 37W
Kabale, *Uganda* **86 C3** 1 15 S 30 0 E
Kabalo, *Dem. Rep. of the Congo* **86 D2** 6 0 S 27 0 E
Kabambare, *Dem. Rep. of the Congo* **86 C2** 4 41 S 27 39 E
Kabango, *Dem. Rep. of the Congo* **87 D2** 8 35 S 28 30 E
Kabanjahe, *Indonesia* **62 D1** 3 6N 98 30 E
Kabankalan, *Phil.* **61 G5** 9 59N 122 49 E
Kabara, *Mali* **82 B4** 16 40N 2 50W
Kabardinka, *Russia* **47 K10** 44 40N 37 57 E
Kabardino-Balkar Republic = Kabardino-Balkaria □, *Russia* **49 J6** 43 30N 43 30 E
Kabardino-Balkaria □, *Russia* **49 J6** 43 30N 43 30 E
Kabarega Falls = Murchison Falls, *Uganda* **86 B3** 2 15N 31 30 E
Kabasalan, *Phil.* **61 H5** 7 47N 122 44 E
Kabba, *Nigeria* **83 D6** 7 50N 6 3 E
Kabetogama, *U.S.A.* **112 A8** 48 28N 92 59W
Kabi, *Niger* **83 C7** 13 30N 12 35 E
Kabin Buri, *Thailand* **64 F3** 13 57N 101 43 E
Kabinakagami L., *Canada* **102 C3** 48 54N 84 25W
Kabinda, *Dem. Rep. of the Congo* **84 F4** 6 19 S 24 20 E
Kabna, *Sudan* **80 D3** 19 6N 32 40 E
Kabompo, *Zambia* **87 E1** 13 36 S 24 14 E
Kabompo →, *Zambia* **85 G4** 14 10 S 23 11 E
Kabondo, *Dem. Rep. of the Congo* **87 D2** 8 58 S 25 40 E
Kabongo, *Dem. Rep. of the Congo* **86 D2** 7 22 S 25 33 E
Kabot, *Guinea* **82 C2** 10 48N 14 57W
Kabou, *Togo* **83 D5** 9 28N 0 55 E
Kabr, *Sudan* **81 E2** 10 54N 26 50 E
Kabūd Gonbad, *Iran* **71 B8** 37 5N 59 45 E
Kabugao, *Phil.* **61 B4** 18 2N 121 11 E
Kābul, *Afghan.* **68 B3** 34 28N 69 11 E
Kābul □, *Afghan.* **66 B6** 34 30N 69 0 E
Kabul →, *Pakistan* **68 C5** 33 55N 72 14 E
Kabunga, *Dem. Rep. of the Congo* **86 C2** 1 38 S 28 3 E
Kaburuang, *Indonesia* **63 D7** 3 50N 126 30 E
Kabushiya, *Sudan* **81 D3** 16 54N 33 41 E
Kabwe, *Zambia* **87 E2** 14 30 S 28 29 E
Kačanik, *Kosovo, Yug.* **40 D5** 42 13N 21 12 E
Kačerginė, *Lithuania* **44 D10** 54 56N 23 42 E
Kachchh, Gulf of, *India* **68 H3** 22 50N 69 15 E
Kachchh, Rann of, *India* **68 H4** 24 0N 70 0 E
Kachchhidhana, *India* **69 J8** 21 44N 78 46 E
Kachebera, *Zambia* **87 E3** 13 50 S 32 50 E
Kachia, *Nigeria* **83 D6** 9 50N 7 55 E
Kachikau, *Botswana* **88 B3** 18 8 S 24 26 E
Kachin □, *Burma* **58 D1** 26 0N 97 30 E
Kachira, L., *Uganda* **86 C3** 0 40 S 31 7 E
Kachiry, *Kazakstan* **50 D8** 53 10N 75 50 E
Kachisi, *Ethiopia* **81 F4** 9 40N 37 50 E
Kachnara, *India* **68 H6** 23 50N 75 6 E
Kachot, *Cambodia* **65 G4** 11 30N 103 3 E
Kaçkar, *Turkey* **73 B9** 40 45N 41 10 E
Kadan, *Czech Rep.* **26 A6** 50 23N 13 16 E
Kadan Kyun, *Burma* **64 F2** 12 30N 98 20 E
Kadanai →, *Afghan.* **68 D1** 31 22N 65 45 E
Kadarkút, *Hungary* **42 D2** 46 13N 17 39 E
Kade, *Ghana* **83 D4** 6 7N 0 56W
Kadi, *India* **68 H5** 23 18N 72 23 E
Kadina, *Australia* **95 E2** 33 55 S 137 43 E
Kadınhanı, *Turkey* **72 C5** 38 14N 32 13 E
Kadiolo, *Mali* **82 C3** 10 35N 7 41W
Kadipur, *India* **69 F10** 26 10N 82 23 E
Kadirli, *Turkey* **70 B3** 37 23N 36 5 E
Kadiyevka = Stakhanov, *Ukraine* **47 H10** 48 35N 38 40 E
Kadodo, *Sudan* **81 E2** 11 4N 29 31 E
Kadoka, *U.S.A.* **112 D4** 43 50N 101 31W
Kadom, *Russia* **48 C6** 54 37N 42 30 E
Kadoma, *Zimbabwe* **87 F2** 18 20 S 29 52 E
Kâdugli, *Sudan* **81 E2** 11 0N 29 45 E
Kaduna, *Nigeria* **83 C6** 10 30N 7 21 E
Kaduna □, *Nigeria* **83 C6** 11 0N 7 30 E
Kaduy, *Russia* **46 C9** 59 12N 37 9 E
Kaédi, *Mauritania* **82 B2** 16 9N 13 28W
Kaélé, *Cameroon* **83 C7** 10 7N 14 27 E
Kaeng Khoï, *Thailand* **64 E3** 14 35N 101 0 E
Kaesŏng, *N. Korea* **57 F14** 37 58N 126 35 E
Kāf, *Si. Arabia* **70 D3** 31 25N 37 29 E
Kafan = Kapan, *Armenia* **70 B5** 39 18N 46 27 E
Kafanchan, *Nigeria* **83 D6** 9 40N 8 20 E
Kafareti, *Nigeria* **83 C7** 10 25N 11 12 E
Kaffrine, *Senegal* **82 C1** 14 8N 15 36W
Kafin, *Nigeria* **83 D6** 9 30N 7 4 E
Kafin Madaki, *Nigeria* **83 C6** 10 41N 9 46 E
Kafinda, *Zambia* **87 E3** 12 32 S 30 20 E
Kafirévs, Ákra, *Greece* **38 C6** 38 9N 24 38 E
Kafr el Battikh, *Egypt* **80 H7** 31 25N 31 44 E
Kafr el Dauwâr, *Egypt* **80 H7** 31 8N 30 8 E
Kafr el Sheikh, *Egypt* **80 H7** 31 15N 30 50 E
Kafue, *Zambia* **87 F2** 15 46 S 28 9 E
Kafue →, *Zambia* **85 H5** 15 30 S 29 0 E
Kafue Flats, *Zambia* **87 F2** 15 40 S 27 25 E
Kafue Nat. Park, *Zambia* **87 F2** 15 0 S 25 30 E
Kafulwe, *Zambia* **87 D2** 9 0 S 29 1 E
Kaga, *Afghan.* **68 B4** 34 14N 70 10 E
Kaga Bandoro, *C.A.R.* **84 C3** 7 0N 19 10 E
Kagan, *Uzbekistan* **50 F7** 39 43N 64 33 E
Kagarko, *Nigeria* **83 D6** 9 28N 7 36 E
Kagawa □, *Japan* **55 G7** 34 15N 134 0 E
Kagera = Ziwa Maghariba □, *Tanzania* **86 C3** 2 0 S 31 30 E
Kagera →, *Uganda* **86 C3** 0 57 S 31 47 E
Kağızman, *Turkey* **70 B4** 40 5N 43 10 E
Kagmar, *Sudan* **81 E3** 14 24N 30 25 E
Kagoshima, *Japan* **55 J5** 31 35N 130 33 E
Kagoshima □, *Japan* **55 J5** 31 30N 130 30 E
Kagul = Cahul, *Moldova* **43 E13** 45 50N 28 15 E
Kahak, *Iran* **71 B6** 36 6N 49 46 E
Kahama, *Tanzania* **86 C3** 4 8 S 32 30 E
Kahan, *Pakistan* **68 E3** 29 18N 68 54 E
Kahang, *Malaysia* **65 L4** 2 12N 103 32 E
Kahayan →, *Indonesia* **62 E4** 3 40 S 114 0 E
Kahe, *Tanzania* **86 C4** 3 30 S 37 25 E
Kahnūj, *Iran* **71 E8** 27 55N 57 40 E
Kahoka, *U.S.A.* **112 E9** 40 25N 91 44W
Kahoolawe, *U.S.A.* **106 H16** 20 33N 156 37W
Kahramanmaraş, *Turkey* **70 B3** 37 37N 36 53 E
Kâhta, *Turkey* **73 D8** 37 46N 38 36 E
Kahuta, *Pakistan* **68 C5** 33 35N 73 24 E
Kai, Kepulauan, *Indonesia* **63 F8** 5 55 S 132 45 E
Kai Besar, *Indonesia* **63 F8** 5 35 S 133 0 E
Kai Is. = Kai, Kepulauan, *Indonesia* **63 F8** 5 55 S 132 45 E
Kai Kecil, *Indonesia* **63 F8** 5 45 S 132 40 E
Kai Xian, *China* **58 B7** 31 11N 108 21 E
Kaiama, *Nigeria* **83 D5** 9 36N 4 1 E
Kaiapoi, *N.Z.* **91 K4** 43 24 S 172 40 E
Kaieteur Falls, *Guyana* **124 B7** 5 1N 59 10W
Kaifeng, *China* **56 G8** 34 48N 114 21 E
Kaihua, *China* **59 C12** 29 12N 118 20 E
Kaijiang, *China* **58 B6** 31 7N 107 55 E
Kaikohe, *N.Z.* **91 F4** 35 25 S 173 49 E
Kaikoura, *N.Z.* **91 K4** 42 25 S 173 43 E
Kaikoura Ra., *N.Z.* **91 J4** 41 59 S 173 41 E
Kailahun, *S. Leone* **82 D2** 8 18N 10 39W
Kaili, *China* **58 D6** 26 33N 107 59 E
Kailu, *China* **57 C11** 43 38N 121 18 E
Kailua Kona, *U.S.A.* **106 J17** 19 39N 155 59W
Kaimana, *Indonesia* **63 E8** 3 39 S 133 45 E
Kaimanawa Mts., *N.Z.* **91 H5** 39 15 S 175 56 E
Kaimganj, *India* **69 F8** 27 33N 79 24 E
Kaimur Hills, *India* **69 G10** 24 30N 82 0 E
Kainab →, *Namibia* **88 D2** 28 32 S 19 34 E
Kaingaroa Forest, *N.Z.* **91 H6** 38 24 S 176 30 E
Kainji Dam, *Nigeria* **83 D5** 9 55N 4 35 E
Kainji Res., *Nigeria* **83 C5** 10 1N 4 40 E
Kainuu, *Finland* **8 D23** 64 30N 29 7 E
Kaipara Harbour, *N.Z.* **91 G5** 36 25 S 174 14 E
Kaiping, *China* **59 F9** 22 23N 112 42 E
Kaipokok B., *Canada* **103 B8** 54 54N 59 47W
Kaira, *India* **68 H5** 22 45N 72 50 E
Kairana, *India* **68 E7** 29 24N 77 15 E
Kaironi, *Indonesia* **63 E8** 0 47 S 133 40 E
Kairouan, *Tunisia* **79 A8** 35 45N 10 5 E
Kaiserslautern, *Germany* **25 F3** 49 26N 7 45 E
Kaiserstuhl, *Germany* **25 G3** 48 4N 7 40 E
Kaitaia, *N.Z.* **91 F4** 35 8 S 173 17 E
Kaitangata, *N.Z.* **91 M2** 46 17 S 169 51 E
Kaithal, *India* **68 E7** 29 48N 76 26 E
Kaitu →, *Pakistan* **68 C4** 33 10N 70 30 E
Kaiwi Channel, *U.S.A.* **106 H16** 21 15N 157 30W
Kaiyang, *China* **58 D6** 27 4N 106 59 E
Kaiyuan, *Liaoning, China* **57 C13** 42 28N 124 1 E
Kaiyuan, *Yunnan, China* **58 F4** 23 40N 103 12 E
Kajaani, *Finland* **8 D22** 64 17N 27 46 E
Kajabbi, *Australia* **94 C3** 20 0 S 140 1 E
Kajana = Kajaani, *Finland* **8 D22** 64 17N 27 46 E
Kajang, *Malaysia* **65 L3** 2 59N 101 48 E
Kajaran, *Armenia* **73 C12** 39 10N 46 7 E
Kajiado, *Kenya* **86 C4** 1 53 S 36 48 E
Kajo Kaji, *Sudan* **81 G3** 3 58N 31 40 E
Kajuru, *Nigeria* **83 C6** 10 15N 7 34 E
Kaka, *Sudan* **81 E3** 10 38N 32 10 E
Kakabeka Falls, *Canada* **102 C2** 48 24N 89 37W
Kakadu Nat. Park, *Australia* **92 B5** 12 30 S 132 5 E
Kakamas, *S. Africa* **88 D3** 28 45 S 20 33 E
Kakamega, *Kenya* **86 B3** 0 20N 34 46 E
Kakanj, *Bos.-H.* **42 F3** 44 4N 18 4 E
Kakanui Mts., *N.Z.* **91 L3** 45 10 S 170 30 E
Kakata, *Liberia* **82 D2** 6 35N 10 20W
Kakdwip, *India* **69 J13** 21 53N 88 11 E
Kake, *Japan* **55 G6** 34 36N 132 19 E
Kake, *U.S.A.* **104 B2** 56 59N 133 57W
Kakegawa, *Japan* **55 G9** 34 45N 138 1 E
Kakeroma-Jima, *Japan* **55 K4** 28 8N 129 14 E
Kakhib, *Russia* **49 J8** 42 28N 46 34 E
Kakhovka, *Ukraine* **47 J7** 46 45N 33 30 E
Kakhovske Vdskh., *Ukraine* **47 J7** 47 5N 34 0 E
Kakinada, *India* **67 L13** 16 57N 82 11 E
Kakisa →, *Canada* **104 A5** 61 3N 118 10W
Kakisa L., *Canada* **104 A5** 60 56N 117 43W
Kakogawa, *Japan* **55 G7** 34 46N 134 51 E
Kakwa →, *Canada* **104 C5** 54 37N 118 28W
Kāl Gūsheh, *Iran* **71 D8** 30 59N 58 12 E
Kal Safīd, *Iran* **70 C5** 34 52N 47 23 E
Kala, *Nigeria* **83 C7** 12 2N 14 40 E
Kalaallit Nunaat = Greenland ■, *N. Amer.* **4 C5** 66 0N 45 0W
Kalabagh, *Pakistan* **68 C4** 33 0N 71 28 E
Kalabahi, *Indonesia* **63 F6** 8 13 S 124 31 E
Kalabáka, *Greece* **38 B3** 39 42N 21 39 E
Kalabana, *Mali* **82 C3** 14 10N 8 35W
Kalach, *Russia* **48 E5** 50 22N 41 0 E
Kalach na Donu, *Russia* **49 F6** 48 43N 43 32 E
Kaladan →, *Burma* **67 J18** 20 20N 93 5 E
Kaladar, *Canada* **102 D4** 44 37N 77 5W
Kalahari, *Africa* **88 C3** 24 0 S 21 30 E
Kalahari Gemsbok Nat. Park, *S. Africa* **88 D3** 25 30 S 20 30 E
Kalajoki, *Finland* **8 D20** 64 12N 24 10 E
Kālak, *Iran* **71 E8** 25 29N 59 22 E
Kalakamati, *Botswana* **89 C4** 20 40 S 27 25 E
Kalakan, *Russia* **51 D12** 55 15N 116 45 E
K'alak'unlun Shank'ou = Karakoram Pass, *Pakistan* **69 B7** 35 33N 77 50 E
Kalam, *Pakistan* **69 B5** 35 34N 72 30 E
Kalama, *Dem. Rep. of the Congo* **86 C2** 2 52 S 28 35 E
Kalama, *U.S.A.* **116 E4** 46 1N 122 51W
Kalámai, *Greece* **38 D4** 37 3N 22 10 E
Kalamariá, *Greece* **40 F6** 40 33N 22 55 E
Kalamata = Kalámai, *Greece* **38 D4** 37 3N 22 10 E
Kalamazoo, *U.S.A.* **108 D3** 42 17N 85 35W
Kalamazoo →, *U.S.A.* **108 D2** 42 40N 86 10W
Kalambo Falls, *Tanzania* **87 D3** 8 37 S 31 35 E
Kálamos, *Attikí, Greece* **38 C5** 38 17N 23 52 E
Kálamos, *Iónioi Nísoi, Greece* **38 C2** 38 37N 20 55 E
Kalan, *Turkey* **70 B3** 39 7N 39 32 E
Kalankalan, *Guinea* **82 C3** 10 7N 8 54W
Kalannie, *Australia* **93 F2** 30 22 S 117 5 E
Kalāntarī, *Iran* **71 C7** 32 10N 54 8 E
Kalao, *Indonesia* **63 F6** 7 21 S 121 0 E
Kalaotoa, *Indonesia* **63 F6** 7 20 S 121 50 E
Kälarne, *Sweden* **10 B10** 62 59N 16 5 E

Kalasin, *Thailand* **64 D4** 16 26N 103 30 E
Kalat, *Pakistan* **66 E5** 29 8N 66 31 E
Kalāteh, *Iran* **71 B7** 36 33N 55 41 E
Kalāteh-ye Ganj, *Iran* **71 E8** 27 31N 57 55 E
Kálathos, *Greece* **39 E10** 36 9N 28 8 E
Kalaus →, *Russia* **49 H7** 45 40N 44 7 E
Kalávrita, *Greece* **38 C4** 38 3N 22 8 E
Kalbarri, *Australia* **93 E1** 27 40 S 114 10 E
Kale, *Antalya, Turkey* **39 E12** 36 14N 30 0 E
Kale, *Denizli, Turkey* **39 D10** 37 27N 28 49 E
Kalecik, *Turkey* **72 B5** 40 4N 33 26 E
Kalegauk Kyun, *Burma* **67 M20** 15 33N 97 35 E
Kalehe, *Dem. Rep. of the Congo* **86 C2** 2 6 S 28 50 E
Kalema, *Tanzania* **86 C3** 1 12 S 31 55 E
Kalemie, *Dem. Rep. of the Congo* **86 D2** 5 55 S 29 9 E
Kalety, *Poland* **45 H5** 50 35N 18 52 E
Kalewa, *Burma* **67 H19** 23 10N 94 15 E
Kaleybar, *Iran* **70 B5** 38 47N 47 2 E
Kalgan = Zhangjiakou, *China* **56 D8** 40 48N 114 55 E
Kalgoorlie-Boulder, *Australia* **93 F3** 30 40 S 121 22 E
Kali →, *India* **69 F8** 27 6N 79 55 E
Kali Sindh →, *India* **68 G6** 25 32N 76 17 E
Kaliakra, Nos, *Bulgaria* **41 C12** 43 21N 28 30 E
Kalianda, *Indonesia* **62 F3** 5 50 S 105 45 E
Kalibo, *Phil.* **61 F5** 11 43N 122 22 E
Kalima, *Dem. Rep. of the Congo* **86 C2** 2 33 S 26 32 E
Kalimantan □, *Indonesia* **62 E4** 0 0 114 0 E
Kalimantan Barat □, *Indonesia* **62 E4** 0 0 110 30 E
Kalimantan Selatan □, *Indonesia* **62 E5** 2 30 S 115 30 E
Kalimantan Tengah □, *Indonesia* **62 E4** 2 0 S 113 30 E
Kalimantan Timur □, *Indonesia* **62 D5** 1 30N 116 30 E
Kálimnos, *Greece* **39 D8** 37 0N 27 0 E
Kalimpong, *India* **69 F13** 27 4N 88 35 E
Kalinin = Tver, *Russia* **46 D8** 56 55N 35 55 E
Kaliningrad, *Russia* **9 J19** 54 42N 20 32 E
Kalininsk, *Russia* **48 E7** 51 30N 44 40 E
Kalinkavichy, *Belarus* **47 F5** 52 12N 29 20 E
Kalinkovichi = Kalinkavichy, *Belarus* **47 F5** 52 12N 29 20 E
Kalinovik, *Bos.-H.* **40 C2** 43 31N 18 29 E
Kalipetrovo, *Bulgaria* **41 B11** 44 5N 27 14 E
Kaliro, *Uganda* **86 B3** 0 56N 33 30 E
Kalirrákhi, *Greece* **41 F8** 40 40N 24 35 E
Kalispell, *U.S.A.* **114 B6** 48 12N 114 19W
Kalisz, *Poland* **45 G5** 51 45N 18 8 E
Kalisz Pomorski, *Poland* **45 E2** 53 17N 15 55 E
Kaliua, *Tanzania* **86 D3** 5 5 S 31 48 E
Kalívia Thorikoú, *Greece* **38 D5** 37 50N 23 55 E
Kalix, *Sweden* **8 D20** 65 53N 23 12 E
Kalix →, *Sweden* **8 D20** 65 50N 23 11 E
Kalka, *India* **68 D7** 30 46N 76 57 E
Kalkan, *Turkey* **39 E11** 36 15N 29 23 E
Kalkarindji, *Australia* **92 C5** 17 30 S 130 47 E
Kalkaska, *U.S.A.* **108 C3** 44 44N 85 11W
Kalkfeld, *Namibia* **88 C2** 20 57 S 16 14 E
Kalkfontein, *Botswana* **88 C3** 22 4 S 20 57 E
Kalkım, *Turkey* **39 B9** 39 48N 27 13 E
Kalkrand, *Namibia* **88 C2** 24 1 S 17 35 E
Kållandsö, *Sweden* **11 F7** 58 40N 13 5 E
Kallavesi, *Finland* **8 E22** 62 58N 27 30 E
Källby, *Sweden* **11 F7** 58 30N 13 8 E
Kållered, *Sweden* **11 G6** 57 32N 12 4 E
Kallimasiá, *Greece* **39 C8** 38 18N 26 6 E
Kallinge, *Sweden* **11 H9** 56 15N 15 18 E
Kallithéa, *Greece* **38 D5** 37 55N 23 41 E
Kallmet, *Albania* **40 E3** 41 51N 19 41 E
Kallmeti = Kallmet, *Albania* **40 E3** 41 51N 19 41 E
Kalloní, *Greece* **39 B8** 39 14N 26 12 E
Kallonís, Kólpos, *Greece* **39 B8** 39 10N 26 10 E
Kallsjön, *Sweden* **8 E15** 63 38N 13 0 E
Kalmalo, *Nigeria* **83 C6** 13 40N 5 20 E
Kalmar, *Sweden* **11 H10** 56 40N 16 20 E
Kalmar län □, *Sweden* **11 G10** 57 25N 16 0 E
Kalmar sund, *Sweden* **11 H10** 56 40N 16 25 E
Kalmyk Republic = Kalmykia □, *Russia* **49 G8** 46 5N 46 1 E
Kalmykia □, *Russia* **49 G8** 46 5N 46 1 E
Kalmykovo, *Kazakstan* **50 E6** 49 0N 51 47 E
Kalna, *India* **69 H13** 23 13N 88 25 E
Kalnai, *India* **69 H10** 22 46N 83 30 E
Kalocsa, *Hungary* **42 D4** 46 32N 19 0 E
Kalofer, *Bulgaria* **41 D8** 42 37N 24 59 E
Kalokhorio, *Cyprus* **36 E12** 34 51N 33 2 E
Kaloko, *Dem. Rep. of the Congo* **86 D2** 6 47 S 25 48 E
Kalol, *Gujarat, India* **68 H5** 22 37N 73 31 E
Kalol, *Gujarat, India* **68 H5** 23 15N 72 33 E
Kalolímnos, *Greece* **39 D9** 37 4N 27 5 E
Kalomo, *Zambia* **87 F2** 17 0 S 26 30 E
Kalonerón, *Greece* **38 D3** 37 20N 21 38 E
Kalpi, *India* **69 F8** 26 8N 79 47 E
Kaltern = Caldaro, *Italy* **29 B8** 46 25N 11 14 E
Kaltungo, *Nigeria* **83 D7** 9 48N 11 19 E
Kalu, *Pakistan* **68 G2** 25 5N 67 39 E
Kaluga, *Russia* **46 E9** 54 35N 36 10 E
Kalulushi, *Zambia* **87 E2** 12 50 S 28 3 E
Kalundborg, *Denmark* **11 J5** 55 41N 11 5 E
Kalush, *Ukraine* **47 H3** 49 3N 24 23 E
Kałuszyn, *Poland* **45 F8** 52 13N 21 52 E
Kalutara, *Sri Lanka* **66 R12** 6 35N 80 0 E
Kalvarija, *Lithuania* **44 D10** 54 24N 23 14 E
Kalyazin, *Russia* **46 D9** 57 15N 37 55 E
Kam, *Albania* **40 D4** 42 17N 20 18 E
Kam →, *Nigeria* **83 D7** 8 15N 1 10 E
Kama, *Dem. Rep. of the Congo* **86 C2** 3 30 S 27 5 E
Kama →, *Russia* **6 D16** 55 45N 52 0 E
Kamachumu, *Tanzania* **86 C3** 1 37 S 31 37 E
Kamaishi, *Japan* **54 E10** 39 16N 141 53 E
Kamalia, *Pakistan* **68 D5** 30 44N 72 42 E
Kaman, *India* **68 F6** 27 39N 77 16 E
Kaman, *Turkey* **72 C5** 39 22N 33 44 E
Kamanjab, *Namibia* **88 B2** 19 35 S 14 51 E
Kamapanda, *Zambia* **87 E1** 12 5 S 24 0 E
Kamaran, *Yemen* **74 D3** 15 21N 42 35 E
Kamativi, *Zimbabwe* **88 B4** 18 20 S 27 6 E
Kamba, *Nigeria* **83 C5** 11 50N 3 45 E
Kambalda, *Australia* **93 F3** 31 10 S 121 37 E
Kambar, *Pakistan* **68 F3** 27 37N 68 1 E
Kambia, *S. Leone* **82 D2** 9 3N 12 53W
Kambolé, *Togo* **83 D5** 8 43N 1 39 E
Kambolé, *Zambia* **87 D3** 8 47 S 30 48 E
Kambos, *Cyprus* **36 D11** 35 2N 32 44 E
Kambove, *Dem. Rep. of the Congo* **87 E2** 10 51 S 26 33 E
Kamchatka, Poluostrov, *Russia* **51 D16** 57 0N 160 0 E
Kamchatka Pen. = Kamchatka, Poluostrov, *Russia* **51 D16** 57 0N 160 0 E
Kamchiya →, *Bulgaria* **41 C11** 43 4N 27 44 E
Kamen, *Russia* **50 D9** 53 50N 81 30 E
Kamen-Rybolov, *Russia* **54 B6** 44 46N 132 2 E
Kamenica, *Serbia, Yug.* **40 C6** 43 27N 22 27 E
Kamenica, *Serbia, Yug.* **40 B3** 44 25N 19 45 E
Kamenice nad Lipou, *Czech Rep.* **26 B8** 49 18N 15 2 E
Kamenjak, Rt., *Croatia* **29 D10** 44 47N 13 55 E
Kamenka = Kaminka, *Ukraine* **47 H7** 49 3N 32 6 E
Kamenka, *Kazakstan* **48 E10** 51 7N 50 19 E
Kamenka, *Penza, Russia* **48 D6** 53 10N 44 5 E
Kamenka, *Voronezh, Russia* **47 G10** 50 47N 39 20 E
Kamenka Bugskaya = Kamyanka-Buzka, *Ukraine* **47 G3** 50 8N 24 16 E
Kamenka Dneprovskaya = Kamyanka-Dniprovska, *Ukraine* **47 J8** 47 29N 34 28 E
Kamennomostskiy, *Russia* **49 H5** 44 18N 40 13 E
Kameno, *Bulgaria* **41 D11** 42 34N 27 18 E
Kamenolomini, *Russia* **49 G5** 47 40N 40 14 E
Kamensk-Shakhtinskiy, *Russia* **49 F5** 48 23N 40 20 E
Kamensk Uralskiy, *Russia* **50 D7** 56 25N 62 2 E
Kamenskiy, *Russia* **48 E7** 50 48N 45 25 E
Kamenskoye, *Russia* **51 C17** 62 45N 165 30 E
Kamenyak, *Bulgaria* **41 C10** 43 24N 26 57 E
Kamenz, *Germany* **24 D10** 51 15N 14 5 E
Kameoka, *Japan* **55 G7** 35 0N 135 35 E
Kami = Kam, *Albania* **40 D4** 42 17N 20 18 E
Kamiah, *U.S.A.* **114 C5** 46 14N 116 2W
Kamień Krajeński, *Poland* **44 E4** 53 32N 17 32 E
Kamień Pomorski, *Poland* **44 E1** 53 57N 14 43 E
Kamienna →, *Poland* **45 G8** 51 6N 21 47 E
Kamienna Góra, *Poland* **45 H3** 50 47N 16 2 E
Kamieńsk, *Poland* **45 G6** 51 12N 19 29 E
Kamieskroon, *S. Africa* **88 E2** 30 9 S 17 56 E
Kamilukuak, L., *Canada* **105 A8** 62 22N 101 40W
Kamin-Kashyrskyy, *Ukraine* **47 G3** 51 39N 24 56 E
Kamina, *Dem. Rep. of the Congo* **87 D2** 8 45 S 25 0 E
Kaminak L., *Canada* **105 A10** 62 10N 95 0W
Kaministiquia, *Canada* **102 C1** 48 32N 89 35W
Kaminka, *Ukraine* **47 H7** 49 3N 32 6 E
Kaminoyama, *Japan* **54 E10** 38 9N 140 17 E
Kamiros, *Greece* **36 C9** 36 20N 27 56 E
Kamituga, *Dem. Rep. of the Congo* **86 C2** 3 2 S 28 10 E
Kamla →, *India* **69 G12** 25 35N 86 36 E
Kamloops, *Canada* **104 C4** 50 40N 120 20W
Kamnik, *Slovenia* **29 B11** 46 14N 14 37 E
Kamo, *Armenia* **49 K7** 40 21N 45 7 E
Kamo, *Japan* **54 F9** 37 39N 139 3 E
Kamoke, *Pakistan* **68 C6** 32 4N 74 4 E
Kamp →, *Austria* **26 C8** 48 23N 15 42 E
Kampala, *Uganda* **86 B3** 0 20N 32 30 E
Kampang Chhnang, *Cambodia* **65 F5** 12 20N 104 35 E
Kampar, *Malaysia* **65 K3** 4 18N 101 9 E
Kampar →, *Indonesia* **62 D2** 0 30N 103 8 E
Kampen, *Neths.* **17 B5** 52 33N 5 53 E
Kampene, *Dem. Rep. of the Congo* **84 E5** 3 36 S 26 40 E
Kamphaeng Phet, *Thailand* **64 D2** 16 28N 99 30 E
Kampolombo, L., *Zambia* **87 E2** 11 37 S 29 42 E
Kampong Saom, *Cambodia* **65 G4** 10 38N 103 30 E
Kampong Saom, Chaak, *Cambodia* **65 G4** 10 50N 103 32 E
Kampong To, *Thailand* **65 J3** 6 3N 101 13 E
Kampot, *Cambodia* **65 G5** 10 36N 104 10 E
Kampti, *Burkina Faso* **82 C4** 10 7N 3 25W
Kampuchea = Cambodia ■, *Asia* **64 F5** 12 15N 105 0 E
Kampung Air Putih, *Malaysia* **65 K4** 4 15N 103 10 E
Kampung Jerangau, *Malaysia* **65 K4** 4 50N 103 10 E
Kampung Raja, *Malaysia* **65 K4** 5 45N 102 35 E
Kampungbaru = Tolitoli, *Indonesia* **63 D6** 1 5N 120 50 E
Kamrau, Teluk, *Indonesia* **63 E8** 3 30 S 133 36 E
Kamsack, *Canada* **105 C8** 51 34N 101 54W
Kamsar, *Guinea* **82 C2** 10 40N 14 36W
Kamskoye Ustye, *Russia* **48 C9** 55 10N 49 20 E
Kamuchawie L., *Canada* **105 B8** 56 18N 101 59W
Kamui-Misaki, *Japan* **54 C10** 43 20N 140 21 E
Kamyanets-Podilskyy, *Ukraine* **47 H4** 48 45N 26 40 E
Kamyanka-Buzka, *Ukraine* **47 G3** 50 8N 24 16 E
Kamyanka-Dniprovska, *Ukraine* **47 J8** 47 29N 34 28 E
Kāmyārān, *Iran* **70 C5** 34 47N 46 56 E
Kamyshin, *Russia* **48 E7** 50 10N 45 24 E
Kamyzyak, *Russia* **49 G9** 46 4N 48 10 E
Kan, *Sudan* **81 F3** 9 1N 31 47 E
Kanaaupscow, *Canada* **102 B4** 54 2N 76 30W
Kanaaupscow →, *Canada* **101 C12** 53 39N 77 9W
Kanab, *U.S.A.* **115 H7** 37 3N 112 32W
Kanab →, *U.S.A.* **115 H7** 36 24N 112 38W
Kanagi, *Japan* **54 D10** 40 54N 140 27 E
Kanairiktok →, *Canada* **103 A7** 55 2N 60 18W
Kanália, *Greece* **38 B4** 39 30N 22 53 E
Kananga, *Dem. Rep. of the Congo* **84 F4** 5 55 S 22 18 E
Kanash, *Russia* **48 C8** 55 30N 47 32 E
Kanaskat, *U.S.A.* **116 C5** 47 19N 121 54W
Kanastraíon, Ákra = Palioúrion, Ákra, *Greece* **40 G7** 39 57N 23 45 E
Kanawha →, *U.S.A.* **108 F4** 38 50N 82 9W
Kanazawa, *Japan* **55 F8** 36 30N 136 38 E
Kanchanaburi, *Thailand* **64 E2** 14 2N 99 31 E
Kanchenjunga, *Nepal* **69 F13** 27 50N 88 10 E
Kanchipuram, *India* **66 N11** 12 52N 79 45 E
Kańczuga, *Poland* **45 J9** 49 59N 22 25 E
Kandaghat, *India* **68 D7** 30 59N 77 7 E
Kandahar = Qandahār, *Afghan.* **66 D4** 31 32N 65 30 E
Kandalaksha, *Russia* **50 C4** 67 9N 32 30 E
Kandalu, *Afghan.* **66 E3** 29 55N 63 20 E
Kandangan, *Indonesia* **62 E5** 2 50 S 115 20 E
Kandanghaur, *Indonesia* **63 G13** 6 21 S 108 6 E
Kandanos, *Greece* **36 D5** 35 19N 23 44 E
Kandava, *Latvia* **44 A9** 57 2N 22 37 E
Kandavu, *Fiji* **91 D8** 19 0 S 178 15 E
Kandhíla, *Greece* **38 D4** 37 46N 22 22 E
Kandhkot, *Pakistan* **68 E3** 28 16N 69 8 E
Kandhla, *India* **68 E7** 29 18N 77 19 E
Kandi, *Benin* **83 C5** 11 7N 2 55 E
Kandi, *India* **69 H13** 23 58N 88 5 E
Kandiaro, *Pakistan* **68 F3** 27 4N 68 13 E
Kandıra, *Turkey* **72 B4** 41 4N 30 9 E
Kandla, *India* **68 H4** 23 0N 70 10 E
Kandos, *Australia* **95 E4** 32 45 S 149 58 E
Kandreho, *Madag.* **89 B8** 17 29 S 46 6 E
Kandy, *Sri Lanka* **66 R12** 7 18N 80 43 E
Kane, *U.S.A.* **110 E6** 41 40N 78 49W
Kane Basin, *Greenland* **4 B4** 79 1N 70 0W
Kanel, *Senegal* **82 B2** 15 30N 13 18W
Kaneohe, *U.S.A.* **106 H16** 21 25N 157 48W
Kanevskaya, *Russia* **49 G4** 46 3N 38 57 E
Kanfanar, *Croatia* **29 C10** 45 7N 13 50 E
Kang, *Botswana* **88 C3** 23 41 S 22 50 E
Kangaba, *Mali* **82 C3** 11 56N 8 25W
Kangal, *Turkey* **72 C7** 39 14N 37 23 E
Kangān, *Fārs, Iran* **71 E7** 27 50N 52 3 E
Kangān, *Hormozgān, Iran* **71 E8** 25 48N 57 28 E
Kangar, *Malaysia* **65 J3** 6 27N 100 12 E
Kangaré, *Mali* **82 C3** 11 36N 8 4W
Kangaroo I., *Australia* **95 F2** 35 45 S 137 0 E
Kangaroo Mts., *Australia* **94 C3** 23 29 S 141 51 E
Kangasala, *Finland* **9 F21** 61 28N 24 4 E
Kangāvar, *Iran* **71 C6** 34 40N 48 0 E
Kangding, *China* **58 B3** 30 2N 101 57 E
Kangdong, *N. Korea* **57 E14** 39 9N 126 5 E
Kangean, Kepulauan, *Indonesia* **62 F5** 6 55 S 115 23 E
Kangean Is. = Kangean, Kepulauan, *Indonesia* **62 F5** 6 55 S 115 23 E
Kangen →, *Sudan* **81 F3** 6 47N 33 9 E
Kanggye, *N. Korea* **57 D14** 41 0N 126 35 E
Kanggyŏng, *S. Korea* **57 F14** 36 10N 127 0 E
Kanghwa, *S. Korea* **57 F14** 37 45N 126 30 E
Kangikajik, *Greenland* **4 B6** 70 7N 22 0W
Kangiqsualujjuaq, *Canada* **101 C13** 58 30N 65 59W
Kangiqsujuaq, *Canada* **101 B12** 61 30N 72 0W
Kangirsuk, *Canada* **101 B13** 60 0N 70 0W
Kangnŭng, *S. Korea* **57 F15** 37 45N 128 54 E
Kangping, *China* **57 C12** 42 43N 123 18 E
Kangra, *India* **68 C7** 32 6N 76 16 E
Kangto, *India* **67 F18** 27 50N 92 35 E
Kanhar →, *India* **69 G10** 24 28N 83 8 E
Kani, *Ivory C.* **82 D3** 8 29N 6 36W
Kaniama, *Dem. Rep. of the Congo* **86 D1** 7 30 S 24 12 E
Kaniapiskau = Caniapiscau →, *Canada* **103 A6** 56 40N 69 30W
Kaniapiskau, Res. = Caniapiscau Rés. de, *Canada* **103 B6** 54 10N 69 55W
Kanin, Poluostrov, *Russia* **50 C5** 68 0N 45 0 E
Kanin Nos, Mys, *Russia* **50 C5** 68 39N 43 32 E
Kanin Pen. = Kanin, Poluostrov, *Russia* **50 C5** 68 0N 45 0 E
Kanina = Kaninë, *Albania* **40 F3** 40 23N 19 30 E
Kaninë, *Albania* **40 F3** 40 23N 19 30 E
Kaniva, *Australia* **95 F3** 36 22 S 141 18 E
Kanjiža, *Serbia, Yug.* **42 D5** 46 3N 20 4 E
Kanjut Sar, *Pakistan* **69 A6** 36 7N 75 25 E
Kankaanpää, *Finland* **9 F20** 61 44N 22 50 E
Kankakee, *U.S.A.* **108 E2** 41 7N 87 52W
Kankakee →, *U.S.A.* **108 E1** 41 23N 88 15W
Kankan, *Guinea* **82 C3** 10 23N 9 15W
Kankendy = Xankändi, *Azerbaijan* **70 B5** 39 52N 46 49 E
Kanker, *India* **67 J12** 20 10N 81 40 E
Kankossa, *Mauritania* **82 B2** 15 54N 11 31W
Kankroli, *India* **68 G5** 25 4N 73 53 E
Kannapolis, *U.S.A.* **109 H5** 35 30N 80 37W
Kannauj, *India* **69 F8** 27 3N 79 56 E
Kannod, *India* **66 H10** 22 45N 76 40 E
Kano, *Nigeria* **83 C6** 12 2N 8 30 E
Kano □, *Nigeria* **83 C6** 11 30N 8 30 E
Kan'onji, *Japan* **55 G6** 34 7N 133 39 E
Kanoroba, *Ivory C.* **82 D3** 9 7N 6 8W
Kanowit, *Malaysia* **62 D4** 2 14N 112 20 E
Kanoya, *Japan* **55 J5** 31 25N 130 50 E
Kanpetlet, *Burma* **67 J18** 21 10N 93 59 E
Kanpur, *India* **69 F9** 26 28N 80 20 E
Kansas □, *U.S.A.* **112 F6** 38 30N 99 0W
Kansas →, *U.S.A.* **112 F7** 39 7N 94 37W
Kansas City, *Kans., U.S.A.* **112 F7** 39 7N 94 38W
Kansas City, *Mo., U.S.A.* **112 F7** 39 6N 94 35W
Kansenia, *Dem. Rep. of the Congo* **87 E2** 10 20 S 26 0 E
Kansk, *Russia* **51 D10** 56 20N 95 37 E
Kansŏng, *S. Korea* **57 E15** 38 24N 128 30 E
Kansu = Gansu □, *China* **56 G3** 36 0N 104 0 E
Kantaphor, *India* **68 H7** 22 35N 76 34 E
Kantchari, *Burkina Faso* **83 C5** 12 37N 1 37 E
Kantché, *Niger* **83 C6** 13 31N 8 30 E
Kanté, *Togo* **83 D5** 9 57N 1 3 E
Kantemirovka, *Russia* **47 H10** 49 43N 39 55 E
Kantharalak, *Thailand* **64 E5** 14 39N 104 39 E
Kantli →, *India* **68 E6** 28 20N 75 30 E
Kantō □, *Japan* **55 F9** 36 15N 139 30 E
Kantō-Sanchi, *Japan* **55 G9** 35 59N 138 50 E
Kanturk, *Ireland* **15 D3** 52 11N 8 54W
Kanuma, *Japan* **55 F9** 36 34N 139 42 E
Kanus, *Namibia* **88 D2** 27 50 S 18 39 E
Kanye, *Botswana* **88 C4** 24 55 S 25 28 E
Kanzenze, *Dem. Rep. of the Congo* **87 E2** 10 30 S 25 12 E
Kanzi, Ras, *Tanzania* **86 D4** 7 1 S 39 33 E
Kaohsiung, *Taiwan* **59 F13** 22 35N 120 16 E
Kaokoveld, *Namibia* **88 B1** 19 15 S 14 30 E
Kaolack, *Senegal* **82 C1** 14 5N 16 8W
Kaoshan, *China* **57 B13** 44 38N 124 50 E
Kapaa, *U.S.A.* **106 G15** 22 5N 159 19W
Kapadvanj, *India* **68 H5** 23 5N 73 0 E
Kapaklı, *Turkey* **41 E11** 41 19N 27 59 E
Kapan, *Armenia* **70 B5** 39 18N 46 27 E
Kapanga, *Dem. Rep. of the Congo* **84 F4** 8 30 S 22 40 E
Kapchagai = Qapshaghay, *Kazakstan* **50 E8** 43 51N 77 14 E
Kapela = Velika Kapela, *Croatia* **29 C12** 45 10N 15 5 E
Kapéllo, Ákra, *Greece* **38 E5** 36 9N 23 3 E
Kapema, *Dem. Rep. of the Congo* **87 E2** 10 45 S 28 22 E
Kapfenberg, *Austria* **26 D8** 47 26N 15 18 E
Kapı Dağı, *Turkey* **41 F11** 40 28N 27 50 E
Kapiri Mposhi, *Zambia* **87 E2** 13 59 S 28 43 E
Kapiskau →, *Canada* **102 B3** 52 47N 81 55W
Kapit, *Malaysia* **62 D4** 2 0N 112 55 E
Kapiti I., *N.Z.* **91 J5** 40 50 S 174 56 E
Kaplan, *U.S.A.* **113 K8** 30 0N 92 17W
Kaplice, *Czech Rep.* **26 C7** 48 42N 14 30 E
Kapoe, *Thailand* **65 H2** 9 34N 98 32 E
Kapoeta, *Sudan* **81 G3** 4 50N 33 35 E
Kápolnásnyék, *Hungary* **42 C3** 47 16N 18 41 E
Kapos →, *Hungary* **42 D3** 46 44N 18 30 E
Kaposvár, *Hungary* **42 D2** 46 25N 17 47 E
Kapowsin, *U.S.A.* **116 D4** 46 59N 122 13W
Kappeln, *Germany* **24 A5** 54 40N 9 55 E
Kappelshamn, *Sweden* **11 G12** 57 52N 18 47 E
Kapps, *Namibia* **88 C2** 22 32 S 17 18 E
Kaprije, *Croatia* **29 E12** 43 42N 15 43 E
Kapsan, *N. Korea* **57 D15** 41 4N 128 19 E
Kapsukas = Marijampolė, *Lithuania* **9 J20** 54 33N 23 19 E
Kapuas →, *Indonesia* **62 E3** 0 25 S 109 20 E
Kapuas Hulu, Pegunungan, *Malaysia* **62 D4** 1 30N 113 30 E
Kapuas Hulu Ra. = Kapuas Hulu, Pegunungan, *Malaysia* **62 D4** 1 30N 113 30 E
Kapulo, *Dem. Rep. of the Congo* **87 D2** 8 18 S 29 15 E
Kapunda, *Australia* **95 E2** 34 20 S 138 56 E
Kapuni, *N.Z.* **91 H5** 39 29 S 174 8 E
Kapurthala, *India* **68 D6** 31 23N 75 25 E
Kapuskasing, *Canada* **102 C3** 49 25N 82 30W
Kapuskasing →, *Canada* **102 C3** 49 49N 82 0W
Kapustin Yar, *Russia* **49 F7** 48 37N 45 40 E
Kaputar, *Australia* **95 E5** 30 15 S 150 10 E
Kaputir, *Kenya* **86 B4** 2 5N 35 28 E
Kapuvár, *Hungary* **42 C2** 47 36N 17 1 E
Kara, *Russia* **50 C7** 69 10N 65 0 E
Karā, W. →, *Si. Arabia* **80 C5** 20 45N 41 42 E
Kara Ada, *Turkey* **39 E9** 36 58N 27 28 E
Kara Bogaz Gol, Zaliv = Garabogazköl Aylagy, *Turkmenistan* **50 E6** 41 0N 53 30 E
Kara Burun, *Turkey* **39 E9** 36 32N 27 58 E
Kara Kalpak Republic = Karakalpakstan □, *Uzbekistan* **50 E6** 43 0N 58 0 E
Kara Kum, *Turkmenistan* **50 F6** 39 30N 60 0 E
Kara Sea, *Russia* **50 B7** 75 0N 70 0 E
Karaadilli, *Turkey* **39 C12** 38 18N 30 37 E
Karabiğa, *Turkey* **41 F11** 40 23N 27 17 E
Karabük, *Turkey* **72 B5** 41 12N 32 37 E
Karaburun, *Albania* **40 F3** 40 25N 19 20 E
Karaburun, *Turkey* **39 C8** 38 41N 26 28 E
Karaburuni = Karaburun, *Albania* **40 F3** 40 25N 19 20 E
Karabutak = Qarabutaq, *Kazakstan* **50 E7** 49 59N 60 14 E
Karacabey, *Turkey* **41 F12** 40 12N 28 21 E
Karacakılavuz, *Turkey* **41 E11** 41 8N 27 21 E
Karacaköy, *Turkey* **41 E12** 41 24N 28 22 E
Karacasu, *Turkey* **39 D10** 37 43N 28 35 E
Karachala = Qaraçala, *Azerbaijan* **49 L9** 39 45N 48 53 E
Karachayevsk, *Russia* **49 J5** 43 50N 41 55 E
Karachev, *Russia* **47 F8** 53 10N 35 5 E
Karachey-Cherkessia □, *Russia* **49 J5** 43 40N 41 30 E
Karachi, *Pakistan* **68 G2** 24 53N 67 0 E
Karad, *India* **66 L9** 17 15N 74 10 E
Karadirek, *Turkey* **39 C12** 38 34N 30 11 E
Karaga, *Ghana* **83 D4** 9 58N 0 28W
Karaganda = Qaraghandy, *Kazakstan* **50 E8** 49 50N 73 10 E
Karagayly, *Kazakstan* **50 E8** 49 26N 76 0 E
Karaginskiy, Ostrov, *Russia* **51 D17** 58 45N 164 0 E
Karagola Road, *India* **69 G12** 25 29N 87 23 E
Karagüney Dağları, *Turkey* **72 B6** 40 30N 34 40 E
Karahallı, *Turkey* **39 C11** 38 21N 29 33 E
Karaikal, *India* **66 P11** 10 59N 79 50 E
Karaikkudi, *India* **66 P11** 10 5N 78 45 E
Karaisali, *Turkey* **72 D6** 37 16N 35 2 E
Karaj, *Iran* **71 C6** 35 48N 51 0 E
Karak, *Malaysia* **65 L4** 3 25N 102 2 E
Karakalpakstan □, *Uzbekistan* **50 E6** 43 0N 58 0 E
Karakelong, *Indonesia* **63 D7** 4 35N 126 50 E
Karakitang, *Indonesia* **63 D7** 3 14N 125 28 E
Karaklis = Vanadzor, *Armenia* **49 K7** 40 48N 44 30 E
Karakoçan, *Turkey* **73 C9** 38 57N 40 2 E
Karakoram Pass, *Pakistan* **69 B7** 35 33N 77 50 E
Karakoram Ra., *Pakistan* **69 B7** 35 30N 77 0 E
Karakurt, *Turkey* **73 B10** 40 10N 42 37 E
Karakuwisa, *Namibia* **88 B2** 18 56 S 19 40 E
Karalon, *Russia* **51 D12** 57 5N 115 50 E
Karama, *Jordan* **75 D4** 31 57N 35 35 E
Karaman, *Balıkesir, Turkey* **39 B9** 39 39N 28 0 E
Karaman, *Konya, Turkey* **70 B2** 37 14N 33 13 E
Karamanlı, *Turkey* **39 D11** 37 23N 29 47 E
Karamay, *China* **60 B3** 45 30N 84 58 E
Karambu, *Indonesia* **62 E5** 3 53 S 116 6 E
Karamea Bight, *N.Z.* **91 J3** 41 22 S 171 40 E
Karamnasa →, *India* **69 G10** 25 31N 83 52 E
Karamürsel, *Turkey* **41 F13** 40 41N 29 36 E
Karand, *Iran* **70 C5** 34 16N 46 15 E
Karangana, *Mali* **82 C3** 12 15N 5 4W
Karanganyar, *Indonesia* **63 G13** 7 38 S 109 37 E
Karanjia, *India* **69 J11** 21 47N 85 58 E
Karankasso, *Burkina Faso* **82 C4** 10 50N 3 53W
Karaova, *Turkey* **39 D9** 37 5N 27 40 E
Karapınar, *Turkey* **72 D5** 37 41N 33 30 E
Karasburg, *Namibia* **88 D2** 28 0 S 18 44 E
Karasino, *Russia* **50 C9** 66 50N 86 50 E
Karasjok, *Norway* **8 B21** 69 27N 25 30 E
Karasu, *Turkey* **72 B4** 41 4N 30 46 E
Karasu →, *Turkey* **39 E12** 36 18N 30 10 E
Karasuk, *Russia* **50 D8** 53 44N 78 2 E
Karasuyama, *Japan* **55 F10** 36 39N 140 9 E
Karataş, *Adana, Turkey* **72 D6** 36 36N 35 21 E
Karataş, *Manisa, Turkey* **39 C10** 38 35N 28 16 E
Karatas Burnu, *Turkey* **72 D6** 36 31N 35 24 E
Karatau = Qarataū, *Kazakstan* **50 E8** 43 10N 70 28 E
Karatau, Khrebet, *Kazakstan* **50 E7** 43 30N 69 30 E
Karatoprak, *Turkey* **39 D9** 37 2N 27 15 E
Karatsu, *Japan* **55 H5** 33 26N 129 58 E
Karaul, *Russia* **50 B9** 70 6N 82 15 E
Karauli, *India* **68 F7** 26 30N 77 4 E
Karavastasë, L. e, *Albania* **40 F3** 40 55N 19 30 E
Karávi, *Greece* **38 E5** 36 49N 23 37 E
Karavostasi, *Cyprus* **36 D11** 35 8N 32 50 E
Karawang, *Indonesia* **63 G12** 6 30 S 107 15 E
Karawanken, *Europe* **26 E7** 46 30N 14 40 E
Karayazı, *Turkey* **73 C10** 39 41N 42 9 E
Karazhal, *Kazakstan* **50 E8** 48 2N 70 49 E
Karbalā', *Iraq* **70 C5** 32 36N 44 3 E
Kårböle, *Sweden* **10 C9** 61 59N 15 22 E
Karcag, *Hungary* **42 C5** 47 19N 20 57 E
Karcha →, *Pakistan* **69 B7** 34 45N 76 10 E
Karchana, *India* **69 G9** 25 17N 81 56 E
Karczew, *Poland* **45 F8** 52 5N 21 15 E
Kardam, *Bulgaria* **41 C12** 43 45N 28 6 E
Kardeljovo = Ploče, *Croatia* **29 E14** 43 4N 17 26 E
Kardhámila, *Greece* **39 C8** 38 35N 26 5 E
Kardhamíli, *Greece* **38 E4** 36 53N 22 13 E
Kardhítsa, *Greece* **38 B3** 39 23N 21 54 E
Kardhítsa □, *Greece* **38 B3** 39 15N 21 50 E
Kärdla, *Estonia* **9 G20** 58 50N 22 40 E
Kareeberge, *S. Africa* **88 E3** 30 59 S 21 50 E
Kareha →, *India* **69 G12** 25 44N 86 21 E
Kareima, *Sudan* **80 D3** 18 30N 31 49 E
Karelia □, *Russia* **50 C4** 65 30N 32 30 E
Karelian Republic = Karelia □, *Russia* **50 C4** 65 30N 32 30 E
Karera, *India* **68 G8** 25 32N 78 9 E
Kārevāndar, *Iran* **71 E9** 27 53N 60 44 E
Kargasok, *Russia* **50 D9** 59 3N 80 53 E
Kargat, *Russia* **50 D9** 55 10N 80 15 E
Kargı, *Turkey* **72 B6** 41 11N 34 30 E
Kargil, *India* **69 B7** 34 32N 76 12 E
Kargopol, *Russia* **46 B10** 61 30N 38 58 E
Kargowa, *Poland* **45 F2** 52 5N 15 51 E
Karguéri, *Niger* **83 C7** 13 27N 10 30 E
Karhal, *India* **69 F8** 27 1N 78 57 E
Kariá, *Greece* **38 C2** 38 45N 20 39 E
Kariaí, *Greece* **41 F8** 40 14N 24 19 E
Karīān, *Iran* **71 E8** 26 57N 57 14 E
Karianga, *Madag.* **89 C8** 22 25 S 47 22 E
Kariba, *Zimbabwe* **87 F2** 16 28 S 28 50 E
Kariba, L., *Zimbabwe* **87 F2** 16 40 S 28 25 E
Kariba Dam, *Zimbabwe* **87 F2** 16 30 S 28 35 E
Kariba Gorge, *Zambia* **87 F2** 16 30 S 28 50 E
Karibib, *Namibia* **88 C2** 22 0 S 15 56 E
Karimata, Kepulauan, *Indonesia* **62 E3** 1 25 S 109 0 E
Karimata, Selat, *Indonesia* **62 E3** 2 0 S 108 40 E
Karimata Is. = Karimata, Kepulauan, *Indonesia* **62 E3** 1 25 S 109 0 E
Karimnagar, *India* **66 K11** 18 26N 79 10 E
Karimunjawa, Kepulauan, *Indonesia* **62 F4** 5 50 S 110 30 E
Karin, *Somali Rep.* **74 E4** 10 50N 45 52 E
Káristos, *Greece* **38 C6** 38 1N 24 29 E
Karīt, *Iran* **71 C8** 33 29N 56 55 E
Kariya, *Japan* **55 G8** 34 58N 137 1 E
Kariyangwe, *Zimbabwe* **89 B4** 18 0 S 27 38 E
Karjala, *Finland* **46 A5** 62 0N 30 25 E
Karkaralinsk = Qarqaraly, *Kazakstan* **50 E8** 49 26N 75 30 E
Karkheh →, *Iran* **70 D5** 31 2N 47 29 E
Karkinitska Zatoka, *Ukraine* **47 K7** 45 56N 33 0 E
Karkinitskiy Zaliv = Karkinitska Zatoka, *Ukraine* **47 K7** 45 56N 33 0 E
Karkur Tohl, *Egypt* **80 C2** 22 5N 25 5 E
Karl Liebknecht, *Russia* **47 G8** 51 40N 35 35 E
Karl-Marx-Stadt = Chemnitz, *Germany* **24 E8** 50 51N 12 54 E
Karlholmsbruk, *Sweden* **10 D11** 60 31N 17 37 E
Karlino, *Poland* **44 D2** 54 3N 15 53 E
Karlivka, *Ukraine* **47 H8** 49 29N 35 8 E
Karlobag, *Croatia* **29 D12** 44 32N 15 5 E
Karlovac, *Croatia* **29 C12** 45 31N 15 36 E
Karlovka = Karlivka, *Ukraine* **47 H8** 49 29N 35 8 E
Karlovo, *Bulgaria* **41 D8** 42 38N 24 47 E
Karlovy Vary, *Czech Rep.* **26 A5** 50 13N 12 51 E
Karlsbad = Karlovy Vary, *Czech Rep.* **26 A5** 50 13N 12 51 E
Karlsborg, *Sweden* **11 F8** 58 33N 14 33 E
Karlshamn, *Sweden* **11 H8** 56 10N 14 51 E
Karlskoga, *Sweden* **10 E8** 59 28N 14 33 E
Karlskrona, *Sweden* **11 H9** 56 10N 15 35 E
Karlsruhe, *Germany* **25 F4** 49 0N 8 23 E
Karlstad, *Sweden* **10 E7** 59 23N 13 30 E

Karlstad, *U.S.A.* **112 A6** 48 35N 96 31W
Karlstadt, *Germany* **25 F5** 49 57N 9 47 E
Karma, *Niger* **83 C5** 13 38N 1 52 E
Karmėlava, *Lithuania* **44 D11** 54 58N 24 4 E
Karmi'el, *Israel* **75 C4** 32 55N 35 18 E
Karnak, *Egypt* **79 C12** 25 43N 32 39 E
Karnal, *India* **68 E7** 29 42N 77 2 E
Karnali →, *Nepal* **69 E9** 28 45N 81 16 E
Karnaphuli Res., *Bangla.* **67 H18** 22 40N 92 20 E
Karnaprayag, *India* **69 D8** 30 16N 79 15 E
Karnataka □, *India* **66 N10** 13 15N 77 0 E
Karnes City, *U.S.A.* **113 L6** 28 53N 97 54W
Karnische Alpen, *Europe* **26 E6** 46 36N 13 0 E
Karnobat, *Bulgaria* **41 D10** 42 39N 26 59 E
Kärnten □, *Austria* **26 E6** 46 52N 13 30 E
Karo, *Mali* **82 C4** 12 16N 3 18W
Karoi, *Zimbabwe* **87 F2** 16 48 S 29 45 E
Karonga, *Malawi* **87 D3** 9 57 S 33 55 E
Karoonda, *Australia* **95 F2** 35 1 S 139 59 E
Karor, *Pakistan* **68 D4** 31 15N 70 59 E
Karora, *Sudan* **80 D4** 17 44N 38 15 E
Káros, *Greece* **39 E7** 36 54N 25 40 E
Karounga, *Mali* **82 B3** 15 20N 7 35W
Karousádhes, *Greece* **38 B1** 39 47N 19 45 E
Karpacz, *Poland* **45 H2** 50 46N 15 46 E
Karpasia □, *Cyprus* **36 D13** 35 32N 34 15 E
Kárpathos, *Greece* **39 F9** 35 37N 27 10 E
Kárpathos, Stenón, *Greece* **39 F9** 36 0N 27 30 E
Karpenísion, *Greece* **38 C3** 38 55N 21 40 E
Karpuz Burnu = Apostolos Andreas, C., *Cyprus* **36 D13** 35 42N 34 35 E
Karpuzlu, *Turkey* **39 D9** 37 33N 27 51 E
Karratha, *Australia* **92 D2** 20 53 S 116 40 E
Kars, *Turkey* **73 B10** 40 40N 43 5 E
Karsakpay, *Kazakstan* **50 E7** 47 55N 66 40 E
Karsha, *Kazakstan* **48 F10** 49 45N 51 35 E
Karshi = Qarshi, *Uzbekistan* **50 F7** 38 53N 65 48 E
Karsiyang, *India* **69 F13** 26 56N 88 18 E
Karsog, *India* **68 D7** 31 23N 77 12 E
Karst = Kras, *Croatia* **29 C10** 45 35N 14 0 E
Kartal, *Turkey* **41 F13** 40 53N 29 11 E
Kartál Óros, *Greece* **41 E9** 41 15N 25 13 E
Kartaly, *Russia* **50 D7** 53 3N 60 40 E
Kartapur, *India* **68 D6** 31 27N 75 32 E
Karthaus, *U.S.A.* **110 E6** 41 8N 78 9W
Kartuzy, *Poland* **44 D5** 54 22N 18 10 E
Karufa, *Indonesia* **63 E8** 3 50 S 133 20 E
Karumba, *Australia* **94 B3** 17 31 S 140 50 E
Karumo, *Tanzania* **86 C3** 2 25 S 32 50 E
Karumwa, *Tanzania* **86 C3** 3 12 S 32 38 E
Kārūn →, *Iran* **71 D6** 30 26N 48 10 E
Karungu, *Kenya* **86 C3** 0 50 S 34 10 E
Karup, *Denmark* **11 H3** 56 19N 9 10 E
Karviná, *Czech Rep.* **27 B11** 49 53N 18 31 E
Karwan →, *India* **68 F8** 27 26N 78 4 E
Karwar, *India* **66 M9** 14 55N 74 13 E
Karwi, *India* **69 G9** 25 12N 80 57 E
Kaş, *Turkey* **39 E11** 36 11N 29 37 E
Kasaba, *Turkey* **39 E11** 36 18N 29 44 E
Kasache, *Malawi* **87 E3** 13 25 S 34 20 E
Kasai →, *Dem. Rep. of the Congo* **84 E3** 3 30 S 16 10 E
Kasaï-Oriental □, *Dem. Rep. of the Congo* **86 D1** 5 0 S 24 30 E
Kasaji, *Dem. Rep. of the Congo* **87 E1** 10 25 S 23 27 E
Kasama, *Zambia* **87 E3** 10 16 S 31 9 E
Kasan-dong, *N. Korea* **57 D14** 41 18N 126 55 E
Kasane, *Namibia* **88 B3** 17 34 S 24 50 E
Kasanga, *Tanzania* **87 D3** 8 30 S 31 10 E
Kasar, Ras, *Sudan* **80 D4** 18 2N 38 36 E
Kasaragod, *India* **66 N9** 12 30N 74 58 E
Kasba L., *Canada* **105 A8** 60 20N 102 10W
Kāseh Garān, *Iran* **70 C5** 34 5N 46 2 E
Kasempa, *Zambia* **87 E2** 13 30 S 25 44 E
Kasenga, *Dem. Rep. of the Congo* **87 E2** 10 20 S 28 45 E
Kasese, *Uganda* **86 B3** 0 13N 30 3 E
Kasewa, *Zambia* **87 E2** 14 28 S 28 53 E
Kasganj, *India* **69 F8** 27 48N 78 42 E
Kashabowie, *Canada* **102 C1** 48 40N 90 26W
Kashaf, *Iran* **71 C9** 35 58N 61 7 E
Kāshān, *Iran* **71 C6** 34 5N 51 30 E
Kashechewan, *Canada* **102 B3** 52 18N 81 37W
Kashi, *China* **60 C2** 39 30N 76 2 E
Kashimbo, *Dem. Rep. of the Congo* **87 E2** 11 12 S 26 19 E
Kashin, *Russia* **46 D9** 57 20N 37 36 E
Kashipur, *India* **69 E8** 29 15N 79 0 E
Kashira, *Russia* **46 E10** 54 45N 38 10 E
Kashiwazaki, *Japan* **55 F9** 37 22N 138 33 E
Kashk-e Kohneh, *Afghan.* **66 B3** 34 55N 62 30 E
Kashkū'īyeh, *Iran* **71 D7** 30 31N 55 40 E
Kāshmar, *Iran* **71 C8** 35 16N 58 26 E
Kashmir, *Asia* **69 C7** 34 0N 76 0 E
Kashmor, *Pakistan* **68 E3** 28 28N 69 32 E
Kashpirovka, *Russia* **48 D9** 53 0N 48 30 E
Kashun Noerh = Gaxun Nur, *China* **60 B5** 42 22N 100 30 E
Kasiari, *India* **69 H12** 22 8N 87 14 E
Kasimov, *Russia* **48 C5** 54 55N 41 20 E
Kasinge, *Dem. Rep. of the Congo* **86 D2** 6 15 S 26 58 E
Kasiruta, *Indonesia* **63 E7** 0 25 S 127 12 E
Kaskaskia →, *U.S.A.* **112 G10** 37 58N 89 57W
Kaskattama →, *Canada* **105 B10** 57 3N 90 4W
Kaskinen, *Finland* **9 E19** 62 22N 21 15 E
Kaslo, *Canada* **104 D5** 49 55N 116 55W
Kasmere L., *Canada* **105 B8** 59 34N 101 10W
Kasongo, *Dem. Rep. of the Congo* **86 C2** 4 30 S 26 33 E
Kasongo Lunda, *Dem. Rep. of the Congo* **84 F3** 6 35 S 16 49 E
Kásos, *Greece* **39 F8** 35 20N 26 55 E
Kásos, Stenón, *Greece* **39 F8** 35 30N 26 30 E
Kaspi, *Georgia* **49 K7** 41 59N 44 26 E
Kaspichan, *Bulgaria* **41 C11** 43 18N 27 11 E
Kaspiysk, *Russia* **49 J8** 42 52N 47 40 E
Kaspiyskiy, *Russia* **49 H8** 45 22N 47 23 E
Kassab ed Doleib, *Sudan* **81 E3** 13 30N 33 35 E
Kassaba, *Egypt* **80 C2** 22 40N 29 55 E
Kassalâ, *Sudan* **81 D4** 15 30N 36 0 E
Kassalâ □, *Sudan* **81 D4** 15 20N 36 26 E
Kassándra, *Greece* **40 F7** 40 0N 23 30 E
Kassándrinon, *Greece* **40 F7** 40 1N 23 27 E
Kassel, *Germany* **24 D5** 51 18N 9 26 E
Kassinger, *Sudan* **80 D3** 18 46N 31 51 E
Kassiópi, *Greece* **36 A3** 39 48N 19 53 E
Kasson, *U.S.A.* **112 C8** 44 2N 92 45W
Kastamonu, *Turkey* **72 B5** 41 25N 33 43 E
Kastav, *Croatia* **29 C11** 45 22N 14 20 E
Kastélli, *Greece* **36 D5** 35 29N 23 38 E
Kastéllion, *Greece* **36 D7** 35 12N 25 20 E
Kastellórizon = Megiste, *Greece* **39 E11** 36 8N 29 34 E
Kástellos, *Greece* **39 E9** 36 16N 27 49 E
Kastellou, Ákra, *Greece* **39 F9** 35 30N 27 15 E
Kasterlee, *Belgium* **17 C4** 51 15N 4 59 E
Kastlösa, *Sweden* **11 H10** 56 26N 16 25 E
Kastóri, *Greece* **38 D4** 37 10N 22 17 E
Kastoría, *Greece* **40 F5** 40 30N 21 19 E
Kastoría □, *Greece* **40 F5** 40 30N 21 15 E
Kastorías, Límni, *Greece* **40 F5** 40 30N 21 20 E
Kastornoye, *Russia* **47 G10** 51 55N 38 2 E
Kastós, *Greece* **38 C2** 38 35N 20 55 E
Kastrosikiá, *Greece* **38 B2** 39 6N 20 36 E
Kastsyukovichy, *Belarus* **46 F7** 53 20N 32 4 E
Kasulu, *Tanzania* **86 C3** 4 37 S 30 5 E
Kasumi, *Japan* **55 G7** 35 38N 134 38 E
Kasumkent, *Russia* **49 K9** 41 47N 48 15 E
Kasungu, *Malawi* **87 E3** 13 0 S 33 29 E
Kasur, *Pakistan* **68 D6** 31 5N 74 25 E
Kataba, *Zambia* **87 F2** 16 5 S 25 10 E
Katagum, *Nigeria* **83 C7** 12 18N 10 21 E
Katahdin, Mt., *U.S.A.* **109 C11** 45 54N 68 56W
Katako Kombe, *Dem. Rep. of the Congo* **86 C1** 3 25 S 24 20 E
Katákolon, *Greece* **38 D3** 37 38N 21 19 E
Katale, *Tanzania* **86 C3** 4 52 S 31 7 E
Katanda, *Katanga, Dem. Rep. of the Congo* **86 D1** 7 52 S 24 13 E
Katanda, *Nord-Kivu, Dem. Rep. of the Congo* **86 C2** 0 55 S 29 21 E
Katanga □, *Dem. Rep. of the Congo* **86 D2** 8 0 S 25 0 E
Katangi, *India* **66 J11** 21 56N 79 50 E
Katanning, *Australia* **93 F2** 33 40 S 117 33 E
Katastári, *Greece* **38 D2** 37 50N 20 45 E
Katavi Swamp, *Tanzania* **86 D3** 6 50 S 31 10 E
Kateríni, *Greece* **40 F6** 40 18N 22 37 E
Katghora, *India* **69 H10** 22 30N 82 33 E
Katha, *Burma* **67 G20** 24 10N 96 30 E
Katherîna, Gebel, *Egypt* **70 D2** 28 30N 33 57 E
Katherine, *Australia* **92 B5** 14 27 S 132 20 E
Katherine Gorge, *Australia* **92 B5** 14 18 S 132 28 E
Kathi, *India* **68 J6** 21 47N 74 3 E
Kathiawar, *India* **68 H4** 22 20N 71 0 E
Kathikas, *Cyprus* **36 E11** 34 55N 32 25 E
Kathua, *India* **68 C6** 32 23N 75 34 E
Kati, *Mali* **82 C3** 12 41N 8 4W
Katihar, *India* **69 G12** 25 34N 87 36 E
Katima Mulilo, *Zambia* **88 B3** 17 28 S 24 13 E
Katimbira, *Malawi* **87 E3** 12 40 S 34 0 E
Katingan = Mendawai →, *Indonesia* **62 E4** 3 30 S 113 0 E
Katiola, *Ivory C.* **82 D3** 8 10N 5 10W
Katlanovo, *Macedonia* **40 E5** 41 52N 21 40 E
Katmandu, *Nepal* **69 F11** 27 45N 85 20 E
Katni, *India* **69 H9** 23 51N 80 24 E
Káto Akhaïa, *Greece* **38 C3** 38 8N 21 33 E
Káto Arkhánai, *Greece* **36 D7** 35 15N 25 10 E
Káto Khorió, *Greece* **36 D7** 35 3N 25 47 E
Káto Pyrgos, *Cyprus* **36 D11** 35 11N 32 41 E
Káto Stavros, *Greece* **40 F7** 40 39N 23 43 E
Katokhí, *Greece* **38 C3** 38 26N 21 15 E
Katompe, *Dem. Rep. of the Congo* **86 D2** 6 2 S 26 23 E
Katonga →, *Uganda* **86 B3** 0 34N 31 50 E
Katoomba, *Australia* **95 E5** 33 41 S 150 19 E
Katoúna, *Greece* **38 C3** 38 47N 21 7 E
Katowice, *Poland* **45 H6** 50 17N 19 5 E
Katrancı Dağı, *Turkey* **39 D12** 37 27N 30 25 E
Katrine, L., *U.K.* **14 E4** 56 15N 4 30W
Katrineholm, *Sweden* **11 E10** 59 9N 16 12 E
Katsepe, *Madag.* **89 B8** 15 45 S 46 15 E
Katsina, *Nigeria* **83 C6** 13 0N 7 32 E
Katsina □, *Nigeria* **83 C6** 12 30N 7 30 E
Katsina Ala, *Nigeria* **83 D6** 7 10N 9 30 E
Katsina Ala →, *Nigeria* **83 D6** 7 10N 9 20 E
Katsumoto, *Japan* **55 H4** 33 51N 129 42 E
Katsuura, *Japan* **55 G10** 35 10N 140 20 E
Katsuyama, *Japan* **55 F8** 36 3N 136 30 E
Kattaviá, *Greece* **36 D9** 35 57N 27 46 E
Kattegat, *Denmark* **11 H5** 56 40N 11 20 E
Katthammarsvik, *Sweden* **11 G12** 57 26N 18 51 E
Katul, J., *Sudan* **81 E2** 14 12N 29 25 E
Katumba, *Dem. Rep. of the Congo* **86 D2** 7 40 S 25 17 E
Katungu, *Kenya* **86 C5** 2 55 S 40 3 E
Katwa, *India* **69 H13** 23 30N 88 5 E
Katwijk, *Neths.* **17 B4** 52 12N 4 24 E
Kąty Wrocławskie, *Poland* **45 G3** 51 2N 16 45 E
Kauai, *U.S.A.* **106 H15** 22 3N 159 30W
Kauai Channel, *U.S.A.* **106 H15** 21 45N 158 50W
Kaub, *Germany* **25 E3** 50 5N 7 46 E
Kaufbeuren, *Germany* **25 H6** 47 53N 10 37 E
Kaufman, *U.S.A.* **113 J6** 32 35N 96 19W
Kauhajoki, *Finland* **9 E20** 62 25N 22 10 E
Kaukauna, *U.S.A.* **108 C1** 44 17N 88 17W
Kaukauveld, *Namibia* **88 C3** 20 0 S 20 15 E
Kaunakakai, *U.S.A.* **106 H16** 21 6N 157 1W
Kaunas, *Lithuania* **9 J20** 54 54N 23 54 E
Kaunia, *Bangla.* **69 G13** 25 46N 89 26 E
Kaunos, *Turkey* **39 E10** 36 49N 28 39 E
Kaura Namoda, *Nigeria* **83 C6** 12 37N 6 33 E
Kauru, *Nigeria* **83 C6** 10 33N 8 12 E
Kautokeino, *Norway* **8 B20** 69 0N 23 4 E
Kauwapur, *India* **69 F10** 27 31N 82 18 E
Kavacha, *Russia* **51 C17** 60 16N 169 51 E
Kavadarci, *Macedonia* **40 E6** 41 26N 22 3 E
Kavaja = Kavajë, *Albania* **40 E3** 41 11N 19 33 E
Kavajë, *Albania* **40 E3** 41 11N 19 33 E
Kavak, *Turkey* **72 B7** 41 4N 36 3 E
Kavak Dağı, *Turkey* **39 D10** 37 10N 28 2 E
Kavaklı, *Turkey* **41 E11** 41 39N 27 10 E
Kavaklıdere, *Turkey* **39 D10** 37 27N 28 21 E
Kavalerovo, *Russia* **54 B7** 44 15N 135 4 E
Kavali, *India* **66 M12** 14 55N 80 1 E
Kavála, *Greece* **41 F8** 40 57N 24 28 E
Kavála □, *Greece* **41 E8** 41 5N 24 30 E
Kavála Kólpos, *Greece* **41 F8** 40 50N 24 25 E
Kavār, *Iran* **71 D7** 29 11N 52 44 E
Kavarna, *Bulgaria* **41 C12** 43 26N 28 22 E
Kavi, *India* **68 H5** 22 12N 72 38 E
Kavimba, *Botswana* **88 B3** 18 2 S 24 38 E
Kavīr, Dasht-e, *Iran* **71 C7** 34 30N 55 0 E
Kavkaz, *Russia* **47 K9** 45 20N 36 40 E
Kävlinge, *Sweden* **11 J7** 55 47N 13 9 E
Kavos, *Greece* **36 B4** 39 23N 20 3 E
Kavoúsi, *Greece* **39 F7** 35 7N 25 51 E
Kaw, *Fr. Guiana* **125 C8** 4 30N 52 15W
Kawa, *Sudan* **81 E3** 13 42N 32 34 E
Kawagama L., *Canada* **110 A6** 45 18N 78 45W
Kawagoe, *Japan* **55 G9** 35 55N 139 29 E
Kawaguchi, *Japan* **55 G9** 35 52N 139 45 E
Kawaihae, *U.S.A.* **106 H17** 20 3N 155 50W
Kawambwa, *Zambia* **87 D2** 9 48 S 29 3 E
Kawanoe, *Japan* **55 G6** 34 1N 133 34 E
Kawardha, *India* **69 J9** 22 0N 81 17 E
Kawasaki, *Japan* **55 G9** 35 35N 139 42 E
Kawasi, *Indonesia* **63 E7** 1 38 S 127 28 E
Kawerau, *N.Z.* **91 H6** 38 7 S 176 42 E
Kawhia Harbour, *N.Z.* **91 H5** 38 5 S 174 51 E
Kawio, Kepulauan, *Indonesia* **63 D7** 4 30N 125 30 E
Kawnro, *Burma* **67 H21** 22 48N 99 8 E
Kawthaung, *Burma* **65 H2** 10 5N 98 36 E
Kawthoolei = Kawthule □, *Burma* **67 L20** 18 0N 97 30 E
Kawthule □, *Burma* **67 L20** 18 0N 97 30 E
Kaxholmen, *Sweden* **11 G8** 57 51N 14 19 E
Kaya, *Burkina Faso* **83 C4** 13 4N 1 10W
Kayah □, *Burma* **67 K20** 19 15N 97 15 E
Kayalıköy Barajı, *Turkey* **41 E11** 41 50N 27 5 E
Kayan →, *Indonesia* **62 D5** 2 55N 117 35 E
Kaycee, *U.S.A.* **114 E10** 43 43N 106 38W
Kayeli, *Indonesia* **63 E7** 3 20 S 127 10 E
Kayenta, *U.S.A.* **115 H8** 36 44N 110 15W
Kayes, *Mali* **82 C2** 14 25N 11 30W
Kayı, *Turkey* **39 B12** 39 12N 30 46 E
Kayima, *S. Leone* **82 D2** 8 54N 11 15W
Kayin = Kawthule □, *Burma* **67 L20** 18 0N 97 30 E
Kaymakçı, *Turkey* **39 C10** 38 10N 28 8 E
Kayoa, *Indonesia* **63 D7** 0 1N 127 28 E
Kayomba, *Zambia* **87 E1** 13 11 S 24 2 E
Kaysatskoye, *Russia* **49 F8** 49 47N 46 49 E
Kayseri, *Turkey* **70 B2** 38 45N 35 30 E
Kaysville, *U.S.A.* **114 F8** 41 2N 111 56W
Kaz Dağı, *Turkey* **39 B8** 39 42N 26 50 E
Kazachye, *Russia* **51 B14** 70 52N 135 58 E
Kazakstan ■, *Asia* **50 E7** 50 0N 70 0 E
Kazan, *Russia* **48 C9** 55 50N 49 10 E
Kazan →, *Canada* **105 A9** 64 3N 95 35W
Kazan-Rettō, *Pac. Oc.* **96 E6** 25 0N 141 0 E
Kazanlŭk, *Bulgaria* **41 D9** 42 38N 25 20 E
Kazanskaya, *Russia* **48 F5** 49 50N 41 10 E
Kazatin = Kozyatyn, *Ukraine* **47 H5** 49 45N 28 50 E
Kazaure, *Nigeria* **83 C6** 12 42N 8 28 E
Kazbek, *Russia* **49 J7** 42 42N 44 30 E
Kāzerūn, *Iran* **71 D6** 29 38N 51 40 E
Kazi Magomed = Qazimämmäd, *Azerbaijan* **49 K9** 40 3N 49 0 E
Kazimierz Dolny, *Poland* **45 G8** 51 19N 21 57 E
Kazimierza Wielka, *Poland* **45 H7** 50 15N 20 30 E
Kazincbarcika, *Hungary* **42 B5** 48 17N 20 36 E
Kazlų Rūda, *Lithuania* **44 D10** 54 46N 23 30 E
Kaztalovka, *Kazakstan* **48 F9** 49 47N 48 43 E
Kazuno, *Japan* **54 D10** 40 10N 140 45 E
Kazym →, *Russia* **50 C7** 63 54N 65 50 E
Kcynia, *Poland* **45 F4** 53 0N 17 30 E
Ké-Macina, *Mali* **82 C3** 13 58N 5 22W
Kéa, *Greece* **38 D6** 37 35N 24 22 E
Keady, *U.K.* **15 B5** 54 15N 6 42W
Kearney, *U.S.A.* **112 E5** 40 42N 99 5W
Kearny, *U.S.A.* **115 K8** 33 3N 110 55W
Kearsarge, Mt., *U.S.A.* **111 C13** 43 22N 71 50W
Keban, *Turkey* **73 C8** 38 50N 38 50 E
Keban Baraji, *Turkey* **70 B3** 38 41N 38 33 E
Kebbi □, *Nigeria* **83 C5** 11 35N 4 0 E
Kébi, *Ivory C.* **82 D3** 9 18N 6 37W
Kebnekaise, *Sweden* **8 C18** 67 53N 18 33 E
Kebri Dehar, *Ethiopia* **74 F3** 6 45N 44 17 E
Kebumen, *Indonesia* **63 G13** 7 42 S 109 40 E
Kecel, *Hungary* **42 D4** 46 31N 19 16 E
Kechika →, *Canada* **104 B3** 59 41N 127 12W
Keçiborlu, *Turkey* **39 D12** 37 57N 30 18 E
Kecskemét, *Hungary* **42 D4** 46 57N 19 42 E
Kedada, *Ethiopia* **81 F4** 5 25N 35 58 E
Kėdainiai, *Lithuania* **9 J21** 55 15N 24 2 E
Kedarnath, *India* **69 D8** 30 44N 79 4 E
Kedgwick, *Canada* **103 C6** 47 40N 67 20W
Kédhros Óros, *Greece* **36 D6** 35 11N 24 37 E
Kediri, *Indonesia* **63 G15** 7 51 S 112 1 E
Kedjebi, *Ghana* **83 D5** 8 12N 0 25 E
Kédougou, *Senegal* **82 C2** 12 35N 12 10W
Kędzierzyn-Koźle, *Poland* **45 H5** 50 20N 18 12 E
Keeler, *U.S.A.* **116 J9** 36 29N 117 52W
Keeley L., *Canada* **105 C7** 54 54N 108 8W
Keeling Is. = Cocos Is., *Ind. Oc.* **96 J1** 12 10 S 96 55 E
Keelung = Chilung, *Taiwan* **59 E13** 25 3N 121 45 E
Keene, *Canada* **110 B6** 44 15N 78 10W
Keene, *Calif., U.S.A.* **117 K8** 35 13N 118 33W
Keene, *N.H., U.S.A.* **111 D12** 42 56N 72 17W
Keene, *N.Y., U.S.A.* **111 B11** 44 16N 73 46W
Keeper Hill, *Ireland* **15 D3** 52 45N 8 16W
Keer-Weer, C., *Australia* **94 A3** 14 0 S 141 32 E
Keeseville, *U.S.A.* **111 B11** 44 29N 73 30W
Keetmanshoop, *Namibia* **88 D2** 26 35 S 18 8 E
Keewatin, *Canada* **105 D10** 49 46N 94 34W
Keewatin →, *Canada* **105 B8** 56 29N 100 46W
Kefa □, *Ethiopia* **81 F4** 6 55N 36 30 E
Kefallinía, *Greece* **38 C2** 38 20N 20 30 E
Kefallinía □, *Greece* **38 C2** 38 20N 20 30 E
Kéfalos, *Greece* **39 E8** 36 45N 26 59 E
Kefamenanu, *Indonesia* **63 F6** 9 28 S 124 29 E
Kefar Sava, *Israel* **75 C3** 32 11N 34 54 E
Keffi, *Nigeria* **83 D6** 8 55N 7 43 E
Keffin Hausa, *Nigeria* **83 C6** 12 13N 9 59 E
Keflavík, *Iceland* **8 D2** 64 2N 22 35W
Keftya, *Ethiopia* **81 E4** 13 54N 37 7 E
Keg River, *Canada* **104 B5** 57 54N 117 55W
Kegaska, *Canada* **103 B7** 50 9N 61 18W
Keheili, *Sudan* **80 D3** 19 25N 32 50 E
Kehl, *Germany* **25 G3** 48 34N 7 50 E
Keighley, *U.K.* **12 D6** 53 52N 1 54W
Keila, *Estonia* **9 G21** 59 18N 24 25 E
Keimoes, *S. Africa* **88 D3** 28 41 S 20 59 E
Keita, *Niger* **83 C6** 14 46N 5 56 E
Keitele, *Finland* **8 E22** 63 10N 26 20 E
Keith, *Australia* **95 F3** 36 6 S 140 20 E
Keith, *U.K.* **14 D6** 57 32N 2 57W
Keizer, *U.S.A.* **114 D2** 44 57N 123 1W
Kejimkujik Nat. Park, *Canada* **103 D6** 44 25N 65 25W
Kejser Franz Joseph Fd., *Greenland* **4 B6** 73 30N 24 30W
Kekri, *India* **68 G6** 26 0N 75 10 E
Kelam, *Ethiopia* **81 G4** 4 48N 35 58 E
Kelamet, *Eritrea* **81 D4** 16 0N 38 30 E
Kelan, *China* **56 E6** 38 43N 111 31 E
Kelang, *Malaysia* **65 L3** 3 2N 101 26 E
Kelantan →, *Malaysia* **65 J4** 6 13N 102 14 E
Këlcyra = Këlcyrë, *Albania* **40 F4** 40 20N 20 12 E
Këlcyrë, *Albania* **40 F4** 40 20N 20 12 E
Kelekçi, *Turkey* **39 D11** 37 15N 29 20 E
Keles, *Turkey* **41 G13** 39 54N 29 14 E
Keleti-főcsatorna, *Hungary* **42 C6** 47 45N 21 20 E
Kelheim, *Germany* **25 G7** 48 54N 11 52 E
Kelkit, *Turkey* **73 B8** 40 7N 39 16 E
Kelkit →, *Turkey* **72 B7** 40 45N 36 32 E
Kellerberrin, *Australia* **93 F2** 31 36 S 117 38 E
Kellett, C., *Canada* **4 B1** 72 0N 126 0W
Kelleys I., *U.S.A.* **110 E2** 41 36N 82 42W
Kellogg, *U.S.A.* **114 C5** 47 32N 116 7W
Kells = Ceanannus Mor, *Ireland* **15 C5** 53 44N 6 53W
Kelmė, *Lithuania* **44 C9** 55 38N 22 56 E
Kelokedhara, *Cyprus* **36 E11** 34 48N 32 39 E
Kelowna, *Canada* **104 D5** 49 50N 119 25W
Kelseyville, *U.S.A.* **116 G4** 38 59N 122 50W
Kelso, *N.Z.* **91 L2** 45 54 S 169 15 E
Kelso, *U.K.* **14 F6** 55 36N 2 26W
Kelso, *U.S.A.* **116 D4** 46 9N 122 54W
Keluang, *Malaysia* **65 L4** 2 3N 103 18 E
Kelvington, *Canada* **105 C8** 52 10N 103 30W
Kem, *Russia* **50 C4** 65 0N 34 38 E
Kema, *Indonesia* **63 D7** 1 22N 125 8 E
Kemah, *Turkey* **70 B3** 39 32N 39 5 E
Kemaliye, *Erzincan, Turkey* **73 C8** 39 16N 38 29 E
Kemaliye, *Manisa, Turkey* **39 C10** 38 27N 28 25 E
Kemalpaşa, *Turkey* **39 C9** 38 25N 27 27 E
Kemaman, *Malaysia* **62 D2** 4 12N 103 18 E
Kemano, *Canada* **104 C3** 53 35N 128 0W
Kemasik, *Malaysia* **65 K4** 4 25N 103 27 E
Kembolcha, *Ethiopia* **81 E4** 11 2N 39 42 E
Kemer, *Antalya, Turkey* **39 E12** 36 36N 30 34 E
Kemer, *Burdur, Turkey* **39 D12** 37 21N 30 4 E
Kemer, *Muğla, Turkey* **39 E11** 36 40N 29 22 E
Kemer Barajı, *Turkey* **39 D10** 37 30N 28 37 E
Kemerovo, *Russia* **50 D9** 55 20N 86 5 E
Kemi, *Finland* **8 D21** 65 44N 24 34 E
Kemi älv = Kemijoki →, *Finland* **8 D21** 65 47N 24 32 E
Kemijärvi, *Finland* **8 C22** 66 43N 27 22 E
Kemijoki →, *Finland* **8 D21** 65 47N 24 32 E
Kemmerer, *U.S.A.* **114 F8** 41 48N 110 32W
Kemmuna = Comino, *Malta* **36 C1** 36 2N 14 20 E
Kemp, L., *U.S.A.* **113 J5** 33 46N 99 9W
Kemp Land, *Antarctica* **5 C5** 69 0 S 55 0 E
Kempsey, *Australia* **95 E5** 31 1 S 152 50 E
Kempt, L., *Canada* **102 C5** 47 25N 74 22W
Kempten, *Germany* **25 H6** 47 45N 10 17 E
Kempton, *Australia* **94 G4** 42 31 S 147 12 E
Kemptville, *Canada* **102 D4** 45 0N 75 38W
Ken →, *India* **69 G9** 25 13N 80 27 E
Kenai, *U.S.A.* **100 B4** 60 33N 151 16W
Kendai, *India* **69 H10** 22 45N 82 37 E
Kendal, *Indonesia* **63 G14** 6 56 S 110 14 E
Kendal, *U.K.* **12 C5** 54 20N 2 44W
Kendall, *Australia* **95 E5** 31 35 S 152 44 E
Kendall, *U.S.A.* **109 N5** 25 41N 80 19W
Kendall →, *Australia* **94 A3** 14 4 S 141 35 E
Kendallville, *U.S.A.* **108 E3** 41 27N 85 16W
Kendari, *Indonesia* **63 E6** 3 50 S 122 30 E
Kendawangan, *Indonesia* **62 E4** 2 32 S 110 17 E
Kende, *Nigeria* **83 C5** 11 30N 4 12 E
Kendervicës, Mal e. = Këndrevicës, Maja e, *Albania* **40 F3** 40 15N 19 52 E
Kendrapara, *India* **67 J15** 20 35N 86 30 E
Këndrevicës, Maja e, *Albania* **40 F3** 40 15N 19 52 E
Kendrew, *S. Africa* **88 E3** 32 32 S 24 30 E
Kene Thao, *Laos* **64 D3** 17 44N 101 10 E
Kenedy, *U.S.A.* **113 L6** 28 49N 97 51W
Kenema, *S. Leone* **82 D2** 7 50N 11 14W
Keng Kok, *Laos* **64 D5** 16 26N 105 12 E
Keng Tawng, *Burma* **67 J21** 20 45N 98 18 E
Keng Tung, *Burma* **58 G2** 21 0N 99 30 E
Kengeja, *Tanzania* **86 D4** 5 26 S 39 45 E
Kenhardt, *S. Africa* **88 D3** 29 19 S 21 12 E
Kéniéba, *Mali* **82 C2** 12 54N 11 17W
Kenitra, *Morocco* **78 B4** 34 15N 6 40W
Kenli, *China* **57 F10** 37 30N 118 20 E
Kenmare, *Ireland* **15 E2** 51 53N 9 36W
Kenmare, *U.S.A.* **112 A3** 48 41N 102 5W
Kenmare River, *Ireland* **15 E2** 51 48N 9 51W
Kennebago Lake, *U.S.A.* **111 A14** 45 4N 70 40W
Kennebec, *U.S.A.* **112 D5** 43 54N 99 52W
Kennebec →, *U.S.A.* **109 D11** 43 45N 69 46W
Kennebunk, *U.S.A.* **111 C14** 43 23N 70 33W
Kennedy, *Zimbabwe* **88 B4** 18 52 S 27 10 E
Kennedy Ra., *Australia* **93 D2** 24 45 S 115 10 E
Kennedy Taungdeik, *Burma* **67 H18** 23 15N 93 45 E
Kenner, *U.S.A.* **113 L9** 29 59N 90 15W
Kennet →, *U.K.* **13 F7** 51 27N 0 57W
Kenneth Ra., *Australia* **93 D2** 23 50 S 117 8 E
Kennett, *U.S.A.* **113 G9** 36 14N 90 3W
Kennewick, *U.S.A.* **114 C4** 46 12N 119 7W
Kenogami →, *Canada* **102 B3** 51 6N 84 28W
Kenora, *Canada* **105 D10** 49 47N 94 29W
Kenosha, *U.S.A.* **108 D2** 42 35N 87 49W
Kensington, *Canada* **103 C7** 46 28N 63 34W
Kent, *Ohio, U.S.A.* **110 E3** 41 9N 81 22W
Kent, *Tex., U.S.A.* **113 K2** 31 4N 104 13W
Kent, *Wash., U.S.A.* **116 C4** 47 23N 122 14W
Kent □, *U.K.* **13 F8** 51 12N 0 40 E
Kent Group, *Australia* **94 F4** 39 30 S 147 20 E
Kent Pen., *Canada* **100 B9** 68 30N 107 0W
Kentau, *Kazakstan* **50 E7** 43 32N 68 36 E
Kentland, *U.S.A.* **108 E2** 40 46N 87 27W
Kenton, *U.S.A.* **108 E4** 40 39N 83 37W
Kentucky □, *U.S.A.* **108 G3** 37 0N 84 0W
Kentucky →, *U.S.A.* **108 F3** 38 41N 85 11W
Kentucky L., *U.S.A.* **109 G2** 37 1N 88 16W
Kentville, *Canada* **103 C7** 45 6N 64 29W
Kentwood, *U.S.A.* **113 K9** 30 56N 90 31W
Kenya ■, *Africa* **86 B4** 1 0N 38 0 E
Kenya, Mt., *Kenya* **86 C4** 0 10 S 37 18 E
Keo Neua, Deo, *Vietnam* **64 C5** 18 23N 105 10 E
Keokuk, *U.S.A.* **112 E9** 40 24N 91 24W
Keonjhargarh, *India* **69 J11** 21 28N 85 35 E
Kep, *Cambodia* **65 G5** 10 29N 104 19 E
Kep, *Vietnam* **64 B6** 21 24N 106 16 E
Kepez, *Turkey* **41 F10** 40 5N 26 24 E
Kepi, *Indonesia* **63 F9** 6 32 S 139 19 E
Kępice, *Poland* **44 D3** 54 16N 16 51 E
Kępno, *Poland* **45 G4** 51 18N 17 58 E
Kepsut, *Turkey* **39 B10** 39 40N 28 9 E
Kerala □, *India* **66 P10** 11 0N 76 15 E
Kerama-Rettō, *Japan* **55 L3** 26 5N 127 15 E
Keran, *Pakistan* **69 B5** 34 35N 73 59 E
Kerang, *Australia* **95 F3** 35 40 S 143 55 E
Keranyo, *Ethiopia* **81 F4** 5 3N 38 18 E
Kerao →, *Sudan* **81 E3** 11 0N 32 41 E
Keratéa, *Greece* **38 D5** 37 48N 23 58 E
Keraudren, C., *Australia* **92 C2** 19 58 S 119 45 E
Kerava, *Finland* **9 F21** 60 25N 25 5 E
Kerch, *Ukraine* **47 K9** 45 20N 36 20 E
Kerchenskiy Proliv, *Black Sea* **47 K9** 45 10N 36 30 E
Kerchoual, *Mali* **83 B5** 17 12N 0 20 E
Kerempe Burnu, *Turkey* **72 A5** 42 2N 33 20 E
Keren, *Eritrea* **81 D4** 15 45N 38 28 E
Kerewan, *Gambia* **82 C1** 13 29N 16 10W
Kerguelen, *Ind. Oc.* **3 G13** 49 15 S 69 10 E
Keri, *Greece* **38 D2** 37 40N 20 49 E
Keri Kera, *Sudan* **81 E3** 12 21N 32 42 E
Kericho, *Kenya* **86 C4** 0 22 S 35 15 E
Kerinci, *Indonesia* **62 E2** 1 40 S 101 15 E
Kerki, *Turkmenistan* **50 F7** 37 50N 65 12 E
Kerkinítis, Límni, *Greece* **40 E7** 41 12N 23 10 E
Kérkira, *Greece* **36 A3** 39 38N 19 50 E
Kérkira □, *Greece* **38 B1** 39 37N 19 50 E
Kerkrade, *Neths.* **17 D6** 50 53N 6 4 E
Kerma, *Sudan* **80 D3** 19 33N 30 32 E
Kermadec Is., *Pac. Oc.* **96 L10** 30 0 S 178 15W
Kermadec Trench, *Pac. Oc.* **96 L10** 30 30 S 176 0W
Kermān, *Iran* **71 D8** 30 15N 57 1 E
Kerman, *U.S.A.* **116 J6** 36 43N 120 4W
Kermān □, *Iran* **71 D8** 30 0N 57 0 E
Kermān, Bīābān-e, *Iran* **71 D8** 28 45N 59 45 E
Kermānshāh = Bākhtarān, *Iran* **70 C5** 34 23N 47 0 E
Kermen, *Bulgaria* **41 D10** 42 30N 26 16 E
Kermit, *U.S.A.* **113 K3** 31 52N 103 6W
Kern →, *U.S.A.* **117 K7** 35 16N 119 18W
Kernhof, *Austria* **26 D8** 47 49N 15 32 E
Kernville, *U.S.A.* **117 K8** 35 45N 118 26W
Keroh, *Malaysia* **65 K3** 5 43N 101 1 E
Kérou, *Benin* **83 C5** 10 50N 2 5 E
Kérouane, *Guinea* **82 D3** 9 15N 9 0W
Kerpen, *Germany* **24 E2** 50 51N 6 41 E
Kerrera, *U.K.* **14 E3** 56 24N 5 33W
Kerrobert, *Canada* **105 C7** 51 56N 109 8W
Kerrville, *U.S.A.* **113 K5** 30 3N 99 8W
Kerry □, *Ireland* **15 D2** 52 7N 9 35W
Kerry Hd., *Ireland* **15 D2** 52 25N 9 56W
Kersa, *Ethiopia* **81 F5** 9 28N 41 48 E
Kerulen →, *Asia* **60 B6** 48 48N 117 0 E
Kerzaz, *Algeria* **78 C5** 29 29N 1 37W
Kesagami →, *Canada* **102 B4** 51 40N 79 45W
Kesagami L., *Canada* **102 B3** 50 23N 80 15W
Keşan, *Turkey* **41 F10** 40 49N 26 38 E
Kesennuma, *Japan* **54 E10** 38 54N 141 35 E
Keshit, *Iran* **71 D8** 29 43N 58 17 E
Keşiş Dağ, *Turkey* **73 C8** 39 47N 39 46 E
Keskin, *Turkey* **72 C5** 39 40N 33 36 E
Kestell, *S. Africa* **89 D4** 28 17 S 28 42 E
Kestenga, *Russia* **50 C4** 65 50N 31 45 E
Keswick, *U.K.* **12 C4** 54 36N 3 8W
Keszthely, *Hungary* **42 D2** 46 50N 17 15 E
Ket →, *Russia* **50 D9** 58 55N 81 32 E
Keta, *Ghana* **83 D5** 5 49N 1 0 E
Keta Lagoon, *Ghana* **83 D5** 5 55N 1 0 E
Ketapang, *Indonesia* **62 E4** 1 55 S 110 0 E
Ketchikan, *U.S.A.* **104 B2** 55 21N 131 39W
Ketchum, *U.S.A.* **114 E6** 43 41N 114 22W
Kete Krachi, *Ghana* **83 D4** 7 46N 0 1W
Ketef, Khalîg Umm el, *Egypt* **70 F2** 23 40N 35 35 E
Keti Bandar, *Pakistan* **68 G2** 24 8N 67 27 E
Kétou, *Benin* **83 D5** 7 25N 2 45 E
Ketri, *India* **68 E6** 28 1N 75 50 E
Kętrzyn, *Poland* **44 D8** 54 7N 21 22 E
Kettering, *U.K.* **13 E7** 52 24N 0 43W
Kettering, *U.S.A.* **108 F3** 39 41N 84 10W
Kettle →, *Canada* **105 B11** 56 40N 89 34W
Kettle Falls, *U.S.A.* **114 B4** 48 37N 118 3W
Kettle Pt., *Canada* **110 C2** 43 13N 82 1W
Kettleman City, *U.S.A.* **116 J7** 36 1N 119 58W
Kęty, *Poland* **45 J6** 49 51N 19 16 E
Keuka L., *U.S.A.* **110 D7** 42 30N 77 9W
Keuruu, *Finland* **9 E21** 62 16N 24 41 E
Kevelaer, *Germany* **24 D2** 51 36N 6 15 E
Kewanee, *U.S.A.* **112 E10** 41 14N 89 56W
Kewaunee, *U.S.A.* **108 C2** 44 27N 87 31W
Keweenaw B., *U.S.A.* **108 B1** 47 0N 88 15W
Keweenaw Pen., *U.S.A.* **108 B2** 47 30N 88 0W
Keweenaw Pt., *U.S.A.* **108 B2** 47 25N 87 43W
Key Largo, *U.S.A.* **109 N5** 25 5N 80 27W
Key West, *U.S.A.* **107 F10** 24 33N 81 48W
Keyala, *Sudan* **81 G3** 4 27N 32 52 E
Keynsham, *U.K.* **13 F5** 51 24N 2 29W
Keyser, *U.S.A.* **108 F6** 39 26N 78 59W
Kezhma, *Russia* **51 D11** 58 59N 101 9 E
Kezi, *Zimbabwe* **89 C4** 20 58 S 28 32 E
Kežmarok, *Slovak Rep.* **27 B13** 49 10N 20 28 E
Khabarovsk, *Russia* **51 E14** 48 30N 135 5 E
Khabr, *Iran* **71 D8** 28 51N 56 22 E
Khābūr →, *Syria* **70 C4** 35 17N 40 35 E
Khachmas = Xaçmaz, *Azerbaijan* **49 K9** 41 31N 48 42 E
Khachrod, *India* **68 H6** 23 25N 75 20 E

Khadari, W. el →, *Sudan* **81 E2** 10 29N 27 15 E
Khadro, *Pakistan* **68 F3** 26 11N 68 50 E
Khadyzhensk, *Russia* **49 H4** 44 26N 39 32 E
Khadzhilyangar, *India* **69 B8** 35 45N 79 20 E
Khaga, *India* **69 G9** 25 47N 81 7 E
Khagaria, *India* **69 G12** 25 30N 86 32 E
Khaipur, *Pakistan* **68 E5** 29 34N 72 17 E
Khair, *India* **68 F7** 27 57N 77 46 E
Khairabad, *India* **69 F9** 27 33N 80 47 E
Khairagarh, *India* **69 J9** 21 27N 81 2 E
Khairpur, *Pakistan* **68 F3** 27 32N 68 49 E
Khairpur Nathan Shah, *Pakistan* **68 F2** 27 6N 67 44 E
Khairwara, *India* **68 H5** 23 58N 73 38 E
Khaisor →, *Pakistan* **68 D3** 31 17N 68 59 E
Khajuri Kach, *Pakistan* **68 C3** 32 4N 69 51 E
Khakassia □, *Russia* **50 D9** 53 0N 90 0 E
Khakhea, *Botswana* **88 C3** 24 48 S 23 22 E
Khalafābād, *Iran* **71 D6** 30 54N 49 24 E
Khalilabad, *India* **69 F10** 26 48N 83 5 E
Khalīlī, *Iran* **71 E7** 27 38N 53 17 E
Khalkhāl, *Iran* **71 B6** 37 37N 48 32 E
Khálki, *Dhodhekánisos, Greece* **39 E9** 36 17N 27 35 E
Khálki, *Thessalía, Greece* **38 B4** 39 36N 22 30 E
Khalkidhikí □, *Greece* **40 F7** 40 25N 23 20 E
Khalkís, *Greece* **38 C5** 38 27N 23 42 E
Khalmer-Sede = Tazovskiy, *Russia* **50 C8** 67 30N 78 44 E
Khalmer Yu, *Russia* **50 C7** 67 58N 65 1 E
Khalūf, *Oman* **74 C6** 20 30N 58 13 E
Kham Keut, *Laos* **64 C5** 18 15N 104 43 E
Khamaria, *India* **69 H9** 23 5N 80 48 E
Khambhaliya, *India* **68 H3** 22 14N 69 41 E
Khambhat, *India* **68 H5** 22 23N 72 33 E
Khambhat, G. of, *India* **66 J8** 20 45N 72 30 E
Khamilonísion, *Greece* **39 F8** 35 50N 26 15 E
Khamīr, *Iran* **71 E7** 26 57N 55 36 E
Khamir, *Yemen* **74 D3** 16 2N 44 0 E
Khamsa, *Egypt* **75 E1** 30 27N 32 23 E
Khan →, *Namibia* **88 C2** 22 37 S 14 56 E
Khān Abū Shāmat, *Syria* **75 B5** 33 39N 36 53 E
Khān Azād, *Iraq* **70 C5** 33 7N 44 22 E
Khān Mujiddah, *Iraq* **70 C4** 32 21N 43 48 E
Khān Shaykhūn, *Syria* **70 C3** 35 26N 36 38 E
Khān Yūnis, *Gaza Strip* **75 D3** 31 21N 34 18 E
Khanai, *Pakistan* **68 D2** 30 30N 67 8 E
Khānaqīn, *Iraq* **70 C5** 34 23N 45 25 E
Khānbāghī, *Iran* **71 B7** 36 10N 55 25 E
Khandrá, *Greece* **39 F8** 35 3N 26 8 E
Khandwa, *India* **66 J10** 21 49N 76 22 E
Khandyga, *Russia* **51 C14** 62 42N 135 35 E
Khāneh, *Iran* **70 B5** 36 41N 45 8 E
Khanewal, *Pakistan* **68 D4** 30 20N 71 55 E
Khangah Dogran, *Pakistan* **68 D5** 31 50N 73 37 E
Khanh Duong, *Vietnam* **64 F7** 12 44N 108 44 E
Khaniá, *Greece* **36 D6** 35 30N 24 4 E
Khaniá □, *Greece* **36 D6** 35 30N 24 0 E
Khaniadhana, *India* **68 G8** 25 1N 78 8 E
Khaníon, Kólpos, *Greece* **36 D5** 35 33N 23 55 E
Khanka, L., *Asia* **51 E14** 45 0N 132 24 E
Khankendy = Xankändi, *Azerbaijan* **70 B5** 39 52N 46 49 E
Khanna, *India* **68 D7** 30 42N 76 16 E
Khanozai, *Pakistan* **68 D2** 30 37N 67 19 E
Khanpur, *Pakistan* **68 E4** 28 42N 70 35 E
Khanty-Mansiysk, *Russia* **50 C7** 61 0N 69 0 E
Khapalu, *Pakistan* **69 B7** 35 10N 76 20 E
Khapcheranga, *Russia* **51 E12** 49 42N 112 24 E
Kharabali, *Russia* **49 G8** 47 25N 47 15 E
Kharaghoda, *India* **68 H4** 23 11N 71 46 E
Kharagpur, *India* **69 H12** 22 20N 87 25 E
Khárakas, *Greece* **36 D7** 35 1N 25 7 E
Kharan Kalat, *Pakistan* **66 E4** 28 34N 65 21 E
Kharānaq, *Iran* **71 C7** 32 20N 54 45 E
Kharda, *India* **66 K9** 18 40N 75 34 E
Khardung La, *India* **69 B7** 34 20N 77 43 E
Khârga, El Wâhât-el, *Egypt* **80 B3** 25 10N 30 35 E
Khargon, *India* **66 J9** 21 45N 75 40 E
Khari →, *India* **68 G6** 25 54N 74 31 E
Kharian, *Pakistan* **68 C5** 32 49N 73 52 E
Kharit, Wadi el →, *Egypt* **80 C3** 24 26N 33 3 E
Khārk, Jazīreh-ye, *Iran* **71 D6** 29 15N 50 28 E
Kharkiv, *Ukraine* **47 H9** 49 58N 36 20 E
Kharkov = Kharkiv, *Ukraine* **47 H9** 49 58N 36 20 E
Kharmanli, *Bulgaria* **41 E9** 41 55N 25 55 E
Kharovsk, *Russia* **46 C11** 59 56N 40 13 E
Kharsawangarh, *India* **69 H11** 22 48N 85 50 E
Kharta, *Turkey* **72 B3** 40 55N 29 7 E
Khartoum = El Khartûm, *Sudan* **81 D3** 15 31N 32 35 E
Khasan, *Russia* **54 C5** 42 25N 130 40 E
Khasavyurt, *Russia* **49 J8** 43 16N 46 40 E
Khāsh, *Iran* **66 E2** 28 15N 61 15 E
Khashm el Girba, *Sudan* **81 E4** 14 59N 35 58 E
Khashum, *Sudan* **81 E2** 12 27N 28 2 E
Khashuri, *Georgia* **49 J6** 42 3N 43 35 E
Khaskovo, *Bulgaria* **41 E9** 41 56N 25 30 E
Khaskovo □, *Bulgaria* **41 E9** 42 0N 25 40 E
Khatanga, *Russia* **51 B11** 72 0N 102 20 E
Khatanga →, *Russia* **51 B11** 72 55N 106 0 E
Khatauli, *India* **68 E7** 29 17N 77 43 E
Khatra, *India* **69 H12** 22 59N 86 51 E
Khātūnābād, *Iran* **71 D7** 30 1N 55 25 E
Khatyrka, *Russia* **51 C18** 62 3N 175 15 E
Khavda, *India* **68 H3** 23 51N 69 43 E
Khaybar, Ḥarrat, *Si. Arabia* **70 E4** 25 45N 40 0 E
Khayelitsha, *S. Africa* **85 L3** 34 5 S 18 42 E
Khāzimiyah, *Iraq* **70 C4** 34 46N 43 37 E
Khazzān Jabal al Awliyā, *Sudan* **81 D3** 15 24N 32 20 E
Khe Bo, *Vietnam* **64 C5** 19 8N 104 41 E
Khe Long, *Vietnam* **64 B5** 21 29N 104 46 E
Khed Brahma, *India* **66 G8** 24 7N 73 5 E
Khekra, *India* **68 E7** 28 52N 77 20 E
Khemarak Phouminville, *Cambodia* **65 G4** 11 37N 102 59 E
Khemisset, *Morocco* **78 B4** 33 50N 6 1W
Khemmarat, *Thailand* **64 D5** 16 10N 105 15 E
Khenāmān, *Iran* **71 D8** 30 27N 56 29 E
Khenchela, *Algeria* **78 A7** 35 28N 7 11 E
Khersān →, *Iran* **71 D6** 31 33N 50 22 E
Khérson, *Greece* **40 E6** 41 5N 22 47 E
Kherson, *Ukraine* **47 J7** 46 35N 32 35 E
Khersónisos Akrotíri, *Greece* **36 D6** 35 30N 24 10 E
Kheta →, *Russia* **51 B11** 71 54N 102 6 E
Khewari, *Pakistan* **68 F3** 26 36N 68 52 E
Khilchipur, *India* **68 G7** 24 2N 76 34 E
Khiliomódhion, *Greece* **38 D4** 37 48N 22 51 E
Khilok, *Russia* **51 D12** 51 30N 110 45 E
Khimki, *Russia* **46 E9** 55 50N 37 20 E
Khíos, *Greece* **39 C8** 38 27N 26 9 E
Khíos □, *Greece* **39 C8** 38 27N 26 9 E
Khirsadoh, *India* **69 H8** 22 11N 78 47 E
Khiuma = Hiiumaa, *Estonia* **9 G20** 58 50N 22 45 E
Khiva, *Uzbekistan* **50 E7** 41 30N 60 18 E
Khīyāv, *Iran* **70 B5** 38 30N 47 45 E
Khlebarovo, *Bulgaria* **41 C10** 43 37N 26 15 E
Khlong Khlung, *Thailand* **64 D2** 16 12N 99 43 E
Khmelnik, *Ukraine* **47 H4** 49 33N 27 58 E
Khmelnitskiy = Khmelnytskyy, *Ukraine* **47 H4** 49 23N 27 0 E
Khmelnytskyy, *Ukraine* **47 H4** 49 23N 27 0 E
Khmer Rep. = Cambodia ■, *Asia* **64 F5** 12 15N 105 0 E
Khoai, Hon, *Vietnam* **65 H5** 8 26N 104 50 E
Khodoriv, *Ukraine* **47 H3** 49 24N 24 19 E
Khodzent = Khudzhand, *Tajikistan* **50 E7** 40 17N 69 37 E
Khojak Pass, *Afghan.* **68 D2** 30 51N 66 34 E
Khok Kloi, *Thailand* **65 H2** 8 17N 98 19 E
Khok Pho, *Thailand* **65 J3** 6 43N 101 6 E
Kholm, *Russia* **46 D6** 57 10N 31 15 E
Kholmsk, *Russia* **51 E15** 47 40N 142 5 E
Khomas Hochland, *Namibia* **88 C2** 22 40 S 16 0 E
Khombole, *Senegal* **82 C1** 14 43N 16 42W
Khomeyn, *Iran* **71 C6** 33 40N 50 7 E
Khomeynī Shahr, *Iran* **71 C6** 32 41N 51 31 E
Khomodino, *Botswana* **88 C3** 22 46 S 23 52 E
Khon Kaen, *Thailand* **64 D4** 16 30N 102 47 E
Khong →, *Cambodia* **64 F5** 13 32N 105 58 E
Khong Sedone, *Laos* **64 E5** 15 34N 105 49 E
Khonuu, *Russia* **51 C15** 66 30N 143 12 E
Khoper →, *Russia* **48 F6** 49 30N 42 20 E
Khor el 'Atash, *Sudan* **81 E3** 13 20N 34 15 E
Khóra, *Greece* **38 D3** 37 3N 21 42 E
Khóra Sfakíon, *Greece* **36 D6** 35 15N 24 9 E
Khorāsān □, *Iran* **71 C8** 34 0N 58 0 E
Khorat = Nakhon Ratchasima, *Thailand* **64 E4** 14 59N 102 12 E
Khorat, Cao Nguyen, *Thailand* **64 E4** 15 30N 102 50 E
Khorixas, *Namibia* **88 C1** 20 16 S 14 59 E
Khorol, *Ukraine* **47 H7** 49 48N 33 15 E
Khorramābād, *Khorāsān, Iran* **71 C8** 35 6N 57 57 E
Khorramābād, *Lorestān, Iran* **71 C6** 33 30N 48 25 E
Khorrāmshahr, *Iran* **71 D6** 30 29N 48 15 E
Khorugh, *Tajikistan* **50 F8** 37 30N 71 36 E
Khosravī, *Iran* **71 D6** 30 48N 51 28 E
Khosrowābād, *Khuzestān, Iran* **71 D6** 30 10N 48 25 E
Khosrowābād, *Kordestān, Iran* **70 C5** 35 31N 47 38 E
Khost, *Pakistan* **68 D2** 30 13N 67 35 E
Khosūyeh, *Iran* **71 D7** 28 32N 54 26 E
Khotyn, *Ukraine* **47 H4** 48 31N 26 27 E
Khouribga, *Morocco* **78 B4** 32 58N 6 57W
Khowai, *Bangla.* **67 G17** 24 5N 91 40 E
Khowst, *Afghan.* **68 C3** 33 22N 69 58 E
Khoyniki, *Belarus* **47 G5** 51 54N 29 55 E
Khrami →, *Georgia* **49 K7** 41 25N 45 0 E
Khrenovoye, *Russia* **48 E5** 51 4N 40 16 E
Khrisoúpolis, *Greece* **41 F8** 40 58N 24 42 E
Khristianá, *Greece* **39 E7** 36 14N 25 13 E
Khrysokhou B., *Cyprus* **36 D11** 35 6N 32 25 E
Khtapodhiá, *Greece* **39 D7** 37 24N 25 34 E
Khu Khan, *Thailand* **64 E5** 14 42N 104 12 E
Khudzhand, *Tajikistan* **50 E7** 40 17N 69 37 E
Khuff, *Si. Arabia* **70 E5** 24 55N 44 53 E
Khūgīānī, *Afghan.* **68 D1** 31 28N 65 14 E
Khuis, *Botswana* **88 D3** 26 40 S 21 49 E
Khuiyala, *India* **68 F4** 27 9N 70 25 E
Khujner, *India* **68 H7** 23 47N 76 36 E
Khulna, *Bangla.* **67 H16** 22 45N 89 34 E
Khulna □, *Bangla.* **67 H16** 22 25N 89 35 E
Khulo, *Georgia* **49 K6** 41 33N 42 19 E
Khumago, *Botswana* **88 C3** 20 26 S 24 32 E
Khūnsorkh, *Iran* **71 E8** 27 9N 56 7 E
Khunti, *India* **69 H11** 23 5N 85 17 E
Khūr, *Iran* **71 C8** 32 55N 58 18 E
Khurai, *India* **68 G8** 24 3N 78 23 E
Khurayṣ, *Si. Arabia* **71 E6** 25 6N 48 2 E
Khureit, *Sudan* **81 E2** 13 59N 26 3 E
Khurīyā Murīyā, Jazā 'ir, *Oman* **74 D6** 17 30N 55 58 E
Khurja, *India* **68 E7** 28 15N 77 58 E
Khūrmāl, *Iraq* **70 C5** 35 18N 46 2 E
Khurr, Wādī al, *Iraq* **70 C4** 32 3N 43 52 E
Khūsf, *Iran* **71 C8** 32 46N 58 53 E
Khush, *Afghan.* **66 C3** 32 55N 62 10 E
Khushab, *Pakistan* **68 C5** 32 20N 72 20 E
Khust, *Ukraine* **47 H2** 48 10N 23 18 E
Khuzdar, *Pakistan* **68 F2** 27 52N 66 30 E
Khūzestān □, *Iran* **71 D6** 31 0N 49 0 E
Khvāf, *Iran* **71 C9** 34 33N 60 8 E
Khvājeh, *Iran* **70 B5** 38 9N 46 35 E
Khvalynsk, *Russia* **48 D9** 52 30N 48 2 E
Khvānsār, *Iran* **71 D7** 29 56N 54 8 E
Khvatovka, *Russia* **48 D8** 52 24N 46 32 E
Khvor, *Iran* **71 C7** 33 45N 55 0 E
Khvorgū, *Iran* **71 E8** 27 34N 56 27 E
Khvormūj, *Iran* **71 D6** 28 40N 51 30 E
Khvoy, *Iran* **70 B5** 38 35N 45 0 E
Khvoynaya, *Russia* **46 C8** 58 58N 34 28 E
Khyber Pass, *Afghan.* **68 B4** 34 10N 71 8 E
Kiabukwa, *Dem. Rep. of the Congo* **87 D1** 8 40 S 24 48 E
Kiama, *Australia* **95 E5** 34 40 S 150 50 E
Kiamba, *Phil.* **61 H6** 6 2N 124 46 E
Kiambi, *Dem. Rep. of the Congo* **86 D2** 7 15 S 28 0 E
Kiambu, *Kenya* **86 C4** 1 8 S 36 50 E
Kiangara, *Madag.* **89 B8** 17 58 S 47 2 E
Kiangsi = Jiangxi □, *China* **59 D11** 27 30N 116 0 E
Kiangsu = Jiangsu □, *China* **57 H11** 33 0N 120 0 E
Kiáton, *Greece* **38 C4** 38 1N 22 45 E
Kibæk, *Denmark* **11 H2** 56 2N 8 51 E
Kibanga Port, *Uganda* **86 B3** 0 10N 32 58 E
Kibara, *Tanzania* **86 C3** 2 8 S 33 30 E
Kibare, Mts., *Dem. Rep. of the Congo* **86 D2** 8 25 S 27 10 E
Kibombo, *Dem. Rep. of the Congo* **86 C2** 3 57 S 25 53 E
Kibondo, *Tanzania* **86 C3** 3 35 S 30 45 E
Kibre Mengist, *Ethiopia* **81 F4** 5 54N 38 59 E
Kibumbu, *Burundi* **86 C2** 3 32 S 29 45 E
Kibungo, *Rwanda* **86 C3** 2 10 S 30 32 E
Kibuye, *Burundi* **86 C2** 3 39 S 29 59 E
Kibuye, *Rwanda* **86 C2** 2 3 S 29 21 E
Kibwesa, *Tanzania* **86 D2** 6 30 S 29 58 E
Kibwezi, *Kenya* **86 C4** 2 27 S 37 57 E
Kicasalih, *Turkey* **41 E10** 41 23N 26 48 E
Kičevo, *Macedonia* **40 E4** 41 34N 20 59 E
Kichha, *India* **69 E8** 28 53N 79 30 E
Kichha →, *India* **69 E8** 28 41N 79 18 E
Kicking Horse Pass, *Canada* **104 C5** 51 28N 116 16W
Kidal, *Mali* **83 B5** 18 26N 1 22 E
Kidderminster, *U.K.* **13 E5** 52 24N 2 15W
Kidete, *Tanzania* **86 D4** 6 25 S 37 17 E
Kidira, *Senegal* **82 C2** 14 28N 12 13W
Kidnappers, C., *N.Z.* **91 H6** 39 38 S 177 5 E
Kidsgrove, *U.K.* **12 D5** 53 5N 2 14W
Kidston, *Australia* **94 B3** 18 52 S 144 8 E
Kidugallo, *Tanzania* **86 D4** 6 49 S 38 15 E
Kiel, *Germany* **24 A6** 54 19N 10 8 E
Kiel Canal = Nord-Ostsee-Kanal, *Germany* **24 A5** 54 12N 9 32 E
Kielce, *Poland* **45 H7** 50 52N 20 42 E
Kielder Water, *U.K.* **12 B5** 55 11N 2 31W
Kieler Bucht, *Germany* **24 A6** 54 35N 10 25 E
Kiembara, *Burkina Faso* **82 C4** 13 15N 2 44W
Kien Binh, *Vietnam* **65 H5** 9 55N 105 19 E
Kien Tan, *Vietnam* **65 G5** 10 7N 105 17 E
Kienge, *Dem. Rep. of the Congo* **87 E2** 10 30 S 27 30 E
Kiessé, *Niger* **83 C5** 13 29N 4 1 E
Kiev = Kyyiv, *Ukraine* **47 G6** 50 30N 30 28 E
Kifaya, *Guinea* **82 C2** 12 10N 13 4W
Kiffa, *Mauritania* **82 B2** 16 37N 11 24W
Kifisiá, *Greece* **38 C5** 38 4N 23 49 E
Kifissós →, *Greece* **38 C5** 38 35N 23 20 E
Kifrī, *Iraq* **70 C5** 34 45N 45 0 E
Kigali, *Rwanda* **86 C3** 1 59 S 30 4 E
Kigarama, *Tanzania* **86 C3** 1 1 S 31 50 E
Kigelle, *Sudan* **81 F3** 8 40N 34 2 E
Kigoma □, *Tanzania* **86 D3** 5 0 S 30 0 E
Kigoma-Ujiji, *Tanzania* **86 C2** 4 55 S 29 36 E
Kigomasha, Ras, *Tanzania* **86 C4** 4 58 S 38 58 E
Kığzı, *Turkey* **70 B4** 38 18N 43 25 E
Kihei, *U.S.A.* **106 H16** 20 47N 156 28W
Kihnu, *Estonia* **9 G21** 58 9N 24 1 E
Kii-Sanchi, *Japan* **55 G8** 34 20N 136 0 E
Kii-Suidō, *Japan* **55 H7** 33 40N 134 45 E
Kikaiga-Shima, *Japan* **55 K4** 28 19N 129 59 E
Kikinda, *Serbia, Yug.* **42 E5** 45 50N 20 30 E
Kikládhes, *Greece* **38 E6** 37 0N 24 30 E
Kikládhes □, *Greece* **38 D6** 37 0N 25 0 E
Kikwit, *Dem. Rep. of the Congo* **84 E3** 5 0 S 18 45 E
Kil, *Sweden* **10 E7** 59 30N 13 20 E
Kilafors, *Sweden* **10 C10** 61 14N 16 36 E
Kilar, *India* **68 C7** 33 6N 76 25 E
Kilauea, *U.S.A.* **106 J14** 22 13N 159 25W
Kilauea Crater, *U.S.A.* **106 J17** 19 25N 155 17W
Kilbrannan Sd., *U.K.* **14 F3** 55 37N 5 26W
Kilchu, *N. Korea* **57 D15** 40 57N 129 25 E
Kilcoy, *Australia* **95 D5** 26 59 S 152 30 E
Kildare, *Ireland* **15 C5** 53 9N 6 55W
Kildare □, *Ireland* **15 C5** 53 10N 6 50W
Kileikli, *Sudan* **81 E2** 11 25N 25 31 E
Kilfinnane, *Ireland* **15 D3** 52 21N 8 28W
Kilgore, *U.S.A.* **113 J7** 32 23N 94 53W
Kilibo, *Benin* **83 D5** 8 32N 2 38 E
Kilifi, *Kenya* **86 C4** 3 40 S 39 48 E
Kilimanjaro, *Tanzania* **86 C4** 3 7 S 37 20 E
Kilimanjaro □, *Tanzania* **86 C4** 4 0 S 38 0 E
Kilimli, *Turkey* **72 B4** 41 28N 31 50 E
Kilindini, *Kenya* **86 C4** 4 4 S 39 40 E
Kilis, *Turkey* **70 B3** 36 42N 37 6 E
Kiliya, *Ukraine* **47 K5** 45 28N 29 16 E
Kilkee, *Ireland* **15 D2** 52 41N 9 39W
Kilkeel, *U.K.* **15 B5** 54 4N 6 0W
Kilkenny, *Ireland* **15 D4** 52 39N 7 15W
Kilkenny □, *Ireland* **15 D4** 52 35N 7 15W
Kilkieran B., *Ireland* **15 C2** 53 20N 9 41W
Kilkís, *Greece* **40 F6** 40 58N 22 57 E
Kilkís □, *Greece* **40 E6** 41 5N 22 50 E
Killala, *Ireland* **15 B2** 54 13N 9 12W
Killala B., *Ireland* **15 B2** 54 16N 9 8W
Killaloe, *Ireland* **15 D3** 52 48N 8 28W
Killaloe Station, *Canada* **110 A7** 45 33N 77 25W
Killarney, *Australia* **95 D5** 28 20 S 152 18 E
Killarney, *Canada* **105 D9** 49 10N 99 40W
Killarney, *Ireland* **15 D2** 52 4N 9 30W
Killary Harbour, *Ireland* **15 C2** 53 38N 9 52W
Killdeer, *U.S.A.* **112 B3** 47 26N 102 48W
Killeberg, *Sweden* **11 H8** 56 29N 14 5 E
Killeen, *U.S.A.* **113 K6** 31 7N 97 44W
Killin, *U.K.* **14 E4** 56 28N 4 19W
Killíni, *Ilía, Greece* **38 D3** 37 55N 21 8 E
Killíni, *Korinthía, Greece* **38 D4** 37 54N 22 25 E
Killorglin, *Ireland* **15 D2** 52 6N 9 47W
Killybegs, *Ireland* **15 B3** 54 38N 8 26W
Kilmarnock, *U.K.* **14 F4** 55 37N 4 29W
Kilmez, *Russia* **48 B10** 56 58N 50 55 E
Kilmez →, *Russia* **48 B10** 56 58N 50 28 E
Kilmore, *Australia* **95 F3** 37 25 S 144 53 E
Kilondo, *Tanzania* **87 D3** 9 45 S 34 20 E
Kilosa, *Tanzania* **86 D4** 6 48 S 37 0 E
Kilrush, *Ireland* **15 D2** 52 38N 9 29W
Kilwa Kisiwani, *Tanzania* **87 D4** 8 58 S 39 32 E
Kilwa Kivinje, *Tanzania* **87 D4** 8 45 S 39 25 E
Kilwa Masoko, *Tanzania* **87 D4** 8 55 S 39 30 E
Kilwinning, *U.K.* **14 F4** 55 39N 4 43W
Kim, *U.S.A.* **113 G3** 37 15N 103 21W
Kim →, *Cameroon* **83 D7** 5 28N 11 7 E
Kimaam, *Indonesia* **63 F9** 7 58 S 138 53 E
Kimamba, *Tanzania* **86 D4** 6 45 S 37 10 E
Kimba, *Australia* **95 E2** 33 8 S 136 23 E
Kimball, *Nebr., U.S.A.* **112 E3** 41 14N 103 40W
Kimball, *S. Dak., U.S.A.* **112 D5** 43 45N 98 57W
Kimberley, *Australia* **92 C4** 16 20 S 127 0 E
Kimberley, *Canada* **104 D5** 49 40N 115 59W
Kimberley, *S. Africa* **88 D3** 28 43 S 24 46 E
Kimberly, *U.S.A.* **114 E6** 42 32N 114 22W
Kimch'aek, *N. Korea* **57 D15** 40 40N 129 10 E
Kimch'ŏn, *S. Korea* **57 F15** 36 11N 128 4 E
Kími, *Greece* **38 C6** 38 38N 24 6 E
Kimje, *S. Korea* **57 G14** 35 48N 126 45 E
Kimmirut, *Canada* **101 B13** 62 50N 69 50W
Kímolos, *Greece* **38 E6** 36 48N 24 37 E
Kimovsk, *Moskva, Russia* **46 E9** 55 21N 37 28 E
Kimovsk, *Tula, Russia* **46 E10** 54 0N 38 29 E
Kimparana, *Mali* **82 C4** 12 48N 5 0W
Kimpese, *Dem. Rep. of the Congo* **84 F2** 5 35 S 14 26 E
Kimry, *Russia* **46 D9** 56 55N 37 15 E
Kimstad, *Sweden* **11 F9** 58 35N 15 58 E
Kinabalu, Gunong, *Malaysia* **62 C5** 6 3N 116 14 E
Kínaros, *Greece* **39 E8** 36 59N 26 15 E
Kinaskan L., *Canada* **104 B2** 57 38N 130 8W
Kinbasket L., *Canada* **104 C5** 52 0N 118 10W
Kincardine, *Canada* **102 D3** 44 10N 81 40W
Kincolith, *Canada* **104 B3** 55 0N 129 57W
Kinda, *Dem. Rep. of the Congo* **87 D2** 9 18 S 25 4 E
Kindberg, *Austria* **26 D8** 47 30N 15 27 E
Kinde, *U.S.A.* **110 C2** 43 56N 83 0W
Kinder Scout, *U.K.* **12 D6** 53 24N 1 52W
Kindersley, *Canada* **105 C7** 51 30N 109 10W
Kindia, *Guinea* **82 D2** 10 0N 12 52W
Kindu, *Dem. Rep. of the Congo* **86 C2** 2 55 S 25 50 E
Kinel, *Russia* **48 D10** 53 15N 50 40 E
Kineshma, *Russia* **48 B6** 57 30N 42 5 E
Kinesi, *Tanzania* **86 C3** 1 25 S 33 50 E
King, L., *Australia* **93 F2** 33 10 S 119 35 E
King, Mt., *Australia* **94 D4** 25 10 S 147 30 E
King City, *U.S.A.* **116 J5** 36 13N 121 8W
King Cr. →, *Australia* **94 C2** 24 35 S 139 30 E
King Edward →, *Australia* **92 B4** 14 14 S 126 35 E
King Frederick VI Land = Kong Frederik VI Kyst, *Greenland* **4 C5** 63 0N 43 0W
King George B., *Falk. Is.* **128 G4** 51 30 S 60 30W
King George I., *Antarctica* **5 C18** 60 0 S 60 0W
King George Is., *Canada* **101 C11** 57 20N 80 30W
King I. = Kadan Kyun, *Burma* **64 F2** 12 30N 98 20 E
King I., *Australia* **94 F3** 39 50 S 144 0 E
King I., *Canada* **104 C3** 52 10N 127 40W
King Leopold Ranges, *Australia* **92 C4** 17 30 S 125 45 E
King of Prussia, *U.S.A.* **111 F9** 40 5N 75 23W
King Sd., *Australia* **92 C3** 16 50 S 123 20 E
King William I., *Canada* **100 B10** 69 10N 97 25W
King William's Town, *S. Africa* **88 E4** 32 51 S 27 22 E
Kingaroy, *Australia* **95 D5** 26 32 S 151 51 E
Kingfisher, *U.S.A.* **113 H6** 35 52N 97 56W
Kingirbān, *Iraq* **70 C5** 34 40N 44 54 E
Kingisepp = Kuressaare, *Estonia* **9 G20** 58 15N 22 30 E
Kingisepp, *Russia* **46 C5** 59 25N 28 40 E
Kingman, *Ariz., U.S.A.* **117 K12** 35 12N 114 4W
Kingman, *Kans., U.S.A.* **113 G5** 37 39N 98 7W
Kingoonya, *Australia* **95 E2** 30 55 S 135 19 E
Kingri, *Pakistan* **68 D3** 30 27N 69 49 E
Kings →, *U.S.A.* **116 J7** 36 3N 119 50W
Kings Canyon National Park, *U.S.A.* **116 J8** 36 50N 118 40W
King's Lynn, *U.K.* **12 E8** 52 45N 0 24 E
Kings Mountain, *U.S.A.* **109 H5** 35 15N 81 20W
Kings Park, *U.S.A.* **111 F11** 40 53N 73 16W
King's Peak, *U.S.A.* **114 F8** 40 46N 110 27W
Kingsbridge, *U.K.* **13 G4** 50 17N 3 47W
Kingsburg, *U.S.A.* **116 J7** 36 31N 119 33W
Kingscote, *Australia* **95 F2** 35 40 S 137 38 E
Kingscourt, *Ireland* **15 C5** 53 55N 6 48W
Kingsford, *U.S.A.* **108 C1** 45 48N 88 4W
Kingsland, *U.S.A.* **109 K5** 30 48N 81 41W
Kingsley, *U.S.A.* **112 D7** 42 35N 95 58W
Kingsport, *U.S.A.* **109 G4** 36 33N 82 33W
Kingston, *Canada* **102 D4** 44 14N 76 30W
Kingston, *Jamaica* **120 C4** 18 0N 76 50W
Kingston, *N.Z.* **91 L2** 45 20 S 168 43 E
Kingston, *N.H., U.S.A.* **111 D13** 42 56N 71 3W
Kingston, *N.Y., U.S.A.* **111 E11** 41 56N 73 59W
Kingston, *Pa., U.S.A.* **111 E9** 41 16N 75 54W
Kingston, *R.I., U.S.A.* **111 E13** 41 29N 71 30W
Kingston Pk., *U.S.A.* **117 K11** 35 45N 115 54W
Kingston South East, *Australia* **95 F2** 36 51 S 139 55 E
Kingston upon Hull, *U.K.* **12 D7** 53 45N 0 21W
Kingston upon Hull □, *U.K.* **12 D7** 53 45N 0 21W
Kingston-upon-Thames, *U.K.* **13 F7** 51 24N 0 17W
Kingstown, *St. Vincent* **121 D7** 13 10N 61 10W
Kingstree, *U.S.A.* **109 J6** 33 40N 79 50W
Kingsville, *Canada* **102 D3** 42 2N 82 45W
Kingsville, *U.S.A.* **113 M6** 27 31N 97 52W
Kingussie, *U.K.* **14 D4** 57 6N 4 2W
Kingwood, *U.S.A.* **113 K7** 29 54N 95 18W
Kınık, *Antalya, Turkey* **39 E11** 36 20N 29 20 E
Kınık, *İzmir, Turkey* **39 B9** 39 6N 27 24 E
Kinistino, *Canada* **105 C7** 52 57N 105 2W
Kinkala, *Congo* **84 E2** 4 18 S 14 49 E
Kinki □, *Japan* **55 H8** 33 45N 136 0 E
Kinleith, *N.Z.* **91 H5** 38 20 S 175 56 E
Kinmount, *Canada* **110 B6** 44 48N 78 45W
Kinna, *Sweden* **11 G6** 57 32N 12 42 E
Kinnairds Hd., *U.K.* **14 D6** 57 43N 2 1W
Kinnared, *Sweden* **11 G7** 57 2N 13 7 E
Kinnarodden, *Norway* **6 A11** 71 8N 27 40 E
Kinnarp, *Sweden* **11 F7** 58 5N 13 32 E
Kinneviken, *Sweden* **11 F7** 58 35N 13 15 E
Kino, *Mexico* **118 B2** 28 45N 111 59W
Kinoje →, *Canada* **102 B3** 52 8N 81 25W
Kinomoto, *Japan* **55 G8** 35 30N 136 13 E
Kinoni, *Uganda* **86 C3** 0 41 S 30 28 E
Kinoosao, *Canada* **105 B8** 57 5N 102 1W
Kinross, *U.K.* **14 E5** 56 13N 3 25W
Kinsale, *Ireland* **15 E3** 51 42N 8 31W
Kinsale, Old Hd. of, *Ireland* **15 E3** 51 37N 8 33W
Kinsha = Chang Jiang →, *China* **59 B13** 31 48N 121 10 E
Kinshasa, *Dem. Rep. of the Congo* **84 E3** 4 20 S 15 15 E
Kinsley, *U.S.A.* **113 G5** 37 55N 99 25W
Kinsman, *U.S.A.* **110 E4** 41 26N 80 35W
Kinston, *U.S.A.* **109 H7** 35 16N 77 35W
Kintampo, *Ghana* **83 D4** 8 5N 1 41W
Kintore Ra., *Australia* **92 D4** 23 15 S 128 47 E
Kintyre, *U.K.* **14 F3** 55 30N 5 35W
Kintyre, Mull of, *U.K.* **14 F3** 55 17N 5 47W
Kinushseo →, *Canada* **102 A3** 55 15N 83 45W
Kinuso, *Canada* **104 B5** 55 20N 115 25W
Kinyangiri, *Tanzania* **86 C3** 4 25 S 34 37 E
Kinyeti, *Sudan* **81 G3** 3 57N 32 54 E
Kinzig →, *Germany* **25 G3** 48 36N 7 49 E
Kinzua, *U.S.A.* **110 E6** 41 52N 78 58W
Kinzua Dam, *U.S.A.* **110 E6** 41 53N 79 0W
Kióni, *Greece* **38 C2** 38 27N 20 41 E
Kiosk, *Canada* **102 C4** 46 6N 78 53W
Kiowa, *Kans., U.S.A.* **113 G5** 37 1N 98 29W
Kiowa, *Okla., U.S.A.* **113 H7** 34 43N 95 54W
Kipahigan L., *Canada* **105 B8** 55 20N 101 55W
Kipanga, *Tanzania* **86 D4** 6 15 S 35 20 E
Kiparissía, *Greece* **38 D3** 37 15N 21 40 E
Kiparissiakós Kólpos, *Greece* **38 D3** 37 25N 21 25 E
Kipawa, L., *Canada* **102 C4** 46 50N 79 0W
Kipembawe, *Tanzania* **86 D3** 7 38 S 33 27 E
Kipengere Ra., *Tanzania* **87 D3** 9 12 S 34 15 E
Kipili, *Tanzania* **86 D3** 7 28 S 30 32 E
Kipini, *Kenya* **86 C5** 2 30 S 40 32 E
Kipling, *Canada* **105 C8** 50 6N 102 38W
Kippure, *Ireland* **15 C5** 53 11N 6 21W
Kipushi, *Dem. Rep. of the Congo* **87 E2** 11 48 S 27 12 E
Kirane, *Mali* **82 B2** 15 20N 10 20W
Kiranomena, *Madag.* **89 B8** 18 17 S 46 2 E
Kiraz, *Turkey* **39 C10** 38 14N 28 13 E
Kirazlı, *Turkey* **41 F10** 40 2N 26 41 E
Kirchhain, *Germany* **24 E4** 50 47N 8 56 E
Kirchheim, *Germany* **25 G5** 48 39N 9 27 E
Kirchheimbolanden, *Germany* **25 F3** 49 40N 8 0 E
Kirchschlag, *Austria* **27 D9** 47 30N 16 19 E
Kireç, *Turkey* **39 B10** 39 33N 28 22 E
Kirensk, *Russia* **51 D11** 57 50N 107 55 E
Kirghizia = Kyrgyzstan ■, *Asia* **50 E8** 42 0N 75 0 E
Kirghizstan = Kyrgyzstan ■, *Asia* **50 E8** 42 0N 75 0 E
Kiribati ■, *Pac. Oc.* **96 H10** 5 0 S 180 0 E
Kırıkhan, *Turkey* **72 D7** 36 31N 36 21 E
Kırıkkale, *Turkey* **72 C5** 39 51N 33 32 E
Kirillov, *Russia* **46 C10** 59 49N 38 24 E
Kirin = Jilin, *China* **57 C14** 43 44N 126 30 E
Kirishi, *Russia* **46 C7** 59 28N 31 59 E
Kiritimati, *Kiribati* **97 G12** 1 58N 157 27W
Kırka, *Turkey* **39 B12** 39 17N 30 33 E
Kırkağaç, *Turkey* **39 B9** 39 8N 27 40 E
Kirkby, *U.K.* **12 D5** 53 30N 2 54W
Kirkby Lonsdale, *U.K.* **12 C5** 54 12N 2 36W
Kirkcaldy, *U.K.* **14 E5** 56 7N 3 9W
Kirkcudbright, *U.K.* **14 G4** 54 50N 4 2W
Kirkee, *India* **66 K8** 18 34N 73 56 E
Kirkenes, *Norway* **8 B23** 69 40N 30 5 E
Kirkfield, *Canada* **110 B6** 44 34N 78 59W
Kirkjubæjarklaustur, *Iceland* **8 E4** 63 47N 18 4W
Kirkkonummi, *Finland* **9 F21** 60 8N 24 26 E
Kirkland Lake, *Canada* **102 C3** 48 9N 80 2W
Kırklareli, *Turkey* **41 E11** 41 44N 27 15 E
Kırklareli □, *Turkey* **41 E11** 41 45N 27 15 E
Kirksville, *U.S.A.* **112 E8** 40 12N 92 35W
Kirkūk, *Iraq* **70 C5** 35 30N 44 21 E
Kirkwall, *U.K.* **14 C6** 58 59N 2 58W
Kirkwood, *S. Africa* **88 E4** 33 22 S 25 15 E
Kirn, *Germany* **25 F3** 49 47N 7 26 E
Kirov, *Kaluga, Russia* **46 E8** 54 3N 34 20 E
Kirov, *Kirov, Russia* **50 D5** 58 35N 49 40 E
Kirovabad = Gäncä, *Azerbaijan* **49 K8** 40 45N 46 20 E
Kirovakan = Vanadzor, *Armenia* **49 K7** 40 48N 44 30 E
Kirovograd = Kirovohrad, *Ukraine* **47 H7** 48 35N 32 20 E
Kirovohrad, *Ukraine* **47 H7** 48 35N 32 20 E
Kirovsk = Babadayhan, *Turkmenistan* **50 F7** 37 42N 60 23 E
Kirovskiy, *Astrakhan, Russia* **49 H9** 45 51N 48 11 E
Kirovskiy, *Kamchatka, Russia* **51 D16** 54 27N 155 42 E
Kirovskiy, *Primorsk, Russia* **54 B6** 45 7N 133 30 E
Kirriemuir, *U.K.* **14 E5** 56 41N 3 1W
Kirsanov, *Russia* **48 D6** 52 35N 42 40 E
Kırşehir, *Turkey* **70 B2** 39 14N 34 5 E
Kirtachi, *Niger* **83 C5** 12 52N 2 30 E
Kirthar Range, *Pakistan* **68 F2** 27 0N 67 0 E
Kirtland, *U.S.A.* **115 H9** 36 44N 108 21W
Kiruna, *Sweden* **8 C19** 67 52N 20 15 E
Kirundu, *Dem. Rep. of the Congo* **86 C2** 0 50 S 25 35 E
Kirya, *Russia* **48 C8** 55 8N 46 55 E
Kiryū, *Japan* **55 F9** 36 24N 139 20 E
Kisa, *Sweden* **11 G9** 58 0N 15 39 E
Kisaga, *Tanzania* **86 C3** 4 30 S 34 23 E
Kisalaya, *Nic.* **120 D3** 14 40N 84 3W
Kisalföld, *Hungary* **42 C2** 47 30N 17 0 E
Kisámou, Kólpos, *Greece* **36 D5** 35 30N 23 38 E
Kisanga, *Dem. Rep. of the Congo* **86 B2** 2 30N 26 35 E
Kisangani, *Dem. Rep. of the Congo* **86 B2** 0 35N 25 15 E
Kisar, *Indonesia* **63 F7** 8 5 S 127 10 E
Kisarawe, *Tanzania* **86 D4** 6 53 S 39 0 E
Kisarazu, *Japan* **55 G9** 35 23N 139 55 E
Kisbér, *Hungary* **42 C3** 47 30N 18 2 E
Kishanganga →, *Pakistan* **69 B5** 34 18N 73 28 E
Kishanganj, *India* **69 F13** 26 3N 88 14 E
Kishangarh, *Raj., India* **68 F6** 26 34N 74 52 E
Kishangarh, *Raj., India* **68 F4** 27 50N 70 30 E
Kishi, *Nigeria* **83 D5** 9 1N 3 52 E
Kishinev = Chişinău, *Moldova* **43 C13** 47 2N 28 50 E
Kishiwada, *Japan* **55 G7** 34 28N 135 22 E
Kishtwar, *India* **69 C6** 33 20N 75 48 E
Kisielice, *Poland* **44 E6** 53 36N 19 16 E
Kisii, *Kenya* **86 C3** 0 40 S 34 45 E
Kisiju, *Tanzania* **86 D4** 7 23 S 39 19 E

Kisir, Turkey 73 B10 41 0N 43 5 E
Kisizi, Uganda 86 C2 1 0 S 29 58 E
Kiskomárom = Zalakomár, Hungary 42 D2 46 33N 17 10 E
Kiskörei-víztároló, Hungary 42 C5 47 31N 20 36 E
Kiskőrös, Hungary 42 D4 46 37N 19 20 E
Kiskundorozsma, Hungary 42 D5 46 16N 20 5 E
Kiskunfélegyháza, Hungary 42 D4 46 42N 19 53 E
Kiskunhalas, Hungary 42 D4 46 28N 19 37 E
Kiskunmajsa, Hungary 42 D4 46 30N 19 48 E
Kislovodsk, Russia 49 J6 43 50N 42 45 E
Kismayu = Chisimaio, Somali Rep. 77 G8 0 22 S 42 32 E
Kiso-Gawa →, Japan 55 G8 35 20N 136 45 E
Kiso-Sammyaku, Japan 55 G8 35 45N 137 45 E
Kisofukushima, Japan 55 G8 35 52N 137 43 E
Kisoro, Uganda 86 C2 1 17 S 29 48 E
Kissidougou, Guinea 82 D2 9 5N 10 5W
Kissimmee, U.S.A. 109 L5 28 18N 81 24W
Kissimmee →, U.S.A. 109 M5 27 9N 80 52W
Kississing L., Canada 105 B8 55 10N 101 20W
Kissónerga, Cyprus 36 E11 34 49N 32 24 E
Kissu, J., Sudan 80 C2 21 37N 25 10 E
Kistanje, Croatia 29 E12 43 58N 15 55 E
Kisújszállás, Hungary 42 C5 47 12N 20 50 E
Kisumu, Kenya 86 C3 0 3 S 34 45 E
Kisvárda, Hungary 42 B7 48 14N 22 4 E
Kiswani, Tanzania 86 C4 4 5 S 37 57 E
Kiswere, Tanzania 87 D4 9 27 S 39 30 E
Kit Carson, U.S.A. 112 F3 38 46N 102 48W
Kita, Mali 82 C3 13 5N 9 25W
Kitaibaraki, Japan 55 F10 36 50N 140 45 E
Kitakami, Japan 54 E10 39 20N 141 10 E
Kitakami-Gawa →, Japan 54 E10 38 25N 141 19 E
Kitakami-Sammyaku, Japan 54 E10 39 30N 141 30 E
Kitakata, Japan 54 F9 37 39N 139 52 E
Kitakyūshū, Japan 55 H5 33 50N 130 50 E
Kitale, Kenya 86 B4 1 0N 35 0 E
Kitami, Japan 54 C11 43 48N 143 54 E
Kitami-Sammyaku, Japan 54 B11 44 22N 142 43 E
Kitangiri, L., Tanzania 86 C3 4 5 S 34 20 E
Kitaya, Tanzania 87 E5 10 38 S 40 8 E
Kitchener, Canada 102 D3 43 27N 80 29W
Kitee, Finland 46 A6 62 5N 30 8 E
Kitega = Gitega, Burundi 86 C2 3 26 S 29 56 E
Kitengo, Dem. Rep. of the Congo 86 D1 7 26 S 24 8 E
Kitgum, Uganda 86 B3 3 17N 32 52 E
Kíthira, Greece 38 E5 36 8N 23 0 E
Kíthnos, Greece 38 D6 37 26N 24 27 E
Kiti, Cyprus 36 E12 34 50N 33 34 E
Kiti, C., Cyprus 36 E12 34 48N 33 36 E
Kitimat, Canada 104 C3 54 3N 128 38W
Kitinen →, Finland 8 C22 67 14N 27 27 E
Kitiyab, Sudan 81 D3 17 13N 33 35 E
Kítros, Greece 40 F6 40 22N 22 34 E
Kitsuki, Japan 55 H5 33 25N 131 37 E
Kittakittaooloo, L., Australia 95 D2 28 3 S 138 14 E
Kittanning, U.S.A. 110 F5 40 49N 79 31W
Kittatinny Mts., U.S.A. 111 F10 41 0N 75 0W
Kittery, U.S.A. 109 D10 43 5N 70 45W
Kittilä, Finland 8 C21 67 40N 24 51 E
Kitui, Kenya 86 C4 1 17 S 38 0 E
Kitwanga, Canada 104 B3 55 6N 128 4W
Kitwe, Zambia 87 E2 12 54 S 28 13 E
Kitzbühel, Austria 26 D5 47 27N 12 24 E
Kitzbühler Alpen, Austria 26 D5 47 20N 12 20 E
Kitzingen, Germany 25 F6 49 44N 10 9 E
Kivarli, India 68 G5 24 33N 72 46 E
Kivertsi, Ukraine 47 G3 50 50N 25 28 E
Kividhes, Cyprus 36 E11 34 46N 32 51 E
Kivik, Sweden 11 J8 55 41N 14 13 E
Kivotós, Greece 40 F5 40 13N 21 26 E
Kivu, L., Dem. Rep. of the Congo 86 C2 1 48 S 29 0 E
Kiyev = Kyyiv, Ukraine 47 G6 50 30N 30 28 E
Kiyevskoye Vdkhr. = Kyyivske Vdskh., Ukraine 47 G6 51 0N 30 25 E
Kıyıköy, Turkey 41 E12 41 38N 28 5 E
Kiziguru, Rwanda 86 C3 1 46 S 30 23 E
Kızıl Adalar, Turkey 41 F13 40 52N 29 5 E
Kızıl Irmak →, Turkey 72 B6 41 44N 35 58 E
Kizil Jilga, India 69 B8 35 26N 78 50 E
Kizil Yurt, Russia 49 J8 43 13N 46 54 E
Kızılcabölük, Turkey 39 D11 37 37N 29 1 E
Kızılcadağ, Turkey 39 D11 37 1N 29 58 E
Kızılcahamam, Turkey 72 B5 40 30N 32 30 E
Kızılhisar, Turkey 72 D3 37 32N 29 17 E
Kızılırmak, Turkey 72 B5 40 21N 33 59 E
Kızılkaya, Turkey 39 D12 37 18N 30 27 E
Kızılören, Turkey 39 C12 38 15N 30 10 E
Kızıltepe, Turkey 70 B4 37 12N 40 35 E
Kizimkazi, Tanzania 86 D4 6 28 S 39 30 E
Kizlyar, Russia 49 J8 43 51N 46 40 E
Kizyl-Arvat = Gyzylarbat, Turkmenistan 50 F6 39 4N 56 23 E
Kjellerup, Denmark 11 H3 56 17N 9 25 E
Kjölur, Iceland 8 D4 64 50N 19 25W
Kladanj, Bos.-H. 42 F3 44 14N 18 42 E
Kladnica, Serbia, Yug. 40 C4 43 23N 20 2 E
Kladno, Czech Rep. 26 A7 50 10N 14 7 E
Kladovo, Serbia, Yug. 40 B6 44 36N 22 33 E
Klaeng, Thailand 64 F3 12 47N 101 39 E
Klagenfurt, Austria 26 E7 46 38N 14 20 E
Klaipėda, Lithuania 9 J19 55 43N 21 10 E
Klaipėda □, Lithuania 44 C8 55 43N 21 7 E
Klaksvík, Færoe Is. 8 E9 62 14N 6 35W
Klamath →, U.S.A. 114 F1 41 33N 124 5W
Klamath Falls, U.S.A. 114 E3 42 13N 121 46W
Klamath Mts., U.S.A. 114 F2 41 20N 123 0W
Klamono, Indonesia 63 E8 1 8 S 131 30 E
Klanjec, Croatia 29 B12 46 3N 15 45 E
Klappan →, Canada 104 B3 58 0N 129 43W
Klarälven →, Sweden 10 E7 59 23N 13 32 E
Klässbol, Sweden 10 E6 59 33N 12 45 E
Klatovy, Czech Rep. 26 B6 49 23N 13 18 E
Klawer, S. Africa 88 E2 31 44 S 18 36 E
Klazienaveen, Neths. 17 B6 52 44N 7 0 E
Klé, Mali 82 C3 12 0N 6 28W
Kłecko, Poland 45 F4 52 38N 17 25 E
Kleczew, Poland 45 F5 52 22N 18 9 E
Kleena Kleene, Canada 104 C4 52 0N 124 59W
Klein-Karas, Namibia 88 D2 27 33 S 18 7 E
Klekovača, Bos.-H. 29 D13 44 25N 16 32 E
Klenoec, Macedonia 40 E4 41 32N 20 49 E
Klenovec, Slovak Rep. 27 C12 48 36N 19 54 E
Klerksdorp, S. Africa 88 D4 26 53 S 26 38 E
Kleszczele, Poland 45 F10 52 35N 23 19 E
Kletnya, Russia 46 F7 53 23N 33 12 E
Kletsk = Klyetsk, Belarus 47 F4 53 5N 26 45 E
Kletskiy, Russia 49 F6 49 16N 43 11 E
Kleve, Germany 24 D2 51 47N 6 7 E
Klickitat, U.S.A. 114 D3 45 49N 121 9W
Klickitat →, U.S.A. 116 E5 45 42N 121 17W
Klidhes, Cyprus 36 D13 35 42N 34 36 E
Klimovichi, Belarus 46 F6 53 36N 32 0 E
Klin, Russia 46 D9 56 20N 36 48 E
Klina, Kosovo, Yug. 40 D4 42 37N 20 35 E
Klinaklini →, Canada 104 C3 51 21N 125 40W
Klintehamn, Sweden 11 G12 57 24N 18 12 E
Klintsy, Russia 47 F7 52 50N 32 10 E
Klip →, S. Africa 89 D4 27 3 S 29 3 E
Klipdale, S. Africa 88 E2 34 19 S 19 57 E
Klippan, Sweden 11 H7 56 8N 13 10 E
Klipplaat, S. Africa 88 E3 33 1 S 24 22 E
Klisura, Bulgaria 41 D8 42 40N 24 28 E
Kljajićevo, Serbia, Yug. 42 E4 45 45N 19 17 E
Ključ, Bos.-H. 29 D13 44 32N 16 48 E
Kłobuck, Poland 45 H5 50 55N 18 55 E
Klockestrand, Sweden 10 B11 62 53N 17 55 E
Kłodawa, Poland 45 F5 52 15N 18 55 E
Kłodzko, Poland 45 H3 50 28N 16 38 E
Klos, Albania 40 E4 41 28N 20 10 E
Klosi = Klos, Albania 40 E4 41 28N 20 10 E
Klosterneuburg, Austria 27 C9 48 18N 16 19 E
Klosters, Switz. 25 J5 46 52N 9 52 E
Klötze, Germany 24 C7 52 37N 11 10 E
Klouto, Togo 83 D5 6 57N 0 44 E
Kluane L., Canada 100 B6 61 15N 138 40W
Kluane Nat. Park, Canada 104 A1 60 45N 139 30W
Kluczbork, Poland 45 H5 50 58N 18 12 E
Klukwan, U.S.A. 104 B1 59 24N 135 54W
Klyetsk, Belarus 47 F4 53 5N 26 45 E
Klyuchevskaya, Gora, Russia 51 D17 55 50N 160 30 E
Knäred, Sweden 11 H7 56 31N 13 19 E
Knaresborough, U.K. 12 C6 54 1N 1 28W
Knee L., Man., Canada 102 A1 55 3N 94 45W
Knee L., Sask., Canada 105 B7 55 51N 107 0W
Knezha, Bulgaria 41 C8 43 30N 24 5 E
Knić, Serbia, Yug. 40 C4 43 53N 20 42 E
Knight Inlet, Canada 104 C3 50 45N 125 40W
Knighton, U.K. 13 E4 52 21N 3 3W
Knights Ferry, U.S.A. 116 H6 37 50N 120 40W
Knights Landing, U.S.A. 116 G5 38 48N 121 43W
Knin, Croatia 29 D13 44 3N 16 17 E
Knislinge, Sweden 11 H8 56 12N 14 5 E
Knittelfeld, Austria 26 D7 47 13N 14 51 E
Knivsta, Sweden 10 E11 59 43N 17 48 E
Knjaževac, Serbia, Yug. 40 C6 43 35N 22 18 E
Knob, C., Australia 93 F2 34 32 S 119 16 E
Knock, Ireland 15 C3 53 48N 8 55W
Knockmealdown Mts., Ireland 15 D4 52 14N 7 56W
Knokke-Heist, Belgium 17 C3 51 21N 3 17 E
Knossós, Greece 36 D7 35 16N 25 10 E
Knowlton, Canada 111 A12 45 13N 72 31W
Knox, U.S.A. 108 E2 41 18N 86 37W
Knox Coast, Antarctica 5 C8 66 30 S 108 0 E
Knoxville, Iowa, U.S.A. 112 E8 41 19N 93 6W
Knoxville, Pa., U.S.A. 110 E7 41 57N 77 27W
Knoxville, Tenn., U.S.A. 109 H4 35 58N 83 55W
Knysna, S. Africa 88 E3 34 2 S 23 2 E
Knyszyn, Poland 44 E9 53 20N 22 56 E
Ko Kha, Thailand 64 C2 18 11N 99 24 E
Koartac = Quaqtaq, Canada 101 B13 60 55N 69 40W
Koba, Indonesia 63 F8 6 37 S 134 37 E
Kobarid, Slovenia 29 B10 46 15N 13 30 E
Kobayashi, Japan 55 J5 31 56N 130 59 E
Kobdo = Hovd, Mongolia 60 B4 48 2N 91 37 E
Kōbe, Japan 55 G7 34 45N 135 10 E
Kobelyaky, Ukraine 47 H8 49 11N 34 9 E
København, Denmark 11 J6 55 41N 12 34 E
Københavns Amtskommune □, Denmark 11 J6 55 42N 12 21 E
Kobenni, Mauritania 82 B3 15 58N 9 24W
Kōbi-Sho, Japan 55 M1 25 56N 123 41 E
Koblenz, Germany 25 E3 50 21N 7 36 E
Kobo, Ethiopia 81 E4 12 2N 39 56 E
Kobryn, Belarus 47 F3 52 15N 24 22 E
Kobuleti, Georgia 49 K5 41 55N 41 45 E
Kobylin, Poland 45 G4 51 43N 17 12 E
Kobyłka, Poland 45 F8 52 21N 21 10 E
Kobylkino, Russia 48 C6 54 8N 43 56 E
Koca →, Turkey 41 F11 40 8N 27 57 E
Kocabaş, Turkey 39 D11 37 49N 29 20 E
Kocaeli, Turkey 41 F13 40 45N 29 50 E
Kocaeli □, Turkey 41 F13 40 45N 29 55 E
Kočane, Serbia, Yug. 40 C5 43 12N 21 52 E
Kočani, Macedonia 40 E6 41 55N 22 25 E
Koçarlı, Turkey 39 D9 37 45N 27 43 E
Koceljevo, Serbia, Yug. 40 B3 44 28N 19 50 E
Kočevje, Slovenia 29 C11 45 39N 14 50 E
Koch Bihar, India 67 F16 26 22N 89 29 E
Kochang, S. Korea 57 G14 35 41N 127 55 E
Kochas, India 69 G10 25 15N 83 56 E
Kocher →, Germany 25 F5 49 13N 9 12 E
Kōchi, Japan 55 H6 33 30N 133 35 E
Kōchi □, Japan 55 H6 33 40N 133 30 E
Kochiu = Gejiu, China 58 F4 23 20N 103 10 E
Kock, Poland 45 G9 51 38N 22 27 E
Kodarma, India 69 G11 24 28N 85 36 E
Kode, Sweden 11 G5 57 57N 11 51 E
Kodiak, U.S.A. 100 C4 57 47N 152 24W
Kodiak I., U.S.A. 100 C4 57 30N 152 45W
Kodinar, India 68 J4 20 46N 70 46 E
Kodok, Sudan 81 F3 9 53N 32 7 E
Kodori →, Georgia 49 J5 42 47N 41 10 E
Koedoesberge, S. Africa 88 E3 32 40 S 20 11 E
Koes, Namibia 88 D2 26 0 S 19 15 E
Kofçaz, Turkey 41 E11 41 58N 27 12 E
Koffiefontein, S. Africa 88 D4 29 30 S 25 0 E
Kofiau, Indonesia 63 E7 1 11 S 129 50 E
Köflach, Austria 26 D8 47 4N 15 5 E
Koforidua, Ghana 83 D4 6 3N 0 17W
Kōfu, Japan 55 G9 35 40N 138 30 E
Koga, Japan 55 F9 36 11N 139 43 E
Kogaluk →, Canada 103 A7 56 12N 61 44W
Køge, Denmark 11 J6 55 27N 12 11 E
Køge Bugt, Denmark 11 J6 55 30N 12 20 E
Kogi □, Nigeria 83 D6 7 45N 6 45 E
Kogin Baba, Nigeria 83 D7 7 55N 11 35 E
Koh-i-Bābā, Afghan. 66 B5 34 30N 67 0 E
Koh-i-Khurd, Afghan. 68 C1 33 30N 65 59 E
Koh-i-Maran, Pakistan 68 E2 29 18N 66 50 E
Kohat, Pakistan 68 C4 33 40N 71 29 E
Kohima, India 67 G19 25 35N 94 10 E
Kohkīlūyeh va Būyer Aḩmadi □, Iran 71 D6 31 30N 50 30 E
Kohler Ra., Antarctica 5 D15 77 0 S 110 0W
Kohlu, Pakistan 68 E3 29 54N 69 15 E
Kohtla-Järve, Estonia 9 G22 59 20N 27 20 E
Koillismaa, Finland 8 D23 65 44N 28 36 E
Koin-dong, N. Korea 57 D14 40 28N 126 18 E
Koinare, Bulgaria 41 C8 43 21N 24 8 E
Koindu, S. Leone 82 D2 8 26N 10 19W
Kojetín, Czech Rep. 27 B10 49 21N 17 20 E
Kojŏ, N. Korea 57 E14 38 58N 127 58 E
Kojonup, Australia 93 F2 33 48 S 117 10 E
Kojūr, Iran 71 B6 36 23N 51 43 E
Koka, Sudan 80 C3 20 5N 30 35 E
Kokand = Qŭqon, Uzbekistan 50 E8 40 30N 70 57 E
Kokas, Indonesia 63 E8 2 42 S 132 26 E
Kokava, Slovak Rep. 27 C12 48 35N 19 50 E
Kokchetav = Kökshetaū, Kazakstan 50 D7 53 20N 69 25 E
Kokemäenjoki →, Finland 9 F19 61 32N 21 44 E
Kokhma, Russia 48 B5 56 57N 41 8 E
Koki, Senegal 82 B1 15 30N 15 59W
Kokkola, Finland 8 E20 63 50N 23 8 E
Koko, Nigeria 83 C5 11 28N 4 29 E
Koko Kyunzu, Burma 67 M18 14 10N 93 25 E
Kokolopozo, Ivory C. 82 D3 5 8N 6 5W
Kokomo, U.S.A. 108 E2 40 29N 86 8W
Kokoro, Niger 83 C5 14 12N 0 55 E
Koksan, N. Korea 57 E14 38 46N 126 40 E
Kökshetaū, Kazakstan 50 D7 53 20N 69 25 E
Koksoak →, Canada 101 C13 58 30N 68 10W
Kokstad, S. Africa 89 E4 30 32 S 29 29 E
Kokubu, Japan 55 J5 31 44N 130 46 E
Kola, Indonesia 63 F8 5 35 S 134 30 E
Kola Pen. = Kolskiy Poluostrov, Russia 50 C4 67 30N 38 0 E
Kolachi →, Pakistan 68 F2 27 8N 67 2 E
Kolahoi, India 69 B6 34 12N 75 22 E
Kolahun, Liberia 82 D2 8 15N 10 4W
Kolaka, Indonesia 63 E6 4 3 S 121 46 E
Kolar, India 66 N11 13 12N 78 15 E
Kolar Gold Fields, India 66 N11 12 58N 78 16 E
Kolaras, India 68 G6 25 14N 77 36 E
Kolari, Finland 8 C20 67 20N 23 48 E
Kolárovo, Slovak Rep. 27 D10 47 54N 18 0 E
Kolašin, Montenegro, Yug. 40 D3 42 50N 19 31 E
Kolayat, India 66 F8 27 50N 72 50 E
Kolbäck, Sweden 10 E10 59 34N 16 15 E
Kolbäcksån →, Sweden 10 E10 59 36N 16 16 E
Kolbermoor, Germany 25 H8 47 51N 12 4 E
Kolbuszowa, Poland 45 H8 50 15N 21 46 E
Kolchugino = Leninsk-Kuznetskiy, Russia 50 D9 54 44N 86 10 E
Kolchugino, Russia 46 D10 56 17N 39 22 E
Kolda, Senegal 82 C2 12 55N 14 57W
Koldegi, Sudan 81 E3 12 3N 30 16 E
Kolding, Denmark 11 J3 55 30N 9 29 E
Kolepom = Dolak, Pulau, Indonesia 63 F9 8 0 S 138 30 E
Kolguyev, Ostrov, Russia 50 C5 69 20N 48 30 E
Kolhapur, India 66 L9 16 43N 74 15 E
Kolia, Ivory C. 82 D3 9 46N 6 28W
Kolín, Czech Rep. 26 A8 50 2N 15 9 E
Kolind, Denmark 11 H4 56 21N 10 34 E
Kolkas rags, Latvia 9 H20 57 46N 22 37 E
Kolkata, India 69 H13 22 36N 88 24 E
Kölleda, Germany 24 D7 51 11N 11 15 E
Kollum, Neths. 17 A6 53 17N 6 10 E
Kolmanskop, Namibia 88 D2 26 45 S 15 14 E
Köln, Germany 24 E2 50 56N 6 57 E
Kolno, Poland 44 E8 53 25N 21 56 E
Koło, Poland 45 F5 52 14N 18 40 E
Kołobrzeg, Poland 44 D2 54 10N 15 35 E
Kolokani, Mali 82 C3 13 35N 7 45W
Koloko, Burkina Faso 82 C3 11 5N 5 19W
Kololo, Ethiopia 81 F5 7 29N 41 58 E
Kolomna, Russia 46 E10 55 8N 38 45 E
Kolomyya, Ukraine 47 H3 48 31N 25 2 E
Kolondiéba, Mali 82 C3 11 5N 6 54W
Kolonodale, Indonesia 63 E6 2 3 S 121 25 E
Kolonowskie, Poland 45 H5 50 39N 18 22 E
Kolosib, India 67 G18 24 15N 92 45 E
Kolpashevo, Russia 50 D9 58 20N 83 5 E
Kolpino, Russia 46 C6 59 44N 30 39 E
Kolpny, Russia 47 F9 52 17N 37 1 E
Kolskiy Poluostrov, Russia 50 C4 67 30N 38 0 E
Kolsva, Sweden 10 E9 59 36N 15 51 E
Kolubara →, Serbia, Yug. 40 B4 44 35N 20 15 E
Koluszki, Poland 45 G6 51 45N 19 46 E
Kolwezi, Dem. Rep. of the Congo 87 E2 10 40 S 25 25 E
Kolyma →, Russia 51 C17 69 30N 161 0 E
Kolymskoye Nagorye, Russia 51 C16 63 0N 157 0 E
Kôm Hamâda, Egypt 80 H7 30 46N 30 41 E
Kôm Ombo, Egypt 80 C3 24 25N 32 52 E
Komadugu Gana →, Nigeria 83 C7 13 5N 12 24 E
Komandorskiye Is. = Komandorskiye Ostrova, Russia 51 D17 55 0N 167 0 E
Komandorskiye Ostrova, Russia 51 D17 55 0N 167 0 E
Komárno, Slovak Rep. 27 D11 47 49N 18 5 E
Komárom, Hungary 42 C3 47 43N 18 7 E
Komárom-Esztergom □, Hungary 42 C3 47 35N 18 20 E
Komatipoort, S. Africa 89 D5 25 25 S 31 55 E
Komatou Yialou, Cyprus 36 D13 35 25N 34 8 E
Komatsu, Japan 55 F8 36 25N 136 30 E
Komatsujima, Japan 55 H7 34 0N 134 35 E
Kombissiri, Burkina Faso 83 C4 12 4N 1 20W
Kombori, Burkina Faso 82 C4 13 26N 3 56W
Kombóti, Greece 38 B3 39 6N 21 5 E
Komen, Slovenia 29 C10 45 49N 13 45 E
Komenda, Ghana 83 D4 5 4N 1 28W
Komi □, Russia 50 C6 64 0N 55 0 E
Komiža, Croatia 29 E13 43 3N 16 11 E
Komló, Hungary 42 D3 46 15N 18 16 E
Kommunarsk = Alchevsk, Ukraine 47 H10 48 30N 38 45 E
Kommunizma, Pik, Tajikistan 50 F8 39 0N 72 2 E
Komodo, Indonesia 63 F5 8 37 S 119 20 E
Komoé →, Ivory C. 82 D4 5 12N 3 44W
Komoran, Pulau, Indonesia 63 F9 8 18 S 138 45 E
Komoro, Japan 55 F9 36 19N 138 26 E
Komotini, Greece 41 E9 41 9N 25 26 E
Komovi, Montenegro, Yug. 40 D3 42 41N 19 39 E
Kompasberg, S. Africa 88 E3 31 45 S 24 32 E
Kompong Bang, Cambodia 65 F5 12 24N 104 40 E
Kompong Cham, Cambodia 65 F5 12 0N 105 30 E
Kompong Chhnang = Kampang Chhnang, Cambodia 65 F5 12 20N 104 35 E
Kompong Chikreng, Cambodia 64 F5 13 5N 104 18 E
Kompong Kleang, Cambodia 64 F5 13 6N 104 8 E
Kompong Luong, Cambodia 65 G5 11 49N 104 48 E
Kompong Pranak, Cambodia 64 F5 13 35N 104 55 E
Kompong Som = Kampong Saom, Cambodia 65 G4 10 38N 103 30 E
Kompong Som, Chhung = Kampong Saom, Chaak, Cambodia 65 G4 10 50N 103 32 E
Kompong Speu, Cambodia 65 G5 11 26N 104 32 E
Kompong Sralao, Cambodia 64 E5 14 5N 105 46 E
Kompong Thom, Cambodia 64 F5 12 35N 104 51 E
Kompong Trabeck, Cambodia 64 F5 13 6N 105 14 E
Kompong Trabeck, Cambodia 65 G5 11 9N 105 28 E
Kompong Trach, Cambodia 65 G5 11 25N 105 48 E
Kompong Tralach, Cambodia 65 G5 11 54N 104 47 E
Komrat = Comrat, Moldova 43 D13 46 18N 28 40 E
Komsberg, S. Africa 88 E3 32 40 S 20 45 E
Komsomolets, Ostrov, Russia 51 A10 80 30N 95 0 E
Komsomolsk, Amur, Russia 51 D14 50 30N 137 0 E
Komsomolsk, Ivanovo, Russia 46 D11 57 2N 40 20 E
Komsomolskiy, Russia 48 C7 54 27N 45 33 E
Kömür Burnu, Turkey 39 C8 38 39N 26 12 E
Kon Tum, Vietnam 64 E7 14 24N 108 0 E
Kon Tum, Plateau du, Vietnam 64 E7 14 30N 108 30 E
Kona, Mali 82 C4 14 57N 3 53W
Konakovo, Russia 46 D9 56 40N 36 51 E
Konarhā □, Afghan. 66 B7 35 30N 71 3 E
Konārī, Iran 71 D6 28 13N 51 36 E
Konch, India 69 G8 26 0N 79 10 E
Konde, Tanzania 86 C4 4 57 S 39 45 E
Kondiá, Greece 39 B7 39 49N 25 10 E
Kondinin, Australia 93 F2 32 34 S 118 8 E
Kondoa, Tanzania 86 C4 4 55 S 35 50 E
Kondókali, Greece 36 A3 39 38N 19 51 E
Kondopaga, Russia 46 A8 62 12N 34 17 E
Kondratyevo, Russia 51 D10 57 22N 98 15 E
Kondrovo, Russia 46 E8 54 48N 35 56 E
Konduga, Nigeria 83 C7 11 35N 13 26 E
Köneürgench, Turkmenistan 50 E6 42 19N 59 10 E
Konevo, Russia 46 A10 62 8N 39 20 E
Kong = Khong →, Cambodia 64 F5 13 32N 105 58 E
Kong, Ivory C. 82 D4 8 54N 4 36W
Kong, Koh, Cambodia 65 G4 11 20N 103 0 E
Kong Christian IX Land, Greenland 4 C6 68 0N 36 0W
Kong Christian X Land, Greenland 4 B6 74 0N 29 0W
Kong Frederik IX Land, Greenland 4 C5 67 0N 52 0W
Kong Frederik VI Kyst, Greenland 4 C5 63 0N 43 0W
Kong Frederik VIII Land, Greenland 4 B6 78 30N 26 0W
Kong Oscar Fjord, Greenland 4 B6 72 20N 24 0W
Kongeå →, Denmark 11 J2 55 23N 8 39 E
Kongerslev, Denmark 11 H4 56 54N 10 6 E
Kongju, S. Korea 57 F14 36 30N 127 0 E
Konglu, Burma 67 F20 27 13N 97 57 E
Kongola, Namibia 88 B3 17 45 S 23 20 E
Kongolo, Kasai-Or., Dem. Rep. of the Congo 86 D1 5 26 S 24 49 E
Kongolo, Katanga, Dem. Rep. of the Congo 86 D2 5 22 S 27 0 E
Kongor, Sudan 81 F3 7 1N 31 27 E
Kongoussi, Burkina Faso 83 C4 13 19N 1 32W
Kongsberg, Norway 9 G13 59 39N 9 39 E
Kongsvinger, Norway 9 F15 60 12N 12 2 E
Kongwa, Tanzania 86 D4 6 11 S 36 26 E
Koni, Dem. Rep. of the Congo 87 E2 10 40 S 27 11 E
Koni, Mts., Dem. Rep. of the Congo 87 E2 10 36 S 27 10 E
Koniakari, Mali 82 C2 14 35N 10 50W
Koniecpol, Poland 45 H6 50 46N 19 40 E
Königs Wusterhausen, Germany 24 C9 52 19N 13 38 E
Königsberg = Kaliningrad, Russia 9 J19 54 42N 20 32 E
Königsbrunn, Germany 25 G6 48 16N 10 54 E
Königslutter, Germany 24 C6 52 15N 10 49 E
Konin, Poland 45 F5 52 12N 18 15 E
Konispol, Albania 40 G4 39 42N 20 10 E
Konispoli = Konispol, Albania 40 G4 39 42N 20 10 E
Kónitsa, Greece 38 A2 40 5N 20 48 E
Konjic, Bos.-H. 42 G2 43 42N 17 58 E
Konkiep, Namibia 88 D2 26 49 S 17 15 E
Konkouré →, Guinea 82 D2 9 50N 13 42W
Könnern, Germany 24 D7 51 41N 11 47 E
Kono, S. Leone 82 D2 8 30N 11 5W
Konongo, Ghana 83 D4 6 40N 1 15W
Konosha, Russia 46 B11 61 0N 40 5 E
Kōnosu, Japan 55 F9 36 3N 139 31 E
Konotop, Ukraine 47 G7 51 12N 33 7 E
Konsankoro, Guinea 82 D3 9 2N 9 0W
Końskie, Poland 45 G7 51 15N 20 23 E
Konstancin-Jeziorna, Poland 45 F8 52 5N 21 7 E
Konstantinovka = Kostyantynivka, Ukraine 47 H9 48 32N 37 39 E
Konstantinovsk, Russia 49 G5 47 33N 41 10 E
Konstantynów Łódźki, Poland 45 G6 51 45N 19 20 E
Konstanz, Germany 25 H5 47 40N 9 10 E
Kont, Iran 71 E9 26 55N 61 50 E
Kontagora, Nigeria 83 C6 10 23N 5 27 E
Kontcha, Cameroon 83 D7 7 59N 12 15 E
Konya, Turkey 70 B2 37 52N 32 35 E
Konya Ovası, Turkey 72 C5 38 9N 33 5 E
Konz, Germany 25 F2 49 42N 6 34 E
Konza, Kenya 86 C4 1 45 S 37 7 E
Koocanusa, L., Canada 114 B6 49 20N 115 15W
Kookynie, Australia 93 E3 29 17 S 121 22 E
Koolyanobbing, Australia 93 F2 30 48 S 119 36 E
Koonibba, Australia 95 E1 31 54 S 133 25 E
Koorawatha, Australia 95 E4 34 2 S 148 33 E
Koorda, Australia 93 F2 30 48 S 117 35 E
Kooskia, U.S.A. 114 C6 46 9N 115 59W
Kootenay →, U.S.A. 104 D5 49 19N 117 39W
Kootenay L., Canada 104 D5 49 45N 116 50W
Kootenay Nat. Park, Canada 104 C5 51 0N 116 0W
Kootjieskolk, S. Africa 88 E3 31 15 S 20 21 E
Kopanovka, Russia 49 G8 47 28N 46 50 E
Kopaonik, Yugoslavia 40 C4 43 10N 20 50 E
Kópavogur, Iceland 8 D3 64 6N 21 55W
Koper, Slovenia 29 C10 45 31N 13 44 E
Kopervik, Norway 9 G11 59 17N 5 17 E
Kopet Dagh, Asia 71 B8 38 0N 58 0 E
Kopi, Australia 95 E2 33 24 S 135 40 E
Köping, Sweden 10 E10 59 31N 16 3 E
Köpingsvik, Sweden 11 H10 56 53N 16 43 E
Kopište, Croatia 29 F13 42 48N 16 42 E
Koplik, Albania 40 D3 42 15N 19 25 E
Kopliku = Koplik, Albania 40 D3 42 15N 19 25 E
Köpmanholmen, Sweden 10 A12 63 10N 18 35 E
Kopparberg, Sweden 10 E9 59 52N 15 0 E
Koppeh Dāgh = Kopet Dagh, Asia 71 B8 38 0N 58 0 E
Koppies, S. Africa 89 D4 27 20 S 27 30 E
Koppom, Sweden 10 E6 59 43N 12 10 E
Koprivlen, Bulgaria 40 E7 41 31N 23 53 E
Koprivnica, Croatia 29 B13 46 12N 16 45 E
Kopřivnice, Czech Rep. 27 B11 49 36N 18 9 E
Koprivshtitsa, Bulgaria 41 D8 42 40N 24 19 E
Köprübaşı, Turkey 39 C10 38 43N 28 23 E
Kopychyntsi, Ukraine 47 H3 49 7N 25 58 E
Korab, Macedonia 40 E4 41 44N 20 40 E
Korakiána, Greece 36 A3 39 42N 19 45 E
Koral, India 68 J5 21 50N 73 12 E
Korarou, L., Mali 82 B4 15 15N 3 15W
Korba, India 69 H10 22 20N 82 45 E
Korbach, Germany 24 D4 51 16N 8 52 E
Korbu, G., Malaysia 65 K3 4 41N 101 18 E
Korça = Korçë, Albania 40 F4 40 37N 20 50 E
Korce = Korçë, Albania 40 F4 40 37N 20 50 E
Korçë, Albania 40 F4 40 37N 20 50 E
Korčula, Croatia 29 F13 42 56N 16 57 E
Korčulanski Kanal, Croatia 29 E13 43 3N 16 40 E
Kord Kūy, Iran 71 B7 36 48N 54 7 E
Kord Sheykh, Iran 71 D7 28 31N 52 53 E
Kordestān □, Iran 70 C5 36 0N 47 0 E
Kordofân, Sudan 79 F11 13 0N 29 0 E
Koré Mayroua, Niger 83 C5 13 18N 3 55 E
Korea, North ■, Asia 57 E14 40 0N 127 0 E
Korea, South ■, Asia 57 G15 36 0N 128 0 E
Korea Bay, Korea 57 E13 39 0N 124 0 E
Korea Strait, Asia 57 H15 34 0N 129 30 E
Korem, Ethiopia 81 E4 12 30N 39 32 E
Korenevo, Russia 47 G8 51 27N 34 55 E
Korenovsk, Russia 49 H4 45 30N 39 22 E
Korets, Ukraine 47 G4 50 40N 27 5 E
Korfantów, Poland 45 H4 50 29N 17 36 E
Korgan, Turkey 72 B7 40 44N 37 13 E
Korgus, Sudan 80 D3 19 16N 33 29 E
Korhogo, Ivory C. 82 D3 9 29N 5 28W
Koribundu, S. Leone 82 D2 7 41N 11 46W
Korienzé, Mali 82 B4 15 22N 3 50W
Korinthía □, Greece 38 D4 37 50N 22 35 E
Korinthiakós Kólpos, Greece 38 C4 38 16N 22 30 E
Kórinthos, Greece 38 D4 37 56N 22 55 E
Korioumé, Mali 82 B4 16 35N 3 0W
Koríssa, Límni, Greece 36 B3 39 27N 19 53 E
Kōriyama, Japan 54 F10 37 24N 140 23 E
Korkuteli, Turkey 39 D12 37 4N 30 13 E
Kormakiti, C., Cyprus 36 D11 35 23N 32 56 E
Körmend, Hungary 42 C1 47 5N 16 35 E
Kornat, Croatia 29 E12 43 50N 15 20 E
Korneshty = Corneşti, Moldova 43 C13 47 21N 28 1 E
Korneuburg, Austria 27 C9 48 20N 16 20 E
Kórnik, Poland 45 F4 52 15N 17 6 E
Koro, Fiji 91 C8 17 19 S 179 23 E
Koro, Ivory C. 82 D3 8 32N 7 30W
Koro, Mali 82 C4 14 1N 2 58W
Koro Sea, Fiji 91 C9 17 30 S 179 45W
Korocha, Russia 47 G9 50 54N 37 19 E
Köroğlu Dağları, Turkey 72 B5 40 38N 33 0 E
Korogwe, Tanzania 86 D4 5 5 S 38 25 E
Koronadal, Phil. 61 H6 6 12N 125 1 E
Koróni, Greece 38 E3 36 48N 21 57 E
Korónia, Limni, Greece 40 F7 40 47N 23 10 E
Koronís, Greece 39 D7 37 12N 25 35 E
Koronowo, Poland 45 E4 53 19N 17 55 E
Koror, Palau 63 C8 7 20N 134 28 E
Körös →, Hungary 42 D5 46 43N 20 12 E
Köröstarcsa, Hungary 42 D6 46 53N 21 3 E
Korosten, Ukraine 47 G5 50 54N 28 36 E
Korostyshev, Ukraine 47 G5 50 19N 29 4 E
Korotoyak, Russia 47 G10 51 1N 39 2 E
Korraraika, Helodranon' i, Madag. 89 B7 17 45 S 43 57 E
Korsakov, Russia 51 E15 46 36N 142 42 E

Korsberga, *Sweden* **11 G9** 57 19N 15 7 E
Korshunovo, *Russia* **51 D12** 58 37N 110 10 E
Korsør, *Denmark* **11 J5** 55 20N 11 9 E
Korsun Shevchenkovskiy, *Ukraine* **47 H6** 49 26N 31 16 E
Korsze, *Poland* **44 D8** 54 11N 21 9 E
Korti, *Sudan* **80 D3** 18 6N 31 33 E
Kortrijk, *Belgium* **17 D3** 50 50N 3 17 E
Korucu, *Turkey* **39 B9** 39 28N 27 22 E
Korwai, *India* **68 G8** 24 7N 78 5 E
Koryakskoye Nagorye, *Russia* **51 C18** 61 0N 171 0 E
Koryŏng, *S. Korea* **57 G15** 35 44N 128 15 E
Koryukovka, *Ukraine* **47 G7** 51 46N 32 16 E
Kos, *Greece* **39 E9** 36 50N 27 15 E
Kosa, *Ethiopia* **81 F4** 7 50N 36 50 E
Kosaya Gora, *Russia* **46 E9** 54 10N 37 30 E
Kościan, *Poland* **45 F3** 52 5N 16 40 E
Kościerzyna, *Poland* **44 D4** 54 8N 17 59 E
Kosciusko, *U.S.A.* **113 J10** 33 4N 89 35W
Kosciuszko, Mt., *Australia* **95 F4** 36 27 S 148 16 E
Kösély ➝, *Hungary* **42 C6** 47 25N 21 5 E
Kosha, *Sudan* **80 C3** 20 50N 30 30 E
Koshava, *Bulgaria* **40 B7** 44 4N 23 2 E
K'oshih = Kashi, *China* **60 C2** 39 30N 76 2 E
Koshiki-Rettō, *Japan* **55 J4** 31 45N 129 49 E
Kosi, *India* **68 F7** 27 48N 77 29 E
Kosi ➝, *India* **69 E8** 28 41N 78 57 E
Košice, *Slovak Rep.* **27 C14** 48 42N 21 15 E
Košický □, *Slovak Rep.* **27 C14** 48 45N 21 0 E
Kosjerić, *Serbia, Yug.* **40 B3** 44 0N 19 55 E
Köşk, *Turkey* **39 D10** 37 50N 28 3 E
Koskhinoú, *Greece* **36 C10** 36 23N 28 13 E
Koslan, *Russia* **50 C5** 63 34N 49 14 E
Kosŏng, *N. Korea* **57 E15** 38 40N 128 22 E
Kosovo □, *Yugoslavia* **40 D4** 42 30N 21 0 E
Kosovo Polje, *Kosovo, Yug.* **40 D5** 42 40N 21 5 E
Kosovska Kamenica, *Kosovo, Yug.* **40 D5** 42 35N 21 35 E
Kosovska Mitrovica, *Kosovo, Yug.* **40 D4** 42 54N 20 52 E
Kossou, L. de, *Ivory C.* **82 D3** 6 59N 5 31W
Kosta, *Sweden* **11 H9** 56 50N 15 24 E
Kostajnica, *Croatia* **29 C13** 45 17N 16 30 E
Kostanjevica, *Slovenia* **29 C12** 45 51N 15 27 E
Kostenets, *Bulgaria* **40 D7** 42 15N 23 52 E
Koster, *S. Africa* **88 D4** 25 52 S 26 54 E
Kôstî, *Sudan* **81 E3** 13 8N 32 43 E
Kostinbrod, *Bulgaria* **40 D7** 42 49N 23 13 E
Kostolac, *Serbia, Yug.* **40 B5** 44 37N 21 15 E
Kostopil, *Ukraine* **47 G4** 50 51N 26 22 E
Kostroma, *Russia* **46 D11** 57 50N 40 58 E
Kostromskoye Vdkhr., *Russia* **46 D11** 57 52N 40 49 E
Kostrzyn, *Lubuskie, Poland* **45 F1** 52 35N 14 39 E
Kostrzyn, *Wielkopolskie, Poland* **45 F4** 52 24N 17 14 E
Kostyantynivka, *Ukraine* **47 H9** 48 32N 37 39 E
Kostyukovichi = Kastsyukovichy, *Belarus* **46 F7** 53 20N 32 4 E
Koszalin, *Poland* **44 D3** 54 11N 16 8 E
Kőszeg, *Hungary* **42 C1** 47 23N 16 33 E
Kot Addu, *Pakistan* **68 D4** 30 30N 71 0 E
Kot Kapura, *India* **68 D6** 30 35N 74 50 E
Kot Moman, *Pakistan* **68 C5** 32 13N 73 0 E
Kot Sultan, *Pakistan* **68 D4** 30 46N 70 56 E
Kota, *India* **68 G6** 25 14N 75 49 E
Kota Baharu, *Malaysia* **65 J4** 6 7N 102 14 E
Kota Barrage, *India* **68 G6** 25 6N 75 51 E
Kota Belud, *Malaysia* **62 C5** 6 21N 116 26 E
Kota Kinabalu, *Malaysia* **62 C5** 6 0N 116 4 E
Kota Kubu Baharu, *Malaysia* **65 L3** 3 34N 101 39 E
Kota Tinggi, *Malaysia* **65 M4** 1 44N 103 53 E
Kotaagung, *Indonesia* **62 F2** 5 38 S 104 29 E
Kotabaru, *Indonesia* **62 E5** 3 20 S 116 20 E
Kotabumi, *Indonesia* **62 E2** 4 49 S 104 54 E
Kotamobagu, *Indonesia* **63 D6** 0 57N 124 31 E
Kotcho L., *Canada* **104 B4** 59 7N 121 12W
Kotdwara, *India* **69 E8** 29 45N 78 32 E
Kotel, *Bulgaria* **41 D10** 42 52N 26 26 E
Kotelnich, *Russia* **48 A9** 58 22N 48 24 E
Kotelnikovo, *Russia* **49 G6** 47 38N 43 8 E
Kotelnyy, Ostrov, *Russia* **51 B14** 75 10N 139 0 E
Kothari ➝, *India* **68 G6** 25 20N 75 4 E
Köthen, *Germany* **24 D7** 51 45N 11 59 E
Kothi, *Mad. P., India* **69 H10** 23 21N 82 3 E
Kothi, *Mad. P., India* **69 G9** 24 45N 80 40 E
Kotiro, *Pakistan* **68 F2** 26 17N 67 13 E
Kotka, *Finland* **9 F22** 60 28N 26 58 E
Kotlas, *Russia* **50 C5** 61 17N 46 43 E
Kotlenska Planina, *Bulgaria* **41 D10** 42 56N 26 30 E
Kotli, *Pakistan* **68 C5** 33 30N 73 55 E
Kotma, *India* **69 H9** 23 12N 81 58 E
Kotmul, *Pakistan* **69 B6** 35 32N 75 10 E
Koton-Karifi, *Nigeria* **83 D6** 8 0N 6 48 E
Kotonkoro, *Nigeria* **83 C6** 11 3N 5 58 E
Kotor, *Montenegro, Yug.* **40 D2** 42 25N 18 47 E
Kotor Varoš, *Bos.-H.* **42 F2** 44 38N 17 22 E
Kotoriba, *Croatia* **29 B13** 46 23N 16 48 E
Kotovo, *Russia* **48 E7** 50 22N 44 45 E
Kotovsk, *Russia* **48 D5** 52 36N 41 32 E
Kotovsk, *Ukraine* **47 J5** 47 45N 29 35 E
Kotputli, *India* **68 F7** 27 43N 76 12 E
Kotri, *Pakistan* **68 G3** 25 22N 68 22 E
Kótronas, *Greece* **38 E4** 36 38N 22 29 E
Kötschach-Mauthen, *Austria* **26 E6** 46 41N 13 1 E
Kottayam, *India* **66 Q10** 9 35N 76 33 E
Kotturu, *India* **66 M10** 14 45N 76 10 E
Kotuy ➝, *Russia* **51 B11** 71 54N 102 6 E
Kotzebue, *U.S.A.* **100 B3** 66 53N 162 39W
Koudougou, *Burkina Faso* **82 C4** 12 10N 2 20W
Koufonísi, *Greece* **36 E8** 34 56N 26 8 E
Koufonísia, *Greece* **39 E7** 36 57N 25 35 E
Kougaberge, *S. Africa* **88 E3** 33 48 S 23 50 E
Kouibli, *Ivory C.* **82 D3** 7 15N 7 14W
Kouilou ➝, *Congo* **84 E2** 4 10 S 12 5 E
Koula Moutou, *Gabon* **84 E2** 1 15 S 12 25 E
Koulen = Kulen, *Cambodia* **64 F5** 13 50N 104 40 E
Koulikoro, *Mali* **82 C3** 12 40N 7 50W
Kouloúra, *Greece* **36 A3** 39 42N 19 54 E
Koúm-bournoú, Ákra, *Greece* **36 C10** 36 15N 28 11 E
Koumala, *Australia* **94 C4** 21 38 S 149 15 E
Koumankou, *Mali* **82 C3** 11 58N 6 6W
Koumbia, *Burkina Faso* **82 C4** 11 10N 3 50W
Koumbia, *Guinea* **82 C2** 11 48N 13 29W
Koumboum, *Guinea* **82 C2** 10 25N 13 0W
Koumpenntoum, *Senegal* **82 C2** 13 59N 14 34W
Koumra, *Chad* **79 G9** 8 50N 17 35 E
Koun-Fao, *Ivory C.* **82 D4** 7 30N 3 15W
Koundara, *Guinea* **82 C2** 12 29N 13 18W
Koundian, *Guinea* **82 C3** 13 10N 10 35W
Koungheul, *Senegal* **82 C2** 14 0N 14 50W
Kounradskiy, *Kazakstan* **50 E8** 46 59N 75 0 E
Kountze, *U.S.A.* **113 K7** 30 22N 94 19W
Koupéla, *Burkina Faso* **83 C4** 12 11N 0 21W
Kouremalé, *Mali* **82 C3** 11 59N 8 42W
Kouris ➝, *Cyprus* **36 E11** 34 38N 32 54 E
Kourou, *Fr. Guiana* **125 B8** 5 9N 52 39W
Kourouba, *Mali* **82 C2** 13 22N 10 57W
Kouroukoto, *Mali* **82 C2** 12 35N 10 5W
Kourouma, *Burkina Faso* **82 C4** 11 35N 4 50W
Kourouninkoto, *Mali* **82 C3** 13 52N 9 35W
Kouroussa, *Guinea* **82 C3** 10 45N 9 45W
Koussanar, *Senegal* **82 C2** 13 52N 14 5W
Koussané, *Mali* **82 C2** 14 53N 11 14W
Koussane, *Senegal* **82 C2** 14 10N 12 22W
Kousseri, *Cameroon* **79 F8** 12 0N 14 55 E
Koutiala, *Mali* **82 C3** 12 25N 5 23W
Kouto, *Ivory C.* **82 D3** 9 53N 6 25W
Kouvé, *Togo* **83 D5** 6 25N 1 25 E
Kouvola, *Finland* **9 F22** 60 52N 26 43 E
Kovačica, *Serbia, Yug.* **42 E5** 45 5N 20 38 E
Kovel, *Ukraine* **47 G3** 51 11N 24 38 E
Kovin, *Serbia, Yug.* **42 F5** 44 44N 20 59 E
Kovrov, *Russia* **48 B5** 56 25N 41 25 E
Kowal, *Poland* **45 F6** 52 32N 19 7 E
Kowalewo Pomorskie, *Poland* **45 E5** 53 10N 18 52 E
Kowanyama, *Australia* **94 B3** 15 29 S 141 44 E
Kowloon, *H.K.* **59 F10** 22 20N 114 15 E
Kowŏn, *N. Korea* **57 E14** 39 26N 127 14 E
Köyceğiz, *Turkey* **39 E10** 36 57N 28 40 E
Köyceğiz Gölü, *Turkey* **39 E10** 36 56N 28 42 E
Koyulhisar, *Turkey* **72 B7** 40 20N 37 52 E
Koyunyeri, *Turkey* **41 F10** 40 50N 26 26 E
Koza, *Japan* **55 L3** 26 19N 127 46 E
Kozak, *Turkey* **39 B9** 39 15N 27 6 E
Kozan, *Turkey* **70 B2** 37 26N 35 50 E
Kozáni, *Greece* **40 F5** 40 19N 21 47 E
Kozáni □, *Greece* **40 F5** 40 18N 21 45 E
Kozara, *Bos.-H.* **29 D14** 45 0N 17 0 E
Kozarac, *Bos.-H.* **29 D13** 44 58N 16 48 E
Kozelets, *Ukraine* **47 G6** 50 55N 31 7 E
Kozelsk, *Russia* **46 E8** 54 2N 35 48 E
Kozhikode = Calicut, *India* **66 P9** 11 15N 75 43 E
Koziegłowy, *Poland* **45 H6** 50 37N 19 8 E
Kozienice, *Poland* **45 G8** 51 35N 21 34 E
Kozje, *Slovenia* **29 B12** 46 5N 15 35 E
Kozloduy, *Bulgaria* **40 C7** 43 45N 23 42 E
Kozlovets, *Bulgaria* **41 C9** 43 30N 25 20 E
Kozlovka, *Russia* **48 C9** 55 52N 48 14 E
Kozlu, *Turkey* **72 B4** 41 26N 31 45 E
Kozluk, *Turkey* **73 C9** 38 11N 41 31 E
Koźmin, *Poland* **45 G4** 51 48N 17 27 E
Kozmodemyansk, *Russia* **48 B8** 56 20N 46 36 E
Kożuchów, *Poland* **45 G2** 51 45N 15 31 E
Kozyatyn, *Ukraine* **47 H5** 49 45N 28 50 E
Kpabia, *Ghana* **83 D4** 9 10N 0 20W
Kpalimé, *Togo* **83 D5** 6 57N 0 44 E
Kpandae, *Ghana* **83 D4** 8 30N 0 2W
Kpessi, *Togo* **83 D5** 8 4N 1 16 E
Kra, Isthmus of = Kra, Kho Khot, *Thailand* **65 G2** 10 15N 99 30 E
Kra, Kho Khot, *Thailand* **65 G2** 10 15N 99 30 E
Kra Buri, *Thailand* **65 G2** 10 22N 98 46 E
Kraai ➝, *S. Africa* **88 E4** 30 40 S 26 45 E
Krabi, *Thailand* **65 H2** 8 4N 98 55 E
Kracheh, *Cambodia* **64 F6** 12 32N 106 10 E
Kragan, *Indonesia* **63 G14** 6 43 S 111 38 E
Kragerø, *Norway* **9 G13** 58 52N 9 25 E
Kragujevac, *Serbia, Yug.* **40 B4** 44 2N 20 56 E
Krajenka, *Poland* **45 E3** 53 18N 16 59 E
Krajina, *Bos.-H.* **29 D13** 44 45N 16 35 E
Krakatau = Rakata, Pulau, *Indonesia* **62 F3** 6 10 S 105 20 E
Krakatoa = Rakata, Pulau, *Indonesia* **62 F3** 6 10 S 105 20 E
Krakor, *Cambodia* **64 F5** 12 32N 104 12 E
Kraków, *Poland* **45 H6** 50 4N 19 57 E
Kralanh, *Cambodia* **64 F4** 13 35N 103 25 E
Králíky, *Czech Rep.* **27 A9** 50 6N 16 45 E
Kraljevo, *Serbia, Yug.* **40 C4** 43 44N 20 41 E
Královský Chlmec, *Slovak Rep.* **27 C14** 48 27N 22 0 E
Kralupy nad Vltavou, *Czech Rep.* **26 A7** 50 13N 14 20 E
Kramatorsk, *Ukraine* **47 H9** 48 50N 37 30 E
Kramfors, *Sweden* **10 B11** 62 55N 17 48 E
Kraniá, *Greece* **40 G5** 39 53N 21 18 E
Kranía Elassónas, *Greece* **38 B4** 39 57N 22 2 E
Kranídhion, *Greece* **38 D5** 37 20N 23 10 E
Kranj, *Slovenia* **29 B11** 46 16N 14 22 E
Kranjska Gora, *Slovenia* **29 B10** 46 29N 13 48 E
Krankskop, *S. Africa* **89 D5** 28 0 S 30 47 E
Krapina, *Croatia* **29 B12** 46 10N 15 52 E
Krapina ➝, *Croatia* **29 C12** 45 50N 15 50 E
Krapkowice, *Poland* **45 H4** 50 29N 17 56 E
Kras, *Croatia* **29 C10** 45 35N 14 0 E
Kraskino, *Russia* **51 E14** 42 44N 130 48 E
Krāslava, *Latvia* **46 E4** 55 54N 27 10 E
Kraslice, *Czech Rep.* **26 A5** 50 19N 12 31 E
Krasnaya Gorbatka, *Russia* **48 C5** 55 52N 41 45 E
Krasnaya Polyana, *Russia* **49 J5** 43 40N 40 13 E
Kraśnik, *Poland* **45 H9** 50 55N 22 15 E
Krasnoarmeisk, *Ukraine* **47 H9** 48 18N 37 11 E
Krasnoarmeysk, *Russia* **48 E7** 51 0N 45 42 E
Krasnoarmeyskiy, *Russia* **49 G6** 47 0N 42 12 E
Krasnobrod, *Poland* **45 H10** 50 33N 23 12 E
Krasnodar, *Russia* **49 H4** 45 5N 39 0 E
Krasnodon, *Ukraine* **47 H10** 48 17N 39 44 E
Krasnogorskiy, *Russia* **48 B9** 56 10N 48 28 E
Krasnograd = Krasnohrad, *Ukraine* **47 H8** 49 27N 35 27 E
Krasnogvardeyskoye, *Russia* **49 H5** 45 52N 41 33 E
Krasnogvardyesk, *Ukraine* **47 K8** 45 32N 34 16 E
Krasnohrad, *Ukraine* **47 H8** 49 27N 35 27 E
Krasnokutsk, *Ukraine* **47 G8** 50 10N 34 50 E
Krasnolesnyy, *Russia* **47 G10** 51 53N 39 35 E
Krasnoperekopsk, *Ukraine* **47 J7** 46 0N 33 54 E
Krasnorechenskiy, *Russia* **54 B7** 44 41N 135 14 E
Krasnoselkup, *Russia* **50 C9** 65 20N 82 10 E
Krasnoslobodsk, *Mordvinia, Russia* **48 C6** 54 25N 43 45 E
Krasnoslobodsk, *Volgograd, Russia* **49 F7** 48 42N 44 33 E
Krasnoturinsk, *Russia* **50 D7** 59 46N 60 12 E
Krasnovodsk = Türkmenbashi, *Turkmenistan* **50 E6** 40 5N 53 5 E
Krasnoyarsk, *Russia* **51 D10** 56 8N 93 0 E
Krasnoye = Krasnyy, *Russia* **46 E6** 54 25N 31 30 E
Krasnozavodsk, *Russia* **46 D10** 56 27N 38 25 E
Krasny Sulin, *Russia* **47 J11** 47 52N 40 8 E
Krasnystaw, *Poland* **45 H10** 50 57N 23 5 E
Krasnyy, *Russia* **46 E6** 54 25N 31 30 E
Krasnyy Kholm, *Russia* **46 C9** 58 10N 37 10 E
Krasnyy Kut, *Russia* **48 E8** 50 50N 47 0 E
Krasnyy Liman, *Ukraine* **47 H9** 48 58N 37 50 E
Krasnyy Luch, *Ukraine* **47 H10** 48 13N 39 0 E
Krasnyy Profintern, *Russia* **46 D11** 57 45N 40 27 E
Krasnyy Yar, *Astrakhan, Russia* **49 G9** 46 43N 48 23 E
Krasnyy Yar, *Samara, Russia* **48 D10** 53 30N 50 22 E
Krasnyy Yar, *Volgograd, Russia* **48 E7** 50 42N 44 45 E
Krasnyye Baki, *Russia* **48 B7** 57 8N 45 10 E
Krasnyyoskolske Vdskh., *Ukraine* **47 H9** 49 27N 37 40 E
Kraszna ➝, *Hungary* **42 B7** 48 4N 22 20 E
Kratie = Kracheh, *Cambodia* **64 F6** 12 32N 106 10 E
Kratovo, *Macedonia* **40 D6** 42 6N 22 10 E
Krau, *Indonesia* **63 E10** 3 19 S 140 5 E
Kravanh, Chuor Phnum, *Cambodia* **65 G4** 12 0N 103 32 E
Krefeld, *Germany* **24 D2** 51 20N 6 33 E
Krémaston, Límni, *Greece* **38 C3** 38 52N 21 30 E
Kremen, *Croatia* **29 D12** 44 28N 15 53 E
Kremenchug = Kremenchuk, *Ukraine* **47 H7** 49 5N 33 25 E
Kremenchuk, *Ukraine* **47 H7** 49 5N 33 25 E
Kremenchuksk Vdskh., *Ukraine* **47 H7** 49 20N 32 30 E
Kremenets, *Ukraine* **47 G3** 50 8N 25 43 E
Kremennaya, *Ukraine* **47 H10** 49 1N 38 10 E
Kremges = Svitlovodsk, *Ukraine* **47 H7** 49 2N 33 13 E
Kremmen, *Germany* **24 C9** 52 45N 13 1 E
Kremmling, *U.S.A.* **114 F10** 40 4N 106 24W
Kremnica, *Slovak Rep.* **27 C11** 48 45N 18 50 E
Krems, *Austria* **26 C8** 48 25N 15 36 E
Kremsmünster, *Austria* **26 C7** 48 3N 14 8 E
Kretinga, *Lithuania* **9 J19** 55 53N 21 15 E
Krettsy, *Russia* **46 C7** 58 15N 32 30 E
Kreuzberg, *Germany* **25 E5** 50 22N 9 58 E
Kreuztal, *Germany* **24 E4** 50 57N 8 0 E
Kría Vrísi, *Greece* **40 F6** 40 41N 22 18 E
Kribi, *Cameroon* **83 E6** 2 57N 9 56 E
Krichem, *Bulgaria* **41 D8** 42 8N 24 28 E
Krichev = Krychaw, *Belarus* **46 F6** 53 40N 31 41 E
Krim, *Slovenia* **29 C11** 45 53N 14 30 E
Kriós, Ákra, *Greece* **36 D5** 35 13N 23 34 E
Krishna ➝, *India* **67 M12** 15 57N 80 59 E
Krishnanagar, *India* **69 H13** 23 24N 88 33 E
Kristdala, *Sweden* **11 G10** 57 24N 16 13 E
Kristiansand, *Norway* **9 G13** 58 8N 8 1 E
Kristianstad, *Sweden* **11 H8** 56 2N 14 9 E
Kristiansund, *Norway* **8 E12** 63 7N 7 45 E
Kristiinankaupunki, *Finland* **9 E19** 62 16N 21 21 E
Kristinehamn, *Sweden* **10 E8** 59 18N 14 7 E
Kristinestad = Kristiinankaupunki, *Finland* **9 E19** 62 16N 21 21 E
Kríti, *Greece* **36 D7** 35 15N 25 0 E
Kritsá, *Greece* **36 D7** 35 10N 25 41 E
Kriva ➝, *Macedonia* **40 D5** 42 5N 21 47 E
Kriva Palanka, *Macedonia* **40 D6** 42 11N 22 19 E
Krivaja ➝, *Bos.-H.* **42 F3** 44 27N 18 9 E
Krivelj, *Serbia, Yug.* **40 B6** 44 10N 22 5 E
Krivoy Rog = Kryvyy Rih, *Ukraine* **47 J7** 47 51N 33 20 E
Križevci, *Croatia* **29 B13** 46 3N 16 32 E
Krk, *Croatia* **29 C11** 45 8N 14 40 E
Krka ➝, *Slovenia* **29 C12** 45 50N 15 30 E
Krkonoše, *Czech Rep.* **26 A8** 50 50N 15 35 E
Krnov, *Czech Rep.* **27 A10** 50 5N 17 40 E
Krobia, *Poland* **45 G3** 51 47N 16 59 E
Krokeaí, *Greece* **38 E4** 36 53N 22 32 E
Krokek, *Sweden* **11 F10** 58 40N 16 24 E
Krokodil ➝, *Mozam.* **89 D5** 25 14 S 32 18 E
Krokom, *Sweden* **10 A8** 63 20N 14 30 E
Krokowa, *Poland* **44 D5** 54 47N 18 9 E
Krolevets, *Ukraine* **47 G7** 51 35N 33 20 E
Kroměříž, *Czech Rep.* **27 B10** 49 18N 17 21 E
Krompachy, *Slovak Rep.* **27 C13** 48 54N 20 52 E
Kromy, *Russia* **47 F8** 52 48N 35 48 E
Kronach, *Germany* **25 E7** 50 14N 11 19 E
Krong Kaoh Kong, *Cambodia* **62 B2** 11 35N 103 0 E
Kronobergs län □, *Sweden* **11 H8** 56 45N 14 30 E
Kronprins Olav Kyst, *Antarctica* **5 C5** 69 0 S 42 0 E
Kronshtadt, *Russia* **46 C5** 59 57N 29 51 E
Kroonstad, *S. Africa* **88 D4** 27 43 S 27 19 E
Kröpelin, *Germany* **24 A7** 54 4N 11 47 E
Kropotkin, *Russia* **49 H5** 45 28N 40 28 E
Kropp, *Germany* **24 A5** 54 24N 9 31 E
Krosna, *Lithuania* **44 D10** 54 23N 23 33 E
Krośniewice, *Poland* **45 F6** 52 15N 19 11 E
Krosno, *Poland* **45 J8** 49 42N 21 46 E
Krosno Odrzańskie, *Poland* **45 F2** 52 3N 15 7 E
Krotoszyn, *Poland* **45 G4** 51 42N 17 23 E
Krotovka, *Russia* **48 D10** 53 18N 51 10 E
Kroussón, *Greece* **36 D6** 35 13N 24 59 E
Krraba = Krrabë, *Albania* **40 E3** 41 13N 20 0 E
Krrabë, *Albania* **40 E3** 41 13N 20 0 E
Krško, *Slovenia* **29 C12** 45 57N 15 30 E
Krstača, *Serbia, Yug.* **40 D4** 42 57N 20 8 E
Kruger Nat. Park, *S. Africa* **89 C5** 23 30 S 31 40 E
Krugersdorp, *S. Africa* **89 D4** 26 5 S 27 46 E
Kruisfontein, *S. Africa* **88 E3** 33 59 S 24 43 E
Kruja = Krujë, *Albania* **40 E3** 41 32N 19 46 E
Krujë, *Albania* **40 E3** 41 32N 19 46 E
Krulevshchina = Krulyewshchyna, *Belarus* **46 E4** 55 5N 27 45 E
Krulyewshchyna, *Belarus* **46 E4** 55 5N 27 45 E
Kruma = Krumë, *Albania* **40 D4** 42 14N 20 28 E
Krumbach, *Germany* **25 G6** 48 13N 10 22 E
Krumë, *Albania* **40 D4** 42 14N 20 28 E
Krumovgrad, *Bulgaria* **41 E9** 41 29N 25 38 E
Krung Thep = Bangkok, *Thailand* **64 F3** 13 45N 100 35 E
Krupanj, *Serbia, Yug.* **40 B3** 44 25N 19 22 E
Krupina, *Slovak Rep.* **27 C12** 48 22N 19 5 E
Krupinica ➝, *Slovak Rep.* **27 C11** 48 4N 18 55 E
Krupki, *Belarus* **46 E5** 54 19N 29 8 E
Kruševac, *Serbia, Yug.* **40 C5** 43 35N 21 28 E
Kruševo, *Macedonia* **40 E5** 41 23N 21 19 E
Kruszwica, *Poland* **45 F5** 52 40N 18 20 E
Krychaw, *Belarus* **46 F6** 53 40N 31 41 E
Krymsk, *Russia* **47 K10** 44 50N 38 0 E
Krymskiy Poluostrov = Krymskyy Pivostriv, *Ukraine* **47 K8** 45 0N 34 0 E
Krymskyy Pivostriv, *Ukraine* **47 K8** 45 0N 34 0 E
Krynica, *Poland* **45 J7** 49 25N 20 57 E
Krynica Morska, *Poland* **44 D6** 54 23N 19 28 E
Krynki, *Poland* **45 E10** 53 17N 23 43 E
Kryvyy Rih, *Ukraine* **47 J7** 47 51N 33 20 E
Krzepice, *Poland* **45 H5** 50 58N 18 50 E
Krzeszów, *Poland* **45 H9** 50 24N 22 21 E
Krzna ➝, *Poland* **45 F10** 52 8N 23 32 E
Krzywiń, *Poland* **45 G3** 51 58N 16 50 E
Krzyż Wielkopolski, *Poland* **45 F2** 52 52N 16 0 E
Ksar el Kebir, *Morocco* **78 B4** 35 0N 6 0W
Ksar es Souk = Ar Rachidiya, *Morocco* **78 B5** 31 58N 4 20W
Ksiąz Wielkopolski, *Poland* **45 F4** 52 4N 17 14 E
Kstovo, *Russia* **48 B7** 56 12N 44 13 E
Ku, W. el ➝, *Sudan* **81 E2** 13 37N 25 15 E
Kuala Belait, *Malaysia* **62 D4** 4 35N 114 11 E
Kuala Berang, *Malaysia* **65 K4** 5 5N 103 1 E
Kuala Dungun = Dungun, *Malaysia* **65 K4** 4 45N 103 25 E
Kuala Kangsar, *Malaysia* **65 K3** 4 46N 100 56 E
Kuala Kelawang, *Malaysia* **65 L4** 2 56N 102 5 E
Kuala Kerai, *Malaysia* **65 K4** 5 30N 102 12 E
Kuala Lipis, *Malaysia* **65 K4** 4 10N 102 3 E
Kuala Lumpur, *Malaysia* **65 L3** 3 9N 101 41 E
Kuala Nerang, *Malaysia* **65 J3** 6 16N 100 37 E
Kuala Pilah, *Malaysia* **65 L4** 2 45N 102 15 E
Kuala Rompin, *Malaysia* **65 L4** 2 49N 103 29 E
Kuala Selangor, *Malaysia* **65 L3** 3 20N 101 15 E
Kuala Sepetang, *Malaysia* **65 K3** 4 49N 100 28 E
Kuala Terengganu, *Malaysia* **65 K4** 5 20N 103 8 E
Kualajelai, *Indonesia* **62 E4** 2 58 S 110 46 E
Kualakapuas, *Indonesia* **62 E4** 2 55 S 114 20 E
Kualakurun, *Indonesia* **62 E4** 1 10 S 113 50 E
Kualapembuang, *Indonesia* **62 E4** 3 14 S 112 38 E
Kualasimpang, *Indonesia* **62 D1** 4 17N 98 3 E
Kuancheng, *China* **57 D10** 40 37N 118 30 E
Kuandang, *Indonesia* **63 D6** 0 56N 123 1 E
Kuandian, *China* **57 D13** 40 45N 124 45 E
Kuangchou = Guangzhou, *China* **59 F9** 23 5N 113 10 E
Kuanshan, *Taiwan* **59 F13** 23 3N 121 9 E
Kuantan, *Malaysia* **65 L4** 3 49N 103 20 E
Kuba = Quba, *Azerbaijan* **49 K9** 41 21N 48 32 E
Kuban ➝, *Russia* **47 K9** 45 20N 37 30 E
Kubenskoye, Ozero, *Russia* **46 C10** 59 40N 39 25 E
Kubokawa, *Japan* **55 H6** 33 12N 133 8 E
Kubrat, *Bulgaria* **41 C10** 43 49N 26 31 E
Kučevo, *Serbia, Yug.* **40 B5** 44 30N 21 40 E
Kucha Gompa, *India* **69 B7** 34 25N 76 56 E
Kuchaman, *India* **68 F6** 27 13N 74 47 E
Kuchenspitze, *Austria* **26 D3** 47 7N 10 12 E
Kuchinda, *India* **69 J11** 21 44N 84 21 E
Kuching, *Malaysia* **62 D4** 1 33N 110 25 E
Kuchino-eruba-Jima, *Japan* **55 J5** 30 28N 130 12 E
Kuchino-Shima, *Japan* **55 K4** 29 57N 129 55 E
Kuchinotsu, *Japan* **55 H5** 32 36N 130 11 E
Kuchl, *Austria* **26 D6** 47 37N 13 9 E
Kucing = Kuching, *Malaysia* **62 D4** 1 33N 110 25 E
Kuçova = Kuçovë, *Albania* **40 F3** 40 47N 19 57 E
Kuçovë, *Albania* **40 F3** 40 47N 19 57 E
Küçükbahçe, *Turkey* **39 C8** 38 33N 26 24 E
Küçükköy, *Turkey* **39 B8** 39 16N 26 42 E
Küçükkuyu, *Turkey* **39 B8** 39 32N 26 36 E
Küçükmenderes ➝, *Turkey* **39 D9** 37 57N 27 16 E
Kud ➝, *Pakistan* **68 F2** 26 5N 66 20 E
Kuda, *India* **66 H7** 23 10N 71 15 E
Kudat, *Malaysia* **62 C5** 6 55N 116 55 E
Kudirkos Naumiestis, *Lithuania* **44 D9** 54 46N 22 53 E
Kudowa-Zdrój, *Poland* **45 H3** 50 27N 16 15 E
Kudus, *Indonesia* **63 G14** 6 48 S 110 51 E
Kudymkar, *Russia* **50 D6** 59 1N 54 39 E
Kueiyang = Guiyang, *China* **58 D6** 26 32N 106 40 E
Kufra Oasis = Al Kufrah, *Libya* **79 D10** 24 17N 23 15 E
Kufstein, *Austria* **26 D5** 47 35N 12 11 E
Kugluktuk, *Canada* **100 B8** 67 50N 115 5W
Kugong I., *Canada* **102 A4** 56 18N 79 50W
Kūhak, *Iran* **66 F3** 27 12N 63 10 E
Kuhan, *Pakistan* **68 E2** 28 19N 67 14 E
Kūhbonān, *Iran* **71 D8** 31 23N 56 19 E
Kūhestak, *Iran* **71 E8** 26 47N 57 2 E
Kuhin, *Iran* **71 B6** 36 22N 49 40 E
Kūhīrī, *Iran* **71 E9** 26 55N 61 2 E
Kuhnsdorf, *Austria* **26 E7** 46 37N 14 38 E
Kūhpāyeh, *Eşfahan, Iran* **71 C7** 32 44N 52 20 E
Kūhpāyeh, *Kermān, Iran* **71 D8** 30 35N 57 15 E
Kūhrān, Kūh-e, *Iran* **71 E8** 26 46N 58 12 E
Kui Buri, *Thailand* **65 F2** 12 3N 99 52 E
Kuiseb ➝, *Namibia* **88 B2** 22 59 S 14 31 E
Kuito, *Angola* **85 G3** 12 22 S 16 55 E
Kuiu I., *U.S.A.* **104 B2** 57 45N 134 10W
Kujang, *N. Korea* **57 E14** 39 57N 126 1 E
Kujawsko-Pomorskie □, *Poland* **44 E5** 53 20N 18 30 E
Kuji, *Japan* **54 D10** 40 11N 141 46 E
Kujū-San, *Japan* **55 H5** 33 5N 131 15 E
Kukavica, *Serbia, Yug.* **40 D5** 42 48N 21 57 E
Kukawa, *Nigeria* **83 C7** 12 58N 13 27 E
Kukës, *Albania* **40 D4** 42 5N 20 27 E
Kukësi = Kukës, *Albania* **40 D4** 42 5N 20 27 E
Kukmor, *Russia* **48 B10** 56 11N 50 54 E
Kukup, *Malaysia* **65 M4** 1 20N 103 27 E
Kukvidze, *Russia* **48 E6** 50 40N 43 0 E
Kula, *Bulgaria* **40 C6** 43 52N 22 36 E
Kula, *Serbia, Yug.* **42 E4** 45 37N 19 32 E
Kula, *Turkey* **39 C10** 38 32N 28 40 E
Kulachi, *Pakistan* **68 D4** 31 56N 70 27 E
Kulai, *Malaysia* **65 M4** 1 44N 103 35 E
Kulal, Mt., *Kenya* **86 B4** 2 42N 36 57 E
Kulaly, Ostrov, *Kazakstan* **49 H10** 45 0N 50 0 E
Kulasekarappattinam, *India* **66 Q11** 8 20N 78 5 E
Kulautuva, *Lithuania* **44 D10** 54 56N 23 36 E
Kuldīga, *Latvia* **9 H19** 56 58N 21 59 E
Kuldīga □, *Latvia* **44 B8** 56 55N 22 0 E
Kuldja = Yining, *China* **50 E9** 43 58N 81 10 E
Kuldu, *Sudan* **81 E2** 12 50N 28 30 E
Kulebaki, *Russia* **48 C6** 55 22N 42 25 E
Kulen, *Cambodia* **64 F5** 13 50N 104 40 E
Kulen Vakuf, *Bos.-H.* **29 D13** 44 35N 16 2 E
Kulgam, *India* **69 C6** 33 36N 75 2 E
Kulgera, *Australia* **94 D1** 25 50 S 133 18 E
Kulim, *Malaysia* **65 K3** 5 22N 100 34 E
Kulin, *Australia* **93 F2** 32 40 S 118 2 E
Kullen, *Sweden* **11 H6** 56 18N 12 26 E
Kulmbach, *Germany* **25 E7** 50 6N 11 26 E
Kŭlob, *Tajikistan* **50 F7** 37 55N 69 50 E
Kulp, *Turkey* **73 C9** 38 29N 41 2 E
Kulpawn ➝, *Ghana* **83 D4** 10 20N 1 5W
Kulsary, *Kazakstan* **50 E6** 46 59N 54 1 E
Kulti, *India* **69 H12** 23 43N 86 50 E
Kulu, *India* **68 D7** 31 58N 77 6 E
Kulu, *Turkey* **72 C5** 39 5N 33 4 E
Kulumbura, *Australia* **92 B4** 13 55 S 126 35 E
Kulunda, *Russia* **50 D8** 52 35N 78 57 E
Kulungar, *Afghan.* **68 C3** 34 0N 69 2 E
Kūlvand, *Iran* **71 D7** 31 21N 54 35 E
Kulwin, *Australia* **95 F3** 35 0 S 142 42 E
Kulyab = Kŭlob, *Tajikistan* **50 F7** 37 55N 69 50 E
Kuma ➝, *Russia* **49 H8** 44 55N 47 0 E
Kumafşarı, *Turkey* **39 D11** 37 19N 29 32 E
Kumaganum, *Nigeria* **83 C7** 13 8N 10 38 E
Kumagaya, *Japan* **55 F9** 36 9N 139 22 E
Kumai, *Indonesia* **62 E4** 2 44 S 111 43 E
Kumalar Dağı, *Turkey* **39 C12** 38 15N 30 20 E
Kumamba, Kepulauan, *Indonesia* **63 E9** 1 36 S 138 45 E
Kumamoto, *Japan* **55 H5** 32 45N 130 45 E
Kumamoto □, *Japan* **55 H5** 32 55N 130 55 E
Kumanovo, *Macedonia* **40 D5** 42 9N 21 42 E
Kumara, *N.Z.* **91 K3** 42 37 S 171 12 E
Kumarina, *Australia* **93 D2** 24 41 S 119 32 E
Kumasi, *Ghana* **82 D4** 6 41N 1 38W
Kumayri = Gyumri, *Armenia* **49 K6** 40 47N 43 50 E
Kumba, *Cameroon* **83 E6** 4 36N 9 24 E
Kumbağ, *Turkey* **41 F11** 40 51N 27 27 E
Kumbakonam, *India* **66 P11** 10 58N 79 25 E
Kumbarilla, *Australia* **95 D5** 27 15 S 150 55 E
Kumbhraj, *India* **68 G7** 24 22N 77 3 E
Kumbia, *Australia* **95 D5** 26 41 S 151 39 E
Kumbo, *Cameroon* **83 D7** 6 15N 10 36 E
Kŭmch'ŏn, *N. Korea* **57 E14** 38 10N 126 29 E
Kumdok, *India* **69 C8** 33 32N 78 10 E
Kume-Shima, *Japan* **55 L3** 26 20N 126 47 E
Kumeny, *Russia* **48 A9** 58 10N 49 47 E
Kumharsain, *India* **68 D7** 31 19N 77 27 E
Kŭmhwa, *S. Korea* **57 E14** 38 17N 127 28 E
Kumi, *Uganda* **86 B3** 1 30N 33 58 E
Kumkale, *Turkey* **41 G10** 39 59N 26 11 E
Kumla, *Sweden* **10 E9** 59 8N 15 10 E
Kumluca, *Turkey* **39 E12** 36 22N 30 20 E
Kummerower See, *Germany* **24 B8** 53 49N 12 51 E
Kumo, *Nigeria* **83 C7** 10 1N 11 12 E
Kumon Bum, *Burma* **67 F20** 26 30N 97 15 E
Kumylzhenskaya, *Russia* **48 F6** 49 51N 42 38 E
Kunágota, *Hungary* **42 D6** 46 26N 21 3 E
Kunashir, Ostrov, *Russia* **51 E15** 44 0N 146 0 E
Kunda, *Estonia* **9 G22** 59 30N 26 34 E
Kunda, *India* **69 G9** 25 43N 81 31 E
Kundar ➝, *Pakistan* **68 D3** 31 56N 69 19 E
Kundian, *Pakistan* **68 C4** 32 27N 71 28 E
Kundla, *India* **68 J4** 21 21N 71 25 E
Kunga ➝, *Bangla.* **69 J13** 21 46N 89 30 E
Kungälv, *Sweden* **11 G5** 57 53N 11 59 E
Kunghit I., *Canada* **104 C2** 52 6N 131 3W
Kungrad = Qŭnghirot, *Uzbekistan* **50 E6** 43 6N 58 54 E
Kungsängen, *Sweden* **10 E11** 59 29N 17 45 E
Kungsbacka, *Sweden* **11 G6** 57 30N 12 5 E
Kungsgården, *Sweden* **10 D10** 60 37N 16 35 E
Kungshamn, *Sweden* **11 F5** 58 22N 11 15 E
Kungsör, *Sweden* **10 E10** 59 25N 16 5 E
Kungur, *Russia* **50 D6** 57 25N 56 57 E
Kunhar ➝, *Pakistan* **69 B5** 34 20N 73 30 E

Kunhegyes, *Hungary* **42 C5** 47 22N 20 36 E
Kuningan, *Indonesia* **63 G13** 6 59 S 108 29 E
Kunlong, *Burma* **58 F2** 23 20N 98 50 E
Kunlun Shan, *Asia* **60 C3** 36 0N 86 30 E
Kunmadaras, *Hungary* **42 C5** 47 28N 20 45 E
Kunming, *China* **58 E4** 25 1N 102 41 E
Kunów, *Poland* **45 H8** 50 57N 21 17 E
Kunsan, *S. Korea* **57 G14** 35 59N 126 45 E
Kunshan, *China* **59 B13** 31 22N 120 58 E
Kunszentmárton, *Hungary* **42 D5** 46 50N 20 20 E
Kunszentmiklós, *Hungary* **42 C4** 47 2N 19 8 E
Kuntaur, *Senegal* **82 C2** 13 40N 14 48W
Kununurra, *Australia* **92 C4** 15 40 S 128 50 E
Kunwari →, *India* **69 F8** 26 26N 79 11 E
Kunya-Urgench = Köneürgench, *Turkmenistan* **50 E6** 42 19N 59 10 E
Künzelsau, *Germany* **25 F5** 49 17N 9 42 E
Kuopio, *Finland* **8 E22** 62 53N 27 35 E
Kupa →, *Croatia* **29 C13** 45 28N 16 24 E
Kupang, *Indonesia* **63 F6** 10 19 S 123 39 E
Kupreanof I., *U.S.A.* **104 B2** 56 50N 133 30W
Kupres, *Bos.-H.* **42 G2** 43 56N 17 15 E
Kupyansk, *Ukraine* **47 H9** 49 52N 37 35 E
Kupyansk-Uzlovoi, *Ukraine* **47 H9** 49 40N 37 43 E
Kuqa, *China* **60 B3** 41 35N 82 30 E
Kür →, *Azerbaijan* **73 C13** 39 29N 49 15 E
Kür Dili, *Azerbaijan* **71 B6** 39 3N 49 13 E
Kura = Kür →, *Azerbaijan* **73 C13** 39 29N 49 15 E
Kuranda, *Australia* **94 B4** 16 48 S 145 35 E
Kuranga, *India* **68 H3** 22 4N 69 10 E
Kurashiki, *Japan* **55 G6** 34 40N 133 50 E
Kurayoshi, *Japan* **55 G6** 35 26N 133 50 E
Kürdämir, *Azerbaijan* **49 K9** 40 25N 48 3 E
Kurdistan, *Asia* **73 D10** 37 20N 43 30 E
Kŭrdzhali, *Bulgaria* **41 E9** 41 38N 25 21 E
Kure, *Japan* **55 G6** 34 14N 132 32 E
Küre, *Turkey* **72 B5** 41 48N 33 43 E
Küre Dağları, *Turkey* **72 B6** 41 50N 34 10 E
Kuressaare, *Estonia* **9 G20** 58 15N 22 30 E
Kurgan, *Russia* **50 D7** 55 26N 65 18 E
Kurganinsk, *Russia* **49 H5** 44 54N 40 34 E
Kurgannaya = Kurganinsk, *Russia* **49 H5** 44 54N 40 34 E
Kuri, *India* **68 F4** 26 37N 70 43 E
Kuria Maria Is. = Khurīyā Murīyā, Jazā 'ir, *Oman* **74 D6** 17 30N 55 58 E
Kuridala, *Australia* **94 C3** 21 16 S 140 29 E
Kurigram, *Bangla.* **67 G16** 25 49N 89 39 E
Kurikka, *Finland* **9 E20** 62 36N 22 24 E
Kuril Is. = Kurilskiye Ostrova, *Russia* **51 E15** 45 0N 150 0 E
Kuril Trench, *Pac. Oc.* **52 E19** 44 0N 153 0 E
Kurilsk, *Russia* **51 E15** 45 14N 147 53 E
Kurilskiye Ostrova, *Russia* **51 E15** 45 0N 150 0 E
Kurino, *Japan* **55 J5** 31 57N 130 43 E
Kurinskaya Kosa = Kür Dili, *Azerbaijan* **71 B6** 39 3N 49 13 E
Kurkur, *Egypt* **80 C3** 23 50N 32 0 E
Kurlovskiy, *Russia* **48 C5** 55 25N 40 40 E
Kurmuk, *Sudan* **81 E3** 10 33N 34 21 E
Kurnool, *India* **66 M11** 15 45N 78 0 E
Kuro-Shima, *Kagoshima, Japan* **55 J4** 30 50N 129 57 E
Kuro-Shima, *Okinawa, Japan* **55 M2** 24 14N 124 1 E
Kuror, J., *Sudan* **80 C3** 20 27N 31 30 E
Kurow, *N.Z.* **91 L3** 44 44 S 170 29 E
Kurów, *Poland* **45 G9** 51 23N 22 12 E
Kurram →, *Pakistan* **68 C4** 32 36N 71 20 E
Kurri Kurri, *Australia* **95 E5** 32 50 S 151 28 E
Kurrimine, *Australia* **94 B4** 17 47 S 146 6 E
Kursavka, *Russia* **49 H6** 44 29N 42 32 E
Kuršėnai, *Lithuania* **44 B9** 56 1N 22 58 E
Kurshskiy Zaliv, *Russia* **9 J19** 55 9N 21 6 E
Kursk, *Russia* **47 G9** 51 42N 36 11 E
Kuršumlija, *Serbia, Yug.* **40 C5** 43 9N 21 19 E
Kuršumlijska Banja, *Serbia, Yug.* **40 C5** 43 3N 21 11 E
Kurşunlu, *Bursa, Turkey* **41 F13** 40 3N 29 40 E
Kurşunlu, *Çankırı, Turkey* **72 B5** 40 51N 33 15 E
Kurtalan, *Turkey* **73 D9** 37 56N 41 44 E
Kurtbey, *Turkey* **41 E10** 41 9N 26 35 E
Kuru, *Sudan* **81 F2** 7 43N 26 31 E
Kuru, Bahr el →, *Sudan* **81 F2** 8 10N 26 50 E
Kurucaşile, *Turkey* **72 B5** 41 49N 32 42 E
Kuruçay, *Turkey* **70 B3** 39 39N 38 29 E
Kuruktag, *China* **60 B3** 41 0N 89 0 E
Kuruman, *S. Africa* **88 D3** 27 28 S 23 28 E
Kuruman →, *S. Africa* **88 D3** 26 56 S 20 39 E
Kurume, *Japan* **55 H5** 33 15N 130 30 E
Kurun →, *Sudan* **81 F3** 5 30N 34 17 E
Kurunegala, *Sri Lanka* **66 R12** 7 30N 80 23 E
Kurya, *Russia* **50 C6** 61 42N 57 9 E
Kus Gölü, *Turkey* **41 F11** 40 10N 27 55 E
Kuşadası, *Turkey* **72 D2** 37 52N 27 15 E
Kuşadası Körfezi, *Turkey* **39 D8** 37 56N 27 0 E
Kusatsu, *Japan* **55 F9** 36 37N 138 36 E
Kusawa L., *Canada* **104 A1** 60 20N 136 13W
Kusel, *Germany* **25 F3** 49 32N 7 24 E
Kushaka, *Nigeria* **83 C6** 10 32N 6 48 E
Kushalgarh, *India* **68 H6** 23 10N 74 27 E
Kushchevskaya, *Russia* **49 G4** 46 33N 39 35 E
Kusheriki, *Nigeria* **83 C6** 10 33N 6 28 E
Kushikino, *Japan* **55 J5** 31 44N 130 16 E
Kushima, *Japan* **55 J5** 31 29N 131 14 E
Kushimoto, *Japan* **55 H7** 33 28N 135 47 E
Kushiro, *Japan* **54 C12** 43 0N 144 25 E
Kushiro-Gawa →, *Japan* **54 C12** 42 59N 144 23 E
Kūshk, *Iran* **71 D8** 28 46N 56 51 E
Kushka = Gushgy, *Turkmenistan* **50 F7** 35 20N 62 18 E
Kūshkī, *Iran* **70 C5** 33 31N 47 13 E
Kushol, *India* **69 C7** 33 40N 76 36 E
Kushtia, *Bangla.* **67 H16** 23 55N 89 5 E
Kushum →, *Kazakstan* **48 F10** 49 20N 50 30 E
Kuskokwim B., *U.S.A.* **100 C3** 59 45N 162 25W
Kusmi, *India* **69 H10** 23 17N 83 55 E
Kussharo-Ko, *Japan* **54 C12** 43 38N 144 21 E
Kustanay = Qostanay, *Kazakstan* **50 D7** 53 10N 63 35 E
Kut, Ko, *Thailand* **65 G4** 11 40N 102 35 E
Kütahya, *Turkey* **39 B12** 39 30N 30 2 E
Kütahya □, *Turkey* **39 B11** 39 10N 29 30 E
Kutaisi, *Georgia* **49 J6** 42 19N 42 40 E
Kutaraja = Banda Aceh, *Indonesia* **62 C1** 5 35N 95 20 E
Kutch, Gulf of = Kachchh, Gulf of, *India* **68 H3** 22 50N 69 15 E
Kutch, Rann of = Kachchh, Rann of, *India* **68 H4** 24 0N 70 0 E
Kutina, *Croatia* **29 C13** 45 29N 16 48 E
Kutiyana, *India* **68 J4** 21 36N 70 2 E
Kutjevo, *Croatia* **42 E2** 45 23N 17 55 E
Kutkashen, *Azerbaijan* **49 K8** 40 58N 47 47 E
Kutná Hora, *Czech Rep.* **26 B8** 49 57N 15 16 E
Kutno, *Poland* **45 F6** 52 15N 19 23 E
Kutse, *Botswana* **88 C3** 21 7 S 22 16 E
Kutu, *Dem. Rep. of the Congo* **84 E3** 2 40 S 18 11 E
Kutum, *Sudan* **81 E1** 14 10N 24 40 E
Kúty, *Slovak Rep.* **27 C10** 48 40N 17 3 E
Kuujjuaq, *Canada* **101 C13** 58 6N 68 15W
Kuujjuarapik, *Canada* **102 A4** 55 20N 77 35W
Kuŭp-tong, *N. Korea* **57 D14** 40 45N 126 1 E
Kuusamo, *Finland* **8 D23** 65 57N 29 8 E
Kuusankoski, *Finland* **9 F22** 60 55N 26 38 E
Kuvshinovo, *Russia* **46 D8** 57 2N 34 11 E
Kuwait = Al Kuwayt, *Kuwait* **70 D5** 29 30N 48 0 E
Kuwait ■, *Asia* **70 D5** 29 30N 47 30 E
Kuwana, *Japan* **55 G8** 35 5N 136 43 E
Kuwana →, *India* **69 F10** 26 25N 83 15 E
Kuybyshev = Samara, *Russia* **48 D10** 53 8N 50 6 E
Kuybyshev, *Russia* **50 D8** 55 27N 78 19 E
Kuybyshevo, *Ukraine* **47 J9** 47 25N 36 40 E
Kuybyshevskoye Vdkhr., *Russia* **48 C9** 55 2N 49 30 E
Kuye He →, *China* **56 E6** 38 23N 110 46 E
Kūyeh, *Iran* **70 B5** 38 45N 47 57 E
Kŭysanjaq, *Iraq* **70 B5** 36 5N 44 38 E
Kuyucak, *Turkey* **39 D10** 37 55N 28 28 E
Kuyumba, *Russia* **51 C10** 60 58N 96 59 E
Kuzey Anadolu Dağları, *Turkey* **72 B7** 41 30N 35 0 E
Kuzmin, *Serbia, Yug.* **42 E4** 45 2N 19 25 E
Kuznetsk, *Russia* **48 D8** 53 12N 46 40 E
Kuzomen, *Russia* **50 C4** 66 22N 36 50 E
Kvænangen, *Norway* **8 A19** 70 5N 21 15 E
Kværndrup, *Denmark* **11 J4** 55 10N 10 31 E
Kvaløy, *Norway* **8 B18** 69 40N 18 30 E
Kvänum, *Sweden* **11 F7** 58 18N 13 11 E
Kvareli = Qvareli, *Georgia* **49 K7** 41 57N 45 47 E
Kvarner, *Croatia* **29 D11** 44 50N 14 10 E
Kvarnerič, *Croatia* **29 D11** 44 43N 14 37 E
Kvicksund, *Sweden* **10 E10** 59 27N 16 19 E
Kvillsfors, *Sweden* **11 G9** 57 24N 15 29 E
Kvismare kanal, *Sweden* **10 E9** 59 11N 15 35 E
Kvissleby, *Sweden* **10 B11** 62 18N 17 22 E
Kwa-Nobuhle, *S. Africa* **85 L5** 33 50 S 25 22 E
Kwabhaca, *S. Africa* **89 E4** 30 51 S 29 0 E
Kwakhanai, *Botswana* **88 C3** 21 39 S 21 16 E
Kwakoegron, *Surinam* **125 B7** 5 12N 55 25W
Kwale, *Kenya* **86 C4** 4 15 S 39 31 E
Kwale, *Nigeria* **83 D6** 5 46N 6 26 E
KwaMashu, *S. Africa* **89 D5** 29 45 S 30 58 E
Kwando →, *Africa* **88 B3** 18 27 S 23 32 E
Kwangdaeri, *N. Korea* **57 D14** 40 31N 127 32 E
Kwangju, *S. Korea* **57 G14** 35 9N 126 54 E
Kwango →, *Dem. Rep. of the Congo* **77 G5** 3 14 S 17 22 E
Kwangsi-Chuang = Guangxi Zhuangzu Zizhiqu □, *China* **58 F7** 24 0N 109 0 E
Kwangtung = Guangdong □, *China* **59 F9** 23 0N 113 0 E
Kwara □, *Nigeria* **83 D6** 8 45N 4 30 E
Kwataboahegan →, *Canada* **102 B3** 51 9N 80 50W
Kwatisore, *Indonesia* **63 E8** 3 18 S 134 50 E
KwaZulu Natal □, *S. Africa* **89 D5** 29 0 S 30 0 E
Kweichow = Guizhou □, *China* **58 D6** 27 0N 107 0 E
Kwekwe, *Zimbabwe* **87 F2** 18 58 S 29 48 E
Kwidzyn, *Poland* **44 E5** 53 44N 18 55 E
Kwiha, *Ethiopia* **81 E4** 13 29N 39 32 E
Kwinana New Town, *Australia* **93 F2** 32 15 S 115 47 E
Kwisa →, *Poland* **45 G2** 51 34N 15 24 E
Kwoka, *Indonesia* **63 E8** 0 31 S 132 27 E
Kwolla, *Nigeria* **83 D6** 9 0N 9 15 E
Kyabra Cr. →, *Australia* **95 D3** 25 36 S 142 55 E
Kyabram, *Australia* **95 F4** 36 19 S 145 4 E
Kyaikto, *Burma* **64 D1** 17 20N 97 3 E
Kyakhta, *Russia* **51 D11** 50 30N 106 25 E
Kyancutta, *Australia* **95 E2** 33 8 S 135 33 E
Kyangin, *Burma* **67 K19** 18 20N 95 20 E
Kyaukpadaung, *Burma* **67 J19** 20 52N 95 8 E
Kyaukpyu, *Burma* **67 K18** 19 28N 93 30 E
Kyaukse, *Burma* **67 J20** 21 36N 96 10 E
Kybartai, *Lithuania* **44 D9** 54 39N 22 45 E
Kyburz, *U.S.A.* **116 G6** 38 47N 120 18W
Kyelang, *India* **68 C7** 32 35N 77 2 E
Kyenjojo, *Uganda* **86 B3** 0 40N 30 37 E
Kyjov, *Czech Rep.* **27 B10** 49 1N 17 7 E
Kyle, *Canada* **105 C7** 50 50N 108 2W
Kyle Dam, *Zimbabwe* **87 G3** 20 15 S 31 0 E
Kyle of Lochalsh, *U.K.* **14 D3** 57 17N 5 44W
Kyll →, *Germany* **25 F2** 49 48N 6 41 E
Kyllburg, *Germany* **25 E2** 50 2N 6 34 E
Kymijoki →, *Finland* **9 F22** 60 30N 26 55 E
Kyneton, *Australia* **95 F3** 37 10 S 144 29 E
Kynuna, *Australia* **94 C3** 21 37 S 141 55 E
Kyō-ga-Saki, *Japan* **55 G7** 35 45N 135 15 E
Kyoga, L., *Uganda* **86 B3** 1 35N 33 0 E
Kyogle, *Australia* **95 D5** 28 40 S 153 0 E
Kyom →, *Sudan* **81 F2** 8 58N 28 13 E
Kyongju, *S. Korea* **57 G15** 35 51N 129 14 E
Kyongpyaw, *Burma* **67 L19** 17 12N 95 10 E
Kyŏngsŏng, *N. Korea* **57 D15** 41 35N 129 36 E
Kyōto, *Japan* **55 G7** 35 0N 135 45 E
Kyōto □, *Japan* **55 G7** 35 15N 135 45 E
Kyparissovouno, *Cyprus* **36 D12** 35 19N 33 10 E
Kyperounda, *Cyprus* **36 E11** 34 56N 32 58 E
Kyrenia, *Cyprus* **36 D12** 35 20N 33 20 E
Kyrgyzstan ■, *Asia* **50 E8** 42 0N 75 0 E
Kyritz, *Germany* **24 C8** 52 56N 12 24 E
Kyrkhult, *Sweden* **11 H8** 56 22N 14 34 E
Kyrönjoki →, *Finland* **8 E19** 63 14N 21 45 E
Kystatyam, *Russia* **51 C13** 67 20N 123 10 E
Kysucké Nové Mesto, *Slovak Rep.* **27 B11** 49 18N 18 47 E
Kythréa, *Cyprus* **36 D12** 35 15N 33 29 E
Kyunhla, *Burma* **67 H19** 23 25N 95 15 E
Kyuquot Sound, *Canada* **104 D3** 50 2N 127 22W
Kyurdamir = Kürdämir, *Azerbaijan* **49 K9** 40 25N 48 3 E
Kyūshū, *Japan* **55 H5** 33 0N 131 0 E
Kyūshū □, *Japan* **55 H5** 33 0N 131 0 E
Kyūshū-Sanchi, *Japan* **55 H5** 32 35N 131 17 E
Kyustendil, *Bulgaria* **40 D6** 42 16N 22 41 E
Kyusyur, *Russia* **51 B13** 70 19N 127 30 E
Kyyiv, *Ukraine* **47 G6** 50 30N 30 28 E
Kyyivske Vdskh., *Ukraine* **47 G6** 51 0N 30 25 E
Kyzyl, *Russia* **51 D10** 51 50N 94 30 E
Kyzyl Kum, *Uzbekistan* **50 E7** 42 30N 65 0 E
Kyzyl-Kyya, *Kyrgyzstan* **50 E8** 40 16N 72 8 E
Kzyl-Orda = Qyzylorda, *Kazakstan* **50 E7** 44 48N 65 28 E

L

La Albuera, *Spain* **35 G4** 38 45N 6 49W
La Alcarria, *Spain* **32 E2** 40 31N 2 45W
La Almarcha, *Spain* **32 F2** 39 41N 2 24W
La Almunia de Doña Godina, *Spain* **32 D3** 41 29N 1 23W
La Asunción, *Venezuela* **124 A6** 11 2N 63 53W
La Baie, *Canada* **103 C5** 48 19N 70 53W
La Banda, *Argentina* **126 B3** 27 45 S 64 10W
La Bañeza, *Spain* **34 C5** 42 17N 5 54W
La Barca, *Mexico* **118 C4** 20 20N 102 40W
La Barge, *U.S.A.* **114 E8** 42 16N 110 12W
La Bastide-Puylaurent, *France* **20 D7** 44 35N 3 55 E
La Baule-Escoubiac, *France* **18 E4** 47 17N 2 24W
La Belle, *U.S.A.* **109 M5** 26 46N 81 26W
La Biche →, *Canada* **104 B4** 59 57N 123 50W
La Biche, L., *Canada* **104 C6** 54 50N 112 5W
La Bisbal d'Empordà, *Spain* **32 D8** 41 58N 3 2 E
La Bomba, *Mexico* **118 A1** 31 53N 115 2W
La Brède, *France* **20 D3** 44 41N 0 32W
La Bresse, *France* **19 D13** 48 2N 6 53 E
La Bureba, *Spain* **34 C7** 42 36N 3 24W
La Calera, *Chile* **126 C1** 32 50 S 71 10W
La Campiña, *Spain* **35 H6** 37 45N 4 45W
La Canal = Sa Canal, *Spain* **37 C7** 38 51N 1 23 E
La Cañiza = A Cañiza, *Spain* **34 C2** 42 13N 8 16W
La Canourgue, *France* **20 D7** 44 26N 3 13 E
La Capelle, *France* **19 C10** 49 59N 3 50 E
La Carlota, *Argentina* **126 C3** 33 30 S 63 20W
La Carlota, *Phil.* **61 F5** 10 25N 122 55 E
La Carlota, *Spain* **35 H6** 37 40N 4 56W
La Carolina, *Spain* **35 G7** 38 17N 3 38W
La Cavalerie, *France* **20 D7** 44 1N 3 10 E
La Ceiba, *Honduras* **120 C2** 15 40N 86 50W
La Chaise-Dieu, *France* **20 C7** 45 18N 3 42 E
La Chapelle d'Angillon, *France* **19 E9** 47 21N 2 25 E
La Chapelle-St-Luc, *France* **19 D11** 48 20N 4 3 E
La Chapelle-sur-Erdre, *France* **18 E5** 47 18N 1 34W
La Charité-sur-Loire, *France* **19 E10** 47 10N 3 1 E
La Chartre-sur-le-Loir, *France* **18 E7** 47 44N 0 34 E
La Châtaigneraie, *France* **20 B3** 46 39N 0 44W
La Châtre, *France* **19 F9** 46 35N 2 0 E
La Chaux-de-Fonds, *Switz.* **25 H2** 47 7N 6 50 E
La Chorrera, *Panama* **120 E4** 8 53N 79 47W
La Ciotat, *France* **21 E9** 43 10N 5 37 E
La Clayette, *France* **19 F11** 46 17N 4 19 E
La Cocha, *Argentina* **126 B2** 27 50 S 65 40W
La Concepción = Ri-Aba, *Eq. Guin.* **83 E6** 3 28N 8 40 E
La Concepción, *Panama* **120 E3** 8 31N 82 37W
La Concordia, *Mexico* **119 D6** 16 8N 92 38W
La Coruña = A Coruña, *Spain* **34 B2** 43 20N 8 25W
La Coruña □, *Spain* **34 B2** 43 10N 8 30W
La Côte-St-André, *France* **21 C9** 45 24N 5 15 E
La Courtine-le-Trucq, *France* **20 C6** 45 41N 2 15 E
La Crau, *Bouches-du-Rhône, France* **21 E8** 43 32N 4 40 E
La Crau, *Var, France* **21 E10** 43 9N 6 4 E
La Crescent, *U.S.A.* **112 D9** 43 50N 91 18W
La Crete, *Canada* **104 B5** 58 11N 116 24W
La Crosse, *Kans., U.S.A.* **112 F5** 38 32N 99 18W
La Crosse, *Wis., U.S.A.* **112 D9** 43 48N 91 15W
La Cruz, *Costa Rica* **120 D2** 11 4N 85 39W
La Cruz, *Mexico* **118 C3** 23 55N 106 54W
La Désirade, *Guadeloupe* **121 C7** 16 18N 61 3W
La Escondida, *Mexico* **118 C5** 24 6N 99 55W
La Esmeralda, *Paraguay* **126 A3** 22 16 S 62 33W
La Esperanza, *Cuba* **120 B3** 22 46N 83 44W
La Esperanza, *Honduras* **120 D2** 14 15N 88 10W
La Estrada = A Estrada, *Spain* **34 C2** 42 43N 8 27W
La Faouët, *France* **18 D3** 48 2N 3 30W
La Fayette, *U.S.A.* **109 H3** 34 42N 85 17W
La Fé, *Cuba* **120 B3** 22 2N 84 15W
La Fère, *France* **19 C10** 49 39N 3 21 E
La Ferté-Bernard, *France* **18 D7** 48 10N 0 40 E
La Ferté-Gaucher, *France* **19 D10** 48 47N 3 19 E
La Ferté-Macé, *France* **18 D6** 48 35N 0 22W
La Ferté-St-Aubin, *France* **19 E8** 47 42N 1 57 E
La Ferté-sous-Jouarre, *France* **19 D10** 48 56N 3 8 E
La Ferté-Vidame, *France* **18 D7** 48 37N 0 53 E
La Flèche, *France* **18 E6** 47 42N 0 4W
La Follette, *U.S.A.* **109 G3** 36 23N 84 7W
La Fregeneda, *Spain* **34 E4** 40 58N 6 54W
La Fuente de San Esteban, *Spain* **34 E4** 40 49N 6 15W
La Gacilly, *France* **18 E4** 47 45N 2 8W
La Gineta, *Spain* **33 F2** 39 8N 2 1W
La Grand-Combe, *France* **21 D8** 44 13N 4 2 E
La Grande, *U.S.A.* **114 D4** 45 20N 118 5W
La Grande →, *Canada* **102 B5** 53 50N 79 0W
La Grande Deux, Rés., *Canada* **102 B4** 53 40N 76 55W
La Grande-Motte, *France* **21 E8** 43 23N 4 5 E
La Grande Quatre, Rés., *Canada* **102 B5** 54 0N 73 15W
La Grande Trois, Rés., *Canada* **102 B4** 53 40N 75 10W
La Grange, *Calif., U.S.A.* **116 H6** 37 42N 120 27W
La Grange, *Ga., U.S.A.* **109 J3** 33 2N 85 2W
La Grange, *Ky., U.S.A.* **108 F3** 38 25N 85 23W
La Grange, *Tex., U.S.A.* **113 L6** 29 54N 96 52W
La Grave, *France* **21 C10** 45 3N 6 18 E
La Guaira, *Venezuela* **124 A5** 10 36N 66 56W
La Guardia = A Guarda, *Spain* **34 D2** 41 56N 8 52W
La Gudiña = A Gudiña, *Spain* **34 C3** 42 4N 7 8W
La Guerche-de-Bretagne, *France* **18 E5** 47 57N 1 16W
La Guerche-sur-l'Aubois, *France* **19 F9** 46 58N 2 56 E
La Habana, *Cuba* **120 B3** 23 8N 82 22W
La Haye-du-Puits, *France* **18 C5** 49 17N 1 33W
La Horra, *Spain* **34 D7** 41 44N 3 53W
La Independencia, *Mexico* **119 D6** 16 31N 91 47W
La Isabela, *Dom. Rep.* **121 C5** 19 58N 71 2W
La Jonquera, *Spain* **32 C7** 42 25N 2 53 E
La Junta, *U.S.A.* **113 F3** 37 59N 103 33W
La Laguna, *Canary Is.* **37 F3** 28 28N 16 18W
La Libertad, *Guatemala* **120 C1** 16 47N 90 7W
La Libertad, *Mexico* **118 B2** 29 55N 112 41W
La Ligua, *Chile* **126 C1** 32 30 S 71 16W
La Línea de la Concepción, *Spain* **35 J5** 36 15N 5 23W
La Loche, *Canada* **105 B7** 56 29N 109 26W
La Londe-les-Maures, *France* **21 E10** 43 8N 6 14 E
La Lora, *Spain* **34 C7** 42 45N 4 0W
La Loupe, *France* **18 D8** 48 29N 1 0 E
La Louvière, *Belgium* **17 D4** 50 27N 4 10 E
La Machine, *France* **19 F10** 46 54N 3 27 E
La Maddalena, *Italy* **30 A2** 41 13N 9 24 E
La Malbaie, *Canada* **103 C5** 47 40N 70 10W
La Mancha, *Spain* **33 F2** 39 10N 2 54W
La Mariña, *Spain* **34 B3** 43 30N 7 40W
La Martre, L., *Canada* **104 A5** 63 15N 117 55W
La Mesa, *U.S.A.* **117 N9** 32 46N 117 3W
La Misión, *Mexico* **118 A1** 32 5N 116 50W
La Mothe-Achard, *France* **18 F5** 46 37N 1 40W
La Motte, *France* **21 D10** 44 20N 6 3 E
La Motte-Chalançon, *France* **21 D9** 44 30N 5 21 E
La Motte-Servolex, *France* **21 C9** 45 35N 5 53 E
La Moure, *U.S.A.* **112 B5** 46 21N 98 18W
La Muela, *Spain* **32 D3** 41 36N 1 7W
La Mure, *France* **21 D9** 44 55N 5 48 E
La Negra, *Chile* **126 A1** 23 46 S 70 18W
La Oliva, *Canary Is.* **37 F6** 28 36N 13 57W
La Orotava, *Canary Is.* **37 F3** 28 22N 16 31W
La Oroya, *Peru* **124** 11 32 S 75 54W
La Pacaudière, *France* **19 F10** 46 11N 3 52 E
La Palma, *Canary Is.* **37 F2** 28 40N 17 50W
La Palma, *Panama* **120 E4** 8 15N 78 0W
La Palma del Condado, *Spain* **35 H4** 37 21N 6 38W
La Paloma, *Chile* **126 C1** 30 35 S 71 0W
La Pampa □, *Argentina* **126 D2** 36 50 S 66 0W
La Paragua, *Venezuela* **124 B6** 6 50N 63 20W
La Paz, *Entre Ríos, Argentina* **126 C4** 30 50 S 59 45W
La Paz, *San Luis, Argentina* **126 C2** 33 30 S 67 20W
La Paz, *Bolivia* **124 G5** 16 20 S 68 10W
La Paz, *Honduras* **120 D2** 14 20N 87 47W
La Paz, *Mexico* **118 C2** 24 10N 110 20W
La Paz, *Phil.* **61 D4** 15 26N 120 45 E
La Paz Centro, *Nic.* **120 D2** 12 20N 86 41W
La Pedrera, *Colombia* **124 D5** 1 18 S 69 43W
La Pérade, *Canada* **103 C5** 46 35N 72 12W
La Perouse Str., *Asia* **54 B11** 45 40N 142 0 E
La Pesca, *Mexico* **119 C5** 23 46N 97 47W
La Piedad, *Mexico* **118 C4** 20 20N 102 1W
La Pine, *U.S.A.* **114 E3** 43 40N 121 30W
La Plata, *Argentina* **126 D4** 35 0 S 57 55W
La Pobla de Lillet, *Spain* **32 C6** 42 16N 1 59 E
La Pocatière, *Canada* **103 C5** 47 22N 70 2W
La Pola de Gordón, *Spain* **34 C5** 42 51N 5 41W
La Porta, *France* **21 F13** 42 25N 9 21 E
La Porte, *Ind., U.S.A.* **108 E2** 41 36N 86 43W
La Porte, *Tex., U.S.A.* **113 L7** 29 39N 95 1W
La Presanella, *Italy* **28 B7** 46 13N 10 40 E
La Puebla = Sa Pobla, *Spain* **32 F8** 39 46N 3 1 E
La Puebla de Cazalla, *Spain* **35 H5** 37 10N 5 20W
La Puebla de los Infantes, *Spain* **35 H5** 37 47N 5 24W
La Puebla de Montalbán, *Spain* **34 F6** 39 52N 4 22W
La Puebla del Río, *Spain* **35 H4** 37 16N 6 3W
La Puerta de Segura, *Spain* **35 G8** 38 22N 2 45W
La Purísima, *Mexico* **118 B2** 26 10N 112 4W
La Push, *U.S.A.* **116 C2** 47 55N 124 38W
La Quiaca, *Argentina* **126 A2** 22 5 S 65 35W
La Réole, *France* **20 D3** 44 35N 0 1W
La Restinga, *Canary Is.* **37 G2** 27 38N 17 59W
La Rioja, *Argentina* **126 B2** 29 20 S 67 0W
La Rioja □, *Argentina* **126 B2** 29 30 S 67 0W
La Rioja □, *Spain* **32 C2** 42 20N 2 20W
La Robla, *Spain* **34 C5** 42 50N 5 41W
La Roche-Bernard, *France* **18 E4** 47 31N 2 19W
La Roche-Canillac, *France* **20 C5** 45 12N 1 57 E
La Roche-en-Ardenne, *Belgium* **17 D5** 50 11N 5 35 E
La Roche-sur-Foron, *France* **19 F13** 46 4N 6 19 E
La Roche-sur-Yon, *France* **18 F5** 46 40N 1 25W
La Rochefoucauld, *France* **20 C4** 45 44N 0 24 E
La Rochelle, *France* **20 B2** 46 10N 1 9W
La Roda, *Spain* **33 F2** 39 13N 2 15W
La Roda de Andalucía, *Spain* **35 H6** 37 12N 4 46W
La Romana, *Dom. Rep.* **121 C6** 18 27N 68 57W
La Ronge, *Canada* **105 B7** 55 5N 105 20W
La Rumorosa, *Mexico* **117 N10** 32 33N 116 4W
La Sabina = Sa Savina, *Spain* **37 C7** 38 44N 1 25 E
La Sagra, *Spain* **33 H2** 37 57N 2 35W
La Salle, *U.S.A.* **112 E10** 41 20N 89 6W
La Sanabria, *Spain* **34 C4** 42 0N 6 30W
La Santa, *Canary Is.* **37 E6** 29 5N 13 40W
La Sarre, *Canada* **102 C4** 48 45N 79 15W
La Scie, *Canada* **103 C8** 49 57N 55 36W
La Selva, *Spain* **32 C7** 42 0N 2 45 E
La Selva Beach, *U.S.A.* **116 J5** 36 56N 121 51W
La Selva del Camp, *Spain* **32 D6** 41 13N 1 8 E
La Serena, *Chile* **126 B1** 29 55 S 71 10W
La Serena, *Spain* **35 G5** 38 45N 5 40W
La Seu d'Urgell, *Spain* **32 C6** 42 22N 1 23 E
La Seyne-sur-Mer, *France* **21 E9** 43 7N 5 52 E
La Sila, *Italy* **31 C9** 39 15N 16 35 E
La Solana, *Spain* **35 G7** 38 59N 3 14W
La Soufrière, *St. Vincent* **121 D7** 13 20N 61 11W
La Souterraine, *France* **19 F8** 46 15N 1 30 E
La Spézia, *Italy* **28 D6** 44 7N 9 50 E
La Suze-sur-Sarthe, *France* **18 E7** 47 53N 0 2 E
La Tagua, *Colombia* **124 C4** 0 3N 74 40W
La Teste, *France* **20 D2** 44 37N 1 8W
La Tortuga, *Venezuela* **121 D6** 11 0N 65 22W
La Tour-du-Pin, *France* **21 C9** 45 33N 5 27 E
La Tranche-sur-Mer, *France* **18 F5** 46 20N 1 27W
La Tremblade, *France* **20 C2** 45 46N 1 8W
La Tuque, *Canada* **102 C5** 47 30N 72 50W
La Unión, *Chile* **128 E2** 40 10 S 73 0W
La Unión, *El Salv.* **120 D2** 13 20N 87 50W
La Unión, *Mexico* **118 D4** 17 58N 101 49W
La Unión, *Spain* **33 H4** 37 38N 0 53W
La Urbana, *Venezuela* **124 B5** 7 8N 66 56W
La Vall d'Uixó, *Spain* **32 F4** 39 49N 0 15W
La Vecilla de Curveño, *Spain* **34 C5** 42 51N 5 27W
La Vega, *Dom. Rep.* **121 C5** 19 20N 70 30W
La Vela de Coro, *Venezuela* **124 A5** 11 27N 69 34W
La Veleta, *Spain* **35 H7** 37 1N 3 22W
La Venta, *Mexico* **119 D6** 18 8N 94 3W
La Ventura, *Mexico* **118 C4** 24 38N 100 54W
La Voulte-sur-Rhône, *France* **21 D8** 44 48N 4 46 E
Laa an der Thaya, *Austria* **27 C9** 48 43N 16 23 E
Laaber, Grosse →, *Germany* **25 G8** 48 55N 12 30 E
Laage, *Germany* **24 B8** 53 55N 12 21 E
Laatzen, *Germany* **24 C5** 52 19N 9 48 E
Laba →, *Russia* **49 H4** 45 11N 39 42 E
Labason, *Phil.* **61 G5** 8 4N 122 31 E
Labastide-Murat, *France* **20 D5** 44 39N 1 33 E
Labastide-Rouairoux, *France* **20 E6** 43 28N 2 39 E
Labbézenga, *Mali* **83 B5** 15 2N 0 48 E
Labe = Elbe →, *Europe* **24 B4** 53 50N 9 0 E
Labé, *Guinea* **82 C2** 11 24N 12 16W
Laberge, L., *Canada* **104 A1** 61 11N 135 12W
Labin, *Croatia* **29 C11** 45 5N 14 8 E
Labinsk, *Russia* **49 H5** 44 40N 40 48 E
Labis, *Malaysia* **65 L4** 2 22N 103 2 E
Łabiszyn, *Poland* **45 F4** 52 57N 17 54 E
Labo, *Phil.* **61 D5** 14 9N 122 51 E
Laboe, *Germany* **24 A6** 54 24N 10 13 E
Laborec →, *Slovak Rep.* **27 C14** 48 37N 21 58 E
Labouheyre, *France* **20 D3** 44 13N 0 55W
Laboulaye, *Argentina* **126 C3** 34 10 S 63 30W
Labrador, *Canada* **103 B7** 53 20N 61 0W
Labrador City, *Canada* **103 B6** 52 57N 66 55W
Labrador Sea, *Atl. Oc.* **101 C14** 57 0N 54 0W
Lábrea, *Brazil* **124 E6** 7 15 S 64 51W
Labruguière, *France* **20 E6** 43 31N 2 16 E
Labuan, *Malaysia* **62 C5** 5 20N 115 14 E
Labuan, Pulau, *Malaysia* **62 C5** 5 21N 115 13 E
Labuha, *Indonesia* **63 E7** 0 30 S 127 30 E
Labuhan, *Indonesia* **63 G11** 6 22 S 105 50 E
Labuhanbajo, *Indonesia* **63 F6** 8 28 S 120 1 E
Labuk, Telok, *Malaysia* **62 C5** 6 10N 117 50 E
Labyrinth, L., *Australia* **95 E2** 30 40 S 135 11 E
Labytnangi, *Russia* **50 C7** 66 39N 66 21 E
Laç, *Albania* **40 E3** 41 38N 19 43 E
Lac Bouchette, *Canada* **103 C5** 48 16N 72 11W
Lac Édouard, *Canada* **102 C5** 47 40N 72 16W
Lac La Biche, *Canada* **104 C6** 54 45N 111 58W
Lac la Martre = Wha Ti, *Canada* **100 B8** 63 8N 117 16W
Lac La Ronge Prov. Park, *Canada* **105 B7** 55 9N 104 41W
Lac-Mégantic, *Canada* **103 C5** 45 35N 70 53W
Lac Seul, Res., *Canada* **102 B1** 50 25N 92 30W
Lac Thien, *Vietnam* **64 F7** 12 25N 108 11 E
Lacanau, *France* **20 D2** 44 58N 1 5W
Lacanau, Étang de, *France* **20 D2** 44 58N 1 7W
Lacantúm →, *Mexico* **119 D6** 16 36N 90 40W
Lacara →, *Spain* **35 G4** 38 55N 6 25W
Lacaune, *France* **20 E6** 43 43N 2 40 E
Lacaune, Mts. de, *France* **20 E6** 43 43N 2 50 E
Laccadive Is. = Lakshadweep Is., *Ind. Oc.* **52 H11** 10 0N 72 30 E
Lacepede B., *Australia* **95 F2** 36 40 S 139 40 E
Lacepede Is., *Australia* **92 C3** 16 55 S 122 0 E
Lacerdónia, *Mozam.* **87 F4** 18 3 S 35 35 E
Lacey, *U.S.A.* **116 C4** 47 7N 122 49W

Lachhmangarh, India 68 F6 27 50N 75 4 E
Lachi, Pakistan 68 C4 33 25N 71 20 E
Lachine, Canada 102 C5 45 30N 73 40W
Lachlan →, Australia 95 E3 34 22 S 143 55 E
Lachute, Canada 102 C5 45 39N 74 21W
Laçi = Laç, Albania 40 E3 41 38N 19 43 E
Lackawanna, U.S.A. 110 D6 42 50N 78 50W
Lackawaxen, U.S.A. 111 E10 41 29N 74 59W
Lacolle, Canada 111 A11 45 5N 73 22W
Lacombe, Canada 104 C6 52 30N 113 44W
Lacona, U.S.A. 111 C8 43 39N 76 10W
Láconi, Italy 30 C2 39 54N 9 4 E
Laconia, U.S.A. 111 C13 43 32N 71 28W
Lacq, France 20 E3 43 25N 0 35W
Ladakh Ra., India 69 C8 34 0N 78 0 E
Lądek-Zdrój, Poland 45 H3 50 21N 16 53 E
Ládhon →, Greece 38 D3 37 40N 21 50 E
Ladik, Turkey 72 B6 40 57N 35 58 E
Ladismith, S. Africa 88 E3 33 28 S 21 15 E
Ladíspoli, Italy 29 G9 41 56N 12 5 E
Lādīz, Iran 71 D9 28 55N 61 15 E
Ladnun, India 68 F6 27 38N 74 25 E
Ladoga, L. = Ladozhskoye Ozero, Russia 46 B6 61 15N 30 30 E
Ladozhskoye Ozero, Russia 46 B6 61 15N 30 30 E
Lady Elliott I., Australia 94 C5 24 7 S 152 42 E
Lady Grey, S. Africa 88 E4 30 43 S 27 13 E
Ladybrand, S. Africa 88 D4 29 9 S 27 29 E
Ladysmith, Canada 104 D4 49 0N 123 49W
Ladysmith, S. Africa 89 D4 28 32 S 29 46 E
Ladysmith, U.S.A. 112 C9 45 28N 91 12W
Lae, Papua N. G. 96 H6 6 40 S 147 2 E
Laem Ngop, Thailand 65 F4 12 10N 102 26 E
Laem Pho, Thailand 65 J3 6 55N 101 19 E
Læsø, Denmark 11 G5 57 15N 11 5 E
Læsø Rende, Denmark 11 G4 57 20N 10 45 E
Lafayette, Colo., U.S.A. 112 F2 39 58N 105 12W
Lafayette, Ind., U.S.A. 108 E2 40 25N 86 54W
Lafayette, La., U.S.A. 113 K9 30 14N 92 1W
Lafayette, Tenn., U.S.A. 109 G2 36 31N 86 2W
Laferte →, Canada 104 A5 61 53N 117 44W
Lafia, Nigeria 83 D6 8 30N 8 34 E
Lafiagi, Nigeria 83 D6 8 52N 5 20 E
Lafleche, Canada 105 D7 49 45N 106 40W
Lafon, Sudan 81 F3 5 5N 32 29 E
Lagan, Sweden 11 H7 56 56N 13 58 E
Lagan →, Sweden 11 H6 56 30N 12 58 E
Lagan →, U.K. 15 B6 54 36N 5 55W
Lagarfljót →, Iceland 8 D6 65 40N 14 18W
Lage, Germany 24 D4 51 59N 8 48 E
Lågen →, Oppland, Norway 9 F14 61 8N 10 25 E
Lågen →, Vestfold, Norway 9 G14 59 3N 10 3 E
Lägerdorf, Germany 24 B5 53 53N 9 34 E
Laghouat, Algeria 78 B6 33 50N 2 59 E
Lagnieu, France 21 C9 45 55N 5 20 E
Lagny-sur-Marne, France 19 D9 48 52N 2 44 E
Lago, Italy 31 C9 39 10N 16 9 E
Lagôa, Portugal 35 H2 37 8N 8 27W
Lagoa Vermelha, Brazil 127 B5 28 13 S 51 32W
Lagoaça, Portugal 34 D4 41 11N 6 44W
Lagodekhi, Georgia 49 K8 41 50N 46 22 E
Lagónegro, Italy 31 B8 40 8N 15 45 E
Lagonoy G., Phil. 61 E5 13 35N 123 50 E
Lagos, Nigeria 83 D5 6 25N 3 27 E
Lagos, Portugal 35 H2 37 5N 8 41W
Lagos □, Nigeria 83 D5 6 28N 3 25 E
Lagos de Moreno, Mexico 118 C4 21 21N 101 55W
Lagrange, Australia 92 C3 18 45 S 121 43 E
Lagrange B., Australia 92 C3 18 38 S 121 42 E
Laguardia, Spain 32 C2 42 33N 2 35W
Laguépie, France 20 D5 44 8N 1 57 E
Laguna, Brazil 127 B6 28 30 S 48 50W
Laguna, U.S.A. 115 J10 35 2N 107 25W
Laguna Beach, U.S.A. 117 M9 33 33N 117 47W
Laguna de Duera, Spain 34 D6 41 35N 4 43W
Laguna Limpia, Argentina 126 B4 26 32 S 59 45W
Lagunas, Chile 126 A2 21 0 S 69 45W
Lagunas, Peru 124 E3 5 10 S 75 35W
Lahad Datu, Malaysia 63 C5 5 0N 118 20 E
Lahad Datu, Teluk, Malaysia 63 D5 4 50N 118 20 E
Lahan Sai, Thailand 64 E4 14 25N 102 52 E
Lahanam, Laos 64 D5 16 16N 105 16 E
Lahar, India 69 F8 26 12N 78 57 E
Laharpur, India 69 F9 27 43N 80 56 E
Lahat, Indonesia 62 E2 3 45 S 103 30 E
Lahewa, Indonesia 62 D1 1 22N 97 12 E
Lāhījān, Iran 71 B6 37 10N 50 6 E
Lahn →, Germany 25 E3 50 19N 7 37 E
Lahnstein, Germany 25 E3 50 19N 7 37 E
Laholm, Sweden 11 H7 56 30N 13 2 E
Laholmsbukten, Sweden 11 H6 56 30N 12 45 E
Lahore, Pakistan 68 D6 31 32N 74 22 E
Lahr, Germany 25 G3 48 20N 7 53 E
Lahri, Pakistan 68 E3 29 11N 68 13 E
Lahti, Finland 9 F21 60 58N 25 40 E
Lahtis = Lahti, Finland 9 F21 60 58N 25 40 E
Laï, Chad 79 G9 9 25N 16 18 E
Lai Chau, Vietnam 58 F4 22 5N 103 3 E
Lai'an, China 59 A12 32 28N 118 30 E
Laibin, China 58 F7 23 42N 109 14 E
Laifeng, China 58 C7 29 27N 109 20 E
L'Aigle, France 18 D7 48 46N 0 38 E
Laignes, France 19 E11 47 50N 4 20 E
L'Aiguillon-sur-Mer, France 20 B2 46 20N 1 18W
Laila = Laylá, Si. Arabia 74 C4 22 10N 46 40 E
Laingsburg, S. Africa 88 E3 33 9 S 20 52 E
Lainio älv →, Sweden 8 C20 67 35N 22 40 E
Lairg, U.K. 14 C4 58 2N 4 24W
Laishui, China 56 E8 39 23N 115 45 E
Laissac, France 20 D6 44 23N 2 50 E
Láives, Italy 29 B8 46 26N 11 20 E
Laiwu, China 57 F9 36 15N 117 40 E
Laixi, China 57 F11 36 50N 120 31 E
Laiyang, China 57 F11 36 59N 120 45 E
Laiyuan, China 56 E8 39 20N 114 40 E
Laizhou, China 57 F10 37 8N 119 57 E
Laizhou Wan, China 57 F10 37 30N 119 30 E
Laja →, Mexico 118 C4 20 55N 100 46W
Lajere, Nigeria 83 C7 12 10N 11 25 E
Lajes, Brazil 127 B5 27 48 S 50 20W
Lajkovac, Serbia, Yug. 40 B4 44 27N 20 14 E
Lajosmizse, Hungary 42 C4 47 3N 19 32 E
Lak Sao, Laos 64 C5 18 11N 104 59 E
Lakaband, Pakistan 68 D3 31 2N 69 15 E
Lakamané, Mali 82 C3 14 35N 9 45W
Lake Alpine, U.S.A. 116 G7 38 29N 120 0W
Lake Andes, U.S.A. 112 D5 43 9N 98 32W
Lake Arthur, U.S.A. 113 K8 30 5N 92 41W
Lake Cargelligo, Australia 95 E4 33 15 S 146 22 E
Lake Charles, U.S.A. 113 K8 30 14N 93 13W
Lake City, Colo., U.S.A. 115 G10 38 2N 107 19W
Lake City, Fla., U.S.A. 109 K4 30 11N 82 38W
Lake City, Mich., U.S.A. 108 C3 44 20N 85 13W
Lake City, Minn., U.S.A. 112 C8 44 27N 92 16W
Lake City, Pa., U.S.A. 110 D4 42 1N 80 21W
Lake City, S.C., U.S.A. 109 J6 33 52N 79 45W
Lake Cowichan, Canada 104 D4 48 49N 124 3W
Lake District, U.K. 12 C4 54 35N 3 20 E
Lake Elsinore, U.S.A. 117 M9 33 38N 117 20W
Lake George, U.S.A. 111 C11 43 26N 73 43W
Lake Grace, Australia 93 F2 33 7 S 118 28 E
Lake Harbour = Kimmirut, Canada 101 B13 62 50N 69 50W
Lake Havasu City, U.S.A. 117 L12 34 27N 114 22W
Lake Hughes, U.S.A. 117 L8 34 41N 118 26W
Lake Isabella, U.S.A. 117 K8 35 38N 118 28W
Lake Jackson, U.S.A. 113 L7 29 3N 95 27W
Lake Junction, U.S.A. 114 D8 44 35N 110 28W
Lake King, Australia 93 F2 33 5 S 119 45 E
Lake Lenore, Canada 105 C8 52 24N 104 59W
Lake Louise, Canada 104 C5 51 30N 116 10W
Lake Mead National Recreation Area, U.S.A. 117 K12 36 15N 114 30W
Lake Mills, U.S.A. 112 D8 43 25N 93 32W
Lake Placid, U.S.A. 111 B11 44 17N 73 59W
Lake Pleasant, U.S.A. 111 C10 43 28N 74 25W
Lake Providence, U.S.A. 113 J9 32 48N 91 10W
Lake St. Peter, Canada 110 A6 45 18N 78 2W
Lake Superior Prov. Park, Canada 102 C3 47 45N 84 45W
Lake Village, U.S.A. 113 J9 33 20N 91 17W
Lake Wales, U.S.A. 109 M5 27 54N 81 35W
Lake Worth, U.S.A. 109 M5 26 37N 80 3W
Lakefield, Canada 102 D4 44 25N 78 16W
Lakehurst, U.S.A. 111 F10 40 1N 74 19W
Lakeland, Australia 94 B3 15 49 S 144 57 E
Lakeland, U.S.A. 109 M5 28 3N 81 57W
Lakemba, Fiji 91 D9 18 13 S 178 47W
Lakeport, Calif., U.S.A. 116 F4 39 3N 122 55W
Lakeport, Mich., U.S.A. 110 C2 43 7N 82 30W
Lakes Entrance, Australia 95 F4 37 50 S 148 0 E
Lakeside, Ariz., U.S.A. 115 J9 34 9N 109 58W
Lakeside, Calif., U.S.A. 117 N10 32 52N 116 55W
Lakeside, Nebr., U.S.A. 112 D3 42 3N 102 26W
Lakeside, Ohio, U.S.A. 110 E2 41 32N 82 46W
Lakeview, U.S.A. 114 E3 42 11N 120 21W
Lakeville, U.S.A. 112 C8 44 39N 93 14W
Lakewood, Colo., U.S.A. 112 F2 39 44N 105 5W
Lakewood, N.J., U.S.A. 111 F10 40 6N 74 13W
Lakewood, N.Y., U.S.A. 110 D5 42 6N 79 19W
Lakewood, Ohio, U.S.A. 110 E3 41 29N 81 48W
Lakewood, Wash., U.S.A. 116 C4 47 11N 122 32W
Lakha, India 68 F4 26 9N 70 54 E
Lakhaniá, Greece 36 D9 35 58N 27 54 E
Lakhimpur, India 69 F9 27 57N 80 46 E
Lakhnadon, India 69 H8 22 36N 79 36 E
Lakhonpheng, Laos 64 E5 15 54N 105 34 E
Lakhpat, India 68 H3 23 48N 68 47 E
Läki, Azerbaijan 49 K8 40 34N 47 22 E
Lakin, U.S.A. 113 G4 37 57N 101 15W
Lakitusaki →, Canada 102 B3 54 21N 82 25W
Lakki, Pakistan 68 C4 32 36N 70 55 E
Lákkoi, Greece 36 D5 35 24N 23 57 E
Lakonía □, Greece 38 E4 36 55N 22 30 E
Lakonikós Kólpos, Greece 38 E4 36 40N 22 40 E
Lakor, Indonesia 63 F7 8 15 S 128 17 E
Lakota, Ivory C. 82 D3 5 50N 5 30W
Lakota, U.S.A. 112 A5 48 2N 98 21W
Laksar, India 68 E8 29 46N 78 3 E
Laksefjorden, Norway 8 A22 70 45N 26 50 E
Lakselv, Norway 8 A21 70 2N 25 0 E
Lakshadweep Is., Ind. Oc. 52 H11 10 0N 72 30 E
Lakshmanpur, India 69 H10 22 58N 83 3 E
Lakshmikantapur, India 69 H13 22 5N 88 20 E
Lala Ghat, India 67 G18 24 30N 92 40 E
Lala Musa, Pakistan 68 C5 32 40N 73 57 E
Lalago, Tanzania 86 C3 3 28 S 33 58 E
Lalapanzi, Zimbabwe 87 F3 19 20 S 30 15 E
Lalapaşa, Turkey 41 E10 41 49N 26 44 E
Lalbenque, France 20 D5 44 19N 1 34 E
L'Albufera, Spain 33 F4 39 20N 0 27W
Lalganj, India 69 G11 25 52N 85 13 E
Lalgola, India 69 G13 24 25N 88 15 E
Lālī, Iran 71 C6 32 21N 49 6 E
Lalibela, Ethiopia 81 E4 12 2N 39 2 E
Lalin, China 57 B14 45 12N 127 0 E
Lalín, Spain 34 C2 42 40N 8 5W
Lalin He →, China 57 B13 45 32N 125 40 E
Lalinde, France 20 D4 44 50N 0 44 E
Lalitapur = Patan, Nepal 67 F14 27 40N 85 20 E
Lalitpur, India 69 G8 24 42N 78 28 E
Lalkua, India 69 E8 29 5N 79 31 E
Lalsot, India 68 F7 26 34N 76 20 E
Lam, Vietnam 64 B6 21 21N 106 31 E
Lam Pao Res., Thailand 64 D4 16 50N 103 15 E
Lama Kara, Togo 83 D5 9 30N 1 15 E
Lamaing, Burma 67 M20 15 25N 97 53 E
Lamar, Colo., U.S.A. 112 F3 38 5N 102 37W
Lamar, Mo., U.S.A. 113 G7 37 30N 94 16W
Lamas, Peru 124 E3 6 28 S 76 31W
Lamastre, France 21 D8 44 59N 4 35 E
Lambach, Austria 26 C6 48 6N 13 51 E
Lamballe, France 18 D4 48 29N 2 31W
Lambaréné, Gabon 84 E2 0 41 S 10 12 E
Lambasa, Fiji 91 C8 16 30 S 179 10 E
Lambay I., Ireland 15 C5 53 29N 6 1W
Lambert Glacier, Antarctica 5 D6 71 0 S 70 0 E
Lambert's Bay, S. Africa 88 E2 32 5 S 18 17 E
Lambesc, France 21 E9 43 39N 5 16 E
Lambeth, Canada 110 D3 42 54N 81 18W
Lambi Kyun, Burma 65 G2 10 50N 98 20 E
Lámbia, Greece 38 D3 37 52N 21 53 E
Lambomakondro, Madag. 89 C7 22 41 S 44 44 E
Lambro →, Italy 28 C6 45 8N 9 32 E
Lame, Nigeria 83 C6 10 30N 9 20 E
Lame Deer, U.S.A. 114 D10 45 37N 106 40W
Lamego, Portugal 34 D3 41 5N 7 52W
Lamèque, Canada 103 C7 47 45N 64 38W
Lameroo, Australia 95 F3 35 19 S 140 33 E
Lamesa, U.S.A. 113 J4 32 44N 101 58W
Lamía, Greece 38 C4 38 55N 22 26 E
Lamitan, Phil. 61 H5 6 39N 122 8 E
Lammermuir Hills, U.K. 14 F6 55 50N 2 40W
Lammhult, Sweden 11 G8 57 10N 14 35 E
Lamoille →, U.S.A. 111 B11 44 38N 73 13W
Lamon B., Phil. 61 D5 14 30N 122 20 E
Lamont, Canada 104 C6 53 46N 112 50W
Lamont, Calif., U.S.A. 117 K8 35 15N 118 55W
Lamont, Wyo., U.S.A. 114 E10 42 13N 107 29W
Lamotte-Beuvron, France 19 E9 47 36N 2 1 E
Lampa, Peru 124 G4 15 22 S 70 22W
Lampang, Thailand 64 C2 18 16N 99 32 E
Lampasas, U.S.A. 113 K5 31 4N 98 11W
Lampazos de Naranjo, Mexico 118 B4 27 2N 100 32W
Lampertheim, Germany 25 F4 49 35N 8 27 E
Lampeter, U.K. 13 E3 52 7N 4 4W
Lampman, Canada 105 D8 49 25N 102 50W
Lamprechtshausen, Austria 26 D5 48 0N 12 58 E
Lampung □, Indonesia 62 F2 5 30 S 104 30 E
Lamta, India 69 H9 22 8N 80 7 E
Lamu, Kenya 86 C5 2 16 S 40 55 E
Lamy, U.S.A. 115 J11 35 29N 105 53W
Lan Xian, China 56 E6 38 15N 111 35 E
Lan Yu = Hungt'ou Hsü, Taiwan 59 F13 22 0N 121 30 E
Lanak La, India 69 B8 34 27N 79 32 E
Lanak'o Shank'ou = Lanak La, India 69 B8 34 27N 79 32 E
Lanao, L., Phil. 61 H6 7 52N 124 15 E
Lanark, Canada 111 A8 45 1N 76 22W
Lanark, U.K. 14 F5 55 40N 3 47W
Lancang, China 58 F2 22 36N 99 58 E
Lancang Jiang →, China 58 G3 21 40N 101 10 E
Lancashire □, U.K. 12 D5 53 50N 2 48W
Lancaster, Canada 111 A10 45 10N 74 30W
Lancaster, U.K. 12 C5 54 3N 2 48W
Lancaster, Calif., U.S.A. 117 L8 34 42N 118 8W
Lancaster, Ky., U.S.A. 108 G3 37 37N 84 35W
Lancaster, N.H., U.S.A. 111 B13 44 29N 71 34W
Lancaster, N.Y., U.S.A. 110 D6 42 54N 78 40W
Lancaster, Ohio, U.S.A. 108 F4 39 43N 82 36W
Lancaster, Pa., U.S.A. 111 F8 40 2N 76 19W
Lancaster, S.C., U.S.A. 109 H5 34 43N 80 46W
Lancaster, Wis., U.S.A. 112 D9 42 51N 90 43W
Lancaster Sd., Canada 101 A11 74 13N 84 0W
Lancelin, Australia 93 F2 31 0 S 115 18 E
Lanchow = Lanzhou, China 56 F2 36 1N 103 52 E
Lanciano, Italy 29 F11 42 14N 14 23 E
Lancun, China 57 F11 36 25N 120 10 E
Łańcut, Poland 45 H9 50 10N 22 13 E
Landau, Bayern, Germany 25 G8 48 40N 12 41 E
Landau, Rhld-Pfz., Germany 25 F4 49 12N 8 6 E
Landeck, Austria 26 D3 47 9N 10 34 E
Lander, U.S.A. 114 E9 42 50N 108 44W
Lander →, Australia 92 D5 22 0 S 132 0 E
Landerneau, France 18 D2 48 28N 4 17W
Landeryd, Sweden 11 G7 57 7N 13 15 E
Landes, France 20 D2 44 0N 1 0W
Landes □, France 20 E3 43 57N 0 48W
Landete, Spain 32 F3 39 56N 1 25W
Landi Kotal, Pakistan 68 B4 34 7N 71 6 E
Landisburg, U.S.A. 110 F7 40 21N 77 19W
Landivisiau, France 18 D2 48 31N 4 6W
Landquart, Switz. 25 J5 46 58N 9 32 E
Landrecies, France 19 B10 50 7N 3 40 E
Land's End, U.K. 13 G2 50 4N 5 44W
Landsberg, Germany 25 G6 48 2N 10 53 E
Landsborough Cr. →, Australia 94 C3 22 28 S 144 35 E
Landsbro, Sweden 11 G8 57 24N 14 56 E
Landshut, Germany 25 G8 48 34N 12 8 E
Landskrona, Sweden 11 J6 55 53N 12 50 E
Landstuhl, Germany 25 F3 49 24N 7 33 E
Landvetter, Sweden 11 G6 57 41N 12 17 E
Lanesboro, U.S.A. 111 E9 41 57N 75 34W
Lanester, France 18 E3 47 46N 3 22W
Lanett, U.S.A. 109 J3 32 52N 85 12W
Lang Qua, Vietnam 64 A5 22 16N 104 27 E
Lang Shan, China 56 D4 41 0N 106 30 E
Lang Son, Vietnam 58 G6 21 52N 106 42 E
Lang Suan, Thailand 65 H2 9 57N 99 4 E
Langå, Denmark 11 H3 56 23N 9 54 E
La'nga Co, China 67 D12 30 45N 81 15 E
Langádhas, Greece 40 F7 40 46N 23 6 E
Langádhia, Greece 38 D4 37 43N 22 1 E
Långan →, Sweden 10 A8 63 19N 14 44 E
Langano, L., Ethiopia 81 F4 7 36N 38 43 E
Langar, Iran 71 C9 35 23N 60 25 E
Langara I., Canada 104 C2 54 14N 133 1W
Långås, Sweden 11 H6 56 58N 12 26 E
Langdai, China 58 D5 26 6N 105 21 E
Langdon, U.S.A. 112 A5 48 45N 98 22W
Långe Jan = Ölands södra udde, Sweden 11 H10 56 12N 16 23 E
Langeac, France 20 C7 45 7N 3 29 E
Langeais, France 18 E7 47 20N 0 24 E
Langeb Baraka →, Sudan 80 D4 17 28N 36 50 E
Langeberg, S. Africa 88 E3 33 55 S 21 0 E
Langeberge, S. Africa 88 D3 28 15 S 22 33 E
Langeland, Denmark 11 K4 54 56N 10 48 E
Langelands Bælt, Denmark 11 K4 54 50N 10 55 E
Langen, Hessen, Germany 25 F4 49 59N 8 40 E
Langen, Niedersachsen, Germany 24 B4 53 36N 8 36 E
Langenburg, Canada 105 C8 50 51N 101 43W
Langeneß, Germany 24 A4 54 38N 8 36 E
Langenlois, Austria 26 C8 48 29N 15 40 E
Langeoog, Germany 24 B3 53 45N 7 32 E
Langeskov, Denmark 11 J4 55 22N 10 35 E
Länghem, Sweden 11 G7 57 36N 13 14 E
Langhirano, Italy 28 D7 44 37N 10 16 E
Langholm, U.K. 14 F5 55 9N 3 0W
Langjökull, Iceland 8 D3 64 39N 20 12W
Langkawi, Pulau, Malaysia 65 J2 6 25N 99 45 E
Langklip, S. Africa 88 D3 28 12 S 20 20 E
Langkon, Malaysia 62 C5 6 30N 116 40 E
Langlade, St- P. & M. 103 C8 46 50N 56 20W
Langley, Canada 116 A4 49 7N 122 39W
Langnau, Switz. 25 J3 46 56N 7 47 E
Langogne, France 20 D7 44 43N 3 50 E
Langon, France 20 D3 44 33N 0 16W
Langøya, Norway 8 B16 68 45N 14 50 E
Langreo, Spain 34 B5 43 18N 5 40W
Langres, France 19 E12 47 52N 5 20 E
Langres, Plateau de, France 19 E12 47 45N 5 3 E
Langsa, Indonesia 62 D1 4 30N 97 57 E
Långsele, Sweden 10 A11 63 12N 17 4 E
Långshyttan, Sweden 10 D10 60 27N 16 2 E
Langtry, U.S.A. 113 L4 29 49N 101 34W
Langu, Thailand 65 J2 6 53N 99 47 E
Languedoc, France 20 E7 43 58N 3 55 E
Languedoc-Roussillon □, France 20 E6 43 25N 3 0 E
Langxi, China 59 B12 31 10N 119 12 E
Langxiangzhen, China 56 E9 39 43N 116 8 E
Langzhong, China 58 B5 31 38N 105 58 E
Lanigan, Canada 105 C7 51 51N 105 2W
Lankao, China 56 G8 34 48N 114 50 E
Länkäran, Azerbaijan 71 B6 38 48N 48 52 E
Lanmeur, France 18 D3 48 39N 3 43W
Lannemezan, France 20 E4 43 8N 0 23 E
Lannilis, France 18 D2 48 35N 4 32W
Lannion, France 18 D3 48 46N 3 29W
L'Annonciation, Canada 102 C5 46 25N 74 55W
Lanouaille, France 20 C5 45 24N 1 9 E
Lanping, China 58 D2 26 28N 99 15 E
Lansdale, U.S.A. 111 F9 40 14N 75 17W
Lansdowne, Australia 95 E5 31 48 S 152 30 E
Lansdowne, Canada 111 B8 44 24N 76 1W
Lansdowne, India 69 E8 29 50N 78 41 E
Lansdowne House, Canada 102 B2 52 14N 87 53W
L'Anse, U.S.A. 108 B1 46 45N 88 27W
L'Anse au Loup, Canada 103 B8 51 32N 56 50W
L'Anse aux Meadows, Canada 103 B8 51 36N 55 32W
Lansford, U.S.A. 111 F9 40 50N 75 53W
Lanshan, China 59 E9 25 24N 112 10 E
Lansing, U.S.A. 108 D3 42 44N 84 33W
Lanslebourg-Mont-Cenis, France 21 C10 45 17N 6 52 E
Lanta Yai, Ko, Thailand 65 J2 7 35N 99 3 E
Lantewa, Nigeria 83 C7 12 16N 11 44 E
Lantian, China 56 G5 34 11N 109 20 E
Lanus, Argentina 126 C4 34 44 S 58 27W
Lanusei, Italy 30 C2 39 52N 9 34 E
Lanuza, Phil. 61 G7 9 14N 126 4 E
Lanxi, China 59 C12 29 13N 119 28 E
Lanzarote, Canary Is. 37 F6 29 0N 13 40W
Lanzhou, China 56 F2 36 1N 103 52 E
Lanzo Torinese, Italy 28 C4 45 16N 7 28 E
Lao →, Italy 31 C8 39 47N 15 48 E
Lao Bao, Laos 64 D6 16 35N 106 30 E
Lao Cai, Vietnam 58 F4 22 30N 103 57 E
Laoag, Phil. 61 B4 18 7N 120 34 E
Laoang, Phil. 61 E6 12 32N 125 8 E
Laoha He →, China 57 C11 43 25N 120 35 E
Laohekou, China 59 A8 32 22N 111 38 E
Laois □, Ireland 15 D4 52 57N 7 36W
Laon, France 19 C10 49 33N 3 35 E
Laona, U.S.A. 108 C1 45 34N 88 40W
Laos ■, Asia 64 D5 17 45N 105 0 E
Lapa, Brazil 127 B6 25 46 S 49 44W
Lapai, Nigeria 83 D6 9 5N 6 32 E
Lapalisse, France 19 F10 46 15N 3 38 E
Lapeer, U.S.A. 108 D4 43 3N 83 19W
Lapeyrade, France 20 D3 44 4N 0 3W
Lapithos, Cyprus 36 D12 35 21N 33 11 E
Lapland = Lappland, Europe 8 B21 68 7N 24 0 E
Laporte, U.S.A. 111 E8 41 25N 76 30W
Lapovo, Serbia, Yug. 40 B5 44 10N 21 7 E
Lappeenranta, Finland 9 F23 61 3N 28 12 E
Lappland, Europe 8 B21 68 7N 24 0 E
Laprida, Argentina 126 D3 37 34 S 60 45W
Lapseki, Turkey 41 F10 40 20N 26 41 E
Laptev Sea, Russia 51 B13 76 0N 125 0 E
Lapua, Finland 8 E20 62 58N 23 0 E
Lăpuş →, Romania 43 C8 47 25N 23 40 E
Lăpuş, Munţii, Romania 43 C8 47 20N 23 50 E
Lăpuşna, Moldova 43 D13 46 53N 28 25 E
Łapy, Poland 45 F9 52 59N 22 52 E
Laqiya Arba'in, Sudan 80 C2 20 1N 28 1 E
Laqiya Umran, Sudan 80 D2 19 55N 28 18 E
L'Áquila, Italy 29 F10 42 22N 13 22 E
Lār, Āzarbājān-e Sharqī, Iran 70 B5 38 30N 47 52 E
Lār, Fārs, Iran 71 E7 27 40N 54 14 E
Larabanga, Ghana 82 D4 9 16N 1 56W
Laragne-Montéglin, France 21 D9 44 18N 5 49 E
Laramie, U.S.A. 112 E2 41 19N 105 35W
Laramie →, U.S.A. 114 F11 42 13N 104 33W
Laramie Mts., U.S.A. 112 E2 42 0N 105 30W
Laranjeiras do Sul, Brazil 127 B5 25 23 S 52 23W
Larantuka, Indonesia 63 F6 8 21 S 122 55 E
Larat, Indonesia 63 F8 7 0 S 132 0 E
L'Arbresle, France 21 C8 45 50N 4 36 E
Lärbro, Sweden 11 G12 57 47N 18 50 E
Larde, Mozam. 87 F4 16 28 S 39 43 E
Larder Lake, Canada 102 C4 48 5N 79 40W
Lardhos, Ákra = Líndhos, Ákra, Greece 36 C10 36 4N 28 10 E
Lardhos, Órmos, Greece 36 C10 36 4N 28 2 E
Laredo, Spain 34 B7 43 26N 3 28W
Laredo, U.S.A. 113 M5 27 30N 99 30W
Laredo Sd., Canada 104 C3 52 30N 128 53W
Largentière, France 21 D8 44 34N 4 18 E
L'Argentière-la-Bessée, France 21 D10 44 47N 6 33 E
Largo, U.S.A. 109 M4 27 55N 82 47W
Largs, U.K. 14 F4 55 47N 4 52W
Lari, Italy 28 E7 43 34N 10 35 E
Lariang, Indonesia 63 E5 1 26 S 119 17 E
Larimore, U.S.A. 112 B6 47 54N 97 38W
Lārīn, Iran 71 C7 35 55N 52 19 E
Larino, Italy 29 G11 41 48N 14 54 E
Lárisa, Greece 38 B4 39 36N 22 27 E
Lárisa □, Greece 38 B4 39 39N 22 24 E
Larkana, Pakistan 68 F3 27 32N 68 18 E
Larnaca, Cyprus 36 E12 34 55N 33 38 E
Larnaca Bay, Cyprus 36 E12 34 53N 33 45 E
Larne, U.K. 15 B6 54 51N 5 51W
Larned, U.S.A. 112 F5 38 11N 99 6W
Laroquebrou, France 20 D6 44 58N 2 12 E
Larose, U.S.A. 113 L9 29 34N 90 23W
Larrimah, Australia 92 C5 15 35 S 133 12 E
Larsen Ice Shelf, Antarctica 5 C17 67 0 S 62 0W
Laruns, France 20 F3 43 0N 0 26W
Larvik, Norway 9 G14 59 4N 10 2 E
Larzac, Causse du, France 20 E7 43 50N 3 17 E
Las Alpujarras, Spain 33 J1 36 55N 3 20W
Las Animas, U.S.A. 112 F3 38 4N 103 13W
Las Anod, Somali Rep. 74 F4 8 26N 47 19 E
Las Arenas, Spain 34 B6 43 17N 4 50W
Las Aves, Is., W. Indies 121 C7 15 45N 63 55W
Las Brenãs, Argentina 126 B3 27 5 S 61 7W
Las Cabezas de San Juan, Spain 35 J5 36 57N 5 58W
Las Cejas, Argentina 128 B4 26 53 S 64 44W
Las Chimeneas, Mexico 117 N10 32 8N 116 5W
Las Cruces, U.S.A. 115 K10 32 19N 106 47W
Las Flores, Argentina 126 D4 36 10 S 59 7W
Las Heras, Argentina 126 C2 32 51 S 68 49W
Las Lajas, Argentina 128 D2 38 30 S 70 25W
Las Lomitas, Argentina 126 A3 24 43 S 60 35W
Las Marismas, Spain 35 H4 37 5N 6 20W
Las Minas, Spain 33 G3 38 20N 1 41W
Las Navas de la Concepción, Spain 35 H5 37 56N 5 30W
Las Navas del Marqués, Spain 34 E6 40 36N 4 20W
Las Palmas, Argentina 126 B4 27 8 S 58 45W
Las Palmas, Canary Is. 37 F4 28 7N 15 26W
Las Palmas →, Mexico 117 N10 32 26N 116 54W
Las Pedroñas, Spain 33 F2 39 26N 2 40W
Las Piedras, Uruguay 127 C4 34 44 S 56 14W
Las Pipinas, Argentina 126 D4 35 30 S 57 19W
Las Plumas, Argentina 128 E3 43 40 S 67 15W
Las Rosas, Argentina 126 C3 32 30 S 61 35W
Las Rozas, Spain 34 E7 40 29N 3 52W
Las Tablas, Panama 120 E3 7 49N 80 14W
Las Termas, Argentina 126 B3 27 29 S 64 52W
Las Toscas, Argentina 126 B4 28 21 S 59 18W
Las Truchas, Mexico 118 D4 17 57N 102 13W
Las Varillas, Argentina 126 C3 31 50 S 62 50W
Las Vegas, N. Mex., U.S.A. 115 J11 35 36N 105 13W
Las Vegas, Nev., U.S.A. 117 J11 36 10N 115 9W
Lasarte, Spain 32 B2 43 16N 2 1W
Lascano, Uruguay 127 C5 33 35 S 54 12W
Lashburn, Canada 105 C7 53 10N 109 40W
Lashio, Burma 67 H20 22 56N 97 45 E
Lashkar, India 68 F8 26 10N 78 10 E
Łasin, Poland 44 E6 53 30N 19 2 E
Lasíthi, Greece 36 D7 35 11N 25 31 E
Lasíthi □, Greece 36 D7 35 5N 25 50 E
Lāsjerd, Iran 71 C7 35 24N 53 4 E
Lask, Poland 45 G6 51 34N 19 8 E
Łaskarzew, Poland 45 G8 51 48N 21 36 E
Laško, Slovenia 29 B12 46 10N 15 16 E
Lassay-les-Châteaux, France 18 D6 48 27N 0 30W
Lassen Pk., U.S.A. 114 F3 40 29N 121 31W
Lassen Volcanic National Park, U.S.A. 114 F3 40 30N 121 20W
Last Mountain L., Canada 105 C7 51 5N 105 14W
Lastchance Cr. →, U.S.A. 116 E5 40 2N 121 15W
Lastoursville, Gabon 84 E2 0 55 S 12 38 E
Lastovo, Croatia 29 F13 42 46N 16 55 E
Lastovski Kanal, Croatia 29 F14 42 50N 17 0 E
Lat Yao, Thailand 64 E2 15 45N 99 48 E
Latacunga, Ecuador 124 D3 0 50 S 78 35W
Latakia = Al Lādhiqīyah, Syria 70 C2 35 30N 35 45 E
Latchford, Canada 102 C4 47 20N 79 50W
Latehar, India 69 H11 23 45N 84 30 E
Laterza, Italy 31 B9 40 37N 16 48 E
Latham, Australia 93 E2 29 44 S 116 20 E
Lathen, Germany 24 C3 52 52N 7 19 E
Lathi, India 68 F4 27 43N 71 23 E
Lathrop Wells, U.S.A. 117 J10 36 39N 116 24W
Latiano, Italy 31 B10 40 33N 17 43 E
Latina, Italy 30 A5 41 28N 12 52 E
Latisana, Italy 29 C10 45 47N 13 0 E
Latium = Lazio □, Italy 29 F9 42 10N 12 30 E
Laton, U.S.A. 116 J7 36 26N 119 41W
Latorytsya →, Slovak Rep. 27 C14 48 28N 21 50 E
Latouche Treville, C., Australia 92 C3 18 27 S 121 49 E
Latrobe, Australia 94 G4 41 14 S 146 30 E
Latrobe, U.S.A. 110 F5 40 19N 79 23W
Latrónico, Italy 31 B9 40 5N 16 1 E
Latvia ■, Europe 9 H20 56 50N 24 0 E
Lau, Nigeria 83 D7 9 11N 11 19 E
Lau Group, Fiji 91 C9 17 0 S 178 30W
Lauchhammer, Germany 24 D9 51 29N 13 47 E
Lauda-Königshofen, Germany 25 F5 49 33N 9 42 E
Lauenburg, Germany 24 B6 53 22N 10 32 E
Lauf, Germany 25 F7 49 30N 11 16 E
Laughlin, U.S.A. 115 J6 35 8N 114 35W
Laujar de Andarax, Spain 33 H2 37 0N 2 54W
Laukaa, Finland 9 E21 62 24N 25 56 E
Launceston, Australia 94 G4 41 24 S 147 8 E
Launceston, U.K. 13 G3 50 38N 4 22W
Laune →, Ireland 15 D2 52 7N 9 47W
Launglon Bok, Burma 64 F1 13 50N 97 54 E
Laupheim, Germany 25 G5 48 14N 9 52 E
Laura, Australia 94 B3 15 32 S 144 32 E
Laureana di Borrello, Italy 31 D9 38 30N 16 5 E
Laurel, Miss., U.S.A. 113 K10 31 41N 89 8W
Laurel, Mont., U.S.A. 114 D9 45 40N 108 46W
Laurencekirk, U.K. 14 E6 56 50N 2 28W
Laurens, U.S.A. 109 H4 34 30N 82 1W
Laurentian Plateau, Canada 103 B6 52 0N 70 0W
Lauria, Italy 31 B8 40 2N 15 50 E
Laurie L., Canada 105 B8 56 35N 101 57W
Laurinburg, U.S.A. 109 H6 34 47N 79 28W
Laurium, U.S.A. 108 B1 47 14N 88 27W
Lausanne, Switz. 25 J2 46 32N 6 38 E

Laut, Indonesia 65 K6 4 45N 108 0 E
Laut, Pulau, Indonesia 62 E5 4 45N 116 10 E
Laut Kecil, Kepulauan, Indonesia 62 E5 4 45 S 115 40 E
Lauterbach, Germany 24 E5 50 37N 9 24 E
Lauterecken, Germany 25 F3 49 38N 7 35 E
Lautoka, Fiji 91 C7 17 37 S 177 27 E
Lauzès, France 20 D5 44 34N 1 35 E
Lavagh More, Ireland 15 B3 54 46N 8 6W
Lavagna, Italy 28 D6 44 18N 9 20 E
Laval, France 18 D6 48 4N 0 48W
Lavalle, Argentina 126 B2 28 15 S 65 15W
Lavant Station, Canada 111 A8 45 3N 76 42W
Lāvar Meydān, Iran 71 D7 30 20N 54 30 E
Lávara, Greece 41 E10 41 19N 26 22 E
Lavardac, France 20 D4 44 12N 0 20 E
Lavaur, France 20 E5 43 40N 1 49 E
Lavelanet, France 20 F5 42 57N 1 51 E
Lavello, Italy 31 A8 41 3N 15 48 E
Laverton, Australia 93 E3 28 44 S 122 29 E
Lavís, Italy 28 B8 46 8N 11 7 E
Lávkos, Greece 38 B5 39 9N 23 14 E
Lavos, Portugal 34 E2 40 6N 8 49W
Lavradio, Portugal 35 G1 38 40N 9 3W
Lavras, Brazil 127 A7 21 20 S 45 0W
Lavre, Portugal 35 G2 38 46N 8 22W
Lávrion, Greece 38 D6 37 40N 24 4 E
Lávris, Greece 36 D6 35 25N 24 40 E
Lavumisa, Swaziland 89 D5 27 20 S 31 55 E
Lawas, Malaysia 62 D5 4 55N 115 25 E
Lawele, Indonesia 63 F6 5 16 S 123 3 E
Lawng Pit, Burma 67 G20 25 30N 97 25 E
Lawqah, Si. Arabia 70 D4 29 49N 42 45 E
Lawra, Ghana 82 C4 10 39N 2 51W
Lawrence, N.Z. 91 L2 45 55 S 169 41 E
Lawrence, Kans., U.S.A. 112 F7 38 58N 95 14W
Lawrence, Mass., U.S.A. 111 D13 42 43N 71 10W
Lawrenceburg, Ind., U.S.A. 108 F3 39 6N 84 52W
Lawrenceburg, Tenn., U.S.A. 109 H2 35 14N 87 20W
Lawrenceville, Ga., U.S.A. 109 J4 33 57N 83 59W
Lawrenceville, Pa., U.S.A. 110 E7 41 59N 77 8W
Laws, U.S.A. 116 H8 37 24N 118 20W
Lawton, U.S.A. 113 H5 34 37N 98 25W
Lawu, Indonesia 63 G14 7 40 S 111 13 E
Lawz, J. al, Si. Arabia 80 B4 28 39N 35 18 E
Laxå, Sweden 11 F8 58 59N 14 37 E
Laxford, L., U.K. 14 C3 58 24N 5 6W
Laxou, France 19 D13 48 41N 6 8 E
Lay →, France 20 B2 46 18N 1 17W
Laylá, Si. Arabia 74 C4 22 10N 46 40 E
Laylān, Iraq 70 C5 35 18N 44 31 E
Layon →, France 18 E6 47 20N 0 45W
Layton, U.S.A. 114 F7 41 4N 111 58W
Laytonville, U.S.A. 114 G2 39 41N 123 29W
Lazarevac, Serbia, Yug. 40 B4 44 23N 20 17 E
Lazarevskoye, Russia 49 J4 43 55N 39 21 E
Lazarivo, Madag. 89 C8 23 54 S 44 59 E
Lazdijai, Lithuania 44 D10 54 14N 23 31 E
Lazio □, Italy 29 F9 42 10N 12 30 E
Lazo, Moldova 43 C13 47 33N 28 2 E
Lazo, Russia 54 C6 43 25N 133 55 E
Le Beausset, France 21 E9 43 12N 5 48 E
Le Blanc, France 20 B5 46 37N 1 3 E
Le Bleymard, France 20 D7 44 30N 3 42 E
Le Bourgneuf-la-Fôret, France 18 D6 48 10N 0 59W
Le Bugue, France 20 D4 44 55N 0 56 E
Le Canourgue = La Canourgue, France 20 D7 44 26N 3 13 E
Le Cateau Cambrésis, France 19 B10 50 7N 3 32 E
Le Caylar, France 20 E7 43 51N 3 19 E
Le Chambon-Feugerolles, France 21 C8 45 24N 4 19 E
Le Châtelet, France 19 F9 46 38N 2 16 E
Le Chesne, France 19 C11 49 30N 4 45 E
Le Cheylard, France 21 D8 44 55N 4 25 E
Le Conquet, France 18 D2 48 21N 4 46W
Le Creusot, France 19 F11 46 48N 4 24 E
Le Croisic, France 18 E4 47 18N 2 30W
Le Donjon, France 19 F10 46 22N 3 48 E
Le Dorat, France 20 B5 46 14N 1 5 E
Le François, Martinique 121 D7 14 38N 60 57W
Le Grand-Lucé, France 18 E7 47 52N 0 28 E
Le Grand-Pressigny, France 18 F7 46 55N 0 48 E
Le Grand-Quevilly, France 18 C8 49 24N 1 3 E
Le Havre, France 18 C7 49 30N 0 5 E
Le Lavandou, France 21 E10 43 8N 6 22 E
Le Lion-d'Angers, France 18 E6 47 37N 0 43W
Le Louroux-Béconnais, France 18 E6 47 30N 0 55W
Le Luc, France 21 E10 43 23N 6 21 E
Le Lude, France 18 E7 47 39N 0 9 E
Le Mans, France 18 E7 48 0N 0 10 E
Le Mars, U.S.A. 112 D6 42 47N 96 10W
Le Mayet-de-Montagne, France 19 F10 46 4N 3 40 E
Le Mêle-sur-Sarthe, France 18 D7 48 31N 0 22 E
Le Monastier-sur-Gazeille, France 20 D7 44 57N 3 59 E
Le Monêtier-les-Bains, France 21 D10 44 58N 6 30 E
Le Mont-Dore, France 20 C6 45 35N 2 49 E
Le Mont-St-Michel, France 18 D5 48 40N 1 30W
Le Moule, Guadeloupe 121 C7 16 20N 61 22W
Le Muy, France 21 E10 43 28N 6 34 E
Le Palais, France 18 E3 47 20N 3 10W
Le Perthus, France 20 F6 42 30N 2 53 E
Le Puy-en-Velay, France 20 C7 45 3N 3 52 E
Le Sueur, U.S.A. 112 C8 44 28N 93 55W
Le Teil, France 21 D8 44 33N 4 40 E
Le Teilleul, France 18 D6 48 32N 0 53W
Le Theil, France 18 D7 48 16N 0 42 E
Le Thillot, France 19 E13 47 53N 6 46 E
Le Thuy, Vietnam 64 D6 17 14N 106 49 E
Le Touquet-Paris-Plage, France 19 B8 50 30N 1 36 E
Le Tréport, France 18 B8 50 3N 1 20 E
Le Val-d'Ajol, France 19 E13 47 55N 6 30 E
Le Verdon-sur-Mer, France 20 C2 45 33N 1 4W
Le Vigan, France 20 E7 43 59N 3 36 E
Lea →, U.K. 13 F8 51 31N 0 1 E
Leach, Cambodia 65 F4 12 21N 103 46 E
Lead, U.S.A. 112 C3 44 21N 103 46W
Leader, Canada 105 C7 50 50N 109 30W
Leadville, U.S.A. 115 G10 39 15N 106 18W
Leaf →, U.S.A. 113 K10 30 59N 88 44W
Leaf Rapids, Canada 105 B9 56 30N 99 59W
Leamington, Canada 102 D3 42 3N 82 36W
Leamington, U.S.A. 114 G7 39 32N 112 17W
Leamington Spa = Royal Leamington Spa, U.K. 13 E6 52 18N 1 31W
Le'an, China 59 D10 27 22N 115 48 E
Leandro Norte Alem, Argentina 127 B4 27 34 S 55 15W
Leane, L., Ireland 15 D2 52 2N 9 32W
Learmonth, Australia 92 D1 22 13 S 114 10 E
Leask, Canada 105 C7 53 5N 106 45W
Leatherhead, U.K. 13 F7 51 18N 0 20W
Leavenworth, Kans., U.S.A. 112 F7 39 19N 94 55W
Leavenworth, Wash., U.S.A. 114 C3 47 36N 120 40W
Łeba, Poland 44 D4 54 45N 17 32 E
Łeba →, Poland 44 D4 54 46N 17 33 E
Lebach, Germany 25 F2 49 25N 6 54 E
Lebak, Phil. 61 H6 6 32N 124 5 E
Lebam, U.S.A. 116 D3 46 34N 123 33W
Lebane, Serbia, Yug. 40 D5 42 56N 21 44 E
Lebanon, Ind., U.S.A. 108 E2 40 3N 86 28W
Lebanon, Kans., U.S.A. 112 F5 39 49N 98 33W
Lebanon, Ky., U.S.A. 108 G3 37 34N 85 15W
Lebanon, Mo., U.S.A. 113 G8 37 41N 92 40W
Lebanon, N.H., U.S.A. 111 C12 43 39N 72 15W
Lebanon, Oreg., U.S.A. 114 D2 44 32N 122 55W
Lebanon, Pa., U.S.A. 111 F8 40 20N 76 26W
Lebanon, Tenn., U.S.A. 109 G2 36 12N 86 18W
Lebanon ■, Asia 75 B5 34 0N 36 0 E
Lebec, U.S.A. 117 L8 34 50N 118 52W
Lebedyan, Russia 47 F10 53 0N 39 10 E
Lebedyn, Ukraine 47 G8 50 35N 34 30 E
Lebel-sur-Quévillon, Canada 102 C4 49 3N 76 59W
Lebomboberge, S. Africa 89 C5 24 30 S 32 0 E
Lębork, Poland 44 D4 54 33N 17 46 E
Lebrija, Spain 35 J4 36 53N 6 5W
Łebsko, Jezioro, Poland 44 D4 54 40N 17 25 E
Lebu, Chile 126 D1 37 40 S 73 47W
Leca da Palmeira, Portugal 34 D2 41 12N 8 42W
Lecce, Italy 31 B11 40 23N 18 11 E
Lecco, Italy 28 C6 45 51N 9 23 E
Lecco, L. di, Italy 28 C6 45 55N 9 19 E
Lécera, Spain 32 D4 41 13N 0 43W
Lech, Austria 26 D3 47 13N 10 9 E
Lech →, Germany 25 G6 48 43N 10 56 E
Lechang, China 59 E9 25 10N 113 20 E
Lechtaler Alpen, Austria 26 D3 47 15N 10 30 E
Lecontes Mills, U.S.A. 110 E6 41 5N 78 17W
Lectoure, France 20 E4 43 56N 0 38 E
Łęczna, Poland 45 G9 51 18N 22 53 E
Łęczyca, Poland 45 F6 52 5N 19 15 E
Ledesma, Spain 34 D5 41 6N 5 59W
Ledong, China 64 C7 18 41N 109 5 E
Leduc, Canada 104 C6 53 15N 113 30W
Lee, U.S.A. 111 D11 42 19N 73 15W
Lee →, Ireland 15 E3 51 53N 8 56W
Lee Vining, U.S.A. 116 H7 37 58N 119 7W
Leech L., U.S.A. 112 B7 47 10N 94 24W
Leechburg, U.S.A. 110 F5 40 37N 79 36W
Leeds, U.K. 12 D6 53 48N 1 33W
Leeds, U.S.A. 109 J2 33 33N 86 33W
Leek, Neths. 17 A6 53 10N 6 24 E
Leek, U.K. 12 D5 53 7N 2 1W
Leeman, Australia 93 E1 29 57 S 114 58 E
Leeper, U.S.A. 110 E5 41 22N 79 18W
Leer, Germany 24 B3 53 13N 7 26 E
Leesburg, U.S.A. 109 L5 28 49N 81 53W
Leesville, U.S.A. 113 K8 31 9N 93 16W
Leeton, Australia 95 E4 34 33 S 146 23 E
Leetonia, U.S.A. 110 F4 40 53N 80 45W
Leeu Gamka, S. Africa 88 E3 32 47 S 21 59 E
Leeuwarden, Neths. 17 A5 53 15N 5 48 E
Leeuwin, C., Australia 93 F2 34 20 S 115 9 E
Leeward Is., Atl. Oc. 121 C7 16 30N 63 30W
Lefka, Cyprus 36 D11 35 6N 32 51 E
Lefkoniko, Cyprus 36 D12 35 18N 33 44 E
Lefroy, Canada 110 B5 44 16N 79 34W
Lefroy, L., Australia 93 F3 31 21 S 121 40 E
Łeg →, Poland 45 H8 50 42N 21 50 E
Leganés, Spain 34 E7 40 19N 3 45W
Legazpi, Phil. 61 E5 13 10N 123 45 E
Lège-Cap-Ferret, France 20 D2 44 48N 1 9W
Lege Hida, Ethiopia 81 F5 7 56N 41 4 E
Legendre I., Australia 92 D2 20 22 S 116 55 E
Leghorn = Livorno, Italy 28 E7 43 33N 10 19 E
Legionowo, Poland 45 F7 52 25N 20 50 E
Legnago, Italy 29 C8 45 11N 11 18 E
Legnano, Italy 28 C5 45 36N 8 54 E
Legnica, Poland 45 G3 51 12N 16 10 E
Legrad, Croatia 29 B13 46 17N 16 51 E
Leh, India 69 B7 34 9N 77 35 E
Lehigh Acres, U.S.A. 109 M5 26 36N 81 39W
Lehighton, U.S.A. 111 F9 40 50N 75 43W
Lehliu, Romania 43 F11 44 29N 26 50 E
Leho, Sudan 81 F3 7 7N 33 52 E
Lehrte, Germany 24 C5 52 22N 9 58 E
Lehututu, Botswana 88 C3 23 54 S 21 55 E
Lei Shui →, China 59 D9 26 55N 112 35 E
Leiah, Pakistan 68 D4 30 58N 70 58 E
Leibnitz, Austria 26 E8 46 47N 15 34 E
Leibo, China 58 C4 28 11N 103 34 E
Leicester, U.K. 13 E6 52 38N 1 8W
Leicester City □, U.K. 13 E6 52 38N 1 8W
Leicestershire □, U.K. 13 E6 52 41N 1 17W
Leichhardt →, Australia 94 B2 17 35 S 139 48 E
Leichhardt Ra., Australia 94 C4 20 46 S 147 40 E
Leiden, Neths. 17 B4 52 9N 4 30 E
Leie →, Belgium 17 C3 51 2N 3 45 E
Leifers = Láives, Italy 29 B8 46 26N 11 20 E
Leigh Creek, Australia 95 E2 30 38 S 138 26 E
Leimen, Germany 25 F4 49 21N 8 41 E
Leine →, Germany 24 C5 52 43N 9 36 E
Leinefelde, Germany 24 D6 51 23N 10 19 E
Leinster, Australia 93 E3 27 51 S 120 36 E
Leinster □, Ireland 15 C4 53 3N 7 8W
Leinster, Mt., Ireland 15 D5 52 37N 6 46W
Leipalingis, Lithuania 44 D10 54 5N 23 51 E
Leipzig, Germany 24 D8 51 18N 12 22 E
Leiria, Portugal 34 F2 39 46N 8 53W
Leiria □, Portugal 34 F2 39 46N 8 53W
Leirvik, Norway 9 G11 59 47N 5 28 E
Leishan, China 58 D7 26 15N 108 20 E
Leisler, Mt., Australia 92 D4 23 23 S 129 20 E
Leith, U.K. 14 F5 55 59N 3 11W
Leith Hill, U.K. 13 F7 51 11N 0 22W
Leitha →, Europe 27 D10 47 50N 17 15 E
Leitrim, Ireland 15 B3 54 0N 8 5W
Leitrim □, Ireland 15 B4 54 8N 8 0W
Leitza, Spain 32 B3 43 5N 1 55W
Leiyang, China 59 D9 26 27N 112 45 E
Leizhou, China 59 G8 20 52N 110 8 E
Leizhou Bandao, China 58 G7 21 0N 110 0 E
Leizhou Wan, China 59 G8 20 50N 110 20 E
Lek →, Neths. 17 C4 51 54N 4 35 E
Leka, Norway 8 D14 65 5N 11 35 E
Lekáni, Greece 41 E8 41 10N 24 35 E
Lekbibaj, Albania 40 D3 42 17N 19 56 E
Lekeitio, Spain 32 B2 43 20N 2 32W
Lekhainá, Greece 38 D3 37 57N 21 16 E
Lekoui, Burkina Faso 82 C4 12 37N 3 40W
Leksand, Sweden 10 D9 60 44N 15 1 E
Lékva Óros, Greece 36 D6 35 18N 24 3 E
Leland, Mich., U.S.A. 108 C3 45 1N 85 45W
Leland, Miss., U.S.A. 113 J9 33 24N 90 54W
Lelång, Sweden 10 E6 59 10N 12 10 E
Leleque, Argentina 128 E2 42 28 S 71 0W
Lelystad, Neths. 17 B5 52 30N 5 25 E
Lem, Denmark 11 H2 56 1N 8 24 E
Lema, Nigeria 83 C5 12 58N 4 13 E
Lema Shilindi, Ethiopia 81 G5 4 50N 42 6 E
Léman, L., Europe 19 F13 46 26N 6 30 E
Lemera, Dem. Rep. of the Congo 86 C2 3 0 S 28 55 E
Lemery, Phil. 61 E4 13 51N 120 56 E
Lemhi Ra., U.S.A. 114 D7 44 30N 113 30W
Lemmer, Neths. 17 B5 52 51N 5 43 E
Lemmon, U.S.A. 112 C3 45 57N 102 10W
Lemon Grove, U.S.A. 117 N9 32 45N 117 2W
Lemoore, U.S.A. 116 J7 36 18N 119 46W
Lempdes, France 20 C7 45 22N 3 17 E
Lemvig, Denmark 11 H2 56 33N 8 20 E
Lena →, Russia 51 B13 72 52N 126 40 E
Lenart, Slovenia 29 B12 46 36N 15 48 E
Lenartovce, Slovak Rep. 27 C13 48 18N 20 19 E
Lencloître, France 18 F7 46 50N 0 20 E
Léndas, Greece 36 E6 34 56N 24 56 E
Lendava, Slovenia 29 B13 46 35N 16 25 E
Lendeh, Iran 71 D6 30 58N 50 25 E
Lendinara, Italy 29 C8 45 5N 11 36 E
Lengerich, Germany 24 C3 52 11N 7 52 E
Lenggong, Malaysia 65 K3 5 6N 100 58 E
Lenggries, Germany 25 H7 47 41N 11 35 E
Lengshuijiang, China 59 D8 27 40N 111 26 E
Lengshuitan, China 59 D8 26 27N 111 35 E
Lengua de Vaca, Pta., Chile 126 C1 30 14 S 71 38W
Lengyeltóti, Hungary 42 D2 46 40N 17 40 E
Lenhovda, Sweden 11 G9 57 0N 15 16 E
Lenina, Kanal →, Russia 49 J7 43 44N 45 17 E
Leninabad = Khudzhand, Tajikistan 50 E7 40 17N 69 37 E
Leninakan = Gyumri, Armenia 49 K6 40 47N 43 50 E
Leningrad = Sankt-Peterburg, Russia 46 C6 59 55N 30 20 E
Lenino, Ukraine 47 K8 45 17N 35 46 E
Leninogorsk, Kazakstan 50 D9 50 20N 83 30 E
Leninsk, Russia 49 F7 48 40N 45 15 E
Leninsk-Kuznetskiy, Russia 50 D9 54 44N 86 10 E
Leninskoye, Russia 48 A8 58 23N 47 3 E
Lenk, Switz. 25 J3 46 27N 7 28 E
Lenkoran = Länkäran, Azerbaijan 71 B6 38 48N 48 52 E
Lenmalu, Indonesia 63 E8 1 45 S 130 15 E
Lenne →, Germany 24 D3 51 25N 7 29 E
Lennestadt, Germany 24 D4 51 8N 8 2 E
Lennox, U.S.A. 112 D6 43 21N 96 53W
Lennoxville, Canada 111 A13 45 22N 71 51W
Leno, Italy 28 C7 45 22N 10 13 E
Lenoir, U.S.A. 109 H5 35 55N 81 32W
Lenoir City, U.S.A. 109 H3 35 48N 84 16W
Lenore L., Canada 105 C8 52 30N 104 59W
Lenox, U.S.A. 111 D11 42 22N 73 17W
Lens, France 19 B9 50 26N 2 50 E
Lensahn, Germany 24 A6 54 13N 10 53 E
Lensk, Russia 51 C12 60 48N 114 55 E
Lentekhi, Georgia 49 J6 42 47N 42 45 E
Lenti, Hungary 42 D1 46 37N 16 33 E
Lentini, Italy 31 E8 37 17N 15 0 E
Lenwood, U.S.A. 117 L9 34 53N 117 7W
Lenya, Burma 62 B1 11 33N 98 57 E
Lenzen, Germany 24 B7 53 5N 11 29 E
Léo, Burkina Faso 82 C4 11 3N 2 2W
Leoben, Austria 26 D8 47 22N 15 5 E
Leodhas = Lewis, U.K. 14 C2 58 9N 6 40W
Leola, U.S.A. 112 C5 45 43N 98 56W
Leominster, U.K. 13 E5 52 14N 2 43W
Leominster, U.S.A. 111 D13 42 32N 71 46W
Léon, France 20 E2 43 53N 1 18W
León, Mexico 118 C4 21 7N 101 40W
León, Nic. 120 D2 12 20N 86 51W
León, Spain 34 C5 42 38N 5 34W
Leon, U.S.A. 112 E8 40 44N 93 45W
León □, Spain 34 C5 42 40N 5 55W
Leon →, U.S.A. 113 K6 31 14N 97 28W
León, Montes de, Spain 34 C4 42 30N 6 18W
Leonardtown, U.S.A. 108 F7 38 17N 76 38W
Leonardville, Namibia 88 C2 23 29 S 18 49 E
Leonberg, Germany 25 G5 48 48N 9 1 E
Leonding, Austria 26 C7 48 16N 14 15 E
Leonessa, Italy 29 F9 42 34N 12 58 E
Leonforte, Italy 31 E7 37 38N 14 23 E
Leongatha, Australia 95 F4 38 30 S 145 58 E
Leonídhion, Greece 38 D4 37 9N 22 52 E
Leonora, Australia 93 E3 28 49 S 121 19 E
Léopold II, Lac = Mai-Ndombe, L., Dem. Rep. of the Congo 84 E3 2 0 S 18 20 E
Leopoldina, Brazil 127 A7 21 28 S 42 40W
Leopoldsburg, Belgium 17 C5 51 7N 5 13 E
Léopoldville = Kinshasa, Dem. Rep. of the Congo 84 E3 4 20 S 15 15 E
Leoti, U.S.A. 112 F4 38 29N 101 21W
Leova, Moldova 43 D13 46 28N 28 15 E
Leoville, Canada 105 C7 53 39N 107 33W
Lepe, Spain 35 H3 37 15N 7 12W
Lepel = Lyepyel, Belarus 46 E5 54 50N 28 40 E
Lepenoú, Greece 38 C3 38 42N 21 17 E
Leping, China 59 C11 28 47N 117 7 E
Lépo, L. do, Angola 88 B2 17 0 S 19 0 E
Lepontine, Alpi, Italy 28 B5 46 22N 8 27 E
Leppävirta, Finland 9 E22 62 29N 27 46 E
Lepsény, Hungary 42 D3 47 0N 18 15 E
Lequeitio = Lekeitio, Spain 32 B2 43 20N 2 32W
Lercara Friddi, Italy 30 E6 37 45N 13 36 E
Lerdo, Mexico 118 B4 25 32N 103 32W
Léré, Chad 83 D7 9 39N 14 13 E
Léré, Mali 82 B4 15 45N 4 55W
Lere, Bauchi, Nigeria 83 D6 9 43N 9 18 E
Lere, Kaduna, Nigeria 83 C6 10 23N 8 35 E
Leribe, Lesotho 89 D4 28 51 S 28 3 E
Lérici, Italy 28 D6 44 4N 9 55 E
Lérida = Lleida, Spain 32 D5 41 37N 0 39 E
Lérins, Îs. de, France 21 E11 43 31N 7 3 E
Lerma, Spain 34 C7 42 0N 3 47W
Léros, Greece 39 D8 37 10N 26 50 E
Lérouville, France 19 D12 48 44N 5 30 E
Lerum, Sweden 11 G6 57 46N 12 16 E
Lerwick, U.K. 14 A7 60 9N 1 9W
Leş, Romania 42 D6 46 58N 21 50 E
Les Abrets, France 21 C9 45 32N 5 35 E
Les Andelys, France 18 C8 49 15N 1 25 E
Les Borges Blanques, Spain 32 D5 41 31N 0 52 E
Les Cayes, Haiti 121 C5 18 15N 73 46W
Les Essarts, France 18 F5 46 47N 1 12W
Les Herbiers, France 18 F5 46 52N 1 1W
Les Minquiers, Plateau des, Chan. Is. 18 D4 48 58N 2 8W
Les Pieux, France 18 C5 49 30N 1 48W
Les Ponts-de-Cé, France 18 E6 47 25N 0 30W
Les Riceys, France 19 E11 47 59N 4 22 E
Les Sables-d'Olonne, France 20 B2 46 30N 1 45W
Les Vans, France 21 D8 44 25N 4 7 E
Lesbos = Lésvos, Greece 39 B8 39 10N 26 20 E
L'Escala, Spain 32 C8 42 7N 3 8 E
Leshan, China 58 C4 29 33N 103 41 E
Lésina, Italy 29 G12 41 52N 15 21 E
Lésina, L. di, Italy 29 G12 41 53N 15 26 E
Lesjöfors, Sweden 10 E8 59 58N 14 11 E
Lesko, Poland 45 J9 49 30N 22 23 E
Leskov I., Antarctica 5 B1 56 0 S 28 0W
Leskovac, Serbia, Yug. 40 C5 43 0N 21 58 E
Leskovik, Albania 40 F4 40 10N 20 34 E
Leskoviku = Leskovik, Albania 40 F4 40 10N 20 34 E
Leśna, Poland 45 G2 51 1N 15 15 E
Lesneven, France 18 D2 48 35N 4 20W
Leśnica, Poland 45 H5 50 26N 18 11 E
Lešnica, Serbia, Yug. 40 B3 44 39N 19 20 E
Lesnoye, Russia 46 C8 58 15N 35 18 E
Lesopilnoye, Russia 54 A7 46 44N 134 20 E
Lesotho ■, Africa 89 D4 29 40 S 28 0 E
Lesozavodsk, Russia 51 E14 45 30N 133 29 E
Lesparre-Médoc, France 20 C3 45 18N 0 57W
Lessay, France 18 C5 49 14N 1 30W
Lesse →, Belgium 17 D4 50 15N 4 54 E
Lessebo, Sweden 11 H9 56 45N 15 16 E
Lesser Antilles, W. Indies 121 D7 15 0N 61 0W
Lesser Slave L., Canada 104 B5 55 30N 115 25W
Lesser Sunda Is., Indonesia 63 F6 7 0 S 120 0 E
Lessines, Belgium 17 D3 50 42N 3 50 E
Lester, U.S.A. 116 C5 47 12N 121 29W
Lestock, Canada 105 C8 51 19N 103 59W
Lesuer I., Australia 92 B4 13 50 S 127 17 E
Lésvos, Greece 39 B8 39 10N 26 20 E
Leszno, Poland 45 G3 51 50N 16 30 E
Letaba, S. Africa 89 C5 23 59 S 31 50 E
Letälven, Sweden 10 E8 59 5N 14 20 E
Létavértes, Hungary 42 C6 47 23N 21 55 E
Letchworth, U.K. 13 F7 51 59N 0 13W
Letea, Ostrov, Romania 43 E14 45 18N 29 20 E
Lethbridge, Canada 104 D6 49 45N 112 45W
Lethem, Guyana 124 C7 3 20N 59 50W
Leti, Kepulauan, Indonesia 63 F7 8 10 S 128 0 E
Leti Is. = Leti, Kepulauan, Indonesia 63 F7 8 10 S 128 0 E
Letiahau →, Botswana 88 C3 21 16 S 24 0 E
Leticia, Colombia 124 D5 4 9 S 70 0W
Leting, China 57 E10 39 23N 118 55 E
Letjiesbos, S. Africa 88 E3 32 34 S 22 16 E
Letlhakane, Botswana 88 C4 21 27 S 25 30 E
Letlhakeng, Botswana 88 C3 24 0 S 24 59 E
Letong, Indonesia 62 D3 2 58N 105 42 E
Letpadan, Burma 67 L19 17 45N 95 45 E
Letpan, Burma 67 K19 19 28N 94 10 E
Letsôk-aw Kyun, Burma 65 G2 11 30N 98 25 E
Letterkenny, Ireland 15 B4 54 57N 7 45W
Leu, Romania 43 F9 44 10N 24 0 E
Leucadia, U.S.A. 117 M9 33 4N 117 18W
Leucate, France 20 F7 42 56N 3 3 E
Leucate, Étang de, France 20 F7 42 50N 3 0 E
Leuk, Switz. 25 J3 46 19N 7 37 E
Leuşeni, Moldova 43 D13 46 49N 28 12 E
Leuser, G., Indonesia 62 D1 3 46N 97 12 E
Leutkirch, Germany 25 H6 47 49N 10 1 E
Leuven, Belgium 17 D4 50 52N 4 42 E
Leuze-en-Hainaut, Belgium 17 D3 50 36N 3 37 E
Lev Tolstoy, Russia 46 F10 53 13N 39 29 E
Levádhia, Greece 38 C4 38 27N 22 54 E
Levan, Albania 40 F3 40 40N 19 28 E
Levanger, Norway 8 E14 63 45N 11 19 E
Levani = Levan, Albania 40 F3 40 40N 19 28 E
Levant, Î. du, France 21 E10 43 3N 6 28 E
Lévanto, Italy 28 D6 44 10N 9 38 E
Lévanzo, Italy 30 D5 38 0N 12 20 E
Levelland, U.S.A. 113 J3 33 35N 102 23W
Leven, U.K. 14 E6 56 12N 3 0W
Leven, L., U.K. 14 E5 56 12N 3 22W
Leven, Toraka, Madag. 89 A8 12 30 S 47 45 E
Leveque C., Australia 92 C3 16 20 S 123 0 E
Leverano, Italy 31 B10 40 17N 18 0 E
Leverkusen, Germany 24 D3 51 1N 7 1 E
Levice, Slovak Rep. 27 C11 48 13N 18 35 E
Levico Terme, Italy 29 C8 46 0N 11 18 E
Levie, France 21 G13 41 40N 9 7 E
Levier, France 19 F13 46 58N 6 8 E
Levin, N.Z. 91 J5 40 37 S 175 18 E
Lévis, Canada 103 C5 46 48N 71 9W
Levis, L., Canada 104 A5 62 37N 117 58W
Levítha, Greece 39 D8 37 0N 26 28 E
Levittown, N.Y., U.S.A. 111 F11 40 44N 73 31W
Levittown, Pa., U.S.A. 111 F10 40 9N 74 51W
Levka, Bulgaria 41 E10 41 52N 26 15 E
Levkás, Greece 38 C2 38 40N 20 43 E
Levkás □, Greece 38 C2 38 40N 20 30 E
Levkímmi, Greece 36 B4 39 25N 20 3 E
Levkímmi, Ákra, Greece 36 B4 39 29N 20 4 E
Levkôsia = Nicosia, Cyprus 36 D12 35 10N 33 25 E
Levoča, Slovak Rep. 27 B13 49 2N 20 35 E
Levroux, France 19 F8 46 59N 1 38 E
Levski, Bulgaria 41 C9 43 21N 25 10 E
Levskigrad = Karlovo, Bulgaria 41 D8 42 38N 24 47 E
Levuka, Fiji 91 C8 17 34 S 179 0 E
Lewes, U.K. 13 G8 50 52N 0 1 E
Lewes, U.S.A. 108 F8 38 46N 75 9W
Lewin Brzeski, Poland 45 H4 50 45N 17 37 E
Lewis, U.K. 14 C2 58 9N 6 40W
Lewis →, U.S.A. 116 E4 45 51N 122 48W
Lewis, Butt of, U.K. 14 C2 58 31N 6 16W
Lewis Ra., Australia 92 D4 20 3 S 128 50 E
Lewis Range, U.S.A. 114 C7 48 5N 113 5W
Lewis Run, U.S.A. 110 E6 41 52N 78 40W
Lewisburg, Pa., U.S.A. 110 F8 40 58N 76 54W
Lewisburg, Tenn., U.S.A. 109 H2 35 27N 86 48W
Lewisburg, W. Va., U.S.A. 108 G5 37 48N 80 27W
Lewisporte, Canada 103 C8 49 15N 55 3W
Lewiston, Idaho, U.S.A. 114 C5 46 25N 117 1W
Lewiston, Maine, U.S.A. 109 C11 44 6N 70 13W
Lewiston, N.Y., U.S.A. 110 C5 43 11N 79 3W
Lewistown, Mont., U.S.A. 114 C9 47 4N 109 26W
Lewistown, Pa., U.S.A. 110 F7 40 36N 77 34W
Lexington, Ill., U.S.A. 112 E10 40 39N 88 47W
Lexington, Ky., U.S.A. 108 F3 38 3N 84 30W
Lexington, Mich., U.S.A. 110 C2 43 16N 82 32W
Lexington, Mo., U.S.A. 112 F8 39 11N 93 52W
Lexington, N.C., U.S.A. 109 H5 35 49N 80 15W
Lexington, N.Y., U.S.A. 111 D10 42 15N 74 22W
Lexington, Nebr., U.S.A. 112 E5 40 47N 99 45W
Lexington, Ohio, U.S.A. 110 F2 40 41N 82 35W
Lexington, Tenn., U.S.A. 109 H1 35 39N 88 24W
Lexington, Va., U.S.A. 108 G6 37 47N 79 27W
Lexington Park, U.S.A. 108 F7 38 16N 76 27W
Leyburn, U.K. 12 C6 54 19N 1 48W
Leye, China 58 E6 24 48N 106 29 E
Leyland, U.K. 12 D5 53 42N 2 43W
Leyre →, France 20 D2 44 39N 1 1W
Leyte □, Phil. 61 F6 11 0N 125 0 E
Leyte Gulf, Phil. 61 F6 10 50N 125 25 E
Leżajsk, Poland 45 H9 50 16N 22 25 E
Lezay, France 20 B3 46 15N 0 1W
Lezha = Lezhë, Albania 40 E3 41 47N 19 39 E
Lezhë, Albania 40 E3 41 47N 19 39 E
Lezhi, China 58 B5 30 19N 104 58 E
Lézignan-Corbières, France 20 E6 43 13N 2 43 E
Lezoux, France 20 C7 45 49N 3 21 E
Lgov, Russia 47 G8 51 42N 35 16 E
Lhasa, China 60 D4 29 25N 90 58 E
Lhazê, China 60 D3 29 5N 87 38 E
Lhokkruet, Indonesia 62 D1 4 55N 95 24 E
Lhokseumawe, Indonesia 62 C1 5 10N 97 10 E
L'Hospitalet de Llobregat, Spain 32 D7 41 21N 2 6 E
Lhuntsi Dzong, India 67 F17 27 39N 91 10 E
Li, Thailand 64 D2 17 48N 98 57 E
Li Shui →, China 59 C9 29 24N 112 1 E
Li Xian, Gansu, China 56 G3 34 10N 105 5 E
Li Xian, Hebei, China 56 E8 38 30N 115 35 E
Li Xian, Hunan, China 59 C8 29 36N 111 42 E
Liádhoi, Greece 39 E8 36 50N 26 11 E
Liancheng, China 59 E11 25 42N 116 40 E
Lianga, Phil. 61 G7 8 38N 126 6 E
Liangcheng, Nei Monggol Zizhiqu, China 56 D7 40 28N 112 25 E
Liangcheng, Shandong, China 57 G10 35 32N 119 37 E
Liangdang, China 56 H4 33 56N 106 18 E
Lianghe, China 58 E2 24 50N 98 20 E
Lianghekou, China 58 C7 29 11N 108 44 E
Liangping, China 58 B6 30 38N 107 47 E
Liangpran, Indonesia 62 D4 1 4N 114 23 E
Lianhua, China 59 D9 27 3N 113 54 E
Lianjiang, Fujian, China 59 D12 26 12N 119 27 E
Lianjiang, Guangdong, China 59 G8 21 40N 110 20 E
Lianping, China 59 E10 24 26N 114 30 E
Lianshan, China 59 E9 24 38N 112 8 E
Lianshanguan, China 57 D12 40 53N 123 43 E
Lianshui, China 57 H10 33 42N 119 20 E
Lianyuan, China 59 D8 27 40N 111 38 E
Lianyungang, China 57 G10 34 40N 119 11 E
Lianzhou, China 59 E9 24 51N 112 22 E
Liao He →, China 57 D11 41 0N 121 50 E
Liaocheng, China 56 F8 36 28N 115 58 E
Liaodong Bandao, China 57 E12 40 0N 122 30 E
Liaodong Wan, China 57 D11 40 20N 121 10 E
Liaoning □, China 57 D12 41 40N 122 30 E
Liaoyang, China 57 D12 41 15N 122 58 E
Liaoyuan, China 57 C13 42 58N 125 2 E
Liaozhong, China 57 D12 41 23N 122 50 E
Liapádhes, Greece 38 B1 39 42N 19 40 E
Liard →, Canada 104 A4 61 51N 121 18W
Liard River, Canada 104 B3 59 25N 126 5W
Liari, Pakistan 68 G2 25 37N 66 30 E
Libau = Liepāja, Latvia 9 H19 56 30N 21 0 E
Libby, U.S.A. 114 B6 48 23N 115 33W
Libenge, Dem. Rep. of the Congo 84 D3 3 40N 18 55 E
Liberal, U.S.A. 113 G4 37 3N 100 55W
Liberec, Czech Rep. 26 A8 50 47N 15 7 E
Liberia, Costa Rica 120 D2 10 40N 85 30W
Liberia ■, W. Afr. 82 D3 6 30N 9 30W
Liberty, Mo., U.S.A. 112 F7 39 15N 94 25W
Liberty, N.Y., U.S.A. 111 E10 41 48N 74 45W
Liberty, Pa., U.S.A. 110 E7 41 34N 77 6W
Liberty, Tex., U.S.A. 113 K7 30 3N 94 48W

Libiąż, Poland 45 H6 50 7N 19 21 E
Lîbîya, Sahrâ', Africa 79 C10 25 0N 25 0 E
Libo, China 58 E6 25 22N 107 53 E
Libobo, Tanjung, Indonesia 63 E7 0 54 S 128 28 E
Libode, S. Africa 89 E4 31 33 S 29 2 E
Libohava = Libohovë, Albania 40 F4 40 3N 20 10 E
Libohovë, Albania 40 F4 40 3N 20 10 E
Libourne, France 20 D3 44 55N 0 14W
Libramont, Belgium 17 E5 49 55N 5 23 E
Librazhd, Albania 40 E4 41 12N 20 22 E
Librazhdi = Librazhd, Albania 40 E4 41 12N 20 22 E
Libreville, Gabon 84 D1 0 25N 9 26 E
Libya ■, N. Afr. 79 C9 27 0N 17 0 E
Libyan Desert = Lîbîya, Sahrâ', Africa 79 C10 25 0N 25 0 E
Libyan Plateau = Ed-Déffa, Egypt 80 A2 30 40N 26 30 E
Licantén, Chile 126 D1 35 55 S 72 0W
Licata, Italy 30 E6 37 6N 13 56 E
Lice, Turkey 73 C9 38 27N 40 39 E
Licheng, China 56 F7 36 28N 113 20 E
Lichfield, U.K. 13 E6 52 41N 1 49W
Lichinga, Mozam. 87 E4 13 13 S 35 11 E
Lichtenburg, S. Africa 88 D4 26 8 S 26 8 E
Lichtenfels, Germany 25 E7 50 8N 11 4 E
Lichuan, Hubei, China 58 B7 30 18N 108 57 E
Lichuan, Jiangxi, China 59 D11 27 18N 116 55 E
Licking →, U.S.A. 108 F3 39 6N 84 30W
Licosa, Punta, Italy 31 B7 40 15N 14 54 E
Lida, Belarus 9 K21 53 53N 25 15 E
Liden, Sweden 10 B10 62 42N 16 48 E
Lidhoríkion, Greece 38 C4 38 32N 22 12 E
Lidhult, Sweden 11 H7 56 50N 13 27 E
Lidköping, Sweden 11 F7 58 31N 13 7 E
Lido, Italy 29 C9 45 25N 12 22 E
Lido, Niger 83 C5 12 54N 3 44 E
Lido di Roma = Ostia, Lido di, Italy 29 G9 41 43N 12 17 E
Lidzbark, Poland 45 E6 53 15N 19 49 E
Lidzbark Warmiński, Poland 44 D7 54 7N 20 34 E
Liebenwalde, Germany 24 C9 52 52N 13 24 E
Lieberose, Germany 24 D10 51 59N 14 17 E
Liebig, Mt., Australia 92 D5 23 18 S 131 22 E
Liebling, Romania 42 E6 45 36N 21 20 E
Liechtenstein ■, Europe 25 H5 47 8N 9 35 E
Liège, Belgium 17 D5 50 38N 5 35 E
Liège □, Belgium 17 D5 50 32N 5 35 E
Liegnitz = Legnica, Poland 45 G3 51 12N 16 10 E
Lienart, Dem. Rep. of the Congo 86 B2 3 3N 25 31 E
Lienyünchiangshih = Lianyungang, China 57 G10 34 40N 119 11 E
Lienz, Austria 26 E5 46 50N 12 46 E
Liepāja, Latvia 9 H19 56 30N 21 0 E
Liepāja □, Latvia 44 B8 56 30N 21 30 E
Liepājas ezers, Latvia 44 B8 56 27N 21 3 E
Lier, Belgium 17 C4 51 7N 4 34 E
Liernais, France 19 E11 47 13N 4 16 E
Liești, Romania 43 E12 45 38N 27 34 E
Liévin, France 19 B9 50 24N 2 47 E
Lièvre →, Canada 102 C4 45 31N 75 26W
Liezen, Austria 26 D7 47 34N 14 15 E
Liffey →, Ireland 15 C5 53 21N 6 13W
Lifford, Ireland 15 B4 54 51N 7 29W
Liffré, France 18 D5 48 12N 1 30W
Lifudzin, Russia 54 B7 44 21N 134 58 E
Ligao, Phil. 61 E5 13 14N 123 32 E
Lightning Ridge, Australia 95 D4 29 22 S 148 0 E
Lignano Sabbiadoro, Italy 29 C10 45 42N 13 9 E
Ligny-en-Barrois, France 19 D12 48 36N 5 20 E
Ligonier, U.S.A. 110 F5 40 15N 79 14W
Ligoúrion, Greece 38 D5 37 37N 23 4 E
Ligueil, France 18 E7 47 2N 0 49 E
Liguria □, Italy 28 D5 44 30N 8 50 E
Ligurian Sea, Medit. S. 6 G7 43 20N 9 0 E
Lihou Reefs and Cays, Australia 94 B5 17 25 S 151 40 E
Lihue, U.S.A. 106 H15 21 59N 159 23W
Lijiang, China 58 D3 26 55N 100 20 E
Likasi, Dem. Rep. of the Congo 87 E2 10 55 S 26 48 E
Likenäs, Sweden 10 D8 60 37N 13 3 E
Likhoslavl, Russia 46 D8 57 12N 35 30 E
Likhovskoy, Russia 47 H11 48 10N 40 10 E
Likoma I., Malawi 87 E3 12 3 S 34 45 E
Likumburu, Tanzania 87 D4 9 43 S 35 8 E
L'Île-Bouchard, France 18 E7 47 7N 0 26 E
L'Île-Rousse, France 21 F12 42 38N 8 57 E
Liling, China 59 D9 27 42N 113 29 E
Lilla Edet, Sweden 11 F6 58 9N 12 8 E
Lille, France 19 B10 50 38N 3 3 E
Lille Bælt, Denmark 11 J3 55 20N 9 45 E
Lillebonne, France 18 C7 49 30N 0 32 E
Lillehammer, Norway 9 F14 61 8N 10 30 E
Lillesand, Norway 9 G13 58 15N 8 23 E
Lillhärdal, Sweden 10 C8 61 51N 14 5 E
Lillian Pt., Australia 93 E4 27 40 S 126 6 E
Lillo, Spain 34 F7 39 45N 3 20W
Lillooet, Canada 104 C4 50 44N 121 57W
Lillooet →, Canada 104 D4 49 15N 121 57W
Lilongwe, Malawi 87 E3 14 0 S 33 48 E
Liloy, Phil. 63 C6 8 4N 122 39 E
Lim →, Bos.-H. 40 C3 43 45N 19 15 E
Lima, Indonesia 63 E7 3 37 S 128 4 E
Lima, Peru 124 F3 12 0 S 77 0W
Lima, Mont., U.S.A. 114 D7 44 38N 112 36W
Lima, Ohio, U.S.A. 108 E3 40 44N 84 6W
Lima →, Portugal 34 D2 41 41N 8 50W
Liman, Indonesia 63 G14 7 48 S 111 45 E
Liman, Russia 49 H8 45 45N 47 12 E
Limanowa, Poland 45 J7 49 42N 20 22 E
Limassol, Cyprus 36 E12 34 42N 33 1 E
Limavady, U.K. 15 A5 55 3N 6 56W
Limay →, Argentina 128 D3 39 0 S 68 0W
Limay Mahuida, Argentina 126 D2 37 10 S 66 45W
Limbach-Oberfrohna, Germany 24 E8 50 52N 12 43 E
Limbang, Brunei 62 D5 4 42N 115 6 E
Limbara, Mte., Italy 30 B2 40 51N 9 10 E
Limbaži, Latvia 9 H21 57 31N 24 42 E
Limbdi, India 68 H4 22 34N 71 51 E
Limbe, Cameroon 83 E6 4 1N 9 10 E
Limburg, Germany 25 E4 50 22N 8 4 E
Limburg □, Belgium 17 C5 51 2N 5 25 E
Limburg □, Neths. 17 C5 51 20N 5 55 E
Limedsforsen, Sweden 10 D7 60 52N 13 25 E
Limeira, Brazil 127 A6 22 35 S 47 28W
Limenária, Greece 41 F8 40 38N 24 32 E
Limerick, Ireland 15 D3 52 40N 8 37W
Limerick, U.S.A. 111 C14 43 41N 70 48W
Limerick □, Ireland 15 D3 52 30N 8 50W
Limestone, U.S.A. 110 D6 42 2N 78 38W
Limestone →, Canada 105 B10 56 31N 94 7W
Limfjorden, Denmark 11 H3 56 55N 9 0 E
Limia = Lima →, Portugal 34 D2 41 41N 8 50W
Limín Khersonísou, Greece 39 F7 35 18N 25 21 E
Limingen, Norway 8 D15 64 48N 13 35 E
Limmared, Sweden 11 G7 57 34N 13 20 E
Limmen Bight, Australia 94 A2 14 40 S 135 35 E
Limmen Bight →, Australia 94 B2 15 7 S 135 44 E
Límni, Greece 38 C5 38 43N 23 18 E
Límnos, Greece 39 B7 39 50N 25 5 E
Limoges, Canada 111 A9 45 20N 75 16W
Limoges, France 20 C5 45 50N 1 15 E
Limón, Costa Rica 120 E3 10 0N 83 2W
Limon, U.S.A. 112 F3 39 16N 103 41W
Limone Piemonte, Italy 28 D4 44 12N 7 34 E
Limousin, France 20 C5 45 30N 1 30 E
Limousin, Plateaux du, France 20 C5 45 45N 1 15 E
Limoux, France 20 E6 43 4N 2 12 E
Limpopo →, Africa 89 D5 25 5 S 33 30 E
Limuru, Kenya 86 C4 1 2 S 36 35 E
Lin Xian, China 56 F6 37 57N 110 58 E
Lin'an, China 59 B12 30 15N 119 42 E
Linapacan I., Phil. 61 F3 11 27N 119 49 E
Linapacan Str., Phil. 61 F3 11 37N 119 56 E
Linares, Chile 126 D1 35 50 S 71 40W
Linares, Mexico 119 C5 24 50N 99 40W
Linares, Spain 35 G7 38 10N 3 40W
Linaro, Capo, Italy 29 F8 42 2N 11 50 E
Línas Mte., Italy 30 C1 39 25N 8 38 E
Lincang, China 58 F3 23 58N 100 1 E
Lincheng, China 56 F8 37 25N 114 30 E
Linchuan, China 59 D11 27 57N 116 15 E
Lincoln, Argentina 126 C3 34 55 S 61 30W
Lincoln, N.Z. 91 K4 43 38 S 172 30 E
Lincoln, U.K. 12 D7 53 14N 0 32W
Lincoln, Calif., U.S.A. 116 G5 38 54N 121 17W
Lincoln, Ill., U.S.A. 112 E10 40 9N 89 22W
Lincoln, Kans., U.S.A. 112 F5 39 3N 98 9W
Lincoln, Maine, U.S.A. 109 C11 45 22N 68 30W
Lincoln, N.H., U.S.A. 111 B13 44 3N 71 40W
Lincoln, N. Mex., U.S.A. 115 K11 33 30N 105 23W
Lincoln, Nebr., U.S.A. 112 E6 40 49N 96 41W
Lincoln City, U.S.A. 114 D1 44 57N 124 1W
Lincoln Hav = Lincoln Sea, Arctic 4 A5 84 0N 55 0W
Lincoln Sea, Arctic 4 A5 84 0N 55 0W
Lincolnshire □, U.K. 12 D7 53 14N 0 32W
Lincolnshire Wolds, U.K. 12 D7 53 26N 0 13W
Lincolnton, U.S.A. 109 H5 35 29N 81 16W
L'Incudine, France 21 G13 41 50N 9 12 E
Lind, U.S.A. 114 C4 46 58N 118 37W
Linda, U.S.A. 116 F5 39 8N 121 34W
Lindau, Germany 25 H5 47 33N 9 42 E
Linden, Guyana 124 B7 6 0N 58 10W
Linden, Ala., U.S.A. 109 J2 32 18N 87 48W
Linden, Calif., U.S.A. 116 G5 38 1N 121 5W
Linden, Tex., U.S.A. 113 J7 33 1N 94 22W
Lindenhurst, U.S.A. 111 F11 40 41N 73 23W
Lindesberg, Sweden 10 E9 59 36N 15 15 E
Lindesnes, Norway 9 H12 57 58N 7 3 E
Líndhos, Greece 36 C10 36 6N 28 4 E
Líndhos, Ákra, Greece 36 C10 36 4N 28 10 E
Lindi, Tanzania 87 D4 9 58 S 39 38 E
Lindi □, Tanzania 87 D4 9 40 S 38 30 E
Lindi →, Dem. Rep. of the Congo 86 B2 0 33N 25 5 E
Lindö, Sweden 11 F10 58 37N 16 15 E
Lindome, Sweden 11 G6 57 35N 12 5 E
Lindoso, Portugal 34 D2 41 52N 8 11W
Lindow, Germany 24 C8 52 58N 12 59 E
Lindsay, Canada 102 D4 44 22N 78 43W
Lindsay, Calif., U.S.A. 116 J7 36 12N 119 5W
Lindsay, Okla., U.S.A. 113 H6 34 50N 97 38W
Lindsborg, U.S.A. 112 F6 38 35N 97 40W
Lindsdal, Sweden 11 H10 56 44N 16 18 E
Linesville, U.S.A. 110 E4 41 39N 80 26W
Linfen, China 56 F6 36 3N 111 30 E
Ling Xian, Hunan, China 59 D9 26 29N 113 48 E
Ling Xian, Shandong, China 56 F9 37 22N 116 30 E
Lingao, China 64 C7 19 56N 109 42 E
Lingayen, Phil. 63 A6 16 1N 120 14 E
Lingayen G., Phil. 61 C4 16 10N 120 15 E
Lingbi, China 57 H9 33 33N 117 33 E
Lingbo, Sweden 10 C10 61 3N 16 41 E
Lingchuan, Guangxi Zhuangzu, China 59 E8 25 26N 110 21 E
Lingchuan, Shanxi, China 56 G7 35 45N 113 12 E
Lingen, Germany 24 C3 52 31N 7 19 E
Lingga, Indonesia 62 E2 0 12 S 104 37 E
Lingga, Kepulauan, Indonesia 62 E2 0 10 S 104 30 E
Lingga Arch. = Lingga, Kepulauan, Indonesia 62 E2 0 10 S 104 30 E
Linghem, Sweden 11 F9 58 26N 15 47 E
Lingle, U.S.A. 112 D2 42 8N 104 21W
Lingqiu, China 56 E8 39 28N 114 22 E
Lingshan, China 58 F7 22 25N 109 18 E
Lingshi, China 56 F6 36 48N 111 48 E
Lingshou, China 56 E8 38 20N 114 20 E
Lingshui, China 64 C8 18 27N 110 0 E
Lingtai, China 56 G4 35 0N 107 40 E
Linguère, Senegal 82 B1 15 25N 15 5W
Lingui, China 59 E8 25 12N 110 2 E
Lingwu, China 56 E4 38 6N 106 20 E
Lingyuan, China 57 D10 41 10N 119 15 E
Lingyun, China 58 E6 25 2N 106 35 E
Linhai, China 59 C13 28 50N 121 8 E
Linhares, Brazil 125 G10 19 25 S 40 4W
Linhe, China 56 D4 40 48N 107 20 E
Linjiang, China 57 D14 41 50N 127 0 E
Linköping, Sweden 11 F9 58 28N 15 36 E
Linkou, China 57 B16 45 15N 130 18 E
Linli, China 59 C8 29 27N 111 30 E
Linnhe, L., U.K. 14 E3 56 36N 5 25W
Linqi, China 56 G7 35 45N 113 52 E
Linqing, China 56 F8 36 50N 115 42 E
Linqu, China 57 F10 36 25N 118 30 E
Linru, China 56 G7 34 11N 112 52 E
Lins, Brazil 127 A6 21 40 S 49 44W
Linshui, China 58 B6 30 21N 106 57 E
Linta →, Madag. 89 D7 25 2 S 44 5 E
Linth →, Switz. 25 H5 47 7N 9 7 E
Linthal, Switz. 25 J5 46 54N 9 0 E
Linton, Ind., U.S.A. 108 F2 39 2N 87 10W
Linton, N. Dak., U.S.A. 112 B4 46 16N 100 14W
Lintong, China 56 G5 34 20N 109 10 E
Linwood, Canada 110 C4 43 35N 80 43W
Linwu, China 59 E9 25 19N 112 31 E
Linxi, China 57 C10 43 36N 118 2 E
Linxia, China 60 C5 35 36N 103 10 E
Linxiang, China 59 C9 29 28N 113 23 E
Linyanti →, Africa 88 B4 17 50 S 25 5 E
Linyi, China 57 G10 35 5N 118 21 E
Linz, Austria 26 C7 48 18N 14 18 E
Linz, Germany 24 E3 50 34N 7 17 E
Linzhenzhen, China 56 F5 36 30N 109 59 E
Linzi, China 57 F10 36 50N 118 20 E
Lion, G. du, France 20 E7 43 10N 4 0 E
Lionárisso, Cyprus 36 D13 35 28N 34 8 E
Lioni, Italy 31 B8 40 52N 15 11 E
Lions, G. of = Lion, G. du, France 20 E7 43 10N 4 0 E
Lion's Den, Zimbabwe 87 F3 17 15 S 30 5 E
Lion's Head, Canada 110 B3 44 58N 81 15W
Liozno = Lyozna, Belarus 46 E6 55 0N 30 50 E
Lipa, Phil. 61 E4 13 57N 121 10 E
Lipali, Mozam. 87 F4 15 50 S 35 50 E
Lipany, Slovak Rep. 27 B13 49 9N 20 58 E
Lípari, Italy 31 D7 38 26N 14 58 E
Lípari, I., Italy 31 D7 38 29N 14 56 E
Lípari, Is. = Eólie, Ís., Italy 31 D7 38 30N 14 57 E
Lipcani, Moldova 43 B11 48 14N 26 48 E
Lipetsk, Russia 47 F10 52 37N 39 35 E
Lipiany, Poland 45 E1 53 2N 14 58 E
Liping, China 58 D7 26 15N 109 7 E
Lipkany = Lipcani, Moldova 43 B11 48 14N 26 48 E
Lipljan, Kosovo, Yug. 40 D5 42 31N 21 7 E
Lipník nad Bečvou, Czech Rep. 27 B10 49 32N 17 36 E
Lipno, Poland 45 F6 52 49N 19 15 E
Lipova, Romania 42 D6 46 8N 21 42 E
Lipovcy Manzovka, Russia 54 B6 44 12N 132 26 E
Lipovets, Ukraine 47 H5 49 12N 29 1 E
Lippe →, Germany 24 D2 51 39N 6 36 E
Lippstadt, Germany 24 D4 51 41N 8 22 E
Lipscomb, U.S.A. 113 G4 36 14N 100 16W
Lipsk, Poland 44 E10 53 44N 23 24 E
Lipsko, Poland 45 G8 51 9N 21 40 E
Lipsói, Greece 39 D8 37 19N 26 50 E
Liptovský Hrádok, Slovak Rep. 27 B12 49 2N 19 44 E
Liptovský Milkuláš, Slovak Rep. 27 B12 49 6N 19 35 E
Liptrap C., Australia 95 F4 38 50 S 145 55 E
Lipu, China 59 E8 24 30N 110 22 E
Lira, Uganda 86 B3 2 17N 32 57 E
Liri →, Italy 30 A6 41 25N 13 52 E
Liria = Llíria, Spain 33 F4 39 37N 0 35W
Lisala, Dem. Rep. of the Congo 84 D4 2 12N 21 38 E
Lisboa, Portugal 35 G1 38 42N 9 10W
Lisboa □, Portugal 35 F1 39 0N 9 12W
Lisbon = Lisboa, Portugal 35 G1 38 42N 9 10W
Lisbon, N. Dak., U.S.A. 112 B6 46 27N 97 41W
Lisbon, N.H., U.S.A. 111 B13 44 13N 71 55W
Lisbon, Ohio, U.S.A. 110 F4 40 46N 80 46W
Lisbon Falls, U.S.A. 109 D10 44 0N 70 4W
Lisburn, U.K. 15 B5 54 31N 6 3W
Liscannor B., Ireland 15 D2 52 55N 9 24W
Liscia →, Italy 30 A2 41 11N 9 9 E
Lishe Jiang →, China 58 E3 24 15N 101 35 E
Lishi, China 56 F6 37 31N 111 8 E
Lishu, China 57 C13 43 20N 124 18 E
Lishui, Jiangsu, China 59 B12 31 38N 119 2 E
Lishui, Zhejiang, China 59 C12 28 28N 119 54 E
Lisianski I., Pac. Oc. 96 E10 26 2N 174 0W
Lisichansk = Lysychansk, Ukraine 47 H10 48 55N 38 30 E
Lisieux, France 18 C7 49 10N 0 12 E
Liski, Russia 47 G10 51 3N 39 30 E
L'Isle-Jourdain, Gers, France 20 E5 43 36N 1 5 E
L'Isle-Jourdain, Vienne, France 20 B4 46 13N 0 31 E
L'Isle-sur-la-Sorgue, France 21 E9 43 54N 5 2 E
Lisle-sur-Tarn, France 20 E5 43 52N 1 49 E
Lismore, Australia 95 D5 28 44 S 153 21 E
Lismore, Ireland 15 D4 52 8N 7 55W
Lista, Norway 9 G12 58 7N 6 39 E
Lister, Mt., Antarctica 5 D11 78 0 S 162 0 E
Liston, Australia 95 D5 28 39 S 152 6 E
Listowel, Canada 102 D3 43 44N 80 58W
Listowel, Ireland 15 D2 52 27N 9 29W
Lit, Sweden 10 A8 63 19N 14 51 E
Lit-et-Mixe, France 20 D2 44 2N 1 15W
Litang, Guangxi Zhuangzu, China 58 F7 23 12N 109 8 E
Litang, Sichuan, China 58 B3 30 1N 100 17 E
Litang Qu →, China 58 C3 28 4N 101 32 E
Litani →, Lebanon 75 B4 33 20N 35 15 E
Litchfield, Calif., U.S.A. 116 E6 40 24N 120 23W
Litchfield, Conn., U.S.A. 111 E11 41 45N 73 11W
Litchfield, Ill., U.S.A. 112 F10 39 11N 89 39W
Litchfield, Minn., U.S.A. 112 C7 45 8N 94 32W
Liteni, Romania 43 C11 47 32N 26 32 E
Lithgow, Australia 95 E5 33 25 S 150 8 E
Líthinon, Ákra, Greece 36 E6 34 55N 24 44 E
Lithuania ■, Europe 9 J20 55 30N 24 0 E
Litija, Slovenia 29 B11 46 3N 14 50 E
Lititz, U.S.A. 111 F8 40 9N 76 18W
Litókhoron, Greece 40 F6 40 8N 22 34 E
Litoměřice, Czech Rep. 26 A7 50 33N 14 10 E
Litomyšl, Czech Rep. 27 B9 49 52N 16 20 E
Litschau, Austria 26 C8 48 58N 15 4 E
Little Abaco I., Bahamas 120 A4 26 50N 77 30W
Little Barrier I., N.Z. 91 G5 36 12 S 175 8 E
Little Belt Mts., U.S.A. 114 C8 46 40N 110 45W
Little Blue →, U.S.A. 112 F6 39 42N 96 41W
Little Buffalo →, Canada 104 A6 61 0N 113 46W
Little Cayman, Cayman Is. 120 C3 19 41N 80 3W
Little Churchill →, Canada 105 B9 57 30N 95 22W
Little Colorado →, U.S.A. 115 H8 36 12N 111 48W
Little Current, Canada 102 C3 45 55N 82 0W
Little Current →, Canada 102 B3 50 57N 84 36W
Little Falls, Minn., U.S.A. 112 C7 45 59N 94 22W
Little Falls, N.Y., U.S.A. 111 C10 43 3N 74 51W
Little Fork →, U.S.A. 112 A8 48 31N 93 35W
Little Grand Rapids, Canada 105 C9 52 0N 95 29W
Little Humboldt →, U.S.A. 114 F5 41 1N 117 43W
Little Inagua I., Bahamas 121 B5 21 40N 73 50W
Little Karoo, S. Africa 88 E3 33 45 S 21 0 E
Little Lake, U.S.A. 117 K9 35 56N 117 55W
Little Laut Is. = Laut Kecil, Kepulauan, Indonesia 62 E5 4 45 S 115 40 E
Little Mecatina = Petit-Mécatina →, Canada 103 B8 50 40N 59 30W
Little Minch, U.K. 14 D2 57 35N 6 45W
Little Missouri →, U.S.A. 112 B3 47 36N 102 25W
Little Ouse →, U.K. 13 E9 52 22N 1 12 E
Little Rann, India 68 H4 23 25N 71 25 E
Little Red →, U.S.A. 113 H9 35 11N 91 27W
Little River, N.Z. 91 K4 43 45 S 172 49 E
Little Rock, U.S.A. 113 H8 34 45N 92 17W
Little Ruaha →, Tanzania 86 D4 7 57 S 37 53 E
Little Sable Pt., U.S.A. 108 D2 43 38N 86 33W
Little Scarcies →, S. Leone 82 D2 8 50N 13 10W
Little Sioux →, U.S.A. 112 E6 41 48N 96 4W
Little Smoky →, Canada 104 C5 54 44N 117 11W
Little Snake →, U.S.A. 114 F9 40 27N 108 26W
Little Valley, U.S.A. 110 D6 42 15N 78 48W
Little Wabash →, U.S.A. 108 G1 37 55N 88 5W
Little White →, U.S.A. 112 D4 43 40N 100 40W
Littlefield, U.S.A. 113 J3 33 55N 102 20W
Littlehampton, U.K. 13 G7 50 49N 0 32W
Littleton, U.S.A. 111 B13 44 18N 71 46W
Litvinov, Czech Rep. 26 A6 50 36N 13 37 E
Liu He →, China 57 D11 40 55N 121 35 E
Liu Jiang →, China 58 F7 23 55N 109 30 E
Liuba, China 56 H4 33 38N 106 55 E
Liucheng, China 58 E7 24 38N 109 14 E
Liugou, China 57 D10 40 57N 118 15 E
Liuhe, China 57 C13 42 17N 125 43 E
Liuheng Dao, China 59 C14 29 40N 122 5 E
Liujiang, China 58 E7 24 26N 109 11 E
Liukang Tenggaja = Sabalana, Kepulauan, Indonesia 63 F5 6 45 S 118 50 E
Liuli, Tanzania 87 E3 11 3 S 34 38 E
Liuwa Plain, Zambia 85 G4 14 20 S 22 30 E
Liuyang, China 59 C9 28 10N 113 37 E
Liuzhou, China 58 E7 24 22N 109 22 E
Liuzhuang, China 57 H11 33 12N 120 18 E
Livada, Romania 42 C8 47 52N 23 5 E
Livadherón, Greece 40 F5 40 2N 21 57 E
Livadhia, Cyprus 36 E12 34 57N 33 38 E
Livádhion, Greece 38 A4 40 8N 22 9 E
Livarot, France 18 D7 48 58N 0 9 E
Live Oak, Calif., U.S.A. 116 F5 39 17N 121 40W
Live Oak, Fla., U.S.A. 109 K4 30 18N 82 59W
Liveras, Cyprus 36 D11 35 23N 32 57 E
Livermore, U.S.A. 116 H5 37 41N 121 47W
Livermore, Mt., U.S.A. 113 K2 30 38N 104 11W
Livermore Falls, U.S.A. 109 C11 44 29N 70 11W
Liverpool, Canada 103 D7 44 5N 64 41W
Liverpool, U.K. 12 D4 53 25N 3 0W
Liverpool, U.S.A. 111 C8 43 6N 76 13W
Liverpool Bay, U.K. 12 D4 53 30N 3 20W
Liverpool Plains, Australia 95 E5 31 15 S 150 15 E
Liverpool Ra., Australia 95 E5 31 50 S 150 30 E
Livigno, Italy 28 B7 46 35N 10 10 E
Livingston, Guatemala 120 C2 15 50N 88 50W
Livingston, U.K. 14 F5 55 54N 3 30W
Livingston, Ala., U.S.A. 109 J1 32 35N 88 11W
Livingston, Calif., U.S.A. 116 H6 37 23N 120 43W
Livingston, Mont., U.S.A. 114 D8 45 40N 110 34W
Livingston, S.C., U.S.A. 109 J5 33 32N 80 53W
Livingston, Tenn., U.S.A. 109 G3 36 23N 85 19W
Livingston, Tex., U.S.A. 113 K7 30 43N 94 56W
Livingston, L., U.S.A. 113 K7 30 50N 95 10W
Livingston Manor, U.S.A. 111 E10 41 54N 74 50W
Livingstone, Zambia 87 F2 17 46 S 25 52 E
Livingstone Mts., Tanzania 87 D3 9 40 S 34 20 E
Livingstonia, Malawi 87 E3 10 38 S 34 5 E
Livno, Bos.-H. 42 G2 43 50N 17 1 E
Livny, Russia 47 F9 52 30N 37 30 E
Livonia, Mich., U.S.A. 108 D4 42 23N 83 23W
Livonia, N.Y., U.S.A. 110 D7 42 49N 77 40W
Livorno, Italy 28 E7 43 33N 10 19 E
Livramento, Brazil 127 C4 30 55 S 55 30W
Livron-sur-Drôme, France 21 D8 44 46N 4 51 E
Liwale, Tanzania 87 D4 9 48 S 37 58 E
Liwiec →, Poland 45 F8 52 36N 21 34 E
Lixi, China 58 D3 26 23N 101 59 E
Lixian, China 58 B4 31 23N 103 13 E
Lixoúrion, Greece 38 C2 38 14N 20 24 E
Liyang, China 59 B12 31 26N 119 28 E
Lizard I., Australia 94 A4 14 42 S 145 30 E
Lizard Pt., U.K. 13 H2 49 57N 5 13W
Lizzano, Italy 31 B10 40 23N 17 27 E
Ljig, Serbia, Yug. 40 B4 44 13N 20 18 E
Ljubija, Bos.-H. 29 D13 44 55N 16 35 E
Ljubinje, Bos.-H. 40 D2 42 58N 18 5 E
Ljubljana, Slovenia 29 B11 46 4N 14 33 E
Ljubno, Slovenia 29 B11 46 25N 14 46 E
Ljubovija, Serbia, Yug. 40 B3 44 11N 19 22 E
Ljugarn, Sweden 11 G12 57 20N 18 43 E
Ljung, Sweden 11 G7 57 59N 13 3 E
Ljungan →, Sweden 10 B11 62 18N 17 23 E
Ljungaverk, Sweden 10 B10 62 30N 16 5 E
Ljungby, Sweden 9 H15 56 49N 13 55 E
Ljungbyholm, Sweden 11 H10 56 39N 16 5 E
Ljungdalen, Sweden 10 B6 62 51N 12 47 E
Ljungsbro, Sweden 11 F9 58 31N 15 30 E
Ljungskile, Sweden 11 F5 58 14N 11 55 E
Ljusdal, Sweden 10 C10 61 46N 16 3 E
Ljusfallshammar, Sweden 11 F9 58 48N 15 30 E
Ljusnan →, Sweden 10 C11 61 12N 17 8 E
Ljusne, Sweden 10 C11 61 13N 17 7 E
Ljutomer, Slovenia 29 B13 46 31N 16 11 E
Llagostera, Spain 32 D7 41 50N 2 54 E
Llancanelo, Salina, Argentina 126 D2 35 40 S 69 8W
Llandeilo, U.K. 13 F4 51 53N 3 59W
Llandovery, U.K. 13 F4 51 59N 3 48W
Llandrindod Wells, U.K. 13 E4 52 14N 3 22W
Llandudno, U.K. 12 D4 53 19N 3 50W
Llanelli, U.K. 13 F3 51 41N 4 10W
Llanes, Spain 34 B6 43 25N 4 50W
Llangollen, U.K. 12 E4 52 58N 3 11W
Llanidloes, U.K. 13 E4 52 27N 3 31W
Llano, U.S.A. 113 K5 30 45N 98 41W
Llano →, U.S.A. 113 K5 30 39N 98 26W
Llano Estacado, U.S.A. 113 J3 33 30N 103 0W
Llanos, S. Amer. 122 C3 5 0N 71 35W
Llanquihue, L., Chile 128 E1 41 10 S 75 50W
Llanwrtyd Wells, U.K. 13 E4 52 7N 3 38W
Llebeig, C. des, Spain 37 B9 39 33N 2 18 E
Lleida, Spain 32 D5 41 37N 0 39 E
Lleida □, Spain 32 C6 42 6N 1 0 E
Llentrisca, C., Spain 37 C7 38 52N 1 15 E
Llera, Mexico 119 C5 23 19N 99 1W
Llerena, Spain 35 G5 38 17N 6 0W
Lleyn Peninsula, U.K. 12 E3 52 51N 4 36W
Llico, Chile 126 C1 34 46 S 72 5W
Llíria, Spain 33 F4 39 37N 0 35W
Llobregat →, Spain 32 D7 41 19N 2 9 E
Llodio, Spain 32 B2 43 9N 2 58W
Lloret de Mar, Spain 32 D7 41 41N 2 53 E
Lloyd B., Australia 94 A3 12 45 S 143 27 E
Lloyd L., Canada 105 B7 57 22N 108 57W
Lloydminster, Canada 105 C7 53 17N 110 0W
Llucena del Cid, Spain 32 E4 40 9N 0 17W
Llucmajor, Spain 37 B9 39 29N 2 53 E
Llullaillaco, Volcán, S. Amer. 126 A2 24 43 S 68 30W
Lo →, Vietnam 64 B5 21 18N 105 25 E
Loa, U.S.A. 115 G8 38 24N 111 39W
Loa →, Chile 126 A1 21 26 S 70 41W
Loaita I., S. China Sea 62 B4 10 41N 114 25 E
Loange →, Dem. Rep. of the Congo 84 E4 4 17 S 20 2 E
Loano, Italy 28 D5 44 8N 8 15 E
Lobatse, Botswana 88 D4 25 12 S 25 40 E
Löbau, Germany 24 D10 51 5N 14 40 E
Lobenstein, Germany 24 E7 50 25N 11 39 E
Lobería, Argentina 126 D4 38 10 S 58 40W
Löberöd, Sweden 11 J7 55 47N 13 31 E
Łobez, Poland 44 E2 53 38N 15 39 E
Lobito, Angola 85 G2 12 18 S 13 35 E
Lobo →, Ivory C. 82 D3 6 2N 6 45W
Lobos, Argentina 126 D4 35 10 S 59 0W
Lobos, I., Mexico 118 B2 27 15N 110 30W
Lobos, I. de, Canary Is. 37 F6 28 45N 13 50W
Łobżenica, Poland 45 E4 53 18N 17 15 E
Loc Binh, Vietnam 64 B6 21 46N 106 54 E
Loc Ninh, Vietnam 65 G6 11 50N 106 34 E
Locarno, Switz. 25 J4 46 10N 8 47 E
Loch Baghasdail = Lochboisdale, U.K. 14 D1 57 9N 7 20W
Loch Garman = Wexford, Ireland 15 D5 52 20N 6 28W
Loch Nam Madadh = Lochmaddy, U.K. 14 D1 57 36N 7 10W
Lochaber, U.K. 14 E3 56 59N 5 1W
Locharbriggs, U.K. 14 F5 55 7N 3 35W
Lochboisdale, U.K. 14 D1 57 9N 7 20W
Loche, L. La, Canada 105 B7 56 30N 109 30W
Lochem, Neths. 17 B6 52 9N 6 26 E
Loches, France 18 E7 47 7N 1 0 E
Lochgilphead, U.K. 14 E3 56 2N 5 26W
Lochinver, U.K. 14 C3 58 9N 5 14W
Lochmaddy, U.K. 14 D1 57 36N 7 10W
Lochnagar, Australia 94 C4 23 33 S 145 38 E
Lochnagar, U.K. 14 E5 56 57N 3 15W
Łochów, Poland 45 F8 52 33N 21 42 E
Lochy, L., U.K. 14 E4 57 0N 4 53W
Lock, Australia 95 E2 33 34 S 135 46 E
Lock Haven, U.S.A. 110 E7 41 8N 77 28W
Lockeford, U.S.A. 116 G5 38 10N 121 9W
Lockeport, Canada 103 D6 43 47N 65 4W
Lockerbie, U.K. 14 F5 55 7N 3 21W
Lockhart, Australia 95 F4 35 14 S 146 40 E
Lockhart, U.S.A. 113 L6 29 53N 97 40W
Lockhart, L., Australia 93 F2 33 15 S 119 3 E
Lockhart River, Australia 94 A3 12 58 S 143 30 E
Lockney, U.S.A. 113 H4 34 7N 101 27W
Lockport, U.S.A. 110 C6 43 10N 78 42W
Locminé, France 18 E4 47 54N 2 51W
Locri, Italy 31 D9 38 14N 16 16 E
Locronan, France 18 D2 48 7N 4 15W
Lod, Israel 75 D3 31 57N 34 54 E
Lodeinoye Pole, Russia 46 B7 60 44N 33 33 E
Lodève, France 20 E7 43 44N 3 19 E
Lodge Bay, Canada 103 B8 52 14N 55 51W
Lodge Grass, U.S.A. 114 D10 45 19N 107 22W
Lodgepole Cr. →, U.S.A. 112 E2 41 20N 104 30W
Lodhran, Pakistan 68 E4 29 32N 71 30 E
Lodi, Italy 28 C6 45 19N 9 30 E
Lodi, Calif., U.S.A. 116 G5 38 8N 121 16W
Lodi, Ohio, U.S.A. 110 E3 41 2N 82 1W
Lodja, Dem. Rep. of the Congo 86 C1 3 30 S 23 23 E
Lodosa, Spain 32 C2 42 25N 2 4W
Lödöse, Sweden 11 F6 58 2N 12 9 E
Lodwar, Kenya 86 B4 3 10N 35 40 E
Łódź, Poland 45 G6 51 45N 19 27 E
Łódzkie □, Poland 45 G6 51 30N 19 30 E
Loei, Thailand 64 D3 17 29N 101 35 E
Loengo, Dem. Rep. of the Congo 86 C2 4 48 S 26 30 E
Loeriesfontein, S. Africa 88 E2 31 0 S 19 26 E
Lofa →, Liberia 83 D2 6 35N 11 8W
Lofer, Austria 26 D5 47 35N 12 41 E
Lofoten, Norway 8 B15 68 30N 14 0 E
Lofsdalen, Sweden 10 B7 62 10N 13 20 E
Lofsen →, Sweden 10 B7 62 7N 13 57 E
Loftahammar, Sweden 11 G10 57 54N 16 41 E
Loga, Niger 83 C5 13 40N 3 15 E
Logan, Iowa, U.S.A. 112 E7 41 39N 95 47W

Logan, *Ohio, U.S.A.* **108 F4** 39 32N 82 25W
Logan, *Utah, U.S.A.* **114 F8** 41 44N 111 50W
Logan, *W. Va., U.S.A.* **108 G5** 37 51N 81 59W
Logan, Mt., *Canada* **100 B5** 60 31N 140 22W
Logandale, *U.S.A.* **117 J12** 36 36N 114 29W
Logansport, *Ind., U.S.A.* **108 E2** 40 45N 86 22W
Logansport, *La., U.S.A.* **113 K8** 31 58N 94 0W
Logirim, *Sudan* **81 G3** 4 43N 33 14 E
Logo, *Sudan* **81 F3** 5 20N 30 18 E
Logone →, *Chad* **79 F9** 12 6N 15 2 E
Logroño, *Spain* **32 C2** 42 28N 2 27W
Logrosán, *Spain* **35 F5** 39 20N 5 32W
Løgstør, *Denmark* **11 H3** 56 58N 9 14 E
Løgumkloster, *Denmark* **11 J2** 55 4N 8 57 E
Lohals, *Denmark* **11 J4** 55 8N 10 55 E
Lohardaga, *India* **69 H11** 23 27N 84 45 E
Loharia, *India* **68 H6** 23 45N 74 14 E
Loharu, *India* **68 E6** 28 27N 75 49 E
Lohja, *Finland* **9 F21** 60 12N 24 5 E
Löhne, *Germany* **24 C4** 52 11N 8 40 E
Lohr, *Germany* **25 F5** 49 59N 9 35 E
Lohri Wah →, *Pakistan* **68 F2** 27 27N 67 37 E
Loi-kaw, *Burma* **67 K20** 19 40N 97 17 E
Loimaa, *Finland* **9 F20** 60 50N 23 5 E
Loir →, *France* **18 E6** 47 33N 0 32W
Loir-et-Cher □, *France* **18 E8** 47 40N 1 20 E
Loire □, *France* **21 C8** 45 40N 4 5 E
Loire →, *France* **18 E4** 47 16N 2 10W
Loire-Atlantique □, *France* **18 E5** 47 25N 1 40W
Loiret □, *France* **19 E9** 47 55N 2 30 E
Loitz, *Germany* **24 B9** 53 58N 13 8 E
Loja, *Ecuador* **124 D3** 3 59 S 79 16W
Loja, *Spain* **35 H6** 37 10N 4 10W
Loji = Kawasi, *Indonesia* **63 E7** 1 38 S 127 28 E
Løjt Kirkeby, *Denmark* **11 J3** 55 7N 9 26 E
Lojung, *China* **58 E7** 24 27N 109 36 E
Loka, *Sudan* **81 G3** 4 13N 31 0 E
Lokandu, *Dem. Rep. of the Congo* **86 C2** 2 30 S 25 45 E
Lokeren, *Belgium* **17 C3** 51 6N 3 59 E
Lokgwabe, *Botswana* **88 C3** 24 10 S 21 50 E
Lokhvitsa, *Ukraine* **47 G7** 50 25N 33 18 E
Lokichokio, *Kenya* **86 B3** 4 19N 34 13 E
Lokitaung, *Kenya* **86 B4** 4 12N 35 48 E
Lokkan tekojärvi, *Finland* **8 C22** 67 55N 27 35 E
Løkken, *Denmark* **11 G3** 57 22N 9 41 E
Loknya, *Russia* **46 D6** 56 49N 30 4 E
Loko, *Nigeria* **83 D6** 8 1N 7 53 E
Lokoja, *Nigeria* **83 D6** 7 47N 6 45 E
Lokot, *Russia* **47 F8** 52 34N 34 36 E
Lol →, *Sudan* **81 F2** 9 13N 26 30 E
Lola, *Guinea* **82 D3** 7 52N 8 29W
Lola, Mt., *U.S.A.* **116 F6** 39 26N 120 22W
Lolibai, Gebel, *Sudan* **81 G3** 3 50N 33 0 E
Lolimi, *Sudan* **81 G3** 4 35N 34 0 E
Loliondo, *Tanzania* **86 C4** 2 2 S 35 39 E
Lolland, *Denmark* **11 K5** 54 45N 11 30 E
Lollar, *Germany* **24 E4** 50 37N 8 43 E
Lolo, *U.S.A.* **114 C6** 46 45N 114 5W
Lolodorf, *Cameroon* **83 E7** 3 16N 10 49 E
Lom, *Bulgaria* **40 C7** 43 48N 23 12 E
Lom →, *Bulgaria* **40 C7** 43 45N 23 15 E
Lom Kao, *Thailand* **64 D3** 16 53N 101 14 E
Lom Sak, *Thailand* **64 D3** 16 47N 101 15 E
Loma, *U.S.A.* **114 C8** 47 56N 110 30W
Loma Linda, *U.S.A.* **117 L9** 34 3N 117 16W
Lomami →, *Dem. Rep. of the Congo* **86 B1** 0 46N 24 16 E
Lomas de Zamóra, *Argentina* **126 C4** 34 45 S 58 25W
Lombadina, *Australia* **92 C3** 16 31 S 122 54 E
Lombárdia □, *Italy* **28 C6** 45 40N 9 30 E
Lombardy = Lombárdia □, *Italy* **28 C6** 45 40N 9 30 E
Lombez, *France* **20 E4** 43 29N 0 55 E
Lomblen, *Indonesia* **63 F6** 8 30 S 123 32 E
Lombok, *Indonesia* **62 F5** 8 45 S 116 30 E
Lomé, *Togo* **83 D5** 6 9N 1 20 E
Lomela, *Dem. Rep. of the Congo* **84 E4** 2 19 S 23 15 E
Lomela →, *Dem. Rep. of the Congo* **84 E4** 0 15 S 20 40 E
Lomianki, *Poland* **45 F7** 52 21N 20 54 E
Lomma, *Sweden* **11 J7** 55 43N 13 6 E
Lommel, *Belgium* **17 C5** 51 14N 5 19 E
Lomond, *Canada* **104 C6** 50 24N 112 36W
Lomond, L., *U.K.* **14 E4** 56 8N 4 38W
Lomphat, *Cambodia* **64 F6** 13 30N 106 59 E
Lompobatang, *Indonesia* **63 F5** 5 24 S 119 56 E
Lompoc, *U.S.A.* **117 L6** 34 38N 120 28W
Łomża, *Poland* **45 E9** 53 10N 22 2 E
Loncoche, *Chile* **128 D2** 39 20 S 72 50W
Londa, *India* **66 M9** 15 30N 74 30 E
Londiani, *Kenya* **86 C4** 0 10 S 35 33 E
Londinières, *France* **18 C8** 49 50N 1 25 E
London, *Canada* **102 D3** 42 59N 81 15W
London, *U.K.* **13 F7** 51 30N 0 3W
London, *Ky., U.S.A.* **108 G3** 37 8N 84 5W
London, *Ohio, U.S.A.* **108 F4** 39 53N 83 27W
London, Greater □, *U.K.* **13 F7** 51 36N 0 5W
Londonderry, *U.K.* **15 B4** 55 0N 7 20W
Londonderry □, *U.K.* **15 B4** 55 0N 7 20W
Londonderry, C., *Australia* **92 B4** 13 45 S 126 55 E
Londonderry, I., *Chile* **128 H2** 55 0 S 71 0W
Londres, *Argentina* **128 B3** 27 43 S 67 7W
Londrina, *Brazil* **127 A5** 23 18 S 51 10W
Lone Pine, *U.S.A.* **116 J8** 36 36N 118 4W
Lonely Mine, *Zimbabwe* **89 B4** 19 30 S 28 49 E
Long B., *U.S.A.* **109 J6** 33 35N 78 45W
Long Beach, *Calif., U.S.A.* **117 M8** 33 47N 118 11W
Long Beach, *N.Y., U.S.A.* **111 F11** 40 35N 73 39W
Long Beach, *Wash., U.S.A.* **116 D2** 46 21N 124 3W
Long Branch, *U.S.A.* **111 F11** 40 18N 74 0W
Long Creek, *U.S.A.* **114 D4** 44 43N 119 6W
Long Eaton, *U.K.* **12 E6** 52 53N 1 15W
Long I., *Australia* **94 C4** 22 8 S 149 53 E
Long I., *Bahamas* **121 B4** 23 20N 75 10W
Long I., *Canada* **102 B4** 54 50N 79 20W
Long I., *Ireland* **15 E2** 51 30N 9 34W
Long I., *U.S.A.* **111 F11** 40 45N 73 30W
Long Island Sd., *U.S.A.* **111 E12** 41 10N 73 0W
Long L., *Canada* **102 C2** 49 30N 86 50W
Long Lake, *U.S.A.* **111 C10** 43 58N 74 25W
Long Point B., *Canada* **110 D4** 42 40N 80 10W
Long Prairie →, *U.S.A.* **112 C7** 46 20N 94 36W
Long Pt., *Canada* **110 D4** 42 35N 80 2W
Long Range Mts., *Canada* **103 C8** 49 30N 57 30W
Long Reef, *Australia* **92 B4** 14 1 S 125 48 E
Long Spruce, *Canada* **105 B10** 56 24N 94 21W
Long Str. = Longa, Proliv, *Russia* **4 C16** 70 0N 175 0 E
Long Thanh, *Vietnam* **65 G6** 10 47N 106 57 E
Long Xian, *China* **56 G4** 34 55N 106 55 E
Long Xuyen, *Vietnam* **65 G5** 10 19N 105 28 E
Longá, *Greece* **38 E3** 36 53N 21 55 E
Longa, Proliv, *Russia* **4 C16** 70 0N 175 0 E
Long'an, *China* **58 F6** 23 10N 107 40 E
Longarone, *Italy* **29 B9** 46 16N 12 18 E
Longbenton, *U.K.* **12 B6** 55 1N 1 31W
Longboat Key, *U.S.A.* **109 M4** 27 23N 82 39W
Longchang, *China* **58 C5** 29 18N 105 15 E
Longchi, *China* **58 C4** 29 25N 103 24 E
Longchuan, *Guangdong, China* **59 E10** 24 5N 115 17 E
Longchuan, *Yunnan, China* **58 E1** 24 23N 97 58 E
Longde, *China* **56 G4** 35 30N 106 20 E
Longeau, *France* **19 E12** 47 47N 5 20 E
Longford, *Australia* **94 G4** 41 32 S 147 3 E
Longford, *Ireland* **15 C4** 53 43N 7 49W
Longford □, *Ireland* **15 C4** 53 42N 7 45W
Longhai, *China* **59 E11** 24 25N 117 46 E
Longhua, *China* **57 D9** 41 18N 117 45 E
Longhui, *China* **59 D8** 27 7N 111 2 E
Longido, *Tanzania* **86 C4** 2 43 S 36 42 E
Longiram, *Indonesia* **62 E5** 0 5 S 115 45 E
Longkou, *Jiangxi, China* **59 D10** 26 8N 115 10 E
Longkou, *Shandong, China* **57 F11** 37 40N 120 18 E
Longlac, *Canada* **102 C2** 49 45N 86 25W
Longli, *China* **58 D6** 26 25N 106 58 E
Longlin, *China* **58 E5** 24 47N 105 20 E
Longling, *China* **58 E2** 24 37N 98 39 E
Longmeadow, *U.S.A.* **111 D12** 42 3N 72 34W
Longmen, *China* **59 F10** 23 40N 114 18 E
Longming, *China* **58 F6** 22 59N 107 7 E
Longmont, *U.S.A.* **112 E2** 40 10N 105 6W
Longnan, *China* **59 E10** 24 55N 114 47 E
Longnawan, *Indonesia* **62 D4** 1 51N 114 55 E
Longobucco, *Italy* **31 C9** 39 27N 16 37 E
Longquan, *China* **59 C12** 28 7N 119 10 E
Longreach, *Australia* **94 C3** 23 28 S 144 14 E
Longshan, *China* **58 C7** 29 29N 109 25 E
Longsheng, *China* **59 E8** 25 48N 110 0 E
Longué-Jumelles, *France* **18 E6** 47 22N 0 8W
Longueau, *France* **19 C9** 49 52N 2 21 E
Longueuil, *Canada* **111 A11** 45 32N 73 28W
Longuyon, *France* **19 C12** 49 27N 5 35 E
Longvic, *France* **19 E12** 47 17N 5 4 E
Longview, *Tex., U.S.A.* **113 J7** 32 30N 94 44W
Longview, *Wash., U.S.A.* **116 D4** 46 8N 122 57W
Longwy, *France* **19 C12** 49 30N 5 46 E
Longxi, *China* **56 G3** 34 53N 104 40 E
Longyan, *China* **59 E11** 25 10N 117 0 E
Longyou, *China* **59 C12** 29 1N 119 8 E
Longzhou, *China* **58 F6** 22 22N 106 50 E
Lonigo, *Italy* **29 C8** 45 23N 11 23 E
Löningen, *Germany* **24 C3** 52 44N 7 46 E
Lonja →, *Croatia* **29 C13** 45 22N 16 40 E
Lonoke, *U.S.A.* **113 H9** 34 47N 91 54W
Lonquimay, *Chile* **128 D2** 38 26 S 71 14W
Lons-le-Saunier, *France* **19 F12** 46 40N 5 31 E
Lönsboda, *Sweden* **11 H8** 56 24N 14 20 E
Looe, *U.K.* **13 G3** 50 22N 4 28W
Lookout, C., *Canada* **102 A3** 55 18N 83 56W
Lookout, C., *U.S.A.* **109 H7** 34 35N 76 32W
Loolmalasin, *Tanzania* **86 C4** 3 0 S 35 53 E
Loon →, *Alta., Canada* **104 B5** 57 8N 115 3W
Loon →, *Man., Canada* **105 B8** 55 53N 101 59W
Loon Lake, *Canada* **105 C7** 54 2N 109 10W
Loongana, *Australia* **93 F4** 30 52 S 127 5 E
Loop Hd., *Ireland* **15 D2** 52 34N 9 56W
Lop Buri, *Thailand* **64 E3** 14 48N 100 37 E
Lop Nor = Lop Nur, *China* **60 B4** 40 20N 90 10 E
Lop Nur, *China* **60 B4** 40 20N 90 10 E
Lopare, *Bos.-H.* **42 F3** 44 39N 18 46 E
Lopatin, *Russia* **49 J8** 43 50N 47 35 E
Lopatina, Gora, *Russia* **51 D15** 50 47N 143 10 E
Lopaye, *Sudan* **81 F3** 6 37N 33 40 E
Lopez, *Phil.* **61 E5** 13 53N 122 15 E
Lopez, *U.S.A.* **111 E8** 41 27N 76 20W
Lopez, C., *Gabon* **84 E1** 0 47 S 8 40 E
Lopphavet, *Norway* **8 A19** 70 27N 21 15 E
Lora →, *Afghan.* **66 D4** 31 35N 65 50 E
Lora, Hāmūn-i-, *Pakistan* **66 E4** 29 38N 64 58 E
Lora Cr. →, *Australia* **95 D2** 28 10 S 135 22 E
Lora del Río, *Spain* **35 H5** 37 39N 5 33W
Lorain, *U.S.A.* **110 E2** 41 28N 82 11W
Loralai, *Pakistan* **68 D3** 30 20N 68 41 E
Lorca, *Spain* **33 H3** 37 41N 1 42W
Lord Howe I., *Pac. Oc.* **96 L7** 31 33 S 159 6 E
Lord Howe Ridge, *Pac. Oc.* **96 L8** 30 0 S 162 30 E
Lordsburg, *U.S.A.* **115 K9** 32 21N 108 43W
Lorestan □, *Iran* **71 C6** 33 30N 48 40 E
Loreto, *Brazil* **125 E9** 7 5 S 45 10W
Loreto, *Italy* **29 E10** 43 26N 13 36 E
Loreto, *Mexico* **118 B2** 26 1N 111 21W
Lorgues, *France* **21 E10** 43 28N 6 22 E
Lorhosso, *Burkina Faso* **82 C4** 10 17N 3 38W
Lorient, *France* **18 E3** 47 45N 3 23W
Lőrinci, *Hungary* **42 C4** 47 44N 19 41 E
Lormi, *India* **69 H9** 22 17N 81 41 E
Lorn, *U.K.* **14 E3** 56 26N 5 10W
Lorn, Firth of, *U.K.* **14 E3** 56 20N 5 40W
Lorne, *Australia* **95 F3** 38 33 S 143 59 E
Loronyo, *Sudan* **81 G3** 4 38N 32 38 E
Lorovouno, *Cyprus* **36 D11** 35 8N 32 36 E
Lörrach, *Germany* **25 H3** 47 36N 7 40 E
Lorraine □, *France* **19 D13** 48 53N 6 0 E
Los, *Sweden* **10 C9** 61 45N 15 10 E
Los, Îles de, *Guinea* **82 D2** 9 30N 13 50W
Los Alamos, *Calif., U.S.A.* **117 L6** 34 44N 120 17W
Los Alamos, *N. Mex., U.S.A.* **115 J10** 35 53N 106 19W
Los Altos, *U.S.A.* **116 H4** 37 23N 122 7W
Los Andes, *Chile* **126 C1** 32 50 S 70 40W
Los Angeles, *Chile* **126 D1** 37 28 S 72 23W
Los Angeles, *U.S.A.* **117 M8** 34 4N 118 15W
Los Angeles, Bahia de, *Mexico* **118 B2** 28 56N 113 34W
Los Angeles Aqueduct, *U.S.A.* **117 K9** 35 22N 118 5W
Los Banos, *U.S.A.* **116 H6** 37 4N 120 51W
Los Barrios, *Spain* **35 J5** 36 11N 5 30W
Los Blancos, *Argentina* **126 A3** 23 40 S 62 30W
Los Chiles, *Costa Rica* **120 D3** 11 2N 84 43W
Los Corrales de Buelna, *Spain* **34 B6** 43 16N 4 4W
Los Cristianos, *Canary Is.* **37 F3** 28 3N 16 42W
Los Gallardos, *Spain* **33 H3** 37 10N 1 57W
Los Gatos, *U.S.A.* **116 H5** 37 14N 121 59W
Los Hermanos Is., *Venezuela* **121 D7** 11 45N 64 25W
Los Islotes, *Canary Is.* **37 E6** 29 4N 13 44W
Los Llanos de Aridane, *Canary Is.* **37 F2** 28 38N 17 54W
Los Loros, *Chile* **126 B1** 27 50 S 70 6W
Los Lunas, *U.S.A.* **115 J10** 34 48N 106 44W
Los Mochis, *Mexico* **118 B3** 25 45N 108 57W
Los Monegros, *Spain* **32 D4** 41 29N 0 13W
Los Nietos, *Spain* **33 H4** 37 39N 0 47W
Los Olivos, *U.S.A.* **117 L6** 34 40N 120 7W
Los Palacios, *Cuba* **120 B3** 22 35N 83 15W
Los Palacios y Villafranca, *Spain* **35 H5** 37 10N 5 55W
Los Reyes, *Mexico* **118 D4** 19 34N 102 30W
Los Roques Is., *Venezuela* **121 D6** 11 50N 66 45W
Los Santos de Maimona, *Spain* **35 G4** 38 27N 6 22W
Los Teques, *Venezuela* **124 A5** 10 21N 67 2W
Los Testigos, Is., *Venezuela* **124 A6** 11 23N 63 6W
Los Vilos, *Chile* **126 C1** 32 10 S 71 30W
Los Yébenes, *Spain* **35 F7** 39 36N 3 55W
Łosice, *Poland* **45 F9** 52 13N 22 43 E
Loskop Dam, *S. Africa* **89 D4** 25 23 S 29 20 E
Løsning, *Denmark* **11 J3** 55 48N 9 42 E
Lossiemouth, *U.K.* **14 D5** 57 42N 3 17W
Lostwithiel, *U.K.* **13 G3** 50 24N 4 41W
Lot □, *France* **20 D5** 44 39N 1 40 E
Lot →, *France* **20 D4** 44 18N 0 20 E
Lot-et-Garonne □, *France* **20 D4** 44 22N 0 30 E
Lota, *Chile* **126 D1** 37 5 S 73 10W
Lotagipi Swamp, *Sudan* **81 G3** 4 36N 34 55 E
Loṭfābād, *Iran* **71 B8** 37 32N 59 20 E
Lothair, *S. Africa* **89 D5** 26 22 S 30 27 E
Lotorp, *Sweden* **11 F9** 58 44N 15 50 E
Lötschbergtunnel, *Switz.* **25 J3** 46 26N 7 43 E
Löttorp, *Sweden* **11 G11** 57 10N 17 0 E
Lotung, *Taiwan* **59 E13** 24 41N 121 46 E
Loubomo, *Congo* **84 E2** 4 9 S 12 47 E
Loudéac, *France* **18 D4** 48 11N 2 47W
Loudi, *China* **59 D8** 27 42N 111 59 E
Loudonville, *U.S.A.* **110 F2** 40 38N 82 14W
Loudun, *France* **18 E7** 47 3N 0 5 E
Loue →, *France* **19 E12** 47 1N 5 28 E
Louga, *Senegal* **82 B1** 15 45N 16 5W
Loughborough, *U.K.* **12 E6** 52 47N 1 11W
Loughrea, *Ireland* **15 C3** 53 12N 8 33W
Loughros More B., *Ireland* **15 B3** 54 48N 8 32W
Louhans, *France* **19 F12** 46 38N 5 12 E
Louis Trichardt, *S. Africa* **89 C4** 23 1 S 29 43 E
Louis XIV, Pte., *Canada* **102 B4** 54 37N 79 45W
Louisa, *U.S.A.* **108 F4** 38 7N 82 36W
Louisbourg, *Canada* **103 C8** 45 55N 60 0W
Louise I., *Canada* **104 C2** 52 55N 131 50W
Louiseville, *Canada* **102 C5** 46 20N 72 56W
Louisiade Arch., *Papua N. G.* **96 J7** 11 10 S 153 0 E
Louisiana, *U.S.A.* **112 F9** 39 27N 91 3W
Louisiana □, *U.S.A.* **113 K9** 30 50N 92 0W
Louisville, *Ky., U.S.A.* **108 F3** 38 15N 85 46W
Louisville, *Miss., U.S.A.* **113 J10** 33 7N 89 3W
Louisville, *Ohio, U.S.A.* **110 F3** 40 50N 81 16W
Loulay, *France* **20 B3** 46 3N 0 30W
Loulé, *Portugal* **35 H3** 37 9N 8 0W
Louny, *Czech Rep.* **26 A6** 50 20N 13 48 E
Loup City, *U.S.A.* **112 E5** 41 17N 98 58W
Loups Marins, Lacs des, *Canada* **102 A5** 56 30N 73 45W
Lourdes, *France* **20 E3** 43 6N 0 3W
Lourenço-Marques = Maputo, *Mozam.* **89 D5** 25 58 S 32 32 E
Lourinhã, *Portugal* **35 F1** 39 14N 9 17W
Lousã, *Portugal* **34 E2** 40 7N 8 14W
Louta, *Burkina Faso* **82 C4** 13 30N 3 10W
Louth, *Australia* **95 E4** 30 30 S 145 8 E
Louth, *Ireland* **15 C5** 53 58N 6 32W
Louth, *U.K.* **12 D7** 53 22N 0 1W
Louth □, *Ireland* **15 C5** 53 56N 6 34W
Loutrá Aidhipsoú, *Greece* **38 C5** 38 54N 23 2 E
Loutráki, *Greece* **38 D4** 37 58N 22 57 E
Louvain = Leuven, *Belgium* **17 D4** 50 52N 4 42 E
Louviers, *France* **18 C8** 49 12N 1 10 E
Louwsburg, *S. Africa* **89 D5** 27 37 S 31 7 E
Lovat →, *Russia* **46 C6** 58 14N 31 28 E
Lovćen, *Montenegro, Yug.* **40 D2** 42 23N 18 51 E
Lovech, *Bulgaria* **41 C8** 43 8N 24 42 E
Lovech □, *Bulgaria* **41 C8** 43 15N 24 55 E
Loveland, *U.S.A.* **112 E2** 40 24N 105 5W
Lovell, *U.S.A.* **114 D9** 44 50N 108 24W
Lovelock, *U.S.A.* **114 F4** 40 11N 118 28W
Lóvere, *Italy* **28 C7** 45 49N 10 4 E
Lövestad, *Sweden* **11 J7** 55 40N 13 53 E
Loviisa, *Finland* **9 F22** 60 28N 26 12 E
Loving, *U.S.A.* **113 J2** 32 17N 104 6W
Lovington, *U.S.A.* **113 J3** 32 57N 103 21W
Lovisa = Loviisa, *Finland* **9 F22** 60 28N 26 12 E
Lovosice, *Czech Rep.* **26 A7** 50 30N 14 2 E
Lovran, *Croatia* **29 C11** 45 18N 14 15 E
Lovrin, *Romania* **42 E5** 45 58N 20 48 E
Lövstabruk, *Sweden* **10 D11** 60 25N 17 53 E
Lövstabukten, *Sweden* **10 D11** 60 35N 17 45 E
Low, L., *Canada* **102 B4** 52 29N 76 17W
Low Pt., *Australia* **93 F4** 32 25 S 127 25 E
Low Tatra = Nízké Tatry, *Slovak Rep.* **27 C12** 48 55N 19 30 E
Lowa, *Dem. Rep. of the Congo* **86 C2** 1 25 S 25 47 E
Lowa →, *Dem. Rep. of the Congo* **86 C2** 1 24 S 25 51 E
Lowell, *U.S.A.* **111 D13** 42 38N 71 19W
Lowellville, *U.S.A.* **110 E4** 41 2N 80 32W
Löwen →, *Namibia* **88 D2** 26 51 S 18 17 E
Lower Alkali L., *U.S.A.* **114 F3** 41 16N 120 2W
Lower Arrow L., *Canada* **104 D5** 49 40N 118 5W
Lower Austria = Niederösterreich □, *Austria* **26 C8** 48 25N 15 40 E
Lower California = Baja California, *Mexico* **118 A1** 31 10N 115 12W
Lower Hutt, *N.Z.* **91 J5** 41 10 S 174 55 E
Lower Lake, *U.S.A.* **116 G4** 38 55N 122 37W
Lower Manitou L., *Canada* **105 D10** 49 15N 93 0W
Lower Post, *Canada* **104 B3** 59 58N 128 30W
Lower Red L., *U.S.A.* **112 B7** 47 58N 95 0W
Lower Saxony = Niedersachsen □, *Germany* **24 C4** 52 50N 9 0 E
Lower Tunguska = Tunguska, Nizhnyaya →, *Russia* **51 C9** 65 48N 88 4 E
Lowestoft, *U.K.* **13 E9** 52 29N 1 45 E
Łowicz, *Poland* **45 F6** 52 6N 19 55 E
Lowville, *U.S.A.* **111 C9** 43 47N 75 29W
Loxton, *Australia* **95 E3** 34 28 S 140 31 E
Loxton, *S. Africa* **88 E3** 31 30 S 22 22 E
Loyalton, *U.S.A.* **116 F6** 39 41N 120 14W
Loyalty Is. = Loyauté, Is., *N. Cal.* **96 K8** 20 50 S 166 30 E
Loyang = Luoyang, *China* **56 G7** 34 40N 112 26 E
Loyauté, Is., *N. Cal.* **96 K8** 20 50 S 166 30 E
Loyev = Loyew, *Belarus* **47 G6** 51 56N 30 46 E
Loyew, *Belarus* **47 G6** 51 56N 30 46 E
Loyoro, *Uganda* **86 B3** 3 22N 34 14 E
Lož, *Slovenia* **29 C11** 45 43N 14 30 E
Lozère □, *France* **20 D7** 44 35N 3 30 E
Loznica, *Serbia, Yug.* **40 B3** 44 32N 19 12 E
Lozova, *Ukraine* **47 H9** 49 0N 36 20 E
Lü Shan, *China* **59 C11** 29 30N 115 55 E
Lü-Tao, *Taiwan* **59 F13** 22 40N 121 30 E
Luachimo, *Angola* **84 F4** 7 23 S 20 48 E
Luajan →, *India* **69 G11** 24 44N 85 1 E
Lualaba →, *Dem. Rep. of the Congo* **86 B2** 0 26N 25 20 E
Luampa, *Zambia* **87 F1** 15 4 S 24 20 E
Lu'an, *China* **59 B11** 31 45N 116 29 E
Luan Chau, *Vietnam* **58 G4** 21 38N 103 24 E
Luan He →, *China* **57 E10** 39 20N 119 5 E
Luan Xian, *China* **57 E10** 39 40N 118 40 E
Luancheng, *Guangxi Zhuangzu, China* **58 F7** 22 48N 108 55 E
Luancheng, *Hebei, China* **56 F8** 37 53N 114 40 E
Luanco, *Spain* **34 B5** 43 37N 5 48W
Luanda, *Angola* **84 F2** 8 50 S 13 15 E
Luang, Thale, *Thailand* **65 J3** 7 30N 100 15 E
Luang Prabang, *Laos* **58 H4** 19 52N 102 10 E
Luangwa, *Zambia* **87 F3** 15 35 S 30 16 E
Luangwa →, *Zambia* **87 E3** 14 25 S 30 25 E
Luangwa Valley, *Zambia* **87 E3** 13 30 S 31 30 E
Luanne, *China* **57 D9** 40 55N 117 40 E
Luanping, *China* **57 D9** 40 53N 117 23 E
Luanshya, *Zambia* **87 E2** 13 3 S 28 28 E
Luapula □, *Zambia* **87 E2** 11 0 S 29 0 E
Luapula →, *Africa* **87 D2** 9 26 S 28 33 E
Luarca, *Spain* **34 B4** 43 32N 6 32W
Luashi, *Dem. Rep. of the Congo* **87 E1** 10 50 S 23 36 E
Luau, *Angola* **84 G4** 10 40 S 22 10 E
Lubaczów, *Poland* **45 H10** 50 10N 23 8 E
Lubań, *Poland* **45 G2** 51 5N 15 15 E
Lubana, Ozero = Lubānas Ezers, *Latvia* **9 H22** 56 45N 27 0 E
Lubānas Ezers, *Latvia* **9 H22** 56 45N 27 0 E
Lubang, *Phil.* **61 E4** 13 52N 120 7 E
Lubang Is., *Phil.* **63 B6** 13 50N 120 12 E
Lubartów, *Poland* **45 G9** 51 28N 22 42 E
Lubawa, *Poland* **44 E6** 53 30N 19 48 E
Lübbecke, *Germany* **24 C4** 52 18N 8 37 E
Lübben, *Germany* **24 D9** 51 56N 13 54 E
Lübbenau, *Germany* **24 D9** 51 52N 13 57 E
Lubbock, *U.S.A.* **113 J4** 33 35N 101 51W
Lübeck, *Germany* **24 B6** 53 52N 10 40 E
Lübecker Bucht, *Germany* **24 A6** 54 3N 10 54 E
Lubefu, *Dem. Rep. of the Congo* **86 C1** 4 47 S 24 27 E
Lubefu →, *Dem. Rep. of the Congo* **86 C1** 4 10 S 23 0 E
Lubelskie □, *Poland* **45 G9** 51 20N 22 50 E
Lubero = Luofu, *Dem. Rep. of the Congo* **86 C2** 0 10 S 29 15 E
Lubersac, *France* **20 C5** 45 26N 1 23 E
Lubicon L., *Canada* **104 B5** 56 23N 115 56W
Lubień Kujawski, *Poland* **45 F6** 52 23N 19 9 E
Lubilash →, *Dem. Rep. of the Congo* **84 F4** 6 2 S 23 45 E
Lubin, *Poland* **45 G3** 51 24N 16 11 E
Lublin, *Poland* **45 G9** 51 12N 22 38 E
Lubliniec, *Poland* **45 H5** 50 43N 18 45 E
Lubnān, Jabal, *Lebanon* **75 B4** 33 45N 35 40 E
Lubniewice, *Poland* **45 F2** 52 31N 15 15 E
Lubny, *Ukraine* **47 G7** 50 3N 32 58 E
Lubomierz, *Poland* **45 G2** 51 1N 15 31 E
Luboń, *Poland* **45 F3** 52 21N 16 51 E
Lubongola, *Dem. Rep. of the Congo* **86 C2** 2 35 S 27 50 E
L'ubotín, *Slovak Rep.* **27 B13** 49 17N 20 53 E
Lubraniec, *Poland* **45 F5** 52 33N 18 50 E
Lubsko, *Poland* **45 G1** 51 45N 14 57 E
Lübtheen, *Germany* **24 B7** 53 18N 11 5 E
Lubuagan, *Phil.* **61 C4** 17 21N 121 10 E
Lubudi, *Dem. Rep. of the Congo* **84 F5** 9 57 S 25 58 E
Lubudi →, *Dem. Rep. of the Congo* **87 D2** 9 0 S 25 35 E
Lubuklinggau, *Indonesia* **62 E2** 3 15 S 102 55 E
Lubuksikaping, *Indonesia* **62 D2** 0 10N 100 15 E
Lubumbashi, *Dem. Rep. of the Congo* **87 E2** 11 40 S 27 28 E
Lubunda, *Dem. Rep. of the Congo* **86 D2** 5 12 S 26 41 E
Lubungu, *Zambia* **87 E2** 14 35 S 26 24 E
Lubuskie □, *Poland* **45 F2** 52 10N 15 20 E
Lubutu, *Dem. Rep. of the Congo* **86 C2** 0 45 S 26 30 E
Luc An Chau, *Vietnam* **64 A5** 22 6N 104 43 E
Luc-en-Diois, *France* **21 D9** 44 36N 5 28 E
Lucan, *Canada* **110 C3** 43 11N 81 24W
Lucania, Mt., *Canada* **100 B5** 61 1N 140 29W
Lucas Channel, *Canada* **110 A3** 45 21N 81 45W
Lucban, *Phil.* **61 D4** 14 6N 121 33 E
Lucca, *Italy* **28 E7** 43 50N 10 29 E
Lucé, *France* **18 D8** 48 26N 1 27 E
Luce Bay, *U.K.* **14 G4** 54 45N 4 48W
Lucea, *Jamaica* **120 C4** 18 25N 78 10W
Lucedale, *U.S.A.* **109 K1** 30 56N 88 35W
Lucena, *Phil.* **61 E4** 13 56N 121 37 E
Lucena, *Spain* **35 H6** 37 27N 4 31W
Lučenec, *Slovak Rep.* **27 C12** 48 18N 19 42 E
Lucera, *Italy* **31 A8** 41 30N 15 20 E
Lucerne = Luzern, *Switz.* **25 H4** 47 3N 8 18 E
Lucerne, *U.S.A.* **116 F4** 39 6N 122 48W
Lucerne Valley, *U.S.A.* **117 L10** 34 27N 116 57W
Lucero, *Mexico* **118 A3** 30 49N 106 30W
Luchena →, *Spain* **33 H3** 37 44N 1 50W
Lucheng, *China* **56 F7** 36 20N 113 11 E
Lucheringo →, *Mozam.* **87 E4** 11 43 S 36 17 E
Lüchow, *Germany* **24 C7** 52 58N 11 8 E
Luchuan, *China* **59 F8** 22 21N 110 12 E
Lucia, *U.S.A.* **116 J5** 36 2N 121 33W
Lucinda, *Australia* **94 B4** 18 32 S 146 20 E
Lucindale, *Australia* **95 F3** 36 58 S 140 26 E
Luckau, *Germany* **24 D9** 51 50N 13 42 E
Luckenwalde, *Germany* **24 C9** 52 5N 13 10 E
Luckhoff, *S. Africa* **88 D3** 29 44 S 24 43 E
Lucknow, *Canada* **110 C3** 43 57N 81 31W
Lucknow, *India* **69 F9** 26 50N 81 0 E
Luçon, *France* **20 B2** 46 28N 1 10W
Lüda = Dalian, *China* **57 E11** 38 50N 121 40 E
Luda Kamchiya →, *Bulgaria* **41 C11** 43 3N 27 29 E
Ludbreg, *Croatia* **29 B13** 46 15N 16 38 E
Lüdenscheid, *Germany* **24 D3** 51 13N 7 37 E
Lüderitz, *Namibia* **88 D2** 26 41 S 15 8 E
Lüderitzbaai, *Namibia* **88 D2** 26 36 S 15 8 E
Ludhiana, *India* **68 D6** 30 57N 75 56 E
Ludian, *China* **58 D4** 27 10N 103 33 E
Luding Qiao, *China* **58 C4** 29 53N 102 12 E
Lüdinghausen, *Germany* **24 D3** 51 46N 7 27 E
Ludington, *U.S.A.* **108 D2** 43 57N 86 27W
Ludlow, *U.K.* **13 E5** 52 22N 2 42W
Ludlow, *Calif., U.S.A.* **117 L10** 34 43N 116 10W
Ludlow, *Pa., U.S.A.* **110 E6** 41 43N 78 56W
Ludlow, *Vt., U.S.A.* **111 C12** 43 24N 72 42W
Ludus, *Romania* **43 D9** 46 29N 24 5 E
Ludvika, *Sweden* **10 D9** 60 8N 15 14 E
Ludwigsburg, *Germany* **25 G5** 48 53N 9 11 E
Ludwigsfelde, *Germany* **24 C9** 52 17N 13 17 E
Ludwigshafen, *Germany* **25 F4** 49 29N 8 26 E
Ludwigslust, *Germany* **24 B7** 53 19N 11 30 E
Ludza, *Latvia* **46 D4** 56 32N 27 43 E
Lueki, *Dem. Rep. of the Congo* **86 C2** 3 20 S 25 48 E
Luena, *Dem. Rep. of the Congo* **87 D2** 9 28 S 25 43 E
Luena, *Zambia* **87 E3** 10 40 S 30 25 E
Lüeyang, *China* **56 H4** 33 22N 106 10 E
Lufeng, *Guangdong, China* **59 F10** 22 57N 115 38 E
Lufeng, *Yunnan, China* **58 E4** 25 0N 102 5 E
Lufira →, *Dem. Rep. of the Congo* **87 D2** 9 30 S 27 0 E
Lufkin, *U.S.A.* **113 K7** 31 21N 94 44W
Lufupa, *Dem. Rep. of the Congo* **87 E1** 10 37 S 24 56 E
Luga, *Russia* **46 C5** 58 40N 29 55 E
Luga →, *Russia* **46 C5** 59 40N 28 18 E
Lugano, *Switz.* **25 J4** 46 1N 8 57 E
Lugano, L. di, *Switz.* **28 C6** 46 0N 9 0 E
Lugansk = Luhansk, *Ukraine* **47 H10** 48 38N 39 15 E
Lugard's Falls, *Kenya* **86 C4** 3 6 S 38 41 E
Lugela, *Mozam.* **87 F4** 16 25 S 36 43 E
Lugenda →, *Mozam.* **87 E4** 11 25 S 38 33 E
Lugh Ganana, *Somali Rep.* **74 G3** 3 48N 42 34 E
Lugnaquilla, *Ireland* **15 D5** 52 58N 6 28W
Lugo, *Italy* **29 D8** 44 25N 11 54 E
Lugo, *Spain* **34 B3** 43 2N 7 35W
Lugo □, *Spain* **34 C3** 43 0N 7 30W
Lugoj, *Romania* **42 E6** 45 42N 21 57 E
Lugovoy, *Kazakstan* **50 E8** 42 55N 72 43 E
Luhansk, *Ukraine* **47 H10** 48 38N 39 15 E
Luhe, *China* **59 A12** 32 19N 118 50 E
Luhe →, *Germany* **24 B6** 53 23N 10 13 E
Luhuo, *China* **58 B3** 31 21N 100 48 E
Luiana, *Angola* **88 B3** 17 25 S 22 59 E
Luimneach = Limerick, *Ireland* **15 D3** 52 40N 8 37W
Luing, *U.K.* **14 E3** 56 14N 5 39W
Luino, *Italy* **28 C5** 45 59N 8 44 E
Luís Correia, *Brazil* **125 D10** 3 0 S 41 35W
Luitpold Coast, *Antarctica* **5 D1** 78 30 S 32 0W
Luiza, *Dem. Rep. of the Congo* **84 F4** 7 40 S 22 30 E
Luizi, *Dem. Rep. of the Congo* **86 D2** 6 0 S 27 25 E
Luján, *Argentina* **126 C4** 34 45 S 59 5W
Lujiang, *China* **59 B11** 31 20N 117 15 E
Lukang, *Taiwan* **59 E13** 24 1N 120 22 E
Lukanga Swamp, *Zambia* **87 E2** 14 30 S 27 40 E
Lukavac, *Bos.-H.* **42 F3** 44 33N 18 32 E
Lukenie →, *Dem. Rep. of the Congo* **84 E3** 3 0 S 18 50 E
Lukhisaral, *India* **69 G12** 25 11N 86 5 E
Lŭki, *Bulgaria* **41 E8** 41 50N 24 43 E
Lukolela, *Dem. Rep. of the Congo* **86 D1** 5 23 S 24 32 E
Lukosi, *Zimbabwe* **87 F2** 18 30 S 26 30 E
Lukovë, *Albania* **40 G3** 39 59N 19 54 E
Lukovit, *Bulgaria* **41 C8** 43 13N 24 11 E
Łuków, *Poland* **45 G9** 51 55N 22 23 E
Lukoyanov, *Russia* **48 C7** 55 2N 44 29 E
Lule älv →, *Sweden* **8 D19** 65 35N 22 10 E
Luleå, *Sweden* **8 D20** 65 35N 22 10 E
Lüleburgaz, *Turkey* **41 E11** 41 23N 27 22 E
Luliang, *China* **58 E4** 25 0N 103 40 E
Luling, *U.S.A.* **113 L6** 29 41N 97 39W
Lulong, *China* **57 E10** 39 53N 118 51 E
Lulonga →, *Dem. Rep. of the Congo* **84 D3** 1 0N 18 10 E

Lulua →, Dem. Rep. of the Congo 84 E4 4 30 S 20 30 E
Luluabourg = Kananga, Dem. Rep. of the Congo 84 F4 5 55 S 22 18 E
Lumajang, Indonesia 63 H15 8 8 S 113 13 E
Lumbala N'guimbo, Angola 85 G4 14 18 S 21 18 E
Lumberton, U.S.A. 109 H6 34 37N 79 0W
Lumbwa, Kenya 86 C4 0 12 S 35 28 E
Lumsden, Canada 105 C8 50 39N 104 52W
Lumsden, N.Z. 91 L2 45 44 S 168 27 E
Lumut, Malaysia 65 K3 4 13N 100 37 E
Lumut, Tanjung, Indonesia 62 E3 3 50 S 105 58 E
Luna, India 68 H3 23 43N 69 16 E
Lunan, China 58 E4 24 40N 103 18 E
Lunavada, India 68 H5 23 8N 73 37 E
Lunca, Romania 43 C10 47 22N 25 1 E
Lunca Corbului, Romania 43 F9 44 42N 24 45 E
Lund, Sweden 11 J7 55 44N 13 12 E
Lundazi, Zambia 87 E3 12 20 S 33 7 E
Lunderskov, Denmark 11 J3 55 29N 9 19 E
Lundi →, Zimbabwe 87 G3 21 43 S 32 34 E
Lundu, Malaysia 62 D3 1 40N 109 50 E
Lundy, U.K. 13 F3 51 10N 4 41W
Lune →, U.K. 12 C5 54 0N 2 51W
Lüneburg, Germany 24 B6 53 15N 10 24 E
Lüneburg Heath = Lüneburger Heide, Germany 24 B6 53 10N 10 12 E
Lüneburger Heide, Germany 24 B6 53 10N 10 12 E
Lunel, France 21 E8 43 39N 4 9 E
Lünen, Germany 24 D3 51 37N 7 32 E
Lunenburg, Canada 103 D7 44 22N 64 18W
Lunéville, France 19 D13 48 36N 6 30 E
Lunga →, Zambia 87 E2 14 34 S 26 25 E
Lungi Airport, S. Leone 82 D2 8 40N 13 17W
Lunglei, India 67 H18 22 55N 92 45 E
Luni, India 68 G5 26 0N 73 6 E
Luni →, India 68 G4 24 41N 71 14 E
Luninets = Luninyets, Belarus 47 F4 52 15N 26 50 E
Luning, U.S.A. 114 G4 38 30N 118 11W
Lunino, Russia 48 D7 53 38N 45 18 E
Luninyets, Belarus 47 F4 52 15N 26 50 E
Lunkaransar, India 68 E5 28 29N 73 44 E
Lunsemfwa →, Zambia 87 E3 14 54 S 30 12 E
Lunsemfwa Falls, Zambia 87 E2 14 30 S 29 6 E
Luo He →, China 56 G6 34 35N 110 20 E
Luocheng, China 58 E7 24 48N 108 53 E
Luochuan, China 56 G5 35 45N 109 26 E
Luoci, China 58 E4 25 19N 102 18 E
Luodian, China 58 E6 25 24N 106 43 E
Luoding, China 59 F8 22 45N 111 40 E
Luofu, Dem. Rep. of the Congo 86 C2 0 10 S 29 15 E
Luohe, China 56 H8 33 32N 114 2 E
Luojiang, China 58 B5 31 18N 104 33 E
Luonan, China 56 G6 34 5N 110 10 E
Luoning, China 56 G6 34 35N 111 40 E
Luoshan, China 59 A10 32 13N 114 30 E
Luotian, China 59 B10 30 46N 115 22 E
Luoxiao Shan, China 59 D10 26 30N 114 1 E
Luoyang, China 56 G7 34 40N 112 26 E
Luoyuan, China 59 D12 26 28N 119 30 E
Luozigou, China 57 C16 43 42N 130 18 E
Lupanshui, China 58 D5 26 38N 104 48 E
Lupeni, Romania 43 E8 45 21N 23 13 E
Lupilichi, Mozam. 87 E4 11 47 S 35 13 E
Łupków, Poland 45 J9 49 15N 22 4 E
Lupoing, China 58 E5 24 53N 104 21 E
Luquan, China 58 E4 25 35N 102 25 E
Luque, Paraguay 126 B4 25 19 S 57 25W
Lúras, Italy 30 B2 40 56N 9 10 E
Luray, U.S.A. 108 F6 38 40N 78 28W
Lure, France 19 E13 47 40N 6 30 E
Lurgan, U.K. 15 B5 54 28N 6 19W
Lusaka, Zambia 87 F2 15 28 S 28 16 E
Lusambo, Dem. Rep. of the Congo 86 C1 4 58 S 23 28 E
Lusangaye, Dem. Rep. of the Congo 86 C2 4 54 S 26 0 E
Luseland, Canada 105 C7 52 5N 109 24W
Lushan, Henan, China 56 H7 33 45N 112 55 E
Lushan, Sichuan, China 58 B4 30 12N 102 52 E
Lushi, China 56 G6 34 3N 111 3 E
Lushnja = Lushnjë, Albania 40 F3 40 55N 19 41 E
Lushnjë, Albania 40 F3 40 55N 19 41 E
Lushoto, Tanzania 86 C4 4 47 S 38 20 E
Lushui, China 58 E2 25 58N 98 44 E
Lüshun, China 57 E11 38 45N 121 15 E
Lusignan, France 20 B4 46 26N 0 8 E
Lusigny-sur-Barse, France 19 D11 48 16N 4 15 E
Lusk, U.S.A. 112 D2 42 46N 104 27W
Lussac-les-Châteaux, France 20 B4 46 24N 0 43 E
Lustenau, Austria 26 D2 47 26N 9 39 E
Lūt, Dasht-e, Iran 71 D8 31 30N 58 0 E
Luta = Dalian, China 57 E11 38 50N 121 40 E
Lutherstadt Wittenberg, Germany 24 D8 51 53N 12 39 E
Luton, U.K. 13 F7 51 53N 0 24W
Luton □, U.K. 13 F7 51 53N 0 24W
Lutselke, Canada 105 A6 62 24N 110 44W
Lutsk, Ukraine 47 G3 50 50N 25 15 E
Lützow Holmbukta, Antarctica 5 C4 69 10 S 37 30 E
Lutzputs, S. Africa 88 D3 28 3 S 20 40 E
Luverne, Ala., U.S.A. 109 K2 31 43N 86 16W
Luverne, Minn., U.S.A. 112 D6 43 39N 96 13W
Luvua, Dem. Rep. of the Congo 87 D2 8 48 S 25 17 E
Luvua →, Dem. Rep. of the Congo 86 D2 6 50 S 27 30 E
Luvuvhu →, S. Africa 89 C5 22 25 S 31 18 E
Luwegu →, Tanzania 87 D4 8 31 S 37 23 E
Luwuk, Indonesia 63 E6 0 56 S 122 47 E
Luxembourg, Lux. 17 E6 49 37N 6 9 E
Luxembourg □, Belgium 17 E5 49 58N 5 30 E
Luxembourg ■, Europe 7 F7 49 45N 6 0 E
Luxeuil-les-Bains, France 19 E13 47 49N 6 24 E
Luxi, Hunan, China 59 C8 28 20N 110 7 E
Luxi, Yunnan, China 58 E4 24 40N 103 55 E
Luxi, Yunnan, China 58 E2 24 27N 98 36 E
Luxor = El Uqsur, Egypt 80 B3 25 41N 32 38 E
Luy-de-Béarn →, France 20 E3 43 39N 0 48W
Luy-de-France →, France 20 E3 43 39N 0 48W
Luyi, China 56 H8 33 50N 115 35 E
Luz-St-Sauveur, France 20 F4 42 53N 0 0W
Luzern, Switz. 25 H4 47 3N 8 18 E
Luzern □, Switz. 25 H3 47 2N 7 55 E
Luzhai, China 58 E7 24 29N 109 42 E
Luzhi, China 58 D5 26 21N 105 16 E
Luzhou, China 58 C5 28 52N 105 20 E
Luziânia, Brazil 125 G9 16 20 S 48 0W
Lužnice →, Czech Rep. 26 B7 49 14N 14 23 E
Luzon, Phil. 61 D4 16 0N 121 0 E
Luzy, France 19 F10 46 47N 3 58 E
Luzzi, Italy 31 C9 39 27N 16 17 E
Lviv, Ukraine 47 H3 49 50N 24 0 E
Lvov = Lviv, Ukraine 47 H3 49 50N 24 0 E
Lwówek, Poland 45 F3 52 28N 16 10 E
Lwówek Śląski, Poland 45 G2 51 7N 15 38 E
Lyakhavichy, Belarus 47 F4 53 2N 26 32 E
Lyakhovskiye, Ostrova, Russia 51 B15 73 40N 141 0 E
Lyaki = Läki, Azerbaijan 49 K8 40 34N 47 22 E
Lyal I., Canada 110 B3 44 57N 81 24W
Lyallpur = Faisalabad, Pakistan 68 D5 31 30N 73 5 E
Lyaskovets, Bulgaria 41 C9 43 6N 25 44 E
Lybster, U.K. 14 C5 58 18N 3 15W
Lycaonia, Turkey 72 D5 38 0N 33 0 E
Lychen, Germany 24 B9 53 12N 13 18 E
Lychkova, Russia 46 D7 57 55N 32 24 E
Lycia, Turkey 39 E11 36 30N 29 30 E
Lyckebyån →, Sweden 11 H9 56 12N 15 39 E
Lycksele, Sweden 8 D18 64 38N 18 40 E
Lycosura, Greece 38 D4 37 20N 22 3 E
Lydda = Lod, Israel 75 D3 31 57N 34 54 E
Lydenburg, S. Africa 89 D5 25 10 S 30 29 E
Lydia, Turkey 39 C10 38 48N 28 19 E
Łydynia →, Poland 45 F7 52 43N 20 26 E
Lyell, N.Z. 91 J4 41 48 S 172 4 E
Lyell I., Canada 104 C2 52 40N 131 35W
Lyepyel, Belarus 46 E5 54 50N 28 40 E
Lygnern, Sweden 11 G6 57 30N 12 15 E
Lykens, U.S.A. 111 F8 40 34N 76 42W
Lyman, U.S.A. 114 F8 41 20N 110 18W
Lyme B., U.K. 13 G4 50 42N 2 53W
Lyme Regis, U.K. 13 G5 50 43N 2 57W
Lymington, U.K. 13 G6 50 45N 1 32W
Łyna →, Poland 9 J19 54 37N 21 14 E
Lynchburg, U.S.A. 108 G6 37 25N 79 9W
Lynd →, Australia 94 B3 16 28 S 143 18 E
Lynd Ra., Australia 95 D4 25 30 S 149 20 E
Lynden, Canada 110 C4 43 14N 80 9W
Lynden, U.S.A. 116 B4 48 57N 122 27W
Lyndhurst, Australia 95 E2 30 15 S 138 18 E
Lyndon →, Australia 93 D1 23 29 S 114 6 E
Lyndonville, N.Y., U.S.A. 110 C6 43 20N 78 23W
Lyndonville, Vt., U.S.A. 111 B12 44 31N 72 1W
Lyngen, Norway 8 B19 69 45N 20 30 E
Lynher Reef, Australia 92 C3 15 27 S 121 55 E
Lynn, U.S.A. 111 D14 42 28N 70 57W
Lynn Lake, Canada 105 B8 56 51N 101 3W
Lynnwood, U.S.A. 116 C4 47 49N 122 19W
Lynton, U.K. 13 F4 51 13N 3 50W
Lyntupy, Belarus 9 J22 55 4N 26 23 E
Lynx L., Canada 105 A7 62 25N 106 15W
Lyon, France 21 C8 45 46N 4 50 E
Lyonnais, France 21 C8 45 45N 4 15 E
Lyons = Lyon, France 21 C8 45 46N 4 50 E
Lyons, Ga., U.S.A. 109 J4 32 12N 82 19W
Lyons, Kans., U.S.A. 112 F5 38 21N 98 12W
Lyons, N.Y., U.S.A. 110 C8 43 5N 77 0W
Lyons →, Australia 93 E2 25 2 S 115 9 E
Lyons Falls, U.S.A. 111 C9 43 37N 75 22W
Lyozna, Belarus 46 E6 55 0N 30 50 E
Lys = Leie →, Belgium 17 C3 51 2N 3 45 E
Lysá nad Labem, Czech Rep. 26 A7 50 11N 14 51 E
Lysekil, Sweden 11 F5 58 17N 11 26 E
Lyskovo, Russia 48 B7 56 0N 45 3 E
Lystrup, Denmark 11 H4 56 14N 10 14 E
Lysvik, Sweden 10 D7 60 1N 13 9 E
Lysychansk, Ukraine 47 H10 48 55N 38 30 E
Lytham St. Anne's, U.K. 12 D4 53 45N 3 0W
Lyttelton, N.Z. 91 K4 43 35 S 172 44 E
Lytton, Canada 104 C4 50 13N 121 31W
Lyuban, Russia 46 C6 59 16N 31 18 E
Lyubertsy, Russia 46 E9 55 39N 37 50 E
Lyubim, Russia 46 C11 58 20N 40 39 E
Lyubimets, Bulgaria 41 E10 41 50N 26 5 E
Lyuboml, Ukraine 47 G3 51 11N 24 4 E
Lyubotyn, Ukraine 47 H8 50 0N 36 0 E
Lyubytino, Russia 46 C7 58 50N 33 16 E
Lyudinovo, Russia 46 F8 53 52N 34 28 E

M

M.R. Gomez, Presa, Mexico 119 B5 26 10N 99 0W
Ma →, Vietnam 58 H5 19 47N 105 56 E
Ma'adaba, Jordan 75 E4 30 43N 35 47 E
Maamba, Zambia 88 B4 17 17 S 26 28 E
Ma'ān, Jordan 75 E4 30 12N 35 44 E
Ma'ān □, Jordan 75 F5 30 0N 36 0 E
Maanselkä, Finland 8 C23 63 52N 28 32 E
Ma'anshan, China 59 B12 31 44N 118 29 E
Maarianhamina, Finland 9 F18 60 5N 19 55 E
Ma'arrat an Nu'mān, Syria 70 C3 35 43N 36 43 E
Maas →, Neths. 17 C4 51 45N 4 32 E
Maaseik, Belgium 17 C5 51 6N 5 45 E
Maasin, Phil. 63 B6 10 8N 124 50 E
Maastricht, Neths. 17 D5 50 50N 5 40 E
Maave, Mozam. 89 C5 21 4 S 34 47 E
Mababe Depression, Botswana 88 B3 18 50 S 24 15 E
Mabalane, Mozam. 89 C5 23 37 S 32 31 E
Mabel L., Canada 104 C5 50 35N 118 43W
Mabenge, Dem. Rep. of the Congo 86 B1 4 15N 24 12 E
Maberly, Canada 111 B8 44 50N 76 32W
Mabian, China 58 C4 28 47N 103 37 E
Mabil, Ethiopia 81 E4 10 26N 36 52 E
Mablethorpe, U.K. 12 D8 53 20N 0 15 E
Mably, France 19 F11 46 5N 4 4 E
Maboma, Dem. Rep. of the Congo 86 B2 2 30N 28 10 E
Mabonto, S. Leone 82 D2 8 53N 11 50W
Mabrouk, Mali 83 B4 19 29N 1 15W
Mac Bac, Vietnam 65 H6 9 46N 106 7 E
Macachín, Argentina 126 D3 37 10 S 63 43W
Macaé, Brazil 127 A7 22 20 S 41 43W
Macael, Spain 33 H2 37 20N 2 18W
McAlester, U.S.A. 113 H7 34 56N 95 46W
McAllen, U.S.A. 113 M5 26 12N 98 14W
MacAlpine L., Canada 100 B9 66 40N 102 50W
Macamic, Canada 102 C4 48 45N 79 0W
Macao = Macau □, China 59 F9 22 16N 113 35 E
Macão, Portugal 35 F3 39 35N 7 59W
Macapá, Brazil 125 C8 0 5N 51 4W
McArthur →, Australia 94 B2 15 54 S 136 40 E
McArthur, Port, Australia 94 B2 16 4 S 136 23 E
Macau, Brazil 125 E11 5 15 S 36 40W
Macau □, China 59 F9 22 16N 113 35 E
McBride, Canada 104 C4 53 20N 120 19W
McCall, U.S.A. 114 D5 44 55N 116 6W
McCamey, U.S.A. 113 K3 31 8N 102 14W
McCammon, U.S.A. 114 E7 42 39N 112 12W
McCauley I., Canada 104 C2 53 40N 130 15W
McCleary, U.S.A. 116 C3 47 3N 123 16W
Macclenny, U.S.A. 109 K4 30 17N 82 7W
Macclesfield, U.K. 12 D5 53 15N 2 8W
M'Clintock Chan., Canada 100 A9 72 0N 102 0W
McClintock Ra., Australia 92 C4 18 44 S 127 38 E
McCloud, U.S.A. 114 F2 41 15N 122 8W
McCluer I., Australia 92 B5 11 5 S 133 0 E
McClure, U.S.A. 110 F7 40 42N 77 19W
McClure, L., U.S.A. 116 H6 37 35N 120 16W
M'Clure Str., Canada 4 B2 75 0N 119 0W
McClusky, U.S.A. 112 B4 47 29N 100 27W
McComb, U.S.A. 113 K9 31 15N 90 27W
McConaughy, L., U.S.A. 112 E4 41 14N 101 40W
McCook, U.S.A. 112 E4 40 12N 100 38W
McCreary, Canada 105 C9 50 47N 99 29W
McCullough Mt., U.S.A. 117 K11 35 35N 115 13W
McCusker →, Canada 105 B7 55 32N 108 39W
McDame, Canada 104 B3 59 44N 128 59W
McDermitt, U.S.A. 114 F5 41 59N 117 43W
McDonald, U.S.A. 110 F4 40 22N 80 14W
Macdonald, L., Australia 92 D4 23 30 S 129 0 E
McDonald Is., Ind. Oc. 3 G13 53 0 S 73 0 E
MacDonnell Ranges, Australia 92 D5 23 40 S 133 0 E
MacDowell L., Canada 102 B1 52 15N 92 45W
Macduff, U.K. 14 D6 57 40N 2 31W
Maceda, Spain 34 C3 42 16N 7 39W
Macedonia, U.S.A. 110 E3 41 19N 81 31W
Macedonia ■, Europe 40 E5 41 53N 21 40 E
Maceió, Brazil 125 E11 9 40 S 35 41W
Maceira, Portugal 34 F2 39 41N 8 55W
Macenta, Guinea 82 D3 8 35N 9 32W
Macerata, Italy 29 E10 43 18N 13 27 E
McFarland, U.S.A. 117 K7 35 41N 119 14W
McFarlane →, Canada 105 B7 59 12N 107 58W
Macfarlane, L., Australia 95 E2 32 0 S 136 40 E
McGehee, U.S.A. 113 J9 33 38N 91 24W
McGill, U.S.A. 114 G6 39 23N 114 47W
Macgillycuddy's Reeks, Ireland 15 E2 51 58N 9 45W
McGraw, U.S.A. 111 D8 42 36N 76 8W
McGregor, U.S.A. 112 D9 43 1N 91 11W
McGregor Ra., Australia 95 D3 27 0 S 142 45 E
Mach, Pakistan 66 E5 29 50N 67 20 E
Māch Kowr, Iran 71 E9 25 48N 61 28 E
Machado = Jiparaná →, Brazil 124 E6 8 3 S 62 52W
Machagai, Argentina 126 B3 26 56 S 60 2W
Machakos, Kenya 86 C4 1 30 S 37 15 E
Machala, Ecuador 124 D3 3 20 S 79 57W
Machanga, Mozam. 89 C6 20 59 S 35 0 E
Machattie, L., Australia 94 C2 24 50 S 139 48 E
Machault, France 19 C11 49 21N 4 29 E
Machava, Mozam. 89 D5 25 54 S 32 28 E
Machece, Mozam. 87 F4 19 15 S 35 32 E
Machecoul, France 18 F5 47 0N 1 49W
Macheke, Zimbabwe 89 B5 18 5 S 31 51 E
Macheng, China 59 B10 31 12N 115 2 E
Machero, Spain 35 F6 39 21N 4 20W
Machhu →, India 68 H4 23 6N 70 46 E
Machias, Maine, U.S.A. 109 C12 44 43N 67 28W
Machias, N.Y., U.S.A. 110 D6 42 25N 78 30W
Machichi →, Canada 105 B10 57 3N 92 6W
Machico, Madeira 37 D3 32 43N 16 44W
Machilipatnam, India 67 L12 16 12N 81 8 E
Machiques, Venezuela 124 A4 10 4N 72 34W
Machupicchu, Peru 124 F4 13 8 S 72 30W
Machynlleth, U.K. 13 E4 52 35N 3 50W
Macia, Mozam. 89 D5 25 2 S 33 8 E
Maciejowice, Poland 45 G8 51 36N 21 33 E
McIlwraith Ra., Australia 94 A3 13 50 S 143 20 E
Măcin, Romania 43 E13 45 16N 28 8 E
Macina, Mali 82 C4 14 50N 5 0W
McInnes L., Canada 105 C10 52 13N 93 45W
McIntosh, U.S.A. 112 C4 45 55N 101 21W
McIntosh L., Canada 105 B8 55 45N 105 0W
Macintosh Ra., Australia 93 E4 27 39 S 125 32 E
Macintyre →, Australia 95 D5 28 37 S 150 47 E
Macizo Galaico, Spain 34 C3 42 30N 7 30W
Mackay, Australia 94 C4 21 8 S 149 11 E
Mackay, U.S.A. 114 E7 43 55N 113 37W
MacKay →, Canada 104 B6 57 10N 111 38W
Mackay, L., Australia 92 D4 22 30 S 129 0 E
McKay Ra., Australia 92 D3 23 0 S 122 30 E
McKeesport, U.S.A. 110 F5 40 21N 79 52W
McKellar, Canada 110 A5 45 30N 79 55W
McKenna, U.S.A. 116 D4 46 56N 122 33W
Mackenzie, Canada 104 B4 55 20N 123 5W
McKenzie, U.S.A. 109 G1 36 8N 88 31W
Mackenzie →, Australia 94 C4 23 38 S 149 46 E
Mackenzie →, Canada 100 B6 69 10N 134 20W
McKenzie →, U.S.A. 114 D2 44 7N 123 6W
Mackenzie Bay, Canada 4 B1 69 0N 137 30W
Mackenzie City = Linden, Guyana 124 B7 6 0N 58 10W
Mackenzie Mts., Canada 100 B6 64 0N 130 0W
Mackinaw City, U.S.A. 108 C3 45 47N 84 44W
McKinlay, Australia 94 C3 21 16 S 141 18 E
McKinlay →, Australia 94 C3 20 50 S 141 28 E
McKinley, Mt., U.S.A. 100 B4 63 4N 151 0W
McKinley Sea, Arctic 4 A7 82 0N 0 0W
McKinney, U.S.A. 113 J6 33 12N 96 37W
Mackinnon Road, Kenya 86 C4 3 40 S 39 1 E
McKittrick, U.S.A. 117 K7 35 18N 119 37W
Macklin, Canada 105 C7 52 20N 109 56W
Macksville, Australia 95 E5 30 40 S 152 56 E
McLaughlin, U.S.A. 112 C4 45 49N 100 49W
Maclean, Australia 95 D5 29 26 S 153 16 E
McLean, U.S.A. 113 H4 35 14N 100 36W
McLeansboro, U.S.A. 112 F10 38 6N 88 32W
Maclear, S. Africa 89 E4 31 2 S 28 23 E
Macleay →, Australia 95 E5 30 56 S 153 0 E
McLennan, Canada 104 B5 55 42N 116 50W
McLeod →, Canada 104 C5 54 9N 115 44W
MacLeod, B., Canada 105 A7 62 53N 110 0W
McLeod, L., Australia 93 D1 24 9 S 113 47 E
MacLeod Lake, Canada 104 C4 54 58N 123 0W
McLoughlin, Mt., U.S.A. 114 E2 42 27N 122 19W
McMechen, U.S.A. 110 G4 39 57N 80 44W
McMinnville, Oreg., U.S.A. 114 D2 45 13N 123 12W
McMinnville, Tenn., U.S.A. 109 H3 35 41N 85 46W
McMurdo Sd., Antarctica 5 D11 77 0 S 170 0 E
McMurray = Fort McMurray, Canada 104 B6 56 44N 111 7W
McMurray, U.S.A. 116 B4 48 19N 122 14W
Macodoene, Mozam. 89 C6 23 32 S 35 5 E
Macomb, U.S.A. 112 E9 40 27N 90 40W
Macomer, Italy 30 B1 40 16N 8 47 E
Mâcon, France 19 F11 46 19N 4 50 E
Macon, Ga., U.S.A. 109 J4 32 51N 83 38W
Macon, Miss., U.S.A. 109 J1 33 7N 88 34W
Macon, Mo., U.S.A. 112 F8 39 44N 92 28W
Macossa, Mozam. 87 F3 17 55 S 33 56 E
Macoun L., Canada 105 B8 56 32N 103 40W
Macovane, Mozam. 89 C6 21 30 S 35 2 E
McPherson, U.S.A. 112 F6 38 22N 97 40W
McPherson Pk., U.S.A. 117 L7 34 53N 119 53W
McPherson Ra., Australia 95 D5 28 15 S 153 15 E
Macquarie →, Australia 95 E4 30 5 S 147 30 E
Macquarie Harbour, Australia 94 G4 42 15 S 145 23 E
Macquarie Is., Pac. Oc. 96 N7 54 36 S 158 55 E
MacRobertson Land, Antarctica 5 D6 71 0 S 64 0 E
Macroom, Ireland 15 E3 51 54N 8 57W
MacTier, Canada 110 A5 45 9N 79 46W
Macubela, Mozam. 87 F4 16 53 S 37 49 E
Macugnaga, Italy 28 C4 45 58N 7 58 E
Macuiza, Mozam. 87 F3 18 7 S 34 29 E
Macusani, Peru 124 F4 14 4 S 70 29W
Macuse, Mozam. 87 F4 17 45 S 37 10 E
Macuspana, Mexico 119 D6 17 46N 92 36W
Macusse, Angola 88 B3 17 48 S 20 23 E
Mada →, Nigeria 83 D6 7 59N 7 55 E
Madadeni, S. Africa 89 D5 27 43 S 30 3 E
Madagali, Nigeria 83 C7 10 56N 13 33 E
Madagascar ■, Africa 89 C8 20 0 S 47 0 E
Madā'in Sālih, Si. Arabia 70 E3 26 46N 37 57 E
Madama, Niger 79 D8 22 0N 13 40 E
Madame I., Canada 103 C7 45 30N 60 58W
Madan, Bulgaria 41 E8 41 30N 24 57 E
Madaoua, Niger 83 C6 14 5N 6 27 E
Madara, Nigeria 83 C7 11 45N 10 35 E
Madaripur, Bangla. 67 H17 23 19N 90 15 E
Madauk, Burma 67 L20 17 56N 96 52 E
Madawaska, Canada 110 A7 45 30N 78 0W
Madawaska →, Canada 102 C4 45 27N 76 21W
Madaya, Burma 67 H20 22 12N 96 10 E
Madbar, Sudan 81 F3 6 17N 30 45 E
Maddalena, Italy 30 A2 41 16N 9 23 E
Maddaloni, Italy 31 A7 41 2N 14 23 E
Madeira, Atl. Oc. 37 D3 32 50N 17 0W
Madeira →, Brazil 122 D5 3 22 S 58 45W
Madeleine, Îs. de la, Canada 103 C7 47 30N 61 40W
Maden, Turkey 73 C8 38 23N 39 40 E
Madera, Mexico 118 B3 29 12N 108 7W
Madera, Calif., U.S.A. 116 J6 36 57N 120 3W
Madera, Pa., U.S.A. 110 F6 40 49N 78 26W
Madha, India 66 L9 18 0N 75 30 E
Madhavpur, India 68 J3 21 15N 69 58 E
Madhepura, India 69 F12 26 11N 86 23 E
Madhubani, India 69 F12 26 21N 86 7 E
Madhupur, India 69 G12 24 16N 86 39 E
Madhya Pradesh □, India 68 J8 22 50N 78 0 E
Madidi →, Bolivia 124 F5 12 32 S 66 52W
Madikeri, India 66 N9 12 30N 75 45 E
Madill, U.S.A. 113 H6 34 6N 96 46W
Madimba, Dem. Rep. of the Congo 84 E3 4 58 S 15 5 E
Ma'din, Syria 70 C3 35 45N 39 36 E
Madina, Mali 82 C3 13 25N 8 50W
Madinani, Ivory C. 82 D3 9 37N 6 57W
Madingou, Congo 84 E2 4 10 S 13 33 E
Madirovalo, Madag. 89 B8 16 26 S 46 32 E
Madison, Calif., U.S.A. 116 G5 38 41N 121 59W
Madison, Fla., U.S.A. 109 K4 30 28N 83 25W
Madison, Ind., U.S.A. 108 F3 38 44N 85 23W
Madison, Nebr., U.S.A. 112 E6 41 50N 97 27W
Madison, Ohio, U.S.A. 110 E3 41 46N 81 3W
Madison, S. Dak., U.S.A. 112 D6 44 0N 97 7W
Madison, Wis., U.S.A. 112 D10 43 4N 89 24W
Madison →, U.S.A. 114 D8 45 56N 111 31W
Madison Heights, U.S.A. 108 G6 37 25N 79 8W
Madisonville, Ky., U.S.A. 108 G2 37 20N 87 30W
Madisonville, Tex., U.S.A. 113 K7 30 57N 95 55W
Madista, Botswana 88 C4 21 15 S 25 6 E
Madiun, Indonesia 63 G14 7 38 S 111 32 E
Madoc, Canada 110 B7 44 30N 77 28W
Madol, Sudan 81 F2 9 3N 27 45 E
Madon →, France 19 D13 48 36N 6 6 E
Madona, Latvia 9 H22 56 53N 26 5 E
Madonie, Italy 30 E6 37 50N 13 50 E
Madonna di Campíglio, Italy 28 B7 46 14N 10 49 E
Madra Dağı, Turkey 39 B9 39 23N 27 12 E
Madrakah, Ra's al, Oman 74 D6 19 0N 57 50 E
Madras = Chennai, India 66 N12 13 8N 80 19 E
Madras = Tamil Nadu □, India 66 P10 11 0N 77 0 E
Madras, U.S.A. 114 D3 44 38N 121 8W
Madre, Laguna, U.S.A. 113 M6 27 0N 97 30W
Madre, Sierra, Phil. 61 C5 17 0N 122 0 E
Madre de Dios →, Bolivia 122 E4 10 59 S 66 8W
Madre de Dios, I., Chile 122 J3 50 20 S 75 10W
Madre del Sur, Sierra, Mexico 119 D5 17 30N 100 0W
Madre Occidental, Sierra, Mexico 118 B3 27 0N 107 0W
Madre Oriental, Sierra, Mexico 118 C5 25 0N 100 0W
Madri, India 68 G5 24 16N 73 32 E
Madrid, Spain 34 E7 40 25N 3 45W
Madrid, U.S.A. 111 B9 44 45N 75 8W
Madrid □, Spain 34 E7 40 30N 3 45W
Madridejos, Spain 35 F7 39 28N 3 33W
Madrigal de las Altas Torres, Spain 34 D6 41 5N 5 0W
Madrona, Sierra, Spain 35 G6 38 27N 4 16W
Madroñera, Spain 35 F5 39 26N 5 42W
Madu, Sudan 81 E2 14 37N 26 4 E
Madura, Australia 93 F4 31 55 S 127 0 E
Madura, Indonesia 63 G15 7 30 S 114 0 E
Madura, Selat, Indonesia 63 G15 7 30 S 113 20 E
Madurai, India 66 Q11 9 55N 78 10 E
Madurantakam, India 66 N11 12 30N 79 50 E
Madzhalis, Russia 49 J8 42 9N 47 47 E
Mae Chan, Thailand 64 B2 20 9N 99 52 E
Mae Hong Son, Thailand 64 C2 19 16N 97 56 E
Mae Khlong →, Thailand 64 F3 13 24N 100 0 E
Mae Phrik, Thailand 64 D2 17 27N 99 7 E
Mae Ramat, Thailand 64 D2 16 58N 98 31 E
Mae Rim, Thailand 64 C2 18 54N 98 57 E
Mae Sot, Thailand 64 D2 16 43N 98 34 E
Mae Suai, Thailand 58 H2 19 39N 99 33 E
Mae Tha, Thailand 64 C2 18 28N 99 8 E
Maebashi, Japan 55 F9 36 24N 139 4 E
Maella, Spain 32 D5 41 8N 0 7 E
Maesteg, U.K. 13 F4 51 36N 3 40W
Maestra, Sierra, Cuba 120 B4 20 15N 77 0W
Maevatanana, Madag. 89 B8 16 56 S 46 49 E
Mafeking = Mafikeng, S. Africa 88 D4 25 50 S 25 38 E
Mafeking, Canada 105 C8 52 40N 101 10W
Maféré, Ivory C. 82 D4 5 30N 3 2W
Mafeteng, Lesotho 88 D4 29 51 S 27 15 E
Maffra, Australia 95 F4 37 53 S 146 58 E
Mafia I., Tanzania 86 D4 7 45 S 39 50 E
Mafikeng, S. Africa 88 D4 25 50 S 25 38 E
Mafra, Brazil 127 B6 26 10 S 49 55W
Mafra, Portugal 35 G1 38 55N 9 20W
Mafungabusi Plateau, Zimbabwe 87 F2 18 30 S 29 8 E
Magadan, Russia 51 D16 59 38N 150 50 E
Magadi, Kenya 86 C4 1 54 S 36 19 E
Magadi, L., Kenya 86 C4 1 54 S 36 19 E
Magaliesburg, S. Africa 89 D4 26 0 S 27 32 E
Magallanes, Estrecho de, Chile 122 J3 52 30 S 75 0W
Magaluf, Spain 33 F7 39 29N 2 32 E
Magangué, Colombia 124 B4 9 14N 74 45W
Magaria, Niger 83 C6 13 4N 9 5 E
Magburaka, S. Leone 82 D2 8 47N 12 0W
Magdalen Is. = Madeleine, Îs. de la, Canada 103 C7 47 30N 61 40W
Magdalena, Argentina 126 D4 35 5 S 57 30W
Magdalena, Bolivia 124 F6 13 13 S 63 57W
Magdalena, Mexico 118 A2 30 50N 112 0W
Magdalena, U.S.A. 115 J10 34 7N 107 15W
Magdalena →, Colombia 122 B3 11 6N 74 51W
Magdalena →, Mexico 118 A2 30 40N 112 25W
Magdalena, B., Mexico 118 C2 24 30N 112 10W
Magdalena, Llano de la, Mexico 118 C2 25 0N 111 30W
Magdeburg, Germany 24 C7 52 7N 11 38 E
Magdelaine Cays, Australia 94 B5 16 33 S 150 18 E
Magdub, Sudan 81 E2 13 42N 25 5 E
Magee, U.S.A. 113 K10 31 52N 89 44W
Magelang, Indonesia 63 G14 7 29 S 110 13 E
Magellan's Str. = Magallanes, Estrecho de, Chile 122 J3 52 30 S 75 0W
Magenta, Italy 28 C5 45 28N 8 53 E
Magenta, L., Australia 93 F2 33 30 S 119 2 E
Magerøya, Norway 8 A21 71 3N 25 40 E
Maggia →, Switz. 25 J4 46 18N 8 36 E
Maggiorasca, Mte., Italy 28 D6 44 33N 9 29 E
Maggiore, Lago, Italy 28 C5 45 57N 8 39 E
Maghâgha, Egypt 80 B3 28 38N 30 50 E
Maghama, Mauritania 82 B2 15 32N 12 57W
Magherafelt, U.K. 15 B5 54 45N 6 37W
Maghreb, N. Afr. 78 B5 32 0N 4 0W
Magione, Italy 29 E9 43 8N 12 12 E
Magistralnyy, Russia 51 D11 56 16N 107 36 E
Maglaj, Bos.-H. 42 F3 44 33N 18 7 E
Magliano in Toscana, Italy 29 F8 42 36N 11 17 E
Máglie, Italy 31 B11 40 7N 18 18 E
Magnac-Laval, France 20 B5 46 13N 1 11 E
Magnetic Pole (North) = North Magnetic Pole, Canada 4 B2 77 58N 102 8W
Magnetic Pole (South) = South Magnetic Pole, Antarctica 5 C9 64 8 S 138 8 E
Magnisía □, Greece 38 B5 39 15N 23 0 E
Magnitogorsk, Russia 50 D6 53 27N 59 4 E
Magnolia, Ark., U.S.A. 113 J8 33 16N 93 14W
Magnolia, Miss., U.S.A. 113 K9 31 9N 90 28W
Magny-en-Vexin, France 19 C8 49 9N 1 47 E
Magog, Canada 103 C5 45 18N 72 9W
Magoro, Uganda 86 B3 1 45N 34 12 E
Magosa = Famagusta, Cyprus 36 D12 35 8N 33 55 E
Magouládhes, Greece 36 A3 39 45N 19 42 E
Magoye, Zambia 87 F2 16 1 S 27 30 E
Magozal, Mexico 119 C5 21 34N 97 59W
Magpie, L., Canada 103 B7 51 0N 64 41W
Magrath, Canada 104 D6 49 25N 112 50W
Magre →, Spain 33 F4 39 11N 0 25W
Magrur, Sudan 81 E3 14 1N 30 27 E
Magrur, Wadi →, Sudan 81 D2 16 5N 26 30 E

Magta Lahjar, *Mauritania* 82 B2 17 28N 13 17W
Maguan, *China* 58 F5 23 0N 104 21 E
Maguarinho, C., *Brazil* 125 D9 0 15 S 48 30W
Magude, *Mozam.* 89 D5 25 2 S 32 40 E
Mağusa = Famagusta, *Cyprus* 36 D12 35 8N 33 55 E
Maguse L., *Canada* 105 A9 61 40N 95 10W
Maguse Pt., *Canada* 105 A10 61 20N 93 50W
Magvana, *India* 68 H3 23 13N 69 22 E
Magwe, *Burma* 67 J19 20 10N 95 0 E
Magwe, *Sudan* 81 G3 4 8N 32 17 E
Maha Sarakham, *Thailand* 64 D4 16 12N 103 16 E
Mahābād, *Iran* 70 B5 36 50N 45 45 E
Mahabharat Lekh, *Nepal* 69 E10 28 30N 82 0 E
Mahabo, *Madag.* 89 C7 20 23 S 44 40 E
Mahadeo Hills, *India* 69 H8 22 20N 78 30 E
Mahaffey, *U.S.A.* 110 F6 40 53N 78 44W
Mahagi, *Dem. Rep. of the Congo* 86 B3 2 20N 31 0 E
Mahajamba →, *Madag.* 89 B8 15 33 S 47 8 E
Mahajamba, Helodranon' i, *Madag.* 89 B8 15 24 S 47 5 E
Mahajan, *India* 68 E5 28 48N 73 56 E
Mahajanga, *Madag.* 89 B8 15 40 S 46 25 E
Mahajanga □, *Madag.* 89 B8 17 0 S 47 0 E
Mahajilo →, *Madag.* 89 B8 19 42 S 45 22 E
Mahakam →, *Indonesia* 62 E5 0 35 S 117 17 E
Mahalapye, *Botswana* 88 C4 23 1 S 26 51 E
Maḩallāt, *Iran* 71 C6 33 55N 50 30 E
Māhān, *Iran* 71 D8 30 5N 57 18 E
Mahan →, *India* 69 H10 23 30N 82 50 E
Mahanadi →, *India* 67 J15 20 20N 86 25 E
Mahananda →, *India* 69 G12 25 12N 87 52 E
Mahanoro, *Madag.* 89 B8 19 54 S 48 48 E
Mahanoy City, *U.S.A.* 111 F8 40 49N 76 9W
Maharashtra □, *India* 66 J9 20 30N 75 30 E
Mahari Mts., *Tanzania* 86 D3 6 20 S 30 0 E
Mahasham, W. →, *Egypt* 75 E3 30 15N 34 10 E
Mahasoa, *Madag.* 89 C8 22 12 S 46 6 E
Mahasolo, *Madag.* 89 B8 19 7 S 46 22 E
Mahattat ash Shīdīyah, *Jordan* 75 F4 29 55N 35 55 E
Mahattat 'Unayzah, *Jordan* 75 E4 30 30N 35 47 E
Mahavavy →, *Madag.* 89 B8 15 57 S 45 54 E
Mahaxay, *Laos* 64 D5 17 22N 105 12 E
Mahbubnagar, *India* 66 L10 16 45N 77 59 E
Maḩḑah, *Oman* 71 E7 24 24N 55 59 E
Mahdia, *Tunisia* 79 A8 35 28N 11 0 E
Mahe, *India* 69 C8 33 10N 78 32 E
Mahendragarh, *India* 68 E7 28 17N 76 14 E
Mahenge, *Tanzania* 87 D4 8 45 S 36 41 E
Maheno, *N.Z.* 91 L3 45 10 S 170 50 E
Mahesana, *India* 68 H5 23 39N 72 26 E
Maheshwar, *India* 68 H6 22 11N 75 35 E
Mahgawan, *India* 69 F8 26 29N 78 37 E
Mahi →, *India* 68 H5 22 15N 72 55 E
Mahia Pen., *N.Z.* 91 H6 39 9 S 177 55 E
Mahilyow, *Belarus* 46 F6 53 55N 30 18 E
Mahmiya, *Sudan* 81 D3 17 12N 33 43 E
Mahmud Kot, *Pakistan* 68 D4 30 16N 71 0 E
Mahmudia, *Romania* 43 E14 45 5N 29 5 E
Mahmudiye, *Turkey* 39 B12 39 48N 30 15 E
Mahmutbey, *Turkey* 41 E12 41 3N 28 49 E
Mahnomen, *U.S.A.* 112 B7 47 19N 95 58W
Mahoba, *India* 69 G8 25 15N 79 55 E
Mahón = Maó, *Spain* 37 B11 39 53N 4 16 E
Mahone Bay, *Canada* 103 D7 44 30N 64 20W
Mahopac, *U.S.A.* 111 E11 41 22N 73 45W
Mahuta, *Nigeria* 83 C5 11 32N 4 58 E
Mahuva, *India* 68 J4 21 5N 71 48 E
Mahya Dağı, *Turkey* 41 E11 41 47N 27 36 E
Mai-Ndombe, L., *Dem. Rep. of the Congo* 84 E3 2 0 S 18 20 E
Mai-Sai, *Thailand* 58 G2 20 20N 99 55 E
Maia, *Portugal* 34 D2 41 14N 8 37W
Maia, *Spain* 32 B3 43 12N 1 29W
Maials, *Spain* 32 D5 41 22N 0 30 E
Maîche, *France* 19 E13 47 16N 6 48 E
Maicurú →, *Brazil* 125 D8 2 14 S 54 17W
Máida, *Italy* 31 D9 38 51N 16 22 E
Maidan Khula, *Afghan.* 68 C3 33 36N 69 50 E
Maidenhead, *U.K.* 13 F7 51 31N 0 42W
Maidstone, *Canada* 105 C7 53 5N 109 20W
Maidstone, *U.K.* 13 F8 51 16N 0 32 E
Maiduguri, *Nigeria* 83 C7 12 0N 13 20 E
Măieruş, *Romania* 43 E10 45 53N 25 31 E
Maigatari, *Nigeria* 83 C6 12 46N 9 27 E
Maignelay Montigny, *France* 19 C9 49 32N 2 30 E
Maigo, *Phil.* 61 G5 8 10N 123 57 E
Maigudo, *Ethiopia* 81 F4 7 30N 37 8 E
Maihar, *India* 69 G9 24 16N 80 45 E
Maijdi, *Bangla.* 67 H17 22 48N 91 10 E
Maikala Ra., *India* 67 J12 22 0N 81 0 E
Mailani, *India* 69 E9 28 17N 80 21 E
Maillezais, *France* 20 B3 46 22N 0 45W
Mailsi, *Pakistan* 68 E5 29 48N 72 15 E
Main →, *Germany* 25 F4 50 0N 8 18 E
Main →, *U.K.* 15 B5 54 48N 6 18W
Mainburg, *Germany* 25 G7 48 38N 11 47 E
Maine, *France* 18 D6 48 20N 0 15W
Maine □, *U.S.A.* 109 C11 45 20N 69 0W
Maine →, *Ireland* 15 D2 52 9N 9 45W
Maine-et-Loire □, *France* 18 E6 47 31N 0 30W
Maïne-Soroa, *Niger* 83 C7 13 13N 12 2 E
Maingkwan, *Burma* 67 F20 26 15N 96 37 E
Mainit, L., *Phil.* 61 G6 9 31N 125 30 E
Mainland, *Orkney, U.K.* 14 C5 58 59N 3 8W
Mainland, *Shet., U.K.* 14 A7 60 15N 1 22W
Mainoru, *Australia* 94 A1 14 0 S 134 6 E
Mainpuri, *India* 69 F8 27 18N 79 4 E
Maintal, *Germany* 25 E4 50 7N 8 52 E
Maintenon, *France* 19 D8 48 35N 1 35 E
Maintirano, *Madag.* 89 B7 18 3 S 44 1 E
Mainz, *Germany* 25 E4 50 1N 8 14 E
Maipú, *Argentina* 126 D4 36 52 S 57 50W
Maiquetía, *Venezuela* 124 A5 10 36N 66 57W
Máira →, *Italy* 28 D4 44 49N 7 38 E
Mairabari, *India* 67 F18 26 30N 92 22 E
Maisí, *Cuba* 121 B5 20 17N 74 9W
Maisí, Pta. de, *Cuba* 121 B5 20 10N 74 10W
Maitland, *N.S.W., Australia* 95 E5 32 33 S 151 36 E
Maitland, *S. Austral., Australia* 95 E2 34 23 S 137 40 E
Maitland →, *Canada* 110 C3 43 45N 81 43W
Maiyema, *Nigeria* 83 C5 12 5N 4 25 E
Maiyuan, *China* 59 E11 25 34N 117 28 E
Maiz, Is. del, *Nic.* 120 D3 12 15N 83 4W
Maizuru, *Japan* 55 G7 35 25N 135 22 E
Majalengka, *Indonesia* 63 G13 6 50 S 108 13 E
Majene, *Indonesia* 63 E5 3 38 S 118 57 E
Majevica, *Bos.-H.* 42 F3 44 45N 18 50 E
Maji, *Ethiopia* 81 F4 6 12N 35 30 E
Majiang, *China* 58 D6 26 28N 107 32 E
Majorca = Mallorca, *Spain* 37 B10 39 30N 3 0 E
Maka, *Senegal* 82 C2 13 40N 14 10W
Makaha, *Zimbabwe* 89 B5 17 20 S 32 39 E
Makak, *Cameroon* 83 E7 3 36N 11 0 E
Makalamabedi, *Botswana* 88 C3 20 19 S 23 51 E
Makale, *Indonesia* 63 E5 3 6 S 119 51 E
Makamba, *Burundi* 86 C2 4 8 S 29 49 E
Makari, *Cameroon* 83 C7 12 35N 10 27 E
Makarikari = Makgadikgadi Salt Pans, *Botswana* 88 C4 20 40 S 25 45 E
Makarovo, *Russia* 51 D11 57 40N 107 45 E
Makarska, *Croatia* 29 E14 43 20N 17 2 E
Makaryev, *Russia* 48 B6 57 52N 43 50 E
Makasar = Ujung Pandang, *Indonesia* 63 F5 5 10 S 119 20 E
Makasar, Selat, *Indonesia* 63 E5 1 0 S 118 20 E
Makasar, Str. of = Makasar, Selat, *Indonesia* 63 E5 1 0 S 118 20 E
Makat, *Kazakstan* 50 E6 47 39N 53 19 E
Makedonija = Macedonia ■, *Europe* 40 E5 41 53N 21 40 E
Makena, *U.S.A.* 106 H16 20 39N 156 27W
Makeni, *S. Leone* 82 D2 8 55N 12 5W
Makeyevka = Makiyivka, *Ukraine* 47 H9 48 0N 38 0 E
Makgadikgadi Salt Pans, *Botswana* 88 C4 20 40 S 25 45 E
Makhachkala, *Russia* 49 J8 43 0N 47 30 E
Makharadze = Ozurgeti, *Georgia* 49 K5 41 55N 42 2 E
Makhmūr, *Iraq* 70 C4 35 46N 43 35 E
Makian, *Indonesia* 63 D7 0 20N 127 20 E
Makindu, *Kenya* 86 C4 2 18 S 37 50 E
Makinsk, *Kazakstan* 50 D8 52 37N 70 26 E
Makiyivka, *Ukraine* 47 H9 48 0N 38 0 E
Makkah, *Si. Arabia* 74 C2 21 30N 39 54 E
Makkovik, *Canada* 103 A8 55 10N 59 10W
Makó, *Hungary* 42 D5 46 14N 20 33 E
Mako, *Senegal* 82 C2 12 52N 12 20W
Makokou, *Gabon* 84 D2 0 40N 12 50 E
Makongo, *Dem. Rep. of the Congo* 86 B2 3 25N 26 17 E
Makoro, *Dem. Rep. of the Congo* 86 B2 3 10N 29 59 E
Maków Mazowiecki, *Poland* 45 F8 52 52N 21 6 E
Maków Podhalański, *Poland* 45 J6 49 43N 19 45 E
Makrá, *Greece* 39 E7 36 15N 25 54 E
Makrai, *India* 66 H10 22 2N 77 0 E
Makran Coast Range, *Pakistan* 66 G4 25 40N 64 0 E
Makrana, *India* 68 F6 27 2N 74 46 E
Mákri, *Greece* 41 F9 40 52N 25 40 E
Makriyialos, *Greece* 36 D7 35 2N 25 59 E
Mākū, *Iran* 70 B5 39 15N 44 31 E
Makunda, *Botswana* 88 C3 22 30 S 20 7 E
Makung, *Taiwan* 59 F12 23 34N 119 34 E
Makurazaki, *Japan* 55 J5 31 15N 130 20 E
Makurdi, *Nigeria* 83 D6 7 43N 8 35 E
Makūyeh, *Iran* 71 D7 28 7N 53 9 E
Makwassie, *S. Africa* 88 D4 27 17 S 26 0 E
Makwiro, *Zimbabwe* 89 B5 17 58 S 30 25 E
Mâl, *Mauritania* 82 B2 16 58N 13 23W
Mal B., *Ireland* 15 D2 52 50N 9 30W
Mala, Pta., *Panama* 120 E3 7 28N 80 2W
Mala Belozërka, *Ukraine* 47 J8 47 12N 34 56 E
Mala Kapela, *Croatia* 29 D12 44 45N 15 30 E
Mała Panew →, *Poland* 45 H4 50 43N 17 54 E
Mala Vyska, *Ukraine* 47 H6 48 39N 31 36 E
Malabang, *Phil.* 61 H6 7 36N 124 3 E
Malabar Coast, *India* 66 P9 11 0N 75 0 E
Malabo = Rey Malabo, *Eq. Guin.* 83 E6 3 45N 8 50 E
Malabon, *Phil.* 61 D4 14 21N 121 0 E
Malabu, *Nigeria* 83 D7 9 32N 12 48 E
Malacca, Str. of, *Indonesia* 65 L3 3 0N 101 0 E
Malacky, *Slovak Rep.* 27 C10 48 27N 17 0 E
Malad City, *U.S.A.* 114 E7 42 12N 112 15W
Maladeta, *Spain* 32 C5 42 39N 0 39 E
Maladzyechna, *Belarus* 46 E4 54 20N 26 50 E
Málaga, *Spain* 35 J6 36 43N 4 23W
Málaga □, *Spain* 35 J6 36 38N 4 58W
Malagarasi, *Tanzania* 86 D3 5 5 S 30 50 E
Malagarasi →, *Tanzania* 86 D2 5 12 S 29 47 E
Malagasy Rep. = Madagascar ■, *Africa* 89 C8 20 0 S 47 0 E
Malagón, *Spain* 35 F7 39 11N 3 52W
Malagón →, *Spain* 35 H3 37 35N 7 29W
Malahide, *Ireland* 15 C5 53 26N 6 9W
Malaimbandy, *Madag.* 89 C8 20 20 S 45 36 E
Malakâl, *Sudan* 81 F3 9 33N 31 40 E
Malakand, *Pakistan* 68 B4 34 40N 71 55 E
Malakwal, *Pakistan* 68 C5 32 34N 73 13 E
Malamala, *Indonesia* 63 E6 3 21 S 120 55 E
Malanda, *Australia* 94 B4 17 22 S 145 35 E
Malang, *Indonesia* 63 G15 7 59 S 112 45 E
Malangen, *Norway* 8 B18 69 24N 18 37 E
Malanje, *Angola* 84 F3 9 36 S 16 17 E
Mälaren, *Sweden* 10 E11 59 30N 17 10 E
Malargüe, *Argentina* 126 D2 35 32 S 69 30W
Malartic, *Canada* 102 C4 48 9N 78 9W
Malaryta, *Belarus* 47 G3 51 50N 24 3 E
Malatya, *Turkey* 70 B3 38 25N 38 20 E
Malawi ■, *Africa* 87 E3 11 55 S 34 0 E
Malawi, L. = Nyasa, L., *Africa* 87 E3 12 30 S 34 30 E
Malay Pen., *Asia* 65 J3 7 25N 100 0 E
Malaya Belozërka = Mala Belozërka, *Ukraine* 47 J8 47 12N 34 56 E
Malaya Vishera, *Russia* 46 C7 58 55N 32 25 E
Malaya Viska = Mala Vyska, *Ukraine* 47 H6 48 39N 31 36 E
Malaybalay, *Phil.* 61 G6 8 5N 125 7 E
Malāyer, *Iran* 71 C6 34 19N 48 51 E
Malaysia ■, *Asia* 65 K4 5 0N 110 0 E
Malazgirt, *Turkey* 70 B4 39 10N 42 33 E
Malbaza, *Niger* 83 C6 13 59N 5 38 E
Malbon, *Australia* 94 C3 21 5 S 140 17 E
Malbooma, *Australia* 95 E1 30 41 S 134 11 E
Malbork, *Poland* 44 D6 54 3N 19 1 E
Malcésine, *Italy* 28 C7 45 46N 10 48 E
Malchin, *Germany* 24 B8 53 44N 12 44 E
Malchow, *Germany* 24 B8 53 28N 12 25 E
Malcolm, *Australia* 93 E3 28 51 S 121 25 E
Malcolm, Pt., *Australia* 93 F3 33 48 S 123 45 E
Malczyce, *Poland* 45 G3 51 14N 16 29 E
Maldah, *India* 69 G13 25 2N 88 9 E
Maldegem, *Belgium* 17 C3 51 14N 3 26 E
Malden, *Mass., U.S.A.* 111 D13 42 26N 71 4W
Malden, *Mo., U.S.A.* 113 G10 36 34N 89 57W
Malden I., *Kiribati* 97 H12 4 3 S 155 1W
Maldives ■, *Ind. Oc.* 52 J11 5 0N 73 0 E
Maldonado, *Uruguay* 127 C5 34 59 S 55 0W
Maldonado, Punta, *Mexico* 119 D5 16 19N 98 35W
Malè, *Italy* 28 B7 46 21N 10 55 E
Malé, *Maldives* 53 J11 4 0N 73 28 E
Malé Karpaty, *Slovak Rep.* 27 C10 48 30N 17 20 E
Maléa, Ákra, *Greece* 38 E5 36 28N 23 7 E
Malegaon, *India* 66 J9 20 30N 74 38 E
Malei, *Mozam.* 87 F4 17 12 S 36 58 E
Malek, *Sudan* 81 F3 6 4N 31 36 E
Malek Kandī, *Iran* 70 B5 37 9N 46 6 E
Malela, *Dem. Rep. of the Congo* 86 C2 4 22 S 26 8 E
Malema, *Mozam.* 87 E4 14 57 S 37 20 E
Maléme, *Greece* 36 D5 35 31N 23 49 E
Maleny, *Australia* 95 D5 26 45 S 152 52 E
Målerås, *Sweden* 11 H9 56 54N 15 34 E
Malerkotla, *India* 68 D6 30 32N 75 58 E
Máles, *Greece* 36 D7 35 6N 25 35 E
Malesherbes, *France* 19 D9 48 15N 2 24 E
Maleshevska Planina, *Europe* 40 E7 41 38N 23 7 E
Malesína, *Greece* 38 C5 38 37N 23 14 E
Malestroit, *France* 18 E4 47 49N 2 25W
Malfa, *Italy* 31 D7 38 35N 14 50 E
Malgobek, *Russia* 49 J7 43 30N 44 34 E
Malgomaj, *Sweden* 8 D17 64 40N 16 30 E
Malgrat = Malgrat de Mar, *Spain* 32 D7 41 39N 2 46 E
Malgrat de Mar, *Spain* 32 D7 41 39N 2 46 E
Malha, *Sudan* 81 D2 15 8N 25 10 E
Malhargarh, *India* 68 G6 24 17N 74 59 E
Malheur →, *U.S.A.* 114 D5 44 4N 116 59W
Malheur L., *U.S.A.* 114 E4 43 20N 118 48W
Mali, *Guinea* 82 C2 12 10N 12 20W
Mali ■, *Africa* 82 B4 17 0N 3 0W
Mali →, *Burma* 67 G20 25 40N 97 40 E
Mali Kanal, *Serbia, Yug.* 42 E4 45 36N 19 24 E
Mali Kyun, *Burma* 64 F2 13 0N 98 20 E
Malibu, *U.S.A.* 117 L8 34 2N 118 41W
Maliku, *Indonesia* 63 E6 0 39 S 123 16 E
Malili, *Indonesia* 63 E6 2 42 S 121 6 E
Målilla, *Sweden* 11 G9 57 23N 15 48 E
Malimba, Mts., *Dem. Rep. of the Congo* 86 D2 7 30 S 29 30 E
Malin Hd., *Ireland* 15 A4 55 23N 7 23W
Malin Pen., *Ireland* 15 A4 55 20N 7 17W
Malindi, *Kenya* 86 C5 3 12 S 40 5 E
Malines = Mechelen, *Belgium* 17 C4 51 2N 4 29 E
Malino, *Indonesia* 63 D6 1 0N 121 0 E
Malinyi, *Tanzania* 87 D4 8 56 S 36 0 E
Malipo, *China* 58 F5 23 7N 104 42 E
Maliq, *Albania* 40 F4 40 45N 20 48 E
Maliqi = Maliq, *Albania* 40 F4 40 45N 20 48 E
Malita, *Phil.* 63 C7 6 19N 125 39 E
Maliwun, *Burma* 62 B1 10 17N 98 40 E
Maliya, *India* 68 H4 23 5N 70 46 E
Maljenik, *Serbia, Yug.* 40 C5 43 54N 21 43 E
Malkara, *Turkey* 41 F10 40 53N 26 53 E
Małkinia Górna, *Poland* 45 F9 52 42N 22 5 E
Malko Tŭrnovo, *Bulgaria* 41 E11 41 59N 27 31 E
Mallacoota Inlet, *Australia* 95 F4 37 34 S 149 40 E
Mallaig, *U.K.* 14 D3 57 0N 5 50W
Mallaoua, *Niger* 83 C6 13 2N 9 36 E
Mallawan, *India* 69 F9 27 4N 80 12 E
Mallawi, *Egypt* 80 B3 27 44N 30 44 E
Mallemort, *France* 21 E9 43 43N 5 11 E
Málles Venosta, *Italy* 28 B7 46 41N 10 32 E
Mállia, *Greece* 36 D7 35 17N 25 32 E
Mallión, Kólpos, *Greece* 36 D7 35 19N 25 27 E
Mallorca, *Spain* 37 B10 39 30N 3 0 E
Mallorytown, *Canada* 111 B9 44 29N 75 53W
Mallow, *Ireland* 15 D3 52 8N 8 39W
Malmbäck, *Sweden* 11 G8 57 34N 14 28 E
Malmberget, *Sweden* 8 C19 67 11N 20 40 E
Malmédy, *Belgium* 17 D6 50 25N 6 2 E
Malmesbury, *S. Africa* 88 E2 33 28 S 18 41 E
Malmköping, *Sweden* 10 E10 59 8N 16 44 E
Malmö, *Sweden* 11 J6 55 36N 12 59 E
Malmslätt, *Sweden* 11 F9 58 27N 15 33 E
Malmyzh, *Russia* 48 B10 56 31N 50 41 E
Malnaş, *Romania* 43 D10 46 2N 25 49 E
Malo Konare, *Bulgaria* 41 D8 42 12N 24 24 E
Maloarkhangelsk, *Russia* 47 F9 52 28N 36 30 E
Malolos, *Phil.* 63 B6 14 50N 120 49 E
Malombe L., *Malawi* 87 E4 14 40 S 35 15 E
Małomice, *Poland* 45 G2 51 34N 15 29 E
Malomir, *Bulgaria* 41 D10 42 16N 26 32 E
Malone, *U.S.A.* 111 B10 44 51N 74 18W
Malong, *China* 58 E4 25 24N 103 34 E
Małopolskie □, *Poland* 45 J7 49 50N 20 20 E
Malorad, *Bulgaria* 40 C7 43 28N 23 41 E
Måløy, *Norway* 9 F11 61 57N 5 6 E
Maloyaroslovets, *Russia* 46 E9 55 2N 36 20 E
Malpartida, *Spain* 35 F4 39 26N 6 30W
Malpaso, *Canary Is.* 37 G1 27 43N 18 3W
Malpelo, I. de, *Colombia* 124 C2 4 3N 81 35W
Malpica de Bergantiños, *Spain* 34 B2 43 19N 8 50W
Malpur, *India* 68 H5 23 21N 73 27 E
Malpura, *India* 68 F6 26 17N 75 23 E
Mals = Málles Venosta, *Italy* 28 B7 46 41N 10 32 E
Malta, *Idaho, U.S.A.* 114 E7 42 18N 113 22W
Malta, *Mont., U.S.A.* 114 B10 48 21N 107 52W
Malta ■, *Europe* 36 D2 35 55N 14 30 E
Maltahöhe, *Namibia* 88 C2 24 55 S 17 0 E
Maltepe, *Turkey* 41 F13 40 55N 29 8 E
Malton, *Canada* 110 C5 43 42N 79 38W
Malton, *U.K.* 12 C7 54 8N 0 49W
Maluku, *Indonesia* 63 E7 1 0 S 127 0 E
Maluku □, *Indonesia* 63 E7 3 0 S 128 0 E
Maluku Sea = Molucca Sea, *Indonesia* 63 E6 2 0 S 124 0 E
Malumfashi, *Nigeria* 83 C6 11 48N 7 39 E
Malung, *Sweden* 10 D7 60 42N 13 44 E
Malungsfors, *Sweden* 10 D7 60 44N 13 33 E
Maluwe, *Ghana* 82 D4 8 40N 2 17W
Malvan, *India* 66 L8 16 2N 73 30 E
Malvern, *U.S.A.* 113 H8 34 22N 92 49W
Malvern Hills, *U.K.* 13 E5 52 0N 2 19W
Malvinas, Is. = Falkland Is. □, *Atl. Oc.* 128 G5 51 30 S 59 0W
Malý Dunaj →, *Slovak Rep.* 27 D11 47 45N 18 9 E
Malya, *Tanzania* 86 C3 3 5 S 33 38 E
Malyn, *Ukraine* 47 G5 50 46N 29 3 E
Malyy Lyakhovskiy, Ostrov, *Russia* 51 B15 74 7N 140 36 E
Mama, *Russia* 51 D12 58 18N 112 54 E
Mamadysh, *Russia* 48 C10 55 44N 51 23 E
Mamanguape, *Brazil* 125 E11 6 50 S 35 4W
Mamarr Mitlā, *Egypt* 75 E1 30 2N 32 54 E
Mamasa, *Indonesia* 63 E5 2 55 S 119 20 E
Mambasa, *Dem. Rep. of the Congo* 86 B2 1 22N 29 3 E
Mamberamo →, *Indonesia* 63 E9 2 0 S 137 50 E
Mambilima Falls, *Zambia* 87 E2 10 31 S 28 45 E
Mambirima, *Dem. Rep. of the Congo* 87 E2 11 25 S 27 33 E
Mambo, *Tanzania* 86 C4 4 52 S 38 22 E
Mambrui, *Kenya* 86 C5 3 5 S 40 5 E
Mamburao, *Phil.* 61 E4 13 13N 120 39 E
Mameigwess L., *Canada* 102 B2 52 35N 87 50W
Mamers, *France* 18 D7 48 21N 0 22 E
Mamfé, *Cameroon* 83 D6 5 50N 9 15 E
Mammoth, *U.S.A.* 115 K8 32 43N 110 39W
Mammoth Cave National Park, *U.S.A.* 108 G3 37 8N 86 13W
Mamoré →, *Bolivia* 122 E4 10 23 S 65 53W
Mamou, *Guinea* 82 C2 10 15N 12 0W
Mampatá, *Guinea-Biss.* 82 C2 11 54N 14 53W
Mampikony, *Madag.* 89 B8 16 6 S 47 38 E
Mampong, *Ghana* 83 D4 7 6N 1 26W
Mamry, Jezioro, *Poland* 44 D8 54 5N 21 50 E
Mamuju, *Indonesia* 63 E5 2 41 S 118 50 E
Mamuno, *Botswana* 88 C3 22 16 S 20 1 E
Mamuras, *Albania* 40 E3 41 34N 19 41 E
Man, *Ivory C.* 82 D3 7 30N 7 40W
Man, I. of, *U.K.* 12 C3 54 15N 4 30W
Man-Bazar, *India* 69 H12 23 4N 86 39 E
Man Na, *Burma* 67 H20 23 27N 97 19 E
Mana →, *Fr. Guiana* 125 B8 5 45N 53 55W
Manaar, G. of = Mannar, G. of, *Asia* 66 Q11 8 30N 79 0 E
Manacapuru, *Brazil* 124 D6 3 16 S 60 37W
Manacor, *Spain* 37 B10 39 34N 3 13 E
Manado, *Indonesia* 63 D6 1 29N 124 51 E
Managua, *Nic.* 120 D2 12 6N 86 20W
Managua, L. de, *Nic.* 120 D2 12 20N 86 30W
Manakara, *Madag.* 89 C8 22 8 S 48 1 E
Manali, *India* 68 C7 32 16N 77 10 E
Manama = Al Manāmah, *Bahrain* 71 E6 26 10N 50 30 E
Manambao →, *Madag.* 89 B7 17 35 S 44 0 E
Manambato, *Madag.* 89 A8 13 43 S 49 7 E
Manambolo →, *Madag.* 89 B7 19 18 S 44 22 E
Manambolosy, *Madag.* 89 B8 16 2 S 49 40 E
Mananara, *Madag.* 89 B8 16 10 S 49 46 E
Mananara →, *Madag.* 89 C8 23 21 S 47 42 E
Mananjary, *Madag.* 89 C8 21 13 S 48 20 E
Manankoro, *Mali* 82 C3 10 28N 7 25W
Manantenina, *Madag.* 89 C8 24 17 S 47 19 E
Manaos = Manaus, *Brazil* 124 D7 3 0 S 60 0W
Manapire →, *Venezuela* 124 B5 7 42N 66 7W
Manapouri, *N.Z.* 91 L1 45 34 S 167 39 E
Manapouri, L., *N.Z.* 91 L1 45 32 S 167 32 E
Manaqil, *Sudan* 81 E3 14 15N 32 59 E
Manār, Jabal, *Yemen* 74 E3 14 2N 44 17 E
Manaravolo, *Madag.* 89 C8 23 59 S 45 39 E
Manas, *China* 60 B3 44 17N 85 56 E
Manas →, *India* 67 F17 26 12N 90 40 E
Manaslu, *Nepal* 69 E11 28 33N 84 33 E
Manasquan, *U.S.A.* 111 F10 40 8N 74 3W
Manassa, *U.S.A.* 115 H11 37 11N 105 56W
Manaung, *Burma* 67 K18 18 45N 93 40 E
Manaus, *Brazil* 124 D7 3 0 S 60 0W
Manavgat, *Turkey* 72 D4 36 47N 31 26 E
Manawan L., *Canada* 105 B8 55 24N 103 14W
Manay, *Phil.* 61 H7 7 17N 126 33 E
Manbij, *Syria* 70 B3 36 31N 37 57 E
Mancha Real, *Spain* 35 H7 37 48N 3 39W
Manche □, *France* 18 C5 49 10N 1 20W
Manchegorsk, *Russia* 50 C4 67 54N 32 58 E
Manchester, *U.K.* 12 D5 53 29N 2 12W
Manchester, *Calif., U.S.A.* 116 G3 38 58N 123 41W
Manchester, *Conn., U.S.A.* 111 E12 41 47N 72 31W
Manchester, *Ga., U.S.A.* 109 J3 32 51N 84 37W
Manchester, *Iowa, U.S.A.* 112 D9 42 29N 91 27W
Manchester, *Ky., U.S.A.* 108 G4 37 9N 83 46W
Manchester, *N.H., U.S.A.* 111 D13 42 59N 71 28W
Manchester, *N.Y., U.S.A.* 110 D7 42 56N 77 16W
Manchester, *Pa., U.S.A.* 111 F8 40 4N 76 43W
Manchester, *Tenn., U.S.A.* 109 H2 35 29N 86 5W
Manchester, *Vt., U.S.A.* 111 C11 43 10N 73 5W
Manchester L., *Canada* 105 A7 61 28N 107 29W
Manchhar L., *Pakistan* 68 F2 26 25N 67 39 E
Manchuria = Dongbei, *China* 57 D13 45 0N 125 0 E
Manchurian Plain, *China* 52 E16 47 0N 124 0 E
Manciano, *Italy* 29 F8 42 35N 11 31 E
Mancifa, *Ethiopia* 81 F5 6 53N 41 50 E
Mand →, *India* 69 J10 21 42N 83 15 E
Mand →, *Iran* 71 D7 28 20N 52 30 E
Manda, *Ludewe, Tanzania* 87 E3 10 30 S 34 40 E
Manda, *Mbeya, Tanzania* 86 D3 7 58 S 32 29 E
Manda, *Mbeya, Tanzania* 87 D3 8 30 S 32 49 E
Mandabé, *Madag.* 89 C7 21 0 S 44 55 E
Mandaguari, *Brazil* 127 A5 23 32 S 51 42W
Mandah = Töhöm, *Mongolia* 56 B5 44 27N 108 2 E
Mandal, *Norway* 9 G12 58 2N 7 25 E
Mandala, Puncak, *Indonesia* 63 E10 4 44 S 140 20 E
Mandalay, *Burma* 67 J20 22 0N 96 4 E
Mandale = Mandalay, *Burma* 67 J20 22 0N 96 4 E
Mandalgarh, *India* 68 G6 25 12N 75 6 E
Mandalgovi, *Mongolia* 56 B4 45 45N 106 10 E
Mandalī, *Iraq* 70 C5 33 43N 45 28 E
Mandan, *U.S.A.* 112 B4 46 50N 100 54W
Mandaon, *Phil.* 61 E5 12 13N 123 17 E
Mandar, Teluk, *Indonesia* 63 E5 3 35 S 119 15 E
Mándas, *Italy* 30 C2 39 40N 9 8 E
Mandaue, *Phil.* 61 F5 10 20N 123 56 E
Mandelieu-la-Napoule, *France* 21 E10 43 34N 6 57 E
Mandera, *Kenya* 86 B5 3 55N 41 53 E
Mandi, *India* 68 D7 31 39N 76 58 E
Mandi Dabwali, *India* 68 E6 29 58N 74 42 E
Mandiana, *Guinea* 82 C3 10 37N 8 39W
Mandimba, *Mozam.* 87 E4 14 20 S 35 40 E
Mandioli, *Indonesia* 63 E7 0 40 S 127 20 E
Mandla, *India* 69 H9 22 39N 80 30 E
Mandø, *Denmark* 11 J2 55 18N 8 33 E
Mandorah, *Australia* 92 B5 12 32 S 130 42 E
Mandoto, *Madag.* 89 B8 19 34 S 46 17 E
Mandoúdhion, *Greece* 38 C5 38 48N 23 29 E
Mándra, *Greece* 38 C5 38 4N 23 30 E
Mandra, *Pakistan* 68 C5 33 23N 73 12 E
Mandrákhi, *Greece* 39 E9 36 36N 27 11 E
Mandrare →, *Madag.* 89 D8 25 10 S 46 30 E
Mandritsara, *Madag.* 89 B8 15 50 S 48 49 E
Mandronarivo, *Madag.* 89 C8 21 7 S 45 38 E
Mandsaur, *India* 68 G6 24 3N 75 8 E
Mandurah, *Australia* 93 F2 32 36 S 115 48 E
Mandúria, *Italy* 31 B10 40 24N 17 38 E
Mandvi, *India* 68 H3 22 51N 69 22 E
Mandya, *India* 66 N10 12 30N 77 0 E
Mandzai, *Pakistan* 68 D2 30 55N 67 6 E
Mané, *Burkina Faso* 83 C4 12 59N 1 21W
Maneh, *Iran* 71 B8 37 39N 57 7 E
Manengouba, Mts., *Cameroon* 83 E6 5 0N 9 50 E
Manera, *Madag.* 89 C7 22 55 S 44 20 E
Manérbio, *Italy* 28 C7 45 21N 10 8 E
Maneroo Cr. →, *Australia* 94 C3 23 21 S 143 53 E
Manfalût, *Egypt* 80 B3 27 20N 30 52 E
Manfredónia, *Italy* 29 G12 41 38N 15 55 E
Manfredónia, G. di, *Italy* 29 G13 41 35N 16 5 E
Manga, *Burkina Faso* 83 C4 11 40N 1 4W
Manga, *Niger* 83 C7 15 0N 11 0 E
Mangabeiras, Chapada das, *Brazil* 125 F9 10 0 S 46 30W
Mangalia, *Romania* 43 G13 43 50N 28 35 E
Mangalore, *India* 66 N9 12 55N 74 47 E
Mangan, *India* 69 F13 27 31N 88 32 E
Mangaung, *S. Africa* 85 K5 29 10 S 26 25 E
Mangawan, *India* 69 G9 24 41N 81 33 E
Mangaweka, *N.Z.* 91 H5 39 48 S 175 47 E
Manggar, *Indonesia* 62 E3 2 50 S 108 10 E
Manggawitu, *Indonesia* 63 E8 4 8 S 133 32 E
Mangindrano, *Madag.* 89 A8 14 17 S 48 58 E
Mangkalihat, Tanjung, *Indonesia* 63 D5 1 2N 118 59 E
Mangla, *Pakistan* 68 C5 33 7N 73 39 E
Mangla Dam, *Pakistan* 69 C5 33 9N 73 44 E
Manglaur, *India* 68 E7 29 44N 77 49 E
Mangnai, *China* 60 C4 37 52N 91 43 E
Mango, *Togo* 83 C5 10 20N 0 30 E
Mangoche, *Malawi* 87 E4 14 25 S 35 16 E
Mangoky →, *Madag.* 89 C7 21 29 S 43 41 E
Mangole, *Indonesia* 63 E6 1 50 S 125 55 E
Mangombe, *Dem. Rep. of the Congo* 86 C2 1 20 S 26 48 E
Mangonui, *N.Z.* 91 F4 35 1 S 173 32 E
Mangoro →, *Madag.* 89 B8 20 0 S 48 45 E
Mangrol, *Mad. P., India* 68 J4 21 7N 70 7 E
Mangrol, *Raj., India* 68 G6 25 20N 76 31 E
Mangualde, *Portugal* 34 E3 40 38N 7 48W
Mangueira, L. da, *Brazil* 127 C5 33 0 S 52 50W
Mangum, *U.S.A.* 113 H5 34 53N 99 30W
Mangyshlak Poluostrov, *Kazakstan* 50 E6 44 30N 52 30 E
Manhattan, *U.S.A.* 112 F6 39 11N 96 35W
Manhiça, *Mozam.* 89 D5 25 23 S 32 49 E
Mania →, *Madag.* 89 B8 19 42 S 45 22 E
Maniago, *Italy* 29 B9 46 10N 12 43 E
Manica, *Mozam.* 89 B5 18 58 S 32 59 E
Manica □, *Mozam.* 89 B5 19 10 S 33 45 E
Manicaland □, *Zimbabwe* 87 F3 19 0 S 32 30 E
Manicoré, *Brazil* 124 E6 5 48 S 61 16W
Manicouagan →, *Canada* 103 C6 49 30N 68 30W
Manicouagan, Rés., *Canada* 103 B6 51 5N 68 40W
Maniema □, *Dem. Rep. of the Congo* 86 C2 3 0 S 26 0 E
Manīfah, *Si. Arabia* 71 E6 27 44N 49 0 E
Manifold, C., *Australia* 94 C5 22 41 S 150 50 E
Maniganggo, *China* 58 B2 31 56N 99 10 E
Manigotagan, *Canada* 105 C9 51 6N 96 18W
Manigotagan →, *Canada* 105 C9 51 7N 96 20W
Manihari, *India* 69 G12 25 21N 87 38 E
Manihiki, *Cook Is.* 97 J11 10 24 S 161 1W
Manika, Plateau de la, *Dem. Rep. of the Congo* 87 E2 10 0 S 25 5 E
Manikpur, *India* 69 G9 25 4N 81 7 E
Manila, *Phil.* 61 D4 14 40N 121 3 E
Manila, *U.S.A.* 114 F9 40 59N 109 43W
Manila B., *Phil.* 61 D4 14 40N 120 35 E
Manilla, *Australia* 95 E5 30 45 S 150 43 E
Manimpé, *Mali* 82 C3 14 11N 5 28W
Maningrida, *Australia* 94 A1 12 3 S 134 13 E
Maninian, *Ivory C.* 82 C3 10 3N 7 52W
Manipur □, *India* 67 G19 25 0N 94 0 E
Manipur →, *Burma* 67 H19 23 45N 94 20 E
Manisa, *Turkey* 39 C9 38 38N 27 30 E
Manisa □, *Turkey* 39 C9 38 40N 28 0 E
Manistee, *U.S.A.* 108 C2 44 15N 86 19W
Manistee →, *U.S.A.* 108 C2 44 15N 86 21W
Manistique, *U.S.A.* 108 C2 45 57N 86 15W
Manito L., *Canada* 105 C7 52 43N 109 43W
Manitoba □, *Canada* 105 B9 55 30N 97 0W

Manitoba, L., *Canada* **105 C9** 51 0N 98 45W
Manitou, *Canada* **105 D9** 49 15N 98 32W
Manitou, L., *Canada* **103 B6** 50 55N 65 17W
Manitou Is., *U.S.A.* **108 C3** 45 8N 86 0W
Manitou Springs, *U.S.A.* **112 F2** 38 52N 104 55W
Manitoulin I., *Canada* **102 C3** 45 40N 82 30W
Manitouwadge, *Canada* **102 C2** 49 8N 85 48W
Manitowoc, *U.S.A.* **108 C2** 44 5N 87 40W
Manizales, *Colombia* **124 B3** 5 5N 75 32W
Manja, *Madag.* **89 C7** 21 26 S 44 20 E
Manjacaze, *Mozam.* **89 C5** 24 45 S 34 0 E
Manjakandriana, *Madag.* **89 B8** 18 55 S 47 47 E
Manjhand, *Pakistan* **68 G3** 25 50N 68 10 E
Manjil, *Iran* **71 B6** 36 46N 49 30 E
Manjimup, *Australia* **93 F2** 34 15 S 116 6 E
Manjra →, *India* **66 K10** 18 49N 77 52 E
Mankato, *Kans., U.S.A.* **112 F5** 39 47N 98 13W
Mankato, *Minn., U.S.A.* **112 C8** 44 10N 94 0W
Mankayane, *Swaziland* **89 D5** 26 40 S 31 4 E
Mankera, *Pakistan* **68 D4** 31 23N 71 26 E
Mankim, *Cameroon* **83 D7** 5 6N 12 3 E
Mankono, *Ivory C.* **82 D3** 8 1N 6 10W
Mankota, *Canada* **105 D7** 49 25N 107 5W
Manlay = Üydzin, *Mongolia* **56 B4** 44 9N 107 0 E
Manlleu, *Spain* **32 C7** 42 2N 2 17 E
Manmad, *India* **66 J9** 20 18N 74 28 E
Mann Ranges, *Australia* **93 E5** 26 6 S 130 5 E
Manna, *Indonesia* **62 E2** 4 25 S 102 55 E
Mannahill, *Australia* **95 E3** 32 25 S 140 0 E
Mannar, *Sri Lanka* **66 Q11** 9 1N 79 54 E
Mannar, G. of, *Asia* **66 Q11** 8 30N 79 0 E
Mannar I., *Sri Lanka* **66 Q11** 9 5N 79 45 E
Mannheim, *Germany* **25 F4** 49 29N 8 29 E
Manning, *Canada* **104 B5** 56 53N 117 39W
Manning, *Oreg., U.S.A.* **116 E3** 45 45N 123 13W
Manning, *S.C., U.S.A.* **109 J5** 33 42N 80 13W
Manning Prov. Park, *Canada* **104 D4** 49 5N 120 45W
Mannu →, *Italy* **30 C2** 39 16N 9 0 E
Mannu, C., *Italy* **30 B1** 40 3N 8 21 E
Mannum, *Australia* **95 E2** 34 50 S 139 20 E
Mano, *S. Leone* **82 D2** 8 3N 12 2W
Mano →, *Liberia* **82 D2** 6 56N 11 30W
Mano River, *Liberia* **82 D2** 7 20N 11 6W
Manoharpur, *India* **69 H11** 22 23N 85 12 E
Manokwari, *Indonesia* **63 E8** 0 54 S 134 0 E
Manolás, *Greece* **38 C3** 38 4N 21 21 E
Manombo, *Madag.* **89 C7** 22 57 S 43 28 E
Manono, *Dem. Rep. of the Congo* **86 D2** 7 15 S 27 25 E
Manoppello, *Italy* **29 F11** 42 15N 14 3 E
Manosque, *France* **21 E9** 43 49N 5 47 E
Manotick, *Canada* **111 A9** 45 13N 75 41W
Manouane →, *Canada* **103 C5** 49 30N 71 10W
Manouane, L., *Canada* **103 B5** 50 45N 70 45W
Manp'o, *N. Korea* **57 D14** 41 6N 126 24 E
Manpojin = Manp'o, *N. Korea* **57 D14** 41 6N 126 24 E
Manpur, *Mad. P., India* **68 H6** 22 26N 75 37 E
Manpur, *Mad. P., India* **69 H10** 23 17N 83 35 E
Manresa, *Spain* **32 D6** 41 48N 1 50 E
Mansa, *Gujarat, India* **68 H5** 23 27N 72 45 E
Mansa, *Punjab, India* **68 E6** 30 0N 75 27 E
Mansa, *Zambia* **87 E2** 11 13 S 28 55 E
Månsåsen, *Sweden* **10 A8** 63 5N 14 18 E
Mansehra, *Pakistan* **68 B5** 34 20N 73 15 E
Mansel I., *Canada* **101 B11** 62 0N 80 0W
Mansfield, *Australia* **95 F4** 37 4 S 146 6 E
Mansfield, *U.K.* **12 D6** 53 9N 1 11W
Mansfield, *La., U.S.A.* **113 J8** 32 2N 93 43W
Mansfield, *Mass., U.S.A.* **111 D13** 42 2N 71 13W
Mansfield, *Ohio, U.S.A.* **110 F2** 40 45N 82 31W
Mansfield, *Pa., U.S.A.* **110 E7** 41 48N 77 5W
Mansfield, Mt., *U.S.A.* **111 B12** 44 33N 72 49W
Mansilla de las Mulas, *Spain* **34 C5** 42 30N 5 25W
Mansle, *France* **20 C4** 45 52N 0 12 E
Mansoa, *Guinea-Biss.* **82 C1** 12 0N 15 20W
Manson Creek, *Canada* **104 B4** 55 37N 124 32W
Manta, *Ecuador* **124 D2** 1 0 S 80 40W
Mantalingajan, Mt., *Phil.* **61 G2** 8 55N 117 45 E
Mantare, *Tanzania* **86 C3** 2 42 S 33 13 E
Manteca, *U.S.A.* **116 H5** 37 48N 121 13W
Manteo, *U.S.A.* **109 H8** 35 55N 75 40W
Mantes-la-Jolie, *France* **19 D8** 48 58N 1 41 E
Manthani, *India* **66 K11** 18 40N 79 35 E
Manti, *U.S.A.* **114 G8** 39 16N 111 38W
Mantiqueira, Serra da, *Brazil* **127 A7** 22 0 S 44 0W
Manton, *U.S.A.* **108 C3** 44 25N 85 24W
Mantorp, *Sweden* **11 F9** 58 21N 15 20 E
Mántova, *Italy* **28 C7** 45 9N 10 48 E
Mänttä, *Finland* **9 E21** 62 0N 24 40 E
Mantua = Mántova, *Italy* **28 C7** 45 9N 10 48 E
Manturovo, *Russia* **48 A7** 58 23N 44 45 E
Manu, *Peru* **124 F4** 12 10 S 70 51W
Manu →, *Peru* **124 F4** 12 16 S 70 55W
Manua Is., *Amer. Samoa* **91 B14** 14 13 S 169 35W
Manuel Alves →, *Brazil* **125 F9** 11 19 S 48 28W
Manui, *Indonesia* **63 E6** 3 35 S 123 5 E
Manukau, *N.Z.* **91 G5** 40 43 S 175 13 E
Manuripi →, *Bolivia* **124 F5** 11 6 S 67 36W
Many, *U.S.A.* **113 K8** 31 34N 93 29W
Manyara, L., *Tanzania* **86 C4** 3 40 S 35 50 E
Manyas, *Turkey* **41 F11** 40 2N 27 59 E
Manych →, *Russia* **49 G5** 47 13N 40 40 E
Manych-Gudilo, Ozero, *Russia* **49 G6** 46 24N 42 38 E
Manyonga →, *Tanzania* **86 C3** 4 10 S 34 15 E
Manyoni, *Tanzania* **86 D3** 5 45 S 34 55 E
Manzai, *Pakistan* **68 C4** 32 12N 70 15 E
Manzala, Bahra el, *Egypt* **80 H7** 31 10N 31 56 E
Manzanares, *Spain* **35 F7** 39 2N 3 22W
Manzaneda, *Spain* **34 C3** 42 12N 7 15W
Manzanillo, *Cuba* **120 B4** 20 20N 77 31W
Manzanillo, *Mexico* **118 D4** 19 0N 104 20W
Manzanillo, Pta., *Panama* **120 E4** 9 30N 79 40W
Manzano Mts., *U.S.A.* **115 J10** 34 40N 106 20W
Manzarīyeh, *Iran* **71 C6** 34 53N 50 50 E
Manzhouli, *China* **60 B6** 49 35N 117 25 E
Manzini, *Swaziland* **89 D5** 26 30 S 31 25 E
Mao, *Chad* **79 F9** 14 4N 15 19 E
Maó, *Spain* **37 B11** 39 53N 4 16 E
Maoke, Pegunungan, *Indonesia* **63 E9** 3 40 S 137 30 E
Maolin, *China* **57 C12** 43 58N 123 30 E
Maoming, *China* **59 G8** 21 50N 110 54 E
Maopi T'ou, *China* **59 G13** 21 56N 120 43 E
Maouri, Dallol →, *Niger* **83 C5** 12 5N 3 30 E
Maoxian, *China* **58 B4** 31 41N 103 49 E
Maoxing, *China* **57 B13** 45 28N 124 40 E
Mapam Yumco, *China* **60 C3** 30 45N 81 28 E
Mapastepec, *Mexico* **119 D6** 15 26N 92 54W
Mapia, Kepulauan, *Indonesia* **63 D8** 0 50N 134 20 E
Mapimí, *Mexico* **118 B4** 25 50N 103 50W
Mapimí, Bolsón de, *Mexico* **118 B4** 27 30N 104 15W
Maping, *China* **59 B9** 31 34N 113 32 E
Mapinga, *Tanzania* **86 D4** 6 40 S 39 12 E
Mapinhane, *Mozam.* **89 C6** 22 20 S 35 0 E
Maple Creek, *Canada* **105 D7** 49 55N 109 29W
Maple Valley, *U.S.A.* **116 C4** 47 25N 122 3W
Mapleton, *U.S.A.* **114 D2** 44 2N 123 52W
Mapuera →, *Brazil* **124 D7** 1 5 S 57 2W
Mapulanguene, *Mozam.* **89 C5** 24 29 S 32 6 E
Maputo, *Mozam.* **89 D5** 25 58 S 32 32 E
Maputo □, *Mozam.* **89 D5** 26 0 S 32 25 E
Maputo, B. de, *Mozam.* **89 D5** 25 50 S 32 45 E
Maqiaohe, *China* **57 B16** 44 40N 130 30 E
Maqnā, *Si. Arabia* **70 D2** 28 25N 34 50 E
Maqueda, *Spain* **34 E6** 40 4N 4 22W
Maquela do Zombo, *Angola* **84 F3** 6 0 S 15 15 E
Maquinchao, *Argentina* **128 E3** 41 15 S 68 50W
Maquoketa, *U.S.A.* **112 D9** 42 4N 90 40W
Mar, Serra do, *Brazil* **127 B6** 25 30 S 49 0W
Mar Chiquita, L., *Argentina* **126 C3** 30 40 S 62 50W
Mar del Plata, *Argentina* **126 D4** 38 0 S 57 30W
Mar Menor, *Spain* **33 H4** 37 40N 0 45W
Mara, *Tanzania* **86 C3** 1 30 S 34 32 E
Mara □, *Tanzania* **86 C3** 1 45 S 34 20 E
Maraã, *Brazil* **124 D5** 1 52 S 65 25W
Marabá, *Brazil* **125 E9** 5 20 S 49 5W
Maracá, I. de, *Brazil* **125 C8** 2 10N 50 30W
Maracaibo, *Venezuela* **124 A4** 10 40N 71 37W
Maracaibo, L. de, *Venezuela* **122 C3** 9 40N 71 30W
Maracaju, *Brazil* **127 A4** 21 38 S 55 9W
Maracay, *Venezuela* **124 A5** 10 15N 67 28W
Maracena, *Spain* **35 H7** 37 12N 3 38W
Maradi, *Niger* **83 C6** 13 29N 7 20 E
Marāgheh, *Iran* **70 B5** 37 30N 46 12 E
Marāh, *Si. Arabia* **70 E5** 25 0N 45 35 E
Marajó, I. de, *Brazil* **122 D6** 1 0 S 49 30W
Marākand, *Iran* **70 B5** 38 51N 45 16 E
Maralal, *Kenya* **86 B4** 1 0N 36 38 E
Maralinga, *Australia* **93 F5** 30 13 S 131 32 E
Maramaraereğlisi, *Turkey* **41 F11** 40 57N 27 57 E
Marampa, *S. Leone* **82 D2** 8 45N 12 28W
Maramureş □, *Romania* **43 C9** 47 45N 24 0 E
Maran, *Malaysia* **65 L4** 3 35N 102 45 E
Marana, *U.S.A.* **115 K8** 32 27N 111 13W
Maranboy, *Australia* **92 B5** 14 40 S 132 39 E
Maranchón, *Spain* **32 D2** 41 6N 2 15W
Marand, *Iran* **70 B5** 38 30N 45 45 E
Marang, *Malaysia* **65 K4** 5 12N 103 13 E
Maranguape, *Brazil* **125 D11** 3 55 S 38 50W
Maranhão = São Luís, *Brazil* **125 D10** 2 39 S 44 15W
Maranhão □, *Brazil* **125 E9** 5 0 S 46 0W
Marano, L. di, *Italy* **29 C10** 45 44N 13 10 E
Maranoa →, *Australia* **95 D4** 27 50 S 148 37 E
Marañón →, *Peru* **122 D3** 4 30 S 73 35W
Marão, *Mozam.* **89 C5** 24 18 S 34 2 E
Maras = Kahramanmaraş, *Turkey* **70 B3** 37 37N 36 53 E
Mărăşeşti, *Romania* **43 E12** 45 52N 27 14 E
Maratea, *Italy* **31 C8** 39 59N 15 43 E
Marateca, *Portugal* **35 G2** 38 34N 8 40W
Marathasa □, *Cyprus* **36 E11** 34 59N 32 51 E
Marathókambos, *Greece* **39 D8** 37 43N 26 42 E
Marathon, *Australia* **94 C3** 20 51 S 143 32 E
Marathon, *Canada* **102 C2** 48 44N 86 23W
Marathón, *Greece* **38 C5** 38 11N 23 58 E
Marathon, *N.Y., U.S.A.* **111 D8** 42 27N 76 2W
Marathon, *Tex., U.S.A.* **113 K3** 30 12N 103 15W
Marathóvouno, *Cyprus* **36 D12** 35 13N 33 37 E
Maratua, *Indonesia* **63 D5** 2 10N 118 35 E
Maravatío, *Mexico* **118 D4** 19 51N 100 25W
Marawi City, *Phil.* **61 G6** 8 0N 124 21 E
Marāwih, *U.A.E.* **71 E7** 24 18N 53 18 E
Marbella, *Spain* **35 J6** 36 30N 4 57W
Marble Bar, *Australia* **92 D2** 21 9 S 119 44 E
Marble Falls, *U.S.A.* **113 K5** 30 35N 98 16W
Marblehead, *U.S.A.* **111 D14** 42 30N 70 51W
Marburg, *Germany* **24 E4** 50 47N 8 46 E
Marcal →, *Hungary* **42 C2** 47 41N 17 40 E
Marcali, *Hungary* **42 D2** 46 35N 17 25 E
Marcaria, *Italy* **28 C7** 45 7N 10 32 E
Mărcăuti, *Moldova* **43 B12** 48 20N 27 14 E
March, *U.K.* **13 E8** 52 33N 0 5 E
Marche, *France* **20 B5** 46 5N 1 20 E
Marche □, *Italy* **29 E10** 43 30N 13 15 E
Marche-en-Famenne, *Belgium* **17 D5** 50 14N 5 19 E
Marchena, *Spain* **35 H5** 37 18N 5 23W
Marches = Marche □, *Italy* **29 E10** 43 30N 13 15 E
Marciana Marina, *Italy* **28 F7** 42 48N 10 12 E
Marcianise, *Italy* **31 A7** 41 2N 14 17 E
Marcigny, *France* **19 F11** 46 17N 4 2 E
Marcillat-en-Combraille, *France* **19 F9** 46 12N 2 38 E
Marck, *France* **19 B8** 50 57N 1 57 E
Marckolsheim, *France* **19 D14** 48 10N 7 30 E
Marco, *U.S.A.* **109 N5** 25 58N 81 44W
Marcos Juárez, *Argentina* **126 C3** 32 42 S 62 5W
Mărculeşti, *Moldova* **43 C13** 47 52N 28 14 E
Marcus I. = Minami-Tori-Shima, *Pac. Oc.* **96 E7** 24 20N 153 58 E
Marcus Necker Ridge, *Pac. Oc.* **96 F9** 20 0N 175 0 E
Marcy, Mt., *U.S.A.* **111 B11** 44 7N 73 56W
Mardan, *Pakistan* **68 B5** 34 20N 72 0 E
Mardin, *Turkey* **70 B4** 37 20N 40 43 E
Mårdsjön, *Sweden* **10 A9** 63 18N 15 35 E
Maréccia →, *Italy* **29 D9** 44 4N 12 34 E
Maree, L., *U.K.* **14 D3** 57 40N 5 26W
Mareeba, *Australia* **94 B4** 16 59 S 145 28 E
Mareetsane, *S. Africa* **88 D4** 26 9 S 25 25 E
Maremma, *Italy* **29 F8** 42 30N 11 30 E
Maréna, *Mali* **82 C2** 14 36N 10 45W
Maréna, *Mali* **82 C3** 13 55N 7 20W
Marengo, *U.S.A.* **112 E8** 41 48N 92 4W
Marennes, *France* **20 C2** 45 49N 1 7W
Marenyi, *Kenya* **86 C4** 4 22 S 39 8 E
Marerano, *Madag.* **89 C7** 21 23 S 44 52 E
Maréttimo, *Italy* **30 E5** 37 58N 12 4 E
Mareuil, *France* **20 C4** 45 26N 0 29 E
Marfa, *U.S.A.* **113 K2** 30 19N 104 1W
Marfa Pt., *Malta* **36 D1** 35 59N 14 19 E
Marganets = Marhanets, *Ukraine* **47 J8** 47 40N 34 40 E
Margaret →, *Australia* **92 C4** 18 9 S 125 41 E
Margaret Bay, *Canada* **104 C3** 51 20N 127 35W
Margaret L., *Canada* **104 B5** 58 56N 115 25W
Margaret River, *Australia* **93 F2** 33 57 S 115 4 E
Margarita, I. de, *Venezuela* **122 B4** 11 0N 64 0W
Margarítion, *Greece* **38 B2** 39 22N 20 26 E
Margaritovo, *Russia* **54 C7** 43 25N 134 45 E
Margate, *S. Africa* **89 E5** 30 50 S 30 20 E
Margate, *U.K.* **13 F9** 51 23N 1 23 E
Margeride, Mts. de la, *France* **20 D7** 44 43N 3 38 E
Margherita di Savóia, *Italy* **31 A9** 41 22N 16 9 E
Marghita, *Romania* **42 C7** 47 22N 22 22 E
Margonin, *Poland* **45 F4** 52 58N 17 5 E
Margosatubig, *Phil.* **61 H5** 7 34N 123 10 E
Mārgow, Dasht-e, *Afghan.* **66 D3** 30 40N 62 30 E
Marguerite, *Canada* **104 C4** 52 30N 122 25W
Marhanets, *Ukraine* **47 J8** 47 40N 34 40 E
Mari El □, *Russia* **48 B8** 56 30N 48 0 E
Mari Indus, *Pakistan* **68 C4** 32 57N 71 34 E
Mari Republic = Mari El □, *Russia* **48 B8** 56 30N 48 0 E
María, Sa. de, *Spain* **33 H2** 37 39N 2 14W
María Elena, *Chile* **126 A2** 22 18 S 69 40W
María Grande, *Argentina* **126 C4** 31 45 S 59 55W
Maria I., *N. Terr., Australia* **94 A2** 14 52 S 135 45 E
Maria I., *Tas., Australia* **94 G4** 42 35 S 148 0 E
Maria van Diemen, C., *N.Z.* **91 F4** 34 29 S 172 40 E
Mariager, *Denmark* **11 H3** 56 40N 9 59 E
Mariager Fjord, *Denmark* **11 H4** 56 42N 10 19 E
Mariakani, *Kenya* **86 C4** 3 50 S 39 27 E
Marian, *Australia* **94 C4** 21 9 S 148 57 E
Marian L., *Canada* **104 A5** 63 0N 116 15W
Mariana Trench, *Pac. Oc.* **52 H18** 13 0N 145 0 E
Marianao, *Cuba* **120 B3** 23 8N 82 24W
Marianna, *Ark., U.S.A.* **113 H9** 34 46N 90 46W
Marianna, *Fla., U.S.A.* **109 K3** 30 46N 85 14W
Mariannelund, *Sweden* **11 G9** 57 37N 15 35 E
Mariánské Lázně, *Czech Rep.* **26 B5** 49 58N 12 41 E
Marias →, *U.S.A.* **114 C8** 47 56N 110 30W
Mariato, Punta, *Panama* **120 E3** 7 12N 80 52W
Mariazell, *Austria* **26 D8** 47 47N 15 19 E
Maribo, *Denmark* **11 K5** 54 48N 11 30 E
Maribor, *Slovenia* **29 B12** 46 36N 15 40 E
Marico →, *Africa* **88 C4** 23 35 S 26 57 E
Maricopa, *Ariz., U.S.A.* **115 K7** 33 4N 112 3W
Maricopa, *Calif., U.S.A.* **117 K7** 35 4N 119 24W
Marîdî, *Sudan* **81 G2** 4 55N 29 25 E
Marîdî, Wadi →, *Sudan* **81 F2** 6 15N 29 21 E
Marié →, *Brazil* **124 D5** 0 27 S 66 26W
Marie Byrd Land, *Antarctica* **5 D14** 79 30 S 125 0W
Marie-Galante, *Guadeloupe* **121 C7** 15 56N 61 16W
Mariecourt = Kangiqsujuaq, *Canada* **101 B12** 61 30N 72 0W
Mariefred, *Sweden* **10 E11** 59 15N 17 12 E
Marieholm, *Sweden* **11 J7** 55 53N 13 10 E
Mariembourg, *Belgium* **17 D4** 50 6N 4 31 E
Marienbad = Mariánské Lázně, *Czech Rep.* **26 B5** 49 58N 12 41 E
Marienberg, *Germany* **24 E9** 50 39N 13 9 E
Mariental, *Namibia* **88 C2** 24 36 S 18 0 E
Marienville, *U.S.A.* **110 E5** 41 28N 79 8W
Mariestad, *Sweden* **11 F7** 58 43N 13 50 E
Marietta, *Ga., U.S.A.* **109 J3** 33 57N 84 33W
Marietta, *Ohio, U.S.A.* **108 F5** 39 25N 81 27W
Marieville, *Canada* **111 A11** 45 26N 73 10W
Mariga →, *Nigeria* **83 C6** 9 40N 5 55 E
Marignane, *France* **21 E9** 43 25N 5 13 E
Marihatag, *Phil.* **61 G7** 8 48N 126 18 E
Mariinsk, *Russia* **50 D9** 56 10N 87 20 E
Mariinskiy Posad, *Russia* **48 B8** 56 10N 47 45 E
Marijampolė, *Lithuania* **9 J20** 54 33N 23 19 E
Marijampolės □, *Lithuania* **44 D10** 54 30N 23 21 E
Marília, *Brazil* **127 A6** 22 13 S 50 0W
Marín, *Spain* **34 C2** 42 23N 8 42W
Marina, *U.S.A.* **116 J5** 36 41N 121 48W
Marinduque, *Phil.* **63 B6** 13 25N 122 0 E
Marine City, *U.S.A.* **110 D2** 42 43N 82 30W
Marineo, *Italy* **30 E6** 37 57N 13 25 E
Marinette, *U.S.A.* **108 C2** 45 6N 87 38W
Maringá, *Brazil* **127 A5** 23 26 S 52 2W
Marinha Grande, *Portugal* **34 F2** 39 45N 8 56W
Marino, *Italy* **29 G9** 41 46N 12 39 E
Marion, *Ala., U.S.A.* **109 J2** 32 38N 87 19W
Marion, *Ill., U.S.A.* **113 G10** 37 44N 88 56W
Marion, *Ind., U.S.A.* **108 E3** 40 32N 85 40W
Marion, *Iowa, U.S.A.* **112 D9** 42 2N 91 36W
Marion, *Kans., U.S.A.* **112 F6** 38 21N 97 1W
Marion, *N.C., U.S.A.* **109 H5** 35 41N 82 1W
Marion, *Ohio, U.S.A.* **108 E4** 40 35N 83 8W
Marion, *S.C., U.S.A.* **109 H6** 34 11N 79 24W
Marion, *Va., U.S.A.* **109 G5** 36 50N 81 31W
Marion, L., *U.S.A.* **109 J5** 33 28N 80 10W
Mariposa, *U.S.A.* **116 H7** 37 29N 119 58W
Mariscal Estigarribia, *Paraguay* **126 A3** 22 3 S 60 40W
Maritime Alps = Maritimes, Alpes, *Europe* **21 D11** 44 10N 7 10 E
Maritimes, Alpes, *Europe* **21 D11** 44 10N 7 10 E
Maritsa = Évros →, *Bulgaria* **72 B2** 41 40N 26 34 E
Maritsá, *Greece* **36 C10** 36 22N 28 8 E
Mariupol, *Ukraine* **47 J9** 47 5N 37 31 E
Marīvān, *Iran* **70 C5** 35 30N 46 25 E
Marj 'Uyūn, *Lebanon* **75 B4** 33 20N 35 35 E
Marka, *Si. Arabia* **80 D5** 18 14N 41 19 E
Markam, *China* **58 C2** 29 42N 98 38 E
Markaryd, *Sweden* **11 H7** 56 28N 13 35 E
Markazī □, *Iran* **71 C6** 35 0N 49 30 E
Markdale, *Canada* **110 B4** 44 19N 80 39W
Marked Tree, *U.S.A.* **113 H9** 35 32N 90 25W
Markelsdorfer Huk, *Germany* **24 A7** 54 33N 11 4 E
Market Drayton, *U.K.* **12 E5** 52 54N 2 29W
Market Harborough, *U.K.* **13 E7** 52 29N 0 55W
Market Rasen, *U.K.* **12 D7** 53 24N 0 20W
Markham, *Canada* **110 C5** 43 52N 79 16W
Markham, Mt., *Antarctica* **5 E11** 83 0 S 164 0 E
Marki, *Poland* **45 F8** 52 20N 21 2 E
Markkleeberg, *Germany* **24 D8** 51 16N 12 23 E
Markleeville, *U.S.A.* **116 G7** 38 42N 119 47W
Markoupoulon, *Greece* **38 D5** 37 53N 23 57 E
Markovac, *Serbia, Yug.* **40 B5** 44 14N 21 7 E
Markovo, *Russia* **51 C17** 64 40N 170 24 E
Markoye, *Burkina Faso* **83 C5** 14 39N 0 2 E
Marks, *Russia* **48 E8** 51 45N 46 50 E
Marksville, *U.S.A.* **113 K8** 31 8N 92 4W
Markt Schwaben, *Germany* **25 G7** 48 11N 11 52 E
Marktoberdorf, *Germany* **25 H6** 47 45N 10 37 E
Marktredwitz, *Germany* **25 E8** 50 1N 12 6 E
Marl, *Germany* **24 D3** 51 39N 7 4 E
Marla, *Australia* **95 D1** 27 19 S 133 33 E
Marlbank, *Canada* **110 B7** 44 26N 77 6W
Marlboro, *Mass., U.S.A.* **111 D13** 42 19N 71 33W
Marlboro, *N.Y., U.S.A.* **111 E11** 41 36N 73 59W
Marlborough, *Australia* **94 C4** 22 46 S 149 52 E
Marlborough, *U.K.* **13 F6** 51 25N 1 43W
Marlborough Downs, *U.K.* **13 F6** 51 27N 1 53W
Marle, *France* **19 C10** 49 43N 3 47 E
Marlin, *U.S.A.* **113 K6** 31 18N 96 54W
Marlow, *Germany* **24 A8** 54 9N 12 33 E
Marlow, *U.S.A.* **113 H6** 34 39N 97 58W
Marmagao, *India* **66 M8** 15 25N 73 56 E
Marmande, *France* **20 D4** 44 30N 0 10 E
Marmara, *Turkey* **41 F11** 40 35N 27 34 E
Marmara, Sea of = Marmara Denizi, *Turkey* **41 F12** 40 45N 28 15 E
Marmara Denizi, *Turkey* **41 F12** 40 45N 28 15 E
Marmara Gölü, *Turkey* **39 C10** 38 37N 28 2 E
Marmaris, *Turkey* **39 E10** 36 50N 28 14 E
Marmaris Limanı, *Turkey* **39 E10** 36 50N 28 19 E
Marmion, Mt., *Australia* **93 E2** 29 16 S 119 50 E
Marmion L., *Canada* **102 C1** 48 55N 91 20W
Marmolada, Mte., *Italy* **29 B8** 46 26N 11 51 E
Marmolejo, *Spain* **35 G6** 38 3N 4 13W
Marmora, *Canada* **102 D4** 44 28N 77 41W
Mármora, La, *Italy* **30 C2** 39 59N 9 20 E
Marnay, *France* **19 E12** 47 16N 5 48 E
Marne, *Germany* **24 B5** 53 56N 9 2 E
Marne □, *France* **19 D11** 48 50N 4 10 E
Marne →, *France* **19 D9** 48 48N 2 24 E
Marneuli, *Georgia* **49 K7** 41 30N 44 48 E
Maroala, *Madag.* **89 B8** 15 23 S 47 59 E
Maroantsetra, *Madag.* **89 B8** 15 26 S 49 44 E
Maroelaboom, *Namibia* **88 B2** 19 15 S 18 53 E
Marofandilia, *Madag.* **89 C7** 20 7 S 44 34 E
Marolambo, *Madag.* **89 C8** 20 2 S 48 7 E
Maromandia, *Madag.* **89 A8** 14 13 S 48 5 E
Marondera, *Zimbabwe* **87 F3** 18 5 S 31 42 E
Maroni →, *Fr. Guiana* **125 B8** 5 30N 54 0W
Marónia, *Greece* **41 F9** 40 53N 25 30 E
Maronne →, *France* **20 C5** 45 5N 1 56 E
Maroochydore, *Australia* **95 D5** 26 29 S 153 5 E
Maroona, *Australia* **95 F3** 37 27 S 142 54 E
Maros →, *Hungary* **42 D5** 46 15N 20 13 E
Marosakoa, *Madag.* **89 B8** 15 26 S 46 38 E
Maroseranana, *Madag.* **89 B8** 18 32 S 48 51 E
Maróstica, *Italy* **29 C8** 45 44N 11 40 E
Marotandrano, *Madag.* **89 B8** 16 10 S 48 50 E
Marotaolano, *Madag.* **89 A8** 12 47 S 49 15 E
Maroua, *Cameroon* **83 C7** 10 40N 14 20 E
Marovato, *Madag.* **89 B8** 15 48 S 48 5 E
Marovoay, *Madag.* **89 B8** 16 6 S 46 39 E
Marquard, *S. Africa* **88 D4** 28 40 S 27 28 E
Marquesas Is. = Marquises, Is., *Pac. Oc.* **97 H14** 9 30 S 140 0W
Marquette, *U.S.A.* **108 B2** 46 33N 87 24W
Marquise, *France* **19 B8** 50 50N 1 40 E
Marquises, Is., *Pac. Oc.* **97 H14** 9 30 S 140 0W
Marra, Djebel, *Sudan* **79 F10** 13 10N 24 22 E
Marra, Gebel, *Sudan* **81 F2** 7 20N 27 35 E
Marracuene, *Mozam.* **89 D5** 25 45 S 32 35 E
Marradi, *Italy* **29 D8** 44 4N 11 37 E
Marrakech, *Morocco* **78 B4** 31 9N 8 0W
Marratxi, *Spain* **32 F7** 39 39N 2 48 E
Marrawah, *Australia* **94 G3** 40 55 S 144 42 E
Marree, *Australia* **95 D2** 29 39 S 138 1 E
Marrero, *U.S.A.* **113 L9** 29 54N 90 6W
Marrimane, *Mozam.* **89 C5** 22 58 S 33 34 E
Marromeu, *Mozam.* **89 B6** 18 15 S 36 25 E
Marroquí, Punta, *Spain* **35 K5** 36 0N 5 37W
Marrowie Cr. →, *Australia* **95 E4** 33 23 S 145 40 E
Marrubane, *Mozam.* **87 F4** 18 0 S 37 0 E
Marrūbiu, *Italy* **30 C1** 39 45N 8 35 E
Marrupa, *Mozam.* **87 E4** 13 8 S 37 30 E
Mars Hill, *U.S.A.* **109 B12** 46 31N 67 52W
Marsá 'Alam, *Egypt* **80 B3** 25 5N 34 54 E
Marsā Matrūh, *Egypt* **80 A2** 31 19N 27 9 E
Marsá Sha'b, *Sudan* **80 C4** 22 52N 35 47 E
Marsabit, *Kenya* **86 B4** 2 18N 38 0 E
Marsala, *Italy* **30 E5** 37 48N 12 26 E
Marsalforn, *Malta* **36 C1** 36 4N 14 15 E
Mârşani, *Romania* **43 F9** 44 1N 24 1 E
Marsberg, *Germany* **24 D4** 51 28N 8 52 E
Marsciano, *Italy* **29 F9** 42 54N 12 20 E
Marsden, *Australia* **95 E4** 33 47 S 147 32 E
Marseillan, *France* **20 E7** 43 23N 3 31 E
Marseille, *France* **21 E9** 43 18N 5 23 E
Marseilles = Marseille, *France* **21 E9** 43 18N 5 23 E
Marsh I., *U.S.A.* **113 L9** 29 34N 91 53W
Marshall, *Liberia* **82 D2** 6 8N 10 22W
Marshall, *Ark., U.S.A.* **113 H8** 35 55N 92 38W
Marshall, *Mich., U.S.A.* **108 D3** 42 16N 84 58W
Marshall, *Minn., U.S.A.* **112 C7** 44 25N 95 45W
Marshall, *Mo., U.S.A.* **112 F8** 39 7N 93 12W
Marshall, *Tex., U.S.A.* **113 J7** 32 33N 94 23W
Marshall →, *Australia* **94 C2** 22 59 S 136 59 E
Marshall Is. ■, *Pac. Oc.* **96 G9** 9 0N 171 0 E
Marshalltown, *U.S.A.* **112 D8** 42 3N 92 55W
Marshbrook, *Zimbabwe* **89 B5** 18 33 S 31 9 E
Marshfield, *Mo., U.S.A.* **113 G8** 37 15N 92 54W
Marshfield, *Vt., U.S.A.* **111 B12** 44 20N 72 20W
Marshfield, *Wis., U.S.A.* **112 C9** 44 40N 90 10W
Marshūn, *Iran* **71 B6** 36 19N 49 23 E
Mársico Nuovo, *Italy* **31 B8** 40 25N 15 44 E
Märsta, *Sweden* **10 E11** 59 37N 17 52 E
Marstal, *Denmark* **11 K4** 54 51N 10 30 E
Marstrand, *Sweden* **11 G5** 57 53N 11 35 E
Mart, *U.S.A.* **113 K6** 31 33N 96 50W
Marta →, *Italy* **29 F8** 42 14N 11 42 E
Martaban, *Burma* **67 L20** 16 30N 97 35 E
Martaban, G. of, *Burma* **67 L20** 16 5N 96 30 E
Martano, *Italy* **31 B11** 40 12N 18 18 E
Martapura, *Kalimantan, Indonesia* **62 E4** 3 22 S 114 47 E
Martapura, *Sumatera, Indonesia* **62 E2** 4 19 S 104 22 E
Marte, *Nigeria* **83 C7** 12 23N 13 46 E
Martel, *France* **20 D5** 44 57N 1 37 E
Martelange, *Belgium* **17 E5** 49 49N 5 43 E
Martellago, *Italy* **29 C9** 45 33N 12 9 E
Martés, Sierra, *Spain* **33 F4** 39 20N 1 0W
Martfű, *Hungary* **42 C5** 47 1N 20 17 E
Martha's Vineyard, *U.S.A.* **111 E14** 41 25N 70 38W
Martigné-Ferchaud, *France* **18 E5** 47 50N 1 20W
Martigny, *Switz.* **25 J3** 46 6N 7 3 E
Martigues, *France* **21 E9** 43 24N 5 4 E
Martin, *Slovak Rep.* **27 B11** 49 6N 18 58 E
Martin, *S. Dak., U.S.A.* **112 D4** 43 11N 101 44W
Martin, *Tenn., U.S.A.* **113 G10** 36 21N 88 51W
Martín →, *Spain* **32 D4** 41 18N 0 19W
Martin, L., *U.S.A.* **109 J3** 32 41N 85 55W
Martina Franca, *Italy* **31 B10** 40 42N 17 20 E
Martinborough, *N.Z.* **91 J5** 41 14 S 175 29 E
Martinez, *Calif., U.S.A.* **116 G4** 38 1N 122 8W
Martinez, *Ga., U.S.A.* **109 J4** 33 31N 82 4W
Martinique ■, *W. Indies* **121 D7** 14 40N 61 0W
Martinique Passage, *W. Indies* **121 C7** 15 15N 61 0W
Martínon, *Greece* **38 C5** 38 35N 23 12 E
Martinópolis, *Brazil* **127 A5** 22 11 S 51 12W
Martins Ferry, *U.S.A.* **110 F4** 40 6N 80 44W
Martinsberg, *Austria* **26 C8** 48 22N 15 9 E
Martinsburg, *Pa., U.S.A.* **110 F6** 40 19N 78 20W
Martinsburg, *W. Va., U.S.A.* **108 F7** 39 27N 77 58W
Martinsicuro, *Italy* **29 F10** 42 54N 13 54 E
Martinsville, *Ind., U.S.A.* **108 F2** 39 26N 86 25W
Martinsville, *Va., U.S.A.* **109 G6** 36 41N 79 52W
Marton, *N.Z.* **91 J5** 40 4 S 175 23 E
Martorell, *Spain* **32 D6** 41 28N 1 56 E
Martos, *Spain* **35 H7** 37 44N 3 58W
Martuni, *Armenia* **49 K7** 40 8N 45 20 E
Maru, *Nigeria* **83 C6** 12 22N 6 22 E
Marudi, *Malaysia* **62 D4** 4 11N 114 19 E
Ma'ruf, *Afghan.* **66 D5** 31 30N 67 6 E
Marugame, *Japan* **55 G6** 34 15N 133 40 E
Marunga, *Angola* **88 B3** 17 28 S 20 2 E
Marungu, Mts., *Dem. Rep. of the Congo* **86 D3** 7 30 S 30 0 E
Marv Dasht, *Iran* **71 D7** 29 50N 52 40 E
Marvast, *Iran* **71 D7** 30 30N 54 15 E
Marvejols, *France* **20 D7** 44 33N 3 19 E
Marvel Loch, *Australia* **93 F2** 31 28 S 119 29 E
Marwar, *India* **68 G5** 25 43N 73 45 E
Mary, *Turkmenistan* **50 F7** 37 40N 61 50 E
Maryborough = Port Laoise, *Ireland* **15 C4** 53 2N 7 18W
Maryborough, *Queens., Australia* **95 D5** 25 31 S 152 37 E
Maryborough, *Vic., Australia* **95 F3** 37 0 S 143 44 E
Maryfield, *Canada* **105 D8** 49 50N 101 35W
Maryland □, *U.S.A.* **108 F7** 39 0N 76 30W
Maryland Junction, *Zimbabwe* **87 F3** 17 45 S 30 31 E
Maryport, *U.K.* **12 C4** 54 44N 3 28W
Mary's Harbour, *Canada* **103 B8** 52 18N 55 51W
Marystown, *Canada* **103 C8** 47 10N 55 10W
Marysville, *Canada* **104 D5** 49 35N 116 0W
Marysville, *Calif., U.S.A.* **116 F5** 39 9N 121 35W
Marysville, *Kans., U.S.A.* **112 F6** 39 51N 96 39W
Marysville, *Mich., U.S.A.* **110 D2** 42 54N 82 29W
Marysville, *Ohio, U.S.A.* **108 E4** 40 14N 83 22W
Marysville, *Wash., U.S.A.* **116 B4** 48 3N 122 11W
Maryville, *Mo., U.S.A.* **112 E7** 40 21N 94 52W
Maryville, *Tenn., U.S.A.* **109 H4** 35 46N 83 58W
Marzūq, *Libya* **79 C8** 25 53N 13 57 E
Masahunga, *Tanzania* **86 C3** 2 6 S 33 18 E
Masai Steppe, *Tanzania* **86 C4** 4 30 S 36 30 E
Masaka, *Uganda* **86 C3** 0 21 S 31 45 E
Masalembo, Kepulauan, *Indonesia* **62 F4** 5 35 S 114 30 E
Masalima, Kepulauan, *Indonesia* **62 F5** 5 4 S 117 5 E
Masallı, *Azerbaijan* **73 C13** 39 3N 48 40 E
Masamba, *Indonesia* **63 E6** 2 30 S 120 15 E
Masan, *S. Korea* **57 G15** 35 11N 128 32 E
Masandam, Ra's, *Oman* **71 E8** 26 30N 56 30 E
Masasi, *Tanzania* **87 E4** 10 45 S 38 52 E
Masaya, *Nic.* **120 D2** 12 0N 86 7W
Masba, *Nigeria* **83 C7** 11 35N 13 1 E
Masbate, *Phil.* **61 E5** 12 21N 123 36 E
Máscali, *Italy* **31 E8** 37 45N 15 12 E
Mascara, *Algeria* **78 A6** 35 26N 0 6 E
Mascota, *Mexico* **118 C4** 20 30N 104 50W
Masela, *Indonesia* **63 F7** 8 9 S 129 51 E
Maseru, *Lesotho* **88 D4** 29 18 S 27 30 E
Mashaba, *Zimbabwe* **87 G3** 20 2 S 30 29 E
Mashābīh, *Si. Arabia* **70 E3** 25 35N 36 30 E
Mashan, *China* **58 F7** 23 40N 108 11 E
Mashar, *Sudan* **81 F2** 8 59N 26 51 E
Mashegu, *Nigeria* **83 D6** 10 0N 5 35 E

Masherbrum, *Pakistan* **69 B7** 35 38N 76 18 E
Mashhad, *Iran* **71 B8** 36 20N 59 35 E
Mashi, *Nigeria* **83 C6** 13 0N 7 54 E
Mashīz, *Iran* **71 D8** 29 56N 56 37 E
Māshkel, Hāmūn-i-, *Pakistan* **66 E3** 28 20N 62 56 E
Mashki Chāh, *Pakistan* **66 E3** 29 5N 62 30 E
Mashonaland, *Zimbabwe* **85 H6** 16 30 S 31 0 E
Mashonaland Central □, *Zimbabwe* **89 B5** 17 30 S 31 0 E
Mashonaland East □, *Zimbabwe* **89 B5** 18 0 S 32 0 E
Mashonaland West □, *Zimbabwe* **89 B4** 17 30 S 29 30 E
Mashrakh, *India* **69 F11** 26 7N 84 48 E
Mashtaga = Maştağa, *Azerbaijan* **49 K10** 40 35N 49 57 E
Masindi, *Uganda* **86 B3** 1 40N 31 43 E
Masindi Port, *Uganda* **86 B3** 1 43N 32 2 E
Maşīrah, *Oman* **74 C6** 21 0N 58 50 E
Maşīrah, Khalīj, *Oman* **74 C6** 20 10N 58 10 E
Masisi, *Dem. Rep. of the Congo* **86 C2** 1 23 S 28 49 E
Masjed Soleyman, *Iran* **71 D6** 31 55N 49 18 E
Mask, L., *Ireland* **15 C2** 53 36N 9 22W
Maskin, *Oman* **71 F8** 23 30N 56 50 E
Maslen Nos, *Bulgaria* **41 D11** 42 18N 27 48 E
Maslinica, *Croatia* **29 E13** 43 24N 16 13 E
Masnou = El Masnou, *Spain* **32 D7** 41 28N 2 20 E
Masoala, Tanjon' i, *Madag.* **89 B9** 15 59 S 50 13 E
Masoarivo, *Madag.* **89 B7** 19 3 S 44 19 E
Masohi = Amahai, *Indonesia* **63 E7** 3 20 S 128 55 E
Masomeloka, *Madag.* **89 C8** 20 17 S 48 37 E
Mason, *Nev., U.S.A.* **116 G7** 38 56N 119 8W
Mason, *Tex., U.S.A.* **113 K5** 30 45N 99 14W
Mason City, *U.S.A.* **112 D8** 43 9N 93 12W
Maspalomas, *Canary Is.* **37 G4** 27 46N 15 35W
Maspalomas, Pta., *Canary Is.* **37 G4** 27 43N 15 36W
Masqat, *Oman* **74 C6** 23 37N 58 36 E
Massa, *Italy* **28 D7** 44 1N 10 9 E
Massa Maríttima, *Italy* **28 E7** 43 3N 10 52 E
Massachusetts □, *U.S.A.* **111 D13** 42 30N 72 0W
Massachusetts B., *U.S.A.* **111 D14** 42 20N 70 50W
Massafra, *Italy* **31 B10** 40 35N 17 7 E
Massakory, *Chad* **79 F9** 13 0N 15 49 E
Massanella, *Spain* **37 B9** 39 48N 2 51 E
Massangena, *Mozam.* **89 C5** 21 34 S 33 0 E
Massango, *Angola* **84 F3** 8 2 S 16 21 E
Massat, *France* **20 F5** 42 53N 1 21 E
Massawa = Mitsiwa, *Eritrea* **81 D4** 15 35N 39 25 E
Massena, *U.S.A.* **111 B10** 44 56N 74 54W
Massénya, *Chad* **79 F9** 11 21N 16 9 E
Masset, *Canada* **104 C2** 54 2N 132 10W
Masseube, *France* **20 E4** 43 25N 0 34 E
Massiac, *France* **20 C7** 45 15N 3 11 E
Massif Central, *France* **20 D7** 44 55N 3 0 E
Massigui, *Mali* **82 C3** 11 48N 6 50W
Massillon, *U.S.A.* **110 F3** 40 48N 81 32W
Massinga, *Mozam.* **89 C6** 23 15 S 35 22 E
Massingir, *Mozam.* **89 C5** 23 51 S 32 4 E
Mässlingen, *Sweden* **10 B6** 62 40N 12 50 E
Masson, *Canada* **111 A9** 45 32N 75 25W
Masson I., *Antarctica* **5 C7** 66 10 S 93 20 E
Maştağa, *Azerbaijan* **49 K10** 40 35N 49 57 E
Mastanli = Momchilgrad, *Bulgaria* **41 E9** 41 33N 25 23 E
Masterton, *N.Z.* **91 J5** 40 56 S 175 39 E
Mastic, *U.S.A.* **111 F12** 40 47N 72 54W
Mástikho, Ákra, *Greece* **39 C8** 38 10N 26 2 E
Mastuj, *Pakistan* **69 A5** 36 20N 72 36 E
Mastung, *Pakistan* **66 E5** 29 50N 66 56 E
Mastūrah, *Si. Arabia* **80 C4** 23 7N 38 52 E
Masty, *Belarus* **46 F3** 53 27N 24 38 E
Masuda, *Japan* **55 G5** 34 40N 131 51 E
Masvingo, *Zimbabwe* **87 G3** 20 8 S 30 49 E
Masvingo □, *Zimbabwe* **87 G3** 21 0 S 31 30 E
Maşyāf, *Syria* **70 C3** 35 4N 36 20 E
Maszewo, *Poland* **44 E2** 53 29N 15 3 E
Mat →, *Albania* **40 E3** 41 40N 19 35 E
Matabeleland, *Zimbabwe* **85 H5** 18 0 S 27 0 E
Matabeleland North □, *Zimbabwe* **87 F2** 19 0 S 28 0 E
Matabeleland South □, *Zimbabwe* **87 G2** 21 0 S 29 0 E
Matachel →, *Spain* **35 G4** 38 50N 6 17W
Matachewan, *Canada* **102 C3** 47 56N 80 39W
Matadi, *Dem. Rep. of the Congo* **84 F2** 5 52 S 13 31 E
Matagalpa, *Nic.* **120 D2** 13 0N 85 58W
Matagami, *Canada* **102 C4** 49 45N 77 34W
Matagami, L., *Canada* **102 C4** 49 50N 77 40W
Matagorda B., *U.S.A.* **113 L6** 28 40N 96 0W
Matagorda I., *U.S.A.* **113 L6** 28 15N 96 30W
Matak, *Indonesia* **65 L6** 3 18N 106 16 E
Mátala, *Greece* **36 E6** 34 59N 24 45 E
Matam, *Senegal* **82 B2** 15 34N 13 17W
Matameye, *Niger* **83 C6** 13 26N 8 28 E
Matamoros, *Campeche, Mexico* **119 D6** 18 50N 90 50W
Matamoros, *Coahuila, Mexico* **118 B4** 25 33N 103 15W
Matamoros, *Tamaulipas, Mexico* **119 B5** 25 50N 97 30W
Ma'ţan as Sarra, *Libya* **79 D10** 21 45N 22 0 E
Matandu →, *Tanzania* **87 D3** 8 45 S 34 19 E
Matane, *Canada* **103 C6** 48 50N 67 33W
Matang, *China* **58 F5** 23 30N 104 7 E
Matankari, *Niger* **83 C5** 13 46N 4 1 E
Matanomadh, *India* **68 H3** 23 33N 68 57 E
Matanzas, *Cuba* **120 B3** 23 0N 81 40W
Matapa, *Botswana* **88 C3** 23 11 S 24 39 E
Matapan, C. = Taínaron, Ákra, *Greece* **38 E4** 36 22N 22 27 E
Matapédia, *Canada* **103 C6** 48 0N 66 59W
Matara, *Sri Lanka* **66 S12** 5 58N 80 30 E
Mataram, *Indonesia* **62 F5** 8 41 S 116 10 E
Matarani, *Peru* **124 G4** 17 0 S 72 10W
Mataranka, *Australia* **92 B5** 14 55 S 133 4 E
Matarma, Râs, *Egypt* **75 E1** 30 27N 32 44 E
Mataró, *Spain* **32 D7** 41 32N 2 29 E
Matarraña →, *Spain* **32 D5** 41 14N 0 22 E
Mataruška Banja, *Serbia, Yug.* **40 C4** 43 40N 20 40 E
Matatiele, *S. Africa* **89 E4** 30 20 S 28 49 E
Mataura, *N.Z.* **91 M2** 46 11 S 168 51 E
Matehuala, *Mexico* **118 C4** 23 40N 100 40W
Mateke Hills, *Zimbabwe* **87 G3** 21 48 S 31 0 E
Matera, *Italy* **31 B9** 40 40N 16 36 E
Matese, Monti del, *Italy* **31 A7** 41 27N 14 22 E
Mátészalka, *Hungary* **42 C7** 47 58N 22 20 E
Matetsi, *Zimbabwe* **87 F2** 18 12 S 26 0 E
Matfors, *Sweden* **10 B11** 62 21N 17 2 E
Matha, *France* **20 C3** 45 52N 0 20W
Mathis, *U.S.A.* **113 L6** 28 6N 97 50W
Mathráki, *Greece* **36 A3** 39 48N 19 31 E
Mathura, *India* **68 F7** 27 30N 77 40 E
Mati, *Phil.* **61 H7** 6 55N 126 15 E
Mati → = Mat →, *Albania* **40 E3** 41 40N 19 35 E
Matiakoali, *Burkina Faso* **83 C5** 12 28N 1 2 E
Matiali, *India* **69 F13** 26 56N 88 49 E
Matías Romero, *Mexico* **119 D5** 16 53N 95 2W
Matibane, *Mozam.* **87 E5** 14 49 S 40 45 E
Matima, *Botswana* **88 C3** 20 15 S 24 26 E
Matiri Ra., *N.Z.* **91 J4** 41 38 S 172 20 E
Matjiesfontein, *S. Africa* **88 E3** 33 14 S 20 35 E
Matla →, *India* **69 J13** 21 40N 88 40 E
Matlamanyane, *Botswana* **88 B4** 19 33 S 25 57 E
Matli, *Pakistan* **68 G3** 25 2N 68 39 E
Matlock, *U.K.* **12 D6** 53 9N 1 33W
Matna, *Sudan* **81 E4** 13 49N 35 10 E
Mato Grosso □, *Brazil* **125 F8** 14 0 S 55 0W
Mato Grosso, Planalto do, *Brazil* **122 E5** 15 0 S 55 0W
Mato Grosso do Sul □, *Brazil* **125 G8** 18 0 S 55 0W
Matochkin Shar, *Russia* **50 B6** 73 10N 56 40 E
Matopo Hills, *Zimbabwe* **87 G2** 20 36 S 28 20 E
Matopos, *Zimbabwe* **87 G2** 20 20 S 28 29 E
Matosinhos, *Portugal* **34 D2** 41 11N 8 42W
Matour, *France* **19 F11** 46 19N 4 29 E
Matroosberg, *S. Africa* **88 E2** 33 23 S 19 40 E
Maţruḩ, *Oman* **74 C6** 23 37N 58 30 E
Matsena, *Nigeria* **83 C7** 13 5N 10 5 E
Matsesta, *Russia* **49 J4** 43 34N 39 51 E
Matsu Tao, *Taiwan* **59 E13** 26 9N 119 56 E
Matsue, *Japan* **55 G6** 35 25N 133 10 E
Matsumae, *Japan* **54 D10** 41 26N 140 7 E
Matsumoto, *Japan* **55 F9** 36 15N 138 0 E
Matsusaka, *Japan* **55 G8** 34 34N 136 32 E
Matsuura, *Japan* **55 H4** 33 20N 129 49 E
Matsuyama, *Japan* **55 H6** 33 45N 132 45 E
Mattagami →, *Canada* **102 B3** 50 43N 81 29W
Mattancheri, *India* **66 Q10** 9 50N 76 15 E
Mattawa, *Canada* **102 C4** 46 20N 78 45W
Matterhorn, *Switz.* **25 K3** 45 58N 7 39 E
Mattersburg, *Austria* **27 D9** 47 44N 16 24 E
Matthew Town, *Bahamas* **121 B5** 20 57N 73 40W
Matthew's Ridge, *Guyana* **124 B6** 7 37N 60 10W
Mattice, *Canada* **102 C3** 49 40N 83 20W
Mattituck, *U.S.A.* **111 F12** 40 59N 72 32W
Mattō, *Japan* **55 F8** 36 31N 136 34 E
Mattoon, *U.S.A.* **108 F1** 39 29N 88 23W
Matuba, *Mozam.* **89 C5** 24 28 S 32 49 E
Matucana, *Peru* **124 F3** 11 55 S 76 25W
Matūn = Khowst, *Afghan.* **68 C3** 33 22N 69 58 E
Maturín, *Venezuela* **124 B6** 9 45N 63 11W
Matveyev Kurgan, *Russia* **47 J10** 47 35N 38 57 E
Matxitxako, C., *Spain* **32 B2** 43 28N 2 47W
Mau, *Mad. P., India* **69 F8** 26 17N 78 41 E
Mau, *Ut. P., India* **69 G10** 25 56N 83 33 E
Mau, *Ut. P., India* **69 G9** 25 17N 81 23 E
Mau Escarpment, *Kenya* **86 C4** 0 40 S 36 0 E
Mau Ranipur, *India* **69 G8** 25 16N 79 8 E
Maubeuge, *France* **19 B10** 50 17N 3 57 E
Maubourguet, *France* **20 E4** 43 29N 0 1 E
Maud, Pt., *Australia* **92 D1** 23 6 S 113 45 E
Maude, *Australia* **95 E3** 34 29 S 144 18 E
Maudin Sun, *Burma* **67 M19** 16 0N 94 30 E
Maués, *Brazil* **124 D7** 3 20 S 57 45W
Mauganj, *India* **67 G12** 24 50N 81 55 E
Maughold Hd., *U.K.* **12 C3** 54 18N 4 18W
Mauguio, *France* **20 E7** 43 37N 4 1 E
Maui, *U.S.A.* **106 H16** 20 48N 156 20W
Maulamyaing = Moulmein, *Burma* **67 L20** 16 30N 97 40 E
Maule □, *Chile* **126 D1** 36 5 S 72 30W
Mauléon-Licharre, *France* **20 E3** 43 14N 0 54W
Maumee, *U.S.A.* **108 E4** 41 34N 83 39W
Maumee →, *U.S.A.* **108 E4** 41 42N 83 28W
Maumere, *Indonesia* **63 F6** 8 38 S 122 13 E
Maumusson, Pertuis de, *France* **20 C2** 45 48N 1 14W
Maun, *Botswana* **88 C3** 20 0 S 23 26 E
Mauna Kea, *U.S.A.* **106 J17** 19 50N 155 28W
Mauna Loa, *U.S.A.* **106 J17** 19 30N 155 35W
Maungmagan Is., *Burma* **64 E1** 14 0N 97 30 E
Maungmagan Kyunzu, *Burma* **67 N20** 14 0N 97 48 E
Maupin, *U.S.A.* **114 D3** 45 11N 121 5W
Maure-de-Bretagne, *France* **18 E5** 47 59N 1 58W
Maurepas, L., *U.S.A.* **113 K9** 30 15N 90 30W
Maures, *France* **21 E10** 43 15N 6 15 E
Mauriac, *France* **20 C6** 45 13N 2 19 E
Maurice, L., *Australia* **93 E5** 29 30 S 131 0 E
Mauricie, Parc Nat. de la, *Canada* **102 C5** 46 45N 73 0W
Maurienne, *France* **21 C10** 45 13N 6 30 E
Mauritania ■, *Africa* **78 E3** 20 50N 10 0W
Mauritius ■, *Ind. Oc.* **77 J9** 20 0 S 57 0 E
Mauron, *France* **18 D4** 48 9N 2 18W
Maurs, *France* **20 D6** 44 43N 2 12 E
Mauston, *U.S.A.* **112 D9** 43 48N 90 5W
Mauterndorf, *Austria* **26 D6** 47 9N 13 40 E
Mauthen, *Austria* **26 E6** 46 40N 13 0 E
Mauvezin, *France* **20 E4** 43 44N 0 53 E
Mauzé-sur-le-Mignon, *France* **20 B3** 46 12N 0 41W
Mavli, *India* **68 G5** 24 45N 73 55 E
Mavrova = Mavrovë, *Albania* **40 F3** 40 26N 19 32 E
Mavrovë, *Albania* **40 F3** 40 26N 19 32 E
Mavuradonha Mts., *Zimbabwe* **87 F3** 16 30 S 31 30 E
Mawa, *Dem. Rep. of the Congo* **86 B2** 2 45N 26 40 E
Mawai, *India* **69 H9** 22 30N 81 4 E
Mawana, *India* **68 E7** 29 6N 77 58 E
Mawand, *Pakistan* **68 E3** 29 33N 68 38 E
Mawk Mai, *Burma* **67 J20** 20 14N 97 37 E
Mawlaik, *Burma* **67 H19** 23 40N 94 26 E
Mawlamyine = Moulmein, *Burma* **67 L20** 16 30N 97 40 E
Mawqaq, *Si. Arabia* **70 E4** 27 25N 41 8 E
Mawson Coast, *Antarctica* **5 C6** 68 30 S 63 0 E
Max, *U.S.A.* **112 B4** 47 49N 101 18W
Maxcanú, *Mexico* **119 C6** 20 40N 92 0W
Maxesibeni, *S. Africa* **89 E4** 30 49 S 29 23 E
Maxhamish L., *Canada* **104 B4** 59 50N 123 17W
Maxixe, *Mozam.* **89 C6** 23 54 S 35 17 E
Maxville, *Canada* **111 A10** 45 17N 74 51W
Maxwell, *U.S.A.* **116 F4** 39 17N 122 11W
Maxwelton, *Australia* **94 C3** 20 43 S 142 41 E
May, C., *U.S.A.* **108 F8** 38 56N 74 58W
May Pen, *Jamaica* **120 C4** 17 58N 77 15W
Maya →, *Russia* **51 D14** 60 28N 134 28 E
Maya Mts., *Belize* **119 D7** 16 30N 89 0W
Mayaguana, *Bahamas* **121 B5** 22 30N 72 44W
Mayagüez, *Puerto Rico* **121 C6** 18 12N 67 9W
Mayahi, *Niger* **83 C6** 13 58N 7 40 E
Mayals = Maials, *Spain* **32 D5** 41 22N 0 30 E
Mayāmey, *Iran* **71 B7** 36 24N 55 42 E
Mayang, *China* **58 D7** 27 53N 109 49 E
Mayanup, *Australia* **93 F2** 33 57 S 116 27 E
Mayapan, *Mexico* **119 C7** 20 30N 89 25W
Mayarí, *Cuba* **121 B4** 20 40N 75 41W
Maybell, *U.S.A.* **114 F9** 40 31N 108 5W
Maybole, *U.K.* **14 F4** 55 21N 4 42W
Maychew, *Ethiopia* **81 E4** 12 50N 39 31 E
Maydān, *Iraq* **70 C5** 34 55N 45 37 E
Maydena, *Australia* **94 G4** 42 45 S 146 30 E
Mayen, *Germany* **25 E3** 50 19N 7 13 E
Mayenne, *France* **18 D6** 48 20N 0 38W
Mayenne □, *France* **18 D6** 48 10N 0 40W
Mayenne →, *France* **18 E6** 47 30N 0 32W
Mayer, *U.S.A.* **115 J7** 34 24N 112 14W
Mayerthorpe, *Canada* **104 C5** 53 57N 115 8W
Mayfield, *Ky., U.S.A.* **109 G1** 36 44N 88 38W
Mayfield, *N.Y., U.S.A.* **111 C10** 43 6N 74 16W
Mayhill, *U.S.A.* **115 K11** 32 53N 105 29W
Maykop, *Russia* **49 H5** 44 35N 40 10 E
Maymyo, *Burma* **64 A1** 22 2N 96 28 E
Maynard, *Mass., U.S.A.* **111 D13** 42 26N 71 27W
Maynard, *Wash., U.S.A.* **116 C4** 47 59N 122 55W
Maynard Hills, *Australia* **93 E2** 28 28 S 119 49 E
Mayne →, *Australia* **94 C3** 23 40 S 141 55 E
Maynooth, *Ireland* **15 C5** 53 23N 6 34W
Mayo, *Canada* **100 B6** 63 38N 135 57W
Mayo □, *Ireland* **15 C2** 53 53N 9 3W
Mayo Daga, *Nigeria* **83 D7** 6 59N 11 25 E
Mayo Faran, *Nigeria* **83 D7** 8 57N 12 4 E
Mayon Volcano, *Phil.* **61 E5** 13 15N 123 41 E
Mayor I., *N.Z.* **91 G6** 37 16 S 176 17 E
Mayorga, *Spain* **34 C5** 42 10N 5 16W
Mayotte, *Ind. Oc.* **85 G9** 12 50 S 45 10 E
Mayraira Pt., *Phil.* **61 B4** 18 39N 120 51 E
Mayskiy, *Russia* **49 J7** 43 47N 44 2 E
Maysville, *U.S.A.* **108 F4** 38 39N 83 46W
Mayu, *Indonesia* **63 D7** 1 30N 126 30 E
Mayville, *N. Dak., U.S.A.* **112 B6** 47 30N 97 20W
Mayville, *N.Y., U.S.A.* **110 D5** 42 15N 79 30W
Mayya, *Russia* **51 C14** 61 44N 130 18 E
Mazabuka, *Zambia* **87 F2** 15 52 S 27 44 E
Mazagán = El Jadida, *Morocco* **78 B4** 33 11N 8 17W
Mazagão, *Brazil* **125 D8** 0 7 S 51 16W
Mazamet, *France* **20 E6** 43 30N 2 20 E
Mazán, *Peru* **124 D4** 3 30 S 73 0W
Māzandarān □, *Iran* **71 B7** 36 30N 52 0 E
Mazapil, *Mexico* **118 C4** 24 38N 101 34W
Mazara del Vallo, *Italy* **30 E5** 37 39N 12 35 E
Mazarrón, *Spain* **33 H3** 37 38N 1 19W
Mazarrón, G. de, *Spain* **33 H3** 37 27N 1 19W
Mazaruni →, *Guyana* **124 B7** 6 25N 58 35W
Mazatán, *Mexico* **118 B2** 29 0N 110 8W
Mazatenango, *Guatemala* **120 D1** 14 35N 91 30W
Mazatlán, *Mexico* **118 C3** 23 13N 106 25W
Mažeikiai, *Lithuania* **9 H20** 56 20N 22 20 E
Māzhān, *Iran* **71 C8** 32 30N 59 0 E
Mazīnān, *Iran* **71 B8** 36 19N 56 56 E
Mazoe, *Mozam.* **87 F3** 16 42 S 33 7 E
Mazoe →, *Mozam.* **87 F3** 16 20 S 33 30 E
Mazowe, *Zimbabwe* **87 F3** 17 28 S 30 58 E
Mazowieckie □, *Poland* **45 F8** 52 40N 21 0 E
Mazrûb, *Sudan* **81 E2** 14 0N 29 20 E
Mazu Dao, *China* **59 D12** 26 10N 119 55 E
Mazurian Lakes = Mazurski, Pojezierze, *Poland* **44 E7** 53 50N 21 0 E
Mazurski, Pojezierze, *Poland* **44 E7** 53 50N 21 0 E
Mazyr, *Belarus* **47 F5** 51 59N 29 15 E
Mbaba, *Senegal* **82 C1** 14 59N 16 44W
Mbabane, *Swaziland* **89 D5** 26 18 S 31 6 E
Mbagne, *Mauritania* **82 B2** 16 6N 14 47W
M'bahiakro, *Ivory C.* **82 D4** 7 33N 4 19W
Mbaïki, *C.A.R.* **84 D3** 3 53N 18 1 E
Mbala, *Zambia* **87 D3** 8 46 S 31 24 E
Mbalabala, *Zimbabwe* **89 C4** 20 27 S 29 3 E
Mbale, *Uganda* **86 B3** 1 8N 34 12 E
Mbalmayo, *Cameroon* **83 E7** 3 33N 11 33 E
Mbam →, *Cameroon* **83 E7** 4 24N 11 17 E
Mbamba Bay, *Tanzania* **87 E3** 11 13 S 34 49 E
Mbandaka, *Dem. Rep. of the Congo* **84 D3** 0 1N 18 18 E
Mbanga, *Cameroon* **83 E6** 4 30N 9 33 E
Mbanza Congo, *Angola* **84 F2** 6 18 S 14 16 E
Mbanza Ngungu, *Dem. Rep. of the Congo* **84 F2** 5 12 S 14 53 E
Mbarara, *Uganda* **86 C3** 0 35 S 30 40 E
Mbashe →, *S. Africa* **89 E4** 32 15 S 28 54 E
Mbatto, *Ivory C.* **82 D4** 6 28N 4 22W
Mbenkuru →, *Tanzania* **87 D4** 9 25 S 39 50 E
Mberengwa, *Zimbabwe* **87 G2** 20 29 S 29 57 E
Mberengwa, Mt., *Zimbabwe* **87 G2** 20 37 S 29 55 E
Mberubu, *Nigeria* **83 D6** 6 10N 7 38 E
Mbesuma, *Zambia* **87 E3** 10 0 S 32 2 E
Mbeya, *Tanzania* **87 D3** 8 54 S 33 29 E
Mbeya □, *Tanzania* **86 D3** 8 15 S 33 30 E
M'bili, *Sudan* **81 F2** 7 35N 28 15 E
Mbinga, *Tanzania* **87 E4** 10 50 S 35 0 E
Mbini □, *Eq. Guin.* **84 D2** 1 30N 10 0 E
Mboki, *C.A.R.* **81 F2** 5 19N 25 58 E
M'bonge, *Cameroon* **83 E6** 4 33N 9 5 E
Mboro, *Senegal* **82 B1** 15 9N 16 54W
M'boukou Res., *Cameroon* **83 D7** 6 23N 12 50 E
Mboune, *Senegal* **82 C2** 14 42N 13 34W
Mbour, *Senegal* **82 C1** 14 22N 16 54W
Mbout, *Mauritania* **82 B2** 16 1N 12 38W
Mbuji-Mayi, *Dem. Rep. of the Congo* **86 D1** 6 9 S 23 40 E
Mbulu, *Tanzania* **86 C4** 3 45 S 35 30 E
Mburucuyá, *Argentina* **126 B4** 28 1 S 58 14W
Mchinja, *Tanzania* **87 D4** 9 44 S 39 45 E
Mchinji, *Malawi* **87 E3** 13 47 S 32 58 E
Mdantsane, *S. Africa* **85 L5** 32 56 S 27 46 E
Mead, L., *U.S.A.* **117 J12** 36 1N 114 44W
Meade, *U.S.A.* **113 G4** 37 17N 100 20W
Meadow Lake, *Canada* **105 C7** 54 10N 108 26W
Meadow Lake Prov. Park, *Canada* **105 C7** 54 27N 109 0W
Meadow Valley Wash →, *U.S.A.* **117 J12** 36 40N 114 34W
Meadville, *U.S.A.* **110 E4** 41 39N 80 9W
Meaford, *Canada* **102 D3** 44 36N 80 35W
Mealhada, *Portugal* **34 E2** 40 22N 8 27W
Mealy Mts., *Canada* **103 B8** 53 10N 58 0W
Meander River, *Canada* **104 B5** 59 2N 117 42W
Meares, C., *U.S.A.* **114 D2** 45 37N 124 0W
Mearim →, *Brazil* **125 D10** 3 4 S 44 35W
Meath □, *Ireland* **15 C5** 53 40N 6 57W
Meath Park, *Canada* **105 C7** 53 27N 105 22W
Meaulne, *France* **19 F9** 46 36N 2 36 E
Meaux, *France* **19 D9** 48 58N 2 50 E
Mebechi-Gawa →, *Japan* **54 D10** 40 31N 141 31 E
Mecanhelas, *Mozam.* **87 F4** 15 12 S 35 54 E
Mecca = Makkah, *Si. Arabia* **74 C2** 21 30N 39 54 E
Mecca, *U.S.A.* **117 M10** 33 34N 116 5W
Mechanicsburg, *U.S.A.* **110 F8** 40 13N 77 1W
Mechanicville, *U.S.A.* **111 D11** 42 54N 73 41W
Mechara, *Ethiopia* **81 F5** 8 36N 40 20 E
Mechelen, *Belgium* **17 C4** 51 2N 4 29 E
Mecheria, *Algeria* **78 B5** 33 35N 0 18W
Mechernich, *Germany* **24 E2** 50 35N 6 39 E
Mechetinskaya, *Russia* **49 G5** 46 45N 40 32 E
Mecidiye, *Turkey* **41 F10** 40 38N 26 32 E
Mecitözü, *Turkey* **72 B6** 40 32N 35 17 E
Mecklenburg-Vorpommern □, *Germany* **24 B8** 53 45N 12 15 E
Mecklenburger Bucht, *Germany* **24 A7** 54 20N 11 40 E
Meconta, *Mozam.* **87 E4** 14 59 S 39 50 E
Mecsek, *Hungary* **42 D3** 46 10N 18 18 E
Meda, *Portugal* **34 E3** 40 57N 7 18W
Medan, *Indonesia* **62 D1** 3 40N 98 38 E
Medanosa, Pta., *Argentina* **128 F3** 48 8 S 66 0W
Mede, *Italy* **28 C5** 45 6N 8 44 E
Médéa, *Algeria* **78 A6** 36 12N 2 50 E
Mededa, *Bos.-H.* **42 G4** 43 44N 19 15 E
Medellín, *Colombia* **124 B3** 6 15N 75 35W
Medelpad, *Sweden* **10 B10** 62 33N 16 30 E
Medemblik, *Neths.* **17 B5** 52 46N 5 8 E
Mederdra, *Mauritania* **82 B1** 17 0N 15 38W
Medford, *Mass., U.S.A.* **111 D13** 42 25N 71 7W
Medford, *Oreg., U.S.A.* **114 E2** 42 19N 122 52W
Medford, *Wis., U.S.A.* **112 C9** 45 9N 90 20W
Medgidia, *Romania* **43 F13** 44 15N 28 19 E
Medi, *Sudan* **81 F3** 5 4N 30 42 E
Media Agua, *Argentina* **126 C2** 31 58 S 68 25W
Media Luna, *Argentina* **126 C2** 34 45 S 66 44W
Medianeira, *Brazil* **127 B5** 25 17 S 54 5W
Mediaş, *Romania* **43 D9** 46 9N 24 22 E
Medicina, *Italy* **29 D8** 44 28N 11 38 E
Medicine Bow, *U.S.A.* **114 F10** 41 54N 106 12W
Medicine Bow Pk., *U.S.A.* **114 F10** 41 21N 106 19W
Medicine Bow Ra., *U.S.A.* **114 F10** 41 10N 106 25W
Medicine Hat, *Canada* **105 D6** 50 0N 110 45W
Medicine Lake, *U.S.A.* **112 A2** 48 30N 104 30W
Medicine Lodge, *U.S.A.* **113 G5** 37 17N 98 35W
Medina = Al Madīnah, *Si. Arabia* **70 E3** 24 35N 39 52 E
Medina, *N. Dak., U.S.A.* **112 B5** 46 54N 99 18W
Medina, *N.Y., U.S.A.* **110 C6** 43 13N 78 23W
Medina, *Ohio, U.S.A.* **110 E3** 41 8N 81 52W
Medina →, *U.S.A.* **113 L5** 29 16N 98 29W
Medina de Pomar, *Spain* **34 C7** 42 56N 3 29W
Medina de Ríoseco, *Spain* **34 D5** 41 53N 5 3W
Medina del Campo, *Spain* **34 D6** 41 18N 4 55W
Medina L., *U.S.A.* **113 L5** 29 32N 98 56W
Medina Sidonia, *Spain* **35 J5** 36 28N 5 57W
Medinaceli, *Spain* **32 D2** 41 12N 2 30W
Medinipur, *India* **69 H12** 22 25N 87 21 E
Mediterranean Sea, *Europe* **6 H7** 35 0N 15 0 E
Médoc, *France* **20 C3** 45 10N 0 50W
Medulin, *Croatia* **29 D10** 44 49N 13 55 E
Medveđa, *Serbia, Yug.* **40 D5** 42 50N 21 32 E
Medvedevo, *Russia* **48 B8** 56 37N 47 47 E
Medveditsa →, *Tver, Russia* **46 D9** 57 5N 37 30 E
Medveditsa →, *Volgograd, Russia* **48 F6** 49 35N 42 41 E
Medvedok, *Russia* **48 B10** 57 20N 50 1 E
Medvezhi, Ostrava, *Russia* **51 B17** 71 0N 161 0 E
Medvezhyegorsk, *Russia* **50 C4** 63 0N 34 25 E
Medway □, *U.K.* **13 F8** 51 25N 0 32 E
Medway →, *U.K.* **13 F8** 51 27N 0 46 E
Medzev, *Slovak Rep.* **27 C13** 48 43N 20 55 E
Medzilaborce, *Slovak Rep.* **27 B14** 49 17N 21 52 E
Medžitlija, *Macedonia* **40 F5** 40 56N 21 26 E
Meekatharra, *Australia* **93 E2** 26 32 S 118 29 E
Meeker, *U.S.A.* **114 F10** 40 2N 107 55W
Meelpaeg Res., *Canada* **103 C8** 48 15N 56 33W
Meersburg, *Germany* **25 H5** 47 41N 9 16 E
Meerut, *India* **68 E7** 29 1N 77 42 E
Meeteetse, *U.S.A.* **114 D9** 44 9N 108 52W
Mega, *Ethiopia* **81 G4** 3 57N 38 19 E
Megálo Khorío, *Greece* **39 E9** 36 27N 27 24 E
Megálo Petalí, *Greece* **38 D6** 38 0N 24 15 E
Megalópolis, *Greece* **38 D4** 37 25N 22 7 E
Meganísi, *Greece* **38 C2** 38 39N 20 48 E
Mégara, *Greece* **38 D5** 37 58N 23 22 E
Megasini, *India* **69 J12** 21 38N 86 21 E
Megdhova →, *Greece* **38 B3** 39 10N 21 45 E
Megève, *France* **21 C10** 45 51N 6 37 E
Meghalaya □, *India* **67 G17** 25 50N 91 0 E
Meghezez, *Ethiopia* **81 F4** 9 18N 39 26 E
Mégiscane, L., *Canada* **102 C4** 48 35N 75 55W
Megiste, *Greece* **39 E11** 36 8N 29 34 E
Megra, *Russia* **46 B9** 60 11N 37 14 E
Mehadia, *Romania* **42 F7** 44 56N 22 23 E
Meharry, Mt., *Australia* **92 D2** 22 59 S 118 35 E
Mehedeby, *Sweden* **10 D11** 60 27N 17 25 E
Mehedinţi □, *Romania* **42 F7** 44 40N 22 45 E
Meheisa, *Sudan* **80 D3** 19 38N 32 57 E
Mehlville, *U.S.A.* **112 F9** 38 30N 90 19W
Mehndawal, *India* **69 F10** 26 58N 83 5 E
Mehr Jān, *Iran* **71 C7** 33 50N 55 6 E
Mehrābād, *Iran* **70 B5** 36 53N 47 55 E
Mehrān, *Iran* **70 C5** 33 7N 46 10 E
Mehrīz, *Iran* **71 D7** 31 35N 54 28 E
Mehun-sur-Yèvre, *France* **19 E9** 47 10N 2 13 E
Mei Jiang →, *China* **59 E11** 24 25N 116 35 E
Mei Xian, *China* **56 G4** 34 18N 107 55 E
Meicheng, *China* **59 C12** 29 29N 119 16 E
Meichengzhen, *China* **59 C8** 28 9N 111 40 E
Meichuan, *China* **59 B10** 30 8N 115 31 E
Meigu, *China* **58 C4** 28 16N 103 20 E
Meiktila, *Burma* **67 J19** 20 53N 95 54 E
Meinerzhagen, *Germany* **24 D3** 51 6N 7 38 E
Meiningen, *Germany* **24 E6** 50 34N 10 25 E
Meira, Serra de, *Spain* **34 B3** 43 15N 7 15W
Meiringen, *Switz.* **25 J4** 46 43N 8 12 E
Meishan, *China* **58 B4** 30 3N 103 23 E
Meissen, *Germany* **24 D9** 51 9N 13 29 E
Meissner, *Germany* **24 D5** 51 14N 9 50 E
Meitan, *China* **58 D6** 27 45N 107 29 E
Meizhou, *China* **59 E11** 24 16N 116 6 E
Meja, *India* **69 G10** 25 9N 82 7 E
Mejillones, *Chile* **126 A1** 23 10 S 70 30W
Mekdela, *Ethiopia* **81 E4** 11 24N 39 10 E
Mekele, *Ethiopia* **81 E4** 13 33N 39 30 E
Mekhtar, *Pakistan* **66 D6** 30 30N 69 15 E
Meknès, *Morocco* **78 B4** 33 57N 5 33W
Meko, *Nigeria* **83 D5** 7 27N 2 52 E
Mekong →, *Asia* **65 H6** 9 30N 106 15 E
Mekongga, *Indonesia* **63 E6** 3 39 S 121 15 E
Mekrou →, *Benin* **83 C5** 12 25N 2 50 E
Mekvari = Kür →, *Azerbaijan* **73 C13** 39 29N 49 15 E
Mel, *Italy* **29 B9** 46 4N 12 5 E
Melagiri Hills, *India* **66 N10** 12 20N 77 30 E
Melaka, *Malaysia* **65 L4** 2 15N 102 15 E
Melalap, *Malaysia* **62 C5** 5 10N 116 5 E
Mélambes, *Greece* **36 D6** 35 8N 24 40 E
Melanesia, *Pac. Oc.* **96 H7** 4 0 S 155 0 E
Melbourne, *Australia* **95 F4** 37 50 S 145 0 E
Melbourne, *U.S.A.* **109 L5** 28 5N 80 37W
Melchor Múzquiz, *Mexico* **118 B4** 27 50N 101 30W
Melchor Ocampo, *Mexico* **118 C4** 24 52N 101 40W
Méldola, *Italy* **29 D9** 44 7N 12 5 E
Meldorf, *Germany* **24 A5** 54 5N 9 5 E
Melegnano, *Italy* **28 C6** 45 21N 9 19 E
Melenci, *Serbia, Yug.* **42 E5** 45 32N 20 20 E
Melenki, *Russia* **48 C5** 55 20N 41 37 E
Mélèzes →, *Qué., Canada* **101 C12** 57 30N 71 0W
Mélèzes →, *Qué., Canada* **102 A5** 57 40N 69 29W
Melfi, *Italy* **31 B8** 41 0N 15 39 E
Melfort, *Canada* **105 C8** 52 50N 104 37W
Melfort, *Zimbabwe* **87 F3** 18 0 S 31 25 E
Melgaço, *Portugal* **34 C2** 42 7N 8 15W
Melgar de Fernamental, *Spain* **34 C6** 42 27N 4 17W
Melhus, *Norway* **8 E14** 63 17N 10 18 E
Melide, *Spain* **34 C2** 42 55N 8 1W
Meligalá, *Greece* **38 D3** 37 15N 21 59 E
Melilla, *N. Afr.* **78 A5** 35 21N 2 57W
Melilli, *Italy* **31 E8** 37 11N 15 7 E
Melipilla, *Chile* **126 C1** 33 42 S 71 15W
Mélissa, Ákra, *Greece* **36 D6** 35 6N 24 33 E
Mélissa Óros, *Greece* **39 D8** 37 32N 26 4 E
Melita, *Canada* **105 D8** 49 15N 101 0W
Mélito di Porto Salvo, *Italy* **31 E8** 37 55N 15 47 E
Melitopol, *Ukraine* **47 J8** 46 50N 35 22 E
Melk, *Austria* **26 C8** 48 13N 15 20 E
Mellan Fryken, *Sweden* **10 E7** 59 45N 13 10 E
Mellansel, *Sweden* **8 E18** 63 25N 18 17 E
Mellbystrand, *Sweden* **11 H6** 56 30N 12 56 E
Melle, *France* **20 B3** 46 14N 0 10W
Melle, *Germany* **24 C4** 52 12N 8 20 E
Mellen, *U.S.A.* **112 B9** 46 20N 90 40W
Mellerud, *Sweden* **11 F6** 58 41N 12 28 E
Mellette, *U.S.A.* **112 C5** 45 9N 98 30W
Mellid = Melide, *Spain* **34 C2** 42 55N 8 1W
Mellieha, *Malta* **36 D1** 35 57N 14 21 E
Mellit, *Sudan* **81 E2** 14 7N 25 34 E
Mellrichstadt, *Germany* **24 E6** 50 25N 10 17 E
Melnik, *Bulgaria* **40 E7** 41 30N 23 25 E
Mělník, *Czech Rep.* **26 A7** 50 22N 14 23 E
Melo, *Uruguay* **127 C5** 32 20 S 54 10W
Melolo, *Indonesia* **63 F6** 9 53 S 120 40 E
Melouprey, *Cambodia* **64 F5** 13 48N 105 16 E
Melrose, *Australia* **95 E4** 32 42 S 146 57 E
Melrose, *U.K.* **14 F6** 55 36N 2 43W
Melrose, *Minn., U.S.A.* **112 C7** 45 40N 94 49W
Melrose, *N. Mex., U.S.A.* **113 H3** 34 26N 103 38W
Melstone, *U.S.A.* **114 C10** 46 36N 107 52W
Melsungen, *Germany* **24 D5** 51 7N 9 32 E
Melton Mowbray, *U.K.* **12 E7** 52 47N 0 54W
Melun, *France* **19 D9** 48 32N 2 39 E
Melut, *Sudan* **81 E3** 10 30N 32 13 E
Melville, *Canada* **105 C8** 50 55N 102 50W
Melville, C., *Australia* **94 A3** 14 11 S 144 30 E
Melville, L., *Canada* **103 B8** 53 30N 60 0W
Melville B., *Australia* **94 A2** 12 0 S 136 45 E
Melville I., *Australia* **92 B5** 11 30 S 131 0 E
Melville I., *Canada* **4 B2** 75 30N 112 0W
Melville Pen., *Canada* **101 B11** 68 0N 84 0W
Mélykút, *Hungary* **42 D4** 46 11N 19 25 E
Memaliaj, *Albania* **40 F3** 40 25N 19 58 E
Memba, *Mozam.* **87 E5** 14 11 S 40 30 E
Memboro, *Indonesia* **63 F5** 9 30 S 119 30 E
Membrilla, *Spain* **35 G7** 38 59N 3 21W
Memel = Klaipėda, *Lithuania* **9 J19** 55 43N 21 10 E
Memel, *S. Africa* **89 D4** 27 38 S 29 36 E
Memmingen, *Germany* **25 H6** 47 58N 10 10 E

Mempawah, Indonesia 62 D3 0 30N 109 5 E
Memphis, Egypt 80 J7 29 52N 31 12 E
Memphis, Mich., U.S.A. 110 D2 42 54N 82 46W
Memphis, Tenn., U.S.A. 113 H10 35 8N 90 3W
Memphis, Tex., U.S.A. 113 H4 34 44N 100 33W
Memphremagog, L., U.S.A. 111 B12 45 0N 72 12W
Mena, Ukraine 47 G7 51 31N 32 13 E
Mena, U.S.A. 113 H7 34 35N 94 15W
Mena →, Ethiopia 81 F5 5 40N 40 50 E
Menai Strait, U.K. 12 D3 53 11N 4 13W
Ménaka, Mali 83 B5 15 59N 2 18 E
Menan = Chao Phraya →, Thailand 64 F3 13 32N 100 36 E
Menarandra →, Madag. 89 D7 25 17 S 44 30 E
Menard, U.S.A. 113 K5 30 55N 99 47W
Menawashei, Sudan 81 E1 12 41N 24 59 E
Mendawai →, Indonesia 62 E4 3 30 S 113 0 E
Mende, France 20 D7 44 31N 3 30 E
Mendebo, Ethiopia 81 F4 7 0N 39 22 E
Menden, Germany 24 D3 51 26N 7 47 E
Menderes, Turkey 39 C9 38 14N 27 8 E
Mendez, Mexico 119 B5 25 7N 98 34W
Mendhar, India 69 C6 33 35N 74 10 E
Mendi, Ethiopia 81 F4 9 47N 35 4 E
Mendip Hills, U.K. 13 F5 51 17N 2 40W
Mendocino, U.S.A. 114 G2 39 19N 123 48W
Mendocino, C., U.S.A. 114 F1 40 26N 124 25W
Mendooran, Australia 95 E4 31 50 S 149 6 E
Mendota, Calif., U.S.A. 116 J6 36 45N 120 23W
Mendota, Ill., U.S.A. 112 E10 41 33N 89 7W
Mendoza, Argentina 126 C2 32 50 S 68 52W
Mendoza □, Argentina 126 C2 33 0 S 69 0W
Mene Grande, Venezuela 124 B4 9 49N 70 56W
Menemen, Turkey 39 C9 38 34N 27 3 E
Menen, Belgium 17 D3 50 47N 3 7 E
Menfi, Italy 30 E5 37 36N 12 58 E
Mengdingjie, China 58 F2 23 31N 98 58 E
Mengeš, Slovenia 29 B11 46 10N 14 35 E
Menggala, Indonesia 62 E3 4 30 S 105 15 E
Menghai, China 58 G3 21 49N 100 55 E
Mengíbar, Spain 35 H7 37 58N 3 48W
Mengjin, China 56 G7 34 55N 112 45 E
Mengla, China 58 G3 21 20N 101 25 E
Menglian, China 58 F2 22 21N 99 27 E
Mengshan, China 59 E8 24 14N 110 55 E
Mengyin, China 57 G9 35 40N 117 58 E
Mengzhe, China 58 F3 22 2N 100 15 E
Mengzi, China 58 F4 23 20N 103 22 E
Menihek, Canada 103 B6 54 28N 56 36W
Menihek L., Canada 103 B6 54 0N 67 0W
Menin = Menen, Belgium 17 D3 50 47N 3 7 E
Menindee, Australia 95 E3 32 20 S 142 25 E
Menindee L., Australia 95 E3 32 20 S 142 25 E
Meningie, Australia 95 F2 35 50 S 139 18 E
Menlo Park, U.S.A. 116 H4 37 27N 122 12W
Menominee, U.S.A. 108 C2 45 6N 87 37W
Menominee →, U.S.A. 108 C2 45 6N 87 36W
Menomonie, U.S.A. 112 C9 44 53N 91 55W
Menongue, Angola 85 G3 14 48 S 17 52 E
Menorca, Spain 37 B11 40 0N 4 0 E
Mentakab, Malaysia 65 L4 3 29N 102 21 E
Mentawai, Kepulauan, Indonesia 62 E1 2 0 S 99 0 E
Menton, France 21 E11 43 50N 7 29 E
Mentor, U.S.A. 110 E3 41 40N 81 21W
Menzies, Australia 93 E3 29 40 S 121 2 E
Meob B., Namibia 88 B2 24 25 S 14 34 E
Me'ona, Israel 75 B4 33 1N 35 15 E
Meoqui, Mexico 118 B3 28 17N 105 29W
Mepaco, Mozam. 87 F3 15 57 S 30 48 E
Meppel, Neths. 17 B6 52 42N 6 12 E
Meppen, Germany 24 C3 52 42N 7 17 E
Mequinenza, Spain 32 D5 41 22N 0 17 E
Mequinenza, Embalse de, Spain 32 D5 41 25N 0 15 E
Mer, France 18 E8 47 42N 1 30 E
Merabéllou, Kólpos, Greece 36 D7 35 10N 25 50 E
Merak, Indonesia 63 F12 6 10N 106 26 E
Meramangye, L., Australia 93 E5 28 25 S 132 13 E
Meran = Merano, Italy 29 B8 46 40N 11 9 E
Merano, Italy 29 B8 46 40N 11 9 E
Merate, Italy 28 C6 45 42N 9 25 E
Merauke, Indonesia 63 F10 8 29 S 140 24 E
Merbein, Australia 95 E3 34 10 S 142 2 E
Merca, Somali Rep. 74 G3 1 48N 44 50 E
Mercato Saraceno, Italy 29 E9 43 57N 12 12 E
Merced, U.S.A. 116 H6 37 18N 120 29W
Merced →, U.S.A. 116 H6 37 21N 120 59W
Merced Pk., U.S.A. 116 H7 37 36N 119 24W
Mercedes, Buenos Aires, Argentina 126 C4 34 40 S 59 30W
Mercedes, Corrientes, Argentina 126 B4 29 10 S 58 5W
Mercedes, San Luis, Argentina 126 C2 33 40 S 65 21W
Mercedes, Uruguay 126 C4 33 12 S 58 0W
Mercedes, U.S.A. 113 M6 26 9N 97 55W
Merceditas, Chile 126 B1 28 20 S 70 35W
Mercer, N.Z. 91 G5 37 16 S 175 5 E
Mercer, U.S.A. 110 E4 41 14N 80 15W
Mercer Island, U.S.A. 116 C4 47 35N 122 15W
Mercury, U.S.A. 117 J11 36 40N 115 58W
Mercy C., Canada 101 B13 65 0N 63 30W
Merdrignac, France 18 D4 48 11N 2 27W
Mere, U.K. 13 F5 51 6N 2 16W
Meredith, C., Falk. Is. 128 G4 52 15 S 60 40W
Meredith, L., U.S.A. 113 H4 35 43N 101 33W
Merefa, Ukraine 47 H9 49 48N 36 4 E
Merei, Romania 43 E11 45 7N 26 43 E
Merga = Nukheila, Sudan 80 D2 19 1N 26 21 E
Mergui, Burma 64 F2 12 26N 98 34 E
Mergui Arch. = Myeik Kyunzu, Burma 65 G1 11 30N 97 30 E
Meriç, Turkey 41 E10 41 11N 26 25 E
Meriç →, Turkey 41 F10 40 52N 26 12 E
Mérida, Mexico 119 C7 20 58N 89 37W
Mérida, Spain 35 G4 38 55N 6 25W
Mérida, Venezuela 124 B4 8 24N 71 8W
Mérida, Cord. de, Venezuela 122 C3 9 0N 71 0W
Meriden, U.K. 13 E6 52 26N 1 38W
Meriden, U.S.A. 111 E12 41 32N 72 48W
Meridian, Calif., U.S.A. 116 F5 39 9N 121 55W
Meridian, Idaho, U.S.A. 114 E5 43 37N 116 24W
Meridian, Miss., U.S.A. 109 J1 32 22N 88 42W
Mérignac, France 20 D3 44 51N 0 39W
Merimbula, Australia 95 F4 36 53 S 149 54 E
Mérinaghène, Senegal 82 B1 15 57N 15 55W
Merinda, Australia 94 C4 20 2 S 148 11 E
Mering, Germany 25 G6 48 16N 10 59 E
Meringa, Nigeria 83 C7 10 44N 12 9 E
Meringur, Australia 95 E3 34 20 S 141 19 E
Merir, Pac. Oc. 63 D8 4 10N 132 30 E
Merirumã, Brazil 125 C8 1 15N 54 50W
Merkel, U.S.A. 113 J5 32 28N 100 1W
Mermaid Reef, Australia 92 C2 17 6 S 119 36 E
Merowe, Sudan 80 D3 18 29N 31 46 E
Merredin, Australia 93 F2 31 28 S 118 18 E
Merrick, U.K. 14 F4 55 8N 4 28W
Merrickville, Canada 111 B9 44 55N 75 50W
Merrill, Oreg., U.S.A. 114 E3 42 1N 121 36W
Merrill, Wis., U.S.A. 112 C10 45 11N 89 41W
Merrimack →, U.S.A. 111 D14 42 49N 70 49W
Merriman, U.S.A. 112 D4 42 55N 101 42W
Merritt, Canada 104 C4 50 10N 120 45W
Merritt Island, U.S.A. 109 L5 28 21N 80 42W
Merriwa, Australia 95 E5 32 6 S 150 22 E
Merry I., Canada 102 A4 55 29N 77 31W
Merryville, U.S.A. 113 K8 30 45N 93 33W
Mersa Fatma, Eritrea 81 E5 14 57N 40 17 E
Mersch, Lux. 17 E6 49 44N 6 7 E
Merse →, Italy 29 E8 43 5N 11 22 E
Mersea I., U.K. 13 F8 51 47N 0 58 E
Merseburg, Germany 24 D7 51 22N 11 59 E
Mersey →, U.K. 12 D4 53 25N 3 1W
Merseyside □, U.K. 12 D4 53 31N 3 2W
Mersin, Turkey 70 B2 36 51N 34 36 E
Mersing, Malaysia 65 L4 2 25N 103 50 E
Merta, India 68 F6 26 39N 74 4 E
Merta Road, India 68 F5 26 43N 73 55 E
Merthyr Tydfil, U.K. 13 F4 51 45N 3 22W
Merthyr Tydfil □, U.K. 13 F4 51 46N 3 21W
Mértola, Portugal 35 H3 37 40N 7 40W
Mertzon, U.S.A. 113 K4 31 16N 100 49W
Méru, France 19 C9 49 13N 2 8 E
Meru, Kenya 86 B4 0 3N 37 40 E
Meru, Tanzania 86 C4 3 15 S 36 46 E
Merville, France 19 B9 50 38N 2 38 E
Méry-sur-Seine, France 19 D10 48 31N 3 54 E
Merzifon, Turkey 72 B6 40 53N 35 32 E
Merzig, Germany 25 F2 49 26N 6 38 E
Mesa, U.S.A. 115 K8 33 25N 111 50W
Mesa Verde National Park, U.S.A. 115 H9 37 11N 108 29W
Mesagne, Italy 31 B10 40 34N 17 48 E
Mesanagrós, Greece 36 C9 36 1N 27 49 E
Mesaoría □, Cyprus 36 D12 35 12N 33 14 E
Mesarás, Kólpos, Greece 36 D6 35 6N 24 47 E
Meschede, Germany 24 D4 51 20N 8 18 E
Mescit, Turkey 73 B9 40 21N 41 11 E
Mesfinto, Ethiopia 81 E4 13 20N 37 22 E
Mesgouez, L., Canada 102 B5 51 20N 75 0W
Meshchovsk, Russia 46 E8 54 22N 35 17 E
Meshed = Mashhad, Iran 71 B8 36 20N 59 35 E
Meshoppen, U.S.A. 111 E8 41 36N 76 3W
Meshra er Req, Sudan 81 F2 8 25N 29 18 E
Mesilinka →, Canada 104 B4 56 6N 124 30W
Mesilla, U.S.A. 115 K10 32 16N 106 48W
Meslay-du-Maine, France 18 E6 47 58N 0 33W
Mesocco, Switz. 25 J5 46 23N 9 12 E
Mesolóngion, Greece 38 C3 38 21N 21 28 E
Mesopotamia = Al Jazirah, Iraq 70 C5 33 30N 44 0 E
Mesopotamia, U.S.A. 110 E4 41 27N 80 57W
Mesopótamon, Greece 38 B2 39 14N 20 32 E
Mesoraca, Italy 31 C9 39 5N 16 48 E
Mésou Volímais = Volímai, Greece 38 D2 37 53N 20 35 E
Mesquite, U.S.A. 115 H6 36 47N 114 6W
Messac, France 18 E5 47 49N 1 50W
Messad, Algeria 78 B6 34 8N 3 30 E
Messalo →, Mozam. 87 E4 12 25 S 39 15 E
Méssaména, Cameroon 83 E7 3 48N 12 49 E
Messeue, Greece 38 D3 37 12N 21 58 E
Messina, Italy 31 D8 38 11N 15 34 E
Messina, S. Africa 89 C5 22 20 S 30 5 E
Messina, Str. di, Italy 31 D8 38 15N 15 35 E
Messíni, Greece 38 D4 37 4N 22 1 E
Messínia □, Greece 38 D3 37 10N 22 0 E
Messiniakós Kólpos, Greece 38 E4 36 45N 22 5 E
Messkirch, Germany 25 H5 47 59N 9 7 E
Messonghi, Greece 36 B3 39 29N 19 56 E
Mesta →, Bulgaria 40 E7 40 54N 24 49 E
Mestá, Ákra, Greece 39 C7 38 16N 25 53 E
Mestanza, Spain 35 G6 38 35N 4 4W
Mestre, Italy 29 C9 45 29N 12 15 E
Mesudiye, Turkey 72 B7 40 28N 37 46 E
Meta →, S. Amer. 122 C4 6 12N 67 28W
Meta Incognita Peninsula, Canada 101 B13 62 40N 68 0W
Metabetchouan, Canada 103 C5 48 26N 71 52W
Metairie, U.S.A. 113 L9 29 58N 90 10W
Metalici, Muntii, Romania 42 D7 46 15N 22 50 E
Metaline Falls, U.S.A. 114 B5 48 52N 117 22W
Metallifere, Colline, Italy 28 E8 43 10N 11 0 E
Metán, Argentina 126 B3 25 30 S 65 0W
Metangula, Mozam. 87 E3 12 40 S 34 50 E
Metauro →, Italy 29 E10 43 50N 13 3 E
Metema, Ethiopia 81 E4 12 56N 36 13 E
Metengobalame, Mozam. 87 E3 14 49 S 34 30 E
Méthana, Greece 38 D5 37 35N 23 23 E
Methóni, Greece 38 E3 36 49N 21 42 E
Methven, N.Z. 91 K3 43 38 S 171 40 E
Metil, Mozam. 87 F4 16 24 S 39 0 E
Metkovets, Bulgaria 40 C7 43 37N 23 10 E
Metković, Croatia 29 E14 43 6N 17 39 E
Metlakatla, U.S.A. 100 C6 55 8N 131 35W
Metlika, Slovenia 29 C12 45 40N 15 20 E
Metropolis, U.S.A. 113 G10 37 9N 88 44W
Métsovon, Greece 38 B3 39 48N 21 12 E
Mettur Dam, India 66 P10 11 45N 77 45 E
Metu, Ethiopia 81 F4 8 18N 35 35 E
Metz, France 19 C13 49 8N 6 10 E
Metzingen, Germany 25 G5 48 31N 9 17 E
Meulaboh, Indonesia 62 D1 4 11N 96 3 E
Meung-sur-Loire, France 19 E8 47 50N 1 40 E
Meureudu, Indonesia 62 C1 5 19N 96 10 E
Meurthe →, France 19 D13 48 47N 6 9 E
Meurthe-et-Moselle □, France 19 D13 48 52N 6 0 E
Meuse □, France 19 C12 49 8N 5 25 E
Meuse →, Europe 17 D5 50 45N 5 41 E
Meuselwitz, Germany 24 D8 51 2N 12 17 E
Mexia, U.S.A. 113 K6 31 41N 96 29W
Mexiana, I., Brazil 125 D9 0 0 49 30W
Mexicali, Mexico 117 N11 32 40N 115 30W
Mexican Plateau, Mexico 98 G9 25 0N 104 0W
Mexican Water, U.S.A. 115 H9 36 57N 109 32W
México, Mexico 119 D5 19 20N 99 10W
Mexico, Maine, U.S.A. 111 B14 44 34N 70 33W
Mexico, Mo., U.S.A. 112 F9 39 10N 91 53W
Mexico, N.Y., U.S.A. 111 C8 43 28N 76 18W
México □, Mexico 119 D5 19 20N 99 10W
Mexico ■, Cent. Amer. 118 C4 25 0N 105 0W
Mexico, G. of, Cent. Amer. 119 C7 25 0N 90 0W
Mexico B., U.S.A. 111 C8 43 35N 76 20W
Meydān-e Naftūn, Iran 71 D6 31 56N 49 18 E
Meydani, Ra's-e, Iran 71 E8 25 24N 59 6 E
Meyenburg, Germany 24 B8 53 18N 12 14 E
Meymac, France 20 C6 45 32N 2 10 E
Meymaneh, Afghan. 66 B4 35 53N 64 38 E
Meyrueis, France 20 D7 44 12N 3 27 E
Meyssac, France 20 C5 45 3N 1 40 E
Meyzieu, France 21 C8 45 46N 4 59 E
Mezdra, Bulgaria 40 C7 43 12N 23 42 E
Mèze, France 20 E7 43 27N 3 36 E
Mezen, Russia 50 C5 65 50N 44 20 E
Mezen →, Russia 50 C5 65 44N 44 22 E
Mézenc, Mt., France 21 D8 44 54N 4 11 E
Mezes, Muntii, Romania 42 C8 47 5N 23 5 E
Mezha →, Russia 46 E6 55 44N 31 33 E
Mezhdurechenskiy, Russia 50 D7 59 36N 65 56 E
Mézidon-Canon, France 18 C6 49 5N 0 1W
Mézières-en-Brenne, France 20 B5 46 49N 1 13 E
Mézilhac, France 21 D8 44 49N 4 21 E
Mézin, France 20 D4 44 4N 0 16 E
Mezőberény, Hungary 42 D6 46 49N 21 3 E
Mezőfalva, Hungary 42 D3 46 55N 18 49 E
Mezőhegyes, Hungary 42 D5 46 19N 20 49 E
Mezőkövácsháza, Hungary 42 D5 46 25N 20 57 E
Mezőkövesd, Hungary 42 C5 47 49N 20 35 E
Mézos, France 20 D2 44 5N 1 10W
Mezőtúr, Hungary 42 C5 47 1N 20 41 E
Mezquital, Mexico 118 C4 23 29N 104 23W
Mezzolombardo, Italy 28 B8 46 13N 11 5 E
Mfolozi →, S. Africa 89 D5 28 25 S 32 26 E
Mgeta, Tanzania 87 D4 8 22 S 36 6 E
Mglin, Russia 47 F7 53 2N 32 50 E
Mhlaba Hills, Zimbabwe 87 F3 18 30 S 30 30 E
Mhow, India 68 H6 22 33N 75 50 E
Miahuatlán, Mexico 119 D5 16 21N 96 36W
Miajadas, Spain 35 F5 39 9N 5 54W
Miami, Fla., U.S.A. 109 N5 25 47N 80 11W
Miami, Okla., U.S.A. 113 G7 36 53N 94 53W
Miami, Tex., U.S.A. 113 H4 35 42N 100 38W
Miami Beach, U.S.A. 109 N5 25 47N 80 8W
Mian Xian, China 56 H4 33 10N 106 32 E
Mianchi, China 56 G6 34 48N 111 48 E
Mīāndarreh, Iran 71 C7 35 37N 53 39 E
Mīāndowāb, Iran 70 B5 37 0N 46 5 E
Miandrivazo, Madag. 89 B8 19 31 S 45 29 E
Mīāneh, Iran 70 B5 37 30N 47 40 E
Mianning, China 58 C4 28 32N 102 9 E
Mianwali, Pakistan 68 C4 32 38N 71 28 E
Mianyang, China 58 B5 31 22N 104 47 E
Mianzhu, China 58 B5 31 22N 104 7 E
Miaoli, Taiwan 59 E13 24 37N 120 49 E
Miarinarivo, Antananarivo, Madag. 89 B8 18 57 S 46 55 E
Miarinarivo, Toamasina, Madag. 89 B8 16 38 S 48 15 E
Miariravaratra, Madag. 89 C8 20 13 S 47 31 E
Miass, Russia 50 D7 54 59N 60 6 E
Miasteczko Krajeńskie, Poland 45 E4 53 7N 17 1 E
Miastko, Poland 44 E3 54 0N 16 58 E
Mica, S. Africa 89 C5 24 10 S 30 48 E
Micăsasa, Romania 43 D9 46 7N 24 7 E
Michalovce, Slovak Rep. 27 C14 48 47N 21 58 E
Michigan □, U.S.A. 108 C3 44 0N 85 0W
Michigan, L., U.S.A. 108 D2 44 0N 87 0W
Michigan City, U.S.A. 108 E2 41 43N 86 54W
Michika, Nigeria 83 C7 10 36N 13 23 E
Michipicoten I., Canada 102 C2 47 40N 85 40W
Michoacan □, Mexico 118 D4 19 0N 102 0W
Michurin, Bulgaria 41 D11 42 9N 27 51 E
Michurinsk, Russia 48 D5 52 58N 40 27 E
Mico, Pta., Nic. 120 D3 12 0N 83 30W
Micronesia, Pac. Oc. 96 G7 11 0N 160 0 E
Micronesia, Federated States of ■, Pac. Oc. 96 G7 9 0N 150 0 E
Midai, Indonesia 65 L6 3 0N 107 47 E
Midale, Canada 105 D8 49 25N 103 20W
Middelburg, Neths. 17 C3 51 30N 3 36 E
Middelburg, Eastern Cape, S. Africa 88 E4 31 30 S 25 0 E
Middelburg, Mpumalanga, S. Africa 89 D4 25 49 S 29 28 E
Middelfart, Denmark 11 J3 55 30N 9 43 E
Middelpos, S. Africa 88 E3 31 55 S 20 13 E
Middelwit, S. Africa 88 C4 24 51 S 27 3 E
Middle Alkali L., U.S.A. 114 F3 41 27N 120 5W
Middle Bass I., U.S.A. 110 E2 41 41N 82 49W
Middle East, Asia 52 F7 38 0N 40 0 E
Middle Fork Feather →, U.S.A. 116 F5 38 33N 121 30W
Middle I., Australia 93 F3 34 6 S 123 11 E
Middle Loup →, U.S.A. 112 E5 41 17N 98 24W
Middle Sackville, Canada 103 D7 44 47N 63 42W
Middleboro, U.S.A. 111 E14 41 54N 70 55W
Middleburg, Fla., U.S.A. 109 K5 30 4N 81 52W
Middleburg, N.Y., U.S.A. 111 D10 42 36N 74 20W
Middleburg, Pa., U.S.A. 110 F7 40 47N 77 3W
Middlebury, U.S.A. 111 B11 44 1N 73 10W
Middlemount, Australia 94 C4 22 50 S 148 40 E
Middleport, N.Y., U.S.A. 110 C6 43 13N 78 29W
Middleport, Ohio, U.S.A. 108 F4 39 0N 82 3W
Middlesboro, U.S.A. 109 G4 36 36N 83 43W
Middlesbrough, U.K. 12 C6 54 35N 1 13W
Middlesbrough □, U.K. 12 C6 54 28N 1 13W
Middlesex, Belize 120 C2 17 2N 88 31W
Middlesex, N.J., U.S.A. 111 F10 40 36N 74 30W
Middlesex, N.Y., U.S.A. 110 D7 42 42N 77 16W
Middleton, Australia 94 C3 22 22 S 141 32 E
Middleton, Canada 103 D6 44 57N 65 4W
Middleton Cr. →, Australia 94 C3 22 35 S 141 51 E
Middletown, U.K. 15 B5 54 17N 6 51W
Middletown, Calif., U.S.A. 116 G4 38 45N 122 37W
Middletown, Conn., U.S.A. 111 E12 41 34N 72 39W
Middletown, N.Y., U.S.A. 111 E10 41 27N 74 25W
Middletown, Ohio, U.S.A. 108 F3 39 31N 84 24W
Middletown, Pa., U.S.A. 111 F8 40 12N 76 44W
Midhurst, U.K. 13 G7 50 59N 0 44W
Midī, Yemen 81 D5 16 20N 42 45 E
Midi, Canal du →, France 20 E5 43 45N 1 21 E
Midi d'Ossau, Pic du, France 20 F3 42 50N 0 26W
Midi-Pyrénées □, France 20 E5 43 55N 1 45 E
Midland, Canada 102 D4 44 45N 79 50W
Midland, Calif., U.S.A. 117 M12 33 52N 114 48W
Midland, Mich., U.S.A. 108 D3 43 37N 84 14W
Midland, Pa., U.S.A. 110 F4 40 39N 80 27W
Midland, Tex., U.S.A. 113 K3 32 0N 102 3W
Midlands □, Zimbabwe 87 F2 19 40 S 29 0 E
Midleton, Ireland 15 E3 51 55N 8 10W
Midlothian, U.S.A. 113 J6 32 30N 97 0W
Midlothian □, U.K. 14 F5 55 51N 3 5W
Midongy, Tangorombohitr' i, Madag. 89 C8 23 30 S 47 0 E
Midongy Atsimo, Madag. 89 C8 23 35 S 47 1 E
Midou →, France 20 E3 43 54N 0 30W
Midouze →, France 20 E3 43 48N 0 51W
Midsayap, Phil. 61 H6 7 12N 124 32 E
Midu, China 58 E3 25 18N 100 30 E
Midway Is., Pac. Oc. 96 E10 28 13N 177 22W
Midway Wells, U.S.A. 117 N11 32 41N 115 7W
Midwest, U.S.A. 114 E10 43 25N 106 16W
Midwest City, U.S.A. 113 H6 35 27N 97 24W
Midyat, Turkey 70 B4 37 25N 41 23 E
Midžor, Bulgaria 40 C6 43 24N 22 40 E
Mie □, Japan 55 G8 34 30N 136 10 E
Miechów, Poland 45 H7 50 21N 20 5 E
Miedwie, Jezioro, Poland 45 E1 53 17N 14 54 E
Międzybórz, Poland 45 G4 51 25N 17 34 E
Międzychód, Poland 45 F2 52 35N 15 53 E
Międzylesie, Poland 45 H3 50 8N 16 40 E
Międzyrzec Podlaski, Poland 45 G9 51 58N 22 45 E
Międzyrzecz, Poland 45 F2 52 26N 15 35 E
Międzyzdroje, Poland 44 E1 53 56N 14 26 E
Miejska Górka, Poland 45 G3 51 39N 16 58 E
Miélan, France 20 E4 43 27N 0 19 E
Mielec, Poland 45 H8 50 15N 21 25 E
Mienga, Angola 88 B2 17 12 S 19 48 E
Miercurea-Ciuc, Romania 43 D10 46 21N 25 48 E
Miercurea Sibiului, Romania 43 E8 45 53N 23 48 E
Mieres, Spain 34 B5 43 18N 5 48W
Mieroszów, Poland 45 H3 50 40N 16 11 E
Mieso, Ethiopia 81 F5 9 15N 40 43 E
Mieszkowice, Poland 45 F1 52 47N 14 30 E
Mifflintown, U.S.A. 110 F7 40 34N 77 24W
Mifraz Hefa, Israel 75 C4 32 52N 35 0 E
Migennes, France 19 E10 47 58N 3 31 E
Migliarino, Italy 29 D8 44 46N 11 56 E
Miguel Alemán, Presa, Mexico 119 D5 18 15N 96 40W
Miguelturra, Spain 35 G7 38 58N 3 53W
Mihăileni, Romania 43 C11 47 58N 26 9 E
Mihăileşti, Romania 43 F10 44 20N 25 54 E
Mihailovca, Moldova 43 D13 46 33N 28 56 E
Mihalgazi, Turkey 39 A12 40 2N 30 34 E
Mihaliççık, Turkey 72 C4 39 53N 31 30 E
Mihara, Japan 55 G6 34 24N 133 5 E
Miheşu de Cîmpie, Romania 43 D9 46 41N 24 9 E
Mijas, Spain 35 J6 36 36N 4 40W
Mikese, Tanzania 86 D4 6 48 S 37 55 E
Mikha-Tskhakaya = Senaki, Georgia 49 J6 42 15N 42 7 E
Mikhailovka = Mykhaylivka, Ukraine 47 J8 47 12N 35 15 E
Mikhaylov, Russia 46 E10 54 14N 39 0 E
Mikhaylovgrad = Montana, Bulgaria 40 C7 43 27N 23 16 E
Mikhaylovka, Russia 48 E6 50 3N 43 5 E
Mikhnevo, Russia 46 E9 55 4N 37 59 E
Mikínai, Greece 38 D4 37 43N 22 46 E
Mikkeli, Finland 9 F22 61 43N 27 15 E
Mikkwa →, Canada 104 B6 58 25N 114 46W
Mikniya, Sudan 81 D3 17 0N 33 45 E
Mikołajki, Poland 44 E8 53 49N 21 37 E
Míkonos, Greece 39 D7 37 30N 25 25 E
Mikrí Préspa, Límni, Greece 40 F5 40 47N 21 3 E
Mikrón Dhérion, Greece 41 E10 41 19N 26 6 E
Mikstat, Poland 45 G4 51 32N 17 59 E
Mikulov, Czech Rep. 27 C9 48 48N 16 39 E
Mikumi, Tanzania 86 D4 7 26 S 37 0 E
Milaca, U.S.A. 112 C8 45 45N 93 39W
Milagro, Ecuador 124 D3 2 11 S 79 36W
Milagros, Phil. 61 E5 12 13N 123 30 E
Milan = Milano, Italy 28 C6 45 28N 9 12 E
Milan, Mo., U.S.A. 112 E8 40 12N 93 7W
Milan, Tenn., U.S.A. 109 H1 35 55N 88 46W
Milang, Australia 95 F2 35 24 S 138 58 E
Milange, Mozam. 87 F4 16 3 S 35 45 E
Milano, Italy 28 C6 45 28N 9 12 E
Milanoa, Madag. 89 A8 13 35 S 49 47 E
Milâs, Turkey 39 D9 37 20N 27 50 E
Milatos, Greece 36 D7 35 18N 25 34 E
Milazzo, Italy 31 D8 38 13N 15 15 E
Milbank, U.S.A. 112 C6 45 13N 96 38W
Milbanke Sd., Canada 104 C3 52 15N 128 35W
Milden, Canada 105 C7 51 29N 107 32W
Mildenhall, U.K. 13 E8 52 21N 0 32 E
Mildmay, Canada 110 B3 44 3N 81 7W
Mildura, Australia 95 E3 34 13 S 142 9 E
Mile, China 58 E4 24 28N 103 20 E
Miléai, Greece 38 B5 39 20N 23 9 E
Miles, Australia 95 D5 26 40 S 150 9 E
Miles City, U.S.A. 112 B2 46 25N 105 51W
Mileşti, Moldova 43 C13 47 13N 28 3 E
Milestone, Canada 105 D8 49 59N 104 31W
Mileto, Italy 31 D9 38 36N 16 4 E
Miletto, Mte., Italy 31 A7 41 27N 14 22 E
Miletus, Turkey 39 D9 37 30N 27 18 E
Milevsko, Czech Rep. 26 B7 49 27N 14 21 E
Milford, Calif., U.S.A. 116 E6 40 10N 120 22W
Milford, Conn., U.S.A. 111 E11 41 14N 73 3W
Milford, Del., U.S.A. 108 F8 38 55N 75 26W
Milford, Mass., U.S.A. 111 D13 42 8N 71 31W
Milford, N.H., U.S.A. 111 D13 42 50N 71 39W
Milford, Pa., U.S.A. 111 E10 41 19N 74 48W
Milford, Utah, U.S.A. 115 G7 38 24N 113 1W
Milford Haven, U.K. 13 F2 51 42N 5 7W
Milford Sd., N.Z. 91 L1 44 41 S 167 47 E
Milḩ, Baḩr al, Iraq 70 C4 32 40N 43 35 E
Milicz, Poland 45 G4 51 31N 17 19 E
Milikapiti, Australia 92 B5 11 26 S 130 40 E
Miling, Australia 93 F2 30 30 S 116 17 E
Militello in Val di Catània, Italy 31 E7 37 16N 14 48 E
Milk →, U.S.A. 114 B10 48 4N 106 19W
Milk, Wadi el →, Sudan 80 D3 17 55N 30 20 E
Milk River, Canada 104 D6 49 10N 112 5W
Mill I., Antarctica 5 C8 66 0 S 101 30 E
Mill Valley, U.S.A. 116 H4 37 54N 122 32W
Millárs →, Spain 32 F4 39 55N 0 1W
Millau, France 20 D7 44 8N 3 4 E
Millbridge, Canada 110 B7 44 41N 77 36W
Millbrook, Canada 110 B6 44 10N 78 29W
Millbrook, U.S.A. 111 E11 41 47N 73 42W
Mille Lacs, L. des, Canada 102 C1 48 45N 90 35W
Mille Lacs L., U.S.A. 112 B8 46 15N 93 39W
Milledgeville, U.S.A. 109 J4 33 5N 83 14W
Millen, U.S.A. 109 J5 32 48N 81 57W
Miller, U.S.A. 112 C5 44 31N 98 59W
Millerovo, Russia 49 F5 48 57N 40 28 E
Millersburg, Ohio, U.S.A. 110 F3 40 33N 81 55W
Millersburg, Pa., U.S.A. 110 F8 40 32N 76 58W
Millerton, U.S.A. 111 E11 41 57N 73 31W
Millerton L., U.S.A. 116 J7 37 1N 119 41W
Millevaches, Plateau de, France 20 C6 45 45N 2 0 E
Millheim, U.S.A. 110 F7 40 54N 77 29W
Millicent, Australia 95 F3 37 34 S 140 21 E
Millington, U.S.A. 113 H10 35 20N 89 53W
Millinocket, U.S.A. 109 C11 45 39N 68 43W
Millmerran, Australia 95 D5 27 53 S 151 16 E
Millom, U.K. 12 C4 54 13N 3 16W
Mills L., Canada 104 A5 61 30N 118 20W
Millsboro, U.S.A. 110 G5 40 0N 80 0W
Milltown Malbay, Ireland 15 D2 52 52N 9 24W
Millville, N.J., U.S.A. 108 F8 39 24N 75 2W
Millville, Pa., U.S.A. 111 E8 41 7N 76 32W
Millwood L., U.S.A. 113 J8 33 42N 93 58W
Milna, Croatia 29 E13 43 20N 16 28 E
Milne →, Australia 94 C2 21 10 S 137 33 E
Milo, U.S.A. 109 C11 45 15N 68 59W
Mílos, Greece 38 E6 36 44N 24 25 E
Miłosław, Poland 45 F4 52 12N 17 32 E
Milot, Albania 40 E3 41 41N 19 43 E
Milparinka, Australia 95 D3 29 46 S 141 57 E
Miltenberg, Germany 25 F5 49 41N 9 16 E
Milton, N.S., Canada 103 D7 44 4N 64 45W
Milton, Ont., Canada 110 C5 43 31N 79 53W
Milton, N.Z. 91 M2 46 7 S 169 59 E
Milton, Calif., U.S.A. 116 G6 38 3N 120 51W
Milton, Fla., U.S.A. 109 K2 30 38N 87 3W
Milton, Pa., U.S.A. 110 F8 41 1N 76 51W
Milton, Vt., U.S.A. 111 B11 44 38N 73 7W
Milton-Freewater, U.S.A. 114 D4 45 56N 118 23W
Milton Keynes, U.K. 13 E7 52 1N 0 44W
Milton Keynes □, U.K. 13 E7 52 1N 0 44W
Miluo, China 59 C9 29 0N 112 59 E
Milverton, Canada 110 C4 43 34N 80 55W
Milwaukee, U.S.A. 108 D2 43 2N 87 55W
Milwaukee Deep, Atl. Oc. 121 C6 19 50N 68 0W
Milwaukie, U.S.A. 116 E4 45 27N 122 38W
Mim, Ghana 82 D4 6 57N 2 33W
Mimizan, France 20 D2 44 12N 1 13W
Mimoň, Czech Rep. 26 A7 50 38N 14 43 E
Min Jiang →, Fujian, China 59 E12 26 0N 119 35 E
Min Jiang →, Sichuan, China 58 C5 28 45N 104 40 E
Min Xian, China 56 G3 34 25N 104 5 E
Mina Pirquitas, Argentina 126 A2 22 40 S 66 30W
Mīnā Su'ud, Si. Arabia 71 D6 28 45N 48 28 E
Mīnā'al Aḩmadī, Kuwait 71 D6 29 5N 48 10 E
Minago →, Canada 105 C9 54 33N 98 59W
Minaki, Canada 105 D10 49 59N 94 40W
Minamata, Japan 55 H5 32 10N 130 30 E
Minami-Tori-Shima, Pac. Oc. 96 E7 24 20N 153 58 E
Minas, Uruguay 127 C4 34 20 S 55 10W
Minas, Sierra de las, Guatemala 120 C2 15 9N 89 31W
Minas Basin, Canada 103 C7 45 20N 64 12W
Minas de Rio Tinto = Minas de Riotinto, Spain 35 H4 37 42N 6 35W
Minas de Riotinto, Spain 35 H4 37 42N 6 35W
Minas Gerais □, Brazil 125 G9 18 50 S 46 0W
Minatitlán, Mexico 119 D6 17 59N 94 31W
Minbu, Burma 67 J19 20 10N 94 52 E
Minchinabad, Pakistan 68 D5 30 10N 73 34 E
Mincio →, Italy 28 C7 45 4N 10 59 E
Minčol, Slovak Rep. 27 B13 49 15N 20 58 E
Mindanao, Phil. 61 H6 8 0N 125 0 E
Mindanao Sea = Bohol Sea, Phil. 63 C6 9 0N 124 0 E
Mindanao Trench, Pac. Oc. 61 F7 12 0N 126 6 E
Mindel →, Germany 25 G6 48 31N 10 23 E
Mindelheim, Germany 25 G6 48 2N 10 29 E
Minden, Canada 110 B6 44 55N 78 43W
Minden, Germany 24 C4 52 17N 8 55 E
Minden, La., U.S.A. 113 J8 32 37N 93 17W
Minden, Nev., U.S.A. 116 G7 38 57N 119 46W

Mindiptana, Indonesia 63 F10 5 55 S 140 22 E
Mindoro, Phil. 61 E4 13 0N 121 0 E
Mindoro Str., Phil. 61 E4 12 30N 120 30 E
Mine, Japan 55 G5 34 12N 131 7 E
Minehead, U.K. 13 F4 51 12N 3 29W
Mineola, N.Y., U.S.A. 111 F11 40 45N 73 39W
Mineola, Tex., U.S.A. 113 J7 32 40N 95 29W
Mineral King, U.S.A. 116 J8 36 27N 118 36W
Mineral Wells, U.S.A. 113 J5 32 48N 98 7W
Mineralnyye Vody, Russia 49 H6 44 15N 43 8 E
Minersville, U.S.A. 111 F8 40 41N 76 16W
Minerva, U.S.A. 110 F3 40 44N 81 6W
Minervino Murge, Italy 31 A9 41 5N 16 5 E
Minetto, U.S.A. 111 C8 43 24N 76 28W
Mingäçevir, Azerbaijan 49 K8 40 45N 47 0 E
Mingäçevir Su Anbarı, Azerbaijan 49 K8 40 57N 46 50 E
Mingan, Canada 103 B7 50 20N 64 0W
Mingechaur = Mingäçevir, Azerbaijan 49 K8 40 45N 47 0 E
Mingechaurskoye Vdkhr. = Mingäçevir Su Anbarı, Azerbaijan 49 K8 40 57N 46 50 E
Mingela, Australia 94 B4 19 52 S 146 38 E
Mingenew, Australia 93 E2 29 12 S 115 21 E
Mingera Cr. →, Australia 94 C2 20 38 S 137 45 E
Minggang, China 59 A10 32 24N 114 3 E
Mingguang, China 59 A11 32 46N 117 59 E
Mingin, Burma 67 H19 22 50N 94 30 E
Mingir, Moldova 43 D13 46 40N 28 20 E
Minglanilla, Spain 33 F3 39 34N 1 38W
Minglun, China 58 E7 25 10N 108 21 E
Mingo Junction, U.S.A. 110 F4 40 19N 80 37W
Mingorria, Spain 34 E6 40 45N 4 40W
Mingshan, China 58 B4 30 6N 103 10 E
Mingxi, China 59 D11 26 18N 117 12 E
Mingyuegue, China 57 C15 43 2N 128 50 E
Minho = Miño →, Spain 34 D2 41 52N 8 40W
Minhou, China 59 E12 26 0N 119 15 E
Minićevo, Serbia, Yug. 42 G7 43 42N 22 18 E
Minidoka, U.S.A. 114 E7 42 45N 113 29W
Minigwal, L., Australia 93 E3 29 31 S 123 14 E
Minilya →, Australia 93 D1 23 45 S 114 0 E
Minilya Roadhouse, Australia 93 D1 23 55 S 114 0 E
Minipi L., Canada 103 B7 52 25N 60 45W
Mink L., Canada 104 A5 61 54N 117 40W
Minkammen, Sudan 81 F3 6 3N 31 32 E
Minna, Nigeria 83 D6 9 37N 6 30 E
Minneapolis, Kans., U.S.A. 112 F6 39 8N 97 42W
Minneapolis, Minn., U.S.A. 112 C8 44 59N 93 16W
Minnedosa, Canada 105 C9 50 14N 99 50W
Minnesota □, U.S.A. 112 B8 46 0N 94 15W
Minnesota →, U.S.A. 112 C8 44 54N 93 9W
Minnewaukan, U.S.A. 112 A5 48 4N 99 15W
Minnipa, Australia 95 E2 32 51 S 135 9 E
Minnitaki L., Canada 102 C1 49 57N 92 10W
Mino, Japan 55 G8 35 32N 136 55 E
Miño, Spain 34 B2 43 21N 8 12W
Miño →, Spain 34 D2 41 52N 8 40W
Minoa, Greece 39 F7 35 6N 25 45 E
Minorca = Menorca, Spain 37 B11 40 0N 4 0 E
Minot, U.S.A. 112 A4 48 14N 101 18W
Minqin, China 56 E2 38 38N 103 20 E
Minqing, China 59 D12 26 15N 118 50 E
Minsen, Germany 24 B3 53 41N 7 58 E
Minsk, Belarus 46 F4 53 52N 27 30 E
Mińsk Mazowiecki, Poland 45 F8 52 10N 21 33 E
Mintabie, Australia 95 D1 27 15 S 133 7 E
Mintaka Pass, Pakistan 69 A6 37 0N 74 58 E
Minteke Daban = Mintaka Pass, Pakistan 69 A6 37 0N 74 58 E
Minto, Canada 103 C6 46 5N 66 5W
Minto, L., Canada 102 A5 57 13N 75 0W
Minton, Canada 105 D8 49 10N 104 35W
Minturn, U.S.A. 114 G10 39 35N 106 26W
Minturno, Italy 30 A6 41 15N 13 45 E
Minûf, Egypt 80 H7 30 26N 30 52 E
Minusinsk, Russia 51 D10 53 43N 91 20 E
Minutang, India 67 E20 28 15N 96 30 E
Minya el Qamh, Egypt 80 H7 30 31N 31 21 E
Mionica, Bos.-H. 42 F3 44 51N 18 29 E
Mionica, Serbia, Yug. 40 B4 44 14N 20 6 E
Miquelon, Canada 102 C4 49 25N 76 27W
Miquelon, St- P. & M. 103 C8 47 8N 56 22W
Mîr, Niger 83 C7 14 5N 11 59 E
Mīr Kūh, Iran 71 E8 26 22N 58 55 E
Mīr Shahdād, Iran 71 E8 26 15N 58 29 E
Mira, Italy 29 C9 45 26N 12 8 E
Mira, Portugal 34 E2 40 26N 8 44W
Mira →, Portugal 35 H2 37 43N 8 47W
Mira por vos Cay, Bahamas 121 B5 22 9N 74 30W
Mirabella Eclano, Italy 31 A7 41 2N 14 59 E
Miraj, India 66 L9 16 50N 74 45 E
Miram Shah, Pakistan 68 C4 33 0N 70 2 E
Miramar, Argentina 126 D4 38 15 S 57 50W
Miramar, Mozam. 89 C6 23 50 S 35 35 E
Miramas, France 21 E8 43 33N 4 59 E
Mirambeau, France 20 C3 45 23N 0 35W
Miramichi, Canada 103 C6 47 2N 65 28W
Miramichi B., Canada 103 C7 47 15N 65 0W
Miramont-de-Guyenne, France 20 D4 44 37N 0 21 E
Miranda, Brazil 125 H7 20 10 S 56 15W
Miranda →, Brazil 124 G7 19 25 S 57 20W
Miranda de Ebro, Spain 32 C2 42 41N 2 57W
Miranda do Corvo, Portugal 34 E2 40 6N 8 20W
Miranda do Douro, Portugal 34 D4 41 30N 6 16W
Mirande, France 20 E4 43 31N 0 25 E
Mirandela, Portugal 34 D3 41 32N 7 10W
Mirándola, Italy 28 D8 44 53N 11 4 E
Mirandópolis, Brazil 127 A5 21 9 S 51 6W
Mirango, Malawi 87 E3 13 32 S 34 58 E
Mirano, Italy 29 C9 45 30N 12 7 E
Miras, Albania 40 F4 40 30N 20 56 E
Mirassol, Brazil 127 A6 20 46 S 49 28W
Mirbāţ, Oman 74 D5 17 0N 54 45 E
Mirear, Egypt 80 C4 23 15N 35 41 E
Mirebeau, Côte-d'Or, France 19 E12 47 25N 5 20 E
Mirebeau, Vienne, France 18 F7 46 49N 0 10 E
Mirecourt, France 19 D13 48 20N 6 10 E
Mirgorod = Myrhorod, Ukraine 47 H7 49 58N 33 37 E
Miri, Malaysia 62 D4 4 23N 113 59 E
Miriam Vale, Australia 94 C5 24 20 S 151 33 E
Miribel, France 19 G11 45 50N 4 57 E
Mirim, L., S. Amer. 127 C5 32 45 S 52 50W
Mirnyy, Russia 51 C12 62 33N 113 53 E
Miroč, Serbia, Yug. 40 B6 44 32N 22 16 E
Mirokhan, Pakistan 68 F3 27 46N 68 6 E
Mirond L., Canada 105 B8 55 6N 102 47W
Mirosławiec, Poland 44 E3 53 20N 16 5 E
Mirpur, Pakistan 69 C5 33 32N 73 56 E
Mirpur Batoro, Pakistan 68 G3 24 44N 68 16 E
Mirpur Bibiwari, Pakistan 68 E2 28 33N 67 44 E
Mirpur Khas, Pakistan 68 G3 25 30N 69 0 E
Mirpur Sakro, Pakistan 68 G2 24 33N 67 41 E
Mirria, Niger 83 C6 13 43N 9 7 E
Mirsk, Poland 45 H2 50 58N 15 23 E
Mirtağ, Turkey 70 B4 38 23N 41 56 E
Miryang, S. Korea 57 G15 35 31N 128 44 E
Mirzaani, Georgia 49 K8 41 24N 46 5 E
Mirzapur, India 69 G10 25 10N 82 34 E
Mirzapur-cum-Vindhyachal = Mirzapur, India 69 G10 25 10N 82 34 E
Misantla, Mexico 119 D5 19 56N 96 50W
Misawa, Japan 54 D10 40 41N 141 24 E
Miscou I., Canada 103 C7 47 57N 64 31W
Mish'āb, Ra's al, Si. Arabia 71 D6 28 15N 48 43 E
Mishan, China 60 B8 45 37N 131 48 E
Mishawaka, U.S.A. 108 E2 41 40N 86 11W
Mishbih, Gebel, Egypt 80 C3 22 38N 34 44 E
Mishima, Japan 55 G9 35 10N 138 52 E
Misión, Mexico 117 N10 32 6N 116 53W
Misiones □, Argentina 127 B5 27 0 S 55 0W
Misiones □, Paraguay 126 B4 27 0 S 56 0W
Miskah, Si. Arabia 70 E4 24 49N 42 56 E
Miskitos, Cayos, Nic. 120 D3 14 26N 82 50W
Miskolc, Hungary 42 B5 48 7N 20 50 E
Misoke, Dem. Rep. of the Congo 86 C2 0 42 S 28 2 E
Misool, Indonesia 63 E8 1 52 S 130 10 E
Misrātah, Libya 79 B9 32 24N 15 3 E
Missanabie, Canada 102 C3 48 20N 84 6W
Missinaibi →, Canada 102 B3 50 43N 81 29W
Missinaibi L., Canada 102 C3 48 23N 83 40W
Mission, Canada 104 D4 49 10N 122 15W
Mission, S. Dak., U.S.A. 112 D4 43 18N 100 39W
Mission, Tex., U.S.A. 113 M5 26 13N 98 20W
Mission Beach, Australia 94 B4 17 53 S 146 6 E
Mission Viejo, U.S.A. 117 M9 33 36N 117 40W
Missirah, Senegal 82 C1 13 40N 16 30W
Missisa L., Canada 102 B2 52 20N 85 7W
Missisicabi →, Canada 102 B4 51 14N 79 31W
Mississagi →, Canada 102 C3 46 15N 83 9W
Mississauga, Canada 110 C5 43 32N 79 35W
Mississippi □, U.S.A. 113 J10 33 0N 90 0W
Mississippi →, U.S.A. 113 L10 29 9N 89 15W
Mississippi L., Canada 111 A8 45 5N 76 10W
Mississippi River Delta, U.S.A. 113 L9 29 10N 89 15W
Mississippi Sd., U.S.A. 113 K10 30 20N 89 0W
Missoula, U.S.A. 114 C7 46 52N 114 1W
Missouri □, U.S.A. 112 F8 38 25N 92 30W
Missouri →, U.S.A. 112 F9 38 49N 90 7W
Missouri City, U.S.A. 113 L7 29 37N 95 32W
Missouri Valley, U.S.A. 112 E7 41 34N 95 53W
Mist, U.S.A. 116 E3 45 59N 123 15W
Mistassibi →, Canada 103 B5 48 53N 72 13W
Mistassini, Canada 103 C5 48 53N 72 12W
Mistassini →, Canada 103 C5 48 42N 72 20W
Mistassini, L., Canada 102 B5 51 0N 73 30W
Mistastin L., Canada 103 A7 55 57N 63 20W
Mistelbach, Austria 27 C9 48 34N 16 34 E
Misterbianco, Italy 31 E8 37 31N 15 1 E
Mistinibi, L., Canada 103 A7 55 56N 64 17W
Mistretta, Italy 31 E7 37 56N 14 22 E
Misty L., Canada 105 B8 58 53N 101 40W
Misurata = Misrātah, Libya 79 B9 32 24N 15 3 E
Mît Ghamr, Egypt 80 H7 30 42N 31 12 E
Mitatib, Sudan 81 D4 15 59N 36 12 E
Mitchell, Australia 95 D4 26 29 S 147 58 E
Mitchell, Canada 110 C3 43 28N 81 12W
Mitchell, Nebr., U.S.A. 112 E3 41 57N 103 49W
Mitchell, Oreg., U.S.A. 114 D3 44 34N 120 9W
Mitchell, S. Dak., U.S.A. 112 D6 43 43N 98 2W
Mitchell →, Australia 94 B3 15 12 S 141 35 E
Mitchell, Mt., U.S.A. 109 H4 35 46N 82 16W
Mitchell Ranges, Australia 94 A2 12 49 S 135 36 E
Mitchelstown, Ireland 15 D3 52 15N 8 16W
Mitha Tiwana, Pakistan 68 C5 32 13N 72 6 E
Mithi, Pakistan 68 G3 24 44N 69 48 E
Míthimna, Greece 39 B8 39 20N 26 12 E
Mithrao, Pakistan 68 F3 27 28N 69 40 E
Mitilíni, Greece 39 B8 39 6N 26 35 E
Mitilinoí, Greece 39 D8 37 42N 26 56 E
Mito, Japan 55 F10 36 20N 140 30 E
Mitrofanovka, Russia 47 H10 49 58N 39 42 E
Mitrovica = Kosovska Mitrovica, Kosovo, Yug. 40 D4 42 54N 20 52 E
Mitsinjo, Madag. 89 B8 16 1 S 45 52 E
Mitsiwa, Eritrea 81 D4 15 35N 39 25 E
Mitsiwa Channel, Eritrea 81 D5 15 30N 40 0 E
Mitsukaidō, Japan 55 F9 36 1N 139 59 E
Mittagong, Australia 95 E5 34 28 S 150 29 E
Mittelberg, Austria 26 D3 47 20N 10 10 E
Mittelfranken □, Germany 25 F6 49 25N 10 40 E
Mittellandkanal →, Germany 24 C4 52 20N 8 28 E
Mittenwalde, Germany 24 C9 52 15N 13 31 E
Mittersill, Austria 26 D5 47 16N 12 29 E
Mitterteich, Germany 25 F8 49 57N 12 14 E
Mittweida, Germany 24 E8 50 59N 12 59 E
Mitú, Colombia 124 C4 1 15N 70 13W
Mitumba, Tanzania 86 D3 7 8 S 31 2 E
Mitumba, Mts., Dem. Rep. of the Congo 86 D2 7 0 S 27 30 E
Mitwaba, Dem. Rep. of the Congo 87 D2 8 2 S 27 17 E
Mityana, Uganda 86 B3 0 23N 32 2 E
Mixteco →, Mexico 119 D5 18 11N 98 30W
Miyagi □, Japan 54 E10 38 15N 140 45 E
Miyāh, W. el →, Egypt 80 C3 25 0N 33 23 E
Miyāh, W. el →, Syria 70 C3 34 44N 39 57 E
Miyake-Jima, Japan 55 G9 34 5N 139 30 E
Miyako, Japan 54 E10 39 40N 141 59 E
Miyako-Jima, Japan 55 M2 24 45N 125 20 E
Miyako-Rettō, Japan 55 M2 24 24N 125 0 E
Miyakonojō, Japan 55 J5 31 40N 131 5 E
Miyani, India 68 J3 21 50N 69 26 E
Miyanoura-Dake, Japan 55 J5 30 20N 130 31 E
Miyazaki, Japan 55 J5 31 56N 131 30 E
Miyazaki □, Japan 55 H5 32 30N 131 30 E
Miyazu, Japan 55 G7 35 35N 135 10 E
Miyet, Bahr el = Dead Sea, Asia 75 D4 31 30N 35 30 E
Miyi, China 58 D4 26 47N 102 9 E
Miyoshi, Japan 55 G6 34 48N 132 51 E
Miyun, China 56 D9 40 28N 116 50 E
Miyun Shuiku, China 57 D9 40 30N 117 0 E
Mizan Teferi, Ethiopia 81 F4 6 57N 35 3 E
Mizdah, Libya 79 B8 31 30N 13 0 E
Mizen Hd., Cork, Ireland 15 E2 51 27N 9 50W
Mizen Hd., Wick., Ireland 15 D5 52 51N 6 4W
Mizhi, China 56 F6 37 47N 110 12 E
Mizil, Romania 43 F11 44 59N 26 29 E
Mizoram □, India 67 H18 23 30N 92 40 E
Mizpe Ramon, Israel 75 E3 30 34N 34 49 E
Mizusawa, Japan 54 E10 39 8N 141 8 E
Mjällby, Sweden 11 H8 56 3N 14 40 E
Mjöbäck, Sweden 11 G6 57 28N 12 53 E
Mjölby, Sweden 11 F9 58 20N 15 10 E
Mjörn, Sweden 11 G6 57 55N 12 25 E
Mjøsa, Norway 9 F14 60 40N 11 0 E
Mkata, Tanzania 86 D4 5 45 S 38 20 E
Mkokotoni, Tanzania 86 D4 5 55 S 39 15 E
Mkomazi, Tanzania 86 C4 4 40 S 38 7 E
Mkomazi →, S. Africa 89 E5 30 12 S 30 50 E
Mkulwe, Tanzania 87 D3 8 37 S 32 20 E
Mkumbi, Ras, Tanzania 86 D4 7 38 S 39 55 E
Mkushi, Zambia 87 E2 14 25 S 29 15 E
Mkushi River, Zambia 87 E2 13 32 S 29 45 E
Mkuze, S. Africa 89 D5 27 10 S 32 0 E
Mladá Boleslav, Czech Rep. 26 A7 50 27N 14 53 E
Mladenovac, Serbia, Yug. 40 B4 44 28N 20 44 E
Mlala Hills, Tanzania 86 D3 6 50 S 31 40 E
Mlange = Mulanje, Malawi 87 F4 16 2 S 35 33 E
Mlanje, Pic, Malawi 85 H7 15 57 S 35 38 E
Mlava →, Serbia, Yug. 40 B5 44 45N 21 13 E
Mława, Poland 45 E7 53 9N 20 25 E
Mlinište, Bos.-H. 29 D13 44 15N 16 50 E
Mljet, Croatia 29 F14 42 43N 17 30 E
Mljetski Kanal, Croatia 29 F14 42 48N 17 35 E
Młynary, Poland 44 D6 54 12N 19 46 E
Mmabatho, S. Africa 88 D4 25 49 S 25 30 E
Mme, Cameroon 83 D7 6 18N 10 14 E
Mnichovo Hradiště, Czech Rep. 26 A7 50 32N 14 59 E
Mo i Rana, Norway 8 C16 66 20N 14 7 E
Moa, Cuba 121 B4 20 40N 74 56W
Moa, Indonesia 63 F7 8 0 S 128 0 E
Moa →, S. Leone 82 D2 6 59N 11 36W
Moab, U.S.A. 115 G9 38 35N 109 33W
Moala, Fiji 91 D8 18 36 S 179 53 E
Moama, Australia 95 F3 36 7 S 144 46 E
Moamba, Mozam. 89 D5 25 36 S 32 15 E
Moapa, U.S.A. 117 J12 36 40N 114 37W
Moate, Ireland 15 C4 53 24N 7 44W
Moba, Dem. Rep. of the Congo 86 D2 7 0 S 29 48 E
Mobārakābād, Iran 71 D7 28 24N 53 20 E
Mobaye, C.A.R. 84 D4 4 25N 21 5 E
Mobayi, Dem. Rep. of the Congo 84 D4 4 15N 21 8 E
Moberley Lake, Canada 104 B4 55 50N 121 44W
Moberly, U.S.A. 112 F8 39 25N 92 26W
Mobile, U.S.A. 109 K1 30 41N 88 3W
Mobile B., U.S.A. 109 K2 30 30N 88 0W
Mobridge, U.S.A. 112 C4 45 32N 100 26W
Mobutu Sese Seko, L. = Albert L., Africa 86 B3 1 30N 31 0 E
Moc Chau, Vietnam 64 B5 20 50N 104 38 E
Moc Hoa, Vietnam 65 G5 10 46N 105 56 E
Mocabe Kasari, Dem. Rep. of the Congo 87 D2 9 58 S 26 12 E
Moçambique, Mozam. 87 F5 15 3 S 40 42 E
Moçâmedes = Namibe, Angola 85 H2 15 7 S 12 11 E
Mocanaqua, U.S.A. 111 E8 41 9N 76 8W
Mochudi, Botswana 88 C4 24 27 S 26 7 E
Mocimboa da Praia, Mozam. 87 E5 11 25 S 40 20 E
Mociu, Romania 43 D9 46 46N 24 3 E
Möckeln, Sweden 11 H8 56 40N 14 15 E
Mockfjärd, Sweden 10 D8 60 30N 14 57 E
Moclips, U.S.A. 116 C2 47 14N 124 13W
Mocoa, Colombia 124 C3 1 7N 76 35W
Mococa, Brazil 127 A6 21 28 S 47 0W
Mocorito, Mexico 118 B3 25 30N 107 53W
Moctezuma, Mexico 118 B3 29 50N 109 0W
Moctezuma →, Mexico 119 C5 21 59N 98 34W
Mocuba, Mozam. 87 F4 16 54 S 36 57 E
Mocúzari, Presa, Mexico 118 B3 27 10N 109 10W
Modane, France 21 C10 45 12N 6 40 E
Modasa, India 68 H5 23 30N 73 21 E
Modder →, S. Africa 88 D3 29 2 S 24 37 E
Modderrivier, S. Africa 88 D3 29 2 S 24 38 E
Módena, Italy 28 D7 44 40N 10 55 E
Modena, U.S.A. 115 H7 37 48N 113 56W
Modesto, U.S.A. 116 H6 37 39N 121 0W
Módica, Italy 31 F7 36 52N 14 46 E
Mödling, Austria 27 C9 48 5N 16 17 E
Modo, Sudan 81 F3 5 31N 30 33 E
Modra, Slovak Rep. 27 C10 48 19N 17 20 E
Modriča, Bos.-H. 42 F3 44 57N 18 17 E
Moe, Australia 95 F4 38 12 S 146 19 E
Moebase, Mozam. 87 F4 17 3 S 38 41 E
Moëlan-sur-Mer, France 18 E3 47 49N 3 38W
Moengo, Surinam 125 B8 5 45N 54 20W
Moffat, U.K. 14 F5 55 21N 3 27W
Moga, India 68 D6 30 48N 75 8 E
Mogadishu = Muqdisho, Somali Rep. 74 G4 2 2N 45 25 E
Mogador = Essaouira, Morocco 78 B4 31 32N 9 42W
Mogadouro, Portugal 34 D4 41 22N 6 47W
Mogalakwena →, S. Africa 89 C4 22 38 S 28 40 E
Mogami-Gawa →, Japan 54 E10 38 45N 140 0 E
Mogán, Canary Is. 37 G4 27 53N 15 43W
Mogaung, Burma 67 G20 25 20N 97 0 E
Mogente = Moixent, Spain 33 G4 38 52N 0 45W
Mogho, Ethiopia 81 G5 4 54N 40 16 E
Mogi das Cruzes, Brazil 127 A6 23 31 S 46 11W
Mogi-Guaçu →, Brazil 127 A6 20 53 S 48 10W
Mogi-Mirim, Brazil 127 A6 22 29 S 47 0W
Mogielnica, Poland 45 G7 51 42N 20 41 E
Mogige, Ethiopia 81 F4 5 24N 36 14 E
Mogilev = Mahilyow, Belarus 46 F6 53 55N 30 18 E
Mogilev-Podolskiy = Mohyliv-Podilskyy, Ukraine 47 H4 48 26N 27 48 E
Mogilno, Poland 45 F4 52 39N 17 55 E
Mogincual, Mozam. 87 F5 15 35 S 40 25 E
Mogliano Véneto, Italy 29 C9 45 33N 12 14 E
Mogocha, Russia 51 D12 53 40N 119 50 E
Mogok, Burma 67 H20 23 0N 96 40 E
Mogollon Rim, U.S.A. 115 J8 34 10N 110 50W
Mógoro, Italy 30 C1 39 41N 8 47 E
Mograt, Sudan 80 D3 19 28N 33 16 E
Moguer, Spain 35 H4 37 15N 6 52W
Mogumber, Australia 93 F2 31 2 S 116 3 E
Mohács, Hungary 42 E3 45 58N 18 41 E
Mohales Hoek, Lesotho 88 E4 30 7 S 27 26 E
Mohall, U.S.A. 112 A4 48 46N 101 31W
Moḩammadābād, Iran 71 B8 37 52N 59 5 E
Mohammedia, Morocco 78 B4 33 44N 7 21W
Mohana →, India 69 G11 24 43N 85 0 E
Mohanlalganj, India 69 F9 26 41N 80 58 E
Mohave, L., U.S.A. 117 K12 35 12N 114 34W
Mohawk →, U.S.A. 111 D11 42 47N 73 41W
Moheda, Sweden 11 G8 57 1N 14 35 E
Mohenjodaro, Pakistan 68 F3 27 19N 68 7 E
Mohicanville Reservoir, U.S.A. 110 F3 40 45N 82 0W
Möhne →, Germany 24 D3 51 29N 7 57 E
Mohoro, Tanzania 86 D4 8 6 S 39 8 E
Mohyliv-Podilskyy, Ukraine 47 H4 48 26N 27 48 E
Moia, Sudan 81 F2 5 3N 28 2 E
Moidart, L., U.K. 14 E3 56 47N 5 52W
Moinești, Romania 43 D11 46 28N 26 31 E
Moira →, Canada 110 B7 44 21N 77 24W
Moirans, France 21 C9 45 20N 5 33 E
Moirans-en-Montagne, France 19 F12 46 26N 5 43 E
Moíres, Greece 36 D6 35 4N 24 56 E
Moisaküla, Estonia 9 G21 58 3N 25 12 E
Moisie, Canada 103 B6 50 12N 66 1W
Moisie →, Canada 103 B6 50 14N 66 5W
Moissac, France 20 D5 44 7N 1 5 E
Moita, Portugal 35 G2 38 38N 8 58W
Moixent, Spain 33 G4 38 52N 0 45W
Möja, Sweden 10 E12 59 26N 18 55 E
Mojácar, Spain 33 H3 37 6N 1 55W
Mojados, Spain 34 D6 41 26N 4 40W
Mojave, U.S.A. 117 K8 35 3N 118 10W
Mojave Desert, U.S.A. 117 L10 35 0N 116 30W
Mojiang, China 58 F3 23 37N 101 35 E
Mojjo →, Ethiopia 81 F5 7 55N 42 0 E
Mojkovac, Montenegro, Yug. 40 D3 42 58N 19 35 E
Mojo, Bolivia 126 A2 21 48 S 65 33W
Mojo, Ethiopia 81 F4 8 35N 39 5 E
Mojokerto, Indonesia 63 G15 7 28 S 112 26 E
Mokai, N.Z. 91 H5 38 32 S 175 56 E
Mokambo, Dem. Rep. of the Congo 87 E2 12 25 S 28 20 E
Mokameh, India 69 G11 25 24N 85 55 E
Mokau, N.Z. 91 H5 38 42 S 174 39 E
Mokelumne →, U.S.A. 116 G5 38 13N 121 28W
Mokelumne Hill, U.S.A. 116 G6 38 18N 120 43W
Mokhós, Greece 36 D7 35 16N 25 27 E
Mokhotlong, Lesotho 89 D4 29 22 S 29 2 E
Möklinta, Sweden 10 D10 60 4N 16 33 E
Mokokchung, India 67 F19 26 15N 94 30 E
Mokolo, Cameroon 83 C7 10 50N 13 55 E
Mokolo →, S. Africa 89 C4 23 14 S 27 43 E
Mokp'o, S. Korea 57 G14 34 50N 126 25 E
Mokra Gora, Yugoslavia 40 D4 42 50N 20 30 E
Mokronog, Slovenia 29 C12 45 57N 15 9 E
Moksha →, Russia 48 C6 54 45N 41 53 E
Mokshan, Russia 48 D7 53 25N 44 35 E
Mokwa, Nigeria 83 D6 9 19N 5 0 E
Mol, Belgium 17 C5 51 11N 5 5 E
Mola di Bari, Italy 31 A10 41 4N 17 5 E
Molale, Ethiopia 81 E4 10 10N 39 41 E
Moláoi, Greece 38 E4 36 49N 22 56 E
Molara, Italy 30 B2 40 52N 9 43 E
Molat, Croatia 29 D11 44 15N 14 50 E
Molchanovo, Russia 50 D9 57 40N 83 50 E
Mold, U.K. 12 D4 53 9N 3 8W
Moldava nad Bodvou, Slovak Rep. 27 C14 48 38N 21 0 E
Moldavia = Moldova ■, Europe 43 C13 47 0N 28 0 E
Moldavia, Romania 43 D12 46 30N 27 0 E
Molde, Norway 8 E12 62 45N 7 9 E
Moldova ■, Europe 43 C13 47 0N 28 0 E
Moldova Nouă, Romania 42 F6 44 45N 21 41 E
Moldoveanu, Vf., Romania 43 E9 45 36N 24 45 E
Moldovița, Romania 43 C10 47 41N 25 32 E
Mole →, U.K. 13 F7 51 24N 0 21W
Mole Creek, Australia 94 G4 41 34 S 146 24 E
Molepolole, Botswana 88 C4 24 28 S 25 28 E
Molfetta, Italy 31 A9 41 12N 16 36 E
Molina de Aragón, Spain 32 E3 40 46N 1 52W
Molina de Segura, Spain 33 G3 38 3N 1 12W
Moline, U.S.A. 112 E9 41 30N 90 31W
Molinella, Italy 29 D8 44 37N 11 40 E
Molinos, Argentina 126 B2 25 28 S 66 15W
Moliro, Dem. Rep. of the Congo 86 D3 8 12 S 30 30 E
Moliterno, Italy 31 B8 40 14N 15 52 E
Molkom, Sweden 10 E7 59 37N 13 44 E
Mölle, Sweden 11 H6 56 17N 12 31 E
Molledo, Spain 34 B6 43 8N 4 6W
Mollendo, Peru 124 G4 17 0 S 72 0W
Mollerin, L., Australia 93 F2 30 30 S 117 35 E
Mollerussa, Spain 32 D5 41 37N 0 54 E
Mollina, Spain 35 H6 37 8N 4 38W
Mölln, Germany 24 B6 53 39N 10 32 E
Mölltorp, Sweden 11 F8 58 30N 14 26 E
Mölnlycke, Sweden 11 G6 57 40N 12 8 E
Molochansk, Ukraine 47 J8 47 15N 35 35 E
Molochnoye, Ozero, Ukraine 47 J8 46 30N 35 20 E
Molodechno = Maladzyechna, Belarus 46 E4 54 20N 26 50 E
Molokai, U.S.A. 106 H16 21 8N 157 0W
Molong, Australia 95 E4 33 5 S 148 54 E
Molopo →, Africa 88 D3 27 30 S 20 13 E
Mólos, Greece 38 C4 38 47N 22 37 E
Molotov = Perm, Russia 50 D6 58 0N 56 10 E
Molsheim, France 19 D14 48 33N 7 29 E
Molson L., Canada 105 C9 54 22N 96 40W
Molteno, S. Africa 88 E4 31 22 S 26 22 E
Molu, Indonesia 63 F8 6 45 S 131 40 E
Molucca Sea, Indonesia 63 E6 2 0 S 124 0 E
Moluccas = Maluku, Indonesia 63 E7 1 0 S 127 0 E
Moma, Dem. Rep. of the Congo 86 C1 1 35 S 23 52 E
Moma, Mozam. 87 F4 16 47 S 39 4 E
Mombasa, Kenya 86 C4 4 2 S 39 43 E
Mombetsu, Japan 54 B11 44 21N 143 22 E
Mombuey, Spain 34 C4 42 3N 6 20W
Momchilgrad, Bulgaria 41 E9 41 33N 25 23 E
Momi, Dem. Rep. of the Congo 86 C2 1 42 S 27 0 E
Mompós, Colombia 124 B4 9 14N 74 26W
Møn, Denmark 11 K6 54 57N 12 20 E
Mon →, Burma 67 J19 20 25N 94 30 E
Mona, Canal de la, W. Indies 121 C6 18 30N 67 45W
Mona, Isla, Puerto Rico 121 C6 18 5N 67 54W
Mona, Pta., Costa Rica 120 E3 9 37N 82 36W
Monaca, U.S.A. 110 F4 40 41N 80 17W
Monaco ■, Europe 21 E11 43 46N 7 23 E
Monadhliath Mts., U.K. 14 D4 57 10N 4 4W
Monadnock, Mt., U.S.A. 111 D12 42 52N 72 7W
Monaghan, Ireland 15 B5 54 15N 6 57W
Monaghan □, Ireland 15 B5 54 11N 6 56W
Monahans, U.S.A. 113 K3 31 36N 102 54W
Monapo, Mozam. 87 E5 14 56 S 40 19 E
Monar, L., U.K. 14 D3 57 26N 5 8W
Monarch Mt., Canada 104 C3 51 55N 125 57W
Monashee Mts., Canada 104 C5 51 0N 118 43W
Monasterevin, Ireland 15 C4 53 8N 7 4W
Monastir = Bitola, Macedonia 40 E5 41 1N 21 20 E
Moncada, Phil. 61 D4 15 44N 120 34 E
Moncalieri, Italy 28 D4 45 0N 7 41 E
Moncalvo, Italy 28 C5 45 3N 8 16 E
Moncão, Portugal 34 C2 42 4N 8 27W
Moncarapacho, Portugal 35 H3 37 5N 7 46W
Moncayo, Sierra del, Spain 32 D3 41 48N 1 50W
Mönchengladbach, Germany 24 D2 51 11N 6 27 E
Monchique, Portugal 35 H2 37 19N 8 38W
Moncks Corner, U.S.A. 109 J5 33 12N 80 1W
Monclova, Mexico 118 B4 26 50N 101 30W
Moncontour, France 18 D4 48 22N 2 38W
Moncton, Canada 103 C7 46 7N 64 51W
Mondariz, Spain 34 C2 42 14N 8 27W
Mondego →, Portugal 34 E2 40 9N 8 52W
Mondego, C., Portugal 34 E2 40 11N 8 54W
Mondeodo, Indonesia 63 E6 3 34 S 122 9 E
Mondeville, France 18 C6 49 10N 0 18W
Mondolfo, Italy 29 E10 43 45N 13 6 E
Mondoñedo, Spain 34 B3 43 25N 7 23W
Mondovì, Italy 28 D4 44 23N 7 49 E
Mondragon, Phil. 61 E6 12 31N 124 45 E
Mondragone, Italy 30 A6 41 7N 13 53 E
Mondrain I., Australia 93 F3 34 9 S 122 14 E
Monemvasía, Greece 38 E5 36 41N 23 3 E
Monessen, U.S.A. 110 F5 40 9N 79 54W
Monesterio, Spain 35 G4 38 6N 6 15W
Monestier-de-Clermont, France 21 D9 44 55N 5 38 E
Monett, U.S.A. 113 G8 36 55N 93 55W
Moneymore, U.K. 15 B5 54 41N 6 40W
Monfalcone, Italy 29 C10 45 49N 13 32 E
Monflanquin, France 20 D4 44 32N 0 47 E
Monforte, Portugal 35 F3 39 6N 7 25W
Monforte de Lemos, Spain 34 C3 42 31N 7 33W
Mong Hsu, Burma 58 G2 21 54N 98 30 E
Mong Kung, Burma 67 J20 21 35N 97 35 E
Mong Nai, Burma 67 J20 20 32N 97 46 E
Mong Pawk, Burma 67 H21 22 4N 99 16 E
Mong Ping, Burma 58 G2 21 22N 99 2 E
Mong Ton, Burma 67 J21 20 17N 98 45 E
Mong Wa, Burma 67 J22 21 26N 100 27 E
Mong Yai, Burma 67 H21 22 21N 98 3 E
Mongalla, Sudan 81 F3 5 8N 31 42 E
Mongers, L., Australia 93 E2 29 25 S 117 5 E
Monghyr = Munger, India 69 G12 25 23N 86 30 E
Mongibello = Etna, Italy 31 E7 37 50N 14 55 E
Mongo, Chad 79 F9 12 14N 18 43 E
Mongo →, S. Leone 82 D2 9 35N 12 10W
Mongolia ■, Asia 51 E10 47 0N 103 0 E
Mongonu, Nigeria 83 C7 12 40N 13 32 E
Mongu, Zambia 85 H4 15 16 S 23 12 E
Môngua, Angola 88 B2 16 43 S 15 20 E
Monifieth, U.K. 14 E6 56 30N 2 48W
Monistrol-sur-Loire, France 21 C8 45 17N 4 11 E
Monkey Bay, Malawi 87 E4 14 7 S 35 1 E
Monkey Mia, Australia 93 E1 25 48 S 113 43 E
Monkey River, Belize 119 D7 16 22N 88 29W
Mońki, Poland 44 E9 53 23N 22 48 E
Monkoto, Dem. Rep. of the Congo 84 E4 1 38 S 20 35 E
Monkton, Canada 110 C3 43 35N 81 5W
Monmouth, U.K. 13 F5 51 48N 2 42W
Monmouth, Ill., U.S.A. 112 E9 40 55N 90 39W
Monmouth, Oreg., U.S.A. 114 D2 44 51N 123 14W
Monmouthshire □, U.K. 13 F5 51 48N 2 54W
Mono L., U.S.A. 116 H7 38 1N 119 1W
Monolith, U.S.A. 117 K8 35 7N 118 22W
Monólithos, Greece 36 C9 36 7N 27 45 E
Monongahela, U.S.A. 110 F5 40 12N 79 56W
Monópoli, Italy 31 B10 40 57N 17 18 E
Monor, Hungary 42 C4 47 21N 19 27 E
Monóvar, Spain 33 G4 38 28N 0 53W

Monreal del Campo, Spain 32 E3 40 47N 1 20W
Monreale, Italy 30 D6 38 5N 13 17 E
Monroe, Ga., U.S.A. 109 J4 33 47N 83 43W
Monroe, La., U.S.A. 113 J8 32 30N 92 7W
Monroe, Mich., U.S.A. 108 E4 41 55N 83 24W
Monroe, N.C., U.S.A. 109 H5 34 59N 80 33W
Monroe, N.Y., U.S.A. 111 E10 41 20N 74 11W
Monroe, Utah, U.S.A. 115 G7 38 38N 112 7W
Monroe, Wash., U.S.A. 116 C5 47 51N 121 58W
Monroe, Wis., U.S.A. 112 D10 42 36N 89 38W
Monroe City, U.S.A. 112 F9 39 39N 91 44W
Monroeton, U.S.A. 111 E8 41 43N 76 29W
Monroeville, Ala., U.S.A. 109 K2 31 31N 87 20W
Monroeville, Pa., U.S.A. 110 F5 40 26N 79 45W
Monrovia, Liberia 82 D2 6 18N 10 47W
Mons, Belgium 17 D3 50 27N 3 58 E
Møns Klint, Denmark 11 K6 54 57N 12 33 E
Monsaraz, Portugal 35 G3 38 28N 7 22W
Monse, Indonesia 63 E6 4 0 S 123 10 E
Monségur, France 20 D4 44 38N 0 4 E
Monsélice, Italy 29 C8 45 14N 11 45 E
Mönsterås, Sweden 11 G10 57 3N 16 26 E
Mont Cenis, Col du, France 21 C10 45 15N 6 55 E
Mont-de-Marsan, France 20 E3 43 54N 0 31W
Mont-Joli, Canada 103 C6 48 37N 68 10W
Mont-Laurier, Canada 102 C4 46 35N 75 30W
Mont-Louis, Canada 103 C6 49 15N 65 44W
Mont-roig del Camp, Spain 32 D5 41 5N 0 58 E
Mont-St-Michel, Le = Le Mont-St-Michel, France 18 D5 48 40N 1 30W
Mont Tremblant, Parc Recr. du, Canada 102 C5 46 30N 74 30W
Montabaur, Germany 24 E3 50 25N 7 50 E
Montagnac, France 20 E7 43 29N 3 28 E
Montagnana, Italy 29 C8 45 14N 11 28 E
Montagu, S. Africa 88 E3 33 45 S 20 8 E
Montagu I., Antarctica 5 B1 58 25 S 26 20W
Montague, Canada 103 C7 46 10N 62 39W
Montague, I., Mexico 118 A2 31 40N 114 56W
Montague Ra., Australia 93 E2 27 15 S 119 30 E
Montague Sd., Australia 92 B4 14 28 S 125 20 E
Montaigu, France 18 F5 46 59N 1 18W
Montalbán, Spain 32 E4 40 50N 0 45W
Montalbano Iónico, Italy 31 B9 40 17N 16 34 E
Montalbo, Spain 32 F2 39 53N 2 42W
Montalcino, Italy 29 E8 43 3N 11 29 E
Montalegre, Portugal 34 D3 41 49N 7 47W
Montalto, Italy 31 D8 38 10N 15 55 E
Montalto di Castro, Italy 29 F8 42 21N 11 37 E
Montalto Uffugo, Italy 31 C9 39 24N 16 9 E
Montalvo, U.S.A. 117 L7 34 15N 119 12W
Montamarta, Spain 34 D5 41 39N 5 49W
Montana, Bulgaria 40 C7 43 27N 23 16 E
Montaña, Peru 124 E4 6 0 S 73 0W
Montana □, Bulgaria 40 C7 43 30N 23 20 E
Montana □, U.S.A. 114 C9 47 0N 110 0W
Montaña Clara, I., Canary Is. 37 E6 29 17N 13 33W
Montánchez, Spain 35 F4 39 15N 6 8W
Montargil, Portugal 35 F2 39 5N 8 10W
Montargis, France 19 E9 47 59N 2 43 E
Montauban, France 20 D5 44 2N 1 21 E
Montauk, U.S.A. 111 E13 41 3N 71 57W
Montauk Pt., U.S.A. 111 E13 41 4N 71 52W
Montbard, France 19 E11 47 38N 4 20 E
Montbarrey, France 19 E12 47 1N 5 39 E
Montbéliard, France 19 E13 47 31N 6 48 E
Montblanc, Spain 32 D6 41 23N 1 4 E
Montbrison, France 21 C8 45 36N 4 3 E
Montcalm, Pic de, France 20 F5 42 40N 1 25 E
Montceau-les-Mines, France 19 F11 46 40N 4 23 E
Montcenis, France 21 B8 46 47N 4 23 E
Montclair, U.S.A. 111 F10 40 49N 74 13W
Montcornet, France 19 C11 49 40N 4 1 E
Montcuq, France 20 D5 44 21N 1 13 E
Montdidier, France 19 C9 49 38N 2 35 E
Monte Albán, Mexico 119 D5 17 2N 96 45W
Monte Alegre, Brazil 125 D8 2 0 S 54 0W
Monte Azul, Brazil 125 G10 15 9 S 42 53W
Monte Bello Is., Australia 92 D2 20 30 S 115 45 E
Monte-Carlo, Monaco 21 E11 43 46N 7 23 E
Monte Caseros, Argentina 126 C4 30 10 S 57 50W
Monte Comán, Argentina 126 C2 34 40 S 67 53W
Monte Cristi, Dom. Rep. 121 C5 19 52N 71 39W
Monte Lindo →, Paraguay 126 A4 23 56 S 57 12W
Monte Patria, Chile 126 C1 30 42 S 70 58W
Monte Quemado, Argentina 126 B3 25 53 S 62 41W
Monte Redondo, Portugal 34 F2 39 53N 8 50W
Monte Rio, U.S.A. 116 G4 38 28N 123 0W
Monte San Giovanni Campano, Italy 30 A6 41 38N 13 31 E
Monte San Savino, Italy 29 E8 43 20N 11 43 E
Monte Sant' Ángelo, Italy 29 G12 41 42N 15 59 E
Monte Santu, C. di, Italy 30 B2 40 5N 9 44 E
Monte Vista, U.S.A. 115 H10 37 35N 106 9W
Monteagudo, Argentina 127 B5 27 14 S 54 8W
Montealegre del Castillo, Spain 33 G3 38 48N 1 17W
Montebello, Canada 102 C5 45 40N 74 55W
Montebello Iónico, Italy 31 E8 37 59N 15 45 E
Montebelluna, Italy 29 C9 45 47N 12 3 E
Montebourg, France 18 C5 49 30N 1 20W
Montecastrilli, Italy 29 F9 42 39N 12 29 E
Montecatini Terme, Italy 28 E7 43 53N 10 46 E
Montecito, U.S.A. 117 L7 34 26N 119 40W
Montecristo, Italy 28 F7 42 20N 10 19 E
Montefalco, Italy 29 F9 42 54N 12 39 E
Montefiascone, Italy 29 F9 42 32N 12 2 E
Montefrío, Spain 35 H7 37 20N 4 0W
Montegiórgio, Italy 29 E10 43 6N 13 33 E
Montego Bay, Jamaica 120 C4 18 30N 78 0W
Montehermoso, Spain 34 E4 40 5N 6 21W
Montejicar, Spain 35 H7 37 33N 3 30W
Montélimar, France 21 D8 44 33N 4 45 E
Montella, Italy 31 B8 40 51N 15 1 E
Montellano, Spain 35 J5 36 59N 5 29W
Montello, U.S.A. 112 D10 43 48N 89 20W
Montemor-o-Novo, Portugal 35 G2 38 40N 8 12W
Montemor-o-Velho, Portugal 34 E2 40 11N 8 40W
Montemorelos, Mexico 119 B5 25 11N 99 42W
Montendre, France 20 C3 45 16N 0 26W
Montenegro, Brazil 127 B5 29 39 S 51 29W
Montenegro □, Yugoslavia 40 D3 42 40N 19 20 E
Montenero di Bisáccia, Italy 29 G11 41 57N 14 47 E
Montepuez, Mozam. 87 E4 13 8 S 38 59 E
Montepuez →, Mozam. 87 E5 12 32 S 40 27 E
Montepulciano, Italy 29 E8 43 5N 11 47 E
Montereale, Italy 29 F10 42 31N 13 15 E
Montereau-Faut-Yonne, France 19 D9 48 22N 2 57 E
Monterey, U.S.A. 116 J5 36 37N 121 55W
Monterey B., U.S.A. 116 J5 36 45N 122 0W
Montería, Colombia 124 B3 8 46N 75 53W
Monteros, Argentina 126 B2 27 11 S 65 30W
Monterotondo, Italy 29 F9 42 3N 12 37 E
Monterrey, Mexico 118 B4 25 40N 100 30W
Montes Claros, Brazil 125 G10 16 30 S 43 50W
Montesano, U.S.A. 116 D3 46 59N 123 36W
Montesano sulla Marcellana, Italy 31 B8 40 16N 15 42 E
Montesárchio, Italy 31 A7 41 4N 14 38 E
Montescaglioso, Italy 31 B9 40 33N 16 40 E
Montesilvano, Italy 29 F11 42 29N 14 8 E
Montevarchi, Italy 29 E8 43 31N 11 34 E
Montevideo, Uruguay 127 C4 34 50 S 56 11W
Montevideo, U.S.A. 112 C7 44 57N 95 43W
Montezuma, U.S.A. 112 E8 41 35N 92 32W
Montfaucon, France 18 E5 47 6N 1 7W
Montfaucon-d'Argonne, France 19 C12 49 16N 5 8 E
Montfaucon-en-Velay, France 21 C8 45 11N 4 20 E
Montfort, France 18 D5 48 9N 1 58W
Montfort-le-Gesnois, France 18 D7 48 3N 0 25 E
Montgenèvre, France 21 D10 44 56N 6 43 E
Montgomery = Sahiwal, Pakistan 68 D5 30 45N 73 8 E
Montgomery, U.K. 13 E4 52 34N 3 8W
Montgomery, Ala., U.S.A. 109 J2 32 23N 86 19W
Montgomery, Pa., U.S.A. 110 E8 41 10N 76 53W
Montgomery, W. Va., U.S.A. 108 F5 38 11N 81 19W
Montgomery City, U.S.A. 112 F9 38 59N 91 30W
Montguyon, France 20 C3 45 12N 0 12W
Monthermé, France 19 C11 49 52N 4 42 E
Monthey, Switz. 25 J2 46 15N 6 56 E
Monthois, France 19 C11 49 19N 4 43 E
Monti, Italy 30 B2 40 49N 9 19 E
Monticelli d'Ongina, Italy 28 C6 45 5N 9 56 E
Monticello, Ark., U.S.A. 113 J9 33 38N 91 47W
Monticello, Fla., U.S.A. 109 K4 30 33N 83 52W
Monticello, Ind., U.S.A. 108 E2 40 45N 86 46W
Monticello, Iowa, U.S.A. 112 D9 42 15N 91 12W
Monticello, Ky., U.S.A. 109 G3 36 50N 84 51W
Monticello, Minn., U.S.A. 112 C8 45 18N 93 48W
Monticello, Miss., U.S.A. 113 K9 31 33N 90 7W
Monticello, N.Y., U.S.A. 111 E10 41 39N 74 42W
Monticello, Utah, U.S.A. 115 H9 37 52N 109 21W
Montichiari, Italy 28 C7 45 25N 10 23 E
Montier-en-Der, France 19 D11 48 30N 4 45 E
Montignac, France 20 C5 45 4N 1 10 E
Montigny-les-Metz, France 19 C13 49 7N 6 10 E
Montigny-sur-Aube, France 19 E11 47 57N 4 45 E
Montijo, Portugal 35 G2 38 41N 8 54W
Montijo, Spain 35 G4 38 52N 6 39W
Montilla, Spain 35 H6 37 36N 4 40W
Montivilliers, France 18 C7 49 33N 0 12 E
Montluçon, France 19 F9 46 22N 2 36 E
Montmagny, Canada 103 C5 46 58N 70 34W
Montmarault, France 19 F9 46 19N 2 57 E
Montmartre, Canada 105 C8 50 14N 103 27W
Montmédy, France 19 C12 49 30N 5 20 E
Montmélian, France 21 C10 45 30N 6 4 E
Montmirail, France 19 D10 48 51N 3 30 E
Montmoreau-St-Cybard, France 20 C4 45 23N 0 8 E
Montmorillon, France 20 B4 46 26N 0 50 E
Montmort-Lucy, France 19 D10 48 55N 3 49 E
Monto, Australia 94 C5 24 52 S 151 6 E
Montoire-sur-le-Loir, France 18 E7 47 45N 0 52 E
Montório al Vomano, Italy 29 F10 42 35N 13 38 E
Montoro, Spain 35 G6 38 1N 4 27W
Montour Falls, U.S.A. 110 D8 42 21N 76 51W
Montoursville, U.S.A. 110 E8 41 15N 76 55W
Montpelier, Idaho, U.S.A. 114 E8 42 19N 111 18W
Montpelier, Vt., U.S.A. 111 B12 44 16N 72 35W
Montpellier, France 20 E7 43 37N 3 52 E
Montpezat-de-Quercy, France 20 D5 44 15N 1 30 E
Montpon-Ménestérol, France 20 D4 45 0N 0 11 E
Montréal, Canada 102 C5 45 31N 73 34W
Montréal, Aude, France 20 E6 43 13N 2 8 E
Montréal, Gers, France 20 E4 43 56N 0 11 E
Montreal →, Canada 102 C3 47 14N 84 39W
Montreal L., Canada 105 C7 54 20N 105 45W
Montreal Lake, Canada 105 C7 54 3N 105 46W
Montredon-Labessonnié, France 20 E6 43 45N 2 18 E
Montrésor, France 18 E8 47 10N 1 10 E
Montret, France 19 F12 46 40N 5 7 E
Montreuil, Pas-de-Calais, France 19 B8 50 27N 1 45 E
Montreuil, Seine-St-Denis, France 19 D9 48 51N 2 27 E
Montreuil-Bellay, France 18 E6 47 8N 0 9W
Montreux, Switz. 25 J2 46 26N 6 55 E
Montrevel-en-Bresse, France 19 F12 46 21N 5 8 E
Montrichard, France 18 E8 47 20N 1 10 E
Montrose, U.K. 14 E6 56 44N 2 27W
Montrose, Colo., U.S.A. 115 G10 38 29N 107 53W
Montrose, Pa., U.S.A. 111 E9 41 50N 75 53W
Monts, Pte. des, Canada 103 C6 49 20N 67 12W
Montsalvy, France 20 D6 44 41N 2 30 E
Montsant, Serra de, Spain 32 D6 41 17N 1 0 E
Montsauche-les-Settons, France 19 E11 47 13N 4 2 E
Montsec, Serra del, Spain 32 C5 42 5N 0 45 E
Montserrat, Spain 32 D6 41 36N 1 49 E
Montserrat ■, W. Indies 121 C7 16 40N 62 10W
Montuenga, Spain 34 D6 41 3N 4 38W
Montuiri, Spain 37 B9 39 34N 2 59 E
Monywa, Burma 67 H19 22 7N 95 11 E
Monza, Italy 28 C6 45 35N 9 16 E
Monze, Zambia 87 F2 16 17 S 27 29 E
Monze, C., Pakistan 68 G2 24 47N 66 37 E
Monzón, Spain 32 D5 41 52N 0 10 E
Mooers, U.S.A. 111 B11 44 58N 73 35W
Mooi →, S. Africa 89 D5 28 45 S 30 34 E
Mooi River, S. Africa 89 D4 29 13 S 29 50 E
Moonah →, Australia 94 C2 22 3 S 138 33 E
Moonda, L., Australia 94 D3 25 52 S 140 25 E
Moonie, Australia 95 D5 27 46 S 150 20 E
Moonie →, Australia 95 D4 29 19 S 148 43 E
Moonta, Australia 95 E2 34 6 S 137 32 E
Moora, Australia 93 F2 30 37 S 115 58 E
Moorcroft, U.S.A. 112 C2 44 16N 104 57W
Moore →, Australia 93 F2 31 22 S 115 30 E
Moore, L., Australia 93 E2 29 50 S 117 35 E
Moore Park, Australia 94 C5 24 43 S 152 17 E
Moore Reefs, Australia 94 B4 16 0 S 149 5 E
Moorefield, U.S.A. 108 F6 39 5N 78 59W
Moores Res., U.S.A. 111 B13 44 45N 71 50W
Moorfoot Hills, U.K. 14 F5 55 44N 3 8W
Moorhead, U.S.A. 112 B6 46 53N 96 45W
Moormerland, Germany 24 B3 53 20N 7 20 E
Moorpark, U.S.A. 117 L8 34 17N 118 53W
Moorreesburg, S. Africa 88 E2 33 6 S 18 38 E
Moosburg, Germany 25 G7 48 27N 11 56 E
Moose →, Canada 102 B3 51 20N 80 25W
Moose →, U.S.A. 111 C9 43 38N 75 24W
Moose Creek, Canada 111 A10 45 15N 74 58W
Moose Factory, Canada 102 B3 51 16N 80 32W
Moose Jaw, Canada 105 C7 50 24N 105 30W
Moose Jaw →, Canada 105 C7 50 34N 105 18W
Moose Lake, Canada 105 C8 53 43N 100 20W
Moose Lake, U.S.A. 112 B8 46 27N 92 46W
Moose Mountain Prov. Park, Canada 105 D8 49 48N 102 25W
Moosehead L., U.S.A. 109 C11 45 38N 69 40W
Mooselookmeguntic L., U.S.A. 109 C10 44 55N 70 49W
Moosilauke, Mt., U.S.A. 111 B13 44 3N 71 40W
Moosomin, Canada 105 C8 50 9N 101 40W
Moosonee, Canada 102 B3 51 17N 80 39W
Moosup, U.S.A. 111 E13 41 43N 71 53W
Mopane, S. Africa 89 C4 22 37 S 29 52 E
Mopeia Velha, Mozam. 87 F4 17 30 S 35 40 E
Mopipi, Botswana 88 C3 21 6 S 24 55 E
Mopoi, C.A.R. 86 A2 5 6N 26 54 E
Mopti, Mali 82 C4 14 30N 4 0W
Moqatta, Sudan 81 E4 14 38N 35 50 E
Moqor, Afghan. 68 C2 32 50N 67 42 E
Moquegua, Peru 124 G4 17 15 S 70 46W
Mór, Hungary 42 C3 47 25N 18 12 E
Mora, Cameroon 83 C7 11 2N 14 7 E
Móra, Portugal 35 G2 38 55N 8 10W
Mora, Spain 35 F7 39 41N 3 46W
Mora, Sweden 10 C8 61 2N 14 38 E
Mora, Minn., U.S.A. 112 C8 45 53N 93 18W
Mora, N. Mex., U.S.A. 115 J11 35 58N 105 20W
Mora →, U.S.A. 113 H2 35 35N 104 25W
Mora de Ebro = Móra d'Ebre, Spain 32 D5 41 6N 0 38 E
Mora de Rubielos, Spain 32 E4 40 15N 0 45W
Móra d'Ebre, Spain 32 D5 41 6N 0 38 E
Móra la Nova, Spain 32 D5 41 7N 0 39 E
Morača →, Montenegro, Yug. 40 D3 42 20N 19 9 E
Moradabad, India 69 E8 28 50N 78 50 E
Morafenobe, Madag. 89 B7 17 50 S 44 53 E
Morąg, Poland 44 E6 53 55N 19 56 E
Moral de Calatrava, Spain 35 G7 38 51N 3 33W
Moraleja, Spain 34 E4 40 6N 6 43W
Moramanga, Madag. 89 B8 18 56 S 48 12 E
Moran, Kans., U.S.A. 113 G7 37 55N 95 10W
Moran, Wyo., U.S.A. 114 E8 43 53N 110 37W
Moranbah, Australia 94 C4 22 1 S 148 6 E
Morano Cálabro, Italy 31 C9 39 50N 16 8 E
Morant Cays, Jamaica 120 C4 17 22N 76 0W
Morant Pt., Jamaica 120 C4 17 55N 76 12W
Morar, India 68 F8 26 14N 78 14 E
Morar, L., U.K. 14 E3 56 57N 5 40W
Moratalla, Spain 33 G3 38 14N 1 49W
Moratuwa, Sri Lanka 66 R11 6 45N 79 55 E
Morava →, Slovak Rep. 27 C9 48 10N 16 59 E
Moravia, U.S.A. 111 D8 42 43N 76 25W
Moravian Hts. = Českomoravská Vrchovina, Czech Rep. 26 B8 49 30N 15 40 E
Moravica →, Serbia, Yug. 40 C4 43 52N 20 8 E
Moravița, Romania 42 E6 45 17N 21 14 E
Moravská Třebová, Czech Rep. 27 B9 49 45N 16 40 E
Moravské Budějovice, Czech Rep. 26 B8 49 4N 15 49 E
Morawa, Australia 93 E2 29 13 S 116 0 E
Morawhanna, Guyana 124 B7 8 30N 59 40W
Moray □, U.K. 14 D5 57 31N 3 18W
Moray Firth, U.K. 14 D5 57 40N 3 52W
Morbach, Germany 25 F3 49 48N 7 6 E
Morbegno, Italy 28 B6 46 8N 9 34 E
Morbi, India 68 H4 22 50N 70 42 E
Morbihan □, France 18 E4 47 55N 2 50W
Mörbylånga, Sweden 11 H10 56 32N 16 22 E
Morcenx, France 20 D3 44 3N 0 55W
Morcone, Italy 31 A7 41 20N 14 40 E
Mordelles, France 18 D5 48 5N 1 52W
Morden, Canada 105 D9 49 15N 98 10W
Mordoğan, Turkey 39 C8 38 30N 26 37 E
Mordovian Republic = Mordvinia □, Russia 48 C7 54 20N 44 30 E
Mordovo, Russia 48 D5 52 6N 40 50 E
Mordvinia □, Russia 48 C7 54 20N 44 30 E
Mordy, Poland 45 F9 52 13N 22 31 E
Morea, Greece 6 H10 37 45N 22 10 E
Moreau →, U.S.A. 112 C4 45 18N 100 43W
Morecambe, U.K. 12 C5 54 5N 2 52W
Morecambe B., U.K. 12 C5 54 7N 3 0W
Moree, Australia 95 D4 29 28 S 149 54 E
Morehead, U.S.A. 108 F4 38 11N 83 26W
Morehead City, U.S.A. 109 H7 34 43N 76 43W
Morel →, India 68 F7 26 13N 76 36 E
Morelia, Mexico 118 D4 19 42N 101 7W
Morella, Australia 94 C3 23 0 S 143 52 E
Morella, Spain 32 E4 40 35N 0 5W
Morelos, Mexico 118 B3 26 42N 107 40W
Morelos □, Mexico 119 D5 18 40N 99 10W
Morena, India 68 F8 26 30N 78 4 E
Morena, Sierra, Spain 35 G7 38 20N 4 0W
Moreni, Romania 43 F10 44 59N 25 36 E
Moreno Valley, U.S.A. 117 M10 33 56N 117 15W
Moresby I., Canada 104 C2 52 30N 131 40W
Morestel, France 21 C9 45 40N 5 28 E
Moreton I., Australia 95 D5 27 10 S 153 25 E
Moreuil, France 19 C9 49 46N 2 30 E
Morey, Spain 37 B10 39 44N 3 20 E
Morez, France 19 F13 46 31N 6 2 E
Morgan, U.S.A. 114 F8 41 2N 111 41W
Morgan City, U.S.A. 113 L9 29 42N 91 12W
Morgan Hill, U.S.A. 116 H5 37 8N 121 39W
Morganfield, U.S.A. 108 G2 37 41N 87 55W
Morganton, U.S.A. 109 H5 35 45N 81 41W
Morgantown, U.S.A. 108 F6 39 38N 79 57W
Morgenzon, S. Africa 89 D4 26 45 S 29 36 E
Morges, Switz. 25 J2 46 31N 6 29 E
Morghak, Iran 71 D8 29 7N 57 54 E
Morgongåva, Sweden 10 E10 59 57N 16 58 E
Morhange, France 19 D13 48 55N 6 38 E
Morhar →, India 69 G11 25 29N 85 11 E
Mori, Italy 28 C7 45 51N 10 59 E
Moriarty, U.S.A. 115 J10 34 59N 106 3W
Moribaya, Guinea 82 D3 9 53N 9 32W
Morice L., Canada 104 C3 53 50N 127 40W
Moriki, Nigeria 83 C6 12 52N 6 30 E
Morinville, Canada 104 C6 53 49N 113 41W
Morioka, Japan 54 E10 39 45N 141 8 E
Moris, Mexico 118 B3 28 8N 108 32W
Morlaàs, France 20 E3 43 21N 0 18W
Morlaix, France 18 D3 48 36N 3 52W
Mörlunda, Sweden 11 G9 57 19N 15 52 E
Mormanno, Italy 31 C8 39 53N 15 59 E
Mormant, France 19 D9 48 37N 2 52 E
Mornington, Australia 95 F4 38 15 S 145 5 E
Mornington, I., Chile 128 F1 49 50 S 75 30W
Mornington I., Australia 94 B2 16 30 S 139 30 E
Mórnos →, Greece 38 C3 38 25N 21 50 E
Moro, Pakistan 68 F2 26 40N 68 0 E
Moro, Sudan 81 E3 10 50N 30 9 E
Moro →, Pakistan 68 E2 29 42N 67 22 E
Moro G., Phil. 61 H5 6 30N 123 0 E
Morocco ■, N. Afr. 78 B4 32 0N 5 50W
Morogoro, Tanzania 86 D4 6 50 S 37 40 E
Morogoro □, Tanzania 86 D4 8 0 S 37 0 E
Moroleón, Mexico 118 C4 20 8N 101 32W
Morombe, Madag. 89 C7 21 45 S 43 22 E
Moron, Argentina 126 C4 34 39 S 58 37W
Morón, Cuba 120 B4 22 8N 78 39W
Morón de Almazán, Spain 32 D2 41 29N 2 27W
Morón de la Frontera, Spain 35 H5 37 6N 5 28W
Morona →, Peru 124 D3 4 40 S 77 10W
Morondava, Madag. 89 C7 20 17 S 44 17 E
Morondo, Ivory C. 82 D3 8 57N 6 47W
Morongo Valley, U.S.A. 117 L10 34 3N 116 37W
Moroni, Comoros Is. 77 H8 11 40 S 43 16 E
Moroni, U.S.A. 114 G8 39 32N 111 35W
Moronou, Ivory C. 82 D4 6 16N 4 59W
Morotai, Indonesia 63 D7 2 10N 128 30 E
Moroto, Uganda 86 B3 2 28N 34 42 E
Moroto Summit, Kenya 86 B3 2 30N 34 43 E
Morozov, Bulgaria 41 D9 42 30N 25 10 E
Morozovsk, Russia 49 F5 48 25N 41 50 E
Morpeth, U.K. 12 B6 55 10N 1 41W
Morphou, Cyprus 36 D11 35 12N 32 59 E
Morphou Bay, Cyprus 36 D11 35 15N 32 50 E
Morrilton, U.S.A. 113 H8 35 9N 92 44W
Morrinhos, Brazil 125 G9 17 45 S 49 10W
Morrinsville, N.Z. 91 G5 37 40 S 175 32 E
Morris, Canada 105 D9 49 25N 97 22W
Morris, Ill., U.S.A. 112 E10 41 22N 88 26W
Morris, Minn., U.S.A. 112 C7 45 35N 95 55W
Morris, N.Y., U.S.A. 111 D9 42 33N 75 15W
Morris, Pa., U.S.A. 110 E7 41 35N 77 17W
Morris, Mt., Australia 93 E5 26 9 S 131 4 E
Morrisburg, Canada 111 B9 44 55N 75 7W
Morristown, Ariz., U.S.A. 115 K7 33 51N 112 37W
Morristown, N.J., U.S.A. 111 F10 40 48N 74 29W
Morristown, N.Y., U.S.A. 111 B9 44 35N 75 39W
Morristown, Tenn., U.S.A. 109 G4 36 13N 83 18W
Morrisville, N.Y., U.S.A. 111 D9 42 53N 75 35W
Morrisville, Pa., U.S.A. 111 F10 40 13N 74 47W
Morrisville, Vt., U.S.A. 111 B12 44 34N 72 36W
Morro, Pta., Chile 126 B1 27 6 S 71 0W
Morro Bay, U.S.A. 116 K6 35 22N 120 51W
Morro del Jable, Canary Is. 37 F5 28 3N 14 23W
Morro Jable, Pta. de, Canary Is. 37 F5 28 2N 14 20W
Morrosquillo, G. de, Colombia 120 E4 9 35N 75 40W
Mörrum, Sweden 11 H8 56 12N 14 45 E
Morrumbene, Mozam. 89 C6 23 31 S 35 16 E
Mörrumsån →, Sweden 11 H8 56 10N 14 45 E
Mors, Denmark 11 H2 56 50N 8 45 E
Morshansk, Russia 48 D5 53 28N 41 50 E
Mörsil, Sweden 10 A7 63 19N 13 40 E
Mortagne →, France 19 D13 48 33N 6 27 E
Mortagne-au-Perche, France 18 D7 48 31N 0 33 E
Mortagne-sur-Gironde, France 20 C3 45 28N 0 47W
Mortagne-sur-Sèvre, France 18 F6 47 0N 0 59W
Mortain, France 18 D6 48 40N 0 57W
Mortara, Italy 28 C5 45 15N 8 44 E
Morteau, France 19 E13 47 3N 6 35 E
Morteros, Argentina 126 C3 30 50 S 62 0W
Mortlach, Canada 105 C7 50 27N 106 4W
Mortlake, Australia 95 F3 38 5 S 142 50 E
Morton, Tex., U.S.A. 113 J3 33 44N 102 46W
Morton, Wash., U.S.A. 116 D4 46 34N 122 17W
Morundah, Australia 95 E4 34 57 S 146 19 E
Moruya, Australia 95 F5 35 58 S 150 3 E
Morvan, France 19 E11 47 5N 4 3 E
Morven, Australia 95 D4 26 22 S 147 5 E
Morvern, U.K. 14 E3 56 38N 5 44W
Morwell, Australia 95 F4 38 10 S 146 22 E
Moryń, Poland 45 F1 52 51N 14 22 E
Morzine, France 19 F13 46 11N 6 42 E
Mosalsk, Russia 46 E8 54 30N 34 55 E
Mosbach, Germany 25 F5 49 21N 9 9 E
Moščenice, Croatia 29 C11 45 17N 14 16 E
Mosciano Sant' Ángelo, Italy 29 F10 42 42N 13 52 E
Moscos Is. = Maungmagan Is., Burma 64 E1 14 0N 97 30 E
Moscow = Moskva, Russia 46 E9 55 45N 37 35 E
Moscow, Idaho, U.S.A. 114 C5 46 44N 117 0W
Moscow, Pa., U.S.A. 111 E9 41 20N 75 31W
Mosel →, Europe 19 B14 50 22N 7 36 E
Moselle = Mosel →, Europe 19 B14 50 22N 7 36 E
Moselle □, France 19 D13 48 59N 6 33 E
Moses Lake, U.S.A. 114 C4 47 8N 119 17W
Mosgiel, N.Z. 91 L3 45 53 S 170 21 E
Moshaweng →, S. Africa 88 D3 26 35 S 22 50 E
Moshi, Tanzania 86 C4 3 22 S 37 18 E
Moshupa, Botswana 88 C4 24 46 S 25 29 E
Mosina, Poland 45 F3 52 15N 16 50 E
Mosjøen, Norway 8 D15 65 51N 13 12 E
Moskenesøya, Norway 8 C15 67 58N 13 0 E
Moskenstraumen, Norway 8 C15 67 47N 12 45 E
Moskva, Russia 46 E9 55 45N 37 35 E
Moskva →, Russia 46 E10 55 5N 38 51 E
Moslavačka Gora, Croatia 29 C13 45 40N 16 37 E
Mosomane, Botswana 88 C4 24 2 S 26 19 E
Moson-magyaróvár, Hungary 42 C2 47 52N 17 18 E
Mošorin, Serbia, Yug. 42 E5 45 19N 20 4 E
Mospino, Ukraine 47 J9 47 52N 38 0 E
Mosquera, Colombia 124 C3 2 35N 78 24W
Mosquero, U.S.A. 113 H3 35 47N 103 58W
Mosqueruela, Spain 32 E4 40 21N 0 27W
Mosquitia, Honduras 120 C3 15 20N 84 10W
Mosquito Coast = Mosquitia, Honduras 120 C3 15 20N 84 10W
Mosquito Creek L., U.S.A. 110 E4 41 18N 80 46W
Mosquito L., Canada 105 A8 62 35N 103 20W
Mosquitos, G. de los, Panama 120 E3 9 15N 81 10W
Moss, Norway 9 G14 59 27N 10 40 E
Moss Vale, Australia 95 E5 34 32 S 150 25 E
Mossbank, Canada 105 D7 49 56N 105 56W
Mossburn, N.Z. 91 L2 45 41 S 168 15 E
Mosselbaai, S. Africa 88 E3 34 11 S 22 8 E
Mossendjo, Congo 84 E2 2 55 S 12 42 E
Mossgiel, Australia 95 E3 33 15 S 144 5 E
Mossingen, Germany 25 G5 48 24N 9 4 E
Mossman, Australia 94 B4 16 21 S 145 15 E
Mossoró, Brazil 125 E11 5 10 S 37 15W
Mossuril, Mozam. 87 E5 14 58 S 40 42 E
Most, Czech Rep. 26 A6 50 31N 13 38 E
Mosta, Malta 36 D1 35 54N 14 24 E
Mostaganem, Algeria 78 A6 35 54N 0 5 E
Mostar, Bos.-H. 42 G2 43 22N 17 50 E
Mostardas, Brazil 127 C5 31 2 S 50 51W
Mostiska = Mostyska, Ukraine 47 H2 49 48N 23 4 E
Móstoles, Spain 34 E7 40 19N 3 53W
Mosty = Masty, Belarus 46 F3 53 27N 24 38 E
Mostyska, Ukraine 47 H2 49 48N 23 4 E
Mosul = Al Mawşil, Iraq 70 B4 36 15N 43 5 E
Mosŭlpo, S. Korea 57 H14 33 20N 126 17 E
Mota, Ethiopia 81 E4 11 5N 37 52 E
Mota del Cuervo, Spain 33 F2 39 30N 2 52W
Mota del Marqués, Spain 34 D5 41 38N 5 11W
Motagua →, Guatemala 120 C2 15 44N 88 14W
Motala, Sweden 11 F9 58 32N 15 1 E
Motaze, Mozam. 89 C5 24 48 S 32 52 E
Moţca, Romania 43 C11 47 15N 26 37 E
Moth, India 69 G8 25 43N 78 57 E
Motherwell, U.K. 14 F5 55 47N 3 58W
Motihari, India 69 F11 26 30N 84 55 E
Motilla del Palancar, Spain 33 F3 39 34N 1 55W
Motnik, Slovenia 29 B11 46 14N 14 54 E
Motovun, Croatia 29 C10 45 20N 13 50 E
Motozintla de Mendoza, Mexico 119 D6 15 21N 92 14W
Motril, Spain 35 J7 36 31N 3 37W
Motru, Romania 42 F7 44 48N 22 59 E
Motru →, Romania 43 F8 44 32N 23 31 E
Mott, U.S.A. 112 B3 46 23N 102 20W
Móttola, Italy 31 B10 40 38N 17 2 E
Motueka, N.Z. 91 J4 41 7 S 173 1 E
Motueka →, N.Z. 91 J4 41 5 S 173 1 E
Motul, Mexico 119 C7 21 0N 89 20W
Mouchalagane →, Canada 103 B6 50 56N 68 41W
Moúdhros, Greece 39 B7 39 50N 25 18 E
Mouding, China 58 E3 25 20N 101 28 E
Moudjeria, Mauritania 82 B2 17 50N 12 28W
Moudon, Switz. 25 J2 46 40N 6 49 E
Mouila, Gabon 84 E2 1 50 S 11 0 E
Moulamein, Australia 95 F3 35 3 S 144 1 E
Moulianá, Greece 36 D7 35 10N 25 59 E
Moulins, France 19 F10 46 35N 3 19 E
Moulmein, Burma 67 L20 16 30N 97 40 E
Moulouya, O. →, Morocco 78 B5 35 5N 2 25W
Moultrie, U.S.A. 109 K4 31 11N 83 47W
Moultrie, L., U.S.A. 109 J5 33 20N 80 5W
Mound City, Mo., U.S.A. 112 E7 40 7N 95 14W
Mound City, S. Dak., U.S.A. 112 C4 45 44N 100 4W
Moúnda, Ákra, Greece 38 C2 38 5N 20 45 E
Moundou, Chad 79 G9 8 40N 16 10 E
Moundsville, U.S.A. 110 G4 39 55N 80 44W
Moung, Cambodia 64 F4 12 46N 103 27 E
Mount Airy, U.S.A. 109 G5 36 31N 80 37W
Mount Albert, Canada 110 B5 44 8N 79 19W

Mount Barker, S. Austral., Australia 95 F2 35 5 S 138 52 E
Mount Barker, W. Austral., Australia 93 F2 34 38 S 117 40 E
Mount Beauty, Australia 95 F4 36 47 S 147 10 E
Mount Brydges, Canada 110 D3 42 54N 81 29W
Mount Burr, Australia 95 F3 37 34 S 140 26 E
Mount Carmel, Ill., U.S.A. 108 F2 38 25N 87 46W
Mount Carmel, Pa., U.S.A. 111 F8 40 47N 76 24W
Mount Charleston, U.S.A. 117 J11 36 16N 115 37W
Mount Clemens, U.S.A. 110 D2 42 35N 82 53W
Mount Coolon, Australia 94 C4 21 25 S 147 25 E
Mount Darwin, Zimbabwe 87 F3 16 47 S 31 38 E
Mount Desert I., U.S.A. 109 C11 44 21N 68 20W
Mount Dora, U.S.A. 109 L5 28 48N 81 38W
Mount Edziza Prov. Park, Canada 104 B2 57 30N 130 45W
Mount Fletcher, S. Africa 89 E4 30 40 S 28 30 E
Mount Forest, Canada 102 D3 43 59N 80 43W
Mount Gambier, Australia 95 F3 37 50 S 140 46 E
Mount Garnet, Australia 94 B4 17 37 S 145 6 E
Mount Holly, U.S.A. 111 G10 39 59N 74 47W
Mount Holly Springs, U.S.A. 110 F7 40 7N 77 12W
Mount Hope, N.S.W., Australia 95 E4 32 51 S 145 51 E
Mount Hope, S. Austral., Australia 95 E2 34 7 S 135 23 E
Mount Isa, Australia 94 C2 20 42 S 139 26 E
Mount Jewett, U.S.A. 110 E6 41 44N 78 39W
Mount Kisco, U.S.A. 111 E11 41 12N 73 44W
Mount Laguna, U.S.A. 117 N10 32 52N 116 25W
Mount Larcom, Australia 94 C5 23 48 S 150 59 E
Mount Lofty Ra., Australia 95 E2 34 35 S 139 5 E
Mount Magnet, Australia 93 E2 28 2 S 117 47 E
Mount Maunganui, N.Z. 91 G6 37 40 S 176 14 E
Mount Molloy, Australia 94 B4 16 42 S 145 20 E
Mount Morgan, Australia 94 C5 23 40 S 150 25 E
Mount Morris, U.S.A. 110 D7 42 44N 77 52W
Mount Pearl, Canada 103 C9 47 31N 52 47W
Mount Penn, U.S.A. 111 F9 40 20N 75 54W
Mount Perry, Australia 95 D5 25 13 S 151 42 E
Mount Pleasant, Iowa, U.S.A. 112 E9 40 58N 91 33W
Mount Pleasant, Mich., U.S.A. 108 D3 43 36N 84 46W
Mount Pleasant, Pa., U.S.A. 110 F5 40 9N 79 33W
Mount Pleasant, S.C., U.S.A. 109 J6 32 47N 79 52W
Mount Pleasant, Tenn., U.S.A. 109 H2 35 32N 87 12W
Mount Pleasant, Tex., U.S.A. 113 J7 33 9N 94 58W
Mount Pleasant, Utah, U.S.A. 114 G8 39 33N 111 27W
Mount Pocono, U.S.A. 111 E9 41 7N 75 22W
Mount Rainier Nat. Park, U.S.A. 116 D5 46 55N 121 50W
Mount Revelstoke Nat. Park, Canada 104 C5 51 5N 118 30W
Mount Robson Prov. Park, Canada 104 C5 53 0N 119 0W
Mount Selinda, Zimbabwe 89 C5 20 24 S 32 43 E
Mount Shasta, U.S.A. 114 F2 41 19N 122 19W
Mount Signal, U.S.A. 117 N11 32 39N 115 37W
Mount Sterling, Ill., U.S.A. 112 F9 39 59N 90 45W
Mount Sterling, Ky., U.S.A. 108 F4 38 4N 83 56W
Mount Surprise, Australia 94 B3 18 10 S 144 17 E
Mount Union, U.S.A. 110 F7 40 23N 77 53W
Mount Upton, U.S.A. 111 D9 42 26N 75 23W
Mount Vernon, Ill., U.S.A. 108 F1 38 19N 88 55W
Mount Vernon, Ind., U.S.A. 112 F10 38 17N 88 57W
Mount Vernon, N.Y., U.S.A. 111 F11 40 55N 73 50W
Mount Vernon, Ohio, U.S.A. 110 F2 40 23N 82 29W
Mount Vernon, Wash., U.S.A. 116 B4 48 25N 122 20W
Mountain Ash, U.K. 13 F4 51 40N 3 23W
Mountain Center, U.S.A. 117 M10 33 42N 116 44W
Mountain City, Nev., U.S.A. 114 F6 41 50N 115 58W
Mountain City, Tenn., U.S.A. 109 G5 36 29N 81 48W
Mountain Dale, U.S.A. 111 E10 41 41N 74 32W
Mountain Grove, U.S.A. 113 G8 37 8N 92 16W
Mountain Home, Ark., U.S.A. 113 G8 36 20N 92 23W
Mountain Home, Idaho, U.S.A. 114 E6 43 8N 115 41W
Mountain Iron, U.S.A. 112 B8 47 32N 92 37W
Mountain Pass, U.S.A. 117 K11 35 29N 115 35W
Mountain View, Ark., U.S.A. 113 H8 35 52N 92 7W
Mountain View, Calif., U.S.A. 116 H4 37 23N 122 5W
Mountain View, Hawaii, U.S.A. 106 J17 19 33N 155 7W
Mountainair, U.S.A. 115 J10 34 31N 106 15W
Mountlake Terrace, U.S.A. 116 C4 47 47N 122 19W
Mountmellick, Ireland 15 C4 53 7N 7 20W
Mountrath, Ireland 15 D4 53 0N 7 28W
Moura, Australia 94 C4 24 35 S 149 58 E
Moura, Brazil 124 D6 1 32 S 61 38W
Moura, Portugal 35 G3 38 7N 7 30W
Mourão, Portugal 35 G3 38 22N 7 22W
Mourdi, Dépression du, Chad 79 E10 18 10N 23 0 E
Mourdiah, Mali 82 C3 14 35N 7 25W
Mourenx, France 20 E3 43 22N 0 38W
Mouri, Ghana 83 D4 5 6N 1 14W
Mourilyan, Australia 94 B4 17 35 S 146 3 E
Mourmelon-le-Grand, France 19 C11 49 8N 4 22 E
Mourne →, U.K. 15 B4 54 52N 7 26W
Mourne Mts., U.K. 15 B5 54 10N 6 0W
Mourniaí, Greece 36 D6 35 29N 24 1 E
Mournies = Mourniaí, Greece 36 D6 35 29N 24 1 E
Mouscron, Belgium 17 D3 50 45N 3 12 E
Moussoro, Chad 79 F9 13 41N 16 35 E
Mouthe, France 19 F13 46 44N 6 12 E
Moutier, Switz. 25 H3 47 16N 7 21 E
Moûtiers, France 21 C10 45 29N 6 32 E
Moutong, Indonesia 63 D6 0 28N 121 13 E
Mouy, France 19 C9 49 18N 2 20 E
Mouzáki, Greece 38 B3 39 25N 21 37 E
Mouzon, France 19 C12 49 36N 5 3 E
Movas, Mexico 118 B3 28 10N 109 25W
Moville, Ireland 15 A4 55 11N 7 3W
Mowandjum, Australia 92 C3 17 22 S 123 40 E
Moy →, Ireland 15 B2 54 8N 9 8W
Moyale, Kenya 81 G4 3 30N 39 0 E
Moyamba, S. Leone 82 D2 8 4N 12 30W
Moyen Atlas, Morocco 78 B4 33 0N 5 0W
Moyne, L. le, Canada 103 A6 56 45N 68 47W
Moyo, Indonesia 62 F5 8 10 S 117 40 E
Moyobamba, Peru 124 E3 6 0 S 77 0W
Moyyero →, Russia 51 C11 68 44N 103 42 E
Moyynty, Kazakstan 50 E8 47 10N 73 18 E
Mozambique = Moçambique, Mozam. 87 F5 15 3 S 40 42 E
Mozambique ■, Africa 87 F4 19 0 S 35 0 E
Mozambique Chan., Africa 89 B7 17 30 S 42 30 E
Mozdok, Russia 49 J7 43 45N 44 48 E
Mozdūrān, Iran 71 B9 36 9N 60 35 E
Mozhaysk, Russia 46 E9 55 30N 36 2 E
Mozhga, Russia 48 B11 56 26N 52 15 E
Mozhnābād, Iran 71 C9 34 7N 60 6 E
Mozirje, Slovenia 29 B11 46 22N 14 58 E
Mozyr = Mazyr, Belarus 47 F5 51 59N 29 15 E
Mpanda, Tanzania 86 D3 6 23 S 31 1 E
Mpésoba, Mali 82 C3 12 31N 5 39W
Mphoengs, Zimbabwe 89 C4 21 10 S 27 51 E
Mpika, Zambia 87 E3 11 51 S 31 25 E
Mpulungu, Zambia 87 D3 8 51 S 31 5 E
Mpumalanga, S. Africa 89 D5 29 50 S 30 33 E
Mpumalanga □, S. Africa 89 B5 26 0 S 30 0 E
Mpwapwa, Tanzania 86 D4 6 23 S 36 30 E
Mqanduli, S. Africa 89 E4 31 49 S 28 45 E
Mqinvartsveri = Kazbek, Russia 49 J7 42 42N 44 30 E
Mrągowo, Poland 44 E8 53 52N 21 18 E
Mramor, Serbia, Yug. 40 C5 43 20N 21 45 E
Mrkonjić Grad, Bos.-H. 42 F2 44 26N 17 4 E
Mrkopalj, Croatia 29 C11 45 21N 14 52 E
Mrocza, Poland 45 E4 53 16N 17 35 E
Msambansovu, Zimbabwe 87 F3 15 50 S 30 3 E
M'sila →, Algeria 78 A6 35 30N 4 29 E
Msoro, Zambia 87 E3 13 35 S 31 50 E
Msta →, Russia 46 C6 58 25N 31 20 E
Mstislavl = Mstsislaw, Belarus 46 E6 54 0N 31 50 E
Mstsislaw, Belarus 46 E6 54 0N 31 50 E
Mszana Dolna, Poland 45 J7 49 41N 20 5 E
Mszczonów, Poland 45 G7 51 58N 20 33 E
Mtama, Tanzania 87 E4 10 17 S 39 21 E
Mtamvuna →, S. Africa 89 E5 31 6 S 30 12 E
Mtilikwe →, Zimbabwe 87 G3 21 9 S 31 30 E
Mtsensk, Russia 46 F9 53 17N 36 36 E
Mtskheta, Georgia 49 K7 41 52N 44 45 E
Mtubatuba, S. Africa 89 D5 28 30 S 32 8 E
Mtwalume, S. Africa 89 E5 30 30 S 30 38 E
Mtwara-Mikindani, Tanzania 87 E5 10 20 S 40 20 E
Mu Gia, Deo, Vietnam 64 D5 17 40N 105 47 E
Mu Us Shamo, China 56 E5 39 0N 109 0 E
Muang Chiang Rai = Chiang Rai, Thailand 58 H2 19 52N 99 50 E
Muang Khong, Laos 64 E5 14 7N 105 51 E
Muang Lamphun, Thailand 64 C2 18 40N 99 2 E
Muang Pak Beng, Laos 58 H3 19 54N 101 8 E
Muar, Malaysia 65 L4 2 3N 102 34 E
Muarabungo, Indonesia 62 E2 1 28 S 102 52 E
Muaraenim, Indonesia 62 E2 3 40 S 103 50 E
Muarajuloi, Indonesia 62 E4 0 12 S 114 3 E
Muarakaman, Indonesia 62 E5 0 2 S 116 45 E
Muaratebo, Indonesia 62 E2 1 30 S 102 26 E
Muaratembesi, Indonesia 62 E2 1 42 S 103 8 E
Muaratewe, Indonesia 62 E4 0 58 S 114 52 E
Mubarakpur, India 69 F10 26 6N 83 18 E
Mubarraz = Al Mubarraz, Si. Arabia 71 E6 25 30N 49 40 E
Mubende, Uganda 86 B3 0 33N 31 22 E
Mubi, Nigeria 83 C7 10 18N 13 16 E
Mubur, Pulau, Indonesia 65 L6 3 20N 106 12 E
Mucajaí →, Brazil 124 C6 2 25N 60 52W
Muchachos, Roque de los, Canary Is. 37 F2 28 44N 17 52W
Mücheln, Germany 24 D7 51 17N 11 47 E
Muchinga Mts., Zambia 87 E3 11 30 S 31 30 E
Muchkapskiy, Russia 48 E6 51 52N 42 28 E
Muchuan, China 58 C5 28 57N 103 55 E
Muck, U.K. 14 E2 56 50N 6 15W
Muckadilla, Australia 95 D4 26 35 S 148 23 E
Mucur, Turkey 72 C6 39 3N 34 22 E
Mucuri, Brazil 125 G11 18 0 S 39 36W
Mucusso, Angola 88 B3 18 1 S 21 25 E
Muda, Canary Is. 37 F6 28 34N 13 57W
Mudanjiang, China 57 B15 44 38N 129 30 E
Mudanya, Turkey 41 F12 40 25N 28 50 E
Muddy Cr. →, U.S.A. 115 H8 38 24N 110 42W
Mudgee, Australia 95 E4 32 32 S 149 31 E
Mudjatik →, Canada 105 B7 56 1N 107 36W
Mudurnu, Turkey 72 B4 40 27N 31 12 E
Muecate, Mozam. 87 E4 14 55 S 39 40 E
Mueda, Mozam. 87 E4 11 36 S 39 28 E
Mueller Ra., Australia 92 C4 18 18 S 126 46 E
Muende, Mozam. 87 E3 14 28 S 33 0 E
Muerto, Mar, Mexico 119 D6 16 10N 94 10W
Mufu Shan, China 59 C10 29 20N 114 30 E
Mufulira, Zambia 87 E2 12 32 S 28 15 E
Mufumbiro Range, Africa 86 C2 1 25 S 29 30 E
Mugardos, Spain 34 B2 43 27N 8 15W
Muge →, Portugal 35 F2 39 8N 8 44W
Múggia, Italy 29 C10 45 36N 13 46 E
Mughal Sarai, India 69 G10 25 18N 83 7 E
Mughayrā', Si. Arabia 70 D3 29 17N 37 41 E
Mugi, Japan 55 H7 33 40N 134 25 E
Mugia = Muxía, Spain 34 B1 43 3N 9 10W
Mugila, Mts., Dem. Rep. of the Congo 86 D2 7 0 S 28 50 E
Muğla, Turkey 39 D10 37 15N 28 22 E
Muğla □, Turkey 39 D10 37 15N 28 0 E
Muglad, Sudan 81 E2 11 1N 27 50 E
Mŭglizh, Bulgaria 41 D9 42 37N 25 32 E
Mugu, Nepal 69 E10 29 45N 82 30 E
Muhammad, Ras, Egypt 70 E2 27 44N 34 16 E
Muhammad Qol, Sudan 80 C4 20 53N 37 9 E
Muhammadabad, India 69 F10 26 4N 83 25 E
Muhesi →, Tanzania 86 D4 7 0 S 35 20 E
Mühlacker, Germany 25 G4 48 57N 8 51 E
Mühldorf, Germany 25 G8 48 14N 12 32 E
Mühlhausen, Germany 24 D6 51 12N 10 27 E
Mühlig Hofmann fjell, Antarctica 5 D3 72 30 S 5 0 E
Mühlviertel, Austria 26 C7 48 30N 14 10 E
Muhos, Finland 8 D22 64 47N 25 59 E
Muhu, Estonia 9 G20 58 36N 23 11 E
Muhutwe, Tanzania 86 C3 1 35 S 31 45 E
Muine Bheag, Ireland 15 D5 52 42N 6 58W
Muir, L., Australia 93 F2 34 30 S 116 40 E
Mujnak, Uzbekistan 50 E6 43 44N 59 10 E
Mukacheve, Ukraine 47 H2 48 27N 22 45 E
Mukachevo = Mukacheve, Ukraine 47 H2 48 27N 22 45 E
Mukah, Malaysia 62 D4 2 55N 112 5 E
Mukandwara, India 68 G6 24 49N 75 59 E
Mukawwa, Geziret, Egypt 80 C4 23 55N 35 53 E
Mukawwar, Sudan 80 C4 20 50N 37 17 E
Mukdahan, Thailand 64 D5 16 32N 104 43 E
Mukden = Shenyang, China 57 D12 41 48N 123 27 E
Mukerian, India 68 D6 31 57N 75 37 E
Mukhtolovo, Russia 48 C6 55 29N 43 15 E
Mukhtuya = Lensk, Russia 51 C12 60 48N 114 55 E
Mukinbudin, Australia 93 F2 30 55 S 118 5 E
Mukishi, Dem. Rep. of the Congo 87 D1 8 30 S 24 44 E
Mukomuko, Indonesia 62 E2 2 30 S 101 10 E
Mukomwenze, Dem. Rep. of the Congo 86 D2 6 49 S 27 15 E
Muktsar, India 68 D6 30 30N 74 30 E
Mukur = Moqor, Afghan. 68 C2 32 50N 67 42 E
Mukutawa →, Canada 105 C9 53 10N 97 24W
Mukwela, Zambia 87 F2 17 0 S 26 40 E
Mula, Spain 33 G3 38 3N 1 33W
Mula →, Pakistan 68 F2 27 57N 67 36 E
Mulange, Dem. Rep. of the Congo 86 C2 3 40 S 27 10 E
Mulanje, Malawi 87 F4 16 2 S 35 33 E
Mulchén, Chile 126 D1 37 45 S 72 20W
Mulde →, Germany 24 D8 51 53N 12 15 E
Mule Creek Junction, U.S.A. 112 D2 43 19N 104 8W
Muleba, Tanzania 86 C3 1 50 S 31 37 E
Mulejé, Mexico 118 B2 26 53N 112 1W
Muleshoe, U.S.A. 113 H3 34 13N 102 43W
Muletta, Gara, Ethiopia 81 F5 9 15N 41 44 E
Mulgrave, Canada 103 C7 45 38N 61 31W
Mulhacén, Spain 35 H7 37 4N 3 20W
Mülheim, Germany 24 D2 51 25N 6 54 E
Mulhouse, France 19 E14 47 40N 7 20 E
Muli, China 58 D3 27 52N 101 8 E
Muling, China 57 B16 44 35N 130 10 E
Mull, U.K. 14 E3 56 25N 5 56W
Mull, Sound of, U.K. 14 E3 56 30N 5 50W
Mullaittivu, Sri Lanka 66 Q12 9 15N 80 49 E
Mullen, U.S.A. 112 D4 42 3N 101 1W
Mullens, U.S.A. 108 G5 37 35N 81 23W
Muller, Pegunungan, Indonesia 62 D4 0 30N 113 30 E
Mullet Pen., Ireland 15 B1 54 13N 10 2W
Mullewa, Australia 93 E2 28 29 S 115 30 E
Müllheim, Germany 25 H3 47 47N 7 36 E
Mulligan →, Australia 94 D2 25 0 S 139 0 E
Mullingar, Ireland 15 C4 53 31N 7 21W
Mullins, U.S.A. 109 H6 34 12N 79 15W
Mullsjö, Sweden 11 G7 57 56N 13 55 E
Mullumbimby, Australia 95 D5 28 30 S 153 30 E
Mulobezi, Zambia 87 F2 16 45 S 25 7 E
Mulroy B., Ireland 15 A4 55 15N 7 46W
Multan, Pakistan 68 D4 30 15N 71 36 E
Mulumbe, Mts., Dem. Rep. of the Congo 87 D2 8 40 S 27 30 E
Mulungushi Dam, Zambia 87 E2 14 48 S 28 48 E
Mulvane, U.S.A. 113 G6 37 29N 97 15W
Mulwad, Sudan 80 D3 18 45N 30 39 E
Mumbai, India 66 K8 18 55N 72 50 E
Mumbwa, Zambia 87 F2 15 0 S 27 0 E
Mumra, Russia 49 H8 45 45N 47 41 E
Mun →, Thailand 64 E5 15 19N 105 30 E
Muna, Indonesia 63 F6 5 0 S 122 30 E
Munabao, India 68 G4 25 45N 70 17 E
Munamagi, Estonia 9 H22 57 43N 27 4 E
Münchberg, Germany 25 E7 50 11N 11 47 E
Müncheberg, Germany 24 C10 52 30N 14 9 E
München, Germany 25 G7 48 8N 11 34 E
Munchen-Gladbach = Mönchengladbach, Germany 24 D2 51 11N 6 27 E
Muncho Lake, Canada 104 B3 59 0N 125 50W
Munch'ŏn, N. Korea 57 E14 39 14N 127 19 E
Muncie, U.S.A. 108 E3 40 12N 85 23W
Muncoonie, L., Australia 94 D2 25 12 S 138 40 E
Mundabbera, Australia 95 D5 25 36 S 151 18 E
Munday, U.S.A. 113 J5 33 27N 99 38W
Münden, Germany 24 D5 51 25N 9 38 E
Mundiwindi, Australia 92 D3 23 47 S 120 9 E
Mundo →, Spain 33 G2 38 30N 2 15W
Mundo Novo, Brazil 125 F10 11 50 S 40 29W
Mundra, India 68 H3 22 54N 69 48 E
Mundrabilla, Australia 93 F4 31 52 S 127 51 E
Munera, Spain 33 F2 39 2N 2 29W
Mungallala, Australia 95 D4 26 28 S 147 34 E
Mungallala Cr. →, Australia 95 D4 28 53 S 147 5 E
Mungana, Australia 94 B3 17 8 S 144 27 E
Mungaoli, India 68 G8 24 24N 78 7 E
Mungari, Mozam. 87 F3 17 12 S 33 30 E
Mungbere, Dem. Rep. of the Congo 86 B2 2 36N 28 28 E
Mungeli, India 69 H9 22 4N 81 41 E
Munger, India 69 G12 25 23N 86 30 E
Munich = München, Germany 25 G7 48 8N 11 34 E
Munising, U.S.A. 108 B2 46 25N 86 40W
Munka-Ljungby, Sweden 11 H6 56 16N 12 58 E
Munkebo, Denmark 11 J4 55 27N 10 34 E
Munkedal, Sweden 11 F5 58 28N 11 40 E
Munkfors, Sweden 10 E7 59 47N 13 30 E
Munku-Sardyk, Russia 51 D11 51 45N 100 20 E
Münnerstadt, Germany 25 E6 50 14N 10 12 E
Muñoz Gamero, Pen., Chile 128 G2 52 30 S 73 5W
Munroe L., Canada 105 B9 59 13N 98 35W
Munsan, S. Korea 57 F14 37 51N 126 48 E
Munster, France 19 D14 48 2N 7 8 E
Munster, Niedersachsen, Germany 24 C6 52 58N 10 5 E
Münster, Nordrhein-Westfalen, Germany 24 D3 51 58N 7 37 E
Munster □, Ireland 15 D3 52 18N 8 44W
Muntadgin, Australia 93 F2 31 45 S 118 33 E
Muntele Mare, Vf., Romania 43 D8 46 30N 23 12 E
Muntok, Indonesia 62 E3 2 5 S 105 10 E
Munyama, Zambia 87 F2 16 5 S 28 31 E
Munzur Dağları, Turkey 73 C8 39 30N 39 10 E
Muong Beng, Laos 58 G3 20 23N 101 46 E
Muong Boum, Vietnam 58 F4 22 24N 102 49 E
Muong Et, Laos 64 B5 20 49N 104 1 E
Muong Hai, Laos 58 G3 21 3N 101 49 E
Muong Hiem, Laos 64 B4 20 5N 103 22 E
Muong Houn, Laos 58 G3 20 8N 101 23 E
Muong Hung, Vietnam 58 G4 20 56N 103 53 E
Muong Kau, Laos 64 E5 15 6N 105 47 E
Muong Khao, Laos 64 C4 19 38N 103 32 E
Muong Khoua, Laos 58 G4 21 5N 102 31 E
Muong Liep, Laos 64 C3 18 29N 101 40 E
Muong May, Laos 64 E6 14 49N 106 56 E
Muong Ngeun, Laos 58 G3 20 36N 101 3 E
Muong Ngoi, Laos 58 G4 20 43N 102 41 E
Muong Nhie, Vietnam 58 F4 22 12N 102 28 E
Muong Nong, Laos 64 D6 16 22N 106 30 E
Muong Ou Tay, Laos 58 F3 22 7N 101 48 E
Muong Oua, Laos 64 C3 18 18N 101 20 E
Muong Peun, Laos 58 G4 20 13N 103 52 E
Muong Phalane, Laos 64 D5 16 39N 105 34 E
Muong Phieng, Laos 64 C3 19 6N 101 32 E
Muong Phine, Laos 64 D6 16 32N 106 2 E
Muong Sai, Laos 58 G3 20 42N 101 59 E
Muong Saiapoun, Laos 64 C3 18 24N 101 31 E
Muong Sen, Vietnam 64 C5 19 24N 104 8 E
Muong Sing, Laos 58 G3 21 11N 101 9 E
Muong Son, Laos 58 G4 20 27N 103 19 E
Muong Soui, Laos 64 C4 19 33N 102 52 E
Muong Va, Laos 58 G4 21 53N 102 19 E
Muong Xia, Vietnam 64 B5 20 19N 104 50 E
Muonio, Finland 8 C20 67 57N 23 40 E
Muonionjoki →, Finland 8 C20 67 11N 23 34 E
Muping, China 57 F11 37 22N 121 36 E
Mupoi, Sudan 81 F2 5 28N 27 40 E
Muqaddam, Wadi →, Sudan 80 D3 18 4N 31 30 E
Muqdisho, Somali Rep. 74 G4 2 2N 45 25 E
Mur →, Austria 27 E9 46 18N 16 52 E
Mur-de-Bretagne, France 18 D4 48 12N 3 0W
Muradiye, Manisa, Turkey 39 C9 38 39N 27 21 E
Muradiye, Van, Turkey 73 C10 39 0N 43 44 E
Murakami, Japan 54 E9 38 14N 139 29 E
Murallón, Cerro, Chile 128 F2 49 48 S 73 30W
Muranda, Rwanda 86 C2 1 52 S 29 20 E
Murang'a, Kenya 86 C4 0 45 S 37 9 E
Murashi, Russia 50 D5 59 30N 49 0 E
Murat, France 20 C6 45 7N 2 53 E
Murat →, Turkey 73 C9 38 46N 40 0 E
Murat Dağı, Turkey 39 C11 38 55N 29 43 E
Muratlı, Turkey 41 E11 41 10N 27 29 E
Murato, France 21 F13 42 35N 9 20 E
Murau, Austria 26 D7 47 6N 14 10 E
Muravera, Italy 30 C2 39 25N 9 34 E
Murayama, Japan 54 E10 38 30N 140 25 E
Murban, U.A.E. 71 F7 23 50N 53 45 E
Murça, Portugal 34 D3 41 24N 7 28W
Murchison →, Australia 93 E1 27 45 S 114 0 E
Murchison, Mt., Antarctica 5 D11 73 0 S 168 0 E
Murchison Falls, Uganda 86 B3 2 15N 31 30 E
Murchison Ra., Australia 94 C1 20 0 S 134 10 E
Murchison Rapids, Malawi 87 F3 15 55 S 34 35 E
Murcia, Spain 33 G3 38 5N 1 10W
Murcia □, Spain 33 H3 37 50N 1 30W
Murdo, U.S.A. 112 D4 43 53N 100 43W
Murdoch Pt., Australia 94 A3 14 37 S 144 55 E
Mürefte, Turkey 41 F11 40 40N 27 14 E
Mureş □, Romania 43 D9 46 45N 24 40 E
Mureş →, Romania 42 D5 46 15N 20 13 E
Mureşul = Mureş →, Romania 42 D5 46 15N 20 13 E
Muret, France 20 E5 43 30N 1 20 E
Murewa, Zimbabwe 89 B5 17 39 S 31 47 E
Murfreesboro, N.C., U.S.A. 109 G7 36 27N 77 6W
Murfreesboro, Tenn., U.S.A. 109 H2 35 51N 86 24W
Murgab = Murghob, Tajikistan 50 F8 38 10N 74 2 E
Murgab →, Turkmenistan 71 B9 38 18N 61 12 E
Murgenella, Australia 92 B5 11 34 S 132 56 E
Murgeni, Romania 43 D13 46 12N 28 1 E
Murgha Kibzai, Pakistan 68 D3 30 44N 69 25 E
Murghob, Tajikistan 50 F8 38 10N 74 2 E
Murgon, Australia 95 D5 26 15 S 151 54 E
Muri, India 69 H11 23 22N 85 52 E
Muria, Indonesia 63 G14 6 36 S 110 53 E
Muriaé, Brazil 127 A7 21 8 S 42 23W
Murias de Paredes, Spain 34 C4 42 52N 6 11W
Muriel Mine, Zimbabwe 87 F3 17 14 S 30 40 E
Müritz, Germany 24 B8 53 25N 12 42 E
Murka, Kenya 86 C4 3 27 S 38 0 E
Murliganj, India 69 G12 25 54N 86 59 E
Murmansk, Russia 50 C4 68 57N 33 10 E
Murnau, Germany 25 H7 47 40N 11 12 E
Muro, France 21 F12 42 34N 8 54 E
Muro, Spain 37 B10 39 44N 3 3 E
Muro, C. de, France 21 G12 41 44N 8 37 E
Muro de Alcoy, Spain 33 G4 38 46N 0 26W
Muro Lucano, Italy 31 B8 40 45N 15 29 E
Murom, Russia 48 C6 55 35N 42 3 E
Muroran, Japan 54 C10 42 25N 141 0 E
Muros, Spain 34 C1 42 45N 9 5W
Muros y de Noya, Ría de, Spain 34 C1 42 45N 9 0W
Muroto, Japan 55 H7 33 18N 134 9 E
Muroto-Misaki, Japan 55 H7 33 15N 134 10 E
Murowana Goślina, Poland 45 F3 52 35N 17 0 E
Murphy, U.S.A. 114 E5 43 13N 116 33W
Murphys, U.S.A. 116 G6 38 8N 120 28W
Murrat, Sudan 80 D2 18 51N 29 33 E
Murrat Wells, Sudan 80 C3 21 3N 32 55 E
Murray, Ky., U.S.A. 109 G1 36 37N 88 19W
Murray, Utah, U.S.A. 114 F8 40 40N 111 53W
Murray →, Australia 95 F2 35 20 S 139 22 E
Murray, L., U.S.A. 109 H5 34 3N 81 13W
Murray Bridge, Australia 95 F2 35 6 S 139 14 E
Murray Harbour, Canada 103 C7 46 0N 62 28W
Murraysburg, S. Africa 88 E3 31 58 S 23 47 E
Murree, Pakistan 68 C5 33 56N 73 28 E
Murrieta, U.S.A. 117 M9 33 33N 117 13W
Murro di Porco, Capo, Italy 31 F8 37 0N 15 20 E
Murrumbidgee →, Australia 95 E3 34 43 S 143 12 E
Murrumburrah, Australia 95 E4 34 32 S 148 22 E
Murrurundi, Australia 95 E5 31 42 S 150 51 E
Murshid, Sudan 80 C3 21 40N 31 10 E
Murshidabad, India 69 G13 24 11N 88 19 E
Murska Sobota, Slovenia 29 B13 46 39N 16 12 E
Murtle L., Canada 104 C5 52 8N 119 38W
Murtoa, Australia 95 F3 36 35 S 142 28 E
Murtosa, Portugal 34 E2 40 44N 8 40W
Murungu, Tanzania 86 C3 4 12 S 31 10 E
Mururoa, Pac. Oc. 97 K14 21 52 S 138 55W
Murwara, India 69 H9 23 46N 80 28 E
Murwillumbah, Australia 95 D5 28 18 S 153 27 E
Mürz →, Austria 26 D8 47 30N 15 25 E
Mürzzuschlag, Austria 26 D8 47 36N 15 41 E
Muş, Turkey 70 B4 38 45N 41 30 E
Mûsa, Gebel, Egypt 70 D2 28 33N 33 59 E
Musa Khel, Pakistan 68 D3 30 59N 69 52 E
Mūsa Qal'eh, Afghan. 66 C4 32 20N 64 50 E
Musafargarh, Pakistan 66 D7 30 10N 71 10 E
Musafirkhana, India 69 F9 26 22N 81 48 E
Musala, Bulgaria 40 D7 42 13N 23 37 E
Musala, Indonesia 62 D1 1 41N 98 28 E
Musan, N. Korea 57 C15 42 12N 129 12 E
Musangu, Dem. Rep. of the Congo 87 E1 10 28 S 23 55 E
Musasa, Tanzania 86 C3 3 25 S 31 30 E
Musay'īd, Qatar 71 E6 25 0N 51 33 E
Muscat = Masqat, Oman 74 C6 23 37N 58 36 E
Muscat & Oman = Oman ■, Asia 74 C6 23 0N 58 0 E
Muscatine, U.S.A. 112 E9 41 25N 91 3W
Musgrave Harbour, Canada 103 C9 49 27N 53 58W
Musgrave Ranges, Australia 93 E5 26 0 S 132 0 E
Mushie, Dem. Rep. of the Congo 84 E3 2 56 S 16 55 E
Mushin, Nigeria 83 D5 6 32N 3 21 E
Musi →, Indonesia 62 E2 2 20 S 104 56 E
Muskeg →, Canada 104 A4 60 20N 123 20W
Muskegon, U.S.A. 108 D2 43 14N 86 16W
Muskegon →, U.S.A. 108 D2 43 14N 86 21W
Muskegon Heights, U.S.A. 108 D2 43 12N 86 16W
Muskogee, U.S.A. 113 H7 35 45N 95 22W
Muskoka, L., Canada 110 B5 45 0N 79 25W
Muskwa →, Canada 104 B4 58 47N 122 48W
Muslīmiyah, Syria 70 B3 36 19N 37 12 E
Musmar, Sudan 80 D4 18 13N 35 40 E
Musofu, Zambia 87 E2 13 30 S 29 0 E
Musoma, Tanzania 86 C3 1 30 S 33 48 E
Musquaro, L., Canada 103 B7 50 38N 61 5W
Musquodoboit Harbour, Canada 103 D7 44 50N 63 9W
Musselburgh, U.K. 14 F5 55 57N 3 2W
Musselshell →, U.S.A. 114 C10 47 21N 107 57W
Mussidan, France 20 C4 45 2N 0 22 E
Mussomeli, Italy 30 E6 37 35N 13 45 E
Mussoorie, India 68 D8 30 27N 78 6 E
Mussuco, Angola 88 B2 17 2 S 19 3 E
Mustafakemalpaşa, Turkey 41 F12 40 2N 28 24 E
Mustang, Nepal 69 E10 29 10N 83 55 E
Musters, L., Argentina 128 F3 45 20 S 69 25W
Musudan, N. Korea 57 D15 40 50N 129 43 E
Muswellbrook, Australia 95 E5 32 16 S 150 56 E
Muszyna, Poland 45 J7 49 22N 20 55 E
Mût, Egypt 80 B2 25 28N 28 58 E
Mut, Turkey 70 B2 36 40N 33 28 E
Mutanda, Mozam. 89 C5 21 0 S 33 34 E
Mutanda, Zambia 87 E2 12 24 S 26 13 E
Mutare, Zimbabwe 87 F3 18 58 S 32 38 E
Muting, Indonesia 63 F10 7 23 S 140 20 E
Mutoko, Zimbabwe 89 B5 17 24 S 32 13 E
Mutoray, Russia 51 C11 60 56N 101 0 E
Mutshatsha, Dem. Rep. of the Congo 87 E1 10 35 S 24 20 E
Mutsu, Japan 54 D10 41 5N 140 55 E
Mutsu-Wan, Japan 54 D10 41 5N 140 55 E
Muttaburra, Australia 94 C3 22 38 S 144 29 E
Muttalip, Turkey 39 B12 39 50N 30 32 E
Mutton I., Ireland 15 D2 52 49N 9 32W
Mutuáli, Mozam. 87 E4 14 55 S 37 0 E
Mutum Biyu, Nigeria 83 D7 8 40N 10 50 E
Muweilih, Egypt 75 E3 30 42N 34 19 E
Muxía, Spain 34 B1 43 3N 9 10W
Muy Muy, Nic. 120 D2 12 39N 85 36W
Muyinga, Burundi 86 C3 3 14 S 30 33 E
Muzaffarabad, Pakistan 69 B5 34 25N 73 30 E
Muzaffargarh, Pakistan 68 D4 30 5N 71 14 E
Muzaffarnagar, India 68 E7 29 26N 77 40 E

Muzaffarpur, *India* **69 F11** 26 7N 85 23 E
Muzafirpur, *Pakistan* **68 D3** 30 58N 69 9 E
Muzhi, *Russia* **50 C7** 65 25N 64 40 E
Muzillac, *France* **18 E4** 47 35N 2 30W
Muzūra, *Egypt* **80 J7** 28 53N 30 48 E
Mvôlô, *Sudan* **81 F2** 6 2N 29 53 E
Mvuma, *Zimbabwe* **87 F3** 19 16 S 30 30 E
Mvurwi, *Zimbabwe* **87 F3** 17 0 S 30 57 E
Mwadui, *Tanzania* **86 C3** 3 26 S 33 32 E
Mwambo, *Tanzania* **87 E5** 10 30 S 40 22 E
Mwandi, *Zambia* **87 F1** 17 30 S 24 51 E
Mwanza, *Dem. Rep. of the Congo* **86 D2** 7 55 S 26 43 E
Mwanza, *Tanzania* **86 C3** 2 30 S 32 58 E
Mwanza, *Zambia* **87 F1** 16 58 S 24 28 E
Mwanza □, *Tanzania* **86 C3** 2 0 S 33 0 E
Mwaya, *Tanzania* **87 D3** 9 32 S 33 55 E
Mweelrea, *Ireland* **15 C2** 53 39N 9 49W
Mweka, *Dem. Rep. of the Congo* **84 E4** 4 50 S 21 34 E
Mwenezi, *Zimbabwe* **87 G3** 21 15 S 30 48 E
Mwenezi →, *Mozam.* **87 G3** 22 40 S 31 50 E
Mwenga, *Dem. Rep. of the Congo* **86 C2** 3 1 S 28 28 E
Mweru, L., *Zambia* **87 D2** 9 0 S 28 40 E
Mweza Range, *Zimbabwe* **87 G3** 21 0 S 30 0 E
Mwilambwe, *Dem. Rep. of the Congo* **86 D2** 8 7 S 25 5 E
Mwimbi, *Tanzania* **87 D3** 8 38 S 31 39 E
Mwinilunga, *Zambia* **87 E1** 11 43 S 24 25 E
My Tho, *Vietnam* **65 G6** 10 29N 106 23 E
Myajlar, *India* **68 F4** 26 15N 70 20 E
Myanaung, *Burma* **67 K19** 18 18N 95 22 E
Myanmar = Burma ■, *Asia* **67 J20** 21 0N 96 30 E
Myaungmya, *Burma* **67 L19** 16 30N 94 40 E
Myeik Kyunzu, *Burma* **65 G1** 11 30N 97 30 E
Myers Chuck, *U.S.A.* **104 B2** 55 44N 132 11W
Myerstown, *U.S.A.* **111 F8** 40 22N 76 19W
Myingyan, *Burma* **67 J19** 21 30N 95 20 E
Myitkyina, *Burma* **67 G20** 25 24N 97 26 E
Myjava, *Slovak Rep.* **27 C10** 48 41N 17 37 E
Mykhaylivka, *Ukraine* **47 J8** 47 12N 35 15 E
Mykines, *Færoe Is.* **8 E9** 62 7N 7 35W
Mykolayiv, *Ukraine* **47 J7** 46 58N 32 0 E
Mymensingh, *Bangla.* **67 G17** 24 45N 90 24 E
Mynydd Du, *U.K.* **13 F4** 51 52N 3 50W
Mýrdalsjökull, *Iceland* **8 E4** 63 40N 19 6W
Myrhorod, *Ukraine* **47 H7** 49 58N 33 37 E
Myrtle Beach, *U.S.A.* **109 J6** 33 42N 78 53W
Myrtle Creek, *U.S.A.* **114 E2** 43 1N 123 17W
Myrtle Point, *U.S.A.* **114 E1** 43 4N 124 8W
Myrtou, *Cyprus* **36 D12** 35 18N 33 4 E
Mysia, *Turkey* **41 G11** 39 50N 27 0 E
Myślenice, *Poland* **45 J6** 49 51N 19 57 E
Myślibórz, *Poland* **45 F1** 52 55N 14 50 E
Mysłowice, *Poland* **45 H6** 50 15N 19 12 E
Mysore = Karnataka □, *India* **66 N10** 13 15N 77 0 E
Mysore, *India* **66 N10** 12 17N 76 41 E
Mystic, *U.S.A.* **111 E13** 41 21N 71 58W
Myszków, *Poland* **45 H6** 50 45N 19 22 E
Myszyniec, *Poland* **44 E8** 53 23N 21 21 E
Mytishchi, *Russia* **46 E9** 55 50N 37 50 E
Mývatn, *Iceland* **8 D5** 65 36N 17 0W
Mže →, *Czech Rep.* **26 B6** 49 46N 13 24 E
Mzimba, *Malawi* **87 E3** 11 55 S 33 39 E
Mzimkulu →, *S. Africa* **89 E5** 30 44 S 30 28 E
Mzimvubu →, *S. Africa* **89 E4** 31 38 S 29 33 E
Mzuzu, *Malawi* **87 E3** 11 30 S 33 55 E

N

Na Hearadh = Harris, *U.K.* **14 D2** 57 50N 6 55W
Na Noi, *Thailand* **64 C3** 18 19N 100 43 E
Na Phao, *Laos* **64 D5** 17 35N 105 44 E
Na Sam, *Vietnam* **58 F6** 22 3N 106 37 E
Na San, *Vietnam* **64 B5** 21 12N 104 2 E
Naab →, *Germany* **25 F8** 49 1N 12 2 E
Na'am, *Sudan* **81 F2** 9 42N 28 27 E
Na'am →, *Sudan* **81 F2** 6 48N 29 57 E
Naantali, *Finland* **9 F19** 60 29N 22 2 E
Naas, *Ireland* **15 C5** 53 12N 6 40W
Nababeep, *S. Africa* **88 D2** 29 36 S 17 46 E
Nabadwip = Navadwip, *India* **69 H13** 23 34N 88 20 E
Nabari, *Japan* **55 G8** 34 37N 136 5 E
Nabawa, *Australia* **93 E1** 28 30 S 114 48 E
Nabberu, L., *Australia* **93 E3** 25 50 S 120 30 E
Nabburg, *Germany* **25 F8** 49 27N 12 11 E
Naberezhnyye Chelny, *Russia* **48 C11** 55 42N 52 19 E
Nabeul, *Tunisia* **79 A8** 36 30N 10 44 E
Nabha, *India* **68 D7** 30 26N 76 14 E
Nabīd, *Iran* **71 D8** 29 40N 57 38 E
Nabire, *Indonesia* **63 E9** 3 15 S 135 26 E
Nabisar, *Pakistan* **68 G3** 25 8N 69 40 E
Nabisipi →, *Canada* **103 B7** 50 14N 62 13W
Nabiswera, *Uganda* **86 B3** 1 27N 32 15 E
Nablus = Nābulus, *West Bank* **75 C4** 32 14N 35 15 E
Naboomspruit, *S. Africa* **89 C4** 24 32 S 28 40 E
Nabou, *Burkina Faso* **82 C4** 11 25N 2 50W
Nabua, *Phil.* **61 E5** 13 24N 123 22 E
Nābulus, *West Bank* **75 C4** 32 14N 35 15 E
Nacala, *Mozam.* **87 E5** 14 31 S 40 34 E
Nacala-Velha, *Mozam.* **87 E5** 14 32 S 40 34 E
Nacaome, *Honduras* **120 D2** 13 31N 87 30W
Nacaroa, *Mozam.* **87 E4** 14 22 S 39 56 E
Naches, *U.S.A.* **114 C3** 46 44N 120 42W
Naches →, *U.S.A.* **116 D6** 46 38N 120 31W
Nachicapau, L., *Canada* **103 A6** 56 40N 68 5W
Nachingwea, *Tanzania* **87 E4** 10 23 S 38 49 E
Nachna, *India* **68 F4** 27 34N 71 41 E
Náchod, *Czech Rep.* **26 A9** 50 25N 16 8 E
Nacimiento L., *U.S.A.* **116 K6** 35 46N 120 53W
Naco, *Mexico* **118 A3** 31 20N 109 56W
Nacogdoches, *U.S.A.* **113 K7** 31 36N 94 39W
Nácori Chico, *Mexico* **118 B3** 29 39N 109 1W
Nacozari, *Mexico* **118 A3** 30 24N 109 39W
Nadi, *Sudan* **80 D3** 18 40N 33 41 E
Nadiad, *India* **68 H5** 22 41N 72 56 E
Nădlac, *Romania* **42 D5** 46 10N 20 50 E
Nador, *Morocco* **78 B5** 35 14N 2 58W
Nadur, *Malta* **36 C1** 36 2N 14 17 E
Nadūshan, *Iran* **71 C7** 32 2N 53 35 E
Nadvirna, *Ukraine* **47 H3** 48 37N 24 30 E
Nadvornaya = Nadvirna, *Ukraine* **47 H3** 48 37N 24 30 E
Nadym, *Russia* **50 C8** 65 35N 72 42 E
Nadym →, *Russia* **50 C8** 66 12N 72 0 E
Nærbø, *Norway* **9 G11** 58 40N 5 39 E
Næstved, *Denmark* **11 J5** 55 13N 11 44 E
Nafada, *Nigeria* **83 C7** 11 8N 11 20 E
Naft-e Safīd, *Iran* **71 D6** 31 40N 49 17 E
Naftshahr, *Iran* **70 C5** 34 0N 45 30 E
Nafud Desert = An Nafūd, *Si. Arabia* **70 D4** 28 15N 41 0 E
Nag Hammâdi, *Egypt* **80 B3** 26 2N 32 18 E
Naga, *Phil.* **61 E5** 13 38N 123 15 E
Nagahama, *Japan* **55 G8** 35 23N 136 16 E
Nagai, *Japan* **54 E10** 38 6N 140 2 E
Nagaland □, *India* **67 G19** 26 0N 94 30 E
Nagano, *Japan* **55 F9** 36 40N 138 10 E
Nagano □, *Japan* **55 F9** 36 15N 138 0 E
Nagaoka, *Japan* **55 F9** 37 27N 138 51 E
Nagappattinam, *India* **66 P11** 10 46N 79 51 E
Nagar →, *Bangla.* **69 G13** 24 27N 89 12 E
Nagar Parkar, *Pakistan* **68 G4** 24 28N 70 46 E
Nagasaki, *Japan* **55 H4** 32 47N 129 50 E
Nagasaki □, *Japan* **55 H4** 32 50N 129 40 E
Nagato, *Japan* **55 G5** 34 19N 131 5 E
Nagaur, *India* **68 F5** 27 15N 73 45 E
Nagda, *India* **68 H6** 23 27N 75 25 E
Nagercoil, *India* **66 Q10** 8 12N 77 26 E
Nagina, *India* **69 E8** 29 30N 78 30 E
Nagīneh, *Iran* **71 C8** 34 20N 57 15 E
Nagir, *Pakistan* **69 A6** 36 12N 74 42 E
Naglarby, *Sweden* **10 D9** 60 25N 15 34 E
Nagod, *India* **69 G9** 24 34N 80 36 E
Nagold, *Germany* **25 G4** 48 32N 8 43 E
Nagold →, *Germany* **25 G4** 48 52N 8 42 E
Nagoorin, *Australia* **94 C5** 24 17 S 151 15 E
Nagorno-Karabakh, *Azerbaijan* **70 B5** 39 55N 46 45 E
Nagornyy, *Russia* **51 D13** 55 58N 124 57 E
Nagoya, *Japan* **55 G8** 35 10N 136 50 E
Nagpur, *India* **66 J11** 21 8N 79 10 E
Nagua, *Dom. Rep.* **121 C6** 19 23N 69 50W
Nagyatád, *Hungary* **42 D2** 46 14N 17 22 E
Nagyecsed, *Hungary* **42 C7** 47 53N 22 24 E
Nagykálló, *Hungary* **42 C6** 47 53N 21 51 E
Nagykanizsa, *Hungary* **42 D2** 46 28N 17 0 E
Nagykáta, *Hungary* **42 C4** 47 25N 19 45 E
Nagykőrös, *Hungary* **42 C4** 47 5N 19 48 E
Naha, *Japan* **55 L3** 26 13N 127 42 E
Nahan, *India* **68 D7** 30 33N 77 18 E
Nahanni Butte, *Canada* **104 A4** 61 2N 123 31W
Nahanni Nat. Park, *Canada* **104 A4** 61 15N 125 0W
Nahargarh, *Mad. P., India* **68 G6** 24 10N 75 14 E
Nahargarh, *Raj., India* **68 G7** 24 55N 76 50 E
Nahariyya, *Israel* **70 C2** 33 1N 35 5 E
Nahāvand, *Iran* **71 C6** 34 10N 48 22 E
Nahe →, *Germany* **25 F3** 49 58N 7 54 E
Nahîya, W. →, *Egypt* **80 B3** 28 55N 31 0 E
Naicá, *Mexico* **118 B3** 27 53N 105 31W
Naicam, *Canada* **105 C8** 52 30N 104 30W
Naikoon Prov. Park, *Canada* **104 C2** 53 55N 131 55W
Naila, *Germany* **25 E7** 50 19N 11 42 E
Naimisharanya, *India* **69 F9** 27 21N 80 30 E
Nain, *Canada* **103 A7** 56 34N 61 40W
Nā'īn, *Iran* **71 C7** 32 54N 53 0 E
Naini Tal, *India* **69 E8** 29 30N 79 30 E
Nainpur, *India* **66 H12** 22 30N 80 10 E
Naintré, *France* **18 F7** 46 46N 0 29 E
Nainwa, *India* **68 G6** 25 46N 75 51 E
Naipu, *Romania* **43 F10** 44 12N 25 47 E
Nairn, *U.K.* **14 D5** 57 35N 3 53W
Nairobi, *Kenya* **86 C4** 1 17 S 36 48 E
Naissaar, *Estonia* **9 G21** 59 34N 24 29 E
Naita, Mt., *Ethiopia* **81 F4** 5 30N 35 18 E
Naivasha, *Kenya* **86 C4** 0 40 S 36 30 E
Naivasha, L., *Kenya* **86 C4** 0 48 S 36 20 E
Najac, *France* **20 D5** 44 14N 1 58 E
Najafābād, *Iran* **71 C6** 32 40N 51 15 E
Najd, *Si. Arabia* **74 B3** 26 30N 42 0 E
Nájera, *Spain* **32 C2** 42 26N 2 48W
Najerilla →, *Spain* **32 C2** 42 32N 2 48W
Najibabad, *India* **68 E8** 29 40N 78 20 E
Najin, *N. Korea* **57 C16** 42 12N 130 15 E
Najmah, *Si. Arabia* **71 E6** 26 42N 50 6 E
Naju, *S. Korea* **57 G14** 35 3N 126 43 E
Nakadōri-Shima, *Japan* **55 H4** 32 57N 129 4 E
Nakalagba, *Dem. Rep. of the Congo* **86 B2** 2 50N 27 58 E
Nakaminato, *Japan* **55 F10** 36 21N 140 36 E
Nakamura, *Japan* **55 H6** 32 59N 132 56 E
Nakano, *Japan* **55 F9** 36 45N 138 22 E
Nakano-Shima, *Japan* **55 K4** 29 51N 129 52 E
Nakashibetsu, *Japan* **54 C12** 43 33N 144 59 E
Nakfa, *Eritrea* **81 D4** 16 40N 38 32 E
Nakhfar al Buşayyah, *Iraq* **70 D5** 30 0N 46 10 E
Nakhichevan = Naxçıvan, *Azerbaijan* **70 B5** 39 12N 45 15 E
Nakhichevan Republic = Naxçıvan □, *Azerbaijan* **50 F5** 39 25N 45 26 E
Nakhl, *Egypt* **75 F2** 29 55N 33 43 E
Nakhl-e Taqī, *Iran* **71 E7** 27 28N 52 36 E
Nakhodka, *Russia* **51 E14** 42 53N 132 54 E
Nakhon Nayok, *Thailand* **64 E3** 14 12N 101 13 E
Nakhon Pathom, *Thailand* **64 F3** 13 49N 100 3 E
Nakhon Phanom, *Thailand* **64 D5** 17 23N 104 43 E
Nakhon Ratchasima, *Thailand* **64 E4** 14 59N 102 12 E
Nakhon Sawan, *Thailand* **64 E3** 15 35N 100 10 E
Nakhon Si Thammarat, *Thailand* **65 H3** 8 29N 100 0 E
Nakhon Thai, *Thailand* **64 D3** 17 5N 100 44 E
Nakhtarana, *India* **68 H3** 23 20N 69 15 E
Nakina, *Canada* **102 B2** 50 10N 86 40W
Nakło nad Notecią, *Poland* **45 E4** 53 9N 17 38 E
Nako, *Burkina Faso* **82 C4** 10 40N 3 4W
Nakodar, *India* **68 D6** 31 8N 75 31 E
Nakskov, *Denmark* **11 K5** 54 50N 11 8 E
Naktong →, *S. Korea* **57 G15** 35 7N 128 57 E
Nakuru, *Kenya* **86 C4** 0 15 S 36 4 E
Nakuru, L., *Kenya* **86 C4** 0 23 S 36 5 E
Nakusp, *Canada* **104 C5** 50 20N 117 45W
Nal, *Pakistan* **68 F2** 27 40N 66 12 E
Nal →, *Pakistan* **68 G1** 25 20N 65 30 E
Nalázi, *Mozam.* **89 C5** 24 3 S 33 20 E
Nalchik, *Russia* **49 J6** 43 30N 43 33 E
Nałęczów, *Poland* **45 G9** 51 17N 22 9 E
Nalerigu, *Ghana* **83 C4** 10 35N 0 25W
Nalgonda, *India* **66 L11** 17 6N 79 15 E
Nalhati, *India* **69 G12** 24 17N 87 52 E
Naliya, *India* **68 H3** 23 16N 68 50 E
Nallamalai Hills, *India* **66 M11** 15 30N 78 50 E
Nallıhan, *Turkey* **72 B4** 40 11N 31 20 E
Nalón →, *Spain* **34 B4** 43 32N 6 4W
Nam Can, *Vietnam* **65 H5** 8 46N 104 59 E
Nam-ch'on, *N. Korea* **57 E14** 38 15N 126 26 E
Nam Co, *China* **60 C4** 30 30N 90 45 E
Nam Dinh, *Vietnam* **58 G6** 20 25N 106 5 E
Nam Du, Hon, *Vietnam* **65 H5** 9 41N 104 21 E
Nam Ngum Dam, *Laos* **64 C4** 18 35N 102 34 E
Nam-Phan, *Vietnam* **65 G6** 10 30N 106 0 E
Nam Phong, *Thailand* **64 D4** 16 42N 102 52 E
Nam Tha, *Laos* **58 G3** 20 58N 101 30 E
Nam Tok, *Thailand* **64 E2** 14 21N 99 4 E
Namacunde, *Angola* **88 B2** 17 18 S 15 50 E
Namacurra, *Mozam.* **89 B6** 17 30 S 36 50 E
Namak, Daryācheh-ye, *Iran* **71 C7** 34 30N 52 0 E
Namak, Kavir-e, *Iran* **71 C8** 34 30N 57 30 E
Namakzār, Daryācheh-ye, *Iran* **71 C9** 34 0N 60 30 E
Namaland, *Namibia* **88 C2** 26 0 S 17 0 E
Namangan, *Uzbekistan* **50 E8** 41 0N 71 40 E
Namapa, *Mozam.* **87 E4** 13 43 S 39 50 E
Namaqualand, *S. Africa* **88 E2** 30 0 S 17 25 E
Namasagali, *Uganda* **86 B3** 1 2N 33 0 E
Namber, *Indonesia* **63 E8** 1 2 S 134 49 E
Nambour, *Australia* **95 D5** 26 32 S 152 58 E
Nambucca Heads, *Australia* **95 E5** 30 37 S 153 0 E
Namche Bazar, *Nepal* **69 F12** 27 51N 86 47 E
Namchonjŏm = Nam-ch'on, *N. Korea* **57 E14** 38 15N 126 26 E
Namecunda, *Mozam.* **87 E4** 14 54 S 37 37 E
Nameponda, *Mozam.* **87 F4** 15 50 S 39 50 E
Náměšť nad Oslavou, *Czech Rep.* **27 B9** 49 12N 16 10 E
Námestovo, *Slovak Rep.* **27 B12** 49 24N 19 25 E
Nametil, *Mozam.* **87 F4** 15 40 S 39 21 E
Namew L., *Canada* **105 C8** 54 14N 101 56W
Namgia, *India* **69 D8** 31 48N 78 40 E
Namhkam, *Burma* **58 E1** 23 50N 97 41 E
Namib Desert = Namibwoestyn, *Namibia* **88 C2** 22 30 S 15 0 E
Namibe, *Angola* **85 H2** 15 7 S 12 11 E
Namibe □, *Angola* **88 B1** 16 35 S 12 30 E
Namibia ■, *Africa* **88 C2** 22 0 S 18 9 E
Namibwoestyn, *Namibia* **88 C2** 22 30 S 15 0 E
Namīn, *Iran* **73 C13** 38 25N 48 30 E
Namlea, *Indonesia* **63 E7** 3 18 S 127 5 E
Namoi →, *Australia* **95 E4** 30 12 S 149 30 E
Nampa, *U.S.A.* **114 E5** 43 34N 116 34W
Nampala, *Mali* **82 B3** 15 20N 5 30W
Namp'o, *N. Korea* **57 E13** 38 52N 125 10 E
Nampō-Shotō, *Japan* **55 J10** 32 0N 140 0 E
Nampula, *Mozam.* **87 F4** 15 6 S 39 15 E
Namrole, *Indonesia* **63 E7** 3 46 S 126 46 E
Namse Shankou, *China* **67 E13** 30 0N 82 25 E
Namsen →, *Norway* **8 D14** 64 28N 11 37 E
Namsos, *Norway* **8 D14** 64 29N 11 30 E
Namtsy, *Russia* **51 C13** 62 43N 129 37 E
Namtu, *Burma* **67 H20** 23 5N 97 28 E
Namtumbo, *Tanzania* **87 E4** 10 30 S 36 4 E
Namu, *Canada* **104 C3** 51 52N 127 50W
Namur, *Belgium* **17 D4** 50 27N 4 52 E
Namur □, *Belgium* **17 D4** 50 17N 5 0 E
Namutoni, *Namibia* **88 B2** 18 49 S 16 55 E
Namwala, *Zambia* **87 F2** 15 44 S 26 30 E
Namwŏn, *S. Korea* **57 G14** 35 23N 127 23 E
Namysłów, *Poland* **45 G4** 51 6N 17 42 E
Nan, *Thailand* **64 C3** 18 48N 100 46 E
Nan →, *Thailand* **64 E3** 15 42N 100 9 E
Nan-ch'ang = Nanchang, *China* **59 C10** 28 42N 115 55 E
Nan Ling, *China* **59 E8** 25 0N 112 30 E
Nan Xian, *China* **59 C9** 29 20N 112 22 E
Nana, *Romania* **43 F11** 44 17N 26 34 E
Nana Kru, *Liberia* **82 E3** 4 55N 8 45W
Nanaimo, *Canada* **104 D4** 49 10N 124 0W
Nanam, *N. Korea* **57 D15** 41 44N 129 40 E
Nanan, *China* **59 E12** 24 59N 118 21 E
Nanango, *Australia* **95 D5** 26 40 S 152 0 E
Nan'ao, *China* **59 F11** 23 28N 117 5 E
Nanao, *Japan* **55 F8** 37 0N 137 0 E
Nanbu, *China* **58 B6** 31 18N 106 3 E
Nanchang, *Jiangxi, China* **59 C10** 28 42N 115 55 E
Nanchang, *Kiangsi, China* **59 C10** 28 34N 115 48 E
Nancheng, *China* **59 D11** 27 33N 116 35 E
Nanching = Nanjing, *China* **59 A12** 32 2N 118 47 E
Nanchong, *China* **58 B6** 30 43N 106 2 E
Nanchuan, *China* **58 C6** 29 9N 107 6 E
Nancy, *France* **19 D13** 48 42N 6 12 E
Nanda Devi, *India* **69 D8** 30 23N 79 59 E
Nanda Kot, *India* **69 D9** 30 17N 80 5 E
Nandan, *China* **58 E6** 24 58N 107 29 E
Nandan, *Japan* **55 G7** 34 10N 134 42 E
Nanded, *India* **66 K10** 19 10N 77 20 E
Nandewar Ra., *Australia* **95 E5** 30 15 S 150 35 E
Nandi, *Fiji* **91 C7** 17 42 S 177 20 E
Nandigram, *India* **69 H12** 22 1N 87 58 E
Nandurbar, *India* **66 J9** 21 20N 74 15 E
Nandyal, *India* **66 M11** 15 30N 78 30 E
Nanfeng, *Guangdong, China* **59 F8** 23 45N 111 47 E
Nanfeng, *Jiangxi, China* **59 D11** 27 12N 115 16 E
Nanga-Eboko, *Cameroon* **83 E7** 4 41N 12 22 E
Nanga Parbat, *Pakistan* **69 B6** 35 10N 74 35 E
Nangade, *Mozam.* **87 E4** 11 5 S 39 36 E
Nangapinoh, *Indonesia* **62 E4** 0 20 S 111 44 E
Nangarhār □, *Afghan.* **66 B7** 34 20N 70 0 E
Nangatayap, *Indonesia* **62 E4** 1 32 S 110 34 E
Nangeya Mts., *Uganda* **86 B3** 3 30N 33 30 E
Nangis, *France* **19 D10** 48 33N 3 0 E
Nangong, *China* **56 F8** 37 23N 115 22 E
Nanhua, *China* **58 E3** 25 13N 101 21 E
Nanhuang, *China* **57 F11** 36 58N 121 48 E
Nanhui, *China* **59 B13** 31 5N 121 44 E
Nanjeko, *Zambia* **87 F1** 15 31 S 23 30 E
Nanji Shan, *China* **59 D13** 27 27N 121 4 E
Nanjian, *China* **58 E3** 25 2N 100 25 E
Nanjiang, *China* **58 A6** 32 28N 106 51 E
Nanjing, *Fujian, China* **59 E11** 24 25N 117 20 E
Nanjing, *Jiangsu, China* **59 A12** 32 2N 118 47 E
Nanjirinji, *Tanzania* **87 D4** 9 41 S 39 5 E
Nankana Sahib, *Pakistan* **68 D5** 31 27N 73 38 E
Nankang, *China* **59 E10** 25 40N 114 45 E
Nanking = Nanjing, *China* **59 A12** 32 2N 118 47 E
Nankoku, *Japan* **55 H6** 33 39N 133 44 E
Nanling, *China* **59 B12** 30 55N 118 20 E
Nanning, *China* **58 F7** 22 48N 108 20 E
Nannup, *Australia* **93 F2** 33 59 S 115 48 E
Nanpan Jiang →, *China* **58 E6** 25 10N 106 5 E
Nanpara, *India* **69 F9** 27 52N 81 33 E
Nanpi, *China* **56 E9** 38 2N 116 45 E
Nanping, *Fujian, China* **59 D12** 26 38N 118 10 E
Nanping, *Henan, China* **59 C9** 29 55N 112 3 E
Nanri Dao, *China* **59 E12** 25 15N 119 25 E
Nanripe, *Mozam.* **87 E4** 13 52 S 38 52 E
Nansei-Shotō = Ryūkyū-rettō, *Japan* **55 M3** 26 0N 126 0 E
Nansen Sd., *Canada* **4 A3** 81 0N 91 0W
Nanshan I., *S. China Sea* **62 B5** 10 45N 115 49 E
Nansio, *Tanzania* **86 C3** 2 3 S 33 4 E
Nant, *France* **20 D7** 44 1N 3 18 E
Nanterre, *France* **19 D9** 48 53N 2 13 E
Nantes, *France* **18 E5** 47 12N 1 33W
Nantiat, *France* **20 B5** 46 1N 1 11 E
Nanticoke, *U.S.A.* **111 E8** 41 12N 76 0W
Nanton, *Canada* **104 C6** 50 21N 113 46W
Nantong, *China* **59 A13** 32 1N 120 52 E
Nantou, *Taiwan* **59 F13** 23 57N 120 35 E
Nantua, *France* **19 F12** 46 10N 5 35 E
Nantucket I., *U.S.A.* **108 E10** 41 16N 70 5W
Nantwich, *U.K.* **12 D5** 53 4N 2 31W
Nanty Glo, *U.S.A.* **110 F6** 40 28N 78 50W
Nanuque, *Brazil* **125 G10** 17 50 S 40 21W
Nanusa, Kepulauan, *Indonesia* **63 D7** 4 45N 127 1 E
Nanutarra Roadhouse, *Australia* **92 D2** 22 32 S 115 30 E
Nanxi, *China* **58 C5** 28 54N 104 59 E
Nanxiong, *China* **59 E10** 25 6N 114 15 E
Nanyang, *China* **56 H7** 33 11N 112 30 E
Nanyi Hu, *China* **59 B12** 31 5N 119 0 E
Nanyuki, *Kenya* **86 B4** 0 2N 37 4 E
Nanzhang, *China* **59 B8** 31 45N 111 50 E
Nao, C. de la, *Spain* **33 G5** 38 44N 0 14 E
Naococane, L., *Canada* **103 B5** 52 50N 70 45W
Náousa, *Imathía, Greece* **40 F6** 40 42N 22 9 E
Náousa, *Kikládhes, Greece* **39 D7** 37 7N 25 14 E
Naozhou Dao, *China* **59 G8** 20 55N 110 20 E
Napa, *U.S.A.* **116 G4** 38 18N 122 17W
Napa →, *U.S.A.* **116 G4** 38 10N 122 19W
Napanee, *Canada* **102 D4** 44 15N 77 0W
Napanoch, *U.S.A.* **111 E10** 41 44N 74 22W
Nape, *Laos* **64 C5** 18 18N 105 6 E
Nape Pass = Keo Neua, Deo, *Vietnam* **64 C5** 18 23N 105 10 E
Napier, *N.Z.* **91 H6** 39 30 S 176 56 E
Napier Broome B., *Australia* **92 B4** 14 2 S 126 37 E
Napier Pen., *Australia* **94 A2** 12 4 S 135 43 E
Napierville, *Canada* **111 A11** 45 11N 73 25W
Naples = Nápoli, *Italy* **31 B7** 40 50N 14 15 E
Naples, *U.S.A.* **109 M5** 26 8N 81 48W
Napo, *China* **58 F5** 23 22N 105 50 E
Napo →, *Peru* **122 D3** 3 20 S 72 40W
Napoleon, *N. Dak., U.S.A.* **112 B5** 46 30N 99 46W
Napoleon, *Ohio, U.S.A.* **108 E3** 41 23N 84 8W
Nápoli, *Italy* **31 B7** 40 50N 14 15 E
Nápoli, G. di, *Italy* **31 B7** 40 43N 14 10 E
Napopo, *Dem. Rep. of the Congo* **86 B2** 4 15N 28 0 E
Naqâda, *Egypt* **80 B3** 25 53N 32 42 E
Naqadeh, *Iran* **73 D11** 36 57N 45 23 E
Naqb, Ra's an, *Jordan* **75 F4** 30 0N 35 29 E
Naqqāsh, *Iran* **71 C6** 35 40N 49 6 E
Nara, *Japan* **55 G7** 34 40N 135 49 E
Nara, *Mali* **82 B3** 15 10N 7 20W
Nara □, *Japan* **55 G8** 34 30N 136 0 E
Nara Canal, *Pakistan* **68 G3** 24 30N 69 20 E
Nara Visa, *U.S.A.* **113 H3** 35 37N 103 6W
Naracoorte, *Australia* **95 F3** 36 58 S 140 45 E
Naradhan, *Australia* **95 E4** 33 34 S 146 17 E
Naraini, *India* **69 G9** 25 11N 80 29 E
Narasapur, *India* **67 L12** 16 26N 81 40 E
Narathiwat, *Thailand* **65 J3** 6 30N 101 48 E
Narayanganj, *Bangla.* **67 H17** 23 40N 90 33 E
Narayanpet, *India* **66 L10** 16 45N 77 30 E
Narbonne, *France* **20 E7** 43 11N 3 0 E
Narcea →, *Spain* **34 B4** 43 33N 6 44W
Nardīn, *Iran* **71 B7** 37 3N 55 59 E
Nardò, *Italy* **31 B11** 40 11N 18 2 E
Narembeen, *Australia* **93 F2** 32 7 S 118 24 E
Narendranagar, *India* **68 D8** 30 10N 78 18 E
Nares Str., *Arctic* **98 A13** 80 0N 70 0W
Naretha, *Australia* **93 F3** 31 0 S 124 45 E
Narew →, *Poland* **45 F7** 52 26N 20 41 E
Nari →, *Pakistan* **68 F2** 28 0N 67 40 E
Narin, *Afghan.* **66 A6** 36 5N 69 0 E
Narindra, Helodranon' i, *Madag.* **89 A8** 14 55 S 47 30 E
Narita, *Japan* **55 G10** 35 47N 140 19 E
Närke, *Sweden* **10 E8** 59 10N 15 0 E
Narmada →, *India* **68 J5** 21 38N 72 36 E
Narman, *Turkey* **73 B9** 40 26N 41 57 E
Narmland, *Sweden* **9 F15** 60 0N 13 30 E
Narnaul, *India* **68 E7** 28 5N 76 11 E
Narni, *Italy* **29 F9** 42 30N 12 30 E
Naro, *Ghana* **82 C4** 10 22N 2 27W
Naro Fominsk, *Russia* **46 E9** 55 23N 36 43 E
Narodnaya, *Russia* **6 B17** 65 5N 59 58 E
Narok, *Kenya* **86 C4** 1 55 S 35 52 E
Narón, *Spain* **34 B2** 43 32N 8 9W
Narooma, *Australia* **95 F5** 36 14 S 150 4 E
Narowal, *Pakistan* **68 C6** 32 6N 74 52 E
Narrabri, *Australia* **95 E4** 30 19 S 149 46 E
Narran →, *Australia* **95 D4** 28 37 S 148 12 E
Narrandera, *Australia* **95 E4** 34 42 S 146 31 E
Narrogin, *Australia* **93 F2** 32 58 S 117 14 E
Narromine, *Australia* **95 E4** 32 12 S 148 12 E
Narrow Hills Prov. Park, *Canada* **105 C8** 54 0N 104 37W
Narsimhapur, *India* **69 H8** 22 54N 79 14 E
Narsinghgarh, *India* **68 H7** 23 45N 76 40 E
Nartes, L. e, *Albania* **40 F3** 40 32N 19 20 E
Nartkala, *Russia* **49 J6** 43 33N 43 51 E
Naruto, *Japan* **55 G7** 34 11N 134 37 E
Narva, *Estonia* **46 C5** 59 23N 28 12 E
Narva →, *Russia* **9 G22** 59 27N 28 2 E
Narvik, *Norway* **8 B17** 68 28N 17 26 E
Narvskoye Vdkhr., *Russia* **46 C5** 59 18N 28 14 E
Narwana, *India* **68 E7** 29 39N 76 6 E
Naryan-Mar, *Russia* **50 C6** 67 42N 53 12 E
Narym, *Russia* **50 D9** 59 0N 81 30 E
Naryn, *Kyrgyzstan* **50 E8** 41 26N 75 58 E
Nasa, *Norway* **8 C16** 66 29N 15 23 E
Nasarawa, *Nigeria* **83 D6** 8 32N 7 41 E
Năsăud, *Romania* **43 C9** 47 19N 24 29 E
Naseby, *N.Z.* **91 L3** 45 1 S 170 10 E
Naselle, *U.S.A.* **116 D3** 46 22N 123 49W
Naser, Buheirat en, *Egypt* **80 C3** 23 0N 32 30 E
Nashua, *Mont., U.S.A.* **114 B10** 48 8N 106 22W
Nashua, *N.H., U.S.A.* **111 D13** 42 45N 71 28W
Nashville, *Ark., U.S.A.* **113 J8** 33 57N 93 51W
Nashville, *Ga., U.S.A.* **109 K4** 31 12N 83 15W
Nashville, *Tenn., U.S.A.* **109 G2** 36 10N 86 47W
Našice, *Croatia* **42 E3** 45 32N 18 4 E
Nasielsk, *Poland* **45 F7** 52 35N 20 50 E
Nasik, *India* **66 K8** 19 58N 73 50 E
Nasipit, *Phil.* **61 G6** 8 57N 125 19 E
Nasir, *Sudan* **81 F3** 8 36N 33 4 E
Nasirabad, *India* **68 F6** 26 15N 74 45 E
Nasirabad, *Pakistan* **68 E3** 28 23N 68 24 E
Naskaupi →, *Canada* **103 B7** 53 47N 60 51W
Naso, *Italy* **31 D7** 38 7N 14 47 E
Naşrābād, *Iran* **71 C6** 34 8N 51 26 E
Naşriān-e Pā'īn, *Iran* **70 C5** 32 52N 46 52 E
Nass →, *Canada* **104 C3** 55 0N 129 40W
Nassarawa □, *Nigeria* **83 D6** 8 30N 8 20 E
Nassau, *Bahamas* **120 A4** 25 5N 77 20W
Nassau, *U.S.A.* **111 D11** 42 31N 73 37W
Nassau, B., *Chile* **128 H3** 55 20 S 68 0W
Nasser, L. = Naser, Buheirat en, *Egypt* **80 C3** 23 0N 32 30 E
Nasser City = Kôm Ombo, *Egypt* **80 C3** 24 25N 32 52 E
Nassian, *Ivory C.* **82 D4** 8 28N 3 28W
Nässjö, *Sweden* **11 G8** 57 39N 14 42 E
Nastapoka →, *Canada* **102 A4** 56 55N 76 33W
Nastapoka, Is., *Canada* **102 A4** 56 55N 76 50W
Nasugbu, *Phil.* **61 D4** 14 5N 120 38 E
Näsum, *Sweden* **11 H8** 56 10N 14 29 E
Näsviken, *Sweden* **10 C10** 61 46N 16 52 E
Nata, *Botswana* **88 C4** 20 12 S 26 12 E
Nata →, *Botswana* **88 C4** 20 14 S 26 10 E
Natal, *Brazil* **125 E11** 5 47 S 35 13W
Natal, *Indonesia* **62 D1** 0 35N 99 7 E
Natal, *S. Africa* **85 K6** 28 30 S 30 30 E
Natalinci, *Serbia, Yug.* **42 F5** 44 15N 20 49 E
Naţanz, *Iran* **71 C6** 33 30N 51 55 E
Natashquan, *Canada* **103 B7** 50 14N 61 46W
Natashquan →, *Canada* **103 B7** 50 7N 61 50W
Natchez, *U.S.A.* **113 K9** 31 34N 91 24W
Natchitoches, *U.S.A.* **113 K8** 31 46N 93 5W
Nathalia, *Australia* **95 F4** 36 1 S 145 13 E
Nathdwara, *India* **68 G5** 24 55N 73 50 E
Nati, Pta., *Spain* **37 A10** 40 3N 3 50 E
Natimuk, *Australia* **95 F3** 36 42 S 142 0 E
Nation →, *Canada* **104 B4** 55 30N 123 32W
National City, *U.S.A.* **117 N9** 32 41N 117 6W
Natitingou, *Benin* **83 C5** 10 20N 1 26 E
Natividad, I., *Mexico* **118 B1** 27 50N 115 10W
Natkyizin, *Burma* **64 E1** 14 57N 97 59 E
Natron, L., *Tanzania* **86 C4** 2 20 S 36 0 E
Natrona Heights, *U.S.A.* **110 F5** 40 37N 79 44W
Natrûn, W. el →, *Egypt* **80 H7** 30 25N 30 13 E
Nättraby, *Sweden* **11 H9** 56 13N 15 31 E
Natukanaoka Pan, *Namibia* **88 B2** 18 40 S 15 45 E
Natuna Besar, Kepulauan, *Indonesia* **65 L7** 4 0N 108 15 E
Natuna Is. = Natuna Besar, Kepulauan, *Indonesia* **65 L7** 4 0N 108 15 E
Natuna Selatan, Kepulauan, *Indonesia* **65 L7** 2 45N 109 0 E
Natural Bridge, *U.S.A.* **111 B9** 44 5N 75 30W
Naturaliste, C., *Australia* **94 G4** 40 50 S 148 15 E
Nau Qala, *Afghan.* **68 B3** 34 5N 68 5 E
Naucelle, *France* **20 D6** 44 13N 2 20 E
Nauders, *Austria* **26 E3** 46 54N 10 30 E
Nauen, *Germany* **24 C8** 52 36N 12 52 E
Naugatuck, *U.S.A.* **111 E11** 41 30N 73 3W
Naujoji Akmenė, *Lithuania* **44 B9** 56 19N 22 54 E
Naumburg, *Germany* **24 D7** 51 9N 11 47 E
Nā'ūr at Tunayb, *Jordan* **75 D4** 31 48N 35 57 E
Nauru ■, *Pac. Oc.* **96 H8** 1 0 S 166 0 E
Naushahra = Nowshera, *Pakistan* **66 C8** 34 0N 72 0 E
Naushahro, *Pakistan* **68 F3** 26 50N 68 7 E
Naushon I., *U.S.A.* **111 E14** 41 29N 70 45W
Nauta, *Peru* **124 D4** 4 31 S 73 35W
Nautanwa, *India* **67 F13** 27 20N 83 25 E
Nautla, *Mexico* **119 C5** 20 20N 96 50W
Nava, *Mexico* **118 B4** 28 25N 100 46W
Nava, *Spain* **34 B5** 43 21N 5 31W
Nava del Rey, *Spain* **34 D5** 41 22N 5 6W
Navadwip, *India* **69 H13** 23 34N 88 20 E
Navahermosa, *Spain* **35 F6** 39 41N 4 28W
Navahrudak, *Belarus* **46 F3** 53 40N 25 50 E
Navajo Reservoir, *U.S.A.* **115 H10** 36 48N 107 36W
Navalcarnero, *Spain* **34 E6** 40 17N 4 5W
Navalmoral de la Mata, *Spain* **34 F5** 39 52N 5 33W
Navalvillar de Pela, *Spain* **35 F5** 39 9N 5 24W
Navan = An Uaimh, *Ireland* **15 C5** 53 39N 6 41W
Navapolatsk, *Belarus* **46 E5** 55 32N 28 37 E
Navarino, I., *Chile* **128 H3** 55 0 S 67 40W
Navarra □, *Spain* **32 C3** 42 40N 1 40W
Navarre, *U.S.A.* **110 F3** 40 43N 81 31W
Navarro →, *U.S.A.* **116 F3** 39 11N 123 45W
Navas de San Juan, *Spain* **35 G7** 38 30N 3 19W
Navasota, *U.S.A.* **113 K6** 30 23N 96 5W
Navassa I., *W. Indies* **121 C5** 18 30N 75 0W
Nävekvarn, *Sweden* **11 F10** 58 38N 16 49 E
Naver →, *U.K.* **14 C4** 58 32N 4 14W
Navia, *Spain* **34 B4** 43 35N 6 42W
Navia →, *Spain* **34 B4** 43 15N 6 50W
Navia de Suarna, *Spain* **34 C3** 42 58N 7 3W
Navibandar, *India* **68 J3** 21 26N 69 48 E
Navidad, *Chile* **126 C1** 33 57 S 71 50W
Naviraí, *Brazil* **127 A5** 23 8 S 54 13W
Navlakhi, *India* **68 H4** 22 58N 70 28 E
Navlya, *Russia* **47 F8** 52 53N 34 30 E

Năvodari, *Romania* **43 F13** 44 19N 28 36 E
Navoi = Nawoiy, *Uzbekistan* **50 E7** 40 9N 65 22 E
Navojoa, *Mexico* **118 B3** 27 0N 109 30W
Navolato, *Mexico* **118 C3** 24 47N 107 42W
Návpaktos, *Greece* **38 C3** 38 24N 21 50 E
Návplion, *Greece* **38 D4** 37 33N 22 50 E
Navrongo, *Ghana* **83 C4** 10 51N 1 3W
Navsari, *India* **66 J8** 20 57N 72 59 E
Nawa Kot, *Pakistan* **68 E4** 28 21N 71 24 E
Nawab Khan, *Pakistan* **68 D3** 30 17N 69 12 E
Nawabganj, *Ut. P., India* **69 F9** 26 56N 81 14 E
Nawabganj, *Ut. P., India* **69 E8** 28 32N 79 40 E
Nawabshah, *Pakistan* **68 F3** 26 15N 68 25 E
Nawada, *India* **69 G11** 24 50N 85 33 E
Nawakot, *Nepal* **69 F11** 27 55N 85 10 E
Nawalgarh, *India* **68 F6** 27 50N 75 15 E
Nawanshahr, *India* **69 C6** 32 33N 74 48 E
Nawar, Dasht-i-, *Afghan.* **68 C3** 33 52N 68 0 E
Nawi, *Sudan* **80 D3** 18 32N 30 50 E
Nawoiy, *Uzbekistan* **50 E7** 40 9N 65 22 E
Naxçıvan, *Azerbaijan* **70 B5** 39 12N 45 15 E
Naxçıvan □, *Azerbaijan* **50 F5** 39 25N 45 26 E
Náxos, *Greece* **39 D7** 37 8N 25 25 E
Nay, *France* **20 E3** 43 10N 0 18W
Nay, Mui, *Vietnam* **62 B3** 12 55N 109 23 E
Nāy Band, *Būshehr, Iran* **71 E7** 27 20N 52 40 E
Nāy Band, *Khorāsān, Iran* **71 C8** 32 20N 57 34 E
Nayakhan, *Russia* **51 C16** 61 56N 159 0 E
Nayarit □, *Mexico* **118 C4** 22 0N 105 0W
Nayé, *Senegal* **82 C2** 14 28N 12 12W
Nayong, *China* **58 D5** 26 50N 105 20 E
Nayoro, *Japan* **54 B11** 44 21N 142 28 E
Nayyāl, W. →, *Si. Arabia* **70 D3** 28 35N 39 4 E
Nazaré, *Brazil* **125 F11** 13 2S 39 0W
Nazaré, *Portugal* **35 F1** 39 36N 9 4W
Nazareth = Nazerat, *Israel* **75 C4** 32 42N 35 17 E
Nazareth, *U.S.A.* **111 F9** 40 44N 75 19W
Nazas, *Mexico* **118 B4** 25 10N 104 6W
Nazas →, *Mexico* **118 B4** 25 35N 103 25W
Nazca, *Peru* **124 F4** 14 50 S 74 57W
Naze, The, *U.K.* **13 F9** 51 53N 1 18 E
Nazerat, *Israel* **75 C4** 32 42N 35 17 E
Nāzīk, *Iran* **70 B5** 39 1N 45 4 E
Nazilli, *Turkey* **39 D10** 37 55N 28 15 E
Nazir Hat, *Bangla.* **67 H17** 22 35N 91 49 E
Nazko, *Canada* **104 C4** 53 1N 123 37W
Nazko →, *Canada* **104 C4** 53 7N 123 34W
Nazret, *Ethiopia* **81 F4** 8 32N 39 22 E
Nazwá, *Oman* **74 C6** 22 56N 57 32 E
Nchanga, *Zambia* **87 E2** 12 30 S 27 49 E
Ncheu, *Malawi* **87 E3** 14 50 S 34 47 E
Ndala, *Tanzania* **86 C3** 4 45 S 33 15 E
Ndalatando, *Angola* **84 F2** 9 12 S 14 48 E
Ndali, *Benin* **83 D5** 9 50N 2 46 E
Ndareda, *Tanzania* **86 C4** 4 12 S 35 30 E
Ndélé, *C.A.R.* **84 C4** 8 25N 20 36 E
Ndikinimeki, *Cameroon* **83 E7** 4 46N 10 50 E
N'Dioum, *Senegal* **82 B2** 16 31N 14 39W
Ndjamena, *Chad* **79 F8** 12 10N 14 59 E
Ndola, *Zambia* **87 E2** 13 0 S 28 34 E
Ndoto Mts., *Kenya* **86 B4** 2 0N 37 0 E
Nduguti, *Tanzania* **86 C3** 4 18 S 34 41 E
Néa Alikarnassós, *Greece* **39 F7** 35 18N 25 13 E
Néa Ankhíalos, *Greece* **38 B4** 39 16N 22 49 E
Néa Epídhavros, *Greece* **38 D5** 37 40N 23 7 E
Néa Flippiás, *Greece* **38 B2** 39 12N 20 53 E
Néa Ionia, *Greece* **38 B4** 39 21N 22 56 E
Néa Kallikrátia, *Greece* **40 F7** 40 21N 23 3 E
Néa Mákri, *Greece* **38 C5** 38 5N 23 59 E
Néa Moudhaniá, *Greece* **40 F7** 40 15N 23 17 E
Néa Péramos, *Attikí, Greece* **38 C5** 38 0N 23 26 E
Néa Péramos, *Kavála, Greece* **41 F8** 40 50N 24 18 E
Néa Víssi, *Greece* **41 E10** 41 34N 26 33 E
Néa Zíkhna, *Greece* **40 E7** 41 2N 23 49 E
Neagh, Lough, *U.K.* **15 B5** 54 37N 6 25W
Neah Bay, *U.S.A.* **116 B2** 48 22N 124 37W
Neale, L., *Australia* **92 D5** 24 15 S 130 0 E
Neamt □, *Romania* **43 C11** 47 0N 26 20 E
Neápolis, *Kozáni, Greece* **40 F5** 40 20N 21 24 E
Neápolis, *Kríti, Greece* **36 D7** 35 15N 25 37 E
Neápolis, *Lakonía, Greece* **38 E5** 36 27N 23 8 E
Near Is., *U.S.A.* **100 C1** 52 30N 174 0 E
Neath, *U.K.* **13 F4** 51 39N 3 48W
Neath Port Talbot □, *U.K.* **13 F4** 51 42N 3 45W
Nebbou, *Burkina Faso* **83 C4** 11 9N 1 51W
Nebelat el Hagana, *Sudan* **81 E2** 13 13N 29 2 E
Nebine Cr. →, *Australia* **95 D4** 29 27 S 146 56 E
Nebitdag, *Turkmenistan* **50 F6** 39 30N 54 22 E
Nebo, *Australia* **94 C4** 21 42 S 148 42 E
Nebolchy, *Russia* **46 C7** 59 8N 33 18 E
Nebraska □, *U.S.A.* **112 E5** 41 30N 99 30W
Nebraska City, *U.S.A.* **112 E7** 40 41N 95 52W
Nébrodi, Monti, *Italy* **31 E7** 37 54N 14 35 E
Necedah, *U.S.A.* **112 C9** 44 2N 90 4W
Nechako →, *Canada* **104 C4** 53 30N 122 44W
Neches →, *U.S.A.* **113 L8** 29 58N 93 51W
Neckar →, *Germany* **25 F4** 49 27N 8 29 E
Necochea, *Argentina* **126 D4** 38 30 S 58 50W
Neda, *Spain* **34 B2** 43 30N 8 9W
Nedelino, *Bulgaria* **41 E9** 41 27N 25 3 E
Nedelišće, *Croatia* **29 B13** 46 23N 16 22 E
Nédha →, *Greece* **38 D3** 37 25N 21 45 E
Needles, *Canada* **104 D5** 49 53N 118 7W
Needles, *U.S.A.* **117 L12** 34 51N 114 37W
Needles, The, *U.K.* **13 G6** 50 39N 1 35W
Ñeembucú □, *Paraguay* **126 B4** 27 0 S 58 0W
Neemuch = Nimach, *India* **68 G6** 24 30N 74 56 E
Neenah, *U.S.A.* **108 C1** 44 11N 88 28W
Neepawa, *Canada* **105 C9** 50 15N 99 30W
Neftçala, *Azerbaijan* **71 B6** 39 19N 49 12 E
Neftegorsk, *Russia* **49 H4** 44 25N 39 45 E
Neftekumsk, *Russia* **49 H7** 44 46N 44 50 E
Nefyn, *U.K.* **12 E3** 52 56N 4 31W
Négala, *Mali* **82 C3** 12 52N 8 30W
Negapatam = Nagappattinam, *India* **66 P11** 10 46N 79 51 E
Negaunee, *U.S.A.* **108 B2** 46 30N 87 36W
Negele, *Ethiopia* **81 F4** 5 20N 39 36 E
Negev Desert = Hanegev, *Israel* **75 E4** 30 50N 35 0 E
Negoiul, Vf., *Romania* **43 E9** 45 38N 24 35 E
Negombo, *Sri Lanka* **66 R11** 7 12N 79 50 E
Negotin, *Serbia, Yug.* **40 B6** 44 16N 22 37 E
Negotino, *Macedonia* **40 E6** 41 29N 22 7 E
Negra, Peña, *Spain* **34 C4** 42 11N 6 30W
Negra, Pta., *Peru* **122 D2** 6 6 S 81 10W
Negrais, C. = Maudin Sun, *Burma* **67 M19** 16 0N 94 30 E
Negrești, *Romania* **43 D12** 46 50N 27 30 E
Negrești-Oaș, *Romania* **43 C8** 47 52N 23 26 E
Negril, *Jamaica* **120 C4** 18 22N 78 20W
Negro →, *Argentina* **122 H4** 41 2 S 62 47W
Negro →, *Brazil* **122 D4** 3 0 S 60 0W
Negro →, *Uruguay* **127 C4** 33 24 S 58 22W
Negros, *Phil.* **61 G5** 9 30N 122 40 E
Negru Vodă, *Romania* **43 G13** 43 47N 28 21 E
Neguac, *Canada* **103 C6** 47 15N 65 5W
Nehalem →, *U.S.A.* **116 E3** 45 40N 123 56W
Nehāvand, *Iran* **71 C6** 35 56N 49 31 E
Nehbandān, *Iran* **71 D9** 31 35N 60 5 E
Nehoiu, *Romania* **43 E11** 45 24N 26 20 E
Nei Monggol Zizhiqu □, *China* **56 D7** 42 0N 112 0 E
Neijiang, *China* **58 C5** 29 35N 104 55 E
Neillsville, *U.S.A.* **112 C9** 44 34N 90 36W
Neilton, *U.S.A.* **114 C2** 47 25N 123 53W
Neiqiu, *China* **56 F8** 37 15N 114 30 E
Neiva, *Colombia* **124 C3** 2 56N 75 18W
Neixiang, *China* **56 H6** 33 10N 111 52 E
Nejanilini L., *Canada* **105 B9** 59 33N 97 48W
Nejd = Najd, *Si. Arabia* **74 B3** 26 30N 42 0 E
Nejo, *Ethiopia* **81 F4** 9 30N 35 28 E
Nekā, *Iran* **71 B7** 36 39N 53 19 E
Nekemte, *Ethiopia* **81 F4** 9 4N 36 30 E
Nêkheb, *Egypt* **80 B3** 25 10N 32 48 E
Neksø, *Denmark* **11 J9** 55 4N 15 8 E
Nelas, *Portugal* **34 E3** 40 32N 7 52W
Nelia, *Australia* **94 C3** 20 39 S 142 12 E
Nelidovo, *Russia* **46 D7** 56 13N 32 49 E
Neligh, *U.S.A.* **112 D5** 42 8N 98 2W
Nelkan, *Russia* **51 D14** 57 40N 136 4 E
Nellore, *India* **66 M11** 14 27N 79 59 E
Nelson, *Canada* **104 D5** 49 30N 117 20W
Nelson, *N.Z.* **91 J4** 41 18 S 173 16 E
Nelson, *U.K.* **12 D5** 53 50N 2 13W
Nelson, *Ariz., U.S.A.* **115 J7** 35 31N 113 19W
Nelson, *Nev., U.S.A.* **117 K12** 35 42N 114 50W
Nelson →, *Canada* **105 C9** 54 33N 98 2W
Nelson, C., *Australia* **95 F3** 38 26 S 141 32 E
Nelson, Estrecho, *Chile* **128 G2** 51 30 S 75 0W
Nelson Bay, *Australia* **95 E5** 32 43 S 152 9 E
Nelson Forks, *Canada* **104 B4** 59 30N 124 0W
Nelson House, *Canada* **105 B9** 55 47N 98 51W
Nelson L., *Canada* **105 B8** 55 48N 100 7W
Nelspoort, *S. Africa* **88 E3** 32 7 S 23 0 E
Nelspruit, *S. Africa* **89 D5** 25 29 S 30 59 E
Néma, *Mauritania* **82 B3** 16 40N 7 15W
Neman, *Russia* **9 J20** 55 2N 22 2 E
Neman →, *Lithuania* **9 J19** 55 25N 21 10 E
Neméa, *Greece* **38 D4** 37 49N 22 40 E
Nemeiben L., *Canada* **105 B7** 55 20N 105 20W
Nemërçkë, Mal, *Albania* **40 F4** 40 15N 20 15 E
Nemërçkës, Mal i = Nemërçkë, Mal, *Albania* **40 F4** 40 15N 20 15 E
Nemira, Vf., *Romania* **43 D11** 46 17N 26 19 E
Némiscau, *Canada* **102 B4** 51 18N 76 54W
Némiscau, L., *Canada* **102 B4** 51 25N 76 40W
Nemours, *France* **19 D9** 48 16N 2 40 E
Nemšová, *Slovak Rep.* **27 C11** 48 58N 18 7 E
Nemunas = Neman →, *Lithuania* **9 J19** 55 25N 21 10 E
Nemuro, *Japan* **54 C12** 43 20N 145 35 E
Nemuro-Kaikyō, *Japan* **54 C12** 43 30N 145 30 E
Nen Jiang →, *China* **57 B13** 45 28N 124 30 E
Nenagh, *Ireland* **15 D3** 52 52N 8 11W
Nenasi, *Malaysia* **65 L4** 3 9N 103 23 E
Nene →, *U.K.* **13 E8** 52 49N 0 11 E
Nénita, *Greece* **39 C8** 38 14N 26 6 E
Nenjiang, *China* **60 B7** 49 10N 125 10 E
Neno, *Malawi* **87 F3** 15 25 S 34 40 E
Neodesha, *U.S.A.* **113 G7** 37 25N 95 41W
Neokhórion, *Aitolía kai Akarnanía, Greece* **38 C3** 38 25N 21 17 E
Neokhórion, *Árta, Greece* **38 B2** 39 4N 21 0 E
Néon Karlovásion, *Greece* **39 D8** 37 45N 26 42 E
Néon Petrítsi, *Greece* **40 E7** 41 16N 23 15 E
Neosho, *U.S.A.* **113 G7** 36 52N 94 22W
Neosho →, *U.S.A.* **113 H7** 36 48N 95 18W
Nepal ■, *Asia* **69 F11** 28 0N 84 30 E
Nepalganj, *Nepal* **69 E9** 28 5N 81 40 E
Nepalganj Road, *India* **69 E9** 28 1N 81 41 E
Nephi, *U.S.A.* **114 G8** 39 43N 111 50W
Nephin, *Ireland* **15 B2** 54 1N 9 22W
Nepi, *Italy* **29 F9** 42 14N 12 21 E
Nepomuk, *Czech Rep.* **26 B6** 49 29N 13 35 E
Neptune, *U.S.A.* **111 F10** 40 13N 74 2W
Nera →, *Italy* **29 F9** 42 26N 12 24 E
Nera →, *Romania* **42 F6** 44 48N 21 25 E
Nérac, *France* **20 D4** 44 8N 0 21 E
Nerang, *Australia* **95 D5** 27 58 S 153 20 E
Neratovice, *Czech Rep.* **26 A7** 50 16N 14 31 E
Nerchinsk, *Russia* **51 D12** 52 0N 116 39 E
Nereju, *Romania* **43 E11** 45 43N 26 43 E
Nerekhta, *Russia* **46 D11** 57 26N 40 38 E
Néret, L., *Canada* **103 B5** 54 45N 70 44W
Neretvanski Kanal, *Croatia* **29 E14** 43 7N 17 10 E
Neringa, *Lithuania* **9 J19** 55 20N 21 5 E
Nerja, *Spain* **35 J7** 36 43N 3 55W
Nerl →, *Russia* **46 D11** 56 11N 40 34 E
Nerpio, *Spain* **33 G2** 38 11N 2 16W
Nerva, *Spain* **35 H4** 37 42N 6 30W
Nervi, *Italy* **28 D6** 44 23N 9 2 E
Neryungri, *Russia* **51 D13** 57 38N 124 28 E
Nescopeck, *U.S.A.* **111 E8** 41 3N 76 12W
Nesebŭr, *Bulgaria* **41 D11** 42 41N 27 46 E
Ness, L., *U.K.* **14 D4** 57 15N 4 32W
Ness City, *U.S.A.* **112 F5** 38 27N 99 54W
Nesterov, *Poland* **47 G2** 50 4N 23 58 E
Nestórion, *Greece* **40 F5** 40 24N 21 5 E
Néstos →, *Greece* **41 E8** 41 20N 24 35 E
Nesvady, *Slovak Rep.* **27 D11** 47 56N 18 7 E
Nesvizh = Nyasvizh, *Belarus* **47 F4** 53 14N 26 38 E
Netanya, *Israel* **75 C3** 32 20N 34 51 E
Netarhat, *India* **69 H11** 23 29N 84 16 E
Nete →, *Belgium* **17 C4** 51 7N 4 14 E
Netherdale, *Australia* **94 C4** 21 10 S 148 33 E
Netherlands ■, *Europe* **17 C5** 52 0N 5 30 E
Netherlands Antilles ■, *W. Indies* **124 A5** 12 15N 69 0W
Neto →, *Italy* **31 C10** 39 12N 17 9 E
Netrang, *India* **68 J5** 21 39N 73 21 E
Nettancourt, *France* **19 D11** 48 51N 4 57 E
Nettetal, *Germany* **24 D2** 51 19N 6 12 E
Nettilling L., *Canada* **101 B12** 66 30N 71 0W
Nettuno, *Italy* **30 A5** 41 27N 12 39 E
Netzahualcoyotl, Presa, *Mexico* **119 D6** 17 10N 93 30W
Neu-Isenburg, *Germany* **25 E4** 50 3N 8 42 E
Neu-Ulm, *Germany* **25 G6** 48 22N 10 0 E
Neubrandenburg, *Germany* **24 B9** 53 33N 13 15 E
Neubukow, *Germany* **24 A7** 54 2N 11 39 E
Neuburg, *Germany* **25 G7** 48 44N 11 11 E
Neuchâtel, *Switz.* **25 J2** 47 0N 6 55 E
Neuchâtel □, *Switz.* **25 J2** 47 0N 6 55 E
Neuchâtel, Lac de, *Switz.* **25 J2** 46 53N 6 50 E
Neudau, *Austria* **26 D9** 47 11N 16 6 E
Neuenhagen, *Germany* **24 C9** 52 30N 13 38 E
Neuenhaus, *Germany* **24 C2** 52 30N 6 58 E
Neuf-Brisach, *France* **19 D14** 48 1N 7 30 E
Neufahrn, *Bayern, Germany* **25 G8** 48 41N 12 11 E
Neufahrn, *Bayern, Germany* **25 G7** 48 18N 11 40 E
Neufchâteau, *Belgium* **17 E5** 49 50N 5 25 E
Neufchâteau, *France* **19 D12** 48 21N 5 40 E
Neufchâtel-en-Bray, *France* **18 C8** 49 44N 1 26 E
Neufchâtel-sur-Aisne, *France* **19 C11** 49 26N 4 1 E
Neuhaus, *Germany* **24 B6** 53 17N 10 56 E
Neuillé-Pont-Pierre, *France* **18 E7** 47 33N 0 33 E
Neuilly-St-Front, *France* **19 C10** 49 10N 3 15 E
Neukalen, *Germany* **24 B8** 53 49N 12 46 E
Neumarkt, *Germany* **25 F7** 49 26N 11 27 E
Neumünster, *Germany* **24 A5** 54 4N 9 58 E
Neung-sur-Beuvron, *France* **19 E8** 47 30N 1 50 E
Neunkirchen, *Austria* **26 D9** 47 43N 16 4 E
Neunkirchen, *Germany* **25 F3** 49 20N 7 9 E
Neuquén, *Argentina* **128 D3** 38 55 S 68 0W
Neuquén □, *Argentina* **126 D2** 38 0 S 69 50W
Neuruppin, *Germany* **24 C8** 52 55N 12 48 E
Neusäss, *Germany* **25 G6** 48 24N 10 50 E
Neuse →, *U.S.A.* **109 H7** 35 6N 76 29W
Neusiedl, *Austria* **27 D9** 47 57N 16 50 E
Neusiedler See, *Austria* **27 D9** 47 50N 16 47 E
Neuss, *Germany* **24 D2** 51 11N 6 42 E
Neussargues-Moissac, *France* **20 C7** 45 9N 3 0 E
Neustadt, *Bayern, Germany* **25 F8** 49 44N 12 10 E
Neustadt, *Bayern, Germany* **25 G7** 48 48N 11 46 E
Neustadt, *Bayern, Germany* **25 F6** 49 34N 10 37 E
Neustadt, *Bayern, Germany* **25 E7** 50 19N 11 7 E
Neustadt, *Brandenburg, Germany* **24 C8** 52 50N 12 27 E
Neustadt, *Hessen, Germany* **24 E5** 50 51N 9 9 E
Neustadt, *Niedersachsen, Germany* **24 C5** 52 30N 9 30 E
Neustadt, *Rhld-Pfz., Germany* **25 F4** 49 21N 8 10 E
Neustadt, *Sachsen, Germany* **24 D10** 51 2N 14 12 E
Neustadt, *Schleswig-Holstein, Germany* **24 A6** 54 6N 10 49 E
Neustadt, *Thüringen, Germany* **24 E7** 50 45N 11 43 E
Neustrelitz, *Germany* **24 B9** 53 21N 13 4 E
Neuvic, *France* **20 C6** 45 23N 2 16 E
Neuville-sur-Saône, *France* **21 C8** 45 52N 4 51 E
Neuvy-le-Roi, *France* **18 E7** 47 36N 0 36 E
Neuvy-St-Sépulchre, *France* **19 F8** 46 35N 1 48 E
Neuvy-sur-Barangeon, *France* **19 E9** 47 20N 2 15 E
Neuwerk, *Germany* **24 B4** 53 55N 8 30 E
Neuwied, *Germany* **24 E3** 50 26N 7 29 E
Neva →, *Russia* **46 C6** 59 50N 30 30 E
Nevada, *Iowa, U.S.A.* **112 D8** 42 1N 93 27W
Nevada, *Mo., U.S.A.* **113 G7** 37 51N 94 22W
Nevada □, *U.S.A.* **114 G5** 39 0N 117 0W
Nevada, Sierra, *Spain* **35 H7** 37 3N 3 15W
Nevada, Sierra, *U.S.A.* **114 G3** 39 0N 120 30W
Nevada City, *U.S.A.* **116 F6** 39 16N 121 1W
Nevado, Cerro, *Argentina* **126 D2** 35 30 S 68 32W
Nevel, *Russia* **46 D5** 56 0N 29 55 E
Nevers, *France* **19 F10** 47 0N 3 9 E
Nevertire, *Australia* **95 E4** 31 50 S 147 44 E
Nevesinje, *Bos.-H.* **40 C2** 43 14N 18 6 E
Neville, *Canada* **105 D7** 49 58N 107 39W
Nevinnomyssk, *Russia* **49 H6** 44 40N 42 0 E
Nevis, *W. Indies* **121 C7** 17 0N 62 30W
Nevrokop = Gotse Delchev, *Bulgaria* **40 E7** 41 36N 23 46 E
Nevşehir, *Turkey* **70 B2** 38 33N 34 40 E
Nevyansk, *Russia* **48 B8** 57 30N 60 13 E
New →, *U.S.A.* **108 F5** 38 10N 81 12W
New Aiyansh, *Canada* **104 B3** 55 12N 129 4W
New Albany, *Ind., U.S.A.* **108 F3** 38 18N 85 49W
New Albany, *Miss., U.S.A.* **113 H10** 34 29N 89 0W
New Albany, *Pa., U.S.A.* **111 E8** 41 36N 76 27W
New Amsterdam, *Guyana* **124 B7** 6 15N 57 36W
New Angledool, *Australia* **95 D4** 29 5 S 147 55 E
New Baltimore, *U.S.A.* **110 D2** 42 41N 82 44W
New Bedford, *U.S.A.* **111 E14** 41 38N 70 56W
New Berlin, *N.Y., U.S.A.* **111 D9** 42 37N 75 20W
New Berlin, *Pa., U.S.A.* **110 F8** 40 50N 76 57W
New Bern, *U.S.A.* **109 H7** 35 7N 77 3W
New Bethlehem, *U.S.A.* **110 F5** 41 0N 79 20W
New Bloomfield, *U.S.A.* **110 F7** 40 25N 77 11W
New Boston, *U.S.A.* **113 J7** 33 28N 94 25W
New Braunfels, *U.S.A.* **113 L5** 29 42N 98 8W
New Brighton, *N.Z.* **91 K4** 43 29 S 172 43 E
New Brighton, *U.S.A.* **110 F4** 40 42N 80 19W
New Britain, *Papua N. G.* **96 H7** 5 50 S 150 20 E
New Britain, *U.S.A.* **111 E12** 41 40N 72 47W
New Brunswick, *U.S.A.* **111 F10** 40 30N 74 27W
New Brunswick □, *Canada* **103 C6** 46 50N 66 30W
New Bussa, *Nigeria* **83 D5** 9 53N 4 31 E
New Caledonia ■, *Pac. Oc.* **96 K8** 21 0 S 165 0 E
New Castile = Castilla-La Mancha □, *Spain* **6 H5** 39 30N 3 30W
New Castle, *Ind., U.S.A.* **108 F3** 39 55N 85 22W
New Castle, *Pa., U.S.A.* **110 F4** 41 0N 80 21W
New City, *U.S.A.* **111 E11** 41 9N 73 59W
New Concord, *U.S.A.* **110 G3** 39 59N 81 54W
New Cumberland, *U.S.A.* **110 F4** 40 30N 80 36W
New Cuyama, *U.S.A.* **117 L7** 34 57N 119 38W
New Delhi, *India* **68 E7** 28 37N 77 13 E
New Denver, *Canada* **104 D5** 50 0N 117 25W
New Don Pedro Reservoir, *U.S.A.* **116 H6** 37 43N 120 24W
New England, *U.S.A.* **112 B3** 46 32N 102 52W
New England Ra., *Australia* **95 E5** 30 20 S 151 45 E
New Forest, *U.K.* **13 G6** 50 53N 1 34W
New Galloway, *U.K.* **14 F4** 55 5N 4 9W
New Glasgow, *Canada* **103 C7** 45 35N 62 36W
New Guinea, *Oceania* **52 K17** 4 0 S 136 0 E
New Hamburg, *Canada* **110 C4** 43 23N 80 42W
New Hampshire □, *U.S.A.* **111 C13** 44 0N 71 30W
New Hampton, *U.S.A.* **112 D8** 43 3N 92 19W
New Hanover, *S. Africa* **89 D5** 29 22 S 30 31 E
New Hartford, *U.S.A.* **111 C9** 43 4N 75 18W
New Haven, *Conn., U.S.A.* **111 E12** 41 18N 72 55W
New Haven, *Mich., U.S.A.* **110 D2** 42 44N 82 48W
New Hazelton, *Canada* **104 B3** 55 20N 127 30W
New Hebrides = Vanuatu ■, *Pac. Oc.* **96 J8** 15 0 S 168 0 E
New Holland, *U.S.A.* **111 F8** 40 6N 76 5W
New Iberia, *U.S.A.* **113 K9** 30 1N 91 49W
New Ireland, *Papua N. G.* **96 H7** 3 20 S 151 50 E
New Jersey □, *U.S.A.* **108 E8** 40 0N 74 30W
New Kensington, *U.S.A.* **110 F5** 40 34N 79 46W
New Lexington, *U.S.A.* **108 F4** 39 43N 82 13W
New Liskeard, *Canada* **102 C4** 47 31N 79 41W
New London, *Conn., U.S.A.* **111 E12** 41 22N 72 6W
New London, *Ohio, U.S.A.* **110 E2** 41 5N 82 24W
New London, *Wis., U.S.A.* **112 C10** 44 23N 88 45W
New Madrid, *U.S.A.* **113 G10** 36 36N 89 32W
New Martinsville, *U.S.A.* **108 F5** 39 39N 80 52W
New Meadows, *U.S.A.* **114 D5** 44 58N 116 18W
New Melones L., *U.S.A.* **116 H6** 37 57N 120 31W
New Mexico □, *U.S.A.* **115 J10** 34 30N 106 0W
New Milford, *Conn., U.S.A.* **111 E11** 41 35N 73 25W
New Milford, *Pa., U.S.A.* **111 E9** 41 52N 75 44W
New Norcia, *Australia* **93 F2** 30 57 S 116 13 E
New Norfolk, *Australia* **94 G4** 42 46 S 147 2 E
New Orleans, *U.S.A.* **113 L9** 29 58N 90 4W
New Philadelphia, *U.S.A.* **110 F3** 40 30N 81 27W
New Plymouth, *N.Z.* **91 H5** 39 4 S 174 5 E
New Plymouth, *U.S.A.* **114 E5** 43 58N 116 49W
New Port Richey, *U.S.A.* **109 L4** 28 16N 82 43W
New Providence, *Bahamas* **120 A4** 25 25N 78 35W
New Quay, *U.K.* **13 E3** 52 13N 4 21W
New Radnor, *U.K.* **13 E4** 52 15N 3 9W
New Richmond, *Canada* **103 C6** 48 15N 65 45W
New Richmond, *U.S.A.* **112 C8** 45 7N 92 32W
New Roads, *U.S.A.* **113 K9** 30 42N 91 26W
New Rochelle, *U.S.A.* **111 F11** 40 55N 73 47W
New Rockford, *U.S.A.* **112 B5** 47 41N 99 8W
New Romney, *U.K.* **13 G8** 50 59N 0 57 E
New Ross, *Ireland* **15 D5** 52 23N 6 57W
New Salem, *U.S.A.* **112 B4** 46 51N 101 25W
New Scone, *U.K.* **14 E5** 56 25N 3 24W
New Siberian I. = Novaya Sibir, Ostrov, *Russia* **51 B16** 75 10N 150 0 E
New Siberian Is. = Novosibirskiye Ostrova, *Russia* **51 B15** 75 0N 142 0 E
New Smyrna Beach, *U.S.A.* **109 L5** 29 1N 80 56W
New South Wales □, *Australia* **95 E4** 33 0 S 146 0 E
New Town, *U.S.A.* **112 B3** 47 59N 102 30W
New Tredegar, *U.K.* **13 F4** 51 44N 3 16W
New Ulm, *U.S.A.* **112 C7** 44 19N 94 28W
New Waterford, *Canada* **103 C7** 46 13N 60 4W
New Westminster, *Canada* **116 A4** 49 13N 122 55W
New York, *U.S.A.* **111 F11** 40 45N 74 0W
New York □, *U.S.A.* **111 D9** 43 0N 75 0W
New York Mts., *U.S.A.* **115 J6** 35 0N 115 20W
New Zealand ■, *Oceania* **91 J6** 40 0 S 176 0 E
Newaj →, *India* **68 G7** 24 24N 76 49 E
Newala, *Tanzania* **87 E4** 10 58 S 39 18 E
Newark, *Del., U.S.A.* **108 F8** 39 41N 75 46W
Newark, *N.J., U.S.A.* **111 F10** 40 44N 74 10W
Newark, *N.Y., U.S.A.* **110 C7** 43 3N 77 6W
Newark, *Ohio, U.S.A.* **110 F2** 40 3N 82 24W
Newark-on-Trent, *U.K.* **12 D7** 53 5N 0 48W
Newark Valley, *U.S.A.* **111 D8** 42 14N 76 11W
Newberg, *U.S.A.* **114 D2** 45 18N 122 58W
Newberry, *Mich., U.S.A.* **108 B3** 46 21N 85 30W
Newberry, *S.C., U.S.A.* **109 H5** 34 17N 81 37W
Newberry Springs, *U.S.A.* **117 L10** 34 50N 116 41W
Newboro L., *Canada* **111 B8** 44 38N 76 20W
Newbridge = Droichead Nua, *Ireland* **15 C5** 53 11N 6 48W
Newburgh, *Canada* **110 B8** 44 19N 76 52W
Newburgh, *U.S.A.* **111 E10** 41 30N 74 1W
Newbury, *U.K.* **13 F6** 51 24N 1 20W
Newbury, *N.H., U.S.A.* **111 B12** 43 19N 72 3W
Newbury, *Vt., U.S.A.* **111 B12** 44 5N 72 4W
Newburyport, *U.S.A.* **109 D10** 42 49N 70 53W
Newcastle, *Australia* **95 E5** 33 0 S 151 46 E
Newcastle, *N.B., Canada* **103 C6** 47 1N 65 38W
Newcastle, *Ont., Canada* **102 D4** 43 55N 78 35W
Newcastle, *S. Africa* **89 D4** 27 45 S 29 58 E
Newcastle, *U.K.* **15 B6** 54 13N 5 54W
Newcastle, *Calif., U.S.A.* **116 G5** 38 53N 121 8W
Newcastle, *Wyo., U.S.A.* **112 D2** 43 50N 104 11W
Newcastle Emlyn, *U.K.* **13 E3** 52 2N 4 28W
Newcastle Ra., *Australia* **92 C5** 15 45 S 130 15 E
Newcastle-under-Lyme, *U.K.* **12 D5** 53 1N 2 14W
Newcastle-upon-Tyne, *U.K.* **12 C6** 54 58N 1 36W
Newcastle Waters, *Australia* **94 B1** 17 30 S 133 28 E
Newcastle West, *Ireland* **15 D2** 52 27N 9 3W
Newcomb, *U.S.A.* **111 C10** 43 58N 74 10W
Newcomerstown, *U.S.A.* **110 F3** 40 16N 81 36W
Newdegate, *Australia* **93 F2** 33 6 S 119 0 E
Newell, *Australia* **94 B4** 16 20 S 145 16 E
Newell, *U.S.A.* **112 C3** 44 43N 103 25W
Newfane, *U.S.A.* **110 C6** 43 17N 78 43W
Newfield, *U.S.A.* **111 D8** 42 18N 76 33W
Newfound L., *U.S.A.* **111 C13** 43 40N 71 47W
Newfoundland, *N. Amer.* **98 E14** 49 0N 55 0W
Newfoundland, *U.S.A.* **111 E9** 41 18N 75 19W
Newfoundland □, *Canada* **103 B8** 53 0N 58 0W
Newhall, *U.S.A.* **117 L8** 34 23N 118 32W
Newhaven, *U.K.* **13 G8** 50 47N 0 3 E
Newkirk, *U.S.A.* **113 G6** 36 53N 97 3W
Newlyn, *U.K.* **13 G2** 50 6N 5 34W
Newman, *Australia* **92 D2** 23 18 S 119 45 E
Newman, *U.S.A.* **116 H5** 37 19N 121 1W
Newmarket, *Canada* **110 B5** 44 3N 79 28W
Newmarket, *Ireland* **15 D2** 52 13N 9 0W
Newmarket, *U.K.* **13 E8** 52 15N 0 25 E
Newmarket, *N.H., U.S.A.* **111 C14** 43 4N 70 56W
Newmarket, *N.H., U.S.A.* **111 C14** 43 5N 70 56W
Newnan, *U.S.A.* **109 J3** 33 23N 84 48W
Newport, *Ireland* **15 C2** 53 53N 9 33W
Newport, *I. of W., U.K.* **13 G6** 50 42N 1 17W
Newport, *Newp., U.K.* **13 F5** 51 35N 3 0W
Newport, *Ark., U.S.A.* **113 H9** 35 37N 91 16W
Newport, *Ky., U.S.A.* **108 F3** 39 5N 84 30W
Newport, *N.H., U.S.A.* **111 C12** 43 22N 72 10W
Newport, *N.Y., U.S.A.* **111 C9** 43 11N 75 1W
Newport, *Oreg., U.S.A.* **114 D1** 44 39N 124 3W
Newport, *Pa., U.S.A.* **110 F7** 40 29N 77 8W
Newport, *R.I., U.S.A.* **111 E13** 41 29N 71 19W
Newport, *Tenn., U.S.A.* **109 H4** 35 58N 83 11W
Newport, *Vt., U.S.A.* **111 B12** 44 56N 72 13W
Newport, *Wash., U.S.A.* **114 B5** 48 11N 117 3W
Newport □, *U.K.* **13 F4** 51 33N 3 1W
Newport Beach, *U.S.A.* **117 M9** 33 37N 117 56W
Newport News, *U.S.A.* **108 G7** 36 59N 76 25W
Newport Pagnell, *U.K.* **13 E7** 52 5N 0 43W
Newquay, *U.K.* **13 G2** 50 25N 5 6W
Newry, *U.K.* **15 B5** 54 11N 6 21W
Newton, *Ill., U.S.A.* **112 F10** 38 59N 88 10W
Newton, *Iowa, U.S.A.* **112 E8** 41 42N 93 3W
Newton, *Kans., U.S.A.* **113 F6** 38 3N 97 21W
Newton, *Mass., U.S.A.* **111 D13** 42 21N 71 12W
Newton, *Miss., U.S.A.* **113 J10** 32 19N 89 10W
Newton, *N.C., U.S.A.* **109 H5** 35 40N 81 13W
Newton, *N.J., U.S.A.* **111 E10** 41 3N 74 45W
Newton, *Tex., U.S.A.* **113 K8** 30 51N 93 46W
Newton Abbot, *U.K.* **13 G4** 50 32N 3 37W
Newton Aycliffe, *U.K.* **12 C6** 54 37N 1 34W
Newton Falls, *U.S.A.* **110 E4** 41 11N 80 59W
Newton Stewart, *U.K.* **14 G4** 54 57N 4 30W
Newtonmore, *U.K.* **14 D4** 57 4N 4 8W
Newtown, *U.K.* **13 E4** 52 31N 3 19W
Newtownabbey, *U.K.* **15 B6** 54 40N 5 56W
Newtownards, *U.K.* **15 B6** 54 36N 5 42W
Newtownbarry = Bunclody, *Ireland* **15 D5** 52 39N 6 40W
Newtownstewart, *U.K.* **15 B4** 54 43N 7 23W
Newville, *U.S.A.* **110 F7** 40 10N 77 24W
Nexon, *France* **20 C5** 45 41N 1 11 E
Neya, *Russia* **48 A6** 58 21N 43 49 E
Neyrīz, *Iran* **71 D7** 29 15N 54 19 E
Neyshābūr, *Iran* **71 B8** 36 10N 58 50 E
Nezhin = Nizhyn, *Ukraine* **47 G6** 51 5N 31 55 E
Nezperce, *U.S.A.* **114 C5** 46 14N 116 14W
Ngabang, *Indonesia* **62 D3** 0 23N 109 55 E
Ngabordamlu, Tanjung, *Indonesia* **63 F8** 6 56 S 134 11 E
N'Gage, *Angola* **84 F3** 7 46 S 15 16 E
Ngala, *Nigeria* **83 C7** 12 20N 14 11 E
Ngambé, *Cameroon* **83 D7** 5 48N 11 29 E
Ngambé, *Cameroon* **83 E7** 4 21N 10 40 E
Ngami Depression, *Botswana* **88 C3** 20 30 S 22 46 E
Ngamo, *Zimbabwe* **87 F2** 19 3 S 27 32 E
Ngangala, *Sudan* **81 G3** 4 42N 31 55 E
Nganglong Kangri, *China* **67 C12** 33 0N 81 0 E
Ngao, *Thailand* **64 C2** 18 46N 99 59 E
Ngaoundéré, *Cameroon* **84 C2** 7 15N 13 35 E
Ngapara, *N.Z.* **91 L3** 44 57 S 170 46 E
Ngara, *Tanzania* **86 C3** 2 29 S 30 40 E
Ngawi, *Indonesia* **63 G14** 7 24 S 111 26 E
Nghia Lo, *Vietnam* **58 G5** 21 33N 104 28 E
Ngoboli, *Sudan* **81 G3** 4 57N 32 37 E
Ngoma, *Malawi* **87 E3** 13 8 S 33 45 E
Ngomahura, *Zimbabwe* **87 G3** 20 26 S 30 43 E
Ngomba, *Tanzania* **87 D3** 8 20 S 32 53 E
Ngop, *Sudan* **81 F3** 6 17N 30 9 E
Ngoring Hu, *China* **60 C4** 34 55N 97 5 E
Ngorkou, *Mali* **82 B4** 15 40N 3 41W
Ngorongoro, *Tanzania* **86 C4** 3 11 S 35 32 E
Ngozi, *Burundi* **86 C2** 2 54 S 29 50 E
Ngudu, *Tanzania* **86 C3** 2 58 S 33 25 E
Nguigmi, *Niger* **79 F8** 14 20N 13 20 E
Nguila, *Cameroon* **83 E7** 4 41N 11 43 E
Nguiu, *Australia* **92 B5** 11 46 S 130 38 E
Ngukurr, *Australia* **94 A1** 14 44 S 134 44 E
Ngulu Atoll, *Pac. Oc.* **63 C9** 8 0N 137 30 E
Ngunga, *Tanzania* **86 C3** 3 37 S 33 37 E

Nguru, *Nigeria* **83 C7** 12 56N 10 29 E
Nguru Mts., *Tanzania* **86 D4** 6 0 S 37 30 E
Nguyen Binh, *Vietnam* **58 F5** 22 39N 105 56 E
Nha Trang, *Vietnam* **65 F7** 12 16N 109 10 E
Nhacoongo, *Mozam.* **89 C6** 24 18 S 35 14 E
Nhamaabué, *Mozam.* **87 F4** 17 25 S 35 5 E
Nhamundá →, *Brazil* **125 D7** 2 12 S 56 41W
Nhangulaze, L., *Mozam.* **89 C5** 24 0 S 34 30 E
Nhill, *Australia* **95 F3** 36 18 S 141 40 E
Nho Quan, *Vietnam* **58 G5** 20 18N 105 45 E
Nhulunbuy, *Australia* **94 A2** 12 10 S 137 20 E
Nia-nia, *Dem. Rep. of the Congo* **86 B2** 1 30N 27 40 E
Niafounké, *Mali* **82 B4** 16 0N 4 5W
Niagara Falls, *Canada* **102 D4** 43 7N 79 5W
Niagara Falls, *U.S.A.* **110 C6** 43 5N 79 4W
Niagara-on-the-Lake, *Canada* **110 C5** 43 15N 79 4W
Niah, *Malaysia* **62 D4** 3 58N 113 46 E
Niamey, *Niger* **83 C5** 13 27N 2 6 E
Niandan-Koro, *Guinea* **82 C3** 11 5N 9 15W
Nianforando, *Guinea* **82 D2** 9 37N 10 36W
Niangara, *Dem. Rep. of the Congo* **86 B2** 3 42N 27 50 E
Niangbo, *Ivory C.* **82 D3** 8 49N 5 10W
Niangoloko, *Burkina Faso* **82 C4** 10 15N 4 55W
Niantic, *U.S.A.* **111 E12** 41 20N 72 11W
Niaro, *Sudan* **81 E3** 10 38N 31 31 E
Nias, *Indonesia* **62 D1** 1 0N 97 30 E
Niassa □, *Mozam.* **87 E4** 13 30 S 36 0 E
Nibāk, *Si. Arabia* **71 E7** 24 25N 50 50 E
Nibe, *Denmark* **11 H3** 56 59N 9 38 E
Nicaragua ■, *Cent. Amer.* **120 D2** 11 40N 85 30W
Nicaragua, L. de, *Nic.* **120 D2** 12 0N 85 30W
Nicastro, *Italy* **31 D9** 38 59N 16 19 E
Nice, *France* **21 E11** 43 42N 7 14 E
Niceville, *U.S.A.* **109 K2** 30 31N 86 30W
Nichicun, L., *Canada* **103 B5** 53 5N 71 0W
Nichinan, *Japan* **55 J5** 31 38N 131 23 E
Nicholás, Canal, *W. Indies* **120 B3** 23 30N 80 5W
Nicholasville, *U.S.A.* **108 G3** 37 53N 84 34W
Nichols, *U.S.A.* **111 D8** 42 1N 76 22W
Nicholson, *Australia* **92 C4** 18 2 S 128 54 E
Nicholson, *U.S.A.* **111 E9** 41 37N 75 47W
Nicholson →, *Australia* **94 B2** 17 31 S 139 36 E
Nicholson L., *Canada* **105 A8** 62 40N 102 40W
Nicholson Ra., *Australia* **93 E2** 27 15 S 116 45 E
Nicholville, *U.S.A.* **111 B10** 44 41N 74 39W
Nicobar Is., *Ind. Oc.* **52 J13** 9 0N 93 0 E
Nicola, *Canada* **104 C4** 50 12N 120 40W
Nicolls Town, *Bahamas* **120 A4** 25 8N 78 0W
Nicopolis, *Greece* **38 B2** 39 2N 20 37 E
Nicosia, *Cyprus* **36 D12** 35 10N 33 25 E
Nicosia, *Italy* **31 E7** 37 45N 14 24 E
Nicótera, *Italy* **31 D8** 38 33N 15 56 E
Nicoya, *Costa Rica* **120 D2** 10 9N 85 27W
Nicoya, G. de, *Costa Rica* **120 E3** 10 0N 85 0W
Nicoya, Pen. de, *Costa Rica* **120 E2** 9 45N 85 40W
Nidd →, *U.K.* **12 D6** 53 59N 1 23W
Nidda, *Germany* **25 E5** 50 23N 9 1 E
Nidda →, *Germany* **25 E4** 50 17N 8 48 E
Nidwalden □, *Switz.* **25 J4** 46 50N 8 25 E
Nidzica, *Poland* **45 E7** 53 25N 20 28 E
Niebüll, *Germany* **24 A4** 54 46N 8 48 E
Nied →, *Germany* **19 C13** 49 23N 6 40 E
Niederaula, *Germany* **24 E5** 50 47N 9 36 E
Niederbayern □, *Germany* **25 G8** 48 40N 12 50 E
Niederbronn-les-Bains, *France* **19 D14** 48 57N 7 39 E
Niedere Tauern, *Austria* **26 D7** 47 20N 14 0 E
Niederlausitz, *Germany* **24 D9** 51 42N 13 59 E
Niederösterreich □, *Austria* **26 C8** 48 25N 15 40 E
Niedersachsen □, *Germany* **24 C4** 52 50N 9 0 E
Niekerkshoop, *S. Africa* **88 D3** 29 19 S 22 51 E
Niellé, *Ivory C.* **82 C3** 10 5N 5 38W
Niemba, *Dem. Rep. of the Congo* **86 D2** 5 58 S 28 24 E
Niemen = Neman →, *Lithuania* **9 J19** 55 25N 21 10 E
Niemodlin, *Poland* **45 H4** 50 38N 17 38 E
Nienburg, *Germany* **24 C5** 52 39N 9 13 E
Niepołomice, *Poland* **45 H7** 50 3N 20 13 E
Niers →, *Germany* **24 D1** 51 43N 5 57 E
Niesky, *Germany* **24 D10** 51 17N 14 49 E
Nieszawa, *Poland* **45 F5** 52 52N 18 50 E
Nieu Bethesda, *S. Africa* **88 E3** 31 51 S 24 34 E
Nieuw Amsterdam, *Surinam* **125 B7** 5 53N 55 5W
Nieuw Nickerie, *Surinam* **125 B7** 6 0N 56 59W
Nieuwoudtville, *S. Africa* **88 E2** 31 23 S 19 7 E
Nieuwpoort, *Belgium* **17 C2** 51 8N 2 45 E
Nieves, Pico de las, *Canary Is.* **37 G4** 27 57N 15 35W
Nièvre □, *France* **19 E10** 47 10N 3 40 E
Niga, *Mali* **82 C3** 13 38N 5 27W
Niğde, *Turkey* **70 B2** 37 58N 34 40 E
Nigel, *S. Africa* **89 D4** 26 27 S 28 25 E
Niger □, *Nigeria* **83 D6** 10 0N 5 30 E
Niger ■, *W. Afr.* **83 B7** 17 30N 10 0 E
Niger →, *W. Afr.* **83 D6** 5 33N 6 33 E
Niger Delta, *Africa* **83 E6** 5 0N 6 0 E
Nigeria ■, *W. Afr.* **83 D6** 8 30N 8 0 E
Nighasin, *India* **69 E9** 28 14N 80 52 E
Nightcaps, *N.Z.* **91 L2** 45 57 S 168 2 E
Nigríta, *Greece* **40 F7** 40 56N 23 29 E
Nii-Jima, *Japan* **55 G9** 34 20N 139 15 E
Niigata, *Japan* **54 F9** 37 58N 139 0 E
Niigata □, *Japan* **55 F9** 37 15N 138 45 E
Niihama, *Japan* **55 H6** 33 55N 133 16 E
Niihau, *U.S.A.* **106 H14** 21 54N 160 9W
Niimi, *Japan* **55 G6** 34 59N 133 28 E
Niitsu, *Japan* **54 F9** 37 48N 139 7 E
Nijar, *Spain* **33 J2** 36 53N 2 15W
Nijil, *Jordan* **75 E4** 30 32N 35 33 E
Nijkerk, *Neths.* **17 B5** 52 13N 5 30 E
Nijmegen, *Neths.* **17 C5** 51 50N 5 52 E
Nijverdal, *Neths.* **17 B6** 52 22N 6 28 E
Nīk Pey, *Iran* **71 B6** 36 50N 48 10 E
Nike, *Nigeria* **83 D6** 6 26N 7 29 E
Nikiniki, *Indonesia* **63 F6** 9 49 S 124 30 E
Nikísiani, *Greece* **41 F8** 40 57N 24 9 E
Níkitas, *Greece* **40 F7** 40 13N 23 43 E
Nikki, *Benin* **83 D5** 9 58N 3 12 E
Nikkō, *Japan* **55 F9** 36 45N 139 35 E
Nikolayev = Mykolayiv, *Ukraine* **47 J7** 46 58N 32 0 E
Nikolayevsk, *Russia* **48 E7** 50 0N 45 35 E
Nikolayevsk-na-Amur, *Russia* **51 D15** 53 8N 140 44 E
Nikolsk, *Russia* **48 D8** 53 49N 46 4 E
Nikolskoye, *Russia* **51 D17** 55 12N 166 0 E
Nikopol, *Bulgaria* **41 C8** 43 43N 24 54 E
Nikopol, *Ukraine* **47 J8** 47 35N 34 25 E
Niksar, *Turkey* **72 B7** 40 31N 37 2 E
Nīkshahr, *Iran* **71 E9** 26 15N 60 10 E
Nikšić, *Montenegro, Yug.* **40 D2** 42 50N 18 57 E
Nîl, Nahr en →, *Africa* **80 H7** 30 10N 31 6 E
Nîl el Abyad →, *Sudan* **81 D3** 15 38N 32 31 E
Nîl el Azraq →, *Sudan* **81 D3** 15 38N 32 31 E
Nila, *Indonesia* **63 F7** 6 44 S 129 31 E
Niland, *U.S.A.* **117 M11** 33 14N 115 31W
Nile = Nîl, Nahr en →, *Africa* **80 H7** 30 10N 31 6 E
Niles, *Mich., U.S.A.* **108 E2** 41 50N 86 15W
Niles, *Ohio, U.S.A.* **110 E4** 41 11N 80 46W
Nilüfer →, *Turkey* **41 F12** 40 18N 28 27 E
Nim Ka Thana, *India* **68 F6** 27 44N 75 48 E
Nimach, *India* **68 G6** 24 30N 74 56 E
Nimbahera, *India* **68 G6** 24 37N 74 45 E
Nîmes, *France* **21 E8** 43 50N 4 23 E
Nimfaíon, Ákra = Pínnes, Ákra, *Greece* **41 F8** 40 5N 24 20 E
Nimmitabel, *Australia* **95 F4** 36 29 S 149 15 E
Nimule, *Sudan* **81 G3** 3 32N 32 3 E
Nin, *Croatia* **29 D12** 44 16N 15 12 E
Nīnawá, *Iraq* **70 B4** 36 25N 43 10 E
Nindigully, *Australia* **95 D4** 28 21 S 148 50 E
Nineveh = Nīnawá, *Iraq* **70 B4** 36 25N 43 10 E
Ning Xian, *China* **56 G4** 35 30N 107 58 E
Ning'an, *China* **57 B15** 44 22N 129 20 E
Ningbo, *China* **59 C13** 29 51N 121 28 E
Ningcheng, *China* **57 D10** 41 32N 119 53 E
Ningde, *China* **59 D12** 26 38N 119 23 E
Ningdu, *China* **59 D10** 26 25N 115 59 E
Ninggang, *China* **59 D9** 26 42N 113 55 E
Ningguo, *China* **59 B12** 30 35N 119 0 E
Ninghai, *China* **59 C13** 29 15N 121 27 E
Ninghua, *China* **59 D11** 26 14N 116 45 E
Ningi, *Nigeria* **83 C6** 10 55N 9 30 E
Ningjin, *China* **56 F8** 37 35N 114 57 E
Ningjing Shan, *China* **58 C2** 30 0N 98 20 E
Ninglang, *China* **58 D3** 27 20N 100 55 E
Ningling, *China* **56 G8** 34 25N 115 22 E
Ningming, *China* **58 F6** 22 8N 107 4 E
Ningnan, *China* **58 D4** 27 5N 102 36 E
Ningpo = Ningbo, *China* **59 C13** 29 51N 121 28 E
Ningqiang, *China* **56 H4** 32 47N 106 15 E
Ningshan, *China* **56 H5** 33 21N 108 21 E
Ningsia Hui A.R. = Ningxia Huizu Zizhiqu □, *China* **56 F4** 38 0N 106 0 E
Ningwu, *China* **56 E7** 39 0N 112 18 E
Ningxia Huizu Zizhiqu □, *China* **56 F4** 38 0N 106 0 E
Ningxiang, *China* **59 C9** 28 15N 112 30 E
Ningyang, *China* **56 G9** 35 47N 116 45 E
Ningyuan, *China* **59 E8** 25 37N 111 57 E
Ninh Binh, *Vietnam* **58 G5** 20 15N 105 55 E
Ninh Giang, *Vietnam* **64 B6** 20 44N 106 24 E
Ninh Hoa, *Vietnam* **64 F7** 12 30N 109 7 E
Ninh Ma, *Vietnam* **64 F7** 12 48N 109 21 E
Ninove, *Belgium* **17 D4** 50 51N 4 2 E
Nioaque, *Brazil* **127 A4** 21 5 S 55 50W
Niobrara, *U.S.A.* **112 D6** 42 45N 98 2W
Niobrara →, *U.S.A.* **112 D6** 42 46N 98 3W
Niono, *Mali* **82 C3** 14 15N 6 0W
Nionsamoridougou, *Guinea* **82 D3** 8 45N 8 50W
Nioro du Rip, *Senegal* **82 C1** 13 40N 15 50W
Nioro du Sahel, *Mali* **82 B3** 15 15N 9 30W
Niort, *France* **20 B3** 46 19N 0 29W
Nipawin, *Canada* **105 C8** 53 20N 104 0W
Nipfjället, *Sweden* **10 C6** 61 59N 12 50 E
Nipigon, *Canada* **102 C2** 49 0N 88 17W
Nipigon, L., *Canada* **102 C2** 49 50N 88 30W
Nipishish L., *Canada* **103 B7** 54 12N 60 45W
Nipissing, L., *Canada* **102 C4** 46 20N 80 0W
Nipomo, *U.S.A.* **117 K6** 35 3N 120 29W
Nipton, *U.S.A.* **117 K11** 35 28N 115 16W
Niquelândia, *Brazil* **125 F9** 14 33 S 48 23W
Nīr, *Iran* **70 B5** 38 2N 47 59 E
Nirasaki, *Japan* **55 G9** 35 42N 138 27 E
Nirmal, *India* **66 K11** 19 3N 78 20 E
Nirmali, *India* **69 F12** 26 20N 86 35 E
Niš, *Serbia, Yug.* **40 C5** 43 19N 21 58 E
Nisa, *Portugal* **35 F3** 39 30N 7 41W
Nişāb, *Si. Arabia* **70 D5** 29 11N 44 43 E
Nişāb, *Yemen* **74 E4** 14 25N 46 29 E
Nišava →, *Serbia, Yug.* **40 C5** 43 20N 21 46 E
Niscemi, *Italy* **31 E7** 37 9N 14 23 E
Nishinomiya, *Japan* **55 G7** 34 45N 135 20 E
Nishino'omote, *Japan* **55 J5** 30 43N 130 59 E
Nishiwaki, *Japan* **55 G7** 34 59N 134 58 E
Nísíros, *Greece* **39 E9** 36 35N 27 12 E
Niška Banja, *Serbia, Yug.* **40 C6** 43 18N 22 1 E
Niskibi →, *Canada* **102 A2** 56 29N 88 9W
Nisko, *Poland* **45 H9** 50 35N 22 7 E
Nisporeni, *Moldova* **43 C13** 47 4N 28 10 E
Nisqually →, *U.S.A.* **116 C4** 47 6N 122 42W
Nissáki, *Greece* **36 A3** 39 43N 19 52 E
Nissan →, *Sweden* **11 H6** 56 40N 12 51 E
Nissum Bredning, *Denmark* **11 H2** 56 40N 8 20 E
Nissum Fjord, *Denmark* **11 H2** 56 20N 8 11 E
Nistru = Dnister →, *Europe* **47 J6** 46 18N 30 17 E
Nisutlin →, *Canada* **104 A2** 60 14N 132 34W
Nitchequon, *Canada* **103 B5** 53 10N 70 58W
Niterói, *Brazil* **127 A7** 22 52 S 43 0W
Nith →, *Canada* **110 C4** 43 12N 80 23W
Nith →, *U.K.* **14 F5** 55 14N 3 33W
Nitra, *Slovak Rep.* **27 C11** 48 19N 18 4 E
Nitra →, *Slovak Rep.* **27 D11** 47 46N 18 10 E
Nitriansky □, *Slovak Rep.* **27 C11** 48 10N 18 30 E
Nittenau, *Germany* **25 F8** 49 12N 12 16 E
Niuafo'ou, *Tonga* **91 B11** 15 30 S 175 58W
Niue, *Cook Is.* **97 J11** 19 2 S 169 54W
Niulan Jiang →, *China* **58 D4** 27 30N 103 5 E
Niut, *Indonesia* **62 D4** 0 55N 110 6 E
Niutou Shan, *China* **59 C13** 29 5N 121 59 E
Niuzhuang, *China* **57 D12** 40 58N 122 28 E
Nivala, *Finland* **8 E21** 63 56N 24 57 E
Nivelles, *Belgium* **17 D4** 50 35N 4 20 E
Nivernais, *France* **19 E10** 47 15N 3 30 E
Niwas, *India* **69 H9** 23 3N 80 26 E
Nixon, *U.S.A.* **113 L6** 29 16N 97 46W
Nizamabad, *India* **66 K11** 18 45N 78 7 E
Nizamghat, *India* **67 E19** 28 20N 95 45 E
Nizhne Kolymsk, *Russia* **51 C17** 68 34N 160 55 E
Nizhnegorskiy = Nyzhnohirskyy, *Ukraine* **47 K8** 45 27N 34 38 E
Nizhnekamsk, *Russia* **48 C10** 55 38N 51 49 E
Nizhneudinsk, *Russia* **51 D10** 54 54N 99 3 E
Nizhnevartovsk, *Russia* **50 C8** 60 56N 76 38 E
Nizhniy Chir, *Russia* **49 F6** 48 22N 43 5 E
Nizhniy Lomov, *Russia* **48 D6** 53 34N 43 38 E
Nizhniy Novgorod, *Russia* **48 B7** 56 20N 44 0 E
Nizhniy Tagil, *Russia* **50 D6** 57 55N 59 57 E
Nizhyn, *Ukraine* **47 G6** 51 5N 31 55 E
Nizina Mazowiecka, *Poland* **45 F8** 52 30N 21 0 E
Nizip, *Turkey* **70 B3** 37 5N 37 50 E
Nízké Tatry, *Slovak Rep.* **27 C12** 48 55N 19 30 E
Nízký Jeseník, *Czech Rep.* **27 B10** 49 50N 17 30 E
Nizza Monferrato, *Italy* **28 D5** 44 46N 8 21 E
Njakwa, *Malawi* **87 E3** 11 1 S 33 56 E
Njanji, *Zambia* **87 E3** 14 25 S 31 46 E
Njegoš, *Montenegro, Yug.* **40 D2** 42 53N 18 45 E
Njinjo, *Tanzania* **87 D4** 8 48 S 38 54 E
Njombe, *Tanzania* **87 D3** 9 20 S 34 50 E
Njombe →, *Tanzania* **86 D4** 6 56 S 35 6 E
Njurundabommen, *Sweden* **10 B11** 62 15N 17 25 E
Nkambe, *Cameroon* **83 D7** 6 35N 10 40 E
Nkana, *Zambia* **87 E2** 12 50 S 28 8 E
Nkandla, *S. Africa* **89 D5** 28 37 S 31 5 E
Nkawkaw, *Ghana* **83 D4** 6 36N 0 49W
Nkayi, *Zimbabwe* **87 F2** 19 41 S 29 20 E
Nkhotakota, *Malawi* **87 E3** 12 56 S 34 15 E
Nkongsamba, *Cameroon* **83 E6** 4 55N 9 55 E
Nkurenkuru, *Namibia* **88 B2** 17 42 S 18 32 E
Nkwanta, *Ghana* **82 D4** 6 10N 2 10W
Nmai →, *Burma* **58 F2** 25 30N 97 25 E
Noakhali = Maijdi, *Bangla.* **67 H17** 22 48N 91 10 E
Nobel, *Canada* **110 A4** 45 25N 80 6W
Nobeoka, *Japan* **55 H5** 32 36N 131 41 E
Noblejas, *Spain* **34 F7** 39 58N 3 26W
Noblesville, *U.S.A.* **108 E3** 40 3N 86 1W
Noce →, *Italy* **28 B8** 46 9N 11 4 E
Nocera Inferiore, *Italy* **31 B7** 40 44N 14 38 E
Nocera Umbra, *Italy* **29 E9** 43 5N 12 47 E
Noci, *Italy* **31 B10** 40 48N 17 7 E
Nocona, *U.S.A.* **113 J6** 33 47N 97 44W
Nocrich, *Romania* **43 E9** 45 55N 24 26 E
Noda, *Japan* **55 G9** 35 56N 139 52 E
Nogales, *Mexico* **118 A2** 31 20N 110 56W
Nogales, *U.S.A.* **115 L8** 31 20N 110 56W
Nogaro, *France* **20 E3** 43 45N 0 2W
Nogat →, *Poland* **44 D6** 54 17N 19 17 E
Nōgata, *Japan* **55 H5** 33 48N 130 44 E
Nogent, *France* **19 D12** 48 1N 5 20 E
Nogent-le-Rotrou, *France* **18 D7** 48 20N 0 50 E
Nogent-sur-Seine, *France* **19 D10** 48 30N 3 30 E
Noggerup, *Australia* **93 F2** 33 32 S 116 5 E
Noginsk, *Moskva, Russia* **46 E10** 55 50N 38 25 E
Noginsk, *Tunguska, Russia* **51 C10** 64 30N 90 50 E
Nogoa →, *Australia* **94 C4** 23 40 S 147 55 E
Nogoyá, *Argentina* **126 C4** 32 24 S 59 48W
Nógrád □, *Hungary* **42 C4** 48 0N 19 30 E
Noguera Pallaresa →, *Spain* **32 D5** 41 55N 0 55 E
Noguera Ribagorzana →, *Spain* **32 D5** 41 40N 0 43 E
Nohar, *India* **68 E6** 29 11N 74 49 E
Nohfelden, *Germany* **25 F3** 49 35N 7 7 E
Nohta, *India* **69 H8** 23 40N 79 34 E
Noia, *Spain* **34 C2** 42 48N 8 53W
Noire, Montagne, *France* **20 E6** 43 28N 2 18 E
Noires, Mts., *France* **18 D3** 48 11N 3 40W
Noirétable, *France* **20 C7** 45 48N 3 46 E
Noirmoutier, Î. de, *France* **18 F4** 46 58N 2 10W
Noirmoutier-en-l'Île, *France* **18 F4** 47 0N 2 14W
Nojane, *Botswana* **88 C3** 23 15 S 20 14 E
Nojima-Zaki, *Japan* **55 G9** 34 54N 139 53 E
Nok Kundi, *Pakistan* **66 E3** 28 50N 62 45 E
Nokaneng, *Botswana* **88 B3** 19 40 S 22 17 E
Nokia, *Finland* **9 F20** 61 30N 23 30 E
Nokomis, *Canada* **105 C8** 51 35N 105 0W
Nokomis L., *Canada* **105 B8** 57 0N 103 0W
Nol, *Sweden* **11 G6** 57 56N 12 5 E
Nola, *C.A.R.* **84 D3** 3 35N 16 4 E
Nola, *Italy* **31 B7** 40 55N 14 33 E
Nolay, *France* **19 F11** 46 58N 4 35 E
Noli, C. di, *Italy* **28 D5** 44 12N 8 25 E
Nolinsk, *Russia* **48 B9** 57 28N 49 57 E
Noma Omuramba →, *Namibia* **88 B3** 18 52 S 20 53 E
Nombre de Dios, *Panama* **120 E4** 9 34N 79 28W
Nome, *U.S.A.* **100 B3** 64 30N 165 25W
Nomo-Zaki, *Japan* **55 H4** 32 35N 129 44 E
Nonacho L., *Canada* **105 A7** 61 42N 109 40W
Nonancourt, *France* **18 D8** 48 47N 1 11 E
Nonda, *Australia* **94 C3** 20 40 S 142 28 E
None, *Italy* **28 D4** 44 56N 7 32 E
Nong Chang, *Thailand* **64 E2** 15 23N 99 51 E
Nong Het, *Laos* **64 C4** 19 29N 103 59 E
Nong Khai, *Thailand* **64 D4** 17 50N 102 46 E
Nong'an, *China* **57 B13** 44 25N 125 5 E
Nongoma, *S. Africa* **89 D5** 27 58 S 31 35 E
Nonoava, *Mexico* **118 B3** 27 28N 106 44W
Nonoava →, *Mexico* **118 B3** 27 29N 106 45W
Nonthaburi, *Thailand* **64 F3** 13 51N 100 34 E
Nontron, *France* **20 C4** 45 31N 0 40 E
Nonza, *France* **21 F13** 42 47N 9 21 E
Noonamah, *Australia* **92 B5** 12 40 S 131 4 E
Noord Brabant □, *Neths.* **17 C5** 51 40N 5 0 E
Noord Holland □, *Neths.* **17 B4** 52 30N 4 45 E
Noordbeveland, *Neths.* **17 C3** 51 35N 3 50 E
Noordoostpolder, *Neths.* **17 B5** 52 45N 5 45 E
Noordwijk, *Neths.* **17 B4** 52 14N 4 26 E
Nootka I., *Canada* **104 D3** 49 32N 126 42W
Nopiming Prov. Park, *Canada* **105 C9** 50 30N 95 37W
Nora, *Eritrea* **81 D5** 16 6N 40 4 E
Nora, *Sweden* **10 E9** 59 32N 15 2 E
Noralee, *Canada* **104 C3** 53 59N 126 26W
Noranda = Rouyn-Noranda, *Canada* **102 C4** 48 20N 79 0W
Norberg, *Sweden* **10 D9** 60 4N 15 56 E
Nórcia, *Italy* **29 F10** 42 48N 13 5 E
Norco, *U.S.A.* **117 M9** 33 56N 117 33W
Nord □, *France* **19 B10** 50 15N 3 30 E
Nord-Kivu □, *Dem. Rep. of the Congo* **86 C2** 1 0 S 29 0 E
Nord-Ostsee-Kanal, *Germany* **24 A5** 54 12N 9 32 E
Nord-Pas-de-Calais □, *France* **19 B9** 50 30N 2 50 E
Nordaustlandet, *Svalbard* **4 B9** 79 14N 23 0 E
Nordborg, *Denmark* **11 J3** 55 5N 9 50 E
Nordby, *Denmark* **11 J2** 55 27N 8 24 E
Norddeich, *Germany* **24 B3** 53 36N 7 9 E
Nordegg, *Canada* **104 C5** 52 29N 116 5W
Norden, *Germany* **24 B3** 53 35N 7 12 E
Nordenham, *Germany* **24 B4** 53 30N 8 30 E
Norderney, *Germany* **24 B3** 53 42N 7 9 E
Norderstedt, *Germany* **24 B6** 53 42N 10 1 E
Nordfjord, *Norway* **9 F11** 61 55N 5 30 E
Nordfriesische Inseln, *Germany* **24 A4** 54 40N 8 20 E
Nordhausen, *Germany* **24 D6** 51 30N 10 47 E
Nordhorn, *Germany* **24 C3** 52 26N 7 4 E
Norðoyar, *Færoe Is.* **8 E9** 62 17N 6 35W
Nordingrå, *Sweden* **10 B12** 62 56N 18 17 E
Nordjyllands Amtskommune □, *Denmark* **11 G4** 57 20N 10 0 E
Nordkapp, *Norway* **8 A21** 71 10N 25 50 E
Nordkapp, *Svalbard* **4 A9** 80 31N 20 0 E
Nordkinn = Kinnarodden, *Norway* **6 A11** 71 8N 27 40 E
Nordkinn-halvøya, *Norway* **8 A22** 70 55N 27 40 E
Nördlingen, *Germany* **25 G6** 48 48N 10 30 E
Nordrhein-Westfalen □, *Germany* **24 D3** 51 45N 7 30 E
Nordstrand, *Germany* **24 A4** 54 30N 8 52 E
Nordvik, *Russia* **51 B12** 74 2N 111 32 E
Nore →, *Ireland* **15 D4** 52 25N 6 58W
Norfolk, *Nebr., U.S.A.* **112 D6** 42 2N 97 25W
Norfolk, *Va., U.S.A.* **108 G7** 36 51N 76 17W
Norfolk □, *U.K.* **13 E8** 52 39N 0 54 E
Norfolk I., *Pac. Oc.* **96 K8** 28 58 S 168 3 E
Norfork L., *U.S.A.* **113 G8** 36 15N 92 14W
Norilsk, *Russia* **51 C9** 69 20N 88 6 E
Norma, Mt., *Australia* **94 C3** 20 55 S 140 42 E
Normal, *U.S.A.* **112 E10** 40 31N 88 59W
Norman, *U.S.A.* **113 H6** 35 13N 97 26W
Norman →, *Australia* **94 B3** 19 18 S 141 51 E
Norman Wells, *Canada* **100 B7** 65 17N 126 51W
Normanby →, *Australia* **94 A3** 14 23 S 144 10 E
Normandin, *Canada* **102 C5** 48 49N 72 31W
Normanhurst, Mt., *Australia* **93 E3** 25 4 S 122 30 E
Normanton, *Australia* **94 B3** 17 40 S 141 10 E
Normétal, *Canada* **102 C4** 49 0N 79 22W
Norquay, *Canada* **105 C8** 51 53N 102 5W
Norquinco, *Argentina* **128 E2** 41 51 S 70 55W
Norra Dellen, *Sweden* **10 C10** 61 53N 16 43 E
Norra Ulvön, *Sweden* **10 A12** 63 3N 18 40 E
Norrahammar, *Sweden* **11 G8** 57 43N 14 7 E
Norrbotten □, *Sweden* **8 C19** 66 30N 22 30 E
Nørre Åby, *Denmark* **11 J3** 55 27N 9 52 E
Nørre Alslev, *Denmark* **11 K5** 54 54N 11 52 E
Nørresundby, *Denmark* **11 G3** 57 5N 9 52 E
Norrhult, *Sweden* **11 G9** 57 7N 15 10 E
Norris Point, *Canada* **103 C8** 49 31N 57 53W
Norristown, *U.S.A.* **111 F9** 40 7N 75 21W
Norrköping, *Sweden* **11 F10** 58 37N 16 11 E
Norrland, *Sweden* **9 E16** 62 15N 15 45 E
Norrsundet, *Sweden* **10 D11** 60 56N 17 8 E
Norrtälje, *Sweden* **10 E12** 59 46N 18 42 E
Norseman, *Australia* **93 F3** 32 8 S 121 43 E
Norsk, *Russia* **51 D14** 52 30N 130 5 E
Norte, Pta. del, *Canary Is.* **37 G2** 27 51N 17 57W
Norte, Serra do, *Brazil* **124** 11 20 S 59 0W
North, C., *Canada* **103 C7** 47 2N 60 20W
North Adams, *U.S.A.* **111 D11** 42 42N 73 7W
North Arm, *Canada* **104 A5** 62 0N 114 30W
North Augusta, *U.S.A.* **109 J5** 33 30N 81 59W
North Ayrshire □, *U.K.* **14 F4** 55 45N 4 44W
North Bass I., *U.S.A.* **110 E2** 41 43N 82 49W
North Battleford, *Canada* **105 C7** 52 50N 108 17W
North Bay, *Canada* **102 C4** 46 20N 79 30W
North Belcher Is., *Canada* **102 A4** 56 50N 79 50W
North Bend, *Oreg., U.S.A.* **114 E1** 43 24N 124 14W
North Bend, *Pa., U.S.A.* **110 E7** 41 20N 77 42W
North Bend, *Wash., U.S.A.* **116 C5** 47 30N 121 47W
North Bennington, *U.S.A.* **111 D11** 42 56N 73 15W
North Berwick, *U.K.* **14 E6** 56 4N 2 42W
North Berwick, *U.S.A.* **111 C14** 43 18N 70 44W
North C., *Canada* **103 C7** 47 5N 64 0W
North C., *N.Z.* **91 F4** 34 23 S 173 4 E
North Canadian →, *U.S.A.* **113 H7** 35 16N 95 31W
North Canton, *U.S.A.* **110 F3** 40 53N 81 24W
North Cape = Nordkapp, *Norway* **8 A21** 71 10N 25 50 E
North Cape = Nordkapp, *Svalbard* **4 A9** 80 31N 20 0 E
North Caribou L., *Canada* **102 B1** 52 50N 90 40W
North Carolina □, *U.S.A.* **109 H6** 35 30N 80 0W
North Cascades National Park, *U.S.A.* **114 B3** 48 45N 121 10W
North Channel, *Canada* **102 C3** 46 0N 83 0W
North Channel, *U.K.* **14 F3** 55 13N 5 52W
North Charleston, *U.S.A.* **109 J6** 32 53N 79 58W
North Chicago, *U.S.A.* **108 D2** 42 19N 87 51W
North Creek, *U.S.A.* **111 C11** 43 41N 73 59W
North Dakota □, *U.S.A.* **112 B5** 47 30N 100 15W
North Downs, *U.K.* **13 F8** 51 19N 0 21 E
North East, *U.S.A.* **110 D5** 42 13N 79 50W
North East Frontier Agency = Arunachal Pradesh □, *India* **67 F19** 28 0N 95 0 E
North East Lincolnshire □, *U.K.* **12 D7** 53 34N 0 2W
North Eastern □, *Kenya* **86 B5** 1 30N 40 0 E
North Esk →, *U.K.* **14 E6** 56 46N 2 24W
North European Plain, *Europe* **6 E10** 55 0N 25 0 E
North Foreland, *U.K.* **13 F9** 51 22N 1 28 E
North Fork, *U.S.A.* **116 H7** 37 14N 119 21W
North Fork American →, *U.S.A.* **116 G5** 38 57N 120 59W
North Fork Feather →, *U.S.A.* **116 F5** 38 33N 121 30W
North Fork Grand →, *U.S.A.* **112 C3** 45 47N 102 16W
North Fork Red →, *U.S.A.* **113 H5** 34 24N 99 14W
North Frisian Is. = Nordfriesische Inseln, *Germany* **24 A4** 54 40N 8 20 E
North Gower, *Canada* **111 A9** 45 8N 75 43W
North Hd., *Australia* **93 F1** 30 14 S 114 59 E
North Henik L., *Canada* **105 A9** 61 45N 97 40W
North Highlands, *U.S.A.* **116 G5** 38 40N 121 23W
North Horr, *Kenya* **86 B4** 3 20N 37 8 E
North I., *Kenya* **86 B4** 4 5N 36 5 E
North I., *N.Z.* **91 H5** 38 0 S 175 0 E
North Kingsville, *U.S.A.* **110 E4** 41 54N 80 42W
North Knife →, *Canada* **105 B10** 58 53N 94 45W
North Koel →, *India* **69 G10** 24 45N 83 50 E
North Korea ■, *Asia* **57 E14** 40 0N 127 0 E
North Lakhimpur, *India* **67 F19** 27 14N 94 7 E
North Lanarkshire □, *U.K.* **14 F5** 55 52N 3 56W
North Las Vegas, *U.S.A.* **117 J11** 36 12N 115 7W
North Lincolnshire □, *U.K.* **12 D7** 53 36N 0 30W
North Little Rock, *U.S.A.* **113 H8** 34 45N 92 16W
North Loup →, *U.S.A.* **112 E5** 41 17N 98 24W
North Magnetic Pole, *Canada* **4 B2** 77 58N 102 8W
North Minch, *U.K.* **14 C3** 58 5N 5 55W
North Moose L., *Canada* **105 C8** 54 11N 100 6W
North Myrtle Beach, *U.S.A.* **109 J6** 33 48N 78 42W
North Nahanni →, *Canada* **104 A4** 62 15N 123 20W
North Olmsted, *U.S.A.* **110 E3** 41 25N 81 56W
North Ossetia □, *Russia* **49 J7** 43 30N 44 30 E
North Pagai, I. = Pagai Utara, Pulau, *Indonesia* **62 E2** 2 35 S 100 0 E
North Palisade, *U.S.A.* **116 H8** 37 6N 118 31W
North Platte, *U.S.A.* **112 E4** 41 8N 100 46W
North Platte →, *U.S.A.* **112 E4** 41 7N 100 42W
North Pole, *Arctic* **4 A** 90 0N 0 0W
North Portal, *Canada* **105 D8** 49 0N 102 33W
North Powder, *U.S.A.* **114 D5** 45 2N 117 55W
North Pt., *U.S.A.* **110 A1** 45 2N 83 16W
North Rhine Westphalia = Nordrhein-Westfalen □, *Germany* **24 D3** 51 45N 7 30 E
North River, *Canada* **103 B8** 53 49N 57 6W
North Ronaldsay, *U.K.* **14 B6** 59 22N 2 26W
North Saskatchewan →, *Canada* **105 C7** 53 15N 105 5W
North Sea, *Europe* **6 D6** 56 0N 4 0 E
North Seal →, *Canada* **105 B9** 58 50N 98 7W
North Somerset □, *U.K.* **13 F5** 51 24N 2 45W
North Sporades = Vóriai Sporádhes, *Greece* **38 B5** 39 15N 23 30 E
North Sydney, *Canada* **103 C7** 46 12N 60 15W
North Syracuse, *U.S.A.* **111 C8** 43 8N 76 7W
North Taranaki Bight, *N.Z.* **91 H5** 38 50 S 174 15 E
North Thompson →, *Canada* **104 C4** 50 40N 120 20W
North Tonawanda, *U.S.A.* **110 C6** 43 2N 78 53W
North Troy, *U.S.A.* **111 B12** 45 0N 72 24W
North Truchas Pk., *U.S.A.* **115 J11** 36 0N 105 30W
North Twin I., *Canada* **102 B4** 53 20N 80 0W
North Tyne →, *U.K.* **12 B5** 55 0N 2 8W
North Uist, *U.K.* **14 D1** 57 40N 7 15W
North Vancouver, *Canada* **104 D4** 49 19N 123 4W
North Vernon, *U.S.A.* **108 F3** 39 0N 85 38W
North Wabasca L., *Canada* **104 B6** 56 0N 113 55W
North Walsham, *U.K.* **12 E9** 52 50N 1 22 E
North-West □, *S. Africa* **88 D4** 27 0 S 25 0 E
North West C., *Australia* **92 D1** 21 45 S 114 9 E
North West Christmas I. Ridge, *Pac. Oc.* **97 G11** 6 30N 165 0W
North West Frontier □, *Pakistan* **68 C4** 34 0N 72 0 E
North West Highlands, *U.K.* **14 D4** 57 33N 4 58W
North West River, *Canada* **103 B7** 53 30N 60 10W
North Western □, *Zambia* **87 E2** 13 30 S 25 30 E
North Wildwood, *U.S.A.* **108 F8** 39 0N 74 48W
North York Moors, *U.K.* **12 C7** 54 23N 0 53W
North Yorkshire □, *U.K.* **12 C6** 54 15N 1 25W
Northallerton, *U.K.* **12 C6** 54 20N 1 26W
Northam, *Australia* **93 F2** 31 35 S 116 42 E

Northam, *S. Africa* **88 C4** 24 56 S 27 18 E
Northampton, *Australia* **93 E1** 28 27 S 114 33 E
Northampton, *U.K.* **13 E7** 52 15N 0 53W
Northampton, *Mass., U.S.A.* **111 D12** 42 19N 72 38W
Northampton, *Pa., U.S.A.* **111 F9** 40 41N 75 30W
Northamptonshire □, *U.K.* **13 E7** 52 16N 0 55W
Northbridge, *U.S.A.* **111 D13** 42 9N 71 39W
Northcliffe, *Australia* **93 F2** 34 39 S 116 7 E
Northeast Providence Chan., *W. Indies* **120 A4** 26 0N 76 0W
Northeim, *Germany* **24 D6** 51 42N 10 0 E
Northern □, *Ghana* **83 D4** 9 30N 1 0W
Northern □, *Malawi* **87 E3** 11 0 S 34 0 E
Northern □, *Uganda* **86 B3** 3 5N 32 30 E
Northern □, *Zambia* **87 E3** 10 30 S 31 0 E
Northern Cape □, *S. Africa* **88 D3** 30 0 S 20 0 E
Northern Circars, *India* **67 L13** 17 30N 82 30 E
Northern Indian L., *Canada* **105 B9** 57 20N 97 20W
Northern Ireland □, *U.K.* **15 B5** 54 45N 7 0W
Northern Light L., *Canada* **102 C1** 48 15N 90 39W
Northern Marianas ■, *Pac. Oc.* **96 F6** 17 0N 145 0 E
Northern Province □, *S. Leone* **82 D2** 9 15N 11 30W
Northern Province □, *S. Africa* **89 C4** 24 0 S 29 0 E
Northern Territory □, *Australia* **92 D5** 20 0 S 133 0 E
Northfield, *Minn., U.S.A.* **112 C8** 44 27N 93 9W
Northfield, *Vt., U.S.A.* **111 B12** 44 9N 72 40W
Northland □, *N.Z.* **91 F4** 35 30 S 173 30 E
Northome, *U.S.A.* **112 B7** 47 52N 94 17W
Northport, *Ala., U.S.A.* **109 J2** 33 14N 87 35W
Northport, *Wash., U.S.A.* **114 B5** 48 55N 117 48W
Northumberland □, *U.K.* **12 B6** 55 12N 2 0W
Northumberland, C., *Australia* **95 F3** 38 5 S 140 40 E
Northumberland Is., *Australia* **94 C4** 21 30 S 149 50 E
Northumberland Str., *Canada* **103 C7** 46 20N 64 0W
Northville, *U.S.A.* **111 C10** 43 13N 74 11W
Northwest Providence Channel, *W. Indies* **120 A4** 26 0N 78 0W
Northwest Territories □, *Canada* **100 B9** 67 0N 110 0W
Northwood, *Iowa, U.S.A.* **112 D8** 43 27N 93 13W
Northwood, *N. Dak., U.S.A.* **112 B6** 47 44N 97 34W
Norton, *U.S.A.* **112 F5** 39 50N 99 53W
Norton, *Zimbabwe* **87 F3** 17 52 S 30 40 E
Norton Sd., *U.S.A.* **100 B3** 63 50N 164 0W
Nortorf, *Germany* **24 A5** 54 10N 9 50 E
Norwalk, *Calif., U.S.A.* **117 M8** 33 54N 118 5W
Norwalk, *Conn., U.S.A.* **111 E11** 41 7N 73 22W
Norwalk, *Iowa, U.S.A.* **112 E8** 41 29N 93 41W
Norwalk, *Ohio, U.S.A.* **110 E2** 41 15N 82 37W
Norway, *Maine, U.S.A.* **109 C10** 44 13N 70 32W
Norway, *Mich., U.S.A.* **108 C2** 45 47N 87 55W
Norway ■, *Europe* **8 E14** 63 0N 11 0 E
Norway House, *Canada* **105 C9** 53 59N 97 50W
Norwegian Sea, *Atl. Oc.* **4 C8** 66 0N 1 0 E
Norwich, *Canada* **110 D4** 42 59N 80 36W
Norwich, *U.K.* **13 E9** 52 38N 1 18 E
Norwich, *Conn., U.S.A.* **111 E12** 41 31N 72 5W
Norwich, *N.Y., U.S.A.* **111 D9** 42 32N 75 32W
Norwood, *Canada* **110 B7** 44 23N 77 59W
Norwood, *U.S.A.* **111 B10** 44 45N 75 0W
Noshiro, *Japan* **54 D10** 40 12N 140 0 E
Nosivka, *Ukraine* **47 G6** 50 50N 31 37 E
Nosovka = Nosivka, *Ukraine* **47 G6** 50 50N 31 37 E
Noşratābād, *Iran* **71 D8** 29 55N 60 0 E
Noss Hd., *U.K.* **14 C5** 58 28N 3 3W
Nossebro, *Sweden* **11 F6** 58 12N 12 43 E
Nossob →, *S. Africa* **88 D3** 26 55 S 20 45 E
Nossombougou, *Mali* **82 C3** 13 5N 7 55W
Nosy Barren, *Madag.* **85 H8** 18 25 S 43 40 E
Nosy Be, *Madag.* **85 G9** 13 25 S 48 15 E
Nosy Boraha, *Madag.* **89 B8** 16 50 S 49 55 E
Nosy Lava, *Madag.* **89 A8** 14 33 S 47 36 E
Nosy Varika, *Madag.* **89 C8** 20 35 S 48 32 E
Noteć →, *Poland* **45 F2** 52 44N 15 26 E
Notikewin →, *Canada* **104 B5** 57 2N 117 38W
Notios Evvoïkos Kólpos, *Greece* **38 C5** 38 20N 24 0 E
Noto, *Italy* **31 F8** 36 53N 15 4 E
Noto, G. di, *Italy* **31 F8** 36 50N 15 12 E
Notodden, *Norway* **9 G13** 59 35N 9 17 E
Notre Dame B., *Canada* **103 C8** 49 45N 55 30W
Notre Dame de Koartac = Quaqtaq, *Canada* **101 B13** 60 55N 69 40W
Notre-Dame-des-Bois, *Canada* **111 A13** 45 24N 71 4W
Notre Dame d'Ivugivic = Ivujivik, *Canada* **101 B12** 62 24N 77 55W
Notre-Dame-du-Nord, *Canada* **102 C4** 47 36N 79 30W
Notsé, *Togo* **83 D5** 7 0N 1 17 E
Nottawasaga B., *Canada* **110 B4** 44 35N 80 15W
Nottaway →, *Canada* **102 B4** 51 22N 78 55W
Nottingham, *U.K.* **12 E6** 52 58N 1 10W
Nottingham, City of □, *U.K.* **12 E6** 52 58N 1 10W
Nottingham I., *Canada* **101 B12** 63 20N 77 55W
Nottinghamshire □, *U.K.* **12 D6** 53 10N 1 3W
Nottoway →, *U.S.A.* **108 G7** 36 33N 76 55W
Notwane →, *Botswana* **88 C4** 23 35 S 26 58 E
Nouâdhibou, *Mauritania* **78 D2** 20 54N 17 0W
Nouâdhibou, Ras, *Mauritania* **78 D2** 20 50N 17 0W
Nouakchott, *Mauritania* **82 B1** 18 9N 15 58W
Nouâmghâr, *Mauritania* **82 B1** 19 20N 16 20W
Nouméa, *N. Cal.* **96 K8** 22 17 S 166 30 E
Nouna, *Burkina Faso* **82 C4** 12 45N 3 52W
Noupoort, *S. Africa* **88 E3** 31 10 S 24 57 E
Nouveau Comptoir = Wemindji, *Canada* **102 B4** 53 0N 78 49W
Nouvelle-Amsterdam, I., *Ind. Oc.* **3 F13** 38 30 S 77 30 E
Nouvelle-Calédonie = New Caledonia ■, *Pac. Oc.* **96 K8** 21 0 S 165 0 E
Nouzonville, *France* **19 C11** 49 48N 4 44 E
Nová Baňa, *Slovak Rep.* **27 C11** 48 28N 18 39 E
Nová Bystřice, *Czech Rep.* **26 B8** 49 2N 15 8 E
Nova Casa Nova, *Brazil* **125 E10** 9 25 S 41 5W
Nova Esperança, *Brazil* **127 A5** 23 8 S 52 24W
Nova Friburgo, *Brazil* **127 A7** 22 16 S 42 30W
Nova Gaia = Cambundi-Catembo, *Angola* **84 G3** 10 10 S 17 35 E
Nova Gorica, *Slovenia* **29 C10** 45 7N 13 39 E
Nova Gradiška, *Croatia* **42 E2** 45 17N 17 28 E
Nova Iguaçu, *Brazil* **127 A7** 22 45 S 43 28W
Nova Iorque, *Brazil* **125 E10** 7 0 S 44 5W
Nova Kakhovka, *Ukraine* **47 J7** 46 42N 33 27 E
Nova Lamego, *Guinea-Biss.* **82 C2** 12 19N 14 11W
Nova Lima, *Brazil* **127 A7** 19 59 S 43 51W
Nova Lisboa = Huambo, *Angola* **85 G3** 12 42 S 15 54 E
Nova Lusitânia, *Mozam.* **87 F3** 19 50 S 34 34 E
Nova Mambone, *Mozam.* **89 C6** 21 0 S 35 3 E
Nova Odesa, *Ukraine* **47 J6** 47 19N 31 47 E
Nová Paka, *Czech Rep.* **26 A8** 50 29N 15 30 E
Nova Pavova, *Serbia, Yug.* **42 F5** 44 56N 20 14 E
Nova Scotia □, *Canada* **103 C7** 45 10N 63 0W
Nova Siri, *Italy* **31 B9** 40 10N 16 35 E
Nova Sofala, *Mozam.* **89 C5** 20 7 S 34 42 E
Nova Varoš, *Serbia, Yug.* **40 C3** 43 29N 19 48 E
Nova Venécia, *Brazil* **125 G10** 18 45 S 40 24W
Nova Zagora, *Bulgaria* **41 D10** 42 32N 26 1 E
Novaci, *Macedonia* **40 E5** 41 5N 21 29 E
Novaci, *Romania* **43 E8** 45 10N 23 42 E
Novafeltria, *Italy* **29 E9** 43 53N 12 17 E
Novaleksandrovskaya = Novoaleksandrovsk, *Russia* **49 H5** 45 29N 41 17 E
Novannenskiy = Novoannenskiy, *Russia* **48 E6** 50 32N 42 39 E
Novar, *Canada* **110 A5** 45 27N 79 15W
Novara, *Italy* **28 C5** 45 28N 8 38 E
Novato, *U.S.A.* **116 G4** 38 6N 122 35W
Novaya Kakhovka = Nova Kakhovka, *Ukraine* **47 J7** 46 42N 33 27 E
Novaya Kazanka, *Kazakstan* **49 F9** 48 56N 49 36 E
Novaya Ladoga, *Russia* **46 B7** 60 7N 32 16 E
Novaya Lyalya, *Russia* **50 D7** 59 4N 60 45 E
Novaya Sibir, Ostrov, *Russia* **51 B16** 75 10N 150 0 E
Novaya Zemlya, *Russia* **50 B6** 75 0N 56 0 E
Nové Město, *Slovak Rep.* **27 C10** 48 45N 17 50 E
Nové Město na Moravě, *Czech Rep.* **26 B9** 49 34N 16 5 E
Nové Město nad Metují, *Czech Rep.* **27 A9** 50 20N 16 10 E
Nové Zámky, *Slovak Rep.* **27 C11** 48 2N 18 8 E
Novelda, *Spain* **33 G4** 38 24N 0 45W
Novellara, *Italy* **28 D7** 44 51N 10 44 E
Noventa Vicentina, *Italy* **29 C8** 45 17N 11 32 E
Novgorod, *Russia* **46 C6** 58 30N 31 25 E
Novgorod-Severskiy = Novhorod-Siverskyy, *Ukraine* **47 G7** 52 2N 33 10 E
Novhorod-Siverskyy, *Ukraine* **47 G7** 52 2N 33 10 E
Novi Bečej, *Serbia, Yug.* **42 E5** 45 36N 20 10 E
Novi Iskar, *Bulgaria* **40 D7** 42 48N 23 21 E
Novi Kneževac, *Serbia, Yug.* **42 D5** 46 4N 20 8 E
Novi Lígure, *Italy* **28 D5** 44 46N 8 47 E
Novi Pazar, *Bulgaria* **41 C11** 43 25N 27 15 E
Novi Pazar, *Serbia, Yug.* **40 C4** 43 12N 20 28 E
Novi Sad, *Serbia, Yug.* **42 E4** 45 18N 19 52 E
Novi Slankamen, *Serbia, Yug.* **42 E5** 45 8N 20 15 E
Novi Travnik, *Bos.-H.* **42 F2** 44 10N 17 40 E
Novi Vinodolski, *Croatia* **29 C11** 45 10N 14 48 E
Novigrad, *Istra, Croatia* **29 C10** 45 19N 13 33 E
Novigrad, *Zadar, Croatia* **29 D12** 44 10N 15 32 E
Novigradsko More, *Croatia* **29 D12** 44 12N 15 33 E
Nôvo Hamburgo, *Brazil* **127 B5** 29 37 S 51 7W
Novo Mesto, *Slovenia* **29 C12** 45 47N 15 12 E
Novo Miloševo, *Serbia, Yug.* **42 E5** 45 42N 20 20 E
Novo Remanso, *Brazil* **125 E10** 9 41 S 42 4W
Novoaleksandrovsk, *Russia* **49 H5** 45 29N 41 17 E
Novoannenskiy, *Russia* **48 E6** 50 32N 42 39 E
Novoataysk, *Russia* **50 D9** 53 30N 84 0 E
Novoazovsk, *Ukraine* **47 J10** 47 15N 38 4 E
Novocheboksarsk, *Russia* **48 B8** 56 5N 47 27 E
Novocherkassk, *Russia* **49 G5** 47 27N 40 15 E
Novodevichye, *Russia* **48 D9** 53 37N 48 50 E
Novogrudok = Navahrudak, *Belarus* **46 F3** 53 40N 25 50 E
Novohrad-Volynskyy, *Ukraine* **47 G4** 50 34N 27 35 E
Novokachalinsk, *Russia* **54 B6** 45 5N 132 0 E
Novokazalinsk = Zhangaqazaly, *Kazakstan* **50 E7** 45 48N 62 6 E
Novokhopersk, *Russia* **48 E5** 51 5N 41 39 E
Novokuybyshevsk, *Russia* **48 D9** 53 7N 49 58 E
Novokuznetsk, *Russia* **50 D9** 53 45N 87 10 E
Novomirgorod, *Ukraine* **47 H6** 48 45N 31 33 E
Novomoskovsk, *Russia* **46 E10** 54 5N 38 15 E
Novomoskovsk, *Ukraine* **47 H8** 48 33N 35 17 E
Novopolotsk = Navapolatsk, *Belarus* **46 E5** 55 32N 28 37 E
Novorossiysk, *Russia* **47 K9** 44 43N 37 46 E
Novorybnoye, *Russia* **51 B11** 72 50N 105 50 E
Novorzhev, *Russia* **46 D5** 57 3N 29 25 E
Novosej, *Albania* **40 E4** 41 56N 20 35 E
Novoselytsya, *Ukraine* **47 H4** 48 14N 26 15 E
Novoshakhtinsk, *Russia* **47 J10** 47 46N 39 58 E
Novosibirsk, *Russia* **50 D9** 55 0N 83 5 E
Novosibirskiye Ostrova, *Russia* **51 B15** 75 0N 142 0 E
Novosil, *Russia* **47 F9** 52 59N 37 2 E
Novosokolniki, *Russia* **46 D6** 56 20N 30 2 E
Novotitarovskaya, *Russia* **49 H4** 45 17N 39 2 E
Novotroitsk, *Russia* **50 D6** 51 10N 58 15 E
Novoukrayinka, *Ukraine* **47 H6** 48 25N 31 30 E
Novouljanovsk, *Russia* **48 C9** 54 8N 48 24 E
Novouzensk, *Russia* **48 E9** 50 32N 48 17 E
Novovolynsk, *Ukraine* **47 G3** 50 45N 24 4 E
Novovoronezhskiy, *Russia* **47 G10** 51 19N 39 13 E
Novozybkov, *Russia* **47 F6** 52 30N 32 0 E
Novska, *Croatia* **29 C14** 45 19N 17 0 E
Novvy Urengoy, *Russia* **50 C8** 65 48N 76 52 E
Nový Bor, *Czech Rep.* **26 A7** 50 46N 14 35 E
Novy Bug = Novyy Buh, *Ukraine* **47 J7** 47 34N 32 29 E
Nový Bydžov, *Czech Rep.* **26 A8** 50 14N 15 29 E
Novy Dwór Mazowiecki, *Poland* **45 F7** 52 26N 20 44 E
Nový Jičín, *Czech Rep.* **27 B11** 49 30N 18 2 E
Novyy Afon, *Georgia* **49 J5** 43 7N 40 50 E
Novyy Buh, *Ukraine* **47 J7** 47 34N 32 29 E
Novyy Oskol, *Russia* **47 G9** 50 44N 37 55 E
Novyy Port, *Russia* **50 C8** 67 40N 72 30 E
Now Shahr, *Iran* **71 B6** 36 40N 51 30 E
Nowa Deba, *Poland* **45 H8** 50 26N 21 41 E
Nowa Ruda, *Poland* **45 H3** 50 35N 16 30 E
Nowa Sarzyna, *Poland* **45 H9** 50 21N 22 21 E
Nowa Sól, *Poland* **45 G2** 51 48N 15 44 E
Nowata, *U.S.A.* **113 G7** 36 42N 95 38W
Nowbarān, *Iran* **71 C6** 35 8N 49 42 E
Nowe, *Poland* **44 E5** 53 41N 18 44 E
Nowe Miasteczko, *Poland* **45 G2** 51 42N 15 42 E
Nowe Miasto, *Poland* **45 G7** 51 38N 20 34 E
Nowe Miasto Lubawskie, *Poland* **44 E6** 53 27N 19 33 E
Nowe Skalmierzyce, *Poland* **45 G4** 51 43N 18 0 E
Nowe Warpno, *Poland* **44 E1** 53 42N 14 18 E
Nowghāb, *Iran* **71 C8** 33 53N 59 4 E
Nowgong, *Assam, India* **67 F18** 26 20N 92 50 E
Nowgong, *Mad. P., India* **69 G8** 25 4N 79 27 E
Nowogard, *Poland* **44 E2** 53 41N 15 10 E
Nowogród, *Poland* **45 E8** 53 14N 21 53 E
Nowogród Bobrzanski, *Poland* **45 G2** 51 48N 15 15 E
Nowogrodziec, *Poland* **45 G2** 51 12N 15 24 E
Nowra-Bomaderry, *Australia* **95 E5** 34 53 S 150 35 E
Nowshera, *Pakistan* **66 C8** 34 0N 72 0 E
Nowy Dwór Gdański, *Poland* **44 D6** 54 13N 19 7 E
Nowy Sącz, *Poland* **45 J7** 49 40N 20 41 E
Nowy Staw, *Poland* **44 D6** 54 13N 19 2 E
Nowy Targ, *Poland* **45 J7** 49 29N 20 2 E
Nowy Tomyśl, *Poland* **45 F3** 52 19N 16 10 E
Nowy Wiśnicz, *Poland* **45 J7** 49 55N 20 28 E
Noxen, *U.S.A.* **111 E8** 41 25N 76 4W
Noxon, *U.S.A.* **114 C6** 48 0N 115 43W
Noyabr'sk, *Russia* **50 C8** 64 34N 76 21 E
Noyant, *France* **18 E7** 47 30N 0 6 E
Noyers, *France* **19 E10** 47 40N 4 0 E
Noyon, *France* **19 C9** 49 34N 2 59 E
Noyon, *Mongolia* **56 C2** 43 2N 102 4 E
Nozay, *France* **18 E5** 47 34N 1 38W
Nqutu, *S. Africa* **89 D5** 28 13 S 30 32 E
Nsanje, *Malawi* **87 F4** 16 55 S 35 12 E
Nsawam, *Ghana* **83 D4** 5 50N 0 24W
Nsomba, *Zambia* **87 E2** 10 45 S 29 51 E
Nsukka, *Nigeria* **83 D6** 6 51N 7 29 E
Ntui, *Cameroon* **83 E7** 4 27N 11 38 E
Nu Jiang →, *China* **58 E2** 29 58N 97 25 E
Nu Shan, *China* **58 E2** 26 0N 99 20 E
Nuba Mts. = Nubah, Jibalan, *Sudan* **81 E3** 12 0N 31 0 E
Nubah, Jibalan, *Sudan* **81 E3** 12 0N 31 0 E
Nubia, *Africa* **76 D7** 21 0N 32 0 E
Nubian Desert = Nûbîya, Es Sahrâ en, *Sudan* **80 C3** 21 30N 33 30 E
Nûbîya, Es Sahrâ en, *Sudan* **80 C3** 21 30N 33 30 E
Nubledo, *Spain* **34 B5** 43 31N 5 52W
Nuboai, *Indonesia* **63 E9** 2 10 S 136 30 E
Nubra →, *India* **69 B7** 34 35N 77 35 E
Nucet, *Romania* **42 D7** 46 28N 22 35 E
Nueces →, *U.S.A.* **113 M6** 27 51N 97 30W
Nueltin L., *Canada* **105 A9** 60 30N 99 30W
Nueva Asunción □, *Paraguay* **126 A3** 21 0 S 61 0W
Nueva Carteya, *Spain* **35 H6** 37 35N 4 28W
Nueva Gerona, *Cuba* **120 B3** 21 53N 82 49W
Nueva Palmira, *Uruguay* **126 C4** 33 52 S 58 20W
Nueva Rosita, *Mexico* **118 B4** 28 0N 101 11W
Nueva San Salvador, *El Salv.* **120 D2** 13 40N 89 18W
Nueva Tabarca, *Spain* **33 G4** 38 17N 0 30W
Nuéve de Julio, *Argentina* **126 D3** 35 30 S 61 0W
Nuevitas, *Cuba* **120 B4** 21 30N 77 20W
Nuevo, G., *Argentina* **128 E4** 43 0 S 64 30W
Nuevo Casas Grandes, *Mexico* **118 A3** 30 22N 108 0W
Nuevo Guerrero, *Mexico* **119 B5** 26 34N 99 15W
Nuevo Laredo, *Mexico* **119 B5** 27 30N 99 30W
Nuevo León □, *Mexico* **118 C5** 25 0N 100 0W
Nuevo Rocafuerte, *Ecuador* **124 D3** 0 55 S 75 27W
Nugget Pt., *N.Z.* **91 M2** 46 27 S 169 50 E
Nugrus, Gebel, *Egypt* **80 C3** 24 47N 34 35 E
Nuhaka, *N.Z.* **91 H6** 39 3 S 177 45 E
Nuits-St-Georges, *France* **19 E11** 47 10N 4 56 E
Nukey Bluff, *Australia* **95 E2** 32 26 S 135 29 E
Nukheila, *Sudan* **80 D2** 19 1N 26 21 E
Nukhuyb, *Iraq* **70 C4** 32 4N 42 3 E
Nuku'alofa, *Tonga* **91 E12** 21 10 S 174 0W
Nukus, *Uzbekistan* **50 E6** 42 27N 59 41 E
Nules, *Spain* **32 F4** 39 51N 0 9W
Nullagine, *Australia* **92 D3** 21 53 S 120 7 E
Nullagine →, *Australia* **92 D3** 21 20 S 120 20 E
Nullarbor, *Australia* **93 F5** 31 28 S 130 55 E
Nullarbor Plain, *Australia* **93 F4** 31 10 S 129 0 E
Numalla, L., *Australia* **95 D3** 28 43 S 144 20 E
Numan, *Nigeria* **83 D7** 9 29N 12 3 E
Numata, *Japan* **55 F9** 36 45N 139 4 E
Numatinna →, *Sudan* **81 F2** 7 38N 27 20 E
Numazu, *Japan* **55 G9** 35 7N 138 51 E
Numbulwar, *Australia* **94 A2** 14 15 S 135 45 E
Numfoor, *Indonesia* **63 E8** 1 0 S 134 50 E
Numurkah, *Australia* **95 F4** 36 5 S 145 26 E
Nunaksaluk I., *Canada* **103 A7** 55 49N 60 20W
Nunap Isua, *Greenland* **4 D5** 59 48N 43 55W
Nunavut □, *Canada* **101 B11** 66 0N 85 0W
Nunda, *U.S.A.* **110 D7** 42 35N 77 56W
Nungarin, *Australia* **93 F2** 31 12 S 118 6 E
Nungo, *Mozam.* **87 E4** 13 23 S 37 43 E
Nungwe, *Tanzania* **86 C3** 2 48 S 32 2 E
Nunivak I., *U.S.A.* **100 B3** 60 10N 166 30W
Nunkun, *India* **69 C7** 33 57N 76 2 E
Nùoro, *Italy* **30 B2** 40 20N 9 20 E
Nūrābād, *Iran* **71 E8** 27 47N 57 12 E
Nure →, *Italy* **28 C6** 45 3N 9 49 E
Nuremberg = Nürnberg, *Germany* **25 F7** 49 27N 11 3 E
Nuri, *Mexico* **118 B3** 28 2N 109 22W
Nuriootpa, *Australia* **95 E2** 34 27 S 139 0 E
Nurlat, *Russia* **48 C10** 54 29N 50 45 E
Nurmes, *Finland* **8 E23** 63 33N 29 10 E
Nürnberg, *Germany* **25 F7** 49 27N 11 3 E
Nurpur, *Pakistan* **68 D4** 31 53N 71 54 E
Nurra, La, *Italy* **30 B1** 40 45N 8 15 E
Nurran, L. = Terewah, L., *Australia* **95 D4** 29 52 S 147 35 E
Nurrari Lakes, *Australia* **93 E5** 29 1 S 130 5 E
Nurri, *Italy* **30 C2** 39 43N 9 14 E
Nürtingen, *Germany* **25 G5** 48 37N 9 19 E
Nurzec →, *Poland* **45 F9** 52 37N 22 25 E
Nus, *Italy* **28 C4** 45 45N 7 28 E
Nusa Barung, *Indonesia* **63 H15** 8 30 S 113 30 E
Nusa Kambangan, *Indonesia* **63 G13** 7 40 S 108 10 E
Nusa Tenggara Barat □, *Indonesia* **62 F5** 8 50 S 117 30 E
Nusa Tenggara Timur □, *Indonesia* **63 F6** 9 30 S 122 0 E
Nusaybin, *Turkey* **73 D9** 37 3N 41 10 E
Nushki, *Pakistan* **68 E2** 29 35N 66 0 E
Nuuk, *Greenland* **101 B14** 64 10N 51 35W
Nuwakot, *Nepal* **69 E10** 28 10N 83 55 E
Nuweiba', *Egypt* **70 D2** 28 59N 34 39 E
Nuwerus, *S. Africa* **88 E2** 31 8 S 18 24 E
Nuweveldberge, *S. Africa* **88 E3** 32 10 S 21 45 E
Nuyts, C., *Australia* **93 F5** 32 2 S 132 21 E
Nuyts, Pt., *Australia* **93 G2** 35 4 S 116 38 E
Nuyts Arch., *Australia* **95 E1** 32 35 S 133 20 E
Nxau-Nxau, *Botswana* **88 B3** 18 57 S 21 4 E
Nyaake, *Liberia* **82 E3** 4 52N 7 37W
Nyabing, *Australia* **93 F2** 33 33 S 118 9 E
Nyack, *U.S.A.* **111 E11** 41 5N 73 55W
Nyagan, *Russia* **50 C7** 62 30N 65 38 E
Nyahanga, *Tanzania* **86 C3** 2 20 S 33 37 E
Nyahua, *Tanzania* **86 D3** 5 25 S 33 23 E
Nyahururu, *Kenya* **86 B4** 0 2N 36 27 E
Nyainqentanglha Shan, *China* **60 C4** 30 0N 90 0 E
Nyakanazi, *Tanzania* **86 C3** 3 2 S 31 10 E
Nyakrom, *Ghana* **83 D4** 5 40N 0 50W
Nyâlâ, *Sudan* **81 E1** 12 2N 24 58 E
Nyamandhlovu, *Zimbabwe* **87 F2** 19 55 S 28 16 E
Nyambiti, *Tanzania* **86 C3** 2 48 S 33 27 E
Nyamlell, *Sudan* **81 F2** 9 7N 26 59 E
Nyamwaga, *Tanzania* **86 C3** 1 27 S 34 33 E
Nyandekwa, *Tanzania* **86 C3** 3 57 S 32 32 E
Nyanding →, *Sudan* **81 F3** 8 40N 32 41 E
Nyandoma, *Russia* **46 B11** 61 40N 40 12 E
Nyangana, *Namibia* **88 B3** 18 0 S 20 40 E
Nyanguge, *Tanzania* **86 C3** 2 30 S 33 12 E
Nyankpala, *Ghana* **83 D4** 9 21N 0 58W
Nyanza, *Rwanda* **86 C2** 2 20 S 29 42 E
Nyanza □, *Kenya* **86 C3** 0 10 S 34 15 E
Nyanza-Lac, *Burundi* **86 C2** 4 21 S 29 36 E
Nyaponges, *Sudan* **81 F3** 5 5N 33 45 E
Nyasa, L., *Africa* **87 E3** 12 30 S 34 30 E
Nyasvizh, *Belarus* **47 F4** 53 14N 26 38 E
Nyazura, *Zimbabwe* **87 F3** 18 40 S 32 16 E
Nyazwidzi →, *Zimbabwe* **87 G3** 20 0 S 31 17 E
Nyborg, *Denmark* **11 J4** 55 18N 10 47 E
Nybro, *Sweden* **11 H9** 56 44N 15 55 E
Nyda, *Russia* **50 C8** 66 40N 72 58 E
Nyeri, *Kenya* **86 C4** 0 23 S 36 56 E
Nyerol, *Sudan* **81 F3** 8 41N 32 1 E
Nyhammar, *Sweden* **10 D8** 60 17N 14 58 E
Nyinahin, *Ghana* **82 D4** 6 43N 2 3W
Nyíradony, *Hungary* **42 C6** 47 41N 21 55 E
Nyírbátor, *Hungary* **42 C7** 47 49N 22 9 E
Nyíregyháza, *Hungary* **42 C6** 47 58N 21 47 E
Nykøbing, *Storstrøm, Denmark* **11 K5** 54 56N 11 52 E
Nykøbing, *Vestsjælland, Denmark* **11 J5** 55 55N 11 40 E
Nykøbing, *Viborg, Denmark* **11 H2** 56 48N 8 51 E
Nyköping, *Sweden* **11 F11** 58 45N 17 1 E
Nykroppa, *Sweden* **10 E8** 59 37N 14 18 E
Nykvarn, *Sweden* **10 E11** 59 11N 17 25 E
Nyland, *Sweden* **10 A11** 63 1N 17 45 E
Nylstroom, *S. Africa* **89 C4** 24 42 S 28 22 E
Nymagee, *Australia* **95 E4** 32 7 S 146 20 E
Nymburk, *Czech Rep.* **26 A8** 50 10N 15 1 E
Nynäshamn, *Sweden* **11 F11** 58 54N 17 57 E
Nyngan, *Australia* **95 E4** 31 30 S 147 8 E
Nyoma Rap, *India* **69 C8** 33 10N 78 40 E
Nyoman = Neman →, *Lithuania* **9 J19** 55 25N 21 10 E
Nyon, *Switz.* **25 J2** 46 23N 6 14 E
Nyong →, *Cameroon* **83 E6** 3 17N 9 54 E
Nyons, *France* **21 D9** 44 22N 5 10 E
Nyou, *Burkina Faso* **83 C4** 12 42N 2 1W
Nýrsko, *Czech Rep.* **26 B6** 49 18N 13 9 E
Nysa, *Poland* **45 H4** 50 30N 17 22 E
Nysa →, *Europe* **24 C10** 52 4N 14 46 E
Nysa Kłodzka →, *Poland* **45 H4** 50 49N 17 40 E
Nysäter, *Sweden* **10 E6** 59 17N 12 47 E
Nyssa, *U.S.A.* **114 E5** 43 53N 117 0W
Nysted, *Denmark* **11 K5** 54 40N 11 44 E
Nyunzu, *Dem. Rep. of the Congo* **86 D2** 5 57 S 27 58 E
Nyurba, *Russia* **51 C12** 63 17N 118 28 E
Nyzhnohirskyy, *Ukraine* **47 K8** 45 27N 34 38 E
Nzébéla, *Guinea* **82 D3** 8 9N 9 7W
Nzega, *Tanzania* **86 C3** 4 10 S 33 12 E
N'zérékoré, *Guinea* **82 D3** 7 49N 8 48W
Nzeto, *Angola* **84 F2** 7 10 S 12 52 E
Nzilo, Chutes de, *Dem. Rep. of the Congo* **87 E2** 10 18 S 25 27 E
Nzo →, *Ivory C.* **82 D3** 6 15N 7 3W
Nzubuka, *Tanzania* **86 C3** 4 45 S 32 50 E

O

O Barco, *Spain* **34 C4** 42 23N 6 58W
O Carballiño, *Spain* **34 C2** 42 26N 8 5W
O Corgo, *Spain* **34 C3** 42 56N 7 25W
O Pino, *Spain* **34 C2** 42 56N 8 20W
O Porriño, *Spain* **34 C2** 42 10N 8 39W
Ō-Shima, *Japan* **55 G9** 34 44N 139 24 E
Oa, Mull of, *U.K.* **14 F2** 55 35N 6 20W
Oacoma, *U.S.A.* **112 D5** 43 48N 99 24W
Oahe, L., *U.S.A.* **112 C4** 44 27N 100 24W
Oahe Dam, *U.S.A.* **112 C4** 44 27N 100 24W
Oahu, *U.S.A.* **106 H16** 21 28N 157 58W
Oak Harbor, *U.S.A.* **116 B4** 48 18N 122 39W
Oak Hill, *U.S.A.* **108 G5** 37 59N 81 9W
Oak Ridge, *U.S.A.* **109 G3** 36 1N 84 16W
Oak View, *U.S.A.* **117 L7** 34 24N 119 18W
Oakan-Dake, *Japan* **54 C12** 43 27N 144 10 E
Oakdale, *Calif., U.S.A.* **116 H6** 37 46N 120 51W
Oakdale, *La., U.S.A.* **113 K8** 30 49N 92 40W
Oakes, *U.S.A.* **112 B5** 46 8N 98 6W
Oakesdale, *U.S.A.* **114 C5** 47 8N 117 15W
Oakey, *Australia* **95 D5** 27 25 S 151 43 E
Oakfield, *U.S.A.* **110 C6** 43 4N 78 16W
Oakham, *U.K.* **13 E7** 52 40N 0 43W
Oakhurst, *U.S.A.* **116 H7** 37 19N 119 40W
Oakland, *U.S.A.* **116 H4** 37 49N 122 16W
Oakley, *Idaho, U.S.A.* **114 E7** 42 15N 113 53W
Oakley, *Kans., U.S.A.* **112 F4** 39 8N 100 51W
Oakover →, *Australia* **92 D3** 21 0 S 120 40 E
Oakridge, *U.S.A.* **114 E2** 43 45N 122 28W
Oakville, *Canada* **110 C5** 43 27N 79 41W
Oakville, *U.S.A.* **116 D3** 46 51N 123 14W
Oamaru, *N.Z.* **91 L3** 45 5 S 170 59 E
Oancea, *Romania* **43 E12** 45 21N 27 42 E
Oasis, *Calif., U.S.A.* **117 M10** 33 28N 116 6W
Oasis, *Nev., U.S.A.* **116 H9** 37 29N 117 55W
Oates Land, *Antarctica* **5 C11** 69 0 S 160 0 E
Oatlands, *Australia* **94 G4** 42 17 S 147 21 E
Oatman, *U.S.A.* **117 K12** 35 1N 114 19W
Oaxaca, *Mexico* **119 D5** 17 2N 96 40W
Oaxaca □, *Mexico* **119 D5** 17 0N 97 0W
Ob →, *Russia* **50 C7** 66 45N 69 30 E
Oba, *Canada* **102 C3** 49 4N 84 7W
Obala, *Cameroon* **83 E7** 4 9N 11 32 E
Obama, *Japan* **55 G7** 35 30N 135 45 E
Oban, *Nigeria* **83 D6** 5 17N 8 33 E
Oban, *U.K.* **14 E3** 56 25N 5 29W
Obbia, *Somali Rep.* **74 F4** 5 25N 48 30 E
Obera, *Argentina* **127 B4** 27 21 S 55 2W
Oberammergau, *Germany* **25 H7** 47 36N 11 4 E
Oberasbach, *Germany* **25 F6** 49 25N 10 57 E
Oberbayern □, *Germany* **25 G7** 48 5N 11 50 E
Oberdrauburg, *Austria* **26 E5** 46 44N 12 58 E
Oberfranken □, *Germany* **25 E7** 50 10N 11 20 E
Oberhausen, *Germany* **24 D2** 51 28N 6 51 E
Oberkirch, *Germany* **25 G4** 48 31N 8 4 E
Oberlausitz, *Germany* **24 D10** 51 16N 14 18 E
Oberlin, *Kans., U.S.A.* **112 F4** 39 49N 100 32W
Oberlin, *La., U.S.A.* **113 K8** 30 37N 92 46W
Oberlin, *Ohio, U.S.A.* **110 E2** 41 18N 82 13W
Obernai, *France* **19 D14** 48 28N 7 30 E
Oberndorf, *Germany* **25 G4** 48 17N 8 34 E
Oberon, *Australia* **95 E4** 33 45 S 149 52 E
Oberösterreich □, *Austria* **26 C7** 48 10N 14 0 E
Oberpfalz □, *Germany* **25 F8** 49 20N 12 10 E
Oberpfälzer Wald, *Germany* **25 F8** 49 30N 12 30 E
Oberstdorf, *Germany* **25 H6** 47 24N 10 15 E
Oberursel, *Germany* **25 E4** 50 11N 8 35 E
Oberwart, *Austria* **27 D9** 47 17N 16 12 E
Obi, Kepulauan, *Indonesia* **63 E7** 1 23 S 127 45 E
Obi Is. = Obi, Kepulauan, *Indonesia* **63 E7** 1 23 S 127 45 E
Obiaruku, *Nigeria* **83 D6** 5 51N 6 9 E
Óbidos, *Brazil* **125 D7** 1 50 S 55 30W
Óbidos, *Portugal* **35 F1** 39 19N 9 10W
Obihiro, *Japan* **54 C11** 42 56N 143 12 E
Obilatu, *Indonesia* **63 E7** 1 25 S 127 20 E
Obilnoye, *Russia* **49 G7** 47 32N 44 30 E
Obing, *Germany* **25 G8** 48 0N 12 24 E
Objat, *France* **20 C5** 45 16N 1 24 E
Obluchye, *Russia* **51 E14** 49 1N 131 4 E
Obninsk, *Russia* **46 E9** 55 8N 36 37 E
Obo, *C.A.R.* **86 A2** 5 20N 26 32 E
Oboa, Mt., *Uganda* **86 B3** 1 45N 34 45 E
Obock, *Djibouti* **81 E5** 12 0N 43 20 E
Oborniki, *Poland* **45 F3** 52 39N 16 50 E
Oborniki Śląskie, *Poland* **45 G3** 51 17N 16 53 E
Oboyan, *Russia* **47 G9** 51 15N 36 21 E
Obozerskaya = Obozerskiy, *Russia* **50 C5** 63 34N 40 21 E
Obozerskiy, *Russia* **50 C5** 63 34N 40 21 E
Obrenovac, *Serbia, Yug.* **40 B4** 44 40N 20 11 E
Obrovac, *Croatia* **29 D12** 44 11N 15 41 E
Obruk, *Turkey* **72 C5** 38 7N 33 12 E
Obrzycko, *Poland* **45 F3** 52 42N 16 32 E
Observatory Inlet, *Canada* **104 B3** 55 10N 129 54W
Obshchi Syrt, *Russia* **6 E16** 52 0N 53 0 E
Obskaya Guba, *Russia* **50 C8** 69 0N 73 0 E
Obuasi, *Ghana* **83 D4** 6 17N 1 40W
Obubra, *Nigeria* **83 D6** 6 8N 8 20 E
Obudu, *Nigeria* **83 D6** 6 38N 9 5 E
Obwalden □, *Switz.* **25 J4** 46 55N 8 15 E
Obzor, *Bulgaria* **41 D11** 42 50N 27 52 E
Ocala, *U.S.A.* **109 L4** 29 11N 82 8W
Ocampo, *Chihuahua, Mexico* **118 B3** 28 9N 108 24W

Ocampo, *Tamaulipas, Mexico* **119 C5** 22 50N 99 20W
Ocaña, *Spain* **34 F7** 39 55N 3 30W
Oconomowoc, *U.S.A.* **112 D10** 43 7N 88 30W
Occidental, Cordillera, *Colombia* **122 C3** 5 0N 76 0W
Ocean City, *Md., U.S.A.* **108 F8** 38 20N 75 5W
Ocean City, *N.J., U.S.A.* **108 F8** 39 17N 74 35W
Ocean City, *Wash., U.S.A.* **116 C2** 47 4N 124 10W
Ocean Falls, *Canada* **104 C3** 52 18N 127 48W
Ocean I. = Banaba, *Kiribati* **96 H8** 0 45 S 169 50 E
Ocean Park, *U.S.A.* **116 D2** 46 30N 124 3W
Oceano, *U.S.A.* **117 K6** 35 6N 120 37W
Oceanport, *U.S.A.* **111 F10** 40 19N 74 3W
Oceanside, *U.S.A.* **117 M9** 33 12N 117 23W
Ochagavía, *Spain* **32 C3** 42 55N 1 5W
Ochakiv, *Ukraine* **47 J6** 46 37N 31 33 E
Ochamchira, *Georgia* **49 J5** 42 46N 41 32 E
Ochil Hills, *U.K.* **14 E5** 56 14N 3 40W
Ochsenfurt, *Germany* **25 F6** 49 40N 10 4 E
Ochsenhausen, *Germany* **25 G5** 48 4N 9 57 E
Ocilla, *U.S.A.* **109 K4** 31 36N 83 15W
Ockelbo, *Sweden* **10 D10** 60 54N 16 45 E
Ocmulgee →, *U.S.A.* **109 K4** 31 58N 82 33W
Ocna Mureș, *Romania* **43 D8** 46 23N 23 55 E
Ocna Sibiului, *Romania* **43 E9** 45 52N 24 2 E
Ocnele Mari, *Romania* **43 E9** 45 8N 24 18 E
Ocnița, *Moldova* **43 B12** 48 25N 27 30 E
Oconee →, *U.S.A.* **109 K4** 31 58N 82 33W
Oconto, *U.S.A.* **108 C2** 44 53N 87 52W
Oconto Falls, *U.S.A.* **108 C1** 44 52N 88 9W
Ocosingo, *Mexico* **119 D6** 17 10N 92 15W
Ocotal, *Nic.* **120 D2** 13 41N 86 31W
Ocotlán, *Mexico* **118 C4** 20 21N 102 42W
Ocotlán de Morelos, *Mexico* **119 D5** 16 48N 96 40W
Ocreza →, *Portugal* **35 F3** 39 32N 7 50W
Ócsa, *Hungary* **42 C4** 47 17N 19 15 E
Octeville, *France* **18 C5** 49 38N 1 40W
Oda, *Ghana* **83 D4** 5 50N 0 51W
Ōda, *Japan* **55 G6** 35 11N 132 30 E
Oda, J., *Sudan* **80 C4** 20 21N 36 39 E
Ódáðahraun, *Iceland* **8 D5** 65 5N 17 0W
Ödåkra, *Sweden* **11 H6** 56 7N 12 45 E
Odate, *Japan* **54 D10** 40 16N 140 34 E
Odawara, *Japan* **55 G9** 35 20N 139 6 E
Odda, *Norway* **9 F12** 60 3N 6 35 E
Odder, *Denmark* **11 J4** 55 58N 10 10 E
Odei →, *Canada* **105 B9** 56 6N 96 54W
Odemira, *Portugal* **35 H2** 37 35N 8 40W
Ödemiș, *Turkey* **39 C9** 38 15N 28 0 E
Odendaalsrus, *S. Africa* **88 D4** 27 48 S 26 45 E
Odensbacken, *Sweden* **10 E9** 59 10N 15 32 E
Odense, *Denmark* **11 J4** 55 22N 10 23 E
Odenwald, *Germany* **25 F5** 49 35N 9 0 E
Oder →, *Europe* **24 B10** 53 33N 14 38 E
Oder-Havel Kanal, *Germany* **24 C10** 52 52N 14 2 E
Oderzo, *Italy* **29 C9** 45 47N 12 29 E
Odesa, *Ukraine* **47 J6** 46 30N 30 45 E
Ödeshög, *Sweden* **11 F8** 58 14N 14 39 E
Odessa = Odesa, *Ukraine* **47 J6** 46 30N 30 45 E
Odessa, *Canada* **111 B8** 44 17N 76 43W
Odessa, *Tex., U.S.A.* **113 K3** 31 52N 102 23W
Odessa, *Wash., U.S.A.* **114 C4** 47 20N 118 41W
Odiakwe, *Botswana* **88 C4** 20 12 S 25 17 E
Odiel →, *Spain* **35 H4** 37 10N 6 55W
Odienné, *Ivory C.* **82 D3** 9 30N 7 34W
Odintsovo, *Russia* **46 E9** 55 39N 37 15 E
Odiongan, *Phil.* **61 E4** 12 24N 121 59 E
Odobești, *Romania* **43 E12** 45 43N 27 4 E
Odolanów, *Poland* **45 G4** 51 34N 17 40 E
O'Donnell, *U.S.A.* **113 J4** 32 58N 101 50W
Odorheiu Secuiesc, *Romania* **43 D10** 46 21N 25 21 E
Odoyevo, *Russia* **46 F9** 53 56N 36 42 E
Odra = Oder →, *Europe* **24 B10** 53 33N 14 38 E
Odra →, *Spain* **34 C6** 42 14N 4 17W
Odžaci, *Serbia, Yug.* **42 E4** 45 30N 19 17 E
Odžak, *Bos.-H.* **42 E3** 45 3N 18 18 E
Odzi, *Zimbabwe* **89 B5** 19 0 S 32 20 E
Odzi →, *Zimbabwe* **89 B5** 19 45 S 32 23 E
Oebisfelde, *Germany* **24 C6** 52 27N 10 57 E
Oeiras, *Brazil* **125 E10** 7 0 S 42 8W
Oeiras, *Portugal* **35 G1** 38 41N 9 18W
Oelrichs, *U.S.A.* **112 D3** 43 11N 103 14W
Oelsnitz, *Germany* **25 E8** 50 24N 12 10 E
Oelwein, *U.S.A.* **112 D9** 42 41N 91 55W
Oenpelli, *Australia* **92 B5** 12 20 S 133 4 E
Oetz, *Austria* **26 D3** 47 13N 10 53 E
Of, *Turkey* **73 B9** 40 59N 40 23 E
Ofanto →, *Italy* **31 A9** 41 22N 16 13 E
Offa, *Nigeria* **83 D5** 8 13N 4 42 E
Offaly □, *Ireland* **15 C4** 53 15N 7 30W
Offenbach, *Germany* **25 E4** 50 6N 8 44 E
Offenburg, *Germany* **25 G3** 48 28N 7 56 E
Offida, *Italy* **29 F10** 42 56N 13 41 E
Ofidhousa, *Greece* **39 E8** 36 33N 26 8 E
Ofotfjorden, *Norway* **8 B17** 68 27N 17 0 E
Ōfunato, *Japan* **54 E10** 39 4N 141 43 E
Oga, *Japan* **54 E9** 39 55N 139 50 E
Oga-Hantō, *Japan* **54 E9** 39 58N 139 47 E
Ogaden, *Ethiopia* **74 F3** 7 30N 45 30 E
Ōgaki, *Japan* **55 G8** 35 21N 136 37 E
Ogallala, *U.S.A.* **112 E4** 41 8N 101 43W
Ogasawara Gunto, *Pac. Oc.* **52 G18** 27 0N 142 0 E
Ogbomosho, *Nigeria* **83 D5** 8 1N 4 11 E
Ogden, *U.S.A.* **114 F7** 41 13N 111 58W
Ogdensburg, *U.S.A.* **111 B9** 44 42N 75 30W
Ogeechee →, *U.S.A.* **109 K5** 31 50N 81 3W
Ogilby, *U.S.A.* **117 N12** 32 49N 114 50W
Oglio →, *Italy* **28 C7** 45 2N 10 39 E
Ogmore, *Australia* **94 C4** 22 37 S 149 35 E
Ognon →, *France* **19 E12** 47 16N 5 28 E
Ogoja, *Nigeria* **83 D6** 6 38N 8 39 E
Ogoki, *Canada* **102 B2** 51 38N 85 58W
Ogoki →, *Canada* **102 B2** 51 38N 85 57W
Ogoki L., *Canada* **102 B2** 50 50N 87 10W
Ogoki Res., *Canada* **102 B2** 50 45N 88 15W
Ogooué →, *Gabon* **84 E1** 1 0 S 9 0 E
Ogosta →, *Bulgaria* **40 C7** 43 48N 23 55 E
Ogowe = Ogooué →, *Gabon* **84 E1** 1 0 S 9 0 E
Ogr = Sharafa, *Sudan* **81 E2** 11 59N 27 7 E
Ogražden, *Macedonia* **40 E6** 41 30N 22 50 E
Ogre, *Latvia* **9 H21** 56 49N 24 36 E
Ogrein, *Sudan* **80 D3** 17 55N 34 50 E
Ogulin, *Croatia* **29 C12** 45 16N 15 16 E
Ogun □, *Nigeria* **83 D5** 7 0N 3 0 E
Ogurchinskiy, Ostrov, *Turkmenistan* **71 B7** 38 55N 53 2 E
Oguta, *Nigeria* **83 D6** 5 44N 6 44 E
Ogwashi-Uku, *Nigeria* **83 D6** 6 15N 6 30 E
Ogwe, *Nigeria* **83 E6** 5 0N 7 14 E
Ohai, *N.Z.* **91 L2** 45 55 S 168 0 E
Ohakune, *N.Z.* **91 H5** 39 24 S 175 24 E
Ohata, *Japan* **54 D10** 41 24N 141 10 E
Ohau, L., *N.Z.* **91 L2** 44 15 S 169 53 E
Ohio □, *U.S.A.* **110 F2** 40 15N 82 45W
Ohio →, *U.S.A.* **108 G1** 36 59N 89 8W
Ohře →, *Czech Rep.* **26 A7** 50 30N 14 10 E
Ohre →, *Germany* **24 C7** 52 18N 11 46 E
Ohrid, *Macedonia* **40 E4** 41 8N 20 52 E
Ohridsko Jezero, *Macedonia* **40 E4** 41 8N 20 52 E
Ohrigstad, *S. Africa* **89 C5** 24 39 S 30 36 E
Öhringen, *Germany* **25 F5** 49 12N 9 31 E
Oi Qu, *China* **58 C2** 28 37N 98 16 E
Oiapoque, *Brazil* **125** 3 50N 51 50W
Oikou, *China* **57 E9** 38 35N 117 42 E
Oil City, *U.S.A.* **110 E5** 41 26N 79 42W
Oil Springs, *Canada* **110 D2** 42 47N 82 7W
Oildale, *U.S.A.* **117 K7** 35 25N 119 1W
Oinousa, *Greece* **39 C8** 38 33N 26 14 E
Oise □, *France* **19 C9** 49 28N 2 30 E
Oise →, *France* **19 C9** 49 0N 2 4 E
Ōita, *Japan* **55 H5** 33 14N 131 36 E
Ōita □, *Japan* **55 H5** 33 15N 131 30 E
Oiticica, *Brazil* **125 E10** 5 3 S 41 5W
Ojacaliente, *Mexico* **118 C4** 22 34N 102 15W
Ojai, *U.S.A.* **117 L7** 34 27N 119 15W
Ojinaga, *Mexico* **118 B4** 29 34N 104 25W
Ojiya, *Japan* **55 F9** 37 18N 138 48 E
Ojos del Salado, Cerro, *Argentina* **126 B2** 27 0 S 68 40W
Oka →, *Russia* **48 B7** 56 20N 43 59 E
Okaba, *Indonesia* **63 F9** 8 6 S 139 42 E
Okahandja, *Namibia* **88 C2** 22 0 S 16 59 E
Okanagan L., *Canada* **104 D5** 50 0N 119 30W
Okanogan, *U.S.A.* **114 B4** 48 22N 119 35W
Okanogan →, *U.S.A.* **114 B4** 48 6N 119 44W
Okány, *Hungary* **42 D6** 46 52N 21 21 E
Okaputa, *Namibia* **88 C2** 20 5 S 17 0 E
Okara, *Pakistan* **68 D5** 30 50N 73 31 E
Okaukuejo, *Namibia* **88 B2** 19 10 S 16 0 E
Okavango Swamps, *Botswana* **88 B3** 18 45 S 22 45 E
Okaya, *Japan* **55 F9** 36 5N 138 10 E
Okayama, *Japan* **55 G6** 34 40N 133 54 E
Okayama □, *Japan* **55 G6** 35 0N 133 50 E
Okazaki, *Japan* **55 G8** 34 57N 137 10 E
Oke-Iho, *Nigeria* **83 D5** 8 1N 3 18 E
Okeechobee, *U.S.A.* **109 M5** 27 15N 80 50W
Okeechobee, L., *U.S.A.* **109 M5** 27 0N 80 50W
Okefenokee Swamp, *U.S.A.* **109 K4** 30 40N 82 20W
Okehampton, *U.K.* **13 G4** 50 44N 4 0W
Okene, *Nigeria* **83 D6** 7 32N 6 11 E
Oker →, *Germany* **24 C6** 52 32N 10 22 E
Okha, *India* **68 H3** 22 27N 69 4 E
Okha, *Russia* **51 D15** 53 40N 143 0 E
Ókhi Óros, *Greece* **38 C6** 38 5N 24 25 E
Okhotsk, *Russia* **51 D15** 59 20N 143 10 E
Okhotsk, Sea of, *Asia* **51 D15** 55 0N 145 0 E
Okhotskiy Perevoz, *Russia* **51 C14** 61 52N 135 35 E
Okhtyrka, *Ukraine* **47 G8** 50 25N 35 0 E
Oki-Shotō, *Japan* **55 F6** 36 5N 133 15 E
Okiep, *S. Africa* **88 D2** 29 39 S 17 53 E
Okigwi, *Nigeria* **83 D6** 5 52N 7 20 E
Okija, *Nigeria* **83 D6** 5 54N 6 55 E
Okinawa □, *Japan* **55 L4** 26 40N 128 0 E
Okinawa-Guntō, *Japan* **55 L4** 26 40N 128 0 E
Okinawa-Jima, *Japan* **55 L4** 26 32N 128 0 E
Okino-erabu-Shima, *Japan* **55 L4** 27 21N 128 33 E
Okitipupa, *Nigeria* **83 D5** 6 31N 4 50 E
Oklahoma □, *U.S.A.* **113 H6** 35 20N 97 30W
Oklahoma City, *U.S.A.* **113 H6** 35 30N 97 30W
Okmulgee, *U.S.A.* **113 H7** 35 37N 95 58W
Oknitsa = Ocnița, *Moldova* **43 B12** 48 25N 27 30 E
Oko, W. →, *Sudan* **80 C4** 21 15N 35 56 E
Okolo, *Uganda* **86 B3** 2 37N 31 8 E
Okolona, *U.S.A.* **113 J10** 34 0N 88 45W
Okombahe, *Namibia* **88 C2** 21 23 S 15 22 E
Okonek, *Poland* **44 E3** 53 32N 16 51 E
Okotoks, *Canada* **104 C6** 50 43N 113 58W
Okrika, *Nigeria* **83 E6** 4 40N 7 10 E
Oksibil, *Indonesia* **63 E10** 4 59 S 140 35 E
Oktabrsk = Oktyabrsk, *Kazakstan* **50 E6** 49 28N 57 25 E
Oktyabrsk, *Kazakstan* **50 E6** 49 28N 57 25 E
Oktyabrsk, *Russia* **48 D9** 53 11N 48 40 E
Oktyabrskiy = Aktsyabrski, *Belarus* **47 F5** 52 38N 28 53 E
Oktyabrskiy, *Russia* **49 G5** 47 30N 40 4 E
Oktyabrskoy Revolyutsii, Ostrov, *Russia* **51 B10** 79 30N 97 0 E
Oktyabrskoye = Zhovtneve, *Ukraine* **47 J7** 46 54N 32 3 E
Okulovka, *Russia* **46 C7** 58 25N 33 19 E
Okuru, *N.Z.* **91 K2** 43 55 S 168 55 E
Okushiri-Tō, *Japan* **54 C9** 42 15N 139 30 E
Okuta, *Nigeria* **83 D5** 9 14N 3 12 E
Okwa →, *Botswana* **88 C3** 22 30 S 23 0 E
Ola, *U.S.A.* **113 H8** 35 2N 93 13W
Ólafsfjörður, *Iceland* **8 C4** 66 4N 18 39W
Ólafsvík, *Iceland* **8 D2** 64 53N 23 43W
Olaine, *Latvia* **44 B10** 56 48N 23 59 E
Olancha, *U.S.A.* **117 J8** 36 17N 118 1W
Olancha Pk., *U.S.A.* **117 J8** 36 15N 118 7W
Olanchito, *Honduras* **120 C2** 15 30N 86 30W
Öland, *Sweden* **11 H10** 56 45N 16 38 E
Ölands norra udde, *Sweden* **11 G11** 57 22N 17 5 E
Ölands södra udde, *Sweden* **11 H10** 56 12N 16 23 E
Olargues, *France* **20 E6** 43 34N 2 53 E
Olary, *Australia* **95 E3** 32 18 S 140 19 E
Olascoaga, *Argentina* **126 D3** 35 15 S 60 39W
Olathe, *U.S.A.* **112 F7** 38 53N 94 49W
Olavarría, *Argentina* **126 D3** 36 55 S 60 20W
Oława, *Poland* **45 H4** 50 57N 17 20 E
Olbernhau, *Germany* **24 E9** 50 40N 13 19 E
Ólbia, *Italy* **30 B2** 40 55N 9 31 E
Ólbia, G. di, *Italy* **30 B2** 40 55N 9 39 E
Olching, *Germany* **25 G7** 48 12N 11 21 E
Olcott, *U.S.A.* **110 C6** 43 20N 78 42W
Old Bahama Chan. = Bahama, Canal Viejo de, *W. Indies* **120 B4** 22 10N 77 30W
Old Baldy Pk. = San Antonio, Mt., *U.S.A.* **117 L9** 34 17N 117 38W
Old Castile = Castilla y Leon □, *Spain* **34 D6** 42 0N 5 0W
Old Crow, *Canada* **100 B6** 67 30N 139 55W
Old Dale, *U.S.A.* **117 L11** 34 8N 115 47W
Old Dongola, *Sudan* **80 D3** 18 11N 30 44 E
Old Forge, *N.Y., U.S.A.* **111 C10** 43 43N 74 58W
Old Forge, *Pa., U.S.A.* **111 E9** 41 22N 75 45W
Old Perlican, *Canada* **103 C9** 48 5N 53 1W
Old Shinyanga, *Tanzania* **86 C3** 3 33 S 33 27 E
Old Speck Mt., *U.S.A.* **111 B14** 44 34N 70 57W
Old Town, *U.S.A.* **109 C11** 44 56N 68 39W
Old Washington, *U.S.A.* **110 F3** 40 2N 81 27W
Old Wives L., *Canada* **105 C7** 50 5N 106 0W
Oldbury, *U.K.* **13 F5** 51 38N 2 33W
Oldcastle, *Ireland* **15 C4** 53 46N 7 10W
Oldeani, *Tanzania* **86 C4** 3 22 S 35 35 E
Oldenburg, *Niedersachsen, Germany* **24 B4** 53 9N 8 13 E
Oldenburg, *Schleswig-Holstein, Germany* **24 A6** 54 17N 10 52 E
Oldenzaal, *Neths.* **17 B6** 52 19N 6 53 E
Oldham, *U.K.* **12 D5** 53 33N 2 7W
Oldman →, *Canada* **104 D6** 49 57N 111 42W
Oldmeldrum, *U.K.* **14 D6** 57 20N 2 19W
Olds, *Canada* **104 C6** 51 50N 114 10W
Oldziyt, *Mongolia* **56 B5** 44 40N 109 1 E
Olean, *U.S.A.* **110 D6** 42 5N 78 26W
Olecko, *Poland* **44 D9** 54 2N 22 31 E
Oléggio, *Italy* **28 C5** 45 36N 8 38 E
Oleiros, *Portugal* **34 F3** 39 56N 7 56W
Oleiros, *Spain* **34 B2** 43 20N 8 19W
Olekma →, *Russia* **51 C13** 60 22N 120 42 E
Olekminsk, *Russia* **51 C13** 60 25N 120 30 E
Oleksandriya, *Kirovohrad, Ukraine* **47 H7** 48 42N 33 3 E
Oleksandriya, *Rivne, Ukraine* **47 G4** 50 37N 26 19 E
Oleksandrovka, *Ukraine* **47 H7** 48 55N 32 20 E
Olema, *U.S.A.* **116 G4** 38 3N 122 47W
Olenek, *Russia* **51 C12** 68 28N 112 18 E
Olenek →, *Russia* **51 B13** 73 0N 120 10 E
Olenino, *Russia* **46 D7** 56 15N 33 30 E
Oléron, Î. d', *France* **20 C2** 45 55N 1 15W
Oleśnica, *Poland* **45 G4** 51 13N 17 22 E
Olesno, *Poland* **45 H5** 50 51N 18 26 E
Olevsk, *Ukraine* **47 G4** 51 12N 27 39 E
Olga, *Russia* **51 E14** 43 50N 135 14 E
Olga, L., *Canada* **102 C4** 49 47N 77 15W
Olga, Mt., *Australia* **93 E5** 25 20 S 130 50 E
Ølgod, *Denmark* **11 J2** 55 49N 8 36 E
Olhão, *Portugal* **35 H3** 37 3N 7 48W
Olib, *Croatia* **29 D11** 44 23N 14 44 E
Oliena, *Italy* **30 B2** 40 16N 9 24 E
Oliete, *Spain* **32 D4** 41 1N 0 41W
Olifants →, *Africa* **89 C5** 23 57 S 31 58 E
Olifants →, *Namibia* **88 C2** 25 30 S 19 30 E
Olifantshoek, *S. Africa* **88 D3** 27 57 S 22 42 E
Ólimbos, *Greece* **39 F9** 35 44N 27 11 E
Ólimbos, Óros, *Greece* **40 F6** 40 6N 22 23 E
Olímpia, *Brazil* **127 A6** 20 44 S 48 54W
Olinda, *Brazil* **125 E12** 8 1 S 34 51W
Olite, *Spain* **32 C3** 42 29N 1 40W
Oliva, *Argentina* **126 C3** 32 0 S 63 38W
Oliva, *Spain* **33 G4** 38 58N 0 9W
Oliva, Punta del, *Spain* **34 B5** 43 37N 5 28W
Oliva de la Frontera, *Spain* **35 G4** 38 17N 6 54W
Olivares, *Spain* **32 F2** 39 46N 2 20W
Olivehurst, *U.S.A.* **116 F5** 39 6N 121 34W
Oliveira de Azeméis, *Portugal* **34 E2** 40 49N 8 29W
Oliveira do Douro, *Portugal* **34 D2** 41 5N 8 2W
Olivenza, *Spain* **35 G3** 38 41N 7 9W
Oliver, *Canada* **104 D5** 49 13N 119 37W
Oliver L., *Canada* **105 B8** 56 56N 103 22W
Olivet, *France* **19 E8** 47 51N 1 55 E
Olkhovka, *Russia* **48 F7** 49 48N 44 32 E
Olkusz, *Poland* **45 H6** 50 18N 19 33 E
Ollagüe, *Chile* **126 A2** 21 15 S 68 10W
Olmedo, *Spain* **34 D6** 41 20N 4 43W
Olmeto, *France* **21 G12** 41 43N 8 55 E
Olney, *Ill., U.S.A.* **108 F1** 38 44N 88 5W
Olney, *Tex., U.S.A.* **113 J5** 33 22N 98 45W
Olofström, *Sweden* **11 H8** 56 17N 14 32 E
Oloma, *Cameroon* **83 E7** 3 29N 11 19 E
Olomane →, *Canada* **103 B7** 50 14N 60 37W
Olomouc, *Czech Rep.* **27 B10** 49 38N 17 12 E
Olonets, *Russia* **46 B7** 61 0N 32 54 E
Olongapo, *Phil.* **61 D4** 14 50N 120 18 E
Olonne-sur-Mer, *France* **20 B2** 46 32N 1 47W
Oloron, Gave d' →, *France* **20 E2** 43 33N 1 5W
Oloron-Ste-Marie, *France* **20 E3** 43 11N 0 38W
Olot, *Spain* **32 C7** 42 11N 2 30 E
Olovo, *Bos.-H.* **42 F3** 44 8N 18 35 E
Olovyannaya, *Russia* **51 D12** 50 58N 115 35 E
Oloy →, *Russia* **51 C16** 66 29N 159 29 E
Olsberg, *Germany* **24 D4** 51 21N 8 31 E
Olshammar, *Sweden* **11 F8** 58 45N 14 48 E
Olshanka, *Ukraine* **47 H6** 48 16N 30 58 E
Olshany, *Ukraine* **47 G8** 50 3N 35 53 E
Olsztyn, *Poland* **44 E7** 53 48N 20 29 E
Olsztynek, *Poland* **44 E7** 53 34N 20 19 E
Olt □, *Romania* **43 F9** 44 20N 24 30 E
Olt →, *Romania* **43 G9** 43 43N 24 51 E
Olten, *Switz.* **25 H3** 47 21N 7 53 E
Olteniţa, *Romania* **43 F11** 44 7N 26 42 E
Olton, *U.S.A.* **113 H3** 34 11N 102 8W
Oltu, *Turkey* **73 B9** 40 35N 41 58 E
Oluanpi, *Taiwan* **59 G13** 21 54N 120 51 E
Olula del Río, *Spain* **33 H2** 37 21N 2 18W
Olur, *Turkey* **73 B10** 40 49N 42 8 E
Olutanga, *Phil.* **61 H5** 7 26N 122 54 E
Olvega, *Spain* **32 D2** 41 47N 2 0W
Olvera, *Spain* **35 J5** 36 55N 5 18W
Olymbos, *Cyprus* **36 D12** 35 21N 33 45 E
Olympia, *Greece* **38 D3** 37 39N 21 39 E
Olympia, *U.S.A.* **116 D4** 47 3N 122 53W
Olympic Dam, *Australia* **95 E2** 30 30 S 136 55 E
Olympic Mts., *U.S.A.* **116 C3** 47 55N 123 45W
Olympic Nat. Park, *U.S.A.* **116 C3** 47 48N 123 30W
Olympus, *Cyprus* **36 E11** 34 56N 32 52 E
Olympus, Mt. = Ólimbos, Óros, *Greece* **40 F6** 40 6N 22 23 E
Olympus, Mt. = Uludağ, *Turkey* **41 F13** 40 4N 29 13 E
Olympus, Mt., *U.S.A.* **116 C3** 47 48N 123 43W
Olyphant, *U.S.A.* **111 E9** 41 27N 75 36W
Om →, *Russia* **50 D8** 54 59N 73 22 E
Om Hajer, *Eritrea* **81 E4** 14 20N 36 41 E
Om Koi, *Thailand* **64 D2** 17 48N 98 22 E
Ōma, *Japan* **54 D10** 41 45N 141 5 E
Ōmachi, *Japan* **55 F8** 36 30N 137 50 E
Omae-Zaki, *Japan* **55 G9** 34 36N 138 14 E
Ōmagari, *Japan* **54 E10** 39 27N 140 29 E
Omagh, *U.K.* **15 B4** 54 36N 7 19W
Omagh □, *U.K.* **15 B4** 54 35N 7 15W
Omaha, *U.S.A.* **112 E7** 41 17N 95 58W
Omak, *U.S.A.* **114 B4** 48 25N 119 31W
Omalos, *Greece* **36 D5** 35 19N 23 55 E
Oman ■, *Asia* **74 C6** 23 0N 58 0 E
Oman, G. of, *Asia* **71 E8** 24 30N 58 30 E
Omaruru, *Namibia* **88 C2** 21 26 S 16 0 E
Omaruru →, *Namibia* **88 C1** 22 7 S 14 15 E
Omate, *Peru* **124 G4** 16 45 S 71 0W
Ombai, Selat, *Indonesia* **63 F6** 8 30 S 124 50 E
Omboué, *Gabon* **84 E1** 1 35 S 9 15 E
Ombrone →, *Italy* **28 F8** 42 42N 11 5 E
Omdurmân, *Sudan* **81 D3** 15 40N 32 28 E
Omegna, *Italy* **28 C5** 45 53N 8 24 E
Omemee, *Canada* **110 B6** 44 18N 78 33W
Omeo, *Australia* **95 F4** 37 6 S 147 36 E
Omeonga, *Dem. Rep. of the Congo* **86 C1** 3 40 S 24 22 E
Ometepe, I. de, *Nic.* **120 D2** 11 32N 85 35W
Ometepec, *Mexico* **119 D5** 16 39N 98 23W
Ominato, *Japan* **54 D10** 41 17N 141 10 E
Omineca →, *Canada* **104 B4** 56 3N 124 16W
Omiš, *Croatia* **29 E13** 43 28N 16 40 E
Omišalj, *Croatia* **29 C11** 45 13N 14 32 E
Omitara, *Namibia* **88 C2** 22 16 S 18 2 E
Ōmiya, *Japan* **55 G9** 35 54N 139 38 E
Omme Å →, *Denmark* **11 J2** 55 56N 8 32 E
Ommen, *Neths.* **17 B6** 52 31N 6 26 E
Ömnögovĭ □, *Mongolia* **56 C3** 43 15N 104 0 E
Omo →, *Ethiopia* **81 F4** 6 25N 36 10 E
Omodeo, L., *Italy* **30 B1** 40 8N 8 56 E
Omodhos, *Cyprus* **36 E11** 34 51N 32 48 E
Omoko, *Nigeria* **83 D6** 5 19N 6 40 E
Omolon →, *Russia* **51 C16** 68 42N 158 36 E
Omono-Gawa →, *Japan* **54 E10** 39 46N 140 3 E
Omsk, *Russia* **50 D8** 55 0N 73 12 E
Omsukchan, *Russia* **51 C16** 62 32N 155 48 E
Ōmu, *Japan* **54 B11** 44 34N 142 58 E
Omul, Vf., *Romania* **43 E10** 45 27N 25 29 E
Omulew →, *Poland* **45 E8** 53 5N 21 33 E
Ōmura, *Japan* **55 H4** 32 56N 129 57 E
Omuramba Omatako →, *Namibia* **88 B2** 17 45 S 20 25 E
Omuramba Ovambo →, *Namibia* **88 B2** 18 45 S 16 59 E
Omurtag, *Bulgaria* **41 C10** 43 8N 26 26 E
Ōmuta, *Japan* **55 H5** 33 5N 130 26 E
Oña, *Spain* **34 C7** 42 43N 3 25W
Onaga, *U.S.A.* **112 F6** 39 29N 96 10W
Onalaska, *U.S.A.* **112 D9** 43 53N 91 14W
Onancock, *U.S.A.* **108 G8** 37 43N 75 45W
Onang, *Indonesia* **63 E5** 3 2 S 118 49 E
Onaping L., *Canada* **102 C3** 47 3N 81 30W
Oñati, *Spain* **32 B2** 43 3N 2 25W
Onavas, *Mexico* **118 B3** 28 28N 109 30W
Onawa, *U.S.A.* **112 D6** 42 2N 96 6W
Oncócua, *Angola* **88 B1** 16 30 S 13 25 E
Onda, *Spain* **32 F4** 39 55N 0 17W
Ondaejin, *N. Korea* **57 D15** 41 34N 129 40 E
Ondangua, *Namibia* **88 B2** 17 57 S 16 4 E
Ondarroa, *Spain* **32 B2** 43 19N 2 25W
Ondava →, *Slovak Rep.* **27 C14** 48 27N 21 48 E
Ondjiva, *Angola* **88 B2** 16 48 S 15 50 E
Ondo, *Nigeria* **83 D5** 7 4N 4 47 E
Ondo □, *Nigeria* **83 D6** 6 45N 5 0 E
Öndörshil, *Mongolia* **56 B5** 45 13N 108 5 E
Öndverðarnes, *Iceland* **8 D1** 64 52N 24 0W
One Tree, *Australia* **95 E3** 34 11 S 144 43 E
Onega, *Russia* **50 C4** 64 0N 38 10 E
Onega →, *Russia* **6 C13** 63 58N 38 2 E
Onega, L. = Onezhskoye Ozero, *Russia* **46 B8** 61 44N 35 22 E
Oneida, *U.S.A.* **111 C9** 43 6N 75 39W
Oneida L., *U.S.A.* **111 C9** 43 12N 75 54W
O'Neill, *U.S.A.* **112 D5** 42 27N 98 39W
Onekotan, Ostrov, *Russia* **51 E16** 49 25N 154 45 E
Onema, *Dem. Rep. of the Congo* **86 C1** 4 35 S 24 30 E
Oneonta, *U.S.A.* **111 D9** 42 27N 75 4W
Onești, *Romania* **43 D11** 46 17N 26 47 E
Onezhskoye Ozero, *Russia* **46 B8** 61 44N 35 22 E
Ongarue, *N.Z.* **91 H5** 38 42 S 175 19 E
Ongers →, *S. Africa* **88 E3** 31 4 S 23 13 E
Ongerup, *Australia* **93 F2** 33 58 S 118 28 E
Ongjin, *N. Korea* **57 F13** 37 56N 125 21 E
Ongkharak, *Thailand* **64 E3** 14 8N 101 1 E
Ongniud Qi, *China* **57 C10** 43 0N 118 38 E
Ongoka, *Dem. Rep. of the Congo* **86 C2** 1 20 S 26 0 E
Ongole, *India* **66 M12** 15 33N 80 2 E
Ongon = Havirga, *Mongolia* **56 B7** 45 41N 113 5 E
Oni, *Georgia* **49 J6** 42 33N 43 26 E
Onida, *U.S.A.* **112 C4** 44 42N 100 4W
Onilahy →, *Madag.* **89 C7** 23 34 S 43 45 E
Onitsha, *Nigeria* **83 D6** 6 6N 6 42 E
Onoda, *Japan* **55 G5** 33 59N 131 11 E
Onpyŏng-ni, *S. Korea* **57 H14** 33 25N 126 55 E
Ons, I. de, *Spain* **34 C2** 42 23N 8 55W
Onslow, *Australia* **92 D2** 21 40 S 115 12 E
Onslow B., *U.S.A.* **109 H7** 34 20N 77 15W
Ontake-San, *Japan* **55 G8** 35 53N 137 29 E
Ontario, *Calif., U.S.A.* **117 L9** 34 4N 117 39W
Ontario, *Oreg., U.S.A.* **114 D5** 44 2N 116 58W
Ontario □, *Canada* **102 B2** 48 0N 83 0W
Ontario, L., *N. Amer.* **102 D4** 43 20N 78 0W
Ontinyent, *Spain* **33 G4** 38 50N 0 35W
Ontonagon, *U.S.A.* **112 B10** 46 52N 89 19W
Ontur, *Spain* **33 G3** 38 38N 1 29W
Onyx, *U.S.A.* **117 K8** 35 41N 118 14W
Oodnadatta, *Australia* **95 D2** 27 33 S 135 30 E
Ooldea, *Australia* **93 F5** 30 27 S 131 50 E
Oombulgurri, *Australia* **92 C4** 15 15 S 127 45 E
Oorindi, *Australia* **94 C3** 20 40 S 141 1 E
Oost-Vlaanderen □, *Belgium* **17 C3** 51 5N 3 50 E
Oostende, *Belgium* **17 C2** 51 15N 2 54 E
Oosterhout, *Neths.* **17 C4** 51 39N 4 47 E
Oosterschelde →, *Neths.* **17 C4** 51 33N 4 0 E
Oosterwolde, *Neths.* **17 B6** 53 0N 6 17 E
Ootacamund = Udagamandalam, *India* **66 P10** 11 30N 76 44 E
Ootsa L., *Canada* **104 C3** 53 50N 126 2W
Opaka, *Bulgaria* **41 C10** 43 28N 26 10 E
Opala, *Dem. Rep. of the Congo* **86 C1** 0 40 S 24 20 E
Opalenica, *Poland* **45 F3** 52 18N 16 24 E
Opan, *Bulgaria* **41 D9** 42 13N 25 41 E
Opanake, *Sri Lanka* **66 R12** 6 35N 80 40 E
Opasatika, *Canada* **102 C3** 49 30N 82 50W
Opasquia Prov. Park, *Canada* **102 B1** 53 33N 93 5W
Opatija, *Croatia* **29 C11** 45 21N 14 17 E
Opatów, *Poland* **45 H8** 50 50N 21 27 E
Opava, *Czech Rep.* **27 B10** 49 57N 17 58 E
Opelika, *U.S.A.* **109 J3** 32 39N 85 23W
Opelousas, *U.S.A.* **113 K8** 30 32N 92 5W
Opémisca, L., *Canada* **102 C5** 49 56N 74 52W
Opheim, *U.S.A.* **114 B10** 48 51N 106 24W
Ophthalmia Ra., *Australia* **92 D2** 23 15 S 119 30 E
Opi, *Nigeria* **83 D6** 6 36N 7 28 E
Opinaca →, *Canada* **102 B4** 52 15N 78 2W
Opinaca, Rés., *Canada* **102 B4** 52 39N 76 20W
Opinnagau →, *Canada* **102 B3** 54 12N 82 25W
Opiscoteo, L., *Canada* **103 B6** 53 10N 68 10W
Opobo, *Nigeria* **83 E6** 4 35N 7 34 E
Opochka, *Russia* **46 D5** 56 42N 28 45 E
Opoczno, *Poland* **45 G7** 51 22N 20 18 E
Opol, *Phil.* **61 G6** 8 31N 124 34 E
Opole, *Poland* **45 H4** 50 42N 17 58 E
Opole Lubelskie, *Poland* **45 G8** 51 9N 21 58 E
Opolskie □, *Poland* **45 H5** 50 30N 18 0 E
Oponono L., *Namibia* **88 B2** 18 8 S 15 45 E
Oporto = Porto, *Portugal* **34 D2** 41 8N 8 40W
Opotiki, *N.Z.* **91 H6** 38 1 S 177 19 E
Opp, *U.S.A.* **109 K2** 31 17N 86 16W
Oppdal, *Norway* **9 E13** 62 35N 9 41 E
Óppido Mamertina, *Italy* **31 D8** 38 16N 15 59 E
Opportunity, *U.S.A.* **114 C5** 47 39N 117 15W
Oprișor, *Romania* **42 F8** 44 17N 23 5 E
Oprtalj, *Croatia* **29 C10** 45 23N 13 50 E
Opua, *N.Z.* **91 F5** 35 19 S 174 9 E
Opunake, *N.Z.* **91 H4** 39 26 S 173 52 E
Opuwo, *Namibia* **88 B1** 18 3 S 13 45 E
Opuzen, *Croatia* **29 E14** 43 1N 17 34 E
Ora, *Cyprus* **36 E12** 34 51N 33 12 E
Oracle, *U.S.A.* **115 K8** 32 37N 110 46W
Oradea, *Romania* **42 C6** 47 2N 21 58 E
Öræfajökull, *Iceland* **8 D5** 64 2N 16 39W
Orahovac, *Kosovo, Yug.* **40 D4** 42 24N 20 40 E
Orahovica, *Croatia* **42 E2** 45 35N 17 52 E
Orai, *India* **69 G8** 25 58N 79 30 E
Oraison, *France* **21 E9** 43 55N 5 55 E
Oral = Zhayyq →, *Kazakstan* **50 E6** 47 0N 51 48 E
Oral, *Kazakstan* **48 E10** 51 20N 51 20 E
Oran, *Algeria* **78 A5** 35 45N 0 39W
Orange, *Australia* **95 E4** 33 15 S 149 7 E
Orange, *France* **21 D8** 44 8N 4 47 E
Orange, *Calif., U.S.A.* **117 M9** 33 47N 117 51W
Orange, *Mass., U.S.A.* **111 D12** 42 35N 72 19W
Orange, *Tex., U.S.A.* **113 K8** 30 6N 93 44W
Orange, *Va., U.S.A.* **108 F6** 38 15N 78 7W
Orange →, *S. Africa* **88 D2** 28 41 S 16 28 E
Orange, C., *Brazil* **122 C5** 4 20N 51 30W
Orange Cove, *U.S.A.* **116 J7** 36 38N 119 19W
Orange Free State = Free State □, *S. Africa* **88 D4** 28 30 S 27 0 E
Orange Grove, *U.S.A.* **113 M6** 27 58N 97 56W
Orange Walk, *Belize* **119 D7** 18 6N 88 33W
Orangeburg, *U.S.A.* **109 J5** 33 30N 80 52W
Orangeville, *Canada* **102 D3** 43 55N 80 5W
Orango, *Guinea-Biss.* **82 C1** 11 5N 16 0W
Orani, *Phil.* **61 D4** 14 49N 120 32 E
Oranienburg, *Germany* **24 C9** 52 45N 13 14 E
Oranje = Orange →, *S. Africa* **88 D2** 28 41 S 16 28 E
Oranje Vrystaat = Free State □, *S. Africa* **88 D4** 28 30 S 27 0 E
Oranjemund, *Namibia* **88 D2** 28 38 S 16 29 E
Oranjerivier, *S. Africa* **88 D3** 29 40 S 24 12 E
Orapa, *Botswana* **85 J5** 21 15 S 25 30 E
Orarak, *Sudan* **81 F3** 6 15N 32 23 E
Oras, *Phil.* **61 E6** 12 9N 125 28 E
Orašje, *Bos.-H.* **42 E3** 45 1N 18 42 E
Orăștie, *Romania* **43 E8** 45 50N 23 10 E
Orașul Stalin = Brașov, *Romania* **43 E10** 45 38N 25 35 E
Orava →, *Slovak Rep.* **27 B12** 49 9N 19 8 E
Orava, Vodna nádrž, *Slovak Rep.* **27 B12** 49 25N 19 35 E
Oravița, *Romania* **42 E6** 45 2N 21 43 E
Orb →, *France* **20 E7** 43 15N 3 18 E
Orba →, *Italy* **28 D5** 44 53N 8 37 E
Ørbæk, *Denmark* **11 J4** 55 17N 10 39 E
Orbe, *Switz.* **25 J2** 46 43N 6 32 E
Orbec, *France* **18 C7** 49 1N 0 23 E
Orbetello, *Italy* **29 F8** 42 27N 11 13 E
Órbigo →, *Spain* **34 C5** 42 5N 5 42W
Orbisonia, *U.S.A.* **110 F7** 40 15N 77 54W
Orbost, *Australia* **95 F4** 37 40 S 148 29 E
Örbyhus, *Sweden* **10 D11** 60 15N 17 43 E
Orcas I., *U.S.A.* **116 B4** 48 42N 122 56W
Orce, *Spain* **33 H2** 37 44N 2 28W
Orce →, *Spain* **33 H2** 37 44N 2 28W
Orchard City, *U.S.A.* **115 G10** 38 50N 107 58W
Orchies, *France* **19 B10** 50 28N 3 14 E
Orchila, I., *Venezuela* **121 D6** 11 48N 66 10W
Órcia →, *Italy* **29 F8** 42 58N 11 21 E
Orco →, *Italy* **28 C4** 45 10N 7 52 E
Orcutt, *U.S.A.* **117 L6** 34 52N 120 27W
Ord, *U.S.A.* **112 E5** 41 36N 98 56W
Ord →, *Australia* **92 C4** 15 33 S 128 15 E
Ord, Mt., *Australia* **92 C4** 17 20 S 125 34 E
Ordenes = Ordes, *Spain* **34 B2** 43 5N 8 29W
Orderville, *U.S.A.* **115 H7** 37 17N 112 38W
Ordes, *Spain* **34 B2** 43 5N 8 29W
Ording = St-Peter-Ording, *Germany* **24 A4** 54 20N 8 36 E

Ordos = Mu Us Shamo, China 56 E5 39 0N 109 0 E
Ordu, Turkey 72 B7 40 55N 37 53 E
Ordubad, Azerbaijan 73 C12 38 54N 46 1 E
Orduña, Álava, Spain 32 C2 42 58N 2 58W
Orduña, Granada, Spain 35 H7 37 20N 3 30W
Ordway, U.S.A. 112 F3 38 13N 103 46W
Ordzhonikidze = Vladikavkaz, Russia 49 J7 43 0N 44 35 E
Ordzhonikidze, Ukraine 47 J8 47 39N 34 3 E
Ore, Dem. Rep. of the Congo 86 B2 3 17N 29 30 E
Ore Mts. = Erzgebirge, Germany 24 E8 50 27N 12 55 E
Orebić, Croatia 29 F14 43 0N 17 11 E
Örebro, Sweden 10 E9 59 20N 15 18 E
Örebro län □, Sweden 10 E8 59 27N 15 0 E
Oregon, U.S.A. 112 D10 42 1N 89 20W
Oregon □, U.S.A. 114 E3 44 0N 121 0W
Oregon City, U.S.A. 116 E4 45 21N 122 36W
Öregrund, Sweden 10 D12 60 21N 18 30 E
Öregrundsgrepen, Sweden 10 D12 60 25N 18 15 E
Orekhov = Orikhiv, Ukraine 47 J8 47 30N 35 48 E
Orekhovo-Zuyevo, Russia 46 E10 55 50N 38 55 E
Orel, Russia 47 F9 52 57N 36 3 E
Orel →, Ukraine 47 H8 48 40N 34 39 E
Orellana, Spain 35 F5 39 1N 5 32W
Orellana, Canal de, Spain 35 F5 39 2N 6 0W
Orellana, Embalse de, Spain 35 F5 39 5N 5 10W
Orem, U.S.A. 114 F8 40 19N 111 42W
Ören, Turkey 39 D9 37 3N 27 57 E
Orenburg, Russia 50 D6 51 45N 55 6 E
Örencik, Turkey 39 B11 39 16N 29 33 E
Orense = Ourense, Spain 34 C3 42 19N 7 55W
Orense □, Spain 34 C3 42 15N 7 51W
Orepuki, N.Z. 91 M1 46 19 S 167 46 E
Orestiás, Greece 41 E10 41 30N 26 33 E
Orestos Pereyra, Mexico 118 B3 26 31N 105 40W
Øresund, Europe 11 J6 55 45N 12 45 E
Orford Ness, U.K. 13 E9 52 5N 1 35 E
Organà = Organyà, Spain 32 C6 42 13N 1 20 E
Organos, Pta. de los, Canary Is. 37 F2 28 12N 17 17W
Organyà, Spain 32 C6 42 13N 1 20 E
Orgaz, Spain 35 F7 39 39N 3 53W
Orgeyev = Orhei, Moldova 43 C13 47 24N 28 50 E
Orhaneli, Turkey 41 G12 39 54N 28 59 E
Orhaneli →, Turkey 41 G12 39 50N 28 55 E
Orhangazi, Turkey 41 F13 40 29N 29 18 E
Orhei, Moldova 43 C13 47 24N 28 50 E
Orhon Gol →, Mongolia 60 A5 50 21N 106 0 E
Ória, Italy 31 B10 40 30N 17 38 E
Oriental, Cordillera, Colombia 122 C3 6 0N 73 0W
Orientale □, Dem. Rep. of the Congo 86 B2 2 20N 26 0 E
Oriente, Argentina 126 D3 38 44 S 60 37W
Orihuela, Spain 33 G4 38 7N 0 55W
Orihuela del Tremedal, Spain 32 E3 40 33N 1 39W
Orikhiv, Ukraine 47 J8 47 30N 35 48 E
Oriku = Orikum, Albania 40 F3 40 20N 19 26 E
Orikum, Albania 40 F3 40 20N 19 26 E
Orillia, Canada 102 D4 44 40N 79 24W
Orinoco →, Venezuela 122 C4 9 15N 61 30W
Orion, Canada 105 D6 49 27N 110 49W
Oriskany, U.S.A. 111 C9 43 10N 75 20W
Orissa □, India 67 K14 20 0N 84 0 E
Orissaare, Estonia 9 G20 58 34N 23 5 E
Oristano, Italy 30 C1 39 54N 8 36 E
Oristano, G. di, Italy 30 C1 39 50N 8 29 E
Orizaba, Mexico 119 D5 18 51N 97 6W
Orizare, Bulgaria 41 D11 42 44N 27 39 E
Orjen, Bos.-H. 40 D2 42 35N 18 34 E
Orjiva, Spain 35 J7 36 53N 3 24W
Orkanger, Norway 8 E13 63 18N 9 52 E
Örkelljunga, Sweden 11 H7 56 17N 13 17 E
Örken, Sweden 11 G9 57 6N 15 1 E
Örkény, Hungary 42 C4 47 9N 19 26 E
Orkla →, Norway 8 E13 63 18N 9 51 E
Orkney, S. Africa 88 D4 26 58 S 26 40 E
Orkney □, U.K. 14 B5 59 2N 3 13W
Orkney Is., U.K. 14 B6 59 0N 3 0W
Orland, U.S.A. 116 F4 39 45N 122 12W
Orlando, U.S.A. 109 L5 28 33N 81 23W
Orlando, C. d', Italy 31 D7 38 10N 14 43 E
Orléanais, France 19 E9 48 0N 2 0 E
Orléans, France 19 E8 47 54N 1 52 E
Orleans, U.S.A. 111 B12 44 49N 72 12W
Orléans, I. d', Canada 103 C5 46 54N 70 58W
Orlice →, Czech Rep. 26 A8 50 13N 15 50 E
Orlov, Slovak Rep. 27 B13 49 17N 20 51 E
Orlov Gay, Russia 48 E9 50 56N 48 19 E
Orlová, Czech Rep. 27 B11 49 51N 18 26 E
Orlovat, Serbia, Yug. 42 E5 45 14N 20 33 E
Ormara, Pakistan 66 G4 25 16N 64 33 E
Ormea, Italy 28 D4 44 9N 7 54 E
Ormília, Greece 40 F7 40 16N 23 39 E
Ormoc, Phil. 61 F6 11 0N 124 37 E
Ormond, N.Z. 91 H6 38 33 S 177 56 E
Ormond Beach, U.S.A. 109 L5 29 17N 81 3W
Ormož, Slovenia 29 B13 46 25N 16 10 E
Ormskirk, U.K. 12 D5 53 35N 2 54W
Ormstown, Canada 111 A11 45 8N 74 0W
Ornans, France 19 E13 47 7N 6 10 E
Orne □, France 18 D7 48 40N 0 5 E
Orne →, France 18 C6 49 18N 0 15W
Orneta, Poland 44 D7 54 8N 20 9 E
Ornö, Sweden 10 E12 59 4N 18 24 E
Örnsköldsvik, Sweden 10 A12 63 17N 18 40 E
Oro, N. Korea 57 D14 40 1N 127 27 E
Oro →, Mexico 118 B3 25 35N 105 2W
Oro Grande, U.S.A. 117 L9 34 36N 117 20W
Oro Valley, U.S.A. 115 K8 32 26N 110 58W
Orobie, Alpi, Italy 28 B6 46 7N 10 0 E
Orocué, Colombia 124 C4 4 48N 71 20W
Orodara, Burkina Faso 82 C4 11 0N 4 55W
Orodo, Nigeria 83 D6 5 34N 7 4 E
Orofino, U.S.A. 114 C5 46 29N 116 15W
Orol Dengizi = Aral Sea, Asia 50 E7 44 30N 60 0 E
Oromocto, Canada 103 C6 45 54N 66 29W
Oron, Nigeria 83 E6 4 48N 8 14 E
Orono, Canada 110 C6 43 59N 78 37W
Orono, U.S.A. 109 C11 44 53N 68 40W
Oronsay, U.K. 14 E2 56 1N 6 15W
Oropesa, Spain 34 F5 39 57N 5 10W
Oroquieta, Phil. 61 G5 8 32N 123 44 E
Orosei, Italy 30 B2 40 23N 9 42 E
Orosei, G. di, Italy 30 B2 40 15N 9 44 E
Orosháza, Hungary 42 D5 46 32N 20 42 E
Oroszlány, Hungary 42 C3 47 29N 18 19 E
Orotukan, Russia 51 C16 62 16N 151 42 E
Oroville, Calif., U.S.A. 116 F5 39 31N 121 33W
Oroville, Wash., U.S.A. 114 B4 48 56N 119 26W
Oroville, L., U.S.A. 116 F5 39 33N 121 29W
Orrefors, Sweden 11 H9 56 50N 15 45 E
Orroroo, Australia 95 E2 32 43 S 138 38 E
Orrviken, Sweden 10 A8 63 6N 14 26 E
Orrville, U.S.A. 110 F3 40 50N 81 46W
Orsa, Sweden 10 C8 61 7N 14 37 E
Orsara di Púglia, Italy 31 A8 41 17N 15 16 E
Orsasjön, Sweden 10 C8 61 7N 14 37 E
Orsha, Belarus 46 E6 54 30N 30 25 E
Örsjö, Sweden 11 H9 56 42N 15 45 E
Orsk, Russia 50 D6 51 12N 58 34 E
Orşova, Romania 42 F7 44 41N 22 25 E
Ørsted, Denmark 11 H4 56 30N 10 20 E
Örsundsbro, Sweden 10 E11 59 44N 17 18 E
Orta, L. d', Italy 28 C5 45 49N 8 24 E
Orta Nova, Italy 31 A8 41 19N 15 42 E
Ortaca, Turkey 39 E10 36 49N 28 45 E
Ortakent, Turkey 39 D9 37 5N 27 21 E
Ortaklar, Turkey 39 D9 37 53N 27 30 E
Ortaköy, Çorum, Turkey 72 B6 40 16N 35 15 E
Ortaköy, Niğde, Turkey 72 C6 38 44N 34 3 E
Orte, Italy 29 F9 42 27N 12 23 E
Ortegal, C., Spain 34 B3 43 43N 7 52W
Orthez, France 20 E3 43 29N 0 48W
Ortigueira, Spain 34 B3 43 40N 7 50W
Orting, U.S.A. 116 C4 47 6N 122 12W
Ortisei, Italy 29 B8 46 34N 11 40 E
Ortles, Italy 28 B7 46 31N 10 33 E
Ortón →, Bolivia 124 F5 10 50 S 67 0W
Ortona, Italy 29 F11 42 21N 14 24 E
Ortonville, U.S.A. 112 C6 45 19N 96 27W
Orūmīyeh, Iran 70 B5 37 40N 45 0 E
Orūmīyeh, Daryācheh-ye, Iran 70 B5 37 50N 45 30 E
Orune, Italy 30 B2 40 24N 9 22 E
Oruro, Bolivia 124 G5 18 0 S 67 9W
Orust, Sweden 11 F5 58 10N 11 40 E
Oruzgān □, Afghan. 66 C5 33 30N 66 0 E
Orvault, France 18 E5 47 17N 1 38W
Orvieto, Italy 29 F9 42 43N 12 7 E
Orwell, N.Y., U.S.A. 111 C9 43 35N 75 50W
Orwell, Ohio, U.S.A. 110 E4 41 32N 80 52W
Orwell →, U.K. 13 F9 51 59N 1 18 E
Orwigsburg, U.S.A. 111 F8 40 38N 76 6W
Oryakhovo, Bulgaria 40 C7 43 40N 23 57 E
Orzinuovi, Italy 28 C6 45 24N 9 55 E
Orzyc →, Poland 45 F8 52 46N 21 14 E
Orzysz, Poland 44 E8 53 50N 21 58 E
Osa →, Poland 44 E5 53 33N 18 46 E
Osa, Pen. de, Costa Rica 120 E3 8 0N 84 0W
Osage, U.S.A. 112 D8 43 17N 92 49W
Osage →, U.S.A. 112 F9 38 35N 91 57W
Osage City, U.S.A. 112 F7 38 38N 95 50W
Ōsaka, Japan 55 G7 34 40N 135 30 E
Osan, S. Korea 57 F14 37 11N 127 4 E
Osawatomie, U.S.A. 112 F7 38 31N 94 57W
Osborne, U.S.A. 112 F5 39 26N 98 42W
Osby, Sweden 11 H7 56 23N 13 59 E
Osceola, Ark., U.S.A. 113 H10 35 42N 89 58W
Osceola, Iowa, U.S.A. 112 E8 41 2N 93 46W
Oschatz, Germany 24 D9 51 17N 13 6 E
Oschersleben, Germany 24 C7 52 2N 11 14 E
Óschiri, Italy 30 B2 40 43N 9 6 E
Oscoda, U.S.A. 110 B1 44 26N 83 20W
Osečina, Serbia, Yug. 40 B3 44 23N 19 34 E
Ösel = Saaremaa, Estonia 9 G20 58 30N 22 30 E
Osery, Russia 46 E10 54 52N 38 28 E
Osgoode, Canada 111 A9 45 8N 75 36W
Osh, Kyrgyzstan 50 E8 40 37N 72 49 E
Oshakati, Namibia 85 H3 17 45 S 15 40 E
Oshawa, Canada 102 D4 43 50N 78 50W
Oshigambo, Namibia 88 B2 17 45 S 16 5 E
Oshkosh, Nebr., U.S.A. 112 E3 41 24N 102 21W
Oshkosh, Wis., U.S.A. 112 C10 44 1N 88 33W
Oshmyany = Ashmyany, Belarus 9 J21 54 26N 25 52 E
Oshnovīyeh, Iran 70 B5 37 2N 45 6 E
Oshogbo, Nigeria 83 D5 7 48N 4 37 E
Oshtorīnān, Iran 71 C6 34 1N 48 38 E
Oshwe, Dem. Rep. of the Congo 84 E3 3 25 S 19 28 E
Osi, Nigeria 83 D6 8 8N 5 14 E
Osieczna, Poland 45 G3 51 55N 16 40 E
Osijek, Croatia 42 E3 45 34N 18 41 E
Ósilo, Italy 30 B1 40 45N 8 40 E
Ósimo, Italy 29 E10 43 28N 13 30 E
Osintorf, Belarus 46 E6 54 40N 30 39 E
Osipenko = Berdyansk, Ukraine 47 J9 46 45N 36 50 E
Osipovichi = Asipovichy, Belarus 46 F5 53 19N 28 33 E
Osiyan, India 68 F5 26 43N 72 55 E
Osizweni, S. Africa 89 D5 27 49 S 30 7 E
Oskaloosa, U.S.A. 112 E8 41 18N 92 39W
Oskarshamn, Sweden 11 G10 57 15N 16 27 E
Oskarström, Sweden 11 H6 56 48N 12 58 E
Oskélanéo, Canada 102 C4 48 5N 75 15W
Öskemen, Kazakstan 50 E9 50 0N 82 36 E
Oskol →, Ukraine 47 H9 49 6N 37 25 E
Oslo, Norway 9 G14 59 55N 10 45 E
Oslob, Phil. 61 G5 9 31N 123 26 E
Oslofjorden, Norway 9 G14 59 20N 10 35 E
Osmanabad, India 66 K10 18 5N 76 10 E
Osmancık, Turkey 72 B6 40 58N 34 50 E
Osmaniye, Turkey 70 B3 37 5N 36 10 E
Osmanlı, Turkey 41 E10 41 35N 26 51 E
Ösmo, Sweden 10 F11 58 58N 17 55 E
Osnabrück, Germany 24 C4 52 17N 8 3 E
Ośno Lubuskie, Poland 45 F1 52 28N 14 51 E
Osoblaha, Czech Rep. 27 A10 50 17N 17 44 E
Osogovska Planina, Macedonia 40 D6 42 10N 22 30 E
Osor, Italy 29 D11 44 42N 14 24 E
Osorio, Brazil 127 B5 29 53 S 50 17W
Osorno, Chile 128 E2 40 25 S 73 0W
Osorno, Spain 34 C6 42 24N 4 22W
Osoyoos, Canada 104 D5 49 0N 119 30W
Osøyro, Norway 9 F11 60 9N 5 30 E
Ospika →, Canada 104 B4 56 20N 124 0W
Osprey Reef, Australia 94 A4 13 52 S 146 36 E
Oss, Neths. 17 C5 51 46N 5 32 E
Ossa, Mt., Australia 94 G4 41 52 S 146 3 E
Óssa, Óros, Greece 38 B4 39 47N 22 42 E
Ossa de Montiel, Spain 33 G2 38 58N 2 45W
Ossabaw I., U.S.A. 109 K5 31 50N 81 5W
Osse →, France 20 D4 44 7N 0 17 E
Osse →, Nigeria 83 D6 6 10N 5 20 E
Ossi, Italy 30 B1 40 40N 8 35 E
Ossining, U.S.A. 111 E11 41 10N 73 55W
Ossipee, U.S.A. 111 C13 43 41N 71 7W
Ossokmanuan L., Canada 103 B7 53 25N 65 0W
Ossora, Russia 51 D17 59 20N 163 13 E
Ostashkov, Russia 46 D7 57 4N 33 2 E
Östavall, Sweden 10 B9 62 26N 15 29 E
Oste →, Germany 24 B5 53 49N 9 2 E
Ostend = Oostende, Belgium 17 C2 51 15N 2 54 E
Oster, Ukraine 47 G6 50 57N 30 53 E
Osterburg, Germany 24 C7 52 47N 11 45 E
Osterburg, U.S.A. 110 F6 40 16N 78 31W
Osterburken, Germany 25 F5 49 25N 9 26 E
Österbybruk, Sweden 10 D11 60 13N 17 55 E
Österbymo, Sweden 11 G9 57 49N 15 15 E
Österdalälven, Sweden 10 C7 61 30N 13 45 E
Østerdalen, Norway 9 F14 61 40N 10 50 E
Österfärnebo, Sweden 10 D10 60 19N 16 48 E
Österforse, Sweden 10 A11 63 9N 17 3 E
Östergötlands län □, Sweden 11 F9 58 35N 15 45 E
Osterholz-Scharmbeck, Germany 24 B4 53 13N 8 47 E
Østerild, Denmark 11 G2 57 2N 8 51 E
Osterode, Germany 24 D6 51 43N 10 15 E
Östersund, Sweden 10 A8 63 10N 14 38 E
Östervåla, Sweden 10 D11 60 11N 17 11 E
Ostfriesische Inseln, Germany 24 B3 53 42N 7 0 E
Ostfriesland, Germany 24 B3 53 20N 7 30 E
Östhammar, Sweden 10 D12 60 16N 18 22 E
Óstia, Lido di, Italy 29 G9 41 43N 12 17 E
Ostíglia, Italy 29 C8 45 4N 11 8 E
Östmark, Sweden 10 D6 60 17N 12 45 E
Östra Husby, Sweden 11 F10 58 35N 16 33 E
Ostrava, Czech Rep. 27 B11 49 51N 18 18 E
Ostróda, Poland 44 E6 53 42N 19 58 E
Ostrogozhsk, Russia 47 G10 50 55N 39 7 E
Ostroh, Ukraine 47 G4 50 20N 26 30 E
Ostrołęka, Poland 45 E8 53 4N 21 32 E
Ostrov, Bulgaria 41 C8 43 40N 24 9 E
Ostrov, Czech Rep. 26 A5 50 18N 12 57 E
Ostrov, Romania 43 F12 44 6N 27 24 E
Ostrov, Russia 46 D5 57 25N 28 20 E
Ostrów Lubelski, Poland 45 G9 51 29N 22 51 E
Ostrów Mazowiecka, Poland 45 F8 52 50N 21 51 E
Ostrów Wielkopolski, Poland 45 G4 51 36N 17 44 E
Ostrowiec-Świętokrzyski, Poland 45 H8 50 55N 21 22 E
Ostrožac, Bos.-H. 42 G2 43 43N 17 49 E
Ostrzeszów, Poland 45 G4 51 25N 17 52 E
Ostseebad Kühlungsborn, Germany 24 A7 54 8N 11 44 E
Osttirol □, Austria 26 E5 46 50N 12 30 E
Ostuni, Italy 31 B10 40 44N 17 35 E
Osum →, Albania 40 F4 40 40N 20 10 E
Osum →, Bulgaria 41 C8 43 40N 24 50 E
Osumi → = Osum →, Albania 40 F4 40 40N 20 10 E
Ōsumi-Kaikyō, Japan 55 J5 30 55N 131 0 E
Ōsumi-Shotō, Japan 55 J5 30 30N 130 0 E
Osun □, Nigeria 83 D5 7 30N 4 30 E
Osuna, Spain 35 H5 37 14N 5 8W
Oswegatchie →, U.S.A. 111 B9 44 42N 75 30W
Oswego, U.S.A. 111 C8 43 27N 76 31W
Oswego →, U.S.A. 111 C8 43 27N 76 30W
Oswestry, U.K. 12 E4 52 52N 3 3W
Oświęcim, Poland 45 H6 50 2N 19 11 E
Otaci, Moldova 43 B12 48 27N 27 47 E
Otago □, N.Z. 91 L2 45 15 S 170 0 E
Otago Harbour, N.Z. 91 L3 45 47 S 170 42 E
Otake, Japan 55 G6 34 12N 132 13 E
Otaki, N.Z. 91 J5 40 45 S 175 10 E
Otaru, Japan 54 C10 43 10N 141 0 E
Otaru-Wan = Ishikari-Wan, Japan 54 C10 43 25N 141 1 E
Otava →, Czech Rep. 26 B7 49 26N 14 12 E
Otavalo, Ecuador 124 C3 0 13N 78 20W
Otavi, Namibia 88 B2 19 40 S 17 24 E
Otchinjau, Angola 88 B1 16 30 S 13 56 E
Otelec, Romania 42 E5 45 36N 20 50 E
Otelnuk L., Canada 103 A6 56 9N 68 12W
Oţelu Roşu, Romania 42 E7 45 32N 22 22 E
Otero de Rey = Outeiro de Rei, Spain 34 B3 43 6N 7 36W
Othello, U.S.A. 114 C4 46 50N 119 10W
Othonoí, Greece 38 B1 39 52N 19 22 E
Óthris, Óros, Greece 38 B4 39 2N 22 37 E
Otjiwarongo, Namibia 88 C2 20 30 S 16 33 E
Otmuchów, Poland 45 H4 50 28N 17 10 E
Otočac, Croatia 29 D12 44 53N 15 12 E
Otoineppu, Japan 54 B11 44 44N 142 16 E
Otok, Croatia 29 E13 43 42N 16 44 E
Otorohanga, N.Z. 91 H5 38 12 S 175 14 E
Otoskwin →, Canada 102 B2 52 13N 88 6W
Otra →, Norway 9 G13 58 9N 8 1 E
Otradnyy, Russia 48 D10 53 22N 51 21 E
Otranto, Italy 31 B11 40 9N 18 28 E
Otranto, C. d', Italy 31 B11 40 7N 18 30 E
Otranto, Str. of, Italy 31 B11 40 15N 18 40 E
Otrokovice, Czech Rep. 27 B10 49 12N 17 32 E
Otse, S. Africa 88 D4 25 2 S 25 45 E
Ōtsu, Japan 55 G7 35 0N 135 50 E
Ōtsuki, Japan 55 G9 35 36N 138 57 E
Ottawa = Outaouais →, Canada 102 C5 45 27N 74 8W
Ottawa, Canada 102 C4 45 27N 75 42W
Ottawa, Ill., U.S.A. 112 E10 41 21N 88 51W
Ottawa, Kans., U.S.A. 112 F7 38 37N 95 16W
Ottawa Is., Canada 101 C11 59 35N 80 10W
Ottélé, Cameroon 83 E7 3 38N 11 19 E
Ottensheim, Austria 26 C7 48 21N 14 12 E
Otter Cr. →, U.S.A. 111 B11 44 13N 73 17W
Otter L., Canada 105 B8 55 35N 104 39W
Otterndorf, Germany 24 B4 53 48N 8 53 E
Otterup, Denmark 11 J4 55 30N 10 22 E
Otterville, Canada 110 D4 42 55N 80 36W
Ottery St. Mary, U.K. 13 G4 50 44N 3 17W
Otto Beit Bridge, Zimbabwe 87 F2 15 59 S 28 56 E
Ottosdal, S. Africa 88 D4 26 46 S 25 59 E
Ottumwa, U.S.A. 112 E8 41 1N 92 25W
Otu, Nigeria 83 D5 8 14N 3 22 E
Otukpa, Nigeria 83 D6 7 9N 7 41 E
Oturkpo, Nigeria 83 D6 7 16N 8 8 E
Otway, B., Chile 128 G2 53 30 S 74 0W
Otway, C., Australia 95 F3 38 52 S 143 30 E
Otwock, Poland 45 F8 52 5N 21 20 E
Ötztaler Ache →, Austria 26 D3 47 14N 10 50 E
Ötztaler Alpen, Austria 26 E3 46 56N 11 0 E
Ou →, Laos 64 B4 20 4N 102 13 E
Ou Neua, Laos 58 F3 22 18N 101 48 E
Ou-Sammyaku, Japan 54 E10 39 20N 140 35 E
Ouachita →, U.S.A. 113 K9 31 38N 91 49W
Ouachita, L., U.S.A. 113 H8 34 34N 93 12W
Ouachita Mts., U.S.A. 113 H7 34 40N 94 25W
Ouagadougou, Burkina Faso 83 C4 12 25N 1 30W
Ouahigouya, Burkina Faso 82 C4 13 31N 2 25W
Ouahran = Oran, Algeria 78 A5 35 45N 0 39W
Oualâta, Mauritania 82 B3 17 20N 6 55W
Ouallam, Niger 83 C5 14 23N 2 10 E
Ouallene, Algeria 78 D6 24 41N 1 11 E
Ouargaye, Burkina Faso 83 C5 11 40N 0 5 E
Ouargla, Algeria 78 B7 31 59N 5 16 E
Ouarkoye, Burkina Faso 82 C4 12 5N 3 40W
Ouarzazate, Morocco 78 B4 30 55N 6 50W
Ouassouas, Mali 83 B5 16 10N 1 23 E
Ouatagouna, Mali 83 B5 15 11N 0 43 E
Oubangi →, Dem. Rep. of the Congo 84 E3 0 30 S 17 50 E
Ouche →, France 19 E12 47 6N 5 16 E
Ouddorp, Neths. 17 C3 51 50N 3 57 E
Oude Rijn →, Neths. 17 B4 52 12N 4 24 E
Oudeïka, Mali 83 B4 17 30N 1 40W
Oudenaarde, Belgium 17 D3 50 50N 3 37 E
Oudon →, France 18 E6 47 41N 0 53W
Oudtshoorn, S. Africa 88 E3 33 35 S 22 14 E
Ouellé, Ivory C. 82 D4 7 26N 4 1W
Ouémé →, Benin 83 D5 6 30N 2 30 E
Ouessa, Burkina Faso 82 C4 11 4N 2 47W
Ouessant, Î. d', France 18 D1 48 28N 5 6W
Ouesso, Congo 84 D3 1 37N 16 5 E
Ouest, Pte. de l', Canada 103 C7 49 52N 64 40W
Ouezzane, Morocco 78 B4 34 51N 5 35W
Ougarou, Burkina Faso 83 C5 12 10N 0 58 E
Oughterard, Ireland 15 C2 53 26N 9 18W
Ouidah, Benin 83 D5 6 25N 2 0 E
Ouidi, Niger 83 C7 14 10N 13 0 E
Ouistreham, France 18 C6 49 17N 0 18W
Oujda, Morocco 78 B5 34 41N 1 55W
Oujeft, Mauritania 82 A2 20 2N 13 0W
Oulainen, Finland 8 D21 64 17N 24 47 E
Ould Yenjé, Mauritania 82 B2 15 38N 12 16W
Oullins, France 21 C8 45 43N 4 49 E
Oulu, Finland 8 D21 65 1N 25 29 E
Oulujärvi, Finland 8 D22 64 25N 27 15 E
Oulujoki →, Finland 8 D21 65 1N 25 30 E
Oulx, Italy 28 C3 45 2N 6 50 E
Oum Chalouba, Chad 79 E10 15 48N 20 46 E
Oum Hadjer, Chad 79 F9 13 18N 19 41 E
Oumé, Ivory C. 82 D3 6 21N 5 27W
Ounasjoki →, Finland 8 C21 66 31N 25 40 E
Ounguati, Namibia 88 C2 22 0 S 15 46 E
Ounianga Sérir, Chad 79 E10 18 54N 20 51 E
Our →, Lux. 17 E6 49 55N 6 5 E
Ouranópolis, Greece 40 F7 40 20N 23 59 E
Ourârene, Niger 83 B6 19 30N 7 10 E
Ouray, U.S.A. 115 G10 38 1N 107 40W
Ourcq →, France 19 C10 49 1N 3 1 E
Ourense, Spain 34 C3 42 19N 7 55W
Ouricuri, Brazil 125 E10 7 53 S 40 5W
Ourinhos, Brazil 127 A6 23 0 S 49 54W
Ourique, Portugal 35 H2 37 38N 8 16W
Ouro Fino, Brazil 127 A6 22 16 S 46 25W
Ouro-Ndia, Mali 82 B4 15 8N 4 50W
Ouro Prêto, Brazil 127 A7 20 20 S 43 30W
Ouro Sogui, Senegal 82 B2 15 36N 13 19W
Oursi, Burkina Faso 83 C4 14 41N 0 27W
Ourthe →, Belgium 17 D5 50 29N 5 35 E
Ouse →, E. Susx., U.K. 13 G8 50 47N 0 4 E
Ouse →, N. Yorks., U.K. 12 D7 53 44N 0 55W
Oust, France 20 F5 42 52N 1 13 E
Oust →, France 18 E4 47 35N 2 6W
Outaouais →, Canada 102 C5 45 27N 74 8W
Outardes →, Canada 103 C6 49 24N 69 30W
Outeiro de Rei, Spain 34 B3 43 6N 7 36W
Outer Hebrides, U.K. 14 D1 57 30N 7 40W
Outes = Serra de Outes, Spain 34 C2 42 52N 8 55W
Outjo, Namibia 88 C2 20 5 S 16 7 E
Outlook, Canada 105 C7 51 30N 107 0W
Outokumpu, Finland 8 E23 62 43N 29 1 E
Outreau, France 19 B8 50 40N 1 36 E
Ouvèze →, France 21 E8 43 59N 4 51 E
Ouyen, Australia 95 F3 35 1 S 142 22 E
Ouzouer-le-Marché, France 19 E8 47 54N 1 32 E
Ovada, Italy 28 D5 44 38N 8 38 E
Ovalau, Fiji 91 C8 17 40 S 178 48 E
Ovalle, Chile 126 C1 30 33 S 71 18W
Ovamboland, Namibia 88 B2 18 30 S 16 0 E
Ovar, Portugal 34 E2 40 51N 8 40W
Overath, Germany 24 E3 50 56N 7 17 E
Overflakkee, Neths. 17 C4 51 44N 4 10 E
Overijssel □, Neths. 17 B6 52 25N 6 35 E
Overland Park, U.S.A. 112 F7 38 55N 94 50W
Overton, U.S.A. 117 J12 36 33N 114 27W
Övertorneå, Sweden 8 C20 66 23N 23 38 E
Överum, Sweden 11 F10 58 0N 16 20 E
Ovid, U.S.A. 111 D8 42 41N 76 49W
Ovidiopol, Ukraine 47 J6 46 15N 30 30 E
Ovidiu, Romania 43 F13 44 16N 28 34 E
Oviedo, Spain 34 B5 43 25N 5 50W
Oviksfjällen, Sweden 10 A7 63 0N 13 49 E
Oviši, Latvia 9 H19 57 33N 21 44 E
Ovoot, Mongolia 56 B7 45 21N 113 45 E
Övör Hangay □, Mongolia 56 B2 45 0N 102 30 E
Ovoro, Nigeria 83 D6 5 26N 7 16 E
Øvre Årdal, Norway 9 F12 61 19N 7 48 E
Övre Fryken, Sweden 10 E7 60 0N 13 7 E
Ovruch, Ukraine 47 G5 51 25N 28 45 E
Owaka, N.Z. 91 M2 46 27 S 169 40 E
Owambo = Ovamboland, Namibia 88 B2 18 30 S 16 0 E
Owasco L., U.S.A. 111 D8 42 50N 76 31W
Owase, Japan 55 G8 34 7N 136 12 E
Owatonna, U.S.A. 112 C8 44 5N 93 14W
Owbeh, Afghan. 66 B3 34 28N 63 10 E
Owego, U.S.A. 111 D8 42 6N 76 16W
Owen Falls Dam, Uganda 86 B3 0 30N 33 5 E
Owen Sound, Canada 102 D3 44 35N 80 55W
Owens →, U.S.A. 116 J9 36 32N 117 59W
Owens L., U.S.A. 117 J9 36 26N 117 57W
Owensboro, U.S.A. 108 G2 37 46N 87 7W
Owerri, Nigeria 83 D6 5 29N 7 0 E
Owl →, Canada 105 B10 57 51N 92 44W
Owo, Nigeria 83 D6 7 10N 5 39 E
Owosso, U.S.A. 108 D3 43 0N 84 10W
Owyhee, U.S.A. 114 F5 41 57N 116 6W
Owyhee →, U.S.A. 114 E5 43 49N 117 2W
Owyhee, L., U.S.A. 114 E5 43 38N 117 14W
Ox Mts. = Slieve Gamph, Ireland 15 B3 54 6N 9 0W
Öxarfjörður, Iceland 8 C5 66 15N 16 45W
Oxbow, Canada 105 D8 49 14N 102 10W
Oxelösund, Sweden 11 F11 58 43N 17 5 E
Oxford, N.Z. 91 K4 43 18 S 172 11 E
Oxford, U.K. 13 F6 51 46N 1 15W
Oxford, Mass., U.S.A. 111 D13 42 7N 71 52W
Oxford, Miss., U.S.A. 113 H10 34 22N 89 31W
Oxford, N.C., U.S.A. 109 G6 36 19N 78 35W
Oxford, N.Y., U.S.A. 111 D9 42 27N 75 36W
Oxford, Ohio, U.S.A. 108 F3 39 31N 84 45W
Oxford L., Canada 105 C9 54 51N 95 37W
Oxfordshire □, U.K. 13 F6 51 48N 1 16W
Oxía, Greece 38 C3 38 16N 21 5 E
Oxie, Sweden 11 J7 55 33N 13 6 E
Oxílithos, Greece 38 C6 38 35N 24 7 E
Oxnard, U.S.A. 117 L7 34 12N 119 11W
Oxsjövålen, Sweden 10 B7 62 34N 13 57 E
Oxus = Amudarya →, Uzbekistan 50 E6 43 58N 59 34 E
Oya, Malaysia 62 D4 2 55N 111 55 E
Oyama, Japan 55 F9 36 18N 139 48 E
Oyem, Gabon 84 D2 1 34N 11 31 E
Oyen, Canada 105 C6 51 22N 110 28W
Oykel →, U.K. 14 D4 57 56N 4 26W
Oymyakon, Russia 51 C15 63 25N 142 44 E
Oyo, Nigeria 83 D5 7 46N 3 56 E
Oyo □, Nigeria 83 D5 8 15N 3 30 E
Oyonnax, France 19 F12 46 16N 5 40 E
Oyster Bay, U.S.A. 111 F11 40 52N 73 32W
Ōyübari, Japan 54 C11 43 1N 142 5 E
Özalp, Turkey 73 C10 38 39N 43 59 E
Ozamiz, Phil. 61 G5 8 15N 123 50 E
Ozark, Ala., U.S.A. 109 K3 31 28N 85 39W
Ozark, Ark., U.S.A. 113 H8 35 29N 93 50W
Ozark, Mo., U.S.A. 113 G8 37 1N 93 12W
Ozark Plateau, U.S.A. 113 G9 37 20N 91 40W
Ozarks, L. of the, U.S.A. 112 F8 38 12N 92 38W
Ożarów, Poland 45 H8 50 53N 21 40 E
Ózd, Hungary 42 B5 48 14N 20 15 E
Ozernoye, Russia 48 E10 51 46N 51 28 E
Ozette L., U.S.A. 116 B2 48 6N 124 38W
Ozieri, Italy 30 B2 40 35N 9 0 E
Ozimek, Poland 45 H5 50 41N 18 11 E
Ozinki, Russia 48 E9 51 12N 49 44 E
Ozona, U.S.A. 113 K4 30 43N 101 12W
Ozorków, Poland 45 G6 51 57N 19 16 E
Ozren, Bos.-H. 42 G3 43 55N 18 29 E
Ozuluama, Mexico 119 C5 21 40N 97 50W
Ozun, Romania 43 E10 45 47N 25 50 E
Ozurgeti, Georgia 49 K5 41 55N 42 2 E

P

Pa, Burkina Faso 82 C4 11 33N 3 19W
Pa-an, Burma 67 L20 16 51N 97 40 E
Pa Mong Dam, Thailand 64 D4 18 0N 102 22 E
Pa Sak →, Thailand 62 B2 15 30N 101 0 E
Paamiut, Greenland 4 C5 62 0N 49 43W
Paar →, Germany 25 G7 48 46N 11 36 E
Paarl, S. Africa 88 E2 33 45 S 18 56 E
Paauilo, U.S.A. 106 H17 20 2N 155 22W
Pab Hills, Pakistan 68 F2 26 30N 66 45 E
Pabbay, U.K. 14 D1 57 46N 7 14W
Pabianice, Poland 45 G6 51 40N 19 20 E
Pabna, Bangla. 67 G16 24 1N 89 18 E
Pabo, Uganda 86 B3 3 1N 32 10 E
Pacaja →, Brazil 125 D8 1 56 S 50 50W
Pacaraima, Sa., S. Amer. 122 C4 4 0N 62 30W
Pacasmayo, Peru 124 E3 7 20 S 79 35W
Paceco, Italy 30 E5 37 59N 12 33 E
Pachhar, India 68 G7 24 40N 77 42 E
Pachino, Italy 31 F8 36 43N 15 5 E
Pachitea →, Peru 124 E4 8 46 S 74 33W
Pachmarhi, India 69 H8 22 28N 78 26 E
Pachpadra, India 66 G8 25 58N 72 10 E
Pachuca, Mexico 119 C5 20 10N 98 40W
Pacific, Canada 104 C3 54 48N 128 28W
Pacific-Antarctic Ridge, Pac. Oc. 97 M16 43 0 S 115 0W
Pacific Grove, U.S.A. 116 J5 36 38N 121 56W
Pacific Ocean, Pac. Oc. 97 G14 10 0N 140 0W
Pacific Rim Nat. Park, Canada 116 B2 48 40N 124 45W
Pacifica, U.S.A. 116 H4 37 36N 122 30W
Pacitan, Indonesia 63 H14 8 12 S 111 7 E
Packwood, U.S.A. 116 D5 46 36N 121 40W
Pacov, Czech Rep. 26 B8 49 27N 15 0 E
Pacy-sur-Eure, France 18 C8 49 1N 1 23 E
Padaido, Kepulauan, Indonesia 63 E9 1 5 S 138 0 E
Padang, Indonesia 62 E2 1 0 S 100 20 E
Padang Endau, Malaysia 65 L4 2 40N 103 38 E
Padangpanjang, Indonesia 62 E2 0 40 S 100 20 E
Padangsidempuan, Indonesia 62 D1 1 30N 99 15 E
Padborg, Denmark 11 K3 54 49N 9 21 E
Paddle Prairie, Canada 104 B5 57 57N 117 29W
Paddockwood, Canada 105 C7 53 30N 105 30W
Paderborn, Germany 24 D4 51 42N 8 45 E
Padeş, Vf., Romania 42 E7 45 40N 22 22 E
Padina, Romania 43 F12 44 50N 27 8 E
Padma, India 69 G11 24 12N 85 22 E
Pádova, Italy 29 C8 45 25N 11 53 E
Padra, India 68 H5 22 15N 73 7 E

Padrauna, *India* **69 F10** 26 54N 83 59 E
Padre I., *U.S.A.* **113 M6** 27 10N 97 25W
Padrón, *Spain* **34 C2** 42 41N 8 39W
Padstow, *U.K.* **13 G3** 50 33N 4 58W
Padua = Pádova, *Italy* **29 C8** 45 25N 11 53 E
Paducah, *Ky., U.S.A.* **108 G1** 37 5N 88 37W
Paducah, *Tex., U.S.A.* **113 H4** 34 1N 100 18W
Padul, *Spain* **35 H7** 37 1N 3 38W
Paengnyŏng-do, *S. Korea* **57 F13** 37 57N 124 40 E
Paeroa, *N.Z.* **91 G5** 37 23 S 175 41 E
Paesana, *Italy* **28 D4** 44 41N 7 16 E
Pafúri, *Mozam.* **89 C5** 22 28 S 31 17 E
Pag, *Croatia* **29 D12** 44 25N 15 3 E
Paga, *Ghana* **83 C4** 11 1N 1 8W
Pagadian, *Phil.* **61 H5** 7 55N 123 30 E
Pagai Selatan, Pulau, *Indonesia* **62 E2** 3 0 S 100 15 E
Pagai Utara, Pulau, *Indonesia* **62 E2** 2 35 S 100 0 E
Pagalu = Annobón, *Atl. Oc.* **77 G4** 1 25 S 5 36 E
Pagara, *India* **69 G9** 24 22N 80 1 E
Pagastikós Kólpos, *Greece* **38 B5** 39 15N 23 0 E
Pagatan, *Indonesia* **62 E5** 3 33 S 115 59 E
Page, *U.S.A.* **115 H8** 36 57N 111 27W
Pagėgiai, *Lithuania* **44 C8** 55 9N 21 54 E
Pago Pago, *Amer. Samoa* **91 B13** 14 16 S 170 43W
Pagosa Springs, *U.S.A.* **115 H10** 37 16N 107 1W
Pagwa River, *Canada* **102 B2** 50 2N 85 14W
Pahala, *U.S.A.* **106 J17** 19 12N 155 29W
Pahang →, *Malaysia* **65 L4** 3 30N 103 9 E
Pahiatua, *N.Z.* **91 J5** 40 27 S 175 50 E
Pahokee, *U.S.A.* **109 M5** 26 50N 80 40W
Pahrump, *U.S.A.* **117 J11** 36 12N 115 59W
Pahute Mesa, *U.S.A.* **116 H10** 37 20N 116 45W
Pai, *Thailand* **64 C2** 19 19N 98 27 E
Paia, *U.S.A.* **106 H16** 20 54N 156 22W
Paicines, *U.S.A.* **116 J5** 36 44N 121 17W
Paide, *Estonia* **9 G21** 58 57N 25 31 E
Paignton, *U.K.* **13 G4** 50 26N 3 35W
Paiho, *Taiwan* **59 F13** 23 21N 120 25 E
Päijänne, *Finland* **9 F21** 61 30N 25 30 E
Pailani, *India* **69 G9** 25 45N 80 26 E
Pailin, *Cambodia* **64 F4** 12 46N 102 36 E
Paimpol, *France* **18 D3** 48 48N 3 4W
Painan, *Indonesia* **62 E2** 1 21 S 100 34 E
Painesville, *U.S.A.* **110 E3** 41 43N 81 15W
Paint Hills = Wemindji, *Canada* **102 B4** 53 0N 78 49W
Paint L., *Canada* **105 B9** 55 28N 97 57W
Painted Desert, *U.S.A.* **115 J8** 36 0N 111 0W
Paintsville, *U.S.A.* **108 G4** 37 49N 82 48W
País Vasco □, *Spain* **32 C2** 42 50N 2 45W
Paisley, *Canada* **110 B3** 44 18N 81 16W
Paisley, *U.K.* **14 F4** 55 50N 4 25W
Paisley, *U.S.A.* **114 E3** 42 42N 120 32W
Paita, *Peru* **124 E2** 5 11 S 81 9W
Paiva →, *Portugal* **34 D2** 41 4N 8 16W
Paizhou, *China* **59 B9** 30 12N 113 55 E
Pajares, *Spain* **34 B5** 43 1N 5 46W
Pajares, Puerto de, *Spain* **34 C5** 42 58N 5 46W
Pajęczno, *Poland* **45 G5** 51 10N 19 0 E
Pak Lay, *Laos* **64 C3** 18 15N 101 27 E
Pak Phanang, *Thailand* **65 H3** 8 21N 100 12 E
Pak Sane, *Laos* **64 C4** 18 22N 103 39 E
Pak Song, *Laos* **64 E6** 15 11N 106 14 E
Pak Suong, *Laos* **58 H4** 19 58N 102 15 E
Pakaur, *India* **69 G12** 24 38N 87 51 E
Pakenham, *Canada* **111 A8** 45 18N 76 18W
Pákhnes, *Greece* **36 D6** 35 16N 24 4 E
Pakhuis, *S. Africa* **88 E2** 32 9 S 19 5 E
Pakistan ■, *Asia* **68 E4** 30 0N 70 0 E
Pakkading, *Laos* **64 C4** 18 19N 103 59 E
Pakokku, *Burma* **67 J19** 21 20N 95 0 E
Pakość, *Poland* **45 F5** 52 48N 18 6 E
Pakowki L., *Canada* **105 D6** 49 20N 111 0W
Pakpattan, *Pakistan* **68 D5** 30 25N 73 27 E
Pakrac, *Croatia* **42 E2** 45 27N 17 12 E
Pakruojis, *Lithuania* **44 C10** 55 58N 23 52 E
Paks, *Hungary* **42 D3** 46 38N 18 55 E
Paktīā □, *Afghan.* **66 C6** 33 0N 69 15 E
Pakwach, *Uganda* **86 B3** 2 28N 31 27 E
Pakxe, *Laos* **64 E5** 15 5N 105 52 E
Pal Lahara, *India* **69 J11** 21 27N 85 11 E
Pala, *Chad* **79 G9** 9 25N 15 5 E
Pala, *Dem. Rep. of the Congo* **86 D2** 6 45 S 29 30 E
Pala, *U.S.A.* **117 M9** 33 22N 117 5W
Palabek, *Uganda* **86 B3** 3 22N 32 33 E
Palacios, *U.S.A.* **113 L6** 28 42N 96 13W
Palafrugell, *Spain* **32 D8** 41 55N 3 10 E
Palagiano, *Italy* **31 B10** 40 35N 17 2 E
Palagonía, *Italy* **31 E7** 37 19N 14 45 E
Palagruža, *Croatia* **29 F13** 42 24N 16 15 E
Palaiókastron, *Greece* **36 D8** 35 12N 26 15 E
Palaiokhóra, *Greece* **36 D5** 35 16N 23 39 E
Pálairos, *Greece* **38 C2** 38 45N 20 51 E
Palaiseau, *France* **19 D9** 48 43N 2 15 E
Palam, *India* **66 K10** 19 0N 77 0 E
Palamás, *Greece* **38 B4** 39 26N 22 4 E
Palamós, *Spain* **32 D8** 41 50N 3 10 E
Palampur, *India* **68 C7** 32 10N 76 30 E
Palamut, *Turkey* **39 C9** 38 59N 27 41 E
Palana, *Australia* **94 F4** 39 45 S 147 55 E
Palana, *Russia* **51 D16** 59 10N 159 59 E
Palanan, *Phil.* **61 C5** 17 8N 122 29 E
Palanan Pt., *Phil.* **61 C5** 17 17N 122 30 E
Palandri, *Pakistan* **69 C5** 33 42N 73 40 E
Palanga, *Lithuania* **9 J19** 55 58N 21 3 E
Palangkaraya, *Indonesia* **62 E4** 2 16 S 113 56 E
Palani Hills, *India* **66 P10** 10 14N 77 33 E
Palanpur, *India* **68 G5** 24 10N 72 25 E
Palapye, *Botswana* **88 C4** 22 30 S 27 7 E
Palas, *Pakistan* **69 B5** 35 4N 73 14 E
Palas de Rei, *Spain* **34 C3** 42 52N 7 52W
Palashi, *India* **69 H13** 23 47N 88 15 E
Palasponga, *India* **69 J11** 21 47N 85 34 E
Palatka, *Russia* **51 C16** 60 6N 150 54 E
Palatka, *U.S.A.* **109 L5** 29 39N 81 38W
Palau, *Italy* **30 A2** 41 11N 9 23 E
Palau ■, *Pac. Oc.* **52 J17** 7 30N 134 30 E
Palauk, *Burma* **64 F2** 13 10N 98 40 E
Palawan, *Phil.* **61 G3** 9 30N 118 30 E
Palayankottai, *India* **66 Q10** 8 45N 77 45 E
Palazzo, Pte., *France* **21 F12** 42 28N 8 30 E
Palazzo San Gervásio, *Italy* **31 B8** 40 56N 15 59 E
Palazzolo Acréide, *Italy* **31 E7** 37 4N 14 54 E
Paldiski, *Estonia* **9 G21** 59 23N 24 9 E
Pale, *Bos.-H.* **42 G3** 43 50N 18 38 E
Paleleh, *Indonesia* **63 D6** 1 10N 121 50 E
Palembang, *Indonesia* **62 E2** 3 0 S 104 50 E
Palencia, *Spain* **34 C6** 42 1N 4 34W
Palencia □, *Spain* **34 C6** 42 31N 4 33W
Palenque, *Mexico* **119 D6** 17 31N 91 58W
Paleokastrítsa, *Greece* **36 A3** 39 40N 19 41 E
Paleometokho, *Cyprus* **36 D12** 35 7N 33 11 E
Palermo, *Italy* **30 D6** 38 7N 13 22 E
Palermo, *U.S.A.* **114 G3** 39 26N 121 33W
Palestina, *Chile* **128 A3** 23 50 S 69 47W
Palestine, *Asia* **75 D4** 32 0N 35 0 E
Palestine, *U.S.A.* **113 K7** 31 46N 95 38W
Palestrina, *Italy* **29 G9** 41 50N 12 53 E
Paletwa, *Burma* **67 J18** 21 10N 92 50 E
Palghat, *India* **66 P10** 10 46N 76 42 E
Palgrave, Mt., *Australia* **92 D2** 23 22 S 115 58 E
Pali, *India* **68 G5** 25 50N 73 20 E
Palikir, *Micronesia* **96 G7** 6 55N 158 9 E
Palinuro, *Italy* **31 B8** 40 2N 15 17 E
Palinuro, C., *Italy* **31 B8** 40 2N 15 16 E
Palioúrion, Ákra, *Greece* **40 G7** 39 57N 23 45 E
Palisades Reservoir, *U.S.A.* **114 E8** 43 20N 111 12W
Paliseul, *Belgium* **17 E5** 49 54N 5 8 E
Palitana, *India* **68 J4** 21 32N 71 49 E
Palizada, *Mexico* **119 D6** 18 18N 92 8W
Palk Bay, *Asia* **66 Q11** 9 30N 79 15 E
Palk Strait, *Asia* **66 Q11** 10 0N 79 45 E
Palkānah, *Iraq* **70 C5** 35 49N 44 26 E
Palkot, *India* **69 H11** 22 53N 84 39 E
Palla Road = Dinokwe, *Botswana* **88 C4** 23 29 S 26 37 E
Pallanza = Verbánia, *Italy* **28 C5** 45 56N 8 33 E
Pallarenda, *Australia* **94 B4** 19 12 S 146 46 E
Pallasovka, *Russia* **48 E8** 50 4N 47 0 E
Pallës, Bishti i, *Albania* **40 E3** 41 24N 19 24 E
Pallinup →, *Australia* **93 F2** 34 27 S 118 50 E
Pallisa, *Uganda* **86 B3** 1 12N 33 43 E
Pallu, *India* **68 E6** 28 59N 74 14 E
Palm Bay, *U.S.A.* **109 L5** 28 2N 80 35W
Palm Beach, *U.S.A.* **109 M6** 26 43N 80 2W
Palm Coast, *U.S.A.* **109 L5** 29 32N 81 10W
Palm Desert, *U.S.A.* **117 M10** 33 43N 116 22W
Palm Is., *Australia* **94 B4** 18 40 S 146 35 E
Palm Springs, *U.S.A.* **117 M10** 33 50N 116 33W
Palma, *Mozam.* **87 E5** 10 46 S 40 29 E
Palma, B. de, *Spain* **37 B9** 39 30N 2 39 E
Palma de Mallorca, *Spain* **37 B9** 39 35N 2 39 E
Palma del Río, *Spain* **35 H5** 37 43N 5 17W
Palma di Montechiaro, *Italy* **30 E6** 37 11N 13 46 E
Palma Soriano, *Cuba* **120 B4** 20 15N 76 0W
Palmares, *Brazil* **125 E11** 8 41 S 35 28W
Palmarola, *Italy* **30 B5** 40 56N 12 51 E
Palmas, *Brazil* **127 B5** 26 29 S 52 0W
Palmas, C., *Liberia* **82 E3** 4 27N 7 46W
Pálmas, G. di, *Italy* **30 D1** 39 0N 8 30 E
Palmdale, *U.S.A.* **117 L8** 34 35N 118 7W
Palmeira das Missões, *Brazil* **127 B5** 27 55 S 53 17W
Palmeira dos Índios, *Brazil* **125 E11** 9 25 S 36 37W
Palmela, *Portugal* **35 G2** 38 32N 8 57W
Palmer, *U.S.A.* **100 B5** 61 36N 149 7W
Palmer →, *Australia* **94 B3** 16 0 S 142 26 E
Palmer Arch., *Antarctica* **5 C17** 64 15 S 65 0W
Palmer Lake, *U.S.A.* **112 F2** 39 7N 104 55W
Palmer Land, *Antarctica* **5 D18** 73 0 S 63 0W
Palmerston, *Canada* **110 C4** 43 50N 80 51W
Palmerston, *N.Z.* **91 L3** 45 29 S 170 43 E
Palmerston North, *N.Z.* **91 J5** 40 21 S 175 39 E
Palmerton, *U.S.A.* **111 F9** 40 48N 75 37W
Palmetto, *U.S.A.* **109 M4** 27 31N 82 34W
Palmi, *Italy* **31 D8** 38 21N 15 51 E
Palmira, *Argentina* **126 C2** 32 59 S 68 34W
Palmira, *Colombia* **124 C3** 3 32N 76 16W
Palmyra = Tudmur, *Syria* **70 C3** 34 36N 38 15 E
Palmyra, *Mo., U.S.A.* **112 F9** 39 48N 91 32W
Palmyra, *N.J., U.S.A.* **111 F9** 40 1N 75 1W
Palmyra, *N.Y., U.S.A.* **110 C7** 43 5N 77 18W
Palmyra, *Pa., U.S.A.* **111 F8** 40 18N 76 36W
Palmyra Is., *Pac. Oc.* **97 G11** 5 52N 162 5W
Palo Alto, *U.S.A.* **116 H4** 37 27N 122 10W
Palo Verde, *U.S.A.* **117 M12** 33 26N 114 44W
Paloich, *Sudan* **81 E3** 10 28N 32 32 E
Palompon, *Phil.* **61 F6** 11 3N 124 23 E
Palopo, *Indonesia* **63 E6** 3 0 S 120 16 E
Palos, C. de, *Spain* **33 H4** 37 38N 0 40W
Palos de la Frontera, *Spain* **35 H4** 37 14N 6 53W
Palos Verdes, *U.S.A.* **117 M8** 33 48N 118 23W
Palos Verdes, Pt., *U.S.A.* **117 M8** 33 43N 118 26W
Pålsboda, *Sweden* **10 E9** 59 3N 15 22 E
Palu, *Indonesia* **63 E5** 1 0 S 119 52 E
Palu, *Turkey* **70 B3** 38 45N 40 0 E
Paluke, *Liberia* **82 D3** 5 2N 8 5W
Paluzza, *Italy* **29 B10** 46 32N 13 1 E
Palwal, *India* **68 E7** 28 8N 77 19 E
Pama, *Burkina Faso* **83 C5** 11 19N 0 44 E
Pamanukan, *Indonesia* **63 G12** 6 16 S 107 49 E
Pamiers, *France* **20 E5** 43 7N 1 39 E
Pamir, *Tajikistan* **50 F8** 37 40N 73 0 E
Pamlico →, *U.S.A.* **109 H7** 35 20N 76 28W
Pamlico Sd., *U.S.A.* **109 H8** 35 20N 76 0W
Pampa, *U.S.A.* **113 H4** 35 32N 100 58W
Pampa de las Salinas, *Argentina* **126 C2** 32 1 S 66 58W
Pampanua, *Indonesia* **63 E6** 4 16 S 120 8 E
Pampas, *Argentina* **126 D3** 35 0 S 63 0W
Pampas, *Peru* **124 F4** 12 20 S 74 50W
Pamphylia, *Turkey* **72 D4** 37 0N 31 20 E
Pamplona, *Colombia* **124 B4** 7 23N 72 39W
Pamplona, *Spain* **32 C3** 42 48N 1 38W
Pampoenpoort, *S. Africa* **88 E3** 31 3 S 22 40 E
Pamukçu, *Turkey* **39 B9** 39 30N 27 54 E
Pamukkale, *Turkey* **39 D11** 37 55N 29 8 E
Pan Xian, *China* **58 E5** 25 46N 104 38 E
Pana, *U.S.A.* **112 F10** 39 23N 89 5W
Panabo, *Phil.* **61 H6** 7 19N 125 42 E
Panaca, *U.S.A.* **115 H6** 37 47N 114 23W
Panagyurishte, *Bulgaria* **41 D8** 42 30N 24 15 E
Panaitan, *Indonesia* **63 G11** 6 36 S 105 12 E
Panaji, *India* **66 M8** 15 25N 73 50 E
Panamá, *Panama* **120 E4** 9 0N 79 25W
Panama ■, *Cent. Amer.* **120 E4** 8 48N 79 55W
Panamá, G. de, *Panama* **120 E4** 8 4N 79 20W
Panama Canal, *Panama* **120 E4** 9 10N 79 37W
Panama City, *U.S.A.* **109 K3** 30 10N 85 40W
Panamint Range, *U.S.A.* **117 J9** 36 20N 117 20W
Panamint Springs, *U.S.A.* **117 J9** 36 20N 117 28W
Panão, *Peru* **124 E3** 9 55 S 75 55W
Panaon I., *Phil.* **61 F6** 10 3N 125 13 E
Panare, *Thailand* **65 J3** 6 51N 101 30 E
Panarea, *Italy* **31 D8** 38 38N 15 4 E
Panaro →, *Italy* **29 D8** 44 55N 11 25 E
Panay, *Phil.* **61 F5** 11 10N 122 30 E
Panay, G., *Phil.* **63 B6** 11 0N 122 30 E
Pančevo, *Serbia, Yug.* **42 F5** 44 52N 20 41 E
Panch'iao, *Taiwan* **59 E13** 25 1N 121 27 E
Panciu, *Romania* **43 E12** 45 54N 27 8 E
Pancorbo, Desfiladero, *Spain* **34 C7** 42 32N 3 5W
Pâncota, *Romania* **42 D6** 46 20N 21 45 E
Panda, *Mozam.* **89 C5** 24 2 S 34 45 E
Pandan, *Antique, Phil.* **61 F5** 11 45N 122 10 E
Pandan, *Catanduanes, Phil.* **61 D6** 14 3N 124 10 E
Pandegelang, *Indonesia* **63 G12** 6 25 S 106 5 E
Pandhana, *India* **68 J7** 21 42N 76 13 E
Pandharpur, *India* **66 L9** 17 41N 75 20 E
Pando, *Uruguay* **127 C4** 34 44 S 56 0W
Pando, L. = Hope, L., *Australia* **95 D2** 28 24 S 139 18 E
Pandokrátor, *Greece* **36 A3** 39 45N 19 50 E
Pandora, *Costa Rica* **120 E3** 9 43N 83 3W
Pandrup, *Denmark* **11 G3** 57 14N 9 40 E
Panevėžys, *Lithuania* **9 J21** 55 42N 24 25 E
Panfilov, *Kazakstan* **50 E8** 44 10N 80 0 E
Panfilovo, *Russia* **48 E6** 50 25N 42 46 E
Pang-Long, *Burma* **67 H21** 23 11N 98 45 E
Pang-Yang, *Burma* **67 H21** 22 7N 98 48 E
Panga, *Dem. Rep. of the Congo* **86 B2** 1 52N 26 18 E
Pangaíon Óros, *Greece* **41 F8** 40 50N 24 0 E
Pangalanes, Canal des = Ampangalana, Lakandranon', *Madag.* **89 C8** 22 48 S 47 50 E
Pangani, *Tanzania* **86 D4** 5 25 S 38 58 E
Pangani →, *Tanzania* **86 D4** 5 26 S 38 58 E
Pangfou = Bengbu, *China* **57 H9** 32 58N 117 20 E
Pangil, *Dem. Rep. of the Congo* **86 C2** 3 10 S 26 35 E
Pangkah, Tanjung, *Indonesia* **63 G15** 6 51 S 112 33 E
Pangkajene, *Indonesia* **63 E5** 4 46 S 119 34 E
Pangkalanbrandan, *Indonesia* **62 D1** 4 1N 98 20 E
Pangkalanbuun, *Indonesia* **62 E4** 2 41 S 111 37 E
Pangkalpinang, *Indonesia* **62 E3** 2 0 S 106 0 E
Pangnirtung, *Canada* **101 B13** 66 8N 65 54W
Pangong Tso, *India* **68 B8** 34 40N 78 40 E
Panguitch, *U.S.A.* **115 H7** 37 50N 112 26W
Pangutaran Group, *Phil.* **61 H4** 6 18N 120 34 E
Panhandle, *U.S.A.* **113 H4** 35 21N 101 23W
Pani Mines, *India* **68 H5** 22 29N 73 50 E
Pania-Mutombo, *Dem. Rep. of the Congo* **86 D1** 5 11 S 23 51 E
Panikota I., *India* **68 J4** 20 46N 71 21 E
Panipat, *India* **68 E7** 29 25N 77 2 E
Panjal Range, *India* **68 C7** 32 30N 76 50 E
Panjang, Hon, *Vietnam* **65 H4** 9 20N 103 28 E
Panjgur, *Pakistan* **66 F4** 27 0N 64 5 E
Panjim = Panaji, *India* **66 M8** 15 25N 73 50 E
Panjin, *China* **57 D12** 41 3N 122 2 E
Panjinad Barrage, *Pakistan* **66 E7** 29 22N 71 15 E
Panjnad →, *Pakistan* **68 E4** 28 57N 70 30 E
Panjwai, *Afghan.* **68 D1** 31 26N 65 27 E
Pankshin, *Nigeria* **83 D6** 9 16N 9 25 E
Panmunjŏm, *N. Korea* **57 F14** 37 59N 126 38 E
Panna, *India* **69 G9** 24 40N 80 15 E
Panna Hills, *India* **69 G9** 24 40N 81 15 E
Pannawonica, *Australia* **92 D2** 21 39 S 116 19 E
Pano Akil, *Pakistan* **68 F3** 27 51N 69 7 E
Pano Lefkara, *Cyprus* **36 E12** 34 53N 33 20 E
Pano Panayia, *Cyprus* **36 E11** 34 55N 32 38 E
Panorama, *Brazil* **127 A5** 21 21 S 51 51W
Pánormon, *Greece* **36 D6** 35 25N 24 41 E
Pansemal, *India* **68 J6** 21 39N 74 42 E
Panshan = Panjin, *China* **57 D12** 41 3N 122 2 E
Panshi, *China* **57 C14** 42 58N 126 5 E
Pantanal, *Brazil* **124 H7** 17 30 S 57 40W
Pantar, *Indonesia* **63 F6** 8 28 S 124 10 E
Pante Macassar, *Indonesia* **63 F6** 9 30 S 123 58 E
Pantelleria, *Italy* **30 F4** 36 50N 11 57 E
Pantón, *Spain* **34 C3** 42 31N 7 37W
Pánuco, *Mexico* **119 C5** 22 0N 98 15W
Panyam, *Nigeria* **83 D6** 9 27N 9 8 E
Panyu, *China* **59 F9** 22 51N 113 20 E
Panzhihua, *China* **58 D3** 26 33N 101 44 E
Páola, *Italy* **31 C9** 39 21N 16 2 E
Paola, *Malta* **36 D2** 35 52N 14 30 E
Paola, *U.S.A.* **112 F7** 38 35N 94 53W
Paonia, *U.S.A.* **115 G10** 38 52N 107 36W
Paoting = Baoding, *China* **56 E8** 38 50N 115 28 E
Paot'ou = Baotou, *China* **56 D6** 40 32N 110 2 E
Paoua, *C.A.R.* **84 C3** 7 9N 16 20 E
Pápa, *Hungary* **42 C2** 47 22N 17 30 E
Papa Stour, *U.K.* **14 A7** 60 20N 1 42W
Papa Westray, *U.K.* **14 B6** 59 20N 2 55W
Papagayo →, *Mexico* **119 D5** 16 36N 99 43W
Papagayo, G. de, *Costa Rica* **120 D2** 10 30N 85 50W
Papakura, *N.Z.* **91 G5** 37 4 S 174 59 E
Papantla, *Mexico* **119 C5** 20 30N 97 30W
Papar, *Malaysia* **62 C5** 5 45N 116 0 E
Pápas, Ákra, *Greece* **38 C3** 38 13N 21 20 E
Papeete, *Tahiti* **97 J13** 17 32 S 149 34W
Papenburg, *Germany* **24 B3** 53 5N 7 23 E
Paphlagonia, *Turkey* **72 B5** 41 30N 33 0 E
Paphos, *Cyprus* **36 E11** 34 46N 32 25 E
Papien Chiang = Da →, *Vietnam* **58 G5** 21 15N 105 20 E
Papigochic →, *Mexico* **118 B3** 29 9N 109 40W
Paposo, *Chile* **126 B1** 25 0 S 70 30W
Papoutsa, *Cyprus* **36 E12** 34 54N 33 4 E
Papua New Guinea ■, *Oceania* **96 H6** 8 0 S 145 0 E
Papudo, *Chile* **126 C1** 32 29 S 71 27W
Papuk, *Croatia* **42 E2** 45 30N 17 30 E
Papun, *Burma* **67 K20** 18 2N 97 30 E
Papunya, *Australia* **92 D5** 23 15 S 131 54 E
Pará = Belém, *Brazil* **125 D9** 1 20 S 48 30W
Pará □, *Brazil* **125 D8** 3 20 S 52 0W
Paraburdoo, *Australia* **92 D2** 23 14 S 117 32 E
Paracale, *Phil.* **61 D5** 14 17N 122 48 E
Paracatu, *Brazil* **125 G9** 17 10 S 46 50W
Paracel Is., *S. China Sea* **62 A4** 15 50N 112 0 E
Parachilna, *Australia* **95 E2** 31 10 S 138 21 E
Parachinar, *Pakistan* **68 C4** 33 55N 70 5 E
Paraćin, *Serbia, Yug.* **40 C5** 43 54N 21 27 E
Paradas, *Spain* **35 H5** 37 18N 5 29W
Paradela, *Spain* **34 C3** 42 44N 7 37W
Paradhísi, *Greece* **36 C10** 36 18N 28 7 E
Paradip, *India* **67 J15** 20 15N 86 35 E
Paradise, *Calif., U.S.A.* **116 F5** 39 46N 121 37W
Paradise, *Nev., U.S.A.* **117 J11** 36 9N 115 10W
Paradise →, *Canada* **103 B8** 53 27N 57 19W
Paradise Hill, *Canada* **105 C7** 53 32N 109 28W
Paradise River, *Canada* **103 B8** 53 27N 57 17W
Paradise Valley, *U.S.A.* **114 F5** 41 30N 117 32W
Parado, *Indonesia* **63 F5** 8 42 S 118 30 E
Paragould, *U.S.A.* **113 G9** 36 3N 90 29W
Paragua →, *Venezuela* **124 B6** 6 55N 62 55W
Paraguaçu →, *Brazil* **125 F11** 12 45 S 38 54W
Paraguaçu Paulista, *Brazil* **127 A5** 22 22 S 50 35W
Paraguaná, Pen. de, *Venezuela* **124 A5** 12 0N 70 0W
Paraguarí, *Paraguay* **126 B4** 25 36 S 57 0W
Paraguarí □, *Paraguay* **126 B4** 26 0 S 57 10W
Paraguay ■, *S. Amer.* **126 A4** 23 0 S 57 0W
Paraguay →, *Paraguay* **126 B4** 27 18 S 58 38W
Paraíba = João Pessoa, *Brazil* **125 E12** 7 10 S 34 52W
Paraíba □, *Brazil* **125 E11** 7 0 S 36 0W
Paraíba do Sul →, *Brazil* **127 A7** 21 37 S 41 3W
Parainen, *Finland* **9 F20** 60 18N 22 18 E
Paraiso, *Mexico* **119 D6** 18 24N 93 14W
Parak, *Iran* **71 E7** 27 38N 52 25 E
Parakhino Paddubye, *Russia* **46 C7** 58 26N 33 10 E
Parakou, *Benin* **83 D5** 9 25N 2 40 E
Paralimni, *Cyprus* **36 D12** 35 2N 33 58 E
Parálion-Astrous, *Greece* **38 D4** 37 25N 22 45 E
Paramaribo, *Surinam* **125 B7** 5 50N 55 10W
Paramithiá, *Greece* **38 B2** 39 30N 20 35 E
Paramushir, Ostrov, *Russia* **51 D16** 50 24N 156 0 E
Paran →, *Israel* **75 E4** 30 20N 35 10 E
Paraná, *Argentina* **126 C3** 31 45 S 60 30W
Paranã, *Brazil* **125 F9** 12 30 S 47 48W
Paraná □, *Brazil* **127 A5** 24 30 S 51 0W
Paraná →, *Argentina* **126 C4** 33 43 S 59 15W
Paranaguá, *Brazil* **127 B6** 25 30 S 48 30W
Paranaíba, *Brazil* **125 G8** 19 40 S 51 11W
Paranaíba →, *Brazil* **125 H8** 20 6 S 51 4W
Paranapanema →, *Brazil* **127 A5** 22 40 S 53 9W
Paranapiacaba, Serra do, *Brazil* **127 A6** 24 31 S 48 35W
Paranas, *Phil.* **61 F6** 11 42N 125 2 E
Paranavaí, *Brazil* **127 A5** 23 4 S 52 56W
Parang, *Maguindanao, Phil.* **63 C6** 7 23N 124 16 E
Parang, *Sulu, Phil.* **61 J4** 5 55N 120 54 E
Parângul Mare, Vf., *Romania* **43 E8** 45 20N 23 37 E
Paraparaumu, *N.Z.* **91 J5** 40 57 S 175 3 E
Parapóla, *Greece* **38 E5** 36 55N 23 27 E
Paraspóri, Ákra, *Greece* **39 F9** 35 55N 27 15 E
Paray-le-Monial, *France* **19 F11** 46 27N 4 7 E
Parbati →, *Mad. P., India* **68 G7** 25 50N 76 30 E
Parbati →, *Raj., India* **68 F7** 26 54N 77 53 E
Parbhani, *India* **66 K10** 19 8N 76 52 E
Parchim, *Germany* **24 B7** 53 26N 11 52 E
Parczew, *Poland* **45 G9** 51 40N 22 52 E
Pardes Hanna-Karkur, *Israel* **75 C3** 32 28N 34 57 E
Pardilla, *Spain* **34 D7** 41 33N 3 43W
Pardo →, *Bahia, Brazil* **125 G11** 15 40 S 39 0W
Pardo →, *Mato Grosso, Brazil* **127 A5** 21 46 S 52 9W
Pardubice, *Czech Rep.* **26 A8** 50 3N 15 45 E
Pare, *Indonesia* **63 G15** 7 43 S 112 12 E
Pare Mts., *Tanzania* **86 C4** 4 0 S 37 45 E
Parecis, Serra dos, *Brazil* **124 F7** 13 0 S 60 0W
Paredes de Nava, *Spain* **34 C6** 42 9N 4 42W
Paren, *Russia* **51 C17** 62 30N 163 15 E
Parent, *Canada* **102 C5** 47 55N 74 35W
Parent, L., *Canada* **102 C4** 48 31N 77 1W
Parentis-en-Born, *France* **20 D2** 44 21N 1 4W
Parepare, *Indonesia* **63 E5** 4 0 S 119 40 E
Parfino, *Russia* **46 D6** 57 59N 31 34 E
Párga, *Greece* **38 B2** 39 15N 20 29 E
Pargo, Pta. do, *Madeira* **37 D2** 32 49N 17 17W
Pariaguán, *Venezuela* **124 B6** 8 51N 64 34W
Paricutín, Cerro, *Mexico* **118 D4** 19 28N 102 15W
Parigi, *Indonesia* **63 E6** 0 50 S 120 5 E
Parika, *Guyana* **124 B7** 6 50N 58 20W
Parikkala, *Finland* **46 B5** 61 33N 29 31 E
Parima, Serra, *Brazil* **124 C6** 2 30N 64 0W
Parinari, *Peru* **124 D4** 4 35 S 74 25W
Pariñas, Pta., *S. Amer.* **122 D2** 4 30 S 82 0W
Parincea, *Romania* **43 D12** 46 27N 27 9 E
Parintins, *Brazil* **125 D7** 2 40 S 56 50W
Pariparit Kyun, *Burma* **67 M18** 14 55N 93 45 E
Paris, *Canada* **110 C4** 43 12N 80 25W
Paris, *France* **19 D9** 48 50N 2 20 E
Paris, *Idaho, U.S.A.* **114 E8** 42 14N 111 24W
Paris, *Ky., U.S.A.* **108 F3** 38 13N 84 15W
Paris, *Tenn., U.S.A.* **109 G1** 36 18N 88 19W
Paris, *Tex., U.S.A.* **113 J7** 33 40N 95 33W
Paris, Ville de □, *France* **19 D9** 48 50N 2 20 E
Parish, *U.S.A.* **111 C8** 43 25N 76 8W
Parishville, *U.S.A.* **111 B10** 44 38N 74 49W
Park, *U.S.A.* **116 B4** 48 45N 122 18W
Park City, *U.S.A.* **114 F8** 40 39N 111 30W
Park Falls, *U.S.A.* **112 C9** 45 56N 90 27W
Park Head, *Canada* **110 B3** 44 36N 81 9W
Park Hills, *U.S.A.* **113 G9** 37 53N 90 28W
Park Range, *U.S.A.* **114 G10** 40 0N 106 30W
Park Rapids, *U.S.A.* **112 B7** 46 55N 95 4W
Park River, *U.S.A.* **112 A6** 48 24N 97 45W
Park Rynie, *S. Africa* **89 E5** 30 25 S 30 45 E
Parkā Bandar, *Iran* **71 E8** 25 55N 59 35 E
Parkano, *Finland* **9 E20** 62 1N 23 0 E
Parker, *Ariz., U.S.A.* **117 L12** 34 9N 114 17W
Parker, *Pa., U.S.A.* **110 E5** 41 5N 79 41W
Parker Dam, *U.S.A.* **117 L12** 34 18N 114 8W
Parkersburg, *U.S.A.* **108 F5** 39 16N 81 34W
Parkes, *Australia* **95 E4** 33 9 S 148 11 E
Parkfield, *U.S.A.* **116 K6** 35 54N 120 26W
Parkhill, *Canada* **110 C3** 43 15N 81 38W
Parkland, *U.S.A.* **116 C4** 47 9N 122 26W
Parkston, *U.S.A.* **112 D6** 43 24N 97 59W
Parksville, *Canada* **104 D4** 49 20N 124 21W
Parla, *Spain* **34 E7** 40 14N 3 46W
Pârliţa, *Moldova* **43 C12** 47 19N 27 52 E
Parma, *Italy* **28 D7** 44 48N 10 20 E
Parma, *Idaho, U.S.A.* **114 E5** 43 47N 116 57W
Parma, *Ohio, U.S.A.* **110 E3** 41 23N 81 43W
Parma →, *Italy* **28 D7** 44 56N 10 26 E
Parnaguá, *Brazil* **125 F10** 10 10 S 44 38W
Parnaíba, *Brazil* **125 D10** 2 54 S 41 47W
Parnaíba →, *Brazil* **122 D6** 3 0 S 41 50W
Parnassós, *Greece* **38 C4** 38 35N 22 30 E
Párnis, *Greece* **38 C5** 38 14N 23 45 E
Párnon Óros, *Greece* **38 D4** 37 15N 22 45 E
Pärnu, *Estonia* **9 G21** 58 28N 24 33 E
Paroo →, *Australia* **95 E3** 31 28 S 143 32 E
Páros, *Greece* **39 D7** 37 5N 25 12 E
Parowan, *U.S.A.* **115 H7** 37 51N 112 50W
Parpaillon, *France* **21 D10** 44 30N 6 40 E
Parral, *Chile* **126 D1** 36 10 S 71 52W
Parras, *Mexico* **118 B4** 25 30N 102 20W
Parrett →, *U.K.* **13 F4** 51 12N 3 1W
Parris I., *U.S.A.* **109 J5** 32 20N 80 41W
Parrsboro, *Canada* **103 C7** 45 30N 64 25W
Parry I., *Canada* **110 A4** 45 18N 80 10W
Parry Is., *Canada* **4 B2** 77 0N 110 0W
Parry Sound, *Canada* **102 C4** 45 20N 80 0W
Parsberg, *Germany* **25 F7** 49 10N 11 43 E
Parsęta →, *Poland* **44 D2** 54 11N 15 34 E
Parsnip →, *Canada* **104 B4** 55 10N 123 2W
Parsons, *U.S.A.* **113 G7** 37 20N 95 16W
Parsons Ra., *Australia* **94 A2** 13 30 S 135 15 E
Partanna, *Italy* **30 E5** 37 43N 12 53 E
Parthenay, *France* **18 F6** 46 38N 0 16W
Partinico, *Italy* **30 D6** 38 3N 13 7 E
Partizánske, *Slovak Rep.* **27 C11** 48 38N 18 23 E
Partridge I., *Canada* **102 A2** 55 59N 87 37W
Paru →, *Brazil* **125 D8** 1 33 S 52 38W
Parvān □, *Afghan.* **66 B6** 35 0N 69 0 E
Parvatipuram, *India* **67 K13** 18 50N 83 25 E
Parvatsar, *India* **68 F6** 26 52N 74 49 E
Påryd, *Sweden* **11 H9** 56 34N 15 55 E
Parys, *S. Africa* **88 D4** 26 52 S 27 29 E
Pas, Pta. des, *Spain* **37 C7** 38 46N 1 26 E
Pas-de-Calais □, *France* **19 B9** 50 30N 2 10 E
Pasada, *Spain* **34 B5** 43 23N 5 46W
Pasadena, *Canada* **103 C8** 49 1N 57 36W
Pasadena, *Calif., U.S.A.* **117 L8** 34 9N 118 9W
Pasadena, *Tex., U.S.A.* **113 L7** 29 43N 95 13W
Pasaje →, *Argentina* **126 B3** 25 39 S 63 56W
Paşalimanı, *Turkey* **41 F11** 40 29N 27 36 E
Pasay, *Phil.* **61 D4** 14 33N 121 0 E
Pascagoula, *U.S.A.* **113 K10** 30 21N 88 33W
Pascagoula →, *U.S.A.* **113 K10** 30 23N 88 37W
Paşcani, *Romania* **43 C11** 47 14N 26 45 E
Pasco, *U.S.A.* **114 C4** 46 14N 119 6W
Pasco, Cerro de, *Peru* **124 F3** 10 45 S 76 10W
Pasco I., *Australia* **92 D2** 20 57 S 115 20 E
Pascoag, *U.S.A.* **111 E13** 41 57N 71 42W
Pascua, I. de, *Pac. Oc.* **97 K17** 27 0 S 109 0W
Pasewalk, *Germany* **24 B9** 53 30N 13 58 E
Pasfield L., *Canada* **105 B7** 58 24N 105 20W
Pasha →, *Russia* **46 B7** 60 29N 32 55 E
Pashiwari, *Pakistan* **69 B6** 34 40N 75 10 E
Pashmakli = Smolyan, *Bulgaria* **41 E8** 41 36N 24 38 E
Pasinler, *Turkey* **73 C9** 39 59N 41 41 E
Pasir Mas, *Malaysia* **65 J4** 6 2N 102 8 E
Pasir Putih, *Malaysia* **65 K4** 5 50N 102 24 E
Pasirian, *Indonesia* **63 H15** 8 13 S 113 8 E
Pasirkuning, *Indonesia* **62 E2** 0 30 S 104 33 E
Påskallavik, *Sweden* **11 G10** 57 10N 16 26 E
Paskūh, *Iran* **71 E9** 27 34N 61 39 E
Pasłęk, *Poland* **44 D6** 54 3N 19 41 E
Pasłęka →, *Poland* **44 D6** 54 26N 19 46 E
Pasley, C., *Australia* **93 F3** 33 52 S 123 35 E
Pašman, *Croatia* **29 E12** 43 58N 15 20 E
Pasni, *Pakistan* **66 G3** 25 15N 63 27 E
Paso Cantinela, *Mexico* **117 N11** 32 33N 115 47W
Paso de Indios, *Argentina* **128 E3** 43 55 S 69 0W
Paso de los Libres, *Argentina* **126 B4** 29 44 S 57 10W
Paso de los Toros, *Uruguay* **126 C4** 32 45 S 56 30W
Paso Robles, *U.S.A.* **115 J3** 35 38N 120 41W
Paspébiac, *Canada* **103 C6** 48 3N 65 17W
Pasrur, *Pakistan* **68 C6** 32 16N 74 43 E
Passage West, *Ireland* **15 E3** 51 52N 8 21W
Passaic, *U.S.A.* **111 F10** 40 51N 74 7W
Passau, *Germany* **25 G9** 48 34N 13 28 E
Passero, C., *Italy* **31 F8** 36 41N 15 10 E
Passo Fundo, *Brazil* **127 B5** 28 10 S 52 20W
Passos, *Brazil* **125 H9** 20 45 S 46 37W
Passow, *Germany* **24 B10** 53 8N 14 6 E
Passy, *France* **21 C10** 45 55N 6 41 E
Pastavy, *Belarus* **9 J22** 55 4N 26 50 E
Pastaza →, *Peru* **124 D3** 4 50 S 76 52W
Pasto, *Colombia* **124 C3** 1 13N 77 17W
Pastrana, *Spain* **32 E2** 40 27N 2 53W
Pasuruan, *Indonesia* **63 G15** 7 40 S 112 44 E
Pasym, *Poland* **44 E7** 53 48N 20 49 E
Pásztó, *Hungary* **42 C4** 47 52N 19 43 E
Patagonia, *Argentina* **122 H4** 45 0 S 69 0W
Patagonia, *U.S.A.* **115 L8** 31 33N 110 45W
Patambar, *Iran* **71 D9** 29 45N 60 17 E
Patan, *Gujarat, India* **66 H8** 23 54N 72 14 E
Patan, *Maharashtra, India* **68 H5** 23 54N 72 14 E
Patan, *Nepal* **67 F14** 27 40N 85 20 E
Patani, *Indonesia* **63 D7** 0 20N 128 50 E
Pătârlagele, *Romania* **43 E11** 45 19N 26 21 E
Pataudi, *India* **68 E7** 28 18N 76 48 E
Patchewollock, *Australia* **95 F3** 35 22 S 142 12 E
Patchogue, *U.S.A.* **111 F11** 40 46N 73 1W
Patea, *N.Z.* **91 H5** 39 45 S 174 30 E
Pategi, *Nigeria* **83 D6** 8 50N 5 45 E
Patensie, *S. Africa* **88 E3** 33 46 S 24 49 E
Paterna, *Spain* **33 F4** 39 30N 0 26W
Paternion, *Austria* **26 E6** 46 43N 13 38 E

Paternò, Italy 31 E7 37 34N 14 54 E
Pateros, U.S.A. 114 B4 48 3N 119 54W
Paterson, U.S.A. 111 F10 40 55N 74 11W
Paterson Ra., Australia 92 D3 21 45 S 122 10 E
Pathankot, India 68 C6 32 18N 75 45 E
Pathfinder Reservoir, U.S.A. 114 E10 42 28N 106 51W
Pathiu, Thailand 65 G2 10 42N 99 19 E
Pathum Thani, Thailand 64 E3 14 1N 100 32 E
Pati, Indonesia 63 G14 6 45 S 111 1 E
Patía →, Colombia 124 C3 2 13N 78 40W
Patiala, Punjab, India 68 D7 30 23N 76 26 E
Patiala, Ut. P., India 69 F8 27 43N 79 1 E
Patine Kouka, Senegal 82 C2 12 45N 13 45W
Patitírion, Greece 38 B5 39 8N 23 50 E
Patkai Bum, India 67 F19 27 0N 95 30 E
Pátmos, Greece 39 D8 37 21N 26 36 E
Patna, India 69 G11 25 35N 85 12 E
Patnos, Turkey 73 C10 39 13N 42 51 E
Pato Branco, Brazil 127 B5 26 13 S 52 40W
Patonga, Uganda 86 B3 2 45N 33 15 E
Patos, Albania 40 F3 40 42N 19 38 E
Patos, Brazil 125 E11 6 55 S 37 16W
Patos, L. dos, Brazil 127 C5 31 20 S 51 0W
Patos, Río de los →, Argentina 126 C2 31 18 S 69 25W
Patos de Minas, Brazil 125 G9 18 35 S 46 32W
Patosi = Patos, Albania 40 F3 40 42N 19 38 E
Patquía, Argentina 126 C2 30 2 S 66 55W
Pátrai, Greece 38 C3 38 14N 21 47 E
Pátraikós Kólpos, Greece 38 C3 38 17N 21 30 E
Patras = Pátrai, Greece 38 C3 38 14N 21 47 E
Patrocínio, Brazil 125 G9 18 57 S 47 0W
Patta, Kenya 86 C5 2 10 S 41 0 E
Pattada, Italy 30 B2 40 35N 9 6 E
Pattani, Thailand 65 J3 6 48N 101 15 E
Pattaya, Thailand 62 B2 12 52N 100 55 E
Patten, U.S.A. 109 C11 46 0N 68 38W
Patterson, Calif., U.S.A. 116 H5 37 28N 121 8W
Patterson, La., U.S.A. 113 L9 29 42N 91 18W
Patterson, Mt., U.S.A. 116 G7 38 29N 119 20W
Patti, Punjab, India 68 D6 31 17N 74 54 E
Patti, Ut. P., India 69 G10 25 55N 82 12 E
Patti, Italy 31 D7 38 8N 14 58 E
Pattoki, Pakistan 68 D5 31 5N 73 52 E
Patton, U.S.A. 110 F6 40 38N 78 39W
Patuakhali, Bangla. 67 H17 22 20N 90 25 E
Patuanak, Canada 105 B7 55 55N 107 43W
Patuca →, Honduras 120 C3 15 50N 84 18W
Patuca, Punta, Honduras 120 C3 15 49N 84 14W
Pătulele, Romania 42 F7 44 21N 22 47 E
Pátzcuaro, Mexico 118 D4 19 30N 101 40W
Pau, France 20 E3 43 19N 0 25W
Pau, Gave de →, France 20 E2 43 33N 1 12W
Pauillac, France 20 C3 45 11N 0 46W
Pauk, Burma 67 J19 21 27N 94 30 E
Paul I., Canada 103 A7 56 30N 61 20W
Paul Smiths, U.S.A. 111 B10 44 26N 74 15W
Paulatuk, Canada 100 B7 69 25N 124 0W
Paulhan, France 20 E7 43 33N 3 28 E
Paulis = Isiro, Dem. Rep. of the Congo 86 B2 2 53N 27 40 E
Paulistana, Brazil 125 E10 8 9 S 41 9W
Paulo Afonso, Brazil 125 E11 9 21 S 38 15W
Paulpietersburg, S. Africa 89 D5 27 23 S 30 50 E
Pauls Valley, U.S.A. 113 H6 34 44N 97 13W
Pauma Valley, U.S.A. 117 M10 33 16N 116 58W
Pauri, India 69 D8 30 9N 78 47 E
Pāveh, Iran 70 C5 35 3N 46 22 E
Pavelets, Russia 46 F10 53 49N 39 14 E
Pavia, Italy 28 C6 45 7N 9 8 E
Pavilion, U.S.A. 110 D6 42 52N 78 1W
Pavilly, France 18 C7 49 34N 0 57 E
Pāvilosta, Latvia 9 H19 56 53N 21 14 E
Pavlikeni, Bulgaria 41 C9 43 14N 25 20 E
Pavlodar, Kazakstan 50 D8 52 33N 77 0 E
Pavlograd = Pavlohrad, Ukraine 47 H8 48 30N 35 52 E
Pavlohrad, Ukraine 47 H8 48 30N 35 52 E
Pavlovo, Russia 48 C6 55 58N 43 5 E
Pavlovsk, Russia 48 E5 50 26N 40 5 E
Pavlovskaya, Russia 49 G4 46 17N 39 47 E
Pavlovskiy-Posad, Russia 46 E10 55 47N 38 42 E
Pavullo nel Frignano, Italy 28 D7 44 20N 10 50 E
Pawayan, India 69 E9 28 4N 80 6 E
Pawhuska, U.S.A. 113 G6 36 40N 96 20W
Pawling, U.S.A. 111 E11 41 34N 73 36W
Pawnee, U.S.A. 113 G6 36 20N 96 48W
Pawnee City, U.S.A. 112 E6 40 7N 96 9W
Pawtucket, U.S.A. 111 E13 41 53N 71 23W
Paximádhia, Greece 36 E6 35 0N 24 35 E
Paxoí, Greece 38 B2 39 14N 20 12 E
Paxton, Ill., U.S.A. 108 E1 40 27N 88 6W
Paxton, Nebr., U.S.A. 112 E4 41 7N 101 21W
Payakumbuh, Indonesia 62 E2 0 20 S 100 35 E
Payerne, Switz. 25 J2 46 49N 6 56 E
Payette, U.S.A. 114 D5 44 5N 116 56W
Paymogo, Spain 35 H3 37 44N 7 21W
Payne Bay = Kangirsuk, Canada 101 B13 60 0N 70 0W
Payne L., Canada 101 C12 59 30N 74 30W
Paynes Find, Australia 93 E2 29 15 S 117 42 E
Paynesville, Liberia 82 D2 6 20N 10 45W
Paynesville, U.S.A. 112 C7 45 23N 94 43W
Pays de la Loire □, France 18 E6 47 45N 0 25W
Paysandú, Uruguay 126 C4 32 19 S 58 8W
Payson, U.S.A. 115 J8 34 14N 111 20W
Paz →, Guatemala 120 D1 13 44N 90 10W
Paz, B. la, Mexico 118 C2 24 15N 110 25W
Pāzanān, Iran 71 D6 30 35N 49 59 E
Pazar, Turkey 73 B9 41 10N 40 50 E
Pazarcık, Turkey 72 D7 37 30N 37 17 E
Pazardzhik, Bulgaria 41 D8 42 12N 24 20 E
Pazarköy, Turkey 39 B9 39 51N 27 24 E
Pazarlar, Turkey 39 C11 39 0N 29 7 E
Pazaryeri, Turkey 39 B11 40 0N 29 56 E
Pazaryolu, Turkey 73 B9 40 21N 40 47 E
Pazin, Croatia 29 C10 45 14N 13 56 E
Pčinja →, Macedonia 40 E5 41 50N 21 45 E
Pe Ell, U.S.A. 116 D3 46 34N 123 18W
Peabody, U.S.A. 111 D14 42 31N 70 56W
Peace →, Canada 104 B6 59 0N 111 25W
Peace Point, Canada 104 B6 59 7N 112 27W
Peace River, Canada 104 B5 56 15N 117 18W
Peach Springs, U.S.A. 115 J7 35 32N 113 25W
Peachland, Canada 104 D5 49 47N 119 45W
Peachtree City, U.S.A. 109 J3 33 25N 84 35W
Peak, The = Kinder Scout, U.K. 12 D6 53 24N 1 52W
Peak District, U.K. 12 D6 53 10N 1 50W
Peak Hill, N.S.W., Australia 95 E4 32 47 S 148 11 E
Peak Hill, W. Austral., Australia 93 E2 25 35 S 118 43 E
Peak Ra., Australia 94 C4 22 50 S 148 20 E
Peake Cr. →, Australia 95 D2 28 2 S 136 7 E
Peal de Becerro, Spain 35 H7 37 55N 3 7W
Peale, Mt., U.S.A. 115 G9 38 26N 109 14W
Pearblossom, U.S.A. 117 L9 34 30N 117 55W
Pearl →, U.S.A. 113 K10 30 11N 89 32W
Pearl City, U.S.A. 106 H16 21 24N 157 59W
Pearl Harbor, U.S.A. 106 H16 21 21N 157 57W
Pearl River, U.S.A. 111 E10 41 4N 74 2W
Pearsall, U.S.A. 113 L5 28 54N 99 6W
Peary Land, Greenland 4 A6 82 40N 33 0W
Pease →, U.S.A. 113 H5 34 12N 99 2W
Peawanuck, Canada 101 C11 55 15N 85 12W
Pebane, Mozam. 87 F4 17 10 S 38 8 E
Pebas, Peru 124 D4 3 10 S 71 46W
Pebble Beach, U.S.A. 116 J5 36 34N 121 57W
Peć, Kosovo, Yug. 40 D4 42 40N 20 17 E
Péccioli, Italy 28 E7 43 33N 10 43 E
Pechea, Romania 43 E12 45 36N 27 49 E
Pechenga, Russia 50 C4 69 29N 31 4 E
Pechenizhyn, Ukraine 47 H3 48 30N 24 48 E
Pechiguera, Pta., Canary Is. 37 F6 28 51N 13 53W
Pechnezhskoye Vdkhr., Ukraine 47 G9 50 5N 36 54 E
Pechora, Russia 50 C6 65 10N 57 11 E
Pechora →, Russia 50 C6 68 13N 54 15 E
Pechorskaya Guba, Russia 50 C6 68 40N 54 0 E
Pecica, Romania 42 D6 46 10N 21 3 E
Pecka, Serbia, Yug. 40 B3 44 18N 19 33 E
Pécora, C., Italy 30 C1 39 27N 8 23 E
Pečory, Russia 9 H22 57 48N 27 40 E
Pecos, U.S.A. 113 K3 31 26N 103 30W
Pecos →, U.S.A. 113 L3 29 42N 101 22W
Pécs, Hungary 42 D3 46 5N 18 15 E
Pedder, L., Australia 94 G4 42 55 S 146 10 E
Peddie, S. Africa 89 E4 33 14 S 27 7 E
Pédernales, Dom. Rep. 121 C5 18 2N 71 44W
Pedieos →, Cyprus 36 D12 35 10N 33 54 E
Pedirka, Australia 95 D2 26 40 S 135 14 E
Pedra Azul, Brazil 125 G10 16 2 S 41 17W
Pedreguer, Spain 33 G5 38 48N 0 3 E
Pedreiras, Brazil 125 D10 4 32 S 44 40W
Pedro Afonso, Brazil 125 E9 9 0 S 48 10W
Pedro Cays, Jamaica 120 C4 17 5N 77 48W
Pedro de Valdivia, Chile 126 A2 22 55 S 69 38W
Pedro Juan Caballero, Paraguay 127 A4 22 30 S 55 40W
Pedro Muñoz, Spain 35 F8 39 25N 2 56W
Pedrógão Grande, Portugal 34 F2 39 55N 8 9W
Pee Dee →, U.S.A. 109 J6 33 22N 79 16W
Peebinga, Australia 95 E3 34 52 S 140 57 E
Peebles, U.K. 14 F5 55 40N 3 11W
Peekskill, U.S.A. 111 E11 41 17N 73 55W
Peel, U.K. 12 C3 54 13N 4 40W
Peel →, Australia 95 E5 30 50 S 150 29 E
Peel →, Canada 100 B6 67 0N 135 0W
Peel Sound, Canada 100 A10 73 0N 96 0W
Peene →, Germany 24 A9 54 9N 13 46 E
Peera Peera Poolanna L., Australia 95 D2 26 30 S 138 0 E
Peerless Lake, Canada 104 B6 56 37N 114 40W
Peers, Canada 104 C5 53 40N 116 0W
Pegasus Bay, N.Z. 91 K4 43 20 S 173 10 E
Peggau, Austria 26 D8 47 12N 15 21 E
Pegnitz, Germany 25 F7 49 44N 11 31 E
Pegnitz →, Germany 25 F6 49 30N 10 59 E
Pego, Spain 33 G4 38 51N 0 8W
Pegu, Burma 67 L20 17 20N 96 29 E
Pegu Yoma, Burma 67 K20 19 0N 96 0 E
Pehčevo, Macedonia 40 E6 41 41N 22 55 E
Pehlıvanköy, Turkey 41 E10 41 20N 26 55 E
Pehuajó, Argentina 126 D3 35 45 S 62 0W
Pei Xian = Pizhou, China 56 G9 34 44N 116 55 E
Peine, Chile 126 A2 23 45 S 68 8W
Peine, Germany 24 C6 52 19N 10 14 E
Peip'ing = Beijing, China 56 E9 39 55N 116 20 E
Peipus, L. = Chudskoye, Ozero, Russia 9 G22 58 13N 27 30 E
Peissenberg, Germany 25 H7 47 48N 11 4 E
Peitz, Germany 24 D10 51 51N 14 24 E
Peixe, Brazil 125 F9 12 0 S 48 40W
Peixe →, Brazil 125 H8 21 31 S 51 58W
Pek →, Serbia, Yug. 40 B5 44 45N 21 29 E
Pekalongan, Indonesia 63 G13 6 53 S 109 40 E
Pekan, Malaysia 65 L4 3 30N 103 25 E
Pekanbaru, Indonesia 62 D2 0 30N 101 15 E
Pekang, Taiwan 59 F13 23 34N 120 18 E
Pekin, U.S.A. 112 E10 40 35N 89 40W
Peking = Beijing, China 56 E9 39 55N 116 20 E
Péla, Guinea 82 D3 7 37N 9 7W
Pelabuhan Kelang, Malaysia 65 L3 3 0N 101 23 E
Pelabuhan Ratu, Teluk, Indonesia 63 G12 7 5 S 106 30 E
Pelabuhanratu, Indonesia 63 G12 7 0 S 106 32 E
Pélagos, Greece 38 B6 39 17N 24 4 E
Pelaihari, Indonesia 62 E4 3 55 S 114 45 E
Pelat, Mt., France 21 D10 44 16N 6 42 E
Pełczyce, Poland 45 E2 53 3N 15 16 E
Peleaga, Vf., Romania 42 E7 45 22N 22 55 E
Pelée, Mt., Martinique 121 D7 14 48N 61 10W
Pelee, Pt., Canada 102 D3 41 54N 82 31W
Pelee I., Canada 102 D3 41 47N 82 40W
Pelekech, Kenya 86 B4 3 52N 35 8 E
Peleng, Indonesia 63 E6 1 20 S 123 30 E
Pélézi, Ivory C. 82 D3 7 17N 6 54W
Pelhřimov, Czech Rep. 26 B8 49 24N 15 12 E
Pelican, U.S.A. 104 B1 57 58N 136 14W
Pelican L., Canada 105 C8 52 28N 100 20W
Pelican Narrows, Canada 105 B8 55 10N 102 56W
Pelješac, Croatia 29 F14 42 55N 17 25 E
Pelkosenniemi, Finland 8 C22 67 6N 27 28 E
Pella, Greece 40 F6 40 46N 22 23 E
Pella, S. Africa 88 D2 29 1 S 19 6 E
Pella, U.S.A. 112 E8 41 25N 92 55W
Pélla □, Greece 40 F6 40 52N 22 0 E
Pello, Finland 8 C21 66 47N 23 59 E
Pellworm, Germany 24 A4 54 31N 8 39 E
Pelly →, Canada 100 B6 62 47N 137 19W
Pelly Bay, Canada 101 B11 68 38N 89 50W
Peloponnese = Pelopónnisos □, Greece 38 D4 37 10N 22 0 E
Pelopónnisos □, Greece 38 D4 37 10N 22 0 E
Peloritani, Monti, Italy 31 D8 38 3N 15 20 E
Pelorus Sd., N.Z. 91 J4 40 59 S 173 59 E
Pelotas, Brazil 127 C5 31 42 S 52 23W
Pelotas →, Brazil 127 B5 27 28 S 51 55W
Pelovo, Bulgaria 41 C8 43 26N 24 17 E
Pelplin, Poland 44 E5 53 55N 18 42 E
Pelvoux, Massif du, France 21 D10 44 52N 6 20 E
Pemalang, Indonesia 63 G13 6 53 S 109 23 E
Pemanggil, Pulau, Malaysia 65 L5 2 37N 104 21 E
Pematangsiantar, Indonesia 62 D1 2 57N 99 5 E
Pemba, Mozam. 87 E5 12 58 S 40 30 E
Pemba, Zambia 87 F2 16 30 S 27 28 E
Pemba Channel, Tanzania 86 D4 5 0 S 39 37 E
Pemba I., Tanzania 86 D4 5 0 S 39 45 E
Pemberton, Australia 93 F2 34 30 S 116 0 E
Pemberton, Canada 104 C4 50 25N 122 50W
Pembina, U.S.A. 112 A6 48 58N 97 15W
Pembroke, Canada 102 C4 45 50N 77 7W
Pembroke, U.K. 13 F3 51 41N 4 55W
Pembrokeshire □, U.K. 13 F3 51 52N 4 56W
Pen-y-Ghent, U.K. 12 C5 54 10N 2 14W
Peña, Sierra de la, Spain 32 C4 42 32N 0 45W
Peña de Francia, Sierra de la, Spain 34 E4 40 32N 6 10W
Penafiel, Portugal 34 D2 41 12N 8 17W
Peñafiel, Spain 34 D6 41 35N 4 7W
Peñaflor, Spain 35 H5 37 43N 5 21W
Peñalara, Spain 34 E7 40 51N 3 57W
Penamacôr, Portugal 34 E3 40 10N 7 10W
Penang = Pinang, Malaysia 65 K3 5 25N 100 15 E
Penápolis, Brazil 127 A6 21 30 S 50 0W
Peñaranda de Bracamonte, Spain 34 E5 40 53N 5 13W
Peñarroya, Spain 32 E4 40 25N 0 40W
Peñarroya-Pueblonuevo, Spain 35 G5 38 19N 5 16W
Penarth, U.K. 13 F4 51 26N 3 11W
Peñas, C. de, Spain 34 B5 43 42N 5 52W
Penas, G. de, Chile 122 H3 47 0 S 75 0W
Peñas de San Pedro, Spain 33 G3 38 44N 2 0W
Peñas del Chache, Canary Is. 37 E6 29 6N 13 33W
Peñausende, Spain 34 D5 41 17N 5 52W
Pench'i = Benxi, China 57 D12 41 20N 123 48 E
Pend Oreille →, U.S.A. 114 B5 49 4N 117 37W
Pend Oreille, L., U.S.A. 114 C5 48 10N 116 21W
Pendálofon, Greece 40 F5 40 14N 21 12 E
Pendembu, Eastern, S. Leone 82 D2 8 10N 10 42W
Pendembu, Northern, S. Leone 82 D2 9 7N 11 14W
Pender B., Australia 92 C3 16 45 S 122 42 E
Pendik, Turkey 41 F13 40 53N 29 13 E
Pendjari →, Benin 83 C5 10 55N 0 50 E
Pendleton, U.S.A. 114 D4 45 40N 118 47W
Pendra, India 69 H9 22 46N 81 57 E
Penedo, Brazil 125 F11 10 15 S 36 36W
Penetanguishene, Canada 102 D4 44 50N 79 55W
Penfield, U.S.A. 110 E6 41 13N 78 35W
Pengalengan, Indonesia 63 G12 7 9 S 107 30 E
Penge, Kasai-Or., Dem. Rep. of the Congo 86 D1 5 30 S 24 33 E
Penge, Sud-Kivu, Dem. Rep. of the Congo 86 C2 4 27 S 28 25 E
Penghu, Taiwan 59 F12 23 34N 119 30 E
Penglai, China 57 F11 37 48N 120 42 E
Pengshan, China 58 B4 30 14N 103 58 E
Pengshui, China 58 C7 29 17N 108 12 E
Penguin, Australia 94 G4 41 8 S 146 6 E
Pengxi, China 58 B5 30 44N 105 45 E
Pengze, China 59 C11 29 52N 116 32 E
Penhalonga, Zimbabwe 87 F3 18 52 S 32 40 E
Peniche, Portugal 35 F1 39 19N 9 22W
Penicuik, U.K. 14 F5 55 50N 3 13W
Penida, Indonesia 62 F5 8 45 S 115 30 E
Peninnes, Alpes = Pennine, Alpi, Alps 25 J3 46 4N 7 30 E
Peninsular Malaysia □, Malaysia 65 L4 4 0N 102 0 E
Peñíscola, Spain 32 E5 40 22N 0 24 E
Penitente, Serra do, Brazil 125 E9 8 45 S 46 20W
Penkridge, U.K. 12 E5 52 44N 2 6W
Penmarch, France 18 E2 47 49N 4 21W
Penmarch, Pte. de, France 18 E2 47 48N 4 22W
Penn Hills, U.S.A. 110 F5 40 28N 79 52W
Penn Yan, U.S.A. 110 D7 42 40N 77 3W
Penna, Punta della, Italy 29 F11 42 10N 14 43 E
Pennant, Canada 105 C7 50 32N 108 14W
Penne, Italy 29 F10 42 27N 13 55 E
Penner →, India 66 M12 14 35N 80 10 E
Pennine, Alpi, Alps 25 J3 46 4N 7 30 E
Pennines, U.K. 12 C5 54 45N 2 27W
Pennington, U.S.A. 116 F5 39 15N 121 47W
Pennington →, Nigeria 83 E6 4 45N 5 35 E
Pennino, Mte., Italy 29 E9 43 6N 12 53 E
Pennsburg, U.S.A. 111 F9 40 23N 75 29W
Pennsylvania □, U.S.A. 108 E7 40 45N 77 30W
Penny, Canada 104 C4 53 51N 121 20W
Peno, Russia 46 D7 57 2N 32 49 E
Penobscot →, U.S.A. 109 C11 44 30N 68 48W
Penobscot B., U.S.A. 109 C11 44 35N 68 50W
Penola, Australia 95 F3 37 25 S 140 48 E
Penong, Australia 93 F5 31 56 S 133 1 E
Penonomé, Panama 120 E3 8 31N 80 21W
Penrith, Australia 95 E5 33 43 S 150 38 E
Penrith, U.K. 12 C5 54 40N 2 45W
Penryn, U.K. 13 G2 50 9N 5 7W
Pensacola, U.S.A. 109 K2 30 25N 87 13W
Pensacola Mts., Antarctica 5 E1 84 0 S 40 0W
Pense, Canada 105 C8 50 25N 104 59W
Penshurst, Australia 95 F3 37 49 S 142 20 E
Penticton, Canada 104 D5 49 30N 119 38W
Pentland, Australia 94 C4 20 32 S 145 25 E
Pentland Firth, U.K. 14 C5 58 43N 3 10W
Pentland Hills, U.K. 14 F5 55 48N 3 25W
Penza, Russia 48 D7 53 15N 45 5 E
Penzance, U.K. 13 G2 50 7N 5 33W
Penzberg, Germany 25 H7 47 45N 11 22 E
Penzhino, Russia 51 C17 63 30N 167 55 E
Penzhinskaya Guba, Russia 51 C17 61 30N 163 0 E
Penzhou, China 58 B4 31 4N 103 32 E
Penzlin, Germany 24 B9 53 30N 13 5 E
Peoria, Ariz., U.S.A. 115 K7 33 35N 112 14W
Peoria, Ill., U.S.A. 112 E10 40 42N 89 36W
Pepacton Reservoir, U.S.A. 111 D10 42 5N 74 58W
Pepani →, S. Africa 88 D3 25 49 S 22 47 E
Pepel, S. Leone 82 D2 8 40N 13 5W
Peqin, Albania 40 E3 41 3N 19 44 E
Peqini = Peqin, Albania 40 E3 41 3N 19 44 E
Pera Hd., Australia 94 A3 12 55 S 141 37 E
Perabumulih, Indonesia 62 E2 3 27 S 104 15 E
Perak →, Malaysia 65 K3 4 0N 100 50 E
Perakhóra, Greece 38 C4 38 2N 22 56 E
Perales de Alfambra, Spain 32 E4 40 38N 1 0W
Perales del Puerto, Spain 34 E4 40 10N 6 40W
Pérama, Kérkira, Greece 36 A3 39 34N 19 54 E
Pérama, Kríti, Greece 36 D6 35 20N 24 40 E
Peräpohjola, Finland 8 C22 66 16N 26 10 E
Perast, Montenegro, Yug. 40 D2 42 31N 18 47 E
Percé, Canada 103 C7 48 31N 64 13W
Perche, France 18 D8 48 31N 1 1 E
Perchtoldsdorf, Austria 27 C9 48 7N 16 16 E
Percival Lakes, Australia 92 D4 21 25 S 125 0 E
Percy, France 18 D5 48 55N 1 11W
Percy Is., Australia 94 C5 21 39 S 150 16 E
Perdido, Mte., Spain 32 C5 42 40N 0 5 E
Perdu, Mt. = Perdido, Mte., Spain 32 C5 42 40N 0 5 E
Pereira, Colombia 124 C3 4 49N 75 43W
Perelazovskiy, Russia 49 F6 49 8N 42 35 E
Perenjori, Australia 93 E2 29 26 S 116 16 E
Peresecina, Moldova 43 C13 47 16N 28 46 E
Pereslavi-Zalesskiy, Russia 46 D10 56 45N 38 50 E
Peretu, Romania 43 F10 44 3N 25 5 E
Pereyaslav-Khmelnytskyy, Ukraine 47 G6 50 3N 31 28 E
Pérez, I., Mexico 119 C7 22 24N 89 42W
Perg, Austria 26 C7 48 15N 14 38 E
Pergamino, Argentina 126 C3 33 52 S 60 30W
Pergau →, Malaysia 65 K3 5 23N 102 2 E
Pérgine Valsugana, Italy 29 B8 46 4N 11 14 E
Pérgola, Italy 29 E9 43 34N 12 50 E
Perham, U.S.A. 112 B7 46 36N 95 34W
Perhentian, Kepulauan, Malaysia 62 C2 5 54N 102 42 E
Periam, Romania 42 D5 46 2N 20 52 E
Péribonca →, Canada 103 C5 48 45N 72 5W
Péribonca, L., Canada 103 B5 50 1N 71 10W
Perico, Argentina 126 A2 24 20 S 65 5W
Pericos, Mexico 118 B3 25 3N 107 42W
Périers, France 18 C5 49 11N 1 25W
Périgord, France 20 D4 45 0N 0 40 E
Périgueux, France 20 C4 45 10N 0 42 E
Perijá, Sierra de, Colombia 124 B4 9 30N 73 3W
Peristéra, Greece 38 B5 39 15N 23 58 E
Peristerona →, Cyprus 36 D12 35 8N 33 5 E
Perito Moreno, Argentina 128 F2 46 36 S 70 56W
Perivol = Dragovishtitsa, Bulgaria 40 D6 42 22N 22 39 E
Perkasie, U.S.A. 111 F9 40 22N 75 18W
Perković, Croatia 29 E13 43 41N 16 10 E
Perlas, Arch. de las, Panama 120 E4 8 41N 79 7W
Perlas, Punta de, Nic. 120 D3 12 30N 83 30W
Perleberg, Germany 24 B7 53 5N 11 52 E
Perlez, Serbia, Yug. 42 E5 45 11N 20 22 E
Perm, Russia 50 D6 58 0N 56 10 E
Përmet, Albania 40 F4 40 15N 20 21 E
Përmeti = Përmet, Albania 40 F4 40 15N 20 21 E
Pernambuco = Recife, Brazil 125 E12 8 0 S 35 0W
Pernambuco □, Brazil 125 E11 8 0 S 37 0W
Pernatty Lagoon, Australia 95 E2 31 30 S 137 12 E
Pernik, Bulgaria 40 D7 42 35N 23 2 E
Peron Is., Australia 92 B5 13 9 S 130 4 E
Peron Pen., Australia 93 E1 26 0 S 113 10 E
Péronne, France 19 C9 49 55N 2 57 E
Perosa Argentina, Italy 28 D4 44 58N 7 10 E
Perow, Canada 104 C3 54 35N 126 10W
Perpendicular Pt., Australia 95 E5 31 37 S 152 52 E
Perpignan, France 20 F6 42 42N 2 53 E
Perris, U.S.A. 117 M9 33 47N 117 14W
Perros-Guirec, France 18 D3 48 49N 3 28W
Perry, Fla., U.S.A. 109 K4 30 7N 83 35W
Perry, Ga., U.S.A. 109 J4 32 28N 83 44W
Perry, Iowa, U.S.A. 112 E7 41 51N 94 6W
Perry, Okla., U.S.A. 113 G6 36 17N 97 14W
Perryton, U.S.A. 113 G4 36 24N 100 48W
Perryville, U.S.A. 113 G10 37 43N 89 52W
Persan, France 19 C9 49 9N 2 16 E
Persberg, Sweden 10 E8 59 47N 14 15 E
Perşembe, Turkey 72 B7 41 5N 37 46 E
Persepolis, Iran 71 D7 29 55N 52 50 E
Pershotravensk, Ukraine 47 G4 50 13N 27 40 E
Persia = Iran ■, Asia 71 C7 33 0N 53 0 E
Persian Gulf = Gulf, The, Asia 71 E6 27 0N 50 0 E
Perstorp, Sweden 11 H7 56 10N 13 25 E
Pertek, Turkey 73 C8 38 51N 39 19 E
Perth, Australia 93 F2 31 57 S 115 52 E
Perth, Canada 102 D4 44 55N 76 15W
Perth, U.K. 14 E5 56 24N 3 26W
Perth & Kinross □, U.K. 14 E5 56 45N 3 55W
Perth Amboy, U.S.A. 111 F10 40 31N 74 16W
Perth-Andover, Canada 103 C6 46 44N 67 42W
Pertuis, France 21 E9 43 42N 5 30 E
Pertusato, C., France 21 G13 41 21N 9 11 E
Peru, Ind., U.S.A. 108 E2 40 45N 86 4W
Peru, N.Y., U.S.A. 111 B11 44 35N 73 32W
Peru ■, S. Amer. 124 D4 4 0 S 75 0W
Peru-Chile Trench, Pac. Oc. 124 G3 20 0 S 72 0W
Perúgia, Italy 29 E9 43 7N 12 23 E
Perušić, Croatia 29 D12 44 40N 15 22 E
Pervomaysk, Russia 48 C6 54 56N 43 58 E
Pervomaysk, Ukraine 47 H6 48 10N 30 46 E
Pervouralsk, Russia 50 D6 56 59N 59 59 E
Pésaro, Italy 29 E9 43 54N 12 55 E
Pescadores = Penghu, Taiwan 59 F12 23 34N 119 30 E
Pescara, Italy 29 F11 42 28N 14 13 E
Pescara →, Italy 29 F11 42 28N 14 13 E
Peschanokopskoye, Russia 49 G5 46 14N 41 4 E
Péscia, Italy 28 E7 43 54N 10 41 E
Pescina, Italy 29 F10 42 2N 13 39 E
Peshawar, Pakistan 68 B4 34 2N 71 37 E
Peshkopi, Albania 40 E4 41 41N 20 25 E
Peshtera, Bulgaria 41 D8 42 2N 24 18 E
Peshtigo, U.S.A. 108 C2 45 4N 87 46W
Peski, Russia 48 E6 51 14N 42 29 E
Pêso da Régua, Portugal 34 D3 41 10N 7 47W
Pesqueira, Brazil 125 E11 8 20 S 36 42W
Pessac, France 20 D3 44 48N 0 37W
Pest □, Hungary 42 C4 47 29N 19 5 E
Pestovo, Russia 46 C8 58 33N 35 42 E
Pestravka, Russia 48 D9 52 28N 49 57 E
Péta, Greece 38 B3 39 10N 21 2 E
Petah Tiqwa, Israel 75 C3 32 6N 34 53 E
Petalídhion, Greece 38 E3 36 57N 21 55 E
Petaling Jaya, Malaysia 65 L3 3 4N 101 42 E
Petaloudhes, Greece 36 C10 36 18N 28 5 E
Petaluma, U.S.A. 116 G4 38 14N 122 39W
Pétange, Lux. 17 E5 49 33N 5 55 E
Petaro, Pakistan 68 G3 25 31N 68 18 E
Petatlán, Mexico 118 D4 17 31N 101 16W
Petauke, Zambia 87 E3 14 14 S 31 20 E
Petawawa, Canada 102 C4 45 54N 77 17W
Petén Itzá, L., Guatemala 120 C2 16 58N 89 50W
Peter I.s Øy, Antarctica 5 C16 69 0 S 91 0W
Peter Pond L., Canada 105 B7 55 55N 108 44W
Peterbell, Canada 102 C3 48 36N 83 21W
Peterborough, Australia 95 E2 32 58 S 138 51 E
Peterborough, Canada 102 D4 44 20N 78 20W
Peterborough, U.K. 13 E7 52 35N 0 15W
Peterborough, U.S.A. 111 D13 42 53N 71 57W
Peterborough □, U.K. 13 E7 52 35N 0 15W
Peterculter, U.K. 14 D6 57 6N 2 16W
Peterhead, U.K. 14 D7 57 31N 1 48W
Peterlee, U.K. 12 C6 54 47N 1 20W
Petermann Bjerg, Greenland 98 B17 73 7N 28 25W
Petermann Ranges, Australia 92 E5 26 0 S 130 30 E
Petersburg, Alaska, U.S.A. 100 C6 56 48N 132 58W
Petersburg, Pa., U.S.A. 110 F6 40 34N 78 3W
Petersburg, Va., U.S.A. 108 G7 37 14N 77 24W
Petersburg, W. Va., U.S.A. 108 F6 39 1N 79 5W
Petersfield, U.K. 13 F7 51 1N 0 56W
Petershagen, Germany 24 C4 52 23N 8 58 E
Petília Policastro, Italy 31 C9 39 7N 16 48 E
Petit Goâve, Haiti 121 C5 18 27N 72 51W
Petit Jardin, Canada 103 C8 48 28N 59 14W
Petit Lac Manicouagan, Canada 103 B6 51 25N 67 40W
Petit-Mécatina →, Canada 103 B8 50 40N 59 30W
Petit-Mécatina, I. du, Canada 103 B8 50 30N 59 25W
Petit Saint Bernard, Col du, Italy 21 C10 45 40N 6 52 E
Petitcodiac, Canada 103 C6 45 57N 65 11W
Petite Baleine →, Canada 102 A4 56 0N 76 45W
Petite Saguenay, Canada 103 C5 48 15N 70 4W
Petitot →, Canada 104 A4 60 14N 123 29W
Petitsikapau L., Canada 103 B6 54 37N 66 25W
Petlad, India 68 H5 22 30N 72 45 E
Peto, Mexico 119 C7 20 10N 88 53W
Petone, N.Z. 91 J5 41 13 S 174 53 E
Petorca, Chile 126 C1 32 15 S 70 56W
Petoskey, U.S.A. 108 C3 45 22N 84 57W
Petra, Jordan 75 E4 30 20N 35 22 E
Petra, Spain 37 B10 39 37N 3 6 E
Petra, Ostrova, Russia 4 B13 76 15N 118 30 E
Petra Velikogo, Zaliv, Russia 54 C6 42 40N 132 0 E
Petrel = Petrer, Spain 33 G4 38 30N 0 46W
Petrella, Monte, Italy 30 A6 41 18N 13 40 E
Petrer, Spain 33 G4 38 30N 0 46W
Petreto-Bicchisano, France 21 G12 41 47N 8 58 E
Petrich, Bulgaria 40 E7 41 24N 23 13 E
Petrified Forest National Park, U.S.A. 115 J9 35 0N 109 30W
Petrijanec, Croatia 29 B13 46 23N 16 17 E
Petrikov = Pyetrikaw, Belarus 47 F5 52 11N 28 29 E
Petrila, Romania 43 E8 45 29N 23 29 E
Petrinja, Croatia 29 C13 45 28N 16 18 E
Petrodvorets, Russia 46 C5 59 52N 29 54 E
Petrograd = Sankt-Peterburg, Russia 46 C6 59 55N 30 20 E
Petrolândia, Brazil 125 E11 9 5 S 38 20W
Petrolia, Canada 102 D3 42 54N 82 9W
Petrolina, Brazil 125 E10 9 24 S 40 30W
Petropavl, Kazakstan 50 D7 54 53N 69 13 E
Petropavlovsk = Petropavl, Kazakstan 50 D7 54 53N 69 13 E
Petropavlovsk-Kamchatskiy, Russia 51 D16 53 3N 158 43 E
Petropavlovskiy = Akhtubinsk, Russia 49 F8 48 13N 46 7 E
Petrópolis, Brazil 127 A7 22 33 S 43 9W
Petroșani, Romania 43 E8 45 28N 23 20 E
Petrova Gora, Croatia 29 C12 45 15N 15 45 E
Petrovac, Montenegro, Yug. 40 D2 42 13N 18 57 E
Petrovac, Serbia, Yug. 40 B5 44 22N 21 26 E
Petrovaradin, Serbia, Yug. 42 E4 45 16N 19 55 E
Petrovsk, Russia 48 D7 52 22N 45 19 E
Petrovsk-Zabaykalskiy, Russia 51 D11 51 20N 108 55 E
Petrovskaya, Russia 47 K9 45 25N 37 58 E
Petrovskoye = Svetlograd, Russia 49 H6 45 25N 42 58 E
Petrozavodsk, Russia 46 B8 61 41N 34 20 E
Petrus Steyn, S. Africa 89 D4 27 38 S 28 8 E

Petrusburg, S. Africa 88 D4 29 4 S 25 26 E
Petzeck, Austria 26 E5 46 57N 12 48 E
Peumo, Chile 126 C1 34 21 S 71 12W
Peureulak, Indonesia 62 D1 4 48N 97 45 E
Pevek, Russia 51 C18 69 41N 171 19 E
Peveragno, Italy 28 D4 44 20N 7 37 E
Peyrehorade, France 20 E2 43 34N 1 7W
Peyruis, France 21 D9 44 1N 5 56 E
Pézenas, France 20 E7 43 28N 3 24 E
Pezinok, Slovak Rep. 27 C10 48 17N 17 17 E
Pfaffenhofen, Germany 25 G7 48 31N 11 31 E
Pfarrkirchen, Germany 25 G8 48 25N 12 56 E
Pfeffenhausen, Germany 25 G7 48 39N 11 58 E
Pforzheim, Germany 25 G4 48 52N 8 41 E
Pfullendorf, Germany 25 H5 47 55N 9 15 E
Pfungstadt, Germany 25 F4 49 48N 8 35 E
Phagwara, India 66 D9 31 10N 75 40 E
Phaistós, Greece 36 D6 35 2N 24 50 E
Phala, Botswana 88 C4 23 45 S 26 50 E
Phalera = Phulera, India 68 F6 26 52N 75 16 E
Phalodi, India 68 F5 27 12N 72 24 E
Phalsbourg, France 19 D14 48 46N 7 15 E
Phan, Thailand 64 C2 19 28N 99 43 E
Phan Rang, Vietnam 65 G7 11 34N 109 0 E
Phan Ri = Hoa Da, Vietnam 65 G7 11 16N 108 40 E
Phan Thiet, Vietnam 65 G7 11 1N 108 9 E
Phanae, Greece 39 C7 38 8N 25 57 E
Phanat Nikhom, Thailand 64 F3 13 27N 101 11 E
Phangan, Ko, Thailand 65 H3 9 45N 100 0 E
Phangnga, Thailand 65 H2 8 28N 98 30 E
Phanom Sarakham, Thailand 64 F3 13 45N 101 21 E
Phaphund, India 69 F8 26 36N 79 28 E
Pharenda, India 69 F10 27 5N 83 17 E
Pharr, U.S.A. 113 M5 26 12N 98 11W
Phatthalung, Thailand 65 J3 7 39N 100 6 E
Phayao, Thailand 64 C2 19 11N 99 55 E
Phelps, U.S.A. 110 D7 42 58N 77 3W
Phelps L., Canada 105 B8 59 15N 103 15W
Phenix City, U.S.A. 109 J3 32 28N 85 0W
Phet Buri, Thailand 64 F2 13 1N 99 55 E
Phetchabun, Thailand 64 D3 16 25N 101 8 E
Phetchabun, Thiu Khao, Thailand 64 E3 16 0N 101 20 E
Phetchaburi = Phet Buri, Thailand 64 F2 13 1N 99 55 E
Phi Phi, Ko, Thailand 65 J2 7 45N 98 46 E
Phiafay, Laos 64 E6 14 48N 106 0 E
Phibun Mangsahan, Thailand 64 E5 15 14N 105 14 E
Phichai, Thailand 64 D3 17 22N 100 10 E
Phichit, Thailand 64 D3 16 26N 100 22 E
Philadelphia, Miss., U.S.A. 113 J10 32 46N 89 7W
Philadelphia, N.Y., U.S.A. 111 B9 44 9N 75 43W
Philadelphia, Pa., U.S.A. 111 G9 39 57N 75 10W
Philip, U.S.A. 112 C4 44 2N 101 40W
Philippeville, Belgium 17 D4 50 12N 4 33 E
Philippi, Greece 41 E8 41 1N 24 16 E
Philippi, U.S.A. 108 F5 39 9N 80 3W
Philippi L., Australia 94 C2 24 20 S 138 55 E
Philippines ■, Asia 61 F5 12 0N 123 0 E
Philippolis, S. Africa 88 E4 30 15 S 25 16 E
Philippopolis = Plovdiv, Bulgaria 41 D8 42 8N 24 44 E
Philipsburg, Canada 111 A11 45 2N 73 5W
Philipsburg, Mont., U.S.A. 114 C7 46 20N 113 18W
Philipsburg, Pa., U.S.A. 110 F6 40 54N 78 13W
Philipstown = Daingean, Ireland 15 C4 53 18N 7 17W
Philipstown, S. Africa 88 E3 30 28 S 24 30 E
Phillip I., Australia 95 F4 38 30 S 145 12 E
Phillips, U.S.A. 112 C9 45 42N 90 24W
Phillipsburg, Kans., U.S.A. 112 F5 39 45N 99 19W
Phillipsburg, N.J., U.S.A. 111 F9 40 42N 75 12W
Philmont, U.S.A. 111 D11 42 15N 73 39W
Philomath, U.S.A. 114 D2 44 32N 123 22W
Phimai, Thailand 64 E4 15 13N 102 30 E
Phitsanulok, Thailand 64 D3 16 50N 100 12 E
Phnom Dangrek, Thailand 62 B2 14 20N 104 0 E
Phnom Penh, Cambodia 65 G5 11 33N 104 55 E
Phnum Penh = Phnom Penh, Cambodia 65 G5 11 33N 104 55 E
Phoenicia, U.S.A. 111 D10 42 5N 74 14W
Phoenix, Ariz., U.S.A. 115 K7 33 27N 112 4W
Phoenix, N.Y., U.S.A. 111 C8 43 14N 76 18W
Phoenix Is., Kiribati 96 H10 3 30 S 172 0W
Phoenixville, U.S.A. 111 F9 40 8N 75 31W
Phon, Thailand 64 E4 15 49N 102 36 E
Phon Tiou, Laos 64 D5 17 53N 104 37 E
Phong →, Thailand 64 D4 16 23N 102 56 E
Phong Saly, Laos 58 G4 21 42N 102 9 E
Phong Tho, Vietnam 64 A4 22 32N 103 21 E
Phonhong, Laos 64 C4 18 30N 102 25 E
Phonum, Thailand 65 H2 8 49N 98 48 E
Phosphate Hill, Australia 94 C2 21 53 S 139 58 E
Photharam, Thailand 64 F2 13 41N 99 51 E
Phra Nakhon Si Ayutthaya, Thailand 64 E3 14 25N 100 30 E
Phra Thong, Ko, Thailand 65 H2 9 5N 98 17 E
Phrae, Thailand 64 C3 18 7N 100 9 E
Phrom Phiram, Thailand 64 D3 17 2N 100 12 E
Phrygia, Turkey 72 C4 38 40N 30 0 E
Phu Dien, Vietnam 64 C5 18 58N 105 31 E
Phu Loi, Laos 64 B4 20 14N 103 14 E
Phu Ly, Vietnam 58 G5 20 35N 105 50 E
Phu Quoc, Dao, Vietnam 65 G4 10 20N 104 0 E
Phu Tho, Vietnam 58 G5 21 24N 105 13 E
Phuc Yen, Vietnam 58 G5 21 16N 105 45 E
Phuket, Thailand 65 J2 7 52N 98 22 E
Phuket, Ko, Thailand 65 J2 8 0N 98 22 E
Phul, India 68 D6 30 19N 75 14 E
Phulad, India 68 G5 25 38N 73 49 E
Phulchari, Bangla. 69 G13 25 11N 89 37 E
Phulera, India 68 F6 26 52N 75 16 E
Phulpur, India 69 G10 25 31N 82 49 E
Phun Phin, Thailand 65 H2 9 7N 99 12 E
Piacenza, Italy 28 C6 45 1N 9 40 E
Pian Cr. →, Australia 95 E4 30 2 S 148 12 E
Piana, France 21 F12 42 15N 8 34 E
Pianella, Italy 29 F11 42 24N 14 2 E
Pianosa, Puglia, Italy 29 F12 42 12N 15 44 E
Pianosa, Toscana, Italy 28 F7 42 35N 10 5 E
Piapot, Canada 105 D7 49 59N 109 8W
Pias, Portugal 35 G3 38 1N 7 29W
Piaseczno, Poland 45 F8 52 5N 21 2 E
Piaski, Poland 45 G9 51 8N 22 52 E
Piastów, Poland 45 F7 52 12N 20 48 E
Piatra, Romania 43 G10 43 51N 25 9 E
Piatra Neamţ, Romania 43 D11 46 56N 26 21 E
Piatra Olt, Romania 43 F9 44 22N 24 16 E
Piauí □, Brazil 125 E10 7 0 S 43 0W
Piaui →, Brazil 125 E10 6 38 S 42 42W
Piave →, Italy 29 C9 45 32N 12 44 E
Piazza Ármerina, Italy 31 E7 37 21N 14 20 E
Pibor →, Sudan 81 F3 7 35N 33 0 E
Pibor Post, Sudan 81 F3 6 47N 33 3 E
Picardie, France 19 C10 49 50N 3 0 E
Picardie, Plaine de, France 19 C9 50 0N 2 0 E
Picardy = Picardie, France 19 C10 49 50N 3 0 E
Picayune, U.S.A. 113 K10 30 32N 89 41W
Picerno, Italy 31 B8 40 38N 15 38 E
Pichhor, India 69 G8 25 58N 78 20 E
Pichilemu, Chile 126 C1 34 22 S 72 0W
Pichor, India 68 G8 25 11N 78 11 E
Pickerel L., Canada 102 C1 48 40N 91 25W
Pickering, U.K. 12 C7 54 15N 0 46W
Pickering, Vale of, U.K. 12 C7 54 14N 0 45W
Pickle Lake, Canada 102 B1 51 30N 90 12W
Pickwick L., U.S.A. 109 H1 35 4N 88 15W
Pico Truncado, Argentina 128 F3 46 40 S 68 0W
Picos, Brazil 125 E10 7 5 S 41 28W
Picton, Australia 95 E5 34 12 S 150 34 E
Picton, Canada 102 D4 44 1N 77 9W
Picton, N.Z. 91 J5 41 18 S 174 3 E
Pictou, Canada 103 C7 45 41N 62 42W
Picture Butte, Canada 104 D6 49 55N 112 45W
Picún Leufú, Argentina 128 D3 39 30 S 69 5W
Pidurutalagala, Sri Lanka 66 R12 7 10N 80 50 E
Piechowice, Poland 45 H2 50 51N 15 36 E
Piedmont = Piemonte □, Italy 28 D5 45 0N 8 0 E
Piedmont, Ala., U.S.A. 109 J3 33 55N 85 37W
Piedmont, S.C., U.S.A. 107 D10 34 0N 81 30W
Piedmonte Matese, Italy 31 A7 41 22N 14 22 E
Piedra →, Spain 32 D3 41 18N 1 47W
Piedrabuena, Spain 35 G6 39 0N 4 10W
Piedrahita, Spain 34 E5 40 28N 5 23W
Piedralaves, Spain 34 E6 40 19N 4 42W
Piedras Blancas, Spain 34 B5 43 33N 5 58W
Piedras Negras, Mexico 118 B4 28 42N 100 31W
Piekary Śląskie, Poland 45 H5 50 24N 18 57 E
Pieksämäki, Finland 9 E22 62 18N 27 10 E
Piemonte □, Italy 28 D5 45 0N 8 0 E
Pienaarsrivier, S. Africa 89 D4 25 15 S 28 18 E
Pieniężno, Poland 44 D7 54 14N 20 8 E
Pieńsk, Poland 45 G2 51 16N 15 2 E
Piercefield, U.S.A. 111 B10 44 13N 74 35W
Pierceland, Canada 105 C7 54 20N 109 46W
Piería □, Greece 40 F6 40 13N 22 25 E
Pierpont, U.S.A. 110 E4 41 45N 80 34W
Pierre, U.S.A. 112 C4 44 22N 100 21W
Pierre-Buffière, France 20 C5 45 41N 1 22 E
Pierre-de-Bresse, France 19 F12 46 54N 5 13 E
Pierrefontaine-les-Varans, France 19 E13 47 14N 6 32 E
Pierrefort, France 20 D6 44 55N 2 50 E
Pierrelatte, France 21 D8 44 23N 4 43 E
Piešťany, Slovak Rep. 27 C10 48 38N 17 55 E
Piesting →, Austria 27 C9 48 6N 16 40 E
Pieszyce, Poland 45 H3 50 43N 16 33 E
Piet Retief, S. Africa 89 D5 27 1 S 30 50 E
Pietarsaari, Finland 8 E20 63 40N 22 43 E
Pietermaritzburg, S. Africa 89 D5 29 35 S 30 25 E
Pietersburg, S. Africa 89 C4 23 54 S 29 25 E
Pietragalla, Italy 31 B8 40 45N 15 53 E
Pietrasanta, Italy 28 E7 43 57N 10 14 E
Pietroşita, Romania 43 E10 45 11N 25 26 E
Pietrosul, Vf., Maramureş, Romania 43 C9 47 35N 24 43 E
Pietrosul, Vf., Suceava, Romania 43 C10 47 12N 25 18 E
Pieve di Cadore, Italy 29 B9 46 26N 12 22 E
Pieve di Teco, Italy 28 D4 44 3N 7 56 E
Pievepélago, Italy 28 D7 44 12N 10 37 E
Pigadhítsa, Greece 40 G5 39 59N 21 23 E
Pigeon L., Canada 110 B6 44 27N 78 30W
Piggott, U.S.A. 113 G9 36 23N 90 11W
Pigna, Italy 28 E4 43 56N 7 40 E
Pigüe, Argentina 126 D3 37 36 S 62 25W
Pihani, India 69 F9 27 36N 80 15 E
Pihlajavesi, Finland 9 F23 61 45N 28 45 E
Pijijiapan, Mexico 119 D6 15 42N 93 14W
Pikalevo, Russia 46 C8 59 37N 34 9 E
Pikangikum Berens, Canada 105 C10 51 49N 94 0W
Pikes Peak, U.S.A. 112 F2 38 50N 105 3W
Piketberg, S. Africa 88 E2 32 55 S 18 40 E
Pikeville, U.S.A. 108 G4 37 29N 82 31W
Pikou, China 57 E12 39 18N 122 22 E
Pikwitonei, Canada 105 B9 55 35N 97 9W
Piła, Poland 45 E3 53 10N 16 48 E
Pila, Spain 33 G3 38 16N 1 11W
Pilaía, Greece 40 F6 40 32N 22 59 E
Pilani, India 68 E6 28 22N 75 33 E
Pilar, Paraguay 126 B4 26 50 S 58 20W
Pilar de la Horadada, Spain 33 H4 37 52N 0 47W
Pilawa, Poland 45 G8 51 57N 21 32 E
Pilaya →, Bolivia 124 H6 20 55 S 64 4W
Pilbara, Australia 92 D2 23 35 S 117 25 E
Pilcomayo →, Paraguay 126 B4 25 21 S 57 42W
Pilgrim's Rest, S. Africa 89 C5 24 55 S 30 44 E
Pilgrimstad, Sweden 10 B9 62 57N 15 2 E
Píli, Greece 39 E9 36 50N 27 15 E
Pilibhit, India 69 E8 28 40N 79 50 E
Pilica →, Poland 45 G8 51 52N 21 17 E
Pilion, Greece 38 B5 39 27N 23 7 E
Pilis, Hungary 42 C4 47 17N 19 35 E
Pilisvörösvár, Hungary 42 C3 47 38N 18 56 E
Pilkhawa, India 68 E7 28 43N 77 42 E
Pilliga, Australia 95 E4 30 21 S 148 54 E
Pílos, Greece 38 E3 36 55N 21 42 E
Pilot Mound, Canada 105 D9 49 15N 98 54W
Pilot Point, U.S.A. 113 J6 33 24N 96 58W
Pilot Rock, U.S.A. 114 D4 45 29N 118 50W
Pilsen = Plzeň, Czech Rep. 26 B6 49 45N 13 22 E
Pilštanj, Slovenia 29 B12 46 8N 15 39 E
Piltene, Latvia 44 A8 57 13N 21 40 E
Pilzno, Poland 45 J8 49 58N 21 16 E
Pima, U.S.A. 115 K9 32 54N 109 50W
Pimba, Australia 95 E2 31 18 S 136 46 E
Pimenta Bueno, Brazil 124 F6 11 35 S 61 10W
Pimentel, Peru 124 E3 6 45 S 79 55W
Pina de Ebro, Spain 32 D4 41 29N 0 33W
Pinamalayan, Phil. 61 E4 13 2N 121 29 E
Pinang, Malaysia 65 K3 5 25N 100 15 E
Pinar, C. des, Spain 37 B10 39 53N 3 12 E
Pinar del Río, Cuba 120 B3 22 26N 83 40W
Pınarbaşı, Çanakkale, Turkey 39 B8 39 53N 26 15 E
Pınarbaşı, Kayseri, Turkey 72 C7 38 43N 36 23 E
Pınarhisar, Turkey 41 E11 41 37N 27 30 E
Pinatubo, Mt., Phil. 61 D3 15 8N 120 21 E
Pincehely, Hungary 42 D3 46 41N 18 27 E
Pinchang, China 58 B6 31 36N 107 3 E
Pincher Creek, Canada 104 D6 49 30N 113 57W
Pinchi L., Canada 104 C4 54 38N 124 30W
Pinckneyville, U.S.A. 112 F10 38 5N 89 23W
Pińczów, Poland 45 H7 50 32N 20 32 E
Pindar, Australia 93 E2 28 30 S 115 47 E
Pindi Gheb, Pakistan 68 C5 33 14N 72 21 E
Pindiga, Nigeria 83 D7 9 58N 10 53 E
Pindos Óros, Greece 38 B3 40 0N 21 0 E
Pindus Mts. = Pindos Óros, Greece 38 B3 40 0N 21 0 E
Pine →, B.C., Canada 104 B4 56 8N 120 43W
Pine →, Sask., Canada 105 B7 58 50N 105 38W
Pine, C., Canada 103 C9 46 37N 53 32W
Pine Bluff, U.S.A. 113 H9 34 13N 92 1W
Pine Bluffs, U.S.A. 112 E2 41 11N 104 4W
Pine City, U.S.A. 112 C8 45 50N 92 59W
Pine Cr. →, U.S.A. 110 E7 41 10N 77 16W
Pine Creek, Australia 92 B5 13 50 S 131 50 E
Pine Falls, Canada 105 C9 50 34N 96 11W
Pine Flat Res., U.S.A. 116 J7 36 50N 119 20W
Pine Grove, U.S.A. 111 F8 40 33N 76 23W
Pine Pass, Canada 104 B4 55 25N 122 42W
Pine Point, Canada 104 A6 60 50N 114 28W
Pine Ridge, U.S.A. 112 D3 43 2N 102 33W
Pine River, Canada 105 C8 51 45N 100 30W
Pine River, U.S.A. 112 B7 46 43N 94 24W
Pine Valley, U.S.A. 117 N10 32 50N 116 32W
Pinecrest, U.S.A. 116 G6 38 12N 120 1W
Pineda de Mar, Spain 32 D7 41 37N 2 42 E
Pinedale, Calif., U.S.A. 116 J7 36 50N 119 48W
Pinedale, Wyo., U.S.A. 114 E9 42 52N 109 52W
Pinega →, Russia 50 C5 64 30N 44 19 E
Pinehill, Australia 94 C4 23 38 S 146 57 E
Pinehouse L., Canada 105 B7 55 32N 106 35W
Pineimuta →, Canada 102 B1 52 8N 88 33W
Pinerolo, Italy 28 D4 44 53N 7 21 E
Pineto, Italy 29 F11 42 36N 14 4 E
Pinetop, U.S.A. 115 J9 34 8N 109 56W
Pinetown, S. Africa 89 D5 29 48 S 30 54 E
Pineville, U.S.A. 113 K8 31 19N 92 26W
Piney, France 19 D11 48 22N 4 21 E
Ping →, Thailand 64 E3 15 42N 100 9 E
Pingaring, Australia 93 F2 32 40 S 118 32 E
Pingba, China 58 D6 26 23N 106 12 E
Pingbian, China 58 F4 23 0N 103 45 E
Pingchuan, China 58 D3 27 35N 101 55 E
Pingding, China 56 F7 37 47N 113 38 E
Pingdingshan, China 56 H7 33 43N 113 27 E
Pingdong, Taiwan 59 F13 22 39N 120 30 E
Pingdu, China 57 F10 36 42N 119 59 E
Pingelly, Australia 93 F2 32 32 S 117 5 E
Pingguo, China 58 F6 23 19N 107 36 E
Pinghe, China 59 E11 24 17N 117 21 E
Pinghu, China 59 B13 30 40N 121 2 E
Pingjiang, China 59 C9 28 45N 113 36 E
Pingle, China 59 E8 24 40N 110 40 E
Pingli, China 58 A7 32 27N 109 22 E
Pingliang, China 56 G4 35 35N 106 31 E
Pinglu, China 56 E7 39 31N 112 30 E
Pingluo, China 56 E4 38 52N 106 30 E
Pingnan, Fujian, China 59 D12 26 55N 119 0 E
Pingnan, Guangxi Zhuangzu, China 59 F8 23 33N 110 22 E
Pingquan, China 57 D10 41 1N 118 37 E
Pingrup, Australia 93 F2 33 32 S 118 29 E
Pingshan, China 58 C5 28 39N 104 3 E
Pingtan, China 59 E12 25 31N 119 47 E
Pingtang, China 58 E6 25 49N 107 17 E
P'ingtung, Taiwan 59 F13 22 38N 120 30 E
Pingwu, China 56 H3 32 25N 104 30 E
Pingxiang, Guangxi Zhuangzu, China 58 F6 22 6N 106 46 E
Pingxiang, Jiangxi, China 59 D9 27 43N 113 48 E
Pingyao, China 56 F7 37 12N 112 10 E
Pingyi, China 57 G9 35 30N 117 35 E
Pingyin, China 56 F9 36 20N 116 25 E
Pingyuan, Guangdong, China 59 E10 24 37N 115 57 E
Pingyuan, Shandong, China 56 F9 37 10N 116 22 E
Pingyuanjie, China 58 F4 23 45N 103 48 E
Pinhal, Brazil 127 A6 22 10 S 46 46W
Pinhal Novo, Portugal 35 G2 38 38N 8 55W
Pinheiro, Brazil 125 D9 2 31 S 45 5W
Pinheiro Machado, Brazil 127 C5 31 34 S 53 23W
Pinhel, Portugal 34 E3 40 50N 7 1W
Pini, Indonesia 62 D1 0 10N 98 40 E
Piniós →, Ilía, Greece 38 D3 37 48N 21 20 E
Piniós →, Tríkkala, Greece 38 B4 39 55N 22 41 E
Pinjarra, Australia 93 F2 32 37 S 115 52 E
Pink Mountain, Canada 104 B4 57 3N 122 52W
Pinkafeld, Austria 27 D9 47 22N 16 9 E
Pinnacles, U.S.A. 116 J5 36 33N 121 19W
Pinnaroo, Australia 95 F3 35 17 S 140 53 E
Pinneberg, Germany 24 B5 53 40N 9 48 E
Pínnes, Ákra, Greece 41 F8 40 5N 24 20 E
Pinon Hills, U.S.A. 117 L9 34 26N 117 39W
Pinos, Mexico 118 C4 22 20N 101 40W
Pinos, Mt., U.S.A. 117 L7 34 49N 119 8W
Pinos Pt., U.S.A. 115 H3 36 38N 121 57W
Pinos Puente, Spain 35 H7 37 15N 3 45W
Pinotepa Nacional, Mexico 119 D5 16 19N 98 3W
Pinrang, Indonesia 63 E5 3 46 S 119 41 E
Pins, Pte. aux, Canada 110 D3 42 15N 81 51W
Pinsk, Belarus 47 F4 52 10N 26 1 E
Pintados, Chile 124 H5 20 35 S 69 40W
Pinyang, China 59 D13 27 42N 120 31 E
Pinyug, Russia 50 C5 60 5N 48 0 E
Pioche, U.S.A. 115 H6 37 56N 114 27W
Piombino, Italy 28 F7 42 55N 10 32 E
Piombino, Canale di, Italy 28 F7 42 53N 10 30 E
Pioner, Ostrov, Russia 51 B10 79 50N 92 0 E
Pionki, Poland 45 G8 51 29N 21 28 E
Piorini, L., Brazil 124 D6 3 15 S 62 35W
Piotrków Trybunalski, Poland 45 G6 51 23N 19 43 E
Piove di Sacco, Italy 29 C9 45 18N 12 2 E
Pīp, Iran 71 E9 26 45N 60 10 E
Pipar, India 68 F5 26 25N 73 31 E
Pipar Road, India 68 F5 26 27N 73 27 E
Piparia, Mad. P., India 68 H8 22 45N 78 23 E
Piparia, Mad. P., India 68 J7 21 49N 77 37 E
Pipéri, Greece 38 B6 39 20N 24 19 E
Pipestone, U.S.A. 112 D6 44 0N 96 19W
Pipestone →, Canada 102 B2 52 53N 89 23W
Pipestone Cr. →, Canada 105 D8 49 38N 100 15W
Piplan, Pakistan 68 C4 32 17N 71 21 E
Piploda, India 68 H6 23 37N 74 56 E
Pipmuacan, Rés., Canada 103 C5 49 45N 70 30W
Pippingarra, Australia 92 D2 20 27 S 118 42 E
Pipriac, France 18 E5 47 59N 1 58W
Piqua, U.S.A. 108 E3 40 9N 84 15W
Piquiri →, Brazil 127 A5 24 3 S 54 14W
Pīr Sohrāb, Iran 71 E9 25 44N 60 54 E
Pira, Benin 83 D5 8 28N 1 48 E
Piracicaba, Brazil 127 A6 22 45 S 47 40W
Piracuruca, Brazil 125 D10 3 50 S 41 50W
Piræus = Piraiévs, Greece 38 D5 37 57N 23 42 E
Piraiévs, Greece 38 D5 37 57N 23 42 E
Pirajuí, Brazil 127 A6 21 59 S 49 29W
Piram I., India 68 J5 21 36N 72 21 E
Piran, Slovenia 29 C10 45 31N 13 33 E
Pirané, Argentina 126 B4 25 42 S 59 6W
Pirano = Piran, Slovenia 29 C10 45 31N 13 33 E
Pirapora, Brazil 125 G10 17 20 S 44 56W
Pirawa, India 68 G7 24 10N 76 2 E
Pirdop, Bulgaria 41 D8 42 40N 24 10 E
Pírgos, Ilía, Greece 38 D3 37 40N 21 27 E
Pírgos, Kríti, Greece 39 F7 35 0N 25 9 E
Pirgovo, Bulgaria 41 C9 43 44N 25 43 E
Piribebuy, Paraguay 126 B4 25 26 S 57 2W
Pirimapun, Indonesia 63 F9 6 45 S 138 0 E
Pirin Planina, Bulgaria 40 E7 41 40N 23 30 E
Pírineos = Pyrénées, Europe 20 F4 42 45N 0 18 E
Piripiri, Brazil 125 D10 4 15 S 41 46W
Pirmasens, Germany 25 F3 49 12N 7 36 E
Pirna, Germany 24 E9 50 57N 13 56 E
Pirot, Serbia, Yug. 40 C6 43 9N 22 33 E
Piru, Indonesia 63 E7 3 4 S 128 12 E
Piru, U.S.A. 117 L8 34 25N 118 48W
Piryatin = Pyryatyn, Ukraine 47 G7 50 15N 32 25 E
Piryí, Greece 39 C7 38 13N 25 59 E
Pisa, Italy 28 E7 43 43N 10 23 E
Pisa →, Poland 45 E8 53 14N 21 52 E
Pisagne, Italy 28 C7 45 45N 10 10 E
Pisagua, Chile 124 G4 19 40 S 70 15W
Pisarovina, Croatia 29 C12 45 35N 15 50 E
Pisco, Peru 124 F3 13 50 S 76 12W
Piscu, Romania 43 E12 45 30N 27 43 E
Písek, Czech Rep. 26 B7 49 19N 14 10 E
Pishan, China 60 C2 37 30N 78 33 E
Pīshīn, Iran 71 E9 26 6N 61 47 E
Pishin, Pakistan 68 D2 30 35N 67 0 E
Pishin Lora →, Pakistan 68 E1 29 9N 64 5 E
Pisidia, Turkey 72 D4 37 30N 31 40 E
Pising, Indonesia 63 F6 5 8 S 121 53 E
Pismo Beach, U.S.A. 117 K6 35 9N 120 38W
Piso, L., Liberia 82 D2 6 50N 11 15W
Pissila, Burkina Faso 83 C4 13 7N 0 50W
Pissis, Cerro, Argentina 126 B2 27 45 S 68 48W
Pissos, France 20 D3 44 19N 0 49W
Pissouri, Cyprus 36 E11 34 40N 32 42 E
Pisticci, Italy 31 B9 40 23N 16 33 E
Pistóia, Italy 28 E7 43 55N 10 54 E
Pistol B., Canada 105 A10 62 25N 92 37W
Pisuerga →, Spain 34 D6 41 33N 4 52W
Pisz, Poland 44 E8 53 38N 21 49 E
Pit →, U.S.A. 114 F2 40 47N 122 6W
Pita, Guinea 82 C2 11 5N 12 15W
Pitarpunga, L., Australia 95 E3 34 24 S 143 30 E
Pitcairn I., Pac. Oc. 97 K14 25 5 S 130 5W
Pite älv →, Sweden 8 D19 65 20N 21 25 E
Piteå, Sweden 8 D19 65 20N 21 25 E
Piterka, Russia 48 E8 50 41N 47 29 E
Piteşti, Romania 43 F9 44 52N 24 54 E
Pithapuram, India 67 L13 17 10N 82 15 E
Pithara, Australia 93 F2 30 20 S 116 35 E
Píthion, Greece 41 E10 41 24N 26 40 E
Pithiviers, France 19 D9 48 10N 2 13 E
Pithoragarh, India 69 E9 29 35N 80 13 E
Pithoro, Pakistan 68 G3 25 31N 69 23 E
Pitigliano, Italy 29 F8 42 38N 11 40 E
Pitkyaranta, Russia 46 B6 61 34N 31 37 E
Pitlochry, U.K. 14 E5 56 42N 3 44W
Pitsilia □, Cyprus 36 E12 34 55N 33 0 E
Pitt I., Canada 104 C3 53 30N 129 50W
Pittsburg, Calif., U.S.A. 116 G5 38 2N 121 53W
Pittsburg, Kans., U.S.A. 113 G7 37 25N 94 42W
Pittsburg, Tex., U.S.A. 113 J7 33 0N 94 59W
Pittsburgh, U.S.A. 110 F5 40 26N 80 1W
Pittsfield, Ill., U.S.A. 112 F9 39 36N 90 49W
Pittsfield, Maine, U.S.A. 109 C11 44 47N 69 23W
Pittsfield, Mass., U.S.A. 111 D11 42 27N 73 15W
Pittsfield, N.H., U.S.A. 111 C13 43 18N 71 20W
Pittston, U.S.A. 111 E9 41 19N 75 47W
Pittsworth, Australia 95 D5 27 41 S 151 37 E
Pituri →, Australia 94 C2 22 35 S 138 30 E
Piura, Peru 124 E2 5 15 S 80 38W
Piva →, Montenegro, Yug. 40 C2 43 20N 18 50 E
Piwniczna, Poland 45 J7 49 27N 20 42 E
Pixley, U.S.A. 116 K7 35 58N 119 18W
Piyai, Greece 38 B3 39 17N 21 25 E
Pizarra, Spain 35 J6 36 36N 4 42W
Pizhou, China 56 G9 34 44N 116 55 E
Pizzo, Italy 31 D9 38 44N 16 10 E
Placentia, Canada 103 C9 47 20N 54 0W
Placentia B., Canada 103 C9 47 0N 54 40W
Placer, Masbate, Phil. 61 F5 11 52N 123 55 E
Placer, Surigao N., Phil. 61 G6 9 36N 125 38 E
Placerville, U.S.A. 116 G6 38 44N 120 48W
Placetas, Cuba 120 B4 22 15N 79 44W
Plačkovica, Macedonia 40 E6 41 45N 22 30 E
Plainfield, N.J., U.S.A. 111 F10 40 37N 74 25W
Plainfield, Ohio, U.S.A. 110 F3 40 13N 81 43W
Plainfield, Vt., U.S.A. 111 B12 44 17N 72 26W
Plains, Mont., U.S.A. 114 C6 47 28N 114 53W
Plains, Tex., U.S.A. 113 J3 33 11N 102 50W
Plainview, Nebr., U.S.A. 112 D6 42 21N 97 47W
Plainview, Tex., U.S.A. 113 H4 34 11N 101 43W
Plainwell, U.S.A. 108 D3 42 27N 85 38W
Plaisance, France 20 E4 43 36N 0 3 E
Plaistow, U.S.A. 111 D13 42 50N 71 6W
Pláka, Greece 39 B7 40 0N 25 24 E
Pláka, Ákra, Greece 36 D8 35 11N 26 19 E
Plakenska Planina, Macedonia 40 E5 41 14N 21 2 E
Planá, Czech Rep. 26 B5 49 50N 12 44 E
Plana Cays, Bahamas 121 B5 22 38N 73 30W
Planada, U.S.A. 116 H6 37 16N 120 19W
Plancoët, France 18 D4 48 32N 2 13W
Plandište, Serbia, Yug. 42 E6 45 16N 21 10 E
Plano, U.S.A. 113 J6 33 1N 96 42W
Plant City, U.S.A. 109 M4 28 1N 82 7W
Plaquemine, U.S.A. 113 K9 30 17N 91 14W
Plasencia, Spain 34 E4 40 3N 6 8W
Plaški, Croatia 29 C12 45 4N 15 22 E
Plaster City, U.S.A. 117 N11 32 47N 115 51W
Plaster Rock, Canada 103 C6 46 53N 67 22W
Plastun, Russia 54 B8 44 45N 136 19 E
Plasy, Czech Rep. 26 B6 49 56N 13 24 E
Plata, Río de la, S. Amer. 126 C4 34 45 S 57 30W
Plátani →, Italy 30 E6 37 23N 13 16 E
Plátanos, Greece 36 D5 35 28N 23 33 E
Plateau □, Nigeria 83 D6 8 30N 9 0 E
Platí, Ákra, Greece 41 F8 40 27N 24 0 E
Platte, U.S.A. 112 D5 43 23N 98 51W
Platte →, Mo., U.S.A. 112 F7 39 16N 94 50W
Platte →, Nebr., U.S.A. 112 E7 41 4N 95 53W
Platteville, U.S.A. 112 D9 42 44N 90 29W
Plattling, Germany 25 G8 48 46N 12 53 E
Plattsburgh, U.S.A. 111 B11 44 42N 73 28W
Plattsmouth, U.S.A. 112 E7 41 1N 95 53W
Plau, Germany 24 B8 53 27N 12 15 E
Plauen, Germany 24 E8 50 30N 12 8 E
Plauer See, Germany 24 B8 53 28N 12 17 E
Plav, Montenegro, Yug. 40 D3 42 38N 19 57 E
Plavinas, Latvia 9 H21 56 35N 25 46 E
Plavnica, Montenegro, Yug. 40 D3 42 20N 19 13 E
Plavno, Croatia 29 D13 44 9N 16 10 E
Plavsk, Russia 46 F9 53 40N 37 18 E
Playa Blanca, Canary Is. 37 F6 28 55N 13 37W
Playa Blanca Sur, Canary Is. 37 F6 28 51N 13 50W
Playa de las Americas, Canary Is. 37 F3 28 5N 16 43W
Playa de Mogán, Canary Is. 37 G4 27 48N 15 47W
Playa del Inglés, Canary Is. 37 G4 27 45N 15 33W
Playa Esmerelda, Canary Is. 37 F5 28 8N 14 16W
Playgreen L., Canada 105 C9 54 0N 98 15W
Pleasant Bay, Canada 103 C7 46 51N 60 48W
Pleasant Hill, U.S.A. 116 H4 37 57N 122 4W
Pleasant Mount, U.S.A. 111 E9 41 44N 75 26W
Pleasanton, Calif., U.S.A. 116 H5 37 39N 121 52W
Pleasanton, Tex., U.S.A. 113 L5 28 58N 98 29W
Pleasantville, N.J., U.S.A. 108 F8 39 24N 74 32W
Pleasantville, Pa., U.S.A. 110 E5 41 35N 79 34W
Pléaux, France 20 C6 45 8N 2 13 E
Plei Ku, Vietnam 64 F7 13 57N 108 0 E
Plélan-le-Grand, France 18 D4 48 0N 2 7W
Pléneuf-Val-André, France 18 D4 48 35N 2 32W
Plenita, Romania 43 F8 44 14N 23 10 E
Plenty →, Australia 94 C2 23 25 S 136 31 E
Plenty, B. of, N.Z. 91 G6 37 45 S 177 0 E
Plentywood, U.S.A. 112 A2 48 47N 104 34W
Plérin, France 18 D4 48 32N 2 46W
Plessisville, Canada 103 C5 46 14N 71 47W
Plestin-les-Grèves, France 18 D3 48 40N 3 39W
Pleszew, Poland 45 G4 51 53N 17 47 E
Pleternica, Croatia 42 E2 45 17N 17 48 E
Plétipi, L., Canada 103 B5 51 44N 70 6W
Pleven, Bulgaria 41 C8 43 26N 24 37 E
Plevlja, Montenegro, Yug. 40 C3 43 21N 19 21 E
Plevna, Canada 110 B8 44 58N 76 59W
Plješevica, Croatia 29 D12 44 45N 15 45 E
Ploaghe, Italy 30 B1 40 40N 8 45 E
Ploče, Croatia 29 E14 43 4N 17 26 E
Płock, Poland 45 F6 52 32N 19 40 E
Plöckenpass, Italy 29 B9 46 37N 12 57 E
Plöckenstein, Germany 25 G9 48 46N 13 51 E
Ploemeur, France 18 E3 47 44N 3 26W
Ploërmel, France 18 E4 47 55N 2 26W
Ploieşti, Romania 43 F11 44 57N 26 5 E
Plomárion, Greece 39 C8 38 59N 26 22 E
Plombières-les-Bains, France 19 E13 47 58N 6 27 E
Plomin, Croatia 29 C11 45 8N 14 10 E
Plön, Germany 24 A6 54 9N 10 24 E
Plonge, Lac la, Canada 105 B7 55 8N 107 20W
Płońsk, Poland 45 F7 52 37N 20 21 E
Plopeni, Romania 43 E10 45 4N 25 59 E
Plopişului, Munţii, Romania 42 C7 47 5N 22 30 E
Płoty, Poland 44 E2 53 48N 15 18 E
Plouaret, France 18 D3 48 37N 3 28W
Plouay, France 18 E3 47 55N 3 21W
Ploučnice →, Czech Rep. 26 A7 50 46N 14 13 E
Ploudalmézeau, France 18 D2 48 34N 4 41W
Plouescat, France 18 D2 48 39N 4 10W
Plougasnou, France 18 D3 48 42N 3 49W
Plougastel-Daoulas, France 18 D2 48 22N 4 17W
Plouguerneau, France 18 D2 48 36N 4 30W
Plouha, France 18 D4 48 41N 2 57W
Plouhinec, France 18 E2 48 0N 4 29W
Plovdiv, Bulgaria 41 D8 42 8N 24 44 E
Plovdiv □, Bulgaria 41 D8 42 15N 24 30 E
Plum, U.S.A. 110 F5 40 29N 79 47W
Plum I., U.S.A. 111 E12 41 11N 72 12W
Plumas, U.S.A. 116 F7 39 45N 120 4W
Plummer, U.S.A. 114 C5 47 20N 116 53W
Plumtree, Zimbabwe 87 G2 20 27 S 27 55 E

Plungė, Lithuania 9 J19 55 53N 21 59 E
Pluvigner, France 18 E3 47 46N 3 1W
Plymouth, U.K. 13 G3 50 22N 4 10W
Plymouth, Calif., U.S.A. 116 G6 38 29N 120 51W
Plymouth, Ind., U.S.A. 108 E2 41 21N 86 19W
Plymouth, Mass., U.S.A. 111 E14 41 57N 70 40W
Plymouth, N.C., U.S.A. 109 H7 35 52N 76 43W
Plymouth, N.H., U.S.A. 111 C13 43 46N 71 41W
Plymouth, Pa., U.S.A. 111 E9 41 14N 75 57W
Plymouth, Wis., U.S.A. 108 D2 43 45N 87 59W
Plynlimon = Pumlumon Fawr, U.K. 13 E4 52 28N 3 46W
Plyusa, Russia 46 C5 58 28N 29 27 E
Plyusa →, Russia 46 C5 59 4N 28 6 E
Plyussa = Plyusa, Russia 46 C5 58 28N 29 27 E
Plyussa → = Plyusa →, Russia 46 C5 59 4N 28 6 E
Plzeň, Czech Rep. 26 B6 49 45N 13 22 E
Pniewy, Poland 45 F3 52 31N 16 16 E
Pô, Burkina Faso 83 C4 11 14N 1 5W
Po →, Italy 29 D9 44 57N 12 4 E
Po, Foci del, Italy 29 D9 44 55N 12 30 E
Po Hai = Bo Hai, China 57 E10 39 0N 119 0 E
Pobé, Benin 83 D5 7 0N 2 56 E
Pobé, Burkina Faso 83 C4 13 53N 1 42W
Pobeda, Russia 51 C15 65 12N 146 12 E
Pobedy, Pik, Kyrgyzstan 50 E8 42 0N 79 58 E
Pobiedziska, Poland 45 F4 52 29N 17 11 E
Pobla de Segur, Spain 32 C5 42 15N 0 58 E
Pobladura del Valle, Spain 34 C5 42 6N 5 44W
Pobra de Trives, Spain 34 C3 42 20N 7 10W
Pocahontas, Ark., U.S.A. 113 G9 36 16N 90 58W
Pocahontas, Iowa, U.S.A. 112 D7 42 44N 94 40W
Pocatello, U.S.A. 114 E7 42 52N 112 27W
Počátky, Czech Rep. 26 B8 49 15N 15 14 E
Pochep, Russia 47 F7 52 58N 33 29 E
Pochinki, Russia 48 C7 54 41N 44 59 E
Pochinok, Russia 46 E7 54 28N 32 29 E
Pöchlarn, Austria 26 C8 48 12N 15 12 E
Pochutla, Mexico 119 D5 15 50N 96 31W
Pocito Casas, Mexico 118 B2 28 32N 111 6W
Pocking, Germany 25 G9 48 23N 13 19 E
Pocomoke City, U.S.A. 108 F8 38 5N 75 34W
Poços de Caldas, Brazil 127 A6 21 50 S 46 33W
Podbořany, Czech Rep. 26 A6 50 14N 13 25 E
Poddębice, Poland 45 G5 51 54N 18 58 E
Poděbrady, Czech Rep. 26 A8 50 9N 15 8 E
Podensac, France 20 D3 44 40N 0 22W
Podenzano, Italy 28 D6 44 57N 9 41 E
Podgorač, Croatia 42 E3 45 27N 18 13 E
Podgorica, Montenegro, Yug. 40 D3 42 30N 19 19 E
Podgorie, Albania 40 F4 40 49N 20 48 E
Podilska Vysochyna, Ukraine 47 H4 49 0N 28 0 E
Podkarpackie □, Poland 45 H9 50 0N 22 10 E
Podkova, Bulgaria 41 E9 41 24N 25 24 E
Podlapača, Croatia 29 D12 44 37N 15 47 E
Podlaskie □, Poland 45 E10 53 10N 23 0 E
Podoleni, Romania 43 D11 46 46N 26 39 E
Podolínec, Slovak Rep. 27 B13 49 16N 20 31 E
Podolsk, Russia 46 E9 55 25N 37 30 E
Podor, Senegal 82 B1 16 40N 15 2W
Podporozhye, Russia 46 B8 60 55N 34 2 E
Podu Iloaiei, Romania 43 C12 47 13N 27 16 E
Podu Turcului, Romania 43 D12 46 11N 27 25 E
Podujevo, Kosovo, Yug. 40 D5 42 54N 21 10 E
Poel, Germany 24 B6 54 0N 11 25 E
Pofadder, S. Africa 88 D2 29 10 S 19 22 E
Poggiardo, Italy 31 B11 40 3N 18 23 E
Poggibonsi, Italy 28 E8 43 28N 11 9 E
Póggio Mirteto, Italy 29 F9 42 16N 12 41 E
Pogoanele, Romania 43 F12 44 55N 27 0 E
Pogorzela, Poland 45 G4 51 50N 17 12 E
Pogradec, Albania 40 F4 40 54N 20 37 E
Pogradeci = Pogradec, Albania 40 F4 40 54N 20 37 E
Pogranitšnyi, Russia 54 B5 44 25N 131 24 E
Poh, Indonesia 63 E6 0 46 S 122 51 E
P'ohang, S. Korea 57 F15 36 1N 129 23 E
Pohjanmaa, Finland 8 E20 62 58N 22 50 E
Pohnpei, Micronesia 96 G7 6 55N 158 10 E
Pohorelá, Slovak Rep. 27 C13 48 50N 20 2 E
Pohořelice, Czech Rep. 27 C9 48 59N 16 31 E
Pohorje, Slovenia 29 B12 46 30N 15 20 E
Pohri, India 68 G6 25 32N 77 22 E
Poiana Mare, Romania 42 G8 43 57N 23 5 E
Poiana Ruscăi, Munții, Romania 42 E7 45 45N 22 25 E
Poiana Stampei, Romania 43 C10 47 19N 25 8 E
Poinsett, C., Antarctica 5 C8 65 42 S 113 18 E
Point Arena, U.S.A. 116 G3 38 55N 123 41W
Point Baker, U.S.A. 104 B2 56 21N 133 37W
Point Edward, Canada 102 D3 43 0N 82 30W
Point Hope, U.S.A. 100 B3 68 21N 166 47W
Point L., Canada 100 B8 65 15N 113 4W
Point Pedro, Sri Lanka 66 Q12 9 50N 80 15 E
Point Pleasant, N.J., U.S.A. 111 F10 40 5N 74 4W
Point Pleasant, W. Va., U.S.A. 108 F4 38 51N 82 8W
Pointe-à-Pitre, Guadeloupe 121 C7 16 10N 61 30W
Pointe-Claire, Canada 111 A11 45 26N 73 50W
Pointe-Gatineau, Canada 111 A9 45 28N 75 42W
Pointe-Noire, Congo 84 E2 4 48 S 11 53 E
Poio, Spain 34 C2 42 28N 8 41W
Poirino, Italy 28 D4 44 56N 7 48 E
Poisonbush Ra., Australia 92 D3 22 30 S 121 30 E
Poissonnier Pt., Australia 92 C2 19 57 S 119 10 E
Poitiers, France 18 F7 46 35N 0 20 E
Poitou, France 20 B3 46 40N 0 10W
Poitou-Charentes □, France 20 B4 46 10N 0 15 E
Poix-de-Picardie, France 19 C8 49 47N 1 58 E
Poix-Terron, France 19 C11 49 38N 4 38 E
Pojoaque, U.S.A. 115 J11 35 54N 106 1W
Pokaran, India 66 F7 27 0N 71 50 E
Pokataroo, Australia 95 D4 29 30 S 148 36 E
Pokhara, Nepal 69 E10 28 14N 83 58 E
Pokhvistnevo, Russia 48 D11 53 36N 52 0 E
Poko, Dem. Rep. of the Congo 86 B2 3 7N 26 52 E
Poko, Sudan 81 F3 5 41N 31 55 E
Pokrov, Russia 46 E10 55 55N 39 7 E
Pokrovsk = Engels, Russia 48 E8 51 28N 46 6 E
Pokrovsk, Russia 51 C13 61 29N 129 0 E
Pokrovskoye, Russia 47 J10 47 25N 38 54 E
Pola = Pula, Croatia 29 D10 44 54N 13 57 E
Pola, Russia 46 D7 57 55N 32 0 E
Pola de Allande, Spain 34 B4 43 16N 6 37W
Pola de Lena, Spain 34 B5 43 10N 5 49W
Pola de Siero, Spain 34 B5 43 24N 5 39W
Pola de Somiedo, Spain 34 B4 43 5N 6 15W
Polacca, U.S.A. 115 J8 35 50N 110 23W
Polan, Iran 71 E9 25 30N 61 10 E
Pol'ana, Slovak Rep. 27 C12 48 38N 19 29 E
Poland ■, Europe 45 G3 52 0N 20 0 E
Polanica-Zdrój, Poland 45 H3 50 24N 16 32 E
Połaniec, Poland 45 H8 50 26N 21 17 E
Polanów, Poland 44 D3 54 7N 16 41 E
Polar Bear Prov. Park, Canada 102 A2 55 0N 83 45W
Polatlı, Turkey 72 C5 39 36N 32 9 E
Polatsk, Belarus 46 E5 55 30N 28 50 E
Polcura, Chile 126 D1 37 17 S 71 43W
Połczyn-Zdrój, Poland 44 E3 53 47N 16 5 E
Polessk, Russia 9 J19 54 50N 21 8 E
Polesye = Pripet Marshes, Europe 47 F5 52 10N 28 10 E
Polgar, Hungary 42 C6 47 54N 21 6 E
Pŏlgyo-ri, S. Korea 57 G14 34 51N 127 21 E
Poli, Cameroon 83 C7 8 34N 13 15 E
Políaigos, Greece 38 E6 36 45N 24 38 E
Policastro, G. di, Italy 31 C8 40 0N 15 35 E
Police, Poland 44 E1 53 33N 14 33 E
Polička, Czech Rep. 27 B9 49 43N 16 15 E
Policoro, Italy 31 B9 40 13N 16 41 E
Polignano a Mare, Italy 31 A9 41 0N 17 13 E
Poligny, France 19 F12 46 50N 5 42 E
Políkhnitas, Greece 39 B8 39 6N 26 10 E
Polillo Is., Phil. 61 D4 14 56N 122 0 E
Polillo Strait, Phil. 61 D4 14 44N 121 51 E
Polis, Cyprus 36 D11 35 2N 32 26 E
Polístena, Italy 31 D9 38 24N 16 4 E
Políyiros, Greece 40 F7 40 23N 23 25 E
Polk, U.S.A. 110 E5 41 22N 79 56W
Polkowice, Poland 45 G3 51 29N 16 3 E
Polla, Italy 31 B8 40 31N 15 29 E
Pollachi, India 66 P10 10 35N 77 0 E
Pollença, Spain 37 B10 39 54N 3 1 E
Pollença, B. de, Spain 37 B10 39 53N 3 8 E
Póllica, Italy 31 B8 40 11N 15 3 E
Pollino, Mte., Italy 31 C9 39 55N 16 11 E
Polna, Russia 46 C5 58 31N 28 5 E
Polnovat, Russia 50 C7 63 50N 65 54 E
Pology, Ukraine 47 J9 47 29N 36 15 E
Polonne, Ukraine 47 G4 50 6N 27 30 E
Polonnoye = Polonne, Ukraine 47 G4 50 6N 27 30 E
Polski Trŭmbesh, Bulgaria 41 C9 43 20N 25 38 E
Polsko Kosovo, Bulgaria 41 C9 43 23N 25 38 E
Polson, U.S.A. 114 C6 47 41N 114 9W
Poltár, Slovak Rep. 27 C12 48 26N 19 48 E
Poltava, Ukraine 47 H8 49 35N 34 35 E
Põltsamaa, Estonia 9 G21 58 41N 25 58 E
Polunochnoye, Russia 50 C7 60 52N 60 25 E
Põlva, Estonia 9 G22 58 3N 27 3 E
Polynesia, Pac. Oc. 97 J11 10 0 S 162 0W
Polynésie française = French Polynesia ■, Pac. Oc. 97 K13 20 0 S 145 0W
Pomarance, Italy 28 E7 43 18N 10 52 E
Pomaro, Mexico 118 D4 18 20N 103 18W
Pombal, Portugal 34 F2 39 55N 8 40W
Pómbia, Greece 36 E6 35 0N 24 51 E
Pomene, Mozam. 89 C6 22 53 S 35 33 E
Pomeroy, Ohio, U.S.A. 108 F4 39 2N 82 2W
Pomeroy, Wash., U.S.A. 114 C5 46 28N 117 36W
Pomézia, Italy 30 A5 41 40N 12 30 E
Pomichna, Ukraine 47 H6 48 13N 31 36 E
Pomona, Australia 95 D5 26 22 S 152 52 E
Pomona, U.S.A. 117 L9 34 4N 117 45W
Pomorie, Bulgaria 41 D11 42 32N 27 41 E
Pomorskie □, Poland 44 D5 54 30N 18 0 E
Pomorskie, Pojezierze, Poland 44 E3 53 40N 16 37 E
Pomos, Cyprus 36 D11 35 9N 32 33 E
Pomos, C., Cyprus 36 D11 35 10N 32 33 E
Pompano Beach, U.S.A. 109 M5 26 14N 80 8W
Pompei, Italy 31 B7 40 45N 14 30 E
Pompey, France 19 D13 48 46N 6 6 E
Pompeys Pillar, U.S.A. 114 D10 45 59N 107 57W
Pompton Lakes, U.S.A. 111 F10 41 0N 74 17W
Ponape = Pohnpei, Micronesia 96 G7 6 55N 158 10 E
Ponask L., Canada 102 B1 54 0N 92 41W
Ponca, U.S.A. 112 D6 42 34N 96 43W
Ponca City, U.S.A. 113 G6 36 42N 97 5W
Ponce, Puerto Rico 121 C6 18 1N 66 37W
Ponchatoula, U.S.A. 113 K9 30 26N 90 26W
Poncheville, L., Canada 102 B4 50 10N 76 55W
Pond, U.S.A. 117 K7 35 43N 119 20W
Pond Inlet, Canada 101 A12 72 40N 77 0W
Pondicherry, India 66 P11 11 59N 79 50 E
Ponds, I. of, Canada 103 B8 53 27N 55 52W
Ponferrada, Spain 34 C4 42 32N 6 35W
Pongo, Wadi →, Sudan 81 F2 8 42N 27 40 E
Poniatowa, Poland 45 G9 51 11N 22 3 E
Poniec, Poland 45 G3 51 48N 16 50 E
Ponikva, Slovenia 29 B12 46 16N 15 26 E
Ponnani, India 66 P9 10 45N 75 59 E
Ponnyadaung, Burma 67 J19 22 0N 94 10 E
Ponoka, Canada 104 C6 52 42N 113 40W
Ponorogo, Indonesia 63 G14 7 52 S 111 27 E
Pons = Ponts, Spain 32 D6 41 55N 1 12 E
Pons, France 20 C3 45 35N 0 34W
Ponsul →, Portugal 34 F3 39 40N 7 31W
Pont-à-Mousson, France 19 D13 48 54N 6 1 E
Pont-Audemer, France 18 C7 49 21N 0 30 E
Pont-Aven, France 18 E3 47 51N 3 47W
Pont Canavese, Italy 28 C4 45 25N 7 36 E
Pont-d'Ain, France 19 F12 46 3N 5 21 E
Pont-de-Roide, France 19 E13 47 23N 6 45 E
Pont-de-Salars, France 20 D6 44 18N 2 44 E
Pont-de-Vaux, France 19 F11 46 26N 4 56 E
Pont-de-Veyle, France 19 F11 46 17N 4 53 E
Pont-du-Château, France 19 G10 45 47N 3 15 E
Pont-l'Abbé, France 18 E2 47 52N 4 15W
Pont-l'Évêque, France 18 C7 49 18N 0 11 E
Pont-St-Esprit, France 21 D8 44 16N 4 40 E
Pont-St-Martin, Italy 28 C4 45 36N 7 48 E
Pont-Ste-Maxence, France 19 C9 49 18N 2 35 E
Pont-sur-Yonne, France 19 D10 48 18N 3 10 E
Ponta do Sol, Madeira 37 D2 32 42N 17 7W
Ponta Grossa, Brazil 127 B5 25 7 S 50 10W
Ponta Pora, Brazil 127 A4 22 20 S 55 35W
Pontacq, France 20 E3 43 11N 0 8W
Pontailler-sur-Saône, France 19 E12 47 13N 5 25 E
Pontarlier, France 19 F13 46 54N 6 20 E
Pontassieve, Italy 29 E8 43 46N 11 26 E
Pontaumur, France 20 C6 45 52N 2 40 E
Pontcharra, France 21 C10 45 26N 6 1 E
Pontchartrain L., U.S.A. 113 K10 30 5N 90 5W
Pontchâteau, France 18 E4 47 25N 2 5W
Ponte da Barca, Portugal 34 D2 41 48N 8 25W
Ponte de Sor, Portugal 35 F2 39 17N 8 1W
Ponte dell'Ólio, Italy 28 D6 44 52N 9 39 E
Ponte di Legno, Italy 28 B7 46 16N 10 31 E
Ponte do Lima, Portugal 34 D2 41 46N 8 35W
Ponte do Pungué, Mozam. 87 F3 19 30 S 34 33 E
Ponte-Leccia, France 21 F13 42 28N 9 13 E
Ponte nelle Alpi, Italy 29 B9 46 11N 12 16 E
Ponte Nova, Brazil 127 A7 20 25 S 42 54W
Ponteareas, Spain 34 C2 42 10N 8 28W
Pontebba, Italy 29 B10 46 30N 13 18 E
Ponteceso, Spain 34 B2 43 15N 8 54W
Pontecorvo, Italy 30 A6 41 27N 13 40 E
Pontedeume, Spain 34 B2 43 24N 8 10W
Ponteix, Canada 105 D7 49 46N 107 29W
Pontevedra, Spain 34 C2 42 26N 8 40W
Pontevedra □, Spain 34 C2 42 25N 8 39W
Pontevedra, R. de →, Spain 34 C2 42 22N 8 45W
Pontevico, Italy 28 C7 45 16N 10 5 E
Pontiac, Ill., U.S.A. 112 E10 40 53N 88 38W
Pontiac, Mich., U.S.A. 108 D4 42 38N 83 18W
Pontian Kecil, Malaysia 65 M4 1 29N 103 23 E
Pontianak, Indonesia 62 E3 0 3 S 109 15 E
Pontine Is. = Ponziane, Ísole, Italy 30 B5 40 55N 12 57 E
Pontine Mts. = Kuzey Anadolu Dağları, Turkey 72 B7 41 30N 35 0 E
Pontínia, Italy 30 A6 41 25N 13 2 E
Pontivy, France 18 D4 48 5N 2 58W
Pontoise, France 19 C9 49 3N 2 5 E
Ponton →, Canada 104 B5 58 27N 116 11W
Pontorson, France 18 D5 48 34N 1 30W
Pontrémoli, Italy 28 D6 44 22N 9 53 E
Pontrieux, France 18 D3 48 42N 3 10W
Ponts, Spain 32 D6 41 55N 1 12 E
Pontypool, Canada 110 B6 44 6N 78 38W
Pontypool, U.K. 13 F4 51 42N 3 2W
Ponza, Italy 30 B5 40 54N 12 58 E
Ponziane, Ísole, Italy 30 B5 40 55N 12 57 E
Poochera, Australia 95 E1 32 43 S 134 51 E
Poole, U.K. 13 G6 50 43N 1 59W
Poole □, U.K. 13 G6 50 43N 1 59W
Poona = Pune, India 66 K8 18 29N 73 57 E
Pooncarie, Australia 95 E3 33 22 S 142 31 E
Poopelloe L., Australia 95 E3 31 40 S 144 0 E
Poopó, L. de, Bolivia 122 E4 18 30 S 67 35W
Popayán, Colombia 124 C3 2 27N 76 36W
Poperinge, Belgium 17 D2 50 51N 2 42 E
Popilta L., Australia 95 E3 33 10 S 141 42 E
Popina, Bulgaria 41 B10 44 7N 26 57 E
Popio L., Australia 95 E3 33 10 S 141 52 E
Poplar, U.S.A. 112 A2 48 7N 105 12W
Poplar →, Canada 105 C9 53 0N 97 19W
Poplar Bluff, U.S.A. 113 G9 36 46N 90 24W
Poplarville, U.S.A. 113 K10 30 51N 89 32W
Popocatépetl, Volcán, Mexico 119 D5 19 2N 98 38W
Popokabaka, Dem. Rep. of the Congo 84 F3 5 41 S 16 40 E
Pópoli, Italy 29 F10 42 10N 13 50 E
Popovača, Croatia 29 C13 45 30N 16 41 E
Popovo, Bulgaria 41 C10 43 21N 26 18 E
Poppberg, Germany 25 F7 49 26N 11 37 E
Poppi, Italy 29 E8 43 43N 11 46 E
Poprad, Slovak Rep. 27 B13 49 3N 20 18 E
Poprad →, Slovak Rep. 27 B13 49 38N 20 42 E
Porali →, Pakistan 68 G2 25 58N 66 26 E
Porbandar, India 66 J6 21 44N 69 43 E
Porcher I., Canada 104 C2 53 50N 130 30W
Porcuna, Spain 35 H6 37 52N 4 11W
Porcupine →, Canada 105 B8 59 11N 104 46W
Porcupine →, U.S.A. 100 B5 66 34N 145 19W
Pordenone, Italy 29 C9 45 57N 12 39 E
Pordim, Bulgaria 41 C8 43 23N 24 51 E
Poreč, Croatia 29 C10 45 14N 13 36 E
Poretskoye, Russia 48 C8 55 9N 46 21 E
Pori, Finland 9 F19 61 29N 21 48 E
Porí, Greece 38 F5 35 58N 23 13 E
Porkhov, Russia 46 D5 57 45N 29 38 E
Porlamar, Venezuela 124 A6 10 57N 63 51W
Porlezza, Italy 28 B6 46 2N 9 7 E
Porma →, Spain 34 C5 42 49N 5 28W
Pornic, France 18 E4 47 7N 2 5W
Poronaysk, Russia 51 E15 49 13N 143 0 E
Póros, Greece 38 D5 37 30N 23 30 E
Poroshiri-Dake, Japan 54 C11 42 41N 142 52 E
Poroszló, Hungary 42 C5 47 39N 20 40 E
Poroto Mts., Tanzania 87 D3 9 0 S 33 30 E
Porpoise B., Antarctica 5 C9 66 0 S 127 0 E
Porquerolles, Î. de, France 21 F10 43 0N 6 13 E
Porrentruy, Switz. 25 H3 47 25N 7 6 E
Porreres, Spain 37 B10 39 31N 3 2 E
Porsangen, Norway 8 A21 70 40N 25 40 E
Porsgrunn, Norway 9 G13 59 10N 9 40 E
Port Alberni, Canada 104 D4 49 14N 124 50W
Port Alfred, S. Africa 88 E4 33 36 S 26 55 E
Port Alice, Canada 104 C3 50 20N 127 25W
Port Allegany, U.S.A. 110 E6 41 48N 78 17W
Port Allen, U.S.A. 113 K9 30 27N 91 12W
Port Alma, Australia 94 C5 23 38 S 150 53 E
Port Angeles, U.S.A. 116 B3 48 7N 123 27W
Port Antonio, Jamaica 120 C4 18 10N 76 30W
Port Aransas, U.S.A. 113 M6 27 50N 97 4W
Port Arthur = Lüshun, China 57 E11 38 45N 121 15 E
Port Arthur, Australia 94 G4 43 7 S 147 50 E
Port Arthur, U.S.A. 113 L8 29 54N 93 56W
Port au Choix, Canada 103 B8 50 43N 57 22W
Port au Port B., Canada 103 C8 48 40N 58 50W
Port-au-Prince, Haiti 121 C5 18 40N 72 20W
Port Augusta, Australia 95 E2 32 30 S 137 50 E
Port Austin, U.S.A. 110 B2 44 3N 83 1W
Port Bell, Uganda 86 B3 0 18N 32 35 E
Port Bergé Vaovao, Madag. 89 B8 15 33 S 47 40 E
Port Blandford, Canada 103 C9 48 20N 54 10W
Port-Bouët, Ivory C. 82 D4 5 16N 3 57W
Port Bradshaw, Australia 94 A2 12 30 S 137 20 E
Port Broughton, Australia 95 E2 33 37 S 137 56 E
Port Burwell, Canada 110 D4 42 40N 80 48W
Port Campbell, Australia 95 F3 38 37 S 143 1 E
Port Canning, India 69 H13 22 23N 88 40 E
Port-Cartier, Canada 103 B6 50 2N 66 50W
Port Chalmers, N.Z. 91 L3 45 49 S 170 30 E
Port Charlotte, U.S.A. 109 M4 26 59N 82 6W
Port Chester, U.S.A. 111 F11 41 0N 73 40W
Port Clements, Canada 104 C2 53 40N 132 10W
Port Clinton, U.S.A. 108 E4 41 31N 82 56W
Port Colborne, Canada 102 D4 42 50N 79 10W
Port Coquitlam, Canada 104 D4 49 15N 122 45W
Port Credit, Canada 110 C5 43 33N 79 35W
Port Curtis, Australia 94 C5 23 57 S 151 20 E
Port d'Alcúdia, Spain 37 B10 39 50N 3 7 E
Port Dalhousie, Canada 110 C5 43 13N 79 16W
Port Darwin, Australia 92 B5 12 24 S 130 45 E
Port Darwin, Falk. Is. 128 G5 51 50 S 59 0W
Port Davey, Australia 94 G4 43 16 S 145 55 E
Port-de-Bouc, France 21 E8 43 24N 4 59 E
Port-de-Paix, Haiti 121 C5 19 50N 72 50W
Port de Pollença, Spain 37 B10 39 54N 3 4 E
Port de Sóller, Spain 37 B9 39 48N 2 42 E
Port Dickson, Malaysia 65 L3 2 30N 101 49 E
Port Douglas, Australia 94 B4 16 30 S 145 30 E
Port Dover, Canada 110 D4 42 47N 80 12W
Port Edward, Canada 104 C2 54 12N 130 10W
Port Elgin, Canada 102 D3 44 25N 81 25W
Port Elizabeth, S. Africa 88 E4 33 58 S 25 40 E
Port Ellen, U.K. 14 F2 55 38N 6 11W
Port-en-Bessin, France 18 C6 49 21N 0 45W
Port Erin, U.K. 12 C3 54 5N 4 45W
Port Essington, Australia 92 B5 11 15 S 132 10 E
Port Etienne = Nouâdhibou, Mauritania 78 D2 20 54N 17 0W
Port Ewen, U.S.A. 111 E11 41 54N 73 59W
Port Fairy, Australia 95 F3 38 22 S 142 12 E
Port Fouâd = Bûr Fuad, Egypt 80 H8 31 15N 32 20 E
Port Gamble, U.S.A. 116 C4 47 51N 122 35W
Port-Gentil, Gabon 84 E1 0 40 S 8 50 E
Port Germein, Australia 95 E2 33 1 S 138 1 E
Port Gibson, U.S.A. 113 K9 31 58N 90 59W
Port Glasgow, U.K. 14 F4 55 56N 4 41W
Port Harcourt, Nigeria 83 E6 4 40N 7 10 E
Port Hardy, Canada 104 C3 50 41N 127 30W
Port Harrison = Inukjuak, Canada 101 C12 58 25N 78 15W
Port Hawkesbury, Canada 103 C7 45 36N 61 22W
Port Hedland, Australia 92 D2 20 25 S 118 35 E
Port Henry, U.S.A. 111 B11 44 3N 73 28W
Port Hood, Canada 103 C7 46 0N 61 32W
Port Hope, Canada 102 D4 43 56N 78 20W
Port Hope, U.S.A. 110 C2 43 57N 82 43W
Port Hope Simpson, Canada 103 B8 52 33N 56 18W
Port Hueneme, U.S.A. 117 L7 34 7N 119 12W
Port Huron, U.S.A. 110 D2 42 58N 82 26W
Port Iliç, Azerbaijan 73 C13 38 53N 48 47 E
Port Jefferson, U.S.A. 111 F11 40 57N 73 3W
Port Jervis, U.S.A. 111 E10 41 22N 74 41W
Port-Joinville, France 18 F4 46 45N 2 23W
Port Katon, Russia 47 J10 46 52N 38 46 E
Port Kelang = Pelabuhan Kelang, Malaysia 65 L3 3 0N 101 23 E
Port Kenny, Australia 95 E1 33 10 S 134 41 E
Port-la-Nouvelle, France 20 E7 43 1N 3 3 E
Port Lairge = Waterford, Ireland 15 D4 52 15N 7 8W
Port Laoise, Ireland 15 C4 53 2N 7 18W
Port Lavaca, U.S.A. 113 L6 28 37N 96 38W
Port Leyden, U.S.A. 111 C9 43 35N 75 21W
Port Lincoln, Australia 95 E2 34 42 S 135 52 E
Port Loko, S. Leone 82 D2 8 48N 12 46W
Port Louis, France 18 E3 47 42N 3 22W
Port Louis, Mauritius 77 H9 20 10 S 57 30 E
Port Lyautey = Kenitra, Morocco 78 B4 34 15N 6 40W
Port MacDonnell, Australia 95 F3 38 5 S 140 48 E
Port McNeill, Canada 104 C3 50 35N 127 6W
Port Macquarie, Australia 95 E5 31 25 S 152 25 E
Port Maria, Jamaica 120 C4 18 25N 76 55W
Port Matilda, U.S.A. 110 F6 40 48N 78 3W
Port Mellon, Canada 104 D4 49 32N 123 31W
Port-Menier, Canada 103 C7 49 51N 64 15W
Port Moody, Canada 116 A4 49 17N 122 51W
Port Morant, Jamaica 120 C4 17 54N 76 19W
Port Moresby, Papua N. G. 96 H6 9 24 S 147 8 E
Port Musgrave, Australia 94 A3 11 55 S 141 50 E
Port-Navalo, France 18 E4 47 34N 2 54W
Port Neches, U.S.A. 113 L8 30 0N 93 59W
Port Nolloth, S. Africa 88 D2 29 17 S 16 52 E
Port Nouveau-Québec = Kangiqsualujjuaq, Canada 101 C13 58 30N 65 59W
Port of Spain, Trin. & Tob. 121 D7 10 40N 61 31W
Port Orange, U.S.A. 109 L5 29 9N 80 59W
Port Orchard, U.S.A. 116 C4 47 32N 122 38W
Port Orford, U.S.A. 114 E1 42 45N 124 30W
Port Pegasus, N.Z. 91 M1 47 12 S 167 41 E
Port Perry, Canada 102 D4 44 6N 78 56W
Port Phillip B., Australia 95 F3 38 10 S 144 50 E
Port Pirie, Australia 95 E2 33 10 S 138 1 E
Port Radium = Echo Bay, Canada 100 B8 66 5N 117 55W
Port Renfrew, Canada 104 D4 48 30N 124 20W
Port Roper, Australia 94 A2 14 45 S 135 25 E
Port Rowan, Canada 110 D4 42 40N 80 30W
Port Safaga = Bûr Safâga, Egypt 70 E2 26 43N 33 57 E
Port Said = Bûr Sa'îd, Egypt 80 H8 31 16N 32 18 E
Port St. Joe, U.S.A. 109 L3 29 49N 85 18W
Port St. Johns = Umzimvubu, S. Africa 89 E4 31 38 S 29 33 E
Port-St-Louis-du-Rhône, France 21 E8 43 23N 4 49 E
Port St. Lucie, U.S.A. 109 M5 27 20N 80 20W
Port-Ste-Marie, France 20 D4 44 15N 0 25 E
Port Sanilac, U.S.A. 110 C2 43 26N 82 33W
Port Severn, Canada 110 B5 44 48N 79 43W
Port Shepstone, S. Africa 89 E5 30 44 S 30 28 E
Port Simpson, Canada 104 C2 54 30N 130 20W
Port Stanley = Stanley, Falk. Is. 128 G5 51 40 S 59 51W
Port Stanley, Canada 102 D3 42 40N 81 10W
Port Sudan = Bûr Sûdân, Sudan 80 D4 19 32N 37 9 E
Port Sulphur, U.S.A. 113 L10 29 29N 89 42W
Port-sur-Saône, France 19 E13 47 42N 6 2 E
Port Talbot, U.K. 13 F4 51 35N 3 47W
Port Taufiq = Bûr Taufiq, Egypt 80 J8 29 54N 32 32 E
Port Townsend, U.S.A. 116 B4 48 7N 122 45W
Port-Vendres, France 20 F7 42 32N 3 8 E
Port Vila, Vanuatu 96 J8 17 45 S 168 18 E
Port Wakefield, Australia 95 E2 34 12 S 138 10 E
Port Washington, U.S.A. 108 D2 43 23N 87 53W
Port Weld = Kuala Sepetang, Malaysia 65 K3 4 49N 100 28 E
Portadown, U.K. 15 B5 54 25N 6 27W
Portaferry, U.K. 15 B6 54 23N 5 33W
Portage, Pa., U.S.A. 110 F6 40 23N 78 41W
Portage, Wis., U.S.A. 112 D10 43 33N 89 28W
Portage La Prairie, Canada 105 D9 49 58N 98 18W
Portageville, U.S.A. 113 G10 36 26N 89 42W
Portalegre, Portugal 35 F3 39 19N 7 25W
Portalegre □, Portugal 35 F3 39 20N 7 40W
Portales, U.S.A. 113 H3 34 11N 103 20W
Portarlington, Ireland 15 C4 53 9N 7 14W
Portbou, Spain 32 C8 42 25N 3 9 E
Portel, Portugal 35 G3 38 19N 7 41W
Porter L., N.W.T., Canada 105 A7 61 41N 108 5W
Porter L., Sask., Canada 105 B7 56 20N 107 20W
Porterville, S. Africa 88 E2 33 0 S 19 0 E
Porterville, U.S.A. 116 J8 36 4N 119 1W
Portes-lès-Valence, France 21 D8 44 52N 4 54 E
Porthcawl, U.K. 13 F4 51 29N 3 42W
Porthill, U.S.A. 114 B5 48 59N 116 30W
Porthmadog, U.K. 12 E3 52 55N 4 8W
Portile de Fier, Europe 42 F7 44 44N 22 30 E
Portimão, Portugal 35 H2 37 8N 8 32W
Portishead, U.K. 13 F5 51 29N 2 46W
Portitei, Gura, Romania 43 F14 44 41N 29 0 E
Portknockie, U.K. 14 D6 57 42N 2 51W
Portland, N.S.W., Australia 95 E5 33 20 S 150 0 E
Portland, Vic., Australia 95 F3 38 20 S 141 35 E
Portland, Canada 111 B8 44 42N 76 12W
Portland, Conn., U.S.A. 111 E12 41 34N 72 38W
Portland, Maine, U.S.A. 101 D12 43 39N 70 16W
Portland, Mich., U.S.A. 108 D3 42 52N 84 54W
Portland, Oreg., U.S.A. 116 E4 45 32N 122 37W
Portland, Pa., U.S.A. 111 F9 40 55N 75 6W
Portland, Tex., U.S.A. 113 M6 27 53N 97 20W
Portland, I. of, U.K. 13 G5 50 33N 2 26W
Portland B., Australia 95 F3 38 15 S 141 45 E
Portland Bill, U.K. 13 G5 50 31N 2 28W
Portland Canal, U.S.A. 104 B2 55 56N 130 0W
Portmadoc = Porthmadog, U.K. 12 E3 52 55N 4 8W
Porto, France 21 F12 42 16N 8 42 E
Porto, Portugal 34 D2 41 8N 8 40W
Porto □, Portugal 34 D2 41 8N 8 20W
Porto, G. de, France 21 F12 42 17N 8 34 E
Pôrto Alegre, Brazil 127 C5 30 5 S 51 10W
Porto Amboim = Gunza, Angola 84 G2 10 50 S 13 50 E
Porto Azzurro, Italy 28 F7 42 46N 10 24 E
Porto Cristo, Spain 37 B10 39 33N 3 20 E
Pôrto de Móz, Brazil 125 D8 1 41 S 52 13W
Porto Empédocle, Italy 30 E6 37 17N 13 32 E
Pôrto Esperança, Brazil 124 G7 19 37 S 57 29W
Pôrto Franco, Brazil 125 E9 6 20 S 47 24W
Pórto Lágos, Greece 41 E9 41 1N 25 6 E
Porto Mendes, Brazil 127 A5 24 30 S 54 15W
Porto Moniz, Madeira 37 D2 32 52N 17 11W
Pôrto Murtinho, Brazil 124 H7 21 45 S 57 55W
Pôrto Nacional, Brazil 125 F9 10 40 S 48 30W
Porto-Novo, Benin 83 D5 6 23N 2 42 E
Porto Petro, Spain 37 B10 39 22N 3 13 E
Porto San Giórgio, Italy 29 E10 43 11N 13 48 E
Porto Sant' Elpídio, Italy 29 E10 43 15N 13 43 E
Porto Santo, Madeira 78 B2 33 45N 16 25W
Porto Santo Stéfano, Italy 28 F8 42 26N 11 7 E
Pôrto São José, Brazil 127 A5 22 43 S 53 10W
Pôrto Seguro, Brazil 125 G11 16 26 S 39 5W
Porto Tolle, Italy 29 D9 44 56N 12 22 E
Porto Tórres, Italy 30 B1 40 50N 8 24 E
Pôrto União, Brazil 127 B5 26 10 S 51 10W
Pôrto Válter, Brazil 124 E4 8 15 S 72 40W
Porto-Vecchio, France 21 G13 41 35N 9 16 E
Pôrto Velho, Brazil 124 E6 8 46 S 63 54W
Portobelo, Panama 120 E4 9 35N 79 42W
Portoferráio, Italy 28 F7 42 48N 10 20 E
Portogruaro, Italy 29 C9 45 47N 12 50 E
Portola, U.S.A. 116 F6 39 49N 120 28W
Portomaggiore, Italy 29 D8 44 42N 11 48 E
Portoscuso, Italy 30 C1 39 12N 8 24 E
Portovénere, Italy 28 D6 44 3N 9 51 E
Portoviejo, Ecuador 124 D2 1 7 S 80 28W
Portpatrick, U.K. 14 G3 54 51N 5 7W
Portree, U.K. 14 D2 57 25N 6 12W
Portrush, U.K. 15 A5 55 12N 6 40W
Portsmouth, Domin. 121 C7 15 34N 61 27W
Portsmouth, U.K. 13 G6 50 48N 1 6W
Portsmouth, N.H., U.S.A. 109 D10 43 5N 70 45W
Portsmouth, Ohio, U.S.A. 108 F4 38 44N 82 57W
Portsmouth, R.I., U.S.A. 111 E13 41 36N 71 15W
Portsmouth, Va., U.S.A. 108 G7 36 50N 76 18W
Portsmouth □, U.K. 13 G6 50 48N 1 6W
Portsoy, U.K. 14 D6 57 41N 2 41W
Portstewart, U.K. 15 A5 55 11N 6 43W

Porttipahtan tekojärvi, Finland 8 B22 68 5N 26 40 E
Portugal ■, Europe 34 F3 40 0N 8 0W
Portugalete, Spain 32 B1 43 19N 3 4W
Portumna, Ireland 15 C3 53 6N 8 14W
Portville, U.S.A. 110 D6 42 3N 78 20W
Porvenir, Chile 128 G2 53 10 S 70 16W
Porvoo, Finland 9 F21 60 24N 25 40 E
Porzuna, Spain 35 F6 39 9N 4 9W
Posada, Italy 30 B2 40 38N 9 43 E
Posada →, Italy 30 B2 40 39N 9 45 E
Posadas, Argentina 127 B4 27 30 S 55 50W
Posadas, Spain 35 H5 37 47N 5 11W
Poschiavo, Switz. 25 J6 46 19N 10 4 E
Posets, Spain 32 C5 42 39N 0 25 E
Poshan = Boshan, China 57 F9 36 28N 117 49 E
Posht-e-Badam, Iran 71 C7 33 2N 55 23 E
Posídhion, Ákra, Greece 40 G7 39 57N 23 30 E
Posidium, Greece 39 F9 35 30N 27 10 E
Poso, Indonesia 63 E6 1 20 S 120 55 E
Posong, S. Korea 57 G14 34 46N 127 5 E
Posse, Brazil 125 F9 14 4 S 46 18W
Possession I., Antarctica 5 D11 72 4 S 172 0 E
Pössneck, Germany 24 E7 50 42N 11 35 E
Possum Kingdom L., U.S.A. 113 J5 32 52N 98 26W
Post, U.S.A. 113 J4 33 12N 101 23W
Post Falls, U.S.A. 114 C5 47 43N 116 57W
Postavy = Pastavy, Belarus 9 J22 55 4N 26 50 E
Poste-de-la-Baleine = Kuujjuarapik, Canada 102 A4 55 20N 77 35W
Postmasburg, S. Africa 88 D3 28 18 S 23 5 E
Postojna, Slovenia 29 C11 45 46N 14 12 E
Poston, U.S.A. 117 M12 34 0N 114 24W
Postville, Canada 103 B8 54 54N 59 47W
Potamós, Andikíthira, Greece 38 F5 35 52N 23 15 E
Potamós, Kíthira, Greece 38 E4 36 15N 22 58 E
Potchefstroom, S. Africa 88 D4 26 41 S 27 7 E
Potcoava, Romania 43 F9 44 30N 24 39 E
Poteau, U.S.A. 113 H7 35 3N 94 37W
Poteet, U.S.A. 113 L5 29 2N 98 35W
Potenza, Italy 31 B8 40 38N 15 48 E
Potenza →, Italy 29 E10 43 25N 13 40 E
Potenza Picena, Italy 29 E10 43 22N 13 37 E
Poteriteri, L., N.Z. 91 M1 46 5 S 167 10 E
Potgietersrus, S. Africa 89 C4 24 10 S 28 55 E
Poti, Georgia 49 J5 42 10N 41 38 E
Potiskum, Nigeria 83 C7 11 39N 11 2 E
Potlogi, Romania 43 F10 44 34N 25 34 E
Potomac →, U.S.A. 108 G7 38 0N 76 23W
Potosí, Bolivia 124 G5 19 38 S 65 50W
Potosi Mt., U.S.A. 117 K11 35 57N 115 29W
Pototan, Phil. 61 F5 10 54N 122 38 E
Potrerillos, Chile 126 B2 26 30 S 69 30W
Potsdam, Germany 24 C9 52 25N 13 4 E
Potsdam, U.S.A. 111 B10 44 40N 74 59W
Pottenstein, Germany 25 F7 49 46N 11 24 E
Pottersville, U.S.A. 111 C11 43 43N 73 50W
Pottery Hill = Abu Ballas, Egypt 80 C2 24 26N 27 36 E
Pottstown, U.S.A. 111 F9 40 15N 75 39W
Pottsville, U.S.A. 111 F8 40 41N 76 12W
Pottuvil, Sri Lanka 66 R12 6 55N 81 50 E
P'otzu, Taiwan 59 F13 23 30N 120 25 E
Pouancé, France 18 E5 47 44N 1 10W
Pouce Coupé, Canada 104 B4 55 40N 120 10W
Poughkeepsie, U.S.A. 111 E11 41 42N 73 56W
Pouilly-sur-Loire, France 19 E9 47 17N 2 57 E
Poulaphouca Res., Ireland 15 C5 53 8N 6 30W
Poulsbo, U.S.A. 116 C4 47 44N 122 39W
Poultney, U.S.A. 111 C11 43 31N 73 14W
Poulton-le-Fylde, U.K. 12 D5 53 51N 2 58W
Pouso Alegre, Brazil 127 A6 22 14 S 45 57W
Pout, Senegal 82 C1 14 45N 17 0W
Pouthisat, Cambodia 64 F4 12 34N 103 50 E
Pouzauges, France 18 F6 46 47N 0 50W
Pova de Sta. Iria, Portugal 35 G1 38 51N 9 4W
Považská Bystrica, Slovak Rep. 27 B11 49 8N 18 27 E
Poverty B., N.Z. 91 H7 38 43 S 178 2 E
Povlen, Serbia, Yug. 40 B3 44 9N 19 44 E
Póvoa de Lanhosa, Portugal 34 D2 41 33N 8 15W
Póvoa de Varzim, Portugal 34 D2 41 25N 8 46W
Povorino, Russia 48 E6 51 12N 42 5 E
Povungnituk = Puvirnituq, Canada 101 B12 60 2N 77 10W
Powassan, Canada 102 C4 46 5N 79 25W
Poway, U.S.A. 117 N9 32 58N 117 2W
Powder →, U.S.A. 112 B2 46 45N 105 26W
Powder River, U.S.A. 114 E10 43 2N 106 59W
Powell, U.S.A. 114 D9 44 45N 108 46W
Powell, L., U.S.A. 115 H8 36 57N 111 29W
Powell River, Canada 104 D4 49 50N 124 35W
Powers, U.S.A. 108 C2 45 41N 87 32W
Powys □, U.K. 13 E4 52 20N 3 20W
Poyang Hu, China 59 C11 29 5N 116 20 E
Poyarkovo, Russia 51 E13 49 36N 128 41 E
Poysdorf, Austria 27 C9 48 40N 16 37 E
Poza de la Sal, Spain 34 C7 42 35N 3 31W
Poza Rica, Mexico 119 C5 20 33N 97 27W
Pozanti, Turkey 72 D6 37 25N 34 50 E
Požarevac, Serbia, Yug. 40 B5 44 35N 21 18 E
Pozazal, Puerto, Spain 34 C6 42 56N 4 10W
Požega, Croatia 42 E2 45 20N 17 40 E
Požega, Serbia, Yug. 40 C4 43 53N 20 2 E
Poznań, Poland 45 F3 52 25N 16 55 E
Pozo, U.S.A. 117 K6 35 20N 120 24W
Pozo Alcón, Spain 35 H8 37 42N 2 56W
Pozo Almonte, Chile 124 H5 20 10 S 69 50W
Pozo Colorado, Paraguay 126 A4 23 30 S 58 45W
Pozoblanco, Spain 35 G6 38 23N 4 51W
Pozzallo, Italy 31 F7 36 43N 14 51 E
Pozzomaggiore, Italy 30 B1 40 24N 8 39 E
Pozzuoli, Italy 31 B7 40 49N 14 7 E
Pra →, Ghana 83 D4 5 1N 1 37W
Prabuty, Poland 44 E6 53 47N 19 15 E
Prača, Bos.-H. 42 G3 43 47N 18 43 E
Prachatice, Czech Rep. 26 B6 49 1N 14 0 E
Prachin Buri, Thailand 64 E3 14 0N 101 25 E
Prachuap Khiri Khan, Thailand 65 G2 11 49N 99 48 E
Pradelles, France 20 D7 44 46N 3 52 E
Prades, France 20 F6 42 38N 2 23 E
Prado, Brazil 125 G11 17 20 S 39 13W
Prado del Rey, Spain 35 J5 36 48N 5 33W
Præstø, Denmark 11 J6 55 8N 12 2 E
Pragersko, Slovenia 29 B12 46 27N 15 42 E
Prague = Praha, Czech Rep. 26 A7 50 5N 14 22 E
Praha, Czech Rep. 26 A7 50 5N 14 22 E
Prahecq, France 20 B3 46 19N 0 26W
Prahova □, Romania 43 E10 45 10N 26 0 E
Prahova →, Romania 43 F10 44 50N 25 50 E
Prahovo, Serbia, Yug. 40 B6 44 18N 22 39 E
Praia, C. Verde Is. 77 E1 14 55N 23 30W
Práia a Mare, Italy 31 C8 39 50N 15 45 E
Praid, Romania 43 D10 46 32N 25 10 E
Prainha, Amazonas, Brazil 124 E6 7 10 S 60 30W
Prainha, Pará, Brazil 125 D8 1 45 S 53 30W
Prairie, Australia 94 C3 20 50 S 144 35 E
Prairie City, U.S.A. 114 D4 44 28N 118 43W
Prairie Dog Town Fork →, U.S.A. 113 H5 34 30N 99 23W
Prairie du Chien, U.S.A. 112 D9 43 3N 91 9W
Prairies, L. of the, Canada 105 C8 51 16N 101 32W
Pramánda, Greece 38 B3 39 32N 21 8 E
Prampram, Ghana 83 D5 5 43N 0 8 E
Pran Buri, Thailand 64 F2 12 23N 99 55 E
Prang, Ghana 83 D4 8 1N 0 56W
Prapat, Indonesia 62 D1 2 41N 98 58 E
Prasonísi, Ákra, Greece 36 D9 35 42N 27 46 E
Prästmon, Sweden 10 A11 63 5N 17 45 E
Praszka, Poland 45 G5 51 5N 18 31 E
Prata, Brazil 125 G9 19 25 S 48 54W
Pratabpur, India 69 H10 23 28N 83 15 E
Pratapgarh, Raj., India 68 G6 24 2N 74 40 E
Pratapgarh, Ut. P., India 69 G9 25 56N 81 59 E
Prato, Italy 28 E8 43 53N 11 6 E
Prátola Peligna, Italy 29 F10 42 6N 13 52 E
Prats-de-Mollo-la-Preste, France 20 F6 42 25N 2 27 E
Pratt, U.S.A. 113 G5 37 39N 98 44W
Prattville, U.S.A. 109 J2 32 28N 86 29W
Pravdinsk, Russia 48 B6 56 29N 43 28 E
Pravets, Bulgaria 40 D7 42 53N 23 55 E
Pravia, Spain 34 B4 43 30N 6 12W
Praya, Indonesia 62 F5 8 39 S 116 17 E
Pré-en-Pail, France 18 D6 48 28N 0 12W
Precordillera, Argentina 126 C2 30 0 S 69 1W
Predáppio, Italy 29 D8 44 6N 11 59 E
Predazzo, Italy 29 B8 46 19N 11 36 E
Predeal, Romania 43 E10 45 30N 25 34 E
Predejane, Serbia, Yug. 40 D6 42 51N 22 9 E
Preeceville, Canada 105 C8 51 57N 102 40W
Preetz, Germany 24 A6 54 14N 10 18 E
Pregrada, Croatia 29 B12 46 11N 15 45 E
Preiļi, Latvia 9 H22 56 18N 26 43 E
Preko, Croatia 29 D12 44 7N 15 10 E
Prelog, Croatia 29 B13 46 18N 16 32 E
Prémery, France 19 E10 47 10N 3 18 E
Premià de Mar, Spain 32 D7 41 29N 2 22 E
Premont, U.S.A. 113 M5 27 22N 98 7W
Premuda, Croatia 29 D11 44 20N 14 36 E
Prenjasi = Prrenjas, Albania 40 E4 41 4N 20 32 E
Prentice, U.S.A. 112 C9 45 33N 90 17W
Prenzlau, Germany 24 B9 53 19N 13 50 E
Preobrazheniye, Russia 54 C6 42 54N 133 54 E
Preparis North Channel, Ind. Oc. 67 M18 15 12N 93 40 E
Preparis South Channel, Ind. Oc. 67 M18 14 36N 93 40 E
Přerov, Czech Rep. 27 B10 49 28N 17 27 E
Prescott, Canada 102 D4 44 45N 75 30W
Prescott, Ariz., U.S.A. 115 J7 34 33N 112 28W
Prescott, Ark., U.S.A. 113 J8 33 48N 93 23W
Prescott Valley, U.S.A. 115 J7 34 40N 112 18W
Preservation Inlet, N.Z. 91 M1 46 8 S 166 35 E
Preševo, Serbia, Yug. 40 D5 42 19N 21 39 E
Presho, U.S.A. 112 D4 43 54N 100 3W
Presicce, Italy 31 C11 39 54N 18 16 E
Presidencia de la Plaza, Argentina 126 B4 27 0 S 59 50W
Presidencia Roque Saenz Peña, Argentina 126 B3 26 45 S 60 30W
Presidente Epitácio, Brazil 125 H8 21 56 S 52 6W
Presidente Hayes □, Paraguay 126 A4 24 0 S 59 0W
Presidente Prudente, Brazil 127 A5 22 5 S 51 25W
Presidio, Mexico 118 B4 29 29N 104 23W
Presidio, U.S.A. 113 L2 29 34N 104 22W
Preslav, Bulgaria 41 C10 43 10N 26 52 E
Preslavska Planina, Bulgaria 41 C10 43 10N 26 45 E
Prešov, Slovak Rep. 27 B14 49 0N 21 15 E
Prešovský □, Slovak Rep. 27 B13 49 10N 21 0 E
Prespa, Bulgaria 41 E8 41 44N 24 55 E
Prespa, L. = Prespansko Jezero, Macedonia 40 F5 40 55N 21 0 E
Prespansko Jezero, Macedonia 40 F5 40 55N 21 0 E
Presque I., U.S.A. 110 D4 42 9N 80 6W
Presque Isle, U.S.A. 109 B12 46 41N 68 1W
Prestatyn, U.K. 12 D4 53 20N 3 24W
Prestea, Ghana 82 D4 5 22N 2 7W
Presteigne, U.K. 13 E5 52 17N 3 0W
Přeštice, Czech Rep. 26 B6 49 34N 13 20 E
Preston, Canada 110 C4 43 23N 80 21W
Preston, U.K. 12 D5 53 46N 2 42W
Preston, Idaho, U.S.A. 114 E8 42 6N 111 53W
Preston, Minn., U.S.A. 112 D8 43 40N 92 5W
Preston, C., Australia 92 D2 20 51 S 116 12 E
Prestonburg, U.S.A. 108 G4 37 39N 82 46W
Prestwick, U.K. 14 F4 55 29N 4 37W
Pretoria, S. Africa 89 D4 25 44 S 28 12 E
Preuilly-sur-Claise, France 18 F7 46 51N 0 56 E
Préveza, Greece 38 C2 38 57N 20 47 E
Préveza □, Greece 38 B2 39 10N 20 40 E
Prey Veng, Cambodia 65 G5 11 35N 105 29 E
Priazovskoye, Ukraine 47 J8 46 44N 35 40 E
Pribilof Is., U.S.A. 100 C2 57 0N 170 0W
Priboj, Serbia, Yug. 40 C3 43 35N 19 32 E
Příbram, Czech Rep. 26 B7 49 41N 14 2 E
Price, U.S.A. 114 G8 39 36N 110 49W
Price I., Canada 104 C3 52 23N 128 41W
Prichard, U.S.A. 109 K1 30 44N 88 5W
Priego, Spain 32 E2 40 26N 2 21W
Priego de Córdoba, Spain 35 H6 37 27N 4 12W
Priekule, Latvia 9 H19 56 26N 21 35 E
Prien, Germany 25 H8 47 51N 12 20 E
Prienai, Lithuania 9 J20 54 38N 23 57 E
Prieska, S. Africa 88 D3 29 40 S 22 42 E
Priest L., U.S.A. 114 B5 48 35N 116 52W
Priest River, U.S.A. 114 B5 48 10N 116 54W
Priest Valley, U.S.A. 116 J6 36 10N 120 39W
Prievidza, Slovak Rep. 27 C11 48 46N 18 36 E
Prignitz, Germany 24 B7 53 6N 11 45 E
Prijedor, Bos.-H. 29 D13 44 58N 16 41 E
Prijepolje, Serbia, Yug. 40 C3 43 27N 19 40 E
Prikaspiyskaya Nizmennost = Caspian Depression, Eurasia 49 G9 47 0N 48 0 E
Prikro, Ivory C. 82 D4 7 40N 3 59W
Prikubanskaya Nizmennost, Russia 49 H4 45 39N 38 33 E
Prilep, Macedonia 40 E5 41 21N 21 32 E
Priluki = Pryluky, Ukraine 47 G7 50 30N 32 24 E
Prime Seal I., Australia 94 G4 40 3 S 147 43 E
Primorsk, Russia 46 B5 60 22N 28 37 E
Primorsko, Bulgaria 41 D11 42 15N 27 44 E
Primorsko-Akhtarsk, Russia 47 J10 46 2N 38 10 E
Primorskoye, Ukraine 47 J9 46 48N 36 20 E
Primrose L., Canada 105 C7 54 55N 109 45W
Prince Albert, Canada 105 C7 53 15N 105 50W
Prince Albert, S. Africa 88 E3 33 12 S 22 2 E
Prince Albert Mts., Antarctica 5 D11 76 0 S 161 30 E
Prince Albert Nat. Park, Canada 105 C7 54 0N 106 25W
Prince Albert Pen., Canada 100 A8 72 30N 116 0W
Prince Albert Sd., Canada 100 A8 70 25N 115 0W
Prince Alfred, C., Canada 4 B1 74 20N 124 40W
Prince Charles I., Canada 101 B12 67 47N 76 12W
Prince Charles Mts., Antarctica 5 D6 72 0 S 67 0 E
Prince Edward I. □, Canada 103 C7 46 20N 63 20W
Prince Edward Is., Ind. Oc. 3 G11 46 35 S 38 0 E
Prince Edward Pt., Canada 110 C8 43 56N 76 52W
Prince George, Canada 104 C4 53 55N 122 50W
Prince of Wales, C., U.S.A. 98 C3 65 36N 168 5W
Prince of Wales I., Australia 94 A3 10 40 S 142 10 E
Prince of Wales I., Canada 100 A10 73 0N 99 0W
Prince of Wales I., U.S.A. 100 C6 55 47N 132 50W
Prince Patrick I., Canada 4 B2 77 0N 120 0W
Prince Regent Inlet, Canada 4 B3 73 0N 90 0W
Prince Rupert, Canada 104 C2 54 20N 130 20W
Princess Charlotte B., Australia 94 A3 14 25 S 144 0 E
Princess May Ranges, Australia 92 C4 15 30 S 125 30 E
Princess Royal I., Canada 104 C3 53 0N 128 40W
Princeton, Canada 104 D4 49 27N 120 30W
Princeton, Calif., U.S.A. 116 F4 39 24N 122 1W
Princeton, Ill., U.S.A. 112 E10 41 23N 89 28W
Princeton, Ind., U.S.A. 108 F2 38 21N 87 34W
Princeton, Ky., U.S.A. 108 G2 37 7N 87 53W
Princeton, Mo., U.S.A. 112 E8 40 24N 93 35W
Princeton, N.J., U.S.A. 111 F10 40 21N 74 39W
Princeton, W. Va., U.S.A. 108 G5 37 22N 81 6W
Principe, I. de, Atl. Oc. 76 F4 1 37N 7 27 E
Principe da Beira, Brazil 124 F6 12 20 S 64 30W
Prineville, U.S.A. 114 D3 44 18N 120 51W
Prins Harald Kyst, Antarctica 5 D4 70 0 S 35 1 E
Prinsesse Astrid Kyst, Antarctica 5 D3 70 45 S 12 30 E
Prinsesse Ragnhild Kyst, Antarctica 5 D4 70 15 S 27 30 E
Prinzapolca, Nic. 120 D3 13 20N 83 35W
Prior, C., Spain 34 B2 43 34N 8 17W
Priozersk, Russia 46 B6 61 2N 30 7 E
Pripet = Prypyat →, Europe 47 G6 51 20N 30 15 E
Pripet Marshes, Europe 47 F5 52 10N 28 10 E
Pripyat Marshes = Pripet Marshes, Europe 47 F5 52 10N 28 10 E
Pripyats = Prypyat →, Europe 47 G6 51 20N 30 15 E
Prislop, Pasul, Romania 43 C9 47 37N 24 48 E
Pristen, Russia 47 G9 51 15N 36 44 E
Priština, Kosovo, Yug. 40 D5 42 40N 21 13 E
Pritzwalk, Germany 24 B8 53 9N 12 10 E
Privas, France 21 D8 44 45N 4 37 E
Priverno, Italy 30 A6 41 28N 13 11 E
Privolzhsk, Russia 48 B5 57 23N 41 16 E
Privolzhskaya Vozvyshennost, Russia 48 E7 51 0N 46 0 E
Privolzhskiy, Russia 48 E8 51 25N 46 3 E
Privolzhye, Russia 48 D9 52 52N 48 33 E
Priyutnoye, Russia 49 G6 46 12N 43 40 E
Prizren, Kosovo, Yug. 40 D4 42 13N 20 45 E
Prizzi, Italy 30 E6 37 43N 13 26 E
Prnjavor, Bos.-H. 42 F2 44 52N 17 43 E
Probolinggo, Indonesia 63 G15 7 46 S 113 13 E
Prochowice, Poland 45 G3 51 17N 16 20 E
Proctor, U.S.A. 111 C11 43 40N 73 2W
Proddatur, India 66 M11 14 45N 78 30 E
Prodhromos, Cyprus 36 E11 34 57N 32 50 E
Proença-a-Nova, Portugal 34 F3 39 45N 7 54W
Profítis Ilías, Greece 36 C9 36 17N 27 56 E
Profondeville, Belgium 17 D4 50 23N 4 52 E
Progreso, Coahuila, Mexico 118 B4 27 28N 101 4W
Progreso, Yucatán, Mexico 119 C7 21 20N 89 40W
Prokhladnyy, Russia 49 J7 43 50N 44 2 E
Prokletije, Albania 40 D3 42 30N 19 45 E
Prokopyevsk, Russia 50 D9 54 0N 86 45 E
Prokuplje, Serbia, Yug. 40 C5 43 16N 21 36 E
Proletarsk, Russia 49 G5 46 42N 41 50 E
Proletarskaya = Proletarsk, Russia 49 G5 46 42N 41 50 E
Prome = Pyè, Burma 67 K19 18 49N 95 13 E
Prophet →, Canada 104 B4 58 48N 122 40W
Prophet River, Canada 104 B4 58 6N 122 43W
Propriá, Brazil 125 F11 10 13 S 36 51W
Propriano, France 21 G12 41 41N 8 52 E
Proserpine, Australia 94 C4 20 21 S 148 36 E
Prosna →, Poland 45 F4 52 6N 17 44 E
Prospect, U.S.A. 111 C9 43 18N 75 9W
Prosser, U.S.A. 114 C4 46 12N 119 46W
Prostějov, Czech Rep. 27 B10 49 30N 17 9 E
Prostki, Poland 44 E9 53 42N 22 25 E
Proston, Australia 95 D5 26 8 S 151 32 E
Proszowice, Poland 45 H7 50 13N 20 16 E
Próti, Greece 38 D3 37 5N 21 32 E
Provadiya, Bulgaria 41 C11 43 12N 27 30 E
Provence, France 21 E9 43 40N 5 46 E
Provence-Alpes-Côte d'Azur □, France 21 D10 44 0N 6 15 E
Providence, Ky., U.S.A. 108 G2 37 24N 87 46W
Providence, R.I., U.S.A. 111 E13 41 49N 71 24W
Providence Bay, Canada 102 C3 45 41N 82 15W
Providence Mts., U.S.A. 117 K11 35 10N 115 15W
Providencia, I. de, Colombia 120 D3 13 25N 81 26W
Provideniya, Russia 51 C19 64 23N 173 18W
Provins, France 19 D10 48 33N 3 15 E
Provo, U.S.A. 114 F8 40 14N 111 39W
Provost, Canada 105 C6 52 25N 110 20W
Prozor, Bos.-H. 42 G2 43 50N 17 34 E
Prrenjas, Albania 40 E4 41 4N 20 32 E
Prudhoe Bay, U.S.A. 100 A5 70 18N 148 22W
Prudhoe I., Australia 94 C4 21 19 S 149 41 E
Prud'homme, Canada 105 C7 52 20N 105 54W
Prudnik, Poland 45 H4 50 20N 17 38 E
Prüm, Germany 25 E2 50 12N 6 25 E
Prundu, Romania 43 F11 44 6N 26 14 E
Pruszcz Gdański, Poland 44 D5 54 17N 18 40 E
Pruszków, Poland 45 F7 52 9N 20 49 E
Prut →, Romania 43 E13 45 28N 28 10 E
Pruzhany, Belarus 47 F3 52 33N 24 28 E
Prvič, Croatia 29 D11 44 55N 14 47 E
Prydz B., Antarctica 5 C6 69 0 S 74 0 E
Pryluky, Ukraine 47 G7 50 30N 32 24 E
Pryor, U.S.A. 113 G7 36 19N 95 19W
Prypyat →, Europe 47 G6 51 20N 30 15 E
Przasnysz, Poland 45 E7 53 2N 20 54 E
Przedbórz, Poland 45 G6 51 6N 19 53 E
Przedecz, Poland 45 F5 52 20N 18 53 E
Przemków, Poland 45 G2 51 31N 15 48 E
Przemyśl, Poland 45 J9 49 50N 22 45 E
Przeworsk, Poland 45 H9 50 6N 22 32 E
Przewóz, Poland 45 G1 51 28N 14 57 E
Przhevalsk, Kyrgyzstan 50 E8 42 30N 78 20 E
Przysucha, Poland 45 G7 51 22N 20 38 E
Psakhná, Greece 38 C5 38 34N 23 35 E
Psará, Greece 39 C7 38 37N 25 38 E
Psathoúra, Greece 38 B6 39 30N 24 12 E
Psel →, Ukraine 47 H7 49 10N 33 37 E
Pserimos, Greece 39 E9 36 56N 27 8 E
Psíra, Greece 36 D7 35 12N 25 52 E
Pskov, Russia 46 D5 57 50N 28 25 E
Pskovskoye, Ozero, Russia 46 D5 58 0N 27 58 E
Psunj, Croatia 42 E2 45 25N 17 19 E
Pteleón, Greece 38 B4 39 3N 22 57 E
Ptich = Ptsich →, Belarus 47 F5 52 9N 28 52 E
Ptolemaís, Greece 40 F5 40 30N 21 43 E
Ptsich →, Belarus 47 F5 52 9N 28 52 E
Ptuj, Slovenia 29 B12 46 28N 15 50 E
Ptujska Gora, Slovenia 29 B12 46 23N 15 47 E
Pu Xian, China 56 F6 36 24N 111 6 E
Pua, Thailand 64 C3 19 11N 100 55 E
Puán, Argentina 126 D3 37 30 S 62 45W
Pu'an, China 58 E5 25 46N 104 57 E
Puan, S. Korea 57 G14 35 44N 126 44 E
Pubei, China 58 F7 22 16N 109 31 E
Pucallpa, Peru 124 E4 8 25 S 74 30W
Pucheng, China 59 D12 27 59N 118 31 E
Pucheni, Romania 43 E10 45 12N 25 17 E
Puchheim, Germany 25 G7 48 9N 11 21 E
Púchov, Slovak Rep. 27 B11 49 8N 18 20 E
Pucioasa, Romania 43 E10 45 5N 25 25 E
Pučišća, Croatia 29 E13 43 22N 16 43 E
Puck, Poland 44 D5 54 45N 18 23 E
Pucka, Zatoka, Poland 44 D5 54 30N 18 40 E
Puçol, Spain 33 F4 39 37N 0 18W
Pudasjärvi, Finland 8 D22 65 23N 26 53 E
Puding, China 58 D5 26 18N 105 44 E
Pudozh, Russia 46 B9 61 48N 36 32 E
Pudukkottai, India 66 P11 10 28N 78 47 E
Puebla, Mexico 119 D5 19 3N 98 12W
Puebla □, Mexico 119 D5 18 30N 98 0W
Puebla de Alcocer, Spain 35 G5 38 59N 5 14W
Puebla de Don Fadrique, Spain 33 H2 37 58N 2 25W
Puebla de Don Rodrigo, Spain 35 F6 39 5N 4 37W
Puebla de Guzmán, Spain 35 H3 37 37N 7 15W
Puebla de la Calzada, Spain 35 G4 38 54N 6 37W
Puebla de Sanabria, Spain 34 C4 42 4N 6 38W
Puebla de Trives = Pobra de Trives, Spain 34 C3 42 20N 7 10W
Pueblo, U.S.A. 112 F2 38 16N 104 37W
Pueblo Hundido, Chile 126 B1 26 20 S 70 5W
Puelches, Argentina 126 D2 38 5 S 65 51W
Puelén, Argentina 126 D2 37 32 S 67 38W
Puente Alto, Chile 126 C1 33 32 S 70 35W
Puente-Genil, Spain 35 H6 37 22N 4 47W
Puente la Reina, Spain 32 C3 42 40N 1 49W
Puenteareas = Ponteareas, Spain 34 C2 42 10N 8 28W
Puentedeume = Pontedeume, Spain 34 B2 43 24N 8 10W
Puentes de Garcia Rodriguez = As Pontes de García Rodríguez, Spain 34 B3 43 27N 7 50W
Pu'er, China 58 F3 23 0N 101 15 E
Puerco →, U.S.A. 115 J10 34 22N 107 50W
Puerto, Canary Is. 37 F2 28 5N 17 20W
Puerto Aisén, Chile 128 F2 45 27 S 73 0W
Puerto Ángel, Mexico 119 D5 15 40N 96 29W
Puerto Arista, Mexico 119 D6 15 56N 93 48W
Puerto Armuelles, Panama 120 E3 8 20N 82 51W
Puerto Ayacucho, Venezuela 124 B5 5 40N 67 35W
Puerto Barrios, Guatemala 120 C2 15 40N 88 32W
Puerto Bermejo, Argentina 126 B4 26 55 S 58 34W
Puerto Bermúdez, Peru 124 F4 10 20 S 74 58W
Puerto Bolívar, Ecuador 124 D3 3 19 S 79 55W
Puerto Cabello, Venezuela 124 A5 10 28N 68 1W
Puerto Cabezas, Nic. 120 D3 14 0N 83 30W
Puerto Cabo Gracias á Dios, Nic. 120 D3 15 0N 83 10W
Puerto Carreño, Colombia 124 B5 6 12N 67 22W
Puerto Castilla, Honduras 120 C2 16 0N 86 0W
Puerto Chicama, Peru 124 E3 7 45 S 79 20W
Puerto Coig, Argentina 128 G3 50 54 S 69 15W
Puerto Cortés, Costa Rica 120 E3 8 55N 84 0W
Puerto Cortés, Honduras 120 C2 15 51N 88 0W
Puerto Cumarebo, Venezuela 124 A5 11 29N 69 30W
Puerto de Alcudia = Port d'Alcúdia, Spain 37 B10 39 50N 3 7 E
Puerto de Andraitx, Spain 37 B9 39 32N 2 23 E
Puerto de Cabrera, Spain 37 B9 39 8N 2 56 E
Puerto de Gran Tarajal, Canary Is. 37 F5 28 13N 14 1W
Puerto de la Cruz, Canary Is. 37 F3 28 24N 16 32W
Puerto de Mazarrón, Spain 33 H3 37 34N 1 15W
Puerto de Pozo Negro, Canary Is. 37 F6 28 19N 13 55W
Puerto de Sóller = Port de Sóller, Spain 37 B9 39 48N 2 42 E
Puerto de Somosierra, Spain 34 D7 41 9N 3 35W
Puerto del Carmen, Canary Is. 37 F6 28 55N 13 38W
Puerto del Rosario, Canary Is. 37 F6 28 30N 13 52W
Puerto Deseado, Argentina 128 F3 47 55 S 66 0W
Puerto Escondido, Mexico 119 D5 15 50N 97 3W
Puerto Heath, Bolivia 124 F5 12 34 S 68 39W
Puerto Inírida, Colombia 124 C5 3 53N 67 52W
Puerto Juárez, Mexico 119 C7 21 11N 86 49W
Puerto La Cruz, Venezuela 124 A6 10 13N 64 38W
Puerto Leguízamo, Colombia 124 D4 0 12 S 74 46W
Puerto Limón, Colombia 124 C4 3 23N 73 30W
Puerto Lobos, Argentina 128 E3 42 0 S 65 3W
Puerto Lumbreras, Spain 33 H3 37 34N 1 48W
Puerto Madryn, Argentina 128 E3 42 48 S 65 4W
Puerto Maldonado, Peru 124 F5 12 30 S 69 10W
Puerto Manotí, Cuba 120 B4 21 22N 76 50W
Puerto Mazarrón = Puerto de Mazarrón, Spain 33 H3 37 34N 1 15W
Puerto Montt, Chile 128 E2 41 28 S 73 0W
Puerto Morazán, Nic. 120 D2 12 51N 87 11W
Puerto Morelos, Mexico 119 C7 20 49N 86 52W
Puerto Natales, Chile 128 G2 51 45 S 72 15W
Puerto Padre, Cuba 120 B4 21 13N 76 35W
Puerto Páez, Venezuela 124 B5 6 13N 67 28W
Puerto Peñasco, Mexico 118 A2 31 20N 113 33W
Puerto Pinasco, Paraguay 126 A4 22 36 S 57 50W
Puerto Plata, Dom. Rep. 121 C5 19 48N 70 45W
Puerto Pollensa = Port de Pollença, Spain 37 B10 39 54N 3 4 E
Puerto Princesa, Phil. 61 G3 9 46N 118 45 E
Puerto Quepos, Costa Rica 120 E3 9 29N 84 6W
Puerto Real, Spain 35 J4 36 33N 6 12W
Puerto Rico, Canary Is. 37 G4 27 47N 15 42W
Puerto Rico ■, W. Indies 121 C6 18 15N 66 45W
Puerto Rico Trench, Atl. Oc. 121 C6 19 50N 66 0W
Puerto San Julián, Argentina 128 F3 49 18 S 67 43W
Puerto Sastre, Paraguay 126 A4 22 2 S 57 55W
Puerto Serrano, Spain 35 J5 36 56N 5 33W
Puerto Suárez, Bolivia 124 G7 18 58 S 57 52W
Puerto Vallarta, Mexico 118 C3 20 36N 105 15W
Puerto Wilches, Colombia 124 B4 7 21N 73 54W
Puertollano, Spain 35 G6 38 43N 4 7W
Pueyrredón, L., Argentina 128 F2 47 20 S 72 0W
Puffin I., Ireland 15 E1 51 50N 10 24W
Pugachev, Russia 48 D9 52 0N 48 49 E
Pugal, India 68 E5 28 30N 72 48 E
Puge, China 58 D4 27 20N 102 31 E
Puge, Tanzania 86 C3 4 45 S 33 11 E
Puget Sound, U.S.A. 114 C2 47 50N 122 30W
Puget-Théniers, France 21 E10 43 58N 6 53 E
Púglia □, Italy 31 A9 41 15N 16 15 E
Pugŏdong, N. Korea 57 C16 42 5N 130 0 E
Pugu, Tanzania 86 D4 6 55 S 39 4 E
Pūgūnzī, Iran 71 E8 25 49N 59 10 E
Pui, Romania 42 E8 45 30N 23 4 E
Puiești, Romania 43 D12 46 25N 27 33 E
Puig Major, Spain 37 B9 39 48N 2 47 E
Puigcerdà, Spain 32 C6 42 24N 1 50 E
Puigmal, Spain 32 C7 42 23N 2 7 E
Puigpunyent, Spain 37 B9 39 38N 2 32 E
Puijiang, China 58 B4 30 14N 103 30 E
Puisaye, Collines de la, France 19 E10 47 37N 3 20 E
Puiseaux, France 19 D9 48 11N 2 30 E
Pujehun, S. Leone 82 D2 7 23N 11 45W
Pujiang, China 59 C12 29 29N 119 54 E
Pujols, France 20 D3 44 48N 0 2W

Pujon-chŏsuji, *N. Korea* **57 D14** 40 35N 127 35 E
Puka = Pukë, *Albania* **40 D3** 42 2N 19 53 E
Pukaki L., *N.Z.* **91 L3** 44 4 S 170 1 E
Pukapuka, *Cook Is.* **97 J11** 10 53 S 165 49W
Pukaskwa Nat. Park, *Canada* **102 C2** 48 20N 86 0W
Pukatawagan, *Canada* **105 B8** 55 45N 101 20W
Pukchin, *N. Korea* **57 D13** 40 12N 125 45 E
Pukch'ŏng, *N. Korea* **57 D15** 40 14N 128 10 E
Pukë, *Albania* **40 D3** 42 2N 19 53 E
Pukekohe, *N.Z.* **91 G5** 37 12 S 174 55 E
Pukhrayan, *India* **69 F8** 26 14N 79 51 E
Pukou, *China* **59 A12** 32 7N 118 38 E
Pula, *Croatia* **29 D10** 44 54N 13 57 E
Pula, *Italy* **30 C1** 39 1N 9 0 E
Pulacayo, *Bolivia* **124 H5** 20 25 S 66 41W
Pulandian, *China* **57 E11** 39 25N 121 58 E
Pularumpi, *Australia* **92 B5** 11 24 S 130 26 E
Pulaski, *N.Y., U.S.A.* **111 C8** 43 34N 76 8W
Pulaski, *Tenn., U.S.A.* **109 H2** 35 12N 87 2W
Pulaski, *Va., U.S.A.* **108 G5** 37 3N 80 47W
Pulau →, *Indonesia* **63 F9** 5 50 S 138 15 E
Puławy, *Poland* **45 G8** 51 23N 21 59 E
Pulga, *U.S.A.* **116 F5** 39 48N 121 29W
Pulicat L., *India* **66 N12** 13 40N 80 15 E
Pullman, *U.S.A.* **114 C5** 46 44N 117 10W
Pulo-Anna, *Pac. Oc.* **63 D8** 4 30N 132 5 E
Pulog, Mt., *Phil.* **61 C4** 16 40N 120 50 E
Pułtusk, *Poland* **45 F8** 52 43N 21 6 E
Pülümür, *Turkey* **73 C8** 39 30N 39 51 E
Pumlumon Fawr, *U.K.* **13 E4** 52 28N 3 46W
Puná, I., *Ecuador* **124 D2** 2 55 S 80 5W
Punakha, *Bhutan* **67 F16** 27 42N 89 52 E
Punasar, *India* **68 F5** 27 6N 73 6 E
Punata, *Bolivia* **124 G5** 17 32 S 65 50W
Punch, *India* **69 C6** 33 48N 74 4 E
Punch →, *Pakistan* **68 C5** 33 12N 73 40 E
Punda Maria, *S. Africa* **89 C5** 22 40 S 31 5 E
Pune, *India* **66 K8** 18 29N 73 57 E
P'ungsan, *N. Korea* **57 D15** 40 50N 128 9 E
Pungue, Ponte de, *Mozam.* **87 F3** 19 0 S 34 0 E
Puning, *China* **59 F11** 23 20N 116 12 E
Punjab □, *India* **68 D7** 31 0N 76 0 E
Punjab □, *Pakistan* **68 E6** 32 0N 74 30 E
Puno, *Peru* **124 G4** 15 55 S 70 3W
Punpun →, *India* **69 G11** 25 31N 85 18 E
Punta Alta, *Argentina* **128 D4** 38 53 S 62 4W
Punta Arenas, *Chile* **128 G2** 53 10 S 71 0W
Punta de Díaz, *Chile* **126 B1** 28 0 S 70 45W
Punta Gorda, *Belize* **119 D7** 16 10N 88 45W
Punta Gorda, *U.S.A.* **109 M5** 26 56N 82 3W
Punta Prieta, *Mexico* **118 B2** 28 58N 114 17W
Punta Prima, *Spain* **37 B11** 39 48N 4 16 E
Punta Umbría, *Spain* **35 H4** 37 10N 6 56W
Puntarenas, *Costa Rica* **120 E3** 10 0N 84 50W
Punto Fijo, *Venezuela* **124 A4** 11 50N 70 13W
Punxsatawney, *U.S.A.* **110 F6** 40 57N 78 59W
Puqi, *China* **59 C9** 29 40N 113 50 E
Puquio, *Peru* **124 F4** 14 45 S 74 10W
Pur →, *Russia* **50 C8** 67 31N 77 55 E
Purace, Vol., *Colombia* **124 C3** 2 21N 76 23W
Puračić, *Bos.-H.* **42 F3** 44 33N 18 28 E
Puralia = Puruliya, *India* **69 H12** 23 17N 86 24 E
Puranpur, *India* **69 E9** 28 31N 80 9 E
Purbeck, Isle of, *U.K.* **13 G6** 50 39N 1 59W
Purcell, *U.S.A.* **113 H6** 35 1N 97 22W
Purcell Mts., *Canada* **104 D5** 49 55N 116 15W
Puri, *India* **67 K14** 19 50N 85 58 E
Purmerend, *Neths.* **17 B4** 52 32N 4 58 E
Purnia, *India* **69 G12** 25 45N 87 31 E
Pursat = Pouthisat, *Cambodia* **64 F4** 12 34N 103 50 E
Purukcahu, *Indonesia* **62 E4** 0 35 S 114 35 E
Puruliya, *India* **69 H12** 23 17N 86 24 E
Purus →, *Brazil* **122 D4** 3 42 S 61 28W
Puruvesi, *Finland* **46 B5** 61 50N 29 30 E
Purvis, *U.S.A.* **113 K10** 31 9N 89 25W
Pŭrvomay, *Bulgaria* **41 D9** 42 8N 25 17 E
Purwa, *India* **69 F9** 26 28N 80 47 E
Purwakarta, *Indonesia* **63 G12** 6 35 S 107 29 E
Purwodadi, *Indonesia* **63 G14** 7 7 S 110 55 E
Purwokerto, *Indonesia* **63 G13** 7 25 S 109 14 E
Puryŏng, *N. Korea* **57 C15** 42 5N 129 43 E
Pusa, *India* **69 G11** 25 59N 85 41 E
Pusan, *S. Korea* **57 G15** 35 5N 129 0 E
Pushkin, *Russia* **46 C6** 59 45N 30 25 E
Pushkino, *Moskva, Russia* **46 D9** 56 2N 37 49 E
Pushkino, *Saratov, Russia* **48 E8** 51 16N 47 0 E
Püspökladány, *Hungary* **42 C6** 47 19N 21 6 E
Pustoshka, *Russia* **46 D5** 56 20N 29 30 E
Puszczykowo, *Poland* **45 F3** 52 18N 16 49 E
Putahow L., *Canada* **105 B8** 59 54N 100 40W
Putao, *Burma* **67 F20** 27 28N 97 30 E
Putaruru, *N.Z.* **91 H5** 38 2 S 175 50 E
Putbus, *Germany* **24 A9** 54 22N 13 28 E
Puthein Myit →, *Burma* **67 M19** 15 56N 94 18 E
Putian, *China* **59 E12** 25 23N 119 0 E
Putignano, *Italy* **31 B10** 40 51N 17 7 E
Puting, Tanjung, *Indonesia* **62 E4** 3 31 S 111 46 E
Putlitz, *Germany* **24 B8** 53 15N 12 2 E
Putna, *Romania* **43 C10** 47 50N 25 33 E
Putna →, *Romania* **43 E12** 45 42N 27 26 E
Putnam, *U.S.A.* **111 E13** 41 55N 71 55W
Putnok, *Hungary* **42 B5** 48 18N 20 26 E
Putorana, Gory, *Russia* **51 C10** 69 0N 95 0 E
Puttalam, *Sri Lanka* **66 Q11** 8 1N 79 55 E
Puttgarden, *Germany* **24 A7** 54 30N 11 10 E
Püttlingen, *Germany* **25 F2** 49 17N 6 53 E
Putumayo →, *S. Amer.* **122 D4** 3 7 S 67 58W
Putuo, *China* **59 C14** 29 56N 122 20 E
Putussibau, *Indonesia* **62 D4** 0 50N 112 56 E
Puvirnituq, *Canada* **101 B12** 60 2N 77 10W
Puy-de-Dôme, *France* **20 C6** 45 46N 2 57 E
Puy-de-Dôme □, *France* **20 C7** 45 40N 3 5 E
Puy-l'Évêque, *France* **20 D5** 44 31N 1 9 E
Puyallup, *U.S.A.* **116 C4** 47 12N 122 18W
Puyang, *China* **56 G8** 35 40N 115 1 E
Puylaurens, *France* **20 E6** 43 35N 2 0 E
Pūzeh Rīg, *Iran* **71 E8** 27 20N 58 40 E
Pwani □, *Tanzania* **86 D4** 7 0 S 39 0 E
Pweto, *Dem. Rep. of the Congo* **87 D2** 8 25 S 28 51 E
Pwllheli, *U.K.* **12 E3** 52 53N 4 25W
Pyana →, *Russia* **48 C8** 55 43N 46 1 E
Pyapon, *Burma* **67 L19** 16 20N 95 40 E
Pyasina →, *Russia* **51 B9** 73 30N 87 0 E
Pyatigorsk, *Russia* **49 H6** 44 2N 43 6 E
Pyatykhatky, *Ukraine* **47 H7** 48 28N 33 38 E
Pydna, *Greece* **40 F6** 40 20N 22 34 E
Pyè, *Burma* **67 K19** 18 49N 95 13 E
Pyetrikaw, *Belarus* **47 F5** 52 11N 28 29 E
Pyhäjoki, *Finland* **8 D21** 64 28N 24 14 E
Pyinmana, *Burma* **67 K20** 19 45N 96 12 E
Pyla, C., *Cyprus* **36 E12** 34 56N 33 51 E
Pymatuning Reservoir, *U.S.A.* **110 E4** 41 30N 80 28W
Pyŏktong, *N. Korea* **57 D13** 40 50N 125 50 E
Pyŏnggang, *N. Korea* **57 E14** 38 24N 127 17 E
P'yŏngt'aek, *S. Korea* **57 F14** 37 1N 127 4 E
P'yŏngyang, *N. Korea* **57 E13** 39 0N 125 30 E
Pyote, *U.S.A.* **113 K3** 31 32N 103 8W
Pyramid L., *U.S.A.* **114 G4** 40 1N 119 35W
Pyramid Pk., *U.S.A.* **117 J10** 36 25N 116 37W
Pyramids, *Egypt* **80 J7** 29 58N 31 9 E
Pyrénées, *Europe* **20 F4** 42 45N 0 18 E
Pyrénées-Atlantiques □, *France* **20 E3** 43 10N 0 50W
Pyrénées-Orientales □, *France* **20 F6** 42 35N 2 26 E
Pyryatyn, *Ukraine* **47 G7** 50 15N 32 25 E
Pyrzyce, *Poland* **45 E1** 53 10N 14 55 E
Pyskowice, *Poland* **45 H5** 50 24N 18 38 E
Pytalovo, *Russia* **46 D4** 57 5N 27 55 E
Pyu, *Burma* **67 K20** 18 30N 96 28 E
Pyzdry, *Poland* **45 F4** 52 11N 17 42 E

Q

Qaanaaq, *Greenland* **4 B4** 77 40N 69 0W
Qabirri →, *Azerbaijan* **49 K8** 41 3N 46 17 E
Qachasnek, *S. Africa* **89 E4** 30 6 S 28 42 E
Qa'el Jafr, *Jordan* **75 E5** 30 20N 36 25 E
Qa'emābād, *Iran* **71 D9** 31 44N 60 2 E
Qā'emshahr, *Iran* **71 B7** 36 30N 52 53 E
Qagan Nur, *China* **56 C8** 43 30N 114 55 E
Qahar Youyi Zhongqi, *China* **56 D7** 41 12N 112 40 E
Qahremānshahr = Bākhtarān, *Iran* **70 C5** 34 23N 47 0 E
Qaidam Pendi, *China* **60 C4** 37 0N 95 0 E
Qajarīyeh, *Iran* **71 D6** 31 1N 48 22 E
Qala, Ras il, *Malta* **36 C1** 36 1N 14 20 E
Qala-i-Jadid = Spīn Búldak, *Afghan.* **68 D2** 31 1N 66 25 E
Qala Viala, *Pakistan* **68 D2** 30 49N 67 17 E
Qala Yangi, *Afghan.* **68 B2** 34 20N 66 30 E
Qal'at al Akhḍar, *Si. Arabia* **70 E3** 28 0N 37 10 E
Qal'at Dīzah, *Iraq* **70 B5** 36 11N 45 7 E
Qal'at Ṣāliḥ, *Iraq* **70 D5** 31 31N 47 16 E
Qal'at Sukkar, *Iraq* **70 D5** 31 51N 46 5 E
Qal'eh Shaharak, *Afghan.* **66 B4** 34 10N 64 20 E
Qalyūb, *Egypt* **80 H7** 30 12N 31 11 E
Qamdo, *China* **58 B1** 31 15N 97 6 E
Qamruddin Karez, *Pakistan* **68 D3** 31 45N 68 20 E
Qandahār, *Afghan.* **66 D4** 31 32N 65 30 E
Qandahār □, *Afghan.* **66 D4** 31 0N 65 0 E
Qapān, *Iran* **71 B7** 37 40N 55 47 E
Qapshaghay, *Kazakstan* **50 E8** 43 51N 77 14 E
Qaqortoq, *Greenland* **4 C5** 60 43N 46 0W
Qâra, *Egypt* **80 B2** 29 38N 26 30 E
Qara Qash →, *India* **69 B8** 35 0N 78 30 E
Qarabutaq, *Kazakstan* **50 E7** 49 59N 60 14 E
Qaraçala, *Azerbaijan* **49 L9** 39 45N 48 53 E
Qaraghandy, *Kazakstan* **50 E8** 49 50N 73 10 E
Qārah, *Si. Arabia* **70 D4** 29 55N 40 3 E
Qarataū, *Kazakstan* **50 E8** 43 10N 70 28 E
Qardud, *Sudan* **81 E2** 10 20N 29 56 E
Qareh →, *Iran* **70 B5** 39 25N 47 22 E
Qareh Tekān, *Iran* **71 B6** 36 38N 49 29 E
Qarqan He →, *China* **60 C3** 39 30N 88 30 E
Qarqaraly, *Kazakstan* **50 E8** 49 26N 75 30 E
Qarrasa, *Sudan* **81 E3** 14 38N 32 5 E
Qarshi, *Uzbekistan* **50 F7** 38 53N 65 48 E
Qartabā, *Lebanon* **75 A4** 34 4N 35 50 E
Qaryat al Gharab, *Iraq* **70 D5** 31 27N 44 48 E
Qaryat al 'Ulyā, *Si. Arabia* **70 E5** 27 33N 47 42 E
Qasr 'Amra, *Jordan* **70 D3** 31 48N 36 35 E
Qaṣr-e Qand, *Iran* **71 E9** 26 15N 60 45 E
Qasr Farâfra, *Egypt* **80 B2** 27 0N 28 1 E
Qataṇā, *Syria* **75 B5** 33 26N 36 4 E
Qatar ■, *Asia* **71 E6** 25 30N 51 15 E
Qatlīsh, *Iran* **71 B8** 37 50N 57 19 E
Qattâra, *Egypt* **80 A2** 30 12N 27 3 E
Qattâra, Munkhafed el, *Egypt* **80 B2** 29 30N 27 30 E
Qattâra Depression = Qattâra, Munkhafed el, *Egypt* **80 B2** 29 30N 27 30 E
Qawām al Ḥamzah, *Iraq* **70 D5** 31 43N 44 58 E
Qāyen, *Iran* **71 C8** 33 40N 59 10 E
Qazaqstan = Kazakstan ■, *Asia* **50 E7** 50 0N 70 0 E
Qazimämmäd, *Azerbaijan* **49 K9** 40 3N 49 0 E
Qazvin, *Iran* **71 B6** 36 15N 50 0 E
Qeissan, *Sudan* **81 E3** 11 4N 34 40 E
Qena, *Egypt* **80 B3** 26 10N 32 43 E
Qena, W. →, *Egypt* **80 B3** 26 12N 32 44 E
Qeqertarsuaq, *Greenland* **4 C5** 69 45N 53 30W
Qeqertarsuaq, *Greenland* **4 C5** 69 15N 53 38W
Qeshlāq, *Iran* **70 C5** 34 55N 46 28 E
Qeshm, *Iran* **71 E8** 26 55N 56 10 E
Qeys, *Iran* **71 E7** 26 32N 53 58 E
Qezel Owzen →, *Iran* **71 B6** 36 45N 49 22 E
Qezi'ot, *Israel* **75 E3** 30 52N 34 26 E
Qi Xian, *China* **56 G8** 34 40N 114 48 E
Qian Gorlos, *China* **57 B13** 45 5N 124 42 E
Qian Xian, *China* **56 G5** 34 31N 108 15 E
Qiancheng, *China* **58 D7** 27 12N 109 50 E
Qianjiang, *Guangxi Zhuangzu, China* **58 F7** 23 38N 108 58 E
Qianjiang, *Hubei, China* **59 B9** 30 24N 112 55 E
Qianjiang, *Sichuan, China* **58 C7** 29 33N 108 47 E
Qianshan, *China* **59 B11** 30 37N 116 35 E
Qianwei, *China* **58 C4** 29 13N 103 56 E
Qianxi, *China* **58 D6** 27 3N 106 3 E
Qianyang, *Hunan, China* **59 D8** 27 18N 110 10 E
Qianyang, *Shaanxi, China* **56 G4** 34 40N 107 8 E
Qianyang, *Zhejiang, China* **59 B12** 30 11N 119 25 E
Qiaojia, *China* **58 D4** 26 56N 102 58 E
Qibā', *Si. Arabia* **70 E5** 27 24N 44 20 E
Qichun, *China* **59 B10** 30 18N 115 25 E
Qidong, *Hunan, China* **59 D9** 26 49N 112 7 E
Qidong, *Jiangsu, China* **59 B13** 31 48N 121 38 E
Qijiang, *China* **58 C6** 28 57N 106 35 E
Qikiqtarjuaq, *Canada* **101 B13** 67 33N 63 0W
Qila Safed, *Pakistan* **66 E2** 29 0N 61 30 E
Qila Saifullāh, *Pakistan* **68 D3** 30 45N 68 17 E
Qilian Shan, *China* **60 C4** 38 30N 96 0 E
Qimen, *China* **59 C11** 29 50N 117 42 E
Qin He →, *China* **56 G7** 35 1N 113 22 E
Qin Jiang →, *Guangxi Zhuangzu, China* **58 F7** 21 53N 108 35 E
Qin Jiang →, *Jiangxi, China* **59 D10** 26 15N 115 55 E
Qin Ling = Qinling Shandi, *China* **56 H5** 33 50N 108 10 E
Qin'an, *China* **56 G3** 34 48N 105 40 E
Qing Xian, *China* **56 E9** 38 35N 116 45 E
Qingcheng, *China* **57 F9** 37 15N 117 40 E
Qingdao, *China* **57 F11** 36 5N 120 20 E
Qingfeng, *China* **56 G8** 35 52N 115 8 E
Qinghai □, *China* **60 C4** 36 0N 98 0 E
Qinghai Hu, *China* **60 C5** 36 40N 100 10 E
Qinghecheng, *China* **57 D13** 41 28N 124 15 E
Qinghemen, *China* **57 D11** 41 48N 121 25 E
Qingjian, *China* **56 F6** 37 8N 110 8 E
Qingjiang = Huaiyin, *China* **57 H10** 33 30N 119 2 E
Qingliu, *China* **59 D11** 26 11N 116 48 E
Qinglong, *China* **58 E5** 25 49N 105 12 E
Qingping, *China* **58 D6** 26 39N 107 47 E
Qingpu, *China* **59 B13** 31 10N 121 6 E
Qingshui, *China* **56 G4** 34 48N 106 8 E
Qingshuihe, *China* **56 E6** 39 55N 111 35 E
Qingtian, *China* **59 C13** 28 12N 120 15 E
Qingtongxia Shuiku, *China* **56 F3** 37 50N 105 58 E
Qingxi, *China* **58 D7** 27 8N 108 43 E
Qingxu, *China* **56 F7** 37 34N 112 22 E
Qingyang, *Anhui, China* **59 B11** 30 38N 117 50 E
Qingyang, *Gansu, China* **56 F4** 36 2N 107 55 E
Qingyi Jiang →, *China* **58 C4** 29 32N 103 44 E
Qingyuan, *Guangdong, China* **59 F9** 23 40N 112 59 E
Qingyuan, *Liaoning, China* **57 C13** 42 10N 124 55 E
Qingyuan, *Zhejiang, China* **59 D12** 27 36N 119 3 E
Qingyun, *China* **57 F9** 37 45N 117 20 E
Qingzhen, *China* **58 D6** 26 31N 106 25 E
Qinhuangdao, *China* **57 E10** 39 56N 119 30 E
Qinling Shandi, *China* **56 H5** 33 50N 108 10 E
Qinshui, *China* **56 G7** 35 40N 112 8 E
Qinyang = Jiyuan, *China* **56 G7** 35 7N 112 57 E
Qinyuan, *China* **56 F7** 36 29N 112 20 E
Qinzhou, *China* **58 G7** 21 58N 108 38 E
Qionghai, *China* **64 C8** 19 15N 110 26 E
Qionglai, *China* **58 B4** 30 25N 103 31 E
Qionglai Shan, *China* **58 B4** 31 0N 102 30 E
Qiongzhou Haixia, *China* **64 B8** 20 10N 110 15 E
Qiqihar, *China* **51 E13** 47 26N 124 0 E
Qiraīya, W. →, *Egypt* **75 E3** 30 27N 34 0 E
Qiryat Ata, *Israel* **75 C4** 32 47N 35 6 E
Qiryat Gat, *Israel* **75 D3** 31 32N 34 46 E
Qiryat Mal'akhi, *Israel* **75 D3** 31 44N 34 44 E
Qiryat Shemona, *Israel* **75 B4** 33 13N 35 35 E
Qiryat Yam, *Israel* **75 C4** 32 51N 35 4 E
Qishan, *China* **56 G4** 34 25N 107 38 E
Qitai, *China* **60 B3** 44 2N 89 35 E
Qiubei, *China* **58 E5** 24 2N 104 12 E
Qixia, *China* **57 F11** 37 17N 120 52 E
Qiyang, *China* **59 D8** 26 35N 111 50 E
Qızılağac Körfäzi, *Azerbaijan* **71 B6** 39 9N 49 0 E
Qojūr, *Iran* **70 B5** 36 12N 47 55 E
Qom, *Iran* **71 C6** 34 40N 51 0 E
Qomolangma Feng = Everest, Mt., *Nepal* **69 E12** 28 5N 86 58 E
Qomsheh, *Iran* **71 D6** 32 0N 51 55 E
Qorveh, *Iran* **73 E12** 35 10N 47 48 E
Qostanay, *Kazakstan* **50 D7** 53 10N 63 35 E
Qoṭūr, *Iran* **73 C11** 38 28N 44 25 E
Qu Jiang →, *China* **58 B6** 30 1N 106 24 E
Qu Xian, *China* **58 B6** 30 48N 106 58 E
Quabbin Reservoir, *U.S.A.* **111 D12** 42 20N 72 20W
Quairading, *Australia* **93 F2** 32 0 S 117 21 E
Quakenbrück, *Germany* **24 C3** 52 41N 7 57 E
Quakertown, *U.S.A.* **111 F9** 40 26N 75 21W
Qualicum Beach, *Canada* **104 D4** 49 22N 124 26W
Quambatook, *Australia* **95 F3** 35 49 S 143 34 E
Quambone, *Australia* **95 E4** 30 57 S 147 53 E
Quamby, *Australia* **94 C3** 20 22 S 140 17 E
Quan Long = Ca Mau, *Vietnam* **65 H5** 9 7N 105 8 E
Quanah, *U.S.A.* **113 H5** 34 18N 99 44W
Quang Ngai, *Vietnam* **64 E7** 15 13N 108 58 E
Quang Tri, *Vietnam* **64 D6** 16 45N 107 13 E
Quang Yen, *Vietnam* **58 G6** 20 56N 106 52 E
Quannan, *China* **59 E10** 24 45N 114 33 E
Quantock Hills, *U.K.* **13 F4** 51 8N 3 10W
Quanzhou, *Fujian, China* **59 E12** 24 55N 118 34 E
Quanzhou, *Guangxi Zhuangzu, China* **59 E8** 25 57N 111 5 E
Qu'Appelle, *Canada* **105 C8** 50 33N 103 53W
Quaqtaq, *Canada* **101 B13** 60 55N 69 40W
Quaraí, *Brazil* **126 C4** 30 15 S 56 20W
Quarré-les-Tombes, *France* **19 E11** 47 21N 4 0 E
Quarteira, *Portugal* **35 H2** 37 4N 8 6W
Quartu Sant'Élena, *Italy* **30 C2** 39 15N 9 10 E
Quartzsite, *U.S.A.* **117 M12** 33 40N 114 13W
Quatsino Sd., *Canada* **104 C3** 50 25N 127 58W
Quba, *Azerbaijan* **49 K9** 41 21N 48 32 E
Qūchān, *Iran* **71 B8** 37 10N 58 27 E
Queanbeyan, *Australia* **95 F4** 35 17 S 149 14 E
Québec, *Canada* **103 C5** 46 52N 71 13W
Québec □, *Canada* **103 C6** 48 0N 74 0W
Quedlinburg, *Germany* **24 D7** 51 47N 11 8 E
Queen Alexandra Ra., *Antarctica* **5 E11** 85 0 S 170 0 E
Queen Charlotte City, *Canada* **104 C2** 53 15N 132 2W
Queen Charlotte Is., *Canada* **104 C2** 53 20N 132 10W
Queen Charlotte Sd., *Canada* **104 C3** 51 0N 128 0W
Queen Charlotte Strait, *Canada* **104 C3** 50 45N 127 10W
Queen Elizabeth Is., *Canada* **98 B10** 76 0N 95 0W
Queen Elizabeth Nat. Park, *Uganda* **86 C3** 0 0 30 0 E
Queen Mary Land, *Antarctica* **5 D7** 70 0 S 95 0 E
Queen Maud G., *Canada* **100 B9** 68 15N 102 30W
Queen Maud Land, *Antarctica* **5 D3** 72 30 S 12 0 E
Queen Maud Mts., *Antarctica* **5 E13** 86 0 S 160 0W
Queens Chan., *Australia* **92 C4** 15 0 S 129 30 E
Queenscliff, *Australia* **95 F3** 38 16 S 144 39 E
Queensland □, *Australia* **94 C3** 22 0 S 142 0 E
Queenstown, *Australia* **94 G4** 42 4 S 145 35 E
Queenstown, *N.Z.* **91 L2** 45 1 S 168 40 E
Queenstown, *S. Africa* **88 E4** 31 52 S 26 52 E
Queets, *U.S.A.* **116 C2** 47 32N 124 20W
Queguay Grande →, *Uruguay* **126 C4** 32 9 S 58 9W
Queimadas, *Brazil* **125 F11** 11 0 S 39 38W
Quelimane, *Mozam.* **87 F4** 17 53 S 36 58 E
Quellón, *Chile* **128 E2** 43 7 S 73 37W
Quelpart = Cheju do, *S. Korea* **57 H14** 33 29N 126 34 E
Queluz, *Portugal* **35 G1** 38 45N 9 15W
Quemado, *N. Mex., U.S.A.* **115 J9** 34 20N 108 30W
Quemado, *Tex., U.S.A.* **113 L4** 28 58N 100 35W
Quemoy = Chinmen, *Taiwan* **59 E13** 24 26N 118 19 E
Quemú-Quemú, *Argentina* **126 D3** 36 3 S 63 36W
Quequén, *Argentina* **126 D4** 38 30 S 58 30W
Querétaro, *Mexico* **118 C4** 20 36N 100 23W
Querétaro □, *Mexico* **118 C5** 20 30N 100 0W
Querfurt, *Germany* **24 D7** 51 23N 11 35 E
Quérigut, *France* **20 F6** 42 42N 2 6 E
Querqueville, *France* **18 C5** 49 40N 1 42W
Quesada, *Spain* **35 H7** 37 51N 3 4W
Queshan, *China* **56 H8** 32 55N 114 2 E
Quesnel, *Canada* **104 C4** 53 0N 122 30W
Quesnel →, *Canada* **104 C4** 52 58N 122 29W
Quesnel L., *Canada* **104 C4** 52 30N 121 20W
Questa, *U.S.A.* **115 H11** 36 42N 105 36W
Questembert, *France* **18 E4** 47 40N 2 28W
Quetico Prov. Park, *Canada* **102 C1** 48 30N 91 45W
Quetta, *Pakistan* **68 D2** 30 15N 66 55 E
Quezaltenango, *Guatemala* **120 D1** 14 50N 91 30W
Quezon City, *Phil.* **61 D4** 14 38N 121 0 E
Qufār, *Si. Arabia* **70 E4** 27 26N 41 37 E
Qui Nhon, *Vietnam* **64 F7** 13 40N 109 13 E
Quibaxe, *Angola* **84 F2** 8 24 S 14 27 E
Quibdo, *Colombia* **124 B3** 5 42N 76 40W
Quiberon, *France* **18 E3** 47 29N 3 9W
Quiberon, Presqu'île de, *France* **18 E3** 47 30N 3 8W
Quickborn, *Germany* **24 B5** 53 42N 9 52 E
Quiet L., *Canada* **104 A2** 61 5N 133 5W
Quiindy, *Paraguay* **126 B4** 25 58 S 57 14W
Quila, *Mexico* **118 C3** 24 23N 107 13W
Quilán, C., *Chile* **128 E2** 43 15 S 74 30W
Quilcene, *U.S.A.* **116 C4** 47 49N 122 53W
Quilimarí, *Chile* **126 C1** 32 5 S 71 30W
Quilino, *Argentina* **126 C3** 30 14 S 64 29W
Quill Lakes, *Canada* **105 C8** 51 55N 104 13W
Quillabamba, *Peru* **124 F4** 12 50 S 72 50W
Quillagua, *Chile* **126 A2** 21 40 S 69 40W
Quillaicillo, *Chile* **126 C1** 31 17 S 71 40W
Quillan, *France* **20 F6** 42 53N 2 10 E
Quillota, *Chile* **126 C1** 32 54 S 71 16W
Quilmes, *Argentina* **126 C4** 34 43 S 58 15W
Quilon, *India* **66 Q10** 8 50N 76 38 E
Quilpie, *Australia* **95 D3** 26 35 S 144 11 E
Quilpué, *Chile* **126 C1** 33 5 S 71 33W
Quilua, *Mozam.* **87 F4** 16 17 S 39 54 E
Quimilí, *Argentina* **126 B3** 27 40 S 62 30W
Quimper, *France* **18 E2** 48 0N 4 9W
Quimperlé, *France* **18 E3** 47 53N 3 33W
Quinault →, *U.S.A.* **116 C2** 47 21N 124 18W
Quincy, *Calif., U.S.A.* **116 F6** 39 56N 120 57W
Quincy, *Fla., U.S.A.* **109 K3** 30 35N 84 34W
Quincy, *Ill., U.S.A.* **112 F9** 39 56N 91 23W
Quincy, *Mass., U.S.A.* **111 D14** 42 15N 71 0W
Quincy, *Wash., U.S.A.* **114 C4** 47 22N 119 56W
Quines, *Argentina* **126 C2** 32 13 S 65 48W
Quinga, *Mozam.* **87 F5** 15 49 S 40 15 E
Quingey, *France* **19 E12** 47 7N 5 52 E
Quinns Rocks, *Australia* **93 F2** 31 40 S 115 42 E
Quintana de la Serena, *Spain* **35 G5** 38 45N 5 40W
Quintana Roo □, *Mexico* **119 D7** 19 0N 88 0W
Quintanar de la Orden, *Spain* **35 F7** 39 36N 3 5W
Quintanar de la Sierra, *Spain* **32 D2** 41 57N 2 55W
Quintanar del Rey, *Spain* **33 F3** 39 21N 1 56W
Quintero, *Chile* **126 C1** 32 45 S 71 30W
Quintin, *France* **18 D4** 48 26N 2 56W
Quinto, *Spain* **32 D4** 41 25N 0 32W
Quípar →, *Spain* **33 G3** 38 15N 1 40W
Quirihue, *Chile* **126 D1** 36 15 S 72 35W
Quirindi, *Australia* **95 E5** 31 28 S 150 40 E
Quirinópolis, *Brazil* **125 G8** 18 32 S 50 30W
Quiroga, *Spain* **34 C3** 42 28N 7 18W
Quissac, *France* **21 E8** 43 55N 4 0 E
Quissanga, *Mozam.* **87 E5** 12 24 S 40 28 E
Quissico, *Mozam.* **89 C5** 24 42 S 34 44 E
Quitilipi, *Argentina* **126 B3** 26 50 S 60 13W
Quitman, *U.S.A.* **109 K4** 30 47N 83 34W
Quito, *Ecuador* **124 D3** 0 15 S 78 35W
Quixadá, *Brazil* **125 D11** 4 55 S 39 0W
Quixaxe, *Mozam.* **87 F5** 15 17 S 40 4 E
Qujing, *China* **58 E4** 25 32N 103 41 E
Qul'ân, Jazâ'ir, *Egypt* **70 E2** 24 22N 35 31 E
Qumbu, *S. Africa* **89 E4** 31 10 S 28 48 E
Quneitra, *Syria* **75 B4** 33 7N 35 48 E
Qŭnghirot, *Uzbekistan* **50 E6** 43 6N 58 54 E
Qu'nyido, *China* **58 B2** 31 15N 98 6 E
Quoin I., *Australia* **92 B4** 14 54 S 129 32 E
Quoin Pt., *S. Africa* **88 E2** 34 46 S 19 37 E
Quorn, *Australia* **95 E2** 32 25 S 138 5 E
Qŭqon, *Uzbekistan* **50 E8** 40 30N 70 57 E
Qurein, *Sudan* **81 E3** 13 30N 34 50 E
Qurnat as Sawdā', *Lebanon* **75 A5** 34 18N 36 6 E
Qûs, *Egypt* **80 B3** 25 55N 32 50 E
Qusar, *Azerbaijan* **49 K9** 41 25N 48 26 E
Quṣaybā', *Si. Arabia* **70 E4** 26 53N 43 35 E
Qusaybah, *Iraq* **70 C4** 34 24N 40 59 E
Quseir, *Egypt* **70 E2** 26 7N 34 16 E
Qūshchī, *Iran* **70 B5** 37 59N 45 3 E
Quthing, *Lesotho* **89 E4** 30 25 S 27 36 E
Qūṭīābād, *Iran* **71 C6** 35 47N 48 30 E
Quwo, *China* **56 G6** 35 38N 111 25 E
Quyang, *China* **56 E8** 38 35N 114 40 E
Quynh Nhai, *Vietnam* **64 B4** 21 49N 103 33 E
Quyon, *Canada* **111 A8** 45 31N 76 14W
Quzhou, *China* **59 C12** 28 57N 118 54 E
Quzi, *China* **56 F4** 36 20N 107 20 E
Qvareli, *Georgia* **49 K7** 41 57N 45 47 E
Qytet Stalin = Kuçovë, *Albania* **40 F3** 40 47N 19 57 E
Qyzylorda, *Kazakstan* **50 E7** 44 48N 65 28 E

R

Ra, Ko, *Thailand* **65 H2** 9 13N 98 16 E
Raab, *Austria* **26 C6** 48 21N 13 39 E
Raahe, *Finland* **8 D21** 64 40N 24 28 E
Raalte, *Neths.* **17 B6** 52 23N 6 16 E
Raasay, *U.K.* **14 D2** 57 25N 6 4W
Raasay, Sd. of, *U.K.* **14 D2** 57 30N 6 8W
Rab, *Croatia* **29 D11** 44 45N 14 45 E
Raba, *Indonesia* **63 F5** 8 36 S 118 55 E
Rába →, *Hungary* **42 C2** 47 38N 17 38 E
Raba →, *Poland* **45 H7** 50 8N 20 30 E
Rabaçal →, *Portugal* **34 D3** 41 30N 7 12W
Rabah, *Nigeria* **83 C6** 13 5N 5 30 E
Rabai, *Kenya* **86 C4** 3 50 S 39 31 E
Rabak, *Sudan* **81 E3** 13 9N 32 44 E
Rabastens, *France* **20 E5** 43 50N 1 43 E
Rabastens-de-Bigorre, *France* **20 E4** 43 23N 0 9 E
Rabat, *Malta* **36 D1** 35 53N 14 25 E
Rabat, *Morocco* **78 B4** 34 2N 6 48W
Rabaul, *Papua N. G.* **96 H7** 4 24 S 152 18 E
Rābigh, *Si. Arabia* **74 C2** 22 50N 39 5 E
Rabka, *Poland* **45 J6** 49 37N 19 59 E
Râbniţa, *Moldova* **43 C14** 47 45N 29 0 E
Rābor, *Iran* **71 D8** 29 17N 56 55 E
Rača, *Serbia, Yug.* **40 B4** 44 14N 21 0 E
Răcăciuni, *Romania* **43 D11** 46 20N 26 59 E
Răcăşdia, *Romania* **42 F6** 44 59N 21 36 E
Racconigi, *Italy* **28 D4** 44 46N 7 46 E
Race, C., *Canada* **103 C9** 46 40N 53 5W
Rach Gia, *Vietnam* **65 G5** 10 5N 105 5 E
Rachid, *Mauritania* **82 B2** 18 45N 11 35W
Raciąż, *Poland* **45 F7** 52 46N 20 10 E
Racibórz, *Poland* **45 H5** 50 7N 18 18 E
Racine, *U.S.A.* **108 D2** 42 41N 87 51W
Rackerby, *U.S.A.* **116 F5** 39 26N 121 22W
Radama, Nosy, *Madag.* **89 A8** 14 0 S 47 47 E
Radama, Saikanosy, *Madag.* **89 A8** 14 16 S 47 53 E
Radan, *Serbia, Yug.* **40 D5** 42 59N 21 29 E
Rădăuţi, *Romania* **43 C10** 47 50N 25 59 E
Rădăuţi-Prut, *Romania* **43 B11** 48 14N 26 48 E
Radbuza →, *Czech Rep.* **26 B6** 49 45N 13 22 E
Radcliff, *U.S.A.* **108 G3** 37 51N 85 57W
Radeberg, *Germany* **24 D9** 51 7N 13 53 E
Radebeul, *Germany* **24 D9** 51 6N 13 39 E
Radeče, *Slovenia* **29 B12** 46 5N 15 14 E
Radekhiv, *Ukraine* **47 G3** 50 25N 24 32 E
Radekhov = Radekhiv, *Ukraine* **47 G3** 50 25N 24 32 E
Radenthein, *Austria* **26 E6** 46 48N 13 43 E
Radew →, *Poland* **44 D2** 54 2N 15 52 E
Radford, *U.S.A.* **108 G5** 37 8N 80 34W
Radhanpur, *India* **68 H4** 23 50N 71 38 E
Radhwa, Jabal, *Si. Arabia* **70 E3** 24 34N 38 18 E
Radika →, *Macedonia* **40 E4** 41 38N 20 37 E
Radisson, *Qué., Canada* **102 B4** 53 47N 77 37W
Radisson, *Sask., Canada* **105 C7** 52 30N 107 20W
Radium Hot Springs, *Canada* **104 C5** 50 35N 116 2W
Radlje ob Dravi, *Slovenia* **29 B12** 46 38N 15 13 E
Radnevo, *Bulgaria* **41 D9** 42 17N 25 58 E
Radnice, *Czech Rep.* **26 B6** 49 51N 13 35 E
Radnor Forest, *U.K.* **13 E4** 52 17N 3 10W
Radolfzell, *Germany* **25 H4** 47 39N 8 59 E
Radom, *Poland* **45 G8** 51 23N 21 12 E
Radomir, *Bulgaria* **40 D6** 42 37N 22 59 E
Radomka →, *Poland* **45 G8** 51 43N 21 28 E
Radomsko, *Poland* **45 G6** 51 5N 19 28 E
Radomyshl, *Ukraine* **47 G5** 50 30N 29 12 E
Radomyśl Wielki, *Poland* **45 H8** 50 14N 21 15 E
Radoszyce, *Poland* **45 G7** 51 4N 20 15 E
Radoviš, *Macedonia* **40 E6** 41 38N 22 28 E
Radovljica, *Slovenia* **29 B11** 46 22N 14 12 E
Radstadt, *Austria* **26 D6** 47 24N 13 28 E
Radstock, C., *Australia* **95 E1** 33 12 S 134 20 E
Răducăneni, *Romania* **43 D12** 46 58N 27 54 E
Raduša, *Macedonia* **40 D5** 42 7N 21 15 E
Radviliškis, *Lithuania* **9 J20** 55 49N 23 33 E
Radville, *Canada* **105 D8** 49 30N 104 15W
Radwā, J., *Si. Arabia* **80 C4** 24 34N 38 18 E
Radymno, *Poland* **45 J9** 49 59N 22 52 E
Radzanów, *Poland* **45 F7** 52 56N 20 8 E
Radziejów, *Poland* **45 F5** 52 40N 18 30 E
Radzyń Chełmiński, *Poland* **44 E5** 53 23N 18 55 E
Radzyń Podlaski, *Poland* **45 G9** 51 47N 22 37 E
Rae, *Canada* **104 A5** 62 50N 116 3W
Rae Bareli, *India* **69 F9** 26 18N 81 20 E
Rae Isthmus, *Canada* **101 B11** 66 40N 87 30W
Raeren, *Belgium* **17 D6** 50 41N 6 7 E
Raeside, L., *Australia* **93 E3** 29 20 S 122 0 E
Raetihi, *N.Z.* **91 H5** 39 25 S 175 17 E
Rafaela, *Argentina* **126 C3** 31 10 S 61 30W
Rafah, *Gaza Strip* **75 D3** 31 18N 34 14 E
Rafai, *C.A.R.* **86 B1** 4 59N 23 58 E

Raffadali, *Italy* **30 E6** 37 24N 13 32 E
Raffili, *Sudan* **81 F2** 6 50N 28 0 E
Rafḥā, *Si. Arabia* **70 D4** 29 35N 43 35 E
Rafsanjān, *Iran* **71 D8** 30 30N 56 5 E
Raft Pt., *Australia* **92 C3** 16 4 S 124 26 E
Râgâ, *Sudan* **81 F2** 8 28N 25 41 E
Raga →, *Sudan* **81 F2** 8 41N 25 52 E
Ragachow, *Belarus* **47 F6** 53 8N 30 5 E
Ragag, *Sudan* **81 E1** 10 59N 24 40 E
Ragama, *Sri Lanka* **66 R11** 7 0N 79 50 E
Ragged, Mt., *Australia* **93 F3** 33 27 S 123 25 E
Raghunathpalli, *India* **69 H11** 22 14N 84 48 E
Raghunathpur, *India* **69 H12** 23 33N 86 40 E
Raglan, *N.Z.* **91 G5** 37 55 S 174 55 E
Ragusa, *Italy* **31 F7** 36 55N 14 44 E
Raha, *Indonesia* **63 E6** 4 55 S 123 0 E
Rahad, Nahr ed →, *Sudan* **81 E3** 14 28N 33 31 E
Rahaeng = Tak, *Thailand* **64 D2** 16 52N 99 8 E
Rahatgarh, *India* **69 H8** 23 47N 78 22 E
Rahden, *Germany* **24 C4** 52 26N 8 36 E
Raheita, *Eritrea* **81 E5** 12 46N 43 4 E
Raḥīmah, *Si. Arabia* **71 E6** 26 42N 50 4 E
Rahimyar Khan, *Pakistan* **68 E4** 28 30N 70 25 E
Rāhjerd, *Iran* **71 C6** 34 22N 50 22 E
Rahon, *India* **68 D7** 31 3N 76 7 E
Raichur, *India* **66 L10** 16 10N 77 20 E
Raiganj, *India* **69 G13** 25 37N 88 10 E
Raigarh, *India* **67 J13** 21 56N 83 25 E
Raijua, *Indonesia* **63 F6** 10 37 S 121 36 E
Raikot, *India* **68 D6** 30 41N 75 42 E
Railton, *Australia* **94 G4** 41 25 S 146 28 E
Rainbow Lake, *Canada* **104 B5** 58 30N 119 23W
Rainier, *U.S.A.* **116 D4** 46 53N 122 41W
Rainier, Mt., *U.S.A.* **116 D5** 46 52N 121 46W
Rainy L., *Canada* **105 D10** 48 42N 93 10W
Rainy River, *Canada* **105 D10** 48 43N 94 29W
Raippaluoto, *Finland* **8 E19** 63 13N 21 14 E
Raipur, *India* **67 J12** 21 17N 81 45 E
Ra'is, *Si. Arabia* **80 C4** 23 35N 38 36 E
Raisen, *India* **68 H8** 23 20N 77 48 E
Raisio, *Finland* **9 F20** 60 28N 22 11 E
Raj Nandgaon, *India* **67 J12** 21 5N 81 5 E
Raj Nilgiri, *India* **69 J12** 21 28N 86 46 E
Raja, Ujung, *Indonesia* **62 D1** 3 40N 96 25 E
Raja Ampat, Kepulauan, *Indonesia* **63 E7** 0 30 S 130 0 E
Rajahmundry, *India* **67 L12** 17 1N 81 48 E
Rajang →, *Malaysia* **62 D4** 2 30N 112 0 E
Rajanpur, *Pakistan* **68 E4** 29 6N 70 19 E
Rajapalaiyam, *India* **66 Q10** 9 25N 77 35 E
Rajasthan □, *India* **68 F5** 26 45N 73 30 E
Rajasthan Canal, *India* **68 F5** 28 0N 72 0 E
Rajauri, *India* **69 C6** 33 25N 74 21 E
Rajgarh, *Mad. P., India* **68 G7** 24 2N 76 45 E
Rajgarh, *Raj., India* **68 F7** 27 14N 76 38 E
Rajgarh, *Raj., India* **68 E6** 28 40N 75 25 E
Rajgir, *India* **69 G11** 25 2N 85 25 E
Rajgród, *Poland* **44 E9** 53 42N 22 42 E
Rajkot, *India* **68 H4** 22 15N 70 56 E
Rajmahal Hills, *India* **69 G12** 24 30N 87 30 E
Rajpipla, *India* **66 J8** 21 50N 73 30 E
Rajpur, *India* **68 H6** 22 18N 74 21 E
Rajpura, *India* **68 D7** 30 25N 76 32 E
Rajshahi, *Bangla.* **67 G16** 24 22N 88 39 E
Rajshahi □, *Bangla.* **69 G13** 25 0N 89 0 E
Rajula, *India* **68 J4** 21 3N 71 26 E
Rakaia, *N.Z.* **91 K4** 43 45 S 172 1 E
Rakaia →, *N.Z.* **91 K4** 43 36 S 172 15 E
Rakan, Ra's, *Qatar* **71 E6** 26 10N 51 20 E
Rakaposhi, *Pakistan* **69 A6** 36 10N 74 25 E
Rakata, Pulau, *Indonesia* **62 F3** 6 10 S 105 20 E
Rakhiv, *Ukraine* **47 H3** 48 3N 24 12 E
Rakhni, *Pakistan* **68 D3** 30 4N 69 56 E
Rakhni →, *Pakistan* **68 E3** 29 31N 69 36 E
Rakitnoye, *Russia* **54 B7** 45 36N 134 17 E
Rakitovo, *Bulgaria* **41 E8** 41 59N 24 5 E
Rakoniewice, *Poland* **45 F3** 52 10N 16 16 E
Rakops, *Botswana* **88 C3** 21 1 S 24 28 E
Rakovica, *Croatia* **29 D12** 44 59N 15 38 E
Rakovník, *Czech Rep.* **26 A6** 50 6N 13 42 E
Rakovski, *Bulgaria* **41 D8** 42 21N 24 57 E
Rakvere, *Estonia* **9 G22** 59 20N 26 25 E
Raleigh, *U.S.A.* **109 H6** 35 47N 78 39W
Ralja, *Serbia, Yug.* **40 B4** 44 33N 20 34 E
Ralls, *U.S.A.* **113 J4** 33 41N 101 24W
Ralston, *U.S.A.* **110 E8** 41 30N 76 57W
Ram →, *Canada* **104 A4** 62 1N 123 41W
Rām Allāh, *West Bank* **75 D4** 31 55N 35 10 E
Ram Hd., *Australia* **95 F4** 37 47 S 149 30 E
Rama, *Nic.* **120 D3** 12 9N 84 15W
Ramacca, *Italy* **31 E7** 37 23N 14 42 E
Ramakona, *India* **69 J8** 21 43N 78 50 E
Ramales de la Victoria, *Spain* **34 B7** 43 15N 3 28W
Raman, *Thailand* **65 J3** 6 29N 101 18 E
Ramanathapuram, *India* **66 Q11** 9 25N 78 55 E
Ramanetaka, B. de, *Madag.* **89 A8** 14 13 S 47 52 E
Ramanujganj, *India* **69 H10** 23 48N 83 42 E
Ramat Gan, *Israel* **75 C3** 32 4N 34 48 E
Ramatlhabama, *S. Africa* **88 D4** 25 37 S 25 33 E
Ramban, *India* **69 C6** 33 14N 75 12 E
Rambervillers, *France* **19 D13** 48 20N 6 38 E
Rambipuji, *Indonesia* **63 H15** 8 12 S 113 37 E
Rambouillet, *France* **19 D8** 48 39N 1 50 E
Ramechhap, *Nepal* **69 F12** 27 25N 86 10 E
Ramenskoye, *Russia* **46 E10** 55 32N 38 15 E
Ramganga →, *India* **69 F8** 27 5N 79 58 E
Ramgarh, *Bihar, India* **69 H11** 23 40N 85 35 E
Ramgarh, *Raj., India* **68 F6** 27 16N 75 14 E
Ramgarh, *Raj., India* **68 F4** 27 30N 70 36 E
Rāmhormoz, *Iran* **71 D6** 31 15N 49 35 E
Ramīān, *Iran* **71 B7** 37 3N 55 16 E
Ramingining, *Australia* **94 A2** 12 19 S 135 3 E
Ramla, *Israel* **75 D3** 31 55N 34 52 E
Ramlu, *Eritrea* **81 E5** 13 32N 41 40 E
Râmna →, *Romania* **43 E12** 45 36N 27 3 E
Ramnad = Ramanathapuram, *India* **66 Q11** 9 25N 78 55 E
Ramnagar, *Jammu & Kashmir, India* **69 C6** 32 47N 75 18 E
Ramnagar, *Ut. P., India* **69 E8** 29 24N 79 7 E
Ramnäs, *Sweden* **10 E10** 59 46N 16 12 E
Râmnicu Sărat, *Romania* **43 E12** 45 26N 27 3 E
Râmnicu Vâlcea, *Romania* **43 E9** 45 9N 24 21 E
Ramon, *Russia* **47 G10** 51 55N 39 21 E
Ramona, *U.S.A.* **117 M10** 33 2N 116 52W
Ramonville-St-Agne, *France* **20 E5** 43 33N 1 28 E
Ramore, *Canada* **102 C3** 48 30N 80 25W
Ramos →, *Nigeria* **83 D6** 5 8N 5 22 E
Ramotswa, *Botswana* **88 C4** 24 50 S 25 52 E
Rampur, *H.P., India* **68 D7** 31 26N 77 43 E
Rampur, *Mad. P., India* **68 H5** 23 25N 73 53 E
Rampur, *Ut. P., India* **69 E8** 28 50N 79 5 E
Rampur Hat, *India* **69 G12** 24 10N 87 50 E
Rampura, *India* **68 G6** 24 30N 75 27 E
Ramrama Tola, *India* **69 J8** 21 52N 79 55 E
Ramree I. = Ramree Kyun, *Burma* **67 K19** 19 0N 94 0 E
Ramree Kyun, *Burma* **67 K19** 19 0N 94 0 E
Rāmsar, *Iran* **71 B6** 36 53N 50 41 E
Ramsey, *U.K.* **12 C3** 54 20N 4 22W
Ramsey, *U.S.A.* **111 E10** 41 4N 74 9W
Ramsey L., *Canada* **102 C3** 47 13N 82 15W
Ramsgate, *U.K.* **13 F9** 51 20N 1 25 E
Ramsjö, *Sweden* **10 B9** 62 11N 15 37 E
Ramstein, *Germany* **25 F3** 49 27N 7 32 E
Ramtek, *India* **66 J11** 21 20N 79 15 E
Ramvik, *Sweden* **10 B11** 62 49N 17 51 E
Rana Pratap Sagar Dam, *India* **68 G6** 24 58N 75 38 E
Ranaghat, *India* **69 H13** 23 15N 88 35 E
Ranahu, *Pakistan* **68 G3** 25 55N 69 45 E
Ranau, *Malaysia* **62 C5** 6 2N 116 40 E
Rancagua, *Chile* **126 C1** 34 10 S 70 50W
Rance →, *France* **18 D5** 48 34N 1 59W
Rancheria →, *Canada* **104 A3** 60 13N 129 7W
Ranchester, *U.S.A.* **114 D10** 44 54N 107 10W
Ranchi, *India* **69 H11** 23 19N 85 27 E
Rancho Cucamonga, *U.S.A.* **117 L9** 34 10N 117 30W
Randalstown, *U.K.* **15 B5** 54 45N 6 19W
Randan, *France* **19 F10** 46 2N 3 21 E
Randazzo, *Italy* **31 E7** 37 53N 14 57 E
Randers, *Denmark* **11 H4** 56 29N 10 1 E
Randers Fjord, *Denmark* **11 H4** 56 37N 10 20 E
Randfontein, *S. Africa* **89 D4** 26 8 S 27 45 E
Randle, *U.S.A.* **116 D5** 46 32N 121 57W
Randolph, *Mass., U.S.A.* **111 D13** 42 10N 71 2W
Randolph, *N.Y., U.S.A.* **110 D6** 42 10N 78 59W
Randolph, *Utah, U.S.A.* **114 F8** 41 40N 111 11W
Randolph, *Vt., U.S.A.* **111 C12** 43 55N 72 40W
Randsburg, *U.S.A.* **117 K9** 35 22N 117 39W
Råne älv →, *Sweden* **8 D20** 65 50N 22 20 E
Rangae, *Thailand* **65 J3** 6 19N 101 44 E
Rangaunu B., *N.Z.* **91 F4** 34 51 S 173 15 E
Rangeley, *U.S.A.* **111 B14** 44 58N 70 39W
Rangeley L., *U.S.A.* **111 B14** 44 55N 70 43W
Rangely, *U.S.A.* **114 F9** 40 5N 108 48W
Ranger, *U.S.A.* **113 J5** 32 28N 98 41W
Rangia, *India* **67 F17** 26 28N 91 38 E
Rangiora, *N.Z.* **91 K4** 43 19 S 172 36 E
Rangitaiki →, *N.Z.* **91 G6** 37 54 S 176 49 E
Rangitata →, *N.Z.* **91 K3** 43 45 S 171 15 E
Rangkasbitung, *Indonesia* **63 G12** 6 21 S 106 15 E
Rangon →, *Burma* **67 L20** 16 28N 96 40 E
Rangoon, *Burma* **67 L20** 16 45N 96 20 E
Rangpur, *Bangla.* **67 G16** 25 42N 89 22 E
Rangsit, *Thailand* **64 F3** 13 59N 100 37 E
Ranibennur, *India* **66 M9** 14 35N 75 30 E
Raniganj, *Ut. P., India* **69 F9** 27 3N 82 13 E
Raniganj, *W. Bengal, India* **67 H15** 23 40N 87 5 E
Ranikhet, *India* **69 E8** 29 39N 79 25 E
Raniwara, *India* **66 G8** 24 50N 72 10 E
Rāniyah, *Iraq* **70 B5** 36 15N 44 53 E
Ranka, *India* **69 H10** 23 59N 83 47 E
Ranken →, *Australia* **94 C2** 20 31 S 137 36 E
Rankin, *U.S.A.* **113 K4** 31 13N 101 56W
Rankin Inlet, *Canada* **100 B10** 62 30N 93 0W
Rankins Springs, *Australia* **95 E4** 33 49 S 146 14 E
Rankweil, *Austria* **26 D2** 47 17N 9 39 E
Rannoch, L., *U.K.* **14 E4** 56 41N 4 20W
Rannoch Moor, *U.K.* **14 E4** 56 38N 4 48W
Ranobe, Helodranon' i, *Madag.* **89 C7** 23 3 S 43 33 E
Ranohira, *Madag.* **89 C8** 22 29 S 45 24 E
Ranomafana, *Toamasina, Madag.* **89 B8** 18 57 S 48 50 E
Ranomafana, *Toliara, Madag.* **89 C8** 24 34 S 47 0 E
Ranomena, *Madag.* **89 C8** 23 25 S 47 17 E
Ranong, *Thailand* **65 H2** 9 56N 98 40 E
Ranotsara Nord, *Madag.* **89 C8** 22 48 S 46 36 E
Ränsa, *Iran* **71 C6** 33 39N 48 18 E
Ransiki, *Indonesia* **63 E8** 1 30 S 134 10 E
Rantabe, *Madag.* **89 B8** 15 42 S 49 39 E
Rantauprapat, *Indonesia* **62 D1** 2 15N 99 50 E
Rantemario, *Indonesia* **63 E5** 3 15 S 119 57 E
Rantoul, *U.S.A.* **108 E1** 40 19N 88 9W
Ranum, *Denmark* **11 H3** 56 54N 9 14 E
Ranyah, W. →, *Si. Arabia* **80 C5** 21 18N 43 20 E
Raon l'Étape, *France* **19 D13** 48 24N 6 50 E
Raoping, *China* **59 F11** 23 42N 117 1 E
Raoyang, *China* **56 E8** 38 15N 115 45 E
Rapa, *Pac. Oc.* **97 K13** 27 35 S 144 20W
Rapallo, *Italy* **28 D6** 44 21N 9 14 E
Rapar, *India* **68 H4** 23 34N 70 38 E
Rāpch, *Iran* **71 E8** 25 40N 59 15 E
Raper, C., *Canada* **101 B13** 69 44N 67 6W
Rapid City, *U.S.A.* **112 D3** 44 5N 103 14W
Rapid River, *U.S.A.* **108 C2** 45 55N 86 58W
Rapla, *Estonia* **9 G21** 59 1N 24 52 E
Rapti →, *India* **69 F10** 26 18N 83 41 E
Rapu Rapu I., *Phil.* **61 E6** 13 12N 124 9 E
Raqaba ez Zarqa →, *Sudan* **81 F2** 9 14N 29 44 E
Raquette →, *U.S.A.* **111 B10** 45 0N 74 42W
Raquette Lake, *U.S.A.* **111 C10** 43 49N 74 40W
Rarotonga, *Cook Is.* **97 K12** 21 30 S 160 0W
Ra's al 'Ayn, *Syria* **70 B4** 36 45N 40 12 E
Ra's al Khaymah, *U.A.E.* **71 E7** 25 50N 55 59 E
Râs el Mâ, *Mali* **82 B4** 16 35N 4 30W
Ras Ghârib, *Egypt* **80 B3** 28 6N 33 18 E
Ras Mallap, *Egypt* **80 B3** 29 18N 32 50 E
Rasca, Pta. de la, *Canary Is.* **37 G3** 27 59N 16 41W
Râşcani, *Moldova* **43 C12** 47 58N 27 33 E
Raseiniai, *Lithuania* **9 J20** 55 25N 23 5 E
Rashad, *Sudan* **81 E3** 11 55N 31 0 E
Rashîd, *Egypt* **80 H7** 31 21N 30 22 E
Rashîd, Masabb, *Egypt* **80 H7** 31 22N 30 17 E
Rashmi, *India* **68 G6** 25 4N 74 22 E
Rasht, *Iran* **71 B6** 37 20N 49 40 E
Rasi Salai, *Thailand* **64 E5** 15 20N 104 9 E
Raška, *Serbia, Yug.* **40 C4** 43 19N 20 39 E
Râsnov, *Romania* **43 E10** 45 35N 25 27 E
Rason L., *Australia* **93 E3** 28 45 S 124 25 E
Raşova, *Romania* **43 F12** 44 15N 27 55 E
Rasovo, *Bulgaria* **40 C7** 43 42N 23 17 E
Rasra, *India* **69 G10** 25 50N 83 50 E
Rasskazovo, *Russia* **48 D5** 52 35N 41 50 E
Rast, *Romania* **43 G8** 43 53N 23 16 E
Rastatt, *Germany* **25 G4** 48 50N 8 11 E
Rastede, *Germany* **24 B4** 53 15N 8 12 E
Răstolita, *Romania* **43 D9** 46 59N 24 58 E
Rasul, *Pakistan* **68 C5** 32 42N 73 34 E
Raszków, *Poland* **45 G4** 51 43N 17 40 E
Rat Buri, *Thailand* **64 F2** 13 30N 99 54 E
Rat Islands, *U.S.A.* **100 C1** 52 0N 178 0 E
Rat L., *Canada* **105 B9** 56 10N 99 40W
Ratangarh, *India* **68 E6** 28 5N 74 35 E
Rätansbyn, *Sweden* **10 B8** 62 29N 14 33 E
Raṭāwī, *Iraq* **70 D5** 30 38N 47 13 E
Ratcatchers L., *Australia* **95 E3** 32 38 S 143 10 E
Rath, *India* **69 G8** 25 36N 79 37 E
Rath Luirc, *Ireland* **15 D3** 52 21N 8 40W
Rathdrum, *Ireland* **15 D5** 52 56N 6 14W
Rathenow, *Germany* **24 C8** 52 37N 12 19 E
Rathkeale, *Ireland* **15 D3** 52 32N 8 56W
Rathlin I., *U.K.* **15 A5** 55 18N 6 14W
Rathmelton, *Ireland* **15 A4** 55 2N 7 38W
Ratibor = Racibórz, *Poland* **45 H5** 50 7N 18 18 E
Rätikon, *Austria* **26 D2** 47 0N 9 55 E
Ratingen, *Germany* **24 D2** 51 18N 6 52 E
Ratlam, *India* **68 H6** 23 20N 75 0 E
Ratnagiri, *India* **66 L8** 16 57N 73 18 E
Ratodero, *Pakistan* **68 F3** 27 48N 68 18 E
Raton, *U.S.A.* **113 G2** 36 54N 104 24W
Rattaphum, *Thailand* **65 J3** 7 8N 100 16 E
Ratten, *Austria* **26 D8** 47 28N 15 44 E
Rattray Hd., *U.K.* **14 D7** 57 38N 1 50W
Rättvik, *Sweden* **10 D9** 60 52N 15 7 E
Ratz, Mt., *Canada* **104 B2** 57 23N 132 12W
Ratzeburg, *Germany* **24 B6** 53 40N 10 46 E
Raub, *Malaysia* **65 L3** 3 47N 101 52 E
Rauch, *Argentina* **126 D4** 36 45 S 59 5W
Raudales de Malpaso, *Mexico* **119 D6** 17 30N 23 30W
Raufarhöfn, *Iceland* **8 C6** 66 27N 15 57W
Raufoss, *Norway* **9 F14** 60 44N 10 37 E
Raukumara Ra., *N.Z.* **91 H6** 38 5 S 177 55 E
Rauma, *Finland* **9 F19** 61 10N 21 30 E
Raurkela, *India* **69 H11** 22 14N 84 50 E
Rausu-Dake, *Japan* **54 B12** 44 4N 145 7 E
Răut →, *Moldova* **43 C14** 47 15N 29 9 E
Rava-Ruska, *Poland* **47 G2** 50 15N 23 42 E
Rava Russkaya = Rava-Ruska, *Poland* **47 G2** 50 15N 23 42 E
Ravalli, *U.S.A.* **114 C6** 47 17N 114 11W
Ravānsar, *Iran* **70 C5** 34 43N 46 40 E
Ravanusa, *Italy* **30 E6** 37 16N 13 58 E
Rāvar, *Iran* **71 D8** 31 20N 56 51 E
Ravena, *U.S.A.* **111 D11** 42 28N 73 49W
Ravenna, *Italy* **29 D9** 44 25N 12 12 E
Ravenna, *Nebr., U.S.A.* **112 E5** 41 1N 98 55W
Ravenna, *Ohio, U.S.A.* **110 E3** 41 9N 81 15W
Ravensburg, *Germany* **25 H5** 47 46N 9 36 E
Ravenshoe, *Australia* **94 B4** 17 37 S 145 29 E
Ravensthorpe, *Australia* **93 F3** 33 35 S 120 2 E
Ravenswood, *Australia* **94 C4** 20 6 S 146 54 E
Ravenswood, *U.S.A.* **108 F5** 38 57N 81 46W
Ravi →, *Pakistan* **68 D4** 30 35N 71 49 E
Ravna Gora, *Croatia* **29 C11** 45 24N 14 50 E
Ravna Reka, *Serbia, Yug.* **40 B5** 44 1N 21 35 E
Ravne na Koroškem, *Slovenia* **29 B11** 46 36N 14 59 E
Rawa Mazowiecka, *Poland* **45 G7** 51 46N 20 12 E
Rawalpindi, *Pakistan* **68 C5** 33 38N 73 8 E
Rawāndūz, *Iraq* **70 B5** 36 40N 44 30 E
Rawang, *Malaysia* **65 L3** 3 20N 101 35 E
Rawene, *N.Z.* **91 F4** 35 25 S 173 32 E
Rawicz, *Poland* **45 G3** 51 36N 16 52 E
Rawka →, *Poland* **45 F7** 52 9N 20 8 E
Rawlinna, *Australia* **93 F4** 30 58 S 125 28 E
Rawlins, *U.S.A.* **114 F10** 41 47N 107 14W
Rawlinson Ra., *Australia* **93 D4** 24 40 S 128 30 E
Rawson, *Argentina* **128 E3** 43 15 S 65 5W
Raxaul, *India* **69 F11** 26 59N 84 51 E
Ray, *U.S.A.* **112 A3** 48 21N 103 10W
Ray, C., *Canada* **103 C8** 47 33N 59 15W
Rayadurg, *India* **66 M10** 14 40N 76 50 E
Rayagada, *India* **67 K13** 19 15N 83 20 E
Raychikhinsk, *Russia* **51 E13** 49 46N 129 25 E
Rāyen, *Iran* **71 D8** 29 34N 57 26 E
Rayleigh, *U.K.* **13 F8** 51 36N 0 37 E
Raymond, *Canada* **104 D6** 49 30N 112 35W
Raymond, *Calif., U.S.A.* **116 H7** 37 13N 119 54W
Raymond, *N.H., U.S.A.* **111 C13** 43 2N 71 11W
Raymond, *Wash., U.S.A.* **116 D3** 46 41N 123 44W
Raymond Terrace, *Australia* **95 E5** 32 45 S 151 44 E
Raymondville, *U.S.A.* **113 M6** 26 29N 97 47W
Raymore, *Canada* **105 C8** 51 25N 104 31W
Rayón, *Mexico* **118 B2** 29 43N 110 35W
Rayong, *Thailand* **64 F3** 12 40N 101 20 E
Rayville, *U.S.A.* **113 J9** 32 29N 91 46W
Raz, Pte. du, *France* **18 D2** 48 2N 4 47W
Razan, *Iran* **71 C6** 35 23N 49 2 E
Ražana, *Serbia, Yug.* **40 B3** 44 6N 19 55 E
Ražanj, *Serbia, Yug.* **40 C5** 43 40N 21 31 E
Razdelna, *Bulgaria* **41 C11** 43 13N 27 41 E
Razdel'naya = Rozdilna, *Ukraine* **47 J6** 46 50N 30 2 E
Razdolnoye, *Russia* **54 C5** 43 30N 131 52 E
Razdolnoye, *Ukraine* **47 K7** 45 46N 33 29 E
Razeh, *Iran* **71 C6** 32 47N 48 9 E
Razgrad, *Bulgaria* **41 C10** 43 33N 26 34 E
Razim, Lacul, *Romania* **43 F14** 44 50N 29 0 E
Razlog, *Bulgaria* **40 E7** 41 53N 23 28 E
Razmak, *Pakistan* **68 C3** 32 45N 69 50 E
Ré, Î. de, *France* **20 B2** 46 12N 1 30W
Reading, *U.K.* **13 F7** 51 27N 0 58W
Reading, *U.S.A.* **111 F9** 40 20N 75 56W
Reading □, *U.K.* **13 F7** 51 27N 0 58W
Realicó, *Argentina* **126 D3** 35 0 S 64 15W
Réalmont, *France* **20 E6** 43 48N 2 10 E
Ream, *Cambodia* **65 G4** 10 34N 103 39 E
Reata, *Mexico* **118 B4** 26 8N 101 5W
Reay Forest, *U.K.* **14 C4** 58 22N 4 55W
Rebais, *France* **19 D10** 48 50N 3 10 E
Rebi, *Indonesia* **63 F8** 6 23 S 134 7 E
Rebiana, *Libya* **79 D10** 24 12N 22 10 E
Rebun-Tō, *Japan* **54 B10** 45 23N 141 2 E
Recanati, *Italy* **29 E10** 43 24N 13 32 E
Recaş, *Romania* **42 E6** 45 46N 21 30 E
Recco, *Italy* **28 D6** 44 22N 9 9 E
Recherche, Arch. of the, *Australia* **93 F3** 34 15 S 122 50 E
Rechna Doab, *Pakistan* **68 D5** 31 35N 73 30 E
Rechytsa, *Belarus* **47 F6** 52 21N 30 24 E
Recife, *Brazil* **125 E12** 8 0 S 35 0W
Recklinghausen, *Germany* **17 C7** 51 37N 7 12 E
Reconquista, *Argentina* **126 B4** 29 10 S 59 45W
Recreo, *Argentina* **126 B2** 29 25 S 65 10W
Recz, *Poland* **45 E2** 53 16N 15 31 E
Red →, *La., U.S.A.* **113 K9** 31 1N 91 45W
Red →, *N. Dak., U.S.A.* **100 C10** 49 0N 97 15W
Red Bank, *U.S.A.* **111 F10** 40 21N 74 5W
Red Bay, *Canada* **103 B8** 51 44N 56 25W
Red Bluff, *U.S.A.* **114 F2** 40 11N 122 15W
Red Bluff L., *U.S.A.* **113 K3** 31 54N 103 55W
Red Cliffs, *Australia* **95 E3** 34 19 S 142 11 E
Red Cloud, *U.S.A.* **112 E5** 40 5N 98 32W
Red Creek, *U.S.A.* **111 C8** 43 14N 76 45W
Red Deer, *Canada* **104 C6** 52 20N 113 50W
Red Deer →, *Alta., Canada* **105 C7** 50 58N 110 0W
Red Deer →, *Man., Canada* **105 C8** 52 53N 101 1W
Red Deer L., *Canada* **105 C8** 52 55N 101 20W
Red Hook, *U.S.A.* **111 E11** 41 55N 73 53W
Red Indian L., *Canada* **103 C8** 48 35N 57 0W
Red L., *Canada* **105 C10** 51 3N 93 49W
Red Lake, *Canada* **105 C10** 51 3N 93 49W
Red Lake Falls, *U.S.A.* **112 B6** 47 53N 96 16W
Red Lake Road, *Canada* **105 C10** 49 59N 93 25W
Red Lodge, *U.S.A.* **114 D9** 45 11N 109 15W
Red Mountain, *U.S.A.* **117 K9** 35 37N 117 38W
Red Oak, *U.S.A.* **112 E7** 41 1N 95 14W
Red Rock, *Canada* **102 C2** 48 55N 88 15W
Red Rock, L., *U.S.A.* **112 E8** 41 22N 92 59W
Red Rocks Pt., *Australia* **93 F4** 32 13 S 127 32 E
Red Sea, *Asia* **74 C2** 25 0N 36 0 E
Red Slate Mt., *U.S.A.* **116 H8** 37 31N 118 52W
Red Sucker L., *Canada* **102 B1** 54 9N 93 40W
Red Tower Pass = Turnu Roşu, P., *Romania* **43 E9** 45 33N 24 17 E
Red Wing, *U.S.A.* **112 C8** 44 34N 92 31W
Reda, *Poland* **44 D5** 54 40N 18 19 E
Redang, *Malaysia* **62 C2** 5 49N 103 2 E
Redange, *Lux.* **17 E5** 49 46N 5 52 E
Redcar, *U.K.* **12 C6** 54 37N 1 4W
Redcar & Cleveland □, *U.K.* **12 C7** 54 29N 1 0W
Redcliff, *Canada* **105 C6** 50 10N 110 50W
Redcliffe, *Australia* **95 D5** 27 12 S 153 0 E
Redcliffe, Mt., *Australia* **93 E3** 28 30 S 121 30 E
Reddersburg, *S. Africa* **88 D4** 29 41 S 26 10 E
Redding, *U.S.A.* **114 F2** 40 35N 122 24W
Redditch, *U.K.* **13 E6** 52 18N 1 55W
Redfield, *U.S.A.* **112 C5** 44 53N 98 31W
Redford, *U.S.A.* **111 B11** 44 38N 73 48W
Redkino, *Russia* **46 D9** 56 39N 36 16 E
Redlands, *U.S.A.* **117 M9** 34 4N 117 11W
Redmond, *Oreg., U.S.A.* **114 D3** 44 17N 121 11W
Redmond, *Wash., U.S.A.* **116 C4** 47 41N 122 7W
Redon, *France* **18 E4** 47 40N 2 6W
Redonda, *Antigua* **121 C7** 16 58N 62 19W
Redondela, *Spain* **34 C2** 42 15N 8 38W
Redondo, *Portugal* **35 G3** 38 39N 7 37W
Redondo Beach, *U.S.A.* **117 M8** 33 50N 118 23W
Redruth, *U.K.* **13 G2** 50 14N 5 14W
Redvers, *Canada* **105 D8** 49 35N 101 40W
Redwater, *Canada* **104 C6** 53 55N 113 6W
Redwood, *U.S.A.* **111 B9** 44 18N 75 48W
Redwood City, *U.S.A.* **116 H4** 37 30N 122 15W
Redwood Falls, *U.S.A.* **112 C7** 44 32N 95 7W
Redwood National Park, *U.S.A.* **114 F1** 41 40N 124 5W
Ree, L., *Ireland* **15 C3** 53 35N 8 0W
Reed, L., *Canada* **105 C8** 54 38N 100 30W
Reed City, *U.S.A.* **108 D3** 43 53N 85 31W
Reedley, *U.S.A.* **116 J7** 36 36N 119 27W
Reedsburg, *U.S.A.* **112 D9** 43 32N 90 0W
Reedsport, *U.S.A.* **114 E1** 43 42N 124 6W
Reedsville, *U.S.A.* **110 F7** 40 39N 77 35W
Reefton, *N.Z.* **91 K3** 42 6 S 171 51 E
Rees, *Germany* **24 D2** 51 46N 6 24 E
Reese →, *U.S.A.* **114 F5** 40 48N 117 4W
Refahiye, *Turkey* **73 C8** 39 54N 38 47 E
Reftele, *Sweden* **11 G7** 57 11N 13 35 E
Refugio, *U.S.A.* **113 L6** 28 18N 97 17W
Rega →, *Poland* **44 D2** 54 10N 15 18 E
Regalbuto, *Italy* **31 E7** 37 39N 14 38 E
Regen, *Germany* **25 G9** 48 58N 13 8 E
Regen →, *Germany* **25 F8** 49 1N 12 6 E
Regensburg, *Germany* **25 F8** 49 1N 12 6 E
Regenstauf, *Germany* **25 F8** 49 7N 12 8 E
Reggello, *Italy* **29 E8** 43 41N 11 32 E
Réggio di Calábria, *Italy* **31 D8** 38 6N 15 39 E
Réggio nell'Emília, *Italy* **28 D7** 44 43N 10 36 E
Reghin, *Romania* **43 D9** 46 46N 24 42 E
Regina, *Canada* **105 C8** 50 27N 104 35W
Regina Beach, *Canada* **105 C8** 50 47N 105 0W
Registro, *Brazil* **127 A6** 24 29 S 47 49W
Reguengos de Monsaraz, *Portugal* **35 G3** 38 25N 7 32W
Rehar →, *India* **69 H10** 23 55N 82 40 E
Rehli, *India* **69 H8** 23 38N 79 5 E
Rehoboth, *Namibia* **88 C2** 23 15 S 17 4 E
Rehovot, *Israel* **75 D3** 31 54N 34 48 E
Reichenbach, *Germany* **24 E8** 50 37N 12 17 E
Reid, *Australia* **93 F4** 30 49 S 128 26 E
Reidsville, *U.S.A.* **109 G6** 36 21N 79 40W
Reigate, *U.K.* **13 F7** 51 14N 0 12W
Reillo, *Spain* **32 F3** 39 54N 1 53W
Reims, *France* **19 C11** 49 15N 4 1 E
Reina Adelaida, Arch., *Chile* **128 G2** 52 20 S 74 0W
Reinbek, *Germany* **24 B6** 53 30N 10 15 E
Reindeer →, *Canada* **105 B8** 55 36N 103 11W
Reindeer I., *Canada* **105 C9** 52 30N 98 0W
Reindeer L., *Canada* **105 B8** 57 15N 102 15W
Reinga, C., *N.Z.* **91 F4** 34 25 S 172 43 E
Reinosa, *Spain* **34 B6** 43 2N 4 15W
Reitz, *S. Africa* **89 D4** 27 48 S 28 29 E
Reivilo, *S. Africa* **88 D3** 27 36 S 24 8 E
Rejaf, *Sudan* **81 G3** 4 45N 31 35 E
Rejmyre, *Sweden* **11 F9** 58 50N 15 55 E
Rejowiec Fabryczny, *Poland* **45 G10** 51 5N 23 17 E
Reka →, *Slovenia* **29 C11** 45 40N 14 0 E
Rekovac, *Serbia, Yug.* **40 C5** 43 51N 21 3 E
Reliance, *Canada* **105 A7** 63 0N 109 20W
Rémalard, *France* **18 D7** 48 26N 0 47 E
Remarkable, Mt., *Australia* **95 E2** 32 48 S 138 10 E
Rembang, *Indonesia* **63 G14** 6 42 S 111 21 E
Remedios, *Panama* **120 E3** 8 15N 81 50W
Remeshk, *Iran* **71 E8** 26 55N 58 50 E
Remetea, *Romania* **43 D10** 46 45N 25 29 E
Remich, *Lux.* **17 E6** 49 32N 6 22 E
Remiremont, *France* **19 D13** 48 2N 6 36 E
Remo, *Ethiopia* **81 F5** 6 48N 41 20 E
Remontnoye, *Russia* **49 G6** 46 34N 43 37 E
Remoulins, *France* **21 E8** 43 55N 4 35 E
Remscheid, *Germany* **17 C7** 51 11N 7 12 E
Ren Xian, *China* **56 F8** 37 8N 114 40 E
Rende, *Italy* **31 C9** 39 20N 16 11 E
Rendína, *Greece* **38 B3** 39 4N 21 58 E
Rendsburg, *Germany* **24 A5** 54 17N 9 39 E
Renfrew, *Canada* **102 C4** 45 30N 76 40W
Renfrewshire □, *U.K.* **14 F4** 55 49N 4 38W
Rengat, *Indonesia* **62 E2** 0 30 S 102 45 E
Rengo, *Chile* **126 C1** 34 24 S 70 50W
Renhua, *China* **59 E9** 25 5N 113 40 E
Renhuai, *China* **58 D6** 27 48N 106 24 E
Reni, *Ukraine* **47 K5** 45 28N 28 15 E
Renk, *Sudan* **81 E3** 11 50N 32 50 E
Renmark, *Australia* **95 E3** 34 11 S 140 43 E
Rennell Sd., *Canada* **104 C2** 53 23N 132 35W
Renner Springs, *Australia* **94 B1** 18 20 S 133 47 E
Rennes, *France* **18 D5** 48 7N 1 41W
Rennie L., *Canada* **105 A7** 61 32N 105 35W
Reno, *U.S.A.* **116 F7** 39 31N 119 48W
Reno →, *Italy* **29 D9** 44 38N 12 16 E
Renovo, *U.S.A.* **110 E7** 41 20N 77 45W
Renqiu, *China* **56 E9** 38 43N 116 5 E
Rens, *Denmark* **11 K3** 54 54N 9 5 E
Renshou, *China* **58 C5** 30 3N 104 9 E
Rensselaer, *Ind., U.S.A.* **108 E2** 40 57N 87 9W
Rensselaer, *N.Y., U.S.A.* **111 D11** 42 38N 73 45W
Rentería, *Spain* **32 B3** 43 19N 1 54W
Renton, *U.S.A.* **116 C4** 47 29N 122 12W
Réo, *Burkina Faso* **82 C4** 12 28N 2 35W
Reocín, *Spain* **34 B6** 43 21N 4 5W
Reotipur, *India* **69 G10** 25 33N 83 45 E
Répcelak, *Hungary* **42 C2** 47 24N 17 1 E
Republic, *Mo., U.S.A.* **113 G8** 37 7N 93 29W
Republic, *Wash., U.S.A.* **114 B4** 48 39N 118 44W
Republican →, *U.S.A.* **112 F6** 39 4N 96 48W
Repulse Bay, *Canada* **101 B11** 66 30N 86 30W
Requena, *Peru* **124 E4** 5 5 S 73 52W
Requena, *Spain* **33 F3** 39 30N 1 4W
Réquista, *France* **20 D6** 44 1N 2 32 E
Reşadiye = Datça, *Turkey* **39 E9** 36 46N 27 40 E
Reşadiye, *Turkey* **72 B7** 40 23N 37 20 E
Reşadiye Yarımadası, *Turkey* **39 E9** 36 40N 27 45 E
Resavica, *Serbia, Yug.* **40 B5** 44 4N 21 31 E
Resen, *Macedonia* **40 E5** 41 5N 21 0 E
Reserve, *U.S.A.* **115 K9** 33 43N 108 45W
Resht = Rasht, *Iran* **71 B6** 37 20N 49 40 E
Resistencia, *Argentina* **126 B4** 27 30 S 59 0W
Reşiţa, *Romania* **42 E6** 45 18N 21 53 E
Resko, *Poland* **44 E2** 53 47N 15 25 E
Resolution I., *Canada* **101 B13** 61 30N 65 0W
Resolution I., *N.Z.* **91 L1** 45 40 S 166 40 E
Ressano Garcia, *Mozam.* **89 D5** 25 25 S 32 0 E
Reston, *Canada* **105 D8** 49 33N 101 6W
Reszel, *Poland* **44 D8** 54 4N 21 10 E
Retalhuleu, *Guatemala* **120 D1** 14 33N 91 46W
Retenue, L. de, *Dem. Rep. of the Congo* **87 E2** 11 0 S 27 0 E
Retezat, Muntii, *Romania* **42 E8** 45 25N 23 0 E
Retford, *U.K.* **12 D7** 53 19N 0 56W
Rethel, *France* **19 C11** 49 30N 4 20 E
Rethem, *Germany* **24 C5** 52 47N 9 22 E
Réthímnon, *Greece* **36 D6** 35 18N 24 30 E
Réthímnon □, *Greece* **36 D6** 35 23N 24 28 E
Reti, *Pakistan* **68 E3** 28 5N 69 48 E
Retiche, Alpi, *Switz.* **25 J6** 46 30N 10 0 E
Retiers, *France* **18 E5** 47 55N 1 23W
Retortillo, *Spain* **34 E4** 40 48N 6 21W
Retournac, *France* **21 C8** 45 12N 4 2 E
Rétság, *Hungary* **42 C4** 47 58N 19 10 E
Réunion ■, *Ind. Oc.* **77 J9** 21 0 S 56 0 E
Reus, *Spain* **32 D6** 41 10N 1 5 E
Reuterstadt Stavenhagen, *Germany* **24 B8** 53 42N 12 54 E
Reutlingen, *Germany* **25 G5** 48 29N 9 12 E
Reutte, *Austria* **26 D3** 47 29N 10 42 E
Reval = Tallinn, *Estonia* **9 G21** 59 22N 24 48 E
Revel, *France* **20 E6** 43 28N 2 1 E
Revelganj, *India* **69 G11** 25 50N 84 40 E
Revelstoke, *Canada* **104 C5** 51 0N 118 10W
Reventazón, *Peru* **124 E2** 6 10 S 80 58W
Revigny-sur-Ornain, *France* **19 D11** 48 49N 4 59 E
Revillagigedo, Is. de, *Pac. Oc.* **118 D2** 18 40N 112 0W
Revin, *France* **19 C11** 49 55N 4 39 E
Revúca, *Slovak Rep.* **27 C13** 48 41N 20 7 E
Revuè →, *Mozam.* **87 F3** 19 50 S 34 0 E
Rewa, *India* **69 G9** 24 33N 81 25 E
Rewari, *India* **68 E7** 28 15N 76 40 E
Rexburg, *U.S.A.* **114 E8** 43 49N 111 47W
Rey, *Iran* **71 C6** 35 35N 51 25 E
Rey, I. del, *Panama* **120 E4** 8 20N 78 30W
Rey Malabo, *Eq. Guin.* **83 E6** 3 45N 8 50 E
Reyðarfjörður, *Iceland* **8 D6** 65 2N 14 13W
Reyes, Pt., *U.S.A.* **116 H3** 38 0N 123 0W
Reyhanlı, *Turkey* **72 D7** 36 16N 36 35 E
Reykjahlið, *Iceland* **8 D5** 65 40N 16 55W
Reykjanes, *Iceland* **8 E2** 63 48N 22 40W
Reykjavík, *Iceland* **8 D3** 64 10N 21 57W
Reynolds Ra., *Australia* **92 D5** 22 30 S 133 0 E
Reynoldsville, *U.S.A.* **110 E6** 41 5N 78 58W

Reynosa, *Mexico* **119 B5** 26 5N 98 18W
Rēzekne, *Latvia* **9 H22** 56 30N 27 17 E
Rezina, *Moldova* **43 C13** 47 45N 28 58 E
Rezovo, *Bulgaria* **41 D12** 42 0N 28 0 E
Reẕvān, *Iran* **71 E8** 27 34N 56 6 E
Rgotina, *Serbia, Yug.* **40 B6** 44 1N 22 17 E
Rhamnus, *Greece* **38 C6** 38 12N 24 3 E
Rhayader, *U.K.* **13 E4** 52 18N 3 29W
Rheda-Wiedenbrück, *Germany* **24 D4** 51 50N 8 20 E
Rhede, *Germany* **24 D2** 51 50N 6 42 E
Rhein →, *Europe* **17 C6** 51 52N 6 2 E
Rhein-Main-Donau-Kanal, *Germany* **25 F7** 49 1N 11 27 E
Rheinbach, *Germany* **24 E2** 50 38N 6 57 E
Rheine, *Germany* **24 C3** 52 17N 7 26 E
Rheinfelden, *Germany* **25 H3** 47 33N 7 47 E
Rheinhessen-Pfalz □, *Germany* **25 F3** 49 20N 8 0 E
Rheinland-Pfalz □, *Germany* **25 E2** 50 0N 7 0 E
Rheinsberg, *Germany* **24 B8** 53 6N 12 54 E
Rhin = Rhein →, *Europe* **17 C6** 51 52N 6 2 E
Rhine = Rhein →, *Europe* **17 C6** 51 52N 6 2 E
Rhinebeck, *U.S.A.* **111 E11** 41 56N 73 55W
Rhineland-Palatinate = Rheinland-Pfalz □, *Germany* **25 E2** 50 0N 7 0 E
Rhinelander, *U.S.A.* **112 C10** 45 38N 89 25W
Rhinns Pt., *U.K.* **14 F2** 55 40N 6 29W
Rhino Camp, *Uganda* **86 B3** 3 0N 31 22 E
Rhir, Cap, *Morocco* **78 B4** 30 38N 9 54W
Rho, *Italy* **28 C6** 45 32N 9 2 E
Rhode Island □, *U.S.A.* **111 E13** 41 40N 71 30W
Rhodes = Ródhos, *Greece* **36 C10** 36 15N 28 10 E
Rhodesia = Zimbabwe ■, *Africa* **87 F3** 19 0S 30 0 E
Rhodope Mts. = Rhodopi Planina, *Bulgaria* **41 E8** 41 40N 24 20 E
Rhodopi Planina, *Bulgaria* **41 E8** 41 40N 24 20 E
Rhön, *Germany* **24 E5** 50 24N 9 58 E
Rhondda, *U.K.* **13 F4** 51 39N 3 31W
Rhondda Cynon Taff □, *U.K.* **13 F4** 51 42N 3 27W
Rhône □, *France* **21 C8** 45 54N 4 35 E
Rhône →, *France* **21 E8** 43 28N 4 42 E
Rhône-Alpes □, *France* **21 C9** 45 40N 6 0 E
Rhum, *U.K.* **14 E2** 57 0N 6 20W
Rhyl, *U.K.* **12 D4** 53 20N 3 29W
Ri-Aba, *Eq. Guin.* **83 E6** 3 28N 8 40 E
Riachão, *Brazil* **125 E9** 7 20S 46 37W
Riangnom, *Sudan* **81 F3** 9 55N 30 1 E
Riaño, *Spain* **34 C6** 42 59N 4 59W
Rians, *France* **21 E9** 43 37N 5 44 E
Riansáres →, *Spain* **35 F7** 39 32N 3 18W
Riasi, *India* **69 C6** 33 10N 74 50 E
Riau □, *Indonesia* **62 D2** 0 0 102 35 E
Riau, Kepulauan, *Indonesia* **62 D2** 0 30N 104 20 E
Riau Arch. = Riau, Kepulauan, *Indonesia* **62 D2** 0 30N 104 20 E
Riaza, *Spain* **34 D7** 41 18N 3 30W
Riaza →, *Spain* **34 D7** 41 42N 3 55W
Riba de Saelices, *Spain* **32 E2** 40 55N 2 17W
Riba-Roja de Turia, *Spain* **33 F4** 39 33N 0 34W
Ribadavia, *Spain* **34 C2** 42 17N 8 8W
Ribadeo, *Spain* **34 B3** 43 35N 7 5W
Ribadesella, *Spain* **34 B5** 43 30N 5 7W
Ribado, *Nigeria* **83 D7** 9 16N 12 47 E
Ribao, *Cameroon* **83 D7** 6 32N 11 30 E
Ribas = Ribes de Freser, *Spain* **32 C7** 42 19N 2 15 E
Ribas do Rio Pardo, *Brazil* **125 H8** 20 27S 53 46W
Ribble →, *U.K.* **12 D5** 53 52N 2 25W
Ribe, *Denmark* **11 J2** 55 19N 8 44 E
Ribe Amtskommune □, *Denmark* **11 J2** 55 35N 8 45 E
Ribeauvillé, *France* **19 D14** 48 10N 7 20 E
Ribécourt-Dreslincourt, *France* **19 C9** 49 30N 2 55 E
Ribeira = Santa Uxía, *Spain* **34 C2** 42 36N 8 58W
Ribeira Brava, *Madeira* **37 D2** 32 41N 17 4W
Ribeirão Prêto, *Brazil* **127 A6** 21 10S 47 50W
Ribemont, *France* **19 C10** 49 47N 3 27 E
Ribera, *Italy* **30 E6** 37 30N 13 16 E
Ribérac, *France* **20 C4** 45 15N 0 20 E
Riberalta, *Bolivia* **124 F5** 11 0S 66 0W
Ribes de Freser, *Spain* **32 C7** 42 19N 2 15 E
Ribnica, *Slovenia* **29 C11** 45 45N 14 45 E
Ribnitz-Damgarten, *Germany* **24 A8** 54 15N 12 27 E
Ričany, *Czech Rep.* **26 B7** 50 0N 14 40 E
Riccarton, *N.Z.* **91 K4** 43 32S 172 37 E
Riccia, *Italy* **31 A7** 41 30N 14 50 E
Riccione, *Italy* **29 E9** 43 59N 12 39 E
Rice, *U.S.A.* **117 L12** 34 5N 114 51W
Rice L., *Canada* **110 B6** 44 12N 78 10W
Rice Lake, *U.S.A.* **112 C9** 45 30N 91 44W
Rich, C., *Canada* **110 B4** 44 43N 80 38W
Richard Toll, *Senegal* **82 B1** 16 25N 15 42W
Richards Bay, *S. Africa* **89 D5** 28 48S 32 6 E
Richardson →, *Canada* **105 B6** 58 25N 111 14W
Richardson Lakes, *U.S.A.* **108 C10** 44 46N 70 58W
Richardson Springs, *U.S.A.* **116 F5** 39 51N 121 46W
Riche, C., *Australia* **93 F2** 34 36S 118 47 E
Richelieu, *France* **18 E7** 47 1N 0 20 E
Richey, *U.S.A.* **112 B2** 47 39N 105 4W
Richfield, *U.S.A.* **115 G8** 38 46N 112 5W
Richfield Springs, *U.S.A.* **111 D10** 42 51N 74 59W
Richford, *U.S.A.* **111 B12** 45 0N 72 40W
Richibucto, *Canada* **103 C7** 46 42N 64 54W
Richland, *Ga., U.S.A.* **109 J3** 32 5N 84 40W
Richland, *Wash., U.S.A.* **114 C4** 46 17N 119 18W
Richland Center, *U.S.A.* **112 D9** 43 21N 90 23W
Richlands, *U.S.A.* **108 G5** 37 6N 81 48W
Richmond, *Australia* **94 C3** 20 43S 143 8 E
Richmond, *N.Z.* **91 J4** 41 20S 173 12 E
Richmond, *U.K.* **12 C6** 54 25N 1 43W
Richmond, *Calif., U.S.A.* **116 H4** 37 56N 122 21W
Richmond, *Ind., U.S.A.* **108 F3** 39 50N 84 53W
Richmond, *Ky., U.S.A.* **108 G3** 37 45N 84 18W
Richmond, *Mich., U.S.A.* **110 D2** 42 49N 82 45W
Richmond, *Mo., U.S.A.* **112 F8** 39 17N 93 58W
Richmond, *Tex., U.S.A.* **113 L7** 29 35N 95 46W
Richmond, *Utah, U.S.A.* **114 F8** 41 56N 111 48W
Richmond, *Va., U.S.A.* **108 G7** 37 33N 77 27W
Richmond, *Vt., U.S.A.* **111 B12** 44 24N 72 59W
Richmond Hill, *Canada* **110 C5** 43 52N 79 27W
Richmond Ra., *Australia* **95 D5** 29 0S 152 45 E
Richwood, *U.S.A.* **108 F5** 38 14N 80 32W
Ricla, *Spain* **32 D3** 41 31N 1 24W
Ridder = Leninogorsk, *Kazakstan* **50 D9** 50 20N 83 30 E
Riddlesburg, *U.S.A.* **110 F6** 40 9N 78 15W
Ridgecrest, *U.S.A.* **117 K9** 35 38N 117 40W
Ridgefield, *Conn., U.S.A.* **111 E11** 41 17N 73 30W
Ridgefield, *Wash., U.S.A.* **116 E4** 45 49N 122 45W
Ridgeland, *U.S.A.* **109 J5** 32 29N 80 59W
Ridgetown, *Canada* **102 D3** 42 26N 81 52W
Ridgewood, *U.S.A.* **111 F10** 40 59N 74 7W
Ridgway, *U.S.A.* **110 E6** 41 25N 78 44W
Riding Mountain Nat. Park, *Canada* **105 C9** 50 50N 100 0W
Ridley, Mt., *Australia* **93 F3** 33 12S 122 7 E
Riebeek-Oos, *S. Africa* **88 E4** 33 10S 26 10 E
Ried, *Austria* **26 C6** 48 14N 13 30 E
Riedlingen, *Germany* **25 G5** 48 9N 9 28 E
Riedstadt, *Germany* **25 F4** 49 45N 8 30 E
Rienza →, *Italy* **29 B8** 46 49N 11 47 E
Riesa, *Germany* **24 D9** 51 17N 13 17 E
Riesi, *Italy* **31 E7** 37 17N 14 5 E
Riet →, *S. Africa* **88 D3** 29 0S 23 54 E
Rietavas, *Lithuania* **44 C8** 55 44N 21 56 E
Rietbron, *S. Africa* **88 E3** 32 54S 23 10 E
Rietfontein, *Namibia* **88 C3** 21 58S 20 58 E
Rieti, *Italy* **29 F9** 42 24N 12 51 E
Rieupeyroux, *France* **20 D6** 44 19N 2 12 E
Riez, *France* **21 E10** 43 49N 6 6 E
Riffe L., *U.S.A.* **116 D4** 46 32N 122 26W
Rifle, *U.S.A.* **114 G10** 39 32N 107 47W
Rift Valley □, *Kenya* **86 B4** 0 20N 36 0 E
Rīga, *Latvia* **9 H21** 56 53N 24 8 E
Riga, G. of, *Latvia* **9 H20** 57 40N 23 45 E
Rigacikun, *Nigeria* **83 C6** 10 40N 7 28 E
Rīgān, *Iran* **71 D8** 28 37N 58 58 E
Rīgas Jūras Līcis = Riga, G. of, *Latvia* **9 H20** 57 40N 23 45 E
Rigaud, *Canada* **111 A10** 45 29N 74 18W
Rigby, *U.S.A.* **114 E8** 43 40N 111 55W
Rīgestān, *Afghan.* **66 D4** 30 15N 65 0 E
Riggins, *U.S.A.* **114 D5** 45 25N 116 19W
Rignac, *France* **20 D6** 44 25N 2 16 E
Rigolet, *Canada* **103 B8** 54 10N 58 23W
Rihand Dam, *India* **69 G10** 24 9N 83 2 E
Riihimäki, *Finland* **9 F21** 60 45N 24 48 E
Riiser-Larsen-halvøya, *Antarctica* **5 C4** 68 0S 35 0 E
Rijau, *Nigeria* **83 C6** 11 8N 5 17 E
Rijeka, *Croatia* **29 C11** 45 20N 14 21 E
Rijeka Crnojevića, *Montenegro, Yug.* **40 D3** 42 24N 19 1 E
Rijssen, *Neths.* **17 B6** 52 19N 6 31 E
Rike, *Ethiopia* **81 E4** 10 50N 39 53 E
Rikuzentakada, *Japan* **54 E10** 39 0N 141 40 E
Rila, *Bulgaria* **40 D7** 42 7N 23 7 E
Rila Planina, *Bulgaria* **40 D7** 42 10N 23 20 E
Riley, *U.S.A.* **114 E4** 43 32N 119 28W
Rima →, *Nigeria* **83 C6** 13 4N 5 10 E
Rimah, Wadi ar →, *Si. Arabia* **70 E4** 26 5N 41 30 E
Rimavská Sobota, *Slovak Rep.* **27 C13** 48 22N 20 2 E
Rimbey, *Canada* **104 C6** 52 35N 114 15W
Rimbo, *Sweden* **10 E12** 59 44N 18 21 E
Rimersburg, *U.S.A.* **110 E5** 41 3N 79 30W
Rimforsa, *Sweden* **11 F9** 58 6N 15 43 E
Rimi, *Nigeria* **83 C6** 12 58N 7 43 E
Rímini, *Italy* **29 D9** 44 3N 12 33 E
Rimouski, *Canada* **103 C6** 48 27N 68 30W
Rimrock, *U.S.A.* **116 D5** 46 38N 121 10W
Rinca, *Indonesia* **63 F5** 8 45S 119 35 E
Rincón de la Victoria, *Spain* **35 J6** 36 43N 4 18W
Rincón de Romos, *Mexico* **118 C4** 22 14N 102 18W
Rinconada, *Argentina* **126 A2** 22 26S 66 10W
Rind →, *India* **69 G9** 25 53N 80 33 E
Ringarum, *Sweden* **11 F10** 58 21N 16 26 E
Ringas, *India* **68 F6** 27 21N 75 34 E
Ringe, *Denmark* **11 J4** 55 13N 10 28 E
Ringim, *Nigeria* **83 C6** 12 13N 9 10 E
Ringkøbing, *Denmark* **11 H2** 56 5N 8 15 E
Ringkøbing Amtskommune □, *Denmark* **11 H2** 56 10N 8 45 E
Ringkøbing Fjord, *Denmark* **11 H2** 56 0N 8 15 E
Ringsjön, *Sweden* **11 J7** 55 55N 13 30 E
Ringsted, *Denmark* **11 J5** 55 25N 11 46 E
Ringvassøy, *Norway* **8 B18** 69 56N 19 15 E
Ringwood, *U.S.A.* **111 E10** 41 7N 74 15W
Rinía, *Greece* **39 D7** 37 23N 25 13 E
Rinjani, *Indonesia* **62 F5** 8 24S 116 28 E
Rinteln, *Germany* **24 C5** 52 10N 9 4 E
Río, Punta del, *Spain* **33 J2** 36 49N 2 24W
Rio Branco, *Brazil* **124 E5** 9 58S 67 49W
Río Branco, *Uruguay* **127 C5** 32 40S 53 40W
Río Bravo del Norte →, *Mexico* **119 B5** 25 57N 97 9W
Rio Brilhante, *Brazil* **127 A5** 21 48S 54 33W
Rio Claro, *Brazil* **127 A6** 22 19S 47 35W
Rio Claro, *Trin. & Tob.* **121 D7** 10 20N 61 25W
Río Colorado, *Argentina* **128 D4** 39 0S 64 0W
Río Cuarto, *Argentina* **126 C3** 33 10S 64 25W
Rio das Pedras, *Mozam.* **89 C6** 23 8S 35 28 E
Rio de Janeiro, *Brazil* **127 A7** 23 0S 43 12W
Rio de Janeiro □, *Brazil* **127 A7** 22 50S 43 0W
Rio do Sul, *Brazil* **127 B6** 27 13S 49 37W
Río Gallegos, *Argentina* **128 G3** 51 35S 69 15W
Rio Grande = Grande, Rio →, *U.S.A.* **113 N6** 25 58N 97 9W
Río Grande, *Argentina* **128 G3** 53 50S 67 45W
Rio Grande, *Brazil* **127 C5** 32 0S 52 20W
Río Grande, *Mexico* **118 C4** 23 50N 103 2W
Río Grande, *Nic.* **120 D3** 12 54N 83 33W
Rio Grande City, *U.S.A.* **113 M5** 26 23N 98 49W
Río Grande de Santiago →, *Mexico* **118 C3** 21 36N 105 26W
Rio Grande do Norte □, *Brazil* **125 E11** 5 40S 36 0W
Rio Grande do Sul □, *Brazil* **127 C5** 30 0S 53 0W
Río Hato, *Panama* **120 E3** 8 22N 80 10W
Río Lagartos, *Mexico* **119 C7** 21 36N 88 10W
Rio Largo, *Brazil* **125 E11** 9 28S 35 50W
Rio Maior, *Portugal* **35 F2** 39 19N 8 57W
Rio Marina, *Italy* **28 F7** 42 49N 10 25 E
Río Mulatos, *Bolivia* **124 G5** 19 40S 66 50W
Río Muni = Mbini □, *Eq. Guin.* **84 D2** 1 30N 10 0 E
Rio Negro, *Brazil* **127 B6** 26 0S 49 55W
Rio Pardo, *Brazil* **127 C5** 30 0S 52 30W
Rio Rancho, *U.S.A.* **115 J10** 35 14N 106 38W
Río Segundo, *Argentina* **126 C3** 31 40S 63 59W
Río Tercero, *Argentina* **126 C3** 32 15S 64 8W
Rio Tinto, *Portugal* **34 D2** 41 11N 8 34W
Rio Verde, *Brazil* **125 G8** 17 50S 51 0W
Río Verde, *Mexico* **119 C5** 21 56N 99 59W
Rio Vista, *U.S.A.* **116 G5** 38 10N 121 42W
Ríobamba, *Ecuador* **124 D3** 1 50S 78 45W
Ríohacha, *Colombia* **124 A4** 11 33N 72 55W
Riom, *France* **20 C7** 45 54N 3 7 E
Riom-ès-Montagnes, *France* **20 C6** 45 17N 2 39 E
Rion-des-Landes, *France* **20 E3** 43 55N 0 56W
Rionero in Vúlture, *Italy* **31 B8** 40 55N 15 40 E
Rioni →, *Georgia* **49 J5** 42 14N 41 44 E
Riós, *Spain* **34 D3** 41 58N 7 16W
Riosucio, *Colombia* **124 B3** 7 27N 77 7W
Riou L., *Canada* **105 B7** 59 7N 106 25W
Rioz, *France* **19 E13** 47 26N 6 5 E
Ripatransone, *Italy* **29 F10** 42 59N 13 46 E
Ripley, *Canada* **110 B3** 44 4N 81 35W
Ripley, *Calif., U.S.A.* **117 M12** 33 32N 114 39W
Ripley, *N.Y., U.S.A.* **110 D5** 42 16N 79 43W
Ripley, *Tenn., U.S.A.* **113 H10** 35 45N 89 32W
Ripley, *W. Va., U.S.A.* **108 F5** 38 49N 81 43W
Ripoll, *Spain* **32 C7** 42 15N 2 13 E
Ripon, *U.K.* **12 C6** 54 9N 1 31W
Ripon, *Calif., U.S.A.* **116 H5** 37 44N 121 7W
Ripon, *Wis., U.S.A.* **108 D1** 43 51N 88 50W
Riposto, *Italy* **31 E8** 37 44N 15 12 E
Risan, *Montenegro, Yug.* **40 D2** 42 32N 18 42 E
Riscle, *France* **20 E3** 43 39N 0 5W
Rishā', W. ar →, *Si. Arabia* **70 E5** 25 33N 44 5 E
Rishiri-Tō, *Japan* **54 B10** 45 11N 141 15 E
Rishon le Ẕiyyon, *Israel* **75 D3** 31 58N 34 48 E
Risle →, *France* **18 C7** 49 26N 0 23 E
Rison, *U.S.A.* **113 J8** 33 58N 92 11W
Risør, *Norway* **9 G13** 58 43N 9 13 E
Rita Blanca Cr. →, *U.S.A.* **113 H3** 35 40N 102 29W
Riti, *Nigeria* **83 D6** 7 57N 9 41 E
Ritter, Mt., *U.S.A.* **116 H7** 37 41N 119 12W
Rittman, *U.S.A.* **110 F3** 40 58N 81 47W
Ritzville, *U.S.A.* **114 C4** 47 8N 118 23W
Riva del Garda, *Italy* **28 C7** 45 53N 10 50 E
Riva Lígure, *Italy* **28 E4** 43 50N 7 50 E
Rivadavia, *Buenos Aires, Argentina* **126 D3** 35 29S 62 59W
Rivadavia, *Mendoza, Argentina* **126 C2** 33 13S 68 30W
Rivadavia, *Salta, Argentina* **126 A3** 24 5S 62 54W
Rivadavia, *Chile* **126 B1** 29 57S 70 35W
Rivarolo Canavese, *Italy* **28 C4** 45 19N 7 43 E
Rivas, *Nic.* **120 D2** 11 30N 85 50W
Rive-de-Gier, *France* **21 C8** 45 32N 4 37 E
River Cess, *Liberia* **82 D3** 5 30N 9 32W
River Jordan, *Canada* **116 B2** 48 26N 124 3W
Rivera, *Argentina* **126 D3** 37 12S 63 14W
Rivera, *Uruguay* **127 C4** 31 0S 55 50W
Riverbank, *U.S.A.* **116 H6** 37 44N 120 56W
Riverdale, *U.S.A.* **116 J7** 36 26N 119 52W
Riverhead, *U.S.A.* **111 F12** 40 55N 72 40W
Riverhurst, *Canada* **105 C7** 50 55N 106 50W
Rivers, *Canada* **105 C8** 50 2N 100 14W
Rivers □, *Nigeria* **83 E6** 4 30N 7 10 E
Rivers Inlet, *Canada* **104 C3** 51 42N 127 15W
Riversdale, *S. Africa* **88 E3** 34 7S 21 15 E
Riverside, *U.S.A.* **117 M9** 33 59N 117 22W
Riverton, *Australia* **95 E2** 34 10S 138 46 E
Riverton, *Canada* **105 C9** 51 1N 97 0W
Riverton, *N.Z.* **91 M2** 46 21S 168 0 E
Riverton, *U.S.A.* **114 E9** 43 2N 108 23W
Riverton Heights, *U.S.A.* **116 C4** 47 28N 122 17W
Rives, *France* **21 C9** 45 21N 5 31 E
Rivesaltes, *France* **20 F6** 42 47N 2 50 E
Riviera, *U.S.A.* **117 K12** 35 4N 114 35W
Riviera di Levante, *Italy* **28 D6** 44 15N 9 30 E
Riviera di Ponente, *Italy* **28 D5** 44 10N 8 20 E
Rivière-au-Renard, *Canada* **103 C7** 48 59N 64 23W
Rivière-du-Loup, *Canada* **103 C6** 47 50N 69 30W
Rivière-Pentecôte, *Canada* **103 C6** 49 57N 67 1W
Rivière-Pilote, *Martinique* **121 D7** 14 26N 60 53W
Rivière St. Paul, *Canada* **103 B8** 51 28N 57 45W
Rivne, *Ukraine* **47 G4** 50 40N 26 10 E
Rívoli, *Italy* **28 C4** 45 3N 7 31 E
Rivoli B., *Australia* **95 F3** 37 32S 140 3 E
Rixheim, *France* **19 E14** 47 40N 7 24 E
Riyadh = Ar Riyāḍ, *Si. Arabia* **70 E5** 24 41N 46 42 E
Rize, *Turkey* **73 B9** 41 0N 40 30 E
Rizhao, *China* **57 G10** 35 25N 119 30 E
Rizokarpaso, *Cyprus* **36 D13** 35 36N 34 23 E
Rizzuto, C., *Italy* **31 D10** 38 53N 17 5 E
Rjukan, *Norway* **9 G13** 59 54N 8 33 E
Ro, *Greece* **39 E11** 36 9N 29 33 E
Roa, *Spain* **34 D7** 41 41N 3 56W
Road Town, *Virgin Is.* **121 C7** 18 27N 64 37W
Roan Plateau, *U.S.A.* **114 G9** 39 20N 109 20W
Roanne, *France* **19 F11** 46 3N 4 4 E
Roanoke, *Ala., U.S.A.* **109 J3** 33 9N 85 22W
Roanoke, *Va., U.S.A.* **108 G6** 37 16N 79 56W
Roanoke →, *U.S.A.* **109 H7** 35 57N 76 42W
Roanoke I., *U.S.A.* **109 H8** 35 55N 75 40W
Roanoke Rapids, *U.S.A.* **109 G7** 36 28N 77 40W
Roatán, *Honduras* **120 C2** 16 18N 86 35W
Robāt Sang, *Iran* **71 C8** 35 35N 59 10 E
Robbins I., *Australia* **94 G4** 40 42S 145 0 E
Róbbio, *Italy* **28 C5** 45 17N 8 35 E
Robe, *Australia* **95 F2** 37 11S 139 45 E
Robe →, *Australia* **92 D2** 21 42S 116 15 E
Röbel, *Germany* **24 B8** 53 22N 12 35 E
Robert Lee, *U.S.A.* **113 K4** 31 54N 100 29W
Robertsdale, *U.S.A.* **110 F6** 40 11N 78 6W
Robertsganj, *India* **69 G10** 24 44N 83 4 E
Robertson, *S. Africa* **88 E2** 33 46S 19 50 E
Robertson I., *Antarctica* **5 C18** 65 15S 59 30W
Robertson Ra., *Australia* **92 D3** 23 15S 121 0 E
Robertsport, *Liberia* **82 D2** 6 45N 11 26W
Robertstown, *Australia* **95 E2** 33 58S 139 5 E
Roberval, *Canada* **103 C5** 48 32N 72 15W
Robeson Chan., *Greenland* **4 A4** 82 0N 61 30W
Robesonia, *U.S.A.* **111 F8** 40 21N 76 8W
Robi, *Ethiopia* **81 F4** 7 52N 39 38 E
Robinson, *U.S.A.* **108 F2** 39 0N 87 44W
Robinson →, *Australia* **94 B2** 16 3S 137 16 E
Robinson Ra., *Australia* **93 E2** 25 40S 119 0 E
Robinvale, *Australia* **95 E3** 34 40S 142 45 E
Robledo, *Spain* **33 G2** 38 46N 2 26W
Roblin, *Canada* **105 C8** 51 14N 101 21W
Roboré, *Bolivia* **124 G7** 18 10S 59 45W
Robson, *Canada* **104 D5** 49 20N 117 41W
Robson, Mt., *Canada* **104 C5** 53 10N 119 10W
Robstown, *U.S.A.* **113 M6** 27 47N 97 40W
Roca, C. da, *Portugal* **35 G1** 38 40N 9 31W
Roca Partida, I., *Mexico* **118 D2** 19 1N 112 2W
Rocamadour, *France* **20 D5** 44 48N 1 37 E
Rocas, I., *Brazil* **125 D12** 4 0S 34 1W
Rocca San Casciano, *Italy* **29 D8** 44 3N 11 50 E
Roccadáspide, *Italy* **31 B8** 40 27N 15 10 E
Roccastrada, *Italy* **29 F8** 43 0N 11 10 E
Roccella Iónica, *Italy* **31 D9** 38 19N 16 24 E
Rocha, *Uruguay* **127 C5** 34 30S 54 25W
Rochdale, *U.K.* **12 D5** 53 38N 2 9W
Rochechouart, *France* **20 C4** 45 50N 0 49 E
Rochefort, *Belgium* **17 D5** 50 9N 5 12 E
Rochefort, *France* **20 C3** 45 56N 0 57W
Rochefort-en-Terre, *France* **18 E4** 47 42N 2 22W
Rochelle, *U.S.A.* **112 E10** 41 56N 89 4W
Rocher River, *Canada* **104 A6** 61 23N 112 44W
Rocheservière, *France* **18 F5** 46 57N 1 30W
Rochester, *U.K.* **13 F8** 51 23N 0 31 E
Rochester, *Ind., U.S.A.* **108 E2** 41 4N 86 13W
Rochester, *Minn., U.S.A.* **112 C8** 44 1N 92 28W
Rochester, *N.H., U.S.A.* **111 C14** 43 18N 70 59W
Rochester, *N.Y., U.S.A.* **110 C7** 43 10N 77 37W
Rociu, *Romania* **43 F10** 44 43N 25 2 E
Rock →, *Canada* **104 A3** 60 7N 127 7W
Rock Creek, *U.S.A.* **110 E4** 41 40N 80 52W
Rock Falls, *U.S.A.* **112 E10** 41 47N 89 41W
Rock Hill, *U.S.A.* **109 H5** 34 56N 81 1W
Rock Island, *U.S.A.* **112 E9** 41 30N 90 34W
Rock Rapids, *U.S.A.* **112 D6** 43 26N 96 10W
Rock Sound, *Bahamas* **120 B4** 24 54N 76 12W
Rock Springs, *Mont., U.S.A.* **114 C10** 46 49N 106 15W
Rock Springs, *Wyo., U.S.A.* **114 F9** 41 35N 109 14W
Rock Valley, *U.S.A.* **112 D6** 43 12N 96 18W
Rockall, *Atl. Oc.* **6 D3** 57 37N 13 42W
Rockdale, *Tex., U.S.A.* **113 K6** 30 39N 97 0W
Rockdale, *Wash., U.S.A.* **116 C5** 47 22N 121 28W
Rockefeller Plateau, *Antarctica* **5 E14** 80 0S 140 0W
Rockford, *U.S.A.* **112 D10** 42 16N 89 6W
Rockglen, *Canada* **105 D7** 49 11N 105 57W
Rockhampton, *Australia* **94 C5** 23 22S 150 32 E
Rockingham, *Australia* **93 F2** 32 15S 115 38 E
Rockingham, *U.S.A.* **109 H6** 34 57N 79 46W
Rockingham B., *Australia* **94 B4** 18 5S 146 10 E
Rocklake, *U.S.A.* **112 A5** 48 47N 99 15W
Rockland, *Canada* **111 A9** 45 33N 75 17W
Rockland, *Idaho, U.S.A.* **114 E7** 42 34N 112 53W
Rockland, *Maine, U.S.A.* **109 C11** 44 6N 69 7W
Rockland, *Mich., U.S.A.* **112 B10** 46 44N 89 11W
Rocklin, *U.S.A.* **116 G5** 38 48N 121 14W
Rockmart, *U.S.A.* **109 H3** 34 0N 85 3W
Rockport, *Mass., U.S.A.* **111 D14** 42 39N 70 37W
Rockport, *Mo., U.S.A.* **112 E7** 40 25N 95 31W
Rockport, *Tex., U.S.A.* **113 L6** 28 2N 97 3W
Rocksprings, *U.S.A.* **113 K4** 30 1N 100 13W
Rockville, *Conn., U.S.A.* **111 E12** 41 52N 72 28W
Rockville, *Md., U.S.A.* **108 F7** 39 5N 77 9W
Rockwall, *U.S.A.* **113 J6** 32 56N 96 28W
Rockwell City, *U.S.A.* **112 D7** 42 24N 94 38W
Rockwood, *Canada* **110 C4** 43 37N 80 8W
Rockwood, *Maine, U.S.A.* **109 C11** 45 41N 69 45W
Rockwood, *Tenn., U.S.A.* **109 H3** 35 52N 84 41W
Rocky Ford, *U.S.A.* **112 F3** 38 3N 103 43W
Rocky Gully, *Australia* **93 F2** 34 30S 116 57 E
Rocky Harbour, *Canada* **103 C8** 49 36N 57 55W
Rocky Island L., *Canada* **102 C3** 46 55N 83 0W
Rocky Lane, *Canada* **104 B5** 58 31N 116 22W
Rocky Mount, *U.S.A.* **109 H7** 35 57N 77 48W
Rocky Mountain House, *Canada* **104 C6** 52 22N 114 55W
Rocky Mountain National Park, *U.S.A.* **114 F11** 40 25N 105 45W
Rocky Mts., *N. Amer.* **114 G10** 49 0N 115 0W
Rocky Point, *Namibia* **88 B2** 19 3S 12 30 E
Rocroi, *France* **19 C11** 49 55N 4 30 E
Rod, *Pakistan* **66 E3** 28 10N 63 5 E
Rødby, *Denmark* **11 K5** 54 41N 11 23 E
Rødbyhavn, *Denmark* **11 K5** 54 39N 11 22 E
Roddickton, *Canada* **103 B8** 50 51N 56 8W
Rødding, *Denmark* **11 J3** 55 23N 9 3 E
Rödeby, *Sweden* **11 H9** 56 15N 15 37 E
Rødekro, *Denmark* **11 J3** 55 4N 9 20 E
Rodenkirchen, *Germany* **24 B4** 53 23N 8 26 E
Rodez, *France* **20 D6** 44 21N 2 33 E
Rodholívas, *Greece* **40 F7** 40 55N 24 0 E
Rodhópi □, *Greece* **41 E9** 41 5N 25 30 E
Rodhopoú, *Greece* **36 D5** 35 34N 23 45 E
Ródhos, *Greece* **36 C10** 36 15N 28 10 E
Rodi Gargánico, *Italy* **29 G12** 41 55N 15 53 E
Rodna, *Romania* **43 C9** 47 25N 24 50 E
Rodnei, Munţii, *Romania* **43 C9** 47 35N 24 35 E
Rodney, *Canada* **110 D3** 42 34N 81 41W
Rodney, C., *N.Z.* **91 G5** 36 17S 174 50 E
Rodniki, *Russia* **48 B5** 57 7N 41 47 E
Rodonit, Kepi i, *Albania* **40 E3** 41 35N 19 27 E
Rodriguez, *Ind. Oc.* **3 E13** 19 45S 63 20 E
Roe →, *U.K.* **15 A5** 55 6N 6 59W
Roebling, *U.S.A.* **111 F10** 40 7N 74 47W
Roebourne, *Australia* **92 D2** 20 44S 117 9 E
Roebuck B., *Australia* **92 C3** 18 5S 122 20 E
Roermond, *Neths.* **17 C6** 51 12N 6 0 E
Roes Welcome Sd., *Canada* **101 B11** 65 0N 87 0W
Roeselare, *Belgium* **17 D3** 50 57N 3 7 E
Rogachev = Ragachow, *Belarus* **47 F6** 53 8N 30 5 E
Rogačica, *Serbia, Yug.* **40 B3** 44 4N 19 40 E
Rogagua, L., *Bolivia* **124 F5** 13 43S 66 50W
Rogaška Slatina, *Slovenia* **29 B12** 46 15N 15 42 E
Rogatec, *Slovenia* **29 B12** 46 15N 15 46 E
Rogatica, *Bos.-H.* **42 G4** 43 47N 19 0 E
Rogatyn, *Ukraine* **47 H3** 49 24N 24 36 E
Rogdhia, *Greece* **36 D7** 35 22N 25 1 E
Rogers, *U.S.A.* **113 G7** 36 20N 94 7W
Rogers City, *U.S.A.* **108 C4** 45 25N 83 49W
Rogersville, *Canada* **103 C6** 46 44N 65 26W
Roggan →, *Canada* **102 B4** 54 24N 79 25W
Roggan L., *Canada* **102 B4** 54 8N 77 50W
Roggeveldberge, *S. Africa* **88 E3** 32 10S 20 10 E
Roggiano Gravina, *Italy* **31 C9** 39 37N 16 9 E
Rogliano, *France* **21 F13** 42 57N 9 30 E
Rogliano, *Italy* **31 C9** 39 10N 16 19 E
Rogoaguado, L., *Bolivia* **124 F5** 13 0S 65 30W
Rogoźno, *Poland* **45 F3** 52 45N 16 59 E
Rogue →, *U.S.A.* **114 E1** 42 26N 124 26W
Rohan, *France* **18 D4** 48 4N 2 45W
Róhda, *Greece* **36 A3** 39 48N 19 46 E
Rohnert Park, *U.S.A.* **116 G4** 38 16N 122 40W
Rohri, *Pakistan* **68 F3** 27 45N 68 51 E
Rohri Canal, *Pakistan* **68 F3** 26 15N 68 27 E
Rohtak, *India* **68 E7** 28 55N 76 43 E
Roi Et, *Thailand* **64 D4** 16 4N 103 40 E
Roja, *Latvia* **9 H20** 57 29N 22 43 E
Rojas, *Argentina* **126 C3** 34 10S 60 45W
Rojiște, *Romania* **43 F8** 44 4N 23 56 E
Rojo, C., *Mexico* **119 C5** 21 33N 97 20W
Rokan →, *Indonesia* **62 D2** 2 0N 100 50 E
Rokel →, *S. Leone* **82 D2** 8 30N 12 48W
Rokiškis, *Lithuania* **9 J21** 55 55N 25 35 E
Rokitno, *Russia* **47 G8** 50 57N 35 56 E
Rokycany, *Czech Rep.* **26 B6** 49 43N 13 35 E
Rolândia, *Brazil* **127 A5** 23 18S 51 23W
Rolla, *U.S.A.* **113 G9** 37 57N 91 46W
Rolleston, *Australia* **94 C4** 24 28S 148 35 E
Rollingstone, *Australia* **94 B4** 19 2S 146 24 E
Rom, *Sudan* **81 F3** 9 54N 32 16 E
Roma, *Australia* **95 D4** 26 32S 148 49 E
Roma, *Italy* **29 G9** 41 54N 12 29 E
Roma, *Sweden* **11 G12** 57 32N 18 26 E
Roma, *U.S.A.* **113 M5** 26 25N 99 1W
Romain C., *U.S.A.* **109 J6** 33 0N 79 22W
Romaine, *Canada* **103 B7** 50 13N 60 40W
Romaine →, *Canada* **103 B7** 50 18N 63 47W
Roman, *Bulgaria* **40 C7** 43 8N 23 57 E
Roman, *Romania* **43 D11** 46 57N 26 55 E
Roman-Kosh, Gora, *Ukraine* **47 K8** 44 37N 34 15 E
Romanche →, *France* **21 C9** 45 5N 5 43 E
Romang, *Indonesia* **63 F7** 7 30S 127 20 E
Români, *Egypt* **75 E1** 30 59N 32 38 E
Romania ■, *Europe* **43 D10** 46 0N 25 0 E
Romanija, *Bos.-H.* **42 G3** 43 50N 18 45 E
Romano, Cayo, *Cuba* **120 B4** 22 0N 77 30W
Romanovka = Basarabeasca, *Moldova* **43 D13** 46 21N 28 58 E
Romans-sur-Isère, *France* **21 C9** 45 3N 5 3 E
Romanshorn, *Switz.* **25 H5** 47 33N 9 22 E
Rombari, *Sudan* **81 G3** 4 33N 31 2 E
Romblon, *Phil.* **61 E5** 12 33N 122 17 E
Rome = Roma, *Italy* **29 G9** 41 54N 12 29 E
Rome, *Ga., U.S.A.* **109 H3** 34 15N 85 10W
Rome, *N.Y., U.S.A.* **111 C9** 43 13N 75 27W
Rome, *Pa., U.S.A.* **111 E8** 41 51N 76 21W
Rometta, *Italy* **31 D8** 38 10N 15 25 E
Romilly-sur-Seine, *France* **19 D10** 48 31N 3 44 E
Romney, *U.S.A.* **108 F6** 39 21N 78 45W
Romney Marsh, *U.K.* **13 F8** 51 2N 0 54 E
Romny, *Ukraine* **47 G7** 50 48N 33 28 E
Rømø, *Denmark* **11 J2** 55 10N 8 30 E
Romodan, *Ukraine* **47 G7** 49 55N 33 15 E
Romodanovo, *Russia* **48 C7** 54 26N 45 23 E
Romont, *Switz.* **25 J2** 46 42N 6 54 E
Romorantin-Lanthenay, *France* **19 E8** 47 21N 1 45 E
Romsdalen, *Norway* **9 E12** 62 25N 7 52 E
Romsey, *U.K.* **13 G6** 51 0N 1 29W
Ron, *Vietnam* **64 D6** 17 53N 106 27 E
Rona, *U.K.* **14 D3** 57 34N 5 59W
Ronan, *U.S.A.* **114 C6** 47 32N 114 6W
Roncador, Cayos, *Caribbean* **120 D3** 13 32N 80 4W
Roncador, Serra do, *Brazil* **125 F8** 12 30S 52 30W
Ronciglione, *Italy* **29 F9** 42 17N 12 13 E
Ronco →, *Italy* **29 D9** 44 24N 12 12 E
Ronda, *Spain* **35 J5** 36 46N 5 12W
Ronda, Serranía de, *Spain* **35 J5** 36 44N 5 3W
Rondane, *Norway* **9 F13** 61 57N 9 50 E
Rondônia □, *Brazil* **124 F6** 11 0S 63 0W
Rondonópolis, *Brazil* **125 G8** 16 28S 54 38W
Rong, Koh, *Cambodia* **65 G4** 10 45N 103 15 E
Rong Jiang →, *China* **58 E7** 24 35N 109 20 E
Rong Xian, *Guangxi Zhuangzu, China* **59 F8** 22 50N 110 31 E
Rong Xian, *Sichuan, China* **58 C5** 29 23N 104 22 E
Rong'an, *China* **58 E7** 25 14N 109 22 E
Rongchang, *China* **58 C5** 29 20N 105 32 E
Ronge, L. la, *Canada* **105 B7** 55 6N 105 17W

Rongjiang, China 58 E7 25 57N 108 28 E
Rongshui, China 58 E7 25 5N 109 12 E
Rønne, Denmark 11 J8 55 6N 14 43 E
Ronne Ice Shelf, Antarctica 5 D18 78 0 S 60 0W
Ronneby, Sweden 11 H9 56 12N 15 17 E
Ronnebyån →, Sweden 11 H9 56 11N 15 18 E
Rönneshytta, Sweden 11 F9 58 56N 15 2 E
Ronsard, C., Australia 93 D1 24 46 S 113 10 E
Ronse, Belgium 17 D3 50 45N 3 35 E
Roodepoort, S. Africa 89 D4 26 11 S 27 54 E
Roof Butte, U.S.A. 115 H9 36 28N 109 5W
Rooiboklaagte →, Namibia 88 C3 20 50 S 21 0 E
Roorkee, India 68 E7 29 52N 77 59 E
Roosendaal, Neths. 17 C4 51 32N 4 29 E
Roosevelt, U.S.A. 114 F8 40 18N 109 59W
Roosevelt →, Brazil 122 D4 7 35 S 60 20W
Roosevelt, Mt., Canada 104 B3 58 26N 125 20W
Roosevelt I., Antarctica 5 D12 79 30 S 162 0W
Ropczyce, Poland 45 H8 50 4N 21 38 E
Roper →, Australia 94 A2 14 43 S 135 27 E
Roper Bar, Australia 94 A1 14 44 S 134 44 E
Roque Pérez, Argentina 126 D4 35 25 S 59 24W
Roquefort, France 20 D3 44 2N 0 20W
Roquemaure, France 21 D8 44 3N 4 48 E
Roquetas de Mar, Spain 33 J2 36 46N 2 36W
Roquetes, Spain 32 E5 40 50N 0 30 E
Roquevaire, France 21 E9 43 20N 5 36 E
Roraima □, Brazil 124 C6 2 0N 61 30W
Roraima, Mt., Venezuela 122 C4 5 10N 60 40W
Røros, Norway 9 E14 62 35N 11 23 E
Rorschach, Switz. 25 H5 47 28N 9 28 E
Rosa, Zambia 87 D3 9 33 S 31 15 E
Rosa, L., Bahamas 121 B5 21 0N 73 30W
Rosa, Monte, Italy 28 C4 45 55N 7 53 E
Rosal de la Frontera, Spain 35 H3 37 59N 7 13W
Rosalia, U.S.A. 114 C5 47 14N 117 22W
Rosamond, U.S.A. 117 L8 34 52N 118 10W
Rosans, France 21 D9 44 24N 5 29 E
Rosario, Argentina 126 C3 33 0 S 60 40W
Rosário, Brazil 125 D10 3 0 S 44 15W
Rosario, Baja Calif., Mexico 118 B1 30 0N 115 50W
Rosario, Sinaloa, Mexico 118 C3 23 0N 105 52W
Rosario, Paraguay 126 A4 24 30 S 57 35W
Rosario de la Frontera, Argentina 126 B3 25 50 S 65 0W
Rosario de Lerma, Argentina 126 A2 24 59 S 65 35W
Rosario del Tala, Argentina 126 C4 32 20 S 59 10W
Rosário do Sul, Brazil 127 C5 30 15 S 54 55W
Rosarito, Mexico 117 N9 32 18N 117 4W
Rosarno, Italy 31 D8 38 29N 15 58 E
Rosas = Roses, Spain 32 C8 42 19N 3 10 E
Roscoe, U.S.A. 111 E10 41 56N 74 55W
Roscoff, France 18 D3 48 44N 3 58W
Roscommon, Ireland 15 C3 53 38N 8 11W
Roscommon □, Ireland 15 C3 53 49N 8 23W
Roscrea, Ireland 15 D4 52 57N 7 49W
Rose →, Australia 94 A2 14 16 S 135 45 E
Rose Blanche, Canada 103 C8 47 38N 58 45W
Rose Pt., Canada 104 C2 54 11N 131 39W
Rose Valley, Canada 105 C8 52 19N 103 49W
Roseau, Domin. 121 C7 15 20N 61 24W
Roseau, U.S.A. 112 A7 48 51N 95 46W
Rosebery, Australia 94 G4 41 46 S 145 33 E
Rosebud, S. Dak., U.S.A. 112 D4 43 14N 100 51W
Rosebud, Tex., U.S.A. 113 K6 31 4N 96 59W
Roseburg, U.S.A. 114 E2 43 13N 123 20W
Rosedale, U.S.A. 113 J9 33 51N 91 2W
Roseland, U.S.A. 116 G4 38 25N 122 43W
Rosemary, Canada 104 C6 50 46N 112 5W
Rosenberg, U.S.A. 113 L7 29 34N 95 49W
Rosendaël, France 19 A9 51 3N 2 24 E
Rosenheim, Germany 25 H8 47 51N 12 7 E
Roses, Spain 32 C8 42 19N 3 10 E
Roses, G. de, Spain 32 C8 42 10N 3 15 E
Roseto degli Abruzzi, Italy 29 F11 42 41N 14 1 E
Rosetown, Canada 105 C7 51 35N 107 59W
Rosetta = Rashîd, Egypt 80 H7 31 21N 30 22 E
Roseville, Calif., U.S.A. 116 G5 38 45N 121 17W
Roseville, Mich., U.S.A. 110 D2 42 30N 82 56W
Rosewood, Australia 95 D5 27 38 S 152 36 E
Roshkhvār, Iran 71 C8 34 58N 59 37 E
Rosières-en-Santerre, France 19 C9 49 49N 2 42 E
Rosignano Maríttimo, Italy 28 E7 43 24N 10 28 E
Rosignol, Guyana 124 B7 6 15N 57 30W
Roșiori de Vede, Romania 43 F10 44 9N 25 0 E
Rositsa, Bulgaria 41 C11 43 57N 27 57 E
Rositsa →, Bulgaria 41 C9 43 10N 25 30 E
Roskilde, Denmark 11 J6 55 38N 12 3 E
Roskilde Amtskommune □, Denmark 11 J6 55 35N 12 5 E
Roskovec, Albania 40 F3 40 44N 19 43 E
Roslavl, Russia 46 F7 53 57N 32 55 E
Rosmaninhal, Portugal 34 F3 39 44N 7 5W
Rosmead, S. Africa 88 E4 31 29 S 25 8 E
Røsnæs, Denmark 11 J4 55 44N 10 55 E
Rosolini, Italy 31 F7 36 49N 14 57 E
Rosporden, France 18 E3 47 57N 3 50W
Ross, Australia 94 G4 42 2 S 147 30 E
Ross, N.Z. 91 K3 42 53 S 170 49 E
Ross Béthio, Mauritania 82 B1 16 15N 16 8W
Ross I., Antarctica 5 D11 77 30 S 168 0 E
Ross Ice Shelf, Antarctica 5 E12 80 0 S 180 0 E
Ross L., U.S.A. 114 B3 48 44N 121 4W
Ross-on-Wye, U.K. 13 F5 51 54N 2 34W
Ross River, Australia 94 C1 23 44 S 134 30 E
Ross River, Canada 104 A2 62 30N 131 30W
Ross Sea, Antarctica 5 D11 74 0 S 178 0 E
Rossall Pt., U.K. 12 D4 53 55N 3 3W
Rossan Pt., Ireland 15 B3 54 42N 8 47W
Rossano, Italy 31 C9 39 36N 16 39 E
Rossburn, Canada 105 C8 50 40N 100 49W
Rosseau, Canada 110 A5 45 16N 79 39W
Rosseau L., Canada 110 A5 45 10N 79 35W
Rosses, The, Ireland 15 A3 55 2N 8 20W
Rossignol, L., Canada 102 B5 52 43N 73 40W
Rossignol Res., Canada 103 D6 44 12N 65 10W
Rossland, Canada 104 D5 49 6N 117 50W
Rosslare, Ireland 15 D5 52 17N 6 24W
Rosslau, Germany 24 D8 51 52N 12 15 E
Rosso, Mauritania 82 B1 16 40N 15 45W
Rosso, C., France 21 F12 42 13N 8 32 E
Rossosh, Russia 47 G10 50 15N 39 28 E
Røssvatnet, Norway 8 D16 65 45N 14 5 E
Røst, Norway 8 C15 67 32N 12 0 E
Rosthern, Canada 105 C7 52 40N 106 20W
Rostock, Germany 24 A8 54 5N 12 8 E
Rostov, Don, Russia 47 J10 47 15N 39 45 E
Rostov, Yaroslavl, Russia 46 D10 57 14N 39 25 E
Rostrenen, France 18 D3 48 14N 3 21W
Roswell, Ga., U.S.A. 109 H3 34 2N 84 22W
Roswell, N. Mex., U.S.A. 113 J2 33 24N 104 32W
Rota, Spain 35 J4 36 37N 6 20W
Rotan, U.S.A. 113 J4 32 51N 100 28W
Rotenburg, Hessen, Germany 24 E5 50 59N 9 44 E
Rotenburg, Niedersachsen, Germany 24 B5 53 6N 9 25 E
Roth, Germany 25 F7 49 15N 11 5 E
Rothaargebirge, Germany 24 D4 51 2N 8 13 E
Rothenburg ob der Tauber, Germany 25 F6 49 23N 10 11 E
Rother →, U.K. 13 G8 50 59N 0 45 E
Rotherham, U.K. 12 D6 53 26N 1 20W
Rothes, U.K. 14 D5 57 32N 3 13W
Rothesay, Canada 103 C6 45 23N 66 0W
Rothesay, U.K. 14 F3 55 50N 5 3W
Roti, Indonesia 63 F6 10 50 S 123 0 E
Rotja, Pta., Spain 33 G6 38 38N 1 35 E
Roto, Australia 95 E4 33 0 S 145 30 E
Rotoroa, L., N.Z. 91 J4 41 55 S 172 39 E
Rotorua, N.Z. 91 H6 38 9 S 176 16 E
Rotorua, L., N.Z. 91 H6 38 5 S 176 18 E
Rott →, Germany 25 G9 48 27N 13 25 E
Rottenburg, Germany 25 G4 48 28N 8 55 E
Rottenmann, Austria 26 D7 47 31N 14 22 E
Rotterdam, Neths. 17 C4 51 55N 4 30 E
Rotterdam, U.S.A. 111 D10 42 48N 74 1W
Rottne, Sweden 11 G8 57 1N 14 54 E
Rottnest I., Australia 93 F2 32 0 S 115 27 E
Rottumeroog, Neths. 17 A6 53 33N 6 34 E
Rottweil, Germany 25 G4 48 9N 8 37 E
Rotuma, Fiji 96 J9 12 25 S 177 5 E
Roubaix, France 19 B10 50 40N 3 10 E
Roudnice nad Labem, Czech Rep. 26 A7 50 25N 14 15 E
Rouen, France 18 C8 49 27N 1 4 E
Rouergue, France 20 D5 44 15N 2 0 E
Rouillac, France 20 C3 45 47N 0 4W
Rouleau, Canada 105 C8 50 10N 104 56W
Round Mountain, U.S.A. 114 G5 38 43N 117 4W
Round Mt., Australia 95 E5 30 26 S 152 16 E
Round Rock, U.S.A. 113 K6 30 31N 97 41W
Roundup, U.S.A. 114 C9 46 27N 108 33W
Rousay, U.K. 14 B5 59 10N 3 2W
Rouses Point, U.S.A. 111 B11 44 59N 73 22W
Rouseville, U.S.A. 110 E5 41 28N 79 42W
Roussillon, Isère, France 21 C8 45 24N 4 49 E
Roussillon, Pyrénées-Or., France 20 F6 42 30N 2 35 E
Rouxville, S. Africa 88 E4 30 25 S 26 50 E
Rouyn-Noranda, Canada 102 C4 48 20N 79 0W
Rovaniemi, Finland 8 C21 66 29N 25 41 E
Rovato, Italy 28 C7 45 34N 10 0 E
Rovenki, Ukraine 47 H10 48 5N 39 21 E
Rovereto, Italy 28 C8 45 53N 11 3 E
Rovigo, Italy 29 C8 45 4N 11 47 E
Rovinj, Croatia 29 C10 45 5N 13 40 E
Rovno = Rivne, Ukraine 47 G4 50 40N 26 10 E
Rovnoye, Russia 48 E8 50 52N 46 3 E
Rovuma = Ruvuma →, Tanzania 87 E5 10 29 S 40 28 E
Row'ān, Iran 71 C6 35 8N 48 51 E
Rowena, Australia 95 D4 29 48 S 148 55 E
Rowley Shoals, Australia 92 C2 17 30 S 119 0 E
Roxa, Guinea-Biss. 82 C1 11 15N 15 45W
Roxas, Capiz, Phil. 61 F5 11 36N 122 49 E
Roxas, Isabela, Phil. 61 C4 17 8N 121 36 E
Roxas, Mind. Or., Phil. 61 E4 12 35N 121 31 E
Roxboro, U.S.A. 109 G6 36 24N 78 59W
Roxburgh, N.Z. 91 L2 45 33 S 169 19 E
Roxbury, U.S.A. 110 F7 40 6N 77 39W
Roxen, Sweden 11 F9 58 30N 15 40 E
Roy, Mont., U.S.A. 114 C9 47 20N 108 58W
Roy, N. Mex., U.S.A. 113 H2 35 57N 104 12W
Roy, Utah, U.S.A. 114 F7 41 10N 112 2W
Royal Canal, Ireland 15 C4 53 30N 7 13W
Royal Leamington Spa, U.K. 13 E6 52 18N 1 31W
Royal Tunbridge Wells, U.K. 13 F8 51 7N 0 16 E
Royan, France 20 C2 45 37N 1 2W
Roye, France 19 C9 49 42N 2 48 E
Royston, U.K. 13 E7 52 3N 0 0W
Rožaj, Montenegro, Yug. 40 D4 42 50N 20 11 E
Różan, Poland 45 F8 52 52N 21 25 E
Rozay-en-Brie, France 19 D9 48 41N 2 58 E
Rozdilna, Ukraine 47 J6 46 50N 30 2 E
Rozhyshche, Ukraine 47 G3 50 54N 25 15 E
Rožmitál pod Třemšínem, Czech Rep. 26 B6 49 36N 13 53 E
Rožňava, Slovak Rep. 27 C13 48 37N 20 35 E
Rozogi, Poland 44 E8 53 28N 21 19 E
Rozoy-sur-Serre, France 19 C11 49 40N 4 8 E
Rozzano, Italy 28 C6 45 22N 9 10 E
Rrëshen, Albania 40 E3 41 47N 19 49 E
Rrësheni = Rrëshen, Albania 40 E3 41 47N 19 49 E
Rrogozhine, Albania 40 E3 41 4N 19 50 E
Rrogozhino = Rrogozhine, Albania 40 E3 41 4N 19 50 E
Rtanj, Serbia, Yug. 40 C5 43 45N 21 50 E
Rtishchevo, Russia 48 D6 52 18N 43 46 E
Rúa = A Rúa, Spain 34 C3 42 24N 7 6W
Ruacaná, Namibia 88 B1 17 27 S 14 21 E
Ruahine Ra., N.Z. 91 H6 39 55 S 176 2 E
Ruapehu, N.Z. 91 H5 39 17 S 175 35 E
Ruapuke I., N.Z. 91 M2 46 46 S 168 31 E
Ruâq, W. →, Egypt 75 F2 30 0N 33 49 E
Rub' al Khālī, Si. Arabia 74 D4 18 0N 48 0 E
Rubeho Mts., Tanzania 86 D4 6 50 S 36 25 E
Rubezhnoye = Rubizhne, Ukraine 47 H10 49 6N 38 25 E
Rubha a' Mhail, U.K. 14 F2 55 56N 6 8W
Rubha Hunish, U.K. 14 D2 57 42N 6 20W
Rubha Robhanais = Lewis, Butt of, U.K. 14 C2 58 31N 6 16W
Rubi, Spain 32 D7 41 29N 2 2 E
Rubicon →, U.S.A. 116 G5 38 53N 121 4W
Rubicone →, Italy 29 D9 44 8N 12 28 E
Rubik, Albania 40 E3 41 46N 19 47 E
Rubino, Ivory C. 82 D4 6 4N 4 18W
Rubio, Venezuela 124 B4 7 43N 72 22W
Rubizhne, Ukraine 47 H10 49 6N 38 25 E
Rubtsovsk, Russia 50 D9 51 30N 81 10 E
Ruby L., U.S.A. 114 F6 40 10N 115 28W
Ruby Mts., U.S.A. 114 F6 40 30N 115 20W
Rubyvale, Australia 94 C4 23 25 S 147 42 E
Rucheng, China 59 E9 25 33N 113 38 E
Ruciane-Nida, Poland 44 E8 53 40N 21 32 E
Rūd Sar, Iran 71 B6 37 8N 50 18 E
Ruda, Sweden 11 G10 57 6N 16 7 E
Ruda Śląska, Poland 45 H5 50 16N 18 50 E
Rudall, Australia 95 E2 33 43 S 136 17 E
Rudall →, Australia 92 D3 22 34 S 122 13 E
Rüdersdorf, Germany 24 C9 52 27N 13 47 E
Rudewa, Tanzania 87 E3 10 7 S 34 40 E
Rudkøbing, Denmark 11 K4 54 56N 10 41 E
Rudna, Poland 45 G3 51 30N 16 17 E
Rudnik, Bulgaria 41 D11 42 36N 27 30 E
Rudnik, Poland 45 H9 50 26N 22 15 E
Rudnik, Serbia, Yug. 40 B4 44 7N 20 35 E
Rudnya, Russia 46 E6 54 55N 31 7 E
Rudnyy, Kazakstan 50 D7 52 57N 63 7 E
Rudo, Bos.-H. 42 G4 43 41N 19 23 E
Rudolfa, Ostrov, Russia 50 A6 81 45N 58 30 E
Rudolstadt, Germany 24 E7 50 44N 11 19 E
Rudong, China 59 A13 32 20N 121 12 E
Rudozem, Bulgaria 41 E8 41 29N 24 51 E
Rudyard, U.S.A. 108 B3 46 14N 84 36W
Rue, France 19 B8 50 15N 1 40 E
Rufa'a, Sudan 81 E3 14 44N 33 22 E
Rufiji →, Tanzania 86 D4 7 50 S 39 15 E
Rufino, Argentina 126 C3 34 20 S 62 50W
Rufisque, Senegal 82 C1 14 40N 17 15W
Rufunsa, Zambia 87 F2 15 4 S 29 34 E
Rugao, China 59 A13 32 23N 120 31 E
Rugby, U.K. 13 E6 52 23N 1 16W
Rugby, U.S.A. 112 A5 48 22N 100 0W
Rügen, Germany 24 A9 54 22N 13 24 E
Rugles, France 18 D7 48 50N 0 40 E
Ruhengeri, Rwanda 86 C2 1 30 S 29 36 E
Ruhla, Germany 24 E6 50 54N 10 23 E
Ruhland, Germany 24 D9 51 27N 13 51 E
Ruhnu, Estonia 9 H20 57 48N 23 15 E
Ruhr →, Germany 24 D2 51 27N 6 43 E
Ruhuhu →, Tanzania 87 E3 10 31 S 34 34 E
Rui'an, China 59 D13 27 47N 120 40 E
Ruichang, China 59 C10 29 40N 115 39 E
Ruidoso, U.S.A. 115 K11 33 20N 105 41W
Ruijin, China 59 E10 25 48N 116 0 E
Ruili, China 58 E1 24 1N 97 43 E
Ruivo, Pico, Madeira 37 D3 32 45N 16 56W
Ruj, Bulgaria 40 D6 42 52N 22 34 E
Rujen, Macedonia 40 D6 42 9N 22 30 E
Rujm Tal'at al Jamā'ah, Jordan 75 E4 30 24N 35 30 E
Ruk, Pakistan 68 F3 27 50N 68 42 E
Rukhla, Pakistan 68 C4 32 27N 71 57 E
Ruki →, Dem. Rep. of the Congo 84 E3 0 5N 18 17 E
Rukwa □, Tanzania 86 D3 7 0 S 31 30 E
Rukwa, L., Tanzania 86 D3 8 0 S 32 20 E
Rulhieres, C., Australia 92 B4 13 56 S 127 22 E
Rum = Rhum, U.K. 14 E2 57 0N 6 20W
Rum Cay, Bahamas 121 B5 23 40N 74 58W
Rum Jungle, Australia 92 B5 13 0 S 130 59 E
Ruma, Serbia, Yug. 42 E4 45 0N 19 50 E
Rumāḥ, Si. Arabia 70 E5 25 29N 47 10 E
Rumania = Romania ■, Europe 43 D10 46 0N 25 0 E
Rumaylah, Iraq 70 D5 30 47N 47 37 E
Rumbêk, Sudan 81 F2 6 54N 29 37 E
Rumburk, Czech Rep. 26 A7 50 57N 14 32 E
Rumford, U.S.A. 109 C10 44 33N 70 33W
Rumia, Poland 44 D5 54 37N 18 25 E
Rumilly, France 21 C9 45 53N 5 56 E
Rumoi, Japan 54 C10 43 56N 141 39 E
Rumonge, Burundi 86 C2 3 59 S 29 26 E
Rumson, U.S.A. 111 F11 40 23N 74 0W
Rumuruti, Kenya 86 B4 0 17N 36 32 E
Runan, China 56 H8 33 0N 114 30 E
Runanga, N.Z. 91 K3 42 25 S 171 15 E
Runaway, C., N.Z. 91 G6 37 32 S 177 59 E
Runcorn, U.K. 12 D5 53 21N 2 44W
Rundu, Namibia 88 B2 17 52 S 19 43 E
Rungwa, Tanzania 86 D3 6 55 S 33 32 E
Rungwa →, Tanzania 86 D3 7 36 S 31 50 E
Rungwe, Tanzania 87 D3 9 11 S 33 32 E
Rungwe, Mt., Tanzania 84 F6 9 8 S 33 40 E
Runka, Nigeria 83 C6 12 28N 7 20 E
Runn, Sweden 10 D9 60 30N 15 40 E
Runton Ra., Australia 92 D3 23 31 S 123 6 E
Ruokolahti, Finland 46 B5 61 17N 28 50 E
Ruoqiang, China 60 C3 38 55N 88 10 E
Rupa, India 67 F18 27 15N 92 21 E
Rupar, India 68 D7 31 2N 76 38 E
Rupat, Indonesia 62 D2 1 45N 101 40 E
Rupea, Romania 43 D10 46 2N 25 13 E
Rupen →, India 68 H4 23 28N 71 31 E
Rupert, U.S.A. 114 E7 42 37N 113 41W
Rupert →, Canada 102 B4 51 29N 78 45W
Rupert B., Canada 102 B4 51 35N 79 0W
Rupert House = Waskaganish, Canada 102 B4 51 30N 78 40W
Rupsa, India 69 J12 21 37N 87 1 E
Rur →, Germany 24 D1 51 11N 5 59 E
Rurrenabaque, Bolivia 124 F5 14 30 S 67 32W
Rus →, Spain 33 F2 39 30N 2 30W
Rusambo, Zimbabwe 87 F3 16 30 S 32 4 E
Rusape, Zimbabwe 87 F3 18 35 S 32 8 E
Ruschuk = Ruse, Bulgaria 41 C9 43 48N 25 59 E
Ruse, Bulgaria 41 C9 43 48N 25 59 E
Ruse □, Bulgaria 41 C10 43 35N 26 20 E
Ruşetu, Romania 43 F12 44 57N 27 14 E
Rush, Ireland 15 C5 53 31N 6 6W
Rushan, China 57 F11 36 56N 121 30 E
Rushden, U.K. 13 E7 52 18N 0 35W
Rushmore, Mt., U.S.A. 112 D3 43 53N 103 28W
Rushville, Ill., U.S.A. 112 E9 40 7N 90 34W
Rushville, Ind., U.S.A. 108 F3 39 37N 85 27W
Rushville, Nebr., U.S.A. 112 D3 42 43N 102 28W
Russas, Brazil 125 D11 4 55 S 37 50W
Russell, Canada 105 C8 50 50N 101 20W
Russell, Kans., U.S.A. 112 F5 38 54N 98 52W
Russell, N.Y., U.S.A. 111 B9 44 27N 75 9W
Russell, Pa., U.S.A. 110 E5 41 56N 79 8W
Russell L., Man., Canada 105 B8 56 15N 101 30W
Russell L., N.W.T., Canada 104 A5 63 5N 115 44W
Russellkonda, India 67 K14 19 57N 84 42 E
Russellville, Ala., U.S.A. 109 H2 34 30N 87 44W
Russellville, Ark., U.S.A. 113 H8 35 17N 93 8W
Russellville, Ky., U.S.A. 109 G2 36 51N 86 53W
Rüsselsheim, Germany 25 F4 49 59N 8 23 E
Russi, Italy 29 D9 44 22N 12 2 E
Russia ■, Eurasia 51 C11 62 0N 105 0 E
Russian →, U.S.A. 116 G3 38 27N 123 8W
Russkoye Ustie, Russia 4 B15 71 0N 149 0 E
Rust, Austria 27 D9 47 49N 16 42 E
Rustam, Pakistan 68 B5 34 25N 72 13 E
Rustam Shahr, Pakistan 68 F2 26 58N 66 6 E
Rustavi, Georgia 49 K7 41 30N 45 0 E
Rustenburg, S. Africa 88 D4 25 41 S 27 14 E
Ruston, U.S.A. 113 J8 32 32N 92 38W
Rutana, Burundi 86 C3 3 55 S 30 0 E
Rute, Spain 35 H6 37 19N 4 23W
Ruteng, Indonesia 63 F6 8 35 S 120 30 E
Ruth, U.S.A. 110 C2 43 42N 82 45W
Rutherford, U.S.A. 116 G4 38 26N 122 24W
Rutland, U.S.A. 111 C12 43 37N 72 58W
Rutland □, U.K. 13 E7 52 38N 0 40W
Rutland Water, U.K. 13 E7 52 39N 0 38W
Rutledge →, Canada 105 A6 61 4N 112 0W
Rutledge L., Canada 105 A6 61 33N 110 47W
Rutqa, W. →, Syria 73 E9 34 30N 41 3 E
Rutshuru, Dem. Rep. of the Congo 86 C2 1 13 S 29 25 E
Ruvo di Púglia, Italy 31 A9 41 7N 16 29 E
Ruvu, Tanzania 86 D4 6 49 S 38 43 E
Ruvu →, Tanzania 86 D4 6 23 S 38 52 E
Ruvuma □, Tanzania 87 E4 10 20 S 36 0 E
Ruvuma →, Tanzania 87 E5 10 29 S 40 28 E
Ruwais, U.A.E. 71 E7 24 5N 52 50 E
Ruwenzori, Africa 86 B2 0 30N 29 55 E
Ruya →, Zimbabwe 89 B5 16 27 S 32 5 E
Ruyigi, Burundi 86 C3 3 29 S 30 15 E
Ruyuan, China 59 E9 24 46N 113 16 E
Ruzayevka, Russia 48 C7 54 4N 45 0 E
Růzhevo Konare, Bulgaria 41 D8 42 23N 24 46 E
Ružomberok, Slovak Rep. 27 B12 49 3N 19 17 E
Rwanda ■, Africa 86 C3 2 0 S 30 0 E
Ryakhovo, Bulgaria 41 C10 43 58N 26 18 E
Ryan, L., U.K. 14 G3 55 0N 5 2W
Ryazan, Russia 46 E10 54 40N 39 40 E
Ryazhsk, Russia 46 F11 53 45N 40 3 E
Rybache = Rybachye, Kazakstan 50 E9 46 40N 81 20 E
Rybachye, Kazakstan 50 E9 46 40N 81 20 E
Rybinsk, Russia 46 C10 58 5N 38 50 E
Rybinskoye Vdkhr., Russia 46 C10 58 30N 38 25 E
Rybnik, Poland 45 H5 50 6N 18 32 E
Rybnitsa = Râbniţa, Moldova 43 C14 47 45N 29 0 E
Rybnoye, Russia 46 E10 54 45N 39 30 E
Rychnov nad Kněžnou, Czech Rep. 27 A9 50 10N 16 17 E
Rychwał, Poland 45 F5 52 4N 18 10 E
Rycroft, Canada 104 B5 55 45N 118 40W
Ryd, Sweden 11 H8 56 27N 14 42 E
Rydaholm, Sweden 11 H8 56 59N 14 18 E
Ryde, U.K. 13 G6 50 43N 1 9W
Ryderwood, U.S.A. 116 D3 46 23N 123 3W
Rydzyna, Poland 45 G3 51 47N 16 39 E
Rye, U.K. 13 G8 50 57N 0 45 E
Rye →, U.K. 12 C7 54 11N 0 44W
Rye Bay, U.K. 13 G8 50 52N 0 49 E
Rye Patch Reservoir, U.S.A. 114 F4 40 28N 118 19W
Ryegate, U.S.A. 114 C9 46 18N 109 15W
Ryki, Poland 45 G8 51 38N 21 56 E
Ryley, Canada 104 C6 53 17N 112 26W
Rylsk, Russia 47 G8 51 36N 34 43 E
Rylstone, Australia 95 E4 32 46 S 149 58 E
Rymanów, Poland 45 J8 49 35N 21 51 E
Ryn, Poland 44 E8 53 57N 21 34 E
Ryn Peski, Kazakstan 49 G9 47 30N 49 0 E
Ryōtsu, Japan 54 E9 38 5N 138 26 E
Rypin, Poland 45 E6 53 3N 19 25 E
Ryssby, Sweden 11 H8 56 52N 14 10 E
Ryūgasaki, Japan 55 G10 35 54N 140 11 E
Ryūkyū Is. = Ryūkyū-rettō, Japan 55 M3 26 0N 126 0 E
Ryūkyū-rettō, Japan 55 M3 26 0N 126 0 E
Rzepin, Poland 45 F1 52 20N 14 49 E
Rzeszów, Poland 45 H8 50 5N 21 58 E
Rzhev, Russia 46 D8 56 20N 34 20 E

S

Sa, Thailand 64 C3 18 34N 100 45 E
Sa Canal, Spain 37 C7 38 51N 1 23 E
Sa Conillera, Spain 37 C7 38 59N 1 13 E
Sa Dec, Vietnam 65 G5 10 20N 105 46 E
Sa Dragonera, Spain 37 B9 39 35N 2 19 E
Sa Mesquida, Spain 37 B11 39 55N 4 16 E
Sa Pobla, Spain 32 F8 39 46N 3 1 E
Sa Savina, Spain 37 C7 38 44N 1 25 E
Sa'ādatābād, Fārs, Iran 71 D7 30 10N 53 5 E
Sa'ādatābād, Hormozgān, Iran 71 D7 28 3N 55 53 E
Sa'ādatābād, Kermān, Iran 71 D7 29 40N 55 51 E
Saale →, Germany 24 D7 51 56N 11 54 E
Saaler Bodden, Germany 24 A8 54 20N 12 27 E
Saalfeld, Germany 24 E7 50 38N 11 21 E
Saalfelden, Austria 26 D5 47 25N 12 51 E
Saane →, Switz. 25 H3 47 8N 7 10 E
Saar →, Europe 17 E6 49 41N 6 32 E
Saarbrücken, Germany 25 F2 49 14N 6 59 E
Saarburg, Germany 25 F2 49 36N 6 32 E
Saaremaa, Estonia 9 G20 58 30N 22 30 E
Saarijärvi, Finland 9 E21 62 43N 25 16 E
Saariselkä, Finland 8 B23 68 16N 28 15 E
Saarland □, Germany 25 F2 49 20N 7 0 E
Saarlouis, Germany 25 F2 49 18N 6 45 E
Sab 'Ābar, Syria 70 C3 33 46N 37 41 E
Saba, W. Indies 121 C7 17 42N 63 26W
Šabac, Serbia, Yug. 40 B3 44 48N 19 42 E
Sabadell, Spain 32 D7 41 28N 2 7 E
Sabah □, Malaysia 62 C5 6 0N 117 0 E
Sabak Bernam, Malaysia 65 L3 3 46N 100 58 E
Sabalān, Kūhhā-ye, Iran 70 B5 38 15N 47 45 E
Sabalana, Kepulauan, Indonesia 63 F5 6 45 S 118 50 E
Sábana de la Mar, Dom. Rep. 121 C6 19 7N 69 24W
Sábanalarga, Colombia 124 A4 10 38N 74 55W
Sabang, Indonesia 62 C1 5 50N 95 15 E
Săbăoani, Romania 43 C11 47 1N 26 51 E
Sabará, Brazil 125 G10 19 55 S 43 46W
Sabarmati →, India 68 H5 22 18N 72 22 E
Sabattis, U.S.A. 111 B10 44 6N 74 40W
Sabáudia, Italy 30 A6 41 18N 13 1 E
Saberania, Indonesia 63 E9 2 5 S 138 18 E
Sabhah, Libya 79 C8 27 9N 14 29 E
Sabi →, India 68 E7 28 29N 76 44 E
Sabidana, J., Sudan 80 D4 18 4N 36 50 E
Sabie, S. Africa 89 D5 25 10 S 30 48 E
Sabinal, Mexico 118 A3 30 58N 107 25W
Sabinal, U.S.A. 113 L5 29 19N 99 28W
Sabiñánigo, Spain 32 C4 42 31N 0 22W
Sabinar, Punta del, Spain 33 J2 36 43N 2 44W
Sabinas, Mexico 118 B4 27 50N 101 10W
Sabinas →, Mexico 118 B4 27 37N 100 42W
Sabinas Hidalgo, Mexico 118 B4 26 33N 100 10W
Sabine →, U.S.A. 113 L8 29 59N 93 47W
Sabine L., U.S.A. 113 L8 29 53N 93 51W
Sabine Pass, U.S.A. 113 L8 29 44N 93 54W
Sabinov, Slovak Rep. 27 B14 49 6N 21 5 E
Sabinsville, U.S.A. 110 E7 41 52N 77 31W
Sabirabad, Azerbaijan 49 K9 40 5N 48 30 E
Sabkhet el Bardawîl, Egypt 75 D2 31 10N 33 15 E
Sablayan, Phil. 61 E4 12 50N 120 50 E
Sable, Canada 103 A6 55 30N 68 21W
Sable, C., Canada 103 D6 43 29N 65 38W
Sable, C., U.S.A. 107 E10 25 9N 81 8W
Sable I., Canada 103 D8 44 0N 60 0W
Sablé-sur-Sarthe, France 18 E6 47 50N 0 20W
Sabonkafi, Niger 83 C6 14 40N 8 45 E
Sabor →, Portugal 34 D3 41 10N 7 7W
Sabou, Burkina Faso 82 C4 12 1N 2 15W
Sabres, France 20 D3 44 9N 0 43W
Sabrina Coast, Antarctica 5 C9 68 0 S 120 0 E
Sabugal, Portugal 34 E3 40 20N 7 5W
Sabulubbek, Indonesia 62 E1 1 36 S 98 40 E
Sabuncu, Turkey 39 B12 39 33N 30 12 E
Sabzevār, Iran 71 B8 36 15N 57 40 E
Sabzvārān, Iran 71 D8 28 45N 57 50 E
Sac City, U.S.A. 112 D7 42 25N 95 0W
Sacedón, Spain 32 E2 40 29N 2 41W
Săcele, Romania 43 E10 45 37N 25 41 E
Sachigo →, Canada 102 A2 55 6N 88 58W
Sachigo, L., Canada 102 B1 53 50N 92 12W
Sachkhere, Georgia 49 J6 42 25N 43 28 E
Sachsen □, Germany 24 E9 50 55N 13 10 E
Sachsen-Anhalt □, Germany 24 D7 52 0N 12 0 E
Sacile, Italy 29 C9 45 57N 12 30 E
Sackets Harbor, U.S.A. 111 C8 43 57N 76 7W
Sackville, Canada 103 C7 45 54N 64 22W
Saco, Maine, U.S.A. 109 D10 43 30N 70 27W
Saco, Mont., U.S.A. 114 B10 48 28N 107 21W
Sacramento, U.S.A. 116 G5 38 35N 121 29W
Sacramento →, U.S.A. 116 G5 38 3N 121 56W
Sacramento Mts., U.S.A. 115 K11 32 30N 105 30W
Sacramento Valley, U.S.A. 116 G5 39 30N 122 0W
Sacratif, C., Spain 35 J7 36 42N 3 28W
Săcueni, Romania 42 C7 47 20N 22 5 E
Sada, Spain 34 B2 43 22N 8 15W
Sada-Misaki, Japan 55 H6 33 20N 132 1 E
Sádaba, Spain 32 C3 42 19N 1 12W
Sadabad, India 68 F8 27 27N 78 3 E
Sadani, Tanzania 86 D4 5 58 S 38 35 E
Sadao, Thailand 65 J3 6 38N 100 26 E
Sadd el Aali, Egypt 80 C3 23 54N 32 54 E
Saddle Mt., U.S.A. 116 E3 45 58N 123 41W
Sade, Nigeria 83 C7 11 22N 10 45 E
Sadimi, Dem. Rep. of the Congo 87 D1 9 25 S 23 32 E
Sadiola, Mali 82 C2 13 50N 11 40W
Sa'dīyah, Hawr as, Iraq 73 F12 32 15N 46 30 E
Sado, Japan 54 F9 38 0N 138 25 E
Sado →, Portugal 35 G2 38 29N 8 55W
Sadon, Burma 67 G20 25 28N 97 55 E
Sadon, Russia 49 J6 42 52N 43 58 E
Sadra, India 68 H5 23 21N 72 43 E
Sadri, India 68 G5 25 11N 73 26 E
Sæby, Denmark 11 G4 57 21N 10 30 E
Saegertown, U.S.A. 110 E4 41 43N 80 9W
Saelices, Spain 32 F2 39 55N 2 49W
Safaalan, Turkey 41 E12 41 26N 28 6 E
Safaga, Egypt 80 B3 26 42N 34 0 E
Şafājah, Si. Arabia 70 E3 26 25N 39 0 E
Šafárikovo = Tornal'a, Slovak Rep. 27 C13 48 25N 20 20 E
Säffle, Sweden 10 E6 59 8N 12 55 E
Safford, U.S.A. 115 K9 32 50N 109 43W
Saffron Walden, U.K. 13 E8 52 1N 0 16 E
Safi, Morocco 78 B4 32 18N 9 20W
Şafīābād, Iran 71 B8 36 45N 57 58 E
Safīd Dasht, Iran 71 C6 33 27N 48 11 E
Safīd Kūh, Afghan. 66 B3 34 45N 63 0 E
Safīd Rūd →, Iran 71 B6 37 23N 50 11 E
Safipur, India 69 F9 26 44N 80 21 E
Safonovo, Russia 46 E7 55 4N 33 16 E
Safranbolu, Turkey 72 B5 41 15N 32 41 E
Saft Rashîn, Egypt 80 J7 28 58N 30 55 E
Safwān, Iraq 70 D5 30 7N 47 43 E
Sag Harbor, U.S.A. 111 F12 41 0N 72 18W
Saga, Japan 55 H5 33 15N 130 16 E
Saga □, Japan 55 H5 33 15N 130 20 E
Sagae, Japan 54 E10 38 22N 140 17 E
Sagala, Mali 82 C3 14 9N 6 38W
Sagamore, U.S.A. 110 F5 40 46N 79 14W
Sagar, Karnataka, India 66 M9 14 14N 75 6 E
Sagar, Mad. P., India 69 H8 23 50N 78 44 E
Sagara, L., Tanzania 86 D3 5 20 S 31 0 E
Sagay, Phil. 61 F5 10 57N 123 25 E
Saginaw, U.S.A. 108 D4 43 26N 83 56W
Saginaw →, U.S.A. 108 D4 43 39N 83 51W
Saginaw B., U.S.A. 108 D4 43 50N 83 40W

Sagleipie, *Liberia* **82 D3** 7 0N 8 52W
Saglouc = Salluit, *Canada* **101 B12** 62 14N 75 38W
Sagŏ-ri, *S. Korea* **57 G14** 35 25N 126 49 E
Sagone, *France* **21 F12** 42 7N 8 42 E
Sagone, G. de, *France* **21 F12** 42 4N 8 40 E
Sagres, *Portugal* **35 J2** 37 0N 8 58W
Sagua la Grande, *Cuba* **120 B3** 22 50N 80 10W
Saguache, *U.S.A.* **115 G10** 38 5N 106 8W
Saguaro Nat. Park, *U.S.A.* **115 K8** 32 12N 110 38W
Saguenay →, *Canada* **103 C5** 48 22N 71 0W
Sagunt, *Spain* **32 F4** 39 42N 0 18W
Sagunto = Sagunt, *Spain* **32 F4** 39 42N 0 18W
Sagwara, *India* **68 H6** 23 41N 74 1 E
Sahaba, *Sudan* **80 D3** 18 57N 30 25 E
Sahagún, *Spain* **34 C5** 42 18N 5 2W
Saḩam al Jawlān, *Syria* **75 C4** 32 45N 35 55 E
Sahamandrevo, *Madag.* **89 C8** 23 15 S 45 35 E
Sahand, Kūh-e, *Iran* **70 B5** 37 44N 46 27 E
Sahara, *Africa* **78 D6** 23 0N 5 0 E
Saharan Atlas = Saharien, Atlas, *Algeria* **78 B6** 33 30N 1 0 E
Saharanpur, *India* **68 E7** 29 58N 77 33 E
Saharien, Atlas, *Algeria* **78 B6** 33 30N 1 0 E
Saharsa, *India* **69 G12** 25 53N 86 36 E
Sahasinaka, *Madag.* **89 C8** 21 49 S 47 49 E
Sahaswan, *India* **69 E8** 28 5N 78 45 E
Sahel, *Africa* **78 E5** 16 0N 5 0 E
Sahel, Canal du, *Mali* **82 C3** 14 20N 6 0W
Sahibganj, *India* **69 G12** 25 12N 87 40 E
Şāḩilīyah, *Iraq* **70 C4** 33 43N 42 42 E
Sahiwal, *Pakistan* **68 D5** 30 45N 73 8 E
Şaḩneh, *Iran* **70 C5** 34 29N 47 41 E
Sahuaripa, *Mexico* **118 B3** 29 0N 109 13W
Sahuarita, *U.S.A.* **115 L8** 31 57N 110 58W
Sahuayo, *Mexico* **118 C4** 20 4N 102 43W
Šahy, *Slovak Rep.* **27 C11** 48 4N 18 55 E
Sai →, *India* **69 G10** 25 39N 82 47 E
Sai Buri, *Thailand* **65 J3** 6 43N 101 45 E
Sa'id Bundâs, *Sudan* **81 F1** 8 24N 24 48 E
Sa'īdābād, *Kermān, Iran* **71 D7** 29 30N 55 45 E
Sa'īdābād, *Semnān, Iran* **71 B7** 36 8N 54 11 E
Sa'īdīyeh, *Iran* **71 B6** 36 20N 48 55 E
Saidpur, *Bangla.* **67 G16** 25 48N 89 0 E
Saidpur, *India* **69 G10** 25 33N 83 11 E
Saidu, *Pakistan* **69 B5** 34 43N 72 24 E
Saignes, *France* **20 C6** 45 20N 2 31 E
Saigon = Thanh Pho Ho Chi Minh, *Vietnam* **65 G6** 10 58N 106 40 E
Saijō, *Japan* **55 H6** 33 55N 133 11 E
Saikanosy Masoala, *Madag.* **89 B9** 15 45 S 50 10 E
Saikhoa Ghat, *India* **67 F19** 27 50N 95 40 E
Saiki, *Japan* **55 H5** 32 58N 131 51 E
Sailana, *India* **68 H6** 23 28N 74 55 E
Saillans, *France* **21 D9** 44 42N 5 12 E
Sailolof, *Indonesia* **63 E8** 1 7 S 130 46 E
Saimaa, *Finland* **9 F23** 61 15N 28 15 E
Saimbeyli, *Turkey* **72 D7** 37 59N 36 6 E
Şa'in Dezh, *Iran* **70 B5** 36 40N 46 25 E
St. Abb's Head, *U.K.* **14 F6** 55 55N 2 8W
St-Affrique, *France* **20 E6** 43 57N 2 53 E
St-Agrève, *France* **21 C8** 45 0N 4 23 E
St-Aignan, *France* **18 E8** 47 16N 1 22 E
St. Alban's, *Canada* **103 C8** 47 51N 55 50W
St. Albans, *U.K.* **13 F7** 51 45N 0 19W
St. Albans, *Vt., U.S.A.* **111 B11** 44 49N 73 5W
St. Albans, *W. Va., U.S.A.* **108 F5** 38 23N 81 50W
St. Alban's Head, *U.K.* **13 G5** 50 34N 2 4W
St. Albert, *Canada* **104 C6** 53 37N 113 32W
St-Amand-en-Puisaye, *France* **19 E10** 47 32N 3 5 E
St-Amand-les-Eaux, *France* **19 B10** 50 27N 3 25 E
St-Amand-Montrond, *France* **19 F9** 46 43N 2 30 E
St-Amarin, *France* **19 E14** 47 54N 7 2 E
St-Amour, *France* **19 F12** 46 26N 5 21 E
St-André-de-Cubzac, *France* **20 D3** 44 59N 0 26W
St-André-les-Alpes, *France* **21 E10** 43 58N 6 30 E
St. Andrew's, *Canada* **103 C8** 47 45N 59 15W
St. Andrews, *U.K.* **14 E6** 56 20N 2 47W
St-Anicet, *Canada* **111 A10** 45 8N 74 22W
St. Ann B., *Canada* **103 C7** 46 22N 60 25W
St. Ann's Bay, *Jamaica* **120 C4** 18 26N 77 15W
St. Anthony, *Canada* **103 B8** 51 22N 55 35W
St. Anthony, *U.S.A.* **114 E8** 43 58N 111 41W
St. Antoine, *Canada* **103 C7** 46 22N 64 45W
St-Antonin-Noble-Val, *France* **20 D5** 44 10N 1 45 E
St. Arnaud, *Australia* **95 F3** 36 40 S 143 16 E
St-Astier, *France* **20 C4** 45 8N 0 31 E
St-Aubin-du-Cormier, *France* **18 D5** 48 15N 1 26W
St-Augustin →, *Canada* **103 B8** 51 16N 58 40W
St-Augustin-Saguenay, *Canada* **103 B8** 51 13N 58 38W
St. Augustine, *U.S.A.* **109 L5** 29 54N 81 19W
St-Aulaye, *France* **20 C4** 45 12N 0 9 E
St. Austell, *U.K.* **13 G3** 50 20N 4 47W
St-Avold, *France* **19 C13** 49 6N 6 43 E
St. Barbe, *Canada* **103 B8** 51 12N 56 46W
St-Barthélemy, *W. Indies* **121 C7** 17 50N 62 50W
St-Béat, *France* **20 F4** 42 55N 0 41 E
St. Bees Hd., *U.K.* **12 C4** 54 31N 3 38W
St-Benoît-du-Sault, *France* **20 B5** 46 26N 1 24 E
St-Bonnet, *France* **21 D10** 44 40N 6 5 E
St-Brévin-les-Pins, *France* **18 E4** 47 14N 2 10W
St-Brice-en-Coglès, *France* **18 D5** 48 25N 1 22W
St. Bride's, *Canada* **103 C9** 46 56N 54 10W
St. Brides B., *U.K.* **13 F2** 51 49N 5 9W
St-Brieuc, *France* **18 D4** 48 30N 2 46W
St-Calais, *France* **18 E7** 47 55N 0 45 E
St-Cast-le-Guildo, *France* **18 D4** 48 37N 2 18W
St. Catharines, *Canada* **102 D4** 43 10N 79 15W
St. Catherines I., *U.S.A.* **109 K5** 31 40N 81 10W
St. Catherine's Pt., *U.K.* **13 G6** 50 34N 1 18W
St-Céré, *France* **20 D5** 44 51N 1 54 E
St-Cergue, *Switz.* **25 J2** 46 27N 6 10 E
St-Cernin, *France* **20 C6** 45 5N 2 25 E
St-Chamond, *France* **21 C8** 45 28N 4 31 E
St. Charles, *Ill., U.S.A.* **108 E1** 41 54N 88 19W
St. Charles, *Mo., U.S.A.* **112 F9** 38 47N 90 29W
St. Charles, *Va., U.S.A.* **108 F7** 36 48N 83 4W
St-Chély-d'Apcher, *France* **20 D7** 44 48N 3 17 E
St-Chinian, *France* **20 E6** 43 25N 2 56 E
St. Christopher-Nevis = St. Kitts & Nevis ■, *W. Indies* **121 C7** 17 20N 62 40W
St-Ciers-sur-Gironde, *France* **20 C3** 45 17N 0 37W
St. Clair, *Mich., U.S.A.* **110 D2** 42 50N 82 30W
St. Clair, *Pa., U.S.A.* **111 F8** 40 43N 76 12W
St. Clair →, *U.S.A.* **110 D2** 42 38N 82 31W
St. Clair, L., *Canada* **102 D3** 42 30N 82 45W
St. Clair, L., *U.S.A.* **110 D2** 42 27N 82 39W
St. Clairsville, *U.S.A.* **110 F4** 40 5N 80 54W
St-Claud, *France* **20 C4** 45 54N 0 28 E
St. Claude, *Canada* **105 D9** 49 40N 98 20W
St-Claude, *France* **19 F12** 46 22N 5 52 E
St-Clet, *Canada* **111 A10** 45 21N 74 13W
St. Cloud, *Fla., U.S.A.* **109 L5** 28 15N 81 17W
St. Cloud, *Minn., U.S.A.* **112 C7** 45 34N 94 10W
St. Cricq, C., *Australia* **93 E1** 25 17 S 113 6 E
St. Croix, *Virgin Is.* **121 C7** 17 45N 64 45W
St. Croix →, *U.S.A.* **112 C8** 44 45N 92 48W
St. Croix Falls, *U.S.A.* **112 C8** 45 24N 92 38W
St-Cyprien, *France* **20 F7** 42 37N 3 2 E
St-Cyr-sur-Mer, *France* **21 E9** 43 11N 5 43 E
St. David's, *Canada* **103 C8** 48 12N 58 52W
St. David's, *U.K.* **13 F2** 51 53N 5 16W
St. David's Head, *U.K.* **13 F2** 51 54N 5 19W
St-Denis, *France* **19 D9** 48 56N 2 22 E
St-Dié, *France* **19 D13** 48 17N 6 56 E
St-Dizier, *France* **19 D11** 48 38N 4 56 E
St-Égrève, *France* **21 C9** 45 14N 5 41 E
St. Elias, Mt., *U.S.A.* **100 B5** 60 18N 140 56W
St. Elias Mts., *Canada* **104 A1** 60 33N 139 28W
St. Elias Mts., *U.S.A.* **100 C6** 60 0N 138 0W
St-Eloy-les-Mines, *France* **19 F9** 46 10N 2 51 E
St-Émilion, *France* **20 D3** 44 53N 0 9W
St-Étienne, *France* **21 C8** 45 27N 4 22 E
St-Étienne-de-Tinée, *France* **21 D10** 44 16N 6 56 E
St-Étienne-du-Rouvray, *France* **18 C8** 49 23N 1 6 E
St. Eugène, *Canada* **111 A10** 45 30N 74 28W
St. Eustatius, *W. Indies* **121 C7** 17 20N 63 0W
St-Fargeau, *France* **19 E10** 47 39N 3 4 E
St-Félicien, *Canada* **102 C5** 48 40N 72 25W
St-Florent, *France* **21 F13** 42 41N 9 18 E
St-Florent, G. de, *France* **21 F13** 42 47N 9 12 E
St-Florent-sur-Cher, *France* **19 F9** 46 59N 2 15 E
St-Florentin, *France* **19 E10** 48 0N 3 45 E
St-Flour, *France* **20 C7** 45 2N 3 6 E
St. Francis, *U.S.A.* **112 F4** 39 47N 101 48W
St. Francis →, *U.S.A.* **113 H9** 34 38N 90 36W
St. Francis, C., *S. Africa* **88 E3** 34 14 S 24 49 E
St. Francisville, *U.S.A.* **113 K9** 30 47N 91 23W
St-François, L., *Canada* **111 A10** 45 10N 74 22W
St-Fulgent, *France* **18 F5** 46 50N 1 10W
St-Gabriel, *Canada* **102 C5** 46 17N 73 24W
St. Gallen = Sankt Gallen, *Switz.* **25 H5** 47 26N 9 22 E
St-Galmier, *France* **19 G11** 45 35N 4 19 E
St-Gaudens, *France* **20 E4** 43 6N 0 44 E
St-Gaultier, *France* **18 F8** 46 39N 1 26 E
St-Gengoux-le-National, *France* **19 F11** 46 37N 4 40 E
St-Geniez-d'Olt, *France* **20 D6** 44 27N 2 58 E
St. George, *Australia* **95 D4** 28 1 S 148 30 E
St. George, *Canada* **103 C6** 45 11N 66 50W
St. George, *S.C., U.S.A.* **109 J5** 33 11N 80 35W
St. George, *Utah, U.S.A.* **115 H7** 37 6N 113 35W
St. George, C., *Canada* **103 C8** 48 30N 59 16W
St. George, C., *U.S.A.* **109 L3** 29 40N 85 5W
St. George Ra., *Australia* **92 C4** 18 40 S 125 0 E
St. George's, *Canada* **103 C8** 48 26N 58 31W
St-Georges, *Canada* **103 C5** 46 8N 70 40W
St. George's, *Grenada* **121 D7** 12 5N 61 43W
St. George's B., *Canada* **103 C8** 48 24N 58 53W
St. Georges Basin, *N.S.W., Australia* **95 F5** 35 7 S 150 36 E
St. Georges Basin, *W. Austral., Australia* **92 C4** 15 23 S 125 2 E
St. George's Channel, *Europe* **15 E6** 52 0N 6 0W
St. Georges Hd., *Australia* **95 F5** 35 12 S 150 42 E
St-Georges-lès-Baillargeaux, *France* **20 B4** 46 41N 0 22 E
St-Germain-de-Calberte, *France* **20 D7** 44 13N 3 48 E
St-Germain-en-Laye, *France* **19 D9** 48 54N 2 6 E
St-Germain-Lembron, *France* **20 C7** 45 27N 3 14 E
St-Gervais-d'Auvergne, *France* **19 F9** 46 4N 2 50 E
St-Gervais-les-Bains, *France* **21 C10** 45 53N 6 42 E
St-Gildas, Pte. de, *France* **18 E4** 47 8N 2 14W
St-Gilles, *France* **21 E8** 43 40N 4 26 E
St-Girons, *Ariège, France* **20 F5** 42 59N 1 8 E
St-Girons, *Landes, France* **20 E2** 43 54N 1 18W
St. Gotthard P. = San Gottardo, P. del, *Switz.* **25 J4** 46 33N 8 33 E
St. Helena, *U.S.A.* **114 G2** 38 30N 122 28W
St. Helena ■, *Atl. Oc.* **76 H3** 15 55 S 5 44W
St. Helena, Mt., *U.S.A.* **116 G4** 38 40N 122 36W
St. Helena B., *S. Africa* **88 E2** 32 40 S 18 10 E
St. Helens, *Australia* **94 G4** 41 20 S 148 15 E
St. Helens, *U.K.* **12 D5** 53 27N 2 44W
St. Helens, *U.S.A.* **116 E4** 45 52N 122 48W
St. Helens, Mt., *U.S.A.* **116 D4** 46 12N 122 12W
St. Helier, *U.K.* **13 H5** 49 10N 2 7W
St-Herblain, *France* **18 E5** 47 13N 1 40W
St-Hilaire-du-Harcouët, *France* **18 D5** 48 35N 1 5W
St-Hippolyte, *France* **19 E13** 47 19N 6 50 E
St-Hippolyte-du-Fort, *France* **20 E7** 43 58N 3 52 E
St-Honoré-les-Bains, *France* **19 F10** 46 54N 3 50 E
St-Hubert, *Belgium* **17 D5** 50 2N 5 23 E
St-Hyacinthe, *Canada* **102 C5** 45 40N 72 58W
St. Ignace, *U.S.A.* **108 C3** 45 52N 84 44W
St. Ignace I., *Canada* **102 C2** 48 45N 88 0W
St. Ignatius, *U.S.A.* **114 C6** 47 19N 114 6W
St-Imier, *Switz.* **25 H2** 47 9N 6 58 E
St. Ives, *U.K.* **13 G2** 50 12N 5 30W
St-James, *France* **18 D5** 48 31N 1 20W
St. James, *U.S.A.* **112 D7** 43 59N 94 38W
St-Jean →, *Canada* **103 B7** 50 17N 64 20W
St-Jean, L., *Canada* **103 C5** 48 40N 72 0W
St-Jean-d'Angély, *France* **20 C3** 45 57N 0 31W
St-Jean-de-Braye, *France* **19 E8** 47 53N 1 58 E
St-Jean-de-Luz, *France* **20 E2** 43 23N 1 39W
St-Jean-de-Maurienne, *France* **21 C10** 45 16N 6 21 E
St-Jean-de-Monts, *France* **18 F4** 46 47N 2 4W
St-Jean-du-Gard, *France* **20 D7** 44 7N 3 52 E
St-Jean-en-Royans, *France* **21 C9** 45 1N 5 18 E
St-Jean-Pied-de-Port, *France* **20 E2** 43 10N 1 14W
St-Jean-Port-Joli, *Canada* **103 C5** 47 15N 70 13W
St-Jean-sur-Richelieu, *Canada* **102 C5** 45 20N 73 20W
St-Jérôme, *Canada* **102 C5** 45 47N 74 0W
St. John, *Canada* **103 C6** 45 20N 66 8W
St. John, *U.S.A.* **113 G5** 38 0N 98 46W
St. John →, *Liberia* **82 D2** 6 40N 9 10W
St. John →, *U.S.A.* **109 C12** 45 12N 66 5W
St. John, C., *Canada* **103 C8** 50 0N 55 32W
St. John's, *Antigua* **121 C7** 17 6N 61 51W
St. John's, *Canada* **103 C9** 47 35N 52 40W
St. Johns, *Ariz., U.S.A.* **115 J9** 34 30N 109 22W
St. Johns, *Mich., U.S.A.* **108 D3** 43 0N 84 33W
St. Johns →, *U.S.A.* **109 K5** 30 24N 81 24W
St. John's Pt., *Ireland* **15 B3** 54 34N 8 27W
St. Johnsbury, *U.S.A.* **111 B12** 44 25N 72 1W
St. Johnsville, *U.S.A.* **111 D10** 43 0N 74 43W
St. Joseph, *La., U.S.A.* **113 K9** 31 55N 91 14W
St. Joseph, *Mo., U.S.A.* **112 F7** 39 46N 94 50W
St. Joseph →, *U.S.A.* **108 D2** 42 7N 86 29W
St. Joseph, I., *Canada* **102 C3** 46 12N 83 58W
St. Joseph, L., *Canada* **102 B1** 51 10N 90 35W
St-Jovite, *Canada* **102 C5** 46 8N 74 38W
St-Juéry, *France* **20 E6** 43 57N 2 12 E
St-Julien-Chapteuil, *France* **21 C8** 45 2N 4 4 E
St-Julien-de-Vouvantes, *France* **18 E5** 47 38N 1 13W
St-Julien-en-Genevois, *France* **19 F13** 46 9N 6 5 E
St-Junien, *France* **20 C4** 45 53N 0 55 E
St-Just-en-Chaussée, *France* **19 C9** 49 30N 2 25 E
St-Just-en-Chevalet, *France* **20 C7** 45 55N 3 50 E
St. Kitts & Nevis ■, *W. Indies* **121 C7** 17 20N 62 40W
St. Laurent, *Canada* **105 C9** 50 25N 97 58W
St-Laurent-de-la-Salanque, *France* **20 F6** 42 46N 2 59 E
St-Laurent-du-Pont, *France* **21 C9** 45 23N 5 45 E
St-Laurent-en-Grandvaux, *France* **19 F12** 46 35N 5 58 E
St-Laurent-Médoc, *France* **20 C3** 45 8N 0 49W
St. Lawrence, *Australia* **94 C4** 22 16 S 149 31 E
St. Lawrence, *Canada* **103 C8** 46 54N 55 23W
St. Lawrence →, *Canada* **103 C6** 49 30N 66 0W
St. Lawrence, Gulf of, *Canada* **103 C7** 48 25N 62 0W
St. Lawrence I., *U.S.A.* **100 B3** 63 30N 170 30W
St. Leonard, *Canada* **103 C6** 47 12N 67 58W
St-Léonard-de-Noblat, *France* **20 C5** 45 49N 1 29 E
St. Lewis →, *Canada* **103 B8** 52 26N 56 11W
St-Lô, *France* **18 C5** 49 7N 1 5W
St-Louis, *France* **19 E14** 47 30N 7 34 E
St. Louis, *Senegal* **82 B1** 16 8N 16 27W
St. Louis, *U.S.A.* **112 F9** 38 37N 90 12W
St. Louis →, *U.S.A.* **112 B8** 47 15N 92 45W
St-Loup-sur-Semouse, *France* **19 E13** 47 53N 6 16 E
St. Lucia ■, *W. Indies* **121 D7** 14 0N 60 50W
St. Lucia, L., *S. Africa* **89 D5** 28 5 S 32 30 E
St. Lucia Channel, *W. Indies* **121 D7** 14 15N 61 0W
St. Maarten, *W. Indies* **121 C7** 18 0N 63 5W
St. Magnus B., *U.K.* **14 A7** 60 25N 1 35W
St-Maixent-l'École, *France* **20 B3** 46 24N 0 12W
St-Malo, *France* **18 D4** 48 39N 2 1W
St-Malo, G. de, *France* **18 D4** 48 50N 2 30W
St-Mandrier-sur-Mer, *France* **21 E9** 43 4N 5 57 E
St-Marc, *Haiti* **121 C5** 19 10N 72 41W
St-Marcellin, *France* **21 C9** 45 9N 5 20 E
St-Marcouf, Îs., *France* **18 C5** 49 30N 1 10W
St. Maries, *U.S.A.* **114 C5** 47 19N 116 35W
St-Martin, *W. Indies* **121 C7** 18 0N 63 0W
St. Martin, L., *Canada* **105 C9** 51 40N 98 30W
St-Martin-de-Crau, *France* **21 E8** 43 38N 4 48 E
St-Martin-de-Ré, *France* **20 B2** 46 12N 1 21W
St-Martin-d'Hères, *France* **21 C9** 45 9N 5 45 E
St-Martin-Vésubie, *France* **21 D11** 44 4N 7 15 E
St-Martory, *France* **20 E4** 43 9N 0 56 E
St. Mary Pk., *Australia* **95 E2** 31 32 S 138 34 E
St. Marys, *Australia* **94 G4** 41 35 S 148 11 E
St. Marys, *Canada* **110 C3** 43 20N 81 10W
St. Mary's, *Corn., U.K.* **13 H1** 49 55N 6 18W
St. Mary's, *Orkney, U.K.* **14 C6** 58 54N 2 54W
St. Marys, *Ga., U.S.A.* **109 K5** 30 44N 81 33W
St. Marys, *Pa., U.S.A.* **110 E6** 41 26N 78 34W
St. Mary's, C., *Canada* **103 C9** 46 50N 54 12W
St. Mary's B., *Canada* **103 C9** 46 50N 53 50W
St. Marys Bay, *Canada* **103 D6** 44 25N 66 10W
St-Mathieu, Pte., *France* **18 D2** 48 20N 4 45W
St. Matthew I., *U.S.A.* **100 B2** 60 24N 172 42W
St. Matthews, I. = Zadetkyi Kyun, *Burma* **65 G1** 10 0N 98 25 E
St-Maurice →, *Canada* **102 C5** 46 21N 72 31W
St-Maximin-la-Ste-Baume, *France* **21 E9** 43 27N 5 52 E
St-Médard-en-Jalles, *France* **20 D3** 44 53N 0 43W
St-Méen-le-Grand, *France* **18 D4** 48 11N 2 12W
St-Mihiel, *France* **19 D12** 48 54N 5 32 E
St. Moritz, *Switz.* **25 J5** 46 30N 9 51 E
St-Nazaire, *France* **18 E4** 47 17N 2 12W
St. Neots, *U.K.* **13 E7** 52 14N 0 15W
St-Nicolas-de-Port, *France* **19 D13** 48 38N 6 18 E
St-Niklaas, *Belgium* **17 C4** 51 10N 4 8 E
St-Omer, *France* **19 B9** 50 45N 2 15 E
St-Palais-sur-Mer, *France* **20 C2** 45 38N 1 5W
St-Pamphile, *Canada* **103 C6** 46 58N 69 48W
St-Pardoux-la-Rivière, *France* **20 C4** 45 29N 0 45 E
St. Pascal, *Canada* **103 C6** 47 32N 69 48W
St. Paul, *Canada* **104 C6** 54 0N 111 17W
St-Paul, *France* **21 D10** 44 31N 6 45 E
St. Paul, *Minn., U.S.A.* **112 C8** 44 57N 93 6W
St. Paul, *Nebr., U.S.A.* **112 E5** 41 13N 98 27W
St-Paul →, *Canada* **103 B8** 51 27N 57 42W
St. Paul →, *Liberia* **82 D2** 6 25N 10 48W
St. Paul, I., *Ind. Oc.* **3 F13** 38 55 S 77 34 E
St-Paul-de-Fenouillet, *France* **20 F6** 42 48N 2 30 E
St. Paul I., *Canada* **103 C7** 47 12N 60 9W
St-Paul-lès-Dax, *France* **20 E2** 43 44N 1 3W
St-Péray, *France* **21 D8** 44 57N 4 50 E
St. Peter, *U.S.A.* **112 C8** 44 20N 93 57W
St-Peter-Ording, *Germany* **24 A4** 54 20N 8 36 E
St. Peter Port, *U.K.* **13 H5** 49 26N 2 33W
St. Peters, *N.S., Canada* **103 C7** 45 40N 60 53W
St. Peters, *P.E.I., Canada* **103 C7** 46 25N 62 35W
St. Petersburg = Sankt-Peterburg, *Russia* **46 C6** 59 55N 30 20 E
St. Petersburg, *U.S.A.* **109 M4** 27 46N 82 39W
St-Philbert-de-Grand-Lieu, *France* **18 E5** 47 2N 1 39W
St-Pie, *Canada* **111 A12** 45 30N 72 54W
St-Pierre, *St- P. & M.* **103 C8** 46 46N 56 12W
St-Pierre, L., *Canada* **102 C5** 46 12N 72 52W
St-Pierre-d'Oléron, *France* **20 C2** 45 57N 1 19W
St-Pierre-en-Port, *France* **18 C7** 49 48N 0 30 E
St-Pierre et Miquelon □, *St- P. & M.* **103 C8** 46 55N 56 10W
St-Pierre-le-Moûtier, *France* **19 F10** 46 47N 3 7 E
St-Pierre-sur-Dives, *France* **18 C6** 49 2N 0 1W
St-Pol-de-Léon, *France* **18 D3** 48 41N 4 0W
St-Pol-sur-Mer, *France* **19 A9** 51 1N 2 20 E
St-Pol-sur-Ternoise, *France* **19 B9** 50 23N 2 20 E
St-Pons, *France* **20 E6** 43 30N 2 45 E
St-Pourçain-sur-Sioule, *France* **19 F10** 46 18N 3 18 E
St-Priest, *France* **21 C8** 45 42N 4 57 E
St-Quay-Portrieux, *France* **18 D4** 48 39N 2 51W
St. Quentin, *Canada* **103 C6** 47 30N 67 23W
St-Quentin, *France* **19 C10** 49 50N 3 16 E
St-Rambert-d'Albon, *France* **21 C8** 45 17N 4 49 E
St-Raphaël, *France* **21 E10** 43 25N 6 46 E
St. Regis, *U.S.A.* **114 C6** 47 18N 115 6W
St-Renan, *France* **18 D2** 48 26N 4 37W
St-Saëns, *France* **18 C8** 49 41N 1 16 E
St-Savin, *France* **20 B4** 46 34N 0 53 E
St-Savinien, *France* **20 C3** 45 53N 0 42W
St. Sebastien, Tanjon' i, *Madag.* **89 A8** 12 26 S 48 44 E
St-Seine-l'Abbaye, *France* **19 E11** 47 26N 4 47 E
St-Sernin-sur-Rance, *France* **20 E6** 43 54N 2 35 E
St-Sever, *France* **20 E3** 43 45N 0 35W
St-Siméon, *Canada* **103 C6** 47 51N 69 54W
St. Simons I., *U.S.A.* **109 K5** 31 12N 81 15W
St. Simons Island, *U.S.A.* **109 K5** 31 9N 81 22W
St. Stephen, *Canada* **103 C6** 45 16N 67 17W
St-Sulpice, *France* **20 E5** 43 46N 1 41 E
St-Sulpice-Laurière, *France* **20 B5** 46 3N 1 29 E
St-Sulpice-les-Feuilles, *France* **20 B5** 46 19N 1 21 E
St-Syprien = St-Cyprien, *France* **20 F7** 42 37N 3 2 E
St-Thégonnec, *France* **18 D3** 48 31N 3 57W
St. Thomas, *Canada* **102 D3** 42 45N 81 10W
St. Thomas I., *Virgin Is.* **121 C7** 18 20N 64 55W
St-Tite, *Canada* **102 C5** 46 45N 72 34W
St-Tropez, *France* **21 E10** 43 17N 6 38 E
St. Troud = St. Truiden, *Belgium* **17 D5** 50 48N 5 10 E
St. Truiden, *Belgium* **17 D5** 50 48N 5 10 E
St-Vaast-la-Hougue, *France* **18 C5** 49 35N 1 17W
St-Valery-en-Caux, *France* **18 C7** 49 52N 0 43 E
St-Valéry-sur-Somme, *France* **19 B8** 50 11N 1 38 E
St-Vallier, *France* **19 F11** 46 38N 4 22 E
St-Vallier-de-Thiey, *France* **21 E10** 43 42N 6 51 E
St-Varent, *France* **18 F6** 46 53N 0 13W
St-Vaury, *France* **20 B5** 46 12N 1 46 E
St. Vincent, *Italy* **28 C4** 45 45N 7 39 E
St. Vincent, G., *Australia* **95 F2** 35 0 S 138 0 E
St. Vincent & the Grenadines ■, *W. Indies* **121 D7** 13 0N 61 10W
St-Vincent-de-Tyrosse, *France* **20 E2** 43 39N 1 19W
St. Vincent Passage, *W. Indies* **121 D7** 13 30N 61 0W
St-Vith, *Belgium* **17 D6** 50 17N 6 9 E
St-Vivien-de-Médoc, *France* **20 C2** 45 25N 1 2W
St. Walburg, *Canada* **105 C7** 53 39N 109 12W
St-Yrieix-la-Perche, *France* **20 C5** 45 31N 1 12 E
Ste-Adresse, *France* **18 C7** 49 31N 0 5 E
Ste-Agathe-des-Monts, *Canada* **102 C5** 46 3N 74 17W
Ste-Anne, L., *Canada* **103 B6** 50 0N 67 42W
Ste-Anne-des-Monts, *Canada* **103 C6** 49 8N 66 30W
Ste-Croix, *Switz.* **25 J2** 46 49N 6 34 E
Ste-Enimie, *France* **20 D7** 44 22N 3 26 E
Ste-Foy-la-Grande, *France* **20 D4** 44 50N 0 13 E
Ste. Genevieve, *U.S.A.* **112 G9** 37 59N 90 2W
Ste-Hermine, *France* **20 B2** 46 32N 1 4W
Ste-Livrade-sur-Lot, *France* **20 D4** 44 24N 0 36 E
Ste-Marguerite →, *Canada* **103 B6** 50 9N 66 36W
Ste-Marie, *Martinique* **121 D7** 14 48N 61 1W
Ste-Marie-aux-Mines, *France* **19 D14** 48 15N 7 12 E
Ste-Marie de la Madeleine, *Canada* **103 C5** 46 26N 71 0W
Ste-Maure-de-Touraine, *France* **18 E7** 47 7N 0 37 E
Ste-Maxime, *France* **21 E10** 43 19N 6 39 E
Ste-Menehould, *France* **19 C11** 49 5N 4 54 E
Ste-Mère-Église, *France* **18 C5** 49 24N 1 19W
Ste-Rose, *Guadeloupe* **121 C7** 16 20N 61 45W
Ste. Rose du Lac, *Canada* **105 C9** 51 4N 99 30W
Ste-Savine, *France* **19 D11** 48 18N 4 3 E
Ste-Sigolène, *France* **21 C8** 45 15N 4 14 E
Saintes, *France* **20 C3** 45 45N 0 37W
Saintes, I. des, *Guadeloupe* **121 C7** 15 50N 61 35W
Stes-Maries-de-la-Mer, *France* **21 E8** 43 26N 4 26 E
Saintfield, *U.K.* **15 B6** 54 28N 5 49W
Saintonge, *France* **20 C3** 45 40N 0 50W
Saipan, *Pac. Oc.* **96 F6** 15 12N 145 45 E
Sairang, *India* **67 H18** 23 50N 92 45 E
Sairecábur, Cerro, *Bolivia* **126 A2** 22 43 S 67 54W
Saitama □, *Japan* **55 F9** 36 25N 139 30 E
Saiteli = Kadınhanı, *Turkey* **72 C5** 38 14N 32 13 E
Saiti, *Moldova* **43 D14** 46 30N 29 24 E
Saiyid, *Pakistan* **68 C5** 33 7N 73 2 E
Sajama, *Bolivia* **124 G5** 18 7 S 69 0W
Sajan, *Serbia, Yug.* **42 E5** 45 50N 20 20 E
Sajó →, *Hungary* **42 C6** 47 56N 21 7 E
Sajószentpéter, *Hungary* **42 B5** 48 12N 20 44 E
Sajum, *India* **69 C8** 33 20N 79 0 E
Sak →, *S. Africa* **88 E3** 30 52 S 20 25 E
Sakaba, *Nigeria* **83 C6** 11 4N 5 35 E
Sakai, *Japan* **55 G7** 34 30N 135 30 E
Sakaide, *Japan* **55 G6** 34 19N 133 50 E
Sakaiminato, *Japan* **55 G6** 35 38N 133 11 E
Sakākah, *Si. Arabia* **70 D4** 30 0N 40 8 E
Sakakawea, L., *U.S.A.* **112 B4** 47 30N 101 25W
Sakami →, *Canada* **102 B4** 53 40N 76 40W
Sakami, L., *Canada* **102 B4** 53 15N 77 0W
Sâkâne, 'Erg i-n, *Mali* **83 A4** 20 30N 1 30W
Sakania, *Dem. Rep. of the Congo* **87 E2** 12 43 S 28 30 E
Sakaraha, *Madag.* **89 C7** 22 55 S 44 32 E
Sakarya, *Turkey* **72 B4** 40 48N 30 25 E
Sakarya →, *Turkey* **72 B4** 41 7N 30 39 E
Sakashima-Guntō, *Japan* **55 M2** 24 46N 124 0 E
Sakassou, *Ivory C.* **82 D3** 7 29N 5 19W
Sakata, *Japan* **54 E9** 38 55N 139 50 E
Sakchu, *N. Korea* **57 D13** 40 23N 125 2 E
Sakeny →, *Madag.* **89 C8** 20 0 S 45 25 E
Sakété, *Benin* **83 D5** 6 40N 2 45 E
Sakha □, *Russia* **51 C13** 66 0N 130 0 E
Sakhalin, *Russia* **51 D15** 51 0N 143 0 E
Sakhalinskiy Zaliv, *Russia* **51 D15** 54 0N 141 0 E
Şaki, *Azerbaijan* **49 K8** 41 10N 47 5 E
Šakiai, *Lithuania* **9 J20** 54 59N 23 2 E
Sakon Nakhon, *Thailand* **64 D5** 17 10N 104 9 E
Sakrand, *Pakistan* **68 F3** 26 10N 68 15 E
Sakri, *India* **69 F12** 26 13N 86 5 E
Sakrivier, *S. Africa* **88 E3** 30 54 S 20 28 E
Sakskøbing, *Denmark* **11 K5** 54 49N 11 39 E
Sakti, *India* **69 H10** 22 2N 82 58 E
Sakuma, *Japan* **55 G8** 35 3N 137 49 E
Sakurai, *Japan* **55 G7** 34 30N 135 51 E
Saky, *Ukraine* **47 K7** 45 9N 33 34 E
Sal →, *Russia* **49 G5** 47 31N 40 45 E
Sala, *Eritrea* **81 D4** 16 53N 37 36 E
Sal'a, *Slovak Rep.* **27 C10** 48 10N 17 50 E
Sala, *Sweden* **10 E10** 59 58N 16 35 E
Sala →, *Eritrea* **81 D4** 16 53N 37 36 E
Sala Consilina, *Italy* **31 B8** 40 23N 15 36 E
Sala-y-Gómez, *Pac. Oc.* **97 K17** 26 28 S 105 28W
Salaberry-de-Valleyfield, *Canada* **102 C5** 45 15N 74 8W
Saladas, *Argentina* **126 B4** 28 15 S 58 40W
Saladillo, *Argentina* **126 D4** 35 40 S 59 55W
Salado →, *Buenos Aires, Argentina* **126 D4** 35 44 S 57 22W
Salado →, *La Pampa, Argentina* **128 D3** 37 30 S 67 0W
Salado →, *Santa Fe, Argentina* **126 C3** 31 40 S 60 41W
Salado →, *Mexico* **113 M5** 26 52N 99 19W
Salaga, *Ghana* **83 D4** 8 31N 0 31W
Şalāḩ, *Syria* **75 C5** 32 40N 36 45 E
Sălaj □, *Romania* **42 C8** 47 15N 23 0 E
Sálakhos, *Greece* **36 C9** 36 17N 27 57 E
Salala, *Liberia* **82 D2** 6 42N 10 7W
Salala, *Sudan* **80 C4** 21 17N 36 16 E
Salālah, *Oman* **74 D5** 16 56N 53 59 E
Salamanca, *Chile* **126 C1** 31 46 S 70 59W
Salamanca, *Spain* **34 E5** 40 58N 5 39W
Salamanca, *U.S.A.* **110 D6** 42 10N 78 43W
Salamanca □, *Spain* **34 E5** 40 57N 5 40W
Salāmatābād, *Iran* **70 C5** 35 39N 47 50 E
Salamis, *Cyprus* **36 D12** 35 11N 33 54 E
Salamís, *Greece* **38 D5** 37 56N 23 30 E
Salar de Atacama, *Chile* **126 A2** 23 30 S 68 25W
Salar de Uyuni, *Bolivia* **124 H5** 20 30 S 67 45W
Sălard, *Romania* **42 C7** 47 12N 22 3 E
Salas, *Spain* **34 B4** 43 25N 6 15W
Salas de los Infantes, *Spain* **34 C7** 42 2N 3 17W
Salatiga, *Indonesia* **63 G14** 7 19 S 110 30 E
Salaverry, *Peru* **124 E3** 8 15 S 79 0W
Salawati, *Indonesia* **63 E8** 1 7 S 130 52 E
Salaya, *India* **68 H3** 22 19N 69 35 E
Salayar, *Indonesia* **63 F6** 6 7 S 120 30 E

Salazar →, Spain 32 C3 42 40N 1 20W
Salbris, France 19 E9 47 25N 2 3 E
Salcia, Romania 43 G9 43 56N 24 55 E
Sălciua, Romania 43 D8 46 24N 23 26 E
Salcombe, U.K. 13 G4 50 14N 3 47W
Saldaña, Spain 34 C6 42 32N 4 48W
Saldanha, S. Africa 88 E2 33 0 S 17 58 E
Saldanha B., S. Africa 88 E2 33 6 S 18 0 E
Saldus, Latvia 9 H20 56 38N 22 30 E
Saldus □, Latvia 44 B9 56 35N 22 30 E
Sale, Australia 95 F4 38 6 S 147 6 E
Sale, Italy 28 D5 44 59N 8 48 E
Salé, Morocco 78 B4 34 3N 6 48W
Sale, U.K. 12 D5 53 26N 2 19W
Salekhard, Russia 50 C7 66 30N 66 35 E
Salem, India 66 P11 11 40N 78 11 E
Salem, Ill., U.S.A. 108 F1 38 38N 88 57W
Salem, Ind., U.S.A. 108 F2 38 36N 86 6W
Salem, Mass., U.S.A. 111 D14 42 31N 70 53W
Salem, Mo., U.S.A. 113 G9 37 39N 91 32W
Salem, N.H., U.S.A. 111 D13 42 45N 71 12W
Salem, N.J., U.S.A. 108 F8 39 34N 75 28W
Salem, N.Y., U.S.A. 111 C11 43 10N 73 20W
Salem, Ohio, U.S.A. 110 F4 40 54N 80 52W
Salem, Oreg., U.S.A. 114 D2 44 56N 123 2W
Salem, S. Dak., U.S.A. 112 D6 43 44N 97 23W
Salem, Va., U.S.A. 108 G5 37 18N 80 3W
Salemi, Italy 30 E5 37 49N 12 48 E
Sälen, Sweden 10 C7 61 15N 13 22 E
Salernes, France 21 E10 43 34N 6 15 E
Salerno, Italy 31 B7 40 41N 14 47 E
Salerno, G. di, Italy 31 B7 40 32N 14 42 E
Salford, U.K. 12 D5 53 30N 2 18W
Salgir →, Ukraine 47 K8 45 38N 35 1 E
Salgótarján, Hungary 42 B4 48 5N 19 47 E
Salgueiro, Brazil 125 E11 8 4 S 39 6W
Salibabu, Indonesia 63 D7 3 51N 126 40 E
Salida, U.S.A. 106 C5 38 32N 106 0W
Salies-de-Béarn, France 20 E3 43 28N 0 56W
Salihli, Turkey 72 C3 38 28N 28 8 E
Salihorsk, Belarus 47 F4 52 51N 27 27 E
Salima, Malawi 85 G6 13 47 S 34 28 E
Salina, Italy 31 D7 38 34N 14 50 E
Salina, Kans., U.S.A. 112 F6 38 50N 97 37W
Salina, Utah, U.S.A. 115 G8 38 58N 111 51W
Salina Cruz, Mexico 119 D5 16 10N 95 10W
Salinas, Brazil 125 G10 16 10 S 42 10W
Salinas, Chile 126 A2 23 31 S 69 29W
Salinas, Ecuador 124 D2 2 10 S 80 58W
Salinas, U.S.A. 116 J5 36 40N 121 39W
Salinas →, Guatemala 119 D6 16 28N 90 31W
Salinas →, U.S.A. 116 J5 36 45N 121 48W
Salinas, B. de, Nic. 120 D2 11 4N 85 45W
Salinas, Pampa de las, Argentina 126 C2 31 58 S 66 42W
Salinas Ambargasta, Argentina 126 B3 29 0 S 65 0W
Salinas de Hidalgo, Mexico 118 C4 22 30N 101 40W
Salinas Grandes, Argentina 126 C3 30 0 S 65 0W
Saline →, Ark., U.S.A. 113 J8 33 10N 92 8W
Saline →, Kans., U.S.A. 112 F6 38 52N 97 30W
Salines, Spain 37 B10 39 21N 3 3 E
Salines, C. de ses, Spain 37 B10 39 16N 3 4 E
Salinópolis, Brazil 125 D9 0 40 S 47 20W
Salins-les-Bains, France 19 F12 46 58N 5 52 E
Salir, Portugal 35 H2 37 14N 8 2W
Salisbury = Harare, Zimbabwe 87 F3 17 43 S 31 2 E
Salisbury, U.K. 13 F6 51 4N 1 47W
Salisbury, Md., U.S.A. 108 F8 38 22N 75 36W
Salisbury, N.C., U.S.A. 109 H5 35 40N 80 29W
Salisbury I., Canada 101 B12 63 30N 77 0W
Salisbury Plain, U.K. 13 F6 51 14N 1 55W
Săliște, Romania 43 E8 45 45N 23 56 E
Salka, Nigeria 83 C5 10 20N 4 58 E
Şalkhad, Syria 75 C5 32 29N 36 43 E
Salla, Finland 8 C23 66 50N 28 49 E
Sallanches, France 21 C10 45 55N 6 38 E
Sallent, Spain 32 D6 41 49N 1 54 E
Salles, France 20 D3 44 33N 0 52W
Salles-Curan, France 20 D6 44 11N 2 48 E
Salling, Denmark 11 H2 56 40N 8 55 E
Salliq, Canada 101 B11 64 8N 83 10W
Sallisaw, U.S.A. 113 H7 35 28N 94 47W
Sallom Junction, Sudan 80 D4 19 17N 37 6 E
Salluit, Canada 101 B12 62 14N 75 38W
Salmās, Iran 70 B5 38 11N 44 47 E
Salmerón, Spain 32 E2 40 33N 2 29W
Salmo, Canada 104 D5 49 10N 117 20W
Salmon, U.S.A. 114 D7 45 11N 113 54W
Salmon →, Canada 104 C4 54 3N 122 40W
Salmon →, U.S.A. 114 D5 45 51N 116 47W
Salmon Arm, Canada 104 C5 50 40N 119 15W
Salmon Gums, Australia 93 F3 32 59 S 121 38 E
Salmon River Mts., U.S.A. 114 D6 45 0N 114 30W
Salo, Finland 9 F20 60 22N 23 10 E
Salò, Italy 28 C7 45 36N 10 31 E
Salobreña, Spain 35 J7 36 44N 3 35W
Salome, U.S.A. 117 M13 33 47N 113 37W
Salon, India 69 F9 26 2N 81 27 E
Salon-de-Provence, France 21 E9 43 39N 5 6 E
Salonica = Thessaloníki, Greece 40 F6 40 38N 22 58 E
Salonta, Romania 42 D6 46 49N 21 42 E
Salor →, Spain 35 F3 39 39N 7 3W
Salou, Spain 32 D6 41 4N 1 8 E
Salou, C. de, Spain 32 D6 41 3N 1 10 E
Saloum →, Senegal 82 C1 13 50N 16 45W
Salpausselkä, Finland 9 F22 61 0N 27 0 E
Salsacate, Argentina 126 C2 31 20 S 65 5W
Salses, France 20 F6 42 50N 2 55 E
Salsk, Russia 49 G5 46 28N 41 30 E
Salso →, Italy 30 E6 37 6N 13 57 E
Salsomaggiore Terme, Italy 28 D6 44 49N 9 59 E
Salt, Spain 32 D7 41 59N 2 47 E
Salt →, Canada 104 B6 60 0N 112 25W
Salt →, U.S.A. 115 K7 33 23N 112 19W
Salt Lake City, U.S.A. 114 F8 40 45N 111 53W
Salt Range, Pakistan 68 C5 32 30N 72 25 E
Salta, Argentina 126 A2 24 57 S 65 25W
Salta □, Argentina 126 A2 24 48 S 65 30W
Saltara, Italy 29 E9 43 45N 12 50 E
Saltash, U.K. 13 G3 50 24N 4 14W
Saltburn by the Sea, U.K. 12 C7 54 35N 0 58W
Saltcoats, U.K. 14 F4 55 38N 4 47W
Saltee Is., Ireland 15 D5 52 7N 6 37W
Saltfjellet, Norway 8 C16 66 40N 15 15 E
Saltfjorden, Norway 8 C16 67 15N 14 10 E
Saltholm, Denmark 11 J6 55 38N 12 43 E
Saltillo, Mexico 118 B4 25 25N 101 0W
Salto, Argentina 126 C3 34 20 S 60 15W
Salto, Uruguay 126 C4 31 27 S 57 50W
Salto del Guaíra, Paraguay 127 A5 24 3 S 54 17W
Salton City, U.S.A. 117 M11 33 29N 115 51W
Salton Sea, U.S.A. 117 M11 33 15N 115 45W
Saltpond, Ghana 83 D4 5 15N 1 3W
Saltsburg, U.S.A. 110 F5 40 29N 79 27W
Saltsjöbaden, Sweden 10 E12 59 15N 18 20 E
Saluda →, U.S.A. 109 J5 34 1N 81 4W
Salûm, Egypt 80 A2 31 31N 25 7 E
Salûm, Khâlig el, Egypt 80 A2 31 35N 25 24 E
Salur, India 67 K13 18 27N 83 18 E
Saluzzo, Italy 28 D4 44 39N 7 29 E
Salvador, Brazil 125 F11 13 0 S 38 30W
Salvador, Canada 105 C7 52 10N 109 32W
Salvador, L., U.S.A. 113 L9 29 43N 90 15W
Salvaterra de Magos, Portugal 35 F2 39 1N 8 47W
Sálvora, I. de, Spain 34 C2 42 30N 8 58W
Salween →, Burma 67 L20 16 31N 97 37 E
Salyan, Azerbaijan 50 F5 39 33N 48 59 E
Salza →, Austria 26 D7 47 40N 14 43 E
Salzach →, Austria 26 C5 48 12N 12 56 E
Salzburg, Austria 26 D6 47 48N 13 2 E
Salzburg □, Austria 26 D6 47 15N 13 0 E
Salzgitter, Germany 24 C6 52 9N 10 19 E
Salzkotten, Germany 24 D4 51 40N 8 37 E
Salzwedel, Germany 24 C7 52 52N 11 10 E
Sam, India 68 F4 26 50N 70 31 E
Sam Neua, Laos 58 G5 20 29N 104 5 E
Sam Ngao, Thailand 64 D2 17 18N 99 0 E
Sam Rayburn Reservoir, U.S.A. 113 K7 31 4N 94 5W
Sam Son, Vietnam 64 C5 19 44N 105 54 E
Sam Teu, Laos 64 C5 19 59N 104 38 E
Sama de Langreo = Langreo, Spain 34 B5 43 18N 5 40W
Samagaltay, Russia 51 D10 50 36N 95 3 E
Samales Group, Phil. 61 J4 6 0N 122 0 E
Samâlût, Egypt 80 B3 28 20N 30 42 E
Samana, India 68 D7 30 10N 76 13 E
Samaná □, Dom. Rep. 121 C6 19 15N 69 27W
Samana Cay, Bahamas 121 B5 23 3N 73 45W
Samandağı, Turkey 72 D6 36 5N 35 59 E
Samandıra, Turkey 41 F13 40 59N 29 13 E
Samanga, Tanzania 87 D4 8 20 S 39 13 E
Samangwa, Dem. Rep. of the Congo 86 C1 4 23 S 24 10 E
Samani, Japan 54 C11 42 7N 142 56 E
Samanli Dağları, Turkey 41 F13 40 32N 29 10 E
Samar, Phil. 61 F6 12 0N 125 0 E
Samara, Russia 48 D10 53 8N 50 6 E
Samara →, Russia 48 D10 53 10N 50 4 E
Samara →, Ukraine 47 H8 48 28N 35 7 E
Samaria = Shōmrōn, West Bank 75 C4 32 15N 35 13 E
Samariá, Greece 36 D5 35 17N 23 58 E
Samarinda, Indonesia 62 E5 0 30 S 117 9 E
Samarkand = Samarqand, Uzbekistan 50 F7 39 40N 66 55 E
Samarqand, Uzbekistan 50 F7 39 40N 66 55 E
Sāmarrā, Iraq 70 C4 34 12N 43 52 E
Samastipur, India 69 G11 25 50N 85 50 E
Şamaxi, Azerbaijan 49 K9 40 38N 48 37 E
Samba, Dem. Rep. of the Congo 86 C2 4 38 S 26 22 E
Samba, India 69 C6 32 32N 75 10 E
Sambalpur, India 67 J14 21 28N 84 4 E
Sambar, Tanjung, Indonesia 62 E4 2 59 S 110 19 E
Sambas, Indonesia 62 D3 1 20N 109 20 E
Sambava, Madag. 89 A9 14 16 S 50 10 E
Sambawizi, Zimbabwe 87 F2 18 24 S 26 13 E
Sambhal, India 69 E8 28 35N 78 37 E
Sambhar, India 68 F6 26 52N 75 6 E
Sambhar L., India 68 F6 26 55N 75 12 E
Sambiase, Italy 31 D9 38 58N 16 17 E
Sambir, Ukraine 47 H2 49 30N 23 10 E
Sambor, Cambodia 64 F6 12 46N 106 0 E
Samborombón, B., Argentina 126 D4 36 5 S 57 20W
Sambuca di Sicília, Italy 30 E6 37 39N 13 7 E
Samch'ŏk, S. Korea 57 F15 37 30N 129 10 E
Samch'onp'o, S. Korea 57 G15 35 0N 128 6 E
Same, Tanzania 86 C4 4 2 S 37 38 E
Samer, France 19 B8 50 38N 1 44 E
Samfya, Zambia 87 E2 11 22 S 29 31 E
Sámi, Greece 38 C2 38 15N 20 39 E
Şamkir, Azerbaijan 49 K8 40 50N 46 0 E
Şamlı, Turkey 39 B9 39 48N 27 51 E
Samnah, Si. Arabia 70 E3 25 10N 37 15 E
Samo Alto, Chile 126 C1 30 22 S 71 0W
Samoa ■, Pac. Oc. 91 B13 14 0 S 172 0W
Samobor, Croatia 29 C12 45 47N 15 44 E
Samoëns, France 19 F13 46 5N 6 45 E
Samokov, Bulgaria 40 D7 42 18N 23 35 E
Šamorín, Slovak Rep. 27 C10 48 2N 17 19 E
Samorogouan, Burkina Faso 82 C4 11 21N 4 57W
Sámos, Greece 39 D8 37 45N 26 50 E
Samoš, Serbia, Yug. 42 E5 45 13N 20 46 E
Samos, Spain 34 C3 42 44N 7 20W
Sámos □, Greece 39 D8 37 45N 26 50 E
Samothráki = Mathráki, Greece 36 A3 39 48N 19 31 E
Samothráki, Évros, Greece 41 F9 40 28N 25 28 E
Samothráki, Évros, Greece 41 F9 40 28N 25 28 E
Samoylovka, Russia 48 E6 51 12N 43 43 E
Sampa, Ghana 82 D4 8 0N 2 36W
Sampacho, Argentina 126 C3 33 20 S 64 50W
Sampang, Indonesia 63 G15 7 11 S 113 13 E
Samper de Calanda, Spain 32 D4 41 11N 0 28W
Sampéyre, Italy 28 D4 44 34N 7 11 E
Sampit, Indonesia 62 E4 2 34 S 113 0 E
Sampit, Teluk, Indonesia 62 E4 3 5 S 113 3 E
Samrong, Cambodia 64 E4 14 15N 103 30 E
Samrong, Thailand 64 E3 15 10N 100 40 E
Samsø, Denmark 11 J4 55 50N 10 35 E
Samsø Bælt, Denmark 11 J4 55 45N 10 45 E
Samsun, Turkey 72 B7 41 15N 36 22 E
Samtredia, Georgia 49 J6 42 7N 42 24 E
Samui, Ko, Thailand 65 H3 9 30N 100 0 E
Samur →, Russia 49 K9 41 53N 48 32 E
Samurskiy Khrebet, Russia 49 K8 41 55N 47 11 E
Samusole, Dem. Rep. of the Congo 87 E1 10 2 S 24 0 E
Samut Prakan, Thailand 64 F3 13 32N 100 40 E
Samut Songkhram →, Thailand 62 B1 13 24N 100 1 E
Samwari, Pakistan 68 E2 28 30N 66 46 E
San, Mali 82 C4 13 15N 4 57W
San →, Cambodia 64 F5 13 32N 105 57 E
San →, Poland 45 H8 50 45N 21 51 E
San Adrián, Spain 32 C3 42 20N 1 56W
San Adrián, C. de, Spain 34 B2 43 21N 8 50W
San Agustin, C., Phil. 61 H7 6 20N 126 13 E
San Agustín de Valle Fértil, Argentina 126 C2 30 35 S 67 30W
San Ambrosio, Pac. Oc. 122 F3 26 28 S 79 53W
San Andreas, U.S.A. 116 G6 38 12N 120 41W
San Andres, Phil. 61 E6 13 36N 124 6 E
San Andrés, I. de, Caribbean 120 D3 12 42N 81 46W
San Andrés del Rabanedo, Spain 34 C5 42 37N 5 36W
San Andres Mts., U.S.A. 115 K10 33 0N 106 30W
San Andrés Tuxtla, Mexico 119 D5 18 30N 95 20W
San Angelo, U.S.A. 113 K4 31 28N 100 26W
San Anselmo, U.S.A. 116 H4 37 59N 122 34W
San Antonio, Belize 119 D7 16 15N 89 2W
San Antonio, Chile 126 C1 33 40 S 71 40W
San Antonio, Phil. 61 D4 14 57N 120 5 E
San Antonio, N. Mex., U.S.A. 115 K10 33 55N 106 52W
San Antonio, Tex., U.S.A. 113 L5 29 25N 98 30W
San Antonio →, U.S.A. 113 L6 28 30N 96 54W
San Antonio, C., Argentina 126 D4 36 15 S 56 40W
San Antonio, C., Cuba 120 B3 21 50N 84 57W
San Antonio, C. de, Spain 33 G5 38 48N 0 12 E
San Antonio, Mt., U.S.A. 117 L9 34 17N 117 38W
San Antonio de los Baños, Cuba 120 B3 22 54N 82 31W
San Antonio de los Cobres, Argentina 126 A2 24 10 S 66 17W
San Antonio Oeste, Argentina 128 E4 40 40 S 65 0W
San Arcángelo, Italy 31 B9 40 14N 16 14 E
San Ardo, U.S.A. 116 J6 36 1N 120 54W
San Augustín, Canary Is. 37 G4 27 47N 15 32W
San Augustine, U.S.A. 113 K7 31 30N 94 7W
San Bartolomé, Canary Is. 37 F6 28 59N 13 37W
San Bartolomé de Tirajana, Canary Is. 37 G4 27 54N 15 34W
San Bartolomeo in Galdo, Italy 31 A8 41 24N 15 1 E
San Benedetto del Tronto, Italy 29 F10 42 57N 13 53 E
San Benedetto Po, Italy 28 C7 45 2N 10 55 E
San Benedicto, I., Mexico 118 D2 19 18N 110 49W
San Benito, U.S.A. 113 M6 26 8N 97 38W
San Benito →, U.S.A. 116 J5 36 53N 121 34W
San Benito Mt., U.S.A. 116 J6 36 22N 120 37W
San Bernardino, U.S.A. 117 L9 34 7N 117 19W
San Bernardino Mts., U.S.A. 117 L10 34 10N 116 45W
San Bernardino Str., Phil. 61 E6 13 0N 125 0 E
San Bernardo, Chile 126 C1 33 40 S 70 50W
San Bernardo, I. de, Colombia 124 B3 9 45N 75 50W
San Blas, Mexico 118 B3 26 4N 108 46W
San Blas, Arch. de, Panama 120 E4 9 50N 78 31W
San Blas, C., U.S.A. 109 L3 29 40N 85 21W
San Bonifacio, Italy 29 C8 45 24N 11 16 E
San Borja, Bolivia 124 F5 14 50 S 66 52W
San Buenaventura, Mexico 118 B4 27 5N 101 32W
San Carlos = Butuku-Luba, Eq. Guin. 83 E6 3 29N 8 33 E
San Carlos = Sant Carles, Spain 37 B8 39 3N 1 34 E
San Carlos, Argentina 126 C2 33 50 S 69 0W
San Carlos, Chile 126 D1 36 10 S 72 0W
San Carlos, Baja Calif. S., Mexico 118 C2 24 47N 112 6W
San Carlos, Coahuila, Mexico 118 B4 29 0N 100 54W
San Carlos, Nic. 120 D3 11 12N 84 50W
San Carlos, Neg. Occ., Phil. 61 F5 10 29N 123 25 E
San Carlos, Pangasinan, Phil. 61 D4 15 55N 120 20 E
San Carlos, Uruguay 127 C5 34 46 S 54 58W
San Carlos, U.S.A. 115 K8 33 21N 110 27W
San Carlos, Venezuela 124 B5 9 40N 68 36W
San Carlos de Bariloche, Argentina 128 E2 41 10 S 71 25W
San Carlos de Bolívar, Argentina 128 D4 36 15 S 61 6W
San Carlos de la Rápita = Sant Carles de la Ràpita, Spain 32 E5 40 37N 0 35 E
San Carlos del Zulia, Venezuela 124 B4 9 1N 71 55W
San Carlos L., U.S.A. 115 K8 33 11N 110 32W
San Cataldo, Italy 30 E6 37 29N 13 59 E
San Celoni = Sant Celoni, Spain 32 D7 41 42N 2 30 E
San Clemente, Chile 126 D1 35 30 S 71 29W
San Clemente, Spain 33 F2 39 24N 2 25W
San Clemente, U.S.A. 117 M9 33 26N 117 37W
San Clemente I., U.S.A. 117 N8 32 53N 118 29W
San Cristóbal = Es Migjorn Gran, Spain 37 B11 39 57N 4 3 E
San Cristóbal, Argentina 126 C3 30 20 S 61 10W
San Cristóbal, Dom. Rep. 121 C5 18 25N 70 6W
San Cristóbal, Venezuela 124 B4 7 46N 72 14W
San Cristóbal de la Casas, Mexico 119 D6 16 50N 92 33W
San Damiano d'Asti, Italy 28 D5 44 50N 8 4 E
San Daniele del Friuli, Italy 29 B10 46 9N 13 1 E
San Diego, Calif., U.S.A. 117 N9 32 43N 117 9W
San Diego, Tex., U.S.A. 113 M5 27 46N 98 14W
San Diego, C., Argentina 128 G3 54 40 S 65 10W
San Diego de la Unión, Mexico 118 C4 21 28N 100 52W
San Dimitri, Ras, Malta 36 C1 36 4N 14 11 E
San Donà di Piave, Italy 29 C9 45 38N 12 34 E
San Estanislao, Paraguay 126 A4 24 39 S 56 26W
San Esteban de Gormaz, Spain 32 D1 41 34N 3 13W
San Felice Circeo, Italy 30 A6 41 14N 13 5 E
San Felice sul Panaro, Italy 29 D8 44 50N 11 8 E
San Felipe, Chile 126 C1 32 43 S 70 42W
San Felipe, Mexico 118 A2 31 0N 114 52W
San Felipe, Venezuela 124 A5 10 20N 68 44W
San Felipe →, U.S.A. 117 M11 33 12N 115 49W
San Felix, Chile 126 B1 28 56 S 70 28W
San Félix, Pac. Oc. 122 F2 26 23 S 80 0W
San Fernando = Sant Ferran, Spain 37 C7 38 42N 1 28 E
San Fernando, Chile 126 C1 34 30 S 71 0W
San Fernando, Baja Calif., Mexico 118 B1 29 55N 115 10W
San Fernando, Tamaulipas, Mexico 119 C5 24 51N 98 10W
San Fernando, La Union, Phil. 61 C4 16 40N 120 23 E
San Fernando, Pampanga, Phil. 61 D4 15 5N 120 37 E
San Fernando, Spain 35 J4 36 28N 6 17W
San Fernando, Trin. & Tob. 121 D7 10 20N 61 30W
San Fernando, U.S.A. 117 L8 34 17N 118 26W
San Fernando de Apure, Venezuela 124 B5 7 54N 67 15W
San Fernando de Atabapo, Venezuela 124 C5 4 3N 67 42W
San Fernando di Púglia, Italy 31 A9 41 18N 16 5 E
San Francisco, Argentina 126 C3 31 30 S 62 5W
San Francisco, U.S.A. 116 H4 37 47N 122 25W
San Francisco →, U.S.A. 115 K9 32 59N 109 22W
San Francisco, Paso de, S. Amer. 126 B2 27 0 S 68 0W
San Francisco de Macorís, Dom. Rep. 121 C5 19 19N 70 15W
San Francisco del Monte de Oro, Argentina 126 C2 32 36 S 66 8W
San Francisco del Oro, Mexico 118 B3 26 52N 105 50W
San Francisco Javier = Sant Francesc de Formentera, Spain 37 C7 38 42N 1 26 E
San Francisco Solano, Pta., Colombia 122 C3 6 18N 77 29W
San Fratello, Italy 31 D7 38 1N 14 36 E
San Gabriel, Chile 126 C1 33 47 S 70 15W
San Gabriel Mts., U.S.A. 117 L9 34 20N 118 0W
San Gavino Monreale, Italy 30 C1 39 33N 8 47 E
San Gimignano, Italy 28 E8 43 28N 11 2 E
San Giórgio di Nogaro, Italy 29 C10 45 50N 13 13 E
San Giórgio Iónico, Italy 31 B10 40 27N 17 23 E
San Giovanni Bianco, Italy 28 C6 45 52N 9 39 E
San Giovanni in Fiore, Italy 31 C9 39 15N 16 42 E
San Giovanni in Persiceto, Italy 29 D8 44 38N 11 11 E
San Giovanni Rotondo, Italy 29 G12 41 42N 15 44 E
San Giovanni Valdarno, Italy 29 E8 43 34N 11 32 E
San Giuliano Terme, Italy 28 E7 43 46N 10 26 E
San Gorgonio Mt., U.S.A. 117 L10 34 7N 116 51W
San Gottardo, P. del, Switz. 25 J4 46 33N 8 33 E
San Gregorio, Uruguay 127 C4 32 37 S 55 40W
San Gregorio, U.S.A. 116 H4 37 20N 122 23W
San Guiseppe Jato, Italy 30 E6 37 57N 13 11 E
San Ignacio, Belize 119 D7 17 10N 89 0W
San Ignacio, Bolivia 124 G6 16 20 S 60 55W
San Ignacio, Mexico 118 B2 27 27N 113 0W
San Ignacio, Paraguay 120 C2 26 52 S 57 3W
San Ignacio, L., Mexico 118 B2 26 50N 113 11W
San Ildefonso, C., Phil. 61 C5 16 0N 122 1 E
San Isidro, Argentina 126 C4 34 29 S 58 31W
San Isidro, Phil. 61 H7 6 50N 126 5 E
San Jacinto, U.S.A. 117 M10 33 47N 116 57W
San Jaime = Sant Jaume, Spain 37 B11 39 54N 4 4 E
San Javier, Misiones, Argentina 127 B4 27 55 S 55 5W
San Javier, Santa Fe, Argentina 126 C4 30 40 S 59 55W
San Javier, Bolivia 124 G6 16 18 S 62 30W
San Javier, Chile 126 D1 35 40 S 71 45W
San Javier, Spain 33 H4 37 49N 0 50W
San Jeronimo Taviche, Mexico 119 D5 16 38N 96 32W
San Joaquin, U.S.A. 116 J6 36 36N 120 11W
San Joaquin →, U.S.A. 116 G5 38 4N 121 51W
San Joaquin Valley, U.S.A. 116 J6 37 20N 121 0W
San Jon, U.S.A. 113 H3 35 6N 103 20W
San Jordi = Sant Jordi, Spain 37 B9 39 33N 2 46 E
San Jorge, Argentina 126 C3 31 54 S 61 50W
San Jorge, Spain 37 C7 38 54N 1 24 E
San Jorge, B. de, Mexico 118 A2 31 20N 113 20W
San Jorge, G., Argentina 128 F3 46 0 S 66 0W
San Jorge, G. of, Argentina 122 H4 46 0 S 66 0W
San José = San Josep, Spain 37 C7 38 55N 1 18 E
San José, Costa Rica 120 E3 9 55N 84 2W
San José, Guatemala 120 D1 14 0N 90 50W
San José, Mexico 118 C2 25 0N 110 50W
San Jose, Mind. Occ., Phil. 61 E4 12 27N 121 4 E
San Jose, Nueva Ecija, Phil. 61 D4 15 45N 120 55 E
San Jose, U.S.A. 116 H5 37 20N 121 53W
San Jose →, U.S.A. 115 J10 34 25N 106 45W
San Jose de Buenavista, Phil. 63 B6 10 45N 121 56 E
San José de Chiquitos, Bolivia 124 G6 17 53 S 60 50W
San José de Feliciano, Argentina 126 C4 30 26 S 58 46W
San José de Jáchal, Argentina 126 C2 30 15 S 68 46W
San José de Mayo, Uruguay 126 C4 34 27 S 56 40W
San José del Cabo, Mexico 118 C3 23 0N 109 40W
San José del Guaviare, Colombia 124 C4 2 35N 72 38W
San Josep, Spain 37 C7 38 55N 1 18 E
San Juan, Argentina 126 C2 31 30 S 68 30W
San Juan, Mexico 118 C4 21 20N 102 50W
San Juan, Phil. 61 F6 10 16N 125 10 E
San Juan, Puerto Rico 121 C6 18 28N 66 7W
San Juan □, Argentina 126 C2 31 9 S 69 0W
San Juan □, Dom. Rep. 121 C5 18 45N 71 25W
San Juan →, Argentina 126 C2 32 20 S 67 25W
San Juan →, Nic. 120 D3 10 56N 83 42W
San Juan →, U.S.A. 115 H8 37 16N 110 26W
San Juan Bautista = Sant Joan Baptista, Spain 37 B8 39 5N 1 31 E
San Juan Bautista, Paraguay 126 B4 26 37 S 57 6W
San Juan Bautista, U.S.A. 116 J5 36 51N 121 32W
San Juan Bautista Valle Nacional, Mexico 119 D5 17 47N 96 19W
San Juan Capistrano, U.S.A. 117 M9 33 30N 117 40W
San Juan Cr. →, U.S.A. 116 J5 35 40N 120 22W
San Juan de Alicante, Spain 33 G4 38 24N 0 26W
San Juan de Guadalupe, Mexico 118 C4 24 38N 102 44W
San Juan de la Costa, Mexico 118 C2 24 23N 110 45W
San Juan de los Morros, Venezuela 124 B5 9 55N 67 21W
San Juan del Norte, Nic. 120 D3 10 58N 83 40W
San Juan del Norte, B. de, Nic. 120 D3 11 0N 83 40W
San Juan del Río, Mexico 119 C5 20 25N 100 0W
San Juan del Sur, Nic. 120 D2 11 20N 85 51W
San Juan I., U.S.A. 116 B3 48 32N 123 5W
San Juan Mts., U.S.A. 115 H10 37 30N 107 0W
San Just, Sierra de, Spain 32 E4 40 45N 0 49W
San Justo, Argentina 126 C3 30 47 S 60 30W
San Kamphaeng, Thailand 64 C2 18 45N 99 8 E
San Lázaro, C., Mexico 118 C2 24 50N 112 18W
San Lázaro, Sa., Mexico 118 C3 23 25N 110 0W
San Leandro, U.S.A. 116 H4 37 44N 122 9W
San Leonardo de Yagüe, Spain 32 D1 41 51N 3 5W
San Lorenzo = Sant Llorenç des Cardassar, Spain 37 B10 39 37N 3 17 E
San Lorenzo, Argentina 126 C3 32 45 S 60 45W
San Lorenzo, Ecuador 124 C3 1 15N 78 50W
San Lorenzo, Paraguay 126 B4 25 20 S 57 32W
San Lorenzo →, Mexico 118 C3 24 15N 107 24W
San Lorenzo, I., Mexico 118 B2 28 35N 112 50W
San Lorenzo, Mte., Argentina 128 F2 47 40 S 72 20W
San Lorenzo de la Parrilla, Spain 32 F2 39 51N 2 22W
San Lorenzo de Morunys = Sant Llorenç de Morunys, Spain 32 C6 42 8N 1 35 E
San Lucas, Bolivia 124 H5 20 5 S 65 7W
San Lucas, Baja Calif. S., Mexico 118 C3 22 53N 109 54W
San Lucas, Baja Calif. S., Mexico 118 B2 27 10N 112 14W
San Lucas, U.S.A. 116 J5 36 8N 121 1W
San Lucas, C., Mexico 118 C3 22 50N 110 0W
San Lúcido, Italy 31 C9 39 18N 16 3 E
San Luis, Argentina 126 C2 33 20 S 66 20W
San Luis, Cuba 120 B3 22 17N 83 46W
San Luis, Guatemala 120 C2 16 14N 89 27W
San Luis, Ariz., U.S.A. 115 K6 32 29N 114 47W
San Luis, Colo., U.S.A. 115 H11 37 12N 105 25W
San Luis □, Argentina 126 C2 34 0 S 66 0W
San Luis, I., Mexico 118 B2 29 58N 114 26W
San Luis, Sierra de, Argentina 126 C2 32 30 S 66 10W
San Luis de la Paz, Mexico 118 C4 21 19N 100 32W
San Luis Obispo, U.S.A. 117 K6 35 17N 120 40W
San Luis Potosí, Mexico 118 C4 22 9N 100 59W
San Luis Potosí □, Mexico 118 C4 22 10N 101 0W
San Luis Reservoir, U.S.A. 116 H5 37 4N 121 5W
San Luis Río Colorado, Mexico 118 A2 32 29N 114 58W
San Manuel, U.S.A. 115 K8 32 36N 110 38W
San Marco, C., Italy 30 C1 39 51N 8 26 E
San Marco Argentano, Italy 31 C9 39 33N 16 7 E
San Marco in Lámis, Italy 29 G12 41 43N 15 38 E
San Marcos, Guatemala 120 D1 14 59N 91 52W
San Marcos, Mexico 118 B2 27 13N 112 6W
San Marcos, Calif., U.S.A. 117 M9 33 9N 117 10W
San Marcos, Tex., U.S.A. 113 L6 29 53N 97 56W
San Marino, San Marino 29 E9 43 55N 12 30 E
San Marino ■, Europe 29 E9 43 56N 12 25 E
San Martín, Argentina 126 C2 33 5 S 68 28W
San Martín →, Bolivia 124 F6 13 8 S 63 43W
San Martín, L., Argentina 128 F2 48 50 S 72 50W
San Martín de la Vega, Spain 34 E7 40 13N 3 34W

San Martin de los Andes, *Argentina* **128 E2** 40 10 S 71 20W
San Martín de Valdeiglesias, *Spain* **34 E6** 40 21N 4 24W
San Mateo = Sant Mateu, *Baleares, Spain* **37 B7** 39 3N 1 23 E
San Mateo = Sant Mateu, *Valencia, Spain* **32 E5** 40 28N 0 10 E
San Mateo, *Phil.* **61 C4** 16 54N 121 33 E
San Mateo, *U.S.A.* **116 H4** 37 34N 122 19W
San Matías, *Bolivia* **124 G7** 16 25 S 58 20W
San Matías, G., *Argentina* **122 H4** 41 30 S 64 0W
San Miguel = Sant Miquel, *Spain* **37 B7** 39 3N 1 26 E
San Miguel, *El Salv.* **120 D2** 13 30N 88 12W
San Miguel, *Panama* **120 E4** 8 27N 78 55W
San Miguel, *U.S.A.* **116 K6** 35 45N 120 42W
San Miguel →, *Bolivia* **124 F6** 13 52 S 63 56W
San Miguel de Tucumán, *Argentina* **126 B2** 26 50 S 65 20W
San Miguel del Monte, *Argentina* **126 D4** 35 23 S 58 50W
San Miguel I., *U.S.A.* **117 L6** 34 2N 120 23W
San Miniato, *Italy* **28 E7** 43 41N 10 51 E
San Nicolás, *Canary Is.* **37 G4** 27 58N 15 47W
San Nicolas, *Phil.* **61 B4** 18 10N 120 36 E
San Nicolás de los Arroyas, *Argentina* **126 C3** 33 25 S 60 10W
San Nicolas I., *U.S.A.* **117 M7** 33 15N 119 30W
San Onofre, *U.S.A.* **117 M9** 33 22N 117 34W
San Pablo, *Bolivia* **126 A2** 21 43 S 66 38W
San Pablo, *Phil.* **61 D4** 14 11N 121 31 E
San Pablo, *U.S.A.* **116 H4** 37 58N 122 21W
San Páolo di Civitate, *Italy* **29 G12** 41 44N 15 15 E
San Pedro, *Buenos Aires, Argentina* **126 C4** 33 40 S 59 40W
San Pedro, *Misiones, Argentina* **127 B5** 26 30 S 54 10W
San Pedro, *Chile* **126 C1** 33 54 S 71 28W
San Pédro, *Ivory C.* **82 E3** 4 50N 6 33W
San Pedro, *Mexico* **118 C2** 23 55N 110 17W
San Pedro □, *Paraguay* **126 A4** 24 0 S 57 0W
San Pedro →, *Chihuahua, Mexico* **118 B3** 28 20N 106 10W
San Pedro →, *Nayarit, Mexico* **118 C3** 21 45N 105 30W
San Pedro →, *U.S.A.* **115 K8** 32 59N 110 47W
San Pedro, Pta., *Chile* **126 B1** 25 30 S 70 38W
San Pedro, Sierra de, *Spain* **35 F4** 39 18N 6 40W
San Pedro Channel, *U.S.A.* **117 M8** 33 30N 118 25W
San Pedro de Atacama, *Chile* **126 A2** 22 55 S 68 15W
San Pedro de Jujuy, *Argentina* **126 A3** 24 12 S 64 55W
San Pedro de las Colonias, *Mexico* **118 B4** 25 50N 102 59W
San Pedro de Macorís, *Dom. Rep.* **121 C6** 18 30N 69 18W
San Pedro del Norte, *Nic.* **120 D3** 13 4N 84 33W
San Pedro del Paraná, *Paraguay* **126 B4** 26 43 S 56 13W
San Pedro del Pinatar, *Spain* **33 H4** 37 50N 0 50W
San Pedro Mártir, Sierra, *Mexico* **118 A1** 31 0N 115 30W
San Pedro Mixtepec, *Mexico* **119 D5** 16 2N 97 7W
San Pedro Ocampo = Melchor Ocampo, *Mexico* **118 C4** 24 52N 101 40W
San Pedro Sula, *Honduras* **120 C2** 15 30N 88 0W
San Pietro, *Italy* **30 C1** 39 8N 8 17 E
San Pietro Vernótico, *Italy* **31 B11** 40 29N 18 0 E
San Quintín, *Mexico* **118 A1** 30 29N 115 57W
San Rafael, *Argentina* **126 C2** 34 40 S 68 21W
San Rafael, *Calif., U.S.A.* **116 H4** 37 58N 122 32W
San Rafael, *N. Mex., U.S.A.* **115 J10** 35 7N 107 53W
San Rafael Mt., *U.S.A.* **117 L7** 34 41N 119 52W
San Rafael Mts., *U.S.A.* **117 L7** 34 40N 119 50W
San Ramón de la Nueva Orán, *Argentina* **126 A3** 23 10 S 64 20W
San Remo, *Italy* **28 E4** 43 49N 7 46 E
San Roque, *Argentina* **126 B4** 28 25 S 58 45W
San Roque, *Spain* **35 J5** 36 17N 5 21W
San Rosendo, *Chile* **126 D1** 37 16 S 72 43W
San Saba, *U.S.A.* **113 K5** 31 12N 98 43W
San Salvador, *El Salv.* **120 D2** 13 40N 89 10W
San Salvador, *Spain* **37 B10** 39 27N 3 11 E
San Salvador de Jujuy, *Argentina* **126 A3** 24 10 S 64 48W
San Salvador I., *Bahamas* **121 B5** 24 0N 74 40W
San Salvo, *Italy* **29 F11** 42 3N 14 44 E
San Sebastián = Donostia-San Sebastián, *Spain* **32 B3** 43 17N 1 58W
San Sebastián, *Argentina* **128 G3** 53 10 S 68 30W
San Sebastian de la Gomera, *Canary Is.* **37 F2** 28 5N 17 7W
San Serra = Son Serra, *Spain* **37 B10** 39 43N 3 13 E
San Severino Marche, *Italy* **29 E10** 43 13N 13 10 E
San Severo, *Italy* **29 G12** 41 41N 15 23 E
San Simeon, *U.S.A.* **116 K5** 35 39N 121 11W
San Simon, *U.S.A.* **115 K9** 32 16N 109 14W
San Stéfano di Cadore, *Italy* **29 B9** 46 34N 12 33 E
San Stino di Livenza, *Italy* **29 C9** 45 44N 12 41 E
San Telmo = Sant Telm, *Spain* **37 B9** 39 35N 2 21 E
San Telmo, *Mexico* **118 A1** 30 58N 116 6W
San Tiburcio, *Mexico* **118 C4** 24 8N 101 32W
San Valentin, Mte., *Chile* **122 H3** 46 30 S 73 30W
San Vicente de Alcántara, *Spain* **35 F3** 39 22N 7 8W
San Vicente de la Barquera, *Spain* **34 B6** 43 23N 4 29W
San Vincente del Raspeig, *Spain* **33 G4** 38 24N 0 31W
San Vincenzo, *Italy* **28 E7** 43 6N 10 32 E
San Vito, *Costa Rica* **120 E3** 8 50N 82 58W
San Vito, *Italy* **30 C2** 39 26N 9 32 E
San Vito, C., *Italy* **30 D5** 38 11N 12 41 E
San Vito al Tagliamento, *Italy* **29 C9** 45 54N 12 52 E
San Vito Chietino, *Italy* **29 F11** 42 18N 14 27 E
San Vito dei Normanni, *Italy* **31 B10** 40 39N 17 42 E
Sana', *Yemen* **74 D3** 15 27N 44 12 E
Sana →, *Bos.-H.* **29 C13** 45 3N 16 23 E
Sanaba, *Burkina Faso* **82 C4** 12 25N 3 47W
Şanāfīr, *Si. Arabia* **80 B3** 27 56N 34 42 E
Sanaga →, *Cameroon* **83 E6** 3 35N 9 38 E
Sanaloa, Presa, *Mexico* **118 C3** 24 50N 107 20W
Sanana, *Indonesia* **63 E7** 2 4 S 125 58 E
Sanand, *India* **68 H5** 22 59N 72 25 E
Sanandaj, *Iran* **70 C5** 35 18N 47 1 E
Sanandita, *Bolivia* **126 A3** 21 40 S 63 45W
Sanary-sur-Mer, *France* **21 E9** 43 7N 5 49 E
Sanawad, *India* **68 H7** 22 11N 76 5 E
Sancellas = Sencelles, *Spain* **37 B9** 39 39N 2 54 E
Sancergues, *France* **19 E9** 47 10N 2 54 E
Sancerre, *France* **19 E9** 47 20N 2 50 E
Sancerrois, Collines du, *France* **19 E9** 47 20N 2 40 E
Sancha He →, *China* **58 D6** 26 48N 106 7 E
Sanchahe, *China* **57 B14** 44 50N 126 2 E
Sánchez, *Dom. Rep.* **121 C6** 19 15N 69 36W
Sanchor, *India* **68 G4** 24 45N 71 55 E
Sancoins, *France* **19 F9** 46 47N 2 55 E
Sancti Spíritus, *Cuba* **120 B4** 21 52N 79 33W
Sancy, Puy de, *France* **20 C6** 45 32N 2 50 E
Sand →, *S. Africa* **89 C5** 22 25 S 30 5 E
Sand Hills, *U.S.A.* **112 D4** 42 10N 101 30W
Sand Springs, *U.S.A.* **113 G6** 36 9N 96 7W
Sanda, *Japan* **55 G7** 34 53N 135 14 E
Sandakan, *Malaysia* **62 C5** 5 53N 118 4 E
Sandan = Sambor, *Cambodia* **64 F6** 12 46N 106 0 E
Sandanski, *Bulgaria* **40 E7** 41 35N 23 16 E
Sandaré, *Mali* **82 C2** 14 40N 10 15W
Sandared, *Sweden* **11 G6** 57 43N 12 47 E
Sandarne, *Sweden* **10 C11** 61 16N 17 9 E
Sanday, *U.K.* **14 B6** 59 16N 2 31W
Sandefjord, *Norway* **9 G14** 59 10N 10 15 E
Sanders, *U.S.A.* **115 J9** 35 13N 109 20W
Sanderson, *U.S.A.* **113 K3** 30 9N 102 24W
Sandersville, *U.S.A.* **109 J4** 32 59N 82 48W
Sandfire Roadhouse, *Australia* **92 C3** 19 45 S 121 15 E
Sandfly L., *Canada* **105 B7** 55 43N 106 6W
Sandfontein, *Namibia* **88 C2** 23 48 S 29 1 E
Sandhammaren, C., *Sweden* **11 J8** 55 23N 14 14 E
Sandía, *Peru* **124 F5** 14 10 S 69 30W
Sandıklı, *Turkey* **39 C12** 38 28N 30 17 E
Sandila, *India* **69 F9** 27 5N 80 31 E
Sandnes, *Norway* **9 G11** 58 50N 5 45 E
Sandnessjøen, *Norway* **8 C15** 66 2N 12 38 E
Sandoa, *Dem. Rep. of the Congo* **84 F4** 9 41 S 23 0 E
Sandomierz, *Poland* **45 H8** 50 40N 21 43 E
Săndominic, *Romania* **43 D10** 46 35N 25 47 E
Sandover →, *Australia* **94 C2** 21 43 S 136 32 E
Sandoway, *Burma* **67 K19** 18 20N 94 30 E
Sandoy, *Færoe Is.* **8 F9** 61 52N 6 46W
Sandpoint, *U.S.A.* **114 B5** 48 17N 116 33W
Sandray, *U.K.* **14 E1** 56 53N 7 31W
Sandringham, *U.K.* **12 E8** 52 51N 0 31 E
Sandstone, *Australia* **93 E2** 27 59 S 119 16 E
Sandu, *China* **58 E6** 26 0N 107 52 E
Sandusky, *Mich., U.S.A.* **110 C2** 43 25N 82 50W
Sandusky, *Ohio, U.S.A.* **110 E2** 41 27N 82 42W
Sandvig, *Sweden* **11 J8** 55 18N 14 47 E
Sandviken, *Sweden* **10 D10** 60 38N 16 46 E
Sandwich, C., *Australia* **94 B4** 18 14 S 146 18 E
Sandwich B., *Canada* **103 B8** 53 40N 57 15W
Sandwich B., *Namibia* **88 C1** 23 25 S 14 20 E
Sandwip Chan., *Bangla.* **67 H17** 22 35N 91 35 E
Sandy, *Oreg., U.S.A.* **116 E4** 45 24N 122 16W
Sandy, *Pa., U.S.A.* **110 E6** 41 6N 78 46W
Sandy, *Utah, U.S.A.* **114 F8** 40 35N 111 50W
Sandy Bay, *Canada* **105 B8** 55 31N 102 19W
Sandy Bight, *Australia* **93 F3** 33 50 S 123 20 E
Sandy C., *Queens., Australia* **94 C5** 24 42 S 153 15 E
Sandy C., *Tas., Australia* **94 G3** 41 25 S 144 45 E
Sandy Cay, *Bahamas* **121 B4** 23 13N 75 18W
Sandy Cr. →, *U.S.A.* **114 F9** 41 51N 109 47W
Sandy L., *Canada* **102 B1** 53 2N 93 0W
Sandy Lake, *Canada* **102 B1** 53 0N 93 15W
Sandy Valley, *U.S.A.* **117 K11** 35 49N 115 36W
Sanford, *Fla., U.S.A.* **109 L5** 28 48N 81 16W
Sanford, *Maine, U.S.A.* **109 D10** 43 27N 70 47W
Sanford, *N.C., U.S.A.* **109 H6** 35 29N 79 10W
Sanford →, *Australia* **93 E2** 27 22 S 115 53 E
Sanford, Mt., *U.S.A.* **100 B5** 62 13N 144 8W
Sang-i-Masha, *Afghan.* **68 C2** 33 8N 67 27 E
Sanga, *Mozam.* **87 E4** 12 22 S 35 21 E
Sanga →, *Congo* **84 E3** 1 5 S 17 0 E
Sangamner, *India* **66 K9** 19 37N 74 15 E
Sangar, *Afghan.* **68 C1** 32 56N 65 30 E
Sangar, *Russia* **51 C13** 64 2N 127 31 E
Sangar Sarai, *Afghan.* **68 B4** 34 27N 70 35 E
Sangaredi, *Guinea* **82 C2** 11 7N 13 52W
Sangarh →, *Pakistan* **68 D4** 30 43N 70 44 E
Sangasso, *Mali* **82 C3** 12 5N 5 35W
Sangatte, *France* **19 B8** 50 56N 1 44 E
Sangay, *Ecuador* **124 D3** 2 0 S 78 20W
Sange, *Dem. Rep. of the Congo* **86 D2** 6 58 S 28 21 E
Sangeang, *Indonesia* **63 F5** 8 12 S 119 6 E
Sângeorz-Băi, *Romania* **43 C9** 47 22N 24 41 E
Sanger, *U.S.A.* **116 J7** 36 42N 119 33W
Sângera, *Moldova* **43 D13** 46 55N 28 58 E
Sangerhausen, *Germany* **24 D7** 51 28N 11 18 E
Sanggan He →, *China* **56 E9** 38 12N 117 15 E
Sanggau, *Indonesia* **62 D4** 0 5N 110 30 E
Sanghar, *Pakistan* **68 F3** 26 2N 68 57 E
Sangihe, Kepulauan, *Indonesia* **63 D7** 3 0N 126 0 E
Sangihe, Pulau, *Indonesia* **63 D7** 3 45N 125 30 E
Sangju, *S. Korea* **57 F15** 36 25N 128 10 E
Sangkapura, *Indonesia* **62 F4** 5 52 S 112 40 E
Sangkhla, *Thailand* **64 E2** 14 57N 98 28 E
Sangkulirang, *Indonesia* **62 D5** 0 59N 117 58 E
Sangla, *Pakistan* **68 D5** 31 43N 73 23 E
Sangli, *India* **66 L9** 16 55N 74 33 E
Sangmélima, *Cameroon* **83 E7** 2 57N 12 1 E
Sangod, *India* **68 G7** 24 55N 76 17 E
Sangre de Cristo Mts., *U.S.A.* **113 G2** 37 30N 105 20W
Sangro →, *Italy* **29 F11** 42 14N 14 32 E
Sangrur, *India* **68 D6** 30 14N 75 50 E
Sangudo, *Canada* **104 C6** 53 50N 114 54W
Sangue →, *Brazil* **124 F7** 11 1 S 58 39W
Sangüesa, *Spain* **32 C3** 42 37N 1 17W
Sanguinaires, Îs., *France* **21 G12** 41 51N 8 36 E
Sangzhi, *China* **59 C8** 29 25N 110 12 E
Sanhala, *Ivory C.* **82 C3** 10 3N 6 51W
Sanibel, *U.S.A.* **109 M4** 26 26N 82 1W
Sanirajak, *Canada* **101 B11** 68 46N 81 12W
Sanjawi, *Pakistan* **68 D3** 30 17N 68 21 E
Sanje, *Uganda* **86 C3** 0 49 S 31 30 E
Sanjiang, *China* **58 E7** 25 48N 109 37 E
Sanjo, *Japan* **54 F9** 37 37N 138 57 E
Sankh →, *India* **69 H11** 22 15N 84 48 E
Sankt Andrä, *Austria* **26 E7** 46 46N 14 50 E
Sankt Augustin, *Germany* **24 E3** 50 45N 7 10 E
Sankt Blasien, *Germany* **25 H4** 47 47N 8 7 E
Sankt Gallen, *Switz.* **25 H5** 47 26N 9 22 E
Sankt Gallen □, *Switz.* **25 H5** 47 25N 9 22 E
Sankt Goar, *Germany* **25 E3** 50 12N 7 43 E
Sankt Ingbert, *Germany* **25 F3** 49 16N 7 6 E
Sankt Johann im Pongau, *Austria* **26 D6** 47 22N 13 12 E
Sankt Johann in Tirol, *Austria* **26 D5** 47 30N 12 25 E
Sankt-Peterburg, *Russia* **46 C6** 59 55N 30 20 E
Sankt Pölten, *Austria* **26 C8** 48 12N 15 38 E
Sankt Ulrich = Ortisei, *Italy* **29 B8** 46 34N 11 40 E
Sankt Valentin, *Austria* **26 C7** 48 11N 14 33 E
Sankt Veit an der Glan, *Austria* **26 E7** 46 47N 14 22 E
Sankt Wendel, *Germany* **25 F3** 49 27N 7 9 E
Sankt Wolfgang, *Austria* **26 D6** 47 43N 13 27 E
Sankuru →, *Dem. Rep. of the Congo* **84 E4** 4 17 S 20 25 E
Sanliurfa, *Turkey* **70 B3** 37 12N 38 50 E
Sanlúcar de Barrameda, *Spain* **35 J4** 36 46N 6 21W
Sanluri, *Italy* **30 C1** 39 34N 8 54 E
Sânmartin, *Romania* **43 D10** 46 19N 25 58 E
Sanmen, *China* **59 C13** 29 5N 121 35 E
Sanmenxia, *China* **56 G6** 34 47N 111 12 E
Sanming, *China* **59 D11** 26 15N 117 40 E
Sannaspos, *S. Africa* **88 D4** 29 6 S 26 34 E
Sannicandro Gargánico, *Italy* **29 G12** 41 50N 15 34 E
Sânnicolau Mare, *Romania* **42 D5** 46 5N 20 39 E
Sannieshof, *S. Africa* **88 D4** 26 30 S 25 47 E
Sannīn, J., *Lebanon* **75 B4** 33 57N 35 52 E
Sanniquellie, *Liberia* **82 D3** 7 19N 8 38W
Sannûr, W. →, *Egypt* **80 B3** 28 59N 31 3 E
Sanok, *Poland* **45 J9** 49 35N 22 10 E
Sanquhar, *U.K.* **14 F5** 55 22N 3 54W
Sansanding, *Mali* **82 C3** 13 48N 6 0W
Sansepolcro, *Italy* **29 E9** 43 34N 12 8 E
Sansha, *China* **59 D13** 26 58N 120 12 E
Sanshui, *China* **59 F9** 23 10N 112 56 E
Sanski Most, *Bos.-H.* **29 D13** 44 46N 16 40 E
Sansui, *China* **58 D7** 26 58N 108 39 E
Sant Antoni Abat, *Spain* **37 C7** 38 59N 1 19 E
Sant Boi de Llobregat, *Spain* **32 D7** 41 21N 2 2 E
Sant Carles, *Spain* **37 B8** 39 3N 1 34 E
Sant Carles de la Ràpita, *Spain* **32 E5** 40 37N 0 35 E
Sant Celoni, *Spain* **32 D7** 41 42N 2 30 E
Sant Feliu de Guíxols, *Spain* **32 D8** 41 45N 3 1 E
Sant Feliu de Llobregat, *Spain* **32 D7** 41 23N 2 2 E
Sant Ferran, *Spain* **37 C7** 38 42N 1 28 E
Sant Francesc de Formentera, *Spain* **37 C7** 38 42N 1 26 E
Sant Jaume, *Spain* **37 B11** 39 54N 4 4 E
Sant Joan Baptista, *Spain* **37 B8** 39 5N 1 31 E
Sant Jordi, *Spain* **37 B9** 39 33N 2 46 E
Sant Jordi, G. de, *Spain* **32 E6** 40 53N 1 2 E
Sant Llorenç de Morunys, *Spain* **32 C6** 42 8N 1 35 E
Sant Llorenç des Cardassar, *Spain* **37 B10** 39 37N 3 17 E
Sant Mateu, *Baleares, Spain* **37 B7** 39 3N 1 23 E
Sant Mateu, *Valencia, Spain* **32 E5** 40 28N 0 10 E
Sant Miquel, *Spain* **37 B7** 39 3N 1 26 E
Sant Telm, *Spain* **37 B9** 39 35N 2 21 E
Sant' Ágata Militello, *Italy* **31 D7** 38 2N 14 8 E
Santa Agnés, *Spain* **37 B7** 39 3N 1 21 E
Santa Ana, *Bolivia* **124 F5** 13 50 S 65 40W
Santa Ana, *El Salv.* **120 D2** 14 0N 89 31W
Santa Ana, *Mexico* **118 A2** 30 31N 111 8W
Santa Ana, *U.S.A.* **117 M9** 33 46N 117 52W
Sant' Ángelo Lodigiano, *Italy* **28 C6** 45 14N 9 25 E
Sant' Antíoco, *Italy* **30 C1** 39 4N 8 27 E
Santa Barbara, *Chile* **126 D1** 37 40 S 72 1W
Santa Bárbara, *Honduras* **120 D2** 14 53N 88 14W
Santa Bárbara, *Mexico* **118 B3** 26 48N 105 50W
Santa Bárbara, *Spain* **32 E5** 40 42N 0 29 E
Santa Barbara, *U.S.A.* **117 L7** 34 25N 119 42W
Santa Bárbara, Mt., *Spain* **33 H2** 37 23N 2 50W
Santa Barbara Channel, *U.S.A.* **117 L7** 34 15N 120 0W
Santa Barbara I., *U.S.A.* **117 M7** 33 29N 119 2W
Santa Catalina, Gulf of, *U.S.A.* **117 N9** 33 10N 117 50W
Santa Catalina, I., *Mexico* **118 B2** 25 40N 110 50W
Santa Catalina I., *U.S.A.* **117 M8** 33 23N 118 25W
Santa Catarina □, *Brazil* **127 B6** 27 25 S 48 30W
Santa Catarina, I. de, *Brazil* **127 B6** 27 30 S 48 40W
Santa Caterina di Pittinuri, *Italy* **30 B1** 40 6N 8 27 E
Santa Caterina Villarmosa, *Italy* **31 E7** 37 35N 14 2 E
Santa Cecília, *Brazil* **127 B5** 26 56 S 50 18W
Santa Clara, *Cuba* **120 B4** 22 20N 80 0W
Santa Clara, *Calif., U.S.A.* **116 H5** 37 21N 121 57W
Santa Clara, *Utah, U.S.A.* **115 H7** 37 8N 113 39W
Santa Clara, El Golfo de, *Mexico* **118 A2** 31 42N 114 30W
Santa Clara de Olimar, *Uruguay* **127 C5** 32 50 S 54 54W
Santa Clarita, *U.S.A.* **117 L8** 34 24N 118 30W
Santa Clotilde, *Peru* **124 D4** 2 33 S 73 45W
Santa Coloma de Farners, *Spain* **32 D7** 41 50N 2 39 E
Santa Coloma de Gramenet, *Spain* **32 D7** 41 27N 2 13 E
Santa Comba, *Spain* **34 B2** 43 2N 8 49W
Santa Croce Camerina, *Italy* **31 F7** 36 50N 14 31 E
Santa Croce di Magliano, *Italy* **29 G11** 41 42N 14 59 E
Santa Cruz, *Argentina* **128 G3** 50 0 S 68 32W
Santa Cruz, *Bolivia* **124 G6** 17 43 S 63 10W
Santa Cruz, *Chile* **126 C1** 34 38 S 71 27W
Santa Cruz, *Costa Rica* **120 D2** 10 15N 85 35W
Santa Cruz, *Madeira* **37 D3** 32 42N 16 46W
Santa Cruz, *Phil.* **61 D4** 14 20N 121 24 E
Santa Cruz, *U.S.A.* **116 J4** 36 58N 122 1W
Santa Cruz →, *Argentina* **128 G3** 50 10 S 68 20W
Santa Cruz de la Palma, *Canary Is.* **37 F2** 28 41N 17 46W
Santa Cruz de Mudela, *Spain* **35 G7** 38 39N 3 28W
Santa Cruz de Tenerife, *Canary Is.* **37 F3** 28 28N 16 15W
Santa Cruz del Norte, *Cuba* **120 B3** 23 9N 81 55W
Santa Cruz del Retamar, *Spain* **34 E6** 40 8N 4 14W
Santa Cruz del Sur, *Cuba* **120 B4** 20 44N 78 0W
Santa Cruz do Rio Pardo, *Brazil* **127 A6** 22 54 S 49 37W
Santa Cruz do Sul, *Brazil* **127 B5** 29 42 S 52 25W
Santa Cruz I., *U.S.A.* **117 M7** 34 1N 119 43W
Santa Cruz Is., *Solomon Is.* **96 J8** 10 30 S 166 0 E
Santa Domingo, Cay, *Bahamas* **120 B4** 21 25N 75 15W
Sant' Egídio alla Vibrata, *Italy* **29 F10** 42 49N 13 42 E
Santa Elena, *Argentina* **126 C4** 30 58 S 59 47W
Santa Elena, C., *Costa Rica* **120 D2** 10 54N 85 56W
Sant' Eufémia, G. di, *Italy* **31 D9** 38 51N 16 4 E
Santa Eulàlia des Riu, *Spain* **37 C8** 38 59N 1 32 E
Santa Fe, *Argentina* **126 C3** 31 35 S 60 41W
Santa Fe, *Spain* **35 H7** 37 11N 3 43W
Santa Fe, *U.S.A.* **115 J11** 35 41N 105 57W
Santa Fé □, *Argentina* **126 C3** 31 50 S 60 55W
Santa Fé do Sul, *Brazil* **125 H8** 20 13 S 50 56W
Santa Filomena, *Brazil* **125 E9** 9 6 S 45 50W
Santa Fiora, *Italy* **29 F8** 42 50N 11 35 E
Santa Gertrudis, *Spain* **37 C7** 39 0N 1 26 E
Santa Giustina, *Italy* **29 B9** 46 10N 12 5 E
Santa Inês, *Brazil* **125 F11** 13 17 S 39 48W
Santa Inés, *Spain* **35 G5** 38 32N 5 37W
Santa Inés, I., *Chile* **122 J3** 54 0 S 73 0W
Santa Isabel = Rey Malabo, *Eq. Guin.* **83 E6** 3 45N 8 50 E
Santa Isabel, *Argentina* **126 D2** 36 10 S 66 54W
Santa Isabel, Pico, *Eq. Guin.* **83 E6** 3 36N 8 49 E
Santa Isabel do Morro, *Brazil* **125 F8** 11 34 S 50 40W
Santa Lucía, *Corrientes, Argentina* **126 B4** 28 58 S 59 5W
Santa Lucía, *San Juan, Argentina* **126 C2** 31 30 S 68 30W
Santa Lucía, *Spain* **33 H4** 37 35N 0 58W
Santa Lucia, *Uruguay* **126 C4** 34 27 S 56 24W
Santa Lucia Range, *U.S.A.* **116 K5** 36 0N 121 20W
Santa Magdalena, I., *Mexico* **118 C2** 24 40N 112 15W
Santa Margarita, *Argentina* **126 D3** 38 28 S 61 35W
Santa Margarita, *Spain* **37 B10** 39 42N 3 6 E
Santa Margarita, *U.S.A.* **116 K6** 35 23N 120 37W
Santa Margarita →, *U.S.A.* **117 M9** 33 13N 117 23W
Santa Margarita, I., *Mexico* **118 C2** 24 30N 111 50W
Santa Margherita, *Italy* **30 D1** 38 58N 8 58 E
Santa Margherita Ligure, *Italy* **28 D6** 44 20N 9 11 E
Santa María, *Argentina* **126 B2** 26 40 S 66 0W
Santa Maria, *Brazil* **127 B5** 29 40 S 53 48W
Santa Maria, *Phil.* **61 C4** 17 22N 120 29 E
Santa Maria, *U.S.A.* **117 L6** 34 57N 120 26W
Santa María →, *Mexico* **118 A3** 31 0N 107 14W
Santa María, B. de, *Mexico* **118 B3** 25 10N 108 40W
Santa Maria, C. de, *Portugal* **35 J3** 36 58N 7 53W
Santa Maria Cápua Vétere, *Italy* **31 A7** 41 5N 14 15 E
Santa Maria da Feira, *Portugal* **34 E2** 40 55N 8 35W
Santa Maria da Vitória, *Brazil* **125 F10** 13 24 S 44 12W
Santa Maria del Camí, *Spain* **37 B9** 39 38N 2 47 E
Santa Maria di Léuca, C., *Italy* **31 C11** 39 47N 18 22 E
Santa María la Real de Nieva, *Spain* **34 D6** 41 4N 4 24W
Santa Marinella, *Italy* **29 F8** 42 2N 11 52 E
Santa Marta, *Colombia* **124 A4** 11 15N 74 13W
Santa Marta, Sierra Nevada de, *Colombia* **122 B3** 10 55N 73 50W
Santa Marta de Tormes, *Spain* **34 E5** 40 57N 5 38W
Santa Marta Grande, C., *Brazil* **127 B6** 28 43 S 48 50W
Santa Marta Ortigueira, Ría de, *Spain* **34 B3** 43 44N 7 45W
Santa Maura = Levkás, *Greece* **38 C2** 38 40N 20 43 E
Santa Monica, *U.S.A.* **117 M8** 34 1N 118 29W
Santa Olalla, *Huelva, Spain* **35 H4** 37 54N 6 14W
Santa Olalla, *Toledo, Spain* **34 E6** 40 2N 4 25W
Santa Paula, *U.S.A.* **117 L7** 34 21N 119 4W
Santa Pola, *Spain* **33 G4** 38 13N 0 35W
Santa Ponsa, *Spain* **37 B9** 39 30N 2 28 E
Santa Rita, *U.S.A.* **115 K10** 32 48N 108 4W
Santa Rosa, *La Pampa, Argentina* **126 D3** 36 40 S 64 17W
Santa Rosa, *San Luis, Argentina* **126 C2** 32 21 S 65 10W
Santa Rosa, *Brazil* **127 B5** 27 52 S 54 29W
Santa Rosa, *Calif., U.S.A.* **116 G4** 38 26N 122 43W
Santa Rosa, *N. Mex., U.S.A.* **113 H2** 34 57N 104 41W
Santa Rosa de Copán, *Honduras* **120 D2** 14 47N 88 46W
Santa Rosa de Río Primero, *Argentina* **126 C3** 31 8 S 63 20W
Santa Rosa del Sara, *Bolivia* **124 G6** 17 7 S 63 35W
Santa Rosa I., *Calif., U.S.A.* **117 M6** 33 58N 120 6W
Santa Rosa I., *Fla., U.S.A.* **109 K2** 30 20N 86 50W
Santa Rosa Range, *U.S.A.* **114 F5** 41 45N 117 40W
Santa Rosalía, *Mexico* **118 B2** 27 20N 112 20W
Santa Sylvina, *Argentina* **126 B3** 27 50 S 61 10W
Santa Tecla = Nueva San Salvador, *El Salv.* **120 D2** 13 40N 89 18W
Santa Teresa, *Argentina* **126 C3** 33 25 S 60 47W
Santa Teresa, *Australia* **94 C1** 24 8 S 134 22 E
Santa Teresa, *Mexico* **119 B5** 25 17N 97 51W
Santa Teresa di Riva, *Italy* **31 E8** 37 57N 15 22 E
Santa Teresa Gallura, *Italy* **30 A2** 41 14N 9 11 E
Santa Uxía, *Spain* **34 C2** 42 36N 8 58W
Santa Vitória do Palmar, *Brazil* **127 C5** 33 32 S 53 25W
Santa Ynez →, *U.S.A.* **117 L6** 35 41N 120 36W
Santa Ynez Mts., *U.S.A.* **117 L6** 34 30N 120 0W
Santa Ysabel, *U.S.A.* **117 M10** 33 7N 116 40W
Santadi, *Italy* **30 C1** 39 5N 8 43 E
Santaella, *Spain* **35 H6** 37 34N 4 51W
Santai, *China* **58 B5** 31 5N 104 58 E
Santana, *Madeira* **37 D3** 32 48N 16 52W
Sântana, *Romania* **42 D6** 46 20N 21 30 E
Santana, Coxilha de, *Brazil* **127 C4** 30 50 S 55 35W
Santana do Livramento, *Brazil* **127 C4** 30 55 S 55 30W
Santander, *Spain* **34 B7** 43 27N 3 51W
Santander Jiménez, *Mexico* **119 C5** 24 11N 98 29W
Santanyí, *Spain* **37 B10** 39 20N 3 5 E
Santaquin, *U.S.A.* **114 G8** 39 59N 111 47W
Santarcángelo di Romagna, *Italy* **29 D9** 44 4N 12 26 E
Santarém, *Brazil* **125 D8** 2 25 S 54 42W
Santarém, *Portugal* **35 F2** 39 12N 8 42W
Santarém □, *Portugal* **35 F2** 39 10N 8 40W
Santaren Channel, *W. Indies* **120 B4** 24 0N 79 30W
Santee, *U.S.A.* **117 N10** 32 50N 116 58W
Santee →, *U.S.A.* **109 J6** 33 7N 79 17W
Santéramo in Colle, *Italy* **31 B9** 40 49N 16 45 E
Santerno →, *Italy* **29 D8** 44 34N 11 58 E
Santhià, *Italy* **28 C5** 45 22N 8 10 E
Santiago, *Brazil* **127 B5** 29 11 S 54 52W
Santiago, *Chile* **126 C1** 33 24 S 70 40W
Santiago, *Panama* **120 E3** 8 0N 81 0W
Santiago, *Phil.* **61 C4** 16 41N 121 33 E
Santiago □, *Chile* **126 C1** 33 30 S 70 50W
Santiago →, *Mexico* **98 G9** 25 11N 105 26W
Santiago →, *Peru* **124 D3** 4 27 S 77 38W
Santiago, Punta de, *Eq. Guin.* **83 E6** 3 12N 8 40 E
Santiago de Compostela, *Spain* **34 C2** 42 52N 8 37W
Santiago de Cuba, *Cuba* **120 C4** 20 0N 75 49W
Santiago de los Cabelleros, *Dom. Rep.* **121 C5** 19 30N 70 40W
Santiago del Estero, *Argentina* **126 B3** 27 50 S 64 15W
Santiago del Estero □, *Argentina* **126 B3** 27 40 S 63 15W
Santiago del Teide, *Canary Is.* **37 F3** 28 17N 16 48W
Santiago do Cacém, *Portugal* **35 G2** 38 1N 8 42W
Santiago Ixcuintla, *Mexico* **118 C3** 21 50N 105 11W
Santiago Papasquiaro, *Mexico* **118 C3** 25 0N 105 20W
Santiaguillo, L. de, *Mexico* **118 C4** 24 50N 104 50W
Santiguila, *Mali* **82 C3** 12 42N 7 25W
Santillana, *Spain* **34 B6** 43 24N 4 6W
Santisteban del Puerto, *Spain* **35 G7** 38 17N 3 15W
Santo Amaro, *Brazil* **125 F11** 12 30 S 38 43W
Santo Anastácio, *Brazil* **127 A5** 21 58 S 51 39W
Santo André, *Brazil* **127 A6** 23 39 S 46 29W
Santo Ângelo, *Brazil* **127 B5** 28 15 S 54 15W
Santo Antônio do Içá, *Brazil* **124 D5** 3 5 S 67 57W
Santo Antônio do Leverger, *Brazil* **125 G7** 15 52 S 56 5W
Santo Domingo, *Dom. Rep.* **121 C6** 18 30N 69 59W
Santo Domingo, *Baja Calif., Mexico* **118 A1** 30 43N 116 2W
Santo Domingo, *Baja Calif. S., Mexico* **118 B2** 25 32N 112 2W
Santo Domingo, *Nic.* **120 D3** 12 14N 84 59W
Santo Domingo de la Calzada, *Spain* **32 C2** 42 26N 2 27W
Santo Domingo de los Colorados, *Ecuador* **124 D3** 0 15 S 79 9W
Santo Domingo Pueblo, *U.S.A.* **115 J10** 35 31N 106 22W
Santo Stéfano di Camastro, *Italy* **31 D7** 38 1N 14 22 E
Santo Tirso, *Portugal* **34 D2** 41 21N 8 28W

Santo Tomás, *Mexico* . **118 A1** 31 33N 116 24W
Santo Tomás, *Peru* ... **124 F4** 14 26 S 72 8W
Santo Tomé, *Argentina* **127 B4** 28 40 S 56 5W
Santo Tomé de Guayana = Ciudad Guayana, *Venezuela* **124 B6** 8 0N 62 30W
Santomera, *Spain* **33 G3** 38 4N 1 3W
Santoña, *Spain* **34 B7** 43 29N 3 27W
Santoríni = Thíra, *Greece* .... **39 E7** 36 23N 25 27 E
Santos, *Brazil* .... **127 A6** 24 0 S 46 20W
Santos, Sierra de los, *Spain* **35 G5** 38 7N 5 12W
Santos Dumont, *Brazil* **127 A7** 22 55 S 43 10W
Sanwer, *India* .... **68 H6** 22 59N 75 50 E
Sanxenxo, *Spain* **34 C2** 42 24N 8 49W
Sanyuan, *China* ...... **56 G5** 34 35N 108 58 E
São Bartolomeu de Messines, *Portugal* . **35 H2** 37 15N 8 17W
São Bernardo do Campo, *Brazil* ..... **127 A6** 23 45 S 46 34W
São Borja, *Brazil* ..... **127 B4** 28 39 S 56 0W
São Brás de Alportel, *Portugal* **35 H3** 37 8N 7 37W
São Carlos, *Brazil* ... **127 A6** 22 0 S 47 50W
São Cristóvão, *Brazil* . **125 F11** 11 1 S 37 15W
São Domingos, *Brazil* . **125 F9** 13 25 S 46 19W
São Domingos, *Guinea-Biss.* .... **82 C1** 12 19N 16 13 E
São Francisco, *Brazil* . **125 G10** 16 0 S 44 50W
São Francisco →, *Brazil* .... **122 E7** 10 30 S 36 24W
São Francisco do Sul, *Brazil* .... **127 B6** 26 15 S 48 36W
São Gabriel, *Brazil* ... **127 C5** 30 20 S 54 20W
São Gonçalo, *Brazil* .. **127 A7** 22 48 S 43 5W
Sao Hill, *Tanzania* ... **87 D4** 8 20 S 35 12 E
São João, *Guinea-Biss.* **82 C1** 11 32N 15 25W
São João da Boa Vista, *Brazil* .... **127 A6** 22 0 S 46 52W
São João da Madeira, *Portugal* **34 E2** 40 54N 8 30W
São João da Pesqueira, *Portugal* **34 D3** 41 8N 7 24W
São João del Rei, *Brazil* **127 A7** 21 8 S 44 15W
São João do Araguaia, *Brazil* .... **125 E9** 5 23 S 48 46W
São João do Piauí, *Brazil* .... **125 E10** 8 21 S 42 15W
São Joaquim, *Brazil* .. **127 B6** 28 18 S 49 56W
São Jorge, Pta. de, *Madeira* **37 D3** 32 50N 16 53W
São José, *Brazil* ...... **127 B5** 27 38 S 48 39W
São José do Norte, *Brazil* .... **127 C5** 32 1 S 52 3W
São José do Rio Prêto, *Brazil* .... **127 A6** 20 50 S 49 20W
São José dos Campos, *Brazil* .... **127 A6** 23 7 S 45 52W
São Leopoldo, *Brazil* . **127 B5** 29 50 S 51 10W
São Lourenço, *Brazil* . **127 A6** 22 7 S 45 3W
São Lourenço →, *Brazil* .... **125 G7** 17 53 S 57 27W
São Lourenço, Pta. de, *Madeira* **37 D3** 32 44N 16 39W
São Lourenço do Sul, *Brazil* .... **127 C5** 31 22 S 51 58W
São Luís, *Brazil* ...... **125 D10** 2 39 S 44 15W
São Luís Gonzaga, *Brazil* .... **127 B5** 28 25 S 55 0W
São Marcos →, *Brazil* **125 G9** 18 15 S 47 37W
São Marcos, B. de, *Brazil* .... **125 D10** 2 0 S 44 0W
São Martinho da Cortiça, *Portugal* ... **34 E2** 40 18N 8 8W
São Mateus, *Brazil* ... **125 G11** 18 44 S 39 50W
São Mateus do Sul, *Brazil* .... **127 B5** 25 52 S 50 23W
São Miguel do Oeste, *Brazil* .... **127 B5** 26 45 S 53 34W
São Paulo, *Brazil* .... **127 A6** 23 32 S 46 37W
São Paulo □, *Brazil* .. **127 A6** 22 0 S 49 0W
São Paulo, I., *Atl. Oc.* . **2 D8** 0 50N 31 40W
São Paulo de Olivença, *Brazil* .... **124 D5** 3 27 S 68 48W
São Pedro do Sul, *Portugal* **34 E2** 40 46N 8 4W
São Roque, *Madeira* .. **37 D3** 32 46N 16 48W
São Roque, C. de, *Brazil* .... **122 D7** 5 30 S 35 16W
São Sebastião, I. de, *Brazil* .... **127 A6** 23 50 S 45 18W
São Sebastião do Paraíso, *Brazil* ..... **127 A6** 20 54 S 46 59W
São Teotónio, *Portugal* **35 H2** 37 30N 8 42W
São Tomé, *Atl. Oc.* ... **76 F4** 0 10N 6 39 E
São Tomé, C. de, *Brazil* **127 A7** 22 0 S 40 59W
São Tomé & Principe ■, *Africa* .. **77 F4** 0 12N 6 39 E
São Vicente, *Brazil* ... **127 A6** 23 57 S 46 23W
São Vicente, *Madeira* . **37 D2** 32 48N 17 3W
São Vicente, C. de, *Portugal* **35 H1** 37 0N 9 0W
Saona, I., *Dom. Rep.* .. **121 C6** 18 10N 68 40W
Saône →, *France* ..... **19 G11** 45 44N 4 50 E
Saône-et-Loire □, *France* .... **19 F11** 46 30N 4 50 E
Saonek, *Indonesia* .... **63 E8** 0 22 S 130 55 E
Sápai, *Greece* .... **41 E9** 41 2N 25 43 E
Sapanca, *Turkey* ..... **72 B4** 40 41N 30 16 E
Saparua, *Indonesia* ... **63 E7** 3 33 S 128 40 E
Sapele, *Nigeria* .... **83 D6** 5 50N 5 40 E
Sapelo I., *U.S.A.* **109 K5** 31 25N 81 12W
Şaphane, *Turkey* ..... **39 B11** 39 1N 29 13 E
Sapiéntza, *Greece* .... **38 E3** 36 45N 21 43 E
Sapone, *Burkina Faso* . **83 C4** 12 3N 1 35W
Saposoa, *Peru* .... **124 E3** 6 55 S 76 45W
Sapouy, *Burkina Faso* . **83 C4** 11 34N 1 44W
Sapozhok, *Russia* .... **48 D5** 53 59N 40 41 E
Sapphire, *Australia* ... **94 C4** 23 28 S 147 43 E
Sappho, *U.S.A.* **116 B2** 48 4N 124 16W
Sapporo, *Japan* ...... **54 C10** 43 0N 141 21 E
Sapri, *Italy* .... **31 B8** 40 4N 15 38 E
Sapulpa, *U.S.A.* **113 H6** 35 59N 96 5W
Saqqez, *Iran* .... **70 B5** 36 15N 46 20 E
Sar Dasht, *Iran* ...... **71 C6** 32 32N 48 52 E
Sar Gachīneh, *Iran* ... **71 D6** 30 31N 51 31 E
Sar Planina, *Macedonia* **40 E4** 42 0N 21 0 E
Sara, *Burkina Faso* ... **82 C4** 11 40N 3 53W
Sara, *Phil.* .... **61 F5** 11 16N 123 1 E
Sara Buri = Saraburi, *Thailand* .... **64 E3** 14 30N 100 55 E
Sarāb, *Iran* .... **70 B5** 37 55N 47 40 E
Sarabadi, *Iraq* .... **70 C5** 33 1N 44 48 E
Saraburi, *Thailand* ... **64 E3** 14 30N 100 55 E
Sarada →, *India* ..... **67 F12** 27 21N 81 23 E
Saradiya, *India* .... **68 J4** 21 34N 70 2 E
Saraféré, *Mali* **82 B4** 15 50N 3 40W
Saragossa = Zaragoza, *Spain* **32 D4** 41 39N 0 53W
Saraguro, *Ecuador* ... **124 D3** 3 35 S 79 16W
Sarai Naurang, *Pakistan* **68 C4** 32 50N 70 47 E
Saraikela, *India* ...... **69 H11** 22 42N 85 56 E
Saraiu, *Romania* ..... **43 F13** 44 43N 28 10 E
Sarajevo, *Bos.-H.* .... **42 G3** 43 52N 18 26 E
Sarakhs, *Turkmenistan* **71 B9** 36 32N 61 13 E
Saran, Gunung, *Indonesia* .... **62 E4** 0 30 S 111 25 E
Saranac L., *U.S.A.* **111 B10** 44 20N 74 10W
Saranac Lake, *U.S.A.* . **111 B10** 44 20N 74 8W
Saranda = Sarandë, *Albania* .... **40 G3** 39 52N 19 55 E
Saranda, *Tanzania* .... **86 D3** 5 45 S 34 59 E
Sarandë, *Albania* ..... **40 G3** 39 52N 19 55 E
Sarandí del Yi, *Uruguay* **127 C4** 33 18 S 55 38W
Sarandí Grande, *Uruguay* .... **126 C4** 33 44 S 56 20W
Sarangani B., *Phil.* ... **61 J6** 6 0N 125 13 E
Sarangani Is., *Phil.* ... **61 J6** 5 25N 125 25 E
Sarangarh, *India* ..... **67 J13** 21 30N 83 5 E
Saransk, *Russia* ...... **48 C7** 54 10N 45 10 E
Sarapul, *Russia* ...... **50 D6** 56 28N 53 48 E
Sarasota, *U.S.A.* **109 M4** 27 20N 82 32W
Saratoga, *Calif., U.S.A.* **116 H4** 37 16N 122 2W
Saratoga, *Wyo., U.S.A.* **114 F10** 41 27N 106 49W
Saratoga Springs, *U.S.A.* **111 C11** 43 5N 73 47W
Saratok, *Malaysia* .... **62 D4** 1 55N 111 17 E
Saratov, *Russia* ...... **48 E7** 51 30N 46 2 E
Saravane, *Laos* ...... **64 E6** 15 43N 106 25 E
Sarawak □, *Malaysia* . **62 D4** 2 0N 113 0 E
Saray, *Tekirdağ, Turkey* **41 E11** 41 26N 27 55 E
Saray, *Van, Turkey* ... **73 C11** 38 38N 44 9 E
Saraya, *Guinea* **82 C2** 12 50N 11 45W
Saraya, *Senegal* **82 C2** 12 50N 11 45W
Saraycık, *Turkey* ..... **39 B11** 39 1N 29 49 E
Sarayköy, *Turkey* ..... **39 D10** 37 55N 28 54 E
Saraylar, *Turkey* ..... **41 F11** 40 39N 27 40 E
Sarayönü, *Turkey* ..... **72 C5** 38 16N 32 24 E
Sarbāz, *Iran* .... **71 E9** 26 38N 61 19 E
Sarbīsheh, *Iran* ...... **71 C8** 32 30N 59 40 E
Sárbogárd, *Hungary* .. **42 D3** 46 50N 18 40 E
Sarca →, *Italy* .... **28 C7** 45 52N 10 52 E
Sarcelles, *France* ..... **19 D9** 48 59N 2 23 E
Sarda = Sarada →, *India* .... **67 F12** 27 21N 81 23 E
Sardarshahr, *India* .... **68 E6** 28 30N 74 29 E
Sardegna □, *Italy* .... **30 B1** 40 0N 9 0 E
Sardhana, *India* ...... **68 E7** 29 9N 77 39 E
Sardina, Pta., *Canary Is.* **37 F4** 28 9N 15 44W
Sardinia = Sardegna □, *Italy* .... **30 B1** 40 0N 9 0 E
Sardis, *Turkey* .... **39 C10** 38 28N 28 2 E
Sārdūīyeh = Dar Mazār, *Iran* .... **71 D8** 29 14N 57 20 E
S'Arenal, *Spain* ...... **37 B9** 39 30N 2 45 E
Sarentino, *Italy* ...... **29 B8** 46 38N 11 21 E
Saréyamou, *Mali* **82 B4** 16 7N 3 10W
Sargasso Sea, *Atl. Oc.* . **97 D20** 27 0N 72 0W
Sargodha, *Pakistan* ... **68 C5** 32 10N 72 40 E
Sarh, *Chad* .... **79 G9** 9 5N 18 23 E
Sarhala, *Ivory C.* **82 D3** 8 22N 6 8W
Sārī, *Iran* .... **71 B7** 36 30N 53 4 E
Sari d'Orcino, *France* . **21 F12** 42 3N 8 49 E
Sária, *Greece* .... **39 F9** 35 54N 27 17 E
Saria, *India* .... **69 J10** 21 38N 83 22 E
Sariab, *Pakistan* ..... **68 D2** 30 6N 66 59 E
Sarıbeyler, *Turkey* .... **39 B9** 39 24N 27 35 E
Sarıgöl, *Turkey* ...... **72 C3** 38 14N 28 41 E
Sarikamiş, *Turkey* .... **73 B10** 40 22N 42 35 E
Sarıkaya, *Turkey* ..... **72 C6** 39 29N 35 22 E
Sarikei, *Malaysia* ..... **62 D4** 2 8N 111 30 E
Sarıköy, *Turkey* ...... **41 F11** 40 12N 27 36 E
Sarila, *India* .... **69 G8** 25 46N 79 41 E
Sarina, *Australia* ..... **94 C4** 21 22 S 149 13 E
Sariñena, *Spain* **32 D4** 41 47N 0 10W
Sarita, *U.S.A.* **113 M6** 27 13N 97 47W
Sariwŏn, *N. Korea* .... **57 E13** 38 31N 125 46 E
Sariyar Baraji, *Turkey* **72 B4** 40 2N 31 33 E
Sarıyer, *Turkey* ...... **41 E13** 41 10N 29 3 E
Sarju →, *India* ...... **69 F9** 27 21N 81 23 E
Sark, *U.K.* **13 H5** 49 25N 2 22W
Sarkad, *Hungary* ..... **42 D6** 46 47N 21 23 E
Sarkari Tala, *India* ... **68 F4** 27 39N 70 52 E
Şarkışla, *Turkey* ..... **72 C7** 39 21N 36 25 E
Şarköy, *Turkey* ...... **41 F11** 40 36N 27 6 E
Sarlat-la-Canéda, *France* .... **20 D5** 44 54N 1 13 E
Sărmăşag, *Romania* .. **42 C7** 47 21N 22 50 E
Sărmaşu, *Romania* ... **43 D9** 46 45N 24 13 E
Sarmi, *Indonesia* ..... **63 E9** 1 49 S 138 44 E
Sarmiento, *Argentina* . **128 F3** 45 35 S 69 5W
Sarmizegetusa, *Romania* .... **42 E7** 45 31N 22 47 E
Särna, *Sweden* .... **10 C7** 61 41N 13 8 E
Sarnano, *Italy* .... **29 E10** 43 2N 13 18 E
Sarnen, *Switz.* .... **25 J4** 46 53N 8 13 E
Sarnia, *Canada* **102 D3** 42 58N 82 23W
Sarno, *Italy* .... **31 B7** 40 49N 14 37 E
Sarnthein = Sarentino, *Italy* .... **29 B8** 46 38N 11 21 E
Särö, *Sweden* .... **11 G5** 57 31N 11 57 E
Sarolangun, *Indonesia* **62 E2** 2 19 S 102 42 E
Saronikós Kólpos, *Greece* .... **38 D5** 37 45N 23 45 E
Saronno, *Italy* .... **28 C6** 45 38N 9 2 E
Saros Körfezi, *Turkey* . **41 F10** 40 30N 26 15 E
Sárospatak, *Hungary* . **42 B6** 48 18N 21 33 E
Sarpsborg, *Norway* ... **9 G14** 59 16N 11 7 E
Sarracín, *Spain* **34 C7** 42 15N 3 45W
Sarralbe, *France* ..... **19 D14** 49 0N 7 1 E
Sarre = Saar →, *Europe* **17 E6** 49 41N 6 32 E
Sarre, *Italy* .... **28 C4** 45 40N 7 15 E
Sarre-Union, *France* .. **19 D14** 48 57N 7 4 E
Sarrebourg, *France* ... **19 D14** 48 43N 7 3 E
Sarreguemines, *France* **19 C14** 49 5N 7 4 E
Sarria, *Spain* **34 C3** 42 49N 7 29W
Sarrión, *Spain* **32 E4** 40 9N 0 49W
Sarro, *Mali* **82 C3** 13 40N 5 15W
Sarstedt, *Germany* .... **24 C5** 52 14N 9 52 E
Sartène, *France* ...... **21 G12** 41 38N 8 58 E
Sarthe □, *France* ..... **18 D7** 48 10N 0 10 E
Sarthe →, *France* **18 E6** 47 33N 0 31W
Sartilly, *France* **18 D5** 48 45N 1 28W
Saruhanlı, *Turkey* .... **39 C9** 38 44N 27 36 E
Sărulești, *Romania* ... **43 F11** 44 25N 26 39 E
Saruna →, *Pakistan* .. **68 F2** 26 31N 67 7 E
Sárvár, *Hungary* ..... **42 C1** 47 15N 16 56 E
Sarvar, *India* .... **68 F6** 26 4N 75 0 E
Sarvestān, *Iran* ...... **71 D7** 29 20N 53 10 E
Särvfjället, *Sweden* ... **10 B7** 62 42N 13 30 E
Sárvíz →, *Hungary* ... **42 D3** 46 24N 18 41 E
Sary-Tash, *Kyrgyzstan* **50 F8** 39 44N 73 15 E
Sarych, Mys, *Ukraine* . **47 K7** 44 25N 33 45 E
Saryshagan, *Kazakstan* **50 E8** 46 12N 73 38 E
Sarzana, *Italy* .... **28 D6** 44 7N 9 58 E
Sarzeau, *France* **18 E4** 47 31N 2 48W
Sasan Gir, *India* ..... **68 J4** 21 10N 70 36 E
Sasaram, *India* ...... **69 G11** 24 57N 84 5 E
Sasebo, *Japan* .... **55 H4** 33 10N 129 43 E
Saser, *India* .... **69 B7** 34 50N 77 50 E
Saskatchewan □, *Canada* **105 C7** 54 40N 106 0W
Saskatchewan →, *Canada* **105 C8** 53 37N 100 40W
Saskatoon, *Canada* ... **105 C7** 52 10N 106 38W
Saskylakh, *Russia* .... **51 B12** 71 55N 114 1 E
Sasolburg, *S. Africa* .. **89 D4** 26 46 S 27 49 E
Sasovo, *Russia* ...... **48 C5** 54 25N 41 55 E
Sassandra, *Ivory C.* ... **82 E3** 4 55N 6 8W
Sassandra →, *Ivory C.* **82 E3** 4 58N 6 5W
Sássari, *Italy* .... **30 B1** 40 43N 8 34 E
Sassnitz, *Germany* .... **24 A9** 54 29N 13 39 E
Sasso Marconi, *Italy* .. **29 D8** 44 24N 11 15 E
Sassocorvaro, *Italy* ... **29 E9** 43 47N 12 30 E
Sassoferrato, *Italy* ... **29 E9** 43 26N 12 51 E
Sasstown, *Liberia* **82 E3** 4 45N 8 27W
Sassuolo, *Italy* .... **28 D7** 44 33N 10 47 E
Sástago, *Spain* **32 D4** 41 19N 0 21W
Sasumua Dam, *Kenya* . **86 C4** 0 45 S 36 40 E
Sasyk, Ozero, *Ukraine* **47 K5** 45 45N 29 20 E
Sata-Misaki, *Japan* ... **55 J5** 31 0N 130 40 E
Satadougou, *Mali* **82 C2** 12 25N 11 25W
Satakunta, *Finland* ... **9 F20** 61 45N 23 0 E
Satama-Soukoura, *Ivory C.* **82 D4** 7 55N 4 27W
Satara, *India* .... **66 L8** 17 44N 73 58 E
Satara, *S. Africa* ..... **89 C5** 24 29 S 31 47 E
Satbarwa, *India* ...... **69 H11** 23 55N 84 16 E
Såtenäs, *Sweden* ..... **11 F6** 58 27N 12 41 E
Säter, *Sweden* .... **10 D9** 60 21N 15 45 E
Satevó, *Mexico* **118 B3** 27 57N 106 7W
Satilla →, *U.S.A.* **109 K5** 30 59N 81 29W
Satmala Hills, *India* .. **66 J9** 20 15N 74 40 E
Satna, *India* .... **69 G9** 24 35N 80 50 E
Šator, *Bos.-H.* .... **29 D13** 44 11N 16 37 E
Sátoraljaújhely, *Hungary* .... **42 B6** 48 25N 21 41 E
Satpura Ra., *India* .... **66 J10** 21 25N 76 10 E
Satrup, *Germany* ..... **24 A5** 54 41N 9 36 E
Satsuna-Shotō, *Japan* . **55 K5** 30 0N 130 0 E
Sattahip, *Thailand* ... **64 F3** 12 41N 100 54 E
Satu Mare, *Romania* .. **42 C7** 47 46N 22 55 E
Satu Mare □, *Romania* **42 C8** 47 45N 23 0 E
Satui, *Indonesia* ..... **62 E5** 3 50 S 115 27 E
Satun, *Thailand* ...... **65 J3** 6 43N 100 2 E
Saturnina →, *Brazil* .. **124 F7** 12 15 S 58 10W
Sauce, *Argentina* ..... **126 C4** 30 5 S 58 46W
Sauceda, *Mexico* **118 B4** 25 55N 101 18W
Saucillo, *Mexico* **118 B3** 28 1N 105 17W
Sauda, *Norway* ...... **9 G12** 59 40N 6 20 E
Sauðarkrókur, *Iceland* **8 D4** 65 45N 19 40W
Saudi Arabia ■, *Asia* . **70 B3** 26 0N 44 0 E
Saugeen →, *Canada* .. **110 B3** 44 30N 81 22W
Saugerties, *U.S.A.* ... **111 D11** 42 5N 73 57W
Saugues, *France* ..... **20 D7** 44 58N 3 32 E
Saugus, *U.S.A.* **117 L8** 34 25N 118 32W
Saujon, *France* **20 C3** 45 41N 0 55W
Sauk Centre, *U.S.A.* .. **112 C7** 45 44N 94 57W
Sauk Rapids, *U.S.A.* .. **112 C7** 45 35N 94 10W
Saulgau, *Germany* ... **25 G5** 48 1N 9 29 E
Saulieu, *France* ...... **19 E11** 47 17N 4 14 E
Sault, *France* .... **21 D9** 44 6N 5 24 E
Sault Ste. Marie, *Canada* **102 C3** 46 30N 84 20W
Sault Ste. Marie, *U.S.A.* **101 D11** 46 30N 84 21W
Saumlaki, *Indonesia* .. **63 F8** 7 55 S 131 20 E
Saumur, *France* **18 E6** 47 15N 0 5W
Saunders C., *N.Z.* .... **91 L3** 45 53 S 170 45 E
Saunders I., *Antarctica* **5 B1** 57 48 S 26 28W
Saunders Point, *Australia* .... **93 E4** 27 52 S 125 38 E
Sauri, *Nigeria* .... **83 C6** 11 42N 6 44 E
Saurimo, *Angola* ..... **84 F4** 9 40 S 20 12 E
Sausalito, *U.S.A.* **116 H4** 37 51N 122 29W
Sauveterre-de-Béarn, *France* **20 E3** 43 24N 0 57W
Sauzé-Vaussais, *France* **20 B4** 46 8N 0 8 E
Savá, *Honduras* **120 C2** 15 32N 86 15W
Sava, *Italy* .... **31 B10** 40 24N 17 33 E
Sava →, *Serbia, Yug.* . **42 F5** 44 50N 20 26 E
Savage, *U.S.A.* **112 B2** 47 27N 104 21W
Savage I. = Niue, *Cook Is.* .... **97 J11** 19 2 S 169 54W
Savage River, *Australia* **94 G4** 41 31 S 145 14 E
Savai'i, *Samoa* ...... **91 A12** 13 28 S 172 24W
Savalou, *Benin* ...... **83 D5** 7 57N 1 58 E
Savane, *Mozam.* ..... **87 F4** 19 37 S 35 8 E
Savanna, *U.S.A.* **112 D9** 42 5N 90 8W
Savanna-la-Mar, *Jamaica* **120 C4** 18 10N 78 10W
Savannah, *Ga., U.S.A.* . **109 J5** 32 5N 81 6W
Savannah, *Mo., U.S.A.* **112 F7** 39 56N 94 50W
Savannah, *Tenn., U.S.A.* **109 H1** 35 14N 88 15W
Savannah →, *U.S.A.* .. **109 J5** 32 2N 80 53W
Savannakhet, *Laos* ... **64 D5** 16 30N 104 49 E
Savant L., *Canada* **102 B1** 50 16N 90 44W
Savant Lake, *Canada* . **102 B1** 50 14N 90 40W
Savanur, *India* .... **66 M9** 14 59N 75 21 E
Săvărşin, *Romania* ... **42 D7** 46 1N 22 14 E
Savaştepe, *Turkey* .... **39 B9** 39 22N 27 42 E
Savé, *Benin* .... **83 D5** 8 2N 2 29 E
Save →, *France* ...... **20 E5** 43 47N 1 17 E
Save →, *Mozam.* ..... **89 C5** 21 16 S 34 0 E
Sāveh, *Iran* .... **71 C6** 35 2N 50 20 E
Savelugu, *Ghana* **83 D4** 9 38N 0 54W
Savenay, *France* **18 E5** 47 20N 1 55W
Săveni, *Romania* ..... **43 C11** 47 57N 26 52 E
Saverdun, *France* .... **20 E5** 43 14N 1 34 E
Saverne, *France* ..... **19 D14** 48 43N 7 20 E
Savigliano, *Italy* ..... **28 D4** 44 38N 7 40 E
Savigny-sur-Braye, *France* .... **18 E7** 47 53N 0 49 E
Sávio →, *Italy* .... **29 D9** 44 19N 12 20 E
Šavnik, *Montenegro, Yug.* .. **40 D3** 42 59N 19 10 E
Savo, *Finland* .... **8 E22** 62 45N 27 30 E
Savoie □, *France* ..... **21 C10** 45 26N 6 25 E
Savona, *Italy* .... **28 D5** 44 17N 8 30 E
Savona, *U.S.A.* **110 D7** 42 17N 77 13W
Savonlinna, *Finland* .. **46 B5** 61 52N 28 53 E
Savoy = Savoie □, *France* .... **21 C10** 45 26N 6 25 E
Şavşat, *Turkey* .... **73 B10** 41 15N 42 20 E
Sävsjö, *Sweden* ...... **11 G8** 57 20N 14 40 E
Savur, *Turkey* .... **70 B4** 37 34N 40 53 E
Sawahlunto, *Indonesia* **62 E2** 0 40 S 100 52 E
Sawai, *Indonesia* ..... **63 E7** 3 0 S 129 5 E
Sawai Madhopur, *India* **68 G7** 26 0N 76 25 E
Sawang Daen Din, *Thailand* .... **64 D4** 17 28N 103 28 E
Sawankhalok, *Thailand* **64 D2** 17 19N 99 50 E
Sawara, *Japan* .... **55 G10** 35 55N 140 30 E
Sawatch Range, *U.S.A.* **115 G10** 38 30N 106 30W
Sawel Mt., *U.K.* **15 B4** 54 50N 7 2W
Sawi, *Thailand* .... **65 G2** 10 14N 99 5 E
Sawla, *Ghana* **82 D4** 9 17N 2 25W
Sawmills, *Zimbabwe* .. **87 F2** 19 30 S 28 2 E
Sawtooth Range, *U.S.A.* **114 E6** 44 3N 114 58W
Sawu, *Indonesia* ..... **63 F6** 10 35 S 121 50 E
Sawu Sea, *Indonesia* .. **63 F6** 9 30 S 121 50 E
Saxby →, *Australia* ... **94 B3** 18 25 S 140 53 E
Saxmundham, *U.K.* ... **13 E9** 52 13N 1 30 E
Saxony = Sachsen □, *Germany* .... **24 E9** 50 55N 13 10 E
Saxony, Lower = Niedersachsen □, *Germany* .... **24 C4** 52 50N 9 0 E
Saxton, *U.S.A.* **110 F6** 40 13N 78 15W
Say, *Mali* **82 C4** 13 50N 4 57W
Say, *Niger* .... **83 C5** 13 8N 2 22 E
Saya, *Nigeria* .... **83 D5** 9 30N 3 18 E
Sayabec, *Canada* **103 C6** 48 35N 67 41W
Sayaboury, *Laos* ..... **64 C3** 19 15N 101 45 E
Sayán, *Peru* .... **124 F3** 11 8 S 77 12W
Sayan, Vostochnyy, *Russia* .... **51 D10** 54 0N 96 0 E
Sayan, Zapadnyy, *Russia* .... **51 D10** 52 30N 94 0 E
Saydā, *Lebanon* ..... **75 B4** 33 35N 35 25 E
Sayhandulaan = Oldziyt, *Mongolia* .. **56 B5** 44 40N 109 1 E
Sayhūt, *Yemen* ...... **74 D5** 15 12N 51 10 E
Saykhin, *Kazakstan* ... **49 F8** 48 50N 46 47 E
Saynshand, *Mongolia* . **60 B6** 44 55N 110 11 E
Sayre, *Okla., U.S.A.* .. **113 H5** 35 18N 99 38W
Sayre, *Pa., U.S.A.* **111 E8** 41 59N 76 32W
Sayreville, *U.S.A.* **111 F10** 40 28N 74 22W
Sayula, *Mexico* **118 D4** 19 50N 103 40W
Sayward, *Canada* **104 C3** 50 21N 125 55W
Sazanit, *Albania* ..... **40 F3** 40 30N 19 20 E
Sázava →, *Czech Rep.* **26 B7** 49 53N 14 24 E
Sazin, *Pakistan* ...... **69 B5** 35 35N 73 30 E
Sazlika →, *Bulgaria* .. **41 E9** 41 59N 25 50 E
Scaër, *France* **18 D3** 48 2N 3 42W
Scafell Pike, *U.K.* **12 C4** 54 27N 3 14W
Scalea, *Italy* .... **31 C8** 39 49N 15 47 E
Scalloway, *U.K.* **14 A7** 60 9N 1 17W
Scalpay, *U.K.* **14 D3** 57 18N 6 0W
Scandia, *Canada* **104 C6** 50 20N 112 0W
Scandiano, *Italy* ..... **28 D7** 44 36N 10 43 E
Scandicci, *Italy* ...... **29 E8** 43 45N 11 11 E
Scandinavia, *Europe* .. **6 C8** 64 0N 12 0 E
Scansano, *Italy* ...... **29 F8** 42 41N 11 20 E
Scapa Flow, *U.K.* **14 C5** 58 53N 3 3W
Scappoose, *U.S.A.* ... **116 E4** 45 45N 122 53W
Scarámia, Capo, *Italy* . **31 F7** 36 47N 14 29 E
Scarba, *U.K.* **14 E3** 56 11N 5 43W
Scarborough, *Trin. & Tob.* **121 D7** 11 11N 60 42W
Scarborough, *U.K.* ... **12 C7** 54 17N 0 24W
Scariff I., *Ireland* **15 E1** 51 44N 10 15W
Scarp, *U.K.* **14 C1** 58 1N 7 8W
Scebeli, Wabi →, *Somali Rep.* .... **74 G3** 2 0N 44 0 E
Šćedro, *Croatia* ..... **29 E13** 43 6N 16 43 E
Schaal See, *Germany* . **24 B6** 53 36N 10 55 E
Schaffhausen, *Switz.* .. **25 H4** 47 42N 8 39 E
Schagen, *Neths.* ..... **17 B4** 52 49N 4 48 E
Schaghticoke, *U.S.A.* . **111 D11** 42 54N 73 35W
Schärding, *Austria* ... **26 C6** 48 27N 13 27 E
Scharhörn, *Germany* .. **24 B4** 53 57N 8 24 E
Scheessel, *Germany* .. **24 B5** 53 10N 9 29 E
Schefferville, *Canada* . **103 B6** 54 48N 66 50W
Scheibbs, *Austria* .... **26 C8** 48 1N 15 9 E
Schelde →, *Belgium* .. **17 C4** 51 15N 4 16 E
Schell Creek Ra., *U.S.A.* **114 G6** 39 15N 114 30W
Schellsburg, *U.S.A.* .. **110 F6** 40 3N 78 39W
Schenectady, *U.S.A.* .. **111 D11** 42 49N 73 57W
Schenevus, *U.S.A.* ... **111 D10** 42 33N 74 50W
Scherfede, *Germany* .. **24 D5** 51 32N 9 2 E
Schesslitz, *Germany* .. **25 F7** 49 58N 11 1 E
Schiedam, *Neths.* .... **17 C4** 51 55N 4 25 E
Schiermonnikoog, *Neths.* .... **17 A6** 53 30N 6 15 E
Schiltigheim, *France* .. **19 D14** 48 35N 7 45 E
Schio, *Italy* .... **29 C8** 45 43N 11 21 E
Schladming, *Austria* .. **26 D6** 47 23N 13 41 E
Schlanders = Silandro, *Italy* .... **28 B7** 46 38N 10 46 E
Schlei →, *Germany* ... **24 A5** 54 40N 10 0 E
Schleiden, *Germany* .. **24 E2** 50 31N 6 28 E
Schleiz, *Germany* .... **24 E7** 50 35N 11 49 E
Schleswig, *Germany* .. **24 A5** 54 31N 9 34 E
Schleswig-Holstein □, *Germany* .... **24 A5** 54 30N 9 30 E
Schlüchtern, *Germany* **25 E5** 50 20N 9 32 E
Schmalkalden, *Germany* .... **24 E6** 50 44N 10 26 E
Schmölln, *Germany* .. **24 E8** 50 54N 12 19 E
Schneeberg, *Austria* .. **26 D8** 47 47N 15 48 E
Schneeberg, *Germany* **24 E8** 50 35N 12 38 E
Schneverdingen, *Germany* .... **24 B5** 53 7N 9 48 E
Schoharie, *U.S.A.* **111 D10** 42 40N 74 19W
Schoharie →, *U.S.A.* . **111 D10** 42 57N 74 18W
Scholls, *U.S.A.* **116 E4** 45 24N 122 56W
Schönberg, *Mecklenburg-Vorpommern, Germany* .... **24 B6** 53 52N 10 56 E
Schönberg, *Schleswig-Holstein, Germany* .... **24 A6** 54 23N 10 21 E
Schönebeck, *Germany* **24 C7** 52 2N 11 44 E
Schongau, *Germany* .. **25 H6** 47 47N 10 53 E
Schöningen, *Germany* **24 C6** 52 8N 10 56 E
Schopfheim, *Germany* **25 H3** 47 38N 7 50 E
Schorndorf, *Germany* . **25 G5** 48 47N 9 32 E
Schortens, *Germany* .. **24 B3** 53 31N 7 56 E
Schouten I., *Australia* . **94 G4** 42 20 S 148 20 E
Schouten Is. = Supiori, *Indonesia* .... **63 E9** 1 0 S 136 0 E
Schouwen, *Neths.* .... **17 C3** 51 43N 3 45 E
Schramberg, *Germany* **25 G4** 48 13N 8 22 E
Schrankogel, *Austria* .. **26 D4** 47 3N 11 7 E
Schreiber, *Canada* ... **102 C2** 48 45N 87 20W
Schrems, *Austria* ..... **26 C8** 48 47N 15 4 E
Schrobenhausen, *Germany* .... **25 G7** 48 34N 11 16 E
Schroffenstein, *Namibia* **88 D2** 27 11 S 18 42 E
Schroon Lake, *U.S.A.* . **111 C11** 43 50N 73 46W
Schruns, *Austria* ..... **26 D2** 47 5N 9 56 E
Schuler, *Canada* **105 C6** 50 20N 110 6W
Schumacher, *Canada* .. **102 C3** 48 30N 81 16W
Schurz, *U.S.A.* **114 G4** 38 57N 118 49W
Schuyler, *U.S.A.* **112 E6** 41 27N 97 4W
Schuylerville, *U.S.A.* . **111 C11** 43 6N 73 35W
Schuylkill →, *U.S.A.* . **111 G9** 39 53N 75 12W
Schuylkill Haven, *U.S.A.* **111 F8** 40 37N 76 11W
Schwabach, *Germany* . **25 F7** 49 19N 11 2 E
Schwaben □, *Germany* **25 G6** 48 15N 10 30 E
Schwäbisch Gmünd, *Germany* .... **25 G5** 48 48N 9 47 E
Schwäbisch Hall, *Germany* .... **25 F5** 49 6N 9 44 E
Schwäbische Alb, *Germany* .... **25 G5** 48 20N 9 30 E
Schwabmünchen, *Germany* .... **25 G6** 48 10N 10 46 E
Schwalmstadt, *Germany* **24 E5** 50 55N 9 10 E
Schwandorf, *Germany* **25 F8** 49 20N 12 7 E
Schwaner, Pegunungan, *Indonesia* .... **62 E4** 1 0 S 112 30 E
Schwanewede, *Germany* .... **24 B4** 53 14N 8 35 E
Schwarmstedt, *Germany* .... **24 C5** 52 39N 9 38 E
Schwarze Elster →, *Germany* .... **24 D8** 51 48N 12 50 E
Schwarzenberg, *Germany* .... **24 E8** 50 32N 12 47 E
Schwarzrand, *Namibia* **88 D2** 25 37 S 16 50 E
Schwarzwald, *Germany* **25 G4** 48 30N 8 20 E
Schwaz, *Austria* ..... **26 D4** 47 20N 11 44 E
Schwechat, *Austria* ... **27 C9** 48 8N 16 28 E
Schwedt, *Germany* ... **24 B10** 53 3N 14 16 E
Schweinfurt, *Germany* **25 E6** 50 3N 10 14 E
Schweizer-Reneke, *S. Africa* .... **88 D4** 27 11 S 25 18 E
Schwenningen = Villingen-Schwenningen, *Germany* .... **25 G4** 48 3N 8 26 E
Schwerin, *Germany* ... **24 B7** 53 36N 11 22 E
Schweriner See, *Germany* .... **24 B7** 53 43N 11 28 E
Schwetzingen, *Germany* **25 F4** 49 23N 8 35 E
Schwyz, *Switz.* ...... **25 H4** 47 2N 8 39 E
Schwyz □, *Switz.* .... **25 H4** 47 2N 8 39 E
Sciacca, *Italy* .... **30 E6** 37 31N 13 3 E
Scicli, *Italy* .... **31 F7** 36 47N 14 42 E
Scilla, *Italy* .... **31 D8** 38 15N 15 43 E
Scilly, Isles of, *U.K.* ... **13 H1** 49 56N 6 22W
Ścinawa, *Poland* ..... **45 G3** 51 25N 16 26 E
Scione, *Greece* ...... **40 G7** 39 57N 23 36 E
Scioto →, *U.S.A.* **108 F4** 38 44N 83 1W
Scituate, *U.S.A.* **111 D14** 42 12N 70 44W
Scobey, *U.S.A.* **112 A2** 48 47N 105 25W
Scone, *Australia* ..... **95 E5** 32 5 S 150 52 E
Scordia, *Italy* .... **31 E7** 37 18N 14 51 E
Scoresbysund = Illoqqortoormiit, *Greenland* **4 B6** 70 20N 23 0W
Scornicești, *Romania* . **43 F9** 44 34N 24 33 E
Scotia, *Calif., U.S.A.* . **114 F1** 40 29N 124 6W
Scotia, *N.Y., U.S.A.* .. **111 D11** 42 50N 73 58W
Scotia Sea, *Antarctica* . **5 B18** 56 5 S 56 0W
Scotland, *Canada* **110 C4** 43 1N 80 22W
Scotland □, *U.K.* **14 E5** 57 0N 4 0W
Scott, C., *Australia* ... **92 B4** 13 30 S 129 49 E
Scott City, *U.S.A.* **112 F4** 38 29N 100 54W
Scott Glacier, *Antarctica* .... **5 C8** 66 15 S 100 5 E
Scott I., *Antarctica* ... **5 C11** 67 0 S 179 0 E
Scott Is., *Canada* **104 C3** 50 48N 128 40W
Scott L., *Canada* **105 B7** 59 55N 106 18W
Scott Reef, *Australia* . **92 B3** 14 0 S 121 50 E
Scottburgh, *S. Africa* . **89 E5** 30 15 S 30 47 E
Scottdale, *U.S.A.* **110 F5** 40 6N 79 35W
Scottish Borders □, *U.K.* **14 F6** 55 35N 2 50W
Scottsbluff, *U.S.A.* ... **112 E3** 41 52N 103 40W
Scottsboro, *U.S.A.* ... **109 H3** 34 40N 86 2W
Scottsburg, *U.S.A.* ... **108 F3** 38 41N 85 47W
Scottsdale, *Australia* .. **94 G4** 41 9 S 147 31 E
Scottsdale, *U.S.A.* ... **115 K7** 33 29N 111 56W
Scottsville, *Ky., U.S.A.* **109 G2** 36 45N 86 11W
Scottsville, *N.Y., U.S.A.* **110 C7** 43 2N 77 47W
Scottville, *U.S.A.* **108 D2** 43 58N 86 17W
Scranton, *U.S.A.* **111 E9** 41 25N 75 40W
Scugog, L., *Canada* ... **110 B6** 44 10N 78 55W
Sculeni, *Moldova* .... **43 C12** 47 20N 27 37 E
Scunthorpe, *U.K.* **12 D7** 53 36N 0 39W
Scuol Schuls, *Switz.* .. **25 J6** 46 48N 10 17 E
Scutari = Üsküdar, *Turkey* .... **41 F13** 41 0N 29 5 E
Seabrook, L., *Australia* **93 F2** 30 55 S 119 40 E
Seaford, *U.K.* .... **13 G8** 50 47N 0 7 E
Seaford, *U.S.A.* **108 F8** 38 39N 75 37W
Seaforth, *Australia* ... **94 C4** 20 55 S 148 57 E
Seaforth, *Canada* **110 C3** 43 35N 81 25W
Seaforth, L., *U.K.* **14 D2** 57 52N 6 36W
Seagraves, *U.S.A.* ... **113 J3** 32 57N 102 34W
Seaham, *U.K.* **12 C6** 54 50N 1 20W
Seal →, *Canada* **105 B10** 59 4N 94 48W
Seal L., *Canada* **103 B7** 54 20N 61 30W
Sealy, *U.S.A.* **113 L6** 29 47N 96 9W
Searchlight, *U.S.A.* .. **117 K12** 35 28N 114 55W
Searcy, *U.S.A.* **113 H9** 35 15N 91 44W
Searles L., *U.S.A.* **117 K9** 35 44N 117 21W
Seascale, *U.K.* **12 C4** 54 24N 3 29W
Seaside, *Calif., U.S.A.* . **116 J5** 36 37N 121 50W
Seaside, *Oreg., U.S.A.* **116 E3** 46 0N 123 56W
Seaspray, *Australia* .. **95 F4** 38 25 S 147 15 E
Seattle, *U.S.A.* **116 C4** 47 36N 122 20W
Seaview Ra., *Australia* **94 B4** 18 40 S 145 45 E
Sebago L., *U.S.A.* **111 C14** 43 52N 70 34W
Sebago Lake, *U.S.A.* .. **111 C14** 43 51N 70 34W
Sebastián Vizcaíno, B., *Mexico* **118 B2** 28 0N 114 30W
Sebastopol = Sevastopol, *Ukraine* **47 K7** 44 35N 33 30 E
Sebastopol, *U.S.A.* ... **116 G4** 38 24N 122 49W
Sebba, *Burkina Faso* .. **83 C5** 13 35N 0 32 E
Sebderat, *Eritrea* .... **81 D4** 15 26N 36 42 E
Sébékoro, *Mali* **82 C3** 12 58N 9 0W
Seben, *Turkey* .... **72 B4** 40 24N 31 34 E

Sebeş, Romania 43 E8 45 58N 23 34 E
Sebeşului, Munţii, Romania 43 E8 45 36N 23 40 E
Sebewaing, U.S.A. 108 D4 43 44N 83 27W
Sebezh, Russia 46 D5 56 14N 28 22 E
Sebha = Sabhah, Libya 79 C8 27 9N 14 29 E
Sébi, Mali 82 B4 15 50N 4 12W
Şebinkarahisar, Turkey 73 B8 40 22N 38 28 E
Sebiş, Romania 42 D7 46 23N 22 13 E
Sebnitz, Germany 24 E10 50 58N 14 15 E
Sebring, Fla., U.S.A. 109 M5 27 30N 81 27W
Sebring, Ohio, U.S.A. 110 F3 40 55N 81 2W
Sebringville, Canada 110 C3 43 24N 81 4W
Sebta = Ceuta, N. Afr. 78 A4 35 52N 5 18W
Sebuku, Indonesia 62 E5 3 30 S 116 25 E
Sebuku, Teluk, Malaysia 62 D5 4 0N 118 10 E
Sečanj, Serbia, Yug. 42 E5 45 25N 20 47 E
Secchia →, Italy 28 C8 45 4N 11 0 E
Sechelt, Canada 104 D4 49 25N 123 42W
Sechura, Desierto de, Peru 124 E2 6 0 S 80 30W
Seclin, France 19 B10 50 33N 3 2 E
Secondigny, France 18 F6 46 37N 0 26W
Sečovce, Slovak Rep. 27 C14 48 42N 21 40 E
Secretary I., N.Z. 91 L1 45 15 S 166 56 E
Secunderabad, India 66 L11 17 28N 78 30 E
Security-Widefield, U.S.A. 112 F2 38 45N 104 45W
Sedalia, U.S.A. 112 F8 38 42N 93 14W
Sedan, France 19 C11 49 43N 4 57 E
Sedan, U.S.A. 113 G6 37 8N 96 11W
Sedano, Spain 34 C7 42 43N 3 49W
Seddon, N.Z. 91 J5 41 40 S 174 7 E
Seddonville, N.Z. 91 J4 41 33 S 172 1 E
Sedé Boqér, Israel 75 E3 30 52N 34 47 E
Sedeh, Fārs, Iran 71 D7 30 45N 52 11 E
Sedeh, Khorāsān, Iran 71 C8 33 20N 59 14 E
Séderon, France 21 D9 44 12N 5 32 E
Sederot, Israel 75 D3 31 32N 34 37 E
Sédhiou, Senegal 82 C1 12 44N 15 30W
Sedico, Italy 29 B9 46 8N 12 6 E
Sedlčany, Czech Rep. 26 B7 49 40N 14 25 E
Sedley, Canada 105 C8 50 10N 104 0W
Sedona, U.S.A. 115 J8 34 52N 111 46W
Sedova, Pik, Russia 50 B6 73 29N 54 58 E
Sedro Woolley, U.S.A. 116 B4 48 30N 122 14W
Šeduva, Lithuania 44 C10 55 45N 23 45 E
Sędziszów, Poland 45 H7 50 35N 20 4 E
Sędziszów Małapolski, Poland 45 H8 50 5N 21 45 E
Seebad Ahlbeck, Germany 24 B10 53 56N 14 10 E
Seefeld in Tirol, Austria 26 D4 47 19N 11 13 E
Seehausen, Germany 24 C7 52 54N 11 45 E
Seeheim, Namibia 88 D2 26 50 S 17 45 E
Seeheim-Jugenheim, Germany 25 F4 49 49N 8 40 E
Seeis, Namibia 88 C2 22 29 S 17 39 E
Seekoei →, S. Africa 88 E4 30 18 S 25 1 E
Seeley's Bay, Canada 111 B8 44 29N 76 14W
Seelow, Germany 24 C10 52 32N 14 23 E
Sées, France 18 D7 48 38N 0 10 E
Seesen, Germany 24 D6 51 54N 10 10 E
Seevetal, Germany 24 B6 53 26N 10 1 E
Sefadu, S. Leone 82 D2 8 35N 10 58W
Seferihisar, Turkey 39 C8 38 10N 26 50 E
Séfeto, Mali 82 C3 14 8N 9 49W
Sefwi Bekwai, Ghana 82 D4 6 10N 2 25W
Segamat, Malaysia 65 L4 2 30N 102 50 E
Şegarcea, Romania 43 F8 44 6N 23 43 E
Ségbana, Benin 83 C5 10 55N 3 42 E
Segbwema, S. Leone 82 D2 8 0N 11 0W
Seget, Indonesia 63 E8 1 24 S 130 58 E
Segonzac, France 20 C3 45 36N 0 14W
Segorbe, Spain 32 F4 39 50N 0 30W
Ségou, Mali 82 C3 13 30N 6 16W
Segovia = Coco →, Cent. Amer. 120 D3 15 0N 83 8W
Segovia, Spain 34 E6 40 57N 4 10W
Segovia □, Spain 34 E6 40 55N 4 10W
Segré, France 18 E6 47 40N 0 52W
Segre →, Spain 32 D5 41 40N 0 43 E
Séguéla, Ivory C. 82 D3 7 55N 6 40W
Séguénéga, Burkina Faso 83 C4 13 25N 1 58W
Seguin, U.S.A. 113 L6 29 34N 97 58W
Segundo →, Argentina 126 C3 30 53 S 62 44W
Segura →, Spain 33 G4 38 3N 0 44W
Segura, Sierra de, Spain 33 G2 38 5N 2 45W
Seh Konj, Kūh-e, Iran 71 D8 30 6N 57 30 E
Seh Qal'eh, Iran 71 C8 33 40N 58 24 E
Sehitwa, Botswana 88 C3 20 30 S 22 30 E
Sehore, India 68 H7 23 10N 77 5 E
Sehwan, Pakistan 68 F2 26 28N 67 53 E
Şeica Mare, Romania 43 D9 46 1N 24 7 E
Seil, U.K. 14 E3 56 18N 5 38W
Seiland, Norway 8 A20 70 25N 23 15 E
Seilhac, France 20 C5 45 22N 1 43 E
Seiling, U.S.A. 113 G5 36 9N 98 56W
Seille →, Moselle, France 19 C13 49 7N 6 11 E
Seille →, Saône-et-Loire, France 19 F11 46 31N 4 57 E
Sein, Î. de, France 18 D2 48 2N 4 52W
Seinäjoki, Finland 9 E20 62 40N 22 51 E
Seine →, France 18 C7 49 26N 0 26 E
Seine, B. de la, France 18 C6 49 40N 0 40W
Seine-et-Marne □, France 19 D10 48 45N 3 0 E
Seine-Maritime □, France 18 C7 49 40N 1 0 E
Seine-St-Denis □, France 19 D9 48 58N 2 24 E
Seini, Romania 43 C8 47 44N 23 21 E
Seirijai, Lithuania 44 D10 54 14N 23 49 E
Seistan = Sīstān, Asia 71 D9 30 50N 61 0 E
Seistan, Daryācheh-ye = Sīstān, Daryācheh-ye, Iran 66 D2 31 0N 61 0 E
Sejerø, Denmark 11 J5 55 54N 11 9 E
Sejerø Bugt, Denmark 11 J5 55 53N 11 15 E
Sejny, Poland 44 D10 54 6N 23 21 E
Seka, Ethiopia 81 F4 8 10N 36 52 E
Sekayu, Indonesia 62 E2 2 51 S 103 51 E
Seke, Tanzania 86 C3 3 20 S 33 31 E
Sekenke, Tanzania 86 C3 4 18 S 34 11 E
Seki, Turkey 39 E11 36 48N 29 33 E
Sekondi-Takoradi, Ghana 82 E4 4 58N 1 45W
Sekota, Ethiopia 81 E4 12 40N 39 2 E
Seksna, Russia 46 C10 59 13N 38 30 E
Sekuma, Botswana 88 C3 24 36 S 23 50 E
Selah, U.S.A. 114 C3 46 39N 120 32W
Selama, Malaysia 65 K3 5 12N 100 42 E
Selárgius, Italy 30 C2 39 16N 9 10 E
Selaru, Indonesia 63 F8 8 9 S 131 0 E
Selb, Germany 25 E8 50 10N 12 7 E
Selby, U.K. 12 D6 53 47N 1 5W
Selby, U.S.A. 112 C4 45 31N 100 2W
Selca, Croatia 29 E13 43 20N 16 50 E
Selçuk, Turkey 39 D9 37 56N 27 22 E
Selden, U.S.A. 112 F4 39 33N 100 34W
Sele →, Italy 31 B7 40 29N 14 56 E
Selebi-Pikwe, Botswana 89 C4 21 58 S 27 48 E
Selemdzha →, Russia 51 D13 51 42N 128 53 E
Selendi, Manisa, Turkey 39 C10 38 43N 28 50 E
Selendi, Manisa, Turkey 39 C9 38 46N 27 53 E
Selenga = Selenge Mörön →, Asia 60 A5 52 16N 106 16 E
Selenge Mörön →, Asia 60 A5 52 16N 106 16 E
Selenica = Selenicë, Albania 40 F3 40 33N 19 39 E
Selenicë, Albania 40 F3 40 33N 19 39 E
Selenter See, Germany 24 A6 54 18N 10 26 E
Sélestat, France 19 D14 48 16N 7 26 E
Seletan, Tanjung, Indonesia 62 E4 4 10 S 114 40 E
Selevac, Serbia, Yug. 40 B4 44 28N 20 52 E
Sélibabi, Mauritania 82 B2 15 10N 12 15W
Seliger, Ozero, Russia 46 D7 57 15N 33 0 E
Seligman, U.S.A. 115 J7 35 20N 112 53W
Şelim, Turkey 73 B10 40 30N 42 46 E
Selîma, El Wâhât el, Sudan 80 C2 21 22N 29 19 E
Selimiye, Turkey 39 D9 37 24N 27 40 E
Selinda Spillway →, Botswana 88 B3 18 35 S 23 10 E
Selinoús, Greece 38 D3 37 35N 21 37 E
Selinsgrove, U.S.A. 110 F8 40 48N 76 52W
Selizharovo, Russia 46 D7 56 51N 33 27 E
Selkirk, Canada 105 C9 50 10N 96 55W
Selkirk, U.K. 14 F6 55 33N 2 50W
Selkirk I., Canada 105 C9 53 20N 99 6W
Selkirk Mts., Canada 104 C5 51 15N 117 40W
Selliá, Greece 36 D6 35 12N 24 23 E
Sellières, France 19 F12 46 50N 5 32 E
Sells, U.S.A. 115 L8 31 55N 111 53W
Sellye, Hungary 42 E2 45 52N 17 51 E
Selma, Ala., U.S.A. 109 J2 32 25N 87 1W
Selma, Calif., U.S.A. 116 J7 36 34N 119 37W
Selma, N.C., U.S.A. 109 H6 35 32N 78 17W
Selmer, U.S.A. 109 H1 35 10N 88 36W
Selongey, France 19 E12 47 36N 5 11 E
Selowandoma Falls, Zimbabwe 87 G3 21 15 S 31 50 E
Selpele, Indonesia 63 E8 0 1 S 130 5 E
Selsey Bill, U.K. 13 G7 50 43N 0 47W
Seltso, Russia 46 F8 53 22N 34 4 E
Seltz, France 19 D15 48 54N 8 4 E
Selu, Indonesia 63 F8 7 32 S 130 55 E
Sélune →, France 18 D5 48 38N 1 22W
Selva = La Selva del Camp, Spain 32 D6 41 13N 1 8 E
Selva, Argentina 126 B3 29 50 S 62 0W
Selvas, Brazil 122 D4 6 30 S 67 0W
Selwyn L., Canada 105 B8 60 0N 104 30W
Selwyn Mts., Canada 100 B6 63 0N 130 0W
Selwyn Ra., Australia 94 C3 21 10 S 140 0 E
Seman →, Albania 40 F3 40 47N 19 30 E
Semani → = Seman →, Albania 40 F3 40 47N 19 30 E
Semarang, Indonesia 63 G14 7 0 S 110 26 E
Sembabule, Uganda 86 C3 0 4 S 31 25 E
Şemdinli, Turkey 73 D11 37 18N 44 35 E
Sémé, Senegal 82 B2 15 4N 13 41W
Semeih, Sudan 81 E3 12 43N 30 53 E
Semenov, Russia 48 B7 56 43N 44 30 E
Semenovka, Chernihiv, Ukraine 47 F7 52 8N 32 36 E
Semenovka, Kremenchuk, Ukraine 47 H7 49 37N 33 10 E
Semeru, Indonesia 63 H15 8 4 S 112 55 E
Semey, Kazakstan 50 D9 50 30N 80 10 E
Semikarakorskiy, Russia 49 G5 47 31N 40 48 E
Semiluki, Russia 47 G10 51 41N 39 2 E
Seminoe Reservoir, U.S.A. 114 F10 42 9N 106 55W
Seminole, Okla., U.S.A. 113 H6 35 14N 96 41W
Seminole, Tex., U.S.A. 113 J3 32 43N 102 39W
Seminole Draw →, U.S.A. 113 J3 32 27N 102 20W
Semipalatinsk = Semey, Kazakstan 50 D9 50 30N 80 10 E
Semirara Is., Phil. 61 F4 12 0N 121 20 E
Semitau, Indonesia 62 D4 0 29N 111 57 E
Semiyarka, Kazakstan 50 D8 50 55N 78 23 E
Semiyarskoye = Semiyarka, Kazakstan 50 D8 50 55N 78 23 E
Semmering P., Austria 26 D8 47 41N 15 45 E
Semnān, Iran 71 C7 35 40N 53 23 E
Semnān □, Iran 71 C7 36 0N 54 0 E
Semporna, Malaysia 63 D5 4 30N 118 33 E
Semuda, Indonesia 62 E4 2 51 S 112 58 E
Semur-en-Auxois, France 19 E11 47 30N 4 20 E
Sen →, Cambodia 62 B3 13 45N 105 12 E
Senā, Iran 71 D6 28 27N 51 36 E
Sena, Mozam. 87 F4 17 25 S 35 0 E
Sena Madureira, Brazil 124 E5 9 5 S 68 45W
Senador Pompeu, Brazil 125 E11 5 40 S 39 20W
Senaki, Georgia 49 J6 42 15N 42 7 E
Senanga, Zambia 85 H4 16 7 S 23 16 E
Senatobia, U.S.A. 113 H10 34 37N 89 58W
Sencelles, Spain 37 B9 39 39N 2 54 E
Sendafa, Ethiopia 81 F4 9 11N 39 3 E
Sendai, Kagoshima, Japan 55 J5 31 50N 130 20 E
Sendai, Miyagi, Japan 54 E10 38 15N 140 53 E
Sendai-Wan, Japan 54 E10 38 15N 141 0 E
Senden, Bayern, Germany 25 G6 48 19N 10 4 E
Senden, Nordrhein-Westfalen, Germany 24 D3 51 52N 7 22 E
Sendhwa, India 68 J6 21 41N 75 6 E
Sene →, Ghana 83 D4 7 30N 0 33W
Senec, Slovak Rep. 27 C10 48 12N 17 23 E
Seneca, U.S.A. 109 H4 34 41N 82 57W
Seneca Falls, U.S.A. 111 D8 42 55N 76 48W
Seneca L., U.S.A. 110 D8 42 40N 76 54W
Senecaville L., U.S.A. 110 G3 39 55N 81 25W
Senegal ■, W. Afr. 82 C2 14 30N 14 30W
Sénégal →, W. Afr. 82 B1 15 48N 16 32W
Senegambia, Africa 76 E2 12 45N 12 0W
Senekal, S. Africa 89 D4 28 20 S 27 36 E
Senftenberg, Germany 24 D10 51 32N 14 0 E
Senga Hill, Zambia 87 D3 9 19 S 31 11 E
Senge Khambab = Indus →, Pakistan 68 G2 24 20N 67 47 E
Sengiley, Russia 48 D9 53 58N 48 46 E
Sengua →, Zimbabwe 87 F2 17 7 S 28 5 E
Senhor-do-Bonfim, Brazil 125 F10 10 30 S 40 10W
Senica, Slovak Rep. 27 C10 48 41N 17 25 E
Senigállia, Italy 29 E10 43 43N 13 13 E
Senio →, Italy 29 D9 44 35N 12 15 E
Senirkent, Turkey 39 C12 38 6N 30 33 E
Senise, Italy 31 B9 40 9N 16 17 E
Senj, Croatia 29 D11 45 0N 14 58 E
Senja, Norway 8 B17 69 25N 17 30 E
Senkaku-Shotō, Japan 55 L1 25 45N 124 0 E
Senlis, France 19 C9 49 13N 2 35 E
Senmonorom, Cambodia 64 F6 12 27N 107 12 E
Sennâr, Sudan 81 E3 13 30N 33 35 E
Sennar □, Sudan 81 E3 13 0N 34 0 E
Senneterre, Canada 102 C4 48 25N 77 15W
Senno, Belarus 46 E5 54 45N 29 43 E
Sénnori, Italy 30 B1 40 47N 8 35 E
Seno, Laos 64 D5 16 35N 104 50 E
Senonches, France 18 D8 48 34N 1 2 E
Senorbì, Italy 30 C2 39 32N 9 8 E
Senožeče, Slovenia 29 C11 45 43N 14 3 E
Sens, France 19 D10 48 11N 3 15 E
Senta, Serbia, Yug. 42 E5 45 55N 20 3 E
Sentani, Indonesia 63 E10 2 36 S 140 37 E
Sentery, Dem. Rep. of the Congo 86 D2 5 17 S 25 42 E
Sentinel, U.S.A. 115 K7 32 52N 113 13W
Šentjur, Slovenia 29 B12 46 14N 15 24 E
Senya Beraku, Ghana 83 D4 5 28N 0 31W
Seo de Urgel = La Seu d'Urgell, Spain 32 C6 42 22N 1 23 E
Seohara, India 69 E8 29 15N 78 33 E
Seonath →, India 69 J10 21 44N 82 28 E
Seondha, India 69 F8 26 9N 78 48 E
Seoni, India 69 H8 22 5N 79 30 E
Seoni Malwa, India 68 H8 22 27N 77 28 E
Seoul = Sŏul, S. Korea 57 F14 37 31N 126 58 E
Sepīdān, Iran 71 D7 30 20N 52 5 E
Sepo-ri, N. Korea 57 E14 38 57N 127 25 E
Sępólno Krajeńskie, Poland 44 E4 53 26N 17 30 E
Sepone, Laos 64 D6 16 45N 106 13 E
Sępopol, Poland 44 D8 54 16N 21 2 E
Sept-Îles, Canada 103 B6 50 13N 66 22W
Septemvri, Bulgaria 41 D8 42 13N 24 6 E
Sepúlveda, Spain 34 D7 41 18N 3 45W
Sequeros, Spain 34 E4 40 31N 6 2W
Sequim, U.S.A. 116 B3 48 5N 123 6W
Sequoia National Park, U.S.A. 116 J8 36 30N 118 30W
Serafimovich, Russia 48 F6 49 36N 42 43 E
Seraing, Belgium 17 D5 50 35N 5 32 E
Seraja, Indonesia 65 L7 2 41N 108 35 E
Serakhis →, Cyprus 36 D11 35 13N 32 55 E
Seram, Indonesia 63 E7 3 10 S 129 0 E
Seram Sea, Indonesia 63 E7 2 30 S 128 30 E
Seranantsara, Madag. 89 B8 18 30 S 49 5 E
Serang, Indonesia 63 G12 6 8 S 106 10 E
Serasan, Indonesia 65 L7 2 29N 109 4 E
Seravezza, Italy 28 E7 43 59N 10 13 E
Şerbettar, Turkey 41 E10 41 27N 26 46 E
Serbia □, Yugoslavia 40 C5 43 30N 21 0 E
Şercaia, Romania 43 E10 45 49N 25 9 E
Serdo, Ethiopia 81 E5 11 56N 41 14 E
Serdobsk, Russia 48 D7 52 28N 44 10 E
Sered', Slovak Rep. 27 C10 48 17N 17 44 E
Seredka, Russia 46 C5 58 12N 28 10 E
Şereflikoçhisar, Turkey 72 C5 38 56N 33 32 E
Seregno, Italy 28 C6 45 39N 9 12 E
Seremban, Malaysia 65 L3 2 43N 101 53 E
Serengeti Plain, Tanzania 86 C4 2 40 S 35 0 E
Serenje, Zambia 87 E3 13 14 S 30 15 E
Sereth = Siret →, Romania 43 E12 45 24N 28 1 E
Sergach, Russia 48 C7 55 30N 45 30 E
Sergen, Turkey 41 E11 41 41N 27 42 E
Sergino, Russia 50 C7 62 25N 65 12 E
Sergipe □, Brazil 125 F11 10 30 S 37 30W
Sergiyev Posad, Russia 46 D10 56 20N 38 10 E
Seria, Brunei 62 D4 4 37N 114 23 E
Serian, Malaysia 62 D4 1 10N 110 31 E
Seriate, Italy 28 C6 45 41N 9 43 E
Seribu, Kepulauan, Indonesia 62 F3 5 36 S 106 33 E
Sérifontaine, France 19 C8 49 20N 1 45 E
Sérifos, Greece 38 D6 37 9N 24 30 E
Sérignan, France 20 E7 43 17N 3 17 E
Sérigny →, Canada 103 A6 56 47N 66 0W
Serik, Turkey 72 D4 36 55N 31 7 E
Seringapatam Reef, Australia 92 B3 13 38 S 122 5 E
Serinhisar, Turkey 39 D11 37 36N 29 18 E
Sermaize-les-Bains, France 19 D11 48 47N 4 54 E
Sermata, Indonesia 63 F7 8 15 S 128 50 E
Sérmide, Italy 29 D8 45 0N 11 18 E
Sernovodsk, Russia 48 D10 53 54N 51 16 E
Sernur, Russia 48 B9 56 52N 49 2 E
Serock, Poland 45 F8 52 31N 21 4 E
Serón, Spain 33 H2 37 20N 2 29W
Serós, Spain 32 D5 41 27N 0 24 E
Serov, Russia 50 D7 59 29N 60 35 E
Serowe, Botswana 88 C4 22 25 S 26 43 E
Serpa, Portugal 35 H3 37 57N 7 38W
Serpeddí, Punta, Italy 30 C2 39 22N 9 18 E
Serpentara, Italy 30 C2 39 8N 9 36 E
Serpentine Lakes, Australia 93 E4 28 30 S 129 10 E
Serpis →, Spain 33 G4 38 59N 0 9W
Serpukhov, Russia 46 E9 54 55N 37 28 E
Serra de Outes, Spain 34 C2 42 52N 8 55W
Serra do Navio, Brazil 125 C8 0 59N 52 3W
Serra San Bruno, Italy 31 D9 38 35N 16 20 E
Serradilla, Spain 34 F4 39 50N 6 9W
Sérrai, Greece 40 E7 41 5N 23 31 E
Sérrai □, Greece 40 E7 41 5N 23 37 E
Serramanna, Italy 30 C1 39 25N 8 55 E
Serrano, Italy 31 B11 40 11N 18 21 E
Serravalle Scrívia, Italy 28 D5 44 43N 8 51 E
Serre-Ponçon, L. de, France 21 D10 44 22N 6 20 E
Serres, France 21 D9 44 26N 5 43 E
Serrezuela, Argentina 126 C2 30 40 S 65 20W
Serrinha, Brazil 125 F11 11 39 S 39 0W
Sersale, Italy 31 C9 39 1N 16 43 E
Sertã, Portugal 34 F2 39 48N 8 6W
Sertanópolis, Brazil 127 A5 23 4 S 51 2W
Sêrtar, China 58 A3 32 20N 100 41 E
Serua, Indonesia 63 F8 6 18 S 130 1 E
Serui, Indonesia 63 E9 1 53 S 136 10 E
Serule, Botswana 88 C4 21 57 S 27 20 E
Sérvia, Greece 40 F6 40 11N 22 0 E
Serzedelo, Portugal 34 D2 41 24N 8 14W
Sese Is., Uganda 86 C3 0 20 S 32 20 E
Sesepe, Indonesia 63 E7 1 30 S 127 59 E
Sesfontein, Namibia 88 B1 19 7 S 13 39 E
Sesheke, Zambia 88 B3 17 29 S 24 13 E
Sésia →, Italy 28 C5 45 5N 8 37 E
Sesimbra, Portugal 35 G1 38 28N 9 6W
S'Espalmador, Spain 37 C7 38 47N 1 26 E
S'Espardell, Spain 37 C7 38 48N 1 29 E
Sessa Aurunca, Italy 30 A6 41 14N 13 56 E
S'Estanyol, Spain 37 B9 39 22N 2 54 E
Sestao, Spain 32 B2 43 18N 3 0W
Sesto Calende, Italy 28 C5 45 44N 8 37 E
Sesto San Giovanni, Italy 28 C6 45 32N 9 14 E
Sestri Levante, Italy 28 D6 44 16N 9 24 E
Sestriere, Italy 28 D3 44 57N 6 53 E
Sestroretsk, Russia 46 B6 60 5N 29 58 E
Sestrunj, Croatia 29 D11 44 10N 15 0 E
Sestu, Italy 30 C2 39 18N 9 5 E
Setana, Japan 54 C9 42 26N 139 51 E
Sète, France 20 E7 43 25N 3 42 E
Sete Lagôas, Brazil 125 G10 19 27 S 44 16W
Sétif, Algeria 78 A7 36 9N 5 26 E
Seto, Japan 55 G8 35 14N 137 6 E
Setonaikai, Japan 55 G6 34 20N 133 30 E
Settat, Morocco 78 B4 33 0N 7 40W
Séttimo Torinese, Italy 28 C4 45 9N 7 46 E
Setting L., Canada 105 C9 55 0N 98 38W
Settle, U.K. 12 C5 54 5N 2 16W
Settlement Pt., Bahamas 109 M6 26 40N 79 0W
Settlers, S. Africa 89 C4 25 2 S 28 30 E
Setúbal, Portugal 35 G2 38 30N 8 58W
Setúbal □, Portugal 35 G2 38 25N 8 35W
Setúbal, B. de, Portugal 35 G2 38 40N 8 56W
Seugne →, France 20 C3 45 42N 0 32W
Seul, Lac, Canada 100 C10 50 20N 92 30W
Seurre, France 19 F12 47 0N 5 8 E
Sevan, Armenia 49 K7 40 33N 44 56 E
Sevan, Ozero = Sevana Lich, Armenia 49 K7 40 30N 45 20 E
Sevana Lich, Armenia 49 K7 40 30N 45 20 E
Sevastopol, Ukraine 47 K7 44 35N 33 30 E
Seven Sisters, Canada 104 C3 54 56N 128 10W
Sever →, Spain 35 F3 39 40N 7 32W
Sévérac-le-Château, France 20 D7 44 20N 3 5 E
Severn →, Canada 102 A2 56 2N 87 36W
Severn →, U.K. 13 F5 51 35N 2 40W
Severn L., Canada 102 B1 53 54N 90 48W
Severnaya Zemlya, Russia 51 B10 79 0N 100 0 E
Severo-Kurilsk, Russia 51 D16 50 40N 156 8 E
Severo-Yeniseyskiy, Russia 51 C10 60 22N 93 1 E
Severočeský □, Czech Rep. 26 A7 50 30N 14 0 E
Severodonetsk = Syeverodonetsk, Ukraine 47 H10 48 58N 38 35 E
Severodvinsk, Russia 50 C4 64 27N 39 58 E
Severomoravský □, Czech Rep. 27 B10 49 38N 17 40 E
Sevier, U.S.A. 115 G7 38 39N 112 11W
Sevier →, U.S.A. 115 G7 39 4N 113 6W
Sevier Desert, U.S.A. 114 G7 39 40N 112 45W
Sevier L., U.S.A. 114 G7 38 54N 113 9W
Sevilla, Spain 35 H5 37 23N 5 58W
Sevilla □, Spain 35 H5 37 25N 5 30W
Seville = Sevilla, Spain 35 H5 37 23N 5 58W
Sevlievo, Bulgaria 41 C9 43 2N 25 6 E
Sevnica, Slovenia 29 B12 46 2N 15 19 E
Sèvre-Nantaise →, France 18 E5 47 12N 1 33W
Sèvre-Niortaise →, France 20 B3 46 28N 0 50W
Sevsk, Russia 47 F8 52 10N 34 30 E
Sewa →, S. Leone 82 D2 7 20N 12 10W
Sewani, India 68 E6 28 58N 75 39 E
Seward, Alaska, U.S.A. 100 B5 60 7N 149 27W
Seward, Nebr., U.S.A. 112 E6 40 55N 97 6W
Seward, Pa., U.S.A. 110 F5 40 25N 79 1W
Seward Peninsula, U.S.A. 100 B3 65 30N 166 0W
Sewell, Chile 126 C1 34 10 S 70 23W
Sewer, Indonesia 63 F8 5 53 S 134 40 E
Sewickley, U.S.A. 110 F4 40 32N 80 12W
Sexsmith, Canada 104 B5 55 21N 118 47W
Seychelles ■, Ind. Oc. 52 K9 5 0 S 56 0 E
Seyðisfjörður, Iceland 8 D6 65 16N 13 57W
Seydişehir, Turkey 72 D4 37 25N 31 51 E
Seydvān, Iran 70 B5 38 34N 45 2 E
Seyhan →, Turkey 70 B2 36 43N 34 53 E
Seyhan Barajı, Turkey 72 D6 37 2N 35 18 E
Seyitgazi, Turkey 39 B12 39 27N 30 43 E
Seyitömer, Turkey 39 B11 39 34N 29 52 E
Seym →, Ukraine 47 G7 51 27N 32 34 E
Seymen, Turkey 41 E11 41 6N 27 57 E
Seymour, Australia 95 F4 37 0 S 145 10 E
Seymour, S. Africa 89 E4 32 33 S 26 46 E
Seymour, Conn., U.S.A. 111 E11 41 24N 73 4W
Seymour, Ind., U.S.A. 108 F3 38 58N 85 53W
Seymour, Tex., U.S.A. 113 J5 33 35N 99 16W
Seyne, France 21 D10 44 21N 6 22 E
Seyssel, France 21 C9 45 57N 5 50 E
Sežana, Slovenia 29 C10 45 43N 13 41 E
Sézanne, France 19 D10 48 40N 3 40 E
Sezze, Italy 30 A6 41 30N 13 3 E
Sfântu Gheorghe, Covasna, Romania 43 E10 45 52N 25 48 E
Sfântu Gheorghe, Tulcea, Romania 43 F14 44 53N 29 36 E
Sfântu Gheorghe, Braţul →, Romania 43 F14 44 51N 29 36 E
Sfax, Tunisia 79 B8 34 49N 10 48 E
Sha Xi →, China 59 D12 26 35N 118 0 E
Sha Xian, China 59 D11 26 23N 117 45 E
Shaanxi □, China 56 G5 35 0N 109 0 E
Shaba = Katanga □, Dem. Rep. of the Congo 86 D2 8 0 S 25 0 E
Shabla, Bulgaria 41 C12 43 31N 28 32 E
Shabogamo L., Canada 103 B6 53 15N 66 30W
Shabunda, Dem. Rep. of the Congo 86 C2 2 40 S 27 16 E
Shache, China 60 C2 38 20N 77 10 E
Shackleton Ice Shelf, Antarctica 5 C8 66 0 S 100 0 E
Shackleton Inlet, Antarctica 5 E11 83 0 S 160 0 E
Shādegān, Iran 71 D6 30 40N 48 38 E
Shadi, China 59 D10 26 7N 114 47 E
Shadi, India 69 C7 33 24N 77 14 E
Shadrinsk, Russia 50 D7 56 5N 63 32 E
Shadyside, U.S.A. 110 G4 39 58N 80 45W
Shaffa, Nigeria 83 C7 10 30N 12 6 E
Shafter, U.S.A. 117 K7 35 30N 119 16W
Shaftesbury, U.K. 13 F5 51 0N 2 11W
Shagamu, Nigeria 83 D5 6 51N 3 39 E
Shagram, Pakistan 69 A5 36 24N 72 20 E
Shah Alizai, Pakistan 68 E2 29 25N 66 33 E
Shah Bunder, Pakistan 68 G2 24 13N 67 56 E
Shahabad, Punjab, India 68 D7 30 10N 76 55 E
Shahabad, Raj., India 68 G7 25 15N 77 11 E
Shahabad, Ut. P., India 69 F8 27 36N 79 56 E
Shahadpur, Pakistan 68 G3 25 55N 68 35 E
Shahba, Syria 75 C5 32 52N 36 38 E
Shahdād, Iran 71 D8 30 30N 57 40 E
Shahdād, Namakzār-e, Iran 71 D8 30 20N 58 20 E
Shahdadkot, Pakistan 68 F2 27 50N 67 55 E
Shahdol, India 69 H9 23 19N 81 26 E
Shahe, China 56 F8 37 0N 114 32 E
Shahganj, India 69 F10 26 3N 82 44 E
Shahgarh, India 66 F6 27 15N 69 50 E
Shahjahanpur, India 69 F8 27 54N 79 57 E
Shahpur, India 68 H7 22 12N 77 58 E
Shahpur, Baluchistan, Pakistan 68 E3 28 46N 68 27 E
Shahpur, Punjab, Pakistan 68 C5 32 17N 72 26 E
Shahpur Chakar, Pakistan 68 F3 26 9N 68 39 E
Shahpura, Mad. P., India 69 H9 23 10N 80 45 E
Shahpura, Raj., India 68 G6 25 38N 74 56 E
Shahr-e Bābak, Iran 71 D7 30 7N 55 9 E
Shahr-e Kord, Iran 71 C6 32 15N 50 55 E
Shāhrakht, Iran 71 C9 33 38N 60 16 E
Shahrig, Pakistan 68 D2 30 15N 67 40 E
Shahukou, China 56 D7 40 20N 112 18 E
Shaikhabad, Afghan. 68 B3 34 2N 68 45 E
Shajapur, India 68 H7 23 27N 76 21 E
Shakargarh, Pakistan 68 C6 32 17N 75 10 E
Shakawe, Botswana 88 B3 18 28 S 21 49 E
Shaker Heights, U.S.A. 110 E3 41 29N 81 32W
Shakhty, Russia 49 G5 47 40N 40 16 E
Shakhunya, Russia 48 B8 57 40N 46 46 E
Shaki, Nigeria 83 D5 8 41N 3 21 E
Shākir, Egypt 80 B3 27 30N 33 59 E
Shala, L., Ethiopia 81 F4 7 30N 38 30 E
Shali, Russia 49 J7 43 9N 45 55 E
Shallow Lake, Canada 110 B3 44 36N 81 5W
Shalqar, Kazakstan 50 E6 47 48N 59 39 E
Shalskiy, Russia 46 B8 61 48N 35 58 E
Shaluli Shan, China 58 B2 30 40N 99 55 E
Shām, Iran 71 E8 26 39N 57 21 E
Shām, Bādiyat ash, Asia 70 C3 32 0N 40 0 E
Shamâl Bahr el Ghazal □, Sudan 81 F2 8 0N 27 30 E
Shamâl Dârfûr □, Sudan 81 E2 15 0N 25 0 E
Shamâl Kordofân □, Sudan 81 E3 15 0N 30 0 E
Shamattawa, Canada 102 A1 55 51N 92 5W
Shamattawa →, Canada 102 A2 55 1N 85 23W
Shambe, Sudan 81 F3 7 8N 30 46 E
Shambu, Ethiopia 81 F4 9 32N 37 3 E
Shamīl, Iran 71 E8 27 30N 56 55 E
Shamkhor = Şämkir, Azerbaijan 49 K8 40 50N 46 0 E
Shāmkūh, Iran 71 C8 35 47N 57 50 E
Shamli, India 68 E7 29 32N 77 18 E
Shammar, Jabal, Si. Arabia 70 E4 27 40N 41 0 E
Shamo = Gobi, Asia 56 C6 44 0N 110 0 E
Shamo, L., Ethiopia 81 F4 5 45N 37 30 E
Shamokin, U.S.A. 111 F8 40 47N 76 34W
Shamrock, U.S.A. 113 H4 35 13N 100 15W
Shamva, Zimbabwe 87 F3 17 20 S 31 32 E
Shan □, Burma 67 J21 21 30N 98 30 E
Shan Xian, China 56 G9 34 50N 116 5 E
Shanan →, Ethiopia 81 F5 8 0N 40 20 E
Shanchengzhen, China 57 C13 42 20N 125 20 E
Shāndak, Iran 71 D9 28 28N 60 27 E
Shandon, U.S.A. 116 K6 35 39N 120 23W
Shandong □, China 57 G10 36 0N 118 0 E
Shandong Bandao, China 57 F11 37 0N 121 0 E
Shang Xian = Shangzhou, China 56 H5 33 50N 109 58 E
Shanga, Nigeria 78 F6 11 12N 4 33 E
Shangalowe, Dem. Rep. of the Congo 87 E2 10 50 S 26 30 E
Shangani, Zimbabwe 89 B4 19 41 S 29 20 E
Shangani →, Zimbabwe 87 F2 18 41 S 27 10 E
Shangbancheng, China 57 D10 40 50N 118 1 E
Shangcheng, China 59 B10 31 47N 115 26 E
Shangchuan Dao, China 59 G9 21 40N 112 50 E
Shangdu, China 56 D7 41 30N 113 30 E
Shanggao, China 59 C10 28 17N 114 55 E
Shanghai, China 59 B13 31 15N 121 26 E
Shanghai □, China 59 B13 31 0N 121 30 E
Shanghai Shi □, China 59 B13 31 0N 121 30 E
Shanghang, China 59 E11 25 2N 116 23 E
Shanghe, China 57 F9 37 20N 117 10 E
Shanglin, China 58 F7 23 27N 108 33 E
Shangnan, China 56 H6 33 32N 110 50 E
Shangqiu, China 56 G8 34 26N 115 36 E
Shangrao, China 59 C11 28 25N 117 59 E
Shangshui, China 60 C6 33 42N 114 35 E
Shangsi, China 58 F6 22 8N 107 58 E
Shangyou, China 59 E10 25 48N 114 32 E
Shangyu, China 59 B13 30 3N 120 52 E
Shangzhi, China 57 B14 45 22N 127 56 E
Shangzhou, China 56 H5 33 50N 109 58 E
Shanhetun, China 57 B14 44 33N 127 15 E
Shani, Nigeria 83 C7 10 14N 12 2 E
Shaniko, U.S.A. 114 D3 45 0N 120 45W
Shannon, N.Z. 91 J5 40 33 S 175 25 E
Shannon →, Ireland 15 D2 52 35N 9 30W
Shannon, Mouth of the, Ireland 15 D2 52 30N 9 55W
Shannon Airport, Ireland 15 D3 52 42N 8 57W
Shansi = Shanxi □, China 56 F7 37 0N 112 0 E

Shantar, Ostrov Bolshoy, Russia 51 D14 55 9N 137 40 E
Shantipur, India 69 H13 23 17N 88 25 E
Shantou, China 59 F11 23 18N 116 40 E
Shantung = Shandong □, China 57 G10 36 0N 118 0 E
Shanwei, China 59 F10 22 48N 115 22 E
Shanxi □, China 56 F7 37 0N 112 0 E
Shanyang, China 56 H5 33 31N 109 55 E
Shanyin, China 56 E7 39 25N 112 56 E
Shaodong, China 59 D8 27 15N 111 43 E
Shaoguan, China 59 E9 24 48N 113 35 E
Shaoshan, China 59 D9 27 55N 112 33 E
Shaowu, China 59 D11 27 22N 117 28 E
Shaoxing, China 59 C13 30 0N 120 35 E
Shaoyang, Hunan, China 59 D8 26 59N 111 20 E
Shaoyang, Hunan, China 59 D8 27 14N 111 25 E
Shap, U.K. 12 C5 54 32N 2 40W
Shapinsay, U.K. 14 B6 59 3N 2 51W
Shaqq el Gi'eifer →, Sudan 81 D2 15 16N 26 0 E
Shaqra', Si. Arabia 70 E5 25 15N 45 16 E
Shaqrā', Yemen 74 E4 13 22N 45 44 E
Sharafa, Sudan 81 E2 11 59N 27 7 E
Sharafkhāneh, Iran 70 B5 38 11N 45 29 E
Sharbot Lake, Canada 111 B8 44 46N 76 41W
Shari, Japan 54 C12 43 55N 144 40 E
Sharjah = Ash Shāriqah, U.A.E. 71 E7 25 23N 55 26 E
Shark B., Australia 93 E1 25 30 S 113 32 E
Sharm el Sheikh, Egypt 80 B3 27 53N 34 18 E
Sharon, Mass., U.S.A. 111 D13 42 7N 71 11W
Sharon, Pa., U.S.A. 110 E4 41 14N 80 31W
Sharon Springs, Kans., U.S.A. 112 F4 38 54N 101 45W
Sharon Springs, N.Y., U.S.A. 111 D10 42 48N 74 37W
Sharp Pt., Australia 94 A3 10 58 S 142 43 E
Sharpe L., Canada 102 B1 54 24N 93 40W
Sharpsville, U.S.A. 110 E4 41 15N 80 29W
Sharq el Istiwa'iya □, Sudan 81 G3 5 0N 33 0 E
Sharya, Russia 48 A7 58 22N 45 20 E
Shasha, Ethiopia 81 F4 6 29N 35 59 E
Shashemene, Ethiopia 81 F4 7 13N 38 33 E
Shashi, Botswana 89 C4 21 15 S 27 27 E
Shashi, China 59 B9 30 25N 112 14 E
Shashi →, Africa 87 G2 21 14 S 29 20 E
Shasta, Mt., U.S.A. 114 F2 41 25N 122 12W
Shasta L., U.S.A. 114 F2 40 43N 122 25W
Shatawi, Sudan 81 E3 14 39N 32 6 E
Shatsk, Russia 48 C5 54 5N 41 45 E
Shatt al Arab = Arab, Shatt al →, Asia 71 D6 30 0N 48 31 E
Shatura, Russia 46 E10 55 33N 39 21 E
Shaumyani = Shulaveri, Georgia 49 K7 41 22N 44 45 E
Shaunavon, Canada 105 D7 49 35N 108 25W
Shaver L., U.S.A. 116 H7 37 9N 119 18W
Shaw →, Australia 92 D2 20 21 S 119 17 E
Shaw I., Australia 94 C4 20 30 S 149 2 E
Shawanaga, Canada 110 A4 45 31N 80 17W
Shawangunk Mts., U.S.A. 111 E10 41 35N 74 30W
Shawano, U.S.A. 108 C1 44 47N 88 36W
Shawinigan, Canada 102 C5 46 35N 72 50W
Shawnee, U.S.A. 113 H6 35 20N 96 55W
Shay Gap, Australia 92 D3 20 30 S 120 10 E
Shayang, China 59 B9 30 42N 112 29 E
Shaybārā, Si. Arabia 70 E3 25 26N 36 47 E
Shayib el Banat, Gebel, Egypt 80 B3 26 59N 33 29 E
Shaykh, J. ash, Lebanon 75 B4 33 25N 35 50 E
Shaykh Miskīn, Syria 75 C5 32 49N 36 9 E
Shaykh Sa'īd, Iraq 70 C5 32 34N 46 17 E
Shchekino, Russia 46 E9 54 1N 37 34 E
Shcherbakov = Rybinsk, Russia 46 C10 58 5N 38 50 E
Shchigry, Russia 47 G9 51 55N 36 58 E
Shchors, Ukraine 47 G6 51 48N 31 56 E
Shchuchinsk, Kazakstan 50 D8 52 56N 70 12 E
She Xian, Anhui, China 59 C12 29 50N 118 25 E
She Xian, Hebei, China 56 F7 36 30N 113 40 E
Shebekino, Russia 47 G9 50 28N 36 54 E
Shebele = Scebeli, Wabi →, Somali Rep. 74 G3 2 0N 44 0 E
Sheboygan, U.S.A. 108 D2 43 46N 87 45W
Shebshi Mts., Nigeria 83 D7 8 30N 12 0 E
Shediac, Canada 103 C7 46 14N 64 32W
Sheelin, L., Ireland 15 C4 53 48N 7 20W
Sheep Haven, Ireland 15 A4 55 11N 7 52W
Sheerness, U.K. 13 F8 51 26N 0 47 E
Sheet Harbour, Canada 103 D7 44 56N 62 31W
Sheffield, U.K. 12 D6 53 23N 1 28W
Sheffield, Ala., U.S.A. 109 H2 34 46N 87 41W
Sheffield, Mass., U.S.A. 111 D11 42 5N 73 21W
Sheffield, Pa., U.S.A. 110 E5 41 42N 79 3W
Shehojele, Ethiopia 81 E4 10 40N 35 9 E
Shehong, China 58 B5 30 54N 105 18 E
Sheikh Idris, Sudan 81 E3 11 43N 33 30 E
Sheikhpura, India 69 G11 25 9N 85 53 E
Shek Hasan, Ethiopia 81 E4 12 5N 35 58 E
Shekhupura, Pakistan 68 D5 31 42N 73 58 E
Sheki = Şaki, Azerbaijan 49 K8 41 10N 47 5 E
Shelburne, N.S., Canada 103 D6 43 47N 65 20W
Shelburne, Ont., Canada 102 D3 44 4N 80 15W
Shelburne, U.S.A. 111 B11 44 23N 73 14W
Shelburne B., Australia 94 A3 11 50 S 142 50 E
Shelburne Falls, U.S.A. 111 D12 42 36N 72 45W
Shelby, Mich., U.S.A. 108 D2 43 37N 86 22W
Shelby, Miss., U.S.A. 113 J9 33 57N 90 46W
Shelby, Mont., U.S.A. 114 B8 48 30N 111 51W
Shelby, N.C., U.S.A. 109 H5 35 17N 81 32W
Shelby, Ohio, U.S.A. 110 F2 40 53N 82 40W
Shelbyville, Ill., U.S.A. 112 F10 39 24N 88 48W
Shelbyville, Ind., U.S.A. 108 F3 39 31N 85 47W
Shelbyville, Ky., U.S.A. 108 F3 38 13N 85 14W
Shelbyville, Tenn., U.S.A. 109 H2 35 29N 86 28W
Sheldon, U.S.A. 112 D7 43 11N 95 51W
Sheldrake, Canada 103 B7 50 20N 64 51W
Shelengo, Khawr →, Sudan 81 E2 10 33N 28 40 E
Shelikhova, Zaliv, Russia 51 D16 59 30N 157 0 E
Shell Lakes, Australia 93 E4 29 20 S 127 30 E
Shellbrook, Canada 105 C7 53 13N 106 24W
Shellharbour, Australia 95 E5 34 31 S 150 51 E
Shelon →, Russia 46 C6 58 13N 30 47 E
Shelter I, U.S.A. 111 E12 41 5N 72 21W
Shelton, Conn., U.S.A. 111 E11 41 19N 73 5W
Shelton, Wash., U.S.A. 116 C3 47 13N 123 6W
Shemakha = Şamaxi, Azerbaijan 49 K9 40 38N 48 37 E
Shëmri, Albania 40 D4 42 7N 20 13 E
Shemsi, Sudan 80 D2 19 2N 29 57 E
Shen Xian, China 56 F8 36 15N 115 40 E
Shenandoah, Iowa, U.S.A. 112 E7 40 46N 95 22W
Shenandoah, Pa., U.S.A. 111 F8 40 49N 76 12W
Shenandoah, Va., U.S.A. 108 F6 38 29N 78 37W
Shenandoah →, U.S.A. 108 F7 39 19N 77 44W
Shenandoah National Park, U.S.A. 108 F6 38 35N 78 22W
Shenchi, China 56 E7 39 8N 112 10 E
Shendam, Nigeria 83 D6 8 49N 9 30 E
Shendî, Sudan 81 D3 16 46N 33 22 E
Shenge, S. Leone 82 D2 7 54N 12 55W
Shengfang, China 56 E9 39 3N 116 42 E
Shëngjergj, Albania 40 E4 41 17N 20 10 E
Shëngjergji = Shëngjergj, Albania 40 E4 41 17N 20 10 E
Shëngjin, Albania 40 E3 41 50N 19 35 E
Shëngjini = Shëngjin, Albania 40 E3 41 50N 19 35 E
Shengzhou, China 59 C13 29 35N 120 50 E
Shenjingzi, China 57 B13 44 40N 124 30 E
Shenmëria = Shëmri, Albania 40 D4 42 7N 20 13 E
Shenmu, China 56 E6 38 50N 110 29 E
Shennongjia, China 59 B8 31 43N 110 44 E
Shenqiu, China 56 H8 33 25N 115 5 E
Shensi = Shaanxi □, China 56 G5 35 0N 109 0 E
Shenyang, China 57 D12 41 48N 123 27 E
Shenzhen, China 59 F10 22 27N 114 10 E
Sheo, India 68 F4 26 11N 71 15 E
Sheopur Kalan, India 66 G10 25 40N 76 40 E
Shepetivka, Ukraine 47 G4 50 10N 27 10 E
Shepetovka = Shepetivka, Ukraine 47 G4 50 10N 27 10 E
Shepparton, Australia 95 F4 36 23 S 145 26 E
Sheppey, I. of, U.K. 13 F8 51 25N 0 48 E
Shepton Mallet, U.K. 13 F5 51 11N 2 33W
Sheqi, China 56 H7 33 12N 112 57 E
Sher Qila, Pakistan 69 A6 36 7N 74 2 E
Sherab, Sudan 81 E1 10 44N 24 41 E
Sherborne, U.K. 13 G5 50 57N 2 31W
Sherbro →, S. Leone 82 D2 7 45N 12 55W
Sherbro I., S. Leone 82 D2 7 30N 12 40W
Sherbrooke, N.S., Canada 103 C7 45 8N 61 59W
Sherbrooke, Qué., Canada 103 C5 45 28N 71 57W
Sherburne, U.S.A. 111 D9 42 41N 75 30W
Shereik, Sudan 80 D3 18 44N 33 47 E
Shergarh, India 68 F5 26 20N 72 18 E
Sherghati, India 69 G11 24 34N 84 47 E
Sheridan, Ark., U.S.A. 113 H8 34 19N 92 24W
Sheridan, Wyo., U.S.A. 114 D10 44 48N 106 58W
Sheringham, U.K. 12 E9 52 56N 1 13 E
Sherkin I., Ireland 15 E2 51 28N 9 26W
Sherkot, India 69 E8 29 22N 78 35 E
Sherman, U.S.A. 113 J6 33 40N 96 35W
Sherpur, India 69 G10 25 34N 83 47 E
Sherridon, Canada 105 B8 55 8N 101 5W
Sherwood Forest, U.K. 12 D6 53 6N 1 7W
Sherwood Park, Canada 104 C6 53 31N 113 19W
Sheslay →, Canada 104 B2 58 48N 132 5W
Shethanei L., Canada 105 B9 58 48N 97 50W
Shetland □, U.K. 14 A7 60 30N 1 30W
Shetland Is., U.K. 14 A7 60 30N 1 30W
Shetrunji →, India 68 J5 21 19N 72 7 E
Shewa □, Ethiopia 81 F4 9 33N 38 10 E
Shewa Gimira, Ethiopia 81 F4 7 4N 35 51 E
Sheyenne →, U.S.A. 112 B6 47 2N 96 50W
Shibām, Yemen 74 D4 16 0N 48 36 E
Shibata, Japan 54 F9 37 57N 139 20 E
Shibecha, Japan 54 C12 43 17N 144 36 E
Shibetsu, Japan 54 B11 44 10N 142 23 E
Shibîn el Kôm, Egypt 80 H7 30 31N 30 55 E
Shibîn el Qanâtir, Egypt 80 H7 30 19N 31 19 E
Shibing, China 58 D7 27 2N 108 7 E
Shibogama L., Canada 102 B2 53 35N 88 15W
Shibushi, Japan 55 J5 31 25N 131 8 E
Shicheng, China 59 D11 26 22N 116 20 E
Shickshinny, U.S.A. 111 E8 41 9N 76 9W
Shickshock Mts. = Chic-Chocs, Mts., Canada 103 C6 48 55N 66 0W
Shidao, China 57 F12 36 50N 122 25 E
Shidian, China 58 E2 24 40N 99 5 E
Shido, Japan 55 G7 34 19N 134 10 E
Shiel, L., U.K. 14 E3 56 48N 5 34W
Shield, C., Australia 94 A2 13 20 S 136 20 E
Shifang, China 58 B5 31 8N 104 10 E
Shiga □, Japan 55 G8 35 20N 136 0 E
Shigu, China 58 D2 26 51N 99 56 E
Shiguaigou, China 56 D6 40 52N 110 15 E
Shihchiachuangi = Shijiazhuang, China 56 E8 38 2N 114 28 E
Shijak, Albania 40 E3 41 21N 19 33 E
Shijaku = Shijak, Albania 40 E3 41 21N 19 33 E
Shijiazhuang, China 56 E8 38 2N 114 28 E
Shijiu Hu, China 59 B12 31 25N 118 50 E
Shikarpur, India 68 E8 28 17N 78 7 E
Shikarpur, Pakistan 68 F3 27 57N 68 39 E
Shikohabad, India 69 F8 27 6N 78 36 E
Shikoku □, Japan 55 H6 33 30N 133 30 E
Shikoku-Sanchi, Japan 55 H6 33 30N 133 30 E
Shiliguri, India 67 F16 26 45N 88 25 E
Shilka, Russia 51 D12 52 0N 115 55 E
Shilka →, Russia 51 D13 53 20N 121 26 E
Shillelagh, Ireland 15 D5 52 45N 6 32W
Shillington, U.S.A. 111 F9 40 18N 75 58W
Shillong, India 67 G17 25 35N 91 53 E
Shilo, West Bank 75 C4 32 4N 35 18 E
Shilong, China 59 F9 23 5N 113 52 E
Shilou, China 56 F6 37 0N 110 48 E
Shilovo, Russia 48 C5 54 25N 40 57 E
Shimabara, Japan 55 H5 32 48N 130 20 E
Shimada, Japan 55 G9 34 49N 138 10 E
Shimane □, Japan 55 G6 35 0N 132 30 E
Shimanovsk, Russia 51 D13 52 15N 127 30 E
Shimen, China 59 C8 29 35N 111 20 E
Shimenjie, China 59 C11 29 29N 116 48 E
Shimian, China 58 C4 29 17N 102 23 E
Shimizu, Japan 55 G9 35 0N 138 30 E
Shimodate, Japan 55 F9 36 20N 139 55 E
Shimoga, India 66 N9 13 57N 75 32 E
Shimoni, Kenya 86 C4 4 38 S 39 20 E
Shimonoseki, Japan 55 H5 33 58N 130 55 E
Shimpuru Rapids, Angola 88 B2 17 45 S 19 55 E
Shimsk, Russia 46 C6 58 15N 30 50 E
Shin, L., U.K. 14 C4 58 5N 4 30W
Shinan, China 58 F7 22 44N 109 53 E
Shinano-Gawa →, Japan 55 F9 36 50N 138 30 E
Shināş, Oman 71 E8 24 46N 56 28 E
Shīndand, Afghan. 66 C3 33 12N 62 8 E
Shinglehouse, U.S.A. 110 E6 41 58N 78 12W
Shingū, Japan 55 H7 33 40N 135 55 E
Shingwidzi, S. Africa 89 C5 23 5 S 31 25 E
Shinjō, Japan 54 E10 38 46N 140 18 E
Shinkafe, Nigeria 83 C6 13 8N 6 29 E
Shinshār, Syria 75 A5 34 36N 36 43 E
Shinyanga, Tanzania 86 C3 3 45 S 33 27 E
Shinyanga □, Tanzania 86 C3 3 50 S 34 0 E
Shio-no-Misaki, Japan 55 H7 33 25N 135 45 E
Shiogama, Japan 54 E10 38 19N 141 1 E
Shiojiri, Japan 55 F8 36 6N 137 58 E
Shipchenski Prokhod, Bulgaria 41 D9 42 45N 25 15 E
Shiping, China 58 F4 23 45N 102 23 E
Shipki La, India 66 D11 31 45N 78 40 E
Shippegan, Canada 103 C7 47 45N 64 45W
Shippensburg, U.S.A. 110 F7 40 3N 77 31W
Shippenville, U.S.A. 110 E5 41 15N 79 28W
Shiprock, U.S.A. 115 H9 36 47N 108 41W
Shiqian, China 58 D7 27 32N 108 13 E
Shiqma, N. →, Israel 75 D3 31 37N 34 30 E
Shiquan, China 56 H5 33 5N 108 15 E
Shiquan He = Indus →, Pakistan 68 G2 24 20N 67 47 E
Shīr Kūh, Iran 71 D7 31 39N 54 3 E
Shiragami-Misaki, Japan 54 D10 41 24N 140 12 E
Shirakawa, Fukushima, Japan 55 F10 37 7N 140 13 E
Shirakawa, Gifu, Japan 55 F8 36 17N 136 56 E
Shirane-San, Gumma, Japan 55 F9 36 48N 139 22 E
Shirane-San, Yamanashi, Japan 55 G9 35 42N 138 9 E
Shiraoi, Japan 54 C10 42 33N 141 21 E
Shīrāz, Iran 71 D7 29 42N 52 30 E
Shirbīn, Egypt 80 H7 31 11N 31 32 E
Shire →, Africa 87 F4 17 42 S 35 19 E
Shiretoko-Misaki, Japan 54 B12 44 21N 145 20 E
Shirinab →, Pakistan 68 D2 30 15N 66 28 E
Shiriya-Zaki, Japan 54 D10 41 25N 141 30 E
Shiroishi, Japan 54 F10 38 0N 140 37 E
Shīrvān, Iran 71 B8 37 30N 57 50 E
Shirwa, L. = Chilwa, L., Malawi 87 F4 15 15 S 35 40 E
Shishi, China 59 E12 24 44N 118 37 E
Shishou, China 59 C9 29 38N 112 22 E
Shitai, China 59 B11 30 12N 117 25 E
Shivpuri, India 68 G7 25 26N 77 42 E
Shixian, China 57 C15 43 5N 129 50 E
Shixing, China 59 E10 24 46N 114 5 E
Shiyan, China 59 A8 32 35N 110 45 E
Shiyata, Egypt 80 B2 29 25N 25 7 E
Shizhu, China 58 C7 29 58N 108 7 E
Shizong, China 58 E5 24 50N 104 0 E
Shizuishan, China 56 E4 39 15N 106 50 E
Shizuoka, Japan 55 G9 34 57N 138 24 E
Shizuoka □, Japan 55 G9 35 15N 138 40 E
Shklov = Shklow, Belarus 46 E6 54 16N 30 15 E
Shklow, Belarus 46 E6 54 16N 30 15 E
Shkoder = Shkodër, Albania 40 D3 42 4N 19 32 E
Shkodër, Albania 40 D3 42 4N 19 32 E
Shkodra = Shkodër, Albania 40 D3 42 4N 19 32 E
Shkumbini →, Albania 40 E3 41 2N 19 31 E
Shmidta, Ostrov, Russia 51 A10 81 0N 91 0 E
Shō-Gawa →, Japan 55 F8 36 47N 137 4 E
Shoal L., Canada 105 D9 49 33N 95 1W
Shoal Lake, Canada 105 C8 50 30N 100 35W
Shōdo-Shima, Japan 55 G7 34 30N 134 15 E
Sholapur = Solapur, India 66 L9 17 43N 75 56 E
Shologontsy, Russia 51 C12 66 13N 114 0 E
Shōmrōn, West Bank 75 C4 32 15N 35 13 E
Shoreham by Sea, U.K. 13 G7 50 50N 0 16W
Shori →, Pakistan 68 E3 28 29N 69 44 E
Shorkot, India 68 D5 30 50N 72 0 E
Shorkot Road, Pakistan 68 D5 30 47N 72 15 E
Shoshone, Calif., U.S.A. 117 K10 35 58N 116 16W
Shoshone, Idaho, U.S.A. 114 E6 42 56N 114 25W
Shoshone L., U.S.A. 114 D8 44 22N 110 43W
Shoshone Mts., U.S.A. 114 G5 39 20N 117 25W
Shoshong, Botswana 88 C4 22 56 S 26 31 E
Shoshoni, U.S.A. 114 E9 43 14N 108 7W
Shostka, Ukraine 47 G7 51 57N 33 32 E
Shou Xian, China 59 A11 32 37N 116 42 E
Shouchang, China 59 C12 29 18N 119 12 E
Shouguang, China 57 F10 37 52N 118 45 E
Shouning, China 59 D12 27 27N 119 31 E
Shouyang, China 56 F7 37 54N 113 8 E
Show Low, U.S.A. 115 J9 34 15N 110 2W
Shpola, Ukraine 47 H6 49 1N 31 30 E
Shreveport, U.S.A. 113 J8 32 31N 93 45W
Shrewsbury, U.K. 13 E5 52 43N 2 45W
Shri Mohangarh, India 68 F4 27 17N 71 18 E
Shrirampur, India 69 H13 22 44N 88 21 E
Shropshire □, U.K. 13 E5 52 36N 2 45W
Shu, Kazakstan 50 E8 43 36N 73 42 E
Shu →, Kazakstan 52 E10 45 0N 67 44 E
Shuangbai, China 58 E3 24 42N 101 38 E
Shuangcheng, China 57 B14 45 20N 126 15 E
Shuangfeng, China 59 D9 27 29N 112 11 E
Shuanggou, China 57 G9 34 2N 117 30 E
Shuangjiang, China 58 F2 23 26N 99 58 E
Shuangliao, China 57 C12 43 29N 123 30 E
Shuangshanzi, China 57 D10 40 20N 119 8 E
Shuangyang, China 57 C13 43 28N 125 40 E
Shuangyashan, China 60 B8 46 28N 131 5 E
Shubra Khit, Egypt 80 H7 31 2N 30 42 E
Shucheng, China 59 B11 31 28N 116 57 E
Shugozero, Russia 46 C8 59 54N 34 10 E
Shuguri Falls, Tanzania 87 D4 8 33 S 37 22 E
Shuiji, China 59 D12 27 13N 118 20 E
Shuiye, China 56 F8 36 7N 114 8 E
Shujalpur, India 68 H7 23 18N 76 46 E
Shukpa Kunzang, India 69 B8 34 22N 78 22 E
Shulan, China 57 B14 44 28N 127 0 E
Shulaveri, Georgia 49 K7 41 22N 44 45 E
Shule, China 60 C2 39 25N 76 3 E
Shumagin Is., U.S.A. 100 C4 55 7N 160 30W
Shumen, Bulgaria 41 C10 43 18N 26 55 E
Shumerlya, Russia 48 C8 55 30N 46 25 E
Shumikha, Russia 50 D7 55 10N 63 15 E
Shunchang, China 59 D11 26 54N 117 48 E
Shunde, China 59 F9 22 42N 113 14 E
Shungay, Kazakstan 49 F8 48 30N 46 45 E
Shuo Xian = Shuozhou, China 56 E7 39 20N 112 33 E
Shuozhou, China 56 E7 39 20N 112 33 E
Shūr →, Fārs, Iran 71 D7 28 30N 55 0 E
Shūr →, Kermān, Iran 71 D8 30 52N 57 37 E
Shūr →, Yazd, Iran 71 D7 31 45N 55 15 E
Shūr Āb, Iran 71 C6 34 23N 51 11 E
Shūr Gaz, Iran 71 D8 29 10N 59 20 E
Shūrāb, Iran 71 C8 33 43N 56 29 E
Shūrjestān, Iran 71 D7 31 24N 52 25 E
Shurugwi, Zimbabwe 87 F3 19 40 S 30 0 E
Shūsf, Iran 71 D9 31 50N 60 5 E
Shūsh, Iran 73 F13 32 11N 48 15 E
Shūshtar, Iran 71 D6 32 0N 48 50 E
Shuswap L., Canada 104 C5 50 55N 119 3W
Shuyang, China 57 G10 34 10N 118 42 E
Shuya, Russia 48 B5 56 50N 41 28 E
Shūzū, Iran 71 D7 29 52N 54 30 E
Shwebo, Burma 67 H19 22 30N 95 45 E
Shwegu, Burma 67 G20 24 15N 96 26 E
Shweli →, Burma 67 H20 23 45N 96 45 E
Shymkent, Kazakstan 50 E7 42 18N 69 36 E
Shyok, India 69 B8 34 13N 78 12 E
Shyok →, Pakistan 69 B6 35 13N 75 53 E
Si Chon, Thailand 65 H2 9 0N 99 54 E
Si Kiang = Xi Jiang →, China 59 F9 22 5N 113 20 E
Si-ngan = Xi'an, China 56 G5 34 15N 109 0 E
Si Prachan, Thailand 64 E3 14 37N 100 9 E
Si Racha, Thailand 64 F3 13 10N 100 48 E
Si Xian, China 57 H9 33 30N 117 50 E
Siahaf →, Pakistan 68 E3 29 3N 68 57 E
Siahan Range, Pakistan 66 F4 27 30N 64 40 E
Siaksriindrapura, Indonesia 62 D2 0 51N 102 0 E
Sialkot, Pakistan 68 C6 32 32N 74 30 E
Siam = Thailand ■, Asia 64 E4 16 0N 102 0 E
Sian = Xi'an, China 56 G5 34 15N 109 0 E
Sianów, Poland 44 D3 54 13N 16 18 E
Siantan, Indonesia 62 D3 3 10N 106 15 E
Sīāreh, Iran 71 D9 28 5N 60 14 E
Siargao I., Phil. 61 G7 9 52N 126 3 E
Siari, Pakistan 69 B7 34 55N 76 40 E
Siasi, Phil. 63 C6 5 34N 120 50 E
Siasi I., Phil. 61 J4 5 33N 120 51 E
Siátista, Greece 40 F5 40 15N 21 33 E
Siau, Indonesia 63 D7 2 50N 125 25 E
Šiauliai, Lithuania 9 J20 55 56N 23 15 E
Šiauliai □, Lithuania 44 C10 55 56N 23 19 E
Siazan = Siyäzän, Azerbaijan 49 K9 41 3N 49 10 E
Sibâi, Gebel el, Egypt 70 E2 25 45N 34 10 E
Sibayi, L., S. Africa 89 D5 27 20 S 32 45 E
Sibdu, Sudan 81 E2 10 57N 26 17 E
Šibenik, Croatia 29 E12 43 48N 15 54 E
Siberia, Russia 4 D13 60 0N 100 0 E
Siberut, Indonesia 62 E1 1 30 S 99 0 E
Sibi, Pakistan 68 E2 29 30N 67 54 E
Sibil = Oksibil, Indonesia 63 E10 4 59 S 140 35 E
Sibiti, Congo 84 E2 3 38 S 13 19 E
Sibiu, Romania 43 E9 45 45N 24 9 E
Sibiu □, Romania 43 E9 45 50N 24 15 E
Sibley, U.S.A. 112 D7 43 24N 95 45W
Sibolga, Indonesia 62 D1 1 42N 98 45 E
Sibsagar, India 67 F19 27 0N 94 36 E
Sibu, Malaysia 62 D4 2 18N 111 49 E
Sibuco, Phil. 61 H5 7 20N 122 10 E
Sibuguey B., Phil. 61 H5 7 50N 122 45 E
Sibut, C.A.R. 84 C3 5 46N 19 10 E
Sibutu, Phil. 63 D5 4 45N 119 30 E
Sibutu Group, Phil. 61 J3 4 45N 119 20 E
Sibutu Passage, E. Indies 63 D5 4 50N 120 0 E
Sibuyan I., Phil. 61 E5 12 25N 122 40 E
Sibuyan Sea, Phil. 61 E5 12 30N 122 20 E
Sic, Romania 43 D8 46 56N 23 53 E
Sicamous, Canada 104 C5 50 49N 119 0W
Siccus →, Australia 95 E2 31 26 S 139 30 E
Sichuan □, China 58 B5 30 30N 103 0 E
Sichuan Pendi, China 58 B5 31 0N 105 0 E
Sicilia, Italy 31 E7 37 30N 14 30 E
Sicilia □, Italy 31 E7 37 45N 14 15 E
Sicily = Sicilia, Italy 31 E7 37 30N 14 30 E
Sicuani, Peru 124 F4 14 21 S 71 10W
Šid, Serbia, Yug. 42 E4 45 8N 19 14 E
Sidamo □, Ethiopia 81 G4 5 0N 37 50 E
Sidaouet, Niger 83 B6 18 34N 8 3 E
Sidári, Greece 36 A3 39 47N 19 41 E
Siddhapur, India 68 H5 23 56N 72 25 E
Siddipet, India 66 K11 18 5N 78 51 E
Sidensjö, Sweden 10 A12 63 18N 18 17 E
Sidéradougou, Burkina Faso 82 C4 10 42N 4 12W
Siderno, Italy 31 D9 38 16N 16 18 E
Sidhauli, India 69 F9 27 17N 80 50 E
Sídheros, Ákra, Greece 36 D8 35 19N 26 19 E
Sidhi, India 69 G9 24 25N 81 53 E
Sidhirókastron, Greece 40 E7 41 13N 23 24 E
Sîdi Abd el Rahmân, Egypt 80 A2 30 55N 29 44 E
Sîdi Barrâni, Egypt 80 A2 31 38N 25 58 E
Sidi-bel-Abbès, Algeria 78 A5 35 13N 0 39W
Sidi Haneish, Egypt 80 A2 31 10N 27 35 E
Sidi Omar, Egypt 80 A1 31 24N 24 57 E
Sidlaw Hills, U.K. 14 E5 56 32N 3 2W
Sidley, Mt., Antarctica 5 D14 77 2 S 126 2W
Sidmouth, U.K. 13 G4 50 40N 3 15W
Sidmouth, C., Australia 94 A3 13 25 S 143 36 E
Sidney, Canada 104 D4 48 39N 123 24W
Sidney, Mont., U.S.A. 112 B2 47 43N 104 9W
Sidney, N.Y., U.S.A. 111 D9 42 19N 75 24W
Sidney, Nebr., U.S.A. 112 E3 41 8N 102 59W
Sidney, Ohio, U.S.A. 108 E3 40 17N 84 9W
Sidney Lanier, L., U.S.A. 109 H4 34 10N 84 4W
Sido, Mali 82 C3 11 37N 7 29W
Sidoarjo, Indonesia 63 G15 7 27 S 112 43 E
Sidon = Saydā, Lebanon 75 B4 33 35N 35 25 E
Sidra, G. of = Surt, Khalīj, Libya 79 B9 31 40N 18 30 E
Siedlce, Poland 45 F9 52 10N 22 20 E
Sieg →, Germany 24 E3 50 46N 7 6 E
Siegburg, Germany 24 E3 50 47N 7 12 E
Siegen, Germany 24 E4 50 51N 8 0 E
Siem Pang, Cambodia 64 E6 14 7N 106 23 E
Siem Reap = Siemreab, Cambodia 64 F4 13 20N 103 52 E
Siemiatycze, Poland 45 F9 52 27N 22 53 E
Siemreab, Cambodia 64 F4 13 20N 103 52 E
Siena, Italy 29 E8 43 19N 11 21 E
Sieniawa, Poland 45 H9 50 11N 22 38 E
Sieradz, Poland 45 G5 51 37N 18 41 E
Sieraków, Poland 45 F3 52 39N 16 2 E
Sierck-les-Bains, France 19 C13 49 26N 6 20 E
Sierning, Austria 26 C7 48 2N 14 18 E
Sierpc, Poland 45 F6 52 55N 19 43 E
Sierra Blanca, U.S.A. 115 L11 31 11N 105 22W
Sierra Blanca Peak, U.S.A. 115 K11 33 23N 105 49W
Sierra City, U.S.A. 116 F6 39 34N 120 38W
Sierra Colorada, Argentina 128 E3 40 35 S 67 50W
Sierra de Yeguas, Spain 35 H6 37 7N 4 52W
Sierra Gorda, Chile 126 A2 22 50 S 69 15W
Sierra Leone ■, W. Afr. 82 D2 9 0N 12 0W
Sierra Madre, Mexico 119 D6 16 0N 93 0W
Sierra Mojada, Mexico 118 B4 27 19N 103 42W
Sierra Nevada, U.S.A. 116 H8 37 30N 119 0W
Sierra Vista, U.S.A. 115 L8 31 33N 110 18W
Sierraville, U.S.A. 116 F6 39 36N 120 22W
Sierre, Switz. 25 J3 46 17N 7 31 E
Sifani, Ethiopia 81 E5 12 18N 40 19 E
Sifié, Ivory C. 82 D3 8 0N 7 5W
Sífnos, Greece 38 E6 37 0N 24 45 E
Sifton, Canada 105 C8 51 21N 100 8W
Sifton Pass, Canada 104 B3 57 52N 126 15W
Sigean, France 20 E6 43 2N 2 58 E
Sighetu-Marmaţiei, Romania 43 C8 47 57N 23 52 E
Sighişoara, Romania 43 D9 46 12N 24 50 E
Sigli, Indonesia 62 C1 5 25N 96 0 E
Siglufjörður, Iceland 8 C4 66 12N 18 55W
Sigmaringen, Germany 25 G5 48 5N 9 12 E
Signa, Italy 28 E8 43 45N 11 10 E
Signakhi = Tsnori, Georgia 49 K7 41 40N 45 57 E
Signal, U.S.A. 117 L13 34 30N 113 38W
Signal Pk., U.S.A. 117 M12 33 20N 114 2W
Signy-l'Abbaye, France 19 C11 49 40N 4 25 E
Sigsig, Ecuador 124 D3 3 0 S 78 50W
Sigüenza, Spain 32 D2 41 3N 2 40W
Siguiri, Guinea 82 C3 11 31N 9 10W
Sigulda, Latvia 9 H21 57 10N 24 55 E
Sihanoukville = Kampong Saom, Cambodia 65 G4 10 38N 103 30 E
Sihora, India 69 H9 23 29N 80 6 E
Sihui, China 59 F9 23 20N 112 40 E
Siikajoki →, Finland 8 D21 64 50N 24 43 E
Siilinjärvi, Finland 8 E22 63 4N 27 39 E
Siirt, Turkey 73 D9 37 57N 41 55 E
Sijarira Ra., Zimbabwe 87 F2 17 36 S 27 45 E
Sika, India 68 H3 22 26N 69 47 E
Sikao, Thailand 65 J2 7 34N 99 21 E
Sikar, India 68 F6 27 33N 75 10 E
Sikasso, Mali 82 C3 11 18N 5 35W
Sikeston, U.S.A. 113 G10 36 53N 89 35W
Sikhote Alin, Khrebet, Russia 51 E14 45 0N 136 0 E
Sikhote Alin Ra. = Sikhote Alin, Khrebet, Russia 51 E14 45 0N 136 0 E
Sikiá, Greece 40 F7 40 2N 23 56 E
Síkinos, Greece 39 E7 36 40N 25 8 E
Sikkani Chief →, Canada 104 B4 57 47N 122 15W
Sikkim □, India 67 F16 27 50N 88 30 E
Siklós, Hungary 42 E3 45 50N 18 19 E
Sikotu-Ko, Japan 54 C10 42 45N 141 25 E
Sil →, Spain 34 C3 42 27N 7 43W
Silacayoapan, Mexico 119 D5 17 30N 98 9W
Šilalė, Lithuania 44 C9 55 28N 22 12 E
Silandro, Italy 28 B7 46 38N 10 46 E
Silawad, India 68 J6 21 54N 74 54 E
Silay, Phil. 61 F5 10 47N 122 58 E
Silba, Croatia 29 D11 44 24N 14 41 E
Silchar, India 67 G18 24 49N 92 48 E
Şile, Turkey 41 E13 41 10N 29 37 E
Siler City, U.S.A. 109 H6 35 44N 79 28W
Silgarhi Doti, Nepal 69 E9 29 15N 81 0 E
Silghat, India 67 F18 26 35N 93 0 E
Sili, Burkina Faso 82 C4 11 37N 2 30W
Silifke, Turkey 70 B2 36 22N 33 58 E
Siliguri = Shiliguri, India 67 F16 26 45N 88 25 E
Siling Co, China 60 C3 31 50N 89 20 E
Silistea Nouă, Romania 43 F10 44 23N 25 1 E
Silistra, Bulgaria 41 B11 44 6N 27 19 E
Silivri, Turkey 41 E12 41 4N 28 14 E
Siljan, Sweden 10 D8 60 55N 14 45 E
Siljansnäs, Sweden 10 D8 60 47N 14 52 E
Silkeborg, Denmark 11 H3 56 10N 9 32 E
Silkwood, Australia 94 B4 17 45 S 146 2 E
Silla, Spain 33 F4 39 22N 0 25W
Sillajhuay, Cordillera, Chile 124 G5 19 46 S 68 40W
Sillamäe, Estonia 9 G22 59 24N 27 45 E
Sillé-le-Guillaume, France 18 D6 48 10N 0 8W
Silleda, Spain 34 C2 42 42N 8 14W
Silloth, U.K. 12 C4 54 52N 3 23W
Sílo, Greece 41 E9 41 10N 25 53 E
Siloam Springs, U.S.A. 113 G7 36 11N 94 32W
Silopi, Turkey 73 D10 37 15N 42 27 E
Silsbee, U.S.A. 113 K7 30 21N 94 11W
Siluko, Nigeria 83 D6 6 35N 5 10 E
Šilutė, Lithuania 9 J19 55 21N 21 33 E
Silva Porto = Kuito, Angola 85 G3 12 22 S 16 55 E
Silvan, Turkey 73 C9 38 7N 41 2 E
Silvani, India 69 H8 23 18N 78 25 E
Silver City, U.S.A. 115 K9 32 46N 108 17W
Silver Cr. →, U.S.A. 114 E4 43 16N 119 13W
Silver Creek, U.S.A. 110 D5 42 33N 79 10W
Silver L., U.S.A. 116 G6 38 39N 120 6W
Silver Lake, Calif., U.S.A. 117 K10 35 21N 116 7W
Silver Lake, Oreg., U.S.A. 114 E3 43 8N 121 3W
Silverdalen, Sweden 11 G9 57 32N 15 45 E
Silverton, Colo., U.S.A. 115 H10 37 49N 107 40W
Silverton, Tex., U.S.A. 113 H4 34 28N 101 19W
Silves, Portugal 35 H2 37 11N 8 26W
Silvi Marina, Italy 29 F11 42 34N 14 5 E
Silvies →, U.S.A. 114 E4 43 34N 119 2W
Silvrettahorn, Switz. 28 B7 46 50N 10 6 E
Silwa Bahari, Egypt 80 C3 24 45N 32 55 E
Silz, Austria 26 D3 47 16N 10 56 E
Simaltala, India 69 G12 24 43N 86 33 E

Simanggang = Bandar Sri Aman, Malaysia 62 D4 1 15N 111 32 E
Simao, China 58 F3 22 47N 101 5 E
Simard, L., Canada 102 C4 47 40N 78 40W
Şimareh →, Iran 73 F12 33 9N 47 41 E
Simav, Turkey 39 B10 39 4N 28 58 E
Simav →, Turkey 41 F12 40 23N 28 31 E
Simav Dağları, Turkey 39 B10 39 10N 28 30 E
Simba, Tanzania 86 C4 2 10 S 37 36 E
Simbach, Germany 25 G9 48 16N 13 2 E
Simbirsk, Russia 48 C9 54 20N 48 25 E
Simbo, Tanzania 86 C2 4 51 S 29 41 E
Simcoe, Canada 102 D3 42 50N 80 20W
Simcoe, L., Canada 102 D4 44 25N 79 20W
Simdega, India 69 H11 22 37N 84 31 E
Simeonovgrad, Bulgaria 41 D9 42 1N 25 50 E
Simeria, Romania 42 E8 45 51N 23 1 E
Simeto →, Italy 31 E8 37 24N 15 6 E
Simeulue, Indonesia 62 D1 2 45N 95 45 E
Simferopol, Ukraine 47 K8 44 55N 34 3 E
Sími, Greece 39 E9 36 35N 27 50 E
Simi Valley, U.S.A. 117 L8 34 16N 118 47W
Simikot, Nepal 69 E9 30 0N 81 50 E
Simitli, Bulgaria 40 E7 41 52N 23 7 E
Simla, India 68 D7 31 2N 77 9 E
Simlångsdalen, Sweden 11 H7 56 43N 13 6 E
Şimleu-Silvaniei, Romania 42 C7 47 17N 22 50 E
Simmern, Germany 25 F3 49 58N 7 30 E
Simmie, Canada 105 D7 49 56N 108 6W
Simmler, U.S.A. 117 K7 35 21N 119 59W
Simnas, Lithuania 44 D10 54 24N 23 39 E
Simojoki →, Finland 8 D21 65 35N 25 1 E
Simojovel, Mexico 119 D6 17 12N 92 38W
Simonette →, Canada 104 B5 55 9N 118 15W
Simonstown, S. Africa 88 E2 34 14 S 18 26 E
Simontornya, Hungary 42 D3 46 45N 18 33 E
Simplonpass, Switz. 25 J4 46 15N 8 3 E
Simplontunnel, Switz. 25 J4 46 15N 8 7 E
Simpson Desert, Australia 94 D2 25 0 S 137 0 E
Simpson Pen., Canada 101 B11 68 34N 88 45W
Simpungdong, N. Korea 57 D15 40 56N 129 29 E
Simrishamn, Sweden 11 J8 55 33N 14 22 E
Simsbury, U.S.A. 111 E12 41 53N 72 48W
Simushir, Ostrov, Russia 51 E16 46 50N 152 30 E
Sin Cowe I., S. China Sea 62 C4 9 53N 114 19 E
Sinabang, Indonesia 62 D1 2 30N 96 24 E
Sinadogo, Somali Rep. 74 F4 5 50N 47 0 E
Sinai = Es Sînâ', Egypt 75 F3 29 0N 34 0 E
Sinai, Mt. = Mûsa, Gebel, Egypt 70 D2 28 33N 33 59 E
Sinai Peninsula, Egypt 75 F3 29 30N 34 0 E
Sinaia, Romania 43 E10 45 21N 25 38 E
Sinaloa □, Mexico 118 C3 25 0N 107 30W
Sinaloa de Leyva, Mexico 118 B3 25 50N 108 20W
Sinalunga, Italy 29 E8 43 12N 11 44 E
Sinan, China 58 D7 27 56N 108 13 E
Sînandrei, Romania 42 E6 45 52N 21 13 E
Sinarádhes, Greece 36 A3 39 34N 19 51 E
Sincan, Turkey 72 B5 39 58N 32 36 E
Sincanlı, Turkey 39 C12 38 45N 30 15 E
Sincelejo, Colombia 124 B3 9 18N 75 24W
Sinch'ang, N. Korea 57 D15 40 7N 128 28 E
Sinchang-ni, N. Korea 57 E14 39 24N 126 8 E
Sinclair, U.S.A. 114 F10 41 47N 107 7W
Sinclair Mills, Canada 104 C4 54 5N 121 40W
Sinclair's B., U.K. 14 C5 58 31N 3 5W
Sinclairville, U.S.A. 110 D5 42 16N 79 16W
Sincorá, Serra do, Brazil 125 F10 13 30 S 41 0W
Sind, Pakistan 68 G3 26 0N 68 30 E
Sind □, Pakistan 68 G3 26 0N 69 0 E
Sind →, Jammu & Kashmir, India 69 B6 34 18N 74 45 E
Sind →, Mad. P., India 69 F8 26 26N 79 13 E
Sind Sagar Doab, Pakistan 68 D4 32 0N 71 30 E
Sindal, Denmark 11 G4 57 28N 10 10 E
Sindangan, Phil. 61 G5 8 10N 123 5 E
Sindangbarang, Indonesia 63 G12 7 27 S 107 1 E
Sinde, Zambia 87 F2 17 28 S 25 51 E
Sindelfingen, Germany 25 G4 48 42N 9 0 E
Sındırgı, Turkey 39 B10 39 13N 28 10 E
Sindou, Burkina Faso 82 C3 10 35N 5 4W
Sindri, India 69 H12 23 45N 86 42 E
Sine →, Senegal 82 C1 14 10N 16 28W
Sinegorskiy, Russia 49 G5 47 55N 40 52 E
Sinekli, Turkey 41 E12 41 14N 28 12 E
Sinelnikovo = Synelnykove, Ukraine 47 H8 48 25N 35 30 E
Sinendé, Benin 83 C5 10 20N 2 22 E
Sines, Portugal 35 H2 37 56N 8 51W
Sines, C. de, Portugal 35 H2 37 58N 8 53W
Sineu, Spain 37 B10 39 38N 3 1 E
Sinfra, Ivory C. 82 D3 6 35N 5 56W
Sing Buri, Thailand 64 E3 14 53N 100 25 E
Singa, Sudan 81 E3 13 10N 33 57 E
Singapore ■, Asia 65 M4 1 17N 103 51 E
Singapore, Straits of, Asia 65 M5 1 15N 104 0 E
Singaraja, Indonesia 62 F5 8 6 S 115 10 E
Singen, Germany 25 H4 47 45N 8 50 E
Singida, Tanzania 86 C3 4 49 S 34 48 E
Singida □, Tanzania 86 D3 6 0 S 34 30 E
Singitikós Kólpos, Greece 40 F7 40 6N 24 0 E
Singkaling Hkamti, Burma 67 G19 26 0N 95 39 E
Singkang, Indonesia 63 E6 4 8 S 120 1 E
Singkawang, Indonesia 62 D3 1 0N 108 57 E
Singkep, Indonesia 62 E2 0 30 S 104 25 E
Singleton, Australia 95 E5 32 33 S 151 0 E
Singleton, Mt., N. Terr., Australia 92 D5 22 0 S 130 46 E
Singleton, Mt., W. Austral., Australia 93 E2 29 27 S 117 15 E
Singö, Sweden 10 D12 60 12N 18 45 E
Singoli, India 68 G6 25 0N 75 22 E
Singora = Songkhla, Thailand 65 J3 7 13N 100 37 E
Singosan, N. Korea 57 E14 38 52N 127 25 E
Sinhung, N. Korea 57 D14 40 11N 127 34 E
Sînî □, Egypt 75 F3 30 0N 34 0 E
Siniátsikon, Óros, Greece 40 F5 40 25N 21 35 E
Siniscóla, Italy 30 B2 40 34N 9 41 E
Sinj, Croatia 29 E13 43 42N 16 39 E
Sinjai, Indonesia 63 F6 5 7 S 120 20 E
Sinjajevina, Montenegro, Yug. 40 D3 42 57N 19 22 E
Sinjār, Iraq 70 B4 36 19N 41 52 E
Sinkat, Sudan 80 D4 18 55N 36 49 E
Sinkiang Uighur = Xinjiang Uygur Zizhiqu □, China 60 B3 42 0N 86 0 E
Sinmak, N. Korea 57 E14 38 25N 126 14 E
Sinnai, Italy 30 C2 39 18N 9 13 E
Sinnamary, Fr. Guiana 125 B8 5 25N 53 0W
Sinni →, Italy 31 B9 40 8N 16 41 E
Sinnuris, Egypt 80 J7 29 26N 30 31 E
Sinoie, Lacul, Romania 43 F13 44 35N 28 50 E
Sinop, Turkey 72 A6 42 1N 35 11 E
Sinor, India 68 J5 21 55N 73 20 E
Sinp'o, N. Korea 57 E15 40 0N 128 13 E
Sinsheim, Germany 25 F4 49 15N 8 52 E
Sinsk, Russia 51 C13 61 8N 126 48 E
Sintang, Indonesia 62 D4 0 5N 111 35 E
Sinton, U.S.A. 113 L6 28 2N 97 31W
Sintra, Portugal 35 G1 38 47N 9 25W
Sinŭiju, N. Korea 57 D13 40 5N 124 24 E
Sinyukha →, Ukraine 47 H6 48 3N 30 51 E
Sinzig, Germany 24 E3 50 32N 7 14 E
Sio →, Hungary 42 D3 46 20N 18 53 E
Siocon, Phil. 61 H5 7 40N 122 10 E
Siófok, Hungary 42 D3 46 54N 18 3 E
Sion, Switz. 25 J3 46 14N 7 20 E
Sion Mills, U.K. 15 B4 54 48N 7 29W
Sioux City, U.S.A. 112 D6 42 30N 96 24W
Sioux Falls, U.S.A. 112 D6 43 33N 96 44W
Sioux Lookout, Canada 102 B1 50 10N 91 50W
Sioux Narrows, Canada 105 D10 49 25N 94 10W
Sipalay, Phil. 61 G5 9 45N 122 24 E
Šipan, Croatia 40 D1 42 45N 17 52 E
Siping, China 57 C13 43 8N 124 21 E
Sipiwesk L., Canada 105 B9 55 5N 97 35W
Šipovo, Bos.-H. 42 F2 44 16N 17 6 E
Sipra →, India 68 H6 23 55N 75 28 E
Sipura, Indonesia 62 E1 2 18 S 99 40 E
Siquia →, Nic. 120 D3 12 10N 84 20W
Siquijor, Phil. 61 G5 9 12N 123 35 E
Siquirres, Costa Rica 120 D3 10 6N 83 30W
Şīr Banī Yās, U.A.E. 71 E7 24 19N 52 37 E
Sir Edward Pellew Group, Australia 94 B2 15 40 S 137 10 E
Sir Graham Moore Is., Australia 92 B4 13 53 S 126 34 E
Sir James MacBrien, Mt., Canada 100 B7 62 8N 127 40W
Sira →, Norway 9 G12 58 23N 6 34 E
Siracusa, Italy 31 E8 37 4N 15 17 E
Sirajganj, Bangla. 69 G13 24 25N 89 47 E
Sirakoro, Mali 82 C3 12 41N 9 14W
Şiran, Turkey 73 B8 40 11N 39 7 E
Sirasso, Ivory C. 82 D3 9 16N 6 6W
Sirathu, India 69 G9 25 39N 81 19 E
Sīrdān, Iran 71 B6 36 39N 49 12 E
Sirdaryo = Syrdarya →, Kazakstan 50 E7 46 3N 61 0 E
Sire, Ethiopia 81 F4 6 55N 35 36 E
Siren, U.S.A. 112 C8 45 47N 92 24W
Sirer, Spain 37 C7 38 56N 1 22 E
Siret, Romania 43 C11 47 55N 26 5 E
Siret →, Romania 43 E12 45 24N 28 1 E
Sirghāyā, Syria 75 B5 33 51N 36 8 E
Siria, Romania 42 D6 46 16N 21 38 E
Sirino, Mte., Italy 31 B8 40 7N 15 50 E
Sirmaur, India 69 G9 24 51N 81 23 E
Sírna, Greece 39 E8 36 22N 26 42 E
Şirnak, Turkey 73 D10 37 32N 42 28 E
Sirohi, India 68 G5 24 52N 72 53 E
Sironj, India 68 G7 24 5N 77 39 E
Síros, Greece 38 D6 37 28N 24 57 E
Sirretta Pk., U.S.A. 117 K8 35 56N 118 19W
Sīrrī, Iran 71 E7 25 55N 54 32 E
Sirsa, India 68 E6 29 33N 75 4 E
Sirsa →, India 69 F8 26 51N 79 4 E
Siruela, Spain 35 G5 38 58N 5 3W
Sisak, Croatia 29 C13 45 30N 16 21 E
Sisaket, Thailand 64 E5 15 8N 104 23 E
Sisante, Spain 33 F2 39 25N 2 12W
Sisargas, Is., Spain 34 B2 43 21N 8 50W
Sishen, S. Africa 88 D3 27 47 S 22 59 E
Sishui, Henan, China 56 G7 34 48N 113 15 E
Sishui, Shandong, China 57 G9 35 42N 117 18 E
Sisipuk L., Canada 105 B8 55 45N 101 50W
Sisophon, Cambodia 64 F4 13 38N 102 59 E
Sisseton, U.S.A. 112 C6 45 40N 97 3W
Sissonne, France 19 C10 49 34N 3 51 E
Sīstān, Asia 71 D9 30 50N 61 0 E
Sīstān, Daryācheh-ye, Iran 66 D2 31 0N 61 0 E
Sīstān va Balūchestān □, Iran 71 E9 27 0N 62 0 E
Sisteron, France 21 D9 44 12N 5 57 E
Sisters, U.S.A. 114 D3 44 18N 121 33W
Siswa Bazar, India 69 F10 27 9N 83 46 E
Sitakili, Mali 82 C2 13 7N 11 14W
Sitamarhi, India 69 F11 26 37N 85 30 E
Sitampiky, Madag. 89 B8 16 41 S 46 6 E
Sitapur, India 69 F9 27 38N 80 45 E
Siteki, Swaziland 89 D5 26 32 S 31 58 E
Sitges, Spain 32 D6 41 17N 1 47 E
Sithoniá, Greece 40 F7 40 0N 23 45 E
Sitia, Greece 36 D8 35 13N 26 6 E
Sitka, U.S.A. 104 B1 57 3N 135 20W
Sitoti, Botswana 88 C3 23 15 S 23 40 E
Sitra, Egypt 80 B2 28 40N 26 53 E
Sittang Myit →, Burma 67 L20 17 20N 96 45 E
Sittard, Neths. 17 C5 51 0N 5 52 E
Sittensen, Germany 24 B5 53 17N 9 32 E
Sittingbourne, U.K. 13 F8 51 21N 0 45 E
Sittona, Eritrea 81 E4 14 25N 37 23 E
Sittoung = Sittang Myit →, Burma 67 L20 17 20N 96 45 E
Sittwe, Burma 67 J18 20 18N 92 45 E
Situbondo, Indonesia 63 G16 7 42 S 114 0 E
Siuna, Nic. 120 D3 13 37N 84 45W
Siuri, India 69 H12 23 50N 87 34 E
Siutghiol, Lacul, Romania 43 F13 44 15N 28 35 E
Sīvand, Iran 71 D7 30 5N 52 55 E
Sivas, Turkey 70 B3 39 43N 36 58 E
Sivaslı, Turkey 39 C11 38 31N 29 42 E
Siverek, Turkey 70 B3 37 50N 39 19 E
Sivrihisar, Turkey 72 C4 39 30N 31 35 E
Sīwa, Egypt 80 B2 29 11N 25 31 E
Sīwa, El Wâhât es, Egypt 80 B2 29 10N 25 30 E
Siwa Oasis, Egypt 76 D6 29 10N 25 30 E
Siwalik Range, Nepal 69 F10 28 0N 83 0 E
Siwan, India 69 F11 26 13N 84 21 E
Siwana, India 68 G5 25 38N 72 25 E
Sixmilebridge, Ireland 15 D3 52 44N 8 46W
Sixth Cataract, Sudan 81 D3 16 20N 32 42 E
Siyâl, Jazâ'ir, Egypt 80 C4 22 49N 36 12 E
Siyäzän, Azerbaijan 49 K9 41 3N 49 10 E
Siziwang Qi, China 56 D6 41 25N 111 40 E
Sjælland, Denmark 11 J5 55 30N 11 30 E
Sjællands Odde, Denmark 11 J5 55 58N 11 24 E
Sjenica, Serbia, Yug. 40 C3 43 16N 20 0 E
Sjöbo, Sweden 11 J7 55 37N 13 45 E
Sjötofta, Sweden 11 G7 57 22N 13 17 E
Sjötorp, Sweden 11 F8 58 50N 14 0 E
Sjumen = Shumen, Bulgaria 41 C10 43 18N 26 55 E
Sjuntorp, Sweden 11 F6 58 12N 12 13 E
Skadarsko Jezero, Montenegro, Yug. 40 D3 42 10N 19 20 E
Skadovsk, Ukraine 47 J7 46 17N 32 52 E
Skælskør, Denmark 11 J5 55 15N 11 18 E
Skærbæk, Denmark 11 J2 55 9N 8 45 E
Skaftafell, Iceland 8 D5 64 1N 17 0W
Skagafjörður, Iceland 8 D4 65 54N 19 35W
Skagastølstindane, Norway 9 F12 61 28N 7 52 E
Skagaströnd, Iceland 8 D3 65 50N 20 19W
Skagen, Denmark 11 G4 57 43N 10 35 E
Skagern, Sweden 11 F8 59 0N 14 20 E
Skagerrak, Denmark 11 G2 57 30N 9 0 E
Skagit →, U.S.A. 116 B4 48 23N 122 22W
Skagway, U.S.A. 100 C6 59 28N 135 19W
Skala-Podilska, Ukraine 47 H4 48 50N 26 15 E
Skala Podolskaya = Skala-Podilska, Ukraine 47 H4 48 50N 26 15 E
Skalat, Ukraine 47 H3 49 23N 25 55 E
Skalbmierz, Poland 45 H7 50 20N 20 25 E
Skälderviken, Sweden 11 H6 56 22N 12 30 E
Skalica, Slovak Rep. 27 C10 48 50N 17 15 E
Skallingen, Denmark 11 J2 55 32N 8 13 E
Skalni Dol = Kamenyak, Bulgaria 41 C10 43 24N 26 57 E
Skanderborg, Denmark 11 H3 56 2N 9 55 E
Skåne, Sweden 11 J7 55 59N 13 30 E
Skåne län □, Sweden 11 H7 56 15N 14 0 E
Skaneateles, U.S.A. 111 D8 42 57N 76 26W
Skaneateles L., U.S.A. 111 D8 42 51N 76 22W
Skänninge, Sweden 11 F9 58 24N 15 5 E
Skanör med Falsterbo, Sweden 11 J6 55 24N 12 50 E
Skantzoúra, Greece 38 B6 39 5N 24 6 E
Skara, Sweden 11 F7 58 25N 13 30 E
Skärblacka, Sweden 11 F9 58 35N 15 54 E
Skardu, Pakistan 69 B6 35 20N 75 44 E
Skåre, Sweden 10 E7 59 26N 13 26 E
Skärhamn, Sweden 11 G5 57 59N 11 34 E
Skarszewy, Poland 44 D5 54 4N 18 25 E
Skaryszew, Poland 45 G8 51 19N 21 15 E
Skarżysko-Kamienna, Poland 45 G7 51 7N 20 52 E
Skattkärr, Sweden 10 E7 59 25N 13 40 E
Skattungbyn, Sweden 10 C8 61 10N 14 56 E
Skawina, Poland 45 J6 49 59N 19 50 E
Skebobruk, Sweden 10 E12 59 58N 18 36 E
Skeena →, Canada 104 C2 54 9N 130 5W
Skeena Mts., Canada 104 B3 56 40N 128 30W
Skegness, U.K. 12 D8 53 9N 0 20 E
Skeldon, Guyana 124 B7 5 55N 57 20W
Skeleton Coast Park, Namibia 88 C1 20 0 S 13 20 E
Skellefte älv →, Sweden 8 D19 64 45N 21 10 E
Skellefteå, Sweden 8 D19 64 45N 20 50 E
Skelleftehamn, Sweden 8 D19 64 40N 21 9 E
Skender Vakuf, Bos.-H. 42 F2 44 29N 17 22 E
Skerries, The, U.K. 12 D3 53 25N 4 36W
Skhíza, Greece 38 E3 36 41N 21 40 E
Skhoinoúsa, Greece 39 E7 36 53N 25 31 E
Ski, Norway 9 G14 59 43N 10 52 E
Skíathos, Greece 38 B5 39 12N 23 30 E
Skibbereen, Ireland 15 E2 51 33N 9 16W
Skiddaw, U.K. 12 C4 54 39N 3 9W
Skidegate, Canada 104 C2 53 15N 132 1W
Skídhra, Greece 40 F6 40 46N 22 10 E
Skien, Norway 9 G13 59 12N 9 35 E
Skierniewice, Poland 45 G7 51 58N 20 10 E
Skikda, Algeria 78 A7 36 50N 6 58 E
Skillingaryd, Sweden 11 G8 57 27N 14 5 E
Skillinge, Sweden 11 J8 55 30N 14 16 E
Skilloura, Cyprus 36 D12 35 14N 33 10 E
Skinári, Ákra, Greece 38 D2 37 56N 20 40 E
Skinnskatteberg, Sweden 10 E9 59 50N 15 42 E
Skipton, U.K. 12 D5 53 58N 2 3W
Skirmish Pt., Australia 94 A1 11 59 S 134 17 E
Skiropoúla, Greece 38 C6 38 50N 24 21 E
Skíros, Greece 38 C6 38 55N 24 34 E
Skivarp, Sweden 11 J7 55 26N 13 34 E
Skive, Denmark 11 H3 56 33N 9 2 E
Skjálfandafljót →, Iceland 8 D5 65 59N 17 25W
Skjálfandi, Iceland 8 C5 66 5N 17 30W
Skjern, Denmark 11 J2 55 57N 8 30 E
Skoczów, Poland 45 J5 49 49N 18 45 E
Škofja Loka, Slovenia 29 B11 46 9N 14 19 E
Skoghall, Sweden 10 E7 59 20N 13 30 E
Skogstorp, Sweden 10 E10 59 19N 16 29 E
Skoki, Poland 45 F4 52 40N 17 11 E
Skole, Ukraine 47 H2 49 3N 23 30 E
Skópelos, Greece 38 B5 39 9N 23 47 E
Skopí, Greece 36 D8 35 11N 26 2 E
Skopin, Russia 46 F10 53 55N 39 32 E
Skopje, Macedonia 40 D5 42 1N 21 26 E
Skórcz, Poland 44 E5 53 47N 18 30 E
Skørping, Denmark 11 H3 56 50N 9 53 E
Skövde, Sweden 11 F7 58 24N 13 50 E
Skovorodino, Russia 51 D13 54 0N 124 0 E
Skowhegan, U.S.A. 109 C11 44 46N 69 43W
Skradin, Croatia 29 E12 43 52N 15 53 E
Skrea, Sweden 11 H6 56 53N 12 34 E
Skrunda, Latvia 44 B9 56 41N 22 1 E
Skrwa →, Poland 45 F6 52 35N 19 32 E
Skull, Ireland 15 E2 51 32N 9 34W
Skultorp, Sweden 11 F7 58 24N 13 51 E
Skultuna, Sweden 10 E10 59 43N 16 25 E
Skunk →, U.S.A. 112 E9 40 42N 91 7W
Skuodas, Lithuania 9 H19 56 16N 21 33 E
Skurup, Sweden 11 J7 55 28N 13 30 E
Skutskär, Sweden 10 D11 60 37N 17 25 E
Skvyra, Ukraine 47 H5 49 44N 29 40 E
Skwierzyna, Poland 45 F2 52 33N 15 30 E
Skye, U.K. 14 D2 57 15N 6 10W
Skykomish, U.S.A. 114 C3 47 42N 121 22W
Skyros = Skíros, Greece 38 C6 38 55N 24 34 E
Skyttorp, Sweden 10 D11 60 5N 17 44 E
Slættaratindur, Færoe Is. 8 E9 62 18N 7 1W
Slagelse, Denmark 11 J5 55 23N 11 19 E
Slamet, Indonesia 63 G13 7 16 S 109 8 E
Slaney →, Ireland 15 D5 52 26N 6 33W
Slangberge, S. Africa 88 E3 31 32 S 20 48 E
Slănic, Romania 43 E10 45 14N 25 58 E
Slano, Croatia 40 D1 42 48N 17 53 E
Slantsy, Russia 46 C5 59 7N 28 5 E
Slaný, Czech Rep. 26 A7 50 13N 14 6 E
Śląskie □, Poland 45 H6 50 30N 19 0 E
Slätbaken, Sweden 11 F10 58 25N 16 45 E
Slate Is., Canada 102 C2 48 40N 87 0W
Slatina, Croatia 42 E2 45 42N 17 45 E
Slatina, Romania 43 F9 44 28N 24 22 E
Slatina Timiş, Romania 42 E7 45 15N 22 17 E
Slatington, U.S.A. 111 F9 40 45N 75 37W
Slaton, U.S.A. 113 J4 33 26N 101 39W
Slave →, Canada 104 A6 61 18N 113 39W
Slave Coast, W. Afr. 83 D5 6 0N 2 30 E
Slave Lake, Canada 104 B6 55 17N 114 43W
Slave Pt., Canada 104 A5 61 11N 115 56W
Slavgorod, Russia 50 D8 53 1N 78 37 E
Slavinja, Serbia, Yug. 40 C6 43 9N 22 50 E
Slavkov u Brna, Czech Rep. 27 B9 49 10N 16 52 E
Slavonija, Europe 42 E2 45 20N 17 40 E
Slavonski Brod, Croatia 42 E3 45 11N 18 1 E
Slavuta, Ukraine 47 G4 50 15N 27 2 E
Slavyanka, Russia 54 C5 42 53N 131 21 E
Slavyanovo, Bulgaria 41 C8 43 28N 24 52 E
Slavyansk = Slovyansk, Ukraine 47 H9 48 55N 37 36 E
Slavyansk-na-Kubani, Russia 47 K10 45 15N 38 11 E
Sława, Poland 45 G3 51 52N 16 2 E
Slawharad, Belarus 46 F6 53 27N 31 0 E
Sławno, Poland 44 D3 54 20N 16 41 E
Sławoborze, Poland 44 E2 53 55N 15 42 E
Sleaford, U.K. 12 D7 53 0N 0 24W
Sleaford B., Australia 95 E2 34 55 S 135 45 E
Sleat, Sd. of, U.K. 14 D3 57 5N 5 47W
Sleeper Is., Canada 101 C11 58 30N 81 0W
Sleepy Eye, U.S.A. 112 C7 44 18N 94 43W
Slemon L., Canada 104 A5 63 13N 116 4W
Ślesin, Poland 45 F5 52 22N 18 14 E
Slide Mt., U.S.A. 111 E10 42 0N 74 25W
Slidell, U.S.A. 113 K10 30 17N 89 47W
Sliema, Malta 36 D2 35 54N 14 30 E
Slieve Aughty, Ireland 15 C3 53 4N 8 30W
Slieve Bloom, Ireland 15 C4 53 4N 7 40W
Slieve Donard, U.K. 15 B6 54 11N 5 55W
Slieve Gamph, Ireland 15 B3 54 6N 9 0W
Slieve Gullion, U.K. 15 B5 54 7N 6 26W
Slieve Mish, Ireland 15 D2 52 12N 9 50W
Slievenamon, Ireland 15 D4 52 25N 7 34W
Sligeach = Sligo, Ireland 15 B3 54 16N 8 28W
Sligo, Ireland 15 B3 54 16N 8 28W
Sligo, U.S.A. 110 E5 41 6N 79 29W
Sligo □, Ireland 15 B3 54 8N 8 42W
Sligo B., Ireland 15 B3 54 18N 8 40W
Slippery Rock, U.S.A. 110 E4 41 3N 80 3W
Slite, Sweden 11 G12 57 42N 18 48 E
Sliven, Bulgaria 41 D10 42 42N 26 19 E
Slivnitsa, Bulgaria 40 D7 42 50N 23 2 E
Sljeme, Croatia 29 C12 45 57N 15 58 E
Sloan, U.S.A. 117 K11 35 57N 115 13W
Sloansville, U.S.A. 111 D10 42 45N 74 22W
Slobodzia, Moldova 43 D14 46 45N 29 42 E
Slobozia, Argeş, Romania 43 F10 44 30N 25 14 E
Slobozia, Ialomiţa, Romania 43 F12 44 34N 27 23 E
Slocan, Canada 104 D5 49 48N 117 28W
Słomniki, Poland 45 H7 50 16N 20 4 E
Slonim, Belarus 47 F3 53 4N 25 19 E
Slough, U.K. 13 F7 51 30N 0 36W
Slough □, U.K. 13 F7 51 30N 0 36W
Sloughhouse, U.S.A. 116 G5 38 26N 121 12W
Slovak Rep. ■, Europe 27 C13 48 30N 20 0 E
Slovakia = Slovak Rep. ■, Europe 27 C13 48 30N 20 0 E
Slovakian Ore Mts. = Slovenské Rudohorie, Slovak Rep. 27 C12 48 45N 20 0 E
Slovenia ■, Europe 29 C11 45 58N 14 30 E
Slovenija = Slovenia ■, Europe 29 C11 45 58N 14 30 E
Slovenj Gradec, Slovenia 29 B12 46 31N 15 5 E
Slovenska Bistrica, Slovenia 29 B12 46 24N 15 35 E
Slovenske Konjice, Slovenia 29 B12 46 20N 15 28 E
Slovenské Rudohorie, Slovak Rep. 27 C12 48 45N 20 0 E
Slovyansk, Ukraine 47 H9 48 55N 37 36 E
Słubice, Poland 45 F1 52 22N 14 35 E
Sluch →, Ukraine 47 G4 51 37N 26 38 E
Sluis, Neths. 17 C3 51 18N 3 23 E
Slŭnchev Bryag, Bulgaria 41 D11 42 40N 27 41 E
Slunj, Croatia 29 C12 45 6N 15 33 E
Słupca, Poland 45 F4 52 15N 17 52 E
Słupia →, Poland 44 D3 54 35N 16 51 E
Słupsk, Poland 44 D4 54 30N 17 3 E
Slurry, S. Africa 88 D4 25 49 S 25 42 E
Slutsk, Belarus 47 F4 53 2N 27 31 E
Slyne Hd., Ireland 15 C1 53 25N 10 10W
Slyudyanka, Russia 51 D11 51 40N 103 40 E
Småland, Sweden 11 G9 57 15N 15 25 E
Smålandsfarvandet, Denmark 11 J5 55 10N 11 20 E
Smålandsstenar, Sweden 11 G7 57 10N 13 25 E
Smalltree L., Canada 105 A8 61 0N 105 0W
Smallwood Res., Canada 103 B7 54 0N 64 0W
Smara, Morocco 78 B4 32 9N 8 16W
Smarhon, Belarus 46 E4 54 20N 26 24 E
Smarje, Slovenia 29 B12 46 15N 15 34 E
Smartt Syndicate Dam, S. Africa 88 E3 30 45 S 23 10 E
Smartville, U.S.A. 116 F5 39 13N 121 18W
Smeaton, Canada 105 C8 53 30N 104 49W
Smedby, Sweden 11 H10 56 41N 16 13 E
Smederevo, Serbia, Yug. 40 B4 44 40N 20 57 E
Smederevska Palanka, Serbia, Yug. 40 B4 44 22N 20 58 E
Smedjebacken, Sweden 10 D9 60 8N 15 25 E
Smela = Smila, Ukraine 47 H6 49 15N 31 58 E
Smerwick Harbour, Ireland 15 D1 52 12N 10 23W
Smethport, U.S.A. 110 E6 41 49N 78 27W
Smidovich, Russia 51 E14 48 36N 133 49 E
Śmigiel, Poland 45 F3 52 1N 16 32 E
Smila, Ukraine 47 H6 49 15N 31 58 E
Smilyan, Bulgaria 41 E8 41 29N 24 46 E
Smith, Canada 104 B6 55 10N 114 0W
Smith Center, U.S.A. 112 F5 39 47N 98 47W
Smith Sund, Greenland 4 B4 78 30N 74 0W
Smithburne →, Australia 94 B3 17 3 S 140 57 E
Smithers, Canada 104 C3 54 45N 127 10W
Smithfield, S. Africa 89 E4 30 9 S 26 30 E
Smithfield, N.C., U.S.A. 109 H6 35 31N 78 21W
Smithfield, Utah, U.S.A. 114 F8 41 50N 111 50W
Smiths Falls, Canada 102 D4 44 55N 76 0W
Smithton, Australia 94 G4 40 53 S 145 6 E
Smithville, Canada 110 C5 43 6N 79 33W
Smithville, U.S.A. 113 K6 30 1N 97 10W
Smoky →, Canada 104 B5 56 10N 117 21W
Smoky Bay, Australia 95 E1 32 22 S 134 13 E
Smoky Hill →, U.S.A. 112 F6 39 4N 96 48W
Smoky Hills, U.S.A. 112 F5 39 15N 99 30W
Smoky Lake, Canada 104 C6 54 10N 112 30W
Smøla, Norway 8 E13 63 23N 8 3 E
Smolensk, Russia 46 E7 54 45N 32 5 E
Smolikas, Óros, Greece 40 F4 40 9N 20 58 E
Smolník, Slovak Rep. 27 C13 48 43N 20 44 E
Smolyan, Bulgaria 41 E8 41 36N 24 38 E
Smooth Rock Falls, Canada 102 C3 49 17N 81 37W
Smoothstone L., Canada 105 C7 54 40N 106 50W
Smorgon = Smarhon, Belarus 46 E4 54 20N 26 24 E
Smulţi, Romania 43 E12 45 57N 27 44 E
Smyadovo, Bulgaria 41 C11 43 2N 27 1 E
Smygehamn, Sweden 11 J7 55 21N 13 22 E
Smyrna = İzmir, Turkey 39 C9 38 25N 27 8 E
Smyrna, U.S.A. 108 F8 39 18N 75 36W
Snæfell, Iceland 8 D6 64 48N 15 34W
Snaefell, U.K. 12 C3 54 16N 4 27W
Snæfellsjökull, Iceland 8 D2 64 49N 23 46W
Snake →, U.S.A. 114 C4 46 12N 119 2W
Snake I., Australia 95 F4 38 47 S 146 33 E
Snake Range, U.S.A. 114 G6 39 0N 114 20W
Snake River Plain, U.S.A. 114 E7 42 50N 114 0W
Snasahögarna, Sweden 10 A6 63 13N 12 21 E
Snåsavatnet, Norway 8 D14 64 12N 12 0 E
Snedsted, Denmark 11 H2 56 55N 8 32 E
Sneek, Neths. 17 A5 53 2N 5 40 E
Sneeuberge, S. Africa 88 E3 31 46 S 24 20 E
Snejbjerg, Denmark 11 H2 56 8N 8 54 E
Snelling, U.S.A. 116 H6 37 31N 120 26W
Snezhnoye, Ukraine 47 J10 48 0N 38 58 E
Snežnik, Slovenia 29 C11 45 36N 14 35 E
Śniadowo, Poland 45 E8 53 2N 22 0 E
Sniardwy, Jezioro, Poland 44 E8 53 48N 21 50 E
Śnieżka, Europe 26 A8 50 44N 15 44 E
Snigirevka = Snihurivka, Ukraine 47 J7 47 2N 32 49 E
Snihurivka, Ukraine 47 J7 47 2N 32 49 E
Snina, Slovak Rep. 27 C15 48 58N 22 9 E
Snizort, L., U.K. 14 D2 57 33N 6 28W
Snøhetta, Norway 9 E13 62 19N 9 16 E
Snohomish, U.S.A. 116 C4 47 55N 122 6W
Snoul, Cambodia 65 F6 12 4N 106 26 E
Snow Hill, U.S.A. 108 F8 38 11N 75 24W
Snow Lake, Canada 105 C8 54 52N 100 3W
Snow Mt., Calif., U.S.A. 116 F4 39 23N 122 45W
Snow Mt., Maine, U.S.A. 111 A14 45 18N 70 48W
Snow Shoe, U.S.A. 110 E7 41 2N 77 57W
Snowbird L., Canada 105 A8 60 45N 103 0W
Snowdon, U.K. 12 D3 53 4N 4 5W
Snowdrift →, Canada 105 A6 62 24N 110 44W
Snowflake, U.S.A. 115 J8 34 30N 110 5W
Snowshoe Pk., U.S.A. 114 B6 48 13N 115 41W
Snowtown, Australia 95 E2 33 46 S 138 14 E
Snowville, U.S.A. 114 F7 41 58N 112 43W
Snowy →, Australia 95 F4 37 46 S 148 30 E
Snowy Mt., U.S.A. 111 C10 43 42N 74 23W
Snowy Mts., Australia 95 F4 36 30 S 148 20 E
Snug Corner, Bahamas 121 B5 22 33N 73 52W
Snyatyn, Ukraine 47 H3 48 27N 25 38 E
Snyder, Okla., U.S.A. 113 H5 34 40N 98 57W
Snyder, Tex., U.S.A. 113 J4 32 44N 100 55W
Soahanina, Madag. 89 B7 18 42 S 44 13 E
Soalala, Madag. 89 B8 16 6 S 45 20 E
Soaloka, Madag. 89 B8 18 32 S 45 15 E
Soamanonga, Madag. 89 C7 23 52 S 44 47 E
Soan →, Pakistan 68 C4 33 1N 71 44 E
Soanierana-Ivongo, Madag. 89 B8 16 55 S 49 35 E
Soanindraniny, Madag. 89 B8 19 54 S 47 14 E
Şoarş, Romania 43 E9 45 56N 24 55 E
Soavina, Madag. 89 C8 20 23 S 46 56 E
Soavinandriana, Madag. 89 B8 19 9 S 46 45 E
Soba, Nigeria 83 C6 10 58N 8 4 E
Sobat, Nahr →, Sudan 81 F3 9 22N 31 33 E
Soběslav, Czech Rep. 26 B7 49 16N 14 45 E
Sobhapur, India 68 H8 22 47N 78 17 E
Sobinka, Russia 46 E11 56 0N 40 0 E
Sobótka, Poland 45 H3 50 54N 16 44 E
Sobra, Croatia 29 F14 42 44N 17 34 E
Sobradinho, Reprêsa de, Brazil 125 E10 9 30 S 42 0 E
Sobral, Brazil 125 D10 3 50 S 40 20W
Sobrance, Slovak Rep. 27 C15 48 45N 22 11 E
Sobreira Formosa, Portugal 34 F3 39 46N 7 51W
Soc Giang, Vietnam 58 F6 22 54N 106 1 E
Soc Trang, Vietnam 65 H5 9 37N 105 50 E
Soča →, Europe 26 E6 46 20N 13 40 E
Socastee, U.S.A. 109 J6 33 41N 79 1W
Sochaczew, Poland 45 F7 52 15N 20 13 E
Soch'e = Shache, China 60 C2 38 20N 77 10 E
Sochi, Russia 49 J4 43 35N 39 40 E
Société, Is. de la, Pac. Oc. 97 J12 17 0 S 151 0W
Society Is. = Société, Is. de la, Pac. Oc. 97 J12 17 0 S 151 0W
Socompa, Portezuelo de, Chile 126 A2 24 27 S 68 18W
Socorro, N. Mex., U.S.A. 115 J10 34 4N 106 54W
Socorro, Tex., U.S.A. 115 L10 31 39N 106 18W
Socorro, I., Mexico 118 D2 18 45N 110 58W
Socotra, Ind. Oc. 74 E5 12 30N 54 0 E
Socovos, Spain 33 G3 38 20N 1 58W
Socuéllamos, Spain 33 F2 39 16N 2 47W

Soda L., *U.S.A.* **115 J5** 35 10N 116 4W
Soda Plains, *India* **69 B8** 35 30N 79 0 E
Soda Springs, *U.S.A.* **114 E8** 42 39N 111 36W
Sodankylä, *Finland* **8 C22** 67 29N 26 40 E
Soddy-Daisy, *U.S.A.* **109 H3** 35 17N 85 10W
Söderala, *Sweden* **10 C10** 61 17N 16 55 E
Söderbärke, *Sweden* **10 D9** 60 5N 15 33 E
Söderfors, *Sweden* **10 D11** 60 23N 17 25 E
Söderhamn, *Sweden* **10 C11** 61 18N 17 10 E
Söderköping, *Sweden* **11 F10** 58 31N 16 20 E
Södermanland, *Sweden* **9 G17** 58 56N 16 55 E
Södermanlands län □, *Sweden* **10 E10** 59 10N 16 30 E
Södertälje, *Sweden* **10 E11** 59 12N 17 39 E
Sodiri, *Sudan* **81 E2** 14 27N 29 0 E
Sodo, *Ethiopia* **81 F4** 7 0N 37 41 E
Södra Dellen, *Sweden* **10 C10** 61 48N 16 43 E
Södra Finnskoga, *Sweden* **10 D6** 60 42N 12 34 E
Södra Sandby, *Sweden* **11 J7** 55 43N 13 21 E
Södra Ulvön, *Sweden* **10 B12** 62 59N 18 38 E
Södra Vi, *Sweden* **11 G9** 57 45N 15 45 E
Sodražica, *Slovenia* **29 C11** 45 45N 14 39 E
Sodus, *U.S.A.* **110 C7** 43 14N 77 4W
Soekmekaar, *S. Africa* **89 C4** 23 30 S 29 55 E
Soest, *Germany* **24 D4** 51 34N 8 7 E
Soest, *Neths.* **17 B5** 52 9N 5 19 E
Sofádhes, *Greece* **38 B4** 39 20N 22 4 E
Sofala □, *Mozam.* **89 B5** 19 30 S 34 30 E
Sofara, *Mali* **82 C4** 13 59N 4 9W
Sofia = Sofiya, *Bulgaria* **40 D7** 42 45N 23 20 E
Sofia →, *Madag.* **89 B8** 15 27 S 47 23 E
Sofievka, *Ukraine* **47 H7** 48 6N 33 55 E
Sofikón, *Greece* **38 D5** 37 47N 23 3 E
Sofiya, *Bulgaria* **40 D7** 42 45N 23 20 E
Sofiya □, *Bulgaria* **40 D7** 42 15N 23 20 E
Sōfu-Gan, *Japan* **55 K10** 29 49N 140 21 E
Sogakofe, *Ghana* **83 D5** 6 2N 0 39 E
Sogamoso, *Colombia* **124 B4** 5 43N 72 56W
Sogār, *Iran* **71 E8** 25 53N 58 6 E
Sögel, *Germany* **24 C3** 52 50N 7 31 E
Sogndalsfjøra, *Norway* **9 F12** 61 14N 7 5 E
Søgne, *Norway* **9 G12** 58 5N 7 48 E
Sognefjorden, *Norway* **9 F11** 61 10N 5 50 E
Söğüt, *Bilecik, Turkey* **39 A12** 40 2N 30 11 E
Söğüt, *Burdur, Turkey* **39 D11** 37 2N 29 50 E
Söğüt Dağı, *Turkey* **39 D11** 37 50N 29 55 E
Söğütköy, *Turkey* **39 E10** 36 40N 28 8 E
Sŏgwipo, *S. Korea* **57 H14** 33 13N 126 34 E
Soh, *Iran* **71 C6** 33 26N 51 27 E
Sohâg, *Egypt* **80 B3** 26 33N 31 43 E
Sohagpur, *India* **68 H8** 22 42N 78 12 E
Sŏhori, *N. Korea* **57 D15** 40 7N 128 23 E
Soignies, *Belgium* **17 D4** 50 35N 4 5 E
Soin, *Burkina Faso* **82 C4** 12 47N 3 50W
Soira, *Eritrea* **81 E4** 14 45N 39 30 E
Soissons, *France* **19 C10** 49 25N 3 19 E
Sōja, *Japan* **55 G6** 34 40N 133 45 E
Sojat, *India* **68 G5** 25 55N 73 45 E
Sok →, *Russia* **48 D10** 53 24N 50 8 E
Sokal, *Ukraine* **47 G3** 50 31N 24 15 E
Söke, *Turkey* **39 D9** 37 48N 27 28 E
Sokelo, *Dem. Rep. of the Congo* **87 D1** 9 55 S 24 36 E
Sokhós, *Greece* **40 F7** 40 48N 23 22 E
Sokhumi, *Georgia* **49 J5** 43 0N 41 0 E
Soko Banja, *Serbia, Yug.* **40 C5** 43 40N 21 51 E
Sokodé, *Togo* **83 D5** 9 0N 1 11 E
Sokol, *Russia* **46 C11** 59 30N 40 5 E
Sokolac, *Bos.-H.* **42 G3** 43 56N 18 48 E
Sokółka, *Poland* **44 E10** 53 25N 23 30 E
Sokolo, *Mali* **82 C3** 10 52N 6 59W
Sokolo, *Mali* **82 C3** 14 53N 6 8W
Sokolov, *Czech Rep.* **26 A5** 50 12N 12 40 E
Sokołów Małpolski, *Poland* **45 H9** 50 12N 22 7 E
Sokołów Podlaski, *Poland* **45 F9** 52 25N 22 15 E
Sokoły, *Poland* **45 F9** 52 59N 22 42 E
Sokoto, *Nigeria* **83 C6** 13 2N 5 16 E
Sokoto □, *Nigeria* **83 C6** 12 30N 6 0 E
Sokoto →, *Nigeria* **83 C5** 11 20N 4 10 E
Sol Iletsk, *Russia* **50 D6** 51 10N 55 0 E
Sola →, *Poland* **45 H6** 50 4N 19 15 E
Solai, *Kenya* **86 B4** 0 2N 36 12 E
Solan, *India* **68 D7** 30 55N 77 7 E
Solano, *Phil.* **61 C4** 16 31N 121 15 E
Solapur, *India* **66 L9** 17 43N 75 56 E
Solca, *Romania* **43 C10** 47 40N 25 50 E
Solda Gölü, *Turkey* **39 D11** 37 33N 29 42 E
Soldănesti, *Moldova* **43 C13** 47 49N 28 48 E
Soldotna, *U.S.A.* **100 B4** 60 29N 151 3W
Soléa □, *Cyprus* **36 D12** 35 5N 33 4 E
Solec Kujawski, *Poland* **45 E5** 53 5N 18 14 E
Soledad, *Colombia* **124 A4** 10 55N 74 46W
Soledad, *U.S.A.* **116 J5** 36 26N 121 20W
Soledad, *Venezuela* **124 B6** 8 10N 63 34W
Solent, The, *U.K.* **13 G6** 50 45N 1 25W
Solenzara, *France* **21 G13** 41 53N 9 23 E
Solesmes, *France* **19 B10** 50 10N 3 30 E
Solfonn, *Norway* **9 F12** 60 2N 6 57 E
Solhan, *Turkey* **70 B4** 38 57N 41 3 E
Soligorsk = Salihorsk, *Belarus* **47 F4** 52 51N 27 27 E
Solihull, *U.K.* **13 E6** 52 26N 1 47W
Solikamsk, *Russia* **50 D6** 59 38N 56 50 E
Solila, *Madag.* **89 C8** 21 25 S 46 37 E
Solimões = Amazonas →, *S. Amer.* **122 D5** 0 5 S 50 0W
Solin, *Croatia* **29 E13** 43 33N 16 30 E
Solingen, *Germany* **24 D3** 51 10N 7 5 E
Sollebrunn, *Sweden* **11 F6** 58 8N 12 32 E
Sollefteå, *Sweden* **10 A11** 63 12N 17 20 E
Sollentuna, *Sweden* **10 E11** 59 26N 17 56 E
Sóller, *Spain* **37 B9** 39 46N 2 43 E
Sollerön, *Sweden* **10 D8** 60 55N 14 37 E
Solling, *Germany* **24 D5** 51 42N 9 38 E
Solnechnogorsk, *Russia* **46 D9** 56 10N 36 57 E
Solo →, *Indonesia* **63 G15** 6 47 S 112 22 E
Solofra, *Italy* **31 B7** 40 50N 14 51 E
Sologne, *France* **19 E8** 47 40N 1 45 E
Solok, *Indonesia* **62 E2** 0 45 S 100 40 E
Sololá, *Guatemala* **120 D1** 14 49N 91 10W
Solomon, N. Fork →, *U.S.A.* **112 F5** 39 29N 98 26W
Solomon, S. Fork →, *U.S.A.* **112 F5** 39 25N 99 12W
Solomon Is. ■, *Pac. Oc.* **96 H7** 6 0 S 155 0 E
Solon, *China* **60 B7** 46 32N 121 10 E
Solon Springs, *U.S.A.* **112 B9** 46 22N 91 49W
Solor, *Indonesia* **63 F6** 8 27 S 123 0 E
Solotcha, *Russia* **46 E10** 54 48N 39 53 E
Solothurn, *Switz.* **25 H3** 47 13N 7 32 E
Solothurn □, *Switz.* **25 H3** 47 18N 7 40 E
Solsona, *Spain* **32 C6** 42 0N 1 31 E
Solt, *Hungary* **42 D4** 46 45N 19 1 E
Šolta, *Croatia* **29 E13** 43 24N 16 15 E
Solṭānābād, *Khorāsān, Iran* **71 C8** 34 13N 59 58 E
Solṭānābād, *Khorāsān, Iran* **71 B8** 36 29N 58 5 E
Soltau, *Germany* **24 C5** 52 59N 9 50 E
Soltsy, *Russia* **46 C6** 58 10N 30 30 E
Solunska Glava, *Macedonia* **40 E5** 41 44N 21 31 E
Solvang, *U.S.A.* **117 L6** 34 36N 120 8W
Solvay, *U.S.A.* **111 C8** 43 3N 76 13W
Sölvesborg, *Sweden* **11 H8** 56 5N 14 35 E
Solway Firth, *U.K.* **12 C4** 54 49N 3 35W
Solwezi, *Zambia* **87 E2** 12 11 S 26 21 E
Sōma, *Japan* **54 F10** 37 40N 140 50 E
Soma, *Turkey* **39 B9** 39 10N 27 35 E
Somabhula, *Zimbabwe* **89 B4** 19 42 S 29 40 E
Somali Pen., *Africa* **76 F8** 7 0N 46 0 E
Somali Rep. ■, *Africa* **74 F4** 7 0N 47 0 E
Somalia = Somali Rep. ■, *Africa* **74 F4** 7 0N 47 0 E
Sombernon, *France* **19 E11** 47 20N 4 40 E
Sombor, *Serbia, Yug.* **42 E4** 45 46N 19 9 E
Sombra, *Canada* **110 D2** 42 43N 82 29W
Sombrerete, *Mexico* **118 C4** 23 40N 103 40W
Sombrero, *Anguilla* **121 C7** 18 37N 63 30W
Şomcuta Mare, *Romania* **43 C8** 47 31N 23 28 E
Somdari, *India* **68 G5** 25 47N 72 38 E
Somers, *U.S.A.* **114 B6** 48 5N 114 13W
Somerset, *Ky., U.S.A.* **108 G3** 37 5N 84 36W
Somerset, *Mass., U.S.A.* **111 E13** 41 47N 71 8W
Somerset, *Pa., U.S.A.* **110 F5** 40 1N 79 5W
Somerset □, *U.K.* **13 F5** 51 9N 3 0W
Somerset East, *S. Africa* **88 E4** 32 42 S 25 35 E
Somerset I., *Canada* **100 A10** 73 30N 93 0W
Somerset West, *S. Africa* **88 E2** 34 8 S 18 50 E
Somersworth, *U.S.A.* **111 C14** 43 16N 70 52W
Somerton, *U.S.A.* **115 K6** 32 36N 114 43W
Somerville, *U.S.A.* **111 F10** 40 35N 74 38W
Someş →, *Romania* **42 C7** 47 49N 22 43 E
Someşul Mare →, *Romania* **43 C8** 47 9N 23 55 E
Somme □, *France* **19 C9** 49 57N 2 20 E
Somme →, *France* **19 B8** 50 11N 1 38 E
Somme, B. de la, *France* **18 B8** 50 14N 1 33 E
Sommen, *Jönköping, Sweden* **11 F8** 58 12N 14 58 E
Sommen, *Östergötland, Sweden* **11 F9** 58 0N 15 15 E
Sommepy-Tahure, *France* **19 C11** 49 15N 4 31 E
Sömmerda, *Germany* **24 D7** 51 9N 11 7 E
Sommesous, *France* **19 D11** 48 44N 4 12 E
Sommières, *France* **21 E8** 43 47N 4 6 E
Somnath, *India* **68 J4** 20 53N 70 22 E
Somogy □, *Hungary* **42 D2** 46 19N 17 30 E
Somogyszob, *Hungary* **42 D2** 46 18N 17 20 E
Somoto, *Nic.* **120 D2** 13 28N 86 37W
Sompolno, *Poland* **45 F5** 52 26N 18 30 E
Somport, Puerto de, *Spain* **32 C4** 42 48N 0 31W
Son →, *India* **69 G11** 25 42N 84 52 E
Son Ha, *Vietnam* **64 E7** 15 3N 108 34 E
Son Hoa, *Vietnam* **64 F7** 13 2N 108 58 E
Son La, *Vietnam* **58 G4** 21 20N 103 50 E
Son Serra, *Spain* **37 B10** 39 43N 3 13 E
Son Servera, *Spain* **32 F8** 39 37N 3 21 E
Son Tay, *Vietnam* **58 G5** 21 8N 105 30 E
Soná, *Panama* **120 E3** 8 0N 81 20W
Sonamarg, *India* **69 B6** 34 18N 75 21 E
Sonamukhi, *India* **69 H12** 23 18N 87 27 E
Sonar →, *India* **69 G8** 24 24N 79 56 E
Sŏnch'ŏn, *N. Korea* **57 E13** 39 48N 124 55 E
Sondags →, *S. Africa* **88 E4** 33 44 S 25 51 E
Sondalo, *Italy* **28 B7** 46 20N 10 19 E
Sondar, *India* **69 C6** 33 28N 75 56 E
Sønder Felding, *Denmark* **11 J2** 55 57N 8 47 E
Sønder Omme, *Denmark* **11 J2** 55 50N 8 54 E
Sønderborg, *Denmark* **11 K3** 54 55N 9 49 E
Sønderjyllands Amtskommune □, *Denmark* **11 J3** 55 10N 9 10 E
Sondershausen, *Germany* **24 D6** 51 22N 10 51 E
Sóndrio, *Italy* **28 B6** 46 10N 9 52 E
Sone, *Mozam.* **87 F3** 17 23 S 34 55 E
Sonepur, *India* **67 J13** 20 55N 83 50 E
Song, *Nigeria* **83 D7** 9 49N 12 39 E
Song, *Thailand* **64 C3** 18 28N 100 11 E
Song Cau, *Vietnam* **64 F7** 13 27N 109 18 E
Song Xian, *China* **56 G7** 34 12N 112 8 E
Songch'ŏn, *N. Korea* **57 E14** 39 12N 126 15 E
Songea, *Tanzania* **87 E4** 10 40 S 35 40 E
Songeons, *France* **19 C8** 49 32N 1 50 E
Songhua Hu, *China* **57 C14** 43 35N 126 50 E
Songhua Jiang →, *China* **60 B8** 47 45N 132 30 E
Songjiang, *China* **59 B13** 31 1N 121 12 E
Songjin, *N. Korea* **57 D15** 40 40N 129 10 E
Songjŏng-ni, *S. Korea* **57 G14** 35 8N 126 47 E
Songkan, *China* **58 C6** 28 35N 106 52 E
Songkhla, *Thailand* **65 J3** 7 13N 100 37 E
Songming, *China* **58 E4** 25 12N 103 2 E
Songnim, *N. Korea* **57 E13** 38 45N 125 39 E
Songo, *Mozam.* **85 H6** 15 34 S 32 38 E
Songo, *Sudan* **79 G10** 9 47N 24 21 E
Songpan, *China* **58 A4** 32 40N 103 30 E
Songtao, *China* **58 C7** 28 11N 109 10 E
Songwe, *Dem. Rep. of the Congo* **86 C2** 3 20 S 26 16 E
Songwe →, *Africa* **87 D3** 9 44 S 33 58 E
Songxi, *China* **59 D12** 27 31N 118 44 E
Songzi, *China* **59 B8** 30 12N 111 45 E
Sonhat, *India* **69 H10** 23 29N 82 31 E
Sonid Youqi, *China* **56 C7** 42 45N 112 48 E
Sonipat, *India* **68 E7** 29 0N 77 5 E
Sonkach, *India* **68 H7** 22 59N 76 21 E
Sonkovo, *Russia* **46 D9** 57 50N 37 5 E
Sonmiani, *Pakistan* **68 G2** 25 25N 66 40 E
Sonmiani B., *Pakistan* **68 G2** 25 15N 66 30 E
Sonnino, *Italy* **30 A6** 41 25N 13 14 E
Sono →, *Brazil* **125 E9** 9 58 S 48 11W
Sonoma, *U.S.A.* **116 G4** 38 18N 122 28W
Sonora, *Calif., U.S.A.* **116 H6** 37 59N 120 23W
Sonora, *Tex., U.S.A.* **113 K4** 30 34N 100 39W
Sonora □, *Mexico* **118 B2** 29 0N 111 0W
Sonora →, *Mexico* **118 B2** 28 50N 111 33W
Sonoran Desert, *U.S.A.* **117 L12** 33 40N 114 15W
Sonoyta, *Mexico* **118 A2** 31 51N 112 50W
Sonqor, *Iran* **73 E12** 34 47N 47 36 E
Sŏnsan, *S. Korea* **57 F15** 36 14N 128 17 E
Sonseca, *Spain* **35 F7** 39 42N 3 57W
Sonsonate, *El Salv.* **120 D2** 13 43N 89 44W
Sonsorol Is., *Pac. Oc.* **63 C8** 5 30N 132 15 E
Sonstorp, *Sweden* **11 F9** 58 44N 15 38 E
Sonthofen, *Germany* **25 H6** 47 30N 10 16 E
Soochow = Suzhou, *China* **59 B13** 31 19N 120 38 E
Sooke, *Canada* **116 B3** 48 13N 123 43W
Sop Hao, *Laos* **58 G5** 20 33N 104 27 E
Sop Prap, *Thailand* **64 D2** 17 53N 99 20 E
Sopelana, *Spain* **32 B2** 43 23N 2 58W
Sopi, *Indonesia* **63 D7** 2 34N 128 28 E
Sopo, Nahr →, *Sudan* **81 F2** 8 40N 26 30 E
Sopot, *Bulgaria* **41 D8** 42 39N 24 45 E
Sopot, *Poland* **44 D5** 54 27N 18 31 E
Sopot, *Serbia, Yug.* **40 B4** 44 29N 20 36 E
Sopotnica, *Macedonia* **40 E5** 41 18N 21 13 E
Sopron, *Hungary* **42 C1** 47 45N 16 32 E
Sopur, *India* **69 B6** 34 18N 74 27 E
Sør-Rondane, *Antarctica* **5 D4** 72 0 S 25 0 E
Sora, *Italy* **29 G10** 41 43N 13 37 E
Sorah, *Pakistan* **68 F3** 27 13N 68 56 E
Söråker, *Sweden* **10 B11** 62 30N 17 32 E
Sorano, *Italy* **29 F8** 42 41N 11 43 E
Soraon, *India* **69 G9** 25 37N 81 51 E
Sorbas, *Spain* **33 H2** 37 6N 2 7W
Sörbygden, *Sweden* **10 B10** 62 48N 16 12 E
Sore, *France* **20 D3** 44 18N 0 35W
Sorel, *Canada* **102 C5** 46 0N 73 10W
Soresina, *Italy* **28 C6** 45 17N 9 51 E
Sörforsa, *Sweden* **10 C10** 61 43N 16 58 E
Sórgono, *Italy* **30 B2** 40 1N 9 6 E
Sorgues, *France* **21 D8** 44 1N 4 53 E
Sorgun, *Turkey* **72 C6** 39 46N 35 11 E
Soria, *Spain* **32 D2** 41 43N 2 32W
Soria □, *Spain* **32 D2** 41 46N 2 28W
Soriano, *Uruguay* **126 C4** 33 24 S 58 19W
Soriano nel Cimino, *Italy* **29 F9** 42 25N 12 14 E
Sorkh, Kuh-e, *Iran* **71 C8** 35 40N 58 30 E
Sorø, *Denmark* **11 J5** 55 26N 11 32 E
Soro, *Guinea* **82 C3** 10 9N 9 48W
Soroca, *Moldova* **43 B13** 48 8N 28 12 E
Sorocaba, *Brazil* **127 A6** 23 31 S 47 27W
Soroki = Soroca, *Moldova* **43 B13** 48 8N 28 12 E
Sorol Atoll, *Pac. Oc.* **63 C10** 7 45N 140 45 E
Sorong, *Indonesia* **63 E8** 0 55 S 131 15 E
Soroní, *Greece* **36 C10** 36 21N 28 1 E
Soroti, *Uganda* **86 B3** 1 43N 33 35 E
Sørøya, *Norway* **8 A20** 70 40N 22 30 E
Sørøysundet, *Norway* **8 A20** 70 25N 23 0 E
Sorraia →, *Portugal* **35 G2** 38 55N 8 53W
Sorrell, *Australia* **94 G4** 42 47 S 147 34 E
Sorrento, *Italy* **31 B7** 40 37N 14 22 E
Sorsele, *Sweden* **8 D17** 65 31N 17 30 E
Sörsjön, *Sweden* **10 C7** 61 24N 13 5 E
Sorso, *Italy* **30 B1** 40 48N 8 34 E
Sorsogon, *Phil.* **61 E6** 13 0N 124 0 E
Sortavala, *Russia* **46 B6** 61 42N 30 41 E
Sortino, *Italy* **31 E8** 37 9N 15 2 E
Sortland, *Norway* **8 B16** 68 42N 15 25 E
Sorvizhi, *Russia* **48 B9** 57 52N 48 32 E
Sos = Sos del Rey Católico, *Spain* **32 C3** 42 30N 1 13W
Sos del Rey Católico, *Spain* **32 C3** 42 30N 1 13W
Sŏsan, *S. Korea* **57 F14** 36 47N 126 27 E
Soscumica, L., *Canada* **102 B4** 50 15N 77 27W
Sösdala, *Sweden* **11 H7** 56 2N 13 41 E
Sosna →, *Russia* **47 F10** 52 42N 38 55 E
Sosnovka, *Kirov, Russia* **48 B10** 56 17N 51 17 E
Sosnovka, *Tambov, Russia* **48 D5** 53 13N 41 24 E
Sosnovyy Bor, *Russia* **46 C5** 59 55N 29 6 E
Sosnowiec, *Poland* **45 H6** 50 20N 19 10 E
Sospel, *France* **21 E11** 43 52N 7 27 E
Sossus Vlei, *Namibia* **88 C2** 24 40 S 15 23 E
Šoštanj, *Slovenia* **29 B12** 46 23N 15 4 E
Sŏsura, *N. Korea* **57 C16** 42 16N 130 36 E
Sot →, *India* **69 F8** 27 27N 79 37 E
Sotkamo, *Finland* **8 D23** 64 8N 28 23 E
Soto del Barco, *Spain* **34 B4** 43 32N 6 4W
Soto la Marina →, *Mexico* **119 C5** 23 40N 97 40W
Soto y Amío, *Spain* **34 C5** 42 46N 5 53W
Sotrondio, *Spain* **34 B5** 43 17N 5 36W
Sotuta, *Mexico* **119 C7** 20 29N 89 43W
Souanké, *Congo* **84 D2** 2 10N 14 3 E
Soubré, *Ivory C.* **82 D3** 5 50N 6 35W
Souderton, *U.S.A.* **111 F9** 40 19N 75 19W
Soúdha, *Greece* **36 D6** 35 29N 24 4 E
Soúdhas, Kólpos, *Greece* **36 D6** 35 25N 24 10 E
Souflíon, *Greece* **41 E10** 41 12N 26 18 E
Soufrière, *St. Lucia* **121 D7** 13 51N 61 3W
Souillac, *France* **20 D5** 44 53N 1 29 E
Souilly, *France* **19 C12** 49 3N 5 17 E
Soukhouma, *Laos* **64 E5** 14 38N 105 48 E
Sŏul, *S. Korea* **57 F14** 37 31N 126 58 E
Soulac-sur-Mer, *France* **20 C2** 45 30N 1 7W
Soulougou, *Burkina Faso* **83 C5** 13 1N 0 25 E
Soultz-sous-Forêts, *France* **19 D14** 48 57N 7 52 E
Sound, The = Øresund, *Europe* **11 J6** 55 45N 12 45 E
Sound, The, *U.K.* **13 G3** 50 20N 4 10W
Soúnion, Ákra, *Greece* **38 D6** 37 37N 24 1 E
Sources, Mt. aux, *Lesotho* **89 D4** 28 45 S 28 50 E
Soure, *Brazil* **125 D9** 0 35 S 48 30W
Soure, *Portugal* **34 E2** 40 4N 8 38W
Souris, *Man., Canada* **105 D8** 49 40N 100 20W
Souris, *P.E.I., Canada* **103 C7** 46 21N 62 15W
Souris →, *Canada* **112 A5** 49 40N 99 34W
Sourou →, *Africa* **82 C4** 12 45N 3 25W
Soúrpi, *Greece* **38 B4** 39 6N 22 54 E
Sousa, *Brazil* **125 E11** 6 45 S 38 10W
Sousel, *Portugal* **35 G3** 38 57N 7 40W
Sousse, *Tunisia* **79 A8** 35 50N 10 38 E
Soustons, *France* **20 E2** 43 45N 1 19W
Sout →, *S. Africa* **88 E3** 31 35 S 18 24 E
South Africa ■, *Africa* **88 E3** 32 0 S 23 0 E
South America **122 E5** 10 0 S 60 0W
South Atlantic Ocean **122 H7** 20 0 S 10 0W
South Aulatsivik I., *Canada* **103 A7** 56 45N 61 30W
South Australia □, *Australia* **95 E2** 32 0 S 139 0 E
South Ayrshire □, *U.K.* **14 F4** 55 18N 4 41W
South Baldy, *U.S.A.* **115 J10** 33 59N 107 11W
South Bass I., *U.S.A.* **110 E2** 41 39N 82 49W
South Bend, *Ind., U.S.A.* **108 E2** 41 41N 86 15W
South Bend, *Wash., U.S.A.* **116 D3** 46 40N 123 48W
South Boston, *U.S.A.* **109 G6** 36 42N 78 54W
South Branch, *Canada* **103 C8** 47 55N 59 2W
South Brook, *Canada* **103 C8** 49 26N 56 5W
South Carolina □, *U.S.A.* **109 J5** 34 0N 81 0W
South Charleston, *U.S.A.* **108 F5** 38 22N 81 44W
South China Sea, *Asia* **62 C4** 10 0N 113 0 E
South Dakota □, *U.S.A.* **112 C5** 44 15N 100 0W
South Deerfield, *U.S.A.* **111 D12** 42 29N 72 37W
South Downs, *U.K.* **13 G7** 50 52N 0 25W
South East C., *Australia* **94 G4** 43 40 S 146 50 E
South East Is., *Australia* **93 F3** 34 17 S 123 30 E
South Esk →, *U.K.* **14 E6** 56 43N 2 31W
South Foreland, *U.K.* **13 F9** 51 8N 1 24 E
South Fork American →, *U.S.A.* **116 G5** 38 45N 121 5W
South Fork Feather →, *U.S.A.* **116 F5** 39 17N 121 36W
South Fork Grand →, *U.S.A.* **112 C3** 45 43N 102 17W
South Fork Republican →, *U.S.A.* **112 E4** 40 3N 101 31W
South Georgia, *Antarctica* **122 J7** 54 30 S 37 0W
South Gloucestershire □, *U.K.* **13 F5** 51 32N 2 28W
South Hadley, *U.S.A.* **111 D12** 42 16N 72 35W
South Haven, *U.S.A.* **108 D2** 42 24N 86 16W
South Henik, L., *Canada* **105 A9** 61 30N 97 30W
South Honshu Ridge, *Pac. Oc.* **96 E6** 23 0N 143 0 E
South Horr, *Kenya* **86 B4** 2 12N 36 56 E
South I., *Kenya* **86 B4** 2 35N 36 35 E
South I., *N.Z.* **91 L3** 44 0 S 170 0 E
South Indian Lake, *Canada* **105 B9** 56 47N 98 56W
South Invercargill, *N.Z.* **91 M2** 46 26 S 168 23 E
South Knife →, *Canada* **105 B10** 58 55N 94 37W
South Koel →, *India* **69 H11** 22 32N 85 14 E
South Korea ■, *Asia* **57 G15** 36 0N 128 0 E
South Lake Tahoe, *U.S.A.* **116 G6** 38 57N 119 59W
South Lanarkshire □, *U.K.* **14 F5** 55 37N 3 53W
South Loup →, *U.S.A.* **112 E5** 41 4N 98 39W
South Magnetic Pole, *Antarctica* **5 C9** 64 8 S 138 8 E
South Milwaukee, *U.S.A.* **108 D2** 42 55N 87 52W
South Molton, *U.K.* **13 F4** 51 1N 3 51W
South Moose L., *Canada* **105 C8** 53 46N 100 8W
South Nahanni →, *Canada* **104 A4** 61 3N 123 21W
South Nation →, *Canada* **111 A9** 45 34N 75 6W
South Natuna Is. = Natuna Selatan, Kepulauan, *Indonesia* **65 L7** 2 45N 109 0 E
South Negril Pt., *Jamaica* **120 C4** 18 14N 78 30W
South Orkney Is., *Antarctica* **5 C18** 63 0 S 45 0W
South Ossetia □, *Georgia* **49 J7** 42 21N 44 2 E
South Pagai, I. = Pagai Selatan, Pulau, *Indonesia* **62 E2** 3 0 S 100 15 E
South Paris, *U.S.A.* **111 B14** 44 14N 70 31W
South Pittsburg, *U.S.A.* **109 H3** 35 1N 85 42W
South Platte →, *U.S.A.* **112 E4** 41 7N 100 42W
South Pole, *Antarctica* **5 E** 90 0 S 0 0W
South Porcupine, *Canada* **102 C3** 48 30N 81 12W
South Portland, *U.S.A.* **109 D10** 43 38N 70 15W
South Pt., *U.S.A.* **110 B1** 44 52N 83 19W
South River, *Canada* **102 C4** 45 52N 79 23W
South River, *U.S.A.* **111 F10** 40 27N 74 23W
South Ronaldsay, *U.K.* **14 C6** 58 48N 2 58W
South Sandwich Is., *Antarctica* **5 B1** 57 0 S 27 0W
South Saskatchewan →, *Canada* **105 C7** 53 15N 105 5W
South Seal →, *Canada* **105 B9** 58 48N 98 8W
South Shetland Is., *Antarctica* **5 C18** 62 0 S 59 0W
South Shields, *U.K.* **12 C6** 55 0N 1 25W
South Sioux City, *U.S.A.* **112 D6** 42 28N 96 24W
South Taranaki Bight, *N.Z.* **91 H5** 39 40 S 174 5 E
South Thompson →, *Canada* **104 C4** 50 40N 120 20W
South Twin I., *Canada* **102 B4** 53 7N 79 52W
South Tyne →, *U.K.* **12 C5** 54 59N 2 8W
South Uist, *U.K.* **14 D1** 57 20N 7 15W
South West Africa = Namibia ■, *Africa* **88 C2** 22 0 S 18 9 E
South West C., *Australia* **94 G4** 43 34 S 146 3 E
South West Rocks, *Australia* **95 E5** 30 52 S 153 3 E
South Williamsport, *U.S.A.* **110 E8** 41 13N 77 0W
South Yorkshire □, *U.K.* **12 D6** 53 27N 1 36W
Southampton, *Canada* **102 D3** 44 30N 81 25W
Southampton, *U.K.* **13 G6** 50 54N 1 23W
Southampton, *U.S.A.* **111 F12** 40 53N 72 23W
Southampton □, *U.K.* **13 G6** 50 54N 1 23W
Southampton I., *Canada* **101 B11** 64 30N 84 0W
Southaven, *U.S.A.* **113 H9** 34 59N 90 2W
Southbank, *Canada* **104 C3** 54 2N 125 46W
Southbridge, *N.Z.* **91 K4** 43 48 S 172 16 E
Southbridge, *U.S.A.* **111 D12** 42 5N 72 2W
Southend, *Canada* **105 B8** 56 19N 103 22W
Southend-on-Sea, *U.K.* **13 F8** 51 32N 0 44 E
Southend-on-Sea □, *U.K.* **13 F8** 51 32N 0 44 E
Southern □, *Malawi* **87 F4** 15 0 S 35 0 E
Southern □, *S. Leone* **82 D2** 8 0N 12 30W
Southern □, *Uganda* **86 C3** 0 15 S 31 30 E
Southern □, *Zambia* **87 F2** 16 20 S 26 20 E
Southern Alps, *N.Z.* **91 K3** 43 41 S 170 11 E
Southern Cross, *Australia* **93 F2** 31 12 S 119 15 E
Southern Indian L., *Canada* **105 B9** 57 10N 98 30W
Southern Ocean, *Antarctica* **5 C6** 62 0 S 60 0 E
Southern Pines, *U.S.A.* **109 H6** 35 11N 79 24W
Southern Uplands, *U.K.* **14 F5** 55 28N 3 52W
Southington, *U.S.A.* **111 E12** 41 36N 72 53W
Southland □, *N.Z.* **91 L1** 45 30 S 168 0 E
Southold, *U.S.A.* **111 E12** 41 4N 72 26W
Southport, *Australia* **95 D5** 27 58 S 153 25 E
Southport, *U.K.* **12 D4** 53 39N 3 0W
Southport, *Fla., U.S.A.* **109 K3** 30 17N 85 38W
Southport, *N.Y., U.S.A.* **110 D8** 42 3N 76 49W
Southwest C., *N.Z.* **91 M1** 47 17 S 167 28 E
Southwold, *U.K.* **13 E9** 52 20N 1 41 E
Soutpansberg, *S. Africa* **89 C4** 23 0 S 29 30 E
Souvigny, *France* **19 F10** 46 33N 3 10 E
Sovata, *Romania* **43 D10** 46 35N 25 3 E
Soverato, *Italy* **31 D9** 38 41N 16 33 E
Sovetsk, *Kaliningd., Russia* **9 J19** 55 6N 21 50 E
Sovetsk, *Kirov, Russia* **48 B9** 57 38N 48 53 E
Sovetskaya Gavan = Vanino, *Russia* **51 E15** 48 50N 140 5 E
Sovicille, *Italy* **29 E8** 43 17N 11 13 E
Soweto, *S. Africa* **89 D4** 26 14 S 27 54 E
Sōya-Kaikyō = La Perouse Str., *Asia* **54 B11** 45 40N 142 0 E
Sōya-Misaki, *Japan* **54 B10** 45 30N 141 55 E
Soyaux, *France* **20 C4** 45 39N 0 12 E
Sozh →, *Belarus* **47 F6** 51 57N 30 48 E
Sozopol, *Bulgaria* **41 D11** 42 23N 27 42 E
Spa, *Belgium* **17 D5** 50 29N 5 53 E
Spain ■, *Europe* **7 H5** 39 0N 4 0W
Spalding, *Australia* **95 E2** 33 30 S 138 37 E
Spalding, *U.K.* **12 E7** 52 48N 0 9W
Spangler, *U.S.A.* **110 F6** 40 39N 78 48W
Spanish, *Canada* **102 C3** 46 12N 82 20W
Spanish Fork, *U.S.A.* **114 F8** 40 7N 111 39W
Spanish Town, *Jamaica* **120 C4** 18 0N 76 57W
Sparks, *U.S.A.* **116 F7** 39 32N 119 45W
Sparreholm, *Sweden* **10 E10** 59 4N 16 49 E
Sparta = Spárti, *Greece* **38 D4** 37 5N 22 25 E
Sparta, *Mich., U.S.A.* **108 D3** 43 10N 85 42W
Sparta, *N.J., U.S.A.* **111 E10** 41 2N 74 38W
Sparta, *Wis., U.S.A.* **112 D9** 43 56N 90 49W
Spartanburg, *U.S.A.* **109 H5** 34 56N 81 57W
Spartansburg, *U.S.A.* **110 E5** 41 49N 79 41W
Spárti, *Greece* **38 D4** 37 5N 22 25 E
Spartivento, C., *Calabria, Italy* **31 E9** 37 55N 16 4 E
Spartivento, C., *Sard., Italy* **30 D1** 38 53N 8 50 E
Sparwood, *Canada* **104 D6** 49 44N 114 53W
Spas-Demensk, *Russia* **46 E7** 54 20N 34 0 E
Spas-Klepiki, *Russia* **46 E11** 55 10N 40 10 E
Spassk Dalniy, *Russia* **51 E14** 44 40N 132 48 E
Spassk-Ryazanskiy, *Russia* **46 E11** 54 24N 40 25 E
Spátha, Ákra, *Greece* **36 D5** 35 42N 23 43 E
Spatsizi →, *Canada* **104 B3** 57 42N 128 7W
Spatsizi Plateau Wilderness Park, *Canada* **104 B3** 57 40N 128 0W
Spean →, *U.K.* **14 E4** 56 55N 4 59W
Spearfish, *U.S.A.* **112 C3** 44 30N 103 52W
Spearman, *U.S.A.* **113 G4** 36 12N 101 12W
Speculator, *U.S.A.* **111 C10** 43 30N 74 25W
Speia, *Moldova* **43 D14** 46 59N 29 19 E
Speightstown, *Barbados* **121 D8** 13 15N 59 39W
Speke Gulf, *Tanzania* **86 C3** 2 20 S 32 50 E
Spello, *Italy* **29 F9** 42 59N 12 40 E
Spencer, *Idaho, U.S.A.* **114 D7** 44 22N 112 11W
Spencer, *Iowa, U.S.A.* **112 D7** 43 9N 95 9W
Spencer, *N.Y., U.S.A.* **111 D8** 42 13N 76 30W
Spencer, *Nebr., U.S.A.* **112 D5** 42 53N 98 42W
Spencer, C., *Australia* **95 F2** 35 20 S 136 53 E
Spencer B., *Namibia* **88 D1** 25 30 S 14 47 E
Spencer G., *Australia* **95 E2** 34 0 S 137 20 E
Spencerville, *Canada* **111 B9** 44 51N 75 33W
Spences Bridge, *Canada* **104 C4** 50 25N 121 20W
Spennymoor, *U.K.* **12 C6** 54 42N 1 36W
Spenser Mts., *N.Z.* **91 K4** 42 15 S 172 45 E
Spentrup, *Denmark* **11 H4** 56 33N 10 2 E
Sperkhiós →, *Greece* **38 C4** 38 57N 22 3 E
Sperrin Mts., *U.K.* **15 B5** 54 50N 7 0W
Spessart, *Germany* **25 F5** 49 56N 9 18 E
Spétsai, *Greece* **38 D5** 37 15N 23 10 E
Spey →, *U.K.* **14 D5** 57 40N 3 6W
Speyer, *Germany* **25 F4** 49 29N 8 25 E
Spezand, *Pakistan* **68 E2** 29 59N 67 0 E
Spezzano Albanese, *Italy* **31 C9** 39 40N 16 19 E
Spiekeroog, *Germany* **24 B3** 53 46N 7 42 E
Spiez, *Switz.* **25 J3** 46 40N 7 40 E
Spíli, *Greece* **36 D6** 35 13N 24 31 E
Spilimbergo, *Italy* **29 B9** 46 7N 12 54 E
Spīn Būldak, *Afghan.* **68 D2** 31 1N 66 25 E
Spinalónga, *Greece* **36 D7** 35 18N 25 44 E
Spinazzola, *Italy* **31 B9** 40 58N 16 5 E
Spineni, *Romania* **43 F9** 44 43N 24 37 E
Spirit Lake, *U.S.A.* **116 D4** 46 15N 122 9W
Spirit River, *Canada* **104 B5** 55 45N 118 50W
Spiritwood, *Canada* **105 C7** 53 24N 107 33W
Spišská Nová Ves, *Slovak Rep.* **27 C13** 48 58N 20 34 E
Spišské Podhradie, *Slovak Rep.* **27 B13** 49 0N 20 48 E
Spital, *Austria* **26 D7** 47 42N 14 18 E
Spithead, *U.K.* **13 G6** 50 45N 1 10W
Spittal an der Drau, *Austria* **26 E6** 46 48N 13 31 E
Spitzbergen = Svalbard, *Arctic* **4 B8** 78 0N 17 0 E
Spjelkavik, *Norway* **9 E12** 62 28N 6 22 E
Split, *Croatia* **29 E13** 43 31N 16 26 E
Split L., *Canada* **105 B9** 56 8N 96 15W
Split Lake, *Canada* **105 B9** 56 8N 96 15W
Splitski Kanal, *Croatia* **29 E13** 43 31N 16 20 E
Splügenpass, *Switz.* **25 J5** 46 30N 9 20 E
Spofford, *U.S.A.* **113 L4** 29 10N 100 25W
Spokane, *U.S.A.* **114 C5** 47 40N 117 24W
Spoleto, *Italy* **29 F9** 42 44N 12 44 E
Spooner, *U.S.A.* **112 C9** 45 50N 91 53W
Sporyy Navolok, Mys, *Russia* **50 B7** 75 50N 68 40 E
Sprague, *U.S.A.* **114 C5** 47 18N 117 59W

Spratly I., *S. China Sea* **62 C4** 8 38N 111 55 E
Spratly Is., *S. China Sea* **62 C4** 8 20N 112 0 E
Spray, *U.S.A.* **114 D4** 44 50N 119 48W
Spreča →, *Bos.-H.* **42 F3** 44 44N 18 6 E
Spree →, *Germany* **24 C9** 52 32N 13 13 E
Spreewald, *Germany* **24 D9** 51 58N 13 51 E
Spremberg, *Germany* **24 D10** 51 34N 14 22 E
Sprengisandur, *Iceland* **8 D5** 64 52N 18 7W
Spring City, *U.S.A.* **111 F9** 40 11N 75 33W
Spring Creek, *U.S.A.* **114 F6** 40 45N 115 38W
Spring Garden, *U.S.A.* **116 F6** 39 52N 120 47W
Spring Hill, *U.S.A.* **109 L4** 28 27N 82 41W
Spring Mts., *U.S.A.* **115 H6** 36 0N 115 45W
Spring Valley, *U.S.A.* **117 N10** 32 45N 117 5W
Springbok, *S. Africa* **88 D2** 29 42 S 17 54 E
Springboro, *U.S.A.* **110 E4** 41 48N 80 22W
Springdale, *Canada* **103 C8** 49 30N 56 6W
Springdale, *U.S.A.* **113 G7** 36 11N 94 8W
Springe, *Germany* **24 C5** 52 13N 9 33 E
Springer, *U.S.A.* **113 G2** 36 22N 104 36W
Springerville, *U.S.A.* **115 J9** 34 8N 109 17W
Springfield, *Canada* **110 D4** 42 50N 80 56W
Springfield, *N.Z.* **91 K3** 43 19 S 171 56 E
Springfield, *Colo., U.S.A.* **113 G3** 37 24N 102 37W
Springfield, *Ill., U.S.A.* **112 F10** 39 48N 89 39W
Springfield, *Mass., U.S.A.* **111 D12** 42 6N 72 35W
Springfield, *Mo., U.S.A.* **113 G8** 37 13N 93 17W
Springfield, *Ohio, U.S.A.* **108 F4** 39 55N 83 49W
Springfield, *Oreg., U.S.A.* **114 D2** 44 3N 123 1W
Springfield, *Tenn., U.S.A.* **109 G2** 36 31N 86 53W
Springfield, *Vt., U.S.A.* **111 C12** 43 18N 72 29W
Springfontein, *S. Africa* **88 E4** 30 15 S 25 40 E
Springhill, *Canada* **103 C7** 45 40N 64 4W
Springhill, *U.S.A.* **113 J8** 33 0N 93 28W
Springhouse, *Canada* **104 C4** 51 56N 122 7W
Springs, *S. Africa* **89 D4** 26 13 S 28 25 E
Springsure, *Australia* **94 C4** 24 8 S 148 6 E
Springvale, *U.S.A.* **111 C14** 43 28N 70 48W
Springville, *Calif., U.S.A.* **116 J8** 36 8N 118 49W
Springville, *N.Y., U.S.A.* **110 D6** 42 31N 78 40W
Springville, *Utah, U.S.A.* **114 F8** 40 10N 111 37W
Springwater, *U.S.A.* **110 D7** 42 38N 77 35W
Spruce-Creek, *U.S.A.* **110 F6** 40 36N 78 9W
Spruce Mt., *U.S.A.* **111 B12** 44 12N 72 19W
Spur, *U.S.A.* **113 J4** 33 28N 100 52W
Spurn Hd., *U.K.* **12 D8** 53 35N 0 8 E
Spuž, *Montenegro, Yug.* **40 D3** 42 32N 19 10 E
Spuzzum, *Canada* **104 D4** 49 37N 121 23W
Squam L., *U.S.A.* **111 C13** 43 45N 71 32W
Squamish, *Canada* **104 D4** 49 45N 123 10W
Square Islands, *Canada* **103 B8** 52 47N 55 47W
Squillace, G. di, *Italy* **31 D9** 38 45N 16 50 E
Squinzano, *Italy* **31 B11** 40 26N 18 2 E
Squires, Mt., *Australia* **93 E4** 26 14 S 127 28 E
Srbac, *Bos.-H.* **42 E2** 45 7N 17 30 E
Srbica, *Kosovo, Yug.* **40 D4** 42 45N 20 47 E
Srbija = Serbia □, *Yugoslavia* **40 C5** 43 30N 21 0 E
Srbobran, *Serbia, Yug.* **42 E4** 45 32N 19 48 E
Sre Ambel, *Cambodia* **65 G4** 11 8N 103 46 E
Sre Khtum, *Cambodia* **65 F6** 12 10N 106 52 E
Sre Umbell = Sre Ambel, *Cambodia* **65 G4** 11 8N 103 46 E
Srebrenica, *Bos.-H.* **42 F4** 44 6N 19 18 E
Sredinny Ra. = Sredinnyy Khrebet, *Russia* **51 D16** 57 0N 160 0 E
Sredinnyy Khrebet, *Russia* **51 D16** 57 0N 160 0 E
Središče, *Slovenia* **29 B13** 46 24N 16 17 E
Sredna Gora, *Bulgaria* **41 D8** 42 40N 24 20 E
Srednekolymsk, *Russia* **51 C16** 67 27N 153 40 E
Sredni Rodopi, *Bulgaria* **41 E8** 41 40N 24 45 E
Srednogorie, *Bulgaria* **41 D8** 42 43N 24 10 E
Śrem, *Poland* **45 F4** 52 6N 17 2 E
Sremska Mitrovica, *Serbia, Yug.* **42 F4** 44 59N 19 38 E
Sremski Karlovci, *Serbia, Yug.* **42 E4** 45 12N 19 56 E
Srepok →, *Cambodia* **64 F6** 13 33N 106 16 E
Sretensk, *Russia* **51 D12** 52 10N 117 40 E
Sri Lanka ■, *Asia* **66 R12** 7 30N 80 50 E
Srikakulam, *India* **67 K13** 18 14N 83 58 E
Srinagar, *India* **69 B6** 34 5N 74 50 E
Środa Śląska, *Poland* **45 G3** 51 10N 16 36 E
Środa Wielkopolski, *Poland* **45 F4** 52 15N 17 19 E
Srpska Crnja, *Serbia, Yug.* **42 E5** 45 38N 20 44 E
Srpski Itebej, *Serbia, Yug.* **42 E5** 45 35N 20 44 E
Staaten →, *Australia* **94 B3** 16 24 S 141 17 E
Staberhuk, *Germany* **24 A7** 54 23N 11 18 E
Stade, *Germany* **24 B5** 53 35N 9 29 E
Stadskanaal, *Neths.* **17 A6** 53 4N 6 55 E
Stadtallendorf, *Germany* **24 E5** 50 48N 9 1 E
Stadthagen, *Germany* **24 C5** 52 19N 9 13 E
Stadtlohn, *Germany* **24 D2** 51 59N 6 55 E
Stadtroda, *Germany* **24 E7** 50 52N 11 44 E
Staffa, *U.K.* **14 E2** 56 27N 6 21W
Staffanstorp, *Sweden* **11 J7** 55 39N 13 13 E
Stafford, *U.K.* **12 E5** 52 49N 2 7W
Stafford, *U.S.A.* **113 G5** 37 58N 98 36W
Stafford Springs, *U.S.A.* **111 E12** 41 57N 72 18W
Staffordshire □, *U.K.* **12 E5** 52 53N 2 10W
Stagnone, *Italy* **30 E5** 37 53N 12 26 E
Staines, *U.K.* **13 F7** 51 26N 0 29W
Stainz, *Austria* **26 E8** 46 53N 15 17 E
Stakhanov, *Ukraine* **47 H10** 48 35N 38 40 E
Stalać, *Serbia, Yug.* **40 C5** 43 43N 21 28 E
Stalingrad = Volgograd, *Russia* **49 F7** 48 40N 44 25 E
Staliniri = Tskhinvali, *Georgia* **49 J7** 42 14N 44 1 E
Stalino = Donetsk, *Ukraine* **47 J9** 48 0N 37 45 E
Stalinogorsk = Novomoskovsk, *Russia* **46 E10** 54 5N 38 15 E
Stalis, *Greece* **36 D7** 35 17N 25 25 E
Stallarholmen, *Sweden* **10 E11** 59 22N 17 12 E
Ställdalen, *Sweden* **10 E8** 59 56N 14 56 E
Stalowa Wola, *Poland* **45 H9** 50 34N 22 3 E
Stalybridge, *U.K.* **12 D5** 53 28N 2 3W
Stamford, *Australia* **94 C3** 21 15 S 143 46 E
Stamford, *U.K.* **13 E7** 52 39N 0 29W
Stamford, *Conn., U.S.A.* **111 E11** 41 3N 73 32W
Stamford, *N.Y., U.S.A.* **111 D10** 42 25N 74 38W
Stamford, *Tex., U.S.A.* **113 J5** 32 57N 99 48W
Stampriet, *Namibia* **88 C2** 24 20 S 18 28 E
Stamps, *U.S.A.* **113 J8** 33 22N 93 30W
Stančevo = Kalipetrovo, *Bulgaria* **41 B11** 44 5N 27 14 E
Standerton, *S. Africa* **89 D4** 26 55 S 29 7 E
Standish, *U.S.A.* **108 D4** 43 59N 83 57W
Stanford, *S. Africa* **88 E2** 34 26 S 19 29 E
Stanford, *U.S.A.* **114 C8** 47 9N 110 13W
Stånga, *Sweden* **11 G12** 57 17N 18 29 E
Stanger, *S. Africa* **89 D5** 29 27 S 31 14 E
Stanišić, *Serbia, Yug.* **42 E4** 45 56N 19 10 E
Stanislaus →, *U.S.A.* **116 H5** 37 40N 121 14W
Stanislav = Ivano-Frankivsk, *Ukraine* **47 H3** 48 40N 24 40 E
Stanisławów, *Poland* **45 F8** 52 18N 21 33 E
Stanley, *Australia* **94 G4** 40 46 S 145 19 E
Stanley, *Canada* **105 B8** 55 24N 104 22W
Stanley, *Falk. Is.* **128 G5** 51 40 S 59 51W
Stanley, *U.K.* **12 C6** 54 53N 1 41W
Stanley, *Idaho, U.S.A.* **114 D6** 44 13N 114 56W
Stanley, *N. Dak., U.S.A.* **112 A3** 48 19N 102 23W
Stanley, *N.Y., U.S.A.* **110 D7** 42 48N 77 6W
Stanovoy Khrebet, *Russia* **51 D13** 55 0N 130 0 E
Stanovoy Ra. = Stanovoy Khrebet, *Russia* **51 D13** 55 0N 130 0 E
Stansmore Ra., *Australia* **92 D4** 21 23 S 128 33 E
Stanthorpe, *Australia* **95 D5** 28 36 S 151 59 E
Stanton, *U.S.A.* **113 J4** 32 8N 101 48W
Stanwood, *U.S.A.* **116 B4** 48 15N 122 23W
Staples, *U.S.A.* **112 B7** 46 21N 94 48W
Stąporków, *Poland* **45 G7** 51 9N 20 31 E
Star City, *Canada* **105 C8** 52 50N 104 20W
Star Lake, *U.S.A.* **111 B9** 44 10N 75 2W
Stará L'ubovňa, *Slovak Rep.* **27 B13** 49 18N 20 42 E
Stara Moravica, *Serbia, Yug.* **42 E4** 45 50N 19 30 E
Stara Pazova, *Serbia, Yug.* **42 F5** 44 58N 20 10 E
Stara Planina, *Bulgaria* **40 C7** 43 15N 23 0 E
Stará Turá, *Slovak Rep.* **27 C10** 48 47N 17 42 E
Stara Zagora, *Bulgaria* **41 D9** 42 26N 25 39 E
Starachowice, *Poland* **45 G8** 51 3N 21 2 E
Staraya Russa, *Russia* **46 D6** 57 58N 31 23 E
Starbuck I., *Kiribati* **97 H12** 5 37 S 155 55W
Starchiojd, *Romania* **43 E11** 45 19N 26 11 E
Stargard Szczeciński, *Poland* **44 E2** 53 20N 15 0 E
Stari Bar, *Montenegro, Yug.* **40 D3** 42 7N 19 10 E
Stari Trg, *Slovenia* **29 C12** 45 29N 15 7 E
Staritsa, *Russia* **46 D8** 56 33N 34 55 E
Starke, *U.S.A.* **109 L4** 29 57N 82 7W
Starnberg, *Germany* **25 H7** 48 0N 11 21 E
Starnberger See, *Germany* **25 H7** 47 54N 11 19 E
Starobilsk, *Ukraine* **47 H10** 49 16N 39 0 E
Starodub, *Russia* **47 F7** 52 30N 32 50 E
Starogard Gdański, *Poland* **44 E5** 53 59N 18 30 E
Starokonstantinov = Starokonstyantyniv, *Ukraine* **47 H4** 49 48N 27 10 E
Starokonstyantyniv, *Ukraine* **47 H4** 49 48N 27 10 E
Starominskaya, *Russia* **47 J10** 46 33N 39 0 E
Staroshcherbinovskaya, *Russia* **47 J10** 46 40N 38 53 E
Start Pt., *U.K.* **13 G4** 50 13N 3 39W
Stary Sącz, *Poland* **45 J7** 49 33N 20 35 E
Staryy Biryuzyak, *Russia* **49 H8** 44 46N 46 50 E
Staryy Chartoriysk, *Ukraine* **47 G3** 51 15N 25 54 E
Staryy Krym, *Ukraine* **47 K8** 45 3N 35 8 E
Staryy Oskol, *Russia* **47 G9** 51 19N 37 55 E
Stassfurt, *Germany* **24 D7** 51 51N 11 35 E
Staszów, *Poland* **45 H8** 50 33N 21 10 E
State College, *U.S.A.* **110 F7** 40 48N 77 52W
Stateline, *U.S.A.* **116 G7** 38 57N 119 56W
Staten, I. = Estados, I. de Los, *Argentina* **122 J4** 54 40 S 64 30W
Staten I., *U.S.A.* **111 F10** 40 35N 74 9W
Statesboro, *U.S.A.* **109 J5** 32 27N 81 47W
Statesville, *U.S.A.* **109 H5** 35 47N 80 53W
Stauffer, *U.S.A.* **117 L7** 34 45N 119 3W
Staunton, *Ill., U.S.A.* **112 F10** 39 1N 89 47W
Staunton, *Va., U.S.A.* **108 F6** 38 9N 79 4W
Stavanger, *Norway* **9 G11** 58 57N 5 40 E
Staveley, *N.Z.* **91 K3** 43 40 S 171 32 E
Stavelot, *Belgium* **17 D5** 50 23N 5 55 E
Stavern, *Norway* **9 G14** 59 0N 10 1 E
Stavoren, *Neths.* **17 B5** 52 53N 5 22 E
Stavropol, *Russia* **49 H6** 45 5N 42 0 E
Stavros, *Cyprus* **36 D11** 35 1N 32 38 E
Stavrós, *Greece* **36 D6** 35 12N 24 45 E
Stavrós, Ákra, *Greece* **36 D6** 35 26N 24 58 E
Stavroúpolis, *Greece* **41 E8** 41 12N 24 45 E
Stawell, *Australia* **95 F3** 37 5 S 142 47 E
Stawell →, *Australia* **94 C3** 20 20 S 142 55 E
Stawiski, *Poland* **44 E9** 53 22N 22 9 E
Stawiszyn, *Poland* **45 G5** 51 56N 18 4 E
Stayner, *Canada* **110 B4** 44 25N 80 5W
Stayton, *U.S.A.* **114 D2** 44 48N 122 48W
Steamboat Springs, *U.S.A.* **114 F10** 40 29N 106 50W
Stebleva = Steblevë, *Albania* **40 E4** 41 23N 20 33 E
Steblevë, *Albania* **40 E4** 41 23N 20 33 E
Steele, *U.S.A.* **112 B5** 46 51N 99 55W
Steelton, *U.S.A.* **110 F8** 40 14N 76 50W
Steen River, *Canada* **104 B5** 59 40N 117 12W
Steenkool = Bintuni, *Indonesia* **63 E8** 2 7 S 133 32 E
Steens Mt., *U.S.A.* **114 E4** 42 35N 118 40W
Steenwijk, *Neths.* **17 B6** 52 47N 6 7 E
Steep Pt., *Australia* **93 E1** 26 8 S 113 8 E
Steep Rock, *Canada* **105 C9** 51 30N 98 48W
Ştefan Vodă, *Moldova* **43 D14** 46 27N 29 42 E
Ştefănesti, *Romania* **43 C12** 47 44N 27 15 E
Stefanie L. = Chew Bahir, *Ethiopia* **81 G4** 4 40N 36 50 E
Stefansson Bay, *Antarctica* **5 C5** 67 20 S 59 8 E
Stege, *Denmark* **11 K6** 54 59N 12 18 E
Ştei, *Romania* **42 D7** 46 32N 22 27 E
Steiermark □, *Austria* **26 D8** 47 26N 15 0 E
Steigerwald, *Germany* **25 F6** 49 44N 10 26 E
Steilacoom, *U.S.A.* **116 C4** 47 10N 122 36W
Steilrandberge, *Namibia* **88 B1** 17 45 S 13 20 E
Steinbach, *Canada* **105 D9** 49 32N 96 40W
Steinfurt, *Germany* **24 C3** 52 9N 7 20 E
Steinhausen, *Namibia* **88 C2** 21 49 S 18 20 E
Steinheim, *Germany* **24 D5** 51 51N 9 5 E
Steinhuder Meer, *Germany* **24 C5** 52 29N 9 21 E
Steinkjer, *Norway* **8 D14** 64 1N 11 31 E
Steinkopf, *S. Africa* **88 D2** 29 18 S 17 43 E
Stellarton, *Canada* **103 C7** 45 32N 62 30W
Stellenbosch, *S. Africa* **88 E2** 33 58 S 18 50 E
Stelvio, Paso dello, *Italy* **28 B7** 46 32N 10 27 E
Stenay, *France* **19 C12** 49 29N 5 12 E
Stendal, *Germany* **24 C7** 52 36N 11 53 E
Stende, *Latvia* **44 A9** 57 11N 22 33 E
Stenhamra, *Sweden* **10 E11** 59 20N 17 41 E
Stenstorp, *Sweden* **11 F7** 58 17N 13 45 E
Stenungsund, *Sweden* **11 F5** 58 6N 11 50 E
Steornabhaigh = Stornoway, *U.K.* **14 C2** 58 13N 6 23W
Stepanakert = Xankändi, *Azerbaijan* **70 B5** 39 52N 46 49 E
Stepanavan, *Armenia* **49 K7** 41 1N 44 23 E
Stephens Creek, *Australia* **95 E3** 31 50 S 141 30 E
Stephens I., *Canada* **104 C2** 54 10N 130 45W
Stephens L., *Canada* **105 B9** 56 32N 95 0W
Stephenville, *Canada* **103 C8** 48 31N 58 35W
Stephenville, *U.S.A.* **113 J5** 32 13N 98 12W
Stepnica, *Poland* **44 E1** 53 38N 14 36 E
Stepnoi = Elista, *Russia* **49 G7** 46 16N 44 14 E
Steppe, *Asia* **52 D9** 50 0N 50 0 E
Stereá Ellas □, *Greece* **38 C4** 38 50N 23 0 E
Sterkstroom, *S. Africa* **88 E4** 31 32 S 26 32 E
Sterling, *Colo., U.S.A.* **112 E3** 40 37N 103 13W
Sterling, *Ill., U.S.A.* **112 E10** 41 48N 89 42W
Sterling, *Kans., U.S.A.* **112 F5** 38 13N 98 12W
Sterling City, *U.S.A.* **113 K4** 31 51N 101 0W
Sterling Heights, *U.S.A.* **108 D4** 42 35N 83 0W
Sterling Run, *U.S.A.* **110 E6** 41 25N 78 12W
Sterlitamak, *Russia* **50 D6** 53 40N 56 0 E
Sternberg, *Germany* **24 B7** 53 42N 11 50 E
Šternberk, *Czech Rep.* **27 B10** 49 45N 17 15 E
Stérnes, *Greece* **36 D6** 35 30N 24 9 E
Sterzing = Vipiteno, *Italy* **29 B8** 46 54N 11 26 E
Stettin = Szczecin, *Poland* **44 E1** 53 27N 14 27 E
Stettiner Haff, *Germany* **24 B10** 53 47N 14 15 E
Stettler, *Canada* **104 C6** 52 19N 112 40W
Steubenville, *U.S.A.* **110 F4** 40 22N 80 37W
Stevenage, *U.K.* **13 F7** 51 55N 0 13W
Stevens Point, *U.S.A.* **112 C10** 44 31N 89 34W
Stevenson, *U.S.A.* **116 E5** 45 42N 121 53W
Stevenson L., *Canada* **105 C9** 53 55N 96 0W
Stevensville, *U.S.A.* **114 C6** 46 30N 114 5W
Stevns Klint, *Denmark* **11 J6** 55 17N 12 28 E
Stewart, *B.C., Canada* **104 B3** 55 56N 129 57W
Stewart, *N.W.T., Canada* **100 B6** 63 19N 139 26W
Stewart, *U.S.A.* **116 F7** 39 5N 119 46W
Stewart, C., *Australia* **94 A1** 11 57 S 134 56 E
Stewart, I., *Chile* **128 G2** 54 50 S 71 15W
Stewart I., *N.Z.* **91 M1** 46 58 S 167 54 E
Stewarts Point, *U.S.A.* **116 G3** 38 39N 123 24W
Stewartville, *U.S.A.* **112 D8** 43 51N 92 29W
Stewiacke, *Canada* **103 C7** 45 9N 63 22W
Steynsburg, *S. Africa* **88 E4** 31 15 S 25 49 E
Steyr, *Austria* **26 C7** 48 3N 14 25 E
Steyr →, *Austria* **26 C7** 48 3N 14 25 E
Steytlerville, *S. Africa* **88 E3** 33 17 S 24 19 E
Stia, *Italy* **29 E8** 43 48N 11 42 E
Stigler, *U.S.A.* **113 H7** 35 15N 95 8W
Stigliano, *Italy* **31 B9** 40 24N 16 14 E
Stigtomta, *Sweden* **11 F10** 58 47N 16 48 E
Stikine →, *Canada* **104 B2** 56 40N 132 30W
Stilfontein, *S. Africa* **88 D4** 26 51 S 26 50 E
Stilís, *Greece* **38 C4** 38 55N 22 47 E
Stillwater, *N.Z.* **91 K3** 42 27 S 171 20 E
Stillwater, *Minn., U.S.A.* **112 C8** 45 3N 92 49W
Stillwater, *N.Y., U.S.A.* **111 D11** 42 55N 73 41W
Stillwater, *Okla., U.S.A.* **113 G6** 36 7N 97 4W
Stillwater Range, *U.S.A.* **114 G4** 39 50N 118 5W
Stillwater Reservoir, *U.S.A.* **111 C9** 43 54N 75 3W
Stilo, Pta., *Italy* **31 D9** 38 25N 16 35 E
Stilwell, *U.S.A.* **113 H7** 35 49N 94 38W
Štip, *Macedonia* **40 E6** 41 42N 22 10 E
Stíra, *Greece* **38 C6** 38 9N 24 14 E
Stirling, *Canada* **110 B7** 44 18N 77 33W
Stirling, *U.K.* **14 E5** 56 8N 3 57W
Stirling □, *U.K.* **14 E4** 56 12N 4 18W
Stirling Ra., *Australia* **93 F2** 34 23 S 118 0 E
Stittsville, *Canada* **111 A9** 45 15N 75 55W
Stjernøya, *Norway* **8 A20** 70 20N 22 40 E
Stjørdalshalsen, *Norway* **8 E14** 63 29N 10 51 E
Stockach, *Germany* **25 H5** 47 50N 9 1 E
Stockaryd, *Sweden* **11 G8** 57 19N 14 36 E
Stockerau, *Austria* **27 C9** 48 24N 16 12 E
Stockholm, *Sweden* **10 E12** 59 20N 18 3 E
Stockholms län □, *Sweden* **10 E12** 59 30N 18 20 E
Stockport, *U.K.* **12 D5** 53 25N 2 9W
Stocksbridge, *U.K.* **12 D6** 53 29N 1 35W
Stockton, *Calif., U.S.A.* **116 H5** 37 58N 121 17W
Stockton, *Kans., U.S.A.* **112 F5** 39 26N 99 16W
Stockton, *Mo., U.S.A.* **113 G8** 37 42N 93 48W
Stockton-on-Tees, *U.K.* **12 C6** 54 35N 1 19W
Stockton-on-Tees □, *U.K.* **12 C6** 54 35N 1 19W
Stockton Plateau, *U.S.A.* **113 K3** 30 30N 102 30W
Stoczek Łukowski, *Poland* **45 G8** 51 58N 21 58 E
Stöde, *Sweden* **10 B10** 62 28N 16 35 E
Stoeng Treng, *Cambodia* **64 F5** 13 31N 105 58 E
Stoer, Pt. of, *U.K.* **14 C3** 58 16N 5 23W
Stogovo, *Macedonia* **40 E4** 41 31N 20 38 E
Stoholm, *Denmark* **11 H3** 56 30N 9 8 E
Stoke-on-Trent, *U.K.* **12 D5** 53 1N 2 11W
Stoke-on-Trent □, *U.K.* **12 D5** 53 1N 2 11W
Stokes Pt., *Australia* **94 G3** 40 10 S 143 56 E
Stokes Ra., *Australia* **92 C5** 15 50 S 130 50 E
Stokksnes, *Iceland* **8 D6** 64 14N 14 58W
Stokmarknes, *Norway* **8 B16** 68 34N 14 54 E
Stolac, *Bos.-H.* **40 C1** 43 5N 17 59 E
Stolberg, *Germany* **24 E2** 50 47N 6 13 E
Stolbovoy, Ostrov, *Russia* **51 B14** 74 44N 135 14 E
Stolbtsy = Stowbtsy, *Belarus* **46 F4** 53 30N 26 43 E
Stolin, *Belarus* **47 G4** 51 53N 26 50 E
Stöllet, *Sweden* **10 D7** 60 26N 13 15 E
Stolnici, *Romania* **43 F9** 44 31N 24 48 E
Stomíon, *Greece* **36 D5** 35 21N 23 32 E
Ston, *Croatia* **29 F14** 42 51N 17 43 E
Stone, *U.K.* **12 E5** 52 55N 2 9W
Stoneboro, *U.S.A.* **110 E4** 41 20N 80 7W
Stonehaven, *U.K.* **14 E6** 56 59N 2 12W
Stonehenge, *Australia* **94 C3** 24 22 S 143 17 E
Stonehenge, *U.K.* **13 F6** 51 9N 1 45W
Stonewall, *Canada* **105 C9** 50 10N 97 19W
Stony L., *Man., Canada* **105 B9** 58 51N 98 40W
Stony L., *Ont., Canada* **110 B6** 44 30N 78 5W
Stony Point, *U.S.A.* **111 E11** 41 14N 73 59W
Stony Pt., *U.S.A.* **111 C8** 43 50N 76 18W
Stony Rapids, *Canada* **105 B7** 59 16N 105 50W
Stony Tunguska = Tunguska, Podkamennaya →, *Russia* **51 C10** 61 50N 90 13 E
Stonyford, *U.S.A.* **116 F4** 39 23N 122 33W
Stopnica, *Poland* **45 H7** 50 27N 20 57 E
Storå, *Sweden* **10 E9** 59 42N 15 6 E
Storå →, *Denmark* **11 H2** 56 20N 8 19 E
Stora Gla, *Sweden* **10 E6** 59 30N 12 30 E
Stora Le, *Sweden* **10 E5** 59 5N 11 55 E
Stora Lulevatten, *Sweden* **8 C18** 67 10N 19 30 E
Storavan, *Sweden* **8 D18** 65 45N 18 10 E
Stord, *Norway* **9 G11** 59 52N 5 23 E
Store Bælt, *Denmark* **11 J4** 55 20N 11 0 E
Store Heddinge, *Denmark* **11 J6** 55 18N 12 23 E
Storebro, *Sweden* **11 G9** 57 35N 15 52 E
Storfors, *Sweden* **10 E8** 59 32N 14 17 E
Storlien, *Sweden* **10 A6** 63 20N 12 5 E
Storm B., *Australia* **94 G4** 43 10 S 147 30 E
Storm Lake, *U.S.A.* **112 D7** 42 39N 95 13W
Stormberge, *S. Africa* **88 E4** 31 16 S 26 17 E
Stormsrivier, *S. Africa* **88 E3** 33 59 S 23 52 E
Stornoway, *U.K.* **14 C2** 58 13N 6 23W
Storo, *Italy* **28 C7** 45 51N 10 35 E
Storozhinets = Storozhynets, *Ukraine* **47 H3** 48 14N 25 45 E
Storozhynets, *Ukraine* **47 H3** 48 14N 25 45 E
Storrs, *U.S.A.* **111 E12** 41 49N 72 15W
Storsjön, *Gävleborg, Sweden* **10 D10** 60 35N 16 45 E
Storsjön, *Jämtland, Sweden* **10 B7** 62 48N 13 7 E
Storsjön, *Jämtland, Sweden* **10 A8** 63 9N 14 30 E
Storstrøms Amtskommune □, *Denmark* **11 J5** 54 50N 11 45 E
Storuman, *Sweden* **8 D17** 65 5N 17 10 E
Storuman, sjö, *Sweden* **8 D17** 65 13N 16 50 E
Storvätteshågna, *Sweden* **10 B6** 62 6N 12 30 E
Storvik, *Sweden* **10 D10** 60 35N 16 33 E
Storvreta, *Sweden* **10 E11** 59 58N 17 44 E
Stouffville, *Canada* **110 C5** 43 58N 79 15W
Stoughton, *Canada* **105 D8** 49 40N 103 0W
Stour →, *Dorset, U.K.* **13 G6** 50 43N 1 47W
Stour →, *Kent, U.K.* **13 F9** 51 18N 1 22 E
Stour →, *Suffolk, U.K.* **13 F9** 51 57N 1 4 E
Stourbridge, *U.K.* **13 E5** 52 28N 2 8W
Stout L., *Canada* **105 C10** 52 0N 94 40W
Stove Pipe Wells Village, *U.S.A.* **117 J9** 36 35N 117 11W
Støvring, *Denmark* **11 H3** 56 54N 9 50 E
Stow, *U.S.A.* **110 E3** 41 10N 81 27W
Stowbtsy, *Belarus* **46 F4** 53 30N 26 43 E
Stowmarket, *U.K.* **13 E9** 52 12N 1 0 E
Strabane, *U.K.* **15 B4** 54 50N 7 27W
Stracin, *Macedonia* **40 D6** 42 13N 22 2 E
Stradella, *Italy* **28 C6** 45 5N 9 18 E
Strahan, *Australia* **94 G4** 42 9 S 145 20 E
Strajitsa, *Bulgaria* **41 C9** 43 14N 25 58 E
Strakonice, *Czech Rep.* **26 B6** 49 15N 13 53 E
Straldzha, *Bulgaria* **41 D10** 42 35N 26 40 E
Stralsund, *Germany* **24 A9** 54 18N 13 4 E
Strand, *S. Africa* **88 E2** 34 9 S 18 48 E
Stranda, *Møre og Romsdal, Norway* **9 E12** 62 19N 6 58 E
Stranda, *Nord-Trøndelag, Norway* **8 E14** 63 33N 10 14 E
Strandby, *Denmark* **11 G4** 57 30N 10 29 E
Strangford L., *U.K.* **15 B6** 54 30N 5 37W
Strängnäs, *Sweden* **10 E11** 59 23N 17 2 E
Stranraer, *U.K.* **14 G3** 54 54N 5 1W
Strasbourg, *Canada* **105 C8** 51 4N 104 55W
Strasbourg, *France* **19 D14** 48 35N 7 42 E
Strasburg, *Germany* **24 B9** 53 30N 13 43 E
Străşeni, *Moldova* **43 C13** 47 8N 28 36 E
Stråssa, *Sweden* **10 E9** 59 44N 15 12 E
Stratford, *Canada* **102 D3** 43 23N 81 0W
Stratford, *N.Z.* **91 H5** 39 20 S 174 19 E
Stratford, *Calif., U.S.A.* **116 J7** 36 11N 119 49W
Stratford, *Conn., U.S.A.* **111 E11** 41 12N 73 8W
Stratford, *Tex., U.S.A.* **113 G3** 36 20N 102 4W
Stratford-upon-Avon, *U.K.* **13 E6** 52 12N 1 42W
Strath Spey, *U.K.* **14 D5** 57 9N 3 49W
Strathalbyn, *Australia* **95 F2** 35 13 S 138 53 E
Strathaven, *U.K.* **14 F4** 55 40N 4 5W
Strathcona Prov. Park, *Canada* **104 D3** 49 38N 125 40W
Strathmore, *Canada* **104 C6** 51 5N 113 18W
Strathmore, *U.K.* **14 E5** 56 37N 3 7W
Strathmore, *U.S.A.* **116 J7** 36 9N 119 4W
Strathnaver, *Canada* **104 C4** 53 20N 122 33W
Strathpeffer, *U.K.* **14 D4** 57 35N 4 32W
Strathroy, *Canada* **102 D3** 42 58N 81 38W
Strathy Pt., *U.K.* **14 C4** 58 36N 4 1W
Strattanville, *U.S.A.* **110 E5** 41 12N 79 19W
Stratton, *U.S.A.* **111 A14** 45 8N 70 26W
Stratton Mt., *U.S.A.* **111 C12** 43 4N 72 55W
Straubing, *Germany* **25 G8** 48 52N 12 34 E
Straumnes, *Iceland* **8 C2** 66 26N 23 8W
Strausberg, *Germany* **24 C9** 52 35N 13 54 E
Strawberry →, *U.S.A.* **114 F8** 40 10N 110 24W
Strážnice, *Czech Rep.* **27 C10** 48 54N 17 19 E
Streaky B., *Australia* **95 E1** 32 48 S 134 13 E
Streaky Bay, *Australia* **95 E1** 32 51 S 134 18 E
Streator, *U.S.A.* **112 E10** 41 8N 88 50W
Středočeský □, *Czech Rep.* **26 B7** 49 55N 14 30 E
Streetsboro, *U.S.A.* **110 E3** 41 14N 81 21W
Streetsville, *Canada* **110 C5** 43 35N 79 42W
Strehaia, *Romania* **43 F8** 44 37N 23 10 E
Strelcha, *Bulgaria* **41 D8** 42 25N 24 19 E
Strelka, *Russia* **51 D10** 58 5N 93 3 E
Streng →, *Cambodia* **64 F4** 13 12N 103 37 E
Stresa, *Italy* **28 C5** 45 52N 8 28 E
Streymoy, *Færoe Is.* **8 E9** 62 8N 7 5W
Strezhevoy, *Russia* **50 C8** 60 42N 77 34 E
Stříbro, *Czech Rep.* **26 A6** 49 44N 13 0 E
Strimón →, *Greece* **40 F7** 40 46N 23 51 E
Strimonikós Kólpos, *Greece* **40 F7** 40 33N 24 0 E
Strofádhes, *Greece* **38 D3** 37 15N 21 0 E
Stroma, *U.K.* **14 C5** 58 41N 3 7W
Strómboli, *Italy* **31 D8** 38 47N 15 13 E
Stromeferry, *U.K.* **14 D3** 57 21N 5 33W
Stromness, *U.K.* **14 C5** 58 58N 3 17W
Strömsbruk, *Sweden* **10 C11** 61 52N 17 18 E
Stromsburg, *U.S.A.* **112 E6** 41 7N 97 36W
Strömsnäsbruk, *Sweden* **11 H7** 56 35N 13 45 E
Strömstad, *Sweden* **11 F5** 58 56N 11 10 E
Strömsund, *Sweden* **8 E16** 63 51N 15 33 E
Strongilí, *Greece* **39 E11** 36 6N 29 42 E
Stróngoli, *Italy* **31 C10** 39 16N 17 3 E
Strongsville, *U.S.A.* **110 E3** 41 19N 81 50W
Stronie Śląskie, *Poland* **45 H3** 50 18N 16 53 E
Stronsay, *U.K.* **14 B6** 59 7N 2 35W
Stropkov, *Slovak Rep.* **27 B14** 49 13N 21 39 E
Stroud, *U.K.* **13 F5** 51 45N 2 13W
Stroud Road, *Australia* **95 E5** 32 18 S 151 57 E
Stroudsburg, *U.S.A.* **111 F9** 40 59N 75 12W
Stroumbi, *Cyprus* **36 E11** 34 53N 32 29 E
Struer, *Denmark* **11 H2** 56 30N 8 35 E
Struga, *Macedonia* **40 E4** 41 11N 20 44 E
Strugi Krasnyye, *Russia* **46 C5** 58 21N 29 1 E
Strumica, *Macedonia* **40 E6** 41 28N 22 41 E
Strumica →, *Europe* **40 E7** 41 20N 23 22 E
Struthers, *Canada* **102 C2** 48 41N 85 51W
Struthers, *U.S.A.* **110 E4** 41 4N 80 39W
Stryama, *Bulgaria* **41 D8** 42 16N 24 54 E
Stryker, *U.S.A.* **114 B6** 48 41N 114 46W
Stryków, *Poland* **45 G6** 51 55N 19 33 E
Stryy, *Ukraine* **47 H2** 49 16N 23 48 E
Strzegom, *Poland* **45 H3** 50 58N 16 20 E
Strzelce Krajeńskie, *Poland* **45 F2** 52 52N 15 33 E
Strzelce Opolskie, *Poland* **45 H5** 50 31N 18 18 E
Strzelecki Cr. →, *Australia* **95 D2** 29 37 S 139 59 E
Strzelin, *Poland* **45 H4** 50 46N 17 2 E
Strzelno, *Poland* **45 F5** 52 35N 18 9 E
Strzybnica, *Poland* **45 H5** 50 28N 18 48 E
Strzyżów, *Poland* **45 J8** 49 52N 21 47 E
Stuart, *Fla., U.S.A.* **109 M5** 27 12N 80 15W
Stuart, *Nebr., U.S.A.* **112 D5** 42 36N 99 8W
Stuart →, *Canada* **104 C4** 54 0N 123 35W
Stuart Bluff Ra., *Australia* **92 D5** 22 50 S 131 52 E
Stuart L., *Canada* **104 C4** 54 30N 124 30W
Stuart Ra., *Australia* **95 D1** 29 10 S 134 56 E
Stubbekøbing, *Denmark* **11 K6** 54 53N 12 9 E
Stuben, *Austria* **26 D3** 47 10N 10 8 E
Studen Kladenets, Yazovir, *Bulgaria* **41 E9** 41 37N 25 30 E
Studenka, *Czech Rep.* **27 B11** 49 44N 18 5 E
Stugun, *Sweden* **10 A9** 63 10N 15 40 E
Stuhr, *Germany* **24 B4** 53 5N 8 44 E
Stull L., *Canada* **102 B1** 54 24N 92 34W
Stung Treng = Stoeng Treng, *Cambodia* **64 F5** 13 31N 105 58 E
Stupart →, *Canada* **102 A1** 56 0N 93 25W
Stupava, *Slovak Rep.* **27 C10** 48 17N 17 2 E
Stupino, *Russia* **46 E10** 54 57N 38 2 E
Sturgeon B., *Canada* **105 C9** 52 0N 97 50W
Sturgeon Bay, *U.S.A.* **108 C2** 44 50N 87 23W
Sturgeon Falls, *Canada* **102 C4** 46 25N 79 57W
Sturgeon L., *Alta., Canada* **104 B5** 55 6N 117 32W
Sturgeon L., *Ont., Canada* **102 C1** 50 0N 90 45W
Sturgeon L., *Ont., Canada* **110 B6** 44 28N 78 43W
Sturgis, *Canada* **105 C8** 51 56N 102 36W
Sturgis, *Mich., U.S.A.* **108 E3** 41 48N 85 25W
Sturgis, *S. Dak., U.S.A.* **112 C3** 44 25N 103 31W
Sturkö, *Sweden* **11 H9** 56 5N 15 42 E
Štúrovo, *Slovak Rep.* **27 D11** 47 48N 18 41 E
Sturt Cr. →, *Australia* **92 C4** 19 8 S 127 50 E
Stutterheim, *S. Africa* **88 E4** 32 33 S 27 28 E
Stuttgart, *Germany* **25 G5** 48 48N 9 11 E
Stuttgart, *U.S.A.* **113 H9** 34 30N 91 33W
Stuyvesant, *U.S.A.* **111 D11** 42 23N 73 45W
Stykkishólmur, *Iceland* **8 D2** 65 2N 22 40W
Styria = Steiermark □, *Austria* **26 D8** 47 26N 15 0 E
Styrsö, *Sweden* **11 G5** 57 37N 11 46 E
Su Xian = Suzhou, *China* **56 H9** 33 41N 116 59 E
Suakin, *Sudan* **80 D4** 19 8N 37 20 E
Suan, *N. Korea* **57 E14** 38 42N 126 22 E
Suaqui, *Mexico* **118 B3** 29 12N 109 41W
Suar, *India* **69 E8** 29 2N 79 3 E
Subang, *Indonesia* **63 G12** 6 34 S 107 45 E
Subansiri →, *India* **67 F18** 26 48N 93 50 E
Subarnarekha →, *India* **69 H12** 22 34N 87 24 E
Subayhah, *Si. Arabia* **70 D3** 30 2N 38 50 E
Subcetate, *Romania* **42 E8** 45 36N 23 0 E
Subi, *Indonesia* **65 L7** 2 58N 108 50 E
Subiaco, *Italy* **29 G10** 41 56N 13 5 E
Subotica, *Serbia, Yug.* **42 D4** 46 6N 19 39 E
Suca, *Ethiopia* **81 F4** 6 31N 39 14 E
Suceava, *Romania* **43 C11** 47 38N 26 16 E
Suceava □, *Romania* **43 C10** 47 37N 25 40 E
Suceava →, *Romania* **43 C11** 47 32N 26 32 E
Sucha-Beskidzka, *Poland* **45 J6** 49 44N 19 35 E
Suchań, *Poland* **45 E2** 53 18N 15 18 E
Suchan, *Russia* **54 C6** 43 8N 133 9 E
Suchedniów, *Poland* **45 G7** 51 3N 20 49 E
Suchitoto, *El Salv.* **120 D2** 13 56N 89 0W
Suchou = Suzhou, *China* **59 B13** 31 19N 120 38 E
Süchow = Xuzhou, *China* **57 G9** 34 18N 117 10 E
Suchowola, *Poland* **44 E10** 53 33N 23 3 E
Suck →, *Ireland* **15 C3** 53 17N 8 3W
Sucre, *Bolivia* **124 G5** 19 0 S 65 15W
Sućuraj, *Croatia* **29 E14** 43 10N 17 8 E
Sucuriú →, *Brazil* **125 H8** 20 47 S 51 38W

Sud, Pte. du, *Canada* **103 C7** 49 3N 62 14W
Sud-Kivu □, *Dem. Rep. of the Congo* **86 C2** 3 30 S 28 0 E
Sud-Ouest, Pte. du, *Canada* **103 C7** 49 23N 63 36W
Suda →, *Russia* **46 C9** 59 0N 37 40 E
Sudak, *Ukraine* **47 K8** 44 51N 34 57 E
Sudan, *U.S.A.* **113 H3** 34 4N 102 32W
Sudan ■, *Africa* **81 E3** 15 0N 30 0 E
Sudbury, *Canada* **102 C3** 46 30N 81 0W
Sudbury, *U.K.* **13 E8** 52 2N 0 45 E
Sûdd, *Sudan* **81 F3** 8 20N 30 0 E
Süderbrarup, *Germany* **24 A5** 54 38N 9 45 E
Süderlügum, *Germany* **24 A4** 54 52N 8 54 E
Süderoogsand, *Germany* **24 A4** 54 27N 8 28 E
Sudeten Mts. = Sudety, *Europe* **27 A9** 50 20N 16 45 E
Sudety, *Europe* **27 A9** 50 20N 16 45 E
Suðuroy, *Færoe Is.* **8 F9** 61 32N 6 50W
Sudi, *Tanzania* **87 E4** 10 11 S 39 57 E
Sudirman, Pegunungan, *Indonesia* **63 E9** 4 30 S 137 0 E
Sudiţi, *Romania* **43 F12** 44 35N 27 38 E
Sudogda, *Russia* **48 C5** 55 55N 40 50 E
Sudr, *Egypt* **80 B3** 29 40N 32 42 E
Sudzha, *Russia* **47 G8** 51 14N 35 17 E
Sue →, *Sudan* **81 F2** 7 41N 28 3 E
Sueca, *Spain* **33 F4** 39 12N 0 21W
Sŭedinenie, *Bulgaria* **41 D8** 42 16N 24 33 E
Suemez I., *U.S.A.* **104 B2** 55 15N 133 20W
Suez = El Suweis, *Egypt* **80 J8** 29 58N 32 31 E
Suez, G. of = Suweis, Khalîg el, *Egypt* **80 J8** 28 40N 33 0 E
Suez Canal = Suweis, Qanâ es, *Egypt* **80 H8** 31 0N 32 20 E
Suffield, *Canada* **104 C6** 50 12N 111 10W
Suffolk, *U.S.A.* **108 G7** 36 44N 76 35W
Suffolk □, *U.K.* **13 E9** 52 16N 1 0 E
Şugag, *Romania* **43 E8** 45 47N 23 37 E
Sugargrove, *U.S.A.* **110 E5** 41 59N 79 21W
Sugarive →, *India* **69 F12** 26 16N 86 24 E
Suğla Gölü, *Turkey* **72 D5** 37 20N 32 0 E
Sugluk = Salluit, *Canada* **101 B12** 62 14N 75 38W
Suhaia, Lacul, *Romania* **43 G10** 43 45N 25 15 E
Şuḩār, *Oman* **71 E8** 24 20N 56 40 E
Sühbaatar □, *Mongolia* **56 B8** 45 30N 114 0 E
Suhl, *Germany* **24 E6** 50 36N 10 42 E
Şuhut, *Turkey* **39 C12** 38 31N 30 32 E
Sui, *Pakistan* **68 E3** 28 37N 69 19 E
Sui Xian, *China* **56 G8** 34 25N 115 2 E
Šuica, *Bos.-H.* **42 G2** 43 52N 17 11 E
Suichang, *China* **59 C12** 28 29N 119 15 E
Suichuan, *China* **59 D10** 26 20N 114 32 E
Suide, *China* **56 F6** 37 30N 110 12 E
Suifenhe, *China* **57 B16** 44 25N 131 10 E
Suihua, *China* **60 B7** 46 32N 126 55 E
Suijiang, *China* **58 C4** 28 40N 103 59 E
Suining, *Hunan, China* **59 D8** 26 35N 110 10 E
Suining, *Jiangsu, China* **57 H9** 33 56N 117 58 E
Suining, *Sichuan, China* **58 B5** 30 26N 105 35 E
Suiping, *China* **56 H7** 33 10N 113 59 E
Suippes, *France* **19 C11** 49 8N 4 30 E
Suir →, *Ireland* **15 D4** 52 16N 7 9W
Suisun City, *U.S.A.* **116 G4** 38 15N 122 2W
Suixi, *China* **59 G8** 21 19N 110 18 E
Suiyang, *Guizhou, China* **58 D6** 27 58N 107 18 E
Suiyang, *Heilongjiang, China* **57 B16** 44 30N 130 56 E
Suizhong, *China* **57 D11** 40 21N 120 20 E
Suizhou, *China* **59 B9** 31 42N 113 24 E
Sujangarh, *India* **68 F6** 27 42N 74 31 E
Sukabumi, *Indonesia* **63 G12** 6 56 S 106 50 E
Sukadana, *Indonesia* **62 E3** 1 10 S 110 0 E
Sukagawa, *Japan* **55 F10** 37 17N 140 23 E
Sukaraja, *Indonesia* **62 E4** 2 28 S 110 25 E
Sukarnapura = Jayapura, *Indonesia* **63 E10** 2 28 S 140 38 E
Sukch'ŏn, *N. Korea* **57 E13** 39 22N 125 35 E
Sukhindol, *Bulgaria* **41 C9** 43 11N 25 10 E
Sukhinichi, *Russia* **46 E8** 54 8N 35 10 E
Sukhona →, *Russia* **50 D4** 61 15N 46 39 E
Sukhothai, *Thailand* **64 D2** 17 1N 99 49 E
Sukhumi = Sokhumi, *Georgia* **49 J5** 43 0N 41 0 E
Sukkur, *Pakistan* **68 F3** 27 42N 68 54 E
Sukkur Barrage, *Pakistan* **68 F3** 27 40N 68 50 E
Sukovo, *Serbia, Yug.* **40 C6** 43 4N 22 37 E
Sukri →, *India* **68 G4** 25 4N 71 43 E
Sukumo, *Japan* **55 H6** 32 56N 132 44 E
Sukunka →, *Canada* **104 B4** 55 45N 121 15W
Sula →, *Ukraine* **47 H7** 49 40N 32 41 E
Sula, Kepulauan, *Indonesia* **63 E7** 1 45 S 125 0 E
Sulaco →, *Honduras* **120 C2** 15 2N 87 44W
Sulaiman Range, *Pakistan* **68 D3** 30 30N 69 50 E
Sulak →, *Russia* **49 J8** 43 20N 47 34 E
Sūlār, *Iran* **71 D6** 31 53N 51 54 E
Sulawesi Sea = Celebes Sea, *Indonesia* **63 D6** 3 0N 123 0 E
Sulawesi Selatan □, *Indonesia* **63 E6** 2 30 S 125 0 E
Sulawesi Utara □, *Indonesia* **63 D6** 1 0N 122 30 E
Sulechów, *Poland* **45 F2** 52 5N 15 40 E
Sulęcin, *Poland* **45 F2** 52 26N 15 10 E
Sulejów, *Poland* **45 G6** 51 26N 19 53 E
Sulejówek, *Poland* **45 F8** 52 13N 21 17 E
Süleymanlı, *Turkey* **39 C9** 38 58N 27 47 E
Sulima, *S. Leone* **82 D2** 6 58N 11 32W
Sulina, *Romania* **43 E14** 45 10N 29 40 E
Sulina, Braţul →, *Romania* **43 E14** 45 10N 29 40 E
Sulingen, *Germany* **24 C4** 52 41N 8 48 E
Suliţa, *Romania* **43 C11** 47 39N 26 59 E
Sulitjelma, *Norway* **8 C17** 67 9N 16 3 E
Sułkowice, *Poland* **45 J6** 49 50N 19 49 E
Sullana, *Peru* **124 D2** 4 52 S 80 39W
Süller, *Turkey* **39 C11** 38 9N 29 29 E
Sullivan, *Ill., U.S.A.* **112 F10** 39 36N 88 37W
Sullivan, *Ind., U.S.A.* **108 F2** 39 6N 87 24W
Sullivan, *Mo., U.S.A.* **112 F9** 38 13N 91 10W
Sullivan Bay, *Canada* **104 C3** 50 55N 126 50W
Sullivan I. = Lambi Kyun, *Burma* **65 G2** 10 50N 98 20 E
Sully-sur-Loire, *France* **19 E9** 47 45N 2 20 E
Sulmierzyce, *Poland* **45 G4** 51 37N 17 32 E
Sulmona, *Italy* **29 F10** 42 3N 13 55 E
Süloğlu, *Turkey* **41 E10** 41 44N 26 53 E
Sulphur, *La., U.S.A.* **113 K8** 30 14N 93 23W
Sulphur, *Okla., U.S.A.* **113 H6** 34 31N 96 58W
Sulphur Pt., *Canada* **104 A6** 60 56N 114 48W
Sulphur Springs, *U.S.A.* **113 J7** 33 8N 95 36W
Sultan, *Canada* **102 C3** 47 36N 82 47W
Sultan, *U.S.A.* **116 C5** 47 52N 121 49W
Sultan Dağları, *Turkey* **72 C4** 38 20N 31 20 E
Sultanhisar, *Turkey* **39 D10** 37 53N 28 9 E
Sultaniça, *Turkey* **41 F10** 40 37N 26 8 E
Sultaniye, *Turkey* **41 F12** 40 11N 28 12 E
Sultanpur, *Mad. P., India* **68 H8** 23 9N 77 56 E
Sultanpur, *Punjab, India* **68 D6** 31 13N 75 11 E
Sultanpur, *Ut. P., India* **69 F10** 26 18N 82 4 E
Sulu Arch., *Phil.* **61 J4** 6 0N 121 0 E
Sulu Sea, *E. Indies* **61 G4** 8 0N 120 0 E
Sülüklü, *Turkey* **72 C5** 38 53N 32 20 E
Sululta, *Ethiopia* **81 F4** 9 10N 38 43 E
Suluova, *Turkey* **72 B6** 40 46N 35 32 E
Suluq, *Libya* **79 B10** 31 44N 20 14 E
Sulzbach, *Germany* **25 F3** 49 18N 7 3 E
Sulzbach-Rosenberg, *Germany* **25 F7** 49 30N 11 44 E
Sulzberger Ice Shelf, *Antarctica* **5 D10** 78 0 S 150 0 E
Sumalata, *Indonesia* **63 D6** 1 0N 122 31 E
Sumampa, *Argentina* **126 B3** 29 25 S 63 29W
Sumatera □, *Indonesia* **62 D2** 0 40N 100 20 E
Sumatera Barat □, *Indonesia* **62 E2** 1 0 S 101 0 E
Sumatera Utara □, *Indonesia* **62 D1** 2 30N 98 0 E
Sumatra = Sumatera □, *Indonesia* **62 D2** 0 40N 100 20 E
Sumba, *Indonesia* **63 F5** 9 45 S 119 35 E
Sumba, Selat, *Indonesia* **63 F5** 9 0 S 118 40 E
Sumbawa, *Indonesia* **62 F5** 8 26 S 117 30 E
Sumbawa Besar, *Indonesia* **62 F5** 8 30 S 117 26 E
Sumbawanga □, *Tanzania* **84 F6** 8 0 S 31 30 E
Sumbe, *Angola* **84 G2** 11 10 S 13 48 E
Sumburgh Hd., *U.K.* **14 B7** 59 52N 1 17W
Sumdeo, *India* **69 D8** 31 26N 78 44 E
Sumdo, *India* **69 B8** 35 6N 78 41 E
Sumedang, *Indonesia* **63 G12** 6 52 S 107 55 E
Sümeg, *Hungary* **42 D2** 46 59N 17 20 E
Sumeih, *Sudan* **81 F2** 9 50N 27 39 E
Šumen = Shumen, *Bulgaria* **41 C10** 43 18N 26 55 E
Sumenep, *Indonesia* **63 G15** 7 1 S 113 52 E
Sumgait = Sumqayıt, *Azerbaijan* **49 K9** 40 34N 49 38 E
Summer L., *U.S.A.* **114 E3** 42 50N 120 45W
Summerland, *Canada* **104 D5** 49 32N 119 41W
Summerside, *Canada* **103 C7** 46 24N 63 47W
Summersville, *U.S.A.* **108 F5** 38 17N 80 51W
Summerville, *Ga., U.S.A.* **109 H3** 34 29N 85 21W
Summerville, *S.C., U.S.A.* **109 J5** 33 1N 80 11W
Summit Lake, *Canada* **104 C4** 54 20N 122 40W
Summit Peak, *U.S.A.* **115 H10** 37 21N 106 42W
Sumner, *Iowa, U.S.A.* **112 D8** 42 51N 92 6W
Sumner, *Wash., U.S.A.* **116 C4** 47 12N 122 14W
Sumoto, *Japan* **55 G7** 34 21N 134 54 E
Šumperk, *Czech Rep.* **27 B9** 49 59N 16 59 E
Sumqayıt, *Azerbaijan* **49 K9** 40 34N 49 38 E
Sumter, *U.S.A.* **109 J5** 33 55N 80 21W
Sumy, *Ukraine* **47 G8** 50 57N 34 50 E
Sun City, *Ariz., U.S.A.* **115 K7** 33 36N 112 17W
Sun City, *Calif., U.S.A.* **117 M9** 33 42N 117 11W
Sun City Center, *U.S.A.* **109 M4** 27 43N 82 18W
Sun Lakes, *U.S.A.* **115 K8** 33 10N 111 52W
Sun Valley, *U.S.A.* **114 E6** 43 42N 114 21W
Sunagawa, *Japan* **54 C10** 43 29N 141 55 E
Sunan, *N. Korea* **57 E13** 39 15N 125 40 E
Sunart, L., *U.K.* **14 E3** 56 42N 5 43W
Sunburst, *U.S.A.* **114 B8** 48 53N 111 55W
Sunbury, *Australia* **95 F3** 37 35 S 144 44 E
Sunbury, *U.S.A.* **111 F8** 40 52N 76 48W
Sunchales, *Argentina* **126 C3** 30 58 S 61 35W
Suncho Corral, *Argentina* **126 B3** 27 55 S 63 27W
Sunch'ŏn, *S. Korea* **57 G14** 34 52N 127 31 E
Suncook, *U.S.A.* **111 C13** 43 8N 71 27W
Sunda, Selat, *Indonesia* **62 F3** 6 20 S 105 30 E
Sunda Is., *Indonesia* **52 K14** 5 0 S 105 0 E
Sunda Str. = Sunda, Selat, *Indonesia* **62 F3** 6 20 S 105 30 E
Sundance, *Canada* **105 B10** 56 32N 94 4W
Sundance, *U.S.A.* **112 C2** 44 24N 104 23W
Sundar Nagar, *India* **68 D7** 31 32N 76 53 E
Sundarbans, The, *Asia* **67 J16** 22 0N 89 0 E
Sundargarh, *India* **67 H14** 22 4N 84 5 E
Sundays = Sondags →, *S. Africa* **88 E4** 33 44 S 25 51 E
Sunderland, *Canada* **110 B5** 44 16N 79 4W
Sunderland, *U.K.* **12 C6** 54 55N 1 23W
Sundre, *Canada* **104 C6** 51 49N 114 38W
Sunds, *Denmark* **11 H3** 56 13N 9 1 E
Sundsvall, *Sweden* **10 B11** 62 23N 17 17 E
Sundsvallsbukten, *Sweden* **10 B11** 62 21N 17 25 E
Sung Hei, *Vietnam* **65 G6** 10 20N 106 2 E
Sungai Kolok, *Thailand* **65 J3** 6 2N 101 58 E
Sungai Lembing, *Malaysia* **65 L4** 3 55N 103 3 E
Sungai Petani, *Malaysia* **65 K3** 5 37N 100 30 E
Sungaigerong, *Indonesia* **62 E2** 2 59 S 104 52 E
Sungailiat, *Indonesia* **62 E3** 1 51 S 106 8 E
Sungaipenuh, *Indonesia* **62 E2** 2 1 S 101 20 E
Sungari = Songhua Jiang →, *China* **60 B8** 47 45N 132 30 E
Sunghua Chiang = Songhua Jiang →, *China* **60 B8** 47 45N 132 30 E
Sungikai, *Sudan* **81 E2** 12 20N 29 51 E
Sungurlu, *Turkey* **72 B6** 40 12N 34 21 E
Sunja, *Croatia* **29 C13** 45 21N 16 35 E
Sunland Park, *U.S.A.* **115 L10** 31 50N 106 40W
Sunnansjö, *Sweden* **10 D8** 60 13N 14 58 E
Sunndalsøra, *Norway* **9 E13** 62 40N 8 33 E
Sunne, *Sweden* **10 E7** 59 52N 13 5 E
Sunnemo, *Sweden* **10 E7** 59 53N 13 44 E
Sunnyside, *U.S.A.* **114 C3** 46 20N 120 0W
Sunnyvale, *U.S.A.* **116 H4** 37 23N 122 2W
Suntar, *Russia* **51 C12** 62 15N 117 30 E
Sunyani, *Ghana* **82 D4** 7 21N 2 22W
Suomenselkä, *Finland* **8 E21** 62 52N 24 0 E
Suomussalmi, *Finland* **8 D23** 64 54N 29 10 E
Suoyarvi, *Russia* **46 A7** 62 3N 32 20 E
Supai, *U.S.A.* **115 H7** 36 15N 112 41W
Supaul, *India* **69 F12** 26 10N 86 40 E
Superior, *Ariz., U.S.A.* **115 K8** 33 18N 111 6W
Superior, *Mont., U.S.A.* **114 C6** 47 12N 114 53W
Superior, *Nebr., U.S.A.* **112 E5** 40 1N 98 4W
Superior, *Wis., U.S.A.* **112 B8** 46 44N 92 6W
Superior, L., *N. Amer.* **102 C2** 47 0N 87 0W
Supetar, *Croatia* **29 E13** 43 25N 16 32 E
Suphan Buri, *Thailand* **64 E3** 14 14N 100 10 E
Suphan Dağı, *Turkey* **70 B4** 38 54N 42 48 E
Supiori, *Indonesia* **63 E9** 1 0 S 136 0 E
Supraśl, *Poland* **45 E10** 53 13N 23 19 E
Supraśl →, *Poland* **45 E9** 53 11N 22 57 E
Supung Shuiku, *China* **57 D13** 40 35N 124 50 E
Sūq Suwayq, *Si. Arabia* **70 E3** 24 23N 38 27 E
Suqian, *China* **57 H10** 33 54N 118 8 E
Sūr, *Lebanon* **75 B4** 33 19N 35 16 E
Sūr, *Oman* **74 C6** 22 34N 59 32 E
Sur, Pt., *U.S.A.* **116 J5** 36 18N 121 54W
Sura →, *Russia* **48 C8** 56 6N 46 0 E
Surab, *Pakistan* **68 E2** 28 25N 66 15 E
Surabaja = Surabaya, *Indonesia* **63 G15** 7 17 S 112 45 E
Surabaya, *Indonesia* **63 G15** 7 17 S 112 45 E
Surahammar, *Sweden* **10 E10** 59 43N 16 13 E
Suraia, *Romania* **43 E12** 45 40N 27 25 E
Surakarta, *Indonesia* **63 G14** 7 35 S 110 48 E
Surakhany, *Azerbaijan* **49 K10** 40 25N 50 1 E
Šurany, *Slovak Rep.* **27 C11** 48 6N 18 10 E
Surat, *Australia* **95 D4** 27 10 S 149 6 E
Surat, *India* **66 J8** 21 12N 72 55 E
Surat Thani, *Thailand* **65 H2** 9 6N 99 20 E
Suratgarh, *India* **68 E5** 29 18N 73 55 E
Suraż, *Poland* **45 F9** 52 57N 22 57 E
Surazh, *Belarus* **46 E6** 55 25N 30 44 E
Surazh, *Russia* **47 F7** 53 5N 32 27 E
Surduc, *Romania* **43 C8** 47 15N 23 25 E
Surduc Pasul, *Romania* **43 E8** 45 21N 23 23 E
Surdulica, *Serbia, Yug.* **40 D6** 42 41N 22 11 E
Surendranagar, *India* **68 H4** 22 45N 71 40 E
Surf, *U.S.A.* **117 L6** 34 41N 120 36W
Surgères, *France* **20 B3** 46 7N 0 47W
Surgut, *Russia* **50 C8** 61 14N 73 20 E
Sùria, *Spain* **32 D6** 41 50N 1 45 E
Suriapet, *India* **66 L11** 17 10N 79 40 E
Surigao, *Phil.* **61 G6** 9 47N 125 29 E
Surigao Strait, *Phil.* **61 F6** 10 15N 125 23 E
Surin, *Thailand* **64 E4** 14 50N 103 34 E
Surin Nua, Ko, *Thailand* **65 H1** 9 30N 97 55 E
Surinam ■, *S. Amer.* **125 C7** 4 0N 56 0W
Suriname = Surinam ■, *S. Amer.* **125 C7** 4 0N 56 0W
Suriname →, *Surinam* **125 B7** 5 50N 55 15W
Sūrmaq, *Iran* **71 D7** 31 3N 52 48 E
Sürmene, *Turkey* **73 B9** 41 0N 40 1 E
Surovikino, *Russia* **49 F6** 48 32N 42 55 E
Surrey □, *U.K.* **13 F7** 51 15N 0 31W
Sursand, *India* **69 F11** 26 39N 85 43 E
Sursar →, *India* **69 F12** 26 14N 87 3 E
Sursee, *Switz.* **25 H4** 47 11N 8 6 E
Sursk, *Russia* **48 D7** 53 3N 45 40 E
Surskoye, *Russia* **48 C8** 54 30N 46 44 E
Surt, *Libya* **79 B9** 31 11N 16 39 E
Surt, Khalīj, *Libya* **79 B9** 31 40N 18 30 E
Surtanahu, *Pakistan* **68 F4** 26 22N 70 0 E
Surte, *Sweden* **11 G6** 57 50N 12 1 E
Surtsey, *Iceland* **8 E3** 63 20N 20 30W
Sürüç, *Turkey* **73 D8** 36 58N 38 25 E
Suruga-Wan, *Japan* **55 G9** 34 45N 138 30 E
Susa, *Italy* **28 C4** 45 8N 7 3 E
Suså →, *Denmark* **11 J5** 55 12N 11 42 E
Sušac, *Croatia* **29 F13** 42 46N 16 30 E
Susak, *Croatia* **29 D11** 44 30N 14 18 E
Susaki, *Japan* **55 H6** 33 22N 133 17 E
Sūsangerd, *Iran* **71 D6** 31 35N 48 6 E
Susanville, *U.S.A.* **114 F3** 40 25N 120 39W
Susch, *Switz.* **25 J6** 46 46N 10 5 E
Suşehri, *Turkey* **73 B8** 40 10N 38 6 E
Sušice, *Czech Rep.* **26 B6** 49 17N 13 30 E
Susleni, *Moldova* **43 C13** 47 25N 28 59 E
Susner, *India* **68 H7** 23 57N 76 5 E
Susong, *China* **59 B11** 30 10N 116 5 E
Susquehanna, *U.S.A.* **111 E9** 41 57N 75 36W
Susquehanna →, *U.S.A.* **111 G8** 39 33N 76 5W
Susques, *Argentina* **126 A2** 23 35 S 66 25W
Sussex, *Canada* **103 C6** 45 45N 65 37W
Sussex, *U.S.A.* **111 E10** 41 13N 74 37W
Sussex, E. □, *U.K.* **13 G8** 51 0N 0 20 E
Sussex, W. □, *U.K.* **13 G7** 51 0N 0 30W
Sustut →, *Canada* **104 B3** 56 20N 127 30W
Susuman, *Russia* **51 C15** 62 47N 148 10 E
Susunu, *Indonesia* **63 E8** 3 20 S 133 25 E
Susurluk, *Turkey* **39 B10** 39 54N 28 8 E
Susuz, *Turkey* **73 B10** 40 46N 43 8 E
Susz, *Poland* **44 E6** 53 44N 19 20 E
Sütçüler, *Turkey* **72 D4** 37 29N 30 57 E
Şuteşti, *Romania* **43 E12** 45 13N 27 27 E
Sutherland, *S. Africa* **88 E3** 32 24 S 20 40 E
Sutherland, *U.S.A.* **112 E4** 41 10N 101 8W
Sutherland Falls, *N.Z.* **91 L1** 44 48 S 167 46 E
Sutherlin, *U.S.A.* **114 E2** 43 23N 123 19W
Suthri, *India* **68 H3** 23 3N 68 55 E
Sutlej →, *Pakistan* **68 E4** 29 23N 71 3 E
Sutter, *U.S.A.* **116 F5** 39 10N 121 45W
Sutter Creek, *U.S.A.* **116 G6** 38 24N 120 48W
Sutton, *Canada* **111 A12** 45 6N 72 37W
Sutton, *Nebr., U.S.A.* **112 E6** 40 36N 97 52W
Sutton, *W. Va., U.S.A.* **108 F5** 38 40N 80 43W
Sutton →, *Canada* **102 A3** 55 15N 83 45W
Sutton Coldfield, *U.K.* **13 E6** 52 35N 1 49W
Sutton in Ashfield, *U.K.* **12 D6** 53 8N 1 16W
Sutton L., *Canada* **102 B3** 54 15N 84 42W
Suttor →, *Australia* **94 C4** 21 36 S 147 2 E
Suttsu, *Japan* **54 C10** 42 48N 140 14 E
Suva, *Fiji* **91 D8** 18 6 S 178 30 E
Suva Gora, *Macedonia* **40 E5** 41 45N 21 3 E
Suva Planina, *Serbia, Yug.* **40 C6** 43 10N 22 5 E
Suva Reka, *Kosovo, Yug.* **40 D4** 42 21N 20 50 E
Suvorov, *Russia* **46 E9** 54 7N 36 30 E
Suvorov Is. = Suwarrow Is., *Cook Is.* **97 J11** 15 0 S 163 0W
Suvorovo, *Bulgaria* **41 C11** 43 20N 27 35 E
Suwałki, *Poland* **44 D9** 54 8N 22 59 E
Suwannaphum, *Thailand* **64 E4** 15 33N 103 47 E
Suwannee →, *U.S.A.* **109 L4** 29 17N 83 10W
Suwanose-Jima, *Japan* **55 K4** 29 38N 129 43 E
Suwarrow Is., *Cook Is.* **97 J11** 15 0 S 163 0W
Suwayq aş Şuqban, *Iraq* **70 D5** 31 32N 46 7 E
Suweis, Khalîg el, *Egypt* **80 J8** 28 40N 33 0 E
Suweis, Qanâ es, *Egypt* **80 H8** 31 0N 32 20 E
Suwŏn, *S. Korea* **57 F14** 37 17N 127 1 E
Suzdal, *Russia* **46 D11** 56 29N 40 26 E
Suzhou, *Anhui, China* **56 H9** 33 41N 116 59 E
Suzhou, *Jiangsu, China* **59 B13** 31 19N 120 38 E
Suzu, *Japan* **55 F8** 37 25N 137 17 E
Suzu-Misaki, *Japan* **55 F8** 37 31N 137 21 E
Suzuka, *Japan* **55 G8** 34 55N 136 36 E
Suzzara, *Italy* **28 D7** 44 59N 10 45 E
Svalbard, *Arctic* **4 B8** 78 0N 17 0 E
Svalöv, *Sweden* **11 J7** 55 57N 13 8 E
Svaneke, *Denmark* **11 J9** 55 8N 15 8 E
Svängsta, *Sweden* **11 H8** 56 16N 14 47 E
Svanskog, *Sweden* **10 E6** 59 11N 12 33 E
Svappavaara, *Sweden* **8 C19** 67 40N 21 3 E
Svärdsjö, *Sweden* **10 D9** 60 45N 15 54 E
Svartå, *Sweden* **10 E8** 59 8N 14 32 E
Svartisen, *Norway* **8 C15** 66 40N 13 50 E
Svartvik, *Sweden* **10 B11** 62 19N 17 24 E
Svatove, *Ukraine* **47 H10** 49 22N 38 15 E
Svatovo = Svatove, *Ukraine* **47 H10** 49 22N 38 15 E
Svay Chek, *Cambodia* **64 F4** 13 48N 102 58 E
Svay Rieng, *Cambodia* **65 G5** 11 9N 105 45 E
Svealand □, *Sweden* **10 D9** 60 20N 15 0 E
Svedala, *Sweden* **11 J7** 55 30N 13 15 E
Sveg, *Sweden* **10 B8** 62 2N 14 21 E
Svendborg, *Denmark* **11 J4** 55 4N 10 35 E
Svenljunga, *Sweden* **11 G7** 57 29N 13 5 E
Svenstavik, *Sweden* **10 B8** 62 45N 14 26 E
Svenstrup, *Denmark* **11 H3** 56 58N 9 50 E
Sverdlovsk = Yekaterinburg, *Russia* **50 D7** 56 50N 60 30 E
Sverdlovsk, *Ukraine* **47 H10** 48 5N 39 47 E
Sverdrup Is., *Canada* **4 B3** 79 0N 97 0W
Svetac, *Croatia* **29 E12** 43 3N 15 43 E
Sveti Nikola, Prokhad, *Europe* **40 C6** 43 27N 22 6 E
Sveti Nikole, *Macedonia* **40 E5** 41 51N 21 56 E
Sveti Rok, *Croatia* **29 D12** 44 22N 15 39 E
Svetlaya, *Russia* **54 A9** 46 33N 138 18 E
Svetlogorsk = Svyetlahorsk, *Belarus* **47 F5** 52 38N 29 46 E
Svetlograd, *Russia* **49 H6** 45 25N 42 58 E
Svetlovodsk = Svitlovodsk, *Ukraine* **47 H7** 49 2N 33 13 E
Svidník, *Slovak Rep.* **27 B14** 49 20N 21 37 E
Svilaja Planina, *Croatia* **29 E13** 43 49N 16 31 E
Svilajnac, *Serbia, Yug.* **40 B5** 44 15N 21 11 E
Svilengrad, *Bulgaria* **41 E10** 41 49N 26 12 E
Svir →, *Russia* **46 B7** 60 30N 32 48 E
Sviritsa, *Russia* **46 B7** 60 29N 32 51 E
Svishtov, *Bulgaria* **41 C9** 43 36N 25 23 E
Svislach, *Belarus* **47 F3** 53 3N 24 2 E
Svitava →, *Czech Rep.* **27 B9** 49 11N 16 37 E
Svitavy, *Czech Rep.* **27 B9** 49 47N 16 28 E
Svitlovodsk, *Ukraine* **47 H7** 49 2N 33 13 E
Svobodnyy, *Russia* **51 D13** 51 20N 128 0 E
Svoge, *Bulgaria* **40 D7** 42 59N 23 23 E
Svolvær, *Norway* **8 B16** 68 15N 14 34 E
Svratka →, *Czech Rep.* **27 B9** 49 11N 16 38 E
Svrljig, *Serbia, Yug.* **40 C6** 43 25N 22 6 E
Svyetlahorsk, *Belarus* **47 F5** 52 38N 29 46 E
Swabian Alps = Schwäbische Alb, *Germany* **25 G5** 48 20N 9 30 E
Swainsboro, *U.S.A.* **109 J4** 32 36N 82 20W
Swakop →, *Namibia* **88 C2** 22 38 S 14 36 E
Swakopmund, *Namibia* **88 C1** 22 37 S 14 30 E
Swale →, *U.K.* **12 C6** 54 5N 1 20W
Swan →, *Australia* **93 F2** 32 3 S 115 45 E
Swan →, *Canada* **105 C8** 52 30N 100 45W
Swan Hill, *Australia* **95 F3** 35 20 S 143 33 E
Swan Hills, *Canada* **104 C5** 54 43N 115 24W
Swan Is., *W. Indies* **120 C3** 17 22N 83 57W
Swan L., *Canada* **105 C8** 52 30N 100 40W
Swan Peak, *U.S.A.* **114 C7** 47 43N 113 38W
Swan Ra., *U.S.A.* **114 C7** 48 0N 113 45W
Swan Reach, *Australia* **95 E2** 34 35 S 139 37 E
Swan River, *Canada* **105 C8** 52 10N 101 16W
Swanage, *U.K.* **13 G6** 50 36N 1 58W
Swansea, *Australia* **94 G4** 42 8 S 148 4 E
Swansea, *Canada* **110 C5** 43 38N 79 28W
Swansea, *U.K.* **13 F4** 51 37N 3 57W
Swansea □, *U.K.* **13 F3** 51 38N 4 3W
Swar →, *Pakistan* **69 B5** 34 40N 72 5 E
Swartberge, *S. Africa* **88 E3** 33 20 S 22 0 E
Swartmodder, *S. Africa* **88 D3** 28 1 S 20 32 E
Swartnossob →, *Namibia* **88 C2** 23 8 S 18 42 E
Swartruggens, *S. Africa* **88 D4** 25 39 S 26 42 E
Swarzędz, *Poland* **45 F4** 52 25N 17 4 E
Swastika, *Canada* **102 C3** 48 7N 80 6W
Swatow = Shantou, *China* **59 F11** 23 18N 116 40 E
Swaziland ■, *Africa* **89 D5** 26 30 S 31 30 E
Sweden ■, *Europe* **9 G16** 57 0N 15 0 E
Swedru, *Ghana* **83 D4** 5 32N 0 41W
Sweet Home, *U.S.A.* **114 D2** 44 24N 122 44W
Sweetgrass, *U.S.A.* **114 B8** 48 59N 111 58W
Sweetwater, *Nev., U.S.A.* **116 G7** 38 27N 119 9W
Sweetwater, *Tenn., U.S.A.* **109 H3** 35 36N 84 28W
Sweetwater, *Tex., U.S.A.* **113 J4** 32 28N 100 25W
Sweetwater →, *U.S.A.* **114 E10** 42 31N 107 2W
Swellendam, *S. Africa* **88 E3** 34 1 S 20 26 E
Swider →, *Poland* **45 F8** 52 6N 21 14 E
Świdnica, *Poland* **45 H3** 50 50N 16 30 E
Świdnik, *Poland* **45 G9** 51 13N 22 39 E
Świdwin, *Poland* **44 E2** 53 47N 15 49 E
Świebodzice, *Poland* **45 H3** 50 51N 16 20 E
Świebodzin, *Poland* **45 F2** 52 15N 15 31 E
Świecie, *Poland* **44 E5** 53 25N 18 30 E
Swierzawa, *Poland* **45 G2** 51 1N 15 54 E
Świętokrzyskie □, *Poland* **45 H7** 50 45N 20 45 E
Świętokrzyskie, Góry, *Poland* **45 H7** 51 0N 20 30 E
Swift Current, *Canada* **105 C7** 50 20N 107 45W
Swiftcurrent →, *Canada* **105 C7** 50 38N 107 44W
Swilly, L., *Ireland* **15 A4** 55 12N 7 33W
Swindon, *U.K.* **13 F6** 51 34N 1 46W
Swindon □, *U.K.* **13 F6** 51 34N 1 46W
Swinemünde = Świnoujście, *Poland* **44 E1** 53 54N 14 16 E
Swinford, *Ireland* **15 C3** 53 57N 8 58W
Świnoujście, *Poland* **44 E1** 53 54N 14 16 E
Switzerland ■, *Europe* **25 J4** 46 30N 8 0 E
Swords, *Ireland* **15 C5** 53 28N 6 13W
Swoyerville, *U.S.A.* **111 E9** 41 18N 75 53W
Syasstroy, *Russia* **46 B7** 60 9N 32 33 E
Sychevka, *Russia* **46 E8** 55 59N 34 16 E
Syców, *Poland* **45 G4** 51 19N 17 40 E
Sydenham →, *Canada* **110 D2** 42 33N 82 25W
Sydney, *Australia* **95 E5** 33 53 S 151 10 E
Sydney, *Canada* **103 C7** 46 7N 60 7W
Sydney L., *Canada* **105 C10** 50 41N 94 25W
Sydney Mines, *Canada* **103 C7** 46 18N 60 15W
Sydprøven = Alluitsup Paa, *Greenland* **4 C5** 60 30N 45 35W
Sydra, G. of = Surt, Khalīj, *Libya* **79 B9** 31 40N 18 30 E
Syeverodonetsk, *Ukraine* **47 H10** 48 58N 38 35 E
Syke, *Germany* **24 C4** 52 55N 8 50 E
Sykesville, *U.S.A.* **110 E6** 41 3N 78 50W
Syktyvkar, *Russia* **50 C6** 61 45N 50 40 E
Sylacauga, *U.S.A.* **109 J2** 33 10N 86 15W
Sylarna, *Sweden* **8 E15** 63 2N 12 13 E
Sylhet, *Bangla.* **67 G17** 24 54N 91 52 E
Sylt, *Germany* **24 A4** 54 54N 8 22 E
Sylvan Beach, *U.S.A.* **111 C9** 43 12N 75 44W
Sylvan Lake, *Canada* **104 C6** 52 20N 114 3W
Sylvania, *U.S.A.* **109 J5** 32 45N 81 38W
Sylvester, *U.S.A.* **109 K4** 31 32N 83 50W
Sym, *Russia* **50 C9** 60 20N 88 18 E
Symón, *Mexico* **118 C4** 24 42N 102 35W
Synelnykove, *Ukraine* **47 H8** 48 25N 35 30 E
Synnott Ra., *Australia* **92 C4** 16 30 S 125 20 E
Syracuse, *Kans., U.S.A.* **113 G4** 37 59N 101 45W
Syracuse, *N.Y., U.S.A.* **111 C8** 43 3N 76 9W
Syracuse, *Nebr., U.S.A.* **112 E6** 40 39N 96 11W
Syrdarya →, *Kazakstan* **50 E7** 46 3N 61 0 E
Syria ■, *Asia* **70 C3** 35 0N 38 0 E
Syrian Desert = Shām, Bādiyat ash, *Asia* **70 C3** 32 0N 40 0 E
Sysslebäck, *Sweden* **10 D6** 60 44N 12 52 E
Syzran, *Russia* **48 D9** 53 12N 48 30 E
Szabolcs-Szatmár-Bereg □, *Hungary* **42 B6** 48 2N 21 45 E
Szadek, *Poland* **45 G5** 51 41N 18 59 E
Szamocin, *Poland* **45 E4** 53 2N 17 7 E
Szamos →, *Hungary* **42 B7** 48 7N 22 20 E
Szamotuły, *Poland* **45 F3** 52 37N 16 33 E
Száraz →, *Hungary* **42 D6** 46 10N 21 15 E
Szarvas, *Hungary* **42 D5** 46 50N 20 38 E
Százhalombatta, *Hungary* **42 C3** 47 20N 18 58 E
Szczawnica, *Poland* **45 J7** 49 26N 20 30 E
Szczebrzeszyn, *Poland* **45 H9** 50 42N 22 59 E
Szczecin, *Poland* **44 E1** 53 27N 14 27 E
Szczecinek, *Poland* **44 E3** 53 43N 16 41 E
Szczeciński, Zalew = Stettiner Haff, *Germany* **24 B10** 53 47N 14 15 E
Szczekociny, *Poland* **45 H6** 50 38N 19 48 E
Szczucin, *Poland* **45 H8** 50 18N 21 4 E
Szczuczyn, *Poland* **44 E9** 53 36N 22 19 E
Szczyrk, *Poland* **45 J6** 49 43N 19 2 E
Szczytna, *Poland* **45 H3** 50 25N 16 28 E
Szczytno, *Poland* **44 E7** 53 33N 21 0 E
Szechwan = Sichuan □, *China* **58 B5** 30 30N 103 0 E
Szécsény, *Hungary* **42 B4** 48 7N 19 30 E
Szeged, *Hungary* **42 D5** 46 16N 20 10 E
Szeghalom, *Hungary* **42 C6** 47 1N 21 10 E
Székesfehérvár, *Hungary* **42 C3** 47 15N 18 25 E
Szekszárd, *Hungary* **42 D3** 46 22N 18 42 E
Szendrő, *Hungary* **42 B5** 48 24N 20 41 E
Szentendre, *Hungary* **42 C4** 47 39N 19 4 E
Szentes, *Hungary* **42 D5** 46 39N 20 21 E
Szentgotthárd, *Hungary* **42 D1** 46 58N 16 19 E
Szentlőrinc, *Hungary* **42 D3** 46 3N 18 1 E
Szerencs, *Hungary* **42 B6** 48 10N 21 12 E
Szigetszentmiklós, *Hungary* **42 C4** 47 21N 19 3 E
Szigetvár, *Hungary* **42 D2** 46 3N 17 46 E
Szikszó, *Hungary* **42 B5** 48 12N 20 56 E
Szklarska Poreba, *Poland* **45 H2** 50 50N 15 33 E
Szkwa →, *Poland* **45 E8** 53 11N 21 43 E
Szlichtyngowa, *Poland* **45 G3** 51 42N 16 15 E
Szob, *Hungary* **42 C3** 47 48N 18 53 E
Szolnok, *Hungary* **42 C5** 47 10N 20 15 E
Szombathely, *Hungary* **42 C1** 47 14N 16 38 E
Szprotawa, *Poland* **45 G2** 51 33N 15 35 E
Sztum, *Poland* **44 E6** 53 55N 19 1 E
Sztutowo, *Poland* **44 D6** 54 20N 19 15 E
Szubin, *Poland* **45 E4** 53 1N 17 45 E
Szydłowiec, *Poland* **45 G7** 51 15N 20 51 E
Szypliszki, *Poland* **44 D10** 54 17N 23 2 E

T

Ta Khli Khok, *Thailand* **64 E3** 15 18N 100 20 E
Ta Lai, *Vietnam* **65 G6** 11 24N 107 23 E
Tab, *Hungary* **42 D3** 46 44N 18 2 E
Tabacal, *Argentina* **126 A3** 23 15 S 64 15W
Tabaco, *Phil.* **61 E5** 13 22N 123 44 E
Tabagné, *Ivory C.* **82 D4** 7 59N 3 4W
Ţābah, *Si. Arabia* **70 E4** 26 55N 42 38 E
Tabankort, *Niger* **83 B5** 17 44N 0 20 E
Ţabas, *Khorāsān, Iran* **71 C9** 32 48N 60 12 E
Ţabas, *Khorāsān, Iran* **71 C8** 33 35N 56 55 E
Tabasará, Serranía de, *Panama* **120 E3** 8 35N 81 40W
Tabasco □, *Mexico* **119 D6** 17 45N 93 30W
Tabāsīn, *Iran* **71 D8** 31 12N 57 54 E
Tabatinga, Serra da, *Brazil* **125 F10** 10 30 S 44 0W
Taber, *Canada* **104 D6** 49 47N 112 8W
Taberg, *Sweden* **11 G8** 57 40N 14 6 E
Taberg, *U.S.A.* **111 C9** 43 18N 75 37W
Tabla, *Niger* **83 C5** 13 46N 3 1 E
Tablas I., *Phil.* **61 E5** 12 25N 122 2 E
Tablas Strait, *Phil.* **61 E4** 12 40N 121 48 E
Table B. = Tafelbaai, *S. Africa* **88 E2** 33 35 S 18 25 E
Table B., *Canada* **103 B8** 53 40N 56 25W
Table Mt., *S. Africa* **88 E2** 34 0 S 18 22 E
Table Rock L., *U.S.A.* **113 G8** 36 36N 93 19W
Tabletop, Mt., *Australia* **94 C4** 23 24 S 147 11 E
Tábor, *Czech Rep.* **26 B7** 49 25N 14 39 E
Tabora, *Tanzania* **86 D3** 5 2 S 32 50 E
Tabora □, *Tanzania* **86 D3** 5 0 S 33 0 E
Tabou, *Ivory C.* **82 E3** 4 30N 7 20W
Tabrīz, *Iran* **70 B5** 38 7N 46 20 E
Tabuaeran, *Pac. Oc.* **97 G12** 3 51N 159 22W
Tabuenca, *Spain* **32 D3** 41 42N 1 33W
Tabūk, *Si. Arabia* **70 D3** 28 23N 36 36 E
Täby, *Sweden* **10 E12** 59 28N 18 4 E

Tacámbaro de Codallos, Mexico 118 D4 19 14N 101 28W
Tacheng, China 60 B3 46 40N 82 58 E
Tach'i, Taiwan 59 E13 24 50N 121 0 E
Tachia, Taiwan 59 E13 24 25N 120 28 E
Tach'ing Shan = Daqing Shan, China 56 D6 40 40N 111 0 E
Tachov, Czech Rep. 26 B5 49 47N 12 39 E
Tácina →, Italy 31 D9 38 57N 16 55 E
Tacloban, Phil. 61 F6 11 15N 124 58 E
Tacna, Peru 124 G4 18 0 S 70 20W
Tacoma, U.S.A. 116 C4 47 14N 122 26W
Tacuarembó, Uruguay 127 C4 31 45 S 56 0W
Tademaït, Plateau du, Algeria 78 C6 28 30N 2 30 E
Tadio, L., Ivory C. 82 D3 5 10N 5 15W
Tadjoura, Djibouti 81 E5 11 50N 42 55 E
Tadjoura, Golfe de, Djibouti 81 E5 11 50N 43 0 E
Tadmor, N.Z. 91 J4 41 27 S 172 45 E
Tadoule, L., Canada 105 B9 58 36N 98 20W
Tadoussac, Canada 103 C6 48 11N 69 42W
Tadzhikistan = Tajikistan ■, Asia 50 F8 38 30N 70 0 E
Taechŏn-ni, S. Korea 57 F14 36 21N 126 36 E
Taegu, S. Korea 57 G15 35 50N 128 37 E
Taegwan, N. Korea 57 D13 40 13N 125 12 E
Taejŏn, S. Korea 57 F14 36 20N 127 28 E
Tafalla, Spain 32 C3 42 30N 1 41W
Tafar, Sudan 81 F2 6 52N 28 15 E
Tafelbaai, S. Africa 88 E2 33 35 S 18 25 E
Tafermaar, Indonesia 63 F8 6 47 S 134 10 E
Tafí Viejo, Argentina 126 B2 26 43 S 65 17W
Tafīhān, Iran 71 D7 29 25N 52 39 E
Tafiré, Ivory C. 82 D3 9 4N 5 4W
Tafo, Ghana 83 D4 6 15N 0 20W
Tafresh, Iran 71 C6 34 45N 49 57 E
Taft, Iran 71 D7 31 45N 54 14 E
Taft, Phil. 61 F6 11 57N 125 30 E
Taft, U.S.A. 117 K7 35 8N 119 28W
Taftān, Kūh-e, Iran 71 D9 28 40N 61 0 E
Taga Dzong, Bhutan 67 F16 27 5N 89 55 E
Taganrog, Russia 47 J10 47 12N 38 50 E
Taganrogskiy Zaliv, Russia 47 J10 47 0N 38 30 E
Tagânt, Mauritania 82 B2 18 20N 11 0W
Tagatay, Phil. 61 D4 14 6N 120 56 E
Tagbilaran, Phil. 61 G5 9 39N 123 51 E
Tággia, Italy 28 E4 43 52N 7 51 E
Tagish, Canada 104 A2 60 19N 134 16W
Tagish L., Canada 104 A2 60 10N 134 20W
Tagliacozzo, Italy 29 F10 42 4N 13 14 E
Tagliamento →, Italy 29 C10 45 38N 13 6 E
Táglio di Po, Italy 29 D9 45 0N 12 12 E
Tago, Phil. 61 G7 9 2N 126 13 E
Tagomago, Spain 37 B8 39 2N 1 39 E
Tagourāret, Mauritania 82 B3 17 45N 7 45W
Taguatinga, Brazil 125 F10 12 16 S 42 26W
Tagudin, Phil. 61 C4 16 56N 120 27 E
Tagum, Phil. 61 H6 7 33N 125 53 E
Tagus = Tejo →, Europe 35 F2 38 40N 9 24W
Tahakopa, N.Z. 91 M2 46 30 S 169 23 E
Tahan, Gunong, Malaysia 65 K4 4 34N 102 17 E
Tahat, Algeria 78 D7 23 18N 5 33 E
Tāherī, Iran 71 E7 27 43N 52 20 E
Tahiti, Pac. Oc. 97 J13 17 37 S 149 27W
Tahlequah, U.S.A. 113 H7 35 55N 94 58W
Tahoe, L., U.S.A. 116 G6 39 6N 120 2W
Tahoe City, U.S.A. 116 F6 39 10N 120 9W
Tahoka, U.S.A. 113 J4 33 10N 101 48W
Taholah, U.S.A. 116 C2 47 21N 124 17W
Tahoua, Niger 83 C6 14 57N 5 16 E
Tahrūd, Iran 71 D8 29 26N 57 49 E
Tahsis, Canada 104 D3 49 55N 126 40W
Tahta, Egypt 80 B3 26 44N 31 32 E
Tahtaköprü, Turkey 41 G13 39 57N 29 39 E
Tahtalı Dağları, Turkey 72 C7 38 20N 36 0 E
Tahulandang, Indonesia 63 D7 2 27N 125 23 E
Tahuna, Indonesia 63 D7 3 38N 125 30 E
Taï, Ivory C. 82 D3 5 55N 7 30W
Tai Hu, China 59 B12 31 5N 120 10 E
Tai Shan, China 57 F9 36 25N 117 20 E
Tai'an, China 57 F9 36 12N 117 8 E
Taibei = T'aipei, Taiwan 59 E13 25 2N 121 30 E
Taibique, Canary Is. 37 G2 27 42N 17 58W
Taibus Qi, China 56 D8 41 54N 115 22 E
Taicang, China 59 B13 31 30N 121 5 E
T'aichung, Taiwan 59 E13 24 9N 120 37 E
Taieri →, N.Z. 91 M3 46 3 S 170 12 E
Taigu, China 56 F7 37 28N 112 30 E
Taihang Shan, China 56 G7 36 0N 113 30 E
Taihape, N.Z. 91 H5 39 41 S 175 48 E
Taihe, Anhui, China 56 H8 33 20N 115 42 E
Taihe, Jiangxi, China 59 D10 26 47N 114 52 E
Taihu, China 59 B11 30 22N 116 20 E
Taijiang, China 58 D7 26 39N 108 21 E
Taikang, China 56 G8 34 5N 114 50 E
Tailem Bend, Australia 95 F2 35 12 S 139 29 E
Tailfingen, Germany 25 G5 48 15N 9 1 E
Tailuko, Taiwan 59 E13 24 9N 121 37 E
Taimyr Peninsula = Taymyr, Poluostrov, Russia 51 B11 75 0N 100 0 E
Tain, U.K. 14 D4 57 49N 4 4W
T'ainan, Taiwan 59 F13 23 0N 120 10 E
Taínaron, Ákra, Greece 38 E4 36 22N 22 27 E
Taining, China 59 D11 26 54N 117 9 E
T'aipei, Taiwan 59 E13 25 2N 121 30 E
Taiping, China 59 B12 30 15N 118 6 E
Taiping, Malaysia 65 K3 4 51N 100 44 E
Taipingzhen, China 56 H6 33 35N 111 42 E
Tairbeart = Tarbert, U.K. 14 D2 57 54N 6 49W
Taishan, China 59 F9 22 14N 112 41 E
Taishun, China 59 D12 27 30N 119 42 E
Taita Hills, Kenya 86 C4 3 25 S 38 15 E
Taitao, Pen. de, Chile 122 H3 46 30 S 75 0W
T'aitung, Taiwan 59 F13 22 43N 121 4 E
Taivalkoski, Finland 8 D23 65 33N 28 12 E
Taiwan ■, Asia 59 F13 23 30N 121 0 E
Taiwan Strait, Asia 59 E12 24 40N 120 0 E
Taixing, China 59 A13 32 11N 120 0 E
Taiyara, Sudan 81 E3 13 12N 30 47 E
Taïyetos Óros, Greece 38 D4 37 0N 22 23 E
Taiyiba, Israel 75 C4 32 36N 35 27 E
Taiyuan, China 56 F7 37 52N 112 33 E
Taizhong = T'aichung, Taiwan 59 E13 24 9N 120 37 E
Taizhou, China 59 A12 32 28N 119 55 E
Taizhou Liedao, China 59 C13 28 30N 121 55 E
Ta'izz, Yemen 74 E3 13 35N 44 2 E
Tājābād, Iran 71 D7 30 2N 54 24 E
Tajikistan ■, Asia 50 F8 38 30N 70 0 E
Tajima, Japan 55 F9 37 12N 139 46 E
Tajo = Tejo →, Europe 35 F2 38 40N 9 24W
Tajrīsh, Iran 71 C6 35 48N 51 25 E
Tak, Thailand 64 D2 16 52N 99 8 E
Takāb, Iran 70 B5 36 24N 47 7 E
Takachiho, Japan 55 H5 32 42N 131 18 E
Takachu, Botswana 88 C3 22 37 S 21 58 E
Takada, Japan 55 F9 37 7N 138 15 E
Takahagi, Japan 55 F10 36 43N 140 45 E
Takaka, N.Z. 91 J4 40 51 S 172 50 E
Takamatsu, Japan 55 G7 34 20N 134 5 E
Takaoka, Japan 55 F8 36 47N 137 0 E
Takapuna, N.Z. 91 G5 36 47 S 174 47 E
Takasaki, Japan 55 F9 36 20N 139 0 E
Takatsuki, Japan 55 G7 34 51N 135 37 E
Takaungu, Kenya 86 C4 3 38 S 39 52 E
Takayama, Japan 55 F8 36 18N 137 11 E
Take-Shima, Japan 55 J5 30 49N 130 26 E
Takefu, Japan 55 G8 35 50N 136 10 E
Takengon, Indonesia 62 D1 4 45N 96 50 E
Takeo, Japan 55 H5 33 12N 130 1 E
Tåkern, Sweden 11 F8 58 22N 14 45 E
Tākestān, Iran 71 C6 36 0N 49 40 E
Taketa, Japan 55 H5 32 58N 131 24 E
Takev, Cambodia 65 G5 10 59N 104 47 E
Takh, India 69 C7 33 6N 77 32 E
Takht-Sulaiman, Pakistan 68 D3 31 40N 69 58 E
Takikawa, Japan 54 C10 43 33N 141 54 E
Takla L., Canada 104 B3 55 15N 125 45W
Takla Landing, Canada 104 B3 55 30N 125 50W
Takla Makan = Taklamakan Shamo, China 52 F12 38 0N 83 0 E
Taklamakan Shamo, China 52 F12 38 0N 83 0 E
Taku →, Canada 104 B2 58 30N 133 50W
Takum, Nigeria 83 D6 7 18N 9 36 E
Tal Halāl, Iran 71 D7 28 54N 55 1 E
Tala, Uruguay 127 C4 34 21 S 55 46W
Talachyn, Belarus 46 E5 54 25N 29 42 E
Talacogan, Phil. 61 G6 8 32N 125 39 E
Talagang, Pakistan 68 C5 32 55N 72 25 E
Talagante, Chile 126 C1 33 40 S 70 50W
Talak, Niger 83 B6 18 0N 5 0 E
Talamanca, Cordillera de, Cent. Amer. 120 E3 9 20N 83 20W
Talant, France 19 E11 47 19N 4 58 E
Talara, Peru 124 D2 4 38 S 81 18W
Talas, Kyrgyzstan 50 E8 42 30N 72 13 E
Talas, Turkey 72 C6 38 41N 35 33 E
Talâta, Egypt 75 E1 30 36N 32 20 E
Talata Mafara, Nigeria 83 C6 12 38N 6 4 E
Talaud, Kepulauan, Indonesia 63 D7 4 30N 127 10 E
Talaud Is. = Talaud, Kepulauan, Indonesia 63 D7 4 30N 127 10 E
Talavera de la Reina, Spain 34 F6 39 55N 4 46W
Talavera la Real, Spain 35 G4 38 53N 6 46W
Talayan, Phil. 61 H6 6 52N 124 24 E
Talayuela, Spain 34 F5 39 59N 5 36W
Talbandh, India 69 H12 22 3N 86 20 E
Talbert, Sillon de, France 18 D3 48 53N 3 5W
Talbot, C., Australia 92 B4 13 48 S 126 43 E
Talbragar →, Australia 95 E4 32 12 S 148 37 E
Talca, Chile 126 D1 35 28 S 71 40W
Talcahuano, Chile 126 D1 36 40 S 73 10W
Talcher, India 67 J14 21 0N 85 18 E
Talcho, Niger 83 C5 14 44N 3 28 E
Taldy Kurgan = Taldyqorghan, Kazakstan 50 E8 45 10N 78 45 E
Taldyqorghan, Kazakstan 50 E8 45 10N 78 45 E
Tālesh, Iran 71 B6 37 58N 48 58 E
Tālesh, Kūhhā-ye, Iran 71 B6 37 42N 48 55 E
Talguharai, Sudan 80 D4 18 19N 35 56 E
Tali Post, Sudan 81 F3 5 55N 30 44 E
Taliabu, Indonesia 63 E6 1 50 S 125 0 E
Talibon, Phil. 63 B6 10 9N 124 20 E
Talibong, Ko, Thailand 65 J2 7 15N 99 23 E
Talihina, U.S.A. 113 H7 34 45N 95 3W
Talisayan, Phil. 61 G6 9 0N 124 55 E
Taliwang, Indonesia 62 F5 8 50 S 116 55 E
Tall 'Afar, Iraq 70 B4 36 22N 42 27 E
Tall Kalakh, Syria 75 A5 34 41N 36 15 E
Talla, Egypt 80 B3 28 5N 30 43 E
Talladega, U.S.A. 109 J2 33 26N 86 6W
Tallahassee, U.S.A. 109 K3 30 27N 84 17W
Tallangatta, Australia 95 F4 36 15 S 147 19 E
Tallard, France 21 D10 44 28N 6 3 E
Tällberg, Sweden 10 D9 60 51N 15 2 E
Tallering Pk., Australia 93 E2 28 6 S 115 37 E
Talli, Pakistan 68 E3 29 32N 68 8 E
Tallinn, Estonia 9 G21 59 22N 24 48 E
Tallmadge, U.S.A. 110 E3 41 6N 81 27W
Tallulah, U.S.A. 113 J9 32 25N 91 11W
Tălmaciu, Romania 43 E9 45 38N 24 19 E
Talmont-St-Hilaire, France 20 B2 46 27N 1 37W
Talne, Ukraine 47 H6 48 50N 30 44 E
Talnoye = Talne, Ukraine 47 H6 48 50N 30 44 E
Talodi, Sudan 81 E3 10 35N 30 22 E
Talovaya, Russia 48 E5 51 6N 40 45 E
Taloyoak, Canada 100 B10 69 32N 93 32W
Talpa de Allende, Mexico 118 C4 20 23N 104 51W
Talsi, Latvia 9 H20 57 10N 22 30 E
Talsi □, Latvia 44 A9 57 20N 22 40 E
Taltal, Chile 126 B1 25 23 S 70 33W
Taltson →, Canada 104 A6 61 24N 112 46W
Talwood, Australia 95 D4 28 29 S 149 29 E
Talyawalka →, Australia 95 E3 32 28 S 142 22 E
Tam Chau, Vietnam 65 G5 10 48N 105 12 E
Tam Ky, Vietnam 64 E7 15 34N 108 29 E
Tam Quan, Vietnam 64 E7 14 35N 109 3 E
Tama, U.S.A. 112 E8 41 58N 92 35W
Tamale, Ghana 83 D4 9 22N 0 50W
Taman, Russia 47 K9 45 14N 36 41 E
Tamani, Mali 82 C3 13 20N 6 50W
Tamano, Japan 55 G6 34 29N 133 59 E
Tamanrasset, Algeria 78 D7 22 50N 5 30 E
Tamaqua, U.S.A. 111 F9 40 48N 75 58W
Tamar →, U.K. 13 G3 50 27N 4 15W
Tamarinda, Spain 37 B10 39 55N 3 49 E
Tamarite de Litera, Spain 32 D5 41 52N 0 25 E
Tamashima, Japan 55 G6 34 32N 133 40 E
Tamási, Hungary 42 D3 46 40N 18 18 E
Tamaské, Niger 83 C6 14 49N 5 43 E
Tamaulipas □, Mexico 119 C5 24 0N 99 0W
Tamaulipas, Sierra de, Mexico 119 C5 23 30N 98 20W
Tamazula, Mexico 118 C3 24 55N 106 58W
Tamazunchale, Mexico 119 C5 21 16N 98 47W
Tamba-Dabatou, Guinea 82 C2 11 50N 10 40W
Tambacounda, Senegal 82 C2 13 45N 13 40W
Tambelan, Kepulauan, Indonesia 62 D3 1 0N 107 30 E
Tambellup, Australia 93 F2 34 4 S 117 37 E
Tambo, Australia 94 C4 24 54 S 146 14 E
Tambo de Mora, Peru 124 F3 13 30 S 76 8W
Tambohorano, Madag. 89 B7 17 30 S 43 58 E
Tambora, Indonesia 62 F5 8 12 S 118 5 E
Tambov, Russia 48 D5 52 45N 41 28 E
Tambre →, Spain 34 C2 42 49N 8 53W
Tambuku, Indonesia 63 G15 7 8 S 113 40 E
Tamburâ, Sudan 81 F2 5 40N 27 25 E
Tâmchekket, Mauritania 82 B2 17 25N 10 40W
Tâmega →, Portugal 34 D2 41 5N 8 21W
Tamenglong, India 67 G18 25 0N 93 35 E
Tamgué, Massif du, Guinea 82 C2 12 0N 12 18W
Tamiahua, L. de, Mexico 119 C5 21 30N 97 30W
Tamil Nadu □, India 66 P10 11 0N 77 0 E
Tamis →, Serbia, Yug. 42 F5 44 51N 20 39 E
Tamluk, India 69 H12 22 18N 87 58 E
Tammerfors = Tampere, Finland 9 F20 61 30N 23 50 E
Tammisaari, Finland 9 F20 60 0N 23 26 E
Tämnaren, Sweden 10 D11 60 10N 17 25 E
Tamo Abu, Pegunungan, Malaysia 62 D5 3 10N 115 5 E
Tampa, U.S.A. 109 M4 27 57N 82 27W
Tampa B., U.S.A. 109 M4 27 50N 82 30W
Tampere, Finland 9 F20 61 30N 23 50 E
Tampico, Mexico 119 C5 22 20N 97 50W
Tampin, Malaysia 65 L4 2 28N 102 13 E
Tamsweg, Austria 26 D6 47 7N 13 49 E
Tamu, Burma 67 G19 24 13N 94 12 E
Tamuja →, Spain 35 F4 39 38N 6 29W
Tamworth, Australia 95 E5 31 7 S 150 58 E
Tamworth, Canada 110 B8 44 29N 77 0W
Tamworth, U.K. 13 E6 52 39N 1 41W
Tamyang, S. Korea 57 G14 35 19N 126 59 E
Tan An, Vietnam 65 G6 10 32N 106 25 E
Tan-Tan, Morocco 78 C3 28 29N 11 1W
Tana →, Kenya 86 C5 2 32 S 40 31 E
Tana →, Norway 8 A23 70 30N 28 14 E
Tana, L., Ethiopia 81 E4 13 5N 37 30 E
Tana River, Kenya 86 C4 2 0 S 39 30 E
Tanabe, Japan 55 H7 33 44N 135 22 E
Tanafjorden, Norway 8 A23 70 45N 28 25 E
Tanaga, Pta., Canary Is. 37 G1 27 42N 18 10W
Tanahbala, Indonesia 62 E1 0 30 S 98 30 E
Tanahgrogot, Indonesia 62 E5 1 55 S 116 15 E
Tanahjampea, Indonesia 63 F6 7 10 S 120 35 E
Tanahmasa, Indonesia 62 E1 0 12 S 98 39 E
Tanahmerah, Indonesia 63 F10 6 5 S 140 16 E
Tanakpur, India 69 E9 29 5N 80 7 E
Tanakura, Japan 55 F10 37 10N 140 20 E
Tanami, Australia 92 C4 19 59 S 129 43 E
Tanami Desert, Australia 92 C5 18 50 S 132 0 E
Tanana →, U.S.A. 100 B4 65 10N 151 58W
Tananarive = Antananarivo, Madag. 89 B8 18 55 S 47 31 E
Tânaro →, Italy 28 D5 44 55N 8 40 E
Tancheng, China 57 G10 34 25N 118 20 E
Tanch'ŏn, N. Korea 57 D15 40 27N 128 54 E
Tanda, Ut. P., India 69 F10 26 33N 82 35 E
Tanda, Ut. P., India 69 E8 28 57N 78 56 E
Tanda, Ivory C. 82 D4 7 48N 3 10W
Tandag, Phil. 61 G7 9 4N 126 9 E
Tandala, Tanzania 87 D3 9 25 S 34 15 E
Tăndărei, Romania 43 F12 44 39N 27 40 E
Tandaué, Angola 88 B2 16 58 S 18 5 E
Tandil, Argentina 126 D4 37 15 S 59 6W
Tandil, Sa. del, Argentina 126 D4 37 30 S 59 0W
Tandlianwala, Pakistan 68 D5 31 3N 73 9 E
Tando Adam, Pakistan 68 G3 25 45N 68 40 E
Tando Allahyar, Pakistan 68 G3 25 28N 68 43 E
Tando Bago, Pakistan 68 G3 24 47N 68 58 E
Tando Mohommed Khan, Pakistan 68 G3 25 8N 68 32 E
Tandou L., Australia 95 E3 32 40 S 142 5 E
Tandragee, U.K. 15 B5 54 21N 6 24W
Tandsjöborg, Sweden 10 C8 61 42N 14 43 E
Tane-ga-Shima, Japan 55 J5 30 30N 131 0 E
Taneatua, N.Z. 91 H6 38 4 S 177 1 E
Tanen Tong Dan, Burma 64 D2 16 30N 98 30 E
Tanew →, Poland 45 H9 50 29N 22 16 E
Tanezrouft, Algeria 78 D6 23 9N 0 11 E
Tang, Koh, Cambodia 65 G4 10 16N 103 7 E
Tang, Ra's-e, Iran 71 E8 25 21N 59 52 E
Tang Krasang, Cambodia 64 F5 12 34N 105 3 E
Tanga, Tanzania 86 D4 5 5 S 39 2 E
Tanga □, Tanzania 86 D4 5 20 S 38 0 E
Tanganyika, L., Africa 86 D3 6 40 S 30 0 E
Tangaza, Nigeria 83 C5 13 19N 4 55 E
Tanger = Tangier, Morocco 78 A4 35 50N 5 49W
Tangerang, Indonesia 63 G12 6 11 S 106 37 E
Tangerhütte, Germany 24 C7 52 26N 11 48 E
Tangermünde, Germany 24 C7 52 33N 11 58 E
Tanggu, China 57 E9 39 2N 117 40 E
Tanggula Shan, China 60 C4 32 40N 92 10 E
Tanghe, China 56 H7 32 47N 112 50 E
Tangier, Morocco 78 A4 35 50N 5 49W
Tangorin, Australia 94 C3 21 47 S 144 12 E
Tangorombohitr'i Makay, Madag. 89 C8 21 0 S 45 15 E
Tangshan, China 57 E10 39 38N 118 10 E
Tangtou, China 57 G10 35 28N 118 30 E
Tanguiéta, Benin 83 C5 10 35N 1 21 E
Tangxi, China 59 C12 29 3N 119 25 E
Tangyan He →, China 58 C7 28 54N 108 19 E
Tanimbar, Kepulauan, Indonesia 63 F8 7 30 S 131 30 E
Tanimbar Is. = Tanimbar, Kepulauan, Indonesia 63 F8 7 30 S 131 30 E
Taninthari = Tenasserim □, Burma 64 F2 14 0N 98 30 E
Tanjay, Phil. 61 G5 9 30N 123 5 E
Tanjong Malim, Malaysia 65 L3 3 42N 101 31 E
Tanjore = Thanjavur, India 66 P11 10 48N 79 12 E
Tanjung, Indonesia 62 E5 2 10 S 115 25 E
Tanjungbalai, Indonesia 62 D1 2 55N 99 44 E
Tanjungbatu, Indonesia 62 D5 2 23N 118 3 E
Tanjungkarang Telukbetung, Indonesia 62 F3 5 20 S 105 10 E
Tanjungpandan, Indonesia 62 E3 2 43 S 107 38 E
Tanjungpinang, Indonesia 62 D2 1 5N 104 30 E
Tanjungredeb, Indonesia 62 D5 2 9N 117 29 E
Tanjungselor, Indonesia 62 D5 2 55N 117 25 E
Tank, Pakistan 68 C4 32 14N 70 25 E
Tankhala, India 68 J5 21 58N 73 47 E
Tännäs, Sweden 10 B6 62 26N 12 42 E
Tannersville, U.S.A. 111 E9 41 3N 75 18W
Tannis Bugt, Denmark 11 G4 57 40N 10 15 E
Tannu-Ola, Russia 51 D10 51 0N 94 0 E
Tannum Sands, Australia 94 C5 23 57 S 151 22 E
Tano →, Ghana 82 D4 5 7N 2 56W
Tanon Str., Phil. 61 F5 10 20N 123 30 E
Tanout, Niger 83 C6 14 50N 8 55 E
Tanshui, Taiwan 59 E13 25 10N 121 28 E
Tansilla, Burkina Faso 82 C4 12 25N 4 23W
Tanta, Egypt 80 H7 30 45N 30 57 E
Tantoyuca, Mexico 119 C5 21 21N 98 10W
Tantung = Dandong, China 57 D13 40 10N 124 20 E
Tanumshede, Sweden 11 F5 58 42N 11 20 E
Tanunda, Australia 95 E2 34 30 S 139 0 E
Tanus, France 20 D6 44 8N 2 19 E
Tanzania ■, Africa 86 D3 6 0 S 34 0 E
Tanzilla →, Canada 104 B2 58 8N 130 43W
Tao, Ko, Thailand 65 G2 10 5N 99 52 E
Tao'an = Taonan, China 57 B12 45 22N 122 40 E
Tao'er He →, China 57 B13 45 45N 124 5 E
Taohua Dao, China 59 C14 29 50N 122 20 E
Taolanaro, Madag. 89 D8 25 2 S 47 0 E
Taole, China 56 E4 38 48N 106 40 E
Taonan, China 57 B12 45 22N 122 40 E
Taormina, Italy 31 E8 37 51N 15 17 E
Taos, U.S.A. 115 H11 36 24N 105 35W
Taoudenni, Mali 78 D5 22 40N 3 55W
Taoyuan, China 59 C8 28 55N 111 16 E
T'aoyüan, Taiwan 59 E13 25 0N 121 4 E
Tapa, Estonia 9 G21 59 15N 25 50 E
Tapa Shan = Daba Shan, China 58 B7 32 0N 109 0 E
Tapachula, Mexico 119 E6 14 54N 92 17W
Tapah, Malaysia 65 K3 4 12N 101 15 E
Tapajós →, Brazil 122 D5 2 24 S 54 41W
Tapaktuan, Indonesia 62 D1 3 15N 97 10 E
Tapanahoni →, Surinam 125 C8 4 20N 54 25W
Tapanui, N.Z. 91 L2 45 56 S 169 18 E
Tapauá →, Brazil 124 E6 5 40 S 64 21W
Tapes, Brazil 127 C5 30 40 S 51 23W
Tapeta, Liberia 82 D3 6 29N 8 52W
Taphan Hin, Thailand 64 D3 16 13N 100 26 E
Tapia de Casariego, Spain 34 B4 43 34N 6 56W
Tapirapecó, Serra, Venezuela 124 C6 1 10N 65 0W
Tapolca, Hungary 42 D2 46 53N 17 29 E
Tapuaenuku, Mt., N.Z. 91 K4 42 0 S 173 39 E
Tapul Group, Phil. 61 J4 5 35N 120 50 E
Tapurucuará, Brazil 124 D5 0 24 S 65 2W
Ţaqţaq, Iraq 70 C5 35 53N 44 35 E
Taquara, Brazil 127 B5 29 36 S 50 46W
Taquari →, Brazil 124 G7 19 15 S 57 17W
Tara, Australia 95 D5 27 17 S 150 31 E
Tara, Canada 110 B3 44 28N 81 9W
Tara, Russia 50 D8 56 55N 74 24 E
Tara, Zambia 87 F2 16 58 S 26 45 E
Tara →, Montenegro, Yug. 40 C2 43 21N 18 51 E
Taraba □, Nigeria 83 D7 8 0N 10 30 E
Taraba →, Nigeria 83 D7 8 30N 10 15 E
Tarabagatay, Khrebet, Kazakstan 50 E9 48 0N 83 0 E
Tarābulus, Lebanon 75 A4 34 31N 35 50 E
Tarābulus, Libya 79 B8 32 49N 13 7 E
Taraclia, Moldova 43 D14 46 34N 29 7 E
Taraclia, Moldova 43 E13 45 54N 28 40 E
Taradehi, India 69 H8 23 18N 79 21 E
Tarajalejo, Canary Is. 37 F5 28 12N 14 7W
Tarakan, Indonesia 62 D5 3 20N 117 35 E
Tarakit, Mt., Kenya 86 B4 2 2N 35 10 E
Tarama-Jima, Japan 55 M2 24 39N 124 42 E
Taran, Mys, Russia 9 J18 54 56N 19 59 E
Taranagar, India 68 E6 28 43N 74 50 E
Taranaki □, N.Z. 91 H5 39 25 S 174 30 E
Taranaki, Mt., N.Z. 91 H5 39 17 S 174 5 E
Tarancón, Spain 32 E1 40 1N 3 1W
Taranga Hill, India 66 H8 24 0N 72 40 E
Taransay, U.K. 14 D1 57 54N 7 0W
Táranto, Italy 31 B10 40 28N 17 14 E
Táranto, G. di, Italy 31 B10 40 8N 17 20 E
Tarapacá, Colombia 124 D5 2 56 S 69 46W
Tarapacá □, Chile 126 A2 20 45 S 69 30W
Tarapoto, Peru 124 E3 6 30 S 76 20W
Tarare, France 21 C8 45 54N 4 26 E
Tararua Ra., N.Z. 91 J5 40 45 S 175 25 E
Tarascon, France 21 E8 43 48N 4 39 E
Tarascon-sur-Ariège, France 20 F5 42 50N 1 36 E
Tarashcha, Ukraine 47 H6 49 30N 30 31 E
Tarauacá, Brazil 124 E4 8 6 S 70 48W
Tarauacá →, Brazil 124 E5 6 42 S 69 48W
Taravo →, France 21 G12 41 42N 8 49 E
Tarawa, Kiribati 96 G9 1 30N 173 0 E
Tarawera, N.Z. 91 H6 39 2 S 176 36 E
Tarawera L., N.Z. 91 H6 38 13 S 176 27 E
Tarazona, Spain 32 D3 41 55N 1 43W
Tarazona de la Mancha, Spain 33 F3 39 16N 1 55W
Tarbat Ness, U.K. 14 D5 57 52N 3 47W
Tarbela Dam, Pakistan 68 B5 34 8N 72 52 E
Tarbert, Arg. & Bute, U.K. 14 F3 55 52N 5 25W
Tarbert, W. Isles, U.K. 14 D2 57 54N 6 49W
Tarbes, France 20 E4 43 15N 0 3 E
Tarboro, U.S.A. 109 H7 35 54N 77 32W
Tărcău, Munţii, Romania 43 D11 46 39N 26 7 E
Tarcento, Italy 29 B10 46 13N 13 13 E
Tarcoola, Australia 95 E1 30 44 S 134 36 E
Tarcoon, Australia 95 E4 30 15 S 146 43 E
Tardets-Sorholus, France 20 E3 43 8N 0 52W
Tardoire →, France 20 C4 45 52N 0 14 E
Taree, Australia 95 E5 31 50 S 152 30 E
Tarfa, W. el →, Egypt 80 B3 28 25N 30 50 E
Tarfaya, Morocco 78 C3 27 55N 12 55W
Târgovişte, Romania 43 F10 44 55N 25 27 E
Târgu Bujor, Romania 43 E12 45 52N 27 54 E
Târgu Cărbuneşti, Romania 43 F8 44 57N 23 31 E
Târgu Frumos, Romania 43 C12 47 12N 27 2 E
Târgu-Jiu, Romania 43 E8 45 5N 23 19 E
Târgu Lăpuş, Romania 43 C8 47 27N 23 52 E
Târgu Mureş, Romania 43 D9 46 31N 24 38 E
Târgu Neamţ, Romania 43 C11 47 12N 26 25 E
Târgu Ocna, Romania 43 D11 46 16N 26 39 E
Târgu Secuiesc, Romania 43 E11 46 0N 26 10 E
Târguşor, Romania 43 F13 44 27N 28 25 E
Târhăus, Vf., Romania 43 D11 46 40N 26 8 E
Ţarif, U.A.E. 71 E7 24 3N 53 46 E
Tarifa, Spain 35 J5 36 1N 5 36W
Tarija, Bolivia 126 A3 21 30 S 64 40W
Tarija □, Bolivia 126 A3 21 30 S 63 30W
Tariku →, Indonesia 63 E9 2 55 S 138 26 E
Tarim Basin = Tarim Pendi, China 60 C3 40 0N 84 0 E
Tarim He →, China 60 C3 39 30N 88 30 E
Tarim Pendi, China 60 C3 40 0N 84 0 E
Taritatu →, Indonesia 63 E9 2 54 S 138 27 E
Tarka →, S. Africa 88 E4 32 10 S 26 0 E
Tarkastad, S. Africa 88 E4 32 0 S 26 16 E
Tarkhankut, Mys, Ukraine 47 K7 45 25N 32 30 E
Tarko Sale, Russia 50 C8 64 55N 77 50 E
Tarkwa, Ghana 82 D4 5 20N 2 0W
Tarlac, Phil. 61 D4 15 29N 120 35 E
Tarm, Denmark 11 J2 55 56N 8 31 E
Tarma, Peru 124 F3 11 25 S 75 45W
Tarn □, France 20 E6 43 49N 2 8 E
Tarn →, France 20 D5 44 5N 1 6 E
Tarn-et-Garonne □, France 20 D5 44 8N 1 20 E
Tarna →, Hungary 42 C4 47 31N 19 59 E
Târnava Mare →, Romania 43 D8 46 10N 23 43 E
Târnava Mică →, Romania 43 D8 46 9N 23 55 E
Târnăveni, Romania 43 D9 46 19N 24 13 E
Tarnica, Poland 45 J9 49 4N 22 44 E
Tarnobrzeg, Poland 45 H8 50 35N 21 41 E
Tarnogród, Poland 45 H9 50 22N 22 45 E
Tarnos, France 20 E2 43 32N 1 28W
Târnova, Moldova 43 B12 48 10N 27 40 E
Târnova, Romania 42 E6 45 23N 21 59 E
Tarnów, Poland 45 H8 50 3N 21 0 E
Tarnowskie Góry, Poland 45 H5 50 27N 18 54 E
Tärnsjö, Sweden 10 D10 60 9N 16 56 E
Táro →, Italy 28 C7 45 2N 10 15 E
Ţārom, Iran 71 D7 28 11N 55 46 E
Taroom, Australia 95 D4 25 36 S 149 48 E
Taroudannt, Morocco 78 B4 30 30N 8 52W
Tarp, Germany 24 A5 54 39N 9 24 E
Tarpon Springs, U.S.A. 109 L4 28 9N 82 45W
Tarquínia, Italy 29 F8 42 15N 11 45 E
Tarragona, Spain 32 D6 41 5N 1 17 E
Tarragona □, Spain 32 D6 41 5N 1 0 E
Tarraleah, Australia 94 G4 42 17 S 146 26 E
Tarrasa = Terrassa, Spain 32 D7 41 34N 2 1 E
Tàrrega, Spain 32 D6 41 39N 1 9 E
Tarrytown, U.S.A. 111 E11 41 4N 73 52W
Târs, Denmark 11 G4 57 23N 10 7 E
Tarshiha = Me'ona, Israel 75 B4 33 1N 35 15 E
Tarso Emissi, Chad 79 D9 21 27N 18 36 E
Tarsus, Turkey 70 B2 36 58N 34 55 E
Tartagal, Argentina 126 A3 22 30 S 63 50W
Tärtär, Azerbaijan 49 K8 40 20N 46 58 E
Tärtär →, Azerbaijan 49 K8 40 26N 47 20 E
Tartas, France 20 E3 43 50N 0 49W
Tartu, Estonia 9 G22 58 20N 26 44 E
Ţarţūs, Syria 70 C2 34 55N 35 55 E
Tarumizu, Japan 55 J5 31 29N 130 42 E
Tarussa, Russia 46 E9 54 44N 37 10 E
Tarutao, Ko, Thailand 65 J2 6 33N 99 40 E
Tarutung, Indonesia 62 D1 2 0N 98 54 E
Tarvísio, Italy 29 B10 46 30N 13 35 E
Taseko →, Canada 104 C4 52 8N 123 45W
Tash-Kömür, Kyrgyzstan 50 E8 41 40N 72 10 E
Tash-Kumyr = Tash-Kömür, Kyrgyzstan 50 E8 41 40N 72 10 E
Tashauz = Dashhowuz, Turkmenistan 50 E6 41 49N 59 58 E
Tashi Chho Dzong = Thimphu, Bhutan 67 F16 27 31N 89 45 E
Ţashk, Daryācheh-ye, Iran 71 D7 29 45N 53 35 E
Tashkent = Toshkent, Uzbekistan 50 E7 41 20N 69 10 E
Tashtagol, Russia 50 D9 52 47N 87 53 E
Tasiilaq, Greenland 4 C6 65 40N 37 20W
Tasikmalaya, Indonesia 63 G13 7 18 S 108 12 E
Tåsinge, Denmark 11 J4 55 0N 10 35 E
Tåsjön, Sweden 8 D16 64 15N 15 40 E
Taskan, Russia 51 C16 62 59N 150 20 E
Tasker, Niger 83 C7 15 8N 10 30 E
Taşköprü, Turkey 72 B6 41 30N 34 15 E
Taşlâc, Moldova 43 C14 47 30N 29 45 E
Tasman B., N.Z. 91 J4 40 59 S 173 25 E
Tasman Mts., N.Z. 91 J4 41 3 S 172 25 E
Tasman Pen., Australia 94 G4 43 10 S 148 0 E
Tasman Sea, Pac. Oc. 96 L8 36 0 S 160 0 E
Tasmania □, Australia 94 G4 42 0 S 146 30 E
Tăşnad, Romania 42 C7 47 30N 22 33 E
Tassili n'Ajjer, Algeria 78 C7 25 47N 8 1 E
Tassili Tin-Rerhoh, Algeria 83 A5 20 5N 3 55 E
Tata, Hungary 42 C3 47 37N 18 19 E
Tatabánya, Hungary 42 C3 47 32N 18 25 E
Tatahouine, Tunisia 79 B8 32 56N 10 27 E
Tatar Republic = Tatarstan □, Russia 48 C10 55 30N 51 30 E

Tatarbunary, Ukraine **47 K5** 45 50N 29 39 E
Tatarsk, Russia **50 D8** 55 14N 76 0 E
Tatarstan □, Russia **48 C10** 55 30N 51 30 E
Tateyama, Japan **55 G9** 35 0N 139 50 E
Tathlina L., Canada **104 A5** 60 33N 117 39W
Tathra, Australia **95 F4** 36 44 S 149 59 E
Tati →, India **66 J8** 21 8N 72 41 E
Tatinnai L., Canada **105 A9** 60 55N 97 40W
Tatla L., Canada **104 C4** 52 0N 124 20W
Tatlısu, Turkey **41 F11** 40 24N 27 55 E
Tatnam, C., Canada **105 B10** 57 16N 91 0W
Tatra = Tatry, Slovak Rep. **27 B13** 49 20N 20 0 E
Tatry, Slovak Rep. **27 B13** 49 20N 20 0 E
Tatshenshini →, Canada **104 B1** 59 28N 137 45W
Tatsuno, Japan **55 G7** 34 52N 134 33 E
Tatta, Pakistan **68 G2** 24 42N 67 55 E
Tatuí, Brazil **127 A6** 23 25 S 47 53W
Tatum, U.S.A. **113 J3** 33 16N 103 19W
Tat'ung = Datong, China **56 D7** 40 6N 113 18 E
Tatvan, Turkey **70 B4** 38 31N 42 15 E
Taubaté, Brazil **127 A6** 23 0 S 45 36W
Tauberbischofsheim, Germany **25 F5** 49 37N 9 39 E
Taucha, Germany **24 D8** 51 23N 12 29 E
Tauern-tunnel, Austria **26 D6** 47 0N 13 12 E
Taufikia, Sudan **81 F3** 9 24N 31 37 E
Taulé, France **18 D3** 48 37N 3 55W
Taumarunui, N.Z. **91 H5** 38 53 S 175 15 E
Taumaturgo, Brazil **124 E4** 8 54 S 72 51W
Taung, S. Africa **88 D3** 27 33 S 24 47 E
Taungdwingyi, Burma **67 J19** 20 1N 95 40 E
Taunggyi, Burma **67 J20** 20 50N 97 0 E
Taungup, Burma **67 K19** 18 51N 94 14 E
Taungup Pass, Burma **67 K19** 18 40N 94 45 E
Taungup Taunggya, Burma **67 K18** 18 20N 93 40 E
Taunsa, Pakistan **68 D4** 30 42N 70 39 E
Taunsa Barrage, Pakistan **68 D4** 30 42N 70 50 E
Taunton, U.K. **13 F4** 51 1N 3 5W
Taunton, U.S.A. **111 E13** 41 54N 71 6W
Taunus, Germany **25 E4** 50 13N 8 34 E
Taupo, N.Z. **91 H6** 38 41 S 176 7 E
Taupo, L., N.Z. **91 H5** 38 46 S 175 55 E
Tauragė, Lithuania **9 J20** 55 14N 22 16 E
Tauragė □, Lithuania **44 C9** 55 15N 22 17 E
Tauranga, N.Z. **91 G6** 37 42 S 176 11 E
Tauranga Harb., N.Z. **91 G6** 37 30 S 176 5 E
Taureau, Rés., Canada **102 C5** 46 46N 73 50W
Taurianova, Italy **31 D9** 38 21N 16 1 E
Taurus Mts. = Toros Dağları, Turkey **70 B2** 37 0N 32 30 E
Tauste, Spain **32 D3** 41 58N 1 18W
Tauz = Tovuz, Azerbaijan **49 K7** 41 0N 45 40 E
Tavas, Turkey **39 D11** 37 34N 29 4 E
Tavda, Russia **50 D7** 58 7N 65 8 E
Tavda →, Russia **50 D7** 57 47N 67 18 E
Tavernes de la Valldigna, Spain **33 F4** 39 5N 0 13W
Taveta, Tanzania **86 C4** 3 23 S 37 37 E
Taveuni, Fiji **91 C9** 16 51 S 179 58W
Taviano, Italy **31 C11** 39 59N 18 5 E
Tavignano →, France **21 F13** 42 7N 9 33 E
Tavira, Portugal **35 H3** 37 8N 7 40W
Tavistock, Canada **110 C4** 43 19N 80 50W
Tavistock, U.K. **13 G3** 50 33N 4 9W
Tavolara, Italy **30 B2** 40 54N 9 42 E
Távora →, Portugal **34 D3** 41 8N 7 35W
Tavoy = Dawei, Burma **64 E2** 14 2N 98 12 E
Tavşanlı, Turkey **39 B11** 39 32N 29 30 E
Taw →, U.K. **13 F3** 51 4N 4 4W
Tawa →, India **68 H8** 22 48N 77 48 E
Tawas City, U.S.A. **108 C4** 44 16N 83 31W
Tawau, Malaysia **62 D5** 4 20N 117 55 E
Taweisha, Sudan **81 E2** 12 19N 26 40 E
Tawitawi, Phil. **63 B6** 5 10N 120 0 E
Tawu, Taiwan **59 F13** 22 30N 120 50 E
Taxco de Alarcón, Mexico **119 D5** 18 33N 99 36W
Taxila, Pakistan **68 C5** 33 42N 72 52 E
Tay →, U.K. **14 E5** 56 37N 3 38W
Tay, Firth of, U.K. **14 E5** 56 25N 3 8W
Tay, L., Australia **93 F3** 32 55 S 120 48 E
Tay, L., U.K. **14 E4** 56 32N 4 8W
Tay Ninh, Vietnam **65 G6** 11 20N 106 5 E
Tayabamba, Peru **124 E3** 8 15 S 77 16W
Tayabas Bay, Phil. **61 E4** 13 45N 121 45 E
Taylakova, Russia **50 D8** 59 13N 74 0 E
Taylakovy = Taylakova, Russia **50 D8** 59 13N 74 0 E
Taylor, Canada **104 B4** 56 13N 120 40W
Taylor, Nebr., U.S.A. **112 E5** 41 46N 99 23W
Taylor, Pa., U.S.A. **111 E9** 41 23N 75 43W
Taylor, Tex., U.S.A. **113 K6** 30 34N 97 25W
Taylor, Mt., U.S.A. **115 J10** 35 14N 107 37W
Taylorville, U.S.A. **112 F10** 39 33N 89 18W
Taymā, Si. Arabia **70 E3** 27 35N 38 45 E
Taymyr, Oz., Russia **51 B11** 74 20N 102 0 E
Taymyr, Poluostrov, Russia **51 B11** 75 0N 100 0 E
Tayport, U.K. **14 E6** 56 27N 2 52W
Tayshet, Russia **51 D10** 55 58N 98 1 E
Taytay, Phil. **61 F3** 10 45N 119 30 E
Taz →, Russia **50 C8** 67 32N 78 40 E
Taza, Morocco **78 B5** 34 16N 4 6W
Tāzah Khurmātū, Iraq **70 C5** 35 18N 44 20 E
Tazawa-Ko, Japan **54 E10** 39 43N 140 40 E
Tazin, Canada **105 B7** 59 48N 109 55W
Tazin L., Canada **105 B7** 59 44N 108 42W
Tazovskiy, Russia **50 C8** 67 30N 78 44 E
Tbilisi, Georgia **49 K7** 41 43N 44 50 E
Tchad = Chad ■, Africa **79 E9** 15 0N 17 15 E
Tchad, L., Chad **79 F8** 13 30N 14 30 E
Tchaourou, Benin **83 D5** 8 58N 2 40 E
Tch'eng-tou = Chengdu, China **58 B5** 30 38N 104 2 E
Tchentlo L., Canada **104 B4** 55 15N 125 0W
Tchetti, Benin **83 D5** 7 50N 1 40 E
Tchibanga, Gabon **84 E2** 2 45 S 11 0 E
Tchien, Liberia **82 D3** 5 59N 8 15W
Tchin Tabaraden, Niger **83 B6** 15 58N 5 56 E
Tch'ong-k'ing = Chongqing, China **58 C6** 29 35N 106 25 E
Tczew, Poland **44 D5** 54 8N 18 50 E
Te Anau, N.Z. **91 L1** 45 25 S 167 43 E
Te Anau, L., N.Z. **91 L1** 45 15 S 167 45 E
Te Aroha, N.Z. **91 G5** 37 32 S 175 44 E
Te Awamutu, N.Z. **91 H5** 38 1 S 175 20 E
Te Kuiti, N.Z. **91 H5** 38 20 S 175 11 E
Te-n-Dghâmcha, Sebkhet, Mauritania **82 B1** 18 30N 15 55W
Te Puke, N.Z. **91 G6** 37 46 S 176 22 E
Te Waewae B., N.Z. **91 M1** 46 13 S 167 33 E
Teaca, Romania **43 D9** 46 55N 24 30 E
Teague, U.S.A. **113 K6** 31 38N 96 17W
Teano, Italy **31 A7** 41 15N 14 4 E
Teapa, Mexico **119 D6** 18 35N 92 56W
Teba, Spain **35 J6** 36 59N 4 55W
Tebakang, Malaysia **62 D4** 1 6N 110 30 E
Teberda, Russia **49 J5** 43 30N 41 46 E
Tébessa, Algeria **78 A7** 35 22N 8 8 E
Tebicuary →, Paraguay **126 B4** 26 36 S 58 16W
Tebingtinggi, Indonesia **62 D1** 3 20N 99 9 E
Tebintingii, Indonesia **62 E2** 1 0N 102 45 E
Tebulos, Georgia **49 J7** 42 36N 45 17 E
Tecate, Mexico **117 N10** 32 34N 116 38W
Tecer Dağları, Turkey **72 C7** 39 27N 37 27 E
Tech →, France **20 F7** 42 36N 3 3 E
Techiman, Ghana **82 D4** 7 35N 1 58W
Techirghiol, Romania **43 F13** 44 4N 28 32 E
Tecka, Argentina **128 E2** 43 29 S 70 48W
Tecomán, Mexico **118 D4** 18 55N 103 53W
Tecopa, U.S.A. **117 K10** 35 51N 116 13W
Tecoripa, Mexico **118 B3** 28 37N 109 57W
Tecuala, Mexico **118 C3** 22 23N 105 27W
Tecuci, Romania **43 E12** 45 51N 27 27 E
Tecumseh, Canada **110 D2** 42 19N 82 54W
Tecumseh, Mich., U.S.A. **108 D4** 42 0N 83 57W
Tecumseh, Okla., U.S.A. **113 H6** 35 15N 96 56W
Tedzhen = Tejen, Turkmenistan **50 F7** 37 23N 60 31 E
Tees →, U.K. **12 C6** 54 37N 1 10W
Tees B., U.K. **12 C6** 54 40N 1 9W
Teeswater, Canada **110 C3** 43 59N 81 17W
Tefé, Brazil **124 D6** 3 25 S 64 50W
Tefenni, Turkey **39 D11** 37 18N 29 45 E
Tegal, Indonesia **63 G13** 6 52 S 109 8 E
Tegernsee, Germany **25 H7** 47 43N 11 46 E
Teggiano, Italy **31 B8** 40 23N 15 32 E
Tegid, L. = Bala, L., U.K. **12 E4** 52 53N 3 37W
Tegina, Nigeria **83 C6** 10 5N 6 11 E
Tegucigalpa, Honduras **120 D2** 14 5N 87 14W
Teguidda i-n-Tessoum, Niger **83 B6** 17 25N 6 37 E
Tehachapi, U.S.A. **117 K8** 35 8N 118 27W
Tehachapi Mts., U.S.A. **117 L8** 35 0N 118 30W
Tehamiyam, Sudan **80 D4** 18 20N 36 32 E
Tehilla, Sudan **80 D4** 17 42N 36 6 E
Téhini, Ivory C. **82 D4** 9 39N 3 40W
Tehoru, Indonesia **63 E7** 3 19 S 129 37 E
Tehrān, Iran **71 C6** 35 44N 51 30 E
Tehri, India **69 D8** 30 23N 78 29 E
Tehuacán, Mexico **119 D5** 18 30N 97 30W
Tehuantepec, Mexico **119 D5** 16 21N 95 13W
Tehuantepec, G. de, Mexico **119 D5** 15 50N 95 12W
Tehuantepec, Istmo de, Mexico **119 D6** 17 0N 94 30W
Teide, Canary Is. **37 F3** 28 15N 16 38W
Teifi →, U.K. **13 E3** 52 5N 4 41W
Teign →, U.K. **13 G4** 50 32N 3 32W
Teignmouth, U.K. **13 G4** 50 33N 3 31W
Teiuş, Romania **43 D8** 46 12N 23 40 E
Teixeira Pinto, Guinea-Biss. **82 C1** 12 3N 16 0W
Tejam, India **69 E9** 29 57N 80 11 E
Tejen, Turkmenistan **50 F7** 37 23N 60 31 E
Tejen →, Turkmenistan **71 B9** 37 24N 60 38 E
Tejo →, Europe **35 F2** 38 40N 9 24W
Tejon Pass, U.S.A. **117 L8** 34 49N 118 53W
Tekamah, U.S.A. **112 E6** 41 47N 96 13W
Tekapo, L., N.Z. **91 K3** 43 53 S 170 33 E
Tekax, Mexico **119 C7** 20 11N 89 18W
Teke, Turkey **41 E13** 41 4N 29 39 E
Tekeli, Kazakstan **50 E8** 44 50N 79 0 E
Tekeze →, Ethiopia **81 E4** 14 20N 35 50 E
Tekija, Serbia, Yug. **40 B6** 44 42N 22 26 E
Tekirdağ, Turkey **41 F11** 40 58N 27 30 E
Tekirdağ □, Turkey **41 E11** 41 0N 27 0 E
Tekirova, Turkey **39 E12** 36 30N 30 32 E
Tekkali, India **67 K14** 18 37N 84 15 E
Tekke, Turkey **72 B7** 40 42N 36 12 E
Tekman, Turkey **73 C9** 39 38N 41 29 E
Tekoa, U.S.A. **114 C5** 47 14N 117 4W
Tel Aviv-Yafo, Israel **75 C3** 32 4N 34 48 E
Tel Lakhish, Israel **75 D3** 31 34N 34 51 E
Tel Megiddo, Israel **75 C4** 32 35N 35 11 E
Tela, Honduras **120 C2** 15 40N 87 28W
Telanaipura = Jambi, Indonesia **62 E2** 1 38 S 103 30 E
Telavi, Georgia **49 J7** 42 0N 45 30 E
Telč, Czech Rep. **26 B8** 49 11N 15 28 E
Telciu, Romania **43 C9** 47 25N 24 24 E
Telde, Canary Is. **37 G4** 27 59N 15 25W
Telegraph Creek, Canada **104 B2** 58 0N 131 10W
Telekhany = Tsyelyakhany, Belarus **47 F3** 52 30N 25 46 E
Telemark, Norway **9 G12** 59 15N 7 40 E
Telén, Argentina **126 D2** 36 15 S 65 31W
Teleneşti, Moldova **43 C13** 47 30N 28 22 E
Teleng, Iran **71 E9** 25 47N 61 3 E
Teleño, Spain **34 C4** 42 23N 6 22W
Teleorman □, Romania **43 G10** 44 0N 25 0 E
Teleorman →, Romania **43 G10** 43 52N 25 26 E
Teles Pires →, Brazil **122 D5** 7 21 S 58 3W
Telescope Pk., U.S.A. **117 J9** 36 10N 117 5W
Teletaye, Mali **83 B5** 16 31N 1 30 E
Telfer Mine, Australia **92 C3** 21 40 S 122 12 E
Telford, U.K. **13 E5** 52 40N 2 27W
Telford and Wrekin □, U.K. **12 E5** 52 45N 2 27W
Telfs, Austria **26 D4** 47 19N 11 4 E
Télimélé, Guinea **82 C2** 10 54N 13 2W
Teljo, J., Sudan **81 E2** 14 42N 25 26 E
Telkwa, Canada **104 C3** 54 41N 127 5W
Tell City, U.S.A. **108 G2** 37 57N 86 46W
Tellicherry, India **66 P9** 11 45N 75 30 E
Telluride, U.S.A. **115 H10** 37 56N 107 49W
Teloloapán, Mexico **119 D5** 18 21N 99 51W
Telpos Iz, Russia **6 C17** 63 16N 59 13 E
Telsen, Argentina **128 E3** 42 30 S 66 50W
Telšiai, Lithuania **9 H20** 55 59N 22 14 E
Telšiai □, Lithuania **44 C9** 55 59N 22 15 E
Teltow, Germany **24 C9** 52 24N 13 15 E
Teluk Anson = Teluk Intan, Malaysia **65 K3** 4 3N 101 0 E
Teluk Betung = Tanjungkarang Telukbetung, Indonesia **62 F3** 5 20 S 105 10 E
Teluk Intan, Malaysia **65 K3** 4 3N 101 0 E
Telukbutun, Indonesia **65 K7** 4 13N 108 12 E
Telukdalem, Indonesia **62 D1** 0 33N 97 50 E
Tema, Ghana **83 D5** 5 41N 0 0W
Temax, Mexico **119 C7** 21 10N 88 50W
Temba, S. Africa **89 D4** 25 20 S 28 17 E
Tembagapura, Indonesia **63 E9** 4 20 S 137 0 E
Tembe, Dem. Rep. of the Congo **86 C2** 0 16 S 28 14 E
Tembleque, Spain **34 F7** 39 41N 3 30W
Temblor Range, U.S.A. **117 K7** 35 20N 119 50W
Teme →, U.K. **13 E5** 52 11N 2 13W
Temecula, U.S.A. **117 M9** 33 30N 117 9W
Temerloh, Malaysia **62 D2** 3 27N 102 25 E
Teminabuan, Indonesia **63 E8** 1 26 S 132 1 E
Temir, Kazakstan **50 E6** 49 1N 57 14 E
Temirtau, Kazakstan **50 D8** 50 5N 72 56 E
Temirtau, Russia **50 D9** 53 10N 87 30 E
Témiscamie →, Canada **103 B5** 50 59N 73 5W
Témiscaming, Canada **102 C4** 46 44N 79 5W
Témiscamingue, L., Canada **102 C4** 47 10N 79 25W
Temnikov, Russia **48 C6** 54 40N 43 11 E
Temo →, Italy **30 B1** 40 17N 8 28 E
Temosachic, Mexico **118 B3** 28 58N 107 50W
Tempe, U.S.A. **115 K8** 33 25N 111 56W
Témpio Pausània, Italy **30 B2** 40 54N 9 6 E
Tempiute, U.S.A. **116 H11** 37 39N 115 38W
Temple, U.S.A. **113 K6** 31 6N 97 21W
Temple B., Australia **94 A3** 12 15 S 143 3 E
Templemore, Ireland **15 D4** 52 47N 7 51W
Templeton, U.S.A. **116 K6** 35 33N 120 42W
Templeton →, Australia **94 C2** 21 0 S 138 40 E
Templin, Germany **24 B9** 53 7N 13 28 E
Tempoal, Mexico **119 C5** 21 31N 98 23W
Temryuk, Russia **47 K9** 45 15N 37 24 E
Temska →, Serbia, Yug. **40 C6** 43 17N 22 33 E
Temuco, Chile **128 D2** 38 45 S 72 40W
Temuka, N.Z. **91 L3** 44 14 S 171 17 E
Tenabo, Mexico **119 C6** 20 2N 90 12W
Tenaha, U.S.A. **113 K7** 31 57N 94 15W
Tenakee Springs, U.S.A. **104 B1** 57 47N 135 13W
Tenali, India **66 L12** 16 15N 80 35 E
Tenancingo, Mexico **119 D5** 19 0N 99 33W
Tenango, Mexico **119 D5** 19 7N 99 33W
Tenasserim, Burma **65 F2** 12 6N 99 3 E
Tenasserim □, Burma **64 F2** 14 0N 98 30 E
Tenby, U.K. **13 F3** 51 40N 4 42W
Tenda, Colle di, France **21 D11** 44 7N 7 36 E
Tendaho, Ethiopia **81 E5** 11 48N 40 54 E
Tende, France **21 D11** 44 5N 7 35 E
Tendelti, Sudan **81 E3** 13 1N 31 55 E
Tendrovskaya Kosa, Ukraine **47 J6** 46 16N 31 35 E
Tendukhera, India **69 H8** 23 24N 79 33 E
Teneida, Egypt **80 B2** 25 30N 29 19 E
Tenenkou, Mali **82 C4** 14 28N 4 55W
Ténéré, Niger **83 B7** 19 0N 10 30 E
Tenerife, Canary Is. **37 F3** 28 15N 16 35W
Tenerife, Pico, Canary Is. **37 G1** 27 43N 18 1W
Teng Xian, Guangxi Zhuangzu, China **59 F8** 23 21N 110 56 E
Teng Xian, Shandong, China **57 G9** 35 5N 117 10 E
Tengah □, Indonesia **63 E6** 2 0 S 122 0 E
Tengah, Kepulauan, Indonesia **62 F5** 7 5 S 118 15 E
Tengchong, China **58 E2** 25 0N 98 28 E
Tengchowfu = Penglai, China **57 F11** 37 48N 120 42 E
Tenggara □, Indonesia **63 E6** 3 0 S 122 0 E
Tenggarong, Indonesia **62 E5** 0 24 S 116 58 E
Tenggol, Pulau, Malaysia **65 K4** 4 48N 103 41 E
Tengiz, Ozero, Kazakstan **50 D7** 50 30N 69 0 E
Tenhult, Sweden **11 G8** 57 41N 14 20 E
Tenino, U.S.A. **116 D4** 46 51N 122 51W
Tenkasi, India **66 Q10** 8 55N 77 20 E
Tenke, Katanga, Dem. Rep. of the Congo **87 E2** 11 22 S 26 40 E
Tenke, Katanga, Dem. Rep. of the Congo **87 E2** 10 32 S 26 7 E
Tenkodogo, Burkina Faso **83 C4** 11 54N 0 19W
Tenna →, Italy **29 E10** 43 14N 13 47 E
Tennant Creek, Australia **94 B1** 19 30 S 134 15 E
Tennessee □, U.S.A. **109 H2** 36 0N 86 30W
Tennessee →, U.S.A. **108 G1** 37 4N 88 34W
Teno, Pta. de, Canary Is. **37 F3** 28 21N 16 55W
Tenom, Malaysia **62 C5** 5 4N 115 57 E
Tenosique, Mexico **119 D6** 17 30N 91 24W
Tenryū-Gawa →, Japan **55 G8** 35 39N 137 48 E
Tenterden, U.K. **13 F8** 51 4N 0 42 E
Tenterfield, Australia **95 D5** 29 0 S 152 0 E
Teo, Spain **34 C2** 42 45N 8 30W
Teófilo Otoni, Brazil **125 G10** 17 50 S 41 30W
Tepa, Indonesia **63 F7** 7 52 S 129 31 E
Tepalcatepec →, Mexico **118 D4** 18 35N 101 59W
Tepecik, Bursa, Turkey **41 F12** 40 7N 28 25 E
Tepecik, Kütahya, Turkey **39 B11** 39 32N 29 28 E
Tepehuanes, Mexico **118 B3** 25 21N 105 44W
Tepelena = Tepelenë, Albania **40 F4** 40 17N 20 2 E
Tepelenë, Albania **40 F4** 40 17N 20 2 E
Tepetongo, Mexico **118 C4** 22 28N 103 9W
Tepic, Mexico **118 C4** 21 30N 104 54W
Teplá, Czech Rep. **26 B5** 49 59N 12 52 E
Teplice, Czech Rep. **26 A6** 50 40N 13 48 E
Tepoca, C., Mexico **118 A2** 30 20N 112 25W
Tequila, Mexico **118 C4** 20 54N 103 47W
Ter →, Spain **32 C8** 42 2N 3 12 E
Ter Apel, Neths. **17 B7** 52 53N 7 5 E
Téra, Niger **83 C5** 14 0N 0 45 E
Tera →, Spain **34 D5** 41 54N 5 44W
Teraina, Kiribati **97 G11** 4 43N 160 25W
Terakeka, Sudan **81 F3** 5 26N 31 45 E
Téramo, Italy **29 F10** 42 39N 13 42 E
Terang, Australia **95 F3** 38 15 S 142 55 E
Terazit, Massif de, Niger **83 A6** 20 2N 8 30 E
Tercan, Turkey **73 C9** 39 47N 40 23 E
Tercero →, Argentina **126 C3** 32 58 S 61 47W
Terebovlya, Ukraine **47 H3** 49 18N 25 44 E
Teregova, Romania **42 E7** 45 10N 22 16 E
Tereida, Sudan **81 E3** 10 35N 31 17 E
Terek →, Russia **49 J8** 44 0N 47 30 E
Tereshka →, Russia **48 E8** 51 48N 46 26 E
Teresina, Brazil **125 E10** 5 9 S 42 45W
Terespol, Poland **45 F10** 52 5N 23 37 E
Terewah, L., Australia **95 D4** 29 52 S 147 35 E
Terges →, Portugal **35 H3** 37 49N 7 41W
Tergnier, France **19 C10** 49 40N 3 17 E
Teridgerie Cr. →, Australia **95 E4** 30 25 S 148 50 E
Terlizzi, Italy **31 A9** 41 8N 16 32 E
Terme, Turkey **72 B7** 41 11N 37 0 E
Termez = Termiz, Uzbekistan **50 F7** 37 15N 67 15 E
Términi Imerese, Italy **30 E6** 37 59N 13 42 E
Términos, L. de, Mexico **119 D6** 18 35N 91 30W
Termiz, Uzbekistan **50 F7** 37 15N 67 15 E
Térmoli, Italy **29 F12** 42 0N 15 0 E
Ternate, Indonesia **63 D7** 0 45N 127 25 E
Terneuzen, Neths. **17 C3** 51 20N 3 50 E
Terney, Russia **51 E14** 45 3N 136 37 E
Terni, Italy **29 F9** 42 34N 12 37 E
Ternitz, Austria **26 D9** 47 43N 16 2 E
Ternopil, Ukraine **47 H3** 49 30N 25 40 E
Ternopol = Ternopil, Ukraine **47 H3** 49 30N 25 40 E
Terowie, Australia **95 E2** 33 8 S 138 55 E
Terpní, Greece **40 F7** 40 55N 23 26 E
Terra Bella, U.S.A. **117 K7** 35 58N 119 3W
Terra Nova Nat. Park, Canada **103 C9** 48 33N 53 55W
Terrace, Canada **104 C3** 54 30N 128 35W
Terrace Bay, Canada **102 C2** 48 47N 87 5W
Terracina, Italy **30 A6** 41 17N 13 15 E
Terralba, Italy **30 C1** 39 43N 8 39 E
Terranova = Ólbia, Italy **30 B2** 40 55N 9 31 E
Terrasini, Italy **30 D6** 38 10N 13 4 E
Terrassa, Spain **32 D7** 41 34N 2 1 E
Terrasson-la-Villedieu, France **20 C5** 45 8N 1 18 E
Terre Haute, U.S.A. **108 F2** 39 28N 87 25W
Terrebonne B., U.S.A. **113 L9** 29 5N 90 35W
Terrell, U.S.A. **113 J6** 32 44N 96 17W
Terrenceville, Canada **103 C9** 47 40N 54 44W
Terry, U.S.A. **112 B2** 46 47N 105 19W
Terryville, U.S.A. **111 E11** 41 41N 73 3W
Terschelling, Neths. **17 A5** 53 25N 5 20 E
Tersko-Kumskiy Kanal →, Russia **49 H7** 44 32N 44 38 E
Tertenía, Italy **30 C2** 39 42N 9 34 E
Terter → = Tärtär →, Azerbaijan **49 K8** 40 26N 47 20 E
Teruel, Spain **32 E3** 40 22N 1 8W
Teruel □, Spain **32 E4** 40 48N 1 0W
Tervel, Bulgaria **41 C11** 43 45N 27 28 E
Tervola, Finland **8 C21** 66 6N 24 49 E
Teryaweyna L., Australia **95 E3** 32 18 S 143 22 E
Tešanj, Bos.-H. **42 F3** 44 38N 18 1 E
Teseney, Eritrea **81 D4** 15 5N 36 42 E
Tesha →, Russia **48 C6** 55 38N 42 9 E
Teshio, Japan **54 B10** 44 53N 141 44 E
Teshio-Gawa →, Japan **54 B10** 44 53N 141 45 E
Tešica, Serbia, Yug. **40 C5** 43 27N 21 45 E
Tesiyn Gol →, Mongolia **60 A4** 50 40N 93 20 E
Teslić, Bos.-H. **42 F2** 44 37N 17 54 E
Teslin, Canada **104 A2** 60 10N 132 43W
Teslin →, Canada **104 A2** 61 34N 134 35W
Teslin L., Canada **104 A2** 60 15N 132 57W
Tessalit, Mali **83 A5** 20 12N 1 0 E
Tessaoua, Niger **83 C6** 13 47N 7 56 E
Tessin, Germany **24 A8** 54 2N 12 26 E
Tessit, Mali **83 B5** 15 13N 0 18 E
Test →, U.K. **13 G6** 50 56N 1 29W
Testa del Gargano, Italy **29 G13** 41 50N 16 10 E
Testigos, Is. Las, Venezuela **121 D7** 11 23N 63 7W
Tét, Hungary **42 C2** 47 30N 17 33 E
Têt →, France **20 F7** 42 44N 3 2 E
Tetachuck L., Canada **104 C3** 53 18N 125 55W
Tetas, Pta., Chile **126 A1** 23 31 S 70 38W
Tete, Mozam. **87 F3** 16 13 S 33 33 E
Tete □, Mozam. **87 F3** 15 15 S 32 40 E
Teterev →, Ukraine **47 G6** 51 1N 30 5 E
Teterow, Germany **24 B8** 53 46N 12 34 E
Teteven, Bulgaria **41 D8** 42 58N 24 17 E
Tethul →, Canada **104 A6** 60 35N 112 12W
Tetiyev, Ukraine **47 H5** 49 22N 29 38 E
Teton →, U.S.A. **114 C8** 47 56N 110 31W
Tétouan, Morocco **78 A4** 35 35N 5 21W
Tetovo, Macedonia **40 D4** 42 1N 20 59 E
Tetyushi, Russia **48 C9** 54 55N 48 49 E
Teuco →, Argentina **126 B3** 25 35 S 60 11W
Teulada, Italy **30 D1** 38 58N 8 46 E
Teulon, Canada **105 C9** 50 23N 97 16W
Teun, Indonesia **63 F7** 6 59 S 129 8 E
Teutoburger Wald, Germany **24 C4** 52 5N 8 22 E
Tevere →, Italy **29 G9** 41 44N 12 14 E
Teverya, Israel **75 C4** 32 47N 35 32 E
Teviot →, U.K. **14 F6** 55 29N 2 38W
Tewantin, Australia **95 D5** 26 27 S 153 3 E
Tewkesbury, U.K. **13 F5** 51 59N 2 9W
Texada I., Canada **104 D4** 49 40N 124 25W
Texarkana, Ark., U.S.A. **113 J8** 33 26N 94 2W
Texarkana, Tex., U.S.A. **113 J7** 33 26N 94 3W
Texas, Australia **95 D5** 28 49 S 151 9 E
Texas □, U.S.A. **113 K5** 31 40N 98 30W
Texas City, U.S.A. **113 L7** 29 24N 94 54W
Texel, Neths. **17 A4** 53 5N 4 50 E
Texline, U.S.A. **113 G3** 36 23N 103 2W
Texoma, L., U.S.A. **113 J6** 33 50N 96 34W
Teykovo, Russia **46 D11** 56 55N 40 30 E
Teza →, Russia **48 B5** 56 32N 41 53 E
Tezin, Afghan. **68 B3** 34 24N 69 30 E
Teziutlán, Mexico **119 D5** 19 50N 97 22W
Tezpur, India **67 F18** 26 40N 92 45 E
Tezzeron L., Canada **104 C4** 54 43N 124 30W
Tha-anne →, Canada **105 A10** 60 31N 94 37W
Tha Deua, Laos **64 D4** 17 57N 102 53 E
Tha Deua, Laos **64 C3** 19 26N 101 50 E
Tha Pla, Thailand **64 D3** 17 48N 100 32 E
Tha Rua, Thailand **64 E3** 14 34N 100 44 E
Tha Sala, Thailand **65 H2** 8 40N 99 56 E
Tha Song Yang, Thailand **64 D1** 17 34N 97 55 E
Thaba Putsoa, Lesotho **89 D4** 29 45 S 28 0 E
Thabana Ntlenyana, Lesotho **89 D4** 29 30 S 29 16 E
Thabazimbi, S. Africa **89 C4** 24 40 S 27 21 E
Thādiq, Si. Arabia **70 E5** 25 18N 45 52 E
Thai Binh, Vietnam **58 G6** 20 35N 106 1 E
Thai Muang, Thailand **65 H2** 8 24N 98 16 E
Thai Nguyen, Vietnam **58 G5** 21 35N 105 55 E
Thailand ■, Asia **64 E4** 16 0N 102 0 E
Thailand, G. of, Asia **65 G3** 11 30N 101 0 E
Thakhek, Laos **64 D5** 17 25N 104 45 E
Thal, Pakistan **68 C4** 33 28N 70 33 E
Thal Desert, Pakistan **68 D4** 31 10N 71 30 E
Thala La, Burma **67 E20** 28 25N 97 23 E
Thalabarivat, Cambodia **64 F5** 13 33N 105 57 E
Thallon, Australia **95 D4** 28 39 S 148 49 E
Thalwil, Switz. **25 H4** 47 17N 8 35 E
Thames, N.Z. **91 G5** 37 7 S 175 34 E
Thames →, Canada **102 D3** 42 20N 82 25W
Thames →, U.K. **13 F8** 51 29N 0 34 E
Thames →, U.S.A. **111 E12** 41 18N 72 5W
Thames Estuary, U.K. **13 F8** 51 29N 0 52 E
Thamesford, Canada **110 C4** 43 4N 81 0W
Thamesville, Canada **110 D3** 42 33N 81 59W
Than, India **68 H4** 22 34N 71 11 E
Than Uyen, Vietnam **64 B4** 22 0N 103 54 E
Thana Gazi, India **68 F7** 27 25N 76 19 E
Thandla, India **68 H6** 23 0N 74 34 E
Thane, India **66 K8** 19 12N 72 59 E
Thanesar, India **68 D7** 30 1N 76 52 E
Thanet, I. of, U.K. **13 F9** 51 21N 1 20 E
Thangool, Australia **94 C5** 24 38 S 150 42 E
Thanh Hoa, Vietnam **64 C5** 19 48N 105 46 E
Thanh Hung, Vietnam **65 H5** 9 55N 105 43 E
Thanh Pho Ho Chi Minh, Vietnam **65 G6** 10 58N 106 40 E
Thanh Thuy, Vietnam **64 A5** 22 55N 104 51 E
Thanjavur, India **66 P11** 10 48N 79 12 E
Thann, France **19 E14** 47 48N 7 5 E
Thano Bula Khan, Pakistan **68 G2** 25 22N 67 50 E
Thaolinta L., Canada **105 A9** 61 30N 96 25W
Thaon-les-Vosges, France **19 D13** 48 15N 6 24 E
Thap Sakae, Thailand **65 G2** 11 30N 99 37 E
Thap Than, Thailand **64 E2** 15 27N 99 54 E
Thar Desert, India **68 F5** 28 0N 72 0 E
Tharad, India **68 G4** 24 30N 71 44 E
Thargomindah, Australia **95 D3** 27 58 S 143 46 E
Tharrawaddy, Burma **67 L19** 17 38N 95 48 E
Tharthār, Mileh, Iraq **70 C4** 34 0N 43 15 E
Tharthār, W. ath →, Iraq **70 C4** 33 59N 43 12 E
Thasopoúla, Greece **41 F8** 40 49N 24 45 E
Thásos, Greece **41 F8** 40 40N 24 40 E
That Khe, Vietnam **58 F6** 22 16N 106 28 E
Thatcher, Ariz., U.S.A. **115 K9** 32 51N 109 46W
Thatcher, Colo., U.S.A. **113 G2** 37 33N 104 7W
Thaton, Burma **67 L20** 16 55N 97 22 E
Thau, Bassin de, France **20 E7** 43 23N 3 36 E
Thaungdut, Burma **67 G19** 24 30N 94 40 E
Thayer, U.S.A. **113 G9** 36 31N 91 33W
Thayetmyo, Burma **67 K19** 19 20N 95 10 E
Thazi, Burma **67 J20** 21 0N 96 5 E
The Alberga →, Australia **95 D2** 27 6 S 135 33 E
The Bight, Bahamas **121 B4** 24 19N 75 24W
The Coorong, Australia **95 F2** 35 50 S 139 20 E
The Dalles, U.S.A. **114 D3** 45 36N 121 10W
The English Company's Is., Australia **94 A2** 11 50 S 136 32 E
The Frome →, Australia **95 D2** 29 8 S 137 54 E
The Great Divide = Great Dividing Ra., Australia **94 C4** 23 0 S 146 0 E
The Hague = 's-Gravenhage, Neths. **17 B4** 52 7N 4 17 E
The Hamilton →, Australia **95 D2** 26 40 S 135 19 E
The Macumba →, Australia **95 D2** 27 52 S 137 12 E
The Neales →, Australia **95 D2** 28 8 S 136 47 E
The Officer →, Australia **93 E5** 27 46 S 132 30 E
The Pas, Canada **105 C8** 53 45N 101 15W
The Range, Zimbabwe **87 F3** 19 2 S 31 2 E
The Rock, Australia **95 F4** 35 15 S 147 2 E
The Salt L., Australia **95 E3** 30 6 S 142 8 E
The Sandheads, India **69 J13** 21 10N 88 20 E
The Stevenson →, Australia **95 D2** 27 6 S 135 33 E
The Warburton →, Australia **95 D2** 28 4 S 137 28 E
The Woodlands, U.S.A. **113 K7** 30 9N 95 27W
Thebes = Thívai, Greece **38 C5** 38 19N 23 19 E
Thebes, Egypt **80 B3** 25 40N 32 35 E
Thedford, Canada **110 C3** 43 9N 81 51W
Thedford, U.S.A. **112 E4** 41 59N 100 35W
Theebine, Australia **95 D5** 25 57 S 152 34 E
Thekulthili L., Canada **105 A7** 61 3N 110 0W
Thelon →, Canada **105 A8** 62 35N 104 3W
Thénezay, France **18 F6** 46 44N 0 2W
Thenon, France **20 C5** 45 9N 1 4 E
Theodore, Australia **94 C5** 24 55 S 150 3 E
Theodore, Canada **105 C8** 51 26N 102 55W
Theodore, U.S.A. **109 K1** 30 33N 88 10W
Theodore Roosevelt National Memorial Park, U.S.A. **112 B3** 47 0N 103 25W
Theodore Roosevelt Res., U.S.A. **115 K8** 33 46N 111 0W
Thepha, Thailand **65 J3** 6 52N 100 58 E
Thérain →, France **19 C9** 49 15N 2 27 E
Theresa, U.S.A. **111 B9** 44 13N 75 48W
Thermaïkós Kólpos, Greece **40 F6** 40 15N 22 45 E
Thermí, Greece **39 B8** 39 11N 26 29 E
Thermopolis, U.S.A. **114 E9** 43 39N 108 13W
Thermopylae P., Greece **38 C4** 38 48N 22 35 E
Thesprotía □, Greece **38 B2** 39 27N 20 22 E
Thessalía □, Greece **38 B4** 39 25N 22 0 E
Thessalon, Canada **102 C3** 46 20N 83 30W
Thessaloníki, Greece **40 F6** 40 38N 22 58 E
Thessaloníki □, Greece **40 F7** 40 45N 23 0 E
Thessaloníki, Gulf of = Thermaïkós Kólpos, Greece **40 F6** 40 15N 22 45 E
Thessaly = Thessalía □, Greece **38 B4** 39 25N 22 0 E
Thetford, U.K. **13 E8** 52 25N 0 45 E

Thetford Mines, Canada 103 C5 46 8N 71 18W
Theun →, Laos 64 C5 18 19N 104 0 E
Theunissen, S. Africa 88 D4 28 26 S 26 43 E
Thevenard, Australia 95 E1 32 9 S 133 38 E
Thiámis →, Greece 38 B2 39 15N 20 6 E
Thiberville, France 18 C7 49 8N 0 27 E
Thibodaux, U.S.A. 113 L9 29 48N 90 49W
Thicket Portage, Canada 105 B9 55 19N 97 42W
Thief River Falls, U.S.A. 112 A6 48 7N 96 10W
Thiel Mts., Antarctica 5 E16 85 15 S 91 0W
Thiene, Italy 29 C8 45 42N 11 29 E
Thiérache, France 19 C10 49 51N 3 45 E
Thiers, France 20 C7 45 52N 3 33 E
Thiès, Senegal 82 C1 14 50N 16 51W
Thiesi, Italy 30 B1 40 31N 8 43 E
Thiet, Sudan 81 F2 7 37N 28 49 E
Thika, Kenya 86 C4 1 1 S 37 5 E
Thikombia, Fiji 91 B9 15 44 S 179 55W
Thille-Boubacar, Senegal 82 B1 16 31N 15 5W
Thimphu, Bhutan 67 F16 27 31N 89 45 E
Þingvallavatn, Iceland 8 D3 64 11N 21 9W
Thionville, France 19 C13 49 20N 6 10 E
Thíra, Greece 39 E7 36 23N 25 27 E
Thirasía, Greece 39 E7 36 26N 25 21 E
Third Cataract, Sudan 80 D3 19 42N 30 20 E
Thirsk, U.K. 12 C6 54 14N 1 19W
Thisted, Denmark 11 H2 56 58N 8 40 E
Thistle I., Australia 95 F2 35 0 S 136 8 E
Thívai, Greece 38 C5 38 19N 23 19 E
Thiviers, France 20 C4 45 25N 0 54 E
Thizy, France 19 F11 46 2N 4 18 E
Þjórsá →, Iceland 8 E3 63 47N 20 48W
Thlewiaza →, Man., Canada 105 B8 59 43N 100 5W
Thlewiaza →, N.W.T., Canada 105 A10 60 29N 94 40W
Thmar Puok, Cambodia 64 F4 13 57N 103 4 E
Tho Vinh, Vietnam 64 C5 19 16N 105 42 E
Thoa →, Canada 105 A7 60 31N 109 47W
Thoen, Thailand 64 D2 17 43N 99 12 E
Thoeng, Thailand 64 C3 19 41N 100 12 E
Thohoyandou, S. Africa 85 J6 22 58 S 30 29 E
Tholdi, Pakistan 69 B7 35 5N 76 6 E
Thomas, U.S.A. 113 H5 35 45N 98 45W
Thomas, L., Australia 95 D2 26 4 S 137 58 E
Thomaston, U.S.A. 109 J3 32 53N 84 20W
Thomasville, Ala., U.S.A. 109 K2 31 55N 87 44W
Thomasville, Ga., U.S.A. 109 K4 30 50N 83 59W
Thomasville, N.C., U.S.A. 109 H5 35 53N 80 5W
Thompson, Canada 105 B9 55 45N 97 52W
Thompson, U.S.A. 111 E9 41 52N 75 31W
Thompson →, Canada 104 C4 50 15N 121 24W
Thompson →, U.S.A. 112 F8 39 46N 93 37W
Thompson Falls, U.S.A. 114 C6 47 36N 115 21W
Thompson Pk., U.S.A. 114 F2 41 0N 123 0W
Thompson Springs, U.S.A. 115 G9 38 58N 109 43W
Thompsontown, U.S.A. 110 F7 40 33N 77 14W
Thomson, U.S.A. 109 J4 33 28N 82 30W
Thomson →, Australia 94 C3 25 11 S 142 53 E
Thomson's Falls = Nyahururu, Kenya 86 B4 0 2N 36 27 E
Thônes, France 21 C10 45 54N 6 18 E
Thonon-les-Bains, France 19 F13 46 22N 6 29 E
Thorez, Ukraine 47 H10 48 4N 38 34 E
Þórisvatn, Iceland 8 D4 64 20N 18 55W
Thornaby on Tees, U.K. 12 C6 54 33N 1 18W
Thornbury, Canada 110 B4 44 34N 80 26W
Thorne, U.K. 12 D7 53 37N 0 57W
Thornhill, Canada 104 C3 54 31N 128 32W
Thorold, Canada 110 C5 43 7N 79 12W
Þórshöfn, Iceland 8 C6 66 12N 15 20W
Thouarcé, France 18 E6 47 17N 0 30W
Thouars, France 18 F6 47 0N 0 15W
Thouet →, France 18 E6 47 17N 0 6W
Thouin, C., Australia 92 D2 20 20 S 118 10 E
Thousand Oaks, U.S.A. 117 L8 34 10N 118 50W
Thrace, Turkey 41 F10 41 0N 27 0 E
Thrakikón Pélagos, Greece 41 F8 40 30N 25 0 E
Three Forks, U.S.A. 114 D8 45 54N 111 33W
Three Gorges Dam, China 59 B8 30 45N 111 15 E
Three Hills, Canada 104 C6 51 43N 113 15W
Three Hummock I., Australia 94 G3 40 25 S 144 55 E
Three Points, C., Ghana 82 E4 4 42N 2 6W
Three Rivers, Calif., U.S.A. 116 J8 36 26N 118 54W
Three Rivers, Tex., U.S.A. 113 L5 28 28N 98 11W
Three Sisters, U.S.A. 114 D3 44 4N 121 51W
Three Springs, Australia 93 E2 29 32 S 115 45 E
Throssell, L., Australia 93 E3 27 33 S 124 10 E
Throssell Ra., Australia 92 D3 22 3 S 121 43 E
Thuan Hoa, Vietnam 65 H5 8 58N 105 30 E
Thubun Lakes, Canada 105 A6 61 30N 112 0W
Thueyts, France 21 D8 44 41N 4 9 E
Thuin, Belgium 17 D4 50 20N 4 17 E
Thuir, France 20 F6 42 38N 2 45 E
Thule = Qaanaaq, Greenland 4 B4 77 40N 69 0W
Thun, Switz. 25 J3 46 45N 7 38 E
Thunder B., U.S.A. 110 B1 45 0N 83 20W
Thunder Bay, Canada 102 C2 48 20N 89 15W
Thunersee, Switz. 25 J3 46 43N 7 39 E
Thung Song, Thailand 65 H2 8 10N 99 40 E
Thunkar, Bhutan 67 F17 27 55N 91 0 E
Thuong Tra, Vietnam 64 D6 16 2N 107 42 E
Thur →, Switz. 25 H5 47 32N 9 10 E
Thurgau □, Switz. 25 H5 47 34N 9 10 E
Thüringen □, Germany 24 D6 51 0N 11 0 E
Thüringer Wald, Germany 24 E6 50 35N 11 0 E
Thurles, Ireland 15 D4 52 41N 7 49W
Thurn P., Austria 26 D5 47 20N 12 25 E
Thurrock □, U.K. 13 F8 51 31N 0 23 E
Thursday I., Australia 94 A3 10 30 S 142 3 E
Thurso, Canada 102 C4 45 36N 75 15W
Thurso, U.K. 14 C5 58 36N 3 32W
Thurso →, U.K. 14 C5 58 36N 3 32W
Thurston I., Antarctica 5 D16 72 0 S 100 0W
Thury-Harcourt, France 18 D6 48 59N 0 30W
Thutade L., Canada 104 B3 57 0N 126 55W
Thy, Denmark 11 H2 56 52N 8 25 E
Thyborøn, Denmark 11 H2 56 42N 8 12 E
Thyolo, Malawi 87 F4 16 7 S 35 5 E
Thysville = Mbanza Ngungu, Dem. Rep. of the Congo 84 F2 5 12 S 14 53 E
Ti-n-Amzi →, Niger 83 B5 18 20N 4 32 E
Ti-n-Barraouene, O. →, Africa 83 B5 18 40N 4 5 E
Ti-n-Zaouatène, Algeria 83 B5 19 55N 2 55 E
Ti Tree, Australia 94 C1 22 5 S 133 22 E
Tiadiaye, Senegal 82 C1 14 25N 16 40W
Tian Shan, Asia 60 B3 42 0N 76 0 E
Tianchang, China 59 A12 32 40N 119 0 E
Tiandeng, China 58 F6 23 6N 107 7 E
Tiandong, China 58 F6 23 36N 107 8 E
Tian'e, China 58 E6 25 1N 107 9 E
Tianhe, China 58 E7 24 48N 108 40 E
Tianjin, China 57 E9 39 8N 117 10 E
Tiankoura, Burkina Faso 82 C4 10 47N 3 17W
Tianlin, China 58 E6 24 21N 106 12 E
Tianmen, China 59 B9 30 39N 113 9 E
Tianquan, China 58 B4 30 7N 102 43 E
Tianshui, China 56 G3 34 32N 105 40 E
Tiantai, China 59 C13 29 10N 121 2 E
Tianyang, China 58 F6 23 42N 106 53 E
Tianzhen, China 56 D8 40 24N 114 5 E
Tianzhu, China 58 D7 26 54N 109 11 E
Tianzhuangtai, China 57 D12 40 43N 122 5 E
Tiaret, Algeria 78 A6 35 20N 1 21 E
Tiassalé, Ivory C. 82 D4 5 58N 4 57W
Tibagi, Brazil 127 A5 24 30 S 50 24W
Tibagi →, Brazil 127 A5 22 47 S 51 1W
Tibati, Cameroon 83 D7 6 22N 12 30 E
Tibe, Ethiopia 81 F4 9 2N 37 12 E
Tiber = Tevere →, Italy 29 G9 41 44N 12 14 E
Tiberias = Teverya, Israel 75 C4 32 47N 35 32 E
Tiberias, L. = Yam Kinneret, Israel 75 C4 32 45N 35 35 E
Tibesti, Chad 79 D9 21 0N 17 30 E
Tibet = Xizang Zizhiqu □, China 60 C3 32 0N 88 0 E
Tibet, Plateau of, Asia 52 F12 32 0N 86 0 E
Tibiao, Phil. 61 F5 11 17N 122 2 E
Tibiri, Niger 83 C6 13 34N 7 4 E
Țibleș, Vf., Romania 43 C9 47 32N 24 15 E
Țibleșului, Muntii, Romania 43 C9 47 38N 24 5 E
Tibnī, Syria 70 C3 35 36N 39 50 E
Tibooburra, Australia 95 D3 29 26 S 142 1 E
Tibro, Sweden 11 F8 58 28N 14 10 E
Tiburón, I., Mexico 118 B2 29 0N 112 30W
Ticao I., Phil. 61 E5 12 31N 123 42 E
Tîchît, Mauritania 82 B3 18 21N 9 29W
Ticho, Ethiopia 81 F4 7 50N 39 32 E
Ticino □, Switz. 25 J4 46 20N 8 45 E
Ticino →, Italy 25 K5 45 9N 9 14 E
Ticleni, Romania 43 F8 44 53N 23 24 E
Ticonderoga, U.S.A. 111 C11 43 51N 73 26W
Ticul, Mexico 119 C7 20 20N 89 31W
Tidaholm, Sweden 11 F7 58 12N 13 58 E
Tidan, Sweden 11 F8 58 34N 14 1 E
Tiddim, Burma 67 H18 23 28N 93 45 E
Tidioute, U.S.A. 110 E5 41 41N 79 24W
Tidjikja, Mauritania 82 B2 18 29N 11 35W
Tidore, Indonesia 63 D7 0 40N 127 25 E
Tiébissou, Ivory C. 82 D3 7 9N 5 10W
Tiel, Neths. 17 C5 51 53N 5 26 E
Tiel, Senegal 82 C1 14 55N 15 5W
Tieling, China 57 C12 42 20N 123 50 E
Tielt, Belgium 17 C3 51 0N 3 20 E
Tien Shan = Tian Shan, Asia 60 B3 42 0N 76 0 E
Tien-tsin = Tianjin, China 57 E9 39 8N 117 10 E
Tien Yen, Vietnam 64 B6 21 20N 107 24 E
T'ienching = Tianjin, China 57 E9 39 8N 117 10 E
Tienen, Belgium 17 D4 50 48N 4 57 E
Tiénigbé, Ivory C. 82 D3 8 11N 5 43W
Tientsin = Tianjin, China 57 E9 39 8N 117 10 E
Tieri, Australia 94 C4 23 2 S 148 21 E
Tierp, Sweden 10 D11 60 20N 17 30 E
Tierra Amarilla, Chile 126 B1 27 28 S 70 18W
Tierra Amarilla, U.S.A. 115 H10 36 42N 106 33W
Tierra Colorada, Mexico 119 D5 17 10N 99 35W
Tierra de Barros, Spain 35 G4 38 40N 6 30W
Tierra de Campos, Spain 34 C6 42 10N 4 50W
Tierra del Fuego, I. Gr. de, Argentina 122 J4 54 0 S 69 0W
Tiétar →, Spain 34 F4 39 50N 6 1W
Tieté →, Brazil 127 A5 20 40 S 51 35W
Tiffin, U.S.A. 108 E4 41 7N 83 11W
Tiflis = Tbilisi, Georgia 49 K7 41 43N 44 50 E
Tifton, U.S.A. 109 K4 31 27N 83 31W
Tifu, Indonesia 63 E7 3 39 S 126 24 E
Tighina, Moldova 43 D14 46 50N 29 30 E
Tigil, Russia 51 D16 57 49N 158 40 E
Tignish, Canada 103 C7 46 58N 64 2W
Tigray □, Ethiopia 81 E4 13 35N 39 15 E
Tigre →, Peru 124 D4 4 30 S 74 10W
Tigre →, Venezuela 124 B6 9 20N 62 30W
Tigris = Dijlah, Nahr →, Asia 70 D5 31 0N 47 25 E
Tigveni, Romania 43 E9 45 10N 24 31 E
Tigyaing, Burma 67 H20 23 45N 96 10 E
Tîh, Gebel el, Egypt 80 B3 29 32N 33 26 E
Tijara, India 68 F7 27 56N 76 31 E
Tijuana, Mexico 117 N9 32 30N 117 10W
Tikal, Guatemala 120 C2 17 13N 89 24W
Tikamgarh, India 69 G8 24 44N 78 50 E
Tikaré, Burkina Faso 83 C4 13 15N 1 43W
Tikhoretsk, Russia 49 H5 45 56N 40 5 E
Tikhvin, Russia 46 C7 59 35N 33 30 E
Tiko, Cameroon 83 E6 4 4N 9 20 E
Tikrīt, Iraq 70 C4 34 35N 43 37 E
Tiksi, Russia 51 B13 71 40N 128 45 E
Tilamuta, Indonesia 63 D6 0 32N 122 23 E
Tilburg, Neths. 17 C5 51 31N 5 6 E
Tilbury, Canada 102 D3 42 17N 82 23W
Tilbury, U.K. 13 F8 51 27N 0 22 E
Tilcara, Argentina 126 A2 23 36 S 65 23W
Tilden, U.S.A. 112 D6 42 3N 97 50W
Tilemses, Niger 83 B5 15 37N 4 44 E
Tilemsi, Vallée du, Mali 83 B5 17 42N 0 15 E
Tilhar, India 69 F8 28 0N 79 45 E
Tilichiki, Russia 51 C17 60 27N 166 5 E
Tílissos, Greece 36 D7 35 20N 25 1 E
Till →, U.K. 12 B5 55 41N 2 13W
Tillabéri, Niger 83 C5 14 28N 1 28 E
Tillamook, U.S.A. 114 D2 45 27N 123 51W
Tillberga, Sweden 10 E10 59 40N 16 39 E
Tillia, Niger 83 B5 16 8N 4 47 E
Tillsonburg, Canada 102 D3 42 53N 80 44W
Tillyeria □, Cyprus 36 D11 35 6N 32 40 E
Tilogne, Senegal 82 B2 16 0N 13 40W
Tílos, Greece 39 E9 36 27N 27 27 E
Tilpa, Australia 95 E3 30 57 S 144 24 E
Tilsit = Sovetsk, Russia 9 J19 55 6N 21 50 E
Tilt →, U.K. 14 E5 56 46N 3 51W
Tilton, U.S.A. 111 C13 43 27N 71 36W
Tiltonsville, U.S.A. 110 F4 40 10N 80 41W
Tim, Denmark 11 H2 56 12N 8 19 E
Timagami, L., Canada 102 C3 47 0N 80 10W
Timaru, N.Z. 91 L3 44 23 S 171 14 E
Timashevo, Russia 48 D10 53 22N 51 9 E
Timashevsk, Russia 49 H4 45 35N 39 0 E
Timau, Kenya 86 B4 0 4N 37 15 E
Timbákion, Greece 36 D6 35 4N 24 45 E
Timbedgha, Mauritania 82 B3 16 17N 8 16W
Timber Creek, Australia 92 C5 15 40 S 130 29 E
Timber Lake, U.S.A. 112 C4 45 26N 101 5W
Timber Mt., U.S.A. 116 H10 37 6N 116 28W
Timbo, Guinea 82 C2 10 35N 11 50W
Timbo, Liberia 82 D3 5 35N 9 45W
Timbuktu = Tombouctou, Mali 82 B4 16 50N 3 0W
Timeiaouine, Algeria 83 A5 20 27N 1 50 E
Timétrine, Mts., Mali 83 B4 19 25N 1 0W
Timfi Óros, Greece 38 B2 39 59N 20 45 E
Timfristós, Óros, Greece 38 C3 38 57N 21 50 E
Timi, Cyprus 36 E11 34 44N 32 31 E
Tîmia, Niger 83 B6 18 4N 8 40 E
Timimoun, Algeria 78 C6 29 14N 0 16 E
Timiris, Râs, Mauritania 82 B1 19 21N 16 30W
Timiș = Tamis →, Serbia, Yug. 42 F5 44 51N 20 39 E
Timiș □, Romania 42 E6 45 40N 21 30 E
Timișoara, Romania 42 E6 45 43N 21 15 E
Timmersdala, Sweden 11 F7 58 32N 13 46 E
Timmins, Canada 102 C3 48 28N 81 25W
Timok →, Serbia, Yug. 40 B6 44 10N 22 40 E
Timor, Indonesia 63 F7 9 0 S 125 0 E
Timor Sea, Ind. Oc. 92 B4 12 0 S 127 0 E
Timor Timur □, Indonesia 63 F7 9 0 S 125 0 E
Timrå, Sweden 10 B11 62 29N 17 18 E
Tin Can Bay, Australia 95 D5 25 56 S 153 0 E
Tin Ethisane, Mali 83 B4 19 3N 0 52W
Tin Gornai, Mali 83 B4 16 38N 0 38W
Tin Mt., U.S.A. 116 J9 36 50N 117 10W
Tina →, S. Africa 89 E4 31 18 S 29 13 E
Tîna, Khalîg el, Egypt 80 A3 31 20N 32 42 E
Tinaca Pt., Phil. 61 J6 5 30N 125 25 E
Tinajo, Canary Is. 37 E6 29 4N 13 42W
Tinca, Romania 42 D6 46 46N 21 58 E
Tindal, Australia 92 B5 14 31 S 132 22 E
Tindouf, Algeria 78 C4 27 42N 8 10W
Tinée →, France 21 E11 43 55N 7 11 E
Tineo, Spain 34 B4 43 21N 6 27W
Ting Jiang →, China 59 E11 24 45N 116 35 E
Tinggi, Pulau, Malaysia 65 L5 2 18N 104 7 E
Tinglev, Denmark 11 K3 54 57N 9 13 E
Tingo Maria, Peru 124 E3 9 10 S 75 54W
Tingrela, Ivory C. 82 C3 10 27N 6 25W
Tingsryd, Sweden 11 H9 56 31N 15 0 E
Tingstäde, Sweden 11 G12 57 44N 18 37 E
Tinh Bien, Vietnam 65 G5 10 36N 104 57 E
Tinnevelly = Tirunelveli, India 66 Q10 8 45N 77 45 E
Tinogasta, Argentina 126 B2 28 5 S 67 32W
Tínos, Greece 39 D7 37 33N 25 8 E
Tiñoso, C., Spain 33 H3 37 32N 1 6W
Tinpahar, India 69 G12 24 59N 87 44 E
Tintina, Argentina 126 B3 27 2 S 62 45W
Tintinara, Australia 95 F3 35 48 S 140 2 E
Tintioulé, Guinea 82 C3 10 13N 9 12W
Tinto →, Spain 35 H4 37 12N 6 55W
Tioga, N. Dak., U.S.A. 112 A3 48 23N 102 56W
Tioga, Pa., U.S.A. 110 E7 41 55N 77 8W
Tioman, Pulau, Malaysia 65 L5 2 50N 104 10 E
Tione di Trento, Italy 28 B7 46 2N 10 43 E
Tionesta, U.S.A. 110 E5 41 30N 79 28W
Tior, Sudan 81 F3 6 26N 31 11 E
Tipongpani, India 67 F19 27 20N 95 55 E
Tipperary, Ireland 15 D3 52 28N 8 10W
Tipperary □, Ireland 15 D4 52 37N 7 55W
Tipton, Calif., U.S.A. 116 J7 36 4N 119 19W
Tipton, Iowa, U.S.A. 112 E9 41 46N 91 8W
Tipton Mt., U.S.A. 117 K12 35 32N 114 12W
Tiptonville, U.S.A. 113 G10 36 23N 89 29W
Tīrān, Iran 71 C6 32 45N 51 8 E
Tīrān, Si. Arabia 80 B3 27 57N 34 32 E
Tirana = Tiranë, Albania 40 E3 41 18N 19 49 E
Tiranë, Albania 40 E3 41 18N 19 49 E
Tirano, Italy 28 B7 46 13N 10 10 E
Tiraspol, Moldova 43 D14 46 55N 29 35 E
Tirdout, Mali 83 B4 16 7N 1 5W
Tire, Turkey 39 C9 38 5N 27 45 E
Tirebolu, Turkey 73 B8 40 58N 38 45 E
Tiree, U.K. 14 E2 56 31N 6 55W
Tiree, Passage of, U.K. 14 E2 56 30N 6 30W
Tîrgoviște = Târgoviște, Romania 43 F10 44 55N 25 27 E
Tîrgu-Jiu = Târgu-Jiu, Romania 43 E8 45 5N 23 19 E
Tîrgu Mureș = Târgu Mureș, Romania 43 D9 46 31N 24 38 E
Tirich Mir, Pakistan 66 A7 36 15N 71 55 E
Tiriolo, Italy 31 D9 38 57N 16 30 E
Tiriro, Guinea 82 C3 10 27N 8 40W
Tírnavos, Greece 38 B4 39 45N 22 18 E
Tirodi, India 66 J11 21 40N 79 44 E
Tirol □, Austria 26 D3 47 3N 10 43 E
Tirschenreuth, Germany 25 F8 49 53N 12 19 E
Tirso →, Italy 30 C1 39 53N 8 32 E
Tirstrup, Denmark 11 H4 56 18N 10 42 E
Tiruchchirappalli, India 66 P11 10 45N 78 45 E
Tirunelveli, India 66 Q10 8 45N 77 45 E
Tirupati, India 66 N11 13 39N 79 25 E
Tiruppur, India 66 P10 11 5N 77 22 E
Tiruvannamalai, India 66 N11 12 15N 79 5 E
Tisa, India 68 C7 32 50N 76 9 E
Tisa →, Serbia, Yug. 42 E5 45 15N 20 17 E
Tisdale, Canada 105 C8 52 50N 104 0W
Tishomingo, U.S.A. 113 H6 34 14N 96 41W
Tisjön, Sweden 10 D7 60 56N 13 0 E
Tisnaren, Sweden 11 F9 58 58N 15 56 E
Tišnov, Czech Rep. 27 B9 49 21N 16 25 E
Tisovec, Slovak Rep. 27 C12 48 41N 19 56 E
Tisza = Tisa →, Serbia, Yug. 42 E5 45 15N 20 17 E
Tiszaföldvár, Hungary 42 D5 46 58N 20 14 E
Tiszafüred, Hungary 42 C5 47 38N 20 50 E
Tiszalök, Hungary 42 B6 48 1N 21 20 E
Tiszavasvári, Hungary 42 C6 47 58N 21 18 E
Tit-Ary, Russia 51 B13 71 55N 127 2 E
Titaguas, Spain 32 F3 39 53N 1 6W
Titao, Burkina Faso 83 C4 13 45N 2 5W
Titel, Serbia, Yug. 42 E5 45 10N 20 18 E
Tithwal, Pakistan 69 B5 34 21N 73 50 E
Titicaca, L., S. Amer. 122 E4 15 30 S 69 30W
Titisee, Germany 25 H4 47 54N 8 10 E
Titiwa, Nigeria 83 C7 12 14N 12 53 E
Tito, Italy 31 B8 40 35N 15 40 E
Titograd = Podgorica, Montenegro, Yug. 40 D3 42 30N 19 19 E
Titova Korenica, Croatia 29 D12 44 45N 15 41 E
Titu, Romania 43 F10 44 39N 25 32 E
Titule, Dem. Rep. of the Congo 86 B2 3 15N 25 31 E
Titusville, Fla., U.S.A. 109 L5 28 37N 80 49W
Titusville, Pa., U.S.A. 110 E5 41 38N 79 41W
Tivaouane, Senegal 82 C1 14 56N 16 45W
Tivat, Montenegro, Yug. 40 D2 42 28N 18 43 E
Tiverton, U.K. 13 G4 50 54N 3 29W
Tívoli, Italy 29 G9 41 58N 12 45 E
Tiyo, Eritrea 81 E5 14 41N 40 15 E
Tizi-Ouzou, Algeria 78 A6 36 42N 4 3 E
Tizimín, Mexico 119 C7 21 0N 88 1W
Tjæreborg, Denmark 11 J2 55 28N 8 36 E
Tjällmo, Sweden 11 F9 58 43N 15 21 E
Tjeggelvas, Sweden 8 C17 66 37N 17 45 E
Tjirebon = Cirebon, Indonesia 63 G13 6 45 S 108 32 E
Tjörn, Sweden 11 F5 58 0N 11 35 E
Tkibuli = Tqibuli, Georgia 49 J6 42 26N 43 0 E
Tkvarcheli = Tqvarcheli, Georgia 49 J5 42 47N 41 42 E
Tlacotalpan, Mexico 119 D5 18 37N 95 40W
Tlahualilo, Mexico 118 B4 26 20N 103 30W
Tlaquepaque, Mexico 118 C4 20 39N 103 19W
Tlaxcala, Mexico 119 D5 19 20N 98 14W
Tlaxcala □, Mexico 119 D5 19 30N 98 20W
Tlaxiaco, Mexico 119 D5 17 18N 97 40W
Tlemcen, Algeria 78 B5 34 52N 1 21W
Tłuszcz, Poland 45 F8 52 25N 21 25 E
Tlyarata, Russia 49 J8 42 9N 46 26 E
To Bong, Vietnam 64 F7 12 45N 109 16 E
Toad →, Canada 104 B4 59 25N 124 57W
Toad River, Canada 104 B3 58 51N 125 14W
Toamasina, Madag. 89 B8 18 10 S 49 25 E
Toamasina □, Madag. 89 B8 18 0 S 49 0 E
Toay, Argentina 126 D3 36 43 S 64 38W
Toba, China 58 B1 31 19N 97 42 E
Toba, Japan 55 G8 34 30N 136 51 E
Toba, Danau, Indonesia 62 D1 2 30N 97 30 E
Toba Kakar, Pakistan 68 D3 31 30N 69 0 E
Toba Tek Singh, Pakistan 68 D5 30 55N 72 25 E
Tobago, W. Indies 121 D7 11 10N 60 30W
Tobarra, Spain 33 G3 38 37N 1 44W
Tobelo, Indonesia 63 D7 1 45N 127 56 E
Tobermory, Canada 102 C3 45 12N 81 40W
Tobermory, U.K. 14 E2 56 38N 6 5W
Tobi, Pac. Oc. 63 D8 2 40N 131 10 E
Tobin, U.S.A. 116 F5 39 55N 121 19W
Tobin, L., Australia 92 D4 21 45 S 125 49 E
Tobin L., Canada 105 C8 53 35N 103 30W
Toblach = Dobbiaco, Italy 29 B9 46 44N 12 14 E
Toboali, Indonesia 62 E3 3 0 S 106 25 E
Tobol →, Russia 50 D7 58 10N 68 12 E
Toboli, Indonesia 63 E6 0 38 S 120 5 E
Tobolsk, Russia 50 D7 58 15N 68 10 E
Tobor, Senegal 82 C1 12 40N 16 15W
Tobruk = Tubruq, Libya 79 B10 32 7N 23 55 E
Tobyhanna, U.S.A. 111 E9 41 11N 75 25W
Tobyl = Tobol →, Russia 50 D7 58 10N 68 12 E
Tocantinópolis, Brazil 125 E9 6 20 S 47 25W
Tocantins □, Brazil 125 F9 10 0 S 48 0W
Tocantins →, Brazil 122 D6 1 45 S 49 10W
Toccoa, U.S.A. 109 H4 34 35N 83 19W
Toce →, Italy 28 C5 45 56N 8 29 E
Tochi →, Pakistan 68 C4 32 49N 70 41 E
Tochigi, Japan 55 F9 36 25N 139 45 E
Tochigi □, Japan 55 F9 36 45N 139 45 E
Tocina, Spain 35 H5 37 37N 5 44W
Töcksfors, Sweden 10 E5 59 31N 11 52 E
Toconao, Chile 126 A2 23 11 S 68 1W
Tocopilla, Chile 126 A1 22 5 S 70 10W
Tocumwal, Australia 95 F4 35 51 S 145 31 E
Tocuyo →, Venezuela 124 A5 11 3N 68 23W
Todd →, Australia 94 C2 24 52 S 135 48 E
Todeli, Indonesia 63 E6 1 38 S 124 34 E
Todenyang, Kenya 86 B4 4 35N 35 56 E
Todgarh, India 68 G5 25 42N 73 58 E
Todi, Italy 29 F9 42 47N 12 24 E
Todos os Santos, B. de, Brazil 125 F11 12 48 S 38 38W
Todos Santos, Mexico 118 C2 23 27N 110 13W
Todtnau, Germany 25 H3 47 49N 7 56 E
Toe Hd., U.K. 14 D1 57 50N 7 8W
Toecé, Burkina Faso 83 C4 11 50N 1 16W
Tofield, Canada 104 C6 53 25N 112 40W
Tofino, Canada 104 D3 49 11N 125 55W
Tofua, Tonga 91 D11 19 45 S 175 5W
Tōgane, Japan 55 G10 35 33N 140 22 E
Togba, Mauritania 82 B2 17 26N 10 12W
Togian, Kepulauan, Indonesia 63 E6 0 20 S 121 50 E
Togliatti, Russia 48 D9 53 32N 49 24 E
Togo ■, W. Afr. 83 D5 8 30N 1 35 E
Togtoh, China 56 D6 40 15N 111 10 E
Tohma →, Turkey 72 C7 38 29N 38 23 E
Tōhoku □, Japan 54 E10 39 50N 141 45 E
Töhöm, Mongolia 56 B5 44 27N 108 2 E
Toinya, Sudan 81 F2 6 17N 29 46 E
Toiyabe Range, U.S.A. 114 G5 39 30N 117 0W
Tojikiston = Tajikistan ■, Asia 50 F8 38 30N 70 0 E
Tojo, Indonesia 63 E6 1 20 S 121 15 E
Tōjō, Japan 55 G6 34 53N 133 16 E
Tok, U.S.A. 100 B5 63 20N 142 59W
Tok-do, Japan 55 F5 37 15N 131 52 E
Tokachi-Dake, Japan 54 C11 43 17N 142 5 E
Tokachi-Gawa →, Japan 54 C11 42 44N 143 42 E
Tokaj, Hungary 42 B6 48 8N 21 27 E
Tokala, Indonesia 63 E6 1 30 S 121 40 E
Tōkamachi, Japan 55 F9 37 8N 138 43 E
Tokanui, N.Z. 91 M2 46 34 S 168 56 E
Tokar, Sudan 80 D4 18 27N 37 56 E
Tokara-Rettō, Japan 55 K4 29 37N 129 43 E
Tokarahi, N.Z. 91 L3 44 56 S 170 39 E
Tokashiki-Shima, Japan 55 L3 26 11N 127 21 E
Tokat, Turkey 72 B7 40 22N 36 35 E
Tŏkch'ŏn, N. Korea 57 E14 39 45N 126 18 E
Tokeland, U.S.A. 116 D3 46 42N 123 59W
Tokelau Is., Pac. Oc. 96 H10 9 0 S 171 45W
Tokmak, Kyrgyzstan 50 E8 42 49N 75 15 E
Tokmak, Ukraine 47 J8 47 16N 35 42 E
Toko Ra., Australia 94 C2 23 5 S 138 20 E
Tokoro-Gawa →, Japan 54 B12 44 7N 144 5 E
Tokuno-Shima, Japan 55 L4 27 56N 128 55 E
Tokushima, Japan 55 G7 34 4N 134 34 E
Tokushima □, Japan 55 H7 33 55N 134 0 E
Tokuyama, Japan 55 G5 34 3N 131 50 E
Tōkyō, Japan 55 G9 35 45N 139 45 E
Tolaga Bay, N.Z. 91 H7 38 21 S 178 20 E
Tolbukhin = Dobrich, Bulgaria 41 C11 43 37N 27 49 E
Toledo, Brazil 127 A5 24 44 S 53 45W
Toledo, Spain 34 F6 39 50N 4 2W
Toledo, Ohio, U.S.A. 108 E4 41 39N 83 33W
Toledo, Oreg., U.S.A. 114 D2 44 37N 123 56W
Toledo, Wash., U.S.A. 114 C2 46 26N 122 51W
Toledo, Montes de, Spain 35 F6 39 33N 4 20W
Toledo Bend Reservoir, U.S.A. 113 K8 31 11N 93 34W
Tolentino, Italy 29 E10 43 12N 13 17 E
Tolfa, Italy 29 F8 42 9N 11 56 E
Tolga, Australia 94 B4 17 15 S 145 29 E
Toliara, Madag. 89 C7 23 21 S 43 40 E
Toliara □, Madag. 89 C8 21 0 S 45 0 E
Tolima, Colombia 124 C3 4 40N 75 19W
Tolitoli, Indonesia 63 D6 1 5N 120 50 E
Tolkmicko, Poland 44 D6 54 19N 19 31 E
Tollarp, Sweden 11 J7 55 55N 13 58 E
Tollensesee, Germany 24 B9 53 30N 13 13 E
Tollhouse, U.S.A. 116 H7 37 1N 119 24W
Tolmachevo, Russia 46 C5 58 56N 29 51 E
Tolmezzo, Italy 29 B10 46 24N 13 1 E
Tolmin, Slovenia 29 B10 46 11N 13 45 E
Tolna, Hungary 42 D3 46 25N 18 48 E
Tolna □, Hungary 42 D3 46 30N 18 30 E
Tolo, Teluk, Indonesia 63 E6 2 20 S 122 10 E
Tolochin = Talachyn, Belarus 46 E5 54 25N 29 42 E
Tolosa, Spain 32 B2 43 8N 2 5W
Tolox, Spain 35 J6 36 41N 4 54W
Toluca, Mexico 119 D5 19 20N 99 40W
Tom Burke, S. Africa 89 C4 23 5 S 28 0 E
Tom Price, Australia 92 D2 22 40 S 117 48 E
Toma, Burkina Faso 82 C4 12 45N 2 53W
Tomah, U.S.A. 112 D9 43 59N 90 30W
Tomahawk, U.S.A. 112 C10 45 28N 89 44W
Tomai, Moldova 43 D13 46 34N 28 19 E
Tomakomai, Japan 54 C10 42 38N 141 36 E
Tomales, U.S.A. 116 G4 38 15N 122 53W
Tomales B., U.S.A. 116 G3 38 15N 123 58W
Tomar, Portugal 35 F2 39 36N 8 25W
Tómaros, Óros, Greece 38 B2 39 29N 20 48 E
Tomarza, Turkey 72 C6 38 27N 35 48 E
Tomaszów Lubelski, Poland 45 H10 50 27N 23 25 E
Tomaszów Mazowiecki, Poland 45 G7 51 30N 20 2 E
Tomatlán, Mexico 118 D3 19 56N 105 15W
Tombadonkéa, Guinea 82 C2 11 0N 14 25W
Tombador, Serra do, Brazil 124 F7 12 0 S 58 0W
Tombe, Sudan 81 F3 5 53N 31 40 E
Tombigbee →, U.S.A. 109 K2 31 8N 87 57W
Tombouctou, Mali 82 B4 16 50N 3 0W
Tombstone, U.S.A. 115 L8 31 43N 110 4W
Tombua, Angola 88 B1 15 55 S 11 55 E
Tomé, Chile 126 D1 36 36 S 72 57W
Tomelilla, Sweden 11 J7 55 33N 13 58 E
Tomelloso, Spain 35 F7 39 10N 3 2W
Tomini, Indonesia 63 D6 0 30N 120 30 E
Tomini, Teluk, Indonesia 63 E6 0 10 S 122 0 E
Tominian, Mali 82 C4 13 17N 4 35W
Tomiño, Spain 34 D2 41 59N 8 46W
Tomintoul, U.K. 14 D5 57 15N 3 23W
Tomislavgrad, Bos.-H. 42 G2 43 42N 17 13 E
Tomkinson Ranges, Australia 93 E4 26 11 S 129 5 E
Tommot, Russia 51 D13 59 4N 126 20 E
Tomnop Ta Suos, Cambodia 65 G5 11 20N 104 15 E
Tomo →, Colombia 124 B5 5 20N 67 48W
Toms Place, U.S.A. 116 H8 37 34N 118 41W
Toms River, U.S.A. 111 G10 39 58N 74 12W
Tomsk, Russia 50 D9 56 30N 85 5 E
Tomtabacken, Sweden 11 G8 57 30N 14 30 E
Tona, Spain 32 D7 41 51N 2 14 E
Tonalá, Mexico 119 D6 16 8N 93 41W
Tonale, Passo del, Italy 28 B7 46 16N 10 35 E
Tonantins, Brazil 124 D5 2 45 S 67 45W
Tonasket, U.S.A. 114 B4 48 42N 119 26W
Tonawanda, U.S.A. 110 D6 43 1N 78 53W
Tonbridge, U.K. 13 F8 51 11N 0 17 E
Tondano, Indonesia 63 D6 1 35N 124 54 E
Tondela, Portugal 34 E2 40 31N 8 5W
Tønder, Denmark 11 K2 54 58N 8 50 E
Tondi Kiwindi, Niger 83 C5 14 28N 2 2 E
Tondibi, Mali 83 B4 16 39N 0 14W
Tondoro, Namibia 88 B2 17 45 S 18 50 E
Tone →, Australia 93 F2 34 25 S 116 25 E
Tone-Gawa →, Japan 55 F9 35 44N 140 51 E
Tonekābon, Iran 71 B6 36 45N 51 12 E
Tong Xian, China 56 E9 39 55N 116 35 E
Tônga, Sudan 81 F3 9 28N 31 3 E
Tonga ■, Pac. Oc. 91 D11 19 50 S 174 30W
Tonga Trench, Pac. Oc. 96 J10 18 0 S 173 0W
Tongaat, S. Africa 89 D5 29 33 S 31 9 E
Tong'an, China 59 E12 24 37N 118 8 E
Tongareva, Cook Is. 97 H12 9 0 S 158 0W
Tongatapu, Tonga 91 E12 21 10 S 174 0W
Tongbai, China 59 A9 32 20N 113 23 E
Tongcheng, Anhui, China 59 B11 31 4N 116 56 E
Tongcheng, Hubei, China 59 C9 29 15N 113 50 E
Tongchŏn-ni, N. Korea 57 E14 39 50N 127 25 E
Tongchuan, China 56 G5 35 6N 109 3 E
Tongdao, China 58 D7 26 10N 109 42 E
Tongeren, Belgium 17 D5 50 47N 5 28 E
Tonggu, China 59 C10 28 31N 114 20 E

Tongguan, *China* **56 G6** 34 40N 110 25 E
Tonghai, *China* **58 E4** 24 10N 102 53 E
Tonghua, *China* **57 D13** 41 42N 125 58 E
Tongjiang, *China* **58 B6** 31 58N 107 11 E
Tongjosŏn Man, *N. Korea* **57 E15** 39 30N 128 0 E
Tongking, G. of = Tonkin, G. of, *Asia* **64 B7** 20 0N 108 0 E
Tongliang, *China* **58 C6** 29 50N 106 3 E
Tongliao, *China* **57 C12** 43 38N 122 18 E
Tongling, *China* **59 B11** 30 55N 117 48 E
Tonglu, *China* **59 C12** 29 45N 119 37 E
Tongnae, *S. Korea* **57 G15** 35 12N 129 5 E
Tongnan = Anyue, *China* **58 B5** 30 9N 105 50 E
Tongobory, *Madag.* **89 C7** 23 32 S 44 20 E
Tongoy, *Chile* **126 C1** 30 16 S 71 31W
Tongren, *China* **58 D7** 27 43N 109 11 E
Tongres = Tongeren, *Belgium* **17 D5** 50 47N 5 28 E
Tongsa Dzong, *Bhutan* **67 F17** 27 31N 90 31 E
Tongue, *U.K.* **14 C4** 58 29N 4 25W
Tongue →, *U.S.A.* **112 B2** 46 25N 105 52W
Tongwei, *China* **56 G3** 35 0N 105 5 E
Tongxiang, *China* **59 B13** 30 39N 120 34 E
Tongxin, *China* **56 F3** 36 59N 105 58 E
Tongyang, *N. Korea* **57 E14** 39 9N 126 53 E
Tongyu, *China* **57 B12** 44 45N 123 4 E
Tongzi, *China* **58 C6** 28 9N 106 49 E
Tonj, *Sudan* **81 F2** 7 20N 28 44 E
Tonj →, *Sudan* **81 F2** 7 31N 28 55 E
Tonk, *India* **68 F6** 26 6N 75 54 E
Tonkawa, *U.S.A.* **113 G6** 36 41N 97 18W
Tonkin = Bac Phan, *Vietnam* **64 B5** 22 0N 105 0 E
Tonkin, G. of, *Asia* **64 B7** 20 0N 108 0 E
Tonle Sap, *Cambodia* **64 F4** 13 0N 104 0 E
Tonnay-Charente, *France* **20 C3** 45 56N 0 55W
Tonneins, *France* **20 D4** 44 23N 0 19 E
Tonnerre, *France* **19 E10** 47 51N 3 59 E
Tönning, *Germany* **24 A4** 54 19N 8 56 E
Tono, *Japan* **54 E10** 39 19N 141 32 E
Tonopah, *U.S.A.* **115 G5** 38 4N 117 14W
Tonosí, *Panama* **120 E3** 7 20N 80 20W
Tons →, *Haryana, India* **68 D7** 30 30N 77 39 E
Tons →, *Ut. P., India* **69 F10** 25 6N 83 33 E
Tønsberg, *Norway* **9 G14** 59 19N 10 25 E
Tonya, *Turkey* **73 B8** 40 53N 39 16 E
Toobanna, *Australia* **94 B4** 18 42 S 146 9 E
Toodyay, *Australia* **93 F2** 31 34 S 116 28 E
Tooele, *U.S.A.* **114 F7** 40 32N 112 18W
Toompine, *Australia* **95 D3** 27 15 S 144 19 E
Toora, *Australia* **95 F4** 38 39 S 146 23 E
Toora-Khem, *Russia* **51 D10** 52 28N 96 17 E
Toowoomba, *Australia* **95 D5** 27 32 S 151 56 E
Top Springs, *Australia* **92 C5** 16 37 S 131 51 E
Topalu, *Romania* **43 F13** 44 31N 28 3 E
Topaz, *U.S.A.* **116 G7** 38 41N 119 30W
Topeka, *U.S.A.* **112 F7** 39 3N 95 40W
Topl'a →, *Slovak Rep.* **27 C14** 48 45N 21 45 E
Topley, *Canada* **104 C3** 54 49N 126 18W
Toplica →, *Serbia, Yug.* **40 C5** 43 15N 21 49 E
Toplița, *Romania* **43 D10** 46 55N 25 20 E
Topocalma, Pta., *Chile* **126 C1** 34 10 S 72 2W
Topock, *U.S.A.* **117 L12** 34 46N 114 29W
Topola, *Serbia, Yug.* **40 B4** 44 17N 20 41 E
Topolčani, *Macedonia* **40 E5** 41 14N 21 25 E
Topol'čany, *Slovak Rep.* **27 C11** 48 35N 18 12 E
Topolnitsa →, *Bulgaria* **41 D8** 42 11N 24 18 E
Topolobampo, *Mexico* **118 B3** 25 40N 109 4W
Topoloveni, *Romania* **43 F10** 44 49N 25 5 E
Topolovgrad, *Bulgaria* **41 D10** 42 5N 26 20 E
Topolvățu Mare, *Romania* **42 E6** 45 46N 21 41 E
Toppenish, *U.S.A.* **114 C3** 46 23N 120 19W
Topraisar, *Romania* **43 F13** 44 1N 28 27 E
Topusko, *Croatia* **29 C12** 45 18N 15 59 E
Torà, *Spain* **32 D6** 41 49N 1 25 E
Tora Kit, *Sudan* **81 E3** 11 2N 32 36 E
Toraka Vestale, *Madag.* **89 B7** 16 20 S 43 58 E
Torata, *Peru* **124 G4** 17 23 S 70 1W
Torbalı, *Turkey* **39 C9** 38 10N 27 21 E
Torbat-e Heydārīyeh, *Iran* **71 C8** 35 15N 59 12 E
Torbat-e Jām, *Iran* **71 C9** 35 16N 60 35 E
Torbay, *Canada* **103 C9** 47 40N 52 42W
Torbay □, *U.K.* **13 G4** 50 26N 3 31W
Torbjörntorp, *Sweden* **11 F7** 58 12N 13 36 E
Tordesillas, *Spain* **34 D6** 41 30N 5 0W
Töreboda, *Sweden* **11 F8** 58 41N 14 7 E
Torekov, *Sweden* **11 H6** 56 26N 12 37 E
Torellò, *Spain* **32 C7** 42 3N 2 16 E
Toreno, *Spain* **34 C4** 42 42N 6 30W
Torfaen □, *U.K.* **13 F4** 51 43N 3 3W
Torgau, *Germany* **24 D8** 51 34N 13 0 E
Torgelow, *Germany* **24 B10** 53 37N 14 1 E
Torhamn, *Sweden* **11 H9** 56 6N 15 50 E
Torhout, *Belgium* **17 C3** 51 5N 3 7 E
Tori, *Ethiopia* **81 F3** 7 53N 33 35 E
Tori-Shima, *Japan* **55 J10** 30 29N 140 19 E
Torigni-sur-Vire, *France* **18 C6** 49 3N 0 58W
Torija, *Spain* **32 E1** 40 44N 3 2W
Torin, *Mexico* **118 B2** 27 33N 110 15W
Torino, *Italy* **28 C4** 45 3N 7 40 E
Torit, *Sudan* **81 G3** 4 27N 32 31 E
Torkamān, *Iran* **70 B5** 37 35N 47 23 E
Torkovichi, *Russia* **46 C6** 58 51N 30 21 E
Tormac, *Romania* **42 E6** 45 30N 21 30 E
Tormes →, *Spain* **34 D4** 41 18N 6 29W
Tornado Mt., *Canada* **104 D6** 49 55N 114 40W
Tornal'a, *Slovak Rep.* **27 C13** 48 25N 20 20 E
Torne älv →, *Sweden* **8 D21** 65 50N 24 12 E
Torneå = Tornio, *Finland* **8 D21** 65 50N 24 12 E
Torneträsk, *Sweden* **8 B18** 68 24N 19 15 E
Tornio, *Finland* **8 D21** 65 50N 24 12 E
Tornionjoki →, *Finland* **8 D21** 65 50N 24 12 E
Tornquist, *Argentina* **126 D3** 38 8 S 62 15W
Toro, *Baleares, Spain* **37 B11** 39 59N 4 8 E
Toro, *Zamora, Spain* **34 D5** 41 35N 5 24W
Torö, *Sweden* **11 F11** 58 48N 17 50 E
Toro, Cerro del, *Chile* **126 B2** 29 10 S 69 50W
Toro Pk., *U.S.A.* **117 M10** 33 34N 116 24W
Törökszentmiklós, *Hungary* **42 C5** 47 11N 20 27 E
Toroníos Kólpos, *Greece* **40 F7** 40 5N 23 30 E
Toronto, *Canada* **102 D4** 43 39N 79 20W
Toronto, *U.S.A.* **110 F4** 40 28N 80 36W
Toropets, *Russia* **46 D6** 56 30N 31 40 E
Tororo, *Uganda* **86 B3** 0 45N 34 12 E
Toros Dağları, *Turkey* **70 B2** 37 0N 32 30 E
Torpa, *India* **69 H11** 22 57N 85 6 E
Torquay, *Australia* **95 F3** 38 20 S 144 19 E
Torquay, *U.K.* **13 G4** 50 27N 3 32W
Torquemada, *Spain* **34 C6** 42 2N 4 19W
Torrance, *U.S.A.* **117 M8** 33 50N 118 19W
Torrão, *Portugal* **35 G2** 38 16N 8 11W
Torre Annunziata, *Italy* **31 B7** 40 45N 14 27 E
Torre de Moncorvo, *Portugal* **34 D3** 41 12N 7 8W
Torre del Campo, *Spain* **35 H7** 37 46N 3 53W
Torre del Greco, *Italy* **31 B7** 40 47N 14 22 E
Torre del Mar, *Spain* **35 J6** 36 44N 4 6W
Torre-Pacheco, *Spain* **33 H4** 37 44N 0 57W
Torre Péllice, *Italy* **28 D4** 44 49N 7 13 E
Torreblanca, *Spain* **32 E5** 40 14N 0 12 E
Torrecampo, *Spain* **35 G6** 38 29N 4 41W
Torrecilla en Cameros, *Spain* **32 C2** 42 15N 2 38W
Torredembarra, *Spain* **32 D6** 41 9N 1 24 E
Torredonjimeno, *Spain* **35 H7** 37 46N 3 57W
Torrejón de Ardoz, *Spain* **34 E7** 40 27N 3 29W
Torrejoncillo, *Spain* **34 F4** 39 54N 6 28W
Torrelaguna, *Spain* **34 E7** 40 50N 3 38W
Torrelavega, *Spain* **34 B6** 43 20N 4 5W
Torremaggiore, *Italy* **29 G12** 41 41N 15 17 E
Torremolinos, *Spain* **35 J6** 36 38N 4 30W
Torrens, L., *Australia* **95 E2** 31 0 S 137 50 E
Torrens Cr. →, *Australia* **94 C4** 22 23 S 145 9 E
Torrens Creek, *Australia* **94 C4** 20 48 S 145 3 E
Torrent, *Spain* **33 F4** 39 27N 0 28W
Torrenueva, *Spain* **35 G7** 38 38N 3 22W
Torreón, *Mexico* **118 B4** 25 33N 103 26W
Torreperogil, *Spain* **35 G7** 38 2N 3 17W
Torres, *Brazil* **127 B5** 29 21 S 49 44W
Torres, *Mexico* **118 B2** 28 46N 110 47W
Torres Novas, *Portugal* **35 F2** 39 27N 8 33W
Torres Strait, *Australia* **96 H6** 9 50 S 142 20 E
Torres Vedras, *Portugal* **35 F1** 39 5N 9 15W
Torrevieja, *Spain* **33 H4** 37 59N 0 42W
Torrey, *U.S.A.* **115 G8** 38 18N 111 25W
Torridge →, *U.K.* **13 G3** 51 0N 4 13W
Torridon, L., *U.K.* **14 D3** 57 35N 5 50W
Torrijos, *Spain* **34 F6** 39 59N 4 18W
Tørring, *Denmark* **11 J3** 55 52N 9 29 E
Torrington, *Conn., U.S.A.* **111 E11** 41 48N 73 7W
Torrington, *Wyo., U.S.A.* **112 D2** 42 4N 104 11W
Torroella de Montgrì, *Spain* **32 C8** 42 2N 3 8 E
Torrox, *Spain* **35 J7** 36 46N 3 57W
Torsås, *Sweden* **11 H9** 56 24N 16 0 E
Torsby, *Sweden* **10 D6** 60 7N 13 0 E
Torshälla, *Sweden* **10 E10** 59 25N 16 28 E
Tórshavn, *Færoe Is.* **8 E9** 62 5N 6 56W
Torslanda, *Sweden* **11 G5** 57 44N 11 45 E
Torsö, *Sweden* **11 F7** 58 48N 13 45 E
Tortola, *Virgin Is.* **121 C7** 18 19N 64 45W
Tórtoles de Esgueva, *Spain* **34 D6** 41 49N 4 2W
Tortolì, *Italy* **30 C2** 39 55N 9 39 E
Tortona, *Italy* **28 D5** 44 54N 8 52 E
Tortorici, *Italy* **31 D7** 38 2N 14 49 E
Tortosa, *Spain* **32 E5** 40 49N 0 31 E
Tortosa, C., *Spain* **32 E5** 40 41N 0 52 E
Tortosendo, *Portugal* **34 E3** 40 15N 7 31W
Tortue, I. de la, *Haiti* **121 B5** 20 5N 72 57W
Tortum, *Turkey* **73 B9** 40 19N 41 35 E
Ţorūd, *Iran* **71 C7** 35 25N 55 5 E
Torul, *Turkey* **73 B8** 40 34N 39 18 E
Toruń, *Poland* **45 E5** 53 2N 18 39 E
Tory I., *Ireland* **15 A3** 55 16N 8 14W
Torysa →, *Slovak Rep.* **27 C14** 48 39N 21 21 E
Torzhok, *Russia* **46 D8** 57 5N 34 55 E
Torzym, *Poland* **45 F2** 52 19N 15 5 E
Tosa, *Japan* **55 H6** 33 24N 133 23 E
Tosa-Shimizu, *Japan* **55 H6** 32 52N 132 58 E
Tosa-Wan, *Japan* **55 H6** 33 15N 133 30 E
Toscana □, *Italy* **28 E8** 43 25N 11 0 E
Toscano, Arcipelago, *Italy* **28 F7** 42 30N 10 30 E
Toshkent, *Uzbekistan* **50 E7** 41 20N 69 10 E
Tosno, *Russia* **46 C6** 59 38N 30 46 E
Tossa de Mar, *Spain* **32 D7** 41 43N 2 56 E
Tösse, *Sweden* **11 F6** 58 58N 12 39 E
Tostado, *Argentina* **126 B3** 29 15 S 61 50W
Tostedt, *Germany* **24 B5** 53 17N 9 42 E
Tostón, Pta. de, *Canary Is.* **37 F5** 28 42N 14 2W
Tosu, *Japan* **55 H5** 33 22N 130 31 E
Tosya, *Turkey* **72 B6** 41 1N 34 2 E
Toszek, *Poland* **45 H5** 50 27N 18 32 E
Totana, *Spain* **33 H3** 37 45N 1 30W
Totebo, *Sweden* **11 G10** 57 38N 16 12 E
Toteng, *Botswana* **88 C3** 20 22 S 22 58 E
Tôtes, *France* **18 C8** 49 41N 1 2 E
Tótkomlós, *Hungary* **42 D5** 46 24N 20 45 E
Totma, *Russia* **50 C5** 60 0N 42 40 E
Totnes, *U.K.* **13 G4** 50 26N 3 42W
Totness, *Surinam* **125 B7** 5 53N 56 19W
Toto, *Nigeria* **83 D6** 8 26N 7 5 E
Totonicapán, *Guatemala* **120 D1** 14 58N 91 12W
Totten Glacier, *Antarctica* **5 C8** 66 45 S 116 10 E
Tottenham, *Australia* **95 E4** 32 14 S 147 21 E
Tottenham, *Canada* **110 B5** 44 1N 79 49W
Tottori, *Japan* **55 G7** 35 30N 134 15 E
Tottori □, *Japan* **55 G7** 35 30N 134 12 E
Touaret, *Niger* **83 A6** 20 17N 7 8 E
Touba, *Ivory C.* **82 D3** 8 22N 7 40W
Touba, *Senegal* **82 C1** 14 50N 15 55W
Toubkal, Djebel, *Morocco* **78 B4** 31 0N 8 0W
Toucy, *France* **19 E10** 47 44N 3 15 E
Tougan, *Burkina Faso* **82 C4** 13 11N 2 58W
Touggourt, *Algeria* **78 B7** 33 6N 6 4 E
Tougouri, *Burkina Faso* **83 C4** 13 20N 0 30W
Tougué, *Guinea* **82 C2** 11 25N 11 50W
Toukoto, *Mali* **82 C3** 13 27N 9 52W
Toul, *France* **19 D12** 48 40N 5 53 E
Toulepleu, *Ivory C.* **82 D3** 6 32N 8 24W
Toulon, *France* **21 E9** 43 10N 5 55 E
Toulouse, *France* **20 E5** 43 37N 1 27 E
Toummo, *Niger* **79 D8** 22 45N 14 8 E
Toumodi, *Ivory C.* **82 D3** 6 32N 5 4W
Tounan, *Taiwan* **59 F13** 23 41N 120 28 E
Toungo, *Nigeria* **83 D7** 8 20N 12 3 E
Toungoo, *Burma* **67 K20** 19 0N 96 30 E
Touques →, *France* **18 C7** 49 22N 0 8 E
Touraine, *France* **18 E7** 47 20N 0 30 E
Tourane = Da Nang, *Vietnam* **64 D7** 16 4N 108 13 E
Tourcoing, *France* **19 B10** 50 42N 3 10 E
Touriñán, C., *Spain* **34 B1** 43 3N 9 17W
Tournai, *Belgium* **17 D3** 50 35N 3 25 E
Tournan-en-Brie, *France* **19 D9** 48 44N 2 46 E
Tournay, *France* **20 E4** 43 13N 0 13 E
Tournon-St-Martin, *France* **18 F7** 46 45N 0 58 E
Tournon-sur-Rhône, *France* **21 C8** 45 4N 4 50 E
Tournus, *France* **19 F11** 46 35N 4 54 E
Tours, *France* **18 E7** 47 22N 0 40 E
Tousidé, Pic, *Chad* **79 D9** 21 1N 16 29 E
Toussora, Mt., *C.A.R.* **84 C4** 9 7N 23 14 E
Touws →, *S. Africa* **88 E3** 33 45 S 21 11 E
Touwsrivier, *S. Africa* **88 E3** 33 20 S 20 2 E
Tovarkovskiy, *Russia* **46 F10** 53 40N 38 14 E
Tovuz, *Azerbaijan* **49 K7** 41 0N 45 40 E
Towada, *Japan* **54 D10** 40 37N 141 13 E
Towada-Ko, *Japan* **54 D10** 40 28N 140 55 E
Towanda, *U.S.A.* **111 E8** 41 46N 76 27W
Towang, *India* **67 F17** 27 37N 91 50 E
Tower, *U.S.A.* **112 B8** 47 48N 92 17W
Towerhill Cr. →, *Australia* **94 C3** 22 28 S 144 35 E
Towner, *U.S.A.* **112 A4** 48 21N 100 25W
Townsend, *U.S.A.* **114 C8** 46 19N 111 31W
Townshend I., *Australia* **94 C5** 22 10 S 150 31 E
Townsville, *Australia* **94 B4** 19 15 S 146 45 E
Towson, *U.S.A.* **108 F7** 39 24N 76 36W
Towuti, Danau, *Indonesia* **63 E6** 2 45 S 121 32 E
Toya-Ko, *Japan* **54 C10** 42 35N 140 51 E
Toyama, *Japan* **55 F8** 36 40N 137 15 E
Toyama □, *Japan* **55 F8** 36 45N 137 30 E
Toyama-Wan, *Japan* **55 F8** 37 0N 137 30 E
Toyohashi, *Japan* **55 G8** 34 45N 137 25 E
Toyokawa, *Japan* **55 G8** 34 48N 137 27 E
Toyonaka, *Japan* **55 G7** 34 50N 135 28 E
Toyooka, *Japan* **55 G7** 35 35N 134 48 E
Toyota, *Japan* **55 G8** 35 3N 137 7 E
Tozeur, *Tunisia* **78 B7** 33 56N 8 8 E
Tqibuli, *Georgia* **49 J6** 42 26N 43 0 E
Tqvarcheli, *Georgia* **49 J5** 42 47N 41 42 E
Trá Li = Tralee, *Ireland* **15 D2** 52 16N 9 42W
Tra On, *Vietnam* **65 H5** 9 58N 105 55 E
Trabancos →, *Spain* **34 D5** 41 36N 5 15W
Traben-Trarbach, *Germany* **25 F3** 49 57N 7 7 E
Trabzon, *Turkey* **73 B8** 41 0N 39 45 E
Tracadie, *Canada* **103 C7** 47 30N 64 55W
Tracy, *Calif., U.S.A.* **116 H5** 37 44N 121 26W
Tracy, *Minn., U.S.A.* **112 C7** 44 14N 95 37W
Tradate, *Italy* **28 C5** 45 43N 8 54 E
Trade Town, *Liberia* **82 D3** 5 40N 9 50W
Trafalgar, C., *Spain* **35 J4** 36 10N 6 2W
Traian, *Brăila, Romania* **43 E12** 45 11N 27 44 E
Traian, *Tulcea, Romania* **43 E13** 45 2N 28 15 E
Trail, *Canada* **104 D5** 49 5N 117 40W
Trainor L., *Canada* **104 A4** 60 24N 120 17W
Trákhonas, *Cyprus* **36 D12** 35 12N 33 21 E
Tralee, *Ireland* **15 D2** 52 16N 9 42W
Tralee B., *Ireland* **15 D2** 52 17N 9 55W
Tramore, *Ireland* **15 D4** 52 10N 7 10W
Tramore B., *Ireland* **15 D4** 52 9N 7 10W
Tran Ninh, Cao Nguyen, *Laos* **64 C4** 19 30N 103 10 E
Tranås, *Sweden* **11 F8** 58 3N 14 59 E
Tranbjerg, *Denmark* **11 H4** 56 6N 10 9 E
Trancas, *Argentina* **126 B2** 26 11 S 65 20W
Trancoso, *Portugal* **34 E3** 40 49N 7 21W
Tranebjerg, *Denmark* **11 J4** 55 51N 10 36 E
Tranemo, *Sweden* **11 G7** 57 30N 13 20 E
Trang, *Thailand* **65 J2** 7 33N 99 38 E
Trangahy, *Madag.* **89 B7** 19 7 S 44 31 E
Trangan, *Indonesia* **63 F8** 6 40 S 134 20 E
Trangie, *Australia* **95 E4** 32 4 S 148 0 E
Trångsviken, *Sweden* **10 A7** 63 19N 13 59 E
Trani, *Italy* **31 A9** 41 17N 16 25 E
Tranoroa, *Madag.* **89 C8** 24 42 S 45 4 E
Tranqueras, *Uruguay* **127 C4** 31 13 S 55 45W
Transantarctic Mts., *Antarctica* **5 E12** 85 0 S 170 0W
Transilvania, *Romania* **43 D9** 46 30N 24 0 E
Transilvanian Alps = Carpații Meridionali, *Romania* **43 E9** 45 30N 25 0 E
Transtrand, *Sweden* **10 C7** 61 6N 13 20 E
Transtrandsfjällen, *Sweden* **10 C6** 61 8N 13 0 E
Transvaal, *S. Africa* **85 K5** 25 0 S 29 0 E
Transylvania = Transilvania, *Romania* **43 D9** 46 30N 24 0 E
Trápani, *Italy* **30 D5** 38 1N 12 29 E
Trapper Pk., *U.S.A.* **114 D6** 45 54N 114 18W
Traralgon, *Australia* **95 F4** 38 12 S 146 34 E
Trarza, *Mauritania* **82 B2** 17 30N 15 0W
Trasacco, *Italy* **29 G10** 41 57N 13 32 E
Trăscău, Muntii, *Romania* **43 D8** 46 14N 23 14 E
Trasimeno, L., *Italy* **29 E9** 43 8N 12 6 E
Träslövsläge, *Sweden* **11 G6** 57 4N 12 16 E
Trasvase Tajo-Segura, Canal de, *Spain* **32 E2** 40 15N 2 55W
Trat, *Thailand* **65 F4** 12 14N 102 33 E
Tratani →, *Pakistan* **68 E3** 29 19N 68 20 E
Traun, *Austria* **26 C7** 48 14N 14 15 E
Traunreut, *Germany* **25 H8** 47 57N 12 36 E
Traunsee, *Austria* **26 D6** 47 55N 13 50 E
Traunstein, *Germany* **25 H8** 47 52N 12 38 E
Travellers L., *Australia* **95 E3** 33 20 S 142 0 E
Travemünde, *Germany* **24 B6** 53 57N 10 52 E
Travers, Mt., *N.Z.* **91 K4** 42 1 S 172 45 E
Traverse City, *U.S.A.* **108 C3** 44 46N 85 38W
Travis, L., *U.S.A.* **113 K5** 30 24N 97 55W
Travnik, *Bos.-H.* **42 F2** 44 17N 17 39 E
Trbovlje, *Slovenia* **29 B12** 46 12N 15 5 E
Trébbia →, *Italy* **28 C6** 45 4N 9 41 E
Trebel →, *Germany* **24 B9** 53 54N 13 2 E
Trébeurden, *France* **18 D3** 48 46N 3 35W
Třebíč, *Czech Rep.* **26 B8** 49 14N 15 55 E
Trebinje, *Bos.-H.* **40 D2** 42 44N 18 22 E
Trebisacce, *Italy* **31 C9** 39 52N 16 32 E
Trebišnjica →, *Bos.-H.* **40 D2** 42 47N 18 8 E
Trebišov, *Slovak Rep.* **27 C14** 48 38N 21 41 E
Trebižat →, *Bos.-H.* **29 E14** 43 15N 17 30 E
Trebnje, *Slovenia* **29 C12** 45 54N 15 1 E
Třeboň, *Czech Rep.* **26 B7** 49 1N 14 50 E
Trebonne, *Australia* **94 B4** 18 37 S 146 5 E
Trebujena, *Spain* **35 J4** 36 52N 6 11W
Trecate, *Italy* **28 C5** 45 26N 8 44 E
Tregaron, *U.K.* **13 E4** 52 14N 3 56W
Tregnago, *Italy* **29 C8** 45 31N 11 10 E
Tregrosse Is., *Australia* **94 B5** 17 41 S 150 43 E
Tréguier, *France* **18 D3** 48 47N 3 16W
Trégunc, *France* **18 E3** 47 51N 3 51W
Treherne, *Canada* **105 D9** 49 38N 98 42W
Tréia, *Italy* **29 E10** 43 19N 13 19 E
Treignac, *France* **20 C5** 45 32N 1 48 E
Treinta y Tres, *Uruguay* **127 C5** 33 16 S 54 17W
Treis-karden, *Germany* **25 E3** 50 10N 7 18 E
Treklyano, *Bulgaria* **40 D6** 42 33N 22 36 E
Trelawney, *Zimbabwe* **89 B5** 17 30 S 30 30 E
Trélazé, *France* **18 E6** 47 26N 0 30W
Trelew, *Argentina* **128 E3** 43 10 S 65 20W
Trélissac, *France* **20 C4** 45 11N 0 47 E
Trelleborg, *Sweden* **11 J7** 55 20N 13 10 E
Tremadog Bay, *U.K.* **12 E3** 52 51N 4 18W
Trémiti, *Italy* **29 F12** 42 8N 15 30 E
Tremonton, *U.S.A.* **114 F7** 41 43N 112 10W
Tremp, *Spain* **32 C5** 42 10N 0 52 E
Trenche →, *Canada* **102 C5** 47 46N 72 53W
Trenčiansky □, *Slovak Rep.* **27 C11** 48 45N 18 20 E
Trenčín, *Slovak Rep.* **27 C11** 48 52N 18 4 E
Trenggalek, *Indonesia* **63 H14** 8 3 S 111 43 E
Trenque Lauquen, *Argentina* **126 D3** 36 5 S 62 45W
Trent →, *Canada* **110 B7** 44 6N 77 34W
Trent →, *U.K.* **12 D7** 53 41N 0 42W
Trentino-Alto Adige □, *Italy* **29 B8** 46 30N 11 20 E
Trento, *Italy* **28 B8** 46 4N 11 8 E
Trenton, *Canada* **102 D4** 44 10N 77 34W
Trenton, *Mo., U.S.A.* **112 E8** 40 5N 93 37W
Trenton, *N.J., U.S.A.* **111 F10** 40 14N 74 46W
Trenton, *Nebr., U.S.A.* **112 E4** 40 11N 101 1W
Trepassey, *Canada* **103 C9** 46 43N 53 25W
Trepuzzi, *Italy* **31 B11** 40 24N 18 4 E
Tres Arroyos, *Argentina* **126 D3** 38 26 S 60 20W
Três Corações, *Brazil* **127 A6** 21 44 S 45 15W
Três Lagoas, *Brazil* **125 H8** 20 50 S 51 43W
Tres Lomas, *Argentina* **126 D3** 36 27 S 62 51W
Tres Marías, Islas, *Mexico* **118 C3** 21 25N 106 28W
Tres Montes, C., *Chile* **128 F1** 46 50 S 75 30W
Tres Pinos, *U.S.A.* **116 J5** 36 48N 121 19W
Três Pontas, *Brazil* **127 A6** 21 23 S 45 29W
Tres Puentes, *Chile* **126 B1** 27 50 S 70 15W
Tres Puntas, C., *Argentina* **128 F3** 47 0 S 66 0W
Três Rios, *Brazil* **127 A7** 22 6 S 43 15W
Tres Valles, *Mexico* **119 D5** 18 15N 96 8W
Tresco, *U.K.* **13 H1** 49 57N 6 20W
Treska →, *Macedonia* **40 E5** 42 0N 21 20 E
Treskavica, *Bos.-H.* **42 G3** 43 40N 18 20 E
Trespaderne, *Spain* **34 C7** 42 47N 3 24W
Trets, *France* **21 E9** 43 27N 5 41 E
Treuchtlingen, *Germany* **25 G6** 48 58N 10 54 E
Treuenbrietzen, *Germany* **24 C8** 52 5N 12 52 E
Trevi, *Italy* **29 F9** 42 52N 12 45 E
Treviglio, *Italy* **28 C6** 45 31N 9 35 E
Trevinca, Peña, *Spain* **34 C4** 42 15N 6 46W
Treviso, *Italy* **29 C9** 45 40N 12 15 E
Trévoux, *France* **21 C8** 45 57N 4 47 E
Trgovište, *Serbia, Yug.* **40 D6** 42 20N 22 10 E
Triabunna, *Australia* **94 G4** 42 30 S 147 55 E
Triánda, *Greece* **36 C10** 36 25N 28 10 E
Triangle, *Zimbabwe* **89 C5** 21 2 S 31 28 E
Triaucourt-en-Argonne, *France* **19 D12** 48 59N 5 2 E
Tribsees, *Germany* **24 A8** 54 5N 12 44 E
Tribulation, C., *Australia* **94 B4** 16 5 S 145 29 E
Tribune, *U.S.A.* **112 F4** 38 28N 101 45W
Tricárico, *Italy* **31 B9** 40 37N 16 9 E
Tricase, *Italy* **31 C11** 39 56N 18 22 E
Trichinopoly = Tiruchchirappalli, *India* **66 P11** 10 45N 78 45 E
Trichur, *India* **66 P10** 10 30N 76 18 E
Trida, *Australia* **95 E4** 33 1 S 145 1 E
Trier, *Germany* **25 F2** 49 45N 6 38 E
Trieste, *Italy* **29 C10** 45 40N 13 46 E
Trieste, G. di, *Italy* **29 C10** 45 40N 13 35 E
Trieux →, *France* **18 D3** 48 43N 3 9W
Triggiano, *Italy* **31 A9** 41 4N 16 55 E
Triglav, *Slovenia* **29 B10** 46 21N 13 50 E
Trigno →, *Italy* **29 F11** 42 4N 14 48 E
Trigueros, *Spain* **35 H4** 37 24N 6 50W
Tríkeri, *Greece* **38 B5** 39 6N 23 5 E
Trikhonis, Límni, *Greece* **38 C3** 38 34N 21 30 E
Tríkkala, *Greece* **38 B3** 39 34N 21 47 E
Tríkkala □, *Greece* **38 B3** 39 41N 21 30 E
Trikomo, *Cyprus* **36 D12** 35 17N 33 52 E
Trikora, Puncak, *Indonesia* **63 E9** 4 15 S 138 45 E
Trilj, *Croatia* **29 E13** 43 38N 16 42 E
Trillo, *Spain* **32 E2** 40 42N 2 35W
Trim, *Ireland* **15 C5** 53 33N 6 48W
Trincomalee, *Sri Lanka* **66 Q12** 8 38N 81 15 E
Trindade, *Brazil* **125 G9** 16 40 S 49 30W
Trindade, I., *Atl. Oc.* **2 F8** 20 20 S 29 50W
Třinec, *Czech Rep.* **27 B11** 49 41N 18 39 E
Trinidad, *Bolivia* **124 F6** 14 46 S 64 50W
Trinidad, *Cuba* **120 B4** 21 48N 80 0W
Trinidad, *Uruguay* **126 C4** 33 30 S 56 50W
Trinidad, *U.S.A.* **113 G2** 37 10N 104 31W
Trinidad, *W. Indies* **121 D7** 10 30N 61 15W
Trinidad →, *Mexico* **119 D5** 17 49N 95 9W
Trinidad & Tobago ■, *W. Indies* **121 D7** 10 30N 61 20W
Trinitápoli, *Italy* **31 A9** 41 21N 16 5 E
Trinity, *Canada* **103 C9** 48 59N 53 55W
Trinity, *U.S.A.* **113 K7** 30 57N 95 22W
Trinity →, *Calif., U.S.A.* **114 F2** 41 11N 123 42W
Trinity →, *Tex., U.S.A.* **113 L7** 29 45N 94 43W
Trinity B., *Canada* **103 C9** 48 20N 53 10W
Trinity Is., *U.S.A.* **100 C4** 56 33N 154 25W
Trinity Range, *U.S.A.* **114 F4** 40 15N 118 45W
Trinkitat, *Sudan* **80 D4** 18 45N 37 51 E
Trino, *Italy* **28 C5** 45 12N 8 18 E
Trinway, *U.S.A.* **110 F2** 40 9N 82 1W
Trionto, C., *Italy* **31 C9** 39 37N 16 43 E
Triora, *Italy* **28 D4** 44 1N 7 46 E
Tripoli = Tarābulus, *Lebanon* **75 A4** 34 31N 35 50 E
Tripoli = Tarābulus, *Libya* **79 B8** 32 49N 13 7 E
Trípolis, *Greece* **38 D4** 37 31N 22 25 E
Tripolitania, *N. Afr.* **79 B8** 31 0N 13 0 E
Tripura □, *India* **67 H18** 24 0N 92 0 E
Tripylos, *Cyprus* **36 E11** 34 59N 32 41 E
Trischen, *Germany* **24 A4** 54 4N 8 40 E
Tristan da Cunha, *Atl. Oc.* **77 K2** 37 6 S 12 20W
Trisul, *India* **69 D8** 30 19N 79 47 E
Trivandrum, *India* **66 Q10** 8 41N 77 0 E
Trivento, *Italy* **29 G11** 41 47N 14 33 E
Trnava, *Slovak Rep.* **27 C10** 48 23N 17 35 E
Trnavský □, *Slovak Rep.* **27 C10** 48 30N 17 45 E
Troarn, *France* **18 C6** 49 11N 0 11W
Trochu, *Canada* **104 C6** 51 50N 113 13W
Trodely I., *Canada* **102 B4** 52 15N 79 26W
Troezen, *Greece* **38 D5** 37 25N 23 15 E
Trogir, *Croatia* **29 E13** 43 32N 16 15 E
Troglav, *Croatia* **29 E13** 43 56N 16 36 E
Tróia, *Italy* **31 A8** 41 22N 15 18 E
Troilus, L., *Canada* **102 B5** 50 50N 74 35W
Troina, *Italy* **31 E7** 37 47N 14 36 E
Trois-Pistoles, *Canada* **103 C6** 48 5N 69 10W
Trois-Rivières, *Canada* **102 C5** 46 25N 72 34W
Troisdorf, *Germany* **24 E3** 50 48N 7 11 E
Troitsk, *Russia* **50 D7** 54 10N 61 35 E
Troitsko Pechorsk, *Russia* **50 C6** 62 40N 56 10 E
Trölladyngja, *Iceland* **8 D5** 64 54N 17 16W
Trollhättan, *Sweden* **11 F6** 58 17N 12 20 E
Trollheimen, *Norway* **8 E13** 62 46N 9 1 E
Trombetas →, *Brazil* **125 D7** 1 55 S 55 35W
Tromsø, *Norway* **8 B18** 69 40N 18 56 E
Trona, *U.S.A.* **117 K9** 35 46N 117 23W
Tronador, Mte., *Argentina* **128 E2** 41 10 S 71 50W
Trøndelag, *Norway* **8 D14** 64 17N 11 50 E
Trondheim, *Norway* **8 E14** 63 36N 10 25 E
Trondheimsfjorden, *Norway* **8 E14** 63 35N 10 30 E
Trönninge, *Sweden* **11 H6** 56 37N 12 51 E
Tronto →, *Italy* **29 F10** 42 54N 13 55 E
Troodos, *Cyprus* **36 E11** 34 55N 32 52 E
Troon, *U.K.* **14 F4** 55 33N 4 39W
Tropea, *Italy* **31 D8** 38 41N 15 54 E
Tropic, *U.S.A.* **115 H7** 37 37N 112 5W
Tropoja = Tropojë, *Albania* **40 D4** 42 23N 20 10 E
Tropojë, *Albania* **40 D4** 42 23N 20 10 E
Trosa, *Sweden* **11 F11** 58 54N 17 33 E
Trostan, *U.K.* **15 A5** 55 3N 6 10W
Trostberg, *Germany* **25 G8** 48 1N 12 33 E
Trostyanets, *Ukraine* **47 G8** 50 33N 34 59 E
Trout →, *Canada* **104 A5** 61 19N 119 51W
Trout L., *N.W.T., Canada* **104 A4** 60 40N 121 14W
Trout L., *Ont., Canada* **105 C10** 51 20N 93 15W
Trout Lake, *Canada* **104 B6** 56 30N 114 32W
Trout Lake, *U.S.A.* **116 E5** 46 0N 121 32W
Trout River, *Canada* **103 C8** 49 29N 58 8W
Trout Run, *U.S.A.* **110 E7** 41 23N 77 3W
Trouville-sur-Mer, *France* **18 C7** 49 21N 0 5 E
Trowbridge, *U.K.* **13 F5** 51 18N 2 12W
Troy, *Turkey* **39 B8** 39 57N 26 12 E
Troy, *Ala., U.S.A.* **109 K3** 31 48N 85 58W
Troy, *Kans., U.S.A.* **112 F7** 39 47N 95 5W
Troy, *Mo., U.S.A.* **112 F9** 38 59N 90 59W
Troy, *Mont., U.S.A.* **114 B6** 48 28N 115 53W
Troy, *N.Y., U.S.A.* **111 D11** 42 44N 73 41W
Troy, *Ohio, U.S.A.* **108 E3** 40 2N 84 12W
Troy, *Pa., U.S.A.* **111 E8** 41 47N 76 47W
Troyan, *Bulgaria* **41 D8** 42 57N 24 43 E
Troyes, *France* **19 D11** 48 19N 4 3 E
Trpanj, *Croatia* **29 E14** 43 1N 17 15 E
Trstenik, *Serbia, Yug.* **40 C5** 43 36N 21 0 E
Trubchevsk, *Russia* **47 F7** 52 33N 33 47 E
Truchas Peak, *U.S.A.* **113 H2** 35 58N 105 39W
Trucial States = United Arab Emirates ■, *Asia* **71 F7** 23 50N 54 0 E
Truckee, *U.S.A.* **116 F6** 39 20N 120 11W
Trudfront, *Russia* **49 H8** 45 56N 47 40 E
Trudovoye, *Russia* **54 C6** 43 17N 132 5 E
Trujillo, *Honduras* **120 C2** 16 0N 86 0W
Trujillo, *Peru* **124 E3** 8 6 S 79 0W
Trujillo, *Spain* **35 F5** 39 28N 5 55W
Trujillo, *U.S.A.* **113 H2** 35 32N 104 42W
Trujillo, *Venezuela* **124 B4** 9 22N 70 38W
Truk, *Micronesia* **96 G7** 7 25N 151 46 E
Trumann, *U.S.A.* **113 H9** 35 41N 90 31W
Trumansburg, *U.S.A.* **111 D8** 42 33N 76 40W
Trumbull, Mt., *U.S.A.* **115 H7** 36 25N 113 8W
Trŭn, *Bulgaria* **40 D6** 42 51N 22 38 E
Trun, *France* **18 D7** 48 50N 0 2 E
Trundle, *Australia* **95 E4** 32 53 S 147 35 E
Trung-Phan = Annam, *Vietnam* **64 E7** 16 0N 108 0 E
Truro, *Canada* **103 C7** 45 21N 63 14W
Truro, *U.K.* **13 G2** 50 16N 5 4W
Truskavets, *Ukraine* **47 H2** 49 17N 23 30 E
Trŭstenik, *Bulgaria* **41 C8** 43 31N 24 28 E
Trustrup, *Denmark* **11 H4** 56 20N 10 46 E
Trutch, *Canada* **104 B4** 57 44N 122 57W
Truth or Consequences, *U.S.A.* **115 K10** 33 8N 107 15W
Trutnov, *Czech Rep.* **26 A8** 50 37N 15 54 E
Truxton, *U.S.A.* **111 D8** 42 45N 76 2W
Truyère →, *France* **20 D6** 44 38N 2 34 E
Tryavna, *Bulgaria* **41 D9** 42 54N 25 25 E
Tryonville, *U.S.A.* **110 E5** 41 42N 79 48W
Trzcianka, *Poland* **45 E3** 53 3N 16 25 E
Trzciel, *Poland* **45 F2** 52 23N 15 50 E
Trzcińsko Zdrój, *Poland* **45 F1** 52 58N 14 35 E
Trzebiatów, *Poland* **44 D2** 54 3N 15 18 E
Trzebiez, *Poland* **44 E1** 53 38N 14 31 E
Trzebnica, *Poland* **45 G4** 51 20N 17 1 E
Trzemeszno, *Poland* **45 F4** 52 33N 17 48 E
Tržič, *Slovenia* **29 B11** 46 22N 14 18 E
Tsagan Aman, *Russia* **49 G8** 47 34N 46 43 E
Tsamandás, *Greece* **38 B2** 39 46N 20 21 E
Tsandi, *Namibia* **88 B1** 17 42 S 14 50 E
Tsaratanana, *Madag.* **89 B8** 16 47 S 47 39 E
Tsaratanana, Mt. de, *Madag.* **89 A8** 14 0 S 49 0 E
Tsarevo = Michurin, *Bulgaria* **41 D11** 42 9N 27 51 E
Tsarevo, *Bulgaria* **41 D9** 42 28N 25 52 E
Tsaritsáni, *Greece* **38 B4** 39 53N 22 14 E
Tsau, *Botswana* **88 C3** 20 8 S 22 22 E
Tsebrykove, *Ukraine* **47 J6** 47 9N 30 10 E

Tselinograd = Astana, *Kazakstan* 50 D8 51 10N 71 30 E
Tses, *Namibia* 88 D2 25 58 S 18 8 E
Tsetserleg, *Mongolia* 60 B5 47 36N 101 32 E
Tsévié, *Togo* 83 D5 6 25N 1 20 E
Tshabong, *Botswana* 88 D3 26 2 S 22 29 E
Tshane, *Botswana* 88 C3 24 5 S 21 54 E
Tshela, *Dem. Rep. of the Congo* 84 E2 4 57 S 13 4 E
Tshesebe, *Botswana* 89 C4 21 51 S 27 32 E
Tshibeke, *Dem. Rep. of the Congo* 86 C2 2 40 S 28 35 E
Tshibinda, *Dem. Rep. of the Congo* 86 C2 2 23 S 28 43 E
Tshikapa, *Dem. Rep. of the Congo* 84 F4 6 28 S 20 48 E
Tshilenge, *Dem. Rep. of the Congo* 86 D1 6 17 S 23 48 E
Tshinsenda, *Dem. Rep. of the Congo* 87 E2 12 20 S 28 0 E
Tshofa, *Dem. Rep. of the Congo* 86 D2 5 13 S 25 16 E
Tshwane, *Botswana* 88 C3 22 24 S 22 1 E
Tsigara, *Botswana* 88 C4 20 22 S 25 54 E
Tsihombe, *Madag.* 89 D8 25 10 S 45 41 E
Tsiigehtchic, *Canada* 100 B6 67 15N 134 0W
Tsimlyansk, *Russia* 49 G6 47 40N 42 6 E
Tsimlyansk Res. = Tsimlyanskoye Vdkhr., *Russia* 49 F6 48 0N 43 0 E
Tsimlyanskoye Vdkhr., *Russia* 49 F6 48 0N 43 0 E
Tsinan = Jinan, *China* 56 F9 36 38N 117 1 E
Tsineng, *S. Africa* 88 D3 27 5 S 23 5 E
Tsínga, *Greece* 41 E8 41 23N 24 44 E
Tsinghai = Qinghai □, *China* 60 C4 36 0N 98 0 E
Tsingtao = Qingdao, *China* 57 F11 36 5N 120 20 E
Tsinjoarivo, *Madag.* 89 B8 19 37 S 47 40 E
Tsinjomitondraka, *Madag.* 89 B8 15 40 S 47 8 E
Tsiroanomandidy, *Madag.* 89 B8 18 46 S 46 2 E
Tsiteli-Tsqaro, *Georgia* 49 K8 41 33N 46 0 E
Tsitondroina, *Madag.* 89 C8 21 19 S 46 0 E
Tsivilsk, *Russia* 48 C8 55 50N 47 25 E
Tsivory, *Madag.* 89 C8 24 4 S 46 5 E
Tskhinvali, *Georgia* 49 J7 42 14N 44 1 E
Tsna →, *Russia* 48 C6 54 55N 41 58 E
Tsnori, *Georgia* 49 K7 41 40N 45 57 E
Tso Moriri, L., *India* 69 C8 32 50N 78 20 E
Tsobis, *Namibia* 88 B2 19 27 S 17 30 E
Tsodilo Hill, *Botswana* 88 B3 18 49 S 21 43 E
Tsogttsetsiy = Baruunsuu, *Mongolia* 56 C3 43 43N 105 35 E
Tsolo, *S. Africa* 89 E4 31 18 S 28 37 E
Tsomo, *S. Africa* 89 E4 32 0 S 27 42 E
Tsu, *Japan* 55 G8 34 45N 136 25 E
Tsu L., *Canada* 104 A6 60 40N 111 52W
Tsuchiura, *Japan* 55 F10 36 5N 140 15 E
Tsuen Wan, *H.K.* 59 F10 22 22N 114 6 E
Tsugaru-Kaikyō, *Japan* 54 D10 41 35N 141 0 E
Tsumeb, *Namibia* 88 B2 19 9 S 17 44 E
Tsumis, *Namibia* 88 C2 23 39 S 17 29 E
Tsuruga, *Japan* 55 G8 35 45N 136 2 E
Tsurugi-San, *Japan* 55 H7 33 51N 134 6 E
Tsuruoka, *Japan* 54 E9 38 44N 139 50 E
Tsushima, *Gifu, Japan* 55 G8 35 10N 136 43 E
Tsushima, *Nagasaki, Japan* 55 G4 34 20N 129 20 E
Tsuyama, *Japan* 55 G7 35 3N 134 0 E
Tsvetkovo, *Ukraine* 47 H6 49 8N 31 33 E
Tsyelyakhany, *Belarus* 47 F3 52 30N 25 46 E
Tua →, *Portugal* 34 D3 41 13N 7 26W
Tual, *Indonesia* 63 F8 5 38 S 132 44 E
Tuam, *Ireland* 15 C3 53 31N 8 51W
Tuamotu Arch. = Tuamotu Is., *Pac. Oc.* 97 J13 17 0 S 144 0W
Tuamotu Is., *Pac. Oc.* 97 J13 17 0 S 144 0W
Tuamotu Ridge, *Pac. Oc.* 97 K14 20 0 S 138 0W
Tuanfeng, *China* 59 B10 30 38N 114 52 E
Tuanxi, *China* 58 D6 27 28N 107 8 E
Tuao, *Phil.* 61 C4 17 55N 121 22 E
Tuapse, *Russia* 49 H4 44 5N 39 10 E
Tuatapere, *N.Z.* 91 M1 46 8 S 167 41 E
Tuba City, *U.S.A.* 115 H8 36 8N 111 14W
Tuban, *Indonesia* 63 G15 6 54 S 112 3 E
Tubani, *Botswana* 88 C3 24 46 S 24 18 E
Tubarão, *Brazil* 127 B6 28 30 S 49 0W
Tūbās, *West Bank* 75 C4 32 20N 35 22 E
Tubas →, *Namibia* 88 C2 22 54 S 14 35 E
Tübingen, *Germany* 25 G5 48 31N 9 4 E
Tubruq, *Libya* 79 B10 32 7N 23 55 E
Tubuai Is., *Pac. Oc.* 97 K13 25 0 S 150 0W
Tuc Trung, *Vietnam* 65 G6 11 1N 107 12 E
Tucacas, *Venezuela* 124 A5 10 48N 68 19W
T'uch'ang, *Taiwan* 59 E13 24 42N 121 25 E
Tuchodi →, *Canada* 104 B4 58 17N 123 42W
Tuchola, *Poland* 44 E4 53 33N 17 52 E
Tuchów, *Poland* 45 J8 49 54N 21 1 E
Tuckanarra, *Australia* 93 E2 27 7 S 118 5 E
Tucson, *U.S.A.* 115 K8 32 13N 110 58W
Tucumán □, *Argentina* 126 B2 26 48 S 66 2W
Tucumcari, *U.S.A.* 113 H3 35 10N 103 44W
Tucupita, *Venezuela* 124 B6 9 2N 62 3W
Tucuruí, *Brazil* 125 D9 3 42 S 49 44W
Tucuruí, Represa de, *Brazil* 125 D9 4 0 S 49 30W
Tuczno, *Poland* 45 E3 53 13N 16 10 E
Tudela, *Spain* 32 C3 42 4N 1 39W
Tudmur, *Syria* 70 C3 34 36N 38 15 E
Tudor, L., *Canada* 103 A6 55 50N 65 25W
Tudora, *Romania* 43 C11 47 31N 26 45 E
Tuella →, *Portugal* 34 D3 41 30N 7 12W
Tugela →, *S. Africa* 89 D5 29 14 S 31 30 E
Tuguegarao, *Phil.* 61 C4 17 35N 121 42 E
Tugur, *Russia* 51 D14 53 44N 136 45 E
Tui, *Spain* 34 C2 42 3N 8 39W
Tuineje, *Canary Is.* 37 F5 28 19N 14 3W
Tukangbesi, Kepulauan, *Indonesia* 63 F6 6 0 S 124 0 E
Tukarak I., *Canada* 102 A4 56 15N 78 45W
Tukayyid, *Iraq* 70 D5 29 47N 45 36 E
Tûkh, *Egypt* 80 H7 30 21N 31 12 E
Tukobo, *Ghana* 82 D4 5 1N 2 47W
Tuktoyaktuk, *Canada* 100 B6 69 27N 133 2W
Tukums, *Latvia* 9 H20 56 58N 23 10 E
Tukums □, *Latvia* 44 B10 56 55N 23 0 E
Tukuyu, *Tanzania* 87 D3 9 17 S 33 35 E
Tula, *Hidalgo, Mexico* 119 C5 20 5N 99 20W
Tula, *Tamaulipas, Mexico* 119 C5 23 0N 99 40W
Tula, *Nigeria* 83 D7 9 51N 11 27 E
Tula, *Russia* 46 E9 54 13N 37 38 E
Tulancingo, *Mexico* 119 C5 20 5N 99 22W
Tulare, *Serbia, Yug.* 40 D5 42 48N 21 28 E
Tulare, *U.S.A.* 116 J7 36 13N 119 21W
Tulare Lake Bed, *U.S.A.* 116 K7 36 0N 119 48W
Tularosa, *U.S.A.* 115 K10 33 5N 106 1W
Tulbagh, *S. Africa* 88 E2 33 16 S 19 6 E
Tulcán, *Ecuador* 124 C3 0 48N 77 43W
Tulcea, *Romania* 43 E13 45 13N 28 46 E
Tulcea □, *Romania* 43 E13 45 0N 28 30 E
Tulchyn, *Ukraine* 47 H5 48 41N 28 49 E
Tūleh, *Iran* 71 C7 34 35N 52 33 E
Tulemalu L., *Canada* 105 A9 62 58N 99 25W
Tulghes, *Romania* 43 D10 46 58N 25 45 E
Tuli, *Zimbabwe* 87 G2 21 58 S 29 13 E
Tulia, *U.S.A.* 113 H4 34 32N 101 46W
Tuliszków, *Poland* 45 F5 52 5N 18 18 E
Tulita, *Canada* 100 B7 64 57N 125 30W
Ṭūlkarm, *West Bank* 75 C4 32 19N 35 2 E
Tulla, *Ireland* 15 D3 52 53N 8 46W
Tullahoma, *U.S.A.* 109 H2 35 22N 86 13W
Tullamore, *Australia* 95 E4 32 39 S 147 36 E
Tullamore, *Ireland* 15 C4 53 16N 7 31W
Tulle, *France* 20 C5 45 16N 1 46 E
Tulln, *Austria* 26 C9 48 20N 16 4 E
Tullow, *Ireland* 15 D5 52 49N 6 45W
Tullus, *Sudan* 81 E1 11 7N 24 31 E
Tully, *Australia* 94 B4 17 56 S 145 55 E
Tully, *U.S.A.* 111 D8 42 48N 76 7W
Tulnici, *Romania* 43 E11 45 51N 26 38 E
Tulovo, *Bulgaria* 41 D9 42 33N 25 32 E
Tulsa, *U.S.A.* 113 G7 36 10N 95 55W
Tulsequah, *Canada* 104 B2 58 39N 133 35W
Tulu Milki, *Ethiopia* 81 F4 9 55N 38 20 E
Tulu Welel, *Ethiopia* 81 F3 8 56N 34 47 E
Tulua, *Colombia* 124 C3 4 6N 76 11W
Tulucești, *Romania* 43 E13 45 34N 28 2 E
Tulun, *Russia* 51 D11 54 32N 100 35 E
Tulungagung, *Indonesia* 63 H14 8 5 S 111 54 E
Tuma, *Russia* 46 E11 55 10N 40 30 E
Tuma →, *Nic.* 120 D3 13 6N 84 35W
Tumaco, *Colombia* 124 C3 1 50N 78 45W
Tumatumari, *Guyana* 124 B7 5 20N 58 55W
Tumba, *Sweden* 10 E11 59 12N 17 48 E
Tumba, L., *Dem. Rep. of the Congo* 84 E3 0 50 S 18 0 E
Tumbarumba, *Australia* 95 F4 35 44 S 148 0 E
Tumbaya, *Argentina* 126 A2 23 50 S 65 26W
Tumbes, *Peru* 124 D2 3 37 S 80 27W
Tumbur, *Sudan* 81 G3 4 20N 31 34 E
Tumbwe, *Dem. Rep. of the Congo* 87 E2 11 25 S 27 15 E
Tumby Bay, *Australia* 95 E2 34 21 S 136 8 E
Tumd Youqi, *China* 56 D6 40 30N 110 30 E
Tumen, *China* 57 C15 43 0N 129 50 E
Tumen Jiang →, *China* 57 C16 42 20N 130 35 E
Tumeremo, *Venezuela* 124 B6 7 18N 61 30W
Tumkur, *India* 66 N10 13 18N 77 6 E
Tump, *Pakistan* 66 F3 26 7N 62 16 E
Tumpat, *Malaysia* 65 J4 6 11N 102 10 E
Tumu, *Ghana* 82 C4 10 56N 1 56W
Tumucumaque, Serra, *Brazil* 122 C5 2 0N 55 0W
Tumut, *Australia* 95 F4 35 16 S 148 13 E
Tumwater, *U.S.A.* 116 C4 47 1N 122 54W
Tuna, *India* 68 H4 22 59N 70 5 E
Tunadal, *Sweden* 10 B11 62 26N 17 22 E
Tunas de Zaza, *Cuba* 120 B4 21 39N 79 34W
Tunbridge Wells = Royal Tunbridge Wells, *U.K.* 13 F8 51 7N 0 16 E
Tunçbilek, *Turkey* 39 B11 39 37N 29 29 E
Tunceli, *Turkey* 73 C8 39 6N 39 31 E
Tuncurry-Forster, *Australia* 95 E5 32 17 S 152 29 E
Tundla, *India* 68 F8 27 12N 78 17 E
Tundubai, *Sudan* 80 D2 18 36N 28 35 E
Tunduru, *Tanzania* 87 E4 11 8 S 37 25 E
Tundzha →, *Bulgaria* 41 E10 41 40N 26 35 E
Tunga Pass, *India* 67 E19 29 0N 94 14 E
Tungabhadra →, *India* 66 M11 15 57N 78 15 E
Tungaru, *Sudan* 81 E3 10 9N 30 52 E
Tungla, *Nic.* 120 D3 13 24N 84 21W
Tungsha Tao, *Taiwan* 59 G11 20 45N 116 43 E
Tungshih, *Taiwan* 59 E13 24 12N 120 43 E
Tungsten, *Canada* 104 A3 61 57N 128 16W
Tunguska, Nizhnyaya →, *Russia* 51 C9 65 48N 88 4 E
Tunguska, Podkamennaya →, *Russia* 51 C10 61 50N 90 13 E
Tunica, *U.S.A.* 113 H9 34 41N 90 23W
Tunis, *Tunisia* 79 A8 36 50N 10 11 E
Tunisia ■, *Africa* 79 A7 33 30N 9 10 E
Tunja, *Colombia* 124 B4 5 33N 73 25W
Tunkhannock, *U.S.A.* 111 E9 41 32N 75 57W
Tunliu, *China* 56 F7 36 13N 112 52 E
Tunnsjøen, *Norway* 8 D15 64 45N 13 25 E
Tunø, *Denmark* 11 J4 55 57N 10 27 E
Tunungayualok I., *Canada* 103 A7 56 0N 61 0W
Tunuyán, *Argentina* 126 C2 33 35 S 69 0W
Tunuyán →, *Argentina* 126 C2 33 33 S 67 30W
Tuo Jiang →, *China* 58 C5 28 50N 105 35 E
Tuolumne, *U.S.A.* 116 H6 37 58N 120 15W
Tuolumne →, *U.S.A.* 116 H5 37 36N 121 13W
Tūp Āghāj, *Iran* 70 B5 36 3N 47 50 E
Tupã, *Brazil* 127 A5 21 57 S 50 28W
Tupelo, *U.S.A.* 109 H1 34 16N 88 43W
Tupik, *Russia* 46 E7 55 42N 33 22 E
Tupinambaranas, *Brazil* 124 D7 3 0 S 58 0W
Tupiza, *Bolivia* 126 A2 21 30 S 65 40W
Tupižnica, *Serbia, Yug.* 40 C6 43 43N 22 10 E
Tupman, *U.S.A.* 117 K7 35 18N 119 21W
Tupper, *Canada* 104 B4 55 32N 120 1W
Tupper Lake, *U.S.A.* 111 B10 44 14N 74 28W
Tupungato, Cerro, *S. Amer.* 126 C2 33 15 S 69 50W
Tuquan, *China* 57 B11 45 18N 121 38 E
Túquerres, *Colombia* 124 C3 1 5N 77 37W
Tura, *Russia* 51 C11 64 20N 100 17 E
Turabah, *Si. Arabia* 70 D4 28 20N 43 15 E
Turabah, *Si. Arabia* 80 C5 21 15N 41 34 E
Tūrān, *Iran* 71 C8 35 39N 56 42 E
Turan, *Russia* 51 D10 51 55N 95 0 E
Ṭurayf, *Si. Arabia* 70 D3 31 41N 38 39 E
Turbacz, *Poland* 45 J7 49 30N 20 8 E
Turbe, *Bos.-H.* 42 F2 44 15N 17 35 E
Turčianske Teplice, *Slovak Rep.* 27 C11 48 52N 18 52 E
Turcoaia, *Romania* 43 E13 45 7N 28 11 E
Turda, *Romania* 43 D8 46 34N 23 47 E
Turek, *Poland* 45 F5 52 3N 18 30 E
Turen, *Venezuela* 124 B5 9 17N 69 6W
Turfan = Turpan, *China* 60 B3 43 58N 89 10 E
Turfan Depression = Turpan Hami, *China* 52 E12 42 40N 89 25 E
Turgeon →, *Canada* 102 C4 50 0N 78 56W
Tŭrgovishte, *Bulgaria* 41 C10 43 17N 26 38 E
Turgut, *Turkey* 39 D10 37 22N 28 4 E
Turgutlu, *Turkey* 39 C9 38 30N 27 43 E
Turgwe →, *Zimbabwe* 89 C5 21 31 S 32 15 E
Turhal, *Turkey* 72 B7 40 24N 36 5 E
Turia →, *Spain* 33 F4 39 27N 0 19W
Turiaçu, *Brazil* 125 D9 1 40 S 45 19W
Turiaçu →, *Brazil* 125 D9 1 36 S 45 19W
Turiec →, *Slovak Rep.* 27 B11 49 7N 18 55 E
Turin = Torino, *Italy* 28 C4 45 3N 7 40 E
Turkana, L., *Africa* 86 B4 3 30N 36 5 E
Türkeli, *Turkey* 41 F11 40 30N 27 30 E
Turkestan = Türkistan, *Kazakstan* 50 E7 43 17N 68 16 E
Túrkeve, *Hungary* 42 C5 47 6N 20 44 E
Turkey ■, *Eurasia* 72 C7 39 0N 36 0 E
Turkey Creek, *Australia* 92 C4 17 2 S 128 12 E
Turki, *Russia* 48 D6 52 0N 43 15 E
Türkistan, *Kazakstan* 50 E7 43 17N 68 16 E
Türkmenbashi, *Turkmenistan* 50 E6 40 5N 53 5 E
Turkmenistan ■, *Asia* 50 F6 39 0N 59 0 E
Türkmenli, *Turkey* 39 B8 39 45N 26 30 E
Türkoğlu, *Turkey* 72 D7 37 23N 36 50 E
Turks & Caicos Is. ■, *W. Indies* 121 B5 21 20N 71 20W
Turks Island Passage, *W. Indies* 121 B5 21 30N 71 30W
Turku, *Finland* 9 F20 60 30N 22 19 E
Turkwel →, *Kenya* 86 B4 3 6N 36 6 E
Turlock, *U.S.A.* 116 H6 37 30N 120 51W
Turnagain →, *Canada* 104 B3 59 12N 127 35W
Turnagain, C., *N.Z.* 91 J6 40 28 S 176 38 E
Turneffe Is., *Belize* 119 D7 17 20N 87 50W
Turner, *U.S.A.* 114 B9 48 51N 108 24W
Turner Pt., *Australia* 94 A1 11 47 S 133 32 E
Turner Valley, *Canada* 104 C6 50 40N 114 17W
Turners Falls, *U.S.A.* 111 D12 42 36N 72 33W
Turnhout, *Belgium* 17 C4 51 19N 4 57 E
Türnitz, *Austria* 26 D8 47 55N 15 29 E
Turnor L., *Canada* 105 B7 56 35N 108 35W
Turnov, *Czech Rep.* 26 A8 50 34N 15 10 E
Tŭrnovo = Veliko Tŭrnovo, *Bulgaria* 41 C9 43 5N 25 41 E
Turnu Măgurele, *Romania* 43 G9 43 46N 24 56 E
Turnu Roșu, P., *Romania* 43 E9 45 33N 24 17 E
Turobin, *Poland* 45 H9 50 50N 22 44 E
Turpan, *China* 60 B3 43 58N 89 10 E
Turpan Hami, *China* 52 E12 42 40N 89 25 E
Turrës, Kala e, *Albania* 40 E3 41 10N 19 28 E
Turrës, Kalaja e = Turrës, Kala e, *Albania* 40 E3 41 10N 19 28 E
Turriff, *U.K.* 14 D6 57 32N 2 27W
Tursāq, *Iraq* 70 C5 33 27N 45 47 E
Tursi, *Italy* 31 B9 40 15N 16 28 E
Turtle Head I., *Australia* 94 A3 10 56 S 142 37 E
Turtle Is., *S. Leone* 82 D2 7 40N 13 0 E
Turtle L., *Canada* 105 C7 53 36N 108 38W
Turtle Lake, *U.S.A.* 112 B4 47 31N 100 53W
Turtleford, *Canada* 105 C7 53 23N 108 57W
Turukhansk, *Russia* 51 C9 65 21N 88 5 E
Turzovka, *Slovak Rep.* 27 B11 49 25N 18 35 E
Tuscaloosa, *U.S.A.* 109 J2 33 12N 87 34W
Tuscánia, *Italy* 29 F8 42 25N 11 52 E
Tuscany = Toscana □, *Italy* 28 E8 43 25N 11 0 E
Tuscarawas →, *U.S.A.* 110 F3 40 24N 81 25W
Tuscarora Mt., *U.S.A.* 110 F7 40 55N 77 55W
Tuscola, *Ill., U.S.A.* 108 F1 39 48N 88 17W
Tuscola, *Tex., U.S.A.* 113 J5 32 12N 99 48W
Tuscumbia, *U.S.A.* 109 H2 34 44N 87 42W
Tuskegee, *U.S.A.* 109 J3 32 25N 85 42W
Tustin, *U.S.A.* 117 M9 33 44N 117 49W
Tuszyn, *Poland* 45 G6 51 36N 19 33 E
Tutak, *Turkey* 73 C10 39 31N 42 46 E
Tutayev, *Russia* 46 D10 57 53N 39 32 E
Tuticorin, *India* 66 Q11 8 50N 78 12 E
Tutin, *Serbia, Yug.* 40 D4 42 58N 20 20 E
Tutóia, *Brazil* 125 D10 2 45 S 42 20W
Tutong, *Brunei* 62 D4 4 47N 114 40 E
Tutova →, *Romania* 43 D12 46 7N 27 30 E
Tutrakan, *Bulgaria* 41 B10 44 2N 26 40 E
Tuttle Creek L., *U.S.A.* 112 F6 39 22N 96 40W
Tuttlingen, *Germany* 25 H4 47 58N 8 48 E
Tutuala, *Indonesia* 63 F7 8 25 S 127 15 E
Tutuila, *Amer. Samoa* 91 B13 14 19 S 170 50W
Tutume, *Botswana* 85 J5 20 30 S 27 5 E
Tutun, *Egypt* 80 J7 29 9N 30 46 E
Tututepec, *Mexico* 119 D5 16 9N 97 38W
Tuva □, *Russia* 51 D10 51 30N 95 0 E
Tuvalu ■, *Pac. Oc.* 96 H9 8 0 S 178 0 E
Tuxer Alpen, *Austria* 26 D4 47 10N 11 45 E
Tuxpan, *Mexico* 119 C5 20 58N 97 23W
Tuxtla Gutiérrez, *Mexico* 119 D6 16 50N 93 10W
Tuy = Tui, *Spain* 34 C2 42 3N 8 39W
Tuy An, *Vietnam* 64 F7 13 17N 109 16 E
Tuy Duc, *Vietnam* 65 F6 12 15N 107 27 E
Tuy Hoa, *Vietnam* 64 F7 13 5N 109 10 E
Tuy Phong, *Vietnam* 65 G7 11 14N 108 43 E
Tuya L., *Canada* 104 B2 59 7N 130 35W
Tuyen Hoa, *Vietnam* 64 D6 17 50N 106 10 E
Tuyen Quang, *Vietnam* 58 G5 21 50N 105 10 E
Tūysarkān, *Iran* 71 C6 34 33N 48 27 E
Tuz Gölü, *Turkey* 72 C5 38 42N 33 18 E
Ṭūz Khurmātū, *Iraq* 70 C5 34 56N 44 38 E
Tuzi, *Montenegro, Yug.* 40 D3 42 22N 19 20 E
Tuzla, *Bos.-H.* 42 F3 44 34N 18 41 E
Tuzlov →, *Russia* 47 J10 47 17N 39 57 E
Tuzluca, *Turkey* 73 B10 40 3N 43 39 E
Tvååker, *Sweden* 11 G6 57 4N 12 25 E
Tvardița, *Moldova* 43 D13 46 9N 28 58 E
Tver, *Russia* 46 D8 56 55N 35 55 E
Tvrdošín, *Slovak Rep.* 27 B12 49 21N 19 35 E
Tvrdošovce, *Slovak Rep.* 27 C11 48 6N 18 4 E
Tvŭrditsa, *Bulgaria* 41 D9 42 42N 25 53 E
Twain, *U.S.A.* 116 E5 40 1N 121 3W
Twain Harte, *U.S.A.* 116 G6 38 2N 120 14W
Twardogóra, *Poland* 45 G4 51 23N 17 28 E
Tweed, *Canada* 110 B7 44 29N 77 19W
Tweed →, *U.K.* 14 F6 55 45N 2 0W
Tweed Heads, *Australia* 95 D5 28 10 S 153 31 E
Tweedsmuir Prov. Park, *Canada* 104 C3 53 0N 126 20W
Twentynine Palms, *U.S.A.* 117 L10 34 8N 116 3W
Twillingate, *Canada* 103 C9 49 42N 54 45W
Twin Bridges, *U.S.A.* 114 D7 45 33N 112 20W
Twin Falls, *Canada* 103 B7 53 30N 64 32W
Twin Falls, *U.S.A.* 114 E6 42 34N 114 28W
Twin Valley, *U.S.A.* 112 B6 47 16N 96 16W
Twinsburg, *U.S.A.* 110 E3 41 18N 81 26W
Twistringen, *Germany* 24 C4 52 48N 8 37 E
Twitchell Reservoir, *U.S.A.* 117 L6 34 59N 120 19W
Two Harbors, *U.S.A.* 112 B9 47 2N 91 40W
Two Hills, *Canada* 104 C6 53 43N 111 52W
Two Rivers, *U.S.A.* 108 C2 44 9N 87 34W
Two Rocks, *Australia* 93 F2 31 30 S 115 35 E
Twofold B., *Australia* 95 F4 37 8 S 149 59 E
Tyachiv, *Ukraine* 47 H2 48 1N 23 35 E
Tychy, *Poland* 45 H5 50 9N 18 59 E
Tyczyn, *Poland* 45 J9 49 58N 22 2 E
Tykocin, *Poland* 45 E9 53 13N 22 46 E
Tyler, *Minn., U.S.A.* 112 C6 44 18N 96 8W
Tyler, *Tex., U.S.A.* 113 J7 32 21N 95 18W
Tyligul →, *Ukraine* 47 J6 47 4N 30 57 E
Týn nad Vltavou, *Czech Rep.* 26 B7 49 13N 14 26 E
Tynda, *Russia* 51 D13 55 10N 124 43 E
Tyndall, *U.S.A.* 112 D6 43 0N 97 50W
Tyne →, *U.K.* 12 C6 54 59N 1 32W
Tyne & Wear □, *U.K.* 12 B6 55 6N 1 17W
Týnec nad Sázavou, *Czech Rep.* 26 B7 49 50N 14 36 E
Tynemouth, *U.K.* 12 B6 55 1N 1 26W
Tyre = Sūr, *Lebanon* 75 B4 33 19N 35 16 E
Tyrifjorden, *Norway* 9 F14 60 2N 10 8 E
Tyringe, *Sweden* 11 H7 56 9N 13 35 E
Tyrnyauz, *Russia* 49 J6 43 21N 42 45 E
Tyrol = Tirol □, *Austria* 26 D3 47 3N 10 43 E
Tyrone, *U.S.A.* 110 F6 40 40N 78 14W
Tyrone □, *U.K.* 15 B4 54 38N 7 11W
Tyrrell →, *Australia* 95 F3 35 26 S 142 51 E
Tyrrell, L., *Australia* 95 F3 35 20 S 142 50 E
Tyrrell L., *Canada* 105 A7 63 7N 105 27W
Tyrrhenian Sea, *Medit. S.* 6 G8 40 0N 12 30 E
Tysfjorden, *Norway* 8 B17 68 7N 16 25 E
Tystberga, *Sweden* 11 F11 58 51N 17 15 E
Tytuvėnai, *Lithuania* 44 C10 55 36N 23 12 E
Tyub Karagan, Mys, *Kazakstan* 49 H10 44 40N 50 19 E
Tyuleni, Ostrova, *Kazakstan* 49 H10 45 2N 50 16 E
Tyuleniy, *Russia* 49 H8 44 28N 47 30 E
Tyuleniy, Mys, *Azerbaijan* 49 K10 40 12N 50 22 E
Tyumen, *Russia* 50 D7 57 11N 65 29 E
Tywi →, *U.K.* 13 F3 51 48N 4 21W
Tywyn, *U.K.* 13 E3 52 35N 4 5W
Tzaneen, *S. Africa* 89 C5 23 47 S 30 9 E
Tzermiádhes, *Greece* 36 D7 35 12N 25 29 E
Tzoumérka, Óros, *Greece* 38 B3 39 30N 21 26 E
Tzukong = Zigong, *China* 58 C5 29 15N 104 48 E

U

U Taphao, *Thailand* 64 F3 12 35N 101 0 E
U.S.A. = United States of America ■, *N. Amer.* 106 C7 37 0N 96 0W
Uatumã →, *Brazil* 124 D7 2 26 S 57 37W
Uaupés, *Brazil* 124 D5 0 8 S 67 5W
Uaupés →, *Brazil* 124 C5 0 2N 67 16W
Uaxactún, *Guatemala* 120 C2 17 25N 89 29W
Ub, *Serbia, Yug.* 40 B4 44 28N 20 6 E
Ubá, *Brazil* 127 A7 21 8 S 43 0W
Uba, *Nigeria* 83 C7 10 29N 13 13 E
Ubaitaba, *Brazil* 125 F11 14 18 S 39 20W
Ubangi = Oubangi →, *Dem. Rep. of the Congo* 84 E3 0 30 S 17 50 E
Ubauro, *Pakistan* 68 E3 28 15N 69 45 E
Ubaye →, *France* 21 D10 44 28N 6 18 E
Ubayyiḍ, W. al →, *Iraq* 70 C4 32 34N 43 48 E
Ube, *Japan* 55 H5 33 56N 131 15 E
Úbeda, *Spain* 35 G7 38 3N 3 23W
Uberaba, *Brazil* 125 G9 19 50 S 47 55W
Uberlândia, *Brazil* 125 G9 19 0 S 48 20W
Überlingen, *Germany* 25 H5 47 46N 9 10 E
Ubiaja, *Nigeria* 83 D6 6 41N 6 22 E
Ubolratna Res., *Thailand* 64 D4 16 45N 102 30 E
Ubombo, *S. Africa* 89 D5 27 31 S 32 4 E
Ubon Ratchathani, *Thailand* 64 E5 15 15N 104 50 E
Ubondo, *Dem. Rep. of the Congo* 86 C2 0 55 S 25 42 E
Ubort →, *Belarus* 47 F5 52 6N 28 30 E
Ubrique, *Spain* 35 J5 36 41N 5 27W
Ubundu, *Dem. Rep. of the Congo* 86 C2 0 22 S 25 30 E
Ucayali →, *Peru* 122 D3 4 30 S 73 30W
Uchab, *Namibia* 88 B2 19 47 S 17 42 E
Uchiura-Wan, *Japan* 54 C10 42 25N 140 40 E
Uchquduq, *Uzbekistan* 50 E7 41 50N 62 50 E
Uchte, *Germany* 24 C4 52 30N 8 54 E
Uchur →, *Russia* 51 D14 58 48N 130 35 E
Uckermark, *Germany* 24 B9 53 5N 13 30 E
Ucluelet, *Canada* 104 D3 48 57N 125 32W
Uda →, *Russia* 51 D14 54 42N 135 14 E
Udagamandalam, *India* 66 P10 11 30N 76 44 E
Udainagar, *India* 68 H7 22 33N 76 13 E
Udaipur, *India* 68 G5 24 36N 73 44 E
Udaipur Garhi, *Nepal* 69 F12 27 0N 86 35 E
Udala, *India* 69 J12 21 35N 86 34 E
Udbina, *Croatia* 29 D12 44 31N 15 47 E
Uddeholm, *Sweden* 10 D7 60 1N 13 38 E
Uddevalla, *Sweden* 11 F5 58 21N 11 55 E
Uddjaur, *Sweden* 8 D17 65 56N 17 49 E
Uden, *Neths.* 17 C5 51 40N 5 37 E
Udgir, *India* 66 K10 18 25N 77 5 E
Udhampur, *India* 69 C6 33 0N 75 5 E
Udi, *Nigeria* 83 D6 6 17N 7 21 E
Údine, *Italy* 29 B10 46 3N 13 14 E
Udmurtia □, *Russia* 50 D6 57 30N 52 30 E
Udon Thani, *Thailand* 64 D4 17 29N 102 46 E
Udupi, *India* 66 N9 13 25N 74 42 E
Udvoy Balkan, *Bulgaria* 41 D10 42 50N 26 50 E
Udzungwa Range, *Tanzania* 87 D4 9 30 S 35 10 E
Ueckermünde, *Germany* 24 B10 53 44N 14 1 E
Ueda, *Japan* 55 F9 36 24N 138 16 E
Uedineniya, Os., *Russia* 4 B12 78 0N 85 0 E
Uele →, *Dem. Rep. of the Congo* 84 D4 3 45N 24 45 E
Uelen, *Russia* 51 C19 66 10N 170 0W
Uelzen, *Germany* 24 C6 52 57N 10 32 E
Uetersen, *Germany* 24 B5 53 40N 9 40 E
Uetze, *Germany* 24 C6 52 28N 10 11 E
Ufa, *Russia* 50 D6 54 45N 55 55 E
Uffenheim, *Germany* 25 F6 49 33N 10 14 E
Ugab →, *Namibia* 88 C1 20 55 S 13 30 E
Ugalla →, *Tanzania* 86 D3 5 8 S 30 42 E
Uganda ■, *Africa* 86 B3 2 0N 32 0 E
Ugento, *Italy* 31 C11 39 56N 18 10 E
Ugep, *Nigeria* 83 D6 5 53N 8 2 E
Ughelli, *Nigeria* 83 D6 5 33N 6 0 E
Ugie, *S. Africa* 89 E4 31 10 S 28 13 E
Ugíjar, *Spain* 35 J7 36 58N 3 7W
Ugine, *France* 21 C10 45 45N 6 25 E
Uglegorsk, *Russia* 51 E15 49 5N 142 2 E
Uglich, *Russia* 46 D10 57 33N 38 20 E
Ugljan, *Croatia* 29 D12 44 12N 15 10 E
Ugljane, *Croatia* 29 E13 43 35N 16 46 E
Ugra →, *Russia* 46 E9 54 30N 36 7 E
Ugŭrchin, *Bulgaria* 41 C8 43 6N 24 26 E
Uh →, *Slovak Rep.* 27 C15 48 37N 22 0 E
Uherské Hradiště, *Czech Rep.* 27 B10 49 4N 17 30 E
Uherský Brod, *Czech Rep.* 27 B10 49 1N 17 40 E
Úhlava →, *Czech Rep.* 26 B6 49 45N 13 24 E
Uhlenhorst, *Namibia* 88 C2 23 45 S 17 55 E
Uhrichsville, *U.S.A.* 110 F3 40 24N 81 21W
Uibhist a Deas = South Uist, *U.K.* 14 D1 57 20N 7 15W
Uibhist a Tuath = North Uist, *U.K.* 14 D1 57 40N 7 15W
Uig, *U.K.* 14 D2 57 35N 6 21W
Uíge, *Angola* 84 F2 7 30 S 14 40 E
Uijŏngbu, *S. Korea* 57 F14 37 48N 127 0 E
Ŭiju, *N. Korea* 57 D13 40 15N 124 35 E
Uinta Mts., *U.S.A.* 114 F8 40 45N 110 30W
Uis, *Namibia* 88 B2 21 8 S 14 49 E
Uitenhage, *S. Africa* 88 E4 33 40 S 25 28 E
Uithuizen, *Neths.* 17 A6 53 24N 6 41 E
Ujazd, *Poland* 45 H5 50 23N 18 21 E
Újfehértó, *Hungary* 42 C6 47 49N 21 41 E
Ujh →, *India* 68 C6 32 10N 75 18 E
Ujhani, *India* 69 F8 28 0N 79 6 E
Uji-guntō, *Japan* 55 J4 31 15N 129 25 E
Ujjain, *India* 68 H6 23 9N 75 43 E
Ujście, *Poland* 45 E3 53 3N 16 45 E
Újszász, *Hungary* 42 C5 47 19N 20 7 E
Ujung Pandang, *Indonesia* 63 F5 5 10 S 119 20 E
Uka, *Russia* 51 D17 57 50N 162 0 E
Ukara I., *Tanzania* 86 C3 1 50 S 33 0 E
Uke-Shima, *Japan* 55 K4 28 2N 129 14 E
Ukerewe I., *Tanzania* 86 C3 2 0 S 33 0 E
Ukholovo, *Russia* 48 D5 53 47N 40 30 E
Ukhrul, *India* 67 G19 25 10N 94 25 E
Ukhta, *Russia* 50 C6 63 34N 53 41 E
Ukiah, *U.S.A.* 116 F3 39 9N 123 13W
Ukki Fort, *India* 69 C7 33 28N 76 54 E
Ukmergė, *Lithuania* 9 J21 55 15N 24 45 E
Ukraine ■, *Europe* 47 H7 49 0N 32 0 E
Ukwi, *Botswana* 88 C3 23 29 S 20 30 E
Ulaan-Uul, *Mongolia* 56 B6 44 13N 111 10 E
Ulaanbaatar, *Mongolia* 51 E11 47 55N 106 53 E
Ulaangom, *Mongolia* 60 A4 50 5N 92 10 E
Ulaanjirem, *Mongolia* 56 B3 45 5N 105 30 E
Ulamba, *Dem. Rep. of the Congo* 87 D1 9 3 S 23 38 E
Ulan Bator = Ulaanbaatar, *Mongolia* 51 E11 47 55N 106 53 E
Ulan Erge, *Russia* 49 G7 46 19N 44 53 E
Ulan Khol, *Russia* 49 H8 45 18N 47 4 E
Ulan Ude, *Russia* 51 D11 51 45N 107 40 E
Ulanów, *Poland* 45 H9 50 30N 22 16 E
Ulaș, *Sivas, Turkey* 72 C7 39 26N 37 2 E
Ulaș, *Tekirdağ, Turkey* 41 E11 41 14N 27 42 E
Ulaya, *Morogoro, Tanzania* 86 D4 7 3 S 36 55 E
Ulaya, *Tabora, Tanzania* 86 C3 4 25 S 33 30 E
Ulcinj, *Montenegro, Yug.* 40 E3 41 58N 19 10 E
Ulco, *S. Africa* 88 D3 28 21 S 24 15 E
Ulefoss, *Norway* 9 G13 59 17N 9 16 E
Ulëz, *Albania* 40 E3 41 46N 19 54 E
Ulëza = Ulëz, *Albania* 40 E3 41 46N 19 54 E
Ulfborg, *Denmark* 11 H2 56 16N 8 20 E
Ulhasnagar, *India* 66 K8 19 15N 73 10 E
Uliastay, *Mongolia* 60 B4 47 56N 97 28 E
Ulithi Atoll, *Pac. Oc.* 63 B9 10 0N 139 30 E
Uljma, *Serbia, Yug.* 42 E6 45 2N 21 10 E
Ulla →, *Spain* 34 C2 42 39N 8 44W
Ulladulla, *Australia* 95 F5 35 21 S 150 29 E
Ullapool, *U.K.* 14 D3 57 54N 5 9W
Ullared, *Sweden* 11 G6 57 8N 12 42 E
Ulldecona, *Spain* 32 E5 40 36N 0 20 E
Ullswater, *U.K.* 12 C5 54 34N 2 52W
Ullŭng-do, *S. Korea* 55 F5 37 30N 130 30 E
Ulm, *Germany* 25 G5 48 23N 9 58 E
Ulmarra, *Australia* 95 D5 29 37 S 153 4 E
Ulmeni, *Buzău, Romania* 43 E11 45 4N 26 40 E
Ulmeni, *Maramureș, Romania* 43 C8 47 28N 23 18 E
Ulonguè, *Mozam.* 87 E3 14 37 S 34 19 E
Ulricehamn, *Sweden* 11 G7 57 46N 13 26 E
Ulrika, *Sweden* 11 F9 58 5N 15 23 E
Ulsan, *S. Korea* 57 G15 35 20N 129 15 E
Ulsta, *U.K.* 14 A7 60 30N 1 9W
Ulster □, *U.K.* 15 B5 54 35N 6 30W
Ulstrem, *Bulgaria* 41 D10 42 1N 26 27 E
Ulubat Gölü, *Turkey* 41 F12 40 9N 28 35 E
Ulubey, *Turkey* 39 C11 38 25N 29 18 E
Uluborlu, *Turkey* 39 C12 38 4N 30 28 E
Uluçinar, *Turkey* 72 D6 36 21N 35 57 E
Uludağ, *Turkey* 41 F13 40 4N 29 13 E
Uludere, *Turkey* 73 D10 37 28N 42 42 E
Uluguru Mts., *Tanzania* 86 D4 7 15 S 37 40 E
Ulukışla, *Turkey* 72 D6 37 33N 34 28 E
Ulungur He →, *China* 60 B3 47 1N 87 24 E
Uluru = Ayers Rock, *Australia* 93 E5 25 23 S 131 5 E
Uluru Nat. Park, *Australia* 93 E5 25 15 S 131 20 E
Ulutau, *Kazakstan* 50 E7 48 39N 67 1 E
Ulva, *U.K.* 14 E2 56 29N 6 13W

Ulverston, U.K. **12 C4** 54 13N 3 5W
Ulverstone, Australia **94 G4** 41 11 S 146 11 E
Ulya, Russia **51 D15** 59 10N 142 0 E
Ulyanovsk = Simbirsk, Russia **48 C9** 54 20N 48 25 E
Ulyasutay = Uliastay, Mongolia **60 B4** 47 56N 97 28 E
Ulysses, U.S.A. **113 G4** 37 35N 101 22W
Umag, Croatia **29 C10** 45 26N 13 31 E
Umala, Bolivia **124 G5** 17 25 S 68 5W
Uman, Ukraine **47 H6** 48 40N 30 12 E
Umaria, India **67 H12** 23 35N 80 50 E
Umarkot, Pakistan **66 G6** 25 15N 69 40 E
Umarpada, India **68 J5** 21 27N 73 30 E
Umatilla, U.S.A. **114 D4** 45 55N 119 21W
Umbagog L., U.S.A. **111 B13** 44 46N 71 3W
Umbakumba, Australia **94 A2** 13 47 S 136 50 E
Umbértide, Italy **29 E9** 43 18N 12 20 E
Umbrella Mts., N.Z. **91 L2** 45 35 S 169 5 E
Umbria □, Italy **29 F9** 42 53N 12 30 E
Ume älv →, Sweden **8 E19** 63 45N 20 20 E
Umeå, Sweden **8 E19** 63 45N 20 20 E
Umera, Indonesia **63 E7** 0 12 S 129 37 E
Umfuli →, Zimbabwe **87 F2** 17 30 S 29 23 E
Umgusa, Zimbabwe **87 F2** 19 29 S 27 52 E
Umim Urūmah, Si. Arabia **80 B4** 25 43N 36 35 E
Umka, Serbia, Yug. **40 B4** 44 40N 20 19 E
Umkomaas, S. Africa **89 E5** 30 13 S 30 48 E
Umlazi, S. Africa **85 L6** 29 59 S 30 54 E
Umm ad Daraj, J., Jordan **75 C4** 32 18N 35 48 E
Umm al Qaywayn, U.A.E. **71 E7** 25 30N 55 35 E
Umm al Qittayn, Jordan **75 C5** 32 18N 36 40 E
Umm Arda, Sudan **81 D3** 15 17N 32 31 E
Umm Bāb, Qatar **71 E6** 25 12N 50 48 E
Umm Badr, Sudan **81 E2** 14 13N 27 58 E
Umm Baiyud, Sudan **81 E3** 12 5N 31 40 E
Umm Bel, Sudan **81 E2** 13 35N 28 0 E
Umm Birkah, Si. Arabia **80 B4** 27 44N 36 31 E
Umm Boim, Sudan **81 E2** 11 43N 25 27 E
Umm Dam, Sudan **81 E3** 13 45N 30 59 E
Umm Debi, Sudan **81 E3** 14 37N 30 23 E
Umm Dubban, Sudan **81 D3** 15 23N 32 52 E
Umm el Fahm, Israel **75 C4** 32 31N 35 9 E
Umm Gafala, Sudan **81 E2** 13 22N 27 15 E
Umm Gimala, Sudan **81 E2** 11 27N 28 12 E
Umm Inderaba, Sudan **80 D3** 15 58N 30 41 E
Umm Keddada, Sudan **81 E2** 13 33N 26 35 E
Umm Koweika, Sudan **81 E3** 13 10N 32 16 E
Umm Lajj, Si. Arabia **70 E3** 25 0N 37 23 E
Umm Merwa, Sudan **80 D3** 18 4N 32 30 E
Umm Qantur, Sudan **81 E3** 14 17N 31 22 E
Umm Qurein, Sudan **81 F2** 9 58N 28 55 E
Umm Ruwaba, Sudan **81 E3** 12 50N 31 20 E
Umm Saiyala, Sudan **81 E3** 14 25N 31 10 E
Umm Shanqa, Sudan **81 E2** 13 14N 27 14 E
Umm Shutur, Sudan **81 F3** 7 17N 33 14 E
Umm Sidr, Sudan **81 E2** 14 29N 25 10 E
Umm Zehetir, Egypt **80 J8** 28 48N 32 31 E
Umnak I., U.S.A. **100 C3** 53 15N 168 20W
Umniati →, Zimbabwe **87 F2** 16 49 S 28 45 E
Umpqua →, U.S.A. **114 E1** 43 40N 124 12W
Umreth, India **68 H5** 22 41N 73 4 E
Umtata, S. Africa **89 E4** 31 36 S 28 49 E
Umuahia, Nigeria **83 D6** 5 31N 7 26 E
Umuarama, Brazil **127 A5** 23 45 S 53 20W
Umurbey, Turkey **41 F10** 40 13N 26 36 E
Umvukwe Ra., Zimbabwe **87 F3** 16 45 S 30 45 E
Umzimvubu, S. Africa **89 E4** 31 38 S 29 33 E
Umzingwane →, Zimbabwe **87 G2** 22 12 S 29 56 E
Umzinto, S. Africa **89 E5** 30 15 S 30 45 E
Una, India **68 J4** 20 46N 71 8 E
Una →, Bos.-H. **29 D13** 45 0N 16 20 E
Unac →, Bos.-H. **29 D13** 44 30N 16 9 E
Unadilla, U.S.A. **111 D9** 42 20N 75 19W
Unalakleet, U.S.A. **100 B3** 63 52N 160 47W
Unalaska, U.S.A. **100 C3** 53 53N 166 32W
Unalaska I., U.S.A. **100 C3** 53 35N 166 50W
'Unayzah, Si. Arabia **70 E4** 26 6N 43 58 E
'Unāzah, J., Asia **70 C3** 32 12N 39 18 E
Uncastillo, Spain **32 C3** 42 21N 1 8W
Uncía, Bolivia **124 G5** 18 25 S 66 40W
Uncompahgre Peak, U.S.A. **115 G10** 38 4N 107 28W
Uncompahgre Plateau, U.S.A. **115 G9** 38 20N 108 15W
Unden, Sweden **11 F8** 58 45N 14 25 E
Underbool, Australia **95 F3** 35 10 S 141 51 E
Undersaker, Sweden **10 A7** 63 19N 13 21 E
Unecha, Russia **47 F7** 52 50N 32 37 E
Ungarie, Australia **95 E4** 33 38 S 146 56 E
Ungarra, Australia **95 E2** 34 12 S 136 2 E
Ungava, Pén. d', Canada **101 C12** 60 0N 74 0W
Ungava B., Canada **101 C13** 59 30N 67 30W
Ungeny = Ungheni, Moldova **43 C12** 47 11N 27 51 E
Unggi, N. Korea **57 C16** 42 16N 130 28 E
Ungheni, Moldova **43 C12** 47 11N 27 51 E
Unguala →, Ethiopia **81 F5** 8 6N 41 9 E
Ungwatiri, Sudan **81 D4** 16 52N 36 10 E
Uni, Russia **48 B10** 57 46N 51 31 E
União da Vitória, Brazil **127 B5** 26 13 S 51 5W
Uničov, Czech Rep. **27 B10** 49 46N 17 8 E
Uniejów, Poland **45 G5** 51 59N 18 46 E
Unije, Croatia **29 D11** 44 40N 14 15 E
Unimak I., U.S.A. **100 C3** 54 45N 164 0W
Union, Miss., U.S.A. **113 J10** 32 34N 89 7W
Union, Mo., U.S.A. **112 F9** 38 27N 91 0W
Union, S.C., U.S.A. **109 H5** 34 43N 81 37W
Union City, Calif., U.S.A. **116 H4** 37 36N 122 1W
Union City, N.J., U.S.A. **111 F10** 40 45N 74 2W
Union City, Pa., U.S.A. **110 E5** 41 54N 79 51W
Union City, Tenn., U.S.A. **113 G10** 36 26N 89 3W
Union Gap, U.S.A. **114 C3** 46 33N 120 28W
Union Springs, U.S.A. **109 J3** 32 9N 85 43W
Uniondale, S. Africa **88 E3** 33 39 S 23 7 E
Uniontown, U.S.A. **108 F6** 39 54N 79 44W
Unionville, U.S.A. **112 E8** 40 29N 93 1W
Unirea, Romania **43 F12** 44 15N 27 35 E
United Arab Emirates ■, Asia **71 F7** 23 50N 54 0 E
United Kingdom ■, Europe **7 E5** 53 0N 2 0W
United States of America ■, N. Amer. **106 C7** 37 0N 96 0W
Unity, Canada **105 C7** 52 30N 109 5W
Universales, Mtes., Spain **32 E3** 40 18N 1 33W
University Park, U.S.A. **115 K10** 32 17N 106 45W
Unjha, India **68 H5** 23 46N 72 24 E
Unna, Germany **24 D3** 51 32N 7 42 E
Unnao, India **69 F9** 26 35N 80 30 E
Uno, Ilha, Guinea-Biss. **82 C1** 11 15N 16 13W
Unst, U.K. **14 A8** 60 44N 0 53W
Unstrut →, Germany **24 D7** 51 10N 11 48 E
Unterfranken □, Germany **25 F5** 50 0N 10 0 E
Unterschleissheim, Germany **25 G7** 48 17N 11 34 E
Unuk →, Canada **104 B2** 56 5N 131 3W
Ünye, Turkey **72 B7** 41 5N 37 15 E
Unzha, Russia **48 A7** 58 0N 44 0 E
Unzha →, Russia **48 B6** 57 49N 43 47 E
Uozu, Japan **55 F8** 36 48N 137 24 E
Upata, Venezuela **124 B6** 8 1N 62 24W
Upemba, L., Dem. Rep. of the Congo **87 D2** 8 30 S 26 20 E
Upernavik, Greenland **4 B5** 72 49N 56 20W
Upington, S. Africa **88 D3** 28 25 S 21 15 E
Upleta, India **68 J4** 21 46N 70 16 E
Upolu, Samoa **91 A13** 13 58 S 172 0W
Upper □, Ghana **83 C4** 10 30N 1 30W
Upper Alkali L., U.S.A. **114 F3** 41 47N 120 8W
Upper Arrow L., Canada **104 C5** 50 30N 117 50W
Upper Austria = Oberösterreich □, Austria **26 C7** 48 10N 14 0 E
Upper Foster L., Canada **105 B7** 56 47N 105 20W
Upper Hutt, N.Z. **91 J5** 41 8 S 175 5 E
Upper Klamath L., U.S.A. **114 E3** 42 25N 121 55W
Upper Lake, U.S.A. **116 F4** 39 10N 122 54W
Upper Musquodoboit, Canada **103 C7** 45 10N 62 58W
Upper Red L., U.S.A. **112 A7** 48 8N 94 45W
Upper Sandusky, U.S.A. **108 E4** 40 50N 83 17W
Upper Volta = Burkina Faso ■, Africa **82 C4** 12 0N 1 0W
Upphärad, Sweden **11 F6** 58 9N 12 19 E
Uppland, Sweden **10 E11** 59 59N 17 48 E
Upplands-Väsby, Sweden **10 E11** 59 31N 17 54 E
Uppsala, Sweden **10 E11** 59 53N 17 38 E
Uppsala län □, Sweden **10 D11** 60 0N 17 30 E
Upshi, India **69 C7** 33 48N 77 52 E
Upstart, C., Australia **94 B4** 19 41 S 147 45 E
Upton, U.S.A. **112 C2** 44 6N 104 38W
Ur, Iraq **70 D5** 30 55N 46 25 E
Urad Qianqi, China **56 D5** 40 40N 108 30 E
Urakawa, Japan **54 C11** 42 9N 142 47 E
Ural = Zhayyq →, Kazakstan **50 E6** 47 0N 51 48 E
Ural, Australia **95 E4** 33 21 S 146 12 E
Ural Mts. = Uralskie Gory, Eurasia **50 D6** 60 0N 59 0 E
Uralla, Australia **95 E5** 30 37 S 151 29 E
Uralsk = Oral, Kazakstan **48 E10** 51 20N 51 20 E
Uralskie Gory, Eurasia **50 D6** 60 0N 59 0 E
Urambo, Tanzania **86 D3** 5 4 S 32 0 E
Urana, Australia **95 F4** 35 15 S 146 21 E
Urandangi, Australia **94 C2** 21 32 S 138 14 E
Uranium City, Canada **105 B7** 59 34N 108 37W
Uraricoera →, Brazil **124 C6** 3 2N 60 30W
Urawa, Japan **55 G9** 35 50N 139 40 E
Uray, Russia **50 C7** 60 5N 65 15 E
'Uray'irah, Si. Arabia **71 E6** 25 57N 48 53 E
Urbana, Ill., U.S.A. **108 E1** 40 7N 88 12W
Urbana, Ohio, U.S.A. **108 E4** 40 7N 83 45W
Urbánia, Italy **29 E9** 43 40N 12 31 E
Urbel →, Spain **34 C7** 42 21N 3 40W
Urbino, Italy **29 E9** 43 43N 12 38 E
Urbión, Picos de, Spain **32 C2** 42 1N 2 52W
Urcos, Peru **124 F4** 13 40 S 71 38W
Urdinarrain, Argentina **126 C4** 32 37 S 58 52W
Urdos, France **20 F3** 42 51N 0 35W
Urdzhar, Kazakstan **50 E9** 47 5N 81 38 E
Ure →, U.K. **12 C6** 54 5N 1 20W
Uren, Russia **48 B7** 57 35N 45 55 E
Ures, Mexico **118 B2** 29 30N 110 30W
Urfa = Sanliurfa, Turkey **70 B3** 37 12N 38 50 E
Urganch, Uzbekistan **50 E7** 41 40N 60 41 E
Urgench = Urganch, Uzbekistan **50 E7** 41 40N 60 41 E
Ürgüp, Turkey **70 B2** 38 38N 34 56 E
Uri, India **69 B6** 34 8N 74 2 E
Uri □, Switz. **25 J4** 46 43N 8 35 E
Uribia, Colombia **124 A4** 11 43N 72 16W
Uricani, Romania **42 E8** 45 20N 23 9 E
Uriondo, Bolivia **126 A3** 21 41 S 64 41W
Urique, Mexico **118 B3** 27 13N 107 55W
Urique →, Mexico **118 B3** 26 29N 107 58W
Urk, Neths. **17 B5** 52 39N 5 36 E
Urla, Turkey **39 C8** 38 20N 26 47 E
Urlați, Romania **43 F11** 44 59N 26 15 E
Urmia = Orūmīyeh, Iran **70 B5** 37 40N 45 0 E
Urmia, L. = Orūmīyeh, Daryācheh-ye, Iran **70 B5** 37 50N 45 30 E
Uroševac, Kosovo, Yug. **40 D5** 42 23N 21 10 E
Urshult, Sweden **11 H8** 56 31N 14 50 E
Uruaçu, Brazil **125 F9** 14 30 S 49 10W
Uruapan, Mexico **118 D4** 19 30N 102 0W
Urubamba →, Peru **124 F4** 10 43 S 73 48W
Uruçara, Brazil **124 D7** 2 32 S 57 45W
Uruçuí, Brazil **125 E10** 7 20 S 44 28W
Uruguai →, Brazil **127 B5** 26 0 S 53 30W
Uruguaiana, Brazil **126 B4** 29 50 S 57 0W
Uruguay ■, S. Amer. **126 C4** 32 30 S 56 30W
Uruguay →, S. Amer. **126 C4** 34 12 S 58 18W
Urumchi = Ürümqi, China **50 E9** 43 45N 87 45 E
Ürümqi, China **50 E9** 43 45N 87 45 E
Urup →, Russia **49 H5** 45 0N 41 10 E
Urup, Ostrov, Russia **51 E16** 46 0N 151 0 E
Uryupinsk, Russia **48 E5** 50 45N 41 58 E
Urzhum, Russia **48 B9** 57 10N 49 56 E
Urziceni, Romania **43 F11** 44 40N 26 42 E
Usa →, Russia **50 C6** 66 16N 59 49 E
Uşak, Turkey **39 C11** 38 43N 29 28 E
Uşak □, Turkey **39 C11** 38 30N 29 0 E
Usakos, Namibia **88 C2** 21 54 S 15 31 E
Ušće, Serbia, Yug. **40 C4** 43 30N 20 39 E
Usedom, Germany **24 B10** 53 55N 14 2 E
Useless Loop, Australia **93 E1** 26 8 S 113 23 E
'Usfān, Si. Arabia **80 C4** 21 58N 39 27 E
Ush-Tobe, Kazakstan **50 E8** 45 16N 78 0 E
Ushakova, Ostrov, Russia **4 A12** 82 0N 80 0 E
Ushant = Ouessant, Î. d', France **18 D1** 48 28N 5 6W
Ushashi, Tanzania **86 C3** 1 59 S 33 57 E
Ushat, Sudan **81 F2** 7 59N 29 28 E
'Ushayrah, Si. Arabia **80 C5** 21 46N 40 42 E
Ushibuka, Japan **55 H5** 32 11N 130 1 E
Ushuaia, Argentina **128 G3** 54 50 S 68 23W
Ushumun, Russia **51 D13** 52 47N 126 32 E
Usk, Canada **104 C3** 54 38N 128 26W
Usk →, U.K. **13 F5** 51 33N 2 58W
Uska, India **69 F10** 27 12N 83 7 E
Üsküdar, Turkey **41 F13** 41 0N 29 5 E
Uslar, Germany **24 D5** 51 39N 9 38 E
Usman, Russia **47 F10** 52 5N 39 48 E
Usoke, Tanzania **86 D3** 5 8 S 32 24 E
Usolye Sibirskoye, Russia **51 D11** 52 48N 103 40 E
Usoro, Nigeria **83 D6** 5 33N 6 11 E
Uspallata, P. de, Argentina **126 C2** 32 37 S 69 22W
Uspenskiy, Kazakstan **50 E8** 48 41N 72 43 E
Ussel, France **20 C6** 45 32N 2 18 E
Usson-du-Poitou, France **20 B4** 46 16N 0 31 E
Ussuri →, Asia **54 A7** 48 27N 135 0 E
Ussuriysk, Russia **51 E14** 43 48N 131 59 E
Ussurka, Russia **54 B6** 45 12N 133 31 E
Ust-Aldan = Batamay, Russia **51 C13** 63 30N 129 15 E
Ust-Amginskoye = Khandyga, Russia **51 C14** 62 42N 135 35 E
Ust-Bolsheretsk, Russia **51 D16** 52 50N 156 15 E
Ust-Buzulukskaya, Russia **48 E6** 50 8N 42 11 E
Ust-Chaun, Russia **51 C18** 68 47N 170 30 E
Ust-Donetskiy, Russia **49 G5** 47 35N 40 55 E
Ust-Ilimpeya = Yukta, Russia **51 C11** 63 26N 105 42 E
Ust-Ilimsk, Russia **51 D11** 58 3N 102 39 E
Ust-Ishim, Russia **50 D8** 57 45N 71 10 E
Ust-Kamchatsk, Russia **51 D17** 56 10N 162 28 E
Ust-Kamenogorsk = Öskemen, Kazakstan **50 E9** 50 0N 82 36 E
Ust-Khayryuzovo, Russia **51 D16** 57 15N 156 45 E
Ust-Kut, Russia **51 D11** 56 50N 105 42 E
Ust-Kuyga, Russia **51 B14** 70 1N 135 43 E
Ust-Labinsk, Russia **49 H4** 45 15N 39 41 E
Ust-Luga, Russia **46 C5** 59 35N 28 20 E
Ust-Maya, Russia **51 C14** 60 30N 134 28 E
Ust-Mil, Russia **51 D14** 59 40N 133 11 E
Ust-Nera, Russia **51 C15** 64 35N 143 15 E
Ust-Nyukzha, Russia **51 D13** 56 34N 121 37 E
Ust-Olenek, Russia **51 B12** 73 0N 120 5 E
Ust-Omchug, Russia **51 C15** 61 9N 149 38 E
Ust-Port, Russia **50 C9** 69 40N 84 26 E
Ust-Tsilma, Russia **50 C6** 65 28N 52 11 E
Ust Urt = Ustyurt Plateau, Asia **50 E6** 44 0N 55 0 E
Ustaritz, France **20 E2** 43 24N 1 27W
Uster, Switz. **25 H4** 47 22N 8 43 E
Ústí nad Labem, Czech Rep. **26 A7** 50 41N 14 3 E
Ústí nad Orlicí, Czech Rep. **27 B9** 49 58N 16 24 E
Ústica, Italy **30 D6** 38 42N 13 11 E
Ustinov = Izhevsk, Russia **50 D6** 56 51N 53 14 E
Ustka, Poland **44 D3** 54 35N 16 55 E
Ustroń, Poland **45 J5** 49 43N 18 48 E
Ustrzyki Dolne, Poland **45 J9** 49 27N 22 40 E
Ustyurt Plateau, Asia **50 E6** 44 0N 55 0 E
Ustyuzhna, Russia **46 C9** 58 50N 36 32 E
Usu, China **60 B3** 44 27N 84 40 E
Usuki, Japan **55 H5** 33 8N 131 49 E
Usulután, El Salv. **120 D2** 13 25N 88 28W
Usumacinta →, Mexico **119 D6** 17 0N 91 0W
Usumbura = Bujumbura, Burundi **86 C2** 3 16 S 29 18 E
Usure, Tanzania **86 C3** 4 40 S 34 22 E
Usutuo →, Mozam. **89 D5** 26 48 S 32 7 E
Uta, Indonesia **63 E9** 4 33 S 136 0 E
Utah □, U.S.A. **114 G8** 39 20N 111 30W
Utah L., U.S.A. **114 F8** 40 10N 111 58W
Utansjö, Sweden **10 B11** 62 46N 17 55 E
Utarni, India **68 F4** 26 5N 71 58 E
Utatlan, Guatemala **120 C1** 15 2N 91 11W
Ute Creek →, U.S.A. **113 H3** 35 21N 103 50W
Utebo, Spain **32 D3** 41 43N 1 0W
Utena, Lithuania **9 J21** 55 27N 25 40 E
Utete, Tanzania **86 D4** 8 0 S 38 45 E
Uthai Thani, Thailand **64 E3** 15 22N 100 3 E
Uthal, Pakistan **68 G2** 25 44N 66 40 E
Utiariti, Brazil **124 F7** 13 0 S 58 10W
Utica, N.Y., U.S.A. **111 C9** 43 6N 75 14W
Utica, Ohio, U.S.A. **110 F2** 40 14N 82 27W
Utiel, Spain **33 F3** 39 37N 1 11W
Utikuma L., Canada **104 B5** 55 50N 115 30W
Utö, Sweden **10 F12** 58 56N 18 16 E
Utopia, Australia **94 C1** 22 14 S 134 33 E
Utraula, India **69 F10** 27 19N 82 25 E
Utrecht, Neths. **17 B5** 52 5N 5 8 E
Utrecht, S. Africa **89 D5** 27 38 S 30 20 E
Utrecht □, Neths. **17 B5** 52 6N 5 7 E
Utrera, Spain **35 H5** 37 12N 5 48W
Utsjoki, Finland **8 B22** 69 51N 26 59 E
Utsunomiya, Japan **55 F9** 36 30N 139 50 E
Uttar Pradesh □, India **69 F9** 27 0N 80 0 E
Uttaradit, Thailand **64 D3** 17 36N 100 5 E
Uttoxeter, U.K. **12 E6** 52 54N 1 52W
Uummannarsuaq = Nunap Isua, Greenland **4 D5** 59 48N 43 55W
Uusikaarlepyy, Finland **8 E20** 63 32N 22 31 E
Uusikaupunki, Finland **9 F19** 60 47N 21 25 E
Uva, Russia **48 B11** 56 59N 52 13 E
Uvac →, Serbia, Yug. **40 C3** 43 35N 19 30 E
Uvalde, U.S.A. **113 L5** 29 13N 99 47W
Uvarovo, Russia **48 E6** 51 59N 42 14 E
Uvat, Russia **50 D7** 59 5N 68 50 E
Uvinza, Tanzania **86 D3** 5 5 S 30 24 E
Uvira, Dem. Rep. of the Congo **86 C2** 3 22 S 29 3 E
Uvs Nuur, Mongolia **60 A4** 50 20N 92 30 E
'Uwairidh, Ḩarrat al, Si. Arabia **70 E3** 26 50N 38 0 E
Uwajima, Japan **55 H6** 33 10N 132 35 E
Uweinat, Jebel, Sudan **80 C1** 21 54N 24 58 E
Uxbridge, Canada **110 B5** 44 6N 79 7W
Uxin Qi, China **56 E5** 38 50N 109 5 E
Uxmal, Mexico **119 C7** 20 22N 89 46W
Üydzin, Mongolia **56 B4** 44 9N 107 0 E
Uyo, Nigeria **83 D6** 5 1N 7 53 E
Üyüklü Tepe, Turkey **39 D9** 37 5N 27 21 E
Uyûn Mûsa, Egypt **75 F1** 29 53N 32 40 E
Uyuni, Bolivia **124 H5** 20 28 S 66 47W
Uzbekistan ■, Asia **50 E7** 41 30N 65 0 E
Uzen, Bolshoi →, Kazakstan **49 F9** 49 6N 49 56 E
Uzen, Mal →, Kazakstan **49 F9** 49 4N 49 44 E
Uzerche, France **20 C5** 45 25N 1 34 E
Uzès, France **21 D8** 44 1N 4 26 E
Uzh →, Ukraine **47 G6** 51 15N 30 12 E
Uzhgorod = Uzhhorod, Ukraine **47 H2** 48 36N 22 18 E
Uzhhorod, Ukraine **47 H2** 48 36N 22 18 E
Užice, Serbia, Yug. **40 C3** 43 55N 19 50 E
Uzlovaya, Russia **46 F10** 54 0N 38 5 E
Üzümlü, Turkey **39 E11** 36 44N 29 14 E
Uzunköprü, Turkey **41 E10** 41 16N 26 43 E
Uzunkuyu, Turkey **39 C8** 38 17N 26 33 E

V

Vaal →, S. Africa **88 D3** 29 4 S 23 38 E
Vaal Dam, S. Africa **89 D4** 27 0 S 28 14 E
Vaalwater, S. Africa **89 C4** 24 15 S 28 8 E
Vaasa, Finland **8 E19** 63 6N 21 38 E
Vabre, France **20 E6** 43 42N 2 24 E
Vác, Hungary **42 C4** 47 49N 19 10 E
Vacaria, Brazil **127 B5** 28 31 S 50 52W
Vacaville, U.S.A. **116 G5** 38 21N 121 59W
Vaccarès, Étang de, France **21 E8** 43 32N 4 34 E
Vach = Vakh →, Russia **50 C8** 60 45N 76 45 E
Vache, Î. à, Haiti **121 C5** 18 2N 73 35W
Väckelsång, Sweden **11 H8** 56 36N 14 58 E
Väddö, Sweden **10 D12** 60 0N 18 50 E
Väderstad, Sweden **11 F8** 58 19N 14 55 E
Vadnagar, India **68 H5** 23 47N 72 40 E
Vado Lígure, Italy **28 D5** 44 17N 8 26 E
Vadodara, India **68 H5** 22 20N 73 10 E
Vadsø, Norway **8 A23** 70 3N 29 50 E
Vadstena, Sweden **11 F8** 58 28N 14 54 E
Vaduz, Liech. **25 H5** 47 8N 9 31 E
Værøy, Norway **8 C15** 67 40N 12 40 E
Vágar, Færoe Is. **8 E9** 62 5N 7 15W
Vaggeryd, Sweden **11 G8** 57 30N 14 10 E
Vagney, France **19 D13** 48 1N 6 43 E
Vagnhärad, Sweden **11 F11** 58 57N 17 33 E
Vagos, Portugal **34 E2** 40 33N 8 42W
Vågsfjorden, Norway **8 B17** 68 50N 16 50 E
Váh →, Slovak Rep. **27 D11** 47 43N 18 7 E
Vahsel B., Antarctica **5 D1** 75 0 S 35 0W
Váï, Greece **36 D8** 35 15N 26 18 E
Vaigach, Russia **50 B6** 70 10N 59 0 E
Vaiges, France **18 D6** 48 2N 0 30W
Vaihingen, Germany **25 G4** 48 54N 8 57 E
Vail, U.S.A. **106 C5** 39 40N 106 20W
Vailly-sur-Aisne, France **19 C10** 49 24N 3 31 E
Vaisali →, India **69 F8** 26 28N 78 53 E
Vaison-la-Romaine, France **21 D9** 44 14N 5 4 E
Vakarel, Bulgaria **40 D7** 42 35N 23 40 E
Vakfıkebir, Turkey **73 B8** 41 2N 39 17 E
Vakh →, Russia **50 C8** 60 45N 76 45 E
Vakhtan, Russia **48 B8** 57 53N 46 47 E
Vál, Hungary **42 C3** 47 22N 18 40 E
Val-de-Marne □, France **19 D9** 48 45N 2 28 E
Val-d'Isère, France **21 C10** 45 27N 6 59 E
Val-d'Oise □, France **19 C9** 49 5N 2 10 E
Val-d'Or, Canada **102 C4** 48 7N 77 47W
Val Marie, Canada **105 D7** 49 15N 107 45W
Valaam, Russia **46 B6** 61 22N 30 57 E
Valadares, Portugal **34 D2** 41 5N 8 38W
Valahia, Romania **43 F9** 44 35N 25 0 E
Valais □, Switz. **25 J3** 46 12N 7 45 E
Valais, Alpes du, Switz. **25 J3** 46 5N 7 35 E
Valandovo, Macedonia **40 E6** 41 19N 22 34 E
Valašské Meziříčí, Czech Rep. **27 B10** 49 29N 17 59 E
Valáxa, Greece **38 C6** 38 50N 24 29 E
Vålberg, Sweden **10 E7** 59 23N 13 11 E
Valbo, Sweden **10 D10** 60 40N 17 0 E
Valbondione, Italy **28 B7** 46 2N 10 1 E
Vălcani, Romania **42 D5** 46 0N 20 26 E
Vâlcea □, Romania **43 F9** 45 0N 24 10 E
Valcheta, Argentina **128 E3** 40 40 S 66 8W
Valdagno, Italy **29 C8** 45 39N 11 18 E
Valdahon, France **19 E13** 47 8N 6 21 E
Valday, Russia **46 D7** 57 58N 33 9 E
Valdayskaya Vozvyshennost, Russia **46 D7** 57 0N 33 30 E
Valdeazogues →, Spain **35 G6** 38 45N 4 55W
Valdecañas, Embalse de, Spain **34 F5** 39 45N 5 25W
Valdemarsvik, Sweden **11 F10** 58 14N 16 40 E
Valdemoro, Spain **34 E7** 40 12N 3 40W
Valdepeñas, Spain **35 G7** 38 43N 3 25W
Valderaduey →, Spain **34 D5** 41 31N 5 42W
Valdérice, Italy **30 D5** 38 4N 12 37 E
Valderrobres, Spain **32 E5** 40 53N 0 9 E
Valdés, Pen., Argentina **122 H4** 42 30 S 63 45W
Valdez, U.S.A. **100 B5** 61 7N 146 16W
Valdivia, Chile **128 D2** 39 50 S 73 14W
Valdobbiádene, Italy **29 C8** 45 54N 12 0 E
Valdosta, U.S.A. **109 K4** 30 50N 83 17W
Valdoviño, Spain **34 B2** 43 36N 8 8W
Valdres, Norway **9 F13** 61 5N 9 5 E
Vale, Georgia **49 K6** 41 30N 42 58 E
Vale, U.S.A. **114 E5** 43 59N 117 15W
Vale of Glamorgan □, U.K. **13 F4** 51 28N 3 25W
Valea lui Mihai, Romania **42 C7** 47 32N 22 11 E
Valea Mărului, Romania **43 E12** 45 49N 27 42 E
Valemount, Canada **104 C5** 52 50N 119 15W
Valença, Brazil **125 F11** 13 20 S 39 5W
Valença, Portugal **34 C2** 42 1N 8 34W
Valença do Piauí, Brazil **125 E10** 6 20 S 41 45W
Valençay, France **19 E8** 47 9N 1 34 E
Valence = Valence d'Agen, France **20 D4** 44 8N 0 53 E
Valence, France **21 D8** 44 57N 4 54 E
Valence d'Agen, France **20 D4** 44 8N 0 53 E
Valencia, Spain **33 F4** 39 27N 0 23W
Valencia, U.S.A. **115 J10** 34 48N 106 43W
Valencia, Venezuela **124 A5** 10 11N 68 0W
Valencia □, Spain **33 F4** 39 20N 0 40W
Valencia, G. de, Spain **33 F5** 39 30N 0 20 E
Valencia de Alcántara, Spain **35 F3** 39 25N 7 14W
Valencia de Don Juan, Spain **34 C5** 42 17N 5 31W
Valencia I., Ireland **15 E1** 51 54N 10 22W
Valenciennes, France **19 B10** 50 20N 3 34 E
Văleni, Romania **43 F9** 44 15N 24 45 E
Vălenii de Munte, Romania **43 E11** 45 11N 26 2 E
Valensole, France **21 E9** 43 50N 5 59 E
Valentigney, France **19 E13** 47 27N 6 51 E
Valentim, Sa. do, Brazil **125 E10** 6 0 S 43 30W
Valentin, Russia **54 C7** 43 8N 134 17 E
Valentine, U.S.A. **113 K2** 30 35N 104 30W
Valenza, Italy **28 C5** 45 1N 8 38 E
Valera, Venezuela **124 B4** 9 19N 70 37W
Valga, Estonia **9 H22** 57 47N 26 2 E
Valguarnera Caropepe, Italy **31 E7** 37 30N 14 23 E
Valier, U.S.A. **114 B7** 48 18N 112 16W
Valinco, G. de, France **21 G12** 41 40N 8 52 E
Valjevo, Serbia, Yug. **40 B3** 44 18N 19 53 E
Valka, Latvia **9 H21** 57 42N 25 57 E
Valkeakoski, Finland **9 F20** 61 16N 24 2 E
Valkenswaard, Neths. **17 C5** 51 21N 5 29 E
Vall de Uxó = La Vall d'Uixó, Spain **32 F4** 39 49N 0 15W
Valla, Sweden **10 E10** 59 2N 16 20 E
Valladolid, Mexico **119 C7** 20 40N 88 11W
Valladolid, Spain **34 D6** 41 38N 4 43W
Valladolid □, Spain **34 D6** 41 38N 4 43W
Vallata, Italy **31 A8** 41 2N 15 15 E
Valldemossa, Spain **37 B9** 39 43N 2 37 E
Valle d'Aosta □, Italy **28 C4** 45 45N 7 15 E
Valle de Arán, Spain **32 C5** 42 50N 0 55 E
Valle de la Pascua, Venezuela **124 B5** 9 13N 66 0W
Valle de las Palmas, Mexico **117 N10** 32 20N 116 43W
Valle de Santiago, Mexico **118 C4** 20 25N 101 15W
Valle de Suchil, Mexico **118 C4** 23 38N 103 55W
Valle de Zaragoza, Mexico **118 B3** 27 28N 105 49W
Valle Fértil, Sierra del, Argentina **126 C2** 30 20 S 68 0W
Valle Hermoso, Mexico **119 B5** 25 35N 97 40W
Valledupar, Colombia **124 A4** 10 29N 73 15W
Vallehermoso, Canary Is. **37 F2** 28 10N 17 15W
Vallejo, U.S.A. **116 G4** 38 7N 122 14W
Vallenar, Chile **126 B1** 28 30 S 70 50W
Vallentuna, Sweden **10 E12** 59 32N 18 5 E
Valleraugue, France **20 D7** 44 6N 3 39 E
Vallet, France **18 E5** 47 10N 1 15W
Valletta, Malta **36 D2** 35 54N 14 31 E
Valley Center, U.S.A. **117 M9** 33 13N 117 2W
Valley City, U.S.A. **112 B6** 46 55N 98 0W
Valley Falls, Oreg., U.S.A. **114 E3** 42 29N 120 17W
Valley Falls, R.I., U.S.A. **111 E13** 41 54N 71 24W
Valley Springs, U.S.A. **116 G6** 38 12N 120 50W
Valley View, U.S.A. **111 F8** 40 39N 76 33W
Valley Wells, U.S.A. **117 K11** 35 27N 115 46W
Valleyview, Canada **104 B5** 55 5N 117 17W
Valli di Comácchio, Italy **29 D9** 44 40N 12 15 E
Vallimanca, Arroyo, Argentina **126 D4** 35 40 S 59 10W
Vallo della Lucánia, Italy **31 B8** 40 14N 15 16 E
Vallon-Pont-d'Arc, France **21 D8** 44 24N 4 24 E
Vallorbe, Switz. **25 J2** 46 42N 6 20 E
Valls, Spain **32 D6** 41 18N 1 15 E
Valmaseda = Balmaseda, Spain **32 B1** 43 11N 3 12W
Valmiera, Latvia **9 H21** 57 37N 25 29 E
Valnera, Spain **34 B7** 43 9N 3 40W
Valognes, France **18 C5** 49 30N 1 28W
Valona = Vlorë, Albania **40 F3** 40 32N 19 28 E
Valongo, Portugal **34 D2** 41 8N 8 30W
Valozhyn, Belarus **46 E4** 54 3N 26 30 E
Valpaços, Portugal **34 D3** 41 36N 7 17W
Valparaíso, Chile **126 C1** 33 2 S 71 40W
Valparaíso, Mexico **118 C4** 22 50N 103 32W
Valparaiso, U.S.A. **108 E2** 41 28N 87 4W
Valparaíso □, Chile **126 C1** 33 2 S 71 40W
Valpovo, Croatia **42 E3** 45 39N 18 25 E
Valréas, France **21 D9** 44 24N 5 0 E
Vals, Switz. **25 J5** 46 39N 9 11 E
Vals →, S. Africa **88 D4** 27 23 S 26 30 E
Vals, Tanjung, Indonesia **63 F9** 8 26 S 137 25 E
Vals-les-Bains, France **21 D8** 44 42N 4 24 E
Valsad, India **66 J8** 20 40N 72 58 E
Valtellina, Italy **28 B6** 46 11N 9 55 E
Valuyki, Russia **47 G10** 50 10N 38 5 E
Valverde, Canary Is. **37 G2** 27 48N 17 55W
Valverde del Camino, Spain **35 H4** 37 35N 6 47W
Valverde del Fresno, Spain **34 E4** 40 15N 6 51W
Vama, Romania **43 C10** 47 34N 25 42 E
Vamdrup, Denmark **11 J3** 55 25N 9 17 E
Våmhus, Sweden **10 C8** 61 7N 14 29 E
Vammala, Finland **9 F20** 61 20N 22 54 E
Vámos, Greece **36 D6** 35 24N 24 13 E
Van, Turkey **70 B4** 38 30N 43 20 E
Van, L. = Van Gölü, Turkey **70 B4** 38 30N 43 0 E
Van Alstyne, U.S.A. **113 J6** 33 25N 96 35W
Van Blommestein Meer, Surinam **125 C7** 4 45N 55 5W
Van Buren, Canada **103 C6** 47 10N 67 55W
Van Buren, Ark., U.S.A. **113 H7** 35 26N 94 21W
Van Buren, Maine, U.S.A. **109 B11** 47 10N 67 58W
Van Buren, Mo., U.S.A. **113 G9** 37 0N 91 1W
Van Canh, Vietnam **64 F7** 13 37N 109 0 E
Van Diemen, C., N. Terr., Australia **92 B5** 11 9 S 130 24 E
Van Diemen, C., Queens., Australia **94 B2** 16 30 S 139 46 E
Van Diemen G., Australia **92 B5** 11 45 S 132 0 E
Van Gölü, Turkey **70 B4** 38 30N 43 0 E
Van Horn, U.S.A. **113 K2** 31 3N 104 50W
Van Ninh, Vietnam **64 F7** 12 42N 109 14 E
Van Rees, Pegunungan, Indonesia **63 E9** 2 35 S 138 15 E
Van Wert, U.S.A. **108 E3** 40 52N 84 35W

Van Yen, Vietnam **58 G5** 21 4N 104 42 E
Vanadzor, Armenia **49 K7** 40 48N 44 30 E
Vanavara, Russia **51 C11** 60 22N 102 16 E
Vancouver, Canada **104 D4** 49 15N 123 10W
Vancouver, U.S.A. **116 E4** 45 38N 122 40W
Vancouver, C., Australia **93 G2** 35 2 S 118 11 E
Vancouver I., Canada **104 D3** 49 50N 126 0W
Vandalia, Ill., U.S.A. **112 F10** 38 58N 89 6W
Vandalia, Mo., U.S.A. **112 F9** 39 19N 91 29W
Vandenburg, U.S.A. **117 L6** 34 35N 120 33W
Vanderbijlpark, S. Africa **89 D4** 26 42 S 27 54 E
Vandergrift, U.S.A. **110 F5** 40 36N 79 34W
Vanderhoof, Canada **104 C4** 54 0N 124 0W
Vanderkloof Dam, S. Africa **88 E3** 30 4 S 24 40 E
Vanderlin I., Australia **94 B2** 15 44 S 137 2 E
Vänern, Sweden **11 F7** 58 47N 13 30 E
Vänersborg, Sweden **11 F6** 58 26N 12 19 E
Vang Vieng, Laos **64 C4** 18 58N 102 32 E
Vanga, Kenya **86 C4** 4 35 S 39 12 E
Vangaindrano, Madag. **89 C8** 23 21 S 47 36 E
Vanguard, Canada **105 D7** 49 55N 107 20W
Vanino, Russia **51 E15** 48 50N 140 5 E
Vânju Mare, Romania **42 F7** 44 25N 22 52 E
Vanna, Norway **8 A18** 70 6N 19 50 E
Vännäs, Sweden **8 E18** 63 58N 19 48 E
Vannes, France **18 E4** 47 40N 2 47W
Vanoise, France **21 C10** 45 25N 6 40 E
Vanrhynsdorp, S. Africa **88 E2** 31 36 S 18 44 E
Vansbro, Sweden **10 D8** 60 32N 14 15 E
Vansittart B., Australia **92 B4** 14 3 S 126 17 E
Vantaa, Finland **9 F21** 60 18N 24 58 E
Vanua Levu, Fiji **91 C8** 16 33 S 179 15 E
Vanua Mbalavu, Fiji **91 C9** 17 40 S 178 57W
Vanuatu ■, Pac. Oc. **96 J8** 15 0 S 168 0 E
Vanwyksvlei, S. Africa **88 E3** 30 18 S 21 49 E
Vanzylsrus, S. Africa **88 D3** 26 52 S 22 4 E
Vapnyarka, Ukraine **47 H5** 48 32N 28 45 E
Var □, France **21 E10** 43 27N 6 18 E
Var →, France **21 E11** 43 39N 7 12 E
Vara, Sweden **11 F6** 58 16N 12 55 E
Varades, France **18 E5** 47 25N 1 1W
Varáita →, Italy **28 D4** 44 49N 7 53 E
Varallo, Italy **28 C5** 45 49N 8 15 E
Varanasi, India **69 G10** 25 22N 83 0 E
Varanger-halvøya, Norway **8 A23** 70 25N 29 30 E
Varangerfjorden, Norway **8 A23** 70 3N 29 25 E
Varano, Lago di, Italy **29 G12** 41 53N 15 45 E
Varaždin, Croatia **29 B13** 46 20N 16 20 E
Varazze, Italy **28 D5** 44 22N 8 34 E
Varberg, Sweden **11 G6** 57 6N 12 20 E
Vardar = Axiós →, Greece **40 F6** 40 57N 22 35 E
Varde, Denmark **11 J2** 55 38N 8 29 E
Varde Å →, Denmark **11 J2** 55 35N 8 19 E
Vardø, Norway **8 A24** 70 23N 31 5 E
Varel, Germany **24 B4** 53 23N 8 8 E
Varella, Mui, Vietnam **64 F7** 12 54N 109 26 E
Varėna, Lithuania **9 J21** 54 12N 24 30 E
Varennes-sur-Allier, France **19 F10** 46 19N 3 24 E
Varennes-Vauzelles, France **19 E10** 47 3N 3 9 E
Vareš, Bos.-H. **42 F3** 44 12N 18 23 E
Varese, Italy **28 C5** 45 48N 8 50 E
Vârfurile, Romania **42 D7** 46 19N 22 31 E
Vårgårda, Sweden **11 F6** 58 2N 12 49 E
Varginha, Brazil **127 A6** 21 33 S 45 25W
Vargön, Sweden **11 F6** 58 22N 12 20 E
Varillas, Chile **126 A1** 24 0 S 70 10W
Varkaus, Finland **9 E22** 62 19N 27 50 E
Värmdölandet, Sweden **10 E12** 59 20N 18 33 E
Värmeln, Sweden **10 E6** 59 35N 12 54 E
Värmlands Bro, Sweden **10 E7** 59 11N 13 0 E
Värmlands län □, Sweden **10 E6** 60 0N 13 20 E
Varna, Bulgaria **41 C11** 43 13N 27 56 E
Varna □, Bulgaria **41 C11** 43 20N 27 30 E
Värnamo, Sweden **11 G8** 57 10N 14 3 E
Varnsdorf, Czech Rep. **26 A7** 50 55N 14 35 E
Várpalota, Hungary **42 C3** 47 12N 18 8 E
Vars, Canada **111 A9** 45 21N 75 21W
Vars, France **21 D10** 44 37N 6 42 E
Varto, Turkey **73 C9** 39 10N 41 27 E
Varvarin, Serbia, Yug. **40 C5** 43 43N 21 20 E
Varysburg, U.S.A. **110 D6** 42 46N 78 19W
Varzaneh, Iran **71 C7** 32 25N 52 40 E
Varzi, Italy **28 D6** 44 49N 9 12 E
Varzo, Italy **28 B5** 46 12N 8 15 E
Varzy, France **19 E10** 47 22N 3 20 E
Vas □, Hungary **42 C1** 47 10N 16 55 E
Vasa Barris →, Brazil **125 F11** 11 10 S 37 10W
Vásárosnamény, Hungary **42 B7** 48 9N 22 19 E
Vascão →, Portugal **35 H3** 37 31N 7 31W
Vaşcău, Romania **42 D7** 46 28N 22 30 E
Vascongadas = País Vasco □, Spain **32 C2** 42 50N 2 45W
Vasht = Khāsh, Iran **66 E2** 28 15N 61 15 E
Vasilevichi, Belarus **47 F5** 52 15N 29 50 E
Vasilikón, Greece **38 C5** 38 25N 23 40 E
Vasilkov = Vasylkiv, Ukraine **47 G6** 50 7N 30 15 E
Vaslui, Romania **43 D12** 46 38N 27 42 E
Vaslui □, Romania **43 D12** 46 30N 27 45 E
Väsman, Sweden **10 D9** 60 9N 15 5 E
Vassar, Canada **105 D9** 49 10N 95 55W
Vassar, U.S.A. **108 D4** 43 22N 83 35W
Västerås, Sweden **10 E10** 59 37N 16 38 E
Västerbotten, Sweden **8 D18** 64 36N 20 4 E
Västerdalälven →, Sweden **10 D8** 60 30N 14 7 E
Västergötland, Sweden **11 F7** 58 0N 13 10 E
Västerhaninge, Sweden **10 E12** 59 7N 18 6 E
Västervik, Sweden **11 G10** 57 43N 16 33 E
Västmanland, Sweden **9 G16** 59 45N 16 20 E
Västmanlands län □, Sweden **10 E10** 59 45N 16 20 E
Vasto, Italy **29 F11** 42 8N 14 40 E
Västra Götalands Län □, Sweden **11 F6** 58 0N 13 0 E
Vasvár, Hungary **42 C1** 47 3N 16 47 E
Vasylkiv, Ukraine **47 G6** 50 7N 30 15 E
Vatan, France **19 E8** 47 4N 1 50 E
Vatersay, U.K. **14 E1** 56 55N 7 32W
Váthia, Greece **38 E4** 36 29N 22 29 E
Vatican City ■, Europe **29 G9** 41 54N 12 27 E
Vaticano, C., Italy **31 D8** 38 37N 15 50 E
Vatili, Cyprus **36 D12** 35 6N 33 40 E
Vatin, Serbia, Yug. **42 E6** 45 12N 21 20 E
Vatnajökull, Iceland **8 D5** 64 30N 16 48W
Vatoa, Fiji **91 D9** 19 50 S 178 13W
Vatólakkos, Greece **36 D5** 35 27N 23 53 E
Vatoloha, Madag. **89 B8** 17 52 S 47 48 E
Vatomandry, Madag. **89 B8** 19 20 S 48 59 E
Vatra-Dornei, Romania **43 C10** 47 22N 25 22 E
Vatrak →, India **68 H5** 23 9N 73 2 E
Vättern, Sweden **11 F8** 58 25N 14 30 E
Vaucluse □, France **21 E9** 43 50N 5 20 E
Vaucouleurs, France **19 D12** 48 37N 5 40 E
Vaud □, Switz. **25 J2** 46 35N 6 30 E
Vaughn, Mont., U.S.A. **114 C8** 47 33N 111 33W
Vaughn, N. Mex., U.S.A. **115 J11** 34 36N 105 13W
Vaujours L., Canada **102 A5** 55 27N 74 15W
Vaupés = Uaupés →, Brazil **124 C5** 0 2N 67 16W
Vaupes □, Colombia **124 C4** 1 0N 71 0W
Vauvert, France **21 E8** 43 42N 4 17 E
Vauxhall, Canada **104 C6** 50 5N 112 9W
Vav, India **68 G4** 24 22N 71 31 E
Vavatenina, Madag. **89 B8** 17 28 S 49 12 E
Vava'u, Tonga **91 D12** 18 36 S 174 0W
Vavoua, Ivory C. **82 D3** 7 23N 6 29W
Vawkavysk, Belarus **47 F3** 53 9N 24 30 E
Vaxholm, Sweden **10 E12** 59 25N 18 20 E
Växjö, Sweden **11 H8** 56 52N 14 50 E
Våxtorp, Sweden **11 H7** 56 25N 13 8 E
Vaygach, Ostrov, Russia **50 C6** 70 0N 60 0 E
Váyia, Greece **38 C5** 38 19N 23 11 E
Váyia, Ákra, Greece **36 C10** 36 15N 28 11 E
Vechelde, Germany **24 C6** 52 16N 10 22 E
Vechta, Germany **24 C4** 52 44N 8 17 E
Vechte →, Neths. **17 B6** 52 34N 6 6 E
Vecsés, Hungary **42 C4** 47 26N 19 19 E
Veddige, Sweden **11 G6** 57 17N 12 20 E
Vedea →, Romania **43 G10** 43 42N 25 41 E
Vedia, Argentina **126 C3** 34 30 S 61 31W
Vedum, Sweden **11 F7** 58 11N 13 0 E
Veendam, Neths. **17 A6** 53 5N 6 52 E
Veenendaal, Neths. **17 B5** 52 2N 5 34 E
Vefsna →, Norway **8 D15** 65 48N 13 10 E
Vega, Norway **8 D14** 65 40N 11 55 E
Vega, U.S.A. **113 H3** 35 15N 102 26W
Vegadeo, Spain **34 B3** 43 27N 7 4W
Vegorrítis, Límni, Greece **40 F5** 40 45N 21 45 E
Vegreville, Canada **104 C6** 53 30N 112 5W
Veinge, Sweden **11 H7** 56 33N 13 4 E
Veisiejai, Lithuania **44 D10** 54 6N 23 42 E
Vejbystrand, Sweden **11 H6** 56 19N 12 45 E
Vejen, Denmark **11 J3** 55 30N 9 9 E
Vejer de la Frontera, Spain **35 J5** 36 15N 5 59W
Vejle, Denmark **11 J3** 55 43N 9 30 E
Vejle Amtskommune □, Denmark **11 J3** 55 45N 9 20 E
Vejle Fjord, Denmark **11 J3** 55 40N 9 50 E
Vela Luka, Croatia **29 F13** 42 59N 16 44 E
Velas, C., Costa Rica **120 D2** 10 21N 85 52W
Velasco, Sierra de, Argentina **126 B2** 29 20 S 67 10W
Velay, Mts. du, France **20 D7** 45 0N 3 40 E
Velbert, Germany **24 D3** 51 20N 7 3 E
Veldrif, S. Africa **88 E2** 32 42 S 18 11 E
Velebit Planina, Croatia **29 D12** 44 50N 15 20 E
Velebitski Kanal, Croatia **29 D11** 44 45N 14 55 E
Veleka →, Bulgaria **41 D11** 42 4N 27 58 E
Velencei-tó, Hungary **42 C3** 47 13N 18 36 E
Velenje, Slovenia **29 B12** 46 23N 15 8 E
Veles, Macedonia **40 E5** 41 46N 21 47 E
Velestínon, Greece **38 B4** 39 23N 22 43 E
Vélez-Málaga, Spain **35 J6** 36 48N 4 5W
Vélez Rubio, Spain **33 H2** 37 41N 2 5W
Velhas →, Brazil **125 G10** 17 13 S 44 49W
Velika, Croatia **42 E2** 45 27N 17 40 E
Velika Gorica, Croatia **29 C13** 45 44N 16 5 E
Velika Kapela, Croatia **29 C12** 45 10N 15 5 E
Velika Kladuša, Bos.-H. **29 C12** 45 11N 15 48 E
Velika Kruša, Kosovo, Yug. **40 D4** 42 19N 20 39 E
Velika Morava →, Serbia, Yug. **40 B5** 44 43N 21 3 E
Velika Plana, Serbia, Yug. **40 B5** 44 20N 21 4 E
Velikaya →, Russia **46 D5** 57 48N 28 10 E
Velikaya Kema, Russia **54 B8** 45 30N 137 12 E
Velikaya Lepetikha, Ukraine **47 J7** 47 2N 33 58 E
Veliké Kapušany, Slovak Rep. **27 C15** 48 34N 22 5 E
Velike Lašče, Slovenia **29 C11** 45 49N 14 45 E
Veliki Jastrebac, Serbia, Yug. **40 C5** 43 25N 21 30 E
Veliki Kanal, Serbia, Yug. **42 E4** 45 45N 19 15 E
Veliki Popović, Serbia, Yug. **40 B5** 44 8N 21 18 E
Velikiye Luki, Russia **46 D6** 56 25N 30 32 E
Veliko Gradište, Serbia, Yug. **40 B5** 44 46N 21 29 E
Veliko Tŭrnovo, Bulgaria **41 C9** 43 5N 25 41 E
Velikonda Range, India **66 M11** 14 45N 79 10 E
Vélingara, Senegal **82 C2** 13 12N 14 5W
Vélingara, Senegal **82 B2** 15 0N 14 40W
Velingrad, Bulgaria **40 D7** 42 4N 23 58 E
Velino, Mte., Italy **29 F10** 42 9N 13 23 E
Velizh, Russia **46 E6** 55 36N 31 11 E
Velké Karlovice, Czech Rep. **27 B11** 49 20N 18 17 E
Velké Meziříčí, Czech Rep. **26 B9** 49 21N 16 1 E
Veľký Javorník, Slovak Rep. **27 B11** 49 19N 18 22 E
Veľký Krtíš, Slovak Rep. **27 C12** 48 12N 19 21 E
Veľký Meder, Slovak Rep. **27 D10** 47 52N 17 46 E
Veľký Tribeč, Slovak Rep. **27 C11** 48 28N 18 15 E
Velletri, Italy **30 A5** 41 41N 12 47 E
Vellinge, Sweden **11 J6** 55 29N 13 0 E
Vellmar, Germany **24 D5** 51 22N 9 28 E
Vellore, India **66 N11** 12 57N 79 10 E
Velsk, Russia **46 B11** 61 10N 42 5 E
Velten, Germany **24 C9** 52 42N 13 10 E
Velva, U.S.A. **112 A4** 48 4N 100 56W
Velvendós, Greece **40 F6** 40 15N 22 6 E
Vemb, Denmark **11 H2** 56 21N 8 21 E
Vemdalen, Sweden **10 B7** 62 27N 13 51 E
Ven, Sweden **11 J6** 55 55N 12 45 E
Venaco, France **21 F13** 42 14N 9 11 E
Venado Tuerto, Argentina **126 C3** 33 50 S 62 0W
Venafro, Italy **31 A7** 41 29N 14 2 E
Venarey-les-Laumes, France **19 E11** 47 32N 4 26 E
Venaría, Italy **28 C4** 45 8N 7 38 E
Venčane, Serbia, Yug. **40 B4** 44 24N 20 28 E
Vence, France **21 E11** 43 43N 7 6 E
Vendas Novas, Portugal **35 G2** 38 39N 8 27W
Vendée □, France **18 F5** 46 50N 1 35W
Vendée →, France **18 F5** 46 20N 1 10W
Vendéen, Bocage, France **20 B2** 46 40N 1 20W
Vendeuvre-sur-Barse, France **19 D11** 48 14N 4 28 E
Vendôme, France **18 E8** 47 47N 1 3 E
Vendrell = El Vendrell, Spain **32 D6** 41 10N 1 30 E
Vendsyssel, Denmark **11 G4** 57 22N 10 0 E
Venelles, France **21 E9** 43 35N 5 28 E
Véneta, L., Italy **29 C9** 45 23N 12 25 E
Véneto □, Italy **29 C9** 45 30N 12 0 E
Venev, Russia **46 E10** 54 22N 38 17 E
Venézia, Italy **29 C9** 45 27N 12 21 E
Venézia, G. di, Italy **29 C10** 45 15N 13 0 E
Venezuela ■, S. Amer. **124 B5** 8 0N 66 0W
Venezuela, G. de, Venezuela **122 B3** 11 30N 71 0W
Vengurla, India **66 M8** 15 53N 73 45 E
Venice = Venézia, Italy **29 C9** 45 27N 12 21 E
Venice, U.S.A. **109 M4** 27 6N 82 27W
Vénissieux, France **21 C8** 45 42N 4 53 E
Venjansjön, Sweden **10 D8** 60 54N 14 0 E
Venkatapuram, India **67 K12** 18 20N 80 30 E
Venlo, Neths. **17 C6** 51 22N 6 11 E
Vennesla, Norway **9 G12** 58 15N 7 59 E
Venosa, Italy **31 B8** 40 58N 15 49 E
Venray, Neths. **17 C6** 51 31N 6 0 E
Venta, Lithuania **44 B9** 56 12N 22 42 E
Venta →, Latvia **44 A8** 57 24N 21 33 E
Venta de Baños, Spain **34 D6** 41 55N 4 30W
Venta de Cardeña = Cardeña, Spain **35 G6** 38 16N 4 20W
Ventana, Punta de la, Mexico **118 C3** 24 4N 109 48W
Ventana, Sa. de la, Argentina **126 D3** 38 0 S 62 30W
Ventersburg, S. Africa **88 D4** 28 7 S 27 9 E
Venterstad, S. Africa **88 E4** 30 47 S 25 48 E
Ventimíglia, Italy **28 E4** 43 47N 7 36 E
Ventnor, U.K. **13 G6** 50 36N 1 12W
Ventotène, Italy **30 B6** 40 47N 13 25 E
Ventoux, Mt., France **21 D9** 44 10N 5 17 E
Ventspils, Latvia **9 H19** 57 25N 21 32 E
Ventspils □, Latvia **44 A8** 57 20N 21 50 E
Ventuarí →, Venezuela **124 C5** 3 58N 67 2W
Ventucopa, U.S.A. **117 L7** 34 50N 119 29W
Ventura, U.S.A. **117 L7** 34 17N 119 18W
Venus B., Australia **95 F4** 38 40 S 145 42 E
Vera, Argentina **126 B3** 29 30 S 60 20W
Vera, Spain **33 H3** 37 15N 1 51W
Veracruz, Mexico **119 D5** 19 10N 96 10W
Veracruz □, Mexico **119 D5** 19 0N 96 15W
Veraval, India **68 J4** 20 53N 70 27 E
Verbánia, Italy **28 C5** 45 56N 8 33 E
Verbicaro, Italy **31 C8** 39 45N 15 55 E
Verbier, Switz. **25 J3** 46 6N 7 13 E
Vercelli, Italy **28 C5** 45 19N 8 25 E
Verchovchevo, Ukraine **47 H8** 48 32N 34 10 E
Verdalsøra, Norway **8 E14** 63 48N 11 30 E
Verde →, Argentina **128 E3** 41 56 S 65 5W
Verde →, Goiás, Brazil **125 G8** 18 1 S 50 14W
Verde →, Mato Grosso do Sul, Brazil **125 H8** 21 25 S 52 20W
Verde →, Chihuahua, Mexico **118 B3** 26 29N 107 58W
Verde →, Oaxaca, Mexico **119 D5** 15 59N 97 50W
Verde →, Veracruz, Mexico **118 C4** 21 10N 102 50W
Verde →, Paraguay **126 A4** 23 9 S 57 37W
Verde →, U.S.A. **106 D4** 33 33N 111 40W
Verde, Cay, Bahamas **120 B4** 23 0N 75 5W
Verde Island Pass, Phil. **61 E4** 13 34N 120 51 E
Verden, Germany **24 C5** 52 55N 9 14 E
Verdhikoúsa, Greece **38 B3** 39 47N 21 59 E
Verdi, U.S.A. **116 F7** 39 31N 119 59W
Verdon →, France **21 E9** 43 43N 5 46 E
Verdun, France **19 C12** 49 9N 5 24 E
Verdun-sur-le-Doubs, France **19 F12** 46 54N 5 2 E
Vereeniging, S. Africa **89 D4** 26 38 S 27 57 E
Verga, C., Guinea **82 C2** 10 30N 14 10W
Vergara, Uruguay **127 C5** 32 56 S 53 57W
Vergato, Italy **28 D8** 44 17N 11 7 E
Vergemont Cr. →, Australia **94 C3** 24 16 S 143 16 E
Vergennes, U.S.A. **111 B11** 44 10N 73 15W
Vergt, France **20 C4** 45 2N 0 43 E
Verín, Spain **34 D3** 41 57N 7 27W
Verkhnedvinsk = Vyerkhnyadzvinsk, Belarus **46 E4** 55 45N 27 58 E
Verkhnevilyuysk, Russia **51 C13** 63 27N 120 18 E
Verkhniy Baskunchak, Russia **49 F8** 48 14N 46 44 E
Verkhovye, Russia **47 F9** 52 55N 37 15 E
Verkhoyansk, Russia **51 C14** 67 35N 133 25 E
Verkhoyansk Ra. = Verkhoyanskiy Khrebet, Russia **51 C13** 66 0N 129 0 E
Verkhoyanskiy Khrebet, Russia **51 C13** 66 0N 129 0 E
Vermenton, France **19 E10** 47 40N 3 42 E
Vermilion, Canada **105 C6** 53 20N 110 50W
Vermilion, U.S.A. **110 E2** 41 25N 82 22W
Vermilion →, Alta., Canada **105 C6** 53 22N 110 51W
Vermilion →, Qué., Canada **102 C5** 47 38N 72 56W
Vermilion, B., U.S.A. **113 L9** 29 45N 91 55W
Vermilion Bay, Canada **105 D10** 49 51N 93 34W
Vermilion L., U.S.A. **112 B8** 47 53N 92 26W
Vermillion, U.S.A. **112 D6** 42 47N 96 56W
Vermont □, U.S.A. **111 C12** 44 0N 73 0W
Vermosh, Albania **40 D3** 42 35N 19 42 E
Vernal, U.S.A. **114 F9** 40 27N 109 32W
Vernalis, U.S.A. **116 H5** 37 36N 121 17W
Vernazza, Italy **28 D6** 44 10N 9 45 E
Verner, Canada **102 C3** 46 25N 80 8W
Verneuil-sur-Avre, France **18 D7** 48 45N 0 55 E
Verneukpan, S. Africa **88 E3** 30 0 S 21 0 E
Vernier, Switz. **25 J2** 46 11N 6 12 E
Vérnio, Italy **28 D8** 44 3N 11 9 E
Vernon, Canada **104 C5** 50 20N 119 15W
Vernon, France **18 C8** 49 5N 1 30 E
Vernon, U.S.A. **113 H5** 34 9N 99 17W
Vernonia, U.S.A. **116 E3** 45 52N 123 11W
Vernouillet, France **18 D8** 48 58N 1 58 E
Vero Beach, U.S.A. **109 M5** 27 38N 80 24W
Véroia, Greece **40 F6** 40 34N 22 12 E
Véroli, Italy **29 G10** 41 41N 13 25 E
Verona, Canada **111 B8** 44 29N 76 42W
Verona, Italy **28 C7** 45 27N 10 59 E
Verona, U.S.A. **112 D10** 42 59N 89 32W
Verrès, Italy **28 C4** 45 40N 7 42 E
Versailles, France **19 D9** 48 48N 2 8 E
Versmold, Germany **24 C4** 52 2N 8 9 E
Vert, C., Senegal **82 C1** 14 45N 17 30W
Vertou, France **18 E5** 47 10N 1 28W
Vertus, France **19 D11** 48 54N 4 2 E
Verulam, S. Africa **89 D5** 29 38 S 31 2 E
Verviers, Belgium **17 D5** 50 37N 5 52 E
Vervins, France **19 C10** 49 50N 3 53 E
Veržej, Slovenia **29 B13** 46 34N 16 13 E
Verzy, France **19 C11** 49 9N 4 10 E
Vescovato, France **21 F13** 42 30N 9 27 E
Veselí nad Lužnicí, Czech Rep. **26 B7** 49 12N 14 43 E
Veselie, Bulgaria **41 D11** 42 18N 27 38 E
Veselovskoye Vdkhr., Russia **49 G5** 46 58N 41 25 E
Veshenskaya, Russia **48 F5** 49 35N 41 44 E
Vesle →, France **19 C10** 49 23N 3 28 E
Vesoul, France **19 E13** 47 40N 6 11 E
Vessigebro, Sweden **11 H6** 56 58N 12 40 E
Vesterålen, Norway **8 B16** 68 45N 15 0 E
Vestfjorden, Norway **8 C15** 67 55N 14 0 E
Vestmannaeyjar, Iceland **8 E3** 63 27N 20 15W
Vestsjællands Amtskommune □, Denmark **11 J5** 55 30N 11 20 E
Vestspitsbergen, Svalbard **4 B8** 78 40N 17 0 E
Vestvågøy, Norway **8 B15** 68 18N 13 50 E
Vesuvio, Italy **31 B7** 40 49N 14 26 E
Vesuvius, Mt. = Vesuvio, Italy **31 B7** 40 49N 14 26 E
Vesyegonsk, Russia **46 C9** 58 40N 37 16 E
Veszprém, Hungary **42 C2** 47 8N 17 57 E
Veszprém □, Hungary **42 C2** 47 5N 17 55 E
Vésztő, Hungary **42 D6** 46 55N 21 16 E
Vetlanda, Sweden **11 G9** 57 24N 15 3 E
Vetluga, Russia **48 B7** 57 53N 45 45 E
Vetlugu →, Russia **48 B8** 56 36N 46 4 E
Vetluzhskiy, Kostroma, Russia **48 A7** 58 23N 45 26 E
Vetluzhskiy, Nizhniy Novgorod, Russia **48 B7** 57 17N 45 12 E
Vetovo, Bulgaria **41 C10** 43 42N 26 16 E
Vetralla, Italy **29 F9** 42 20N 12 2 E
Vetren, Bulgaria **41 D8** 42 15N 24 3 E
Vettore, Mte., Italy **29 F10** 42 49N 13 16 E
Veurne, Belgium **17 C2** 51 5N 2 40 E
Veveno →, Sudan **81 F3** 6 40N 32 58 E
Vevey, Switz. **25 J2** 46 28N 6 51 E
Vévi, Greece **40 F5** 40 47N 21 38 E
Veynes, France **21 D9** 44 32N 5 49 E
Veys, Iran **71 D6** 31 30N 49 0 E
Vézelay, France **19 E10** 47 27N 3 45 E
Vézelise, France **19 D13** 48 30N 6 5 E
Vézère →, France **20 D4** 44 53N 0 53 E
Vezhen, Bulgaria **41 D8** 42 50N 24 20 E
Vezirköprü, Turkey **72 B6** 41 8N 35 27 E
Vezzani, France **21 F13** 42 10N 9 15 E
Vi Thanh, Vietnam **65 H5** 9 42N 105 26 E
Viacha, Bolivia **124 G5** 16 39 S 68 18W
Viadana, Italy **28 D7** 44 56N 10 31 E
Viamão, Brazil **127 C5** 30 5 S 51 0W
Viana, Brazil **125 D10** 3 13 S 44 55W
Viana, Spain **32 C2** 42 31N 2 22W
Viana do Alentejo, Portugal **35 G3** 38 17N 7 59W
Viana do Bolo, Spain **34 C3** 42 11N 7 6W
Viana do Castelo, Portugal **34 D2** 41 42N 8 50W
Viana do Castelo □, Portugal **34 D2** 41 50N 8 30W
Vianden, Lux. **17 E6** 49 56N 6 12 E
Vianópolis, Brazil **125 G9** 16 40 S 48 35W
Viar →, Spain **35 H5** 37 36N 5 50W
Viaréggio, Italy **28 E7** 43 52N 10 14 E
Viaur →, France **20 D5** 44 8N 1 58 E
Vibble, Sweden **11 G12** 57 37N 18 16 E
Vibo Valéntia, Italy **31 D9** 38 40N 16 6 E
Viborg, Denmark **11 H3** 56 27N 9 23 E
Viborg Amtskommune □, Denmark **11 H3** 56 30N 9 30 E
Vibraye, France **18 D7** 48 3N 0 44 E
Vic, Spain **32 D7** 41 58N 2 19 E
Vic, Étang de, France **20 E7** 43 29N 3 50 E
Vic-en-Bigorre, France **20 E4** 43 24N 0 3 E
Vic-Fézensac, France **20 E4** 43 47N 0 19 E
Vic-le-Comte, France **19 G10** 45 39N 3 14 E
Vic-sur-Cère, France **20 D6** 44 59N 2 38 E
Vícar, Spain **33 J2** 36 50N 2 38W
Vicenza, Italy **29 C8** 45 33N 11 33 E
Vich = Vic, Spain **32 D7** 41 58N 2 19 E
Vichada →, Colombia **124 C5** 4 55N 67 50W
Vichuga, Russia **48 B5** 57 12N 41 55 E
Vichy, France **19 F10** 46 9N 3 26 E
Vicksburg, Ariz., U.S.A. **117 M13** 33 45N 113 45W
Vicksburg, Miss., U.S.A. **113 J9** 32 21N 90 53W
Vico, France **21 F12** 42 10N 8 49 E
Vico, L. di, Italy **29 F9** 42 19N 12 10 E
Vico del Gargano, Italy **29 G12** 41 54N 15 57 E
Vicovu de Sus, Romania **43 C10** 47 56N 25 41 E
Victor, India **68 J4** 21 0N 71 30 E
Victor, U.S.A. **110 D7** 42 58N 77 24W
Victor Harbor, Australia **95 F2** 35 30 S 138 37 E
Victoria = Labuan, Malaysia **62 C5** 5 20N 115 14 E
Victoria, Argentina **126 C3** 32 40 S 60 10W
Victoria, Canada **104 D4** 48 30N 123 25W
Victoria, Chile **128 D2** 38 13 S 72 20W
Victoria, Guinea **82 C2** 10 50N 14 32W
Victoria, Malta **36 C1** 36 2N 14 14 E
Victoria, Phil. **61 D4** 15 35N 120 41 E
Victoria, Romania **43 E9** 45 44N 24 41 E
Victoria, Kans., U.S.A. **112 F5** 38 52N 99 9W
Victoria, Tex., U.S.A. **113 L6** 28 48N 97 0W
Victoria □, Australia **95 F3** 37 0 S 144 0 E
Victoria →, Australia **92 C4** 15 10 S 129 40 E
Victoria, Grand L., Canada **102 C4** 47 31N 77 30W
Victoria, L., Africa **86 C3** 1 0 S 33 0 E
Victoria, L., Australia **95 E3** 33 57 S 141 15 E
Victoria Beach, Canada **105 C9** 50 40N 96 35W
Victoria de Durango = Durango, Mexico **118 C4** 24 3N 104 39W
Victoria de las Tunas, Cuba **120 B4** 20 58N 76 59W
Victoria Falls, Zimbabwe **87 F2** 17 58 S 25 52 E
Victoria Harbour, Canada **110 B5** 44 45N 79 45W
Victoria I., Canada **100 A8** 71 0N 111 0W
Victoria L., Canada **103 C8** 48 20N 57 27W
Victoria Ld., Antarctica **5 D11** 75 0 S 160 0 E
Victoria Nile →, Uganda **86 B3** 2 14N 31 26 E
Victoria River, Australia **92 C5** 16 25 S 131 0 E
Victoria Str., Canada **100 B9** 69 30N 100 0W
Victoria Taungdeik, Burma **67 J18** 21 15N 93 55 E
Victoria West, S. Africa **88 E3** 31 25 S 23 4 E
Victorias, Phil. **61 F5** 10 54N 123 5 E
Victoriaville, Canada **103 C5** 46 4N 71 56W
Victorica, Argentina **126 D2** 36 20 S 65 30W
Victorville, U.S.A. **117 L9** 34 32N 117 18W
Vicuña, Chile **126 C1** 30 0 S 70 50W
Vicuña Mackenna, Argentina **126 C3** 33 53 S 64 25W
Vidal, U.S.A. **117 L12** 34 7N 114 31W
Vidal Junction, U.S.A. **117 L12** 34 11N 114 34W
Vidalia, U.S.A. **109 J4** 32 13N 82 25W
Vidauban, France **21 E10** 43 25N 6 27 E
Videbæk, Denmark **11 H2** 56 6N 8 38 E
Videle, Romania **43 F10** 44 17N 25 31 E
Vídho, Greece **36 A3** 39 38N 19 55 E
Vidigueira, Portugal **35 G3** 38 12N 7 48W
Vidin, Bulgaria **40 C6** 43 59N 22 50 E
Vidio, C., Spain **34 B4** 43 35N 6 14W
Vidisha, India **68 H7** 23 28N 77 53 E
Vidra, Romania **43 E11** 45 56N 26 55 E
Viduša, Bos.-H. **40 D2** 42 55N 18 21 E
Vidzy, Belarus **9 J22** 55 23N 26 37 E
Viechtach, Germany **25 F8** 49 4N 12 53 E
Viedma, Argentina **128 E4** 40 50 S 63 0W
Viedma, L., Argentina **128 F2** 49 30 S 72 30W
Vieira do Minho, Portugal **34 D2** 41 38N 8 8W
Vielha, Spain **32 C5** 42 43N 0 44 E
Viella = Vielha, Spain **32 C5** 42 43N 0 44 E
Vielsalm, Belgium **17 D5** 50 17N 5 54 E
Vienenburg, Germany **24 D6** 51 57N 10 34 E
Vieng Pou Kha, Laos **58 G3** 20 41N 101 4 E
Vienna = Wien, Austria **27 C9** 48 12N 16 22 E
Vienna, Ill., U.S.A. **113 G10** 37 25N 88 54W
Vienna, Mo., U.S.A. **112 F9** 38 11N 91 57W
Vienne, France **21 C8** 45 31N 4 53 E
Vienne □, France **20 B4** 46 30N 0 42 E
Vienne →, France **18 E7** 47 13N 0 5 E
Vientiane, Laos **64 D4** 17 58N 102 36 E
Vientos, Paso de los, Caribbean **121 C5** 20 0N 74 0W
Viernheim, Germany **25 F4** 49 31N 8 35 E
Viersen, Germany **24 D2** 51 15N 6 23 E
Vierwaldstättersee, Switz. **25 J4** 47 0N 8 30 E
Vierzon, France **19 E9** 47 13N 2 5 E
Vieste, Italy **29 G13** 41 53N 16 10 E
Vietnam ■, Asia **64 C6** 19 0N 106 0 E
Vieux-Boucau-les-Bains, France **20 E2** 43 48N 1 23W
Vif, France **21 C9** 45 5N 5 41 E
Vigan, Phil. **61 C4** 17 35N 120 28 E
Vigévano, Italy **28 C5** 45 19N 8 51 E
Vigia, Brazil **125 D9** 0 50 S 48 5W
Vigía Chico, Mexico **119 D7** 19 46N 87 35W
Víglas, Ákra, Greece **36 D9** 35 54N 27 51 E
Vignemale, France **20 F3** 42 47N 0 10W
Vigneulles-lès-Hattonchâtel, France **19 D12** 48 59N 5 43 E
Vignola, Italy **28 D8** 44 29N 11 1 E
Vigo, Spain **34 C2** 42 12N 8 41W
Vigo, Ría de, Spain **34 C2** 42 15N 8 45W
Vigsø Bugt, Denmark **11 G2** 57 8N 8 47 E
Vihiers, France **18 E6** 47 10N 0 30W
Vihowa, Pakistan **68 D4** 31 8N 70 30 E
Vihowa →, Pakistan **68 D4** 31 8N 70 41 E
Vijayawada, India **67 L12** 16 31N 80 39 E
Vijosë →, Albania **40 F3** 40 37N 19 24 E
Vík, Iceland **8 E4** 63 25N 19 1W
Vika, Sweden **10 D8** 60 57N 14 28 E
Vikarbyn, Sweden **10 D9** 60 55N 15 1 E
Vikeke, Indonesia **63 F7** 8 52 S 126 23 E
Viken, Skåne, Sweden **11 H6** 56 9N 12 34 E
Viken, Västra Götaland, Sweden **11 F8** 58 39N 14 20 E
Viking, Canada **104 C6** 53 7N 111 50W
Vikmanshyttan, Sweden **10 D9** 60 18N 15 50 E
Vikna, Norway **8 D14** 64 55N 10 58 E
Vila da Maganja, Mozam. **87 F4** 17 18 S 37 30 E
Vila de João Belo = Xai-Xai, Mozam. **89 D5** 25 6 S 33 31 E
Vila de Rei, Portugal **34 F2** 39 41N 8 9W
Vila do Bispo, Portugal **35 H2** 37 5N 8 53W
Vila do Conde, Portugal **34 D2** 41 21N 8 45W
Vila Franca de Xira, Portugal **35 G2** 38 57N 8 59W
Vila Gamito, Mozam. **87 E3** 14 12 S 33 0 E
Vila Gomes da Costa, Mozam. **89 C5** 24 20 S 33 37 E
Vila Machado, Mozam. **87 F3** 19 15 S 34 14 E
Vila Mouzinho, Mozam. **87 E3** 14 48 S 34 25 E
Vila Nova de Famalicão, Portugal **34 D2** 41 25N 8 32W
Vila Nova de Fos Côa, Portugal **34 D3** 41 5N 7 9W
Vila Nova de Foscôa = Vila Nova de Fos Côa, Portugal **34 D3** 41 5N 7 9W
Vila Nova de Gaia, Portugal **34 D2** 41 4N 8 40W
Vila Nova de Ourém, Portugal **34 F2** 39 40N 8 35W
Vila Pouca de Aguiar, Portugal **34 D3** 41 30N 7 38W
Vila Real, Portugal **34 D3** 41 17N 7 48W
Vila Real □, Portugal **34 D3** 41 36N 7 35W
Vila-real de los Infantes, Spain **32 F4** 39 55N 0 3W

Vila Real de Santo António, *Portugal* **35 H3** 37 10N 7 28W
Vila Vasco da Gama, *Mozam.* **87 E3** 14 54 S 32 14 E
Vila Velha, *Brazil* **127 A7** 20 20 S 40 17W
Vila Viçosa, *Portugal* **35 G3** 38 45N 7 27W
Vilafranca del Maestrat, *Spain* **32 E4** 40 26N 0 16W
Vilafranca del Penedès, *Spain* **32 D6** 41 21N 1 40 E
Vilagarcía de Arousa, *Spain* **34 C2** 42 34N 8 46W
Vilaine →, *France* **18 E4** 47 30N 2 27W
Vilanandro, Tanjona, *Madag.* **89 B7** 16 11 S 44 27 E
Vilanculos, *Mozam.* **89 C6** 22 1 S 35 17 E
Vilanova de Castelló, *Spain* **33 F4** 39 5N 0 31W
Vilanova i la Geltrú, *Spain* **32 D6** 41 13N 1 40 E
Vilar Formosa, *Portugal* **34 E4** 40 38N 6 45W
Vilaseca, *Spain* **32 D6** 41 7N 1 9 E
Vilaseca-Salou = Vilaseca, *Spain* **32 D6** 41 7N 1 9 E
Vilbjerg, *Denmark* **11 H2** 56 12N 8 46 E
Vilches, *Spain* **35 G7** 38 12N 3 30W
Vileyka, *Belarus* **46 E4** 54 30N 26 53 E
Vilhelmina, *Sweden* **8 D17** 64 35N 16 39 E
Vilhena, *Brazil* **124 F6** 12 40 S 60 5W
Viliga, *Russia* **51 C16** 61 36N 156 56 E
Viliya →, *Lithuania* **9 J21** 55 8N 24 16 E
Viljandi, *Estonia* **9 G21** 58 28N 25 30 E
Vilkaviškis, *Lithuania* **44 D10** 54 39N 23 2 E
Vilkija, *Lithuania* **44 C10** 55 3N 23 35 E
Vilkitskogo, Proliv, *Russia* **51 B11** 78 0N 103 0 E
Vilkovo = Vylkove, *Ukraine* **47 K5** 45 28N 29 32 E
Villa Abecia, *Bolivia* **126 A2** 21 0 S 68 18W
Villa Ahumada, *Mexico* **118 A3** 30 38N 106 30W
Villa Ana, *Argentina* **126 B4** 28 28 S 59 40W
Villa Ángela, *Argentina* **126 B3** 27 34 S 60 45W
Villa Bella, *Bolivia* **124 F5** 10 25 S 65 22W
Villa Bens = Tarfaya, *Morocco* **78 C3** 27 55N 12 55W
Villa Cañás, *Argentina* **126 C3** 34 0 S 61 35W
Villa Cisneros = Dakhla, *W. Sahara* **78 D2** 23 50N 15 53W
Villa Colón, *Argentina* **126 C2** 31 38 S 68 20W
Villa Constitución, *Argentina* **126 C3** 33 15 S 60 20W
Villa de María, *Argentina* **126 B3** 29 55 S 63 43W
Villa del Rio, *Spain* **35 H6** 37 59N 4 17W
Villa Dolores, *Argentina* **126 C2** 31 58 S 65 15W
Villa Frontera, *Mexico* **118 B4** 26 56N 101 27W
Villa Guillermina, *Argentina* **126 B4** 28 15 S 59 29W
Villa Hayes, *Paraguay* **126 B4** 25 5 S 57 20W
Villa Iris, *Argentina* **126 D3** 38 12 S 63 12W
Villa Juárez, *Mexico* **118 B4** 27 37N 100 44W
Villa María, *Argentina* **126 C3** 32 20 S 63 10W
Villa Mazán, *Argentina* **126 B2** 28 40 S 66 30W
Villa Minozzo, *Italy* **28 D7** 44 22N 10 28 E
Villa Montes, *Bolivia* **126 A3** 21 10 S 63 30W
Villa Ocampo, *Argentina* **126 B4** 28 30 S 59 20W
Villa Ocampo, *Mexico* **118 B3** 26 29N 105 30W
Villa Ojo de Agua, *Argentina* **126 B3** 29 30 S 63 44W
Villa San Giovanni, *Italy* **31 D8** 38 13N 15 38 E
Villa San José, *Argentina* **126 C4** 32 12 S 58 15W
Villa San Martín, *Argentina* **126 B3** 28 15 S 64 9W
Villa Santina, *Italy* **29 B9** 46 24N 12 55 E
Villa Unión, *Mexico* **118 C3** 23 12N 106 14W
Villablino, *Spain* **34 C4** 42 57N 6 19W
Villacarlos, *Spain* **37 B11** 39 53N 4 17 E
Villacarriedo, *Spain* **34 B7** 43 14N 3 48W
Villacarrillo, *Spain* **35 G7** 38 7N 3 3W
Villacastín, *Spain* **34 E6** 40 46N 4 25W
Villach, *Austria* **26 E6** 46 37N 13 51 E
Villacidro, *Italy* **30 C1** 39 27N 8 44 E
Villada, *Spain* **34 C6** 42 15N 4 59W
Villadiego, *Spain* **34 C6** 42 31N 4 1W
Villadóssola, *Italy* **28 B5** 46 4N 8 16 E
Villafeliche, *Spain* **32 D3** 41 10N 1 30W
Villafranca, *Spain* **32 C3** 42 17N 1 46W
Villafranca de los Barros, *Spain* **35 G4** 38 35N 6 18W
Villafranca de los Caballeros, *Baleares, Spain* **37 B10** 39 34N 3 25 E
Villafranca de los Caballeros, *Toledo, Spain* **35 F7** 39 26N 3 21W
Villafranca del Cid = Vilafranca del Maestrat, *Spain* **32 E4** 40 26N 0 16W
Villafranca del Panadés = Vilafranca del Penedès, *Spain* **32 D6** 41 21N 1 40 E
Villafranca di Verona, *Italy* **28 C7** 45 21N 10 50 E
Villafranca Tirrena, *Italy* **31 D8** 38 20N 15 25 E
Villagrán, *Mexico* **119 C5** 24 29N 99 29W
Villaguay, *Argentina* **126 C4** 32 0 S 59 0W
Villaharta, *Spain* **35 G6** 38 9N 4 54W
Villahermosa, *Mexico* **119 D6** 17 59N 92 55W
Villahermosa, *Spain* **33 G2** 38 46N 2 52W
Villaines-la-Juhel, *France* **18 D6** 48 21N 0 20W
Villajoyosa, *Spain* **33 G4** 38 30N 0 12W
Villalba, *Spain* **34 B3** 43 26N 7 40W
Villalba de Guardo, *Spain* **34 C6** 42 42N 4 49W
Villalón de Campos, *Spain* **34 C5** 42 5N 5 4W
Villalpando, *Spain* **34 D5** 41 51N 5 25W
Villaluenga, *Spain* **34 E7** 40 2N 3 54W
Villamanán, *Spain* **34 C5** 42 19N 5 35W
Villamartín, *Spain* **35 J5** 36 52N 5 38W
Villamayor de Santiago, *Spain* **32 F2** 39 50N 2 59W
Villamblard, *France* **20 C4** 45 2N 0 32 E
Villanova Monteleone, *Italy* **30 B1** 40 30N 8 28 E
Villanueva, *U.S.A.* **113 H2** 35 16N 105 22W
Villanueva de Castellón = Vilanova de Castelló, *Spain* **33 F4** 39 5N 0 31W
Villanueva de Córdoba, *Spain* **35 G6** 38 20N 4 38W
Villanueva de la Fuente, *Spain* **33 G2** 38 42N 2 42W
Villanueva de la Serena, *Spain* **35 G5** 38 59N 5 50W
Villanueva de la Sierra, *Spain* **34 E4** 40 12N 6 24W
Villanueva de los Castillejos, *Spain* **35 H3** 37 30N 7 15W
Villanueva de los Infantes, *Spain* **35 G7** 38 43N 3 1W
Villanueva del Arzobispo, *Spain* **33 G2** 38 10N 3 0W
Villanueva del Fresno, *Spain* **35 G3** 38 23N 7 10W
Villanueva y Geltrú = Vilanova i la Geltrú, *Spain* **32 D6** 41 13N 1 40 E
Villaputzu, *Italy* **30 C2** 39 26N 9 34 E
Villaquilambre, *Spain* **34 C5** 42 39N 5 33W
Villar del Arzobispo, *Spain* **32 F4** 39 44N 0 50W
Villar del Rey, *Spain* **35 F4** 39 7N 6 50W
Villard-de-Lans, *France* **21 C9** 45 3N 5 33 E
Villarramiel, *Spain* **34 C6** 42 2N 4 55W
Villarreal = Vila-real de los Infantes, *Spain* **32 F4** 39 55N 0 3W
Villarrica, *Chile* **128 D2** 39 15 S 72 15W
Villarrica, *Paraguay* **126 B4** 25 40 S 56 30W
Villarrobledo, *Spain* **33 F2** 39 18N 2 36W
Villarroya de la Sierra, *Spain* **32 D3** 41 27N 1 46W
Villarrubia de los Ojos, *Spain* **35 F7** 39 14N 3 36W
Villars-les-Dombes, *France* **19 F12** 46 0N 5 3 E
Villasayas, *Spain* **32 D2** 41 24N 2 39W
Villaseca de los Gamitos = Villaseco de los Gamitos, *Spain* **34 D4** 41 2N 6 7W
Villaseco de los Gamitos, *Spain* **34 D4** 41 2N 6 7W
Villasimíus, *Italy* **30 C2** 39 8N 9 31 E
Villastar, *Spain* **32 E3** 40 17N 1 9W
Villatobas, *Spain* **34 F7** 39 54N 3 20W
Villavicencio, *Argentina* **126 C2** 32 28 S 69 0W
Villavicencio, *Colombia* **124 C4** 4 9N 73 37W
Villaviciosa, *Spain* **34 B5** 43 32N 5 27W
Villazón, *Bolivia* **126 A2** 22 0 S 65 35W
Ville-Marie, *Canada* **102 C4** 47 20N 79 30W
Ville Platte, *U.S.A.* **113 K8** 30 41N 92 17W
Villedieu-les-Poêles, *France* **18 D5** 48 50N 1 13W
Villefort, *France* **20 D7** 44 28N 3 56 E
Villefranche-de-Lauragais, *France* **20 E5** 43 25N 1 44 E
Villefranche-de-Rouergue, *France* **20 D6** 44 21N 2 2 E
Villefranche-du-Périgord, *France* **20 D5** 44 38N 1 5 E
Villefranche-sur-Saône, *France* **21 C8** 45 59N 4 43 E
Villel, *Spain* **32 E3** 40 14N 1 12W
Villemur-sur-Tarn, *France* **20 E5** 43 51N 1 31 E
Villena, *Spain* **33 G4** 38 39N 0 52W
Villenauxe-la-Grande, *France* **19 D10** 48 35N 3 33 E
Villenave-d'Ornon, *France* **20 D3** 44 46N 0 33W
Villeneuve-d'Ascq, *France* **19 B10** 50 38N 3 9 E
Villeneuve-l'Archevêque, *France* **19 D10** 48 14N 3 32 E
Villeneuve-lès-Avignon, *France* **21 E8** 43 58N 4 49 E
Villeneuve-sur-Allier, *France* **19 F10** 46 40N 3 13 E
Villeneuve-sur-Lot, *France* **20 D4** 44 24N 0 42 E
Villeneuve-sur-Yonne, *France* **19 D10** 48 5N 3 18 E
Villeréal, *France* **20 D4** 44 38N 0 45 E
Villers-Bocage, *France* **18 C6** 49 3N 0 40W
Villers-Cotterêts, *France* **19 C10** 49 15N 3 4 E
Villers-sur-Mer, *France* **18 C6** 49 21N 0 2W
Villersexel, *France* **19 E13** 47 33N 6 26 E
Villerupt, *France* **19 C12** 49 28N 5 55 E
Villeurbanne, *France* **21 C8** 45 46N 4 55 E
Villiers, *S. Africa* **89 D4** 27 2 S 28 36 E
Villingen-Schwenningen, *Germany* **25 G4** 48 3N 8 26 E
Vilna, *Canada* **104 C6** 54 7N 111 55W
Vilnius, *Lithuania* **9 J21** 54 38N 25 19 E
Vils, *Austria* **26 D3** 47 33N 10 38 E
Vils →, *Bayern, Germany* **25 G9** 48 37N 13 11 E
Vils →, *Bayern, Germany* **25 F7** 49 10N 11 57 E
Vilsbiburg, *Germany* **25 G8** 48 26N 12 22 E
Vilshofen, *Germany* **25 G9** 48 37N 13 11 E
Vilusi, *Montenegro, Yug.* **40 D2** 42 44N 18 34 E
Vilvoorde, *Belgium* **17 D4** 50 56N 4 26 E
Vilyuy →, *Russia* **51 C13** 64 24N 126 26 E
Vilyuysk, *Russia* **51 C13** 63 40N 121 35 E
Vimianzo, *Spain* **34 B1** 43 7N 9 2W
Vimioso, *Portugal* **34 D4** 41 35N 6 31W
Vimmerby, *Sweden* **11 G9** 57 40N 15 55 E
Vimoutiers, *France* **18 D7** 48 57N 0 10 E
Vimperk, *Czech Rep.* **26 B6** 49 3N 13 46 E
Viña del Mar, *Chile* **126 C1** 33 0 S 71 30W
Vinarós, *Spain* **32 E5** 40 30N 0 27 E
Vincennes, *U.S.A.* **108 F2** 38 41N 87 32W
Vincent, *U.S.A.* **117 L8** 34 33N 118 11W
Vinchina, *Argentina* **126 B2** 28 45 S 68 15W
Vindelälven →, *Sweden* **8 E18** 63 55N 19 50 E
Vindeln, *Sweden* **8 D18** 64 12N 19 43 E
Vinderup, *Denmark* **11 H2** 56 29N 8 45 E
Vindhya Ra., *India* **68 H7** 22 50N 77 0 E
Vineland, *U.S.A.* **108 F8** 39 29N 75 2W
Vineuil, *France* **18 E8** 47 35N 1 22 E
Vinga, *Romania* **42 D6** 46 1N 21 14 E
Vingåker, *Sweden* **10 E9** 59 2N 15 52 E
Vinh, *Vietnam* **64 C5** 18 45N 105 38 E
Vinh Linh, *Vietnam* **64 D6** 17 4N 107 2 E
Vinh Long, *Vietnam* **65 G5** 10 16N 105 57 E
Vinh Yen, *Vietnam* **58 G5** 21 21N 105 35 E
Vinhais, *Portugal* **34 D3** 41 50N 7 5W
Vinica, *Croatia* **29 B13** 46 20N 16 9 E
Vinica, *Macedonia* **40 E6** 41 53N 22 30 E
Vinica, *Slovenia* **29 C12** 45 28N 15 16 E
Vinita, *U.S.A.* **113 G7** 36 39N 95 9W
Vinkovci, *Croatia* **42 E3** 45 19N 18 48 E
Vinnitsa = Vinnytsya, *Ukraine* **47 H5** 49 15N 28 30 E
Vinnytsya, *Ukraine* **47 H5** 49 15N 28 30 E
Vinslöv, *Sweden* **11 H7** 56 7N 13 55 E
Vintjärn, *Sweden* **10 D10** 60 50N 16 4 E
Vinton, *Calif., U.S.A.* **116 F6** 39 48N 120 10W
Vinton, *Iowa, U.S.A.* **112 D8** 42 10N 92 1W
Vinton, *La., U.S.A.* **113 K8** 30 11N 93 35W
Vintu de Jos, *Romania* **43 D8** 46 0N 23 30 E
Viöl, *Germany* **24 A5** 54 34N 9 11 E
Vipava, *Slovenia* **29 C10** 45 51N 13 58 E
Vipiteno, *Italy* **29 B8** 46 54N 11 26 E
Vir, *Croatia* **29 D12** 44 17N 15 3 E
Virac, *Phil.* **61 E6** 13 30N 124 20 E
Virachei, *Cambodia* **64 F6** 13 59N 106 49 E
Virago Sd., *Canada* **104 C2** 54 0N 132 30W
Viramgam, *India* **68 H5** 23 5N 72 0 E
Viranşehir, *Turkey* **70 B3** 37 13N 39 45 E
Virawah, *Pakistan* **68 G4** 24 31N 70 46 E
Virbalis, *Lithuania* **44 D9** 54 39N 22 49 E
Virden, *Canada* **105 D8** 49 50N 100 56W
Vire, *France* **18 D6** 48 50N 0 53W
Vire →, *France* **18 C5** 49 20N 1 7W
Vírgenes, C., *Argentina* **128 G3** 52 19 S 68 21W
Virgin →, *U.S.A.* **115 H6** 36 28N 114 21W
Virgin Gorda, *Virgin Is.* **121 C7** 18 30N 64 26W
Virgin Is. (British) ■, *W. Indies* **121 C7** 18 30N 64 30W
Virgin Is. (U.S.) ■, *W. Indies* **121 C7** 18 20N 65 0W
Virginia, *S. Africa* **88 D4** 28 8 S 26 55 E
Virginia, *U.S.A.* **112 B8** 47 31N 92 32W
Virginia □, *U.S.A.* **108 G7** 37 30N 78 45W
Virginia Beach, *U.S.A.* **108 G8** 36 51N 75 59W
Virginia City, *Mont., U.S.A.* **114 D8** 45 18N 111 56W
Virginia City, *Nev., U.S.A.* **116 F7** 39 19N 119 39W
Virginia Falls, *Canada* **104 A3** 61 38N 125 42W
Virginiatown, *Canada* **102 C4** 48 9N 79 36W
Virje, *Croatia* **29 B13** 46 4N 16 59 E
Viroqua, *U.S.A.* **112 D9** 43 34N 90 53W
Virovitica, *Croatia* **42 E2** 45 51N 17 21 E
Virpazar, *Montenegro, Yug.* **40 D3** 42 14N 19 6 E
Virpur, *India* **68 J4** 21 51N 70 42 E
Virserum, *Sweden* **11 G9** 57 20N 15 35 E
Virton, *Belgium* **17 E5** 49 35N 5 32 E
Virudunagar, *India* **66 Q10** 9 30N 77 58 E
Vis, *Croatia* **29 E13** 43 4N 16 10 E
Visalia, *U.S.A.* **116 J7** 36 20N 119 18W
Visayan Sea, *Phil.* **61 F5** 11 30N 123 30 E
Visby, *Sweden* **11 G12** 57 37N 18 18 E
Viscount Melville Sd., *Canada* **4 B2** 74 10N 108 0W
Visé, *Belgium* **17 D5** 50 44N 5 41 E
Višegrad, *Bos.-H.* **42 G4** 43 47N 19 17 E
Viseu, *Brazil* **125 D9** 1 10 S 46 5W
Viseu, *Portugal* **34 E3** 40 40N 7 55W
Viseu □, *Portugal* **34 E3** 40 40N 7 55W
Vişeu de Sus, *Romania* **43 C9** 47 45N 24 25 E
Vishakhapatnam, *India* **67 L13** 17 45N 83 20 E
Vişina, *Romania* **43 G9** 43 52N 24 27 E
Vişineşti, *Moldova* **43 D13** 46 20N 28 27 E
Visingsö, *Sweden* **11 F8** 58 2N 14 20 E
Viskafors, *Sweden* **11 G6** 57 37N 12 50 E
Viskan →, *Sweden* **11 G6** 57 14N 12 12 E
Viški Kanal, *Croatia* **29 E13** 43 4N 16 5 E
Vislanda, *Sweden* **11 H8** 56 46N 14 30 E
Visnagar, *India* **68 H5** 23 45N 72 32 E
Višnja Gora, *Slovenia* **29 C11** 45 58N 14 45 E
Viso, Mte., *Italy* **28 D4** 44 38N 7 5 E
Viso del Marqués, *Spain* **35 G7** 38 32N 3 34W
Visoko, *Bos.-H.* **42 G3** 43 58N 18 10 E
Visokoi I., *Antarctica* **5 B1** 56 43 S 27 15W
Visp, *Switz.* **25 J3** 46 17N 7 52 E
Vissefjärda, *Sweden* **11 H9** 56 32N 15 35 E
Visselhövede, *Germany* **24 C5** 52 59N 9 34 E
Vissenbjerg, *Denmark* **11 J4** 55 23N 10 7 E
Vista, *U.S.A.* **117 M9** 33 12N 117 14W
Vistonikos, Ormos = Vistonís, Límni, *Greece* **41 E9** 41 0N 25 7 E
Vistonís, Límni, *Greece* **41 E9** 41 0N 25 7 E
Vistula = Wisła →, *Poland* **44 D5** 54 22N 18 55 E
Vit →, *Bulgaria* **41 C8** 43 30N 24 30 E
Vitanje, *Slovenia* **29 B12** 46 25N 15 18 E
Vitebsk = Vitsyebsk, *Belarus* **46 E6** 55 10N 30 15 E
Viterbo, *Italy* **29 F9** 42 25N 12 6 E
Vitez, *Bos.-H.* **42 F2** 44 10N 17 48 E
Viti Levu, *Fiji* **91 C7** 17 30 S 177 30 E
Vitigudino, *Spain* **34 D4** 41 1N 6 26W
Vitim, *Russia* **51 D12** 59 28N 112 35 E
Vitim →, *Russia* **51 D12** 59 26N 112 34 E
Vitina, *Bos.-H.* **29 E14** 43 17N 17 29 E
Vitina, *Greece* **38 D4** 37 40N 22 10 E
Vítkov, *Czech Rep.* **27 B10** 49 46N 17 45 E
Vitória, *Brazil* **125 H10** 20 20 S 40 22W
Vitória da Conquista, *Brazil* **125 F10** 14 51 S 40 51W
Vitória de São Antão, *Brazil* **125 E11** 8 10 S 35 20W
Vitoria-Gasteiz, *Spain* **32 C2** 42 50N 2 41W
Vitré, *France* **18 D5** 48 8N 1 12W
Vitry-le-François, *France* **19 D11** 48 43N 4 33 E
Vitry-sur-Seine, *France* **19 D9** 48 47N 2 24 E
Vitsand, *Sweden* **10 D7** 60 20N 13 0 E
Vitsi, Óros, *Greece* **40 F5** 40 40N 21 25 E
Vitsyebsk, *Belarus* **46 E6** 55 10N 30 15 E
Vittaryd, *Sweden* **11 H7** 56 58N 13 57 E
Vitteaux, *France* **19 E11** 47 24N 4 30 E
Vittel, *France* **19 D12** 48 12N 5 57 E
Vittória, *Italy* **31 F7** 36 57N 14 32 E
Vittório Véneto, *Italy* **29 C9** 45 59N 12 18 E
Vittsjö, *Sweden* **11 H7** 56 20N 13 40 E
Viveiro, *Spain* **34 B3** 43 39N 7 38W
Vivian, *U.S.A.* **113 J8** 32 53N 93 59W
Viviers, *France* **21 D8** 44 30N 4 40 E
Vivonne, *France* **20 B4** 46 25N 0 15 E
Vizcaíno, Desierto de, *Mexico* **118 B2** 27 40N 113 50W
Vizcaíno, Sierra, *Mexico* **118 B2** 27 30N 114 0W
Vizcaya □, *Spain* **32 B2** 43 15N 2 45W
Vize, *Turkey* **41 E11** 41 34N 27 45 E
Vizianagaram, *India* **67 K13** 18 6N 83 30 E
Vizille, *France* **21 C9** 45 5N 5 46 E
Viziňada, *Croatia* **29 C10** 45 20N 13 46 E
Viziru, *Romania* **43 E12** 45 0N 27 43 E
Vizzini, *Italy* **31 E7** 37 10N 14 45 E
Vjosa → = Vijosë →, *Albania* **40 F3** 40 37N 19 24 E
Vlaardingen, *Neths.* **17 C4** 51 55N 4 21 E
Vlădeasa, Vf., *Romania* **42 D7** 46 47N 22 50 E
Vladičin Han, *Serbia, Yug.* **40 D6** 42 42N 22 1 E
Vladikavkaz, *Russia* **49 J7** 43 0N 44 35 E
Vladimir, *Russia* **46 D11** 56 15N 40 30 E
Vladimir Volynskiy = Volodymyr-Volynskyy, *Ukraine* **47 G3** 50 50N 24 18 E
Vladimirci, *Serbia, Yug.* **40 B3** 44 36N 19 50 E
Vladimirovac, *Serbia, Yug.* **42 E5** 45 1N 20 53 E
Vladimirovka, *Russia* **49 F8** 48 27N 46 10 E
Vladimirovo, *Bulgaria* **40 C7** 43 32N 23 22 E
Vladimorvka, *Kazakstan* **48 E10** 50 51N 51 8 E
Vladislavovka, *Ukraine* **47 K8** 45 12N 35 29 E
Vladivostok, *Russia* **51 E14** 43 10N 131 53 E
Vlăhiţa, *Romania* **43 D10** 46 21N 25 31 E
Vlakhiótis, *Greece* **38 E4** 36 52N 22 42 E
Vlasenica, *Bos.-H.* **42 F3** 44 11N 18 59 E
Vlašić, *Bos.-H.* **42 F2** 44 19N 17 37 E
Vlašim, *Czech Rep.* **26 B7** 49 40N 14 53 E
Vlasinsko Jezero, *Serbia, Yug.* **40 D6** 42 44N 22 22 E
Vlasotince, *Serbia, Yug.* **40 D6** 42 59N 22 7 E
Vlieland, *Neths.* **17 A4** 53 16N 4 55 E
Vlissingen, *Neths.* **17 C3** 51 26N 3 34 E
Vlóra = Vlorë, *Albania* **40 F3** 40 32N 19 28 E
Vlorë, *Albania* **40 F3** 40 32N 19 28 E
Vlorës, Gjiri i, *Albania* **40 F3** 40 29N 19 27 E
Vltava →, *Czech Rep.* **26 A7** 50 21N 14 30 E
Vo Dat, *Vietnam* **65 G6** 11 9N 107 31 E
Vobarno, *Italy* **28 C7** 45 39N 10 30 E
Voćin, *Croatia* **42 E2** 45 37N 17 33 E
Vöcklabruck, *Austria* **26 C6** 48 1N 13 39 E
Vodice, *Croatia* **29 E12** 43 47N 15 47 E
Vodňany, *Czech Rep.* **26 B7** 49 9N 14 11 E
Vodnjan, *Croatia* **29 D10** 44 59N 13 52 E
Voe, *U.K.* **14 A7** 60 21N 1 16W
Vogel Pk., *Nigeria* **83 D7** 8 24N 11 47 E
Vogelkop = Doberai, Jazirah, *Indonesia* **63 E8** 1 25 S 133 0 E
Vogelsberg, *Germany* **24 E5** 50 31N 9 12 E
Voghera, *Italy* **28 D6** 44 59N 9 1 E
Vohibinany, *Madag.* **89 B8** 18 49 S 49 4 E
Vohilava, *Madag.* **89 C8** 21 4 S 48 0 E
Vohimarina = Iharana, *Madag.* **89 A9** 13 25 S 50 0 E
Vohimena, Tanjon' i, *Madag.* **89 D8** 25 36 S 45 8 E
Vohipeno, *Madag.* **89 C8** 22 22 S 47 51 E
Voi, *Kenya* **86 C4** 3 25 S 38 32 E
Void-Vacon, *France* **19 D12** 48 40N 5 36 E
Voineşti, *Iaşi, Romania* **43 C12** 47 5N 27 27 E
Voineşti, *Prahova, Romania* **43 E10** 45 5N 25 14 E
Voïotía □, *Greece* **38 C5** 38 20N 23 0 E
Voiron, *France* **21 C9** 45 22N 5 35 E
Voisey B., *Canada* **103 A7** 56 15N 61 50W
Voitsberg, *Austria* **26 D8** 47 3N 15 9 E
Vojens, *Denmark* **11 J3** 55 16N 9 18 E
Vojmsjön, *Sweden* **8 D17** 64 55N 16 40 E
Vojnić, *Croatia* **29 C12** 45 19N 15 43 E
Vojnik, *Italy* **29 B12** 46 18N 15 19 E
Vojvodina □, *Serbia, Yug.* **42 E5** 45 20N 20 0 E
Vokhtoga, *Russia* **46 C11** 58 46N 41 8 E
Volary, *Czech Rep.* **26 C6** 48 54N 13 52 E
Volborg, *U.S.A.* **112 C2** 45 51N 105 41W
Volcano Is. = Kazan-Rettō, *Pac. Oc.* **96 E6** 25 0N 141 0 E
Volchansk = Vovchansk, *Ukraine* **47 G9** 50 17N 36 58 E
Volchya →, *Ukraine* **47 H8** 48 32N 36 0 E
Volda, *Norway* **9 E12** 62 9N 6 5 E
Volga, *Russia* **46 C10** 57 58N 38 16 E
Volga →, *Russia* **49 G9** 46 0N 48 30 E
Volga Hts. = Privolzhskaya Vozvyshennost, *Russia* **48 E7** 51 0N 46 0 E
Volgo-Baltiyskiy Kanal, *Russia* **46 B9** 60 0N 38 0 E
Volgo-Donskoy Kanal, *Russia* **49 F7** 48 40N 43 37 E
Volgodonsk, *Russia* **49 G6** 47 33N 42 5 E
Volgograd, *Russia* **49 F7** 48 40N 44 25 E
Volgogradskoye Vdkhr., *Russia* **48 E8** 50 0N 45 20 E
Volgorechensk, *Russia* **48 B5** 57 28N 41 14 E
Volímai, *Greece* **38 D2** 37 53N 20 35 E
Volintiri, *Moldova* **43 D14** 46 26N 29 37 E
Volissós, *Greece* **39 C7** 38 29N 25 54 E
Volkach, *Germany* **25 F6** 49 52N 10 14 E
Völkermarkt, *Austria* **26 E7** 46 39N 14 39 E
Volkhov, *Russia* **46 C7** 59 55N 32 15 E
Volkhov →, *Russia* **46 B7** 60 8N 32 20 E
Völklingen, *Germany* **25 F2** 49 15N 6 50 E
Volkovysk = Vawkavysk, *Belarus* **47 F3** 53 9N 24 30 E
Volksrust, *S. Africa* **89 D4** 27 24 S 29 53 E
Volnansk, *Ukraine* **47 H8** 48 2N 35 29 E
Volnovakha, *Ukraine* **47 J9** 47 35N 37 30 E
Volochanka, *Russia* **51 B10** 71 0N 94 28 E
Volodarsk, *Russia* **48 B6** 56 12N 43 15 E
Volodymyr-Volynskyy, *Ukraine* **47 G3** 50 50N 24 18 E
Vologda, *Russia* **46 C10** 59 10N 39 45 E
Volokolamsk, *Russia* **46 D8** 56 5N 35 57 E
Volokonovka, *Russia* **47 G9** 50 33N 37 52 E
Vólos, *Greece* **38 B4** 39 24N 22 59 E
Volosovo, *Russia* **46 C5** 59 27N 29 32 E
Volovets, *Ukraine* **47 H2** 48 43N 23 11 E
Volovo, *Russia* **46 F10** 53 35N 38 1 E
Volozhin = Valozhyn, *Belarus* **46 E4** 54 3N 26 30 E
Volsk, *Russia* **48 D8** 52 5N 47 22 E
Volta □, *Ghana* **83 D5** 7 0N 0 30 E
Volta →, *Ghana* **83 D5** 5 46N 0 41 E
Volta, L., *Ghana* **83 D5** 7 30N 0 0W
Volta Blanche = White Volta →, *Ghana* **83 D4** 9 10N 1 15W
Volta Redonda, *Brazil* **127 A7** 22 31 S 44 5W
Voltaire, C., *Australia* **92 B4** 14 16 S 125 35 E
Volterra, *Italy* **28 E7** 43 24N 10 51 E
Voltri, *Italy* **28 D5** 44 26N 8 45 E
Volturno →, *Italy* **30 A6** 41 1N 13 55 E
Vólvi, L., *Greece* **40 F7** 40 40N 23 34 E
Volyně, *Czech Rep.* **26 B6** 49 10N 13 53 E
Volzhsk, *Russia* **48 C9** 55 57N 48 23 E
Volzhskiy, *Russia* **49 F7** 48 56N 44 46 E
Vondrozo, *Madag.* **89 C8** 22 49 S 47 20 E
Vónitsa, *Greece* **38 C2** 38 53N 20 58 E
Vopnafjörður, *Iceland* **8 D6** 65 45N 14 50W
Vorarlberg □, *Austria* **26 D2** 47 20N 10 0 E
Vóras Óros, *Greece* **40 F5** 40 57N 21 45 E
Vorbasse, *Denmark* **11 J3** 55 39N 9 6 E
Vorchdorf, *Austria* **26 C6** 48 0N 13 55 E
Vorderrhein →, *Switz.* **25 J5** 46 49N 9 25 E
Vordingborg, *Denmark* **11 J5** 55 0N 11 54 E
Vorë, *Albania* **40 E3** 41 23N 19 40 E
Voreppe, *France* **21 C9** 45 18N 5 39 E
Vóriai Sporádhes, *Greece* **38 B5** 39 15N 23 30 E
Vórios Aiyaíon □, *Greece* **39 C7** 38 50N 25 30 E
Vórios Evvoïkos Kólpos, *Greece* **38 C5** 38 45N 23 15 E
Vorkuta, *Russia* **50 C7** 67 48N 64 20 E
Vormsi, *Estonia* **9 G20** 59 1N 23 13 E
Vorona →, *Russia* **48 E6** 51 22N 42 3 E
Voronezh, *Russia* **47 G10** 51 40N 39 10 E
Voronezh, *Ukraine* **47 G7** 51 47N 33 28 E
Voronezh →, *Russia* **47 G10** 51 32N 39 10 E
Vorontsovo-Aleksandrovskoye = Zelenokumsk, *Russia* **49 H6** 44 24N 44 0 E
Voroshilovgrad = Luhansk, *Ukraine* **47 H10** 48 38N 39 15 E
Voroshilovsk = Alchevsk, *Ukraine* **47 H10** 48 30N 38 45 E
Vórroi, *Greece* **38 F6** 35 4N 24 49 E
Vorskla →, *Ukraine* **47 H8** 48 50N 34 10 E
Võrts Järv, *Estonia* **9 G22** 58 16N 26 3 E
Vöru, *Estonia* **9 H22** 57 48N 26 54 E
Vosges, *France* **19 D14** 48 20N 7 10 E
Vosges □, *France* **19 D13** 48 12N 6 20 E
Voskopoja = Voskopojë, *Albania* **40 F4** 40 35N 20 33 E
Voskopojë, *Albania* **40 F4** 40 35N 20 33 E
Voskresensk, *Russia* **46 E10** 55 19N 38 43 E
Voskresenskoye, *Russia* **48 B7** 56 51N 45 30 E
Voss, *Norway* **9 F12** 60 38N 6 26 E
Vostok I., *Kiribati* **97 J12** 10 5 S 152 23W
Votice, *Czech Rep.* **26 B7** 49 38N 14 39 E
Votsuri-Shima, *Japan* **55 M1** 25 45N 123 29 E
Vouga →, *Portugal* **34 E2** 40 41N 8 40W
Vouillé, *France* **18 F7** 46 38N 0 10 E
Voúxa, Ákra, *Greece* **36 D5** 35 37N 23 32 E
Vouzela, *Portugal* **34 E2** 40 43N 8 7W
Vouziers, *France* **19 C11** 49 22N 4 40 E
Vovchansk, *Ukraine* **47 G9** 50 17N 36 58 E
Vozhe, Ozero, *Russia* **46 B10** 60 45N 39 0 E
Vozhega, *Russia* **46 B11** 60 29N 40 12 E
Voznesensk, *Ukraine* **47 J6** 47 35N 31 21 E
Voznesenye, *Russia* **46 B8** 61 0N 35 28 E
Vrå, *Denmark* **11 G3** 57 21N 9 56 E
Vráble, *Slovak Rep.* **27 C11** 48 15N 18 16 E
Vraćevšnica, *Serbia, Yug.* **40 B4** 44 2N 20 34 E
Vrakhnéïka, *Greece* **38 C3** 38 10N 21 40 E
Vrancea □, *Romania* **43 E11** 45 50N 26 45 E
Vrancei, Munţii, *Romania* **43 E11** 46 0N 26 30 E
Vrangelya, Ostrov, *Russia* **51 B19** 71 0N 180 0 E
Vranica, *Bos.-H.* **42 G2** 43 55N 17 50 E
Vranje, *Serbia, Yug.* **40 D5** 42 34N 21 54 E
Vranjska Banja, *Serbia, Yug.* **40 D6** 42 34N 22 1 E
Vranov nad Topľou, *Slovak Rep.* **27 C14** 48 53N 21 40 E
Vransko, *Slovenia* **29 B11** 46 17N 14 58 E
Vransko Jezero, *Croatia* **29 E12** 43 53N 15 34 E
Vrapčište, *Macedonia* **40 E4** 41 50N 20 53 E
Vratsa, *Bulgaria* **40 C7** 43 15N 23 30 E
Vrbas, *Serbia, Yug.* **42 E4** 45 40N 19 40 E
Vrbas →, *Bos.-H.* **42 E2** 45 8N 17 29 E
Vrbnik, *Croatia* **29 C11** 45 4N 14 40 E
Vrbovec, *Croatia* **29 C13** 45 53N 16 28 E
Vrbovsko, *Croatia* **29 C12** 45 24N 15 5 E
Vrchlabí, *Czech Rep.* **26 A8** 50 38N 15 37 E
Vrede, *S. Africa* **89 D4** 27 24 S 29 6 E
Vredefort, *S. Africa* **88 D4** 27 0 S 27 22 E
Vreden, *Germany* **24 C2** 52 2N 6 50 E
Vredenburg, *S. Africa* **88 E2** 32 56 S 18 0 E
Vredendal, *S. Africa* **88 E2** 31 41 S 18 35 E
Vretstorp, *Sweden* **10 E8** 59 1N 14 53 E
Vrgorac, *Croatia* **29 E14** 43 12N 17 20 E
Vrhnika, *Slovenia* **29 C11** 45 58N 14 15 E
Vridi, *Ivory C.* **82 D4** 5 15N 4 3W
Vrigstad, *Sweden* **11 G8** 57 22N 14 28 E
Vrindavan, *India* **68 F7** 27 37N 77 40 E
Vríses, *Greece* **36 D6** 35 23N 24 13 E
Vrnograč, *Bos.-H.* **29 C12** 45 10N 15 57 E
Vrondádhes, *Greece* **39 C8** 38 25N 26 7 E
Vrpolje, *Croatia* **42 E3** 45 13N 18 24 E
Vršac, *Serbia, Yug.* **42 E6** 45 8N 21 20 E
Vrsacki Kanal, *Serbia, Yug.* **42 E5** 45 15N 21 0 E
Vrútky, *Slovak Rep.* **27 B11** 49 7N 18 55 E
Vryburg, *S. Africa* **88 D3** 26 55 S 24 45 E
Vryheid, *S. Africa* **89 D5** 27 45 S 30 47 E
Vsetín, *Czech Rep.* **27 B11** 49 20N 18 0 E
Vu Liet, *Vietnam* **64 C5** 18 43N 105 23 E
Vůcha →, *Bulgaria* **41 D8** 42 10N 24 26 E
Vučitrn, *Kosovo, Yug.* **40 D4** 42 49N 20 59 E
Vukovar, *Croatia* **42 E3** 45 21N 18 59 E
Vulcan, *Canada* **104 C6** 50 25N 113 15W
Vulcan, *Romania* **43 E8** 45 23N 23 17 E
Vulcaneşti, *Moldova* **43 E13** 45 41N 28 18 E
Vulcano, *Italy* **31 D7** 38 24N 14 58 E
Vůlchedruma, *Bulgaria* **40 C7** 43 42N 23 27 E
Vulkaneshty = Vulcaneşti, *Moldova* **43 E13** 45 41N 28 18 E
Vunduzi →, *Mozam.* **87 F3** 18 56 S 34 1 E
Vung Tau, *Vietnam* **65 G6** 10 21N 107 4 E
Vŭrbitsa, *Bulgaria* **41 D10** 42 59N 26 40 E
Vurshets, *Bulgaria* **40 C7** 43 13N 23 23 E
Vutcani, *Romania* **43 D12** 46 26N 27 59 E
Vuya, *Sudan* **81 F2** 5 21N 29 40 E
Vyartsilya, *Russia* **46 A6** 62 8N 30 45 E
Vyatka = Kirov, *Russia* **50 D5** 58 35N 49 40 E
Vyatka →, *Russia* **48 C10** 55 37N 51 28 E
Vyatskiye Polyany, *Russia* **48 B10** 56 14N 51 5 E
Vyazemskiy, *Russia* **51 E14** 47 32N 134 45 E
Vyazma, *Russia* **46 E8** 55 10N 34 15 E
Vyazniki, *Russia* **48 B6** 56 10N 42 10 E
Vyborg, *Russia* **46 B5** 60 43N 28 47 E
Vychegda →, *Russia* **50 C5** 61 18N 46 36 E
Východné Beskydy, *Europe* **27 B15** 49 20N 22 0 E
Východočeský □, *Czech Rep.* **26 E8** 50 20N 15 45 E

Vyerkhnyadzvinsk, Belarus **46 E4** 55 45N 27 58 E
Vyksa, Russia **48 C6** 55 19N 42 11 E
Vylkove, Ukraine **47 K5** 45 28N 29 32 E
Vynohradiv, Ukraine **47 H2** 48 9N 23 2 E
Vyrnwy, L., U.K. **12 E4** 52 48N 3 31W
Vyshniy Volochek, Russia **46 D8** 57 30N 34 30 E
Vyshzha = imeni 26 Bakinskikh Komissarov, Turkmenistan **71 B7** 39 22N 54 10 E
Vyškov, Czech Rep. **27 B9** 49 17N 17 0 E
Vysoké Mýto, Czech Rep. **27 B9** 49 58N 16 10 E
Vysokovsk, Russia **46 D9** 56 22N 36 30 E
Vyšší Brod, Czech Rep. **26 C7** 48 37N 14 19 E
Vytegra, Russia **46 B9** 61 0N 36 27 E

W

W.A.C. Bennett Dam, Canada **104 B4** 56 2N 122 6W
Wa, Ghana **82 C4** 10 7N 2 25W
Waal →, Neths. **17 C5** 51 37N 5 0 E
Waalwijk, Neths. **17 C5** 51 42N 5 4 E
Waat, Sudan **81 F3** 8 10N 32 7 E
Wabana, Canada **103 C9** 47 40N 53 0W
Wabasca →, Canada **104 B5** 58 22N 115 20W
Wabasca-Desmarais, Canada **104 B6** 55 57N 113 56W
Wabash, U.S.A. **108 E3** 40 48N 85 49W
Wabash →, U.S.A. **108 G1** 37 48N 88 2W
Wabi →, Ethiopia **81 F5** 7 45N 40 50 E
Wabigoon L., Canada **105 D10** 49 44N 92 44W
Wabowden, Canada **105 C9** 54 55N 98 38W
Wąbrzeźno, Poland **45 E5** 53 16N 18 57 E
Wabu Hu, China **59 A11** 32 20N 116 50 E
Wabuk Pt., Canada **102 A2** 55 20N 85 5W
Wabush, Canada **103 B6** 52 55N 66 52W
Wąchock, Poland **45 G8** 51 4N 21 1 E
Wächtersbach, Germany **25 E5** 50 14N 9 17 E
Waco, U.S.A. **113 K6** 31 33N 97 9W
Waconichi, L., Canada **102 B5** 50 8N 74 0W
Wad Ban Naqa, Sudan **81 D3** 16 32N 33 9 E
Wad Banda, Sudan **81 E2** 13 10N 27 56 E
Wad el Haddad, Sudan **81 E3** 13 50N 33 30 E
Wad en Nau, Sudan **81 E3** 14 10N 33 34 E
Wad Hamid, Sudan **81 D3** 16 30N 32 45 E
Wad Medanî, Sudan **81 E3** 14 28N 33 30 E
Wad Thana, Pakistan **68 F2** 27 22N 66 23 E
Wadai, Africa **76 E5** 12 0N 19 0 E
Wadayama, Japan **55 G7** 35 19N 134 52 E
Waddeneilanden, Neths. **17 A5** 53 20N 5 10 E
Waddenzee, Neths. **17 A5** 53 6N 5 10 E
Waddington, U.S.A. **111 B9** 44 52N 75 12W
Waddington, Mt., Canada **104 C3** 51 23N 125 15W
Waddy Pt., Australia **95 C5** 24 58 S 153 21 E
Wadebridge, U.K. **13 G3** 50 31N 4 51W
Wadena, Canada **105 C8** 51 57N 103 47W
Wadena, U.S.A. **112 B7** 46 26N 95 8W
Wädenswil, Switz. **25 H4** 47 14N 8 40 E
Wadern, Germany **25 F2** 49 32N 6 53 E
Wadeye, Australia **92 B4** 14 28 S 129 52 E
Wadhams, Canada **104 C3** 51 30N 127 30W
Wādī as Sīr, Jordan **75 D4** 31 56N 35 49 E
Wadi Gemâl, Egypt **80 C4** 24 35N 35 10 E
Wadi Halfa, Sudan **80 C3** 21 53N 31 19 E
Wadian, China **59 A9** 32 42N 112 29 E
Wadlew, Poland **45 G6** 51 31N 19 23 E
Wadowice, Poland **45 J6** 49 52N 19 30 E
Wadsworth, Nev., U.S.A. **114 G4** 39 38N 119 17W
Wadsworth, Ohio, U.S.A. **110 E3** 41 2N 81 44W
Waegwan, S. Korea **57 G15** 35 59N 128 23 E
Wafangdian, China **57 E11** 39 38N 121 58 E
Wafrah, Si. Arabia **70 D5** 28 33N 47 56 E
Wageningen, Neths. **17 C5** 51 58N 5 40 E
Wager B., Canada **101 B11** 65 26N 88 40W
Wagga Wagga, Australia **95 F4** 35 7 S 147 24 E
Waghete, Indonesia **63 E9** 4 10 S 135 50 E
Wagin, Australia **93 F2** 33 17 S 117 25 E
Wagner, U.S.A. **112 D5** 43 5N 98 18W
Wagon Mound, U.S.A. **113 G2** 36 1N 104 42W
Wagoner, U.S.A. **113 H7** 35 58N 95 22W
Wągrowiec, Poland **45 F4** 52 48N 17 11 E
Wah, Pakistan **68 C5** 33 45N 72 40 E
Wahai, Indonesia **63 E7** 2 48 S 129 35 E
Wahiawa, U.S.A. **106 H15** 21 30N 158 2W
Wâḥid, Egypt **75 E1** 30 48N 32 21 E
Wahnai, Afghan. **68 C1** 32 40N 65 50 E
Wahni, Ethiopia **81 E4** 12 40N 36 39 E
Wahoo, U.S.A. **112 E6** 41 13N 96 37W
Wahpeton, U.S.A. **112 B6** 46 16N 96 36W
Wai, Koh, Cambodia **65 H4** 9 55N 102 55 E
Waiau →, N.Z. **91 K4** 42 47 S 173 22 E
Waibeem, Indonesia **63 E8** 0 30 S 132 59 E
Waiblingen, Germany **25 G5** 48 49N 9 18 E
Waidhofen an der Thaya, Austria **26 C8** 48 49N 15 17 E
Waidhofen an der Ybbs, Austria **26 D7** 47 57N 14 46 E
Waigeo, Indonesia **63 E8** 0 20 S 130 40 E
Waihi, N.Z. **91 G5** 37 23 S 175 52 E
Waihou →, N.Z. **91 G5** 37 15 S 175 40 E
Waika, Dem. Rep. of the Congo **86 C2** 2 22 S 25 42 E
Waikabubak, Indonesia **63 F5** 9 45 S 119 25 E
Waikari, N.Z. **91 K4** 42 58 S 172 41 E
Waikato →, N.Z. **91 G5** 37 23 S 174 43 E
Waikerie, Australia **95 E3** 34 9 S 140 0 E
Waikokopu, N.Z. **91 H6** 39 3 S 177 52 E
Waikouaiti, N.Z. **91 L3** 45 36 S 170 41 E
Wailuku, U.S.A. **106 H16** 20 53N 156 30W
Waimakariri →, N.Z. **91 K4** 43 24 S 172 42 E
Waimate, N.Z. **91 L3** 44 45 S 171 3 E
Wainganga →, India **66 K11** 18 50N 79 55 E
Waingapu, Indonesia **63 F6** 9 35 S 120 11 E
Waini →, Guyana **124 B7** 8 20N 59 50W
Wainwright, Canada **105 C6** 52 50N 110 50W
Waiouru, N.Z. **91 H5** 39 28 S 175 41 E
Waipara, N.Z. **91 K4** 43 3 S 172 46 E
Waipawa, N.Z. **91 H6** 39 56 S 176 38 E
Waipiro, N.Z. **91 H7** 38 2 S 178 22 E
Waipu, N.Z. **91 F5** 35 59 S 174 29 E
Waipukurau, N.Z. **91 J6** 40 1 S 176 33 E
Wairakei, N.Z. **91 H6** 38 37 S 176 6 E
Wairarapa, L., N.Z. **91 J5** 41 14 S 175 15 E
Wairoa, N.Z. **91 H6** 39 3 S 177 25 E
Waitaki →, N.Z. **91 L3** 44 56 S 171 7 E
Waitara, N.Z. **91 H5** 38 59 S 174 15 E
Waitsburg, U.S.A. **114 C5** 46 16N 118 9W
Waiuku, N.Z. **91 G5** 37 15 S 174 45 E
Wajima, Japan **55 F8** 37 30N 137 0 E
Wajir, Kenya **86 B5** 1 42N 40 5 E
Waka, Ethiopia **81 F4** 7 2N 37 20 E
Wakasa, Japan **55 G7** 35 20N 134 24 E
Wakasa-Wan, Japan **55 G7** 35 40N 135 30 E
Wakatipu, L., N.Z. **91 L2** 45 5 S 168 33 E
Wakaw, Canada **105 C7** 52 39N 105 44W
Wakayama, Japan **55 G7** 34 15N 135 15 E
Wakayama □, Japan **55 H7** 33 50N 135 30 E
Wake Forest, U.S.A. **109 H6** 35 59N 78 30W
Wake I., Pac. Oc. **96 F8** 19 18N 166 36 E
WaKeeney, U.S.A. **112 F5** 39 1N 99 53W
Wakefield, N.Z. **91 J4** 41 24 S 173 5 E
Wakefield, U.K. **12 D6** 53 41N 1 29W
Wakefield, Mass., U.S.A. **111 D13** 42 30N 71 4W
Wakefield, Mich., U.S.A. **112 B10** 46 29N 89 56W
Wakema, Burma **67 L19** 16 30N 95 11 E
Wakkanai, Japan **54 B10** 45 28N 141 35 E
Wakkerstroom, S. Africa **89 D5** 27 24 S 30 10 E
Wakool, Australia **95 F3** 35 28 S 144 23 E
Wakool →, Australia **95 F3** 35 5 S 143 33 E
Wakre, Indonesia **63 E8** 0 19 S 131 5 E
Wakuach, L., Canada **103 A6** 55 34N 67 32W
Walamba, Zambia **87 E2** 13 30 S 28 42 E
Wałbrzych, Poland **45 H3** 50 45N 16 18 E
Walbury Hill, U.K. **13 F6** 51 21N 1 28W
Walcha, Australia **95 E5** 30 55 S 151 31 E
Walcheren, Neths. **17 C3** 51 30N 3 35 E
Walcott, U.S.A. **114 F10** 41 46N 106 51W
Wałcz, Poland **45 E3** 53 17N 16 27 E
Waldbröl, Germany **24 E3** 50 52N 7 37 E
Waldburg Ra., Australia **93 D2** 24 40 S 117 35 E
Waldeck, Germany **24 D5** 51 12N 9 4 E
Walden, Colo., U.S.A. **114 F10** 40 44N 106 17W
Walden, N.Y., U.S.A. **111 E10** 41 34N 74 11W
Waldkirch, Germany **25 G3** 48 5N 7 58 E
Waldkirchen, Germany **25 G9** 48 43N 13 36 E
Waldkraiburg, Germany **25 G8** 48 11N 12 24 E
Waldport, U.S.A. **114 D1** 44 26N 124 4W
Waldron, U.S.A. **113 H7** 34 54N 94 5W
Waldviertel, Austria **26 C8** 48 30N 15 30 E
Walebing, Australia **93 F2** 30 41 S 116 13 E
Walembele, Ghana **82 C4** 10 30N 1 58W
Walensee, Switz. **25 H5** 47 7N 9 13 E
Wales □, U.K. **13 E3** 52 19N 4 43W
Walewale, Ghana **83 C4** 10 21N 0 50W
Walgett, Australia **95 E4** 30 0 S 148 5 E
Walgreen Coast, Antarctica **5 D15** 75 15 S 105 0W
Walker, U.S.A. **112 B7** 47 6N 94 35W
Walker, L., Canada **103 B6** 50 20N 67 11W
Walker L., Canada **105 C9** 54 42N 95 57W
Walker L., U.S.A. **114 G4** 38 42N 118 43W
Walkerston, Australia **94 C4** 21 11 S 149 8 E
Walkerton, Canada **102 D3** 44 10N 81 10W
Wall, U.S.A. **112 D3** 44 0N 102 8W
Walla Walla, U.S.A. **114 C4** 46 4N 118 20W
Wallace, Idaho, U.S.A. **114 C6** 47 28N 115 56W
Wallace, N.C., U.S.A. **109 H7** 34 44N 77 59W
Wallaceburg, Canada **102 D3** 42 34N 82 23W
Wallachia = Valahia, Romania **43 F9** 44 35N 25 0 E
Wallal, Australia **95 D4** 26 32 S 146 7 E
Wallam Cr. →, Australia **95 D4** 28 40 S 147 20 E
Wallambin, L., Australia **93 F2** 30 57 S 117 35 E
Wallan, Australia **95 F3** 37 26 S 144 59 E
Wallangarra, Australia **95 D5** 28 56 S 151 58 E
Wallaroo, Australia **95 E2** 33 56 S 137 39 E
Walldürn, Germany **25 F5** 49 34N 9 22 E
Wallenhorst, Germany **24 C4** 52 21N 8 1 E
Wallenpaupack, L., U.S.A. **111 E9** 41 25N 75 15W
Wallingford, U.S.A. **111 E12** 41 27N 72 50W
Wallis & Futuna, Is., Pac. Oc. **96 J10** 13 18 S 176 10W
Wallowa, U.S.A. **114 D5** 45 34N 117 32W
Wallowa Mts., U.S.A. **114 D5** 45 20N 117 30W
Walls, U.K. **14 A7** 60 14N 1 33W
Wallula, U.S.A. **114 C4** 46 5N 118 54W
Wallumbilla, Australia **95 D4** 26 33 S 149 9 E
Walmsley, L., Canada **105 A7** 63 25N 108 36W
Walney, I. of, U.K. **12 C4** 54 6N 3 15W
Walnut Creek, U.S.A. **116 H4** 37 54N 122 4W
Walnut Ridge, U.S.A. **113 G9** 36 4N 90 57W
Walpole, Australia **93 F2** 34 58 S 116 44 E
Walpole, U.S.A. **111 D13** 42 9N 71 15W
Wals, Austria **26 D5** 47 47N 12 58 E
Walsall, U.K. **13 E6** 52 35N 1 58W
Walsenburg, U.S.A. **113 G2** 37 38N 104 47W
Walsh, U.S.A. **113 G3** 37 23N 102 17W
Walsh →, Australia **94 B3** 16 31 S 143 42 E
Walsrode, Germany **24 C5** 52 51N 9 35 E
Walterboro, U.S.A. **109 J5** 32 55N 80 40W
Walters, U.S.A. **113 H5** 34 22N 98 19W
Waltershausen, Germany **24 E6** 50 54N 10 33 E
Waltham, U.S.A. **111 D13** 42 23N 71 14W
Waltman, U.S.A. **114 E10** 43 4N 107 12W
Walton, U.S.A. **111 D9** 42 10N 75 8W
Walton-on-the-Naze, U.K. **13 F9** 51 51N 1 17 E
Walvis Bay, Namibia **88 C1** 23 0 S 14 28 E
Walvisbaai = Walvis Bay, Namibia **88 C1** 23 0 S 14 28 E
Wamba, Dem. Rep. of the Congo **86 B2** 2 10N 27 57 E
Wamba, Kenya **86 B4** 0 58N 37 19 E
Wamba, Nigeria **83 D6** 8 57N 8 42 E
Wamego, U.S.A. **112 F6** 39 12N 96 18W
Wamena, Indonesia **63 E9** 4 4 S 138 57 E
Wamsutter, U.S.A. **114 F9** 41 40N 107 58W
Wamulan, Indonesia **63 E7** 3 27 S 126 7 E
Wan Xian, China **56 E8** 38 47N 115 7 E
Wana, Pakistan **68 C3** 32 20N 69 32 E
Wanaaring, Australia **95 D3** 29 38 S 144 9 E
Wanaka, N.Z. **91 L2** 44 42 S 169 9 E
Wanaka L., N.Z. **91 L2** 44 33 S 169 7 E
Wan'an, China **59 D10** 26 26N 114 49 E
Wanapitei L., Canada **102 C3** 46 45N 80 40W
Wandel Sea = McKinley Sea, Arctic **4 A7** 82 0N 0 0W
Wandérama, Ivory C. **82 D4** 8 37N 4 25W
Wanderer, Zimbabwe **87 F3** 19 36 S 30 1 E
Wandhari, Pakistan **68 F2** 27 42N 66 48 E
Wanding, China **58 E2** 24 5N 98 4 E
Wandoan, Australia **95 D4** 26 5 S 149 55 E
Wanfu, China **57 D12** 40 8N 122 38 E
Wang →, Thailand **64 D2** 17 8N 99 2 E
Wang Kai, Sudan **81 F2** 9 3N 29 23 E
Wang Noi, Thailand **64 E3** 14 13N 100 44 E
Wang Saphung, Thailand **64 D3** 17 18N 101 46 E
Wang Thong, Thailand **64 D3** 16 50N 100 26 E
Wanga, Dem. Rep. of the Congo **86 B2** 2 58N 29 12 E
Wangal, Indonesia **63 F8** 6 8 S 134 9 E
Wanganella, Australia **95 F3** 35 6 S 144 49 E
Wanganui, N.Z. **91 H5** 39 56 S 175 3 E
Wangaratta, Australia **95 F4** 36 21 S 146 19 E
Wangary, Australia **95 E2** 34 35 S 135 29 E
Wangcang, China **58 A6** 32 18N 106 20 E
Wangcheng, China **59 C9** 28 22N 112 49 E
Wangdu, China **56 E8** 38 40N 115 7 E
Wangen, Germany **25 H5** 47 41N 9 50 E
Wangerooge, Germany **24 B3** 53 47N 7 54 E
Wangi, Kenya **86 C5** 1 58 S 40 58 E
Wangiwangi, Indonesia **63 F6** 5 22 S 123 37 E
Wangjiang, China **59 B11** 30 10N 116 42 E
Wangmo, China **58 E6** 25 11N 106 5 E
Wangolodougou, Ivory C. **82 D3** 9 55N 5 10W
Wangqing, China **57 C15** 43 12N 129 42 E
Wankaner, India **68 H4** 22 35N 71 0 E
Wanless, Canada **105 C8** 54 11N 101 21W
Wannian, China **59 C11** 28 42N 117 4 E
Wanning, Taiwan **64 C8** 23 15N 121 17 E
Wanon Niwat, Thailand **64 D4** 17 38N 103 46 E
Wanquan, China **56 D8** 40 50N 114 40 E
Wanrong, China **56 G6** 35 25N 110 50 E
Wanshan, China **58 D7** 27 30N 109 12 E
Wanshengchang, China **58 C6** 28 57N 106 53 E
Wantage, U.K. **13 F6** 51 35N 1 25W
Wanyuan, China **58 A7** 32 4N 108 3 E
Wanzai, China **59 C10** 28 7N 114 30 E
Wapakoneta, U.S.A. **108 E3** 40 34N 84 12W
Wapato, U.S.A. **114 C3** 46 27N 120 25W
Wapawekka L., Canada **105 C8** 54 55N 104 40W
Wapikopa L., Canada **102 B2** 52 56N 87 53W
Wapiti →, Canada **104 B5** 55 5N 118 18W
Wappingers Falls, U.S.A. **111 E11** 41 36N 73 55W
Wapsipinicon →, U.S.A. **112 E9** 41 44N 90 19W
Warab □, Sudan **81 F2** 7 30N 28 30 E
Warangal, India **66 L11** 17 58N 79 35 E
Waraseoni, India **69 J9** 21 45N 80 2 E
Waratah, Australia **94 G4** 41 30 S 145 30 E
Waratah B., Australia **95 F4** 38 54 S 146 5 E
Warburg, Germany **24 D5** 51 28N 9 11 E
Warburton, Vic., Australia **95 F4** 37 47 S 145 42 E
Warburton, W. Austral., Australia **93 E4** 26 8 S 126 35 E
Warburton Ra., Australia **93 E4** 25 55 S 126 28 E
Ward, N.Z. **91 J5** 41 49 S 174 11 E
Ward →, Australia **95 D4** 26 28 S 146 6 E
Ward Mt., U.S.A. **116 H8** 37 12N 118 54W
Warden, S. Africa **89 D4** 27 50 S 29 0 E
Wardha, India **66 J11** 20 45N 78 39 E
Wardha →, India **66 K11** 19 57N 79 11 E
Ware, Canada **104 B3** 57 26N 125 41W
Ware, U.S.A. **111 D12** 42 16N 72 14W
Waregem, Belgium **17 D3** 50 53N 3 27 E
Wareham, U.S.A. **111 E14** 41 46N 70 43W
Waremme, Belgium **17 D5** 50 43N 5 15 E
Waren, Germany **24 B8** 53 31N 12 40 E
Warendorf, Germany **24 D4** 51 57N 8 1 E
Warialda, Australia **95 D5** 29 29 S 150 33 E
Wariap, Indonesia **63 E8** 1 30 S 134 5 E
Warin Chamrap, Thailand **64 E5** 15 12N 104 53 E
Warka, Poland **45 G8** 51 47N 21 12 E
Warkopi, Indonesia **63 E8** 1 12 S 134 9 E
Warm Springs, U.S.A. **115 G5** 38 10N 116 20W
Warman, Canada **105 C7** 52 19N 106 30W
Warmbad, Namibia **88 D2** 28 25 S 18 42 E
Warmbad, S. Africa **89 C4** 24 51 S 28 19 E
Warmińsko-Mazurskie □, Poland **44 D8** 54 0N 21 0 E
Warminster, U.K. **13 F5** 51 12N 2 10W
Warminster, U.S.A. **111 F9** 40 12N 75 6W
Warnemünde, Germany **24 A8** 54 10N 12 5 E
Warner Mts., U.S.A. **114 F3** 41 40N 120 15W
Warner Robins, U.S.A. **109 J4** 32 37N 83 36W
Warnow →, Germany **24 A8** 54 6N 12 9 E
Waroona, Australia **93 F2** 32 50 S 115 58 E
Warracknabeal, Australia **95 F3** 36 9 S 142 26 E
Warragul, Australia **95 F4** 38 10 S 145 58 E
Warrego →, Australia **95 E4** 30 24 S 145 21 E
Warrego Ra., Australia **94 C4** 24 58 S 146 0 E
Warren, Australia **95 E4** 31 42 S 147 51 E
Warren, Ark., U.S.A. **113 J8** 33 37N 92 4W
Warren, Mich., U.S.A. **108 D4** 42 30N 83 0W
Warren, Minn., U.S.A. **112 A6** 48 12N 96 46W
Warren, Ohio, U.S.A. **110 E4** 41 14N 80 49W
Warren, Pa., U.S.A. **110 E5** 41 51N 79 9W
Warrenpoint, U.K. **15 B5** 54 6N 6 15W
Warrensburg, Mo., U.S.A. **112 F8** 38 46N 93 44W
Warrensburg, N.Y., U.S.A. **111 C11** 43 29N 73 46W
Warrenton, S. Africa **88 D3** 28 9 S 24 47 E
Warrenton, U.S.A. **116 D3** 46 10N 123 56W
Warri, Nigeria **83 D6** 5 30N 5 41 E
Warrina, Australia **95 D2** 28 12 S 135 50 E
Warrington, U.K. **12 D5** 53 24N 2 35W
Warrington, U.S.A. **109 K2** 30 23N 87 17W
Warrington □, U.K. **12 D5** 53 24N 2 35W
Warrnambool, Australia **95 F3** 38 25 S 142 30 E
Warroad, U.S.A. **112 A7** 48 54N 95 19W
Warruwi, Australia **94 A1** 11 36 S 133 20 E
Warsa, Indonesia **63 E9** 0 47 S 135 55 E
Warsak Dam, Pakistan **68 B4** 34 11N 71 19 E
Warsaw = Warszawa, Poland **45 F8** 52 13N 21 0 E
Warsaw, Ind., U.S.A. **108 E3** 41 14N 85 51W
Warsaw, N.Y., U.S.A. **110 D6** 42 45N 78 8W
Warsaw, Ohio, U.S.A. **110 F3** 40 20N 82 0W
Warstein, Germany **24 D4** 51 26N 8 22 E
Warszawa, Poland **45 F8** 52 13N 21 0 E
Warta, Poland **45 G5** 51 43N 18 38 E
Warta →, Poland **45 F1** 52 35N 14 39 E
Warthe = Warta →, Poland **45 F1** 52 35N 14 39 E
Waru, Indonesia **63 E8** 3 30 S 130 36 E
Warwick, Australia **95 D5** 28 10 S 152 1 E
Warwick, U.K. **13 E6** 52 18N 1 35W
Warwick, N.Y., U.S.A. **111 E10** 41 16N 74 22W
Warwick, R.I., U.S.A. **111 E13** 41 42N 71 28W
Warwickshire □, U.K. **13 E6** 52 14N 1 38W
Wasaga Beach, Canada **110 B4** 44 31N 80 1W
Wasagaming, Canada **105 C9** 50 39N 99 58W
Wasatch Ra., U.S.A. **114 F8** 40 30N 111 15W
Wasbank, S. Africa **89 D5** 28 15 S 30 9 E
Wasco, Calif., U.S.A. **117 K7** 35 36N 119 20W
Wasco, Oreg., U.S.A. **114 D3** 45 36N 120 42W
Wase, Nigeria **83 D6** 9 4N 9 54 E
Waseca, U.S.A. **112 C8** 44 5N 93 30W
Wasekamio L., Canada **105 B7** 56 45N 108 45W
Wash, The, U.K. **12 E8** 52 58N 0 20 E
Washago, Canada **110 B5** 44 45N 79 20W
Washburn, N. Dak., U.S.A. **112 B4** 47 17N 101 2W
Washburn, Wis., U.S.A. **112 B9** 46 40N 90 54W
Washim, India **66 J10** 20 3N 77 0 E
Washington, U.K. **12 C6** 54 55N 1 30W
Washington, D.C., U.S.A. **108 F7** 38 54N 77 2W
Washington, Ga., U.S.A. **109 J4** 33 44N 82 44W
Washington, Ind., U.S.A. **108 F2** 38 40N 87 10W
Washington, Iowa, U.S.A. **112 E9** 41 18N 91 42W
Washington, Mo., U.S.A. **112 F9** 38 33N 91 1W
Washington, N.C., U.S.A. **109 H7** 35 33N 77 3W
Washington, N.J., U.S.A. **111 F10** 40 46N 74 59W
Washington, Pa., U.S.A. **110 F4** 40 10N 80 15W
Washington, Utah, U.S.A. **115 H7** 37 8N 113 31W
Washington □, U.S.A. **114 C3** 47 30N 120 30W
Washington, Mt., U.S.A. **111 B13** 44 16N 71 18W
Washington Court House, U.S.A. **108 F4** 39 32N 83 26W
Washington I., U.S.A. **108 C2** 45 23N 86 54W
Washougal, U.S.A. **116 E4** 45 35N 122 21W
Wasian, Indonesia **63 E8** 1 47 S 133 19 E
Wasilków, Poland **45 E10** 53 12N 23 13 E
Wasilla, U.S.A. **100 B5** 61 35N 149 26W
Wasior, Indonesia **63 E8** 2 43 S 134 30 E
Waskaganish, Canada **102 B4** 51 30N 78 40W
Waskaiowaka, L., Canada **105 B9** 56 33N 96 23W
Waskesiu Lake, Canada **105 C7** 53 55N 106 5W
Wasserburg, Germany **25 G8** 48 3N 12 14 E
Wasserkuppe, Germany **24 E5** 50 29N 9 55 E
Wassy, France **19 D11** 48 30N 4 58 E
Waswanipi, Canada **102 C4** 49 40N 76 29W
Waswanipi, L., Canada **102 C4** 49 35N 76 40W
Watampone, Indonesia **63 E6** 4 29 S 120 25 E
Water Park Pt., Australia **94 C5** 22 56 S 150 47 E
Water Valley, U.S.A. **113 H10** 34 10N 89 38W
Waterberge, S. Africa **89 C4** 24 10 S 28 0 E
Waterbury, Conn., U.S.A. **111 E11** 41 33N 73 3W
Waterbury, Vt., U.S.A. **111 B12** 44 20N 72 46W
Waterbury L., Canada **105 B8** 58 10N 104 22W
Waterdown, Canada **110 C5** 43 20N 79 53W
Waterford, Canada **110 D4** 42 56N 80 17W
Waterford, Ireland **15 D4** 52 15N 7 8W
Waterford, Calif., U.S.A. **116 H6** 37 38N 120 46W
Waterford, Pa., U.S.A. **110 E5** 41 57N 79 59W
Waterford □, Ireland **15 D4** 52 10N 7 40W
Waterford Harbour, Ireland **15 D5** 52 8N 6 58W
Waterhen L., Canada **105 C9** 52 10N 99 40W
Waterloo, Belgium **17 D4** 50 43N 4 25 E
Waterloo, Ont., Canada **102 D3** 43 30N 80 32W
Waterloo, Qué., Canada **111 A12** 45 22N 72 32W
Waterloo, S. Leone **82 D2** 8 26N 13 8W
Waterloo, Ill., U.S.A. **112 F9** 38 20N 90 9W
Waterloo, Iowa, U.S.A. **112 D8** 42 30N 92 21W
Waterloo, N.Y., U.S.A. **110 D8** 42 54N 76 52W
Watersmeet, U.S.A. **112 B10** 46 16N 89 11W
Waterton Lakes Nat. Park, U.S.A. **114 B7** 48 45N 115 0W
Watertown, Conn., U.S.A. **111 E11** 41 36N 73 7W
Watertown, N.Y., U.S.A. **111 C9** 43 59N 75 55W
Watertown, S. Dak., U.S.A. **112 C6** 44 54N 97 7W
Watertown, Wis., U.S.A. **112 D10** 43 12N 88 43W
Waterval-Boven, S. Africa **89 D5** 25 40 S 30 18 E
Waterville, Canada **111 A13** 45 16N 71 54W
Waterville, Maine, U.S.A. **109 C11** 44 33N 69 38W
Waterville, N.Y., U.S.A. **111 D9** 42 56N 75 23W
Waterville, Pa., U.S.A. **110 E7** 41 19N 77 21W
Waterville, Wash., U.S.A. **114 C3** 47 39N 120 4W
Watervliet, U.S.A. **111 D11** 42 44N 73 42W
Wates, Indonesia **63 G14** 7 51 S 110 10 E
Watford, Canada **110 D3** 42 57N 81 53W
Watford, U.K. **13 F7** 51 40N 0 24W
Watford City, U.S.A. **112 B3** 47 48N 103 17W
Wathaman →, Canada **105 B8** 57 16N 102 59W
Wathaman L., Canada **105 B8** 56 58N 103 44W
Watheroo, Australia **93 F2** 30 15 S 116 0 E
Wating, China **56 G4** 35 40N 106 38 E
Watkins Glen, U.S.A. **110 D8** 42 23N 76 52W
Watling I. = San Salvador I., Bahamas **121 B5** 24 0N 74 40W
Watonga, U.S.A. **113 H5** 35 51N 98 25W
Watrous, Canada **105 C7** 51 40N 105 25W
Watrous, U.S.A. **113 H2** 35 48N 104 59W
Watsa, Dem. Rep. of the Congo **86 B2** 3 4N 29 30 E
Watseka, U.S.A. **108 E2** 40 47N 87 44W
Watson, Australia **93 F5** 30 29 S 131 31 E
Watson, Canada **105 C8** 52 10N 104 30W
Watson Lake, Canada **104 A3** 60 6N 128 49W
Watsontown, U.S.A. **110 E8** 41 5N 76 52W
Watsonville, U.S.A. **116 J5** 36 55N 121 45W
Wattiwarriganna Cr. →, Australia **95 D2** 28 57 S 136 10 E
Wattwil, Switz. **25 H5** 47 18N 9 6 E
Watuata = Batuata, Indonesia **63 F6** 6 12 S 122 42 E
Watubela, Kepulauan, Indonesia **63 E8** 4 28 S 131 35 E
Watubela Is. = Watubela, Kepulauan, Indonesia **63 E8** 4 28 S 131 35 E
Wau = Wâw, Sudan **81 F2** 7 45N 28 1 E
Waubamik, Canada **110 A4** 45 27N 80 1W
Waubay, U.S.A. **112 C6** 45 20N 97 18W
Wauchope, N.S.W., Australia **95 E5** 31 28 S 152 45 E
Wauchope, N. Terr., Australia **94 C1** 20 36 S 134 15 E
Wauchula, U.S.A. **109 M5** 27 33N 81 49W
Waukarlycarly, L., Australia **92 D3** 21 18 S 121 56 E
Waukegan, U.S.A. **108 D2** 42 22N 87 50W
Waukesha, U.S.A. **108 D1** 43 1N 88 14W
Waukon, U.S.A. **112 D9** 43 16N 91 29W
Waupaca, U.S.A. **112 C10** 44 21N 89 5W
Waupun, U.S.A. **112 D10** 43 38N 88 44W
Waurika, U.S.A. **113 H6** 34 10N 98 0W
Wausau, U.S.A. **112 C10** 44 58N 89 38W
Wautoma, U.S.A. **112 C10** 44 4N 89 18W
Wauwatosa, U.S.A. **108 D2** 43 3N 88 0W
Waveney →, U.K. **13 E9** 52 35N 1 39 E
Waverley, N.Z. **91 H5** 39 46 S 174 37 E
Waverly, Iowa, U.S.A. **112 D8** 42 44N 92 29W
Waverly, N.Y., U.S.A. **111 E8** 42 1N 76 32W
Wavre, Belgium **17 D4** 50 43N 4 38 E
Wâw, Sudan **81 F2** 7 45N 28 1 E
Wāw al Kabīr, Libya **79 C9** 25 20N 16 43 E
Wawa, Canada **102 C3** 47 59N 84 47W
Wawa, Nigeria **83 D5** 9 54N 4 27 E
Wawa, Sudan **80 C3** 20 30N 30 22 E
Wawanesa, Canada **105 D9** 49 36N 99 40W
Wawona, U.S.A. **116 H7** 37 32N 119 39W
Waxahachie, U.S.A. **113 J6** 32 24N 96 51W
Way, L., Australia **93 E3** 26 45 S 120 16 E
Waycross, U.S.A. **109 K4** 31 13N 82 21W
Wayi, Sudan **81 F3** 5 8N 30 10 E
Wayland, U.S.A. **110 D7** 42 34N 77 35W
Wayne, Nebr., U.S.A. **112 D6** 42 14N 97 1W
Wayne, W. Va., U.S.A. **108 F4** 38 13N 82 27W
Waynesboro, Ga., U.S.A. **109 J4** 33 6N 82 1W
Waynesboro, Miss., U.S.A. **109 K1** 31 40N 88 39W
Waynesboro, Pa., U.S.A. **108 F7** 39 45N 77 35W
Waynesboro, Va., U.S.A. **108 F6** 38 4N 78 53W
Waynesburg, U.S.A. **108 F5** 39 54N 80 11W
Waynesville, U.S.A. **109 H4** 35 28N 82 58W
Waynoka, U.S.A. **113 G5** 36 35N 98 53W
Wazirabad, Pakistan **68 C6** 32 30N 74 8 E
Wda →, Poland **44 E5** 53 25N 18 29 E
We, Indonesia **62 C1** 5 51N 95 18 E
Weald, The, U.K. **13 F8** 51 4N 0 20 E
Wear →, U.K. **12 C6** 54 55N 1 23W
Weatherford, Okla., U.S.A. **113 H5** 35 32N 98 43W
Weatherford, Tex., U.S.A. **113 J6** 32 46N 97 48W
Weaverville, U.S.A. **114 F2** 40 44N 122 56W
Webb City, U.S.A. **113 G7** 37 9N 94 28W
Webequie, Canada **102 B2** 52 59N 87 21W
Webo = Nyaake, Liberia **82 E3** 4 52N 7 37W
Webster, Mass., U.S.A. **111 D13** 42 3N 71 53W
Webster, N.Y., U.S.A. **110 C7** 43 13N 77 26W
Webster, S. Dak., U.S.A. **112 C6** 45 20N 97 31W
Webster City, U.S.A. **112 D8** 42 28N 93 49W
Webster Springs, U.S.A. **108 F5** 38 29N 80 25W
Weda, Indonesia **63 D7** 0 21N 127 50 E
Weda, Teluk, Indonesia **63 D7** 0 30N 127 50 E
Weddell I., Falk. Is. **128 G4** 51 50 S 61 0W
Weddell Sea, Antarctica **5 D1** 72 30 S 40 0W
Wedderburn, Australia **95 F3** 36 26 S 143 33 E
Wedel, Germany **24 B5** 53 34N 9 42 E
Wedemark, Germany **24 C5** 52 32N 9 43 E
Wedgeport, Canada **103 D6** 43 44N 65 59W
Wedza, Zimbabwe **87 F3** 18 40 S 31 33 E
Wee Waa, Australia **95 E4** 30 11 S 149 26 E
Weed, U.S.A. **114 F2** 41 25N 122 23W
Weed Heights, U.S.A. **116 G7** 38 59N 119 13W
Weedsport, U.S.A. **111 C8** 43 3N 76 35W
Weedville, U.S.A. **110 E6** 41 17N 78 30W
Weenen, S. Africa **89 D5** 28 48 S 30 7 E
Weener, Germany **24 B3** 53 9N 7 20 E
Weert, Neths. **17 C5** 51 15N 5 43 E
Węgierska-Górka, Poland **45 J6** 49 36N 19 7 E
Węgliniec, Poland **45 G2** 51 18N 15 10 E
Węgorzewo, Poland **44 D8** 54 13N 21 43 E
Węgorzyno, Poland **44 E2** 53 32N 15 33 E
Węgrów, Poland **45 F9** 52 24N 22 0 E
Wehda □, Sudan **81 F3** 9 30N 30 0 E
Wei He →, Hebei, China **56 F8** 36 10N 115 45 E
Wei He →, Shaanxi, China **56 G6** 34 38N 110 15 E
Weichang, China **57 D9** 41 58N 117 49 E
Weichuan, China **56 G7** 34 20N 113 59 E
Weida, Germany **24 E8** 50 46N 12 3 E
Weiden, Germany **25 F8** 49 41N 12 10 E
Weifang, China **57 F10** 36 44N 119 7 E
Weihai, China **57 F12** 37 30N 122 6 E
Weil, Germany **25 H3** 47 35N 7 37 E
Weilburg, Germany **24 E4** 50 28N 8 17 E
Weilheim, Germany **25 H7** 47 50N 11 9 E
Weimar, Germany **24 E7** 50 58N 11 19 E
Weinan, China **56 G5** 34 31N 109 29 E
Weingarten, Germany **25 F4** 49 3N 8 31 E
Weinheim, Germany **25 F4** 49 32N 8 39 E
Weining, China **58 D5** 26 50N 104 17 E
Weipa, Australia **94 A3** 12 40 S 141 50 E
Weir →, Australia **95 D4** 28 20 S 149 50 E
Weir →, Canada **105 B10** 56 54N 93 21W
Weir River, Canada **105 B10** 56 49N 94 6W
Weirton, U.S.A. **110 F4** 40 24N 80 35W
Weiser, U.S.A. **114 D5** 44 10N 117 0W
Weishan, Shandong, China **57 G9** 34 47N 117 5 E
Weishan, Yunnan, China **58 E3** 25 12N 100 20 E
Weissenburg, Germany **25 F6** 49 2N 10 58 E
Weissenfels, Germany **24 D7** 51 11N 12 0 E
Weisswasser, Germany **24 D10** 51 30N 14 36 E
Wéitra, Austria **26 C7** 48 41N 14 54 E
Weixi, China **58 D2** 27 10N 99 10 E
Weixin, China **58 D5** 27 48N 105 3 E
Weiyuan, China **56 G3** 35 7N 104 10 E
Weiz, Austria **26 D8** 47 13N 15 39 E
Weizhou Dao, China **58 G7** 21 0N 109 5 E
Wejherowo, Poland **44 D5** 54 35N 18 12 E
Wekusko L., Canada **105 C9** 54 40N 99 50W
Welch, U.S.A. **108 G5** 37 26N 81 35W
Weldya, Ethiopia **81 E4** 11 50N 39 34 E
Welega □, Ethiopia **81 F3** 9 25N 34 20 E

Welkite, Ethiopia 81 F4 8 15N 37 42 E
Welkom, S. Africa 88 D4 28 0S 26 46 E
Welland, Canada 102 D4 43 0N 79 15W
Welland →, U.K. 13 E7 52 51N 0 5W
Wellesley Is., Australia 94 B2 16 42 S 139 30 E
Wellingborough, U.K. 13 E7 52 19N 0 41W
Wellington, Australia 95 E4 32 35 S 148 59 E
Wellington, Canada 110 C7 43 57N 77 20W
Wellington, N.Z. 91 J5 41 19 S 174 46 E
Wellington, S. Africa 88 E2 33 38 S 19 1 E
Wellington, Somst., U.K. 13 G4 50 58N 3 13W
Wellington, Telford & Wrekin, U.K. 13 E5 52 42N 2 30W
Wellington, Colo., U.S.A. 112 E2 40 42N 105 0W
Wellington, Kans., U.S.A. 113 G6 37 16N 97 24W
Wellington, Nev., U.S.A. 116 G7 38 45N 119 23W
Wellington, Ohio, U.S.A. 110 E2 41 10N 82 13W
Wellington, Tex., U.S.A. 113 H4 34 51N 100 13W
Wellington, I., Chile 122 H3 49 30 S 75 0W
Wellington, L., Australia 95 F4 38 6 S 147 20 E
Wells, U.K. 13 F5 51 13N 2 39W
Wells, Maine, U.S.A. 111 C14 43 20N 70 35W
Wells, N.Y., U.S.A. 111 C10 43 24N 74 17W
Wells, Nev., U.S.A. 114 F6 41 7N 114 58W
Wells, L., Australia 93 E3 26 44 S 123 15 E
Wells, Mt., Australia 92 C4 17 25 S 127 8 E
Wells Gray Prov. Park, Canada 104 C4 52 30N 120 15W
Wells-next-the-Sea, U.K. 12 E8 52 57N 0 51 E
Wells River, U.S.A. 111 B12 44 9N 72 4W
Wellsboro, U.S.A. 110 E7 41 45N 77 18W
Wellsburg, U.S.A. 110 F4 40 16N 80 37W
Wellsville, N.Y., U.S.A. 110 D7 42 7N 77 57W
Wellsville, Ohio, U.S.A. 110 F4 40 36N 80 39W
Wellsville, Utah, U.S.A. 114 F8 41 38N 111 56W
Wellton, U.S.A. 115 K6 32 40N 114 8W
Welmel, Wabi →, Ethiopia 81 F5 5 38N 40 47 E
Welo □, Ethiopia 81 E4 11 50N 39 48 E
Wels, Austria 26 C7 48 9N 14 1 E
Welshpool, U.K. 13 E4 52 39N 3 8W
Welwyn Garden City, U.K. 13 F7 51 48N 0 12W
Wem, U.K. 12 E5 52 52N 2 44W
Wembere →, Tanzania 86 C3 4 10 S 34 15 E
Wemindji, Canada 102 B4 53 0N 78 49W
Wen Xian, China 56 G7 34 55N 113 5 E
Wenatchee, U.S.A. 114 C3 47 25N 120 19W
Wenchang, China 64 C8 19 38N 110 42 E
Wencheng, China 59 D13 27 46N 120 4 E
Wenchi, Ghana 82 D4 7 46N 2 8W
Wenchow = Wenzhou, China 59 D13 28 0N 120 38 E
Wenchuan, China 58 B4 31 22N 103 35 E
Wenden, U.S.A. 117 M13 33 49N 113 33W
Wendeng, China 57 F12 37 15N 122 5 E
Wendesi, Indonesia 63 E8 2 30 S 134 17 E
Wendo, Ethiopia 81 F4 6 40N 38 27 E
Wendover, U.S.A. 114 F6 40 44N 114 2W
Weng'an, China 58 D6 27 5N 107 25 E
Wengcheng, China 59 E9 24 22N 113 50 E
Wengyuan, China 59 E10 24 20N 114 9 E
Wenjiang, China 58 B4 30 44N 103 55 E
Wenling, China 59 C13 28 21N 121 20 E
Wenlock →, Australia 94 A3 12 2 S 141 55 E
Wenshan, China 58 F5 23 20N 104 18 E
Wenshang, China 56 G9 35 45N 116 30 E
Wenshui, China 56 F7 37 26N 112 1 E
Wensleydale, U.K. 12 C6 54 17N 2 0W
Wensu, China 60 B3 41 15N 80 10 E
Wensum →, U.K. 12 E8 52 40N 1 15 E
Wentworth, Australia 95 E3 34 2 S 141 54 E
Wentzel L., Canada 104 B6 59 2N 114 28W
Wenut, Indonesia 63 E8 3 11 S 133 19 E
Wenxi, China 56 G6 35 20N 111 10 E
Wenxian, China 56 H3 32 43N 104 36 E
Wenzhou, China 59 D13 28 0N 120 38 E
Weott, U.S.A. 114 F2 40 20N 123 55W
Wepener, S. Africa 88 D4 29 42 S 27 3 E
Werda, Botswana 88 D3 25 24 S 23 15 E
Werdau, Germany 24 E8 50 44N 12 22 E
Werder, Germany 24 C8 52 23N 12 55 E
Werdohl, Germany 24 D3 51 15N 7 46 E
Wereilu, Ethiopia 81 E4 10 40N 39 28 E
Weri, Indonesia 63 E8 3 10 S 132 38 E
Werneck, Germany 25 F6 49 58N 10 5 E
Wernigerode, Germany 24 D6 51 50N 10 47 E
Werra →, Germany 24 D5 51 24N 9 39 E
Werrimull, Australia 95 E3 34 25 S 141 38 E
Werris Creek, Australia 95 E5 31 18 S 150 38 E
Wertach →, Germany 25 G6 48 22N 10 54 E
Wertheim, Germany 25 F5 49 45N 9 32 E
Wertingen, Germany 25 G6 48 33N 10 41 E
Wesel, Germany 24 D2 51 39N 6 37 E
Weser →, Germany 24 B4 53 36N 8 28 E
Weser-Ems □, Germany 24 C3 53 0N 7 30 E
Weserbergland, Germany 24 C5 52 12N 9 7 E
Wesiri, Indonesia 63 F7 7 30 S 126 30 E
Weslemkoon L., Canada 110 A7 45 2N 77 25W
Wesleyville, Canada 103 C9 49 8N 53 36W
Wesleyville, U.S.A. 110 D4 42 9N 80 0W
Wessel, C., Australia 94 A2 10 59 S 136 46 E
Wessel Is., Australia 94 A2 11 10 S 136 45 E
Wesselburen, Germany 24 A4 54 13N 8 54 E
Wessington Springs, U.S.A. 112 C5 44 5N 98 34W
West, U.S.A. 113 K6 31 48N 97 6W
West →, U.S.A. 111 D12 42 52N 72 33W
West Baines →, Australia 92 C4 15 38 S 129 59 E
West Bank □, Asia 75 C4 32 6N 35 13 E
West Bend, U.S.A. 108 D1 43 25N 88 11W
West Bengal □, India 69 H13 23 0N 88 0 E
West Berkshire □, U.K. 13 F6 51 25N 1 17W
West Beskids = Západné Beskydy, Europe 27 B12 49 30N 19 0 E
West Branch, U.S.A. 108 C3 44 17N 84 14W
West Branch Susquehanna →, U.S.A. 111 F8 40 53N 76 48W
West Bromwich, U.K. 13 E6 52 32N 1 59W
West Burra, U.K. 14 A7 60 5N 1 21W
West Canada Cr. →, U.S.A. 111 C10 43 1N 74 58W
West Cape Howe, Australia 93 G2 35 8 S 117 36 E
West Chazy, U.S.A. 111 B11 44 49N 73 28W
West Chester, U.S.A. 111 G9 39 58N 75 36W
West Columbia, U.S.A. 113 L7 29 9N 95 39W
West Covina, U.S.A. 117 L9 34 4N 117 54W
West Des Moines, U.S.A. 112 E8 41 35N 93 43W
West Dunbartonshire □, U.K. 14 F4 55 59N 4 30W
West End, Bahamas 120 A4 26 41N 78 58W
West Falkland, Falk. Is. 122 J4 51 40 S 60 0W
West Fargo, U.S.A. 112 B6 46 52N 96 54W
West Farmington, U.S.A. 110 E4 41 23N 80 58W
West Fjord = Vestfjorden, Norway 8 C15 67 55N 14 0 E
West Fork Trinity →, U.S.A. 113 J6 32 48N 96 54W
West Frankfort, U.S.A. 112 G10 37 54N 88 55W
West Hartford, U.S.A. 111 E12 41 45N 72 44W
West Haven, U.S.A. 111 E12 41 17N 72 57W
West Hazleton, U.S.A. 111 F9 40 58N 76 0W
West Helena, U.S.A. 113 H9 34 33N 90 38W
West Hurley, U.S.A. 111 E10 41 59N 74 7W
West Ice Shelf, Antarctica 5 C7 67 0S 85 0 E
West Indies, Cent. Amer. 121 D7 15 0N 65 0W
West Jordan, U.S.A. 114 F8 40 36N 111 56W
West Lorne, Canada 110 D3 42 36N 81 36W
West Lothian □, U.K. 14 F5 55 54N 3 36W
West Lunga →, Zambia 87 E1 13 6 S 24 39 E
West Memphis, U.S.A. 113 H9 35 9N 90 11W
West Midlands □, U.K. 13 E6 52 26N 2 0W
West Mifflin, U.S.A. 110 F5 40 22N 79 52W
West Milton, U.S.A. 110 E8 41 1N 76 50W
West Monroe, U.S.A. 113 J8 32 31N 92 9W
West Newton, U.S.A. 110 F5 40 14N 79 46W
West Nicholson, Zimbabwe 87 G2 21 2 S 29 20 E
West Palm Beach, U.S.A. 109 M5 26 43N 80 3W
West Plains, U.S.A. 113 G9 36 44N 91 51W
West Point, N.Y., U.S.A. 111 E11 41 24N 73 58W
West Point, Nebr., U.S.A. 112 E6 41 51N 96 43W
West Point, Va., U.S.A. 108 G7 37 32N 76 48W
West Pt. = Ouest, Pte. de l', Canada 103 C7 49 52N 64 40W
West Pt., Australia 95 F2 35 1 S 135 56 E
West Road →, Canada 104 C4 53 18N 122 53W
West Rutland, U.S.A. 111 C11 43 38N 73 5W
West Schelde = Westerschelde →, Neths. 17 C3 51 25N 3 25 E
West Seneca, U.S.A. 110 D6 42 51N 78 48W
West Siberian Plain, Russia 52 C11 62 0N 75 0 E
West Sussex □, U.K. 13 G7 50 55N 0 30W
West-Terschelling, Neths. 17 A5 53 22N 5 13 E
West Valley City, U.S.A. 114 F8 40 42N 111 57W
West Virginia □, U.S.A. 108 F5 38 45N 80 30W
West-Vlaanderen □, Belgium 17 D2 51 0N 3 0 E
West Walker →, U.S.A. 116 G7 38 54N 119 9W
West Wyalong, Australia 95 E4 33 56 S 147 10 E
West Yellowstone, U.S.A. 114 D8 44 40N 111 6W
West Yorkshire □, U.K. 12 D6 53 45N 1 40W
Westall Pt., Australia 95 E1 32 55 S 134 4 E
Westbrook, U.S.A. 109 D10 43 41N 70 22W
Westbury, Australia 94 G4 41 30 S 146 51 E
Westby, U.S.A. 112 A2 48 52N 104 3W
Westend, U.S.A. 117 K9 35 42N 117 24W
Westerland, Germany 9 J13 54 54N 8 17 E
Westerly, U.S.A. 111 E13 41 22N 71 50W
Western □, Ghana 82 D4 5 30N 2 30W
Western □, Kenya 86 B3 0 30N 34 30 E
Western □, S. Leone 82 D2 8 30N 13 20W
Western □, Uganda 86 B3 1 45N 31 30 E
Western □, Zambia 87 F1 15 0 S 24 4 E
Western Australia □, Australia 93 E2 25 0 S 118 0 E
Western Cape □, S. Africa 88 E3 34 0 S 20 0 E
Western Dvina = Daugava →, Latvia 9 H21 57 4N 24 3 E
Western Ghats, India 66 N9 14 0N 75 0 E
Western Isles □, U.K. 14 D1 57 30N 7 10W
Western Sahara ■, Africa 78 D3 25 0N 13 0W
Western Samoa = Samoa ■, Pac. Oc. 91 B13 14 0 S 172 0W
Westernport, U.S.A. 108 F6 39 29N 79 3W
Westerschelde →, Neths. 17 C3 51 25N 3 25 E
Westerstede, Germany 24 B3 53 15N 7 55 E
Westerwald, Germany 24 E3 50 38N 7 56 E
Westfield, Mass., U.S.A. 111 D12 42 7N 72 45W
Westfield, N.Y., U.S.A. 110 D5 42 20N 79 35W
Westfield, Pa., U.S.A. 110 E7 41 55N 77 32W
Westhill, U.K. 14 D6 57 9N 2 19W
Westhope, U.S.A. 112 A4 48 55N 101 1W
Westland Bight, N.Z. 91 K3 42 55 S 170 5 E
Westlock, Canada 104 C6 54 9N 113 55W
Westmar, Australia 95 D4 27 55 S 149 44 E
Westmeath □, Ireland 15 C4 53 33N 7 34W
Westminster, U.S.A. 108 F7 39 34N 76 59W
Westmont, U.S.A. 110 F6 40 19N 78 58W
Westmorland, U.S.A. 117 M11 33 2N 115 37W
Weston, Oreg., U.S.A. 114 D4 45 49N 118 26W
Weston, W. Va., U.S.A. 108 F5 39 2N 80 28W
Weston I., Canada 102 B4 52 33N 79 36W
Weston-super-Mare, U.K. 13 F5 51 21N 2 58W
Westover, U.S.A. 110 F6 40 45N 78 40W
Westport, Canada 111 B8 44 40N 76 25W
Westport, Ireland 15 C2 53 48N 9 31W
Westport, N.Z. 91 J3 41 46 S 171 37 E
Westport, N.Y., U.S.A. 111 B11 44 11N 73 26W
Westport, Oreg., U.S.A. 116 D3 46 8N 123 23W
Westport, Wash., U.S.A. 116 D2 46 53N 124 6W
Westray, Canada 105 C8 53 36N 101 24W
Westray, U.K. 14 B5 59 18N 3 0W
Westree, Canada 102 C3 47 26N 81 34W
Westville, U.S.A. 116 F6 39 8N 120 42W
Westwood, U.S.A. 114 F3 40 18N 121 0W
Wetar, Indonesia 63 F7 7 30 S 126 30 E
Wetaskiwin, Canada 104 C6 52 55N 113 24W
Wete, Tanzania 84 F7 5 4 S 39 43 E
Wetherby, U.K. 12 D6 53 56N 1 23W
Wethersfield, U.S.A. 111 E12 41 42N 72 40W
Wetteren, Belgium 17 D3 51 0N 3 53 E
Wetzlar, Germany 24 E4 50 32N 8 31 E
Wewoka, U.S.A. 113 H6 35 9N 96 30W
Wexford, Ireland 15 D5 52 20N 6 28W
Wexford □, Ireland 15 D5 52 20N 6 25W
Wexford Harbour, Ireland 15 D5 52 20N 6 25W
Weyburn, Canada 105 D8 49 40N 103 50W
Weyer Markt, Austria 26 D7 47 51N 14 40 E
Weyhe, Germany 24 C4 52 58N 8 49 E
Weyib →, Ethiopia 81 F5 7 15N 40 15 E
Weymouth, Canada 103 D6 44 30N 66 1W
Weymouth, U.K. 13 G5 50 37N 2 28W
Weymouth, U.S.A. 111 D14 42 13N 70 58W
Weymouth, C., Australia 94 A3 12 37 S 143 27 E
Wha Ti, Canada 100 B8 63 8N 117 16W
Whakatane, N.Z. 91 G6 37 57 S 177 1 E
Whale →, Canada 103 A6 58 15N 67 40W
Whale Cove, Canada 105 A10 62 11N 92 36W
Whales, B. of, Antarctica 5 D12 78 0 S 165 0W
Whalsay, U.K. 14 A8 60 22N 0 59W
Whangamomona, N.Z. 91 H5 39 8 S 174 44 E
Whangarei, N.Z. 91 F5 35 43 S 174 21 E
Whangarei Harb., N.Z. 91 F5 35 45 S 174 28 E
Wharfe →, U.K. 12 D6 53 51N 1 9W
Wharfedale, U.K. 12 C5 54 6N 2 1W
Wharton, N.J., U.S.A. 111 F10 40 54N 74 35W
Wharton, Pa., U.S.A. 110 E6 41 31N 78 1W
Wharton, Tex., U.S.A. 113 L6 29 19N 96 6W
Wheatland, Calif., U.S.A. 116 F5 39 1N 121 25W
Wheatland, Wyo., U.S.A. 112 D2 42 3N 104 58W
Wheatley, Canada 110 D2 42 6N 82 27W
Wheaton, Md., U.S.A. 108 F7 39 3N 77 3W
Wheaton, Minn., U.S.A. 112 C6 45 48N 96 30W
Wheelbarrow Pk., U.S.A. 116 H10 37 26N 116 5W
Wheeler, Oreg., U.S.A. 114 D2 45 41N 123 53W
Wheeler, Tex., U.S.A. 113 H4 35 27N 100 16W
Wheeler →, Canada 103 A6 57 2N 67 13W
Wheeler L., U.S.A. 109 H2 34 48N 87 23W
Wheeler Pk., N. Mex., U.S.A. 115 H11 36 34N 105 25W
Wheeler Pk., Nev., U.S.A. 115 G6 38 57N 114 15W
Wheeler Ridge, U.S.A. 117 L8 35 0N 118 57W
Wheeling, U.S.A. 110 F4 40 4N 80 43W
Whernside, U.K. 12 C5 54 14N 2 24W
Whiskey Jack L., Canada 105 B8 58 23N 101 55W
Whistleduck Cr. →, Australia 94 C2 20 15 S 135 18 E
Whistler, Canada 104 C4 50 7N 122 58W
Whitby, Canada 110 C6 43 52N 78 56W
Whitby, U.K. 12 C7 54 29N 0 37W
White →, Ark., U.S.A. 113 J9 33 57N 91 5W
White →, Ind., U.S.A. 108 F2 38 25N 87 45W
White →, S. Dak., U.S.A. 112 D5 43 42N 99 27W
White →, Tex., U.S.A. 113 J4 33 14N 100 56W
White →, Utah, U.S.A. 114 F9 40 4N 109 41W
White →, Vt., U.S.A. 111 C12 43 37N 72 20W
White →, Wash., U.S.A. 116 C4 47 12N 122 15W
White, L., Australia 92 D4 21 9 S 128 56 E
White B., Canada 103 C8 50 0N 56 35W
White Bird, U.S.A. 114 D5 45 46N 116 18W
White Butte, U.S.A. 112 B3 46 23N 103 18W
White City, U.S.A. 114 E2 42 26N 122 51W
White Cliffs, Australia 95 E3 30 50 S 143 10 E
White Hall, U.S.A. 112 F9 39 26N 90 24W
White Haven, U.S.A. 111 E9 41 4N 75 47W
White Horse, Vale of, U.K. 13 F6 51 37N 1 30W
White I., N.Z. 91 G6 37 30 S 177 13 E
White L., Canada 111 A8 45 18N 76 31W
White L., U.S.A. 113 L8 29 44N 92 30W
White Mountain Peak, U.S.A. 115 G4 37 38N 118 15W
White Mts., Calif., U.S.A. 116 H8 37 30N 118 15W
White Mts., N.H., U.S.A. 111 B13 44 15N 71 15W
White Nile = Nîl el Abyad →, Sudan 81 D3 15 38N 32 31 E
White Nile Dam = Khazzān Jabal al Awliyā, Sudan 81 D3 15 24N 32 20 E
White Otter L., Canada 102 C1 49 5N 91 55W
White Pass, U.S.A. 116 D5 46 38N 121 24W
White Plains, U.S.A. 111 E11 41 2N 73 46W
White River, Canada 102 C2 48 35N 85 20W
White River, S. Africa 89 D5 25 20 S 31 0 E
White River, U.S.A. 112 D4 43 34N 100 45W
White Rock, Canada 116 A4 49 2N 122 48W
White Russia = Belarus ■, Europe 46 F4 53 30N 27 0 E
White Sea = Beloye More, Russia 50 C4 66 30N 38 0 E
White Sulphur Springs, Mont., U.S.A. 114 C8 46 33N 110 54W
White Sulphur Springs, W. Va., U.S.A. 108 G5 37 48N 80 18W
White Swan, U.S.A. 116 D6 46 23N 120 44W
White Volta →, Ghana 83 D4 9 10N 1 15W
Whitecliffs, N.Z. 91 K3 43 26 S 171 55 E
Whitecourt, Canada 104 C5 54 10N 115 45W
Whiteface Mt., U.S.A. 111 B11 44 22N 73 54W
Whitefield, U.S.A. 111 B13 44 23N 71 37W
Whitefish, U.S.A. 114 B6 48 25N 114 20W
Whitefish L., Canada 105 A7 62 41N 106 48W
Whitefish Point, U.S.A. 108 B3 46 45N 84 59W
Whitegull, L., Canada 103 A7 55 27N 64 17W
Whitehall, Mich., U.S.A. 108 D2 43 24N 86 21W
Whitehall, Mont., U.S.A. 114 D7 45 52N 112 6W
Whitehall, N.Y., U.S.A. 111 C11 43 33N 73 24W
Whitehall, Wis., U.S.A. 112 C9 44 22N 91 19W
Whitehaven, U.K. 12 C4 54 33N 3 35W
Whitehorse, Canada 104 A1 60 43N 135 3W
Whitemark, Australia 94 G4 40 7 S 148 3 E
Whiteplains, Liberia 82 D2 6 28N 10 40W
Whiteriver, U.S.A. 115 K9 33 50N 109 58W
Whitesand →, Canada 104 A5 60 9N 115 45W
Whitesands, S. Africa 88 E3 34 23 S 20 50 E
Whitesboro, N.Y., U.S.A. 111 C9 43 7N 75 18W
Whitesboro, Tex., U.S.A. 113 J6 33 39N 96 54W
Whiteshell Prov. Park, Canada 105 D9 50 0N 95 40W
Whitesville, U.S.A. 110 D7 42 2N 77 46W
Whiteville, U.S.A. 109 H6 34 20N 78 42W
Whitewater, U.S.A. 108 D1 42 50N 88 44W
Whitewater Baldy, U.S.A. 115 K9 33 20N 108 39W
Whitewater L., Canada 102 B2 50 50N 89 10W
Whitewood, Australia 94 C3 21 28 S 143 30 E
Whitewood, Canada 105 C8 50 20N 102 20W
Whithorn, U.K. 14 G4 54 44N 4 26W
Whitianga, N.Z. 91 G5 36 47 S 175 41 E
Whitman, U.S.A. 111 D14 42 5N 70 56W
Whitney, Canada 102 C4 45 31N 78 14W
Whitney, Mt., U.S.A. 116 J8 36 35N 118 18W
Whitney Point, U.S.A. 111 D9 42 20N 75 58W
Whitstable, U.K. 13 F9 51 21N 1 3 E
Whitsunday I., Australia 94 C4 20 15 S 149 4 E
Whittier, U.S.A. 117 M8 33 58N 118 3W
Whittlesea, Australia 95 F4 37 27 S 145 9 E
Wholdaia L., Canada 105 A8 60 43N 104 20W
Whyalla, Australia 95 E2 33 2 S 137 30 E
Wiarton, Canada 102 D3 44 40N 81 10W
Wiawso, Ghana 82 D4 6 10N 2 25W
Wiay, U.K. 14 D1 57 24N 7 13W
Wiązów, Poland 45 H4 50 50N 17 10 E
Wibaux, U.S.A. 112 B2 46 59N 104 11W
Wichian Buri, Thailand 64 E3 15 39N 101 7 E
Wichita, U.S.A. 113 G6 37 42N 97 20W
Wichita Falls, U.S.A. 113 J5 33 54N 98 30W
Wick, U.K. 14 C5 58 26N 3 5W
Wicked Pt., Canada 110 C7 43 52N 77 15W
Wickenburg, U.S.A. 115 K7 33 58N 112 44W
Wickepin, Australia 93 F2 32 50 S 117 30 E
Wickham, Australia 92 D2 20 42 S 117 11 E
Wickham, C., Australia 94 F3 39 35 S 143 57 E
Wickliffe, U.S.A. 110 E3 41 36N 81 28W
Wicklow, Ireland 15 D5 52 59N 6 3W
Wicklow □, Ireland 15 D5 52 57N 6 25W
Wicklow Hd., Ireland 15 D6 52 58N 6 0W
Wicklow Mts., Ireland 15 C5 52 58N 6 26W
Widawa, Poland 45 G5 51 27N 18 51 E
Widawka →, Poland 45 G5 51 27N 18 52 E
Widgeegoara Cr. →, Australia 95 D4 28 51 S 146 34 E
Widgiemooltha, Australia 93 F3 31 30 S 121 34 E
Widnes, U.K. 12 D5 53 23N 2 45W
Więcbork, Poland 45 E4 53 21N 17 30 E
Wiehl, Germany 24 E3 50 56N 7 34 E
Wiek, Germany 24 A9 54 37N 13 17 E
Wielbark, Poland 44 E7 53 24N 20 55 E
Wieleń, Poland 45 F3 52 53N 16 9 E
Wielichowo, Poland 45 F3 52 7N 16 22 E
Wieliczka, Poland 45 J7 50 0N 20 5 E
Wielkopolskie □, Poland 45 F4 52 10N 17 30 E
Wieluń, Poland 45 G5 51 15N 18 34 E
Wien, Austria 27 C9 48 12N 16 22 E
Wiener Neustadt, Austria 27 D9 47 49N 16 16 E
Wieprz →, Poland 45 G8 51 34N 21 49 E
Wieprza →, Poland 44 D3 54 26N 16 25 E
Wieruszów, Poland 45 G5 51 19N 18 9 E
Wiesbaden, Germany 25 E4 50 4N 8 14 E
Wiesental, Germany 25 F4 49 13N 8 31 E
Wiesloch, Germany 25 F4 49 18N 8 41 E
Wiesmoor, Germany 24 B3 53 24N 7 47 E
Wieżyca, Poland 44 D5 54 14N 18 8 E
Wigan, U.K. 12 D5 53 33N 2 38W
Wiggins, Colo., U.S.A. 112 E2 40 14N 104 4W
Wiggins, Miss., U.S.A. 113 K10 30 51N 89 8W
Wight, I. of □, U.K. 13 G6 50 40N 1 20W
Wigry, Jezioro, Poland 44 D10 54 2N 23 8 E
Wigston, U.K. 13 E6 52 35N 1 6W
Wigton, U.K. 12 C4 54 50N 3 10W
Wigtown, U.K. 14 G4 54 53N 4 27W
Wigtown B., U.K. 14 G4 54 46N 4 15W
Wil, Switz. 25 H5 47 28N 9 3 E
Wilamowice, Poland 45 J6 49 55N 19 9 E
Wilber, U.S.A. 112 E6 40 29N 96 58W
Wilberforce, Canada 110 A6 45 2N 78 13W
Wilberforce, C., Australia 94 A2 11 54 S 136 35 E
Wilburton, U.S.A. 113 H7 34 55N 95 19W
Wilcannia, Australia 95 E3 31 30 S 143 26 E
Wilcox, U.S.A. 110 E6 41 35N 78 41W
Wildbad, Germany 25 G4 48 44N 8 33 E
Wildeshausen, Germany 24 C4 52 54N 8 27 E
Wildon, Austria 26 E8 46 52N 15 31 E
Wildrose, U.S.A. 117 J9 36 14N 117 11W
Wildspitze, Austria 26 E3 46 53N 10 53 E
Wilga →, Poland 45 G8 51 52N 21 18 E
Wilge →, S. Africa 89 D4 27 3 S 28 20 E
Wilhelm II Coast, Antarctica 5 C7 68 0 S 90 0 E
Wilhelmsburg, Austria 26 C8 48 6N 15 36 E
Wilhelmshaven, Germany 24 B4 53 31N 8 7 E
Wilhelmstal, Namibia 88 C2 21 58 S 16 21 E
Wilkes-Barre, U.S.A. 111 E9 41 15N 75 53W
Wilkie, Canada 105 C7 52 27N 108 42W
Wilkinsburg, U.S.A. 110 F5 40 26N 79 53W
Wilkinson Lakes, Australia 93 E5 29 40 S 132 39 E
Willandra Creek →, Australia 95 E4 33 22 S 145 52 E
Willapa B., U.S.A. 114 C2 46 40N 124 0W
Willapa Hills, U.S.A. 116 D3 46 35N 123 25W
Willard, N.Y., U.S.A. 110 D8 42 40N 76 50W
Willard, Ohio, U.S.A. 110 E2 41 3N 82 44W
Willcox, U.S.A. 115 K9 32 15N 109 50W
Willemstad, Neth. Ant. 121 D6 12 5N 69 0W
Willet, U.S.A. 111 D9 42 28N 75 55W
William →, Canada 105 B7 59 8N 109 19W
William 'Bill' Dannely Res., U.S.A. 109 J2 32 10N 87 10W
William Creek, Australia 95 D2 28 58 S 136 22 E
Williams, Australia 93 F2 33 2 S 116 52 E
Williams, Ariz., U.S.A. 115 J7 35 15N 112 11W
Williams, Calif., U.S.A. 116 F4 39 9N 122 9W
Williams Harbour, Canada 103 B8 52 33N 55 47W
Williams Lake, Canada 104 C4 52 10N 122 10W
Williamsburg, Ky., U.S.A. 109 G3 36 44N 84 10W
Williamsburg, Pa., U.S.A. 110 F6 40 28N 78 12W
Williamsburg, Va., U.S.A. 108 G7 37 17N 76 44W
Williamson, N.Y., U.S.A. 110 C7 43 14N 77 11W
Williamson, W. Va., U.S.A. 108 G4 37 41N 82 17W
Williamsport, U.S.A. 110 E7 41 15N 77 0W
Williamston, U.S.A. 109 H7 35 51N 77 4W
Williamstown, Australia 95 F3 37 51 S 144 52 E
Williamstown, Ky., U.S.A. 108 F3 38 38N 84 34W
Williamstown, Mass., U.S.A. 111 D11 42 41N 73 12W
Williamstown, N.Y., U.S.A. 111 C9 43 26N 75 53W
Willimantic, U.S.A. 111 E12 41 43N 72 13W
Willingboro, U.S.A. 108 E8 40 3N 74 54W
Willis Group, Australia 94 B5 16 18 S 150 0 E
Williston, S. Africa 88 E3 31 20 S 20 53 E
Williston, Fla., U.S.A. 109 L4 29 23N 82 27W
Williston, N. Dak., U.S.A. 112 A3 48 9N 103 37W
Williston L., Canada 104 B4 56 0N 124 0W
Willits, U.S.A. 114 G2 39 25N 123 21W
Willmar, U.S.A. 112 C7 45 7N 95 3W
Willoughby, U.S.A. 110 E3 41 39N 81 24W
Willow Bunch, Canada 105 D7 49 20N 105 35W
Willow L., Canada 104 A5 62 10N 119 8W
Willow Wall, The, China 57 C12 42 10N 122 0 E
Willowick, U.S.A. 110 E3 41 38N 81 28W
Willowlake →, Canada 104 A4 62 42N 123 8W
Willowmore, S. Africa 88 E3 33 15 S 23 30 E
Willows, U.S.A. 116 F4 39 31N 122 12W
Willowvale = Gatyana, S. Africa 89 E4 32 16 S 28 31 E
Wills, L., Australia 92 D4 21 25 S 128 51 E
Wills Cr. →, Australia 94 C3 22 43 S 140 2 E
Willsboro, U.S.A. 111 B11 44 21N 73 24W
Willunga, Australia 95 F2 35 15 S 138 30 E
Wilmette, U.S.A. 108 D2 42 5N 87 42W
Wilmington, Australia 95 E2 32 39 S 138 7 E
Wilmington, Del., U.S.A. 108 F8 39 45N 75 33W
Wilmington, N.C., U.S.A. 109 H7 34 14N 77 55W
Wilmington, Ohio, U.S.A. 108 F4 39 27N 83 50W
Wilmington, Vt., U.S.A. 111 D12 42 52N 72 52W
Wilmslow, U.K. 12 D5 53 19N 2 13W
Wilpena →, Australia 95 E2 31 25 S 139 29 E
Wilsall, U.S.A. 114 D8 45 59N 110 38W
Wilson, N.C., U.S.A. 109 H7 35 44N 77 55W
Wilson, N.Y., U.S.A. 110 C6 43 19N 78 50W
Wilson, Pa., U.S.A. 111 F9 40 41N 75 15W
Wilson →, Australia 92 C4 16 48 S 128 16 E
Wilson Bluff, Australia 93 F4 31 41 S 129 0 E
Wilson Inlet, Australia 93 G2 35 0 S 117 22 E
Wilsons Promontory, Australia 95 F4 38 55 S 146 25 E
Wilster, Germany 24 B5 53 55N 9 23 E
Wilton, U.S.A. 112 B4 47 10N 100 47W
Wilton →, Australia 94 A1 14 45 S 134 33 E
Wiltshire □, U.K. 13 F6 51 18N 1 53W
Wiltz, Lux. 17 E5 49 57N 5 55 E
Wiluna, Australia 93 E3 26 36 S 120 14 E
Wimborne Minster, U.K. 13 G6 50 48N 1 59W
Wimereux, France 19 B8 50 45N 1 37 E
Wimmera →, Australia 95 F3 36 8 S 141 56 E
Winam G., Kenya 86 C3 0 20 S 34 15 E
Winburg, S. Africa 88 D4 28 30 S 27 2 E
Winchendon, U.S.A. 111 D12 42 41N 72 3W
Winchester, U.K. 13 F6 51 4N 1 18W
Winchester, Conn., U.S.A. 111 E11 41 53N 73 9W
Winchester, Idaho, U.S.A. 114 C5 46 14N 116 38W
Winchester, Ind., U.S.A. 108 E3 40 10N 84 59W
Winchester, Ky., U.S.A. 108 G3 38 0N 84 11W
Winchester, N.H., U.S.A. 111 D12 42 46N 72 23W
Winchester, Nev., U.S.A. 117 J11 36 6N 115 10W
Winchester, Tenn., U.S.A. 109 H2 35 11N 86 7W
Winchester, Va., U.S.A. 108 F6 39 11N 78 10W
Wind →, U.S.A. 114 E9 43 12N 108 12W
Wind River Range, U.S.A. 114 E9 43 0N 109 30W
Windau = Ventspils, Latvia 9 H19 57 25N 21 32 E
Windber, U.S.A. 110 F6 40 14N 78 50W
Winder, U.S.A. 109 J4 34 0N 83 45W
Windermere, U.K. 12 C5 54 23N 2 55W
Windhoek, Namibia 88 C2 22 35 S 17 4 E
Windischgarsten, Austria 26 D7 47 42N 14 21 E
Windom, U.S.A. 112 D7 43 52N 95 7W
Windorah, Australia 94 D3 25 24 S 142 36 E
Window Rock, U.S.A. 115 J9 35 41N 109 3W
Windrush →, U.K. 13 F6 51 43N 1 24W
Windsor, Australia 95 E5 33 37 S 150 50 E
Windsor, N.S., Canada 103 D7 44 59N 64 5W
Windsor, Ont., Canada 102 D3 42 18N 83 0W
Windsor, U.K. 13 F7 51 29N 0 36W
Windsor, Colo., U.S.A. 112 E2 40 29N 104 54W
Windsor, Conn., U.S.A. 111 E12 41 50N 72 39W
Windsor, Mo., U.S.A. 112 F8 38 32N 93 31W
Windsor, N.Y., U.S.A. 111 D9 42 5N 75 37W
Windsor, Vt., U.S.A. 111 C12 43 29N 72 24W
Windsor & Maidenhead □, U.K. 13 F7 51 29N 0 40W
Windsorton, S. Africa 88 D3 28 16 S 24 44 E
Windward Is., W. Indies 121 D7 13 0N 61 0W
Windward Passage = Vientos, Paso de los, Caribbean 121 C5 20 0N 74 0W
Winefred L., Canada 105 B6 55 30N 110 30W
Winejok, Sudan 81 F2 9 1N 27 30 E
Winfield, U.S.A. 113 G6 37 15N 96 59W
Wingate Mts., Australia 92 B5 14 25 S 130 40 E
Wingham, Australia 95 E5 31 48 S 152 22 E
Wingham, Canada 102 D3 43 55N 81 20W
Winisk, Canada 102 A2 55 20N 85 15W
Winisk →, Canada 102 A2 55 17N 85 5W
Winisk L., Canada 102 B2 52 55N 87 22W
Wink, U.S.A. 113 K3 31 45N 103 9W
Winkler, Canada 105 D9 49 10N 97 56W
Winklern, Austria 26 E5 46 52N 12 52 E
Winlock, U.S.A. 116 D4 46 30N 122 56W
Winneba, Ghana 83 D4 5 25N 0 36W
Winnebago, L., U.S.A. 108 D1 44 0N 88 26W
Winnecke Cr. →, Australia 92 C5 18 35 S 131 34 E

Winnemucca, *U.S.A.* **114 F5** 40 58N 117 44W
Winnemucca L., *U.S.A.* **114 F4** 40 7N 119 21W
Winnett, *U.S.A.* **114 C9** 47 0N 108 21W
Winnfield, *U.S.A.* **113 K8** 31 56N 92 38W
Winnibigoshish, L., *U.S.A.* **112 B7** 47 27N 94 13W
Winnipeg, *Canada* **105 D9** 49 54N 97 9W
Winnipeg →, *Canada* **105 C9** 50 38N 96 19W
Winnipeg, L., *Canada* **105 C9** 52 0N 97 0W
Winnipeg Beach, *Canada* **105 C9** 50 30N 96 58W
Winnipegosis, *Canada* **105 C9** 51 39N 99 55W
Winnipegosis L., *Canada* **105 C9** 52 30N 100 0W
Winnipesaukee, L., *U.S.A.* **111 C13** 43 38N 71 21W
Winnisquam L., *U.S.A.* **111 C13** 43 33N 71 31W
Winnsboro, *La., U.S.A.* **113 J9** 32 10N 91 43W
Winnsboro, *S.C., U.S.A.* **109 H5** 34 23N 81 5W
Winnsboro, *Tex., U.S.A.* **113 J7** 32 58N 95 17W
Winokapau, L., *Canada* **103 B7** 53 15N 62 50W
Winona, *Minn., U.S.A.* **112 C9** 44 3N 91 39W
Winona, *Miss., U.S.A.* **113 J10** 33 29N 89 44W
Winooski, *U.S.A.* **111 B11** 44 29N 73 11W
Winooski →, *U.S.A.* **111 B11** 44 32N 73 17W
Winschoten, *Neths.* **17 A7** 53 9N 7 3 E
Winsen, *Germany* **24 B6** 53 22N 10 13 E
Winsford, *U.K.* **12 D5** 53 12N 2 31W
Winslow, *Ariz., U.S.A.* **115 J8** 35 2N 110 42W
Winslow, *Wash., U.S.A.* **116 C4** 47 38N 122 31W
Winsted, *U.S.A.* **111 E11** 41 55N 73 4W
Winston-Salem, *U.S.A.* **109 G5** 36 6N 80 15W
Winter Garden, *U.S.A.* **109 L5** 28 34N 81 35W
Winter Haven, *U.S.A.* **109 M5** 28 1N 81 44W
Winter Park, *U.S.A.* **109 L5** 28 36N 81 20W
Winterberg, *Germany* **24 D4** 51 11N 8 33 E
Winterhaven, *U.S.A.* **117 N12** 32 47N 114 39W
Winters, *U.S.A.* **116 G5** 38 32N 121 58W
Wintersville, *U.S.A.* **110 F4** 40 23N 80 42W
Winterswijk, *Neths.* **17 C6** 51 58N 6 43 E
Winterthur, *Switz.* **25 H4** 47 30N 8 44 E
Winthrop, *U.S.A.* **114 B3** 48 28N 120 10W
Winton, *Australia* **94 C3** 22 24 S 143 3 E
Winton, *N.Z.* **91 M2** 46 8 S 168 20 E
Wipper →, *Germany* **24 D7** 51 16N 11 12 E
Wirrulla, *Australia* **95 E1** 32 24 S 134 31 E
Wisbech, *U.K.* **13 E8** 52 41N 0 9 E
Wisconsin □, *U.S.A.* **112 C10** 44 45N 89 30W
Wisconsin →, *U.S.A.* **112 D9** 43 0N 91 15W
Wisconsin Rapids, *U.S.A.* **112 C10** 44 23N 89 49W
Wisdom, *U.S.A.* **114 D7** 45 37N 113 27W
Wishaw, *U.K.* **14 F5** 55 46N 3 54W
Wishek, *U.S.A.* **112 B5** 46 16N 99 33W
Wisła, *Poland* **45 J5** 49 38N 18 53 E
Wisła →, *Poland* **44 D5** 54 22N 18 55 E
Wisłok →, *Poland* **45 H9** 50 13N 22 32 E
Wisłoka →, *Poland* **45 H8** 50 27N 21 23 E
Wismar, *Germany* **24 B7** 53 54N 11 29 E
Wisner, *U.S.A.* **112 E6** 41 59N 96 55W
Wissant, *France* **19 B8** 50 52N 1 40 E
Wissembourg, *France* **19 C14** 49 2N 7 57 E
Wisznice, *Poland* **45 G10** 51 48N 23 13 E
Witbank, *S. Africa* **89 D4** 25 51 S 29 14 E
Witdraai, *S. Africa* **88 D3** 26 58 S 20 48 E
Witham, *U.K.* **13 F8** 51 48N 0 40 E
Witham →, *U.K.* **12 E7** 52 59N 0 2W
Withernsea, *U.K.* **12 D8** 53 44N 0 1 E
Witkowo, *Poland* **45 F4** 52 26N 17 45 E
Witney, *U.K.* **13 F6** 51 48N 1 28W
Witnica, *Poland* **45 F1** 52 40N 14 54 E
Witnossob →, *Namibia* **88 D3** 23 55 S 18 45 E
Wittdün, *Germany* **24 A4** 54 38N 8 23 E
Witten, *Germany* **24 D3** 51 26N 7 20 E
Wittenberge, *Germany* **24 B7** 53 0N 11 45 E
Wittenburg, *Germany* **24 B7** 53 31N 11 4 E
Wittenheim, *France* **19 E14** 47 44N 7 20 E
Wittenoom, *Australia* **92 D2** 22 15 S 118 20 E
Wittingen, *Germany* **24 C6** 52 44N 10 44 E
Wittlich, *Germany* **25 F2** 49 59N 6 53 E
Wittmund, *Germany* **24 B3** 53 34N 7 46 E
Wittow, *Germany* **24 A9** 54 38N 13 20 E
Wittstock, *Germany* **24 B8** 53 10N 12 28 E
Witvlei, *Namibia* **88 C2** 22 23 S 18 32 E
Witzenhausen, *Germany* **24 D5** 51 20N 9 51 E
Wkra →, *Poland* **45 F7** 52 27N 20 44 E
Władysławowo, *Poland* **44 D5** 54 48N 18 25 E
Wleń, *Poland* **45 G2** 51 2N 15 39 E
Wlingi, *Indonesia* **63 H15** 8 5 S 112 25 E
Włocławek, *Poland* **45 F6** 52 40N 19 3 E
Włodawa, *Poland* **45 G10** 51 33N 23 31 E
Włoszczowa, *Poland* **45 H6** 50 50N 19 55 E
Woburn, *U.S.A.* **111 D13** 42 29N 71 9W
Wodian, *China* **56 H7** 32 50N 112 35 E
Wodzisław Śląski, *Poland* **45 H5** 50 1N 18 26 E
Woerth, *France* **19 D14** 48 57N 7 45 E
Woinbogoin, *China* **58 A2** 32 51N 98 39 E
Woippy, *France* **19 C13** 49 10N 6 8 E
Wojcieszow, *Poland* **45 H2** 50 58N 15 55 E
Wokam, *Indonesia* **63 F8** 5 45 S 134 28 E
Woking, *U.K.* **13 F7** 51 19N 0 34W
Wokingham □, *U.K.* **13 F7** 51 25N 0 51W
Wolbrom, *Poland* **45 H6** 50 24N 19 45 E
Wołczyn, *Poland* **45 G5** 51 1N 18 3 E
Woldegk, *Germany* **24 B9** 53 27N 13 34 E
Wolf →, *Canada* **104 A2** 60 17N 132 33W
Wolf Creek, *U.S.A.* **114 C7** 47 0N 112 4W
Wolf L., *Canada* **104 A2** 60 24N 131 40W
Wolf Point, *U.S.A.* **112 A2** 48 5N 105 39W
Wolfe I., *Canada* **102 D4** 44 7N 76 20W
Wolfeboro, *U.S.A.* **111 C13** 43 35N 71 13W
Wolfen, *Germany* **24 D8** 51 39N 12 15 E
Wolfenbüttel, *Germany* **24 C6** 52 10N 10 33 E
Wolfratshausen, *Germany* **25 H7** 47 54N 11 24 E
Wolfsberg, *Austria* **26 E7** 46 50N 14 52 E
Wolfsburg, *Germany* **24 C6** 52 25N 10 48 E
Wolgast, *Germany* **24 A9** 54 3N 13 44 E
Wolhusen, *Switz.* **25 H4** 47 4N 8 4 E
Wolin, *Poland* **44 E1** 53 50N 14 37 E
Wollaston, Is., *Chile* **128 H3** 55 40 S 67 30W
Wollaston L., *Canada* **105 B8** 58 7N 103 10W
Wollaston Lake, *Canada* **105 B8** 58 3N 103 33W
Wollaston Pen., *Canada* **100 B8** 69 30N 115 0W
Wollongong, *Australia* **95 E5** 34 25 S 150 54 E
Wolmaransstad, *S. Africa* **88 D4** 27 12 S 25 59 E
Wolmirstedt, *Germany* **24 C7** 52 14N 11 37 E
Wołomin, *Poland* **45 F8** 52 19N 21 15 E
Wołów, *Poland* **45 G3** 51 20N 16 38 E
Wolseley, *S. Africa* **88 E2** 33 26 S 19 7 E
Wolsey, *U.S.A.* **112 C5** 44 24N 98 28W
Wolstenholme, C., *Canada* **98 C12** 62 35N 77 30W
Wolsztyn, *Poland* **45 F3** 52 8N 16 5 E
Wolvega, *Neths.* **17 B6** 52 52N 6 0 E
Wolverhampton, *U.K.* **13 E5** 52 35N 2 7W
Wondai, *Australia* **95 D5** 26 20 S 151 49 E
Wongalarroo L., *Australia* **95 E3** 31 32 S 144 0 E
Wongan Hills, *Australia* **93 F2** 30 51 S 116 37 E
Wŏnju, *S. Korea* **57 F14** 37 22N 127 58 E
Wonosari, *Indonesia* **63 G14** 7 58 S 110 36 E
Wonosobo, *Indonesia* **63 G13** 7 22 S 109 54 E
Wonowon, *Canada* **104 B4** 56 44N 121 48W
Wŏnsan, *N. Korea* **57 E14** 39 11N 127 27 E
Wonthaggi, *Australia* **95 F4** 38 37 S 145 37 E
Wood Buffalo Nat. Park, *Canada* **104 B6** 59 0N 113 41W
Wood Is., *Australia* **92 C3** 16 24 S 123 19 E
Wood L., *Canada* **105 B8** 55 17N 103 17W
Woodah I., *Australia* **94 A2** 13 27 S 136 10 E
Woodbourne, *U.S.A.* **111 E10** 41 46N 74 36W
Woodbridge, *Canada* **110 C5** 43 47N 79 36W
Woodbridge, *U.K.* **13 E9** 52 6N 1 20 E
Woodburn, *U.S.A.* **114 D2** 45 9N 122 51W
Woodenbong, *Australia* **95 D5** 28 24 S 152 39 E
Woodend, *Australia* **95 F3** 37 20 S 144 33 E
Woodford, *Australia* **95 D5** 26 58 S 152 47 E
Woodfords, *U.S.A.* **116 G7** 38 47N 119 50W
Woodlake, *U.S.A.* **116 J7** 36 25N 119 6W
Woodland, *Calif., U.S.A.* **116 G5** 38 41N 121 46W
Woodland, *Maine, U.S.A.* **109 C12** 45 9N 67 25W
Woodland, *Pa., U.S.A.* **110 F6** 40 59N 78 21W
Woodland, *Wash., U.S.A.* **116 E4** 45 54N 122 45W
Woodland Caribou Prov. Park, *Canada* **105 C10** 51 0N 94 45W
Woodridge, *Canada* **105 D9** 49 20N 96 9W
Woodroffe, Mt., *Australia* **93 E5** 26 20 S 131 45 E
Woods, L., *Australia* **94 B1** 17 50 S 133 30 E
Woods, L. of the, *Canada* **105 D10** 49 15N 94 45W
Woodside, *Australia* **95 F4** 38 31 S 146 52 E
Woodstock, *Australia* **94 B4** 19 35 S 146 50 E
Woodstock, *N.B., Canada* **103 C6** 46 11N 67 37W
Woodstock, *Ont., Canada* **102 D3** 43 10N 80 45W
Woodstock, *U.K.* **13 F6** 51 51N 1 20W
Woodstock, *Ill., U.S.A.* **112 D10** 42 19N 88 27W
Woodstock, *Vt., U.S.A.* **111 C12** 43 37N 72 31W
Woodsville, *U.S.A.* **111 B13** 44 9N 72 2W
Woodville, *N.Z.* **91 J5** 40 20 S 175 53 E
Woodville, *Miss., U.S.A.* **113 K9** 31 6N 91 18W
Woodville, *Tex., U.S.A.* **113 K7** 30 47N 94 25W
Woodward, *U.S.A.* **113 G5** 36 26N 99 24W
Woody, *U.S.A.* **117 K8** 35 42N 118 50W
Woody →, *Canada* **105 C8** 52 31N 100 51W
Woolamai, C., *Australia* **95 F4** 38 30 S 145 23 E
Wooler, *U.K.* **12 B5** 55 33N 2 1W
Woolgoolga, *Australia* **95 E5** 30 6 S 153 11 E
Woomera, *Australia* **95 E2** 31 5 S 136 50 E
Woonsocket, *R.I., U.S.A.* **111 E13** 42 0N 71 31W
Woonsocket, *S. Dak., U.S.A.* **112 C5** 44 3N 98 17W
Wooramel →, *Australia* **93 E1** 25 47 S 114 10 E
Wooramel Roadhouse, *Australia* **93 E1** 25 45 S 114 17 E
Wooster, *U.S.A.* **110 F3** 40 48N 81 56W
Worcester, *S. Africa* **88 E2** 33 39 S 19 27 E
Worcester, *U.K.* **13 E5** 52 11N 2 12W
Worcester, *Mass., U.S.A.* **111 D13** 42 16N 71 48W
Worcester, *N.Y., U.S.A.* **111 D10** 42 36N 74 45W
Worcestershire □, *U.K.* **13 E5** 52 13N 2 10W
Wörgl, *Austria* **26 D5** 47 29N 12 3 E
Workington, *U.K.* **12 C4** 54 39N 3 33W
Worksop, *U.K.* **12 D6** 53 18N 1 7W
Workum, *Neths.* **17 B5** 52 59N 5 26 E
Worland, *U.S.A.* **114 D10** 44 1N 107 57W
Wormhout, *France* **19 B9** 50 52N 2 28 E
Worms, *Germany* **25 F4** 49 37N 8 21 E
Worsley, *Canada* **104 B5** 56 31N 119 8W
Wörth, *Germany* **25 F8** 49 1N 12 24 E
Wortham, *U.S.A.* **113 K6** 31 47N 96 28W
Wörther See, *Austria* **26 E7** 46 37N 14 10 E
Worthing, *U.K.* **13 G7** 50 49N 0 21W
Worthington, *Minn., U.S.A.* **112 D7** 43 37N 95 36W
Worthington, *Pa., U.S.A.* **110 F5** 40 50N 79 38W
Wosi, *Indonesia* **63 E7** 0 15 S 128 0 E
Wou-han = Wuhan, *China* **59 B10** 30 31N 114 18 E
Wousi = Wuxi, *China* **59 B13** 31 33N 120 18 E
Wowoni, *Indonesia* **63 E6** 4 5 S 123 5 E
Wrangel I. = Vrangelya, Ostrov, *Russia* **51 B19** 71 0N 180 0 E
Wrangell, *U.S.A.* **104 B2** 56 28N 132 23W
Wrangell Mts., *U.S.A.* **100 B5** 61 30N 142 0W
Wrath, C., *U.K.* **14 C3** 58 38N 5 1W
Wray, *U.S.A.* **112 E3** 40 5N 102 13W
Wrekin, The, *U.K.* **13 E5** 52 41N 2 32W
Wrens, *U.S.A.* **109 J4** 33 12N 82 23W
Wrexham, *U.K.* **12 D4** 53 3N 3 0W
Wrexham □, *U.K.* **12 D5** 53 1N 2 58W
Wriezen, *Germany* **24 C10** 52 42N 14 7 E
Wright = Paranas, *Phil.* **61 F6** 11 42N 125 2 E
Wright, *U.S.A.* **112 D2** 43 47N 105 30W
Wright Pt., *Canada* **110 C3** 43 48N 81 44W
Wrightson Mt., *U.S.A.* **115 L8** 31 42N 110 51W
Wrightwood, *U.S.A.* **117 L9** 34 21N 117 38W
Wrigley, *Canada* **100 B7** 63 16N 123 37W
Wrocław, *Poland* **45 G4** 51 5N 17 5 E
Wronki, *Poland* **45 F3** 52 41N 16 21 E
Września, *Poland* **45 F4** 52 21N 17 36 E
Wschowa, *Poland* **45 G3** 51 48N 16 20 E
Wu Jiang →, *China* **58 C6** 29 40N 107 20 E
Wu'an, *China* **56 F8** 36 40N 114 15 E
Wubin, *Australia* **93 F2** 30 6 S 116 37 E
Wubu, *China* **56 F6** 37 28N 110 42 E
Wuchang, *China* **57 B14** 44 55N 127 5 E
Wucheng, *China* **56 F9** 37 12N 116 20 E
Wuchuan, *Guangdong, China* **59 G8** 21 33N 110 43 E
Wuchuan, *Guizhou, China* **58 C7** 28 25N 108 3 E
Wuchuan, *Nei Monggol Zizhiqu, China* **56 D6** 41 5N 111 28 E
Wudi, *China* **57 F9** 37 40N 117 35 E
Wuding, *China* **58 E4** 25 24N 102 21 E
Wuding He →, *China* **56 F6** 37 2N 110 23 E
Wudinna, *Australia* **95 E2** 33 0 S 135 22 E
Wudu, *China* **56 H3** 33 22N 104 54 E
Wufeng, *China* **59 B8** 30 12N 110 42 E
Wugang, *China* **59 D8** 26 44N 110 35 E
Wugong Shan, *China* **59 D9** 27 30N 114 0 E
Wuhan, *China* **59 B10** 30 31N 114 18 E
Wuhe, *China* **57 H9** 33 10N 117 50 E
Wuhsi = Wuxi, *China* **59 B13** 31 33N 120 18 E
Wuhu, *China* **59 B12** 31 22N 118 21 E
Wujiang, *China* **59 B13** 31 10N 120 38 E
Wukari, *Nigeria* **83 D6** 7 51N 9 42 E
Wulajie, *China* **57 B14** 44 6N 126 33 E
Wulanbulang, *China* **56 D6** 41 5N 110 55 E
Wular L., *India* **69 B6** 34 20N 74 30 E
Wulehe, *Ghana* **83 D5** 8 39N 0 0W
Wulian, *China* **57 G10** 35 40N 119 12 E
Wuliang Shan, *China* **58 E3** 24 30N 100 40 E
Wuliaru, *Indonesia* **63 F8** 7 27 S 131 0 E
Wuling Shan, *China* **58 C7** 30 0N 110 0 E
Wulong, *China* **58 C6** 29 22N 107 43 E
Wulumuchi = Ürümqi, *China* **50 E9** 43 45N 87 45 E
Wum, *Cameroon* **83 D7** 6 24N 10 2 E
Wuming, *China* **58 F7** 23 12N 108 18 E
Wun Rog, *Sudan* **81 F2** 9 0N 28 20 E
Wundowie, *Australia* **93 F2** 31 47 S 116 23 E
Wuning, *China* **59 C10** 29 17N 115 5 E
Wunnummin L., *Canada* **102 B2** 52 55N 89 10W
Wunsiedel, *Germany* **25 E8** 50 2N 12 0 E
Wunstorf, *Germany* **24 C5** 52 25N 9 26 E
Wuntho, *Burma* **67 H19** 23 55N 95 45 E
Wuping, *China* **59 E11** 25 5N 116 5 E
Wuppertal, *Germany* **24 D3** 51 16N 7 12 E
Wuppertal, *S. Africa* **88 E2** 32 13 S 19 12 E
Wuqing, *China* **57 E9** 39 23N 117 4 E
Wurtsboro, *U.S.A.* **111 E10** 41 35N 74 29W
Würzburg, *Germany* **25 F5** 49 46N 9 55 E
Wurzen, *Germany* **24 D8** 51 22N 12 44 E
Wushan, *China* **56 G3** 34 43N 104 53 E
Wushishi, *Nigeria* **83 D6** 9 46N 6 7 E
Wusuli Jiang = Ussuri →, *Asia* **54 A7** 48 27N 135 0 E
Wutach →, *Germany* **25 H4** 47 37N 8 15 E
Wutai, *China* **56 E7** 38 40N 113 12 E
Wuting = Huimin, *China* **57 F9** 37 27N 117 28 E
Wutong, *China* **59 E8** 25 24N 110 4 E
Wutonghaolai, *China* **57 C11** 42 50N 120 5 E
Wutongqiao, *China* **58 C4** 29 22N 103 50 E
Wuwei, *Anhui, China* **59 B11** 31 18N 117 54 E
Wuwei, *Gansu, China* **60 C5** 37 57N 102 34 E
Wuxi, *Jiangsu, China* **59 B13** 31 33N 120 18 E
Wuxi, *Sichuan, China* **58 B7** 31 23N 109 35 E
Wuxiang, *China* **56 F7** 36 49N 112 50 E
Wuxuan, *China* **58 F7** 23 34N 109 38 E
Wuxue, *China* **59 C10** 29 52N 115 30 E
Wuyang, *China* **56 H7** 33 25N 113 35 E
Wuyi, *Hebei, China* **56 F8** 37 46N 115 56 E
Wuyi, *Zhejiang, China* **59 C12** 28 52N 119 50 E
Wuyi Shan, *China* **59 D11** 27 0N 117 0 E
Wuyishan, *China* **59 D12** 27 45N 118 0 E
Wuyo, *Nigeria* **83 C7** 10 23N 11 50 E
Wuyuan, *Jiangxi, China* **59 C11** 29 15N 117 50 E
Wuyuan, *Nei Monggol Zizhiqu, China* **56 D5** 41 2N 108 20 E
Wuzhai, *China* **56 E6** 38 54N 111 48 E
Wuzhi Shan, *China* **64 C7** 18 45N 109 45 E
Wuzhong, *China* **56 E4** 38 2N 106 12 E
Wuzhou, *China* **59 F8** 23 30N 111 18 E
Wyaaba Cr. →, *Australia* **94 B3** 16 27 S 141 35 E
Wyalkatchem, *Australia* **93 F2** 31 8 S 117 22 E
Wyalusing, *U.S.A.* **111 E8** 41 40N 76 16W
Wyandotte, *U.S.A.* **108 D4** 42 12N 83 9W
Wyandra, *Australia* **95 D4** 27 12 S 145 56 E
Wyangala Res., *Australia* **95 E4** 33 54 S 149 0 E
Wyara, L., *Australia* **95 D3** 28 42 S 144 14 E
Wycheproof, *Australia* **95 F3** 36 5 S 143 17 E
Wye →, *U.K.* **13 F5** 51 38N 2 40W
Wyemandoo, *Australia* **93 E2** 28 28 S 118 29 E
Wyk, *Germany* **24 A4** 54 41N 8 33 E
Wymondham, *U.K.* **13 E9** 52 35N 1 7 E
Wymore, *U.S.A.* **112 E6** 40 7N 96 40W
Wyndham, *Australia* **92 C4** 15 33 S 128 3 E
Wyndham, *N.Z.* **91 M2** 46 20 S 168 51 E
Wynne, *U.S.A.* **113 H9** 35 14N 90 47W
Wynyard, *Australia* **94 G4** 41 5 S 145 44 E
Wynyard, *Canada* **105 C8** 51 45N 104 10W
Wyola L., *Australia* **93 E5** 29 8 S 130 17 E
Wyoming, *Canada* **110 D2** 42 57N 82 7W
Wyoming □, *U.S.A.* **114 E10** 43 0N 107 30W
Wyomissing, *U.S.A.* **111 F9** 40 20N 75 59W
Wyong, *Australia* **95 E5** 33 14 S 151 24 E
Wyrzysk, *Poland* **45 E4** 53 10N 17 17 E
Wyśmierzyce, *Poland* **45 G7** 51 37N 20 50 E
Wysoka, *Poland* **45 E4** 53 13N 17 2 E
Wysokie, *Poland* **45 H9** 50 55N 22 40 E
Wysokie Mazowieckie, *Poland* **45 F9** 52 55N 22 30 E
Wyszków, *Poland* **45 F8** 52 36N 21 25 E
Wyszogród, *Poland* **45 F7** 52 23N 20 9 E
Wytheville, *U.S.A.* **108 G5** 36 57N 81 5W
Wyżyna Małopolska, *Poland* **45 H7** 50 45N 20 0 E

X

Xaçmaz, *Azerbaijan* **49 K9** 41 31N 48 42 E
Xai-Xai, *Mozam.* **89 D5** 25 6 S 33 31 E
Xainza, *China* **60 C3** 30 58N 88 35 E
Xangongo, *Angola* **88 B2** 16 45 S 15 5 E
Xankändi, *Azerbaijan* **70 B5** 39 52N 46 49 E
Xanlar, *Azerbaijan* **49 K8** 40 37N 46 12 E
Xanten, *Germany* **24 D2** 51 39N 6 26 E
Xánthi, *Greece* **41 E8** 41 10N 24 58 E
Xánthi □, *Greece* **41 E8** 41 10N 24 58 E
Xanthos, *Turkey* **39 E11** 36 19N 29 18 E
Xanxerê, *Brazil* **127 B5** 26 53 S 52 23W
Xapuri, *Brazil* **124 F5** 10 35 S 68 35W
Xar Moron He →, *China* **57 C11** 43 25N 120 35 E
Xarrë, *Albania* **40 G4** 39 44N 20 3 E
Xátiva, *Spain* **33 G4** 38 59N 0 32W
Xau, L., *Botswana* **88 C3** 21 15 S 24 44 E
Xavantina, *Brazil* **127 A5** 21 15 S 52 48W
Xenia, *U.S.A.* **108 F4** 39 41N 83 56W
Xeropotamos →, *Cyprus* **36 E11** 34 42N 32 33 E
Xertigny, *France* **19 D13** 48 3N 6 24 E
Xhora, *S. Africa* **89 E4** 31 55 S 28 38 E
Xhumo, *Botswana* **88 C3** 21 7 S 24 35 E
Xi Jiang →, *China* **59 F9** 22 5N 113 20 E
Xi Xian, *Henan, China* **59 A10** 32 20N 114 43 E
Xi Xian, *Shanxi, China* **56 F6** 36 41N 110 58 E
Xia Xian, *China* **56 G6** 35 8N 111 12 E
Xiachengzi, *China* **57 B16** 44 40N 130 18 E
Xiachuan Dao, *China* **59 G9** 21 40N 112 40 E
Xiaguan, *China* **60 D5** 25 32N 100 16 E
Xiajiang, *China* **59 D10** 27 30N 115 10 E
Xiajin, *China* **56 F9** 36 56N 116 0 E
Xiamen, *China* **59 E12** 24 25N 118 4 E
Xi'an, *China* **56 G5** 34 15N 109 0 E
Xian Xian, *China* **56 E9** 38 12N 116 6 E
Xianfeng, *China* **58 C7** 29 40N 109 8 E
Xiang Jiang →, *China* **59 C9** 28 55N 112 50 E
Xiangcheng, *Henan, China* **56 H8** 33 29N 114 52 E
Xiangcheng, *Henan, China* **56 H7** 33 50N 113 27 E
Xiangcheng, *Sichuan, China* **58 C2** 28 53N 99 47 E
Xiangdu, *China* **58 F6** 23 13N 106 58 E
Xiangfan, *China* **59 A9** 32 2N 112 8 E
Xianggang = Hong Kong □, *China* **59 F10** 22 11N 114 14 E
Xianghuang Qi, *China* **56 C7** 42 2N 113 50 E
Xiangning, *China* **56 G6** 35 58N 110 50 E
Xiangquan, *China* **56 F7** 36 30N 113 1 E
Xiangquan He = Sutlej →, *Pakistan* **68 E4** 29 23N 71 3 E
Xiangshan, *China* **59 C13** 29 29N 121 51 E
Xiangshui, *China* **57 G10** 34 12N 119 33 E
Xiangtan, *China* **59 D9** 27 51N 112 54 E
Xiangxiang, *China* **59 D9** 27 43N 112 28 E
Xiangyin, *China* **59 C9** 28 38N 112 54 E
Xiangyun, *China* **58 E3** 25 34N 100 35 E
Xiangzhou, *China* **58 F7** 23 58N 109 40 E
Xianju, *China* **59 C13** 28 51N 120 44 E
Xianning, *China* **59 C10** 29 51N 114 16 E
Xianshui He →, *China* **58 B3** 30 10N 100 59 E
Xiantao, *China* **59 B9** 30 25N 113 25 E
Xianyang, *China* **56 G5** 34 20N 108 40 E
Xianyou, *China* **59 E12** 25 22N 118 38 E
Xiao Hinggan Ling, *China* **60 B7** 49 0N 127 0 E
Xiao Xian, *China* **56 G9** 34 15N 116 55 E
Xiaofeng, *China* **59 B12** 30 35N 119 32 E
Xiaogan, *China* **59 B9** 30 52N 113 55 E
Xiaojin, *China* **58 B4** 30 59N 102 21 E
Xiaolan, *China* **59 F9** 22 38N 113 13 E
Xiaoshan, *China* **59 B13** 30 12N 120 18 E
Xiaoyi, *China* **56 F6** 37 8N 111 48 E
Xiapu, *China* **59 D12** 26 54N 119 59 E
Xiawa, *China* **57 C11** 42 35N 120 38 E
Xiayi, *China* **56 G9** 34 15N 116 10 E
Xichang, *China* **58 D4** 27 51N 102 19 E
Xichong, *China* **58 B5** 30 57N 105 54 E
Xichou, *China* **58 E5** 23 25N 104 42 E
Xichuan, *China* **56 H6** 33 0N 111 30 E
Xide, *China* **58 C4** 28 8N 102 19 E
Xiemahe, *China* **59 B8** 31 38N 111 12 E
Xieng Khouang, *Laos* **64 C4** 19 17N 103 25 E
Xifei He →, *China* **56 H9** 32 45N 116 40 E
Xifeng, *Gansu, China* **56 G4** 35 40N 107 40 E
Xifeng, *Guizhou, China* **58 D6** 27 7N 106 42 E
Xifeng, *Liaoning, China* **57 C13** 42 42N 124 45 E
Xifengzhen = Xifeng, *China* **56 G4** 35 40N 107 40 E
Xigazê, *China* **60 D3** 29 5N 88 45 E
Xihe, *China* **56 G3** 34 2N 105 20 E
Xihua, *China* **56 H8** 33 45N 114 30 E
Xiliao He →, *China* **57 C12** 43 32N 123 35 E
Xilin, *China* **58 E5** 24 30N 105 6 E
Xilókastron, *Greece* **38 C4** 38 5N 22 38 E
Xime, *Guinea-Biss.* **82 C2** 11 59N 14 57W
Ximeng, *China* **58 F2** 22 50N 99 27 E
Xin Jiang →, *China* **59 C11** 28 45N 116 35 E
Xin Xian = Xinzhou, *China* **56 E7** 38 22N 112 46 E
Xinavane, *Mozam.* **89 D5** 25 2 S 32 47 E
Xinbin, *China* **57 D13** 41 40N 125 2 E
Xincai, *China* **59 A10** 32 43N 114 58 E
Xinchang, *China* **59 C13** 29 28N 120 52 E
Xincheng, *Guangxi Zhuangzu, China* **58 E7** 24 5N 108 39 E
Xincheng, *Jiangxi, China* **59 D10** 26 48N 114 6 E
Xindu, *China* **58 B5** 30 50N 104 10 E
Xinfeng, *Guangdong, China* **59 E10** 24 5N 114 16 E
Xinfeng, *Jiangxi, China* **59 D11** 27 7N 116 11 E
Xinfeng, *Jiangxi, China* **59 E10** 25 27N 114 58 E
Xinfengjiang Skuiku, *China* **59 F10** 23 52N 114 30 E
Xing Xian, *China* **56 E6** 38 27N 111 7 E
Xing'an, *Guangxi Zhuangzu, China* **59 E8** 25 38N 110 40 E
Xingan, *Jiangxi, China* **59 D10** 27 46N 115 20 E
Xingcheng, *China* **57 D11** 40 40N 120 45 E
Xingguo, *China* **59 D10** 26 21N 115 21 E
Xinghe, *China* **56 D7** 40 55N 113 55 E
Xinghua, *China* **57 H10** 32 58N 119 48 E
Xinghua Wan, *China* **59 E12** 25 15N 119 20 E
Xinglong, *China* **57 D9** 40 25N 117 30 E
Xingning, *China* **59 E10** 24 3N 115 42 E
Xingping, *China* **56 G5** 34 20N 108 28 E
Xingren, *China* **58 E5** 25 24N 105 11 E
Xingshan, *China* **59 B8** 31 15N 110 45 E
Xingtai, *China* **56 F8** 37 3N 114 32 E
Xingu →, *Brazil* **122 D5** 1 30 S 51 53W
Xingwen, *China* **58 C5** 28 22N 104 50 E
Xingyang, *China* **56 G7** 34 45N 112 52 E
Xinhe, *China* **56 F8** 37 30N 115 15 E
Xinhua, *China* **59 D8** 27 42N 111 13 E
Xinhuang, *China* **58 D7** 27 21N 109 12 E
Xinhui, *China* **59 F9** 22 25N 113 0 E
Xining, *China* **60 C5** 36 34N 101 40 E
Xinjian, *China* **59 C10** 28 37N 115 46 E
Xinjiang, *China* **56 G6** 35 34N 111 11 E
Xinjiang Uygur Zizhiqu □, *China* **60 B3** 42 0N 86 0 E
Xinjie, *China* **58 D3** 26 48N 101 15 E
Xinjin = Pulandian, *China* **57 E11** 39 25N 121 58 E
Xinjin, *China* **58 B4** 30 24N 103 47 E
Xinkai He →, *China* **57 C12** 43 32N 123 35 E
Xinle, *China* **56 E8** 38 25N 114 40 E
Xinlitun, *China* **57 D12** 42 0N 122 8 E
Xinlong, *China* **58 B3** 30 57N 100 12 E
Xinmin, *China* **57 D12** 41 59N 122 50 E
Xinning, *China* **59 D8** 26 28N 110 50 E
Xinping, *China* **58 E3** 24 5N 101 59 E
Xinshao, *China* **59 D8** 27 21N 111 26 E
Xintai, *China* **57 G9** 35 55N 117 45 E
Xintian, *China* **59 E9** 25 55N 112 13 E
Xinxian, *China* **59 B10** 31 36N 114 51 E
Xinxiang, *China* **56 G7** 35 18N 113 50 E
Xinxing, *China* **59 F9** 22 35N 112 15 E
Xinyang, *China* **59 A10** 32 6N 114 3 E
Xinye, *China* **59 A9** 32 30N 112 21 E
Xinyi, *China* **59 F8** 22 25N 111 0 E
Xinyu, *China* **59 D10** 27 49N 114 58 E
Xinzhan, *China* **57 C14** 43 50N 127 18 E
Xinzheng, *China* **56 G7** 34 20N 113 45 E
Xinzhou, *Hubei, China* **59 B10** 30 50N 114 48 E
Xinzhou, *Shanxi, China* **56 E7** 38 22N 112 46 E
Xinzo de Limia, *Spain* **34 C3** 42 3N 7 47W
Xiongyuecheng, *China* **57 D12** 40 12N 122 5 E
Xiping, *Henan, China* **56 H8** 33 22N 114 5 E
Xiping, *Henan, China* **56 H6** 33 25N 111 8 E
Xiping, *Zhejiang, China* **59 C12** 28 16N 119 29 E
Xique-Xique, *Brazil* **125 F10** 10 50 S 42 40W
Xisha Qundao = Paracel Is., *S. China Sea* **62 A4** 15 50N 112 0 E
Xishui, *Guizhou, China* **58 C6** 28 19N 106 9 E
Xishui, *Hubei, China* **59 B10** 30 30N 115 15 E
Xitole, *Guinea-Biss.* **82 C2** 11 43N 14 50W
Xiu Shui →, *China* **59 C10** 29 13N 116 0 E
Xiuning, *China* **59 C12** 29 45N 118 10 E
Xiuren, *China* **59 E8** 24 27N 110 12 E
Xiushan, *China* **58 C7** 28 25N 108 57 E
Xiushui, *China* **59 C10** 29 2N 114 33 E
Xiuwen, *China* **58 D6** 26 49N 106 32 E
Xiuyan, *China* **57 D12** 40 18N 123 11 E
Xixabangma Feng, *China* **67 E14** 28 20N 85 40 E
Xixia, *China* **56 H6** 33 25N 111 29 E
Xixiang, *China* **56 H4** 33 0N 107 44 E
Xiyang, *China* **56 F7** 37 38N 113 38 E
Xizang Zizhiqu □, *China* **60 C3** 32 0N 88 0 E
Xlendi, *Malta* **36 C1** 36 1N 14 12 E
Xu Jiang →, *China* **59 D11** 28 0N 116 25 E
Xuan Loc, *Vietnam* **65 G6** 10 56N 107 14 E
Xuan'en, *China* **58 C7** 30 0N 109 30 E
Xuanhan, *China* **58 B6** 31 18N 107 38 E
Xuanhua, *China* **56 D8** 40 40N 115 2 E
Xuanwei, *China* **58 C5** 26 15N 103 59 E
Xuanzhou, *China* **59 B12** 30 56N 118 43 E
Xuchang, *China* **56 G7** 34 2N 113 48 E
Xudat, *Azerbaijan* **49 K9** 41 38N 48 41 E
Xuefeng Shan, *China* **59 D8** 27 5N 110 35 E
Xuejiaping, *China* **59 B8** 31 39N 110 16 E
Xun Jiang →, *China* **59 F8** 23 35N 111 30 E
Xun Xian, *China* **56 G8** 35 42N 114 33 E
Xundian, *China* **58 E4** 25 36N 103 15 E
Xunwu, *China* **59 E10** 24 54N 115 37 E
Xunyang, *China* **56 H5** 32 48N 109 22 E
Xunyi, *China* **56 G5** 35 8N 108 20 E
Xupu, *China* **59 D8** 27 53N 110 32 E
Xúquer →, *Spain* **33 F4** 39 5N 0 10W
Xushui, *China* **56 E8** 39 2N 115 40 E
Xuwen, *China* **59 G8** 20 20N 110 10 E
Xuyen Moc, *Vietnam* **65 G6** 10 34N 107 25 E
Xuyong, *China* **58 C5** 28 10N 105 22 E
Xuzhou, *China* **57 G9** 34 18N 117 10 E
Xylophagou, *Cyprus* **36 E12** 34 54N 33 51 E

Y

Ya Xian, *China* **64 C7** 18 14N 109 29 E
Yaamba, *Australia* **94 C5** 23 8 S 150 22 E
Ya'an, *China* **58 C4** 29 58N 103 5 E
Yaapeet, *Australia* **95 F3** 35 45 S 142 3 E
Yabassi, *Cameroon* **83 E6** 4 30N 9 57 E
Yabelo, *Ethiopia* **81 G4** 4 50N 38 8 E
Yablanitsa, *Bulgaria* **41 C8** 43 2N 24 5 E
Yablonovyy Ra. = Yablonovyy Khrebet, *Russia* **51 D12** 53 0N 114 0 E
Yablonovyy Khrebet, *Russia* **51 D12** 53 0N 114 0 E
Yabrai Shan, *China* **56 E2** 39 40N 103 0 E
Yabrūd, *Syria* **75 B5** 33 58N 36 39 E
Yacheng, *China* **64 C7** 18 22N 109 6 E
Yacuiba, *Bolivia* **126 A3** 22 0 S 63 43W
Yacuma →, *Bolivia* **124 F5** 13 38 S 65 23W
Yadgir, *India* **66 L10** 16 45N 77 5 E
Yadkin →, *U.S.A.* **109 H5** 35 29N 80 9W
Yadrin, *Russia* **48 C8** 55 57N 46 12 E
Yaeyama-Rettō, *Japan* **55 M1** 24 30N 123 40 E
Yagaba, *Ghana* **83 C4** 10 14N 1 20W
Yağcılar, *Turkey* **39 B10** 39 25N 28 23 E
Yagodnoye, *Russia* **51 C15** 62 33N 149 40 E
Yahila, *Dem. Rep. of the Congo* **86 B1** 0 13N 24 28 E
Yahk, *Canada* **104 D5** 49 6N 116 10W
Yahotyn, *Ukraine* **47 G6** 50 17N 31 46 E
Yahuma, *Dem. Rep. of the Congo* **84 D4** 1 0N 23 10 E
Yahyalı, *Turkey* **72 C6** 38 5N 35 2 E
Yaita, *Japan* **55 F9** 36 48N 139 56 E
Yaiza, *Canary Is.* **37 F6** 28 57N 13 46W
Yajiang, *China* **58 B3** 30 2N 100 57 E
Yajua, *Nigeria* **83 C7** 11 27N 12 49 E
Yakima, *U.S.A.* **114 C3** 46 36N 120 31W
Yakima →, *U.S.A.* **114 C3** 47 0N 120 30W
Yako, *Burkina Faso* **82 C4** 12 59N 2 15W
Yakobi I., *U.S.A.* **104 B1** 58 0N 136 30W
Yakoruda, *Bulgaria* **40 D7** 42 1N 23 39 E
Yakovlevka, *Russia* **54 B6** 44 26N 133 28 E
Yaku-Shima, *Japan* **55 J5** 30 20N 130 30 E
Yakumo, *Japan* **54 C10** 42 15N 140 16 E
Yakutat, *U.S.A.* **100 C6** 59 33N 139 44W
Yakutia = Sakha □, *Russia* **51 C13** 66 0N 130 0 E
Yakutsk, *Russia* **51 C13** 62 5N 129 50 E
Yala, *Thailand* **65 J3** 6 33N 101 18 E
Yale, *U.S.A.* **110 C2** 43 8N 82 48W
Yalgoo, *Australia* **93 E2** 28 16 S 116 39 E
Yalinga, *C.A.R.* **84 C4** 6 33N 23 10 E
Yalkubul, Punta, *Mexico* **119 C7** 21 32N 88 37W
Yalleroi, *Australia* **94 C4** 24 3 S 145 42 E
Yalobusha →, *U.S.A.* **113 J9** 33 33N 90 10W
Yalong Jiang →, *China* **58 D3** 26 40N 101 55 E
Yalova, *Turkey* **41 F13** 40 41N 29 15 E
Yalta, *Ukraine* **47 K8** 44 30N 34 10 E
Yalu Jiang →, *China* **57 E13** 40 0N 124 22 E
Yalvaç, *Turkey* **72 C4** 38 17N 31 10 E
Yam Ha Melaḥ = Dead Sea, *Asia* **75 D4** 31 30N 35 30 E

Yam Kinneret, Israel **75 C4** 32 45N 35 35 E
Yamada, Japan **55 H5** 33 33N 130 49 E
Yamagata, Japan **54 E10** 38 15N 140 15 E
Yamagata □, Japan **54 E10** 38 30N 140 0 E
Yamaguchi, Japan **55 G5** 34 10N 131 32 E
Yamaguchi □, Japan **55 G5** 34 20N 131 40 E
Yamal, Poluostrov, Russia **50 B8** 71 0N 70 0 E
Yamal Pen. = Yamal, Poluostrov, Russia **50 B8** 71 0N 70 0 E
Yamanashi □, Japan **55 G9** 35 40N 138 40 E
Yamba, Australia **95 D5** 29 26 S 153 23 E
Yambarran Ra., Australia **92 C5** 15 10 S 130 25 E
Yambéring, Guinea **82 C2** 11 50N 12 18 E
Yâmbiô, Sudan **81 G2** 4 35N 28 16 E
Yambol, Bulgaria **41 D10** 42 30N 26 30 E
Yamdena, Indonesia **63 F8** 7 45 S 131 20 E
Yame, Japan **55 H5** 33 13N 130 35 E
Yamethin, Burma **67 J20** 20 29N 96 18 E
Yamma-Yamma, L., Australia **95 D3** 26 16 S 141 20 E
Yamoussoukro, Ivory C. **82 D3** 6 49N 5 17W
Yampa →, U.S.A. **114 F9** 40 32N 108 59W
Yampi Sd., Australia **92 C3** 16 8 S 123 38 E
Yampil, Moldova **47 H5** 48 15N 28 15 E
Yampol = Yampil, Moldova **47 H5** 48 15N 28 15 E
Yamrat, Nigeria **83 C6** 10 11N 9 55 E
Yamrukchal = Botev, Bulgaria **41 D8** 42 44N 24 52 E
Yamuna →, India **69 G9** 25 30N 81 53 E
Yamunanagar, India **68 D7** 30 7N 77 17 E
Yamzho Yumco, China **60 D4** 28 48N 90 35 E
Yan, Nigeria **83 C7** 10 5N 12 11 E
Yana →, Russia **51 B14** 71 30N 136 0 E
Yanagawa, Japan **55 H5** 33 10N 130 24 E
Yanai, Japan **55 H6** 33 58N 132 7 E
Yan'an, China **56 F5** 36 35N 109 26 E
Yanbian, China **58 D3** 26 47N 101 31 E
Yanbu 'al Baḩr, Si. Arabia **70 F3** 24 0N 38 5 E
Yanchang, China **56 F6** 36 43N 110 1 E
Yancheng, Henan, China **56 H8** 33 35N 114 0 E
Yancheng, Jiangsu, China **57 H11** 33 23N 120 8 E
Yanchep Beach, Australia **93 F2** 31 33 S 115 37 E
Yanchi, China **56 F4** 37 48N 107 20 E
Yanchuan, China **56 F6** 36 51N 110 10 E
Yanco, Australia **95 E4** 34 38 S 146 27 E
Yanco Cr. →, Australia **95 F4** 35 14 S 145 35 E
Yandoon, Burma **67 L19** 17 0N 95 40 E
Yanfeng, China **58 E3** 25 52N 101 8 E
Yanfolila, Mali **82 C3** 11 11N 8 9W
Yang Xian, China **56 H4** 33 15N 107 30 E
Yang-Yang, Senegal **82 B1** 15 30N 15 20W
Yangambi, Dem. Rep. of the Congo **86 B1** 0 47N 24 24 E
Yangbi, China **58 E2** 25 41N 99 58 E
Yangcheng, China **56 G7** 35 28N 112 22 E
Yangch'ü = Taiyuan, China **56 F7** 37 52N 112 33 E
Yangchun, China **59 F8** 22 11N 111 48 E
Yanggao, China **56 D7** 40 21N 113 55 E
Yanggu, China **56 F8** 36 8N 115 43 E
Yangjiang, China **59 G8** 21 50N 111 59 E
Yangliuqing, China **57 E9** 39 2N 117 5 E
Yangon = Rangoon, Burma **67 L20** 16 45N 96 20 E
Yangping, China **59 B8** 31 12N 111 25 E
Yangpingguan, China **56 H4** 32 58N 106 5 E
Yangquan, China **56 F7** 37 58N 113 31 E
Yangshan, China **59 E9** 24 30N 112 40 E
Yangshuo, China **59 E8** 24 48N 110 29 E
Yangtse = Chang Jiang →, China **59 B13** 31 48N 121 10 E
Yangtze Kiang = Chang Jiang →, China **59 B13** 31 48N 121 10 E
Yangxin, China **59 C10** 29 50N 115 12 E
Yangyang, S. Korea **57 E15** 38 4N 128 38 E
Yangyuan, China **56 D8** 40 1N 114 10 E
Yangzhong, China **59 A12** 32 22N 119 22 E
Yangzhou, China **59 A12** 32 21N 119 26 E
Yanhe, China **58 C7** 28 31N 108 29 E
Yanji, China **57 C15** 42 59N 129 30 E
Yanjin, China **58 C5** 28 5N 104 18 E
Yanjing, China **58 C2** 29 7N 98 33 E
Yankton, U.S.A. **112 D6** 42 53N 97 23W
Yanonge, Dem. Rep. of the Congo **86 B1** 0 35N 24 38 E
Yanqi, China **60 B3** 42 5N 86 35 E
Yanqing, China **56 D8** 40 30N 115 58 E
Yanshan, Hebei, China **57 E9** 38 4N 117 22 E
Yanshan, Jiangxi, China **59 C11** 28 15N 117 41 E
Yanshan, Yunnan, China **58 F5** 23 35N 104 20 E
Yanshou, China **57 B15** 45 28N 128 22 E
Yantabulla, Australia **95 D4** 29 21 S 145 0 E
Yantai, China **57 F11** 37 34N 121 22 E
Yanting, China **58 B5** 31 11N 105 24 E
Yantra →, Bulgaria **41 C9** 43 40N 25 37 E
Yanwa, China **58 D2** 27 35N 98 55 E
Yanyuan, China **58 D3** 27 25N 101 30 E
Yanzhou, China **56 G9** 35 35N 116 49 E
Yao Xian, China **56 G5** 34 55N 108 59 E
Yao Yai, Ko, Thailand **65 J2** 8 0N 98 35 E
Yao'an, China **58 E3** 25 31N 101 18 E
Yaodu, China **58 A5** 32 45N 105 22 E
Yaoundé, Cameroon **83 E7** 3 50N 11 35 E
Yaowan, China **57 G10** 34 15N 118 3 E
Yap I., Pac. Oc. **96 G5** 9 30N 138 10 E
Yapen, Indonesia **63 E9** 1 50 S 136 0 E
Yapen, Selat, Indonesia **63 E9** 1 20 S 136 10 E
Yapero, Indonesia **63 E9** 4 59 S 137 11 E
Yappar →, Australia **94 B3** 18 22 S 141 16 E
Yaqui →, Mexico **118 B2** 27 37N 110 39W
Yar-Sale, Russia **50 C8** 66 50N 70 50 E
Yaraka, Australia **94 C3** 24 53 S 144 3 E
Yaransk, Russia **48 B8** 57 22N 47 49 E
Yarbasan, Turkey **39 C10** 38 59N 28 49 E
Yardımcı Burnu, Turkey **39 E12** 36 13N 30 25 E
Yare →, U.K. **13 E9** 52 35N 1 38 E
Yaremcha, Ukraine **47 H3** 48 27N 24 33 E
Yarensk, Russia **50 C5** 62 11N 49 15 E
Yarfa, Si. Arabia **80 C4** 24 37N 38 35 E
Yarí →, Colombia **124 D4** 0 20 S 72 20W
Yarkand = Shache, China **60 C2** 38 20N 77 10 E
Yarker, Canada **111 B8** 44 23N 76 46W
Yarkhun →, Pakistan **69 A5** 36 17N 72 30 E
Yarmouth, Canada **103 D6** 43 50N 66 7W
Yarmūk →, Syria **75 C4** 32 42N 35 40 E
Yaroslavl, Russia **46 D10** 57 35N 39 55 E
Yarqa, W. →, Egypt **75 F2** 30 0N 33 49 E
Yarra Yarra Lakes, Australia **93 E2** 29 40 S 115 45 E
Yarram, Australia **95 F4** 38 29 S 146 39 E
Yarraman, Australia **95 D5** 26 50 S 152 0 E
Yarras, Australia **95 E5** 31 25 S 152 20 E
Yartsevo, Sib., Russia **51 C10** 60 20N 90 0 E
Yartsevo, Smolensk, Russia **46 E7** 55 6N 32 43 E
Yarumal, Colombia **124 B3** 6 58N 75 24W
Yasawa Group, Fiji **91 C7** 17 0 S 177 23 E
Yaselda, Belarus **47 F4** 52 7N 26 28 E
Yashi, Nigeria **83 C6** 12 23N 7 54 E
Yashikera, Nigeria **83 D5** 9 44N 3 29 E
Yashkul, Russia **49 G7** 46 11N 45 21 E
Yasin, Pakistan **69 A5** 36 24N 73 23 E
Yasinovataya, Ukraine **47 H9** 48 7N 37 57 E
Yasinski, L., Canada **102 B4** 53 16N 77 35W
Yasinya, Ukraine **47 H3** 48 16N 24 21 E
Yasothon, Thailand **64 E5** 15 50N 104 10 E
Yass, Australia **95 E4** 34 49 S 148 54 E
Yatağan, Turkey **39 D10** 37 20N 28 10 E
Yatakala, Niger **83 C5** 14 50N 0 22 E
Yates Center, U.S.A. **113 G7** 37 53N 95 44W
Yathkyed L., Canada **105 A9** 62 40N 98 0W
Yatsushiro, Japan **55 H5** 32 30N 130 40 E
Yatta Plateau, Kenya **86 C4** 2 0 S 38 0 E
Yavari →, Peru **124 D4** 4 21 S 70 2W
Yávaros, Mexico **118 B3** 26 42N 109 31W
Yavatmal, India **66 J11** 20 20N 78 15 E
Yavne, Israel **75 D3** 31 52N 34 45 E
Yavoriv, Ukraine **47 H2** 49 55N 23 20 E
Yavorov = Yavoriv, Ukraine **47 H2** 49 55N 23 20 E
Yavuzeli, Turkey **72 D7** 37 18N 37 24 E
Yawatahama, Japan **55 H6** 33 27N 132 24 E
Yawri B., S. Leone **82 D2** 8 22N 13 0W
Yaxi, China **58 D6** 27 33N 106 41 E
Yazd, Iran **71 D7** 31 55N 54 27 E
Yazd □, Iran **71 D7** 32 0N 55 0 E
Yazd-e Khväst, Iran **71 D7** 31 31N 52 7 E
Yazıköy, Turkey **39 E9** 36 40N 27 20 E
Yazman, Pakistan **68 E4** 29 8N 71 45 E
Yazoo →, U.S.A. **113 J9** 32 22N 90 54W
Yazoo City, U.S.A. **113 J9** 32 51N 90 25W
Ybbs, Austria **26 C8** 48 12N 15 4 E
Yding Skovhøj, Denmark **11 J3** 55 59N 9 46 E
Ye Xian = Laizhou, China **57 F10** 37 8N 119 57 E
Ye Xian, China **56 H7** 33 35N 113 25 E
Yebyu, Burma **64 E2** 14 15N 98 13 E
Yechŏn, S. Korea **57 F15** 36 39N 128 27 E
Yecla, Spain **33 G3** 38 35N 1 5W
Yécora, Mexico **118 B3** 28 20N 108 58W
Yedintsy = Edinet, Moldova **43 B12** 48 9N 27 18 E
Yedseram →, Nigeria **83 C7** 12 30N 14 5 E
Yefremov, Russia **46 F10** 53 8N 38 3 E
Yeghegnadzor, Armenia **73 C11** 39 44N 45 19 E
Yegorlyk →, Russia **49 G5** 46 35N 41 57 E
Yegorlykskaya, Russia **49 G5** 46 35N 40 35 E
Yegoryevsk, Russia **46 E10** 55 27N 38 55 E
Yegros, Paraguay **126 B4** 26 20 S 56 25W
Yehuda, Midbar, Israel **75 D4** 31 35N 35 15 E
Yei, Sudan **81 G3** 4 9N 30 40 E
Yei, Nahr →, Sudan **81 F3** 6 15N 30 13 E
Yejmiadzin, Armenia **49 K7** 40 12N 44 19 E
Yekaterinburg, Russia **50 D7** 56 50N 60 30 E
Yekaterinodar = Krasnodar, Russia **49 H4** 45 5N 39 0 E
Yelabuga, Russia **48 C11** 55 45N 52 4 E
Yelan, Russia **48 E6** 50 55N 43 43 E
Yelarbon, Australia **95 D5** 28 33 S 150 38 E
Yelatma, Russia **48 C5** 55 0N 41 45 E
Yelets, Russia **47 F10** 52 40N 38 30 E
Yélimané, Mali **82 B2** 15 9N 10 34W
Yelizavetgrad = Kirovohrad, Ukraine **47 H7** 48 35N 32 20 E
Yell, U.K. **14 A7** 60 35N 1 5W
Yell Sd., U.K. **14 A7** 60 33N 1 15W
Yellow Sea, China **57 G12** 35 0N 123 0 E
Yellowhead Pass, Canada **104 C5** 52 53N 118 25W
Yellowknife, Canada **104 A6** 62 27N 114 29W
Yellowknife →, Canada **104 A6** 62 31N 114 19W
Yellowstone →, U.S.A. **112 B3** 47 59N 103 59W
Yellowstone L., U.S.A. **114 D8** 44 27N 110 22W
Yellowstone National Park, U.S.A. **114 D9** 44 40N 110 30W
Yelnya, Russia **46 E7** 54 35N 33 15 E
Yelsk, Belarus **47 G5** 51 50N 29 10 E
Yelwa, Nigeria **83 C5** 10 49N 4 41 E
Yemen ■, Asia **74 E3** 15 0N 44 0 E
Yen Bai, Vietnam **58 G5** 21 42N 104 52 E
Yenagoa, Nigeria **83 E6** 4 58N 6 16 E
Yenakiyeve, Ukraine **47 H10** 48 15N 38 15 E
Yenakiyevo = Yenakiyeve, Ukraine **47 H10** 48 15N 38 15 E
Yenangyaung, Burma **67 J19** 20 30N 95 0 E
Yenbo = Yanbu 'al Baḩr, Si. Arabia **70 F3** 24 0N 38 5 E
Yenda, Australia **95 E4** 34 13 S 146 14 E
Yende Millimou, Guinea **82 D2** 8 55N 10 10W
Yendéré, Burkina Faso **82 C4** 10 12N 4 59W
Yendi, Ghana **83 D4** 9 29N 0 1W
Yéni, Niger **83 C5** 13 30N 3 1 E
Yenice, Ankara, Turkey **72 C5** 39 14N 32 42 E
Yenice, Aydın, Turkey **39 D10** 37 49N 28 35 E
Yenice, Çanakkale, Turkey **39 B9** 39 55N 27 17 E
Yenice, Edirne, Turkey **41 F10** 40 42N 26 9 E
Yenice →, Turkey **72 D6** 37 37N 35 33 E
Yenifoça, Turkey **39 C8** 38 44N 26 51 E
Yenihisar, Turkey **39 D9** 37 22N 27 16 E
Yeniköy, Bursa, Turkey **41 F13** 40 31N 29 22 E
Yeniköy, Çanakkale, Turkey **39 B8** 39 55N 26 10 E
Yeniköy, Kütahya, Turkey **39 C11** 38 52N 29 17 E
Yenipazar, Turkey **39 D10** 37 49N 28 11 E
Yenisaía, Greece **41 E8** 41 1N 24 57 E
Yenişehir, Turkey **41 F13** 40 16N 29 38 E
Yenisey →, Russia **50 B9** 71 50N 82 40 E
Yeniseysk, Russia **51 D10** 58 27N 92 13 E
Yeniseyskiy Zaliv, Russia **50 B9** 72 20N 81 0 E
Yennádhi, Greece **36 C9** 36 2N 27 56 E
Yenne, France **21 C9** 45 43N 5 44 E
Yenotayevka, Russia **49 G8** 47 15N 47 0 E
Yenyuka, Russia **51 D13** 57 57N 121 15 E
Yeo →, U.K. **13 G5** 51 2N 2 49W
Yeo, L., Australia **93 E3** 28 0 S 124 30 E
Yeo I., Canada **110 A3** 45 24N 81 48W
Yeola, India **66 J9** 20 2N 74 30 E
Yeoryioúpolis, Greece **36 D6** 35 20N 24 15 E
Yeovil, U.K. **13 G5** 50 57N 2 38W
Yepes, Spain **34 F7** 39 55N 3 39W
Yeppoon, Australia **94 C5** 23 5 S 150 47 E
Yeráki, Greece **38 D4** 37 0N 22 42 E
Yerbent, Turkmenistan **50 F6** 39 30N 58 50 E
Yerbogachen, Russia **51 C11** 61 16N 108 0 E
Yerevan, Armenia **49 K7** 40 10N 44 31 E
Yerington, U.S.A. **114 G4** 38 59N 119 10W
Yerkesik, Turkey **39 D10** 37 7N 28 19 E
Yerköy, Turkey **72 C6** 39 38N 34 28 E
Yermak, Kazakstan **50 D8** 52 2N 76 55 E
Yermo, U.S.A. **117 L10** 34 54N 116 50W
Yerólakkos, Cyprus **36 D12** 35 11N 33 15 E
Yeropol, Russia **51 C17** 65 15N 168 40 E
Yeropótamos →, Greece **36 D6** 35 3N 24 50 E
Yeroskipos, Cyprus **36 E11** 34 46N 32 28 E
Yershov, Russia **48 E9** 51 23N 48 27 E
Yerushalayim = Jerusalem, Israel **75 D4** 31 47N 35 10 E
Yerville, France **18 C7** 49 40N 0 53 E
Yes Tor, U.K. **13 G4** 50 41N 4 0W
Yesan, S. Korea **57 F14** 36 41N 126 51 E
Yeşilhisar, Turkey **72 C6** 38 20N 35 5 E
Yeşilırmak →, Turkey **72 B7** 41 22N 36 37 E
Yeşilkent, Turkey **72 D7** 36 57N 36 12 E
Yeşilköy, Turkey **41 F12** 40 57N 28 49 E
Yeşilova, Turkey **39 D11** 37 31N 29 46 E
Yeşilyurt, Manisa, Turkey **39 C10** 38 22N 28 40 E
Yeşilyurt, Muğla, Turkey **39 D10** 37 10N 28 20 E
Yesnogorsk, Russia **46 E9** 54 32N 37 38 E
Yeso, U.S.A. **113 H2** 34 26N 104 37W
Yessentuki, Russia **49 H6** 44 5N 42 53 E
Yessey, Russia **51 C11** 68 29N 102 10 E
Yeste, Spain **33 G2** 38 22N 2 19W
Yetman, Australia **95 D5** 28 56 S 150 48 E
Yeu, Î. d', France **18 F4** 46 42N 2 20W
Yevlakh = Yevlax, Azerbaijan **49 K8** 40 39N 47 7 E
Yevlax, Azerbaijan **49 K8** 40 39N 47 7 E
Yevpatoriya, Ukraine **47 K7** 45 15N 33 20 E
Yeya →, Russia **47 J10** 46 40N 38 40 E
Yeysk, Russia **47 J10** 46 40N 38 12 E
Yezd = Yazd, Iran **71 D7** 31 55N 54 27 E
Yezerishche, Belarus **46 E5** 55 50N 29 59 E
Yhati, Paraguay **126 B4** 25 45 S 56 35W
Yhú, Paraguay **127 B4** 25 0 S 56 0W
Yi →, Uruguay **126 C4** 33 7 S 57 8W
Yi 'Allaq, G., Egypt **75 E2** 30 22N 33 32 E
Yi He →, China **57 G10** 34 10N 118 8 E
Yi Xian, Anhui, China **59 C11** 29 55N 117 57 E
Yi Xian, Hebei, China **56 E8** 39 20N 115 30 E
Yi Xian, Liaoning, China **57 D11** 41 30N 121 22 E
Yialí, Greece **39 E9** 36 41N 27 11 E
Yialiás →, Cyprus **36 D12** 35 9N 33 44 E
Yi'allaq, G., Egypt **80 A3** 30 21N 33 31 E
Yialousa, Cyprus **36 D13** 35 32N 34 10 E
Yiáltra, Greece **38 C4** 38 51N 22 59 E
Yianisádhes, Greece **36 D8** 35 20N 26 10 E
Yiannitsa, Greece **40 F6** 40 46N 22 24 E
Yibin, China **58 C5** 28 45N 104 32 E
Yichang, China **59 B8** 30 40N 111 20 E
Yicheng, Henan, China **59 B9** 31 41N 112 12 E
Yicheng, Shanxi, China **56 G6** 35 42N 111 40 E
Yichuan, China **56 F6** 36 2N 110 10 E
Yichun, Heilongjiang, China **60 B7** 47 44N 128 52 E
Yichun, Jiangxi, China **59 D10** 27 48N 114 22 E
Yidu, China **57 F10** 36 43N 118 28 E
Yidun, China **58 B2** 30 22N 99 21 E
Yifag, Ethiopia **81 E4** 12 4N 37 46 E
Yifeng, China **59 C10** 28 22N 114 45 E
Yihuang, China **59 D11** 27 30N 116 12 E
Yijun, China **56 G5** 35 28N 109 8 E
Yıldız Dağları, Turkey **41 E11** 41 48N 27 36 E
Yıldızeli, Turkey **72 C7** 39 51N 36 36 E
Yiliang, Yunnan, China **58 D5** 27 38N 104 2 E
Yiliang, Yunnan, China **58 E4** 24 56N 103 11 E
Yilong, China **58 B6** 31 34N 106 23 E
Yimen, China **58 E4** 24 40N 102 10 E
Yimianpo, China **57 B15** 45 7N 128 2 E
Yinchuan, China **56 E4** 38 30N 106 15 E
Yindarlgooda, L., Australia **93 F3** 30 40 S 121 52 E
Ying He →, China **56 H9** 32 30N 116 30 E
Ying Xian, China **56 E7** 39 32N 113 10 E
Yingcheng, China **59 B9** 30 56N 113 35 E
Yingde, China **59 E9** 24 10N 113 25 E
Yingjiang, China **58 E1** 24 41N 97 55 E
Yingjing, China **58 C4** 29 41N 102 52 E
Yingkou, China **57 D12** 40 37N 122 18 E
Yingshan, Henan, China **59 B9** 31 35N 113 50 E
Yingshan, Hubei, China **59 B10** 30 41N 115 32 E
Yingshan, Sichuan, China **58 B6** 31 4N 106 35 E
Yingshang, China **59 A11** 32 38N 116 12 E
Yingtan, China **59 C11** 28 12N 117 0 E
Yining, China **50 E9** 43 58N 81 10 E
Yinjiang, China **58 C7** 28 1N 108 21 E
Yinmabin, Burma **67 H19** 22 10N 94 55 E
Yiofiros →, Greece **36 D7** 35 20N 25 6 E
Yioúra, Nótios Aiyaíon, Greece **38 D6** 37 32N 24 40 E
Yioúra, Thessalía, Greece **38 B6** 39 23N 24 10 E
Yipinglang, China **58 E3** 25 10N 101 52 E
Yirba Muda, Ethiopia **81 F4** 6 12N 38 42 E
Yirga Alem, Ethiopia **81 F4** 6 48N 38 22 E
Yirol, Sudan **81 F3** 6 33N 30 30 E
Yirrkala, Australia **94 A2** 12 14 S 136 56 E
Yishan, China **58 E7** 24 28N 108 38 E
Yishui, China **57 G10** 35 47N 118 30 E
Yíthion, Greece **38 E4** 36 46N 22 34 E
Yitong, China **57 C13** 43 13N 125 20 E
Yiwu, China **59 C13** 29 20N 120 3 E
Yixing, China **59 B12** 31 21N 119 48 E
Yiyang, Henan, China **56 G7** 34 27N 112 10 E
Yiyang, Hunan, China **59 C9** 28 35N 112 18 E
Yiyang, Jiangxi, China **59 C11** 28 22N 117 20 E
Yizhang, China **59 E9** 25 27N 112 57 E
Yizheng, China **59 A12** 32 18N 119 10 E
Yli-Kitka, Finland **8 C23** 66 8N 28 30 E
Ylitornio, Finland **8 C20** 66 19N 23 39 E
Ylivieska, Finland **8 D21** 64 4N 24 28 E
Yngaren, Sweden **11 F10** 58 50N 16 35 E
Yoakum, U.S.A. **113 L6** 29 17N 97 9W
Yobe □, Nigeria **83 C7** 12 0N 11 30 E
Yog Pt., Phil. **63 B6** 14 6N 124 12 E
Yogan, Togo **83 D5** 6 23N 1 30 E
Yoğuntaş, Turkey **41 E11** 41 50N 27 4 E
Yogyakarta, Indonesia **63 G14** 7 49 S 110 22 E
Yoho Nat. Park, Canada **104 C5** 51 25N 116 30W
Yojoa, L. de, Honduras **120 D2** 14 53N 88 0W
Yŏju, S. Korea **57 F14** 37 20N 127 35 E
Yokadouma, Cameroon **84 D2** 3 26N 14 55 E
Yokkaichi, Japan **55 G8** 34 55N 136 38 E
Yoko, Cameroon **83 D7** 5 32N 12 20 E
Yokohama, Japan **55 G9** 35 27N 139 28 E
Yokosuka, Japan **55 G9** 35 20N 139 40 E
Yokote, Japan **54 E10** 39 20N 140 30 E
Yola, Nigeria **83 D7** 9 10N 12 29 E
Yolaina, Cordillera de, Nic. **120 D3** 11 30N 84 0W
Yoloten, Turkmenistan **71 B9** 37 18N 62 21 E
Yom →, Thailand **62 A2** 15 35N 100 1 E
Yonago, Japan **55 G6** 35 25N 133 19 E
Yonaguni-Jima, Japan **55 M1** 24 27N 123 0 E
Yŏnan, N. Korea **57 F14** 37 55N 126 11 E
Yonezawa, Japan **54 F10** 37 57N 140 4 E
Yong Peng, Malaysia **65 L4** 2 0N 103 3 E
Yong Sata, Thailand **65 J2** 7 8N 99 41 E
Yongamp'o, N. Korea **57 E13** 39 56N 124 23 E
Yong'an, China **59 E11** 25 59N 117 25 E
Yongcheng, China **56 H9** 33 55N 116 20 E
Yŏngch'ŏn, S. Korea **57 G15** 35 58N 128 56 E
Yongchuan, China **58 C5** 29 17N 105 55 E
Yongchun, China **59 E12** 25 16N 118 20 E
Yongde, China **58 E2** 24 5N 99 25 E
Yongdeng, China **56 F2** 36 38N 103 25 E
Yongding, China **59 E11** 24 43N 116 45 E
Yŏngdŏk, S. Korea **57 F15** 36 24N 129 22 E
Yŏngdŭngpo, S. Korea **57 F14** 37 31N 126 54 E
Yongfeng, China **59 D10** 27 20N 115 22 E
Yongfu, China **58 E7** 24 59N 109 59 E
Yonghe, China **56 F6** 36 46N 110 38 E
Yŏnghŭng, N. Korea **57 E14** 39 31N 127 18 E
Yongji, China **56 G6** 34 52N 110 28 E
Yongjia, China **59 C13** 28 10N 120 45 E
Yŏngju, S. Korea **57 F15** 36 50N 128 40 E
Yongkang, Yunnan, China **58 E2** 24 9N 99 20 E
Yongkang, Zhejiang, China **59 C13** 28 55N 120 2 E
Yongnian, China **56 F8** 36 47N 114 29 E
Yongning, Guangxi Zhuangzu, China **58 F7** 22 44N 108 28 E
Yongning, Ningxia Huizu, China **56 E4** 38 15N 106 14 E
Yongping, China **58 E2** 25 27N 99 38 E
Yongqing, China **56 E9** 39 25N 116 28 E
Yongren, China **58 D3** 26 4N 101 40 E
Yongshan, China **58 C4** 28 11N 103 35 E
Yongsheng, China **58 D3** 26 38N 100 46 E
Yongshun, China **58 C7** 29 2N 109 51 E
Yongtai, China **59 E12** 25 49N 118 58 E
Yŏngwŏl, S. Korea **57 F15** 37 11N 128 28 E
Yongxin = Jinggangshan, China **59 D10** 26 58N 114 15 E
Yongxing, China **59 D9** 26 9N 113 8 E
Yongxiu, China **59 C10** 29 2N 115 42 E
Yongzhou, China **59 D8** 26 17N 111 37 E
Yonibana, S. Leone **82 D2** 8 30N 12 19W
Yonkers, U.S.A. **111 F11** 40 56N 73 54W
Yonne □, France **19 E10** 47 50N 3 40 E
Yonne →, France **19 D9** 48 23N 2 58 E
York, Australia **93 F2** 31 52 S 116 47 E
York, U.K. **12 D6** 53 58N 1 6W
York, Ala., U.S.A. **113 J10** 32 29N 88 18W
York, Nebr., U.S.A. **112 E6** 40 52N 97 36W
York, Pa., U.S.A. **108 F7** 39 58N 76 44W
York, C., Australia **94 A3** 10 42 S 142 31 E
York, City of □, U.K. **12 D6** 53 58N 1 6W
York, Kap, Greenland **4 B4** 75 55N 66 25W
York, Vale of, U.K. **12 C6** 54 15N 1 25W
York Haven, U.S.A. **110 F8** 40 7N 76 46W
York Sd., Australia **92 C4** 15 0 S 125 5 E
Yorke Pen., Australia **95 E2** 34 50 S 137 40 E
Yorketown, Australia **95 F2** 35 0 S 137 33 E
Yorkshire Wolds, U.K. **12 C7** 54 8N 0 31W
Yorkton, Canada **105 C8** 51 11N 102 28W
Yorkville, U.S.A. **116 G3** 38 52N 123 13W
Yoro, Honduras **120 C2** 15 9N 87 7W
Yoron-Jima, Japan **55 L4** 27 2N 128 26 E
Yorosso, Mali **82 C4** 12 17N 4 55W
Yos Sudarso, Pulau = Dolak, Pulau, Indonesia **63 F9** 8 0 S 138 30 E
Yosemite National Park, U.S.A. **116 H7** 37 45N 119 40W
Yosemite Village, U.S.A. **116 H7** 37 45N 119 35W
Yoshkar Ola, Russia **48 B8** 56 38N 47 55 E
Yŏsu, S. Korea **57 G14** 34 47N 127 45 E
Yotvata, Israel **75 F4** 29 55N 35 2 E
You Jiang →, China **58 F6** 22 50N 108 6 E
You Xian, China **59 D9** 27 1N 113 17 E
Youbou, Canada **116 B2** 48 53N 124 13W
Youghal, Ireland **15 E4** 51 56N 7 52W
Youghal B., Ireland **15 E4** 51 55N 7 49W
Youkounkoun, Guinea **82 C2** 12 35N 13 11W
Young, Australia **95 E4** 34 19 S 148 18 E
Young, Canada **105 C7** 51 47N 105 45W
Young, Uruguay **126 C4** 32 44 S 57 36W
Younghusband, L., Australia **95 E2** 30 50 S 136 5 E
Younghusband Pen., Australia **95 F2** 36 0 S 139 25 E
Youngstown, Canada **105 C6** 51 35N 111 10W
Youngstown, N.Y., U.S.A. **110 C5** 43 15N 79 3W
Youngstown, Ohio, U.S.A. **110 E4** 41 6N 80 39W
Youngsville, U.S.A. **110 E5** 41 51N 79 19W
Youngwood, U.S.A. **110 F5** 40 14N 79 34W
Youxi, China **59 D12** 26 10N 118 13 E
Youyang, China **58 C7** 28 47N 108 42 E
Youyu, China **56 D7** 40 10N 112 20 E
Yozgat, Turkey **72 C6** 39 51N 34 47 E
Ypané →, Paraguay **126 A4** 23 29 S 57 19W
Yport, France **18 C7** 49 45N 0 15 E
Ypres = Ieper, Belgium **17 D2** 50 51N 2 53 E
Yreka, U.S.A. **114 F2** 41 44N 122 38W
Yssingeaux, France **21 C8** 45 9N 4 8 E
Ystad, Sweden **11 J7** 55 26N 13 50 E
Ysyk-Köl, Ozero, Kyrgyzstan **50 E8** 42 25N 77 15 E
Ythan →, U.K. **14 D7** 57 19N 1 59W
Ytterhogdal, Sweden **10 B8** 62 12N 14 56 E
Ytyk Kyuyel, Russia **51 C14** 62 30N 133 45 E
Yu Jiang →, China **58 F7** 23 22N 110 3 E
Yu Xian = Yuzhou, China **56 G7** 34 10N 113 28 E
Yu Xian, Hebei, China **56 E8** 39 50N 114 35 E
Yu Xian, Shanxi, China **56 E7** 38 5N 113 20 E
Yuan Jiang →, Hunan, China **59 C8** 28 55N 111 50 E
Yuan Jiang →, Yunnan, China **58 F4** 22 20N 103 59 E
Yuan'an, China **59 B8** 31 3N 111 34 E
Yuanjiang, Hunan, China **59 C9** 28 47N 112 21 E
Yuanjiang, Yunnan, China **58 F4** 23 32N 102 0 E
Yüanli, Taiwan **59 E13** 24 27N 120 39 E
Yüanlin, Taiwan **59 F13** 23 58N 120 30 E
Yuanling, China **59 C8** 28 29N 110 22 E
Yuanmou, China **58 E3** 25 42N 101 53 E
Yuanqu, China **56 G6** 35 18N 111 40 E
Yuanyang, Henan, China **56 G7** 35 3N 113 58 E
Yuanyang, Yunnan, China **58 F4** 23 10N 102 43 E
Yuba →, U.S.A. **116 F5** 39 8N 121 36W
Yuba City, U.S.A. **116 F5** 39 8N 121 37W
Yūbari, Japan **54 C10** 43 4N 141 59 E
Yubdo, Ethiopia **81 F4** 8 58N 35 24 E
Yūbetsu, Japan **54 B11** 44 13N 143 50 E
Yubo, Sudan **81 F2** 5 23N 27 25 E
Yucatán □, Mexico **119 C7** 21 30N 86 30W
Yucatán, Canal de, Caribbean **120 B2** 22 0N 86 30W
Yucatán, Península de, Mexico **98 H11** 19 30N 89 0W
Yucatán Basin, Cent. Amer. **98 H11** 19 0N 86 0W
Yucatan Str. = Yucatán, Canal de, Caribbean **120 B2** 22 0N 86 30W
Yucca, U.S.A. **117 L12** 34 52N 114 9W
Yucca Valley, U.S.A. **117 L10** 34 8N 116 27W
Yucheng, China **56 F9** 36 55N 116 32 E
Yuci, China **56 F7** 37 42N 112 46 E
Yudu, China **59 E10** 25 59N 115 30 E
Yuechi, China **58 B6** 30 34N 106 25 E
Yuendumu, Australia **92 D5** 22 16 S 131 49 E
Yueqing, China **59 C13** 28 9N 120 59 E
Yueqing Wan, China **59 D13** 28 5N 121 20 E
Yuexi, Anhui, China **59 B11** 30 50N 116 20 E
Yuexi, Sichuan, China **58 C4** 28 37N 102 26 E
Yueyang, China **59 C9** 29 21N 113 5 E
Yugan, China **59 C11** 28 43N 116 37 E
Yugoslavia ■, Europe **40 C4** 43 20N 20 0 E
Yuhuan, China **59 C13** 28 9N 121 12 E
Yuhuan Dao, China **59 C13** 28 5N 121 15 E
Yujiang, China **59 C11** 28 10N 116 43 E
Yukhnov, Russia **46 E8** 54 44N 35 15 E
Yukon →, U.S.A. **100 B3** 62 32N 163 54W
Yukon Territory □, Canada **100 B6** 63 0N 135 0W
Yüksekova, Turkey **73 D11** 37 34N 44 16 E
Yukta, Russia **51 C11** 63 26N 105 42 E
Yukuhashi, Japan **55 H5** 33 44N 130 59 E
Yulara, Australia **93 E5** 25 10 S 130 55 E
Yule →, Australia **92 D2** 20 41 S 118 17 E
Yuleba, Australia **95 D4** 26 37 S 149 24 E
Yuli, Nigeria **83 D7** 9 44N 10 12 E
Yuli, Taiwan **59 F13** 23 20N 121 18 E
Yulin, Guangxi Zhuangzu, China **59 F8** 22 40N 110 8 E
Yülin, Hainan, China **65 C7** 18 10N 109 31 E
Yulin, Shaanxi, China **56 E5** 38 20N 109 30 E
Yuma, Ariz., U.S.A. **117 N12** 32 43N 114 37W
Yuma, Colo., U.S.A. **112 E3** 40 8N 102 43W
Yuma, B. de, Dom. Rep. **121 C6** 18 20N 68 35W
Yumbe, Uganda **86 B3** 3 28N 31 15 E
Yumbi, Dem. Rep. of the Congo **86 C2** 1 12 S 26 15 E
Yumen, China **60 C4** 39 50N 97 30 E
Yumurtalık, Turkey **72 D6** 36 45N 35 43 E
Yun Gui Gaoyuan, China **58 E3** 26 0N 104 0 E
Yun Ho →, China **57 E9** 39 10N 117 10 E
Yun Ling, China **58 D2** 27 0N 99 20 E
Yun Xian, Hubei, China **59 A8** 32 50N 110 46 E
Yun Xian, Yunnan, China **58 E3** 24 27N 100 8 E
Yuna, Australia **93 E2** 28 20 S 115 0 E
Yunak, Turkey **72 C4** 38 49N 31 43 E
Yunan, China **59 F8** 23 12N 111 30 E
Yuncheng, Henan, China **56 G8** 35 36N 115 57 E
Yuncheng, Shanxi, China **56 G6** 35 2N 111 0 E
Yunfu, China **59 F9** 22 50N 112 5 E
Yungas, Bolivia **124 G5** 17 0 S 66 0W
Yungay, Chile **126 D1** 37 10 S 72 5W
Yunhe, China **59 C12** 28 8N 119 33 E
Yunkai Dashan, China **59 F8** 22 30N 111 0 E
Yunlin, Taiwan **59 F13** 23 42N 120 30 E
Yunlong, China **58 E2** 25 57N 99 13 E
Yunmeng, China **59 B9** 31 2N 113 43 E
Yunnan □, China **58 E4** 25 0N 102 0 E
Yunquera de Henares, Spain **32 E1** 40 47N 3 11W
Yunt Dağı, Turkey **39 C9** 38 56N 27 13 E
Yunta, Australia **95 E2** 32 34 S 139 36 E
Yunxi, China **56 H6** 33 0N 110 22 E
Yunxiao, China **59 F11** 23 59N 117 18 E
Yuping, China **58 D7** 27 13N 108 56 E
Yupyongdong, N. Korea **57 D15** 41 49N 128 53 E
Yuqing, China **58 D6** 27 13N 107 53 E
Yurga, Russia **50 D9** 55 42N 84 51 E
Yurimaguas, Peru **124 E3** 5 55 S 76 7W
Yuryev-Polskiy, Russia **46 D10** 56 30N 39 40 E
Yuryevets, Russia **48 B6** 57 25N 43 2 E
Yuryung Kaya, Russia **51 B12** 72 48N 113 23 E
Yuscarán, Honduras **120 D2** 13 58N 86 45W
Yushan, China **59 C12** 28 42N 118 10 E
Yushanzhen, China **58 C7** 29 28N 108 22 E
Yushe, China **56 F7** 37 4N 112 58 E
Yushu, Jilin, China **57 B14** 44 43N 126 38 E
Yushu, Qinghai, China **60 C4** 33 5N 96 55 E
Yusufeli, Turkey **73 B9** 40 50N 41 33 E
Yutai, China **56 G9** 35 0N 116 45 E
Yutian, China **57 E9** 39 53N 117 45 E
Yuxarı Qarabağ = Nagorno-Karabakh, Azerbaijan **70 B5** 39 55N 46 45 E
Yuxi, China **58 E4** 24 30N 102 35 E

Yuyao, *China* **59 B13** 30 3N 121 10 E
Yuzawa, *Japan* **54 E10** 39 10N 140 30 E
Yuzha, *Russia* **48 B6** 56 34N 42 1 E
Yuzhno-Sakhalinsk, *Russia* **51 E15** 46 58N 142 45 E
Yuzhou, *China* **56 G7** 34 10N 113 28 E
Yvelines □, *France* **19 D8** 48 40N 1 45 E
Yverdon-les-Bains, *Switz.* **25 J2** 46 47N 6 39 E
Yvetot, *France* **18 C7** 49 37N 0 44 E
Yzeure, *France* **19 F10** 46 33N 3 22 E

Z

Zaanstad, *Neths.* **17 B4** 52 27N 4 50 E
Zāb al Kabīr →, *Iraq* **70 C4** 36 1N 43 24 E
Zāb aş Şagīr →, *Iraq* **70 C4** 35 17N 43 29 E
Žabalj, *Serbia, Yug.* **42 E5** 45 21N 20 5 E
Žabari, *Serbia, Yug.* **40 B5** 44 22N 21 15 E
Zabarjad, *Egypt* **80 C4** 23 40N 36 12 E
Zabaykalsk, *Russia* **51 E12** 49 40N 117 25 E
Zabki, *Poland* **45 F8** 52 17N 21 7 E
Ząbkowice Śląskie, *Poland* **45 H3** 50 35N 16 50 E
Žabljak, *Montenegro, Yug.* **40 C3** 43 18N 19 5 E
Zabłudów, *Poland* **45 F9** 53 0N 23 19 E
Żabno, *Poland* **45 H7** 50 9N 20 53 E
Zābol, *Iran* **71 D9** 31 0N 61 32 E
Zābolī, *Iran* **71 E9** 27 10N 61 35 E
Zabré, *Burkina Faso* **83 C4** 11 12N 0 36W
Zábřeh, *Czech Rep.* **27 B9** 49 53N 16 52 E
Zabrze, *Poland* **45 H5** 50 18N 18 50 E
Zabzuga, *Ghana* **83 D5** 9 20N 0 30 E
Zacapa, *Guatemala* **120 D2** 14 59N 89 31W
Zacapu, *Mexico* **118 D4** 19 50N 101 43W
Zacatecas, *Mexico* **118 C4** 22 49N 102 34W
Zacatecas □, *Mexico* **118 C4** 23 30N 103 0W
Zacatecoluca, *El Salv.* **120 D2** 13 29N 88 51W
Zachary, *U.S.A.* **113 K9** 30 39N 91 9W
Zachodnio-Pomorskie □, *Poland* **44 E2** 53 40N 15 50 E
Zacoalco, *Mexico* **118 C4** 20 14N 103 33W
Zacualtipán, *Mexico* **119 C5** 20 39N 98 36W
Zadar, *Croatia* **29 D12** 44 8N 15 14 E
Zadawa, *Nigeria* **83 C7** 11 33N 10 19 E
Zadetkyi Kyun, *Burma* **65 G1** 10 0N 98 25 E
Zadonsk, *Russia* **47 F10** 52 25N 38 56 E
Zafarqand, *Iran* **71 C7** 33 11N 52 29 E
Zafora, *Greece* **39 E8** 36 5N 26 24 E
Zafra, *Spain* **35 G4** 38 26N 6 30W
Żagań, *Poland* **45 G2** 51 39N 15 22 E
Zagaoua, *Chad* **79 E10** 15 30N 22 24 E
Žagarė, *Lithuania* **44 B10** 56 21N 23 15 E
Zagazig, *Egypt* **80 H7** 30 40N 31 30 E
Zāgheh, *Iran* **71 C6** 33 30N 48 42 E
Zaglivérion, *Greece* **40 F7** 40 36N 23 15 E
Zagnanado, *Benin* **83 D5** 7 18N 2 28 E
Zagorá, *Greece* **38 B5** 39 27N 23 6 E
Zagorje, *Slovenia* **29 B11** 46 8N 15 0 E
Zagórów, *Poland* **45 F4** 52 10N 17 54 E
Zagorsk = Sergiyev Posad, *Russia* **46 D10** 56 20N 38 10 E
Zagórz, *Poland* **45 J9** 49 30N 22 14 E
Zagreb, *Croatia* **29 C12** 45 50N 15 58 E
Zāgros, Kūhhā-ye, *Iran* **71 C6** 33 45N 48 5 E
Zagros Mts. = Zāgros, Kūhhā-ye, *Iran* **71 C6** 33 45N 48 5 E
Žagubica, *Serbia, Yug.* **40 B5** 44 15N 21 47 E
Zaguinaso, *Ivory C.* **82 C3** 10 1N 6 14W
Zagyva →, *Hungary* **42 C5** 47 5N 20 4 E
Zāhedān, *Fārs, Iran* **71 D7** 28 46N 53 52 E
Zāhedān, *Sīstān va Balūchestān, Iran* **71 D9** 29 30N 60 50 E
Zahlah, *Lebanon* **75 B4** 33 52N 35 50 E
Zahna, *Germany* **24 D8** 51 55N 12 49 E
Záhony, *Hungary* **42 B7** 48 25N 22 11 E
Zainsk, *Russia* **48 C11** 55 18N 52 4 E
Zaïre = Congo →, *Africa* **84 F2** 6 4 S 12 24 E
Zaječar, *Serbia, Yug.* **40 C6** 43 53N 22 18 E
Zaka, *Zimbabwe* **89 C5** 20 20 S 31 29 E
Zakamensk, *Russia* **51 D11** 50 23N 103 17 E
Zakataly = Zaqatala, *Azerbaijan* **49 K8** 41 38N 46 35 E
Zakháro, *Greece* **38 D3** 37 30N 21 39 E
Zakhodnaya Dzvina = Daugava →, *Latvia* **9 H21** 57 4N 24 3 E
Zākhū, *Iraq* **70 B4** 37 10N 42 50 E
Zákinthos, *Greece* **38 D2** 37 47N 20 57 E
Zákinthos □, *Greece* **38 D2** 37 47N 20 57 E
Zakopane, *Poland* **45 J6** 49 18N 19 57 E
Zakroczym, *Poland* **45 F7** 52 26N 20 38 E
Zákros, *Greece* **36 D8** 35 6N 26 10 E
Zala, *Ethiopia* **81 F4** 6 28N 37 13 E
Zala □, *Hungary* **42 D1** 46 42N 16 50 E
Zala →, *Hungary* **42 D2** 46 43N 17 16 E
Zalaegerszeg, *Hungary* **42 D1** 46 53N 16 47 E
Zalakomár, *Hungary* **42 D2** 46 33N 17 10 E
Zalalövő, *Hungary* **42 D1** 46 51N 16 35 E
Zalamea de la Serena, *Spain* **35 G5** 38 40N 5 38W
Zalamea la Real, *Spain* **35 H4** 37 41N 6 38W
Zalău, *Romania* **42 C8** 47 12N 23 3 E
Žalec, *Slovenia* **29 B12** 46 16N 15 10 E
Zaleshchiki = Zalishchyky, *Ukraine* **47 H3** 48 45N 25 45 E
Zalew Wiślany, *Poland* **44 D6** 54 20N 19 50 E
Zalewo, *Poland* **44 E6** 53 50N 19 41 E
Zalingei, *Sudan* **79 F10** 12 51N 23 29 E
Zalishchyky, *Ukraine* **47 H3** 48 45N 25 45 E
Zama L., *Canada* **104 B5** 58 45N 119 5W
Zambeke, *Dem. Rep. of the Congo* **86 B2** 2 8N 25 17 E
Zambeze →, *Africa* **87 F4** 18 35 S 36 20 E
Zambezi = Zambeze →, *Africa* **87 F4** 18 35 S 36 20 E
Zambezi, *Zambia* **85 G4** 13 30 S 23 15 E
Zambezia □, *Mozam.* **87 F4** 16 15 S 37 30 E
Zambia ■, *Africa* **87 F2** 15 0 S 28 0 E
Zamboanga, *Phil.* **61 H5** 6 59N 122 3 E
Zambrów, *Poland* **45 F9** 52 59N 22 14 E
Zametchino, *Russia* **48 D6** 53 30N 42 30 E
Zamfara □, *Nigeria* **83 C6** 12 10N 6 0 E
Zamfara →, *Nigeria* **83 C5** 12 5N 4 2 E
Zamora, *Mexico* **118 D4** 20 0N 102 21W
Zamora, *Spain* **34 D5** 41 30N 5 45W
Zamora □, *Spain* **34 D5** 41 30N 5 46W
Zamość, *Poland* **45 H10** 50 43N 23 15 E
Zamtang, *China* **58 A3** 32 26N 101 6 E
Zan, *Ghana* **83 D4** 9 26N 0 17W
Záncara →, *Spain* **33 F1** 39 18N 3 18W
Zandvoort, *Neths.* **17 B4** 52 22N 4 32 E
Zanesville, *U.S.A.* **110 G2** 39 56N 82 1W
Zangābād, *Iran* **70 B5** 38 26N 46 44 E
Zangue →, *Mozam.* **87 F4** 17 50 S 35 21 E
Zanjān, *Iran* **71 B6** 36 40N 48 35 E
Zanjān □, *Iran* **71 B6** 37 20N 49 30 E
Zanjān →, *Iran* **71 B6** 37 8N 47 47 E
Zannone, *Italy* **30 B6** 40 58N 13 3 E
Zante = Zákinthos, *Greece* **38 D2** 37 47N 20 57 E
Zanthus, *Australia* **93 F3** 31 2 S 123 34 E
Zanzibar, *Tanzania* **86 D4** 6 12 S 39 12 E
Zaouiet El-Kala = Bordj Omar Driss, *Algeria* **78 C7** 28 10N 6 40 E
Zaouiet Reggane, *Algeria* **78 C6** 26 32N 0 3 E
Zaoyang, *China* **59 A9** 32 10N 112 45 E
Zaozhuang, *China* **57 G9** 34 50N 117 35 E
Zap Suyu = Zāb al Kabīr →, *Iraq* **70 C4** 36 1N 43 24 E
Zapadna Morava →, *Serbia, Yug.* **40 C5** 43 38N 21 30 E
Zapadnaya Dvina = Daugava →, *Latvia* **9 H21** 57 4N 24 3 E
Zapadnaya Dvina, *Russia* **46 D7** 56 15N 32 3 E
Západné Beskydy, *Europe* **27 B12** 49 30N 19 0 E
Zapadni Rodopi, *Bulgaria* **40 E7** 41 50N 24 0 E
Západočeský □, *Czech Rep.* **26 B6** 49 35N 13 0 E
Zapala, *Argentina* **128 D2** 39 0 S 70 5W
Zapaleri, Cerro, *Bolivia* **126 A2** 22 49 S 67 11W
Zapata, *U.S.A.* **113 M5** 26 55N 99 16W
Zapatón →, *Spain* **35 F4** 39 0N 6 49W
Zaporizhzhya, *Ukraine* **47 J8** 47 50N 35 10 E
Zaporozhye = Zaporizhzhya, *Ukraine* **47 J8** 47 50N 35 10 E
Zaqatala, *Azerbaijan* **49 K8** 41 38N 46 35 E
Zara, *Turkey* **70 B3** 39 58N 37 43 E
Zaragoza, *Coahuila, Mexico* **118 B4** 28 30N 101 0W
Zaragoza, *Nuevo León, Mexico* **119 C5** 24 0N 99 46W
Zaragoza, *Spain* **32 D4** 41 39N 0 53W
Zaragoza □, *Spain* **32 D4** 41 35N 1 0W
Zarand, *Kermān, Iran* **71 D8** 30 46N 56 34 E
Zarand, *Markazī, Iran* **71 C6** 35 18N 50 25 E
Zărandului, Muntii, *Romania* **42 D7** 46 14N 22 7 E
Zaranj, *Afghan.* **66 D2** 30 55N 61 55 E
Zarasai, *Lithuania* **9 J22** 55 40N 26 20 E
Zarate, *Argentina* **126 C4** 34 7 S 59 0W
Zarautz, *Spain* **32 B2** 43 17N 2 10W
Zaraysk, *Russia* **46 E10** 54 48N 38 53 E
Zard, Kūh-e, *Iran* **71 C6** 32 22N 50 4 E
Zāreh, *Iran* **71 C6** 35 7N 49 9 E
Zari, *Nigeria* **83 C7** 13 4N 12 45 E
Zaria, *Nigeria* **83 C6** 11 0N 7 40 E
Żarki, *Poland* **45 H6** 50 38N 19 23 E
Zárkon, *Greece* **38 B4** 39 38N 22 6 E
Zarneh, *Iran* **70 C5** 33 55N 46 10 E
Zărnești, *Romania* **43 E10** 45 33N 25 18 E
Zarós, *Greece* **36 D6** 35 8N 24 54 E
Żarów, *Poland* **45 H3** 50 56N 16 29 E
Zarqā', Nahr az →, *Jordan* **75 C4** 32 10N 35 37 E
Zarrīn, *Iran* **71 C7** 32 46N 54 37 E
Zaruma, *Ecuador* **124 D3** 3 40 S 79 38W
Żary, *Poland* **45 G2** 51 37N 15 10 E
Zarza de Granadilla, *Spain* **34 E4** 40 14N 6 3W
Zarzis, *Tunisia* **79 B8** 33 31N 11 2 E
Zas, *Spain* **34 B2** 43 4N 8 53W
Zaskar →, *India* **69 B7** 34 13N 77 20 E
Zaskar Mts., *India* **69 C7** 33 15N 77 30 E
Zastron, *S. Africa* **88 E4** 30 18 S 27 7 E
Žatec, *Czech Rep.* **26 A6** 50 20N 13 32 E
Zaterechnyy, *Russia* **49 H7** 44 48N 45 11 E
Zator, *Poland* **45 J6** 49 59N 19 28 E
Zavala, *Bos.-H.* **40 D1** 42 50N 17 59 E
Zavāreh, *Iran* **71 C7** 33 29N 52 28 E
Zave, *Zimbabwe* **89 B5** 17 6 S 30 1 E
Zavetnoye, *Russia* **49 G6** 47 13N 43 50 E
Zavidovići, *Bos.-H.* **42 F3** 44 27N 18 10 E
Zavitinsk, *Russia* **51 D13** 50 10N 129 20 E
Zavodovski, I., *Antarctica* **5 B1** 56 0 S 27 45W
Zavolzhsk, *Russia* **48 B6** 57 30N 42 0 E
Zavolzhye, *Russia* **48 B6** 56 37N 43 26 E
Zawadzkie, *Poland* **45 H5** 50 37N 18 28 E
Zawichost, *Poland* **45 H8** 50 48N 21 51 E
Zawidów, *Poland* **45 G2** 51 1N 15 1 E
Zawiercie, *Poland* **45 H6** 50 30N 19 24 E
Zāwiyat al Bayḍā = Al Bayḍā, *Libya* **79 B10** 32 50N 21 44 E
Zâwyet Shammas, *Egypt* **80 A2** 31 30N 26 37 E
Zâwyet Um el Rakham, *Egypt* **80 A2** 31 18N 27 1 E
Zâwyet Ungeîla, *Egypt* **80 A2** 31 23N 26 42 E
Zāyā, *Iraq* **70 C5** 33 33N 44 13 E
Zāyandeh →, *Iran* **71 C7** 32 35N 52 0 E
Zaysan, *Kazakstan* **50 E9** 47 28N 84 52 E
Zaysan, Oz., *Kazakstan* **50 E9** 48 0N 83 0 E
Zayü, *China* **58 C1** 28 48N 97 27 E
Zazafotsy, *Madag.* **89 C8** 21 11 S 46 21 E
Zázrivá, *Slovak Rep.* **27 B12** 49 16N 19 7 E
Zbarazh, *Ukraine* **47 H3** 49 43N 25 44 E
Zbąszyń, *Poland* **45 F2** 52 14N 15 56 E
Zbąszynek, *Poland* **45 F2** 52 16N 15 51 E
Zblewo, *Poland* **44 E5** 53 56N 18 19 E
Žďár nad Sázavov, *Czech Rep.* **26 B8** 49 34N 15 57 E
Zdolbuniv, *Ukraine* **47 G4** 50 30N 26 15 E
Ždrelo, *Serbia, Yug.* **40 B5** 44 16N 21 28 E
Zduńska Wola, *Poland* **45 G5** 51 37N 18 59 E
Zduny, *Poland* **45 G4** 51 39N 17 21 E
Zeballos, *Canada* **104 D3** 49 59N 126 50W
Zebediela, *S. Africa* **89 C4** 24 20 S 29 17 E
Zebila, *Ghana* **83 C4** 10 55N 0 30W
Zeebrugge, *Belgium* **17 C3** 51 19N 3 12 E
Zeehan, *Australia* **94 G4** 41 52 S 145 25 E
Zeeland □, *Neths.* **17 C3** 51 30N 3 50 E
Zeerust, *S. Africa* **88 D4** 25 31 S 26 4 E
Zefat, *Israel* **75 C4** 32 58N 35 29 E
Zege, *Ethiopia* **81 E4** 11 43N 37 18 E
Zeggerene, Iracher, *Mali* **83 B5** 16 49N 2 16 E
Zégoua, *Mali* **82 C3** 10 32N 5 35W
Zehdenick, *Germany* **24 C9** 52 58N 13 20 E
Zeil, Mt., *Australia* **92 D5** 23 30 S 132 23 E
Zeila, *Somali Rep.* **74 E3** 11 21N 43 30 E
Zeist, *Neths.* **17 B5** 52 5N 5 15 E
Zeitz, *Germany* **24 D8** 51 2N 12 7 E
Zelechów, *Poland* **45 G8** 51 49N 21 54 E
Zelengora, *Bos.-H.* **40 C2** 43 22N 18 30 E
Zelenodolsk, *Russia* **48 C9** 55 55N 48 30 E
Zelenogorsk, *Russia* **46 B5** 60 12N 29 43 E
Zelenograd, *Russia* **46 D9** 56 1N 37 12 E
Zelenogradsk, *Russia* **9 J19** 54 53N 20 29 E
Zelenokumsk, *Russia* **49 H6** 44 24N 44 0 E
Železná Ruda, *Czech Rep.* **26 B6** 49 8N 13 15 E
Železnik, *Serbia, Yug.* **40 B4** 44 43N 20 23 E
Zelienople, *U.S.A.* **110 F4** 40 48N 80 8W
Želiezovce, *Slovak Rep.* **27 C11** 48 3N 18 40 E
Zelina, *Croatia* **29 C13** 45 57N 16 16 E
Zell, *Baden-W., Germany* **25 H3** 47 42N 7 52 E
Zell, *Rhld-Pfz., Germany* **25 E3** 50 1N 7 10 E
Zell am See, *Austria* **26 D5** 47 19N 12 47 E
Zella-Mehlis, *Germany* **24 E6** 50 39N 10 40 E
Zelów, *Poland* **45 G6** 51 28N 19 14 E
Zeltweg, *Austria* **26 D7** 47 11N 14 45 E
Zémio, *C.A.R.* **86 A2** 5 2N 25 5 E
Zempléni-hegység, *Hungary* **42 B6** 48 25N 21 25 E
Zemplínska šírava, *Slovak Rep.* **27 C15** 48 48N 22 0 E
Zemun, *Serbia, Yug.* **40 B4** 44 51N 20 25 E
Zengbé, *Cameroon* **83 D7** 5 46N 13 4 E
Zengcheng, *China* **59 F9** 23 13N 113 52 E
Zenica, *Bos.-H.* **42 F2** 44 10N 17 57 E
Žepče, *Bos.-H.* **42 F3** 44 28N 18 2 E
Zeraf, Bahr ez →, *Sudan* **81 F3** 9 42N 30 52 E
Zerbst, *Germany* **24 D8** 51 58N 12 5 E
Żerków, *Poland* **45 F4** 52 4N 17 32 E
Zermatt, *Switz.* **25 J3** 46 2N 7 46 E
Zernez, *Switz.* **25 J6** 46 42N 10 7 E
Zernograd, *Russia* **49 G5** 46 52N 40 19 E
Zerqan, *Albania* **40 E4** 41 27N 20 20 E
Zerqani = Zerqan, *Albania* **40 E4** 41 27N 20 20 E
Zestaponi, *Georgia* **49 J6** 42 6N 43 0 E
Zetel, *Germany* **24 B3** 53 25N 7 58 E
Zeulenroda, *Germany* **24 E7** 50 39N 11 59 E
Zeven, *Germany* **24 B5** 53 17N 9 16 E
Zevenaar, *Neths.* **17 C6** 51 56N 6 5 E
Zévio, *Italy* **28 C8** 45 22N 11 8 E
Zeya, *Russia* **51 D13** 53 48N 127 14 E
Zeya →, *Russia* **51 D13** 51 42N 128 53 E
Zeytinbağı, *Turkey* **41 F12** 40 24N 28 47 E
Zeytindağ, *Turkey* **39 C9** 38 58N 27 4 E
Zghartā, *Lebanon* **75 A4** 34 21N 35 53 E
Zgierz, *Poland* **45 G6** 51 50N 19 27 E
Zgorzelec, *Poland* **45 G2** 51 10N 15 0 E
Zgurița, *Moldova* **43 B13** 48 8N 28 1 E
Zhabinka, *Belarus* **47 F3** 52 13N 24 2 E
Zhailma, *Kazakstan* **50 D7** 51 37N 61 33 E
Zhambyl, *Kazakstan* **50 E8** 42 54N 71 22 E
Zhangaly, *Kazakstan* **49 G10** 47 1N 50 37 E
Zhangaqazaly, *Kazakstan* **50 E7** 45 48N 62 6 E
Zhangbei, *China* **56 D8** 41 10N 114 45 E
Zhangguangcai Ling, *China* **57 B15** 45 0N 129 0 E
Zhangjiakou, *China* **56 D8** 40 48N 114 55 E
Zhangping, *China* **59 E11** 25 17N 117 23 E
Zhangpu, *China* **59 E11** 24 8N 117 35 E
Zhangshu, *China* **59 C10** 28 4N 115 29 E
Zhangwu, *China* **57 C12** 42 43N 123 52 E
Zhangye, *China* **60 C5** 38 50N 100 23 E
Zhangzhou, *China* **59 E11** 24 30N 117 35 E
Zhanhua, *China* **57 F10** 37 40N 118 8 E
Zhanjiang, *China* **59 G8** 21 15N 110 20 E
Zhannetty, Ostrov, *Russia* **51 B16** 76 43N 158 0 E
Zhanyi, *China* **58 E4** 25 38N 103 48 E
Zhanyu, *China* **57 B12** 44 30N 122 30 E
Zhao Xian, *China* **56 F8** 37 43N 114 45 E
Zhao'an, *China* **59 F11** 23 41N 117 10 E
Zhaocheng, *China* **56 F6** 36 22N 111 38 E
Zhaojue, *China* **58 C4** 28 1N 102 49 E
Zhaoping, *China* **59 E8** 24 11N 110 48 E
Zhaoqing, *China* **59 F9** 23 0N 112 20 E
Zhaotong, *China* **58 D4** 27 20N 103 44 E
Zhaoyuan, *Heilongjiang, China* **57 B13** 45 27N 125 0 E
Zhaoyuan, *Shandong, China* **57 F11** 37 20N 120 23 E
Zharkovskiy, *Russia* **46 E7** 55 56N 32 19 E
Zhashkiv, *Ukraine* **47 H6** 49 15N 30 5 E
Zhashui, *China* **56 H5** 33 40N 109 8 E
Zhayyq →, *Kazakstan* **50 E6** 47 0N 51 48 E
Zhdanov = Mariupol, *Ukraine* **47 J9** 47 5N 37 31 E
Zhecheng, *China* **56 G8** 34 7N 115 20 E
Zhegao, *China* **59 B11** 31 46N 117 45 E
Zhejiang □, *China* **59 C13** 29 0N 120 0 E
Zheleznogorsk, *Russia* **47 F8** 52 22N 35 23 E
Zheleznogorsk-Ilimskiy, *Russia* **51 D11** 56 34N 104 8 E
Zheltyye Vody = Zhovti Vody, *Ukraine* **47 H7** 48 21N 33 31 E
Zhen'an, *China* **56 H5** 33 27N 109 9 E
Zhenba, *China* **56 H3** 32 34N 107 58 E
Zhenfeng, *China* **58 E5** 25 22N 105 40 E
Zheng'an, *China* **58 C6** 28 32N 107 27 E
Zhengding, *China* **56 E8** 38 8N 114 32 E
Zhenghe, *China* **59 D12** 27 20N 118 50 E
Zhengyang, *China* **59 A10** 32 37N 114 22 E
Zhengyangguan, *China* **59 A11** 32 30N 116 29 E
Zhengzhou, *China* **56 G7** 34 45N 113 34 E
Zhenhai, *China* **59 C13** 29 59N 121 42 E
Zhenjiang, *China* **59 A12** 32 11N 119 26 E
Zhenkang, *China* **58 F2** 23 58N 99 0 E
Zhenlai, *China* **57 B12** 45 50N 123 5 E
Zhenning, *China* **58 D5** 26 4N 105 45 E
Zhenping, *Henan, China* **56 H7** 33 10N 112 16 E
Zhenping, *Shaanxi, China* **58 B7** 31 59N 109 31 E
Zhenxiong, *China* **58 D5** 27 27N 104 50 E
Zhenyuan, *Gansu, China* **56 G4** 35 35N 107 30 E
Zhenyuan, *Guizhou, China* **58 D7** 27 4N 108 21 E
Zherdevka, *Russia* **48 E5** 51 56N 41 29 E
Zherong, *China* **59 D12** 27 15N 119 52 E
Zhetiqara, *Kazakstan* **50 D7** 52 11N 61 12 E
Zhezqazghan, *Kazakstan* **50 E7** 47 44N 67 40 E
Zhicheng, *China* **59 B8** 30 25N 111 27 E
Zhidan, *China* **56 F5** 36 48N 108 48 E
Zhigansk, *Russia* **51 C13** 66 48N 123 27 E
Zhigulevsk, *Russia* **48 D9** 53 28N 49 30 E
Zhijiang, *Hubei, China* **59 B8** 30 28N 111 45 E
Zhijiang, *Hunan, China* **58 D7** 27 27N 109 42 E
Zhijin, *China* **58 D5** 26 37N 105 45 E
Zhilinda, *Russia* **51 C12** 70 0N 114 20 E
Zhirnovsk, *Russia* **48 E7** 50 57N 44 49 E
Zhitomir = Zhytomyr, *Ukraine* **47 G5** 50 20N 28 40 E
Zhizdra, *Russia* **46 F8** 53 45N 34 40 E
Zhlobin, *Belarus* **47 F6** 52 55N 30 0 E
Zhmerinka = Zhmerynka, *Ukraine* **47 H5** 49 2N 28 2 E
Zhmerynka, *Ukraine* **47 H5** 49 2N 28 2 E
Zhob, *Pakistan* **68 D3** 31 20N 69 31 E
Zhob →, *Pakistan* **68 C3** 32 4N 69 50 E
Zhodino = Zhodzina, *Belarus* **46 E5** 54 5N 28 17 E
Zhodzina, *Belarus* **46 E5** 54 5N 28 17 E
Zhokhova, Ostrov, *Russia* **51 B16** 76 4N 152 40 E
Zhongdian, *China* **58 D2** 27 48N 99 42 E
Zhongdong, *China* **58 F6** 22 48N 107 47 E
Zhongdu, *China* **58 E7** 24 40N 109 40 E
Zhongning, *China* **56 F3** 37 29N 105 40 E
Zhongshan, *Guangdong, China* **59 F9** 22 26N 113 20 E
Zhongshan, *Guangxi Zhuangzu, China* **59 E8** 24 29N 111 18 E
Zhongtiao Shan, *China* **56 G6** 35 0N 111 10 E
Zhongwei, *China* **56 F3** 37 30N 105 12 E
Zhongxiang, *China* **59 B9** 31 12N 112 34 E
Zhongyang, *China* **56 F6** 37 20N 111 11 E
Zhoucun, *China* **57 F9** 36 47N 117 48 E
Zhouning, *China* **59 D12** 27 12N 119 20 E
Zhoushan, *China* **59 B14** 30 1N 122 6 E
Zhoushan Dao, *China* **59 C14** 30 5N 122 10 E
Zhouzhi, *China* **56 G5** 34 10N 108 12 E
Zhovti Vody, *Ukraine* **47 H7** 48 21N 33 31 E
Zhovtneve, *Ukraine* **47 J7** 46 54N 32 3 E
Zhovtnevoye = Zhovtneve, *Ukraine* **47 J7** 46 54N 32 3 E
Zhu Jiang →, *China* **59 F9** 22 45N 113 37 E
Zhuanghe, *China* **57 E12** 39 40N 123 0 E
Zhucheng, *China* **57 G10** 36 0N 119 27 E
Zhugqu, *China* **56 H3** 33 40N 104 30 E
Zhuhai, *China* **59 F9** 22 15N 113 30 E
Zhuji, *China* **59 C13** 29 40N 120 10 E
Zhukovka, *Russia* **46 F7** 53 35N 33 50 E
Zhumadian, *China* **56 H8** 32 59N 114 2 E
Zhuo Xian = Zhuozhou, *China* **56 E8** 39 28N 115 58 E
Zhuolu, *China* **56 D8** 40 20N 115 12 E
Zhuozhou, *China* **56 E8** 39 28N 115 58 E
Zhuozi, *China* **56 D7** 41 0N 112 25 E
Zhushan, *China* **59 A8** 32 15N 110 13 E
Zhuxi, *China* **58 A7** 32 25N 109 40 E
Zhuzhou, *China* **59 D9** 27 49N 113 12 E
Zhytomyr, *Ukraine* **47 G5** 50 20N 28 40 E
Zi Shui →, *China* **59 C9** 28 40N 112 40 E
Žiar nad Hronom, *Slovak Rep.* **27 C11** 48 35N 18 53 E
Zīārān, *Iran* **71 B6** 36 7N 50 32 E
Ziarat, *Pakistan* **68 D2** 30 25N 67 49 E
Zibo, *China* **57 F10** 36 47N 118 3 E
Zichang, *China* **56 F5** 37 18N 109 40 E
Zidarovo, *Bulgaria* **41 D11** 42 20N 27 24 E
Ziębice, *Poland* **45 H4** 50 37N 17 2 E
Zielona Góra, *Poland* **45 G2** 51 57N 15 31 E
Zierikzee, *Neths.* **17 C3** 51 40N 3 55 E
Ziesar, *Germany* **24 C8** 52 16N 12 17 E
Zifta, *Egypt* **80 H7** 30 43N 31 14 E
Zigey, *Chad* **79 F9** 14 43N 15 50 E
Zigong, *China* **58 C5** 29 15N 104 48 E
Ziguinchor, *Senegal* **82 C1** 12 35N 16 20W
Zihuatanejo, *Mexico* **118 D4** 17 38N 101 33W
Zijin, *China* **59 F10** 23 33N 115 8 E
Zile, *Turkey* **72 B6** 40 15N 35 52 E
Žilina, *Slovak Rep.* **27 B11** 49 12N 18 42 E
Žilinský □, *Slovak Rep.* **27 B12** 49 10N 19 0 E
Zillah, *Libya* **79 C9** 28 30N 17 33 E
Zillertaler Alpen, *Austria* **26 D4** 47 6N 11 45 E
Zima, *Russia* **51 D11** 54 0N 102 5 E
Zimapán, *Mexico* **119 C5** 20 54N 99 20W
Zimba, *Zambia* **87 F2** 17 20 S 26 11 E
Zimbabwe, *Zimbabwe* **87 G3** 20 16 S 30 54 E
Zimbabwe ■, *Africa* **87 F3** 19 0 S 30 0 E
Zimi, *S. Leone* **82 D2** 7 20N 11 20W
Zimnicea, *Romania* **43 G10** 43 40N 25 22 E
Zimovniki, *Russia* **49 G6** 47 10N 42 25 E
Zinder, *Niger* **83 C6** 13 48N 9 0 E
Zinga, *Tanzania* **87 D4** 9 16 S 38 49 E
Zingst, *Germany* **24 A8** 54 26N 12 39 E
Ziniaré, *Burkina Faso* **83 C4** 12 35N 1 18W
Zinnowitz, *Germany* **24 A9** 54 4N 13 54 E
Zion National Park, *U.S.A.* **115 H7** 37 15N 113 5W
Zirbitzkogel, *Austria* **26 D7** 47 4N 14 34 E
Zirc, *Hungary* **42 C2** 47 17N 17 52 E
Žiri, *Slovenia* **29 B11** 46 5N 14 5 E
Žirje, *Croatia* **29 E12** 43 39N 15 42 E
Zirl, *Austria* **26 D4** 47 17N 11 14 E
Zirndorf, *Germany* **25 F6** 49 27N 10 57 E
Ziros, *Greece* **36 D8** 35 5N 26 8 E
Zisterdorf, *Austria* **27 C9** 48 33N 16 45 E
Zitácuaro, *Mexico* **118 D4** 19 28N 100 21W
Žitava →, *Slovak Rep.* **27 C11** 48 14N 18 21 E
Žitište, *Serbia, Yug.* **42 E5** 45 30N 20 32 E
Zitong, *China* **58 B5** 31 37N 105 10 E
Zítsa, *Greece* **38 B2** 39 47N 20 40 E
Zittau, *Germany* **24 E10** 50 53N 14 48 E
Zitundo, *Mozam.* **89 D5** 26 48 S 32 47 E
Živinice, *Bos.-H.* **42 F3** 44 27N 18 36 E
Ziwa Maghariba □, *Tanzania* **86 C3** 2 0 S 31 30 E
Ziway, L., *Ethiopia* **81 F4** 8 0N 38 50 E
Zixi, *China* **59 D11** 27 45N 117 4 E
Zixing, *China* **59 E9** 25 59N 113 21 E
Ziyang, *Shaanxi, China* **56 H5** 32 32N 108 31 E
Ziyang, *Sichuan, China* **58 B5** 30 6N 104 40 E
Ziyuan, *China* **59 D8** 26 2N 110 40 E
Ziyun, *China* **58 E6** 25 45N 106 5 E
Zizhong, *China* **58 C5** 29 48N 104 47 E
Zlarin, *Croatia* **29 E12** 43 42N 15 49 E
Zlatar, *Croatia* **29 B13** 46 5N 16 3 E
Zlatar, *Serbia, Yug.* **40 C3** 43 25N 19 47 E
Zlataritsa, *Bulgaria* **41 C9** 43 2N 25 55 E
Zlaté Moravce, *Slovak Rep.* **27 C11** 48 23N 18 24 E
Zlatibor, *Serbia, Yug.* **40 C3** 43 45N 19 43 E
Zlatitsa, *Bulgaria* **41 D8** 42 41N 24 7 E
Zlatna, *Romania* **43 D8** 46 8N 23 11 E
Zlatna Panega, *Bulgaria* **41 C8** 43 5N 24 9 E
Zlatni Pyasŭtsi, *Bulgaria* **41 C12** 43 17N 28 3 E
Zlatograd, *Bulgaria* **41 E9** 41 22N 25 7 E
Zlatoust, *Russia* **50 D6** 55 10N 59 40 E
Zletovo, *Macedonia* **40 E6** 41 59N 22 17 E
Zlín, *Czech Rep.* **27 B10** 49 14N 17 40 E
Złocieniec, *Poland* **44 E3** 53 30N 16 1 E
Złoczew, *Poland* **45 G5** 51 24N 18 35 E
Zlot, *Serbia, Yug.* **40 B5** 44 1N 21 58 E
Złotoryja, *Poland* **45 G2** 51 8N 15 55 E
Złotów, *Poland* **44 E4** 53 22N 17 2 E
Zmeinogorsk, *Kazakstan* **50 D9** 51 10N 82 13 E
Żmigród, *Poland* **45 G3** 51 28N 16 53 E
Zmiyev, *Ukraine* **47 H9** 49 39N 36 27 E
Znamenka = Znamyanka, *Ukraine* **47 H7** 48 45N 32 30 E
Znamyanka, *Ukraine* **47 H7** 48 45N 32 30 E
Żnin, *Poland* **45 F4** 52 51N 17 44 E
Znojmo, *Czech Rep.* **26 C9** 48 50N 16 2 E
Zobeyrī, *Iran* **70 C5** 34 10N 46 40 E
Zobia, *Dem. Rep. of the Congo* **86 B2** 3 0N 25 59 E
Zoetermeer, *Neths.* **17 B4** 52 3N 4 30 E
Zogang, *China* **58 C1** 29 55N 97 42 E
Zogno, *Italy* **28 C6** 45 48N 9 40 E
Zogqên, *China* **58 A2** 32 13N 98 47 E
Zolochev = Zolochiv, *Ukraine* **47 H3** 49 45N 24 51 E
Zolochiv, *Ukraine* **47 H3** 49 45N 24 51 E
Zolotonosha, *Ukraine* **47 H7** 49 39N 32 5 E
Zomba, *Malawi* **87 F4** 15 22 S 35 19 E
Zongo, *Dem. Rep. of the Congo* **84 D3** 4 20N 18 35 E
Zonguldak, *Turkey* **72 B4** 41 28N 31 50 E
Zongyang, *China* **59 B11** 30 42N 117 12 E
Zonqor Pt., *Malta* **36 D2** 35 51N 14 34 E
Zonza, *France* **21 G13** 41 45N 9 11 E
Zorgo, *Burkina Faso* **83 C4** 12 15N 0 35W
Zorita, *Spain* **35 F5** 39 17N 5 39W
Zorleni, *Romania* **43 D12** 46 14N 27 44 E
Zornitsa, *Bulgaria* **41 D10** 42 23N 26 58 E
Zorritos, *Peru* **124 D2** 3 43 S 80 40W
Żory, *Poland* **45 H5** 50 3N 18 44 E
Zorzor, *Liberia* **82 D3** 7 46N 9 28W
Zossen, *Germany* **24 C9** 52 13N 13 27 E
Zou Xiang, *China* **56 G9** 35 30N 116 58 E
Zouan-Hounien, *Ivory C.* **82 D3** 6 55N 8 15W
Zouar, *Chad* **79 D9** 20 30N 16 32 E
Zouérate = Zouîrât, *Mauritania* **78 D3** 22 44N 12 21W
Zouîrât, *Mauritania* **78 D3** 22 44N 12 21W
Zourika, *Niger* **83 B6** 19 15N 7 50 E
Zourma, *Burkina Faso* **83 C4** 11 20N 0 50W
Zoushan Dao, *China* **59 B14** 30 5N 122 10 E
Zoutkamp, *Neths.* **17 A6** 53 20N 6 18 E
Zrenjanin, *Serbia, Yug.* **42 E5** 45 22N 20 23 E
Zuarungu, *Ghana* **83 C4** 10 49N 0 46W
Zuba, *Nigeria* **83 D6** 9 11N 7 12 E
Zubayr, *Yemen* **81 D5** 15 3N 42 10 E
Zubtsov, *Russia* **46 D8** 56 10N 34 34 E
Zuénoula, *Ivory C.* **82 D3** 7 34N 6 3W
Zuera, *Spain* **32 D4** 41 51N 0 49W
Zufār, *Oman* **74 D5** 17 40N 54 0 E
Zug □, *Switz.* **25 H4** 47 9N 8 35 E
Zugdidi, *Georgia* **49 J5** 42 30N 41 55 E
Zugersee, *Switz.* **25 H4** 47 7N 8 35 E
Zugspitze, *Germany* **25 H6** 47 25N 10 59 E
Zuid-Holland □, *Neths.* **17 C4** 52 0N 4 35 E
Zuidbeveland, *Neths.* **17 C3** 51 30N 3 50 E
Zuidhorn, *Neths.* **17 A6** 53 15N 6 23 E
Zújar, *Spain* **35 H8** 37 34N 2 50W
Zújar →, *Spain* **35 G5** 39 1N 5 47W
Żukowo, *Poland* **44 D5** 54 21N 18 22 E
Zula, *Eritrea* **81 D4** 15 17N 39 40 E
Zülpich, *Germany* **24 E2** 50 41N 6 39 E
Zumaia, *Spain* **32 B2** 43 19N 2 15W
Zumárraga, *Spain* **32 B2** 43 5N 2 19W
Zumbo, *Mozam.* **87 F3** 15 35 S 30 26 E
Zummo, *Nigeria* **83 D7** 9 51N 12 59 E
Zumpango, *Mexico* **119 D5** 19 48N 99 6W
Zungeru, *Nigeria* **83 D6** 9 48N 6 8 E
Zunhua, *China* **57 D9** 40 18N 117 58 E
Zuni, *U.S.A.* **115 J9** 35 4N 108 51W
Zunyi, *China* **58 D6** 27 42N 106 53 E
Zuo Jiang →, *China* **58 F6** 22 50N 108 6 E
Zuozhou, *China* **58 F6** 22 42N 107 27 E
Županja, *Croatia* **42 E3** 45 4N 18 43 E
Žur, *Kosovo, Yug.* **40 D4** 42 13N 20 34 E
Zurbātīyah, *Iraq* **70 C5** 33 9N 46 3 E
Zürich, *Switz.* **25 H4** 47 22N 8 32 E
Zürich □, *Switz.* **25 H4** 47 26N 8 40 E
Zürichsee, *Switz.* **25 H4** 47 18N 8 40 E
Żuromin, *Poland* **45 E6** 53 4N 19 51 E
Žut, *Croatia* **29 E12** 43 52N 15 17 E
Zutphen, *Neths.* **17 B6** 52 9N 6 12 E
Zuwārah, *Libya* **79 B8** 32 58N 12 1 E
Zūzan, *Iran* **71 C8** 34 22N 59 53 E
Žužemberk, *Slovenia* **29 C11** 45 52N 14 56 E
Zvenigorodka = Zvenyhorodka, *Ukraine* **47 H6** 49 4N 30 56 E
Zvenyhorodka, *Ukraine* **47 H6** 49 4N 30 56 E
Zverinogolovskoye, *Russia* **50 D7** 54 26N 64 50 E
Zvezdets, *Bulgaria* **41 D11** 42 6N 27 26 E
Zvishavane, *Zimbabwe* **87 G3** 20 17 S 30 2 E
Zvolen, *Slovak Rep.* **27 C12** 48 33N 19 10 E
Zvonce, *Serbia, Yug.* **40 D6** 42 57N 22 34 E
Zvornik, *Bos.-H.* **42 F4** 44 26N 19 5 E
Zwedru = Tchien, *Liberia* **82 D3** 5 59N 8 15W
Zweibrücken, *Germany* **25 F3** 49 15N 7 21 E
Zwenkau, *Germany* **24 D8** 51 13N 12 20 E
Zwettl, *Austria* **26 C8** 48 35N 15 9 E
Zwickau, *Germany* **24 E8** 50 44N 12 30 E
Zwierzyniec, *Poland* **45 H9** 50 36N 22 58 E
Zwiesel, *Germany* **25 F9** 49 1N 13 13 E
Zwoleń, *Poland* **45 G8** 51 21N 21 36 E
Zwolle, *Neths.* **17 B6** 52 31N 6 6 E
Zwolle, *U.S.A.* **113 K8** 31 38N 93 39W
Zychlin, *Poland* **45 F6** 52 15N 19 37 E
Żyrardów, *Poland* **45 F7** 52 3N 20 28 E
Zyryan, *Kazakstan* **50 E9** 49 43N 84 20 E
Zyryanka, *Russia* **51 C16** 65 45N 150 51 E
Zyryanovsk = Zyryan, *Kazakstan* **50 E9** 49 43N 84 20 E
Żywiec, *Poland* **45 J6** 49 42N 19 10 E
Zyyi, *Cyprus* **36 E12** 34 43N 33 20 E

Afghanistan · Albania · Algeria · Andorra · Angola · Antigua & Barbuda · Argentina

Barbados · Belarus · Belgium · Belize · Benin · Bhutan · Bolivia

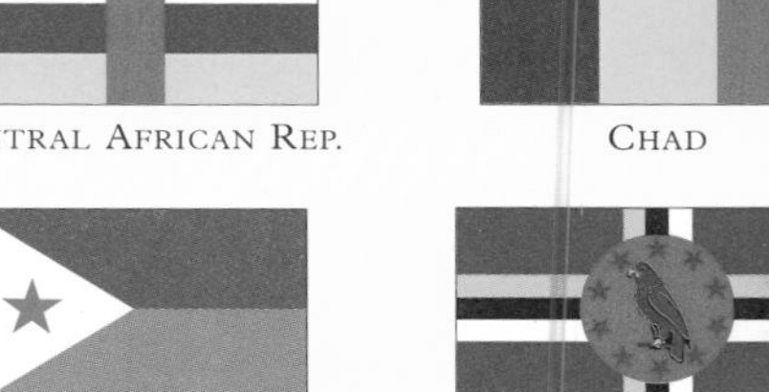

Burundi · Cambodia · Cameroon · Canada · Cape Verde · Central African Rep. · Chad

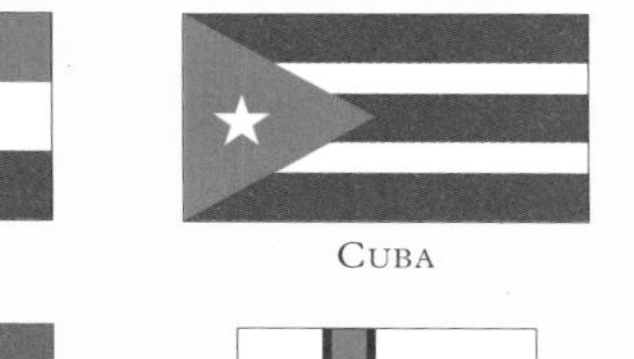

Croatia · Cuba · Cyprus · Czech Republic · Denmark · Djibouti · Dominica

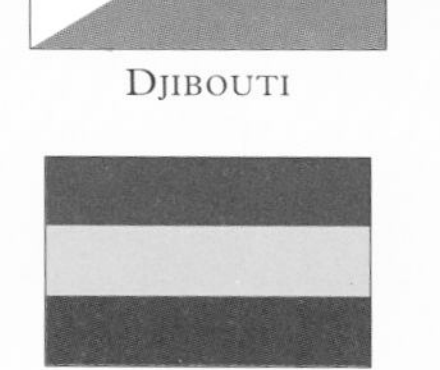

Ethiopia · Faroe Islands · Fiji · Finland · France · Gabon · Gambia

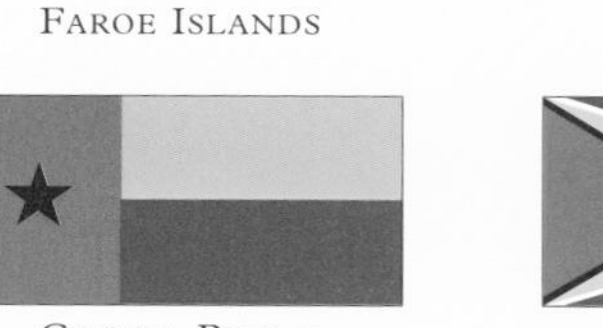

Guinea · Guinea-Bissau · Guyana · Haiti · Honduras · Hong Kong · Hungary

Italy · Ivory Coast · Jamaica · Japan · Jordan · Kazakstan · Kenya

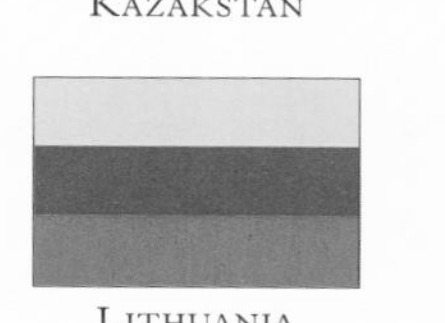

Lebanon · Lesotho · Liberia · Libya · Liechtenstein · Lithuania · Luxembourg

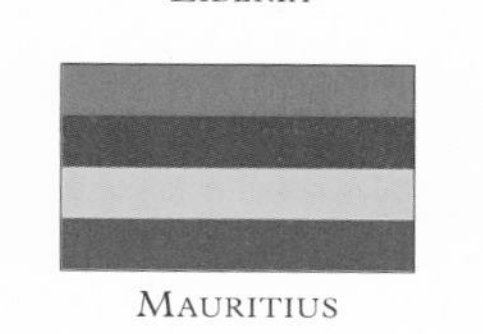
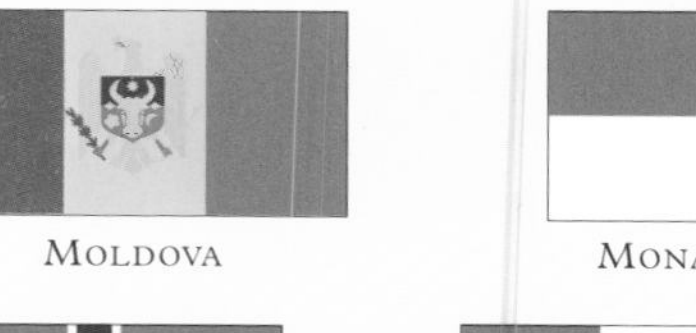

Malta · Mauritania · Mauritius · Mexico · Micronesia · Moldova · Monaco

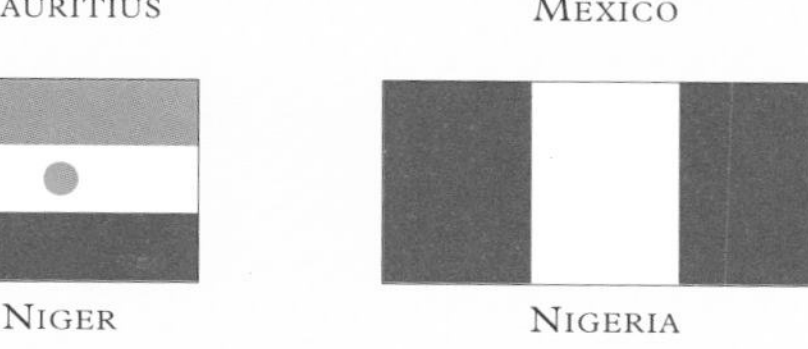

New Zealand · Nicaragua · Niger · Nigeria · Northern Marianas · Norway · Oman

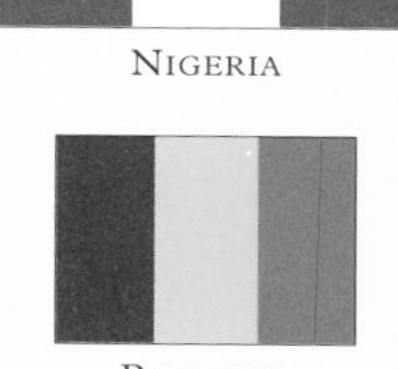
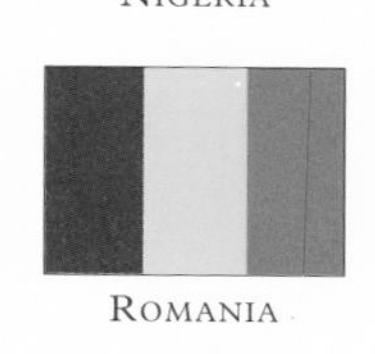

Portugal · Puerto Rico · Qatar · Romania · Russia · Rwanda · Samoa

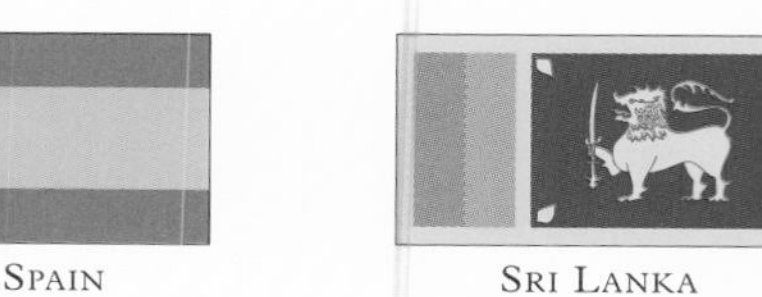

Slovak Republic · Slovenia · Solomon Islands · Somalia · South Africa · Spain · Sri Lanka

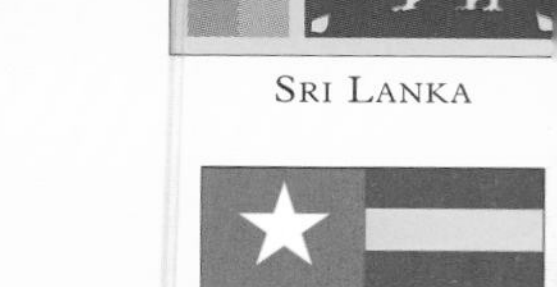

Switzerland · Syria · Taiwan · Tajikistan · Tanzania · Thailand · Togo

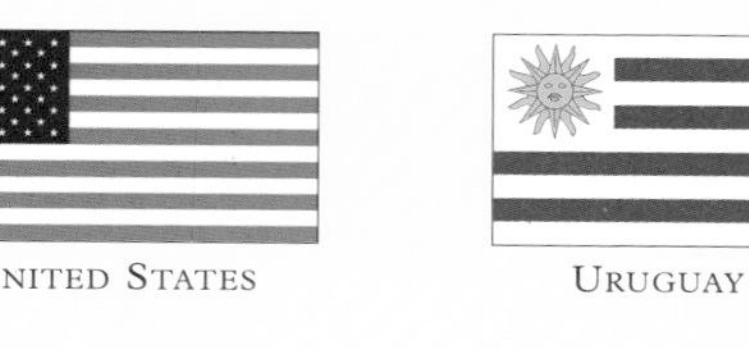

Ukraine · United Arab Emirates · United Kingdom · United States · Uruguay · Uzbekistan · Vanuatu